THEOLOGICAL DICTIONARY

OF THE

NEW TESTAMENT

EDITED BY

GERHARD KITTEL

Translator and Editor

GEOFFREY W. BROMILEY, D. LITT., D. D.

Volume III

Θ—Κ

WM. B. EERDMANS PUBLISHING COMPANY

GRAND RAPIDS, MICHIGAN

THEOLOGICAL DICTIONARY OF THE NEW TESTAMENT

Translated from
THEOLOGISCHES WÖRTERBUCH ZUM NEUEN TESTAMENT
Dritter Band: Θ—K, herausgegeben von Gerhard Kittel
Published by
W. KOHLHAMMER VERLAG
Stuttgart, Germany

Printed in the Netherlands
by Drukkerij Holland N.V., Amsterdam

Editor's Preface

From the publication of the first volume, and during the years of its long and arduous composition, the *Theologisches Wörterbuch zum Neuen Testament*, familiarly known as Kittel or abbreviated as *TWNT*, has secured for itself a solid place in biblical scholarship, not only as a reference work or a starting-point for further research, but also as a formative contribution to theology.

There has, of course, been some misunderstanding of its role. While it is not a simple lexicon, it obviously cannot replace either the full commentary or the biblical theology. Its task is to mediate between ordinary lexicography and the specific task of exposition, more particularly at the theological level. For this reason attention is concentrated on theologically significant terms, and on the theologically significant usage of these terms.

When this is understood, Kittel is safeguarded against the indiscriminate enthusiasm which would make it a sole and absolute authority in lexical and exegetical matters. It is also safeguarded against the resultant criticism that it involves an illegitimate task for which it uses improper means. Its more limited, yet valid and invaluable role, can be appreciated, and its learning and insights incorporated into the great task of New Testament interpretation.

Hitherto access to the great bulk of *TWNT* has been only in the original language. Some of the more important articles have been translated in the *Key Words* series, and by virtue of the significance of the words selected this series has performed a most useful service. Yet even the chosen articles have undergone some abridgment and editorial redaction, quite apart from the fact that the main part of Kittel has not been translated at all.

By contrast, the present rendering aims to present the whole of *TWNT* in a faithful reproduction of the original. At the cost of less felicity, for German scholarship is no guarantee of stylistic elegance, the rendering is more closely tied to the German. Quotations are fully given in the original Hebrew, Greek and Latin, and the references are left as they are apart from essential changes. For scholars who may wish to consult the original, even the pagination is retained except for a slight fluctuating variation of no more than two or three pages either way. The external size of the volumes has been much reduced, however, and costs have been trimmed so as to provide the student with maximum material at minimum price.

It need hardly be said that the translation and publication of Kittel is no necessary endorsement of everything contained in it. Written by many scholars over a long period, Kittel naturally contains articles of unequal value and varying outlook. Indeed, there are internal disagreements as regards basic presuppositions, historical assumptions and specific interpretations. The ultimate worth of the undertaking lies in its fundamental orientation and its objective findings; for these it is now presented in translation.

In the preparation of the volumes particular thanks are due to Professor F. F. Bruce of the University of Manchester for his many valuable suggestions and corrections in the course of laborious proof-reading. Also deserving of mention in this instance are the publishers for the courage and helpfulness which they have displayed in so monumental an enterprise, and the printers for the skill with which they have handled such difficult material. In spite of every effort, it would be presumptuous to suppose that all errors have been avoided, and the help of readers will be appreciated in detecting and eliminating those that remain.

Pasadena, California, 1965.

G. W. Bromiley

Contents

Contents

Contents IX

Contributors

Editor:

Gerhard Kittel, Tübingen.

Contributors:

Otto Bauernfeind, Tübingen.
Friedrich Baumgärtel, Göttingen.
Johannes Behm, Berlin.
Georg Bertram, Giessen.
Hermann Wolfgang Beyer, Leipzig.
Günther Bornkamm, Königsberg/Bethel.
Friedrich Büchsel, Rostock.
Rudolf Bultmann, Marburg.
Albert Debrunner, Bern.
Kurt Deissner, Greifswald.
Gerhard Delling, Glauchau.
Werner Foerster, Münster.
Gerhard Friedrich, Gross-Heydekrug (East Prussia).
Ernst Fuchs, Winzershausen (Württemberg).
Heinrich Greeven, Greifswald/Heidelberg.
Walter Grundmann, Jena.
Walter Gutbrod, Tübingen.
Hermann Hanse, Bismarck (Altmark).
Friedrich Hauck, Erlangen.
Hans Wolfgang Heidland, Mannheim.
Volkmar Herntrich, Bethel.
Johannes Herrmann, Münster.
Johannes Horst, Posen.
Joachim Jeremias, Göttingen.
Hermann Kleinknecht, Halle.
Karl Georg Kuhn, Tübingen.
Rudolf Meyer, Leipzig.
Wilhelm Michaelis, Bern.
Otto Michel, Halle.
Hugo Odeberg, Lund.
Albrecht Oepke, Leipzig.
Erik Peterson, Rome.
Herbert Preisker, Breslau.
Otto Procksch, Erlangen.
Gottfried Quell, Rostock.
Gerhard von Rad, Jena.
Karl Heinrich Rengstorf, Loccum (Hannover).

Oskar Rühle, Stuttgart.
Hermann Sasse, Erlangen.
Hans Heinrich Schaeder, Berlin.
Heinrich Schlier, Elberfeld.
Lothar Schmid, Maulbronn (Württemberg).
Karl Ludwig Schmidt, Basel.
Otto Schmitz, Bethel.
Carl Schneider, Königsberg.
Johannes Schneider, Berlin/Breslau.
Julius Schniewind, Halle.
Gottlob Schrenk, Zürich.
Heinrich Seesemann, Riga/Berlin.
Hans Freiherr von Soden, Marburg.
Gustav Stählin, Leipzig (and Madras, India).
Ethelbert Stauffer, Bonn.
Hermann Strathmann, Erlangen.
Albrecht Stumpff, Tübingen.
Artur Weiser, Tübingen.
Hans Windisch, Halle.
Ernst Würthwein, Tübingen.

Abbreviations

Bacher Term. = W. Bacher, *Die exegetische Terminologie der jüdischen Traditionsliteratur,* I (1899), II (1905).

bibl. = biblical.

class. = classical.

CPG = Corpus Paroemiographorum Graecorum, ed. E. L. v. Leutsch-F. G. Schneidewin, I (1839), II (1851).

Darembg.-Saglio = C. Daremberg-E. Saglio, *Dictionnaire des Antiquités Grecques et Romaines* (1877 ff.).

Diels⁵ = H. Diels, *Die Fragmente der Vorsokratiker,* 5th ed. by W. Kranz (1934 ff.).

Eichr. Theol. AT = W. Eichrodt, *Die Theologie des AT,* I (1933), II (1935).

hist. = history.

Hndbch (Kl.) AW = *Handbuch der klassischen Altertumswissenschaft,* ed. by I. v. Müller (1886 ff.), in revised form under the title *Handbuch der Altertumswissenschaft* by W. Otto.

HThR = *The Harvard Theological Review* (1908 ff.).

P. Par. = *Notices et Extraits des Manuscrits Grecs de la Bibliothèque Impériale,* XVIII, 2 (1865), ed. by W. Brunet de Presle.

P. Strassb. = *Griechische Papyrus der Kaiserlichen Universitäts u. Landesbibliothek zu Strassburg,* ed. by F. Preisigke, I (1912), II (1920).

Plut.

    Adulat. = Quomodo Adulator ab Amico internoscatur.

    Athen. = Bellone an Pace clariores fuerint Athenienses.

    Aud. Poet. = Quomodo Adolescens Poetas audire debeant.

    Laud. s. Inv. = Qua quis Ratione seipse sine Invidia laudet.

Plac. Phil. = De Placitis Philosophorum.

PRE = Pirqe de Rabbi Eliezer.

Pr.-Bauer³ = W. Bauer, *Griechisch-Deutsches Wörterbuch zu den Schriften des NT u. der übrigen urchristlichen Literatur,* 3rd and completely revised ed. (1937).

Rabbinovicz VL = R. Rabbinovicz, Variae Lectiones in Mischnam et in Talmud Babylonicum (1867 ff.).

rec. = recensuit.

Rec. IG = *Recueil d'Inscriptions Grecques,* ed. C. Michel (1900), Suppl. (1912).

Riessler = P. Riessler, *Altjüdisches Schrifttum ausserhalb der Bibel, übersetzt u. erläutert* (1928).

Suppl. Epigr. Graec. = Supplementum Epigraphicum Graecum, adiuvantibus P. Roussel et aliis curavit J. J. E. Hondius (1923 ff.).

Tac. = Cornelius Tacitus, the historian, contemporary of Plutarch, ed. C. Halm-G. Andresen⁵ (1929/30).

    Ann. = Annales.

Theophr.

    Hist. Plant. = Historia Plantarum.

Vg = Vulgate.

Waddington = P. Le Bas-W. H. Waddington-P. Foucart, *Voyage Archéologique en Grèce et en Asie Mineure* (1847 ff.), III : *Inscriptions.*

ZSem = *Zeitschrift für Semitistik u. verwandte Gebiete* (1922 ff.).

ZVglSpr = *Zeitschrift f. vergleichende Sprachforschung auf dem Gebiete des Deutschen, Griechischen und Lateinischen* (later, *auf dem Gebiete der indogermanischen Sprachen*) (1852 ff. ; 1877 ff.).

---
† Θαμάρ, † Ῥαχάβ, † Ῥούθ,
† ἡ τοῦ Οὐρίου

The very fact that the genealogy of Jesus in Matthew includes women is surprising, since women's names are rare in Jewish genealogies.[1] It is even more surprising that, if Mt. regards it as necessary to mention certain women as the ancestors of Jesus, he does not follow the custom attested elsewhere of mentioning (or inventing)[2] the mothers of leading patriarchs like Abraham or David, or introduce the four famous matriarchs whose names are handed down in other places as the ancestral mothers of Israel,[3] but rather accepts the traditional number and yet substitutes four other women (Mt. 1:3, 5, 6).

The number and the choice are intentional, not accidental. The Evangelist has a point to make through them. He wishes to show that the genealogy of Christ, embracing the whole history of Israel, bears witness not only to its high points but also to the sin and unworthiness which run through this history even at its high points, i.e., in the age of the patriarchs and the house of David. These four women, the very opposites of the other four, are regarded by God as worthy to be ancestresses of His Messiah even though they are unworthy as sinners and aliens.[4] This means, however, that the history of the people elected to be the people of the Messiah is one of grace rather than glory.[5] It also means that the manner of this grace is to fulfil its work through the fall of man.[6] Thus the genealogy embraces a basic thought which runs through the whole Gospel, namely, that the last shall be first, that God can raise up of these stones children to Abraham, or, in Pauline terms, that God has chosen τὰ ἀσθενῆ τοῦ κόσμου, ... τὰ ἀγενῆ τοῦ κόσμου καὶ τὰ ἐξουθενημένα ..., ἵνα καταισχύνῃ τὰ ἰσχυρά, ... ὅπως μὴ καυχήσηται πᾶσα σάρξ ἐνώπιον τοῦ θεοῦ (1 Cor. 1:27 ff.).

Θ α μ ά ρ κ τ λ. [1] Str.-B., I, 15.
[2] bBB, 91a; cf. G. Kittel, "Die γενεαλογίαι der Past.," ZNW, 20 (1931), 49 ff., esp. 65.
[3] Schl. Erl., I, 6 f.; Str.-B., I, 29.
[4] F. W. Grosheide, *Het Heilig Evangelie volgens Mattheus* (1922), 4, points out that Rahab the Canaanite and Bathsheba the wife of a Hittite are aliens as well as Ruth the Moabitess.
[5] How strong this emphasis is may be seen from the fact that the Evangelist is not even interested in the name of the wife of Uriah. The essential point is that David had a son by another man's wife and therefore that there is adultery within the genealogy. Δαυὶδ δὲ ἐγέννησεν τὸν Σολομῶνα ἐκ τῆς τοῦ Οὐρίου, Mt. 1:6. It should also be noted that in Mt. the child of this union, Solomon, stands at one of the high points in the sacred history : Mt. 6:29; 12:42. The fact that strictly Solomon was born in wedlock (2 S. 12:24) after the child of adultery died (2 S. 12:14) does not alter the case as Mt. sees it. Even after she marries David Bathsheba is still the wife of Uriah, and the fruit of the marriage is still illegitimate.
[6] Schl. Erl., I, 7.

If it is objected that we ought not to see in Mt. any particular reference to the sin or illegitimacy of these women, since Synagogue tradition excuses and even glorifies them, or the sin of the men connected with them, [7] this is to mistake the situation. For one thing, Rabbinic tradition is by no means unanimous in this matter. At the older levels in particular there is no such reversal of moral concepts (→ 3). Again, the hypothesis that Mt. is accepting some such glorification has nothing to support it and is quite improbable (→ n. 5).

We may hardly deduce that the strange introduction of these four women into the genealogy is designed to prepare the ground for the extraordinary nature of the last in the series, as though the four were *typi Mariae*. [8] For wherein does the type consist? Mary is a true Israelite and therefore the comparison would have to be in terms of illegitimate conception rather than alien status. But this would imply acceptance of the Jewish charge that Jesus was born illegitimately as the son of Panthera. [9] It would be quite grotesque for the Evangelist to try to justify the Virgin Birth by reference to admitted harlots or adulteresses. In any case, this whole view falls to the ground for the simple reason that to the best of our knowledge the Jewish attack had not yet been launched in the days of Mt. It is true that older Rabb. texts (T. Chul., 2, 22 ff.) contain the name Jeshua' ben Panthera. But there is here no polemical intention. [10] The probability is that Jacob, the father of Joseph, did in fact bear the surname Πανθήρ. [11] Only later in passages in the Babylonian Talmud (Shab., 104b; Sanh., 67a) and in Celsus (Orig. Cels., I, 32 ff., cf. 28 and 39) do we find the assertion that Panthera was the lover of Mary and therefore the illegitimate father of Jesus. [12]

2. Jewish exegesis is unanimous in its estimation of these women and of the men concerned. Especially in later traditions there is a strong tendency in each of the four cases to mitigate the sin or illegitimacy reported in the OT, or even to transform it into its opposite. [13]

a. Thamar, who acc. to Gn. 38 was twice widowed by sons of Judah without children, has in accordance with the custom of Levirate marriage a claim to the third brother, who is withheld from her by her father-in-law. To assert her right to children, she dresses as a harlot and entices her father-in-law, who out of wedlock and in fornication begets by her the twins Pharez and Zara, Pharez being the ancestor of David (Ju. 4:18).

The OT itself attributes the sin to Judah rather than to Thamar (Gn. 38:26). Almost without exception, however, later Rabb. exegesis seeks to exculpate Judah too on the ground that he acted under the compulsion of God, who had appointed him the fore-father of David and of the Messiah. Gn. r., 85 on 38:15 f.: "R. Jochanan said: He (Judah) wanted to pass by, but God sent to him the angel who is set over the sexual impulse. This angel said to him: Judah, where are you going? Whence shall come kings and great men? And he turned unto her by the way (38:16), not voluntarily, but under

---

[7] Kl. Mt.², 2, appealing to Str.-B., and earlier H. A. W. Meyer⁶ (1876) appealing to Wettstein, *ad loc*. It is worth noting that Str.-B. does not draw this conclusion.

[8] So already H. Grotius, *Annotationes ad NT* (1641) on Mt. 1:3. So also Meyer and Kl. Mt.², *ad loc*.

[9] So Wettstein, I, 226 f.

[10] Cf. Str.-B., I, 38. The absence of any reference to the illegitimate birth of Jesus in these oldest texts makes it unlikely that "son of Panthera" arose out of "son of the *parthenos*" (J. Klausner, *Jesus von Nazareth* [1930], 24 f.).

[11] Epiph. Haer., 78, 7, 5; cf. Zn. Forsch., VI, 267, who surmises that Hegesipp. was the source of Epiph.

[12] On this whole question cf. esp. H. L. Strack, *Jesus, die Häretiker und die Christen nach den ältesten jüd. Angaben* (1910); also H. Windisch, "Die Legende von Panthera," *Christliche Welt*, 49 (1935), 689-694.

[13] On what follows cf. the exhaustive review in Str.-B., I, 15-29.

compulsion." Tanch. וישב, 13 (Buber, 92b): "A lover who was rewarded was Judah, for from him sprang Pharez and Hezron, who were to give us David and the King Messiah who will redeem Israel. See what devious ways God must follow before He can cause the King Messiah to arise from Judah." Tg. J., II on Gn. 38:26 : "You are both innocent, for the matter is of Me." [14]

This glorifying of Judah seems to belong, of course, to the Amoraean and therefore to the later tradition. So far as we can see, the Tannait. period took a different view. T. Ber., 4, 17 f. has two discussions from the circles of R. Tarphon and R. Akiba concerning the question how Judah merited the kingdom. The first, without trying to excuse his sin, points to his confession in Gn. 38:26 as a reason for his acknowledgment. But the second rejects this view : "Is a sin rewarded ?" Other events in the life of Judah must be sought as the basis of his reward (e.g., his humility in Gn. 44:33).

b. Rahab, [15] the harlot of Jericho, saved the Hebrew spies according to Jos. 2. She is extolled as a proselyte (M. Ex., 18, 1) and a tool of the Holy Spirit (S. Dt., 22 on 1:24). The NT magnifies her for her faith (Hb. 11:31) and for her works (Jm. 2:25). Acc. to the OT her reward was that she and her family were spared in the sack of Jericho (Jos. 6:22 ff.). Acc. to a widespread Rabb. tradition she was the ancestress of many priests and prophets, esp. Jeremiah and Ezekiel and the prophetess Huldah (S. Nu., 78 on 10:29; Pesikt., 115a). Only occasionally is Joshua mentioned as her husband in the passages known to us, [16] and it is assumed that he had only sons, not daughters. There is no known support for the suggestion in Mt. 1:5 that she bore Boaz of Salmon, and that she was thus the ancestress of David, though this version may rest on older exegesis.

c. That Ruth, a Moabitess and therefore an alien, was the ancestress of David is from the natural standpoint a serious family blemish which opponents of David might hold against him. [17] Sometimes we find the view expressed that it was the implied humiliation which made the house of David more lasting than that of Saul (bJoma, 22b). But the predominant reference is to the meritorious nature of Ruth's coming over to Judaism and to the reward which this brought her. [18] There is also stress on the providential divine overruling which appointed her from the very beginning an ancestress of the Messiah. [19]

d. The wife of Uriah. In bShab., 56a; bQid., 43a we have quotations from several 3rd century rabbis which summarise the grounds on which David's act might be excused and justified, e.g., that men divorced their wives on going to war and that Bathsheba was thus free, or that Uriah rebelled against David and was thus put to death justly. On the other hand, there are in bQid., 43a other statements which go back to R. Shammai and in which David's guilt is unequivocally admitted in Rabb. exposition. [20]

Kittel

---

[14] This and other examples may be found in Str.-B., I, 15 ff.

[15] Mas.: רָחָב; LXX and Hb. 11:31; Jm. 2:25 : Ῥαάβ; Mt. 1:5 : Ῥαχάβ. Cf. further Zn. Mt., 57 ff. (text and n. 26).

[16] bMeg., 14b (Str.-B., I, 23).

[17] bJeb., 76b (Str.-B., I, 24): "Then said the Edomite Doeg: ... Ask concerning him, whether he is fit to enter the congregation of Israel or not, since he springs from Ruth, the Moabitess."

[18] For instances cf. Str.-B., I, 25c/d.

[19] *Ibid.,* 26 f.

[20] *Ibid.,* 28 f.

> † θάμβος, † θαμβέω,
> † ἔκθαμβος, † ἐκθαμβέομαι

1. θάμβος,[1] θαμβεῖν (from the time of Homer), also θάμβησις and the compounds ἔκθαμβος, ἐκθαμβεῖν are connected with the Indo-germanic root *dhabh*, "to strike," "to be struck." Cf. also τάφος, τέθηπα, θῆπος, "astonishment." "To be amazed, astonished," is the basic meaning of the group. From this developed the trans. "terror" and the pass. "to be affrighted" which later become predominant, e.g., in the LXX.[2] The compound ἐκθαμβεῖν, -εῖσθαι is to be understood as an intensive form in the sense of "strong amazement or fear" (like the older ἐκφοβεῖσθαι). ἔκθαμβος is constructed from the verb (like the older ἔκφοβος) and means "astounded" and "dreadful." Eustath. Thessal. Comm. in Il., 4, 79 (Stallbaum, I, 358, 12 f.) gives the following definition: θάμβος is ἡ διὰ θέας ἐμβιβαζομένη ἔκπληξις εἰς ψυχήν. The trembling arises from both amazement and fear. The presupposition of the emotion is the direct impression of an event which suddenly takes place before one. Both gods and men awaken this rigid astonishment with their appearance and acts. There are many examples in Homer. The individual battles of heroes, the miraculous appearances and disappearances of gods and signs in heaven can cause inquisitive or startled astonishment.[3] Nor do we have to have something visible. Priam asking for the body of his son in Achilles' tent awakens astonishment by his tragic fate.[4] Thus a miracle may cause amazement and fear not merely in virtue of what is seen but also in virtue of the thought of the miraculous power manifested in it. Cf., e.g., Aesch. Suppl., 570: τέρας δ᾽ ἐθάμβουν. Hence θάμβος acquires the sense of fear as it may be found, e.g., in Plat. Phaedr., 254c. The attitude of ἔκθαμβος is finely characterised in the passage sometimes quoted in NT comm., namely, Polyb., 20, 10, 9: ἔκθαμβοι γεγονότες ἔστασαν ἄφωνοι πάντες, οἱονεὶ (as) παραλελυμένοι καὶ τοῖς σώμασι καὶ ταῖς ψυχαῖς διὰ τὸ παράδοξον τῶν ἀπαντωμένων. Plutarch thinks θάμβος is a result of superstition (e.g., Pericl., VI, 1 [I, 154e/f]); cf. also Arat. Phaen., 32, 2, where we read: αὐτοῖς δὲ τοῖς πολίταις θέαμα σεμνότερον ἢ κατ᾽ ἄνθρωπον ἐφάνη, καὶ τοῖς πολεμίοις φάσμα θεῖον ὁρᾶν δοκοῦσι φρίκην (trembling) ἐνέβαλε καὶ θάμβος, ὥστε μηδένα τρέπεσθαι πρὸς ἀλκήν. There is a similar passage in Heliod. Aeth., X, 9. Acc. to Plutarch man is tormented on his way of death by τὰ δεινὰ πάντα, φρίκη καὶ τρόμος καὶ ἱδρὼς καὶ θάμβος, before he may enter the sphere of φῶς τι θαυμάσιον (Fr., VI: Ex Opere de Anima, II, 6 [Doehner-Dübner, V, p. 9, 40 ff.]). In Pericl., VI, 1 (I, 154e f) Plutarch links superstition (δεισιδαιμονία) and astonishment. θάμβος in this sense is the root of all superstition, while true piety can flourish only on the soil of clear and rational knowledge. On the whole there was no essential change in the Gk. use of the word group in question. In every age it denotes emotions between astonishment and fear as these are evoked by things seen. Thus ἐκθαμβεῖσθαι, e.g., is found in its old connection with seeing in the Orphic Argonaut epic, 1218 f. (*c.* 400 A.D.; ed. E. Abel, 1885). Inscriptions and the pap. bear witness to its use in the *koine*. We have an inscr. from the temple of Serapis of Delos which speaks of the θαμβητὰ ἔργα of Serapis and on which we also read: ὃ θαμβήσας ἀνηγέρετο (awakened) ...[5]

Particularly interesting is the inscr. on a pagan temple in Gerasa which was taken over for use by Christians. This inscr. dates from the time of Justinian. It says con-

---

θ ά μ β ο ς κ τ λ.   [1] We find both ὁ and τὸ θάμβος. Cf. Bl.-Debr.[6] § 51, 2.
[2] Bl.-Debr.[6] § 78; Helbing Kasussyntax, 79; Wbg. Mk. on 1:27. Three stages may be distinguished in the development of the verb: a. intr. θαμβῶ; b. θαμβοῦμαι, ἐθαμβήθην (the transition of intr. actives in verbs of emotion to deponential inflection, Bl.-Debr.[6] § 307); c. the resultant trans. θαμβῶ.
[3] Il., 23, 728 and 815; 4, 79; 8, 77; Od., 3, 372; 17, 367.
[4] Il., 24, 483 f.
[5] IG, XI, 4, No. 1299, line 60, cf. 30 and 91. Cf. BCH, 37 (1913), 319 ff.

cerning the temple : θάμβος όμοῦ καὶ θαῦμα, παρερχομένοισι ἐτύχθην. [6] Examples from the magic pap. are found in the so-called 8th Book of Moses, XI, 478 ff., [7] where we read : ἡ Γῆ ἀκούσασα ἤχους καὶ ἰδοῦσα Αὐγὴν ἐθαμβήθη καὶ ἐκύρτανε. Relevant in the great Paris magic pap. is the admonition not to be afraid of phenomena which follow incantations. There is a corresponding prayer to the deity : "Manifest thyself … and affright not mine eyes …" [8]

2. θάμβος and its cognates are not common in the Gk. Bible. Nor is there any certain Heb. basis for the group. It is used for several Heb. words which denote a physical movement occasioned by terror, and then the emotion itself. Thus for בעת, "to fall upon," 2 Βασ. 22:5 : χείμαρροι ἀνομίας ἐθάμβησάν με (vl.: περιέπνιξάν με, ψ 17:4 : ἐξετάραξάν με) in the LXX, and more often in ᾿Α (ἐκθαμβεῖν, ᾿Ιωβ 3:5; 15:24; 33:7). Also for חפז and נחפז, cf. LXX 4 Βασ. 7:15; ᾿Α 1 Βασ. 23:26; Ex. 12:11; Dt. 16:3; ᾿ΑΣ Is. 52:12 (ἐκθάμβησις, ἔκθαμβος). The LXX often has σπεύδειν, σπουδή, σαλεύεσθαι etc. for these. Also for רגז, "to quake," ταράσσειν, ὀργίζειν etc. 1 Βασ. 14:15 : וַתִּרְגַּז הָאָרֶץ = ἐθάμβησεν (vl. the psychologised ἐθαμβήθησαν) (πᾶς ὁ λαὸς ἐν τῇ γῇ ἐκείνῃ. For חרד "to tremble," and the derivatives חָרֵד, "experiencing holy awe," חֲרָדָה, "fear," "terror," the LXX usually has ἐξιστάναι, ἔκστασιν ἐκφοβεῖν. Our word group is sometimes found for it in ᾿Α ᾿Ιερ. 37(30):5, also Ez. 21:14(19), and in Σ 1 Βασ. 4:13 (ἔκθαμβος). It is also found for פחד, "to be afraid," cf. LXX Cant. 3:8 and Θ ψ 52:5; Is. 44:8, and for בהל "to be startled," cf. Σ ᾿Ιερ. 51(28):32 (ἔκθαμβος) and the rare words פַּלָּצוּת, "quaking," "terror" (LXX Ez. 7:18 : θάμβος, but ἀνομία in Is. 21:4, σκότος in ψ 54:5 [᾿Α εἰλίνδησις, Σ φρίκη] and ὀδύνη in ᾿Ιωβ 21:6); חִתְחַת, "horror" (only Qoh. 12:5 [᾿Α : τρόμος]), אֹים, "terrible" (Cant. 6:4, 10 [Hab. 1:7: φοβερός]) and אֵימְתָן Aram., "terrible" (Θ Da. 7:7 [LXX φόβος]). Rather different is the rendering of תמה, "to be amazed," "to be speechless with fright," by θαμβεῖσθαι at Σ ᾿Ιωβ 26:11 and the anonym. rendering of תִּמָּהוֹן, "confusion," "delusion," by θάμβος at Dt. 28:28. Here and in the other passage in which this occurs in the Mas. (Zech. 12:4) the LXX has ἐξιστάναι or ἔκστασις. רדם and תַּרְדֵּמָה, "to sleep," "magical sleep," are also often translated ἐξιστάναι, ἔκστασις in the Gk., though sometimes we find θαμβεῖν, θάμβος instead. Thus LXX 1 Βασ. 26:12; Θ Da. 8:18 (A). When the root פחז, "to be frivolous," "arrogant," is translated by derivatives of θάμβος at LXX Ju. 9:4 (A), ᾿Α Gn. 49:4 and ᾿ΑΣ Jer. 23:32, the link is that frivolity and arrogance cause a divinely effected confusion, a terror of God, in the sense of quem deus perdere vult, prius dementat. Occasionally the Gk. word group can be referred to a physical process in accordance with the original sense of the underlying Heb. (cf. 1 Βασ. 14:15 supra). In general, however, the psychological understanding increasingly tends to predominate. As distinct from the class. use, the element of the occasional is less noticeable in bibl. Gk. It is a mysterious and impalpable factor which proves operative as mysterium tremendum in the θάμβος of man. [9]

3. In the NT astonishment is often linked with sight : Mk. 9:15 (ἐκθαμβεῖσθαι); [10] 16:5, 6; Ac. 3:10, 11; cf. Apc. Pt. 3:8; 4:11. In the miracle story in

---

[6] Epigr. Graec., 1068.
[7] Preis. Zaub., XIII, 478 ff.
[8] Ibid., IV, 210 and 237.
[9] Sir. 30:9 (no Heb.) uses ἐκθαμβεῖν in the secular sense for "to terrify." In Wis. 11:19; 17:3, however, the reference is to the fear of God. In the long run 1 Macc. 6:8 is to be explained along similar lines.
[10] ἐκθαμβεῖν and ἔκθαμβος are rare in the OT. In the LXX the verb is found only at Sir. 30:9 and the adj. only at Wis. 10:19 א: ἐκθάμβους (acc. plur.) (or ἐκ θάμβους ?)

Ac. 3:10, 11 θάμβος and ἔκθαμβοι — the only occurrence in the NT — or the θαμβηθέντες of D are used with ἔκστασις and θαυμάζειν [11] more in the sense of astonishment than fear. In Apc. Pt. 3:8; 4:11 the suddenness of the appearance (4:11) or its glory (3:8) is the basis of the fear. There is perhaps a similar external conception in Mk. 16:5, 6. But here the μὴ ἐκθαμβεῖσθε [12] on the lips of the angel indicates a revelation. Hence the terror is not really grounded externally in the form and occurrence of the appearance. What is represented is not physical reaction to the miraculous. Nor may it be regarded as a kind of numinous experience of the participant. The terror of man is rather a typical element in a revelation or epiphany. The use of θαμβεῖν is thus a sign that for the author the account relates to a theophany. Thus in Mk. 9:15 the astonishment of the people is a means used by the narrator to describe the coming of Jesus as an epiphany of the Lord for believers. [13] Expressions of fear and astonishment (→ φοβεῖσθαι, → ἐκπλήττεσθαι, → θορυβεῖσθαι, → θαυμάζειν, → ἐξίστασθαι) serve to emphasise the revelatory content and christological significance of many incidents in the Synoptic Gospels. Mk. 1:27: ἐθαμβήθησαν (-βησαν), vl. ἐθαύμαζον (-μάσθησαν), is also to be understood in this sense. Here the reference is to the διδαχὴ καινὴ κατ' ἐξουσίαν and the preceding exorcism. The term also serves, as customarily in ancient miracle stories, to indicate the accreditation of the miracle by the spectators. [14] The expression ἐγένετο θάμβος (D + μέγας) ἐπὶ πάντας seems to have a similar significance in Lk. 4:36. Mk. 10:24 refers to the fear which the words of Jesus arouse in the disciples. It may be seen from v. 26 that this does not relate merely to the salvation of the rich, which does not affect the disciples personally, but to the general claim of Jesus which men do not meet. In His demand for discipleship the Lord kindles fear and terror even among the disciples. Humanly speaking, even they are unable to meet this claim. The effect of the Lord is also expressed in the saying reported of Peter in Lk. 5:8 : ἔξελθε ἀπ' ἐμοῦ. This is described in terms of θάμβος in v. 9, and it is met by the gracious declaration : μὴ φοβοῦ, in v. 10. [15] The person of Jesus is also central in the little scene in Mk. 10:32a. What awakens terror in the disciples and fear in those who follow is not the way to Jerusalem nor what is to be expected there. Rather the power of the Lord, who holds His own and their fate in His hands, is manifested for the Evangelist and his readers in the awe and dread which characterise the attitude of those around Him.

---

instead of ἐκ βάθους ἀβύσσου. To these should be added the passages from 'Α, Σ and Θ already mentioned above. ἐκθαμβεῖσθαι is found only in Mk.

[11] What is meant acc. to Zn. Ac., ad loc. is an "astonishment at the palpable working of supernatural powers which is akin to rapturous enthusiasm." Cf. also E. Jacquier, Les Actes des Apôtres (1926), 100 f. θάμβος is a poetic expression much used by Lk. but rare in class. Gk.

[12] Mt. 28:5 has μὴ φοβεῖσθε ὑμεῖς. This formal greeting, often used to introduce epiphanies (cf. Mt. 14:27), is enough, with its emphatic ὑμεῖς, to distinguish the attitude of the women from that of the guards.

[13] We are not to think here of the radiance of transfiguration, as in Ex. 34:29 f. Nor are we to seek external reasons, plentifully suggested in the comm. Cf. also Cramer Cat., ad loc. : ἀλλ' αἰφνίδιον αὐτὸν θεασάμενοι, μᾶλλον δὲ οὐκ αὐτοὶ (οὐδὲ γὰρ εἰσιν ἄξιοι τὸν Σωτῆρα θεωρεῖν) ἀλλ' ὁ πᾶς ὄχλος ἐξεθαμβήθη, τῆς θέας αὐτοὺς εἰς ἔκπληξιν ἀγαγούσης.

[14] Cf. Kl. Mk., ad loc.; Bultmann Trad., 241 and E. Peterson, Εἷς θεός (1926), 193 ff., who distinguishes between religious and aesthetic astonishment.

[15] Cf. Zn. Lk., ad loc.

This pious awe is proper to the righteous acc. to the Oxyrhynchus logion deriving from Ev. Hebr. and preserved in Cl. Al.Strom., V, 14, 96. [16] In this apocryphal saying of the Lord the concepts of seeking, finding, astonishment, kingly rule and rest are all combined in a climax. The pious attitude, which in the canonical tradition is an indirect portrayal of the Lord by way of reflection, has here taken on autonomous significance in the sense of numinous experience. It denotes a preparatory stage in the Christian possession of salvation. This is true of the attitude of astonishment before the Lord in general. Astonishment is the attitude of those who are without, who are not yet believers. Those who are astonished lack the final certainty of the children of God, who in faith know that they possess salvation. Astonishment is the product of a sense of distance. It can be overcome only by the gracious saying : μή ἐκθαμβεῖσθε (→ n. 12).

In the Gethsemane story in Mk. 14:33 ἐκθαμβεῖσθαι is again found with ἀδημονεῖν and as a parallel to the λυπεῖσθαι of Mt. (26:37).

Ἀδημονεῖν is found in Σ at ψ 115:2 for בהל, where Ἀ has θαμβεῖσθαι and the LXX uses the concept of ἔκστασις. [17] The LXX uses the same term for the same Heb. word at ψ 30:22 to introduce a verse which is a parallel to and a continuation of ψ 21:1. The christological understanding of these OT statements, which is to be presumed in the Gethsemane story, sees in them not merely a description of the spiritual condition of Jesus at this hour but also a characterisation of Gethsemane as an epiphany by means of established forms in OT revelation (cf. esp. ψ 115). The theological significance of the incident has always been found in its antidocetic character. [18] To modern historical judgment it is also one of the firm pillars of the historical character of Jesus. The "fearful" [19] Christ is the Bearer of divine revelation for us.

Bertram

θάνατος, θνήσκω, ἀποθνήσκω, συναποθνήσκω, θανατόω, θνητός, ἀθανασία (ἀθάνατος)	→ ζωή.

θάνατος, θνήσκω, ἀποθνήσκω, συναποθνήσκω.

Contents : A. θάνατος in Greek Usage : 1. Classical Usage ; 2. Hellenistic Usage : a. Stoicism ; b. Neo-Platonism ; c. Gnosticism ; d. Philo. B. The Concept of Death in the NT. On the thought of death in the OT and Judaism → ζωή, II, 851; 855 f.

---

[16] Cf. on this pt. the observations of B. Grenfell and A. Hunt in their edition of the Oxyrhynchus pap. (IV, 654, 1 ff.); also Zahn Kan., II, 657; A. v. Harnack, SAB, 1904, 175 ff.; Deissmann LO, 363 f. Zn. tries to find a Semitic basis to yield θορυβηθείς/συντετριμμένος acc. to Lk. 4:18. Harnack defends the existing form. The reference is to astonishment for joy, as in Mt. 13:44.

[17] The LXX uses θαμβεῖν at 1 Βασ. 14:15 and λυπεῖν at Is. 32:11 and Ez. 16:43 for רגז "to quake."

[18] Cf. Cramer Cat., ad loc.

[19] Cf. Luther Ps. 31:23; 116:11; Mt. 26:37; Mk. 14:33. τρέμων and θαμβῶν are also found together at Ac. 9:6 ς; cf. the transl. of Vg and Luther. Here again we have a theophany.

θ ά ν α τ ο ς κτλ. → ζάω Bibl., esp. Rohde. Cf. also W. F. Otto, *Die Götter Griechenlands* (1929), 175-191; K. Sauer, *Untersuchungen zur Darstellung des Todes in der griech.-röm. Geschichtsschreibung* (Diss. Frankf., 1930); Stob. Ecl. IV, 1066-1073 : περὶ θανάτου, καὶ ὡς εἴη ἄφυκτος, 1074-78 : ἔπαινος ζωῆς; 1079-1096 : ἔπαινος θανάτου; 1079-1112 : σύγκρισις ζωῆς καὶ θανάτου. Τὸ ζάω, ζωή B (→ II, 832 Bibl.) should be added K. F. Müller, *Die israelitischen Anschauungen über die Beziehungen der Toten zu den Lebenden in der Zeit des Jahvismus* (unpubl. Diss. Kiel, 1920).

A. θάνατος in Greek Usage.

1. Classical Usage.

If according to a popular Greek view death does not end human existence to the degree that the dead lead a shadowy existence in Hades, this cannot be regarded as a life. For what is called life is destroyed by death, and none can talk away the terror of death (Hom. Od., 11, 487 ff.). Life is the supreme good.[1] Except for the idea of the translation of individual heroes to the isles of the blessed, for the belief in Orphic and Pythagorean circles that death is the liberation of the soul imprisoned in the body, and for the idea of the transmigration of the soul in the same circles, death is accepted as the end of life and therefore as something terrible,[2] for otherwise why should not the blessed gods die? (Sappho acc. to Aristot. Rhet., II, 23, p. 1398b, 27 ff.). That death is the general lot of men (as in the old saying, θανάτῳ πάντες ὀφειλόμεθα) is no comfort. The necessity of death casts its shadow on life and calls its meaning into question.[3] There is better comfort in the thought that life itself is a questionable good with its toil and

---

[1] Hes. Theog., 758 ff. on sleep and death. Sleep is described as a friend of man, τοῦ δὲ (sc. τοῦ θανάτου) σιδηρέη μὲν κραδίη, χάλκεον δέ οἱ ἦτορ νηλεὲς ἐν στήθεσσιν· ἔχει δ' ὃν πρῶτα λάβῃσιν ἀνθρώπων· ἐχθρὸς δὲ καὶ ἀθανάτοισι θεοῖσιν. Op., 116 of men of the Golden Age: θνῇσκον δ' ὥς θ' ὕπνῳ δεδμημένοι, 152 ff. of those of the Bronze Age: καὶ τοὶ μὲν χείρεσσιν ὕπο σφετέρῃσι δαμέντες βῆσαν ἐς εὐρώεντα δόμον κρυεροῦ Ἀΐδαο νώνυμνοι· θάνατος δὲ καὶ ἐκπάγλους (fearful) περ ἐόντας εἷλε μέλας, λαμπρὸν δ' ἔλιπον φάος ἠελίοιο. Cf. Sappho Fr., 58; Soph. Fr., 64: τὸ ζῆν γάρ, ὦ παῖ, παντὸς ἥδιστον γέρας. θανεῖν γὰρ οὐκ ἔξεστι τοῖς αὐτοῖσι δίς; Fr., 275: τὸν Ἀΐδαν γὰρ οὐδὲ γῆρας οἶδε φιλεῖν (TGF). Eur. Fr., 816, 10 f.: τὸ ζῆν γὰρ ἴσμεν, τοῦ θανεῖν δ' ἀπειρίᾳ πᾶς τις φοβεῖται φῶς λιπεῖν τόδ' ἡλίου (TGF). Iph. Aul., 1251 f.: μαίνεται δ' ὃς εὔχεται θανεῖν. κακῶς ζῆν κρεῖσσον ἢ καλῶς θανεῖν; 1416: ὁ θάνατος δεινὸν κακόν. Aristoph. Ra., 1394: θάνατος as βαρύτατον κακόν. On the Homeric conception of death as the realm of what has been, and on the sublimation of sorrow unto death, cf. W. F. Otto, op. cit.

[2] As distinct from → ζωή, n. 3, θάνατος is personified and represented in art. The depiction of ὕπνος and θάνατος as brothers (cf. Hom. Il., 16, 671 f., also 14, 231; Hes. Theog., 211 f., 756 ff.), which Lessing discusses in his Wie die Alten den Tod gebildet, is not characteristic of popular belief. In the well-known Lekythe representation ὕπνος is probably giving up the dead to the demon of the grave. Typical of popular belief is the conception of death as a terrifying demon in Eur. Alc., and the artistic representation of death is to be sought not merely in the rare direct presentation but also in depictions of the terrors and shades of the underworld which appear also on Etruscan vases. On the iconography of death, cf. C. Robert, Thanatos (Winckelmann-Programm) (1879); A. Adamek, Die Darstellung des Todes in der griech. Kunst und Lessings Schrift ... (1885); H. Ubell, Vier Kapitel vom Thanatos (1903); K. Heinemann, Thanatos in Poesie und Kunst der Griechen (Diss. München, 1913); F. P. Weber, Aspects of Death and Correlated Aspects of Life in Art, Epigram and Poetry⁴ (1922); also A. Man, Katalog der Bibliothek des Deutschen Archäol. Instituts in Rom (1932), II, 1093 f. J. Martha, L'Art Etrusque, II (1889), 394; P. Jacobsthal, "Göttinger Vasen," AGG, NF, XIV, 1 (1912), 8-10; F. Weege, Etrusk. Malerei (1921), 42 ff.; J. Kroll, Tod und Teufel in der Antike, Verhandlungen d. Versammlung deutscher Philologen u. Schulmänner, 56 (1927), 44 f.; L. Malten, "Das Pferd im Totenglauben," Jahrbuch des Kaiserlich. Deutsch. Archäol. Instituts, 29 (1914), 179-256. On the demon Eurynomos (Paus., X, 28, 7), cf. C. Robert, Die Nekyia des Polygnot (1892) and O. Kern in Pauly-W., VI (1909), s.v. Eurynomos.

[3] Pind. Pyth., 8, 96 f.: ... σκιᾶς ὄναρ ἄνθρωπος. Soph. Ai., 125 f.: ὁρῶ γὰρ ἡμᾶς οὐδὲν ὄντας ἄλλο πλὴν εἴδωλ', ὅσοιπερ ζῶμεν, ἢ κούφην σκιάν. Eur. Fr., 532 (TGF): The dead is γῆ and σκιά· τὸ μηδὲν εἰς οὐδὲν ῥέπει (sinks), cf. Fr., 638 (TGF) → ζωή II, 835. Rather different is Plat. Phileb., 51b on the mixture of joy and sorrow μὴ τοῖς δράμασι μόνον ἀλλὰ καὶ τῇ τοῦ βίου ξυμπάσῃ τραγῳδίᾳ καὶ κωμῳδίᾳ. The brevity of life is emphasised, e.g., on epitaphs, Epigr. Graec., 303, 3 f.; 699, 5 f.

tribulation, so that it can seem to be better never to have been born or, having been born, to die again. [4] Death does at least bring rest, [5] and suicide can be represented as a liberation from ignominy and suffering. [6] Yet when death comes, no one wants to die. [7] Nor is there any knowledge of what will come after death. [8]

But as the Homeric heroes hazard their lives for fame, [9] so κλέος (δόξα) offers the opportunity of bringing death as an act into life. Those who fall in glorious battle live on immortally in their renown on earth, [10] and perhaps the dead hear something of this renown. [11] But the ἀρετή (ἀνδρεία) which brings death upon itself does not always have to be accompanied by reflection concerning δόξα: οὐδὲ ζῆν ἂν ἐγὼ δεξαίμην δειλὸς ὤν, Plat. Alc., 115d. [12] Above all death is a great thing for the πόλις in which the κλέος lives on. [13] Thus καλῶς ἀποθνῄσκειν becomes the typically Greek conquest of θάνατος. [14]

If it thus appears that in Greek thought death is not originally understood as a natural phenomenon but as the particular lot of human existence with which we have all to reckon, it is equally typical of Greek thought that it tries to reckon with it by interpreting it as a natural phenomenon.

> For Ionic philosophy the vital force, the ψυχή, is immortal, but only as the force which indwells the κόσμος and which is the same in all the forms and changes in which it appears, among which are to be counted human life and death (→ ζωή, II, 833). The birth of one is the death of another, so that Heracl. Fr., 62 expressly relativises the antitheses life and death: ἀθάνατοι θνητοί, θνητοὶ ἀθάνατοι, ζῶντες τὸν ἐκείνων θάνατον, τὸν δὲ ἐκείνων βίον τεθνεῶτες (I, 89, 14 f., Diels).

The problem of death is treated by Euripides and Plato in a way which is representative of all Greek thinking.

---

[4] Rohde, II, 200; R. Hirzel, ARW, XI (1908), 86; esp. Theogn., 425 ff. Cf. the much varied statement: ὃν οἱ θεοὶ φιλοῦσιν ἀποθνῄσκει νέος.
[5] Aesch. Fr., 255 (TGF); Soph. Trach., 1173; Oed. Col., 955, 1225 ff.; Eur. Tro., 606 f., 634 ff.
[6] R. Hirzel, ARW, XI (1908), 75-104; 243-284; 417-476. Primarily Theogn., 173 ff.
[7] Eur. Alc., 669 ff.; Iph. Aul., 1252 f.; Lycophron Fr., 5 (TGF); Aesopicae Fabulae, 90, p. 44 (C. Halm, 1868): ὅτι πᾶς ἄνθρωπος φιλόζωος ἐν τῷ βίῳ, κἂν δυστυχῇ (vl. 90b, p. 44 f.: ὅτι πᾶς ἄνθρωπος, φιλόζωος ὤν, κἂν μυρίοις κινδύνοις περιπεσὼν δοκῇ θανάτου ἐπιθυμεῖν, ὅμως τὸ ζῆν πολὺ πρὸ τοῦ θανάτου αἱρεῖται).
[8] Eur. Hipp., 189 ff.; Fr., 816, 10 f.
[9] Hom. Il., 18, 115 ff.; 19, 420 ff.
[10] Tyrtaeus, 9, 31 f. (Diehl, I, 15); Pind. Isthm., 7, 27 ff.; 8, 56 ff.; Heracl. Fr., 24 and 25 (Diels, I, 82, 14 f.; 16 f.); Eur. Tro., 393 f.; Hel., 841.
[11] Rohde, II, 201, n. 4.
[12] Plat. Menex., 247d: It is better to be ἀγαθός than ἀθάνατος; cf. Eur. Iph. Taur., 502 and 674.
[13] Plat. Menex., 248c; Thuc., II, 41-44; Tyrtaeus, 6, 1 ff. (Diehl, I, 9 f.): τεθνάμεναι γὰρ καλὸν ἐνὶ προμάχοισι πεσόντα ἄνδρ' ἀγαθὸν περὶ ἧι πατρίδι μαρνάμενον.
[14] Soph. Ai., 473 ff.; Eur. Iph. Taur., 321 f.; Plat. Menex., 246d; Leg., 944c; Aristot. Eth. Nic., I, 8, p. 1169a, 18 ff.; Xenoph. Resp. Lac., 9, 1: αἱρετώτερον εἶναι τὸν καλὸν θάνατον ἀντὶ τοῦ αἰσχροῦ βίου. Hence suicide can acquire a heroic character, cf. Hirzel, op. cit.; F. Dornseiff, ARW, 22 (1923/24), 146 f. The way in which later scepticism dissolves this view may be seen, e.g., in Luc. Dialogi Mortuorum, 15, 2: Death levels all distinctions: ἰσηγορία δὲ ἀκριβὴς καὶ νεκρὸς ὅμοιος "ἠμὲν κακὸς ἠδὲ καὶ ἐσθλός". It remains: σιωπᾶν γὰρ καὶ φέρειν καὶ ἀνέχεσθαι δέδοκται ἡμῖν. In the Gk. world the thought is also widespread that the dead man lives on in his children, cf. Mimnermus Fr., 2, 13 ff. (Diehl, I, 40 f.), and for παῖδες alongside fame Hypereides, 6, 42 (p. 113, 9 ff., Jensen [1917]).

If Eur., too, not infrequently reproduces the natural view of the immortal world soul into which the individual soul passes at death,[15] he is also aware that this does not resolve the problem posed by individual death. He treats of this specifically in Alcestis, in which it is especially made plain that death is always my death in which none can represent me, which I cannot master by means of general considerations, for whose terror there is no comfort and which makes all life of doubtful value. The question introduced by this poem is whether death and life are values at all by which human conduct can be orientated and which determine its meaning.

A positive answer is given in Platonic philosophy. In the Apology it is first expressly denied that death and life are such values and that man can know whether death is an ἀγαθόν or a κακόν (29a). The problem of death is thus lifted into another sphere. We must ask concerning right or wrong (28b, 29b) rather than good or evil, and as this question is put to man's conduct he himself must answer it. Thus dying rather than death is what matters. It becomes an act. For it gives man another chance to show that he is good or bad and thus to pass the final test of obedience which God demands (28d; 38e ff.; 41d ff.). The Phaedo [16] goes even further, stating that the true philosophical outlook is a μελετᾶν ἀποθνῄσκειν (64a; 67e; 80e). It is thus clear how far death can be a test of life, i.e., not to the degree that it must be accepted as an inexplicable destiny at the end of a righteous life, but positively in the sense that the righteous life finds its fulfilment in the death towards which it constantly strives. For death affects only the σῶμα. The life of the philosopher consists, however, in liberation of the ψυχή from the σῶμα. If Plato finally adopts the figures of speech of the Orphic and Pythagorean tradition, he does not have in view the dualism of this tradition, since philosophical κάθαρσις is not asceticism but a positive attitude to life. The significance of that tradition is thus that it offers a means of expressing the thought that the true life of man is not a natural phenomenon. The distinctive character of this life is to be won in the battle against ἐπιθυμίαι and ἡδοναί and in the service of ἀρετή (φρόνησις) (82c; 107c d; 114c). True ζωή is not given; it is proposed. Death, however, is a natural process and belongs to the sphere of the given. If, then, true life is a liberation from the body, the philosopher need not fear the end of physical existence in death. He has no certainty that the soul will live on, but there is a μεγάλη ἐλπίς (114c d). This hope, and therefore the attempts to prove immortality, are not the basis of the philosophical attitude to death. They derive from it. The belief in immortality is thus a venture (κίνδυνος, 114d). What is unconditionally binding, however, is the demand for ἀρετή, and this forbids us to regard the soul as something corporeal, life as a natural process and death as a mere phenomenon of nature.

These motifs all exert an influence in the period which follows. When Aristot. analyses ζωή as a natural phenomenon (→ ζωή, II, 833), this means that for him death can only be a natural phenomenon. In it the ψυχή is extinguished, i.e., the vital force of the physical organism. Since this can exist only with the organism, it comes to an end in death. But the νοῦς which has come θύραθεν into the ψυχή is immortal. This separates itself from the σῶμα and the ψυχή at death. There is complete obscurity,

---

[15] Rohde, II, 247 ff.
[16] A. Tumarkin, *Rheinisches Museum*, NF, 75 (1926), 58-83. I cannot wholly accept the view (cf. P. Natorp, *Platos Ideenlehre*[2] [1921]) that for Plato the immortality of the soul is only a figure for the supratemporality of the idea. Cf. P. Friedländer, *Platon*, II (1930), 321-344.

however, concerning the nature of its continued existence. [17] Yet this does not prevent Aristot., too, from understanding death as an act. [18]

2. Hellenistic Usage.

a. Stoicism. In Stoicism death is expressly regarded as a natural phenomenon, though in the same inconsistent manner as ζωή (→ II, 837 f.).

As a natural phenomenon it is an ἀδιάφορον. But each individual must accept it as such. Death becomes an ethical problem or an ethical act. [19] Here again death is always my own, and if the admonition to μελετᾶν ἀποθνήσκειν is again adopted and developed, it is with the distinctive feature that the μελετᾶν consists for the most part in the fact that man must be aware of himself as a natural creature and of death as an indifferent natural process. [20] This self-education is made easier by the fact that natural ζωή and its apparent goods are not merely characterised as ἀδιάφορα but that, in a readoption of older motifs, the goods of life, and the body in its worthlessness and shame and with all its toil and tribulation, are regarded pessimistically, a pessimistic view of history being also developed. [21] This conception finds clear expression in the justification of suicide. [22] But when it is demanded that this ἐξαγωγή must be an εὔλογος, [23] and when philosophy is defined as the art of right living and dying, [24] an ethical view competes with the materialistic and pessimistic. For ζωή and θάνατος are again regarded as mine, so that I am responsible for them, and Epict. especially can warn against light-hearted suicide. [25] This μελετᾶν can again be given a positive sense in Epict. and M. Ant., as in Plato. Death is the test of right conduct, [26] and the μελετᾶν is accomplished in turning from external things and ἐπιστρέφειν εἰς ἑαυτόν, [27] which leads to the grateful acceptance of destiny, by which God blesses and instructs man, and to the acceptance of moral responsibility in the exercise of ἀρετή and (esp. in M. Ant.) in the knowledge ὅτι ἀλλήλων ἕνεκεν γεγόναμεν, [28] in εὔνοια and εὐμένεια to neighbours. [29] Thus the death which awaits us and which casts its shadow over the whole of life serves the positive purpose of giving direction to life. [30] For οὐδεὶς ἄλλον ἀποβάλλει βίον ἢ τοῦτον, ὃν ζῇ, οὐδὲ ἄλλον ζῇ ἢ ὃν ἀποβάλλει (M. Ant., 2, 14, p. 18, 14 ff.; cf. Sen. Ep., 69, 6). Regard for death, therefore, leads to the resolute acceptance of ἐν χερσί, of παρόν, [31] and it is of no consequence how long life is. In this case man is well-prepared when death strikes, [32] and this readiness is expressly opposed by M. Ant., 11, 3 (p. 137, 22 ff.) to the Christian readiness for death.

---

[17] Rohde, II, 301-309.
[18] Eth. Nic., I, 8, p. 1169a, 18 ff. (ὑπεραποθνήσκειν for πατρίς or φίλοι is a καλόν).
[19] E. Benz, Das Todesproblem in der stoischen Philosophie (1929).
[20] R. Bultmann, ZNW, 13 (1912), 108 f.; cf. M. Ant., 2, 12 and 17; 4, 5; 8, 25; 11, 20 (p. 17, 15 ff.; 20, 7 ff.; 34, 12 ff.; 98, 13 ff.; 146, 1 ff.); also Epic. in Diog. L., X, 126, 126 and 139.
[21] Benz, op. cit., 59 ff.
[22] Ibid., 54 ff.
[23] Ibid., 68 ff.; Hirzel, op. cit., 281.
[24] Benz, op. cit., 83 ff.
[25] Ibid., 76 ff.; Diss., I, 9, 24.
[26] Benz, op. cit., 86 ff.
[27] Ibid., 79 ff.; cf. Sen. Ep., 1, 1 (vindica te tibi).
[28] M. Ant., 8, 56; 11, 18 (p. 106, 18 f.; 143, 4).
[29] οἱ πλησίον, cf. M. Ant., 11, 1 (p. 137, 9): ἴδιον δὲ λογικῆς ψυχῆς καὶ τὸ φιλεῖν τοὺς πλησίον. 6, 30 (p. 69, 13 ff.): βραχὺς ὁ βίος· εἷς καρπὸς τῆς ἐπιγείου ζωῆς διάθεσις ὁσία καὶ πράξεις κοινωνικαί.
[30] M. Ant., 2, 5 and 11; 5, 29; 7, 56 (p. 14, 16 ff.; 16, 13 ff.; 59, 1 ff.; 88, 16 f.).
[31] M. Ant., 2, 5 and 14; 3, 10 and 12; 6, 2; 10, 1; 12, 35 (p. 14, 12 ff.; 18, 17 ff.; 28, 5; 29, 11; 62, 8; 122, 12 ff.; 158, 21 ff.).
[32] Epict. Diss., III, 5, 5-11; IV, 1, 103-110; 10, 8-17; M. Ant., 6, 30 (p. 70, 7 f.), etc. Cf. also Bultmann, ZNW, 13 (1912), 108-110.

One can hardly say that here in Epict. and M. Ant. the present in which life is to acquire its distinctive quality dissolves into timelessness. It is characteristic, however, that the present is never regarded here in its relationship to the past, to my past. Since man is not seen to be bound by guilt and sin, he is free in respect of death. He can master its terrors, because death need never assume the character of a judgment on him.

If the true reality of life is not threatened by death, it is menaced by the perversion which consists in an unphilosophical outlook, in the abandonment of ἀρετή and in surrender to external life and its goods. And since this constitutes a threat to real life, it can be described as death or dying and the body and external goods as dead. Indeed, men who are not awakened to the philosophical life are called dead (νεκρός), as are also their relationships to life. [33]

b. Neo-Platonism. This usage is also proper to Hellen. dualism. For Plotinus bodily life is θάνατος for the ψυχή : αὐτῇ καὶ ἔτι ἐν τῷ σώματι βεβαπτισμένη ἐν ὕλῃ ἐστὶ καταδῦναι καὶ πλησθῆναι αὐτῆς, i.e., to sink in wickedness. [34] Plotin. is not, of course, a consistent dualist, since he ascribes positive tasks to the ψυχή in its connection with the σῶμα. Only for the φαῦλος is this earthly ζωή an absolute κακόν. [35] But in any case corporeal ζωή is only a shadow (ἴχνος) of ἀληθινὴ ζωή, [36] and the body is for the soul a chain and a grave. [37] The soul attains to its true life as it is progressively released from the body. [38] For this reason physical death is the objective disjunction of σῶμα and ψυχή. [39] Far from being a κακόν, it is an ἀγαθόν, for (as in Plato) it completes that for which the soul strives. [40] Nevertheless, suicide is rejected as an illegitimate means of helping oneself towards this goal. [41]

c. Gnosticism. In the dualistic parts of the Corp. Herm. physical life is regarded far more radically as true death in which true ζωή cannot develop, so that physical death is release, as in Gnosticism generally. [42] Here, however, true life is not understood in the philosophical sense ; it is simply the immortality of divine life (→ ζωή, II, 838 f.). Hence the transition to this ζωή is an organic transition only in so far as earthly life

---

[33] The σωμάτιον of man is a νεκρόν (Epict. Diss., II, 9, 27); the false philosopher is dead like his word (Diss., III, 23, 28). Earthly νόμοι are νόμοι τῶν νεκρῶν (Diss., I, 13, 5), and those who cling to bodily life are νεκροί (Diss., I, 9, 19; cf. also I, 3, 3; 5, 7; M. Ant., 2, 12; 4, 41: ψυχάριον εἶ, βαστάζον νεκρόν; 9, 24 : πνευμάτια νεκροὺς βαστάζοντα; 10, 33; 12, 33). We have the image of the chaining of the soul to a corpse in Cicero's Hortensius in Aug. Contra Julianum Pelagianum, V, 78 (MPL, 44, 778). This usage, which is prefigured in Orphic and Pythagorean mysticism and varied in Plato (σῶμα-σῆμα), is particularly developed in Sen., cf. Sen. Ep., 1, 2 : Who is it *qui intellegat se cotidie mori?* *in hoc enim fallimur, quod mortem prospicimus : magna pars eius iam praeteriit. quicquid aetatis retro est, mors tenet.* Benz, 98 ff.; J. Kroll, *Die Lehren des Hermes Trismegistos* (1914), 345, → ζωή, II, 838. A different point is made, of course, when Eur. Hel., 285 f. says that the unhappy are as good as dead.
[34] Enn., I, 8, 13, p. 112, 15 ff.
[35] I, 7, 3, p. 98, 12 ff.
[36] VI, 9, 9, p. 521, 2.
[37] IV, 8, 3 and 4, p. 146, 6; 148, 4.
[38] I, 7, 3, cf. P. O. Kristeller, *Der Begriff der Seele in der Ethik des Plot.* (1929), 16 ff.; cf. also Porphyr. Abst., I, 41.
[39] I, 6, 6; I, 9, p. 92, 1 f.; 115, 18 ff. etc.
[40] I, 6, 6; I, 7, 3, p. 92, 1 ff.; 98, 12 ff.; cf. also Ps.-Plat. Ax., 366a b.
[41] I, 9.
[42] Corp. Herm., I, 28, 29 (those who do not understand the preaching of repentance are τῇ τοῦ θανάτου ὁδῷ ἑαυτοὺς ἐκδεδωκότες); VII, 2 (πρῶτον δὲ δεῖ σε περιρρήξασθαι ὃν φορεῖς χιτῶνα ... τὸν ζῶντα θάνατον, τὸν αἰσθη<τι>κὸν νεκρόν, τὸν περιφόρητον τάφον ...).

is mortified by asceticism. [43] As in the mystery religions, which to a large extent underlie Gnosticism, ἀθανασία or ἀφθαρσία is secured through sacraments, i.e., through mystical and ecstatic experiences in which original sacraments are spiritualised. [44] When the soul puts off the σῶμα in the mystery of παλιγγενεσία [45] or in the ascent to heaven, [46] it attains to ζωή. [47]

d. Philo. On the OT and Jewish conception of death → ζωή, II, 849, 855. In Philo we often find Stoic and Neo-Platonic usage as in the case of ζωή. Τὸ ἀψευδῶς ζῆν corresponds πρὸς ἀλήθειαν τεθνάναι. [48] This is falling victim to αἰσθητὰ σώματα and πράγματα which are "not alive." [49] Thus Cain dies continually in his bodily life [50] because he is the victim of λύπη and φόβος. Similarly θάνατος is the result of ἡδονή; [51] the wicked are ἔτι ζῶντες νεκροί. [52]

On the other hand physical death, χωρισμὸς ψυχῆς ἀπὸ σώματος, [53] is an ἀγαθόν or an ἀδιάφορον. [54] In this sense Philo distinguishes a διττὸς θάνατος. [55] In fact, however, he uses ζωή and θάνατος in three senses, [56] since he also speaks of the ascetic ἀποθνήσκειν θνητῆς ζωῆς which corresponds to the attainment of ἄφθαρτος βίος. [57] Γένεσις γὰρ τῶν καλῶν θάνατος αἰσχρῶν ἐπιτηδευμάτων ἐστίν (Deus Imm., 123). And in this sense Philo varies the Platonic μελετᾶν ἀποθνήσκειν and characterises the souls of true philosophers: μελετῶσαι τὸν μετὰ σωμάτων ἀποθνήσκειν βίον, ἵνα τῆς ἀσωμάτου καὶ ἀφθάρτου παρὰ τῷ

---

[43] On asceticism cf. Corp. Herm., IV, 5 f.; VI, 3; VII, 2 f.; X, 15; XI, 20 f.; Ascl. 22 (Scott, I, 336, 15 ff.). J. Kroll, op. cit., 341 f.; 347, n. 4; Reitzenstein Hell. Myst. passim (v. Index).

[44] This is factually so even when acc. to cosmological and anthropological theory man carries within him from the very first a divine spark (Corp. Herm., I, 15; cf. Jul. Or., 7, 234 C: μέμνησο οὖν ὅτι τὴν ψυχὴν ἀθάνατον ἔχεις ...). He must come to see again that he is ἀθάνατος by divine revelation. On the rivalry of anthropological motifs cf. W. Bousset, GGA, 1914, 724-732. On belief in immortality in the mysteries, magic and Gnosticism, cf. Reitzenstein, op. cit., 11 ff., 19 ff., 27, 30 f., 39 ff., 109 f., 220 ff., 253, 289 f. etc.; F. Cumont, Die orient. Religionen im röm. Heidentum³ (1931), 39 ff. etc.

[45] Corp. Herm., XIII, 3; cf. 14: τὸ αἰσθητὸν τῆς φύσεως σῶμα πόρρωθέν ἐστι [τῆς] <τοῦ> οὐσιώδους [γενέσεως]· τὸ μὲν γάρ ἐστι διαλυτόν, τὸ δὲ ἀδιάλυτον, καὶ τὸ μὲν θνητόν, τὸ δὲ ἀθάνατον. Cf. Κόρη κόσμου, § 41 (Scott, I, 478, 29 ff.).

[46] Corp. Herm., I, 24-26. J. Kroll, op. cit. (Index: "Himmelfahrt der Seele"); Die Himmelfahrt der Seele in der Antike (1930); Gott u. Hölle (1932) (Index: "Ascensus"); W. Bousset, ARW, 4 (1901), 136 ff., 229 ff.; Mithr. Liturg., 179 ff.

[47] There then comes the καρποφορεῖν of the ἀγαθὰ ἐκ τῆς ἀληθείας, of ἀθάνατα γεννήματα, Corp. Herm., XIII, 22.

[48] Rer. Div. Her., 201.

[49] Ibid., 242; Gig., 15: ἐπὶ τὸν συμφυᾶ νεκρὸν ἡμῶν, τὸ σῶμα; cf. Leg. All., I, 108. Hence νεκροφορεῖν of the ψυχή which is borne by the νεκρὸν σῶμα, Leg. All., III, 69 and 74; Agric., 25 etc. → ζωή, II, 860.

[50] Ζῆν ἀποθνήσκοντα ἀεί, Praem. Poen., 70 f., also the paradoxical θάνατος ἀθάνατος, cf. Poster. C., 44 f.: ἀεὶ τὸν πρὸς ἀρετὴν βίον θνήσκοντα. In this sense the variation of the saying of Heraclitus, → II, 860.

[51] Agric., 98.

[52] Som., II, 66; Rer. Div. Her., 290. Spec. Leg., I, 345: ὄντως γὰρ οἱ μὲν ἄθεοι τὰς ψυχὰς τεθνᾶσιν.

[53] Leg. All., I, 105 etc.; cf. Leisegang, s.v. θάνατος 1.

[54] Praem. Poen., 70.

[55] Leg. All., I, 105; Praem. Poen., 70, cf. Benz, 95 ff.

[56] Sometimes, indeed, he can use θάνατος in yet another sense, Conf. Ling., 36 f. on Ex. 14:30: θάνατον λέγων οὐ τὴν ἀπὸ σώματος ψυχῆς διάκρισιν, ἀλλὰ τὴν ἀνοσίων δογμάτων καὶ λόγων φθοράν ... λόγου δὲ θάνατός ἐστιν ἡσυχία.

[57] Fug., 59; Det. Pot. Ins., 49: ὁ μὲν δὴ σοφὸς τεθνηκέναι δοκῶν τὸν φθαρτὸν βίον ζῇ τὸν ἄφθαρτον, ὁ δὲ φαῦλος ζῶν τὸν ἐν κακίᾳ τέθηκε τὸν εὐδαίμονα.

ἀγεννήτῳ καὶ ἀφθάρτῳ ζωῆς μεταλάχωσιν (Gig., 14; 56).[58] For this reason true ζωή (→ II, 860) is for Philo not merely virtuous life in an ideal eternity but life which is temporally incorruptible. It is thus natural that true θάνατος should be eternal destruction.[59]

B. The Concept of Death in the NT.

1. In the NT ἀποθνήσκειν (perf.: τέθνηκα without ἀπο-) and τελευτᾶν are first and most often used for the process of dying (pres. "to be dying," aor. "to die," perf. "to be dead"), and θάνατος (once τελευτή, Mt. 2:15)[60] means dying (e.g., Hb. 7:23) or being dead (e.g., Phil. 1:20). Death is the lot of all men,[61] being remote only from God and His world (1 Tm. 6:16; 1 C. 15:53 f.). It is a dreadful thing[62] which man fears[63] and which he will seek only in the most terrible circumstances (Rev. 9:6). It is never portrayed in heroic terms, and if Paul recognises that there may be heroic death and that this stands in some analogy to Christ's death (R. 5:7), Christ's death is not interpreted as a heroic achievement (→ 18), nor is the sacrifice of death which the apostle brings for others (2 C. 4:12), nor the faithfulness of martyrs unto death (Rev. 2:10; 12:11). For it is not suggested that the one who makes the offering neutralises death so far as he personally is concerned. It is characteristic that suicide is never treated as a problem.[64] Death is always the terrible thing which makes ζωή improper ζωή (→ ζωή, II, 863)[65] and the work of Christ is to have destroyed death (2 Tm. 1:10; → 19). Death is the ἔσχατος ἐχθρός with whose definitive destruction the work of salvation is fully accomplished (1 C. 15:26; Rev. 20:14).

[58] Sometimes there emerges (as in the case of ζωή) a dualistic conception which goes beyond that of Stoicism, e.g., Leg. All., I, 108, where the saying of Heraclitus (→ II, 834, n. 12) is expounded: ὡς νῦν μέν, ὅτε ζῶμεν, τεθνηκυίας τῆς ψυχῆς καὶ ὡς ἂν ἐν σήματι, τῷ σώματι ἐντετυμβευμένης (buried), εἰ δὲ ἀποθάνοιμεν, τῆς ψυχῆς ζώσης τὸν ἴδιον βίον καὶ ἀπηλλαγμένης κακοῦ καὶ νεκροῦ συνδέτου τοῦ σώματος.

[59] Ἀΐδιος θάνατος, Poster. C., 39; cf. Plant., 37; 45; Migr. Abr., 189 etc.

[60] The NT also uses κοιμᾶσθαι for "to die," e.g., Jn. 11:11; Ac. 7:60; 13:36; 1 C. 7:39 etc. (also the post-apost. fathers), v. Pr.-Bauer; similarly οἱ κοιμώμενοι (1 Th. 4:13) or οἱ κεκοιμημένοι (1 C. 15:20) means those who have passed away. In Gk. κοιμᾶσθαι is used for the sleep of death from the time of Homer; cf. also inscr. and the pap. (v. Liddell-Scott; Pr.-Bauer, s.v.; Radermacher², 108). It is also used in the LXX in the same sense for שָׁכַב ("to lie down," "to lay oneself down"), e.g., Gn. 47:30; 2 Βασ. 7:12; 3 Βασ. 2:10. The Rabbis have a similar expression for those who have passed away, i.e., "to sleep" (usually יָדַם, v. Str.-B., I, 1040 on Mt. 27:45; Schl. Mt., 784; Schl. J., 249) or "those who have fallen on sleep" (דְמִכַיָּא, Str.-B., III, 634). The subst., which Jn. 11:13 uses both of the κοίμησις τοῦ ὕπνου and of death, is also used in Gk. for the sleep of death (Audollent Def. Tab., 242, 30; R. Wünsch, Antike Fluchtafeln = Kl. T., 20 [1907], 4, 30). Cf. also LXX Sir. 46:19; 48:13;; Roman Jewish graves; Herm. v., 3, 11, 3; s., 9, 15, 6 (Pr.-Bauer). Cf. also Lidz. Joh., 168, 6 f.

[61] Jn. 6:49, 58; 8:52 f.; Hb. 7:8; 9:27. We are enslaved to death acc. to Barn., 16, 9. Exceptions are Enoch in Hb. 11:5 and Melchisedec in Hb. 7:3, 16 f. The human σῶμα is a θνητόν, R. 6:12; 8:11; 1 C. 15:53 f.; cf. 2 C. 4:11; 5:4; 1 Cl., 39, 2 : τί γὰρ δύναται θνητός; ἢ τίς ἰσχὺς γηγενοῦς; Death is also mentioned in respect of animals (Mt. 8:32 etc.) and plants (Jn. 12:24; 1 C. 15:36, though cf. Jd. 12).

[62] Rev. 6:8; 18:8; Herm. s., 6, 2, 4 : ὁ δὲ θάνατος ἀπώλειαν ἔχει αἰώνιον. We find old expressions like "sickness unto death" (Phil. 2:27, 30; Jn. 11:4; cf. Rev. 13, 3, 12), "sorrowful unto death" (Mk. 14:34 and par.) and "persecution unto death" (Ac. 22:4; 1 Cl., 4, 9; cf. 5, 2). Naturally death can also be imposed as a human punishment (Mk. 10:33 f. etc.). For θάνατος in the sense of mortal peril cf. 2 C. 1:10; 11:23.

[63] Hb. 2:15; cf. R. 8:15.

[64] On Augustine's criticism of the Stoic conception of suicide cf. Benz, 119 ff.

[65] We find the antithesis θάνατος/ἀλήθεια in Ign. Sm., 5, 1.

No attempt is made to interpret death as a natural process and thus to neutralise it. Even where it is seen to be defeated by the resurrection and death and resurrection are described in terms of an analogy from nature (1 C. 15:36; Jn. 12:24), it is no more regarded as a natural process than is the resurrection. The process in view in the analogy is not to be regarded as a natural process in the sense of Greek science. The Whence? and Wherefore? of death can be understood mythologically with death as a demonic person (1 C. 15:26; Rev. 6:8; 20:13 f.) or the devil as the lord of death (Hb. 2:14; on both → ζωή, II, 858). But the point of these mythologoumena, [66] which are not aetiological, is to express the fact that death is opposed to life as the true being of God (→ ζωή, II, 863) and therewith also that sin and death belong together.

2. Death is the consequence and punishment of sin. [67] The question of the origin of death is thus the question of the origin of sin, and, as in the corresponding understanding of → ἁμαρτία, this question is not treated speculatively. It is true, of course, that some of the statements of Paul in which he adopts the Gnostic *anthropos* myth (→ ζωή, II, 866 f.) have a speculative tendency. In his conception of Adam and Christ as the original men who determine humanity he goes beyond the Jewish conception of Adam (→ ζωή, II, 856; → 'Αδάμ), and death (and sin) and life are presented as cosmic powers. Nevertheless, the speculative conception is diverted to a different end in R. 5:12 ff., for sin is consistently regarded as a responsible act and death as its consequence. 1 C. 15:21 f. must be taken in the same sense. In 1 C. 15:44-49, however, it sounds as though Adamic humanity was created subject to death from the very first. Adam was only ψυχὴ ζῶσα, whereas Christ is πνεῦμα ζωοποιοῦν; Adam was ἐκ γῆς χοϊκός, Christ ἐξ οὐρανοῦ ἐπουράνιος. If Paul means this strictly, he is distinguishing true θάνατος from mere mortality, which does not have the character of θάνατος. He does not say this expressly, but he certainly says that death came into the world through Adam (1 C. 15:22), i.e., through Adam's sin (R. 5:12, 17 f.). [68] This cannot be taken speculatively, since Paul is not trying to excuse the individual by this statement. He insists that for each man death is the punishment of his own sin. [69] And if in R. 5:14, in at least formal contradiction of R. 1:18 ff., he speaks as if men in the time from Adam to Moses were responsible only for their death as the consequence of their sin but not for their ἁμαρτάνειν after the manner of Adam, since they did not transgress any specific command (→ ἁμαρτάνω, → ἐλλογέω), it is clear 1. that Paul is not attributing sin to something which is not sin (e.g., matter, sensuality etc.) but that he is saying that sin came into the world through sin,

---

[66] There is perhaps a mythical allusion in 2 C. 11:3, cf. Ltzm. K. and Wnd. 2 K., *ad loc.* It is worth noting that there is no reference to the mythical figures of death and the devil in R. 5:12 ff.

[67] This conviction is common to the NT and Judaism, → ζωή, II, 856. Cf. R. 1:32; 6:16, 21, 23; 7:5 (καρποφορῆσαι τῷ θανάτῳ); 8:6, 13; 1 C. 15:56 (τὸ δὲ κέντρον τοῦ θανάτου ἡ ἁμαρτία); Jm. 1:15 (ἡ δὲ ἁμαρτία ἀποτελεσθεῖσα ἀποκύει θάνατον); cf. Gl. 6:7 f.; 2 C. 7:10; Jn. 8:21, 24; 1 Jn. 5:16 f.; Barn., 12, 2 and 5; 1 Cl., 3, 4; 2 Cl., 1, 6; Herm. v., 2, 3, 1; m., 2, 1; 12, 6, 2; s., 8, 8, 5; 8, 11, 3 etc. Individual sins are called παγὶς θανάτου in Did., 2, 4; Barn., 19, 7 f.; cf. in the OT Prv. 14:27; 21:6 etc.

[68] There is allusion in 2 C. 11:3 and 1 Tm. 2:14 (cf. also Barn., 12, 5) to the thought of the guilt of Eve, which is also found in Judaism (→ ζωή, n. 191).

[69] The ἐφ' ᾧ πάντες ἥμαρτον of R. 5:12 must bear this sense; cf. → n. 67 and on R. 5:12-21 generally cf. J. Freundorfer, "Erbsünde und Erbtod" (*Nt.liche Abhandlungen,* XIII, 1/2 [1927], 216 ff.).

and 2. that Paul in his preaching has in view only men who are responsible for their sin and therefore for their death. To the extent that speculative thoughts are applied in R. 5 and 1 C. 15 they serve only to bring out the ineluctability of sin and death for man and the fact that there is salvation only in Christ. They do not take away man's responsibility but show rather that man cannot stand by himself in his responsibility before God, → ἀμαρτία.

This is shown also by the second answer which Pl. gives to the Whence? of death. If sin is the κέντρον τοῦ θανάτου, it is also true that ἡ δὲ δύναμις τῆς ἀμαρτίας ὁ νόμος (1 C. 15:56). The Law is what actually effects death (→ νόμος). Its letter kills (2 C. 3:6), so that the office of the Law is called the διακονία τοῦ θανάτου (2 C. 3:7; v. 9: διακονία τῆς κατακρίσεως). As Adam's disobedience to God's command caused death (R. 5:12 ff.), and as pagan humanity fell victim to the mortal wrath of God because it knew and transgressed His just requirement (δικαίωμα, R. 1:32), so it is true of post-Mosaic Israel that the Law brought death because by it the sin slumbering in man was awakened (R. 7:5, 10, 13). Pl. undoubtedly means to establish man's responsibility and the penal character of death without making it appear that liberation from death is a human possibility. For this reason he traces back mortal sin to the σάρξ, which characterises the actual being of man. The → σάρξ, however, is not evil matter in the Gnostic sense. It is not a prison of the soul or a demonic power to which man is subject with no personal responsibility. It is man himself in his lost and guilty state, namely, man in so far as he understands himself in terms of the sphere of the σάρξ, i.e., of the visible and demonstrable (R. 2:28 f.; 2 C. 4:18), whether in the form of natural phenomena, of historical circumstances or of palpable achievements. [70] Since all these are corruptible and under the sway of death, so the man who seeks life in them is from the very outset subject to death. But this is the manner of man. He wants to live of himself and not of God. Hence he can only be of the σάρξ. In this way Paul establishes the relationship between flesh, sin and death and therewith the relationship between the Law and death. Every attempt of man to effect his own escape from death and to merit life by his achievements is simply another effort to live of himself, and it thus entangles him the more in sin and death, so that even the Law, which ought to lead him to life, leads him to death (R. 7:10). He cannot liberate himself. [71]

Though we do not find in Jn. the same explicit lines of thought as in Pl., his teaching is implicitly the same. Outside revelation in Jesus the human race is given up to death, and it is responsible for this because it is sinful. Its sin is simply that it will not understand itself in its creatureliness from the standpoint of its Creator (Jn. 1:4 f., → ζωή, II, 870). It seeks rather to understand itself in terms of itself. This is shown in the fact that in relation to God it thinks it has criteria by which His revelation must be proved (5:31 ff.; 8:13 ff.), that it thinks it is free (8:33) and that instead of asking concerning God's glory it establishes its own standards of glory (5:41 ff.). It is thus in sin and death (8:21-24, 34-47).

3. There is not complete unanimity in NT statements on the question how far death finds its true character in the fact that it destroys, and how far in the fact that it involves future torment. Sometimes traditional Jewish conceptions of the punishments of hell predominate (Mk. 9:48; Lk. 16:23 etc., → ᾅδης, γέεννα). In any case, however, it is accepted that God or Christ is the κριτὴς ζώντων καὶ

---

[70] Cf. R. Bultmann, RGG², IV, 1034 f.

[71] R. 7:24, cf. R. Bultmann in *Imago Dei, Festschr. f. G. Krüger* (1932), 53-62.

νεκρῶν (→ ζωή, II, 862), that physical death is not the final end but is followed by the judgment (Hb. 9:27) and that physical death is thus either reversed by the resurrection or, if only the resurrection of the righteous is expected, it is followed by a period of torment in hell.[72] Pl. seems to have expected more than a resurrection of the righteous, for, though 1 C. 15:22-24; 1 Th. 4:15 ff. could be taken in that sense, it is refuted by R. 2:5-13, 16; 2 C. 5:10. On the intermediate state between death and the resurrection the NT gives us no explicit information. It is thought of as a sleep (→ n. 60) unless the various authors suggest other conceptions.[73] In any case physical death becomes quite definitively death through God's judgment. Hence we sometimes find the expression δεύτερος θάνατος (Rev. 2:11; 20:6, 14; 21:8).[74] Implied are the torments of hell (Rev. 21:8 : ἐν τῇ λίμνῃ τῇ καιομένῃ πυρὶ καὶ θείῳ). Where these are regarded as the true judgment of death, they are never depicted along the lines of Jewish or Orphic conceptions of the underworld. The true curse of death is always destruction, and φθορά and ἀπώλεια characterise this end.[75]

More important is the fact that the destructive power of death is thought to rule life even now and to rob it of its true quality (→ ζωή, II, 863). The death which awaits us holds life in φόβος (Hb. 2:15; R. 8:15) and those to whom Jesus is sent are regarded as καθήμενοι ἐν χώρᾳ καὶ σκιᾷ θανάτου (Mt. 4:16; Lk. 1:79 quoting Is. 9:1). Life is always a life "for" (→ ζωή, II, 863) — whether for God or for death (R. 6:13-23). Only of the believer is it true that he lives and dies to the Lord (R. 14:7). But θάνατος finally reigns over what is carnal (R. 8:6), so that where there is no hope grounded in Christ the slogan is : φάγωμεν καὶ πίωμεν, αὔριον γὰρ ἀποθνήσκομεν (1 C. 15:32). The uncertainty of the morrow makes all concern useless (Mt. 6:25-34). No one knows whether he will be alive tomorrow (Lk. 12:16-21). Death stands not only behind hope and care but also behind the λύπη of the κόσμος (2 C. 7:10), and all the works of men are from the very first νεκρά (Hb. 9:14, → ζωή, II, 863). Thus men may be described in advance as νεκροί (Mt. 8:22 and par.). For they are sinners,[76] so that Pl. can say

---

[72] There is similar vacillation in Judaism (→ ζωή, II, 856 f.) whether the resurrection is general or partial. The latter is the view in Lk. 14:14, → ἀνάστασις, → ᾅδης, I, 147; cf. H. Molitor, "Die Auferstehung der Christen und Nichtchristen nach dem Ap. Pls." (Nt.liche Abhandlungen, XVI, 1 [1933], 53 ff.).

[73] → ᾅδης.

[74] On the conception of the second death in Judaism → ζωή, n. 198. There may be some influence of Egyptian ideas, G. Roeder, Urkunden zur Religion des alten Ägypten (1923), Index, s.v. sterben and Tod; F. Boll, Aus der Offenbarung Joh. (1914), 49, n. 1. It is common among the Mandaeans, cf. Lidz. Ginza, Index. Acc. to Oecumenius Comm. on Rev., p. 221 (ed. H. C. Hoskier, 1928) the πρῶτος θάνατος is ὁ αἰσθητός, ὁ χωρισμὸν ἔχων ψυχῆς καὶ σώματος, δεύτερος δὲ ὁ νοητὸς ὁ τῆς ἁμαρτίας (and shortly before : ὁ τῆς ἁμαρτίας καὶ τῆς τότε κολάσεως).

[75] → φθορά, e.g., Gl. 6:8; → ἀπώλεια, e.g., Phil. 3:19. Barn., 20, 1 speaks of the ὁδὸς ... θανάτου αἰωνίου μετὰ τιμωρίας, ἐν ᾗ ἐστιν τὰ ἀπολλύντα τὴν ψυχὴν αὐτῶν. Acc. to Herm. v., 1, 1, 18 the wicked bring down θάνατον καὶ αἰχμαλωτισμόν upon themselves.

[76] R. 6:11, 13; Col. 2:13; Eph. 2:1, 5; 5:14; though the usage is figur. in Lk. 15:24. For the use of νεκρός → ζωή, n. 267. When we read in Jm. 2:26 : ὥσπερ γὰρ τὸ σῶμα χωρὶς πνεύματος νεκρόν ἐστιν, this rests on a naive anthropological dichotomy, namely, that the σῶμα is dead if not filled with vital force. On the other hand, we find Hell. dualism in the νεκροφόρος of Ign. Sm., 5, 2, → n. 33 and 49. For this reason Ign. can also ask the Romans (R., 6, 2): μὴ ἐμποδίσητέ μοι ζῆσαι, μή θελήσητέ με ἀποθανεῖν, they are not to prevent his martyrdom. Hell. terminology also underlies the opposing of ὄντως θάνατος to δοκῶν ἐνθάδε θάνατος in Dg., 10, 7.

in R. 7:10 : (ἐλθούσης δὲ τῆς ἐντολῆς) ἡ ἁμαρτία ἀνέζησεν, ἐγὼ δὲ ἀπέθανον, and in 7:24 he can call his σῶμα a σῶμα τοῦ θανάτου. Again, in 1 Jn. 3:14 it can be said of the false Christian who has no love that he abides in death. Men are dead outside revelation (Jn. 5:21, 25).

4. Death as a destroying power is thus suspended over human life and there is no evading it outside revelation. But in revelation, i.e., through Christ, God has destroyed death (2 Tm. 1:10; Hb. 2:14; → ζωή, II, 865). Christ's death and resurrection are the eschatological event. His death differed from the ordinary lot of men. It was the death which God caused Him to die for us. It was not His debt to sin. God made Him to be sin for us and He was condemned as such (2 C. 5:21; R. 8:3; Gl. 3:13 f.). Hence He died for us. [77] In this context we need not discuss the question how far the ideas of sin-offering and substitution are normative in such statements, nor what may be the influence of the mystery religions (cf. the commentaries). The controlling thought is that God deals with the world through Christ (2 C. 5:19), and that inasmuch as in this action God took death to Himself in Christ it lost its destructive character and became a creative divine act. Thus the resurrection is grounded in Christ's death. This death removed sin and it therefore removed death. [78] Life grew out of it. As Christ was dead, so He became alive (R. 8:34; 14:9; 1 Th. 4:14). Death could not hold Him (Ac. 2:24). He now has the keys of death and of Hades (Rev. 1:18). As He gave His life freely, so He took it again (Jn. 10:18). Because He humbled Himself to the death of the cross, God has highly exalted Him (Phil. 2:6-11). Death is overcome for those who make this death their own in faith, so that Christ can be called the πρωτότοκος (ἐκ) τῶν νεκρῶν (Col. 1:18; Rev. 1:5; cf. R. 8:29).

Believers are still subject, of course, to physical death, though in the early days of imminent expectation of the *parousia* it is seen that this fate will not overtake all Christians (Mk. 9:1; 1 Th. 4:15 ff.; 1 C. 15:51 f.). The destruction of death will come with the resurrection or with the change which comes with the *parousia*. When the expected events of the last time are completed, there will be no more death (1 Cor. 15:26; Rev. 21:4). Even now death has lost its sting for believers. They already have the victory (1 C. 15:55). As impending death negates the whole life of unbelievers, so the awaiting resurrection gives a new character to the whole of life. Thus we find in Jn. the strong expressions that believers will not die (6:50;

---

[77] Christ's death ὑπὲρ ἀσεβῶν, R. 5:6; ὑπὲρ ἡμῶν (ὑμῶν), R. 5:8; (1 C. 1:13; 11:24); 2 C. 5:21; Gl. 3:13; Eph. 5:2; Tt. 2:14; 1 Pt. (2:21); 4:1; 1 Jn. 3:16; Ign. R., 6, 1; Pol., 9, 2. ὑπὲρ ἐμοῦ, Gl. 2:20 (cf. R. 14:15). ὑπὲρ πολλῶν, Mk. 14:24 (cf. 10:45). ὑπὲρ ἀδίκων, 1 Pt. 3:18. ὑπὲρ πάντων, R. 8:32; 2 C. 5:14 f.; 1 Tm. 2:6 (cf. Hb. 2:9). ὑπὲρ αὐτῆς (τῆς ἐκκλησίας), Eph. 5:25 (cf. Col. 1:24). ὑπὲρ (τῶν) ἁμαρτιῶν (ἡμῶν), 1 C. 15:3; Gl. 1:4; Hb. 10:12 (cf. 1 Pt. 3:18 : περὶ ἁμαρτιῶν). Various phrases with ὑπέρ, Jn. 6:51; 10:11, 15; 11:51 f.; 15:13; 17:19; 18:14. For a formal catena of such expressions, Dg., 9, 2. Corresponding phrases with περί (often as vl.), Mt. 26:28; R. 8:3; 1 Th. 5:10; 1 Pt. 3:18; 1 Jn. 2:2; 4:10. Expressions with διά, R. 3:25; 4:25; 1 C. 8:11; 2 C. 8:9; (1 Pt. 1:20); Ign. Tr., 2, 1. For other descriptions of the saving significance of the death of Christ, R. 3:24; Col. 1:20-22; 2:13 f. etc. → αἷμα, I, 174; → σταυρός. Cf. also Barn., 5, 6; 7, 2 (ἵνα ἡ πληγὴ αὐτοῦ ζωοποιήσῃ ἡμᾶς) and the variations on the theme in Ign. Mg., 9, 1; Tr., 2, 1; 9, 1 f.; Phld., 8, 2; — Pol., 1, 2. If sometimes the death and resurrection of Christ are described as two separate and accompanying events, they both belong to the unity of the one event. The separation is only rhetorical, as in R. 4:25. Or it serves to bring out the unity of the event, as in R. 5:10; 8:32-35.

[78] R. 6:7-10; 8:3. On formulation acc. to Jewish legal principle, v. Str.-B., III, 232 (on R. 6:7), 234 (on R. 7:3); K. G. Kuhn, R. 6:7 in ZNW, 30 (1931), 305 ff.; H. Windisch, *Taufe und Sünde* (1908), 173.

11:25 f.), that they have passed from death to life (5:24; 1 Jn. 3:14, → ζωή, II, 870). And Paul uses the *anthropos* myth to make it plain that ζωή is present (→ ζωή, II, 866). Against the misunderstanding of this thought in a Gnostic sense, as though the reference were to the secure possession of an immortal nature, there is obvious polemic in 2 Tm. 2:18, and already in some sense in 1 C. 15. For the view of the Corinthians which Paul contests is obviously not that death ends everything — a view refuted in v. 29. It is rather that they do not believe in a coming new life imparted by the miracle of the resurrection, but in the accomplished transformation of their own nature. This is in keeping with the general threat that Gnostic ideas will disrupt the community (→ γνῶσις, I, 709). For faith, however, the destruction of death is now present only in ἐλπίς (→ II, 531). This is based on the Gospel, so that it can be said that ζωή is present and that death is destroyed in the preached Gospel (2 Tm. 1:10). This ἐλπίς belongs organically to → πίστις, and in this the new life is present (→ ζωή, II, 867). This means, however, that the destruction of death is not, as it were, apart from faith. It takes place in the obedience of faith. As this is reception into the ζωή of Christ, so acceptance of the death of Christ, of the cross, is part of it. The believer has died with Christ.[79] Paul can thus borrow from the mystery religions to express the fact that baptism is for him a baptism into Christ's death, a burial with Him (R. 6:3 f.; cf. 2 Tm. 2:11), a being planted together with Him.[80] That he does not adopt the view of the mysteries is shown, of course, by the change of image (R. 6:6): ὅτι ὁ παλαιὸς ἡμῶν ἄνθρωπος συνεσταυρώθη, ἵνα καταργηθῇ τὸ σῶμα τῆς ἁμαρτίας, τοῦ μηκέτι δουλεύειν ἡμᾶς τῇ ἁμαρτίᾳ, i.e., the acceptance of death is worked out in a new way of life. This must be grasped with the intelligent resolve (6:11): οὕτως καὶ ὑμεῖς λογίζεσθε ἑαυτοὺς εἶναι νεκροὺς μὲν τῇ ἁμαρτίᾳ, ζῶντας δὲ τῷ θεῷ ἐν Χριστῷ Ἰησοῦ (cf. v. 2), and it must be fulfilled in ὑπακοή under God, or the δικαιοσύνη of those who are ἐκ νεκρῶν ζῶντες (6:12 ff.). The destruction of sin and death effected by the death of Christ must manifest itself in a walk which fulfils the righteous demands of the Law (8:2-4), in which death to sin is worked out in mortification of the πράξεις τοῦ σώματος (8:10,13), in καρποφορεῖν τῷ θεῷ and δουλεύειν ἐν καινότητι πνεύματος (7:4-6). Thus the point of death and resurrection for the believer is that he no longer lives for himself but that his life and death stand in the service of the κύριος (14:7-9). Christ has died for all; hence all are dead with Him, ἵνα ... μηκέτι ἑαυτοῖς ζῶσιν, ἀλλὰ τῷ ὑπὲρ αὐτῶν ἀποθανόντι καὶ ἐγερθέντι (2 C. 5:14 f.; cf. R. 15:1-3). The fact that the old is past must be reflected in the exclusion of γινώσκειν κατὰ σάρκα (2 C. 5:16 f.). Acceptance of the cross is worked out in the life of faith (Gl. 2:19 f.) in such sort

---

[79] The ἀποθνήσκειν σὺν Χριστῷ of R. 6:8 and Col. 2:20 has this sense, also the συναποθνήσκειν of 2 Tm. 2:11 and the συσταυρωθῆναι of R. 6:6; Gl. 2:19. Quite different is the συναποθνήσκειν of erotic male friendship, of marital love and of faithful allegiance, which is discussed by R. Hirzel, ARW, 11 (1908), 79, n. 1 and in terms of which F. Olivier, Συναποθνήσκω (1929), tries to explain ἀποθνήσκειν σὺν Χριστῷ. On the fellow-dying of a liegeman we have only the non-technical use in Mk. 14:31 and par. and Jn. 11:16, and the only reference to that of a friend is in 2 C. 7:3.
[80] R. 6:5: εἰ γὰρ σύμφυτοι γεγόναμεν τῷ ὁμοιώματι τοῦ θανάτου αὐτοῦ. The likeness (ὁμοίωμα) of His death is baptism. τῷ ὁμοιώματι is perhaps dependent on σύμφυτοι to yield the abbreviated expression: "We are planted together with his death by its ὁμοίωμα, i.e., baptism." But perhaps an αὐτῷ should be added to σύμφυτοι and then τῷ ὁμοιώματι is a dat. instrum.; cf. the comm. and also Bl.-Debr.⁶ § 194, 2; W. Schauf, Sarx (*Nt.liche Abhandlungen*, XI, 1/2 [1924]), 48, n. 1; K. Mittring, *Heilswirklichkeit bei Pls.* (1929), 75 f.

that in the cross of Christ the world is crucified for the believer and he for the world (Gl. 6:14). [81] If the celebration of the Lord's Supper by the community proclaims the death of the κύριος (1 C. 11:26, → I, 71 f., καταγγέλλω), this must be taken seriously in the lives of believers, i.e., in the form of worthy conduct (1 C. 11:27 ff.) and of the purging out of the old leaven (1 C. 5:7 f.). His death has made us men of the day who must walk accordingly (1 Th. 5:6-10). [82] This new walk is not designed, however, to overcome death; it has already reached this goal; there can be no attempt to attain it in one's own strength; with the death of Christ the Law has been set aside and all καύχησις is excluded (R. 3:27). Part of the acceptance of the cross is to know that the Law is set aside (R. 7:1-6; Gl. 3:13). To re-establish the Law to which the believer is dead (R. 7:6; Gl. 2:19; Col. 2:20) would be to make the death of Christ of none effect (Gl. 2:19-21). Participation in His death is worked out in constant movement which realises that it is never at the goal but which is always looking ahead (Phil. 3:9; 14).

Acceptance of the death of Christ is worked out in conduct not only in the fact that the believer lives for the Lord and therewith for others but also in the fact that in communion with Christ he has a new understanding of the sufferings which afflict him, accepting them as the cross, as the νέκρωσις τοῦ 'Ιησοῦ. That death is overcome may be seen in the fact that διὰ 'Ιησοῦν he gives himself up to daily death and that this self-giving to death leads to life for others through the bringing of the message to them. [83] Thus the sufferings of the apostle fill up the suffering of Christ (Col. 1:24). The thought of union with Christ in suffering also underlies the simple admonition that slaves should be obedient (1 Pt. 2:18-21) and that there should be bravery in persecution (1 Pt. 3:13-18). The thought of this union is also a consolation. Believers who die are νεκροὶ ἐν Χριστῷ (1 Th. 4:16; cf. v. 14; 1 C. 15:18). This is especially true of martyrs (Rev. 14:13). The death of the apostle is an ἀποθνήσκειν ὑπὲρ τοῦ ὀνόματος τοῦ κυρίου 'Ιησοῦ (Ac. 21:13). [84] God is glorified thereby (Jn. 21:19). The same thought recurs in a different and even more radical formulation (Jn. 13:34 f.; 15:11-14) when the command to love the brethren is based on the experience of the love of Jesus which led Him to death (cf. 13:1).

θάνατος is no more understood idealistically than ζωή. The new walk and the new understanding of suffering and death as man's spiritual attitude are not themselves the conquest of death. This acceptance of the death of Christ, which is no mere embracing of an idea of Christ but attachment to a historical event, is part of an ongoing historical movement which is conquest of death only because it moves forward to consummation. We are dead, but our ζωή is still hidden (Col. 3:3). Since our present life is provisional, it gives rise to longing for the *parousia* and therefore for physical death which will take us out of this provisional stage (2 C. 5:1-8; Phil. 1:21-23; 3:9-14; cf. R. 8:18-30; Phil. 3:20 f.), [85] though this longing is limited by the positive understanding of this provisional life as service for the Lord (2 C. 5:9; Phil. 1:24), yet always with the awareness: τὸ ἀποθανεῖν κέρδος

---

[81] Imitated in Ign. R., 7, 2: ὁ ἐμὸς ἔρως ἐσταύρωται.

[82] Cf. also Col. 1:22 ff.; 3:5; Eph. 5:2, 25 f.; Tt. 2:14; 1 Pt. 4:1 f.; Jn. 17:19; 1 Jn. 3:16.

[83] 2 C. 4:7-12; 6:9; 11:23; cf. R. 8:36; 1 C. 15:31: καθ' ἡμέραν ἀποθνήσκειν, and therefore in a very different sense from the *cotidie mori* of Sen. → n. 33.

[84] In Ign. this thought is expressed by ἀποθνήσκειν εἰς 'Ιησοῦν Χριστόν (R., 6, 1, vl. ἐν, διὰ) and εἰς τὸ αὐτοῦ πάθος (Mg., 5, 2) or ὑπὲρ θεοῦ (R., 4, 1).

[85] In Ign. this has already developed into longing for martyrdom, R., 6, 1: καλόν μοι ἀποθανεῖν εἰς Χριστόν; 7, 2: ἐρῶν τοῦ ἀποθανεῖν.

(Phil. 1:21). In this sense both death and life are relativised (R. 8:38; 1 C. 3:22). If the event of salvation has not destroyed death, it has certainly made it final for the ἀπολλύμενοι (→ ἀπώλεια). For them the Gospel spreads death (2 C. 2:16; 4:3 f.; Phil. 1:28; 1 C. 1:18); they abide in death (1 Jn. 3:14; cf. Jn. 3:36; 9:41; 15:22).

† θανατόω.

θανατοῦν is an old Attic word [1] meaning "to kill," "to deliver up to death," "to condemn to death." In the sense of "to kill" it is used in the LXX for הֵמִית and הָרַג, e.g., Ex. 21:12 ff.; 1 Macc. 1:57; and of God, 1 Βασ. 2:6; 4 Βασ. 5:7 (→ II, 874). It does not occur in Jos. but is used by Philo. In the NT θανατοῦν means "to kill" (with men as subj.), Mk. 13:12 and par.; 2 C. 6:9; cf. also Barn., 12, 2; 1 Cl., 12, 2. [2] It is used hyperbolically for "to be given up to danger of death" in R. 8:36 (quoting ψ 43:22). Of Christ, 1 Pt. 3:18 : θανατωθεὶς μὲν σαρκί, ζωοποιηθεὶς δὲ πνεύματι. [3] To the degree that believers participate in the death of Christ (→ θάνατος, 19) it can be said of them : καὶ ὑμεῖς ἐθανατώθητε τῷ νόμῳ διὰ τοῦ σώματος τοῦ Χριστοῦ, R. 7:4. θανατοῦν means "condemn to death" at Mk. 14:55 and par.; Mt. 27:1.

θανατοῦν is often used figuratively in Philo, [4] and there is a similar use at R. 8:13 : εἰ δὲ πνεύματι τὰς πράξεις τοῦ σώματος θανατοῦτε, ζήσεσθε.

Cf. 1 Cl., 39, 7 (quoting Job 5:2 : πεπλανημένον δὲ θανατοῖ ζῆλος); Herm. m., 12, 1, 3 : ἐν ποίοις ἔργοις θανατοῖ ἡ ἐπιθυμία ἡ πονηρὰ τοὺς δούλους τοῦ θεοῦ; [5] also m., 12, 2, 2; s., 9, 20, 4 of vices.

† θνητός.

θνητός in the sense of "mortal" was early used in Gk. to characterise men, so that θνητοί are men in contrast to gods as ἀθάνατοι. [1] There are typical instances of a similar use in the LXX : Job 30:23 : οἰκία γὰρ παντὶ θνητῷ γῆ (לְכָל־חָי); Prv. 3:13 (for אָדָם in parallelism with ἄνθρωπος); 20:24(18) (for אָדָם in par. with ἀνήρ); Wis. 9:14 : λογισμοὶ γὰρ θνητῶν δειλοί. [2] Joseph. uses θνητός for "mortal" at Bell., 6, 84; he speaks of the θνητὴ φύσις at Bell., 7, 345 and Ant., 19, 345, and he characterises the σῶμα as θνητόν at Bell., 3, 372 and 7, 344. [3] The term is very common in Philo. He uses it as an attribute of ἀνήρ (Cher., 43) and ἄνθρωπος (Op. Mund., 77; Spec. Leg.,

---

θ α ν α τ ό ω. [1] W. Schmid, Der Attizismus, I (1887), 384; IV (1896), 251, 651.
[2] Common in Just., e.g., Ap., I, 60, 2; Dial., 39, 6; 46, 7. θανατώδη of ἑρπετά, Herm. s., 9, 1, 9 (vl. θανάσιμα).
[3] It is also used of Christ's death in Just. Dial., 94, 2; 99, 3; 102, 2.
[4] Leg. All., II, 87 (of ἡδοναί); Fug., 53 ff. (allegor. exposition of the θανάτῳ θανατούσθω of Ex. 21:12-14).
[5] So also θανατώδεις of ἐπιθυμίαι in Herm. m., 12, 2, 3.
θ ν η τ ό ς. [1] Hence the admonition to consider that man is θνητός in Epict. Diss., III, 24, 4; IV, 1, 95 and 104; M. Ant., 4, 3; 8, 44.
[2] At Gn. 2:17 the θνητὸς ἔσῃ of Σ (instead of θανάτῳ ἀποθανεῖσθε, for מוֹת תָּמוּת) is a correction in accordance with the usual exegesis that mortality rather than death is the result of eating the forbidden fruit.
[3] Cf. Wis. 9:15 : φθαρτὸν σῶμα.

IV, 14); man is ὁ θνητός (Sacr. AC, 76; Mut. Nom., 181 etc.; plur. Leg. All., I, 5, 18; II, 80 etc.). As αἰσθητὸς ἄνθρωπος, man is φύσει θνητός acc. to Philo (Op. Mund., 134), but as bearer of the divine πνεῦμα he stands between θνητή and ἀθάνατος φύσις. [4]

Pl. uses θνητός as a comprehensive description of human nature in 1 C. 15:53 f.: δεῖ γὰρ τὸ φθαρτὸν τοῦτο ἐνδύσασθαι ἀφθαρσίαν καὶ τὸ θνητὸν τοῦτο ἐνδύσασθαι ἀθανασίαν ... He yearns to be clothed upon with the heavenly body, ἵνα καταποθῇ τὸ θνητὸν ὑπὸ τῆς ζωῆς 2 C. 5:4. He specifically defines the σάρξ or the σῶμα (like Philo and Joseph.) as θνητόν (2 C. 4:11; R. 6:12; 8:11).

In the post-apost. fathers, too, θνητός is a characteristic attribute of man, as in 1 Cl., 39, 2 : τί γὰρ δύναται θνητός; ἢ τίς ἰσχὺς γηγενοῦς; Acc. to Dg., 9, 2 God has given up His Son τὸν ἄφθαρτον ὑπὲρ τῶν φθαρτῶν, τὸν ἀθάνατον ὑπὲρ τῶν θνητῶν. Dg., 6, 8 describes the body as θνητὸν σκήνωμα, and in 7, 1 human thought is θνητὴ ἐπίνοια (par. ἐπίγειος and ἀνθρώπινος). In Did., 4, 8 the whole sphere of the earthly is called θνητόν: εἰ γὰρ ἐν τῷ ἀθανάτῳ κοινωνοί ἐστε, πόσῳ μᾶλλον ἐν τοῖς θνητοῖς. In the Apol., too, the human is called θνητός (Arist. Apol., 9, 6; Athenag. Suppl., 28, 4) and the word is also applied to pagan deities in polemical sections (Tat., 21, 2; Athenag. Suppl., 21, 3). Man, or his ψυχή, is mortal because God's πνεῦμα has left him (Tat., 7, 3; 8, 1; 13, 1). Christ was θνητός in His πρώτη παρουσία (Just. Dial., 14, 8).

† ἀθανασία (ἀθάνατος) → ζωή, θάνατος.

1. Ἀθανασία is primarily a literary term found in Greek from the time of Plato and Isocrates. [1] It means "immortality." According to Gk. belief this is proper to the gods, the ἀθάνατοι. Whether it is also true of the human soul is a matter of debate. Plato tries to prove that it is, [2] and in his school the immortality of the soul becomes a characteristic dogma, [3] so that later Christian Apologists refer to Plato and claim that he took his teaching from Moses. [4] In Hellenism the demand for immortality is great but belief in it meagre. [5] Apart from the διὰ τῆς δόξης ἀθανατισμός, [6] an attempt is made through Pantheistic Stoic speculation to show that the individual belongs organically to the living cosmos and has im-

---

[4] For θνητός as an attribute of φύσις cf. also Det. Pot. Ins., 87; Deus Imm., 77 etc.; of ζωή, Fug., 39; 59 etc.; of βίος, Op. Mund., 152; Leg. All., II, 57 etc.; of γένος, Op. Mund., 61; 135 etc.; of δόγμα, Leg. All., III, 35; of δόξα, Deus Imm., 120; of ἔννοια, Det. Pot. Ins., 87; of νοῦς, Op. Mund., 165; of σῶμα, Mut. Nom., 36; 187 etc.

ἀ θ α ν α σ ί α (ἀ θ ά ν α τ ο ς), → ζωή, Bibl.
[1] Nägeli, 18.
[2] → θάνατος, 10. Plat. Phaedr., 246a : περὶ μὲν οὖν ἀθανασίας αὐτῆς (τῆς ψυχῆς) ἱκανῶς.
[3] Max. Tyr. Diss., 41, 5 f., p. 482, 19 f., Hobein : ὃν γὰρ καλοῦσιν οἱ πολλοὶ θάνατον, αὐτὸ τοῦτο ἦν ἀθανασίας ἀρχὴ καὶ γένεσις μέλλοντος βίου. In Enn., IV, 7 Plot. treats περὶ ἀθανασίας ψυχῆς; cf. → ζωή, II, 838.
[4] Just. Ap., I, 44, 9.
[5] Cf. M. Ant., 4, 48 : πόσοι δὲ φιλόσοφοι, περὶ θανάτου ἢ ἀθανασίας μύρια διατεινόμενοι (make assertions).
[6] Diod. S., I, 1, 5, p. 3, 22 f., Vogel, cf. I, 2, 4 : Heracles has undergone great πόνοι, ἵνα τὸ γένος τῶν ἀνθρώπων εὐεργετήσας τύχῃ τῆς ἀθανασίας. Also other men μεγάλων ἐπαίνων ἠξιώθησαν, τὰς ἀρετὰς αὐτῶν τῆς ἱστορίας ἀπαθανατιζούσης.

personal immortality in it.[7] To some extent ἀθανασία is also sought in the mysteries,[8] in magic[9] or in mystical contemplation.[10]

This ἀθανασία is naturally more than simple duration. It is participation in the blissful divine nature, and therefore divinisation.[11] Hence, in so far as something superhuman and divine may be attributed to a man, this element is called "immortal." Acc. to Vett. Val. there is revealed in the power to foresee the future a μέρος ἀθανασίας (p. 221, 24, Kroll), an ἀπόρροια καιρική ἀθανασίας (p. 330, 20; cf. 242, 16; 346, 19 f.). This type of usage is found esp. in the ruler cult. The decision of Antiochus I of Commagene is an ἀθάνατος κρίσις (Ditt. Or., I, 383, 207). The divine majesty of the emperor (Gaius) is called τὸ μεγαλεῖον τῆς ἀθανασίας (Ditt. Syll.[3], 798, 4) and his clemency is ἀθάνατος χάρις (ibid., 7 f.). Similarly, anything pneumatic may be called ἀθάνατος. Where Pl. uses πνευματικός in R. 15:27; 1 C. 9:11, Did., 4, 8 (→ 22) has ἀθάνατος. Christian γνῶσις is called ἀθάνατος at 1 Cl., 36, 2.[12] On a 5th cent. pap. Holy Scripture is described as καλλίνικος καὶ ἀθάνατος (Preis. Sammelbuch, 5273, 8). We find ὕμνοι ἀθάνατοι in P. Oxy., I, 130, 21 (6th cent.).

The old idea that there is a food of immortality[13] plays a great role in the imaginary notion of a φάρμακον ἀθανασίας (or ζωῆς).

Acc. to legend, Isis is supposed to have found this elixir, and physicians also believe

---

[7] Rohde, II, 310 ff. and cf. the pantheistic parts of the Corp. Herm.: VIII, 3 deals with the ἀθανασία of the κόσμος as a ζῷον ἀθάνατον; XII, 15 ff.: the κόσμος is a πλήρωμα τῆς ζωῆς (15), πᾶν ἄρα ζῷον ἀθάνατον ... πάντων δὲ μᾶλλον ὁ ἄνθρωπος (18 f.) ὑπὸ τίνος οὖν ζωοποιεῖται τὰ πάντα ζῷα; ὑπὸ τίνος ἀθανατίζεται τὰ ἀθάνατα; ... καὶ τοῦτό ἐστιν ὁ θεός, τό πᾶν (22). Cf. also XIV, 10.

[8] On the ancient Gk. mysteries and Orphism, Rohde, I, 278 ff.; II, 103 ff.; G. Anrich, Das antike Mysterienwesen (1894), 6 ff.; W. Kroll, RGG¹, IV, 585 ff.; H. Leisegang, RGG², IV, 326 ff.; O. Kern, ibid., 789 ff. On the myst. of the Hell. period, Anrich, op. cit., 34 ff.; Leisegang, op. cit.; F. Cumont, Die orientalischen Religionen im röm. Heidentum (1931); ibid., 36 ff. and passim on the demand for and belief in immortality; Reitzenstein Hell. Myst., passim, esp. 102, n. 3; 222, 253 (also JHSt, 4 [1883], 419-421), → σωτηρία. For an example cf. esp. Apul. Met., XI, 21.

[9] → ζωή, n. 62; Reitzenstein, op. cit., passim, esp. 169 ff., 185 ff.; T. Schermann, Gr. Zauberpap. (TU, 34, 2b [1909]), 40-44. The portion of the great Paris magic pap. (Preis. Zaub., IV, 475-722 or 834) treated by A. Dieterich (1910) under the title Eine Mithrasliturgie is an ἀπαθανατισμός (Diet., 16, line 15); ἀθανασία is promised to the initiate (3, 3; cf. 4, 7 ff. and 18 ff.; 10, 4 ff.; 12:2 ff.: ἀπαθανατισθείς).

[10] Mithr. Liturg., 4, 10 and 18; the contemplation which leads to immortality is linked with Gnostic speculation and asceticism in the dualistic parts of Corp. Herm.: I, 20 and 28 (τί ἑαυτοὺς ... εἰς θάνατον ἐκδεδώκατε, ἔχοντες ἐξουσίαν τῆς ἀθανασίας μεταλαβεῖν; ... μεταλάβετε τῆς ἀθανασίας, καταλείψαντες τὴν φθοράν); IV, 5 (ὅσοι δὲ τῆς ἀπὸ τοῦ θεοῦ δωρεᾶς μετέσχον ... ἀθάνατοι ἀντὶ θνητῶν εἰσι; X, 4 (the radiance contemplated in mystic θέα is πάσης ἀθανασίας ἀνάπλεως); XI, 20; XIII, 3 (ἐμαυτὸν <δι>εξελήλυθα εἰς ἀθάνατον σῶμα); Ascl., 12 and 22 (Scott, I, 308, 20 f.; 336, 9 ff.), also 27-29 (Scott, I, 364-370).

[11] On ἀποθεωθῆναι cf. Reitzenstein, op. cit., 221 f.; magic gives ἰσόθεος φύσις, Preis. Zaub., IV, 220.

[12] On the other hand Wis. 1:15: δικαιοσύνη γὰρ ἀθάνατός ἐστιν, means that the righteous are immortal. But cf. Jos. Ant., 9, 222 (Jeroboam χαυνωθεὶς [puffed up] θνητῇ περιουσίᾳ τῆς ἀθανάτου ... ὠλιγώρησεν) and 11, 56 (all other things are θνητὰ καὶ ὠκύμορα [transitory], ἀλήθεια is an ἀθάνατον χρῆμα καὶ ἀίδιον); cf. 4 Macc. 7:3 א.

[13] → ζωή, n. 63; H. Schlier, Religionsgeschichtliche Untersuchungen zu den Ignatius-briefen (1929), 168, n. 1. There was already an ἀθανατοποιὸν φάρμακον in Gk. legend, E. Maass, ARW, 21 (1922), 265. Mockingly Aristoph. Fr., 86 (CAF): ὁ δὲ λιμός ἐστιν ἀθανασίας φάρμακον. Acc. to Luc. Dial. Deorum, 4, 3 and 5 Ganymede, when he tastes ambrosia, is οὐκέτι ἄνθρωπος ἀλλ᾽ ἀθάνατος; he drinks immortality in the nectar.

they can administer it. [14] But the idea also plays a part in mysticism and magic. Acc. to the alchemistic writing *The Teaching of Queen Cleopatra* the φάρμακον τῆς ζωῆς brings life to the dead. [15] The κόρη κόσμου (8, Scott, I, 460, 13) speaks of ἱεραὶ βίβλοι which are (stocked ?) with the τῆς ἀφθαρσίας φάρμακον. The idea also made its way into Jewish tradition; in a Jewish Christian legend the angel says to Asenath, after giving her a honeycomb from Paradise : ἰδοὺ δὴ ἔφαγες ἄρτον ζωῆς καὶ ποτήριον ἔπιες ἀθανασίας καὶ χρίσματι κέχρισαι ἀφθαρσίας. [16] One may see from Sir. 6:16 : φίλος πιστὸς φάρμακον ζωῆς, [17] that the legend must have been familiar. Ign. Eph., 20, 2 applies the expression to the Lord's Supper : ἕνα ἄρτον κλῶντες, ὅς ἐστιν φάρμακον ἀθανασίας, ἀντίδοτος [18] τοῦ μὴ ἀποθανεῖν, ἀλλὰ ζῆν ἐν Ἰησοῦ Χριστῷ διὰ παντός. [19] Iren. also tells us in Haer., V, 2, 2 f. how the cup and the bread in the Lord's Supper contain the Logos and therefore ζωὴ αἰώνιος. Acc. to Iren., I, 4, 1 the Valentinians speak of Christ leaving behind an ὀδμὴ ἀφθαρσίας for fallen Achamoth. [20]

2. We have already spoken of the influence of syncretistic ideas on Judaism and Christianity. There is little to say about the remaining use. The OT has no equivalent for ἀθανασία.

Only in the LXX apocr. is ἀθανασία used to describe the expected eternal life of the righteous (Wis. 3:4; 15:3; 4 Macc. 14:5), [21] and only here is the ψυχή described as ἀθάνατος (4 Macc. 14:6; 18:23, → ζωή, II, 859). Naturally ἀθανασία is common in Philo, like ἀθάνατος and (ἀπ)αθανατίζειν. [22] In Jos. Bell., 7, 340 Eleazar gives an address περὶ ψυχῆς ἀθανασίας (cf. 348) and in Bell., 6, 46 Titus speaks of the ἀθανασία of those fallen in battle. [23] It is said of the Essenes in Ant., 18:18 : ἀθανατίζουσι δὲ τὰς ψυχάς, and of the Pharisees in Ant., 18, 14 : ἀθάνατον ἰσχὺν ταῖς ψυχαῖς πίστις αὐτοῖς εἶναι.

3. ἀθάνατος does not occur in the NT and ἀθανασία is found only in two passages. In 1 Cor. 15:53 f. the incorruptible mode of existence of the resurrected is called (ἀφθαρσία and) ἀθανασία as in Hellenistic Judaism, the thought being not merely that of eternal duration but of a mode of existence different from that of σάρξ and αἷμα (→ ζωή, II, 869) and equivalent to what is elsewhere

---

[14] Diod. S., I, 25, 6, p. 40, 23 f.: εὑρεῖν δ᾽ αὐτὴν (τὴν Ἴσιδα) καὶ τὸ τῆς ἀθανασίας φάρμακον, δι᾽ οὗ τὸν υἱὸν Ὧρον, ὑπὸ τῶν Τιτάνων ἐπιβουλευθέντα καὶ νεκρὸν εὑρεθέντα καθ᾽ ὕδατος, μὴ μόνον ἀναστῆσαι, δοῦσαν τὴν ψυχήν, ἀλλὰ καὶ τῆς ἀθανασίας ποιῆσαι μεταλαβεῖν. Cf. R. Reitzenstein, *Hell. Wundererzählungen* (1906), 104-106; ARW, 7 (1904), 402; T. Schermann, *Theol. Quartalschrift*, 92 (1910), 6-19; Bau. Ign. on Eph., 20, 2.

[15] Reitzenstein Hell. Myst., 314.

[16] Cf. Schürer, III, 400, 126.

[17] The Heb. has צְרוֹר חַיִּים, which Smend renders magic of life in allusion to 1 S. 25:29. The opp. is φάρμακον ὀλέθρου, Wis. 1:14, or θανάσιμον φάρμακον, Ign. Tr., 6, 2. Philo has the notion when in Fug., 199 he describes God, the πηγὴ τοῦ ζῆν (Jer. 2:13), as τὸ τῆς ἀθανασίας ποτόν.

[18] ἀντίδοτος is also a technical medical term, Schermann, *op. cit.*

[19] Is there a connection here with the description of Christ as the Physician ? → ἰατρός.

[20] → ζωή, n. 59.

[21] Through the Gk. transl. ἀθάνατος has also come into the text of Sir. 17:30; 51:9 A in the sense of immortal. The meaning of ἀθανασία in Wis. 8:13, 17 is not wholly clear; in 4:1 it is "mnemonic" immortality, → n. 6.

[22] Cf., e.g., Virt., 9 and Leisegang.

[23] In the speech of Joseph. himself in Bell., 3, 372 : τὰ μέν γε σώματα θνητὰ πᾶσιν καὶ ἐκ φθαρτῆς ὕλης δεδημιούργηται, ψυχὴ δὲ ἀθάνατος ἀεὶ καὶ θεοῦ μοῖρα τοῖς σώμασιν ἐνοικίζεται.

called δόξα. In 1 Tm. 6:16 ἀθανασία is used of God : ὁ μόνος ἔχων ἀθανασίαν, in a context which displays the influence of Hellenistic Jewish terminology. [24]

Both uses occur in later literature. On Did., 4, 8 → 22. In the eucharistic prayer in Did., 10, 2 there is thanksgiving ὑπὲρ τῆς γνώσεως καὶ πίστεως καὶ ἀθανασίας, ἧς ἐγνώρισας ἡμῖν διὰ Ἰησοῦ τοῦ παιδός σου (cf. 9:3 : ὑπὲρ τῆς ζωῆς καὶ γνώσεως). [25] Of the δῶρα of God in 1 Cl., 35, 2 the first is ζωὴ ἐν ἀθανασίᾳ, and in 2 Cl., 19, 3 consolation is found in the ἀθάνατος τῆς ἀναστάσεως καρπός. [26]

Acc. to Athenag. Suppl., 22, 5 ἀθάνατον is the character of the θεῖον. Dg., 9, 2 describes Christ as ἀθάνατος. The Apologists treat of the ἀθανασία of the soul, → ζωή, n. 281; Dg., 6, 8 calls it ἀθάνατος.

Bultmann

---

† θαρρέω (θαρσέω)

1. The term occurs in the two forms θαρρέω and θαρσέω, of which θαρσέω is attested to be the earlier. [1] It has the basic sense of "to dare," "to be bold," and thence "to be of good courage," "to be cheerful," "to be confident," e.g., θάρρει, Xenoph. Cyrop., V, 1, 6; also V, 1, 17; Jos. Ant., 7, 266 : θάρρει καὶ δείσῃς μηδὲν ὡς τεθνηξόμενος. This gives us the further main senses of a. "to trust in something or someone," "to rely on," e.g., with the dat. : τεθαρσηκότες τοῖς ὄρνισι, Hdt., III, 76; θαρρεῖν τοῖς χρήμασι αὐτοῦ, Greek Pap. from the Cairo Museum (ed. E. J. Goodspeed, 1902), 15, 19 (4th cent. A.D.); with the acc. : οὔτε Φίλιππος ἐθάρρει τούτους οὔθ᾽ οὗτοι Φίλιππον, Demosth., 3, 7; with prep.: ἅμα δὲ θαρρεῖν ἐφ᾽ ἑαυτῷ καὶ τῇ διαθέσει, Plut. Adulat., 28 (II, 69d); b. "to be bold against someone or something," "to go out bravely to" : θάρσει τὸ τοῦδέ γ᾽ ἀνδρός, Soph. Oed. Col., 649 : κρέσσον δὲ πάντα θαρσέοντα, Hdt., VII, 50. Except at Prv. 31:11 (θαρσεῖ ἐπ᾽ αὐτῇ ἡ καρδία τοῦ ἀνδρὸς αὐτῆς, θαρσεῖν = בָּטַח) the LXX uses the term in the absol. [2] In the twelve passages in which it is a rendering from the Mas. it is used ten times for יָרֵא *cum negatione* and once for בָּטַח. It always means "to be of good courage," "to be confident," "not to be afraid." Almost always we have θαρσεῖν, θαρρεῖν being found only in Da. and 4 Macc. [3] In the NT the Evangelists and Ac. have θαρσεῖν, and Pl. and Hb. θαρρεῖν.

---

[24] Cf. Dib. Past., ad loc.

[25] Cf. T. Schermann, *Gr. Zauberpapyri* (→ n. 9), 41-43.

[26] Ἀθανασία can also be used in the purely formal sense of eternal duration, so that is can be applied not only to the saved (Just. Dial., 45, 4; Tat., 20, 3) but also to the lost (Tat., 13, 1; 14, 2).

θαρρέω. [1] θαρσέω is certainly much older in Attic than the oldest instance of θαρρέω; this appears later only because Attic lit. is not so old as non-Attic. θαρσέω (from the time of Homer), whence the Attic (and Boeotian) θαρρέω (attested from the time of Soph. and Plato). The koine has both, though ρσ is on the whole more common ; cf. on this pt. J. Wackernagel, *Hellenistica* (1907), 13 ff.; Bl.-Debr.⁶ § 34, 2 [Debrunner].

[2] Prv. 1:21 is uncertain, though the θαρροῦσα λέγει is probably intended to correspond to what is thought to be a strengthening אָמְרֶיהָ תֹאמֵר. Cf. 1:20: קוֹלָהּ תִּתֵּן = παρρησίαν ἄγει, as also the common combination in Philo θαρρῶν λέγειν etc.: Poster. C., 38; Rer. Div. Her., 28, 71 (λέγε θαρροῦσα ἡμῖν, ὦ διάνοια); Fug., 82. Also Σ 1 Βασ. 30:6 : ἐθάρσησεν = יִּתְחַזֵּק (LXX : ἐκραταιώθη, Ἀ : ἐνίσχυσεν [ἐν κυρίῳ θεῷ]), where the verb is not used in the absol. Apart from the two passages in Prv. and that in Σ, θαρρεῖν is always used in the imp. in the OT and NT [Bertram].

[3] There is some uncertainty as to Bar. 4:21, 27.

The term plays some part in Plato's Phaed. with reference to the question of death as the severest threat to man. Cebes, one of those who take part in the discussion, has the following statement: ... οὐδενὶ προσήκει θάνατον θαρροῦντι μὴ οὐκ ἀνοήτως θαρρεῖν, ὃς ἂν μὴ ἔχῃ ἀποδεῖξαι, ὅτι ἔστι ψυχὴ παντάπασιν ἀθάνατόν τε καὶ ἀνώλεθρον, Phaed., 88b. The question at issue is this: θαρρεῖν ἢ δεδιέναι ὑπὲρ τῆς ἡμετέρας ψυχῆς, 78b. The discussion takes place with reference to the imminent death of Socrates, and Socrates maintains: φαίνεται εἰκότως ἀνὴρ τῷ ὄντι ἐν φιλοσοφίᾳ διατρίψας τὸν βίον θαρρεῖν μέλλων ἀποθανεῖσθαι καὶ εὔελπις εἶναι μέγιστα οἴσεσθαι ἀγαθὰ ἐπειδὰν τελευτήσῃ. The dialogue hinges on the immortality of the soul, which secures θαρρεῖν (87e, 95c), and it closes with the insight: τούτων δὴ ἕνεκα θαρρεῖν χρὴ περὶ τῇ ἑαυτοῦ ψυχῇ ἄνδρα, 114d, i.e., in face of death, the severest threat to human existence, θαρρεῖν is possible through awareness of the immortality of the soul.

In Philo θαρρεῖν is combined with → εὐλάβεια (II, 752 f.) in face of God: σκόπει ... ὅτι εὐλαβείᾳ τὸ θαρρεῖν ἀνακέκραται, τὸ μὲν γὰρ "τί μοι δώσεις"; θάρσος ἐμφαίνει, Rer. Div. Her., 22. If εὐλάβεια expresses the sense of distance, the *tremendum*, θαρρεῖν expresses the *fascinosum*. [4]

In the LXX θαρρεῖν is a summons which men issue to one another in times of emergency and stress and anxiety (e.g., Moses to Israel in Ex. 14:13; 20:20; Elijah to the widow of Sarepta in 3 Βασ. 17:13; on the lips of the prophet in Zeph. 3:16; Bar. 4:5, 21, 27, 30). The basis of the summons is the readiness of Yahweh to help, cf. also Philo: θαρρεῖτε, μὴ ἀποκάμητε, ... προσδοκᾶτε τὴν ἀήττητον ἐκ τοῦ θεοῦ βοήθειαν, Vit. Mos., II, 252, and Joseph.: οὐδὲ ἄλλῳ τινὶ θαρσήσας ἢ τῇ παρ' αὐτοῦ βοηθείᾳ, Ant., 8, 293. It may also take the form of a divine summons to the people (Hag. 2:5; Zech. 8:13, 15) in which God stakes His own existence by way of guarantee.

2. In the NT it is a summons on the lips of Jesus. He says to the man sick of the palsy: θάρσει, τέκνον, ἀφίενταί σου αἱ ἁμαρτίαι, Mt. 9:2; to the woman with an issue of blood: θάρσει, θύγατερ· ἡ πίστις σου σέσωκέν σε, Mt. 9:22; to the fearful disciples in the storm and on His appearance: θαρσεῖτε, ἐγώ εἰμι, Mt. 14:27; Mk. 6:50. Sometimes men are summoned to θαρρεῖν in respect of what Jesus gives them or is to them. [5] Behind the summons lies the claim of Jesus to give the necessary assurance in His life and work. The summons is dynamic evidence of the fact that in encounter with Jesus God's action is accomplished as a liberating action. The Gospel of Jesus, which consists in both His proclamation and His action, gives joy and confidence. It chases away anxiety and distress. It brings men into the goodness of the God whom they call Father. The exalted Lord comes to Paul in prison with the same summons: θάρσει. He may do this because Christ tells him to (Ac. 23:11). The basis is clearer in the more frequently attested summons linked with μὴ φοβοῦ or μὴ φοβεῖσθε (→ φοβεῖσθαι), as in Jn. 16:33: ἐν τῷ κόσμῳ θλῖψιν ἔχετε, ἀλλὰ θαρσεῖτε, ἐγὼ νενίκηκα τὸν κόσμον. The disciples are constantly threatened by persecution and martyrdom in the world. They live in the situation of the parting discourses before Gethsemane. Hence they live always in anxiety. Yet they are summoned to θαρσεῖν in every respect. This summons is based on reference to Christ: ἐγὼ νενίκηκα τὸν κόσμον. They are in the hands of the Victor over the cosmos. Hence they need have no fear what the cosmos will bring. This passage is highly significant. The Greek

---

[4] Cf. the combination in Epict. Diss., II, 1, which contains no reference to God and which is thus quite humanistic: ὅτι οὐ μάχεται τὸ θαρρεῖν τῷ εὐλαβεῖσθαι, esp.: πρὸς τὰ ἀπροαίρετα θαρρεῖν εὐλαβεῖσθαι τὰ προαιρετικά, II, 1, 29.

[5] It is in this sense that those who accompany Jesus use the expression to the blind man who is calling to Jesus for help: θάρσει, ἔγειρε, φωνεῖ σε (Mk. 10:49).

faced by the ultimate threat to existence, draws θαρρεῖν from what lies in himself, i.e., the immortality of his higher part, the soul, whose immortality must first
be proved, however, by philosophical considerations. The Christian, on the
other hand, derives θαρρεῖν from the victory of Christ which overcomes the
cosmos. Yet the passage is also significant from another standpoint. It has certain
features comparable with the language of the mysteries. Firmicus Maternus hands
down the saying of the mysteries wherein the priest announces the rising again
of the deity and the deliverance assured therein: θαρρεῖτε μύσται τοῦ θεοῦ
σεσωσμένου· ἔσται γὰρ ἡμῖν ἐκ πόνων σωτηρία, Firm. Mat. Err. Prof. Rel., 22.
Here what gives θαρρεῖν is the mystical process which the initiate imitates and
which deifies him. The difference is that in Jn. it is Christ Himself who, on the
basis of His victory over the world achieved through His crucifixion and resurrection, issues the summons to θαρρεῖν. Here is history instead of myth, fulfilment
instead of yearning. The passages in Plato and Firmicus Maternus as well as Jn.
show how important is the question of θαρρεῖν in the religious life and what
different answers can be given.

Paul tells us in 2 C. 5:6, 8 that in the Christian situation characterised by separation from Christ (→ ἐκδημεῖν, II, 63) the possibility of θαρρεῖν is given. Christians
are in the world as θαρροῦντες, for through the earnest of the Spirit they are
linked with the Lord and they know of the consummation in περιπατεῖν διὰ
εἴδους.

The author of Hb. bases his θαρρεῖν on the promised help of the *Kyrios* when
he comforts his readers undergoing persecution: ... θαρροῦντας ἡμᾶς λέγειν·
κύριος ἐμοὶ βοηθός, οὐ φοβηθήσομαι· τί ποιήσει μοι ἄνθρωπος; Hb. 13:6.

θαρρεῖν, "to rely on," "to trust in," is found at 2 C. 7:16: χαίρω ὅτι ἐν παντὶ
θαρρῶ ἐν ὑμῖν. In the sense of "to be bold against," "to approach boldly," θαρρεῖν
is used at 2 C. 10:1, 2: ... ἀπὼν ... θαρρῶ εἰς ὑμᾶς· δέομαι δὲ τὸ μὴ παρὼν
θαρρῆσαι ...

Grundmann

---

† θαῦμα, † θαυμάζω, † θαυμάσιος, † θαυμαστός

Contents: A. The Use of the Word Group in Secular Greek; B. The Use of the Word
Group in Greek Judaism: 1. The Greek OT; 2. Philo and Josephus; C. The Use of the
Word Group in the NT: 1. Synoptics; 2. Acts; 3. Jn.; 4. Paul; 5. Catholic Epistles;
6. Revelation; D. The Use of the Word Group in Early Christianity.

A. The Use of the Word Group in Secular Greek.

θαυμάζειν and the underlying θαῦμα, whose root is linked with θέα, "vision," and
θεάομαι, "contemplate," are common from the time of Homer and Hesiod. The adj.
θαυμάσιος, attested from the time of Hesiod, is preferred by Atticists to the verbal
adj. θαυμαστός, which is found from the time of the Homeric hymns. In Hell. Gk.,
including the LXX, there is no material difference between them in spite of Plut.
Terrestriane an Aquatilia sint Callidiora, 21 (II, 974d): ἧττον δὲ ταῦτα θαυμαστά,

---

θ α ῦ μ α, κτλ. → θάμβος, δύναμις, ἔργον, esp. II, 640, 642, and the bibl. given
there. Moult.-Mill., *s.v.*; Preisigke, 50; Trench § 59.

καίπερ ὄντα θαυμάσια, *minus miranda quamvis mirabilia*. In the first instance the verb means "to be astonished," and it often expresses an attitude of criticism, doubt or even censure and rejection, thought it may also express inquisitiveness and curiosity. It is followed by εἰ when the cause is uncertain and by ὅτι when it is known. Secondly, the verb means "to wonder at," "to look on with astonishment," followed by a subsidiary clause with ὡς or εἰ or τινά, τί, τινός τι, περί (in the LXX also ἐν, ἐπί) and rarely τινί (in the LXX at Sir. 43:24[26]; 4 Macc. 6:11).[1] From this derive the senses of "to esteem," "to admire," "to honour." θαῦμα can mean both "admiration" (Hom. Od., 10, 326; Soph. El., 897: ἰδοῦσα ἔσχον θαῦμα, 928) and also "miracle" (Hom. Od., 9, 190). Miracle as a sudden and unexpected phenomenon evokes astonishment, often a sceptical surprise and critical and receptive observation (Hesych.: θαυμάζειν, θεάσασθαι καὶ μανθάνειν, cf. Hdt., 8, 37). But there is also an element of fear, of awe at the unknown and of respect for the mysterious (Soph. Oed. Tyr., 777: τύχη θαυμάσαι μὲν ἀξία). Thus the adj. often expresses that which is surprising or noteworthy or incomprehensible. The word group is thus of frequent occurrence in accounts of travels (Paus., II, 5, 7; III, 26, 3; VI, 2, 10; X, 18, 5),[2] in stories of extraordinary events like the acts of Hercules, in the aetiological narrations of a Callimachus, in the accounts of natural marvels in the history of a Theopompus,[3] and in encomiums and epinicia.[4] In the religious sphere it is particularly the epiphany of deity which arouses wonder (Hom. Od., 1, 323; 19, 36; Il., 3, 398; Hom. Hymn. Ap., 135;[5] Vergil. Aen., III, 172; Lk. 24:41). The same feeling is kindled by miracles[6] and by the teachings of priests and prophets as the mediators of revelation (Plat. Phaedr., 257c). Astonishment at the δύναμις and ἀρετή of the deity is the basis of worship. There are innumerable examples of religious usage in Aelius Aristides. Here, too, the idea of wonder is linked with the different phenomena of the religious life and especially with the mighty acts of deity (48, 30 : καί τινα κλίμακα, οἶμαι, ἐξήγγελλεν ἱερὰν καὶ παρουσίαν καὶ δυνάμεις τινὰς τοῦ θεοῦ θαυμαστάς; cf. 48, 15 : θαυμαστά ... σημαίνων οὐ μόνον εἰς τὸ σῶμα ἔχοντα, ἀλλὰ καὶ ἄλλα πολλά, and 48, 74 : ταῦτ' ἐστὶ τὰ πρῶτα τοῦ θαύματος). But wondering belief is also directed to providence (48, 55 : θαυμαστότερον τὸ τοῦ θεοῦ ... τὴν αὐτοῦ δύναμιν καὶ πρόνοιαν ἐμφανίζοντος), to accurate prophecies (51, 18 : οἱ δ' ἐθαύμαζον τῆς προρρήσεως τὴν ἀκρίβειαν) and to dreams (51, 50 : θαυμάσαι τε δὴ τοῦ ἐνυπνίου ἀκρίβειαν). Naturally the deities themselves have the attribute of θαυμαστός, e.g., Serapis and Aesculapius. A healing formula can also be described as an ἔργον τοῦ θεοῦ θαυμαστόν (50, 17). From the sphere of religion the group sinks into that of magic. Thus in the pap.[7] the words are often used of magical acts or media (VII, 643 : ποτήριον λίαν θαυμαστόν; VII, 919 : νικητικὸν θαυμαστὸν τοῦ Ἑρμοῦ; XXXVI, 134 : ἀγωγὴ θαυμαστή) as phenomena which cause astonishment, and they are also used for the wonder of those making use of these media (IV, 160 ff.: καὶ <σὺ> δοκιμάσας θαυμάσεις τὸ παράδοξον τῆς οἰκονομίας (magical formula) ταύτης; IV, 233 : ὃς τῷδε αὐτῷ λόγῳ χρώμενος θαυμάσεις, "if you use this prayer, you will be astonished"; cf. XIII, 252).

In philosophy, too, the group is basic. This emerges particularly in Plato. The chief question in Prot., 326e is: θαυμάσεις ... καὶ ἀπορεῖς, εἰ διδακτόν ἐστιν ἀρετή. Cf. also Xenoph. Mem., I, 2, 7: ἐθαύμαζε δ' εἴ τις ἀρετὴν ἐπαγγελλόμενος ἀργύριον πράττοιτο. θαυμάζειν denotes the philosophical doubt which must be overcome,

---

[1] Helbing, *Kasussyntax*, 265 f.
[2] It is used of artistic monuments and of natural wonders. The deity Thaumas expresses mythologically the wonder of the sea and is supposed to be the son of Pontos and Gaia.
[3] U. v. Wilamowitz-Moellendorff, *Antigonos von Karystos* (1881), 23 ff.
[4] O. Pfister in Pauly-W., Suppl. Vol. IV (1924), 317.
[5] θαμβεῖν is often used in this sense in the passages mentioned.
[6] Thus Philostr. Vit. Ap., IV, 45 introduces a resurrection by Apollonius of Tyana in Rome with the words κἀκεῖνο Ἀπολλωνίου θαῦμα.
[7] The references are from Preis. Zaub.

so that we finally read : θαυμάσιον ἔσται μὴ διδακτὸν ὄν (Plat. Prot., 361b). Fundamentally this means that θαυμάζειν is seen to be the beginning of philosophy. Thus we read in Theaet., 155d : Μάλα γὰρ φιλοσόφου τοῦτο τὸ πάθος τὸ θαυμάζειν. In this light it is natural on the one side that an attitude of wonder should still mark the philosopher in face of certain phenomena, Symp., 178a : μέγας θεὸς ... ὁ "Ερως καὶ θαυμαστός; Leg., XII, 957c : ὁ θεῖος καὶ θαυμαστὸς νόμος. But no less natural on the other hand is the view ascribed to Pythagoras : ἐκ φιλοσοφίας ἔφησεν αὐτῷ περιγεγονέναι τὸ μηδὲν θαυμάζειν (Plut. Aud., 13 [II, 44b]). This is widespread among the Stoics and acc. to Diog. L., VII, 123 may be found already in Zeno : τὸν σοφὸν οὐδὲν θαυμάζειν τῶν δοκούντων παραδόξων.[8] To Plato for his part sophistic dialectics seems to be a θαῦμα, an artifice (Soph., 233a), and in Gk. rhetoric the word is more or less a mere means of transition (Demosth., 19, 26).[9] Basically Aristot. agrees with Plato, Metaph., I, 2, p. 982b, 12 : διὰ γὰρ τὸ θαυμάζειν οἱ ἄνθρωποι ... ἤρξαντο φιλοσοφεῖν. Wonder ceases as soon as the cause of a phenomenon is discovered, Mechanica, 1, p. 847a, 11 : θαυμάζεται τῶν κατὰ φύσιν συμβαινόντων, ὅσων ἀγνοεῖται τὸ αἴτιον. Aristot., too, keeps the term to denote remarkable phenomena.[10]

In the language of the inscr. and pap. θαυμασιώτατος is a title of honour.[11] θαῦμα, too, is sometimes found on burial inscriptions.[12]

B. The Use of the Word Group in Greek Judaism.

1. The Greek OT.

How varied is the use of the group in the Gk. Bible may be seen from the relatively large number of Heb. words rendered by θαυμάζειν etc. even though in some measure these Heb. words have not the slightest connection with one another. Naturally the content of the terms is partly determined by these words, not only in the LXX, but also in the NT. In particular, the word is a distinctive expression for the anthropocentrically determined piety of experience in the LXX, especially where it characterises the object of experience as something which transcends all human possibilities. It thus embraces *miraculum* and *mirabile*[13] and may express any degree of wonder or astonishment.

a. The purely rhetorical introductory formula : οὐ θαυμαστὸν ἐάν ... occurs at Prv. 6:30, where there is no Mas. original, and at Sir. 16:11: θαυμαστὸν τοῦτο εἰ ... (תמה זה אם). The admonition μὴ θαυμάσῃς also has a formal character at Qoh. 5:7; Sir. 26:11. This introduction with the negative is designed to emphasise the self-evident nature of a statement, while the positive form represents something as impossible or unlikely. In this case it is used of a position which is presupposed to be generally recognised. Materially, it is often used in the Gk. OT with reference to questions of average morality such as are particularly common in the Wisdom lit. It has a religious and moral character only at Sir. 16:11, where we read that an obstinate and unyielding man will not go unpunished, the fear of God and submission being the self-evident content of piety.

---

[8] Cf. also Cic. Tusc., III, 14 : *nihil admirari cum acciderit, nihil antequam evenerit non evenire posse arbitrari,* and Horat. Ep., I, 6, 1 f.: *nil admirari prope res est una ... solaque, quae possit facere et servare beatum.*

[9] Cf. also F. W. Sturz, *Lexicon Xenophonteum,* II (1802), 511.

[10] Cf. A. Bonitz, *Index Aristotelicus* (1870), *s.v.*

[11] Preisigke Wört., *s.v.*

[12] Epigr. Graec., 591, 2 : ἐνθάδε Νεῖλος κεῖται, ἀνὴρ προφερέστατος ἀνδρῶν, ῥητορικός, μέγα θαῦμα.

[13] Cf. on this pt. R. Seeberg in RE³, XXI, 567.

Another example of the less profound use of the word group is to be seen in θαυμά-ζειν πρόσωπον as a translation of נָשָׂא פָנִים, which is to be understood in terms of oriental court etiquette. This phrase is twice used to express the theological concept that God shows no respect of persons, Dt. 10:17; 2 Ch. 19:7 (cf. Job 34:19). But it can also denote the acceptance of the righteous by God and His intention to receive their requests, Gn. 19:21. In the main, however, it refers to human relationships. Here the emphasis often falls on the recognition and respect which men owe one another, as in the secular use of θαυμάζειν for "to esteem." Cf. Sir. 7:29: ἐν ὅλῃ ψυχῇ σου εὐλαβοῦ τὸν κύριον καὶ τοὺς ἱερεῖς αὐτοῦ θαύμαζε (הקדיש); also 7:31: φοβοῦ τὸν κύριον καὶ δόξασον ἱερέα כבד אל והדר כהן. When used for נָשָׂא פָנִים, it can mean "to regard" (Dt. 28:50) or "to be respected" (4 Βασ. 5:1). Elsewhere the phrase expresses a demand directed specifically to judges. As God shows no respect of persons, neither should the judge. This theological basis of equal rights for all should not be confused with the line of thought in secular ethics which begins with the Utopian idea of human equality. The LXX is thinking of the unjust judge who does have respect of persons in Is. 9:14, where it introduces the active θαυμάζειν πρόσωπον. The Mas. has a pass. part. (Σ: αἰδέσιμος) and thus refers generally to the "respected" without grounding the threatened judgment on a negative ethical evaluation. A further reference to partiality is to be seen in the law of Lv. 19:15, where we have: οὐ λήμψῃ (נָשָׂא) πρόσωπον πτωχοῦ οὐδὲ θαυμάσεις (vl. δοξάσεις) [14] πρόσωπον δυνάστου, cf. Ex. 23:3: הדר = ἐλεεῖν, Σ: τιμᾶν, elsewhere mostly δοξάζειν, and Dt. 1:17: ἐπιγινώσκειν πρόσω-πον. The principle expressed in Prv. 18:5 displays the same usage: θαυμάσαι πρόσω-πον ἀσεβοῦς οὐ καλόν. The phrase is also used in the same sense in the LXX addition to Da. 6:13. In Job it occurs three times in addition to the passage already mentioned. In Job 13:10 we have a literal rendering of the original. In Job 22:8 there is an inter-change of active and passive as in Is. 9:14. In Job 32:22 we have θαυμάζειν πρόσωπα for כנה pi, "to flatter." The literal rendering of נָשָׂא פָנִים as λαμβάνειν → πρόσωπον is rare in the LXX, cf. Mal. 1:8; Sir. 4:22 (cf. 42:1); 42:1; 1 ῎Εσδρ. 4:39. The rendering πρόσωπον θαυμάζειν is not so much a literal translation of הָדַר פָּנִים, since it cor-responds to a stronger Gk. linguistic sense. It is also to be found in Ass. Mos. 5:5; Ps. Sol. 2:18 and in the NT at Jd. 16. [15] Apart from 4 Βασ. 5:1, with its clumsy Hebraic rendering of נָשָׂא פָנִים, the LXX only once translates the pass. part. according to its sense, namely, in Is. 3:3, [16] where θαυμαστός with σοφός and συνετός is used of the leading people who come under the judgment of divine destruction (cf. Is. 2:11, 17). Est. 4:17 p (14:10): θαυμασθῆναι βασιλέα σάρκινον εἰς αἰῶνα, is to be understood similarly of the heathen deification of men. On the other hand, ἐκθαυμάζειν in Sir. 27:23 denotes the attitude of the flatterer who praises a man's opinions to his face but vilifies them behind his back.

b. Even where the group denotes astonishment in the deeper sense, it is often used as a stylistic device in the Gk. Bible, being employed by a narrator or author to emphasise the greatness or significance of a fact or event by showing its effect on those who saw it. This usage is less frequent in the Gk. OT, however, than in the NT.

Expression of astonishment indirectly emphasises a fact in Tob. 11:16 and perhaps Jdt. 10:23, though in Jdt. 10:7, 19; 11:20 the element of astonishment has direct significance in the context. In Job 42:11 ἐθαύμασαν reminds us of the choruses which conclude the

---

[14] Acc. to Field, ad loc.

[15] Cf. Wnd. Kath. Br., ad loc.

[16] J. Ziegler, *Untersuchungen zur LXX des Buches Isaias* (1934), 136, derives the θαυ-μαστὸς σύμβουλος from 9:5, but fails to note that it is there secondary to μεγάλης βουλῆς ἄγγελος.

miracle stories in the Gospels (→ 37). Here as elsewhere the LXX introduces this literary device independently of the original. In the Mas. this is : וַיָּנֻדוּ לוֹ וַיְנַחֲמוּ אֹתוֹ עַל כָּל־הָרָעָה אֲשֶׁר־הֵבִיא יְהֹוָה עָלָיו, "they showed their sympathy and comforted him over all the evil that Yahweh had allowed to come on him." The LXX combines the two verbs and leaves out הָרָעָה: ἐθαύμασαν ἐπὶ πᾶσιν οἷς ἐπήγαγεν αὐτῷ ὁ κύριος. The sentence is thus given a new and self-contained sense. In accordance with Hell. Jewish belief in providence, the wonderful direction which Job has experienced is the focal point of interest. A similar destiny seems to be presupposed in Job 11:13 : "He raises him out of his lowliness and lifts up his head, and many are astonished at him." [17] In Wis. 11:14 the same line of thought achieves more basic theological precision : ἐπὶ τέλει τῶν ἐκβάσεων ἐθαύμασαν.

Herein lies a wholly this-worldly solution of the problem of theodicy, though one which both positively and negatively has exercised persistent influence in Christian piety. Our word group has terminological significance as an expression of this faith in the wonderful ways of God which in the first instance man cannot understand. [18]

The subst. θαῦμα is used three times in Job, at 17:8 and 21:5 for שָׁמֵם and at 18:20 for שָׁעַר. It here expresses, like the Heb. words, the horror which grips those who, without being directly involved, must watch the judgment of God fall. This corresponds to the use of the verb in Lv. 26:32 (שָׁמֵם) and to the concept πληγαὶ θαυμασταί in Dt. 28:59, which the LXX introduces into the text independently, while θαυμαστὰ ἔργα in Ex. 34:10 refers to Yahweh's wonderful direction of His people. In the Mas. we here have נוֹרָא, which alludes to the fearfulness of these acts for the enemies of the people. The adj. θαυμαστά in Job 42:3 refers to the wonderful acts of God in the guidance of Job, although in a much broader sense.

The thought of the direction of the pious corresponds chiefly to the piety of the Psalms. In ψ 44:4 the LXX has the express formulation : "Thy right hand shall guide thee wonderfully," while the Mas. has : "Thy right hand shall teach thee fearful acts." [19] The verb θαυμαστοῦν is used in the same way, as in ψ 16:7; ψ 30:21. ψ 138:6, 14 belongs to this context. When we have φοβερῶς ἐθαυμαστώθην in v. 14, the adv. shows that the element of the fearful is not lacking in the guidance of the righteous. Man cannot evade God's working — this is the fearful and blessed experience of the psalmist. In ψ 4:4 the verb means "to lead wonderfully," while in ψ 15:3 it is to be rendered "to accomplish wonderfully." Outside the Psalter the verb occurs only at 2 Βασ. 1:26 and 2 Ch. 26:15. The former speaks of the wonderful experience of the love of friends, while the latter is to be referred to the miraculous help of God. In all instances apart from ψ 15:3 we have in the Heb. forms of the stem פלא or פלה, between which the LXX does not distinguish. Nor does the LXX pay any attention to the different senses of פלא, 1. "to be wonderful" and 2. "to fulfil a vow." The Heb. stem פלא, which does not occur in the qal, is notably never translated θαυμάζειν. It thus refers, not to the subjective experience of wonder, but to the objective fact. The verb, which is most common in the part. ni, is rendered θαυμάσιος, θαυμαστός and θαυμαστοῦν (causative) in the LXX. θαυμάσιος corresponds almost always (41 times)

---

[17] V. 13b is a quotation from Is. 52:14 (LXX : ἐκστήσονται, Θ : ἐθαύμασαν, quoted in Augustine, De Consensu Evangelistarum : *mirabuntur*). Like Sir., Θ has in view a righteous sufferer. Cf. K. F. Euler, *Die Verkündigung vom leidenden Gottesknecht aus Js. 53 in der griech. Bibel* (1934), 39 ff., 48.

[18] In 2 Macc. 1:22 the miraculous preservation and recapture of the fire of the altar for the second temple brings us into the sphere of legend. Cf. also 3 Macc. 5:39.

[19] Cf. the translation of H. Schmidt (1934), *ad loc.*

to a form of פלא. Only at Nu. 14:11 in A (B : σημεῖον) is it used for אוֹת, which elsewhere in the LXX (some 80 times) is translated σημεῖον, τέρας being used only at Sir. 45:19 and ὑπόδειγμα at 44:16. Once, at Dt. 34:12, θαυμάσιος corresponds to the Heb. מוֹרָא.²⁰ This mostly denotes the wonder which arouses terror, but apart from this passage it is rendered ὅραμα²¹ at Dt. 4:34; 26:8; Ιερ. 39(32):21. מוֹפֵת is also used for miracle. At Sir. 36:5 (33:6) it is translated θαυμάσιος, but σημεῖον at Ex. 7:9; 11:9, 10; 2 Ch. 32:24, and mostly (34 times) τέρας. Only once at Hab. 1:5 do we have θαυμάσατε θαυμάσια for הִתַּמְהוּ תְמָהוּ, where obviously the second form of the stem תמה, which is difficult to fit in syntactically, is taken to be an inner acc. The rendering of the root פלא (פלה) by other words than θαυμάσιος shows us the objective character of the concept of "wonder" herein expressed. A wonder is a mighty act, δύναμις (→ II, 301), Job 37:14, but it is also that which is impossible or extraordinarily difficult for man, and it can thus be translated ἀδυνατεῖν, Gn. 18:14; Dt. 17:8 (for a judicial process which is too difficult for judgment at the gate); Zech. 8:6; ἀδύνατος, Prv. 30:18 (24:53) or χαλεπώτερα, βάθυτερα at Sir. 3:21 B א. ὑπέρογκος is also used in this sense at Dt. 30:11; 2 Βασ. 13:2; Lam. 1:9. θαυμάσιος is used for נפלא וחזק at Sir. 39:20 : Nothing is incomprehensible or difficult for God.²² The same observation applies to the Heb. אַדִּיר, which denotes strength and greatness, but which in the LXX Psalter is often rendered θαυμαστός or θαυμαστοῦν, 8:2, 10; (41:5 ?); 15:3; 75:5; 92:4. The passages speak of God and His work.²³

In such cases the wonder is what is difficult or impossible,²⁴ or possible only for God. In other cases, however, it is something powerful and glorious. Thus μέγας and μεγαλύνειν are used for it in the LXX. In Job 42:3, of course, μεγάλα is only epexegetical to θαυμαστά, but in Is. 9:5 μεγάλης βουλῆς ἄγγελος is obviously the original rendering of פֶּלֶא יוֹעֵץ אֵל גִּבּוֹר and θαυμαστὸς σύμβουλος, θεὸς ἰσχυρός is only a later attempt at a philologically more accurate and literal translation. In Sir. 50:22, too, μεγαλοποιεῖν is used for the wonderful rule of God (פלא). In Nu. 6:2; 15:3, 8 the original פלא has the second sense of "to fulfil a vow," but the LXX fails to see this and the μεγάλως or μεγαλύνειν thus serves to strengthen the main concept εὐχή.²⁵ The term μεγαλεῖον often occurs in the OT and the NT in the sense of a miraculous

²⁰ Cf. P. Churgin, "The Targum and the Septuagint," *American Journal of Semitic Languages and Literature*, 50 (1933), 58, where Dt. 34:12 is regarded as the only passage in which the original translation has undergone later emendations, in part of an exegetical nature (Ιερ. 39[32]:21).

²¹ Elsewhere it is rendered τρόμος (Gn. 9:2; Dt. 11:25 vl.), φοβερός (ψ 75:12) and φόβος (Dt. 11:25; Mal. 1:6; 2:5; Is. 8:12, 13; Sir. 45:2 marg.). In ψ 9:20 the LXX has obviously read מוֹרֶה "teacher" = νομοθέτης.

²² Cf. the transl. of R. Smend, *Die Weisheit des Jesus Sirach* (1906). In Ju. 13:18 ὄνομα θαυμαστόν (ἀγγέλου) implies the name which is ineffable to man.

²³ In the Psalter it is only at ψ 135:18 that אַדִּיר is translated κραταιός (as an adj. with βασιλεύς).

²⁴ In the use of תמה in the Tg. the thought of the impossible is predominant. There is astonishment when something cannot be believed (Abraham, Tg. J., II, Gn. 17:17; Sara, Tg. J., I, Gn. 18:12 etc.). But תִּימְהָא can also mean wonder (= מופת e.g., Tg. J., I, Ex. 7:9). In Rabb. lit. תמה has primarily the sense of astonishment, with more of the element of surprise than of admiration (e.g., M. Ex. 14:29 of angels). Linked with this is the fact that in discussions of the Law it is often used for astonishment on the one side or the other (e.g., jPes., 33b, 53 ff.; also Pes., 6, 2; Zeb., 7, 4), but that the term can also denote expectant surprise (as in Keritot, 4, 3) [Rengstorf].

²⁵ The second meaning of פלא is rightly perceived by the LXX at Lv. 22:21 (διαστέλλειν) and 27:2 (εὔχεσθαι).

act.[26] In Ex. 34:10 ἔνδοξα,[27] and in Job 5:9;[28] 9:10 ἔνδοξα καὶ ἐξαίσια, denote the glorious acts of Yahweh. ἐξαίσια, which in Job 37:16 is used with reference to the fall of the ungodly, contains a suggestion of the monstrous outside all human norms. This element is also present in παραδοξάζειν πληγάς (הַפְלֵא) in Dt. 28:59 and in παράδοξα καὶ θαυμάσια ἔργα with reference to the works of creation in Sir. 43:25. ὑπεραίρειν in Sir. 48:13 is to be taken in the same way, being related to τέρατα and θαυμάσια ἔργα in 48:14 (cf. v. 4). The mystery accompanying the miracle sometimes determines the Gk. rendering. κρύπτειν is to be taken in this way at ʼΙερ. 39(32):27, though it involves a complete alteration of the meaning of the sentence, which in the Mas. is a par. to Gn. 18:14. The context does not support the emendation of יִפָּלֵא to יְכָּסֶה or יִכָּלֵא.[29] Μετατιθέναι in Is. 29:14 means "to act marvellously."

Finally and supremely there is in miracle or wonder an element of the dreadful, the *tremendum*. This seldom appears in the rendering of פלא in the LXX. It is present, however, in Job 10:16, where in accordance with both sense and content the hitp of פלא is rendered δεινῶς με ὀλέκεις. It is also plainly apparent behind the usage of the Gk. Bible inasmuch as Heb. words which contain this element are usually the originals of θαυμάζειν and its cognates.

We have already referred to שׁמם and שׁער (→ 31). Apart from the passages mentioned, the former also occurs at Da. Θ 8:27;[30] LXX 4:19; Sir. 43:24, as the original of θαυμάζειν. It means "to be startled," "to be rigid with terror," and with its wide range of meaning it has been variously rendered in the LXX. שׁער, which is much rarer, is rendered ἀποθαυμάζειν only at Sir. 47:17; elsewhere we find ἐξιστάναι at Ez. 27:35; 32:10; φρίττειν at Jer. 2:12. The rendering of מול ho at Job 41:1 as θαυμάζειν is on the basis of the sense "to fall down for fear." The same applies to מְהוּמָה, "disquiet," "alarm." The LXX has ἔκστασις for this at 2 Ch. 15:5; Zech. 14:13 and θαυμαστά at Am. 3:9. At Job 20:8 חִזְיוֹן x* is rendered θαῦμα. This is to be understood in relation to the vl. φάσμα, φάντασμα and to the par. passage in Job 7:14 : ἐν ὁράμασίν με καταπλήσσεις. Conversely, the use of ὅραμα for מוֹרָא (→ 32) points in the same direction.[31] Finally and supremely, however, נוֹרָא, the part. ni of יָרֵא, forms a common original of the adj. θαυμαστός (Ex. 15:11; 34:10; Dt. 28:58; ψ 44:5; 64:5; 67:35; Da. Θ 9:4; Sir. 43:2, 8).[32] In all these passages the reference is to God, to His name, to His temple or to His works.

Naturally there are other nuances of the terms expressing astonishment, surprise, admiration or the element of miracle or marvel. Those discussed must be taken into account, however, even where the Heb. or Gk. expresses the concept less precisely or where there is a conventional use.[33]

---

[26] On the OT cf. Hatch-Redp.; in the NT Lk. 1:49 (?) and esp. Ac. 2:11.

[27] To the same context belong ἐνδοξάζεσθαι for פלה at Ex. 33:16 and παραδοξάζειν for the same word at Ex. 8:18; 9:4; 11:7.

[28] In the introduction to the hymn to God's mighty power.

[29] Cf. BHK², ad loc.

[30] At Da. 8:27 the LXX has ἐκλύεσθαι and at Da. 4:19 Θ has ἀπονεοῦσθαι. Θ has θαυμάζειν at Ez. 27:35 and 28:19 (LXX in both cases στυγνάζειν), also at Is. 52:14 (LXX ἐξιστάναι). At Is. 52:5, too, the LXX perhaps reads שׁמם instead of משׁל (Duhm⁴ [1922], ad loc.). ʼΑΣΘ all construe משׁל as "to rule."

[31] The hapaxlegomenon תָּוַהּ ("astonish," "startle") is rendered θαυμάζειν at Da. 3:24 (91) LXX and Θ.

[32] At 2 Macc. 15:13 the figure of Jeremiah is described as wonderful in a vision. The emphasis is on its superhuman aspect.

[33] These observations are most important in writings where there is no Heb. original.

The element of the fearful may be detected even in the Heb. and Aram. stem תמה with its generally weak signification. Thus the verb is par. to שמם at Jer. 4:9 in a context of prophetic threatening. The LXX has : ἀπολεῖται ἡ καρδία τοῦ βασιλέως καὶ ἡ καρδία τῶν ἀρχόντων, καὶ οἱ ἱερεῖς ἐκστήσονται, καὶ οἱ προφῆται θαυμάσονται. The element of startled astonishment is also implied in the context of Is. 14:16. If the Heb. original suggests optical perception (שגה), this is a reminder that θαυμάζειν originally denotes the reaction of man to sudden sensual impressions. This element is also present in relation to the שעה hitp of Is. 41:23, which means "to look around," and which is rendered θαυμάζειν in the LXX. The basic sensual significance is also, perhaps, present in Sir. 43:18, where גהה "to blind" (?) [34] is rendered ἐκθαυμάζειν. That תמה denotes startled astonishment may also be seen from the above-mentioned passage in Hab. 1:5, where a verb of seeing is again linked with θαυμάζειν. In ψ 47:5 the combination of ἐθαύμασαν, ἐταράχθησαν and ἐσαλεύθησαν shows that the three terms are related. A translates ἐθαμβήθησαν. [35] Here, too, there is an introductory reference to seeing. At Jl. 2:26 the usage is different. Here the word refers to the wonderful guidance and preservation of the people by Yahweh. The same usage occurs at Sir. 11:13 [36] except that here the reference is to an individual visited by salvation. Is. 61:6 is to be understood of attainment of salvation and corresponding recognition before the world. Here the LXX has θαυμάζειν for the hapaxlegomenon ימר hitp, "to exchange." That it must have conjectured or had before it a form of אמר or הדר, as suggested in OT textual criticism, is most unlikely. [37] The understanding of the text is certainly plain enough in the LXX : ἰσχὺν ἐθνῶν κατέδεσθε καὶ ἐν τῷ πλούτῳ αὐτῶν θαυμασθήσεσθε. The verb here is used with reference to the fact that the wonderful acts of Yahweh are manifested in and to the holy people. There is a similar usage at Sir. 38:3 : ἐπιστήμη ἰατροῦ ... θαυμασθήσεται, cf. v. 6 : καὶ αὐτὸς ἔδωκεν ἀνθρώποις ἐπιστήμην ἐνδοξάζεσθαι ἐν τοῖς θαυμασίοις αὐτοῦ (גבורתיו). The LXX itself invented the concept of the Creator's wonderful gift of means of medicine, and the Heb. יתיצב is not a true equivalent of θαυμάζεσθαι. In Sir. 36:3 א ἐθαυμάσθης ἐν ἡμῖν is similarly used of God Himself. A B follow the Heb. with ἡγιάσθης ἐν ἡμῖν. Cf. also ψ 138:14, where God magnifies Himself among the nations by the miracle of redeeming His people. The prayer expressed here finds its fulfilment in the revelation of the παῖς θεοῦ in Is. 52:15. The LXX certainly formulated this thought independently of the Heb.: οὕτως θαυμάσονται ἔθνη πολλὰ ἐπ᾽ αὐτῷ.

Here θαυμάζεσθαι hardly signifies more than the ἐξιστάναι of Is. 52:14 (Θ : ἐθαύμασαν). It denotes the offence which nations and kings take at the revelation of the Servant of God and at His wonderful recognition by those who did not know Him. [38] This offence is caused by God, and in this sense θαυμάζειν denotes man's reaction to the revelation of the divine — a reaction which humanly speaking

---

[34] Acc. to Smend, op. cit.; cf. גהה, "to heal," Hos. 5:13.

[35] Job 26:11 Σ has θαμβεῖσθαι for תמה. The LXX has ἐξιστάναι. θαυμάζειν is found 4 times in the LXX for תמה. So, too, is ἐξιστάναι. θαυμάσιος occurs once at Hab. 1:5; ἀνα- or ἀποθαυμάζειν once at Sir. 11:13 and θαυμαστός once at Sir. 16:11. The similarity between תמה and θαυμάζειν may have played some part in the selection. (Perhaps א תמהא, המיּת. in the Rabbinic tradition corresponds to the Gk. θαῦμα; cf. Tg. Jer. 5:30 etc. [Rengstorf]).

[36] With the simple form we here have as vl. compounds with ἀπο and ἀνα. Like ἐκθαυμάζειν they have intensive significance, cf. also Sir. 40:7.

[37] BHK², ad loc.

[38] Cf. K. F. Euler, op. cit. (→ n. 17), 49 f., 107 ff.; also on יזּה: = vg. asperget, ᾽ΑΘ. ῥαντίσει, or (acc. to Field) = exsilire (prae admiratione) faciet.

is in the first instance inevitably negative. That θαυμάζειν can have this negative sense may perhaps be seen most clearly in Sir. 11:21, where it refers to the offence which the righteous take at the life and conduct of the wicked, and therefore to their failure to discern God's rule in the world : μὴ θαύμαζε (תמה) ἐν ἔργοις ἁμαρτωλοῦ. Obviously the word has more than this negative sense. God's works bear witness to His gracious will for His creatures. This is expressed in the use of θαυμάσιος and θαυμαστός in the LXX when the reference is to God's wonderful guidance of the righteous (→ 31) and when God, His works and His operation in general are called wonderful.

The LXX mostly took the root פלא in this sense. God performs miracles of punishment and salvation (Ex. 3:20; Jos. 3:5; Ju. 13:18, 19; ψ 39:5; 71:18; 76:14; 77:4, 12; 85:10; 87:10; 97:1; 105:22; 135:4; Est. 4:17c; Job 37:5; Jer. 21:2; Da. 3:43; 8:24; 12:6 LXX, Θ; 4:37a LXX). [39] The righteous have the task of proclaiming these. This is stated again and again in many different ways : διηγεῖσθαι, ψ 9:1; 25:7; 74:1; 104:2; 144:5; Ju. 6:13; 1 Ch. 16:9; ἐκδιηγεῖσθαι, Sir. 42:17; ἐξηγεῖσθαι, 1 Ch. 16:24 (Sixtina, 1587); ἐξομολογεῖσθαι, ψ 88:5; 106:8, 15, 21, 31; 138:14; ἀπαγγέλλειν, ψ 70:17; ἀναγγέλλειν, ψ 95:3; ἀδολεσχεῖν, ψ 118:27; ὁρᾶν, Amos 3:9; Mi. 7:15; εἰδέναι, ψ 106:24; γινώσκειν, ψ 87:12; ἐπίστασθαι, Job 42:3; κατανοεῖν, ψ 118:18; συνιέναι, ψ 105:7; μνημονεύειν, 1 Ch. 16:12; μιμνήσκεσθαι, ψ 76:11; 104:5; ἀναμιμνήσκεσθαι, 2 Εσδρ. 19:17; μνείαν ποιεῖσθαι, ψ 110:4; ἐπιλανθάνεσθαι, ψ 77:11; πιστεύειν, ψ 77:32; καυχᾶσθαι, Sir. 17:8; ἐξιχνιάζειν, Sir. 18:6; (ἐν-)δοξάζεσθαι, Sir. 38:6; 48:4; cf. also ψ 138:6 : ἐθαυμαστώθη ἡ γνῶσίς σου. God Himself is wonderful in His works : ψ 67:35 (ירא ni); 92:4 (אדיר); Jdt. 16:13. Hence all His works can have the attribute of the wonderful : ὄνομα κυρίου, ψ 8:1, 9 (אדיר); σκηνή, ψ 41:4 (אדיר?); ναός, ψ 64:5 (ירא); δυναστεία, Sir. 43:29 (פלא); ἔργα, Tob. 12:22; Sir. 11:4 (פלא); πράγματα, Is. 25:1 (פלא); μαρτύρια, ψ 118:129 (פלא); ὁδός, Wis. 10:17; τέρατα, Wis. 19:8; ἡμέρα, ψ 117:23 (פלא); μετεωρισμοὶ θαλάσσης, ψ 92:4 (אדיר); σελήνη αὐξανομένη, Sir. 43:8 (ירא); σκεῦος, Sir. 43:2 (ירא).

c. To the degree that all God's works may be called wonderful, the attribute applies also to man as the creature of God, and especially to those in whom He specifically manifests His power, i.e., His people, the saints and righteous, and especially martyrs. But it is only in the Hellenistic writings of the OT that this deduction is drawn, and the implied danger of profanation is not avoided. It is directly evident in an exaggerated utterance like Jdt. 10:19 with its heroine cult. It also occurs in Jdt. 11:8, Est. 5:2a and 3 Macc. 1:10. Wis. 8:11 over-emphasises the wise king's sense of his own piety. Above all, the martyr piety of the books of Maccabees sets secular heroic motifs in place of the wonderful testimony to the power of God in martyrdom.

This is true already in 2 Macc. 7:20 and it is everywhere present in the depiction of martyrdom in 4 Macc., e.g., 1:11; 6:11, 13; 7:13; 8:5; 9:26; 17:16, 17; 18:3. This suppression of the concept of revelation in connection with the miracle corresponds to the religious outlook of 4 Macc. and it occurs, e.g., even when the miracle of heredity is emphasised in 15:4 or when finally it is rightly stated from the standpoint of autonomous reason in 14:11: "You do not need to regard it as something particularly wonderful that reason had power over those men in tortures ..." [40] Opposed to this profanation

---

[39] In 2 Macc. 7:18 ἄξια θαυμασμοῦ γέγονεν refers to the divinely effected punishment of the Jewish people.

[40] On the basis of A. Deissmann's translation, ad loc. (Kautzsch Apkr. u. Pseudepigr.). E. T. "Nay, count it not a marvellous thing that reason prevailed over tortures in the case of those men" (M. Hadas, New York, 1953).

and dissolution of miracle in Hellenistic Judaism is the concept of OT revelation that man cannot and should not enter of himself into the sphere of the divine wonder. Cf. Ex. 19:12, 13, 24 (Hb. 12:18 ff.); Ex. 34:30; 1 K. 19:13. In Is. 7 Ahaz represents an intrinsically legitimate view when he rejects as a temptation the offer of a miracle through the prophet. But in so doing he despises the miraculous power of God. On the other hand, the opponents of Jesus in the NT (Mt. 12:38 ff.; Lk. 11:29; Mt. 16:1 ff.; Mk. 8:11 ff.) try to make miracle into an experiment. Their desire for miracle derives from human *hybris*. The Psalmist, on the other hand, avoids the sin of arrogance, ψ 130:1: οὐδὲ ἐπορεύθην ἐν μεγάλοις οὐδὲ ἐν θαυμασίοις ὑπὲρ ἐμέ. And the Heb. אלפ sometimes expresses the same thought (Da. 11:36), for which the Gk. has ἔξαλλος (LXX) or ὑπέρογκος (Θ). The title θαυμαστός is also unbiblical. It is found only once in the Gk. OT at 1 Εσδρ. 4:29, with no Heb. original.

2. Philo and Josephus hardly add anything new in their usage, but they strengthen the secular and legendary motifs.

Above all they emphasise certain wonderful events in OT history, e.g., the miracles of Elisha (Jos. Ant., 9, 182) or miraculous disposings and providences like the deliverance of Saul from David (Ant., 6, 290). The story of the exodus and the wilderness wandering is rightly set under the sign of the miraculous (Philo Vit. Mos., I, 180 and 206). Philo uses the concept of the miraculous supremely in relation to the order of creation, Op. Mund., 49; 90; 95; 106; 78; 172; Vit. Mos., I, 213; Spec. Leg., III, 188, and also in relation to the nature of the Law which everywhere commands recognition, Vit. Mos., II, 10 and 17, and which is unalterable, Spec. Leg., IV, 143, cf. also Vit. Mos., II, 290. Naturally the attribute can be used of details in the story and in the giving of the Law. There are numerous examples. [41]

For Philo, with his Gk. outlook (Plant., 80, cf. Plato → 28), θαυμάζειν has theological significance. The basis of a religious and moral outlook is : μὴ θαυμάζειν . . . χρήματα, . . . δόξαν, . . . σωμάτων δύναμιν, Gig., 37, but : τὸ μόνον θαυμάζετε τίμιον, Agric., 129, cf. 54 and 116; Poster. C., 133; Abr., 103. But it is true of men in general that they value σοφιστείαν πρὸ σοφίας (Op. Mund., 45; here, as often in Philo, θαυμάζειν is used in the sense of "to value"). Wonder in the world can lead to a true admiration of the Creator, but it may also remain fixed on the creature, Op. Mund., 7: τὸν κόσμον ἢ τὸν κοσμοποιόν; Virt., 180; Praem. Poen., 34 and 42; Som., II, 228. He who causes all wonders is the νοῦς ὁ ἐν σοὶ εἴτε ὁ τῶν συμπάντων, Fug., 46. God Himself is θαυματοποιός, Plant., 3. We do not have here, however, the *mysterium tremendum* of divine rule. The terms are used within a rational explanation of the world. They serve, not to glorify God, but to magnify the Jewish religion and those who profess it. Thus Philo does not hesitate to describe wise men and prophets as θαυμασιώτατοι, Abr., 38; Ebr., 210. Even when suffering and evil are declared to be βέλτιστα and θαυμασιώτατα, Leg. All., II, 16, or when the praise of patience is called θαυμασιωτάτη καὶ περιμάχητος, Migr. Abr., 210, we have secular conceptions similar to those of 4 Macc. Thus there is in Philo no true religious use of the word group. On the basis of certain philosophical notions of the Hell. world he uses it apologetically in the sense of propaganda for Judaism.

C. The Use of the Word Group in the NT.

In the religious life of Hellenistic Judaism we obviously miss the deep and obscure undertones which can still be heard in the translation Greek of the LXX. Little of the *mysterium tremendum* is to be found in the admiration of martyrs in the books of Maccabees or in Philo's astonishment at the works of the Creator. There is little sense of man's confrontation by divine revelation. The philosophical element has suppressed or even destroyed the element of revelation present in miracle.

---

[41] Cf. Leisegang, *s.v.*

The result is that it is difficult to find a straight line of continuity from the OT use of this word group to its use in the NT. Externally, to be sure, the NT use agrees with that of the OT in general and it even manifests dependence in many points of detail. But the OT concept of revelation, which had been linked with the concept of wonder in the Greek translation, had now been secularised by Hellenistic Judaism, philosophically weakened and robbed of its theological content. Hence the group could not maintain or recapture in the NT the linguistic significance which it had in the OT. Both the number and the importance of the passages declined, and distinction has to be made between the different literary strata. The Synoptists and Acts, the Johannine writings, Paul and Revelation reveal strong differences in the use of the word group. Regard for these is a prerequisite in the theological understanding of the term "wonderful" within the sphere of the NT revelation.

1. a. Most of the passages occur in the Synoptists, and especially Luke. Here the word is primarily linked with miracle stories. With ἐκπλήσσειν, θαμβεῖσθαι and ἐξιστάναι, θαυμάζειν is used at the end to depict the effect of the miracles on spectators. [42] Thus we read at the end of the story of the Gerasene demoniac in Mk. 5:20 : ἤρξατο κηρύσσειν ἐν τῇ Δεκαπόλει ὅσα ἐποίησεν αὐτῷ ὁ Ἰησοῦς, καὶ πάντες ἐθαύμαζον. The last three words are not found in Lk. 8:39, and in Mt. 8:34 the story closes with the request of the inhabitants that Jesus would leave their district. In Lk. 11:14 we find the observation : ἐθαύμασαν οἱ ὄχλοι, at the end of the account of the healing of the dumb demoniac. Mt. has ἐξίσταντο at the corresponding point (12:23), and he has ἐθαύμασαν οἱ ὄχλοι in the parallel story in chapter 9 (9:33). In the latter passage the astonishment is not so much at the healing itself as at the extraordinary nature of the proceeding. Here, as in similar cases, it is obvious that the purpose of the narrator and author is not to describe the historical and psychological impression made by Jesus on the crowd but rather to use the motif of astonishment as a provisional means to direct the interest of the reader to the significance of the event. Thus exegesis cannot be content merely to interpret the expression of astonishment : οὐδέποτε ἐφάνη οὕτως ἐν τῷ Ἰσραήλ, from the standpoint of those who experienced this history as Jews. It has rather to adopt the standpoint of the Christian community considering the whole history of salvation. This is finely done by Hugo Grotius, [43] who says of Mt. 9:33 : *tot signa, tam admirabilia, tam celeriter, neque contactu tantum, sed et verbo et in omni morborum genere, a nemine antehac edita, ne a Mose quidem.* The θαυμάσαι of Mt. 15:31 is also to be explained with reference to NT salvation history ; here is the fulfilment of Is. 35:5. Mk., which does not have the total account but only the story of the healing of a deaf mute, has for θαυμάσαι the much stronger expression : ὑπερπερισσῶς ἐξεπλήσσοντο (7:37). In Mt. 9:8, at the end of the story of the healing of the man sick of the palsy, ἐθαύμασαν is a vl. for ἐφοβήθησαν. Mk. 2:12 has ἐξίστασθαι (→ II, 459 f.) and Lk. 5:26 ἔκστασις and φόβος. The material point here, of course, is remission of sins rather than healing. The Christian community shares in the joyous astonishment since it recognises here that Jesus does not merely give Himself as a sacrifice for the sins of men but that He personally forgives us our sins. [44] The expressions of astonishment in Lk. 9:43b : πάντων δὲ θαυμαζόντων, and Mt. 21:15 : τὰ θαυ-

---

[42] Cf. M. Dibelius, *Formgeschichte* (1919), 29.
[43] *Annotationes in NT* (ed. C. E. de Windheim, 1755 f.) on Mt. 9:33.
[44] Cf. Grotius, *op. cit.* on Mt. 9:8.

μάσια, are also linked with stories of healing. Elsewhere in the Synoptic tradition θαυμάζειν is found in the story of the epiphany during the storm on the lake, Mt. 8:27: οἱ δὲ ἄνθρωποι ἐθαύμασαν, Lk. 8:25 : φοβηθέντες ἐθαύμασαν. Mk. 4:41 has ἐφοβήθησαν, and in the story of the walking on the water in Mk. 6:51 it is said of the disciples : λίαν ἐκ περισσοῦ ἐν ἑαυτοῖς ἐξίσταντο (καὶ ἐθαύμαζον being almost certainly a later addition). Mt. 14:33 deliberately uses προσκυνεῖν instead. It is here plain that at the most astonishment can be regarded only as a "preliminary stage of the faith which is pleasing to God."[45] Mt. was not satisfied with mere astonishment on the part of the disciples and he therefore changed the text at this point. He could still speak of astonishment in the story of the barren fig-tree in Mt. 21:20. The reply of Jesus shows that this astonishment contains an element of critical questioning, of enquiry and even of doubt. Early exegesis warns us against this by understanding θαυμάζειν here in the sense of "to admire" or even "to magnify" :[46] μόνον δὲ τὸ θαῦμα διόρα καὶ θαύμαζε τὸν θαυματουργόν.[47]

θαυμάζειν is used in accounts of the teaching of Jesus in much the same way as in the miracle stories. It occurs in Lk. 4:22 at the conclusion of the so-called sermon at Nazareth. The hearers are surprised at His eloquence, which they hardly think it possible to expect from a man of His origin. But λόγοι τῆς χάριτος does not refer only to the outward charm of the address.[48] It refers also to its inward content as a proclamation of grace.[49] The attitude of the hearers remains critical : *admirantes hoc dicebant, sed vi veritatis perculsi magis, quam sincero pietatis studio.*[50] Hb. 4:2 is true of them : "The word which they came to hear was of no value to them, because it did not intertwine firmly with the hearers through faith."[51] A second instance is in the debate about taxes. Mt. 22:22, Mk. 12:17 and Lk. 20:26 all wind up this story with an account of the astonishment of His opponents. According to א B Mk. has the stronger compound ἐξεθαύμαζον ἐπ' αὐτῷ, Lk. has θαυμάσαντες ἐπὶ τῇ ἀποκρίσει and Mt. simply ἐθαύμασαν. Early exegesis saw here astonishment at the divine wisdom with which He saw through and refuted His enemies.[52] Rather different is the surprise of the Pharisee that He does not respect Jewish rites of purification before eating (Lk. 11:38). From his own standpoint the Pharisee is here offended by the Lord's attitude. In Mk. 15:5 and Mt. 27:14 Pilate is astonished that Jesus does not defend Himself. But here θαυμάζειν expresses more than mere surprise that one under such serious accusation should not protect himself against charges which are so manifestly false. The μᾶλλον ἐφοβήθη of Jn. 19:8 and the dream of Pilate's wife in Mt. 27:19 show that Pilate senses the mystery of the divine in Jesus, though he cannot formulate it and it does not affect his decision. Naturally this attempt to understand the attitude of the procurator psychologically is made from the standpoint of the

---

[45] Wbg. Mk., 157. It is obviously to be taken in the same way in the reading of D E etc. at Ac. 13:12 : ὁ ἀνθύπατος ... ἐθαύμασεν καὶ ἐπίστευσεν (B etc. only ἐπίστευσεν).
[46] E. Peterson, ΕΙΣ ΘΕΟΣ (1926), 195. Θαυμάζειν can indeed be used of cultic adoration. → 41 on Rev. 13:3; 17:8 and Orig. Cels., III, 77: προσκυνεῖν καὶ θαυμάζειν καὶ σέβειν. Christ is for Celsus ὁ ὑπὸ Χριστιανῶν προσκυνούμενος καὶ θαυμαζόμενος θεός (I, 51).
[47] Cramer Cat., *ad loc.*
[48] Zn. Lk., *ad loc.*
[49] Hck. Lk., *ad loc.*
[50] Grotius, *ad loc.*
[51] On the basis of the translation of H. Menge.
[52] Cramer Cat., *ad loc.*

Christian community. In faith the community sees the majesty of Christ in His lowliness in terms of Is. 49:7. [53] It is thus understandable that the heathen ruler, seized by superstitious awe, should become insecure in his proud and self-conscious attitude. [54] Neither here nor in Mk. 15:44 is there any apologetic motif. [55] In Mk. 15:44 the astonishment of Pilate contains an element of doubt. He cannot believe that the Lord has died with such miraculous speed, since the punishment of crucifixion involved a lingering and agonising death in slow stages. He has to be convinced by the centurion, from whom the nature of Christ's death forced the confession: "Truly this man was the Son of God." The centurion regarded the loud death-cry as a miracle: *accelerata quippe mors erat divino consilio antequam vires eius naturales defecissent, alioqui nondum mors expectari poterat.* [56] θαυμά- ζειν is also found in Lk. 24:12, which corresponds to the narrative in Jn. 20:3-10. In Jn., however, the disciple referred to believes, while here it is said of Peter only that he marvels. The same term occurs at Lk. 24:41 in immediate proximity to ἀπιστεῖν; ἔτι δὲ ἀπιστούντων αὐτῶν ἀπὸ τῆς χαρᾶς καὶ θαυμα- ζόντων is said in respect of the appearance of the risen Lord to the disciples at Jerusalem. Doubt and fear are combined in this θαυμάζειν, as in the well-known conclusion of the story of the empty tomb in Mk. 16:8: ἐφοβοῦντο γάρ.

There are four occurrences of θαυμάζειν in the infancy stories in Lk. The astonishment of the crowd at the extraordinarily long time that Zacharias tarried in the temple (Lk. 1:21) serves as a literary device to prepare readers or hearers for the events which follow. Similarly, the astonishment of the crowd at the miraculous concurrence of the two parents in naming the child (1:63) gives us a sense of the divine action in this story. [57] Again, in Lk. 2:18, 33 the astonishment of the hearers and the parents is a means to prepare the ground for the fact that the story of Jesus has the character of revelation. The marvellous element in this story corresponds to OT prophecy. Jesus Himself applied the saying in Ps. 118:22 f. to Himself in the parable of the wicked husbandmen, Mk. 12:11; Mt. 21:42, in keeping with its Messianic exposition in Judaism. [58] The feminine θαυμαστή does not relate to γωνία [59] or to κεφαλή γωνίας. [60] It is a slavish imitation of the feminine זֹאת, which is really meant as a neuter. [61] As the θαυμάζειν corresponds to OT prophecy, it expresses man's attitude to the divine from the standpoint of religious psychology. This is always present in the background in the Synoptic stories already mentioned, though it may take the various forms of an awesome sense of astonishment at the divine, of a critical surprise which resists or which fails to understand, or of honest and acceptable admiration. But even if there is for the reader at least some expression of the divine mystery which awakens dread, those who know astonishment are still in the forecourt. The human attitude of astonishment at the numinous is not yet faith. At the most it is only a preliminary stage to faith, or, in psychological terms, the impulse which may awaken faith but which may also give rise to doubt.

---

[53] Grotius on Mt. 27:14.
[54] Cf. G. Bertram, *Die Leidensgeschichte Jesu und der Christuskult* (1922), 63 f.
[55] P. Wernle deliberately emphasises the apologetic motifs in ZNW, 1 (1900), 50 ff.
[56] Grotius on Mt. 27:50.
[57] Hck. Lk., *ad loc.*
[58] Str.-B. on Mt. 21:42.
[59] Wettstein in B. Weiss, Mt.[10] (1910), *ad loc.*
[60] B. Weiss, *op. cit.*
[61] Zn. Mt., 632. Kl. Mk. on 12:11.

b. Twice there is reference to astonishment on the part of Jesus. In Mk. 6:6 it is caused by the unbelief with which He meets in Nazareth. If the Evangelist intended a break in his narrative at this point, the statement has the special significance of a conclusion. [62] In Mt. 8:10; Lk. 7:9 it is the faith of the Capernaum centurion which provokes His astonishment: καὶ ζωῆς καὶ θανάτου εἶχεν ὁ ἑκατοντάρχης τὸν Ἰησοῦν ἐξουσιαστήν· διὸ καὶ ἐθαυμάσθη, as Origen says. [63]

2. Acts follows the usage of the Synoptic Gospels. In Ac. 2:7 and 3:12 θαυμάζειν is linked with wonderful events. In Ac. 4:13 there is a parallel to Lk. 4:22 and Jn. 7:15. In Ac. 7:31 the term is used of the OT miracle of the burning bush, which is described as a vision. מַרְאֶה in Ex. 3:3 is ὅραμα. [64] And in Ac. 13:41 there is an OT citation from Hab. 1:5 (→ 32; 34). It serves here as a final admonition and warning to doubters and to despisers of the Word. The negative element seems to be predominant. This is generally true of θαυμάζειν in the NT. Fear and terror are experienced in face of the divine revelation by the man who is not, or not yet, a believer. This is evident in early exegesis in so far as θαυμάζειν is represented by synonyms which particularly express the element of terror. [65]

3. The usage of John's Gospel is different from that of the Synoptics. Above all, θαυμάζειν is not now related directly to individual miracles. Nor is it ever used of the attitude of believers, of disciples, or of the community. It is rather a term for the impact made by the works of Jesus. It is to be understood in this way particularly in Jn. 5:20 [66] and 7:21. [67] In Jn. 4:27 it serves to indicate the disciples' misunderstanding of the conduct of Jesus, in line with other Johannine references to the carnal misunderstandings of the disciples (4:33). The admonition of John's Gospel to the disciples, however is: μὴ θαυμάσῃς (3:7) [68] in the story of Nicodemus, and: μὴ θαυμάζετε (Jn. 5:28) in the saying concerning the hour of revelation, cf. also the saying concerning the hatred of the world in 1 Jn. 3:13. The disciples are to beware of intellectual doubt; they are not to be offended by the message of faith; they are not to be led astray by the hatred of the world (cf. 1 Pt. 4:12: μὴ ξενίζεσθε), which always turns against the good as Cain did against Abel. [69] Materially different is Jn. 9:30. Here the blind man says: "This is the offence (θαυμαστόν) which I take at you, that you do not know whence he is who has opened my eyes." The usage corresponds, however, to that found in other Johannine passages.

4. In Paul θαυμάζειν is used actively only as a literary form. It is thus used in Gl. 1:6 to express surprise at the conduct of the Galatians and corresponds to a usage often found in Greek rhetoricians. [70] The οὐ θαῦμα of 2 C. 11:14 is also a transitional formula found in the Hellenistic diatribe. [71] In 2 Th. 1:10, on the

---

[62] Hck. Mk., ad loc.
[63] Cramer Cat., ad loc.
[64] More often for מוֹרָא → 32.
[65] Cf. Cramer Cat., e.g., Chrysostom on Ac. 3:12; 4:13; 13:41.
[66] Unbelieving opponents are in view; hence πιστεύειν is avoided (B. Weiss, op. cit., ad loc.).
[67] Cf. the usage in Qoh. 5:7; Sir. 11:21.
[68] On Jn. 3:7 cf. Dg., 10, 4: μὴ θαυμάσῃς εἰ δύναται μιμητὴς ἄνθρωπος γενέσθαι θεοῦ. Here a doubt similar to that of Nicodemus is repudiated.
[69] Cf. Bü. J., ad loc.
[70] F. Sieffert⁹ (1899) on Gl. 1:6.
[71] Wnd. 2 K. on 11:14.

other hand, we find the verb in the passive, as often in the LXX. [72] Here the reference is to the eschatological manifestation of the glory of God among saints and believers. It is obvious that the community shares in this glory, as is attested in many eschatological passages in the NT. Both materially and formally θαυμασθῆναι is here parallel to ἐνδοξασθῆναι.

Early exegesis interprets the passage as follows : δι' ἐκείνων (τῶν πιστευόντων) γὰρ θαυμαστὸς ἐπιδείκνυται, ὅταν τοὺς οἰκτροὺς τοὺς ταλαιπώρους καὶ μυρία παθόντας δεινὰ καὶ πιστεύσαντας εἰς τοσαύτην ἄγει λαμπρότητα. δείκνυται αὐτοῦ ἡ ἰσχύς τότε. [73] Grotius attempts to link the glory of Christ with that of believers rather differently : tum id fiet, quum Christus, credentes eosdemque sanctos in summam claritatem evehendo, admirandam ex hoc facto claritatem consequetur. [74]

5. Elsewhere the word is found once at Jd. 16 in the familiar OT phrase θαυμάζειν πρόσωπον. Usually the NT has instead πρόσωπον λαμβάνειν, βλέπειν εἰς πρόσωπον or the new construct προσωπολημπτεῖν. In 1 Pt. 2:9 we have a formulation which is strongly reminiscent of Hellenistic style : ὅπως τὰς ἀρετὰς ἐξαγγείλητε τοῦ ἐκ σκότους ὑμᾶς καλέσαντος εἰς τὸ θαυμαστὸν αὐτοῦ φῶς.

The same expression is found in 1 Cl., 36, 2, which reads : διὰ τούτου ἡ ἀσύνετος καὶ ἐσκοτωμένη διάνοια ἡμῶν ἀναθάλλει εἰς τὸ θαυμαστὸν αὐτοῦ φῶς. In the Dionysian mysteries the way of the initiate goes through the darkness with φρίκη, τρόμος, ἱδρώς, θάμβος, ἐκ δὲ τούτου φῶς τι θαυμαστὸν ἀπήντησε ... [75] That these mystical speculations penetrated into the Church may be seen from the occasional understanding of 1 Pt. 2:9 as a revelation of the mystical sense of Is. 42:6, 7 and Job 37:21. [76]

6. Finally the word group is found 6 times in Rev. At Rev. 13:3, where ἐθαυμάσθη is to be read as a pass. aorist with intr. significance, [77] the startled wonder refers to the return of Nero and the ἐξουσία of the beast. [78] As may be seen from v. 4 and from 17:8, the thought is one of cultic adoration, which was already a historical reality in the imperial cult. The astonishment is a "typical human reaction to the appearance of an anti-godly being." [79] Astonishment is the first step to prostration before the beast. It is for this reason that the angel forbids the "marvelling" of the seer in Rev. 17:6, 7, though this is a natural reaction in his soul to the fearful nature of what he sees. [80] We thus have here the same view of astonishment as in Jn. In another passage (15:1) Rev. calls a sign from heaven great and wonderful, and in 15:3, in a hymn to God, His works are called great and wonderful. This usage corresponds to that of the Psalms, and there is nothing new or distinctive about it.

---

[72] E.g., Sir. 38:3, 6; Is. 61:6; 4 Βασ. 5:1; Wis. 8:11.
[73] Cramer Cat., ad loc.
[74] Grotius, ad loc.
[75] Cf. R. Perdelwitz, Die Mysterienreligion und das Problem des I. Petrusbriefes = RVV, 11, 3 (1911), 78. Plut. Fr., VI : Ex Opere de Anima, 2, 6.
[76] Grotius, ad loc.
[77] Bl.-Debr.[6] § 78.
[78] Bousset, ad loc., cf. also E. B. Allo, St. Jean L'Apocalypse[2] (1921), 187.
[79] Loh. Apk., ad loc.
[80] Cf. Cramer Cat., ad loc.: ὑπερβαλλούσῃ ἐκπλήξει κατάσχετον γενέσθαι τοῦτο γὰρ τὸ μέγα θαῦμα ἐμφαίνει.

D. The Word Group in Early Christian Usage.

The same is true in general of the use of the group in early Christian literature. At one point, however, there is a radical departure from the biblical framework, namely, in the saying of Jesus from the Ev. Hebr. preserved in Cl. Al. Strom., II, 9, 45, 4.

It is also found in Clement himself (Strom., V, 14, 96, 3) and in the second Oxyrhynchus logion [81] in a similar form, though with the key-word θαμβεῖν (→ 7). In the present form ὁ θαυμάσας βασιλεύσει, the word obviously echoes the basic motif in Platonic philosophy sometimes found in Philo, and in this respect it threatens a mystical and speculative misunderstanding of the biblical concept of wonder. Thus it is a mistake to set Jn. 5:20 alongside the logion and thereby to rob the concept in the NT of its suggestion of the imperfect and provisional. The clear insight that the religious experience of wonder is provisional is particularly threatened when the attribute or predicate of the wonderful is arbitrarily and in a weakened sense linked with various Christian blessings, as in Hell. Judaism. Thus, e.g., in 1 Cl., 1, 2 : τήν τε σώφρονα καὶ ἐπιεικῆ ... εὐσέβειαν; 35, 1: ὡς μακάρια καὶ θαυμαστὰ τὰ δῶρα τοῦ θεοῦ; 50, 1: ἡ ἀγάπη. The case is different in 2 Cl., 13, 3 and 4, where the element of the provisional remains when wonder is ascribed to the Gentiles : τὰ ἔθνη γὰρ ἀκούοντα ... τὰ λόγια τοῦ θεοῦ ὡς καλὰ καὶ μεγάλα θαυμάζει ... θαυμάζουσι τὴν ὑπερβολὴν τῆς ἀγαθότητος (Lk. 6:32 ff., cf. Just. Apol., 16, 2). Theological particularity also characterises the thought in 2 Cl., 2, 6 : ἐκεῖνο γάρ ἐστιν μέγα καὶ θαυμαστόν, οὐ τὰ ἑστῶτα στηρίζειν ἀλλὰ τὰ πίπτοντα. In Hermes v., 1, 3, 3 θαυμαστῶς refers to heavenly revelations which man can neither apprehend nor sustain. The usage in early Christian martyrology does not differ essentially from that of 4 Macc. Cf., e.g., Mart. Pol., 3, 2 : τὸ πλῆθος, θαυμάσαν τὴν γενναιότητα τοῦ θεοφιλοῦς ... γένους τῶν Χριστιανῶν; 7, 2 : θαυμαζόντων ... τὴν ἡλικίαν αὐτοῦ καὶ τὸ εὐσταθές; 15, 1 ff.: θαῦμα εἴδομεν, οἷς ἰδεῖν ἐδόθη ... τὸ γὰρ πῦρ ... ὥσπερ ὀθόνη πλοίου; 16, 1: θαυμάσαι πάντα τὸν ὄχλον εἰ; 16, 2: θαυμασιώτατος μάρτυς. The word group occurs several times in Just. and Ep. Dg., but there are no distinctive features. Ref. may be made to Just. Dial., 10, 2 which speaks of παραγγέλματα, θαυμαστὰ οὕτως καὶ μεγάλα ... ὡς ὑπολαμβάνειν, μηδένα δύνασθαι φυλάξαι αὐτά, and to Dial., 100, 1, where in allusion to Ps. 22:3 it is said of the resurrection of Jesus: ἐπαίνου ἄξιον καὶ θαυμασμοῦ μέλλει ποιεῖν ... ἀνίστασθαι.

Bertram

θεάομαι → ὁράω.

| † θέατρον, † θεατρίζομαι |

θέατρον (from the time of Hdt., not in the LXX): a. the "theatre" (or "amphitheatre") which serves for the presentation of dramatic and other spectacles and also for public assemblies (Ac. 19:29, 31); [1] b. collectively the "spectators" (Plat. Symp., 194b

---

[81] Deissmann LO, 363 ff.
θ έ α τ ρ ο ν κ τ λ. Joh. W., 1 K, Ltzm. K on 1 C. 4:9; A. Bonhöffer, *Epiktet u. das NT* (1911), 170; Wendland Hell. Kult., 357, n. 1; M. Dibelius, *Die Geisterwelt im Glauben des Pls.* (1909), 28 ff.; H. J. Cadbury, "θεατρίζω no longer a NT Hapax Legomenon," ZNW, 29 (1930), 60-63; A. Schweitzer, *Die Mystik des Ap. Pls.* (1930), 149.
[1] Cf. the interesting inscr. in two languages from the same theatre in Ephesus (103/104 A.D.): ἵνα τίθηνται κατ᾽ ἐκκλησίαν ἐν τῷ (sic) θεάτρῳ (sic) ἐπὶ τῶν βάσεων, Deissmann LO, 90 f.

etc.); c. (= θέαμα) the "play" or "spectacle" seen in a theatre (Aeschines Socraticus, Dialogi, 3, 20; Achill. Tat., I, 16). θεατρίζω, "to make a spectacle of someone." It was once thought that this word did not occur in non-Christian literature, [2] but it has now been found on a Gerasenic inscr. from the reign of Trajan. [3] Cf. also Polyb., 3, 91, 10; 5, 15, 2; 11, 8, 7: ἐκθεατρίζω.

Sense c., like θέαμα, is a favourite Stoic image to express the fact that the "wise man in conflict with fate is a spectacle for gods and men." [4] Sen., De Providentia, 2, 9 (cf. Ep., 64, 4-6): To see a brave man fighting misfortune is a spectaculum deo dignum. Epict. especially calls "the true philosopher generally, but particularly in conflict with misfortune, a θέαμα which gives pleasure to both gods and men," [5] Diss., II, 19, 25; III, 22, 59. It is a proud fight and a joyful spectacle. Jupiter takes pleasure in the sight of Cato, iam partibus non semel fractis stantem nihilominus inter ruinas publicas rectum (Sen., op. cit.). [6]

There is an external echo of this usage in 1 C. 4:9 : ὅτι θέατρον ἐγενήθημεν τῷ κόσμῳ καὶ ἀγγέλοις [7] καὶ ἀνθρώποις; [8] cf. also Hb. 10:33 : ὀνειδισμοῖς τε καὶ θλίψεσιν θεατριζόμενοι. [9] It is naturally conceivable [10] that Paul adopted a popular philosophical slogan current in his age and communities. [11] But 1. there are also reminiscences of Job, whose sufferings were a spectacle to angels (Satan: one of the בְּנֵי הָאֱלֹהִים; → I, 78), and to men (the friends); 2. the θέατρον is by human standards, not a proud one, but a sorry (→ ἀσθένεια, I, 490 ff.) and contemptible; [12] and 3. the emphasis is on the θεὸς ἀπέδειξεν from 9a. To put the subject thus is to give to the whole process a very different character from that of the Stoic image. In the Stoic use deity is a spectator of the battle which man himself fights in the proud autonomy of his heroism. Here, however, God is the author of the weakness of His apostles, which, because it is of God, is true, i.e., divine, power, so that the spectators think they see something quite different from that which is really enacted in this θέατρον.

Kittel

θεῖος, θειότης → θεός.

---

[2] So also Pr.-Bauer, 551.

[3] This inscr. has been published as No. 14 by A. H. M. Jones, *Journal of Roman Studies*, 18 (1928), 144 ff.; cf. also Cadbury, op. cit. for the key sentences.

[4] Schweitzer ; Lietzmann, op. cit.

[5] Bonhöffer, op. cit.

[6] Elsewhere without the philosophical note and therefore of man who feels himself to be *infelix*, Sallust., De Bello Iugurthino, 14, 23; Plin. Panegyricus (M. Schuster, 1933), 33; Polyb., 3, 91, 10.

[7] 1 Pt. 1:12 (εἰς ἃ ἐπιθυμοῦσιν ἄγγελοι παρακύψαι) is often quoted as a par. but it refers to something quite different, i.e., not to the suffering but to the glory of Christ, which the angels desire to see because they have nothing comparable (→ I, 85).

[8] Different again is Slav. En. 62:9-12 : The angels of punishment take charge of the wicked and punish them for their misdeeds. "They (the wicked) will provide a spectacle for the righteous and His elect (the good), who will rejoice over them because the wrath of God rests on them and His sword is intoxicated with their blood."

[9] Perhaps the vl. ὀνειδ- arose because the verb is unusual (D*). It is hardly necessary to refer to the torches of Nero, e.g., Wnd., ad loc.

[10] As against Bonhöffer, who sharply resists this view.

[11] Pre-Pauline examples may be found in Jewish martyrology. Cf. Philo Flacc., 72 : ὥσπερ ἐν τοῖς θεατρικοῖς μίμοις καθυπεκρίνοντο τοὺς πάσχοντας; Leg. Gaj., 368 : τοιοῦτον ἀντὶ δικαστηρίου θέατρον ὁμοῦ καὶ δεσμωτήριον ἐκφυγόντες. οἰκτροτάτη θεωρία is found in a similar context in 3 Macc. 5:24 [Bertram].

[12] So correctly Bonhöffer.

θέλω, θέλημα, θέλησις

θέλω.

Contents: A. The Common Greek Meaning of (ἐ)θέλω; B. Significant Features in the NT Use of θέλω from the Standpoint of Biblical Theology: 1. The θέλειν of God; 2. The θέλειν of Jesus; 3. The θέλειν of Paul in His Authoritative Apostolic Dealings with the Churches; 4. Religious θέλειν and its Opposite in the NT.

On the distinction between (ἐ)θέλω and βούλομαι → I, 629 ff. The usage must be investigated in epochs, since the two terms mostly express the same thing. On the predominance of ἐθέλω in Hom. → I, 630, and on its replacement by βούλομαι from the time of Hdt., and often in the prose writers → I, 630. The inter-relation is much the same in the LXX → I, 630 f. In Polyb. I have counted βούλομαι 450 times and θέλω 29, and in the seven books of Diod. S. βούλομαι 88 times and θέλω 4. The meanings of θέλω in Polyb. and the LXX are distributed as follows: Polyb. "to purpose" 17, "to be ready or willing" 4, and very rarely "to resolve," "to wish"; LXX "to find pleasure in" 14, "to have a desire for" 11, "to wish" 14, "to desire" 2, "to purpose" 9, and of "resolution" 7, "to be ready or inclined" 6, "to be on the point of" 1, "to prefer" 1, and negatively "to refuse" 31, of the divine will 21 and the royal will 3. The inter-relation is different again in the NT → I, 632. The usage in Epict. Diss. corresponds to that of the NT, with 433 instances of θέλω and 42 of βούλομαι (including the Fr.).

θέλειν is very commonly used in the OT in a negative sense. Thus it is usually negative as a rendering of אבה. Only חפץ = θέλειν has mostly a positive sense. Since אבה is predominantly the original in Gn. and 4 Βασ., and חפץ in the Ps. and other writings, the positive θέλειν is found esp. in the writings and in the Hell. books, and sometimes in the prophets, though not in Jeremiah, who simply has οὐ θέλειν for the root מאן. Only in the Gk. translation is there introduced more commonly the concept of volition. The Heb. refers rather to desiring or taking pleasure in (→ θέλημα, 54).[1]

On the verbal forms of (ἐ)θέλω, which sometimes vary in the dialects, cf. Liddell-Scott. ἐθέλω is Homeric Attic. Hom. and Hes. never have θέλω (Il., 1, 277; Od., 15, 317 are doubtful). Early Attic inscr. also have ἐθέλω. θέλω is still rare in the early epic and lyric literature of the 6th cent. It is more common in the 5th. Attic prose writers use it sparingly. On Ionic inscr. cf. Ditt. Syll.³, 45, 16 (4th cent. B.C.); 1037, 7 (4th cent. B.C.). From the 2nd cent. θέλω is used on Attic inscr. and it then becomes general. θέλω predominates in the pap., and it is normal in the *koine* except in augmented forms. ἐθέλω does not occur in the LXX or the NT.

A. The Common Greek Meaning of (ἐ)θέλω.

We may obviously assume as the original and basic meanings:[2]

1. The category of approach in the sense of a. "to be ready or inclined." This readiness need not derive from inclination. It may involve agreement[3] or even compulsion.[4] Thus there is often the nuance of "to consent to."[5] Negatively we have "not

---

θ έ λ ω. R. Rödiger in *Glotta*, 8 (1917), 1 ff. with bibl. → βούλομαι, I, 629. On the Attic ἐθέλω cf. K. Meisterhans-E. Schwyzer, *Grammatik der Attischen Inschriften*³ (1900), 178; θέλω in the pap., Mayser, 350 f. C. H. Turner, "The Verb θέλω as Auxiliary," JThSt, 28 (1927), 355-357. θέλημα: A. W. Slaten, *Qualitative Nouns in the Pauline Epistles*, 2nd Series, Vol. IV, Part 1 (1918), 52 ff.

[1] This paragraph is by G. Bertram.
[2] Rödiger, 14 ff. In the NT Mt. 26:15.
[3] Hom. Il., 7, 364; Jos. Ant., 13, 257; Philo Jos., 228; Jm. 2:20.
[4] Polyb., 30, 31, 8.
[5] Philo Spec. Leg., III, 31; Epict. Diss., I, 1, 19; Mt. 11:14; Ac. 26:5.

to be inclined," in the first instance with no basic resolution. [6] b. "To take pleasure in," "to like," on the basis of inclination or pleasure. Hence "it is agreeable to me," "it pleases me," with no great stress on the activity of wishing or desiring. [7]

2. The motive of desire. a. "Express desire" [8] which can have the character of "wanting" or a strong "desire to have." [9] b. In this respect θέλειν can be used in the most varied ways in a sexual and erotic sense, "to take pleasure in," "to experience desire or impulse," "to come together" and even "to conceive." [10] In Gnosticism it is used of the generation which produces emanation. [11] But it also signifies love for sons, brothers or friends. [12] c. With no erotic suggestion it is used in the LXX for "to like," "to take pleasure in someone or something," primarily with man as subj. [13] In Ign. we have θέλειν absol. in the sense of "to experience love." [14] This is linked with b. (spiritualised) and also with c. in view of the closeness of Ign. to Palestinian usage. The LXX mainly has this θέλειν with God as subject. It is a rendering of חָפֵץ בְּ or c. acc. or of רָצָה בְּ, for which εὐδοκεῖν is often used, → II, 738. It is usually construed with the acc. [15] or with ἐν c. dat. [16] or very occasionally with the dat. [17]

---

[6] Test. L. 9:2; Gn. 24:8 (לֹא אָבָה); 37:35 (מֵאֵן לְ).

[7] Hom. Il., 23, 894; Plat. Theaet., 143d; Cant. 2:7; Jos. Ant., 1, 236; Philo Op. Mund., 88. Very common in Epict., Diss., II, 14, 16. But he can also use βούλομαι instead, II, 24, 6 and 9. The impulsive θέλειν of taste and appetite, Lk. 5:39; perhaps also Mt. 27:34 negatively, unless there is here deliberate rejection of the opiate. "Not to like," "to have no desire for," 2 Th. 3:10; Mt. 23:4. Arbitrary, capricious or indifferent choice or pleasure, Mk. 9:13; Jn. 5:35; 21:18.

[8] Soph. El., 80; Hdt., 2, 2; Diod. S., I, 36, 2; LXX for חפץ: 3 Βασ. 10:13; ψ 34:27; 2 Macc. 12:4; θέλειν εἰ: Sir. 23:14; Jos. Ant., 17, 137; frequ. in Epict. Diss., I, 1, 18, though βούλομαι in IV, 1, 156 f. Corp. Herm., I, 30; P. Giess., I, 40, col. II, 25 (2nd cent. A.D.). This activity of wishing is strong in the NT. For an urgent, demanding θέλειν which takes the form of a request, cf. Jn. 9:27; 12:21; Mt. 5:42; 12:38; Mk. 6:22, 25 (ἵνα); 1 C. 14:35. For θέλειν followed by ποιεῖν cf. Mk. 14:7. For wish as a direction, Ac. 10:10. More rarely we have a pure wish, Gl. 4:20; 2 C. 12:20. In 1 C. 7:7 it has a fictional character. In 1 C. 14:5 it is simply the acceptance of a possibility worth striving after. In many cases it may not be granted, Lk. 8:20, or cannot be granted, Hb. 12:17; Lk. 10:24. As natural human desire it may be directed to religious ends, though without including the certainty of ἐλπίζειν, 2 C. 5:4.

[9] Hom. Od., 11, 566; ψ 33:12; Mal. 3:1; Jos. Bell., 3, 370; P. Tebt., 423, 21 (3rd cent. A.D.). Noteworthy in the NT are Mk. 9:35; 10:43 f.; Mt. 20:26 f., where it denotes the natural desire for power, the impulsive search after greatness and rank, which in the next sentences are contrasted with the true goal of the disciple to be a δοῦλος and διάκονος.

[10] Hom. Il., 9, 397; Od., 3, 272; 8, 316. LXX Dt. 21:14 (חפץ); Diod. S., IV, 36, 4; Philo Vit. Mos., I, 297, 300; Sobr., 32; Poster. C., 175. Cf. 1 Tm. 5:11: γαμεῖν θέλουσιν, of young widows, → 61.

[11] Iren. Haer., I, 12, 1; Hipp. Ref., VI, 38, 5; Epiph. Haer., 33, 1, 4 → 53.

[12] Epict. Diss., III, 24, 85. Rarely βούλομαι instead, II, 18, 18.

[13] For חפץ בְּ, 1 Βασ. 18:22; 2 Βασ. 15:26; 3 Βασ. 10:9; 1 Ch. 28:4; ψ 111:1; 146:10. Cf. Tob. 4:5. Col. 2:18: θέλων ἐν ταπεινοφροσύνῃ καὶ θρησκείᾳ τῶν ἀγγέλων is to be construed along these lines as "to take pleasure in." Cf., however, the uncertain reading Test. A. 1:6: ἐὰν οὖν ἡ ψυχὴ θέλει ἐν καλῷ. A. Fridrichsen, ZNW, 21 (1922),135-137 takes θέλων as an adv. more closely defining καταβραβευέτω, "willingly," "after mature reflection." But the LXX usage is more natural. The conjectures of Ew. Gefbr., Cr.-Kö., 483 are unnecessary.

[14] Ign. R., 8, 1 and 3 (opp. μισεῖν).

[15] For חפץ בְּ: ψ 17:19; 40:11; Ez. 18:23, 32; Tob. 13:8. For חפץ c. acc., ψ 36:23.

[16] 2 Βασ. 15:26; ψ 146:10 (חפץ בְּ).

[17] 2 Ch. 9:8.

3. Intention. a. In this sense, often related to that of wishing, θέλειν has the distinctive sense of the determined and active fixing of the will on action.[18] In Hom. it often carries the suggestion of a venture.[19] b. The element of intention is carried a step further when it acquires the sense of "to be on the point of doing something." This cannot be expressed by βούλεσθαι.[20] c. It is even more expressive of action when it means "to be used to doing something."[21] In this sense it is often linked with an impersonal subject.[22] d. Very frequently, though less so than in the case of βούλεσθαι, the θέλειν of material subject occurs with the addition λέγειν, σημαίνειν, εἶναι, προφαίνειν, and in such cases it means "to purpose," "to intend," "to aim."[23] e. The idea of purpose is also present when it implies "to maintain in opposition to the true facts," as esp. in the form θέλοντες εἶναι.[24]

4. The category of resolve, decision and choice. a. Here are the following nuances: the maturely weighed decision,[25] the decision which is resolute but which is self-constraining,[26] and free resolve.[27] b. The latter may involve choice or selection[28] (→ II, 740). The θέλειν of choice is often accompanied by an ἤ or a μᾶλλον: "to prefer something in choice."[29] c. For "resolute willingness in the religious sense" θέλειν is used not only in the LXX but also commonly elsewhere.[30] d. An important role is played by the negative conception of considered or resolute refusal or resistance.[31]

---

[18] Hom. Il., 1, 549; Test. S. 2:10. LXX: Ju. 20:5 (דְּמָה pi); 2 Ch. 7:11 A (כָּל־הַבָּא עַל־לֵב); ψ 39:14 (חפץ c. acc.); 2 Macc. 15:38; Jos. Ant., 2, 204 etc. Philo Conf. Ling., 5; Epict. Diss., I, 24, 2 etc. (βούλεσθαι, prooem., 7). Very often with purpose of action in the NT, Lk. 13:31; 14:28; Ac. 7:28; Jn. 6:67; of the radical striving which attains a goal, Gl. 1:7; 6:13. As a desire in conversation, Jn. 16:19; Lk. 10:29; 2 C. 12:6. More strongly, "to champion something in speech," Ac. 17:18. Sometimes the purpose is not achieved, Jn. 7:44; Ac. 19:33; 1 Th. 2:18. In 1 C. 16:7 attainment is dependent on the Lord's permission.

[19] Hom. Od., 8, 223; Il., 2, 247. Cf. Lk. 18:13.

[20] Hom. Il., 6, 336; Tob. 3:10 א; Jos. Bell., 5, 99; Philo Gig., 39; Cher., 115. NT: Mk. 6:48; Mt. 5:40; Jn. 1:43; 6:21; Ac. 14:13; Gl. 4:9.

[21] Mk. 12:38. Lk. 20:46 τῶν θελόντων ἐν στολαῖς περιπατεῖν, "they desire to walk ...," cf. φιλεῖν in Mt. 23:6; Lk. 20:46. Related is Gl. 6:12. The usage is also influenced by the sense "it pleases them." Cf. Epict. Diss., IV, 9, 7: ἐσθῆτα ἐπιδεικνύειν θέλεις στιλπνήν.

[22] Antiphon Fr., 49 (II, 300, 8, Diels); Hdt., I, 74, 21; Xenoph. Mem., III, 12, 8. Cf. Rödiger, 18 f.

[23] Hdt., I, 78; II, 13; IV, 131; Lk. 15:26 D; Ac. 2:12; 17:20.

[24] Epict. Diss., I, 19, 12; IV, 2, 10; Herodian, V, 3, 11; Paus., I, 4, 6. "To maintain," 2 Pt. 3:5; "to claim to be teachers of the law," 1 Tm. 1:7.

[25] Plat. Resp., X, 604d; Jos. Ant., 2, 69; Philo Vit. Mos., I, 249; Migr. Abr., 11. For definite will in the NT cf. Jn. 5:6; for will grounded in solid motives, Mk. 6:26; Phlm. 14. Resolution as a mature attitude of will, Mt. 1:19, where βούλεσθαι is the practical intention (→ I, 632, n. 53). Resolute refusal for definite reasons is commonly expressed by οὐ θέλειν, Mt. 2:18 (Ιερ. 38:15); Jn. 7:1; Mt. 18:30; Lk. 15:28; 18:4.

[26] Thuc., III, 56, 5; Philo Ebr., 167; Spec. Leg., III, 154.

[27] Plat. Prot., 335b; Philo Sobr., 20.

[28] Jos. Ant., 8, 311; Philo Sacr. AC, 37. For the θέλειν of choice or decision in the NT cf. Mk. 15:9; Mt. 27:15, 17, 21 (cf. ἤ in 17); Ac. 25:9; 1 C. 7:39; 10:27.

[29] Cf. Rödiger, 20 f., 22. ἤ : Hos. 6:6 B (חפץ); ἤπερ : 2 Macc. 14:42; μᾶλλον ἤ : Jos. Ant., 9, 240; Bell., 7, 12; Epict. Diss., IV, 1, 50 etc.; BGU, III, 846, 15. θέλειν ἤ in the NT as "to prefer," 1 C. 4:21; 14:19.

[30] 1 Ch. 28:9 (וּבְנֶפֶשׁ חֲפֵצָה); 2 Εσδρ. 11:11 (חפץ); Sir. 15:15; Is. 1:19 (אבה); Test. A. 1:6; Jos. Ant., 19, 284; Philo Abr., 5; Corp. Herm., XI, 21b; 2 Cl., 6, 1.

[31] Hdt., 6, 12; Polyb., VI, 37, 12. In the LXX mostly for לֹא אָבָה: 1 Βασ. 26:23; Prv. 1:30; Is. 28:12, or for מֵאֵן: Nu. 20:21; ψ 77:10; Hos. 11:5. Cf. Jos. Bell., 7, 51; Philo Leg. All., III, 81; Epict. Diss., II, 20, 28.

5. θέλειν as commanding will. a. Expressly of God and His purposes and rule. The formula ἐὰν θεὸς (θεοἰ) θέλῃ (θέλωσιν) is a common legacy of antiquity. [32] In the LXX this θέλειν is used of God's sovereign rule in creation and human history, [33] for His control manifested in individual events. [34] Josephus made much use of the very common expression θεοῦ θέλοντος, or θελήσαντος. [35] Philo uses θέλειν in dealing with God's creation, His direction of the world structure and His revelation. [36] But he can also ascribe this to φύσις. [37] Epict., too, can say ὡς ἡ τύχη θέλει instead of ὡς ὁ θεὸς θέλει. [38] For him the true θέλειν of the man who is trained philosophically is agreement with the θέλειν of God, while τὰ μὴ θελητὰ θέλειν means θεομαχεῖν. [39] He has in view the willing of what is attainable or possible, the non-willing of what is not possible, the acceptance of the inevitable. Thus everything depends upon the μὴ θέλειν of unprofitable wishes. He who accepts the foreordination of life by fate is completely subject to God. [40] The Corp. Herm. has its own distinctive use of θέλειν in relation to God. The will of the νοῦς at creation, i.e., of the demiurge, is that the cosmos should be living. God wills that all things should be. The existence of all things consists in this. [41] Ign., too, treats of the divine will which is orientated to all that is. 1 Cl. refers to the will of God which sustains, which directs and which encloses all gnosis in Christ. [42] b. There is a human analogy to the authoritative utterance of God's will in the rule of princes and administrators, in the directions of the royal will, [43] also in the desires of officials, in military commands, [44] and in the promulgation of law. [45]

B. Significant Features in the NT Use of θέλειν from the Standpoint of Biblical Theology.

1. The θέλειν of God.

God's θέλειν is always characterised by absolute definiteness, sovereign self-assurance and efficacy. It is resolute and complete willing. Only once is θέλειν used for the OT חפץ in the sense of elective and loving good-pleasure in the Son (→ II, 740): Mt. 27:43 quoting ψ 21:8. Elsewhere it refers either to the divine will in creation (1 C. 12:18; 15:38) or to the divine sovereignty in disposing to salvation (Jn. 3:8 of the Spirit in regeneration; 1 Tm. 2:4 of God's gracious and majestic will to save all). In Mt. 20:14 f., on the lips of the owner of the vineyard, it

---

[32] Cf. Rödiger, 16 f. Hom. Il., 1, 554; 14, 120; 19, 274; ἐὰν θεὸς θέλῃ : Xenoph. Cyrop., II, 4, 19; Plat. Phaed., 80d; Stobaei Hermetica, Excerptum, II, A, 2 (Scott, I, 382, 16); P. Petr., I, 2, 3 (3rd cent. B.C.).
[33] ψ 113:10 (חפץ); 134:6, cf. Mt. 6:10; Job 23:13; Da. LXX 4:17; Jdt. 8:15; Wis. 11:25; 12:18; Sir. 39:6. For His will in His Word, Is. 55:11; for His will as a secret, Wis. 9:13.
[34] אָבָה לֹא : Dt. 10:10; 4 Βασ. 13:23; 24:4.
[35] Jos. Ant., 2, 333; 7, 209; 18, 119 etc. Cf. P. Oxy., III, 533, 10 (2nd cent. A.D.); P. Giess., I, 18, 10 f. (reign of Hadrian) etc.
[36] Philo Conf. Ling., 175; Op. Mund., 46; Sacr. AC, 40; Decal., 43.
[37] Philo Gig., 43.
[38] Epict. Diss., I, 1, 17; IV, 6, 21; cf. with II, 7, 9.
[39] Ibid., IV, 1, 89 f., cf. IV, 1, 100.
[40] Ibid., II, 17, 21 f., 28; II, 16, 42; 47; III, 10, 5 f.; III, 24, 96-99; IV, 1, 100.
[41] Corp. Herm., I, 11b; IV, 2, 3; XII, 15b; X, 2; Stobaei Hermetica, Excerptum VII (Scott, I, 418, 25 ff.).
[42] Ign. R., prooem.; 1 Cl., 21, 9; 27, 5; 36, 2.
[43] Pind. Pyth., 2, 128; LXX : Est. 1:8; 6:6 f., 11; Qoh. 8:3; 2 Macc. 7:16; Mt. 18:23 of the king's reckoning.
[44] Da. LXX 1:13; Epict. Diss., III, 24, 35; Mt. 13:28 of the command of the householder; Lk. 1:62 of the wish of the father; Rev. 11:6 of the effective authority of the witnesses.
[45] Plato Leg., IX, 923a; cf. the formula for asking to be accepted, θέλησον, etc. in the pap. (examples in Preisigke Wört.). Cf. also Rödiger, 17.

denotes the independent and self-efficacious power of disposal in the hands of God, who is free to do what He wills with His own. In R. 9:18, 22 Paul shows how the θέλειν of free and sovereign disposal is declared in the event of salvation. It finds expression as a demonstration of wrath and power both in having mercy and in hardening. If the antithesis of Gentile Church and Jews here determines the profound seriousness of the theme of a twofold disposing will, the presentation in Col. 1:27 stops at the glory of the mystery among the Gentiles. This divine θέλειν is declared to the Gentiles. In contrast to the sovereign divine will which characterises revelation, Lk. 4:6 introduces the disruptive picture of the pseudo-sovereignty of the Satanic claim. Other statements with reference to God use θέλειν to denote that which God requires of the righteous. In this respect there is recurrent reference (Mt. 9:13; 12:7; Hb. 10:5, 8) to the prophetic statement that God requires ἔλεος and not θυσία (Hos. 6:6; ψ 39:6).

1 Pt. 3:17 refers to God's will in the direction of believers. Thus they have to suffer for doing what is right. The tribulation of persecution is appointed by God's will. But τοῦ θεοῦ θέλοντος or ἐὰν ὁ κύριος θελήσῃ (Ac. 18:21; 1 C. 4:19; Jm. 4:15 → 47) also applies in the detailed decisions of life, in resolves to plan and do things.

2. The θέλειν of Jesus.

It is to be noted that the expression may be used here both for the incomparable will of the Son who is sent and also for the simple share which Jesus has in ordinary human θέλειν.

a. The disciples' acceptance of the power of His will may be seen not only in erroneous expectation of a miracle of punishment (Lk. 9:54), or in fantastic imaginings (Mt. 17:4), but also in readiness to follow His simple commands (Mk. 14:12 and par.). Mt. 15:32 is the definite decision which sets in motion an action intended to prepare the way for a miraculous occurrence. This θέλειν of Jesus as decision and action in unique omnipotence is displayed in another series of passages: Mk. 3:13, in His election of the disciples; Mk. 1:40 f.; Mt. 8:2 f.; Lk. 5:12 f., in His work as the Redeemer from sickness. θέλω καθαρίσθητι as an answer to ἐὰν θέλῃς, δύνασαί με καθαρίσαι gives the action significance as the execution of liberating power. The omnipotent will of the Son is particularly emphasised in John. According to Jn. 5:21 it extends to the resurrection of the dead. His majestic will, which is also efficacious action, is in harmony with the resurrecting work of the Father. John testifies with solemn emphasis that this almighty θέλειν of the Son expresses itself with reference to the disciples as a declaration of His will in prayer which irresistibly makes His own participants in His glory (17:24). This will determines the whole path of the disciple, so that it alone is at issue in the question whether John will experience the *parousia* (21:22 f.).

The reading at Ac. 9:6 vg^{cl} h p t syhcl : *quid me vis facere* (cf. 22:10 : τί ποιήσω), expresses the same conviction that the will of the risen Lord directs the apostle.

b. At the same time the will of the Son in the lowliness of His earthly calling attests to His share in the incompleteness of earthly existence. Thus the Synoptic record speaks of the frustration of His will in Mk. 7:24. That His θέλειν can be crossed is part of His humiliation. On another occasion it can be successful, Mk. 9:30 in the negative. More important than the occasional thwarting of His wishes in daily life is the frustration of His gracious purpose to save by the refusal of men, Mt. 23:37; Lk. 13:34. The longing, in accordance with God's appointment, that fire should be kindled on earth, cannot be fulfilled at once (Lk. 12:49). This synthesis in His life of omnipotent and effective will on the one side and patient obedience in lowliness on the other is most clearly and radically expressed in the balanced ἀλλ' (πλὴν) οὐ τί (οὐχ ὡς) ἐγὼ θέλω ἀλλ' ὡς σύ of His prayer in Gethsemane (Mk. 14:36; Mt. 26:39; cf. θέλημα in Lk. 22:42 : → 59). Here the position of the Son is as follows. Humanly He has the possibility of an independent will, but this will exists only to be negated in face of the divine will. Its perfect agreement with the divine will finds expression in the declaration of this negation.

3. The θέλειν of Paul in His Authoritative Apostolic Dealings with the Churches.

Paul is fond of θέλειν, especially when he wishes to emphasise an important point of doctrine in instructing the community. His favourite expressions in this respect are οὐ θέλομεν (θέλω) ὑμᾶς ἀγνοεῖν (1 Th. 4:13; 1 C. 10:1; 1 C. 12:1; R. 11:25) or θέλω ὑμᾶς εἰδέναι (1 C. 11:3). But the first formula is also used in personal statements concerning his relation to the community (R. 1:13; [46] 2 C. 1:8; Col. 2:1). It may also denote his intention in controversy, carrying with it the demand for a reply (Gl. 3:2). θέλειν may also be used to express his apostolic will as a teacher in pastoral directions (1 C. 7:32; R. 16:19; in the negative 1 C. 10:20). [47] In sum, θέλειν denotes in Paul the weighty and authoritative discharge of office. In this form it always implies resolute will (though cf. the sense "to wish," → 45, n. 8).

4. Religious θέλειν and its Opposite in the NT.

a. In the Synoptic records θέλειν can express resolute religious striving which characterises Jewish piety in the best sense as θέλειν εἰς τὴν ζωὴν εἰσελθεῖν, Mt. 19:17, 21. [48] θέλειν ὀπίσω μου ἐλθεῖν (Mk. 8:34; cf. Mt. 16:24; Lk. 9:23 : ἔρχεσθαι) is used for the new direction of will which is ready for discipleship. On the other hand, the mistaken though definitely religious wish of the mother of the sons of Zebedee is expressed in the form θέλομεν ἵνα (Mk. 10:35, cf. Mt. 20:21). The answer of Jesus in Mk. 10:36 treats the θέλειν as a mere question. It deals only with the content of the request and ignores the inappropriate form in which it is put.

The οἱ ὑπὸ νόμον θέλοντες εἶναι of Gl. 4:21 also refers to a basic resolve (→ 46, n. 25) of the misdirected will. On the other hand, πιστεύειν is found in the form of a will orientated to the revelation of divine power in Christ (Mt. 15:28). To this corresponds Mk. 10:51 and par., for the θέλειν of the blind man is a request for sight directed to the Son of David. Jn. 7:17: ἐάν τις θέλῃ τὸ θέλημα αὐτοῦ ποιεῖν (→ 58), implies resolute readiness to do the will of God. Jn. 15:7 implies the directed will which becomes a prayer. There is here no mere arbitrary wish, but something grounded in the spirit. The direction of the will of believers to sanctification is the theme of Hb. 13:18; 2 Tm. 3:12. On the other hand, 1 Pt. 3:10 has in view a basic orientation under the influence of wisdom (cf. ψ 33:12). [49] The same source in a general moral principle is to be seen in Mt. 7:12 (constr. with

---

[46] Cf. BGU, I, 27, 5 : γινώσκειν σε θέλω.
[47] On 1 C. 10:20 : Ign. R., 2, 1.
[48] Cf. Epict. Diss., III, 1, 7: εἰ θέλεις καλὸς εἶναι (with βούλεσθαι, II, 14, 10, but cf. also II, 18, 19).
[49] Cr.-Kö. rightly sees in the alteration from ὁ θέλων ζωήν to ὁ θέλων ζωὴν ἀγαπᾶν evidence of estrangement from the use of חפץ.

ἵνα). This θέλειν implies a claim which determines all conduct. Cf. Lk. 6:31. On the other hand the θέλειν which seeks salvation in Rev. 22:7 by demanding the water of life reflects the same equation of θέλειν and πιστεύειν as we find in the Synoptists.

b. In Pl. religious θέλειν is always linked with ποιεῖν, ἐνεργεῖν, πράσσειν, κατεργάζεσθαι. When he says in Phil. 2:13 that God works in believers τὸ θέλειν καὶ τὸ ἐνεργεῖν ὑπὲρ τῆς εὐδοκίας, → II, 746, the meaning may be amply elucidated from parallels. In 2 C. 8:10 f., too, there is a combination of θέλειν and ποιεῖν. According to 8:11 fulfilment of the act, i.e., giving to the collection, follows ἡ προθυμία τοῦ θέλειν. Here θέλειν obviously has the sense of willingness or readiness. In 1 C. 7:36 it is said of him who loves the virgin (→ 60) that he should do what he wills, i.e., carry out his purpose. Thus Phil. 2:13 implies that God effects in believers both a ready purpose and achievement. Both are related to the attainment of the goal of final salvation. Purpose and action are also linked in Gl.5:17. Flesh and Spirit are in conflict. The flesh seeks to hinder the execution of the purpose fixed by spiritual impulse, namely, the achievement of love (cf. v. 14 f.), which can be attained only by walking in the Spirit.

R. 7:14-25 belongs to a different context,[50] though here again θέλειν is linked with κατεργάζεσθαι, v. 15, 18, 20, πράσσειν, v. 15, 19, ποιεῖν, v. 15, 16, 19, 20, 21. θέλειν here denotes definite purpose and readiness to do the divine will. But the conflict is not now between flesh and Spirit, as in Gl. 5:17. This is the θέλειν of man under the Law, who as αὐτὸς ἐγώ (v. 25), without redemption and grace (v. 24 f.), without the power of the Spirit (c. 8), faces alone the demands of the Law and attempts to translate them into action. In no sense are the validity and dignity of the Law as the holy will of God impugned. Only thus does it show that man is carnal, sold under sin. This is seen in the fact that no true action corresponding to the θέλειν is achieved. The only result is something which the doer himself finds alien and abhorrent. θέλειν and ποιεῖν are irreconcilably opposed. There is done what is not willed. To define this θέλειν more closely it is important to consider the σύμφημι τῷ νόμῳ ὅτι καλός in v. 16 and the συνήδομαι τῷ νόμῳ τοῦ θεοῦ κατὰ τὸν ἔσω ἄνθρωπον in v. 22. To be sure, θέλειν here is more than εὐδοκεῖν. But because it never goes beyond readiness and purpose, these expressions of pleasure and consent elucidate its positive content. This impotent θέλειν, which in its isolation is stamped by powerlessness, is at least consent. This is significant, because it shows that even the carnal man acknowledges that the Law of God is righteous. Value is placed on this. The reason is not that there remains an unshaken remnant of human ethos. Everything is under σάρξ, including the νοῦς and ἔσω ἄνθρωπος. The consent is an impotent gesture. Nevertheless, even this gesture recognises that God and His Law are righteous in the midst of bondage. Thus the θέλειν of R. 7 is the inner intention of man to keep the Law which, grounded though it is in pleasure in the Law, never goes beyond the stage of intention. It is the θέλειν of the σάρκινος in whose existence there is cleavage.

Bultmann[51] does not agree that the cleavage of R. 7 is that the will affirms the demand of the Law and the act violates it. For him the object of θέλειν is not

---

[50] On the impotence of θέλειν cf. Philo Decal., 135; Poster. C., 156; Migr. Abr., 211; "to will and not to be able" is found in another connection in Ep. Ar., 224.
[51] R. Bultmann, "R. 7 und die Anthropologie des Pls." in *Imago Dei, Festschr. f. G. Krüger* (1932), 55 ff.

fulfilment of the ἐντολαί but ζωή as the final result. θέλειν is not a movement of the will in the sphere of subjectivity. It is the trans-subjective tendency of human existence. κατεργάζεσθαι does not refer to the empirical act of transgression. It refers to the result of the action which proceeds from every act of legal existence, namely, death. Again, συμφάναι and συνήδεσθαι do not imply current acceptance of a specific demand of the Law. They denote rather the affirmation of its basic intention to lead to life. It is correctly seen here that R. 7 cannot be understood simply in terms of moral shortcoming. It depicts the cleavage in the existence of the whole man who does not follow the true way of salvation. Because the way of salvation is at issue, it is a matter of life and death, not of this or that concrete point. Nevertheless, it must not be overlooked that θέλειν takes place in face of the specific demand. The wrong way of salvation is disclosed in the volitional sphere. Concrete transgression and trans-subjective existence are not separated by Paul. If we say that the real sin of the Jews is not concrete transgression but persistence in legal existence as a way of salvation, we run the risk of making sin into no more than a wrong standpoint. If it involves perversion of being, it is also concrete transgression. Paul has to separate the way of the Law from the new way of salvation because the Law cannot prevent transgression. According to R. 8:4 the δικαίωμα of the Law finds fulfilment in life in the Spirit.

A similar thesis is that θέλειν is not subjectively conscious volition. Since humanity transcends the sphere of consciousness, it is volition under the dominion of the σάρξ. It is thus a trans-subjective tendency of all human existence, comparable with the φρονεῖν of R. 8 and the ἐπιθυμεῖν of Gl. 5:17. Now it is true that Gl. 5:17 speaks expressly of the ἐπιθυμεῖν of the σάρξ and R. 8:5-7, 27 of the φρόνημα τῆς σαρκός and the φρόνημα τοῦ πνεύματος. Similarly, R. 8:5 shows that this φρονεῖν under the dominion of the Spirit or the flesh can be expressed personally. There is certainly in Pl. no subjectivity without the trans-subjective which conditions all existence. Nevertheless, this does not imply the abolition of subjectivity. The θέλειν of R. 7 is certainly that of a subjectivity enslaved and broken by the σάρξ. But Pl. does not abstract his view of existence from the concreteness of willing and non-willing, of doing and not doing. It is when man agrees to a specific demand of the νόμος that he accepts its basic intention to lead to life. It is when he concretely transgresses that he shows that he is under the dominion of the σάρξ. Keeping to the way of law, he is also a transgressor in detail.

R. 7 and Epictet. [52] In Epictet., too, we read of a θέλειν τι καὶ μὴ γίνεσθαι, Diss., I, 27, 10; IV, 8, 25; cf. II, 1, 31; IV, 1, 18. But this means that something in life does not conform with what is desired. The ethical depth of the conflict of R. 7 is missing. On the other hand, there is some parallel in the discovery that man wills to be free but finds that he is bound too closely to the body: IV, 1, 151, cf. the formally similar τί γάρ εἰμι; ταλαίπωρον ἀνθρωπάριον καὶ τὰ δύστηνά μου σαρκίδια in I, 3, 5. Nevertheless, the σάρξ is not the metaphysical power which enslaves, as in Pl.; it is the lower side of human nature in comparison with προαίρεσις, νοῦς, λόγος, something which is really secondary and which the man who is truly free can leave out of account. The cleavage in the ἁμαρτάνων who does not do what he wills, and does what he does not will (Diss., II, 26, 1 f., 4), is logical. Thus the thief wills what is useful to him, and does the opposite. If we can show the ἁμαρτάνων the contradiction he will abandon it (II, 26, 7). It is simply a matter of ἄγνοια, of wrong ideas. Cf. Diss., IV, 1, 1;

---

[52] On this whole question cf. A. Bonhöffer, *Epiktet und das NT* (1911), 66, 160, 162. For another view cf. K. Kuiper, *Epictetus en de Christelijke Moraal* (1906).

I, 28, 4; IV, 9, 16. If ἁμαρτάνειν is the perversion of ἡγεμονικόν, or aberration from rational thinking, sin is a rational defect. Hence ποιεῖν ἃ θέλομεν is the true use of the terms, the acceptance of things in the situation and connection in which they really are : Diss., II, 17, 17-21. μετάνοια is critically reckoned, however, among the πάθη. [53] It should not be overlooked, of course, that for the Gks. ἄγνοια, or erroneous knowledge, is not a mere lack of understanding. The central Socratic and Platonic saying : πάντες βούλονται τὸ εὖ, includes within it the fact that true volition is present only where an ἀγαθόν is sought.

Thus we see in R. 7 the impotence of legal man according to Paul. This man wills and fails to do, and does what he does not will (v. 18, cf. 16, 19). For the sin implied in the Law renders his will powerless. Only walking in the Spirit (→ 50; Gl. 5) can bring about the unity of θέλειν and ἐνεργεῖν referred to in Phil. 2:13. This will is the fruit of the Spirit in the believer. Unconditionally linked with the true fulfilment of the will of God, it is to be strictly separated from the impotent θέλειν of R. 7. Paul thus distinguishes between the will of the spiritual man and the will of the legal man. Only the former will is effective.

In R. 9:16, with its contrast between the human will and the divine (cf. v. 18, 22), there is again mention of τρέχειν (for ποιεῖν) along with θέλειν. What is meant is man's concern for salvation. But this denies the prospect and goal of salvation, since only the divine mercy and will can make it possible.

c. Determined refusal as the opposite of religious volition is found parabolically in the disobedient son of Mt. 21:30 and factually in the resistance of Jerusalem to the loving concern of Jesus in Mt. 23:37. Cf. Lk. 13:34. In Lk. 19:14 the blunt and rude message of the subjects : οὐ θέλομεν, is the sharpest conceivable form of this self-destructive antithesis. In Jn. 5:40 rejection of Christ again takes the form of οὐ θέλειν. Cf. also Mt. 22:3. It is used of the fathers' refusal to obey in Ac. 7:39 and of the refusal to repent in Rev. 2:21. In Jn. 8:44 it occurs positively to denote a resolute evil will. The basic orientation of the soul which clings wilfully to purely earthly values and decides against Christ is described as θέλειν, Mk. 8:35 (par. Mt. 16:25; Lk. 9:24).

† θέλημα.

Contents : A. θέλημα in the Greek World, in Hellenism and in the Synagogue. B. θέλημα in the NT. 1. θέλημα as God's Will : a. Christ as the Doer of the divine will ; b. The conception of the will of God as the basis and purpose of salvation ; c. The new life of believers as a doing of the divine will. 2. θέλημα as Human and Demonic Will. C. θέλημα in the Early Church.

A. θέλημα in the Greek World, in Hellenism and in the Synagogue.

1. Θέλημα occurs once in the Sophist Antiphon (5th cent. B.C.), Fr., 58 (II, 302, 27, Diels) in the sense of "purpose" or "wish" in the plur., in the 4th cent. in Aristot. De Plantis, I, 1, p. 815b, 21, where, in contrast to plants which have neither ἐπιθυμία nor αἴσθησις, it is said of man that τὸ τοῦ ἡμετέρου θελήματος τέλος orientates itself πρὸς τὴν αἴσθησιν. Here ἐπιθυμία and θέλημα are interchangeable. The latter is used quite neutrally, with no moral implication, for the human impulse of desire. Cf. also Aen. Tact. (4th cent. B.C.), Poliorcetica (ed. L. W. Hunter, S.A, Handford, 1927), 2, 8; 18, 19. This early use helps us to see why the term could also be used for sexual desire and specifically for the θέλησις of the male (→ 62). There are clear traces of this in

---

[53] A. Bonhöffer, 252, 371.

Preis. Zaub., IV (Paris), where the wish is expressed concerning the desired paramour who is placed under magic : τὰ ἐμὰ θελήματα πάντα ποιείτω, 1521 f., cf. 1532 f. To this corresponds the use in the Ptolemaic doctrine of the two σύζυγοι = διαθέσεις, ῎Εννοια and Θέλημα, the deity Bythos : Iren. Haer., I, 12, 1; Hipp. Ref., VI, 38, 5-7; Epiph. Haer., 33, 1, 2-7. Here θέλημα is the male force of procreation, whereas ἔννοια is simply the activity of conception. Similarly in the Barbelognostics in Iren. Haer., I, 29, 1 f. the will of God the Father is the begetting force which forms a syzygy with ζωὴ αἰώνιος. (Cf. Ign., Just., Tat. → 61, where this sense stands in the background.)

2. A deeper or more explicit moral and especially religious use is in evidence in the LXX. Here it is a translation of חֵפֶץ as subst., verb and adj., and of חֵפֶץ, also רָצוֹן, with a few other special cases (→ infra). There is here a notable tendency to use the plur. both when this is present in the Heb.: Jer. 23:17, 26; ψ 102:6, and also when it is not : Is. 44:28; 58:13; ψ 15:2; 2 Ch. 9:12, and even when there is the sense of pleasure rather than directions, or when the Mas. has a verb, Ιερ. 9:23. In terms of distribution the usage is as follows.

Of God : a. of the divine "will." Sir. 43:16 (freely translated) of His majestic rule in creation. For a voluntarist conception the rendering of ψ 29:5 is important, since here the divine delight becomes will, along with passion. The word is used for God's rule in creation in Da. Θ 4:35 (צְבָא). The formula : עָשָׂה רָצוֹן, for the doing of the divine will, is often rendered ποιεῖν τὸ θέλημά σου, αὐτοῦ, ψ 39:9; 102:21; 142:10, cf. 1 Εσδρ. 9:9; 4 Macc. 18:16. There is an important par. to the Lord's Prayer in 1 Macc. 3:60 : ὡς δ' ἂν ᾖ θέλημα ἐν οὐρανῷ, οὕτως ποιήσει. As a divine direction, 1 Εσδρ. 8:16, plur. ψ 102:6 (עֲלִילוֹת, great acts); Is. 44:28 (חֵפֶץ, purpose); 2 Macc. 1:3. b. "Delight," "pleasure" : ψ 29:8 (רָצוֹן); Ιερ. 9:23 (חָפֵץ verb). Here the ἐν is kept, as with בְּ חֵפֶץ (θέλειν ἐν). Thus also Mal. 1:10 (חֵפֶץ subst.); ψ 15:2. In Is. 62:4 LXX there is an erotic nuance : θέλημα ἐμόν (חֶפְצִי־בָהּ), of the spouse, though this is ennobled by the application of the metaphor to God (→ supra).

Of man. Here the most common sense is a. "desire," "wish." There is again a voluntarist alteration in ψ 27:7, which has ἐκ θελήματος for לִבִּי instead of ἐκ καρδίας. In 2 Βασ. 23:5 the reference is to David's desire (חֵפֶץ). It is used in the plur. in 3 Βασ. 5:22 etc. (cf. also 2 Ch. 9:12) with reference to the treaty between Hiram and Solomon. In ψ 106:30 it is used of the desired haven (חֵפֶץ) and in ψ 144:19 (רָצוֹן) of the desire of those who fear God. Related is the "interest" or "share in" denoted by חֵפֶץ in Job 21:21, cf. Job 22:3 Mas. חֵפֶץ = "advantage." But the LXX seems to have translated mechanically here. [1] b. Of the "royal will," Is. 48:14, where the LXX makes of God's will the despotic will of Cyrus. Similarly of the capricious will of the despot, Da. Θ 11:3, 16, 36 (LXX 11:16, 36). In Est. 1:8 the LXX has the royal will in spite of the Heb. c. Included in this is the use of the word for man's "obstinacy," "self-will" or "caprice" in general. This is particularly instructive, since in such cases θέλημα is not usually a rendering of חֵפֶץ or רָצוֹן but of a whole list of other words : Jer. 23:17 (שְׁרִרוּת) plur. "stubbornness'; Sir. 8:15 (נוֹכַח פָּנָיו) "self-will." In Jer. 23:26 (תַּרְמִת לִבָּם) the LXX has τὰ θελήματα τῆς καρδίας instead of "deceit of their hearts." It has in view "caprice," which is quite plain in Sir. 32:17 (21) (צָרְכוֹ). d. "Pleasure," "good-pleasure," "delight," of man : ψ 1:2 (חֵפֶץ). So also Is. 58:13, which can hardly have the sense of the Mas. עֲשׂוֹת חֲפָצֶךָ "to do business" (cf. "interest," "share" in Job 21:21 → supra). The Gk. πραγματεία, ἐργασία, ἐμπορία, would best correspond to this. Related is the sense of "pleasantness," "attractiveness," Qoh. 12:10. From this review it is clear that θέλημα

θέλημα. [1] Instead of ὅτι τὸ θέλημα αὐτοῦ ἐν οἴκῳ αὐτοῦ μετ᾽ αὐτόν, we should read ὅτι τί θέλημα αὐτοῦ.

in the LXX emphasises the element of will and represses that of love or inclination. Both are found expressly in חפץ and רצון (→ θέλω, 44).

3. The plentiful use in the Hermetica gives evidence of biblical and Christian influence. θέλημα is often used here synon. with or alongside → βουλή, I, 634. In a song of praise : Corp. Herm., XIII, 19 f. God's will is eternal : Ascl., III, 26a b (Scott, I, 346, 7 ff.). It is ἀγαθόν (cf. R. 12:2): Corp. Herm., X, 2; Ascl., III, 20b (Scott, I, 332, 13); 26a b. In Ascl. esp. there is speculation how God's will is achieved. It proceeds from thought and is a possession whose execution follows naturally, *voluisse* and *perfecisse* being one in God : III, 26b (Scott, I, 346, 10 ff.); I, 8 (Scott, I, 300, 9 f.). God is always *praegnans,* abounding (→ 53), full of *bonitas* and *voluntas.* He must always will : Ascl., III, 20b. Everything depends on this will : III, 34c (Scott, I, 326, 12 ff.); 17c (Scott, I, 316, 25 ff.). Corp. Herm. treats esp. of the will of God as unlimited creative power : X, 2; V, 7, and as the conceptual seed of regeneration : Corp. Herm., XIII, 2; 4; 20. Worth noting in comparison with θέλημα as the sexual power to beget and conceive (→ 52) is XIII, 2 : τίνος σπείραντος; τοῦ θελήματος τοῦ θεοῦ, which is characteristically different from Jn. 1:13. The regenerate can thus say : δυνάμεις αἱ ἐν ἐμοὶ τὸ σὸν θέλημα τελοῦσι, Corp. Herm., XIII, 19. Of human will, XIII, 17.

4. When we turn to the Rabb. use so far as it influenced the NT, we find that in the Rabbis God's will is Heb. רצון, Aram. רְעוּתָא, st. abs. רְעֵוָא → II, 743. A standing formula in the Palestinian synagogue is עֲשֵׂה רְצוֹנוֹ or עֲשֵׂה מָקוֹם שֶׁל רְצוֹנוֹ [2] "to do His, God's will" : Ket., 66b (R. Jochanan b. Zakkai); Ab., 2, 4 (R. Gamaliel III); M. Ex. 15:1 (ed. Friedmann, 36a); T. Nazir, 4, 7; Sch. E., 13. "To do the will of the Father in heaven" is a common mode of expression : Ab., 5, 14; S. Dt. § 306 on 32:3. [3] On Mt. 18:14: Ex. r., 46, 2 on 34:1. [4] On Mt. 21:31: jBer., 5c, 3 f. [5] On Jn. 6:38 : S. Dt. § 306 on 32:1. [6] On Gl. 1:4 : κατὰ τὸ θέλημα τοῦ θεοῦ, the opening of the Qaddish prayer : כרעותה.

On the Lord's Prayer : the will and the name of God are linked in M. Ex. 15:2, [7] the name, the will, and the royal dominion in the opening of the Qaddish prayer. On "thy will be done," S. Nu. § 107 on 15:7. [8] Elsewhere the formula is always יהי רצון or יהי רצון לפניך. In the Tg. . . . . רעוא קדם. "As in heaven, so also on earth," the prayer of R. Eliezer (90-100 A.D.): "Do Thy will in heaven above, and give rest of spirit to those who fear Thee below" : bBer., 29b; [9] prayer of R. Saphra (c. 300 A.D.); bBer., 16b. [10]

B. θέλημα in the NT.

The plural form is almost completely absent from the NT. Except in LXX quotations as in Ac. 13:22 (Is. 44:28), it is used of God's will only at vl. Mk. 3:35 B (cf. Ev. Eb., 7) and of carnal desires at Eph. 2:3 (→ 61). God's will is expressed in the singular because the concept is shaped, not by individual legal directions, but by the conviction that this θέλημα of God is a powerful unity.

---

[2] For examples cf. Str.-B., I, 467, 653; cf. 219 ff., 664. On the formula "it is the will before Yahweh" → II, 745; Dalman WJ, I, 173.
[3] Schl. Mt. on 7:21; P. Fiebig, *Jesu Bergpredigt* (1924), 147; Str.-B., I, 467.
[4] Schl. Mt., 553.
[5] *Ibid.,* 625.
[6] Schl. J., 175.
[7] Fiebig, I, 114 f.; II, 114 f.; II, 53.
[8] Schl. Mt., 209. On this pt. cf. K. G. Kuhn's transl. of S. Nu. (1933 ff.), *ad loc.* (p. 293, n. 70).
[9] Fiebig, I, 116; II, 53; Str.-B., I, 419 f.
[10] Str.-B., I, 420.

1. θέλημα as God's Will.

a. Christ as the Doer of the divine will.

(i). The third petition of the Lord's Prayer:[11] γενηθήτω[12] τὸ θέλημά σου ὡς ἐν οὐρανῷ καὶ ἐπὶ γῆς (→ 54) expresses not merely submission but consent to a comprehensive fulfilment of God's will in keeping with the hallowing of His name and the coming of His kingdom. It thus implies an ultimate and basic attitude on the part of the one who prays. It agrees exactly with the petition of the Son in Gethsemane, Mt. 26:42 (on the Lucan form in 22:42 → 59). If this expresses particularly willing submission in suffering, the presupposition in the Lord's Prayer is the basic attitude. According to Mk. 3:35; Mt. 12:50 (→ 58) this attitude is necessarily demanded of the followers of Jesus because Jesus Himself is wholly rooted and lives in the divine will.

(ii). This truth is most commonly expressed in Jn. with great christological depth. If Mt. links θέλημα with the Father in heaven (→ 56 f.), Jn. links it with the divine Sender: 4:34; 5:30; 6:38 f. (→ 54); 7:16 f.; cf. 6:40. He who is sent as God's organ is the One who bears and mediates the will of Him that sent Him. He is the One who totally receives and who is totally at disposal. He simply hears and executes. It is true, of course, that these sayings concerning the θέλημα of the Sender are only a portion of what John has to say about the sonship of Christ.

This is expressed equally by phrases like 8:29: ἐγὼ τὰ ἀρεστὰ αὐτῷ ποιῶ πάντοτε, or 8:55: οἶδα αὐτὸν καὶ τὸν λόγον αὐτοῦ τηρῶ. Cf. also the ἐντολή of the Father, → II, 553, and the related statements concerning the love of the Father: 14:31; 15:10. For the sake of completeness we should also mention what is said concerning dependence on the "hour" and the total direction of the life and suffering of the Son.

Nevertheless, what is said about the θέλημα of the Father is particularly significant since it expresses decisively the voluntarism of the Evangelist in the christological field. As the whole ethics of John is volitional rather than mystical, so the Christology of Jn. is simply the will, act and obedience of the Son. There is a constant union of the metaphysical and ethical aspects of sonship. As a whole person, Jesus is from the very first the Son and therefore the One who is sent: 7:28; 8:42. He is in the bosom of the Father and one with Him: 1:18; 10:38; 14:10; cf. 10:30. Hence the Father shows Him all things and He hears the words of God: 5:20; 8:47. With this being of His, however, is most closely related His ever new and resolute readiness for active obedience, His constant openness to the will of the Father, by which He shows Himself to be the Son. In this context the sayings concerning the θέλημα of Him that sent Him are a most comprehensive description of the being and work of the Son. According to Jn. 4:34 it is His means of life and nourishment to do the will of the One who sent Him. There is here exact correspondence between ποιεῖν τὸ θέλημα and τελειοῦν τὸ ἔργον. The will is done by accomplishing the works. The basis, power and goal of the life of the Son are to be found in this effective execution.

According to 6:39 f. the content of the will of the Sender is the working out of this life to its final goal. He leads all who see and believe in Him, who are

---

[11] Did. as Mt. In Lk. 11:2 the words are not found in B vg^cl sy^s c Marc. Orig. as opp. to א C D it vg^s vl. Tert. has the sequence name, will, kingdom. D abc k Tert Cypr simplify by omitting ὡς. The threefold form of opening corresponds to the Qaddish (→ 54).

[12] On γενηθήτω cf. Ac. 21:14. The formula may be traced back to the synagogue: יהי רצון (→ 54; cf. → II, 745).

given to Him, even now to eternal life and ultimately to the resurrection. The will is thus described as consummated future salvation, but in such a way that the whole way which leads thereto is included. The doing of the divine will by the Son is also conceived, however, in terms of a sacrifice of His own will. It thus implies an act of will on His part.[13] Cf. the denial of His own will in Lk. 22:42. His obedience is not just a natural process which can be taken for granted. Nor is it a magical miracle. It is a denial of self-will accomplished by the Son in the σάρξ (6:38).[14] This explains His opposition to the arbitrary demand for signs raised by the Galilaeans. This act of self-will is opposed by the One who with His coming into the world sacrifices His own will to the One who sends Him. This corresponds to the recurrent denial of ἀφ' ἑαυτοῦ, ἀπ' ἐμαυτοῦ (5:19, 30; 7:28; 8:28, 42; 14:10; ἐξ ἐμαυτοῦ, 12:49), which constantly implies that the life, mission, word and work of Jesus derive, not from His own will, but from the will of God. According to Jn. 5:30 the fact that He seeks the will of the Sender rather than His own will[15] is a guarantee that His κρίσις is just. This saving work of Jesus is not an arbitrary desecration of the Sabbath; it is a mission. This basic distinction from all human work, including that of self-styled opponents, sheds a light on the action of the Son, which constantly implies renunciation of His own will, cf. the saying in 12:25 concerning the μισεῖν of the ψυχή and the sayings concerning the rejection of human δόξα in 5:41; 7:18; 8:50. The only difference in Jn. 9:31 is that here it is explained, in terms familiar to all Jews from their instruction in the Torah, that the work performed by Jesus is a "hearing" by God, i.e., God's answer to the doing of His will.

(iii). In Hb. 10:7, 9, and especially v. 10, where we have a quotation from ψ 39:7-9, though without the characteristic LXX emphasis on the σῶμα, the ministry of Christ is regarded as a self-offering of His whole personal life to the divine will in contrast to animal sacrifices and material offerings. Since the will of God is fully done through the body of Christ, through His human life, we are consecrated to God in this will. This leads us to the next point.

b. The conception of the will of God as the basis and purpose of salvation.

(i). Only once in the NT (Rev. 4:11) does θέλημα (διά, propter, in the sense of "by virtue of") denote the will of the Creator of all things. Elsewhere it is always used for His will to save. In Mt. 18:14 this will (→ 54) stands protectively over the μικροί. It is distinctive of Mt. that he consistently links it with the title Father: 6:10; 7:21; 12:50; 18:14; also in the parable in 21:31 (→ 54). Cf. the characteristic differences in Mk. 3:35; Lk. 22:42. His usage is here fixed by synagogue forms (→ 54) and by the new estimation of the name of Father, which is very much on his heart. The child stands under the commanding will of the father (21:31). But the reference is to the Father in heaven. In heaven this will of His is carried out in a way which is normative. On the saving purpose of the will of the Sender in Jn. → 55 f.

(ii). In Paul this approach is usually indicated by κατά: Gl. 1:4[16] (→ 54). The sacrifice for our sins, the redemption of Christ which frees the community, cor-

---

[13] Cf. the τελειοῦν of Jn. 4:34; 5:36; 17:4
[14] The mention of Christ's denial of His own will, of its subjection to the will of God, caused difficulty to the Monothelites. Cf. what the Roman bishop Honorius writes to Sergius in J. D. Mansi, *Sacrorum Conciliorum Nova et Amplissima Collectio*, XI (1765), 538 ff.
[15] On ζητεῖν cf. ψ 4:2; Mi. 3:2.
[16] On κατὰ τὸ θέλημά σου, P. Oxy., VI, 924, 8 (4th cent. A.D.).

responds to the will of the Father. In understanding this κατά in Eph. 1:5, 9, 11 [17] it is to be noted that the division of the hymn in 1:3-14 into three sections dealing with election, redemption and inheritance is not the only norm by which to explain the structure of the passage. There is another basic scheme running through all the statements. This is brought out by the prepositions ἐν (in Christ as the Mediator), κατά (according to the will of God as the pre-temporal basis) and εἰς (to the praise of His glory as the final goal). θέλημα here is always linked with προ- statements which define God's will as His eternal decree of salvation, and it occurs in all three sections (4-6; 7-10; 11-14). It is more precisely defined in terms of εὐδοκία as free estimation, or of βουλή [18] as counsel or plan, and in v. 9 it is declared to be a published μυστήριον. The threefold θέλημα does not seem to the author to be adequate to express what he has in view. This is in keeping with the need felt by Mt. to define it more precisely in terms of the Father of heaven, and by John in terms of the Sender. θέλημα, or θέλημα θεοῦ, is a phrase common to antiquity. Alone, it cannot express the distinctive Christian content. If, however, we combine all the elucidations in Eph. 1, θέλημα is obviously the ultimate basis, the supreme norm, the only source of the whole work of salvation. It is its final, pre-temporal foundation. What is meant is the active divine resolve which cannot remain in the sphere of thought but demands action. Everywhere we have the impression that nothing human, but only this divine will, can provide the impulse for the execution of the plan of salvation.

c. The new life of believers and the divine will.

(i). The basic attitude to the divine will. α. The recognition and testing of this will. Paul says in R. 2:18 that the Jew does not merely claim to know the will [19] as recognition of the requirement of the Law, but that he actually knows it and is treated as one to whom the divine demand is evident. But it is in NT instruction that the will of God is really seen to be declared and open. In Lk. 12:47 the servant knows the will of his lord, i.e., Jesus, and it is for this reason that he will be so sternly judged at the *parousia*. Those outside the band of disciples do not know the will of Jesus (v. 48), and will thus be judged more leniently. According to Ac. 22:14 the revolutionary outworking of the election of Paul at his conversion has as its result: γνῶναι τὸ θέλημα αὐτοῦ. But this new knowledge of the will of God in Christ, and its effects on the whole of life and ministry, are something new compared with the requirement of the Law in Rom. 2:18. They are the declared secret of God's will (→ *supra*). According to R. 12:2, [20] however, this state of knowledge demands constant δοκιμάζειν. The presupposition for true testing of the will of God is nonconformity to this aeon and readiness for the renewal of the νοῦς. The reference here is obviously to conduct. Only the renewed νοῦς knows the will of God in order thereby to set up its goal and to fashion its service. The request to be filled with knowledge of His will ἐν πάσῃ σοφίᾳ καὶ συνέσει

---

[17] On the arrangement of Eph. 1 cf. E. Lohmeyer, ThBl, 5 (1926), 120 ff.; A. Debrunner, *ibid.*, 231 ff.

[18] θέλημα and βουλή, used synon. of God, Corp. Herm., XIII, 19; 20.

[19] On R. 2:18 cf. O. Olivieri, "Sintassi, Senso e Rapporto col Contesto di Rom. 2:17-24," *Biblica*, 11 (1930), 188 ff. Cf. on the Rabb. use of θέλημα alone (→ 54; cf. → II, 745), 1 C. 16:12 → 59, n. 24 and Ign. → 61.

[20] For the combination of ἀγαθόν, θέλημα, εὐάρεστον in an obvious formula, cf. Hb. 13:21. On ἀγαθόν cf. Corp. Herm. → 54. The words may be adj. attributes, for (as against Zn., *ad loc.*) εὐάρεστον θέλημα is the correct rendering of εὐδοκία.

πνευματικῇ (Col. 1:9) is also concerned with a *gnosis* relating to the practical goal of life (v. 10, περιπατῆσαι). It comes when the Spirit influences the capacity for knowledge and permanently determines and deepens the understanding. We are to think here of the formation and correction of the gait for proper walking. In Eph. 5:17 the reference is again to clear insight into what is conformable to God's will in individual cases.

β. Prayer according to His will. Prayer κατὰ τὸ θέλημα αὐτοῦ (→ 54) is again modelled on Jesus, Mk. 14:36; Jn. 9:31. In 1 Jn. 5:14 (cf. 3:21) stress is laid on the joy which this attitude brings to us in prayer.

(ii). The new life of believers as a doing of the divine will. α. The doing of the will as the basic condition of an essential goal. In Mt. 12:50 the doing of the divine will is decisive for following Jesus (Mk. 3:35, the will of God, Mt. of my Father in heaven; Mk. 3:35 B, Ev. Eb., 7 θελήματα, with a legalistic trend). In Jn. 7:17 serious resolve or readiness to do it is necessary to know the διδαχή of Jesus, since self-will, which is opposed to the οὐκ ἀπ' ἐμαυτοῦ of Jesus, prevents any insight into the ἐκ τοῦ θεοῦ of Jesus. If doing of the will is not here separated from what is plain to Jews from the Law and the prophets, [21] the reference is to the will of the One who sent Jesus (v. 16b). The true attitude of will demanded is so constituted that it has regard to the harmony between Scripture and the sending of Jesus (cf. 5:46). Doing of the will is a condition of entry into the βασιλεία in Mt. 7:21, also 21:31, cf. 31b. To this corresponds what is said in 1 Jn. 2:17 about the antithesis to the ἐπιθυμία of the κόσμος, which is as transitory as the cosmos itself, whereas he who does the will of God μένει εἰς τὸν αἰῶνα. [22] The κόσμος does not do God's will. There is a similar goal in the κομίζεσθαι τὴν ἐπαγγελίαν of Hb. 10:36, except that here the explicit content of patience is linked with doing the will in view of the particular situation of the readers.

β. Apart from these sayings which call it a condition, doing the will of God is constantly called the simple content of the Christian life. Hb. 13:21 (→ 57, n. 20) is a material parallel not merely to R. 12:2 but also to Phil. 2:12 f. inasmuch as it is God Himself who works in us that which is well-pleasing. [23] 1 Pt. 4:2 speaks of θελήματι θεοῦ βιῶσαι, the opp. being their prior life in lusts. Suffering in the flesh is the way in which the break is made with sin and life is divided into two halves (cf. τὸν ἐπίλοιπον ἐν σαρκὶ ... χρόνον). In the admonition to slaves in Eph. 6:6 there is the addition ἐκ ψυχῆς, opp. ὀφθαλμοδουλία. Even in this special situation this doing is the epitome which provides the impulse for the whole conduct of life.

γ. Basic and explicit definitions of the content of the divine will for the community. Only comparatively rarely are we told specifically what God wills, since it is presupposed that this will is no secret. If the content of the divine will is described as ἁγιασμός in 1 Th. 4:3 and εὐχαριστεῖν in 1 Th. 5:18 — an εἰς ὑμᾶς expresses the direction of the requirement — in both cases the lack of article indicates that an important part of the total will is intended. A particular task to be observed in fulfilling the divine will is mentioned in 1 Pt. 2:15 in the admonition

---

[21] Chrys. (MPG, 57, 466), Euthymius Zigabenus (MPG, 129, 393), Bengel, B. Weiss⁹ (1898), Zn. Mt., *ad loc.*

[22] Par. from Philo and Ginza in Wnd. 1 Jn., *ad loc.*

[23] Cf. the three par. from Ep. Ar. in Wnd. Hb., *ad loc.*

to be subject to rulers and to reduce opponents to silence by well-doing. The διὰ θελήματος θεοῦ of 2 C. 8:5 has as its content total submission to the κύριος and the apostle. All these individual statements may be reduced, however, to the common denominator of glorifying God.

δ. θέλημα as divine direction and orientation in the detailed questions of life. According to Col. 4:12 — the prayer of Epaphras — the will of God is viewed as a stance, and the ἐν παντί indicates that there is to be specific application in detail. This express emphasising of detailed direction is most solemnly expressed in the Pauline epistles by the formula Παῦλος (κλητὸς) ἀπόστολος Χριστοῦ Ἰησοῦ διὰ θελήματος θεοῦ. This expresses with striking brevity and force the complete subjection of his ministry to his commission. It is not he himself, nor a human authority, but the unrestricted act of God's will which is the only ultimate cause of his apostolic power, of both the commencement and the continuation of his ministry: 1 C. 1:1; 2 C. 1:1; Col. 1:1; Eph. 1:1; 2 Tm. 1:1. As an apostle he declares the will of God. This determines his ministry even down to such details as his plans (R. 1:10; 15:32) and those of his fellow-workers (1 C. 16:12). [24] This will also rules over the whole life of the community by apportioning suffering to it. This is emphasised in 1 Pt. 3:17 (with the singular expression εἰ θέλοι τὸ θέλημα τοῦ θεοῦ) and 4:19 (on κατά → 54; 58).

2. θέλημα as Human and Demonic Will.

Apart from Mt. 21:31, where the parable speaks of the will of the father, Lk. is the only Synoptist who expressly uses the word of human will: Lk. 12:47. Both these passages (→ 56 f.) refer ultimately, of course, to the will of God or of Jesus. But the singularity of Luke's usage is confirmed by the fact that he twice has an unqualified θέλημα quite unambiguously for man's own will or preference: Lk. 22:42, where Jesus negates His own will in Gethsemane (→ 49), and 23:25, where Pilate delivers up Jesus to the θέλημα of the Jews, θέλημα having here the special implication of caprice. Cf. θέλειν in this sense (→ 45). There is also reference to arbitrary and autonomous will in 2 Pt. 1:21. Here arbitrary interpretation of Scripture is the point of departure. The only true exposition through the Spirit is grounded in the origin of Scripture, for prophecy was not brought forth, as the Gnostics expound it, by human desire or caprice, but holy men "spake as they were moved" by the Spirit.

The vl. in 1 Pt. 4:3: τὸ θέλημα τῶν ἐθνῶν κατειργάσθαι, P 𝔖 al (on the reading τὸ βούλημα → I, 636 f.) speaks of the sinful will of the pagan masses [25] as an orientation of life, in opp. to ποιεῖν τὸ θέλημα τοῦ θεοῦ.

Along the lines of the meaning mentioned earlier (→ 52 f.), θέλημα is also used in the NT for sexual desire. ἐκ θελήματος σαρκός has this sense in Jn. 1:13, and the following phrase: ἐκ θελήματος ἀνδρός, if it is not a mere repetition, perhaps refers to the conscious and superior will of the male seeking a son and heir. [26] This θέλημα corresponds to θέλειν in its erotic sense (→ 45).

---

[24] The οὐκ ἦν θέλημα denotes, not the will of Apollos (Ltzm. K., W. Bousset in Schr. NT³, Bchm. K., ad loc.), but the will of God (Joh. W. 1 K. and Schl. K., ad loc.), cf. the Rabb. use of יהי רצון alone (→ 57, n. 19) and Ign. (→ 61).

[25] Cf. Kn. Pt., ad loc.

[26] Cf. Schl. Jn., ad loc.

Cadbury (→ n. 27) thinks it likely that ἐξ αἱμάτων describes the female contribution to procreation, so that 1:13 comprehensively negates human conception and birth. If so, however, there can be no reference here to Jesus. Yet the reading ἐγεννήθη (Blass, Zahn, R. Seeberg → n. 27) is attested early, for Iren. Haer., III, 16, 2; III, 19, 2; III, 21, 5; V, 1, 3, has the sing. with reference to Christ, and probably Just. Dial., 63, 2. Cf. Tert. De carne Christi, 19; 24 : natus est. Hipp. Ref., VI, 9, 2. Aug. Confess., VII, 9, 14. Also b : qui natus est. syᶜ has a plur. subj. and a sing. predicate, which is rather awkwardly retained in syᴾ also. In Tert., op. cit., 19 the Valentinians are accused of falsifying the text by introducing a plur., which they then refer to their own pneumatics. Cl. Al. and Orig. have the plur., but may be influenced by the Valentinian text. From the middle of the 4th cent. this oriental οἳ ἐγεννήθησαν carries the day in the Lat. Thus Aug. on Jn. 1 has the plur. Harnack regards the sing. as an early gloss from within the Johannine circle. [27]

The same sense is found at 1 C. 7:37, [28] where ἐξουσίαν δὲ ἔχει περὶ τοῦ ἰδίου θελήματος must be translated : "to have power over one's own sexual impulse."

If the τις of v. 36 is referred to the father or guardian — though there is no actual reference to father and daughter — it is difficult to make satisfactory sense of v. 37. In v. 36 ἀσχημονεῖν (unseemly conduct) does not seem to fit, and γαμείτωσαν is also surprising, since it suddenly introduces a twofold relation, whereas prior reference has been only to the determinative authority and the virgin. And does not this make v. 37 very hard to understand ? If it is referred to that authority, Paul is justifying an unheard of tyranny, for to impose asceticism on oneself is rather different from imposing it on marriageable children. Can an instructed Jew say that he who allows his daughter to marry is not sinning (v. 36)? According to the Jewish view it is a sin to place her under this eschatological asceticism. Moreover, the οὐχ ἁμαρτάνει of v. 36 corresponds to v. 28, where it is said that to marry by one's own decision is not sin. If we find in v. 37 a magnifying of patriarchal and family authority, what is said is the height of pretension and does not correspond to any helpful situation. The case is different if we think of those who are actually marrying. Then v. 37 is quite clear. What is said in these verses refers to sexual necessity in the sense of the ὑπέρακμος of v. 36. On ἀκμή in this sense cf. Delling, 88, n. 194. Cf. also Method. Symp., III, 14 (G. N. Bonwetsch [1917], p. 44, 4 [GCS]). With Ltzm., ad loc. (as against Delling) we are to refer ὑπέρακμος to the man. The μὴ ἔχων ἀνάγκην is a repetition of ἐὰν ᾖ ὑπέρακμος in negative form. It certainly refers to male impulse. Cf. the corresponding definition of ἀνάγκη in Method. Symp., III, 14 (Bonwetsch, 44, 15). The saying concerning the power of the impulse reminds us of 1 C. 7:4, where ἐξουσιάζειν is used of marital intercourse. If the guardian thesis breaks down, the interpretation in terms of purely formal marriage offers supreme difficulty. How can the Jew Paul, whose judgments concerning marriage questions we know from this chapter, countenance uneasy "spiritual" unions ? This was not how the early Church took the passage. Appeal was never made to the early Church for this view. But the hypothesis has so captivated expositors that they have not considered the simplest solution (van Manen) in terms of a purpose of marriage. It is true that ἡ παρθένος αὐτοῦ can mean a virgin daughter. [29] But the question is what it

---

[27] Lit.: C. H. Cadbury in Exp. 9th Series, Vol. 2 (1924), 430 ff.; F. Blass, Ev. secundum Johannem (1902), XII; Zn. J., ad loc. and Exc. II; Bau. J., ad loc.; M. J. Lagrange, Ev. selon St. Jean² (1925), 15 f. A. v. Harnack, SAB, 1915, 542-552, also Studien z. Geschichte des NT und der alten Kirche, I (1931), 115-127; R. Seeberg, Festgabe f. Harnack (1921), 267-269; C. F. Burney, The Aramaic Origin of the Fourth Gospel (1922), 34.

[28] Lit. on 1 C. 7 under → παρθένος. In what is said here we lean on W. C. van Manen, ThT, 8 (1874), 612 ff.; G. Delling, Pls' Stellung zu Frau und Ehe (1931), 86-91; J. Sickenberger, BZ, 3 (1905), 44 ff.; A. Juncker, Die Ethik des Ap. Pls., II (1919), 191-200; Ltzm. 1 K., ad loc.

[29] Cf. Sickenberger, 66; Juncker, 197.

means to a Corinthian contemplating marriage with a παρθένος. This need not be a νύμφη or μνηστευθεῖσα; hence the expression. If Paul is calling celibacy desirable, then there arises for every serious relation of love a case of conscience, especially when there is engagement to a young girl. The reference is thus to a man and his prospective fiancée. τηρεῖν need not mean "to keep her with him as his daughter"; [30] it can also mean : "renouncing marriage, to allow her to serve the Lord alone" in the sense of v. 34. It is presupposed that the question comes from the man. On the ancient view he is the one who proposes. Hence the reference is to his decision alone. [31]

On this view θέλημα in both Jn. 1:13 and 1 C. 7:37 means sexual impulse in the psychological and non-derogatory sense. In Eph. 2:3, however, it is used synon. with ἐπιθυμίαι τῆς σαρκός (cf. the sing. in 1 Jn. 2:16) in a hostile sense : ποιοῦντες τὰ θελήματα τῆς σαρκὸς καὶ τῶν διανοιῶν, to describe the former manner of pagan conversation. If here θελήματα τῆς σαρκός goes rather beyond sexual lust to embrace the Pauline sense of → σάρξ, the expression includes not only διάνοιαι, "sensual inclinations," but also the irrational impulses of physical life and especially those of an unbridled sex life. The exact parallels with ποιεῖν from the Paris magic pap. (→ 53) are worth noting in this connection.

2 Tm. 2:26 refers to the θέλημα of Satan. The Gnostics in their intoxication are caught in Satan's net and they are brought into bondage to his will as into (εἰς) a sphere of captivity. The word is well adapted to portray the captivating and enslaving force of the satanic θέλημα. [32]

C. θέλημα in the Early Church.

In the post-apostolic fathers the use of θέλημα in completely under the influence of biblical usage and unequivocally denotes the will of God. It expresses predominantly (→ 59) the divine direction to and commissioning for service : Ign. Eph., 20, 1; R. 1, 1; Ign. Pol., 8, 1; Tr., 1, 1. It also underlies the state of salvation : Ign. Sm., 11, 1; Eph. prooem. (the προωρισμένη reminds us of Pl. Eph. 1); Pol. Phil., 1, 3; 1 Cl., 42, 2 : Christ from God and the apostles from Christ, εὐτάκτως ἐκ θελήματος θεοῦ. Especially significant in Ign. Eph., 20, 1; R., 1, 1; Sm., 11, 1; Pol., 8, 1, is the use of θέλημα for God's will without mentioning God, cf. the Rabb. רצון and → 57; 59. ποιεῖν αὐτοῦ τὸ θέλημα is found in Pol. Phil., 2, 2. Cf. also πρὸς τὸ ἐκείνου θέλημα in Herm. s., 9, 5, 2. In connection with God's will as the power which begets Christ we should note Ign. Sm., 1, 1: υἱὸν θεοῦ κατὰ θέλημα καὶ δύναμιν θεοῦ, γεγεννημένον ἀληθῶς ἐκ παρθένου. Just. Dial., 61, 1 also causes the Logos ἐκ τοῦ ἀπὸ τοῦ πατρὸς θελήσει γεγεννῆσθαι. Tat. Or. Graec., 5, 1: θελήματι προπηδᾷ λόγος, later ἔργον πρωτότοκον τοῦ πατρός.

---

[30] Van Manen, 616.

[31] On γαμίζειν cf. Ltzm. K., ad loc. Apollon Dyscol. Synt. (Grammatici Graeci, II [1910], 400, 5 f.) understands it as a correct grammarian : "to give in marriage." But in the Gospels γαμίζεσθαι is used of the woman for "to be married" : Mk. 12:25; Mt. 22:30; Lk. 20:35 (vl. γαμίσκονται). The act. form in Mt. 24:38 is ambiguous, though the par. in Lk. 17:27 uses it of the woman in the sense of "to marry." Method. Symp., III, 14 also uses γαμίζειν simply for "to marry."

[32] We here assume the identity of αὐτοῦ and ἐκείνου and the reference of both to διάβολος. So vg., Luther, Calvin, Cocceius, and among recent scholars de Wette, J. T. Beck, Schl. Erl., E. Riggenbach in Komm.² (1898), Dib. Past., ad loc. Beza and Grotius, and among more recent scholars B. Weiss in Komm.⁷ (1902), suggest God's will, but in Gk. αὐτός and ἐκεῖνος often occur in the same sentence for the same subject, cf. Plat. Phaed., 106b; Crat., 430e. Bengel's reference back to δοῦλος κυρίου is quite impossible.

The terms θέλημα, θέλησις, ἐνέργεια occur in the Monothelite controversy. On the terminology cf. already Apollinaris of Laodicaea, Ad Julianum Fr. (ed. J. Dräseke, TU, VII 3/4 [1892], 400). [33] The psychological presuppositions are that the νοῦς is active in the θέλημα and that what is willed is then expressed in words and acts (ἐνεργεῖται). [34] The NT itself has no interest in this type of psychology, which is Greek in source. The Monothelite and Dyothelite discussion always regards θέλημα as an organ of volition, whereas in the NT θέλημα is what is willed, and the whole emphasis falls on the content of volition. The Gospels take quite seriously the existence of a will which is conditioned by the σάρξ of Christ but which is constantly offered up as a sacrifice (→ 49).

† θέλησις.

θέλησις is a late *koine* word, closely related to θέλημα but much less frequent. In the LXX it is similarly used for חפץ and רצון, but also for צבי and אֲרֶשֶׁת. a. of God: Tob. 12:18, Raphael has come at God's command. 2 Macc. 12:16: they took the city by the will of God. Of God's good-pleasure: Ez. 18:23: μὴ θελήσει θελήσω (הֶחָפֹץ אֶחְפֹּץ), Prv. 8:35: θέλησις παρὰ κυρίου (רצון), quoted by Just. at Dial., 61, 5. b. Of man: "demand," "desire," "wish." 2 Ch. 15:15: ἐν πάσῃ θελήσει (רצון) to seek God with one's whole heart. ψ 20:2 א c.a R: τὴν θέλησιν τῶν χειλέων (אֲרֶשֶׁת). Wis. 16:25: desire expressed in prayer. As the royal will, 3 Macc. 2:26, of Ptolemy, here in the bad sense of ordering the calumniation of his friends. A special instance is the translation of אֶרֶץ־הַצְּבִי, "land of glory or splendour," as χώρα τῆς θελήσεως in Da. 11:16 Syr., and of הַר צְבִי־קֹדֶשׁ, "mountain of sacred glory," as τὸ ὄρος τῆς θελήσεως in Da. LXX 11:45 B. Here θέλησις means "glory," "sweetness," "pleasantness." Stob. Ecl., 87, 22 defines θέλησις as ἑκούσιος βούλησις, but this is for him εὔλογος ὄρεξις. [1] θέλησις does not occur in Epict. It is used in Corp. Herm., IV, 1a, 1b, however, of the creative will of the demiurge, and in X, 2 of the Godhead: ἡ γὰρ τούτου ἐνέργεια ἡ θέλησίς ἐστι καὶ ἡ οὐσία αὐτοῦ τὸ θέλειν πάντα εἶναι. In Preis. Zaub., IV, 1428 ff. the sense is "female desire": δότε αὐτῇ ... θέλησιν τῶν ἐμῶν θελημάτων, "give her desire for my desire." But cf. → supra. In the accounts of the Ptolemaeans in Iren. Haer., I, 12, 1; Hipp. Ref., VI, 38, 5 f.; Epiph. Haer., 33, 1; 5, θέλησις is synon. with θέλημα (→ 53), as also in the Monothelite controversy. It is used with σύνεσις, φρόνησις in Iren. Haer., I, 29, 1 f. In 2 Cl., 1, 6 it signifies God's will which dispels the mist of idolatry.

In the NT θέλησις occurs only at Hb. 2:4. With the preaching of the Gospel, testimony was given to God through signs and wonders κατὰ τὴν αὐτοῦ θέλησιν.

Schrenk

---

[33] On this pt. cf. F. Loofs RE³, IV, 47, 56 ff.
[34] Cf. βουλή and ἐνέργεια in Corp. Herm., I, 14.
θ έ λ η σ ι ς. [1] Cf. A. Dyroff, *Die Ethik der alten Stoa* (1897), 23 f.; A. Bonhöffer, *Epiktet und die Stoa* (1890), 261.

† θεμέλιος, † θεμέλιον, † θεμελιόω

1. θεμέλιος occurs from the time of Homer (for metrical reasons θεμείλια; cf. the equivalent θέμεθλα. Neither construction is clear. Relation to the root θε [cf. the later θέμα] is perhaps secondary, the assumption being that this is a loan word).[1] The substant. adj. ὁ θεμέλιος (add λίθος, cf. Rev. 21:14, 19) and τὸ θεμέλιον mean the "basic stone" or "foundation." In the NT, as elsewhere in Gk., the masc. use (definite in 1 C. 3:12; 2 Tm. 2:19; Hb. 11:10; Rev. 21:19) is more common than the neuter (definite in Ac. 16:26). There are 16 instances in the NT, and in most of these the case does not allow us to determine the gender.[2]

Also in keeping with ordinary Gk. usage is the fact that the term is employed both lit., e.g., for the foundation of a house, tower or city (cf. Lk. 6:48, 49; 14:29; Ac. 16:26; Hb. 11:10; Rev. 21:14, 19) and metaph. (in the other passages). As there is reference to θεμέλιος τῆς τέχνης (Macho, 2, 1 f. [CAF, III, 325]), as the figure of the θεμέλιος and of building thereon is used for philosophical doctrines (Epict., II, 15, 8), so the NT refers to laying the foundations of the communities (Rom. 15:20;[3] 1 C. 3:10 ff.) or to fundamental Christian doctrines (Hb. 6:1). To the same group belongs 1 Tm. 6:19, unless we are to read κειμέλιον ("treasure") for θεμέλιον.[4]

There is a deeper Christological and ecclesiological content in R. 15:20 : Christ as the foundation ; 1 C. 3:11: the same ;[5] and Eph. 2:20 : τῷ θεμελίῳ τῶν ἀποστό-λων καὶ προφητῶν, ὄντος ἀκρογωνιαίου αὐτοῦ Χριστοῦ Ἰησοῦ, the apostles and prophets as the foundation and Christ as the corner stone (gen. of apposition) in this foundation.[6] 2 Tm. 2:19 is to be expounded along the same lines : ὁ ... στερεὸς θεμέλιος τοῦ θεοῦ ἕστηκεν.

This Christological and ecclesiological use arises naturally from a combination of the figurative sense[7] of θεμέλιος with the fact that in the NT Christ and the Church are always the logical subject to which such figures must refer. The thought of building or edification (→ οἰκοδομή) is a familiar one in the NT. The Church or community is a house which is built by God or Christ, and which is constantly to be built with God in Christ by the community and its leaders (→ οἰκία). Christ is the foundation of this house, as He is the Head of His Church. With Christ are some of the chief apostles, especially Peter. Eph. 2:20 — note the express reference to οἰκοδομή in v. 21 — should be compared with Mt. 16:18 : ἐπὶ ταύτῃ

θ ε μ έ λ ι ο ς κτλ. [1] Cf. Bl.-Debr.⁶ § 109, 3. Cf. also P. Chantraine, *La Formation des Noms en Grec Ancien* (1933), 43, 375, which refers to H. Güntert, "Labyrinth" (SAH, 1932/3, 1), 30 [Debrunner].

[2] Moult.-Mill. *s.v.*: "... the gender is indeterminable, as in a number of the NT passages." Cf. also Bl.-Debr.⁶ § 49, 3.

[3] On the inter-relationship of R. 15:20 and 1 C. 3:10 cf. M. J. Lagrange, *St. Paul, Epître aux Romains*² (1922), 354.

[4] Cf. Nestle.

[5] Cf. on this pt. certain Rabb. traditions in which Abraham is presented as the foundation of the world, Str.-B., III, 333; on the idea as such, Joach. Jeremias, *Golgotha* (1926), 73 f.; cf. also Str.-B., I, 733.

[6] → ἀκρογωνιαῖος, I, 792.

[7] The common tendency to use θεμέλιος figur. may be seen from legal pap. in which the word means not only "foundation" but the "right of possession from foundation to roof" or even the "purchase," *v.* Preisigke Wört., *s.v.*

τῇ πέτρᾳ οἰκοδομήσω (→ οἰκοδομέω) μου τὴν ἐκκλησίαν, where the → πέτρα is regarded as θεμέλιος (v).[8] 2 Tm. 2:19 : στερεὸς θεμέλιος τοῦ θεοῦ, is similarly followed in v. 20 by a reference to the οἰκία, which, as the οἶκος θεοῦ, is equivalent to the ἐκκλησία θεοῦ, 1 Tm. 3:15.[9]

As this conception of the → ἐκκλησία as the οἶκος θεοῦ betrays OT influence, so there are OT roots for the idea of the θεμέλιος (v). In the LXX the word occurs dozens of times for various Heb. terms.[10] It is not used figur. but lit. for the foundations of houses or cities, and cosmologically for the foundations of the mountains, of lands, of the earth and of heaven. The θεμέλια Σιών in Is. 28:16 (cf. Is. 54:11) refer to the holy city, the city of God,[11] with allusion also to the people of God, the Church, and its foundations. It is on this basis that the passages in Rev. (21:14, 19), though literal rather than figurative, acquire a Christological and ecclesiological significance.

2. What is true of θεμέλιος (v) is no less true of the verb θεμελιόω (from the time of Xenoph., also on inscr.). Mt. 7:25; Lk. 6:48;[12] Hb. 1:10 use the term literally : "to provide with a foundation." To understand the usage in Eph. 3:17 (ἐν ἀγάπῃ ἐρριζωμένοι καὶ τεθεμελιωμένοι) = Col. 1:23 (τῇ πίστει τεθεμελιωμένοι καὶ ἑδραῖοι); 1 Pt. 5:10 (ὁ θεὸς ... ὑμᾶς ... στηρίξει, σθενώσει, θεμελιώσει), we need only consider the figur. sense of "to strengthen," "to confirm."[13] Nevertheless, it is as well to take into account all that we have said concerning θεμέλιος (v), since it is only thus that we can do justice to the comprehensive and distinctive meaning of these statements. When God confirms believers, or when believers are confirmed in faith and love, this is implicitly the assuring of the house or Church of God through its foundation, Christ.

K. L. Schmidt

θεοδίδακτος → θεός.
θεόπνευστος → πνεῦμα.

θεόμαχος, θεομαχέω → μάχομαι.

---

[8] These links make it plain that one cannot find such divergence between Eph. 2:20 and 1 C. 3:11 as often accompanies the thesis that Eph. is not Pauline. Cf. Holtzmann NT, II, 721. A more cautious judgment is that of Dibelius in Gefbr. on Eph. 2:20. In this respect the Roman Catholic exegetes are right. Cf. esp. C. Trossen, "Erbauen" in *Theologie und Glaube*, 6 (1914), 804 ff. Trossen rejects the exposition of Thomas Aquinas that the foundation of the apostles and prophets is that on which the apostles and prophets themselves rest, but he comes to the right conclusion that "there is no contradiction with 1 C. 3:11; for the same figure can be used at different times in different ways. The apostles uphold the temple of God as Peter is the rock of the Church." Meinertz Gefbr. on Eph. 2:20 follows Trossen.

[9] Cf. Wilke-Grimm, *s.v.*: θεμ. *dici videtur ecclesia tamquam civitatis divinae fundamentum*, 2 Tim. 2:19 *coll.* vs. 20 *et* 1 Tim. 3:15.

[10] V. Hatch-Redp., *s.v.*

[11] In the Heb. the reference is hardly to the city, but to a new sanctuary, since we have בְּצִיֹּן (unlike the LXX); cf. H. Gressmann, *Der Messias* (1929), 174; O. Procksch, Js. I (1930), 357 [v. Rad].

[12] In place of διὰ τὸ καλῶς οἰκοδομῆσθαι αὐτήν there is also the well-attested reading τεθεμελίωτο γὰρ ἐπὶ τὴν πέτραν.

[13] Cf. on this pt. Thes. Steph.: Chrysost. Ὅπερ γάρ ἐστιν ἐν οἰκίᾳ θεμέλιος, τοῦτο ἐν ψυχῇ προσευχή. Cl. Al. Prot., VIII, 77, 1 says in the figur. sense : θεμελιόω τὴν ἀλήθειαν. Cf. also Diod. S., 11, 68, 7: βασιλεία καλῶς θεμελιωθεῖσα.

θεός, θεότης, ἄθεος, θεοδίδακτος,
θεῖος, θειότης

θεός → κύριος, → πατήρ.

Contents : A. The Greek Concept of God : 1. θεός in the Usage of Secular Gk.; 2. The Content of the Gk. Concept of God ; 3. The Development of the Gk. Concept of God. B. El and Elohim in the OT : 1. The Usage of the LXX : 2. The OT Belief in God in the Form of Faith in Yahweh ; 3. The Traditions concerning Belief in God prior to the

---

θεός κτλ. Note : The original art. prepared by Stauffer on θεός κτλ. had to be revised. Because of other commitments the author could not do this himself, and at his own request the revision was made by G. Friedrich, who also checked most of the quotations. Friedrich contributed some independent paragraphs on → 96 and 109, and these, with the contributions of Quell, Kleinknecht and Kuhn, are solely the work of the authors designated.

Bibl. On the whole field, H. Usener, *Götternamen, Versuch einer Lehre von der religiösen Begriffsbildung* [1](1896), [2](1929); N. Söderblom, *Das Werden des Gottesglaubens* [2](1926); Art. "God" in ERE, VI, 243-306; Art. "Gottesglaube" in RGG², III, 1356-1377; E. Lehmann, „Götter u. Gottheiten" in Bertholet-Leh., I, 64-87. On A : Doxographic review of the concept of God in philosophy and gen. in Stob. Ecl., I, 23-51; cf. H. Diels, *Doxographi Graeci* (1879), p. 297-307 and Cic. Nat. Deor., I, 10-15; on psychological theology: Sext. Emp. Math., IX, 13-194 (p. 215-255, Mutschmann): Περὶ Θεῶν; W. F. Otto, *Die altgriech. Gottesidee* (1926); *Die Götter Griechenlands* (1929), [2](1934); U. v. Wilamowitz, *Der Glaube der Hellenen*, I (1931), 12 ff. and passim ; K. Lehrs, "Gott, Götter und Dämonen" in *Populäre Aufsätze* [2](1875), 143 ff.; E. Rohde, "Die Religion der Griechen" in *Kleine Schriften* (1901), II, 320 ff.; W. Nestle, *Griech. Religiosität*, I-III (1930-1933); K. F. Nägelsbach, *Homerische Theologie* [3](1884); *Die nachhomerische Theologie* (1857); E. Caird, *The Evolution of Theology in the Greek Philosophers* (1904); O. Gilbert, *Griechische Religionsphilosophie* (1911); H. Schwarz, *Der Gottesgedanke in der Geschichte der Philosophie, Synthesis* 4 (1913); J. Stenzel, *Metaphysik des Altertums* (1931); W. Theiler, "Die Vorbereitung des Neuplatonismus" in *Problemata*, I (1930); E. Norden, *Agnostos Theos* (1913), 13 ff. and passim ; E. Zeller, "Die Entwicklung des Monotheismus bei den Griechen" in *Vorträge und Abhandlungen*, I (1865), 1 ff.; W. Weber, "Die Vereinheitlichung der religiösen Welt" in *Probleme der Spätantike* (1930); K. Keyssner, "Gottesvorstellung und Lebensauffassung im gr. Hymnus," *Würzburger Studien zur Altertumswissenschaft*, II (1932), 9-127; E. Peterson, *Der Monotheismus als politisches Problem* (1935); K. Prümm, *Der christliche Glaube und die altheidnische Welt*, I and II (1935); Harnack Dg., I, 138 n. On B : A. Alt, *Der Gott der Väter* (1929); B. Baentsch, *Altorientalischer und israelitischer Monotheismus* (1906); F. Baethgen, *Beiträge zur semitischen Religionsgeschichte, I* (1888); W. W. Graf Baudissin, *Kyrios als Gottesname im Judentum*, I-IV (1929); *Adonis und Esmun* (1911); *Studien zur semitischen Religionsgeschichte*, I (1876), 49 ff.; F. Baumgärtel, *Elohim ausserhalb des Pentateuch* (1914); *Die Eigenart der at.lichen Frömmigkeit* (1932), 26-35; 63-93; G. Beer, *Welches war die älteste Religion Israels?* (1927); E. Brügelmann, *Der Gottesgedanke bei Ezechiel* (1935); M. Buber, *Königtum Gottes* (1932); H. Duhm, *Der Verkehr Gottes mit den Menschen im AT* (1926); O. Eissfeldt, *Vom Werden der biblischen Gottesanschauung* (1929); H. Ewald, *Die Lehre der Bibel von Gott* (1873); J. Hehn, *Die biblische und die babylonische Gottesidee* (1913); P. Kleinert, "El" in *Baudissin-Festschrift* (1918), 26 ff.; E. Meyer, Art. "El" in Roscher, I, 1 (1890), 1223 ff.; E. Sellin, *Beiträge zur israelitischen u. jüdischen Religionsgeschichte*, I : "Jahwes Verhältnis zum israelitischen Volk u. Individuum nach altisraelitischer Vorstellung" (1896), passim ; C. Steuernagel, "Jahwe, Der Gott Israels" in *Wellhausen-Festschr.*, ZAW, Beiheft, 27 (1914), 331 ff.; P. Volz, *Mose und sein Werk* [2](1932), 27-36; 58-71; W. Eichrodt, *Theologie des AT*, I (1933), 86 ff. On C in general : I. A. Maynard, "Judaism and Mazdayasna," JBL, 44 (1925), 163-170; K. Holl, "Urchristentum u. Religionsgeschichte" in *Ges. Aufsätze*, II : *Der Osten* (1928), 1 ff.; G. Kittel, *Die Religionsgeschichte u. das Urchristentum* (1932), 123 ff.; A. v. Harnack, *Die Entstehung der christlichen Theologie und des kirchlichen Dogmas* (1927);

Rise of the Community of Yahweh ; 4. El and Elohim as Appellatives ; 5. The Content of the OT Belief in God ; 6. The Historical Continuation of the OT Belief in God. C. The Early Christian Fact of God and Its Conflict with the Concept of God in Judaism : 1. The Usage ; 2. The Uniqueness of God : a. Prophetic Monotheism as the Starting-point of True Monotheism ; b. Dynamic Monotheism in Later Judaism ; c. θεοί in the NT ; d. Εἷς θεός in the Confession and Practice of Early Christianity ; e. God and His Angels in the NT ; f. Monotheism and Christology in the NT ; g. Christ as θεός in Early Christianity ; h. The Threefold Relation of God, Christ and Spirit ; 3. The Personal Being of God : a. The Conflict against Anthropomorphism in the Jewish World ; b. The Personal God of the NT ; 4. The Transcendence of God : a. The Power of God as Ruler in Semitic Religions ; b. God and the World in Later Judaism ; c. The Transcendent God of the NT.

P. Feine, *Jesus* (1930), 115 ff.; H. E. Weber, *Die Vollendung des nt.lichen Glaubensbekenntnisses durch Joh.* (1912); E. Stauffer, "Grundbegriffe einer Morphologie des nt.lichen Denkens" = BFTh, 33, 2 (1929), 57-64; E. v. Dobschütz, "Rationales und irrationales Denken über Gott im Urchristentum, Eine Studie insbes. zum Hb.," ThStKr, 97 (1924), 235 ff.; "Die fünf Sinne im NT," JBL, 48 (1929), 378 ff.; J. Leipoldt, *Das Gotteserlebnis Jesu* (1927); G. Kuhlmann, "*Theologia naturalis* bei Pls. u. Philon" = *Nt.liche Forschungen*, I, 7 (1930); O. Michel, "Luthers *deus absconditus* und der Gottesgedanke bei Pls.," ThStKr, 103 (1931), 199 ff.; E. Fascher, "*Deus invisibilis*" in *Marburger Studien, R. Otto Festgruss* (1931), 41 ff. On C 1.: H. Gressmann, "Die Aufgaben der Wissenschaft des nachbiblischen Judentums," ZAW, NF, 2 (1925), 1 ff.; Art "Gott" in EJ, VII (1931), 548-571; O. Michel, "Wie spricht der Aristeasbrief über Gott ?" in ThStKr, 102 (1930), 302 ff.; Moore, I, 357 ff.; R. Marcus, "Divine Names and Attributes in Hellenistic Jewish Literature" in *Proceedings of the American Academy for Jewish Research* (1931/2), 43-120; A. Marmorstein, *The Old Rabbinic Doctrine of God*, I (1927); Dalman WJ, I, 157 ff.; Schl. Theol. d. Judt., 1-45; Schl. Jos., *passim*; W. H. S. Jones, "A Note on the Vague Use of θεός" in Class. Rev., 27 (1913), 252 ff.; W. F. Albright, "The Name Jahveh," JBL, 43 (1924), 370-378 and 44 (1925), 158-162; B. Weiss, "Der Gebrauch des Artikels bei den Gottesnamen," ThStKr, 84 (1911), 319-392, 503-538. On C 2.: H. Zimmern, *Vater, Sohn u. Fürsprecher in der babylonischen Gottesvorstellung* (1896); H. Usener, "Dreiheit," *Rheinisches Museum für Philologie*, NF, 58 (1903), 1 ff.; N. Söderblom, *Vater, Sohn und Geist unter den heiligen Dreiheiten* (1909); D. Nielsen, *Der dreieinige Gott in religionshistorischer Beleuchtung*, I (1922); Clemen, 125 ff.; J. Hehn, *Wege zum Monotheismus* (1913); H. Hommel, "Der allgegenwärtige Himmelsgott," ARW, 23 (1925), 193 ff.; E. A. W. Budge, *Tutankhamen, Amenism, Atenism and Egyptian Monotheism* (1923); W. W. Graf Baudissin, *Studien z. semit. Religionsgeschichte*, I (1876), 47 ff.; W. Smith, *Lectures on the Religion of the Semites* [3](1927); J. Wellhausen, *Reste arabischen Heidentums* [2](1897), 208-242; J. Guidi, *L'Arabie Antéislamique* (1921); A. Jeremias, *Monotheistische Strömungen innerhalb der babylonischen Religion* (1904); R. H. Pfeiffer, "The Dual Origin of Hebrew Monotheism," JBL, 46 (1927), 193-206; Str.-B., II, 28 ff. (εἷς θεός); III, 48-60 (*Götter der Heiden*); E. Rohde, "Gottesglaube u. Kyriosglaube bei Pls.," ZNW, 22 (1923), 43-57; A. Nock, *Harvard Theol. Review*, 23 (1930), 261 f.; F. J. A. Hort, "Two Dissertations on μονογενὴς θεός" in *Scripture and Tradition* (1876); Bau. Ign., 193 f.; E. Peterson, Εἷς Θεός (1926); A. Seeberg, *Der Katechismus der Urchristenheit* (1903); J. Kunze, *Das apostolische Glaubensbekenntnis u. das NT* (1911); J. Haussleiter, *Trinitarischer Glaube u. Christusbekenntnis in der alten Kirche* (1920); P. Feine, *Die Gestalt des apostolischen Glaubensbekenntnisses in der Zeit des NT* (1925); Wnd. 2 K., 429 ff.; O. Moe, "Hat Pls. ... ein trinitarisches Taufbekenntnis gekannt ?" in *Festschrift f. R. Seeberg*, I (1929), 179 ff.; E. v. Dobschütz, "Zwei- u. dreigliedrige Formeln," JBL, 50 (1931), 117-147; *Das Apostolikum in biblisch-theologischer Beleuchtung* (1932). On C. 3.: R. Sander, *Furcht u. Liebe im palästinischen Judentum* (1935), Index, *s.v.* "Gottesanschauung"; H. Preisker, *Die urchr. Botschaft von der Liebe Gottes* (1930); C. A. Bernoulli, "Le Dieu-Père de Jésus d'après les Synoptiques," in *Actes du Congrès International d'Histoire des Religions*, II (1923), 211 ff.; C. Fabricius, "Urbekenntnisse der Christenheit," *Festschr. f. R. Seeberg*, I (1929), 21 ff. On C. 4.: W. W. Graf Baudissin in *Festschr. f. K. Marti* (1925), 1-11; O. Eissfeldt, ZMR, 42 (1927), 161-186; W. Grundmann, *Der Begriff der Kraft in der nt.lichen Gedankenwelt* (1932), 11 ff.

A. The Greek Concept of God.

1. θεός in the Usage of Secular Gk.

The question of the etym. of θεός has never been solved. It can thus tell us nothing about the nature of the Gk. concept of God. [1] θεός [2] is originally a predicative term ; [3] hence its use is as broad and varied as the religious interpretation of the world and of life by the Gks. Homer already uses both the plur. (οἱ) θεοί and the indefinite sing. θεός (τις). [4] In this use he is sometimes thinking of divine being and work in general, [5] sometimes of a particular god, [6] and sometimes specifically of Zeus. [7] There is similar variation between θεός and ὁ θεός with no obvious distinction of sense. We also have variations, often close together, between "the gods," "the god," "god," and "the godhead," as though they were all monistic terms referring to a single power. [8]

Yet (ὁ) θεός does not denote the unity of a specific personality in the monotheistic sense. It rather expresses what is felt to be the unity of the religious world in spite of its multiplicity. The Greek concept of God is essentially polytheistic, not in the sense of many individual gods, but in that of an ordered totality of gods, of a world of gods, which, e.g., in the divine state of Homer, forms an integrated nexus. This view naturally gave strong support to the term θεός. Indeed, it brought it into prominence, and it found its finest expression in the person of Zeus, the πατὴρ ἀνδρῶν τε θεῶν τε (Hom. Il., 15, 47), the monarchical θεῶν ὕπατος καὶ ἄριστος (Hom. Od., 19, 303), the exponent of divine rule in general. [9]

---

[1] Cf. the etym. lexicons, which suggest different stems ; more recently cf. F. Pfister, *Die Religion der Griechen u. Römer* (1930), 113; Walde-Pok., I, 867.

[2] On the manifoldness of the Gk. concept of θεός, cf. Harnack Dg., I, 138 n.; → II, 1 ff.

[3] Hes. Op., 764 of the φήμη : θεός νύ τίς ἐστι καὶ αὐτή. Aesch. Choeph., 59 f.: τόδ' εὐτυχεῖν, τόδ' ἐμ βροτοῖς θεός τε καὶ θεοῦ πλέον. Eur. Hel., 560; cf. U. v. Wilamowitz, *Der Glaube der Hellenen,* I (1931), 17 f.

[4] Hom. Il., 13, 729 f. (θεός) and Il., 4, 320 (θεοί).

[5] On Homeric usage, cf. H. Ebeling, *Lexicon Homericum,* I (1880), s.v. θεός.

[6] Hom. Od., 7, 286.

[7] Hom. Od., 14, 440/444.

[8] Pind. Pyth., 10, 30; 5, 158; Soph. Fr., 226 (TGF).

[9] But the basic polytheism, according to which there arose from the divine plenitude of life — θεῶν πλήρη πάντα, acc. to the classic polytheistic formulation of the religious significance of reality by Thales in Plat. Leg., X, 899b — a cosmos of gods, clearly maintained itelf in spite of the strongest attempts at unity made by the philosophical concept, from which anthropomorphism had long since disappeared. We have only to think of the worlds of Anaximander (No. 15 : I, 17, 29 ff., Diels), which proceeded from original Godhead, and which are themselves θεοί; or of Plato's θεοὶ ὁρατοὶ καὶ γεννητοί (Tim., 40d; 41a ff.) alongside the one invisible God ; or of the polytheism of Stoicism, which rejected monotheism as a diminution of God, cf. Onatas in Stob. Ecl., I, 48 f.: Δοκίει δέ μοι καὶ μὴ εἷς εἶμεν ὁ θεός, ἀλλ' εἷς μὲν ὁ μέγιστος καὶ καθυπέρτερος καὶ ὁ κρατέων τῶ παντός, τοὶ δ' ἄλλοι πολλοὶ διαφέροντες κατὰ δύναμιν· βασιλεύεν δὲ πάντων αὐτῶν ὁ καὶ κράτει καὶ μεγέθει καὶ ἀρετᾷ μέζων. Οὗτος δέ κ' εἴη θεὸς ὁ περιέχων τὸν σύμπαντα κόσμον ... Τοὶ δὲ λέγοντες ἕνα θεὸν εἶμεν, ἀλλὰ μὴ πολλὼς ἁμαρτάνοντι (cf. Norden, *Agnostos Theos* [1913], 39, n. 4); or of Plotinus (against Christian Gnosticism), Enn., II, 9, 9 : "One must laud the gods of the intelligible world, and among them the great king. His greatness is displayed through the plurality of the gods. For it is not compressing the divine into a single point, but expounding it in its plurality and extension, which shows knowledge of the power of God, when He, remaining who He is, creates many things, which are still all dependent on Him, which are by Him and of Him" (ἐντεῦθεν δὲ ἤδη καὶ τοὺς νοητοὺς ὑμνεῖν θεούς, ἐφ' ἅπασι δὲ ἤδη τὸν μέγαν τῶν ἐκεῖ βασιλέα καὶ ἐν τῷ πλήθει μάλιστα τῶν θεῶν τὸ μέγα αὐτοῦ ἐνδεικνυμένους· οὐ γὰρ τὸ συστεῖλαι εἰς ἕν, ἀλλὰ τὸ δεῖξαι πολὺ τὸ θεῖον, ὅσον ἔδειξεν αὐτός, τοῦτό ἐστι δύναμιν θεοῦ

Zeus takes the first decision and has the final word. Hence piety often equates him quite simply with God (cf. Hom. Od., 4, 236; Demosth. Or., 18, 256; Aesch. Suppl., 524 ff.; 720 ff.; Ag., 160 ff.). Under the influence of rational theological speculation along causal lines there develops out of the original plurality of gods a divine genealogy and hierarchy (cf. Hesiod's theogony). We read of higher and lower gods, of families of gods, and finally of a pantheon. In Greece and Rome there is not only a trinity etc., but also a group of twelve gods (οἱ δώδεκα θεοί), [10] and this expression comes to be used for the unity and totality of the gods who rule the world (cf. Pind. Olymp., 5, 5; Plat. Phaedr., 247a).

For the most part θεός is used for such well-known deities as Zeus, Apollos, Athena, Eros etc. But to call the cosmos God is also good Gk. (Plat. Tim., 92c: ὅδε ὁ κόσμος ... θεός, Orig. Cels., V, 7); the φθόνος is a κάκιστος κἀδικώτατος θεός, Hippothoon Fr., 2 (TGF, p. 827), and in Eur. even meeting again is a god: Hel., 560: ὦ θεοί· θεὸς γὰρ καὶ τὸ γιγνώσκειν φίλους. In Aesch. Choeph., 60 εὐτυχεῖν is for men θεός τε καὶ θεοῦ πλέον. Similarly, original forces (→ δίκη II, 181), both inward and outward, may be furnished with the predicate θεός, and later abstract concepts, cosmic magnitudes and divine attributes such as → αἰών (→ I, 198), → λόγος, → νοῦς (Corp. Herm., II, 12), are personified in the cultus and philosophy and hypostatised as gods. εὐλάβεια is an ἄδικος θεός, Eur. Phoen., 560; 782, [11] and λύπη is a δεινὴ θεός, Eur. Or., 399.

This brings us to a further vital point in the Greek concept of God. In face of the deepest reality, of great, sustaining being in all its glory, the Greek can only say that this, and not the Wholly Other, is God. Where we read in 1 Jn. 4:16 that θεὸς ἀγάπη ἐστίν, classical Greek would have to reverse this and say that ἀγάπη θεός ἐστιν. This shift of subject and predicate expresses a whole world of religious difference. The Greek gods are simply basic forms of reality, whether this be conceived in the forms of myth (Homer), in a final, unifying ἀρχή (Ionic physics), [12] or in the ἰδέα of philosophers. Reality, however, is manifold, and it advances on man the most varied claims, which are free and unbound in the world of the gods, but which in many cases tragically intersect in the human breast. Hence the plural θεοί, or polytheism.

Also described as gods are heroes like Chiron (Soph. Trach., 714) and Colonos (Soph. Oed. Col., 65). Homer speaks of extraordinary men as ἴσα θεοῖς, ἴσα (ἴσος) θεῷ or θεὸς ὥς (Hom. Il., 5, 440; 5, 78 etc.).

In the Hellenistic period an outstanding ruler may be called a θεός as the creator of a new political order: ὥσπερ γὰρ θεὸν ἐν ἀνθρώποις εἰκὸς εἶναι τὸν τοιοῦτον Aristot. Pol., III, 13, p. 1284a, 11; Plut. Lysander, 18 (I, 443b); Demetrius Poliorketes and his father Antigonos are celebrated as θεοὶ σωτῆρες in Athens (307 B.C.), cf. the hymn in Athen., VI, 63 (p. 253d): ὡς οἱ μέγιστοι τῶν θεῶν καὶ φίλτατοι | τῇ πόλει πάρεισιν. In the Hell. cult of the ruler and the Roman cult of the emperor [13] θεός becomes a designation of office (→ εὐεργέτης, κύριος, σωτήρ). Ptolemaeus in Ditt. Or., I, 90, 10; Antiochus of Commagene in Ditt. Or., I, 383, 1: Ἀντίοχος θεὸς δίκαιος

εἰδότων, ὅταν μένων ὃς ἔστι πολλοὺς ποιῇ πάντας εἰς αὐτὸν ἀνηρτημένους καὶ δι' ἐκεῖνον καὶ παρ' ἐκείνου ὄντας); or finally Julian (of Helios), Or., 4, 149a: τὴν δὲ τοσαύτην στρατιὰν τῶν θεῶν εἰς μίαν ἡγεμονικὴν ἕνωσιν συντάξας), cf. 138b; 139c.

[10] Cf. O. Weinreich, "Zwölfgötter," Aus Unterricht und Forschung (1935), 327 ff.

[11] Cf. W. Nestle, Griech. Religiosität, II (1933), 21 ff. Plentiful material may be found in Roscher, III, 2, 2127 ff., s.v. "Personifikationen," e.g., Plut. Cleomenes, 9 (I, 808e).

[12] Anaximand. No. 15 (I, 85, 14 ff., Diels); Hipp. Ref., I, 21, 1.

[13] Cf. Deissmann LO, 291 ff.; P. Oxy., VIII, 1143, 4: ὑπὲρ τοῦ θεοῦ καὶ κυρίου Αὐτοκράτορος.

ἐπιφανής ... ὁ ἐκ ... βασιλίσσης Λαοδίκης θεᾶς. Ptolemaeus XIII τοῦ κυρίου βασιλέος θεοῦ, Ditt. Or., I, 186, 8. The dictator Caesar, Ditt. Syll.³, 760, 7: θεὸν ἐπιφανῆ καὶ κοινὸν τοῦ ἀνθρωπίνου βίου σωτῆρα. Augustus is θεὸς ἐκ θεοῦ, Ditt. Or., I, 655, 2; ὁ θεὸς Καῖσαρ, Strabo, IV, 177; 193; 199. The emperor is called θεὸς ἡμῶν καὶ δεσπότης, Dominus et Deus noster (Suet. Caes. Domitianus, 13). In spite of oriental models and later oriental influence, the idea of divine humanity and of human deification is genuinely Greek. [14]

Finally, in the world of religious philosophy θεός is used increasingly to denote impersonal metaphysical powers and forces, and it is thus often replaced by general and neutral terms like the divine ([τὸ] → θεῖον), destiny, or even the good, the existent, the one. [15] This is linked with the total development of the Greek concept, which might be regarded as a process of progressive refinement [16] in the sense that the palpable divine figures of myth are increasingly spiritualised and moralised, thus gaining in dignity, spirituality and purity, but to the same degree losing in proximity, in relationship to man and in mythical presence. The Greek concept of God, which achieved its first enduring form in the myth of Homer, ends in the philosophical idea, in religious philosophy. It must be immediately emphasised, however, that this does not imply a change in the essence, the inner structure or the substance of the concept, but a constant shift in the form of the divine in accordance with the attitude of man to the world and to life. This change in the form of the divine constitutes the development in the Greek idea of God.

2. The Content of the Greek Concept of God.

The gods are a given factor for Homer and Hesiod. Although eternal (αἰὲν ἐόντες, Hom. Od., I, 263; αἰειγενέται, Hom. Il., 2, 400; Od., 23, 81), they have come into being like men. They are, indeed, of the same origin (ὁμόθεν γεγάασι θεοὶ θνητοί τ' ἄνθρωποι, Hes. Op., 108). Both have life from a common mother (ἐκ μιᾶς δὲ πνέομεν ματρὸς ἀμφότεροι, Pind. Nem., 6, 1 ff.). The gods have not created the world out of nothing [17] (→ κόσμον ... τὸν αὐτὸν ἀπάντων, οὔτε τις θεῶν οὔτε ἀνθρώπων ἐποίησεν, ἀλλ' ἦν ἀεὶ καὶ ἔστιν καὶ ἔσται πῦρ ἀείζωον, ἁπτόμενον μέτρα καὶ ἀποσβεννύμενον μέτρα, Heracl. Fr., 30 [I, 84, 1 ff., Diels]). They are rather the order and form (and therefore the meaning of the world) which have struggled out of chaos and formed and harnessed the original titanic forces of being. They are the "creators of a sensually intelligible nexus, of an order of things, which must be thus because it can always be so again." [18] Hence they are not related to nature or to the world as Creator to creature. God is the attainment of order. He is form and totality, intrinsic meaning. The Greek world never aban-

---

[14] Cf. the Orphic verse of Empedocles concerning himself, Fr. 112, 4 (I, 264, 15 f., Diels): ἐγὼ δ' ὑμῖν θεὸς ἄμβροτος, οὐκέτι θνητὸς πωλεῦμαι. Cf. O. Weinreich, "Antikes Gottmenschentum," NJbch. Wiss. u. Jugendbildung, 2 (1926), 633 ff.

[15] Cf. already Heracl. Fr., 32 (I, 159, 1 f., Diels): ἓν τὸ σοφὸν μοῦνον λέγεσθαι οὐκ ἐθέλει καὶ ἐθέλει Ζηνὸς ὄνομα. Then the prayer of Hecabe, Eur. Tro., 884 ff.: ὅστις ποτ' εἶ σύ, δυστόπαστος εἰδέναι (difficult to search out) Ζεύς, εἴτ' ἀνάγκη φύσεος εἴτε νοῦς βροτῶν, Plot. Enn., V, 4, 1.

[16] J. Stenzel, Platon der Erzieher (1928), 21.

[17] Cf. Wilamowitz, Glaube der Hellenen, I, 349.

[18] Stenzel, op. cit., 16. Cf. Hes. Theog., 70 ff. on Zeus: ὃ δ' οὐρανῷ ἐμβασιλεύει ... κάρτει νικήσας πατέρα Κρόνον· εὖ δὲ ἕκαστα ἀθανάτοις διέταξε ὁμῶς καὶ ἐπέφραδε τιμάς. Cf. Op., 276 ff.

doned this basic Homeric conception. [19] It is one of the constitutive elements in Platonic philosophy (→ ψυχή), and ever after it has been an essential mark of the classical Greek concept of God. Thus the gods are also gods of the state, [20] i.e., of the most essential order of human life which gives direct proof of its divinity in → νόμος (cf. Heracl. Fr., 114 [I, 176, 7 ff., Diels]) and the oath.

To the Gk. ἀθάνατος is synon. with θεός. The gods are called the immortals (ἀθάνατοι, Hom. Il., 1, 503; Od., 1, 31 etc.). This does not mean eternal pre-existence. It means only that they have no end, that they are not subject to death. [21] Another point of importance for the Hellenic concept of God is that eternity includes eternal youth, the Greeks finding it distasteful to think of the gods ever growing old : ἡ μὲν (Penelope) γὰρ βροτός ἐστι, σὺ (the goddess) δ' ἀθάνατος καὶ ἀγήρως : Hom. Od., 5, 215 ff. Beauty is also included : Hom. Hymn. Cer., 275 ff.; Heracl. Fr., 83 (I, 169, 17 ff., Diels): ἀνθρώπων ὁ σοφώτατος πρὸς θεὸν πίθηκος φανεῖται καὶ σοφίᾳ καὶ κάλλει καὶ τοῖς ἄλλοις πᾶσιν, also great power and knowledge : God is τῷ ὄντι σοφός, Plat. Ap., 23a; cf. Heracl. Fr., 78 and 79 (I, 168, 16 ff., Diels). Legitimate power, κρατοῦν, superiority — the gods are, and are often called, κρείττονες — is a constant feature of θεός, cf. Menand. Fr., 257 (CAF): τὸ κρατοῦν γὰρ πᾶν νομίζεται θεός. They are also the μάκαρες, the blessed ones, who in eternal splendour and glory (Οὐρανίωνες, Hom. Il., I, 570) live out their days in pleasure high above human need and distress (Hom. Od., 6, 42 : θεοὶ ῥεῖα ζώοντες; Od., 5, 122). We find no trace of moral seriousness or of what is for us the characteristic trait of holiness. [22] The relation of gods and men finds classical Greek expression in Pindar Nem., 6, 1 ff.: They are separated by an eternal and unbridgeable gulf, and yet they are originally related : ἓν ἀνδρῶν, | ἓν θεῶν γένος· ἐκ μιᾶς δὲ πνέομεν | ματρὸς ἀμφότεροι· διείργει δὲ πᾶσα κεκριμένα | δύναμις, ὡς τὸ μὲν οὐδέν, ὁ δὲ | χάλκεος ἀσφαλὲς αἰὲν ἕδος | μένει οὐρανός. ἀλλά τι προσφέρομεν ἔμπαν ἢ μέγαν | νόον ἤτοι φύσιν ἀθανάτοις. "God stands before us ... not as an infinite being of another kind, but simply as an infinite being of the same kind." [23]

What the gods are, or are not, as the genii of life, may first be seen with full clarity when we compare them with the autonomous, independently operating and impersonal μοῖρα or αἶσα, the Greek concept of fate, as an eternal and ineluctable order by which an end, or death, is appointed for all things and all men. The idea of the Godhead is confronted by that of fate, which the gods know but are unable to alter (Hom. Il., 16, 431 ff.; Hdt., I, 9). Here the power of the gods, which is elsewhere said to be infinite (Hom. Od., 4, 236 ff.), reaches its limit (Hom. Od., 3, 238). "But with the thought of foreordination by Zeus or the gods (Hom. Od., 9, 52; 3, 269) the idea changes from that of obscure destiny to one of meaningful plan and purpose." [24] Behind and above both is the totality of being.

[19] Cf. H. Heyse, Idee und Existenz (1935), 34 ff.
[20] Cf. Tyrtaeus Fr., 2, 2 (Diehl): Ζεὺς ... τήνδε δέδωκε πόλιν; Solon Fr., 3, 4 (Diehl); Xenoph. Mem., IV, 3, 16 : ὁ ἐν Δελφοῖς θεός, ὅταν τις αὐτὸν ἐπερωτᾷ πῶς ἄν τοῖς θεοῖς χαρίζοιτο, ἀποκρίνεται· νόμῳ πόλεως, cf. Ditt. Syll.³, 1268; Plat. Prot., 322a-d; Plut. Col., 31 (II, 1125e). Thus later systematisation could advance a threefold theology of the φυσικόν, μυθικόν and νομικόν : Plut. De Placitis Philosophorum, I, 6, 9 (H. Diels, Doxographi Graeci [1879], p. 295, 6 ff.).
[21] There is a contradiction in the oldest Gk. concept of God. In Homer and Hesiod the gods have come into being. But there is a new concept of eternity in Ionic physics. Thus it is said of Thales in Diog. L., I, 35 (I, 71, 10 f., Diels) πρεσβύτατον τῶν ὄντων θεός· ἀγένητον γάρ, I, 36 : τί τὸ θεῖον; τὸ μήτε ἀρχὴν ἔχον μήτε τελευτήν. Cf. Anaximand., A 15 (I, 85, 14 ff., Diels). The element of the personal, of anthropomorphism, disappears in consequence.
[22] Cf. W. F. Otto, Die Götter Griechenlands² (1934).
[23] H. Schwarz, op. cit.
[24] Cf. W. F. Otto, op. cit., 366 f.; cf. Zeus Μοιραγέτης in Paus., V, 15, 5; it is worth

A highly distinctive feature of the early Gk. idea of God is anthropomorphism. The gods have for the most part human qualities, emotions and customs. Above all, they have a human form. ἄνθρωποι ἀΐδιοι, Aristotle says of them (Metaph., II, 2, p. 997b, 11). The Gks. could not find majesty except in the form of the highest living creature. Thus the Stoic Dio Chrys. Or., 12, 59 (I, 171, 27 ff., v. Arnim) solemnly vindicates the human form of the gods : Νοῦν γὰρ καὶ φρόνησιν αὐτὴν μὲν καθ᾽ αὑτὴν οὔτε τις πλάστης οὔτε τις γραφεὺς εἰκάσαι δυνατὸς ἔσται· ἀθέατοι γὰρ τῶν τοιούτων καὶ ἀνιστόρητοι παντελῶς πάντες. τὸ δὲ ἐν ᾧ τοῦτο γιγνόμενόν ἐστιν οὐχ ὑπονοοῦντες, ἀλλ᾽ εἰδότες, ἐπ᾽ αὐτὸ καταφεύγομεν, ἀνθρώπινον σῶμα ὡς ἀγγεῖον φρονήσεως καὶ λόγου θεῷ προσάπτοντες, ἐνδείᾳ καὶ ἀπορίᾳ παραδείγματος τῷ φανερῷ τε καὶ εἰκαστῷ τὸ ἀνείκαστον καὶ ἀφανὲς ἐνδείκνυσθαι ζητοῦντες, συμβόλου δυνάμει χρώμενοι, κρεῖττον ἤ φασιν τῶν βαρβάρων τινὰς ζῴοις τὸ θεῖον ἀφομοιοῦν . . . [25] This is in contrast to the second commandment in the OT, which is one of the roots of the NT view.

3. The Development of the Greek Concept of God.

a. The development of the Gk. concept is determined by two motifs which are both present in Homer. These are the natural motif and the ethical. There is thus development 1. in the direction of nature mysticism (cf. Thales, A 22 [I, 79, 27, Diels]: πάντα πλήρη θεῶν), and 2. in the direction of rational ethics, which leads from Hesiod's Δίκη through Solon and the city-state to Plato. The Homeric world is dissolved by rational criticism, causal thinking and philosophical reflection. Xenophanes can find in the individual gods of his world no more than a reflection of those who worship them (Fr., 15 : I, 132, 19 ff., Diels), and he sets against these childish self-reflections his own purer concept, which is greatly influenced by ratio : εἷς θεός, ἔν τε θεοῖσι — as men represent themselves — καὶ ἀνθρώποισι μέγιστος, | οὔτι δέμας θνητοῖσιν ὁμοίιος οὐδὲ νόημα (Fr., 23 : I, 135, 4 f., Diels ; cf. Antisthenes in Philodem. Philos., De Pietate, 7a, p. 72, Gomperz [1866]; Cic. Nat. Deor., I, 13). It is fitting (ἐπιτρέπει) [26] that the supreme being should be at rest rather than in movement (Fr., 26). Ethical thinking attacks the anthropomorphic concept. The God of Xenophanes is cosmomorphic. In spite of the severest criticism of Homer, none of these early Gk. philosophers denies the presence of the divine in the world or eliminates the divine from it. With advancing rationalism, however, the mode of the divine being is more rationally understood along the lines of the unity of the divine. The source of the new conception of God is the revolutionary reconstruction of the world by Milesian physics. God is the living essence of the world : οὖλος ὁρᾶι, οὖλος δὲ νοεῖ, οὖλος δέ τ᾽ ἀκούει (Xenophanes Fr., 24 : I, 135, 7, Diels); "effortlessly he impels all things by the power of thought, himself unmoved" (Fr., 25 : I, 135, 8, Diels). [27] A process of rationalising

---

noting that in Iambl. this is a name for the θεοί in general, v. the lexicons.

[25] On this pt. cf. Otto, Die altgriechische Gottesidee (1926), 19.

[26] The θεοπρεπές (cf. Pr. Bauer, s.v.) became important for Christian thinkers in their assertion of monotheism. Hence Xenophanes is significant here. Stoicism gave a distinctive turn to the concept of the θεοπρεπές, of what is truly majestic, of the divine, Plut. Tranq. An., 20 (II, 477c); ἱερὸν μὲν γὰρ ἁγιώτατον ὁ κόσμος ἐστὶ καὶ θεοπρεπέστατον, Ad Principem Ineruditum, 2 and 3 (II, 780a f.); Dio Chrys. Or., 12, 52; Ditt. Or., I, 385, 57; common in Plato, v. Leisegang, s.v.

[27] Cf. J. Stenzel, Die Metaphysik des Altertums (1931), 38 f.

and ethicising transforms the Gk. concept of God. Naturally, there does not enter into the Gk. mind any thought of a "deity whose innermost essence is love, love for man and not merely for individual elect."[28] God is rather found in the unshakable regularity of being, in the righteousness immanent in the world, in → δίκη, the great principle of compensation. The idea of God is closely bound up with the thought of cosmic righteousness. Righteousness is the nature and essence of God, to whom prayer in the true sense is inconceivable.[29]

This throws light on the φθόνος θεῶν of Herodotus[30] and also on the concept of God in Gk. tragedy. Like all human action, reality, or God,[31] is ambiguous and equivocal, threatening on the one side and yet also protective on the other. This is expressed even linguistically in the juxtaposition of θεός and δαίμων.[32] What is evident in tragedy is not merely the instability of human fortune and its ultimate dependence on God, but also the way in which the righteousness of God, which is beyond human understanding, rules in the tragic dialectic of existence. With Zeus, the all-embracing God,[33] is linked a riddle. Thus in Aeschylus there is in Zeus an element that man cannot understand, though what we might call the side which is turned to man everywhere causes its light to shine on man, even in the obscurity of a dark destiny (Aesch. Suppl., 87 ff.). Perhaps there is no more typical revelation of the tragic concept of God than in the famous prayer to Zeus in Aesch. Ag., 160-183 : Ζεὺς ὅστις ποτ' ἐστίν, εἰ τόδ' αὐτῷ φίλον κεκλημένῳ, τοῦτό νιν προσεννέπω. οὐκ ἔχω προσεικάσαι πάντ' ἐπισταθμώμενος πλὴν Διός, εἰ τὸ μάταν ἀπὸ φροντίδος ἄχθος χρὴ βαλεῖν ἐτητύμως ... Ζῆνα δέ τις προφρόνως ἐπινίκια κλάζων τεύξεται φρενῶν τὸ πᾶν· τὸν φρονεῖν βροτοὺς ὁδώσαντα, τῷ πάθει μάθος θέντα κυρίως ἔχειν ... δαιμόνων δέ που χάρις βιαίως σέλμα (helm) σεμνὸν ἡμένων. Zeus is the power which gives meaning and which redeems. Redemption is to know "the way of true moderation." Man cannot do this alone, not even by thought. Only Zeus can give it to him, and the law in accordance with which he does so is that of learning through suffering. Χάρις, grace, is this powerful action (βία) of the gods.[34]

The Gk. concept of God comes to fruition in a solemnising objectivity and righteousness sensed in this life. There is, of course, no direct I-Thou relationship

---

[28] E. Rohde, "Die Religion der Griechen," Kleine Schriften, II (1901), 327.
[29] Plat. Theaet., 176b: θεὸς οὐδαμῆ οὐδαμῶς ἄδικος, ἀλλ' ὡς οἷόν τε δικαιότατος. Aesch. Ag., 772 ff.; Solon Fr., 1, 31 ff. (Diehl).
[30] Hdt., VII, 10 ε : ... φιλέει γὰρ ὁ θεὸς τὰ ὑπερέχοντα πάντα κολούειν ... οὐ γὰρ ἐᾷ φρονέειν μέγα ὁ θεὸς ἄλλον ἢ ἑωυτόν.
[31] Cf. Heracl. Fr., 67 (I, 165, 8 ff., Diels): ὁ θεὸς ἡμέρη εὐφρόνη, χειμὼν θέρος, πόλεμος εἰρήνη, κόρος λιμός, and Soph. Trach., 1276 ff.: μεγάλους μὲν ἰδοῦσα νέους θανάτους, | πολλὰ δὲ πήματα καὶ καινοπαθῆ, | κοὐδὲν τούτων ὅτι μὴ Ζεύς.
[32] Cf. W. Nestle, "Menschliche Existenz und politische Erziehung in der Tragödie des Aischylos," Tübinger Beiträge zur Altertumswissenschaft, 23 (1934), 74 ff.
[33] Cf. Aesch. Fr., 70 (TGF): Ζεύς ἐστιν αἰθήρ, Ζεὺς δὲ γῆ, Ζεὺς δ' οὐρανός, Ζεύς τοι τὰ πάντα χὤτι τῶνδ' ὑπέρτερον. For other predicates of Zeus in Aesch., cf. W. Nestle, Griech. Religiosität, I (1930), 123; on predicates of the gods generally, cf. C. F. H. Bruchmann, Epitheta Deorum, Suppl. 1 to Roscher (1893); for the Gk. hymn, K. Keyssner, Gottesvorstellung, 9-127; special note should be taken of predicates used in the cultus predominantly of alien deities → μέγας (cf. μεγάλη Ἄρτεμις Ἐφεσίων, Ac. 19:34; cf. B. Müller, Μέγα Θεός, Diss. Halle, 1913); Hom. Il., 18, 292; Soph. El., 174 ff.; Eur. Andr., 37; or μέγιστος, Eur. Ion, 1606; → ὕψιστος, Pind. Nem., 1, 90 ff.; Soph. Phil., 1289; and → κύριος, Epict. Diss., II, 16, 13 : κύριε ὁ θεός.
[34] Cf. E. Fränkel, Philol., 86 (1931), 1 ff.

between God and man. Between the two stands always society, the state, or the "developed world of the divine." [35] For the classical Greek the divine is always such that he thinks he encounters it only in direct apprehension through the νοῦς and in the overpowering of all the true reality in which he stands. God Himself is invisible, but we know Him from His works, [36] from nature and from history.

b. If in the earlier Gk. view everything is said to come from the gods, including guilt and suffering, misfortune and destruction (Hom. Il., 24, 525 ff.), and if in the middle period a distinction was made between merited and divinely sent ἄτη (Hom. Od., 1, 32 ff.; Solon Fr., 3, Diehl), the ethicising and spiritualising of the concept has gone so far in Plato that he attacks the kind of religiosity which finds almost exaggerated expression in the recently discovered Niobe verse (cf. Plat. Resp., II, 380a): θεὸς μὲν αἰτίαν φύει βροτοῖς, ὅταν κακῶσαι δῶμα παμπήδην θέλῃ (Aesch. Fr., 56, TGF), and in the theological chapter [37] of the Resp. (II, 380d) he can say: μὴ πάντων αἴτιον τὸν θεὸν ἀλλὰ τῶν ἀγαθῶν (cf. X, 617e: ἀρετὴ δὲ ἀδέσποτον, ἣν τιμῶν καὶ ἀτιμάζων πλέον καὶ ἔλαττον αὐτῆς ἕκαστος ἕξει· αἰτία ἑλομένου· θεὸς ἀναίτιος). If the Homeric Greeks, with their way of thought which did not separate nature and spirit, could conceive of the constant intervention of divine power in this world — and this is the point of divine existence — only in terms of physical intercourse between the gods and elect mortals (Ps.-Hesiod., Scutum, 27 ff., ed. P. Mazon, 1928), in Plato there is complete separation between God and man (Symp., 203a: θεὸς ἀνθρώπῳ οὐ μείγνυται). There is no fellowship in the sense of becoming one with this God; there is only a distant resemblance, the ὁμοίωσις τῷ θεῷ κατὰ τὸ δυνατόν· ὁμοίωσις δὲ δίκαιον καὶ ὅσιον μετὰ φρονήσεως γενέσθαι, Plat. Theaet., 176b.

If the tragic concept of God still found expression in myth and its images, Plato [38] also degrades the mythical form of presentation to the position of a mere elucidation of philosophical themes. Final reality, τὸ πάντα συνέχον, that which first gives and reveals full being and becoming, τάξις and εἶδος, order and form — this is impersonal and non-individual, the ἰδέα τοῦ ἀγαθοῦ. This is not, of course, equated directly with the supreme deity, since for Plato "that which is proper to the divine is given in the actualisation of being." [39] This is how we are to understand the creation myth and the concept of God in Tim., 28c ff. As δημιουργός, ποιητής and πατήρ (28c; 30b; 41a) τοῦδε τοῦ παντός, as an architect following the eternal παράδειγμα of the νοητὸς κόσμος, God has fashion-

---

[35] Stenzel, Platon der Erzieher, 281.

[36] Xenoph. Mem., IV, 3, 13; Ps.-Aristot. Mund., 6, p. 399b, 14 ff.: God, the absolutely perfect πάσῃ θνητῇ φύσει γενόμενος ἀθεώρητος ἀπ' αὐτῶν τῶν ἔργων θεωρεῖται.

[37] Cf. Plat. Resp., II, 382e: πάντῃ ἄρα ἀψευδὲς τὸ δαιμόνιόν τε καὶ τὸ θεῖον ... ὁ θεὸς ἁπλοῦν (opp. ἀλλάττοντα τὸ ἑαυτοῦ εἶδος εἰς πολλὰς μορφάς) καὶ ἀληθὲς ἔν τε ἔργῳ καὶ λόγῳ, καὶ οὔτε αὐτὸς μεθίσταται οὔτε ἄλλους ἐξαπατᾷ, 381b: ὁ θεὸς γε καὶ τὰ τοῦ θεοῦ πάντῃ ἄριστα ἔχει. In his perfection he is πάντων χρημάτων μέτρον, Plat. Leg., IV, 716c; cf. Protagoras Fr., 1 (II, 228, 3 ff., Diels).

[38] On the Platonic concept of God cf. the Summa Theologiae Platonis in Leg., X; cf., e.g., 901d/e: πρῶτον μὲν θεοὺς ... γιγνώσκειν καὶ ὁρᾶν καὶ ἀκούειν πάντα, λαθεῖν δὲ αὐτοὺς οὐδὲν δυνατὸν εἶναι τῶν ὁπόσων εἰσὶν αἱ αἰσθήσεις τε καὶ ἐπιστῆμαι ... δύνασθαι πάντα ὁπόσων αὖ δύναμίς ἐστιν θνητοῖς τε καὶ ἀθανάτοις ... καὶ μὴν ἀγαθούς γε καὶ ἀρίστους ... αὐτοὺς εἶναι. 903b: τῷ τοῦ παντὸς ἐπιμελουμένῳ πρὸς τὴν σωτηρίαν καὶ ἀρετὴν τοῦ ὅλου πάντ' ἐστὶ συντεταγμένα, ὧν καὶ τὸ μέρος εἰς δύναμιν ἕκαστον τὸ προσῆκον πάσχει καὶ ποιεῖ. Cf. C. Ritter, "Platons Gedanken über Gott u. d. Verhältnis der Welt u. d. Menschen zu ihm," ARW, 19 (1918/19), 233 ff., 466 ff.

[39] J. Stenzel, Metaphysik des Altertums, 148.

ed the world in space and time as the moving reflection of eternity. The αἰτία, δι᾽ ἥντινα γένεσιν καὶ τὸ πᾶν τόδε ὁ συνιστὰς συνέστησεν: ἀγαθὸς ἦν (29d), wherewith the quality of God is constantly described in Plato. God is no Creator God in the Timaeus. He has not made the world out of nothing. He is simply the Architect of the world: Tim., 30: βουληθεὶς γὰρ ὁ θεὸς ἀγαθὰ μὲν πάντα, φλαῦρον δὲ μηδὲν εἶναι κατὰ δύναμιν, οὕτω δὴ πᾶν ὅσον ἦν ὁρατὸν παραλαβὼν οὐχ ἡσυχίαν ἄγον ἀλλὰ κινούμενον πλημμελῶς καὶ ἀτάκτως, εἰς τάξιν αὐτὸ ἤγαγεν ἐκ τῆς ἀταξίας, ἡγησάμενος ἐκεῖνο τούτου πάντως ἄμεινον. Of the ψυχή (world-soul) we read in Plat. Leg., X, 897b that it νοῦν προσλαβοῦσα ἀεὶ θεὸν ... ὀρθὰ καὶ εὐδαίμονα παιδαγωγεῖ πάντα. Thus the ancient Hellenic principle of παιδεία is a final factor to play a determinative role in Plato's concept of God.

The religious element in Platonism remains an inviolable reality in Aristotle too. For him, too, God is essentially the final necessary and adequate condition of the existence of a world order: [40] ἡ ἑνοποιὸς αὐτοῦ καὶ δημιουργικὴ δύναμις πάντων τῶν ὄντων αἰτία ἐστὶ τοῦ ἔχειν ὥσπερ ἔχει. "The creative power of God, which establishes unity, is the cause of every existent thing's being in the state that it is." This is how a later commentator on the Metaphysics (Alexandri Aphrodisiensis in Aristotelis Metaphysica Commentaria, p. 564, 20, M. Hayduck [1891]) [41] formulates the Aristotelian experience of God. God is Spirit (νοῦς), if not something higher than Spirit (Fr., 49, Rose). [42] One cannot pray to this deity. Similarly, there can be no "God so loved the world" (Jn. 3:16) in the case of a God who αὐτὸ ἀκίνητον ὄν, ἐνεργείᾳ ὄν, Met., XI, 7, p. 1072b, 7, moves the world by the fact that he is loved, through eros (κινεῖ δὴ ὡς ἐρώμενον, Met., XI, 7, p. 1072b, 3), the striving for a higher form of existence, which he begets [43] through the power of attraction residing in his perfection. [44] It is in love for God that everything achieves its true being. But God does not will anything, for he is perfect being beyond the world (Cael., I, 9, p. 279a, 18 ff.). What man can bring him is the active recognition of this being, namely, → τιμή (Aristot. Eth. Nic., IV, 7, p. 1123b, 18 ff.: μέγιστον δὲ τοῦτ᾽ ἂν θείημεν ὃ τοῖς θεοῖς ἀπονέμομεν ... τοιοῦτον δ᾽ ἡ τιμή).

c. In Hellenism Stoicism allegorically transforms the mythical figures of the gods into metaphysical and cosmic concepts.

---

[40] Cf. Aristot. Met., XI, 7, p. 1072b, 14: ἐκ τοιαύτης ἄρα ἀρχῆς ἤρτηται ὁ οὐρανὸς καὶ ἡ φύσις, to the degree that order and form come into the world through God.

[41] Acc. to Stenzel, op. cit., 162 f.

[42] Cf. Diog. L., VII, 135; also H. Diels, Doxographi Graeci (1879), p. 301 ff. God is πνεῦμα in a very different sense in Jn. 4:24.

[43] Cf. H. Scholz, Eros u. Caritas (1929), 37 ff., 55 ff. For a very different concept cf. 1 Jn. 4:19: ἡμεῖς ἀγαπῶμεν, ὅτι αὐτὸς πρῶτος ἠγάπησεν ἡμᾶς.

[44] Cf. the theological chapter Met., XI, 7, p. 1072b, 26 ff.: καὶ → ζωὴ δέ γε ὑπάρχει· ἡ γὰρ νοῦ ἐνέργεια ζωή, ἐκεῖνος δὲ ἡ ἐνέργεια· ἐνέργεια δὲ ἡ καθ᾽ αὑτὴν ἐκείνου ζωὴ ἀρίστη καὶ ἀΐδιος. φαμὲν δὴ τὸν θεὸν εἶναι ζῷον ἀΐδιον ἄριστον, ὥστε ζωὴ καὶ αἰὼν συνεχὴς καὶ ἀΐδιος ὑπάρχει τῷ θεῷ· τοῦτο γὰρ ὁ θεός. Cf. also Aristot. Fr., 16, Rose: ἄριστον (a supremely perfect being) ὅπερ εἴη ἂν τὸ θεῖον. The thought of God's autarchy became a philosophical commonplace: Eur. Herc. Fur., 1345: δεῖται γὰρ ὁ θεός, εἴπερ ἐστ᾽ ὀρθῶς θεός, οὐδενός; Plat. Tim., 34b: αὔταρκες καὶ οὐδενὸς ἑτέρου προσδεόμενον of the world as realised deity; Tim., 68d; Aristot. Cael., I, 9, p. 279a, 18 ff.; Ac. 17:25. Cf. E. Norden, Agn. Theos, 14.

Cf. Chrysipp. (II, 315, 3 ff. v. Arnim): Δία ... (εἶναι τὸ)ν ἅπαντ(α διοικοῦ)ντα λόγον κ(αὶ τὴν) τοῦ ὅλου ψυχὴ(ν κα)ὶ τῇ τούτου μ(ετοχ)ῇ πάντα (ζῆν)? ... (δ)ιὸ καὶ Ζῆνα καλε(ῖσ)θαι, Δία δ'(ὅ)τι (πάν)των αἴτ(ι)ος (καὶ κύ)ριος· τόν τε κόσμον ἔμψ(υ)χον εἶναι καὶ θεό(ν, κ)αὶ τὸ ἡ(γεμονι)κὸν (κ)αὶ τὴν ὅ(λην ψ)υχ(ή)ν· καὶ ... ὀν(ομάζεσ)θαι τὸν Δία καὶ τὴν κοινὴν πάντων φύσιν καὶ εἱμαρμ(έ)νην καὶ ἀνά(γ)κην. Here the gods are at root only elements of a world which goes its way ineluctably according to irrevocable laws. Conscious adaptation to necessity is here the fulfilment of being. [45] Stoicism understands Zeus as the comprehensive law of the world, → λόγος. [46] God is the active, fashioning form alive and operative in all things, the πνεῦμα διῆκον δι' ὅλου τοῦ κόσμου, defined by Poseidonios (acc. to Aetius in Stob. Ecl., I, 34, 26 ff.) as follows: πνεῦμα νοερὸν καὶ πυρῶδες, οὐκ ἔχον μὲν μορφήν, μεταβάλλον δὲ εἰς ὃ βούλεται καὶ συνεξομοιούμενον πᾶσιν. [47]

God and the cosmos are identical (οὐσίαν δὲ θεοῦ ... τὸν ὅλον κόσμον, II, 305, 26 ff., v. Arnim). A philosophical concept of God, pantheistic and full of belief in providence, [48] arises to put to older views the question of what it is fitting to think. In this way it banishes or refashions all personal features from the conception of God. [49] But later Stoicism becomes more personal again, [50] and above all it has a strong ethical colouring (Epict. Diss., II, 8, 11-14), God is the Father and Provider (Epict. Diss., I, 3, 1; τὸ δὲ τὸν θεὸν ποιητὴν ἔχειν καὶ πατέρα καὶ κηδεμόνα, Diss., I, 9, 7), ὁ θεὸς ὠφέλιμος (Diss., II, 8, 1), φιλάνθρωπος (M. Ant., 12, 5), the original of all virtues (Diss., II, 14, 11 f.); on the purity of the view of God cf. Plut. Ei Delph., 19 f. (II, 392 E ff.); Is. et Os., 53 f. (II, 372 E ff.); Def. Orac., 24 (II, 423 C ff.).

On the other hand, by way of the νοῦς in man (cf. M. Ant., 5, 27) there followed increasingly an "inwardising" of the concept of God which begins already in Eur. Fr., 1018 TGF (cf. the apparat. ad loc.) and which leads to the concept of God in us in Epict. Diss., I, 14, 13; II, 8, 12, M. Ant., 3, 5 (ὁ ἐν σοὶ θεός), Plotin. Enn., VI, 5, 1 (τὸν ἐν ἑκάστῳ ἡμῶν θεόν) etc.

If Stoicism equated the world with God, no place is left for God at all in the atomistic philosophy of Epicurus.

Yet he did not deny religious experience (θεοὶ μὲν γάρ εἰσίν· ἐναργὴς γὰρ αὐτῶν ἐστιν ἡ γνῶσις· οἵους δ' αὐτοὺς οἱ πολλοὶ νομίζουσιν, οὐκ εἰσίν, Men., 123). As ζῷον ἄφθαρτον καὶ μακάριον (Men., 123, Sententiae 1) the deity exists apart ἐν τοῖς μετακοσμίοις (Fr., 359, Usener) without influencing the world and its course, with no concern for man or destiny, a blessed picture of the inner freedom and εὐδαιμονία with a view to which philosophical βίος actualises and fulfils itself. This psychological theology, which no longer asks concerning the divine as something which really is, but is more concerned about men's views of it, about man's consciousness of God (cf. Epic. Men., 123/4), takes its place in a line of spiritual development which begins in Sophism

---

[45] Epict. Ench., 53, 1: ἄγου δέ μ', ὦ Ζεῦ, καὶ σύ γ' ἡ Πεπρωμένη, ὅποι ποθ' ὑμῖν εἰμι διατεταγμένος· ὡς ἕψομαι γ' ἄοκνος· ἢν δέ γε μὴ θέλω, κακὸς γενόμενος οὐδὲν ἧττον ἕψομαι.
[46] Cf. the hymn to Zeus in Cleanthes I, 121, 34 ff., v. Arnim.
[47] On this pt. cf. K. Reinhardt, Kosmos u. Sympathie (1926), 276 ff.
[48] πρόνοια cannot be separated from the concept of God, cf. Theon Rhetor. Progymnasmata, 8, 49 (Rhet. Graec., II, 127, 4): ὅτι ἀναγκαῖόν ἐστιν τὸ πρόνοιαν εἶναι· εἰ γάρ τις τὸ προνοεῖν περιέλοι τοῦ θεοῦ ἀνήρηκε καὶ ἣν ἔχομεν περὶ αὐτοῦ ἔννοιαν. M. Ant., 2, 3.
[49] Cf. Diog. L., VII, 147: θεὸν δὲ εἶναι ζῷον ἀθάνατον λογικόν, τέλειον ἢ νοερὸν ἐν εὐδαιμονίᾳ, κακοῦ παντὸς ἀνεπίδεκτον, προνοητικὸν κόσμου τε καὶ τῶν ἐν κόσμῳ· μὴ εἶναι μέντοι ἀνθρωπόμορφον. εἶναι δὲ τὸν μὲν δημιουργὸν τῶν ὅλων καὶ ὥσπερ πατέρα πάντων κοινῶς τε καὶ τὸ μέρος αὐτοῦ τὸ διῆκον διὰ πάντων, ὃ πολλαῖς προσηγορίαις προσονομάζεται κατὰ τὰς δυνάμεις. There is added a reinterpretation of a whole series of popular gods.
[50] Epict. Diss., II, 14, 11.

with Prodicos of Ceos (Fr., 5, II, 274 f., Diels), Protagoras (Fr. 1, II, 228 f., Diels), Democrit. and Critias (Fr., 25, II, 320 f., Diels) and which leads by way of Plat. Leg., XII, 966e [51] to Aristotle Fr., 10 (Rose).

In face of the constant increase in the number of gods, Hellenism attempts a certain unification by the equation of different deities on the ground that only the ὀνόματα differ and the underlying realities are everywhere the same (Dio Chrys. Or., 31, 11 [I, 322, 14 ff., v. Arnim]); Plut. Is. et Os., 67 ff. [II, 377 f ff.]). In this syncretistic interfusion of deities, the non-Greek deities take on great and even predominant significance, although only in Hellenised form. Thus the supreme goddess Isis is equated with Athene and Aphrodite, Artemis and Persephone, Demeter and Hera, Hecate and the Phrygian mother of the gods. Una, quae es omnia dea Isis — even the mistress of destiny (Apul. Met., XI, 15) — is the way in which she is invoked on a Latin inscr. [52] Finally, syncretistic and monarchical trends often work together and lead to the worship of a deity which is also the chief of gods or the universal God.

In this sense Jupiter is sometimes called Optimus Maximus and sometimes Jupiter Pantheus. [53] Zeus-Asclepius is the universal God in the discourses of Aelius Aristides : οὗτός ἐσθ' ὁ τὸ πᾶν ἄγων καὶ νέμων σωτὴρ τῶν ὅλων καὶ φύλαξ τῶν ἀθανάτων ... "ἔφορος οἰάκων," σῴζων τά τε ὄντα ἀεὶ καὶ τὰ γιγνόμενα ... πάλιν δὲ αὐτὸν ἀποφαίνουσιν ὄντα τῶν ὄντων πατέρα καὶ ποιητήν (Or., 42, 4 [Keil]). In the same sense we also find in the later Hell. period the Helios cult of Julian and esp. Zeus-Sarapis. [54] The desire and need for unity in the polytheistic speculation of later antiquity sought fulfilment supremely in the cult of this god. [55] In the Zeus discourse of Aelius Aristides Or., 43 (Keil) he is called αὐτοπάτωρ, [56] σωτήρ, προστάτης, ἔφορος, πρύτανις, ἡγεμών, ταμίας, δοτήρ, ποιητής, εὐεργέτης, ὅλων ἀπάντων κρατῶν, ἀρχηγέτης. Similarly, we very frequently encounter in this cultic sphere the μόνος and πάντα motifs, and henotheistic formulae like Εἷς θεός. [57] But Zeus-Sarapis is not the only God. Neither fusion nor the conjunction of syncretistic and monarchical thinking led to real monotheism in the biblical sense.

d. Philo's concept of God [58] seeks to mediate between the OT conception of Yahweh and the Gk. idea found in Platonism and Stoicism. Thus God is wholly transcendent on the one side. He is beyond the world, thought, and being. He is not in time or space. He cannot be compared with anything earthly. He confronts the creature as Creator (Gig., 42 : ὁ θεὸς οὐδὲ τῷ ἀρίστῳ τῶν φύντων ὅμοιος ... ὁ δ' ἐστὶν ἀγένητός τε καὶ ποιῶν ἀεί). He can be defined only by negatives (Sacr. AC, 101: ἀπὸ ἐννοίας τῆς περὶ θεοῦ τοῦ ἀγενήτου καὶ ἀφθάρτου καὶ

---

[51] The ἀέναος οὐσία of the human ψυχή and the φορά, ὡς ἔχει τάξεως, ἄστρων as the two sources of belief in God.

[52] CIL, X, 3800; cf. P. Oxy., XI, 1380; Apul. Met., XI, 5; 15.

[53] CIL, II, 2008; also Serapis Pantheus, II, 46.

[54] Cf. O. Weinreich, Neue Urkunden zur Sarapisreligion (1919), 24 ff., Suppl. I.

[55] Cf. (Sarapis) Or., 45, 24 (Keil): πάντα αὐτὸς εἰς ὤν, ἅπασιν εἰς ταὐτὸν δυνάμενος; cf. also 45, 21 (Keil), and the conclusion of the hymn to Zeus, 43, 31 (Keil): τὸν ἀπάντων κρατοῦντα ἀρχηγέτην καὶ τέλειον μόνον αὐτὸν ὄντα τῶν πάντων. On these discourses cf. J. Amann, "Die Zeusrede des Ailios Aristeides," Tübinger Beiträge zur Altertumswissenschaft, 12 (1931) and A. Höfler, "Der Sarapishymnus des Ailios Aristeides," ibid., 27 (1935).

[56] As a predicate of the Christian God in Synesius of Cyrene, Hymnus, 3, 145 ff. (ed. J. Flach, 1875).

[57] P. Oxy., XI, 1382, 20; cf. also E. Peterson, Εἷς Θεός (1926), 227; Jul. Or., 4, 136a, Hertlein.

[58] → 90; 109. Cf. Leisegang, s.v. θεός.

ἀτρέπτου καὶ ἁγίου καὶ μόνου μακαρίου). He is incomprehensible spirituality and yet also the effective power in all things (Vit. Mos., 111: θεὸς δ' ἡ ἀνωτάτω καὶ μεγίστη δύναμις ὤν; Decal., 52: ἀρχὴ δ' ἀρίστη πάντων μὲν τῶν ὄντων θεός; Gig., 47: πάντα γὰρ πεπληρωκὼς ὁ θεὸς ἐγγύς ἐστιν). Philo is able to bring together Jewish and Greek cosmogony, the Creator God who made the world out of nothing and the Platonic Artificer, by regarding God first as the One who gives birth to the original world of ideas, and then as the One who fashions ideas into the visible world (cf. Op. Mund., 16: προλαβὼν γὰρ ὁ θεὸς ἅτε θεὸς ὅτι μίμημα καλὸν οὐκ ἄν ποτε γένοιτο δίχα καλοῦ παραδείγματος οὐδέ τι τῶν αἰσθητῶν ἀνυναίτιον, ὃ μὴ πρὸς ἀρχέτυπον καὶ νοητὴν ἰδέαν ἀπεικονίσθη, βουληθεὶς τὸν ὁρατὸν κόσμον τουτονὶ δημιουργῆσαι προεξετύπου τὸν νοητόν, ἵνα χρώμενος ἀσωμάτῳ καὶ θεοειδεστάτῳ παραδείγματι τὸν σωματικὸν ἀπεργάσηται). This second, derived deity, which is begotten by God in eternity and which remains with Him, is the → λόγος (Op. Mund., 24: οὐδὲν ἂν ἕτερον εἴποι τὸν νοητὸν κόσμον εἶναι ἢ θεοῦ λόγον ἤδη κοσμοποιοῦντος, cf. also 25). As God begets the λόγος of Himself, the λόγος begets ideas within itself. The God-λόγος idea strongly depersonalises the national Jewish God and sets Him in a sphere of distant transcendence. On the other hand, the Greek concept of God has here undergone a basic reconstruction in terms of the principle of creation in the theology of revelation. The idea, which in Greek thinking expresses the deepest reality of being itself, is here a creation and emanation from God (cf. Aug. De Diversis Quaestionibus, 46 [MPL, 40, 29 ff.]). [59] The work of the Greek God is simply the interrelating of idea and being, the actualisation of being as a totality complete in itself.

e. In Neo-Platonism religion combines with philosophy in natural theology, which asks concerning an ultimate, impersonal one. [60] The intellectual starting-point of this movement is the ancient Orphic idea of unity: "All things have come out of one, and all things flow back into one." [61] Its crowning conclusion is the monistic metaphysics of Plotinus, which reaches its climax in the idea of the ἕν. This is the metaphysical unity in which the all has its origin and basis of possibility, and it is thus called πατήρ and πρῶτος θεός. From it proceeds νοῦς, which operates as δημιουργός and βασιλεύς; and it is from this that ψυχή proceeds, the μεταξύ between the world of ideas and that of experience, between heaven and earth.

The ancient twofold formula ἕν καὶ πᾶν is justified in this sense. The ἕν itself, however, does not merge into the πᾶν. God is what lies without, above all being and

---

[59] For a comparison with the myth of the formation of the world in the Timaeus, and for the further development of the thought, cf. H. Heyse, *Idee und Existenz* (1935), 115 ff.; also W. Theiler, *op. cit.*, 15 ff.

[60] M. Ant., 7, 9: κόσμος τε γὰρ εἷς ἐξ ἁπάντων καὶ θεὸς εἷς διὰ πάντων καὶ οὐσία μία καὶ νόμος εἷς, λόγος κοινὸς πάντων τῶν νοερῶν ζῴων, καὶ ἀλήθεια μία.

[61] On this formula: ἐξ ἑνὸς πάντα καὶ εἰς ἓν πάντα etc., cf. H. Diels, *Doxographi Graeci* (1879), 179 and E. Norden, *Agnostos Theos,* 247 f. Cf. the Orphic hymn to Zeus in Plat. Leg., IV, 715e: ὁ μὲν δὴ θεὸς (the demiurge) ὥσπερ καὶ ὁ παλαιὸς λόγος, ἀρχήν τε καὶ τελευτὴν καὶ μέσα τῶν ὄντων ἁπάντων ἔχει (= Orph. Fr., 21, Kern), and in a Hell. Stoic version in Ps.-Aristot. Mund., 7, p. 401a, 25 ff. = Orph. Fr., 21a, Kern; cf. also Orph. Fr., 239b, Kern: εἷς Ζεύς, εἷς ᾍδης, εἷς Ἥλιος, εἷς Διόνυσος, εἷς θεὸς ἐν πάντεσσι.

thought,[62] and yet He is also the underlying force of all that is, τὸ ἀγαθόν, τὸ ἄπειρον and the πρώτη δύναμις.[63] Being, eternal creating and begetting are one and the same with Him : ἒν γὰρ τῇ ποιήσει καὶ οἷον γεννήσει ἀιδίῳ τὸ εἶναι, Enn., VI, 8, 20. The nature of the Godhead is to be defined only *via eminentiae* and *negationis :* δεῖ μὲν γάρ τι πρὸ πάντων εἶναι ἁπλοῦν τοῦτο καὶ πάντων ἕτερον τῶν μετ' αὐτό, ἐφ' ἑαυτοῦ ὄν, οὐ μεμειγμένον τοῖς ἀπ' αὐτοῦ, καὶ πάλιν ἕτερον τρόπον τοῖς ἄλλοις παρεῖναι δυνάμενον, ὂν ὄντως ἕν, οὐχ ἕτερον ὄν, εἶτα ἕν, καθ' οὖ ψεῦδος καὶ τὸ ἓν εἶναι, οὗ μὴ λόγος μηδὲ ἐπιστήμη, ὃ δὴ καὶ ἐπέκεινα λέγεται εἶναι οὐσίας (Enn., V, 4, 1). He can thus say that the ἕν is οὐδὲν τῶν πάντων, ἀλλὰ πρὸ πάντων, and yet the statement is also true : οὐ γὰρ δὴ ἄπεστιν οὐδενὸς ἐκεῖνο (Enn., VI, 9, 4). For ἡ ἀρχὴ αὐτῶν ... μένει ... ὅλη μένουσα ... οὐ γὰρ ἀπο- τετμήμεθα οὐδὲ χωρὶς ἐσμέν, ... ἀλλ' ἐμπνέομεν καὶ σῳζόμεθα ... ἐκείνου ... ἀεὶ χορηγοῦντος ἕως ἂν ᾖ ὅπερ ἔστι (Enn., VI, 9, 9).

Herewith the basic metaphysical and religious question of the history of ancient thought, namely, the problem of the world and the upper world, is in some sense resolved in the idea that God becomes the world. (The idea of God becoming man was always alien in the Gk. world. The distinctively Gk. experience of God demands that we assume the divine mode of being, not that God assume the human.) Of His own superfluity (ὑπερπλῆρες), God necessarily evolves the world eternally and timelessly out of Himself in the form of an outshining (ἔκλαμψις) in which God always remains unchanged, like light shining in darkness. For in spite of every reservation, the system of Plotinus envisages this world as the objectification and actualisation of God, and indeed as the only, and the only possible, form of this actualisation.[64] There is thus no point in prayer. Prayer is possible as self-reflection, as the return of the soul to the origin, as its elevation to purer heights. But there is no invasion of the reality of this world by that of the world above.

f. An extreme mystical pantheism is to be found in the Hermetic writings with their mystical extolling of the greatness and omnipresence of God : Corp. Herm., 16, 3 : τὸν θεὸν ... τὸν τῶν ὅλων δεσπότην καὶ ποιητὴν καὶ πατέρα καὶ περίβολον (All-embracer), [καὶ πάντα ὄντα] τὸν [ἕνα] καὶ ἕνα ὄντα < καὶ > τὰ πάντα.[65] God is everything. Everything is filled by Him. There is nothing in the universe which is not God, *ibid.*, V, 9 : οὐδὲν γάρ ἐστιν ἐν παντὶ ἐκείνῳ (sc. κόσμῳ) ὃ οὐκ ἔστιν αὐτός. ἔστιν αὐτὸς καὶ τὰ ὄντα καὶ τὰ μὴ ὄντα. He is bi-sexual, the Father and Mother of the universe ; creating, He creates Himself (αὐτοπάτωρ, Iambl. Myst., 8, 2), Corp. Herm., V, 7 f.: τίς πάντα ταῦτα ἐποίησε; ποία μήτηρ, ποῖος πατήρ, εἰ μὴ ὁ ἀφανὴς θεός, < ὁ > τῷ ἑαυτοῦ θελήματι πάντα δημιουργήσας. 9 : ἢ γὰρ < οὐ > μόνος οὗτος; καὶ τοῦτο αὐτῷ τὸ ἔργον ἐστί, < τὸ > πατέρα εἶναι, indeed, τὸ κυεῖν πάντα καὶ ποιεῖν.[66] God is the one and all, the μονάς, the beginning and root. Here the point of cosmic unity merges into the transcendental unity of the pneumatic

---

[62] Plot. Enn., I, 7, 1: ἐπέκεινα οὐσίας, ἐπέκεινα καὶ ἐνεργείας καὶ ἐπέκεινα νοῦ καὶ νοήσεως. Enn., I, 8, 2 : αὐτός τε γὰρ ὑπέρκαλος καὶ ἐπέκεινα τῶν ἀρίστων βασι-λεύων ἐν τῷ νοητῷ, and yet the middle point of the world : Enn., VI, 9, 7; the world seeks God, not God the world : Enn., VI, 8, 15 : καὶ ἐράσμιον καὶ ἔρως ὁ αὐτὸς καὶ αὐτοῦ ἔρως. On the Neo-Platonic concept of God cf. also Porphyr. Marc., 16-23.
[63] Plot. Enn., VI, 2, 17; II, 9, 1; IV, 3, 8; V, 4, 1.
[64] Cf. the aesthetic rational theodicy in Enn., III, 23.
[65] Cf. Mart., V, 24, 15 : *Hermes omnia solus et ter unus.*
[66] Cf. Corp. Herm., V, 10 : οὗτος ὁ θεὸς ὀνόματος κρείττων· οὗτος ὁ ἀφανής, οὗτος ὁ φανερώτατος. οὗτος ὁ τῷ νοῒ θεωρητός, οὗτος ὁ τοῖς ὀφθαλμοῖς ὁρατός· οὗτος ὁ ἀσώματος, [οὗτος] ὁ πολυσώματος.

ego. The mystic who reflects on this unity is not only the παῖς θεοῦ, κατὰ πάνθ' ὁμοούσιος; he is himself θεός [67] — an impossible idea for Plato (→ 73). The soil of the Gk. concept of God is thus abandoned.

In the intellectual history of antiquity there is thus a progressive refinement of the conception of God in human terms, but a personal, monotheistic view of God as the Creator of heaven and earth is plainly rejected, as is only natural in a form of religious experience and thought which is constantly orientated to eternal being and law and which thus thinks of God as the power or essence which ensures permanence as being. Neither in the anthropomorphism of Homer nor in the later metaphysics of ideas is there a personal conception of God or even a personal relation of the individual soul to God. The early and later views are merely different but not mutually exclusive forms of the same basic religious attitude in religion, art and philosophy, which as a self-contained unity is absolutely different from the NT concept of God.

Kleinknecht

B. El and Elohim in the OT. [68]

1. The Usage of the LXX.

With comparatively few exceptions θεός in the LXX corresponds to the Heb. words אֵל, אֱלוֹהַ and אֱלֹהִים, which for their part are only rarely translated by κύριος or other terms. Apart from θεός and κύριος, ἰσχυρός is used some 20 times for אֵל, and elsewhere δύναμις (Neh. 5:5) or δυνάστης (Sir. 46:7, 16). In these cases etymological considerations can hardly have carried much weight (→ 5. a. and n. 88), and the same is true in relation to ἄρχων, ἐπίσκοπος, ἄγγελος (Job 20:15), οὐρανός, ὕψιστος, εἴδωλον, ἅγιος etc. The picture is less varied but essentially the same in respect of אֱלֹהִים (Zech. 11:4 : παντοκράτωρ) and אֱלָהּ. For the divine names יהוה and יָהּ we usually have → κύριος; θεός occurs only some 330 times.

2. The OT Belief in God in the Form of Faith in Yahweh.

The belief in God held by the OT authors is plainly expressed in what they say about God and to God. The nature of their statements is thus the source of exegetical knowledge of the religious reality which is essentially the same in basic character, though varied in individual experience and teaching, and from which the divine community of Israel receives its vital powers.

To convey the basic character, we should note the simplest expressions, often stereotyped and unaffected by the immediate situation of the speaker, which the Israelite uses to describe his God, and we should also try so far as possible to trace the history of their use. In this connection a first point to notice is that the total picture of OT usage is distinguished and yet also complicated by the fact that in all parts of the canon the radically related terms for God, אֵל, אֱלוֹהַ and אֱלֹהִים, along with the interchangeable individual and personal name יהוה, for which we

---

[67] Ibid., 13, 14 : ἀγνοεῖς ὅτι θεὸς πέφυκας καὶ τοῦ ἑνός παῖς; G. Heinrici, Die Hermesmystik und das NT (1918); on the concept of God in the Herm. lit. cf. J. Kroll, Die Lehren des Hermes Trismegistos (1914), 1-110.

[68] For the sake of order, it is best, following the usage of the LXX under 1., to give first the exposition of belief in Yahweh under κύριος, while under θεός we shall deal with the questions which arise out of the more comprehensive use of אֵל etc.

now use the scientifically reconstructed form Yahweh (→ κύριος), are used more or less at random. This makes it perfectly clear that Yahweh and God are synonyms and that the concept of God includes the concept of person and is shaped by it. Yet if we look away from the theological terms to the sense of reality concealed in the forms of expression, we can detect an active tension in which the strongly emotional confession of the divine person of Yahweh is confronted by the equally strong experience of the world as a sum of divine communities and of the greater and smaller spheres of influence of numinous forces of all degrees. It may thus be seen how, with the passage of generations, under the initially sharp and then more gradual operation of the prophetic message, and also under the weighty pressure of national destiny, belief in Yahweh was irresistibly consolidated, in spite of the severest crises, into confidence in Yahweh as the Creator and Ruler of the world, in whom divine essence and power are concentrated into a resolute and omnipotent will, to the exclusion of all other gods or conceptions of the gods. The canon depicts the rise and effect of this tension in the portrayal of the outer and inner history of the community of Yahweh which was founded by Moses. For, in a movement characterised at times by ignorant resistance, and at other times by clear perception of the one Lord of all things, this community presses on from experience of the greatness of the tribal and national God of the covenant to recognition and acknowledgment of the power of God which fashions and rules the world.

The history of Israel's belief in God is thus essentially the history of the faith in Yahweh established by Moses. With this begins the inner life of the community pledged to its God in the covenant (→ διαθήκη), and only in the confession of Yahweh may it be seen what the concept of God means for the consciousness of the Israelite. But this concept had already been formed by a long pre-history when Moses, by emphatically and exclusively referring it to Yahweh, the God of the fathers (Ex. 3:15), the jealous God (Ex. 20:5; 34:14 etc.), gave to it the impelling power which constitutes the inimitable and unparalleled characteristic of the whole of the biblical message concerning God. The questions which arise in relation to this prior history relate for the most part to the significance of the older terms for God adopted by the community of Yahweh, and to their application in cultic life.

3. The Tradition concerning Belief in God prior to the Rise of the Community of Yahweh.

For the most part it is impossible to state with confidence, or to evaluate theologically, either the terms for God or the ideas about Him which were current in the days before Moses among the tribes of which Israel was later made up, and among related and neighbouring groups. The literary tradition concerning this period, when Israel did not yet have the measure of cohesion to be found increasingly from the time of Moses, is limited to the transmission of sagas which do not seem to have been preserved with any great care so far their religious content is concerned. It need only be pointed out that the so-called J tradition speaks naively of the cult of Yahweh in the pre-Mosaic period (Gn. 4:26), and that it has tried to suppress the distinguishing marks of the knowledge of God preceding Yahweh worship either by adding the name of Yahweh or by excising the original forms of expression. There can be little doubt, however, that in the oral saga, and perhaps in written versions prior to those now extant, these individual features were clear enough. This conjecture is supported particularly by old cultic names formed with אל, which constituted the heart of legends relating to local shrines. The fact that P tells us expressly in Ex. 6:3 that God had not revealed Himself to the fathers under the name of Yahweh also shows us that in the community of Yahweh there was an awareness of the difference between the pre-Mosaic and the post-Mosaic epochs, although it was part of the unassailable content of faith that the God who acted in the earlier period was the same as the God who acted in the later.

In Gn. this is particularly clear in the expression יהוה אֱלֹהִים used in Gn. 2 and 3. Whatever the literary origin may be, an obvious explanatory apposition is intended: "Yahweh, i.e., God." [69] Thus the reader of the canon is given immediate help in respect of the problem of the distinctive divine name, Yahweh being identified with the God of all ages, with the unique bearer of divine essence who has made the world. [70] אֲדֹנָי יֱהוִֹה, which is very common in Ez. and fairly frequent elsewhere, is to be understood in the same way, as may be seen expressly from the Mas. pointing. [71] On the other hand, the plerophoric אֵל אֱלֹהִים יְהוָֹה, "God, Godhead, Yahweh" (Ps. 50:1; Jos. 22:22), which is probably intended as a climax, has the evident nature of a confession of faith.

4. El and Elohim as Appellatives.

At the same time, it is fairly obvious that neither אֵל nor אֱלֹהִים has originally the same meaning as is contained in the name Yahweh. These words denote a divine person by species rather than an individual divine person. As genetic terms for "God" they have their roots in polytheistic religion. The divine individual, the numinous Thou, is as little denoted by them as is an individual person by the generic "man."

The plurals אֵלִים and אֱלֹהִים may thus be specifically defined in terms of בְּנֵי אֵלִים (Ps. 29:1; 89:7) and בְּנֵי אֱלֹהִים (Gn. 6:2, 4; Job 1:6; 38:7), "sons of God," as general terms for individual beings which possess the quality אֵל and which belong to the species אֱלֹהִים. [72]

At any rate, in the OT אֵל and אֱלֹהִים are not names but appellatives, which need to be defined by a gen. (e.g., אֱלֹהֵי יִשְׂרָאֵל or אֵל עוֹלָם) or by apposition (e.g., אֵל שַׁדַּי or אֵל אֱלֹהֵי יִשְׂרָאֵל) if they are to be taken to denote individuals.

It is true that אֵל is sometimes found as a name outside Israel. [73] But these cases do not make it likely that the predicative function of the word is to be regarded as secon-

---

[69] On the transl. cf. O. Procksch, Die Genesis [2, 3] (1924) on Gn. 2:4b and M. Buber, op. cit., 213.

[70] The same theological tendency, though with no reference to the earlier period, is to be found in Jon. 4:6, whether this is original or not. It certainly fits the main theme of the book. In passages like Ps. 72:18; 84:11, we have obvious glosses.

[71] In Ez. the expression is strikingly preferred with the many formulae of audition כֹּה אָמַר and נְאֻם. In Gn. it is found only at Gn. 15:2, 8 (JE).

[72] Cf. also Dt. 32:8 LXX: the number of nations corresponds to the number of the sons of God, i.e., to the numerical constitution of the pantheon.

[73] Cf. Baudissin, Kyrios, III, 11. Along with later documents like the Hadad and Panammu inscr. (Hadad, lines 2, 11, 18; Panammu, line 22; cf. proper names like רפאל, אלמלך, חיאל, etc. in M. Lidzbarski, Handbuch der nordsemit. Epigraphik [1898], 214 f.) we now have the Ras Shamra tablets, which are much nearer the time of Moses (cf. H. Bauer, ZAW, NF, 10 [1933], 81 ff.). Whether אֵל is originally a name in the sayings attributed to the alien Balaam (Nu. 23:8, 19, 22, 23; 24:4, 8, 16, 23) is uncertain in view of editorial revision.

dary, [74] and they contribute nothing to our understanding of biblical usage. A place-name like מִגְדַּל אֵל (Jos. 19:38) may certainly be taken to mean "the tower of El," and verbal names like יִפְתַּח אֵל (Jos. 19:14) can be similarly explained, [75] but there is no need to interpret them thus, since the predicative function of nouns denoting the divine is on the whole the rule.

When אֵל without addition, or הָאֵל (Ps. 68:20), is used in the sense of Yahweh (e.g., Is. 40:18; Ps. 16:1; 17:6; Job 5:8; 8:5; 9:2 etc.), or when it is used as a parallel to Yahweh (Nu. 23:8; Is. 42:5; Ps. 85:8 etc.), this can only be an emphatic way of stating that for those who speak the species אֵל is exhausted in Yahweh. There need be no intentional polemic against other gods. Scores of examples of the **promiscuity** of אֱלֹהִים and יהוה shows that this was hardly felt, though it is the root of the expression. For in practice this kind of statement is always understood monolatrously, as may be seen from the first sentence of the Decalogue, and in theory it is not always easy to distinguish between henotheism and monotheism in individual writers, quite apart from the fact that this question has little bearing on our understanding of the substance of what is said.

5. The Content of the OT Belief in God.

The statement that Yahweh is the אֱלֹהֵי יִשְׂרָאֵל, the God who belongs to Israel, is the fundamental principle of OT religion, no matter what may be our view concerning the origin of the formula. [76] It carries with it the basic insight that the manner of Yahweh is the manner אֱלֹהִים. For specific reasons this is sometimes emphasised, [77] as when He is called God absolutely (1 K. 18:21, 37; Dt. 4:35; 7:9), i.e., the One apart from whom none other has the property of God. It thus follows that in the words אֵל and אֱלֹהִים we have the vital heritage of faith whose significance increases to the degree that the name merges into the appellatives. We may thus say that Israel's belief in God is pushed beyond the basic statement יְהוָה אֱלֹהֵי יִשְׂרָאֵל by the intentional and conscious application of these appellatives. A good deal of conjecture is obviously involved in the interpretation of the appellatives. Nevertheless, what may be said concerning them forms a not wholly unserviceable foundation on which to evaluate the spiritual experience reflected in the usage.

a. As concerns אֵל, it is not peculiar to Israel even in the OT.

Ishmael, the Arab, has the word in his name no less than Israel, and Balaam and the Easterner Job both use it. It was used in very early times, as may be seen from the names Mehujael, Methusael (Gn. 4:18) and Mahalaleel (Gn. 5:12). In fact, it is one of the religious terms common to most Semites. Perfect parallels may be found to the Heb. name, not only in the Accadian *ilu*, fem. *iltu*, but also in the אֵל which is attested in many theophorous personal names amongst the Phoenicians, Canaanites, Ammonites, Edomites and Southern Arabians. [78] The usage is perhaps even richer than thus far shown by the epigraphical evidence.

---

[74] The converse is more likely, cf. M. Noth, *Die israelitischen Personennamen im Rahmen der gemeinsemitischen Namengebung* (1929), 96 f.

[75] *V.* the list in Baudissin, *Kyrios*, III, 133; W. Borée, *Die alten Ortsnamen Palästinas* (1930), 99.

[76] Cf. on this pt. Steuernagel, *op. cit.*

[77] Cf. also אֵל אֱלֹהֵי יִשְׂרָאֵל (Gn. 33:20) and the instances of אֵל given *supra* under 4.

[78] *V.* the examples in Baudissin, *Kyrios*, III, 8 ff.

In Heb., as elsewhere, אֵל is the simplest term for what is divine as distinct from what is human. The emphasis laid on this antithesis in many passages in the prophets is most instructive. Ez. 28:2 contrasts אֵל and אָדָם as mutually exclusive concepts : אַתָּה אָדָם וְלֹא אֵל. Hos. 11:9 has the same contrast with אִישׁ. The אֵל is thus a being which is completely different in nature from man, so that there can be no comparison. It is a person of non-human structure. To express the positive characteristic of אֵל we may again refer to Hos. 11:9. The אֵל is holy, and as such He is not man. [79] Alternatively, in Is. 31:3 the distinction between אָדָם and אֵל is to be understood in analogy with that between בָּשָׂר and רוּחַ. The concreteness of אֵל is blurred by mystery, like that of the wind or breath. [80] Ethically the אֵל is absolutely superior to what is human : לֹא אִישׁ אֵל וִיכַזֵּב וּבֶן־אָדָם וְיִתְנֶחָם (Nu. 23:19). In His quality as אֵל He is thus worthy of absolute trust.

These various statements may contain very different nuances, but there can be no doubt that אֵל is a personal object of religious perception and pious awe. This is self-evident throughout the total usage. But it does not on this account fix the thought originally and independently contained in the word. It may be asked whether the translation "God," which includes the personal character, really gives us the original sense. Is the concept of God as person originally and radically implied in the term, or is it first introduced into it by usage ? What is the original meaning of the word ?

This question is directly raised in the OT by the expression יֶשׁ לְאֵל יָדִי, which occurs five times and which is usually translated : "It is in the power of mine hand." [81]

> This translation fits the context in all the passages concerned, and it is undoubtedly simpler, and more natural not merely to modern taste, than one which dismisses in advance the strong possibility that in this expression the word אֵל is used in a sense unaffected by religious conceptions, or at least in a sense different from that found elsewhere, and which thus tries to understand it here also in terms of a divine being. If we adopt the latter course, יָדִי is not a gen. dependent on אֵל, but the predicate of a nominal clause formed with יֶשׁ, in which לְאֵל is a more precise definition of the statement : "My hand is present for an ēl." This means that I am making a gesture connected with an oath, i.e., stretching out my hand to the god or to his image : "My hand is stretched out to God." [82] Apart from the fact that this explanation does not fit (→ n. 82), however, it argues too much in a circle to be convincing, and we thus do better to stick to the compelling sense of "power" : "It is at the command of the power

---

[79] אֱלֹהִים and אָדָם are also diametric opposites ; Ps. 82:6 f.

[80] In this light it is most unlikely that the אֵלִם who are to judge אָדָם in Ps. 58:1 are men.

[81] Linked with the ensuing infin. in Gn. 31:29; Prv. 3:27; abs. Mi. 2:1; negat. Dt. 28:32; Neh. 5:5; (אֵין לְאֵל יָדִי). Occurrence in texts of such divergent nature and origin shows that it is part of the ancient heritage of popular usage.

[82] So O. Procksch, NKZ, 35 (1924), 20 ff. The transl. "My hand belongs to a god" (Baudissin, Kyrios, III, 17) in the sense of "I have a fortunate hand" (E. Sellin, Theologie des AT [1933], 4) makes nonsense of Dt. 28:32 and also of Mi. 2:1. It also presupposes poor Heb. It would be correct enough if we had יֶשׁ יָדִי לְאֵל. But אֵל comes first because it is the dominant noun. The expression הֵבִיא אֱלוֹהַּ בְּיָדוֹ in Job 12:6 is perhaps a theological interpretation of the proverb.

of my hand," i.e., "I am able." [83] Nevertheless, it is difficult to believe that this was taken in a purely secular sense. The word ēl had a different ring for the Semite from that which "power" has for us. If we have no option but to use "power" in a proverbial expression of this kind, we are to think in terms of the epitome of what is incomprehensible to men of simple culture, namely, of a power whose origin they are unable to grasp with the means of knowledge at their disposal, and therefore of what the science of religion places under the category of *mana*. [84] אֶל יְדִי is thus to be regarded as an expression which belongs to the sphere of magical ideas. Man is trying to gain control of "power." Perhaps when related to אֵל "power" denotes the strong and impressive tree which the Canaanites customarily worship and which is called אֵלָה, "the tree of power," in Heb. [85]

Our conclusion, then, in no way contradicts the general result to which we are led with a high degree of probability by our general survey of the usage, namely, that the word is rooted in religious soil. We may list it among the most primitive terms of piety, and there is no need to regard it as a metaphor transferred from the secular sphere to the religious. אֵל is the power which man cannot master, and which fills his religious consciousness. The listed cases of a secular use of ēl in the practical sense are too few to affect this judgment, and their secular character is too questionable, since it may be only an appearance due to misunderstanding. If we cannot say that our conclusion is established beyond doubt, neither linguistically nor materially is there any decisive objection to it. We are thus to take it as highly probable that for Semites the concept of power was the basic one in terms of which they understood the divine being. [86]

This assumption is strongly supported by parallel appellatives which are used to denote deity and which also imply possession of power, e.g., בַּעַל, "Owner," אָדוֹן, "Lord," and מֶלֶךְ "King," [87] although this is, of course, only indirect confirmation. The combination אֵל גִּבּוֹר used in Is. 9:5 (cf. also Is. 10:21) for the Saviour King is too uncertain to allow of any conclusions in respect of the meaning of אֵל. [88]

b. A separate question is that of the root and the root meaning of אֵל.

אֵל is hardly a word of analogous structure to עֵד ,גֵּר, מֵת etc., with אוּל as the root. [89] For אֵל has made a long ē of the short i found in the Accadian *ilu* (fem. *iltu*) and the

---

[83] Cf. A. Bertholet, *Das Dynamistische im AT* (1926), 10 f.; Beer, op. cit., 34; J. Hänel, *Die Religion der Heiligkeit* (1931), 135. Hehn, op. cit., 211, takes a different view (="sphere").

[84] A similar view is found in C. Brockelmann, ZAW, 26 (1906), 30 and K. Beth, ZAW, 36 (1916), 152. Kleinert strongly emphasises the incompleteness of the analogy, op. cit., 270 ff.

[85] The variants אֵלוֹן and אַלּוֹן may also be mentioned as terms for the "tree of God," the terebinth, cf. Baudissin, *Adonis und Esmun*, 433.

[86] On this whole complex of questions cf. R. Kittel, *Geschichte des Volkes Israel*, I [5, 6] (1923), 165 ff. A bibl. is given in this work, to which we should add M. Noth, *Die israelitischen Personennamen im Rahmen der gemeinsemitischen Namengebung* (1928), p. 82 ff.

[87] The God worshipped in Shechem can be called both בַּעַל בְּרִית and אֵל בְּרִית (Ju. 9:4, 46). As personal names we find, e.g., אלידע and בעלידע, אליאל and מלכיאל, אליה and אדניה.

[88] Eus. Praep. Ev., XI, 6, 19 quotes a tradition to the effect that אֵל is elucidated by ἰσχὺς καὶ δύναμις; Aquila has ἰσχυρός (Hier. Ad Marcellam, 25).

[89] So esp. T. Nöldeke, *Monatsberichte der Königlich. Preuss. Akademie der Wissenschaften zu Berlin*, 1880, 773; STB, 1882, 1190 f.

Arab. *ilah,* cf. in Heb. the reduction of vowels in cases like אֱלִימֶלֶךְ, אֶלְקָנָה etc. [90] If, then, אוּל means "to be pre-eminent," [91] "to be strong," this has no bearing on the meaning of אֵל. Nor is it any help to presuppose the root אלל [92] in comparison with אֱלִיל, "idol," "non-god," "little god," since this is most unlikely in view of the plur. אֵלִים and other forms which avoid the strong articulation of the ל. In any case the word אלל, which is nearer the neg. particle אַל than the noun אֵל, is of doubtful meaning, so that even if a connection is rightly seen it gives us no clue to the true sense. A final possibility is to assume that the third radical has disappeared and that it comes from a root *tertiae* י אלי (אלה). [93] This seems to be supported by אֱלֹהִים, but it is of little practical value. For, apart from the doubtfulness of ה as part of the root in אֱלֹהִים (→ *infra*), the basic אלה sheds little real light on the meaning of אֵל. Since אלה, "to curse," as a denominative of אֵל and אלה, which is not found in Heb., are of little value in explaining the derivation on account of the strong ה, we can only look to the אלה underlying the preposition אֵל (אֱלֵי) as a possible root, and this would leave us in the sphere of imagination so far as meaning is concerned, as well as causing us to lose sight of the obvious connection between אֵל and *ilu.* [94]

c. If there is no etymological basis for the meanings "power" and "God" suggested by the usage of אֵל, the linguistic data cannot be clearly explained in terms of אֱלֹהִים and אֱלוֹהַּ. It seems to be unquestionable, though even this is contested, [95] that we have a plural and the related sing. [96] If this is so, then we might perhaps argue that, if there is a root relationship between אֱלוֹהַּ and אֵל, the vocative has become fixed as an independent name, [97] giving us the plur. אֱלֹהִים. The construction is similar to the epigraphically well attested אלה (*ĕlāh*) of the Aramaeans, Southern Arabians and Nabateans, and might therefore be accepted with some measure of justification as an Aramaism.

There are not sufficient grounds on which to dispute or deny the root relationship with אֵל and to postulate an independent basis like, e.g., the Arab. *'aliha,* "to shudder," "to be fearful," [98] since the strong ה in אֱלוֹהַּ is adequately explained by the purpose of the Mas. to make the word a clearly recognisable sing. of אֱלֹהִים, the ה serving to avoid the hiatus as a rough breathing. Hence there is little probability in attempts to

---

[90] Cf. H. Bauer-P. Leander, *Historische Grammatik der hbr. Sprache,* I (1922), § 61 i, 69 m.

[91] Whence perhaps אַיִל, "ram," "bell-weather," which like עַתּוּד (Is. 14:9) is sometimes used of leaders: אֵל גּוֹיִם, Ez. 31:11; אֵילֵי מוֹאָב Ex. 15:15; אוּלֵי הָאָרֶץ, 2 K. 24:15 Q. The accidental similarity of sound often enabled the Mas. to dedivinise offensive statements about אֵל, cf. A. Geiger, *Urschrift und Übersetzungen der Bibel*[2] (1928), 292 ff.

[92] O. Procksch, NKZ, 35 (1924), 20 ff.

[93] So esp. Hehn, *op. cit.,* 209 f.

[94] To assume *ilu iliu* (Hehn, *op. cit.,* 208) is too forced to carry conviction.

[95] Acc. to L. Venetianer, ZAW, 40 (1922), 157 ff. אֱלֹהִים arose by Hebraising of the cuneiform *ilu-IM,* so that the plur. is not original.

[96] C. Brockelmann, *Grundriss der vergleichenden Grammatik der semitischen Sprachen,* I (1907), 334 and others consider the possibility that אֱלוֹהַּ for its part already expresses a plur. to אֵל.

[97] Cf. Bauer-Leander, *op. cit.* § 78e f (analogy אָמָה, "maid"); Procksch, *op. cit.,* 26; Noth, *op. cit.,* 83, n. 1. אֲדֹנָי (→ κύριος) also seems to derive from address in prayer.

[98] This theory has often been advanced since the days of A. Fleischer (cf. F. Delitzsch, *Genesis*[4] [1872], 57).

ascribe to אֱלֹהִים or אֱלוֹהַּ a basic sense like "He who is to be feared," and to support this by other than linguistic considerations. [99]

d. If, then, the three terms for God are to be regarded as one in origin, and if it seems probable that the original meaning is that of power, the further question arises how we are to understand the differentiation into sing. and plur. if this is not to be given numerical significance.

In discussing this problem אֱלוֹהַּ may be treated separately, since its use seems to be closely restricted. It is not found in older parts of the canon, so that, apart from poetical use (Dt. 32:15, 17; Ps. 18:30; 50:22; 114:7; 139:19), which is difficult to date, it might be said to belong to the post-exilic literature, and even here it is restricted almost entirely to its plentiful use in Job (41 times). [100] The use of אֱלוֹהַּ thus arises only when we have already fixed the precise sense of אֵל and אֱלֹהִים. There can be no question of any different sense. We need only assume that the need for more emphatic expression provides occasion for the use of the more resonant word, unless we are to assume Aramaic influence.

Quite unambiguous is the use of אֵלִים as a numerical plur., of which the only real instance in the OT is Ex. 15:11 (מִי כָמֹכָה בָּאֵלִים). [101] A smaller number of the occurrences of אֱלֹהִים is to be taken along the same lines (Ju. 9:13: אֱלֹהִים וַאֲנָשִׁים; [102] Ex. 18:11: כָּל־הָאֱלֹהִים; 12:12; Dt. 10:17: אֱלֹהֵי הָאֱלֹהִים וַאֲדֹנֵי הָאֲדֹנִים etc.). [103] But this use is not the rule. A single heathen god, e.g., can be denoted by the plur. אֱלֹהִים (e.g., Ju. 11:24 Kemoš; 1 K. 11:5, the goddess Ištar of Sidon; 2 K. 1:2, the Baal Zebub of Ekron), like the Phoenician אלם אלם נרגל, the god Nergal; אלם אדרת אס אלם עשתרת, the mighty god Isis, the goddess Ištar) or the Accadian ilanu when this is applied to a specific divine person [104] or when it involves the transfer of divine predication to a man. [105] If the Heb. expression is the same at this point as that of neighbouring peoples, including the Canaanites, the application of אֱלֹהִים to the person of Yahweh cannot be regarded as the result of theological or mythological speculations which were common among worshippers of Yahweh and which were designed to throw light on the relation of Yahweh to the gods. In Israel as elsewhere the practical need for pious reverence led to the use of the plur. of amplitude (Böhl, op. cit., 36) in addressing God, and thus underlay the development of the nominative expression in the sing. (on אֲדֹנִי → κύριος). [106] In אֱלֹהִים, therefore, the polytheistic idea of

---

[99] Cf. e.g., Kleinert, op. cit., p. 277 f.

[100] Cf. also Is. 44:8; Hab. 1:11; 3:3; Prv. 30:5; Da. 11:37 ff.; Neh. 9:17; 2 Ch. 32:15. Sometimes in Job there are signs of redaction in the use of the divine names, so that it is doubtful whether the text gives a correct picture of the usage of the author; cf. F. Baumgärtel, *Der Hiobdialog* (1933), 151 ff.

[101] בְּנֵי אֵלִים (Ps. 29:1; 89:6) emphasises the number by pleonastic mention of the individuality בֵּן. → 81.

[102] Cf. the Ras Shamra texts. H. Bauer, ZAW, NF, 10 (1933), 85.

[103] Ex. 22:8 takes a middle position to the extent that it refers to two parties.

[104] Cf., e.g., the older Babylonian names Idin-ilum with the newer Ilani-iddin, Hehn, op. cit., 169, with many other examples.

[105] So often in the Amarna texts, Hehn, op. cit., 172; F. Böhl, *Die Sprache der Amarnabriefe* (1909), 35 f.

[106] The "we" in the sayings of God in Gn. 1:26; 3:22; 11:7 seems to be numerical, and it thus seems to be taken over from polytheism, as plainly shown by כְּאַחַד מִמֶּנּוּ (3:22); → κύριος.

God is only an accompanying undertone. He who says אֱלֹהִים of his God, or who addresses Him as אֱלֹהָי, is occupied with many gods only inasmuch as he certifies that he has knowledge of them. His practical relation to them is decided by the fact that he honours in the person of his God that which constitutes a god. The אֱלֹהִים possesses the אֵל quality in full measure.

6. The Historical Continuation of the OT Belief in God.

If, then, Yahweh is an אֵל or אֱלֹהִים, this does not imply merely a more precise conception of a general idea of God, as may be achieved by a genitive (אֵל עוֹלָם, אֵל בֵּית־אֵל etc.) or by apposition (אֵל עֶלְיוֹן, אֵל שַׁדַּי). In accordance with the content of the terms it implies that we have in Yahweh a concrete manifestation of divine reality. For the concept God does not have the strong dynamism of the name but it does form the presupposition for its development in statements concerning the divine name, since it is fashioned by a basic religious experience.

This basic experience is not the same thing for the community of Yahweh as it is for the Gentiles, and on this distinction is built up biblical religion as faith in one God who is truly God in the full sense, in sharp differentiation from all other numinous experience which cannot penetrate to the heart of the divine and which is called heathenism in faithful paraphrase of the OT use of the word "Gentiles." God's sovereign independence of man, His all-conditioning creative power and His urgent utterance in revelation to His people constitute the essential difference between the faith of the OT community of God and the beliefs of the Gentiles, who are marked by the fact that they make gods, fashioning in wood and stone, or in cultic actions, symbols of natural forces numinously conceived. These gods cannot help or avail (הוֹעִיל, Is. 44:9 etc.). They are a silent mystery. They cannot release any impulses of will. They are inoperative, and therefore they are to be regarded as nought (cf. expressions like תֹּהוּ, הֶבֶל, אַיִן etc., 1 S. 12:21; Is. 59:4; 40:17 etc.). Rationally, they can be easily explained as that which is "in heaven above (Gn. 1:14 מְאֹרֹת, "lamps"), or in the earth beneath, or in the water under the earth" (Ex. 20:4; Dt. 5:8). Or they can be explained in terms of the sexual impulse in men or beasts. But reason cannot wholly encompass numinous feelings, and it cannot explain them away for those who experience them. Thus the prophetic attack seeks to break the power of heathen piety by kindling the basic motive of faith in Yahweh, the experience of God's commanding will. It seeks to overcome it by issuing a summons to obedience. When there is no activation of will, there is no God. God has created man in His own likeness (Gn. 1:26). Man cannot make God. [107] The Word of God finds lodging only where the creative caprice of man is expelled by the manifestation of a reality which transcends and fashions human will and action. This reality may be modest and inadequate. Even a materialised spirit of the dead can be called אֱלֹהִים in 1 S. 28:13. But it always constitutes the strongly felt meaning of the appellatives even where there is some question as to their use. If the reality of אֱלִים is to be challenged or denied, this cannot be merely in the light of rational considerations. It is possible only if there is experience of the activity of the God who commands, directs and helps. This experience is basic to the religion established by Moses. But it goes through several crises. One reason

---

[107] Jer. 2:28; Is. 44:9 ff. etc. The man who has made a god (Ju. 18:24) plays a comic role, since it has cost him a good deal of money. Similar ideas are to be found in the description of the manufacture of idols in Dt. Is., esp. Is. 44:13 f.

for this is that it cannot be counted on with any regularity. God is accustomed to hide Himself (אֵל מִסְתַּתֵּר, Is. 45:15; cf. Ps. 89:46 etc.). Mystery envelops His actions (פֶּלֶא, Is. 25:1; Ps. 88:12). This mystery is revealed only to believing worship (Ps. 139:14), and even in hymns there is still an element of awe (cf. נוֹרָא תְהִלֹּת, Ex. 15:11). A second reason is the constriction and confusion caused by the actuality of experiences in other cults which set themselves alongside the knowledge of God based on the tradition of the people of God. Heathenism as the recognition of mysterious power is a genuine human phenomenon rooted in creaturely feeling. It influences Israel as such, and it has other attractions than its moral laxity. We read in the Decalogue of the divinity of other gods (אֵל נֵכָר, Dt. 32:12), and if we have here only a breath (הַבְלֵי שָׁוְא, Ps. 31:6; cf. Jer. 10:15; 16:19 etc.) or puny gods (אֱלִילִים, 1 Ch. 16:26), this is not obvious to those who contemplate with astonishment the triumphs of the people of the queen of heaven (Jer. 7:18; 44:17 ff.) or of Sakkut and Kewan (Am. 5:26), or who see the bounty of the land of milk and honey lavished on people who find and celebrate the deity in growth and impulse on every hill and under every green tree (Dt. 12:2; Jer. 2:20; 3:6 etc.). The result is allegiance to the alien god (Jer. 5:7). Those who caused sons and daughters to pass through the fire for a god (Dt. 18:10; 2 K. 16:3 etc.) can hardly have done so with a light heart. They must have been under the compelling pressure of a numinous experience which they tried to escape by sacrifice. Religion was thus brought into opposition to religion if the אֵל נֵכָר could prove and maintain his divinity. That he could do so, Israel learned from the great anger of the god of the Moabites, who frustrated the campaign against Mesha (2 K. 3:27), or from the gods of Damascus, who showed their power in the wars against the Syrians (2 Ch. 28:23). Even Dt., with its frequent warning against the אֱלֹהִים אֲחֵרִים, does not clearly challenge the belief that these are real divine powers to which a man can fall victim if he forgets Yahweh (Dt. 6:12, 14). That this is so seems to be clearly expressed in the statement that Yahweh must militantly establish Himself as אֵל קַנָּא, as a jealous God (Dt. 6:15 and the extended Decalogue in Ex. 20:5; Dt. 5:9).[108] If it is pointed out that Yahweh's jealousy is directed against Israelites who turn to other gods (cf. also Jos. 24:19), there can be no disguising the fact that the jealousy or wounded love is basically caused by the false gods themselves and by their power of attraction, even though they are only graven images (Dt. 4:24). The reality of the territorial and national pantheon imposed itself no less forcibly on men in covenant with Yahweh than on resident aliens and strangers, especially when, in accordance with custom, they participated in local cultic fellowship (Ex. 34:15) or in external politics (cf. e.g., 1 K. 16:31; 11:7 f.; 2 K. 23:13). Only the certainty that Yahweh was אֵל אֱלֹהִים (Jos. 22:22), that He was אֵל עֶלְיוֹן (Ps. 78:35 etc.) who dominated the pantheon and surpassed all others in power, could authoritatively prevent participation in the worship of idols and the recognition of alien myths. In the pre-exilic community this certainty was not much stronger than that of a rational form of monarchical monotheism rather along the lines of 1 K. 22:19. Jeremiah, with his intense experience of God and his anger at the disloyalty of the divine community, was perhaps the first to venture the bold statement of faith: הֵמָּה לֹא אֱלֹהִים, "which are yet no gods" (2:11), and in the very

---

[108] It is another matter whether such a motif is present in the name יִשְׂרָאֵל (deriv. from שׂרה, "to fight").

same breath even he can express his high regard for the integrity and sincerity of paganism: "Hath a nation changed their gods?" Yet behind these courteous words, which almost sound as though he is magnifying the Gentiles, there is no longer any religious particularism. There stands rather a clear recognition of the full greatness of the one Lord, as in the saying of Isaiah: "The whole earth is full of his glory" (6:3). There can be no exchange of gods, because there are no gods. Hence Gentiles who are faithful to their gods are sincere, but they are mistaken. On the other hand, when members of the people of God look to other gods, they are guilty of infidelity, and they fall victim to the fatal inner discord (כְּבֹשֶׁת גַּנָּב כִּי יִמָּצֵא, Jer. 2:26) which Jeremiah, with perhaps greater sorrow than any other prophet, sees in his people.

It is instructive to note that in the OT this certainty of the divine uniqueness of Yahweh to the exclusion of all other deity does not seem to be attained speculatively, though there is perhaps an excess of rational argument in the complaints of the prophets, and though we find some more arid, theoretical statements in the later literature. Among these we may mention chiefly Da. 11:36, where there is a correct differentiation between אֵל אֵלִים and כָּל־אֵל, and Mal. 2:10, where אֵל אֶחָד loses its full sense in such close proximity to the אֵל נֵכָר of 2:11. Ps. 82 causes the אֱלֹהִים κατ' ἐξοχήν to hold judgment among the אֱלֹהִים, and this ends with the degradation of beings which can be regarded as אֱלֹהִים only in delusion. These thoughts may easily give a wrong impression of the OT perception of the reality denoted by the word "God," for they do not bring out the impelling force of faith in God or the emotional strength of experience of God's acts to His people. Hence statements which take the form of spontaneous adoration or the confession of unbounded confidence are more revealing. He who prays: אֵלִי, "my God," has experienced the divine act as help (Ex. 15:2; Ps. 89:26), deliverance (מְפַלְטִי, Ps. 18:2), faithfulness (Ps. 63:1, 3: חֶסֶד; Ps. 140:7) or consolation (Ps. 22:10: מִבֶּטֶן אִמִּי אֵלִי אָתָּה). The hymnal motif "my God" magnifies the deity of God as living and active deity, and the motif of trust directs hope upon this. That we do not have here questions of cultic rank, or a monarchical monotheism, but the free confession of the heritage of faith, may be seen with compelling clarity from the inwardness of the address. God is the living and active God: אֵל חַי (Hos. 2:1), and the promise that He will be the God of the children of Israel (וְהָיִיתִי לָהֶם לֵאלֹהִים, Lv. 26:12 etc.) simply means that He is active on their behalf. If a being wishes to be God, he must do that which is worthy of God: Ju. 6:31; 10:14; 1 K. 18:21, 27. The proofs of God in Dt. Is. are all based on this premise. The poem in Is. 40:21-31 often seems to lead in the direction of a cosmological proof.[109] There is certainly no doubt that contemplation of the starry heaven is presumed to give an answer to the question of the Creator. Yet the answer is not simply that Yahweh has created it, and none else. It goes beyond mere reflection. It is to this effect: So great is God! Remember this, and you will see that you are forced to take God much more seriously than you normally do. To take God seriously is to be aware of His power, and to hope for His act in affliction. He constantly gives new power (Is. 40:31). How does the prophet know this? Almost indignantly he answers: "Hast thou not known? hast thou not heard?" (40:28). The truth in a hundred hymnal motifs extolling God's power is to be found in these words.

Quell

---

[109] Cf. v. 26: "Lift up your eyes on high, and behold who hath created these things."

C. The Early Christian Fact of God and Its Conflict with the Concept of God in Judaism.

1. The Usage.

(i). In the LXX θεός is usually the equivalent of the Heb. אֱלֹהִים, → 79. [110] The def. ὁ θεός refers to the one God of Israel, θεός without the art. seems to be almost always appellative. [111] τὸ θεῖον, the favourite Gk. term for the Godhead, is not found at all in the LXX.

Judaism avoids the term God. It prefers to speak of the Lord, the Almighty, the Most High, heaven, and only rarely of God or the God of heaven. This may be seen in 1 Macc., which usually speaks of heaven, and has θεός only twice, at 5:68 and 3:18. On the usage of Rabb. Judaism, → 92 f.

Hell. Judaism prefers to avoid θεός in order not to seem uncultured. It adopts the style of religious philosophy and speaks of the deity, of providence, or of the divine. This can be seen in 4 Macc. Here the good Gk. adj. θεῖος, which occurs only 9 times in LXX (including the Apoc.), is found 25 times. We also have θεία πρόνοια (4 Macc. 17:22), θεία δίκη (4 Macc. 4:21), and τὰ θεῖα (4 Macc. 1:17) in the absol. Philo has ὁ θεός in the OT sense for the God of Israel. [112] He distinguishes between ὁ θεός and κύριος. ὁ θεός is used for the goodness and kindness of God the Creator. ὁ κύριος denotes God's kingly power as ruler (Leg. All., III, 73). [113] θεός without the art. can be used for the δεύτερος θεός, the λόγος. [114] θεοί may denote men. [115] In the main, however, he likes the philosophical τὸ θεῖον and similar abstractions which are never found in LXX (→ θεῖος, 122). Joseph. uses θεός and ὁ θεός interchangeably with no apparent distinction and in the most diverse connections, [116] but he prefers ὁ θεός. [117] Along with the term for God, [118] which is also used ingenuously in the oath ὄμνυμι

---

[110] In individual sections of the Pentateuch, however, θεός is often used for Yahweh, cf. Ex. 16 (5 times), Ex. 19 (10 times), Nu. 22 (11 or 12 times). In Prv. 1-22 this equation is the rule except for 2:15 f., though only in LXX. 'Α, Σ, Αλλ often use κύριος instead.

[111] Baudissin, Kyrios, I, 19 f., 25, 50-60 etc.

[112] Som., I, 62, 65 f., 228-230. On the tetragrammaton, v. Vit. Mos., II, 132.

[113] Cf. on this pt. the constant principle of Rabb. exegesis of the OT that the word אלהים denotes the righteous, judicial God and יהוה the loving, gracious and merciful God, e.g., Gn. r., 33 on 8:1; Ex. r., 3 on 3:14: "When I judge men, I am called אלהים . . . when I have mercy on them I am called יהוה." אלהים = מדת הדין, "the principle of righteousness," and יהוה = מדת הרחמים, "the principle of love" (in God's activity). V. on this pt. K. G. Kuhn, S. Nu. übersetzt (1933 ff.), 551, n. 89, and the bibl. given there [Kuhn].

[114] Som., I, 229 f.; Leg. All., III, 207 f. Cf. Eus. Praep. Ev., VII, 13, 1.

[115] Pr.-Bauer refers to Som., I, 229; Det. Pot. Ins., 161 f.; Mut. Nom., 128; Omn. Prob. Lib., 43; Vit. Mos., I, 158; Decal., 120; Leg. All., I, 40; Migr. Abr., 84. The ref. to Som., I, 229 is mistaken. One might add passages like AC, 9 and Mut. Nom., 19. Obviously Philo does not mean that Moses, to whom he mainly refers on the basis of Ex. 7:1, is really God. He insists on the unity of God: ὁ μὲν ἀληθείᾳ θεὸς εἷς ἐστιν, οἱ δ' ἐν καταχρήσει λεγόμενοι πλείους, Som., I, 229. Moses is not God πρὸς ἀλήθειαν, but only δόξῃ: θεὸς πρὸς φαντασίαν καὶ δόκησιν, οὐ πρὸς ἀλήθειαν καὶ τὸ εἶναι, Det. Pot. Ins., 161 f.

[116] θεός and ὁ θεός are interchangeable in Ap. 2, 168; περὶ θεοῦ in Ap. 2, 179; 2, 169; 2, 256. περὶ τοῦ θεοῦ in Ap., 2, 254. Also ὁ θεός in Ant., 3, 97; 4, 292; 4, 287; 4, 294; 7, 72; 9, 2; 9, 8; 9, 27.

[117] Ant., 5, 109: πανταχοῦ δ' ἐν τοῖς τούτου (sc. τοῦ θεοῦ) ἐστέ. (Cf. 8, 145 of Menander: τόν τε χρυσοῦν κίονα [pillar] τὸν ἐν τοῖς τοῦ Διός); 9, 236: εὐσεβὴς τὰ πρὸς τὸν θεόν; 3, 211: τὴν εἰς τὸν θεὸν τιμήν.

[118] On the tetragrammaton, v. Ant., 2, 276: καὶ ὁ θεὸς αὐτῷ σημαίνει τὴν αὐτοῦ προσηγορίαν οὐ πρότερον εἰς ἀνθρώπους παρελθοῦσαν, περὶ ἧς οὔ μοι θεμιτὸν εἰπεῖν.

τὸν θεόν, [119] we have the paraphrases οἱ οὐρανοί and esp. the metaphysical τὸ θεῖον (→ θεῖος, 122). κύριος is very rare in Joseph., since it was allowed as a transl. of יהוה only in the reading of Scripture and in invocation. [120] Joseph. also uses θεία φύσις etc. θεότης is not found in his writings. But it is used of men (→ θειότης, 123, n. 1).

Although Judaism was very careful to avoid the divine name, it is noteworthy that in the comparatively late apocryphal and pseudepigraphical writings we do find κύριος (Heb. יהוה). The reason for this is that works like the Ps. Sol. intentionally keep the older forms of expression in order to achieve the same style as the genuine Psalms. Jubilees [121] uses both terms for God quite freely, interchanging them according to no fixed pattern [122] and using hardly any other expressions. [123] The same is true of the Assumptio Mosis, [124] of the Vita Adae, of the Apoc. of Moses, and of Pseudo-Philo. [125] The Damascus document almost always has God. [126] The older books of Enoch occupy a special position. [127] They usually have God or the Lord, but they like liturgical amplitude and they thus offer a whole range of other divine predications. [128] 4 Esr. and S. Bar. are more modest, and along with God and the Lord they simply have the Most High, the Creator, the Almighty, the Most Merciful etc. [129] Even simpler is Slav. En., which for the most part is content with God and the Lord. [130] The Apoc. of Abraham, which betrays Gnostic influence, has a welter of high-sounding and mysterious names both old and new. Among these we may mention God, [131] God of gods, Holy One, Mighty, Creator, Sole Ruler, also Light, Unbegotten, Incorruptible, Lover of men, finally Sabaoth, Eli, El, Jaoel. [132] The simple "the Lord" [133] is very rare; instead there is reference to the power of the ineffable name (10), and the older name Yahweh finds an echo in Jao-el. [134] In general, the usage in Apoc. Abr. is a model of later subjection to alien influence.

---

[119] Ant., 4, 287 (ὀμνύτω τὸν θεόν); 7, 353 (ὄμνυμι τὸν μέγιστον θεόν); Bell., 4, 543 (θεὸν ὄμνυσιν τὸν πάντων ἔφορον).

[120] Cf. Schl. Jos., 9-11.

[121] Baudissin (Kyrios, II) has tried to prove that the LXX gave the impulse towards the suppression of the divine name by its term kyrios. But it is most unlikely that this development really began on Alexandrian soil. In any case, the usage of Jubilees (and the older Enoch texts) is independent of, and perhaps even older than, the LXX. This suggests that the suppression of the divine name and its replacement by "Lord" began on Semitic soil and then found its way into the Alexandrian translation (→ n. 149).

[122] We have both together in 1:19 : Lord, my God.

[123] E.g., 50:13 in some MSS : Lord of all creation, King of kings.

[124] Ass. Mos. 1:11: Lord of the world ; 4:2 : Lord of all ; 2:4 : God of heaven.

[125] The Biblical Antiquities of Philo, trans. M. R. James (1917).

[126] Also the Only One, the First, the Last. Swearing by El or Adonai is expressly forbidden.

[127] Cf. Bousset-Gressm., 307 f., n. 1, 310 ff.

[128] Eth. En. 1:4 : The everlasting God ; 14:20 : The great Glory ; 61:13 : Lord of spirits ; 12:3 : Lord of majesty and King of the world ; 25:7: Lord of glory, King of eternity; 10:1: The Most High, the Holy One and the Great One ; 9:4 : Lord of lords, God of gods, King of kings ; 25:3 : The Holy One, the Great One, the One, the Lord of glory, the eternal King.

[129] 4 Esr. 11:46; 6:32; 7:132 ff.; S. Bar. passim.

[130] Slav. En. 22 : Lord God. Slav. En. 4 like Eth. En. 71:10 : He that sitteth on the throne, cf. Da. 7:9.

[131] Apc. Abr. (Bonwetsch), 10. In 3 f. Terah is called the "God" of the idols which he has made. Cf. also Joseph and Asenath, XXII (p. 62 ff., Brooks).

[132] Apc. Abr. 8:10, and esp. the great hymn to God in 17.

[133] In 16 the old Trishagion.

[134] In 17 Jaoel is a divine name, in 10 it is the name of the angel which has its name from God, which goes out in the power of His inexpressible name, and which blesses in this name. On Jao v. H. Gressmann, ZAW, NF, 2 (1925), 13 ff.

Jesus uses the term θεός quite freely (though cf. Mt. 5:34 f.; 23:16 ff.). More rarely He has → κύριος or expressions like → οὐρανός, [135] δύναμις (→ II, 306) Mk. 14:61 f., σοφία Lk. 7:35, cf. 11:49. The most common word of all is → πατήρ. This is the true name for God on the lips of Jesus, and it characterises His unique message concerning God, which far surpasses the OT and especially Apocalyptic (→ ἀββᾶ, I, 5 f.).

θεός [136] is the normal word for God, and it is one of the commonest terms in the NT. Sometimes we have Lord, though from Pl. onwards this is increasingly applied to Jesus. In the nomin. θεός is used almost always with the art. [137] In other cases [138] it is sometimes def., sometimes without the art., according to the demands of rhythm and style, and with no discernible distinction. [139] θεός is not restricted to the God and Father of Jesus Christ. It is also used occasionally of Jesus Himself. [140] It is also used fairly frequently of the gods and goddesses [141] of heathenism and of other so-called deities. [142] Finally, it can also denote men (Jn. 10:34 f.).

Stauffer

2. The Rabbinic terms for God.

Later Rabb. Judaism was very scrupulous in avoiding the divine name, and it thus constructed a whole system of substitutes. This system is purely formal; it implies no change in the concept. To understand it, we must realise that later Judaism distinguishes closely between 1. the tetragrammaton יהוה as the proper name (שם המיוחד) of God; [143] 2. the words אל, אלוה, אלהים as generic names which, as it were, denote His title and office; and 3. words which describe God in terms of attributes, e.g., the Holy One, the Gracious One, the Most High (עליון), or nouns such as King, Lord, or Father, some of these being common in the OT and some being newly invented by later Judaism.

The commandment not to take God's name in vain was thus referred by later Judaism only to the proper name, the tetragrammaton. To avoid misuse of this name, even before the Christian era it had come to discontinue its use altogether, in the spirit of the saying in Ab., 1, 1: "Make a hedge about the Law." [144] Its use was allowed on certain specific occasions, e.g., in the cultus, when it could not be avoided. But even on these occasions there were special regulations to avoid any possible misuse. [145] Avoidance of the name

---

[135] E.g., Lk. 15:7, 18, 21. The expression → βασιλεία τῶν οὐρανῶν is to be attributed to Mt., who is inclined elsewhere to adopt Rabb. style and expressions. Cf. E. v. Dobschütz, "Mt. als Rabbi und Katechet," ZNW, 27 (1928), 338 ff. Jesus Himself used βασιλεία τοῦ θεοῦ, as we learn from Mk., confirmed by Lk., Ac., Jn. and Pl.

[136] Often instead of (Jn.) or in combination with (Pl.) πατήρ. τὸ → θεῖον only at Ac. 17:29.

[137] Exceptions like Jn. 8:54 or R. 8:33 are for syntactical reasons.

[138] Vocative ὁ θεός, e.g., Hb. 1:9.

[139] Cf. e.g., R. 7:22 (νόμος τοῦ θεοῦ) with 7:25 (νόμος θεοῦ). Cf. B. Weiss, "Gebrauch des Artikels bei den Gottesnamen" (→ Lit. n.); Bl.-Debr.⁶ § 254, 1.

[140] Jn. 1:1; 20:28 etc.

[141] ἡ θεός in Ac. 19:37 (cf. Jos. Ant., 9, 19) interchangeably with ἡ θεά in Ac. 19:27 (cf. Herm. v., 1, 1, 7). Cf. Bl.-Debr.⁶ § 44, 2.

[142] 1 C. 8:5; Gl. 4:8; Phil. 3:19.

[143] → I, 98, n. 32.

[144] The Ps. Sol. in the immediate pre-Christian period freely use κύριος (יהוה, Heb.), but this is because they deliberately copy the style of the original Psalms. On the other hand, there is already a careful avoidance of the divine name in Qoh. and Esther.

[145] Cf. the examples in Str.-B., II, 311-313.

of Yahweh was carried through so consistently in later Judaism that soon after the destruction of the temple all recollection of the correct enunciation of the tetragrammaton was erased. This name for God continued to exist only as a written symbol, not as a living word.

In the system of substitutes for the proper name of God, we are to distinguish between 1. the occurrence of the name of God in Holy Scripture, i.e., its utterance in Scripture reading, and 2. its use in free speech outside quotations from Scripture. In the second case, the customary use in pre-Christian times [146] was always to employ הַשָּׁמַיִם ("heaven") as a substitute for the name of God. [147, 148] In the former case, even prior to the LXX translation of the Pentateuch [149] it had become customary to put אֲדוֹנָי for יהוה in reading of Scripture and quotation from it. Only exceptionally, e.g., when יהוה and אֲדוֹנָי came together, do we find אֱלֹהִים instead.

Both substitutes, שָׁמַיִם and אֲדוֹנָי, were themselves replaced later. [150] The reading of אֲדוֹנָי for יהוה came to apply only in cultic reading in synagogue worship. In other cases, e.g., private reading, study, or quotation, the very general הַשֵּׁם [151] was always used for יהוה, הַשֵּׁם, "the name" κατ᾽ ἐξοχήν, was the proper name of God, the tetragrammaton. The common הַשָּׁמַיִם was also avoided later in general speech. It remained only in certain stereotyped phrases and expressions, [152] e.g., בִּידֵי שָׁמַיִם "through God," or לְשֵׁם שָׁמַיִם, "for God's sake," or מַלְכוּת שָׁמַיִם, "the royal dominion of God." [153] Except in these traditional expressions, שָׁמַיִם was always replaced by the more general הַמָּקוֹם, [151] הַמָּקוֹם, "the place" κατ᾽ ἐξοχήν, being heaven, i.e., שָׁמַיִם as a term for God. [154]

As we have emphasised, it was only in the case of the substitution of אֲדוֹנָי or שָׁמַיִם for Yahweh that a legal compulsion, i.e., that imposed by the commandment, underlay the development of substitute terms. The other expressions cannot be explained along these lines. They probably answer to a primitive taboo. In time even the substitutes became more and more precise words for God, and therefore, in terms of the primitive thinking at work, they were felt to be more and more identical with God, they were increasingly filled with God Himself, with His essence and person, and therefore they came to be too holy (→ I, 98) to be used in profane speech. Thus they were themselves replaced by הַשֵּׁם or הַמָּקוֹם.

The divine names in the second group, אֵל, אֱלוֹהַּ, and אֱלֹהִים, were probably not used any longer in free, secular speech. On the other hand, their utterance in reading and

---

[146] Cf. 1 Macc.

[147] Obviously group 3. → 92 was used even more widely and indeed much earlier, when the name of Yahweh could still be freely uttered.

[148] The origin of this substitute term is probably to be found in the phrase אֱלָהּ שְׁמַיָּא, "God of heaven," which is common in Da. and Ezr., and also in the Elephantine pap., which show us that this had become a stereotyped expression, perhaps under Persian influence, and that it was very common in the Judaism of the 5th century. There had always been a sense that God and heaven were very closely related, and therefore it was not a very great step to use heaven alone as a term for God. Cf. M. A. Beek, Das Danielbuch (Leiden, 1935), 68 f.

[149] The LXX already uses κύριος (= אֲדוֹנָי) as the natural rendering of יהוה, → n. 121.

[150] When this happened, it is impossible to say. It certainly belonged to the early Rabb. period, and we may thus suggest the turn of the 1st and 2nd cent. A.D.

[151] Whether and how far these substitute phrases came into common use, or whether they remained limited to the scholarly language of the Rabb. schools, is an open question.

[152] They are collected in Str.-B., I, 172 and 862 ff.

[153] → I, 571.

[154] The decisive proof of the development as here presented is that הַשֵּׁם is found only in Scripture quotations (instead of יהוה), whereas הַמָּקוֹם is found only outside quotations, in free speech.

even in secular quotation of the OT caused no offence. Nor did their use in liturgical and more general religious texts. Thus they are used quite freely in the prayers of later Judaism. [155] It is only in the Middle Ages that the custom develops of avoiding the taboo word by substituting the artificial אלקים for אלהים in written and later in printed texts. [156]

The third group of expressions, i.e., terms or nouns expressing qualities, was always used quite freely in Judaism. Indeed, these are not really to be viewed as substitutes for the divine names. They have their own life alongside the divine names or the various substitutes. Thus הקדוש, the Holy One, is always linked with the eulogy, ברוך הוא, one of the most common terms for God, probably coming into use only in the later Rabb. period. [157] The nouns are also of frequent occurrence, as אדון Lord, also רבון Lord, esp. in the combination רבונו של עולם, Lord of the world; מלך King, esp. in the form מלך מלכי המלכים, King of kings; [158] אב, Father, esp. in אב שבשמים or אבי שבשמים, Father in heaven, and also with מלך: אבינו מלכנו our Father, our King. Another common phrase for God amongst the Rabbis is מי שאמר והיה העולם, "He who spake, and the world was."

In later Judaism there also arises another group, namely, that of abstract concepts such as כבוד, holiness, גבורה, power, and esp. שכינה, the dwelling of God, i.e., His gracious presence (for the concrete fact that God dwells in the temple or among His people), [159] and in the Targumim מימרא, God's speaking [160] (for the fact that He spoke → λόγος).

This third group of terms for God, including the abstract designations, became very popular in Judaism and was developed with great wealth, [161] as may best be seen from the instances collected by A. Marmorstein. [162]

Kuhn

2. The Uniqueness of God.

a. Prophetic Monotheism as the Starting-Point of True Monotheism.

True monotheism is not a more or less necessary end product of the history of polytheistic religion and its motifs of unity. It arises as a strict negation of all polytheism. Its God is not a new idea of unity which is more satisfying than other ideas. He is not a hitherto unknown power. He is ultimate and true reality.

Thus the one God became the decisive reality for Moses. He claimed sole validity among the people of Moses: "I am Yahweh thy God ... Thou shalt have no other gods before me" (Ex. 20:2 f.). In Dt. Is. the same God is revealed as the only God in the whole world. Not merely in Israel, but in the vast Gentile world, there is no other God, the idols of the heathen being things of nought. This radical monotheism overcame the appearance of monolatry in the earlier period. But of course the one God reveals Himself only in Israel, and is worshipped only there. Even in Israel His uniqueness must not merely assert itself against the false

---

[155] Hence, even in the orthodox Rabb. sense, there is nothing offensive in the use of θεός or ὁ θεός = אל, אלהים in the religious texts of the apocr. and pseudepigr.

[156] Cf. the analogous *Deixel* for *Teufel* and *Sapperment* for *Sakrament* in German.

[157] V. A. Marmorstein, *The Old Rabbinic Doctrine of God*, I (1927) 97 and 108-147 passim.

[158] The threefold form is a further development of the common Persian and oriental title "King of kings." God has royal power even over kings of kings.

[159] → I, 571, n. 33.

[160] Str.-B., II, 313 ff. On שכינה and מימרא v. esp. G. F. Moore in *Harvard Theological Review*, 15 (1922), 41-59.

[161] As later in Islam.

[162] *Op. cit.*, I, 56-107.

concepts of ancient superstition and alien religion; it must also maintain itself continually against the real powers which dominate and threaten the people. "O Lord our God, other lords beside thee have had dominion over us; but we will make mention only of thee and thy name." [163] The uniqueness of God can only be believed in this age.

A later triumph of monotheism in the Semitic world is to be found in Islam. Even in older Arabia, alongside the tribal deities and other cults, we find a recognition of Allah [164] as Ruler of the world, [165] But the prophet Mohammed. who appealed to a revelation of God which reminds us in many respects of the call of Moses, was the first to achieve sole recognition for Allah. [166] Since his day the main tenet of Islamic religion has been the confession that there is no God save Allah, and that Mohammed is his prophet. The deities of an older period become mere representatives of Allah. [167]

The development of Mohammedan monotheism took place under the influence of biblical concepts. [168] Elsewhere in the ancient world we occasionally find echoes of biblical monotheism, e.g., in formulae like μόνος θεός or μόνος θεός ἀληθινός. [169] But these have exerted no historical influence. Living monotheism seems to be possible only as prophetic monotheism. But not all prophetic religion leads necessarily to monotheism.

A prophet also arose in the Indo-germanic world, namely, Zoroaster. But his message was dualistic. Zoroastrian dualism is naturally not the same thing as philosophical or mythological speculation. [170] Zoroaster is passionately and exclusively the prophet of Ahura Mazda, who has called him. But he is conscious of being called by his God to fight against the ungodly powers whose head is Angra Mainyu, the opponent of Ahura Mazda. His whole life and work stands under the sign of this conflict of creation. His message is a summons to enter this conflict and to strengthen the power of light against that of darkness. As the reality of the ungodly world becomes more evident in the seriousness of the prophetic battle, so a dualistic picture of the world emerges from his prophetic faith: "I will speak of the two spirits at the beginning of life, of which the holy one said to the wicked: Neither our thoughts nor our works will agree." [171] Sometimes these two spirits seem to be elemental powers of equal strength: "The two spirits at the beginning, which revealed themselves in a vision to be a pair of twins, are the better and the evil spirit in thought, word and deed." [172] But in the poetic preaching of Zoroaster there are hints that Ahura Mazda will emerge from the conflict and that he will thus show himself to be of greater age and power. [173] At any rate, the final victory of light over darkness is certain. Thus the freedom of prophetic faith finds expression in a dualistically grounded, but monotheistically orientated, theology of history.

---

[163] Is. 26:13. On the interchangeability of my God and our God, cf. Baudissin, Kyrios, III, 555 ff., and P. Feine, Theologie des NT⁶ (1934), 20, n. 2, where our attention is directed to Is. 7:13 ("ye weary my God") and Jer. 42:2-5 ("thy God, your God").

[164] Allah = "the God" (ὁ θεός).

[165] Cf. C. Snouck-Hurgronje in Bertholet-Leh., I, 649 ff.

[166] Like the God of the OT, He is the God of revelation, but His revelation is that of a book, as in later Judaism; v. Sura, 96: "Read in the name of thy Lord, who created ... who instructed with the pen."

[167] Koran, Sura, 10 and 19.

[168] V. also Baudissin, Kyrios, III, 675 ff.

[169] Cf. Norden, Theos, 145.

[170] Like the Egyptian myth of the conflict between Horus and Seth, and the settling of the conflict by Atum.

[171] Yasna, 45, 2 in C. Bartholomae, Die Gatha's des Avesta (1905).

[172] Yasna, 30, 3 (Bartholomae). Cf. F. C. Andreas in NGG, 1909, 48.

[173] Bartholomae, op. cit., 124 f. Cf. also Yasna, 30, 6, later Yäšt, 13, 77 (H. Lommel, 1927), and esp. Bundehesh (F. Justi, 1868), passim.

b. Dynamic Monotheism in Later Judaism.

Later Judaism a. occasionally used the term for God of men, and even of the θεοί of the Gentiles, but it was strongly opposed to heathen polytheism. b. It gave a primary place to its confession of one God in formulae, faith and practice. But c. it sees the one God at work through a wealth of intermediary or angelic beings. It sees Him d. in conflict with demonic forces. In this conflict e. the Son of Man or the Messiah plays a decisive role, though without claiming divine dignity. Thus apocalyptic, by accepting dualistic motifs, develops the basic monotheistic conviction of the OT into a dynamic monotheism.

a. The passages in the OT in which men are called אלהים are infrequent, and their interpretation is debated. In Ps. 45:6 the אֱלֹהִים undoubtedly refers to a man, i.e., the king, and not to Yahweh. [174] The case is rather different in Ps. 82:1, 6; Ex. 21:6; 22:7 ff. From these passages it has been thought that we may conclude that judges are called θεοί. [175] ψ 81:1: ὁ θεὸς ἔστη ἐν συναγωγῇ θεῶν, ἐν μέσῳ δὲ θεοὺς διακρίνει, is to be understood as a judgment scene with gods. If they die like men and fall like princes (v. 7), this implies that they are not men or princes, but that they are like them. Ex. 21:6 means "to bring before God," as may be seen from what follows. The man is to be brought to the entrance of the house, to the cultic place where sacrifices were offered in earlier days, and where God was thus present and pronounced His judgment. In Ex. 22:7 ff. judicial cases are to be "brought before God." This does not mean before the judges as θεοί. The judges authoritatively proclaim the divine sentence in the sacred place. The statement of R. Akiba is to be interpreted along the same lines : "Thou standest before Him who spake and the world was" (→ II, 347, n. 49). The ordained rabbi acts with divine authority. The meaning of Ex. 22:28 is unmistakable in the Mas.: "Thou shalt not blaspheme God, nor curse a prince in thy people." The LXX has θεούς for the appellative אלהים. At this point there is probably an error in translation. Certainly the θεοί who are not to be blasphemed cannot be identified with men, e.g., judges, as by R. Israel in M. Ex. 22:28. M. Ex. also refers Ex. 22:7 and 21:6 to judges. The Rabbis were interested to try to give to אלהים the artificial sense of judges in many passages, since they wished to avoid the offence to their view of God contained in a literal understanding. Especially they had to give a different sense to the בני אלהים of Gn. 6:2, since it was unthinkable for Rabb. thought that these should be sons of God. Hence we read of sons of judges or of leaders. [176] In Ex. 4:16 God says to Moses : "He shall be to thee the mouth, and thou shalt be to him God." The LXX weakens this : σὺ δὲ αὐτῷ ἔσῃ τὰ πρὸς τὸν θεόν. But the Mas. does not here deify Moses. It is simply comparing the relation between Moses and Aaron to that of the nabi and his God. The comparison is altered by P in Ex. 7:1, where Moses is God to Pharaoh.

Woe to a man who calls himself God ! [177] This is a Gentile title, and it is supreme blasphemy, to which God will make a terrible reply : ὁ βασιλεύς ... ὑψωθήσεται ἐπὶ πάντα θεὸν καὶ ἐπὶ τὸν θεὸν τῶν θεῶν ἔξαλλα λαλήσει, καὶ εὐοδωθήσεται ἕως ἂν συντελεσθῇ ἡ ὀργή· εἰς αὐτὸν γὰρ συντέλεια γίνεται (Da. 11:36 f.; cf. 13:5). In the Syrian and Roman period Judaism often experienced this self-glorification and

---

[174] Attempts have been made to avoid this explanation by adding a כְּסֵא acc. to the sense : Thy throne is a divine throne. Others have suggested that אלהים is an alteration of an original יהוה, which was confused with יִהְיֶה.

[175] Cr.-Kö., 485.

[176] I owe this reference to Kuhn.

[177] Cf. Gn. 3:5 and Apc. Mos. 18; 21. Polemically against Christ, jTaan., 65b, 70 f. (Str.-B., I, 486): "If a man should say to thee, 'I am God,' he lies ; 'I am the Son of Man,' he will finally rue it ; 'I ascend to heaven,' he has said it, but he shall not fulfil it." → II, 348.

saw the divine answer, as may be seen in 2 and 3 Macc. and Ps. Sol. [178] The Haggada has gathered together a whole list of OT examples of human pretension. [179] Nimrod makes this claim to be God: "I am he who has created heaven and earth and all their hosts." [180]

Heavenly beings, too, are sometimes called אלהים in the OT. In these cases, however, the LXX goes its own way and usually has ἄγγελοι or υἱοὶ θεοῦ [181] in order to avoid any suggestion of polytheism. [182] But this is only one aspect of the great conflict against polytheism and idolatry which from the time of Dt. Is. becomes a powerful stream in apocalyptic, Hellenistic and Rabbinic literature. The stories of Bel and the Dragon portray the folly of idolatry with graphic realism. The book of Baruch laughs at the helplessness of images. [183] We find the same motifs in Jubilees and later in the Testament of Job and the Apc. Abr. Wisdom seeks the origin of polytheism in the worship of the dead, [184] and investigates the connection between religious and ethical corruption (Wis. 13:1 ff.; 14:22 ff.). The Sib. lashes the cult of animals, which worships the creature instead of the Creator (Sib., 3, 9 ff., 27 ff.). Ps.-Phokylides (194) exclaims: "Eros is not a God, but the most unbridled of all passions." [185] The radical Hellenists attack polytheism with the weapons of religious philosophy. [186] The Rabbis, too, sometimes use similar proofs in their battle against the worship of stars, the cult of animals and emperor worship. [187] Some of them perceive demonic forces in the gods of the heathen. [188] Other declare them to be things of nought along the lines of Dt. Is. [189] The weapons used against polytheism vary, but there is a united front. This was demanded by the fundamental confession of Judaism.

---

[178] Cf. the motive for the building of the tower and Abraham's protest in Pseudo-Philo, VI (M. R. James, The Biblical Antiquities of Philo [1917], 89 ff.). Ps. Sol. 2:28 f. (Pompey): οὐκ ἐλογίσατο ὅτι ἄνθρωπός ἐστιν, καὶ τὸ ὕστερον οὐκ ἐλογίσατο. εἶπεν Ἐγὼ κύριος γῆς καὶ θαλάσσης ἔσομαι· καὶ οὐκ ἐπέγνω ὅτι ὁ θεὸς μέγας κραταιὸς ἐν ἰσχύι αὐτοῦ τῇ μεγάλῃ.

[179] M. Ex. 15:11 (49a). Pharaoh (Ez. 29:9), Sennacherib (2 K. 18:35), Nebuchadnezzar (Is. 14:14) and the prince of Tyre (Ez. 28:2) all called themselves gods.

[180] Ma'ase-Abraham in Str.-B., III, 35 (acc. to M. Horowitz, Sammlung kleiner Midraschim [1888], 43).

[181] ψ 96:7: προσκυνήσατε αὐτῷ, πάντες οἱ ἄγγελοι αὐτοῦ (= כל־אלהים); Job 1:6: ἄγγελοι τοῦ θεοῦ (= בני האלהים), cf. ἄγγελοι in Job 38:7. Dt. 32:43: προσκυνησάτωσαν αὐτῷ πάντες υἱοὶ θεοῦ ... καὶ ἐνισχυσάτωσαν αὐτῷ πάντες ἄγγελοι θεοῦ (no Mas. original).

[182] The same motif could even help toward the elimination of the name of Yahweh, v. H. Gunkel, RGG², II, 1369; Eissfeldt, op. cit., 16.

[183] Ep. Jer. (= Bar. 6); cf. also Ma'ase-Abraham in Str.-B., III, 35: "Nimrod said to Abram, why hast thou burnt the gods of thy father? Abraham answered and said, Forsooth, I saw the smallest lying feebly on the ground, and I asked my mother to make me a fine cake, and I brought it to the smallest. Then the wrath of the greatest was kindled, and it consumed the smallest and itself with fire. Nimrod said to him, They cannot do anything. He said to him, My lord king, perceive and accept what thou hast said out of thine own mouth, namely, that they cannot do anything, and wilt thou abandon the living God and the eternal King, who made heaven and earth and all the hosts of them, to serve idols of wood?"

[184] Wis. 14:15, cf. Ep. Ar., 135 ff.; Sib. 3, 554, 588, 723.

[185] T. Bergk, Poetae Lyrici Graeci, II (1915), 106.

[186] V. Eus. Praep. Ev., XIII, 13, 40 (Ps.-Soph.); 13, 60 (Ps.-Aesch.). R. Hercher, Epistolographi Graeci (1873), 280 ff.: Ps.-Heracl. Ep., 4 (→ 121, n. 8). Cf. also Jos. Ant., 10, 50: τῆς περὶ τῶν εἰδώλων δόξης (!) ὡς οὐχὶ θεῶν ὄντων ἀποστάντας.

[187] A. Marmorstein, EJ, VII (1931), 561 ff.

[188] Str.-B., III, 48 ff.

[189] Ibid., 53 ff.

b. At no point is later Judaism more united than in fidelity to the confession Εἷς ὁ θεός. [190] Sometimes the formula appears as in Dt. 6:4, [191] sometimes in two and three-membered extensions, [192] sometimes in the form μόνος θεός and other variations, [193] sometimes in the short form εἷς θεός, [194] or in the name, the Only One. [195] The sense of the formula also varies. On later inscriptions it perhaps has apotropaic significance. [196] In the Sib. and other Hell. pseudepigrapha it has a polemical and propagandist ring. [197] In Jos. Ant., 3, 91 the statement θεός ἐστιν εἷς is seen to contain the content of the first commandment. The original meaning is most vitally preserved where there is greatest fidelity to the original form, e.g., in the prayers of the synagogue, or in the schᵉma: "Hear, O Israel, the Lord thy God is one Lord." This is how those who confess the one and only God pray in the midst of a world which despises this God, which persecutes His people because of this confession, and which puts its leaders to death. Hence the uniqueness of God is often brought into juxtaposition with the uniqueness of the people of God. Both belong together. [198] One day God will be the only God for the whole earth. [199] Now He is so only for Israel. [200] There is a readiness to die for the confession of His uniqueness. This is shown in the faithfulness of Rabbi Akiba, who acc. to tradition was brought to the place of execution at the time of the reading of the schᵉma, and who murmured the words of Dt. 6:4 throughout his tortures, breathing his last on the decisive אחד. [201] The oneness of God as orthodox Judaism understood it was not just a point of doctrine. It was a confession. For in Jewish thinking it referred, not to God in Himself, but to God for us.

c. Theocentric thinking is safeguarded even in later Jewish conceptions of intermediary and angelic beings. Indeed, it reaches its full force in this thinking. We encounter a plenitude of hypostases in apocal. and Philo: [202] God's Word, Spirit, truth, glory, presence, Law, name, dwelling etc. But they are not independent magnitudes alongside God. They cannot dispute His rank. They are subordinate to Him. They are His instruments or deputies in creation and history. The Word is His Word, the Spirit His Spirit, no less inconceivable without Him than is daylight without the sun.

God acts with and through the hosts of His angels, which in later Judaism often take the place of the OT אלהים (→ n. 181). From Daniel to the Heb. Enoch[203] these

---

[190] Jos. Ant., 5, 112: θεὸν ἕνα γινώσκειν τὸν Ἑβραίοις ἅπασι κοινόν.

[191] Cf. Str.-B., II, 28 ff. (on Mk. 12:29).

[192] With two members in parallelism, Zech. 14:9: ἐν τῇ ἡμέρᾳ ἐκείνῃ ἔσται κύριος εἷς καὶ τὸ ὄνομα αὐτοῦ ἕν. But also Jos. Ap., 2, 193: εἷς ναὸς ἑνὸς θεοῦ. Three members: one God, one Israel, one temple, or one God, one name, one Israel, ERE, VI, 295.

[193] Da. 3:45; Philo Leg. All., II, 1 f.; Jos. Ant., 8, 335: ὃς μόνος ἐστὶ θεός, 8, 337: θεὸν ἀληθῆ καὶ μόνον.

[194] Jos. Ant., 4, 201; Peterson, Εἷς Θεός, 277, 281 f. (with βοήθῃ), 285 ff.

[195] Damasc., passim יחיד (e.g., 20, 1); Apc. Abr. 17.

[196] So Peterson, op. cit., 280 ff.

[197] Eus. Praep. Ev., XIII, 12, 1 f. (Aristobul.); XIII, 12, 5 (Ps.-Orpheus); XIII, 13, 40 (Ps.-Soph.). Sib., 3, 11; 718; 760.

[198] → n. 192. ERE, VI, 295. Cf. the saying of Akiba: "God has redeemed himself when he redeemed Israel" (Bacher, Tannaiten, I², 281).

[199] Tg. J. I on Ex. 17:15 f.: "... when idolatry is rooted out, when God is alone in the world and his kingdom is established for all eternity ... then the Eternal will be one, and his name one" (Bacher, op. cit., 142).

[200] Cf. formulae like ὁ θεὸς τοῦ πατρός σου, θεὸς Ἀβραὰμ καὶ θεὸς Ἰσαὰκ καὶ θεὸς Ἰακώβ in Ex. 3:6; θεός σου in Dt. 6:5, 13, 16. M. Ex. on 13:3: "Our God, and the God of our fathers, the God of Abraham, the God of Isaac and the God of Jacob." Jos. Ant., 9, 20: ὁ τῶν Ἑβραίων θεός; 9, 21: ὁ Ἰσραηλιτῶν θεός. Cf. also Baudissin, Kyrios, III, 675 ff.

[201] → I, 42; II, 526; II, 801.

[202] S. Mowinckel, Art. Hypostase in RGG², II, 2065 ff.; Bousset-Gressm., 342 ff.

[203] The chief figure in Heb. En. (passim) is the angel Metatron, who is closest to the thone of God. In Jeb., 16b he is called "the prince of the world." → θρόνος, n. 30.

gain steadily in numbers and importance. The angels, too, are instruments of God. But they are not involuntary, like the hypostases. They are free and independent creatures with wills of their own. But they have completely integrated their wills into the will of God. Daily they receive orders and execute them with blind obedience. It may sometimes happen that their hearts are heavy, or even that they assail God with petitions, but this in itself shows us that God has the last word. They can proclaim God's will in the first person, but they do so in the name of God. They can be called "Lord," [204] but only as God's representatives. [205] In all that they are and do, they refer back to the one and only God. They can represent men before God, but they do not accept the worship of men. This belongs to God alone. And in an extreme emergency their mediatorship between God and man is of no avail. "If distress comes on a man, he must not call on Michael or Gabriel, but he must call upon me, and I will answer him," says the one God. [206]

d. Satan, who was originally an angel closely linked with God (→ διάβολος), becomes an independent force in later Judaism. He abuses the freedom which God gives him, revolts against God and demands divine worship (Vit. Ad., 14; Mt. 4:9). A host of demons stands in his service. Does this destroy monotheism? By no means, for Satan is a creature of God, and his rebellion ends with a fearful fall from heaven. He is still powerful, but his operations are held in check by God, and in the last days he will be finally destroyed (Jub. 23:29; 50:5). Above all, whatever demonic powers attempt against God in the intervening period will finally serve to advance God's plans and to bring about their own ruin. For in His superior power and wisdom God directs their evil action to a good end. Thus the demons themselves tremble before the εἷς θεός. [207] This implies the rejection both of a mechanical monotheism and of a static dualism. [208] Both are overcome by a dynamic monotheism.

e. Apocalyptic also speaks of the great leader whom God will send to meet all the forces arrayed against Him. This is the Saviour King of the last time, the Son of Man or the Messiah. [209] In natural subjection to the will of God, He fulfils His task with the same unreserved devotion as loyal angels display in the discharge of their ministry. [210] Whether He be a heavenly [211] or an earthly [212] being, He is certainly the representative of God, no more and no less. He is no more, for He is not called God, nor is He revered nor worshipped as God. But He is also no less, for He is armed by God with a power to which all hostile powers must submit. Thus the Saviour King is the decisive representative of God, not replacing Him, but representing Him, and in the name of God causing the divine glory, honour and uniqueness to be acknowledged throughout the world. The dynamic monotheism of Jewish apocalyptic found its most forceful expression in expectation of the Saviour King.

---

[204] So the angelus interpres in 4 Esr. (passim).

[205] They are not called θεοί, but υἱοὶ θεοῦ, → n. 181.

[206] Judan in jBer., 13a, 69-71.

[207] Peterson, op. cit., 280, 296 ff. suggests an apotropaic use of the εἷς θεός formula.

[208] The Rabbis also rejected, of course, the kind of dualism found in Marcion, v. S. Dt. § 329 (p. 139b, Friedmann) in A. Marmorstein, EJ, VII (1931), 564.

[209] Bibl. on both in P. Feine, Theologie⁶ (1934), 44, 56; → Χριστός, → υἱὸς τοῦ ἀνθρώπου.

[210] The Messiah as the Son of God, v. Str.-B., I, 11; cf. III, 17, 19 ff., 673 ff. → υἱός.

[211] Cf. Da. 7:13.

[212] The Rabbis laid particular stress on the non-metaphysical character of the "son" concept, and on the humanity of the Messiah, in their debate with Christianity, v. Str.-B., II, 335 ff.; → ἐγώ, II, 348.

c. θεοί in the New Testament.

The NT gives us in Ac. a colourful picture of the polytheistic impulse encountered by the apostles. In Ephesus flourishes the cult of Artemis, τῆς μεγάλης θεᾶς (Ac. 19:27; cf. 26, 37), and the fashioning of little silver temples (→ ναός) is an important industry. In Athens Paul comes up against an altar with the inscription ἀγνώστῳ θεῷ (Ac. 17:23). In Caesarea Herod causes himself to be acclaimed and honoured as God : θεοῦ φωνὴ καὶ οὐκ ἀνθρώπου.[213] In Malta Paul himself is regarded as a god because he does not succumb to the bite of the viper (Ac. 28:6). In Lystra he works a miracle along with Barnabas, and the crowd shouts : οἱ θεοὶ ὁμοιωθέντες ἀνθρώποις κατέβησαν πρὸς ἡμᾶς. ἐκάλουν τε τὸν Βαρναβᾶν Δία, τὸν δὲ Παῦλον Ἑρμῆν, ἐπειδὴ αὐτὸς ἦν ὁ ἡγούμενος τοῦ λόγου. ὅ τε ἱερεὺς τοῦ Διὸς τοῦ ὄντος πρὸ τῆς πόλεως ταύρους καὶ στέμματα ἐπὶ τοὺς πυλῶνας ἐνέγκας σὺν τοῖς ὄχλοις ἤθελεν θύειν (Ac. 14:11 ff.). But Paul and Barnabas intervene : καὶ ἡμεῖς ὁμοιοπαθεῖς ἐσμεν ὑμῖν ἄνθρωποι (Ac. 14:15). To Herod's self-glorification God Himself makes answer παραχρῆμα, smiting him with a loathsome and fatal disease (Ac. 12:23). In Ac. 17 Paul says concerning the altar inscription : ὃ οὖν ἀγνοοῦντες εὐσεβεῖτε, τοῦτο ἐγὼ καταγγέλλω ὑμῖν (17:23 f.). The message of the one true God necessarily goes hand in hand with conflict against idolatry in Athens,[214] Lystra,[215] and Ephesus.[216]

Paul refers to polytheism in the same way in his epistles : οὐκ εἰδότες θεὸν ἐδουλεύσατε τοῖς φύσει μὴ οὖσιν θεοῖς.[217] Idols are nothing in themselves (1 C. 8:4; 10:19). Idolatry, however, is not an indifferent matter. It is a sin (1 C. 10:7; Ac. 7:40 ff.; 1 Jn. 5:21). For it involves a failure to worship the one true God, and it inevitably leads to bondage to demonic powers :[218] ἃ θύουσιν, δαιμονίοις καὶ οὐ θεῷ θύουσιν· οὐ θέλω δὲ ὑμᾶς κοινωνοὺς τῶν δαιμονίων γίνεσθαι.[219] This is what gives Paul's battle against idolatry its seriousness and what distinguishes it from the rationalistic arguments of Hellenism. There are not only so-called gods ; there are also real demonic forces which have brought the heathen under their power and which constantly threaten Christians too (cf. 2 C. 4:4) — θεοὶ πολλοί. But these are not gods for us. For us there is only one God (1 C. 8:5 f.): εἴπερ εἰσὶν λεγόμενοι θεοὶ εἴτε ἐν οὐρανῷ εἴτε ἐπὶ γῆς, ὥσπερ εἰσὶν θεοὶ πολλοί ... ἀλλ' ἡμῖν εἷς θεός.

---

[213] Ac. 12:22. Similar motifs under the influence of Da. 11:36 f. etc. are to be found in 2 Th. 2:4 concerning the coming Antichrist : ὁ ἀντικείμενος καὶ ὑπεραιρόμενος ἐπὶ πάντα λεγόμενον θεὸν ἢ σέβασμα, ὥστε αὐτὸν εἰς τὸν ναὸν τοῦ θεοῦ καθίσαι, ἀποδεικνύντα ἑαυτὸν ὅτι ἐστὶν θεός. → ἄθεος, 120. But cf. Jn. 10:34 ff., where the θεοί ἐστε of Ps. 82:6 is acknowledged and given a christological evaluation.
[214] Ac. 17:24 f.: οὐκ ἐν χειροποιήτοις ναοῖς κατοικεῖ, οὐδὲ ὑπὸ χειρῶν ἀνθρωπίνων θεραπεύεται.
[215] Ac. 14:15 : εὐαγγελιζόμενοι ὑμᾶς ἀπὸ τούτων τῶν ματαίων ἐπιστρέφειν ἐπὶ θεὸν ζῶντα.
[216] Ac. 19:26 : ὁ Παῦλος οὗτος πείσας μετέστησεν ἱκανὸν ὄχλον, λέγων ὅτι οὐκ εἰσὶν θεοὶ οἱ διὰ χειρῶν γινόμενοι. The sharpness of the polemic is wrongly blunted again in 19:37: ἠγάγετε τοὺς ἄνδρας τούτους οὔτε ἱεροσύλους οὔτε βλασφημοῦντας τὴν θεὸν (D* : θεὰν) ἡμῶν.
[217] Gl. 4:8 f.; 1 Th. 1:9 : ἐπεστρέψατε πρὸς τὸν θεὸν ἀπὸ τῶν εἰδώλων δουλεύειν θεῷ ζῶντι καὶ ἀληθινῷ. 1 Th. 4:5 : τὰ ἔθνη τὰ μὴ εἰδότα τὸν θεόν, quoting Jer. 10:25.
[218] Gl. 4:8; R. 1:23, 25; Eph. 2:2.
[219] 1 C. 10:20 ff., cf. 10:7, 14. On this pt. cf. H. Gressmann, Ἡ κοινωνία τῶν δαιμονίων, ZNW, 20 (1921), 224-230.

d. Εἷς θεός in the Confession and Practice of Early Christianity.

According to Mk. 12:29 f. Jesus Himself quotes the sch^ema : "Ακουε, 'Ισραήλ, κύριος ὁ θεὸς ἡμῶν κύριος εἷς ἐστιν. The scribe can only endorse this confession of the faith of the fathers, again in words taken from the OT : εἷς ἐστιν καὶ οὐκ ἔστιν ἄλλος πλὴν αὐτοῦ (Mk. 12:32 f.; cf. 10:18). Elsewhere, too, the men of the NT [220] mostly think of the traditional formulae when they speak of the εἷς θεός [221] or μόνος θεός. [222] Monotheism is a firm part of the tradition, and therefore confession of the one God can be introduced by πιστεύειν ὅτι (Jm. 2:19; Hb. 11:6) or even εἰδέναι ὅτι (1 C. 8:4 : οἴδαμεν ... ὅτι οὐδεὶς θεὸς εἰ μὴ εἷς). Nevertheless, there is awareness in the NT, too, that recognition of this one God has not penetrated to all parts of the world, so that in a special sense God is the God of His own people. There are θεοὶ πολλοὶ καὶ κύριοι πολλοί (→ 100) ἀλλ' ἡμῖν εἷς θεός (1 C. 8:5). Hence the men of the NT favour the ancient formulae which speak of the God of the fathers, [223] of Israel, [224] of Abraham, Isaac and Jacob, [225] or even, in OT fashion, of our God [226] or my God. [227] The former promises are now fulfilled : ἔσομαι αὐτῶν θεός, καὶ αὐτοὶ ἔσονταί μου λαός. [228] As God was once the God of the ancient people of God, [229] so He is now ὁ θεὸς τῆς ἐκκλησίας. [230]

In this Church, however, there is need not merely to believe that God is one, as the devils also do (Jm. 2:19, cf. Hb. 11:6), but also to believe in God. [231] There is need not merely to believe that God repays (Hb. 11:6), but also to hope in God. [232] There is need not merely of knowledge of God but of the control of the will by a passionate zeal for Him (cf. R. 3:11; 10:2). Finally, there is need not merely of a clear realisation that God cannot be hindered (Ac. 11:17) but also of a realisation that God is not to be tempted. [233] Only in this faith and hope, this zeal and rest, can there be a living confession of the oneness of God.

In its outworking, however, this monotheistic confession implies a wholly new seriousness in relation to the first commandment. For only thus can it be shown whether the one God is really God, whether He is truly the one God for those who confess Him. They are not to have any gods alongside Him, whether mammon, [234] the belly, [235] idols, [236] the forces of the cosmos (Gl. 4:8 ff.), local author-

---

[220] On the form and use of this formula in the early Church, cf. Peterson, *op. cit.*, 1 ff.
[221] R. 3:29 f.; Gl. 3:20; Eph. 4:6; 1 Tm. 2:5, cf. Jn. 8:41.
[222] 1 Tm. 1:17; Jd. 25; Jn. 17:3 : μόνον ἀληθινὸν θεόν, R. 16:27: μόνῳ σοφῷ θεῷ.
[223] Ac. 3:13; 5:30; 22:14.
[224] Mt. 15:31; Lk. 1:68, cf. Lk. 1:16; Ac. 13:17; 2 C. 6:16; Hb. 11:16.
[225] Ac. 3:13; 7:32; Mt. 22:32; Mk. 12:26; Lk. 20:37.
[226] Mk. 12:29; Lk. 1:78; Ac. 2:39; Rev. 4:11; 2 Pt. 1:1; Rev. 7:12; 19:5.
[227] Lk. 1:47; R. 1:8; 2 C. 12:21; Phil. 1:3; 4:19; Phlm. 4; Rev. 3:12; cf. "thy God," Mt. 4:7; 22:37; Mk. 12:30; Lk. 4:8; 10:27.
[228] 2 C. 6:16b, cf. Hb. 8:10b; Rev. 21:7, 3.
[229] Jn. 8:41 f.; Ac. 13:17; Hb. 11:16.
[230] Ac. 20:28, cf. Lk. 7:16; Ac. 15:14; Hb. 4:9; 11:25; 1 Pt. 2:10.
[231] R. 4:3; Gl. 3:6; Jm. 2:23; Tt. 3:8; Hb. 6:1; 1 Pt. 1:21; Ac. 27:25.
[232] 1 Pt. 1:21; 3:5; Ac. 24:15; R. 4:18; 2 C. 3:4.
[233] Mt. 4:7; Ac. 15:10; 1 C. 10:9, 22 → πειράζειν.
[234] Mt. 6:24 : οὐ δύνασθε θεῷ δουλεύειν καὶ μαμωνᾷ. Cf. Mk. 10:21; Ac. 5.
[235] Lk. 12:19 ff. (οὕτως ὁ θησαυρίζων αὐτῷ καὶ μὴ εἰς θεὸν πλουτῶν, v. 21); Phil. 3:19 (ὧν ὁ θεὸς ἡ κοιλία). Moses censures the Israelites : τὴν ἡδονὴν προτιμήσαντες τοῦ θεοῦ καὶ τοῦ κατὰ τοῦτον βίου (Jos. Ant., 4, 143).
[236] 2 C. 6:16 : τίς δὲ συγκατάθεσις ναῷ θεοῦ μετὰ εἰδώλων; 1 C. 10:21: οὐ δύνασθε τραπέζης κυρίου μετέχειν καὶ τραπέζης δαιμονίων, cf. 1 Th. 1:9; 1 C. 12:2 etc.

ity, [237] or the emperor in Rome. [238] It is necessary to serve God, to give God what is His, to obey Him and to build on Him alone, to be faithful to Him through every threat even to the point of martyrdom. This is the meaning of the εἷς θεός according to Jesus and early Christianity. Monotheism can be taken for granted as a confession in the NT, but its practice is a task which is ever new.

e. God and His Angels in the New Testament.

Angelic beings (→ I, 83 ff.) do not play so great as role in the NT as in later Judaism. God has sent them (Ac. 12:11), they come ἀπὸ τοῦ θεοῦ, He acts through them (Ac. 7:35; Rev. 1:1), they fulfil His commands with His omnipotent power. [239] They are in every respect executive organs of the divine will.

They have nothing of their own in independence of the divine power.

Hence the oneness of God is not affected by the idea of angels. [240] The ἄγγελος θεοῦ is nothing without God and everything in His name. He will not allow the divine to fall down before him : ὅρα μή· σύνδουλός σού εἰμι ... τῷ θεῷ προσκύνησον (Rev. 19:10).

f. Monotheism and Christology in the New Testament.

Early Christian monotheism is confirmed rather than shattered by the Christology of the NT. For by His coming Christ deprives the prince of the world of his power.

According to the Gospels Jesus Himself sharpens the monotheistic confession. He rejects the address διδάσκαλε ἀγαθέ with the explanation : οὐδεὶς ἀγαθὸς εἰ μὴ εἷς ὁ θεός (Mk. 10:18). He takes obedience to God more seriously than any before or after Him. Even His enemies must agree that He cares for no man, [241] and they mock at Him for building on God in vain. [242] The zeal of God's house consumes Him. [243] He consults God alone in all decisions and actions. He prays to Him in His most difficult hours, and even in the cry or dereliction : "My God." [244] God is God for Him as for none else. He never calls Him "our Father." He makes an emphatic distinction : τὸν πατέρα μου καὶ πατέρα ὑμῶν καὶ θεόν μου καὶ θεὸν ὑμῶν (Jn. 20:17). God is His Father, and He the Son, absolutely.

As the Son of God He has ἐξουσία (→ II, 568). He has the power to remit sins, which according to Jewish tradition God alone enjoyed. [245] He will sit on the throne of God and judge the world. [246] He appropriates the offices and to

---

[237] Ac. 4:19; 5:29 : πειθαρχεῖν δεῖ θεῷ μᾶλλον ἢ ἀνθρώποις.

[238] Mk. 12:17: τὰ Καίσαρος ἀπόδοτε Καίσαρι καὶ τὰ τοῦ θεοῦ τῷ θεῷ.

[239] Rev. 18:1: ἐξουσία, Rev. 6:4; 8:2 : ἐδόθη.

[240] On such questions as fallen angels, Satan etc. → 99.

[241] Mk. 12:14 : οὐ μέλει σοι περὶ οὐδενός, ... ἀλλ' ἐπ' ἀληθείας τὴν ὁδὸν τοῦ θεοῦ διδάσκεις.

[242] Mt. 27:43 : πέποιθεν ἐπὶ τὸν θεόν, ῥυσάσθω νῦν, εἰ θέλει αὐτόν, words based on the scorning of the martyr and his πίστις in Ps. 22:8; Wis. 2:13.

[243] Jn. 2:17: ὁ ζῆλος τοῦ οἴκου σου καταφάγεταί με, from the martyr psalm, 69:9.

[244] Lk. 6:12; Mk. 14:35 ff.; Mk. 15:34 : ὁ θεός μου ..., from the complaint of the martyr, Ps. 22:1.

[245] Mk. 2:7: βλασφημεῖ· τίς δύναται ἀφιέναι ἁμαρτίας εἰ μὴ εἷς ὁ θεός (Lk. 5:21: μόνος ὁ θεός).

[246] R. 14:10 (βῆμα τοῦ θεοῦ); 2 C. 5:10 (βῆμα τοῦ Χριστοῦ); both together in 1 C. 4:4 f. Cf. the saying : "As I find you, so will I judge you," which in Jewish Apocalyptic is a saying of God, but which is a saying of the Lord in Christian tradition. V. Cl. Al. Quis Div. Salv., 40, 2 and Hennecke, 35.

some degree the names (e.g., Logos) of intermediary beings, and in their place He is the Mediator of creation [247] and of salvation history (1 C. 10:4; Hb. 1:1). He stands high and predominant above the angels (→ I, 84 f.). [248]

Jesus wages God's battle against the prince of this world, who constantly attacks Him from the first to the last of His activity, and indeed of His life (Lk. 22:28). Εἰς τοῦτο ἐφανερώθη ὁ υἱὸς τοῦ θεοῦ, ἵνα λύσῃ τὰ ἔργα τοῦ διαβόλου (1 Jn. 3:8). From the very first He refuses to worship him, and He resists his temptations with a threefold reference to God and His exclusive claim. He enters the house of the strong man and hurls him from his throne. [249] He drives out demons with the finger of God and rules them with the power of God. [250] ἔρχεται γὰρ ὁ τοῦ κόσμου ἄρχων· καὶ ἐν ἐμοὶ οὐκ ἔχει οὐδέν (Jn. 14:30). The opponent of God seems to win only one victory over his invincible enemy, namely, at the cross (Lk. 22:53). But the crushing blow recoils on himself (1 C. 2:8). Satan is judged, and the victory of the βασιλεία τοῦ θεοῦ is assured. Thus in and with Jesus the sole dominion of the εἷς θεός is established rather than challenged (1 C. 15:28).

The unique relationship herein displayed between God and Jesus, His Representative, is expressed in many different ways in the NT. God has named (προσαγορεύω, Hb. 5:10), sent (→ ἀποστέλλω, I, 404; Jn. 3:34; Ac. 7:35), brought (ἄγω, Ac. 13:23; vl. ἐγείρω: C D sy, from v. 22), made (ποιέω, Ac. 2:36), instituted (→ ὁρίζω, Ac. 10:42), accredited (ἀποδείκνυμι, Ac. 2:22), confirmed (→ σφραγίζω, Jn. 6:27), anointed (→ χρίω, Hb. 1:9), and exalted Jesus (→ ὑψόω, Ac. 5:31; ὑπερυψόω, Phil. 2:9). Jesus comes from God, ἐκ (Jn. 8:42; 16:28), παρά (Jn. 9:16, 33; 16:27), ἀπὸ θεοῦ (Jn. 3:2; 13:3). God is with Him (Mt. 1:23; Jn. 3:2). He works in Him. [251] He gives Him all power. [252] "God was in Christ, reconciling the world unto himself." [253] Indeed, ἐν αὐτῷ κατοικεῖ πᾶν τὸ πλήρωμα τῆς θεότητος σωματικῶς. [254] He returns πρὸς τὸν θεόν (Jn. 13:3; 17:11). In Jn's Gospel faith in God and faith in Christ are thus one and the same thing. "He that hath seen me hath seen the Father." "I and the Father are one." [255]

The most important formulae, however, are the least noticeable. In Mal. 3:1 God promises a forerunner who will prepare His way: ἰδοὺ ἐξαποστέλλω τὸν ἄγγελόν μου, καὶ ἐπιβλέψεται ὁδὸν πρὸ προσώπου μου. In Mk. 1:2 this saying of God is made into a promise to Jesus that He will have a forerunner to prepare His way: ἰδοὺ ἀποστέλλω τὸν ἄγγελόν μου πρὸ προσώπου σου, ὃς κατασκευάσει τὴν ὁδόν σου. The μου after προσώπου is changed into a σου, [256] so that in this whole question of a forerunner the reference is to Jesus instead of God. In, with and under Jesus, God Himself comes. In the Synoptists, and especially in John, Jesus also uses the divine I. He can even use ἐγώ εἰμι without a

---

[247] 1 C. 8:6; Jn. 1:3; Hb. 1:2b; Col. 1:16 f.

[248] Phil. 2:10 f.; Col. 1:19; 2:10; 2 Th. 1:7; Mk. 1:13; 13:27; Jn. 1:51; Mt. 26:53; Lk. 22:43; Mk. 8:38; 1 Pt. 3:22; Hb. 1:4 ff. etc.

[249] Mk. 3:27; Lk. 10:18; Jn. 12:31; 16:11.

[250] Lk. 11:20 : ἐν δακτύλῳ θεοῦ → II, 626. The demon itself says : ὁρκίζω σε τὸν θεόν, Mk. 5:7.

[251] Eph. 4:32 : θεὸς ἐν Χριστῷ ἐχαρίσατο ἡμῖν.

[252] Mt. 28:18; Jn. 3:35; 5:22; 13:3; Eph. 1:21.

[253] 2 C. 5:19 : θεὸς ἦν ἐν Χριστῷ κόσμον καταλλάσσων ἑαυτῷ. The nomin. θεός has no article, and is thus predicative.

[254] Col. 2:9; cf. 1:19 → θεότης.

[255] Jn. 14:1, 9; 10:30; 17:11, 21 f.

[256] Cf. also Lk. 7:27; Mt. 11:10.

predicate, which is the self-declaration of God in the OT (→ ἐγώ, II, 352). In 1 C. 4:4 f. Christ is first the Judge and then God. In R. 5:8 there is a similar change of subject from God to Christ: συνίστησιν ... τὴν ἑαυτοῦ ἀγάπην ... ὁ θεός, ὅτι ... Χριστὸς ... ἀπέθανεν. In R. 11:36 it is said of God: ἐξ αὐτοῦ καὶ δι' αὐτοῦ καὶ εἰς αὐτὸν τὰ πάντα; in 1 C. 8:6 the δι' οὗ τὰ πάντα is referred to Christ, whereas the ἐξ and εἰς are still said of God, and in Col. 1:16 the final εἰς is also referred to Christ. In Rev. 1:13 ff. the appearance of the Son of Man (Jesus) is described in terms taken from the depiction of the Most High (God) in Da. 7, and I-formulae such as ἐγώ εἰμι ὁ πρῶτος καὶ ὁ ἔσχατος are sometimes put on the lips of God and sometimes on the lips of Jesus (→ ἐγώ, II, 351). In these various ways the very highest is said of Jesus that can be said. He takes over the functions of God, and represents Him to the greatest possible extent.

But He does not crowd Him out. This is confirmed by many statements of relationship which may be found alongside the formulae quoted. God is ὁ θεὸς τοῦ κυρίου ἡμῶν Ἰησοῦ Χριστοῦ (Eph. 1:17), His κεφαλή (1 C. 11:3), His → πατήρ (Jn. 5:18). We learn that the Pre-existent was ἐν μορφῇ θεοῦ, [257] but that He resisted the temptation to seize equality. [258] The Post-existent is again exalted to the right hand of God. [259] The reference back to the εἷς θεός is perhaps expressed most simply and plainly in the statement that Christ is of God (1 C. 3:23). The gen. τοῦ θεοῦ, which elsewhere in the NT refers things and events to God as their final Author and decisive origin (cf. Col. 2:19; 1 Th. 4:16; Rev. 2:7), gives plain expression to the fact that Christ belongs unconditionally to the θεός, ἐξ οὗ τὰ πάντα.

The titles of dignity, which the NT uses to express His significance and work, also characterise Him as the Representative of God: ἅγιος (→ I, 102), → ἐκλεκτός, → χριστός, → υἱός, → μονογενής, → μεσίτης, εἰκών (→ II, 395), ἄρτος, ἀμνός (→ I, 338), ἀρνίον (→ I, 341), → ἀρχιερεύς, [260] etc. They are given absolute signification by the use of the article, e.g., ὁ ἅγιος, and they thus denote the uniqueness of Jesus. But the use of the *Theos* genitive keeps them in line with the designations of relationship to which we referred above. The person and work of Jesus are still referred back to the εἷς θεός: ὁ Χριστὸς τοῦ θεοῦ. [261]

There is one title, however, which by its specific nature does not allow of this genitive, namely, κύριος. This is the most important of all, for it is the chief title and the representative name of God in the OT and apocalyptic, and the absolute name of God in the LXX. This name is now transferred from God to Christ. Is the term θεός also used of Christ in the NT?

g. Christ as θεός in Early Christianity.

To the statement of Jesus: ἐγὼ καὶ ὁ πατὴρ ἕν ἐσμεν, the Jews answer with the accusation (Jn. 10:30 ff.): σὺ ἄνθρωπος ὢν ποιεῖς σεαυτὸν θεόν (→ II, 350). Jesus then shows them from the θεοί ἐστε of Ps. 82:6 that to use this term of men is not inconsistent with biblical thinking, so that a title which seems to be

---

[257] Phil. 2:6, though cf. Jn. 1:1; 1:18.
[258] Phil. 2:6, though cf. Jn. 5:18; A. Nock, *Harvard Theological Review*, 23 (1930), 261 f.
[259] R. 8:34: ὅς ἐστιν ἐν δεξιᾷ τοῦ θεοῦ, → δεξιός, II, 39.
[260] Hb. 2:17: πιστὸς ἀρχιερεὺς τὰ πρὸς τὸν θεόν, cf. 5:1.
[261] ὁ ἅγιος τοῦ θεοῦ in Mk. 1:24; Jn. 6:69; ὁ Χριστὸς τοῦ θεοῦ in Lk. 9:20; ὁ Χριστὸς τοῦ θεοῦ ὁ ἐκλεκτός in Lk. 23:35; ἀμνὸς τοῦ θεοῦ in Jn. 1:29; ἄρτος τοῦ θεοῦ in Jn. 6:33; εἰκὼν τοῦ θεοῦ in 2 C. 4:4.

applied to men in Ps. 82 (→ 96) cannot be denied in principle to the Holy One who is sent by God. But the only title which He himself claims, of course, is that of υἱὸς τοῦ θεοῦ. In Hb. 1:8 f. the way which is entered here is trodden to the very end, and an OT *Theos* predication is applied typologically to the υἱός — the twofold ὁ θεός of Ps. 45:7 f., which in the psalm is addressed to the divinely anointed king (→ 96): ὁ θρόνος σου, ὁ θεός, εἰς τὸν αἰῶνα, and διὰ τοῦτο ἔχρισέν σε, ὁ θεός, ὁ θεός σου. Thus the supreme OT designation of office is transferred to Christ, and ¡Christ is exalted to be the only legitimate bearer of this title. Moreover, Christ is also called θεός quite independently of OT sayings and concepts.

Paul is probably making a start when in R. 9:4 f. he lists the advantages of Israel in salvation history, and at the end he says: ἐξ ὧν ὁ Χριστὸς τὸ κατὰ σάρκα, ὁ ὢν ἐπὶ πάντων θεὸς εὐλογητὸς εἰς τοὺς αἰῶνας, ἀμήν. It is most probable that the final clause ὁ ὢν ... is to be understood in apposition to the last preceding nominative, i.e., ὁ Χριστός. If so, Christ is not only called *Theos*, but He is also the subject of a sonorous benediction normally reserved in Judaism, and in Paul himself, for God alone. [262]

From the time of Eus. attempts have been made to avoid the implied difficulty by stronger punctuation after σάρκα. [263] This gives an independent doxology to God the Father. But this is a typical attempt at softening, and though it is formally unobjectionable it is materially no more reliable than the ἀμήν which a later scribe added to strengthen the break. Others try to avoid offence by a slight change in the order. They put ΩΝΟ for ΟΩΝ, and then instead of ὧν οἱ πατέρες they read the like-sounding ὧν ὁ ἐπὶ πάντων θεός ... But this formally brilliant conjecture is shattered materially by R. 3:29, where Paul expressly declares that God is not just the God of the Jews. Hence the reference of the concluding benediction to Christ, which is syntactically the most likely, is still the best. It is finally confirmed by the morphological observation that Paul is here speaking of Christ in the current schema of the διπλοῦν κήρυγμα. In R. 1:3 f. he calls Christ the Son of David κατὰ σάρκα and the Son of God κατὰ πνεῦμα. In R. 9:5 he has spoken of Christ as the Son of Israel κατὰ σάρκα, and he now logically pursues his thinking in that schema to the final conclusion of calling Him the θεός who is over all things. [264]

Nevertheless, this ascription of divine majesty is isolated in Paul, [265] and open to question. A similar ascription is more common in the Johannine writings, and for the most part incontestable. Jn. 1:1 says of the Pre-existent: καὶ θεὸς ἦν ὁ λόγος. In Jn. 1:18 the best MSS and the older fathers [266] have: μονογενὴς θεὸς ... ἐκεῖνος ἐξηγήσατο, which is difficult, but which is to be maintained for this very reason. The lack of article, which is grammatically necessary in 1:1, [267] is striking here, and reminds us of Philonic usage (→ n. 114). The Logos who became flesh

---

[262] Cf. R. 1:25: The Creator, ὅς ἐστιν εὐλογητὸς εἰς τοὺς αἰῶνας. 2 C. 11:31: God the Father, ὁ ὢν εὐλογητὸς εἰς τοὺς αἰῶνας. Eph. 4:6: εἷς θεός ... ὁ ἐπὶ πάντων.

[263] Or at the very latest after πάντων, though this seems to conflict with Eph. 4:6.

[264] The same twofold schema as the framework of *Theos* predication is to be found in Ign. Eph., 7, 2; 18, 2, → 106.

[265] We can hardly adduce 2 Th. 1:12: κατὰ τὴν χάριν τοῦ θεοῦ ἡμῶν καὶ κυρίου Ἰησοῦ Χριστοῦ. The first attribute (θεός) is separated from the second by ἡμῶν, and therefore it is not to be related to Christ (like κύριος).

[266] For further details cf. Cr.-Kö., 489 f.

[267] On the predicative use cf. Jn. 8:54; 2 C. 5:19; Jos. Ant., 10, 61: ἵνα πεισθῶσιν ὅτι θεός ἐστιν.

and revealed the invisible God was a divine being, God by nature. The man born blind has some sense of this when, after his healing, he falls down in believing adoration before Christ, who addresses him with the divine "I" (Jn. 9:38 f.). The final veil is removed, however, when the Risen Lord discloses Himself to Thomas, and the astonished disciple exclaims : ὁ κύριός μου καὶ ὁ θεός μου (Jn. 20:28). In Jn. 1:1 we have Christology : He is God in Himself. Here we have the revelation of Christ : He is God for believers. At the end of the First Epistle of John this faith is given the established form of a confession : οὗτός ἐστιν ὁ ἀληθινὸς θεός (1 Jn. 5:20).

Among other examples of the attributing of the term *Theos* to Christ we may mention Tt. 2:13, which speaks of the δόξα τοῦ μεγάλου θεοῦ καὶ σωτῆρος ἡμῶν Χριστοῦ Ἰησοῦ. [268] Presumably the cry Ὡσαννὰ τῷ θεῷ Δαυίδ, which is found alongside μαρὰν ἀθά in Did., 10, 6, also applies to Christ. [269] The statement in Pliny's letter (Ep. X, 96, 7, M. Schuster, 1933): *carmen Christo quasi deo dicere,* apparently bears witness to the addressing of Christ as θεός in liturgical usage. [270] Christ is also called θεός in several inscriptions in Syria and elsewhere. [271] The apocryphal writings know the designation, [272] and it finds its way into later texts of the NT. [273]

> Above all, Ignatius of Antioch bears witness and gives currency to this description of Christ as *Theos.* Within the schema of R. 9:5 he can say : ὁ γὰρ θεὸς ἡμῶν Ἰησοῦς ὁ Χριστὸς ἐκυοφορήθη ὑπὸ Μαρίας ... ἐκ σπέρματος μὲν Δαβίδ, πνεύματος δὲ ἁγίου. [274] Along the lines of Jn. 20:28 he emphasises the deity of Christ for believers. [275] We also find formal expressions like Ἰησοῦς Χριστὸς ὁ θεὸς ἡμῶν (R. prooem ; 3, 3), or simply Χριστὸς θεός, [276] or even θεός alone with unambiguous reference to Christ : πάθος θεοῦ μου (R., 6, 3). In many cases there is an undeniable tendency towards modalism. [277] But it is emphasised that He is sent by God [278] and that He returns to God. What takes place in relation to Him is κατ' οἰκονομίαν θεοῦ (Ign. Eph., 18, 2), and ἐν Χριστῷ we are ἐν ἑνότητι θεοῦ (Ign. Pol., 8, 3).

Thus the basic christological ideas of Paul and John are faithfully preserved. Christ is the Representative of God. But the Christology of the NT is carried to its logical conclusion with the thorough-going designation of Christ as θεός. He is not merely a Representative of God. He is *the* Representative of God in the world and in history. For He is instituted and equipped by God the Father. He is Himself the Bearer of the divine office.

---

[268] The two attributes are here linked by the concluding ἡμῶν, so that they both refer to Christ. On the other hand, in 2 Pt. 1:1, as in 2 Th. 1:12, the ἡμῶν separates the attributes : ἐν δικαιοσύνῃ τοῦ θεοῦ ἡμῶν καὶ σωτῆρος Ἰησοῦ Χριστοῦ.

[269] We can see from Mk. 12:36 f. that the early Church preferred to call Christ the Son of David. Did. is carrying this a step further.

[270] On invocation and worship of Christ, cf. 1 C. 1:2; Mart. Pol., 17, 3 etc.; Just. Apol., I, 6.

[271] V. Peterson, op. cit., 13.

[272] V. Hennecke[1] (1904), 78 : Abgar to Jesus : "Thou art either God Himself come down from heaven, or the Son of God." The former alternative leans in the direction of Patripassianism, → n. 273.

[273] Ac. 20:28, θεός ... διὰ τοῦ ἰδίου αἵματος.

[274] Eph., 18, 2, cf. 7, 2 : σαρκικός τε καὶ πνευματικός ... ἐν σαρκὶ γενόμενος θεός.

[275] Eph., 15, 3 : ἵνα ... αὐτὸς ᾖ ἐν ἡμῖν θεὸς ἡμῶν, ὅπερ καὶ ἔστιν καὶ φανήσεται.

[276] Ign. Sm., 10, 1; Tr., 7, 1; Sm., 1, 1: δοξάζω Ἰησοῦν Χριστὸν τὸν θεόν.

[277] Eph., 1, 1: ἐν αἵματι θεοῦ; 19, 3 : θεοῦ ἀνθρωπίνως φανερουμένου.

[278] Eph. prooem : ἐν θελήματι τοῦ πατρὸς καὶ Ἰησοῦ Χριστοῦ τοῦ θεοῦ ἡμῶν.

h. The Threefold Relation of God, Christ and Spirit.

From the very first early Christianity was concerned to express the mutual relation between God and Christ in twofold formulae which would give equal expression to the unity of the two on the one side and to their distinctness and individuality on the other. It was also felt necessary to establish the primacy of God over Christ.

The most common solution is to be found in the titles Father (→ πατήρ) and Son (→ υἱός), the uniqueness of the Son being emphasised by the addition → μονογενής. θεός and μονογενὴς θεός are found only in Jn. 1:18. The singularity of both can also be stressed by the twofold use of εἷς. Thus in 1 C. 8:6 [279] Paul says : ἡμῖν εἷς θεὸς ὁ πατήρ, ἐξ οὗ τὰ πάντα καὶ ἡμεῖς εἰς αὐτόν, καὶ εἷς κύριος Ἰησοῦς Χριστός, δι' οὗ τὰ πάντα καὶ ἡμεῖς δι' αὐτοῦ, and in 1 Tm. 2:5 we have : εἷς γὰρ θεός, εἷς καὶ μεσίτης θεοῦ καὶ ἀνθρώπων, ἄνθρωπος Χριστὸς Ἰησοῦς. Even in the threefold formula in Mt. 23:8-10 the reference seems to be simply to God and to Christ : εἷς ... διδάσκαλος, [280] ... εἷς ... πατὴρ ὁ οὐράνιος, ... καθηγητὴς ὑμῶν εἷς ὁ Χριστός.

Already the influence of Jewish models may be discerned. This is even clearer in the triadic formula, God, Christ, angel, [281] and especially in Rev. 1:4 f.: χάρις ὑμῖν καὶ εἰρήνη ἀπὸ ὁ ὢν καὶ ὁ ἦν καὶ ὁ ἐρχόμενος, καὶ ἀπὸ τῶν ἑπτὰ πνευμάτων, ἃ ἐνώπιον τοῦ θρόνου αὐτοῦ, καὶ ἀπὸ Ἰησοῦ Χριστοῦ, ὁ μάρτυς ὁ πιστός. But these formulae are isolated, and they are of little significance compared with the decisive triad of God, Christ, and the Spirit.

The Word, wisdom and other intermediaries, with their titles and offices, are either crowded out or taken over by the NT figure of Christ. But the Spirit retains His independence. He stands in a distinctive and special relation to God : ὁ δὲ κύριος τὸ πνεῦμά ἐστιν, as Paul can sometimes put it (2 C. 3:17), or πνεῦμα ὁ θεός, in the fundamental statement of Jn. (4:24). On the other hand, there is a certain significant interchangeability between Christ and the Spirit. In the Synoptic tradition the blaspheming of Jesus is equated with the sin against the Holy Ghost. [282] Later Jesus is said to be conceived of the Spirit. [283] In R. 8 it is sometimes the Spirit (v. 27) and sometimes Christ (v. 34) who does the work of intercession. According to 1 C. 6:17 the πιστός is ἓν πνεῦμα with Christ. In Jn. the earthly Christ is the bearer of the Spirit in full measure (3:34), but only with His exaltation is the Spirit released and transferred to the disciples. [284] The Spirit has a certain independence as the → παράκλητος (14:26; 15:26), but He is again

---

[279] On later development → n. 285.

[280] syc Byz here add ὁ Χριστός, and thus bring out the oldest and truest interpretation. F. Blass thinks of the heavenly διδάσκαλος in distinction from 10b, and he thus attains a certain justification of the threefold structure ; v. Nestle in the apparatus.

[281] Lk. 9:36 (Mk. 13:32); 1 Tm. 5:21.

[282] Mk. 3:29 f.: ὃς δ' ἂν βλασφημήσῃ εἰς τὸ πνεῦμα τὸ ἅγιον, ... ἔνοχος ἔσται αἰωνίου ἁμαρτήματος. ὅτι ἔλεγον· πνεῦμα ἀκάθαρτον ἔχει. The two larger Gospels (Mt. 12:32; Lk. 12:10) wrongly introduce a differentiation here, deducing from the sins against men which may be forgiven (Mk. 3:28) a forgivable sin against the Son of Man. Against this interpretation stands the threat which is found both in the Marcan tradition and in that of the sayings, and which finds fourfold attestation : ὃς ... ἐπαισχυνθῇ με ... καὶ ὁ υἱὸς τοῦ ἀνθρώπου ἐπαισχυνθήσεται αὐτόν, Mk. 8:38; cf. Lk. 9:26, also Lk. 12:9, Mt. 10:33.

[283] Lk. 1:35; Mt. 1:18; Ign. Eph., 18, 2 etc.

[284] Jn. 7:39; 20:22; → II, 536 f.

linked with Christ: ἐκ τοῦ ἐμοῦ λήμψεται (16:14). Finally, in 1 Jn. 2:1 Jesus Himself is called the παράκλητος πρὸς τὸν πατέρα. Thus in Jn. there is a final interchangeability of Christ and the Spirit, as in R. 8. In both, Christ takes precedence of the Spirit as God does of Christ.

Behind the individual relationships is the total context of salvation history as this may be seen most clearly and succinctly in Gl. 4:4 ff.: God first sends the Son, and then, to continue the work, τὸ πνεῦμα τοῦ υἱοῦ αὐτοῦ. The divine work of salvation is thus prosecuted in the historical threefold relation of Father, Son and Spirit.

This threefold relation soon found fixed expression in the triadic formulae κύριος, θεός, πνεῦμα in 2 C. 13:13, and πνεῦμα, κύριος, θεός in 1 C. 12:4-6.[285] The form πατήρ, υἱός, πνεῦμα is first found in the baptismal formula in Mt. 28:19; Did., 7, 1 and 3.[286]

Perhaps recollection of the many triads of the surrounding polytheistic world contributed to the formation of these threefold formulae.[287] More likely, however, is the influence of Jewish models. For in Judaism, as in the early Church, we find triadic formulae,[288] and even formulae with four or more members. Justin combines the triad God, Christ and angel, with that of Father, Son and Spirit, to produce the fourfold πατήρ, υἱός, ἄγγελοι, πνεῦμα (Apol., I, 6). Eph. 4:4 ff. has ἓν σῶμα, ἓν πνεῦμα and μία ἐλπίς, and then εἷς κύριος, μία πίστις, ἓν βάπτισμα and εἷς θεός. This is even more complicated than the formula in S. Bar. 85:14: One law through one, one world, one end. In 1 Cl., 46, 6: ἕνα θεὸν ἔχομεν καὶ ἕνα Χριστὸν καὶ ἓν πνεῦμα — καὶ μία κλῆσις, the narrower triad is more clearly distinguished from the fourth and additional member.

In these later examples, as in the twofold formulae in 1 C. 8:6 etc., the singularity and individuality of the two factors is emphasised by means of the preceding εἷς. Yet it is self-evident that Father, Son and Spirit are here linked in an indissoluble threefold relationship. On the other hand, the NT does not actually speak of triunity. We seek this in vain in the triadic formulae of the NT. The Spanish texts of the 6th century are the first to offer a clear-cut trinitarian formula in the so-called Comma Johanneum of 1 Jn. 5:7 f.

The original there, according to the unanimous testimony of the Egyptian and Syrian texts, the earliest fathers and all the Orientals, is as follows: τρεῖς εἰσιν οἱ μαρτυροῦντες, τὸ πνεῦμα καὶ τὸ ὕδωρ καὶ τὸ αἷμα, καὶ οἱ τρεῖς εἰς τὸ ἕν εἰσιν. The Spanish Catholics made of this a trinitarian formula by continuing after μαρτυροῦντες: ἐν τῷ οὐρανῷ, ὁ πατήρ, ὁ λόγος καὶ τὸ ἅγιον πνεῦμα· καὶ

---

[285] 2 Th. 2:13 is less definite. The twofold εἷς of 1 C. 8:6 was given triadic form in the early Catholic period by the addition of ἓν πνεῦμα, cf. Nestle apparatus.

[286] πατήρ, Ἰησοῦς, πνεῦμα in 1 Pt. 1:2; Ac. 2:33; cf. 2 C. 1:21 f.: θεός, Χριστός, πνεῦμα. Cf. Jd. 20 f.

[287] In the Gospel of the Hebrews or Nazarenes there is a very likely influence of Semitic syncretism. Here the Spirit is feminine in the sense of the Heb. *ruach*, and in plain contradiction of the NT is regarded as the mother of Jesus (→ n. 283): ἔλαβέ με ἡ μήτηρ μου τὸ ἅγιον πνεῦμα, and: *descendit fons omnis spiritus sancti ... et dixit: ... tu es filius meus primogenitus*, Orig. Hom. XV, 4 in Jer. 15:10 (MPG, 13, 433 B) and Hier. Comm. in Is. 11:2 (MPL, 24, 145 B). Thus we have the common family triad of antiquity, i.e., father, mother and son.

[288] Triadic formulae in the NT cover faith, love and hope as well as Father, Son and Spirit. Triads were also favoured in Judaism, and they are basically independent of the notion of divine triads.

οὗτοι οἱ τρεῖς ἕν εἰσι ... [289] They thus imported a conclusion of early dogma into the NT. Early Christianity itself, however, does not yet have the problem of the Trinity in view.

3. The Personal Being of God.

a. The Conflict with Anthropomorphism in the Jewish World.

In Jewish apocalyptic we find both the older terms θεός and κύριος, and also several hypostases of God, λόγος, σοφία, δόξα etc. (→ 98). Yet these are all referred back to God, and it is only thus that they have any meaning.

The LXX is concerned for a pure concept of God. It tries to achieve its goal by minor alterations in the text. [290] Thus it seeks to take the offence out of Yahweh's attack on Moses in Ex. 4:24 by introducing the messenger of God in place of God Himself. Often by adding a word or two it avoids too anthropomorphic a view of God. In Ex. 4:20 the divine rod of Moses is made into a rod which God puts at the disposal of Moses : τὴν ῥάβδον τὴν παρὰ τοῦ θεοῦ. Again, in Ex. 19:3 Moses does not go up to God Himself, but to the mount of God. The hand of Yahweh in Jos. 4:24 becomes the δύναμις τοῦ κυρίου. In Ex. 21:6 we have πρὸς τὸ κριτήριον τοῦ θεοῦ προσάγειν instead of "to bring before God." In Is. 6:1 the δόξα of God rather than His train fills the temple. In Dt. 14:23 we read of the "dwelling" of His name, but the LXX changes this into : ἐπικληθῆναι τὸ ὄνομα αὐτοῦ. In Ex. 15:3 and Is. 42:13, where God is called אִישׁ מִלְחָמָה, the LXX translates συντρίβων πολέμους. The passages in which the Mas. speaks of seeing God are all changed. God cannot be literally seen. Hence the 70 elders in Ex. 24:10(11) do not see God Himself ; they see only the place where He stands. In Is. 38:11 σωτήριον is added : to see the salvation of God. In Job 19:27 the LXX has the more general ἃ ὁ ὀφθαλμός μου ἑόρακεν, and it thus avoids the view that God can be seen like a creature. That God might repent is also inconceivable in the LXX. Thus the Heb. texts which refer to God's repentance are altered. In Gn. 6:6, 7 God is angry that He has made man, but He does not repent. In Ex. 32:12 the prayer is, not that God should repent, but that He should be gracious. In many cases the LXX traces back events to man's sin rather than to God's wrath. It does violence to Nu. 1:53 : "That there be no wrath on Israel" ; LXX : οὐκ ἔσται ἁμάρτημα ἐν υἱοῖς Ἰσραηλ, and also to Job 42:7 : "My wrath is kindled" ; LXX : "Thou hast sinned." In 1 Εσδρ. 6:14 (5:12) "to provoke God" is changed into "to sin against God."

The later LXX writings use rational weapons in their fight against the dissipation of the thought of God in polytheistic cults. They themselves begin to speak in Gk. fashion of the divine, of → θειότης and → πρόνοια. Radical Hellenists from Aristobulus to Philo tread this path to the end, and handle the OT writings as do the Stoics their secret religious tradition. [291] They expound allegorically, and find a supposed abstract content in anthropomorphic expressions. [292] In the battle against polytheism and mythology, theology is not only decked out in more sophisticated language. [293] It is also put into philosophical concepts and controlled by the fundamental critical principle that the idea of God must be kept pure, and undefiled by unsuitable conceptions (Philo Leg. All., II, 1 f.) (τὸ ὄν ...) αὐτὸ γὰρ ἑαυτοῦ πλῆρες καὶ αὐτὸ ἑαυτῷ ἱκανόν ... ἄτρεπτον γὰρ καὶ ἀμετάβλητον, χρῇζον ἑτέρου τὸ παράπαν οὐδενός. [294] Thus we must think of God in a befitting manner.

---

[289] For further details cf. Nestle apparatus and Wnd. Kath. Br., ad loc.

[290] Cf. A. F. Dähne, Geschichtliche Darstellung der jüd.-alexandrinischen Religions-Philosophie, II (1834), 33 f.; H. B. Swete, An Introduction to the OT in Greek (1900), 327.

[291] Ep. Ar., 16 appeals to the Stoic interpretation of Zeus.

[292] Eus. Praep. Ev., VII, 10; XIII, 12 (Aristobulus); XIII, 13, 60 (Ps.-Aesch.).

[293] Ep. Ar., 95 : ἡ μεγάλη θειότης; Philo Decal., 63; Fug., 99 : τὸ θεῖον.

[294] Philo Mut. Nom., 27; Virt., 9 f.: ἔστι γὰρ ὁ μὲν θεὸς ἀνεπιδεής, οὐδενὸς χρεῖος ὤν, ἀλλ᾽ αὐτὸς αὐταρκέστατος ἑαυτῷ. Also Cher., 46; Mut. Nom., 46; Spec. Leg., II, 38

In all these struggles and movements, however, Hellenistic Judaism did not surrender its faith in a personal God. [295] Josephus is an example. He speaks as loftily as possible of the God of the OT. He prefers εὐσέβεια εἰς τὸ θεῖον [296] to fear of God, and ὀργὴ ἦν ... τὸ θεῖον ... ἔχει (Ant., 3, 321) to the wrath of God. He coins the pseudo-philosophical sentence : μεθ' ὧν γὰρ τὸ δίκαιόν ἐστιν, μετ' ἐκείνων ὁ θεός (Ant., 15, 138). He, too, despises mythology, though he is thinking of pagan mythology. [297] He, too, is convinced that God needs nothing, [298] and his ideal is : ταῦτα περὶ θεοῦ φρονεῖν ... ὅτι δ' ἐστὶ καλὰ καὶ πρέποντα τῇ τοῦ θεοῦ φύσει καὶ μεγαλειό-τητι. [299] But he is certain that this ideal is fulfilled in the OT doctrine of God, and in spite of the alien garb the God of whom he speaks is the living God of his fathers. [300]

The Synagogue has no philosophical bias. In the main it keeps itself from Hell. allegorising (→ I, 262). But the Rabbis, too, found difficulty in the anthropomorphism of the OT. They tried to solve it by theological explanation. The Torah has to make the Eternal smaller to speak of Him. It must use comparisons and images in adaptation to our world of thought. It does so for our sake. [301] The Rabbis, too, like comparisons, and they sometimes use anthropomorphic forms of expression. But they do so with great care, usually prefixing a phrase like "so to speak," or "in human terms." [302] The great Rabbis were great men of prayer. [303] They called their God "Father" (→ πα-τήρ), [304] and were certain that He had an ear and a hand for their needs, [305] and no less certain that the God of the Word would answer them (→ n. 206). God Himself weeps daily for Jerusalem. Indeed, He prays to Himself that His grace may prevail over His severity. [306] The Rabbis conceived of the personality of God more radically than any before them. Neither the wisdom of God nor His righteousness is God's true essence. The final and decisive thing in God is His will, which is irrational even to the point of seeming caprice, and absolutely contingent in all its resolves.

Thus the great movement against anthropomorphism embraced both the Gk. and the Jewish worlds. Yet the basic results differed. In the Gk. world the idea of a personal God was regarded as a final relic of the anthropomorphic thinking which had to be overcome. In the Jewish world the distinction between anthropomorphic conceptions and faith in the personal God was not only maintained but grasped with increasing clarity. God is not as a man. But He is a God who wills and speaks and hears.

b. The Personal God of the New Testament.

The battle against anthropomorphism is long since over when we come to early Christianity. The NT writers do not waste words on it. But the personal nature

---

and 174; Conf. Ling., 175 etc. The same idea is found in Ep. Ar., 211: ὁ θεὸς δὲ ἀπροσδεής ἐστιν καὶ ἐπιεικής.

[295] Joseph and Asenath, VIII (E. W. Brooks, Translations of Early Texts, II, 7 [1917], 32 f.).

[296] Vit., 14; cf. Ant., 18, 127; Bell., 2, 128; Vit., 48 : τὸ θεῖον.

[297] Ant., 1, 15 : πάσης καθαρὸν τὸν περὶ αὐτοῦ (sc. θεοῦ) φυλάξας λόγον τῆς παρ' ἄλλοις ἀσχήμονος μυθολογίας.

[298] Ant., 8, 111: ἀπροσδεὲς τὸ θεῖον ἀπάντων.

[299] Ap., 2, 168, cf. Ant., 8, 107; Bell., 7, 344.

[300] Ap., 2, 197: δέησις ἔστω πρὸς τὸν θεόν.

[301] Cf. Strack, Einleitung, 99 : "The Torah speaks in the language of the children of men," S. Nu., 112 on 15:31.

[302] כאן or כביכול, v. ERE, VI, 295.

[303] P. Fiebig, "Das Vaterunser" in BFTh, 30, 3 (1927), 28 ff. → II, 801 f.

[304] Yoma, 8, 9; Sota, 9, 15 (Str.-B., I, 394 f.).

[305] Cf. רחמנא for (the merciful) God, and on this M. Ex. 18:12 (59a): God provides all creatures with nourishment, both good and bad.

[306] V. ERE, VI, 296; Ber., 7a; 59a. Cf. Gn. r., 33 on 8:1; Ex. r., 3 on 3:14 : Yahweh is the God of grace, Elohim of judgment. The same problems arise in Heb. En. (Odeberg), passim.

of God is to them a living reality. It has revealed itself to them ἐν προσώπῳ Χριστοῦ (2 C. 4:6). It discloses itself to them ἐν πνεύματι, for the pneumatic realises that he is known by his God, and he knows his God. [307] That God is personal finds fresh certainty in the cry 'Αββά in prayer (→ I, 6; → πατήρ). The countless attestations of living prayer in the NT (→ αἰτέω, I, 191; → βοάω, I, 625; → εὔχομαι, II, 803) are so many testimonies to the personal God in whom early Christianity believed. They also attest to us in what sense the concept of God's personal nature is here understood. The God of the NT is a God to whom man may say Thou, as to a personal being. This Thou of man to God, however, is the response to God's Thou to man. [308]

God is a living God (→ ζάω) who deals as such with the realities of the world and the forces in man, and who allows Himself to be invoked by prayers and cries for help. His sovereign will (→ θέλω) is revealed to those who set their own wills against it, His mysterious decree (→ βούλομαι, I, 632) to those who integrate their wills with His. The NT does not venture any doctrine of the qualities of God, but it bears testimony to the purpose of God as this is declared to those who pray and believe in the overruling (2 C. 1:3 ff.) of their own lives and of human history. Only in these testimonies do we see the fulness of what the thought of the personal God embraces in the NT.

πιστὸς ὁ θεός is the first and final thing, especially in Paul. [309] ἀμεταμέλητα τὰ χαρίσματα τοῦ θεοῦ (R. 11:29). He is ἀληθής, we read in Jn. 3:33. ἀψευδής, says Tt. in much the same sense. [310] He is a God of mercy, says the NT with reference to the Christ event. We read of God's love and grace, of His kindness (R. 2:4), and even of His φιλανθρωπία in writings which betray Hellenistic influence. [311] But early Christianity can also discern the righteous wrath [312] of God in history: ἴδε οὖν χρηστότητα καὶ ἀποτομίαν θεοῦ (R. 11:22). Only later writings can venture to say what is impossible for God by nature. [313] More rarely the language of the NT speaks of the holiness of God which awakens fear. On one occasion (Mt. 5:48) God is called τέλειος, not in the sense of metaphysical speculation, but in terms of moral perfection. Here too, then, the personal being of God is the presupposition. Above all, however, these statements about God are never alone, nor are they ever made for their own sake. They are always linked with thanksgiving or petition, with proclamation or demand. In the NT we do not have a doctrine of the personal nature of God; we have the historical attestation and fulfilment of the will of God.

The mode of expression is varied enough. God's purpose is most simply expressed by an attributive or predicative adjective: μόνος σοφὸς θεός (R. 16:27), or θεὸς ἀληθής ἐστιν (Jn. 3:33). But Paul also likes to speak of the χρηστόν (R. 2:4), μωρόν (1 C. 1:25), ἀσθενὲς τοῦ θεοῦ (1 C. 1:25). Very common and

---

307 2 C. 11:11 etc.: ὁ θεὸς οἶδεν; R. 8:27: ὁ δὲ ἐρευνῶν τὰς καρδίας οἶδεν τί τὸ φρόνημα τοῦ πνεύματος. Cf. Lk. 16:15 etc.: ὁ θεὸς γινώσκει τὰς καρδίας ὑμῶν; Ac. 1:24; 15:8: ὁ καρδιογνώστης θεός.
308 K. Heim, "Das Gebet" in *Leben aus dem Glauben* (1934), 122 ff.
309 1 C. 1:9; 10:13; 2 C. 1:18 → πιστός.
310 Tt. 1:2: (ἐλπίς ...) ἣν ἐπηγγείλατο ὁ ἀψευδὴς θεὸς πρὸ χρόνων αἰωνίων.
311 Tt. 3:4: ἡ χρηστότης καὶ ἡ φιλανθρωπία ἐπεφάνη τοῦ σωτῆρος ἡμῶν θεοῦ.
312 → ὀργή, → θυμός. R. 1:18; 1 Th. 2:16.
313 Jm. 1:13: θεὸς ἀπείραστός ἐστιν; Hb. 6:10: οὐ γὰρ ἄδικος ὁ θεός; 6:18: ἀδύνατον ψεύσασθαι θεόν. Cf. however R. 3:4; 9:14, 19; Jn. 9:31.

very natural is the combining of a *Theos* genitive with a substantive : [314] → πίστις τοῦ θεοῦ (R. 3:3). Paul likes to invert this in a way reminiscent of the OT : ὁ θεὸς τῆς εἰρήνης, [315] ὑπομονῆς, [316] ἐλπίδος, [317] παρακλήσεως, [318] ἀγάπης. [319] 1 Jn. 4:8 ventures the bold equation : ὁ θεὸς ἀγάπη ἐστίν. This does not mean that God is thought of in terms of an impersonal force. He is rather declared to be the origin and norm of all that can or should be called love. [320] It is not that love is a deity. On the contrary, the personal God is love in all His will and work, and decisively in the work of Christ (Jn. 3:16).

Yet the NT, and especially the later writings, can also offer predications of God which refer rather to the manner or φύσις of God than to His disposition and purpose. In this connection we may mention what are not yet necessarily attributes like αἰώνιος (→ I, 208; R. 16:26), ἀόρατος, also ἄφθαρτος, [321] and especially the strongly Hellenistic μακάριος (1 Tm. 1:11). Fully along the lines of Hellenistic tradition is Ac. 17:25 : οὐδὲ ὑπὸ χειρῶν ἀνθρωπίνων θεραπεύεται προσδεόμενός τινος. This is the same spirit which later gave rise to the addition τὸ → θεῖον in 17:27, i.e., the spirit of natural theology.

A separate problem is that of the Johannine equation of ὁ θεός with a neutral predication. We have referred already (→ 107) to the πνεῦμα ὁ θεός of Jn. 4:24. This does not go decisively beyond 1 Jn. 4:8. On the other hand, in 1 Jn. 1:5 a purely natural concept is equated with God : ὁ θεὸς → φῶς ἐστιν. [322] Here the same thinking seems to be at work as in the dual constructions of Persian theology. But what is elementary there is here fully worked out. All that may be called light in the world, whether in a natural, intellectual, or moral sense, refers back to the personal God as its Author and Norm. God's form of manifestation and operation is light. Hence ὁ θεὸς φῶς ἐστιν.

4. The Transcendence of God.

a. The Power of God as Ruler in Semitic Religions.

i. In the Semitic world the tribal deities are Baal, Malk, Sar, Mar, Adon, [323] on Syrian soil κύριος, δεσπότης, βασιλεύς, and on Arab Rabb, Shayyim (Lord, Protector) etc. [324] These titles are so essential to the Semites that they often replace the original proper names and are themselves used as such. [325] What makes the gods into

---

[314] Lk. 1:78 : σπλάγχνα ἐλέους θεοῦ ἡμῶν. R. 12:1: διὰ τῶν οἰκτιρμῶν τοῦ θεοῦ. Phil. 4:7: εἰρήνη τοῦ θεοῦ.
[315] R. 15:33; 16:20; 1 Th. 5:23; Phil. 4:9; 1 C. 14:33 : οὐ γάρ ἐστιν ἀκαταστασίας ὁ θεός, ἀλλὰ εἰρήνης. Cf. Hb. 13:20.
[316] R. 15:5 : θεὸς τῆς ὑπομονῆς καὶ τῆς παρακλήσεως.
[317] R. 15:13 : ὁ δὲ θεὸς τῆς ἐλπίδος πληρώσαι ὑμᾶς πάσης χαρᾶς καὶ εἰρήνης.
[318] 2 C. 1:3 : ὁ πατὴρ τῶν οἰκτιρμῶν καὶ θεὸς πάσης παρακλήσεως. Cf. 1 Pt. 5:10 : ὁ θεὸς πάσης χάριτος. → also n. 316.
[319] 2 C. 13:11: ὁ θεὸς τῆς ἀγάπης καὶ εἰρήνης.
[320] 1 Jn. 4:7: ἡ ἀγάπη ἐκ τοῦ θεοῦ ἐστιν, cf. 1 Jn. 3:16.
[321] 1 Tm. 1:17: ἀφθάρτῳ ἀοράτῳ μόνῳ θεῷ.
[322] Hb. 12:29: ὁ θεὸς ἡμῶν πῦρ καταναλίσκον, is simply an OT figure for God's final work.
[323] Baudissin, *Kyrios*, III, 19 ff.
[324] *Ibid.*, 70 ff.; S. Margoliouth in ERE, VI, 248 : Shayyim in inscr. in S. Arabia, Rabb in the Koran, under biblical influence, and cf. also Ilah (inscr.) and Allah (the chief term in the Koran).
[325] O. Eissfeldt, *Vom Werden der biblischen Gottesanschauung* (1929), 7. On Baal, v. Baudissin, III, 246 ff. On Marduk, v. *Babylonisches Weltschöpfungsepos*, II, 131 in Ungnad, *Religion*, 34.

gods is not that they are immortal or blessed, as in Homer. This may be a presupposition, but no more. God is God in virtue of His power to rule. [326]

This is primarily true of His relation to men, whether the nation or individuals. [327] God is the Lord, and man His slave [328] (→ δοῦλος). But God is also the Protector to whom man entrusts himself in every need or danger. [329] God is Judge, [330] but also Father. [331] In a word, He is King. Hereby God's superiority to man and man's subordination to Him are established in a single term.

When the same relationship is transferred from God and man to God and the world, [332] God is neither an immanent God, nor a transcendent God, nor a combination of the two. He is rather the Ruler of the world, and above it in this sense. Hence the Semites like designations such as Bel Shamin, μέγας, μέγιστος, ὕψιστος, [333] which primarily denote the majesty of God, but which also emphasise His superiority over all powers. In short, these names are not definitions of His being, like similar concepts in Gk. religion. In the genuine Semitic sense, they are definitions of relationship. They denote the power of God as Ruler.

This power is decisively confirmed by His control of destiny. Anshar means both "Ruler" and "Destiny" of the great gods, [334] and appeal is made to Shamash because it is in his hand to shape the destiny of life. [335] It is because of this power over destiny that the gods can be protectors and helpers in times of need [336] and under all the threats of the powers and chances of this world.

ii. Other Semitic religions draw additional vitality from magical beliefs, fertility cults, astral mythologies and astrology. They thus contain within themselves the seed of decay, and are swallowed up in the fatalistic beliefs of syncretism. The prophets, however, renew the original Mosaic belief, and they thus deepen the concept of God and safeguard it against alienation. At the end of the prophetic period the God of Israel is the absolute Ruler, [337] and His power as such has no limits. He is the Creator who has called forth the world out of nothing, who can at any moment plunge it back into nothing, and who can always intervene with power in the events of this world. There can be no independent fate alongside or above Him.

The LXX carried this train of thought to its final conclusion, and decided the path taken by later Judaism, when it took the most prominent of God's ancient titles, Κύριος, and made it the representative proper name of God. Other titles such as δεσπότης, βασιλεύς etc. complete the picture of the divine Ruler who is above the world and who holds all things in His firm hands. [338] Prayer now becomes truly serious as man's

---

[326] On related phenomena in the Egyptians and Sumerians, v. Baudissin, III, 284 ff. The same usage entered the Hell. world, v. Pr.-Bauer, s.v. θεός (P. Lond., I, 121, III, 529 κύριε θεὲ μέγιστε. Preisigke Sammelbuch, I, 159, 2 f.: τῷ κυρίῳ θεῷ Ἀσκληπιῷ. Ditt. Or., II, 655, 3 f.: τῷ θεῶι καὶ κυρίῳ Σοκνοπαίωι. Epict. Diss., II, 16, 13 : κύριε ὁ θεός). In Plotin. the κύριος is the one who determines himself freely. On this whole question → κύριος.

[327] Enlil as the Lord who summons His people, in Ungnad, op. cit., 196. On God as first the Father of the people, then of the individual, v. Baudissin, III, 347 ff.

[328] Margoliouth, ERE, VI, 249.

[329] Eissfeldt, op. cit., 7.

[330] Also Lawgiver, cf. Baudissin, III, 379 ff.; Eissfeldt, 8.

[331] Baudissin, III, 309 ff.

[332] On God and nature, v. Baudissin, III, 463 ff., also 523 for the assimilation of nature gods to the national God.

[333] A. E. Suffrin in ERE, VI, 296; Baudissin, III, 70 ff.

[334] The Babyl. creation epic, II, 133 in Ungnad, op. cit., 34.

[335] Ungnad, 168.

[336] Marduk as Helper, Ungnad, 182.

[337] Man is God's image in so far as he is instituted as ruler, v. Gn. 1:26 and Baudissin, III, 233.

[338] Baudissin, II; Eissfeldt, op. cit., 16.

cry to Him who alone can help because He is outside and above the world, yet powerful within it.

b. God and the World in Later Judaism.

The God of later Judaism has sometimes been called a remote God, and the hypostases
and angels have been regarded as mediators between God and the world. [339] A more
accurate view is that God is above the world and that the hypostases and angels are
executives who carry out the will of God in His world (→ 98). This is brought out
by the many names for God which under the influence of the Heb. and Gk. OT are
found throughout later Jewish writings, e.g., Adonai and → κύριος, El Elyon and θεός
ὕψιστος, [340] μέγας, δεσπότης, [341] βασιλεύς, βασιλεὺς βασιλέων etc. [342]

There may be reference to God's immortality, but this is simply a presupposition of
His lordship, which is the true theme. The emphasis is on the dynamic definition rather
than the metaphysical. [343] We necessarily find many terms for God which stress His
distance from the world, especially Shamayim, also Makom etc. (→ 93). Yet these
denote, not a sphere outside the world, but the place above the world which enables
God to keep His hand on all that happens [344] (→ θρόνος). The God of heaven is also
the Father in heaven. [345] Makom is used of the omnipresent God. Why is the Holy One
called Makom? Because He is the place for the world, not because the world is His
place. Hence the God whose glory can find no place in the whole world can deal with
man by means of the hair on his head. [346] Of the Shechina, however, it is said that
it stays in the midst of Israel wherever the people of God may be driven. [347]

On the other hand, God may denote the all: τὸ πᾶν ἐστιν αὐτός. But this dangerous
word has nothing to do with ideas of emanation or with pantheism: αὐτὸς γὰρ ὁ
μέγας παρὰ πάντα τὰ ἔργα αὐτοῦ ... δοξάζοντες κύριον ὑψώσατε καθ' ὅσον
ἂν δύνησθε, ὑπερέξει γὰρ καὶ ἔτι ... οὐ γὰρ μὴ ἀφίκησθε. [348] God is not the
epitome or the origin of the all; He is its Creator. He who spake, and the world was,
is greater than His works, and He remains the Lord over them. [349] Hence later Judaism
considers it supremely important to exclude any idea of an intermingling or interfusion
of the divine and the human. [350] There is here no place for an ἐν θεῷ in the sense
of natural or ecstatic union. [351] The more common, however, are expressions like παρὰ

---

[339] So Gunkel in RGG², II, 1369.

[340] Eth. En. 10:1 f. etc.; Sib., 3, 702 ff.; Asenath, VIII (p. 32 f., Brooks). In Joseph. only
in the edict of Augustus in Ant., 16, 163: ἐπὶ Ὑρκανοῦ ἀρχιερέως θεοῦ ὑψίστου. Cf.
bRH, 18b: כהן גדול לאל עליון.

[341] Jos. Ant., 20, 90 δέσποτα κύριε (→ II, 44).

[342] V. Baudissin, op. cit., III, 675 ff.; Suffrin in ERE, VI, 296; → I, 568 ff.

[343] Sib., 3, 717 ff., cf. Ps.-Phokylides, 54 in T. Bergk, Poetae Lyrici Graeci, II (1915),
74 ff.

[344] Sib., 3, 1 ff., 704 f.; Eus. Praep. Ev., VI, 8, 10; Asenath, VIII, XI (p. 32 f., 37 ff.,
Brooks).

[345] Yoma, 8, 9; Sota, 9, 15; cf. ERE, VI, 297. Cf. Jos. Ant., 4, 318: τοῦ θεοῦ ... ᾧ
μελήσει καὶ πρὸς τὸ μέλλον ὑμῶν. Ant., 7, 45: θεὸς ... ᾧ μέλει πάντων.

[346] Pesikt. r., 21; Gn. r., 4 on 1:7. Cf. ERE, VI, 296 f.

[347] Cf. the rabb. passages quoted in → n. 354. The indirectness of God's working in a
godless world is emphasised in the Amoraic theory of the Bath kol. This is the echo of
the voice of God, v. W. Bacher, Die exegetische Terminologie der jüd. Traditionslit., II
(1905), 206.

[348] Sir. 43:27 ff.

[349] Sib., 3, 20 ff.

[350] Eus. Praep. Ev., XIII, 13, 60 (Ps.-Aesch.). Jos. Bell., 7, 344: κοινωνία θείῳ πρὸς
θνητὸν ἀπρεπής ἐστιν.

[351] Very different is the ἐν in Jos. Ant., 3, 23: ἐν αὐτῷ (God) εἶναι τὴν σωτηρίαν
αὐτοῦ καὶ οὐκ ἐν ἄλλῳ. Or 8, 282: τὰς ἐλπίδας ἔχειν ἐν τῷ θεῷ.

θεοῦ, [352] ὑπὸ θεοῦ. [353] What we see before us comes from God and is set in motion by Him. Above all, the important OT formula "God with us" is still used in many connections. [354] God is not like a man. He is not entangled in the world or tied to it. But He has made a covenant with His people, and He is their strong Protector. [355] Israel may pray to this Protector in all its needs. There is no situation over which He is not the Lord. For He is Lord of all the elements of the world and the forces of destiny. The people of God is not subject to fortune ; it is subject to the Lord of heaven and earth. [356]

Hence the later Jewish texts often speak of the גבורה, the δύναμις τοῦ θεοῦ. [357] God is compared to a ruler who remains invisible but who is always present to the world in his acts of power, his laws and his officers, and who enforces his will thereby. [358] The angels surround Him like a heavenly court. [359] Jewish apocalyptic in particular worked out even the details of the image of the great monarch, comparing the relation of God and the world to that of the ruler and his kingdom.

Apocalyptic realises, of course, that God's will as ruler is not asserted in His creation without opposition. It is hampered by opposing powers, so that there is tension between the reality of the world and the divine will. [360] Here then, as in Gk. idealism, there seems to be an antithesis between this world and the world above. *Finitum incapax infiniti?* Not at all. What separates our world from God is not spatial distance, nor essential distinction, but opposition of will, though this opposition has, of course, perverted the whole form of this world. Hence apocalyptic thought sees neither division nor union between the divine and human worlds in the Gk. sense. It sees only conflict — the battle for dominion.

With all later Judaism, Jewish apocalyptic believes firmly in the omnipotent God. But it is not thinking of omnicausality. The very fact of sin makes this impossible. It believes rather in God's ability to do all things in the sense of dynamic monotheism (→ 96). God is not the only one at work, but He can bend all that happens to His own purpose. Often the goal of this overruling is not visible. Indeed, God often seems to hold aloof and to leave the course of the world to alien and hostile powers. Apocalyptic is careful not to speak of God's sole rule in the world. But it believes in the superior power of God, in His final victory in the struggle for dominion, and in His final rule. Hence expectation of the final βασιλεία τοῦ θεοῦ is the last word of Judaism on the theme of God and the world, and the most vital testimony to Jewish belief in the transcendence of God.

c. The Transcendent God of the New Testament.

When early Christianity speaks of the relation of God and the world, it begins with the ideas and concepts of later Judaism. In the NT, too, God is called

---

[352] Jos. Ant., 1, 14; 2, 137; 3, 222; 15, 136.
[353] Jos. Ant., 1, 106; 9, 182. Particularly worth noting is the restriction by διά in Ant., 8, 223 : κωλυθεὶς ὑπὸ τοῦ θεοῦ διὰ τοῦ προφήτου, and 9, 2 : τὰ νόμιμα τὰ διὰ Μωυσέως ὑπὸ τοῦ θεοῦ δοθέντα.
[354] Ant., 6, 181: μετ' ἐμοῦ; 6, 231: μετά σου; 15, 138; μετ' ἐκείνων. Cf. M. Ex. 20:24 עמהם שכינה. S. Nu. § 84 on 10:35 (Trans. K. G. Kuhn, [1933 ff.], 226 f.).
[355] Cf. also Ant., 2, 152 : φυλαχθησόμενος ὑπὸ τοῦ θεοῦ.
[356] Shabb., 156b.
[357] A. Marmorstein, EJ, VII, 565; Jos. Ant., 10, 242 : τὸν θεὸν ὡς τὴν ἅπασαν ἔχοντα δύναμιν; cf. 5, 109 : μὴ νομίσητε ... τῆς τοῦ θεοῦ δυνάμεως ἔξω γεγονέναι· πανταχοῦ δ' ἐν τοῖς τούτου ἐστέ. Cf. Asenath, VIII (p. 32 f., Brooks).
[358] V. the monarchical proof of God, Marmorstein, EJ, VII, 562.
[359] S. Bar. 51; Sanh., 38a; BB, 74a in Suffrin, ERE, VI, 297.
[360] This relation between God and the world is revealed in the destiny of wisdom (or the Shechina), which finds no place on earth, or at best only in Israel. Cf. the variations on the motif in Job 28:23 ff.; Sir. 24:4 ff.; Eth. En. 42; cf. Heb. En. (Odeberg), s.v. Shekinah.

→ κύριος, [361] βασιλεύς, μέγας, [362] ὕψιστος, [363] and we also read of the → θρόνος θεοῦ, [364] and the βασιλεία θεοῦ or the βασιλεία τῶν οὐρανῶν (→ I, 581 f.). [365] The God of the NT is neither in the world nor outside the world, but above the world.

He is above the world, or transcendent, in exactly the same sense as in Jewish apocalyptic. This is most evident in the early Christian conception of the relation of heaven and earth. ὁ → οὐρανὸς καὶ ἡ γῆ belong together. [366] As thus linked, they constitute the totality of God's creation. [367] Cf. → γῆ, I, 678. Yet normally the two spheres are intentionally distinguished (Lk. 2:14; Mt. 28:18; 23:9). The earthly sphere has no future worth (Col. 3:2; Mt. 6:19 f.). Heaven is superior to it as the place and starting-point of God's rule. Heaven is God's throne, earth His foot-stool. [368] This distinction is made into an actual antithesis by the fact that there are at work in the earthly world forces which oppose the lordship of heaven. It is not self-evident that God's will is done on earth as it is in heaven (Mt. 6:10). Thus the fundamental apocalyptic conviction that there is a twofold relation of interconnection and tension between heaven and earth is a basic assumption of early Christian thinking.

On the basis of this assumption the Christ event is regarded in the NT as the decisive encounter between the heavenly world and the earthly, as the encounter which apocalyptic awaited as an eschatological event. Jesus Himself said to the Pharisees: "Behold, the kingdom of God is among you," [369] though naturally they will not see it. Mt. follows Is. 7 in calling Him Immanuel, and He translates with emphasis: μεθ᾽ ἡμῶν ὁ θεός. [370] In this way Christ is the encounter between God and the world of man. In Phil. 2:6 ff. Paul stresses the contrast between the μορφὴ θεοῦ and the μορφὴ δούλου, between His heavenly lordship and His earthly manifestation ἐν ὁμοιώματι σαρκὸς ἁμαρτίας, between His heavenly being and His earthly destiny ἕως θανάτου τοῦ σταυροῦ (→ II, 278). The Johannine Prologue summarises all these motifs in a few sentences: θεὸς ἦν ὁ λόγος — ὁ κόσμος δι᾽ αὐτοῦ ἐγένετο — ὁ λόγος σὰρξ ἐγένετο καὶ ἐσκήνωσεν ἐν ἡμῖν — τὸ φῶς ἐν τῇ σκοτίᾳ φαίνει καὶ ἡ σκοτία αὐτὸ οὐ κατέλαβεν. [371] The encounter between

---

[361] E.g., Rev. 4:11: ὁ κύριος καὶ ὁ θεὸς ἡμῶν. On the early Christian view man is also His δοῦλος, → II, 273. But Jesus usually bears the name of *Kyrios*, and therefore the term δοῦλος is predominantly brought into relation to Him, esp. by Paul, → II, 274.

[362] μεγάλου βασιλέως in Mt. 5:35 (ψ 47:2). → I, 579.

[363] Lk. 1:32, 35, 76; 6:35; Ac. 7:48. θεὸς ὕψιστος in Mk. 5:7; Ac. 16:17; Hb. 7:1 (Gn. 14:18); ἐν ὑψίστοις, Mk. 11:10; Lk. 2:14 etc.

[364] Esp. Rev. 7:15; 12:5 etc.

[365] Cf. Rev. 21:2, 10 : ἐκ τοῦ οὐρανοῦ = ἀπὸ τοῦ θεοῦ.

[366] Lk. 10:21; Ac. 17:24.

[367] Ac. 4:24; Rev. 10:6; 2 Pt. 3:5 ff.

[368] Mt. 5:34 f.; 23:22; Ac. 7:49, quoting Is. 66:1 f.

[369] Lk. 17:21: ἰδοὺ γὰρ ἡ βασιλεία τοῦ θεοῦ ἐντὸς ὑμῶν ἐστιν. The transl. "within you" is linguistically possible (cf. Mt. 23:26). But "among you" is suported by 1. the ἰδού at the beginning of the saying, 2. other sayings of Jesus like Lk. 11:20; 3. the oldest interpretation of the saying in its setting, according to which it is not addressed tc the disciples (to whom He turns only in v. 22), but to the Pharisees, who certainly do not bear God's kingdom in their hearts acc. to Jesus' opinion ; and 4. the oldest translations, cf. the Syrian, which is nearest to the original, "between" (*bainath*), and the Lat., *intra vos* rather than *in vobis* or *in cordibus vestris*. Lk. 11:20 makes it very likely that the kingdom "among you" refers to the present and to Jesus, though cf. R. Bultmann, *Jesus* (1926), 39 : "At a stroke among you."

[370] Mt. 1:23 (Is. 7:14). But cf. Ac. 10:38 : ὁ θεὸς ἦν μετ᾽ αὐτοῦ (Jesus). → 117.

[371] Jn. 1:1, 10, 14, 5. Cf. 14:17.

the two worlds has taken place, not in the form of an illumination or deification of the human, nor in the form of a marriage or union of the heavenly world and the earthly, but in the form of an explosion. The encounter between the two worlds in the Christ event does not lead to a lessening of the tension between them. On the contrary, it leads to a heightening and an overcoming of the tension. This is the unanimous conviction of early Christianity.

This tension bears no relation to the metaphysical antithesis between phenomenon and idea, the finite and the infinite, time and eternity, which is a theme of Hellenistic philosophy. Later pseudo-theology has made the attempt to understand the Christ event in terms of this prior conception of religious philosophy, but in so doing it has had to deny the realistic seriousness of the incarnation, being forced to do this by the metaphysical preconception: *finitum non capax infiniti.* Jn. himself experienced the beginnings of this confusion, and he saw his way clearly through it. 1 Jn. 4:2 f. makes serious acceptance of the message of the historical incarnation of the eternal Logos a yardstick of the divine authority of a theology; [372] and 2 Jn. 7 says: πολλοὶ πλάνοι ἐξῆλθον εἰς τὸν κόσμον, οἱ μὴ ὁμολογοῦντες Ἰησοῦν Χριστὸν ἐρχόμενον ἐν σαρκί· οὗτός ἐστιν ὁ πλάνος καὶ ὁ ἀντίχριστος.

The living God of the NT is neither conditioned nor restricted in His action by basic metaphysical relations. The men of the NT believe that God can do all things. As the Baptist proclaimed in Lk. 3:8, He can raise up children of the stones. Jesus Himself impressed upon His disciples the fact that nothing is impossible with God (Mk. 10:27). The κραταιὰ χεὶρ τοῦ θεοῦ (1 Pt. 5:6) is the ultimately decisive power in the world. God can destroy Israel or exalt it as He pleases — and no natural or historical right can hinder it (R. 11:23 f.). His work cannot be hampered or destroyed. Only in appearance can man resist or thwart it (Ac. 5:39; 2 Tm. 2:9). His Word means life or death (Lk. 12:20). Power (R. 13:1 f.) and weakness, wealth and poverty (2 C. 9:8; 1 Tm. 6:17; Jm. 1:17), distress and deliverance, and all the changes and chances of life come from Him. With ἀπὸ θεοῦ, the NT likes to use θεὸς μεθ' ἡμῶν (→ 116), which has been fulfilled in the Christ event, and which on this basis finds self-actualisation in a new way. The Ruler of the world is the Protector of the Christian community. Corresponding to this μεθ' ἡμῶν we find in Ac. 23:1 the dative θεῷ: πεπολίτευμαι τῷ θεῷ ἄχρι ταύτης τῆς ἡμέρας. Jm. 4:8 (cf. Hb. 7:19, 25) coins the saying: ἐγγίσατε τῷ θεῷ, καὶ ἐγγίσει ὑμῖν. Man remains a δοῦλος of the κύριος God (→ n. 361). In Eph. Christians are called συμπολῖται τῶν ἁγίων καὶ οἰκεῖοι τοῦ θεοῦ. [373] These are very largely OT thoughts, and early Christianity spoke of the protective relation of God to the community in much the same way as the men of the OT. But what was previously intimated has now become a fact once and for all in and with and through Jesus Christ. This is most plainly expressed in the ὑπέρ of R. 8:31 f.: εἰ ὁ θεὸς ὑπὲρ ἡμῶν, τίς καθ' ἡμῶν; Whence and in what sense this ὑπέρ? ὑπὲρ ἡμῶν πάντων παρέδωκεν αὐτόν (the Son). On this fact, however, there is established a certainty of victory which not only goes beyond anything in the OT but which also gives an answer to the extreme urgency of the ancient search for God as it is betrayed in statements concerning the power of Isis over human destiny: πέπεισμαι γὰρ ὅτι οὔτε θάνατος οὔτε ζωή ... οὔτε ἀρχαὶ ...

---

[372] ἐν τούτῳ γινώσκετε τὸ πνεῦμα τοῦ θεοῦ. πᾶν πνεῦμα ὃ ὁμολογεῖ Ἰησοῦν Χριστὸν ἐν σαρκὶ ἐληλυθότα ἐκ τοῦ θεοῦ ἐστιν. Cf. 1 Jn. 1:1 f. Perhaps Jn. 1:14 is already meant in this sense, cf. Jn. 6:41, 51, 58.
[373] Eph. 2:19 (cf. 22: κατοικητήριον τοῦ θεοῦ). On this pt. cf. Phil. 3:20.

οὔτε δυνάμεις ... οὔτε τις κτίσις ἑτέρα δυνήσεται ἡμᾶς χωρίσαι ἀπὸ τῆς ἀγάπης τοῦ θεοῦ τῆς ἐν Χριστῷ. [374] No destiny has power, validity or meaning before God. Words like εἱμαρμένη or μοῖρα are never found in the NT. The NT has overcome both the cosmic anxiety of the world of antiquity, and the very concept of fate itself.

The transcendence of the living God, which here shows itself to be an indispensable presupposition of the early Christian assurance of faith, seems to be challenged by certain statements which indicate an interfusion between God and the world or man. We need not mention among these the idea that the community is the temple in which God dwells, since this implies little more than the concept of the divine household. Even the description of the individual as the temple or dwelling-place of God moves in the same framework. The θεὸς ἐν ὑμῖν of 1 C. 14:25 is an OT expression, and like the ἐντὸς ὑμῶν of Lk. 17:20 it denotes that God is among them. [375] On the other hand, Ephesians seems to approximate closer to immanentism when it calls God the πατὴρ πάντων, ὁ ἐπὶ πάντων καὶ διὰ πάντων καὶ ἐν πᾶσιν (4:6). Yet this is only an appearance, since the third clause is to be understood in the light of the first, and it is thus a development of the Pauline θεὸς ὁ ἐνεργῶν τὰ πάντα ἐν πᾶσιν (1 C. 12:6) and a counterpart to the Pauline τὰ πάντα ἐν αὐτῷ (Christ) συνέστηκεν of Col. 1:17. There is a more mystical ring about the Johannine ἐν formulae like ὁ θεὸς ἀγάπη ἐστίν, καὶ ὁ μένων ἐν τῇ ἀγάπῃ ἐν τῷ θεῷ μένει καὶ ὁ θεὸς ἐν αὐτῷ μένει. [376] But the personal nature of God is firmly established in the main sentence, and ἀγάπη is declared to be the principle by which God asserts Himself in the world, so that abiding in love is understood simply as faithfulness to this principle, and abiding in God as faithfulness to God (→ I, 52). But this faithfulness to God stands in reciprocal relation to the faithfulness of God to which the concluding statement refers with the counterbalancing formula: θεὸς μένει ἐν αὐτῷ. In short, this is not a metaphysical relation of immanence. What is actualised in the μένειν is a historical Thou-relationship. The Jn. who argued against a God outside the world (→ n. 372) shows the same unerring instinct in avoiding the idea of a God inside the world. [377]

This interpretation is decisively confirmed by the fact that in Jn., as in the NT generally, there are abundant examples of living prayer, and in Jn. particularly the prayer of petition plays the chief role. [378] But where the idea of a God inside or outside the world is dominant, the Thou-relationship which constitutes the essence of true prayer is impossible. Prayer makes sense only if we presuppose a God who is above the world. Hence the petitionary prayers of the NT are our most direct and powerful testimonies to early Christian belief in the transcendent God who in

---

[374] R. 8:38 f. Note esp. the piling up and use of the term δύναμις.

[375] For this reason the ἄπιστος should not worship the enthusiasts, but fall down before God: προσκυνήσει θεῷ.

[376] 1 Jn. 4:16, cf. 3:24; 4:12 ff.; Jn. 5:19 f.; 2 Jn. 9 → ἐν II, 543. On θεὸν ἔχειν → II, 822; cf. also ἐπιτυχεῖν θεοῦ in Ign.; Pr.-Bauer, s.v. ἐπιτυγχάνω.

[377] Only at one point in the NT do we seem to have an incursion of immanentist ideas, i.e., in the Areopagus address in Ac. 17:27 f. This gives evidence of other Hell. ideas (→ 123), and it is not by accident that we have here a plain quotation from the poets: θεὸν ... οὐ μακρὰν ἀπὸ ἑνὸς ἑκάστου ἡμῶν ὑπάρχοντα — ἐν αὐτῷ γὰρ ζῶμεν καὶ κινούμεθα καὶ ἐσμέν, ὡς καί τινες τῶν καθ' ὑμᾶς ποιητῶν εἰρήκασιν· τοῦ γὰρ καὶ γένος ἐσμέν. Cf. v. 29: τὸ θεῖον.

[378] Jn. 11:22; 14:13; 16:23 ff.; 1 Jn. 5:15 ff. etc.

the Christ event has declared that He can do all things and that He relieves all the distresses of this world.

The expressions for prayer vary. We have προσεύχεσθαι (→ II, 807) and αἰτεῖν (→ I, 191), also αἴρειν τὴν φωνήν (→ I, 185), and the more urgent → κράζειν and βοᾶν (→ I, 625), the cry of distress to the κύριος βοηθός[379] and → σωτήρ. The address to a Thou outside and above the one who prays is almost always indicated by an unequivocal πρός (τὸν θεόν).[380] Often the prayer seems to be referred back to the event in which God's supremacy over the world is decisively and instructively revealed. Prayer is made to God in the name of Jesus (→ ὄνομα). This gives to prayer not only its assurance and confidence but also its meaning and purpose. For all early Christian prayer culminates with the request for the final demonstration of the power of God in this world (→ ἵνα), for the definitive actualisation of the rule of God whose victory is decided with Christ: ἐλθάτω ἡ βασιλεία σου (Lk. 11:2). Thus the petitionary prayer of the NT is ultimately an expression of the fact that even after the Christ event the supremacy of God and His power as Ruler can only be believed until the final dominion of God is manifested. For the first encounter between heaven and earth will be transcended and completed[381] with the removal of all conflict, and the world will be the sphere of God: ἰδοὺ ἡ σκηνὴ τοῦ θεοῦ μετὰ τῶν ἀνθρώπων — καὶ αὐτὸς ὁ θεὸς μετ᾽ αὐτῶν ἔσται (Rev. 21:3, cf. 4 f., 7). In the coming creation, but only then, God will be πάντα ἐν πᾶσιν (1 C. 15:28, cf. R. 11:36).

† θεότης → θειότης.

"Divinity," "Godhead," in Plutarch, Lucian, Themistios etc., common in Hermas.[1]

It occurs only once in the NT, Col. 2:9: ἐν αὐτῷ (Christ) κατοικεῖ πᾶν τὸ πλήρωμα τῆς θεότητος σωματικῶς, cf. 1:19 f. The Εἷς θεός of the OT has attracted to Himself all divine power in the cosmos, and on the early Christian view He has given this fulness of power to Christ as the Bearer of the divine office.

---

[379] → βοήθεια, βοηθεῖν, I, 628. Cf. Peterson, Εἷς θεός, 3, 63 f. and Preisigke Sammelbuch, I, 159, 1.

[380] αἰτήματα πρὸς θεόν in Phil. 4:6. προσευχὴ πρὸς θεόν etc. in Ac. 12:5; 2 C. 13:7. εὔχεσθαι θεῷ in Ac. 26:29.

[381] Rev. 7:10; 12:10: ἄρτι ἐγένετο ἡ σωτηρία καὶ ἡ δύναμις καὶ ἡ βασιλεία τοῦ θεοῦ ἡμῶν.

θεότης. H. S. Nash, θειότης — θεότης (R. 1:20; Col. 2:9), JBL, 18 (1899), 1-34.

[1] V. Plut. Def. Orac., 10 (II, 415c): οὕτως ἐκ μὲν ἀνθρώπων εἰς ἥρωας, ἐκ δὲ ἡρώων εἰς δαίμονας αἱ βελτίονες ψυχαὶ τὴν μεταβολὴν λαμβάνουσιν. ἐκ δὲ δαιμόνων ὀλίγαι μὲν ἔτι χρόνῳ πολλῷ δι᾽ ἀρετῆς καθαρθεῖσαι παντάπασι θεότητος μετέσχον. Cf. also Luc. Icaromenipp., 9: διελόμενοι τὸν μέν τινα πρῶτον θεὸν ἐκάλουν, τοῖς δὲ τὰ δεύτερα καὶ τρίτα ἔνεμον τῆς θεότητος. R. Reitzenstein, "Zur Geschichte der Alchemie und des Mystizismus" in NGG, 1919, 14 ff. (lines 62, 117, 137); cf. Pr.-Bauer,³ s.v. Also Themist., XV, 193d (p. 237, 30 Dindorf). E. J. Goodspeed, Index Patristicus (1907), s.v. Joseph. does not use θεότης, but has θειότης.

ἄθεος.

In Aeschylus, the Stoics, Philo, Josephus, not in the LXX, once in the NT (Eph. 2:12; → 121), then in the post-apost. fathers, the Apologists, Sib., etc.[1] in the sense of "godless."

Seven basic forms of atheism may be distinguished in antiquity.

1. The practical atheism of the ignorant, short-sighted, self-sufficient, hedonistic or careless is attacked in the OT at Is. 22:13; Jer. 5:4 ff.; Ps. 10:4; 14:1 ff., and also in the NT at R. 1:30; 3:10 ff.; 1 C. 15:32; Eph. 2:12.[2]

2. The self-glorification of the state or its head leads, if not to a denial of the gods, at least to a secularisation of religion. In the east, and later in Rome, the cult of the state becomes a cult of the ruler which both OT and NT regard as the summit of demonic self-glorification and as violation of the honour of the Εἷς θεός, cf. Ez. 28:2; Da. 11:36; 2 Th. 2:4; Rev. 13 etc. (→ ἐγώ, II, 346b; → θεός, 96).

3. Plato mentions ἄθεοι who lay emphasis on mysterious rites, Leg., X, 908d; cf. 909b; cf. also the three forms of atheism in X, 885b and the term ἄθεος in XII, 966e, 967a; ἀθεότης, XII, 967c. In the Hell. period, belief in God is swallowed up in much wider circles by a belief in fate which sometimes has a heroic and fatalistic, sometimes a magical and astrological character. It is out of such belief that there springs the fear of the → στοιχεῖα τοῦ κόσμου to which Paul opposes his message of the cosmic supremacy of Christ and of the all-embracing scope of His death (Col. 1 f. → θεότης).

4. The replacement of traditional belief in God by philosophical enlightenment, which sometimes involves a metaphysical reinterpretation of the old ideas and new forms of piety,[3] plays no very significant role in the NT.[4]

5. Very different from philosophical scepticism is the shattering of faith by religious doubt, which is evoked by the contradiction between belief and the course of the world, and which can lead to despair of God. The different degrees of this shattering, which is evident already in Euripides, may be seen in Kerkidas,[5] Ps.-Diphilus,[6] Qohelet, Is. 45:15; Ps. 73. In these works we may also see the various means taken to overcome it. Kerkidas ends with the assertion that there is neither justice nor equity, neither meaning nor purpose, in the course of things. Ps.-Diphilus points to the later punishment of sinners and to future retribution. Qohelet saves himself from the ultimate consequences of his observation and reflection with the practical solution: "Fear God." The gloss on Is. 45:15 tries to secure the reader against the idea of a Deus absconditus. Ps. 73 is led by doubt to prayer, and by prayer to a deeper understanding of God and His ways. This is the train of thought which leads to the early Christian theology of the ways of God and to the theodicy of Paul in R. 9-11.

6. In the OT the sense of absolute dependence can sometimes take the form of im-potent avoidance and rejection of the omnipotent God. Jeremiah complains that God is

---

ἄθεος. Cr.-Kö., s.v.; A. B. Drachmann, Atheism in Pagan Antiquity (1922); A. Nock (1926), p. LXXXVIII on Sallust § 18; T. Mommsen, "Der Religionsfrevel nach röm. Recht," Hist. Zschr., 64 = NF, 28 (1890), 389 ff., esp. 407; A. Harnack, "Der Vorwurf des Atheismus in den drei ersten Jahrhunderten," in TU, NF, XIII, 4 (1905).

[1] V. Pr.-Bauer, s.v.; E. J. Goodspeed, op. cit., and also Index Apologeticus (1912), s.v.
[2] Cf. also Jos. Bell., 5, 566 : ἤνεγκε γενεὰν ἀθεωτέραν.
[3] Cf. the personal piety of the Platonic Socrates with the caricature of Aristophanes, who accepts the popular view and ascribes to him the atheism of nature philosophy.
[4] Philo Som., I, 43 f. contests the atheistic view that the cosmos is uncreated and eternal.
[5] P. Oxy., VIII, 1082 (→ θεός).
[6] Eus. Praep. Ev., XIII, 13, 47.

too strong for him. Moses opposes God when He plans to destroy the people.[7] When the enigma of providence obscures everything, and man can see only caprice and terror in the course of events, belief in God can turn into hatred of God. Job and the seer in 4 Esr. are in this danger, and they can be rescued from it, not by the warnings of their friends or the arguments of the angel, but only by encounter with God and by the Nevertheless of faith. The Gospel cuts the ground from under this attitude. Yet one may see from Ac. 9:5; 1 C. 15:9; R. 9:3, 20 that the defiance of the prophets and apocalyptists still lived on in Paul. Behind and above this defiance, however, stands his passion for God, and without this tension neither Paul himself nor R. 9-11 could be understood. The NT also speaks of a defiance of God which springs from self-glory. This is the demonic hatred of God which seeks to destroy all His works and which brings the Christ of God to the cross.

7. Charges of blasphemy, demonism and atheism are favourite weapons in the conflict between different faiths. They are particularly used by champions of the old faith against heralds or prophets of the new. This is how Plato represents the mission and rejection of Socrates (→ n. 3). This is how a Jew can interpret Heraclitus, seeing in him a preacher of the one true God who has constantly to meet the charge of atheism.[8] This is why Jewish monotheism, denying polytheism and emptying the world of gods, can be proscribed as atheism.[9] The Jews themselves accuse and hand over Jesus as a messenger of the devil and a blasphemer of God,[10] and they bring the same charges against His community.[11] Yet the early Church adopted Jewish monotheism, and among pagans it thus came under the old anti-Semitic charge of atheism, now intensified by reason of its passionate rejection of the imperial cult.[12] Αἶρε τοὺς ἀθέους was the anti-Christian battle-cry of the heathen mob.[13] The Christian community did not merely reject this charge; it threw it back. Thus we read already in Eph. 2:11 f.: μνημονεύετε ὅτι ποτὲ ὑμεῖς τὰ ἔθνη ... ἦτε ἄθεοι ἐν τῷ κόσμῳ.[14] But the plainest example is in Mart. Pol., 9, 2. The martyr bishop is asked to renounce his faith with the cry: Αἶρε τοὺς ἀθέους. But Polycarp, εἰς πάντα τὸν ὄχλον τὸν ἐν τῷ σταδίῳ ἀνόμων ἐθνῶν ἐμβλέψας ... καὶ ἀναβλέψας εἰς τὸν οὐρανόν, εἶπεν· Αἶρε τοὺς ἀθέους!

† θεοδίδακτος.

While θεόπνευστος (→ πνεῦμα) is referred in the NT to the γραφή (2 Tm. 3:16), and is later used regularly of the canonical Scriptures and their authors, the related θεοδίδακτος ("taught of God") is used in 1 Th. 4:9 of Christians generally[1] as members of the new covenant of Jer. 31:34; Is. 54:13; cf. Jn. 6:45 (→ II, 165).

Stauffer

---

[7] Ex. 32:32, cf. Ps.-Philo, XII, 9 f. (James [→ 97, n. 178] p. 113), etc.
[8] V. R. Hercher, *Epistolographi Graeci* (1873), 280 ff. E. Norden, "Der vierte heraklitische Brief," in *Beitr. zur Gesch. der griech. Philosophie, Jbch. f. Phil.*, Suppl. 19 (1893), 365 ff., cf. 386, n. 2.
[9] Jos. Ap., 2, 148 of the anti-Semitism of Apollonius: ἡμᾶς ὡς ἀθέους καὶ μισανθρώπους λοιδορεῖ. For a distinctive adaptation in Pl. cf. 1 Th. 2:15.
[10] Jn. 10:20: δαιμόνιον ἔχει — the same reproach as is brought against the Baptist in Lk. 7:33.
[11] V. Ac. 5:39; 9:5; 23:9 vl. (θεομαχέω).
[12] On the rejection of polytheism v. Just. Apol., I, 6: καὶ ὁμολογοῦμεν τῶν πάντων νομιζομένων θεῶν ἄθεοι εἶναι, ἀλλ᾽ οὐχὶ τοῦ ἀληθεστάτου ... θεοῦ. On the repudiation of idolatry and its influence v. Ac. 19 etc. On the rejection of the imperial cult, v. Rev. 13; Mart. Pol., 9, 2.
[13] Mart. Pol., 3, 2; Just. Apol., I, 13, 1; Ditt. Or., II, 569, 22; cf. also Pr.-Bauer and Mommsen. The Docetic heretics are called ἄθεοι in Ign. Trall., 10.
[14] Cf. 1 Th. 4:5; Gl. 4:8 f.

θ ε ο δ ί δ α κ τ ο ς [1] Barn., 21, 6: γίνεσθε δὲ θεοδίδακτοι. Not in Joseph.

† θεῖος.

a. Adj. for θεός, as δαιμόνιος for δαίμων, "divine," all that bears the stamp of a θεός,[1] whether by derivation or relation (θεῖον γένος, Hom. Il., 6, 180; θείη ὀμφή, ibid., 2, 41), whether there is seen in it the nature of a god or something superhuman, a predominant power, a final reality, a supreme meaning, which defies direct rational conception, like the Socratic θεῖόν τι καὶ δαιμόνιον, Plat. Ap., 31c; cf. Aristot. Eth. Nic., VII, 1, p. 1145a, 19 ff.: θεία ἀρετή. The abundance and nature of the use of the term are characteristic of Gk. religion, which sees traces of God in almost everything (Hippocr. Morb. Sacr., VI, 394, Littré; De Aëribus, Aquis, Locis, II, 76 f., Littré: οὐδὲν ἕτερον ἑτέρου θειότερον οὐδὲ ἀνθρωπινώτερον, ἀλλὰ πάντα ὁμοῖα καὶ πάντα θεῖα). It is a favourite expression of educated authors in class. and esp. in Hell. Gk.,[2] but also in the LXX,[3] Philo,[4] and Josephus.[5] Instead of reference to God, we have more general and impersonal reference to the θεία φύσις (Diod. S., V, 31, 4; Jos. Ap., 1, 232: θείας δοκοῦντα μετεσχηκέναι φύσεως), or θεία (opp. ἀνθρώπινος) δύναμις (Plat. Leg., III, 691e: φύσις τις ἀνθρωπίνη μεμειγμένη θεία τινὶ δυνάμει). Diog. L., III, 63: θεία σοφία.

If ἀνθρώπινος is often the antonym of θεῖος, man[6] as the bearer of creative and socially constructive power can also be called θεῖος. The typically Gk. conception of the θεῖος ἀνήρ, which is not found in the NT, is as early as Homer's θεῖος ἀοιδός ("singer") (Hom. Od., 8, 43; 1, 336; 4, 17 etc.). Θεῖοι ἄνδρες (or ἄνθρωποι) include seers, priests, religious heroes, workers of miracles like Apollonius of Tyana, and esp. the great law-givers of the past (Epimenides in Plat. Leg., I, 642d), rulers and kings (Plat. Men., 99d: καὶ τοὺς πολιτικοὺς οὐχ ἥκιστα ... ἂν θείους τε εἶναι καὶ ἐνθουσιάζειν. Resp., 500c/d: θείῳ δὴ καὶ κοσμίῳ ὅ γε φιλόσοφος ὁμιλῶν κόσμιός τε καὶ θεῖος εἰς τὸ δυνατὸν [!] ἀνθρώπῳ γίγνεται). In Stoicism θεῖος is a predicate of the wise (Diog. L., VII, 119 f.), and in Luc. Cynicus, 13 Heracles, the bringer of salvation to men, is called θεῖος ἀνὴρ καὶ θεός. Finally, θεῖος is a fixed term in the imperial cult (= divinus): τοῦ θειοτάτου ἡμῶν δεσπότου.[7] Dio C., 56, 35: ἐπὶ τῷ θείῳ ἐκείνῳ Αὐγούστῳ (→ θειότης).

b. The subst. τὸ θεῖον (→ θεός), "the divine," "the deity," is very common in Gk. from the middle of the 5th cent. B.C. (Hdt., 1, 32; Thuc., V, 70; Plat. Soph., 254b: τὸ ὄν = τὸ θεῖον;[8] Luc., also pap. and inscr., Keil-Premerstein, op. cit., No. 30; Ditt. Syll.³, 695, 16; 1268, 20; IG, V, 2, No. 266, 6; Ditt. Or., I, 90, 35 (2nd cent. B.C.); P.

θεῖος. J. Keil-A. v. Premerstein, Bericht über eine 3. Reise in Lydien (1914), 29; R. Mugnier, Le Sens du Mot θεῖος chez Platon (1930); Deissmann LO, 295 f.; H. Windisch, "Pls. u. Christus" = UNT, 24 (1934), 24 ff.; L. Bieler, ΘΕΙΟΣ ΑΝΗΡ. Das Bild des göttlichen Menschen in Spätantike und Frühchristentum, I (1935).

[1] As distinct from → ἱερός, "peculiar to a god."
[2] Salt is called θεῖος (Hom. Il., 9, 214); Aristot. Eth. Nic., VII, 13, p. 1153b, 32: πάντα γὰρ φύσει ἔχει τι θεῖον. Cf. Iambl. Vit. Pyth. (ed. A. Nauck [1884]), Index, s.v.
[3] Very occasionally in Ez., Job, Prv.; more frequently in later writers (Sir., 2 and 3 Macc.); a favourite word in 4 Macc.: θεία πρόνοια, θεία δίκη, θεῖα καὶ ἀνθρώπινα πράγματα, 1:16.
[4] Cf. Leisegang, Index, s.v.
[5] Bell., 7, 343: θεῖοι λόγοι; Ant., 1, 189; 3, 108 etc., Ap., 1, 232.
[6] On this view, which springs from belief in man's relationship to God (συγγένεια), cf. the fine materials and bibl. in Windisch, op. cit., 24 ff.; also Bieler, op. cit., 10 ff.; Reitzenstein Hell. Myst.³ (1927), 26.
[7] Cf. Deissmann LO, 295 f.
[8] It is a mark of the basic distinction between the concepts of God in the Gk. and Jewish worlds that Plato and Plutarch (Ei Delph., 19/20 [II, 392e/393b]) can use the impersonal τὸ ὄν as an equivalent of θεῖον or θεός, whereas the divine name of Gk. speaking Jews is the personal → ὁ ὤν (→ II, 398). Philo, standing between the two worlds, has both ὁ ὤν and τὸ ὄν (cf. Leisegang, Index, 226 ff.).

Lond., V, 1703, 17. It is worth noting that we do not find it in the LXX, but it does occur in Jos. Ant., 3, 321; 8, 111; 18, 167; Vit., 14, 48, and Philo Fug., 99; Decal., 63.

In the NT θεῖος occurs only in works or passages which betray Hellenistic influence. But the impersonal expression implies no surrender of personal faith in God. 2 P. 1:3 f.: τῆς θείας δυνάμεως αὐτοῦ ... δεδωρημένης ... ἵνα γένησθε θείας κοινωνοὶ φύσεως; Ac. 17:29: γένος ὑπάρχοντες τοῦ θεοῦ οὐκ ὀφείλομεν νομίζειν ... χαράγματι τέχνης ... τὸ θεῖον εἶναι ὅμοιον (cf. Ac. 17:27 vl.: ζητεῖν τὸ θεῖον).

† θειότης.

Subst. of θεῖος, "divinity" in the sense that something is θεῖον, or has the quality of the divine; that which shows God to be God, and gives Him the right to worship. Thus θειότης is first used of the deity: Plut. Convivalium Disputationum, IV, 2, 2 (II, 665a); Pyth. Or., 8 (II, 398a): ... πεπλῆσθαι πάντα θειότητος; Ditt. Syll.[3], 867, 31: Artemis has made Ephesus famous διὰ τῆς ἰδίας θειότητος. But also of men:[1] in the imperial cult θειότης is a term for the divinity of imperial majesty[2] (Ditt. Syll.[3], 900, 20: ἡ θειότης τοῦ δεσπότου ἡμῶν [Maximinus Daza] ... ἐπέλαμψεν. Ditt. Syll.[3], 888, 10 [238 A.D.]; P. Lond., II, 233, 8 [4th cent.]). It is rare in later Jewish texts (Ep. Ar., 95; Philo Op. Mund., 172 vl.). It occurs once in the LXX (Wis. 18:9: παῖδες ἀγαθῶν ... τὸν τῆς θειότητος νόμον ἐν ὁμονοίᾳ διέθεντο).

In the NT it occurs only at R. 1:20: ἡ ἀΐδιος αὐτοῦ δύναμις καὶ θειότης (→ θεός).

Kleinknecht

---

† θεοσεβής, † θεοσέβεια

Contents: A. Usage outside the NT; B. NT Usage; C. Early Church Usage.

A. Usage outside the NT.

1. Of the innumerable Gk. combinations of which θεός is the first part, the Gk. Bible has only θεοσεβής, θεοσέβεια, and once each in the NT we have θεοστυγής (R. 1:30), θεομάχος (Ac. 5:39), θεομαχεῖν (Ac. 23:9), → θεοδίδακτος (1 Th. 4:9) and → θεόπνευστος (2 Tm. 3:16). θεοσεβής is found from the time of Sophocles. Cf. Oed. Col., 260: Ἀθήνας φασὶ θεοσεβεστάτας εἶναι.[1] It denotes true piety. "To honour the gods" is the essence, kernel and goal of Gk. religion. On the other hand, → δεισιδαιμονία is often used in a critical or even a condemnatory sense. It can even denote superstition, as in Appian Rom. Hist. Ἐκ τῆς Σαυνιτικῆς, 12: Πύρρος οὐδὲ τῶν ἀναθημάτων τῆς Περσεφόνης ἀπέσχετο, ἐπισκώψας (scornfully noting) τὴν ἄκαιρον θεοσέβειαν εἶναι δεισιδαιμονίαν, τὸ δὲ συλλέξαι πλοῦτον ἄπονον εὐβουλίαν. The two terms are related in Xenoph. Cyrop., III, 3, 58, though here the

---

θ ε ι ό τ η ς. Pr.-Bauer³; Cr.-Kö., *s.v.* H. S. Nash → θεότης, Bibl.
[1] From Da. in Jos. Ant., 10, 268: δόξαν θειότητος παρὰ τοῖς ὄχλοις ἀποφέρεσθαι.
[2] Preisigke Wört., *s.v.*

θ ε ο σ ε β ή ς κτλ. Moult.-Mill., 288; Trench, 104 f. Cf. also → σέβομαι.
[1] Cf. Ac. 17:22: δεισιδαιμονεστέρους; Jos. Ap., 2, 11: εὐσεβέστατοι πάντων Ἑλλήνων. In Hdt., II, 37 we find a similar judgment of the Egyptians: θεοσεβέες δὲ περισσῶς ἐόντες μάλιστα πάντων ἀνθρώπων νόμοισι τοιοῖσδε χρέωνται.

author is obviously recording with a certain reserve some expressions of piety which he finds remarkable: οἱ δὲ θεοσεβῶς πάντες συνεπήχησαν (παιᾶνα) μεγάλῃ τῇ φωνῇ· ἐν τῷ τοιούτῳ γὰρ δὴ οἱ δεισιδαίμονες ἧττον τοὺς ἀνθρώπους φοβοῦνται. θεοσέβεια is a narrower concept than the more common εὐσέβεια. Thus the Lat. *pietas*, according to Augustine, corresponds to the Gk. εὐσέβεια or to the richer and more precise θεοσέβεια. [2] θεοσέβεια denotes, not so much an inner attitude or disposition, but rather pious conduct in the form of religious exercise or achievement, or of worship. Like its synonyms δεισιδαιμονία and εὐσέβεια, it finally corresponds in most instances to our modern "religion." [3] The practical side is seen in a text from the second century B.C. (Ditt. Syll.[3], II, 708, 18), in which we read: προαγόμενος εἰς τὸ θεοσεβεῖν ... πρῶτον μὲν ἐτείμησεν τοὺς θεούς. Cf. also Dio C., 54, 30, 1, where the reference is to cultic exercises: Ὁ Αὔγουστος ... θυμιᾶν τοὺς βουλευτὰς ἐν τῷ συνεδρίῳ ... ἵνα θεοσεβῶσι ... ἐκέλευσε. In the so-called Mithras Liturgy θεοσεβής, like εὐσεβής, is used as a self-description in prayer. [4] The term has more an ethical than a cultic bearing when it is linked with expressions from the ethical sphere, such as truth, righteousness, goodness, e.g., Plat. Crat., 394d: ὅταν ἐξ ἀνδρὸς ἀγαθοῦ καὶ θεοσεβοῦς ἀσεβὴς γένηται, Xenoph. An., II, 6, 26: ἀγάλλεται ἐπὶ θεοσεβείᾳ καὶ ἀληθείᾳ καὶ δικαιότητι. A more ethical understanding is also presupposed in Ps.-Plat. Epin., 985c: ἐπὶ θεοσέβειαν τρέψαι πόλιν ἑαυτοῦ. The same is true in pap. from 158/157 B.C., in which the help of the Egyptian king Ptolemy Philometor is invoked on the following grounds in favour of a certain Apollonius: ἧς ἔχετε πρὸς πάντας τοὺς τοιούτους θεοσεβουάς. [5] Similarly, in Iambl. Protr., 20 wisdom is seen to be the presupposition of true reverence: ὡς δεῖ θεοσέβειαν ἀσκεῖν, αὐτὴ δὲ οὐκ ἂν παραγένοιτο, εἰ μή τις ἀφομώσειε (equated) τῷ θεραπευομένῳ τὸ θεραπεῦον, τὴν δὲ ὁμοιότητα ταύτην οὐκ ἄλλη τις ἢ φιλοσοφία παρέχει. That fear of God underlies a particularly close relationship to God, and establishes a claim to His help, is a widespread belief in the pagan world, proof of which Cyrus seeks in Croesus according to an anecdote recounted in Hdt., I, 86: πυθόμενος τὸν Κροῖσον εἶναι θεοσεβέα τοῦδε εἵνεκεν ἀνεβίβασε ἐπὶ τὴν πυρήν, βουλόμενος εἰδέναι, εἴ τίς μιν δαιμόνων ῥύσεται. In general θεοσεβής is used of persons, and only rarely of things, e.g., Aristoph. Av., 897 of μέλος.

The word group does not occur frequently, but it has a certain material significance. It denotes the righteous κατ᾽ ἐξοχήν, whether they themselves advance this claim, or whether they are singled out in this way by those around. It denotes true religion as distinct from superstition.

2. This is how we are to understand the application of the group to the Jews and to their religion as the only true faith. It is true that the group is rare in the Gk. OT. The term religion — cf. → εὐσέβεια, which is generally rare, though surprisingly common in 4 Macc. — is basically alien in the biblical sphere, and has found its way into only a few passages. A lack of fear of God, and therefore moral deficiency, is presupposed in the story of Abimelech in Gn. 20:11. In the Heb. we have יִרְאַת אֱלֹהִים, which elsewhere in the LXX (2 Βασ. 23:3; 2 Εσδρ. 15:9, 15) is rendered φόβος θεοῦ

---

[2] *Pietatem, quam Graeci uel* εὐσέβειαν *uel expressius et plenius* θεοσέβειαν *vocant*: Aug. Ep., 167, 3 (CSEL, 44, 598); De Trinitate, XIV, 1; Civ. D., X, 1; Enchiridion, 1 and 2. In the last passage we have the following comment on Job 28:28: *Pietas est sapientia: si quaeras, inquit, quam dixerit eo loco pietatem, distinctius in Graeco reperies* θεοσέβειαν, *qui est Dei cultus.* Similarly the Vulg. translates Jdt. 11:17: *Deum colo,* and Jn. 9:31: *Deus cultor;* otherwise it usually has *timor Dei,* or *pietas.*

[3] Cf. G. Bertram, "Der Begriff 'Religion' in der Septuaginta," ZDMG, NF, 12 (1933), 1 ff. → εὐλάβεια, and cf. the cultic terms adduced in A. Deissmann, *Paulus*[2] (1925), 92.

[4] Preis. Zaub., IV, 683/684.

[5] P. Lond., I, 23 (p. 38), col. 2, 20.

(Κυρίου), but here θεοσέβεια. In Job 28:28 יִרְאַת אֲדֹנָי הִיא חָכְמָה is translated ἡ θεοσέβειά ἐστιν σοφία. Cf. Prv. 1:7; 9:10 : ἀρχὴ σοφίας φόβος Κυρίου. Cf. also Sir. 1:25, where we again have θεοσέβεια with σοφία : ἐν θησαυροῖς σοφίας παραβολαὶ ἐπιστήμης, βδέλυγμα δὲ ἁμαρτωλῷ θεοσέβεια. In Bar. 5:4 δόξα θεοσεβείας is used along with εἰρήνη δικαιοσύνης in an eschatological description of Jerusalem. The reference is usually to persons, but in general the adj. θεοσεβής is rare. It is used of Abraham in 4 Macc. 15:28, and of the mother of the martyrs in 16:12. Judith (11:17) says of herself : ἡ δούλη σου θεοσεβής ἐστι καὶ θεραπεύουσα νυκτὸς καὶ ἡμέρας τὸν θεὸν τοῦ οὐρανοῦ. This obviously refers to her religious attitude, and to her consequent claim to be heard by God in prayer, as in the above story of Croesus. [6] θεοσεβής is also used three times of Job at 1:1, 8; 2:3, being used with ἀληθινός, ἄμεμπτος, δίκαιος, ἄκακος. It is also found at Ex. 18:21 as one of the qualities demanded in the judges appointed by Moses. In the OT, too, the word has a strong ethical flavour. Even 4 Macc. understands θεοσέβεια, religion, in the sense of wisdom or philosophy. Thus we read in 7:21 f.: ἐπεὶ τίς πρὸς ὅλον τὸν τῆς φιλοσοφίας κανόνα [7] φιλοσοφῶν καὶ πεπιστευκὼς θεῷ καὶ εἰδώς, ὅτι διὰ τὴν ἀρετὴν πάντα πόνον ὑπομένειν μακάριόν ἐστιν, οὐκ ἂν περικρατήσειεν τῶν παθῶν διὰ τὴν θεοσέβειαν. [8] In 7:6 θεοσέβεια denotes the pure worship of God as opposed to impure heathen cults. This purity is symbolised in the regulations concerning meats. θεοσέβεια has the sense of true religion in the statement which characteristically concludes the story of the martyrs in 17:15 : θεοσέβεια δὲ ἐνίκα τοὺς ἑαυτῆς ἀθλητὰς στεφανοῦσα. In formulation, and in its estimation of Jewish religion, this may be compared with the statement with which Zerubbabel triumphs in the contest of the three youths before Darius (1 Εσδρ. 3:12): ὑπὲρ δὲ πάντα νικᾷ ἡ ἀλήθεια (cf. 4:41: μεγάλη ἡ ἀλήθεια καὶ ὑπερισχύει). There is a similar saying in Wis. 10:12 : παντὸς δυνατωτέρα ἐστὶν εὐσέβεια, and here, too, εὐσέβεια is very closely related to σοφία. [9] In other Gk. trans. of the OT θεοσέβεια occurs only once at Prv. 1:29. In Ep. Ar., 179 θεοσεβεῖς ἄνδρες is an address to the Jews used by the heathen king. Philo uses the term in the same way as the translators of the OT with reference to the true, i.e., the Jewish religion. He presupposes a philosophical, ethico-ascetic understanding of the biblical revelation. Thus θεοσέβεια is for him the supreme ἀρετή, δι' ἧς ἀθανατίζεται ἡ ψυχή (Op. Mund., 154; cf. Abr., 114), or the ἀγαθὸν τέλειον (Congr., 130) and κάλλιστον κτῆμα (Fug., 150). Here, too, θεοσέβεια is closely linked with φρόνησις, δικαιοσύνη and δύναμις (Spec. Leg., IV, 134 and 170). The σοφός is τείχει πεφραγμένος ἀκαθαιρέτῳ, θεοσεβείᾳ (Virt., 186). [10]

3. The same usage is even more pronounced in inscriptions which give evidence of Judaism in the Hell. and Roman period. Here the term is used to describe the Jews. Thus θεοσέβιοι is found in a much discussed inscr. in the theatre at Miletus : [11] Ἰουδαίων τῶν καὶ θεοσεβίων, which we are not so to amend by altering the order : καὶ τῶν, that it is made to refer to Jews and proselytes. The Jews prefer to call themselves "God-fearers" in an exclusive sense. This corresponds to the terms for God which are either common in Hellenistic Judaism or coined by it : κύριος, παντοκράτωρ, θεὸς ὕψιστος. [12] Here, as in the designation of Jews as "God-fearers," we have appellatives with a universalistic claim which have replaced the more strictly national proper name Yahweh. A syncretistic Jewish sect is expressly called the Hypsistarians after the cult of the θεὸς ὕψιστος. This is particularly common in the Hellenistic cities of the Crimea,

---

[6] Cf. infra on Jn. 9:31.
[7] A : + εὐσεβῶς.
[8] A : εὐσέβειαν.
[9] Cf. supra on Job 28:28.
[10] For further examples cf. Leisegang.
[11] Deissmann LO, 391 f.; Schürer, III, 174, 70.
[12] Bertram in G. Rosen-G. Bertram, Juden und Phönizier (1929), 50 ff.

and it makes use of the self-designation σεβόμενοι θεὸν ὕψιστον. [13] In the case of Lydia θεοσεβής is attested on a synagogue inscription. [14] In Phoenicia and Palestine Cyril of Alexandria refers to a half-Jewish and half-Hellenistic society of θεοσεβεῖς. [15] A Gk. burial inscription from Rome uses θεοσεβής to describe a certain Agrippa of Phaena, the chief city of Trachonitis in Transjordan. [16]

These examples, which could easily be multiplied, show that Jewish and half-Jewish societies called themselves "God-fearers" and were known by this name. Materially this self-designation is to be estimated in the same way as, e.g., ἅγιοι in the NT, or as the general use of appellatives denoting piety for religious societies. [17]

B. NT Usage.

If we may assume that in the NT period and the NT sphere the designation of Jews as "God-fearers" was widespread, it is natural that the NT should avoid the term. In any case the whole concept of "religion" is alien to the Bible. At all events, we find θεοσεβής and θεοσέβεια only once each in the Bible. In Jn. 9:31 the quality of fearing God is a presupposition of being heard by Him: ἐάν τις θεοσεβὴς ᾖ καὶ τὸ θέλημα αὐτοῦ ποιῇ, τούτου ἀκούει. The second part of the qualifying clause is to be regarded as an elucidation of what it means to fear God, i.e., to do His will. The idea itself is common, and there are many examples adduced in the commentaries from biblical, Jewish and Hellenistic sources. [18] Cf. Prv. 15:29; Job 27:9; ψ 33:15; Qoh. 12:13 according to the interpretation of the Midrash: "The end of the matter is that he is heard who fears God." [19] In some of these parallels we have the righteous in place of those who fear God, but in the saying of the man born blind it is obvious that θεοσεβής has an ethical sense after the manner of the OT.

The substantive θεοσέβεια is found in 1 Tm. 2:10. In accordance with established Hellenistic and Jewish usage, though naturally from the standpoint of the NT, it here denotes true religion. Women who confess Christianity must adorn themselves with good works. This is the meaning of the statement. It is not that good works are to serve to give primary evidence of Christianity, but rather that those who confess it must substantiate this confession of their religion by good works. [20]

---

[13] E. Schürer, "Die Juden im bosporanischen Reiche und die Genossenschaften der σεβόμενοι τὸν θεὸν ὕψιστον ebendaselbst" (SAB, 1897, XIII).

[14] Deissmann LO, 392, 2. The reference in this inscr. is undoubtedly to a proselyte.

[15] E. Schürer, op. cit. (→ n. 13), 23 f.

[16] G. Kaibel, Inscriptiones Graecae Siciliae et Italiae (1890), 1325. Cf. also Epigr. Graec., 729: Ἐνθάδε ἐν εἰρήνῃ κεῖτε Ῥουφεῖνος ἀμύμων, θεοσεβής. In a broader sense Jos. Ant., 20, 195 uses the term of the empress Poppaea. But here, too, it denotes a connection with Jewish monotheism.

[17] Cf. e.g., Cathari, Puritans, Pietists.

[18] C. F. Nägelsbach, Die nachhomerische Theologie (1857), 223; Bau. J., ad loc.

[19] Str.-B., ad loc.

[20] On ἐπαγγέλλεσθαι → II, 579. H. Grotius, Annotationes in NT (ed. C. E. de Windheim, 1755), ad loc.: bene sensum expressit Syrus: ... sed per opera bona (nempe 'se ornant' ex praecedentibus) ut decet feminas pietatem (Christianam scilicet) professas. Calvin translates and expounds the verse rather differently in his comm. (ed. A. Tholuck, 1831): quod decet mulieres profitentes pietatem per bona opera: si operibus testanda est pietas in vestitu etiam casto apparere haec professio debet. On our view a comma should come after θεοσέβειαν, as in Nestle. H. v. Soden omits it, cf. also H. H. Mayer, Über die Pastoralbriefe (1913), 31.

C. Early Church Usage.

In early Christian literature, too, θεοσεβής and cognates are infrequent. In Mart. Pol., 3 we have a reference to the γενναιότης τοῦ θεοφιλοῦς καὶ θεοσεβοῦς γένους τῶν Χριστιανῶν. Even though there is no explicit reference, θεοσέβεια is obviously used of the Christian religion in this work. Cf. also 2 Cl., 20, 4 : εἰ γὰρ τὸν μισθὸν τῶν δικαίων ὁ θεὸς συντόμως ἀπεδίδου, εὐθέως ἐμπορίαν ἠσκοῦμεν καὶ οὐ θεοσέβειαν. The word is more common in the Apologists. Cf. Just. Dial., 91, 3 of the heathen : εἰς τὴν θεοσέβειαν ἐτράπησαν ἀπὸ τῶν ματαίων εἰδώλων καὶ δαιμόνων (cf. 52, 4; 53, 6). Christians are the ἔθνος θεοσεβὲς καὶ δίκαιον (119, 6; cf. Melito in Eus. Hist. Eccl., IV, 26, 5). Knowledge of the true religion (θεοσέβεια) comes only through the preaching of the apostles (110, 2; cf. 44, 2). [21] Again, in Athenag. Suppl., 37, 1 the God-fearers are Christian, and if in 14, 2 the corresponding verb θεοσεβεῖν is first used as a comprehensive term for Christian and heathen worship, more exact exposition of the μὴ κοινῶς ἐκείνοις θεοσεβοῦμεν leads to the basic distinction which prescribes the use of fear of God for pagan cults. The term θεοσέβεια is used in a similar comprehensive fashion in Diognetus. This charming 2nd century work derives from the wish of a man in high position to know more of Christianity (τὴν θεοσέβειαν τῶν Χριστιανῶν μαθεῖν, 1, 1). Its content is first described negatively. It is not to be compared with the Jewish religion (3, 1). Sacrificial cults and astrology are folly in the eyes of Christians, and have nothing to do with true religion (3, 3; 4, 5). In words that have become famous the work then lays great emphasis upon the practical piety and morality of Christians. The true secret of the Christian religion is not to be learned from men (4, 6). For Christian reverence for God cannot be perceived with the senses (6, 4).

The normal Apologetic usage is also to be found in the debate between Origen and Celsus. [22] The main point here is to delimit the uniqueness and particularity of κατὰ τὸν Ἰησοῦν θεοσέβεια (III, 59 and 81) against the assertion : οὕτω τοι σέβειν μᾶλλον δόξεις τὸν μέγαν θεόν, ἐὰν καὶ τούσδε (τὸν Ἥλιον ἢ τὴν Ἀθηνᾶν) ὑμνῇς, τὸ γὰρ θεοσεβὲς διὰ πάντων διεξιὸν τελεώτερον γίνεται. This view of Celsus that the way to worship of the great God can and must lead through the variety of cults can be refuted only if the uniqueness of the biblical revelation is recognised in distinction from all human religion. But the use of the expression κατὰ τὸν Ἰησοῦν θεοσέβεια, the religion of Jesus, shows that Origen is not finally in a position to do this. By the use of a general term for religion the character of Christianity as revelation is surrendered. [23]

The use of θεοσέβεια and θεοσεβέστατος as epithets and titles, [24] especially in letters, is also the result of an anthropocentric view which is orientated rather to piety as a human attitude than to revelation as the gift of God. There are many examples of this. Cf., for example, the correspondence of Paphnutius in the 4th century. Here we find in P. Lond., VI, 1923, 1 ff.: τῷ ἀγαπητῷ καὶ θεοσεβεστάτῳ καὶ θεοφιλῆ καὶ εὐλογημένῳ πατρὶ Παπνουθίῳ Ἀμμώνιος ἐν κυρίῳ θεῷ χαίρειν, [25] or VI, 1924, 2, 3 : Μεμνημένος τῶν ἐντολῶν τῆς σῆς θεοσεβίας. From the 4th century we have a letter which is thought to be by St. Anthony (d. 356) and which might be addressed to the monk Ammonius, one of the hermits of the Nitric Mtns. It contains the following formulation (P. Lond., V, 1658, 3 ff.): [26] χάρις τῷ πάντων δεσπότῃ παρασχόντι ἡμῖν

---

[21] Cf. E. J. Goodspeed, *Index Apologeticus* (1912), *s.v.*
[22] A. Miura-Stange, *Celsus und Origenes* (1926), 30, 90 ff.
[23] G. Bertram, *Der anthropozentrische Charakter der Septuaginta-Frömmigkeit*, *Forschungen und Fortschritte*, 8 (1932), 219.
[24] Cf. Preisigke Wört., III, 190.
[25] H. I. Bell, *Jews and Christians in Egypt* (1924), cf. also P. Lond., V, 1925, 3 and 17; 1928, 11; 1929, 3.
[26] G. Ghedini, *Lettere Cristiane dai Papiri Greci del III e IV Secolo* (1923), 150 ff.

καιρὸν ἐπιτήδιον προσειπεῖν τὴν ἀναμίλλητόν (insurpassable) σου θεοσέβειαν, ἀγαπητὲ υἱέ. [27] In P. Giess., I, 55, 1 (6th cent.) the recipient is addressed as follows: τῷ ἀγαπητῷ καὶ θεοσεβεστάτῳ ἀδελφῷ.

On the whole the history of the term θεοσέβεια displays the penetration into the biblical sphere of a word group alien to the biblical revelation. This is why it is necessary to carry beyond the confines of the NT, where it is almost non-existent, the story of this term which has its source in an anthropocentrically orientated spiritual attitude. As claimed in Judaism and early Christianity it does at least denote the true worship of God in contrast to pagan superstition and idolatry. But it still stands in the stream of the development of an anthropocentrically orientated concept of religion and piety which had its source in Hellenistic Judaism, and it becomes stereotyped as an ecclesiastical title.

G. Bertram

> **θεραπεία, θεραπεύω,
> θεράπων**

---

† **θεραπεύω.**

1. In secular Gk. θεραπεύω means a. "to serve," "to be serviceable." It thus has much the same meaning as → διακονέω, → δουλεύω, → λατρεύω, → λειτουργέω, ὑπηρετέω. On the distinction between these terms → II, 81. The specific feature of θεραπεύω is that it expresses willingness to serve and the personal relation of him who serves to the one served by him, whether of respect in the case of a more powerful master, or of solicitude in the case of someone in need. [1] All θεραπεύειν "has in view something good and the advancement of the subject to which it applies," says Plat. Euthyphr., 13a ff., where the different senses of θεραπεύω are clearly set out. Thus we read in 13d: δοῦλοι τοὺς δεσπότας θεραπεύουσιν. This ministry of slaves to their masters is compared by Plato with ministering worship of the gods, though Socrates, of course, sees objections to this. As there is a ἵππους θεραπεύειν of the master of horse and a κύνας θεραπεύειν of the huntsman, so ὁσιότης and εὐσέβεια are a θεραπεία τῶν θεῶν, Euthyphr., 13a ff. This consists mainly in cultic action. θεραπεύοντες καὶ ἁγνεύοντες θύομεν, Lys., 6, 51. The religious significance of the word is more common in the inscr. and pap. Ditt. Syll.[3], III, 996, 28 ff. (1st cent. A.D.): τῶν ἱεροδούλων καὶ τὸν θεὸν θεραπευόντων, Ditt. Syll.[3], III, 1042, 11 f. (2nd/3rd cent. A.D.): καὶ εὐείλατος γένοιτο ὁ θεὸς τοῖς θεραπεύουσιν ἀπλῇ τῇ ψυχῇ. But doctors also render service in Euthyphr., 13d, and therefore θεραπεύειν acquires the sense b. "to care for the sick," "to treat medically," "to cure": Plat. Leg., IV, 720d:

---

[27] For further examples cf. Ghedini No. 23, 1; 41, 5.

θ ε ρ α π ε ύ ω. K. Bornhäuser, *Das Wirken des Christus durch Taten und Worte*[2] (1924); K. Heim, "Zur Frage der Wunderheilungen" in *Zeitwende*, III, 1 (1927), 410 ff.; "Gebetswunder und Wunderheilungen" in *Leben aus dem Glauben* (1932), 150 ff.; W. K. Hobart, *The Medical Language of St. Luke* (1882), 16 f.; F. Fenner, *Die Krankheit im NT* (1930).

[1] That it can be a title of honour to be called θεράπων of someone may be seen from Il., 23, 89 f., where the spirit of Patroclos says to Achilles: ἔνθα με δεξάμενος ἐν δώμασιν ἱππότα Πηλεὺς ἔτραφέ τ' ἐνδυκέως (solicitously) καὶ σὸν θεράποντ' ὀνόμηνεν.

(ὁ ἰατρός) τὰ νοσήματα θεραπεύει, e.g., Aristot. Eth. Nic., I, 13, p. 1102a, 19 f.: ὀφθαλμούς. Usually the reference is to actual medical treatment : P. Oxy., VIII, 1088, 28 ff. (1st cent. A.D.): ὕπτιον (backwards) κατακλίνας τὸν ἄνθρωπον θεράπευε. Metaphorically, however, it may be used of the healing of body and soul, Plat. Gorg., 513d. The healing may be divine, Strabo, VIII, 8, 15 : διὰ τὴν ἐπιφάνειαν τοῦ ᾿Ασκληπιοῦ θεραπεύειν νόσους παντοδαπάς.

2. Greek-speaking Judaism gives evidence of the same senses. In the LXX, too, θεραπεύω means a. "to serve," even in a secular sense, Est. 1:1b; 2:19; 6:10 : θεραπεύων ἐν τῇ αὐλῇ τοῦ βασιλέως, or, indeed, in the figurative sense of "to be obsequious to," Prv. 19:6; 29:26, and also in the religious sense of "to serve God," Jdt. 11:17: θεραπεύουσα νυκτὸς καὶ ἡμέρας τὸν θεὸν τοῦ οὐρανοῦ; Is. 54:17: κύριον, or idols, Ep. Jer. 25, 38. We also find the sense b. "to heal" in Tob. 2:10;[2] 12:3; Wis. 16:12; Sir. 18:19; 38:7. The facts are much the same in Philo except that his usage includes not only medical healing (Vit. Cont., 2 : ἡ [ἰατρική] μὲν γὰρ σώματα θεραπεύει) but also very prominently the healing of the soul, Leg. All., III, 118 : θεραπεύων (τὸν θυμόν), Spec. Leg., II, 239 : ἀφροσύνη δ' οὐκ ἄλλῳ ἢ φόβῳ θεραπεύεται.

3. The important role of miracles of healing in the ministry of Jesus might lead us to suspect that there would be parallels among the rabbis in His day. This is not so. Schlatter has made this quite plain :[3] "In Palestinian Judaism of the time there were no workers of miracles, nor were there any who were honoured as such." We have only isolated accounts of healings by rabbis. In the 1st century we simply read that R. Chanina b. Dosa accomplished cures at a distance by prayer : jBer., 9d, 22-25 ; bBer., 34b. In this case it is quite evident that the pious man of prayer brings about the cure rather than the rabbi. Around 200 R. Jehuda cures two dumb people, bChag., 3a, and for the 3rd century cf. bBer., 5b. The religious basis of the surprisingly few healings recorded in this early period is that the righteous may claim from God answers to their prayers. This is logical in the sphere of a religion of law and merit, but it has nothing whatever to do with the attitude of Jesus in His struggle against the sinister powers of this world.

4. a. In the NT θεραπεύω is never used in the secular sense of "to serve," and only once in the religious sense of cultic worship, namely, at Ac. 17:25 : ὁ θεὸς ὁ ποιήσας τὸν κόσμον καὶ πάντα τὰ ἐν αὐτῷ, οὗτος οὐρανοῦ καὶ γῆς ὑπάρχων κύριος οὐκ ἐν χειροποιήτοις ναοῖς κατοικεῖ, οὐδὲ ὑπὸ χειρῶν ἀνθρωπίνων θεραπεύεται προσδεόμενός τινος. Paul brings out the antithesis between the Creator of heaven and earth and the Greek gods by showing 1. that the true God has no cultic dwelling, that He is not linked to a temple, and 2. that He does not need a cultic ministry. The θεραπεύειν which is suitable for idols, but not for God, consists in the bringing of sacrificial gifts and in any cultic action which might give the impression that the deity is referred to some human performance (→ II, 41).

b. θεραπεύω is used much more often in the sense of "to heal," and always in such a way that the reference is not to medical treatment, which might fail, but to real healing.[4] Among the full powers of the Messiah is His power to heal the sick (Lk. 7:21 ff. and par.). The δύναμις (→ II, 301) at work in Jesus, which

---

[2] The reading in S.
[3] "Das Wunder in der Synagoge" (BFTh, 16 [1912], 498 ff.), as against P. Fiebig, ZwTh, 54 (1912), 160 ff. Cf. also Bultmann Trad., 247 ff.
[4] Cf. Leisegang, s.v. θεραπεία and θεραπεύω.

makes Him Lord of every spirit, gives rise constantly to new δυνάμεις, or acts of power.[5] These take particularly the form of healings. They are so much a part of His activity that they can be mentioned along with the preaching of the Gospel in depictions of His work : Mt. 4:23; 9:35 : καὶ περιῆγεν ἐν ὅλῃ τῇ Γαλιλαίᾳ, διδάσκων ἐν ταῖς συναγωγαῖς αὐτῶν καὶ κηρύσσων τὸ εὐαγγέλιον τῆς βασιλείας καὶ θεραπεύων πᾶσαν νόσον καὶ πᾶσαν μαλακίαν ἐν τῷ λαῷ (→ II, 720). There is no sickness or weakness which Jesus cannot master. This is the basic thought in all the stories of His healings. Sometimes there is a general reference to them, but in some cases the process is described in detail, e.g., Mt. 8:7 (the centurion's servant), Jn. 5:1 ff. (the man at the pool of Bethesda). Men come from all sides to be cured of their sufferings, Lk. 5:15; 6:18, and Jesus heals them, Mt. 4:24; 14:14; 19:2,[6] heals many, Mk. 3:10, heals all, Mt. 12:15, the lame, the maimed, the blind, the dumb, Mt. 15:30; 21:14. The contrast between the moral conceptions of the Pharisees and the attitude of Jesus is brought into sharp relief by the fact that there can be conflict on the question whether one should heal on the Sabbath, Mt. 12:10; Mk. 3:2; Lk. 6:7; 13:14; 14:3.

Two great groups of healings are to be distinguished, namely, the exorcism of evil spirits and the curing of defects like blindness, lameness etc. Hence we read in Mt. 8:16 : ἐξέβαλεν τὰ πνεύματα λόγῳ καὶ πάντας τοὺς κακῶς ἔχοντας ἐθεράπευσεν. The conflict with demons is often a powerful struggle between the divine power of Christ and Satanic forces, as in Lk. 4:40 f.; 8:2; Mk. 1:34; 3:10 f.; Mt. 12:22; 17:18. Christ wins the victory, not through techniques such as those used by the exorcists of His day, but through His word. This also cures defects, though often He will touch the sick, Mk. 1:41; 8:22, or take their hand, Mk. 1:31; 5:41; Lk. 14:4; Ac. 3:7, or lay on His hands,[7] Mk. 5:23; 6:5; 7:32; 8:23, 25; Lk. 4:40; 13:13, or even perform acts similar to those of doctors, Mk. 7:33; 8:23; cf. also James 5:14. Indeed, in popular belief it is enough for the sick person simply to touch the healer or his garment, Mk. 3:10; 5:28; 6:56; Lk. 6:19; 8:44 f. (the woman with an issue of blood). Healing power is ascribed even to Peter's shadow (Ac. 5:15) or to parts of Paul's clothing (Ac. 19:12). The result of the intervention of Jesus is always that the sick person is fully cured even though he has been sick from birth or for many years. As the Bringer of the age of salvation Jesus is the great Physician. Mt. 8:17 sees in this a fulfilment of the saying in Isaiah concerning the Servant of the Lord (Is. 53:4), which is quoted as follows : αὐτὸς τὰς ἀσθενείας ἡμῶν ἔλαβεν καὶ τὰς νόσους ἐβάστασεν, λαμβάνειν and βαστάζειν being taken to imply a bearing away of sicknesses.[8]

There is no point in asking what particular capacities of soul Jesus might have commanded, though He certainly possessed these. Nor is there any point in investigating the historicity of the various incidents. The essential feature is that in a wonderful "already" the light shines in which Jesus will perfect His victory over all dark, Satanic powers. This biblical understanding of the miracles of healing does not preclude the possibility that the form in which they are recounted will display many points of agreement with similar accounts from the Greek and Jewish

---

[5] Cf. W. Grundmann, *Der Begriff der Kraft in der nt.lichen Gedankenwelt* (1932).
[6] In the corresponding passage Mk. has καὶ ἐδίδασκεν αὐτούς, which fits the context better.
[7] Cf. J. Behm, *Die Handauflegung im Urchristentum* (1911), 8 ff., 102 ff.
[8] Cf. Kl. Mt., *ad loc.* and Str.-B., I, 481 f.

world, especially in connection with the figure of Aesculapius.[9] The only thing is that in the NT the process itself is never the important point, but the demonstration of the power of Jesus by which He makes it plain that with Him the kingdom of God has broken into this suffering world. The miracle does not consist in the breaking of the causal nexus of natural law. This does not come within the purview of the NT. The real miracle is victory in the conflict with forces which struggle for mastery over this cosmos. The NT thus looks into the depths of world occurrence.

Only in this light can we understand why Jesus could authoritatively commission His disciples to heal the sick (→ II, 310). That this is not a matter of magic may be seen from the fact that there is no transmission of power from the Master to the disciples. He simply issues to them the command: ἀσθενοῦντας θεραπεύετε, ... δαιμόνια ἐκβάλλετε, Mt. 10:8; Lk. 10:9. This command, received in faith, gives them power over spirits. Full power is herewith given to them, Mt. 10:1; Lk. 9:1; Mk. 3:15.[10] The disciples act accordingly, Mk. 6:13; Lk. 9:6. The Risen Lord again gave power to His apostles to do mighty works when He sent them forth. In His name, but only thus, they heal the sick who throng around them, Ac. 5:16. Healings are reported of Peter, Ac. 3:1 ff.; 5:14 f.; 9:32 ff., Philip, Ac. 8:7, Paul and Luke, Ac. 28:8 f.

Worth noting are the few instances when the disciples (Mt. 17:16), and in Nazareth Jesus (Mk. 6:5), cannot heal. In both cases the reason is a false attitude in men. The healing power is not to serve as a miracle for unbelievers or miracle-seekers. In Nazareth Jesus attributes to His doubting hearers the reproach: "Physician, heal thyself" (Lk. 4:23), which must have been a well-known utterance of ancient scepticism.[11]

c. In the healing of the mortal wound of the beast in Rev. 13:3, 12 the allusion is to a historical event which we cannot now identify but in which the power of Antichrist receives a serious blow from which it later recovers.[12]

† θεραπεία.

In the NT this means a. "household," like οἰκετεία, at Mt. 24:45; Lk. 12:42; and b. "healing," whether in the medical sense at Lk. 9:11 or in the eschatological of the healing of the nations at Rev. 22:2.

The word θεραπεία is occasionally used in the LXX for the "worship of God" or "cultic action," e.g., at Est. 5:1; Jl. 1:14; 2:15. In the last two passages it is used for עֲצָרָה, which elsewhere is translated differently. Intrinsically, however, the term is more compatible with the usage of paganism than with that of the OT religion of revelation (cf. Ac. 17:25). Hence it is never used in the NT in this sense.

---

[9] R. Reitzenstein, Hellenistische Wundererzählungen (1906); Weinreich AH, 119 ff.; P. Fiebig, Jüd. Wundergeschichten im nt.lichen Zeitalter (1911); Antike Wundergeschichten (1911); Rabb. Wundergeschichten (1911); S. Herrlich, Antike Wunderkuren (1911); A. Schlatter, Das Wunder in der Synagoge (1912); R. Herzog, Die Wunderheilungen von Epidauros (1931).

[10] Only AD it sys have θεραπεύειν τὰς νόσους at Mk. 3:15.

[11] Eur. Fr., 1086 (TGF): ἄλλων ἰατρὸς αὐτὸς ἕλκεσιν βρύων, Cic. Ep., IV, 5, 5: malos medicos, qui in alienis morbis profitentur tenere se medicinae scientiam, ipsi se curare non possunt. Gn. r., 23 on 4:23: "Physician, heal thy lameness"; G. Dalman, Jesus-Jeschua (1922), 207; Kl. Lk. on 4:23.

[12] Cf. Loh. Apk., ad loc.; Had. Apk., ad loc.; E. B. Allo, L'Apocalypse de St. Jean⁴ (1932), 186, 190.

† θεράπων.

Though this word is common in the LXX, it is used in the NT only of Moses at Hb. 3:5 (cf. Nu. 12:7),[1] and the important point here is the contrast with Jesus, who is the Son where Moses is the servant. Cf. Gl. 4:1 ff.

Beyer

θερίζω, θερισμός

† θερίζω.

a. Lit. "to reap" (from θέρος, "summer"); b. figur. of the "reaping of a harvest," esp. of the consequences of an act.[1] In accordance with the image, there is often emphasis on the moral righteousness or normativeness of the event.[2] This is particularly so in proverbial speech.[3]

In the OT it is almost always used for צָר, a. lit. at Ruth 2:3 ff.; b. figur. of sowing and reaping, of the correspondence between moral action and its consequences, at Prv. 22:8: ὁ σπείρων φαῦλα, θερίσει κακά, Job 4:8; Sir. 7:3. The horizon here is still in this world. In prophecy, however, the harvest is the eschatological action of God (→ θερισμός).

Similarly Hellen. and Palestinian Judaism later uses the image of reaping (→ θερισμός, καρπός) both with reference to this world[4] and also eschatologically.[5] Philo avoids eschatology; his use is ethical and psychological.[6]

The NT uses θερίζειν a. literally at Mt. 6:26 and par.; James 5:4, and b. figuratively, especially in an eschatological context. God makes of the end of the world the harvest of the world (→ θερισμός) in which the results of human action are established and the decision of salvation or judgment is taken, Rev. 14:15 f. (cf. Mt. 3:12; 13:30). Man thus reaps the fruit of what he has done, with emphasis upon the correspondence between what is sown and what is reaped. The inevita-

---

θ ε ρ ά π ω ν. [1] Cf. e.g., Rgg. Hb., *ad loc.* Hb. 3:5 naturally follows the OT designation of Moses as עֶבֶד יְהוָה. In the LXX Moses is called θεράπων at Ex. 4:10; Nu. 12:7; Wis. 10:16.

θ ε ρ ί ζ ω. [1] Proverbially at Gregorius Cyprius, 57 (Corpus Paroemiographorum Graecorum, ed. E. L. Leutsch, II [1851], 77: καρπὸν ὃν ἔσπειρας, θέριζε· (Explanation) ἐπὶ τῶν τοιαῦτα πασχόντων οἷα ἔδρασαν.

[2] Gorgias in Aristot. Rhet., III, 3, p. 1406b, 10: αἰσχρῶς μὲν ἔσπειρας, κακῶς δὲ ἐθέρισας. Plat. Phaedr., 260d.

[3] Gregorius Cyprius, 57: ὃς δὲ κακὰ σπείρει, θεριεῖ κακὰ κήδεα παισίν, → n. 1; Cic. De Orat. (ed. J. Bake, 1868), II, 261: *Ut sementem feceris, ita metes*; Plaut. Mercator, I, 71; Plaut. Epidicus, 265; Epict. Diss., II, 6, 11 f.; III, 24, 91: θερίζομαι as an image of human dying.

[4] Test. L. 13:6: ἐὰν σπείρητε πονηρά, πᾶσαν ταραχὴν καὶ θλίψιν θερίσετε.

[5] 4 Esr. 4:28 ff.; S. Bar. 70:2 ff. (Str.-B., IV, 980); Midr. Cant., 8, 14 (I, 672): Redemption is compared with four things, grain harvest, vintage, balsam, and a woman in travail.

[6] Deus Imm., 166: τὸν τῆς ψυχῆς αὐτοῦ καρπόν; Conf. Ling., 152: ἀδικίαν μὲν σπείραντες, ἀσέβειαν δὲ θερίσαντες. Mut. Nom., 269.

bility and the righteousness of this assessment are expressed at Gl. 6:7 ff. (ὅ/τοῦτο, σάρξ/φθοράν, πνεῦμα/ζωήν); [7] 2 C. 9:6 (φειδομένως, ἐπ' εὐλογίαις). The obvious law of correspondence between what is sown and what is reaped provides a motive for human conduct in the present aeon.

The results of mission are also described as the harvest which Christian workers reap on the basis of prior sowing in Jn. 4:36-38. The case of the apostles is particularly favourable, since they have the full joy of reaping without the same degree of preliminary labour in sowing. [8]

The material support which Christian workers receive from the community is also regarded as a harvest in relation to the spiritual seed which they have planted in the community (1 C. 9:11).

† θερισμός.

"The harvest." In the LXX this word is used almost exclusively for קָצִיר, a. in the lit. sense at Gn. 8:22, and b. figur. (→ θερίζω), esp. in eschatological contexts as the image of the judgment which God will exercise on the nations at the end of the world (Jl. 4:1 ff., LXX 4:13; Is. 27:11). The standpoint here is national. God rejects the nations and gathers Israel as valuable wheat from the Gentile chaff, Is. 27:12. Later Jewish apocalyptic sometimes uses the eschatological figure of harvest in an ethical sense, cf. 4 Esr. 4:28 ff.; 9:17, 31. Philo uses the metaphor ethically and psychologically in his rational and non-eschatological manner, Som., II, 23 f.

In the NT it is used a. literally at Jn. 4:35; b. figuratively as a similitude of the eschatological decision of God at Mt. 13:30, 39; Mk. 4:29; Rev. 14:15. The distinctive feature of NT proclamation is that this hour of decision is regarded as imminent, Mt. 9:37 f.; Jn. 4:35, and that the image is understood in a purely moral sense, Mt. 13:41 ff. The figure carries with it both threat and promise, especially in accompanying explanations, Mt. 3:12; 13:30. It impels man to decision by showing what will be the consequences of his action. The divine harvest entails definitive separation.

Hauck

θεωρέω → ὁράω.

θηρίον

θηρίον, as a diminutive of θήρ, originally means a "wild animal," or in pre-Hell. Gk. an "animal living wild" (Plat. Menex., 237d: θηρία along with βοτά [a "pastured beast"]), occasionally including insects and birds (Xenoph. Cyrop., I, 6, 39), and later any "animal": Plat. Resp., IX, 1 (571d): ἄνθρωποι καὶ θεοὶ καὶ θηρία. So Ac. 28:4 f. of a snake. In the LXX it is restricted to land animals, usually those living wild, and

---

[7] Zn. Gl., 275 f.
[8] This thought, too, is proverbial, cf. Diogenian, II, 62 (Corp. Par. [→ n. 1], II, 98): ἄλλοι μὲν σπείρουσιν, ἄλλοι δ' ἀμήσονται ("gather," "harvest"). Cf. Mt. 25:24, 26.

it is distinguished from ἰχθύες, πετεινά, ἑρπετά and κτήνη : Gn. 7:14, 21; 8:1, 17, 19; 9:2; Hos. 4:3. So Ac. 11:6; Jm. 3:7; Tt. 1:12; Rev. 6:8. If in Tt. the adj. κακός gives the clear sense of "beasts of prey," and if the addition of the OT τῆς γῆς gives the same sense in Rev., the original sense of θηρίον maintains such vitality that even in the Hell. period no addition is needed to convey the sense of a wild animal to readers. When Apollonius of Tyana (Philostr. Vit. Ap., IV, 38) calls Nero a θηρίον, the context shows that he is thinking of a beast of prey with claws and teeth, a carnivorous animal, like a lion or panther. There is an exact equivalent in the Heb. חיה. Cant. r. on 2:15 compares the חיות, which represent world powers, with the fox, which stands for the less dangerous Egypt, and on a mosaic in the synagogue at Gerasa the birds which go out of the ark (Gn. 8:17b), tame animals (בְּהֵמוֹת) and beasts of burden are surrounded by wild animals (חיות),[1] How easily θηρίον as a wild animal can be used figur. may be seen from Sib., 8, 157, where Nero is θὴρ μέγας, and from Plin. (the younger) Panegyricus (ed. M. Schuster, 1933), 48, 3, where Domitian is called immanissima belua, cf. also the above-mentioned passage from Philostr.[2]

We find θηρίον in theologically important passages in the NT at Mk. 1:13 and in Rev. In the story of the temptation in Mk. (→ I, 141) it is said of Jesus : καὶ ἦν μετὰ τῶν θηρίων, καὶ οἱ ἄγγελοι διηκόνουν αὐτῷ. Attempts to find here remnants of a mythological divine conflict[3] or indications of a return to the age of Paradise[4] impose too great a strain on the text. Anyone living in the wilderness of Judaea, which is the setting of the story, will be among wild beasts, and the ministry of angels forms a counterpart to this abandonment by men.[5]

Mention of the θηρίον in Rev. 13:2 links Rev. to Da. 7. For Rabb. exegesis[6] up to the 1st cent. A.D. the fourth beast of Da. 7 is Edom = Rome. The beast which in Rev. 13 rises out of the sea (i.e., the abyss, 11:7) at the glance of the dragon unites all the features of the four beasts of Da. and cannot, therefore, be identified with Rome. In Rev. there is, rather, an obvious antithetical parallelism between God and the dragon, Jesus Christ and the beast, the seven spirits and the second beast of Rev. 13:11 ff., which is interpreted as the ψευδοπροφήτης (16:13; 19:20; 20:10).[7] It is thus clear that the beast is Antichrist. The antithetical parallelism is also to be noted in the contrast between the ἀρνίον ὡς ἐσφαγμένον of 5:6 and the mortal wound of the beast. For the primary significance of the image of

---

θ η ρ ί ο ν. [1] Ill. in E. L. Sukenik, Ancient Synagogues in Palestine and Greece (1934), plate IX. For details cf. A. Barrois in Rev. Bibl., 39 (1930), 257-265.

[2] For this reason the passages adduced are no proof that the beast of Rev. has to be Nero, as R. Schütz believes in Die Offenbarung des Joh. und Kaiser Domitian (1933), 8 f.

[3] H. Gunkel, Zum religionsgeschichtlichen Verständnis des NT (1903), 70; A. Meyer, "Die evang. Berichte über die Versuchung Jesu Christi" in Festgabe f. H. Blümner (1914), 434-468.

[4] F. Spitta, "Die Tiere in der Versuchungsgeschichte," ZNW, 5 (1904), 323 ff.; "Steine und Tiere in der Versuchungsgeschichte," ibid., 8 (190), 66-68, with reference to various passages from the OT and the Test. XII; J. Jeremias, Das Ev. nach Mk. (1928), 30 f.; Bultmann Trad., 271. The thought is weakened in Hck. Mk., ad loc., where it is seen to be a reward of piety that the beasts do not harm Jesus. Cf. also S. Hirsch, Taufe, Versuchung und Verklärung Jesu (1933).

[5] So also Clemen, 215. Similarly, Schl. Mk., 35 rejects any reference back to the age of Paradise in view of the total content of Mk.

[6] Str.-B., IV, 1002 f. Rabb. tradition always distinguishes the four animal kingdoms.

[7] May it be also that the red colour of the beast in Rev. 17:3 indicates the blood shed by it in murder, in contrast to the outpoured blood of the horseman in the ἱμάτιον βεβαμμένον αἵματι of 19:13 ? On the antithetical parallelism cf. E. B. Allo, Saint Jean, L'Apocalypse² (1921), 182 f.; Loh. Apk. on 17:4; Had. Apk. on 13:2.

the θηρίον is in contrast to the Lamb. If → ἀρνίον denotes Jesus Christ as the One who, by the self-surrender of His life even to the point of death in an act of service, is worthy to receive power (Rev. 5:12), θηρίον denotes the Antichrist as the one who uses the power given by "the murderer from the beginning" to commit acts of violence (11:7), and who causes himself to be worshipped because of this power (13:3 ff.). The beast has not actually suffered death; he has simply been given a mortal wound. The dragon, which has also been mortally wounded and cast out of heaven, has divine permission to give "life" to this beast which is mortally stricken under the divine judgment, and as a beast of prey it persecutes those who belong to the Lamb. If Jesus can say of Himself as the Lamb that He honours the Father, the whole point of the existence of the beast is to dishonour God by causing itself to be worshipped as God (13:4 f.). The divine indicates this by saying of the beast that it was, is not, and will be — a blasphemous parody of the name of God as He who was, is and will be, and of the ἐν ἀρχῇ ἦν ὁ λόγος. If Jesus Christ is the Shepherd of the community, Antichrist as θηρίον is its persecutor, and this persecution causes the community to tread the way of its Lord through death to glory, 11:7-12; 13:7-10; 15:2-4.

The other beast, which is always called ψευδοπροφήτης except in Rev. 13:11, is the false prophet of the last time from whom proceeds the temptation to worship the first beast (13:11 ff.). He has the external appearance of a genuine prophet (εἶχεν κέρατα δύο ὅμοια ἀρνίῳ), but his prophecy is devilish (ἐλάλει ὡς δράκων). [8] There is here an independent development of the thought of Mt. 7:15. The figure of the θηρίον shows that the activity of this false prophet is that of a beast of prey.

While ζῷον (→ II, 873) is used for a living creature, and can thus include man, [9] even the more general sense of θηρίον extends only to the animal kingdom in distinction from man. In the imagery of Rev. satanic and demonic powers are consistently represented as beasts. Thus we have the locusts of 9:1 ff., the horses of 9:16 ff., [10] the dragon, the frogs of 16:13 f., and the two θηρία. Linked with man and yet distinct from him, the animal world with its domination of instincts seems to have in fallen creation the significance of a perversion of that whereto man is called as the image of God. This fact is evident throughout the animal kingdom, but is particularly clear in wild animals. Hence individual animals, and especially the θηρία, can serve as a figure of the demonic which perverts the divine similitude of man into that which is sub-human (→ II, 19). [11]

Foerster

---

[8] B. Murmelstein, ThStKr, 101 (1929), 447-457, is surely wrong when he equates the second beast, which comes up out of the earth, speaks as a dragon, is seated on Babylon, and will allow no buying or selling without the mark of the first beast, with Herod, who comes from the land of Palestine, speaks Greek, bases his power on Rome, and is the first to introduce into Palestine coins bearing the Roman eagle.

[9] Corp. Herm., VIII, e.g., calls man τὸ λογικὸν ζῷον and the κόσμος a ζῷον ἀθάνατον (§ 1). Cf. Rev. 4:6 f.

[10] Cf. the colour of the horsemen in v. 17 and the corresponding mention of fire and smoke and brimstone in v. 17 f.

[11] For bibl. on the beasts in Rev., v. W. Foerster, ThStKr, 104 (1932), 279-310 and E. Lohmeyer, ThR, NF, 6 (1934), 269-314; also 7 (1935), 28-62. We need not list the literature here, where our concern is with the theological content of the image, for most of the works quoted do not tackle the theological question, but assume a historical interpretation. Theologically, this is based on the view that biblical prophecies always have concrete,

---

θησαυρός, θησαυρίζω

† θησαυρός.

a. "What is deposited," "store," esp. of what is valuable, "treasure"; figur. σοφίας, Plat. Phileb., 15e; τῶν πάλαι σοφῶν ἀνδρῶν; Xenoph. Mem., I, 6, 14; Epic. Sententiae Vaticanae, Fr. 44 : μᾶλλον ἐπίσταται μεταδιδόναι ἢ μεταλαμβάνειν· τηλικοῦτον αὐταρκείας εὗρε θησαυρόν. Philo Congr., 127: σοφίας. b. "The place where a thing is stored," the "treasure chamber, chest, or house," e.g., state warehouse, P. Lond., I, 31, [1] temple treasury, or temple storehouse for offerings in kind. [2] Payments into the θησαυρός are temple offerings, [3] sacrificial and guilt offerings, [4] or thank offerings, e.g., for successful cures. [5] The erection of a θησαυρός in the temple seems to have spread to Greece from Egypt. [6] The cultic treasuries provided an impulse for private money boxes (1 C. 16:2). [7]

---

contemporary significance, indeed, R. Schütz (ThStKr, 105 [1933], 460) takes the view that prophecy in Rev. is written at the time when the author thinks the great turning point must come. Historically this interpretation is based on the suggestion that apocalyptic lit. is always written with contemporary reference at times when some turning point was expected in view of the urgency of the need. The eschatological discourses of Jesus, however, are not spoken in the "need of the present" which has become "the boiling-point of history" (Schütz, 459) in which "everything ungodly ... is concentrated in the temporal kingdom or the contemporary ruler" (459 f.). Nor is this true of 2 Th. 2:3 ff. Similarly, it cannot be postulated of Rev. Otherwise we shall either have to follow Schütz (463) in referring 17:10 : ὁ ἄλλος οὔπω ἦλθεν, καὶ ὅταν ἔλθῃ ὀλίγον αὐτὸν δεῖ μεῖναι to the past, or else we shall threaten the unity of the book. Rev. also speaks of the hour of testing which is to come (3:10) without detriment to its actuality. NT prophecy has permanent significance because no one knows the hour and the mystery of iniquity is already at work, as expressed in Rev. by the fact that Babylon sits on the beast, i.e., has a lasting connection with it which is not dependent on the manifestation of the beast (cf. Foerster, op. cit., 299 ff.). The historical argument for the contemporary interpretation of Rev., and esp. of the beasts, namely, that apocalyptic literature demands such an interpretation, rests on the petitio principii that Rev. is to be interpreted in terms of this literature. It is well known to what difficulties application of this interpretation leads. Similarly, the view of Schütz (464) that the images of Rev. could be known to the author only from apocalyptic literature is another petitio principii. Every page of Rev. shows how immersed its speech and imagery are in the OT. Every page shows also how free the author is from the letter of the OT and from any attested apocalyptic tradition. This is why the question of the theological significance of the images must be raised.

θ η σ α υ ρ ό ς. Str.-B., I, 429 f.; III, 657; Dalman WJ, I, 169 f.

[1] For further details cf. W. Otto, Priester und Tempel im hell. Ägypten (1905 ff.), Index, s.v. θησαυρός.

[2] P. Par., 60, 31: θησαυρὸς τοῦ ἱεροῦ; P. Amh., II, 41; θησαυρὸς θεοῦ P. Tebt., II, 445 (storehouse). Cf. Otto, II, 123.

[3] Heron of Alexandria (2nd cent. B.C.), Pneumatika, I, 21; II, 32 concerning collection boxes with an automatic contrivance to pay the entrance money, Otto, I, 395 f.

[4] Ditt. Syll.[3], III, 736, 87: the θύοντες should cast in ; III, 1004, 12 f.: ἂν δ' ἐκτίνει τὸ ἀργύριον, παρεόντος τοῦ ἱερέος ἐμβα(λ)λέτω εἰς τὸν θησαυρόν.

[5] Ditt. Syll.[3], III, 982, 13 f.: τῶν εἰς τὸν [θ]ησαυρὸν ἐμβαλλομένων εὐχ[αριστηρίων], III, 1004, 21 f.: τὸν μέλλοντα θεραπεύεσθαι ὑπὸ τοῦ θεοῦ μὴ ἔλαττον ἐννεοβόλου δοκίμου ἀργυρίου καὶ ἐμβάλλειν εἰς τὸν θησαυρὸν παρεόντος τοῦ νεωκόρου.

[6] H. Graeven, "Die thönerne Sparbüchse im Altertum," Jahrbuch des Kaiserl. Deutschen Archäologischen Instituts, XVI (1901), 160 ff., 162. On the finances of Gk. temples cf. K. F. Hermann, Lehrbuch der griech. Privatalterthümer (1882), 456. In the Jewish temple there was already a treasury in the time of Josiah (2 K. 12:10).

[7] Graeven, 167; cf. the illustrations.

In the LXX θησαυρός is almost always used for אוֹצָר a. lit. for material "treasures," Jos. 6:19, 24 (εἰς θησαυρὸν κυρίου); 3 Βασ. 7:37 (51) (εἰς τοὺς θησαυροὺς οἴκου κυρίου); 14:26;[8] 15:18 (τοῦ οἴκου τοῦ βασιλέως); Prv. 10:2; Ιερ. 30:20 (warning against false trust in them). Fig. Is. 33:6, wisdom and the fear of God as treasures. b. "Treasure chest" or "storehouse," Am. 8:5 (ἀνοίξομεν θησαυρόν), esp. of the heavenly storehouse from which God dispenses, Ιερ. 27:25 (50:25), e.g., the θησαυρός of light (Jer. 51:16 [Ιερ. 28:16]), of snow (Job 38:22) etc.; cf. Eth. En. 17:3. This thought is spiritualised in Philo.[9]

The idea of payment to God is distinctively extended in later Judaism. The good works of the righteous, esp. his almsgiving, are regarded as a θησαυρός which is laid up with God in heaven. While the interest on this (פְּרִי → καρπός) may accrue to man in this life in the form of happy results, the capital will be kept in heaven to the day of judgment, and then it will be paid back, Tob. 4:8 ff.; 4 Esr. 6:5 ff. (to lay up treasures of faith); 7:77; T. Pea, 4, 18 : "My fathers have laid up treasures for below, I have laid up treasures for above ... My fathers have laid up treasures which pay no interest, I have laid up treasures which pay interest."[10] A common Jewish saying speaks of laying up (as treasures) fulfilments of the Law or good works סגל מצות ומעשים טובים e.g., Dt. r. 1 on Dt. 1:1: "All that Israel lays up in the form of fulfilments of the Law and good works, it lays up for its Father in heaven."[11]

In another expression Judaism can speak of the treasure house of eternal life (גנזי חיי עלמא). The seventh heaven is the place where the souls of those who are not yet born reside (→ 138).[12] During the lifetime of man these are in the hand of the Creator (Job 12:10). At death they mount up to heaven. The souls of the righteous go into a treasure house (אוֹצָר) of life and are preserved by God, being bound in the bundle (δεσμός) of the living (1 S. 25:29), while the ungodly are rejected.[13] On this whole notion, cf. the commending of the spirit to God at death (Lk. 23:46), and the reserving of the souls of martyrs under the heavenly altar, i.e., in immediate proximity to God (Rev. 6:9).[14]

In the NT 1. the word is used literally for "treasure" at Mt. 13:44; Hb. 11:26, and figuratively of the inner store in the heart of man at Mt. 12:35. It is normally used in the NT in contexts in which there is contrast between heavenly and earthly treasure. Thus Jesus takes up the Jewish image and teaching that man should not assemble earthly and material things, but that he should do good actions by which the righteous lay up treasure in heaven (Mt. 6:19-21; Mk. 10:21 and par.; Lk. 12:33 f.). The difference from later Judaism is that imminent eschatological expectation gives added exclusiveness to the demand, and that there is now no thought of merit. In Col. 2:3 Paul speaks of the treasures of wisdom and knowledge which are hidden in Christ, as distinct from illusory, earthly wisdom (2:4, 8). In 2 C. 4:7 he describes the glory of the new life of Christians as θησαυρός which is carried in the fragile and coarse vessels of the earthly body.

---

[8] On deposits in the temple which were laid out profitably, cf. R. Eisler, Ιησους βασιλευς, II (1930), 491.

[9] Fug., 79 : ἐν ἡμῖν αὐτοῖς ... οἱ τῶν κακῶν εἰσι θησαυροί, παρὰ θεῷ δὲ οἱ μόνων ἀγαθῶν, Rer. Div. Her., 76 : ἐξ οὗ (sc. οὐρανοῦ) δὴ τὰς τελεωτάτας εὐφροσύνας ὁ χορηγὸς ἀδιαστάτως ὕει (on Dt. 28:12), Leg. All., III, 105.

[10] Str.-B., I, 430.

[11] Ibid., 431.

[12] For examples cf. Moore, I, 368.

[13] Str.-B., II, 268; S. Nu. § 139 on 27:16 (cf. K. G. Kuhn, S. Nu. übersetzt [1933], 569, n. 7).

[14] Str.-B., III, 803; Bss. Apk., 270.

2. "Receptacles for treasures," Mt. 2:11; 13:52. θησαυρός in the sense of "treasure" plays an important role in Gnostic religion. Here the land of light is described as treasure. From it are the emanations which fill the 60 treasures of light in various τάξεις. The soul comes from the sphere of light, and its redemption consists in return to the treasure of light. Cf. the Pistis Sophia, the books of Jeû, [15] and also the Mandaean writings. [16] According to the 2nd book of Jeû, p. 319, 2 (ed. C. Schmidt in GCS, XIII, 1 [1905]), Jeû, the original man, is the father of the treasure of light. In Ac. Pt., 20, in which there are Gnostic overtones, Christ Himself is called *margarita* (→ μαργαρίτης) and *thesaurus*. It is not impossible that the expression chosen in Col. 2:3 : ἐν ᾧ εἰσιν πάντες οἱ θησαυροὶ τῆς σοφίας καὶ γνώσεως ἀπόκρυφοι, is influenced by current Gnostic terminology, though it is also reminiscent of Is. 45:3. The implication is that not merely the natural glory of light is in Christ, but the fulness of all σοφία and γνῶσις, i.e., of the supreme religious values.

† θησαυρίζω.

"To keep, hoard, lay up as treasure (in the treasury)," esp. of valuable things, both lit. and figur. Diod. S., XX, 36 : τεθησαυρισμένον κατ' αὐτοῦ ... τὸν φθόνον; Philo Leg. All., III, 36 : τὰς φαύλας δόξας ... θησαυρίζεις, ὦ διάνοια; Det. Pot. Ins., 35 : τῶν γὰρ ἐπιτηδευόντων ἀρετὴν οἱ μὲν ἐν ψυχῇ μόνῃ τὸ καλὸν ἐθησαύρισαν πράξεων ἐπαινετῶν ἀσκηταὶ γενόμενοι. Poster. C., 57. In the LXX, lit. at 4 Βασ. 20:17; ψ 38:6; Zech. 9:3; figur. at Am. 3:10; Prv. 1:8 (θησαυρίζουσιν ἑαυτοῖς κακά); 16:27. In later Judaism esp. of the laying up of the treasure which the righteous store up in heaven by good works (→ θησαυρός), Tob. 4:8 ff.; Ps. Sol. 9:5; 4 Esr. 6:5.

The piety of Jesus is distinguished by His definite repudiation of the laying up of earthly goods. High estimation of acts of love as such, and obedience with a view to the last hour, will determine the judgment. Is so far as the heaping up of earthly goods expresses a this-worldly and egotistic attitude, it is a contradiction of God (Lk. 12:21; Jm. 5:3). At times earthly goods have to be given up, especially when the concrete situation makes this unavoidable (Mt. 6:19-21 and par.; Lk. 12:33; Mk. 10:17 ff.; 1:16 ff.). [1] In accordance with the Jewish image, acts of love are described as a laying up of treasure in heaven (→ θησαυρός).

Paul uses θησαυρίζω literally in the sense of the setting aside of monetary offerings in the service of love, 2 C. 12:14; 1 C. 16:2. He also uses it figuratively of the unrepentant who lay up divine wrath against themselves to the day of judgment, R. 2:5. In 2 Pt. 3:7 θησαυρίζω is used for the preservation of the present world for the final judgment of God.

Hauck

---

[15] Pist. Soph., p. 123, 1; 1st Book of Jeû, p. 260, 25 ff.; 261, 9 ff., 24 f.; 265, 4; 296, 18; 303, 17 ff. (cf. Od. Sol. 16:15; 1 Tm. 6:16); on relations with Manichaeanism, cf. W. Bousset, *Die Hauptprobleme der Gnosis* (1907), 348 f.

[16] Lidz. Ginza R., XV, 16, 345 (p. 360, 28); L., I, 3, 24 (p. 442, 14 ff.) (return of the soul to the treasure of the Father); L., II, 6, 45 (p. 462, 30); L., II, 22, 66 (p. 493) (*Mana* is first located in the hidden treasure-house under the most loyal keepers). Cf. also Lidz. Ginza, Index *s.v. Schatz, Schatzhaus, Schatz des Lebens* etc.

θ η σ α υ ρ ί ζ ω. [1] Acc. to Mt. Jesus requires the gathering of heavenly treasures instead of earthly, but acc. to Lk. He demands the surrender of all earthly goods. Lk. has thus made the saying of Jesus more extreme and more general in accordance with the ancient ideal of poverty current in his day, cf. P. Feine, *Theologie des NT*[2] (1911), 687 ff. (abbreviated in the 3rd ed.); J. Behm, "Kommunismus und Urchristentum," NKZ, 31 (1920), 282 ff.

θλίβω, θλῖψις [1]

A. θλίβω, θλῖψις in Secular Greek.

Contents : A. θλίβω, θλῖψις in Secular Greek. B. θλίβω, θλῖψις in the LXX. C. θλίβω, θλῖψις in the NT : 1. The Nature of Tribulation ; 2. The Experience of Tribulation.

1. θλίβω in the lit. sense : "to press," "squash," "rub," "hem in" : Hom. Od., 17, 221; Aristoph. Pax, 1239 : (ὁ θώραξ) θλίβει τὸν ὄρρον, Lys., 314; Theocr. Idyll., 20, 4 : χείλεα θλίβειν, "to kiss"; Demosth. Or., 18, 260 : τοὺς ὄφεις θλίβων, Mk. 3:9 : ἵνα μὴ θλίβωσιν αὐτόν ("crush"); "to press together": Plat. Tim., 60c : σφόδρα ἔθλιψε ... αὐτόν (sc. τὸν τῆς γῆς ὄγκον), cf. Wis. 15:7 ... κεραμεὺς ἁπαλὴν γῆν θλίβων. This leads in the past part. to the sense of "to be small or narrow": Luc. Alex., 49 : τῆς πόλεως θλιβομένης ὑπὸ τοῦ πλήθους; Theocr. Idyll., 21, 18 : θλιβομένα καλύβα (hut), cf. Mt. 7:13 : στενὴ ἡ πύλη καὶ τεθλιμμένη ἡ ὁδὸς ἡ ἀπάγουσα εἰς τὴν ζωήν (antonym : πλατεῖα καὶ εὐρύχωρος), but also Dion. Hal. Ant. Rom., VIII, 73 : βίοι τεθλιμμένοι (slender competence); Ditt. Syll.[3], II, 708, 28; Diog. L., II, 109 : τοῖς ἐφοδίοις θλίβεσθαι ("to be in want"), IV, 37. Similarly θλῖψις has the lit. meaning of "pressure" in the physical sense, Epic. Ep., 2 (p. 49, Usener): θλίψεως τῶν νεφῶν γενομένης, Strabo, I, 3, 6 : διὰ τὴν ἐξ ἴσης ἀντέρεισιν (resistance, opposition) καὶ θλῖψιν (τοῦ ὕδατος). In medical terminology, Oribasius Fr., 42 (CMG): θλῖψις στομάχου, Gal. De Differentiis Febrium, I, 9 (VII, 306, Kühn): pressure of the pulse ; Soranus Gynaecia (CMG, IV), I, 42 : ὑστερικαὶ θλίψεις.

2. θλίβω in the figur, sense, "to afflict," "oppress," "harass." Though it is not always possible to distinguish between external and internal affliction, the following main meanings may be discerned : a. "to afflict" or "to discomfit," Polyb., 18, 24, 3 (in battle); Aristot. Polit., V, 7, p. 1307a, 1: διὰ τὸν πόλεμον; Ditt. Syll.[3], II, 731, 3 : ἐπειδὴ διὰ τὰς τῶν καιρῶν περιστάσεις βαρέως ἀπορῶν καὶ θλιβόμενος ὁ δῆμος ἐν τῇ μεγίστῃ καθέστηκεν δυσελπιστίᾳ; cf. II, 685, 39; 700, 15. θλίβεσθαι ὑπὸ τῆς νόσου also occurs, Anth. Pal., III, 314, 354; Plut. Apophth. Philippi, 6 (II, 177d): ὑπὸ πενίας. We have θλίψεις in the sense of "afflictions" in BGU, IV, 1139, 4 : διὰ τὰς τῶν πόλεων θλίψεις, Catal. Cod. Astr. Graec., VIII, 3, p. 175, 5 f.: ἔννοιαι (ἔσονται) καὶ θλῖψις ; p. 178, 8 : ἀφανία ἀνθρώπων μεγάλων καὶ θλῖψις; VII, p. 169, 12 : λύπαι καὶ πένθη καὶ κλαυθμοὶ ἔσονται ἐν ἐκείνῳ τῷ τόπῳ καὶ στοναχαὶ (groaning) καὶ θλίψεις. b. "to oppress," "to trouble," "to vex" : Philodem. Philos. Περὶ Παρρησίας Libellus Fr., 88, col. 22, 3 f. (A. Olivieri [1914], p. 61): θλίβεσθαι ὑπὸ τῆς ἀδοξίας, Philo Migr. Abr., 157; Virt., 146; Jos., 179; Decal., 145 : ὅταν δὲ τὸ κακὸν μήπω μὲν εἰσῳκισμένον θλίβῃ; Callim. Hymn., IV (Εἰς Δῆλον), 35 (ed. U. v. Wilamowitz-Moellendorff, 1897): σὲ δ᾽ οὐκ ἔθλιψεν ἀνάγκη, Vett. Val., II, 16 : πολλῶν ἐναντιωμάτων αἴτιος τῇ τε μητρὶ θλίψεις καὶ ταπεινώσεις ἀποτελεῖ, Plut. Alc., 25 (I, 204d): ἀλλὰ γλίσχρως χορηγοῦντα θλίβειν καὶ ἀποκναίειν ἀτρέμα καὶ ποιεῖν ἀμφοτέρους βασιλεῖ χειροήθεις καὶ καταπόνους ὑπ᾽ ἀλλήλων, Aristot. Eth. Nic., I, 11, p. 1100b, 28 : θλίβει καὶ λυμαίνεται τὸν μακάριον. While the terms θλίβειν and θλῖψις are not elsewhere very common in the philosophical terminology of Hellenism, they play a certain role in Epict. in his doctrine of the self-assertion of man. τὰ θλίβοντα (Diss., IV, 1, 45), τὸ θλῖβον (I, 27, 2 f.) and the θλιβῆναι ὑπὸ τῶν γενομένων (I, 25, 17; III, 13, 8), the afflictions of life, of which the last and strongest is death,

---

θ λ ί β ω. A. Steubing, *Der paul. Begriff Christusleiden* (1905); J. Schneider, *Die Passionsmystik des Pls.* (1929); W. Wichmann, *Die Leidenstheologie* (1930); K. F. Euler, *Die Verkündigung vom leidenden Gottesknecht aus Js. 53 in der griech. Bibel* (1934); Wnd. 2 K., 40 f.; Meinertz Gefbr., 27 f.

[1] On the accent cf. Winer (Schmiedel) § 6, 3c; Bl.-Debr.[6] § 13.

must be overcome by the philosopher. And they are overcome when we see that we bring this θλῖψις on ourselves by our δόγματα (Diss., I, 25, 28 : καθόλου γὰρ ἐκείνου μέμνησο, ὅτι ἑαυτοὺς θλίβομεν, ἑαυτοὺς στενοχωροῦμεν, τοῦτ' ἔστιν τὰ δόγματα ἡμᾶς θλίβει καὶ στενοχωρεῖ, cf. Epict. Ench., 16; 24, 1). It seems that in this general and figurative sense θλίβειν and θλῖψις represent a popular concept. As examples show, στενοχωρεῖν, στενοχωρία are synon. with θλίβειν, θλῖψις. Cf. Luc. Nigrinus, 13 : ὀχληρὸς ἦν θλίβων τοῖς οἰκέταις καὶ στενοχωρῶν τοὺς ἀπαντῶντας; Artemid. Oneirocr., I, 66 : πάσης θλίψεως καὶ στενοχωρίας λύσιν ὑπισχνεῖται; II, 4 : θλίψεις καὶ στενοχωρίας καὶ τοῖς δικαζομένοις καταδίκην μαντεύεται, cf. I, 79; II, 37, 50.

B. θλίβω, θλῖψις in the LXX.

1. In the LXX the use of θλίβειν, θλῖψις in the figur. sense, which is alone of theological significance, is very widespread. In the Gk. translation θλίβειν, θλῖψις are used for several Hebrew terms which all more or less express the afflictions of life in various nuances.

Thus θλίβω is used a. for צָרַר hi, "to constrict someone," Dt. 28:52; Ju. 10:9; 3 Βασ. 8:37; 2 Ch. 6:28; 28:22; 33:12; Neh. 9:27 etc.; for צַר subst., "distress," "affliction" in passive formulations, ψ 17:6 : ἐν τῷ θλίβεσθαί με = בַּצַּר־לִי, "in my distress"; Ju. 11:7; 1 Βασ. 28:15; 2 Βασ. 22:19; Lam. 1:20 etc.

It is also used b. for צָרַר, "to treat someone with hostility," Is. 11:13 : Ἰούδας οὐ θλίψει Ἐφραΐμ; ψ 22:5; 41:9; 68:19; 142:12. Elsewhere the LXX renders צָרַר in this sense by ἐχθραίνειν, Nu. 25:17; Dt. 2:9; ἐχθρεύειν, Ex. 23:22; Nu. 33:55; πολεμεῖν, ψ 128:1 etc.; καταπατεῖν : Am. 5:12; μισεῖν, ψ 73:3, or ἐχθρός, ψ 6:7; 7:5; 8:2 etc.; צַר, "the enemy," "adversary," "oppressor" (ἐχθρός, ψ 43:5) in the fixed formula : οἱ θλίβοντες, ψ 3:1; 12:4; 26:2 : οἱ θλίβοντές με καὶ οἱ ἐχθροί μου = צָרַי וְאֹיְבַי לִי (in the sing. at Lam. 4:12 : ἐχθρὸς καὶ ἐκθλίβων), ψ 26:12; 43:7 Bᵇ (vid) א ART; 118:157: πολλοὶ οἱ ἐκδιώκοντές με καὶ οἱ ἐκθλίβοντές με = רֹדְפַי וְצָרָי, Mi. 5:8; Lam. 1:5, 7, 17; 2:17 etc.

c. לָחַץ, "to afflict," "to oppress"; Ex. 3:9; 22:20; 23:9; Ju. 4:3; 6:9; 10:12; 4 Βασ. 13:4; ψ 55:1; 105:42; Is. 19:20; Ιερ. 37:20. ἐκθλίβειν is another rendering at Ju. 2:18 B; Am. 6:14.

d. יָנָה hi, "to oppress," Lv. 19:33; 25:14, 17; Dt. 23:17; Is. 49:26. Transl. κακοῦν at Ex. 22:20; καταδυναστεύειν, Jer. 22:3; Ez. 18:12.

e. In addition to these four words, of which the first two are by far the most common, we also find as the Heb. originals צוק hi, "to constrict or harass someone," Dt. 28:53, 55, 57; Is. 29:7; 51:13; עָשַׁק, "to press down," Ez. 18:18; Jer. 7:6; Hos. 5:11; Am. 4:1; Jer. 7:6 etc. transl. καταδυναστεύειν; ψ 104:14; 118:121 ἀδικεῖν. Also אָיַב, "to be hostile to," Ju. 8:34B and רַעַע, "to destroy," Ju. 10:8B. [2]

θλῖψις is the usual rendering of a. צָרָה, "distress," "evil," "oppression," "trouble," Gn. 35:3; 42:21; Dt. 31:17, 21A; Ju. 10:14; 1 Βασ. 1:6; 10:19; 26:24; 4 Βασ. 19:3; 2 Ch.

[2] λαὸς τεθλιμμένος, Is. 18:7 is not a transl. of עַם מְמֻשָּׁךְ, any more than ἄνδρες τεθλιμμένοι at Is. 28:14 is of אַנְשֵׁי לָצוֹן. In both cases the LXX presupposes a different text from the Mas. Cf. also Job 36:15. Lv. 26:26 : ἐν τῷ θλῖψαι ὑμᾶς σιτοδείᾳ ἄρτων is a free rendering of what is elsewhere transl. καὶ συντρίψω στήριγμα ἄρτου σου, Ez. 5:16; ψ 104:16.

15:6; 20:9; ψ 9:9, 21; 19:1; Zeph. 1:15. But this צָרָה can also be rendered differently, e.g., by ἀνάγκη at Job 27:9, in the plur. by ἀνάγκαι at ψ 30:7; Prv. 17:17. At Jer. 4:31 we have στεναγμός for צָרָה.

b. צַר, "distress," "tribulation," Dt. 4:29; ψ 4:1; 31:7; 58:16; 59:11; 65:14; Hos. 5:15; Zech. 8:10; Is. 26:16; 30:20. We find ἀνάγκη for צַר at Job 7:11.

c. Occasionally לַחַץ, "tribulation," 3 Βασ. 22:27; 4 Βασ. 13:4; 2 Ch. 18:26; ψ 43:24 (= Dt. 26:7: θλιμμός); מְצוּקָה, "oppression," Job 15:24 along with צַר, ἀνάγκη. In Zeph. 1:15 we find מְצוּקָה, ἀνάγκη along with צָרָה, θλῖψις. Cf. ψ 24:17; ψ 106:13, 19, 28, ἀνάγκαι. מְצוּק (מָצוֹר?), "tribulation," Dt. 28:53, 55, 57. אֵיד, "disaster," "distress," "catastrophe," 2 Βασ. 22:19, transl. ἀπώλεια at Job 30:12; 31:3; Prv. 6:15, κάκωσις at ψ 17:18, ὄλεθρος at Prv. 1:26 f., ἀδικία at Ez. 35:5. עֳנִי, "distress," "misery," "plight," Ex. 4:31, transl. κάκωσις at Ex. 3:17, ταπείνωσις at 4 Βασ. 14:26; ψ 9:13; ψ 118:50; Lam. 1:3, 7, 9; πτωχεία at ψ 87:9; Lam. 3:19. מוּעָקָה, "heavy burden," ψ 65:11 (θλίψεις). עֹצֶר, "oppression," "affliction," ψ 106:39 (Is. 53:8, ταπείνωσις). רָעָה, "evil," "calamity," ψ 33:19 (θλίψεις), κακία at Am. 3:6; κακά at 1 Βασ. 10:19, πονηρία at Neh. 1:3. דְּאָגָה, "carefulness," Ez. 12:18. עֹשֶׁק, "oppression," "violence," Ez. 18:18 (Jer. 6:6, καταδυναστεία; ψ 72:8, πονηρία). עָקָה, "mourning," "complaint," ψ 54:3. שׁוֹאָה, "destruction," "ruin," Is. 10:3 (Is. 47:11: ἀπώλεια).

If the many Hebrew terms are in some sense formally unified in the LXX by their common translation as θλῖψις, materially there are still nuances in meaning. For θλῖψις (θλίβειν) is used for the most varied forms of distress or oppression in the LXX.

Purely schematically, we can differentiate, as in secular Gk., between external and internal affliction, and in the case of the latter between distress and anxiety. In relation to external afflictions, θλῖψις, θλίβειν might denote political constriction by encircling enemies, as at Ju. 10:8 f., 14; 3 Βασ. 8:37; 4 Βασ. 13:4; Ob. 1, 12, 14; Neh. 9:27; the scourge of war, Dt. 28:53 ff.; ψ 9:9; 45:1; 107:13; 1 Macc. 5:16; 12:13; oppression, Ex. 3:9; 4:31; ψ 80:7; exile, Dt. 4:29; mortal danger, ψ 85:7; 114:3; the affliction of slaves, Dt. 23:17, or of aliens, Ex. 22:20; 23:9, or of the πλησίον generally, Lv. 25:14, 17; injury caused by personal enemies, ψ 49:15; 53:7; 58:16. There is a typical combination in 2 Ch. 20:9: Ἐὰν ἐπέλθῃ ἐφ' ἡμᾶς κακά, ῥομφαία, κρίσις, θάνατος, λιμός ... βοησόμεθα πρὸς σὲ ἀπὸ τῆς θλίψεως, καὶ ἀκούσῃ καὶ σώσεις. Cf. also ψ 106, where the θλίβεσθαι is successively wandering in the desert (v. 6), imprisonment (v. 13), sickness (v. 19), ship-wreck (v. 28). Again we often have the phrase ἐκ πασῶν τῶν θλίψεων αὐτοῦ ἔσωσεν αὐτόν, ψ 33:6, 17, or there is reference to πολλαὶ αἱ θλίψεις, ψ 33:19. The plentiful use of synon. together with θλῖψις, θλίβειν helps to confirm the manifoldness of the meaning of the term. For example, at Ex. 22:20 we have: οὐ κακώσετε οὐδὲ μὴ θλίψητε; at Ju. 10:8 B: καὶ ἔθλιψαν καὶ ἔθλασαν τοὺς υἱοὺς Ἰσραήλ; at Ez. 18:18: ἐὰν θλίψει θλίψῃ καὶ ἁρπάσῃ ἅρπαγμα; at Dt. 31:17: καὶ εὑρήσουσιν αὐτὸν κακὰ πολλὰ καὶ θλίψεις; at Jer. 15:11: ἐν καιρῷ τῶν κακῶν αὐτῶν καὶ ἐν καιρῷ θλίψεως αὐτῶν; at Prv. 1:27: καὶ ὅταν ἔρχηται ὑμῖν θλῖψις καὶ πολιορκία, ἢ ὅταν ἔρχεται ὑμῖν ὄλεθρος; at 4 Βασ. 19:3: ἡμέρα θλίψεως καὶ ἐλεγμοῦ καὶ παροργισμοῦ ἡ ἡμέρα αὕτη; at ψ 77:49: ἐξαπέστειλεν εἰς αὐτοὺς ὀργὴν θυμοῦ αὐτοῦ, θυμὸν καὶ ὀργὴν καὶ θλῖψιν; at ψ 43:24: ἐπιλανθάνῃ τῆς πτωχείας ἡμῶν καὶ τῆς θλίψεως ἡμῶν. More often we have θλῖψις καὶ ὀδύνη, ψ 106:39; 114:3; Ez. 12:18; θλῖψις καὶ ἀνάγκη, ψ 118:143; Job 15:24; Zeph. 1:15; cf. ψ 24:17 f.

αἱ θλίψεις τῆς καρδίας μου ἐπλατύνθησαν,
ἐκ τῶν ἀναγκῶν μου ἐξάγαγέ με.
ἴδε τὴν ταπείνωσίν μου καὶ τὸν κόπον μου
καὶ ἄφες πάσας τὰς ἁμαρτίας μου.

θλῖψις καὶ στενοχωρία, Dt. 28:53, 55, 57; Is. 8:22; 30:6; Est. 1:1g. ἀνάγκη and στενοχωρία can be called synon. of θλῖψις in the narrower sense. [3]

3. It is also to be noted, of course, that θλῖψις can be used for the distress or
fear which arises in ἀνάγκη and στενοχωρία, Job 15:24; Zeph. 1:15; Is. 8:22;
30:6 (?). θλῖψις thus expresses an inner affliction. When it bears the sense of
inner fear or trouble, θλῖψις is more frequently used alone.

Gn. 42:21 is a notable example : ὅτι ὑπερείδομεν τὴν θλῖψιν τῆς ψυχῆς αὐτοῦ,
ὅτε κατεδέετο ἡμῶν, καὶ οὐκ εἰσηκούσαμεν αὐτοῦ· ἕνεκεν τούτου ἐπῆλθεν ἐφ'
ἡμᾶς ἡ θλῖψις αὕτη. θλῖψις, which in both cases is used for צָרָה, refers first to the
anguish of Joseph and then to the distress of his brothers. Cf. also Jer. 6:24; Ez. 12:18;
1 Macc. 6:11; or the verb in 2 Βασ. 22:7: ἐν τῷ θλίβεσθαί με ἐπικαλέσομαι κύριον;
2 Ch. 33:12; ψ 17:6; 30:9; 68:17; Lam. 1:20. The sense of trouble or even sorrow is often
present, e.g., 1 Βασ. 1:6; 30:6 : ἐθλίβη Δαυὶδ σφόδρα; 2 Βασ. 13:2.

4. This term which is so common and which has so many senses in the LXX
acquires its theological significance from the fact that it predominantly denotes the
oppression and affliction of the people of Israel or of the righteous who represent Israel. To be sure, we never find the general statement that θλῖψις necessarily belongs to the history of Israel as the people chosen and guided by God.
Yet Israel does in fact constantly experience θλῖψις in its history, and it is aware
that this θλῖψις is significant in the history of salvation. The oppression in Egypt,
which is called θλῖψις in Ex. 4:31 (cf. 3:9), and the affliction of the exile, for
which θλῖψις is used in Dt. 4:29 (cf. 28:47 ff.), are both events of salvation history.
The same is true of almost all the other θλῖψις in the life of the people which
is occasioned by its enemies, Ju. 6:9; 10:6-16; 1 Βασ. 10:18 ff.; 4 Βασ. 19:3. For
almost all these real threats to the historical existence of the chosen people come
from God as a punishment for its unfaithfulness and serve to fashion an obedient
people, 2 Ch. 20:9 ff.; Hos. 5:15; Neh. 9:26 f.; Is. 26:16; 37:3; 63:9; 65:16; Jer. 10:18
etc. In the real tribulations experienced ἐν ἡμέρᾳ (or ἐν καιρῷ) θλίψεως (4 Βασ.
19:3 = Is. 37:3; Ob. 1, 12, 14; Is. 33:2; Nah. 1:7 etc.) we have the continual visitation of the chosen people by God. To these days of affliction, according to Da. 12:1,
belongs also a future ἡμέρα θλίψεως, οἵα οὐκ ἐγενήθη ἀφ' οὗ ἐγενήθησαν ἕως
τῆς ἡμέρας ἐκείνης. The judgment fulfilled in the history of Israel will be totally
revealed in the eschatological θλῖψις. In Hab. 3:16 also the promised ἡμέρα
θλίψεως has an eschatological character.

Cf. also Zeph. 1:15, where the ἡμέρα κυρίου ἡ μεγάλη, which is near and which
will come very quickly, is described as ἡμέρα ὀργῆς ... ἡμέρα θλίψεως καὶ ἀνάγκης, ἡμέρα ἀωρίας καὶ ἀφανισμοῦ, ἡμέρα σκότους καὶ γνόφου, ἡμέρα νεφέλης
καὶ ὁμίχλης ...

5. Along with the θλῖψις of the people of Israel there is also in the Psalms [4]
the affliction of righteous individuals whose sufferings have paradigmatic significance. Great tribulation is only to be expected by the righteous : πολλαὶ αἱ
θλίψεις τῶν δικαίων : ψ 33:19 (4 Macc. 18:15). They walk ἐν μέσῳ θλίψεως
(ψ 137:7). They know all about the ἡμέρα θλίψεως, the καιρὸς θλίψεως (ψ 36:39;
49:15; 76:2 etc.). In constant hostility and persecution by their enemies (οἱ θλί-

---

[3] For στενοχωρία, cf. Trench, 124 f.
[4] θλῖψις is not used in this connection in Job, nor does it appear at all in Is. 53.

βοντες, ψ 3:1; 12:4; 22:5 etc.), in sickness and mortal peril (ψ 65:11; 70:20), God brings θλῖψις upon them. But God is also the One who hears their prayer and delivers them out of their distress, ψ 9:9; 31:7; 33:6, 17; 36:39 f.; 53:7; 58:16; 90:15 etc. Thus the righteous regard the oppressions and troubles which they meet in life as experiences in a personal salvation history which are typical in character. The term θλῖψις is thus significant as a religious concept in the LXX.

The further development of the general concept of suffering in Rabbinic and Jewish Apocryphal literature evaluates צָרָה, or, more commonly, יִסּוּרִין (chastisements), mainly as sufferings which serve as punishments, which bring about repentance, and which increase human merits, or as sufferings which are means of expiation for sin and which have a representative character for the blotting out of the guilt of others.[5] θλῖψις, however, is no longer of great significance as the Gk. equivalent (→ κρίμα, παιδεύειν, also πάσχειν).

C. θλίβω, θλῖψις in the New Testament.

I. The Nature of Tribulation.

1. There are many references to θλῖψις or θλίβειν in the NT, especially in Paul.[6] Except for two passages in the Synoptists (→ 139), θλῖψις (θλίβειν) is always used in a figurative sense. Those who experience affliction are members of the Church, and exemplarily the apostles. This tribulation is not merely factual, though it is such in Ac. 11:19; 2 C. 1:4 ff.; Phil. 4:14; 1 Th. 1:6; 3:7; 2 Th. 1:4; Hb. 10:33; Rev. 2:9 f., and this may be self-evidently presupposed in Mk. 4:17; R. 5:3; Rev. 1:9. According to the understanding of the NT, however, θλῖψις is also necessary, Jn. 16:33 : ἐν τῷ κόσμῳ θλῖψιν ἔχετε; Ac. 14:22 : παρακαλοῦντες ἐμμένειν τῇ πίστει, καὶ ὅτι διὰ πολλῶν θλίψεων δεῖ ἡμᾶς εἰσελθεῖν εἰς τὴν βασιλείαν τοῦ θεοῦ; 1 Th. 3:2 f.: εἰς τὸ στηρίξαι ὑμᾶς ... τὸ μηδένα σαίνεσθαι ἐν ταῖς θλίψεσιν ταύταις. αὐτοὶ γὰρ οἴδατε ὅτι εἰς τοῦτο κείμεθα, cf. also Barn., 7, 11: οὕτω, φησίν, οἱ θέλοντές με ἰδεῖν καὶ ἅψασθαί μου τῆς βασιλείας ὀφείλουσιν θλιβέντες καὶ παθόντες λαβεῖν με. The constant tribulation of Israel in the OT has become the necessary tribulation of the Church in the NT. The former is thus an indication of the latter. Along with and within the community the apostle, too, suffers θλῖψις. The ὅτι εἰς τοῦτο κείμεθα of 1 Th. 3:3 includes him. He tells the Thessalonians : ὅτι μέλλομεν θλίβεσθαι (3:4). In Ac. 20:23 all that he knows of his future is the δεσμὰ καὶ θλίψεις attested to him by the Holy Spirit. This affliction is distinguished from that of other Christians by the excess of sorrows. A common phrase of his is : ἐπί πάσῃ τῇ θλίψει ἡμῶν (2 C. 1:4; 7:4; 1 Th. 3:7), or : ἐν παντὶ θλιβόμενοι (2 C. 4:8; 7:5). The sufferings of Christ overwhelm him (2 C. 1:5). He exhausts them (Col. 1:24).

2. In the NT these necessary afflictions of the Church and the apostle are regarded as the sufferings of Christ which are not yet filled up, Col. 1:24 : νῦν χαίρω ἐν τοῖς παθήμασιν ὑπὲρ ὑμῶν, καὶ ἀνταναπληρῶ τὰ ὑστερήματα τῶν θλίψεων τοῦ Χριστοῦ ἐν τῇ σαρκί μου ὑπὲρ τοῦ σώματος αὐτοῦ, ὅ ἐστιν ἡ ἐκκλησία. Cf. 2 C. 1:5. The θλίψεις τοῦ Χριστοῦ, which are identical with the

---

[5] Cf. Str.-B., Index, s.v. Leiden; esp. II, 274 ff.

[6] θλῖψις is used 45 times in the NT, 22 or 24 times in Paul. The corresponding figures for θλίβειν are 10 and 6.

παθήματα τοῦ Χριστοῦ, [7] are the sufferings which were endured by Christ (cf. Phil. 3:10; 1 Pt. 4:13). But obviously the sufferings of Christ are not yet exhausted, and the apostle now experiences and fulfils them on behalf of the Church, which is the body of Christ. In the θλίψεις which come upon the apostle there is a continuation of the sufferings which Christ has already suffered.

We are led to the same conclusion by 2 C. 4:10 f., where the ἐν παντὶ θλιβόμενοι ... of 4:8 is taken up and completed as follows : πάντοτε τὴν νέκρωσιν τοῦ Ἰησοῦ ἐν τῷ σώματι περιφέροντες, ἵνα καὶ ἡ ζωὴ τοῦ Ἰησοῦ ἐν τῷ σώματι ἡμῶν φανερωθῇ. ἀεὶ γὰρ ἡμεῖς οἱ ζῶντες εἰς θάνατον παραδιδόμεθα διὰ Ἰησοῦν, ἵνα καὶ ἡ ζωὴ τοῦ Ἰησοῦ φανερωθῇ ἐν τῇ θνητῇ σαρκὶ ἡμῶν. The apostle experiences in his own physical existence the death suffered by Jesus. For he is given up to death for Jesus' sake. For Jesus' sake, however, his sufferings take place in the wholly concrete sense — the context shows this quite plainly — that they are experienced for the sake of preaching His Gospel, in which Jesus is present. The apostle sets himself under the Word of the death of Christ. He represents this by giving up his own life to the claims of men. The Lord present in the Word is thus set among men through the obedient apostle, who bears the afflictions suffered by Jesus Christ, who fulfils here and now the tribulation experienced by Him. [8]

Rev. 7:14 should also be quoted in this context. The martyrs before the throne of God, whom the divine sees coming out of great tribulation, have also suffered the sufferings of Christ. They are the host of those who in the tribulation of the last time have been washed, not in their own blood, but in the blood of the Lamb, i.e., who in their own suffering for Jesus Christ have borne witness to the sufferings which He Himself endured. The sufferings of the apostle, or of members of the Church, are thus called θλίψεις τοῦ Χριστοῦ in the sense that they represent in the members of the exalted Lord the suffering which He Himself has already suffered in His humiliation. Hence the suffering is not just similar to that of Christ, nor is the genitive merely a general characterisation. This is a suffering of Christ in His messengers according to, and on the basis of, the θλῖψις of Jesus, of the humiliated Christ, and the genitive is subjective.

3. If we thus see that it belongs to the nature of θλῖψις in the NT, first, that it is inseparable from Christian life in this world, and secondly, that it is the suffering of Christ, who is afflicted in His members, a third characteristic is that this is eschatological tribulation. This eschatological character of θλῖψις may be deduced generally from the fundamentally eschatological nature of the time in which it is endured. This time is to be understood in terms of the end which has come upon it in Jesus Christ (1 C. 10:11). Yet the eschatological significance of θλῖψις may also be gathered from relevant texts. Thus Paul in 1 C. 7:26 alludes to the ἐνεστῶσα ἀνάγκη, the present distress, which is occasioned by the fact that we remain in the existing relationships of one man to another. But he then continues in v. 28 f.: ἐὰν δὲ καὶ γαμήσῃς, οὐχ ἥμαρτες, καὶ ἐὰν γήμῃ ἡ παρθένος, οὐχ ἥμαρτεν· θλῖψιν δὲ τῇ σαρκὶ ἕξουσιν οἱ τοιοῦτοι, ἐγὼ δὲ ὑμῶν

---

[7] Steubling, 10 tries to draw a distinction between παθήματα and θλίψεις on the basis of 2 C. 1:4 ff., παθήματα being the category of suffering and θλίψεις personal suffering — a more significant term preferred by Paul. But this distinction is hardly tenable, at least with reference to the παθήματα or θλίψεις τοῦ Χριστοῦ. That there can be a distinction between θλίβεσθαι and πάσχειν may be seen from Herm. s., 8, 3, 7.

[8] The power of the Word to bring suffering may also be seen in Mk. 4:17 and 1 Th. 1:6.

φείδομαι. τοῦτο δέ φημι, ἀδελφοί, ὁ καιρὸς συνεσταλμένος ἐστίν. With his awareness of the shortening of the time, Paul obviously sees the afflictions of the last time breaking into the present, and his advice is designed to lessen the related θλῖψις for his community. [9]

Similarly in Mt. 24 (Mk. 13) Jesus speaks of the sufferings before the *parousia*, of their first beginnings (ἀρχὴ ὠδίνων) in the form of a shaking of the historical and natural cosmos (24:4-8), of their continuation in the form of θλίψεις, or persecutions of the disciples (24:9-14), and of their consummation at the end of the age (24:15-28) in the θλῖψις μεγάλη, οἵα οὐ γέγονεν ἀπ᾽ ἀρχῆς κόσμου ἕως τοῦ νῦν οὐδ᾽ οὐ μὴ γένηται (v. 21). In Rev. 1:9 : Ἐγὼ Ἰωάννης, ὁ ἀδελφὸς ὑμῶν καὶ συγκοινωνὸς ἐν τῇ θλίψει καὶ βασιλείᾳ καὶ ὑπομονῇ ἐν Ἰησοῦ we find the same conviction that the tribulation has already begun in the days of the author. The sufferings of the churches bear witness to this. The divine knows of the θλῖψις of the community at Smyrna, and he sees in it, and in a shorter period of suffering which is still to come, the work of Satan, Rev. 2:9 f. These sufferings will lead to the μεγάλη θλῖψις (Rev. 7:14; cf. 3:10). But from the standpoint of the triumphant Church all the affliction of this present time is set in the light of the μεγάλη θλῖψις which has already opened : "These are they which came out of great tribulation, and have washed their robes, and made them white in the blood of the Lamb."

This idea of an eschatological θλῖψις is linked with thoughts which strongly affected the historical consciousness of Judaism. In both Rabb. and apocalyptic texts we read that before the dawn of the Messianic kingdom the Jewish people, or the cosmos, must pass through a period of mounting affliction. [10] The last of these last times is the "final, evil time," which the Rabbis often call the woes of the Messiah (→ ὠδίν). According to Da. 12:1 Θ it is already the καιρὸς θλίψεως (עֵת־צָרָה), θλῖψις οἵα οὐ γέγονεν ἀφ᾽ οὗ γεγένηται ἔθνος ἐπὶ τῆς γῆς ἕως τοῦ καιροῦ ἐκείνου. On the phrase, cf. Jl. 2:2; 1 Macc. 9:27; Ass. Mos. 8:1. 4 Esr. 13:16-19 is typical : "Woe to those who remain in those days ! But even more so to those who do not ! For those who do not remain are (then) sad ; for they see what is reserved for the last time, but they do not attain to it. Yet to those who remain, woe ! For they will experience great dangers and many distresses (acc. to Violet [1924], ad loc.: necessitates = ἀνάγκας = צָרוֹת or מְצוּקוֹת; cf. 4 Esr. 4:12), as these visions show." S. Bar. 25:1 ff.: "Then he (the angel) answered and said to me (Baruch): You, too, will be kept unto that time, unto that sign that the Most High will create for dwellers on earth at the end of the days. This, then, will be the sign : when severe terrors will seize the dwellers on earth, they will fall into many tribulations and into acute sufferings. And when in consequence of their afflictions they then say in their thoughts, 'The Almighty no longer remembers the earth,' and when they give up hope, then the new time will come. Then I answered and said : Will, then, this tribulation which is to come last a long time, this affliction endure for many years ?" [11] Cf. 48:20 : "The time which brings affliction"; 68:2; Sib., II, 154 ff.:

ἀλλ᾽ ὁπόταν τόδε σῆμα φανῇ κατὰ κόσμον ἅπαντα
....
θλίψεις δ᾽ ἀνθρώπων λιμοὶ λοιμοὶ πολεμοί τε
καιρῶν δ᾽ ἀλλαγή, πενθήματα δάκρυα πολλά.

Cf. Sib., VIII, 85 : θλῖψις ἄελπτος. Cf. also Herm. v., 2, 2, 7: μακάριοι ὑμεῖς ὅσοι ὑπομένετε τὴν θλῖψιν τὴν ἐρχομένην τὴν μεγάλην, καὶ ὅσοι οὐκ ἀρνήσονται τὴν

[9] Cf. Joh. W. 1 C., ad loc.
[10] Cf. the catena in Str.-B., IV, 977-986, and the exposition in Volz. Esch., 147-163.
[11] Str.-B., IV, 979.

ζωὴν αὐτῶν, 2, 3, 4; 4, 1, 1; m., 2, 5; 3, 6. From Rabb. literature we might quote bSanh., 97a: [12] "... Thus spake R. Jochanan: In the generation in which the Son of David comes there will be few Rabbinic pupils and the eyes of the rest will be swollen for sorrow and sighing; many afflictions and severe calamities will continually come; before one affliction is over, the next will hurry on." Cf. bSanh., 98, 99a; Midr. Ps. 20:4 (88a).

The basic distinction between the Jewish and the Christian understanding of the eschatological θλῖψις is to be found, of course, in the fact that this tribulation, which is still future in Judaism, has already begun according to the early Christian view. The great tribulation has already begun. A second distinction is to be found in the fact that eschatological suffering began with the suffering of the Messiah, so that all the suffering of the age is simply a repetition of that which has already taken place in Him. A third distinction is that the manifested eschatological suffering of Christ is experienced by the new people scattered in the world, namely, the Church, though naturally within the painful relationships of the cosmos. Hence the NT concept of θλῖψις is not simply an adoption or development of the Jewish idea of eschatological suffering. We have here an understanding of the whole question of eschatology which has been newly disclosed in the concrete history of Jesus Christ. The nature of NT θλῖψις, and therefore of the concept of NT θλῖψις, is determined by the historical event of the death of Jesus Christ.

4. Finally, θλῖψις occurs in the NT in connection with statements concerning the last judgment. In the revelation of the decision of divine righteousness the unrighteous come definitively under θλῖψις (R. 2:9). So, too, do those who in the last days bring θλῖψις on the Church (2 Th. 1:6). As the ὀργή of God which rests on the cosmos of the Gentiles has within it something of the terror of world judgment, so the θλῖψις which the Church undergoes in the last days has within it something of the affliction of the last judgment. For in the tribulation which is suffered by him the believing Christian takes up the divine judgment executed on Jesus Christ. The last judgment is thus anticipated by him in company with Jesus Christ. For faith, the tribulation of the last time is a real demonstration of the "righteous judgment of God" (2 Th. 1:5), because an execution of this righteous judgment is already manifested in it.

II. The Experience of Tribulation.

1. The θλίψεις which the Christian necessarily undergoes as eschatological sufferings consist of afflictions of different kinds.

This may be seen from the fact that the NT uses a comparatively large number of synon. for θλῖψις. Thus we have a. στενοχωρία. This does not always overlap, though cf. R. 2:9; 8:35; 2 C. 6:4. But even when it does not, as in 2 C. 4:8, στενοχωρεῖν is simply θλίβειν which has reached its goal: ἐν παντὶ θλιβόμενοι ἀλλ' οὐ στενοχωρούμενοι. b. ἀνάγκη, 1 Th. 3:7; 2 C. 6:4; cf. 2 C. 12:10: διὸ εὐδοκῶ ἐν ἀσθενείαις, ἐν ὕβρεσιν, ἐν ἀνάγκαις, ἐν διωγμοῖς καὶ στενοχωρίαις, ὑπὲρ Χριστοῦ; in 1 C. 7:26 the θλῖψις which is still to come is called ἐνεστῶσα ἀνάγκη; cf. Lk. 21:23. c. λύπη, Jn. 16:21; cf. Jn. 16:22 with 16:33; Herm. m., 10, 2, 4 ff. If we disregard πάθημα (πάθος, πάσχειν, → 143), d. διωγμός is particularly common along with θλῖψις, Mk. 4:17: θλῖψις ἢ διωγμός; 2 Th. 1:4: ἐν πᾶσιν τοῖς διωγμοῖς ὑμῶν καὶ ταῖς θλίψεσιν αἷς ἀνέχεσθε, cf. Ac. 11:19 with 8:1; 2 C. 4:8 f.; R. 8:35. θλῖψις is the broader term in this combination.

---

[12] *Ibid.*, 981.

Among the concrete afflictions generally signified by θλῖψις, the reference is to persecution in 1 Th. 1:6; 3:3 f. (= 2:14 f.). Imprisonment is meant in Ac. 20:23; Eph. 3:13 (cf. 3:1); Rev. 2:10 (2 C. 6:4), and derision in Hb. 10:33; 11:37. In 2 C. 8:13; 1 Tm. 5:10 (?) we have poverty. Cf. also Rev. 2:9 : οἶδά σου τὴν θλῖψιν καὶ τὴν πτωχείαν ... καὶ τὴν βλασφημίαν. [13] In Rev. 2:22 the reference may be to sickness. The rhetorical series in R. 8:35 lists seven θλίψεις, of which θλῖψις is the first : θλῖψις ἢ στενοχωρία ἢ διωγμὸς ἢ λιμὸς ἢ γυμνότης ἢ κίνδυνος ἢ μάχαιρα. [14] Materially the sufferings listed in 2 C. 11:23 ff. are also θλίψεις. In addition to external afflictions there is also reference to inner distress and sorrow, as in Phil. 1:17; 2 C. 2:4 : ἐκ γὰρ πολλῆς θλίψεως καὶ συνοχῆς καρδίας; Jm. 1:27; cf. also Act. Jn. 22 and 23, or to anxiety or fear, as in 2 C. 7:5 : καὶ γὰρ ἐλθόντων ἡμῶν εἰς Μακεδονίαν οὐδεμίαν ἔσχηκεν ἄνεσιν ἡ σὰρξ ἡμῶν, ἀλλ' ἐν παντὶ θλιβόμενοι· ἔξωθεν μάχαι, ἔσωθεν φόβοι, cf. Act. Phil. 34. As may be seen from 2 C. 7:5 the opposite of external and internal θλῖψις is ἄνεσις, cf. 2 Th. 1:7; 2 C. 8:13; Act. Pl. et Thecl. 37; Act. Pt. 2; Act. Thom. 39.

2. The power common to all θλῖψις is that of death at work in it. [15] The apostle sees death in the almost intolerable weight of his sufferings, 2 C. 1:8 f. In palpable afflictions he experiences the νέκρωσις τοῦ Ἰησοῦ in his own body, 2 C. 4:10. He regards these sufferings as an abandonment to death, 2 C. 4:11, as the ἐνεργεῖσθαι of death in us, 2 C. 4:12. Thus at the end of his list of afflictions in R. 8:36 he quotes ψ 43:22 : ἕνεκεν σοῦ θανατούμεθα ὅλην τὴν ἡμέραν, ἐλογίσθημεν ὡς πρόβατα σφαγῆς. The θλίψεις are θάνατοι, in the pregnant expression of 2 C. 11:23. And it is clear that in this last time the necessary suffering of Christ in His members is an experience of the concrete effects of the power of death which Christ has already broken in His death and resurrection. κοινωνία παθημάτων αὐτοῦ is by συμμορφιζόμενος τῷ θανάτῳ αὐτοῦ, Phil. 3:10. The power of death in θλίψεις affects man in his carnal existence, 2 C. 7:5 f. The apostle fulfils the sufferings of Christ in his own σάρξ, Col. 1:24. He bears the marks of the νέκρωσις τοῦ Ἰησοῦ in his σῶμα, 2 C. 4:10, in his total psycho-physical constitution, 2 C. 7:5. In θλίψεις death shatters the earthen vessel, 2 C. 4:7. It destroys our outward man, the outwardly orientated and outwardly experienced life with its essential contingency and corruptibility, 2 C. 4:16.

The mortal threat in θλίψεις is thus a constant temptation for the Christian, 1 Th. 3:3 ff.; Rev. 2:10; cf. 1 Pt. 4:12. In Lk. 8:13 the εἶτα γενομένης θλίψεως ἢ διωγμοῦ διὰ τὸν λόγον of Mk. 4:17 is characteristically rendered καὶ ἐν καιρῷ πειρασμοῦ. Sufferings are a test whether the Christian will champion the Gospel at the risk of his life or not, which means finally whether he will understand his own life in terms of its own possibilities or in terms of the divine promise and the possibilities opened up by it. This is evident in 2 C. 1:8 f. Paul resists the temptation of overwhelming afflictions by accepting the death operative in them as a divine judgment, and by thus offering up his life in faith to the God who raises the dead. This faith which offers life back to God, and which overcomes the temptation of mortal tribulation, is active in patience, 2 Th. 1:4 : ὑπὲρ τῆς ὑπομονῆς ὑμῶν καὶ πίστεως ἐν πᾶσιν τοῖς διωγμοῖς ὑμῶν καὶ ταῖς θλίψεσιν αἷς

[13] Cf. Test. Iss. 3:8 : πάντα γὰρ πένησι καὶ θλιβομένοις παρεῖχον. θλίβεσθαι is "to starve" in Test. Jos. 17:6. In Test. B. 5:1 the θλιβόμενοι are the poor; cf. Herm. s., 1, 8; Ign. Sm., 6, 2; Barn., 20, 2 = Did., 5, 2; 1 Cl., 59, 4.

[14] Acc. to Test. B. 7:2 μάχαιρα is the mother of seven evils : φθόνος, ἀπώλεια, θλῖψις, αἰχμαλωσία, ἔνδεια, ταραχή, ἐρήμωσις, cf. Test. Jos. 2:4 : οὐ γὰρ ἐγκαταλείπει κύριος τοὺς φοβουμένους αὐτόν, οὐκ ἐν σκότει ἢ δεσμοῖς ἢ θλίψεσιν ἢ ἀνάγκαις.

[15] Cf. also A. Schweitzer, Die Mystik des Apostels Pls. (1930), 142.

ἀνέχεσθε, cf. R. 12:12; Rev. 1:9; Herm. v., 2, 2, 7; Act. Andr. et Matth. 18; Act. Pt. et Pl. 2.

For in patience the hope is sustained which sees the invisible rather than the visible, so that the present tribulation which consumes man is reduced to a small affliction for a brief period as compared with the coming glory, 2 C. 4:17 f. In patience (of the φωτισθέντες in Hb. 10:32) there is also the comfort which comes to those who suffer through Christ, 2 C. 1:5 f. Hence suffering creates patience, and by the way of confirmation it strengthens again the hope in which faith lives, R. 5:3 f. There is thus a causal nexus of events. Under the promise of Christ, which orientates faith to hope, suffering calls for patience. The patience of suffering, however, brings proof and this augments hope, which does not make ashamed. Thus the patience with which suffering is accepted by faith is fulfilled in the joy which is wrought by the promise of the Holy Spirit, 1 Th. 1:6; Col. 1:24. In the superabundant joy of the Holy Spirit, 2 C. 8:2, θλῖψις is radically accepted by faith. For in it there is victory over the spirit of the death which hangs over us in θλίψεις, namely, anxiety.

3. With this acceptance of θλίψεις by faith the Christian promotes the edification of the community. For in patient and indeed joyful advocacy of the Gospel even in the midst of the afflictions which it brings, the Word of God becomes a personally relevant promise of comfort to others, cf. 2 C. 1:4 ff.; 4:10 f.; Col. 1:24; Eph. 3:13; 1 Th. 1:6 f. Through the consolation of His own sufferings, Christ accomplishes in the patiently borne afflictions of believers the edification of His Church, and He thus causes the world to experience even now the fact that the power of afflictions has been broken.

Schlier

θνῄσκω, θνητός → 7; 21.

| † θρηνέω, † θρῆνος | (→ κλαίω, κλαυθμός, κόπτω, κοπετός, λυπέω, λύπη, πενθέω, πένθος). |

Contents : A. θρῆνος in Graeco-Roman Culture. B. θρῆνος in Near Eastern Culture : 1. The OT ; 2. Judaism. C. θρηνέω and θρῆνος in the NT : 1. Jewish Mourning Customs at the Time of Jesus ; 2. The Continuation of OT Trends in the NT.

From the time of Homer to the NT, and on into modern Gk., θρῆνος is a technical term for "mourning" (i.e., on bereavement). Sometimes it bears the even more restricted sense of a "lament" or "funeral dirge." [1] On the other hand the verb θρηνέω is often used even when the lamentation does not refer specifically to the dead. [2]

θ ρ η ν έ ω, θ ρ ῆ ν ο ς. Pr.-Bauer, 566; Moult.-Mill., 292 f.; Liddell-Scott, Pape, Pass., *s.v.* On A : *Handbuch der klass. Altertumswiss.*, IV, 1, 2; I. Müller, *Die griech. Privataltertümer*[2] (1893), 214; *ibid.*, IV, 2, 2; H. Blümner, *Die römischen Privataltertümer*[3] (1911), 486; C. Sittl, *Die Gebärden der Griechen und Römer* (1890), 65-78; Rohde, I, 220-223. On B : RE[3], 20 (1908), 83, 36-90, 50 (R. Zehnpfund, "Trauer und Trauergebräuche bei den Hebräern"); H. Jahnow, *Das hb. Leichenlied im Rahmen der Völkerdichtung* ⚌ *Beihefte* ZAW, 36 (1923); A. Bertholet, *Kulturgeschichte Israels* (1919), 96, 139, 269; Str.-B., I, 521-523, IV, 582-590.

[1] On the distinction between θρῆνος and ἐπικήδειον cf. Etym. M., *s.v.*; Eustath. Thessal. Comm. in Od., 11, 75 (I, 400, 16 f., Stallbaum).

A. θρῆνος in Graeco-Roman Culture.

1. In Greece γόοι and θρῆνοι were an essential part of the γέρας θανόντων (cf. Hom. Il., 24, 721) [3] and even of the cult of souls. For the departed soul receives cries of lamentation and funeral dirges as homage to itself in which it takes pleasure. Immediately after placing the corpse on the bier in the house, the true purpose of which was to provide a space for the lament, [4] the θρῆνοι were struck up. So long as the body was open to view, these were renewed each day, [5] and they mounted to a climax with the burial rites.

Women played a special role in the funeral dirges, as may be seen from the depiction of the Muses as mourners in Homer (Od., 24, 60 f.: θρήνεον!) and especially from the description of the lamentations of women at the bier of Hector (Il., 24, 720 ff.). Yet here there is also reference to θρήνων ἔξαρχοι, to men who sing funeral dirges, and similarly the later references are not merely to θρηνήτριαι, Schol. Eur. Phoen., 1489 (ed. E. Schwartz, 1887) but also to their male counterpart, the θρηνητήρ, θρηνητής or θρηνήτωρ (cf. Manetho Apotelesmatica, IV, 190 [ed. A. Koechly in Poetae Bucolici et Didactici (1862)]; BGU, I, 34 recto col., IV, 3 f.: εἰς πεῖν τοῖς παιδίοις ᾱ, θρηνητῇ ᾱ, sc. probably pots of wine). [6] Here there is no doubt that we have professional men or women mourners who are paid for their services.

Solon tried to remedy some of the abuses connected with mourning customs and to limit mourning to women who were closely related [7] to the dead person. [8] With other extreme expressions of grief (→ κοπετός), he forbade τὸ θρηνεῖν πεποιημένα, the intonation of poems (Plut. Solon, 21 [I, 90c]). Obviously there had grown up in connection with burial customs a real industry which, like the theatre, provided a living for poets as well as actors. It is likely that Homer had formal songs in view in his descriptions (e.g., Il., 24, 720 ff.), but these were longer and less impromptu, and they were probably composed by θρήνων σοφισταί and then formally declaimed by these professional mourners. [9]

2. The simplification and purification of burial customs attempted by Solon seems to have been only partially successful (→ κόπτω). For these customs were constantly reinforced from the east, the more so as later Gk. culture came under oriental influence. At one point in particular there is a development in the Hellenistic use of the θρῆνος which gives clear evidence of this influence. This is the use of the cultic lamentation in the mystery rites, in which the violent death of a cultic god is bewailed. Thus in P. Tebt., I, 140 (p. 598) (72 B.C.) we read of θρηνώματα [10] εἰς τὸν Ὄσιριν, and in Ps.-Luc. (Syr. Dea, 6) of cultic mourning for Adonis: (The inhabitants of Byblos) μνήμην τοῦ πάθεος (sc. of Adonis) τύπτονταί τε ἑκάστου ἔτεος καὶ θρηνέουσι. There is perhaps an echo of the Attic mystery in the Gnostic hymn preserved in Act. Joh., 95: θρηνῆσαι θέλω· κόψασθε πάντες. [11]

---

[2] Cf. the general descriptions given by Hesych., s.v. θρῆνος· γόος and θρηνεῖ· πενθεῖ, ὀλολύζει, ὀλοφύρεται.

[3] Müller, 214; K. F. Ameis-C. Hentze, Anhang z. Homers Ilias, VIII (1886), 136 ff.

[4] Rohde, 221.

[5] Müller, loc. cit.

[6] V. Moult.-Mill., s.v. θρηνέω.

[7] Cf. on this pt. Epigr. Graec., 345, 3 f.: μῆτερ ἐμή, θρήν[ων ἀ]ποπαύεο κτλ.

[8] Cf. Rohde, 221.

[9] Ibid., n. 3.

[10] Other forms of θρῆνος are θρήνωμα and θρήνημα (cf. Moult.-Mill., 293, s.v. θρηνέω).

[11] Cf. H. Schlier, Religionsgeschichtliche Untersuchungen zu den Ignatiusbriefen (1929), 164, n. 3 and → κόπτω.

3. Among the Romans, [12] whose burial customs and laws were directly influenced by the Gks. according to Cicero, [13] funeral dirges were sung by close female relatives of the family both at the showing of the corpse and at the actual burial. Men played a much less active role than women in this case. [14]

B. θρῆνος in Near Eastern Culture.

The real home of violent lamentation, and perhaps of the formal θρῆνος in the narrower sense, of the lament, is probably the east. Persian burial customs were famous (Aesch. Choeph., 411 ff.; Pers., 683; → κόπτω). There is perhaps a similar reminiscence in the description by Nonnus (Dionysiaca, 24, 179 ff. [Ludwich, 1911]) of the funeral lament in the barbaric Indies. If he refers to the φιλόθρηνοι γυναῖκες (v. 181), there is reflected here the fact that in the orient, too, women played, and still play, a more prominent role in mourning than men.

1. The Old Testament.

The OT gives us a picture of Hebrew funeral customs which forms an interesting parallel and contrast to Greek mourning.

The Hebrew lament is the קִינָה, which is the home of the qina metre. [15] The LXX has θρῆνος for קִינָה, and sometimes for נְהִי, and similarly it uses forms of θρηνέω for קוֹנֵן, also הֵילִיל and נהה. As distinct from the NT, however, the LXX normally uses θρῆνος and θρηνέω more generally for the lament than for more spontaneous mourning.

In Israel, too, mourning first takes place in the house with the deceased on the bier, and then during the actual ceremonies of interment. The mourning of family relatives, who are naturally the first to engage in lamentation, becomes more general national mourning in the case of outstanding figures (cf. Gn. 50:3, 10; 2 Βασ. 1:17 f.; 3:34). At a later date we find professional mourners in Israel too, and at the same time spontaneous lamentation (κόπτεσθαι, κλαίειν, πενθεῖν, e.g., Gn. 23:2; 50:1, 3, 10) is replaced by the more or less formal dirge (θρῆνος) (cf. Ιερ. 9:19 : διδάξατε τὰς θυγατέρας ὑμῶν οἶκτον καὶ γυνὴ τὴν πλησίον αὐτῆς θρῆνον, also 3 Macc. 4:6, where we have θρῆνον as opposed to ὑμέναιος). At this stage we find that εἰδότες θρῆνον (Am. 5:6) in Israel correspond to the θρήνων ἔξαρχοι of Homer and αἱ θρηνοῦσαι (Ιερ. 9:16) to Greek θρηνήτριαι. But inspired poets like David (cf. 2 Βασ. 1:17-27; 3:33 f.) and Jeremiah (cf. 9:9 Mas.; 7:29 LXX) are found instead of the paid θρήνων σοφισταί of the Greeks. It is no accident that in Jeremiah, to whom Lamentations is ascribed, [16] the words θρῆνος and θρηνέω are particularly common. [17]

In the OT, too, women are particularly prominent in the exercise of θρῆνος. Jeremiah arranges for mourning women to accompany his θρῆνος (Ιερ. 9:16 f.), and he also calls all the women of the nation to θρῆνος (v. 19). Similarly, Ezekiel declares that the daughters of the Gentiles will accompany his lament for Egypt (Ez. 32:16). In national mourning virgins play a predominant role (cf. Jl. 1:8; Ju. 11:40; 3 Macc. 4:6 ff.), as may also be seen from the symbolism of the weeping daughter of Sion (Jer. 7:29 Mas.)

---

[12] Cf. Blümner, 486; Sittl, 69 f. and the examples in Ovid, Amores, 3, 9, 50 ff.; Petronius Arbiter, Satiricon, 111 (ed. A. Ernout, 1922); P. Papinius Statius, Thebais, VI, 178 (ed. A. Klotz, 1908); Silvae, II, 1, 23 (ed. A. Klotz, 1911), also artistic representations like the Haterii relief (v. Blümner, op. cit., n. 4).

[13] Cf. Rohde, 222, n. 2.

[14] Sittl, 70.

[15] Cf. the basic essay of K. Budde in ZAW, 2 (1882), 1 ff.

[16] Cf. Lam. 1:1: ἐκάθισεν Ἰερεμίας κλαίων καὶ ἐθρήνησεν τὸν θρῆνον τοῦτον ἐπὶ Ἰερουσαλήμ.

[17] Cf. W. Baumgartner, Die Klagegedichte des Jeremia (1917).

and the mourning virgin of Samaria (Mi. 1:8 LXX); cf. also the mourning of Rachel in Jer. 31:15.

In the OT there is naturally no cultic lamentation along the lines of oriental religion. Attempts have been made to find something of this nature in the four-day lamentation annually devoted to the recollection of Jephthah's daughter (Ju. 11:40). But this takes place in a circle in which there can be no true veneration of heroes or heroines, so that there is only a formal parallel to the annual festivals of lamentation for Adonis (cf. Ps.-Luc. Syr. Dea, 6) or for Achilles in Elis (Paus., VI, 23, 3). On the contrary, the prophetic θρῆνος of the OT stands in sharp contrast to the cultic θρῆνος of heathenism. There is no bewailing of a dead god. The living God Himself summons the prophets to θρῆνος on account of the rejection of the people of God (Ιερ. 7:29 LXX) or on account of the impending destruction of other nations like the Egyptians (cf. Ez. 32:18), and the prophets pass on this summons to θρῆνος. There is a fourfold call of Joel (1:5, 8, 11, 13) to priests and drunkards, to the city and the land, to lament because of the threat of destruction on the day of the Lord. There is also a fourfold call of Jeremiah to θρῆνος on account of the divine threat of devastation and death among the people (Ιερ. 9:9 LXX, 16 f., 19). In keeping with this is the fact that the intimation of θρῆνος occupies a special position in the foretellings of the prophets, whether it be the θρῆνος of the prophet himself (cf. Mi. 1:8 Mas.; Jer. 9:9 Mas.), or that of those who are affected (Am. 5:16; Ιερ. 38:15), or that of contemporary spectators (Is. 14:4; Ez. 32:16). For the circle of those who lament widens out in accordance with the more universal character of the disasters proclaimed until it covers all the people or all the peoples (cf. Am. 5:16; Jl. 1 f.; Jer. 9:19; Ez. 32:16), and the scene of θρῆνος is the whole land, streets and market-places, houses and vineyards (Am. 5:16), and especially the high places (cf. Jer. 7:29; Ιερ. 38:15 [31:15] A : ἐν τῇ ὑψηλῇ).

Examples of the contents of Hebrew θρῆνοι may be found in Lamentations and also in 2 Βασ. 1:19-27; Jer. 9:18, 20; Am. 5:1 ff.; Is. 14:4 ff.

2. Judaism.

In post-biblical Judaism the mourning customs of the OT are codified, and in detail they are defined and fixed along various lines.

There are two kinds of θρῆνοι : עֱנוּי, or common lamentation, and קִינָה, which denotes an antiphonal lament (cf. Jer. 9:19). The corresponding verbs are עֱנָּה and קוֹנֵן, cf. MQ, 3, 8 and 9; Str.-B., I, 522c, e.

As in all other parts of the ancient world, lamentation took place in the house of the deceased [18] and then especially at the burial. But there were certain restrictions. Thus laments with flutes were not allowed in houses or on the way to the tomb on the day of the new moon, on the festivals of the Dedication or of Purim, or on intermediate feast-days. At these times עֱנוּי was ordained instead, and after the interment even this was forbidden on the first of the feasts mentioned, as was also → κοπετός, cf. TMQ, 2, 17; Str.-B., I, 522d.

Dirges in the strict sense [19] were sung by mourning women (מְקוֹנֶנֶת or אַלְיָתָא, e.g., Ket., 4, 4; Kelim, 16, 7). Flute-players (מְחַלְּלִים בַּחֲלִילִים. Ket., 4, 4; Str.-B., I, 521a with n. 1) accompanied them (Jos. Bell., 3, 437: αὐληταὶ οἳ θρήνων αὐτοῖς ἐξῆρχον, cf. Mt. 9:23):

---

[18] Cf. Str.-B., I, 522d.
[19] For fragments of such θρῆνοι cf. ibid., I, 523i; also Meg., 6a; Str.-B., II, 469.

flutes are also used at Roman interments, along with tubas.[20] The women themselves accompanied their laments with clapping of the hands (אירוס), with what was called רְבִיעִית,[21] and with → κοπετός.

Women relatives played little part in the public lamentation, but the men engaged in panegyrics in which the virtues of the dead were extolled (קִלּוּס),[22] and they accompanied these by beating their hands on their breasts and heads and by stamping their feet (Gn. r., 100 on 50:10; cf. Str.-B., IV, 584c).

There thus arose a third form of formal lamentation, the oration (הֶסְפֵּד)[23] which was usually delivered by a paid speaker (סַפְדָן) in the vicinity of the grave.[24]

In all laments, which often contained extravagant praise of the deceased,[25] the thought in the background was that the deceased heard them (Shab., 152b; 153a; j AZ, 42c, 4; Str.-B., IV, 586t; → 149), and the belief that in some way the words of lamentation would make it known whether or not the deceased was a son of the עולם הבא (Shab., 153a; Str.-B., IV, 586r).

Apart from sung or intoned θρῆνοι there were also burial inscriptions called ἐπιτάφιοι θρῆνοι (Jos. Ant., 7, 42).

C. θρηνέω and θρῆνος in the New Testament.

The subst. θρῆνος is found only once in the NT, and even here the attestation is not certain (Mt. 2:18).[26] The verb occurs three times at Mt. 11:17 = Lk. 7:32; Lk. 23:27; Jn. 16:20. In three of these four instances the reference is to mourning (Mt. 2:18; 11:17 and par.; Lk. 23:27), but always to general lamentation rather than to the formal lament.

1. The NT use of θρηνέω attests first the persistence of Jewish mourning customs at the time of Jesus. The grumbling words of children playing at marriages and funerals (Mt. 11:17 and par.),[27] and accusing their playmates of spoiling the game, are a reflection of contemporary customs, with the music of flutes inviting to the dance on the one side, and the θρῆνος accompanied by weeping (Lk.) and beating on the breast (Mt.)[28] on the other. The same link between κόπτεσθαι and θρηνεῖν is seen to be an established custom in the lamentation of the women who accompany Jesus on the way from Gabbatha to Golgotha (Lk. 23:27).

The special emphasis on women corresponds to the prominence which they are given elsewhere in connection with mourning (→ A. and B.).

There is a similar relation between θρῆνος and κοπετός in all ancient cultures, and among the Gks. in both private (Epigr. Graec., 345, 3 f.) and cultic mourning (Ps.-Luc.

---

[20] Cf. Blümner, 486.

[21] Cf. Str.-B., I, 522g, h.

[22] Cf. Str.-B., IV, 582, 584 f., d-h.

[23] Ibid., 583m-590.

[24] With the Jews as with the Gks. there are two professional groups, the mourning women and the orators.

[25] Cf. the Rabb. discussion of this pt. in Str.-B., IV, 584 f.

[26] θρῆνος is found only in ℵCD pl sy; cf. Zn. Mt., 107 f., n. 11.

[27] For a material par. to Mt. 11:16 f. cf. Jeb., 16, 5: "Even when we hear children say: 'We are now going to hold mourning for NN (לספור) and to bury him'" (this is in certain circumstances a valid testimony to his death). I owe this reference to K. H. Rengstorf.

[28] As thus used with θρηνεῖν, → κόπτεσθαι must here be understood in its literal sense (as against Zn., ad loc.). On the other hand, in the children's game θρηνεῖν obviously has the general sense of "to mourn." It seems to me very doubtful whether the participation of men in lamentation for the dead can be deduced from Mt. 11:17, as in Sittl, 68, n. 1.

Syr. Dea, 6). In the prophetic lamentation of the OT we also find the two together, both materially and metrically (e.g., Mi. 1:8, cf. esp. the parallelism in Jer. 9:9; Jl. 1:13). In Jewish mourning both the dirges of the women and the lamentations of the men are accompanied by κοπετός, cf. esp. MQ, 3, 8, where נהה and ספד (→ κόπτω) stand in the same close connection as the verbs θρηνεῖν and κόπτεσθαι in Mt. 11:17 and Lk. 23:27. But the Church, too, continues both κοπετός and θρῆνος as the integrated gestures and words of mourning (cf. Chrys. Hom. in Acta Apostolorum, 21, 3 = MPG, 60, 168).

The link between θρηνεῖν and → κλαίειν, which is found in the Lucan form of the children's saying (Lk. 7:32), is obviously very general; cf. also Jn. 16:20; Mt. 2:18, and in the OT Jl. 1:5; Ιερ. 38:15 etc.

2. More important, however, is the inner continuation of OT trends. In 2:17 f. Mt. quotes Jer. 38:15 (→ 151), and in spite of the difference in place, and the LXX aorist, he claims that this is fulfilled in the mourning of the women of Bethlehem: φωνὴ ἐν 'Ραμὰ ἠκούσθη, θρῆνος καὶ κλαυθμὸς καὶ ὀδυρμὸς πολύς (cf. n. 26). In fact we here have the LXX aorist which corresponds to a prophetic perfect in the Hebrew. But the decisive point is that there is a striking similarity between the OT prophecy and the NT fulfilment. In both cases the saying concerning lamentation is embedded in a context of salvation. In both cases there seems to be complete destruction, but God accomplishes a miraculous deliverance. The salvation of Israel from the mortal distress of national destruction, which Jeremiah foresees, is a τύπος of the deliverance of Jesus from the mortal distress of the slaughter of the innocents. The OT θρῆνος of the mother of Israel (Rachel) is applied to the mothers of Israel in the NT. But already in the OT the voice of the ἔλεος of God rings out above the θρῆνος of Israel, and in the NT the divine redemption, the Saviour Himself, arises out of the depths of the sorrow. By referring to the prophecy of the sorrow of Rachel, which is changed into salvation and joy, Mt. was seeking to turn the point of the Jewish accusation that Jesus had brought death to those of his own generation.

The θρῆνος of the women of Israel is found not only at the beginning of the life of Jesus, but also at its end. But now it applies to Jesus Himself. His march to the place of execution takes on the form of a burial procession, Lk. 23:27: ἠκολούθει δὲ αὐτῷ πολὺ πλῆθος τοῦ λαοῦ καὶ γυναικῶν αἳ ἐκόπτοντο καὶ ἐθρήνουν αὐτόν. Where paid mourners usually bewail the respected dead with eulogies, the women of Jerusalem freely bewail Jesus on His way to a criminal's death. This is a kind of anticipated mourning for which there is a prophetic parallel in the anointing at Bethany (→ κόπτω). Jesus, however, knows that He himself is on the threshold of life, whereas those who bewail Him are really on the threshold of destruction. He thus forbids θρῆνος for Himself, and demands instead, after the manner of the prophets, that they should engage in proleptic mourning for themselves and their children (cf. the self-lamentation of 3 Macc. 4:8).

In Lk. 23:28, then, Jesus takes up the prophetic demand for general θρῆνος (→ 151 on Jer. 9; Jl. 1 f. etc.). But He also uses another prophetic form, i.e., that of intimation of θρῆνος, not merely for the old Israel, which now moves towards a destruction that it has brought upon itself, but also for the new Israel, i.e., for His disciples, who must also pass through mortal afflictions. Jn. 16:20: ἀμὴν ἀμὴν λέγω ὑμῖν ὅτι κλαύσετε καὶ θρηνήσετε ὑμεῖς, ὁ δὲ κόσμος χαρήσεται. θρηνεῖν, along with → κλαίειν and → λυπεῖσθαι, will characterise the situation of the disciples to the very last. It is true, of course, that the reference of the verb here is to lamentation in the general sense, not to lamentation for the dead. On the other hand, we might think in terms of the latter (again with reference to Jesus Himself), since the ambiguous statement of the Johannine Jesus does not allow us to conclude with certainty whether He is referring to the two days before the resurrection or to the whole period up to the *parousia*. The second thought is obviously predominant, however, [29] for the use of the picture of the woman in travail (v. 21), which is often found in Jewish eschatology, is an indication that Jesus has in view the time of the woes of the Messiah prior to His definitive manifestation. But as the woes of earthly Israel on Christ's first appearance are ultimately only the prelude to the consolation and salvation which will come forth out of them (→ 153 on Mt. 2:18), so Jesus intimates a great transformation of the tribulation of the new Israel: the λύπη of the disciples is to be turned into χαρά, their θρῆνος into χορός (to borrow from ψ 29:11). The prophecy of Jesus takes the same lines as that of the OT prophets, who trace the way of their people through the night of sorrow and death to the endless day of salvation and divine joy.

Not finally clear is the point which Jesus is making when he uses the figure of children playing in the market-place. Mt. (11:17) and Lk. (7:32) put the grumbling accusation of one of the two groups of children into almost identical verse form:

> ηὐλήσαμεν ὑμῖν καὶ οὐκ ὡρχήσασθε·
> ἐθρηνήσαμεν καὶ οὐκ ἐκόψασθε (Lk. ἐκλαύσατε).

In both the accusing party is compared with the corrupt generation of the present which brings no more understanding and faith to Jesus than to John the Baptist. The parable would be easier to understand if the messengers of God were compared to the accusers. [30] But for Jesus the point of the parable is different. As children at play always want to choose the game and to be the leaders, and the rest must be ready to comply with their choice, so this generation, and especially those who believe themselves to be the leaders of God's people in the time of Jesus, take it for granted that all men, including the divine messengers, should dance to their tune. In open self-contradiction, they thus demand that the ascetic preacher of repentance should show a more agreeable openness to the world (cf. Mt. 11:8), and that the Bearer of the good news should show more of the seriousness of the ascetic (cf. Mk. 2:18 ff. and par.). Sharing the attitude which brought Ahab to ruin (1 K. 22:8 ff.), they believe that they can tell God what He ought to say through His messengers, and they fail to note that they are thereby forcing their own will on God instead of acknowledging His sovereign will. The serious charge of Jesus is thus that the piping and mourning of the leaders of the people is basically an attempt to give orders to God. It is fully in keeping that they do not believe in the true Word of God any more than Ahab did. They misinterpret the divine singularity of the messengers as demonic or sinful, and in either case ungodly. They thus evade the claim of God by this most serious sin (cf. Mk. 3:22, 29 f.).

The assured justification of the divine messengers (Mt. 11:19) carries with it the no less certain rejection of this generation.

The acts of God are accompanied by the θρῆνος of men. In the OT θρῆνος is the answer to His judicial action, in the NT it is centred on Jesus, the Messenger of joy. The entry of Jesus into this world brings not only personal suffering but

---

[29] Cf. G. Stählin, ZNW, 33 (1934), 241, 242, 243.
[30] This is how F. Köster (ThStKr, 35 [1862], 347) interprets the parable.

also the accompanying lamentation of fellow-citizens of Bethlehem who suffer on His account (Mt. 2:18). His death is accompanied by the θρῆνος of fellow-citizens of Jerusalem (Lk. 23:27). Moreover, His death is the reason for the final judgment of Israel which He calls upon men to bewail like a prophet of disaster. Indeed, the life of His own people on earth is one of fellow-suffering with Him (R. 8:17), and it is thus filled with θρῆνος (Jn. 16:20). Nevertheless, Christ is the Messenger of joy. Those who expect or demand θρῆνος in Him personally are resisting God (Mt. 11:17 and par.). But those who accept a life of suffering for His sake will find that at the end the θρῆνος of the Church Militant is turned into the χαρά of the Church Triumphant (Jn. 16:20, 22; → ἡδονή, II, 926).

Stählin

> † θρησκεία, † θρῆσκος, [1]
> † ἐθελοθρησκεία

1. The data are as follows. There is only sparse attestation in the NT, θρησκεία 4 times (2 in the same passage), θρῆσκος once, and ἐθελοθρησκεία once. This paucity is quite striking in relation to the whole sphere of Gk. literature. For elsewhere words with the stem θρησκ- are fairly common. Thus we never find the verb θρησκεύω in the NT, though it comes twice in rapid succession in the LXX. The LXX does not have θρῆσκος, but θρησκεία occurs 4 times, twice in the same passage. In Philo[2] and Josephus[3] θρησκεία is common (also θρησκεύω in Joseph.), as in Gk. literature generally, in which we also find θρήσκευμα, θρήσκευσις, θρησκεύσιμος, θρησκευτήριον, θρησκευτής, (τά) θρήσκια, θρησκώδης. θρησκεία is first found in Ionic (Herodotus), and it then passes, not only into the LXX and the NT, but also into the literary (Dion. Hal., Plut., Herodian, the fathers) and non-literary *koine* (inscr., pap.). [4]

2. The etymology is uncertain. Acc. to Plut. Alex., 2, 5 (I, 665d) (ταῖς περὶ τὸν Αἷμον Θρήσσαις ὅμοια δρῶσιν, ἀφ᾽ ὧν δοκεῖ καὶ τὸ θρησκεύειν ὄνομα ταῖς κατακόροις ("sated," "excessive") γενέσθαι καὶ περιέργοις ἱερουργίαις) derives the word θρησκεία from Θρῇσσα because the Thracian women dedicated to the Bacchic and Orphic cult inclined to religious fanaticism and superstition. [5] Later there came a derivation from θρέομαι, θροέω, "to tremble"; [6] this helps us to understand the form

---

θρησκεία κτλ. J. C. A. van Herten, Θρησκεία, Εὐλάβεια, ʿΙκέτης, *Bijdrage tot de Kennis der religieuze terminologie in het Grieksch,* with a summary in English (Diss. Utrecht, 1934), 2-27, 95 f.; A. Kraemer, *Philol. Wochenschr.,* 54 (1935), 409 ff.; K. Prümm, DLZ, 56 (1935), 1075 ff. The thesis of van Herten is : *De woorden* θρησκεία *c.s. zijn door een griek vooral gebruikt om die cultusvormen aan te duiden, welke van de algemeenaanvaarde afweken* ("The word θρησκεία and its cognates were used above all by the Gks. to denote cultic forms which deviated from those which were generally valid"). The thesis itself, and much of the material, is in agreement with 1.-4. of this article, but the questions discussed under 5. are not dealt with by van Herten.

[1] Most lexicographers prefer θρησκός; but cf. Bl.-Debr.[6] § 118, 2 : "θρῆσκος, Jm. 1:26, is formed from θρησκεία, -εύειν;" hence the above order. Liddell-Scott also have θρῆσκος.
[2] Cf. Leisegang, *s.v.*
[3] Cf. Schl. Jos., 77.
[4] Cf. Preisigke Wört. and Moult.-Mill.
[5] Hence the form θρῆσκος.
[6] Wilke-Grimm, *s.v.*: θρησκός, religiosus (*uti videtur a* τρέω, *tremo, ergo propr.* tremens, pavidus ...).

θρεσκός in Hesych. More recent Indo-Germanic students are inclined to link the stem θρησκ- with θεραπ-, thus giving to θρησκεύω the sense of "to serve." [7]

3. It might be asked whether etymological discussion has any bearing on the actual sense. It has a certain value in our own case, however, because the etymological conflict is also a conflict of signification. If Plutarch is right, we have a term which is used in a bad sense ; if the others are right, it is used in a good sense. Furthermore, there has always been a distinction in meaning apart from the etymology. Hdt. writes in II, 37: ἄλλας τε θρησκηίας ἐπιτελέουσι μυρίας. If these words are set in the context of what precedes them (θεοσεβέες δὲ περισσῶς ἐόντες μάλιστα πάντων ἀνθρώπων), the meaning is that of "religious conduct or practice" in general, with particular emphasis on the zealousness of such practice. Cf. θρησκεύω in the sense of "to practise religion," "to keep a religious statute," Hdt., II, 64, 65; Dion. Hal. Ant. Rom., I, 76; II, 23, 67. With θρησκεία the being to whom the practice refers is in the obj. gen. So Herodian Hist., IV, 8, 17: θρησκεία τοῦ θεοῦ, "worship of God." Particularly instructive is Corp. Herm., XII, 23 : καὶ τοῦτό ἐστιν ὁ θεός, τὸ πᾶν ... τοῦτον τὸν λόγον, ὦ τέκνον, προσκύνει καὶ θρήσκευε. θρησκεία δὲ τοῦ θεοῦ μία ἐστί, μὴ εἶναι κακόν. In the famous Gallio inscr. [8] we read: ἀεὶ [δ'] ἐτήρη[σα τὴ]ν θρησκεί[αν τ]οῦ Ἀπό[λλωνος τοῦ Πυθίου]. There is an exact par. in a letter of Hadrian to Delphi: καὶ εἰς τὴν ἀρ[χαιότητα τῆ]ς πόλεως καὶ εἰς τὴν τοῦ κατέχοντος α[ὐτὴν θεοῦ θρησ]κείαν ἀφορῶν. In his letter to the Jews of Alexandria Claudius refers to πάτριος θρησκεία, Jos. Ant., 19, 5, 2, and there is a similar expression in his letter to the authorities at Jerusalem, Jos. Ant., 20, 1, 2. [9] The expressions θρησκεία τοῦ θεοῦ and θρησκεύω are favourites with Joseph., who has transmitted these two imperial letters. Thus in Ant., 13, 8, 2 he speaks of the respect of Antiochus VII for the Jewish religion ; θρησκεία πρὸς τὸν θεόν in Ant., 1, 13, 1 is the same as pietas ; θρησκεία κοσμική in Bell., 4, 5, 2 is roughly equivalent to world "religion." [10] Cf. 4 Macc. 5:7, 13 (Jewish "religion").

Under this head we may group Ac. 26:5 and Jm. 1:26 f. As Joseph. mostly uses θρησκεία (τοῦ θεοῦ) for Jewish worship of God, so Paul says in Ac. 26:5 : κατὰ τὴν ἀκριβεστάτην αἵρεσιν τῆς ἡμετέρας θρησκείας ἔζησα Φαρισαῖος. In Jm. 1:26 f. θρῆσκος means "god-fearing," "pious," and θρησκεία means "fear of God" : εἴ τις δοκεῖ θρῆσκος εἶναι, μὴ χαλιναγωγῶν γλῶσσαν ἑαυτοῦ ..., τούτου μάταιος ἡ θρησκεία. θρησκεία καθαρὰ ... αὕτη ἐστίν, ἐπισκέπτεσθαι ὀρφανοὺς κτλ. Along similar lines the reference in 1 Cl., 45, 7 is to Christian worship : θρησκεύειν τὴν θρησκείαν τοῦ ὑψίστου; cf. 62, 1.

---

[7] So esp. J. Wackernagel in the Zeitschrift f. vergleichende Sprachforschung auf dem Gebiete der indogermanischen Sprachen, 33 (1895), 41: "... it is fairly obvious that the Ionic, and later the koine, θρησκεύω, 'to pay divine honour,' θρησκεία, 'worship of God,' is to be derived from *θρήπσκω, an inchoate of θεραπ-, 'to serve.'" Cf. also Prellwitz Etym. Wört., 186 : "... cf. the Sanskrit dhar, 'to keep,' 'to submit to' (vratam, a law)." F. Pfister follows both in his art. Kultus in Pauly-W., XI (1922), 2124 : "θεραπεία and θρησκεία go back to the same root, ... θεραπεία, like the Lat. cultus (from colo) means 'nurture,' Sansk. dhar, 'to keep,' 'to support,' 'to keep alive.'" Reference is made to Pfister by A. Deissmann, Paulus² (1925), 92, who translates θρησκεία "concern for," "respect." Acc. to L. Meyer, Handbuch der griech. Etymologie, III (1901), 470 f. "θρησκεία is thought to be closely linked with the concluding part of ἀ-θερίζειν." A. Debrunner refers to O. Hoffmann, Festschr. A. Bezzenberger (1921), 79: on θρήσκω· νοῶ (Hesych., s.v.). Walde-Pok., I, 857 also mentions θράσκειν (ᾱ)· ἀναμιμνήσκειν (Hesych., s.v.).

[8] Cf. A. Deissmann, op. cit., 203 ff., esp. 212.

[9] Ibid., 217.

[10] For further examples (from Joseph.) cf. Schlatter, op. cit.

4. On the other hand θρησκεία or θρησκεύω can be used in a bad sense. Plut. Praec. Coniug., 19 (II, 140d): περιέργοις δὲ θρησκείαις καὶ ξέναις δεισιδαιμονίαις, has in view an excessive practice of religion with a bad implication. Hesych. links θρησκ- with → δεισιδαίμων, → δεισιδαιμονία in this sense. It is open to question whether the implication is always bad (→ II, 20). [11] But this is quite clear in two passages in Philo: Spec. Leg., I, 315: κἂν μέντοι τις ὄνομα καὶ σχῆμα προφητείας ὑποδὺς ... ἄγῃ πρὸς τὴν τῶν νενομισμένων κατὰ πόλεις θρησκείαν θεῶν ... γόης, ἀλλ' οὐ προφήτης ἔστιν τοιοῦτος; Det. Pot. Ins., 21: πεπλάνηται καὶ οὗτος τῆς πρὸς εὐσέβειαν ὁδοῦ, θρησκείαν ἀντὶ ὁσιότητος ἡγούμενος. There is a sharp attack on idolatry in Wis. 11:15: πλανηθέντες ἐθρήσκευον ἄλογα ἑρπετὰ etc.; 14:17: τυράννων ἐπιταγαῖς ἐθρησκεύετο τὰ γλυπτά; 14:18: εἰς ἐπίτασιν (straining, intensifying) δὲ θρησκείας καὶ τοὺς ἀγνοοῦντας ἢ τοῦ τεχνίτου προετρέψατο φιλοτιμία, 14:27: ἡ γὰρ τῶν ἀνωνύμων εἰδώλων θρησκεία παντὸς ἀρχὴ κακοῦ καὶ αἰτία καὶ πέρας ἐστίν.

In this regard reference may be made to Col. 2:18 with its attack on the θρησκεία τῶν ἀγγέλων, the wrong worship or cult of angels. Cf. also the reference to the θρησκεία τῶν δαιμονίων in Eus. Hist. Eccl., VI, 41, 2. [12]

5. To point out that θρησκεία and θρῆσκος can sometimes be used in a good sense, and sometimes in a bad, and that the few NT passages may be divided along these lines, is hardly to touch the decisive point from the standpoint of biblical theology. In a passage like Col. 2:18, where we are confronted by ancient and modern attempts to establish the etymology and significance of the term, it needs to be emphasised that the bad sense is not intrinsically necessary. If this θρησκεία is objectionable, it is because of the added obj. genitive, i.e., the worship of angels as contrasted with the worship of God. The distinctive colouring of the more or less colourless θρησκεία is sometimes sought in the fact that the reference is to the external ceremonies of religious worship. [13] In fact, when we compare the Christian

---

[11] H. Kleinknecht is more cautious: "In the passage in Plut. Praec. Coniug., 19 (II, 140d), θρησκεία has a neutral sense. The bad sense is brought to light only by the adjective περίεργος. The term does not bear it of itself." In such a case individual judgment may differ as to the feel of a word. All the clearer, then, are the passages in Philo. A. Debrunner is of the view that the word first comes to be used contemptuously by intellectuals, especially philosophers, who have abandoned the popular cultus. The word "religion" can be given a similar nuance.

[12] Cf. Meinertz Gefbr. on Col. 2:18: "It is open to question whether the phrase 'worship of angels' denotes a specific cult, and whether confirmation of this is to be seen in the prohibition of idolatrous angel worship at the Council of Laodicaea (360). The general references of the apostle simply enable us to say with some probability that the heretics were paying to spirits a reverence which was no longer compatible with the supreme significance of Jesus." On this matter of the worship of angels at Colossae cf. esp. A. L. Williams, JThSt, 10 (1909), 413-438, and Dib. Gefbr., Excursus after Col. 2:23.

[13] So, e.g., Wilke-Grimm, s.v.: "cultus religiosus, potissimum externus, qui caeremoniis continetur"; Liddell-Scott: "religious worship," "cult ritual." Acc. to Trench θρησκεία denotes more specifically the ceremonial worship of religion. Cf. also K. Kerényi, Εὐλάβεια, Byzantin-Neugriech. Jahrbücher, 8 (1931), 307, 313. Van Herten, op. cit., 95 f.: "... it should be noted that where we do find the words, they are often used with reference to religious worship that deviates from the traditional and generally accepted forms of veneration of the national gods of the Greeks. Thus in connection with religious observances and rites, we find the words used of ceremonies which are unusual and strange ... From this usage arises their function to signify orgiastic rites ... they occur, however, in the usual normal sense of cult, the worship of the gods ... The meaning of piety we find ... and that of religious sense ... They are also used to denote the worship of men ... In Jewish authors we find the words ... used of the worship of animals and images (LXX) and of strange gods (Philo, Josephus), but also of the Jewish religion, sometimes as religious

and the non-Christian cultus, the biblical and the non-biblical worship of God, we do find a contrast between the inward and the outward. It should be remembered, however, that even if the Colossian error of angel worship was wholly inward, with no external ceremonies, it was still, potentially, an outward work. We thus see once more that everything depends on the object to which the θρησκεία refers. What the use of this term implies is finally a matter of taste. The same is true of such words, or concepts, as "cult" and "cultus." According to our own attitude to the human service of God thereby denoted, the terms have either a good sense or a bad. Our reflection thereupon is rooted elsewhere.

We noted at the outset that the rare occurrence of θρησκεία in the NT is at a first glance surprising. It is particularly surprising for those who try to understand early Christianity as a cult. No matter what term we might prefer for "cult," it can and must be stated that none of the possible alternatives is particularly emphasised in the NT or the Bible generally. We have seen that in the LXX θρησκεία, θρησκεύω occur only a few times in Wis. and once in 4 Macc., i.e., in works which are more specifically under Greek influence. [14] The Hellenist Josephus likes the word θρησκεία; the OT and NT hardly use it at all. Nor is there much difference when we turn to the synonyms : θεραπεία is rare in the OT and does not occur at all in the NT, while → θεραπεύω finds a religious use only in Ac. 17:25 (the Areopagus address); → λατρεία; ἐπιμέλεια is found only in Ac. 27:3, where neither God nor Christ is the object; → λειτουργία is common in the LXX in a specifically priestly sense, and it is found esp. in Hb., where we also have → λειτουργός and → λειτουργικός; ἱερουργία occurs at 4 Macc. 3:20 and not at all in the NT, while there is one occurrence of → ἱερουργέω at R. 15:16 (cf. 4 Macc. 7:8, and more frequently in Philo). [15]

These lexical statistics are of decisive significance from the standpoint of biblical theology. 1. In the Bible only a subordinate role is played by expressions which denote a specific religious or cultic attitude towards God, alongside which there might be some other attitude. [16] 2. In the Bible the attitude of man towards God is primarily the answer to God's call, the decision in face of God's claim. The cult or *cultus* (from *colo*) easily leads to synergism. [17] The Bible speaks of → πίστις

---

formalism, opposed to ὁσιότης (Philo), but also as inward piety, adherence to religion as opposed to external rites and ceremonies (Josephus). In the writings of Christian authors the words occur with reference of pagan gods ..., images ..., angels ..., but in the same time in the sense of Christian religiousness ... θρῆσκος ... in the sense of pious may, however, have the unfavourable meaning of ἑτερόδοξος and περιττός ..."

[14] We may also list Sir. 22:5, unless, with Tischendorf, we read ἡ θρασεῖα for ἡ θρησκεία.

[15] These are all the Greek synon. for "cult" as listed by Deissmann, *op. cit.*, 92. We naturally take a different view of them than does Deissmann with his veneration with or, as one might almost say, his cult of the cult. (His supposed essential difference between "cult" and "cultus" is again a matter of taste, and cannot be regarded as authoritatively binding.)

[16] Cf. → ἐκκλησία, which is not a cultic word like, e.g., θίασος; θίασος does not occur in the Bible and is rare in early Christianity (cf. K. L. Schmidt, *Die Kirche des Urchristentums*² [1932], 266 f.).

[17] Cf. a synergistic statement like that of Pfister, *op. cit.*: "Both words, θεραπεύω and *colo*, point to man's concern for the deity, to man's care for the deity, which has need of man ; they imply concerning oneself about the deity, caring for it, in some sense keeping it alive and nourishing it. The etymology of *religio* points in the same direction." This may be a relevant description of pagan cults, but it certainly does not apply to God's history with His people, the Church, as it is described in the Bible, in the old covenant and the new. The reference to *religio* is also correct, but "this word is alien to the canonical writings of Christianity" (J. G. Müller, "Über Bildung und Gebrauch des Wortes *Religio*" in ThStKr, 8 [1835], 121 ff.).

in the sense of the obedience of the whole man to God. Cf. the use of πίστις alongside the cultic term in Phil. 2:17: λειτουργία τῆς πίστεως. It is perhaps worth noting that θρησκεία can also be referred to men. [18]

In view of these basic factors, it is hardly worth trying to distinguish between θρησκεία and its synonyms. [19]

6. ἐθελοθρησκεία occurs only at Col. 2:23. It may be accepted as a Pauline construct [20] which later passed into the Greek of the early Church. [21]

> Some MSS have θρησκία. The signification of ἐθελοθρησκεία is a "cultus which is freely chosen, which is not commanded or forbidden." The ἐθελο- follows the example of the more common φιλο-. Similar constructs are ἐθελόπονος ("one who is willing to work"), ἐθελόκωφος ("one who pretends to be deaf"), ἐθελοφιλόσοφος ("one who alleges that he is a philosopher"), ἐθελοδιδάσκαλος ("one who alleges that he is a teacher"). [22]

In terms of these analogies, "the addition (sc. ἐθελο-) ... is in contrast to the situation posited by the facts or relationships. Hence it is not just an affected piety. It is a piety which does not keep to the reality and to what is implied in it, which does not keep to the true head, Christ. It is a piety which orders its own nature." [23]

K. L. Schmidt

---

† θριαμβεύω

θρίαμβος: an unrestrained hymn to Bacchus, and hence a name for Bacchus himself. By way of Etruscan [1] it becomes the Lat. *triumphus* (Liddell-Scott); θριαμβεύω

---

[18] Cf. the inscr. from Samaria in the time of Augustus which sharply prohibits the violation of graves and protects the θρησκεία προγόνων (lines 2, 15 f.: τὰς τῶν ἀνθρώπων θρησκίας). Cf. F. M. Abel, "Un Rescrit Impérial sur la Violation de Sépulture et le Tombeau trouvé vide," *Rev. Bibl.*, 39 (1930), 567 ff.; J. Zeller, "L'Inscription dite de Nazareth," *Recherches de Science religieuse*, 21 (1931), 570 ff. There is also reference to a θρησκεία ἀνθρώπων in Da. 2:46 Σ (Mas. יְהִיב, LXX σπονδάς, Θ εὐωδίας). Elsewhere (Jer. 3:19; Ez. 20:6, 15) Σ has θρησκεία for צְבִי [Bertram].

[19] Cr.-Kö., 499: "It (sc. θρησκεία) was perhaps the only word which could express the general concept of religion in the objective sense, so that neither Israel nor the Christian Church had any need to give it a specific meaning, and yet which could also express the concept of perverted religion." The central clause in this judgment discloses a sound insight into the facts from the standpoint of biblical theology.

[20] Moult.-Mill.: "Apparently a Pauline coinage." Cf. Dib. Gefbr. on Col. 2:23, where the word is translated "Eigenkult" ("individual cult").

[21] Acc. to the evidence of Thes. Steph. we also find in the fathers ἐθελοθρησκευτός, ἐθελοθρησκεύω, ἐθελοθρησκέω. A unique verbal monstrosity is to be found in Epiph. Haer., 16, 1, 7, where the Pharisees are accused of ἐθελοπερισσοθρησκεία. Cf. van Herten, *op. cit.*, 22.

[22] Cf. Bl.-Debr.[6] § 118, 2.

[23] So quite correctly Cr.-Kö., 499. Some Lat. texts (it Vg) miss the real meaning with their renderings *religio, observatio* or *simulatio religionis*. Cf. Tischendorf's large edition of the NT.

θ ρ ι α μ β ε ύ ω. Wnd. 2 K. on 2:14a. Less convincing Exp. T., XXI (1909/10), 19-21, 282 f. and Exp. 7th Series, Vol. VII (1909), 473.

[1] A. Walde, *Lateinisches etymologisches Wörterbuch*[2] (1910), 793. A. Ernout-A. Meillet, *Dictionnaire Etymologique de la Langue Latine* (1932), 1016. P. Kretschmer in A. Gercke-E. Norden, *Einleitung in die Altertumswiss.*, I[3], 6 (1923), 112.

thus comes to be a transl. of *triumphare*. a. "To triumph over (ἀπό, κατά τινος, ἐπί τινι); b. "to lead in a triumphal procession," τινά (Plut.).[2] It does not occur in the LXX.

In the NT it is used with the acc. in sense b. The way of Jesus to the cross is paradoxically the triumphal procession of God in which, as *imperator mundi*, He leads the ἀρχαί as a Roman emperor leads his prisoners, Col. 2:15. In 2 C. 2:14 Paul describes himself as one of these prisoners. But he regards it as a grace that in his fetters he can accompany God always and everywhere (πάντοτε — ἐν παντὶ τόπῳ, in his missionary work) in the divine triumphant march through the world, even though it be only as the δοῦλος Χριστοῦ. This statement has the same tension between δουλεία and ἐλευθερία as we find in the designation δοῦλος.

Delling

θρόνος

Contents: A. The Throne outside the New Testament: 1. On the Usage; 2. The Throne in the Greek World; 3. The Throne in the Old Testament; 4. The Throne in Hellenistic Judaism; 5. The Throne in Palestinian Judaism. B. The Throne in the New Testament: 1. Heaven as God's Throne; 2. The Throne of David; 3. The Throne of Glory; 4. The Throne of Grace; 5. The Throne of God and of the Lamb; 6. The Throne of Satan and of the Beast; 7. The Throne as a Class of Angels.

A. The Throne outside the New Testament.

1. On the Usage.

The word θρόνος is related to θρᾶνος, "seat," "bench," and θρῆνυς "foot-stool." It means "in general a high stool with back and arms, and with an accompanying foot-stool."[1] As distinct from *thronus*, which is rare and is used only for the seat of deity, the seat denoted by θρόνος is only later reserved for kings and gods. From the time of Plato (Prot., 315c) θρόνος can also be used for the teaching chair of the philosopher (Philostr. Vit. Soph., I, 23, 1; I, 25, 15; I, 30, 1; Anth. Pal., IX, 174). The LXX mostly uses θρόνος for אסכ.[2] Luther in most cases has *Stuhl* for the Semitic equivalents. In the NT he has *Thron* only at Col. 1:16, where the synonyms make this rendering necessary.[3] In all other cases we find *Stuhl*. With reference to Col. 1:16 the use of the plur. θρόνοι is interesting. In the tragic poets it is used for the power of kings and gods[4] (Aesch. Eum., 912; Prom., 220; Soph. Oed. Col., 426), but also for the divinatory throne of Apollo (Aesch. Eum., 18; 30; 606), along with the sing. (Eur. Iph. Taur., 1254; 1282). We find a figur. use in Plat. Resp., VIII, 553b/c, where there is reference to a θρόνος in one's own soul. Peculiar to biblical Gk. are the many gen. combinations with

[2] θριαμβεύω τινά, "I deride": Vita Euripidis, p. 137, 89 (Westermann). I owe this ref. to Debrunner, who found it in W. Schmid, *Philologische Wochenschrift*, 54 (1934), 961. On other meanings, cf. Wnd. 2 K.

θ ρ ό ν ο ς. Liddell-Scott, *s.v.*; Pr.-Bauer³, *s.v.*; C. Daremberg-E. Saglio, *Dictionnaire des Antiquités Grecques et Romaines*, XV (1919), 278-283; A. Hug, Art. Θρόνος in Pauly-W., VI, A (1935), 613-618.

[1] A. Hug, *op. cit.*
[2] For more details cf. Hatch-Redp., I, 655 f.
[3] Cf. Calwer, *Bibelkonkordanz* (1893), 1142 f.; 1173.
[4] On the throne as a metaphor for political and judicial power in Rabb. Judaism, cf. Str.-B., I, 979.

θρόνος, in which the gen. defines the noun in a logically very general way.[5] A list is as follows: θρόνος δόξης, 1 Βασ. 2:8; Is. 22:23; Jer. 14:21; 17:12; Sir. 47:11; Wis. 9:10; θρόνος βασιλείας, 3 Βασ. 9:5; 1 Ch. 22:10; 28:5; 2 Ch. 7:18; Est. 5:1c (τῆς); Da. 3:54 (τῆς) Θ LXX (acc. to 88 LXX has θρόνος δόξης τῆς βασιλείας); 4:27 (τῆς) LXX; 5:20 Θ; Bar. 5:6; 1 Macc. 2:57; 7:4; 10:53, 55; 11:52; θρόνος ἀρχῆς Prv. 16:12; θρόνος ἀτιμίας, Prv. 11:16; θρόνος ἀνομίας, ψ 93:20; cf. also in the NT: θρόνος δόξης, Mt. 19:28; 25:31;[6] ὁ θρόνος τῆς χάριτος, Hb. 4:16.[7] In the linking of → δόξα and → χάρις with θρόνος, which is only possible in biblical speech, there is also reflected a material distinction between the world of the Bible and that of Greece.

2. The Throne in the Greek World.

The royal throne was not originally a Greek institution. It "comes from the orient, where the absolute ruler sat on a magnificently decorated throne, which usually stood on a base with several steps, and which thus expressed the power of the ruler over his subjects."[8] The divine throne, to which there are many references in Greek poetry and superstition, is often a prerogative of Zeus. But plastic art also portrays a double throne for two deities, especially Zeus and Hera. A model for depicting a god on its throne was the throne of Zeus in Olympia fashioned by Pheidias. Worth noting is the influence of the Asiatic "custom of representing the throne of an invisible deity without the image of the god."[9] Reference may also be made to the use of thrones in the cult of the dead.[10]

These facts stand out all the more sharply by comparison with the Bible. On the soil of revelation there are obviously no divine thrones. The session of the Messiah on the right hand of God is no real parallel to the session of two deities on a common throne. However, the description of heaven as the Διὸς θρόνος[11] (Aesch. Eum., 229; cf. Theocr. Idyll., 7, 93) does remind us of corresponding statements in the Bible. Those who believe that the ark was the throne of Yahweh[12] naturally think also of the empty thrones of the gods.[13] But this analogy is alien to the OT itself, and there is nothing corresponding to the use of thrones in the cult of the dead.

---

[5] Cf. on this pt. O. Schmitz, Die Christusgemeinschaft des Pls. im Lichte seines Genetivgebrauchs (1924), 232, where several parallels from the LXX are given.

[6] For θρόνος in connection with δόξα cf. also Pol., 2, 1 (δόξαν καὶ θρόνον); cf. also θρόνος αἰώνιος in doxologies which begin with δόξα, Mart. Pol., 21, 1 and 1 Cl., 65, 2.

[7] We do not include in this list Hb. 8:1: ὁ θρόνος τῆς μεγαλωσύνης, where the gen. denotes the majesty of God as the One who sits on the throne, so that μεγαλωσύνη is to be taken as an equivalent of the divine name; cf. Rgg. Hb.[2,3], 219, n. 7. Similarly, θρόνος αἰσθήσεως in Prv. 12:23 seems to have in view a throne which is occupied by αἴσθησις. The construction is "formed independently by the LXX with no basis in the Mas. The Mas. has כָּסֶה דַּעַת, "conceals the knowledge," whereas the LXX reads כִּסֵּא דַּעַת" [Bertram].

[8] Pauly-W., VI, n. 613.

[9] Ibid., n. 616.

[10] On θρόνωσις in the mysteries of the Corybants, in which the initiate became a hypostasis of Dionysus, and on the role of the throne of Mnemosyne in the Trophonios oracle at Lebadeia, cf. ibid., n. 617.

[11] Cf. also F. Boll, Aus der Offenbarung Johannis (1914), 31.

[12] M. Dibelius, Die Lade Jahwes (1906), also F. Münzer, ARW, 9 (1906), 517 f.

[13] Cf. W. Eichrodt, Theologie des AT, II (1935), 102: "The earthly counterpart to the heavenly throne ... is the ark of Yahweh with the cherubim; this belongs to the category of empty divine thrones, and as the God of the ark Yahweh bears the name יוֹשֵׁב הַכְּרוּבִים = "he who is seated between the cherubim" (1 S. 4:4; 2 S. 6:2; 2 K. 19:15; Ps. 80:1 etc.).

3. The Throne in the Old Testament.

In the OT the throne is the privilege of the king (Gn. 41:40). But the word is also used for the seat of the queen mother (1 K. 2:19) and for the judicial seat of the governor (Neh. 3:7). How closely the king and the throne are linked may be seen from passages like 2 S. 14:9 and 1 K. 16:11. The first born son of Pharaoh shares his throne (Ex. 11:5; 12:29). The throne of Solomon is called the throne of his father David (1 K. 1:13, 35, 46; 2:12, 24, 33, 45; though cf. also 1 K. 1:37). But the reference here is not so much to the actual throne constructed by Solomon with unparalleled magnificence (1 K. 10:18-20; 2 Ch. 9:17-19; cf. also 1 K. 7:7) as to the throne as a symbol of government (2 S. 3:10; cf. also Is. 14:13) which transcends the present occupant of the throne. Thus there are many references to the throne of David in the sense of the eternal duration of his dynasty promised in 2 S. 7:12 ff. (1 Ch. 17:11 ff.; cf. 1 Macc. 2:57; cf. also 2 S. 7:16; Jer. 13:13; 17:25; 22:30; 36:30; Ps. 89:4, 29, 36; 132:11-12). On one occasion there is a similar reference to the throne of Israel (1 K. 2:4). It is in similar terms that the throne of David is called the throne of the Messiah in Is. 9:6. This throne is distinguished not merely by power but also by justice (Is. 16:5; Ps. 122:5).[14] To the degree that this kingship of the Davidic dynasty implies the kingship of Yahweh (2 Ch. 13:8; cf. also 9:8), the throne of David on which Solomon is to sit can also be called "the throne of the kingdom of Yahweh over Israel" (1 Ch. 28:5) or "the throne of Yahweh" (1 Ch. 29:23).[15]

That the OT conception of the throne of God takes its imagery from the earthly throne is shown by the intentional juxtaposition of the two in 1 K. 22:10, 19 (cf. 2 Ch. 18:9, 18). When Is. sees the king, Yahweh of hosts (6:5), in the temple, seated on a high and lofty throne (6:1), when Ez., on the manifestation of the divine glory above the firmament, sees the likeness of a throne (1:26; 10:1),[16] when in Tr. Is. Yahweh calls heaven rather than an earthly seat His throne (Is. 66:1; cf. also Job 26:9), or when in the Psalms this throne is to be found in heaven (11:4; 103:19), what is expressed is always the overwhelming majesty of the divine Ruler. But in self-revelation this majesty has made itself present on earth. Thus Jeremiah can claim, not only the name and covenant of God, but also the throne of God's glory as a sign of His gracious will concerning Israel (14:21). It is in keeping that in the future age of national salvation Jerusalem is to be called the throne of Yahweh (Jer. 3:17),[17] and that in the new temple the throne of God will be seen as the seat of His abiding presence among the sons of Israel (Ez. 43:7). The transcendent majesty and the immanent presence by revelation are brought together when Jeremiah ventures the address: "O throne of glory, exalted from the beginning, the place of our sanctuary, thou Hope of Israel, Yahweh" (17:12 f.).

---

[14] On the general link between the throne and righteousness, cf. Prv. 20:28; 25:5; 29:14 (20:8).

[15] → I, 569. On Rabb. exegesis, cf. Str.-B., 24, 979.

[16] Cf. W. Eichrodt, op. cit., II, 102: "In the moving throne with the cherubim there is obviously a reminiscence of Yahweh enthroned on the ark, at least in idealised form. The platform of the throne, called רָקִיעַ, is the reflection of the heavenly רָקִיעַ, of the arch of heaven, and it conceals as in a hollow space lightnings and thunders. The one who is throned on this raki'a is a demuth or mar'eh, a reflection of Yahweh enthroned on the crown of the arch of heaven. There is obviously expressed here the transcendence of God."

[17] This passage (cf. v. 16) undoubtedly seems to support the view that "in earlier times especially the ark was regarded as the throne of Yahweh, invisibly present" (v. Rad).

The power of His sacred throne extends over the Gentiles (Ps. 47:8). It is obvious, but it is also stated, that the throne of God is from eternity (Ps. 93:2) and endures for eternity (Lam. 5:19). As with an earthly ruler, so with God, the throne is a symbol of judicial power. The righteousness of God's judgment is frequently emphasised (Ps. 9:4, 7; 97:2). Once (Ps. 45:6 f.) the eternity and the righteousness of the throne of God are transferred to the throne of the king of Israel in predicates which transcend any earthly rule. Finally, in the visions of the night in Daniel we have a picture of the four empires and of the setting up of the Messianic kingdom when "judgment" will be seated on thrones (7:9 ff.; cf. Rev. 20:4). In this connection the throne of the Ancient of Days, by whom judgment is passed on the four beasts, is described as aflame with fire and encircled by the angelic hosts.

4. The Throne in Hellenistic Judaism.

Hellenistic Judaism finds no place for this eschatological throne of divine judgment. On the contrary, judgment is executed on the first born of Egypt by the operation of the omnipotent Word of God which comes down from the throne of God in heaven like a fierce warrior leaping into the land which is doomed to destruction (Wis. 18:15). Wisdom, too, is described as an "occupant" (πάρεδρος) of the throne (9:4) [18] from which it can be sent to the assistance of men (9:10). [19] The throne of the glory of God is synonymous with the holy heaven. The martyrs extolled in 4 Macc. are near to this divine throne in virtue of their endurance. They live out there a blessed eternity (17:18). It is noteworthy that there is no description of the divine throne in Hellenistic Judaism. It is mentioned in Josephus in his account of the cherubim. These are living, winged creatures which Moses, as he says, saw fastened to the throne (Ant., 3, 137). Schlatter points out that, although Joseph. follows 1 K. 22 clause by clause, he misses out vv. 19-22, in which God is seated on His throne with the council of heaven around him (Ant., 8, 406). [20] He avoided the idea of God's throne as too anthropomorphic. Similarly, Philo never spoke of the throne of God. [21]

5. The Throne in Palestinian Judaism.

By contrast, Palestinian, and esp. Rabbinic, Judaism shows a pronounced interest in the throne of glory. On the basis of Ps. 93:2 or Jer. 17:12 the throne is one of the pre-cosmic works of God. [22] Along the lines of Daniel there are descriptions esp. in Eth. En. 14:9 ff.; 71:5 ff.; and Slav. En. 20-22. As Billerbeck notes, these are comparatively rare in older Jewish literature, because "this material belonged to the secret theosophical doctrines concerning the appearance of the chariot in Ez. 1 and 10 מֶרְכָּבָה or מַעֲשֵׂה מֶרְכָּבָה, and public discussion was not allowed." [23] The throne of glory is borne by four living creatures (חַיּוֹת) which, in spite of their proximity to the throne of God, do not know the "habitation of His glory." [24] Acc. to R. Eliezer (c. 90) the souls of the righteous dead are kept under the throne. [25] But even they cannot see it because it is surrounded by a dark cloud as by a curtain. [26] The place of the martyrs is closest to the throne of God. [27] Of the hosts of angels who are about the throne, the nearest are

---

[18] Wisdom already has a throne in Sir. 24:4.
[19] The thrones of earthly rulers in particular need the counsel of wisdom if they are to endure (9:12; 6:21; cf. also 7:8).
[20] Schl. Theol. d. Jdt., 9.
[21] Schl. Mt., 182.
[22] Str.-B., I, 974 f.; II, 335, 353.
[23] Ibid., I, 975.
[24] Str.-B., I, 976; III, 799 f.
[25] Shab., 152b; cf. Str.-B., I, 977.
[26] For examples, v. Str.-B., I, 976; II, 266.
[27] Ibid., III, 803; cf. I, 224, 225.

the angels of the throne, of whom there were seven (six) according to one group in the early Synagogue, and four according to another. [28] The Rabbis were naturally interested in exegesis of the plur. "thrones" in Da. 7:9. The final conclusion was that they were reserved for the great men of Israel with whom God as presiding Judge would judge the nations of the world. [29] It is worth noting that the "sitting of Messiah on the throne of the divine glory is found only in the figurative imagery of the Book of Enoch, which belongs to the pre-Christian period." [30] Here the essential function of the Son of Man whom God has chosen is the same as in Da., namely, to execute eschatological judgment (Eth. En. 45:3; 51:3; 55:4; 61:8; 62:2, 3, 5; 69:27, 29) in the name of the "Lord of spirits." Acc. to Eth. En. 108:12, of those who loved God's holy name, only He will finally come to sit on the throne of His glory.

B. The Throne in the New Testament.

In the NT there is free reference to the throne of God, but with no speculative interpretations. The stream of Messianic eschatology in the OT issues finally in the saving event of the NT, and is then orientated to the ultimate consummation. It is typical of the new redemptive situation that there is another throne alongside the throne of God.

1. Heaven as God's Throne.

On the basis of Is. 66:1 ff., heaven is for Jesus the throne of God, so that in swearing by heaven we swear by God as the One who sits on the throne (Mt. 5:34; 23:22). The OT passage which Jesus adduces with no fear of anthropomorphism is quoted in Stephen's speech (Ac. 7:49) as prophetic witness to the fact that God cannot be enclosed in a building made with the hands of men.

2. The Throne of David.

In the NT the only real reference to earthly thrones is in Lk. 1:52. [31] The throne of David in Lk. 1:32 is the throne of the Messianic king. God has granted it to the Son of Mary as the throne of David, His father, that He may exercise eternal dominion over the house of Jacob, according to the prophecy of 2 S. 7:12 ff. (cf. Is. 9:6), which is referred to Him in Ac. 2:30. There is also reference to the throne of the king of the last days in Ps. 45:6a, which is used in Hb. 1:8 to prove the superiority of the Son over the angels. What is meant is the sovereign majesty of Him who sits on the throne with God (cf. 1:3). Here "the idea of the Davidic monarchy achieves its definitive realisation." [32]

3. The Throne of Glory.

The expression θρόνος δόξης is often found in Synoptic sayings of the Lord. It is used for the sovereign seat of the Son of Man when He is manifested in His

---

[28] *Ibid.,* III, 805 ff.

[29] Tanch קדשים 1 (36a); cf. Str.-B., IV, 871.

[30] Str.-B., I, 978. The remarkable word *metatron* or *metator,* which is found in later Jewish lit., has mostly been linked with θρόνος by Christian theologians from the time of J. H. Maius (*Synopsis Theologiae Judaicae* [1698]) (μετάθρονος in the sense of σύνθρονος). It is supposed to denote a heavenly being which shares the throne of God. In reality it is the Lat. *metator* in the sense of the one who prepares the way; cf. G. F. Moore, *Harvard Theological Review,* 15 (1922), 62-85.

[31] καθεῖλεν δυνάστας ἀπὸ θρόνων, cf. Sir. 10:14.

[32] Rgg. Hb. [2], [3], 22.

Messianic glory to judge and to rule. The reference is to His future rule over the twelve tribes of Israel. In this rule the twelve disciples will have a part. They will sit on twelve thrones and judge (Mt. 19:28). [33] There is also reference to the judgement exercised on all nations by the Son of Man from this throne, though it is not said that others will share in this judgment (Mt. 25:31 f.). The same distinction is to be found in Rev. At the beginning of the millennial reign of Christ on earth, the divine sees thrones, and those who sit on them, to whom judgment is given (20:4; cf. Da. 7:9, 22, 26, and the promise to those who overcome that they will share the throne with the exalted Lord, Rev. 3:21). At the conclusion of the millennium, however, he sees only the great white throne of world judgment, and Him that sits thereon (20:11). [34]

4. The Throne of Grace.

Hebrews calls the throne of God the θρόνος τῆς χάριτος in view of the fact that Jesus, the great High-priest, having undergone every temptation in the days of His flesh, has now entered heaven (4:14), and is seated at the right hand of the throne of the majesty on high (8:1), or of God (12:2). It is called the throne of grace instead of כָּרְסֵא־דִין, inasmuch as "pardoning grace rather than pitiless judgment now streams forth from it." [35] Even as the throne of grace the throne of God is still the symbol of His sovereign majesty.

5. The Throne of God and of the Lamb.

As a symbolical expression of God's sovereign majesty, the throne of God stands at the heart of the vision of the throne in Rev. (c. 4). It is located in heaven, [36] and in the vision it is inseparably linked with Him that sits on it. The throne as such is not described. Yet everything else in the heavenly throne room is orientated to it (4:3-7). [37] In the vision, the worship of the living creatures (4:8-9) and of the elders (4:10-11) is concentrated on Him that sits on the throne. This expression is almost a name for God in terms of His illimitable glory as the Creator (4:9, 10: 5:1, 7, 13; 7:15; 21:5; cf. also 19:4). It is thus the more significant that the adoration of all creation (5:13) is addressed "unto him that sitteth upon the throne, and unto the Lamb" (cf. also 7:10), as also that the dwellers on earth, in their fear of judgment, seek to hide "from the face of him that sitteth on the throne, and from the wrath of the Lamb" (6:16). For the author of Rev. the exalted Christ shares the throne of God. This is most plainly expressed in the vision of the new Jerusalem in the last chapter. Whereas in 7:15 the host clothed in white garments is said to be "before the throne of God," where "the Lamb which is in the midst of the throne shall feed them" (7:17), in 22:1 the stream of living water proceeds "out of

---

[33] At Lk. 22:30, in the parting words of Jesus at the Last Supper, this participation of the disciples in the Messianic reign is linked with the promise of table fellowship with the parting Lord in His coming kingdom.

[34] Session on the throne, to which there is reference elsewhere, indicates entry upon His judicial activity.

[35] Rgg. Hb. [2,3], 122, and cf. the Jewish par. quoted there in n. 21.

[36] 4:2; cf. also 12:5, where the Messianic child is taken up to God and His throne, and 8:2, where the 7 angels stand before the throne of God; acc. to Str.-B., III, 805 ff. these are "identical with the throne angels of the ancient Synagogue."

[37] Cf. E. Peterson, *Das Buch von den Engeln* (1935), 22 f. Acc. to Peterson, 104, "the detailed description of the heavenly throne room" is designed "to express the power of dominion" in the symbol of the throne.

the throne of God and of the Lamb," and in 22:3 it is explicitly said of the city of God that "the throne of God and of the Lamb shall be in it." When the throne of God has "descended to earth" [38] at the consummation, it is called the throne both of God and of the Lamb. Already in 3:21 Jesus shares the throne of His Father, and He promises the fellowship of the throne to those who overcome. But this participation of the company of overcomers in the throne of Christ is not depicted in the visions of Rev. For the thrones of the 24 elders in 4:4 are the seats of powers which bear rule in heaven. That their dominion is in no sense autonomous in relation to the majesty of God as the Creator is overwhelmingly expressed in the fact that they fall down before Him that sits on the throne and cast their crowns before the throne (4:9, 10). The more telling, then, is the fact that in the new world of God at the end of the days the seat of God's rule is also the throne of the Lamb. This twofold throne, which represents one and the same dominion, has its anti-godly counterpart.

6. The Throne of Satan and of the Beast.

In the letter to the community at Pergamos, with reference to persecutions which may in some cases lead to martyrdom, we read of the θρόνος τοῦ σατανᾶ which is found in this city ὅπου ὁ σατανᾶς κατοικεῖ (Rev. 2:13). This strong expression can hardly refer either to the imperial suzerainty of Rome (notwithstanding 2:9) or to the Jewish Synagogue. It is also unlikely that the temple of Augustus and Roma, as the centre of the imperial cult, should be called the throne of Satan, since the headquarters of this cult in Asia Minor were at Ephesus. More is to be said for the view that there is here a reference to the characteristic Pergamos cult of the σωτήρ Aesculapius, whose symbol was the serpent, and whose miraculous cures represented devilish imitations of the saving acts of Jesus. [39] Such a place of pilgrimage, saturated in paganism, was in fact a location for the throne of the adversary of God. If we are to think of an actual structure in which this hostile Satanic power had its dwelling, the most likely suggestion is the huge altar to Zeus in the castle at Pergamos. [40] It is possible that the expression refers to the "imposing totality" of these religious symbols. [41] That Satan has a throne is presupposed in Rev. 13:2, where the dragon gives to the first beast, i.e., Antichrist, "his power, and his seat, and great authority." Similarly, the fifth angel pours out his vial upon the throne of the beast (16:10). That throne and dominion are closely related here is seen in the sentence which follows: "And his kingdom was full of darkness."

7. The Throne as a Class of Angels.

In the christological exposition of Colossians, the invisible powers, which like all other creatures were created "in him," i.e., "in the Son of his love," include not only κυριότητες, ἀρχαί and ἐξουσίαι, but also, and first of all, θρόνοι (1:16). This title is found in Slav. En. 20:1 in a list of supraterrestrial powers which the author sees in the seventh heaven. Similarly, in Test. L. 3 we find in the seventh heaven θρόνοι (καὶ) ἐξουσίαι, ἐν ᾧ ἀεὶ ὕμνοι τῷ θεῷ προσφέρονται. The re-

---

[38] Loh. Apk., 173.
[39] Zn. Apk., 253 ff.; Had. Apk., 48.
[40] Loh. Apk., 23. For bibl., cf. Pr.-Bauer³, s.v.
[41] R. Kraemer, *Die Offenbarung des Johannes in überzeitl. Deutung* (1930), 161; E. B. Allo, *Saint Jean. L'Apocalypse²* (1921), 28, 30-31.

ference seems to be to one of the highest classes of angels, [42] though no precise distinction is possible. [43] The name might indicate that they have thrones at their disposal like the 24 elders of Rev. 4:4, who are certainly to be regarded as angelic powers. [44]

Schmitz

θυμός, ἐπιθυμία, ἐπιθυμέω,
ἐπιθυμητής,
ἐνθυμέομαι, ἐνθύμησις

θυμός → ὀργή.

θύω originally denotes a violent movement of air, water, the ground, animals, or men. [1] From the sense of "to well up," "to boil up," there seems to have developed that of "to smoke," and then "to cause to go up in smoke," "to sacrifice." [2] The basic meaning of θυμός is thus similar to that of πνεῦμα, namely, "that which is moved and which moves," "vital force." [3] In Homer θυμός is the vital force of animals and men, θυμὸν ἀποπνείειν: Il., 13, 654; λίπε δ᾽ ὀστέα θυμός: Il., 16, 743. θυμός then takes on the sense of a. desire, impulse, inclination, b. spirit, c. anger, d. sensibility, e. disposition or mind, f. thought, consideration. [4] This richly developed usage in Homer and the tragic dramatists is no longer present in the prose writers, e.g., Plato, Thucydides. For them θυμός means spirit, anger, rage, agitation. In Jewish Gk. θυμός is common in this sense. The LXX uses it for אַף, חֵמָה, חָרוֹן, כַּעַס etc. Philo makes frequent use of θυμός, [5] and Joseph. often has it for anger. [6]

In the NT θυμός occurs 5 times in Paul (R. 2:8; 2 C. 12:20; Gl. 5:20; Eph. 4:31; Col. 3:8); once in Hb. (11:27); twice in Lk. (Lk. 4:28; Ac. 19:28); 10 times in Rev., 5 of these with the addition τοῦ θεοῦ. Everywhere in the NT it means "wrath." In Pl., Hb., Lk. it is always human wrath except at R. 2:8; in Rev. it is always

---

[42] Cf. Str.-B., III, 581 ff. and Loh. Kol., 58, n. 1.
[43] Meinertz Gefbr., 21.
[44] Instructive for the conception of the thrones is the Gnostically coloured description of the visionary ascent to the seventh heaven in Asc. Is., esp. 7:14-35; 8:7-9, 16, 26; 9:10-18, 24 f.; 11:40; cf. Hennecke, 309 ff.

θ υ μ ό ς. Pape, Cr.-Kö., *s.v.*
[1] Cf. Pape, *s.v.* The Indo-Germ. root *dheuā-dhū* (Walde-Pok., I, 835 ff.) means "to start up suddenly," "to swirl up," esp. of dust, smoke, or steam. θυμός is Indo-Germ., cf. Lat. *fumus*.
[2] Aristarch. notes on Il. 9, 219 that θύω in Hom. does not mean σφάξαι, "to immolate," but θυμιάσαι, "to cause to go up in smoke" (K. Lehrs, De Aristarchi Studiis Homericis [1865], 82).
[3] If in Plat. Crat., 419e θυμός is derived ἀπὸ τῆς θύσεως καὶ ζέσεως τῆς ψυχῆς "from the heaving and tossing of the soul," this is not correct etymology, but there is more to it than the play on words usually found in Crat.
[4] Cf. Pape, *s.v.* and specialised dictionaries on Homer.
[5] Cf. Leisegang, 394. Philo follows the Platonic tradition acc. to which θυμός is one of the three parts of the ψυχή (with λόγος and ἐπιθυμία): Spec. Leg., IV, 92; cf. Leg. All., III, 116-118. He advises the control of θυμός, Jos., 73; 222.
[6] Ant., 20, 108: ὀργὴ καὶ θυμός; Bell., 2, 135: (the Essenes) θυμοῦ καθεκτικοί; 5, 489: δι᾽ ὑπερβολὴν θυμῶν; Vit., 143: τοῖς θυμοῖς ἐπέμενον; 393: μὴ καὶ λάβῃ τέλος ἅπαξ ὁ θυμός.

divine except for the wrath of the dragon at 12:12. The wrath of God is objectified as wine in Rev. 14:10; 16:19; 19:15, and there is reference to vials of wrath in 15:7; 16:1, and to the cup of wrath in 14:19. The idea of a cup of wrath, or of wine of wrath, comes from the OT. The suffering which man brings on himself is represented as a drink, a cup, or wine, which God hands to him in His anger : Jer. 25:15-17, 27 ff.; Ps. 60:4; 75:8 etc. [7] In Rev. 14:8; 18:3 the wine of the wrath of fornication which Babylon has made the nations drink is the godlessness with which it has ensnared the nations, so that they have fallen into sin and under the wrath of God. θυμός here is not poison or passion. [8] ὀργή and θυμός are often found together, and we also find θυμὸς τῆς ὀργῆς at Rev. 16:19; 19:15. There is no material difference between them.

ἐπιθυμία, ἐπιθυμέω → ἡδονή.

A. The Usage outside the NT.

1. ἐπιθυμία, ἐπιθυμέω [1] are not found in Homer, but they are pre-Socratic, and common later. The words denote the direct impulse towards food, sexual satisfaction etc., and also desire in general. [2] In the first instance there is nothing morally objectionable or even suspicious about them. From the time of Plato, and esp. the Stoics, the term acquires a distinctive sense in Gk. philosophy. This is not found in the pre-Socratics, though they took note of ἐπιθυμία. [3] In Plato ἐπιθυμία is still generally *vox media*. Reprehensible desire is called ἐπιθυμία κακή. [4] To true philosophy, however, belongs theoretical and practical aloofness from the sensual world. Hence the true philosopher keeps his soul from τῶν ἡδονῶν τε καὶ ἐπιθυμιῶν καὶ λυπῶν καὶ φόβων. [5] ἐπιθυμία plays no essential part in Aristot. ethics. [6] In Stoicism from the time of Zeno's Περὶ παθῶν, [7] ἐπιθυμία is listed with ἡδονή, φόβος and λύπη [8] as one of the four chief passions. These arise out of a wrong attitude to possessions, with desire and anxiety when these are present and with cupidity and fear when they are future. Along the same lines Cicero, following Chrysippus, defines (ἐπιθυμία) *cupiditas, libido : opinio venturi boni, quod sit ex usu iam praesens esse atque adesse*, or *inmoderata adpetitio opinati magni boni rationi non obtemperans*. [9] With ἐπιθυμία Stoicism reckons ὀργή, ἔρως etc. πᾶν μὲν γὰρ πάθος ἁμαρτία κατ᾽ αὐτούς ἐστιν καὶ πᾶς ὁ λυπούμενος ἢ φοβούμενος ἢ ἐπιθυμῶν ἁμαρτάνει, [10] *in libidine esse peccatum est etiam sine*

---

[7] Cf. P. Volz, *Der Prophet Jeremia* (1922), 388 f.
[8] Cf. Loh. Apk. 14:8 against Pr.-Bauer, *s.v.*, 1.

ἐ π ι θ υ μ ί α, ἐ π ι θ υ μ έ ω. [1] On the deriv. cf. θυμός; the adj. ἐπίθυμος "desirous," "greedy," is rare and late, cf. Liddell-Scott, *s.v.* Plut. Quaest. Conv., VIII, 6, 1 (II, 726a) has ἐπιθυμό-δειπνος, "desirous of meal-time." If this is a (humorous) imitation of φιλό-δειπνος, the first part is verbal (Debr. Griech. Wortb., 37 f.) and thus comes from ἐπι-θυμέω.
[2] Cf. the examples in Pape, *s.v.*
[3] Cf. Index to Diels² (1906-10), col. 227 f., and the passages adduced there.
[4] Leg., IX, 854a; Resp., I, 328d : αἱ περὶ τοὺς λόγους ἐπιθυμίαι. Cf. also Xenoph. Mem., I, 2, 64 : πονηρὰς ἐπιθυμίας ἔχων ... τῆς ἀρετῆς προτρέπων ἐπιθυμεῖν.
[5] Phaed., 83b. The meaning is that ἐπιθυμία is not wrong in itself, or else restraint would be self-evident.
[6] Like ὀργή, φόβος, but also χαρά and φιλία, it is one of the πάθη of the soul in Eth. Nic., II, 4, p. 1105b, 21. It is divided into κοιναὶ (καὶ φυσικαί), ἴδιοι καὶ ἐπίθετοι, *ibid.*, III, 13, p. 1118b, 8 f., strong and weak, *ibid.*, VII, 3, p. 1146a, 15, the beautiful and the ugly, *ibid.*, VII, 6, p. 1148a, 22 f. Cf. also χρησταὶ ἐπιθυμίαι.
[7] Diog. L., VII, 110, cf. VII, 4.
[8] → n. 5.
[9] Tusc., IV, 7, 14 and III, 11, 24.
[10] Plut. De Virtute Morali, 10 (II, 449d).

effectu. [11] Along these lines there is a strict distinction between ἐπιθυμία and βούλησις, *cupere* and *velle.* [12] Epictetus often refers to ἐπιθυμία, and he calls for a struggle against it, as against λύπη, φόβος, φθόνος etc. [13] But he can also use ἐπιθυμία as *vox media.* [14] Epicurus divides ἐπιθυμίαι into φυσικαί, or natural, and κεναί, illegitimate. The first may be divided again into purely natural and those that are necessary to happiness, to freedom from bodily pain, and to life. The ἀπλανὴς θεωρία knows how to divide them, and how to attain thereby to physical health and to inviolability of soul. [15]

In Greek philosophy ἐπιθυμία is the waywardness of man in conflict with his rationality. It is estimated ethically rather then religiously.

2. In Hebrew and Jewish religion there is condemnation not merely of the evil act but also of the evil will. The Decalogue forbids stealing and the desire for the goods of others, including their wives. The inability in obedience to God to renounce what may be in themselves natural and legitimate desires, the longing for sexual satisfaction outside marriage, is called sin in both J and E in Nu. 11 and Gn. 39. Self-discipline in the sexual sphere even to the control of one's glances is a duty of the righteous from the time of 2 S. 11:2 and Job 31:1. The demand for renunciation and for obedience for God's sake increases in the post-exilic period with the tightening of legalism and the rise of ethical reflection, in both of which may be seen the influence of Hellenism. Regular ascetic practices like fasting, scrupulosity in keeping the Sabbath, and the regulation of meats, become constituent elements in piety. Sexual asceticism takes on significance at different levels. The consciousness of sin becomes more profound, and with it attention to the impulsive, passionate desire which withstands renunciation and obedience for the sake of God. [16] There are moving complaints concerning the evil heart which will not renounce or obey. [17] The view is reached that desire is the chief of all sins. [18] The will of God can be expressed in the single formula: not to desire. [19]

In the OT and Judaism ἐπιθυμία is an offence against God, who demands of man total obedience and love from the whole heart, Dt. 5:5.

3. In Jewish Greek ἐπιθυμία and ἐπιθυμεῖν can denote a sin. This usage is plainly dependent in part on the Stoic usage, and in part a result of the above development in Judaism. The lines converge. The LXX uses ἐπιθυμία and ἐπιθυμεῖν predominantly for constructs of the stems אוה and חמד. [20] ἐπιθυμία is mostly *vox media.* [21] But without

---

[11] Cic. Fin., III, 9, 32.

[12] Diog. L., VII, 116; Sen. ep., 116, 1. On this whole pt. cf. v. Arnim in Index, *s.v.* ἐπιθυμία, and E. Zeller, *Die Philosophie der Griechen,* III, 1⁴ (1909), 235 ff.

[13] Diss., II, 16, 45; II, 18, 8.

[14] *Ibid.,* III, 9, 21.

[15] Letter to Menoikeus, Diog. L., X, 127.

[16] On the development in detail, cf. J. Köberle, *Sünde und Gnade im religiösen Leben des Volkes Israel* (1905), 118, 449 ff. etc.

[17] 4 Esr. 3:20-27 etc., cf. Bousset-Gressm., 402 ff.

[18] Vit. Ad., 19 (Kautzsch Apkr. u. Pseudepigr., II, 521). (Even though the Gk. Book of Adam may be Christian, the thought can be claimed as Jewish.)

[19] 4 Macc. 2:6; cf. Rm. 7:7; 13:9.

[20] Along with ἐπιθυμία and ἐπιθυμεῖν: ἐπιθύμημα, ἐπιθυμητής, ἐπιθυμητός.

[21] E.g., Gn. 31:30; Dt. 12:20, 21. We read of the ἐπιθυμία of the righteous, Prv. 11:23; the ungodly, 12:12; the pious, 13:19; also of the ἐπιθυμία σοφίας, Wis. 6:20; Sir. 6:37 etc.

addition ἐπιθυμία is also used for base and ungodly desire, e.g., at Nu. 11:4, 34; 33:16, 17; Dt. 9:22; ψ 105:14. [22] ἐπιθυμία κάλλους is sinful sexual desire in the male, Prv. 6:25; Susanna 32; cf. Sir. 40:22. ἐπιθυμεῖν is also used of pious striving, and sometimes of eschatological expectation, Is. 58:2; ψ 118:20; Am. 5:18. ἐπιθυμία is very common in Philo. [23] In Platonic fashion it is used along with λόγος and θυμός to denote the lowest part of the soul, [24] and after the manner of the Stoics it is also used for the four passions, [25] which in constant warnings and admonitions Philo summons us to combat, combining Stoic moralism and the strictest Jewish legalism, and breaking forth in powerful declamations. We find a similar combination of Stoic and Jewish elements in the use of ἐπιθυμία and ἐπιθυμεῖν in 4 Macc. The theme here is that what rules over the impulsive in man is reason, [26] and the impulsive includes first of all ἐπιθυμία, with which are ranged ἡδονή, φόβος and λύπη (1:22, 23), and which arises out of sensuality (1:3; 3:11-16) and sexuality (2:4, 5). In Josephus ἐπιθυμία is mostly *vox media*, [27] but it can also be used for sinful desire. [28]

4. In Rabbinic theology the equivalents of NT ἐπιθυμεῖν are הִתְאַוָּה and חמד, [29] and for ἐπιθυμία we have יֵצֶר הָרַע, [30] except that this denotes a general disposition in man rather than the actual impulse in concrete individuality. For this the term is תַּאֲוָה. M. Ex. 15:1: כדי לעשות תאותם ("to work their desire"); Tanch. נשא § 6 (15a): of the adulterer and adulteress אינם מבקשים... אלא שיעשו תאותן ("they seek only to do their desire"); Tanch. ויגש § 1 (102b): ויצר הרע אומר נאכל ונשתה ונעשה כל תאותינו ("evil impulse says: We will eat and drink and do all our desire").

B. The Usage in the New Testament.

In the NT ἐπιθυμία and ἐπιθυμεῖν are rare in the Gospels, more common in the Epistles. As in current speech, they are often *vox media*. Hence they may be used for the natural desire of hunger, Lk. 15:16; 16:21, or longing, Lk. 22:15; 1 Th. 2:17, also Rev. 9:6 (ἐπιθυμήσουσιν ἀποθανεῖν); Ac. 20:33; Jm. 4:2, or a desire for the **divine mysteries**, Mt. 13:17; Lk. 17:22; 1 Pt. 1:12, [31] or for anything good, Phil. 1:23; [32] 1 Tm. 3:1; Hb. 6:11. [33] Mostly, however, they indicate evil desire in accordance with the Greek and Jewish development considered under A. They may be characterised as such by information as to the object: Mt. 5:28: αὐτήν (a woman); Mk. 4:19: περὶ τὰ λοιπά; 1 C. 10:6: κακῶν, or the direction: Gl. 5:17: κατὰ τοῦ πνεύματος, or the vehicle: 1 C. 10:6; Jd. 16; R. 1:24: τῶν καρδιῶν;

---

[22] Since the LXX is here using ἐπεθύμησαν ἐπιθυμίαν simply for the Heb. הִתְאַוּוּ תַּאֲוָה, Stoic influence is unlikely.

[23] Cf. the detailed and carefully systematised examples in Leisegang.

[24] Conf. Ling., 21 etc.; v. Leisegang.

[25] ἐπιθυμία ὄρεξις ἄλογος, Leg. All., III, 115, ἐπιθυμία δὲ ἀλόγους ἐμποιοῦσα ὀρέξεις ἐκ τοῦ σώματος; Poster. C., 26 etc.

[26] 1:13; cf. 2:6; 5:23.

[27] ἐπιθυμία γάμων: Ant., 17, 352; ὑπὸ τῆς περὶ τὸ ἔργον ἐπιθυμίας; Ant., 11, 176: τῆς ἀρχῆς ἐπιθυμίαν ἔχων; Vit., 70: ἐπιθυμοῦντες ἐγκρατεῖς γενέσθαι κἀκείνου; Bell., 6, 112.

[28] προσκαίρῳ τῆς ἐπιθυμίας ἡδονῇ; Ant., 2, 51 of adulterous desire.

[29] Cf. Str.-B., III, 234 ff.

[30] → ἡδονή, II, 917 f.; also Str.-B., IV, 1, 464 ff.; also Köberle, Sünde und Gnade, esp. 510 ff.

[31] Cf. the desire for divine wisdom in Sap. 6:11-13; Sir. 1:26; 6:37.

[32] ἐπιθυμίαν ἔχων also in Jos. Vit., 70.

[33] Thus far ἐπιθυμία and ἐπιθυμεῖν are par. with ἐπιποθία and ἐπιποθεῖν, which always indicate natural longing in the NT.

R. 6:12 : τοῦ σώματος; Gl. 5:16; Eph. 2:3; 1 Jn. 2:16; 2 Pt. 2:18 : τῆς σαρκός;
1 Jn. 2:16 : τῶν ὀφθαλμῶν; Jn. 8:44 : τοῦ πατρός (the devil); 1 Jn. 2:17, the world ;
1 Pt. 4:2 : ἀνθρώπων; Rev. 18:14 : τῆς ψυχῆς, or the manner: σαρκικαί, 1 Pt.
2:11; κοσμικαί, Tt. 2:12; νεωτερικαί, 2 Tm. 2:22; κακή, Col. 3:5; τῆς ἀπάτης,
Eph. 4:22; ἀνοήτους, 1 Tm. 6:9; ἰδίας, 2 Tm. 4:3; 2 Pt. 3:3; ταῖς πρότερον, 1 Pt.
1:14; φθορᾶς, 2 Pt. 1:4; μιασμοῦ, 2 Pt. 2:10. But ἐπιθυμία (R. 7:7, 8; Gl. 5:24;
1 Th. 4:5; 2 Tm. 3:6; Tt. 3:3; Jm. 1:14, 15; 1 Pt. 4:3) and ἐπιθυμεῖν (R. 7:7; 13:9;
1 C. 10:6) can be used for sinful desire without any such addition. In this regard
1 C. 10:6 plainly follows Nu. 11:4. The compression and extension of the tenth
commandment into a simple οὐκ ἐπιθυμήσεις in R. 7:7; 13:9 finds a parallel in
4 Macc. 2:6 : μὴ ἐπιθυμεῖν εἴρηκεν ἡμᾶς ὁ νόμος, and it is thus pre-Pauline.
There is no point in asking whether Paul is here following Jewish or Stoic usage.
The two had long since merged in respect of the use of ἐπιθυμία and ἐπιθυμεῖν.
Apart from πάθος ἐπιθυμίας at 1 Th. 4:5 there is nothing distinctively Stoic in
Paul. The antithesis of λογισμός and ἐπιθυμία is not found in him. ἐπιθυμία is
evil, not because it is irrational, but because it is disobedience to the command
of God. Basically, then, his conception of ἐπιθυμία is OT and Jewish, not Stoic.
For Paul, who alone in the NT offers an explicit doctrine of sinful man, ἐπιθυμία
is a manifestation of the sin which dwells in man and which controls him, but
which is dead apart from the ἐπιθυμία stirred up by the Law, R. 7:7, 8. That desire
is a result of the prohibition of sin reveals the carnality of man, Gl. 5:16, 24,
his separation from God, his subjection to divine wrath, R. 1:18 ff. In James
(1:14, 15) ἐπιθυμία is regarded as the constant root in man of the individual acts
of sin to which the author's attention is mainly directed. The special feature in
Jn. is the connection between desire and the world, 1 Jn. 2:15-17. Desire arises out
of the world, constitutes its essence and perishes with it. [34]

What the NT has to say concerning ἐπιθυμία is not based on the reflection
which seeks to dissect the nature of man. It is part of the preaching of repentance.
The seriousness of man's God-given duty has to be fully impressed upon him in
order to stir his will to resolution in self-denial. There is here taken seriously that
which moral self-observation cannot establish of itself. The essential point in ἐπιθυμία is that it is desire as impulse, as a motion of the will. [35] It is, in fact, lust,
since the thought of satisfaction gives pleasure and that of non-satisfaction pain. [36]
ἐπιθυμία is anxious self-seeking. Only exceptionally do we read of an ἐπιθυμεῖν
of love ; [37] ἐπιποθεῖν is normally used. In ἐπιθυμεῖν man is seen as he really is,
the more so because ἐπιθυμία bursts upon him with the force of immediacy. Even
after the reception of the divine Spirit, ἐπιθυμία is always a danger against which
man must be warned and must fight. [38]

---

[34] What perishes is not the object of desire, nor the pleasure which it gives, but desire
itself. He who constantly desires cannot participate in the eternity of God, cf. Bü. J., ad loc.
Cf. also Tt. 2:12 : τὰς κοσμικὰς ἐπιθυμίας.

[35] Cf. Eph. 2:3, where ἐπιθυμίαι τῆς σαρκός and θελήματα τῆς σαρκός are exact par.

[36] The word for pleasure is ἡδονή, Lk. 8:14; Tt. 3:3; Jm. 4:1, 3; 2 Pt. 2:13. ἡδονή and
ἐπιθυμία are closely related, cf. Tt. 3:3 : when ἐπιθυμία is satisfied we have ἡδονή, and
when ἡδονή is sought we have ἐπιθυμία.

[37] Lk. 22:15; Gl. 5:17, inasmuch as ἐπιθυμεῖ must be supplied as the predicate of πνεῦμα.

[38] Those who think they can deduce the NT statements concerning ἐπιθυμία from the
self-soiling and self-destroying decline of instinct through racial corruption merely show
that they are not capable of taking moral self-observation seriously.

† ἐπιθυμητής.

In the NT this occurs only at 1 C. 10:6, with obvious allusion to Nu. 10:34 : ἐκεῖ ἔθαψαν τὸν λαὸν τὸν ἐπιθυμητήν.

The word is found from the time of Hesiod. [1] It is rare in the LXX, more common in Joseph., [2] predominantly in an approving sense.

† ἐνθυμέομαι.

This derives from ἔνθυμος, which is used in the sense of "brave," "spirited." [1] It is attested from the time of Epicharmos, [2] also in the pap., [3] likewise in Philo [4] and Josephus. [5] The LXX uses it for a variety of words. [6]

Of its many senses [7] we find only "to weigh," "to consider," in the NT. We find ἐνθυμέομαι only at Mt. 1:20; 9:4. [8] The par. to 9:4 in Mk. 2:8; Lk. 5:22 have διαλογίζεσθαι.

Qoh. r. on 5:2 furnishes for ἐνθυμεῖσθε πονηρὰ ἐν ταῖς καρδίαις ὑμῶν the striking par. הן חושבין רעות בלבבם (on the ungodly). [9]

† ἐνθύμησις.

ἐνθύμησις is rare. It is found from the time of Euripides, also in the pap., [1] but not in the LXX, Philo, or Josephus. [2] It means "consideration," "reflection."

In the NT ἐνθύμησις at Mt. 9:4; 12:25 and Hb. 4:12 is the unexpressed and hidden thing in man which God's omniscience sees and judges. ἔννοια is par. in Heb. 4:12, and τέχνη in Acts 17:29. It can also imply what is foolish or wicked.

Schlatter [3] mentions מַחֲשָׁבוֹת as the Heb. equivalent.

Büchsel

ἐ π ι θ υ μ η τ ή ς.   [1] Cf. Pape, s.v.
[2] Jos. Ap., 2, 45 : Philadelphos ἐπιθυμητὴς ἐγένετο τοῦ γνῶναι τοὺς ἡμετέρους νό-μους, 2, 151: νόμου κοινωνίας ἐπιθυμηταί; Ant., 11, 85 : τῆς θρησκείας ... ἐπιθυμη-ταί; Ant. 8:209 : μεγάλων ἐπιθυμητὴς πραγμάτων.
ἐ ν θ υ μ έ ο μ α ι.   Cf. the dictionaries of Pape, Pr.-Bauer etc. Schl. Mt., 299 f.
[1] Aristot. Pol., VII, 7 (p. 1327b, 30); cf. ἄθυμος, "spiritless."
[2] I, 119, 16 and 20 (Diels).
[3] Cf. Preisigke, s.v.
[4] Cf. Leisegang, s.v.
[5] Ant., 11, 155 : ἐνθυμούμενοι πρὸς αὐτούς.
[6] Cf. the concord. and G. Bertram, "Der Begriff der 'Religion' in der Septuaginta," ZDMG, NF, XII (1933), 1 ff. For Bertram ἐνθυμεῖσθαι is one of the many words in which the psychologising attitude of the LXX seeks expression; hence there is no fixed Heb. equivalent.
[7] Cf. Pape, s.v. The basic meaning is intrans. "to be in a passionate mood" (Hippocrates, De Aere, 22 [Kühlewein, 1894, p. 65, 11]), hence "to take something to heart" either in the sense of "to take badly" (Aesch. Eum., 213) or "to ponder" (in the majority of instances).
[8] At Acts 10:19 we find the compound δι-ενθυμέομαι.
[9] Cf. Schl. Mt. on 9:4. ἐνθυμηθείς ... πονηρά, also Wis. 3:14.
ἐ ν θ ύ μ η σ ι ς.   [1] Cf. Pr.-Bauer, s.v.
[2] Σ has it at Job 21:27; Ez. 11:21. LXX, Philo (cf. Leisegang), Joseph. (cf. Schl. Mt. on 9:4) have ἐνθύμημα, which is not found in the NT.
[3] Schl. Mt., 299.

| † θύρα | (→ κλείς, πύλη).

Contents : A. The Literal and Figurative Use. B. The Door-Miracles of the New Testament. C. The Heavenly Door. D. The Eschatological Use of the Image of the Door. E. 'Εγώ εἰμι ἡ θύρα (John 10:7, 9).

A. The Literal and Figurative Use.

1. In the strict sense ἡ θύρα is used in the NT a. for "the door,"[1] especially the "house-door" (Mk. 1:33; 2:2; 11:4; Mt. 25:10; Lk. 11:7; 13:25; Ac. 5:9), also the "outer door"[2] (Jn. 18:16; Ac. 12:13 : the door of the passage leading from the street into the courtyard; Jn. 10:1 f., the door of the walled fold), or the "door" into a single room (Mt. 6:6 : the closet; Ac. 5:23; 12:6 : the prison cell),[3] or the "door of heaven" (→ C). Occasionally it may denote b. the "gate of the temple"[4] (= ἡ πύλη), as in Ac. 3:2 : "the beautiful gate of the temple,"[5] or in Ac. 21:30, where the plur. denotes the gates of the inner court.[6] It can also be used c. for the "entrance into a sepulchre" (Mk. 15:46; 16:3; Mt. 27:60; 28:2 vl.; Ev. Pt. 8:32; 9:37; 12:53 f.).[7]

2. Figuratively θύρα is used as follows in the NT : a. "to stand before the door," i.e., to be about to enter, to be very near (Mk. 13:29; Mt. 24:33 : ἐγγύς ἐστιν ἐπὶ θύραις; Jm. 5:9 : ὁ κριτὴς πρὸ τῶν θυρῶν ἔστηκεν; Ac. 5:9). The use

---

θ ύ ρ α. On A : Pr.-Bauer³, s.v.; Bl.-Debr.⁶ § 141, 4; Str.-B., Index, s.v. On B : G. Rudberg, "Zu den Bacchen des Euripides," *Symbolae Osloenses*, 4 (1926), 29-35; S. Lönborg, "En Dionysosmyt i Acta Apostolorum," *Eranos*, 24 (1926), 73-80; O. Weinreich, "Gebet und Wunder" in *Tübinger Beiträge z. Altertumswissenschaft*, 5 (1929), 169-464. On C : W. Köhler, "Die Schlüssel des Petrus," ARW, 8 (1905), 214-243; A. Dell, ZNW, 15 (1914), 33-35; A. Jacoby, "Das Bild vom 'Tor des Lichtes,' " *Byzantinisch-neugr. Jahrbücher*, 2 (1921), 277-284; H. Odeberg, *The Fourth Gospel* (1929), 319 ff.; Bau. J., Excursus on Jn. 10:21. On E : F. Spitta, *Das Joh.-Ev. als Quelle der Geschichte Jesu* (1910), 213 ff.; H. Odeberg, *op. cit.*, 313 ff.; 319 ff.; the Comm. on Jn. 10:7, 9, esp. Schl. J. and Bau. J., Exc. on Jn. 10:21.

[1] On the use of the plur. for a single door → n. 8.
[2] The plur. in Jn. 20:19, 26 embraces both the outer gate and the door.
[3] The plur. in Ac. 5:19; 16:26 f. embraces both the gate of the prison and the cell-doors.
[4] Elsewhere infrequent : Jos. Ant., 15, 424 (θύρα is usually the "wing of a door" in Jos.).
[5] Prob. identical with the Nicanor gate (Mid., 1, 4; 2, 6 etc.) which is called the Corinthian (Bell., 5, 204) or bronze (*ibid.*, 2, 411; cf. 6, 293) gate by Jos. Its situation is uncertain. Jos. sets it at the east of the court of women (Bell., 5, 204), Rabb. lit. at the west (G. Dalman, PJB, 5 [1909], 42; *Orte und Wege Jesu*³ [1924], 318, n. 1; J. Jeremias, *Jerusalem z. Zeit Jesu*, II, B [1929], 21, n. 6; for a different view of the Rabb. material cf. Schürer, II, 64; Str.-B., II, 622-624; K. G. Kuhn, S. Nu. [1933], 12, n. 94). More recent research rightly follows Jos. for the most part, locating the Nicanor gate to the east of the court of women (Schürer, II, 64 f., 342; Dalman, *Orte und Wege Jesu*, 315, 318, n. 1; Str.-B., II, 622 ff.; Jeremias, *op. cit.*, II, A [1924], 33; K. G. Kuhn, *op. cit.*; Pr. Ag. and Zn. Ag. on Ac. 3:2). This busy spot was particularly suitable for a beggar. But there is always the possibility that the beautiful gate was an outer gate.
[6] G. Dalman, PJB, 5 (1909), 42; *Orte und Wege Jesu*, 314, n. 3.
[7] This usage is foreign to the OT, though the entrance to the cave is פֶּתַח in 1 K. 19:13 and θύρα in 2 Macc. 2:5.

of a spatial image to denote time is Hellenistic.[8] b. In many cases we have a figurative use of "to open the door," which is both later Jewish[9] and Hellenistic.[10] The religious colouring of the image in the NT is distinctive of later Judaism, which speaks of both God and man as opening the door; man opens the door to God by repenting,[11] and God opens the door to man by giving him opportunities (e.g., for intercession[12] or repentance),[13] or by granting grace.[14] Man opens the door to Christ in a religious sense in Rev. 3:20, i.e., by penitent obedience.[15] In relation to God the expression finds a place in missionary usage[16] in the twofold sense that God opens a door for the missionary (Col. 4:3, for the Word), through which he can enter, by giving him a field in which to work (1 C. 16:9; 2 C. 2:12; Col. 4:3),[17] and also that he opens a door of faith to those who come to believe (Ac. 14:27: ἤνοιξεν τοῖς ἔθνεσιν θύραν → πίστεως)[18] by giving them the possibility of believing.[19] If God's opening of the door signifies the giving of grace,[20] the opposite figure of c. closing the door,[21] which expresses the irrevocable loss of an opportunity (Rev. 3:7; cf. Is. 22:22; in the parable, Mt. 25:10; Lk. 13:25), carries the sense of judgment. The power of Christ to open and to shut (Rev. 3:7)

---

[8] Cf. Joannes Philoponus, In Aristotelis Meteorologicorum Librum Primum Commentarium, 130, 25 (M. Hayduck, 1901): χειμῶνος ἐπὶ θύραις ὄντος. The non-Semitic origin of the expression is confirmed by the formal use of the plur. for one door. This usage is class. (Bl.-Debr.[6] § 141, 4, examples in Liddell-Scott, s.v. θύρα). In the NT it is sometimes found in the expression "before the door" (Mk. 13:29; Mt. 24:33; Jm. 5:9), for the plur. is really meant in Jn. 20:19, 26; Ac. 5:19; 16:26 f. → n. 2, 3. There is doubt only at Ac. 5:23, where ἐπὶ τῶν θυρῶν could be either a formal plur. or a true plur. (Bl.-Debr., op. cit.).

[9] Str.-B., I, 458; II, 728; III, 484 f., 631.

[10] Epict. (Schenkl, Index, s.v. θύρα) often uses ἡ θύρα ἤνοικται in the sense of "I am free to go anywhere" (Ltzm. K. on 1 C. 16:9). Luc. Hermot., 15 has πολλῶν σοι θυρῶν ἀναπεπταμένων of the various philosophical schools available for those who desire knowledge. Serenus Gnomologus (Stob. Ecl., III, 284, 15 f.) of the senses: τὸ ... σῶμα ... πολλαῖς θυρίσι καὶ θύραις ἀνοίγοντες. "Opened doors" is also a figure of literary activity (Weinreich, 294).

[11] Midr. Cant., 5, 2: "God spake to the Israelites, My children, open to me a door of repentance."

[12] S. Dt. § 27 on 3:24.

[13] 4 Esr. 9:12; Gn. r., 38 on 11:6.

[14] bMeg., 12b etc.

[15] → n. 11.

[16] It is no accident that similar missionary expressions are found in Luke the missionary. He speaks of the opening of eyes (Lk. 24:31; Ac. 26:18), of the understanding (Lk. 24:45), of the heart (Ac. 16:14), of Scripture (Lk. 24:32; Ac. 17:3). Cf. also Barn., 16, 9, where God opens the door of the temple, i.e., the mouth; Ps.-Clem. Hom., 1, 18; Ps.-Clem. Recog., 1, 15 (Hennecke, 156): Christ opens the door of the fumigated house (i.e., the world), so that the sunlight may come in.

[17] Rev. 3:8 hardly belongs to this group; → 178.

[18] On θύρα πίστεως cf. Ps. 118:19: "the gates of righteousness" (LXX: πύλας δικαιοσύνης); 118:20: "the gate of the Lord" (LXX: ἡ πύλη τοῦ κυρίου); Ign. Phld., 9, 1 of Christ: θύρα τοῦ πατρός (vl. ἡ θύρα τῆς γνώσεως, ianua scientiae et agnitionis; Hipp. Ref., V, 8, 20: ἡ πύλη ἡ ἀληθινή; also Gn. r., 38 on 11:6: "the door of repentance"; jShab., 9c, 9 f.: "the door of the Law"; Corp. Herm., VII, 2a: ἐπὶ τὰς τῆς γνώσεως θύρας. On the other hand, there is no parallel in the question in the account of the slaying of James, the Lord's brother, in Hegesippus: τίς ἡ θύρα τοῦ Ἰησοῦ (Eus. Hist. Eccl., 23, 8 and 12), since the text seems to be corrupt. Perhaps we should read θωρα (= תּוֹרָה) instead of θύρα (cf. J. Weiss-R. Knopf, Das Urchristentum (1917), 554, n. 1).

[19] On the meaning of πίστις in this expression cf. Pr.-Bauer, s.v. πίστις 2d.

[20] On the eschatological use of the image of the open door → 178.

[21] Cf. the proverb in bBQ, 80b: "A closed door is not so easily opened," i.e., it is hard to get what is once refused.

shows that He possesses full authority, since grace and judgment are both in His hand.

B. The Door-Miracles of the New Testament.

1. Three times in Acts (5:19; 12:6-11; 16:26 f.) we read of liberation from prison through the miraculous opening of the prison doors by night.

The motif of a door which opens of itself [22] is common in the Orient (Babylon, Egypt, India, OT, later Judaism). [23] It is also found in many different connections in Gk. literature from the time of Homer, e.g., in epiphanies, belief in prodigies, miracles of liberation, magic, prayer, ordeal. [24] It enjoys extraordinary popularity in later Christian legends. [25] Yet its special application to liberation from prison is much more limited. In the Orient we find it for certain only in India, [26] which is perhaps its home. [27] It comes into Greece with the Dionysus myth, [28] in which it occurs in various forms (freeing of the god himself, [29] of the Bacchantes, [30] of the companion of the god, Acoetes [31]). The brilliant description of the Dionysiac miracle of liberation in the Bacchae of Eur., 443 ff., 576 ff. contributed especially to its popularity. In antiquity outside the Dionysiac circle, the independent and miraculous opening of prison doors is found only [32] in the βίος of the θεῖος ἀνήρ. In the story of the miraculous freeing of Apollonius of Tyana, [33] there is reference only to the falling off of his chains, not the independent opening of the prison doors. The latter is found, however, in the story of Moses by Artapanus. [34] But it is the apocryphal acts and early Christian hagiographical literature [35] which attest the widespread nature of the theme in the βίος of the θεῖος ἀνήρ. For the constant new features and variations make it impossible for us to trace back all the miracles of liberation in this literature to the three miracles in Ac. The *topos* is alien to later Palestinian Judaism. [36] Only once do we hear of the miraculous opening of prison doors, namely, to make possible the burial of the body of R. Akiba, who died in prison. [37] But this is not really a miracle of liberation, since Akiba is dead. Moreover, the reference is found in a midrash of the early Middle Ages, so that we may assume that it is influenced by Christian legends of the saints. The spread of the motif is thus restricted in the world outside the NT; it occurs only in the Dionysus myth and in the βίοι of the god-men of antiquity.

---

[22] There is a comprehensive collection of material in Weinreich, 200 ff. Cf. also the bibl., 205, n. 5.

[23] Weinreich, 411-420; also 271 ff.

[24] *Ibid.,* 207-410.

[25] *Ibid.,* 420-434.

[26] *Ibid.,* 403, 414.

[27] But cf. *ibid.,* 310, where it is suggested that there is historical convergence rather than dependence on India.

[28] *Ibid.,* 280-295.

[29] Eur. Ba., 576 ff.

[30] *Ibid.,* 443 ff.; Nonnus, Dionysiaca (ed. A. Ludwich, 1911), 45, 274 ff.

[31] Pacuvius, Pentheus (acc. to Servius Danielis on Aen., 4, 469 [v. Weinreich, 291]) and Ovid. Met., III, 695 ff., cf. Weinreich, 291.

[32] Liberation by magical opening (magical ἄνοιξις θύρας) — cf. Weinreich, 342 ff. — is closely related to the miracle of liberation, but it cannot be discussed in this context, since there is a difference between magic and miracle.

[33] Philostr. Vit. Ap., 8, 30; cf. 7, 38. Cf. Weinreich, 295-298.

[34] Eus. Praep. Ev., IX, 27, 12 : νυκτὸς δὲ ἐπιγενομένης τάς τε θύρας πάσας αὐτομάτως ἀνοιχθῆναι τοῦ δεσμωτηρίου (in which Moses is imprisoned by the Egyptian king); par. Cl. Al. Strom., 1, 23, 151, 1 ff.

[35] Weinreich, 422-429.

[36] On Hell. Judaism → *supra* and n. 34.

[37] Midr. Prv., 9 on 9:2 (Str.-B., II, 635 f.).

The threefold repetition of the motif of the miraculous opening of prison doors in Ac., its distribution between the apostles in Ac. 5:19, Peter in 12:6-11, and Paul in 16:26 f., and the agreement with ancient parallels in many details, e.g., liberation by night, the role of the guards, the falling off of chains, the bursting open of the doors, the shining of bright light, earthquake, [38] all suggest that in form at least Lk. is following an established *topos*. It has often been argued that in his stylisation of the miracles he was influenced by the Bacchae of Eur. [39] or by the Dionysus myth, [40] but this has not been proved. [41] More probable is the suggestion that the spread of the *topos* in the βίοι of god-men exerted some influence on Lk., [42] since in both cases the miracles of liberation serve to demonstrate the claim to divine sending. [43]

Whatever may be our judgment of the facts from the standpoint of the history of religion, the three door-miracles in Acts certainly express the certainty that the course of the Gospel cannot be hindered by prisons or bonds, since God's arm is strong enough to burst the locks of prison doors.

2. According to Jn. the risen Lord twice appears to His disciples τῶν θυρῶν κεκλεισμένων (Jn. 20:19, 26). In this case, the doors are not miraculously opened, as in Acts. The Lord comes through closed doors. [44] The transfigured corporeality of the risen Lord is no longer subject to the limitations of earthly corporeality. [45]

C. The Heavenly Door.

When heaven is regarded as a solid firmament, it may have one or many doors, like the underworld (→ κλείς, πύλη). This conception is part of the ancient oriental picture of the world. [46] In the OT we have only two references to the door of heaven, at Gn. 28:17: "This is none other but the house of God, and this is the gate of heaven," and Ps. 78:23. But this is purely accidental. The notion is found also in class. literature, [47] and it plays an important part in Gnosticism, mysticism, and the magic literature of Hellenistic syncretism, which frequently refers to the gates of heaven, of life, of light,

---

[38] Weinreich, 329 f., 422 ff.; Rudberg, 30.

[39] W. Nestle, Philol., 59 (1900), 46 ff.; P. Fiebig, *Angelos*, 2 (1926), 157 f.; Weinreich, 280 f., 332 ff., esp. 340. Nestle and Weinreich appeal esp. to the fact that Ac. reveals the influence of the usage of Euripides at two points: 5:39 (θεομάχος) and 26:14 (πρὸς κέντρα λακτίζειν, → κέντρον).

[40] Rudberg, 35.

[41] So also Jackson-Lake, I, 4 (1933), 135, 196 f.

[42] Orig. Cels., II, 34 says that Celsus, if he had known the Acts miracles, would have said: καὶ γόητές τινες ἐπῳδαῖς δεσμοὺς λύουσι καὶ θύρας ἀνοίγουσιν.

[43] Hell. Judaism, which knew the *topos* (Artapanus → 175), might have mediated it.

[44] F. Spitta, *Die Auferstehung Jesu* (1918), 71 rejects the miracle, and claims that the doors were opened to the risen Lord when He knocked. But if this is so, why is there the twofold mention of the fact that the doors were closed? The motif of passing through closed doors is fairly common in later hagiographical lit. (Weinreich, 429, cf. 428, n. 38).

[45] Cf. Lk. 24:31, 36.

[46] A. Jeremias, *Handbuch der altorientalischen Geisteskultur*[2] (1929), 133; *Das AT im Lichte des alten Orients*[4] (1930), 65, 90, 360 ff.; Weinreich, 207, 411-413. The Indo-Aryans also show acquaintance with the idea of gates of heaven, cf. J. Hertel, *Die Himmelstore im Veda und im Awesta* (1924) = *Indo-Iranische Quellen und Forschungen*, Heft II [Debrunner].

[47] First found in Hom. Il., 5, 749 = 8, 393; cf. Weinreich, 207 ff. For Pind. and Parm. cf. H. Fränkel, "Parmenidesstudien," NGG, 1930, 153 f.; on the Epicurean school, Reitzenstein Hell. Myst., 133 f. and K. Kerényi, "Religionsgeschichtliches zur Erklärung römischer Dichter," ARW, 28 (1930), 392-395.

of glory and of knowledge which the soul of the elect has to go through either during life or on the heavenly journey after death. [48]

Later Judaism speaks of the gates of the lower heaven through which the sun, moon and stars come, [49] of the gates of fire, earthquake, wind and hail, [50] dew and rain, [51] and the clouds. [52] From these are to be distinguished the heavenly gates which lead to the throne of God regarded as a temple [53] or a palace. [54] Under the influence of current syncretism, it was assumed that there are many heavens, so that the gates are almost always plural. [55] As may be seen from Gr. Bar. 11, [56] these gates leading to God's throne are in view when there is reference to the gates of prayer, [57] mercy, [58], tears, [59] or affliction, [60] e.g., bBM, 59a : "All gates are closed apart from the gates of affliction," i.e., the ear of God is always open to the afflicted. [61] These gates open when God reveals Himself in deliverance (3 Macc. 6:18) or causes His voice to be heard (S. Bar. 22:1). Only a few chosen ones can look (Gn. 28:17; Ez. 1:1 ff.) or enter (Test. L. 2-5; Eth. En. 14:15; Gr. Bar. 2 ff. etc.) through the opened gates of heaven during their lifetime. On the other hand — and this is not accidental, → 178 — the picture of the heavenly gates is used only in Eth. En. 104:2 to describe eternal bliss. [62]

The NT has only one express reference to the door of heaven, at Rev. 4:1. But the figure underlies passages which speak of the opening and closing of heaven, i.e., of its door. The reference is to the lower heaven when we read that heaven, or its door, was or will be shut (Lk. 4:25; cf. Rev. 11:6). [63] All the other references are to the opening of the door which leads to the throne of God [64] in the twofold sense 1. that God opens it to reveal Himself as the God who gives, instructs, judges and redeems (Mk. 1:10 par.; Jn. 1:51; Ac. 10:11; Rev. 19:11), so that opened heaven declares the eschatological redemption; and 2. that for the saints there is vision (Ac. 7:55 f.) or access ἐν πνεύματι (Rev. 4:1 f.; cf. 2 C. 12:2 ff.) to the hidden recesses of God's heavenly seat or palace, [65] so that they are granted the vision of God and disclosure of the mysteries of the world to come.

---

[48] Bau. J., Excursus on 10:21; Köhler, 224 ff.; Odeberg, 319 ff.; Weinreich, 228, 345 ff., 364 ff.

[49] Eth. En. 72-75; Slav. En. 13 f.; Damasc. 10:16; cf. Ps. 19:4-6. Acc. to Eth. En. 72:2 ff. there are 6 each in east and west; acc. to Gr. Bar. 6 there are 365 gates of heaven, which the angels open early in the morning.

[50] 4 Esr. 3:19. Gates of the winds also in Eth. En. 34-36; 76; there are 3 each in the 4 quarters.

[51] Eth. En. 36. Cf. the windows of heaven through which the water of the heavenly ocean flows down, Gn. 7:11; 8:2, and the opening of the heavenly chambers which dispense rain, Dt. 28:12; Eth. En. 60:21.

[52] Ps. 78:23; LXX Sir. 43:14.

[53] Test. L. 5:1.

[54] Eth. En. 14:10 ff.

[55] Test. L. 5:1; 3 Macc. 6:18; Gr. Bar. 2 ff.; Asc. Is. 10:24 ff.

[56] Michael, the keeper of the heavenly keys, opens the gates of the 5th heaven at a certain hour to receive the prayers of men, cf. Rev. 8:3.

[57] bBer., 32b.

[58] bMeg., 12b.

[59] bBer., 32b.

[60] bBM, 59a. Cf. Eth. En. 9:2, 10; earth resounds even to the gates of heaven with the cry of innocent sufferers (9:2) and of the dead (esp. the murdered, 9:1; 9:10).

[61] Cf. also jBer., 2d, 60 : prayer is knocking at the door of the heavenly king.

[62] This passage should be added in Str.-B., I, 460, 463.

[63] → n. 51.

[64] → supra.

[65] Rev. 4:2 : θρόνος (→ 165).

D. The Eschatological Use of the Image of the Door.

Eschatologically, the opened or closed door denotes the granting or refusal of a share in eternal salvation (→ 174). In the passages which follow, the reference is not to the door of heaven, as is often erroneously assumed. For, although the consummation of salvation embraces both heaven and earth, the main reference in its depiction in the NT is to the transfigured earth. We have in view first the sayings concerning entry into the kingdom of God. [66] Whether the door is expressly mentioned (Mt. 25:10; Lk. 13:24 f.) or not, in the Gospels the image of the door into the festive hall, in which the eschatological banquet is held, seems almost always [67] to be presupposed (cf. Mt. 7:7 f.; 22:12; 25:10, 21, 23; Lk. 13:24 f.; 14:23). It is in terms of access to eschatological glory [68] (rather than of the promise of missionary success, → 174), [69] that the opened door of Rev. 3:8 seems to be used according to the context (esp. v. 7): ἰδοὺ δέδωκα ἐνώπιόν σου θύραν ἠνεῳγμένην, ἣν οὐδεὶς δύναται κλεῖσαι αὐτήν. Concretely, the thought is that of access to the eschatological palace of God, [70] as may be seen especially from the quotation of Is. 22:22 in Rev. 3:7 (→ κλείς). The exalted Christ alone has power to grant this, and His promise is irrefragable, 3:8.

In Rev. 3:20 (ἰδοὺ ἕστηκα ἐπὶ τὴν θύραν καὶ κρούω) we do not have the believer standing before the door of God; we have Christ knocking at His disciple's. This has constantly given rise to the rather mystical idea of the Saviour knocking at the heart's door. [71] Against this understanding, however, there must be set the eschatological nature of the image of the eschatological feast and also of the promises in the letters from 2:1 ff., → II, 34. Thus 3:20 is also to be understood eschatologically of the returning Saviour (cf. Lk. 12:37 etc.) [72] who desires entry as a guest into the house of His disciple in order that He may enjoy table fellowship with him in a festive meal.

E. Ἐγώ εἰμι ἡ θύρα (John 10:7, 9).

This I-predication of the Johannine Christ (→ ἐγώ, II, 349 f.) is found twice in the address on the Good Shepherd in Jn. 10. The context seems to force us to take the image in different ways in v. 7 and v. 9. If we understand v. 7 f. in terms of v. 1 f., the sense is that "I am the door to the sheep," [73] while in the light of v. 9b the meaning in v. 9a is that "I am the door for the sheep." [74] But this distinction does not seem very probable, and there is the further difficulty that along these lines there has to be added to v. 7 f. a thought which is alien to the rest of the context, namely, that I am the door to the sheep i.e., for the shepherds, the spiritual leaders of the community. These difficulties have justifiably led to suspicion as to

---

[66] → II, 677, and H. Windisch, "Die Sprüche vom Eingehen in das Reich Gottes," ZNW, 27 (1928), 163-192, esp. 183. The passages are listed in → II, 677 and need not be repeated here.

[67] Cf. Mt. 7:13 f. → πύλη.

[68] So Bss. Apk.; Loh. Apk.; Holtzmann NT; J. Behm, NT Deutsch, ad loc.

[69] So Had. Apk. and E. B. Allo, Saint Jean. L'Apocalypse³ (1933), ad loc.

[70] Not to the future Jerusalem (Mt. 7:13 f.; Rev. 22:14), in which case we should expect πύλη.

[71] E. B. Allo (→ n. 69), ad loc.

[72] Bss. Apk.; A. Holtzmann NT; Had. Apk.; J. Behm, NT Deutsch, ad loc.

[73] Analogous gen. constructions: ψ 117:20: ἡ πύλη τοῦ κυρίου; Mk. 15:46 etc.: ἡ θύρα τοῦ μνημείου; Ign. Phld., 9, 1: αὐτὸς ὢν θύρα τοῦ πατρός.

[74] For a different view cf. Zn. J. and M. J. Lagrange, L'Évangile selon Saint Jean² (1925), who take v. 9 also in the sense of "I am the door to the sheep." But this harmonising of v. 7 and v. 9 demands the forced application of v. 9b to the shepherds.

the original integrity of the text. [75] In fact, vv. 7-10 seem to come from a different pen. In allegorical interpretation of vv. 1-5, they give prominence to the concept of the door, which is not important in vv. 1-5. An expositor who did not pay sufficiently careful attention to the text found the metaphor, not in the shepherd, but rather in the door, notwithstanding the reference to the porter in v. 3. [76] If this is correct, then the ambiguous v. 7 is to be interpreted solely in terms of v. 9, and the meaning of the expositor in both verses is that "I am the door for the sheep." [77]

What has been said also answers the question as to the origin of the I-predication. Four answers are possible. 1. The figure is due to a misreading of the Aram. original. The original רָעֲיָהוֹן דִּי עָנָא (shepherd of the sheep) is misread as תַּרְעֲהוֹן דִּי עָנָא (door of the sheep). [78] While v. 8 and v. 10 fit in smoothly on this assumption, v. 9 is still difficult, and recourse has to be had to the further conjecture that a false reading and interpretation of v. 7 led to the intrusion of this verse. [79] 2. A second, but rather dubious, explanation [80] assumes that the comparison of the Redeemer with the door was already current in pre-Christian Gnosticism, and was taken over from it. [81] Hence the door is the door of heaven [82] and the fold is the divine and spiritual world. [83] 3. It is more probable that the image of the shepherd in Jn. 10 (→ ποιμήν) derives from the OT. Going in and out, and finding pasture (v. 9), are also common expressions in the OT; indeed, the former is a Semitism, as is also the place of the verb in v. 7a. [84] Hence it is more natural to explain the door-predication in terms of the same world of thought. We may thus agree with Schl. J., 235 that it rests on a Messianic interpretation of Ps. 118:20 : זֶה הַשַּׁעַר לַיהֹוָה (זֶה) = the Messiah). In favour of this view it may be argued that Jesus gives an analogous Messianic sense to the concluding words of the psalm concerning the stone which the builders rejected (Ps. 118:22; Mk. 12:10 f. par.), and that He also relates Ps. 118:26 to Himself (Mt. 23:39). [85] 4. Nearer the mark is the explanation of the

---

[75] J. Wellhausen, Das Ev. Joh. (1908), 48 f.; E. Schwartz, NGG, 1908, 163 ff.; W. Heitmüller, Schr. NT[3] ad loc.; E. Hirsch, Das vierte Ev. (1936), 33 regard the text of the Sahidic transl. as the original of v. 7 (ποιμήν for θύρα), and v. 9 as an addition; but the Sah. seems to be an obvious correction. Cf. also Spitta, 209 ff.; Bau. J., ad loc.

[76] Spitta, 215.

[77] This is how the figure of the door is taken in Herm. s., 9, 12, 3 : Jesus is the πύλη, the gate, to the kingdom of God for all who are to be saved, and in Ign. Phld., 9, 1: Jesus is the θύρα to the Father for patriarchs, prophets, apostles and the Church.

[78] C. C. Torrey, The Four Gospels (1933), 323 f.

[79] Torrey, loc. cit.

[80] Other instances are all post-Christian, and in spite of variations show the influence of Jn. 10:7, 9 (Bau. J., Excursus on 10:21). Ign. Phld., 9, 1 of Christ : αὐτὸς ὢν θύρα τοῦ πατρός (vl. → n. 18); Herm. s., 9, 12, 1: ἡ πύλη ὁ υἱὸς τοῦ θεοῦ ἐστι; cf. 12, 6. In the Christian additions to the pagan Preaching of the Naassenes, Hipp. Ref., V, 8, 20, Jesus says : ἐγώ εἰμι ἡ πύλη (on πύλη instead of θύρα cf. the neighbouring quotation of LXX Gn. 28:17) ἡ ἀληθινή; cf. 9, 21; Ps.-Clem. Hom., 3, 52, where Jesus says : ἐγώ εἰμι ἡ πύλη τῆς ζωῆς (on πύλη τῆς ζωῆς cf. Mt. 7:13 f.), cf. 3, 18; Act. Joh., 95, θύρα εἰμί σοι κρούοντί με, cf. 98 and 109; Syrian Doxology of the Apostle Thomas (E. Hennecke, Handbuch zu den nt.lichen Apkr. [1904], 593 f.): "Son, fruit, Thou who art the door of light . . ."; Manichean tractate, ed. E. Chavannes and P. Pelliot, Journal Asiatique, Series 10, Tome 18 (1911), 586 of the ambassador of light : "He is also the gate of light"; Lidz. Ginza R. XII, 4, 277 (p. 275, 21), where the one who is sent is called the "precious door" (תורא באסימא). We cannot refer in this connection to 1 Cl., 48, 4 : πολλῶν οὖν πυλῶν ἀνεῳγυιῶν ἡ ἐν δικαιοσύνῃ αὕτη ἐστὶν ἡ ἐν Χριστῷ, because here Christ is not equated with the door. The same is true of Od. Sol. 17:10 (cf. Odeberg, 320 f.).

[81] Bau. J., Excursus on 10:21; R. Bultmann, ZNW, 24 (1925), 134 f.

[82] Odeberg, 321 ff.

[83] Ibid., 313.

[84] The difficulty of the expression εἰσελεύσεται καὶ ἐξελεύσεται may be explained by the fact that the Semitic has no compound verbs.

[85] On the Messianic interpretation of Ps. 118, cf. also Mk. 11:9-10 par. (= Ps. 118:25 f.).

origin of the door-predication given above (→ 179), namely, that it arose out of Jn. 10:1-2. If the expositor saw here the figure of Christ as the door, it is not surprising that he should formulate it in an I-saying when the Gospel offers a parallel in 14:6 : ἐγώ εἰμι ἡ ὁδός. [86]

In content the idea that Christ is the door for the sheep carries the lesson that Jesus mediates membership of the Messianic community and reception of the promised blessings of salvation, i.e., deliverance from judgment (σωθήσεται), citizenship in the divine community of salvation (εἰσελεύσεται καὶ ἐξελεύσεται), and eternal life (νομήν; cf. on the metaphor ἄρτος τῆς ζωῆς, → I, 477). The absolute claim of Jesus to be the only Mediator, to the exclusion of all other mediation, is emphasised by the emphatic, preceding δι' ἐμοῦ (10:9). [87]

In the present context this thought is stated only at v. 9. At v. 7 f. the further thought is added that Jesus alone mediates the true pastoral office. [88] Those who do not have His authorisation are disturbers of the flock.

On the later history of the image, → n. 80.

J. Jeremias

θυρεός → ὅπλον, πανοπλία.

| θύω, θυσία, θυσιαστήριον |

Contents : A. Linguistic : 1. θύω; 2. θυσία; 3. θυσιαστήριον = Altar of the God of the Bible. B. The Concept of Sacrifice in the New Testament : 1. Old Testament Presuppositions ; 2. The New Testament Evidence ; 3. The Historical Background : Later Judaism and Hellenism ; 4. The New Testament Concept of Sacrifice and the Early Church.

A. Linguistic.

1. θύω.

a. The basic meaning, "to sacrifice," is used only of burnt offerings in the earliest literature, [1] Hom. Il., 9, 219 : θεοῖσι δὲ θῦσαι ἀνώγει Πάτροκλον (cf. Aristarch. in the Schol., ad loc. [K. Lehrs, 1865, p. 82]: θῦσαι does not mean σφάξαι, but θυμιᾶσαι, Phryn. Soph. Prop. [p. 74, de Borries]: θῦσαι ἀντὶ τοῦ θυμιᾶσαι), Od., 14, 446 : ἄργματα (firstfruits) θῦσε θεοῖς, then all kinds of offerings, Plat. Euthyphr., 14c :

---

[86] Cf. Spitta, 215.

[87] The idea that Christ is the only gate (πύλη) into the kingdom of God is common in the vision of the tower, Herm. s., 9.

[88] Cf. Jn. 21:15-17; Eph. 4:11; 1 Pt. 5:2-4 → ποιμήν.

θ ύ ω, θ υ σ ί α, θ υ σ ι α σ τ ή ρ ι ο ν. On A : Thes. Steph., IV, 466 ff.; Pass., I, 1444 f.; Cr.-Kö., 504 ff.; Liddell-Scott, 812 f.; Pr.-Bauer, 570 ff.; Moult.-Mill., 295; Preisigke Wört., III, 373. B : A. Seeberg, Der Tod Christi in seiner Bedeutung für die Erlösung (1895); O. Schmitz, Die Opferanschauung des späteren Judentums und die Opferaussagen des NTs (1910); Art. "Opfer" II, B : "Im NT," RGG², IV, 717 ff.; P. Fiebig, "Das kultische Opfer im NT," ZwTh, 53 (1911), 253 ff.; W. Bötticher, "Der at.liche Sühnopfergedanke im NT," ZwTh, 55 (1914), 230 ff.; A. Loisy, Essai Historique sur le Sacrifice (1920); W. F. Lofthouse, Altar, Cross and Community (1920); H. Wenschkewitz, "Die Spiritualisierung der Kultusbegriffe Tempel, Priester und Opfer im NT," in Angelos, 4 (1932), 71 ff.; W. v. Loewenich, "Zum Verständnis des Opfergedankens in Hb.," ThBl, 12 (1933), 167 ff.; J. W. F. Höfling, Die Lehre der ältesten Kirche vom Opfer im Leben und Kultus des Christen (1851); F. Kattenbusch, RE³, XII, 669 ff.; F. Wieland, Mensa und Confessio, I (1906); Der vorirenäische Opferbegriff (1909); J. Brinktrine, "Der Messopferbegriff in den ersten 2 Jahrhunderten," Freiburger Theol. Studien, 21 (1918); O. Casel, "Die λογικὴ θυσία der antiken Mystik in christlich-liturgischer Umdeutung," Jbch. für Liturgiewissenschaft, 4 (1924), 37 ff.

[1] In accordance with the basic meaning of the Indo-germ. root, "to swirl, esp. of dust, mist, or smoke," cf. Walde-Pok., I, 835 [Debrunner].

τὸ θύειν δωρεῖσθαί ἐστι τοῖς θεοῖς, Xenoph. Cyrop., VIII, 7, 3 : λαβὼν ἱερεῖα ἔθυε Διί; Luc. Dialogi Deorum, 4, 2 : ᾧ τὸν κριὸν ὁ πατὴρ ἔθυσεν; BGU, I, 287, 7: ἀεὶ θύων τοῖς θεοῖς διετέλεσα; Philo Vit. Mos., II, 147: ἵνα θύσῃ περὶ ἀφέσεως ἁμαρτημάτων; Decal., 72 : ἤδη γάρ τινας οἶδα τῶν πεποιηκότων τοῖς πρὸς ἑαυτῶν γεγονόσιν εὐχομένους τε καὶ θύοντας; Jos. Ant., 12, 362 : τοὺς ἀναβαίνοντας εἰς τὸ ἱερὸν καὶ θῦσαι βουλομένους; cf. 1, 54; 10, 212. In the LXX it is used for זבח, in honour of Yahweh, Gn. 31:54; 3 Βασ. 8:63; in honour of alien gods, Ex. 34:15; Dt. 32:17; 3 Βασ. 11:7(8); in the NT only of pagan sacrifices, 1 C. 10:20; Ac. 14:13 (D : ἐπιθύειν), 18, cf. 2 Cl., 3, 1; Mart. Pol., 12, 2; Just. Dial., 19, 6; 136, 3.

b. Since parts of the sacrificed animal were burned, it is also used for "to immolate" for a cultic or profane purpose, which is from the very first very close to ancient concepts, Hdt., I, 216 : θύουσι ... πρόβατα ..., ἐψήσαντες δὲ τὰ κρέα κατευωχέονται ("to feast"), Aristoph. Lys., 1061 ff.: δελφάκιον (sucking pig) ... τέθυχ', ὥστε κρέ' ἔδεσθ' ἁπαλὰ καὶ καλά, Thuc., I, 126 : πανδημεὶ θύουσιν πολλὰ ... θύματα ἐπιχώρια, Jos. Ant., 4, 74 : τοῖς κατ' οἶκον θύουσιν εὐωχίας ἕνεκα; cf. 1, 197: μόσχον θύσας. In the LXX for זבח, 1 Βασ. 28:24; Ez. 39:17, for שחט, Ju. 12:6; Is. 22:13 (σφάζω is more common for שחט). In the NT Lk. 15:23, 27, 30; Ac. 10:13; 11:7; Mt. 22:4; Mk. 14:12 (cf. Lk. 22:7): θύειν τὸ πάσχα, "to slay the passover lamb" [2] (cf. Ex. 12:21; Dt. 16:2, 5 f.; 1 Εσδρ. 7:12; Philo Migr. Abr., 25; Leg. All., III, 94, 165; Jos. Ant., 9, 271; Just. Dial., 40, 1). Cf. 1 C. 5:7: καὶ γὰρ τὸ πάσχα ἡμῶν ἐτύθη, Χριστός, "for Christ, our passover lamb, is slain for us."

c. "To slay," "to murder" : Eur. Iph. Taur., 621: αὐτὴ ξίφει θύουσα θῆλυς ἄρσενας, 1 Macc. 7:19; Jn. 10:10.

2. θυσία.

a. "Sacrifice," "the act of sacrifice," Hdt., IV, 60 : θυσίη ἡ αὐτὴ πᾶσι κατέστηκε, "the act of sacrifice is conducted in the same way by all," cf. I, 132; II, 39; VIII, 99; Xenoph. Cyrop., III, 3, 34 : τέλος εἶχεν ἡ θυσία, BGU, I, 287, 1: τοῖς ἐπὶ τῶν θυσιῶν ᾑρημένοις, cf. P. Oxy., XII, 1464, 1 etc. In temple accounts, P. Oxy., VIII, 1143, 6; 1144, 15, there is expenditure εἰς τὰς θυσίας or εἰς θυσίαν, cf. the list of things necessary for sacrifice in P. Oxy., IX, 1211, 1 f. as τὰ πρὸς τὴν θυσίαν τοῦ ἱερωτάτου Νείλου. [3]

b. "Sacrifice," a. literally : Aesch. Sept. c. Theb., 701: ὅταν ἐκ χερῶν θεοὶ θυσίαν δέχωνται; Ag., 151: σπευδομένα θυσίαν ἑτέραν; Thuc., VIII, 70 : εὐχαῖς καὶ θυσίαις; Philo Spec. Leg., I, 162 ff. passim; 269 : τοὺς μέλλοντας φοιτᾶν εἰς τὸ ἱερὸν ἐπὶ μετουσίᾳ θυσίας; Jos. Bell., 2, 30 : τῷ πλήθει τῶν περὶ τὸν ναὸν φονευθέντων, οὓς ... παρὰ ταῖς ἰδίαις θυσίαις ὠμῶς ἀπεσφάχθαι. In the LXX for זבח, Hos. 6:6; 1 Βασ. 6:15 etc., and מנחה Gn. 4:3, 5; Lv. 2:1, 7 ff. etc. [4] θυσία σωτηρίου, Dt. 27:7; 2 Ch. 33:16; cf. Philo Spec. Leg., I, 247, or θυσία εἰρηνική, Prv. 7:14; 1 Βασ. 10:8 is used for the שלמים offering, θυσία τῆς αἰνέσεως, Lv. 7:12; 2 Ch. 33:16 (cf. Hb. 13:15) for the זבח התודה, while θυσία is only occasionally used for עליה, חטאת and אשם (cf. Hb. 10:26 : περὶ ἁμαρτιῶν θυσία). In the NT θυσία is used for Jewish offerings at Mt. 9:13 = 12:7 (Hos. 6:6); Mk. 9:49 vl. (Lv. 2:13); 12:33; Lk. 2:24; 13:1; 1 C. 10:18; Hb. 5:1; 8:3; 10:1, 5, 8, 11, of pagan offerings at Ac. 7:41. θυσίαν (-ας) ἀνάγειν is a tt. for "to offer sacrifice," Hdt., II, 60 : ὁρτάζουσι μεγάλας ἀνάγοντες θυσίας; VI, 111; 3 Βασ. 3:15; Philo Spec. Leg., I, 166 : τοῖς ἀνάγουσι τὰς θυσίας

---

[2] On the rite cf. Ex. 12:6 ff.; Dt. 16:6 f.; Pes., 5. Cf. J. Benzinger, Hebräische Archäologie[3] (1927), 382 f.; Str.-B., IV, 47 ff.; G. Dalman, Jesus-Jeschua (1922), 102 ff.

[3] Dib. Phil. and Loh. Phil. assign this sense to Phil. 2:17, but cf. → 182.

[4] προσφορά, in LXX only at ψ 39:6 for מנחה, is interchangeable with θυσία or δῶρον at Sir. 14:11; 34:18 (31:21); Eph. 5:2; Hb. 10:5, 8 etc. There is an attempt to distinguish between θυσία and δῶρον in the Philo fragment in P. Wendland, Neu entdeckte Fragmente Philos (1891), 38.

etc.; Ac. 7:41. προσάγειν is used at Nu. 6:12; Mal. 2:12; Philo Spec. Leg., I, 291: κελεύων πᾶσαν θυσίαν ... προσάγεσθαι, φέρειν at Gn. 4:3 f.; Philo Sacr. AC, 88; 1 Cl., 4, 1; Just. Dial., 19, 6, ἀναφέρειν at Is. 57:6; 2 Macc. 1:18; Jos. Ant., 11, 76 : ὅπως τὰς νομίμους ἀναφέρωσι θυσίας ... τῷ θεῷ; 7, 86 : θυσίας τελείας καὶ εἰρηνικὰς ἀνήνεγκε; Hb. 7:27; 1 Pt. 2:5, προσφέρειν at Ex. 32:6; Jos. Ant., 12, 251: τὰς καθημερινὰς θυσίας, ἃς προσέφερον τῷ θεῷ κατὰ τὸν νόμον, ἐκώλυσεν αὐτοὺς προσφέρειν; 20, 49 : χαριστηρίους θυσίας προσενεγκεῖν, Ac. 7:42 (Am. 5:25); Hb. 5:1; 8:3; 10:11; 11:4 etc., ἐπιτελεῖν, Hdt., II, 63 : θυσίας μούνας ἐπιτελέουσι; Philo Spec. Leg., I, 221: τῶν τὴν θυσίαν ἐπιτελούντων, ibid., III, 56 : τὴν θυσίαν μέλλειν ἐπιτελεῖσθαι; Dg., 3, 5: οἱ ... θυσίας αὐτῷ ἐπιτελεῖν οἰόμενοι, Ps.-Luc. Syr. Dea, 44: θυσίη δὶς ἑκάστης ἡμέρης ἐπιτελέεται — παριστάναι, [5] Polyb., 16, 25, 7: ἐπὶ πᾶσι θύματα τοῖς βωμοῖς παραστήσαντες; Ditt. Syll.[3], 736, 70 : παριστάτω τὰ θύματα εὔιερα καθαρὰ ὁλόκληρα; Ditt. Or., 332, 17: παρασταθείσης θυσίας; 764:23 : παραστήσας θυσίαν αὐτοῖς; Jos. Ant., 7, 382 : θυσίας τῷ θεῷ παρέστησαν μόσχους χιλίους; R. 12:1, ποιεῖσθαι at Hdt., I, 132 : ἄνευ ... μάγου οὔ σφι νόμος ἐστὶ θυσίας ποιέεσθαι; Plat. Symp., 174c : θυσίαν ποιουμένου καὶ ἑστιῶντος; BGU, IV, 1198, 12 : ποιεῖσθαι ἁγνείας καὶ θυσίας; Philo Sacr. AC, 88 : τὴν θυσίαν ποιήσασθαι κατὰ τὸ ἱερώτατον διάταγμα, more rarely ἐπιφέρειν, Jos. Ant., 8, 231: ἐπιφέρειν τὰς θυσίας καὶ τὰς ὁλοκαυτώσεις, or (ἀπο-)διδόναι, 7, 196 : θυσίαν ἀποδοῦναι τῷ θεῷ; Lk. 2:24; 1 C. 10:18 : οἱ ἐσθίοντες (→ II, 693) τὰς θυσίας, "those who eat the sacrifices," the participants in the OT sacrifices, the priests and Levites (Nu. 18:8 ff.; Dt. 18:1 ff.; cf. 1 C. 9:13), but also the laity (1 S. 1:4; 9:19 ff.; 16:3, 5).

b. Figuratively : i. of the death of Christ in which He has offered Himself to God, Eph. 5:2 : παρέδωκεν ἑαυτὸν ὑπὲρ ἡμῶν προσφορὰν καὶ θυσίαν τῷ θεῷ; Hb. 10:12 : μίαν ὑπὲρ ἁμαρτιῶν προσενέγκας θυσίαν; cf. 7:27: ἐφάπαξ ἑαυτὸν ἀνενέγκας; 9:23, 26; Barn., 7, 3. ii. of the life of Christians as a self-offering to God, R. 12:1: παραστῆσαι τὰ σώματα ὑμῶν θυσίαν ζῶσαν (→ ζάω) ἁγίαν (→ I, 107) τῷ θεῷ εὐάρεστον (→ I, 457); Phil. 2:17: ἐπὶ τῇ θυσίᾳ καὶ → λειτουργίᾳ τῆς πίστεως ὑμῶν χαίρω; [6] Phil. 4:18 : τὰ παρ' ὑμῶν (the gift of the community) ... θυσίαν δεκτήν (→ II, 59), εὐάρεστον τῷ θεῷ, 1 Pt. 2:5 : ἀνενέγκαι → πνευματικὰς θυσίας εὐπροσδέκτους (→ II, 59) θεῷ διὰ Ἰησοῦ Χριστοῦ, Hb. 13:15 f.: the θυσία αἰνέσεως of Christians is the fruit of their lips (Hos. 14:3) which praise God's name ; the sacrifices pleasing to God are sharing and doing good. Cf. the use of ψ 50:19 : θυσία τῷ θεῷ πνεῦμα συντετριμμένον in 1 Cl., 18, 17; 52, 4; Barn., 2, 10.

3. θυσιαστήριον [7] = Altar of the God of the Bible. [8]

a. Literally i. the altars in the temple at Jerusalem, [9] the altar of burnt offering, Lv. 4:7 etc.; Mt. 5:23 f.; 23:18 ff., 35; Lk. 11:51; 1 C. 9:13; 10:18 (→ κοινωνός); Hb.

---

[5] Cf. Deissmann NB, 82; Ltzm. R. on 12:1.

[6] On the construction and exegesis of this difficult passage cf. Chrys. Hom. in Phil., VIII, 3 (MPG, 62, 243); T. Zahn, "Altes und Neues zum Verständnis des Phil.," ZWL, 6 (1885), 290 ff.; Haupt Gefbr., ad loc.; Ew. Gefbr., ad loc.

[7] Derived from θυσιάζω; adj. θυσιαστήριος sc. ὕμνος once in Timaeus (FHG, I, 232 : Fr., 153). On the form, cf. Winer-Schmiedel § 16, 2b; Moulton-Howard, Grammar of the NT Greek, II (1929), 342 f. The subst. τὸ θυσιαστήριον occurs first in the LXX, and prior to the Codex Justinianus, I, 12, 3, 1 ff. (p. 97 f., Krueger) it is found only in Jewish and Christian literature. On the history of the term, cf. B. F. Westcott, The Epistle to the Hebrews (1889), 453 ff.

[8] For altars of alien gods in the LXX and NT βωμός is always used (for a typical distinction between θυσιαστήριον and βωμός, 1 Macc. 1:59, cf. 54). This consistent distinction is no longer observed in Philo and Joseph., who regularly use βωμός for the altar of the OT and Jewish cultus, and more rarely θυσιαστήριον, e.g., Philo Spec. Leg., I, 285 ff.; Jos. Ant., 8, 88 and 230. Philo Vit. Mos., II, 106, cf. Spec. Leg., I, 290, etymological play : θυσιαστήριον = τηρητικὸν θυσιῶν (παρὰ τὸ διατηρεῖν τὰς θυσίας).

[9] Cf. Benzinger, op. cit., 329 ff.; K. Galling, Biblisches Reallexikon (Handbuch z. AT, I, 1 [1934], 20 ff.).

7:13; Rev. 11:1; 1 Cl., 32, 2; 41, 2; the altar of incense, Ex. 30:1; 40:5; Lv. 4:7; Lk. 1:11 (though cf. Jos. Ant., 9, 223 : ἐπὶ τοῦ χρυσοῦ βωμοῦ); ii. other altars of the OT cultus, Jm. 2:21 (Gn. 22:9 f.); R. 11:3 (3 Βασ. 19:10, 14); iii. the altar (or altars ?) [10] which the divine saw in the heavenly sanctuary, Rev. 6:9; 8:3, 5; 9:13; 14:18; 16:7; cf. Herm. m., 10, 3, 2 f.; s., 8, 2, 5.

b. Figuratively : Hb. 13:10 : ἔχομεν θυσιαστήριον ἐξ οὗ φαγεῖν (→ II, 693) οὐκ ἔχουσιν ἐξουσίαν οἱ τῇ σκηνῇ λατρεύοντες, where it is impossible to fix any specific sense (the context does not allow of a reference either to the cross [11] or to the Lord's Table [12]), and the only point which is clear is that there are no sacrificial meals in the sacrificial order of the NT. [13] θυσιαστήριον is used in various ways as a figure in Ign. Eph., 5, 2; Tr., 7, 2; Mg., 7, 2; Phld., 4; R., 2, 2; Pol., 4, 3 → n. 41.

B. The Concept of Sacrifice in the New Testament.

1. Old Testament Presuppositions. [14]

The concept of sacrifice in the OT is rooted in the reality of the covenant order into which God's historical revelation has integrated the people of Israel. Whatever religious ideas may underlie the OT view, [15] its characteristic distinctiveness, which is significant for the NT, is due to the manner in which the God self-revealed in history has ordered the relationship between Himself and the people. In the sacrificial order of the old covenant God wills to have personal and active dealings with His people. Sacrifice, whether it be the gift of man to God, the expression of spiritual fellowship between God and man, or a means of atonement, is always orientated to the presence of God in grace and judgment. If prophets fight against sacrifice (Am. 5:21 ff.; Hos. 6:6; Is. 1:10 ff.; Jer. 7:21 f.; 1 S. 15:22 etc.) and psalms reject it (Ps. 40:6 ff.; 50:8 ff.; 51:16 f.; 69:31), this is not because of any basic opposition to the cultus. It is because in practice the original purpose of the cultus has been abandoned. Material human achievement has replaced personal, spiritual encounter with the God of salvation. The occasional recognition that humble worship and praise, the doing of God's will, and faithfulness and love are the true sacrifices (Ps. 40:6 ff.; 50:14; 51:17; 119:108; Prv. 16:6; 21:3), does not lead to any radical reconstruction of the concept of sacrifice. In the legalistic religion of post-exilic Judaism cultic sacrifice tends to be an *opus operatum* which is achieved in scrupulous obedience to the command of a distant God, and it is integrated into a series of similar meritorious forms of legal observance which survive the end of sacrifice with the destruction of the temple.

---

[10] V. the Comm.

[11] So Bengel, ad loc.; F. Bleek in Komm., III (1840), ad loc.; A. Seeberg, Komm., ad loc.; Wieland, Der vorirenäische Opferbegriff, 16 f., 20 f.

[12] So Theophylact, ad loc. (MPG, 125, 393) and Roman Cath. expositors, e.g., J. Rohr, Komm., ad loc. (1932); cf. A. Médebielle, "Sacrificium Expiationis et Communionis (Hb. 13:10)," in Verbum Domini, 5 (1925), 168 ff.; 203 ff.; 238 ff.; also F. Spitta, Zur Geschichte und Lit. des Urchristentums, I (1893), 326 ff.; K. G. Goetz, Die Abendmahlsfrage² (1907), 195 f.; T. Haering, Der Brief an die Hebräer (1925), 103.

[13] Cf. Rgg. Hb. and Wnd. Hb., ad loc.

[14] For further details cf. such works in OT theology and the history of religion as E. König, Theologie des AT⁴ (1923); W. Eichrodt, Theologie des AT, I (1933); E. Sellin, At.liche Theologie auf religionsgeschichtlicher Grundlage, I/II (1933) and the bibl. in the art. "Opfer," II A : "Im AT," RGG², IV, 711 ff.; also Benzinger, op. cit., 358 ff.; Jüd. Lex., IV, 578 ff.; A. Bertholet, "Zum Verständnis des at.lichen Opfergedankens," JBL, 49 (1930), 218 ff.

[15] Cf. Loisy, op. cit.; F. Pfister, Art. "Kultus," Pauly-W., XI (1922), 2180 ff. etc.; A. Bertholet, Art. "Opfer" I : "Religionsgeschichtlich," RGG², IV, 704 ff.; G. v. d. Leeuw, Phänomenologie der Religion (1933), 327 ff. etc.

In criticism of sacrifice the LXX [16] sometimes goes beyond the Mas. This may be seen from the use of the relevant passages in the NT. In Ac. 7:41 f. θυσία is a pagan concept. Cf. also ψ 105:28 : ἔφαγον θυσίας νεκρῶν. At Job 20:5 f. the LXX (not the Mas.) has : ... χαρμονὴ δὲ παρανόμων ἀπώλεια, ἐὰν ἀναβῇ εἰς οὐρανὸν αὐτοῦ τὰ δῶρα (not Cain !), ἡ δὲ θυσία αὐτοῦ νεφῶν ἅψηται. But sometimes the Mas. is the more critical : Qoh. 5:1 Mas. "Be more ready to hear than to give the sacrifice of fools"; LXX : ὑπὲρ δόμα τῶν ἀφρόνων θυσία σου. Expressions like θυσία δικαιοσύνης (ψ 4:5), ἀλαλαγμοῦ, 26:6; αἰνέσεως, 49:14 (= Mas. Ps. 50:14); 106:22; 115:17 are meant figuratively, and were thus understood by readers of the LXX. Yet θυσία δικαιοσύνης (50:19) and θυσία αἰνέσεως (Lv. 7) can also be used of actual sacrifices in the LXX.

2. The New Testament Evidence. [17]

In the canonical Gospels Jesus does not pronounce any judgment on Jewish sacrifices (by contrast cf. the saying from Ev. Eb. according to Epiph. Haer., 30, 16, 5 : ἦλθον καταλῦσαι τὰς θυσίας, καὶ ἐὰν μὴ παύσησθε τοῦ θύειν, οὐ παύσεται ἀφ' ὑμῶν ἡ ὀργή). According to Mt. 5:23 f.; 23:18 ff. the altar and sacrifices are accepted factors in the traditional worship of God. [18] It is true that in Mt. 9:13; 12:7 Jesus quotes against the Pharisees the saying that God desires mercy and not sacrifice (Hos. 6:6), but there is here no more rejection of the sacrificial ministry than in the prophets. It is also true that in His sayings concerning the temple in Mt. 12:6; 26:61, cf. 27:40; Jn. 2:19; 4:21 ff. (→ ἱερός, → ναός) Jesus makes it clear that sacrifices are of secondary value and are doomed to perish. Yet this is not because of their cultic or ritual character. It is because they belong to the old order which He has come to replace as God's plenipotentiary. It is because He establishes the new διαθήκη (→ II, 133) that the sacrificial cultus ends. There is no sacrifice in the new διαθήκη. Jesus does not set under the perspective of sacrifice the actualisation of the καινὴ διαθήκη by His death (→ I, 174).

Paul is familiar with both the sacrificial cult of the OT and Judaism on the one side, and that of paganism on the other, 1 C. 9:13; 10:18 ff. He realises that communion with the deity is the goal of sacrificial meals. But when he compares with this communion the → κοινωνία τοῦ αἵματος and τοῦ σώματος τοῦ Χριστοῦ in the Lord's Supper (1 C. 10:16 ff.), this is not because he links the concept of sacrifice with the Lord's Supper. In his discussion of the Lord's Supper in 1 C. 10:11 there is not the least basis for the conjecture that "the celebration of the Eucharist is for Paul a sacred sacrificial meal." [19] The idea of sacrifice is present in the religious thinking of Paul in the figurative sense, as an edifying picture of the self-offering of Christ to death and of the Christian's task of self-offering to God. It is in keeping with Paul's theology of history, which uses the schema of the old divine order and the new (→ II, 129 f.), that in 1 C. 5:7 Christ as the slain Paschal lamb of the new community is compared with the Paschal lamb of the old. As deliverance formerly came through the sacrificial death of the lamb, so it now comes through the antitypical event of the death of Christ. In Eph. 5:2 the loving

---

[16] This paragraph is by Bertram.

[17] Cf. esp. Schmitz, op. cit., 196 ff.; Wenschkewitz, op. cit., 152 ff.

[18] Mt. 23:19 : τὸ θυσιαστήριον τὸ ἁγιάζον τὸ δῶρον, agrees with the Rabb. doctrine of Zeb., 9, 1: "The altar sanctifies that which is appointed for it," Str.-B., I, 932.

[19] Brinktrine, op. cit., 38. Cf. also W. Heitmüller, Taufe und Abendmahl bei Pls. (1903), 40 ff.

self-sacrifice of Christ for Christians is viewed, both in its nature and its results, from the standpoint of an offering which is pleasing to God. But in the Christology of Paul the figurative concept of sacrifice is no more than a help towards the understanding of the basic saving fact of the death of Christ.[20] Similarly, in his attempt to portray the nature of the Christian life he chooses metaphors from the sphere of the sacrificial cultus. Because they have known the mercy of God, Christians are to bring sacrifices of thanksgiving. That is to say, they themselves, in all the vitality of a being which is determined by God, are to give themselves to God, to live for Him as He would have it. This is their → λογικὴ → λατρεία, R. 12:1. All that faith does (cf. Gl. 5:6), whether it be ministry in the spread of the Gospel (Phil. 2:17b; cf. 16a; also the apostle's own work and calling, R. 15:16; Phil. 2:17a; 2 Tm. 4:6), or the giving of material assistance (Phil. 4:18), becomes θυσία and → λειτουργία. Life is a sacrifice — the direct opposite of the offering of the life of another in cultic sacrifice.

We are in much the same sphere as Paul's thinking when it is said in First Peter that Christians are a holy priesthood (→ ἱεράτευμα) which is ordained, ἀνενέγκαι → πνευματικὰς θυσίας εὐπροσδέκτους θεῷ διὰ 'Ιησοῦ Χριστοῦ (2:5). The gifts which Christians bring, and whose acceptance by God is guaranteed by Christ, are no longer cultic offerings in the true sense. They are spiritual offerings. That is, they have the nature of the Spirit of God who works in Christians. A life which is received from God is offered back to God (cf. 1:15).

Hebrews[21] returns to the cultic concept of the OT. On the basis of its distinctive comparison of Christ with the high-priest (→ ἀρχιερεύς), it revives especially the thought of expiation, which is linked supremely with the offering of the high-priest on the day of atonement, 9:7. The bloody sacrifice through which the high-priest expiated the sin of the people is a type of the high-priestly self-sacrifice of Christ, 8-10. By a comparison of the two offerings, which is strengthened by subsidiary glances at other offerings, e.g., 9:9 f., 13, 18, the cultic concept of sacrifice in the strictest sense (cf. 9:22) seems to be of central significance for a theological estimation of the work of Christ. In reality, however, the comparison posits not merely a quantitative superiority of the high-priestly ministry of the NT over that of the OT, but also a qualitative distinction between them. The sacrifice of Christ is not a prescribed, material achievement which must be continually repeated by sinful men. It is a free, personal act of self-giving which the sinless and eternal Son accomplishes once for all (ἐφάπαξ, → I, 381; 10:11 ff.; 7:23 ff., 27 f.; 9:6 f., 11 f., 25 f.). For this reason it has power to effect not merely outward cleansing but the cleansing of the conscience (9:13 f., cf. 9). It is no vain attempt at expiation (10:1 ff.); it achieves eternal redemption (9:12; 10:14). When Hb. compares the atoning sacrifice of Christ with its OT model, it does not present us with a caricature which remains within the sphere of a religion of law. It goes back to the original conception and purpose of sacrifice in the OT, namely, that it is a means of personal intercourse between God and man (→ 183). This original purpose of sacrifice is finally fulfilled in the personal act of Christ, in the voluntary and unique offering up of His life. Sacrifice is thus brought to an end in Him. Cultic sacrifice is not merely transcended but ended by the unique self-offering of Christ (10:18; cf. 9:8) because the person of Christ as High-priest is unique. The

---

[20] Cf. the Comm. on 1 C. 5:7 and Eph. 5:2, also A. Seeberg, op. cit., 203 ff.
[21] Cf. for Hb. Schmitz, op. cit., 259 ff.; Rgg. Hb.[2,3], 459 ff.; Wnd. Hb., Excursus on 10:18 and 9:14, also on 9:22; Wenschkewitz, op. cit., 195 ff.; von Loewenich, op. cit., 167 ff.

NT experience of salvation frees the author of Hb. from the cultic conception of sacrifice which dominates his world of thought. Yet, in spite of the constantly emphasised differentiation between the image and the reality, it provides him also with a means to portray the saving work of Christ. We can thus understand the spiritualisation of the concept of sacrifice which he carries through with the express help of Ps. 40 and 50, → 183, when he finds the meaning of sacrifice in fulfilment of the will of God, 10:5 ff., and when he demands of Christians the sacrificial ministry of unceasing worship of God and performance of acts of brotherly love, 13:15 f. In the sphere of the new διαθήκη, whose establishment by Christ brings the old διαθήκη to an end, 8:6 ff. etc. (→ II, 132), there is no more sacrifice in the literal sense. To bring oneself, one's will, one's action, wholly to God, is the new meaning which the concept of sacrifice acquires in Hb., as in Paul and 1 Pt.

3. The Historical Background : Later Judaism and Hellenism.

a. Though sacrifice is strictly practised in later Judaism, there is no clear or simple view of it. [22] The standpoint of strict cultic legalism is espoused, e.g., by Jub. 50:11: "That day by day they should constantly offer the sin offering for Israel as a remembrance which is pleasing to God, and that He should accept it day by day for ever, as is commanded (thee)"; Sib., III, 574-579, where the last time is extolled as the time of the glorious fulfilment of the Jewish sacrificial ministry, which is now only partial (III, 570):

βουλαῖς ἠδὲ νόῳ προσκείμενοι Ὑψίστοιο,
οἳ ναὸν μεγάλοιο θεοῦ περικυδανέουσιν
λοιβῇ τε κνίσσῃ τ᾽ ἠδ᾽ αὖθ᾽ ἱεραῖς ἑκατόμβαις
ταύρων ζατρεφέων θυσίαις κριῶν τε τελείων
πρωτοτόκων ὀίων τε καὶ ἀρνῶν πίονα μῆλα
βωμῷ ἐπὶ μεγάλῳ ἁγίως ὁλοκαρπεύοντες,

or 1 Macc., with its depiction of the stubborn resistance of the Jews to any violation of the ritual of sacrifice (e.g., 1:45), which belongs to the προστάγματα τοῦ νόμου (2:68), or 2 Macc. with its glorification of the temple and the sacrificial cultus, 1:19 ff.; 3:1 ff., esp. 32 ff. etc. Yet there are also voices of radical criticism which reject the temple cultus, and specifically the bloody sacrifices, e.g., Sib., IV, 27-30 :

οἳ νηοὺς μὲν ἅπαντας ἀπαρνήσονται ἰδόντες
καὶ βωμούς, εἰκαῖα λίθων ἀφιδρύματα κωφῶν,
αἵμασιν ἐμψύχων μεμιασμένα καὶ θυσίῃσιν
τετραπόδων, [23]

or Slav. En. 45:3 f. (echoing Ps. 51:16 f., 19); Jos. Ant., 18, 19 (E lat): (The Essenes) θυσίας οὐκ ἐπιτελοῦσιν διαφορότητι ἁγνειῶν, ἃς νομίζοιεν. [24] The predominant view of sacrifices is that they are Godward actions which are commanded by the Law and whose obedient observance God rewards if he who offers them also lives in obedience to the Law in other respects, e.g., Sir. 34:18-35:13. To keep the commandments, to shun evil, to exercise benevolence, is just as good a proof of fidelity to the Law as sacrifice ;

---

[22] Cf. Schmitz, op. cit., 55 ff.; Wenschkewitz, op. cit., 77 ff.
[23] Or is the reference here to the pagan cultus, as in Sib. Fr., 1, 22 (p. 229, Geffcken [1902] in GCS), cf. Sib., VIII, 390 f.?
[24] Cf. also Philo Omn. Prob. Lib., 75 : οὐ ζῷα καταθύοντες, ἀλλ᾽ ἱεροπρεπεῖς τὰς ἑαυτῶν διανοίας κατασκευάζειν ἀξιοῦντες. On the problem of the position of the Essenes, cf. W. Bauer, Pauly-W., Suppl. IV (1924), 396, 398 f. According to Epiph. Haer., 18, 1, 4, the Jewish sect of the Nazarenes was hostile to sacrifice, though we have no other information concerning them.

indeed, these things are sacrifice : ὁ συντηρῶν νόμον πλεονάζει προσφοράς, Sir. 35:1, cf. 2 ff.; Tob. 4:10 f.: ἐλεημοσύνη ἐκ θανάτου ῥύεται ... δῶρον γὰρ ἀγαθόν ("a good sacrifice") ἐστιν ἐλεημοσύνη πᾶσι τοῖς ποιοῦσιν αὐτὴν ἐνώπιον τοῦ ὑψίστου, cf. 12:9. This transformation of the concept of sacrifice, in terms of which any religious or moral action in accordance with the Law (e.g., prayer, Ps. 141:2; Tob. 12:12; 2 Macc. 12:43 f.; Da. 3:40 LXX; Jub. 2:22, [25] or the fear of God, Jdt. 16:16, or the sufferings of martyrs, 4 Macc. 6:29; 17:22) can be regarded as sacrifice in a higher sense, deprives cultic sacrifice of its special position, and finally allows it to disappear from the Jewish religion of the dispersion and the Rabbis without shaking it to the very foundations. In Rabbinic Judaism [26] a minutely elaborated theory of sacrifice bears the marks of antiquarian pedantry now that the cultus itself has perished (Tractate of the Seder Qodashim). But the religious meaning of sacrifice in a religion of the Law is not forgotten. Sacrifices were offered in the temple because God had commanded them. They were a fulfilment of the commandments of the Torah, an exercise in obedience. This finds illustration [27] in the Tannaitic midrash, in which the OT phrase "a burnt offering for a sweet savour to the Lord" is consistently changed into "to the good-pleasure of the Lord," "since God has commanded the bringing of this sacrifice in the Torah, and since His will is thus done by it." [28] Ab., 1, 2 [29] in a very early tradition (Simon the Just) mentions the cultus as one of the three things on which the world rests ; it comes second after the Torah. The piety of the Synagogue is a substitute for sacrifices, and thus the following especially are called sacrifices: repentance (cf. Yoma, 8, 8 f., also Lv. r., 7 on 6:9 : "How can we prove that he who repents is viewed as if he offered the prescribed offerings of the Torah ? From the verse, The sacrifices of God are a broken spirit, Ps. 51:17"); the study of the Torah (bMen., 110a : "A pure offering — that is the study of the Torah in purity ... ; he who is occupied with the Torah is like one who brings burnt offerings and meat offerings and sin offerings and guilt offerings"); [30] works of love (Ab. R. Nat., 2d [Jochanan ben Zakkai]: "We have an atonement equivalent to that, i.e., the offering in the sanctuary) ... the doing of works of love" (Hos. 6:6; [31] bSukka, 49b : "Greater is he who exercises benevolence than all sacrifices"); [32] and prayer (S. Dt., 41 on 11:13): "As the ministry of the altar is called a עֲבוֹדָה, so also prayer is called a עֲבוֹדָה "; [33] cf. also bBer., 26a b : prayer takes the place of sacrifice ; Pesikt., 79a : "In the future all sacrifices will cease, but the sacrifice of thanksgiving will not cease to all eternity; similarly, all confessions will cease, but the confession of thanksgiving will not cease to all eternity." [34]

b. As regards the attitude of Hellenism to sacrifice, [35] it is worth noting that it

---

[25] Cf. the (Christian ?) description of the worship of the angels in heaven in Test. L. (α): 3:6 : προσφέροντες τῷ κυρίῳ ὀσμὴν εὐωδίας λογικὴν καὶ ἀναίμακτον θυσίαν, ibid., 8 : ἀεὶ ὕμνον τῷ θεῷ προσφέροντες.

[26] Cf. also Moore, I, 504 ff., II, 14 f.

[27] I owe this reference to Kuhn.

[28] E.g., S. Nu., 107 on 15:7 (S. Nu., ed. K. G. Kuhn in Rabb. Texte [ed. G. Kittel], II, 2 [1933], 293; ibid., 143 on 28:8) etc. Cf. C. Albeck, Untersuchungen über die halakischen Midraschim (1927), 12, and A. Schlatter, "Jochanan Ben Zakkai," BFTh, III, 4 (1899), 41 ff.

[29] I owe this reference to Rengstorf.

[30] Str.-B., III, 152, 607.

[31] Ibid., IV, 555; cf. I, 500; Schl. Mt., 308.

[32] Str.-B., IV, 541.

[33] Ibid., III, 26.

[34] Ibid., I, 246.

[35] Cf. P. Stengel, Die griech. Kultusaltertümer³ (1920), 95 ff.; F. Pfister, Art. "Kultus," Pauly-W., XI (1922), 2164 ff.; "Die Religion der Griechen und Römer" in Jahresbericht über die Fortschritte der klass. Altertumswissenschaft, Supplementband, Bd., 229 (1930), 180 ff. etc.; A. Bonhoeffer, Epiktet und das NT (1911), 361 etc.; Reitzenstein Hell. Myst., 328 f.; Wenschkewitz, op. cit., 113 ff.; Ltzm. R. on 12:1; J. Geffcken, Zwei griech. Apologeten (1907), XXII, n. 5; Casel, op. cit., 37 ff.

inherits from the classical Greek world, [36] not the ancient concept of sacrifice, nor even a religious and ethical development of the concept, but the hostile mood of the later period in which the original religious awareness was shattered. That sacrifices are more than man's gifts to the gods to propitiate them; that deity demands more than sacrifice (Aesch. Ag., 1296 ff.); that only the good man is worthy to sacrifice to the gods (cf. Plat. Leg., IV, 716d : . . . τῷ μὲν ἀγαθῷ θύειν καὶ προσομιλεῖν ἀεὶ τοῖς θεοῖς εὐχαῖς καὶ ἀναθήμασιν καὶ συμπάσῃ θεραπείᾳ θεῶν κάλλιστον καὶ ἄριστον καὶ ἀνυσιμώτατον πρὸς τὸν εὐδαίμονα βίον καὶ δὴ καὶ διαφερόντως πρέπον, τῷ δὲ κακῷ τούτων τἀναντία πέφυκεν, Theophr. acc. to Porphyr. Abst., II, 32 : . . . οὐκ ἀξιόχρεως δ᾽ εἰς τὸ θύειν θεοῖς πάντας ἡμᾶς ἡγουμένους. καθάπερ γὰρ οὐ πᾶν θυτέον αὐτοῖς, οὕτως οὐδ᾽ ὑπὸ παντὸς ἴσως κεχάρισται τοῖς θεοῖς); that the pious life of him who offers is pleasing to God rather than the greatness of the offering (cf. Xenoph. Mem., I, 3, 3 on Socrates : θυσίας δὲ θύων μικρὰς ἀπὸ μικρῶν οὐδὲν ἡγεῖτο μειοῦσθαι τῶν ἀπὸ πολλῶν καὶ μεγάλων πολλὰ καὶ μεγάλα θυόντων. οὔτε γὰρ τοῖς θεοῖς ἔφη καλῶς ἔχειν, εἰ ταῖς μεγάλαις θυσίαις μᾶλλον ἢ ταῖς μικραῖς ἔχαιρον· πολλάκις γὰρ ἂν αὐτοῖς τὰ παρὰ τῶν πονηρῶν μᾶλλον ἢ τὰ παρὰ τῶν χρηστῶν εἶναι κεχαρισμένα· οὔτ᾽ ἂν τοῖς ἀνθρώποις ἄξιον εἶναι ζῆν, εἰ τὰ παρὰ τῶν πονηρῶν μᾶλλον ἦν κεχαρισμένα τοῖς θεοῖς ἢ τὰ παρὰ τῶν χρηστῶν· ἀλλ᾽ ἐνόμιζε τοὺς θεοὺς ταῖς παρὰ τῶν εὐσεβεστάτων τιμαῖς μάλιστα χαίρειν, also Xenoph. An., V, 7, 32 : πῶς . . . θεοῖς θύσομεν ἡδέως ποιοῦντες ἔργα ἀσεβῆ . . . ; Isoc., 2, 20 : τὰ πρὸς τοὺς θεοὺς ποίει μὲν ὡς οἱ πρόγονοι κατέδειξαν, ἡγοῦ δὲ θῦμα τοῦτο κάλλιστον εἶναι καὶ θεραπείαν μεγίστην, ἂν ὡς βέλτιστον καὶ δικαιότατον σαυτὸν παρέχῃς· μᾶλλον γὰρ ἐλπὶς τοὺς τοιούτους ἢ τοὺς ἱερεῖα πολλὰ καταβάλλοντας πράξειν τι παρὰ τῶν θεῶν ἀγαθόν, Eur. Fr., 329 etc.) — all these are ancient Greek thoughts which, as they are now re-echoed, bear no inner relation to literal sacrifice. The philosophical criticism of sacrifice (e.g., Ps.-Plat. Alc., II, 149e : καὶ γὰρ ἂν δεινὸν εἴη, εἰ πρὸς τὰ δῶρα καὶ τὰς θυσίας ἀποβλέπουσιν ἡμῶν οἱ θεοί, ἀλλὰ μὴ πρὸς τὴν ψυχήν, ἄν τις ὅσιος καὶ δίκαιος ὢν τυγχάνῃ, Anaximenes Ars Rhetorica, 2, ed. L. Spengel and C. Hammer in Rhetores Graeci, I [1894], 20 : οὐκ εἰκὸς τοὺς θεοὺς χαίρειν ταῖς δαπάναις τῶν θυομένων, ἀλλὰ ταῖς εὐσεβείαις τῶν θυόντων) continues in Hellenism alongside an unreflecting sacrificial practice at the official level. For Stoicism cf. Sen. Fr., 123 (Lact. Inst., VI, 25, 3): *non immolationibus nec sanguine multo colendum* (*sc. deum*) . . . *sed mente pura, bono honestoque proposito*, Ben., I, 6, 3 : in sacrifice it is a matter of *recta ac pia voluntas venerantium* ; Epict. Diss., I, 19, 25 : τίς οὖν πώποτε ὑπὲρ τοῦ ὀρεχθῆναι καλῶς ἔθυσεν; ὑπὲρ τοῦ ὁρμῆσαι κατὰ φύσιν; cf. Ench., 31, 5. Apollonius of Tyana is a strong opponent of sacrifice in Περὶ Θυσιῶν (Fr. in Eus. Praep. Ev., IV, 13 = Dem. Ev., III, 3, 11); he sets the worship of God in the sphere of the νοῦς : οὕτως τοίνυν μάλιστα ἄν τις τὴν προσήκουσαν ἐπιμέλειαν ποιοῖτο τοῦ θείου . . ., εἰ . . . μὴ θύοι τι τὴν ἀρχὴν μήτε ἀνάπτοι πῦρ μήτε τι καθόλου τῶν αἰσθητῶν ἐπονομάζοι . . ., μόνῳ δὲ χρῷτο πρὸς αὐτὸν ἀεὶ τῷ κρείττονι λόγῳ (λέγω δὲ τῷ μὴ διὰ στόματος ἰόντι) . . .· νοῦς δέ ἐστιν οὗτος ὀργάνου μὴ δεόμενος, cf. Porphyr. Abst., II, 34 : δεῖ ἄρα συναφθέντας καὶ ὁμοιωθέντας αὐτῷ τὴν αὐτῶν ἀναγωγὴν θυσίαν ἱερὰν προσάγειν τῷ θεῷ, τὴν αὐτὴν δὲ καὶ ὕμνον οὖσαν καὶ ἡμῶν σωτηρίαν, ἐν ἀπαθείᾳ ἄρα τῆς ψυχῆς, τοῦ δὲ θεοῦ θεωρίᾳ ἡ θυσία αὕτη τελεῖται. Here, as also in Corp. Herm., mystical prayer takes the place of sacrifice, cf. I, 31: δέξαι λογικὰς θυσίας ἁγνὰς ἀπὸ ψυχῆς καὶ καρδίας πρὸς σὲ ἀνατεταμένης, ἀνεκλάλητε, ἄρρητε, σιωπῇ φωνούμενε, XIII, 18 : ὁ σὸς λόγος δι᾽ ἐμοῦ ὑμνεῖ σέ· δι᾽ ἐμοῦ δέξαι τὸ πᾶν λόγῳ λογικὴν θυσίαν, XIII, 21: Τὰτ θεῷ πέμπω λογικὰς θυσίας . . . Εὖ, ὦ τέκνον, ἔπεμψας δεκτὴν θυσίαν τῷ πάντων πατρὶ θεῷ, Ascl. (41a, p. 372, 13 ff.): *hoc enim sacrilegii simile est, cum deum roges, tus ceteraque incendere . . . nos agentes gratias adoremus ; haec sunt enim summi incensiones dei, gratiae cum aguntur a*

---

[36] On the ancient Gk. view of sacrifice cf. Stengel, *op. cit.*; Pfister, *op. cit.*; F. Schwenn, *Gebet und Opfer* (1927); W. F. Otto, *Dionysos* (1934), 11 ff.

mortalibus. Both the ethical criticism of literal sacrifice and the coining of a figurative and mystical concept of sacrifice are to be found in Hellenistic Judaism. [37] In Jewish authors who estimate obedience to the moral law higher than the fulfilment of cultic duties (e.g., Ep. Ar., 234: τί μέγιστόν ἐστι δόξης; ... τὸ τιμᾶν τὸν θεόν· τοῦτο δ' ἐστὶν οὐ δώροις οὐδὲ θυσίαις, ἀλλὰ ψυχῆς καθαρότητι καὶ διαλήψεως ὁσίας, Jos. Ant., 6, 147 ff. (on the basis of 1 S. 15:22): ὁ δὲ προφήτης οὐχὶ θυσίαις ἔλεγεν ἥδεσθαι τὸ θεῖον, ἀλλὰ τοῖς ἀγαθοῖς καὶ δικαίοις ... τοῖς δ' ἓν καὶ μόνον τοῦθ', ὅτι περ ἂν φθέγξηται καὶ κελεύσῃ ὁ θεὸς διὰ μνήμης ἔχουσι καὶ τεθνάναι μᾶλλον ἢ παραβῆναί τι τούτων αἱρουμένοις ἐπιτέρπεται, καὶ οὔτε θυσίαν ἐπιζητεῖ παρ' αὐτῶν), [38] there is perhaps a fusion of philosophical and prophetic influence. Philo allegorises the OT Torah of sacrifice, and he is thus able to spiritualise the concept along the lines of Hellenistic mysticism. [39] He also considers the point that a right attitude of soul in necessary in cultic offering, e.g., Spec. Leg., I, 283: δεῖ δὴ τὸν μέλλοντα θύειν σκέπτεσθαι μὴ εἰ τὸ ἱερεῖον ἄμωμον, ἀλλ' εἰ ἡ διάνοια ὁλόκληρος αὐτῷ καὶ παντελὴς καθέστηκε; *ibid.,* 191: ἄτοπον γὰρ ἕκαστον μὲν τῶν ὁλοκαυτουμένων ἀσινὲς καὶ ἀβλαβὲς ἀνευρισκόμενον καθιεροῦσθαι, τὴν δὲ τοῦ θύοντος διάνοιαν μὴ οὐ κεκαθάρθαι πάντα τρόπον καὶ πεφαιδρύνθαι λουτροῖς καὶ περιρραντηρίοις χρησαμένην, ἅπερ ὁ τῆς φύσεως ὀρθὸς λόγος δι' ὑγιαινόντων καὶ ἀδιαφόρων ὤτων ψυχαῖς φιλοθέοις ἐπαντλεῖ, *ibid.,* 277: παρὰ θεῷ ... εἶναι τίμιον ... τὸ καθαρώτατον τοῦ θύοντος πνεῦμα λογικόν, cf. 68, 293; II, 35; Deus Imm., 8. But Philo's true interest is in the inward mystic sacrifice, not in the outward form, which points beyond itself. *V.* Plant., 108: βωμοῖς γὰρ ἀπύροις, περὶ οὓς ἀρεταὶ χορεύουσι, γέγηθεν ὁ θεός, ἀλλ' οὐ πυρὶ πολλῷ φλέγουσιν, Vit. Mos., II, 108: ἡ γὰρ ἀληθὴς ἱερουργία τίς ἂν εἴη πλὴν ψυχῆς θεοφιλοῦς εὐσέβεια; Det. Pot. Ins., 21: The true θεραπεῖαι are αἱ ψυχῆς ψιλὴν καὶ μόνην θυσίαν φερούσης ἀλήθειαν, cf. Som., II, 73 f.; Spec. Leg., I, 290: οὐ τὰ ἱερεῖα θυσίαν ἀλλὰ τὴν διάνοιαν καὶ προθυμίαν ὑπολαμβάνει (sc. God) τοῦ καταθύοντος εἶναι, ἐν ᾗ τὸ μόνιμον καὶ βέβαιον ἐξ ἀρετῆς, *ibid.,* 201: νοῦς ..., ὃς ἄμωμος ὢν καὶ καθαρθεὶς καθάρσεσι ταῖς ἀρετῆς τελείας αὐτός ἐστιν ἡ εὐαγεστάτη θυσία καὶ ὅλη δι' ὅλων εὐάρεστος θεῷ, *ibid.,* 272: αὐτοὺς φέροντες πλήρωμα καλοκἀγαθίας τελειότατον τὴν ἀρίστην ἀνάγουσι θυσίαν, ὕμνοις καὶ εὐχαριστίαις τὸν εὐεργέτην καὶ σωτῆρα θεὸν γεραίροντες, τῇ μὲν διὰ τῶν φωνητηρίων ὀργάνων, τῇ δὲ ἄνευ γλώττης καὶ στόματος, μόνῃ ψυχῇ τὰς νοητὰς ποιούμενοι διεξόδους καὶ ἐκβοήσεις, ὧν ἓν μόνον οὖς ἀντιλαμβάνεται τὸ θεῖον· αἱ γὰρ τῶν ἀνθρώπων οὐ φθάνουσιν ἀκοαὶ συναισθέσθαι, cf. Ebr., 152; Plant., 126: θεῷ δὲ οὐκ ἔνεστι γνησίως εὐχαριστῆσαι δι' ὧν νομίζουσιν οἱ πολλοὶ κατασκευῶν ἀναθημάτων θυσιῶν ... ἀλλὰ δι' ἐπαίνων καὶ ὕμνων, οὐχ οὓς ἡ γεγωνὸς ᾄσεται φωνή, ἀλλὰ οὓς ὁ ἀειδὴς καὶ καθαρώτατος νοῦς ἐπηχήσει καὶ ἀναμέλψει, Spec. Leg., I, 287: the altar of God is in truth ἡ εὐχάριστος τοῦ σοφοῦ ψυχὴ παγεῖσα ἐκ τελείων ἀρετῶν ἀτμήτων καὶ ἀδιαιρέτων, cf. Leg. All., I, 50.

Everywhere in the world around early Christianity we see the literal concept of sacrifice disappearing. But the motives differ from those found in the NT.

4. The New Testament Concept of Sacrifice and the Early Church. [40]

In the first Christian literature after the NT sacrifice is a plastic image for the thought of self-giving to God. In a rather cruder spiritualising than that of Hb., Barn. regards

---

[37] Cf. Schmitz, *op. cit.,* 119 ff.; Wenschkewitz, *op. cit.,* 131 ff.

[38] Cf. also the Jewish verses interposed among Gk. poets in Cl. Al. Strom., V, 14, 119, 2 (406, 9 ff. Stählin) == Ps.-Just. De Monarchia (ed. J. C. T. v. Otto, Justini Opera, II³ [1879] p. 140, 6 ff.) == Eus. Praep. Ev., XIII, 13, 57 f.

[39] *V.* also I. Heinemann, *Philons griech. und jüd. Bildung* (1932), 66 f.

[40] Cf. R. Seeberg, *Lehrbuch der Dogmengeschichte,* I³ (1922), 150, 171 f., 457 ff., 655 ff. etc.; Harnack Dg., I, 225 ff., 231 ff. etc.; F. Loofs, *Leitfaden zum Studium der Dogmengeschichte*⁴ (1906), 213 ff.; Höfling, *op. cit., passim*; Kattenbusch, *op. cit.,* 671 ff.; Wieland,

the atoning death of Christ as the NT counterpart of the OT sacrifices (7:3 : αὐτὸς ὑπὲρ τῶν ἡμετέρων ἁμαρτιῶν ἔμελλεν τὸ σκεῦος τοῦ πνεύματος προσφέρειν θυσίαν, cf. 8:2 f.). Mart. Pol., 14, 2 compares the death of martyrs with a θυσία πίων καὶ προσδεκτή. Where the new law of Christ rules, there is no longer any material sacrifice, any ἀνθρωποποίητος προσφορά, Barn., 2, 6 (cf. Cl. Al. Strom., VII, 3, 14, 5 f.). Christians draw near to their God with the sacrifice of the heart, Barn., 2, 10; 1 Cl., 52, 2 ff. (Ps. 51:17), cf. O. Sol. 20 : "(To the Lord) I offer His spiritual sacrifice ; ... the sacrifice of the Lord is righteousness, and purity of the heart and lips"; Martyrium Apollonii, 8 : θυσίαν ἀναίμακτον καὶ καθαρὰν ἀναπέμπω κἀγὼ καὶ πάντες Χριστιανοὶ τῷ παντοκράτορι θεῷ etc. Prayer is a sacrifice, Herm. m., 10, 3, 2 f., cf. Cl. Al. Strom., VII, 6, 31, 7: ἡμεῖς δι' εὐχῆς τιμῶμεν τὸν θεόν, καὶ ταύτην τὴν θυσίαν ἀρίστην καὶ ἁγιωτάτην μετὰ δικαιοσύνης ἀναπέμπομεν, ibid., 32, 4 : καὶ γάρ ἐστιν ἡ θυσία τῆς ἐκκλησίας λόγος τῶν ἁγίων ψυχῶν ἀναθυμιώμενος, ἐκκαλυπτομένης ἅμα τῇ θυσίᾳ καὶ τῆς διανοίας ἁπάσης τῷ θεῷ, cf. ibid., 34, 2. So, too, are fasting and acts of love, Herm. s., 5, 3, 7 f., cf. Ptolemaeus, Epistle to Flora, 3 (Iren. Haer., ed. A. Stieren, I, 931)ʹ προσφορὰς προσφέρειν προσέταξεν ἡμῖν ὁ σωτήρ ... τὰς ... διὰ πνευματικῶν αἴνων καὶ δοξῶν καὶ εὐχαριστίας καὶ διὰ τῆς εἰς τὸν πλησίον κοινωνίας καὶ εὐποιίας. Prayers in worship (1 Cl., 40, 2 f.; 36, 1), including especially the eucharistic prayer (1 Cl., 44, 4; Ign. Eph., 5, 2; Phld., 4),[41] are sacrifices. There is also reference to the eucharistic prayer in Did., 14, 1: κλάσατε ἄρτον καὶ εὐχαριστήσατε προεξομολογησάμενοι τὰ παραπτώματα ὑμῶν, ὅπως καθαρὰ ἡ θυσία ὑμῶν ᾖ, in accordance with the injunction in 14, 14 that we should make the right preparation for prayer by confession of sin. The reminiscence of Mt. 5:23 f. and Mal. 1:11 in Did., 14, 2 does not compel us to think of the bringing of bread and wine for communion by the congregation, or of its offering up in the sacred feast. [42] Justin, too, can speak of the sacramental elements as θυσίαι in the light of his typological view of OT and NT worship (Dial., 41: περὶ τῶν ... ὑφ' ἡμῶν ... προσφερομένων αὐτῷ θυσιῶν, τοῦτ' ἔστι τοῦ ἄρτου τῆς εὐχαριστίας καὶ τοῦ ποτηρίου ὁμοίως τῆς εὐχαριστίας, cf. 117). But he emphasises that in Christianity only prayers really bear the character of sacrifice, Dial., 117: καὶ εὐχαὶ καὶ εὐχαριστίαι ... τέλειαι μόναι καὶ εὐάρεστοί εἰσι τῷ θεῷ θυσίαι ... ταῦτα γὰρ μόνα καὶ Χριστιανοὶ παρέλαβον ποιεῖν, καὶ ἐπ' ἀναμνήσει δὲ τῆς τροφῆς αὐτῶν ξηρᾶς τε καὶ ὑγρᾶς, ἐν ᾗ καὶ τοῦ πάθους, ὃ πέπονθε δι' αὐτοὺς ὁ υἱὸς τοῦ θεοῦ, μέμνηνται, cf. 28 f.; Apol., 9; 13; 65 ff.; Athenag. Suppl., 13 (after it has been shown that the praise of creation is the supreme sacrifice to God): δέον ἀναίμακτον θυσίαν τὴν λογικὴν προσάγειν λατρείαν. Only with Irenaeus is there relapse into pre-NT ideas of material sacrifices and true cultic offering (the sacrifice of the mass, cf. Haer., 18, 1 ff. etc.).

Behm

θώραξ → ὅπλον, πανοπλία.

Mensa und Confessio, 47 ff.; *Der vorirenäische Opferbegriff,* 34 ff.; Brinktrine, *op. cit.,* 60 ff.; Casel, *op. cit.,* 40 ff.

[41] On the figurative conception of θυσιαστήριον in Ignatius cf. Wieland, *Mensa und Confessio,* 40 ff.; *Der vorirenäische Opferbegriff,* 51 ff.; Brinktrine, *op. cit.,* 77 ff.; K. Völker, *Mysterium und Agape* (1927), 117 f.; C. C. Richardson, *The Christianity of Ignatius of Antioch* (1935), 56, 101 f., n. 9. It lives on in Cl. Al. Strom., VII, 6, 31, 8: ἔστι γοῦν τὸ παρ' ἡμῖν θυσιαστήριον ἐνταῦθα τὸ ἐπίγειον <τὸ> ἄθροισμα τῶν ταῖς εὐχαῖς ἀνακειμένων, μίαν ὥσπερ ἔχον φωνὴν τὴν κοινὴν καὶ μίαν γνώμην, or Chrys. Hom. in J., XIII, 4 (MPG, 59, 90): ἐκεῖνο μὲν γὰρ ἄψυχον τὸ θυσιαστήριον (sc. the altar of burnt offerings), τοῦτο δὲ ἔμψυχον· κἀκεῖ μὲν τὸ ἐπικείμενον ἅπαν τοῦ πυρὸς γίνεται δαπάνη ...· ἐνταῦθα δὲ οὐδὲν τοιοῦτον, ἀλλ' ἑτέρους φέρει τοὺς καρπούς ... εἰς εὐχαριστίαν ... καὶ αἶνον τοῦ θεοῦ ... θύωμεν τοίνυν ... εἰς ταῦτα τὰ θυσιαστήρια καθ' ἑκάστην ἡμέραν etc., cf. Westcott, *op. cit.,* → n. 7.

[42] So Kn. Did. on 9.

'Ιακώβ

1. In the NT the formula "Abraham, Iaac and Jacob" denotes the special relationship to God which was the boast of the Jews and which they regarded as their own prerogative. Abraham, Isaac and Jacob were the three patriarchs with whom, as representatives of Israel, God concluded His covenant. Hence the expression is a symbol of faithful or true Israel. It is thus a symbol which the Pharisees could apply especially to themselves, for they particularly had adapted themselves to the divine will and accepted "the yoke of heaven." In virtue of the covenant, the faithful Jew was sure of the coming kingdom of God; he had his citizenship. Hence "Abraham, Isaac and Jacob" might be regarded as a phrase for "sons of the kingdom." More precisely, those who had Abraham, Isaac and Jacob as their fathers were "sons of the kingdom" (→ 'Αβραάμ). Hence the saying in Mt. 8:11 par. must have seemed an unheard of paradox in the ears of the Pharisees. For it spoke of many who were outside the covenant (the ungodly) becoming sons of the kingdom, while the sons themselves were cast out.

Later Judaism found the formula "Abraham, Isaac and Jacob" in the Torah and the prophets. [1] The ideas which it linked with the expression are pregnantly expressed in 2 Macc. 1:2: "God will do you good, and will be mindful of His covenant with Abraham, Isaac and Jacob, His faithful servants." In the three patriarchs there is a prototype and guarantee of God's dealings with Israel, the covenant people, which is truly included in the patriarchs: "... let us thank the Lord our God, who tempts us as He did our fathers. Remember what He did to Abraham, and how greatly He tempted Isaac, and all that befell Jacob ..." (Jdt. 8:26).

The formula is so common in Rabbinic lit. that there is no need to adduce individual instances. It is presupposed as self-evident that God's dealings with Abraham, Isaac and Jacob are a prototype and guarantee of His relationship to the covenant people. [2]

This idea is also presupposed in the hermeneutical appeal to Ex. 3:2, 6 in Mk. 12:26; Mt. 22:32; Lk. 20:37, cf. also Ac. 3:13. The conclusion is that, as we must assume the resurrection of Abraham, Isaac and Jacob from the dead, so it is certain for their children. [3] The point of Ac. 3:13 is that it is the God of Israel who has transfigured Jesus and made Him the prince of life, so that if the Jews deny Christ they deny their own God.

The combination of the three names serves a restrictive purpose. All Jews are, and call themselves, the children of Abraham, and they are thereby drawn into the promises which were given to Abraham. But not all the descendants of Abraham or Isaac are the people of God, Israel. It is the name of Jacob which defines the

---

'Ι α κ ώ β. [1] Cf. Ex. 2:24; 3:6, 15 f.; Dt. 1:8; 6:10; 9:27; Jer. 33:26 etc.
[2] E.g., M. Ex. on 12:1: It is shown from Ex. 3:6 that Abraham, Isaac and Jacob are equivalent, and can be counted as one.
[3] Cf. 4 Macc. 7:19; 16:25.

people of the covenant. [4] Thus in Hb. 11:9 Isaac and Jacob are heirs of the promise along with Abraham. This successive limitation is reflected in Ac. 7:2-8.

Cf. Tob. 4:12: "We are descendants of the prophets: Noah, Abraham, Isaac and Jacob."

2. Paul abandons this idea that the true Israel, the true children of God, are the descendants of Jacob. For him Christians, whether Jews or Gentiles, are the true children of Abraham and the heirs of the promise made to him ($\rightarrow$ 'Αβραάμ). Quoting the OT, he does once use Jacob to indicate Israel after the flesh (R. 11:26). But in contrast to the Jewish conception he uses the OT story of the election of Jacob and the rejection of Esau to show that the counsel of God is not dependent on the right of birth (R. 9:13; $\rightarrow$ 'Ησαῦ).

3. The expression "house of Jacob" for Israel (Lk. 1:33; Ac. 7:46), for which there is precedent in the OT, is again linked with the restrictive use of the name of Jacob.

4. 1 Cl., 31, 4 f. remains within the circle of the above ideas: "Jacob fled humbly out of his country for the sake of his brother . . ., and the twelve tribes of Israel were given to him. If this is more narrowly considered, the greatness of the gifts with which he was endowed will be perceived. For from him derive all the priests and Levites who serve the altar of God. From him derives the Lord Jesus according to the flesh, from him come kings and rulers and princes through Judah." To the author, Jacob is the epitome of carnal Israel, to which belongs also Jesus according to the flesh and as High-priest. It is also worth noting that the author (32, 2) relates at once to Jacob the promise which was given to Abraham according to Gn. 15:5; 22:17. Jacob and his children, and they alone, are the true children of Abraham.

Odeberg

---

† 'Ιάννης, † 'Ιαμβρῆς [1]

1. In Jewish writings these two names are corrupt even in the texts which have come down to us. The original forms have obviously been lost in the course of the centuries. We find such different renderings of Jannes as יניס,[2] יוניס,[3] יונוס,[4] יוחנא,[5] יוחני,[6] and of Jambres as ימריס,[2] ימבריס,[3] יומברוס,[7] ממרא.[8] In the first case we can see a twofold original, the Aram. Yoḥannā, and the Gk. Iannes (cf. Shim'on, Simon). In the second we can hardly work back past the original Gk. form Iambres.

---

[4] Cf. the statement: "For three generations impurity did not disappear from our fathers: Abraham begot Ishmael, Isaac Esau, and only Jacob the twelve tribes in which there was no spot," bShab., 146a. The expression "God of Jacob" is the most important of the three expressions, "God of Abraham, God of Isaac and God of Jacob," bBer., 64a (in allusion to Ps. 20:1). Thus it can even be said that Abraham was saved only for the sake of Jacob. Abraham was preserved from death because it was foreseen that Jacob and Israel would come forth from him, Gn. r., 63 on 25:19.

'Ι α ν ν η ς κ τ λ. [1] In both cases the stress is uncertain.

[2] Tg. J., I on Ex. 1:15; 7:11; Nu. 22:22.

[3] A variant in Tg. I, *loc. cit.*

[4] Yalkut Shim'oni on Ex. 2, No. 168; Tanch. כי תשא 19 on Ex. 32:1.

[5] bMen., 85a.

[6] Ex. r., 9 on Ex. 7:11; Midrash ויושע on Ex. 15:10 (J. D. Eisenstein, *Ozar Midraschim* [1928], I, 154a).

[7] Tanch., *loc. cit.*

[8] bMen., 85a; Ex. r., *loc. cit.*; Midrash ויושע, *loc. cit.*

According to the remnants of the tradition preserved in surviving Rabb. texts, Jannes and Jambres were the magicians, or chief magicians, [9] of Pharaoh who according to Ex. 7:11 ff. deployed their magical arts against Moses and Aaron. [10] They are supposed to have cried out to Moses: "You are bringing straw to 'Afārávim," i.e., you believe that you can do something in Egypt, the home of magical arts. [11] They have been linked with Balaam as his companions, servants, [12] or sons. [13] They are supposed to have continued their opposition to Moses and Israel even after their defeat in Ex. 7. They tried to destroy Israel in its passage through the Red Sea by practising magical arts against the angels sent by God in order to restrict their miraculous power. [14] They also went with Israel through the wilderness to fight against Moses and to lead Israel astray. They were the real instigators of the apostasy of Israel at the making of the golden calf (Ex. 32). [15]

The statements concerning them are never attributed to a known author. This is an indication that they derive from a collected tradition, e.g., from a writing dealing with the story of Jannes and Jambres. It is true that there is no reference to any such work, but this applies equally to all the pseudepigraphical works from which many anonymous statements in the Rabbinic writings derive. That the traditions concerning these opponents of Moses go back to the pre-Christian era is obvious in view of their attestation in the NT.

2. 2 Tm. 3:8. The general way in which Jannes and Jambres are mentioned is in keeping with the references in Jewish sources. It cannot be said for certain to what situation there is supposed to be allusion. That the readers of the epistle know the story of Jannes and Jambres is presupposed. The reference may be to incidents developed out of Ex. 7, or to an opposition to the truth which lasted over a longer period, as in the Rabbinic accounts already mentioned. Probably the stories at issue were contained in a work which is now lost but which was numbered with the OT writings at the time of 2 Tm.

3. Later traces of a work which contained the tales of Jannes and Jambres have been detected in Origen, who mentions τὴν περὶ Μωϋσέως καὶ Ἰαννοῦ καὶ Ἰαμβροῦ ἱστορίαν, [16] and who also speaks of a Book of Jannes and Jambres. [17] Pope Gelasius in his *Decretum De Libris Recipiendis et Non Recipiendis* also mentions an apocryphal Book of Jannes and Jambres (*liber qui appellatur Paenitentia Jamne et Mambre apocryphus*). [18]

Odeberg

---

[9] Tg. J., I, on Ex. 1:15.

[10] Tg. J., I on Ex. 7:11; 1:15; bMen., 85a; Ex. r., 7 on 7:11.

[11] bMen., 85a; Ex. r., 9 on 7:12.

[12] Tg. J., I, on Nu. 22:22.

[13] Yalkut Shim'oni on Ex. 2:15, No. 168.

[14] Midrash ויושע, loc. cit.; Yalkut Shim'oni on Ex. 14:24, No. 235.

[15] Tanch. כי תשא, 15 on Ex. 32.

[16] Orig. Cels., IV, 51 (I, p. 324, 27, Koetschau).

[17] Orig. on Mt. 27:9 (only in the Lat. translation: *Item quod ait: "Sicut Iamnes et Mambres restiterunt Moysi," non invenitur in publicis libris, sed in libro secreto qui suprascribitur liber Iamnes et Mambres*).

[18] Line 303, ed. E. v. Dobschütz, TU, 3. Reihe, 8, 4 (1912), 12.

ἰάομαι, ἴασις, ἴαμα, ἰατρός → δύναμις, → θεραπεύω, → σωτήρ, → ὑγιής.

Contents : A. Sickness and Healing outside the Bible : 1. Primitive Views ; 2. Rationalisation of the Art of Healing in Ancient Medicine ; 3. Miracles of Healing, Gods of Healing and Saviour Gods in Hellenism ; 4. The Literal and Figurative Use of the Words. B. Sickness and Healing in the Old Testament and in Judaism : 1. The Religious Evaluation of Sickness ; 2. Magic and Medicine ; God the Healer (in the literal sense); 3. Healing in the

ἰ ά ο μ α ι κ τ λ. On A. 1: RGG², III, 1277 ff.; V, 1677 ff.; M. Bartels, *Die Medizin der Naturvölker* (1893); H. Vorwahl, *Geschichte der Medizin unter Berücksichtigung der Volksmedizin* (1928); J. Koty, *Die Behandlung der Alten u. Kranken bei den Naturvölkern* (1934); E. Stemplinger, *Sympathieglaube und Sympathiekuren in Altertum und Neuzeit* (1919); *Antiker Aberglaube in modernen Ausstrahlungen* (1922), esp. 19 ff., 59 ff., 75 ff.; T. Canaan, *Dämonenglaube im Lande der Bibel* (1929). On A. 2-4 : Sources : CMG (Hippocrates, Aretaeus, Galenus, Oribasius etc.); Corpus Medicorum Latinorum, ed. F. Merx and others (1915 ff.); Ael. Arist. Or. Sacr.; Philostr. Vit. Ap.; Preis. Zaub.; for the steles of Epidauros and other accounts cf. R. Herzog, "Die Wunderheilungen von Epidauros," *Philologus*, Suppl. XXII, 3 (1931), with bibl.; votive inscr., IG, II, 3, 1440 ff.; III, 1, 132 (cf. addenda 132a ff., p. 485) and IG², II/III, 3, 4351 (Athens); IG, IV, 978 ff. and IG², IV, 1, 121 ff., 236 ff., 439 ff. (Epidauros); for the Cos inscriptions cf. IG, XII, 4 and W. R. Paton and E. L. Hicks, *The Inscriptions of Cos* (1891); also R. Herzog, "Heilige Gesetze von Kos," AAB, 1928, No. 6; an Aesculapius hymn of Aristides of Smyrna has been published by R. Herzog, SAB, 1934, No. 23. Cf. Pauly-W., II, 1642 ff., esp. 1686 ff.; VI, 46 ff.; VIII, 1801 ff.; L. Friedländer, *Darstellungen aus der Sittengesch. Roms*¹⁰, I (1922), 190 ff.; C. Schneider, *Einführung in die nt.liche Zeitgesch.* (1934), 55 f., 59, 68 ff., 75, 138 ff.; I. L. Heilberg, *Geschichte der Mathematik und Naturwissenschaften im Altertum (Handbuch der Altertumswissenschaft*, V, 1, 2 [1925]); A. Rehm and K. Vogel, *Exakte Wissenschaften. Einleitung in d. Altertumswiss.*⁴, II, 5 (1933); R. Reitzenstein, *Hellenistische Wundererzählungen* (1906); O. Weinreich, *Antike Heilungswunder* (1909); K. Kerényi, *Die griechisch-orientalische Romanliteratur in religionsgeschichtlicher Beleuchtung* (1927); R. Söder, "Die apokryphen Apostelgeschichten u. die romanhafte Lit. in der Antike," *Würzburger Studien z. Altertumswiss.*, 3 (1932); P. Cavvadias, *Fouilles d'Epidaure*, I (1891); Τὸ ἱερὸν τοῦ Ἀσκληπιοῦ ἐν Ἐπιδαύρῳ (1900); *Kos, Ergebnisse der deutschen Ausgrabungen*, ed. R. Herzog, I : *Asklepieion* (1932); *Koische Forschungen und Funde* (1899), esp. 202 ff. (cf. → δύναμις, II, 284, Bibl.). On B. : "Auszüge aus den ausserbiblischen Quellen in deutscher Übersetzung" (also covering A. in part) in P. Fiebig, *Die Umwelt des NT* (1926), 38 ff., 49 ff.; P. Fiebig, *Jüdische Wundergeschichten* (1911); Kl. T., No. 78/79 (in the originals, also covering A.); Str.-B., *passim*; cf. also RE³, XI, 64 ff.; I. Benzinger, *Hebräische Archäologie* (1927), 187 ff.; B. Stade-A. Bertholet, *Biblische Theologie des AT* (1905/ 11), Index, *s.v.*, "Krankheit," "Leiden," "Heilkunst," "Ärzte"; E. Balla, "Das Problem des Leidens in der Geschichte der israelitisch-jüdischen Religion," in *Eucharisterion für H. Gunkel* (1923), 214 ff.; S. Krauss, *Talmudische Archäologie*, I (1910), 252 ff.; M. Neubauer, *Die Medizin im Flavius Josephus* (1919); L. Blau, *Das altjüdische Zauberwesen*² (1914); A. Schlatter, *Das Wunder in der Synagoge* (1912). On C. : F. Fenner, *Die Krankheit im NT* (1930, with additional bibl.); M. Dibelius, *Die Formgeschichte des Evangeliums*² (1933), esp. 51 ff., 69 ff., 166 ff., 290 f. (cf. Index); Bultmann Trad., 223 ff.; *Jesus* (1926), 158 ff.; K. Beth, *Die Wunder Jesu* (1914); M. Goguel, *Das Leben Jesu* (1934), 124 ff.; F. Barth, *Die Hauptprobleme des Lebens Jesu*⁵ (1918), sctn. 3 : K. Knur, *Christus Medicus ?* (1905); R. Jelke, *Die Wunder Jesu* (1922); J. Ninck, *Jesus als Charakter*³ (1925), Index, *s.v.* "Krankenheilungen;" H. Schlingensiepen, "Die Wunder des NT," BFTh, 2. Reihe, 28 (1933); O. Perels, *Die Wunder-Überlieferung . . .* = BWANT, IV, 12 (1934); H. Seng, *Zur Frage der religiösen Heilungen* (1926); "Die Heilungen Jesu in medizinischer Beleuchtung" (*Arzt und Seelsorger*, 4, 1926); H. Grossmann, *Die nt.lichen Wunder* (1927); W. Beyer, *Gibt es Heilungen von körperlicher Krankheit durch Geisteskraft ?* (1921); *Jesus und seine Wunder im Lichte der kommenden Naturwissenschaft* (1922); E. Liek, *Das Wunder in der Heilkunde* (1930); B. Aschner, *Die Krise der Medizin* (1928); E. R. Micklem, *Miracles and the New Psychology. A Study on the Healing Miracles of the NT* (1922); A. Fridrichsen, "Le Problème du Miracle dans le Christianisme Primitif" (*Études d'Histoire et de Philosophie Religieuses*, 12 [1925]). → θεραπεύω, 128 ff. On D. : A. Harnack, "Medizinisches

Figurative Sense. C. Sickness and Healing in the New Testament: 1. Sickness and the Art of Healing in the Light of the New Testament; 2. Jesus the Physician. The Use of the Terms in the Gospels; 3. Jesus' Miracles of Healing in the Light of the History of Religion: a. Tradition; b. The Nature of the Miracles; c. The Accomplishment of the Cure; d. Concluding Theological Appraisal; the Uniqueness of Jesus' Miracles of Healing; 4. The Transmission of the Gift of Healing to the Disciples. Healing in the Apostolic Age. D. The Gospel of the Healer and of Healing in the Early Church.

A. Sickness and Healing outside the Bible.

1. Primitive Views.

At all stages of life sickness makes a profound and at first incomprehensible incision. About the only thing that primitive man can understand as a cause of physical ailment is the wound received in battle. By way of analogy he comes to regard sicknesses which he cannot understand as "attacks." The assailants suspected are more or less personally conceived evil powers which either strike man down, bombard him with less powerful but more artful shots, or even take possession of him. He expects healing through the overcoming of these hostile powers by magic, if necessary by countermagic, or by propitiatory offerings. The former is exercised through analogical magic or through substances which are regarded as conveying superior vital force or powerful mana, e.g., spittle (→ ἐκπτύω), blood (→ αἷμα) etc. Along with the luxuriant imagination which contributed to this view we have also to reckon with the actual experience of the healing properties of plants and animals, which plays an increasing role. The beginnings of rational treatment, however, are not linked with magic. It would thus be exaggerated to describe magic as the root of medicine.

2. Rationalisation of the Art of Healing in Ancient Medicine.

Medicine was first developed among the ancient Egyptians in the third millennium. But it was the Greeks who first established the art of healing on an empirical and rational foundation.

Our knowledge of Egyptian medicine is derived from seven papyri (1900-1250 B.C.). [1] The most important of these is the Ebers Papyrus (c. 1550 B.C., now in Leipzig). But the underlying texts are older than the collections, and the main development came between 2600 and 1600. The anatomical views of the ancient Egyptians rest on a strange blend of research and theory. Doctors apparently played no part in mummifying, though the removal of the entrails took place through the abdominal cavity without affecting the breast. Therapy was rated quite highly. The lancing of sores, the setting of broken bones, the stitching of wounds and the filling of teeth were all practised. Several drugs were more or less purposefully used, especially, though not exclusively, those of animal origin. The Ebers pap. also describes a primitive inhalation apparatus. In a prescription against worms we do also find an exorcism. Often the chief physician to the king will also be the high-priest and the chief of the magicians as well. But Grapow observes: "It is obvious that Egyptian medicine degenerates into magic, not that it develops out of it." [2] Egyptian doctors were highly esteemed among the Greeks (Hom. Od., 4, 220-

---

in der ältesten Kirchengeschichte," TU, VIII, 4 (1892); *Mission und Ausbreitung*[4] (1924), I, 129 ff.; J. Ott, "Die Bezeichnung Christi als ἰατρός in der urchristlichen Literatur," in *Der Katholik,* 90 (1910), 454 ff.

[1] H. Grapow, *Untersuchungen über die altägyptischen medizinischen Papyri,* I (1935); "Über die anatomischen Kenntnisse der altägyptischen Ärzte," *Morgenland,* 26 (1935); an excellent general review of Egyptian medicine by the same author may also be found in the *Münchener Medizinische Wochenschrift,* 82 (1935), 958 ff., 1002 ff. (also printed separately).

[2] Grapow, *Münchener Med. Wochenschrift,* 960.

232; Hdt., II, 84; also Diodorus). We do not have sufficient information as to the connections between Egyptian and Greek medicine. These exist, for a primitive means of establishing pregnancy is almost identical in pap. Berlin and Hippocrates.

Homer values the physician very highly (Il., 11, 514 : ἰητρὸς γὰρ ἀνὴρ πολλῶν ἀντάξιος ἄλλων). But there is a still a carefree mixture of medicine and magic even in the treatment of wounds. True medicine arises from the 6th century onwards in the colonies of Asia Minor, Greater Greece and Africa, as the doctors themselves develop into a kind of guild. Doctors are publicly appointed and a special levy is raised to pay them. The Hippocratic oath bears fine witness to the growing ethics of the profession. The decisive sentences are as follows : "I will follow that method of treatment which, according to my ability and judgment, I consider for the benefit of my patients, and abstain from whatever is deleterious and mischievous. I will give no deadly medicine to anyone if asked, nor suggest any such counsel ; furthermore, I will not give to a woman an instrument to produce abortion. With purity and with holiness (ἁγνῶς δὲ καὶ ὁσίως) I will pass my life and practise my art. I will not cut a person who is suffering with a stone, but will leave this to be done by practitioners of this work. Into whatever houses I enter, I will go into them for the benefit of the sick and will abstain from every voluntary art of mischief and corruption ; and further from the seduction of females or males, bond or free. Whatever, in connection with my professional practice, or not in connection with it, I may see or hear in the lives of men which ought not to be spoken abroad, I will not divulge, as reckoning that all such should be kept secret." Alcmaion of Croton (c. 500 B.C.) and Hippocrates of Cos (c. 420 B.C.) were not only pioneers and discoverers ; they also founded famous schools. Six schools may be distinguished in the 5th century, the Crotonic, the Coic, the Cnidic, the Sicilian, the Athenian and the Aeginetic. Empiricism reached its highest point under the Ptolemies with dissection, and even the vivisection of condemned criminals. Under the Roman empire the specialisation introduced in Egypt at the time of Herodot. was further developed with specialists in eyes, teeth, ears and women etc.[3] The skilful doctor was highly esteemed and wealthy. The brother of the physician of Claudius, Q. Stertinius, estimated his practice at 600,000 sesterces. Galen (d. 199 A.D.) carried on part of his practice by letter. He was the last great medical writer and was astonishingly productive. Oribasius (4th century) was merely a compiler.

3. Miracles of Healing, Gods of Healing and Saviour Gods in Hellenism.

We must not form exaggerated ideas as to the general spread of scientific medicine. Alongside it there flourished in every age superstition and religion. The boundaries are fluid. Religion was recognised as an independent force by medicine, nor did it wholly scorn to make alliance with the latter. From around the 1st century A.D. the scientific enlightenment was checked by a new growth of religion, and also of superstition.

Plato had some strange anatomical ideas (Tim., 91). From the standpoint of natural science Barn., 10, 6 ff. is not very profound for its age. C. 138 A.D. Aesculapius prescribed for blindness a salve composed of the blood of a white hen and honey (Ditt. Syll.[3], 1173, 15 ff.).

Often sickness is regarded as a punishment sent by angry gods. In sickness there might even be resort to unknown gods, as may be seen from the reported sacrifice of

---

[3] In Papias Fr., III (Catena in Acta SS Apostt., ed. J. A. Cramer [1838], 12) there is reference to the διόπτρα as an instrument of the doctor. Magnifying glasses and microscopes are in use even amongst the Jews c. 150 A.D. according to Gn. r., 4 on Gn. 1:6 (Str.-B., I, 559). Rich Jewesses have artificial teeth of gold or silver (Shab., 6, 5; bShab., 65a), and even more so other women.

Epimenides in Athens τῷ προσήκοντι θεῷ (Diog. L., I, 110). Serapis sends sickness because insufficient attention is paid to his command to build the temple (P. Greci e Latini, IV [1917], No. 435). In ancient times the real Greek god both of pestilence and of healing is Apollo (cf. Hom. Il., I, 42 ff.; → I, 397). Later Aesculapius is particularly popular as a god of healing. How highly regarded he was may be seen from the fact that Augustine caused Turullius, one of the murderers of Caesar, to be executed because he chopped down the cypress grove of the Coic Aesculapieion in order to build the fleet of Antonius (Dio C., 51, 8, 2). Xenophon of Cos dedicated a temple to Nero as Aesculapius. Among the sanctuaries of the god, Epidauros — an ancient Lourdes — was easily the most renowned. [4] There were others at Athens, Cos, Pergamos, where Aelius Aristides stayed in the 2nd century, on the island in the Tiber at Rome etc.; the Amphiareion at Oropos served a similar purpose. Since incubation, the temple sleep, was supposed to be of therapeutic value, there were places in which to lie down within the precincts. At Epidauros there stood in the midst the *tholos* of the yr. Polycletus (c. 350 B.C.) mentioned by Pausanias (II, 27, 3). This was neither a covered spring nor a cage of serpents, let alone a music pavilion ; it was a round temple for processions and sacrifices, with labyrinthine foundations and a ramp at the entrance. A stadium and theatre catered for the entertainment of guests. Pregnant women and the dying were not admitted within the walls of the sacred precincts. Only in Roman days were premises built for them outside. Innumerable votive offerings (representations of healed limbs) [5] and inscriptions [6] bear witness of the gratitude to the god, and to the priests, [7] of those who were cured, though Aristophanes lashes their conduct in his Plutos. Less imposing, but particularly functional, was the Aesculapieion at Cos excavated by R. Herzog. The terraces and broad staircases must have been especially charming. Regard for health and healing was here more important than the cultus. Particular stress was laid on an open situation, on large rooms, and on abundant water. Pillared halls, long corridors and several subsidiary buildings provided accommodation for the guests. A system of piped water was installed by Nero's physician, Xenophon of Cos. The sinter with its rich deposit suggests that mineral waters were used. In later Roman times there was a toilet, with running water, and also a thermal installation. In view of the proximity of the city there was no need for a gymnasium, stadium or theatre. A library existed from the 1st century. Herond. Mim., 4 gives us a fine depiction of the visit of a family to offer sacrifice at Cos, with a tour of the magnificent sanctuary.

The Aesculapieion at Pergamos has also been discovered. The mineral spring was found in 1931 and is again a place of healing.

The relationship between the practice of medicine and miraculous healing is more complicated that might appear at a first glance. [8]

The discovery of medical instruments makes it quite certain that doctors took part in the healing procedures at the Aesculapieion at Cos. On the other hand, there are here no inscriptions referring to miraculous cures. Yet there is no confirmation of the older view that surgical operations were undertaken at Epidauros during the temple sleep. The inscriptions provide no trace either of doctors or of priestly charlatanry.

---

[4] Cf. the works in the bibl. on this point.
[5] Cf. for examples Haas, 13/14 (1928): a leg with varicose veins (140), ears and hands (142).
[6] Examples in Cavvadias, *Fouilles d'Epidaure*, 32 ff.; cf. also → 194, Bibl. A. 2-4 : Sources. In the votive inscriptions we often find mention not only of Aesculapius, but also of his daughter Hygieia, and on one occasion there is the significant dedication Ἀσκληπιῶι καὶ Ὑγιείαι καὶ τῶι Ὕπνωι (Athens, Ditt. Syll.³, III, 1143).
[7] Cf. the thanksgiving stele of someone cured at Athens (2nd cent. A.D. : Εὔνεικος Γαΐῳ Πεινσρίῳ χαριστήριον εἰσθείς. BCH, 51 (1927), 281.
[8] Herzog, *Wunderheilungen*, 149.

In the case of Oropos, the votive relief of Archinos [9] does not point in this direction. The supposed knife is really a spatula with which the god applies salve to cure the bite of the sacred snake. At Piraeus, however, surgical knives and clippers are listed in the inventory, not as votive offerings, but for use in the sanctuary (Ditt. Syll.[3], I, 144, 16 f.).

Obviously no clear-cut distinction can be made between the two systems. The fact that doctors saw in Aesculapius their patron saint bears witness to the presence of a religious impulse in them too. [10] A particularly difficult problem is raised by epilepsy, which was popularly regarded as ἱρὴ νοῦσος. Hippocrates, or a like-minded pupil, explained it in terms of a sickness of the brain which could be cured by medicine. But he does not exclude divine aid, for he recommends ἱκετεύειν τοὺς θεούς (incubation) and combines natural and supernatural therapy in the beautiful and basically significant sentence: πάντα θεῖα καὶ πάντα ἀνθρώπινα. The physician Menecrates of Syracuse, who seems to have been surprisingly successful in curing epilepsy, apparently through suggestion, regarded himself as Zeus. [11] The ἰάματα of Epidauros (23), perhaps deliberately, did not accept the Hippocratic view, but argued in favour of exorcism by means of a ring held at the openings of the head (→ II, 7). Nevertheless, their polemic against the unskilled "sons of the god" who could not bind up again a head which had been cut open for a tape-worm operation, is not really directed against professional doctors, as was once supposed, but against priestly competition at Troas. [12] And the god increasingly gives dietetic directions of a medical character (→ 208 f.).

Miraculous healings are also reported of high-placed personages.

The emperors Vespasian and Hadrian are supposed to have cured the blind and the lame by touch and by spittle. [13] A typical thaumaturge (θεῖος ἄνθρωπος), to be understood as an independent development of vanishing antiquity rather than as a rival, pagan saviour, [14] is Apollonius of Tyana. The healing stories of antiquity have their own distinctive features (→ 206).

In Greek religion, however, the concept of healing is much broader and deeper. The gods are doctors and saviours both in a cosmic and universal sense and also in an inward sense. The typically Greek thought form of analogy leads here to a particular conception of divine rule in the world. The gods become mediators between Zeus and men, and as such they dispense healing. This is particularly true of Aesculapius. The spiritualised religion of Aesculapius may be compared to some extent with Christianity. Its victorious march begins with Plato and reaches its climax with Aelius Aristides. [15] Even with Julian this enthusiastic religiosity fructifies the opposition to Christianity by way of reaction against it.

In Plato the doctor Eryximachos sings the praises of his tutelary lord, Aesculapius, who according to the poets is the founder of medicine (Symp., 186e). Plato, however, finds an even more comprehensive embodiment of the divine power to heal in Eros.

---

[9] Op. cit.
[10] The Aesculapieion at Cos was founded only after the death of Hippocrates in the 4th century. This disposes of the later legend that Hippocrates learned his medicine from the pinakes of those cured in the Aesculapieion. But the Coic Aesculapiads had a hereditary cult of Aesculapius long before, Herzog, op. cit., 141.
[11] O. Weinreich, "Menekrates, Zeus und Salmoneus," Tübinger Beiträge zur Altertumswissenschaft, 18 (1933).
[12] There seems to be here the clever exploitation of a malicious rumour which was circulating concerning Epidauros. Herzog, Wunderheilungen, 78.
[13] Weinreich AH, 112 f., 66, 68, 73 f.
[14] Cf. C. Schneider, op. cit., 10.
[15] Cf. O. Kern, Die Religion der Griechen, II (1935), 303 ff.

On Eros depend gymnastics, agriculture and music as well as medicine. Among the gods Eros is man's greatest friend (θεῶν φιλανθρωπότατος), a helper and physician who liberates from those evils whose curing is the greatest boon for man (ἐπίκουρός τε ὢν τῶν ἀνθρώπων καὶ ἰατρὸς τούτων, ὧν ἰαθέντων μεγίστη εὐδαιμονία ἂν τῷ ἀνθρωπείῳ γένει εἴη, Symp., 189d). He it is who puts together again the separated parts, male, female, and androgynous, of original man, and who thus restores wholeness to human nature (καταστήσας ἡμᾶς εἰς τὴν ἀρχαίαν φύσιν καὶ ἰασάμενος μακαρίους καὶ εὐδαίμονας ποιῆσαι, Symp., 193d). Heavenly, i.e., chaste love [16] is the spiritual and physical fulfilment of human nature.

Aelius Aristides [17] discerned the help of his special god Aesculapius in the curing of a persistent neurasthenia. With other healing gods, the god was for him a kind of mediating figure who embodied the healing presence of the supreme god, Zeus. Apollo declares to men the infallible pronouncement of Zeus καὶ 'Ασκληπιὸς ἰᾶται οὓς ἰᾶσθαι Διὶ φίλτερον, along with Athene, Hera and Artemis (Or., 43, 25 [Keil]). An inscription from Asia Minor in honour of an unnamed god of healing bears witness to genuine fervour: Δαίμονι φιλανθρώπῳ νέῳ 'Ασκληπιῷ ἐπιφανεῖ μεγίστῳ. [18]

For Julian, Aesculapius is a conscious and deliberate alternative to the Saviour of Christianity. Zeus begot Aesculapius of himself in the intelligible world (ἐν τοῖς νοητοῖς), and caused him to appear on earth through the vital force of Helios-Mithra. When Aesculapius had come from heaven to earth, he appeared at Epidauros in the form of a man (ἐν ἀνθρώπου μορφῇ, cf. Phil. 2:7), and from there, by missionary extension, he established his healing sway over the whole earth (πληθυνόμενος ταῖς προόδοις ἐπὶ πᾶσαν ὤρεξε τὴν γῆν τὴν σωτήριον ἑαυτοῦ δεξιάν). Hence he is now omnipresent on land and sea. He does not come to every one of us individually, but he cures sick souls and bodies (ἐπανορθοῦται ψυχὰς πλημμελῶς διακειμένας καὶ τὰ σώματα ἀσθενῶς ἔχοντα, Contra Christianos, 200a b). Cf. Or., 4, 144b: ἐπεὶ δὲ καὶ ὅλην ἡμῖν τὴν τῆς εὐταξίας ζωὴν συμπληροῖ, γεννᾷ μὲν ἐν κόσμῳ τὸν 'Ασκληπιόν, ἔχει δὲ αὐτὸν καὶ πρὸ τοῦ κόσμου παρ' ἑαυτῷ. A pagan counterpart of Jn. 1:1!

The goal of this healing activity of the gods is human happiness. This is predominantly understood in natural terms.

4. The Literal and Figurative Use of the Words.

a. For the words as a whole the literal use is predominant.

ἰᾶσθαι etc. are used lit. in Homer, Plato and Galen; Ditt. Syll.³, 1168, 108, 113 and 117; 1169, 7 and 53; P. Oxy., VIII, 1151, 25; ἴασις, Hippocr. Aphorismi, 2, 17; ἰατρός, Hom. Il., 11, 514; ἰατρὸς ὀφθαλμῶν, κεφαλῆς, ὀδόντων, Hdt., II, 84 etc.

b. It is in keeping with the Greek tendency to think analogically that these terms which are originally medical should be extended to other fields in the sense of "to restore," "to make good."

As we have said above (→ 198), ἰατρός is an appellation attached to several deities, Apollo (Aristoph. Av., 584, the Hippocratic oath, coins from Asia Minor), Aesculapius (Stob. Ecl., I, 38, 20: θείῳ ἰατρὸς τ' 'Ασκληπιοῦ ὀλβιοδῶτα), Dionysus (Plut. Convivalium Disputationum, III, 1, 3 [II, 647a]), Aphrodite (Plut. Praec. Coniug., 38

---

[16] In the first instance what is meant is pederasty. Plato idealises it, and seeks safeguards against licentiousness in every form. True Eros is the impulse which draws man upwards. The dubious features in this view have been much discussed in modern theology. There is a defence of Plato in C. Ritter, *Platonische Liebe, Übersetzung und Erläuterung des Symposions* (1931) → ἀγάπη, I, 35 ff.

[17] O. Weinreich, "Typisches und Individuelles in der Religion des Aelius Aristides," N. Jbch. Kl. Alt., 17 (1914), 597 ff.

[18] Weinreich, *op. cit.*, 599.

[II, 143d]), the nymphs in Elis (Hesych., *s.v.*) etc.[19] Selene, under the right sign, brings good fortune : τῶν φαύλων (πραγμάτων) ἴασιν ἀποτελεῖ (Vett. Val., IV, 18). The Greeks also seem to have brought the name Jason into etymological connection with ἰᾶσθαι. This is shown by its feminine counterpart, the name of the daughter of Aesculapius and the healing goddess Iaso (Ion. Ἰησώ, Herond. Mim., 4, 6). That Aesculapius himself was called Iasios[20] cannot be substantiated.[21] On the similarity to Ἰησοῦς → 214 f.

Often the reference is to the removal of intellectual deficiencies : δύσγνοιαν ἰᾶσθαι, Eur. Herc. Fur., 1107; ἴασιν ποιήσασθαι τῆς ... ἀδυναμίας ἐν τοῖς λόγοις, Luc. Jup. Trag., 28; sometimes also to the avenging of wrongs. Thus in Eur. Or., 650 Orestes says to Menelaus that Agamemnon went to Troy οὐκ ἐξαμαρτὼν αὐτός, ἀλλ᾽ ἁμαρτίαν | τῆς σῆς γυναικὸς ἀδικίαν τ᾽ ἰώμενος. The politician can be the ἰατρὸς τῆς πόλεως (Thuc., VI, 14). In Platonic philosophy the medical argumentation is constitutive of what Plato understands by philosophy, Gorg., 521c/522a. Only thus can we understand the constant parallels drawn between gymnastics and legislation, ἰατρική and the penal code (Gorg., 464b), also music (Symp., 187a ff.). Plato ascribes to the lawgiver the task of healing, if possible, the unlawful pursuit of gain, which is a sickness of the soul (ἴασις τῆς ἀδικίας, Leg., IX, 862c). Epictetus describes the philosophical school as ἰατρεῖον. We should not come out of it merrily, but full of sorrow (Diss., III, 23, 30). In such contexts man is usually the subject.

B. Sickness and Healing in the Old Testament and Judaism.

1. The Religious Evaluation of Sickness.

The primitive explanation of sickness applies specifically in Israel to mental sickness, sexual discharge, leprosy and death. These things are originally unclean because they are ascribed to the work of demons. Fear of demons becomes especially strong again in Judaism, probably under the influence of Persian dualism and in connection with the purification of the concept of God.[22] In the first instance recognition of the natural causes of disease is little developed. But it is not lacking altogether, as may be seen from the beginnings of rational hygiene. The two modes of approach are present without any sharp lines of differentiation. The conviction steadily gains ground that it is Yahweh who sends or withholds sickness. Through this religious evaluation sickness is brought into a positive context. To the righteous in times of severe affliction it is a sign of God's wrath. Experience of such affliction, and of deliverance from it, is reflected in many psalms, though the usage may sometimes be figurative (32; 38; 51; 88; 91; 107:17-22). Particularly impressive is the story of Hezekiah's sickness, and the accompanying psalm, which arose out of personal experience, even though it was perhaps transferred later to Hezekiah (Is. 38, esp. 10-20; cf. 2 K. 20:1 ff.).[23] Leprosy (צָרַעַת, which literally denotes being smitten [by God], and is often used with נֶגַע, "stroke,"

---

[19] ἰατρός (or ἰητήρ) is often a predicate of deity in hymns, in which there are also many requests for healing. Many examples are given by H. Keyssner, "Gottesvorstellung und Lebensauffassung im griech. Hymnus," *Würzburger Studien z. Altertumswiss.,* II (1932), 113 f.

[20] A. Drews, *Die Christusmythe* (1924), 34, though no instances are given.

[21] Cf. Roscher, II, 1 *s.v.* Iasion, Iasios, Iaso, Iason, Iasos. Iasion is the beloved of Demeter and the father of Pluto.

[22] For a review of older Jewish demonology cf. Str.-B., IV, 501 ff. On the cause of sicknesses, 524 f. For parallels from more modern Palestine, cf. T. Canaan, and from Eastern Europe, G. M. Löwen, *Ein Tag aus dem Leben eines gesetzestreuen Juden* (1911). Rab is supposed to have derived 99% of all sicknesses from the evil eye.

[23] J. Begrich, *Der Psalm des Hiskia* (1926).

"mark"), is regarded as a mark of divine shame, as though a father were to spit in the face of his child (Nu. 12:14). The question of its origin is particularly tormenting for the righteous if the cause of divine displeasure cannot be seen. In part, this is the problem of the Book of Job. Things are easier when a particular cause can be assigned. This may be removed, or there may be repentance (2 S. 12:15 ff.; 24:15).

Judaism was able to apply its central doctrine of retribution with great virtuosity even to sickness (cf. Jn. 9:2). It can ascribe a particular fault to each sickness, and to each fault a punishment. Ulcers and dropsy are on account of immorality and licentiousness, quinsy on account of neglecting tithes, leprosy on account of blasphemy, bloodshed and perjury, epilepsy and the crippling of children on account of marital infidelity. Even the sins of infants in their mothers' wombs might be causes of sickness. [24] The law of cause and effect was applied in a way which was particularly oppressive and devastating. But Judaism could also allow that some sicknesses helped to alleviate eternal pains or were chastisements of love (יִסּוּרִין שֶׁל אַהֲבָה) which had no particular cause but which, if borne with humility and resignation, would confirm the knowledge of the Torah and lead to the remission of all sins. [25]

2. Magic and Medicine; God the Healer (in the literal sense).

Belief in Yahweh quickly discredited magic in Israel, but it was not completely eradicated.

Even in Judaism of the Talmudic period conjurations, exorcisms and sympathetic cures play a significant role. [26] In this originally animistic context spittle also appears as a means of healing. [27]

The first beginnings of rational medicine in early days probably go back to Egyptian (Gn. 50:2) and later Greek influences. The great prophets presuppose that there are doctors and balsam to help wounds to heal (Is. 3:7: חֹבֵשׁ, Jer. 8:22 : רֹפֵא ﬩ ἰατρός). Rules of hygiene are given in the Wisdom literature (Sir. 19:2 f.; 30:14 ff., 23 f.; 31 (34): 20 ff.; 37:27 ff.). Rabbinic Judaism attaches high value to vegetable means of healing, including oil (→ ἔλαιον) and wine (Lk. 10:34). Anatomy (embryo section) and surgery (settings, trepanation etc.) are also regarded with respect.

But the true and only doctor is Yahweh. To define the relationship between His creative power and human skill is more difficult than in the non-biblical world. Yet the tendency is towards a both-and rather than an either-or, with the accent on the ultimately omnicausal power of Yahweh.

The man of God, originally a medicine man charged with an impersonal *mana*, becomes the commissioned agent of Yahweh (2 K. 5; Is. 38:21 etc.). Alongside him is the priest, who for cultic reasons is put in charge of health in the Torah (Lv. 13:49 ff.; 14:2 ff.; cf. Mt. 8:4 par.; Lk. 17:14). Ex. 15:26 : אֲנִי יהוה רֹפְאֶךָ, is not meant exclusively, but it approaches exclusiveness. Asa is blamed for resorting to physicians rather than to Yahweh in his sickness (2 Ch. 16:12). The ways in which the wise are able to commend the art of the physician in Sir. 38 are singular enough. God has made him, v. 1, 12; sometimes he can help us because he prays to God, v. 13 f.; the apothecary is included in v. 7; scriptural proof is adduced in v. 5. Notwithstanding the high position of medicine in Ptolemaic Egypt, the attitude of the LXX is not wholly positive. It repeatedly ex-

---

[24] Str.-B., II, 193 ff., 527 ff.; Jn. 9:2.
[25] Str.-B., II, 193; I, 495.
[26] *Ibid.*, I, 627; II, 15, 17; IV, 773; I, 652; IV, 527 ff. → ἐξορκίζω.
[27] *Ibid.*, I, 216; II, 15 ff.; IV, 773.

presses its view in remarkable misreadings of the Heb. ψ 87:10 : μὴ τοῖς νεκροῖς ποιήσεις θαυμάσια; ἢ ἰατροὶ ἀναστήσουσιν . . . ; "Wilt thou (God) show wonders to the dead? can the physicians awaken them?" Mas. אִם־רְפָאִים יָקוּמוּ, "Will the spirits of the dead arise?" The LXX reads אִם־רֹפְאִים יְקִימוּ. Cf. also Is. 26:14 : οὐδὲ ἰατροὶ οὐ μὴ ἀναστήσωσιν, Mas. רְפָאִים בַּל יָקֻמוּ. In the positive statement in Is. 26:19 : ἡ γὰρ δρόσος (dew) ἡ παρὰ σοῦ ἴαμα αὐτοῖς ἐστιν, ἡ δὲ γῆ τῶν ἀσεβῶν πεσεῖται, it cannot be said with certainty whether the expression ἴαμα is due to the undoubted misunderstanding of רְפָאִים. At Sir. 43:22 we have the equation δρόσος = ἴαμα in respect of dew in the literal sense. There is genuine recognition in Sir. 38:7 f., which tells us that through the physician εἰρήνη comes on the earth (cf. 1:18 : εἰρήνη καὶ ὑγίεια ἰάσεως in the figur. sense).

Philo, too, gives occasional recognition, e.g., to good doctors who gladly render their services even when they see that the sick are incurable (Sacr. AC, 123). On the other hand, he blames those who, instead of trusting in God the Saviour, resort to means of help in creation : ἰατρούς, βοτάνας, φαρμάκων συνθέσεις, δίαιταν ἠκριβωμένην, τἆλλα πάνθ' ὅσα παρὰ τῷ θνητῷ γένει βοηθήματα. He also blames those who mock the one who points the sick to the μόνος ἰατρός (Sacr. AC, 70).

Later Palestinian Judaism has even stronger, though not insuperable, reservations in respect of doctors. "Do not dwell in a city whose leader is a doctor," and even : "Do not drink any medicines. Do not jump over streams. Do not allow your teeth to be pulled. Do not irritate any snake or Aramaean" (bPes., 113a). On the other hand : "Woe to the city whose doctor suffers from gout" (Lv. r., 5, 6 on Lv. 4:3). One should seek to live in a place where there is a worthy doctor, and one should call him in when there is sickness. There is a doctor in the temple for priests who are sick with abdominal complaints. Many rabbis were doctors by profession, and even practised as such. A Jewish prayer at blood-letting runs : "May it be Thy will, O Lord my God, that this action may serve to heal me, and do Thou heal me, for Thou, O God, art the true Physician, and Thine healing is true. The practice of men to let themselves be healed is followed only because it is a custom" (bBer., 60a).

Prayer is thus the chief means of healing. That it was originally linked with the cultus seems to be proved by many references to place, to time, to dress and to penitential exercises in the psalms of complaint (Ps. 5:3, 7; 28:2; 38:6; 42:9; 88:13 etc.). Yet most of these psalms contain free utterances of the individual who thus prays. There is a regular pattern of complaint, of petition for healing, and of thanksgiving that God has heard (Ps. 6; 16:10; 30:2; 32:3 f.; 38; 41:4; 51:7 f.; 103:3; 107:17 ff. 147:3). The context often shows that the concept of healing is carried over into other spheres (→ 3.). But the literal use is the original one.

The Rabbis, too, make it a duty that the sick should pray and that the healthy should intercede for them, which is no less meritorious a work than visiting the sick.

The frontier between the hearing of prayer and miraculous healing is fluid. OT examples of the latter are the account of the brazen serpent (Nu. 21:8 f.) and the cleansing of Naaman (2 K. 5). The raising of the dead at 1 K. 17:20 ff. and 2 K. 4:33 f. is in answer to prayer. The healings of the most famous thaumaturge of the Synagogue, Chanina ben Dosa (c. 70 A.D.) seem to be recorded only as answers to prayer.

Cf. bBer., 34b (Str.-B., II, 441): Chanina sees from the fluency of his prayer whether it is heard. It was later said of him : "After Chanina ben Dosa died, men of deeds (i.e., thaumaturges) ceased" (T. Sot., 15, 5). There is no record of the gift of healing among the rabbis at the time of Jesus (though cf. Mt. 12:27 par.). This gift is not an indispensable rabbinic qualification (→ 129).

3. Healing in the Figurative Sense.

Yahweh is in general the One who heals by withdrawing His judgment in the form of sickness or of personal or national calamity (Gn. 20:17; Ex. 15:26; Hos. 6:1; 7:1; 11:3, and frequently in the psalms). ἰάομαι and its alternatives are common in the figurative sense in Jer.: 3:22; 17:14; 37(30):17 etc. Cf. also Is. 7:4 LXX and Zech. 10:2. In the latter verse the LXX introduces, without any basis in the Mas. (it reads רֹפֵא for רֹעֶה), the formula οὐκ ἦν ἴασις, which is found elsewhere (e.g., Jer. 14:19; Prv. 29:1), mostly in a figurative sense.[28] An indispensable prerequisite of healing is the remission of sins, which for its part is dependent on repentance and conversion. Hence healing and remission are closely linked (Is. 6:10; ψ 6:2; 29:2; 40:4: ἴασαι τὴν ψυχήν μου, ὅτι ἥμαρτόν σοι, ψ 102:3: τὸν εὐιλατεύοντα πάσαις ταῖς ἀνομίαις σου, τὸν ἰώμενον πάσας τὰς νόσους σου). ἰᾶσθαι can even be a technical term for God's gracious turning to save. Behind this is the idea of binding up a wound; hence the combination of ἰᾶσθαι with συντετριμμένος at ψ 146:3; Is. 61:1, or with σύντριμμα at ψ 59:2. What is at issue here is not so much the removal of intellectual, or even, in the first instance, moral deficiencies. This is partly a presupposition and partly a consequence. The crucial thing is the restoration of fellowship with God, with all the comfort which flows from this and all the help that derives from it. At Sir. 28:3 ἴασις can even mean forgiveness. ἰᾶσθαι in the sense of "to forgive" is also found at Dt. 30:3: ἰάσεται τὰς ἁμαρτίας σου, Mas. God will turn thy fate (שׁוּב שְׁבוּת). Cf. also its use as a vl. for ἱλάσκεσθαι at 2 Ch. 6:30 AB. In the same connection we should also refer finally to Job 12:21, where the Mas. is obscure and the LXX goes its own way: ταπεινοὺς δὲ ἰάσατο.[29] In the last analysis the subject is always God. While the ungodly leaders of the people neglect their divinely given task of binding up the wounded (Zech. 11:6; Jer. 6:14), the prophet, the true Servant of God, knows that he is anointed by the Spirit of Yahweh to bind up the broken in heart (Is. 61:1: לַחֲבֹשׁ לְנִשְׁבְּרֵי לֵב, ἰάσασθαι τοὺς συντετριμμένους τῇ καρδίᾳ). This takes place in the first instance through the glad tidings which he brings: לְבַשֵּׂר עֲנָוִים, εὐαγγελίσασθαι πτωχοῖς. To the work of the Servant of God belongs also vicarious suffering in expiation of the sins of his people. Though at first unbelieving, those who look on make the paradoxical confession: "By his stripes we are healed" (Is. 53:5: בַּחֲבֻרָתוֹ נִרְפָּא לָנוּ, τῷ μώλωπι αὐτοῦ ἡμεῖς ἰάθημεν). In this pregnant saying OT religion transcends itself and reaches its climax.

Philo uses the terms in the literal sense (especially ἰατρός, though apparently not ἴασις), but more often in the figurative. Greek influence may be seen in the fact that healing is the overcoming of moral defects rather than forgiveness. Yet Philo is still true to the OT and Judaism in so far as he attributes the healing of the soul to God, to the divine λόγος or to the divine ἔννοια. Leg. All., III, 215: ἐὰν ἔλθῃ εἰς τὴν διάνοιαν ἔννοια θεοῦ, εὐθὺς εὐλογιστεῖ τε καὶ πάσας τὰς νόσους αὐτῆς ἰᾶται. Ibid., 124: ... λόγος (in the first instance human) σὺν ἀρεταῖς ἀληθότητι καὶ σαφηνείᾳ (clarity) θυμὸν νόσημα χαλεπὸν ψυχῆς ἰώμενος ... God is the μόνος ἰατρὸς ψυχῆς ἀρρωστημάτων to whom men usually resort when all other means of help have been exhausted (Sacr. AC, 70 f.).

---

[28] I owe the last three sentences to Bertram.
[29] I owe the last four sentences to Bertram.

C. Sickness and Healing in the New Testament.

1. Sickness and the Art of Healing in the Light of the New Testament.

That the primitive assessment of sickness is still present in the NT may be seen not only from the many references to the possessed but also from the causation of physical suffering in Mt. 12:22 par.; Lk. 13:11; Ac. 12:23; 1 C. 10:10; 2 C. 12:7; Rev. 16:2. Yet this view is not the only one. [30] It is linked with faith in God in such a way that it brings to light both the resistance of the powers which control this aeon (Mk. 3:27) and also the judgment of God (Rev. 6:8, θάνατος LXX = דֶּבֶר, plague). Although Jesus recognises the connection between sickness and sin (Mk. 2:5 par.; Jn. 5:14), He breaks through the rigid dogma of retribution and thus sets sickness in a completely new light (Jn. 9:3 f.; 11:4; cf. Lk. 13:1 ff.). Its sharpest sting is thus removed. Paul, then, can group it with all other sufferings (R. 8:28; 2 C. 4:17). The apostle maintains this view even under the severe burden of personal sickness (2 C. 12:7 ff.).

Paul's thorn in the flesh can hardly have been epilepsy or an eye affliction (cf. Gl. 4:13 ff.). It was more likely severe neuralgia or hysteria accompanied by depression. [31]

On the other hand, the NT is quite clear that diseases and handicaps are evils which contradict God's plan for creation. Hence it does not allow religious narrowness or ascetic fanaticism to bring it into opposition to disrespectful attempts to liberate us from these ills. Mk. 5:26 par. is no proof to the contrary. The medical action of the Good Samaritan in Lk. 10:34 is typical. [32] Col. 4:14 has fundamental significance. [33] Even 1 Tm. 5:23 is quite uninhibited.

2. Jesus the Physician. The Use of the Terms in the Gospels.

Hardly another image impressed itself so deeply on early Christian tradition as that of Jesus as the great Physician. All the Gospels use ἰᾶσθαι of the work of Jesus, especially Luke (5:17; 6:19; Ac. 10:38 etc.). ἴασις is used literally at Lk. 13:32. The figurative use occurs in the Gospels only in quotation (Mt. 13:15; Jn. 12:40 = Is. 6:10). How little feeling there is for it may be seen from the application of Is. 53:4 in Mt. 8:17. The substance is present, but physical healings dominate the field of vision. Jesus Himself uses the self-designation "physician" on quite a few occasions. In its profoundest sense this must be understood, within the framework of oriental symbolism, as a reference to the time of salvation. [34] It is used figuratively of the Saviour of sinners in a parabolic saying compounded of seriousness and irony at Mk. 2:17 par. At Lk. 4:23 it is linked with a current expression which impresses upon us the fact that what is primarily demanded is the fulfilment of the most immediate duties.

---

[30] The fact that rabbis sometimes speak of a spirit of asthma does not justify us in postulating a spirit of fever at Mk. 1:30 or of haemorrhage at Mk. 5:25 par.

[31] For the different views and bibl. cf. Wnd. 2 C., Exc. on 12:7; Fenner, 33 ff.; F. R. Montgomery Hitchcock, "St. Paul's Malady," *Church Quarterly Review,* 107 (1929), No. 214.

[32] On oil and wine as salves and means of healing, Str.-B., I, 428. → ἔλαιον.

[33] Attempts to show by linguistic means that the author of Luke and Acts was a qualified doctor can only be regarded as more or less forced combinations. W. K. Hobart, *The Medical Language of St. Luke* (1882); A. Harnack, *Lukas der Arzt* (1906); A. C. Clark, *The Acts of the Apostles* (1933), 405 ff.: "Supposed Medical Language in Lk. and Acts."

[34] J. Jeremias, "Jesus als Weltvollender," BFTh, 33, 4 (1930), 34.

Gn. r., 23 on 4:23 : [35] אָ֫סְיָא אַסִי אַגִּירוּתָך, "Physician, heal thine own halting"; cf. Eur. Fr., 1086 (TGF): ἄλλων ἰατρὸς αὐτὸς ἕλκεσιν βρύων. On Mk. 2:17 cf. Stob. Ecl., III, 462, 14 : οὐδὲ γὰρ ἰατρὸς ... ὑγιείας ὢν ποιητικὸς ἐν τοῖς ὑγιαίνουσι τὴν δια- τριβὴν ποιεῖται. [36]

3. Jesus' Miracles of Healing in the Light of the History of Religion.

Historically considered, the miraculous cures of Jesus are not isolated phenomena. There are many parallels from both ancient and modern times. A wealth of material may be found on the steles of Epidauros, and fresh light is shed by the votive records of modern healing centres. The parallels raise many questions.

a. Tradition.

When Epidauros was excavated by Cavvadias, there were brought to light, though not in perfect condition, four of the six steles on which Pausanias (II, 27, 3) read (c. 165 A.D.) the accounts of those who were healed. These steles, which were no longer complete even at the time of Pausanias, had been committed to the priests by order of the city authorities. The beautiful and careful writing goes back to the 4th century B.C. From that time onwards changes in the records are excluded.

Illustration may be given of the way in which the wooden votive tablets (πίνακες) were edited for reproduction on the steles. Thus the healing of a supposedly five-year pregnancy is said to have resulted in the birth of a boy who was already four years old. The world of antiquity found in this "completion" of the miracle a source of pious awe rather than scepticism. Along these lines grotesque accounts could easily arise (→ 209). It would be foolish, however, to contest the objectivity of the records on these grounds. Many of the persons mentioned can be identified, e.g., the son of Arybbas of Epeiros, who was supposedly born with miraculous help c. 350, or the rhetor Aischines (d. c. 320 B.C.), whose epigram (Anth. Pal., VI, 330; → 206) once adorned his *pinax* and formed the basis of one of the records. The dreams recorded must also have been true in essentials. Real healings did take place, as to-day at Lourdes, Kevelaer or Gall-spach. But many of the sick must have gone away unhelped or only temporarily cured, and of these there is no record. Miracles of which we have only written accounts are not too satisfactory, since there is no means of controlling the origin of the accounts. For all our criticism, however, we cannot throw them out altogether.

There are no written accounts in respect of the Jewish tradition. The fixed Tannaitic tradition concerning the works of, e.g., Chanina ben Dosa (c. 70) is at least a hundred years later. Even an unbroken chain of authorities does not preclude the possibility of legendary accretion. Many Jewish stories of miracles bear the obvious mark of exaggeration. In other cases the essentials may be historical. Has Josephus simply invented his well-known account of the exorcism performed by Eleazar in the presence of the emperor Vespasian (Ant., 8, 46 ff.)? The Jewish stories are particularly instructive from the standpoint of form criticism when they are present in more than one recension. On the whole they confirm the tenacity of popular tradition.

We have no original testimony to the miracles of Jesus, whether on inscriptions or in any other way. In spite of the well-known statements of Papias concerning the authors of the Gospels, we cannot establish with full certainty an unbroken chain of tradition. As form criticism has shown in detail, expansion of original outlines is as little excluded as the development of completely new accounts. In this respect we are reminded of the passages which Dibelius has called "short stories" (*Novellen*).

---

[35] To be read instead of חיגרותך.

[36] For further parallels cf. Wettstein, I, 358 f., 681; Str.-B., II, 156; Schl. Mt., 306; Zn. Lk. and Kl. Lk. on 4:23.

We can almost trace the possibility in the texts. It is tradition which tells us that Jesus healed the smitten ear of the high-priest's servant on the night of the Passion (Lk. 22:51). Mk. 5:21 ff. par., Lk. 7:11 ff. and Jn. 11:1 ff. plainly work up to a climax (cf. also Mt. 8:5 ff. and Jn. 4:46 ff., Mk. 2:1 ff. par. and Jn. 5:1 ff.). This is not to discredit any particular tradition, but it calls for notice. It could be that alien material has been attributed to Jesus in some cases (Mk. 5:1 ff. par.?).

In their present form the accounts are three or four decades after the events. Apart from minor corrections, however, they can hardly have been changed substantially after the final decade of the first century. It should also be added that there are several signs that the tradition received its basic form long before the written records, and that it did so on Palestinian soil (cf. 1 C. 15:6),[37] so that we are brought back to eye-witnesses. Many of the accounts authenticate themselves by their vividness and simplicity (Mk. 1:29 ff. par.; 10:46 ff. etc.). We can see from the Gospel of Thomas and the apocryphal Acts what shape miracles take when they owe their origin to literary imagination. If there had been nothing outstanding in the story of Jesus, the rise of the community would itself be inexplicable. But if the followers of Jesus lived through great acts, it is hard to see how the record of real events could perish and be replaced by a completely different tradition. Nor should we imagine that early Christianity was too uncritical or avid for miracles. Though the Baptist was regarded as a prophet, no miracles were ascribed to him (cf. Jn. 10:41). Events such as those of Ac. 14:20; 20:10; 28:5 may have a mysterious aspect, but they are recounted as "natural" events.

The features of the miracle stories of antiquity[38] are also significant in the Gospels. The following are the most important. 1. Medical skill is unavailing. Cf. Aischines, Anth. Pal., VI, 330 :

Θνητῶν μὲν τέχναις ἀπορούμενος, εἰς δὲ τὸ θεῖον
ἐλπίδα πᾶσαν ἔχων, προλιπὼν εὔπαιδας Ἀθήνας
ἰάθην ἐλθών, Ἀσκληπιέ, πρὸς τὸ σὸν ἄλσος
ἕλκος ἔχων κεφαλῆς ἐνιαύσιον, ἐν τρισὶ μησίν.

The doctors cannot cure Tobit's blindness (2:10, א even has : ὅσῳ ἐνεχρίοσάν με τὰ φάρμακα, τοσούτῳ μᾶλλον ἐξετυφλοῦντο οἱ ὀφθαλμοί μου, cf. Mk. 5:26; Lk. 8:43; also Jn. 5:7; Mk. 9:18, 28 f. par.). 2. The miracle often takes place on an encounter, e.g., Philostr. Vit. Ap., IV, 45, a story of resurrection which reminds us strongly of Lk. 7:11 ff. Cf. also Lk. 17:12 ff.; Mk. 10:46 etc. 3. It takes place suddenly, swiftly and surely, cf. No. 5 in Herzog, op. cit. (a dumb boy): ἐξ]απίνας ... ἔφα, also No. 38 (a lame man): ἐγκρατῆ τῶν γονάτων γε]νέσθαι εὐθύς; Lk. 8:47; Mk. 10:52. But cf. Mk. 8:24 ff. In Mk. 7:35 the vacillating tradition εὐθέως or εὐθύς is instructive ; there is obvious unwillingness to dispense with such an addition. The healed man carres his bed back home in proof of his cure. Luc. Philops., 11: ὁ Μίδας ἀράμενος τὸν σκίμποδα (bed, mattress) ἐφ' οὗ ἐκεκόμιστο, ᾤχετο ἐς τὸν ἀγρὸν ἀπιών. Mk. 2:12 par.; Jn. 5:8 f. 4. The miracle is paradoxical. Ael. Arist. Or., 42, 8 (Keil): Τό γε παράδοξον πλεῖστον ἐν τοῖς ἰάμασι. Lk. 5:26. Cf. Mk. 2:12 par.; 7:37 etc. (→ 457). 5. The miracles are more numerous than can be recounted. Ael. Arist. Or., 47, 1 (Keil): Κἀγὼ πάντα μὲν

---

[37] Dibelius, Formgeschichte, 27 ff. underrates the contribution of the earliest Palestinian communities. On the other hand, he rightly stresses the fact that "the earliest tradition concerning Jesus was directed with majestic stringency towards the passing on of things essential to salvation." Details like the technique of healing, the story of the sick persons, the confirmation of success, are no proof of originality but may well be imaginative additions, DLZ, 57 (1936), 4 on Fragments of an Unknown Gospel, ed. H. Idris Bell and T. C. Skeat (1935).
[38] Weinreich AH, 171 ff., 195 ff.

οὐκ ἂν εἴποιμι τὰ τοῦ Σωτῆρος ἀγωνίσματα; Jn. 20:30 f.; 21:25. Cf. Mt. 8:16; 12:15 ff.

There is always a motive in miracle stories. The motives may vary. If they can affect the tradition, they do not have to do so. The NT finds certain precautions against the unchecked growth of fantasy in its simple glorification of Jesus and the Holy Spirit, and in the strongly historical interest of its piety.

The ἰάματα of Epidauros are designed to give confidence to those who seek healing, to shorten the time of waiting with humour, and to promote the fame and income of the shrine. The Rabbinic stories serve to show what merits individual observers of the Law can attain and how profitable this is in every situation of life; their purpose is thus to enflame to keeping of the Torah. The point of the Gospels is to lead to saving faith in Jesus Christ, the Saviour, and to strengthen this faith. In the Fourth Gospel the miracles are greater, but the stories are in some sense transparencies which receive their meaning from the discourses which follow. To some degree there is here a conscious antithesis to Aesculapius and Dionysus.

b. The Nature of the Miracles.

In Epidauros there are some nature miracles as well as the predominant miracles of healing. Thus a broken cup is put together again (Herzog, No. 10). Antiquity sees no sharp line of demarcation here. The Dionysus stories and practices are particularly rich in nature miracles of an extravagant kind. [39] Here as elsewhere there is a measure of priestly deception (→ II, 452, n. 14). Judaism has some nature miracles (rain, sun, the giving of water), and miracles of punishment, [40] but for all the element of fantasy there is a restraint against extravagance such as we do not find in the pagan world. [41]

In the case of Jesus nature miracles are found in the oldest strata of the tradition (Mk. 4:35 ff. par.; 6:35 ff. par., 45 ff. par.), though miracles of healing are much more frequent. Where there might seem to be an element of extravagance (Lk. 5:1 ff., cf. with Jn. 21:1 ff.; Mt. 17:24 ff.; Jn. 2:1 ff.), we seem to have a secondary tradition, and there is an underlying pastoral or didactic purpose.

The diseases are much the same at Epidauros and in the Gospels. To try to attribute all the illnesses of the NT to nervous causes, [42] even if it could be substantiated medically, would be contrary to the intention of the stories. Why should Jesus have encountered only people with nervous disorders?

There are no exorcisms at Epidauros, perhaps because those who were mentally ill were not allowed within the sacred precincts. [43] Apollonius of Tyana healed in India a boy who was possessed by the spirit of a fallen warrior whose wife had married again after three days (Philostr. Vit. Ap., III, 38 ff.). He also healed in Athens a youth who had lived a licentious life (ibid., IV, 20). For Judaism → 205.

The miracle stories of the Gospels are distinguished from the ἰάματα in respect of their depiction of sickness. Jesus helps where there is real need. The stories of healing at Epidauros are told from the standpoint of the sick persons, who are

---

[39] For examples v. Bau. J., Exc. on 2:1-12.
[40] Examples in Fiebig, Umwelt, 38 ff.
[41] Worth noting is the story of R. Jose of Joqeret (bTaan., 24a, Str.-B., II, 26), who put his son to death by a curse because he had blasphemed his Creator by a superfluous miracle. The reserve of the better Greek novel in respect of such blatant aretology is on grounds of reason and taste rather than religion. Cf. Kerényi, op. cit.
[42] Fenner, op. cit. in the interests of a natural explanation.
[43] Herzog, No. 62 is an exception for special reasons (→ 198).

full of their sufferings and unfulfilled desires, and of the priests, who seek to magnify
the fame of the sanctuary. But the NT stories are seen from the standpoint of the
mercy of Jesus. At Epidauros egoism is the central force, in the Gospels love.

In Hellenism there are several stories of the healing of animals, which then demonstrate
their gratitude. [44] There are no parallels in the Gospels. Aesculapius heals sciatica, gout,
headaches, goitres, stones, and baldness, which, when accompanied by a beard, exposes
to ridicule. He frees from lice, worms and tape-worms. He helps in child labour, and
gives the blessing of children to women who undergo incubation for this purpose. Desires
in respect of the sex of children are promptly met (Herzog, No. 34: male, cf. 31, 42;
but No. 2: female). He can find lost children and even buried treasure.

When Aesculapius has rendered help, he demands a fee which has often been agreed
beforehand, a silver pig, a gold statuette, 200 drachmas or up to 2000 gold staters.
But he will also take ten marbles with a smile from a poor boy (Herzog, No. 8). Those
who try to snap their fingers at the god can expect a miracle of punishment. Some
of these are skilfully interwoven into the collection of ἰάματα. The priests are behind
this, of course, yet not out of pure egoism. The magnificent facilities of Epidauros would
never have been possible if they had not been exploited.

A man who tried to contest his own payment by virtue of that of someone else
entrusted to him gets the other's mole on his face in addition to his own (Herzog,
No. 6/7). The fish carrier who does not pay to the god the premium for his lung begins
to be consumed on the market square at Tegea by his turbots and eels (No. 47; for similar
miracles → 210). In most cases, however, those who are punished quickly realise their
fault. When this is so, the god takes the punishment from them by a new miracle. At
this point the humour in ancient miracle stories often emerges. It can take the form of
burlesque. At the conclusion of the story of resurrection to which we have referred
already (→ 206), Apollonius of Tyana gives back the 150,000 drachmas donated to
him as a dowry for the restored girl. Even stranger is the very Hellenistic bug miracle
recounted in Act. Joh. (60 f.), which itself treats it as a joke. The fairly common miracles
of punishment in Judaism are much more serious. Here the point at issue is no mere
mine and thine, but the directly or indirectly violated honour of God. The end is usually
sudden death, and the punishment is not remitted. [45]

The miracles of Jesus belong to another world. There are no punishments. [46]
But the burlesque element is also lacking. We certainly cannot imagine the story of
the young man at Nain ending in the same way as the parallel story in Aesculapius.
Again, there is no egotistic motive. Jesus regularly refuses to do miracles either
to save Himself or to accredit His mission (Mt. 4:1 ff. par.; 12:38 ff. par.; 26:53 f.;
27:39 ff.). Similarly, He will not use His miracles to cause a sensation (cf.
especially Mk., perhaps with a measure of stylisation, but not without historical
basis, 1:44; 3:12; 5:43; 7:36; 8:26). Instead of asking for payment, He demands
of His disciples unconditional unselfseeking (Mt. 10:8, cf. 2 C. 5:16 ff.). What
Jesus desires is gratitude, not for His own sake, but for that of God and of those
healed by Him, in order that the physical benefit may not be unaccompanied by
spiritual blessing (Lk. 17:17 ff.).

c. The Accomplishment of the Cure.

The god of Epidauros increasingly gives therapeutical directions which are open to
rational criticism. Thus on the stele of Apelles (c. 160 A.D., Ditt. Syll.[3], III, 1170; the
cures of Lebena in Crete are more peculiar, *ibid.*, 1171 f.) the prescription against

---

[44] Weinreich AH, 120 f., 125 ff.
[45] Examples in Str. -B., 858 f., II, 26.
[46] Mk. 11:12 ff. par. is to be regarded as a symbolic miracle of punishment.

digestive troubles is not to become irritated, to go on a vegetarian diet of cheese, bread, celery, lettuce, slices of citrus fruit softened in water, milk and honey, to go barefoot, to engage in running and gymnastics, massage, rubbing with wine, salt and mustard, warm baths without service, oil against congestions, and finally not to forget a thank-offering to the god and a tip to the manager of the baths (1 drachma). Epidauros becomes more and more a luxury sanatorium, like the Aesculapieion at Cos (→ 197).

In comparison, the mode of healing practised by Jesus is infinitely simple, externally unimpressive, but inwardly so much the more powerful. It hardly contains the first beginnings of rational therapy. Jesus heals without φάρμακα and βοτάναι (Ep. Abgari in Eus. Hist. Eccl., I, 13, 6). The use of spittle in Mk. 7:33; 8:23; Jn. 9:6 is much more primitive than medicine. There may have been some special reasons for it when those in need of healing did not have the use of all their senses, unless we are to see here a later addition. The use of oil is mentioned only with reference to the disciples (Mk. 6:13, → II, 472).

There is no incubation in the NT. We find a faint analogy in Jn. 5:2 ff. But here Jesus is the one who makes incubation unnecessary. Perhaps there is a certain polemic against Aesculapius at this point. At Epidauros the healing sleep is a kind of state of trance in which things happen which are later found to be real, e.g., the opening of sores without the usual medical burning or cutting, the opening of the cavity of the breast or abdomen, the cutting open of the head and hanging by the feet until the water flows out (Herzog, No. 21). [47] When it is a question of the birth of children, the processes of betrothal are more or less decently suggested (No. 31, 39, 42, 71). In one case liberation from a calculus stuck in the member is accomplished by means of imaginary pederasty (No. 14). Such things would be quite unthinkable in the Gospels. For here everything takes place in a state of wakefulness, in the clear light of day, and the air is pure.

An important healing factor in Hellenism is touch, [48] e.g., the kiss (Herzog, No. 41). [49] At Epidauros laying on of hands is found only once in a case of deficient fertility (No. 31). [50] We read more often of the foot-step [51] of the god (No. 3) or his horses (No. 38) on the sick member, though naturally in a dream. We also read of the licking or biting of sacred geese, dogs or snakes (No. 17, 26, 43, 45). The complete lack of such crude contacts is just as characteristic of the Gospels as in the predominance of the laying on of hands (→ χείρ). The conveyance of virtue through touching garments occurs only rarely (Mk. 5:27 ff. par.; Lk. 6:19; cf. Ac. 5:15; 19:12).

In the ἰάματα, as in the Gospels, there are some healings at a distance (Mt. 8:5 ff.; Jn. 4:46 ff.; Mt. 15:21 ff.; cf. Herzog, No. 21: ἀγχωρήσασα εἰς Λακεδαί-μονα καταλαμβάνε[ι τ]ἀν θυγατέρα ὑγιαίνουσαν, which is almost word for word the same as Mk. 7:30; Lk. 7:10). Rabbinic tradition has a similar report of Chanina ben Dosa which reminds us of Jn. 4:46 ff. (bBer., 34b; Str.-B., II, 441).

---

[47] That mother and daughter have the same dream reminds us of the not infrequent motif of double vision. Cf. Angelos, I (1925), 37 f.

[48] There is a remarkable account of mutual healing by touch in Vita Hadriani (Script. Hist. Aug.), 25 : Venit de Pannonia quidam vetus caecus ad febrientem Hadrianum eumque conti[n]git, quo facto et ipse oculos recepit, et Hadrianum febris reliquit. Previously we are told how a woman who had been blinded because she did not carry out an order given in a dream had her sight restored by kissing the knee of the emperor and by washing in temple water.

[49] For further details cf. Weinreich AH, 73 ff.

[50] For other examples, ibid., 14 ff.

[51] Ibid., 67 ff.

Apart from certain promises of Aesculapius, healings by word are found in paganism only in the form of magic. In Judaism they occur as answers to prayer (→ 202). Hellenism presupposes prayer on the part of those who seek healing (Herzog, No. 2, 4). At Epidauros, Pergamos (Ael. Arist.) etc. much prayer is undoubtedly offered to Aesculapius. Appeals are often made to Jesus for help. It is not said that He for His part demanded prayer on the part of those who sought healing. Mk. 7:34 is not to be understood in this way. It refers to the prayer of Jesus Himself. There are no magic formulae in the Gospels. The most common means of healing is Jesus' word of power, His command (Mk. 1:25, 27, 41 par.; Mt. 8:9 par., 13; Mk. 2:10 f. par.; 5:41; 7:34 etc.). Attempts have been made to show that this is a distinctive mark of the miracles of Jesus as compared with the Synagogue. [52] But in the Rabbis, too, we find words of power which are not magical formulae. [53] Nor does Jesus make a sharp distinction between His own miracles and those of others. There are indications that, like others who work miracles (Mk. 9:29; 11:23 f.), He receives His power in prayer and exercises it from case to case (Mk. 7:34; 9:29). At any rate, He has special power in virtue of His special commission (→ 211; 213; Mt. 12:29 par.).

A pre-condition and consequence of miracle is faith.

The god of Epidauros demands this stringently. Those who do not believe in his healing power (ἀπιστεῖν, No. 3) will be shamed and punished. To be given the name of unbeliever (Ἄπιστος, No. 3) is only the beginning. A mocker will be lamed by his own "Bucephalus" [54] and then generously healed again (No. 36). The god helps even unbelievers, but he demands of them a specially high reward (No. 4). [55]

Jesus annexes the greatest promises to faith, particularly to that of one who performs miracles (Mk. 11:23 par.). He Himself has a faith which moves mountains. But He will not use it to provide spectacles. He constantly repudiates such tempting of God (Mt. 4:5 ff.; 12:38 ff.; 16:1 ff. par.). Nevertheless, He demands faith of those who would receive the blessing of the miracle (Mk. 5:36 par.; Mt. 15:28; Mt. 8:10; Mk. 6:5 par. etc.; both are linked in Mk. 9:23 f.). [56] For all the formal similarity, however, the structure of faith is quite different from that of Epidauros → πίστις.

In the case of Aesculapius the emphasis falls primarily on the credibility of the miracle stories and of the power of the god. To doubt this is a punishable offence. The disposition of the god is generally benevolent, but not without an element of caprice. It is in keeping that faith is closely linked with courage. When the god has broken the staff of a lame man, he is required in a dream to climb the temple on a ladder. If he is afraid, the god scolds him and then laughs at him (No. 35) until he does it, and the work of healing is complete. In other cases the pool in which they are to bathe is too cold. Aesculapius tells them that he will not heal the timid (δειλούς) but only those who come to him in his sanctuary in good hope that he will not harm them, but send them away cured (No. 37).

For Jesus, too, faith implies courage. Cowardice and unbelief belong together (Mt. 8:26 par.: τί δειλοί ἐστε, ὀλιγόπιστοι). But there is no humorous appeal

---

[52] A. Schlatter, Das Wunder in der Synagoge (1912).
[53] Str.-B., I, 127.
[54] The use of this name of Alexander's horse implies an element of parody.
[55] A silver pig. In this there is perhaps a malicious thrust at the rationalistic Athenians, who coined the nickname Βοιωτία ὕς for the ἀπαιδευσία of their neighbours.
[56] Kl. Mk., ad loc.

to one's own power. A deep seriousness forms the background. Faith includes the conviction of the power of God and of Jesus. But it is also a personal relationship of trust. Trust in the merciful love of God, humble surrender, obedience and self-giving are inseparable from it. This is particularly plain in Mt. 8:5 ff. Aesculapius demands strict belief in the miracle. Jesus does not (Jn. 4:48). Under severe temptation He Himself maintains His faith even where the miraculous help of God is not displayed (Mt. 26:36 ff. par., 52 ff.). Similarly, He acknowledges particularly the faith which maintains itself victoriously in spite of all opposition (Mt. 15:21 ff. par.; cf. Jn. 20:29). Faith is thus a decisive condition of fellowship with God. It receives, not merely healing of the body, but full health or salvation for the whole personality (Mk. 5:34 par.; Mk. 10:52; Lk. 7:50; 17:19).

d. Concluding Theological Appraisal; the Uniqueness of Jesus' Miracles of Healing.

Whether in the form of plain rejection, of reinterpretation, or of the evaluation of what is recounted in terms of myth, religious history, or symbol, a threadbare rationalism may indulge in radical criticism of all miracle stories. On the other hand, an exclusive supernaturalism may press for a complete schematic isolation of the miracles of Jesus. These are two modes of approach which are more or less equally ruled out by the actual data. Many miracles of healing from many different sources, both ancient and modern, are well attested. Furthermore, recent scientific research has shown us how relative are natural laws. [57] Greater elasticity is thus demanded as regards our view of what is possible or not possible. At the same time, very difficult problems are raised from a theological standpoint. These are posed by the proximity of the obscure and even uncanny depths of the being of man. The extent to which the efficacy of the miraculous power of Jesus is dependent on the faith of those who seek healing may be seen from the primitive observation in Mk. 6:5, even though this could also refer to a moral and religious impossibility. We have seen "that in many cases the miracles of Jesus are conditioned and mediated processes in which divine efficacy and human receptivity meet in the action of Jesus." [58] We are confronted by the fact of the tremendous impact of the personality of Jesus on those around Him. If we speak of this in terms of "suggestion," we are using the feeblest of all conceivable analogies. We should think rather of the healing influences, by no means merely suggestive, which flow from great doctors and other particularly gifted people. [59] Modern medicine has overcome the abstract separation of soul and body and the isolated material or psychological treatment of an earlier day. If this helps to explain many things in Jesus, it need cause no theological difficulty so long as we can bring the realities described into harmony with Christian faith in God. The endowment of Jesus may well have included some such powers in unique perfection. That such endowment may have a spiritual and moral aspect can be seen particularly clearly in His dealings with the mentally deranged who are so prominent amongst those with whom He comes in contact. But in the Gospels the endowment stands in the service of God's offering of Himself in fellowship. And where God intervenes so expressly in human history, who is to measure His work by ordinary standards?

---

[57] We have in view the work of men like August Mie and Werner Heisenberg.
[58] F. Barth, *Die Hauptprobleme des Lebens Jesu*⁵ (1918), 110.
[59] Cf. Liek, *op. cit.*

There can be a more precise definition of the revelational aspects of the miracles of Jesus only when we see their uniqueness in incisive comparison with analogies. Our previous deliberations have already given us some hints in this respect (→ 206; 207; 208; 209; 210; 211). We may now bring these into focus by saying that at the heart of all the individual miracle stories of the Gospels stands the person of Jesus. In all the varied literature of ancient and modern miracle stories we do not find anything which even remotely approaches, let alone surpasses, the holy and merciful love of Jesus. The uniqueness of this love lies both in its intensity and in its comprehensiveness. But it is to be found particularly in the fact that in a unique way it embraces both the outer and the inner man.

The philosophical and mystical separation of soul and body is almost as completely remote from popular Greek thinking as it is from Judaism. In paganism the sick have the sense that they are singled out and punished by the deity. [60] Hence their whole striving is for liberation from sin. But this is understood in a ritual sense, and it is essentially a means to an end. The essential thing is the removal of the bodily suffering. This whole view is eudaemonistically orientated. Jesus breaks through the schema of retribution, though He does not completely sever the connection between evil and sin. Sin in the moral sense is for Him the source of evil. It is itself the greatest evil. Jesus' true concern is to liberate from it. In many cases He tries to do this by first bringing physical healing and then moving on from this point (Mt. 8:1 ff.; Lk. 17:11 ff. etc.). But sometimes He first speaks the more urgent word of remission to the trembling heart, and then follows this up with external healing (Mt. 9:2 par.). Even when the situation does not demand physical healing, forgiveness of sins can still be imparted as the greatest gift of all (Lk. 7:47 ff.; 15).

Jesus cares for the soul as well as the body. It is true that Aesculapius insists on his reputation and encourages the fainthearted (→ 210). It is also true that Apollonius of Tyana heals demoniacs and restores them to an honourable life (→ 207). But these are only remote and isolated analogies to the pastoral work of Jesus. In general, non-Christian miracles are performed for their own sake. The Gospel miracles, however, have a material point outside the miracle itself. This is usually pastoral. The miracles are set in the context of a dispute, e.g., concerning the Sabbath (Mt. 12:9 ff. par.; Lk. 13:10 ff.), or the remission of sins (Mt. 9:1 ff.). They issue in a significant saying of the Lord (Mt. 8:4, 10 ff.; Lk. 17:17 ff. etc.). Or they make it evident that there has also been an inner change in the life of those who are healed (Mk. 10:52 par.; cf. Jn. 5:14). Normally, the healing is not the end. It provides the "impulse towards an eternal movement."

The miracles of Jesus are signs, but they are not spectacles (→ 210). Only in Jn. are they called → σημεῖα and → τέρατα (Jn. 2:11, 23; 4:48; 6:2 etc.). Apart from the non-genuine Marcan ending (16:17, 20), the Synoptists use these terms almost always in a reproving sense. The miracles of Jesus are simple and yet powerful signs that the prophecies of the age of salvation are beginning to be fulfilled (cf. Mt. 11:5 with Is. 35:5 f.; 61:1). In face of them the Baptist ought to see, and even opponents are forced to recognise, that the royal dominion of God has come to them (Mt. 12:28; Lk. 17:21). If they do not do so, this is unpardonable obtuseness (Lk. 12:54 ff.; in the par. in Mt. 16:3, which may not be genuine, we

---

[60] Less in Greece than in the Orient. In Asia Minor sores may be attributed to the eating of anchovies sacred to Atargatis. For further examples cf. Steinleitner, op. cit., 98 f.

have the phrase σημεῖα τῶν καιρῶν). The miracles are themselves partial victories of God's rule. The host of demons flees. When Jesus extends help, the kingdom of God is achieved at a specific point, though completely so only when there is comprehension of the miracle in this sense. Each partial victory is a foretaste and guarantee of the final victory. As the Hero of God who perfects creation, Jesus invades the kingdom of Satan with power (Lk. 10:18; 11:21 ff. par.). He conquers, and nothing can resist Him. Even though He is put to death, the kingdom of God comes thereby. This Messianic and eschatological context gives to the earliest records (Mk., and perhaps Mt. 8:29) the distinctive impetus for which there are not the slightest parallels in Aesculapius or Dionysus.

In spite of every analogy, the miraculous healings of Jesus thus occupy a unique position in religious history. They are inseparably connected with the uniqueness of Jesus and with His unparalleled sense of mission.

4. The Transmission of the Gift of Healing to the Disciples. Healing in the Apostolic Age.

The fact that Jesus transmits the power to heal to the disciples whom He sends out (Mk. 3:14 f.; 6:7 par.) does not mean that there is put at their disposal, for their own self-glorification, a natural gift inherent in their own persons. The intention of the Lord is rather to equip them to be effective witnesses of the imminent kingdom of God by word and act. In some cases the disciples come up against the limits of their power (Mk. 9:18). Jesus warns them against a self-seeking use (Mt. 10:8) which misses the essential point (Lk. 10:20; Mt. 7:22). Although the conduct of the strange exorcist of Mk. 9:38 ff. par. is rooted in a superstitious use of the name so far as he himself and those around him are concerned, Jesus endorses him. His answer implies neither approval nor condemnation of the superstition. With the patience of the truly great He is seeking to lead the disciples out of their self-seeking narrowness.

These points are to be noted in relation to the understanding of the gift of healing in the community which handed down these traditions. In a triumphant confidence which stemmed from eschatological faith in Christ, the apostolic age took up the struggle even against the sufferings of the body (cf. Ac. 3:1 ff.; 8:7; 9:32 ff.; 14:7 ff.; 28:8 f.). [61] Here, too, there are primitive aspects (Ac. 5:15; 19:12). [62] These relate primarily to the attitude of the people, though the author of Ac. recounts them with a certain satisfaction. Nevertheless, it is clear that Christianity differentiates itself from magic (Ac. 8:18 ff.; 19:13 ff., 19), materially, if not with formal rationalism. [63] The essential thing for the community is never healing alone. The acts of power (→ δύναμις) are signs. If they confer benefits on individuals, in this very quality they awaken faith and further the progress of preaching (→ σημεῖον, τέρας, R. 15:18 f. [1 C. 2:4 f.; 1 Th. 1:5 ?]; 2 C. 12:12; also Ac. 2:43; 5:12; 6:8; 14:3; 15:12; with ἴασις 4:22, 30). Along the same lines missionary preaching appeals to the healing acts of Jesus (Ac. 2:22; 10:38). The gift of healing is an operation of the name of the exalted Christ (Ac. 3:16). To put

---

[61] Critical doubts as to individual narratives do not affect their significance as a contribution to the general depiction.

[62] For anointing with oil cf. Mk. 6:13 (in essential distinction from Lk. 10:34) and Jm. 5:14 → ἔλαιον, II, 472, and esp. ἀλείφω, → I, 230.

[63] Cf. J. Leipoldt, "Gebet und Zauber im Urchristentum," ZKG, 54 (1935), 1 ff.

the same thing in another way, it is an operation of the ascended Lord through the Spirit (Ac. 9:34; R. 15:18 f.). It does not belong to the essence of the Christian state. It is an individual gift of grace (χαρίσματα ἰαμάτων, 1 C. 12:9, 28, 30). In particular, it is part of the endowment of the commissioned witness. It gives neither the prospect nor the privilege of claiming or enforcing help, so that, quite apart from cases where there is specific guilt (1 C. 11:30), the onset and persistence of illness cannot be ruled out even in the case of believers (Phil. 2:26; 2 Tm. 4:20; 2 C. 12:8 ff.). Early Christianity may be conscious of its power to heal, but healing is still a theme of godly prayer (2 C. 12:8). In Jm. 5:13 ff. the intercession of the elders is commended as particularly efficacious. [64] But intercession is not restricted to this narrower circle. It is strongly emphasised that the forgiveness of sins is a pre-condition of healing.

> In the literature of the apostolic age the figurative use of the terms is restricted to OT quotations apart from the single instance at Hb. 12:13. Is. 6:10 (→ 204) is used in Ac. 28:27 as a warning of judgment against unreceptive Judaism. In 1 Pt. 2:24, Is. 53:5 is referred to the atoning work of Christ. In such passages ἰᾶσθαι denotes the restoration of divine fellowship through the forgiveness of sins, and all the saving benefits which accompany it. In contrast, Hb. 12:13 : ἵνα μὴ τὸ χωλὸν ἐκτραπῇ, ἰαθῇ δὲ μᾶλλον, is more generally ethical; that the lame man should not be turned out of the way, but should rather be healed — an exhortation to definitely Christian conduct.

D. The Gospel of the Healer and of Healing in the Early Church.

The unparalleled missionary vigour of Christianity in the first centuries derives not least of all from the bold supremacy, continually confirmed by striking experiences, with which the new religion brought freedom to those who were enslaved by demons and destiny (Εἱμαρμένη), and from the selfless love with which it took up the cause of all who were in need, including the sick. It was not forgotten that healing in the deepest sense consists in the forgiveness of sins. But this became increasingly subsidiary to actual liberation from sin and its consequences. In some measure under OT influence, the figurative use of the terms came into its own again.

> There is a fusion of Hellenistic modes of expression with evangelical motifs when, in a predominantly figurative sense, Jesus is described as ἰατρός (Ign. Eph., 7, 2 : εἷς ἰατρός ἐστιν; Cl. Al. Quis Div. Salv., 29; Or. Cels., II, 67 etc.), and when God is also called ἰατρός as well as τροφεύς, πατήρ, διδάσκαλος (Dg., 9, 6). [65] It is possible that Greeks were reminded of ἰᾶσθαι by the mere sound of the name of Jesus (→ 200). [66] If the statue of Christ (cf. Eus. Hist. Eccl., VII, 18) before the supposed house of the woman with an issue of blood in Caesarea Philippi (cf. the depiction of her healing on a relief in the Lateran) [67] was really a monument to Aesculapius, there is a palpable

---

[64] Possibly on the basis of a Jewish source. A. Meyer, *Das Rätsel des Jk.*, Beih. 10 (1930), ZNW.

[65] There is excellent material on Cl. Al. in J. M. Tsermoulas, *Die Bildersprache des Klemens von Alexandrien* (Cairo, 1934; Diss. Würzburg, 1933), 84 ff.

[66] Cf. H. Lamer, "Jüdische Namen im griechisch-römischen Altertum. Der Name Jesu," Philol. Wochenschr., 50 (1930), 763 ff., esp. 765. But it is not convincing that the Greek Ἰησοῦς is to be derived thus. We find it already in the LXX (Jos. *passim*), and in Joseph. (Index). It might be argued that this is based on the meaning of the name Joshua : "Yahweh is healing," but this is very artificial and has no bearing on Christianity.

[67] Cf. the illustration in F. Wolter, *Wie sah Jesus aus?* (1930).

transferring of Hellenistic motifs to Jesus. ἰᾶσθαι and ἴασις are often found in quotations (1 Cl., 16, 5 and Barn., 5, 2 = Is. 53:5; Barn., 14, 9 = Is. 61:1; 1 Cl., 56, 7 = Job 5:18). They are seldom used literally (Barn., 8, 6 medically; 12, 7; 1 Cl., 59, 4 of God), more often figur. (2 Cl., 9, 7). Figur. they are favourite words of Hermas: v., 1, 1, 9; 1, 3, 1; m., 4, 1, 11; 12, 6, 2; s., 5, 7, 3 and 4; 7, 4; 8, 11, 3; 9, 28, 5. Though there is here no sharp distinction between the remission of sins and the infusion of grace, the emphasis begins to fall on the latter. Hermas stresses the former in the sense of the setting aside of the pre-Christian past.

Oepke

---

† ἰδιώτης

A. ἰδιώτης and הֶדְיוֹט outside the New Testament.

1. In Greek usage ἰδιώτης bears the following senses.

a. It means a "private individual" as distinct from a public person or official, e.g., the simple citizen as compared with the ruler: Hdt., VII, 3; Lys., 5, 3; Plat. Polit., 259b; Aeschin., 3, 125, 233; Jos. Bell., 2, 182: ἐξ ἰδιώτου βασιλέα πεποίηκεν, 1, 665; 2, 178; Dio Chrys., 1, 43; Epict. Diss., III, 24, 99; Epict. Ench., 17; Prv. 6:8b; P. Oxy., XII, 1409, 14; Ditt. Syll.³, 305, 71; Ditt. Or., I, 383, 186 ff.: ἀλλ' ἐπιμελείσθωσαν μὲν αὐτῶν ἱερεῖς, ἐπαμυνέτωσαν δὲ βασιλεῖς τε καὶ ἄρχοντες ἰδιῶταί τε πά[ν]τες. Hence ἰδιώτης can come to be used simply for a citizen: Plat. Symp., 185b; Aeschin., 3, 46, 110 and 158; Aristoph. Ra., 458 f.: περὶ τοὺς ξένους καὶ τοὺς ἰδιώτας; Ditt. Syll.³, 37, 3; Ditt. Or., II, 483, 71.¹ Cf. also Thuc., I, 124: ξυμφέροντα καὶ πόλεσι καὶ ἰδιώταις, where ἰδιώτης is the individual, the citizen, as distinct from the whole state. ἰδιώτης can also mean the average man. Plut. Thes., 24 (I, 10 f.): οἱ ἰδιῶται καὶ οἱ πένητες. Herodian Hist., IV, 10, 2.

b. It also means the "layman" as compared with the expert, e.g., in relation to the judge: Antiphon Or., 6, 24; the doctor: Thuc., II, 48, 3; Plat. Theaet., 178c; Leg., XI, 933d; the private as distinct from the officer: Thuc., IV, 2; Xenoph. An., I, 3, 11; Polyb., I, 69, 11: καὶ πολλοὺς ... καὶ ... τῶν ἡγεμόνων καὶ τῶν ἰδιωτῶν διέφθειρον; P. Hibeh, 1, 30, 21; but also the civilian as distinct from the soldier: Xenoph. Eq. Mag., VIII, 1; Ditt. Or., II, 609, 12; the layman in relation to the orator: Isoc., 4, 11; Aeschin., 1, 7 and 8; Hyperides Or., 3, 27 (ed. C. Jensen, 1917); Luc. Jup. Trag., 27; or the philosopher or sophist: Aristot. Polit., II, 7, p. 1266a, 31; Philodem. Philos. Περὶ Παρρησίας (ed. A. Olivieri, 1914), 51: Περὶ θεῶν, 1, 25 (Diels [SAB, 1915]); Epict. Diss., II, 12, 2 and 11; II, 13, 3 etc.; Dio Chrys. Or., 12, 16; the prose writer as distinct from the poet, Plat. Phaedr., 258d; Symp., 178b; the man without charismatic gifts as compared with the μάντις: Paus., II (Korinthiaca), 13, 7: τέως δὲ ἦν 'Αμφιάραος τῷ ἐκείνων λόγῳ ἰδιώτης τε καὶ οὐ μάντις; the layman as distinct from the priest: Ditt. Or., I, 90, 52; Ditt. Syll.³, 736, 16 ff.: οἱ τελούμενοι τὰ μυστήρια ἀνυπόδετοι ἔστωσαν καὶ ἐχόντω τὸν εἱματισμὸν λευκόν, αἱ δὲ γυναῖκες ... καὶ αἱ μὲν ἰδιώτιες ἐχόντω χιτῶνα λίνεον ... αἱ δὲ παῖδες ... αἱ δὲ δοῦλαι ... αἱ δὲ ἱεραί ..., Scholia Graeca in Hom. Od., 3, 332 (W. Dindorf [1855], I, 153): καὶ ὅτι τὰ μυστικὰ καὶ θεοῖς ἁρμόζοντα οὐ χρὴ πρὸς τοὺς ἀμυήτους καὶ ἰδιώτας λέγειν ἀνθρώπους, Philo Omn.

ἰ δ ι ώ τ η ς. Liddell-Scott, *s.v.*; Bchm. K. on 1 C. 14:16; Joh. W. 1 K. on 14:16.
¹ The LXX uses the adj. ἰδιωτικός in the same sense: 4 Macc. 4:3, 6: ἰδιωτικὰ χρήματα, "private means."

Prob. Lib., 3; Spec. Leg., III, 134. On this basis ἰδιώτης comes to have the general sense of "unskilled," Xenoph. Mem., III, 7, 7; III, 12, 1; "immature," Epict. Ench., 51, 1; "uneducated," "inexperienced," Luc. Indoct., 29 : ἀμαθής καὶ ἰδιώτης, Philo Ebr., 126; Som., II, 21: ἐκεῖνο μὲν ἰδιωτῶν καὶ ὑπηρετῶν (!) ἔργον, τοῦτο δ' ἡγεμόνων καὶ γεωργίας ἐμπειροτάτων τὸ ἐπιτήδευμα; Agric., 4; Jul. Or., 5, 170b: τοῖς μὲν ἰδιώταις ἀρκούσης ... τῆς ἀλόγου καὶ διὰ τῶν συμβόλων μόνων ὠφελείας.

c. It means finally the "outsider" or "alien" as distinct from a member : [2] Inscr. in P. Foucart, *Des Associations Religieuses chez les Grecs* ... (1873), 189, Inscr. 2, lines 2 ff.: ἐὰν δέ τις θύηι τῆι θεῶι τῶν ὀργεώνων οἷς μέτεστιν τοῦ ἱεροῦ, ἀτελεῖς αὐτοὺς θύειν· ἂν δὲ ἰδιώτης τις θύηι τῆι θεῶι, διδόναι τῆι ἱερέαι, Ditt. Syll.³, 1013, 2 ff.: ὅταν τὸ γένος θύῃ ... ὅταν δὲ ἰδιώτης θύῃ, 987, 28 : φρατρίαν δὲ μηδὲ ἰδιώτη[ν μ]ηθένα τῶι οἴκωι τούτωι χρῆσθαι.

In general it is evident that the term ἰδιώτης takes on its concrete sense from the context or the specific contrast. There can be no fixed rendering, though it always maintains the basic sense of one who represents his own interests as compared with the official or public interest. Even the professional or the expert is broadly concerned with the public interest of society at large. [3]

2. The same is true of the loan word הֶדְיוֹט, which is the form taken by ἰδιώτης in Rabbinic usage. [4] In Rabbinic literature הֶדְיוֹט also has the following senses.

a. It means the "private citizen" as compared with the king : Sanh., 10, 2; M. Ex., 17, 14; Tg. 1 S. 18:23.

b. It can also be the "layman" as compared with the expert, e.g., the tailor: MQ, 1, 8 : "A layman הדיוט (who is not a tailor by profession) may sew as usual (on days between festivals). But the professional tailor אוּמָּן may make only unequal stitches"; or the prophet: bSanh., 67a: "Who leads astray. The reference is to a layman." The reason (why he is stoned) is because he is a layman. If he were a prophet, he would be put to death by strangling ; and especially the expert in the Law : jJeb, 15d, 60 f. הֶדְיוֹט as distinct from חָכָם; S. Nu., 103 on 12:8 : "So write also the unlearned and common people" (קלי הדעת וההדיוטות). In this kind of context the הדיוט often = עַם הָארֶץ, T. Taan., 4, 12.

c. Finally, it can denote "man" as distinct from the deity : T. Qid., 1, 6 and 9 גבוה : הדיוט; T. Meg., 3, 2.

B. ἰδιώτης in the New Testament.

1. In the NT the word ἰδιώτης is used in the general sense of "uneducated" at Ac. 4:13 (θεωροῦντες δὲ τὴν τοῦ Πέτρου παρρησίαν καὶ Ἰωάννου, καὶ καταλαβόμενοι, ὅτι ἄνθρωποι ἀγράμματοί εἰσιν καὶ ἰδιῶται, ἐθαύμαζον ...), and 2 C. 11:6 : εἰ δὲ καὶ ἰδιώτης τῷ λόγῳ, ἀλλ' οὐ τῇ γνώσει, ἀλλ' ἐν παντὶ φανερώσαντες ἐν πᾶσιν εἰς ὑμᾶς. At 2 C. 11:6 the dative indicates that in which Paul is not skilled, i.e., in eloquence. [5]

---

[2] Cf. W. Bauer, *Der Wortgottesdienst der ältesten Christen* (1930), 17 f.

[3] Cf. δημιουργός [Debrunner].

[4] Cf. Str.-B., III, 454-456; Schürer, II, 468, n. 54; Weber, 126.

[5] Elsewhere we find the gen.: ἰδιώτης ἔργου, Xenoph. Oec., 3, 9; ἰδιώτης ἰατρικῆς Plat. Prot., 345a; cf. Tim., 20a; or the acc.: Herodian Hist., IV, 12, 1; Just. Apol., I, 60, 11; Hipp. Philos., VIII, 18, 1: ἰδιῶται τὴν γνῶσιν.

Cf. on these two passages Just. Apol., I, 39, 3: καὶ οὗτοι ἰδιῶται, λαλεῖν μὴ δυνά-μενοι, διὰ δὲ θεοῦ δυνάμεως ἐμήνυσαν παντὶ γένει ἀνθρώπων; Apol., I, 60, 11: παρ' ἡμῖν οὖν ἔστι ταῦτα ἀκοῦσαι καὶ μαθεῖν παρὰ τῶν οὐδὲ τοὺς χαρακτῆρας τῶν στοιχείων ἐπισταμένων, ἰδιωτῶν μὲν καὶ βαρβάρων τὸ φθέγμα, σοφῶν δὲ καὶ πιστῶν τὸν νοῦν ὄντων, καὶ πηρῶν καὶ χήρων τινῶν τὰς ὄψεις, Hipp. Philos., IX, 11, 1: τὸν Ζεφυρῖνον, ἄνδρα ἰδιώτην καὶ ἀγράμματον καὶ ἄπειρον τῶν ἐκ-κλησιαστικῶν ὅρων, Just. Apol., II, 10, 8; Athenag. Suppl., 11, 3.

2. At 1 C. 14:16 the meaning of ἰδιῶται may be gathered from the distinction in view. The reference of the ἀναπληρῶν τὸν τόπον⁶ τοῦ ἰδιώτου is to the one who does not have the gift of tongues or the interpretation of tongues. He is ex-pressly described as one who "does not know what thou sayest," and who con-sequently cannot say Amen to the charismatic thanksgiving of the man who speaks with tongues. At 1 C. 14:23 f.: ἐὰν οὖν συνέλθῃ ἡ ἐκκλησία ὅλη ἐπὶ τὸ αὐτὸ καὶ πάντες λαλῶσιν γλώσσαις, εἰσέλθωσιν δὲ ἰδιῶται ἢ ἄπιστοι, οὐκ ἐροῦσιν ὅτι μαίνεσθε; ἐὰν δὲ πάντες προφητεύωσιν, εἰσέλθῃ δέ τις ἄπιστος ἢ ἰδιώτης, ἐλέγχεται ὑπὸ πάντων, ... light is shed on the meaning of ἰδιώτης by its com-bination with ἄπιστος, once before it and once after it. The ἰδιῶται are those who do not belong to the community though they join in its gatherings. They are first characterised as such by the fact that they do not understand speaking with tongues, and then by the fact that they are not members (v. 24). In each case the context demands a reference to non-Christians. Here, then, the ἰδιώτης is the unbeliever who does not possess the *charisma* of speaking with tongues or interpretation of tongues. ⁷ That the ἰδιῶται are not a middle group between ἄπιστοι and πιστοί⁸ is shown by the fact that the context does not demand such a distinction, and that there are thus no grounds for it.

Schlier

---

† Ἰεζάβελ

Jezebel is very seldom mentioned in later Jewish writings. What is said about her is simply repetition of what is found in the OT stories (1 K. 16:31; 18:4, 13; 21:5 ff.; 2 K. 9:7 ff.). She is the one who leads Ahab into idolatry, ¹ or for whose sake the balances tip in favour of evil in the life of Ahab. ² Legendary embellishments of the story of Jezebel occur only in non-Rabbinic writings. ³ There is no trace of any symbolical use of the name.

In the NT there is very likely a symbolical use of the name at Rev. 2:20. The allusion to the OT story of Queen Jezebel is plain. With reference to the concrete situation which the name denotes, many explanations are possible. Perhaps the

---

⁶ Cf. Ac. 1:25.
⁷ Ltzm. 1 K., *ad loc.*
⁸ W. Bauer, *op. cit.*
Ἰ ε ζ ά β ε λ. ¹ jSanh., 28b, 19 ff.
² Yalkut Shimoni (on bSanh., 102, 103).
³ PRE¹, 17.

name represents a trend or party in the community at Thyatira. Or it may denote a particular individual, e.g., a prophetess of the shrine of the Chaldean Sibyl in Thyatira. Again, it may stand for the woman leader of "a movement within the Christian congregation." The final assumption is the most likely. We are to see in Jezebel "a false, i.e., libertinistic, Christian prophetess who pursues her course within the community." [4]

Odeberg

ἱερατεία, ἱερατεύω, ἱεράτευμα → ἱερός.

---

† Ἰερεμίας

A. The Prophet Jeremiah in Later Judaism.

Sources of the later Jewish Jeremiah tradition are 2 Ch. 35:25; 36:12, 21 f.; Ezr. 1:1; Da. 9:2; Sir. 49:6 f.; to Eupolemos probably belongs a fragment about Jeremiah which has been transmitted anonymously in Eus. Praep. Ev., 9, 39; [1] 2 Macc. 2:1-8; 15:12-16; 1 Εσδρ. 1:26, 30, 45, 54; Philo Cher., 49; Jos. with his free rendering of the biblical narratives in Ant., 10, 78-80, 89-95, 104-107, 112-130, 141, 156-158, 176-179; 11, 1-2; Bell., 5, 391 f.; S. Bar. 2:1; 5:5; 9:1 f.; 10:2, 4; 33:1 f.; on a Jewish foundation Prophetarum Vitae, ed. T. Schermann (1907), 9, 11 ff.; 43, 6 ff.; 61, 11 ff.; 71, 3 ff.; 104, 19 f.; 106, 1 ff.; 157, 13 ff.; representative Rabb. materials in A. Rosmarin and M. Guttmann, EJ, VIII, 1088-1092, "Jeremia in der Agada."

We should also mention the Jeremiah apocr.: 1. Ep. Jer.; 2. Paralipomena Jeremiae ; [2] 3. On the basis of the Paralipomena, an apocryphon which A. Mingana edited in 1927 from an Arab version in Syrian letters. [3] 4. A lost Heb. Apocryphum Jeremiae, which contained Mt. 27:9b-10, was shown to Jerome by a Jewish Christian. [4] This work was

---

[4] Bss. Apk., ad loc. Cf. Loh. Apk., R. H. Charles (ICC, 1920), ad loc.

Ἰερεμίας. On A: J. A. Fabricius, Codex Pseudepigraphicus Veteris Testamenti (1713), 1102-1116; Weber, 298, 354; Schürer, II, 612; III, 362, 365 f., 369 f., 393-395, 465, 467 f., 475, 486; Str.-B., I, 644, 730, 755, 1029 f.; Hennecke, 388, 391, 393, 419; EJ, VIII, 1088-1092. On B: J. Hänel, "Der Schriftbegriff Jesu," BFTh, 24, 5-6 (1919), 95 f. and the comm. on Mt.

[1] J. Freudenthal, Alexander Polyhistor. = *Hellenistische Studien*, 1-2 (1875), 208 f.; Schürer, III, 475; O. Stählin, *Die hellenistisch-jüdische Literatur* = offprint from W. v. Christ, *Griech. Literaturgeschichte*, II, 1⁶ (1921), 589, n. 4; Schl. Gesch. Isr., 191.

[2] For an ed. of the Gk. text cf. J. R. Harris, *The Rest of the Words of Baruch* (1889); cf. P. Riessler, *Altjüd. Schrifttum* (1928), 903-919. For the Eth. text cf. F. Prätorius in ZwTh, 15 (1872), 230-247; E. König in ThStKr, 50 (1877), 318-338. For bibl. cf. Schürer, III, 393-395.

[3] "A New Jeremiah Apocryphon," in *Bulletin of the John Rylands Library*, XI, 2 (July, 1927), 352-437, with a preface by J. R. Harris, 329-342. Reprinted in *Woodbrooke Studies*, I (1927), 125-138, 148-233. Cf. A. Marmorstein, ZNW, 27 (1928), 327-337; J. Gutmann, EJ, VIII, 1092-1094.

[4] In Mt. 27:9 (MPL, 26, 205b): *Legi nuper in quodam Hebraico volumine, quod Nazaraenae sectae mihi Hebraeus obtulit, Jeremiae apocryphum, in quo haec* (= Mt. 27:9b-10) *ad verbum scripta reperi.*

probably of Jewish Christian origin, and arose out of a desire to have a text of Jeremiah containing the quotation from Zechariah erroneously ascribed to Jeremiah in Mt. 27:9 (→ 220). [5] 5. Euthalius and Georgius Syncellus claim to have read the quotation at Eph. 5:14 in an Apocryphum Jeremiae. [6] 6. For individual sayings attributed to Jeremiah, cf. V. Ryssel in Kautzsch Pseudepigr., 404; Hennecke, 388. 7. From the time of Iren. Jeremiah was often regarded as the author of Gr. Bar. [7]

Unlike the statements concerning → Elijah and → Enoch, those concerning Jeremiah in later Jewish literature are almost exclusively concerned with the historic personage. The distinction is bound up with the attachment of later Judaism to Scripture. What Scripture says about Jeremiah gives little occasion for going beyond his earthly life. There is a rich accretion of legends concerning his birth, his prophetic work, his fate both before and after the destruction of Jerusalem and during the exile, and his death. This was obviously the prophet of whom it was said that "his heart was found pure from sins," [8] that he saved and hid the ark and the vessels of the temple, [9] and that he sealed his witness by martyrdom (stoning) [10] — one of the favourite prophets of the people.

An odd passage which does go beyond his earthly life is 2 Macc. 15:12-16. [11] To Judas Maccabaeus there appears, with the high-priest Onias, a figure of supraterrestrial majesty who hands him a golden sword. Onias says to him: ὁ φιλάδελφος οὗτός ἐστιν ὁ πολλὰ προσευχόμενος περὶ τοῦ λαοῦ καὶ τῆς ἁγίας πόλεως [12] Ιερεμιας ὁ τοῦ θεοῦ προφήτης (15:14).

B. The Prophet Jeremiah in the New Testament.

1. In the NT the prophet Jeremiah is mentioned expressly only by Mt. (2:17; 16:14; 27:9). [13] But the passages in Mt. 23:37 par. and Hb. 11:37, which speak of the stoning of the divine messenger and witness, both refer to Jeremiah. For in Mt. 23:37 the plural makes it likely that there is reference to the legendary stoning

---

[5] On other attempts to show that Mt. 27:9b-10 really comes from Jer., cf. Schürer, III, 369, n. 104 and Kl. Mt. on 27:9.

[6] Schürer, III, 362, 365 f.

[7] Ibid., 465.

[8] S. Bar. 9:1. So long as he was in Jerusalem, the city could not be destroyed (S. Bar. 2:1-2; Paral. Jerem. 1:1-3; Pesikt., 13 [Buber, 1868, 115b, 28]).

[9] The ark : Eupolemos Fragment (→ 218); 2 Macc. 2:4-7; Vitae Prophetarum, 10, 9 ff.; 45, 14 ff.; 62, 15 ff.; 72, 13 ff.; Josephus Gorionides → n. 17. The tent and the altar of incense : 2 Macc. 2:4-7. The vessels : Paral. Jerem. 3:7 f., 14. The garment and mitre of the high-priest and other temple property: Jeremiah Apocryphon, ed. Mingana (Bulletin of the John Rylands Lib., XI [1927], 375-377 = Woodbrooke Studies, I [1927], 171-173). The curtains : Josephus Gorionides → n. 17.

[10] Paral. Jerem. 9:21 ff.; Vitae Prophetarum, 9, 13; 44, 7 ff.; 61, 12; 71, 4; 104, 20; 106, 3 f. For the NT → supra. Early Christian references from the time of Tertullian, Adversus Gnosticos Scorpiace, 8 (MPL, 2, 137b) in Rgg. Hb., 380, n. 95. That the Eupolemus Fragm. is garbled, and that the original reference is not to the burning of the prophet by King Jonachim (!), but to the burning of his book, has been shown by A. Schlatter, "Der Märtyrer in den Anfängen der Kirche," BFTh, 19, 3 (1915), 68, n. 38.

[11] Different in nature is the dream omen in bBer., 57b: "Whoever sees Jeremiah in a dream, let him fear punishment."

[12] Even in his lifetime, his prayers were a "strong (Paral. Jerem. "steel") wall" for Jerusalem (S. Bar. 2:2; Paral. Jerem. 1:2). Cf. also Jeremiah Apocr., ed. Mingana → n. 3 (Bulletin, 364 = Woodbrooke Studies, 160).

[13] The vl. of Lk. 9:19 ἄλλοι (ἕτεροι φ) δὲ 'Ιερεμίαν (λφ) is based on Mt. 16:14.

of Jeremiah as well as to Zechariah the son of Jehoiada (2 Ch. 24:20-22), and in Hb. 11:37 (ἐλιθάσθησαν) the ensuing reference to the martyrdom of Isaiah by sawing asunder makes it probable that Jeremiah is primarily in view.

NT "parallels" (in the broadest possible sense of mere allusions as well as literal quotations) to the Book of Jeremiah, Lamentations and the Epistle of Jeremiah have been collected by W. Dittmar, Vetus Testamentum in Novo (1903), 321-324, 344, 352. Particular emphasis is to be laid on the significance of the prophecy of the new → διαθήκη (Jer. 31:31-34) for the NT.

2. At Mt. 2:17 the quotation from Jer. 31:15 is introduced by the words τότε ἐπληρώθη τὸ ῥηθὲν διὰ 'Ιερεμίου τοῦ προφήτου λέγοντος.

3. The same words are used at Mt. 27:9 to introduce Zech. 11:13. This is probably a slip of memory occasioned by recollection of Jer. 32:9 (the purchase of the field).[14]

4. Only in Mt. are we told that the people found in Jesus a re-appearance of the prophet Jeremiah ('Ιερεμίαν ἢ ἕνα τῶν προφητῶν, 16:14). This report is striking, since later Jewish literature does not speak of any eschatological mission of the prophet Jeremiah.[15] Expectation of his return is first found in the Christian 5 Esr. 2:18,[16] in a reading of Josephus Gorionides, 1, 21,[17] and probably also in an addition to the section on Jeremiah in the Vitae Prophetarum.[18] All three are probably dependent on Mt. 16:14. It is possible, if not very likely, that Mt. 16:14 refers to an otherwise unattested expectation of later Jewish eschatology that Jeremiah will return prior to the end.[19] On the other hand, there may be a much simpler explanation of the mention of Jeremiah. According to bBB, 14b Bar. the place of the Book of Jeremiah in the Canon was at the head of the latter prophets.[20] When Mt. puts the fuller 'Ιερεμίαν ἢ ἕνα τῶν προφητῶν (Mt. 16:14) in place of εἷς τῶν προφητῶν (Mk. 8:28) or προφήτης τις τῶν ἀρχαίων (Lk. 9:19), he is obviously introducing the name of the first of the prophets as an example, possibly in order to express the fact that the popular idea of Jesus as a prophet was thinking in terms of one of the later prophets. Hence the mention of Jeremiah

---

[14] Schl. Mt. and Kl. Mt., ad loc.; Pr.-Bauer, s.v. Str.-B., I, 1030 considers the possibility that Jeremiah the prophet denotes "very generally the prophetic writings," "at the head of which the Book of Jer. previously stood" (→ infra). This solution derives from J. Lightfoot, Opera Omnia, II (1686), 384 f. It is rightly rejected as improbable by J. A. Fabricius, 1103 f.

[15] Str.-B., I, 730. Bousset-Gressm., 233 wrongly appeal to 2 Macc. 2:1 ff.; 15:13 in support of the opposite view.

[16] The mother of the sons, i.e., the congregation, is promised: Mittam tibi adiutorium pueros meos Isaiam et Jeremiam. This is a variant on Rev. 11:3 ff. and Mk. 9:4 par.

[17] Acc. to the text of J. F. Breithaupt (Gothae [1707], 64, line 1) and the Amsterdam ed., 1723 (fol. 13b, line 4), Jeremiah says that the place where he hid the ark and the curtains is to remain unknown עַד בּוֹא אֵלִיָּהוּ. But the Codex Munsterianus, with which Breithaupt compares, reads עַד בּוֹאִי אֲנִי וָאֵלִיָּה (op. cit., p. 63, n. 11).

[18] The addition is found in three recensions: Dorothei Recensio, 46, 9 ff.; Epiphanii Recensio Altera, 63, 7 ff.; Recensio Anonyma, 73, 17 ff. The shortest of the three texts (the second) runs: καὶ ἔδωκεν ὁ θεὸς τῷ 'Ιερεμίᾳ χάριν, ἵνα τὸ τέλος τοῦ μυστηρίου αὐτοῦ αὐτὸς ποιήσῃ, ὅπως γένηται κοινωνὸς Μωϋσέως. The concluding words are to be taken eschatologically according to the context.

[19] Weber, 354; Schürer, II, 612; Kl. Mt. on 16:14; Pr.-Bauer, 580.

[20] "Our teachers taught that the sequence of the prophets is Joshua, Judges, Samuel, Kings: Jeremiah, Ezekiel, Isaiah and the Twelve."

in Mt. 16:14 does not refer to an expectation of his return for which we have no other attestation. It is simply due to the place of the Book of Jeremiah in the Canon. [21]

J. Jeremias

ἱερός, τὸ ἱερόν, ἱερωσύνη, ἱερατεύω,
ἱεράτευμα, ἱερατεία (-ία), ἱερουργέω,
ἱερόθυτος, ἱεροπρεπής, ἱεροσυλέω,
ἱερόσυλος, ἱερεύς, ἀρχιερεύς

---

† ἱερός.

Contents: A. Etymology. B. ἱερός in Common Greek Usage: 1. Synonyms and Antonyms; 2. The Mains Groups of Usage: a. In Relation to Things; b. In Relation to Persons. C. ἱερός in the Septuagint. D. ἱερός in the Rest of Hellenistic Judaism: 1. Generally in Josephus; 2. Generally in Philo; 3. The Usage in the Apocrypha and in Josephus and Philo; 4. In Speculative Connections in Philo and 4 Maccabees; 5. ἱερός for Persons. E. ἱερός in the New Testament. F. ἱερός in the Early Church.

A. Etymology.

Ionic, and often in Hom. ἱρός: Il., 2, 420; 4, 46; Od., 1, 66; 3, 278; Doric only ἱαρός. Etymology. [1] a. The Gk. ἱερός is usually linked originally with the Sanskrit *isirá*: "invigorating," "strong," "lively," and the Celtic **isaros*, fem. as the name of a river, **Isarā* (*Isar, Isère*). This is formally acceptable if we assume a basic Indo-Germanic form **isᵊrós*, but it is unsatisfactory as regards the meaning, since the Sanskrit term does not belong to the religious sphere, and no decision can be reached in respect of the Celtic word. b. As regards the Greek term, especially in Homer, two or three

---

[21] Cf. Hänel, 95 f., though he gives priority to Mt.

ἱ ε ρ ό ς. The def. in Hesych., who explains ἱερός by σεμνός, ἥμερος, ἀγαθός, cannot be sustained. But Suid. is important, for he goes to the heart of the concept: τῷ θεῷ ἀνατεθειμένος (Lat. *sacer, sacrosanctus, consecratus*). But cf. → 225. For bibl. on "holy," "holiness," → I, 88, ἅγιος. Cf. also art. "Holiness" in ERE, VI, 731-759; art. "*heilig*," in LexThK, IV, 881-884; RGG², II, 1714 ff. (with bibl.); E. Fehrle, *Die kultische Keuschheit im Altertum* (1910); T. Wächter, *Reinheitsvorschriften im griech. Kult* (1910); M. Schumpp, "Das Heilige in der Bibel" in *Theologie und Glaube*, 22 (1930), 331-343; R. Kittel, "Heiligkeit Gottes im AT," RE³, VII, 566-573; I. Benzinger, *Hbr. Archäologie³* (1927), 395-402; J. Dillersberger, *Das Heilige im NT* (1926). On ἱερός: Pass., Pape, Liddell-Scott, *s.v.*; Trench, 206 f., 241; Moult.-Mill., Preisigke Wört., *s.v.*; D. Magie, *De Romanorum Juris Publici Sacrique Vocabulis Sollemnibus in Graecum Sermonem Conversis* (1905), Index; E. Williger, "Hagios," RVV, 19 (1922), 54, n. 1. Cf. also H. Delehaye, "Sanctus" in *Analecta Bollandiana*, 28 (1909), 145-200; W. Sickel in GGA, 1901, 387 ff. (review of G. Waitz, *Deutsche Verfassungsgeschichte*, VI [1896]); F. Poland, *Geschichte des gr. Vereinswesens* (1909), Index; G. Thieme, *Die Inschriften von Magnesia am Maeander und das NT* (1905), 36; Deissmann LO, 321 f.; Schl. Theol. d. Judt., 64, 80. On *sanctus*: W. Link, *De Vocis Sanctus Usu Pagano Quaestiones Selectae*, Diss. Königsberg (1910).

[1] For this section I am indebted to M. Leumann, Zürich.

homonyms have been suspected, a first in the sense of "powerful" corresponding to the above etymology (Sanskrit *isirá-*), and a second in the sense of "holy." The second is composed as follows. In Western Indo-Germanic there is a root *ais*, which produces *Ehre* etc. in New High German, and from which we have the Oscan-Umbrian *ais* ("God") and also an Etruscan *aesar* ("God"). [2] The connection of ἱερός with *ais*, however, is by no means certain. c. More recent linkings suggests that the Oscan-Umbrian *ais* is a loan word from a pre-Indo-Germanic language (whence also the Etruscan *aesar*). There is thus a tendency to regard ἱερός as pre-Greek. On the other hand, the shift from *ais* to *is* (as in **isᵌrós* ἱερός) demands very bold speculations concerning this pre-Indo-Germanic people, since it is as such an Indo-Germanic change.

The present state of research suggests that the word is pre-Greek, and that we are thus unable to trace its etymology. If it is true that one part of Homer's usage (→ 225) suggests the sense of "powerful" and thus leads in the direction indicated above, investigation will show that the isolation of Homer's ἱερός from the basic religious significance is very questionable (→ 225). [3]

B. ἱερός in Common Greek Usage.

1. Synonyms and Antonyms. [4]

ἱερός is constantly combined with the synonyms θεῖος, → ἅγιος (less frequently ἁγνός), ὅσιος, σεμνός, ἄσυλος. [5] There is no hard and fast distinction from these terms. Even → θεῖος can mean "coming from the gods," "posited by them," "belonging or dedicated to them," "standing under their protection." It is thus used of superhuman heroes and in imperial times of Caesar: *sacer, divinus*. The less frequent ἅγιος can also mean "consecrated to deity," whether of things or persons, although, unlike ἱερός, it can also express personal holiness in the moral sense. The element of separation in consecration and dedication to deity made ἅγιος more suitable as a translation of קדשׁ and for use in the NT sense, quite apart from the fact that it is less frequent, more fluid and less firmly fixed than ἱερός. ἁγνός is used also of places and things consecrated to the gods. Nevertheless, it can also mean "chaste," "innocent," "pure," "unspotted," whether as a personal quality or in the sense of ceremonial purity; it thus bears a flavour of its own. ὅσιος can mean sanctified or consecrated by divine or natural law, especially in juxtaposition to → δίκαιος. But it can also mean "pious" or "religious" of persons, and it is thus markedly different from ἱερός. Finally, σεμνός is used of the gods and divine things in the sense of "holy" or "exalted," but its distinctive sense is that of "honourable," "worthy of regard," "majestic" or "pre-eminent." Now ἱερός itself is not uniform. It has two main senses, a. "filled with the divine power of deity," and b. "consecrated to deity." But these two senses are linked by the thought of belonging to the divine sphere, and to this degree ἱερός is absolute in meaning. It can never have a negative sense like ἅγιος ("accursed" or "worthy to be cursed"), or

---

[2] Cf. Walde-Pok., I, 13 *s.v. ais* "to be respectful," "to honour." On c.: J. Schrijnen, *Bulletin de la Société de Linguistique de Paris,* 32 (1931), 54-64.

[3] Cf. Debrunner (e.g., *Indogermanische Forschungen,* 21 [1907], 31 f.), who argues that no matter how we interpret the examples in Homer there is a ἱαρός (ἱερός) in the sense of "vigorous," "vital," and that this stems from ἱαίνω, which is related to ἱαρός as μιαίνω to μιαρός. I suspect an intermingling of the Indo-Germ. **isᵌrós* and a borrowed (*a*)*isr-*.

[4] Cf. also H. H. Schmidt, *Synonymik der griech. Sprache,* IV (1886), 321 ff.

[5] With θεῖος: Plat. Tim., 45a; Philo Conf. Ling., 59; Jos. Ant., 4, 285. With ἅγιος: Philo Det. Pot. Ins., 133 f.; Som., I, 149; Spec. Leg., I, 234. With ὅσιος: Conf. Ling., 27. With ἄσυλος: Plut. Gen. Socr., 24 (II, 593a); Philo Gig., 16; Rer. Div. Her., 108; Sobr., 66; Jos. Ant., 15; 136. In Philo σεμνός is often used with ἅγιος: Decal., 133; Som., I, 234; Spec. Leg., I, 151. On the distinction between θεῖος and ἱερός cf. the comprehensive survey in U. v. Wilamowitz, *Glaube der Hellenen,* I (1931), 18 ff.

ὅσιος (profane in distinction to ἱερός), or σεμνός ("proud," "pompous" in an ironical sense). Of the terms mentioned, the closest are θεῖος and ἅγιος, and the most distant is ἁγνός, since ἱερός does not denote personal piety. If Oedipus says of himself in Soph. Oed. Col., 287: ἱερὸς εὐσεβής τε, strictly speaking the second word is not a synonym but a consequence of the first. He is pious as one who is dedicated to God. The ἱερός is *sacer;* he is not unconditionally *sanctus* (ὅσιος). He is *destinatus diis.* He bears the *character divinus indelebilis.* Hence the ἱερόν is an ἄσυλον. Along with ἄσυλος other expressions like καθωσιωμένος, παναγής, ἱεροπρεπής, ἀφιερωμένος, καθιερωμένος confirm the almost technical definition [6] of ἱερός as "sacrosanct." The best antonym is βέβηλος (with ἀνίερος), which means "profane." [7]

On the one hand, ἱερός denotes the divine power of the sphere which belongs to the gods. On the other, it expresses the supernatural power and sanctity which something has when it belongs and is consecrated to deity. This consecration may be by primal laws, by natural factors, or by the specific divine and human definition and institution of the cultus, of custom, or of law. The character of divine consecration is a fact of divine operation, yet only in the sense of consecration and not in the moral sense. Thus ἱερός is the most common sacral and cultic term in the Greek world.

2. The Main Groups of Usage.

ἱερός is very rarely used in a statement concerning the person of the gods, as in Hes. Theog., 21: ἱερὸν γένος ἀθανάτων. [8] For this reason, we need not regard this as a separate group, but may consider it under a.

a. In Relation to Things. i. ἱερός denotes that which belongs, or is very closely related, to the divine sphere, with no question of human action.

Hence it is used of the form (Hom. Il., 15, 39, the head of Zeus), the dwelling (Aristoph. Nu., 270 of the snowy regions of Olympus, Hom. Od., 10, 426 of the house of Circe), the resting-place (Hes. Theog., 57, the couch of Zeus), and the weapons (Soph. Phil., 943, the bow of Heracles) of the gods. It is also used of the scales in the hand of Kronion, Hom. Il., 16, 658, and of the divine steeds before the chariot of Achilles, which are a gift of Kronion, Hom. Il., 17, 464, and which make the chariot holy, i.e., victoriously strong, because they are a gift from the divine hand. In more sophisticated formulae the case is the same as in these apparently primitive and mythological materials. The ἱερὰ γράμματα (Ditt. Or., I, 56, 36 [3rd cent. B.C.]) (→ γράμμα, I, 763 f.) bear this name because they rest on a divine declaration. This applies similarly to oracular scrolls with their designs, Aristoph. Eq., 116; 1017. Once we enter the sphere of the gods, we have to do with the holy, so that even a war against Zeus can be called a ἱερὸς πόλεμος, Aristoph. Av., 556.

ii. Yet the chief use of ἱερός begins only when this divine aspect may be felt and experienced by men in the form of consecration. Hence the word is used of nature as that which is divinely filled, dispensed and consecrated.

Light (Hes. Op., 337), the aether (Aristoph. Thes., 1068), the half-personified periods of darkness and day (Hom. Il., 8, 66; Od., 9, 56; Il., 11, 194 and 209) are all regarded as

[6] Delehaye, *op. cit.,* 146 f. On καθιερωμένος, Magie, *op. cit.,* 92.
[7] Cf. the synon. ἀβέβηλος, ἄβατος, in Plut. Quaest. Rom., 27 (II, 271a). On βέβηλος, Philo Poster. C., 110.
[8] Pind. Olymp., 7, 60; Pyth., 9, 64 calls the gods ἁγνοί. Cf. W. Nestle, *Griech. Religiosität,* I (1930), 110.

powers which are determined by and proceed from the deity. So, too, the earth (Soph. Phil., 706), the land which abounds in fruits (Aristoph. Nu., 282), and the streams and rivers which flow from Zeus are all filled with deity and are consequently holy (Hom. Od., 10, 351; Soph. Phil., 1215). This finds specific expression in the fact that certain deities rule over the forces of nature. The threshing-floor is ἱερός (Hom. Il., 5, 499) because it is sacred to Demeter ; corn has divine power because it is her gift (11, 631); the olive-tree in the grotto of the nymphs (Hom. Od., 13, 372), the fish which is consecrated to Poseidon (Hom. Il., 16, 407) and the bees (Pind. Fr., 123) are all called ἱεροί because they are bearers and dispensers of the divine.

iii. Lands, islands, cities and straits which are sacred to protective deities share the same consecration.

We may refer to Ilion with Pergamos (Hom. Il., 4, 46; 5, 446), or Thebes (Il., 4, 378), or Athens (Aristoph. Eq., 1037), or the strongholds of Pylos (Hom. Od., 21, 108) and Sunion (Od., 3, 278), Euboea (Il., 2, 535), or πόρος Ἑλλάς (Aristoph. Vesp., 308).

iv. Consecration to the deity finds its true centre in the cultus.

In narrower cultic usage the temple is called ἱερὸς δόμος or ναός, Hom. Il., 6, 89; Aristoph. Lys., 775; the altar, Hom. Il., 2, 305; Soph. Trach., 994 f.; the sacrifice, ἑκατόμβη in Hom. Il., 1, 99; Od., 3, 144; the table of sacrifice, Aristoph. Pl., 678; also the temple precincts, Soph. Oed. Col., 16 and 54, and the temple grove, Hom. Il., 2, 506 : all are called ἱερός. This sacral term is also used of the feasts. Thus the ἱεραὶ ὧραι are festivals, Aristoph. Thes., 948, and the word can even be used of the torches, Thes., 101. Particularly instructive is Plat. Leg., VIII, 841d; cf. Resp., V, 458e, for here a true marriage festival which stands under divine blessing can be called ἱερός (cf. the cultic fact of the ἱερὸς γάμος, → I, 653). The ἀγῶνες and ἄθλοι are ἱεροί because they take place in honour of the gods, Pind. Nem., 2, 4; Olymp., 8, 64. Orations dedicated to the gods are ἱεροὶ λόγοι, Iambl. Vit. Pyth. (A. Nauck, 1884), 111, 6; 182, 6. The deity to which something is consecrated is put in the genit.: Hom. Od., 6, 322 : Ἀθηναίης; 13, 104 : Νυμφάων; Xenoph. An., V, 3, 13 : Ἀρτέμιδος; cf. Plat. Leg., V, 741c : τῶν πάντων θεῶν; Athenag. Suppl., 28, 3 : τῆς Ἴσιδος.

v. But the term can be used of anything consecrated in a religious way to God, quite apart from worship.

Hence it can be applied to dramatic choruses, because they intimate divine things, Aristoph. Ra., 674, 686, and esp. to songs which resound to the gods, Plat. Leg., VIII, 829e, or to the circle of judgment, because it is sacred to Zeus, Hom. Il., 18, 504, to graves and burial mounds, which are particularly sacred, Soph. Oed. Col., 1545, 1763, or even to the couch on which Strepsiades is to sit at the behest of Socrates, since this is to be the place of his initiation into divine things (Aristoph. Nu., 254).

vi. There are several abstract uses, [9] e.g., ἱερὰ ἄγκυρα, the final refuge, or ἱερὰ συμβουλή, the ultimate resolve. These are religious inasmuch as they suggest that help and counsel are to be found with the gods alone.

That all these uses are common to Greek in every age may be seen from the pap., where all these connections and formulae recur. [10]

b. Persons are called ἱεροί i. in Pindar and Homer, as kings or warriors who stand under special divine protection or who satisfy the divine character in the discharge of their official tasks.

---

[9] Cf. Pass., *s.v.*
[10] Cf. Preisigke Wört., III, section 20 (p. 378 f.), *s.v.*

When Pind. Pyth., 5, 97 speaks of βασιλέες ἱεροί, there is a reminder that their dignity comes from deity. We are to understand in the same way the ἱερὸν μένος Ἀλκινόοιο and the ἱερὴ ἷς Τηλεμάχοιο in Hom. Od., 7, 167; 2, 409 etc. Alkinoos has his office from Zeus, and Telemachus stands under the protection of Athene. They thus represent supernatural power no less than the πυλαωροὶ ἱεροί, Il., 24, 681, the φυλάκων ἱερὸν τέλος, Il., 10, 56 and the host of Achaian spearmen, Od., 24, 81. Because they are selected by the deity, their task and commission are also therefrom. In this case ἱερός might well be translated "august" or "exalted," but we cannot weaken this to "stately," "manly," "strong," or "worthy of regard," [11] for the relation to the deity bears on the origin of the expression. On the other hand, there is no moral sense.

ii. The description of the king as ἱερός has a powerful influence at a later period. Augustus is called ἱερός, σεβάσμιος : Corpus Glossariorum Latinorum, II (1888), 26, 21 and 25, [12] ὁ ἱερώτατος Καῖσαρ : Preisigke Sammelbuch, 5136, 19 (3rd cent. A.D.). The emperor is sacrosanct in virtue of the power which he has taken over from the people's tribune, and he stands inviolably under the protection of the gods. Not merely his person, but everything imperial, shares in this character.

Hence the expression ἱερὰ γράμματα is used of imperial edicts, Inscr. Graecae ad Res Romanas Pertinentes (ed. R. Cagnat, 1900), IV, 571, 13 (2nd cent. A.D.) (→ γράμμα, I, 763). We also read of τὸ ἱερώτατον βῆμα of the prefect of Egypt, P. Hamb., 4, 8 (1st cent. A.D.); cf. P. Fay, Class. Philol., I (1906), 172, pap. 5, line 26 (154-159 A.D.), P. Lond., II, 358, 19 (2nd cent. A.D.). The same character can be ascribed to the senate : populus sanctusque senatus : Cic. Divin., I, 12; Just. Apol., I, 1, 1: ἱερᾷ τε συγκλήτῳ of the senate. The word can also be used of city councils and people, and especially of the fiscus : ὁ ἱερώτατος φίσκος, Cagnat, op. cit., III, 727, or τὸ ἱερώτατον ταμιεῖον, Ditt. Syll.³, 888, 10 (3rd cent. A.D.); P. Lond., II, 214, 5. But it can be used of other exalted officials, [13] and of various unions (mystery and agonistic) and guilds, some of which receive the title ἱερὸς or ἱερώτατος because they stand under imperial patronage. [14]

iii. The ἄνθρωπος ἱερός of the Mysteries etc.

Already in Aristoph. Ra., 652 the initiate in the Mysteries is called ἄνθρωπος ἱερός. In the Messenian mystery law, Ditt. Syll.³, 736 (Andania) the initiates are an organised official body between the priests and lesser cultic officials, and they are called ἱεροί (-αί). [15] Similarly Plut. Alex. Fort. Virt., I, 10 (II, 332b) calls the Indian gymnosophists ἄνδρες ἱεροὶ καὶ αὐτόνομοι because they are θεῷ σχολάζοντες, cf. the ἱεροὶ καὶ δαιμόνιοι ἄνθρωποι in Gen. Socr., 20 (II, 589d). At this point we are strongly reminded of a supplementary definition of Suid. : ἱερὸς λέγεται καὶ ὁ εὐσεβής, though here there is a natural enough shift of meaning, since ἱερός now means "with reference to the divine or the religious," cf. Orig. Cels., IV, 89, where Celsus calls the conversations of animals : ἐννοίας τοῦ θείου ἱερωτέρας ἡμῶν. The common ascription to Plato of the title ὁ ἱερός, ὁ ἱερώτατος points in a similar, if not the same, direction. According to Plat. Ion, 534b the ποιητής is ἱερός because his spirit is ἔνθεος, cf. Democr. Fr., 18 (I, 146, Diels): The poet writes μετ' ἐνθουσιασμοῦ καὶ ἱεροῦ πνεύματος (inspiration). [16] But the cultic officials or freed men who are under the protection of a shrine are also called ἱεροί. In the imperial period members of the priest's family, who

---

[11] → 222.
[12] Cf. D. Magie, 64. On sacer, sanctus, ἅγιος etc. cf. also GGA, 163 (1901), 387 ff.
[13] Poland, 391.
[14] Poland, 169 f.
[15] Cf. Pauly-W., VIII (1913), 1472.
[16] It is in terms of this general view of ἐνθουσιασμός that the impression of epilepsy as ἡ ἱερὰ νόσος is to be understood, Plat. Leg., XI, 916a etc.

are implicated in the service of God, are also given the title, [17] cf. the expression ἱεροὶ παῖδες. [18] If this is an extension of the sacrosanct character of the priest to his family, there is a notable parallel to the ἅγιοι of 1 C. 7:14.

C. ἱερός in the Septuagint.

For קֹדֶשׁ and its derivatives קָדוֹשׁ and מִקְדָּשׁ the Gk. Bible has ἅγιος rather than ἱερός, and we also find ἁγιάζειν, ἁγνίζειν, ἁγίασμα, ἁγιασμός and ἁγιωσύνη. ἱερός is found as an adj. only twice.

At Jos. 6:8 it is used for יוֹבֵל; the trumpets of rams' horns are called σάλπιγγες ἱεραί. At Da. 1:2 LXX the temple vessels are called ἱερὰ σκεύη → 227. [19] The influence of this decision of the LXX on Hellenistic Judaism is considerable. Ep. Ar., Test. XII, Ps. Sol. and even Test. Sol. all use ἅγιος rather than ἱερός.

This reserve of the LXX in respect of ἱερός is striking and eloquent. One may assume that prior to the existence of the LXX Hellenistic Jews used ἱερός for קֹדֶשׁ (cf. the influence of this usage under D.). But the LXX translators felt strongly the pagan and cultic sense of the term. It was too freighted to allow of its usage as an equivalent of קֹדֶשׁ. On the other hand, the rarer and less definite ἅγιος, with its more fluid meaning, was better adapted to take on a distinctive new sense. [20]

D. ἱερός in the Rest of Hellenistic Judaism.

ἱερός found more ready access into a restricted circle of Jewish writers who had no suspicions in relation to the Hellenistic spirit. This circle includes 1, 2, and 3 Esr., 1, 2 and 4 Maccabees, and to a large degree Josephus and Philo.

Since their usage is much the same, these works may be treated together, though the speculative peculiarities of Philo and 4 Macc. demand independent consideration.

1. Generally in Josephus. Josephus has a sense of the distinctiveness of ἅγιος in the substantive use, e.g., in relation to the temple, → 234. Yet he has no scruples in preferring ἱερός as an adj.; indeed, he uses it lavishly. This is a characteristic difference between Joseph. and the translators of the LXX. It is conscious deviation. Thus in Ant., 13, 51 (decree of King Demetrius) he intentionally amends 1 Macc. 10:31: καὶ Ἰερουσαλὴμ ἔστω ἁγία, to: καὶ τὴν Ἰεροσολυμιτῶν πόλιν ἱερὰν καὶ ἄσυλον εἶναι βούλομαι. He explicitly returns to the more general form of expression. And he understands ἱερός after the Gk. pattern, e.g., in Bell., 1, 465, where he causes Herod to appeal to ἱερὰ φύσις, the bonds of nature; cf. 4 Macc. 15:13, → 229. Again, in Bell., 2, 401 he does not call the angels the angels of God, or of the Lord, as in the OT, but οἱ ἱεροὶ ἄγγελοι τοῦ θεοῦ (found in the NT, though not common: → ἅγιοι, Mk. 8:38; Ac. 10:22; Rev. 14:10). Directing his work to the cultured world, Josephus simply adopts the ordinary literary usage. [21]

---

[17] Poland, 301.
[18] Poland, 302. The expression is also used for the temple slave. Cf. Pauly-W., VIII (1913), 1475. O. Kern, *Hermes,* 46 (1911), 302 favours a view similar to → 225, line 32.
[19] 2 Εσδρ. 17:72 S † has it by mistake for ἱερέων.
[20] Cf. Delehaye, 146 f.
[21] Cf. Schl. Jos., 28, n. 1; Schl. Mt., 12.

2. Generally in Philo. For Philo the LXX itself is a ἱερὸν γράμμα. He uses ἅγιος much more frequently than Josephus, but in the development of his thought his cultured interests give him a strong preference for ἱερός. He defines the word in Rer. Div. Her., 171: The commandment to honour parents is ἱερός because it relates basically to God rather than to men. In good Gk. fashion, then, ἱερός expresses relationship to the divine world. Yet under OT influence he draws the moral consequences of this relationship much more resolutely than is customary in the Gk. world. This aspect is not altogether lacking even in the Gk. sphere after the criticism of the immorality of myths by Xenophanes. But biblical influences enable Philo to press it much more radically. This is plain in the revaluation of the formula ἱερὸς ἀγών, → 224. He calls secular games ἀνίεροι because they involve roughness and brutality. Only truly Olympian struggles for the possession of virtue deserve the earlier epithet, for ψεκτὸν δ' οὐδὲν τῶν ἱερῶν, Agric., 91; 113-119. Here, then, ἱερός has a decided moral significance, though it still retains the basic sense of relationship to deity. But the divine is now that which is free from censure. [22]

3. The Usage in the Apocrypha and in Josephus and Philo.

a. Scripture and the Law are ἱεροί. Philo esp. likes the superlative here. βίβλος of the Book of the Law → I, 616, n. 10 : 2 Macc. 8:23 → I, 615 f.; Jos. Ant., 4, 303; Philo Migr. Abr., 14 (of Ex.). βίβλοι : Jos. Ant., 1, 82; Philo Rer. Div. Her., 258 — very common in Philo — superlative, Sobr., 17. βιβλία : Jos. Vit., 418. γραφαί : Philo Congr., 34; superlative, Abr., 4. γράμμα (→ I, 763 f.): Migr. Abr., 139. γράμματα : Jos. Ant., 10, 210 etc. [23] ἀναγραφαί : Philo Som., I, 48. Philo often uses ὁ ἱερὸς λόγος for all Scripture or for a single text : Sacr. AC, 55 and 76; Ebr., 95; Rer. Div. Her., 259 etc. The divine sayings are also called ἱερώτατοι χρησμοί : Philo Mut. Nom., 152; Leg. All., III, 129; the individual precept: διάταγμα : Sacr. AC, 88 f. The songs χοροί, παλινῳδίαι: Conf. Ling., 35; Poster. C., 179 are also ἱεροί. Of the νόμος (Pentateuch): Jos. Bell., 2, 229, or the νόμοι : Bell., 1, 108; Philo Abr., 1. Of the Decalogue : Congr., 120 : ἡ ἱερὰ καὶ θεία νομοθεσία. Of the statutes : Jos. Bell., 4, 182 : τὰ ἱερὰ ἔθη. More abstractly in 4 Macc. 5:29 of the ὅρκοι of the forefathers to preserve the Law.

b. The same agreement, more pronounced in the apocrypha, is found in respect of the holy things belonging to the tabernacle and the temple. Of the many instances we may note particularly those in the apocrypha and parallels for the different groups. The tabernacle is called ἡ ἱερὰ σκηνή only at Jos. Ant., 5, 68 (after Eupolemos); cf. Philo Rer. Div. Her., 112. At 2 Εσδρ. 6:3 B the temple itself is called οἶκος ἱερός, and at 4 Macc. 4:12 its site is ἱερὸς τόπος. The courts in the temple precincts are χωρία ἱερά in Philo Plant., 61; Sobr., 40. The precincts themselves are more generally called holy (2 Macc. 1:34), the περίβολοι (2 Macc. 6:4), the πυλῶνες (1 Εσδρ. 9:41; 2 Macc. 8:33; Jos. Bell., 4, 191) or πύλαι (Bell., 5, 7), the γαζοφυλάκιον or θησαυρός (1 Εσδρ. 5:44; 4 Macc. 4:7). There are many instances in Jos. and Philo when such things as the table for the showbread, the lamps, etc. are called holy. Eight times in 1 Εσδρ. we have τὰ ἱερὰ σκεύη for the temple vessels, e.g., 1:39; 6:17; and the same phrase occurs three times in 2 Macc. 4:48 → Da., 226. Jos., too, uses it : Ant., 3, 258. Like 1 Εσδρ. 8:70 he and Philo call the priestly vestment στολή or ἐσθὴς ἱερά : Ant., 3, 211; 20, 6; 12; Philo Leg. Gaj., 296. For σάλπιγγες cf. 1 Macc. 16:8, → 226; Jos. 6:8. The building of the temple and the works of the temple are τὰ ἱερὰ ἔργα in

---

[22] On ἱερὸς ἀγών, cf. also Migr. Abr., 200; Mut. Nom., 81 and 106; Abr., 48; Cher., 73. Par. from the diatribe, P. Wendland, "Philo und die kynisch-stoische Diatribe" in P. Wendland-O. Kern, Beiträge zur Geschichte der griech. Philosophie und Religion (1895), 43. Cf. also Pauly-W., II (1896), 2051 f.

[23] On ἱερὰ γράμματα as written signs (the band round the forehead of the high priest), Jos. Ant., 3, 178 → I, 761. The language of Egyptian hieroglyphics → I, 761 is also called ἱερὰ γλῶσσα : Jos. Ap., 1, 82.

1 Εσδρ. 7:2 f., [24] Jos. Ant., 11, 105 and Philo Plant., 26. Examples might be multiplied indefinitely. Anything relating to the temple is ἱερός: expenditure on the sanctuary, Jos. Ant., 16, 28; Philo Rer. Div. Her., 195; the archives, Jos. Ap., 1, 11; the edict concerning the temple, Ant., 12, 145.

c. Finally, the term applies to the holy days, esp. the Sabbath: Jos. Ant., 13, 168; Bell., 7, 99; Philo Vit. Mos., I, 205; to Jerusalem, ἡ ἱερὰ πόλις: Jos. Ant., 4, 70; ἱερωτάτη: Bell., 7, 328; and to Israel as ἐκκλησία: Philo Migr. Abr., 69, and as a land: Som., I, 27.

In relation to b. and c. we should add, in view of → n. 25, that in these connections Philo and Jos. occasionally have ἅγιος instead of ἱερός: Sacr. AC, 134 (primogeniture); Gig., 23 (temple works); Rer. Div. Her., 186 (double drachma); Op. Mund., 89; Som., II, 123 (Sabbath); Praem. Poen., 123 (the people of God); Jos. Bell., 4, 163 (ἅγιαι χῶραι of the temple); Bell., 5, 384 (the ark); Bell., 2, 321 (the vessels); Ant., 12, 320 (temple ministry); 8, 100 (feast of tabernacles); Ant., 14, 227 (convocations); Bell., 5, 400 (the holy land). But these individual instances are rare compared with the overwhelming use of ἱερός.

4. In Speculative Connections in Philo and 4 Maccabees.

a. Nature and the cosmos. When Philo raises his song to the aether as the habitation of the stars, of the visible and invisible deities which are established in heaven as in a temple; when he extols them as θέατρον, as a sacred chorus, as the flock which the divine shepherd pastures, then ἱερώτατος alone usually suffices: Conf. Ling., (156) 174; Op. Mund., 27, (55,) 78; Gig., 6 ff.; Plant., 118 (Agric., 51). Even of the human body he says in Op. Mund., 137: οἶκος γάρ τις ἢ νεὼς ἱερὸς ἐτεκταίνετο ψυχῆς λογικῆς. This reminds us of 1 C. 6:19, but it is very different in content.

b. λόγος ἱερός, ἱερὸς νοῦς and the doctrine of virtue in Philo and 4 Macc. In Philo esp. the logos is called ἱερός or ἱερώτατος as the formless similitude and reflection of God, Conf. Ling., 147, or of being, ibid., 97. It conditions true knowledge, Poster C., 153. On the expression: Aaron the high-priest ἱερὸς λόγος, as the symbol of the divine word, Leg. All., I, 76. Rer. Div. Her., 201 → ἀρχιερεύς. οἱ ἱεροὶ λόγοι are rational concepts whose main weapon is in ἐπιστήμη, Sacr. AC, 130; cf. the sacred goods, Rer. Div. Her., 105 and 129. The human νοῦς, like a coin impressed by God, is also ἱερώτατος, Deus Imm., 105. Similarly, in his doctrine of virtue Philo uses ἱερός of the main goals of his ethics. The Stoic καθήκοντα are called ἱεραὶ δόξαι into which the νοῦς enters, Leg. All., III, 126. Above all, Philo uses ἱερός when dominion over the senses is extolled. This goal is reached by the soul which dwells in the holy house of virtue, Leg. All., III, 152. It goes through ἁγνεία ἱερά, Det. Pot. Ins., 170. Contempt for the physical is ἱερωτέρα τάξις, Migr. Abr., 23. And cosmopolitan equanimity is the goal of ἱερὸν γένος σοφίας inasmuch as it is an ἀνθρώπινον, Rer. Div. Her., 182. 4 Macc. also uses ἱερός to show that the victory of reason over the sensual world is divine. Here there is a strong influence of the OT קדשׁ, for basically this victory is legal piety in the form of a strict observance of rules concerning meats; all the examples are from this sphere. But this observance is reinterpreted along Stoic lines. The connection is clearest in 4 Macc. 2:22. At creation God set τὸν ἱερὸν ἡγεμόνα νοῦν on the throne. This shows itself to be ἱερός by its lordship over impulses and passions. This is the basic concept. Eleazar, the seven brothers and their mother are examples. The seven fight a ἱερὰ στρατεία for piety in 9:24. They constitute a ἱερὰ συμφωνία περὶ τῆς εὐσεβείας (14:3) through their common mastery of sensual impulses.

---

[24] Worth noting in relation to 1 Εσδρ. is the fact that the Gk. translator has consistently added the attribute ἱερός. It is completely lacking in the Heb. and in the corresponding passages in 2 Ch. and 2 Εσδρ. [Bertram].

c. The mystical in the broadest sense is ἱερόν. To this belongs the favourite mysticism of numbers : Op. Mund., 97 of the κάλλος ἱερώτατον of the number seven ; Mut. Nom., 191 f. of the δεκάτη ἱερά, etc. There also belongs here the allegorical meaning of words and things. Thus Plant., 139 calls husbandry ἱερωτάτη because it has a higher, spiritual significance. Similarly, the dogmas of philosophy are holy, Vit. Cont., 26. In particular, Philo uses ἱερός with reference to the mysteries. The secret doctrines which initiates take into their souls are ἱερὰ μυστήρια (Cher., 48); the τελεταί are initiation into them, and are called ἱερώταται, Cher., 42, Gig., 54, Leg. All., III, 219; Sacr. AC, 60 : ὁ ἱερὸς μύστης λόγος. [25]

5. ἱερός for Persons. In Jos. it is used only of those consecrated to God's service in the temple : the Levites, Ant., 3, 287; cf. 3, 258; the temple servants, Ant., 11, 70; Det. Pot. Ins., 62. Philo can also call God the ἱερώτατος νομοθέτης, Rer. Div. Her., 21, and the angels are ἱεροὶ καὶ ἄσυλοι on account of their ministry (Gig., 16, cf. Abr., 115). He often calls Moses ὁ ἱερώτατος, Abr., 181 etc., and his staff is holy, Vit. Mos., I, 210. In Virt., 119 we find ἱερώτατος προφήτης, and Plato is holy in Omn. Prob. Lib., 13 → 225. But only rarely is the term used of the virtuous or pious, Mut. Nom., 60; Fug., 83. On the other hand, 4 Macc. applies it often to people. When Eleazar dies for the Law in a triumph of reason (6:30) he is ὁ ἱερὸς ἀνήρ; cf. τὴν ἱερὰν ψυχήν in 7:4. The seven are οἱ ἱεροὶ μείρακες (14:6) and their mother is ἡ ἱερὰ καὶ θεοσεβὴς μήτηρ (16:12). It is worth noting that her motherly love (φύσις ἱερά) is surpassed by λογισμός at 15:13. In 7:6 Eleazar did not not soil τοὺς ἱεροὺς ὀδόντας with unclean food. The teeth remain cultically clean and are thus holy to God.

There can be no question that with this usage 4 Macc. influenced the later development in the Church of ideas relating to *sanctus*. In this respect one may ignore the fusion of the Jewish קדש and the Stoic λογισμός which derives from God and is thus the superior element in man. The whole emphasis may be laid on the martyrdom through which those who are faithful to the Law are holy. Yet in 4 Macc. itself ἱερός is not one-sidedly linked with martyrdom. It is also linked with the triumph of νοῦς.

E. ἱερός in the New Testament.

The fact that ἱερός occurs so seldom in the NT is a sign that primitive Christianity shared the linguistic sense of the LXX and was afraid of the sacral words of paganism. This basic term is avoided because it is anchored in Greek mythology, because it reflects the whole religious world bound up with the ancient conception of deity and nature, and especially because it is a painful reminder of all that the Christian must reject as idolatrous. The only small concession to Hellenistic usage is in 2 Tm. 3:15 : ἱερὰ γράμματα, in relation to OT Scripture.

This is a favourite formula of Philo and Joseph. → I, 763 f.; III, 227. But it is not found elsewhere in Paul. The Law is ἅγιος in R. 7:12. In the shorter Marcan ending supported by L ψ 099, 579, 0112, 274 mg sy hcl mg sa codd b codd k, also B we find the expression : τὸ ἱερὸν καὶ ἄφθαρτον κήρυγμα τῆς αἰωνίου σωτηρίας, but this is a sign of late and non-apostolic style. The phrase probably originated in the 3rd cent. in Egypt, and,

---

[25] On ἱερός in mystery expressions in Philo, cf. Williger, *Hagios,* 102 f. But the usage is varied. In more explicit speculative connections (4. a-c) Philo has ἅγιος more often than in 3. a-c → 227 f.: κόσμος, Plant., 50; Rer. Div. Her., 199; λόγος: Leg. All., I, 16; Migr. Abr., 202; νοῦς, Leg. All., I, 17; number mysticism, Vit. Mos., II, 80; Spec. Leg., II, 194; Migr. Abr., 169; τελεταί, Som., I, 82. That ἅγιος has for him a more exalted ring than ἱερός may be seen from expressions like Rer. Div. Her., 75 : τῶν πανιέρων τεμενῶν ἁγιώτερον, cf. Spec. Leg., I, 275. ἅγιος of God, Praem. Poen., 123; Sacr. AC, 101; Som., I, 254.

although an attempt is made to adapt it to the style of the NT, it stands out by reason of this word and of its rhetorical pathos. On τὰ ἱερά at 1 C. 9:13 → 232.

F. ἱερός in the Early Church.

Post-apostolic fathers and apologists. In 1 Cl., 33, 4 there is reference to ταῖς ἱεραῖς καὶ ἀμώμοις χερσίν (of God). Elsewhere in the post-apost. fathers, however, ἱερός is not used of God. In Herm. s., 1, 10 the right use of money in brotherly love is ἡ πολυτέλεια καλὴ καὶ ἱερά. From 1 Cl. on (43, 1; 45, 2; 53, 1) the Scriptures are called ἱεραὶ βίβλοι, γραφαί, → I, 751.

Clement of Alexandria. Clement has ὁ ἱερὸς ὄντως Μωυσῆς once at Prot., VI, 69, 2. In Strom., I, 12, 4 he calls Moses νόμων ἱερῶν ἑρμηνεύς, and in Prot., II, 25, 1 ἱερο-φάντης τῆς ἀληθείας. But ἱερός as an epithet is rare in Clement. David and Plato are not ἱεροί. In Paed., I, 55, 2 Jesus is ἅγιος θεός, in Strom., I, 11, 3 the apostles are οἱ ἅγιοι ἀπόστολοι; and in Strom., V, 65, 4 Paul is ὁ ἅγιος ἀπόστολος.

On the other hand, ἱερός is highly estimated by Origen, especially in Cels., VII, 52 in opposition to τοὺς ἐπὶ τὰ νομιζόμενα ἱερὰ ὡς ἀληθινὰ ἱερὰ σπεύδοντας who do not see that no product of human handiwork can be ἱερόν. Origen's love for ἱερός is obviously influenced by Philo, → γράμμα, I, 764. Thus we find phrases like οἱ ἱεροὶ τῶν θείων γραμμάτων λόγοι and ὁ ἱερὸς νοῦς τῶν γραφῶν, Cels., VI, 47; Comm. in Joh., 28, 22; cf. ὁ ἱερὸς λόγος, Comm. in Joh., 2, 25. Of OT religion he can say ἡ τῶν πάλαι θεοσέβεια ἱερὰ ἦν, Comm. in Joh., 2, 34. He calls the incense of the temple cultus ἱερός in Hom., 18, 9 in Jer. 18. The resurrection is also ἱερός, Comm. in Joh., 32, 9, and so are the δόγματα with which Jesus was filled, Exhortatio ad Marty-rium, 29. Particularly strong is his inclination to use the term of people. Angels, souls and spirits which intercede for Christians are δυνάμεις ἱεραί, Cels., VIII, 64, and the authors of the OT and NT are ἱεροὶ ἄνδρες, VI, 18. In Cels., IV, 33 the question is raised whether the patriarchs deserve this title. It is accorded to inspired poets, sages and philosophers in Cels., VII, 41. Moses is the ἱερὸς θεράπων, Comm. in Joh., 20, 36. Jesus was θεῖόν τι καὶ ἱερὸν χρῆμα. His incarnate soul is called ἱερά, Cels., VII, 17. The genuinely divine uses the most pure and holy (ἱερωτάταις) of the souls of men. The apostles are οἱ ἱεροὶ ἀπόστολοι, Comm. in Joh., 10, 29. In his writings he often addresses his friend and patron as ἱερὲ ἀδελφὲ Ἀμβρόσιε, Cels., VII, 1, or ἱερὲ Ἀμβρόσιε, Cels., IV, 1.[26] This can hardly mean pious alone, but one who is devoted to the holy, or to sacred study. All in all, Philo finds here a means of entry into the early Church.

τὸ ἱερόν.

Contents: A. τὸ ἱερόν, τὰ ἱερά as General Cultic Terms. B. The Use of τὸ ἱερόν for Temple: 1. General Greek Usage; 2. The Jerusalem Temple in Judaism: a. The Septuagint and Apocrypha; b. Josephus and Philo: i. In General; ii. The Usage; 3. The Use of τὸ

---

[26] Cf. the address ἱερὲ υἱέ, P. Oxy., XII, 1492, 1 (3/4 cent. A.D.) to a Christian.

τὸ ἱερόν. On the background: P. Stengel, Die griech. Kultusaltertümer (1920), 10-31; S. Wide, M. P. Nilsson, "Griech. und röm. Religion" in A. Gercke and E. Norden, Einleitung in die Altertumswissenschaft, II, 2⁴ (1933). W. F. Otto, Priester und Tempel im hellenisti-schen Ägypten, I (1905), 258-405; F. Poland, Geschichte des griech. Vereinswesens (1909), 457 ff. The different temples in Israel's history: R. Kittel, "Tempel von Jerusalem," RE³, 19, 488-500; W. Nowack, Lehrbuch der hbr. Archäologie, II (1894), 25-83; I. Benzinger, Hbr. Archäologie³ (1927), 312-337; K. Möhlenbrink, Der Tempel Salomos (1932). The Herodian temple: Schürer, I, 15-17, 392 f.; RE³, 19, 488. Plans of the temple, P. Volz, Die biblischen Altertümer² (1925), 50; G. Dalman, Orte und Wege Jesu³ (1924), 288; C. Watzinger, Denk-mäler Palästinas, II (1935), Ill. 24-28; On Middot: O. Holtzmann, Middot, Giessener Misch-na (1913). Descriptions: Schürer, II, 342 ff. The cultus: Schürer, II, 336-363; P. Volz, Die biblischen Altertümer, 46-55; Kl. Mk., 129 f.; cf. RGG², V, 1040-1046. For Middot (c. 150

ἱερόν for the Temple in the NT : a. The General Usage ; b. τὸ ἱερόν as a General Term ; c. As the Temple Hill ; d. τὸ πτερύγιον τοῦ ἱεροῦ; e. The Teaching of Jesus and the Apostles in the ἱερόν; f. The Beautiful Gate ; g. τὸ ἱερόν as the Court of Women ; h. As the Inner Court ; i. As the Temple Proper. C. Impulses towards a Spiritualisation of the Temple in the Greek World : 1. The Enlightenment ; 2. The Spiritualising of the Concept of the Temple. D. The Way from Old Testament Prophecy to Jewish Apocalyptic and Hellenistic Judaism : 1. The Temple in Old Testament Prophecy ; 2. The Temple in Apocalyptic : a. Sayings prior to 70 ; b. The New Temple ; c. The Heavenly Temple ; d. The Catastrophe of 70 ; e. The Spiritualising and Criticism of Sacrifice. 3. The Temple in Josephus and Philo : a. Josephus ; b. Philo. E. The Attitude of Jesus and Early Christianity towards the Temple ; 1. The Record of the Witness of Jesus and of the early Christian Attitude in the Gospels : a. The Twofold Attitude of Jesus ; b. The Temple as the Place of the Divine Presence ; c. The Cleansing of the Temple ; d. The Saying concerning the Destruction and Rebuilding of the Temple ; e. The Prophecy of Its Destruction ; f. Sayings from the Later Strata of the Tradition ; 2. The Attitude of the Other New Testament Writings towards the Temple as τὸ ἱερόν; a. Acts ; b. Other New Testament References ; c. The Images of Revelation.

A. τὸ ἱερόν, τὰ ἱερά as General Cultic Terms.

τὸ ἱερόν and the plur. can mean a. the "sacrifice," Hom. Il., 1, 147; Hdt., VIII, 54, also Soph., Thuc., Plat., Philo Spec. Leg., III, 40; Jos. Ant., 2, 275. These are mostly burnt offerings, but they may sometimes be others, Hdt., IV, 33. Then the animal sacrificed is called τὸ ἱερόν, Hom. Il., 2, 420. In Jos. often ἱερεῖον, Ant., 1, 227 etc. Also the "entrails" of animals and the oracles deduced therefrom, Xenoph. An., I, 8, 15. The "sacrificial meal" after the θυσία, Jos. Ant., 6, 158. Finally in the imperial period "sacrificial customs" at society festivals [1] and the part of the members in the sacrifice. [2] b. τὰ ἱερά also means res sacrae, i.e., cultic objects and actions generally, Demosth. Or., 57, 3.

A.D.), Holtzmann ; English Trans. with Commentary, Palestine Exploration Fund Quarterly Statement (1886), 224 ff.; (1887), 60 ff., 116 ff.; Maimonides, Bet-hab-bechira : Engl. Trans. with Exposition, ibid. (1885), 29 ff., 140 ff., 184 ff. Comparison of Josephus with Middot . J. Hildesheimer, "Die Beschreibung des herodianischen Tempels im Traktat Middot und bei Flavius Jos.", Jahresbericht des Rabbiner-Seminars für das orthodoxe Jdt. zu Berlin für 5637 (1876/77); Pal. Expl. Fund Quart. Statement (1886), 92-111; O. Holtzmann, op. cit., 15-44. On the chronology and archaeology of Herod's temple cf. also W. Otto, Herodes (1913), 83 f. (Art. in Pauly-W., VIII [1913], 918 ff. and Suppl. 2, 1 ff.); Schürer, I, 392; F. Spiess, Das Jerusalem des Josephus (1881), 49-94; O. Wolff, Der Tempel von Jerusalem und seine Masse (1887); A. Schlatter, Zur Topographie und Geschichte Palästinas (1893), 166-202; A. Büchler, Die Priester und der Kultus im letzten Jahrzehnt des jerusalemischen Tempels (1895); A. R. S. Kennedy, Exp. T., 20 (1908/1909), 24 ff., 66 ff., 191 ff., 270 ff.; G. Dalman, PJB, 5 (1909), 29-57; Neue Petraforschungen und der heilige Felsen von Jerusalem (1912); Orte und Wege Jesu³ (1923), 301-324; J. Jeremias, "Golgotha," Angelos-Beiheft, 1 (1926), Index s.v. Tempelplatz ; Jerusalem z. Zt. Jesu, II, B, 1 (1929); H. Schmidt, Der heilige Fels in Jerusalem (1933); C. Watzinger, op. cit., 33-45; E. Schürer, "Die θύρα oder πύλη ὡραία Ac. 3:2, 10", ZNW, 7 (1906), 51-68; O. Holtzmann, ZNW, 9 (1908), 71-74. Views of the temple. The cultus in the Hell. period: Bousset-Gressm., 97-118; H. Wenschkewitz, "Die Spiritualisierung der Kultusbegriffe," Angelos-Beiheft, 4 (1932). On the Messianic temple hope in the Synagogue : Weber, 375 f.; Str.-B., 1, 1003-1005; IV, 885, 929-937. Apocalyptic : Volz Esch., 172, 217, 371-378. Philo : I. Heinemann, Philons griech. und jüd. Bildung (1932), 45-58; P. Krüger, Philo und Jos. als Apologeten des Jdts. (1906); Wenschkewitz, op. cit., 82-87. Josephus : Schl. Jos., 72 f.; Theol. d. Jdt. (1932), 72-80; O. Schmitz, Die Opferanschauung des späten Jdts. und die Opferaussagen des NT (1910), 180 ff.; H. Guttmann, Die Darstellung der jüd. Religion bei Flavius Jos. (1928); Wenschkewitz, op. cit., 21-24. NT : R. A. Hoffmann, "Das Wort Jesu von der Zerstörung des Tempels" in Nt.liche Studien f. G. Heinrici (1914); J. Jeremias, "Jesus als Weltvollender," BFTh, 33 (1930), 38-44; 79-81; J. Klausner, Jesus v. Nazareth (1930), 429-435.

[1] Poland, 255 ff.
[2] Ibid., 258.

Also "cultic pictures," Inscr. Graecae ad Res Romanas Pertinentes (ed. R. Cagnat, 1900), III, 800 (Syllium). The gold decoration on statues, Thuc., II, 13, 5. Sacred furnishings like the "altar of burnt offering," Da. 9:27, LXX Θ. Both read קִדְשׁ for the Heb. כְּנַף (wings) and related this to the altar on which the βδέλυγμα comes to stand. Cf. Orig. Hom., 26, 3 in Librum Jesu Nave. But also the ark, vestments etc., Philo Ebr., 85 (elsewhere τὰ ἅγια). Also the temple property, Philo Spec. Leg., I, 234. c. More generally and comprehensively the "cultus," Hdt., I, 172; 3 Macc. 3:21 that of Dionysus. Jos. Ant., 14, 234; 237; 240 : ἱερὰ ποιεῖν ᾽Ιουδαϊκά, "to live according to the Jewish cultus," cf. 245 : τὰ ἱερὰ τὰ πάτρια τελεῖν, and the Roman edict, 14, 213 f. Orig. Cels., VIII, 48 calls the expositors of the mysteries τῶν ἱερῶν ἐξηγηταί. Philo uses it more abstractly for the sacred as opposed to the profane.

When Paul writes (1 C. 9:13): οὐκ οἴδατε, ὅτι οἱ τὰ ἱερὰ ἐργαζόμενοι [τὰ] ἐκ τοῦ ἱεροῦ ἐσθίουσιν, this means "those who discharge the ministry of the temple" (qui sacris operantur).

This use with ἐργάζεσθαι is unique. Philo has δρᾶν τὰ ἅγια, Det. Pot. Ins., 64 of the ministry of the Levites, or τὰ ἅγια κατασκευάζεσθαι of artistic work for the temple, Som., I, 207, but never ἐργάζεσθαι with τὰ ἱερά, though he often uses ἐργάζεσθαι in other connections. At 1 Ch. 6:34; 9:13; 28:13 we find πᾶσα ἐργασία of the ministry of the priests, at Nu. 3:7; 8:15 ἐργάζεσθαι τὰ ἔργα τῆς σκηνῆς, cf. 8:11, 19 of that of the Levites. Paul combined this LXX use of ἐργάζεσθαι with the customary use of τὰ ἱερά for the cultus in the surrounding world. He is thinking, not merely of sacrifices, but more comprehensively of the temple ministry. The reference to sacrifices is expressed in the following sentence with θυσιαστήριον. But τὰ ἱερὰ ἐργάζεσθαι corresponds exactly to ἐκ τοῦ ἱεροῦ ἐσθίουσιν. He could hardly use the unaccustomed τὰ ἱερά here if ordinary usage, including Christian, did not have τὸ ἱερόν for the temple, thus suggesting the allusion naturally. Like the adjectival use in 2 Tm. 3:15, this τὰ ἱερά is highly exceptional. We cannot conclude from this, however, that 1 C. 9:13 refers to a pagan cult, since the context suggests the OT.

B. The Use of τὸ ἱερόν for Temple.

1. General Greek Usage.

The distinctive nature of τὸ ἱερόν becomes clearer when we compare it with other terms for cultic sites. ναός is aedes, the temple proper, or the inner shrine with the image of the god, Hdt., I, 183, which can be carried in processions, Hdt., II, 63. The guild of Demetrius, Ac. 19:24 makes ναοὶ ἀργυροῖ of the ἱερόν (v. 27) of Artemis. The father of the Baptist, Lk. 1:9, 21 f. performs his service in the ναός, i.e., the sanctuary. But ναός is flexible. Joseph. normally uses it for the temple building, Bell., 5, 207; 209; 211; Ant., 15, 391, but also for the precincts, Ap., 2, 119; Bell., 6, 293. Otherwise τέμενος, consecrated and separated land, is normally used for the precincts. It could often be a grove with a temple or just an altar, Hom. Il., 2, 696; Od., 8, 363; Pind. Nem., 6, 63; Hdt., III, 142; Soph. Oed. Col., 135. Cf. Pap.[3] Hdt. uses ἱρόν, νηός and τέμενος interchangeably, II, 170, cf. 155. In 2 Macc. 11:3 τέμενος is used generally for the sanctuary. The same is true during the empire.[4]

ἱερόν (Ionic ἱρόν) is not merely the temple proper. It can also be a consecrated grove (Hdt., V, 119), or any place of sacrifice,[5] or the inner portion of the τέμενος, the place of worship. It is distinguished from ναός and τέμενος by its comprehensiveness. From the very first, and not merely by a shift of meaning,

---

[3] Preisigke Wört.
[4] Poland, 455.
[5] Poland, 457.

it can also denote both τέμενος and ναός in their original senses. Hence the definition of Ammonius is possible : τοὺς περιβόλους τῶν ναῶν. Nor is it merely the most general word for the cultic place and building with all their accessories. It is also the most solemn. And it is wholly inter-confessional.

Polyb. uses it at XVI, 39, 4 of the Jerusalem temple. Jewish and Christian writers very frequently use it of pagan shrines. Thus Ez. 27:6; 28:18 LXX (not the Heb.), τὰ ἱερά σου of Tyre. The temple of Astarte, Jos. Ant., 6, 374; of Dagon, 1 Macc. 10:84; 11:4; of Isis, Jos. Ant., 18, 65; Bell., 7, 123; of Bel at Babylon, Bel 8 LXX, 22 Θ; Jos. Ant., 10, 224; of Nanaia (Persian Anahid), 2 Macc. 1:13; the Gk. temples of Zeus, Jos. Ant., 14, 36; 19, 4; Bell., 4, 661; of Apollo, Ant., 13, 364; Bell., 2, 81; of Artemis, Ant., 12, 354; Ac. 19:27; of Dionysus, 2 Macc. 14:33. Philo often uses τὰ ἱερά with reference to the cult in the πόλεις, Deus Imm., 17; Op. Mund., 17. But in Leg. Gaj. (cf. esp. 232 : τὸ ἡμέτερον ἱερόν) τὸ ἱερόν can be used once or twice for the synagogue at Alexandria. [6]

2. The Jerusalem Temple in Judaism.

a. The Septuagint and Apocrypha.

i. In accordance with the decision of the Greek Bible in respect of ἱερός → 226, τὸ ἱερόν is practically never used for the Jewish temple, though the priest is constantly called ὁ ἱερεύς. As Ez. shows (→ supra), ἱερόν is used for pagan shrines. It thus expresses opposition to idolatry.

For the Jerusalem temple the usual word is simply οἶκος, or οἶκος ἅγιος, τοῦ θεοῦ, κυρίου, or → ναός, ναὸς ἅγιος. The simple term "house of God" has an inner nobility. Nor is ναός too burdened with false associations, for fundamentally ἱερόν alone is a religious word. We find the latter almost by accident at Ez. 45:19 in a wrong translation of עֲזָרָה (setting of the altar), at 1 Ch. 29:4 : τοὺς τοίχους τοῦ ἱεροῦ for בַּיִת; 1 Ch. 9:27: τὰς θύρας τοῦ ἱεροῦ (בֵּית־הָאֱלֹהִים); 2 Ch. 6:13 : αὐλὴ τοῦ ἱεροῦ (no Heb.). Thus only Chronicles offers rare exceptions to the basic attitude.

ii. The case is very different in 1 Εσδρ., 1, 2, 3, 4 Macc., which in contrast to the LXX make frequent use of ἱερόν. Here the temple is either τὸ ἱερόν, 1 Εσδρ. 1:8; 1 Macc. 15:9; 2 Macc. 2:9; 3 Macc. 3:16; 4 Macc. 4:3 etc., or τὸ ἱερὸν τοῦ θεοῦ, 1 Εσδρ. 8:18, perhaps with ἐν Ἰερουσαλήμ added, 1 Macc. 10:43; 1 Εσδρ. 5:43. Or τὸ ἱερὸν τοῦ κυρίου, 1 Εσδρ. 8:64 etc. It is always a comprehensive term for the whole. The reference may be to the forecourt, 1 Εσδρ. 1:5 A; 2 Macc. 6:4, for this is where the violent desecration by Antiochus took place.

b. Josephus and Philo.

i. In General. In Bell., 5, 184-227, cf. Ant., 15, 380-425, Jos. describes the temple of Herod before his account of its destruction. He places the commencement of its construction in the 18th year of the reign of Herod, i.e., 19 B.C. (Ant., 15, 380). The reckoning in Bell., I, 401 (the 15th year) is incorrect. [7] The whole work was only finished in 63/64 A.D., just before its destruction. The 46 years of Jn. 2:20 would give us a date of 27 A.D. The tractate Middot offers the best material for comparison with Jos. This work gives us the measurements and lays down the various duties in respect of the temple should it be rebuilt. Like Ez. 40-44 it is an ideal rather than a strictly historical depiction. But it does at least preserve the scribal tradition. The total plan is very largely in agreement with that of Jos. The differences, e.g., contested questions as to the gates of the temple hill, do not affect the general plan. [8] It is probable that Philo

---

[6] Cf. Leisegang, s.v.
[7] Cf. W. Otto, Art. "Herodes," op. cit., 84. Schl. J., 80.
[8] More recently C. Watzinger, op. cit., II (1935), 41 favours the Mishnah against Joseph.

saw Herod's temple : De providentia in Eus. Praep. Ev., VIII, 14, 64. [9] In his description
in Spec. Leg., I, 67-78 in 70 there is perhaps a reflection of what he saw. The fact that
he had the temple before his eyes (on Spec. Leg., I, 71 περίβολος, cf. Jos. Bell., I, 401;
5, 190 and 401; Ant., 15, 396) is not contradicted by inexactitudes or exaggerations
(e.g., Spec. Leg., I, 72). His regard for the Torah causes him to make considerable use
of OT sayings regarding the tabernacle in his allegorising. [10]

ii. The Usage. Joseph. can use ἱερόν for the tabernacle, for Solomon's temple, for
Zerubabbel's and for Herod's. Philo, too, uses ἱερόν both for pagan temples (→ 233)
and frequently for the tabernacle and for the temple in Jerusalem. [11] It is the most
common term. In general, however, only the usage of Joseph. is of interest from the
NT standpoint. Rare expressions in Joseph. are ἱερὸν τοῦ θεοῦ, Ant., 18, 8; 20, 49, or
τὸ Ἰουδαίων ἱερόν, Ant., 18, 297. ἱερόν can be used for the whole court, including the
court of the Gentiles, or for the temple hill : τὸ ἔξωθεν ἱερόν, Bell., 6, 244; 277; 324.
To it belongs, e.g., the porch of Solomon, Ant., 20, 220-222; Bell., 6, 283; cf. 151 (Jn.
10:23). The temple proper stands ἐν τῷ ἔνδον ἱερῷ, in the inner precincts, Bell., 2, 411;
5, 565; 6, 248 and 299; cf. Bell., 6, 292 : ἐν τῷ ἱερῷ μέσῳ. There Zechariah was killed by
the Zealots (Bell., 4, 343). The precincts begin with the inner court beyond the Nicanor
gate. Up to this point is τὸ ἔξωθεν ἱερόν, Bell., 6, 151, cf. 5, 187: τὸ κάτω ἱερόν.
Here is the stone boundary with the warning inscription to the Gentiles in Greek and
Latin that they should not cross it : Bell., 5, 193; 6, 124-126; Philo Leg. Gaj., 31; Mishnah
Kelim, 1, 8; cf. the accusation against Paul in Ac. 21:27-30; also the similar inscr. in Ditt.
Or., II, 598 (1st cent. A.D.). It runs as follows (→ I, 266): Μηθένα ἀλλογενῆ εἰσπο-
ρεύεσθαι ἐντὸς τοῦ περὶ τὸ ἱερὸν τρυφάκτου καὶ περιβόλου. ὃς δ' ἂν ληφθῇ,
ἑαυτῶι αἴτιος ἔσται διὰ τὸ ἐξακολουθεῖν θάνατον. In Jos. Bell., 5, 194; cf. 6, 125;
Ant., 15, 417 a shorter version is given → I, 762. With τὸ ἱερόν Joseph. mostly has ὁ
ναός for the temple proper. Worth noting is Bell., 5, 201: μία δ' ἡ ἔξωθεν τοῦ νεώ
(of the Nicanor gate): it is outside the sanctuary in the narrower sense. On the broader
use of ναός → 232. It is common in more precise descriptions, Bell., 5, 207: αὐτὸς δ' ὁ
ναός, of the temple proper ; cf. Philo Spec. Leg., I, 72 : αὐτὸς ὁ νεώς. τὸ ἅγιον, τὰ
ἅγια are also normally reserved for the temple proper, esp. in Bell., 4, 5 and 6, though
also in 1, 2 and 3. τὸ ἅγιον may be the whole of the inner sanctuary, τὸ δεύτερον
ἱερόν, which begins with the inner court beyond the Nicanor gate, Bell., 5, 194. Or it
may be the holy place (הֵיכָל) with the lamps, the table and the censer, Bell., 5, 215 f.
(as distinct from the holiest of all : τοῦ ἁγίου τὸ ἅγιον) — whether in the tabernacle
(Ant., 3, 125) or Herod's temple (Bell., 5, 219). Worth noting is the plur. use as demanded by the distinction between the holy and the holy of holies, cf. the formula ὁ
ναὸς μετὰ τῶν ἁγίων, Bell., 2, 400, or Bell., 1, 354 = Ant., 14, 482 : τὸ ἱερὸν καὶ τὰ
κατὰ τὸν ναὸν ἅγια. Finally, τὸ ἅγιον, τὰ ἅγια is used of the whole, including the
walls, Ant., 12, 413 (→ I, 97); Bell., 4, 388. In all cases τὸ ἅγιον implies a particularly
solemn evaluation : Bell., 1, 152, Pompey hesitates to enter it, cf. Bell., 4, 151, the advance
from νεὼς τοῦ θεοῦ to τὸ ἅγιον, which the Zealots make into a fortress. The same
advance in estimation is to be seen in Bell., 6, 95. This term is never used unless there
is a desire to emphasise the holiness of the site. Philo in his allegorical treatment of the
temple prefers τὸ ἅγιον, τὰ ἅγια. For him τὰ ἅγια includes everything in the temple
precincts or commited to priestly care, Det. Pot. Ins., 62; Fug., 93; Leg. All., III, 135;
Som., I, 207; Spec. Leg., I, 115; Vit. Mos., II, 114 and 155. The first sanctuary is τὰ
ἅγια, Rer. Div. Her., 226; Spec. Leg., I, 296. The Holy of Holies is also plural : τὰ
ἅγια τῶν ἁγίων, Leg. All., II, 56; Mut. Nom., 192, or τὰ ἐσωτάτω τῶν ἁγίων, Som.,
I, 216; τὸ ἄδυτον καὶ ἄβατον, Vit. Mos., II, 95.

---

[9] Cf. Schürer, III, 148, n. 37.
[10] Heinemann, *op. cit.*, 539 conjectures that he made use of monographs on the temple
ministry.
[11] Cf. Leisegang, *s.v.*

3. The Use of τὸ ἱερόν for the Temple in the New Testament.

a. The General Usage. Whereas the LXX carefully avoids ἱερόν, and thereby emphasises the particularity of Israel's sanctuary, the NT does not object to ἱερόν, even though it almost completely shuns the adjective ἱερός in relation to its concept of holiness. Early Christianity is not concerned solemnly to emphasise revelation in the cultus by studied terms. For when the message of the NT was first preached the time of cultic involvement was already past. It is thus logical that ἱερόν should be used for the outdated shrine, with no attempt to mark it off from the religious world around.

Only seldom do we find more solemn descriptions like ἱερὸν τοῦ θεοῦ, Mt. 21:12 C אּ D (ἱερόν alone, ﬡΘ). Parallel to the LXX is οἶκος τοῦ θεοῦ at Mt. 12:4 (of the tabernacle in David's time), cf. Jos. Bell., 4, 281; 6, 104. Jn. 2:16 : οἶκος τοῦ πατρός μου is a distinctive Johannine elaboration of the same usage. Otherwise the temple is almost always τὸ ἱερόν, Heb. בית המקדש, jSukka, 55c, Aram. בית מקדשא, jMS, 56a; Pea, 20b; Ber., 5a; Tg. Cant., 3, 11. This means all the temple precincts, including the temple hill. We also find → ναός, Heb. היכל, Aram. היכלא, bQid, 71a for the temple proper. This is particularly used in the NT in the context of spiritual reinterpretation. The thesis of G. Dalman [12] that in the Gospels there is a normative distinction between ἱερόν for the whole sanctuary and ναός for the temple proper can hardly be sustained in the light of Mt. 27:5 and Jn. 2:19. [13] Judas had no access to the temple proper, and yet he cast the pieces of silver in the ναός. Mt. 12:5 : "The priests in the ἱερόν profane the sabbath," refers to their ministry both in the forecourt and in the temple proper.

b. τὸ ἱερόν as a General Term. ἱερόν is used very generally of the temple, Mt. 12:6; Ac. 24:6; 25:8; 1 C. 9:13, in basic expositions and in passages which do not permit of more exact topographical description, Lk. 22:53; Jn. 5:14. It is also used generally when the reference is to the whole complex (Mk. 13:3, from the Mount of Olives) which the disciples admire, exclaiming at the stones and at the costly gifts which adorn it, Mk. 13:1; Lk. 21:5.

c. As the Temple Hill. To begin on the outside, ἱερόν is used for the hill of the house, הר הבית, for the outermost court to which even the Gentiles have access. [14] Here the blind and the lame come to Jesus (Mt. 21:14). Here the children greet him with rejoicing (v. 15). Here is where He drives out those who buy and sell (Mt. 21:12; cf. Mk. 11:15; Lk. 19:45; Jn. 2:14).

G. Dalman believes that the selling of doves took place in the basilica of Herod (not the porch of Solomon → infra) at the south end of the outer court. [15] It is certainly to be located in the outer court. The sheep and oxen of Jn. are regarded by Dalman as a later addition. But according to jYom. Tob., 61c, 13 [16] Baba bButa, a contemporary of Herod the Great, drove a herd of 3000 sheep into the temple court. [17] There are references to stores on the temple hill. Opinions vary as to the booths of the house of Chanan (Hanna) and their location, S. Dt., 14, 22 § 105 (95b). [18] They were either on

---

[12] Orte und Wege Jesu³ (1924), 301.
[13] Cf. Schl. J. on 2:20.
[14] Cf. 1 Macc. 13:52 : τὸ ὄρος τοῦ ἱεροῦ; 16:20; Jos. Ant., 1, 226. The temple is also called αὐλὴ τοῦ ἱεροῦ : 1 Εσδρ. 9:1; the temple square : 1 Εσδρ. 9:6 etc. εὐρύχωρος. At 4 Macc. 4:11 the court of the Gentiles is ὁ πάμφυλος τοῦ ἱεροῦ περίβολος.
[15] Op. cit., 309 f.
[16] Str.-B., I, 852 (= jBeza, 61c, 15 ff.).
[17] On this whole pt. cf. Str.-B., I, 850-853.
[18] Cf. J. Dérenbourg, Histoire de la Palestine (1867), 459; G. Dalman, op. cit., 309, n. 6; J. Jeremias, Jerusalem zur Zeit Jesu, I (1923), 21, 55; "Jesus als Weltvollender" (1930), 42; Str.-B., I, 1000; II, 570 f. (d).

the Mount of Olives or they are identical with those of Beth Hino (Jeremias, Str.-B.). On the mercantile spirit of the high-priest Hanna, cf. Jos. Ant., 20, 205.

d. τὸ πτερύγιον τοῦ ἱεροῦ. It is doubtful where the πτερύγιον τοῦ ἱεροῦ of Mt. 4:5; Lk. 4:9 is to be located.

Elsewhere in Gk. the word can mean tower, rampart, or pinnacle. [19] Schlatter suggests a balcony of the temple wall overhanging the street, and quotes jPes., 35b. [20] Dalman is in favour of "corner" rather than "spire," and he suggests the south-east corner of the outer court, which jutted out into the vale of Kedron. [21] Reference has also been made to Jos. Ant., 15, 412, which mentions the pinnacle of the στοὰ βασιλική, to the south of the outer precincts, where people often turned giddy: ἀπ' ἄκρου τοῦ ταύτης τέγους (τῆς στοᾶς). According to Eus. Hist. Eccl., II, 23, 12 James was set by the authorities ἐπὶ τὸ πτερύγιον τοῦ ναοῦ, and then thrown over.

e. The Teaching of Jesus and the Apostles in the ἱερόν. When we read of the teaching of Jesus and the apostles in the ἱερόν, Mk. 14:49; Mt. 26:55; Lk. 19:47; 21:37; 22:53; Jn. 7:14, 28; 18:20; Ac. 5:20, or of the 12 year old Jesus sitting among the doctors, Lk. 2:46, the site is either the house of instruction in the temple [22] or one of the pillared halls in the outer court, e.g., Solomon's porch to the east of the sanctuary hill. [23] This is the στοὰ τοῦ Σολομῶνος of Jn. 10:23; cf. Ac. 3:11; 5:12; Jos. Ant., 8, 96; 15, 401; 20, 220-222; Bell., 5, 185. It was a remnant of the temple of Zerubbabel. [24]

f. The Beautiful Gate. The beautiful gate where the lame man lay who was healed by Peter and John (Ac. 3:2, 10) is the bronze Corinthian gate of Jos. Bell., 2, 411; 5, 198 and 201-206; 6, 293. It is located at the eastern entrance to the court of women and thus forms an entry from the outer court into the true precincts of the sanctuary (τοῦ ἔνδον ἱεροῦ, Bell., 2, 411).

It must be insisted against Schürer [25] that Jos. Bell., 5, 201 makes good sense, → 234. O. Holtzmann's interpretation of Jos. [26] is based on a mistranslation of Bell., 5, 204, which refers to the high inner gate, beyond the Corinthian, which leads from the court of women into the inner court. The Mishnah confuses these two gates. As distinct from Jos., it locates the Nicanor gate (the Corinthian of Jos. and the beautiful gate of Ac.) between the court of women and the court of men, and the great gate between the temple square and the court of women. Cf. the mention of the Nicanor gate, Mid., 1, 4-5; 2, 6; Sheq., 6, 3; Sota, 1, 5; Neg., 14, 8; T. Yoma, 2, 4; jYoma, 41a; bYoma, 38a. Here Jos. is surely right as against the Rabb. tradition. He knew the temple as a priest, whereas tradition was probably affected by ritual considerations and ideal dreams of the future. [27]

g. τὸ ἱερόν as the Court of Women. ἱερόν can also be used for the court of women. This is so called because women may come here but must not go beyond. Here Anna prays, Lk. 2:37. Here Jesus watches the widow at one of the 13 γαζοφυλακεῖα, Mk. 12:41 ff.; Lk. 21:1 ff. Here he teaches according to Jn. 8:20. Here there probably takes place the encounter with the adulterous woman, Jn. 8:2 f.

---

[19] Cf. Liddell-Scott, s.v.
[20] Schl. Mt., ad loc.
[21] Op. cit., 311 f.
[22] Dalman, op. cit., 317.
[23] Dalman, 310 f.; Str.-B., II, 625 f.
[24] A. Schlatter, Zur Topographie und Geschichte Palästinas (1893), 197-202 places it in the inner court. But cf. E. Schürer, ZNW, 7 (1906) 66; also Dalman, op. cit., 315, n. 4.
[25] ZNW, 7 (1906), 55.
[26] ZNW, 9 (1908), 72.
[27] Cf. Str.-B., II, 620-625. Dalman, op. cit., 315. On this whole pt. → 173, n. 5.

Mothers who brought their offering after purification (Lk. 2:24) stood here at the great gate, → 236, where they could see the altar and the temple proper. Perhaps the publican prayed here (Lk. 18:13), if he did not stay on the hill of the house. [28]

h. As the Inner Court. ἱερόν means the inner court, with the altar and the temple proper, when we read of the Pharisee praying (Lk. 18:11), of the disciples praying (Lk. 24:53), and of Jesus standing before the altar (cf. Mk. 11:11). This is also the reference on the seventh day of the feast of tabernacles in Jn. 7:37 f. and in Ac. 21:26, when Paul offers with the men the concluding sacrifice of his vow. [29]

i. As the Temple Proper. Only the priest could enter into the ἱερόν = the temple proper. The layman fixed his gaze on the costly curtain above the temple door with its encircling tendrils of gold. Was this the veil that was rent on the death of Jesus, or was it the curtain before the Holy of Holies (Mt. 27:51)? The second is more likely in view of the general symbolism, → 246. [30]

C. Impulses towards a Spiritualisation of the Temple in the Greek World.

1. The Enlightenment. The Ionic enlightenment, which was remote from a Pindar or Aeschylus, achieved its real break-through with Xenophon of Colophon (570-480). It raised the objection that Homer and Hesiod ascribe to the gods all the faults and abuses of men. [31] But it does not merely protest against viewing the gods anthropomorphically. It also speaks of a single God in nature, and shows some understanding of more inward prayer. [32] There is then a criticism of cultic piety which prepares the way for developing spiritualisation. Heraclitus at the turn of the 6th and 5th centuries takes up arms against sacrifices and images. [33] Sacrifice is a purification, yet in it one is defiled with blood, and prayer to images is like "chattering with houses." The one only Wise does not will — and yet he does will — to be called Zeus. [34] This pioneer is followed by Zeno of Cition (300 B.C.), the founder of Stoicism. He is the first express critic of the whole idea of the temple: μήτε ναοὺς δεῖν ποιεῖν μήτε ἀγάλματα· μηδὲν γὰρ εἶναι τῶν θεῶν ἄξιον κατασκεύασμα ... ἱερά τε οἰκοδομεῖν οὐδὲν δεήσει· ἱερὸν γὰρ μὴ πολλοῦ ἄξιον καὶ ἅγιον οὐδὲν χρὴ νομίζειν· οὐδὲν δὲ πολλοῦ ἄξιον καὶ ἅγιον οἰκοδόμων ἔργον καὶ βαναύσων. [35] It is not insignificant that his pupil Cleanthes (4th/3rd cent. B.C.), whose hymn to Zeus "popularised the Stoic equation of Zeus, fate, and cosmic reason," [36] and Aratos (3rd cent. B.C.), who be-

---

[28] Cf. Mid., 2, 5-7a; Jos. Bell., 5, 198 f., 204; Ant., 15, 418 f.; Ap., 2, 104. On Lk. 2:37: Tanch., 17, 15. Cf. also Str.-B., II, 37 ff.; Dalman, op. cit., 313, 315 ff. The half-shekel tribute was also paid in this court, Dalman, 308. Dalman, 318 rejects as unsupported the account given in Lk., but cf. Str.-B., II, 120 ff. and Volz, Biblische Altertümer, 145. On Lk. 18:13, Dalman, 319. The stairs from which Paul addressed the people in Ac. 21:35, 40 are either those of the Antonia castle or the steps which lead from the court of women to the place of Israel and the place of the priests in the inner court. For the latter, Dalman, 314, n. 3.
[29] On Lk. 18:11, Str.-B., II, 246; Dalman, 319. On Jn. 7, Dalman, 320; Str.-B., II, 490 f. and Exc. on the feast of tabernacles.
[30] On the outer curtain, cf. Sheq., 8, 4; Tamid, 7, 1; Jos. Bell., 5, 212-214; Ep. Ar., 86; cf. Dalman, 323; Str.-B., I, 1043-1046; Schl. Mt., ad loc. Dalman favours the outer veil, Str.-B. and Schlatter the inner. Cf. H. Laible in Str.-B., III, 733-736.
[31] Fr., 11 (I, 132, 2 ff., Diels).
[32] Fr., 1 (I, 127, 11 ff., Diels).
[33] Fr., 5 (I, 151, 12 ff., Diels); cf. Fr., 128 (I, 180, 10 ff., Diels) (doubtful).
[34] Fr., 32 (I, 159, 1 f., Diels).
[35] v. Arnim, I, 61, 264. Cf. Cl. Al. Strom., V, 12, 76; Orig. Cels., VII, 35.
[36] W. Nestle, Griech. Religiosität von Alexander dem Grossen bis auf Proklos (1934) 109.

longed to the same circle, were the authors of the saying concerning our divine generation which is used in the Areopagus address — an address that also takes up the Stoic criticism of the temple (Ac. 17:18-28).

Later Stoicism developed this criticism. Seneca (cf. Aug. Civ. D., VI, 10) says in De Superstitione that the wise man observes cultic actions *tamquam legibus iussa non tamquam diis grata* and bears in mind : *cultum eius magis ad morem quam ad rem pertinere.* The cultus is necessary and salutary for the people. But the philosophical enlightenment seeks the way of reflection against this popular background. It establishes a mediating religion for the educated, who can ascribe to images a value which the people cannot, i.e., as depictions of the divine. Thus Stoicism maintains contact with popular feeling. No revolutionary changes are attempted. The cultic is reinterpreted and spiritualised by the sage, Cic. Nat. Deor., II, 17, 45; Dio Chrys., 12, 59 f.

2. The Spiritualising of the Concept of the Temple. In this respect there are two motifs in Seneca which are taken up more explicitly in Philo, namely, the suggestion that the world is the temple of God, and also the soul.

Sen. Ben., VII, 7, 3 : *totum mundum deorum esse immortalium templum.* Ep., 90, 28 (influenced by Poseidonius ?): the conclusion of philosophy is : not *municipale sacrum, sed ingens deorum omnium templum, mundus ipse.* Cf. also Plut. Tranq. An., 20 (II, 477c): ἱερὸν γὰρ ἁγιώτατον ὁ κόσμος ἐστὶ καὶ θεοπρεπέστατον (borrowed from the Stoic Panaitios). [37] For the soul as a temple cf. Sen. Fr., 123 in Lact. Inst., VI, 25, 3 : *non templa illi, congestis in altitudinem saxis exstruenda sunt, in suo cuique consecrandus est pectore.* If Seneca does not specifically describe the soul as a temple, the inward part of the *animus* is a shrine for deity, cf. Ep., 41, 1: *prope est a te deus, tecum est, intus est.* [38] Ep., 95, 47 ff. On the other hand, dualistic contempt for the body does not allow the Stoic to declare the body to be the temple of God. Epictetus is still friendly towards the cultus and forbearing with popular religion, Diss., I, 18, 15; II, 22, 17 ff.; III, 21, 12 ff.; Ench., 31, 5. Cf. also Musonius and Marcus Aurelius. Their true piety goes its own way. [39] But they do not deduce complete freedom from the cultus. Stoic religion is a mixture of the philosophical substitute for religion and of acknowledgment of popular religion. Epictetus speaks of the relationship of the soul to God. But he does not use the image of a spiritual temple. The Neo-Pythagorean Apollonius of Tyana is more ruthless than the Stoics in rejecting bloody sacrifices, Philostr. Vit. Ap., I, 31; V, 25. According to Eus. Praep. Ev., IV, 13; Dem. Ev., III, 3, he said of the deity : δεῖται γὰρ οὐδενός. Wordless prayer is the best worship. Cf. also the attack on temples in Sib., IV, 8 ff., 27 ff.

Later the image of the temple is often related to the indwelling of the spirit or of magical power, cf. Valerius Maximus (31 A.D.), Factorum et Dictorum Memorabilium, IV, 7, Ext., 1 (p. 209, 1 f., C. Halm [1865]): *fida hominum pectora quasi quaedam sancto spiritu referta templa sunt.* Apul. Apologia, 43 (ed. J. v. d. Vliet [1900]): *ut in eo divina potestas quasi bonis aedibus digne diversetur.*

D. The Way from Old Testament Prophecy to Jewish Apocalyptic and Hellenistic Judaism.

1. The Temple in Old Testament Prophecy.

Unlike the nebiim of the shrines, Amos, Hosea, Isaiah and Micah do not stand in any cultic tradition. Hence it is difficult to say what practical attitude they take towards the cultus. A leading motif of prophetic admonition is that observance of

---

[37] E. Norden, *Agnostos Theos* (1913), 22. The cosmos as a temple is a favourite motif, cf. Ps.-Heracl. Ep., 4, lines 47 ff. (ed. J. Bernays, 1869). Cf. Cic. Rep., III, 14.

[38] Cf. Wenschkewitz, 59-61. Ep. 41 also goes back to Poseidonius : *sacer intra nos sedet spiritus* is equivalent to πνεῦμα ἱερόν, cf. Williger, *Hagios,* 96.

[39] Cf. A. Bonhöffer, *Die Ethik des Stoikers Epiktet* (1894), 82 f.; Wenschkewitz, 55.

the cultus is displeasing to God if there is injustice, lack of love, or failure to walk humbly before Yahweh the Holy One, Am. 5:21 ff.; Hos. 6:6; Is. 1:10 ff., Mi. 6:6 ff. This thought recurs in post-exilic prophecy, Zech. 7:5 ff. But it is hard to prove any attempt to set aside the cultus or to spiritualise it. In Is. 66:1 ff. there is a profound sense that no temple can embrace the lofty majesty of Yahweh. Here the antithesis is not a protest against the contradiction of the cultus and disobedience. The two sides of the antithesis are the building and the broken spirit which God sees. Yet in Is. 60:1 ff., and especially v. 13, Sion and its temple are the place to which the nations come.

The Wisdom literature repeats the ancient prophetic antithesis (Prv. 21:27). But it also sets prayer over against sacrifice (Prv. 15:8). In the Psalter stress is laid on the inward law instead of sacrifice, 40:6, 8, 9 (cf. 1 S. 15:22), or on thanksgiving and right conduct instead of sacrifice, Ps. 50. In Ps. 50:8 ff. the statement that Yahweh does not want meat offerings reminds us of the basic treatment of the concept of the temple in Is. 66:1 ff. In v. 14 the thankoffering of prayer is regarded as true sacrifice. Cf. Ps. 141:2; 69:30 f. Even one who is zealous for the temple (v. 9) may say this. The prophetic insight that brokenness before God is better than sacrifice (Is. 66) exerts a profound influence (Ps. 51:16 ff.).

Mi. 3:12 prophesies that Jerusalem shall be heaps and the temple hill as a high place of the forest. Jer. 26:18 repeats the prophecy. [40] Ez. 40-48 gives us a vision of the new temple of the Messianic era; it thus nourishes hope with pictures which can never be fulfilled in any actual temple here below. A prophecy like Is. 2:1-4 directs attention to the temple as the focal point of all nations. Hag. 2:9, cf. 14:8 ff., contains a significant prophecy. The glory of the latter house is to be greater than that of the former. Apart from these prophecies, there were after the erection of the Zerubbabel temple three elements which affected temple prophecy up to the commencement of the Herodian phase, the littleness of the Zerubbabel temple, the absence of the ark, and the desecration of the temple by Antiochus Epiphanes. [41] The sayings concerning the cessation of the sacrifice and the desecration of the site in Da. 8:11 ff.; 11:31; 12:11 are the prelude to all further temple apocalyptic. They are still influential after the Maccabean period, and they constantly give rise to fresh expectation.

2. The Temple in Apocalyptic.

a. Sayings prior to 70. If we try to date apocalyptic sayings concerning the temple, we find that the decisive foundations are laid prior to 70.

The experience of destruction gave fresh point to them, but was not creative. The impressive image in the shepherd vision of Eth. En. 90:28 f., which tells us that the old house was taken down and transferred to a new site, and that "the Lord of the sheep" brings a completely new and bigger house in place of the first, is earlier than the death of Judas Maccabaeus. It is to the effect that the unpretentious house of Zerubbabel, which has now been desecrated by the Syrian, will be replaced in the Messianic period.

The relationship of the Messiah to temple expectation is hard to unravel. After 70

---

[40] For later prophecy of destruction prior to 70, jYoma, 43c, 61 Bar. (Str.-B., I, 1045) and bYoma, 39b; Jos. Bell., 6, 300-309 (62 A.D.). The shekinah departs prior to the destruction, 6, 299. Cf. Schl. Mt., 477, 16-19.

[41] For the glorification of the temple cf. esp. 2 Macc. 3:30. It is πανυπέρτατον, 3 Macc. 1:20. It is esteemed and praised throughout the world, 2 Macc. 2:22; 3:12. The desecrated temple is reconsecrated after the Maccabean rebellion, 165 B.C.

we only rarely find the view that the Messiah will be the builder of the future temple. [42]
But already in Tg. on Is. 53:5 (Str.-B., I, 482) the Messiah builds the house of the
sanctuary, cf. also Tg. on Zech. 6:12 f. (Str.-B., I, 94). As against J. Jeremias, Volz has
pointed out that the new house of En. 90 includes the city as well as the temple. But
there is no Jerusalem without the temple. It should be noted that the white bull (the
Messiah) comes only when Jerusalem is built, En. 90:37. But the Son of 4 Esr. 9:38-10:27
is also the Messiah. It is also expected that the Taeb of the Samaritans will rediscover
the temple vessels which Moses buried at Gerizim, and that he will restore the sanctuary. [43]

b. The new temple. The legend that the sanctuary is concealed and buried prior to
its restoration is found already at 2 Macc. 2:4 f., 8 (c. 125 B.C.). The expectation that
when Israel is liberated from the yoke of the kingdoms a new and glorious and much
extended Jerusalem will arise, with a new temple within it, occurs already in Eth. En.
89:73 (135 B.C.); 91:13 (prior to 167 B.C.); Tob. 14:5 (2nd/1st cent. B.C.); Jub. 1:17, 27,
29 (Maccabean). The prophecy of the universal sanctuary of the nations (Is. 2:2 ff.;
Mi. 4:1 ff.) is also at work in this whole period (Eth. En. 90:33; Tob. 13:13; Jub. 4:26).

c. The heavenly temple. Alongside the restored earthly temple are also the
heavenly Jerusalem and temple.

This idea is also current prior to 70. The sanctuary of Ex. 26:30; Ez. 40 ff. has a
heavenly pattern. [44] Cf. Wis. 9:8. This idea of a pre-existent σκηνή is linked with the
ancient oriental view that the heavenly and the earthly places of God must correspond.
This helps us to understand why Rabb. literature and Rev., also apocalyptic, cf. Slav.
En. 55:2, [45] speak of the heavenly Jerusalem, which is also the abode of the blessed.

d. The Catastrophe of 70. All these motifs are intensified by the catastrophe
of 70.

The destruction of the temple and the altar cause 4 Esr. 10:21, 45 and S. Bar., 35 to
bewail the ruins of the temple. According to bBB, 60b a great and sustained fast begins
with the disaster. Legend develops further, S. Bar. 6:7 f.; 80:2. The future restoration of
Jerusalem and the sanctuary becomes a true object of hope: Akiba: Pes., 10, 6; Nu. r.,
29, 26, cf. bPes., 5a, as a reward for Israel. Longing is kept alive by daily prayers for
the renewal of the temple site, Sh. E : (p) petitions 14 and 16; (b) petition 17; Habinenu :
Taanit., 4, 8; Derek Eres Zuta, 9, 6. [46] The only new point in 4 Esr. is that the pre-
existent Jerusalem will appear here and will be manifested at the end of the days : 7:26;
10:54 f.; 13:36; cf. v. 6; 8:52. Worth noting are the accounts in 10:27 ff. and 42-44, since
here the temple and the cultus are linked with the reconstructed city, whereas in other
passages there is not the same emphasis on the supraterrestrial temple as on the supraterrestrial city. Even in 4 Esr., however, these is no descent of the city as in Rev. On
the other hand, the thought of a Jerusalem in heaven must have been a great consolation
after the destruction.

e. The spiritualising and criticism of sacrifice. While there is at this period
satisfaction with the cultus, there is also in Judaism a spiritualising and even
criticism of sacrifice.

---

[42] Cf. Str.-B., I, 1005; also Volz Esch., 217 (and J. Jeremias, "Jesus als Weltvollender,"
38 f.).
[43] Cf. M. Gaster, *Samaritan Eschatology* (1932), 218, 271. Bousset-Gressm., 239 f.
[44] Cf. the later form of this idea in S. Bar. 4:2-6.
[45] P. Riessler, *Altjüd. Schrifttum* (1928), 469.
[46] Cf. Volz Esch., 377; Wenschkewitz, 28. On apocalyptic temple expectation after 70
cf. Apk. Abr., 29 (G. N. Bonwetsch, p. 39 in *Studien z. Geschichte der Theologie und
der Kirche*, ed. N. Bonwetsch and R. Seeberg, I, 1 [1897]); Sib., III, 573-579, 657 f., 725;
V, 432 f. For the universal temple hope, cf. Sib., III, 718, 772 f., 776; V, 424 ff.

Jdt. 16:16. According to Tob. 4:10 f., cf. 12:9; Jub. 2:22, alms and observance of the commandments are sacrifices. After 70 some Rabb. statements find a substitute for the lost cultus in acts of love, Jochanan Ab. R. Nat., 4, 5. The view is even advanced that there will be no more sacrifices in the world to come, Dt. r., 16, 18 (Simon b. Chalafta). Even earlier there is interaction with the elements of the Greek enlightenment known to us from Stoicism. This leads to such fusions as we find in Josephus and Philo.

3. The Temple in Josephus and Philo.

a. Josephus. Josephus values the temple highly. This may be seen from his whole historical presentation. Everything culminates in the destiny of the sanctuary. The right of a free exercise of the cultus is for him more important than political freedom. [47] His magnifying of the temple in Ap., 2, 193 is magnifying of the one God and the one people. On the one side he constantly expresses his conviction concerning the shekinah: the temple is οἰκητήριον τοῦ θεοῦ, Ant., 8, 114 and 131; 20, 166. When God prepared it, 8, 117, He resolved to send into it a portion of His Spirit, 8, 114. Cf. Bell., 5, 459; Ant., 8, 102 and 106; 3, 100, 202 and 290. But this comes into conflict with his Greek sense that God cannot be localised. We thus have ambiguous expressions [48] such as "it appears to the people," Ant., 3, 129 and 219; 8, 102, 106 and 114 f. There is also evidence of the Greek enlightenment when in Ap., 2, 192 he calls virtue the worthiest service of God in an apology for Judaism which changes the prophetic antithesis into a moralistic criticism of sacrifice, Ant., 6, 147-150. He joins forces with Philo in love for the cosmological interpretation of the house and its customs, Ant., 3, 123 and 180 ff.; cf. Bell., 5, 212-217. The κόσμος is God's eternal house, Ant., 8, 107. Whether the Zealots actually told Titus that if this temple perished God had a better one, τὸν κόσμον, is very doubtful. This is Josephus' own conception. Yet it betrays no hostility to the temple. By adaptation to cultured style, it serves rather to make the purpose of such institutions more intelligible to Greek readers. It is certainly not Pharisaical. [49]

b. Philo's cultured religion fuses very heterogeneous elements. What is his main ethical concern? He protests against the cultic conception of a perverted religiosity which forgets purification of the soul, Cher., 94 f. He who adorns the temple but pollutes the διάνοια is not of the εὐσεβεῖς, Det. Pot. Ins., 20. Here ancient prophetic strands are interwoven into a distinctively Platonic and Stoic piety. No Jew can fail to note the ancient themes which are mediated through the synagogue even though he may have no personal acquaintance with the prophetic writings. But there are also sayings which directly negate the cultus, Cher., 97 ff. To make God a house of wood or stone is an idea which it is sin even to utter. The ἱερόν which truly honours God is σύμπας ὁ κόσμος, Plant., 126. Philo thus makes rich use of the temple in cosmic allegorising, Vit. Mos., II, 101-104. [50] Apart from the κόσμος, the λογικὴ ψυχή, the νοῦς, the λογισμός, the διάνοια of the wise are called the θεοῦ οἶκος, the ἱερὸν ἅγιον, Som., II, 248; I, 149; Virt., 188. The logos reigns as a true priest in the soul, Deus Imm., 135 (cf. 8). But this is not a spatial indwelling. The reference is to supervisory care, Sobr., 63. There is a singular use of the temple image in Op. Mund., 137, where in spite of his basic dualism he calls the body of Adam the οἶκος, νεὼς ἱερός of the ψυχὴ λογική. He can do this only because the corporeality of Adam is something far superior to that of his descendants.

Philo can also do justice to the temple worship of Israel. His symbolical and allegorical reinterpretation does not involve negation, Migr. Abr., 92. Along with the ἱερόν of the cosmos there is a χειρόκμητον, Spec. Leg., I, 66 f. This is defended as follows (67).

---

[47] Cf. Schl. Jos., 72.

[48] Ibid., 72 f.

[49] Ibid., 75. On the attitude of Josephus to the temple in Gerizim and in Egypt, ibid., 75-80.

[50] On the further development of the idea of the cosmic temple in Philo cf. Wenschkewitz, 72. Cf. also Cl. Al. Strom., V, 6, 32-38.

We are not to check the impulse (ὁρμή) in man which impels him to bring thank-offerings and to seek expiation.[51] God does not need or receive anything, but He stimulates us to piety. Hence He declares His acceptance, Rer. Div. Her., 123. Naturally this can be regarded as an alien body in Philo's total religious understanding,[52] as the inconsistency of a Jew who would not be a Jew at all apart from these traditions. But fundamentally Philo is only doing the same as the Stoic does with popular religion (→ 237). The fusion of incompatible elements is his distinctiveness. His divided soul lives by this synthesis. A man of culture, he is both a Jew and a Hellenist, using each aspect to explain, to complement and to support the other.

E. The Attitude of Jesus and Early Christianity towards the Temple.

1. The Emphasis of the Witness of Jesus and the Early Christian Attitude in the Gospels.

The evangelical sayings concerning the temple are not just testimony to the Church's recollection of Jesus. They also reflect the Church's own conflict in respect of the temple. As the new motifs of Jesus are drawn into this situation of conflict, the kerygma becomes confession. The Spirit of Jesus has a profound effect on the decision of the Church. What Jesus Himself said is often hard to ascertain in detail. But there can be no doubt as to the attitude of the early community under His influence. In its depiction of the attitude of Jesus we have thus to take into account the confessional character of the sayings.

a. The twofold attitude of Jesus. Throughout the Synoptic portrayal we find in Jesus both an affirmation of temple worship as the divinely appointed way to worship God and also a superiority of Christ over the temple. It is in the sacred precincts that Jesus is tempted to prove His sonship by a striking miracle, Mt. 4:5; Lk. 4:9. Like all who fear God, He prays in the temple. Here rather than in His activity in the synagogues, at the very focus and centre of the expression of religious life, He meets the various types of Jewish piety, e.g., the widow at the offertory box, Mk. 12:41 ff. par., or the two men who pray, Lk. 18:10 ff., and whose very different attitudes are so keenly perceived. It is an important feature of the passion narrative that He taught daily in the temple, Mk. 14:49; Mt. 26:55; Lk. 22:53; cf. 19:47; 21:37 f. Jn. 18:20 brings out most clearly the purpose of this. What happened did not take place ἐν κρυπτῷ, but at the place where all the Jews were assembled. The motif of publicity is not worked out in the same way as in the case of John, the preacher in the wilderness. Judaism is now visited at its main sacramental centre. The whole presentation also draws attention to the fact that important self-witness is given in the holy place. It is here that the questions of His Davidic sonship and His authority are raised (Mk. 12:35; 11:27; Mt. 21:23; Lk. 20:1: εὐαγγελιζομένου). Not by accident the questioning, the concern of the people regarding Him, and His most solemn self-declarations are all located in the temple precincts, Jn. 7:14, 28; 8:20, 59; 10:23; 11:56. Emphasis is laid on the location in the healing in Jn. 5:14 and in the μοιχαλίς story in 8:2. Mt. speaks of the healing of the blind and the lame in the temple, 21:14. That the lips of children praise him as the Son of David in the forecourt of the temple is divine irony by which Ps. 8:2 is fulfilled; this is demonstrated by the protest of the leaders in the background.

---

[51] Heinemann, 54 shows that the expression is also found in Dio Chrys., 12, 60.

[52] Cf. Heinemann, 57 as opposed to Krüger; Wenschkewitz, 87. Philo transcends and universalises the nationalistic element by arguing that the sacrifices in the temple at Jerusalem are for the whole human race, Spec. Leg., I, 168, 190; II, 167; Vit. Mos., I, 149.

b. The Temple as the Place of the Divine Presence.

By setting the new revelation at the centre of the cultic religion, the depiction in the Gospels expresses the fact that Christ does His work on the basis and in fulfilment of the previous divine history. He affirms and transcends the former revelation in a unique relationship of tension and reciprocity. In the action and witness which involve wrestling with the question of the temple it is particularly obvious that transcending the cultus is not intended as an act of irreligion. In the express sayings concerning the temple, the temple is viewed on the one hand as the specific place of the divine presence. The tabernacle is the οἶκος τοῦ θεοῦ, Mt. 12:4; Lk. 6:4. In militant confirmation of an OT saying, the Herodian temple is called an οἶκος προσευχῆς (as distinct from a den of thieves), Mk. 11:17; Mt. 21:13; Lk. 19:46. The Johannine form is even more personal; it is the house of the Father, Jn. 2:16. The customary introduction of the temple into the casuistry of oaths gives rise to two further sayings. The one (Mt. 23:21) emphasises the fact that he who swears by the temple swears by God, because God dwells in the temple. The other (Mt. 23:16 f.) goes so far as to extend the concept of holiness to the temple in such a way that the temple, as the locus of the shekinah of God, sanctifies (ἁγιάσας) everything in it, even the gold decorations. This is a strong affirmation of the conviction that God is sacramentally present in the sanctuary. In keeping is the fact that prior to 70 the Palestinian Church tolerantly paid the temple tax (cf. Mt. 17:24-27) [53] in spite of its conviction that there was no compulsion, and that in all its discussions of the question [54] it appealed to the example of Jesus Himself. Even if this is simply to avoid giving offence to Judaism, it does at least point to a deliberate attachment to the common sanctuary.

c. The Cleansing of the Temple.

The cleansing of the temple (Mk. 11:15-17; Mt. 21:12 f.; Lk. 19:45 f.; Jn. 2:14-17) [55] is not an interruption of the worship of God. It is an attempt to purify the cultus from a profane and calculating spirit. It should not be overlooked that the act took place in the court of the Gentiles, on the hill of the house. The total holiness of the ἱερόν is thus ascribed to this district. The protest is against the mercantile activity of the Sadducees, and in spite of the resort to violent action it reflects a similar view of the temple to that of the Pharisees. [56] If the onslaught bears witness to a claim to authority, this is not more than was found among the prophets. The basis is prophetic, namely, the belief that this is no place for gain (Jer. 7:11), and the universal hope that the temple is to be a place of prayer for all nations (Mk.; cf. Is. 56:7 LXX; also Is. 2:2 f.). Prophetic, too, is the conviction that prayer (οἶκος προσευχῆς) takes precedence of sacrifice, unless prayer negates sacrifice. The view that this is something revolutionary is refuted by the fact that the act as such plays no part in the trial of Jesus.

We go rather beyond a prophetic interpretation of the event if we see in it a conscious

---

[53] τὸ δίδραχμον: Jos. Ant., 18, 312; Bell., 5, 187. Cf. Schl. Jos., 92.

[54] So Kl. Mt.; also Schl. Mt.; *Die Kirche des Mt.* (1929), 13 f.; Bultmann Trad., 235.

[55] Here the pericope is linked with the first appearance of Jesus in the temple. The chronological question is hard to decide.

[56] Dalman, *Orte und Wege*³, 309. Klausner, 433. Mk. 11:16 refers to the carrying of vessels of household use through the forecourt as a short-cut. This is the kind of profanation which is a violation of decorum. Here, too, His action would evoke the applause of the stricter party, cf. Schl. Mk., *ad loc.*; Str.-B., II, 27; Klausner, 434, n. 26.

Messianic demonstration on the part of Jesus. [57] J. Jeremias lays particular stress on the Messianic aspect of the event. [58] He tries to show that the renewal of the temple and the enthronement of the Messiah are combined in apocalyptic. Volz argues against this. [59] R. Eisler is the most resolute champion of a religio-political interpretation. [60] He appeals to the seizure of the temple and the attack on the temple treasury in Slav. Jos. But there is here no cleansing of the temple. [61] If this view were correct, it would be inconceivable that the Romans did not attack at once. We should also expect early Christianity to display political aspirations in consequence of this action.

d. The Saying concerning the Destruction and Rebuilding of the Temple.

When we turn to traditional sayings of Jesus which speak of absolute renewal rather than the honoured past, we have first to consider the *mashal* concerning the destruction and rebuilding of the temple → ναός : Mk. 14:57 f.; 15:29 f.; Mt. 26:61; 27:40; Jn. 2:18-22. Cf. also Ac. 6:14. It is taken up in the trial, garbled by His opponents, and related to destruction by Jesus Himself. What Jesus is really reported to have said is that in the future there will be a new temple worship in the Messianic sense, and that the old will be set aside in the coming time of salvation. He is also said to have linked this with His own person. This is extremely likely in view of the strong chain of tradition to this effect and against the apocalyptic background of the conception, Eth. En., 90, 28 f. → 239. The importance of the saying is that it constitutes an uneffaced sign that Jesus did not merely affirm the sanctity of the cultus, but that He also looked forward to a perfected worship in the coming time of the Messianic Son of Man. [62] This is how Jn. understood it. He has the form : "Destroy this temple." This refutes the assertion of the false witness that Jesus Himself will destroy it. The saying is also referred to the body of Jesus, which His enemies can put to death. Jesus is also reported to have said that "in three days I will build it again." Jn. relates this to the resurrection body, and he also says that the *mašal* only took on relevance for the disciples after the resurrection. The exposition is thus a confession of the primitive Christian community. In a further development in Jn. 1:14b : ἐσκήνωσεν ἐν ἡμῖν, the community can bear witness, after the destruction of the temple, that it has the true temple in the glorified Christ Himself. Jn. 4:21-24 (cf. Rev. 21:22) shows conclusively that Jn. linked this christological interpretation of the saying with the idea of the new worship. [63] On the other hand, his interpretation differs from the general apostolic conception that the new temple is the new community, [64] → 246. With this antithesis of the old temple on the one side and the temple newly given in the risen Lord on the other we should link the christological saying at Mt. 12:6 : λέγω δὲ ὑμῖν ὅτι τοῦ ἱεροῦ μεῖζόν ἐστιν ὧδε. [65] This is important both as a record of Jesus' own attestation of His superiority to the cultus and also as a confession of Palestinian Christians, after the overthrow of the sanctuary, that

---

[57] Meyer Ursprung, I, 162 f.; Klausner, 432.

[58] "Jesus als Weltvollender" (1930), 35-44.

[59] Esch., 217 → 240.

[60] Ἰησοῦς βασιλεύς, II (1930).

[61] Cf. A. Berendts, "Die Zeugnisse vom Christentum im slavischen De Bello Judaico des Jos.," TU, NF, 14, 4 (1906).

[62] At 14:58 Mk. has the antithesis χειροποίητος and ἀχειροποίητος (earthly and heavenly). This is supported by Rev., cf. Wenschkewitz, 98.

[63] On Jn. 4 cf. from the Tannaitic period, Str.-B., IV, 936 f. (aω).

[64] This is how Jeremias takes the saying, *op. cit.*, 39.

[65] The reference of μεῖζον is to Jesus Himself (as against Zn. Mt., *ad loc.*). Cf. with the μεῖζον the πλεῖον of 6:25; 12:41 f.

they have in Jesus something better than the ancient cultus. Here early Christianity completes the inner process of emancipation. [66]

e. The Prophecy of Its Destruction.

If the destruction in the *mašal* is not identical with the actual overthrow, there is an express prediction of the overthrow in the Synoptic apocalypse, Mk. 13:2 f.; Mt. 24:1; Lk. 21:5 f.; also Mk. 13:14; Mt. 24:15; Lk. 21:20. This word of judgment is a continuation of ancient prophecy, → 239. The destruction of the city and the temple is a sign of judgment and a warning sign of the *parousia*. The discourse begins with the astonishment of the disciples at the glory of the temple. [67] Mk. 11:11 tells us that Jesus, too, inspected the temple. But His answer to the admiration of the disciples — and His only recorded statement on architecture — is the prophecy of utter devastation. He Himself will not accomplish this. It is coming. But this sorrowful word opens the way for the liberation of the community from the ἱερόν. [68]

The βδέλυγμα τῆς ἐρημώσεως of Da. 12:11 LXX (→ I, 598; 600; II, 660) refers originally to the fact that an abominable object (the altar to Zeus in the Syrian period) causes the temple community to abandon the sanctuary. The prophecy in Da. is not regarded as completely fulfilled in the days of the Maccabees. It takes on wider significance. What is in the first instance a general reference comes to have specialised meaning. Lk. 21:20 thinks in terms of armies, 2 Th. 2:3 f. in terms of Antichrist. The new application of βδέλυγμα underlies the Christian prophecy. Perhaps it arose at the time when Caligula declared his intention of setting up an image to himself in the temple. [69]

f. Sayings from the Later Strata of the Tradition.

Sayings from the later strata of the Gospel tradition reflect the same twofold attitude of the Palestinian community, namely, reverence for the temple on the one side and the superiority of Christ on the other. The infancy stories in Lk. give us prophecies from within the circle of temple devotees. Under the leading of the Spirit, Simeon and Anna meet the child within the sacred precincts, 2:27, 37. Perhaps we have here an echo of the magnifying of Jesus by Jerusalem Christians to whom it was significant that the new revelation (τὸ σωτήριον, 2:30) should be given on the site of the ancient worship, → 242. In the story of the childhood visit to Jerusalem attention is drawn to the fact that Jesus showed reverence for the temple even as a boy (2:46). There is also a tacit reference to His later witness in this place, for even when He was a boy the Word which could be heard and expounded in the temple occupied a central position. It is worth noting that the piety which recounts this episode lays chief emphasis on the Word in the temple. Two elements in the passion narrative bear witness to the conviction that the death of Jesus makes possible a transformation of the cultus. The fact that

---

[66] Form criticism believes that this is a secondary proof from Scripture added to the original debate, Bultmann Trad., 51; M. Albertz, *Die synpt. Streitgespräche* (1921), 10. Schlatter too (*Die Kirche des Mt.* [1929], 31 f.) regards this as a confession of the community, though in Schl. Mt., 396 it is accepted as a saying of Jesus.

[67] Cf. Sukka, 51 bBar.; BB 4a in Str.-B., I, 944, and the exaggerations of Joseph., Schl. Mt., 694.

[68] The prediction is literally fulfilled in respect of the ναός. The walls of the *ḥaram esh-sherif*, the temple precincts, are still standing to-day.

[69] Cf. Schl. Mt., 706; Gesch. d. Chr., 479, n. 1.

Judas casts the rejected pieces of silver into the temple (Mt. 27:5) indicates the permanent defilement of the sanctuary by the death of Jesus. The symbolism of the rending of the temple veil on the death of Jesus (Mk. 15:38; Mt. 27:51; Lk. 23:45) shows us that access to God is now by the death of Christ and not by the former ministry. [70]

2. The Attitude of Other New Testament Writings towards the Temple as τὸ ἱερόν.

a. Acts. In Acts we note first the same favourable attitude as in Jesus. The apostles go up to the temple to pray, cf. Ac. 2:46; 3:1-10 with Lk. 24:52 f. Neither the crucifixion nor Pentecost makes any difference in this respect. At Ac. 22:17 Paul has a revelation of the risen Lord while he is praying in the temple. [71] The apostles teach in the temple as Jesus did (Ac. 5:12, 20 f., 25, 42). Paul shows regard for the cultus by bringing the offering of Nazirite purification, 21:26; 24:6, 12, 18; 25:8; 26:21. [72] In this connection he is falsely accused of profaning the temple, → 234. Neither his epistles nor Acts show us how he viewed the emancipated attitude of Stephen with its radical repudiation of the cultus. The reason for this is that separation was not yet complete. At this point emancipation from the community of Israel took place only very slowly. It certainly cannot be contested that a more radical depreciation both of the Law and also of the cultus was first found in the Hellenistic portion of the Church, Ac. 6:13 f., and that it was this group which first gave cause for complaint. The formula used in false witness at the trial, namely, that Jesus the Nazarene will destroy this place (Lk. brings it in here rather than at the trial) is clearly enunciated in 7:44-50. According to Stephen, it is to be taken in the sense of Is. 66:1 f., that the Most High does not dwell ἐν χειροποιήτοις. [73] If this link with the prophetic saying is important, the reminiscence of similar Stoic sayings is not accidental in a Hellenist. The OT statement appeals to something which he himself brings by temperament and upbringing. On the other hand, the same theme in the Areopagus address of Paul at Ac. 17:24 (οὐκ ἐν χειροποιήτοις ναοῖς κατοικεῖ), and the related statement which again reminds us of Stoicism: οὐδὲ ... προσδεόμενός τινος, refer in this instance to pagan cults.

b. Other New Testament References. In all the other NT sayings which treat of the significance of the temple, which use the image of the temple to denote the new relationship to God given in Christ, and which transfer the image to the community, the term is → ναός or, in Hb., τὰ ἅγια → ἅγιος rather than ἱερόν. This is not without significance as regards the estimation of the word, since ναός and τὰ ἅγια are contrasting LXX terms. The basic and essential point in all these sayings is the conviction that the ancient predicates of people, temple, priesthood and city all apply to the new and universal community. This is linked with the missionary task of the community. The first three predicates are all found in

---

[70] Cf. Kl. Mk., ad loc.; Hb. 10:20; Jerome Ep., 18 ad Damasum : aditum ad deum ipsum per Christi mortem apertum significare videtur.

[71] The story raises certain difficulties in view of Gl. 1:22.

[72] Cf. Str.-B., III, 755-761. The basic attitude described in 1 C. 9:19-21 explains this course of action, which cannot be dismissed as a mere matter of politics (Meyer Ursprung, III, 71, 479). Even though the cultus cannot be regarded as a way of salvation, loyalty to the temple implies loyalty to hereditary Judaism.

[73] Cf. Is. 21:9; Jdt. 8:18; Bel. Θ 5, of idols. Hb. 9:24 χειροποίητα ἅγια of the OT temple. On this whole pt. cf. Wenschkewitz, 49-67.

1 Pt. 2:4-10. Here the image of the temple → οἶκος is combined with that of the living stone, i.e., Christ. [74] That the community is itself the temple (→ ναός) is a belief common to the whole of the NT witness: 1 C. 3:9, 16 f.; cf. 6:19 f. (the body); 2 C. 6:16 f.; Eph. 2:19-22. It is only from the time of Paul that we have certain evidence for the conception. Perhaps the Stoic use of the temple image had some influence. [75] On the other hand, οἶκος θεοῦ is used in the sense of the household, the *familia dei*, in 1 Tm. 3:15; 1 Pt. 4:17; Hb. 3:6; 10:21.

c. The Images of Revelation. In Rev. the reference of the image to the community, and the complete emancipation from the earthly sanctuary, take on a distinctive form → ναός. Those who overcome will be pillars in the temple of God. On them is inscribed the name of the new Jerusalem, 3:12. There is no longer a distinction between Jerusalem above and Jerusalem below, as in older Rabbinic writings. The Jerusalem which is above comes down, 3:12; 21:2, not in a nationalistic eschatological sense, as in 4 Esr. and the later midrashim, but as the universal and perfected city. [76] The temple is the eternal presence of God on the throne, 7:15; 11:19; 14:15, 17; 15:5 f., 8; 16:1, 17. [77] This reinterpretation carries with it the conviction of salvation history that the throne and the place of revelation have become one. Rev. 11:1 ff. seems to contradict this when it says that only the inner sanctuary is inviolate and that the outer court of the Gentiles is to be surrendered. But the temple is here an image of the community which through Jesus becomes the temple after the destruction of the earthly sanctuary. [78] In the consummation there will be no more temple, 21:22: ὁ γὰρ κύριος ὁ θεὸς ὁ παντοκράτωρ ναὸς αὐτῆς ἐστιν καὶ τὸ ἀρνίον. [79] → ναός.

† ἱερωσύνη.

1. ἱερωσύνη, by way of ἱερεωσύνη (Attic), e.g., Ditt. Syll.[3] 1068, 22: τοῦ Ἑρμοῦ, is formed from ἱερεύς by the reduction of ε to a semi-vowel and then by its elimination. [1]

ἱερωσύνη is more abstract than the later Greek ἱερατεία. It can mean "priesthood," "priestly office," "priestly dignity," or, more rarely, "priestly ministry."

a. Hdt., III, 142: ἱερωσύνην Διός, IV, 161 as the "income of the priest." More rarely in Plat., Demosth., Aristot. Pol., VII, 8, p. 1329a, 34: τὰς ἱερωσύνας. Diod. S., I, 73, 5: "priestly ministry"; I, 88, 2, plur.: πατρικὰς ἱερωσύνας, of hereditary "priesthood," cf. V, 58, 2. Plut. De Numa, 14, 1 (I, 69b) of "endowed priesthood," plur. Appian Bell. Civ., II, 132; V, 72; 131: ἡ μεγίστη ἱερωσύνη for the *pontificatus maximus* of the emperor. Egypt, Heliodor. Aeth., VII, 8. On inscr. for "priestly office," 3rd and 2nd cent. B.C.; E. Michel, *Recueil d'Inscriptions Grecques*, I (1900), 977, 13; 981, 7; 704, 15; Ditt. Or., I, 56, 23; Inscr. Priene, 174; 2nd and 3rd cent. A.D.; Inscr. Priene, 205, 2. Astrological, Class. Philol., 22 (1927), 14, line 34: ἀρχὰς ἱερωσύνας. b. It occurs only

---

[74] Cf. Jeremias, *Golgotha*, 85: the symbolism of the cosmic rock.
[75] Cf. Wenschkewitz, 100 ff., 116. → λατρεία (R. 12:1).
[76] Cf. A. Schlatter, *Das AT in der joh. Apk.* (1912), 29 f. Str.-B., III, 796.
[77] Cf. Hb. 9:1, 12, 24. Cf. 8:2; 9:12 f.
[78] Cf. Loh. Apk., *ad loc.*; Schlatter, *Das AT in der joh. Apk.*, 81; *Gesch. d. erst. Chr.*, 336 f.
[79] Cf. Str.-B., III, 852; IV, 884; Wenschkewitz, 155.
ἱ ε ρ ω σ ύ ν η. D. Magie, *De Romanorum Juris Publici Sacrique Vocabulis Sollemnibus in Graecum Sermonem Conversis* (1905), Index; E. Schweizer, *Grammatik der Pergamenischen Inschriften* (1898), 93 n.; F. Poland, *Geschichte des Griechischen Vereinswesens* (1909), 347**.
[1] Cf. Schweizer, *op. cit.*, 93 n., with many examples; Mayser, I, 15, 154. On ἱερωσύνη instead of ἱερωσύνη, cf. Schweizer, *op. cit.*, 102.

once in the OT canon at 1 Ch. 29:22 for the priestly office of Zadok (Heb. concretely כהן). But it is common in the Apocr., 1 Εσδρ. 5:38. Sir. 45:24 : ἱερωσύνης μεγαλεῖον, "high-priesthood." 1 Macc. 2:54; 3:49 : garments of the "priestly office"; 7:9, of the "office of the high-priest." Cf. 7:21; 4 Macc. 5:35; 7:6. In Test. XII : Test. L. 8:13; 9:7; 14:7; 16:1; 17:1-3; 18:1,9. c. In Joseph. Ant., 2, 216 of the "priestly office" of Aaron. But also of Baal worship, Ant., 9, 154. Of the "high-priestly office," Ant., 5, 350; 15, 36, 56; 16, 187; 17, 341. But the general sense of "priestly dignity" is always basic. Joseph. himself, being related to the royal house of the Hasmonaeans, has τὴν ἱερωσύνην, Ant., 16, 187; Vit., 198. He emphasises the high estimation of the priestly dignity among his people, Vit., 1; Ap., 1, 31. d. Philo, too, uses the term frequently for the "office or dignity of the priest," and sometimes for the "priesthood," Abr., 98; Leg. All., III, 242; Plant., 63; Vit. Mos., I, 304; II, 71. In the sense of "priestly activity" (also ἱερουργία, Vit. Mos., II, 174): Vit. Mos., II, 66. *Ibid.*, II, 5 : ἡ πρώτη ἱερωσύνη instead of ἀρχιερωσύνη. Philo, too, stresses the fact that this office is a supreme honour, Ebr., 65ᵢ and 126; Sacr. AC, 132. At the Passover it may be said of the whole people : ἱερωσύνης ἀξιώματι τετιμημένοι (Spec. Leg., II, 145).

2. In the NT it is found only at Hb. 7:11 f., 24. The Levitical priesthood has not achieved any τελείωσις. There is thus a change of ἱερωσύνη. Christ becomes a priest after the order of Melchisedec. Because He remains for ever, He possesses the priesthood as ἀπαράβατον. The point at issue here is the character of the institution rather than the specific dignity → ἀρχιερεύς.

1 Cl., 43, 2 speaks of the ἱερωσύνη of the tribe of Levi, for which Moses is jealous. Athenag. Suppl., 28, 3, however, uses it of pagan priesthood. Orig. Comm. in Joh., I, 28, 191 follows Hb. in applying it to the priesthood of Christ, which is set alongside His kingly office : βασιλεία. Chrys. in περὶ ἱερωσύνης, MPG, 47, 623-692 deals with the lofty nature of the priestly and episcopal office, whose dignity surpasses that of kings and even angels, and whose authority culminates in the eucharistic sacrifice, which implies mediatorship between God and humanity.

† ἱερατεύω.

1. ἱερατεύω (Ionic ἱερητεύω, Lesbian ἱρητεύω) is formed from ἱεράομαι after a verbal adj. ἱερατός, which is no longer extant. It means "to discharge the priestly office." Hesych. *Verbum Alexandrinum est et Macedonicum : sacerdotio fungi. Graecis hoc veteribus dicebatur* ἱερᾶσθαι.[1]

a. It occurs first in the *koine* and then in later writers like Herodian, Heliodorus,[2] and in inscriptions[3] of the 4th/3rd cent. B.C.: Ditt. Syll.³, 1044, 19, in the 2nd cent. B.C.: Inscr. Magn., 178, 6. The only example in the pap. seems to be P. Giess., I, 11, 10 (118 A.D.): εἱερατεύειν. b. It is found in the LXX. Though ἱερός is avoided → 226, this technical pagan term is accepted, since it is a verbal form of the indispensable

---

ἱ ε ρ α τ ε ύ ω. A. Thumb, *Die griech. Sprache im Zeitalter des Hellenismus* (1889), 68; H. Anz, *Subsidia* (Diss. Halle, 1894); 370 f.; Deissmann B, 215 f.; Deissmann NB, 42 f.; E. Schweizer, *Grammatik der Pergamenischen Inschriften* (1898), 39 f.; E. Fraenkel, *Griechische Denominativa* (1906), 218; F. Poland, *Geschichte des griech. Vereinswesens* (1909), 347**; J. Rouffiac, *Recherches sur les Caractères du Grec dans le NT d'après les Inscriptions de Priène* (1911), 66 f.

[1] Acc. to Suid., Phot. Lex., Hesych., ἱερᾶσθαι = ἱερουργεῖν, "to be a priest." Cf. Schweizer, 39 f. Pap.: Preisigke Wört., III, 373. Joseph. uses it for the discharge of the priestly office, Ant., 5, 354; Bell., 6, 438. Thus the priest can be called ὁ ἱερασάμενος, Ant., 4, 23 and 28. Philo has the same usage at Vit. Mos., I, 149 etc., but he prefers ὁ ἱερώμενος, esp. applied allegorically, Leg. All., III, 125; Poster. C., 184.

[2] Cf. Pr.-Bauer, *s.v.*

[3] Cf. Deissmann NB, 43; Schweizer, 39 f.

ἱερεύς. It is used for כֹּהֵן pi, mostly in Ex., e.g., 28:1-4; 40:15; also Lv., Nu., Dt., e.g., Lv. 16:32; Nu. 3:4; Dt. 10:6; cf. 1 Ch. 5:36; Hos. 4:6; Ez. 44:13; Sir. 45:15. It is also used for כֹּהֵן kal : 1 Βασ. 2:28; 2 Ch. 31:19. Finally it is used for כְּהֻנָּה: Nu. 16:10. Cf. Is. 61:10 'A. c. In the Apocrypha : 1 Εσδρ. 5:39; 8:45; 1 Macc. 7:5. d. Like → ἱερωσύνη (→ supra) it is found in Test. XII at L. 8:10; 12:5. Joseph. has it at Ant., 3, 189; 15, 253; 20, 242. It does not occur in Philo.

2. The only NT instance at Lk. 1:8 is influenced by LXX usage. It treats of the discharge of the priestly office by Zacharias after the order of his course.

In 1 Cl., 43, 4 it is used with λειτουργεῖν of the priestly ministry of the tribe of Levi, in Just. Apol., I, 62, 2 of pagan priests, and cf. Eus. Dem. Ev., IV, 15, 16-15, 18 : τῷ θεῷ ἱερατεύεσθαι.

† ἱεράτευμα.

So far as modern investigation shows, ἱεράτευμα occurs only in the LXX and dependent writings. The Greek Bible ventures this construction in the basic exposition of the revelation at Sinai, Ex. 19:6 : ὑμεῖς δὲ ἔσεσθέ μοι βασίλειον ἱεράτευμα καὶ ἔθνος ἅγιον, cf. also Ex. 23:22.

1. The Hebrew text [1] is מַמְלֶכֶת כֹּהֲנִים, "kingdom of priests." Ex. 19:1 ff. seems to be drawn from many sources, since there are various themes and a change of usage. It is perhaps a part of the Yahwistic redaction JE. The main strand is J, but there are clear traces of E, e.g., v. 3 : בֵּית יַעֲקֹב for Israel. There is no trace of P. Thus מַמְלֶכֶת כֹּהֲנִים comes from E. Such theologising phrases are alien to J, whereas E can call Abraham a prophet, Gn. 20:7. The expression "kingdom of priests" comes from a period in which it can mean that all members of the people of Israel should be priests, i.e., a kingdom consisting of priests. In E, therefore, a general outpouring of the Spirit is at least regarded as possible, Nu. 11:29. [2]

Cf. later Is. 61:6, though here the reference is to Israel's relation to the nations. The words do not mean a kingdom represented by the priesthood, i.e., a hierocracy, [3] as apparently in P and Ezekiel.

2. The LXX translation is surprisingly free. Σ and Θ, also b (108), have the literal βασιλεί(α) ἱερῶν. 'A has regnum sacerdotum. The Syrohexapla has regnum sacerdotes, the Peshitto βασιλεία καὶ ἱερεῖς, [4] cf. Rev. 1:6; 5:10. Tg. O. and J., II have "kings, priests," cf. Tg. J., I : "Kings adorned with crowns and ministering priests." [5] This branch of the tradition influences Rev. → ἱερεύς at Rev. 1:6. βασίλειον ἱεράτευμα brings out the priestly side more strongly than the Heb., not merely in the sense of individual priests, but of the priesthood as a corporation, in analogy to τεχνίτευμα as a guild of artists, Ditt. Or., I, 51. [6] βασίλειον means belonging to a king, but in such a way that after this adjectival definition all the emphasis falls on the priestly fellowship. Thus

---

ἱεράτευμα. [1] Cf. E. König, Theologie des AT (1923), 91, n. 1; W. Eichrodt, Theologie des AT, I (1933), 9, n. 5. In the second paragraph I am much indebted to L. Köhler of Zürich.
[2] One might also compare the expression "kingdom of priests" with the theology of Dt., for which all Israel is עַם קָדוֹשׁ (Dt. 7:6; 14:2, 21; 26:19; 28:9), or with the oldest stratum of the story of Korah, i.e., with the rebellious slogan כָּל־הָעֵדָה כֻּלָּם קְדֹשִׁים, Nu. 16:3 [v. Rad].
[3] Cf. H. Holzinger, Komm. (1900) on Ex. 19:1 ff. This conception of priestly kingship seems to be present in Jub. 16:18, and it corresponds to the spirit of the Maccabean period.
[4] Cf. A. E. Brooke-N. McLean, The Old Testament in Greek (1909), ad loc.
[5] Str.-B., III, 789.
[6] Moult.-Mill., ad loc.

ἱεράτευμα is the chief concept. βασίλειον does not mean that they are all kings. This idea is first found in the exposition represented by the Tg., which seems to reflect the vacillating interpretation of the Synagogue, → ἱερεύς.

3. At 2 Macc. 2:17, in a letter from the Jews in Jerusalem to those in Egypt, a statement is made concerning that which God has conferred upon the Jewish people : ὁ δὲ θεὸς ὁ σώσας τὸν πάντα λαὸν αὐτοῦ καὶ ἀποδοὺς τὴν κληρονομίαν πᾶσιν καὶ τὸ βασίλειον καὶ τὸ ἱεράτευμα καὶ τὸν ἁγιασμόν ... Here there is express allusion to Ex. 19:6, for we find all the basic concepts of that passage : λαός (v. 5), βασίλειον, ἱεράτευμα, ἁγιασμός (= ἔθνος ἅγιον). Once again it should be noted that βασίλειον and ἱεράτευμα are separated. This goes back to a different tradition from that of the LXX → 249. βασίλειον, which means "royal palace," does not really fit this context, and the only possibility is to construe it as "royal diadem" or "royal dignity." But if we do this, then ἱεράτευμα must mean "priestly dignity" rather than "priesthood," as in the LXX. ἁγιασμός, "consecration," refers to the temple ministry. We again see how the detailed terms of Ex. 19:6 were variously applied in Synagogue usage ; each employed them in his own way to describe the dignity conferred upon Israel. Here, too, ἱεράτευμα is a quality which belongs to the whole people.

In Philo too, Abr., 56; Sobr., 66 we find in quotations the same separation of the concepts βασίλειον καὶ ἱεράτευμα (θεοῦ). βασίλειον is viewed as a "royal residence," and if the word is taken independently this is a correct translation. But Abr., 56 does not make the same express use of this interpretation as Sobr., 66. The Philo passages do not help us towards a more precise definition of ἱεράτευμα. It is obvious, however, that Philo must have had a Greek text which did not have βασίλειον ἱεράτευμα, like the LXX, but which belonged to the same tradition (Syrohexapla, Peshitto, Tg. O.) as that which influenced 2 Macc. Joseph. does not use ἱεράτευμα.

In M. Ex. 19:6 (71a) the passage provides occasion for reflection on the peaceful nature of Jewish world dominion : "If princes, then perhaps merchant princes ?" The word priest can be used to express the peaceful nature of Jewish dominion as compared with oppressive rule. [7]

4. 1 Pt. 2:5, 9. The distinctive feature of the whole section 1 Pt. 2:1-10 is that the predicates of salvation and dignity, namely, possession, temple and priesthood (with a sacrificial ministry) are consistently transferred from Israel to the Gentile Christian community. On the living stone, Christ, this is built up as living stones into an οἶκος πνευματικός, i.e., a spiritual temple, εἰς ἱεράτευμα ἅγιον. In this context the latter phrase must have the sense of a consecrated priesthood. If we ask concerning its distinctive priestly ministry, the answer is that spiritual sacrifices are offered through the community. It is ἱεράτευμα inasmuch as it offers these sacrifices. And it offers them to God through Jesus Christ. It is noteworthy that in this application the image of the temple is made less static and more dynamic by intermingling it with the metaphor of the body. The community is alive by the Spirit. It is edified by constant growth. But ἱεράτευμα denotes priestly corporation in the LXX sense. While Ex. 19:6 is taken literally, the thought is also present that as a priestly company the community is "immediate to God." This truth casts an astonishing light on Ex. 19:6. But it is a fulfilment which is granted only to the Gentile Christian community through Christ. If elsewhere the priest is aloof from the people, here the whole new people of God is a priestly fellowship. True to the LXX sense, βασίλειον means that it belongs to the King. [8] The priesthood serves the King. Belonging to Him, it shares His glory. The continuation in

---

[7] Cf. Str.-B., III, 789. The sparse attestation seems to justify the conclusion that exposition of Ex. 19:6 had no great influence. Cf. Wenschkewitz, op. cit., 43 f.

[8] The usage in Rev. → ἱερεύς, i.e., "kings," is not to be confused with this passage. So T. Spörri, Der Gemeindegedanke im 1 Pt. (1925), 36.

v. 9 speaks of proclamation. This makes it clear that the preceding descriptions, including ἱεράτευμα, cannot be restricted to the inner life of the Christian community, e.g., as a general priesthood, though this is how the passage is customarily treated. What is really meant is a ministry of witness to all humanity along the lines of Is. 61:6 (cf. v. 9). [9]

† ἱερατεία (-ία).

1. This is another word which belongs to the sphere of ἱερεύς. It is only thus that we can understand its use in the LXX in spite of the avoidance of ἱερός. It derives from ἱερατεύω. Though commonly used in later Greek, and cf. Aristot. → infra, it is designed to fill the gap left by the lack of any Greek word for the priestly state, office or dignity (elsewhere expressed by ἡ ἱερατική or occasionally ἱερωσύνη, → 247).

a. In Aristot. Pol., 7, 8, p. 1328b, 12 f. we have ἡ περὶ τὸ θεῖον ἐπιμέλεια, ἥν καλοῦσιν ἱερατείαν, "the priestly ministry and work" (ἔργον), which is the fifth and yet also the first thing in a state. Here the word carries the sense of active ministry, [1] but this is a nuance which cannot be definitely established elsewhere. It is in any case rare in literature. We might mention Dion. Hal., II, 73; Dio C., 55, 22 : ἡ τῆς Ἑστίας ἱερατεία = sacerdotium Vestae. It is more common on inscr. as early as the 4th cent. B.C.: Inscr. Priene, 139, 7 περὶ τῆς ἱερατείης τοῦ Διός; 3rd and 2nd cent. B.C.: Ditt. Syll.[3], 1014, 14; 1015, 5 : ὁ πριάμενος τὴν ἱερατείαν τῆς Ἀρτέμιδος. Here it always means "priestly office." [2] Pap. in the 2nd cent. A.D.: P. Tebt., II, 298, 14; P. Giess., I, 23, 19. b. In the LXX the term vacillates between "priestly office" and "priestly ministry"; indeed, it can also denote "priesthood." It is mostly used for כְּהֻנָּה. At Ex. 29:9 the vestments, and at Ex. 40:15 the anointing, express the office. Nu. 3:10; 18:1. Nu. 25:13: διαθήκη ἱερατείας. In Jos. 18:7 it is hereditary to the Levites. At 1 Βασ. 2:36 it brings with it bread. 2 Εσδρ. 2:62; Neh. 13:29. In Apocr. only Sir. 45:7: ἱερατείαν λαοῦ. For the infin. pi of כהן: Ex. 35:19; 39:18 : clothes for the priestly ministry. For אֵפוֹד: Hos. 3:4 along with θυσιαστήριον. The "priestly office" is also in view in Test. L. 5:2 (cf. Test. Iss. 5:7); 8:2, 9 f., 14; but "priesthood" in Test. Jud. 21:2, 4 : this surpasses the monarchy. [3] Jos. and Philo do not use the Word.

2. The reference in Lk. 1:9 is to the discharge of the priestly ministry. In this case it is more precisely defined as the burning of incense. At Hb. 7:5, however, it denotes those of the sons of Levi who receive the priestly office. [4]

† ἱερουργέω.

1. ἱερουργέω, from ἱερουργός, a compound of ἱερός and a subsidiary -εργός, cf. κακοῦργος, δημιουργός (for the verb cf. θαυματουργέω, κακουργέω etc.), is

---

[9] Orig. Comm. in Joh., X, 39, 266; XIII, 13, 84 quotes 1 Pt. 2. On the use of ἱεράτευμα in the Christian Church, cf. RE[3], 16, 47-52. H. Behm, Der Begriff des allgemeinen Priestertums (1912); A. v. Harnack, Entstehung und Entwicklung der Kirchenverfassung und des Kirchenrechts in den zwei ersten Jahrhunderten (1910), 81 ff.; RGG[2], IV, 1492 f.

ἱερατεία. D. Magie (→ 221, Bibl.), Index ; F. Poland, Geschichte des griech. Vereinswesens (1909), 347**.

[1] Moult.-Mill., s.v.

[2] For the imperial period cf. Schweizer (→ 248, Bibl.), 39 (Ionic form ἱερητεία).

[3] Cf. E. Schnapp, Die Testamente der zwölf Patriarchen (1884), 45.

[4] Cl. Al. Fr., 61 (III, p. 227, 28, Stählin) along with θυσία. Orig. Princ., IV, 1, 3 (p. 297, 11 f., Koetschau) along with θυσιαστήριον.

ἱερουργέω. C. F. A. Fritzsche, Pauli ad Romanos Epistola, III (1843), 256-258; C. L. W. Grimm, Kurzgefasstes exegetisches Handbuch zu den Apkr. (1857), 329 f. on 4 Macc. 7:8.

a late Greek word and means *sacris operari, sacras res tractare,* "to perform holy or sacrificial ministry."

a. Herodian Hist., V, 5, 6; V, 6, 1. In Plut. Alex., 31, 4 (I, 683b) med.: ἱερουργίας τινὰς ἀπορρήτους ἱερουργούμενος, as an object to the verb (cf. R. 15:16); cf. also CIG Addenda to 4528 (III, p. 1175, Boeckh): ἱεροὐργησε τὴν κλείνην, *lectisternium fecit,* of the preparation of a meal for the gods, when their images were put on cushions and dishes were set before them. Closer to R. 15:16, however, is the vl. [1] at 4 Macc. 7:8 : τοὺς ἱερουργοῦντας (for δημιουργοῦντας) τὸν νόμον, "to discharge priestly ministry towards the Law," i.e., to protect this with one's own blood and noble sweat even to the death. [2] Here, too, ἱερουργεῖν τι, "to discharge something priestly." b. Josephus and Philo do not have this usage. In them ἱερουργεῖν always means "to offer sacrifice." It is often used without object : Jos. Ant., 7, 333; 14, 65; 17, 166; Bell., 5, 14 and 16; Philo Cher., 96; Ebr., 138; Migr. Abr., 98; Plant., 164. Particularly in Jos. it is often used as a participial definition : Jos. Ant., 3, 237; 11, 110; 14, 67; Philo Abr., 198. When it has an object, this usually tells us what is sacrificed : Ant., 5, 263 : τί; 6, 102 : εὐχὰς καὶ θυσίας; 9, 43 : τῶν υἱῶν τὸν πρεσβύτατον; Philo Conf. Ling., 124 : τὰ πρωτότοκα; Migr. Abr., 67: θυσίας; 140 : υἱόν; Som., II, 72 : ψυχήν etc. Pass., Leg. All., III, 130; Spec. Leg., I, 254; Migr. Abr., 202. c. ἱερουργία is also used for "sacrifice," Plat. Leg., VI, 774e, dedicatory offering at weddings. Joseph. and Philo use it frequently, Jos. Ant., 1, 225 and 231 (with prayer), 236; 4, 37. ἱεροὐργημα also occurs for the act of sacrifice, Ant., 8, 123. ἱερουργία in Philo, Abr., 170; Ebr., 130; Spec. Leg., I, 162. With ἐπιτελεῖν, P. Tebt., II, 292, 20 f. Orig. Orat., 11, 1 of Raphael's offering of prayer. But it is more common for cultus or divine worship, Hdt., V, 83; 4 Macc. 3:20 SR : temple ministry ; Jos. Ant., 3, 150; Bell., 6, 389; Philo Plant., 107; Eus. Dem. Ev., I, 8, 2. With θυσίαι as the more comprehensive term, Jos. Ant., 8, 105; Philo Spec. Leg., I, 21; Vit. Mos., II, 73. Of circumcision, P. Tebt., I, 293, 20 (2nd cent. A.D.). Eus. Vit. Const., IV, 45, 2 : μυστικαὶ ἱερουργίαι.

2. When Paul uses ἱερουργοῦντα τὸ εὐαγγέλιον τοῦ θεοῦ in R. 15:16, he is describing his service of the Gospel as service of a cultus, which he discharges as λειτουργὸς Χριστοῦ ᾽Ιησοῦ εἰς τὰ ἔθνη. In the development of the metaphor the preparation and offering of the sacrifice is emphasised as the chief thing. By being brought εἰς ὑπακοὴν (λόγῳ καὶ ἔργῳ, v. 18), the Gentiles become a προσφορὰ εὐπρόσδεκτος. This use of the image is protected against pagan, sacral misunderstanding by the fact that the offering of personal life in comprehensive obedience is the sacrifice, sanctified by the Holy Spirit (v. 16).

† ἱερόθυτος.

1. ἱερόθυτος, from ἱερός and θυτός, the verbal adj. of θύω, cf. θεόθυτος [1] (for ἱερεῖον) and εἰδωλόθυτος, 4 Macc. 5:2, NT → II, 378. It means "consecrated or sacrificed to deity." In Pind. Fr., 78 ἱρόθυτος θάνατος is used of man's sacrificial death regarded as an offering to the gods, cf. Plut. Bellone an Pace Clariores Fuerint Athenienses, 7 (II, 349c). Elsewhere the term is exclusively cultic. Aristoph. Av., 1266 f.: ἱερόθυτον καπνόν of sacrificial smoke. Of the flesh of sacrificial animals, Aristot. De Mirabilibus Auscultationibus, 123, p. 842b, 1 f.; Plut. Convivalium Disputationum, VIII, 8, 3 (II, 729c); Athen., XIV, 79 (p. 660c); Aristot. Oec., II, p. 1349b, 13 : ἱερόθυτα ἐποίουν. Ditt. Syll.[3], 624, 42 (2nd cent. B.C.): οἶν (sheep) ἱερόθυτον alongside οἶνον. Of the

---

[1] Cf. Fritzsche, *ad loc.* Swete and Rahlfs do not mention the vl. in their editions of the LXX.

[2] Cf. Grimm, *ad loc.,* though he does not connect "with one's own blood" to ἱερουργοῦντας (Deissmann in Kautzsch, *Apkr. u. Pseudepigr., ad loc.*).

ἱερόθυτος. [1] Classicist criticism in Phryn. Ecl. (Lobeck, p. 159): ἱερόθυτον οὐκ ἐρεῖς, ἀλλ᾽ ἀρχαῖον θεόθυτον.

skin of the sacrificial animal, Ditt. Syll.³, 736, 23 (91 B.C., mystery inscr., Andania): the ἱεραὶ γυναῖκες should carry at the mysteries ὑποδήματα ... πίλινα ἤ δερμάτινα ἱερόθυτα, "shoes of felt or leather from an animal immolated as a sacrifice." The word does not occur in Jos. and Philo.[2]

2. The point raised in 1 C. 10:28[3] is as follows. An invitation is received to a feast, most probably from a Christian, though perhaps from a non-Christian as a test. It is stated that the meat which will be eaten is ἱερόθυτον, i.e., that it derives from the cultus, and that it has come to the table of the host by way of the μάκελλον. We cannot be sure that the vl. εἰδωλόθυτον here is original; it makes good sense as a Christian correction. In the invitation to a pagan house the formula is selected which fits in with the cultic conceptions of paganism. For Paul himself the meat is certainly εἰδωλόθυτον rather than ἱερόθυτον, 1 C. 8:1, 4, 7, 10; 10:19.

† ἱεροπρεπής.

1. ἱεροπρεπής, which is made up of ἱερόν and πρέπει, does not mean that which befits a saint, but that which corresponds to the ἱερόν, the temple precincts and ministry, the sacred action, the religious, and finally the deity. It thus means that which is sacred or reverend. Hence Hesych. rightly defines it as θεοπρεπῶς.

a. In the primary sense ἱεροπρεπής is well adapted to express the fact that the cultus corresponds to sacred determinations and represents consecration to the divine. Xenoph. Symp., 8, 40 of priestly dignity: δοκεῖς ἱεροπρεπέστατος εἶναι. Frequently of sacrifice, Luc. De Sacrificiis, 13: κνῖσα (incense) θεσπέσιος καὶ ἱεροπρεπής. Iambl. Myst., V, 3: ἡ ἱεροπρεπῶς ἀναθυμίασις. In inscr.: proper to the ministry of the temple or the sacred use, Inscr. Priene, 109, 215 f. (c. 120 B.C.); Ditt. Syll.³, 708, 23 f.: πομπαῖς ἱεροπρεπέσιν, of the solemn procession, as Jos. Ant., 11, 329, here too in the sense of what is proper to the religious or cultic. More generally, Luc. Vit. Auct., 6, corresponding to holy, or even to oracularly superstitious things, though here with a cynical twist. b. Particular note should be taken of 4 Macc. 9:25, where he who is faithful unto death according to the statutes is ἱεροπρεπής, and 11:20 א R, where the same militant attitude is described as a ἱεροπρεπὴς ἀγών. c. In addition to the cultus or the Law, the inescapable demand of morality can be that to which the use of the term is orientated. In Plut. Lib. Educ., 14 (II, 11c) it is called ἱεροπρεπέστατον (a most sacred duty) to accustom boys to the truth. What is meant is that which is consonant with virtue, i.e., the divine. d. There is a distinctive use in Philo. Very occasionally he might use the term in the broad popular sense of "solemn," e.g., of the theatre in Deus Imm., 102. But in the main it is integrated into his basic religious understanding. A definition is given in Spec. Leg., III, 83; Decal., 175: that which is θεοειδές, ἁρμόττον αὐτοῦ (θεοῦ) τῇ φύσει (man; the Decalogue), that which corresponds to God, is ἱεροπρεπές. But there can also be a cultic connection, i.e., that which is in keeping with the temple, Plant., 162. Even here, however, allegorical interpretation brings us back to the final divine signification, Congr., 114; Vit. Mos., II, 85. What is consonant with God is explicitly declared by the simultaneous use of ἅγιος, σεμνός, θεῖος, τελεώτατος, Rer. Div. Her., 110; Spec. Leg., I, 317; Abr., 101; Migr. Abr., 98. The absolutely miraculous is a mark of God's action, Decal., 33. So, too, is the incorporeal, Decal., 60; Abr., 101.

---

[2] ἱεροθύται: P. Fay., 22, 8 (1st cent. A.D.), the name of a priest who acts in marriages and divorces, attested from Rhodes, Arcadia, Alexandria, Ptolemais. W. Schubart, APF, 5 (1909), 78 f.; W. F. Otto, *Priester und Tempel im hell. Ägypten* (1905), I, 164; II, 295; F. Poland, *Geschichte des griech. Vereinswesens* (1909), 41, 309; Preisigke Fachwörter, s.v.; Pauly-W., VIII (1913), 1590 f.

[3] Cf. Joh. W. 1 K.; Ltzm. K.; Schl. K., *ad loc.*; Bchm. K., 303, n. 1.

What is consonant with God is demonstrated in the θεσμοί, the νομοθεσία, the ἐντολαί, Leg. All., III, 204; Vit. Mos., II, 25; Praem. Poen., 101, in the Sabbath, Decal., 51;
Spec. Leg., II, 70, in the number 7, Op. Mund., 99. The true cultus, which consists in
the offering of the διάνοια, is ἱεροπρεπῶς, Omn. Prob. Lib., 75, where the Essenes,
named for ὁσιότης and as θεραπευταὶ θεοῦ, are ἱεροπρεπεῖς in this sense. Cf. also
on ἀρετή, Sacr. AC, 45; Migr. Abr., 98. True prayers and hymns also correspond to
God, Plant., 90; Praem. Poen., 84; Spec. Leg., I, 185; also the mysteries, Som., I, 82. [1]
The constellations are also holy and in this sense divine, Spec. Leg., III, 187; Plant., 25.
The translation "sublime," "solemn," "reverend," is hardly adequate in the case of
Philo. The standpoint is always that of corresponding to God. e. A rather weaker sense
is "worthy of respect," Ps.-Plat. Theag., 122d, with a play on the name Theages, which
indicates the divine. Joseph., in a quotation from Berosus, also uses the word in the
sense of "costly" with reference to the decoration of the gates of Babylon by Nebuchadnezzar, Ant., 10, 225 == Ap., 1, 140.

2. In Tt. 2:3 it is said of the old ladies in the community that they should be
ἱεροπρεπεῖς in their conduct. This usage corresponds to the fondness of the Past.
for compounds, [2] and to their preference for a solemn and cultic style. Like
R. 15:16 it involves a Christian reinterpretation of the cultic metaphor. The basis is
ἱερόν, so that there is no exact parallel to the use of ἱερός in 2 Tm. 3:15. We can
finally see such a parallel only if we take the ἱερόν which is in view in a very
general sense for the divine, cf. Philo. But allusion to the figure of the temple is
more natural. What is meant is best explained by 1 Tm. 2:10 : ὃ πρέπει γυναιξὶν
ἐπαγγελλομέναις θεοσέβειαν. ἱεροπρεπεῖς is an abbreviation of this description.
There, too, we have πρέπει. The women are reminded what it means that they
confess fear of God. The ἱεροπρεπεῖς of Tt. 2:3 can be expounded in a Christian
sense only if we take it to refer to the fact that we truly belong to God
by faith in Jesus Christ, i.e., that this is the reality expressed in the image of the
temple. To live worthy of this will alone keep us from unworthy conversation. If
we translate "in keeping with holiness," we fail to do justice to the author's lack
of concern lest his hieratic borrowing should be misunderstood. For such a rendering leads us, in fact, into a dubious sacral sphere. The simple meaning is that we
must take seriously the fact that we belong to God. [3]

There is even greater freedom in the use of the term in Orig. Comm. in Joh., X, 39, 266,
where ἱεροπρεπῶς νοῆσαι is employed for spiritual understanding. Cf. also Eus. Laus
Constantini, 16, 10 : νοερῶν τε καὶ λογικῶν θυσιῶν ἱεροπρεπεῖς λειτουργίαι.

ἱεροπρεπής. [1] Cf. Iambl. Myst., III, 31: τῶν ἱεροπρεπῶν δρωμένων ἐξήγησις,
rerum sacrarum explicatio.

[2] Nägeli, 87.

[3] "Ehrwürdig" is used in the Zürich Bible, but it emphasises too strongly the human
character and too little the relation to the divine background. "Priestly" is better. Dib. Past.,
ad loc. or Schl. Erl., ad loc.: "as is becoming in the sanctuary." Materially, translation must
bring out the fact that dedication to God, belonging to Him, is to be taken seriously.

† ἱεροσυλέω.

1. The robbery of temples,[1] originally the removal of sacred property from a sacred site, is a. in Greek, Roman and Egyptian eyes[2] one of the most serious of offences. At times of amnesty, murderers and robbers of temples are often excluded. Temple robbery is generally classified with treason and murder. Those convicted are denied burial in consecrated ground. In Plat. Phaed., 113e criminals of these categories are regarded as ἀνιάτως and are plunged into Tartarus. Philo in Spec. Leg., III, 83 describes ἀνδροφονία as ἱεροσυλιῶν ἡ μεγίστη. Cf. Decal., 133, where the murderer is guilty of robbing the temple, since he has plundered the most sacred possession of God. This mode of expression reflects Philo's view of the nobility of man. But it also testifies to the broader use of ἱεροσυλία. The term *sacrilegium,* which originally meant temple robbery and then any sacral offence, is now used of religious transgression generally.[3] It is impossible to think of anything more heinous.

b. In the OT we are reminded of Dt. 7:25 f. With special reference to relationships with the heathen peoples of Canaan, and their definitive extirpation, the possession of idols and their reception into houses are forbidden. They are an offence to God and fall under the ban. Even the silver and the gold in them must be rejected lest it become a snare. Everything must be burned.

c. Of particular interest is the treatment of this subject in Josephus. In Ant., 4, 207 he does not scruple to find in the Torah the new law that we are not to scorn the gods of other nations. He adopts a free translation to bring Dt. 7:25 f. under this rule of tolerance, suppressing the true argument of the passage. His purpose is to show to the cultured reader that the Jewish people is tolerant. In Ap., 1, 249, 310 and 318 he is also meeting the slanders of a Manetho and Lysimachus, who accuse the Jews of robbing temples in Egypt, and who allow themselves the witticism that Jerusalem arose out of Ἱερόσυλα, i.e., that it took its name originally from temple robbery.

d. The attitude of the Rabbis is much laxer than one would expect from Dt. 7. They have no legal term for intentional temple robbery. Whipping is an adequate punishment. According to bSanh., 84a it is only the violation of a prohibition. It is thus judged more leniently than murder. Capital punishment by God, but not by human courts, may also be the punishment. The softening of Dt. 7:25 f. is astonishing. Thus we read in AZ 53b, Bar. that "taking" is if an Israelite comes into possession of an idol, and since it is valuable, he sells it to a Gentile, who will worship it. This is a ref. to Dt. 7. R. Samuel says in 52a that an idol may be accepted if it is deconsecrated. But the Mishnah AZ,

---

ἱεροσυλέω. T. Thalheim in Pauly-W., VIII (1913), 1589 f.; M. H. E. Meier-G. F. Schömann-J. H. Lipsius, *Der attische Prozess* (1883-1887), 366 ff.; J. H. Lipsius, *Das attische Recht und Rechtsverfahren* (1905-1915), 362, 401, 442; R. Taubenschlag, *Das Strafrecht im Rechte der Papyri* (1916), 51 ff.; F. v. Woess, *Das Asylwesen Ägyptens in der Ptolemaeerzeit* (1923), 110; J. Juster, *Les Juifs dans l'Empire Romain* (1914), 382 f.; I. Heinemann, *Philons griech. u. jüd. Bildung* (1932), 38 f.; F. Cumont in *Rev. Hist.,* 163 (1930), 263; L. Wenger in *Zeitschrift der Savigny-Stiftung für Rechtsgeschichte, Romanistische Abtlg.,* 51 (1931), 381; F. R. Tonneau in *Revue Biblique,* 40 (1931), 557. On the question of the danger and possibility of robbing the temple in Judaism, F. Delitzsch, *Pls. des Ap. Brief an die Römer* (1870), 77; A. Bischoff, ZNW, 9 (1908), 167; Str.-B., III, 113-115.

[1] Materially, though without the word ἱεροσυλεῖν, Xenophon Hist. Graec., VI, 4, 30; VII, 3, 8; VII, 4, 33. Diod. S., XVI, 25, 2 mentions that ἀτάφους ῥίπτεσθαι is a common Greek law in respect of robbers of temples.

[2] Cf. Heinemann, 39.

[3] Thalheim, *op. cit.*: the violation of a pillar of Zeus, the misuse of educational funds, coining, absence from the torch-light procession of Demeter. Violation of graves falls under τιμωρία ἱεροσυλίας, F. Cumont, L. Wenger, F. R. Tonneau, *op. cit.*

4, 4 has the qualification that only a Gentile and not a Jew may deconsecrate it. In 4, 2 the gold, clothing or vessels found on the head of an idol may be put to positive use. 4, 5 mentions the case of a Gentile selling or pledging his idol. [4]

2. The usage. ἱεροσυλέω, deriving from → ἱερόσυλος, means "to commit temple robbery." It occurs also as συλάω τὰ ἱερά, τὸ ἱερόν; Jos. Ant., 4, 207; 8, 258; Ap., 1, 310. It is mostly used a. in the literal sense. [5] Aristoph. Vesp., 845; Polyb., 30, 26, 9 (with ἱερά); Ditt. Syll.[3], 417, 8 and 10 (3rd cent. B.C.); 2 Macc. 9:2 (Antiochus in Persepolis). Jos. Ant., 17, 163, where Herod uses this word for the alienation of consecrated gifts from the temple on the part of the Jews. b. Figuratively, it occurs in Jos. Ant., 16, 45 for Nicolaus' complaint before Agrippa, in which the taking of temple gold from the Jews is called ἱεροσυλεῖν. c. Note should be taken of the usual lists in which ἱεροσυλεῖν is one of the offences : Plat. Resp., IX, 575b, with stealing, breaking in, picking pockets, stealing clothes, kidnapping, cf. Xenoph. Mem., I, 2, 62; Ps.-Heracl. Ep., 7 (J. Bernays, *Die Heraklitischen Briefe* [1869], p. 64) with poisoning. Philo Conf. Ling., 163, with stealing, committing adultery, and murder, cf. Leg. All., III, 241. Ceb. Tab., IX, 4 with robbery, perjury etc. Cf. the lists under → ἱερόσυλος, *infra*.

3. In R. 2:22 Paul accuses the Jews of despising idolaters and yet of robbing temples themselves. That he is using ἱεροσυλεῖν in the strict sense may be concluded from his association of various sins in a kind of catalogue (cf. especially stealing, committing adultery and robbing temples, → *supra*). Any contemporary reader would take such a list literally. Moreover, all the other terms have their exact antithesis, so that we have full correspondence only if those who despise the εἴδωλα of the Gentiles are not ashamed to lay violent hands on the same objects. This probably means making profit out of such costly articles, e.g., votive offerings. The pregnant expression ἱεροσυλεῖν is probably used because the stern warning of the Law (Dt. 7:25 f.) stands in the background. Chrys., Theophylact. and Oecumen take the word literally for the robbing of pagan temples. In view of the technical term, it is unlikely that there is reference to the Jerusalem temple. The weak suggestion that what is meant is refusal to pay the temple tax, which cuts down the lawful revenues of the temple, [6] is ruled out by the antithesis : ὁ βδελυσσόμενος τὰ εἴδωλα.

† ἱερόσυλος.

1. ἱερόσυλος (from ἱερόν and συλάω) means τὰ ἱερὰ κλέπτων acc. to Hesychius. a. It is used of the removal of gold vessels from the Jerusalem temple by Lysimachus, 2 Macc. 4:42. Acc. to the edict of Augustus, Jos. Ant., 16, 164 and 168, anyone who steals sacred books or funds from the Jews is ἱερόσυλος. Bell., 1, 654 of those who destroyed the golden eagle above the temple gate. b. Also in the literal sense we are to think of the lists of offences (→ *supra*). Aristoph. Pl., 30 along with συκοφάνται, πονηροί; Plat. Resp., I, 344b with ἀνδραποδισταί, τοιχωρύχοι (rogues), ἀποστερηταί, κλέπται. If the ἱερόσυλος is here grouped with the robber, he is grouped with murderers and adulterers by Philo, Jos., 84, and with murderers in Plut. De Solone, 17, 1 (I, 87e). Cf. also Orig. Cels., III, 59, 61. c. The noun is more common than the verb for sacrilege in general, Ditt. Syll.[3], 1016, 8 (4th/3rd cent. B.C.). d. ὡς ἱερόσυλος is also

---

[4] On the buying of idols by Jews as receivers, cf. Str.-B., III, 114 (f).

[5] ἱεροσυλία, the technical term for a sacral offence, is often used in the lit. sense, Xenoph. Ap., 25 (a list of vices); Diod. S., XVI, 30, 2, cf. 32, 1; 2 Macc. 13:6; Jos. Ap., 1, 318; Bell., 5, 562; Philo Spec. Leg., II, 13; IV, 87; ἱεροσύλημα : 2 Macc. 4:39.

[6] So J. C. K. v. Hofmann in his comm. (1868), *ad loc.*

ἱ ε ρ ό σ υ λ ο ς. Bibl. → ἱεροσυλέω. J. B. Lightfoot, *The Contemporary Review* (1878), 294 f.

used to denote the category of punishment applying to other offences meriting the same penalty, Plat. Leg., IX, 856c (the rebel). Cf. Ditt. Syll.³, 578, 47 ff. (3rd cent. B.C.). e. In later comedy the word is used very loosely and generally and with great exaggeration as a term of abuse, Menander Comicus, Epitrepontes, 630 : ἱερόσυλε γραῦ : "horsethief"; De Samia, 333 (ed. C. Jensen, Auctarium Weidmannianum, I [1929]): ἱερόσυλε παῖ : "rascal."

2. In the riot at Ephesus (Ac. 19:37) the town clerk takes the apostles under his protection. They are neither ἱερόσυλοι nor do they blaspheme Artemis. Here the term is general. They are not offenders against religion, and have not committed sacrilege.

ἱερεύς.

Contents : A. The Priest in the Greek World : 1. The Facts of Religious History ; 2. Philosophical Reflections on the Priesthood in Stoicism ; 3. The Particular Form of such Reflection in Hellenistic Judaism (Philo). B. The Priest in the History of Israel : 1. From the Early Period to Josiah's Reform ; 2. From Josiah to Ezra ; 3. The Priests and Levites at the Time of Jesus ; 4. The Priest after the Destruction of the Temple. C. The Use of ἱερεύς in Jewish and Christian Writings. D. ἱερεύς in the New Testament.

A. The Priest in the Greek World.

1. The Facts of Religious History.

a. ἱερεύς[1] is found in Homer almost as a synonym of μάντις, Il., 1, 62 μάντιν ἤ ἱερῆα, also 24, 221. The difference is hard to see. The frontiers between the priest and the mantic are fluid. The reason for this link is not adequately presented in the strongly constructive definition of Hesychius : ἱερεύς : ὁ διὰ θυσιῶν μαντευόμενος. It goes back to an important connection in religious history. The Greek world, too, yields the original conception that, by virtue of a specific indwelling power, seers and priests are

---

ἱ ε ρ ε ύ ς. For the Gk. world : D. Magie, De Romanorum Juris Publici Sacrique Vocabulis Sollemnibus in Graecum Sermonem Conversis (1905), Index; Hastings ERE, X, 302-307; G. Plaumann, Art. ἱερεῖς in Pauly-W., VIII (1913), 1411-1457; F. Pfister, Die Religion der Griechen und Römer (1930), Index ; J. Toepfer Attische Genealogie (1889), 24-112; P. Stengel, Die griech. Kultusaltertümer³ (1920), 32-48; S. Wide-M. P. Nilsson, "Griech. u. römische Religion" in A. Gercke und E. Norden, Einl. in die Altertumswissenschaft, II, 2⁴ (1933); Landmann, Origin of Priesthood (1905); W. Otto, Priester und Tempel im hell. Ägypten, I (1905), 17-172, 200-257; II (1908), 167-260; F. Poland, Geschichte des griech. Vereinswesens (1909), 338 ff. For Stoicism : E. Zeller, Philosophie der Griechen, III, 1⁵ (1923), 257; H. Wenschkewitz, "Die Spiritualisierung der Kultbegriffe," Angelos-Beiheft, 4 (1932), 63-65. For Israel : Hastings ERE, X, 307-311, 322-325; J. Köberle, Art. "Priestertum im AT" in RE³, 16, 32-47; S. Mowinckel in RGG², IV, 1488 ff.; G. Hölscher, Art. "Levi" in Pauly-W., XII (1920), 2155 ff.; RE³, 11, 417 ff.; W. Nowack, Lehrbuch der hbr. Archäologie³, II (1894), 87-130; I. Benzinger, Hbr. Archäologie³ (1927), 341-356 (bibl. on the priesthood prior to the monarchy, 341); J. Wellhausen, Prolegomena zur Geschichte Israels⁴ (1895), 118 ff.; W. Graf Baudissin, Geschichte des at.lichen Priestertums (1889); R. H. Kennett, "The Jewish Priesthood" in Old Testament Essays (1928); W. Eichrodt, Theologie des AT, I (1933), 209-235. The NT age and the later period : Schürer II, 277-363; Str.-B., I, 2-5, 762 f.; II, 66, 69 f., 182, 569; IV, 351 (priesthood); II, 55-68 (classes of ministry); II, 33 f., 76, 89, 281, 366, 794 f.; III, 4, 456, 645; IV, 150, 238, 244 f., 646-650, 664 (ministry of the priest); A. Büchler, Die Priester und der Cultus im letzten Jahrzehnt des jerusalemischen Tempels (1895); J. Jeremias, Jerusalem z. Zeit Jesu, II, B, 1 (1929), 2-87. On Philo and Josephus : L. Cohn, "Kritisch-Exegetische Beiträge zu Philo," Hermes, 32 (1897), 122 f.; H. Wenschkewitz, op. cit.; W. Schmidt, De Flavii Josephi Elocutione Observationes Criticae (1893); Schl. Theol. d. Judt., 91, 195, 253.

[1] ἱερεύς (Ionic) at Hom. Il., 5, 10; 16, 604; Od., 9, 198. On the form ἱερέως for ἱερεύς cf. E. Schweizer, Grammatik der Pergamenischen Inschriften (1898), 151, n. 2.

specially equipped to mediate intercourse with deity. If manticism can be learned, we cannot escape the original notion of a special divine endowment for sacred things (→ infra).[2]

b. Alongside this hieratic[3] conception, however, is the idea of general priesthood, that each may draw near to God in sacrifice and prayer. The head of the family sacrifices for the family, the leader for the race, the demarch for the community and the magistrates for the city.[4] Without any special priestly training, the layman can see to purifications and expiatory offerings. This penetrating and far-reaching conception is expressed in Isocr., 2, 6 as follows: τὴν βασιλείαν ὥσπερ ἱερωσύνην παντὸς ἀνδρὸς εἶναι νομί-ζουσιν. Cf. Demost. Prooemia, 55, 3 (p. 1461). If the abrupt formulation of Isocr. is primarily an ideal which is not historically binding, it is still important.

c. On the other hand, the practice of the existing shrines demands an official priest-hood. Yet one can see clearly at this point that a man would not be a priest in the general sense, but the priest of a particular sanctuary. It is to be noted already in Homer that we usually read of the priests of a specific deity, of Zeus, Il., 16, 604, Apollo, Il., 1, 370; Od., 9, 198 (so also Il., 1, 23 = 377), Hephaestus, Il., 5, 10. Cf. Plut. Numa, 7 (I, 64c): ἱερεῖς Διὸς καὶ Ἄρεως. Ac. 14:13, Zeus. Cf. Orig. Cels., VIII, 40.

d. There is thus a priestly vocation. Is there also a separate and self-enclosed priestly class? This is usually denied. But an absolute generalisation is not tenable.[5] To be sure, there is no priesthood in the Jewish sense. Nevertheless, certain priestly functions are the hereditary prerogative of aristocratic families.[6] Hence, if there is no hereditary priestly caste, there are hereditary priesthoods. In most cases, these are allotted by selection, lot, or purchase.[7] But this does not imply an enclosed priestly caste with a hierarchical sense of status, such as would arise through the linking of the priests of different shrines. In many cases the priestly office is discharged only for a period. We do, of course, find mention of a priestly caste in theoretical and ideal discussions, e.g., Plat. Polit., 290c d and Aristot. Pol., VII, 8, p. 1328b, 12 f. Plato, who champions a tightly-knit class system in his state, allots to τῶν ἱερέων γένος the task of offering sacrifices and prayers. Aristot. appoints for the ἱερατεία τὴν περὶ τὸ θεῖον ἐπιμέλειαν. These principles have some basis in the political life of Greece. The cultus is linked up with the state. Its exercise is a matter of state. Hence Aeschin Or., 3, 18 can emphasise as the priestly function: τὰς εὐχὰς ὑπὲρ τοῦ δήμου πρὸς τοὺς θεοὺς εὔχεσθαι.

2. Philosophical Reflections on the Priesthood in Stoicism.

a. Worth noting is the older Stoic definition of the priest in Zeno, Stob. Ecl., II, 67, 20 (v. Arnim, III, 604). Here reference is first made to his cultic knowledge and experience. He is ἔμπειρος νόμων τῶν περὶ θυσίας. Then we read of ethical qualities, of the piety required. He needs ἁγιστεία, εὐσέβεια. At root this means that he must be within the divine nature.[8] This is the pantheistic Stoic formula in explanation of manticism. The innermost equipment of the priest is his union with the powers at work in all things. εὐσέβεια, however, is also the way to ἐπιστήμη θεῶν θεραπείας. Thus cultic know-ledge and piety are not two separate things; they are correlative. Finally, there is the

---

[2] On these facts cf. the older presentations, also Stengel, op. cit.

[3] Cf. G. Plaumann in Pauly-W., VIII (1913), loc. cit.

[4] Stengel, op. cit.

[5] Cf. Pfister, op. cit., 78: "It is thus assumed that the characteristic of Greek religion is the lack of any common doctrine, religious instruction, or priestly caste. But this generalisation is not wholly correct. It is truer to say that there is no comprehensive church with a common dogma (though there are impulses in this direction), no common priesthood to teach this dogma, and no common religious instruction in which it is taught."

[6] Cf. J. Toepffer, op. cit., 24-112: The Eleusinian priestly aristocracy, the Εὐμολπίδαι, Κήρυκες, etc. This is something which goes back to the Homeric period.

[7] On the sacral functions of the king → 267.

[8] (τοῦ supplied by H. Usener) ἐντὸς εἶναι τῆς φύσεως τῆς θείας.

essential antithesis : the φαῦλος is wicked and impious ; he knows nothing of θεραπεία.

b. In the same passage we find the thesis : ἱερέα μόνον εἶναι τὸν σοφόν, φαῦλον δὲ μηδένα. Orig. Comm. in Joh. on 1:4 (Preuschen, 72, 29-33) adduces this as τινὰ δόγματα παρ᾽ "Ελλησι; cf. Diog. L. on Chrysippus and his school, VII, 119 (v. Arnim, III, 157, 608). The principle is extended in Stob. Ecl., II, 114, 16 (v. Arnim, III, 157, 605) to embrace the sage as the true μαντικός. The principle must be viewed in the context of the general glorification of the σοφός which is so common in older Stoicism. According to the witty parody of Luc. Vit. Auct., 20 the Stoic ascribes each and everything to the sage, and denies them all to the φαῦλος. The sage alone is the true king, ruler, administrator, judge, orator, official, business-man and subject. [9] But this does not yield a true spiritualisation, (e.g., in terms of the priest of an inner cult etc.). This is clear already from the fact that in parallel expositions we should have to speak of a spiritualisation of the king, the official, the business-man etc. What is really meant is that only the sage is truly equipped for what a priest properly is and should be. But this is no less true in other spheres. Only when a sage takes an office in hand can we really see justice done to it. Only then is the idea behind it realised. By this exaggerated moralising the human attainment of virtue is made the basis of the priesthood.

c. Though ἱερεύς is not used, the figure of the priest is employed for the philosophical ministry of the true Cynic in Epict. Diss., III, 22, 82 : τοῦ κοινοῦ πατρὸς ὑπηρέτης τοῦ Διός. Cf. Apul. Apologia, 41 (ed. J. v. d. Vliet, 1900). It is said of the good man (rather than the sage) in M. Ant., III, 4, 4 that he is a ἱερεύς τις καὶ ὑπουργὸς θεῶν to the degree that he uses τὸ ἔνδον ἱδρυμένον (= προαίρεσιν). Rather different is the correction of the priestly cult in the Neo-Pythagorean Apollonius of Tyana, Philostr. Vit. Ap., I, 16 → 238.

3. The Particular Form of Such Reflection in Hellenistic Judaism (Philo).

a. In Philo the ἱερεύς is a symbol of the logos or reason. Philo is thus very fond of the phrase ὁ ἱερεὺς λόγος. [10] In Deus Imm., 131-135 the ἱερεύς is allegorised as ὁ θεῖος λόγος. In 134 he is ἐπίτροπος ἢ πατὴρ ἢ διδάσκαλος. In 135 he is also ὁ ἱερεὺς ὄντως ἔλεγχος, persuasive conscience. Cf. also Som., I, 215, where we read that in the temple of the soul the true man reigns as priest, i.e., what Philo elsewhere calls the "man in us," or the reflective divine power of the soul, Congr., 97; Agric., 9 and 108; Rer. Div. Her., 231. [11]

b. It is only logical that the ideal of the Stoic sage should wholly determine the concept of the priest. The priestly office is the supreme one for Philo, Ebr., 126. He can read into it his supreme philosophical ideal, his ascetic concept, and thus idealise the priests and the Levites. [12] The priest must lead a completely blameless life, Spec. Leg., I, 102. The demand that he be free from physical blemish is a symbol of spiritual perfection, Spec. Leg., I, 80 f. The Levites represent the image of true priesthood (Ebr., 76 : ἱερεὺς πρὸς ἀλήθειαν) in the sense that they must follow the ὀρθὸς λόγος, renounce the sphere of the corruptible, keep themselves from impurity in νοῦς and αἴσθησις, Fug., 109, avoid entanglement with the sensual world and the passions, Ebr., 63, and fix their regard on God. Cf. Det. Pot. Ins., 62 ff.; Sacr. AC, 128 f. It is thus that

---

[9] Cf. the variegated list with the constantly recurring μόνος, v. Arnim, III, 611-624.

[10] Aaron is the representative of the λογισμός, Ebr., 128. Melchisedec as ἱερεὺς λόγος, Leg. All., III, 82, cf. 79. Cf. also ἱερεὺς λόγος in Cher., 17; Det. Pot. Ins., 132; ὁ ἀρχιερεὺς λόγος, Gig., 52; Migr. Abr., 102. Abraham as priest, Abr., 198. Moses, Vit. Mos., II, 66. Phinehas, Leg. All., III, 242; Poster. C., 182; Mut. Nom., 108. Priests and prophets, Gig., 61 (as men of God). ὁ ἱερεὺς καὶ προφήτης λόγος, Cher., 16 f. Priests and prophets in Joseph., Ant., 6, 262 and 268.

[11] Cf. I. Heinemann, Philons griech. u. jüd. Bildung (1932), 51. L. Cohn, Hermes, 32 (1897), 122.

[12] On what follows cf. H. Wenschkewitz, op. cit., 70-76.

Philo uses the traditional equation of the sage alone with the priest (→ 259). He can number amongst the priests anyone who no longer treads the path of sin (Spec. Leg., I, 243).

c. But there are still national traits. The Jewish people has priestly rank within the human race in virtue of its purification and consecration through the Law (Spec. Leg., II, 163 f.). The giving of the Law is a preparatory school for the priesthood (*ibid.*, 164). And yet finally it is the sage rather than the Jew who is the true priest (Rer. Div. Her., 82 f. cf. with 303).

B. The Priest in the History of Israel.

1. From the Early Period to Josiah's Reform.

The first traces of the priesthood [13] in the earliest sources make it plain that originally the primary function of the priest is the delivery of oracles rather than sacrifice. The oracular casting of lots is found already in the time of Moses and the judges (Ex. 17:9; 33:7-11; Ju. 17:5 f.; 18:30; 1 S. 14:41; 28:6). In Dt. 33:8-11 the task of the Levites is primarily administration of the Urim and Thummim (cf. the oracle of the arrows in Ez. 21:21). Then follows instruction in the rights and Law of Yahweh. Only finally is there reference to the ministry of sacrifice.

This fact is reflected in the derivation of כֹּהֵן from the Arabic *kahin,* "seer," "prophet." The probable etymology of the word לֵוִי, Arabic *lawa (y),* points in the same direction. [14] Cf. Heb. יָרָה "to throw," thence הוֹרָה, "to give an oracle." The Levite is primarily one who dispenses the oracle. This is in keeping with parallel evidence in the history of religion, → 257. In the history of Israel, too, the oldest form of the priesthood is mantic. The priest is the charismatic, the vehicle of higher powers, who has visionary insight into the will of deity.

Sacrifices can be brought by any *pater familias.* Hence they do not denote a particular caste. There are priests prior to the Sinai revelation, Ex. 19:22, 24. Moses is a Levite, and discharges priestly service. Aaron is a Levite, Ex. 4:14. The Levites are linked with the priestly clan in the steppes of South Palestine at Kadesh. It is there that the ancient cultic traditions, and even the Levites themselves, are perhaps incorporated into the new religion.

Cf. Ex. 32:25 ff.; Dt. 33:8. It is thus understandable that the Levites should be a guest tribe in the national organism. The family relations of Moses to the Midianite priest, Jethro, are worth noting in this connection, Ex. 2:18, 21; Ex. 18; Nu. 10:29; Ju. 4:11. We can see why basic sagas should later derive the Levitical caste from the tribe of Levi. The historical existence of such a tribe is a separate question. [15] But the tribe and the caste are two different things. Questions relating to the person of Aaron as the first priest are wrapped in obscurity. In Ex. 32 he is the priest of the golden calf. In Nu. 12 he withstands Moses. His historicity is questioned by some. His figure is obviously used to anchor the vindication of a priestly caste more firmly in the Mosaic tradition.

In the first instance the cultus is decentralised. There is a covenant sanctuary where the Levites consult the oracle, offer sacrifice and minister to the ark. But the individual tribes have their own shrines, where Levites also serve. The ark is brought to Shiloh. The Levites are also active as house priests. Our sources for the period of the judges and the monarchy prove that the head of the household also discharged a sacrificial ministry.

---

[13] Cf. on B. 1-2 : W. Eichrodt, *op. cit.,* I, 209-214.
[14] On the Minaean term for the priest, cf. the bibl. in Eichrodt, *op. cit.,* I, 209, n. 4.
[15] Cf. M. Noth, *Das System der zwölf Stämme Israels* (1930).

A firmly established priesthood could arise only with the development of the cultus in the temples of the two kingdoms under royal protection. This opens the way for official control under cultic ordinances, and for priestly law. Throne and altar work together. This alliance demands cultic centres, suppresses the shrines and elevates the residentiary priest at the expense of the rural Levite. At the same time sacrifice becomes more important than the oracle or instruction in the Torah. But there is still no reference to concentration of the sacrificial ministry in the priesthood. Apart from the Levites there are other hereditary priesthoods like that of Eli, or that of Zadok in Jerusalem.

2. From Josiah to Ezra.

Unconditional requirement of cultic centralisation is first found in the reforms of Josiah in the year 622. Here something which had been championed both by the Levites as representatives of the Mosaic tradition, and also by the prophets, is radically demanded, namely, the suppression of images, of cultic licence, of the cult of the dead, and of witchcraft. Solution is found in the complete abolition of idolatry and of the priests of the high places. For this purpose, the temple of Yahweh at Zion is declared to be the only legitimate cultic centre. These principles, which are represented in the book of instruction, do not merely strengthen the exclusiveness of the cultus which has no images. They also promote the establishment of the priests of the one sanctuary. The income of these priests is assured. Levites outside Jerusalem are disowned in favour of the Zadokites, and their legitimacy is challenged. From this time onwards they can be considered only for lesser duties in the temple. But this development carries with it great dangers. Instruction in the Law of Yahweh is overshadowed by sacrifice. The attitude of the prophets, with their criticism of the cultus, throws a sharp light on the position. Yet prophetism could not check this whole cultic development. It could only present within this sphere deeper reflection on the basic requirements of Yahweh. It was at one with the priesthood in its rejection of Canaanite influences on Yahweh religion.

The period between the destruction of the state and the return from Exile (586-538) is marked by decisive intellectual activity. In an intensive literary effort the priesthood collects and re-edits the sacred writings, subjecting all references to the cultus to a thorough and deliberate rearrangement. All ritual is assembled for future use under the guiding principle of a centralised cultus. The historical depiction of the origins of Israel is also subjected to thorough reconstruction from a priestly angle. What we find in the future Torah of Ezekiel or the Holiness Code is the result of this priestly codification of the Law during these fateful decades. In Ezekiel and Chronicles the official cultus is for the priests alone. As we can see from P (Lv. 1-7), private sacrifice continues, but it is relegated to the background. The Exile confirms the priesthood in its exclusive right to control the cultus.

After the return from Exile, Ezra achieves the firm reconstruction of the community on the basis of this Torah. Now the one sacrifice in the central sanctuary is no longer a mere programme. It is purposefully established. On the basis of the codified Law, the priesthood becomes a self-enclosed order. Its task is to watch over the statutes of Yahweh. But this task also calls for scribes. The scribe takes his place alongside the priest. He sets the priesthood under the control of a Law which is fixed in writing but which also needs exposition by scholars.

On the high-priesthood, which arose after the Exile, and which represented priestly dominion, → 268.

If all further development is characterised by the partnership of ἱερεύς and γραμματεύς, we should also note the growing authority of the scribe over the priest. [16] The priest retains his importance as the organ of the temple ministry. Politically active and socially elevated, the aristocratic priestly caste is influential in the Sanhedrin. But the scribes declare the Torah. They are in charge of religious instruction and direction. They even teach the priests, [17] who are only cultic ministers. Hence they become rivals of the priesthood. In time the priest is reduced to comparative insignificance. The poor reputation of the priesthood contributes to this process. [18]

3. The Priests and Levites at the Time of Jesus.

a. Ordinary priests (כהן הדיוט) are distinguished from the higher priests (→ 270) by a social gulf. They form a closed profession and constitute a particular group in the Jewish people. Priestly dignity is traced back to Aaron and is hereditary. Already in 4 Βασ. 19:2 (= Is. 37:2) we read of a priestly organisation with elders. The period which follows brings with it a tightly knit organisation. In 445 B.C. 21 priestly names or classes are recorded in subscription to the Law (Neh. 10:3-9). Further lists are given in Neh. 12:1-7, 12-21. 24 classes are mentioned in 1 Ch. 24:1-19. Cf. Jos. Ant., 7, 365. [19] In the days of Jesus the priesthood was divided into 24 classes or courses (מִשְׁמָר = "watch"). In Jos. Vit., 2; Ant., 12, 265 they are called ἐφημερίς or πατριά, in Lk. 1:5, 8 ἐφημερία. [20] The Greek term is misleading. Each class served in the temple a week at a time ; hence מִשְׁמָר denotes a weekly rather than a daily period. The ἐφημερία of Abia in Lk. 1:5 is one of these weekly divisions. The individual מִשְׁמָרוֹת are then sub-divided into 4-9 houses (בָּתֵּי אָבוֹת). Each of these usually ministers one day in the temple. Thus πατριά (Jos. φυλή) corresponds to the daily rota. [21] The priests pursue a secular calling in their own home towns. Their duties are restricted to two weeks in the year and to the three festivals. [22]

b. The Levites. The basic formula in the Deuteronomic portion of the Law is "the priests, the Levites," i.e., the Levitical priests, Dt. 17:9; 24:8; 27:9; Jos. 21:4 etc.; cf. also 1 Ch. 9:2; 1 Εσδρ. 5:54, 60; Ez. 43:19; 44:15. The co-existence of two classes, "priests and Levites," is a mark of later strata, Ez. 44-48; Ezr.; Neh.; 1 and 2 Chr. But cf. also 1 K. 8:4; Is. 66:21; Jer. 33:18, 21, and then 1 Εσδρ. 7:9 f.; 9:37. The phrase "priests and Levites" is very common in Josephus, Ant., 7, 78 and 363; 8, 169; 10, 62 etc. The descendants of the earlier rural priests (and disinherited high-priests?) were now in charge of the more lowly temple duties and the temple music. They had no access to the altar or the sanctuary. Their rank, too, was hereditary.

4. The Priest after the Destruction of the Temple.

After the destruction of the temple the scribe becomes the true centre of the community. The priest still has the privilege of a certain respect. He takes part in the reading of

---

[16] On the scribe → γραμματεύς, I, 740-742. J. Jeremias, op. cit., 101-114.
[17] Cf. Jos. Ant., 12, 142 : γραμματεῖς τοῦ ἱεροῦ.
[18] Cf. Str.-B., I, 853; II, 45, 66 ff., 182, 569; Wenschkewitz, op. cit., 39 f.
[19] Cf. J. Jeremias, 60.
[20] LXX has ἐφημερία for מַחֲלֹקֶת, cf. 1 Ch. 28:13, 21; 2 Ch. 8:14 : διαιρέσεις τῶν ἱερέων. The ἄρχοντες τῶν πατριῶν, 1 Ch. 24:6; 2 Εσδρ. 8:29.
[21] Cf. Schürer, II, 286 ff.; Str.-B., II, 55-68.
[22] J. Jeremias, 67 tries to work out the numbers. On the basis of Ep. Ar., 95 he estimates the priests and Levites, with their wives and children, to be about 50,000 to 60,000 out of a total Palestinian population of about 500,000 to 600,000.

Scripture. He imparts the blessing. [23] He also receives the first-fruits. [24] But the expert in the Law is now much more important for the life of Judaism. The Torah itself is more than either the priesthood or the monarchy : Ab., 5, 5. [25] The שכינה is regarded as closely bound up with study of the Torah and the precepts. Here is a substitute for the sanctuary and for the sacrifices which can no longer be offered : Ber., 33a; Jeb., 105a; Tanch. אחרי 10 (33b). [26] It is the equivalent of a sacrifice to receive and entertain a scribe, Ber., 10b. To be sure, we do not have a complete spiritualisation of the concept of the priest. The literal cultus is still a force which occupies the mind. The hope of a restoration of the temple and priesthood never dies. But the Tannaim and Amoraeans serve the unqualified lordship of the Torah and revere its sovereign authority. To follow the Torah brings a reward. In practice the Torah has taken the place of the temple, the sacrifice and the priest.

C. The Use of ἱερεύς in Jewish and Christian Writings.

1. In the LXX ἱερεύς is used for כֹּהֵן and כֹּהֵן. Since there is no alternative, the term is employed without reservation. λειτουργός cannot be used, since it has a political and general as well as a cultic connotation. LXX also uses ἱερεύς for the high-priest, cf. its use for *pontifex* in the pagan world (→ 266 f.). ὁ ἱερεὺς πρῶτος and ἱερεὺς ὁ μέγας are also used for ἀρχιερεύς (→ 278, n. 57).

2. In Jewish and Christian writings the pagan as well as the Jewish priest is ἱερεύς. Yet there is need to make some distinction between them, cf. Jos. Ant., 10, 65; Barn., 9, 6 : ἱερεῖς τῶν εἰδώλων, or Orig. Cels., VIII, 37: ἱερεῖς ἀγαλμάτων. Cf. 3 Βασ. 12:32; 4 Βασ. 17:32 etc.: ἱερεῖς τῶν ὑψηλῶν. Cf. also the distinction between οἱ Αἰγυπτίων ἱερεῖς, Orig. Cels., V, 49 and οἱ Ἰουδαίων ἱερεῖς, ibid., V, 44. But in most cases the context explains the reference.

3. In the acc. Josephus vacillates between the Atticistic ἱερέας, Ant., 2, 242 etc., and the Hellenistic ἱερεῖς, Ant., 2, 285 etc. He often distinguishes ordinary priests from the ἀρχιερεύς as οἱ πολλοί, πάντες, ἄλλοι, λοιποὶ ἱερεῖς, Ant., 3, 158, 172 and 277.

D. ἱερεύς in the New Testament.

In comparison with the high-priest or high-priests (→ ἀρχιερεύς, C. IV, 2), and especially with the scribe, the ἱερεύς plays only a minor role in the NT. Quite apart from the word, it is striking that the cultus and the figure of the priest are found so little in the sayings of Jesus. Jesus does not call either Himself (cf. Ps. 110 and Mt. 22:44) or His disciples priests. He takes His images from the secular world rather than from that of priestly ministry. [27] In this respect we are tempted to see in Him a fulfilment of prophetism. Nevertheless, He does not display towards the cultus the same critical attitude as the prophets, even though His Word as a whole is closer to the prophetic than the priestly type, and He imbibes of the prophetic spirit and brings it to a new height.

---

[23] Str.-B., II, 76; III, 456, 645; IV, 238, 244 f.

[24] Ibid., 646-650, 664.

[25] The saying of R. Meir : "A non-Jew who occupies himself with the Torah is as a high-priest," has been recorded three times, Sanh., 59a; BB, 38a; AZ, 3a. Cf. Wenschkewitz, 41 f. We might add to Wenschkewitz' appraisal the suggestion that we have here polemic against a high-priesthood that does not keep strictly to the Torah. In any case, the saying gives us palpable evidence of the replacement of the cultus by the Torah.

[26] Weber, 331; cf. 39 f.

[27] Cf. the outstanding expositions in Schl. Gesch. d. Chr., 111 f., 161. The conclusion of Wenschkewitz from Mt. 12:6 that Jesus compares His disciples with priests goes rather too far (op. cit., 94).

1. In the Synoptic witness stress should be laid on the "show thyself to the priest" of Mt. 8:4; Mk. 1:44; Lk. 5:14; plur. Lk. 17:14; cf. Lv. 13:49. Jesus accepts the regulation established by the Mosaic Law. He does not challenge the authority of the priest in matters connected with the protection of public health or ritual purity. He expressly requires that the ordinance be observed. His command also refers to the offering of a gift. The εἰς μαρτύριον αὐτοῖς indicates the significance which His work of healing has for the priest. The work is an eloquent testimony to the authority of Jesus. The priest himself must share in this testimony by giving his endorsement. [28]

2. Two further sayings show how Jesus supports His freedom in respect of the Sabbath by examples from the Torah. They imply the abolition of slavish legalism. In Mt. 12:4 par. David and his companions violate priestly privileges (cf. Lv. 24:5-9) in an emergency, cf. 1 Βασ. 21:7. [29] In Mt. 12:5 f. it is emphasised that the ministry of the priest in the temple is a regular and justifiable violation of the Sabbath. Both sayings illustrate the traditional early Christian synthesis between regard for and superiority to cultic law. In both cases the breach of the commandment is grounded on Scripture. In both cases we read that there is One present who is greater, i.e., greater than the theocratic king and the temple (→ 244).

3. The priest motif is particularly prominent in Lk. Lk. has a searching criticism of the priestly caste in 10:31 f., where it is shown that the heretical Samaritan is superior to the priest and Levite by virtue of his display of love. Priests and Levites are linked elsewhere only at Jn. 1:19. At the very commencement in Lk. 1:5 we have a ἱερεύς who receives on the ancient cultic site the new revelation (→ 245. On ἐφημερία, 262). At Ac. 6:7 it is noted that many priests became obedient to the faith. This shows that Lk. has in view the transformation of the priesthood by the Gospel.

4. On ἱερεύς in Hb. → 277, n. 54. The translation of Ex. 19:6 mentioned under ἱεράτευμα (→ 249) influenced Rev. 1:6; 5:10, [30] and cf. the even freer 20:6 and the βασιλεύσουσιν of 22:5. In the first two references we are to prefer βασιλείαν to βασιλεῖς, but the continuation shows that the share of believers in this royal dominion is deduced from this βασιλεία. Together with the stress on the priestly dignity which is conferred on the new community, this gives us a striking emphasis on the royal and priestly elements in close interrelation, as in the ἀρχιερεύς (→ 268; 281). [31] According to 1:6 and 5:10 Christians are priests as they are re-

---

[28] As regards the payment of the priest, Schl. Mt., *ad loc.* quotes the כהן אחד of S. Dt., 208. The priest would not be in Jerusalem. Acc. to T. Neg., 8, 2 (cf. J. Jeremias, *op. cit.,* 69, n. 3) the man cured of leprosy has first to show himself to the local priest before being declared clean in Jerusalem.

[29] On the expression εἰ μὴ μόνοις cf. Jos. Ant., 13, 373; 14, 72; 15, 419. Materially cf. also Jdt. 11:12 f.

[30] On 1:6 cf. H. C. Hoskier, *Concerning the Text of the Apc.,* II (1929), 34 : h reads *regnum nostrum sacerdotes ;* Tertullian *regnum quoque nos et sacerdotes deo ;* gig, Pseud.-Ambr *regnum et sacerdotes ;* most minusc. and ℵ* C A B βασιλείαν ἱερεῖς, cf. Peshitto Ex. 19:6. On 5:10 (Hoskier, 156): βασιλείαν ἱερεῖς in A 56 111* etc. sah boh Prim Cypr, and only ℵ βασιλείαν καὶ ἱερατείαν.

[31] Cf. Loh. Apk., *ad loc.* : Is this "overweening pride on the part of the divine"? Certainly the Heb. is not thinking of the rule of the community, but the idea of a share of the community in the βασιλεύειν is not peculiar to Rev. The ascription of priesthood to all is already present in Ex. 19:6.

deemed and purchased by the blood of Christ. As in 1 Pt. 2:5, the promise to Israel is transferred to the new community. This consists wholly of priests of God and of Christ. Its differentiation from the old covenant is to be seen here. This is the only saying in the NT in which the priestly image in a personal sense is used of Christianity. This usage occurs in passages which are full of the spirit of consummation, and yet also in the very book which sees no temple in future glory (→ 247).

ἀρχιερεύς.

Contents : A. Linguistic Observations. B. The ἀρχιερεύς in the Greek and Hellenistic World : 1. The Chief Priest in the Religion of Egypt and Tyre, and in Theoretical Discussions ; 2. The Office of the ἀρχιερεύς under the Seleucids and Ptolemies ; 3. The ἀρχιερεῖς after Augustus ; 4. The ἀρχιερεύς as Pontifex Maximus. C. The High-priest and Chief Priests in Judaism and in the New Testament : 1. The History of the High-priesthood ; 2. The Dignity, Rights and Tasks of the High-priest ; 3. The ἀρχιερεύς in the New Testament ; 4. The ἀρχιερεῖς as Chief Priests : a. The Significance of the Higher Priestly Offices ; b. The ἀρχιερεῖς in the New Testament. D. Speculation concerning the High-priest in Philo : 1. The Concept of Mediator ; 2. The Concept of Sinlessness ; 3. Cosmos Speculation. E. The High-priest in Hebrews : 1. The Basic Elements in the Scheme ; 2. The Levitical High-priest ; 3. Christ the Exalted High-priest ; 4. Radical Deductions from the Christological Interpretation of the Cultus ; 5. The Saving Efficacy and Practical Implications of the Truth Proclaimed. F. ἀρχιερεύς and ἱερεύς in the Early Church.

A. Linguistic Observations.

1. In general Greek usage. ἀρχιερεύς is formed from ἱερεύς by way of the older ἀρχιέρεως (cf. ἀρχέ-νεως from ναῦς).[1] There are several derivatives : ἀρχιέρεια high-priestess (inscr.); ἀρχιεράομαι (inscr., 4 Macc., Jos.); ἀρχιερατεύω (pap., inscr., 1 Macc., Jos.); ἀρχιερατικός (inscr., Jos.); ἀρχιερωσύνη (inscr., 1 and 2 and 4 Macc., very common in Jos., Plut., Appian); ἀρχιερατεία (inscr.). None of these is found in the NT. ἀρχιερεύς and derivatives are found in inscr. only from the 3rd cent. B.C. Most examples in Preisigke Wört. are from the 2nd and 3rd cent. A.D. ἀρχιερεύς seems to have been adopted by the Jews between 150 B.C. and 50 A.D.

ἀ ρ χ ι ε ρ ε ύ ς. D. Magie, op. cit. (→ 257, Bibl.), Index ; E. Schweizer, Grammatik der Pergamenischen Inschriften (1898), Index : G. Thieme, Die Inschriften von Magnesia am Mäander und das NT (1906), 21 f.; J. Rouffiac, Recherches sur les Caractères du Grec dans le NT d'après les Inscriptions de Priène (1911), 73 f.; Moult.-Mill., 82; C. G. Brandis in Pauly-W., II (1896), 471-483; P. Stengel, Die griech. Kultusaltertümer³ (1920), 43 (cf. 47, n. 6 for earlier literature); W. Otto, Priester und Tempel im hell. Ägypten, I (1905), 134-137; 172 ff.; G. Wissowa, Religion und Kultus der Römer² (1912), 501-523 (the pontifical collegium); G. Rohde, Die Kultsatzungen der römischen Pontifices. On the Rex Sacrorum cf. Wissowa, op. cit., 503 f.; T. Mommsen, Das röm. Staatsrecht² (1877), 14, 3. E. v. Dobschütz in ThStKr, 104 (1932), 240; C. B. Welles, Royal Correspondence in the Hellenistic Period (1934), 318 f. The high-priest in later Judaism, Schürer, II, 267-277; "Die ἀρχιερεῖς im NT," ThStKr, 45 (1872), 597-607; Str.-B., Index "Hohepriester," esp. III, 696-700 (the plur. II, 56, 626, 634 f.); J. Jeremias, Jerusalem zur Zeit Jesu, II, B, 1 (1929), 3-59. On Philo, J. Heinemann, Philons griech. u. jüd. Bildung (1932), 59-62; H. Wenschkewitz, Die Spiritualisierung der Kultusbegriffe (1932), 71-73. On Hb.: Wnd. Hb., Exc. on 7:27; 8:2; 9:14; Str.-B., IV, 1, Exc. 18, 452-465 (esp. 460 ff.): "Der 110. Psalm in der altrabbinischen Lit."; E. K. A. Riehm, Der Lehrbegriff des Hb. (1859), 431-488; O. Kluge, Die Idee des Priestertums in Israel-Juda und im Urchristentum (1906), 40 ff.; A. Nairne, The Epistle of Priesthood (1913), 135 ff.; W. v. Loewenich, "Zum Verständnis des Opfergedankens im Hb." in ThBl, 12 (1933), 167-172; R. Gyllenberg, "Die Christologie des Hb.," ZSTh, 11 (1934), 662-690; H. Wenschkewitz, op. cit., 131-149.
[1] Cf. E. Schweizer, op. cit., 151; Bl.-Debr. § 44, 1.

2. In the Heb. OT the high-priest is הַכֹּהֵן הַגָּדוֹל, Lv. 21:10; Nu. 35:25, or later כֹּהֵן הָרֹאשׁ, 2 K. 25:18; 2 Ch. 19:11; Ezr. 7:5 (of Aaron). Rarely הַכֹּהֵן הַמָּשִׁיחַ, Lv. 4:5. כֹּהֵן alone from Dt. onwards.

3. ἀρχιερεύς is practically never found in the LXX. The word was adopted by the Jews from without. a. It occurs only 5 times (for כֹּהֵן) at Lv. 4:3; Jos. 22:13; 24:33; 3 Βασ. 1:25 A†; 1 Ch. 15:14 S*†. b. Normally the high-priest is called ὁ ἱερεὺς ὁ μέγας (cf. Hb. 10:21): Nu. 35:25; Jos. 20:6 A; 4 Βασ. 22:4, 8; 2 Ch. 24:11; Jdt. 4:6, 8; Sir. 50:1. Without the art. 1 Macc. 14:20; 15:2. c. Elsewhere he is simply ὁ ἱερεύς, Ex. 35:19 (Aaron), cf. the same at LXX 36:8 (Mas. 39:1). Zadok is ὁ ἱερεύς at 3 Βασ. 1:8 and Simon at 1 Macc. 15:1. Cf. Jos. Ant., 5, 24; 6, 242; 8, 9 f.; 9, 144, and in many cases ἱερωσύνη for ἀρχιερωσύνη. d. ὁ ἱερεὺς ὁ χριστός, Lv. 4:5, 16 → supra. Cf. ὁ ἀρχιερεὺς ὁ κεχρισμένος, Lv. 4:3. e. ἱερεὺς πρῶτος, 3 Βασ. 2:35; 4 Βασ. 25:18.

4. On the other hand ἀρχιερεύς occurs 41 times in the Apocrypha, mostly in 1 Εσδρ., 1 and 2 Macc., 4 times in 3 and 4 Macc.: 1 Εσδρ. 5:40 AR; 9:40, 49; 1 Macc. 10:20; 12:3; 13:36; 2 Macc. 3:1; 3 Macc. 1:11; 4 Macc. 4:13. Cf. 1 Macc. 13:42: ἀρχιερέως μεγάλου, in connection with Hb. 4:14.

B. The ἀρχιερεύς in the Greek and Hellenistic World.

1. The Chief Priest in the Religion of Egypt and Tyre, and in Theoretical Discussions. ἀρχιερεύς is first found in Herodotus, who uses the term for the hereditary or chief priest in ancient Egypt. He stresses his high rank next to the king, II, 142. His image is set up in the temples during his lifetime, II, 143. The succession is treated in II, 37, 3. Cf. also II, 151. An extract from a Phoenician document in Jos. Ap., I, 157 speaks of an Ἄββαρος ἀρχιερεύς in connection with Tyre.

Plato incorporates this office into his ideal state, Leg., XII, 947a. Each year there is to be a chief priest at the head of the priests who officiate for that year. Time is to be kept by his name, which is recorded annually.

2. The Office of the ἀρχιερεύς under the Seleucids and Ptolemies. In the Hellenistic period under the Seleucids the official ἀρχιερεύς is the chief priest of the individual satrapies, and he is appointed by the crown. The name is also used for the chief priests of shrines at a single place. Cf. the letters of Antiochus the Great, Ditt. Or., I, 224, 24, 28 (Welles, 36, 12 and 17), 204 B.C., and 244, 29 f., 33 f. (Welles, 44, 28, 33), Daphne, 189 B.C.; also the missive of Attalos to the chief priest of Apollos in Tarsus (Welles, 47, 2), 185 B.C. We also hear of ἀρχιερεῖς under the Ptolemies, e.g., under Ptolemy V Epiphanes (205-181 B.C.), Ditt. Or., I, 93, 4. Thus in Cyprus the στρατηγός, i.e., the supreme military commander under the Egyptian monarch, is accompanied by the ἀρχιερεὺς τῆς νήσου, or the ἀρχιερεὺς τῶν κατὰ τὴν νήσον, Ditt. Or., I, 105 (Paphos, 2nd cent. B.C.). These are royal high-priests. On Cyprus there are also ἀρχιερεῖς without this addition.

Among Egyptian priests in the age of the Ptolemies we meet various classes, e.g., οἱ ἀρχιερεῖς, προφῆται, ἱερογραμματεῖς,[2] Ditt. Or., I, 56, 3 f., 73 (3rd cent. B.C.); 90, 6 (2nd cent. B.C.). Whether the ἐπιστάτης τοῦ ἱεροῦ at the head of the temple, Ditt. Or., I, 56, 73, is identical with, or different from, the ἀρχιερεύς[3] is open to debate.

3. The ἀρχιερεῖς after Augustus.

a. Priests of the imperial cult. Impulses already found in the Hellenistic kingdoms are further developed in the Roman period. The provincial chief priests of the imperial cult

---

[2] Cf. for the imperial period (Caracalla) from Asia Minor, G. Thieme, Die Inschriften von Magnesia (1905), 21 f.: ἀρχιερεῖς καὶ γραμματεῖς. The words are common in the sing. Mostly the same person is meant, not different groups, as in Judaism and the NT.

[3] W. Otto, op. cit., I, 23 ff. Mitteis-Wilcken, I, 1 (1912), 111, with bibl.

are ἀρχιερεῖς τοῦ Σεβαστοῦ or τῶν Σεβαστῶν. They are leaders of the assemblies (κοινά). They offer sacrifice to the emperor and take vows for him and the imperial house. P. Ryl., 149, 2 (1st cent. A.D.): Γαίου Καίσαρος Σεβαστοῦ Γερμανικοῦ ἀρχιερεὺς Γάιος Ἰούλιος Ἀσκλᾶς κτλ. Cf. also Ditt. Or., II, 458, 31 (Asia). [4]

b. The ἀρχιερεὺς Ἀλεξανδρείας καὶ Αἰγύπτου πάσης. In the Roman period the temple organisation is increasingly nationalised and centralised. Thus there is in Egypt a chief priest (ἀρχιερεύς) whose position is combined with that of a Roman procurator, the idiologos, CIL, III, 5900, 1 = CIG, XIV, 1085, 1; cf. τῷ ἰδίῳ λόγῳ; BGU, I, 250 (Mitteis-Wilcken, I, 2, 215, 21 (after 130 A.D.). It is debatable whether this ἀρχιερεύς is also the head of the imperial cult. [5] He seems to be distinguished from the provincial imperial priests by the fact that Greek and Egyptian cults are all subject to him. [6]

c. The provincial temples in Pergamos, Smyrna, Cyzicos, Ephesus, Sardis etc. are all under ἀρχιερεῖς, i.e., provincial chief priests who are elected each year by the assembly. [7]

d. The hereditary priests of artistic and other societies meeting in a common sanctuary are also called ἀρχιερεῖς. [8]

e. The term is also used of local chief priests of a Sebasteion, of the chief priests of the Achaean or Lycian league, of the chief priests of specific gods, and of other local chief priests. In the case of Egypt at least the term seems to be a titular eponym which does not have to be linked with oversight of a temple or of other priests. [9]

4. The ἀρχιερεύς as Pontifex Maximus.

The linking of the kingly office with sacral functions is very ancient. A long history stands behind the combination of imperial dignity with that of the pontifex maximus. [10] The original significance of the pontifex has not yet been explained. [11] But there is rich attestation for the rendering of pontifex maximus by ἀρχιερεύς and without μέγιστος. Polybius seems to be the first to use the term for the Roman pontifex. He has it for the consul M. Aemilius Lepidus, 22, 3, 2; 32, 6, 5. We find the same usage in Plut. De Numa, 9 (I, 65e ff.). He tells us that there was allotted to Numa the appointing τῶν ἀρχιερέων, which the Romans call pontifices.

The dictator Caesar bears this title in IG, VII, 1835, 2; Appian Bell. Civ., I, 16.

In the imperial style at the time of Augustus, and especially after Nero, ἀρχιερεύς is richly attested in inscriptions and authors, very frequently (as distinct from 3. a-e) with μέγιστος. Ditt. Syll.³, 832, 3 (Hadrian), but also earlier, Jos. Ant., 14, 190, 192; 16, 162. [12]

---

[4] Cf. D. Magie, op. cit., 21, 40; C. G. Brandis in Pauly-W., op. cit.; Stengel, op. cit. For Claudius, Poland, Vereinswesen, 145**.

[5] T. Mommsen, Röm. Geschichte, V (1904), 558, 569; U. Wilcken, Hermes, 23 (1888), 601 ff.; C. G. Brandis in Pauly-W., II, 474; P. Meyer, Festschrift f. O. Hirschfeld (1903), 157 ff.; though cf. W. Otto, op. cit., I, 58, 71. On this whole subject v. Mitteis-Wilcken, I, 1, 114; W. Otto, op. cit., I, 62; APF, 5 (1909), 181; W. Weber, Untersuchungen zur Geschichte des Kaisers Hadrian (1907), 114.

[6] A list of such ἀρχιερεῖς, W. Otto, I, 172 ff.

[7] Cf. C. G. Brandis in Pauly-W., op. cit.

[8] Cf. Brandis; Poland, 343, 421; Preisigke Sammelbuch, 623.

[9] Cf. Otto, I, 135 ff.

[10] Cf. M. P. Nilsson, The Minoan-Mycenaean Religion and its Survival in Greek Religion (1927), 415 ff.; cf. also L. Deubner, Attische Feste (1932), 100: The ἱερὸς γάμος of Dionysus with the consort of the ἄρχων βασιλεύς.

[11] F. Pfister, op. cit., 384.

[12] For further examples, cf. D. Magie, op. cit., 142.

C. The High-priest and Chief Priests in Judaism and in the New Testament.

1. The History of the High-priesthood.

a. From the Exile to the Hasmoneans.

The post-exilic rank διὰ βίου, 4 Macc. 4:1, which ideally is heir to the lapsed monarchy, and which claims civil rule in the priestly state, as symbolised by anointing and the diadem, is at first forced to set aside this unrealised goal in view of the fact that civil power is vested in the Persian governor. But the high-priest stands alongside the governor, and when the latter office ceases his temporal powers are enhanced. His rank is augmented by the exalted past which the priestly presentation of history ascribes to his office. The claim is that Israel has had an unbroken line of high-priests from Aaron by way of Zadok, the high-priest in the time of Solomon. [13]

The last Zadokites are Onias II (to 175 B.C.) in legitimate succession, and Jason, who is arbitrarily appointed by Antiochus IV Epiphanes (175-172 B.C.). Antiochus then appoints Menelaus (172-162 B.C.) of a non-priestly family, and he is followed by the non-Zadokite Jakim (Alkimos, 162-160 B.C.). A revolution thus takes place (→ 239) in the fateful year 175. Onias III, the son of the last legitimate high-priest (Onias II), goes to Egypt in 170 B.C. and there receives permission to build a temple at Leontopolis (which lasts up to 73 A.D.). From the death of Jakim (160) to 153 B.C. Jerusalem is without a high-priest. [14]

b. From the Hasmoneans to the Time of Jesus and the Apostles.

When Jonathan the Hasmonean took the high-priestly robes in 153 B.C., he did so, not as a Zadokite, but as the son of an ordinary priestly house. Only the services of the Maccabeans made this venture possible. The Pharisees contested its legality. [15] Later the Hasmoneans also assumed the royal title. [16] They filled the office until the time of Aristobulus, and there were 8 high-priests during this period of 116 years.

The Herodian-Roman period brought decisive changes. Anointing was abandoned and consecration was only by investiture — a significant loss of prestige. Herod destroyed the Hasmoneans. The hereditary and permanent character of the office was disregarded by the political rulers, and arbitrary depositions and appointments followed. The rights of the Zadokites were ignored. Representatives of other priestly families were accepted. In the 106 years between 37 B.C. and 70 A.D. 28 high-priests discharged the office, and 25 of these were of non-legitimate priestly families. The most influential families were those of Boethus, Annas, Phiabi and Kamith, especially Boethus and then Annas (→ 270). But legal opponents still maintained the legitimacy of the Zadokites. Thus the Zealots, when they occupied Jerusalem in 67 A.D., declared all these houses illegitimate and introduced selection by lot. The lot was drawn among the Zadokites, so that Palestine again saw a member of this race as high-priest. [17]

By the time of Jesus this confusion had broken the influence of the high-priest beyond repair, and political caprice, assisted by simony and competition, and the growing power of the scribes and Pharisees in the cultus and the Sanhedrin (→ 269), had further

---

[13] Zadok: 2 S. 8:17; 15:24; 1 K. 1:8; 2:35. There is a list from Aaron to the Exile in 1 Ch. 6:3-15. Cf. Jos. Ant., 10, 151-153. Cf. 1 Ch. 6:3 ff. with 1 Ch. 6:50-53 for the period up to Solomon. In Ant., 20, 224-251 Jos. reviews the high-priests from Aaron to the destruction of the temple. Cf. also J. Jeremias, op. cit., II, B, 1 (1929), 41.

[14] Jos. Ant., 20, 237.

[15] Cf. Jeremias, op. cit., 12 f., 49 f.

[16] Acc. to Jos. Bell., 1, 70; Ant., 13, 301 Aristobulus I (104-103 B.C.) is the first to do this, but acc. to coins and Strabo, 16, 2, 40 Alexander Jannaeus (103-76 B.C.) is the first; cf. Jeremias, 49, n. 2 for an attempted reconciliation.

[17] Cf. Jos. Bell., 4, 148. According to Bell., 4, 155 the Zealots summoned μίαν τῶν ἀρχιε-ρατικῶν (masc.) φυλήν. On their view there was only one φυλή of ἀρχιερατικοί.

undermined it. Nevertheless, the high-priest was still the supreme religious representative of the Jewish people.

2. The Dignity, Rights and Tasks of the High-priest.

a. The Dignity. Jos. in Ap., 2, 185 describes the Jewish priesthood as the most excellent and logical order. God, the Ruler of the cosmos, is at the head. The whole rule of the state is committed to the priests. Cf. Ap., 2, 193. Here the כֹּהֵן גָּדוֹל is regarded as the supreme head of the priesthood. [18] As such he is also the chief representative of the people [19] after the lapse of the monarchy. But he is also the plenipotentiary of God, [20] and he has the קְדוּשַׁת עוֹלָם, the character of eternal holiness, which is shown to be indelible by the fact that even those who are deposed still possess it. [21] After the abolition of anointing, this character is transmitted by investiture with the eight-fold garments. [22] In all their parts these are able to atone for certain sins. They are so much a symbol of the office that in the Roman period the struggle for the vestments is a struggle for religion itself. Even the death of the high-priest has atoning efficacy for man-slayers who have fled to the cities of refuge (Nu. 35:25 ff.).

b. The rights of the high-priest include prerogatives in relation to sacrifices, the privilege of always being able to take part in sacrifices, and even of offering when sick, as priests cannot do, and the right to a seat in the Sanhedrin (Mt. 26:3; Ac. 22:5; 23:1 f.), which is made up of 71 chief priests, scribes and elders. This is the only court competent to try the high-priests in case of a capital offence.

c. The duties of the high-priest are primarily cultic. His unique and supreme prerogative, which distinguishes him from all other men, is that once a year he can go into the Holy of Holies to offer sacrifice on the great Day of Atonement. [23] Rabbinic tradition speaks of heavenly voices granted to the officiating high-priest in the innermost sanctuary. Perhaps there is a reference to this in Jn. 11:51, where the ἀρχιερεύς is a prophet. [24] According to the Mishnah he ministers in the week prior to the Day of Atonement, and must carefully guard his Levitical purity during this period. There is also a tradition in the Mishnah concerning his function at the burning of the red heifer. [25]

d. Ritual regulations are particularly strict in his case. He must not come into contact with a corpse, or enter a house where there is death, or take part in a funeral procession, or wear mourning. This applies even in the case of the decease of close relatives. [26]

e. The inviolate succession of this hereditary office is safeguarded by strict marriage rules. The Law is that he should marry only a virgin, and Rabbinic exposition further lays down that she must be between 12 and 12½, that she must not be betrothed, that she must not be the child of an illegitimate priestly marriage, that she must not be a proselyte or deflowered, that she must not have been a prisoner of war, and that she

---

[18] Also in Jos. Ant., 3, 151, where we should read ἀραβάρχην = ἀραβχαναίαν = *rab kahanaia*, the high-priest is called the head of the priesthood.

[19] Cf. Ac. 23:5: ἄρχοντα τοῦ λαοῦ σου.

[20] ἀρχιερεὺς τοῦ θεοῦ, Ac. 23:4; Jos. Ant., 15, 22; Philo → 272; Orig. Cels., V, 44.

[21] That the title, the official character, the atoning efficacy of his death, the marriage regulations and the prohibition of impurity by contact with the dead or by mourning all applied to the deposed high-priest (Jeremias, 14 f.) is important if we are to understand the role of Annas alongside Caiaphas.

[22] Cf. Ex. 28; 29; Sir. 45:6-13; Ep. Ar., 96-99; Jos. Ant., 3, 151, 159-187; Bell., 5, 231-236; Ant., 15, 403-409; 18, 90-95; 20, 6-14; Yoma, 7, 5. Cf. Jeremias, 3 f. Herod Archelaus and the Romans held them in safekeeping, and Claudius handed them back in 45.

[23] Jos. Ant., 3, 242 f.; Phil. Spec. Leg., I, 72. Cf. Jeremias, 6 f.

[24] Jeremias, 5.

[25] Examples in Jeremias, 6 f., 9 f. Cf. Philo Spec. Leg., I, 268; Jos. Ant., 4, 79.

[26] Cf. Jeremias 8 f., where there is also an account of the debate between the Sadducees and the Pharisees on the issue.

must be the daughter of a priest, or Levite, or Israelite of unblemished descent. [27] That the mother of the Hasmonean John Hyrcanus had been a prisoner of war was one of the charges brought by the Pharisees against him and against his grandson Alexander Jannaeus, and they regarded it as sufficient ground or pretext on which to reject the whole Hasmonean dynasty as illegitimate. [28]

3. The ἀρχιερεύς [29] (singular) in the New Testament.

a. The high-priest most frequently mentioned in the NT is Caiaphas (c. 18-37 A.D.), [30] the son-in-law of Annas, who in Jn. 11:49 f., 51; 18:13 f. is emphatically called ἀρχιερεὺς τοῦ ἐνιαυτοῦ ἐκείνου, i.e., of the memorable year of the death of Jesus. It is inconceivable that a book so knowledgeable in Jewish matters as John's Gospel should be suggesting that the high-priesthood was a yearly office.

Cf. also Mt. 26:57, 62 f., 65; Mk. 14:53, 60 f.; Jn. 18:24, though vv. 19-24 seem to refer to Annas. [31] The αὐλή, Mt. 26:58; Mk. 14:54, is that of Caiaphas. There is again doubt in Jn. 18:15 (cf. 24). The παιδίσκη of Mk. 14:66 belongs to the household of Caiaphas.

b. Annas (6-15 A.D.) had been replaced at the time of Jesus, but he was still influential, Lk. 3:2; Ac. 4:6; Jn. 18:13, 24. Apart from his son-in-law (→ supra) five of his sons and his grandson Matthias (65 A.D.) held the office. He was thus the head of a γένος ἀρχιερατικόν (→ 272).

The servants of the ἀρχιερεύς in Mt. 26:51; Mk. 14:47; Lk. 22:50; Jn. 18:10, 26 belong either to a. or b.

c. Ananias the high-priest, Ac. 23:2; 24:1. No name is given at Ac. 5:17, 21, 27; 7:1; 9:1 f.

d. The ἀρχιερεύς is president of the Sanhedrin, which also includes γραμμα-τεῖς καὶ πρεσβύτεροι, at Mt. 26:57; Mk. 14:53; Lk. 22:54.

Cf. Jos. Ant., 4, 224 with οἱ γερουσιασταί instead of γερουσία, but always with ἀρχιερεύς: Ant., 4, 218; 5, 55, 57, 103, 353.

4. The ἀρχιερεῖς (plural) as Chief Priests. [32]

a. The Significance of Higher Priestly Offices.

The chief priests seem to be an established college with oversight of the cultus, control of the temple, administration of the temple treasury, and supervision of priestly discipline. They have a seat and voice in the Sanhedrin.

We should distinguish i. the ruler of the temple סְגַן, סְגַן הַכֹּהֲנִים = στρατηγὸς τοῦ ἱεροῦ, Ac. 4:1; 5:24, 26; Jos. Ant., 20, 131 etc. He has the highest rank next to the high-priest, who in many cases was the ruler of the temple. [33] In emergencies the סְגָן represented the כֹּהֵן גָּדוֹל on the Day of Atonement. He assisted him in the cultus, and

---

[27] Philo Fug., 114, only the daughter of a priest. Cf. Jeremias, 11.

[28] Jeremias, 12 f., with other examples.

[29] On the ἐπὶ ἀρχιερέως Ἅννα καὶ Καιαφᾶ of Lk. 3:2 and the ἐπὶ Ἀβιαθὰρ ἀρ-χιερέως of Mk. 2:26 as means of fixing the date, cf. Mart. Pol., 21, 1; Pauly-W., VIII (1913), 1426, 1429.

[30] On the dating of the replacement of Caiaphas, Jeremias, 55, n. 8.

[31] Though cf. Zn. Jn., ad loc. F. Spitta, Das Joh.-Ev. (1910), 364 f. thinks that there has been conflation.

[32] Cf. Str.-B., II, 56, 626-631, 634 f. Jeremias, op. cit., 17-25, 33-40.

[33] This is a principle according to jYoma, 41a, 5 (Jeremias, 19 f., 58, n. 6).

took the place of honour at his right hand. He was chosen from the highest priestly aristocracy. He had oversight of the cultus and the priesthood, and also of the temple guard. ii. The heads of the weekly courses. iii. The leaders of the daily courses. iv. The אֲמַרְכְּלִין or στρατηγοί, i.e., the temple proctors (no less than 7), Lk. 22:4, 52. [34] v. The גִּזְבָּרִים, i.e., the temple treasurers (no less than 3). These controlled the income and expenditure of the temple. [35]

b. The ἀρχιερεῖς in the New Testament.

i. It is astonishing that ἀρχιερεῖς is found 62 times, and ἀρχιερεύς only 38 times, in the Gospels and Acts.

The results are similar when we examine Josephus and Rabbinic sources. Nor can we explain them by supposing that the reference is to past and present high-priests, for often the names given are not found on the high-priestly lists. [36] Nor is the view tenable that ἀρχιερεῖς denotes members of the high-priestly families. [37] This is destroyed by the fact that many of them are members of the Sanhedrin, whereas not all members of even the privileged families could be included among the 71 members. This formula refers to the holders of priestly offices under a. i-v, among whom we may perhaps number the high-priest and previous high-priests.

ii. Often in the NT we have ἀρχιερεῖς alone.

Here there are two possible references, first, to office-holders within the college under a. i-v, Mt. 26:3 f., 14 f.; 27:6; 28:11; Mk. 14:10 f.; Lk. 22:4 f.; Ac. 5:17, 21, 24; 9:14, 21; 26:10, 12, and secondly, to the whole Sanhedrin of which these are the most prominent members, Mk. 15:3, 10 f., cf. with 15:1; Jn. 12:10; 18:35; 19:6, 15, 21; Ac. 22:30. In this sense ἀρχιερεῖς is used very frequently by Jos.: Ant., 20, 180 f., 207; Bell., 2, 316-322, 331, 336, 342, 410 f. etc.; Bell., 4, 151, 238; Vit., 197.

iii. In another category the ἀρχιερεῖς are mentioned along with other groups of the Sanhedrin, or with one such group.

All the groups are mentioned together (chief priests, elders and scribes) in the sonorous Mt. 27:1 (cf. Lk. 22:66); cf. Mt. 16:21; 27:41; Mk. 8:31; 11:27; 14:43; Lk. 9:22; 20:1 (Alexandrian text); Ac. 4:5 (ἄρχοντες = ἀρχιερεῖς). Cf. Jos. Bell., 2, 411, where we have δυνατοί (elders), ἀρχιερεῖς and οἱ τῶν Φαρισαίων γνώριμοι (scribes). In more abbreviated form cf. Mt. 26:59; Mk. 14:55; Ac. 22:30; also Jos. Bell., 2, 331, 336.

The phrase ἀρχιερεῖς καὶ γραμματεῖς denotes the religious authorities, Mt. 2:4; 20:18; 21:15; Mk. 10:33; 11:18; 15:11 f.; Lk. 19:47; 20:19; 22:2; 23:10; cf. also ἀρχιερεῖς καὶ Φαρισαῖοι, Mt. 21:45; 27:62; and esp. Jn., i.e., 7:32, 45; 11:47, 57; 18:3. Cf. Jos. Vit., 5 and 21.

ἀρχιερεῖς καὶ πρεσβύτεροι, Mt. 21:23; 26:3, 47; 27:3, 12; 28:11 f.; Mk. 14:1. Ac. 4:23; 23:14; 25:15 (though cf. Ac. 22:5). Cf. 1 Macc. 1:26; Jos. Bell., 2, 422.

On ἀρχιερεῖς καὶ οἱ πρῶτοι τῶν Ἰουδαίων, Ac. 25:2, cf. Jos. Ant., 20, 6 and 180; Vit., 9.

The οἱ ἀρχιερεῖς καὶ οἱ ἄρχοντες of Lk. 23:13; 24:20 is unusual, since the archontes are normally the chief priests. [38]

---

[34] Jeremias, 24, 33.
[35] *Ibid.,* 24 f., 33.
[36] *Ibid.,* 34, n. 2-8.
[37] This view, predominant in Schürer, ThStKr (1872), 368 ff. and Schürer, II, 275-277, has been overthrown by the researches of Jeremias, 34 ff. Schürer's exposition cannot be supported from Ac. 4:6 or Ket., 13, 1 f.; Oholot, 17, 5, for בְּנֵי כֹהֲנִים here denotes class rather than descent. On Jos. Bell., 6, 114 cf. Jeremias, 34 f.
[38] Cf. Jeremias, 58, n. 2; 88 ff.; 90.

iv. γένος ἀρχιερατικόν [39] in Ac. 4:6, as in Jos. Ant., 15, 40, denotes membership of the legitimate priestly nobility (in the strictest and most proper sense the Zadokites) — a concept which on the Sadducean view had broadened at the time of Jesus.

This priestly aristocracy occupied the higher priestly posts to which we have referred [40] and was socially distinct from the ordinary priesthood. [41] Wealth contributed no little to their success. [42]

v. In the case of the chief priest (ἀρχιερεύς) Sceva in Ephesus (Ac. 19:14) we have a chief priest in the diaspora.

Cf. Jos. Ap., 1, 32 f., 187; Ant., 12, 108. The last two passages refer to Jewish chief priests in Egypt, and ἀρχιερεύς is used at Ap., 1, 187.

The very common use of ἀρχιερεῖς forces the reader of the NT records to ask for an explanation. This is not given in the texts, but it speaks the more eloquently as a fact. The findings show that when opposition arose against Jesus, it was not the work of a single individual, nor of the supreme holder of priestly rank alone, but of the religious authorities in general. Along with the scribes, the main opponents were the chief priests as a whole, i.e., the priestly aristocracy, the leading official representatives of the sacral life of the nation. As a body, they rejected Christ as a transgressor. One of the eloquent and radical revelations of the cross is that it does not merely show scribal learning to be a human craft, but that it also brings the ἱερόν of men to judgment as a religious institution, and that it does so through its supreme representatives (ἀρχι — ἱερεῖς).

D. Speculation concerning the High-priest in Philo.

1. The Concept of Mediator. [43]

a. In Philo we still find relics of the basic historical Jewish view in the depiction of the high-priest.

He is the representative of the people. As ἔθνους ὑπηρέτης, Spec. Leg., I, 229, he must be identified with his people in expiation. To this there corresponds on the other hand, Spec. Leg., I, 114, the divine relationship of the προσκεκληρωμένος θεῷ. As thus stated, the mediator concept seems to stand within correct limits. The emphasis on the dignity of the ταξίαρχος τῆς ἱερᾶς τάξεως, which in Vit. Mos., II, 131 is greater than that of kings as well as laity during the sacred action, is also completely consonant with the Jewish conception.

b. Yet this aspect is non-essential. The mediator concept receives its chief determination and distinctiveness from Logos speculation.

---

[39] Jos. Ant., 12, 387: ἡ τῶν ἀρχιερέων γενεά; Just. Dial., 116, 3 uses the expression in Ac. 4:6 of Christians (τὸ ἀληθινόν) → 283. ἱερατικὸν γένος is very common, also of the high-priestly house. It occurs in Philo, Orig., also Jos., along with γενεά or φυλή.

[40] On the nepotism of the priestly nobility, cf. bPes., 57 (Bar.) and T. Men., 13, 21; Jeremias, 56, 58 f.

[41] For examples, Jeremias, 40.

[42] Acc. to T. Yoma, 1, 6 the high-priest must be wealthier than the others, Jeremias, 59, n. 5.

[43] On the origin of the doctrine of mediation cf. Heinemann, op. cit., 62, who recalls Plat. Symp., 202e, that the daemonic is between God and mortals. W. W. Jäger, Nemesios von Emesa (1914), 102 traces back to Poseidonios the doctrine that man is an intermediary between God and creation.

The concept is linked with Moses as well as Aaron. Moses is ἀρχιερεύς in Rer. Div. Her., 182. βασιλεία, νομοθεσία, ἀρχιερωσύνη, προφητεία can all be related to him, Vit. Mos., I, 334; II, 2, 187, 292; Sacr. AC, 130. It is he who directs Aaron in his sacred ministry, Vit. Mos., II, 153. Moses is the primary Logos who stands on the frontier between God and the creature, ἱκέτης of mortals and also πρεσβευτής of the Ruler towards His subjects, μέσος τῶν ἄκρων, Rer. Div. Her., 205 f. Aaron is normally the λόγος προφητικός. But the place of contact is not the essential thing. Basically, we are concerned with the ἀρχιερεὺς λόγος, Gig., 52; Migr. Abr., 102; in Rer. Div. Her., 201 Aaron, too, is ὁ ἱερὸς λόγος.

This Logos speculation underlies the exaggerated statements concerning the ἀρχιερεύς, who is exalted beyond all human measure.

It is deduced from Lv. 16:17 that he who enters into the Holiest of all is no longer a man. We again find the ἑκατέρων τῶν ἄκρων, Som., II, 189, cf. 231. According to Spec. Leg., I, 116 the Logos as mediator is μείζονος φύσεως ἢ κατ' ἄνθρωπον. Thus the μεθόριος ἀμφοῖν implies basically a severing of identification with humanity. Thus we read in Fug., 108: λέγομεν γὰρ τὸν ἀρχιερέα οὐκ ἄνθρωπον ἀλλὰ λόγον θεῖον εἶναι.

2. The Concept of Sinlessness.

a. The mediator is also sinless. Here, too, Philo goes far beyond Lv. 16:6, which states that the high-priest has also to offer for his own sins.

This point is not completely ignored. In brief and unemphatic form it may be found in Spec. Leg., I, 228. But it does not play the slightest role. Other considerations immediately deprive it of significance. We can see this in Spec. Leg., I, 230. If the high-priest makes a mistake, this falls back on the people which commissions him, [44] and it is easily made good.

b. It is the Stoic ideal of the sage which determines the ethical *habitus* of the ἀρχιερεύς.

As in the Stoic doctrine of stages, we now have a confusing interplay of concepts, since all the stages are projected into him. The basic concern that the σοφός should be reflected in the ἀρχιερεύς emerges in Spec. Leg., II, 164. He who lives according to the Law may be accepted as a high-priest before the judgment of truth. Aaron is the προκόπτων according to Som., II, 234 ff. If he were τέλειος, death would cease through his mediatorial work among mortals, Nu. 17:13. Rer. Div. Her., 82 also refers to the possibility of a μὴ τέλειος ἀρχιερεύς. But the drift is towards an ideal sage, e.g., Fug., 106-118. He does not incur impurity through contact with corpses, i.e., νοῦς (father) and αἴσθησις (mother), Fug., 109. His father is God, his mother σοφία. He turns from everything created (the ties of family), Spec. Leg., I, 113-115. He is aloof from all sorrow, i.e., he is ἄλυπος εἰς ἀεὶ διατελῆ, *ibid.*, 115. He is thus an impassible Stoic. When he enters the sanctuary, he sets aside his magnificent vestments, i.e., earthly ideas and imaginations, Leg. All., II, 56; Som., I, 216. He is guided by the ἡγεμονικόν and the virtues, Fug., 110.

c. The formulation of absolute sinlessness is again determined by the Logos doctrine.

In the first instance this is again linked with cultic purity. He is ἀμίαντος, Fug.,118; Spec. Leg., I, 113, ἄμωμος, Som., II, 185. But the thought of absolute perfection is also present, Fug., 108 (cf. already Spec. Leg., III, 134 f.). As οὐκ ἄνθρωπος ἀλλὰ

---

[44] ὥστε τὸν λαὸν ἁμαρτεῖν. According to L. Cohn on Spec. Leg., I, 230 (*Philos Werke, deutsch,* II [1910]), this is also present in Rashi.

λόγος θεῖος, he is πάντων οὐκ ἑκουσίων μόνον ἀλλὰ καὶ ἀκουσίων ἀδικημάτων ἀμέτοχος, cf. Fug., 117; Spec. Leg., I, 230.

d. The shifting category of the ἄνθρωπος θεοῦ, which has every possible implication, is again useful at this point to subjugate everything to the ideal.

It is used of Moses in Mut. Nom., 25 and 125. It can also denote man on the frontier between mortal and immortal nature, Op. Mund., 135. Or it can be equated with the Logos, Conf. Ling., 41 ff., or with the archetypal man, ibid., 146, or with the priest and prophet as an ecstatic, [45] Gig., 61; Deus Imm., 138 f., or with the sage as the possessor of prophetic power, as the vocal instrument of God.

3. Cosmos Speculation.

The high-priest Logos in the temple of the cosmos, Som., I, 214 f., Spec. Leg., I, 66 → 241. In Philo this concept is a development of the mediator concept. But it is more. For the cosmos is not merely that which is to be represented before God. It is also the divine itself, the exalted world of God, into which the ἀρχιερεύς is taken and which divinely ennobles him. His vestments are at all points a faithful reflection of the cosmos, [46] Spec. Leg., I, 82-97; Vit. Mos., II, 109-135 and they symbolise its orders and relationships.

Since the high-priest bears this reflection of the cosmos, the mediator concept is brought out in such a way that he who is consecrated to the service of the father brings the cosmos, the son (Deus Imm., 31; Vit. Mos., II, 134), into this service, Spec. Leg., I, 96. The ἀρχιερεύς prays and gives thanks not merely for the community, for humanity, but also for his country, for the cosmos, ibid., 97. But he does so in such a way (Vit. Mos., II, 133) that the universe enters with him into the sanctuary. Hence the mediator concept merges into the Poseidonios motif of universal worship. In accordance with our findings under 2., the Stoic telos formula occurs at a prominent place in Spec. Leg., I, 96. Bearing the reflection of the universe, the high-priest should fashion his own life in a way which is worthy of universal nature, and himself become a βραχὺς κόσμος, Vit. Mos., II, 135. [47]

E. The High-priest in Hebrews.

1. The Basic Elements in the Scheme.

a. The powerful conception of the ἀρχιερεύς in Hb. rests on the deep impression made by the obedient, merciful and dedicated life and death of the Son in the light of His exaltation. There is hardly any reference to the resurrection (only at 13:20), obviously because everything is strictly integrated into the image of the high-priest who goes into the sanctuary to offer sacrifice. The vividness of the cultic imagery has suppressed this feature, although the essential glorification of Christ necessarily presupposes a strong conviction of His resurrection. [48]

---

[45] On the mystical features of the image of the high-priest, cf. Spec. Leg., III, 134 f.; the ἀρχιερεύς as hierophant.

[46] That Philo here stands in the nexus of well-loved traditions is shown by Wis. 18:24; Jos. Ant., 3, 183 ff., cf. Bell., 5, 213 and → 241. The estimation of the glory of the robe in Sir. 45:8 ff., and the poetic exaggeration in glorification of officiating Simon in 50:5 ff. may not display the cosmic motifs, but they help us to see how such poetry can become speculation.

[47] Expiation for manslayers by the death of the ἀρχιερεύς may be linked with such cosmic ideas, Fug., 110 and 113; cf. 87, 106 and 116.

[48] Cf. G. Bertram, "Die Himmelfahrt Jesu vom Kreuz aus und der Glaube an seine Auferstehung" in Festgabe f. A. Deissmann (1927), 213-215. The statement that "Hb. teaches an ascension from the cross" (Wnd. Hb., 79, cf. 70 f.) is hardly correct. The most that can be said is that there is such an "ascension" in 7:26: ὑψηλότερος τῶν οὐρανῶν γενόμενος.

b. The truth of the high-priesthood of Christ is illuminated by specific texts of Scripture.

i. Particularly significant as the underlying basis is ψ 109:4, which is quoted in 5:6, 10; 6:20. This verse appears so often before its final explanation that the reader waits impatiently for the solution.

ii. It introduces us to the story of Melchisedec in Gn. 14, which is expounded strictly in terms of this basic text. In both sayings (cf. Gn. 14:18) the reference is to priestly character. The point of the Melchisedec story is not to glorify a mythological Melchisedec but to glorify Christ Himself (7:1-28). The dignity of Christ is above that of the Levitical priesthood, for the biblical Melchisedec is superior to this priesthood (7:1-10).

The etymological and allegorical exposition (the king of righteousness or Salem, 7:2), which we already find wholly or in part in Philo Leg. All., III, 79-82 [49] and Jos. Ant., 1, 180, is not so important as that which Scripture does not say concerning Melchisedec (7:3). In Scripture he is treated as supratemporal, whereas in other circles priestly genealogy is of supreme importance. The saying in 7:3 : μένει ἱερεὺς εἰς τὸ διηνεκές, is greatly affected by the basic text. Is this mythological, as might be suggested by Melchisedec speculation in the early Church, in which the concept of the incarnation and that of the Logos are brought together ? No, Hb. itself refutes this. According to 5:1-4 the priest is taken from among men. How, then, can a mythological *alter ego* of Jesus [50] come between Aaron and the incarnate Son ? Such a divinisation would rob the priesthood of Jesus of its value, and make Melchisedec useless as a type of Christ. What we have are simply typological deductions from ψ 109:4. In Scripture Melchisedec does not leave the scene. But this can be said only when he has been equated with the Son of God (7:3). Chrys. (MPG, 63, 97) finely observes that there is a distinction between not being written and not being. Scripture does not fix our regard on Melchisedec as a historical or mythological figure but on Melchisedec as a type. The description thus takes over features from Christ, just as the meaning shines through the story in parables. The basic text shapes the narrative. Thus the Antiochenes [51] rightly say that that Melchisedec's is an eternal priesthood in the Lord. In the light of the fulfilment, the truth of Christ is read back into the OT ; it lays its impress upon the sayings of Scripture by way of ψ 109:4. The main thought is that of superiority to the Levitical priesthood. This is shown in 7:4-10. Abraham pays tithes to this priest and is blessed by him. Levi himself thus pays tithes in the loins of his ancestor. Hence Levi is demoted.

iii. The basic concepts → διαθήκη (as covenant and testament) and → ἐπαγγελία, 8:6-13; 9:15-22, set the high-priestly image within the framework of a great historical conception. They do this by adducing passages in the prophets which are critical of the cultus, Jer. 31:31 ff.; ψ 39:6 ff. These passages reject external offerings. They give a central place to pneumatic internalisation in the fulfilment of the will of God, to fellowship with God, and to forgiveness. The use of the cultic image is thus protected against lifelessness and rigidity. Whereas it would otherwise lack historical dynamism, this link enables it to achieve both a dynamic and a static quality, and thereby to do justice both to the basic saving action and to the eternal character. Clarification is thus brought in the following matters.

---

[49] The story of Melchisedec has no significance for Philo in respect of the ἀρχιερεὺς λόγος. Philo regards Melchisedec as ὀρθὸς λόγος in contrast to τύραννος νοῦς. Here as elsewhere his concern is the conflict against sensuality. His application is ethico-psychological.

[50] Wnd. Hb., 61.

[51] Rgg. Hb., 187, n. 9.

c. With regard to the historical conception of Hb. (cf. the express temporal references in 9:9-11, 26, 28), it should be noted that the high-priesthood of Christ is first described as a way. He treads this in order that we may now do so, 10:20. He penetrates through the curtain (διά, local, through His flesh). He thus attains to the throne of God and makes access for the covenant community. This is the new and living way (as distinct from the way of death in the Law), 10:20; cf. 7:19 : ἐπεισαγωγή. It is a way inasmuch as it leads to the throne by way of and through the sacrificial death. The crucifixion belongs to the high-priestly office of Christ as well as His present rule in the sanctuary. His office comprises both the penetrating movement of His saving action and the lofty calm of His constant giving. His present ministry is no longer on earth, 8:4. But the contrast here is between heaven and earth (→ 278), which is the site of the priesthood of the Law. That an essential part of His high-priestly work is done on earth is shown by the word ἐφάπαξ, which gives a central place to the crucifixion.

Although the treatment of the νόμος is restricted to the cultus, in this respect, and in the historical presentation, there are surprising parallels to Paul. In the story of Abraham the priesthood of Melchisedec is an extraordinary one which cannot be integrated into anything else. This corresponds to the ἐπαγγελία in Paul (cf. the oath in Hb. 7:28). Hb. does not say, of course, that the priesthood of Melchisedec is prior in time to the Levitical. ψ 109:4 is later than the Law, and it replaces it : 7:28. We should also compare the ἐφάπαξ of 7:27 with R. 6:10, and νόμου μετάθεσις at 7:12 with R. 10:4. Above all, the cultus is incapable of atoning for sin (→ 278), cf. 1 C. 15:56; R. 7:13; R. 8:3. Salvation comes from elsewhere than the Law, cf. 7:13 f., 18 with R. 3:21; 4:13; 5:20; 7. Basic agreement goes hand in hand with the distinction of cultic concentration in Hb.

d. Fundamental, too, is the supplementation of the image of the high-priest by the transcendent truth of the Son and by His eternal character. The new thing is that the Son both fulfils and transcends the cultus as High-priest. The epistle begins with an exposition of His sonship. Even before we enter on the first main section (4:14-10:31) there is a statement of the basic theme that He Himself in person is the full revelation of God, higher than the angels, more than the OT bearers of God's self-declaration, faithful in His house, ἀρχηγός in suffering, Mediator of σαββατισμός. All this is simply confirmed by the ensuing exposition of His high-priesthood. If the supreme value of the personal representation of cultic truth is used to show that the ancient cultus is fulfilled and transcended in Christ, [52] this is possible only because the truth of the Son augments and controls the truth of the High-priest. The basic concept, [53] which carries with it the predicate of eternity, is always the main truth in the background. The equation of the Son and the High-priest permeates the whole. It is thus that the use of the cultic image is prevented from becoming static and unfruitful. And it is just because the saying concerning the Son gives to the saying concerning the High-priest its decisive impress and eternal character (cf. 5:5 f., and also 3:1: ἀπόστολος with ἀρχιερεύς) that the latter acquires its force. Cf. the καίπερ ὢν υἱός of 5:8, which combines majesty with lowliness. Only the designation as Son, and not as High-priest, can be all-comprehensive.

---

[52] 5:1 ff., and later the grandiose comparison with the revelation at Sinai in 12:18-29.
[53] In Hb. the Son is the Mediator of creation, the Heir of all things, the One who sits on the throne → υἱός. The designation as Son is so basic to all the rest that one may well say with F. Büchsel, "Die Christologie des Hb.," BFTh, 27 (1922), 15 that "the high-priesthood is a part of His divine sonship," though the epistle itself does not subsume it thus.

Yet the basic elements of the prophetic view of history (→ 275, διαθήκη) are also used to emphasise the character of eternity in the new revelation. The new covenant is attested by oath, 7:19 f. But an oath has the character of an ἐπαγγελία which is unconditional and unbreakable.

e. Justification for concentration on the cultic image is not merely found in the particular danger that the readers of Hb. might flirt again with the ancient cultus. There is the deeper point that the whole of the ancient theocracy was built up on the foundation of the Levitical priesthood. Cf. 7:11 with what is probably the true reading ἐπ' αὐτῇ. That which is of abiding significance in the figure is thus the basis of the whole comparison (cf. 2. and 3.). In both cases we find δικαιώματα λατρείας, 9:1. The heavenly sanctuary, too, is consecrated by a sacrifice, 9:23. But it is all seen from the central standpoint of the high-priestly office. This is the climax and comprehensive personal representation of the cultus.

2. The Levitical High-priest. [54]

a. The Deepest and Eternally Significant Definitions and Tasks of the Priestly Ministry.

The priest is called by God, 5:4-6. He does not presume to snatch at such a dignity. He represents the people before God, and stands before Him in this ministry, 2:17; 5:1, cf. the fulfilment in 7:25. But even before God he is in solidarity with men, 5:1 ff. He who is taken ἐξ ἀνθρώπων has to intercede ὑπὲρ ἀνθρώπων as one among others, 5:1. He is enabled to fulfil his office by his own qualification as circumdatus infirmitate (vg.). Hence he can μετριοπαθεῖν; he can moderate the impact of wrath on human sin, 5:2. His own weakness gives him a right official outlook on the weakness displayed in sin. But he must also offer for his own sin (→ infra, cf. 273).

This offering of unbloody and bloody sacrifices for sins is his true task, 5:1; 8:3 (10:11 of every priest). It takes place in expiation, 2:17. Over it there stands the sacred principle: οὐ χωρὶς αἵματος, 9:7, cf. 18-21, and the comprehensive statement that without shedding of blood is no remission (v. 22) — a Jewish principle which is particularly common in the Mishnah.

What has been said is enough to bring out the general character of the priest. It has eternal validity for Christ too, except in so far as He transcends the obvious limitations of the OT cultus.

b. The Office of the OT High-priest finds its Limit in Sin.

The priest offers for his own sins and for those of the people, 7:27 (ἰδίων). The Law places in this office men who are themselves weak, 7:28; cf. 9:7. But wilful sin is not covered by the expiation. On the basis of Lv. 4:2; 5:15, we are told in 5:2 that it refers only to the ἀγνοοῦντες and πλανώμενοι, and not to calculated wickedness, which comes under the destruction pronounced in Nu. 15:30. [55]

---

[54] The passages which speak of the ἱερεύς rather than the ἀρχιερεύς do not carry any particular emphasis. If, in accordance with ψ 109:4 and Gn. 14:18, ἱερεύς is not used of Melchisedec (5:6; 7:3, 11, 17, 21; though cf. 7:15 with reference to Christ Himself), it is constantly used for the Levitical priest, 7:14, 20, 23; 8:4; 9:6; 10:11). It occurs most frequently in c. 7, but the reference is always to the specific function of the ἀρχιερεύς on the Day of Atonement. ἱερεύς is thus a generic word; the exposition always has the ἀρχιερεύς in view.

[55] At this point we may rightly ask why Hb. does not go on to say that the atoning sacrifice of Christ deals with wilful sin. This is surely a logical deduction. It is not expressly drawn, however, in the interests of the motive of fear. The sacrifice of Christ is very seriously used as such a motive in 10:26.

Thus the Levitical priesthood cannot really deal with sin. It does not set it aside, and therefore it does not bring fellowship with God or τελείωσις. Hence it does not accomplish its final goal, 7:11, 19. The sense of guilt is not removed, 9:9; 10:2 f. The continuing conviction of sin creates a constant need for fresh offerings. Thus the cultus (10:3) becomes ἀνάμνησις, i.e., an objective reminder of sins. It keeps the wound open.[56]

c. This failure in the basic concern of both priest and sacrifice is deeply rooted in the carnal, earthly and mortal nature of the ancient cultus and its exponents. In a word, it is to be explained by the fact that this cultus does not have the character of eternity. It cannot do away with sin because it does not have eternal force.

The priests who practise it are mortal. This is why they are a changing plurality, 7:23. Similarly, the sacrifices lack the character of eternity and consequently they have to be continually repeated. The sacrifice on the Day of Atonement is offered only once a year, but it is offered once every year. This πολλάκις, κατ᾽ ἐνιαυτόν shows by the endless repetition that such offerings do not bring purification, 9:6 f., 12; 10:1 f. The ministry of the priest may have some purifying power (9:13), but it can lead only to a καθαρότης σαρκός, i.e., to an external and cultic purification. The blood of animals cannot take away sin, 10:4. At this stage everything is transitory. The cultus is κατὰ νόμον ἐντολῆς σαρκίνης, 7:16. It is concerned with δικαιώματα σαρκός, 9:10 (→ II, 553; 221).

We have a similar declaration when the ancient sanctuary in which the priest ministers is called κοσμικόν, 9:1. The antonym is ἐπουράνιος. κοσμικός here does not have the same meaning as in Philo (→ 241), though Chrys. and Thdrt. borrow this thought in their exposition of Hb. It does not denote a reflection of the universe. Its implication is that of imperfection. It is that which is old, which is a product of the hands of men (9:11), and which derives from this corruptible creation. A parallel concept is that the ministry of the priest is rendered only to the ὑπόδειγμα, σκία or τύπος of the heavenly, 8:5; 9:23; 10:1. This idea of ministry to a sketch or shadow or copy of the original goes back to Ex. 25:40 (→ 240). The true tabernacle is above, 8:5. The original, the σῶμα, the true actualisation, is not in this corruptible sphere but in glory. A specific indication of the fact that the old covenant cannot give access to the throne of grace is to be found in the division between the forecourt and the inner court, 8:2; 9:3, 8, 24. This is done away in the new covenant. It expresses the indirect, mediate and provisional nature of the relationship to God, cf. 9:9 → supra.

3. Christ the Exalted High-priest.

The synthesis of Son and High-priest (→ 276)[57] gives rise to the following lines of thought.

a. Solidarity with Humanity (→ 277).

The opening expositions in 2:17 and 4:15 do not begin with the majesty but with the lowliness into which Christ was thrust by this office. This is not merely because this aspect of the life of the Redeemer is what causes offence to the readers.

---

[56] Cf. the statements of Paul concerning the way in which sin is provoked by the Law.
[57] With ἀρχιερεύς, 2:17; 3:1; 4:15; 5:5, 10; 6:20; 7:26; 8:1; 9:11, we also have for Christ ἀρχιερεὺς μέγας, 4:14, and ἱερεὺς μέγας, 10:21, → 263.

Nor is there any desire to awaken human sympathy. It is rather that this constitutes the abiding centre of consideration in the light of which there can be true understanding of the majesty. Everything depends on this commencement with the earthly life. Hence the high-priestly representation of Hb. begins with historical Jesus. He who is in all points like His human brothers, and is tempted as they are, corresponds (→ 277) to the OT high-priest in the *circumdatus infirmitate*. He wins an objective right to make expiation [58] and to offer help in virtue of His own victory and perseverance. His loftiness (4:14) does not make Him remote and unapproachable (4:15). It does not deprive Him of the ability to sympathise with our human weaknesses. This trait of merciful συμπαθῆσαι is closely related to the μετριοπαθεῖν (cf. 5:2, → 277). The κατὰ πάντα καθ᾽ ὁμοιότητα emphasises the similarity as strongly as possible. But the χωρὶς ἁμαρτίας indicates the radical distinction from the OT μετριοπαθεῖν. 5:7-10 must also be seen in connection with the thought of συμπαθῆσαι. In this participation He is called merciful and faithful, 2:17. If this high-priestly solidarity indicates the tension between majesty and fellowship with humanity, the point of division or distinction is brought out with particular care and strictness. There is no more acute expression of the abiding distinction than in the juxtaposition of the two statements: κατὰ πάντα τοῖς ἀδελφοῖς ὁμοιωθῆναι (2:17, cf. 4:15), and: κεχωρισμένος ἀπὸ τῶν ἁμαρτωλῶν, 7:26. [59]

b. The Eternal High-priesthood Arises by Attestation of the Sonship.

5:1-10 shows how He becomes High-priest (γενηθῆναι, v. 5), namely, by fidelity to the One who has appointed Him in His incarnation, 3:2, by learning obedience through suffering, 5:8, by enduring the severest tests with εὐλάβεια, with holy fear, 5:7 (→ 280, n. 63), and therefore by being made perfect in obedience, 5:9. τελειωθείς implies both that He has proved Himself to be the victor through obedience (cf. the contrast to the weak high-priest of the OT, 7:28 alongside 5:1-10), and also that He is exalted to all eternity: υἱὸς εἰς τὸν αἰῶνα τετελειωμένος, 7:28. [60] He thus becomes High-priest by proving and accrediting Himself as the Son. In so doing He also becomes the perfected Son. He thus maintains His calling as supreme Priest. His whole way is thus characterised by the fulfilment of His Sonship. If at other points it is stated that like the Levitical priest He does not attain to the office on His own account, but is called and instituted (→ 277), His calling and institution are grounded in the declaration concerning the Son in ψ 2:7.

---

[58] The ἐν ᾧ of 2:18 is a simple causal conjunction, "because." It usually introduces psychological reflection. In terms of the total Christology of Hb., however, it would be an odd consideration that the Son must first attain to the subjective capacity of experiencing sympathy (is God incapable of sympathy?), and that He can be truly merciful only inasmuch as He has human experience behind Him. As in 4:15 f. and 5:7 f., the real thought is that only He who is righteous and obedient can make atonement.

[59] To be sure, 7:26 does not apply to His earthly existence in the same way as 2:17 or 4:15. But this is not the decisive point. The similarity acquires eternal validity, since He who is glorified bears the countenance of man. The χωρὶς ἁμαρτίας of 4:15 is wholly in keeping with 7:26.

[60] On τελειόω cf. J. Kögel, "Der Begriff τελειοῦν im Hb.," *Theologische Studien*, *M. Kähler dargebracht* (1905), 35 ff.; T. Häring, *Monatsschrift für Pastoraltheologie*, 17 (1921), 264 ff.; E. Riggenbach, NKZ, 34 (1923), 184 ff.; T. Häring, *ibid.*, 386 ff.; F. Büchsel, "Die Christologie des Hb.," BFTh, 27, 2 (1922), 56 ff.; Wnd. Hb., 44-46; Rgg. Hb., *ad loc.*; Pr.-Bauer, *s.v.*

c. The Sinless High-priest (→ 278).

There is another analogy to the Levitical ἀρχιερεύς in 7:26, where Jesus is described as ὅσιος (wholly orientated in thought and act to God and His service), ἄκακος (untouched by evil), and ἀμίαντος (unspotted), and therefore as separate from sinners. [61] In this respect He is linked with the cultic preparation of the כֹּהֵן גָּדוֹל, though ἄκακος and ἀμίαντος cannot be applied to the latter in the full sense. A deep cleft between the two is revealed, however, in 7:27. All priestly sacrifice is first for the sins of the priest, and it takes place καθ' ἡμέραν. [62] But this is unnecessary in the case of Christ. His sinlessness is not, of course, a static predicate. It is demonstrated in active conflict and decision as continually attested ὑπακοή, 2:18; 4:15; 5:7-9. His successful conflict carries with it the right to represent, to help and to save. He who obeys delivers those who obey through Him, 5:9. At this decisive point the link with the concept of the Son is again the crucial thing. Exaltation is granted to Him who in conflict maintains the fear of God. He who shows reverence, i.e., the Son, is strengthened for definitive execution of the divine will (5:7: ἀπὸ τῆς εὐλαβείας). [63]

d. The Contrast with the Carnal Offering (→ 278).

The sacrifice of the great High-priest in substitutionary expiation (9:28, quoting Is. 53:11) is no mere equivalent. It is full personal self-giving (ἑαυτόν, 7:27). In this case the victim is the priest himself. This unity of the priest and sacrifice brings the old offerings to an end, cf. 9:12, 25. The blood which is shed is not the alien blood of beasts, but His own blood. That this blood is not regarded, however, as a sacred "thing" is impressively brought out in 10:5, where it is shown from the LXX that with the coming of the Messiah into the world the σῶμα which is offered up to God, i.e., His whole personal life, is the means to fulfil the will of God. The concept of sacrifice is thus deepened. The emphasis is now placed, not on cultic and material sacrifice, but on the fulfilment of the will of God in a human life.

But only the intervention of the eternal Spirit makes this a complete and total offering. Christ offered Himself through the eternal Spirit (the more difficult reading αἰωνίου rather than ἁγίου), 9:14. Thus the sacrifice which remains in the

---

[61] It is perhaps recalled here that prior to the Day of Atonement the high-priest had to live eight days in the temple and take particular care to avoid cultic impurity. Cf. Jeremias, op. cit., 9.

[62] The καθ' ἡμέραν does not refer to the sacrifice on the Day of Atonement. It has a more general reference to the whole sacrificial ministry, and specifically perhaps to the meal offerings of Lv. 6:12-16. Cf. F. Bleek, Komm., III (1840); H. v. Soden, Komm.³ (1899); Rgg. Hb., ad loc.

[63] The presentation is here coloured by Gethsemane. To sure, Lk. 22:43 f., which is closest to Hb., is not found in א A B sy^s, and may not be genuine. But it could have been rejected because it gives rise to dogmatic problems, cf. A. v. Harnack, Studien zur Geschichte des NT und der alten Kirche, I (1931), 244 ff. It is defended by L. Brun in ZNW, 32 (1933), 265-276. The Greek fathers construe ἀπὸ τῆς εὐλαβείας as "reverent fear" before God (ἀπό = "on account of"). The other meaning, "mortal anguish" (ἀπό as a prep. of separation) yields a much weaker sense, namely, that He is not kept from death, but from anxious fear : Bengel, Hofmann, B. Weiss, Comm. ad loc.; Zn. Lk., ad loc. Harnack, op. cit., 246 ff. considers only this sense of εὐλάβεια, and he thus conjectures that an οὐκ has been deleted from before εἰσακουσθείς on dogmatic grounds. But how can we have an ἀρχιερεύς who is not heard by God ? The decisive point, however, is that εὐλάβεια certainly means reverent fear in Hb. 12:28. This sense alone fits what follows in 5:9. Cf. on this whole question Harnack, op. cit., 244-252. For Harnack's proposal cf. also → II, 753 (R. Bultmann).

carnal sphere is replaced by a pneumatic offering which is made definitive and unique by the Spirit of eternity. Cf. the enduring force of His priesthood in 7:16, 23 f. His αἷμα does not operate as a substance. The new thing springs forth from the eternal spiritual root.

The unique offering (→ 278). → ἅπαξ or ἐφάπαξ is one of the most important and illuminating words in the epistle. It is contrasted with the καθ' ἡμέραν, πολλάκις, or κατ' ἐνιαυτόν of the Levitical offering. The sacrifice of the High-priest Jesus Christ takes place once, unrepeatably, and once for all, 7:27; 9:24-28; 10:10, cf. 12: μίαν θυσίαν, 14: μιᾷ προσφορᾷ. If in 9:27 f. the starting-point is the experience and event of the one destiny of man, this shows how seriously the ἅπαξ is taken in a historical sense. Nevertheless, it is no less clear that here, too, the unique thing becomes significant only by virtue of the manifested power of eternity. The one offering becomes once-for-all because it is the Son who takes to Himself the one destiny of man. In the case of the OT כֹּהֵן גָּדוֹל once means once a year (→ 278) [64] and in fact once a day (→ 280, n. 62). But in the case of Christ it means once and for all, or definitively.

e. The High-priest Christ Effects Access to the Throne, to the Full Presence of God (→ 278).

He who has suffered the misery of man (4:14-16) has "passed through the heavens" as the Levitical ἀρχιερεύς passes through the forecourt and the sanctuary into the Holy of Holies. Hope has thus been anchored beyond the veil (6:17-20). That is, the place of God's presence is now accessible to hope. This world is linked with the world to come. For the πρόδρομος (6:20) has penetrated into that world for us. Cf. 7:26; 9:11, 24. This is a leading and essential theme in the presentation. The unique offering has opened heaven, 9:23; 10:19 f.

Thus the κήρυγμα declared in the image of the high-priest reaches its true goal. It links up with that of the King on the throne. [65] Priest and king are one. Christ is the abiding λειτουργός in the true tabernacle (8:2) as the One who has taken His place at the right hand of majesty. Hence His sacrifice is decisive for all time, 10:12 f. He is enthroned in virtue of it. Whereas the OT priest can never find rest, He enjoys the rest of eternity. He waits until His enemies are made His footstool. The main battle has been fought, and everything else follows.

In contrast with the mortal Levite (→ 278), there thus stands the eternal High-priest (7:8-10) who has neither beginning nor end, ὅτι ζῇ. He is established (7:15) as a Priest with the character of eternity and omnipotence, for what He was, He is, 7:16: κατὰ δύναμιν ζωῆς ἀκαταλύτου. Thus change and chance are remote from His priesthood. No death can interrupt His work. He remains to eternity, 7:24 f.

4. Radical Deductions from the Christological Interpretation of the Cultus.

The νόμου μετάθεσις, the alteration of the law, the change in the priesthood (μετατίθεσθαι), does not mean that the old is replaced by something inferior, 7:12. As the basic text shows us (→ 275), the Aaronic priesthood is now set aside.

---

[64] Even then he went three or four times into the Holy of Holies, three times according to Yoma, 5, 1-4, and four according to Nu. r., 7 on 5:1.

[65] Cf. F. Büchsel, op. cit., 11-14: Messiah and High-priest.

A priest is brought in after the order of Melchisedec. This divinely attested fact involves a radical break with the ancient order. If it is indisputable that the κύριος is of Judah and not of Levi, 7:13 f., the decisive nature of the change is realised only when we are confronted by the eternal validity of the High-priest who brings fulfilment (1. d). The first sacrifice is set aside in order that the second may come into force, 10:9. There thus takes place an ἀθέτησις, a legal annulment of the earlier commandment, 7:18. [66] God Himself declares in Jer. 31 that the first covenant is outmoded, and He promises a new one. The first covenant is now a venerable institution with all the signs of age and decay. It has no more right to existence, 8:13.

5. The Saving Efficacy and Practical Implications of the Truth Proclaimed.

a. The essential nature of this truth is not perceived unless our exposition presents the following insights in terms of the discussion in Hb. The real future benefits at issue (10:1) consist in total, definitive and sufficient redemption, cf. 10:18. The effect of this high-priestly sacrifice, intercession and rule is eternal λύτρωσις, 9:12; ἀπολύτρωσις τῶν παραβάσεων, 9:15; ἄφεσις, 10:18; purging of the sense of guilt, 9:14, or of the heart, 10:22. It brings ἁγιάζεσθαι to God, 10:10 (ἁγιαζομένους, 10:14, durative, cf. 13:12); cf. also τετελείωκεν in 10:14 as a completed fact, and also what is said in 7:19, 25 about drawing near to God.

b. This saving state is a possession, 4:14; 8:1; cf. 10:21, ἔχομεν ἀρχιερέα. It is an access, 12:22. For the community it is thus the confession (ὁμολογία) of an impregnable reality, 3:1; 4:14; 10:23. With free and unhampered joy the community makes use of its new access, 4:16; 10:19, 22. Everything thus stands in the living address of admonition, and presents itself as an incisive and liberating hope.

c. But the final deduction from this cultic consideration is also a new and practical fact in the situation of the community. If the old cultus has been done away, this means that only the sacrifice of the true High-priest can lead it to the new and true cultus, 9:14: εἰς τὸ λατρεύειν θεῷ ζῶντι. [67] The only θυσίαι which remain are those of thanksgiving, well-doing and loving fellowship, 13:15 ff. But this situation is one of actual conflict. There is a duty to break away from the former cultic bondage. Attachment to Jesus, who suffered before the camp, implies a break with the Jewish way of cultic salvation. The ancient priest has no more place at the altar (of the atoning sacrifice of Christ). This is brought out with great seriousness and point in 13:10-13. And in this respect there is a final, comprehensive reference to the will of God, 13:21.

The final result of this incisive interpretation of the Israelite cultus is thus as follows. Christ Himself is He who definitively fulfils the truth of priesthood. Hence He alone remains.

---

[66] Cf. Pl. in R. 7:1-6.
[67] Cf. Pl. in R. 6:12 ff.; 12:1.

F. ἀρχιερεύς and ἱερεύς in the Early Church.

1. Christ as High-priest or Priest. The language and thinking of Hb. are reflected in Ign. Phld., 9, 1; 1 Cl., 61, 3. Worth noting is 1 Cl., 36, 1: τὸν ἀρχιερέα τῶν προσφορῶν ἡμῶν. He presents the prayers of the community before God. ἀρχιερεὺς αἰώνιος, Mart. Pol., 14, 3. Just. Dial., 42, 1 sees the twelve apostles in the bells on the garment of the high-priest. The Alexandrians make rich use of the image of the high-priest. Cl. Al. Strom., VI, 153, 4 and Orig. Comm. in Joh., VI, 53, 275 use μέγας, but we also find ἀληθινός in Hom. in Jos., 26, 3 and τέλειος ἀρχιερεύς in Comm. in Joh., 28, 1, 6. The most extended treatment is in Comm. in Joh., I, 2, 9 f. Cf. II, 34 and 209. The Philonic ἀρχιερεὺς λόγος is also found in Orig., even as a general formula, Hom. XIX in Jer., 20, Klostermann, 167, 19; Hom. No. 27 in Lam. 1:10, Klostermann, 248, 2. Cf. also Cels., V, 4. The Scriptures which speak of Melchisedec are much quoted in Just. Dial., 19, 4; 32, 6 etc., and also in Cl. Al. Strom. Χριστὸς ἱερεύς is also common, Just. Dial., 86, 3; Orig. Hom. in Jos., 18, 2, Baehrens, 406, 27; ἐξαίρετος ἱερεύς, Just. Dial., 118, 2, or ὁ ἱερεὺς μέγας, ibid., 115, 2; Orig. Comm. in Joh., I, 2, 11, or αἰώνιος ἱερεύς, Just. Dial., 19, 4; 33, 2 etc.

2. The General Priesthood of the Community. Just. Dial., 116, 3 can even call believers (→ 272, n. 39) ἀρχιερατικὸν τὸ ἀληθινὸν γένος. It is also stated in Iren. Haer., IV, 8, 3 : omnes justi sacerdotalem habent ordinem. According to Tert. Exhortatio ad Castitatem, VII the priestly laws of the Torah have something to say to Christians, i.e., as regards the prohibition of second marriage. Tertullian continues : nonne et laici sacerdotes sumus ? Only the authority of the Church established the distinction between clergy and people. But emergency baptism proves the right of all to act as priests in the hour of need. This brings all under priestly discipline. According to Orig. Exhortatio ad Martyrium, 30 Christians are priests under the ἀρχιερεύς Christ, their Head. They offer themselves as He does. Cf. Orat., 28, 9 : οἱ τοῖς ἀποστόλοις ὡμοιωμένοι are, like them, priests κατὰ τὸν μέγαν ἀρχιερέα. The priestly law of the OT thus applies to us, Hom. in Lv. 9:1. This is, of course, interpreted allegorically. Christians are also ἱερεῖς as those who pray for their earthly countries, Cels., VIII, 74. Others take to the field, but they participate in the campaigns as priests, i.e., in prayer, Cels., VIII, 73. They keep themselves pure from sexual intercourse ὡς καὶ τρόπον τελείων ἱερέων, Cels., VII, 48. In Aug. Civ. D., 20, 10 it is deduced from Rev. 20:6 that Christians are omnes sacerdotes, quoniam membra sunt unius sacerdotis.

3. But the description of the clergy as priests is also early. Of the prophets Did., 13, 3 ventures the astonishing saying : οἱ ἀρχιερεῖς ὑμῶν. 1 Cl., 40 f. values highly the cultic orders of Judaism as a model for the cultus of the Christian community. Tertullian Bapt., 17 calls the bishop summus sacerdos. Hipp. Ref., I, 6 prooem. also says : ὧν (of the apostles) ἡμεῖς διάδοχοι τυγχάνοντες τῆς τε αὐτῆς χάριτος μετέχοντες ἀρχιερατείας. In the festal address in Eus. Hist. Eccl., X, 4, 2 the clergy are again addressed as ἱερεῖς. [68]

Schrenk

ἱερόθυτος, ἱεροπρεπής, ἱεροσυλέω, ἱερόσυλος, ἱερουργέω → 251-257.
Ἰερουσαλήμ, Ἰεροσόλυμα → Σιών.   ἱερωσύνη → 247.

---

[68] On later development, cf. RE³, 16, 47 ff.; RGG², IV, 1492 f.

| Ἰησοῦς | → ὄνομα.

1. The Greek form of a list of OT characters who in pre-exilic Hebrew are called יְהוֹשֻׁעַ and usually after the Exile יֵשׁוּעַ.

Joshua the son of Nun is יְהוֹשֻׁעַ in Ex., Nu., Dt., Jos., Ju., 1 K. 16:34, 1 Ch. 7:27 and the Heb. of Sir. 46:1, but יֵשׁוּעַ in Neh. 8:17. The high-priest Joshua, the son of Josedech, who returned with Zerubbabel from exile, is always called יְהוֹשֻׁעַ in Hag. and Zech. and always יֵשׁוּעַ in Ezr. and Neh. יְהוֹשֻׁעַ is the name of two men in 1 S. 6:14, 18; 2 K. 23:8, while 2 Ch. 31:15 calls a Levite under Hezekiah יֵשׁוּעַ, and this form of the name is also found in post-exilic priestly and Levitical families and in the references to their return from exile under Zerubbabel and Joshua. The full form thus prevails up to c. 500, and after that (up to 1 Ch. 7:27 and Sir. 46:1) the shorter.

The reason for the vowel shift from ō to ē seems to be the desire to avoid having ō and û together, [1] and perhaps there was a general tendency for the cholem to become ö. [2]

The LXX retained the later form יֵשׁוּעַ, and made it declinable by adding a nominative ς. [3]

Gen. Ἰησοῦ, [4] Dat. 19 times Ἰησοῖ (only in Ex., Dt. and Jos.), 7 times Ἰησοῦ

Ἰ η σ ο ῦ ς. F. Delitzsch in *Zeitschrift für lutherische Theol. u. Kirche*, 37 (1876), 209-214; F. Philippi in *Zeitschrift f. Völkerpsychologie und Sprachwissenschaft*, 14 (1883), 175-190; S. Fraenkel in *Wiener Zeitschrift f. die Kunde des Morgenlandes*, 4 (1890), 332-333; A. Müller in ThStKr, 65 (1892), 177 f.; E. Nestle, *ibid.*, 573 f.; M. Lidzbarski, *Handbuch der nordsemitischen Epigraphik*, I (1898), 291; F. Praetorius in ZDMG, 59 (1905), 341 f.; E. Nestle in DCG¹, I (1906), 859-861; S. Krauss in REJ, 55 (1908), 148-151; F. X. Steinmetzer in BZ, 14 (1916), 193-197; Zn. Mt. on 1:21; Str.-B. on Mt. 1:21; A. Deissmann in *Mysterium Christi* (1931), 13-41; J. Klausner, *Jesus von Nazareth²* (1934), 311. On 5 : NN, in *Antiqua mater* (1887), 229; J. van Loon in ThT, 29 (1895), 484-487; G. J. P. J. Bolland, *Der evangelische Jozua* (1907); A. Drews, *Die Christusmythe*, I (1909), 16-25; II (1911), 300-314; *Die Entstehung des Christentums* (1924), 102-106, 118-120; W. B. Smith, *Der vorchristliche Jesus²* (1911), 1-41; J. M. Robertson, *Pagan Christs²* (1911), 162-168, 315 ; C. Guignebert, *Jésus* (1913), 76 ff.; E. Dujardin, *Le Dieu Jésus* (1927), 203-206; H. Windisch in ThR, 13 (1910), 163 ff.; W. Bousset, *ibid.*, 14 (1911), 373-385; M. Goguel, *Jésus de Nazareth, Mythe ou Histoire?* (1925), 56 ff.; *Das Leben Jesu* (1934), 104 f.; O. Graber, *Im Kampfe um Christus* (1927), 142-144, 184.

[1] So Philippi, Fraenkel, Nestle, Müller, Steinmetzer. There are many examples of this dissimilation : יְהוָֹה from *יוֹהוּא, מוֹשֶׁה to מִישָׁא in Mandaean lit. etc. Delitzsch derives the form from the middle form *Isua*, Praetorius by way of יְהוֹ + יְשׁוּעַ with the deletion of the first part. Acc. to K. G. Kuhn (*Festschrift f. E. Littmann* [1935], 36 ff.) יוֹשׁוּעַ existed from the very first alongside יְהוֹשֻׁעַ, and יֵשׁוּעַ arose from it by dissimilation.

[2] H. Grimme, "Die jemenische Aussprache des Hebräischen" in *Festschrift f. E. Sachau* (1915), 125-142 draws attention to the fact (p. 132) that Jews in the Yemen, whose pronunciation is old, pronounce the cholem like an open ö or even e, and he points to the vacillation in the pointing of the Berlin Ms. qu 680 (140). Fraenkel, too, refers to the pronunciation of modern Jews in Aden.

[3] On the declension cf. Moulton, 72; Bl.-Debr.⁶ § 55.

[4] Only at 2 Ch. 31:15 Ἰησοῦς as gen. (A Ἰησοῦ).

(Ex. 17:9; Jos. 10:17; 17:14; 1 Ch. 24:11; 1 Εσδρ. 5:65; 2 Εσδρ. 2:36 (B Ἰησοῖ); 21:26 (a city name); acc. Ἰησοῦν, voc. Ἰησοῦ. [5]

Only at 1 Ch. 7:27 is Joshua the son of Nun Ἰησουε, and here alone his father is Νουμ. The MSS shows further variations in the Gk. form of the name. B has Ἰησουε at 2 Εσδρ. 2:40; A alone has Ἰησοῦ at 1 Βασ. 6:14, 18 (B Ὠσηε) and the Luc recension also has Ἰωσηε at 4 Βασ. 23:8. There is a great variety in the rendering of יֵשׁוּעַ at 1 Εσδρ. 5:26: A Ἰησουε, B Ἰησουεις, and the others Ἰησοῦ. In B, too, Ἰησοῦς is used for several other OT names: 2 Βασ. 20:25 (for שִׁיָא); 1 Ch. 2:38 (for יֵהוּא); 1 Ch. 2:47 (for יַהְדָּי); 1 Ch. 18:16 (שִׁוְשָׁא); 2 Ch. 20:34 (יֵהוּא). At Sir. 48:20 א and V have Ἰησοῦ instead of Ἠσαΐου.

2. Up to the beginning of the 2nd century A.D. the name יֵשׁוּעַ or Ἰησοῦς was very common among the Jews.

Among the 72 translators of the LXX according to Ep. Ar. (48, 49), three bear the name of Ἰησοῦς. Jos. mentions some 20 of the name, including ten contemporaries of Jesus. [6] The ossuary inscr. from the vicinity of Jerusalem (at the beginning of the 2nd cent. A.D. at the very latest) yield us ישוע once, [7] ישוע בר נתי once, [8] שמעון בר ישוע once, [9] and once ישוע בר יהוסף and ישו, [10] with perhaps also the imperfect שוע. [11] In the sepulchre of a Jew of the dispersion on Mount Scopus near Jerusalem [12] we also find the inscription Ἰησοῦς. [13]

The first certain example of Ἰησοῦς in Gk. is on a burial inscr. of the year 1 B.C.-A.D. 1, [14] though there is probably an instance in P. Oxy., IV, 816 (6th-5th cent. B.C.). The pap. of the Jewish colony of Apollonopolis Magna (1st-2nd cent. A.D.) yield many examples. [15]

The evidence of the NT is to the same effect. In Ac. 7:45 and Hb. 4:8 there is reference to Ἰησοῦς, i.e., Joshua the son of Nun. Many others bear the name as

---

[5] We also find the gen. Ἰησοῦτος, → n. 15 and Ἰησοῖ, Ex. 17:14 B; 2 Εσδρ. 2:36 B; 22:7 BA. Cf. Helbing, 60; Thackeray, 164 f.

[6] Deissmann, 19.

[7] S. Klein, Jüdisch-palästinisches Corpus Inscriptionum (1920), 24, No. 44.

[8] Ibid., No. 45.

[9] Ibid., 27, No. 67.

[10] E. L. Sukenik, Jüdische Gräber Jerusalems um Christi Geburt (1931), 19; cf. A. Deissmann in Archäologischer Anzeiger, 1931 (Beiblatt zum Jahrbuch des deutschen Archäologischen Instituts, 46 [1931], 316 f.); G. Dalman in AELKZ, 64 (1931), 186 f.; MK in Νέα Σιών, 23 (1931), 333-345. ישו with ישוע on the same ossuary is to be explained by lack of space, though Sukenik (19, n. 1) suggests also the possibility of a shorter form of the name.

[11] C. Clermont-Ganneau in Revue Archéologique, III, 1 (1883), 264, No. 18.

[12] Klein, 31, No. 94. Whether the Ιεσους which twice occurs on a Jerusalem ossuary should be mentioned in this connection (Klein, No. 46) is doubted by Deissmann (18 f.).

[13] Clermont-Ganneau, Mission en Palestine et en Phénice, entreprise en 1881, 5th report (1884), 99, No. 26: ישוע בר מתי is another reading of the inscr. mentioned under → n. 8.

[14] Ἰησοῦς Σαμβαίου ἄωρε ἄτεκνε χρηστὲ χαῖρε, Seymour de Ricci in Revue épigraphique, NS, I (1913), 146 ff., No. 12.

[15] Cf. C. Wessely in Studien zur Palaeographie und Papyruskunde, 13 (1913), 8 ff., No. 2, 7, 9, 11, 13, 20; the gen. Ἰησοῦτος in No. 2; cf. also P. Lond., III (1907), No. 1119a (105 A.D.). The name also appears on a pap. (103-104 A.D.) published in the Archiv f. Papyrusforschung, 6 (1913-1920), 220, No. 6, and on a metrical burial inscr., Annales du Service des Antiquités de l'Égypte, 22 (1922), 10 f. = Deissmann, 21 = ZNW, 22 (1923), 283, No. 22.

well as Jesus. Thus we find a pre-exilic example in the genealogy in Lk. 3:29. In Mt. 27:16 (Θλ) Barabbas is also called 'Ιησοῦς Βαραββᾶς. [16] In Ac. 13:6 the sorcerer in Cyprus is called Βαριησοῦς = בַּר יֵשׁוּעַ, [17] and in Col. 4:11 the helper of Paul is 'Ιησοῦς ὁ λεγόμενος 'Ιοῦστος. [18]

Once the Jews came under Greek influence, we note a tendency to replace or to translate Jewish names by similar sounding Greek names. For an example of the latter, cf. the family of Dositheos, whose son and nephew are both called Mattathias (Matthias). [19] For the former, cf. אֶסְתֵּר/'Αστήρ [20] or שָׁאוּל/Παῦλος. יֵשׁוּעַ is often rendered 'Ιάσων, e.g., the brother of the high-priest Onias in the Syrian period, Jos. Ant., 12, 239. Among the translators of the LXX we twice find 'Ιάσων in Ep. Ar., 49, and the name is also found twice in the records of Apollonopolis Magna. [21]

With the 2nd century A.D. יֵשׁוּעַ or 'Ιησοῦς disappears as a proper name. In Rabbinic literature ישוע is found only as the name of the 9th priestly class; [22] elsewhere we always have the full יְהוֹשׁוּעַ, which is borne by quite a number of rabbis. [23] In the Greek field, however, 'Ιάσων may still be found in the catacombs. [24] 'Ιησοῦς, on the other hand, is not found there, although the form Gesua and the feminine Gesues occur in Venusia in the 6th century A.D. [25] At a later date the name Jesus is rare as a proper name. [26] When we add to this the fact that Jesus of Nazareth is almost always called יֵשׁוּ in Rabbinic writings, [27] we are confronted by a problem which demands explanation. The full form in the Rabbis

---

[16] Kl. and Zn. Mt., ad loc., and Deissmann, 32 ff., regard this reading as original, Nestle-Dobsch., 137 rejects it.

[17] The MSS vacillate as to the form of the name, as in other cases in which others than Jesus bear the name, Deissmann, 29 ff.

[18] Deissmann, 35 f. concludes that in Mk. 15:7 a 'Ιησοῦς has dropped out before ὁ λεγόμενος Βαραββᾶς, cf. Kl. Mt. on 27:17; at 36 ff., acc. to Zn. Einl., I, 321, he reads ἀσπάζεταί σε 'Επαφρᾶς ὁ συναιχμάλωτός μου ἐν Χριστῷ, 'Ιησοῦς (instead of ἐν Χριστῷ 'Ιησοῦ) at Phlm. 23; that is, in Phlm. there is a greeting to the Jesus Justus mentioned in Col. So also E. Amling in ZNW, 10 (1909), 261 f. When we consider how much the Jesus passages have been worked over in the MS tradition, these conjectures are very likely.

[19] E. L. Sukenik, The Journal of the Palestinian Oriental Society, 8 (1927), 113-121.

[20] N. Müller/N. A. Bees, Die Inschr. der jüd. Katakombe am Monteverde zu Rom (1919), No. 47, n. 1.

[21] → n. 15.

[22] M. Jastrow, A Dictionary of the Targumim, the Talmud Babli and Yerushalmi ... (1926), s.v. יֵשׁוּעַ.

[23] Cf. Strack Einl., Index III. The name יוחנן בן ישוע (brother-in-law of Akiba) is found only in some MSS at Yad., 3, 5, and יישוע at jMQ, 82 c, 30, Krauss, op. cit., 149 f., 150, n. 2. For the former cf. Delitzsch and Zn. Mt. on 1:21. Zn. also conjectures that the יהושע בן פרחיה mentioned in Ab., 1, 6 was also called יֵשׁוּעַ by his contemporaries. It is worth noting that while the necropolis of Jerusalem yields only the form ישוע from the 1st century B.C., that of Jaffa has an example of the form יהושוע (Klein, op. cit., No. 116).

[24] H. Vogelstein/P. Rieger, Geschichte der Juden in Rom, I (1896), 465, No. 43; N. Müller/N. A. Bees, op. cit., No. 53: Αισω; H. W. Beyer/H. Lietzmann, Die jüd. Katakombe der Villa Torlonia zu Rom (1930), No. 15.

[25] CIL, IX, 6224, 1 f., 4. J. B. Frey, editor of the Corpus Inscriptionum Iudaicarum, told me that neither ישוע nor 'Ιησοῦς is found in the ancient Jewish inscriptions of Europe.

[26] Deissmann, 24 ff. Deissmann does not mention a אהרון בן ישוע c. 900 in Jerusalem (J. Winter-A. Wünsche, Jüd. Literatur, II [1894], 78) (Rengstorf).

[27] Str.-B., I, 63 f. The full name יֵשׁוּעַ is found only in T. Chul., 2, 22 and 24 (ibid., I, 64).

might be a return to the biblical form, but the short form יוֹסִי instead of the biblical יוֹסֵף maintained itself some centuries longer. To regard יֵשׁוּ as merely a transcription of the Greek 'Ιησοῦς creates both linguistic and material difficulties. σ is usually transcribed ס, and the ς ending is usually carried over; it is also hard to suppose that the Rabbis had to learn the name Jesu from the Greek Church. The common conjecture [28] that in both the Greek and the Hebrew spheres the Jews deliberately avoided the name 'Ιησοῦς/יֵשׁוּעַ because of their rejection of Jesus is confronted by the difficulty that 'Α, Σ and Θ do not avoid 'Ιησοῦς, [29] although the Jews should have altered the LXX in view of its use by Christians, and although Christian apologetic often used as a Scripture proof against the Jews the presence of 'Ιησοῦς for Joshua in the Greek Bible (→ 292). Nevertheless, the three facts that 'Ιησοῦς begins to drop out of the Greek sphere after the beginning of the 2nd century A.D., that the Rabbis return to the older form of the name, and that in the Talmud the singular form יֵשׁוּ[30] is used only for Jesus of Nazareth, cannot be separated from one another, and they seem to be explained best by the theory that the name of Jesus is consciously avoided. יֵשׁוּ instead of יֵשׁוּעַ is an assimilation to the Greek 'Ιησοῦς.

3. The name borne by Jesus is in the first instance an expression of His humanity. The three Gospels speak of One who bears this common name. It is by this name that He is discussed among the people. This is the name by which He is addressed. To distinguish Him from others of the same name there is added ἀπὸ Ναζαρὲτ τῆς Γαλιλαίας, or ὁ Ναζαρηνός, or ὁ Ναζωραῖος. The phrase υἱὸς Δαυείδ is also added to show that He belongs to the house of David.

At Mt. 21:11 the people says: οὗτός ἐστιν ὁ προφήτης 'Ιησοῦς ὁ ἀπὸ Ναζαρὲθ τῆς Γαλιλαίας; at Mk. 14:67 and par. (cf. Mt. 26:71) the maid says to Peter: καὶ σὺ μετὰ τοῦ Ναζαρηνοῦ ἦσθα τοῦ 'Ιησοῦ; at Mk. 10:47 and par. the blind man says: ἀκούσας ὅτι 'Ιησοῦς ὁ Ναζαρηνός ἐστιν; at Mt. 27:37 Pilate causes to be written on the cross: οὗτός ἐστιν 'Ιησοῦς ὁ βασιλεὺς τῶν 'Ιουδαίων (ὁ Ναζωραῖος is added to 'Ιησοῦς at Jn. 19:19); at Jn. 1:45 Philip tells Nathanael: εὑρήκαμεν 'Ιησοῦν υἱὸν τοῦ 'Ιωσὴφ τὸν ἀπὸ Ναζαρέτ; at Jn. 18:5, 7 the guard seeks 'Ιησοῦν τὸν Ναζωραῖον; at Lk. 24:19 Cleophas tells the stranger τὰ περὶ 'Ιησοῦ τοῦ Ναζαρηνοῦ; at Mk. 16:6 the angel says: 'Ιησοῦν ζητεῖτε τὸν Ναζαρηνόν. Where the Evangelists tell us briefly what others think or say about Jesus, they do not give an addition to distinguish Him from others of the same name (Lk. 7:3; Mk. 5:27; Mt. 14:1; Mk. 5:20 and par.; cf. Lk. 6:11). He is most commonly addressed as διδάσκαλε, ῥαββεί, ἐπιστάτα, or κύριε, but we also find 'Ιησοῦ Ναζαρηνέ at Mk. 1:24 and par. and υἱὲ Δαυείδ 'Ιησοῦ at Mk. 10:47 f. (cf. Lk. 18:38). The penitent thief uses only His name at Lk. 23:42 and the lepers have 'Ιησοῦ ἐπιστάτα at Lk. 17:13.

Of this 'Ιησοῦς who was born under Herod the Great and crucified under Pontius Pilate, it is confessed by the early Church and the whole Christian world

---

[28] Zn. Mt. on 1:21 ([4][1922], 78, n. 48); Deissmann, 25 f.

[29] 'Α has 'Ιησουά only at Dt. 1:38.

[30] But → n. 10. In the Bibl. Antiquities of Ps.-Philo Jesus is occasionally used for the more common Jesue (20, 9; 22, 2 and 7). The Gesua of the Venusia inscr. (→ n. 25) is an exact transcription of יֵשׁוּעַ which avoids reminiscence of the Greek 'Ιησοῦς. The explanation of the name of Jesus which Irenaeus (II, 24, 2) owes to the *periti*: *Dominus, qui continet caelum et terram*, also goes back to יֵשׁוּ: יהוה שמים וארץ, and the Aram. dedication formula of the Marcosites (Iren., I, 21, 3) also has יֵשׁוּ, if the transcription is reliable.

that He was raised again from the dead as the ἀρχηγὸς τῆς ζωῆς (Ac. 3:15), that He has been made the Messiah of His people and the Lord of the whole world, and that this Ἰησοῦς ἀπὸ Ναζαρὲτ τῆς Γαλιλαίας is God's only-begotten Son and the only Saviour of all men. Ἰησοῦς ὁ Χριστός, Ἰησοῦς ὁ κύριος, is the confession of Christianity, which sees in Him who ἐν ὁμοιώματι ἀνθρώπων γενόμενος καὶ σχήματι εὑρεθεὶς ὡς ἄνθρωπος the εἰκὼν τοῦ θεοῦ τοῦ ἀοράτου (Phil. 2:7). There is no separation between an earthly body and a Christ who put on this body, as in Christian Gnosticism. Ἰησοῦς is ὁ κύριος, and not something apart from Him. Hence the Gospels, the missionary preaching of Acts and Paul (Gl. 3:1) present this Jesus of Nazareth and say that God has made this man the Lord and the Judge : ἐν ἀνδρὶ ᾧ ὥρισεν, Ac. 17:31 (D : ἐν ἀνδρὶ Ἰησοῦ).

What has been said throws light on the usage of the four Gospels and Acts. Where Mk. uses a designation — he usually speaks of Jesus in the third person — he normally has Ἰησοῦς. When he mentions Jesus for the first time in 1:9, he has the more precise Ἰησοῦς ἀπὸ Ναζαρὲτ τῆς Γαλιλαίας. [31] Mt. and Lk. follow Mk., except that Mt. uses the name much more frequently, e.g., to introduce stories or sayings, whereas Lk. often has ὁ κύριος (up to Lk. 22:61b only in the distinctive Lucan material). [32] Only in the first sentence does Mk. add Χριστός to Ἰησοῦς (cf. also Mt. 1:1). Χριστός alone instead of the name is found only at Mk. 9:41 and Mt. 11:2, perhaps deliberately in the latter case. Jn. uses Ἰησοῦς more often than Mt., and sometimes κύριος.

In Acts the simple Ἰησοῦς is common, nor is this used merely in references to the life of Jesus (1:1, 14, 16) or in the sayings of non-Christians concerning Him (4:18; 5:40; 17:7, 18; 19:13, 15; 25:19; 26:9). It is by this name that He declares Himself to Saul (9:5; 22:8; 26:15). The angels also use it at the ascension (1:11). Stephen is supposed to have said that Jesus the Nazarene would destroy this place (6:14), and Stephen also sees Jesus standing at the right hand of God (7:55).

Nevertheless, Acts clearly proclaims that Jesus is the Christ, and the addition ὁ Ναζωραῖος is sometimes made in order to point plainly to the historical figure and to show what the Jews did to this Jesus in Jerusalem, 2:22, 32, 36; 3:13, 20; 5:30; 10:38; 13:23 and 33; 17:3; 18:5, 28; cf. also 4:10; 9:27. This is how Jesus is proclaimed in Ac., 8:35; 9:20; 18:25; 28:23. But we also find expressions like εὐαγγελίζεσθαι τὸν κύριον Ἰησοῦν, 11:20; 28:31 (+ Χριστός), or on Palestinian soil τὸν Χριστὸν Ἰησοῦν, 5:42, or simply τὸν Χριστόν, 8:5, or περὶ τοῦ ὀνόματος Ἰησοῦ Χριστοῦ, 8:12, or in missionary preaching references to Ἰησοῦς Χριστός (Χριστός without art.), 9:34; 10:36; 16:18. For the simple Ἰησοῦς, cf. also 9:17. This all goes to show that in Acts the preaching of the first community and its messengers is to the effect that a specific bearer of this well-known name is the Lord, the Messiah. Where the reference is less to the content of the message, Ac. uses other phrases which derive from the usage of the community, e.g., sayings of the κύριος (11:16; 20:35); the word of the κύριος, 8:25; 12:24; 13:12, 48 f.; 15:35 f.; 19:10; to be converted to, or to believe in, the κύριος (κύριος Ἰησοῦς Χριστός). [33] In Ac. 19:4 the simple Ἰησοῦς naturally denotes this specific bearer of the name. Special reference should be made to Ac. 16:7: οὐκ εἴασεν αὐτοὺς τὸ πνεῦμα Ἰησοῦ.

---

[31] The comm. link the reference to place with ἦλθεν, but the important thing here is not that He came from Nazareth. Like Jesus, John is called Ἰωάννης ὁ βαπτίζων when he is first mentioned in Mk. (1:4).

[32] For details cf. W. Foerster, Herr ist Jesus (1924), 213, n. 1. On Jn. ibid., 219 n. 1 and 2. On the whole subject, 212 ff.; for the apocr. Gospels, 266 f. The more recently discovered Gospel in H. I. Bell and T. C. Skeat, Fragments of an Unknown Gospel, 1935, has ὁ Ἰησοῦς (v. 17, 50, 65) and ὁ κύριος (30, 37, 39) in the narrative, and διδάσκαλε Ἰησοῦ (33 and 45) as an address.

[33] Examples in Foerster, op. cit., 251, No. 17.

If Acts, like the special Lucan material, illustrates the usage of the community, for which ὁ κύριος was a sufficient designation of Jesus and Ἰησοῦς Χριστός and ὁ κύριος (ἡμῶν) Ἰησοῦς Χριστός were fixed expressions, it is still astonishing that the simple Ἰησοῦς is so rare in the NT epistles. Half of the passages in which Paul uses the simple Ἰησοῦς are to be found in 1 Th. 4:14 and 2 C. 4:11-14. The substance of these passages makes it plain that Paul is thinking especially of the historical Jesus, as the simple Ἰησοῦς itself suggests. This is also true in Phil. 2:10 : ἵνα ἐν τῷ ὀνόματι Ἰησοῦ πᾶν γόνυ κάμψῃ, to the one who has passed through the lowliness of humanity and suffering God has granted that every knee should bow at this name of humility. Similarly the death and resurrection of Jesus are at issue in most of the other passages in which Paul has the simple Ἰησοῦς, 1 Th. 4:14a; Gl. 6:17; 2 C. 4:10 a and b, 11 a and b, 14b; R. 8:11a. Ἰησοῦς is also found at 2 C. 4:5; 11:4; R. 3:26; Eph. 4:21. The second of these passages reminds us of Acts. Ἰησοῦς also occurs in Hb. and Rev. in external expression of the fact that it is the one Jesus of Nazareth whose history is the basis of Christian faith, Hb. 2:9; 3:1; 6:20; 7:22; 10:19; 12:2, 24; Rev. 1:9b; 14:12; 17:6; 20:4; 22:16.[34]

4. According to Mt. and Lk. the name יֵשׁוּעַ = Ἰησοῦς is not accidental. It is given to the child of Mary by virtue of the divine promise. Mt. 1:21 explains this as follows : καλέσεις τὸ ὄνομα αὐτοῦ Ἰησοῦν· αὐτὸς γὰρ σώσει τὸν λαὸν αὐτοῦ ἀπὸ τῶν ἁμαρτιῶν αὐτῶν. This shows that the important thing in the name יֵשׁוּעַ is the verb ישׁע.[35] On the material significance of the name as thus expounded, → σῴζω.

The full form יְהוֹשֻׁעַ is a sentence name,[36] in which the subject comes first and represents a form of the divine name יהוה, and in which the verb is a subsidiary form of the verb ישׁע which is also found in names like אֲבִישׁוּעַ, אֱלִישׁוּעַ and מַלְכִּישׁוּעַ, and which means "to help." Philo's explanation, while not wholly accurate, recognises the two parts (Mut. Nom., 121): Ἰησοῦς σωτηρία κυρίου. More exact is the interpretation in a pap. of the 3rd to 4th cent. A.D.: Ἰησοῦς Ἰω σωτηρία.[37] The Rabbis, too, were aware of the two parts of the name, Nu. r., 16 on 13:2 (Str.-B., I, 64): הושׁע is called יהושׁע (Nu. 13:6), i.e., י is added, because in view of the wickedness of the spies Moses said : י"ה יושׁיעך מן הדור הזה : The י thus indicates the tetragrammaton (or its abbreviation י"ה). The shortened form יֵשׁוּעַ no longer expresses the theophoric element clearly, directing attention simply to the verb ישׁע, cf., Sir. 46:1 with reference to Joshua : ὃς ἐγένετο κατὰ τὸ ὄνομα αὐτοῦ μέγας ἐπὶ σωτηρίᾳ ἐκλεκτῶν αὐτοῦ. Cl. Al. and Cyril[38] also link the name Ἰησοῦς with the Gk. ἰάομαι, but the scholarship of Eusebius enables him to interpret it in the light of the full Hebrew form: Ἰσουὰ μὲν γὰρ παρ' Ἑβραίοις σωτηρία, Ἰησοῦς δὲ παρὰ τοῖς αὐτοῖς Ἰωσουὲ ὀνομάζεται: Ἰωσουὲ δέ ἐστιν

---

[34] Typical of the way in which Ἰησοῦς as the proper name of a historical figure was made more precise by a geographical designation is the message which according to Just. Dial., 108 the Jews send out to their congregations in the world: ὅτι αἵρεσίς τις ἄθεος καὶ ἄνομος ἐγήγερται ἀπὸ Ἰησοῦ τινος Γαλιλαίου πλάνου.

[35] Delitzsch relates the αὐτός to God.

[36] On what follows cf. M. Noth, Die israelitischen Personennamen (1928), 16, 18, 106, 154 f. The combination of the second part of the name with ישׁע has not been uncontested, cf. E. Nestle, ThStKr, 65 (1892), 573 f.

[37] Cf. Deissmann LO, 344 f. for text and illustration.

[38] Cf. E. Nestle in DCG, I, 859-861; Cl. Al. Paed., III, 12, 98 ad loc.; Cyr. Cat. Myst., X, 13 (MPG, 33, 677): Ἰησοῦς τοίνυν ἐστὶ κατὰ μὲν Ἑβραίους σωτήρ, κατὰ δὲ τὴν Ἑλλάδα γλῶσσαν ὁ ἰώμενος.

Ἰαὼ σωτηρία, τοῦτ' ἔστιν θεοῦ σωτήριον. [39] Chrysostom [40] simply attaches to Ἰησοῦς the meaning of σωτηρία. [41]

H. Lamer believes that the Gk. Jesu is a masculine form of Ἰασώ, the goddess of salvation, for which we have the form Ἰησώ in Herond. Mim., IV, 6. [42] But assimilation to Gk. mythology in the Greek forms of Jewish names leads us into Hellenised Jewish circles, i.e., into circles which approximate culturally, socially and religiously to Hellenism, and which do not participate in the early Christian mission. In any case, the formation of Ἰησοῦς for יֵשׁוּעַ is centuries older than the Christian period. Early Christianity simply adopts the current Gk. form of the Hebrew name יֵשׁוּעַ. It does this quite naturally and with no deliberate policy of choosing related and intelligible Gk. names after the manner of small Hellenising groups.

5. The name Jesus is finally important from the standpoint of the historicity of Jesus. Those who try to contest the historical existence of the figure of Jesus as portrayed in the Gospels, and to understand the Gospels as the historicising myths of a deity, must support their thesis by showing that there is a Jewish myth of a dying and rising God, and also by producing a schema which makes the individual stories non-historically intelligible in their concrete form and succession, whether this schema be the starry heaven of Drews or the early Christian mission of Raschke. In this connection the name Jesus must also be proved to be the name of a mythological figure, and evidence must be given of a pre-Christian Jesus cult. There are no direct or unequivocal testimonies to any such cult. The most that is possible is deduction. Attention is first drawn to the OT יְהוֹשֻׁעַ, Joshua, the son of Nun, in whom an earlier period of OT research found a saga-like figure who had perhaps been invested with mythological features (Jos. 10:12). Thus for Robertson, to whom Drews appeals, [43] Joshua has characteristics of the Sun God. Furthermore, by linking Ex. 23:20-23 with Jos. 24:11, Joshua may be equated with the angel in whom is God's name, since the nations which in the one place are driven out by the angel are the same as those driven out by God through Joshua. In later Jewish tradition this angel is equated with Metatron (→ θρόνος, 164, n. 30), and in the liturgy for the New Year festival there is reference to Joshua as the prince of the presence of God. [44] From this is deduced an ancient equation of Joshua/Jesus with Metatron, [45] and Joshua is thus made the name of a mythical liberator. [46] The same mythical position of Joshua is supposedly reflected at Jd. 5 according to the reading in BA vg. Or.: ὑπομνῆσαι δὲ ὑμᾶς βούλομαι, εἰδότας ἅπαξ πάντα, ὅτι Ἰησοῦς (other readings: [ὁ] κύριος or ὁ

---

[39] Dem. Ev., IV, 17, 23.

[40] Chrys. Hom. in Mt., II, 2 (MPG, 57, 26).

[41] S. Poznanski in REJ, 54 (1907), 279 points out that in Jewish-Arabic double names יֵשׁוּעַ corresponds to the Arabic Faraǧ and the Syrian-Arabic Furqân, and according to S. Krauss, ibid., 55 (1908), 150 f. this is understood Messianically under Christian influence: Syr. פורקנא = redemption.

[42] Philol. Wochenschr., 50 (1930), 764 f. The goddess Ἰασώ is the only figure in Gk. mythology which can be brought into relation with Jesus. A. Drews suggests impossible combinations with Cadmillos on the basis of Ezr. 2:40 and with Jason and Jasios (sic!) in terms of an Aesculapius-Hermes-Jason equation, Entstehung, 105 f. and cf. Pauly-W., IX (1906), 752-777, s.v. Jasion, Jaso, Jason.

[43] J. M. Robertson, Pagan Christs² (1911), 163; Drews, Christusmythe, I, 21; cf. II, 311 f. II, 311 f.

[44] Robertson, 165, n. 4.

[45] Ibid., 163; Drews, I, 21.

[46] Robertson, 90.

θεός) λαὸν ἐκ γῆς Αἰγύπτου σώσας τὸ δεύτερον, (this is where Drews puts the comma) τοὺς μὴ πιστεύσαντας ἀπώλεσεν.[47] In Sib., V, 256-259, according to the traditional text, Joshua, ὃς ἥλιόν ποτε στῆσεν, is equated with the returning Christ, ὃς παλάμας ἥπλωσεν ἐπὶ ξύλου πολυκάρπου,[48] and Drews asks whether Enoch, Melchisedek, Noah, Joseph and Cain would all be objects of cultic worship and not Joshua.[49] But this whole line of reasoning is quite unsound. Joshua is never depicted as a mythical figure in the OT. There is no trace of a Joshua myth in later Judaism. The combining of Ex. 23:20-23 and Jos. 24:11 is an exact reproduction of the methods of Rabbinic exegesis, which takes words out of their context and uses similarities to prove similarities in the context. Without this arbitrary combination, however, the examples culled from the Jewish literature of later antiquity and the Middle Ages are irrelevant. For none of them equates Joshua with Metatron. Robertson is the one to substitute Joshua for Metatron in the passages adduced.[50] The Jude passage does not refer to Joshua. Whether we read κύριος or Ἰησοῦς, it refers to the Lord Himself active in OT history. In any case, the allusion is to the wilderness wandering rather than the entry into the promised land. The Sib. passage is disputed, and we should perhaps follow Geffcken in reading στήσει instead of στῆσεν.[51] It is quite valueless to suggest that יושע echoes יצחק, whom Abraham was to sacrifice.[52] There is no such similarity, so that this is no proof of the pre-Christian combination of a Jesus figure with the concept of sacrifice. Equally valueless is the suggestion of Drews (on the basis of Epiphanius) that the sect of the Jessaeans was perhaps named after Jesus, or His ancestor Jesse, or Isaiah, who wrote of the Suffering Servant.[53] Valueless again is the argument that, because Epiphanius once calls Jesus θεραπευτής, the Jewish society of Therapeutae or the Essenes — the connection is not very clear — worshipped their cultic god under the name of Jesus.[54] And we can raise the question whether the sorcerer Bar-jesus was the son of one of the many יושע of the time or whether he belonged to a Jesus sect[55] only if there is evidence elsewhere for the existence of such a pre-Christian sect. For Smith the reference to Apollos in Ac. 18:24-28 is highly important. If Apollos knows only the baptism of John, he knows nothing of a historical Jesus. Hence here and everywhere else the phrase used of Apollos in Ac. 18:25 : ἐδίδασκεν ἀκριβῶς τὰ περὶ τοῦ Ἰησοῦ, denotes material rather than historical instruction.[56] Goguel expressly refutes this argument and proves the very opposite.[57] Indeed, we have already seen that Ac. always uses Ἰησοῦς for the historical Jesus. The provisional aspect in the position of Apollos is precisely his limited knowledge of the historical Jesus.

---

[47] Drews, II, 306 f.; *Entstehung*, 108 ff.
[48] Drews, II, 307.
[49] *Ibid.*, 312.
[50] On Metatron, *v.* G. F. Moore in *The Harvard Theological Review*, 15 (1922), 62-85. Metatron is not linked with Joshua in the Metatron speculations of Hb. En. (Windisch).
[51] In his edition of the Sib. (1902), ad loc., with a reference to the par. in Lactant. Str.-B., I, 12 f., who is followed by Volz Esch., 57, refers the passage in its original form to a Joshua who will return as the Messiah, but this would be highly singular.
[52] Robertson, 162.
[53] Drews, I, 21; II, 302.
[54] *Ibid.*, I, 21.
[55] Smith, 17 f.
[56] *Ibid.*, 1 ff.
[57] 70 ff.

This negative demonstration must be supplemented by positive exposition. For later Judaism the period of the Exodus, along with the figure of Abraham, was the central point in world history. The reception of the Law by the people of Israel brought a return of the age of Paradise. This is not restricted to the actual giving of the Law; it embraces the whole Exodus. The coming age of salvation is depicted in the colours of the Exodus period. The period of the entry into the land, however, does not share in this glory, though the technical term for possession, נחל or ירש, → κληρονομεῖν, is also used for inheritance of eternal life. The future inheritance of the land is not depicted in terms of the entry under Joshua. Hence Joshua is not a prototype of the Messiah in later Judaism. Naturally, later Judaism does not ignore Joshua. He is one of the righteous heroes of the history of Israel. He is a meritorious figure. But for the Rabbis only a few aspects of his story are significant, as in the case of many other OT characters. [58]

In the NT the giving of the Law is no longer the crucial point in world history. For Paul it is an interim act between the commencement of salvation history with Abraham and its completion in Jesus Christ. Thus the period of the Exodus no longer has the glory of Paradise on the basis of reception of the Law. But the events of the Exodus are still important as written for us, 1 C. 10:1 ff.; Hb. 11:27 ff.; Rev. 15:2-4. Also written for us is the story of Joshua. That is to say, it is written to show the power of faith, Hb. 11:30 f. But the OT events here retain their historical place and singularity. The same is true in Hb. 3:7-4:13 and Hb. 4:8, where Joshua is mentioned. Here the entry into the promised land ought to have brought fulfilment of the divine promises. What is emphasised, however, is that history did not bring about this fulfilment. The figure of Joshua is mentioned with no typological implications. Similarly, Ac. 7:45 refers to him only incidentally. The fact that the story of Joshua is so little mentioned in the NT is not due to the accidental nature of surviving early Christian documents. It is due to the fact that Joshua does not occupy a decisive place either in later Judaism or in the NT understanding of salvation history. Apologists like Barnabas (12, 7) and Justin (Dial., 75; 113, 2-4; 132) [59] could not fail to see the LXX equation of the names Joshua and Jesus, but even here there is no continuous chain of understanding to support the conjecture of a pre-Christian Joshua-Jesus cult.

We are on theoretically possible ground only when we come to the reference to Jesus in the so-called Naassene Psalm [60] and to the frequent occurrence of the name Jesus in some magic papyri. For the Naassenes make use of a pre-Christian legacy, and there are many ancient things in the magic papyri. In the great Paris magic papyrus we find the words: ὁρκίζω σε κατὰ τοῦ θεοῦ τῶν Ἑβραίων 'Ιησοῦ, [61] and in another place, in a Coptic magic papyrus, we find the address: "God of Abraham, God of Isaac, God of Jacob, Jesus Christos, Holy Spirit, Son of the Father ..." [62] Elsewhere we find 'Ιησοῦς ἄνουι, [63] and also ['Ιησοῦ]ς,

---

[58] 1 Macc. 2:55; 2 Macc. 12:15; Sir. 46:1; Pesikt. r., 11 (ZNW, 32 [1933] 38); bSukka, 28a; for Samaritan eschatology, cf. Volz Esch., 176.

[59] For the later period, v. Wnd. Barn. on 12, 7.

[60] Hipp. Ref., V, 10, 2.

[61] Preis. Zaub., IV, 3019 f.

[62] Ibid., 1231 f.

[63] Ibid., XII, 192. Not 'Ιησοῦς "Ανου[βις], as A. Dieterich reads, Jbch. f. class. Philol. Suppl., 16 (1888), 805. Cf. W. W. Baudissin, Kyrios als Gottesname, II (1929), 120.

᾽Ιησοῦς, ᾽Ιησοῦς ΑΩ ᾽Αδωναί ᾽Ελωαί ᾽Ελωέ. [64] If these texts were pre-Christian, they would point to a pre-Christian cult of Jesus. The first and last would also equate Jesus with the God of the OT, and in virtue of the concluding formula — φύλασσε καθαρός· ὁ γὰρ λόγος ἐστὶν ῾Εβραϊκὸς καὶ φυλασσόμενος παρὰ καθαροῖς ἀνδράσιν — [65] Drews concurs with A. Dieterich in ascribing the first directly to the Therapeutae or related circles, [66] though there is no evidence whatever for this. Indeed, the texts all belong to a later period, [67] and they show what an impression Christian faith in Jesus Christ made on the surrounding world, and yet how external this impression was, since the authors of these magic texts are concerned only to find magically powerful names which they can bend to their own arbitrary purposes.

At root the attempt to prove a pre-Christian Jesus sect depends upon making speculative combinations in two spheres in which the sources are most obscure, namely, the history of Jewish sects and the history of magic texts. Such combinations are possible only because they are constructed in an empty and dark place. No substantial evidence is adduced in support of a pre-Christian Jesus cult. We have only to note how the people use the name Jesus in the Gospels, or how the Gospels and Acts speak of Jesus without further addition (→ 288), and we find natural and by no means conscious or intentional support for the historicity of Jesus of Nazareth.

Foerster

> ἱκανός, † ἱκανότης,
> † ἱκανόω

ἱκανός, from the root ἱκ- (ἵκω, ἱκνέομαι, ἱκόμην), "to reach (with the hand)," "to attain" (Walde-Pok., II, 465), has been variously used from the time of the tragic dramatists in the basic sense of "adequate," "sufficient," "enough" or "large enough." NT usage corresponds to the secular. [1] Hence the word is used to indicate a large group of people (e.g., Mk. 10:46: ὄχλου ἱκανοῦ, cf. Mt. 20:29: ὄχλος πολύς), or to describe a longish period of time (e.g., Lk. 8:27: χρόνῳ ἱκανῷ), or to denote a quality (Mt. 3:11 and par.). The statistics are interesting. Of the 40 occurrences of ἱκανός in the NT, 3 are in Mt., 3 in Mk., 6 in Pl. (also 2 Tm. 2:2), 27 in the Lucan writings, and none in the Catholic Epistles, Hb. or the Johannine literature. This distribution shows that it is a typical Hellenistic word in the NT, and this is supported by the fact that in Lk., as in the non-biblical writings of the time, it does not usually have any particular emphasis. In this respect Josephus offers some good parallels to Luke; cf. [2] Ap., 1, 237: ὡς χρόνος ἱκανὸς διῆλθεν, with Ac. 27:9: ἱκανοῦ δὲ χρόνου διαγενομένου; Ant., 9, 45: κατέ-

---

[64] *Ibid.*, II, p. 199.
[65] *Ibid.*, IV, 3084 f.
[66] *Christusmythe*, II, 304 f.; A. Dieterich, *Abraxas* (1891), 143 ff.; cf. Mithr. Liturg., 44 f.
[67] Preis. Zaub., IV belongs to the first half of the 4th cent. A.D.

ἱ κ α ν ό ς. A. Schlatter, "Die beiden Schwerter Lukas 22:35-38" in BFTh, 20, 6 (1916).
[1] Cf. the examples in Pr.-Bauer, *s.v.*
[2] According to Schl. Lk.

λιπε δὲ καὶ παῖδας ἱκανούς, with Ac. 11:26 : διδάξαι ὄχλον ἱκανόν; Ant., 14, 231: προσκαλεσάμενος ... ἱκανοὺς τῶν πολιτῶν, with Ac. 19:19 : ἱκανοὶ τῶν τὰ περίεργα πραξάντων. On the other hand, neither Jos. nor Luke has the designation of God as ὁ ἱκανός, which is often the LXX rendering of שַׁדַּי.[3] At this point, however, the two differ in the sense that Jos. makes a concession to the philosophical religion[4] of his non-Jewish readers by calling God (τὸ θεῖον) ἀπροσδεὲς ἀπάντων (Ant., 8, 111),[5] whereas in Luke, or in his source, emphasis is placed upon the fact that God wills men, that He seeks after them, that He does His work on them, just because He is God and as such the Creator (cf. Lk. 2:14; 20:38 etc.). On Rabb. exegesis of שׁדּי, → I, 467, αὐτάρκης.

As used in the NT the word group is of theological significance in the following passages.

1. At Mt. 3:11 the Baptist says with reference to Him who is to come : ὁ δὲ ὀπίσω μου ἐρχόμενος ἰσχυρότερός μού ἐστιν, οὗ οὐκ εἰμὶ ἱκανὸς τὰ ὑποδήματα βαστάσαι. Here the οὐκ εἰμὶ ἱκανός[6] is designed to measure John by Christ and His greatness, and to show that his authority is only that of service to Christ. The office which John discharges is comparable with that of a slave who takes his master's shoes, or unties his shoelaces (Mk.; Lk.), and who thereby shows that he is a slave.[7] Thus the Baptist is neither the independent precursor of Christ, nor His fellow, nor Christ in person, but the servant of Christ who simply does what he is under obligation to do. The saying also contains an impressive confession that He who is to come is the absolute κύριος. For if even the Baptist, who offers the people forgiveness of sins in the name of God, is yet a servant of this Other, how can the rest, whether sinners (→ ἁμαρτωλός) or righteous (→ δίκαιος), raise any kind of claim before Him?

If this οὐκ εἰμὶ ἱκανός implies confidence that God will act beyond all human measure in His Anointed, in Mt. 8:8; Lk. 7:6 it denotes the impression made by the person of Jesus upon the Gentile centurion. When this man says with reference to Jesus : οὐκ εἰμὶ ἱκανὸς ἵνα μου ὑπὸ τὴν στέγην εἰσέλθῃς (Mt.), he is not thinking of the ritual uncleanness which Jesus as a Jew would incur by entering a non-Jewish house. What he has in view is the majesty and authority of Jesus which lift Him above everything human, especially in the non-Jewish sphere. This is expressed supremely in the way in which he goes on to speak of his own authority and of the ἐξουσία of Jesus (Mt. 8:9). On the lips of the centurion the οὐκ εἰμὶ ἱκανός is thus a confession of the Messiahship of Jesus. This is how Jesus

---

[3] Cf. Ἰωβ 21:15; 31:2; 40:2; Ἰεζ. 1:24 ΑΣ; Ju. 1:20, 21, and many passages from Aquila, Symmachus and Theodotion. The transl. was partly influenced by דַּי (שׁדי was divided into דַּי + שׁ, → I, 467), which resembles שַׁדַּי and which finds its Gk. equivalent in ἱκανός, as attested by the LXX. But it was also influenced by the desire of the translator to express God's independence of man and absolute transcendence.

[4] For material from Euripides to Stoicism, cf. E. Norden, Agnostos Theos (1913), 13 f.

[5] Material par. from Philo in Schl. Theol. d. Judt., 5, n. 2. ἱκανός also occurs in this sense in Philo : ἱκανὸς αὐτὸς ἑαυτῷ ὁ θεός (Leg. All., I, 44; Mut. Nom., 46; cf. Cher., 46; Mut. Nom., 27).

[6] Linguistically there are Rabb. par. for the formula in אֵינִי כְדַאי or אֵינִי כְדַי; cf. the passages in Str.-B., II, 217. But cf. also Εξ. 4:10, where Moses says to God : οὐχ ἱκανός εἰμι ...· ἰσχνόφωνος καὶ βραδύγλωσσος ἐγώ εἰμι. This is an interpretation rather than a translation of the original.

[7] Cf. the Rabb. passages in Str.-B., I, 121.

Himself understands it, and He thus grants to the centurion what He always grants where there is faith in Him : ὕπαγε, ὡς ἐπίστευσας γενηθήτω σοι.

Paul's attitude is the same as that of the centurion when he says of himself in 1 C. 15:9 : οὐκ εἰμὶ ἱκανὸς καλεῖσθαι ἀπόστολος. The only difference is that he is measuring himself by the exalted Lord who has sovereignly called him to be His plenipotentiary (→ ἀπόστολος, I, 437). The words imply that he has no qualifications of his own for this office. There here applies to him as the ἀπόστολος ἐθνῶν (R. 11:13) that which is of more general application in 2 C. 2:16 : καὶ πρὸς ταῦτα τίς ἱκανός. If this is certain, it is also certain that God's mercy (1 C. 7:25; 2 C. 4:1), trust (Gl. 2:7; 2 Th. 1:10) and grace (1 C. 15:10) have made of the persecutor of the community a witness who labours more than all the rest on His behalf. Confession of personal incapacity is thus accompanied by confession of God as the basis of all personal capacity : ἡ ἱκανότης ἡμῶν ἐκ τοῦ θεοῦ, ὃς καὶ ἱκάνωσεν ἡμᾶς διακόνους καινῆς διαθήκης (2 C. 3:5 f.; cf. Col. 1:12), and by praise of His χάρις (1 C. 15:10) which can set its powerful affirmation above all human incapacity.

2. In the story of the passion Lk. (22:39 ff.) alone records a saying of Jesus to His disciples concerning the coming emergency (22:35 ff.). In this saying He counsels them to buy swords (v. 36). When they produce two swords, He answers : ἱκανόν ἐστιν. This answer is not very clear [8] in the context, [9] and various explanations have been offered. Does He mean that two swords are adequate for what is ahead ? [10] Or does His saying imply censure rather than reassurance, i.e., that His disciples have completely misunderstood Him, that they have construed the metaphor of v. 36 as a command, and that they have met it by producing two swords ? Even if we take this view, there are still three possible interpretations, since the censure can be related either to the general incomprehension of the disciples, to their particular misunderstanding in this case, or to their folly in relying, not merely on the two swords which they have produced, but on weapons of any kind, i.e., on their own power. In the first case, Jesus breaks off the discussion as useless [11] (cf. Dt. 3:26 : ἱκανούσθω σοι, μὴ προσθῇς ἔτι λαλῆσαι τὸν λόγον τοῦτον); [12] the only difficulty is that we lack the necessary linguistic support for this view. [13] The second possibility imparts an ironic tone to the saying: This is more than enough = satis superque, with the implication that two swords are absurdly inadequate in the present situation. But this raises the difficulty that there is no irony in the parables, [14] and that Jesus always takes seriously even those who resist Him in

---

[8] The OT usage at Gn. 30:15; 1 K. 16:31; Ez. 34:18 is different, and is thus of no help. Nor are we helped by extra-biblical quotations like the otherwise very interesting Epict. Diss., I, 2, 36 : Ἐπίκτητος κρείσσων Σωκράτου οὐκ ἔσται· εἰ δὲ μή, οὐ χείρων, τοῦτό μοι ἱκανόν ἐστιν (cf. H. Windisch, Paulus und Christus [1934], 50).

[9] Doubt has been raised as to the integrity of the passage, cf. Kl. Lk., ad loc.

[10] So B. Weiss and J. Weiss, Die Evangelien des Mk. u. Lk. = Meyer⁸ (1892), ad loc., and also D it, which read ἀρκεῖ for ἱκανόν ἐστιν.

[11] So Chrysostom, ad loc.; v. Cramer Cat., II, 159.

[12] Cf. also 3 Βασ. 19:4; Ιεζ. 45:9.

[13] The OT term רַב־לָךְ (Dt. 3:26) or רַב־לָכֶם (Ez. 45:9), which is greatly stressed by A. Merx, Die vier kanonischen Evangelien, II, 2 (1905), 455, ad loc., is no more an exact parallel of the absolute ἱκανόν ἐστιν than the usual רַי with suffix (ibid., 455 f.).

[14] This may be seen most clearly from the way in which Jesus not only deals with the righteous but also speaks concerning them to His listeners (→ I, 330 and the bibl. in n. 95; → also II, 189).

order to be able to help them to a right relationship to God and to right conduct. We are thus left with the third possibility, namely, that the ἱκανόν ἐστιν is designed to shake the naive self-confidence of the disciples and to free them from hoping in the sword.[15] That this is how the Evangelist himself probably understood the saying is perhaps suggested by the fact that immediately prior to this scene he places the saying to Peter which warns him of a severe impending πειρασμός and which points him to the patience and intercession of Jesus alone for preservation (22:31 ff.). The two swords are really enough for Jesus; He does not need any other weapons. But when He who knows His situation says this, He hereby reveals the patience with which He both goes to death and also suffers the misplaced love and loyalty of His disciples. The swords are not forbidden, for they play their part in the arrest (22:49 ff. par.). But He tries to make it clear to those who own them that their calculations are erroneous. What takes place in Gethsemane[16] is a significant ending to the discussion of the swords in the hands of the disciples. It shows that in spite of the readiness of His disciples to intervene, Jesus must tread His divinely appointed path alone, since none of those who have been under His teaching has yet learned to orientate his own will to the will of God.[17] Yet the ἱκανόν ἐστιν tells us that His fellowship with them continues even when they break off their fellowship with Him.

The bull *Unam Sanctam* (Boniface VIII, 1302) appeals to this passage. It sees in the two swords the spiritual and temporal powers, and on the basis of the saying of Jesus to Peter it argues that these powers are united in the vicar of Christ. It need hardly be said that there is no exegetical basis for this theory, which goes back to Gregory VII.

Rengstorf

┌─────────────┐
│ † ἱκετηρία │
└─────────────┘

ἱκετήριος derives from ἱκτήριος, which itself derives from ἱκτήρ, "he who asks for protection" (both words are attested in the dramatists). Under the influence of the par. ἱκέτης,[1] ἱκτήριος changed its form to ἱκετήριος.[2] ἱκτήρ, ἱκέτης (from ἵκω [cf. ἱκνέομαι] "to come") means a "stranger" ("new-comer") who, pursued for a fault, esp. blood-guiltiness, sought help or protection by casting himself down at the altar or hearth of a strange house, in order that through the law of hospitality he might win back what he had lost in his own land. An olive-branch, which he bore in his right hand,

---

[15] Schlatter, *op. cit.*, 72.

[16] Other signs of the great patience of Jesus are the saying ἐᾶτε ἕως τούτου (v. 51) and tne healing of the wounded servant of the high-priest.

[17] Cf. the quotation of Is. 53:12 by Jesus (Lk. 22:37).

ἱ κ ε τ η ρ ί α. Pape, Pr.-Bauer, Preisigke Wört., Moult.-Mill., Cr.-Kö., *s.v.* ἱκετηρία.

[1] Cf. ἱκετία (-εία), which is used in the LXX and in the Rheneia prayers for vengeance (Deissmann LO⁴, 351 ff.). Cf. also E. Schlesinger, *Die griech. Asylie* (Diss. Giessen, 1933), esp. 32 ff., 38 ff. on the judicial aspects of ἱκετεία.

[2] E. Fraenkel, *Gesch. d. gr. Nomina agentis auf* -τηρ, -τωρ, -της, I (1910), 52 f.

marked him off as such. [3] ἱκετηρία, to which we should add ῥάβδος or ἐλαία, is the feminine of a denominative adj. used to denote this request for protection. [4] Since the olive-branch symbolises the request, ἱκετηρία can also be used for the request, and then more generally for urgent supplication to men and gods. So Isoc., 8, 138 : πολλὰς ἱκετηρίας καὶ δεήσεις ποιούμενοι; cf. Polyb., [5] Philo. [6] But ἱκετηρία can still have the specific meaning of seeking protection, [7] and it can even be used for the olive branch carried by those who seek it. [8]

At Hb. 5:7 it is said of the Son of God that He offered to God δεήσεις καὶ ἱκετηρίας. Here we can hardly insist on the original sense of ἱκετηρία. δεήσεις τε καὶ ἱκετηρίας is a traditional phrase [9] which helps to show that Hb. is written in the cultivated language of educated circles.

Büchsel

---

† ἱλαρός, † ἱλαρότης

1. In both classical and later Gk. (also pap.) ἱλαρός means "glad," "merry," "cheerful." The word can be used of daylight (φέγγος, Aristoph. Ra., 455), songs (ᾄσματα, Athen., XV, 53, p. 697d, III, 544, 18, Kaibel), ἐλπίς (Kritias in Diels, II, 315, 11), a message (Ephesus inscr., *Jahreshefte d. österr. arch. Inst.*, 23 [1926], 283), but esp. men. ἱλαρός is a physiognomic characteristic; the antonym is σκυθρωπός (Xenoph. Mem., II, 7, 12; Ps.-Aristot. Physiognomica, 4, p. 808b, 16), but also μεμψίμοιρος (Theophr. Char., 17, 9); along with ἱλαρῶς βλέπειν (Anth. Pal., XII, 159, 6) we find ῥᾳδίως καὶ ἱλαρῶς φέρειν (Plut. Ages., II, 3 [I, p. 596e]). ἱλαρός is linked with εὔελπις and εὔθυμος in Xenoph. Ag., 8, 2, and the rarer ἱλαρότης with τὸ εὔθυμον in Plut. Ages., II, 4 (I, 596 f.) and with εὐφροσύνη (at the symposium) in Alciphr. Ep., 3, 7 vl. (p. 65). According to Plut. Tranq. An., 19 (II, 477b) the ἐνέργεια of a pure soul is ἐνθουσιώδης καὶ ἱλαρά. ἱλαρός is a predicate of the deity in the hymn to Demetrius Poliorketes as God, Athen., VI, 63, p. 253d (II, 65, 21, Kaibel): ὁ δ᾽ ἱλαρός, ὥσπερ τὸν θεὸν δεῖ. [1]

---

[3] P. Stengel, *Griech. Kultusaltertümer*³ (1920), 30, 80, 244.

[4] Aesch. Suppl., 191-196: ἀλλ᾽ ὡς τάχιστα βᾶτε καὶ λευκοστεφεῖς | ἱκτηρίας, ἀγάλματ᾽ αἰδοίου Διός, | σεμνῶς ἔχουσαι διὰ χερῶν εὐωνύμων, | αἰδοῖα καὶ γοεδνὰ καὶ ζαχρεῖ᾽ ἔπη | ξένους ἀμείβεσθ᾽, ὡς ἐπήλυδας πρέπει, | τορῶς λέγουσαι τάσδ᾽ ἀναιμάκτους φυγάς. For other examples cf. Pape.

[5] 2, 6, 1: δεόμενοι μεθ᾽ ἱκετηρίας ...; 3, 112, 8 : εὐχαὶ καὶ θυσίαι καὶ θεῶν ἱκετηρίαι καὶ δεήσεις ἐπεῖχον τὴν πόλιν.

[6] Leg.Gaj., 228 : προσπίπτουσιν εἰς ἔδαφος ὀλολυγὴν θρηνώδη τινὰ μεθ᾽ ἱκετηριῶν ἀφιεῖσαι.

[7] Jos. Bell., 5, 317-321: συνυπεκρίνοντο τὴν ἱκετηρίαν; 318: ὡς ἱκετεύων; 319 : ἱκέτας; cf. also 7, 203. Cf. also Schl. Theol. d. Judt., 113.

[8] Philo Leg. Gaj., 276 : γραφὴ δὲ μηνύσει μου τὴν δέησιν, ἣν ἀνθ᾽ ἱκετηρίας προτείνω.

[9] Isoc., 8, 138. Job 40:27: λαλήσει δέ σοι δεήσει, ἱκετηρίᾳ μαλακῶς. Also Philo Cher., 47: χωρὶς ἱκετείας καὶ δεήσεως.

ἱ λ α ρ ό ς κτλ. Nägeli, 65 f.

[1] → I, 660; cf. also P. Friedländer in *Die Antike,* 10 (1934), 209 ff. In the cosmogony of the Paris magic pap. (XIII, 186 or 507 f.) we read of the creating God : ἐκάκχασε (he laughed) ... καὶ ἱλαρύνθη πολύ.

In later usage ἱλαρός is influenced by ἵλεως and can have the sense of "benevolent." [2] In magic the deity is invoked: ἐλθέ μοι ἱλαρῷ τῷ προσώπῳ (Preis. Zaub., III, 575), and ἱλαρός is linked with εὐμενής and πραΰς or with πρόθυμος (ibid., IV, 1042; XIII, 608). P. Oxy., XI, 1380, 127 speaks of the ἱλαρὰ ὄψις of Isis in this sense. [3] It is open to question whether this shift of meaning can be explained merely by external influences. May there not be a sense of the inner connection between cheerfulness and benevolence? There is a hint of this in Cornut. Theol. Graec., 15 (p. 20, 5 ff., Lang), where the reason for the derivation of the name Χάριτες from χαρά is given as follows: ἱλαρῶς δὲ εὐεργετεῖν δέοντος καὶ ἱλαροὺς ποιουσῶν τοὺς εὐεργετουμένους τῶν Χαρίτων...

2. In the LXX ἱλαρός is never an attribute of God. It is often used of the πρόσωπον, Job 33:26 (vl.); Est. 5:1b; Sir. 13:26; 26:4 (in the first two and the last with no Heb. equivalent; at Sir. 13:26 for פָּנִים אוֹרִים). The meaning is "cheerful," though "favourable" at Job 33:26. This corresponds to the older Gk. usage, as does ἱλαρῶς εἰς τὸν οὐρανὸν ἀναβλέπειν at Job 22:26 (no Heb.) and ἱλαρῶς διεξάγειν at Ep. Ar., 182 (opp. δυσχεραίνειν). Cf. 3 Macc. 6:35 (ἐν ἐξομολογήσεσιν ἱλαραῖς καὶ ψαλμοῖς); Test. Jos. 8:5 (ἐν ἱλαρᾷ φωνῇ δοξάζων τὸν θεόν, vl. ἐν ἱλαρότητι φωνῆς). At Prv. 19:12 τὸ ἱλαρόν is used for רָצוֹן (the favour of the king), and we read in Prv. 22:8: ἄνδρα ἱλαρὸν καὶ δότην εὐλογεῖ ὁ θεός; ἱλαρός is here a rendering of the טוֹב־עַיִן of Heb. v. 9. Hence ἱλαρός has the sense of "kindly disposed." At Prv. 18:22 ἱλαρότης is used for רָצוֹן, but the reference is to man's ἱλαρότης rather than God's, as in the Heb. The meaning seems to be "cheerfulness," as in Test. N. 9:2 (φαγὼν καὶ πιὼν ἐν ἱλαρότητι ψυχῆς); Test. Jos. 8:5 vl. (→ supra). Once in the Ps. (ψ 103:15 for צָהַל hi) and more often in Sir. (and elsewhere in Σ) ἱλαρύνειν or ἱλαροῦν is used in the sense of "to make radiant or merry," Sir. 7:24; 35:8 (32:11) for אוֹר hi; 36:22(27) for הלל hi; 43:22 for דשׁן. Except at Sir. 43:22, πρόσωπον is always the object. Ep. Ar., 108 uses ἱλαροῦσθαι (τὸ κατὰ ψυχήν) in the sense of "to be glad or cheerful."

In the OT the "kindly eye" is not a physiognomic characteristic. It is a term for outgoing benevolence. Hence the combination of the two senses of ἱλαρός rests on the insight that a cheerful countenance reflects a kind heart. This may be seen from Sir. 35:8 (32:11), where the ἱλαροῦν literally means "to make radiant or cheerful," but where the admonition to do all things with a cheerful countenance is accompanied by an appeal for generosity (v. 7 and 9: ἐν ἀγαθῷ ὀφθαλμῷ: v. 7 is missing in the Heb.; v. 9: בְּטוֹב עַיִן). Similarly the gracious glance of the king is ἱλαρὸν πρόσωπον at Ep. Ar., 18. The Rabbis especially emphasise the connection between generosity and cheerfulness: "He who gives alms, let him do so with a cheerful heart." [4]

In Philo ἱλαρός usually means "cheerful" and ἱλαρότης "cheerfulness." The word is used of the κίνησις of dogs (Praem. Poen., 89), of βίος (Spec. Leg., II, 48), δίαιτα (Leg. Gaj., 83), διαγωγαί (Vit. Cont., 40), ἄνεσις (Vit. Cont., 58), more frequently εὐθυμία(ι) (Som., II, 144; Jos., 245; Spec. Leg., II, 43; Flacc., 118; Congr., 161: ἱλαραὶ εὐφροσύναι καὶ εὐθυμίαι; Vit. Mos., II, 211 and Spec. Leg., I, 69: ἐν ἱλαραῖς διάγειν εὐθυμίαις. Cf. I, 134: ἱλαρώτερον τρυφᾶν. This cheerfulness characterises the symposium (Vit. Cont., 40 and 58) and feasts in general (Congr., 161; Som., II, 167; Vit. Mos., II, 211; Spec. Leg., I, 69; Jos., 204: ἱλαρότητα γὰρ ἐπιζητοῦσιν εὐωχίαι, σεμνὸν ἄγαν καὶ αὐστηρὸν συμπότην ἥκιστα προσδεχόμεναι). For this reason ἱλαρότης is also a characteristic of the sage, whose λογισμός: μεθίεται εἰς ἀνέσεως καὶ εὐθυμίας καὶ ἱλαρότητος ἀπόλαυσιν (Plant., 166). For ὅτι οὐ σκυθρωπὸν καὶ

---

[2] Probably there is also an etymological connection between ἱλαρός and ἵλεως; root sel- "favourably disposed." Boisacq, s.v.; Walde-Pok., II, 506 f.

[3] For further material cf. Nägeli and the lexicons.

[4] Lv. r., 34 on 25:39; Str.-B., III, 296; cf. Str.-B., I, 459 on Mt. 7:9; III, 524 on 2 C. 9:7.

αὐστηρὸν τὸ τῆς σοφίας εἶδος, ὑπὸ συννοίας καὶ κατηφείας ἐσταλμένον, ἀλλ' ἔμπαλιν ἱλαρὸν καὶ γαληνίζον, μεστὸν γηθοσύνης καὶ χαρᾶς (Plant., 167).[5]

As Vit. Cont., 77 speaks of the ἱλαρότης of the countenance, so ἱλαρός is an attribute of ὄψεις at Virt., 67: ἱλαραῖς ὄψεσιν ἐκ τῆς κατὰ ψυχὴν εὐθυμίας φαιδρὸς καὶ γεγηθώς. That it may here take on the sense of "benevolent" may be seen from Leg. Gaj., 12 : εὐμένειαν ἐξ ἱλαρᾶς τῆς ὄψεως προφαίνοντες; cf. 180 : τῷ δοκεῖν φαιδρῷ τῷ βλέμματι καὶ ἱλαρωτέραις ταῖς προσρήσεσι. Only once does ἱλαρός occur in the specifically Jewish sense as an attribute of μεταδόσεις, Spec. Leg., IV, 74.

3. At 2 C. 9:7 Paul quotes loosely from Prv. 22:9 : ἱλαρὸν γὰρ δότην ἀγαπᾷ ὁ θεός. Unlike the LXX, he makes ἱλαρός an attribute of δότης. It thus has the sense of "cheerful," as ἱλαρότης obviously means "cheerfulness" at R. 12:8 (ὁ ἐλεῶν ἐν ἱλαρότητι). In both passages the freedom and authenticity of generous giving are marked by the symptom of cheerfulness. ἱλαρότης almost has the sense of ἁπλότης (→ I, 387), which is used alongside it at R. 12:8 (ὁ μεταδιδοὺς ἐν ἁπλότητι) and which is elsewhere regarded as the true mark of benevolence. This cheerfulness is contrasted with the γογγυσμοί (→ I, 736) and διαλογισμοί (Phil. 2:14) which destroy the unity of the act and falsify it.

Cf. the admonition of 1 Pt. 4:9 : φιλόξενοι εἰς ἀλλήλους ἄνευ γογγυσμοῦ. Similarly we have γογγυστής alongside μεμψίμοιρος at Jd. 16, → 297.

Judaism and the Gentile world, as well as Christianity, believe that cheerfulness belongs to the inner freedom of generosity (→ 298 and cf. Sen. Ben., II, 1 f.; 7, 1).[6] What is Christian is not the thought itself but the new motivation suggested by the context in R. 12:8 (cf. 12:1 ff.) and 2 C. 9:7 (cf. 8:9; 9:8 ff.) and expressly stated in 1 Pt. 4:9 f. Reception of the gift of God makes us cheerful and drives out γογγυσμός.

4. Of the post-apostolic fathers only Hermas has ἱλαρός and ἱλαρότης, but he uses them frequently. Nature is described as ἱλαρός (the πρόσοψις of a mountain, s., 9, 1, 10, a τόπος, s., 9, 10, 3, βοτάναι, s., 9, 1, 8; 24, 1, sheep, s., 6, 1, 6; 2, 3);[7] the countenance of a man (v., 1, 2, 3, opp. στυγνός and κατηφής) especially heavenly figures (v., 1, 4, 3; 3, 10, 4 f. etc.),[8] cf. the ʿΙλαρότης of a personified virtue (s., 9, 15, 2); also the disposition (v., 3, 3, 1; 9, 10; s., 9, 2, 4, combined with πρόθυμος, → 298 etc.).[9] If m., 12, 4, 2 (ἤρξατό μοι ἐπιεικέστερον < καὶ ἱλαρώτερον > λαλεῖν) is largely Greek, the Jewish tradition may be seen elsewhere. Generosity is a λειτουργία which is καλὴ καὶ ἱλαρά; according to s., 1, 10 it is a prodigality which is καλὴ καὶ ἱλαρά (MS ἱερά), λύπην μὴ ἔχουσα μηδὲ φόβον, ἔχουσα δὲ χαράν. Obviously under Gk. influence, the significance of cheerfulness is broadened. As the ἐντολαί are described as ἱλαραί, s., 6, 1, 1, so in the σεμνότης linked with ἁπλότης, v., 3, 9, 1: πάντα ὁμαλά καὶ ἱλαρά, m., 2, 4.[10] According to m., 5, 2, 3 μακροθυμία is ἱλαρὰ καὶ ἀγαλλιωμένη. Μ., 10, 3 deals specifically with ἱλαρότης, as distinct from λύπη.

---

[5] This is the more remarkable because according to the ancient view the philosopher is σκυθρωπός and is marked by σεμνότης, though → 297.

[6] Wnd. 2 C. on 2 C. 9:7.

[7] This is not the earlier Gk. usage, but it is typical of the Hellenistic novel, which had much influence on Hermas.

[8] Cf. Act. Joh., 88 (II, 1, p. 194, 16): John sees Jesus as ἄνδρα εὔμορφον καλὸν ἱλαρόπρόσωπον.

[9] Cf. Act. Thom., 14 (p. 12, 18): ἐν ἱλαρότητι (vl. : ἱλαρίᾳ) καὶ χαρᾷ ὑπάρχω. Passio Bartholomaei, 2 (Act. II, 1, p. 132, 18 f.): πάντοτε τὸ πρόσωπον αὐτοῦ καὶ ἡ ψυχὴ καὶ ἡ καρδία ἱλαρύνεται καὶ ἀγάλλεται.

[10] Here, then, σεμνότης with ἱλαρός, → n. 5.

If in § 1, along the lines of Jewish tradition, we have : πᾶς γὰρ ἱλαρὸς ἀνὴρ ἀγαθὰ ἐργάζεται καὶ ἀγαθὰ φρονεῖ καὶ καταφρονεῖ τῆς λύπης, in §§ 2-4 we find the rather different view [11] that λύπη is incompatible with the Holy Spirit, and that the λυπηρός cannot pray. But : πάντες ζήσονται τῷ θεῷ, ὅσοι ἂν ἀποβάλωσιν ἀφ' ἑαυτῶν τὴν λύπην καὶ ἐνδύσωνται πᾶσαν ἱλαρότητα.

Bultmann

ἵλεως, ἱλάσκομαι, ἱλασμός, ἱλαστήριον

† ἵλεως.

ἵλεως is the Attic form [1] of ἵλαος, which is common from the time of Homer. ἵλεως-ἵλαος is related in stem and meaning to → ἱλαρός, "cheerful." It is a predicate of persons, men and gods, originally "happy," cf. Plat. Symp., 206d : ὅταν μὲν καλῷ προσπελάζῃ τὸ κυοῦν, ἵλεων τε γίγνεται καὶ εὐφραινόμενον διαχεῖται ... ὅταν δὲ αἰσχρῷ, σκυθρωπόν τε καὶ λυπούμενον ..., and Leg., I, 649a, where it is said of wine, in relation to him who drinks it, that it ποιεῖ ... ἵλεων. Hence ἵλεως comes to mean "friendly," "gracious," "favourable." It is often combined with εὐμενής, e.g., Xenoph. Cyrop., I, 6, 2; II, 1, 1; III, 3, 21; Plat. Phaed., 257a; Leg., IV, 712b; Jos. Ant., 5, 213; common in Philo, e.g., Jos., 104; Plant., 171; Spec. Leg., III, 193; Vit. Mos., II (III), 238. It is preferably used of those of high estate, especially rulers or gods. [2] To make the gods gracious (ἵλεω ποιεῖν) is one of the tasks of the cultus, Plat. Leg., X, 910a.

In the LXX ἵλεως is used only as a predicate of God. It is used in phrases like ἵλεως γίγνεσθαι, ἵλεως εἶναι, which are mostly used for סָלַח, "to forgive," or occasionally נָחַם, "to accept hurt," כִּפֶּר‎, נָשָׂא, "to forgive," רָחַם "to have pity on." ἵλεων ποιεῖν and similar phrases do not occur. The LXX also uses ἵλεως for the emphatic rejection חָלִילָה and for the greeting שָׁלוֹם, Gn. 43:23. The expression ἵλεως ... is elliptic ; we need to supply εἴη ὁ κύριός σοι (μοι). [3] Hence the LXX substitutes a religious

---

[11] There seems to be reflected here a Hellenistic tradition, perhaps of Persian origin, → λύπη ; cf. Dib. Herm. on m., 10, 1, 1.

ἵ λ ε ω ς. Cr.-Kö., *s.v.*; Kl. Mt.; Str.-B., Schl. Mt. on 16:22.

[1] Liddell-Scott also has examples of ἵλεος, ἵληƒος, ἵλλαος. On the derivation, cf. Boisacq, 372, and Walde-Pok., II, 506. In the NT ἵλεως is the only instance of the 2nd Attic declension, which dies out in popular Hellenistic speech, Bl.-Debr.⁶, § 44, 1.

[2] As is known, Hellenism speaks a great deal about the goodness of deity, and is the root of over-emphasis on this point. That it could influence Judaism here is strikingly shown by Ep. Ar., 254 : God rules the whole world with favour, not with wrath.

[3] In favour of this cf. the use of the optative μὴ γένοιτο elsewhere in the LXX for the Heb. חָלִילָה (Jos. 24:16), and the corresponding conjunctive *absit a te* in the Vulgate. Schl. Mt., *ad loc.* supplies an indicative : "God is gracious to thee." He is right inasmuch as the expression is now a fixed formula of rejection or negative protestation, so that the element of wishing is no longer present. The Targums all translate חָלִילָה by חַס : 'holding off," "sparing." In Rabb. writings we also find the stereotyped חַס וְשָׁלוֹם "God forbid"; cf. Str.-B., I, 748.

formula for the non-religious Heb. ῐλεως σοι (μοι) with the names of gods is also found in pagan Gk. in invocations, petitions and greetings, [4] though there are no examples of its use in refusals or negative protestations. [5] Probably this type of use arose through adaptation of pagan greetings in Hellenistic Judaism. The suppression of the divine name favours this view. [6] ῐλεως is common in Philo, predominantly as a predicate of God, Exsecr., 163, or of His δύναμις, Spec. Leg., I, 229, Vit. Mos., II (III), 96 and 132, ἀρετή, Vit. Mos., II (III), 189, φύσις, Spec. Leg., II, 196. This is natural inasmuch as benevolence is a basic feature in Philo's view of God. ῐλεως can also be used for God's grace towards the sinner, Leg. All., III, 174; Spec. Leg., I, 242. Philo can call God the μόνος ῐλεως, Som., I, 90. ῐλεως is also a predicate of God in Jos, cf. Ant., 4, 222 etc.

It occurs in the NT only in the quotation from Jer. 31:34 at Hb. 8:12 : ῐλεως ἔσομαι ταῖς ἀδικίαις αὐτῶν, and in the negative protestation at Mt. 16:22. The almost complete absence of ῐλεως in the NT corresponds to the sparseness of ἱλάσκομαι, ἱλασμός and ἱλαστήριον.

Büchsel

† ἱλάσκομαι, † ἱλασμός.

Contents : A. Expiation and Forms of Expiation in the OT : 1. כִּפֶּר in the LXX ; 2. The Meaning of the Root כפר ; 3. כִּפֶּר and כֹּפֶר ; 4. The Use of כִּפֶּר outside the Priestly Document ; 5. The Use of כִּפֶּר in the Priestly Document and in Related Parts of the Old Testament ; 6. Conclusion. B. ἱλασμός and καθαρμός in the Greek World. C. Ideas of Expiation in Judaism : 1. Rabbinic Judaism ; 2. Hellenistic Judaism. D. ἱλάσκομαι. E. ἱλασμός.

---

[4] Cf. Bl.-Debr.[6] § 128, 5, also Kl. Mt. on 16:22, with bibl.

[5] J. H. Moulton in Class. Rev., 15 (1901), 436, shows clearly that the passages adduced for ῐλεως σοι ... (A. J. Letronne, *Recueil des Inscriptions Grecques et Latines de l'Égypte*, II [1848], 286, 221 etc.) do not display "the deprecatory use in the biblical passages," and this is the decisive point which is only too often disregarded. That pagan Greek, like other languages, might have developed a formula of rejection or negative protestation out of expressions of religious desire is incontestable, but so far no one has proved that it actually did.

[6] The Heb. חָלִילָה and the Aram. חַס cannot be rendered literally, and Jews who moved from Aram. or Heb. to Gk. would not wish to abandon this emphatic form of expression. This is how the Jewish Greek formula arose out of the existing pagan formula.

ἱ λ ά σ κ ο μ α ι κ τ λ. On A.: J. Herrmann, *Die Idee der Sühne im AT* (1905), with bibl. up to 1905 ; N. Messel, "Die Komposition von Lv. 16," ZAW, 27 (1907), 1 ff.; C. v. Orelli, "Versöhnungstag," RE³, XX (1908), 576-582 ; O. Kirn, "Versöhnung," RE³, XX (1908), 554-556; W. Schrank, *Babylonische Sühneriten* = *Leipziger semitistische Studien*, III, 1 (1908); A. Bertholet, *Biblische Theologie des AT*, II (1911), 30-44; E. Kautzsch, *Biblische Theologie des AT* (1911), 345-347; P. Volz, *Die Biblischen Altertümer*² (1914), 124-143; E. König, *Theologie des AT* (1922), 301-309; S. Landersdorfer, *Studien zum biblischen Versöhnungstag* (1924); M. Löhr, *Das Ritual von Lv. 16* = *Schriften der Königsberger Gelehrten Gesellschaft, geisteswissenschaftl. Klasse* 2. Jahr, Heft 1 (1925); G. B. Gray, *Sacrifice in the OT* (1925); D. Schötz, *Schuld- und Sündopfer im AT* = *Breslauer Studien zur historischen Theologie*, 18 (1930); A. Bertholet, "Entsündigung," RGG, II, 171-174; "Opfer," I, RGG, IV, 704-711; O. Eissfeldt, "Opfer," II, A, RGG, IV, 711-717; A. Bertholet, "Sühne," RGG, V, 873-875; H. Gunkel, "Sünde und Schuld," II, A, RGG, V, 881; A. Bertholet, "Versöhnung," I, RGG, V, 1558-1559; O. Procksch, "Versöhnung," II, A, RGG, V, 1559-1561; J. Hänel, *Die Religion der Heiligkeit* (1931), 298-300; S. Landersdorfer, "Keilinschriftliche Parallelen zum biblischen Sündenbock" in BZ, 19 (1931), 20; W. Eichrodt, *Theologie des AT,* I (1933), 74-80; H. H. B. Ayles, "The OT Doctrine of the Atonement" in *Interpreter*, 14 (1917/18), 206-209. On B : P. Stengel, *Die griech. Kultusaltertümer*³ (1920); O. Kern, *Die Religion der Griechen*, I (1926); II (1935); M. P. Nilsson in Bertholet-Leh. (1925), II; K. Latte, "Schuld und Sünde in der griech. Religion," ARW, 20 (1921), 254 ff. On C : Weber, 313-335 (partly out of date); Str.-B. on the passages mentioned in

A. Expiation and Forms of Expiation in the Old Testament.

1. כָּפֶּר in the LXX.

The proper Heb. verb for "to expiate" is כפר. The predominant LXX translation is ἐξιλάσκομαι (83 times out of 100). This includes almost all the passages in which כפר is a cultic term in P (Lv. and Nu.) and in other priestly writings, Ez. 40-48, Neh. and Ch. In the few passages in which another word is used it is either by way of variation or because of the peculiar content of the passage, as at Ex. 29:33, 36 ἁγιάζω, Ex. 29:37; Ex. 30:10 καθαρίζω. In the three passages in which we find כפר in the surviving Heb. of Sir. it is rendered ἐξιλάσκομαι (3:30; 45:16, 23). Of the other 6 occurrences of ἐξιλάσκομαι in Sir. the original probably had כפר in at least two passages (3:3; 20:28). In the circles which produced the Alexandrian translation כפר was thus predominantly coupled with ἐξιλάσκομαι. Where there is non-cultic use, ἱλάσκομαι occurs three times (Ps. 65:3; 78:38; 79:9) and ἵλεως γίγνομαι once (Dt. 21:8). In the remaining 8 passages the LXX renders the non-cultic כפר, by ἐκκαθαρίζω, Dt. 32:43; περικαθαρίζω (Is. 6:7); καθαρὸς γίγνομαι (Is. 47:11, inaccurately); ἀφίημι (Is. 22:14); ἀθῳόω ("to leave unpunished," Jer. 18:23); and finally ἀφαιρέω ("to take away," Is. 27:9); ἀποκαθαίρω ("to wash away," Prv. 16:6); ἀπαλείφω ("to wash away," Da. 9:24). The last three bring us to the question of the basic meaning of כפר, which they alone of all the 100 indicate.

2. The Meaning of the Root כפר

"The question of the etymological meaning of the Hebrew root כפר is obscure." We must accept this judgment of Robertson Smith, [1] since the various Semitic analogies do not permit us to make a definitive distinction between "to cover" and "to wash away." There are Semitic analogies for regarding forgiveness of sins both in terms of covering and in terms of washing away. [2]

In Heb. Gn. 32:21 seems to incline in favour of "to cover," [3] especially if we are justified in appealing to Gn. 20:16; Job 9:24. "To wash away" can certainly be ruled out. Yet it may be asked whether the sense of "to propitiate" does not fit the context. The cultic term kuppuru in the expiation ritual of Babylon has a similar sound to כפר, and it yields the sense, not of "to cover," but of "to wash," "to set aside," "to cancel." [4] Of the derivatives כִּפֻּרִים does not help, since it derives from the technical כפר. It should be emphasised that the same is true of כַּפֹּרֶת, which does not mean "cover." On the other hand, כֹּפֶר testifies in favour of "to cover," and it is of such significance in relation to the meaning of כפר that one is inclined to take it as the starting-point of investigation. All in all, the solution of the problem is perhaps that the root leaves etymological play for both "to cover" and "to wash away." [5]

---

the Index, IV, 1264; J. Köberle, *Sünde und Gnade* (1905), 592 ff.; Bousset-Gressm., 404 ff.; W. Wichmann, *Die Leidenstheologie, eine Form der Leidensdeutung im Spätjudentum* = BWANT, IV, 2 (1930); K. G. Kuhn in ZNW, 32 (1931), 305 ff. On D and E: Cr.-Kö., s.v.; Rgg. Hb.², 61, n. 59; Helbing, *Kasussyntax,* 213 ff.; C. H. Dodd, "ἱλάσκεσθαι, Its Cognates, Derivates and Synonyms in the Septuagint," JThSt, 33 (1930), 31, 128, 352 f.

[1] Robertson Smith, *The Old Testament in the Jewish Church.*
[2] *Loc. cit.*
[3] Cf. J. Wellhausen, *Die Composition des Hexateuch*³ (1899), 336-338.
[4] W. Schrank, *op. cit.* 86.
[5] Cf. Ges.-Buhl, *s.v.*; also J. Herrmann.

3. כֹּפֶר and כִּפֶּר.

Many students rightly assume that there is a close connection between כפר and כֹּפֶר.[6] כֹּפֶר does not have its seat in cultic life. It denotes a material expiation by which injury is made good and the injured party is reconciled, i.e., by which the hurt is covered and the guilty party is released from obligation.

Thus the Book of the Covenant (Ex. 21:30) lays down that a man whose ox has gored another through the negligence of the owner shall have laid on him a כֹּפֶר instead of the death penalty, and that he shall pay this as a פִּדְיֹן, i.e., a "ransom," for his life (נֶפֶשׁ). The LXX has τὰ λύτρα for both words. פִּדְיֹן occurs only here and at Ps. 49:8 in this sense, and in the latter passage it is parallel to כֹּפֶר.[7] פִּדוּיִם has the same meaning at Nu. 3:46, 48, 49, 51; 18:16 (LXX: τὰ λύτρα).[8] פִּדוּיִם denotes release by payment, or ransom for the lives of the firstborn which are claimed by Yahweh. At Nu. 35:31, 32 כֹּפֶר is the ransom for the life (נֶפֶשׁ)[9] of the murderer. According to Ex. 30:12 every numbered Israelite must pay כֹּפֶר נַפְשׁוֹ (LXX: λύτρα τῆς ψυχῆς αὐτοῦ) lest plague fall upon him, i.e., lest his life be forfeit. This payment is also called כֶּסֶף הַכִּפֻּרִים, since it is paid to make expiation (כפר) for the life of the Israelites. כֹּפֶר is again a ransom for the life of man at Job 33:24 and 36:18,[10] and also at Prv. 13:8; 6:35; 21:18. In the last verse, and also in Is. 43:3, 4, the idea of substitution is plainly coupled with כֹּפֶר; Egypt and the neighbouring kingdoms serve as a substitutionary ransom[11] (כֹּפֶר, LXX ἄλλαγμα) for Israel. It is expressly stated in v. 4 that what is meant is life for life. At 1 S. 12:3 the aged Samuel bears witness that he has taken no כֹּפֶר (LXX: ἐξίλασμα). Here the context leaves it uncertain whether he means an expiatory ransom for a forfeited life, but there is nothing to rule out this view.[12] The same is true in Am. 5:12 (LXX: ἀνταλλάγματα).

Investigation of כֹּפֶר thus leads us to an almost unanimous conclusion.

4. The Use of כִּפֶּר outside the Priestly Document.

a. We now turn to the non-cultic use of כִּפֶּר, i.e., the use outside P, with which we have also grouped Ez. 40-48, Neh. and Ch.

At Is. 47:11 כפר means "to pay" כֹּפֶר, "to raise a כֹּפֶר," "to avert by כֹּפֶר." It is a parallel of < שׁחד > ("to raise or to avert by שֹׁחַד"), to which it seems to be related as

---

[6] Herrmann, 38-43.

[7] LXX: ἐξίλασμα αὐτοῦ for כָּפְרוֹ, τιμὴ τῆς λυτρώσεως τῆς ψυχῆς αὐτοῦ for פִּדְיֹן נַפְשָׁם.

[8] Or פִּדְיֹם at Nu. 3:49, פדים at Nu. 3:51 K.

[9] LXX: λύτρα περὶ ψυχῆς.

[10] In both cases the text is uncertain, cf. the comm.

[11] F. Delitzsch, Jesaja⁴ (1889), ad loc.

[12] For MT וְאַעֲלִים עֵינַי בּוֹ the LXX (BA[L]) and Vetus Latina read וְנַעֲלַיִם עֲנוּ בִי, a text for which there is also attestation in the Heb. original of Sir. 46:19. If with K. Budde, Die Bücher Samuel (1902), ad loc.; R. Kittel in Kautzsch, ad loc.; W. Caspari, Die Samuelbücher (1926), ad loc., we keep to the Mas., the כֹּפֶר would be taken to conceal his eyes (from the transgression). But A. Schulz, Die Bücher Samuel, I (1919), ad loc., finds good reasons for accepting the LXX, for which there are parallels at Am. 2:6; 8:6; Gn. 14:23; he points out particularly that the expression in the MT is used in a different sense in passages like Lv. 20:4; Ez. 22:26; Prv. 28:27. R. Kittel in BHK³ (Liber Samuelis, 1933) now regards the LXX as fortasse recte.

שַׁחַד to שָׁחֵד. [13] What is at issue is the averting of complete destruction. At Gn. 32:20 Jacob tries to ward off what he fears to be threatened destruction at the hands of Esau [14] by making costly presents: אֲכַפְּרָה פָנָיו בַּמִּנְחָה (LXX: ἐξιλάσομαι). This can hardly mean "to cover his face," since he says goes on to say: "And afterward I will see his face." Its meaning is "to propitiate," "to make him friendly." At Prv. 16:14 כפר means to appease the destructive wrath of a king (LXX: ἐξιλάσεται). According to 2 S. 21:3 blood-guiltiness rests on the house of Saul because he slew the Gibeonites. Since no payment is possible (v. 4), David makes atonement (כפר בְּ) by slaying seven men of the house of Saul. Slaying expiates slaying. [15] According to Dt. 32:43 the enemies of Israel have defiled the land by shedding blood in it; Yahweh cleanses the land by destroying these enemies (v. 41, 42). According to Dt. 21:8 the innocent blood of a man anonymously slain is to be purged from the midst of the people by the killing (not the offering) of a heifer with accompanying washings and prayers. Prayer is made to Yahweh that He will grant expiation to the people (כפר לְ), and assurance is given that the blood will be regarded as expiated (נְכַפֵּר לְ). [16] There can be no doubt that this expiation is by substitution. At Ex. 32:30 Moses desires to make atonement for (בְּעַד) the sin of his people by offering, if necessary, his own life on behalf of the guilty who are threatened by destruction. At Is. 6:7 the sin of Isaiah is purged by an extraordinary rite; the result is that he need not be afraid of dying because he has seen the holy God. At Prv. 16:6 guilt can be expiated by חֶסֶד and אֱמֶת, so that men depart from evil. [17] When God is the subject, כפר takes on the sense "to make expiation," "to grant expiation or remission," "to forgive." Hence Jeremiah prays for the destruction of his enemies: "Forgive not their iniquity, neither blot out their sin from my sight" (18:23). [18] The result is that his enemies will be destroyed. Ps. 78:38 gives thanks that the merciful God is accustomed to expiate guilt (par. "to withdraw his anger"), i.e., not to destroy. At Ps. 65:3 our guilt is stronger than we are, and He purges it. In these passages the sense is almost "to forgive," as at Is. 22:14 in the passive and at Ez. 16:63 with a different construction. [19]

When we survey the material, it is evident that כפר involves expiation for life. Blood-guiltiness is expiated by the substitution of human life (2 S. 21:3; Dt. 32:43; Ex. 32:30) or animal life (Dt. 21:8). The destruction which threatens because of guilt is averted by expiatory gifts (Is. 47:11; Gn. 32:20). The wise man can appease the wrath of the king with its threat of death (Prv. 16:14). It is possible to expiate guilt by goodness and faithfulness and thus to escape destruction (Prv. 16:6). If God does not atone, if He does not make or grant expiation, if He does not forgive, the sinful man must die (Jer. 18:23; Is. 22:14). If God atones, man lives (Ps. 78:38) and is saved (Ps. 79:9). Only in the vision at the call of Isaiah is this (life-sustaining) expiation effected by a ceremonial act in the cultic sphere

---

[13] So K. Marti (Das Buch Js. [1900], ad loc.), who refers to Hdt., I, 105. Cf. שַׁחַד at Job 6:22: "to raise a שָׁחֵד." Prv. 6:35: כֹּפֶר par. of שֹׁחַד.

[14] Gn. 27:41-45; 32:9, 12.

[15] Herrmann, 45, 46.

[16] On the form cf. H. Bauer and P. Leander, Historische Grammatik des Hebräischen, I (1922), § 38s, 283.

[17] F. Delitzsch, Das salomonische Spruchbuch (1873), ad loc.

[18] The same sentence occurs word for word at Neh. 3:37, except that we have תְּכַס for תְּכַפֵּר (in terms of which the כפר על of Jer. 18:23 might mean "to cover something"!) and תִּמָּחֶה for תֶּמְחִי.

[19] Is. 27:9 can be left out of account, since the text and context are uncertain. So, too, can Da. 9:24, where the subject of כפר is doubtful. At Is. 28:18 כפר is due to textual corruption, cf. O. Procksch, Jesaja, I (1930), 361.

(Is. 6:7). This is extraordinary and symbolical, but it does indicate the possibility of cultic expiation.

b. We have refrained from mentioning one passage which undoubtedly shows that the possibility of atoning for guilt by sacrifice must have been very old, namely, 1 S. 3:14. The sons of Eli have committed such serious offences against God (2:17, 25) that God Himself declares that there can be no expiation by sacrifice. Except in this passage, כפר is never the result of sacrifice outside the priestly writings. It is naturally perceived, of course, that sacrifice is pleasing and acceptable to God, and that it is thus calculated to propitiate. Hence we find at 1 S. 26:19 the firm statement that when God is unfriendly the savour of sacrifice will propitiate Him. The element of expiation seems to be lacking here, since this isolated primitive statement provides no motive for the wrath of the deity. Gn. 8:20 ff. is to be understood along the same lines. Here it is said that God is propitiated when He smells the "savour of pacification" [20] (רֵיחַ הַנִּיחֹחַ) from the burnt offering, and that He gives a promise which rules out a second flood. But the context makes it clear that this is not expiation, and so, too, does the expression ריח הניחח (or ריח ניחח), which occurs 43 times, but which is never used in relation to כפר or to the sin and guilt offerings, [21] except once in a secondary and figurative sense. [22] One might also refer to 2 S. 24:25, where we read that, when God is angered by the census, He accepts prayer on behalf of the people, and the plague is stayed, after David built an altar and offered burnt offerings and peace offerings. It should be noted, however, that David is ordered to do this by the prophet Gad (24:17 ff.).

That sacrifices were offered quite early with a view to expiation is proved beyond question by 1 S. 3:14. The ordinary sacrifices זֶבַח and מִנְחָה (or עֹלָה and שְׁלָמִים at 2 S. 24:25) are used for this.

5. The Use of כִּפֶּר in the Priestly Document and in Related Parts of the Old Testament.

a. As we now turn to the use of כִּפֶּר in P, we shall first consider those passages which display closest similarity to the use of כֹּפֶּר and of כפר outside P. This will help us in the further course of our enquiry.

We have already had to consider Ex. 30:15, 16 under the כֹּפֶר passages (→ 303). Alongside this we may set Nu. 31:48-54, where the returning officers, who had to number the people, bring with them an oblation (קָרְבָּן) of gold jewels, chains etc. "to make an atonement for (עַל) our souls." In connection with כֹּפֶר as expiation for the life of the murderer (→ 303) we should mention Nu. 35:33, 34; acceptance of כֹּפֶר for the life of the murderer is refused on the significant ground : "Ye shall not pollute the land wherein ye are : for blood it defileth the land : and there can be no expiation for the land on account of the blood that is shed therein, but by the blood of him that shed it." Here it is plainly stated that expiation can be made only by blood for blood. In Nu. 25 the wrath of God is kindled against Israel because of the transgression with Baal Peor. Phinehas and his companions thrust through the guilty Israelites. "Then the

---

[20] This is how we are to construe ניחח.

[21] The burnt offerings, עֹלָה, מִנְחָה and שְׁלָמִים, contribute to ריח ניחח.

[22] Lv. 4:31. What is said about the fat of the שְׁלָמִים offering at Lv. 3:5 is transferred to the sin offering, as the text itself shows.

plague was stayed from the children of Israel." Phinehas acted according to the word of Yahweh, and consequently the wrath of God which had sent the plague and which threatened the people with destruction was turned away from them. Through the godly zeal of Phinehas expiation was made for (עַל) the Israelites (vv. 11-13). Here the atoning act of Phinehas averted the annihilating wrath of God and life was preserved. In Nu. 17:6-15 the destructive wrath of God is again kindled, and the plague has begun. At the command of Moses, Aaron carries a censer of incense from the altar among the people; through the incense atonement is made for (עַל) the people, and the plague is arrested.

These P passages suggest that even the cultic and sacrificial expiation found in P may be coupled with the views which we have found in relation to כֹּפֶר and כִּפֶּר outside P.

b. About three quarters of all the occurrences of כִּפֶּר are in connection with specific sacrifices prescribed by P. The word is here an established term along with חטא, "to free from sin," טהר pi, "to purge," קדש, "to sanctify or consecrate." It seems to be used interchangeably with these words, though it naturally preserves its distinctive meaning, and the other words are not exact equivalents. When we ask what is effected by כִּפֶּר, and how it is effected, the problem is complicated by the fact that the need for expiation continually expands, so that the usage becomes loose and imprecise. There can be no doubt, however, that expiation is linked with the manipulation of blood. This blood is the blood of animals. In particular, although not exclusively, there are two specific offerings, of which the one, אָשָׁם, is much less prominent than the other, חַטָּאת. This must be our starting-point.

Prior to P (or Ez. 40-48) there are no sacrifices of this name, though אָשָׁם and חַטָּאת are used in another sense in connection with the cultus. In the decrees of Joash concerning the administration of the temple revenues (2 K. 12:17) we read that the אָשָׁם money and the חַטָּאת money are not to be put with the rest, but belong to the priests. So far as can be seen, אָשָׁם and חַטָּאת seem to be here expiatory payments to the sanctuary for אָשָׁם ("guilt") and חַטָּאת ("sin"), though it is not clear what the offences were which could be expiated in this way. That expiation is involved is proved in the case of אָשָׁם by 1 S. 6. Here the Philistines are returning the ark, and they are advised by their priests and seers to send with it a costly אָשָׁם as compensation (הֵשִׁיב), i.e., to make reparation, and indeed to offer an expiatory gift, which will appease the divine anger and arrest the plague which God has sent among them. For the linguistic and material development of the expression we may also refer to the P passage Nu. 5:6-8, which seems to be supplementary to the law of guilt offering in Lv. 5:20-26, but which gives evidence of representing an earlier stage. When a man is guilty of fraud (מַעַל) against Yahweh (by fraud against his neighbour, Lv. 5:21), he incurs guilt (אשם). The fraud is his guilt (אשם), and he must clear it by paying the principal (הֵשִׁיב) and an extra fifth, which is to be given to the one whom he has defrauded (אשם). Only at the end (v. 8), and almost incidentally, do we find a reference to the אָשָׁם ram. "whereby an atonement shall be made for him (כפר)." This gives us a clear glimpse into the history of אָשָׁם as a guilt offering. Earlier, as may be seen from 2 K. 12:17, אָשָׁם payments were made, and only later was a special אָשָׁם offering added by way of expiation. In 2 K. 12:17 חַטָּאתas well as אָשָׁם payments are made to the temple or to the priests, and we may thus assume that a similar development took place in the case of חַטָּאת. Only gradually did a clear distinction come to be made between אָשָׁם and חַטָּאת. This may be seen in Lv. 5:1-6. Here the one who is guilty (אשם) of certain offences must confess his fault (as in Nu. 5:7) and then bring his אָשָׁם to Yahweh on account of the sin, a female of the flock, a lamb or a kid of the goats, for a חַטָּאת, and the priest shall make expiation for him in respect of his sin. Here, and in Lv. 5:17-19, it does not seem that אָשָׁם is an independent offering alongside חַטָּאת. Only later is the חַטָּאת offering which is brought for אָשָׁם also called אָשָׁם. Certainly חַטָּאת remains much more important than אָשָׁם, since it is compendiously said of חַטָּאת at Lv. 10:17 that Yahweh has given it "to take away (לָשֵׂאת) guilt and to make atonement for (עַל) your sin before Yahweh."

At this point we may legitimately adduce the well-known text Lv. 17:11. The strict prohibition of eating blood (v. 10) is here supported as follows: "For the נֶפֶשׁ of the flesh is in the blood, [23] and I have given it to you for (עַל) the altar to make atonement for your souls. For the blood it is that makes atonement through (בְּ) the נֶפֶשׁ." Here expiation is made with the blood that Yahweh has given for the altar, and this is brought about by the fact that in the blood is the נֶפֶשׁ, the soul or the life. We shall now see whether our individual findings concerning cultic expiation in P support these statements in Lv. 17:11.

    c. In the fourfold ritual of the sin-offering in Lv. 4 (for the priest, the congregation, the prince and the ordinary Israelite) the climax of the action is incontestably the manipulation of the blood of the sin offering by the priest (the sevenfold sprinkling before the veil of the sanctuary, the sprinkling on the horns of the altar, and the pouring out of the rest of the blood at the foot of the altar), and the burning of the fat upon the altar. It is here that we find the statements concerning the purpose and result of the sacrifice: "and the priest shall make an atonement for him, and it shall be forgiven him" (vv. 20, 26, 31, 35). In the supplement concerning the sin offerings of the poor (Lv. 5:7-13) the mere offering of flour in expiation is sufficient for the very poor (11-13), but here the life has gone out of the ritual and all that remains is the observance of a priestly action which makes expiation because it is ordained by God. Manipulation of blood is also found in the ritual of the trespass offering (Lv. 7:1 ff.), though here it is less complicated. In the law of guilt offering in Lv. 5:14-16, 20-26 the repayment of six fifths of the estimated damage, which originally constitutes the אָשָׁם, is subordinated in time (v. 15) to the offering. The priest makes expiation for the guilty party (אשׁם) through the sacrificial lamb or kid of the goats, and he is thus forgiven. Both the sin offering and the trespass offering are most holy. They are thus surrounded by strict taboos, as may be seen in the supplementary regulations in Lv. 6:17 ff.; 7:1 ff.

Apart from these rituals and the supplementary regulations, tradition has brought down to us several rituals of consecration in which the sin offering plays an important role. Ex. 29 gives us the ritual of priestly consecration. After the purification, investiture and anointing, this includes a threefold offering: the sin offering with manipulation of blood at the altar; the burnt offering with a simpler manipulation; and the offering of institution with manipulation of blood both on the altar and on the one who is being consecrated. It is worth noting that there is no reference to כפר in the ritual itself. Only in supplementary notes do we read that expiation is made by the consecration offerings (v. 33) and that the consecration, which lasts seven days, must be accompanied by a seven-day purification (חטא) and consecration (קדשׁ) of the altar where atonement is made by sin offerings (v. 36 f.). Lv. 8 tells us, with additions, how Ex. 28 and 29 were carried out. Here the consecration of the altar by atoning action is incorporated into the ritual. Here, too, there is a concluding reference to the seven-day offerings of priestly consecration. Appended to this chapter (Lv. 9) is a description of the first solemn act of sacrificial worship. Expiation is here said to be the purpose and result of the sin offerings and burnt offerings (v. 7). The same is true at Nu. 8:5-22, where sin offerings

---

[23] Cf. Dt. 12:23; Gn. 9:4.

and burnt offerings are brought to make atonement for the Levites (who are themselves the sacrificial gift of the people to God), to cleanse and purify them, in order that they may fulfil their ministry. [24]

It is in keeping that the description of the ritual of burnt offering in Lv. 1 tells us that the purpose and result of the offering of the bullock (v. 4) is atonement. If we do not find a similar statement in respect of the smaller offerings of sheep or doves, if we are not told that these, too, are a sweet savour to Yahweh, this is surely accidental. In all three forms there is manipulation of blood. This is equally true of the peace offerings (שְׁלָמִים); if there is no reference to expiation in the threefold ritual of Lv. 3 this is probably because the peace offerings are of subsidiary importance and value in P. [25] From what has been said, it is only natural that there should be no mention of expiation in the ritual of meal offerings in Lv. 2.

Sin offerings are sacrificed at purification as well as consecration. In Lv. 12 we have burnt offerings and sin offerings after child birth. Atonement is made for the mother that she may be clean again. Similarly there are purificatory offerings in Lv. 15:2-15 for those with an issue of flesh, in Lv. 15:25-30 for those with an issue of blood, and in Nu. 6:9-12 for Nazirites who become unclean through contact with a dead body. The ritual for the purification of lepers is very complicated, Lv. 14. In addition to purificatory rites with the blood of birds (vv. 10-32), a threefold offering is required: first (and strangely) אָשָׁם with manipulation of blood and oil; then חַטָּאת; and finally עֹלָה with מִנְחָה. All three have an atoning purpose. No true sacrifice is offered according to the curious law of leprosy in houses, Lv. 14:33-53, but there is a rite of purification with the blood of birds whereby the house is cleansed (חִטֵּא) and expiation is made. It is evident that very different religious motives are expressed in these rituals. In the present tradition these have been combined with the concept of expiation.

The concepts of purification, cleansing and consecration are all found in the ritual of the great Day of Atonement (Lv. 16).

We cannot attempt a literary analysis of this complicated passage. [26] As in other rituals, burnt offerings are brought as well as sin offerings; it is quite evident, however, that expiation is here linked with the sin offerings. It is also more evident here than elsewhere that the true rites of expiation are the manipulations of the blood of the sin offering, which are here to be seen in their richest and most varied form. On the one hand Aaron is to make atonement for himself and his house (vv. 6, 11, 17); on the other hand he is to make atonement for the congregation of Israel (vv. 5, 17). But he is also to make atonement for the inner sanctuary "because of the uncleanness of the children of Israel, and because of their transgression in all their sins." Similarly, he is to make atonement for the tent of revelation and for the altar. Manipulation of blood is now of supreme importance. Whereas the blood is in other rituals sprinkled before the veil of the sanctuary, it is here brought into the sanctuary and sprinkled upon the mercy seat and seven times before it. Together with the offerings and manipulations we also have in vv. 21 ff. the strange action in relation to the second of the two goats which are required for the congregation. This is not sacrificed. It is driven into the wilderness to Azazel, where it is to carry all the transgressions of the whole congregation according

---

[24] In this account there is an interjection (vv. 16-19; cf. Nu. 3:11-13) to the effect that the ministry of Levites in the tabernacle is designed to make atonement for Israel lest it should be smitten by plague. Cf. also, though without כפר, Nu. 1:53; 18:5 ("that there be no wrath any more upon the children of Israel"). כפר is here added to these passages.

[25] V. P. Volz, Die biblischen Altertümer[2] (1925), 122 f. This is expressed already in the fact that females of the flock may be used.

[26] This is a subject of much debate, cf. Herrmann, Sühne, 89-91.

to the preceding ceremony of transferral. There is a parallel to this in Lv. 14:7, 53. But this rite is not the true act of expiation, which is completed in v. 20. [27] Supplementary statements in conclusion emphasise once again that "on that day shall the priest make an atonement for you, to cleanse you, that you may be clean from all your sins before Yahweh" (vv. 30, 34). The day is called the day of atonement (יוֹם הַכִּפֻּרִים) in the law of feasts in Lv. 23 (vv. 26 ff.); cf. also, though without the name, Nu. 28 and 29. We are told again in Ex. 30:10 that expiation is made with the blood of the חַטַּאת הַכִּפֻּרִים. In Ez. 40-48 the regulations for feasts and sacrifices (45:18-25) include a purification of the sanctuary, and this involves sprinkling of blood, though it is to take place twice a year.

The material on cultic expiation in Ez. 40-48 has been left to the last because many recent Ezekiel scholars doubt its authenticity. [28] The sin offerings laid down by P seem to be known here already. The ritual for the consecration of the altar in Ez. 43:18-27 seems to build on the ritual legislation of P. [29] When Ez. 45:13 ff. states that atonement is the purpose and result of all the cultic actions of the people or the prince, including the meat offerings and meal offerings (15, 17), this goes much further than the sacrificial ritual of Lv. 1 ff. On the other hand, the requirement of two days of atonement in the calendar of Ez. 45:18 ff. might well be older than the demand for a single day of atonement in Lv. 16. In the present state of research, we can hardly make any authoritative use of Ez. 40-48 in tracing the history of cultic expiation. [30]

How strongly the idea of expiation permeated the whole cultus may be seen not only from the fact that the great Day of Atonement has come to have such overwhelming significance amongst the Israelite feasts but also from the fact that in the calendar of sacrifices in Nu. 28 and 29, which is supplementary to the calendar of feasts in Lv. 23, the expiatory sin offering (Nu. 28:22, 30; 29:5) is now offered along with the burnt offering, not just at the daily and Sabbath offerings, but at all others. [31] The goat which is here demanded is also one of the sacrificial offerings of each of the twelve princes in Nu. 7. Twelve goats are also offered as sin offerings at the dedication of the temple in Ezr. 6:17, and they are also among the offerings of the returned exiles in Ezr. 8:35. At 1 Ch. 6:49 one of the tasks of the priests is as follows: "Aaron and his sons offered upon the altar of the burnt offering and on the altar of incense, for all the work of the Most Holy, and to make an atonement for Israel." [32]

Reviewing the laws of sin offering, we see that there can be expiation and forgiveness for all transgressions of the commandments of Yahweh (Lv. 4:2; Nu. 15:22 ff.) or for all injuries caused by offences (Lv. 5:16) as long as the offence is committed בִּשְׁגָגָה. The reference (cf. the meaning and use of the verb שָׁגָה, "to go astray," → I, 274) is to faults committed unintentionally and unwittingly. The distinction is brought out clearly in Nu. 15:30. Sins committed בְּיָד רָמָה, with deliberately evil intent (→ I, 280), cannot be expiated by sin offerings; they demand extirpation from the people. This makes it plain that what is in view applies only to the community and to offences within it. In the laws of sin offerings as we have them it is quite possible to make atonement and to procure forgiveness for all sins which are not wifully committed with evil intent. Our findings do not

---

[27] This seems to be contradicted by v. 10, but the לכפר עליו there is unintelligible in the light of 21 ff. and is most likely an addition.

[28] From the time of J. Herrmann, *Ezechielstudien* (1908).

[29] J. Herrmann, *Ezechiel* (1924), 279.

[30] For details v. Herrmann, *Sühne*, 61 ff.; *Ezechiel*, XXXI ff. and *ad loc.*

[31] Nu. 28:15, 22, 30; 29:5, 11, 16, 19, 22, 25, 28, 31, 34, 38.

[32] A literal translation; the construction is loose.

enable us to say how broad the sphere of such sins is; we are certainly not justified in restricting it to the cultic field.

In P the idea of expiation is also coupled with the consecration and purification of both persons and objects. The connecting point is that what is unclean, or what makes unclean, is in need of atonement.

6. Conclusion.

When we assemble all the material on cultic expiation in P, it is easy to discern a single religious concern. In the community of Yahweh nothing which needs expiation is to be left unexpiated. Through cultic ordinances Yahweh Himself has provided the possibility of expiating what needs expiation. There is no such possibility for those who transgress the commands of Yahweh with evil intent, and who thus cut themselves off from the community. But apart from this, within the community, the disturbed relationship between God and the community can always be restored, both on a small scale and on a great, by the fulfilment of the laws of expiation which Yahweh Himself has given. The need became constantly greater in the post-exilic period; the material reflects an increasing concern which permeates the whole cultic life of Israel.

Anything affected by sin or uncleanness needs expiation. It cannot stand before the holy God. The destructive reaction of God, with its mortal threat, is provoked against that which needs expiation and is not expiated. Expiation is effected supremely by sprinkling or marking with the blood of animals, and particularly by the blood of the sin offerings חַטָּאת and אָשָׁם. The theological interpretation of these rites has often been influenced by partisan doctrinal considerations which do not derive from the actual material and which incline our evaluation of it either to the one side or to the other. [33] By contrast, it is essential to keep to the material itself. Certainly it would be a mistake to treat this uniformly. Behind the rites are varied ideas and motifs which lead us into areas beyond the distinctive sphere of the revealed religion of the OT. Nevertheless, there can be no doubt that Yahweh has provided and ordained blood as a means of atonement, and that blood is suitable and effective as such in virtue of the נֶפֶשׁ, the soul or the life, which is contained in it. The material has shown us again and again that the life of man is threatened if expiation is not made, and that it is preserved if forgiveness is secured through expiation. It is thus incontestable that the blood of animals used in expiatory rites is thought to effect the preservation of the life of man, which would otherwise be doomed, by reason of the animal life which is contained in it. In the light of כֹּפֶר and the non-cultic כפר, it would be useless to deny that the idea of substitution is present to some degree.

Herrmann

B. ἱλασμός and καθαρμός in the Greek World.

To understand what the pagan Hellenic and Hellenistic world denoted by ἱλάσκεσθαι and ἱλασμός, we must first be clear on the relation between ἱλασμός and καθαρμός.

καθαρμός is purification from cultic and moral defects, ἱλασμός the propitiation of gods, demons, or the departed, from whom demonstrations of favour are

---

[33] In my view this is true, e.g., of A. Ritschl's expositions in *Rechtfertigung und Versöhnung*, II⁴ (1900), 68 ff.

sought, or whose wrath has been provoked. Not all ἱλασμοί are καθαρμοί, and *vice versa*. But in fact καθαρμός and ἱλασμός denote the same process, which may be described as the purification of man on the one side or the propitiation of supernatural beings on the other. In Hellenic and Hellenistic religion cleansing is on the whole more important than propitiation (→ I, 254). As a rule, cleansing is essential to the restoration of the relationship with the deity. Whether the rites of purification go back to the taboos which are found in all religion, and which are older than belief in the gods, [34] is a question which we cannot pursue in the present context. Nor can we investigate the possibility that they arose outside Greece in Crete. [35] They certainly assumed a place of importance in the cultic religion of the Greeks. [36] The καθαρμοί may consist in the removal of physically conceived stains by washings with water, blood etc., or by rubbings with clay etc., or by the fumigation of rooms etc.; in this case they are not true sacrifices even though animals are slaughtered to secure their blood. But we also find true sacrifices, and even human sacrifices (→ περικάθαρμα), in which the stains of guilt, which are now conceived less physically, are transferred to the victim and washed away by means of it. In the case of such sacrifices we are naturally not to think in terms of the feasting of gods or men. The essential thing is the offering up of the life and the blood.

ἱλασμός includes various cultic acts such as prayers, sacrifices, purifications dances and games. These may be repeated annually. Since the deities are the guardians of order, of law and morality, offences against this demand ἱλασμός of the deity. These offences include especially murder, violation of the right of refuge etc., but also ritual transgressions, e.g., by the priests. In such cases ἱλασμός and καθαρμός merge into one another. For ἱλασμός does not merely reconcile; it also expiates guilt and cleanses men and cultic objects. ἱλασμός also arises when man desires a revelation or an oracle, or when he wishes to protect himself against the envy of the deity. The wrath of the deity may be quite capricious. Some deities, even though they are not angry, demand crude and even barbaric cultic rites, e.g., Artemis. Propitiatory sacrifices and actions may be required for the most varied reasons. The cult of the departed and of heroes is significant in this respect. To deities which are particularly jealous in upholding the moral order euphemistic names are given, e.g., the εὐμενίδες or the μειλίχιοι. Apollo is the καθάρσιος. He understands the art of purifying those who are stained. In times of emergency, or when there are other reasons for detecting the anger of the gods, cities call in men who are skilled in discovering the reason for this anger and in suggesting and applying ways of averting it, like Epimenides of Crete, who was brought in by the Athenians to make expiation for the Cylonic outrage. Oracles may also be consulted in such cases. Such things play a considerable role in the Orphic rites.

Along with the belief that such cultic means are necessary to win, or to win back, the divine favour, we have early evidence of the conviction that what matters is moral conduct or disposition. The enlightenment shattered mythical ideas of the gods and the departed. The idea of divine envy was expressly rejected by

---

[34] Nilsson, *op. cit.*, 285, 295.
[35] Kern, *op. cit.*, 48, 139 f.
[36] We must empasise this point because there are still those who idealise Greek religion, as though it were far more serene, and unaffected by such elements. It is true that a more realistic view has now been established, but such idealisation still persists, cf. Stengel and Nilsson.

Plato. The deity came to be regarded as benevolent by nature. Hence καθαρμοί and ἱλασμοί lost their significance, or maintained it only by way of ethical and psychological reinterpretation. This process was already far advanced in the time of the NT writings, although to different degrees in the different strata. On the other hand, barbaric and bloody rites of expiation had come into Greek religion from the Orient. Fear of the gods and their judgment was not yet dead by a long way.

C. Ideas of Expiation in Judaism.

1. The consciousness of sin was very much alive in Rabbinic piety and theology. Hence the question of removing sin was important. Reconciliation, i.e., the restoration of peace between the sinner and God (→ I, 254), is rather a different thing from the removal of sin, both in term and concept. Yet the two cannot be separated in fact. [37] For the Rabbis sin is the only thing to provoke God's wrath. All sin destroys fellowship with God. Cleansing from sin is denoted by כִּפֶּר, "to expiate," and the derived noun כַּפָּרָה. Yet it is also denoted by נָשָׂא עָוֹן and similar expressions. [38] Men are usually the subjects when verbs are used, but God may also be the subject.

Expiation of sins is accomplished by the cultus on the one side and by personal achievements and experiences on the other. Among the cultic means of reconciliation the Day of Atonement is pre-eminent. It expiates the sins of all Jews. The sacrifices, especially the daily burnt offerings, have the same significance. [39] Rabbinic theology also ascribes varying expiatory significance to the various objects used in the cultus, e.g., the priestly vestments, [40] the little bell on the robe of the high-priest, the frontal on his turban, [41] or the temple tax, which is the contribution of individual Israelites. [42] Many personal experiences and expressions of piety bring atonement, e.g., penitence, suffering, death, works of love and especially almsgiving, restitution for wrongs, study of the Torah, fasting and prayer. [43] An important question is what means cleanse from what sins. The ripest answer of Rabbinic casuistry if that of Rabbi Israel (d. 135), T. Joma, 5, 6 ff.: [44] "There is a fourfold expiation. If a man has transgressed the commandments, and repents, he does not go forth (from the place of penitence) without being forgiven, as we read in Jer. 3:22: 'Return, ye backsliding children, and I will heal your backsliding.' If a man has transgressed the prohibitions, and repents, this holds off (the punishment), and the Day of Atonement makes expiation, as we read in Lv. 16:30: 'For on that day shall one make atonement for you.' If a man has committed sins which incur excommunication or a capital sentence, and he repents, this and the Day of Atonement will hold off (the punishment), and suffering will make atonement, as we read in Ps. 89:32: 'Then will I visit their transgression with the rod, and their iniquity with plagues.' But if a man defiles the name of God and has repented, neither this has power to hold off (the punishment) nor the Day of Atonement to make expiation, but repentance and the Day of Atonement will supply one third of the expiation, and suffering

---

[37] The two are mentioned together at T. Sheq., 1, 6: The offerings of the congregation bring reconciliation and expiation מרצין ומכפרין between Israel and its Father in heaven.
[38] Str.-B., II, 363 ff.
[39] Joma, 8, 8 f.
[40] J. Joma, 44b, 53; Lv. r., 10 on 8:1, cf. Str.-B., I, 229 f.
[41] Pes., 7, 7 (cf. Str.-B., II, 365).
[42] T. Sheq., 1, 6 (Str.-B., I, 761 f.).
[43] Examples in Str.-B., IV, 2, cf. Index, "Sühnmittel."
[44] Cf. Str.-B., I, 169.

for the rest of the year a third, and the day of death will bring full expiation, as at Is. 22:14 : 'Surely this iniquity shall not be purged from you till ye die,' which teaches us that the day of death makes full atonement." The atoning power of death is thus particularly great. We also find statements such as this : "All the dead are cleansed from sin by death." [45] "He who comes into mortal jeopardy by entering the baths should say : May death be an expiation for all my sins." [46] Penitence is always presupposed. Rabbi Ishmael taught that sin offerings and guilt offerings and death and the Day of Atonement can make expiation only in conjunction with penitence, for it is said in Lv. 23:27: " 'Nevertheless' : if he returns (in penitence), he will have expiation ; if not, he will not." [47] On the other hand, there is also the principle that without shedding of blood there is no expiation. [48] That the actual offering of blood became impossible with the burning of the temple did not affect the Rabbis. Their theology expounded the statements of Scripture in a fully Scholastic manner, [49] i.e., without reference to the realities of life. Their piety found in good works a substitute for the temple cultus. [50] For the main point of this had long since been that of representing a punctilious fulfilment of the statutes of the Law, [51] i.e., of offering an opportunity for good works.

The idea that the righteous who suffer without being guilty, or who suffer more than their guilt requires, thereby atone for the sins of the people and ward off suffering from others, is very common among the Rabbis. [52] The sufferings of the patriarchs, Moses, David etc., and the sufferings of more recent figures, especially the martyrs, are evaluated thus. To overcome a gnawing sense of guilt this estimation of the suffering of others could assume great significance. In some cases it might be perverted into a petty calculation of the value of such expiatory suffering. [53] How cheaply its achievement could be rated may be seen from the practice of proffering oneself as an expiation for others in expression of one's love and piety. [54]

2. The views of the Judaism of the Greek Dispersion concerning expiation are essentially the same as those of the Rabbis.

It should not be assumed that the Jews of the Dispersion were generally cut loose from the temple cultus. The rites of the Day of Atonement were for the whole people, not just for those present in the temple. The whole Dispersion thus had a part in it, and it also paid the temple tax. [55] Repentance, good works and sufferings were accorded the same significance in the Dispersion as in Palestine. The Books of Maccabees often

---

[45] S. Nu § 112 on 15:31: כל המתים במיתה מתכפרים, cf. R. 6:7, and K. G. Kuhn in ZNW, 32 (1931), 305 ff. and Ber., 19a : "If one has repented and then dies, death destroys sin."

[46] T. Ber., 7, 17.

[47] → n. 44; cf. Kuhn, loc. cit.

[48] bJoma, 5a etc., cf. Str.-B., III, 742.

[49] Schl. Gesch. Isr., 346.

[50] R. Josua said (when he saw the ruined sanctuary): "Woe to us, because the place is destroyed where they atoned the sins of Israel." (Jochanan b. Zakkai said to him : "Do not grieve, my son. We have an atonement כַּפָּרָה similar to it. What is it ? It is almsgiving, for it is said : 'I desire mercy and not sacrifice' (Hos. 6:6)," Ab. R. Nat. (I), 5, 4 (Schechter, 11a).

[51] R. Jochanan b. Zakkai : "Neither a dead body makes unclean, nor does water make clean, but the Holy One, blessed be He, has said : 'I have established a law, I have taken a decision, and thou hast no power to transgress my decision,' " S. Nu. § 123 on 19:2; Pesikt., 40b (Buber); T. Joma, 5, 6 ff.

[52] Cf. Str.-B., II, 275 ff.

[53] Ibid., 281 under k.

[54] Ibid., III, 261; the formula used is אֲנִי כַפָּרָה.

[55] → n. 42.

speak of the vicarious force of martyrdom. [56] Philo, too, speaks of vicarious suffering. [57]

D. ἱλάσκομαι.

1. Related to the same root as ἵλεως are the verbs ἵλημι, "to be gracious," [58] ἱλάσκομαι (ἱλάομαι, also ἱλέομαι, ἱλεόομαι) with the causative significance, "to make gracious," [59] and in much the same sense, and particularly common in the LXX, ἐξιλάσκομαι.

ἱλάσκομαι is frequently used from the time of Homer [60] with man as the subject and a god or a deceased person as object ; [61] the sense is "to make gracious," "to placate." We do not have to assume that the god is angry or that the man has committed sin. [62] A deity which at first refuses to hear may be made gracious. [63] ἱλάσκεσθαι can be parallel to θεραπεύειν. [64] In this sense of "to make gracious" ἱλάσκεσθαι is used up to a later period among pagans, [65] Jews [66] and Christians. [67] This is the main meaning. But though ἱλάσκεσθαι is for the most part a cultic action, it can sometimes be applied to men and can even be used on occasion in the surprising sense of "to bribe." [68] Between the cultic and the secular use it can denote the placating of the emperor or his anger. [69] The one placated can later be put in the dat. [70] The pass. aor. has the significance that the deity allowed itself to be made gracious, i.e., showed mercy. This is found specifically in the invocation ἱλάσθητι, "Be merciful." Grammatically the form ἱλάσθη is

---

[56] 2 Macc. 7:37, 38 : "We pray that God may soon be gracious to the people ... that the wrath of the Almighty, which is rightly kindled against our whole race, may cease towards me and my brethren." On 4 Macc. → ἱλαστήριον.

[57] Sacr. AC, 121 → λύτρον; also ἱλάσκομαι and ἱλασμός.

[58] Cf. Boisacq, 372 f.

[59] The σ in the aor. pass. ἱλάσθην is secondary as in ἐσπά-σ-θην.

[60] Od., 3, 419 : ὄφρ' ἤτοι πρώτιστα θεῶν ἱλάσσομ' Ἀθήνην. Il., 1, 386; 2, 550.

[61] Hdt., V, 47: ἐπὶ γὰρ τοῦ τάφου αὐτοῦ ἡρώιον ἱδρυσάμενοι θυσίῃσι αὐτὸν ἱλάσκονται. Plut. Ser. Num. Pun., 17 (II, 560e f): ἱλάσκεσθαι τὴν τοῦ Ἀρχιλόχου ψυχήν.

[62] Hdt., VI, 105 : καὶ αὐτὸν (Pan) ἀπὸ ταύτης τῆς ἀγγελίης θυσίῃσι ἐπετείοισι καὶ λαμπάδι ἱλάσκονται; Pan expressly calls himself εὔνους to the Athenians, and simply misses his cult in Athens. Cf. also the description of the cult of Aphrodite in Empedocles Fr., 128 (I, 271, Diels): εὐσεβέεσσιν ἀγάλμασιν ἱλάσκοντο. Epigr. Graec., 1027, 4 : οἳ πολλὰ γεγηθότης ἱλάσκονται σὸν σθένος (Aesculapius).

[63] Xenoph. Cyrop., VII, 2, 19 : πάμπολλα δὲ θύων ἐξιλασάμην ποτὲ αὐτόν (Apollo for the reception of an oracle).

[64] Xenoph. Oec., 5, 20, where τοὺς θεοὺς ἱλάσκεσθαι is parallel to τοὺς θεοὺς θεραπεύειν in the sentence which follows.

[65] Dio Chrys. Or., 4, 90 : μῆνιν Ἑκάτης ἱλασκόμενοι; Paus., III, 13, 3 : θυσίαις ἱλάσκονται (Apollo); cf. Polyb., 3, 112, 9 : καὶ θεοὺς ἐξιλάσασθαι καὶ ἀνθρώπους; 1, 68, 4 : σπουδάζοντες ἐξιλάσασθαι τὴν ὀργὴν αὐτῶν; 32, 15 (27, 25), 7: διὰ τούτων (sacrifices) ἐξιλάσασθαι τὸ θεῖον. In the Asia Minor inscr. collected by Steinleitner ἱλάσκομαι is found in this sense in 4, 6; 5, 6; 6, 16; 8, 9; 10, 9; 25, 6 and 7; 33, 5; cf. also the Menander Fr. on p. 73 : τὴν θεὸν ἐξιλάσαντο.

[66] Jos. Ant., 6, 124 : τὸν θεὸν οὕτως ἐξιλάσασθαι etc. Schl. Theol. d. Judt., 115; also the Philo passages in 3.

[67] 1 Cl., 7, 7: οἱ δὲ μετανοήσαντες ἐπὶ τοῖς ἁμαρτήμασιν αὐτῶν ἐξιλάσαντο τὸν θεόν ...; Herm. v., 1, 2, 1: πῶς ἐξιλάσομαι τὸν θεὸν ἐπὶ τῶν ἁμαρτιῶν μου τῶν τελείων.

[68] Hdt. VIII, 112, 2 : Πάριοι δὲ Θεμιστοκλέα χρήμασιν ἱλασάμενοι διέφυγον τὸ στράτευμα.

[69] Plut. Anton., 67, 3 (I, 947d): ἱλάσασθαι Καίσαρα. Cato Minor, 61, 3 (I, 789e): ἱλασάμενοι τὴν πρὸς αὐτοὺς ὀργὴν τοῦ Καίσαρος.

[70] Plut. Poplicola, 21, 3 (I, 108a): ἱλασάμενος τῷ Ἅιδῃ.

passive, but the deity is regarded as active rather than passive. Prayer is used, not coercion. [71]

2. In the LXX ἱλάσκομαι occurs only 12 times. In the aor. pass. the meaning is that God showed mercy (Ex. 32:14; 4 Βασ. 24:4), or "Be merciful" (Est. 4:17h; Lam. 3:42; Da. 9:19 Θ; ψ 78[79]:9). The mid. forms ἱλάσεται, ἱλάση mean "to be or to become gracious" [72] (4 Βασ. 5:18 twice ; 2 Ch. 6:30; ψ 24[25]:11; 64[65]:4; 77[78]:38). This is shown by the context, and particularly by the fact that the words rendered ἱλάσεται and ἱλάση are כַּפֶּר and סְלַח, which elsewhere are translated ἵλεως ἔση or γενοῦ. ἱλάσεται and ἱλάση cannot be derived from a causative ἱλάσκομαι, since God is the subject and men or sins are the dat. object. [73] Here ἵλημι, "to be gracious," can hardly have affected the meaning of ἱλάση and ἱλάσεται. These forms are probably wrested a little in translation. On the other hand, ἐξιλάσκομαι is common in the LXX. It is mostly used for כַּפֶּר and denotes the action of the priest as he nullifies, purges or expiates sin before God. It is normally construed with περί (τῶν υἱῶν Ἰσραήλ etc. or τῆς ἁμαρτίας) (cf. the Heb. עַל) or with ἀπό (τῆς ἁμαρτίας etc.) (Heb. מִן). A personal as well as a cultic sense arises : "to make gracious." Men are the subject and God the object (Zech. 7:2; 8:22; Mal. 1:9; Heb. חִלָּה, "to placate by prayer"), or in one case a man (Gn. 32:21; Heb. כַּפֶּר). ἐξιλάσασθαι can also mean "to cleanse or purge the stain of sin or guilt," with men as subject and cultic objects as object (Ez. 43:20, 22, 26; 45:18, 20, Heb. כַּפֶּר, חִטֵּא). The usage of Sir. deserves notice. Here ἐξιλάσκομαι means "to pardon," "to expiate," with sin as the object and the subject either God (5:6; 34:19 [31:23] "to pardon") or man (3:3, 30; 20:28 = "to atone"). Without the accus. obj. we find it with περί (τοῦ λαοῦ); God (16:7) and men (45:16, 23) are the subject ("to make expiation"). Man's expiation usually consists in moral achievement (3:3, 30; 45:23). The references to God's ἐξιλάσκεσθαι are negative. At 20:28 ἐξιλάσεται denotes the nullifying of wrong before men.

3. Philo makes only infrequent use of ἱλάσκομαι and ἐξιλάσκομαι. ἱλάσκομαι usually means "to placate," "to make gracious." Men are the subject and God (Plant., 162; Abr., 129; Vit. Mos., II [III], 24; Spec. Leg., I, 116) or a man (Spec. Leg., I, 237) the object. ἐξευμενίζεσθαι τὸν θεόν is a parallel (Spec. Leg., II, 196). ἱλάσκεσθαι can also mean "to make expiation," "to cleanse from sin," "to atone," with man as subject (Mut. Nom., 235; Vit. Mos., II [III], 201; Spec. Leg., I, 234; Praem. Poen., 56); cf. also ἐξιλάσασθαι (Poster C., 72). Expiation is made through cultic or moral actions. In Leg. All., III, 174, on the basis of Dt. 8:3 (ἐκάκωσέ σε), we read : "The act of violence is expiation (ἱλασμός). For He makes atonement (ἱλάσκεται) on the 10th day, by doing violence to our soul. For when He robs us of our sin, we think that we are roughly handled. But in truth this is to experience the grace of God (ἵλεων τὸν θεὸν ἔχειν)." Philo gives a deeper and more religious turn to the moralistic idea that good works atone for sin (Sir. 3:3, 30). God Himself acts on man to effect true purity from sin. God is here the Redeemer from the bond of sin. By way of the ethical view the older cultic understanding has here led to a religious and personal.

4. In the NT ἱλάσκομαι occurs only at Lk. 18:13; Hb. 2:17; ἐξιλάσκομαι is not used at all. At Lk. 18:13 ἱλάσθητι is the cry to God for mercy, as at Est. 4:17 h; ψ 78(19):9; Da. Θ 9:19. At Hb. 2:17 the task of Jesus as High-priest is ἱλάσκεσθαι

---

[71] The pass. and mid. are close in such cases, but are to be distinguished. Cf. Bl.-Debr.[6] § 314 and 317. ἀδικεῖσθε at 1 C. 6:7 is pass.: "Let wrong be done you ; suffer it." κείρασθαι at 1 C. 11:6 is mid. "Cause her to be shorn."

[72] Cf. Helbing, 213.

[73] ψ 64(65):4 Β : τὰς ἀσεβείας ; א : ταῖς ἀσεβείαις.

τὰς ἁμαρτίας τοῦ λαοῦ, [74] to expiate the sins of His people, to rob them of their validity and significance before God. We are not to think here either of making God gracious or of an ethical conquest of sin in man.

5. When we consider the striking changes in the construction and meaning of ἱλάσκομαι and ἐξιλάσκομαι, the most surprising thing is that alongside the sense of "to propitiate" we now have the senses "to purge from sin" and "to expiate." The first of these is construed with the acc. of the person propitiated, and it gives us in the aorist the sense "to let oneself be propitiated," "to be merciful," construed with the dat. of the person who finds mercy. The second is construed with the acc. of the person or object which is purged. The third is construed with the acc. of the guilt expiated or with such prepositions as περί or ἀπό. The first meaning and construction for ἱλάσκομαι and ἐξιλάσκομαι are found everywhere in pagan Greek, in the LXX, in Philo and in the NT, though in the LXX and the NT ἱλάσκομαι occurs only in the aor. pass. Behind the second and third constructions and meanings the use of כִּפֶּר is plainly evident in the case of ἐξιλάσκομαι in the LXX, though this is not so true of ἱλάσκομαι. What may be said of the LXX applies equally to Sir., Philo and the NT. But did the LXX or its forerunners initiate this change in the use of ἐξιλάσκομαι and ἱλάσκομαι with the literal translation of the Hebrew text? Or had these words already acquired the second and third senses along with the first? We can hardly suppose that ἐξιλάσκομαι was chosen for כִּפֶּר if it only meant "to propitiate." On the other hand, we can easily see how it took on the further meanings. Through cultic use, this expansion of meaning was quite natural. The cultic action denoted by the words was designed to make God gracious again to the sinner. Hence it also cleansed him from sin, or expiated his sin. Materially the effect on God could not be separated from the effect on man or his sin. The two were sought and achieved together. In purpose and effect the cleansing of the sinner and the expiation of his sin are so essential a part of the cultic action that they came to be expressed along with propitiation in the term used for this action. Hence the meaning of the term, though complex, is ultimately consistent. It is true that there are no examples of the senses "to cleanse" or "to expiate" prior to the LXX. [75] On the other hand, we may conjecture that when the LXX used

---

[74] On the reading ταῖς ἁμαρτίαις א 33, cf. the variant readings in → n. 73.

[75] Plat. Leg., VIII, 862c : τὸ ἀποίνοις ἐξιλασθὲν τοῖς δρῶσιν καὶ πάσχουσιν ἑκάστας τῶν βλάψεων ἐκ διαφορᾶς εἰς φιλίαν ἀεὶ πειρατέον καθιστάναι τοῖς νόμοις. Here one might construe ἐξιλασθέν as "purged," since the offender is freed from guilt by repayment to the injured party, but it is better to render it "placated," since the injured party is moved by the repayment to let go his anger against the offender, and friendship can be restored. That the reference of ἐξιλασθέν is to a person rather than an object may be seen from the preceding parallel. From the time of Deissmann NB, 52 allusion has often been made to the inscr. IG, II², 1366, 16 (Ditt. Syll.³, 1042, 16), cf. 1365, 32 : ἁμαρτίαν ὀφιλέτω Μηνὶ Τυράννῳ ἣν οὐ μὴ δύνηται ἐξειλάσασθαι. But these belong to the 2nd or 3rd century A.D. and are thus 3-400 years later than the LXX. As the twofold repetition shows, the formula is traditional in the Men cultus ; it thus derives from Asia Minor. It is worth noting that Dittenberger alleges foedissima sermonis vitia in these inscriptions. Bl.-Debr.⁶ § 148, 2 explains ἱλάσκεσθαι ἁμαρτίας according to the rule that the original intr. of an affective verb can become a trans. In my view this is mistaken. ἱλάσκομαι originally means "to make someone gracious," trans. mid. There thus develops in the pass. an intr. use, "to let oneself be propitiated," "to be gracious." According to the above rule the intr. could thus be used as a trans. But the forms which have ἁμαρτίαν as object in the LXX

ἐξιλάσκομαι for כְּפֶר in the sense of "to make gracious" at Gn. 32:21, and when it also used ἐξιλάσκομαι for כְּפֶר in the sense of "to make atonement," it was simply following a usage of ἐξιλάσκομαι which existed already in the surrounding Jewish world. [76]

The most striking thing about the development of the terms, however, is that words which were originally used to denote man's action in relation to God cease to be used in this way in the NT and are used instead of God's action in relation to man.

E. ἱλασμός.

ἱλασμός (formed from → ἱλάσκομαι) is the action in which God is propitiated and sin expiated. The word is not very common in literature. [77] Plutarch uses it often, Fab. Max., 18, 3 (I, 184e): πρὸς ἱλασμοὺς θεῶν ἢ τεράτων ἀποτροπάς, De Solone, 12 (I, 84e): ἱλασμοῖς τισι καὶ καθαρμοῖς καὶ ἱδρύσεσι κατοργιάσας καὶ καθοσιώσας τὴν πόλιν, De Camillo, 7 (I, 133a): θεῶν μῆνιν ἱλασμοῦ καὶ χαριστηρίων δεομένην. These passages show that what is in view is both cultic propitiation of the gods and expiatory action in general, De Solone, 12. Behind the use of ἱλασμός stands the twofold sense of ἱλάσκομαι as both "to propitiate" and "to expiate," → ἱλάσκομαι, 5.

Along with ἱλασμός the LXX has ἐξιλασμός, ἐξίλασμα, ἐξίλασις. It uses these words for derivatives of כָּפַר, specifically כִּפֻּרִים. ἱλασμός is usually the cultic expiation by which sin is made ineffective. In Ez. ἱλασμός and ἐξιλασμός are the sin offering חַטָּאת, 44:27; 45:19. God is not the object of ἱλασμός (ἐξιλασμός, ἐξίλασις). It is expressly stated that man cannot offer Him an ἐξίλασμα (ψ 48:7). ἱλασμός, however, is also God's forgiveness סְלִיחָה, ψ 129:4. This usage corresponds to that of ἱλάσκομαι and ἐξιλάσκομαι → ἱλάσκομαι, 2. The word is not found in Josephus. In Philo it mostly has the sense of sacrificial expiation, Plant., 61; Rer. Div. Her., 179; Congr., 89 and 107, though it can also mean purging from sin as God's work in man, Leg. All., III, 174; Poster. C., 48. Here, too, the use of the noun is like that of the verb.

The only NT passages are 1 Jn. 2:2 and 4:10: ἱλασμὸς περὶ τῶν ἁμαρτιῶν ἡμῶν. The construction corresponds to that used with ἱλάσκεσθαι in the LXX. John is obviously following the OT. ἱλασμός does not imply the propitiation of God. It refers to the purpose which God Himself has fulfilled by sending the Son. Hence it rests on the fact that God is gracious, i.e., on His love, cf. 4:10. The meaning, then, is the setting aside of sin as guilt against God. This is shown by the combination of ἱλασμός in 2:2 with παράκλητος in 2:1 and with the confession of sin in 1:8, 10. The subjective result of ἱλασμός in man is παρρησία, confidence before the divine judgment, 4:17; 2:28, or victory over the consciousness of sin. As a demonstration of love, 4:9, 10, ἱλασμός begets love (for the brethren), 4:7, 11, 20 f. The overcoming of sin as guilt cannot be separated in fact from the overcoming of sin as transgression, which in John is lack of love. In this respect John can even say that he who is born of God cannot sin, 3:9, 6. He deduces this

---

and the Men inscr. are middle, not pass. The mid. ἱλάσκεσθαι does occur intr. in the LXX. But this would give the confused development : a. trans. mid. with acc. obj. of person : "to cause someone to be gracious"; b. intr. mid.: "to be gracious"; c. trans. mid. with acc. obj. of object : "to expiate." It is thus better to assume for the mid. a complex meaning arising out of cultic use : "to propitiate a deity" and "to expiate a sin," cf. the Lat. *expiare*.

[76] Helbing, 215.

[77] Acc. to the indexes it is not found in the Attic orators, Sophocles, Thucydides, Epictetus, the Orphic fragments, the pre-Socratics, the older Stoics.

impossibility of sin in the regenerate from the fact that Jesus, who is sinless, is manifested for the putting away of sin (i.e., as ἱλασμός),[78] 3:5 (→ I, 305). If Christians do still sin — and to deny this is to sin against the truth, 1:8, 10 — this simply forces them to look again to Him who is the ἱλασμός. The line from 1:8, 10 leads directly to 2:2. John does not say how Jesus accomplished the ἱλασμός. But it is worth noting that neither in 2:2 nor 4:10 does he refer to the death of Christ. He simply speaks of the risen Lord (2:1, πρὸς τὸν πατέρα) and of the total mission of Jesus (4:10). The ἱλασμός is not one-sidedly linked with the single achievement of the death, but with the total person and work of Jesus, of which His death is, of course, an indissoluble part, 5:6; cf. 3:16; 1:7. Jesus is our expiation as the One who has fulfilled the purpose of His sending, who has been kept in perfect love (3:17) and who is perfectly righteous, 2:2.[79] John does not speak of any necessity of expiation. He sees the day of judgment approaching, 4:17, and it is thus unnecessary to establish the necessity of expiation. For John the ἱλασμός is much more than a concept of Christian doctrine; it is the reality by which he lives.

Büchsel

† ἱλαστήριον.

1. ἱλαστήριον = כַּפֹּרֶת.

a. According to Ex. 25:17-22 there is to be set up on the ark of the covenant a כַּפֹּרֶת of pure gold. Like the ark, this is to be two cubits and a half long and one cubit and a half wide. The other dimension is not given. At both ends are to be cherubim; in the older account in 1 K. 8, which does not mention the כַּפֹּרֶת, these stand in no material connection with the ark. The cherubim are protectively to cover the כַּפֹּרֶת, their faces towards it (Ex. 25:20). There Yahweh will meet Moses (יעד niphal).[1] From above the כַּפֹּרֶת, from the space between the two cherubim (v. 22), He will speak with him and give His commandments. Nu. 7:89 is in accord with this, and at Lv. 16:2 we learn that Yahweh will "appear in the cloud upon the כַּפֹּרֶת." In the ritual of the Day of Atonement it is also laid down that Aaron should burn incense before the כַּפֹּרֶת and that the cloud of incense should cover the כַּפֹּרֶת, "that he die not" (Lv. 16:13). The presence of God above the כַּפֹּרֶת is evidently assumed. The ensuing sprinkling of blood on and before the כַּפֹּרֶת brings the blood

---

[78] On the material identity of כִּפֶּר and נָשָׂא עָוֹן in the Rabbis → 312.

[79] The equation of Jesus and atonement corresponds on the one side to the equation of Jesus and His gifts, which is very common in John's Gospel, 6:35; 11:25; 14:6, and on the other hand to statements like the sons of the Torah who are atonement for the world שֶׁהֵן לְעוֹלָם כפרה, TBQ, 7, 6, or to the formula which expresses readiness to atone for the sins of others: אֲנִי כַּפָּרָה → n. 54.

ἱ λ α σ τ ή ρ ι ο ν. On 1.: The bibl. under ἱλάσκομαι κτλ. (→ 301, n.). On 2-4: The comm. on R. 3:25: Zn. R., Khl. R., Ltzm. R., Str.-B., III, P. Althaus in NT Deutsch, *ad loc.*; the NT theologies: H. Weinel⁴ (1928), 232 f.; H. J. Holtzmann, II² (1911), 112. A. Ritschl, *Die christ. Lehre von der Rechtfertigung und Versöhnung*⁴, II (1900), 170; A. Deissmann, ZNW, 4 (1903), 193 ff.; C. Bruston, *ibid.*, 7 (1906), 77 ff.; W. Bleibtreu, ThStKr, 56, 1 (1883), 548 ff.; C. Bruston, *Revue de Théologie et des Questions Religieuses*, 8 (1904) (Montauban).

[1] With this is linked the description of the tabernacle as אֹהֶל מוֹעֵד׃

of the sin offering as near as possible to Him (Lv. 16:14). In 1 Ch. 28:11 the Holy of Holies is described as בֵּית הַכַּפֹּרֶת, and in Ex. 30:6 the כַּפֹּרֶת is more important than the ark.

b. The כַּפֹּרֶת cannot be regarded merely as a cover over the ark. According to Ex. 25:21 it is to be put above the chest as the tables of the Law are put in it. According to passages like Ex. 26:34; 35:12; 39:35 it is no part of the ark. It is called "the כַּפֹּרֶת that is over the ark of the law" (Ex. 30:6; Nu. 7:89); never is it the כַּפֹּרֶת of the ark. When it is first mentioned at Ex. 25:17 (and at the parallel Ex. 37:6), the LXX calls it ἱλαστήριον ἐπίθεμα, an atoning headpiece. [2] After that it simply has ἱλαστήριον, which can mean a means or place of expiation. Once (1 Ch. 28:11) it has ἐξιλασμός. [3] Philo [4] is aware that what is called ἱλαστήριον in Holy Scripture is an ἐπίθεμα, a kind of πῶμα (cover). The term is thus derived from כִּפֶּר, "to expiate." But Saadya, Rashi and Kimchi derive it from כפר "to cover," and most modern scholars accept this. [5] One might say that the reference in Ex. 25:17, [6] in close proximity to technical expressions, argues in favour of an original technical significance. On the other hand, the way in which 1 Ch. 28:11 describes the Holy of Holies as בֵּית הַכַּפֹּרֶת favours the view that the OT itself here understood כַּפֹּרֶת as ἱλαστήριον. The exegetical tradition uniformly supports this understanding for a long period after the LXX.

Herrmann

2. τὸ ἱλαστήριον is a neuter noun from the adj. ἱλαστήριος. This adj. is related to ἱλαστής as σωτήριος to σωτήρ or κριτήριος to κριτής (1 Εσδρ. 8:53 according to A²). It is also linked with → ἱλάσκομαι and ἵλαος → ἵλεως, and denotes someone or something related to the ἱλαστής. The adj. is rare. In the LXX it is found at Ex. 25:16 (also in a variant of Ex. 37:6): ἱλαστήριον ἐπίθεμα; 4 Macc. 17:22 : διὰ τοῦ ἱλαστηρίου θανάτου αὐτῶν. [7] We also find it on a pap. of the 2nd cent. A.D. : εἰλαστηρίους θυσίας, [8] in Nicephorus Vita Sym. Stylit. : [9] χεῖρας ἱκετηρίους εἰ βούλει δὲ ἱλαστηρίους, in Jos. Ant., 16, 182 : τοῦ δέους ἱλαστήριον μνῆμα. [10] At R. 3:25 ἱλαστήριον could be the acc. masc., and the older Latins, who have *propitiatorem*, favour this view. But there are no other instances of a masc. noun ; hence we do better to assume the neuter.

3. The neuter noun occurs often in the LXX as a rendering of כַּפֹּרֶת Ex. 25:16-21 (17-23); 31:7; 35:12; 38:5-8 (37:6-9); Lv. 16:2-15; Nu. 7:89. Though neuter nouns can often denote the place where the relevant action takes place, [11] the LXX uses the term for a headpiece or vessel of expiation rather than for the place of expiation. For in the

---

[2] This shows that the LXX does not regard the ἱλαστήριον as a cover for the ark.

[3] The only other LXX use of ἱλαστήριον is for עֲזָרָה (Ez. 43:14, 17, 20), which is part of the altar of burnt offering in Ezekiel, and at which something is done by the blood of the sin offering in cleansing and expiation (v. 20).

[4] Cf. Str.-B., III, 165.

[5] Cf. E. König, *Wörterbuch z. AT* ², ³ (1922), *s.v.*

[6] "A כפרת of pure gold, two cubits and a half long and a cubit and a half broad."

[7] The reading διὰ τοῦ ἱλαστηρίου τοῦ θανάτου αὐτῶν is not to be preferred.

[8] *Fayûm Towns and Their Papyri*, ed. B. P. Grenfell-A. S. Hunt (1900), p. 313, No. 337.

[9] Act. SS Mai V, 355.

[10] Usually rendered "a memorial to calm his fear" (Herod had opened and despoiled the grave of David, and feared the wrath of the deceased or of God), obj. gen. (cf. Schl. Theol. d. Judt., 116). Perhaps a better rendering would be "occasioned by his fear," gen. auct.

[11] βουλευτήριον, council house ; δικαστήριον, κριτήριον, place of judgment.

first reference at Ex. 25:16(17) it renders וְעָשִׂיתָ כַפֹּרֶת זָהָב טָהוֹר by καὶ ποιήσεις ἱλαστήριον ἐπίθεμα χρυσίου καθαροῦ. That is, it introduces its rendering of כַפֹּרֶת as ἱλαστήριον by first using as an adj. the term which will later be a neuter noun, and by sup-
plying the noun ἐπίθεμα. It is thus evident that the reference of τὸ ἱλαστήριον is not
to a place. It is employed generally for "that which makes expiation." In Ez. 43:14,
17, 20 the עֲזָרָה of the altar of burnt offering is called τὸ ἱλαστήριον, probably because
it is sprinkled by the blood in expiation.[12] In the LXX, then, the original general use
of ἱλαστήριον for "that which expiates" is plain. On the other hand, ἱλαστήριον
becomes a technical term for the כַפֹּרֶת, and this usage is highly influential. We see this
in Philo. He uses τὸ ἱλαστήριον exclusively for the כַפֹּרֶת in Cher., 25 : (τὰ χερουβὶμ)
νεύοντα πρὸς τὸ ἱλαστήριον πτεροῖς, Vit. Mos., II (III), 95 : ἐπίθεμα ὡσανεὶ
πῶμα τὸ λεγόμενον ἐν ἱεραῖς βίβλοις ἱλαστήριον; Vit. Mos., II (III), 97: ἐπίθεμα
τὸ προσαγορευόμενον ἱλαστήρον. These passages show that in Philo ἱλαστήριον
is the technical scriptural term for the כַפֹּרֶת. Yet the word is also used in his time for
oblations etc., and he is obviously aware that it does not evoke a concrete image of
the כַפֹּרֶת, so that before mentioning the name he describes it as ἐπίθεμα ὡσανεὶ πῶμα
(headpiece as a cover). In Jos. ἱλαστήριον is used only as an attributive adj. and not
as a technical term for the כַפֹּרֶת.[13] What Symmachus had in view when he called Noah's
ark, Gn. 6:16(15), ἱλαστήριον is not very clear. Outside biblical and Jewish Greek the
neuter noun ἱλαστήριον is used in the sense of "oblation": ὁ δᾶμος ὑπὲρ τῆς
τοῦ Αὐτοκράτορος Καίσαρος θεοῦ υἱοῦ Σεβαστοῦ σωτηρίας θεοῖς ἱλαστήριον, [14]
and : ἱλαστήριον οἱ Ἀχαιοὶ τῇ Ἰλιάδι. [15] That ἱλαστήριον has here the sense of
oblation rather than vessel of expiation is in keeping with the sense of ἱλάσκομαι
= θεραπεύειν, → 128. [16]

4. R. 3:25.

a. It is hard to say with any clarity whether Paul in R. 3:25 is thinking of the
ἱλαστήριον in particular or a means of expiation in general. Paul does not elaborate
his meaning but is content with this summary statement. Moreover, we cannot be
absolutely sure as to the meaning of προέθετο or the reference of ἐν τῷ αὐτοῦ
αἵματι. Nevertheless, whatever the final meaning of ἱλαστήριον, it certainly
denotes that which expiates sins. By means of it is the ἀπολύτρωσις or redemption
of the sinner and therewith the revelation of God's righteousness. The ἱλάσκομαι
contained in ἱλαστήριον naturally does not mean "to propitiate," as though God
were an object. This is excluded by the fact that it is God who has made the
ἱλαστήριον what it is. In this whole context God is subject, not object. This is in
keeping with Paul's doctrine of reconciliation (→ I, 255). Only men, or the sins
of men, can be object of ἱλάσκομαι (→ 314 ff.). To sure, we cannot support this

---

[12] It does not greatly matter how the LXX interpreted the obscure עֲזָרָה, whether as a
cornice, as the rim of the altar, or as an enclosure. The important thing is the cultic significance.

[13] Jos. in his description of the ark (Ant., 3, 134-138) does not refer to the ἱλαστήριον
but only to an ἐπίθεμα with the cherubim. In his description of the Day of Atonement
(Ant., 3, 240-243) he does not mention the ark at all. Is he describing the common custom
of his own time ?

[14] W. R. Paton and E. L. Hicks, The Inscriptions of Cos (1891), 81, from the time of
Augustus ; cf. 347: Διὶ Στρατίῳ ἱλαστήριον.

[15] Dio Chrys. Or., 11, 121 (I, 185, G. de Budé [1916]) has ἱλαστήριον in parallelism
with ἀνάθημα κάλλιστον καὶ μέγιστον.

[16] On the later use of ἱλαστήριον cf. A. Deissmann, ZNW, 7 (1906) under I, 4, and
the examples given in Ltzm. R. on 3:25.

statement by Paul's use of ἱλάσκομαι elsewhere, since there is in Paul no other instance of the word or its derivatives. Nevertheless, the statement is incontestable. Furthermore, in Paul's use of the כַּפֹּרֶת conception, the only significant point is that the כַּפֹּרֶת is an atonement for human sin. The other points, namely, that it covers the tables of the Law, that it is sprinkled with blood once every year, or even that it is the place of divine revelation (Ex. 25:22),[17] are all unimportant. If these details were really relevant, Paul would surely have alluded to them. The distinction between the two main interpretations of ἱλαστήριον is in the event very small. It boils down to the question whether Paul has in mind the Jewish view of the expiation of sins in general, or whether he is thinking of a specific form of this expiation.

διὰ πίστεως is undoubtedly to be taken with ἱλαστήριον, not προέθετο. This is supported by the parallel in v. 22 : δικαιοσύνη θεοῦ διὰ πίστεως. Through the faith which He awakens, Jesus is ἱλαστήριον. Those who believe are justified, vv. 22, 26. The object of faith is Jesus crucified and risen, 4:24, 25. He is thus ἱλαστήριον as the crucified and risen Lord, as the object of the λόγος καταλλαγῆς, 2 C. 5:19, 21. We may thus conclude that προέθετο denotes the apostolic preaching which sets Jesus before the eyes of men, Gl. 3:1. The dative object which completes it is not αὐτῷ or θεῷ, but ἡμῖν or τῷ κόσμῳ. The common rendering "to propose" or "to select"[18] is not possible here. For the point is, not that God has chosen Him as ἱλαστήριον, but that He has given Him to men as the basis of their faith. What is at issue is not God's secret counsel, but His action before and on men by which He reveals His righteousness. If this ἱλαστήριον is so only διὰ πίστεως, it is so only in the revealing action of God which gives birth to faith. To make ἐν τῷ αὐτοῦ αἵματι dependent on πίστεως is hardly apposite, since Paul does not speak of faith in the blood of Jesus. This, too, must be related to ἱλαστήριον. He is ἱλαστήριον for believers in His blood, i.e., as the One who died for them.

The revelation of divine righteousness which takes place in the ἱλαστήριον is obviously set by Paul in juxtaposition to the earlier πάρεσις τῶν ... ἁμαρτημάτων, v. 25. Witness is borne to it not merely by the prophets but also by the Law, v. 21. The indisputable centre of the earlier expiations of the Law is the Day of Atonement, when the ἱλαστήριον, or כַּפֹּרֶת, must be sprinkled with blood to mediate the remission of all sins. Paul obviously assumes that the church to which he writes is acquainted with the Mosaic Law, 7:1. Hence it is natural that He should depict Jesus in this context as a higher כַּפֹּרֶת [19] which is efficacious through faith rather than through purely external observance (R. 2:28, 29; 2 C. 3:6), which is sprinkled, not with the blood of animals, but with His own blood, and which is exposed to public view rather than concealed in the inaccessible Holy of Holies. Paul spiritualises the concept כַּפֹּרֶת, as he spiritualises λογικὴ λατρεία in R. 12:1 and circumcision in Col. 2:11. In so doing he changes it. We say too much if we argue that he should have added to ἱλαστήριον the καινῆς διαθήκης of 2 C. 3:6

---

[17] Cf. Str.-B., III, 174 f.

[18] Orig., Chrys., Ambrst., cf. Zn. R., ad loc., n. 72; C. Bruston, ZNW, 7 (1906), 77 ff.; it is quite incorrect that the mid. in προέθετο demands this interpretation. The mid. is common in the sense of "to display publicly," Pape, s.v.

[19] Luther, ad loc.; Cr.-Kö., s.v. ἱλαστήριον. Ritschl, Weinel, Bleibtreu, op. cit.; Schl. R., ad loc.; older literature in B. Weiss, Komm.⁹ (1899), ad loc.

or some other antithetical attribute. The way in which he speaks of ἱλαστήριον is enough to show his obvious antithesis to the OT. This interpretation has in its favour the fact that ἱλαστήριον can still take on concrete and even plastic significance. It is no more "out of taste" than the designation of the community as a temple, which describes the personal in terms of an object. [20] Naturally it is possible that Paul is simply following the usage of his time and taking ἱλαστήριον in the sense of something that ἱλάσκεται, that cleanses from sin. [21] But in my view this interpretation is too weak and abstract to correspond fully to the context or to Pauline forms of expression. Paul's letters are saturated with references and allusions to the LXX. Hence it is hard to think that in this case he was simply following the general usage of the day. It is incorrect to say that, except in theological circles, the Jewish communities did not have the presupposed acquaintance with the כַּפֹּרֶת now that it no longer existed. [22]

> Paul's thorough-going reorientation of the ἱλαστήριον concept completes the development of OT views of expiation which had been advanced by Philo and the Rabbis (→ 313). Closest to it is 4 Macc. 17:21 f.: ὥσπερ ἀντίψυχον γεγονότας (the martyrs of the Maccabean period) τῆς τοῦ ἔθνους ἁμαρτίας, καὶ διὰ τοῦ αἵματος τῶν εὐσεβῶν ἐκείνων καὶ τοῦ ἱλαστηρίου τοῦ θανάτου αὐτῶν ἡ θεία πρόνοια τὸν Ἰσραὴλ προκακωθέντα διέσωσεν. [23] In 4 Macc. 17, too, God creates the means of expiation and consequently brings deliverance. The community is purged, not by the temple cultus with its sacrificial animals, but only by substitutionary death, by personal self-sacrifice. Here, of course, the deliverance is only from temporal judgment; in Paul it is from eternal judgment. Furthermore, 4 Macc. 17 does not refer to the Day of Atonement.

b. In this light the theological root of Paul's view of ἱλαστήριον is clear. For Paul ἱλαστήριον is not something which makes God gracious. This expiation for human sin presupposes the grace of God. For Paul even those who fall victim to the wrath of God are also set under His patience, kindness and long-suffering, R. 2:4. The ἱλαστήριον serves the revelation or the righteousness of God, cf. vv. 25, 26: εἰς ἔνδειξιν, v. 21: πεφανέρωται. But revelation and substitution are not antithetical. Revelation comes to men only as substitution is made. God in His righteousness reveals more than a patience which leaves sin unpunished, v. 26. He also reveals a holiness which is at one and the same time both grace and judgment, which distinguishes between a sinner and his sin, which separates him from his sin, which brings him to a faith that is also repentance, i.e., self-judgment and true conversion. The revelation of a grace which is also judgment, and which establishes a faith that is also repentance, is no mere declaration of a transcendent attitude of God. It is a real fulfilment of grace and judgment on the human race. This demands, not only One to reveal God to the race, but also One to represent the race before God, to bear the divine judgment vicariously in order that the race might be brought thereby to self-judgment. A revelation without representation

---

[20] Cf. the Johannine designation of Jesus as the door: 10:9, or the way: 14:6.

[21] B. Weiss, Komm., Zn., Ltzm. R., ad loc.; Deissmann, op. cit., etc.

[22] The Law, including the sections on the Day of Atonement, was regularly read in the synagogues; and the Law was more important than what was found in the temple.

[23] Cf. 1:11: ὥστε καθαρισθῆναι ("purged from sin," not "refined") δι᾽ αὐτῶν τὴν πατρίδα; 6:28 f.: ἵλεως γενοῦ τῷ ἔθνει σου ἀρκεσθεὶς τῇ ἡμετέρᾳ περὶ αὐτῶν δίκῃ. καθάρσιον αὐτῶν ποίησον τὸ ἐμὸν αἷμα καὶ ἀντίψυχον αὐτῶν λάβε τὴν ἐμὴν ψυχήν ("make my blood an expiation for them, and take my soul vicariously for their souls").

would be no more effective than the Law in terms of judgment. Hence it could not bring men true ἀπολύτρωσις.[24] In this unity of the revelation of God to men and the representation of men before God, which really frees men from sin by self-release, redemption, and union with God, Jesus is ἱλαστήριον διὰ πίστεως ἐν τῷ αὐτοῦ αἵματι.

5. Hb. 9:5 simply follows LXX usage in its description of the ark of the covenant: χερουβὶν δόξης κατασκιάζοντα τὸ ἱλαστήριον.

Büchsel

| ἵνα | → εἰς, διά.

Contents: A. Theological Final Clauses: 1. In Judaism; 2. In the New Testament. B. Ethical Final Clauses: 1. In Judaism; 2. In the New Testament.

ἵνα, "in order that,"[1] is used in the NT alongside ὅπως and εἰς with the infinitive, often after εἰς τοῦτο, διὰ τοῦτο etc.; sometimes with the indicative, as in Gl. 2:4; 4:17. The final significance is not always too strict. In John ἵνα often introduces an explicative subsidiary clause after a preceding demonstrative (οὗτος etc.). This is in keeping with the generally explicative mode of thinking in the Johannine writings.[2] In the *koine* ἵνα can take on consecutive and even causal significance.[3] In the NT, however, this shift of meaning is less common, and it is of no theological importance.[4] The main passages which can be adduced for consecutive or causal significance, Mk. 4:11 f. etc., are robbed of their σκάνδαλον, but also of their

---

[24] It would simply bring a condemnation of sin which shows that it ought to be, not a victory over sin such as takes place when He who reveals God takes the place of the sinner and dies for him, Gl. 2:20: τοῦ ἀγαπήσαντός με καὶ δόντος ἑαυτὸν ὑπὲρ ἐμοῦ → ὑπέρ.

ἵνα. C. H. Dodd, JThSt, 23 (1922), 62 f.; D. C. Hesseling and H. Pernot in *Neophilologus*, 12 (1927), 41 ff.; H. Windisch, "Die Verstockungsidee in Mk. 4:12 und das kausale ἵνα der späteren Koine," ZNW, 26 (1927), 203 ff.; E. Stauffer, "'Ἵνα und das Problem des teleologischen Denkens bei Pls.," ThStKr, 102 (1930), 232 ff.; "Vom λόγος τοῦ σταυροῦ und seiner Logik," *ibid.*, 103 (1931), 179 ff.; J. A. F. Gregg, " 'Therefore ... because' and Parallel Uses," Exp. T., 39 (1927/28), 308 ff.; E. Molland, "ΔΙΟ, Einige syntaktische Beobachtungen," *Serta Rudbergiana* (1931), 49 ff., *Symbolae Osloenses Suppl.* IV; H. Preisker, *Geist und Leben, Das Telos-Ethos des Urchr.* (1933), 5 ff.; G. Stählin, "V. d. Dynamik der urchristlichen Mission" in *Festgabe f. K. Heim* (1934), 99 ff.; E. Schlink, "Zum Begriff des Teleologischen und seiner augenblicklichen Bdtg. für die Theologie," ZSTh, 10 (1933), 94 ff.

[1] V. Pr.-Bauer, Liddell-Scott, *s.v.* Bau. J.[3] on Jn. 15:8.

[2] Jn. 6:39 f.; 15:8, 12 f.; 17:3 etc.

[3] ἵνα = because: not found in literature, but cf. the anon. Apollon Dyscol. Synt., 266, 5 etc. Liddell-Scott, *s.v.* Cf. Dodd, Hesseling and Pernot, also A. T. Robertson. "The Causal Use of ἵνα," *Studies in Early Christianity* (1927), 49 ff.; Bl.-Debr.[6], 312. On the teleological ἵνα of consequence, *ibid.* § 391, 5 and suppl., 314.

[4] E.g., Jn. 9:2; Mk. 9:12. In Mk. the particular frequency of ἵνα clauses is for linguistic rather than theological reasons.

σοφία, by this weaker interpretation. They display their ultimate theological seriousness only when they are understood as final clauses in the strictest sense. The NT is particularly fond of clauses with ἵνα. But the decisive reason for this preference is not to be found in a linguistic softening of the conjunction ἵνα or in an extension of its meaning. This is shown by the common alternation of ἵνα clauses with other final constructions (ὅπως, εἰς with inf., διά with acc.). The reason is to be sought in the teleological understanding of the ways of God and the destiny of man as this is promoted in the NT. This is proved on the one hand by the prior history of ἵνα and its Semitic equivalents in the OT and later Judaism, and on the other hand by the fact that in the NT itself ἵνα and its synonyms are most common where there is the strongest teleological thinking, i.e., in the Pauline and Johannine writings.

A. Theological Final Clauses.

1. In Judaism.

a. The LXX normally has ἵνα, sometimes ὅπως or εἰς, for the purposes which determine God's action. In spite of Israel's sins, God does not abandon His people to their enemies lest the nations should fall into arrogant forgetfulness of God. God takes up the sufferer who is faithful to Him in order to bring him comfort and to bring shame to his enemies. [5] ἕνεκεν τούτου διετηρήθης, ἵνα ἐνδείξωμαι ἐν σοὶ τὴν ἰσχύν μου, καὶ ὅπως διαγγελῇ τὸ ὄνομά μου ἐν πάσῃ τῇ γῇ. [6] The revelation of His divine nature, power and glory is the constant aim of His actions, and this belief is basic for an understanding of God right on into NT days.

In the Wisdom literature the use of final conjunctions increases and becomes an indication of the increasing permeation of theological thought by the teleological motif. [7] The thinking of this literature is guided by the conviction that the purposeful activity of God is at work in all reality and events, and its aim is to unfold the plans which lie behind this divine work. In Sir. 39 the teleological character of creation, of natural events and of human history is underlined. [8] Final clauses play a decisive role especially in the great chapters of theological history in Wis. 16 [9] and Sir. 44 ff. [10] The fundamental importance of these clauses is emphasised by the preceding διά τοῦτο. [11] We understand the ways of God only if we ask, not why, but to what end. διὰ τοῦτο ... ὑπηρέτει πρὸς τὴν τῶν δεομένων θέλησιν, ἵνα μάθωσιν ... [12] God's historical action serves very different ends. But here, as in the OT, the final goal is that God should be acknowledged and glorified.

b. In Apocalyptic this teleological understanding is both deepened and broadened to comprise all history. Final clauses are predominant in Eth. En., Ps. Sol., Ass. Mos., Ps.-Philo, S. Bar., and the later Syrian Treas. Combinations like διά τοῦτο ... ἵνα are particularly common in these writings. In answer to the question as to the purpose of

---

[5] Dt. 32:27: ἵνα, ἵνα. ψ 83:7: εἰς. ψ 85:17: εἰς.
[6] Ex. 9:16. The context is permeated by the thought that God has raised up Pharaoh, and spares or blames, preserves or finally destroys, only to prove His omnipotence thereby.
[7] ῞Ινα is rare in the Psalter, common in Gn., even more common in Ex., Dt. and Is., and most common in Prv., Wis. and Sir.
[8] Sir. 39:16, 21, 26 f., 33. Cf. Menandri Sapientis Sententiae, ed. J. P. N. Land, *Anecdota Syriaca*, I (1862), p. 164.
[9] Wis. 16:3, 19, 23.
[10] Sir. 45:26; 46:6; 47:13.
[11] Sir. 45:24; cf. 44:17 f., 21.
[12] Wis. 16:25 f., cf. 16:11, 18, 22; Paral. Jer. 7.

creation, we are told : *propter plebem suam creavit orbem.* [13] Institutions and events both in heaven and on earth are scrutinised from the standpoint of teleology. [14] A model of teleological enactment is the Torah, which tells man what he should do and not do, [15] and which prepares him for the coming times. [16] In later ages much takes place *ut completur verbum* [17] which was previously spoken in Scripture. Even the *vaticinia ex eventu* of the Apocalypses serve this proof from prophecy in their own way. Very typical of Apocalyptic is the question as to the teleological office which God has assigned to individual figures and forces in the great plan of universal history, and especially the problem of human destiny. [18] This line of investigation led to the development and fixing of certain final clauses which might briefly be called formulae of commission : the archangel, king, seer, or man in general is created and sent, and has come, in order that he may fulfil this or that commission. This may be a commission which is essentially and permanently bound up with the office, e.g., of a king, [19] or it may be a special task which is divinely given to this particular king at this particular moment in history. [20] Apocalyptic also raises the question of the destiny of nations, and its answer is again in terms of a ἵνα. [21] In particular, the destiny of God's people continually poses this urgent question. [22] Here the final clause is sometimes preceded by a preparatory οὐχ ἵνα or οὐκ εἰς. The present visitation of God's people is not εἰς ἀπώλειαν, but εἰς νουθεσίαν. It must be understood, not as the final end, but as a means to the end. [23]

The distinctive inwardness and depth of this teleological thinking is displayed at the point where the loyal servant of God recognises in his own life the teleological direction of the living God. The stories of Joseph are dominated by the guiding principle that the reverses of Joseph serve a divine goal and that God pursues His aim of deliverance even when it seems that the human will to destroy is triumphant. [24] In Est. 4:14 Mordecai raises the question whether Esther has not been exalted in order that in her high station she may hazard her own life for her people (τίς οἶδεν εἰ εἰς τὸν καιρὸν τοῦτον ἐβασίλευσας). In the same stereotyped formula the children of Israel put the same question to Jephthah in his exile : *Quis enim scit, si propterea servatus es in dies istos, aut propterea liberatus es de manibus fratrum tuorum, ut principeris in tempore hoc populo tuo,* Ps.-Philo, 39, 3 (ed. princ., p. 40). Similar phrases and motifs are found in 1 Macc., Tob., Jdt. and the Test. Jos. They show how those who were faithful to God reflected on the mysterious ways of providence in times of darkness, and how they came to discern the paradoxical teleology latent within them.

---

[13] Ass. Mos. 1:12 (cf. *ut* in 1:13). Apc. Sedrach in M. R. James, *Apocrypha Anecdota,* TSt, II, 3 (1893), p. 131, 3 f. : διὰ τί . . . ; διὰ τὸν ἄνθρωπον.

[14] Eth. En. 27:1; 61:5; 100:11; 101:2; Slav. En. 30:5, 15; Ps.-Philo, 32, 10 (*v. Philonis Iudaei Ant. Bibl. liber incerto interprete,* Basel, 1527).

[15] 4 Esr. 7:21; abbreviated and moralised in Ep. Ar., 168.

[16] Ps.-Philo, 19, 4; cf. also Ass. Mos. 1:13 ff.; Eth. En. 108:7.

[17] Ps.-Philo, 12, 3 (ed. princ., p. 13); cf. *ut compleret verba sua,* 46, 1 (p. 46); cf. 21, 5; 28, 6.

[18] Eth. En. 69:10 f.

[19] Cf. the final clauses in defining the office of the accusing angels in Apc. Eliae, 4 (G. Steindorff, 41).

[20] Ex. 9:16 (Pharaoh); Sir. 45:24 (Phinehas); Apc. Abr., 10 (angels), 27 (kings); S. Bar. 3:1; 13:3 ff. Baruch); Apc. Eliae, 31 (king); Eth. En. 61:3 ff. angels); Ps.-Philo, 19, 4 (witness); Ass. Mos. 1:14 (Moses); Jub. 48:15 f. (Mastema).

[21] Eth. En. 15:5 ff.; Ps. Sol. 2:17 ff.

[22] S. Bar. 6:8; 7:1; 80:3; Ps. Sol. 2:16 ff.; 9:2 f.; Sib., 3, 282.

[23] Jdt. 8:27; 9:14; Bar. 4:5 f.; Ps.-Philo, 11, 14; Ps. Sol. 3:3 ff.; 2 Macc. 6:12 ff.; cf. Prv. 24:16.

[24] Gn. 45:4 ff.; 50:20. God brings good out of evil. The counterpart is the formulation of Aristobulus in Eus. Praep. Ev., 13, 12 : αὐτὸς (God) δ' ἐξ ἀγαθῶν θνητοῖς κακὸν οὐκ ἐπιτέλλει.

The *telos* idea reaches its extreme point when the teleological understanding of universal history broadens out into eschatology. The eschatological final clause is the frontier of the teleological ἵνα. For on the Apocalyptic view all historical goals point beyond themselves to the final goal of the ways of God which can be attained only when history itself reaches its end (→ τέλος). Only then will the faithfulness and righteousness and majesty of God, which continually manifest themselves in history, come to their final triumph. Only in the coming world will the ultimate goal of creation be realised. The world is created for man's sake. But what happens to this end if God allows man to perish? The world which is created for man's sake is the coming world, and the man for whom God has even now prepared it is the righteous. [25]

Here as everywhere the impelling problem of Apocalyptic teleology is that of theodicy. This drives teleological thinking into eschatology, but it does not allow it to rest content with eschatological solutions. Sirach has to fight doubts concerning the purposeful fulfilment of the cosmic plan, and these finally become dominant. Hence 4 Esr. presents us with a combination of teleology and the principle of selection. Its terrible thesis is that the multitude is *sine causa nata,* i.e., that the mass of creatures, and of men in particular, is simply placed in the world to fall victim to destruction or corruption. [26] Only a small minority reaches the divine goal, i.e., the future world. Thus 4 Esr. thinks through Apocalyptic eschatology to its end, and betrays Jewish theology into a crisis in which it must transcend itself.

Judaism evaded this terrible logic and revoked the dysteleology of 4 Esr. by opposing to it the pious correction of S. Bar. Here the better solution is reached that the nations are now let loose in order that they may later be disciplined, whereas the people of God is now disciplined in order that it may enter forgiven into the coming world. The end of the days will manifest the purpose of all God's ways. [27]

c. The ancient confidence of Wisdom literature in the future can thus reassert itself, and the way is charted for Rabbinic theology. [28] At much the same period as S. Bar. Nachum of Gimzo achieved fame through the saying which he used to utter in times of crisis: "Even this is for good." [29] His pupil Akiba built up this saying into a theological principle, namely, that man should always accustom himself to say that all that God does is for good. [30] For those who lived between the fall of Jerusalem in 70 A.D. and the catastrophe of 135 A.D. this was in some sense a defiant Nevertheless. [31] Later, however, it became a facile slogan [32] and empty schematism. [33] The phrase "that it might be fulfilled" also found a counterpart among the Rabbis. [34] Final constructions were used, but the theological content dissolved only too easily in speculative frivolities. Even the epigones of Apocalyptic surprisingly pursue a similar course and are overtaken by the same fate. Sanh., 4, 5 says: "only one man was created, in order to teach thee that

---

[25] S. Bar. 4:1 ff. Cf. the question of theodicy in Gr. Bar. 1.

[26] 4 Esr. 9:22; 10:34. Cf. the same teleological question in aetiological form, Ps.-Philo, 18, 11; 23, 13.

[27] S. Bar. 13:3 f., 9 f.; 20:2.

[28] My view of the relation between Apocalyptic and the Synagogue is the opposite of that of F. Rosenthal, *Vier apocryphische Bücher aus der Zeit und Schule R. Akiba's* (1885), 115 etc.

[29] bTaan., 21a.

[30] bBer., 60b; cf. S. Dt. § 32 on 6:5; bSanh., 101b.

[31] Cf. Stauffer in ThStKr, 102 (1930), 236, n. 1; 245, n. 1.

[32] We find rudimentary teleological proofs of God in Gn. r., 12 on 2:4; Ex. r., 26 on 17:8.

[33] Cf. ThStKr, 102 (1930), 232 ff., with details on the linguistic form and theological use of final clauses among the Rabbis.

[34] לקים מה שנאמר, v. W. Bacher, *Die exegetische Terminologie der jüdischen Traditionslit.,* I (1905), 170 f. ThStKr, *op. cit.,* 238, n. 2; 244, n. 1.

he who destroys a single soul from Israel is accounted by Scripture to have destroyed the whole world ; and for the sake of peace among the creatures, that one man should not say to another : My ancestor was greater than yours. And that the Minim should not be able to say that there are several original forces in heaven. And to declare the greatness of the Holy One, blessed be He ; [35] for when a man impresses many coins with the same form, they are all alike. But the King of kings, blessed be He, impresses each man with the form of the first man, yet none is like his neighbour. Hence each is obliged to say : The world was created for my sake." We also read : "Why did God create Adam out of the four cosmic elements ?" and the answer is : "In order that everything in the world might thereby be subjected to him. He took a speck of earth that all natures made of dust might serve Adam, a drop of water that all inhabitants of the seas and rivers might belong to him, a breath of air that all kinds of birds might be set under his control, and heat from the fire that all fiery creatures and forces might be available to help him." [36]

2. In the New Testament.

a. The Christ event was the decisive impulse which brought new life and significance to older teleological thinking. Jesus Himself spoke of His unique office in terms of the commission formula of Apocalyptic : "I am come ..." [37] John took up these formulae and developed them in the most varied ways. [38] The Synoptic Jesus says that His miracles are not an end in themselves. Their purpose is not exhausted by the momentary deliverance from need. They are to serve the revelation of Christ. [39] The Johannine Christ [40] puts the aetiological question : τίς ἥμαρτεν ... ἵνα τυφλὸς γεννηθῇ; and this receives the teleological answer : οὔτε οὗτος ἥμαρτεν οὔτε οἱ γονεῖς αὐτοῦ, ἀλλ᾽ ἵνα φανερωθῇ τὰ ἔργα τοῦ θεοῦ ἐν αὐτῷ. Here a final ἵνα corresponds to the consecutive ἵνα of the question. [41] But where no faith is kindled, unbelief is hardened by the very same act or word of revelation. For the Word and work of Jesus put an end to secret uncertainty in the world. They bring on the crisis of decision for or against Him. From the very first [42] the twofold goal of His mission is to bring about faith or hardening according to the predestined decision of God. Hence ἵνα clauses must be taken in a final sense no less when the reference is to hardening than to the awakening of faith : ἐν παραβολαῖς τὰ πάντα γίνεται, ἵνα βλέποντες βλέπωσιν καὶ μὴ ἴδωσιν ... μήποτε ἐπιστρέψωσιν καὶ ἀφεθῇ αὐτοῖς. [43] Here, too, John states the thoughts of Jesus in fixed theological formulae. Εἰς κρίμα ἐγὼ εἰς τὸν κόσμον τοῦτον ἦλθον, says Jesus when He cures the man born blind, ἵνα οἱ μὴ βλέποντες βλέ-

---

35 Cf. ThStKr, 102 (1930), 247, n. 1.
36 C. Bezold, *Die Schatzhöhle* (1883), p. 3. The passage is not in all the MSS, but there is a parallel in Ps.-Epiphanius, *v.* Bezold, *op. cit.*, p. 72, n. 14.
37 Mt. 5:17 ff. Similar forms in everyday use, Ac. 9:21; 16:36; Eph. 6:22.
38 Of the Baptist, 1:7 f., 31 (ἦλθον). Of Jesus, 3:17 (ἀπέστειλεν); 10:10; 12:46 f.; 18:37 (ἐλήλυθα); 6:38, 50 (καταβέβηκα); 5:36 (δέδωκεν); 1 Jn. 4:9 (ἀπέσταλκεν). There are 35 commission formulae in Rev. (δίδωμι, τίθημι, ἑτοιμάζω ...), and some 25 of these are followed by ἵνα.
39 Mk. 2:10; Lk. 5:24; Mt. 9:6 (→ n. 12); the malicious perversion of this thought by blasphemers, Mk. 15:32 : καταβάτω, ἵνα ἴδωμεν καὶ πιστεύσωμεν.
40 The witness to Christ and the depiction of the ways and works of Jesus, also serve to awaken faith (Lk. 1:4) Jn. 1:7; 19:35; 20:31; 1 Jn. 1:3 f.
41 Jn. 9:2 f. Cf. 11:4, but also 5:14 : μηκέτι ἁμάρτανε, ἵνα μὴ χεῖρόν σοί τι γένηται.
42 Lk. 2:34 : οὗτος κεῖται εἰς πτῶσιν καὶ ἀνάστασιν πολλῶν.
43 Mk. 4:11 f.; cf. Lk. 8:10; 9:45.

πωσιν καὶ οἱ βλέποντες τυφλοὶ γένωνται. [44] Finally, in His sayings concerning the necessity of the passion Jesus takes up again the motifs and formulae of the proof from prophecy (→ n. 17, 34), and in so doing He sets an example followed by Mt. and his successors : τοῦτο δὲ ὅλον γέγονεν ἵνα πληρωθῶσιν αἱ γραφαὶ τῶν προφητῶν. [45] The decisive point, however, is that in these sayings concerning the passion He lays the foundation for a teleological understanding of the cross. [46]

b. The oldest Christian kerygma known to us, which like Ac. we may link with Peter, borrows from the formulae of the Joseph stories and glorifies the planned and purposeful divine overruling which at the cross gained the victory over the counter-attack of the enemies of God, Ac. 2:36 etc. Yet the teleological concept is not yet given final form. This is the contribution of Paul, who works up the antithetical passion formula into a paradoxical formula of incarnation which gives a confessional form to the saying about the cross : δι' ὑμᾶς ἐπτώχευσεν πλούσιος ὤν, ἵνα ὑμεῖς τῇ ἐκείνου πτωχείᾳ πλουτήσητε. [47] Here there is built on the basis of an interpretation of the death of Jesus in terms of martyrdom theology [48] a soteriological understanding of the cross, [49] namely, that Jesus does not die merely to be exalted, but finally to accomplish the world's salvation. The cross is thus interpreted in terms of its *telos*, and the teleological principle has penetrated to the very heart of the Christian message and Christian theology.

From this central point the *telos* concept permeated the general Christian understanding of God, the world and history. [50] The starting-point of all creation and history — prescience, predestination and preparation — implies a teleological orientation. Abraham, [51] the giving of the Law at Sinai, [52] the destinies of the people of God in the days of the old covenant, all point beyond themselves and can be understood only in the light of their *telos*, the Christ event. [53] The martyrs of the pre-Christian period received no ἀπολύτρωσις, ἵνα κρείττονος ἀναστάσεως τύχωσιν. The faithful witnesses of the ancient covenant people did not experience the fulfilment of the promise, τοῦ θεοῦ περὶ ἡμῶν κρεῖττόν τι προβλεψαμένου, ἵνα μὴ χωρὶς ἡμῶν τελειωθῶσιν. [54]

But the Church of Christ also looks forward to the final consummation. Here particularly the fate of martyrs keeps alive the teleological understanding of the present, R. 8:17. For the elect are fated above all others to suffer, ἵνα τὸ δοκί-

---

[44] Jn. 9:39. Cf. 12:38, 40.

[45] Mt. 26:56, cf. Jn. 19:28 : ἵνα τελειωθῇ ἡ γραφή. Also Mt. 1:22; 2:15; 4:14; 12:17; 21:4; Jn. 13:18; 15:25; 17:12; 19:24, 36. In 18:9 the same formula occurs with reference to an earlier saying of Jesus.

[46] Behind the strictly final ἵνα of Lk. 11:50 is a conception of the murder of the righteous common to the theology of martyrdom, namely, that by such murder the enemies of God fill up the measure of their sins and bring the judgment day upon themselves. Cf. Ass. Mos. 9 f.; Mk. 12:7 ff.

[47] 2 C. 8:9, cf. 5:21; Gl. 3:13 f.; 4:5; R. 8:3 f. For an analysis of these formulae cf. Stauffer, ThStKr, 103 (1931), 179 ff. There are echoes of this paradoxical incarnation formula in 1 Pt. 2:24; 3:18; Hb. 2:14 f.; Barn., 5, 11; 7, 2; 14, 5.

[48] Cf. Lk. 24:26; Jn. 10:17; Hb. 2:9; Phil. 2:6 ff.

[49] Hb. 13:12, cf. 2:14 etc.

[50] Cf. the examination of Paul in ThStKr, 102 (1930), 232 ff.

[51] R. 4:16; cf. 9:11 f.

[52] R. 5:20; 7:13; though cf. 2 Tm. 3:17.

[53] 1 C. 10:11; 2 C. 3:13 f.; Gl. 3:22 ff.; R. 4:23 f.; 5:21; 8:4; 10:4; 15:4; Hb. 10:9.

[54] Hb. 11:35, 40; cf. the ἵνα in Jn. 4:36.

μιον ... τῆς πίστεως ... εὑρεθῇ εἰς ... δόξαν ... ἐν ἀποκαλύψει ... Χριστοῦ, 1 Pt. 1:6 f.; 5:6. The way through conflict is the way which God continually treads with men, with His apostle, [55] His community, [56] and all who love Him: τοῖς ἀγαπῶσιν τὸν θεὸν πάντα συνεργεῖ εἰς ἀγαθόν, τοῖς κατὰ πρόθεσιν κλητοῖς οὖσιν. In this saying in R. 8:28 Paul provides a predestinarian basis and an eschatological perspective for the motifs of the Joseph stories; he thus anticipates the formulae of Nahum and Akiba. When Paul considers the events in the lives of Philemon and Onesimus, he arrives at a formula very similar to that found in the Book of Esther and also in the pseudo-Philonic Antiquities (→ 325): τάχα γὰρ διὰ τοῦτο ἐχωρίσθη πρὸς ὥραν, ἵνα αἰώνιον αὐτὸν ἀπέχῃς, Phlm. 15.

But Paul finds the same paradoxical teleology in the puzzling dealings of God with His ancient people. Paul has no doubt but that it is God who has hardened the heart of Israel, and in R. 9:17 he quotes in this sense the terrible saying of Ex. 9:16: εἰς αὐτὸ τοῦτο ἐξήγειρά σε, ὅπως ἐνδείξωμαι ... (→ 324). But this hardening and rejection are not God's final purpose. They are only the means to an end: μὴ ἔπταισαν, ἵνα πέσωσιν; μὴ γένοιτο· ἀλλὰ τῷ αὐτῶν παραπτώματι ἡ σωτηρία τοῖς ἔθνεσιν, εἰς τὸ παραζηλῶσαι αὐτούς. [57] Thus final clauses crowd in upon one another in R. 11 until the final purpose of God is revealed in 11:32: συνέκλεισεν ... τοὺς πάντας εἰς ἀπείθειαν, ἵνα τοὺς πάντας ἐλεήσῃ.

c. But what is the *telos* to which the ways of God lead? Justification by faith alone, [58] the salvation of the world, [59] the self-revelation of God, [60] all these and other answers are found in the NT. [61] But the ultimate answer is the glorification of God. [62] This is the ancient answer of apocalyptic, but it is now pronounced with a new certainty and unparalleled confidence, namely, with the confidence that God's glory will not be achieved in the revelation of His righteous anger, but in the final manifestation of His all-conquering grace. [63] At the last all things will be subject to Him as at the first, ἵνα ᾖ ὁ θεὸς πάντα ἐν πᾶσιν, 1 C. 15:28. ὅτι ἐξ αὐτοῦ ... καὶ εἰς αὐτὸν τὰ πάντα, R. 11:36. For finally the original purpose of creation will be achieved, and all creation will realise its original destiny in the eschatological hymn of thanksgiving: αὐτῷ ἡ δόξα εἰς τοὺς αἰῶνας. [64]

This is how Paul views the eschatological *telos* of the ways of God — a different goal from the view of the future in 4 Esr. Is Paul so confident because he takes a less serious and stringent view of God and man than does the seer of 4 Esr.? No, he is confident because he confesses the cross, because he sees at work in the Christ event the God who carries forward His history to its goal even through

---

55 Phil. 1:12 f.; 2:27; 2 C. 4:10 f.; 12:9. Cf. 1 Tm. 1:15 f.

56 1 C. 11:19; 12:25; 2 C. 7:9. On 1 C. 11:32 cf. n. 27. On teleology in the life of the community v. 1 C. 1:26 ff.; 2 C. 8:6 ff.; 2 Th. 1:11 f.

57 R. 11:11; cf. 11:14; 10:19; Ps.-Philo, 20, 4; Gr. Bar. 16.

58 Gl. 2:16; R. 4:16; 9:11 f.; Eph. 2:9.

59 Mt. 18:14; Jn. 3:14-17 (ἵνα 4 times); 5:34; 6:38-40 (ἵνα 3 times); 15:11; 16:24, 33; 17:11, 13, 21 ff.; 1 Jn. 3:5, 8; Eph. 2:15; 4:10.

60 Jn. 5:20; 9:3; 10:38; 13:19; 14:31; Eph. 2:6 f.; 3:10, 18 f.

61 Cf. the teleological understanding of the course of the world in Mk. 4:22; Jn. 4:36 etc.

62 Jn. 5:23; 11:4; 14:13; 17:1; Phil. 2:10 f.

63 1 Th. 5:9 f.; R. 3:19 ff.; 9:23.

64 R. 11:36; cf. the eschatological doxologies of Rev., though here the expectation is somewhat different.

conflict, destroying the self-glorification of man in order that He may magnify His own glory. Salvation history is thus a merciless war of attrition against all καύ-χησις — ἵνα πᾶν στόμα φραγῇ καὶ ὑπόδικος γένηται πᾶς ὁ κόσμος τῷ θεῷ [65] — and it is salvation history for this very reason. For God is not fighting man. He is fighting man's self-glorification. When this self-glorification is overcome and the glory of God is re-established, i.e., in justification, there is σωτηρία. [66] Thus the paradoxical teleology of the ways of God leads through the destruction of all καύχησις to the δόξα θεοῦ, though *iustitia dei passiva* (Luther) to the *gloria dei* (Calvin), through the cross to the *soli deo gloria* of the new creation.

B. Ethical Final Clauses.

1. In Judaism.

a. Alongside theological final clauses we very quickly find ethical : Honour thy father and thy mother, ἵνα εὖ σοι γένηται, καὶ ἵνα μακροχρόνιος γένῃ. [67] In such imperatives with ensuing positive or negative final clauses the wisdom of Proverbs found the form of exhortation which best suited its basic ethical attitude. The final clause is often a firm moral indication of the good or bad results which we should seek or avoid in our conduct. [68] But in the last resort the fear of God is the epitome of wisdom, and to seek God's good pleasure is the goal of conduct : τήρησον ... ἐμὴν βουλήν ... ἵνα ζήσῃ ἡ ψυχή σου ... ἵνα πορεύῃ πεποιθώς ... The trust of those who fear God is not in their own action, but in God's : κύριος ... ἐρείσει σὸν πόδα, ἵνα μὴ σαλευ-θῇς. [69] The basic orientation and form of blessings is in keeping with this. Here the main clause does not speak imperatively of our task, but indicatively or optatively of God's action. Only in the concluding final clause is there reference to man's way and action. The divine rule is the presupposition of will and destiny. But God's action is directed to man's will and way. The work of God demands and makes possible the work of man.

b. Apocalyptic made these theological concepts the basis of its ethics. The starting-point of all ethical reflection is the question of the divinely willed and created orientation of man. God has not made man to seek out many arts. He has made him that he may remain righteous and blameless as the angels. [70] After the aberrations of Adam and his descendants, He gave His people the Law in order that it should recognise and fulfil its purpose more seriously and thereby regain the divine favour. In promises and threats He has shown it the way of life and the way of death, → n. 15 f. In special acts and words and tasks God also intervenes in the life of His people to keep it from evil and to lead it in the way of righteousness. [71] But God does not act merely in order that man may act. He also shows to man the goals of his ethical action. Every individual commandment is a contribution to the teleological direction of our conduct. The final motivations attached to the imperatives no longer express the short-sighted teleology of per-

---

[65] R. 3:19, 27; 1 C. 1:26 ff. On Paul's view this war of attrition is basically more pitiless than in 4 Esr. For there (7:92 ff.) we have a righteous remnant which will take its place in heaven with the pride of victory, whereas here (R. 3:27) we read : ποῦ οὖν ἡ καύχησις; ἐξεκλείσθη ! Here all stand ὑφ' ἁμαρτίαν, and none is great save God alone.

[66] Eph. 2:8 f.; 1 Tm. 1:16.

[67] Ex. 20:12; cf. Dt. 5:16; Eph. 6:3.

[68] Prv. 24:13; 30:4, 6, 9; 31:5, 7; Sir. 22:13, 23, 27.

[69] Prv. 3:21 ff., 26. Cf. also Ep. Ar., 251.

[70] Eth. En. 69:10 f.; Slav. En. 65:3 f. On commission formulae which refer to the orientation of man, → n. 20.

[71] Ass. Mos. 1:10; Ps.-Philo, 11, 12; 26, 1; Apc. Eliae, 22.

forming moral actions for specific results. [72] They are insights into the final goals of God. Hence the teleological ethics of Apocalyptic is in every sense theological ethics. Its nature is most clearly displayed in the prayers with concluding final clauses which are now found along with blessings. Prayer is made that God will keep us from the evil which threatens the human heart, that God Himself will lead us to the goal which He has set for man and his action. Nor is this mere petition. It is also intercession for those who know nothing of God or have no hope of His help and mercy. [73]

c. In the Synagogue the understanding of the teleological connection between divine and human action lost its depth and became stereotyped. Why did God create man on the last day of creation? "In order that when man should become arrogant, he might be told that even a gnat preceded him in the work of creation." Why did He create men with different faces? In order that they should not steal each other's wives. [74] At every point we find similar statements which, in answer to questions as to the purpose of creation and the motives of the Creator, reply in terms of the will of the Creator and the duty of the creature. [75] But the mechanical application of this method is very different from the theological penetration of ethics along the lines of Apocalyptic. In contrast, it leads to the moralistic dissolution of theology. Hence imperatives with ensuing final clauses again become dominant, and they express a very utilitarian spirit : "Exercise the duties of love in order that others should exercise them towards you ..." [76]

2. In the New Testament.

a. Jesus is fond of imperatives with final clauses. But these final clauses direct the regard and will and action of man quite radically to the one thing which is necessary (Mk. 10:21; Lk. 10:42 sy^c), to the eschatological goal of salvation. Our whole life's conduct must be orientated to this goal; it must be preparation and conflict, resignation and sacrifice, διὰ τὴν βασιλείαν, Mt. 19:12, 23 ff. The question : τί ποιήσω ἵνα ζωὴν αἰώνιον κληρονομήσω, is the question of all questions, Mk. 10:17, cf. Ac. 16:30. The answer is : ἀγωνίζεσθε εἰσελθεῖν (→ ἀγών, I, 137), ποιήσατε φίλους, ἵνα δέξωνται ὑμᾶς, [77] and especially : ἀφίετε, ἵνα καὶ ὁ πατὴρ ἀφῇ ὑμῖν τὰ παραπτώματα, Mk. 11:25, cf. Mt. 7:1. In thus setting the goal of ethics, Jesus tells us that the *telos* which decides the basic thinking of the NT is the glory of God. Λαμψάτω τὸ φῶς ὑμῶν ἔμπροσθεν τῶν ἀνθρώπων, ὅπως ἴδωσιν ὑμῶν τὰ καλὰ ἔργα [78] καὶ δοξάσωσιν τὸν πατέρα ὑμῶν τὸν ἐν τοῖς οὐρανοῖς. [79]

b. But the impulse which makes all human action possible is the divine action. In Jesus this is the theological presupposition of all ethical imperatives, and it is worked out in detail by Paul and his followers. Here the guiding theological concepts of Apocalyptic ethics are worked out consistently. The divine creation is a calling forth in the original sense of the term. God's historical work has the character of word. It is a word or summons directed to the will of man. [80] In this

---

[72] Eschatological ethics of reward, Test. L. 13.
[73] Ps. Sol. 5:6; Apc. Sedrach (→ n. 13) 14; Ps.-Philo, 12, 9; Gr. Bar., 16 (Slav. addition).
[74] Sanh., 38a; from the Gemara on Sanh., 4, 5 (→ 326 f.). Comparison shows that moralisation increases at a later period.
[75] ThStKr, 102 (1930), 242, n. 1; also Ass. Mos. 1:13 : *ut in ea gentes arguantur.*
[76] ThStKr, 102 (1930), 255, n. 1.
[77] Lk. 16:9 → n. 72.
[78] Cf. Mt. 5:15; Lk. 11:33.
[79] Mt. 5:16, cf. Jn. 3:20 f.; 1 Pt. 2:12; 4:11.
[80] Gl. 1:16; R. 15:15 f.

sense statements concerning God's will and act lead on to final clauses which speak of the possibilities and tasks that are posited of man. [81] In this sense predestination stands at the beginning of all history, pointing to the final goal of the ways of man, R. 8:29; 9:11 f., 17, 23. But this determination of the goal is no mere fatalism. Predestination is orientated to the will of man. Nor is this determination of will a deterministic enslavement. It is a voluntaristic awakening of the will. God wills the will of man. It is the will of man which He directs to His goals according to His purposes. He is not directing a mere vessel with no will of its own. God's will calls forth the will of man, and liberates it by taking possession of it.

This predestinating will of God is fulfilled in the Christ event. This is again both God's work and God's word. It is directed to the will of man and it calls forth his action. τῇ χάριτί ἐστε σεσωσμένοι, οὐκ ἐξ ἔργων, ἵνα μή τις καυχήσηται· αὐτοῦ γάρ ἐσμεν ποίημα, κτισθέντες ἐν Χριστῷ Ἰησοῦ ἐπὶ ἔργοις ἀγαθοῖς, οἷς προητοίμασεν ὁ θεὸς ἵνα ἐν αὐτοῖς περιπατήσωμεν, Eph. 2:8 f. Hence the indicatives with which Paul speaks of the Christ event will often lead to imperatives with οὖν, ὥστε or διό. [82] Paul is particularly fond of concluding a kerygmatic main clause with the final clause which refers to God's will for us and to us. [83] The basic formula of the word of the cross can lead directly from the soteriological to the ethical: ὁ θεὸς τὸν ἑαυτοῦ υἱὸν πέμψας ἐν ὁμοιώματι σαρκὸς ἁμαρτίας καὶ περὶ ἁμαρτίας κατέκρινεν τὴν ἁμαρτίαν ἐν τῇ σαρκί, ἵνα τὸ δικαίωμα τοῦ νόμου πληρωθῇ ἐν ἡμῖν τοῖς μὴ κατὰ σάρκα περιπατοῦσιν ἀλλὰ κατὰ πνεῦμα, Rom. 8:3 f. To take the λόγος τοῦ σταυροῦ seriously is to put it into practice. Hence Paul models his basic ethical formula on the paradoxical incarnation formula: ὑμεῖς ἐθανατώθητε τῷ νόμῳ διὰ τοῦ σώματος τοῦ Χριστοῦ, εἰς τὸ γενέσθαι ὑμᾶς ἑτέρῳ, τῷ ἐκ νεκρῶν ἐγερθέντι, ἵνα καρποφορήσωμεν τῷ θεῷ. [84] The final εἰς and ἵνα refer emphatically to the typical force which the cross of Christ must have for the lives of Christians. [85] Above all, the apostolic life and office must stand under the sign of the cross, and Paul accepts this necessity. He accepts the conflict through which he must reach the goal of his life and calling: πάντοτε τὴν νέκρωσιν τοῦ Ἰησοῦ ἐν τῷ σώματι περιφέροντες, ἵνα καὶ ἡ ζωὴ τοῦ Ἰησοῦ ἐν τῷ σώματι ἡμῶν φανερωθῇ. [86]

c. The final clauses in Pauline and post-Pauline epistles, however, do not refer merely to the human attitude which lies in the purpose of the divine work of salvation. They refer also to the goals which God has set for human action: πᾶσιν γέγονα πάντα, ἵνα πάντως τινὰς σώσω· πάντα δὲ ποιῶ διὰ τὸ εὐαγγέλιον, ἵνα συγκοινωνὸς αὐτοῦ γένωμαι, says Paul of himself, [87] and he then turns to his readers with the admonition: τρέχετε ἵνα καταλάβητε. [88] This has nothing whatever to do with a cheap morality of ends. For the goal, which demands of us

---

[81] 1 Th. 5:8 ff.; 1 C. 12:24 ff.; 2 C. 9:8.
[82] Cf. also R. Bultmann, "Das Problem der Ethik bei Paulus," ZNW, 23 (1924), 123 ff.; H. Windisch, "Das Problem des paul. Imperativs," *ibid.*, 265 ff.
[83] 1 C. 5:7; (15:49;) 2 C. 5:15; R. 6:4 ff. Cf. Eph. 4:14; 5:26 f. (ἵνα 3 times).
[84] R. 7:4, anal. Gl. 2:19. Analysis in ThStKr, 103 (1931), 184 f.
[85] 1 C. 1:17; 2:5; Phil. 2:30; 1 Pt. 2:21; 3:9.
[86] 2 C. 4:10, cf. 7:8 ff.; 11:7; 1 C. 3:18.
[87] 1 C. 9:22 ff.; cf. R. 1:11 ff.; 1 C. 1:15.
[88] 1 C. 9:12-27 (ἵνα 15 times); 7:5; 2 C. 2:11. Cf. Eph. 6:13.

the very utmost in effort and readiness for self-sacrifice, is eschatological salvation in the sense of Jesus. [89] Thus even the most refined religious utilitarianism is excluded. There can be no mere pursuit of personal salvation. For Paul perceives a whole hierarchy of goals in which the provisional must serve the definitive and the salvation of the individual the salvation of the whole. [90] The final goal which must permeate all our conduct and impress all lesser goals into its service is again the glorifying of God : τὰ γὰρ πάντα δι' ὑμᾶς, ἵνα ἡ χάρις πλεονάσασα διὰ τῶν πλειόνων τὴν εὐχαριστίαν περισσεύσῃ εἰς τὴν δόξαν τοῦ θεοῦ. [91]

This ultimate goal cannot be reached apart from the will of man. But the whole of the NT is agreed that the high *telos* of early Christian ethics transcends the will and power of man. Hence the ethics of the NT is an ethics of prayer. Ἀγωνίζεσθαι ἵνα means that we are both to fight and to pray for the goal which is set before us. It is thus the quintessence of Christian conduct and a guarantee of the insight that the work of Christians must finally be prayer. Final exhortations merge into blessings and prayers which are introduced by a ἵνα. Jesus Himself prays the Father that the faith of Peter fail not, [92] and He admonishes the disciples : ἀγρυπνεῖτε ... ἐν παντὶ καιρῷ δεόμενοι ἵνα κατισχύσητε ἐκφυγεῖν ταῦτα πάντα ... καὶ σταθῆναι ἔμπροσθεν τοῦ υἱοῦ τοῦ ἀνθρώπου. [93] Paul does not take a single step on his divinely appointed way which is not prayer and which is not grounded in prayer ; and he expects the same of his churches. For it is only in prayer that the will of man experiences its constant integration into the will of God. It is only here that the work of man finds its fullest possibilities (→ ἀγών, I, 138 f.). The most powerful prayer, however, is intercession. Hence the community must intercede for the apostle, ἵνα ὁ θεὸς ἀνοίξῃ θύραν τοῦ λόγου ... ἵνα φανερώσω (τὸ μυστήριον) ὡς δεῖ με λαλῆσαι. [94] And the apostle prays for the community. Prayer is for him the beginning and the end of exhortation. [95] It is no mere stylistic habit that he opens his epistles with thanksgivings and requests and that he closes them with blessings. He puts more trust in intercessions than in admonitions. He has more faith in God than in the good will and power of the churches. And if Jesus teaches His disciples to begin their prayers with the petition : ἁγιασθήτω τὸ ὄνομά σου, Paul opens his letters with the request : προσεύχομαι, ἵνα ... εἰς ... ἵνα ἦτε εἰλικρινεῖς καὶ ἀπρόσκοποι εἰς ἡμέραν Χριστοῦ, πεπληρωμένοι καρπὸν δικαιοσύνης τὸν διὰ ... Χριστοῦ, εἰς δόξαν καὶ ἔπαινον θεοῦ. [96] The final goal of prayer can only be the same as that of all our ways, and as the great end of the ways of God, the *gloria dei*.

Stauffer

Ἰορδάνης → ποταμός.

---

[89] Cf. Rev. 3:18 : συμβουλεύω σοι ἀγοράσαι ... ἵνα πλουτήσῃς, καὶ ... ἵνα περιβάλῃ καὶ μὴ φανερωθῇ ... καὶ ... ἵνα βλέπῃς.

[90] 1 Th. 2:16; 4:12; 2 Th. 3:9; 1 C. 7:5; 8:13; 10:33; 14:1 ff.; 2 C. 2:4; 6:3; Gl. 2:5; Phil. 2:15 f.; Col. 1:28.

[91] 2 C. 4:15; 5:15; R. 15:16; cf. 1 Pt. 2:12; 4:11.

[92] Lk. 22:32; cf. Jn. 17:15. ἐρωτᾶν ἵνα in the everyday sense at Jn. 4:47; 19:31, 38.

[93] Lk. 21:36; Mt. 24:20; 26:41. → βοάω, I, 627.

[94] Col. 4:3 f.; cf. R. 15:30 ff.; 2 Th. 3:1 f.; also Eph. 6:18 ff.

[95] Col. 1:9 ff.; 2 C. 13:7; cf. Eph. 1:17 ff.; 3:16 ff.

[96] Phil. 1:9 ff.; cf. 2 Th. 1:11 f.; 2 C. 1:8 ff. Δόξα as a motif of intercession in Eph. 1:17 ff.; 3:16.

---

† ἰός, † κατιόομαι

Distinction must be made between ὁ ἰός, "the arrow" (Lam. 3:13 : εἰσήγαγεν τοῖς νεφροῖς μου ἰοὺς φαρέτρας αὐτοῦ) and the different word ὁ ἰός, "flux," "sap," "poison," "rust." The former (since Hom.) is connected with the Indo-iranian *isu* "arrow," [1] while the latter (since Theogn., Pind. and Aesch., cf. also the pap. and LXX) is related to the Lat. *virus* and the Sanskrit *viša*. [2] Only the second of the two words is found in the NT. It has the sense of 1. "poison" in R. 3:13; Jm. 3:8, and 2. "rust" in Jm. 5:3. In Jm. 5:3 we also find the verb κατιοῦσθαι (ὁ χρυσὸς ὑμῶν καὶ ὁ ἄργυρος κατίωται), of which there are other instances; κατιοῦν is also found at Sir. 12:11: γνώσῃ ὅτι οὐκ εἰς τέλος κατίωσεν. The comparison ὡς γὰρ ὁ χαλκὸς ἰοῦται occurs at Sir. 12:10, and at Sir. 29:10 we find the admonition : ἀπόλεσον ἀργύριον δι' ἀδελφὸν καὶ φίλον, καὶ μὴ ἰωθήτω ὑπὸ τὸν λίθον εἰς ἀπώλειαν.

1. ἰός, "Poison."

The OT refers first to the poison of snakes (ἰὸς ἀσπίδων, ψ 139:3; ψ 13:3, in R. 3:13, in translation of the Heb. חֲמַת עַכְשׁוּב).The Psalmist sees in the poison of snakes a figure of the malicious words of his opponents, who try to entrap the righteous. The tongue of snakes contains poison as a treacherous weapon of attack ; similarly the wicked sharpen their tongues and have poison under their lips (ὑπὸ τὰ χείλη). It has been suggested that behind the metaphor there lurks the fear of evil magic and of curses (cf. also ψ 57:4 : θυμὸς αὐτοῖς κατὰ τὴν ὁμοίωσιν τοῦ ὄφεως, חֲמַת־נָחָשׁ). [3] The righteous do not feel that they are a match for this kind of hostility, and they turn to God for help in prayer. According to Job 20:12-16 evil may taste sweet in the mouth, but it changes into the gall of asps in the body (20:14 : χολὴ ἀσπίδος). The same image is used of the effects of wine at Prv. 23:32. It is attractive and pleasant to drink, but then it bites like a serpent (τὸ δὲ ἔσχατον ὥσπερ ὑπὸ ὄφεως πεπληγὼς ἐκτείνεται καὶ ὥσπερ ὑπὸ κεράστου διαχεῖται αὐτῷ ὁ ἰός).

In the NT Paul uses OT terms to describe the bondage of our human members under the dominion of sin (R. 3:10-18). Our tongues are deceitful, our lips have the poison of serpents (ἰὸς ἀσπίδων, ψ 139, 3), our mouths are full of cursing and bitterness (3:13-14). Sin drives men into mutual enmity and makes their words treacherous weapons. When they proceed from sin, words are like the poison of serpents and bring destruction. Here, too, the member embodies man's activity, and λάρυγξ, γλῶσσαι, χείλη and στόμα represent his word. If R. 3:10-18 builds up to a climax, we are impressed by the comprehensiveness of the depiction. In

---

ἰός κτλ. [1] Walde-Pok., I, 107.

[2] *Ibid.*, 243 f.

[3] Cf. S. Mowinckel, *Psalmenstudien,* I (1921), 19 : "The tongue and the powerful word as an instrument of the magician"; 23 : "Experience of a death-dealing reality is the source of this traditional image"; cf. 46 on Ps. 58:4. H. Birkeland, *Die Feinde des Individuums in der israelitischen Psalmenliteratur* (1933) thinks that Ps. 140 refers to war and foreign enemies, and he describes it as a psalm of protection (pp. 228-230).

this heaping up of members which serve the word, there is on the one side a recognition of the importance of the word itself and on the other a particular shrinking from the sinister power of sins of the tongue. Other members are mentioned more briefly (πόδες, 3:15; ὀφθαλμοί, 3:18). The destructive power of the dominion of sin is the negative counterpart of the saving message of Christ (R. 10:15).

In his recognition of the dangerous nature of the tongue Paul is at one with James, especially Jm. 3:8, where the tongue is described as a member which no men can tame, a restless evil full of deadly poison (μεστὴ ἰοῦ θανατηφόρου).[4] As compared with Prv. 10:19 f. the perception of sin is heightened and radicalised. It is not just that evil comes into the world through the tongue. The very nature of the tongue is manifested in its poisonous character. As we fear the violence (ψ 57:4 : θυμός) and treachery of the serpent, so death lurks in the violent and treacherous word of the tongue. This has been known since the story of Paradise, in which sin and death are connected.[5] The divine requirement aims at the overcoming of malice and division (Jm. 3:10-12).

> There is a reference to cunning and slanderous men in Herm. s., 9, 26, 7: "For as the beasts with their poison (τῷ ἑαυτῶν ἰῷ) slay man and brings him to corruption, so the words of such people slay man and bring him to corruption." Ign. Tr., 6, 2 warns us against being poisoned by false teachers. These are like men who mix deadly poison (θανάσιμον φάρμακον) in the wine and thereby entice the unwary to drink to themselves death in their lust.

2. ἰός, "Rust."

As rust which corrupts gold and silver and thereby indicts its owner, ἰός is in Jm. 5:2 f. a warning against the danger of riches and earthly treasures (ὁ πλοῦτος ὑμῶν σέσηπεν ..., ὁ χρυσὸς ὑμῶν καὶ ὁ ἄργυρος κατίωται). There is an apocalyptic ring about the warning that the rust of riches will bear testimony against their owner and sear his flesh like fire (we should take ὡς πῦρ with φάγεται). The fact that gold and silver rust is in the Bible a repeated warning against false confidence in possessions (Mt. 6:19-20).[6] Does the rust bear witness to the impermanent nature of both the possession and its owner?[7] Or does it accuse the rich of preferring to let things rot rather than give them to the poor?[8] The context favours the latter interpretation. In the apocalyptic image rust is almost a living avenging force.

> Ezekiel is given the task of setting on the fire a pot with pieces of flesh (24:3 ff.). But he perceives that the inside is eaten with rust (חֶלְאָה, LXX ἰός : 24:6; 24:11-12). Perhaps he is alluding to the blood-guiltiness of Jerusalem. Increasing heat should purge the impurity and rust, but there is reason to doubt whether it will succeed. Jerusalem

---

[4] Cf. Sib. Fr., 3, 33 : τῶν δὴ κἀκ στόματος χεῖται θανατηφόρος ἰός; cf. also Test. R. 5:3; G. 6:3 (τὸν ἰὸν τοῦ μίσους).

[5] "It is distinctive of James as compared with the Test. XII that he alludes far less to Satan as the author of evil. He speaks in more psychological terms," Hck. Jk., 169, n. 86.

[6] Sir. 29:10 : καὶ μὴ ἰωθήτω ὑπὸ τὸν λίθον εἰς ἀπώλειαν; Ep. Jer., 10, 23; Cl. Al. Paed., II, 38, 2; though cf. Philo Rer. Div. Her., 217: ὁ χρυσὸς ἰὸν οὐ παραδέχεται. This general view that gold and silver do not rust is contested in the Bible.

[7] J. C. K. v. Hofmann : Der Brief Jakobi (D. hl. Schrift. NTs, VII, 3 [1876]), ad loc.

[8] Dib. Jk., Hck. Jk., ad loc.

falls victim to judgment as the pot to the fire. Here, too, rust is an indictment of the owner, and it indicates the imminent intervention of God. In Ep. Jer. rust and corruption denote the helplessness and impermanence of silver, gold and wooden idols which cannot save themselves nor preserve their splendour (v. 10, 23). Similarly Dg., 2, 2 pours scorn on gods of iron which are eaten up by rust (ὁ δὲ σίδηρος ὑπὸ ἰοῦ διεφθαρμένος).

The apocalyptic warning (Ez.; Jm.) is thus accompanied by apologetic rationalism (Ep. Jer.; Dg.). The image of rust (ἰός) can be used in both connections.

Michel

’Ιουδαία, ’Ιουδαῖος, ἰουδαΐζω, ’Ιουδαϊσμός → ’Ισραήλ.

ἵππος[1]

1. The Horse in Palestine, the OT and Judaism.

From the time of the Hyksos (c. 1700) the horse is of military importance in Egypt for drawing chariots, and in this capacity it is capable of limited use on the Palestinian plains. According to the OT it is first found in Egypt and then in Canaan (Gn. 47:17; Ex. 9:3; 14:9; Dt. 17:16; Ez. 17:15). Egypt introduced horses to Palestine at an early period, though horses from Asia Minor may also have been known and used for warlike purposes in Palestine. The chariot seems to have been used first in the reign of Solomon ; David was still crippling enemy horses that were captured (2 S. 8:4). Solomon's stables and chariot cities (cf. archaeological discoveries at Megiddo) were renowned (1 K. 5:6; 2 Ch. 9:25). He received horses as presents (1 K. 10:25) and also bought them from Egypt (1 K. 10:29). Horses and chariots, and later horses and riders (Assyrians and Persians), were an established part, and indeed the core and centre, of ancient armies (Israel, 1 K. 18:5; 22:4; the Syrians, 1 K. 20:1 ff.; 2 K. 5:9; 6:14; 7:7 ff.; the Assyrians : 2 K. 18:23, riders). Horses were extolled for their speed (Jer. 4:13) and strength (2 Εσδρ. 4:23 LXX : ἐν ἵπποις καὶ δυνάμει). There is an admiring description of their strength and courage in Job 39:19-25. God is the Lord of hosts (Sabaoth). He thus controls heavenly messengers and forces who can also come in military array.[2] Thus horses and chariots of fire take the prophet Elijah to heaven (2 K. 2:11), and along the same lines God reveals His military power to Elisha and his servant (2 K. 6:17). We learn from

---

ἵ π π ο ς. Cf. M. Ebert, *Reallexikon der Vorgeschichte*, 10 (1927-28), 109-115; K. Galling, *Biblisches Reallexikon* (1934 ff.), *s.v.* Pferd ; for bibl. of the horsemen of the Apocalypse cf. M. W. Müller, ZNW, 8 (1907), 290 ff.; G. Hoennicke in *Studierstube*, 19 (1921), 3 ff.; A. v. Harnack, *Erforschtes und Erlebtes* (1923), 53 ff.; L. Köhler, *Die Offenbarung des Joh.* (1924), 59-68; cf. also Pr.-Bauer³, *s.v.*

[1] ἵππος belongs to the common Gk.-Indogerm. inheritance (Lat. *equus*), cf. Walde-Pok., I, 113.

[2] The point of the OT and NT accounts is not that God disposes of horses and chariots of fire, or of horsemen, but that God specifically equips His messengers for definite functions. We are to view the Messianic battle in the same light (Rev. 19:11-15).

Est. 6:8 ff. (Ez. 23:6 ff.) that the horse is the steed of kings. At a later period there is reference to a horse gate in Jerusalem (Jer. 31:40; Neh. 3:28). [3]

It is never forgotten, however, that the horse is a symbol of alien power. In the prophets and the Psalter there are many warnings against trusting in chariots and horses. "At thy rebuke, O God of Jacob, both the chariot and the horse are put into a dead sleep" (ψ 75:6; cf. Hos. 1:7; Am. 2:15). The LXX often introduces this thought even where it is not present in the Heb. (Na. 2:4; Am. 6:7). It is fighting against ungodly ὕβρις. The horse is a symbol of the flesh and of fleshly confidence (Is. 30:16; 31:1-3; ψ 19:7; 32:16 f.; 146:10). Alien military power cannot save. Carnal confidence brings into enmity against God. The faith and hope demanded by Yahweh imply renunciation of all false security or human calculation (Is. 30:15). Intentionally the king of peace in Zech. chooses an ass rather than a horse (9:9). Perhaps this is in keeping with a primitive motif. [4]

Apocalyptic occupies a special place. Joel describes the plague of locusts in terms of chariots and horses (2:4-5; cf. the equation with demons in Rev. 9:7 ff.). [5] In the visions of the night in Zech. a man rides on a red horse, and behind him are speckled horses which are charged to walk through the earth (1:8-10; 6:1-8). The colours of the animals are related to the four corners of heaven to which they are sent. Heavenly chariots are despatched to declare the will of God everywhere. [6] 2 Macc. 3:25-29 tells of a heavenly horse with a terrible rider who in alliance with two youths punishes the usurper Heliodorus (θεομάχος). [7] In battle (10:29-30) five glorious figures appear on horses with golden bridles, place themselves at the head of the Jews, protect Judas Maccabeus and launch thunderbolts and strokes of lightning against the enemy. The enemy are blinded and routed.

2. The Horse in the NT.

a. Jesus rides into Jerusalem on an ass, not on the warlike horse of a king (Mk. 11:1-10). Mt. sees here an express fulfilment and confirmation of the prophecy of the king of peace and a visible testimony to the meekness of Christ (πραΰς, Mt. 5:5; 11:29; 21:5). According to Jn. this royal action of Christ is prophesied in the ancient saying (ὁ βασιλεύς σου, Jn. 12:15). Faith recognises the coming king of the last time, and perceives in the manner of His entry the fulfilment of Scripture and the disclosure of the Messianic secret. [8]

---

[3] In 2 K. 23:11 we read that chariots and horses of the sun were destroyed as part of the reform under Josiah.

[4] E. Sellin, Das Zwölfprophetenbuch, II², ³ (1930), 551: "As may be seen from the continuation in v. 10, the author sees in this a sign of the king's love of peace. He is distinguished by his steed from other earthly kings, who ride on horses to battle (Jer. 17:25; 22:4). In reality, however, the ass is an established part of the very earliest expectation of the coming king. For in the earliest period of folk history princes generally rode on asses, and this is how the king of Paradise is depicted." Cf. Ju. 5:10; 10:4; 12:14; 2 S. 19:27; Gn. 49:11.

[5] Jl. 2:4 : ὡς ὅρασις ἵππων ἡ ὄψις αὐτῶν καὶ ὡς ἱππεῖς οὕτως καταδιώξονται.

[6] Sellin, op. cit., 515 : "The heavenly chariots are about to move to all the quarters of heaven to take God's Spirit there and to gather the scattered Jews in order that they may share in the building of the temple."

[7] Cf. on the Heliodorus legend in connection with the view of the θεομάχος, H. Windisch, "Die Christusepiphanie vor Damaskus (Ac. 9; 22; 26) und ihre religionsgesch. Parallelen," ZNW, 31 (1932), 1-23.

[8] Cf. bSanh., 98a : R. Alexandrei (c. 270) has said : R. Jehoshua b. Levi (c. 250) brought into contrast Da. 7:13 : "Lo, there came with the clouds of heaven one like a son of man," and Zech. 9:9 : "Poor and riding on an ass." If they (Israel) have merits (are worthy), he comes with the clouds of heaven ; if they have no merits, he comes poor and riding on

b. Occasionally the OT emphasised the fact that horses and mules were wild and needed to be tamed by bridle, bit and whip (ψ 31:9; Prv. 26:3). Wisdom literature makes a good deal of use of this metaphor and refers in different senses to the one who directs (ἡνίοχος) or steers (κυβερνήτης) the chariot. [9] According to James the perfect man (τέλειος ἀνήρ) can control the whole body (3:2: χαλιναγωγεῖν; 3:3: χαλινός). James has in view the control of the word or the tongue (3:2, 4). As he sees it, part of perfection (τελειότης) as the goal of Christian sanctification is mastery over every member of the body and its activity. This is his contribution to the doctrine of creation and sanctification.

c. Like OT Apocalyptic, Rev. refers in various ways to horses. Best known are the four horses with their avenging and destroying riders (6:1-8). Each horse follows the other and constitutes a separate seal. There is no special connection between the quarters of heaven, or the winds, and the colours of the horses. [10] The white horse represents the conqueror (νικῶν) who comes from without with an alien host (τόξον) and oppresses the kingdom. [11] It is followed by the fiery red horse (πυρρός) which takes away peace and unleashes civil strife (ἵνα ἀλλήλους σφάξουσιν). There logically follows the black horse with the one who carries scales (ζυγός); this third rider taxes the necessities of life (wheat and barley), but leaves the oil and wine untouched. In the rear comes the pale horse whose rider, pestilence (דֶּבֶר, Rev. 2:23), completes the sum of horrors, with Hades for his squire. In Rev. 9 a wild swarm of demonic locusts bursts upon the earth and its inhabitants (cf. Ex. 10; Jl. 1-2). These are like horses prepared for battle (9:7). The rustling of their wings is like the thunder of chariots and horses rushing into battle (9:9). This host consists of myriads and myriads (9:16). The riders wear multi-coloured breastplates (9:17). The heads of the horses are like the heads of lions, and they smite and slay with both head and tail (9:19). Various OT pests and animals (locusts, scorpions and leviathan) unite their demonic forces and enhance the terrible nature of this apocalyptic host.

Rev. often speaks of the terrible battle, and one of the most grisly descriptions is that of the blood which flows as a result of the judgment of the angel: "Blood came out …

---

an ass. King Shabor (I) says to Shemuel († 254): You say that Messiah will come on an ass; I will send him a glorious horse such as I have. He answered: Do you then have one of a thousand colours (as his ass will be of a thousand colours)? Midr. Qoh., 1, 9: As the first redeemer, so the last redeemer: As it was said of the first redeemer in Ex. 4:20 that Moses took his wife and sons and caused them to ride on an ass, so it is said of the last redeemer in Zech. 9:9: Poor and riding on an ass. PRE, 31 on Gn. 22:3 (Abraham's ass): This was the ass on which Moses rode when he came to Egypt (Ex. 4:20), and this will be the ass on which the Son of David will one day ride (Zech. 9:9).

[9] The image of the ἡνίοχος, either alone or along with the κυβερνήτης, is often used in Philo, Op. Mund., 88; Leg. All., II, 104; III, 223; Spec. Leg., I, 14. Cf. also Dio Chrys. Or., 12, 34; 36, 50; Stob., III, 493; and Plato's well-known metaphor of the charioteer and the horses (Phaedr., 246 f.). Cf. also Ab. R. Nat., 24: The man whose study is coupled with good deeds is a rider whose horse has a bridle (χαλινός). Mere knowledge is like an unbridled horse which suddenly throws its rider. For further instances cf. Dib. Jk., ad loc.; Wnd. Kath. Br., ad loc. In Hellenism the application may be secular ("small causes, great effects"), or religious (God's direction of the world), or ethical (the mastery of man's soul over his body).

[10] North = red; south = black; east and west = white and yellow (indefinite).

[11] We misunderstand the destructive activity of the horsemen if we identify the first with the avenging or warring Messiah of 19:11-16, or with the Gospel in its incursion into the world (Mk. 13:10).

even unto the horse bridles, by the space of 1600 furlongs" (14:20). Cf. the prophecy in En. 100:2-3 : "(In those days) sinners will slay one another from the first dawn to sundown : a horse will wade in the blood of sinners up to its breast, and a chariot will sink up to its full height." [12] In the lament which merchants raise over the fall of Babylon (18:11-14) they speak of the things they used to import into the city, and these include "beasts, and sheep, and horses, and chariots, and slaves, and souls of men" (18:13). [13]

In opposition to the wild demonic host Messiah Himself and His army appear at the end of Rev. on white horses (19:11-16). White is the colour of the Victor (6:2), of the new purity attained through Christ (7:14; 19:14), and of heavenly splendour (Mk. 9:3). The earlier emphasis on many colours is here replaced. Again a heavenly host goes out to battle and conflict, but only Messiah Himself fights (κρίνει καὶ πολεμεῖ, 19:11), and He does so with the sword of His mouth (19:15). [14]

Michel

---

† ἶρις

A. The position outside the New Testament.

1. From the time of Homer ἶρις is the customary word for a "rainbow" (e.g., Il., 17, 547); Theophr., De Signis Tempestatum, 22 : ὅταν ἶρις γένηται, ἐπισημαίνει (sc. rain), or for a rainbow round the moon (Aristot. Meteor., III, 4, p. 375a, 18 : μέγιστον δὲ σημεῖον τούτων ἡ ἀπὸ τῆς σελήνης ἶρις). Figur. it can be used for a "halo," for the "circle" round a light (Theophr., op. cit., 13), for the "iris" of the human eye, or even for the "play of colours" around the eyes on the feathers of a peacock (Luc. De Domo, 11). Even when used figur. the word still retains the original notion of the coloured ring or bow. Along with many other natural phenomena, the bow around heaven and earth was personified for the Greeks in the messenger goddess Iris (Hom. Il., 15, 144; 24, 77 ff.), who also found a place in Roman mythology (Vergil Aen., 4, 693 ff.). [1] In this figure are

---

[12] Cf. the description of the massacre of Beth-ter in Rabbinic sources (Str.-B., III, 817). It is a common oriental image, cf. Lidz. Ginza, XVIII, 390 f. (p. 417, 15): "Then comes that king, looses his horse, and the horse strides above them up to its saddle in blood, and the swirl of the blood reaches to its nostrils."

[13] The reference here seems to be to horses in general rather than specifically to war-horses. The horse is not an apocalyptic creature but an earthly animal which symbolises the culture of this demonic metropolis.

[14] As in military history, horses which draw chariots (e.g., in earlier narratives) yield before horses with riders. Worth noting, too, is the statement which follows : "The armies which were in heaven followed him" (τὰ στρατεύματα τὰ ἐν τῷ οὐρανῷ); the whole host of heaven is mobilised. In this passage the horse is simply at the service of its rider ; it has no function of its own in the battle.

ἶ ρ ι ς. Pr.-Bauer and Liddell-Scott, s.v.

[1] Cf. on Iris the mythological and archaeological data in W. Ruge, Pauly-W., IX (1916), 2037 ff.

reflected the religious experiences and concepts which the sight of a rainbow kindled in the men of antiquity. The rainbow was thought to typify the ancient connection between the world of the gods and the world of men.

2. The biblical conception of the rainbow does not greatly deviate from that of classical antiquity. The rainbow appears for the first time in Gn. 9:13. It is here a sign of the covenant between God and the earth. It bears witness to the gracious will of God towards men. How the bow can be such a sign is not explained by the author, though he does try to explain the sign, namely, that the bow in and above the rain-clouds is a guarantee that God will spare humanity a second flood (9:14 ff.). Underlying the whole idea is perhaps the belief that the bow of the god of war or the god of thunderstorms is set in the clouds and is thus robbed of its force.[2] In support of this kind of historicising of a mythological feature[3] it might be pointed out that the original speaks of the קֶשֶׁת of God, and that basically this term signifies the bow of the warrior or the hunter.

This usage is common in the OT. We find it at Ez. 1:28, and it dominates the LXX, though at Gn. 9:13; Ez. 1:28, also Sir. 43:11; 50:7, τόξον is used for קֶשֶׁת.[4] ἶρις occurs only at Ex. 30:24 in translation of קִדָּה, a plant used for ointment which perhaps came from Arabia or India. Why ἶρις is used here is not clear, since קִדָּה is not rendered ἶρις at LXX Ez. 27:19. There is perhaps some textual corruption. If not, the best explanation of the confusion is that קִדָּה was not unambiguous but could be used for several plants.[5]

In the OT the rainbow is a demonstration not merely of God's grace but also of His glory. In Ez. 1:28 comparison with it is used in describing the greatness of the כְּבוֹד־יְהוָה. At Sir. 43:11 it bears witness with all creation to the wonderful power of the Creator, and at Sir. 50:7 it is used with the morning star and the sun to suggest the impression made by the high-priest Simon.

3. The later Rabbis[6] carried this thought further in their warning not to look at the rainbow. Resh Laqish (c. 250 A.D.) saw in this a threat to the eyesight (bChag., 16a), since man cannot bear to look on God's glory (Ez. 1:28; Is. 6:5), and Rabba († 331 A.D.) regarded it as an insult to the Creator and consequently as a desecration of the divine name (→ ὄνομα, bQid., 40a). The idea of merit, which dominates Rabbinic piety, is here introduced into the consideration and appraisal of the rainbow. This shatters the unity of the revelation of God's glory on the one side and His grace on the other — two things which cannot be separated, since the one God is manifested in both and His

---

[2] Cf. the comm. on Gn. 9:8 ff.; cf. also Jos. Ant., 1, 103 (v. S. Rappaport, *Agada und Exegese bei Flavius Josephus* [1930], 63) and cf. P. Riessler, *Altjüd. Schrifttum* (1928), 965.

[3] Cf. the discussion in M. Noth, "Die Historisierung des Mythus im AT" in *Christentum und Wissenschaft*, 4 (1928), 265 ff., 301 ff.; A. Weiser, "Glaube und Geschichte im AT," BWANT, IV, 4 (1931), 23 ff.

[4] At Ez. 1:4 ἶρις is found only in the Heb. of the Hexapla : φῶς γὰρ ἐν μέσῳ αὐτοῦ ὡς ὅρασις ἴριδος. The Mas. has חַשְׁמַל, which is rendered ἤλεκτρον in the LXX and which means a bright metal.

[5] A. Socin considers this possibility in BW, 358 under *Kasia*. In Ex. 30:24 ἶρις means the iris, which was used in popular cosmetics in Southern Europe and the Near East (the root of Florentine iris). Cf. P. Tebt., II, 414, 11 (2nd cent.): πέμψω τῇ θυγατρί σου κοτύλην ἶρις (read ἴριδος), "a little dish of orris-root" (cf. Moult.-Mill.). The κρίνον of Mt. 6:28 perhaps belongs to the same species [Bertram].

[6] Str.-B., IV, Index under *Regenbogen*.

whole activity is directed to one and the same goal. This unity has to be dissolved, however, because a religion of attainment makes grace dependent on human conduct. The question now is not whether one is strong enough to bear the vision of the divine glory which is vouchsafed (Is. 6:5), but whether one may contemplate the sign of the gracious will of God which also declares His omnipotence. For who knows, and who can know, whether this grace is of personal application? The lack of assurance of salvation in later Judaism (→ II, 526 f.) is also manifested in another way in connection with the rainbow. We often find the view (Gn. r., 35 on 9:12; bKet, 77b) that the rainbow appears only when there is none completely righteous on earth, since the existence of such an one would guarantee the preservation of the world and an express indication of divine grace through the rainbow would be unnecessary. [7] This is a complete departure from the outlook of the author of Gn. 9:8 ff. and of the OT generally.

B. The New Testament.

1. Only an OT reader can see what is meant when τόξον is used for rainbow. Josephus took this into account when he explained to non-Jewish readers that the τοξεία of the biblical narrative signifies ἶρις (Ant., 1, 103). This makes the meaning clear. The word ἶρις and its associated ideas were also indispensable to Philo. [8] Similarly the NT had to use it in order to speak intelligibly. This is the basic reason why ἶρις is used in the ordinary sense of Greek antiquity in Rev.

2. The term occurs in very different contexts in Rev. 4:3 and 10:1, and it is a legitimate question whether the meaning and the theological application are the same in the two passages. [9] At 4:3 the ἶρις [10] encircles the throne of God which is set up for judgment, and it has for those who see it the appearance of an emerald, i.e., it is bright green. Allusion to Ez. 1:27 f. is proved by the κυκλόθεν. But in Ez. 1:28 the bow is only a means to describe the nature and greatness of the divine δόξα. If, then, Rev. 4:3 speaks only of a circular radiance which is emerald green in colour, does not this imply that the reference is simply to the presence of a halo like a rainbow, not to an actual rainbow? [11] At 10:1, on the other hand, ἶρις [12] is one of the emblems of the angel with the book which contains a prophecy known only in heaven (cf. Ez. 3:1 ff.). By consuming the book the divine is able to become a mediator of the divine prophecy, which relates to the destiny of the whole race (10:8 ff.). But the one from whom he receives it is not God. He is an angel. Yet it is worth noting that the ἶρις is about his head. With the cloud which is his vesture, and the resemblance of his countenance to the sun in splendour, this can only be the rainbow. [13] In this case the original meaning is proved by the context,

---

[7] Cf. Str.-B., IV, 1133, n. 1.

[8] Quaest. in Gn., II, 64, p. 148 (ed. Aucher) in Philonis Iudaei Paralipomena Armena (1876).

[9] Pr.-Bauer, 593 takes the word literally at 10:1 and figur. at 4:3.

[10] There is no art. in the text.

[11] Pr.-Bauer thus translates "a halo, to look at like an emerald." Cf. also Loh. Apk., 43 ad loc.; J. Behm in NT Deutsch, ad loc. For a good survey and assessment of older exegesis cf. F. Düsterdieck (in Meyers Komm.)[2] (1865), 218 f., ad loc. On the remarkable reading ἱερεῖς אA, cf. Zn. Apk., 319, n. 4.

[12] The more important texts have the art.

[13] For the psychological and historical background of the vision, which need not be treated here, cf. the comm. ad loc.

even though it may have been thought that the ἶρις had to be included as a traditional feature in theophanies. [14]

Nevertheless, it is perhaps better to take the two passages together and to construe the term in the same way in both verses. The main reason for so doing is to be found in the concern of Rev. to give to believers impregnable assurance of the divine grace and salvation even in and with the intimation of God's judgment on the race. This assurance is given to the community of Jesus because in His Word and work, and especially in His death and resurrection, it has come to know the grace of God as the basis of its existence (cf. 1:17 f.). At 10:1 this finds expression in the fact that the message of the divine is regarded as the conclusion and epitome of all prophetic proclamation. The constant theme of prophecy, however, is the contemporaneous revelation of the judgment and the grace of God (cf. the juxtaposition of Is. 3 and 4). For the manifestation of God's power and glory implies judgment for His enemies and the dawn of the age of salvation for His servants (Rev. 1:1 etc.). To show this, the ancient covenant sign (Gn. 9:13) is used in the form of the ἶρις around the head of the angel (10:1) as an indication of the good and gracious will of God. [15] But if it is used thus in 10:1, the same is surely true of its use at 4:3 in the introduction to the great depiction of judgment. The θρόνος (→ III, 165) of God and the θρόνοι of the πρεσβύτεροι leave us in no doubt that a judicial process of unparalleled significance is about to begin. It is thus the more important that the author should bear witness to the Church that even as Judge God is still gracious to His people. This is shown by the ἶρις which encircles His throne of judgment (cf. Gn. 9:13). [16] In this passage the assurance gains its particular significance from v. 6, which tells us that the throne of God, and with it God Himself, is separated from His entourage by a θάλασσα ὑαλίνη. This is a powerful description of God's transcendence or remoteness (cf. 1 Tm. 6:16). But the ἶρις around the throne bears witness that this distant God is also near. [17] The implication comes to light in chapter 5, where only the Lamb that was slain is able and willing to declare the will of God to the world. For the divine, the saying of God in Gn. 9:9 ff. is thus fulfilled in God's historical action in the crucified and risen Jesus. Through Him God as Judge is near to His servants and related to them.

In view of the linguistic and material background of the word ἶρις, we may thus say in conclusion that this term, which is not itself biblical, is given in Rev. the content of the OT nψ̣ρ/τόξον, and that with this content it is set in the light of the revelation in Christ. Its non-Greek character rests on the first fact, and on the second rests its nature as the sign, not of promised grace, but of grace already given. In this connection the principle of self-attainment which characterises the Rabbinic view of the rainbow (→ 340) is completely transcended. For the witness of this sign is that one alone brings salvation, namely, God. The goodness and patience of God precede all the good works of man.

Rengstorf

Ἰσαάκ → 191 f.   ἰσάγγελος → I, 87.

---

[14] Cf. esp. Loh. and Behm, *ad loc.*

[15] In spite of W. Hadorn (Apk., 70, cf. 114) we must insist on an allusion to Gn. 9:13 both at 10:1 and 4:3 if we are to do full justice to the text.

[16] It seems to be alien to the text to describe the ἶρις as an attribute of the world Judge on His throne, Bss. Apk.[5] (1896), 361 on 10:1.

[17] Discussion of the question whether the κύκλος is horizontal or vertical is thus irrelevant. Cf. the pertinent remarks of Düsterdieck on 4:3.

| † ἴσος, † ἰσότης, † ἰσότιμος | → δίκαιος, II, 182; → εἷς, II, 434; → ὅμοιος. |

Contents : A. ἰσότης as Equality : 1. Quantitative Equality ; 2. Equality of Content or Meaning ; 3. Equality among Men : the Greeks ; 4. Equality among Men : Christians ; 5. Equality by Nature and Equality with God outside the New Testament ; 6. The Equality of Jesus with God in the New Testament. B. ἰσότης as Equity.

A. ἰσότης as Equality.

1. Quantitative Equality.

a. The equality expressed by ἴσος and its derivatives is primarily an equality of size or number, or perhaps of value [1] or force, though not so much in a qualitative sense, for which originally ὅμοιος and its cognates are mostly used [2] (the basis of this word, -οιος, as in ποῖος, *qualis,* carries with it the suggestion of quality).

The distinction and relationship of the two words may be seen in Hom. Il., 187: ἴσον ἐμοὶ φάσθαι καὶ ὁμοιωθήμεναι ἄντην, "to raise the claim to equality with me, and to regard himself as like in essence." Aristotle gives a more precise definition, Cat., 6, p. 6a, 26 (cf. line 33 f.): τὸ ἴσον as ἴδιον τοῦ ποσοῦ; [3] or Metaph., III, 2, p. 1004b, 11: ἰσότης as πάθος ἴδιον ἀριθμοῦ ἢ ἀριθμός. [4] ἴσος is accordingly used to denote equal sums of money, or payments, or pieces, or an equal voice, or equal lengths of space or time, or equal shares, or other equal quantities.

This is often the meaning in the LXX : Ex. 30:34 (ἴσον ἴσῳ ἔσται, mixture in equal parts); Lv. 7:10 (6:40 : ἑκάστῳ τὸ ἴσον, in distribution); Ez. 40:5 ff. (→ 344); 4 Macc. 13:20 f. (of equal lengths of time); cf. also the two NT passages Rev. 21:16 and Lk. 6:34.

ἴσος, ἰσότης. Cr.-Kö., 790 f. (*s.v.* ὅμοιος); Moult.-Mill., 307; Bl.-Debr.⁶ § 194, 1 (on ἴσος); 434, 1; 453, 4 (on ἴσον); J. B. Lightfoot, *St. Paul's Epistles to the Colossians and to Philemon* (1892) on Col. 4:1; Loh. Kol., 159 and n. 5; → ἁρπαγμός, I, 473; T. K. Abbott Col., 296 (ICC, XXXV, 1916); R. Hirzel, *Themis, Dike, und Verwandtes. Ein Beitrag zur Geschichte der Rechtsidee bei den Griechen* (1907), 228 ff., 421 ff. (Excursus VII), esp. on the relation between ἴσος and ὅμοιος.

[1] For the connection between equality of number and of value in the use of ἴσος, the division of booty may have played some part at an early stage, since this involves equal value (not similarity) as well as amount. The same connection comes out particularly clearly in the exchange of money.

[2] Cr.-Kö., 790; cf. also T. Zahn in ZWL, 6 (1885), 254.

[3] Similarly Eustath. Thessal. Comm. on Il., 5, 432 ff. (II, 44, Stallbaum) maintains that ὅμοιος is related to ποιότης, ἴσος to ποσότης (Hirzel, 422).

[4] Cf. Plat. Resp., IV, 441c : ἴσα τὸν ἀριθμόν; Philo Rer. Div. Her., 144 : λέγεται γὰρ ἴσον καθ᾽ ἕνα μὲν τρόπον ἐν ἀριθμοῖς ..., καθ᾽ ἕτερον δὲ ἐν μεγέθεσιν. There are many instances of such equality in amount or size in the pap. (cf. Preisigke Wört., *s.v.*) and inscr. (cf. F. Hiller de Gaertringen, Index to Ditt. Syll.³, *s.v.*). Above all, cf. the examples in Liddell-Scott, *s.v.*

b. Rev. 21:16 (of the heavenly Jerusalem): τὸ μῆκος καὶ τὸ πλάτος καὶ τὸ ὕψος αὐτῆς ἴσα ἐστίν.

There are several parallels for the equality of two dimensions or of lengths within the same dimension; cf. Xenoph. An., V, 4, 32 : ἴσος τὸ πλάτος καὶ τὸ μῆκος. Ditt. Syll.³, 969, 45 ff.: πλάτος καὶ ὕψος ἴσα τοῖς ἐπιστυλίοις. Jos. Ant., 10, 131: χώματα τοῖς τείχεσι τὸ ὕψος ἴσα. Ex. 26:24; and esp. Ez. 40, where the measurement of the heavenly Jerusalem is in terms of the κάλαμος as a unit, cf. v. 5 : τὸ πλάτος (i.e., of the wall) ἴσον τῷ καλάμῳ καὶ τὸ ὕψος αὐτοῦ ἴσον τῷ καλάμῳ, and many of the verses that follow.

The surprising thing in Rev. 21:16 is that the three dimensions are equal. We thus have a cube of which each side is about 2000 kilometres long. The equality of the sides, and especially the threefold twelve, is a sign of perfection.

Perhaps this is enough to explain the strange idea of a city in the form of a cube, which is probably based on a theory of perfection rather than a realistic conception. If this is true, there is no need to recall similar examples such as the cubic tower of the god Marduk in the heavenly Babylon of the Babylonians, [6] or the similar shape of the Holy of Holies in the temple of Solomon [7] and its successors, or the similarly shaped Kaaba in Mecca. It may be that cosmological speculations underlie all these ideas and structures. [8] The fantastic measurements in terms of the present world can only denote that the new Jerusalem fills both heaven and earth.

For this, even for the extraordinary height, there are Jewish parallels. According to BB, 75b (Str.-B., III, 849 f.) God will make Jerusalem some 17 kilometers high, and this will correspond (cf. Zech. 14:10) to the size of the other two dimensions; cf. also Pesikt., 137b (Str.-B., III, 852). The dimensions of Jerusalem are to be twelve miles square, though here the height is obviously not to be the same. [9] According to Pesikt., 143a (Str.-B., III, 849) Jerusalem will one day rise up and mount up to the very throne of glory etc.; cf. also Cant. r., 7, 5 (127b).

c. Lk. 6:34 : ἁμαρτωλοὶ ἁμαρτωλοῖς δανείζουσιν ἵνα ἀπολάβωσιν τὰ ἴσα. In this and the accompanying sentences the basic thought of Jesus is clear, but not the exact sense. The problem of the passage is this : When we lend money, what is meant by τὰ ἴσα, the goal of the worldly attitude which Jesus rejects ?

It could mean 1. the same sum, i.e., the capital without interest ; [10] 2. the corresponding total, i.e., the capital with interest, [11] in which case ἀπολαμβάνω is both times used in the sense of "to receive back"; 3. if ἀπολαμβάνω simply means "to receive," τὰ ἴσα would signify the same service in the case of need ; [12] 4. there is also the possibility that ἀπολαμβάνω τὰ ἴσα is a technical term [13] for receiving an amount of interest as

---

[5] Loh. Apk., ad loc. → δώδεκα, II, 323.
[6] Cf. B. Meissner, Babylonien u. Assyrien, I (1920), 312 f.
[7] Cf. Bss. Apk., ad loc.
[8] Cf. K. Galling, Art. Tempel, II in RGG², V, 1044.
[9] → δώδεκα, II, 325.
[10] Pr.-Bauer, s.v.; Hck. Lk., 87; Schl. Lk., ad loc. Pr.-Bauer refers to P. Ryl., 65, 7: εἰς τὸ βασιλικὸν τὰ ἴσα. But this is not an exact parallel, since τὰ ἴσα is here related to an amount already mentioned, whereas it is used absol. at Lk. 6:34, and the correspondence can only be deduced indirectly from δανείζουσιν.
[11] E.g., in mediaeval exegesis (cf. H. J. Holtzmann Komm.³ [1901], 341 ad loc.) and also A. Plummer Lk. (ICC)³ (1907), 187. Plummer argues from δανείζω, "to lend at interest" (as compared with κίχρημι), but this argument is exploded by v. 35, unless the use of δανείζω is one of the paradoxical elements in the words of Jesus.
[12] Cf. Kl. Lk., ad loc., and especially the intricate discussion of F. Godet, Lk.² (1890), ad loc.
[13] Pr.-Bauer, s.v., No. 1.

high as the original capital, cf. ἴσοι τόκοι in the pap. [14] for interest which finally comes to as much as the capital outlay.

It is hard to decide between these meanings, since, apart from ἀπολαμβάνω, → ἀπελπίζω in v. 35 is used in a singular manner and might mean either to expect back or to hope for.

The whole section makes it clear that Jesus has in view a *do ut des* attitude which is inconsistent with unselfseeking Christian love. In the type of love which seeks a return, as often in the thought of vengeance (cf. Mt. 5:38), an important part is played by the principle of exact correspondence, whereas such calculation is alien to the Christian attitude (cf. 1 C. 13:5).

On the use of ἴσος to denote exact correspondence in retribution (whether in a good sense or a bad), cf. Hdt., I, 2 : ταῦτα δὴ ἴσα πρὸς ἴσα [15] σφι γενέσθαι; Plat. Leg., VI, 774c : ἴσα ἀντὶ ἴσων λαβεῖν or ἐκδοῦναι; Ditt. Syll.³, 798, 5 : ἴσας ἀμοιβὰς οἷς εὐηργέτηνται; 971, 9 : ἀμειβόμενα τὸ ἴσον.

2. Equality of Content or Meaning.

When ἴσος is used of quantity, especially in mathematics (cf. Aristot. Metaph., IX, 3, p. 1054a, 31 ff.), great emphasis is placed on exact equality. This is no less true, however, in respect of its use for agreement in content ; cf. Aristot. Pol., V, 1, p. 1301b, 31 : ταὐτὸ καὶ ἴσον.

τὸ ἴσον can thus be used technically for a duplicate (P. Tebt., II, 397, 19 [2nd cent. A.D.]) or for an attested transcript (P. Lond., III, 1222, 5 [138 A.D.]; P. Tebt., II, 301, 21 [190 A.D.]). It can also be used in the sense of checking entries by the facts, P. Tebt., I, 120, 127 (1st cent. A.D.): τὰ ἴσα (πιττάκια) ἔχω παρὰ τοῦ δεῖνα, "I have a promissory note which is in precise agreement" ; cf. also P. Oxy., I, 78, 27 (3rd cent. A.D.): τὰ ἴσα ἐπιστέλλειν, "to give direction in the same sense."

Along these lines ἴσος is also used of consistent witness at Mk. 14:56 : καὶ ἴσαι αἱ μαρτυρίαι οὐκ ἦσαν; 14:59 : καὶ οὐδὲ οὕτως ἴση ἦν ἡ μαρτυρία αὐτῶν. In spite of v. 57 f. the witnesses obviously do not agree in detail as required ; cf. the same requirement in Sus. 51 ff.

The rules were as follows (Sanh., 5, 2, Str.-B., I, 1002): If the two (witnesses) contradict one another, their witness is invalid ; (5, 4) if they agree, the facts are established, and the verdict can be given on the guilt of the accused, and sentence can be passed, though arguments in favour of acquittal will first be heard. [16]

Concern for the ἰσότης of the μαρτυρίαι is part of the formal justice which concealed the injustice of the trial of Jesus and which lent a cloak under which injustice could triumph.

3. Equality among Men : the Greeks.

The concept of equality is most important in Greek law and politics. [17] There is hardly a term which is so common as this in discussions of law, and nowhere

---

[14] Preisigke Wört., *s.v.*
[15] Liddell-Scott, *s.v.* ("tit for tat").
[16] According to the paraphrase of K. G. Kuhn.
[17] Cf. on this section the important discussion in Hirzel, 228 ff., on which the above remarks are based.

has the close connection between equality and law found such clear and full expression, such plain recognition, as among the Greeks. Above all, we must insist that the Greeks saw much more fully than the Romans that equality is necessary in legal relationships. Law is based on equality. Only equals can enter into legal relationships. In the state the legal equality of ἴσοι increasingly comes to be differentiated from the natural equality of ὅμοιοι. Different by nature, ἴσοι are equal by acknowledgment of the same rights. The high regard of the Greeks for ἰσότης is reflected in its personification by Euripides (Phoen., 536) and in its evaluation by Aristotle as a means of fostering unity and solidarity in the state, Pol., II, 2, p. 1261a, 30 f.: τὸ ἴσον τὸ ἀντιπεπονθὸς σῴζει τὰς πόλεις; Ps.-Aristot. Mund., 5, p. 397a, 3 f.: τὸ ἴσον σωστικὸν ὁμονοίας; cf. Philo Rer. Div. Her., 162 : ἰσότης εἰρήνην ἔτεκε. Hence Cicero (De Legibus, I, 18, 48, ed. J. Vahlen³ [1883]) can say : societas quoque hominum et aequalitas et iustitia per se <est>expetenda.

The Greek ideal of ἰσότης among men is a reflection or a part of the cosmic equality of which Plato speaks (Gorg., 507d ff.; cf. esp. 508a): ἀλλὰ λέληθέν σε ὅτι ἡ ἰσότης ἡ γεωμετρικὴ καὶ ἐν θεοῖς καὶ ἐν ἀνθρώποις μέγα δύναται. [18] This ἰσότης γεωμετρική, as a law of proportion, is an essential δύναμις of the κόσμος; it creates order, and consequently it is divine. Its opposite is → πλεονεξία, i.e., always wanting more than one's position and attainments warrant; cf. also Menand. Mon., 259 : ἰσότητα τίμα καὶ πλεονέκτει μηδένα.

a. In the Greek states equality is a basic principle of democracy along with freedom (cf. Aristot. Pol., IV, 4, p. 1291b, 35 : ἐλευθερία καὶ ἰσότης). ἰσότης πολιτική [19] (Pol., VI, VIII, IV), πολιτεία συνεστηκυῖα κατ᾽ ἰσότητα τῶν πολιτῶν (ibid., III, 6, p. 1279a, 9), is the pride of Greek democracy.

The essence of this ἰσότης consists in enjoyment of ἴσα καὶ ὅμοια (Demosth. Or., 21, 112 → n. 19). All citizens have the same position and rights, and they are thus ἴσοι καὶ ὅμοιοι (cf. Xenoph. Hist. Graec., VII, 1, 1). The cell of democracy is the πολίτης ἐφ᾽ ἴσῃ καὶ ὁμοίᾳ (Ditt. Syll.³, 333, 25; 742, 45), or, more briefly, πολίτης ἴσος καὶ ὅμοιος (ibid., 421, 13). One's position is equal in value (ἴσος) and in nature (ὅμοιος) to that of others. Thus democracy itself is a πολιτεία ἐπ᾽ ἴσῃ καὶ ὁμοίῃ (ibid., 312, 25), or a πολιτεία ἐν τοῖς ἴσοις καὶ ὁμοίοις (Xenoph. Hist. Graec., VII, 1, 45), or again (→ supra) πολιτεία ἴση καὶ ὁμοία (Ditt. Syll.³, 254, 6; cf. Aeschin. Or., 1, 5 : ἴση καὶ ἔννομος πολιτεία).

It will be noted that ἴσος and ὅμοιος constantly occur together in this connection. The distinction between them has all but disappeared, as also in such expressions as αἱ ἰσότητες καὶ αἱ ὁμοιότητες (Isoc., 7, 61) and ἡ ὁμοιότης καὶ ἰσότης (Plat. Leg., V, 741a). But this twofold phrase does not denote essential equality. It denotes equality of status and significance. Democratic equality is an equality in which each has the same position and rights as the other. [20]

---

[18] Cf. Ditt. Syll.³, 526, 28 : πολιτεό[σομ]αι (sic) ἐπ᾽ ἴσᾳ καὶ ὁμοίᾳ καὶ θί[νων κ]αὶ ἀνθρωπίνων. Here we have the archetype of Greek democracy (→ infra).

[19] In the first instance this implies legal equality; cf. Thuc., II, 37, 1: μέτεστι δὲ κατὰ μὲν τοὺς νόμους πρὸς τὰ ἴδια διάφορα (private cases) πᾶσι τὸ ἴσον (the same law). On the other hand, Demosthenes brings the censure (21, 112): οὐ μέτεστι τῶν ἴσων οὐδὲ τῶν ὁμοίων πρὸς τοὺς πλουσίους τοῖς πολλοῖς ἡμῶν, "the great majority does not have equal rights with the wealthy" (Pape, s.v. ἴσος). In democracy, too, practice does not always tally with theory.

[20] Cf. H. v. Sybel, Vorträge und Abhandlungen (1897), 54, 1 (in Hirzel, 251).

The LXX uses ἴσος once in the sense of equality before the law, namely, at 2 Macc. 9:15 : πάντας αὐτοὺς (sc. the Jews) ἴσους (with the same political rights) [21] Ἀθηναίοις ποιήσειν. Cf. also ἰσοπολίτης (3 Macc. 2:30).

b. As ἰσότης is basic to society in Greek political and legal theory, so in Greek philosophy the personal society of friends rests on the same fundamental principle.

According to the Pythagoreans friendship is the ἐναρμόνιος ἰσότης of two men (Diog. L., VIII, 33), and Aristotle has the definition (Eth. Nic., VIII, 10, p. 1159b, 2 f.): ἡ δ' ἰσότης καὶ ὁμοιότης φιλότης. The true friend is ἴσος καὶ ὅμοιος (Pol., III, 16, p. 1287b, 33). One may venture to say, however, that this is a different and more perfect equality than in the state, though in the latter the ideal of the πολίτης ἴσος καὶ ὅμοιος is not so far removed from the φίλος ἴσος καὶ ὅμοιος. In true friendship the one is to the other not merely φίλος ἴσος τῆς ψυχῆς (LXX Dt. 13:6[7]): "a friend as dear to him as his own life"; there is also achieved here, in a true blending of spirits, the ἰσότης which the state claims for its citizens with its ideal of equality.

c. The concept of legal equality can itself be deepened to the point where it becomes a principle of judicial righteousness. In the first instance this implies simply that the judge will dispense the same law without respect of persons (e.g., Ditt. Syll.[3], 426, 14 : ἀφ' ἴσου πᾶσι ποιησάμενος τὰς κρίσεις).

This is what Aristotle means when he says (Eth. Nic., V, 1, p. 1129a, 34): τὸ δίκαιόν ἐστι τὸ ἴσον. Δικαιοσύνη is for him the observance and preservation of ἰσότης, or equality (ibid., V, p. 1129 ff.). It is ἕξις ἰσότητος ποιητικὴ ἢ διανεμητικὴ τοῦ ἴσου (Topica, VI, 5, p. 143a, 16). This genuinely Greek concept is also present in the ἰσονομεῖν of 4 Macc. 5:24. To assign what is equal (suum cuique), and consequently to act quite impartially, is a sign of true (Greek) righteousness. The same understanding of righteousness led the Pythagoreans to adopt the square, the product of equal factors, as the symbol of righteousness ; [22] cf. Aristot. Eth. M., I, 1, p. 1182a, 14; also Philo Op. Mund., 51: (ὁ τέτταρα) μέτρον δικαιοσύνης καὶ ἰσότητος; also the ἰσότης γεωμετρική of Plato (Gorg., 508a) as the cosmic principle of righteousness (→ 346).

This is how we are also to understand the ἰσότης with which the Messiah leads the elect people of God (Ps. Sol. 17:41[46]): ἐν ἰσότητι πάντας αὐτοὺς ἄξει. But there is also dimly intimated here the hope of the glorious ἰσότης of all the fellow-citizens of the Messiah (→ 349).

The term ἴσος thus undergoes a development which brings it much closer to the concept of δίκαιος (→ B.). This means that gradually the definition (legal ἰσότης is the granting of the same rights to all) is filled out or corrected by the insight that true righteousness consists in giving to each, not what is equal, but what is proper to him.

This is expressed already in the apparently paradoxical statement of Xenophon (Cyrop., II, 2, 18): καίτοι ἔγωγε οὐδὲν ἀνισότερον (nothing more unjust) νομίζω ἐν ἀνθρώποις εἶναι ἢ τοῦ ἴσου τόν τε κακὸν καὶ τὸν ἀγαθὸν ἀξιοῦσθαι.

d. ἰσότης plays a special role in legal contracts or treaties in which the partners equally accept both rights and obligations.

---

[21] A. Kamphausen (in Kautzsch Apkr. u. Pseudepigr., 104) translates "just as free," but this brings out only one aspect of the underlying ἰσότης.
[22] Hirzel, 229.

Cf. Hdt., IX, 7: συμμάχους ἐπ' ἴσῃ τε καὶ ὁμοίῃ ποιήσασθαι (the same prepositional phrase is found also in Ditt. Syll.[3], 312, 27 (4th cent. B.C.); cf. Thuc., I, 99, 2 : (the Athenians in the Athenian Maritime League) ... οὔτε ξυνεστράτευον ἀπὸ τοῦ ἴσου.

4. Equality among Men : Christians.

These secular forms of equality, which are determined by earthly law and righteousness, are confronted in the NT by another kind of equality which is established by the love of Christians and by the divine gifts of grace. This two-sided equality with its twofold foundation is anchored in the very centre of the Gospel. It also constitutes a single whole. For the inner equality in spiritual possessions (Ac. 11:17) and eternal salvation (Mt. 20:12), which God in His sovereign grace establishes between Christians without regard for origin or prior history (Ac. 11:17), for achievement or merit (Mt. 20:12), by inner necessity demands of their love an equality even in external matters (2 C. 8:13).

a. Paul is obviously making a conscious appeal to the strongly developed Greek sense of equality when in his admonition to the Corinthians concerning the Jerusalem collection he uses the motive of ἰσότης (2 C. 8:13 f.): οὐ γὰρ ἵνα ἄλλοις ἄνεσις, ὑμῖν θλῖψις, ἀλλ' ἐξ ἰσότητος ἐν τῷ νῦν καιρῷ τὸ ὑμῶν περίσσευμα εἰς τὸ ἐκείνων ὑστέρημα, ἵνα καὶ τὸ ἐκείνων περίσσευμα γένηται εἰς τὸ ὑμῶν ὑστέρημα, ὅπως γένηται ἰσότης.

In such motivation ἰσότης is the criterion (ἐξ ἰσότητος) and goal (ὅπως γένηται ἰσότης) [23] of action. We may thus ask whether this is not a concession to secular, i.e., Greek *do ut des* thinking. As compared with R. 15:27, which offers a rather different reason for liberality, do we not have the suggestion of ministry for reward rather than ministry out of gratitude, so that there is at least approximation to the attitude which Jesus plainly rejected in Lk. 6:32 ff. (→ 344)?[24] On the other hand, may it not be that the ἰσότης commended by Paul is an application of the Golden Rule of Lk. 6:31, especially if we do not link the ἵνα of v. 14 too closely with what precedes, but see in it the indication of a divinely given objective rather than of human purposes, as in the concluding ὅπως clause ?[25] Such an interpretation undoubtedly corresponds very closely to the characteristic movement of Pauline thinking.

If this is so, the closely-knit argument is as follows. ἰσότης on the part of Christians, as a regulative principle of mutual assistance, as in the ideal picture of Ac. 2:44 f.; 4:36 f.; 5, should serve the divine goal of ἰσότης. [26] An example of the balance between need on the one side and superfluity on the other is provided by the distribution of the manna (Ex. 16:18), in which the divine objective of ἰσότης is clearly displayed in the equality which God Himself plans and effects. [27]

b. But God Himself sees to it that ἰσότης is established also in the people of the new covenant. As in the type or shadow of the old covenant (→ *supra*), so in the reality of the new there is displayed the glorious equality[28] of gifts of grace which

---

[23] Cf. Demosth. Or., 5, 17: ἄχρι τῆς ἴσης, "until equality is reached."
[24] Cf. Ltzm. K., 134 f.
[25] Cf. E. Stauffer in ThStKr, 102 (1930), 235 and n. 1 and 2.
[26] Ltzm. K., *ad loc.*
[27] Cf. Schl. K., *ad loc.*
[28] In spite of remaining, and divinely posited, inequalities (→ 350).

bridges even the deepest clefts between men, e.g., the gulf between Jews and Gentiles. This is a miracle both for Peter and also for Paul (cf. esp. Eph. 2:14 f.). The fact that (Ac. 11:17) τὴν ἴσην δωρεὰν ἔδωκεν[29] αὐτοῖς ὁ θεὸς ὡς καὶ ἡμῖν brought about a second μετάνοια in the prince of the apostles. The very same gift of the greatest thing that man can receive, the gift of the Holy Spirit, accomplishes and bears witness to the equality of the recipients before God, and establishes the unity of the Church (→ εἷς, II, 438 ff.).[30]

This fact of the endowment of all Christians with the same spiritual gift is described even more specifically in the second letter attributed to the same prince of the apostles. 2 Pt. 1:1: Συμεὼν Πέτρος ... τοῖς ἰσότιμον ἡμῖν λαχοῦσιν πίστιν ἐν δικαιοσύνῃ τοῦ θεοῦ ἡμῶν κτλ.

In secular Greek the words ἰσότιμος and ἰσοτιμία[31] are used to denote the same status and rank in civic life, cf. Thdrt. on Col. 4:1 (MPG, 82, 621); also Plut. Sull., 6 (I, 454d/e); Jos. Ant., 12, 119 : Σέλευκος ὁ Νικάτωρ ... αὐτοὺς (sc. τοὺς ᾿Ιουδαί-ους) ... τοῖς ἐνοικισθεῖσιν ἰσοτίμους ἀπέφηνεν Μακεδόσιν καὶ ῞Ελλησιν (cf. 2 Macc. 9:15; 8:2 f.).

If in the world the reference is to equal status and rights, in the kingdom of God it is to the same spiritual allotment (λαχοῦσιν). Each Christian receives from the gracious righteousness of God, which acts impartially towards all, an equal faith which makes all equally righteous before God.[32]

c. Equality in what is most essential to the Christian in this age, namely, equality in blessing by the Spirit, is not the real point made by Jesus in the parable of the labourers in the vineyard (Mt. 20:12). Here those who began to work first complain at the favour accorded to those who came last : ἴσους αὐτοὺς ἡμῖν ἐποίησας.[33] The reference, however, is to the eschatological equality which will be effected in the eternal kingdom established at the end of the age.

---

[29] Cf. the related expressions in Ditt. Syll.³, 982, 25 : duabus κοινῇ τὸ ἴσον διδόναι; Jos. Ant., 9, 3 (Schl. Mt., 589): βραβεύειν ἅπασιν τὸ ἴσον; Philo Decal., 61 f.: ἴσα διδοὺς ἀνίσοις ... μηδὲ τὸ ἴσον ἀποδιδόντες. But in distinction from these expressions, and from the ἴση μοῖρα of Hom. Il., 9, 318; Od., 20, 282, the ἴσον μέρος of Aristoph. Pl., 225 etc., ἴση δωρεά denotes a gift which is the same, not in size, but by nature. On the construction with ὡς καί cf. 1 Th. 2:14 : ὁ αὐτὸς καθὼς καί, and on this cf. Bl.-Debr.⁶ § 194, 1; Kühner-Blass-Gerth, I, 413, n. 11.

[30] The equal love of Christians for one another should reflect the equal gift of God, 1 Cl., 21, 7: τὴν ἀγάπην ... μὴ κατὰ προσκλίσεις, ἀλλὰ πᾶσιν ... ὁσίως ἴσην παρεχέτωσαν. Cf. Pol., 4, 2 : ... ἀγαπῶσας πάντας ἐξ ἴσου ἐν πάσῃ ἐγκρατείᾳ. In practice, then, this love must keep equality in the external things of life (→ 348).

[31] On ἰσότιμος Moult.-Mill., 307; Bl.-Debr.⁶ § 118, 1; Kn. Pt., ad loc.; Wnd. Kath. Br., ad loc.; J. B. Mayor (1907), ad loc.; F. Field, Notes on the Translation of the NT (1899), 240. Cf. also the instances given in Moult.-Mill., Pr.-Bauer and Pape, s.v.

[32] Wnd. Pt., ad loc. thinks that the apostle to the Jews is here greeting adopted but fully equal brethren in faith, in terms of Ac. 11:17; 15:9. It is more likely, however, that he has in view the equality of all Christians with the apostles, who in 2 Pt. are already high above the rest (cf. the solemn title which precedes). In faith, which in the long run is all that really counts, all believers are equal through the righteous grace of our God.

[33] On the expression ἴσον ποιεῖν cf. Hes. Op., 705 : μηδὲ κασιγνήτῳ ἴσον ποιεῖσθαι ἑταῖρον. Griech. Papyrus der Kaiserlichen Universitäts- und Landesbibliothek zu Strassburg (ed. F. Preisigke), I (1912), 32, 14 (261 A.D.): τὸν ἴσον σεαυτῷ ποιήσας εἰς τὰ παρά σοι ἔργα.

At a first glance one might suppose that the parable confirms the Greek equation of δικαιοσύνη and ἰσότης, for the master of the vineyard promises at least to the second group (v. 4), and perhaps also to those that follow, including the last (cf. v. 7 text rec), that he will give them in payment that ὅ ἐὰν ἦ δίκαιον, and he fulfils this promise by treating them all alike. But this ἰσότης in the kingdom of God is quite different from democratic equality. It is not a legal principle in terms of which each can insist on his rights. It is a wholly sovereign action of divine grace. Nor does it rest on equality of achievement. It is a reward of pure grace. [34] In this sense Mt. 20:12 is an answer to Lk. 6:32-34, where what matters is the correspondence of achievement and payment. The equality of grace in which the righteousness of God triumphs is thus opposed to the Aristotelian or any other human concept of righteousness (→ 347). This can be seen clearly from the fact that the secular sense of righteousness regards it as unrighteous (v. 11 f.). [35] The equal reward which God grants is, however, eternal life, or equal felicity. [36]

In the Gk. world there are only formal parallels, e.g., BGU, III, 747, II, 5 (2nd cent. A.D.): κατὰ τὸ ἴσον τοῖς ἐγχωρίοις ἴστασθαι, "made equal with the natives" (in rights and obligations, cf. Jos. Ant., 12, 119).

On the other hand, Judaism contains the same thoughts, e.g., Philo Spec. Leg., II, 34 : παρὰ μὲν ἡμῖν ἀνισότης, ἰσότης δὲ παρὰ θεῷ τίμιον. Eschatological ἰσότης, though more in the sense of righteousness (→ 347), is at issue in Ps. Sol. 17:41 (46): (the Messiah) ἐν ἰσότητι πάντας αὐτοὺς (sc. the whole company of the Lord) ἄξει.

In later Judaism we even find the idea of eschatological equality in spite of differences of attainment, and this arouses just as great astonishment as in the parable of Jesus. In Tanch. כי תשא, 110a (on Qoh. 5:11, Str.-B., IV, 498 f.) the heart of the story is that the reward of him who dies after only 20 years of study of the Torah will be equal to that of one who dies at 80 years of age after devoting 70 years to the study of the Torah. AZ, 10b, 17a, 18a (Str.-B., I, 832 f.). The insight which results from the various stories (here recounted) is that there are many who attain to God's world in an hour and many who attain to it over many, many years.

Nevertheless, a paradox remains. Christian are equal on earth and in heaven. This is confirmed by the gift of the Spirit and the Word of Jesus. But there is also inequality in the community both on earth and in heaven. In addition to outward differences, e.g., between slaves and free men, rich and poor, Greeks and barbarians etc., there are also inward differences. Even in the gifts of grace which are granted there are essential differences (cf. Mt. 25:14 ff.; 1 C. 12, esp. v. 28 ff.; R. 12:6 ff.; also Eph. 4:16). Even receptivity to Jesus and His Word (cf. Mk. 4:24) [37] and faith itself (cf. esp. R. 12:3 : ὡς ὁ θεὸς ἐμέρισεν μέτρον πίστεως, though cf. 2 Pt. 1:1) point to different levels in individual Christians.

---

[34] Cf. Str.-B., IV, 484 ff.

[35] The main interest of the parable, of course, is not in the established equality but in contesting the Jewish principle of rewards. We must always remember to be very cautious in the interpretation of details even where we do not completely rule out such interpretation as allegorising.

[36] Zn. Mt., 598 f. Cf. Cl. Al. Paed., I, 28, 5 : ἰσότης τῆς σωτηρίας; Strom., V, 30, 4 : καινὴ ἡ κτίσις καὶ ἰσότης δικαία : The world of the new creation and the equality established by the gracious righteousness of God belong together. Cf. also Strom., VII, 20, 7: πᾶσι πάντα ἴσα κεῖται παρὰ τοῦ θεοῦ.

[37] Cf. J. Schniewind, NT Deutsch, ad loc.

Indeed, the NT expects distinctions in the new life. In the parable of Mt. 20:1 ff. the established equality is also inequality. It is an inequality different from that expected (v. 16). In other places, too, the NT often mentions or presupposes differences in the kingdom of God, cf. Mt. 5:19; 10:41 f.; 11:11; 19:28; 20:23; 25:19 ff.; Lk. 19:17, 19. [38]

5. Equality by Nature and Equality with God outside the NT.

As we have seen, the original reference of ἴσος is to equality of size or number. But along with this first sense there also develops quite early in relation to the term a concept of qualitative equality. This finds its purest expression in the Aristotelian expression (Pol., II, 2, p. 1261b, 1): ἴσοι πάντες τὴν φύσιν.

> Homer's phrase (Il. 13, 704): ἴσον θυμὸν ἔχειν is along these lines. Similarly, when Thuc. (II, 65, 10) says of the successors of Pericles that they were ἴσον μᾶλλον αὐτοὶ πρὸς ἀλλήλους, he has in mind equality of character or capabilities. We may also mention in this respect the originally very rigorous Stoic doctrine that all sins [39] and good actions are basically equal, Diog. L., VII, 120; Cic. Paradoxa Stoicorum (ed. O. Plasberg [1908]), III : ἴσα τὰ ἁμαρτήματα καὶ τὰ κατορθώματα. Diog. L., VII, 101 (v. Arnim, III, 23, 3): δοκεῖ δὲ πάντα τὰ ἀγαθὰ ἴσα εἶναι. An echo of this view in biblical form is heard at 4 Macc. 5:20 : τὸ γὰρ ἐπὶ μικροῖς καὶ μεγάλοις παρανομεῖν ἰσοδύναμόν ἐστιν (though cf. also n. 39).

The LXX, too, uses ἴσος to express the equality of all men by nature (cf. Jdt. 1:11: ὡς ἀνὴρ ἴσος, "like any ordinary man"). On the biblical view, however, the natural equality of Aristotle (→ 346) is concentrated upon two vital and painful points in human life, namely, birth (Wis. 7:3 : πᾶσιν ἴσα κλαίων; cf. v. 6 : μία πάντων εἴσοδος) and death (Wis. 7:6 : ... ἔξοδός τε ἴση), and it finds its most fundamental expression in the confession (1:7): εἰμὶ ... κἀγὼ θνητὸς ἴσος ἅπασιν. [40]

On biblical soil the equality of all men [41] before God stands in contrast to God, who is equal only to Himself, cf. Philo Aet. Mund., 43 : ἴσος ... αὐτὸς ἑαυτῷ καὶ ὅμοιος ὁ θεός, Sacr. AC, 10 : (ὁ θεὸς) πλήρης καὶ ἰσαίτατος ὢν ἑαυτῷ. The OT echoes with majestic monotony the question : "Who is like God?", whether in the form of the prophetic challenge : "Who is like unto me?" (Is. 44:7; 40:25; 46:5; Jer. 49:19), or in the form of adoration : "Lord, who is like unto thee?" (Ex. 15:11; Ps. 35:10; 71:19; 89:6), or "None is like unto thee" (1 K. 8:23; 2 Ch. 6:14; 1 Ch. 17:20; Ps. 40:5; 86:8; Jer. 10:6).

Man is created in the divine image (Gn. 1:26), so that he is like God, but only as a copy resembles the original (cf. Wis. 2:23). This rules out equality by nature. Only to the end does there apply the great promise (1 Jn. 3:2): ὅμοιοι αὐτῷ ἐσόμεθα, which is found also in Judaism, cf. S. Lv. 26:12 : God says to the righteous

---

[38] Cf. Kl. Mt., 159; Zn. Mt., 598 f.; Str.-B., IV, 486. For Rabbinic par. referring to distinctions in the glory of the righteous and differences of rank among the blessed, v. Str.-B., I, 249 f., 774; III, 476; IV, 491, 499 f., 1138-1142.

[39] As a biblical par. one might mention the rigorous principle of the Law (cf. Gl. 3:10; Jm. 2:10) that to offend at one point is to be guilty in respect of the whole Law.

[40] Cf. what Cl. Al. Exc. Theod., 10, 3 says of the ἑνότης καὶ ἰσότης καὶ ὁμοιότης of the πρωτόκτιστοι.

[41] Cf. also Str.-B., III, 562 f.

who delight to walk with Him : Why do you fear ? I am as one of you. The *eritis sicut deus* is brought to pass by God. [42] Until then, to desire and to strive after it is a devilish temptation (cf. Gn. 3:5) which is condemned in the Bible, e.g., in the fall of the king of Babylon (Is. 14:14), who says : "I will be like the most High," and who is thus plunged into *sheol*. [43] Cf. Philo Leg. All., I, 49 : φίλαυτος καὶ ἄθεος ὁ νοῦς οἰόμενος ἴσος εἶναι θεῷ, and conversely 2 Macc. 9:12 : δίκαιον ὑποτάσσεσθαι τῷ θεῷ καὶ μὴ — θνητὸν ὄντα — ἰσόθεα φρονεῖν. In Greek literature man is often compared to God, and we constantly find such expressions as "god-like" or "divine," but these are avoided in the Bible. In spite of warnings against ὕβρις, the Greek world made far too free with such terms, and it easily took the further step of maintaining actual likeness with God, and even divinisation. We have only to consider how common are such terms as δαίμονι ἴσος (Il., 5, 438) and flattering epithets like ἰσόθεος (from Homer, cf. Ditt. Syll.³, 390, 28; 624, 4) and ἰσοδαίμων (Aesch. Pers., 633; Pind. Nem., 4, 137; Plat. Resp., II, 360c) even outside epic and dramatic poetry. [44] Indeed, for Plato (Theaet.,176a) the supreme goal of human striving is ὁμοιοῦσθαι τῷ θεῷ κατὰ τὸ δυνατόν. [45] Apollonius of Tyana (Ep., 44) [46] maintains that some regard him as ἰσόθεος and others as θεός, and similar claims have often been made for outstanding personalities. [47] Particularly important is Corp. Herm., I, 12 (Reitzenstein Poim., 331): The divine Ἄνθρωπος is ἴσος to God.

6. The Equality of Jesus with God in the New Testament.

a. It is against the background of these assumptions that we are to view the claim of the NT that Jesus is equal to God.

Jn. 5:18 : The Jews bring against Jesus the accusation : πατέρα ἴδιον ἔλεγεν τὸν θεόν, ἴσον ἑαυτὸν ποιῶν τῷ θεῷ. The basis of the charge [48] is not just the emphatic "my Father," but the related teaching of Jesus that He is identical with the divine Law-giver and that His works are the same as God's works. [49] Augustine remarks on this that the Jews understand what the Arians cannot grasp, namely, that Jesus claims to be truly God. Now it is true that Jesus Himself does not make this express claim. Indeed, He seems to emphasise the contrary : ὁ πατὴρ μείζων μού ἐστιν (14:28). He answers the accusation of the Jews along similar lines in 5:19. It sounds as if He is repudiating, or at least modifying, the ἴσος. The emphasis is all on the identity of His works : ἃ γὰρ ἂν ἐκεῖνος ποιῇ, ταῦτα καὶ ὁ υἱὸς ὁμοίως ποιεῖ. Nevertheless, John accepts the paradox that He is the

---

[42] P. Volz., *Jüd. Eschatologie von Daniel bis Akiba* (1903), 357.

[43] The punishment of those who seek to be equal with God is a feature common to many religions, cf. B. Duhm, *Komm.*⁴ (1922) on Is. 14:14; for Rabbinic statements on this theme, v. Str.-B., II, 462 ff.

[44] Cf. also Hom. Il., 5, 441; 9, 603; Od., 15, 520; Thuc., III, 14. A Gk. sense of language is also responsible for the use of the flattering ἰσαστήρ at 4 Macc. 17:5.

[45] This sounds like Mt. 5:48 and Lv. 19:2, but it rests on different presuppositions and is really quite different.

[46] C. L. Kayser, Philostr. (1870), 354, 11.

[47] Cf. Wettstein on Jn. 5:18.

[48] Cf. the similar accusation which Eliphaz (Tanch. ויישלח, 8 [83b, Buber]) brings against Job : "Dost thou believe that He (God) has made thee equal to him (Abraham)?" (Schl. Mt., 589).

[49] Cf. Zn. J., *ad loc.*

Son who is both subject to the Father and yet also one with Him (10:30; 1:1). In other words, He is equal to the Father [50] (cf. also 10:33, where we have the even stronger accusation : σὺ ἄνθρωπος ὢν ποιεῖς σεαυτὸν θεόν).

In 5:18 ἴσος expresses neither likeness not identity, but the equality of dignity, will and nature which the later term ὁμοούσιος was designed to defend. Like many other terms, ἰσότης thus acquires in the NT a depth and fulness which it never had before. Because of the character of exactness which clung to it as a term of quantitative equality, it was better adapted than ὅμοιος [51] to express what the NT has in view, the more so as it had already taken on qualitative significance as well. In other words, it denotes an equality which is both essential and perfect.

b. This is also the meaning of ἴσα [52] in the famous and difficult verse Phil. 2:6 : [53] ὃς ἐν μορφῇ θεοῦ ὑπάρχων οὐχ ἁρπαγμὸν ἡγήσατο τὸ εἶναι ἴσα θεῷ, ἀλλὰ ἑαυτὸν ἐκένωσεν μορφὴν δούλου λαβών.

Among the many problems posed by this verse the following are our main concern. First, does τὸ εἶναι ἴσα θεῷ denote something which Christ already had, or something which He could seek after, i.e., which He did not have prior to His way through lowliness to glory? No light is shed on this question by ἁρπαγμὸν ἡγεῖσθαι, since this can mean both "to use something which is already present" and also "to grasp a possibility" (→ ἁρπαγμός, I, 474). Secondly, is the action that of the pre-existent or the historical Christ? And finally, what is the reference of ἐκένωσεν ἑαυτόν?

These questions can be answered only in the light of the ἴσα εἶναι θεῷ. Christ was and is equal to God by nature. [54] This equality is a possession which He can neither renounce nor lose. It is the beginning of His way (v. 6) and it will also be the end (vv. 9-11). It is the fixed and ultimate background from which His way leads and to which it returns. [55] But He does not make use of His divine equality [56] by retaining the form of God or of divine existence which He had (ὑπάρχων instead of an imperfect). On the contrary, He temporarily divests Himself of it, and in place of the form of God He takes the form of a servant. He who Himself is κύριος (יהוה) becomes עבד יהוה. To be equal with God is to be κύριος. [57] He remains κύριος even in the form of a servant, even in His full humanity. But it is

---

[50] Cf. Schl. J., ad loc.

[51] ὅμοιος and derivates are never actually used of the equality of Jesus with God in the NT, and they are later rejected for this purpose, Trench, 34.

[52] ἴσα is here an adverbial neut. plur. used as a predic. adj. (like οὕτως in R. 4:18), Bl.-Debr.⁶ § 434, 1. M. R. Vincent (ICC, 1911), ad loc. (p. 59 f.) thinks that it is used adverbially rather than predicatively : "to exist in a manner of equality." Though ἴσα is in itself an adverb, however, we can hardly construe it thus in this passage (→ infra). It is to be interpreted as often in the LXX (12-13 times in Job alone), where it introduces a comparison. At Phil. 2:6 the ἴσα has all the significance of the concept of equality in Jn. 5:18. Cf. also Winer § 27, 3; Buttmann § 129, 11; Pr.-Bauer, s.v.

[53] Cf. K. Barth, Erklärung des Phil. (1928), ad loc.; Dib. Phil., Ew. Gefbr., ad loc.; J. B. Lightfoot, Comm.³ (1873), ad loc.; Loh. Phil., ad loc. and the bibl. there, and also in Pr.-Bauer, s.vv. ἁρπαγμός, κενόω, μορφή; → ἁρπαγμός, I, 472 ff.

[54] We must accept this meaning in spite of the objections of Lightfoot, ad loc. and F. Godet on Jn. 5:19.

[55] K. Barth, ad loc.

[56] Cf. also J. Kögel, "Christus der Herr," BFTh, 12 (1908), 46.

[57] Loh. Phil., 92 f.

by this divestiture or humiliation that He moves to His manifest dignity as κύριος. Because He does not have regard to Himself on this way — this (v. 4) [58] rather than humility (v. 3) [59] is the main point of the parenetic comparison — He regains everything even more gloriously than before (vv. 9-11). If we may put it thus, this is the unintended result of the work of redemption for Christ. His divine nature is demonstrated through the *status exinanitionis,* and it is confirmed by God in His public glorification. It is in a certain sense both *res rapta* and *res rapienda,* the one by eternal possession, the other by humble action. [60]

In the NT the thought of equality finds its centre in two trains of thought, that of the equality of Christians among themselves on the one side, and that of the equality of Jesus with God on the other.

B. ἰσότης as Equity.

The claim that ἰσότης is essential to δικαιοσύνη (→ 345 f.) leads to the concept of equity; equality becomes equity. [61]

The righteous judge, who is impartial towards all, is ἴσος; cf. Plat. Leg., XII, 957c: ἴσος δικαστής; Polyb., 24, 15, 3: κριταὶ ἴσοι καὶ δίκαιοι; Inscr. Priene, 61, 9 f. (before 200 B.C.): ἴσους (impartial) [αὑτοὺς παρασχ]όμενοι τοῖς διαφερομένοις. In the sphere of law the ἴσος thus comes to be the same as the δίκαιος, and it goes through the same development, first as a designation of the judge, [62] then of the just or righteous man. [63] The relationship of ἰσότης to righteousness (cf. Plut. Convivialium Disputationum, VIII, 2, 2 f. [II, 719]) is differently defined by the ancients. According to Stoic ethics, for which ἰσότης is uprightness (cf. Stob. Ecl., II, 104 ff.), ἕπεται ... τῇ δικαιοσύνῃ ἰσότης καὶ εὐγνωμοσύνη (Diog. L., VII, 125, v. Arnim, III, 73, 6). [64] According to Philo, who wrote a special tractate περὶ ἰσότητος (Rer. Div. Her., 141-206), the relation is the very opposite: Spec. Leg., IV, 231: ἰσότης μήτηρ δικαιοσύνης; Plant., 122: ἰσότης δικαιοσύνην ... ἔτεκεν; Rer. Div. Her., 163: ἰσότης δικαιοσύνης τροφός, or in another image. Leg. Gaj., 85: ἰσότης πηγὴ δικαιοσύνης. Often the two terms are treated as synonyms, Aristot. Eth. Nic., V, 1, p. 1129a, 1 ff.), or are regarded as a double concept, e.g., Demosth. Or., 14, 3; 19, 15, 21, 67; also 12, 9 (ἴσον ἢ δίκαιον). Ditt. Or., I, 339, 51 praises as ἴσος καὶ δίκαιος the man who is found to be righteous in various public offices or actions on behalf of the state. [65]

---

[58] Perhaps we may agree with Barth (51 f.) that the καί is here an untranslatable, strengthening particle.

[59] In this sense the comparison is not "baroque" (as against W. Lütgert in BFTh, 13 [1909], 39 [591]). It may be added that the multiplication of expressions in v. 7 (μορφὴν δούλου λαβών, ἐν ὁμοιώματι ἀνθρώπων γενόμενος καὶ σχήματι εὑρεθεὶς ὡς ἄνθρωπος) plainly shows that the reference is not to triumph in temptation but to the incarnation. Interpretation in terms of an act of the historical Christ is thus ruled out.

[60] Cf. on this point the excellent discussion in Loh. Phil., 93.

[61] The transitional stage between the two senses may be seen in the paradoxical juxtaposition of ἄνισος (unjust) and ἴσος (equal) in Xenoph. Cyrop., II, 2, 18 (→ 347; Hirzel, 276³). Cf. also the imprecision of meaning in Cl. Al. Strom., VII, 69, 1; ὁ γνωστικὸς πρὸς τοὺς πέλας ἴσος καὶ ὅμοιος.

[62] Cf. Hirzel, 228, n. 5.

[63] *Ibid.,* 273 f.

[64] *Ibid.,* 230, n. 1.

[65] *Ibid.,* 229, n. 4.

A similar combination [66] of these two Hellenistically influenced [67] terms is to be found in Paul's exhortation in Col. 4:1: οἱ κύριοι, τὸ δίκαιον καὶ τὴν ἰσότητα τοῖς δούλοις παρέχεσθε. [68]

ἰσότης does not mean here an equal social position [69] which masters are to accord to their servants, cf. Melanchthon : *Non vult servos fieri aequales vel pares domino, sed vult servari aequalitatem geometrica proportione.* [70] ἰσότης is what is equitable ; [71] δίκαιον and ἰσότης may be rendered "just and fair." [72] It can hardly be maintained that masters alone are allowed to judge what is just and fair. [73] We do better to say that ἰσότης denotes "what cannot be brought under positive rules, but is in accordance with the judgment of a fair mind" (Abbott), and as an illustration we might quote the ἰσότης of the par. passage in Eph. 6:9 : both masters and slaves are to be guided by the same principles. [74] Or we might follow the exposition of Theodoret, *ad loc.* (MPG, 82, 621): ἰσότητα· οὐ τὴν ἰσοτιμίαν, ἀλλὰ τὴν προσήκουσαν ἐπιμέλειαν ἧς παρὰ τῶν δεσποτῶν ἀπολαύειν χρὴ τοὺς οἰκέτας.

In any case, it will be left to the one Lord and Judge to say whether earthly masters have accorded and maintained δίκαιον καὶ ἰσότητα, [75] and this Lord and Judge is unconditionally δίκαιος καὶ ἴσος.

On ἴσος as an attribute of God, cf. Cl. Al. Paed., I, 30, 2 : ἡ ἰσότης καὶ κοινωνία τοῦ θεοῦ ἡ αὐτὴ πρὸς πάντας; Strom., III, 6, 1 (cf. III, 7, 1; 8, 1): ἡ δικαιοσύνη τοῦ θεοῦ κοινωνία τις μετ' ἰσότητος; Strom., VI, 47, 4 : ὁ κύριος σῴζει μετὰ δικαιοσύνης καὶ ἰσότητος τῆς πρὸς τοὺς ἐπιστρέφοντας. The reference here is not to judicial ἰσότης; it is to that of the grace which establishes fellowship with those who resort to it.

Stählin

---

[66] The combination chosen by Paul (δίκαιον καὶ ἰσότης) is rare, though cf. P. Lond., IV, 1345, 2 (VIII): φυλάσσειν τὸ δίκαιον καὶ τὴν ἰσότητα.

[67] Loh. Kol., 159, n. 5.

[68] Cf. T. K. Abbott in ICC (1916); Ew. Gefbr., Lightfoot Col.; Loh. Kol., *ad loc.*

[69] In spite of the clever suggestions of Schlatter, *ad loc.,* it does not mean equality in any sense.

[70] Cf. Ew. Gefbr., *ad loc.*

[71] → δίκαιος, II, 188; cf. also Loh. Kol., 159, n. 5; also Ep. Ar., 263, and passages in which ἰσότης is set against πλεονεξία, e.g., Archytas in Stob., IV, 88, 14 f.; cf. Menand. Mon., 259 : ἰσότητα τίμα καὶ πλεονέκτει μηδένα. On the other hand the two terms bear a different sense in Xenoph. Cyrop., I, 6, 28 : εἰς τὸ ἴσον — "on equal (level) ground" — καθιστάμενοι μάχεσθαι, as distinct from μετὰ πλεονεξίας ἀγωνίζεσθαι ("to be at an advantage in battle").

[72] Abbott, *ad loc.* (296).

[73] Loh. Kol., 159.

[74] Abbott, 296.

[75] ἰσότης as an attribute of masters also in Philo Omn. Prob. Lib., 12 : καταγινώσκουσί τε τῶν δεσποτῶν, οὐ μόνον ὡς ἀδίκων, ἰσότητα λυμαινομένων, ἀλλὰ καὶ ὡς ἀσεβῶν κτλ. This means, of course, "mocking all equity" (cf. Polyb., 18, 26, 4 : λυμαίνεσθαι τὴν χάριτά τινος). Cf. also Cl. Al. Paed., III, 74, 2 : ἡ ἰσότης τοῖς δεσπόταις εὐάρμοστος.

Ἰσραήλ, Ἰσραηλίτης, Ἰουδαῖος,
Ἰουδαία, Ἰουδαϊκός, ἰουδαΐζω,
Ἰουδαϊσμός, Ἑβραῖος, Ἑβραϊκός,
ἑβραΐς, ἑβραϊστί

Contents : A. Israel, Judah and Hebrews in the Old Testament : 1. Israel and Judah ;
2. Hebrews. B. Ἰσραήλ, Ἰουδαῖος, Ἑβραῖος, in Jewish Literature after the Old Testament : 1. Ἰσραήλ-Ἰουδαῖος : i. The Basis ; ii. The Usage of Palestinian Judaism ; iii. The
Usage of Hellenistic Judaism ; 2. Ἑβραῖος ; i. As a Term for the Language and Script ;
ii. As an Archaic Name and Lofty Expression for the People of Israel. C. Ἰουδαῖος,
Ἰσραήλ, Ἑβραῖος in Greek Hellenistic Literature : 1. Ἰουδαῖος : i. In Pagan Writers ;
ii. Among Jews and Jewish Writers ; 2. Ἰσραήλ : i. Pagan Writers ; ii. In Philo and
Josephus ; 3. Ἑβραῖος : i. In Pagan Writers ; ii. Among Jews-Philo and Josephus. D. Ἰουδαῖος, Ἰσραήλ, Ἑβραῖος in the New Testament : 1. Ἰουδαῖος, Ἰουδαία, Ἰουδαϊκός,
ἰουδαΐζω, Ἰουδαϊσμός : i. Ἰουδαῖος in the Synoptists ; ii. In John ; iii. In Acts ; iv. In
Paul ; v. In Revelation ; vi. Ἰουδαία, Ἰουδαϊκός ; vii. ἰουδαΐζω, Ἰουδαϊσμός.
2. Ἰσραήλ, Ἰσραηλίτης : i. Of the Patriarch Israel ; ii. Israel as the People of God :
a. In the Synoptists ; b. In John ; c. In Acts ; d. In Paul. 3. Ἑβραῖος, ἑβραΐς, ἑβραϊστί :
i. The Derived Forms ; ii. Ἑβραῖος.

A. Israel, Judah and Hebrews in the Old Testament.

1. Israel and Judah.

Israel[1] in the oldest time known to us[2] is not the name of a tribe or place or
individual[3] but of a sacral league of tribes, an amphictyonic league of twelve, whose

---

Ἰουδαῖος κτλ. On A. : E. Sachsse, *Die Bedeutung des Namens Israel,* I (1910),
II (1922); A. Alt, *Die Landnahme der Israeliten in Palästina (Reformationsprogramm der
Universität Leipzig,* 1925); *Die Staatenbildung der Israeliten in Palästina (ibid.,* 1930);
M. Noth, "Das System der zwölf Stämme Israels," BWANT, IV, 1 (1930); "Erwägungen
zur Hebräerfrage," *Festschr.* Procksch (1934), 99-112; "Die Ansiedlung des Stammes Juda
auf dem Boden Palästinas," *Palästinajahrbuch,* 30 (1934), 31-46; M. Naor, "Jakob und
Israel," ZAW, 49 (1931), 317-321; W. Caspari, "Die sprachl. u. religionsgeschichtl. Be-
deutung des Namens Israel," *Zeitschr. für Semitistik,* 3 (1924), 194-211; W. F. Albright,
"The Name 'Israel' and 'Judah'" in JBL, 46 (1927), 151-185. On B. and C. : Liddell-Scott,
Moult.-Mill., Pape III (Proper Names), Preisigke Wört., III, Pr.-Bauer, Schleusner, *s.vv.*;
Schürer, esp. III § 31; Schl. Theol. d. Judt., 46 ff.; T. Reinach, *Textes d'Auteurs Grecs et
Romains relatifs au Judaïsme* (1895); J. Juster, *Les Juifs dans l'Empire Romain* (1914);
F. M. T. Böhl, "Die Juden im Urteil der griech. u. röm. Schriftsteller" in ThT, 48 (1914),
371 ff.; Trench, 79 ff. On D. : Bau. J., Excursus on Jn. 1:19; H. J. Cadbury, Note VII : "The
Hellenists," in *The Beginnings of Christianity,* I, 5 (1933), 59 ff.; W. Lütgert, "Die Juden
im Joh. Ev." in *Nt.liche Studien f. G. Heinrici* (1914), 147 ff.; "Die Juden im NT" in *Aus
Schrift und Geschichte, Abhandlungen f. A. Schlatter* (1922), 137 ff.; Schl. Mt. on 2:2; Str.-
B., II, 442 ff.; Zahn. Einl., I § 1, n. 12; Zn. Ag., Excursus on 18:4.
[1] On the question of the etymology of the name Israel cf. M. Noth, "Die israelitischen
Personennamen," BWANT, III, 10 (1928), 207 ff. (older bibl. in E. Sachse, ZAW, 34
[1914], 1 ff.). יִשְׂרָאֵל is one of the names built out of a clause. The theophoric element אֵל
is the subject, and the verbal predicate is the imperf. of a verb שָׂרָה, which probably means
"to rule," i.e., "God rules." More recently a derivation from שׂרה, "to shine," has been
advocated by H. Bauer, OLZ, 38 (1935), 477, ZAW, 10 (1933), 83 f., 101. Cf. also K. Vol-
lers in ARW, 9 (1906), 184.
[2] So already in the Song of Deborah, Ju. 5:2, 7 ff.
[3] The transfer of the name to the ancestor Jacob is a secondary process acc. to Sachsse,
Die Bedeutung . . ., I, 73.

establishment is narrated in Jos. 24. [4] Whether the name was already used of an older league, i.e., of tribes which were not in Egypt, is uncertain. The reference on the Merneptah stele (c. 1220) seems to support this view. [5] At any rate, Israel is originally a sacral term. It denotes the totality of the elect of Yahweh and of those united in the Yahweh cult. It thus embraces the central beliefs of the league. The rise of the monarchy puts an end to the sacral league. It thus brings about a change in the use of the name Israel.

The kingdom of Saul includes the south, [6] but with the crowning of David in Hebron the name Israel is separated from the southern tribes, and we have the commencement of the opposition of Israel and Judah, which already led to some dangerous crises even in the time of David. [7] The Leah group, especially Judah and Simeon, had always led a separate existence, even in respect of its sacral traditions. [8] Hence it was only a manifestation of underlying tensions in the structure of the Davidic kingdom, of tensions which only the masterly politics of the founder could overcome, when in 932 the northern tribes broke away from Rehoboam and formed the kingdom of Israel. The southern tribes returned to their separate existence, except that they now took the form of the kingdom of Judah under the Davidic dynasty.

Judah is the name of a tribe, and it remains an essentially political name by which the southern kingdom is known a parte potiori. Neither in its earlier nor its later use does it have sacral significance. Throughout the whole range of OT literature it is the secular name for a tribe.

The fall of the northern kingdom and the deportation of 722 introduced a new change in the significance and use of the name Israel, and the third phase dates from this point. Israel is now adopted by the southern kingdom and it is used again for the whole of God's people as a spiritual designation which transcends such political titles as the house of Judah [9] or the province of Judah. [10] This use of Israel even for the southern kingdom had deep roots, for Judah was once a member of the great tribal league, [11] and then part of the greater Davidic kingdom. Even in the later monarchy the prophets could still refer to the two houses (kingdoms) of Israel, Is. 8:14. It was thus logical that after 722 the name Israel should come to the southern kingdom with all its doctrinal implications. Both Isaiah and Micah — immediately after 722 — see that the situation has altered and use Israel for the southern kingdom. [12] This use of the term, not as a political title, but as the name of the people of God as such, becomes normative for subsequent generations in spite of political and geographical changes. It is to be noted, however, that the

---

[4] Noth, *System,* 65 ff.

[5] Cf. AOT, 20-25.

[6] 1 S. 11:8; 15:4; cf. also Noth, *op. cit.,* 110.

[7] E.g., 2 S. 19:42 ff.; 20:1 ff.

[8] On the separate political and sacral existence of the Leah group cf. Noth, *op. cit.,* 26, 32 f., 75 ff., 88 ff.

[9] בֵּית יְהוּדָה 1 K. 12:21, 23; 2 K. 19:30; Is. 22:21.

[10] מְדִינָה Ezr. 2:1; Neh. 1:3; 7:6; 11:3.

[11] As against E. Meyer, *Die Israeliten und ihre Nachbarstämme* (1906), 75, 233; cf. also A. Alt, Art. "Juda," RGG², III, 458 f.

[12] Is. 5:7; 8:18; Mi. 2:12; 3:1, 8, 9; 4:14; 5:1. The name Jacob was also transferred from the northern to the southern kingdom, Mi. 2:7; 3:1, 8, 9; 5:6; Na. 2:3; Is. 2:5, 6; 29:22.

concept of a greater Israel, [13] i.e., recollection of the ideal compass of the Davidic kingdom, is never lost. King Josiah was the last who by his actions, and by exploiting a unique situation in world politics, tried to restore the full Davidic kingdom. This attempt failed. [14] But faith in a greater Israel was still maintained as a theological postulate. This may be seen in the genealogical derivation of the twelve tribes in the later work of the Chronicler, and in the emphatic use of the name Israel in Chronicles. [15] For the Chronicler the twelve tribes constitute Israel according to the divine will, though the actual compass of the Persian province in the time of Ezra and Nehemiah forms a blatant contradiction. [16] This means, however, that in the post-exilic period Israel increasingly becomes the object of a hope that God will perform an eschatological act of salvation, [17] sometimes in the form of a reconstitution of the twelve tribes. [18]

2. Hebrews.

The name Hebrews (עִבְרִי) is very different from Israel and Judah. As scholars have realised for some time, the problem of this name cannot be solved apart from the great Ḥabiru question. Only recently, however, has there developed the certainty that ḥabiru/עִבְרִי is not the name of a people but an appellative which tells us something concerning the legal and social position of those who bear it. Thus in the 2nd and 3rd millennia we hear of ḥabiru in the great states of Asia Minor, Mesopotamia and Egypt, or on their borders. These are partly engaged in forced service, partly in voluntary slavery, and partly in rebellious activity. [19] There can be no doubt that they do not constitute an ethnic unity. On the other hand, we cannot fix with any precision their social and legal position. Noth thinks that they are nomads who move into civilisation but who live in tents and have no settled property. [20] Alt, on the other hand, thinks that עִבְרִי is a purely legal term to describe the position of those who decide to make themselves slaves. In this case the antonym of עִבְרִי would be חׇפְשִׁי, "free." [21]

In the OT עִבְרִי is in fact a legal term in the first instance. This may be seen from the law of slavery in Ex. 21:2 ff., where עִבְרִי is not an ethnic term, and from the

---

[13] K. Galling, "Die Erwählungstraditionen Israels," *Beih. 48 zur ZAW* (1928), 68 ff.

[14] O. Procksch, "König Josia" in *Festgabe f. T. Zahn* (1929), 19 ff.

[15] For details cf. G. v. Rad, "Geschichtsbild des chronistischen Werkes," BWANT, 4, 3 (1930), 18-37.

[16] The great territorial compression of Israel to roughly the older tribal lands of Judah made it natural that the members of God's people should also be called Jews, though this is hardly an OT usage; there are a few instances in the Chronicler and cf. Zech. 8:23; Da. 3:8, 12.

[17] Is. 49:3; 56:8; 66:20; Jl. 2:27; 4:2, 16; Ob. 20; Zech. 12:1. Cf. also in Psalms the hope that Yahweh will redeem Israel, 25:22; 53:6; 130:7 f. It is striking, however, that the name Israel fades into the background in post-exilic prophecy. On the other hand, the restoration of the people of God is to a great extent the theme of this prophecy. Hence no great significance can be attached to the nomenclature.

[18] Ez. 47:13-48:29; Is. 49:5 f.; Sir. 48:10; later esp. Ps. Sol. 17.

[19] Cf. M. Noth in *Festschr. f. O. Procksch* (1934), 99 ff.; for older material A. Jirku, "Die Wanderungen der Hebräer im 3. und 2. vorchristlichen Jahrtausend" (1934), op. cit., 24, 2.

[20] Noth, *op. cit.*, 111.

[21] A. Alt, "Die Ursprünge des israelitischen Rechts" (1934), 21, *Sächsische Akademie der Wissenschaften, Phil. hist. Klasse, 86, 1.*

passage concerning the manumission of slaves in Jer. 34:8-11, where עִבְרִי recurs
(v. 9, 14). Again, the Hebrews of 1 S. 14:21 are men who lived in dependence and
who now dissolve the relationship.

But the term עִבְרִי takes on a sense wider than the legal, and becomes more
general. Especially on the lips of non-Israelites it is used as a more or less critical
term for Israel. [22] Israelites also use it of themselves in distinction from foreigners. [23]
It carries with it a sense, not of national pride, but of humility and even contempt. [24]
Furthest from the original sense are Gn. 14:13 and Jon. 1:9, which are both late.
Here there is still distinction from foreigners, but the word is almost used in a
national sense ; the OT certainly prepares the way for the use of עִבְרִי to describe
an ethnic group. [25]

von Rad

B. 'Ἰσραήλ, 'Ἰουδαῖος, 'Εβραῖος in Jewish Literature after the OT.

1. 'Ἰσραήλ — 'Ἰουδαῖος.

i. The Basis.

After the collapse of Northern Israel in 722 B.C., only the comparatively small
territory around Jerusalem, the kingdom of יהודה, was left to maintain the ancient
tradition and name of what was once the whole people ישראל. Thus in pre-exilic
times the total designation ישראל can be used in passages where strictly the reference is only to the kingdom of יהודה.[26] After the return from exile the people
is even more exclusively restricted to the province of Judah, and all those who
live in Palestine outside this province are non-Israelites. It is thus quite natural that
the name which derives from the territory, Heb. יְהוּדִי, Aram. יְהוּדָי (יהודאי), or Greek
'Ἰουδαῖος, which originally denotes an inhabitant of the kingdom or province of
Judah, should come to be used more generally for a member of the people of Israel.
To denote, not a member of the Jewish state or an inhabitant of Judaea, but a
member of this people, two terms can thus be used, namely, ישׂרלא-'Ἰσραήλ,
"Israel(ite)" and יהודי-'Ἰουδαῖος, "Jew." [27]

Both terms denote a people. That is to say, they describe individuals in terms
of their genealogical membership of this people irrespective of their national
allegiance or residence. The decisive characteristic of the Jews, however, is that the
two terms denote the specifically religious confession of these individuals. As
this people, Israel is the fellowship of all those who worship the one true God.
Thus this people describes itself as the chosen people, i.e., the people whom the

---

[22] Gn. 39:14, 17; 41:12; Ex. 1:16; 2:6; 1 S. 4:6, 9; 13:19; 14:11; 29:3.

[23] Gn. 40:15; Ex. 1:19; 2:7; 3:18; 5:3; 7:16; 9:1, 13.

[24] Alt, *op. cit.,* → n. 21.

[25] The "Hebrew" tongue is שְׂפַת כְּנַעַן at Is. 19:18; "Hebrew" (adj.) is יְהוּדִית at 2 K. 18:26;
Neh. 13:24.

[26] → 357 and n. 12.

[27] יהודי/'Ἰουδαῖος is always used, then, for a member of the Jewish people, whether he
lives in Palestine, Babylon, Egypt, or anywhere else. I have not been able to detect any
post-exilic use of יהודי/'Ἰουδαῖος for an inhabitant of Judah as distinct from other countries.

one true God has chosen to worship and confess Him as distinct from the rest of the world. Every Jew, by virtue of his physical descent, inherits this one true religion, stands in a right relationship with God and partakes of the salvation which is granted to believers. [28] On the other hand, one who is not a Jew by physical descent can confess the one true God, and partake of eternal salvation, only if he becomes a member of this people. [29]

The terms ישראל and יהודי-Ἰουδαῖος thus express both national and religious allegiance. The two are always implied, though the emphasis may fall sometimes on the one and sometimes on the other according to the context.

Yet there is an element of selectivity in the use of the alternatives ישראל-Ἰσραήλ and יהודי-Ἰουδαῖος. The observable distinctions may be expressed as follows. ישראל is the name which the people uses for itself, whereas יהודים-Ἰουδαῖοι is the non-Jewish name for it. Thus ישראל always emphasises the religious aspect, namely, that "we are God's chosen people," whereas Ἰουδαῖος may acquire on the lips of non-Jews a disrespectful and even contemptuous sound, though this is not usual, since Ἰουδαῖος is used quite freely without any disparagement. This is shown by the fact that the Judaism of the *diaspora*, especially Hellenistic Judaism, finds no difficulty in adopting this non-Jewish usage, employing οἱ Ἰουδαῖοι of itself and reserving Ἰσραήλ for special religious use, primarily in prayers and biblical or liturgical expressions.

In detail, we do best to take the Palestinian and the Hellenistic usage separately.

ii. The Usage of Palestinian Judaism.

a. The usage of Palestinian Jews is best seen in 1 Macc. In the true historical presentation of this book, where the author himself speaks, there is a consistent use of Ἰσραήλ. But there is also a consistent and exclusive use of Ἰουδαῖοι (1) when non-Jews are speaking.

Cf. Demetrius at 10:23 or the Antiochenes at 11:50.

Ἰουδαῖοι is also used (2) in diplomatic correspondence, letters and treaties with non-Jewish states and rulers.

Thus the treaty of friendship between Judas Maccabaeus and the Romans (8:21-32) refers only to the Jews or to the people of Judah, not Israel. Cf. also the renewal of the treaty with the Romans and the Spartans by Jonathan (12:1-23); the letter of the Spartans to Simon on its renewal (14:20-23); the diplomatic circular of the Romans in favour of Simon (15:16-24). Similarly, the Syrian kings always speak of the Ἰουδαῖοι in their speeches and writings. Thus at 10:25-45 Demetrius uses it in his message to Jonathan, and the author himself adds in v. 46 that "Jonathan and the people put no trust in the promises of Demetrius, ... because they remembered the great wickedness which he had perpetrated against Israel." Similarly, the document of Demetrius in favour of Jonathan speaks only of the people of the Jews (11:30-37), while just before (11:23) the author says that Jonathan went to see Demetrius with some of the leaders of Israel. Similarly, we read in the letter at 13:36 that Demetrius sends greetings to the people of the Jews. Cf. also the missive of Antiochus VII to Simon at 15:1-9.

---

[28] Sanh., 10, 1: All Israel has a share in the future world.

[29] → προσήλυτος; on this whole question cf. K. G. Kuhn, "Die inneren Voraussetzungen der jüdischen Ausbreitung" in DTh, 2 (1935), 9 ff.

(3) ʼΙουδαῖοι, not ʼΙσραήλ, is also used by the Jews themselves in diplomatic communications with non-Jewish states.

Cf. the Jewish envoys before the Roman senate at 8:20, though just before at v. 18 the author himself says : "... when the Romans see that the kingdom of the Hellenes enslaves Israel."

(4) Not merely in external affairs, but also in official domestic documents ʼΙουδαῖοι is always used for the people, not Israel.

Cf. the great national charter which vested the dignity of high-priest and prince in the family of Simon, 14:27-46. In this there are many references to ʼΙουδαῖοι (14:33, 34, 37, 40, 41) and none to ʼΙσραήλ, though in 14:26 the author records the people as saying that "Simon and his brothers ... have repulsed the enemies of Israel," whereas in the document at 14:19 the reference is simply to "the enemies of their people." ʼΙουδαῖοι is also used in official titles ; thus Simon is the commander and prince of the Jews (e.g., 14:47 etc.).

Particularly instructive for this official use of ʼΙουδαῖος in place of the otherwise exclusive use of ʼΙσραήλ in self-designation is the statement at 1 Macc. 13:42 : "The people of Israel[30] began to write in documents and treaties : In the first year of Simon, the leader of the Jews."

Hasmonean coins bear out this conclusion. Here היהודים is consistently used, since the reference is to official titles.[31] It is of interest to compare the shekel which was probably minted during the great revolt of 66-70 A.D.[32] This bears the inscription שקל ישראל, Cf. also the coins minted under Bar Cochba in 132-135 A.D., which carry the inscriptions לחרות ישראל and לגאלת ישראל.[33] היהודים on Hasmonean coins is the correct official inscription ; the ישראל of the rebellions proclaims a religio-political programme, namely, that we, the people of God, now throw off the yoke of the Gentiles, that the Messianic age is dawning, and that it brings with it the redemption (גאלה!) and freedom (חרות!),[34] the dominion and glory, of the people of God.

b. The Palestinian usage reflected in 1 Maccabees[35] is fully confirmed in other writings of Palestinian Judaism. When we turn to works which, unlike 1 Maccabees, are religious rather than historical and political, and are written from a purely

---

[30] Following the reading in A ; the author also uses Israel at v. 41.

[31] V. Schürer, I, 269, 275, 285.

[32] Ibid., 762 ff.

[33] Ibid., 767.

[34] For the eschatological implications of these two terms cf. Shemone-Esre, 7th and 10th benedictions.

[35] The only possible exceptions to this usage in 1 Macc. are (a) 2:23 : A "Jewish man" will offer on the Gentile altar. One would expect here the more common "apostate from Israel." The expression denotes purely formal membership of the Jewish people, as in the usage of the diaspora (→ 363). Cf. the addition to Est. 1:1b : ἄνθρωπος ʼΙουδαῖος, of Mordecai = איש יהודי, Est. 2:5 (cf. → 363). (b) 1 Macc. 4:2 : Gorgias moves to fall on the camp of the Jews. This is probably a stereotyped expression ; cf. the many place-names (in Egypt) called castra Judaeorum and ʼΙουδαίων στρατόπεδον, Schürer, III, 42 f. (c) 11:42-53 is not a true exception, since the reference here is to Jewish troops in Antioch and their fighting for Demetrius. The consistent use of the name ʼΙουδαῖοι thus indicates that it is not Israel which is fighting, and that they are not fighting for Israel. These are Jewish mercenaries of the Syrian king. Cf. 11:41, where we read that the Syrian garrisons of fortresses in the land constantly made war upon Israel.

Jewish standpoint to edify members of the people, it is not surprising to find that 'Ισραήλ is always used in such works and never 'Ιουδαῖοι. For Israel implies the religious claim of this people to be God's chosen people even when it is used in secular contexts, with no religious emphasis, as the accepted designation, e.g., at Jdt. 4:1; 5:1; 7:1 etc. Examples of this type of writing are Sir., Jdt.,[36] Tob., Bar., Ps. Sol., 4 Esr., Test. XII, 3 En. 'Ισραήλ is found on innumerable occasions in these works, but never 'Ιουδαῖος.

The whole of Rabb. literature confirms this usage. The name ישראל occurs on every page. Nor is it restricted to religious contexts. As in 1 Macc. and the works mentioned above, it is also used as a consistent self-designation even in the secular field.

ישראל can denote either the people as a whole or individual Israelites. To take only one of countless examples, we read in T. Pea, 2, 9, in a comparison of Jew and non-Jew, that "if a גוי has sold his standing corn to an ישראל to reap, the latter is obligated to the Pea, but if an ישראל and a גוי own the standing corn in common, the ישראל is obligated for his share, but the גוי is free" etc. ישראל is often used for the ordinary Israelite as compared with the higher classes of priests and Levites, though it can also be used for full Israelites as compared with the lower classes of נתינים (lower temple servants) and ממזרים (bastards) etc. Very occasionally we find יִשְׂרְאֵלִי instead of ישראל for the individual Israelite, but always the fem. יִשְׂרְאֵלִית for Israelitess.

c. As compared with this constant use of ישראל, throughout the whole range of Rabb. literature it is only very rarely that we find יהודי = 'Ιουδαῖος, and this is mostly on the lips of non-Jews. We can see that the Rabbis were very conscious of the profound scorn and contempt with which other nations could treat the name יהודים-'Ιουδαῖοι.

Thus a motif which is variously exploited in several stories is that of a ruler or eminent man standing up to honour a Jew, and of those around him asking with astonishment: "Dost thou stand for a Jew?"[37] Again, R. Abbahu (c. 300 A.D.) in Eka r. Intr., No. 17 (33b)[38] tells us of the way in which Jews were mocked and scorned in Greek comedies and pantomimes. Again, the most grievous and unpardonable insult for a woman in Ascalon (Eka r., 1, 11[55a])[39] was to be told: "You have a face like a Jewess (יהודאיתא)." This causes the Rabbis to add the saying from Lam. 1:11: "See, O Lord, how I am despised."

But יהודי does not always have this contemptuous accent. Cf. the way in which it is used by a pagan in Rome in jSheb., 35b, 1; or by a Roman prefect in Gn. r., 11 on 2:3;[40] or by a pagan in jBM, 8c, 30 f. and 34: בריך אלההון דיהודאי, "Blessed be the God of the Jews!"; or by the Samaritans in Meg. Taan., 9, where they introduce the Jewish embassy to King Alexander: "These are the Jews ...";[41] or by pagans in Ex. r., 42 on 32:7,[42]

---

[36] On Jdt. v. also Ἑβραῖος → 368.
[37] jBer., 9a, 30 (Str.-B., II, 666) and 9a, 32 (Str.-B., III, 97); Lv. r., 13 on 11:1 (Str.-B., III, 393); Pesikta, 40 b (Str.-B., III, 394); Meg. Taan., 9 (Str.-B., I, 555).
[38] Str.-B., I, 615.
[39] Ibid., III, 97.
[40] Ibid., I, 614.
[41] Str.-B., I, 555.
[42] Ibid., III, 96 f.

when they put before the Jews the choice of either abandoning Judaism or suffering martyrdom in the words : אוֹ יְהוּדִי אוֹ צָלוּב.

Very rarely יהודי is also used by Jews or even by the Rabbis themselves (i.e., not on the lips of non-Jews). But this is not an independent usage of the Rabbis. They are simply imitating the usage of non-Jews or of the *diaspora* (→ 360).

> This is undoubtedly so in Ned., 11, 12, where the question is raised whether a wife must or can leave her husband because she has taken a vow which prohibits all marital intercourse with יהודים. Cf. also Ket., 7, 6, which refers to דָּת יְהוּדִית, the "(good) Jewish custom,"[43] and bMeg., 13a, where we find מאכל יהודי, "Jewish food," i.e., food which Jews are allowed to eat, as distinct from swine's flesh. Cf. again Gn. r., 63 on 25:23, where R. Chelbo says : Whereas the names of the peoples agree with the names of their progenitors according to Gn., this is not true of the peoples which derive from Jacob and Esau ; for they are called יהודאין וארמאין, "Jews and Romans." Here the name יהודאין (in Gentile fashion) is appropriate, because the true name ישראל does in fact agree with the name of the progenitor Jacob-Israel. To my mind there is also imitation, this time of the *diaspora*, in the few instances where יהדות is used for Judaism or the Jewish religion (in translation of ᾽Ιουδαϊσμός, → 364): Esther r., § 7, 11 (ed. Vilna, 1921, Fol., p. 12b): The Jews in Babylon did not change their God or their religious laws, but held on fast ביהדותן[44] to their Judaism.

But it was striking and unusual for Jews, and especially Rabbis, to call a Jew יהודי. This may best be seen from the exegesis of the term איש יהודי for Mordecai in Est. 2:5.[45] Attempts were first made to construe יהודי as a member of the tribe of Judah, but unfortunately Mordecai was a Benjamite. How then could he be called יהודי? The Rabbis found a play of words יחידי < יהודי (monotheist). It was thus a title of honour.[46] Mordecai was called יהודי because he confessed the one God.

iii. The Usage of Hellenistic Judaism.

a. If 1 Macc. is the best example of Palestinian Judaism, 2 Macc. is the best example of Hellenistic. Here ᾽Ισραήλ is used only 5 times in all, and always in strongly religious contexts : the prayer of 1:25 : "Thou, God, redeemest Israel"; 1:26 : "Thy people Israel" ; 10:38 : Praise of the Lord who has shown Israel such favours ; 11:6 : Request to the Lord for the salvation of Israel; and 9:5, in the biblically and liturgically current formula, "the Lord, the God of Israel." ᾽Ιουδαῖος is much more common, and it is used quite freely as a self-designation for the Jews.[47] Hence the usage is the very reverse of that of 1 Macc. In 1 Macc. ᾽Ισραήλ is always used except on the lips of non-Jews or as an official name, where we

---

[43] The two passages mentioned, Ned. 11, 12 and Ket., 7, 6, are the only two in the Mishnah where יהודי occurs. (איש יהודי at Meg., 2, 3 is a quotation from Est. 2:5.)

[44] So correctly the emendation of Levy Wört., *s.v.* for the ביהודתן of the text.

[45] Midr. Est. 2:5 (93a); cf. also bMeg., 13a (Str.-B., III, 96).

[46] There is thus a conscious antithesis here to the contempt with which the name can meet elsewhere. The very fact that the name gives rise to a special interpretation shows how strange and alien it was as a self-designation.

[47] Also ῾Εβραῖος 3 times (→ 368).

have 'Ιουδαῖος. In 2 Macc. 'Ιουδαῖοι is always used except in prayers and in biblical and liturgical formulae, where we have 'Ισραήλ.

Cf. 2 Macc. 1:1-10: A communication from the ἐν 'Ιεροσολύμοις 'Ιουδαῖοι, who call themselves ἡμεῖς οἱ 'Ιουδαῖοι,[48] to their ἀδελφοί, namely, οἱ ἐν Αἰγύπτῳ 'Ιουδαῖοι. Particularly instructive is a comparison with corresponding passages in 1 Macc. Thus we read in 2 Macc. 8:32: "Who had caused the Jews much trouble," whereas in 1 Macc. we read: "Who had caused Israel much trouble," cf. 1 Macc. 3:15, 35, 41; 5:3; 7:23; 8:18; 10:46 etc. Similarly, at 2 Macc. 6:1, 6, 8; 10:14, 15 we have 'Ιουδαῖοι as compared with 'Ισραήλ in 1 Macc. 5:3; 6:18 etc. 2 Macc. 10:8 is also quite clear: The community (in Jerusalem) resolves that the whole people of the Jews should annually celebrate the feast of the dedication. In 1 Macc. 4:59, however, Judas ... and the whole community of Israel ordain that the feast of the dedication should be observed annually.

It is thus natural that in 2 Macc. we should also find 'Ιουδαϊσμός for Judaism or the Jewish religion, e.g., 8:1: Judas and his friends gathered around them for battle τοὺς μεμενηκότας ἐν τῷ 'Ιουδαϊσμῷ. Here 1 Macc. 2:42 says that there gathered around them ... brave men of Israel who were ready to sacrifice themselves for the Law. 'Ιουδαϊσμός is thus an expression of Hellenistic Judaism. Characteristically, the Palestinian Jew has no equivalent.[49]

The usage of 3 Macc. is analogous to that of 2 Macc. Here, too, 'Ισραήλ occurs only in a specifically religious context, e.g., in prayers at 2:6, 10, 16; 6:4, 9, and in the current liturgical expression[50] ὁ θεὸς ὁ σωτὴρ 'Ισραήλ (6:32; 7:16), or ῥύστης 'Ισραήλ (7:23). Elsewhere οἱ 'Ιουδαῖοι is very frequently used as the normal name. Highly characteristic is 3 Macc. 4:21: "This was the work of providence, which came to the help of the Jews from heaven." Palestinian Jews could not possibly have spoken thus.

b. In agreement with this established usage of 2 and 3 Macc. are Greek inscriptions which either come from or mention Jews. Schürer has collected many Graeco-Roman inscriptions (III, 13-70), and in all these we never find 'Ισραήλ or 'Ισραηλίτης. The Jew is consistently called 'Ιουδαῖος, and the Jews οἱ 'Ιουδαῖοι, even by Jews themselves.[51]

The usage is thus the same as in BGU, VI, 1282, 2-3, where a Σαββαταῖος and his son call themselves 'Ιουδαῖοι. Similarly, in the burial inscriptions of the Jewish catacomb of Villa Torlonia in Rome[52] a Jewess is called 'Ιουδαία (28) and Cresces Sinicerius is called Judeus proselitus (47).[53]

Examples of the same usage may also be found in the Aram. letters and documents of

---

[48] We have only to consider how impossible it would be for a rabbi to say „we Jews (היהודים)," → 363.

[49] On what is, to my knowledge, the only passage in Rabb. lit., and perhaps in Palestinian usage, where we find יהדות = 'Ιουδαϊσμός, → 363.

[50] Cf. Shemone-Esre, 7th benediction: ברוך אתה יהוה גואל ישראל.

[51] Occasionally also Ἑβραῖος, → 368 f.

[52] H. W. Beyer-H. Lietzmann, Die jüdische Katakombe der Villa Torlonia in Rom (1930).

[53] Inscr. 44 is the only exception. Here a three-year old girl is θρεπτὴ προσήλυτος πατρὸς καὶ μητρὸς Εἰουδαία 'Ισδραηλίτης. The editors take this to mean an Israelitess of the tribe of Judah, but they give no examples of such a singular use of 'Ιουδαῖος; one could only point to the Rabb. exegesis of Est. 2:5, → 363. A better interpretation seems to be that she was a Jewess ('Ιουδαία), and then 'Ισραηλίτης is added to emphasise that she was a member of the chosen people of God.

the Jewish colonists in Persian service on the Nile island of Elephantine (5th century B.C.). [54] These people always call themselves יְהוּדִי (e.g., No. 6, 3 מחסיה בר ידניה יהודי), plur. יהודיא. There is no trace of the name יִשְׂרָאֵל in these pap. [55]

c. A few other writings call for notice. 4 Macc. and Susanna illustrate the usage in Hellenistic synagogue preaching. The use of Ἰουδαῖος in Sus. v. 4 and v. 22 (LXX), and of Ἰουδαϊσμός in 4 Macc. 4:26, agrees with Hellenistic Jewish usage elsewhere. On the other hand, the fact that this is preaching means that Ἰσραήλ is used much more commonly than among other Hellenistic Jews, since the vocabulary of preaching draws much more heavily on the style of the Greek Bible and liturgy. [56]

So Sus. v. 28 (LXX): οἱ ὄντες ἐκεῖ πάντες οἱ υἱοὶ Ἰσραήλ were gathered in the synagogue. Cf. v. 48 in address to the congregation: υἱοὶ Ἰσραήλ. Cf. again 4 Macc. 17:22: Through the blood of the martyrs ἡ θεία πρόνοια τὸν Ἰσραὴλ προκακωθέντα διέσωσεν. The language generally is Hellenistic (θεία πρόνοια) but the preaching style demands the use of Ἰσραήλ; cf. also Ἰσραηλῖται at 4 Macc. 18:1. [57, 58]

Relevant in this connection is the addition to Est. 6:5 (Εσθ. 10:3e-3f) in exposition of Mordecai's dream. Here we have the Greek τὰ δὲ ἔθνη, τὰ ἐπισυναχθέντα ἀπολέσαι τὸ ὄνομα τῶν Ἰουδαίων, and then immediately after (6:6[10:3 f.]) the accentuated τὸ δὲ ἔθνος τὸ ἐμόν, οὗτός ἐστιν Ἰσραήλ. Another example of the preaching style of Hellenistic Judaism is the addition to Est. 3:11 (Εσθ. 4:17i): "Let πᾶς Ἰσραήλ cry to God for help." [59]

Finally, we may refer to the Jewish Sib., which, with Ἑβραῖοι → 367, uses only Ἰουδαῖοι, 4, 127; 11, 45 = 11, 239; 12, 152; 14, 340. This is true even when there is a religious emphasis, 5, 249: In the last days Ἰουδαίων μακάρων θεῖον γένος οὐράνιόν τε. Ἰσραήλ is not found at all in the Jewish Sib.; this is an indication of its Hellenistic origin. We find it only in a later Christian part, Sib., 1, 360 and 366 (with Ἑβραῖοι).

2. Ἑβραῖος.

Along with Ἰσραήλ and Ἰουδαῖος we also find the much less common Ἑβραῖος. This is used in two very different ways.

i. As a Term for the Language and Script.

a. This is the exclusive use of עִבְרִי in Rabbinic literature. [60] As regards the

---

[54] A. Cowley, *Aramaic Papyri of the Fifth Century B.C.* (Oxford, 1923), Index, *s.v.*

[55] In this case the name יהודי might be used, even in self-designation, as an official name, as in Palestinian usage (→ 361), since the letters and documents are all official.

[56] In analogy to the use of Ἰσραήλ, not Ἰουδαῖοι, in the prayers and liturgical formulae of Hellenistic Judaism, → 363.

[57] For 4 Macc. cf. also Ἑβραῖος → 368.

[58] Cf. the normal description of Susanna as ἡ Ἰουδαία at v. 22 (LXX) and θυγάτηρ Ἰσραήλ of v. 48 (in address to the community in LXX style). It is interesting that we have θυγάτηρ Ἰούδα at v. 57, apparently synon. to θυγάτηρ Ἰσραήλ in the same verse. For the sake of variety the author has θυγάτηρ Ἰούδα in analogy to θυγάτηρ Ἰσραήλ. Ἰούδα fits his preaching style better than the more usual Ἰουδαία.

[59] The other passages in the additions to Est. (3:2, 14, 16; 6:10 = Εσθ. 4:17b, 17k, 17m; 10:3k) give us Ἰσραήλ in prayers and liturgical formulae. The ordinary use of Ἰουδαῖος is found in additions at 1:2; 5:15, 19 (= Εσθ. 1:1b, 8:12p, 12s) and Bel and the Dragon, v. 28.

[60] The only other use of עברי here is in עבד עברי and העבריה (or אמה) שפחה, "the Hebrew boy or girl." But this has no bearing whatever on Rabbinic usage, since it is simply a scholarly use in quotations from or allusions to the corresponding expressions at Ex. 21:2.

language עברי is used in Rabbinic Hebrew for what is often called לשון הקודש, the
sacred language, i.e., what we call Hebrew, as distinct from ארמי, what we call
Aramaic (also called תרגום by the Rabbis), and, of course, from יוני, Greek. As
regards the script, עברי denotes the old Hebrew script[61] as distinct from אשורי,
the Assyrian, i.e., square characters, and, of course, יוני, the Greek.

The main instances of this usage are as follows. jMeg., 71b, 13 ff.: "Four languages are
particularly apt ... Greek for poetry ..., Hebrew (עברי) for speech (דיבור, i.e., the divine
address in the OT). And many say: Also אשורי, Assyrian, i.e., square characters, for
writing. For אשורי has a script and no language, while עברי has a language and no
script. Hence the Jews at the time of Ezra chose for the Bible the כתב אשורי and the
לשון עברי. Why is this script called אשורי? ... R. Levi says: Because it came to them
(the Jews) from Assyria (Babylon) ... R. Nathan says: The Torah was given (to
Moses on Sinai) in רעץ, i.e., in the script of the Samaritans, or old Hebrew ... Rabbi
says: The Torah was given (to Moses on Sinai) in אשורית, i.e., square characters. But
the Israelites sinned, and it was altered to רעץ, the script of the Samaritans, or old
Hebrew. Then when they earned merit at the time of Ezra it was changed back into
אשורית, or square characters ..." etc. bSanh., 21b: "Mar Zutra ... said: Originally
the Torah was given to the Israelites in כתב עברי the old Hebrew script, and in
לשון הקודש, the Hebrew language. Later, at the time of Ezra, it was given to them
again in כתב אשורית, square characters, and לשון ארמית, Aramaic. Finally, there was
chosen for the Israelites כתב אשורית, square characters, and לשון הקודש, the Hebrew
language, though כתב עברי, the old Hebrew script, and לשון ארמית, Aramaic, were left
for the common people (ἰδιῶται). What is meant here by ἰδιῶται? R. Chisda says:
The Samaritans ..." Jad., 4, 5: "תרגום, the Aram. parts of Ezra and Da., are Holy
Scripture[62] ... and כתב עברי, the old Hebrew script, i.e., the biblical books written in
this script, are not Holy Scripture. A copy of the biblical books is Holy Scripture only
when it is written in אשורית, in square characters ..." Many further examples and
parallels may be found in Str.-B., II, 442-451, though some of these are misunderstood.[63]

In all these passages the Rabbis make a precise distinction between עברי, Hebrew,
and ארמי or תרגום, Aramaic. Only rarely are the two lumped together. That is to
say, only rarely is Aramaic, the popular language of Palestinian and Babylonian
Jews at the time of the Rabbis, described as עברי.

Cf. Git., 9, 6 and 9, 8, where we read of bills of divorce written in עברית as distinct
from those written in יונית (Greek), or of signatures in עברית as distinct from those in
יונית (Greek). Since bills of divorce, like other official documents (e.g., promissory
notes), were always written in Aramaic, עברית must obviously mean the popular Aramaic

---

[61] This was current in Israel up to the Exile. During the Exile the Jews adopted the Aram.
script, which they developed into the artificial and decorative square characters. But the old
Hebrew script was still used for some years, e.g., on Jewish coins and among the Samaritans,
who still used it in copies of the Pentateuch and consequently in other writings. The Rabbis
call this script רעץ or רַעַץ as thus used by the Samaritans.

[62] I do not understand the beginning of the sentence which follows: תרגום שכתבו עברית
ועברית שכתבו תרגום. So far as I can see, the various interpretations and translations of the
Mishnah ad loc. are all mere expedients.

[63] Cf. esp. Ep. Ar. § 11, Str.-B., II, 448 under e.

of Palestinian and Babylonian Jews. Along the same lines there is a reference to עדים עברים, i.e., to Jews whose mother tongue is Aramaic, and who thus add their signature in this language, as distinct from עדים יונים, i.e., Jews whose mother tongue is Greek, and who thus subscribe in Greek. We find the same use of עברי for Aramaic in TBB, 11, 8, which speaks of the translation of documents from עברית (Aram.) into Greek and *vice versa*.[64]

b. In the OT apocrypha and pseudepigrapha we have the common use of עברי-'Εβραῖος for Hebrew, Sir. Prol. 22 ('Εβραϊστί, the earliest attestation of this use) and 4 Macc. 12:7 = 16:15 ἐν τῇ 'Εβραΐδι φωνῇ. In the latter passage it is possible that the reference is to Aram. rather than Hebrew. If so, this usage, along with that in the few Rabbinic passages mentioned → *supra,* would agree with the usage of Josephus[65] and the NT,[66] where 'Εβραῖος and 'Εβραϊστί are used on various occasions for Aram.

There is in Josephus[67] an extension of the use of 'Εβραῖος for Hebrew or Aramaic. He does not think merely of the script and language. He also uses the term for measures, coins, names of the month, or national characteristics of the Palestinian Jews in general. There is no trace of any such extension in the literature which here concerns us.

ii. As an Archaic Name and Lofty Expression for the People of Israel.

a. A completely different use of the term derives from its use in the OT, particularly for the most primitive period. On this basis 'Εβραῖος comes to be used as an archaic name for Israel when the reference is to its distant past.

For examples cf. esp. Josephus;[68] also Test. Jos. 12:2 and 13:3 in the story of Joseph: νέος 'Εβραῖος and ὁ παῖς ὁ 'Εβραῖος of Joseph; also 12:2: ὁ θεὸς τῶν 'Εβραίων;[69] cf. also Jub. 47:5.

This use then led to the employment of 'Εβραῖοι for the Jewish people of the present and future in works which deliberately cultivated an archaic style.

Thus in the Jewish Sib. books, which often use 'Εβραῖοι synon. with 'Ιουδαῖοι,[70] e.g., 2, 175: ἐκλεκτοὶ πιστοὶ 'Εβραῖοι (also 3, 69); 5, 161: 'Εβραίων ἅγιοι πιστοὶ καὶ λαὸς ἀληθής; 5, 258: 'Εβραίων ὁ ἄριστος of Joshua. On this basis the later Christian parts almost always have 'Εβραῖοι for the Jews[71] (1, 346, 362, 387, 395; 2, 248, 250; 7, 135; 8, 141 [11, 38]).

b. In a few Jewish writings the final step is taken of using this archaic term for the Jews as a lofty expression. 'Εβραῖος becomes the more dignified, select

---

[64] Whether we have this use of עברי in the two passages quoted in Str.-B., II, 447 under c (i.e., bMeg., 18a and bShab., 115a), is open to question. In both of these עברית is probably just a textual corruption.

[65] → 374.

[66] → 388 f.

[67] → 374.

[68] On this pt. → 374; cf. also Philo → 373.

[69] This is the only use of 'Εβραῖος in Test. XII. 'Ιουδαῖος does not occur at all, but 'Ισραήλ on innumerable occasions → 362. On ὁ θεὸς τῶν 'Εβραίων cf. → 374 (Jos. Ant., 9, 20).

[70] 'Ιουδαῖοι also occurs in many passages, → 365.

[71] There are two instances of 'Ισραήλ, → 365.

and polite term as compared with the common 'Ιουδαῖος, which may often be used in a derogatory or even contemptuous sense. [72] 'Εβραῖος is thus used to denote Jewish nationality or religion in passages which wish to avoid the depreciatory element that clings so easily to 'Ιουδαῖος. It is supposed to carry with it the very opposite nuance of high esteem and respect. [73]

This is plain in the martyrdom stories in 4 Macc. Here the martyrs are always called 'Εβραῖοι (5:2, 4; 8:2; 9:6, 18). 'Εβραῖος is a title of honour (9:18 : μόνοι παῖδες 'Εβραίων ὑπὲρ ἀρετῆς εἰσιν ἀνίκητοι). Only once is 'Ιουδαῖος used (5:7), [74] and typically this is in the scornful words of the persecuting tyrant Antiochus to a martyr. 'Εβραῖοι is often used of the Jews in general (4:11; 17:9). The honourable nature of the term is particularly clear in 4:11. Apollonius wants to rob the temple treasury and is prevented by an angel. He then falls down and τοὺς 'Εβραίους παρεκάλει that they should pray for him.

'Εβραῖοι occurs in the same sense at 2 Macc. 7:31 in the speech of a martyr. It is found three times in 2 Macc. (7:31; 11:13; 15:37), but here the glorifying aspect is not so plain, since 'Ιουδαῖος is used quite freely along with it, with no derogatory accent. [75] Hence in the very similar passages 11:13 and 8:36 'Εβραῖος can be used on the one occasion and 'Ιουδαῖος on the other (11:13 : ἀνικήτους εἶναι τοὺς 'Εβραίους τοῦ δυναμένου θεοῦ συμμαχοῦντος αὐτοῖς; 8:36 : ὑπέρμαχον (sc. God) ἔχειν τοὺς 'Ιουδαίους καὶ διὰ τὸν τρόπον τοῦτον ἀτρώτους εἶναι τοὺς 'Ιουδαίους).

On the other hand, the magnifying trend is plainly apparent in Judith. Here the consistent use of Israel for the people (→ 362) is clear evidence of Palestinian Jewish usage. Nevertheless, at three points where Palestinian usage would lead us to expect 'Ιουδαῖος, i.e., 12:11 and 14:18 on the lips of Holofernes and Bagoas, and 10:12 on the lips of Judith when she confesses to the Assyrian sentries that she is a Jewess, and obviously cannot use Israel but must employ a non-Jewish designation for her people, [76] 'Ιουδαῖος is not used, but 'Εβραῖος; 'Ιουδαῖος is not used at all throughout the book. The only explanation is that the author feels 'Ιουδαῖος to be a derogatory and contemptuous term which he cannot use for the heroine of his book even when it is a non-Jew who is speaking. In such cases he prefers the more lofty and non-derogatory 'Εβραῖος.

c. It is perhaps along these lines that we are to understand the use of 'Εβραῖος on some Greek inscriptions. [77] Here 'Ιουδαῖος is consistently used both for individuals and for the whole people. [78] But those who used 'Εβραῖοι may have felt that 'Ιουδαῖος was a derogatory and contemptuous term. Hence, to avoid the contemptuous undertone, they chose the more lofty 'Εβραῖος.

On the other hand, it is more likely that we have here the use under i., i.e., for language and script, and particularly in the extended usage found in Joseph. [79]

---

[72] Zn. Ag. [1, 2] (1919), 642 ff. thinks that this latter use of 'Εβραῖος, which he groups with that for the script and language, arose only in the Christian community because of its need for a new expression in place of the disliked 'Ιουδαῖος. But it is plainly attested already in Jewish lit.

[73] As we have said, this use occurs in only a few writings. In most OT apoc. and pseudepigr. 'Εβραῖος does not occur.

[74] And once each 'Ισραήλ, 'Ισραηλῖται, 'Ιουδαϊσμός, → 365.

[75] → 363.

[76] Analogous to the usage under (3), → 361.

[77] Collected by Schürer, III, 83, n. 29.

[78] → 364.

[79] → 374.

and some pagan writers, [80] i.e., for the national characteristics of Palestinian Jews. If this is so, the Ἑβραῖοι of Greek inscriptions are Jews who have maintained their Palestinian traits, primarily by using Aramaic as their mother tongue, in distinction from Jews of the *diaspora* who had fully adapted themselves to the surrounding world in language and manner of life.

K. G. Kuhn

C. Ἰουδαῖος, Ἰσραήλ, Ἑβραῖος in Greek Hellenistic Literature.

1. Ἰουδαῖος.

i. In Pagan Writers.

a. In distinction from classical Greek literature, the post-classical period contains many references to the Jews. The usual term is Ἰουδαῖος [81, 82] for the individual Jew and οἱ Ἰουδαῖοι for the whole people. Ἑβραῖοι is less common. Historians in particular take note of this people, and they are naturally interested in the political and historical side.

So first Hecataeus of Abdera (FHG, II, 392 f., No. 13): ἀεὶ τὸ γένος τῶν Ἰουδαίων ὑπῆρχε πολυάνθρωπον. Here there is, of course, a picture of the religious situation of the Jews, but only as one would describe any other people. Cf. also Agatharchides (Jos. Ap., 1, 209): οἱ καλούμενοι Ἰουδαῖοι πόλιν οἰκοῦντες ὀχυρωτάτην πασῶν, ἣν καλεῖν Ἱεροσόλυμα συμβαίνει τοὺς ἐγχωρίους. The name is also common in the pap. in this sense. P. Oxy., II, 335 speaks of a house in the Jewish quarter (ἐπ᾽ ἀμφόδου Ἰουδα[ϊ]κ[οῦ]) built by a member τῶν ἀπ᾽ Ὀξ(υρύγχων) πόλ(εως) Ἰου(δ)αίων (cf. also IX, 1189, 9; 1205, 7); P. Fay., 123, 15 f.: ἐλήλυθεν γὰρ Τεύφιλος Ἰουδαῖος λέγων. [83] According to the remains preserved in Jos., Polybius, too, writes of τὸ Ἰουδαίων ἔθνος and τῶν Ἰουδαίων οἱ περὶ τὸ ἱερὸν τὸ προσαγορευόμενον Ἱεροσόλυμα κατοικοῦντες (Polyb., 16, 39, 1 and 4). In these instances the historical or national side is always to the fore.

b. Alongside the political, historical and national aspect of the name Ἰουδαῖος there is always the religious, and this plays a decisive role in the attention devoted to this people.

This aspect is present already in the very first examples of Ἰουδαῖος, i.e., in Clearch., Theophrast. and Megasthenes. Thus Aristotle says in Clearch. (acc. to Jos.): οὗτοι δέ εἰσιν (sc. the Jews) ἀπόγονοι τῶν ἐν Ἰνδοῖς φιλοσόφων, καλοῦνται ... οἱ φιλόσοφοι ... παρὰ Σύροις Ἰουδαῖοι (Jos. Ap., 1, 179). Cf. Megasthenes (FHG, II, 437, No. 41): ... τὰ μὲν παρ᾽ Ἰνδοῖς ὑπὸ τῶν Βραχμάνων, τὰ δὲ ἐν τῇ Συρίᾳ ὑπὸ τῶν καλουμένων Ἰουδαίων (sc. λέγεται). Dio C., 67, 14: τὰ τῶν Ἰουδαίων ἔθη,

---

[80] → 372 f.; 374 f.

[81] Naturally the Gks. did not pronounce the ι in Ἰουδαῖος as a consonant, but purely as a vowel; cf. the occasional form Εἰουδαῖος: Beyer-Lietzmann, *op. cit.* (→ n. 52), No. 44, CIG, IV, 9916. In contrast to older Hebrew, this corresponds with Aram. pronunciation, cf. Dalman Gr., 62 f. (§ 10, 3) ī for יְ; in Jewish Aram. the ה in יְהוּדָה also lost its value as a consonant, *ibid.*, 75 ff. (§ 10, 1).

[82] National names in -ιος had long since been used both as nouns and adjectives; for the latter cf. Jos. Ant., 10, 265; Philo Flacc., 29; 1 Macc. 2:23; Ac. 10:28 etc.

[83] For further examples cf. Preisigke Wört., III, 14, *s.v.*

"the Jewish religion." *Ibid.*, 68, 1 refers to the 'Ιουδαϊκὸς βίος; the reference here is to members of the Christian Church, of whom it is said that they will be condemned or accused on account of Jewish customs or a Jewish way of life.

Further representative examples may be taken from Plutarch. In Superst., 8 (II, 169c) he says that οἱ 'Ιουδαῖοι σαββάτων ὄντων ... οὐκ ἀνέστησαν, and this he attributes to their δεισιδαιμονία. Again, in Quaest. Conv., IV, 5 (II, 669f-671c) the question is raised whether it is due to reverence or to loathing that the 'Ιουδαῖοι do not eat swine's flesh. [84] Again, *ibid.*, IV, 6, (II, 671c-672c) τίς ὁ παρὰ 'Ιουδαίοις θεός is discussed, and there is also reference to the Jewish festivals. The religious aspect is here to the fore. Nor is the relationship of these 'Ιουδαῖοι to their Palestinian homeland and its distinctive features overlooked. Thus in the last passage we read of such special Palestinian elements as the vestments of the high-priest. In many cases individuals are described by the appositive 'Ιουδαῖος, Anton., 36 (I, 932b), 61 (I, 944b), 71 (I, 949b). All this shows that, while attention focuses primarily on the religious character of the Jew, the term 'Ιουδαῖος may also refer to nationality or to a connection with the Palestinian homeland.

c. Particularly significant is the fact that 'Ιουδαῖος can sometimes be used to denote religious adherence irrespective of nationality.

Thus in Plut. Cic., 7 (I, 864c) a man who is ἔνοχος τῷ ἰουδαΐζειν is called 'Ιουδαῖος by Cicero simply to denote his religion. It is true that we have here a witticism (a χαρίεν). But reference may also be made to Dio C., 37, 17: φέρει δὲ (sc. the ἐπίκλησις '"Ιουδαῖος") καὶ ἐπὶ τοὺς ἄλλους ἀνθρώπους ὅσοι τὰ νόμιμα αὐτῶν καίπερ ἀλλοεθνεῖς ὄντες ζηλοῦσι. Cf. also Arrian of Nicomedia (Epict. Diss., II, 9, 20): ὅταν τινὰ ἐξαμφοτερίζοντα ἴδωμεν, εἰώθαμεν λέγειν 'οὐκ ἔστιν 'Ιουδαῖος, ἀλλ' ὑποκρίνεται'. ὅταν δ' ἀναλάβῃ τὸ πάθος τὸ τοῦ βεβαμμένου καὶ ᾑρημένου, τότε καὶ ἔστι τῷ ὄντι καὶ καλεῖται 'Ιουδαῖος. Occasionally, then, 'Ιουδαῖος may have a purely religious sense.

ii. Among Jews and Jewish Writers.

a. Since the name 'Ιουδαῖος was the normal term used by foreigners for the Jewish people, the Jews of the *diaspora* soon adopted it as a name for themselves (→ 363).

Cf. a lease of the 2nd-1st cent. B.C. (BGU, VI, 1282, cf. 1272, 22), also inscr. (Ditt. Or., I, 73 : εὐλογεῖ τὸν θεὸν Πτολεμαῖος Διονυσίου 'Ιουδαῖος; cf. I, 74; 96, 5; II, 726; also CIG, 9916, 9926). This usage is particularly common in Philo and Joseph.

---

[84] This is not the place to speak of the anti-semitism of antiquity, but a few points may be made. Prior to NT days anti-semitism does not seem to have been racial — this was a cosmopolitan age — nor economic. It had its root in the aloofness (ἀμιξία, cf. 2 Macc. 14:38) of official Judaism from all other forms of life, especially in the religious sphere. Particularly important was the refusal to recognise or worship other gods as true gods. (It should be noted, however, that on the first contact between the Jewish world and the Greek the Jewish concept of God made a great impression and furthered the spread of Judaism.) The religious separation also involved social. Jews did not eat with Gentiles, did not attend the games, had as far as possible their own administration of justice, would not contract mixed marriages and avoided military service (because of the Sabbath) etc. Religious customs such as the Sabbath, circumcision, the laws of meats, and especially the refusal to eat swine's flesh, caused particular scorn or annoyance. The many strange distortions and calumnies (e.g., that they worshipped the head of an ass, or were driven out of Egypt as lepers) need not be listed in detail. On this whole question cf. esp. J. Leipold, *Antisemitismus in der alten Welt* (1933; bibl. on p. 3); Schürer, III, 150 ff.; Reinach, *op. cit.*, Preface.

b. In Philo 'Ιουδαῖος occurs most frequently in Flacc. and Leg. Gaj., where contemporary Jews are almost always 'Ιουδαῖοι, with no restriction of the term to inhabitants of Palestine (Flacc., 49 : οἱ πανταχόθι τῆς οἰκουμένης 'Ιουδαῖοι). The Jews are a national as well as a religious unity, cf. the discussion of the origin τοῦ τῶν 'Ιουδαίων ἔθνους in Virt., 212. In Philo, however, the emphasis is usually on the religious side. An enemy τοῦ τῶν 'Ιουδαίων ἔθνους is one who teaches them to renounce obedience in confidence in their noble descent and the merits of the patriarchs (Virt., 226).

Hence Philo can also speak of a μεταλλάξασθαι πρὸς τὴν 'Ιουδαίων πολιτείαν (Virt. 108), and the context makes it plain that this must imply adherence to the Jewish religion and the Jewish community. The Jewish people is also a totality in the religious sense : ὃν λόγον ἔχει πρὸς πόλιν ἱερεύς, τοῦτον πρὸς ἅπασαν τὴν οἰκουμένην τὸ 'Ιουδαίων ἔθνος (Spec. Leg., II, 163). It would be too much to say that Philo makes a complete distinction between the national and the religious aspect, or that he speaks of Jews who do not belong to the Jewish nation. Nevertheless, the main emphasis in his use of 'Ιουδαῖος is on the distinctive religion of the man thus described.

c. Josephus rarely uses 'Ιουδαῖοι of early Israel (→ 'Εβραῖος, 374 and → 'Ισραηλίτης, 372). In Ant., 6, 30 Samuel wrests from the Philistines the land ἣν τῶν 'Ιουδαίων ἀπετέμνοντο. When he comes to the post-exilic and contemporary period, however, Joseph. uses nothing else but 'Ιουδαῖοι.

On the introduction of the term cf. Ant., 11, 173 : οἱ 'Ιουδαῖοι ... ἐκλήθησαν δὲ τὸ ὄνομα ἀφ᾽ ἧς ἡμέρας ἐκ Βαβυλῶνος ἀνέβησαν ἐκ τῆς 'Ιούδα φύλης ἧς πρώτης ἐλθούσης εἰς ἐκείνους τοὺς τόπους αὐτοί τε καὶ ἡ χώρα τὴν προσηγορίαν αὐτοῖς μετέλαβον (→n. 16).

It is unnecessary to show in detail how closely the national and religious aspects are interwoven in Joseph. In Vit., 16 a man is 'Ιουδαῖος τὸ γένος if he is a Jew by nationality. On the other hand, the religious aspect comes out in the enumeration and discussion of the αἱρέσεις τῶν 'Ιουδαίων in Ant., 13, 171 f. [85]

Joseph. can sometimes call proselytes 'Ιουδαῖοι (cf. → 364, also n. 53 : 'Ιουδαῖος προσήλυτος as a correct Jewish burial inscr.): Ant., 13, 258. For love of their homeland subjugated Idumaeans accept circumcision etc., κἀκείνοις αὐτοῖς χρόνος ὑπῆρχεν ὥστε εἶναι τὸ λοιπὸν 'Ιουδαίους.

2. 'Ισραήλ.

i. In Pagan Writers.

In pagan writers 'Ισραήλ is never used for the Jewish people either past or present, nor should we expect this, since 'Ισραήλ is a specifically Jewish term which is not based primarily on nationality or external factors.

Israhel as a king of the Jews, i.e., the patriarch Jacob, is found once in Trogus Pompeius (cf. M. J. Justin, XXXVI, 2, 4 ff., ed. F. Rühl-O. Seel, 1935) in a presentation which mixes fact and fantasy. This Israhel calls his 10 sons Judaeos after the one who died first, i.e. Judah, whom the rest were all to revere. Alexander Polyhistor is also acquainted with the second name of Jacob (FHG, III, 215b, No. 8). After the angelic annunciation Jacob is called 'Ισραήλ, and so this name is often used : καὶ φάναι αὐτῷ τὸν ἄγγελον, ἀπὸ τοῦδε μηκέτι 'Ιακώβ, ἀλλ᾽ 'Ισραὴλ ὀνομασθήσεσθαι.

When 'Ισραήλ occurs in the pap. this is obviously due to direct Jewish or Christian influence, e.g., in the great Paris magic pap. (Preis. Zaub., I, 4, 3034, 3055 etc.), where the use is the same as in corresponding passages in the OT. In the formula θεὸς τοῦ

---

[85] Cf. also Schl. Theol. d. Judt., 87 f.

"Ισραμα (R. Wünsch, *Antike Fluchtafeln* [1907], 5, 3, KIT, 20) we have a corruption of 'Ισραήλ, but the context reveals a general influence of Alexandrian Judaism and especially of the OT. [86] Cf. also CIG, IV, 9270; P. Masp., Vol. I (1911), 67002, I, 18; P. Oxy., XIII, 1602, 3.

ii. In Philo and Josephus.

a. When referring to the early period, Philo uses 'Ισραήλ according to the sense and usage of the OT, quite frequently in quotations, more rarely independently.

> Rer. Div. Her., 203 compares the Egyptian and the 'Ισραηλιτικὴ στρατιά (cf. Poster. C., 54). 'Ισραήλ is often used for the patriarch Jacob, usually in allegorising, but 'Ιακώβ is more common. The metaphorical implication of 'Ισραήλ is in terms of Philo's translation of the term: ἄνθρωπος ὁρῶν θεόν. The privilege of Israel (as Is-ra-el) is that he sees God; for he who sees has a share in what he sees (Poster. C., 92). The vision of God expressed in the name is the essential thing for Philo (Abr., 57-59; Leg. Gaj., 4). But this means that 'Ισραήλ may easily come to transcend the limits of the Jewish people. All οἱ τοῦ ὁρατικοῦ γένους μετέχοντες are 'Ισραήλ (Deus Imm., 144; Sacr. AC, 134). This extension is not directly stated; nevertheless, the way is clearly prepared for it.

b. Joseph. uses 'Ισραηλίτης for members of the people of God in past days. He does not use it for present members. This use is in keeping with the biblical text and is also suitable for the readers whom he has in view.

> The name is not used after Ant., 12. No special account is given of its derivation, as in the case of Ἑβραῖος (→ 374) and 'Ιουδαῖος (→ 371). But he is aware of the derivation, e.g., when he causes Moses to address the people ὦ παῖδες 'Ισραήλου (Ant., 4, 180). Only once does he mention 'Ισραήλ as the second name of the patriarch Jacob, and he here gives the translation ὁ ἀντιστάτης ἀγγέλῳ θεοῦ (Ant., 1, 333). This rendering shows a better grasp of Hebrew than that of Philo. [87]

> It is interesting that Joseph. often shows knowledge of the Palestinian use of 'Ισραηλίτης for ordinary members of the people (alongside priests and Levites): Ἔζδρας ἐποίησεν ὁμόσαι τοὺς φυλάρχας τῶν ἱερέων καὶ τῶν Λευιτῶν καὶ 'Ισραηλιτῶν (Ant., 11, 146, cf. 151, 312; → 362).

> It is not evident that the name 'Ισραήλ has any particular significance for Joseph. as denoting the religious situation of the Jewish people. In Ant., 9, 20, when ὁ τῶν Ἑβραίων θεός has appeared to Elijah, he asks εἰ θεὸν 'Ισραηλιτῶν λαὸς ἴδιον οὐκ ἔχει, but we can hardly be sure that the term is used in this sense here. Certainly, the concept is not indissolubly tied to it. This is linked with the fact that Joseph. does not use 'Ισραήλ to denote the whole people; he employs only 'Ισραηλῖται.

3. Ἑβραῖος.

i. In Pagan Writers.

a. The word Ἑβραῖος [88] is rare in Greek literature. It is usually employed in the narrower sense of geographical, national, or linguistic definition. In the main

---

[86] Cf. also Deissmann B, 23-54.

[87] Cf. Schl. Theol. d. Judt., 56, n. 2.

[88] It is to be noted that, though a soft breathing is often used (cf. Bl.-Debr.[6] § 39, 3), we are keeping to the normal rough breathing, as also in such subsidiary forms as ἁβραϊκός or Αἰβρέος.

it occurs in passages where Ἰουδαῖος could be used but where it is avoided because it is normally used for the Jews in general, and also particularly in a religious sense.

Thus Antonius Diogenes (Porphyr. Vit. Pyth., 11) mentions Ἑβραῖοι along with Ἄραβες and Χαλδαῖοι. He means inhabitants of Palestine irrespective of their religion, cf. Porphyr. Abst., II, 61, Plut. Anton., 27 (I, 927e). This is particularly plain in Tacitus : According to some accounts *Judaei colunt proprias urbes hebraeasque terras et prop(r)iora Syriae* (Historiarum, V, 2). *Judaei* is the general term which can be used for Jews in Rome or anywhere else ; *hebraeae terrae* denotes Palestine.

b. Occasionally Ἑβραῖος seems to be regarded as a more ancient term which is selected because of its force as such.

Thus Damascius (Phot. Cod., 242) [89] says : Ἄβραμος ὁ τῶν πάλαι Ἑβραίων πρόγονος, or Charax of Pergamon (FHG, III, 644b, No. 49): Ἑβραῖοι ... οὕτως Ἰουδαῖοι ἀπὸ Ἀβραμῶνος (cf. also Alexander Polyhistor in FHG, III, 206a).

Ἑβραῖος seems to be used similarly, or just as a more selective term, in Plut. (Quaest. Conv., IV, 6 [II, 671c]): Διόνυσον ἐγγράφεις καὶ ὑπονοεῖς τοῖς Ἑβραίων ἀπορρήτοις (the mysterious God of the Jews). [90]

c. Once Ἑβραῖος plainly denotes the speech : Luc. Alex., 13 : All the people run together on account of the deceiver Alexander, who φωνάς τινας φθεγγόμενος, οἷαι γένοιντ' ἂν Ἑβραίων ἢ Φοινίκων. Ἑβραίων φωνή is thus the particular language spoken by the Ἑβραῖοι as Phoenician is by the Phoenicians.

d. Ἑβραῖος is often used by Pausanias, whose usage demands brief treatment. In I, 5, 5 he says that Hadrian subdued τοὺς Ἑβραίους τοὺς ὑπὲρ Σύρων ἀποστάντας. He also compares the βύσσος ἡ ἐν τῇ Ἠλείᾳ with the βύσσος τῶν Ἑβραίων (V, 5, 2), and speaks of something which is ἐν τῇ Ἑβραίων χώρᾳ (V, 7, 4; VI, 28, 8). The Ἑβραῖοι live there (VIII, 16, 4 f.). For Paus., then, a Ἑβραῖος springs from the land of the Hebrews. (He does not always have to be a Jew ; no religious definition is primarily in view.) Paus. seems to avoid the name Ἰουδαῖοι. He thus uses Ἑβραῖος with geographical reference to Palestine. There is no express reference to the speech of these Ἑβραῖοι, though this would be quite conceivable.

ii. Among Jews-Philo and Josephus.

a. Following the LXX, Philo uses Ἑβραῖος for the people Israel in ancient times.

Αἰγύπτιον καλοῦσι Μωϋσῆν, τὸν οὐ μόνον Ἑβραῖον, ἀλλὰ καὶ τοῦ καθαρωτάτου γένους ὄντα Ἑβραίων (Mut. Nom., 117; cf. also Vit. Mos., I, 243). Sometimes the name is allegorised : a Ἑβραῖος is a περάτης (cf. the LXX at Gn. 14:13), and indeed ἀπὸ τῶν αἰσθητῶν ἐπὶ τὰ νοητά (Migr. Abr., 20). But normally Ἑβραῖος is used for the ancient people. [91]

As regards the present, Philo uses the term for that which, though Jewish, is not common to all Jews, especially the Hebrew or Aramaic language.

---

[89] Quoted from Reinach, *op. cit.*, 212.
[90] We misread the situation if we think we detect the slightly derogatory tone which the name usually has in the OT (→ 359). This nuance is no longer present in NT times (→ 367).
[91] → 367.

He compares the ῾Εβραίων γλῶττα with the ῾Ελλήνων γλῶττα (Conf. Ling., 68), and also, very pertinently, ἔστι δὲ ὡς μὲν ῾Εβραῖοι λέγουσι ... ὡς δὲ ἡμεῖς (ibid., 129). Philo is a Jew, but he does not speak ὡς ῾Εβραῖοι λέγουσιν. This aspect is particularly clear in the story in Vit. Mos., II, 31 f., where we are told that the king (Ptolemy Philadelphus) resolved to have the "Chaldean" text of the OT translated into Greek, and that for this purpose there were sent to him ῾Εβραῖοι from Judaea who were acquainted both with their native and with Hellenic culture, particularly the languages. As ῾Εβραῖοι they understood the text of the OT. In such cases Philo is naturally not thinking only of a specific locality whose inhabitants are called ῾Εβραῖοι because they speak Aramaic; but it is only a short step to this usage (cf. Som., II, 250; Abr., 28).

b. Like Philo, Josephus normally uses ῾Εβραῖος for the people in ancient times. Hence the term is particularly common in Ant., 1-9 (alongside ᾿Ισραηλίτης, with no obvious distinction between them, e.g., Ant., 2, 201/2).

Josephus derives the name from Heber, ἀφ᾽ οὗ τοὺς ᾿Ιουδαίους ῾Εβραίους ἄρχηθεν ἐκάλουν (Ant., 1, 146). This statement is characteristic. ᾿Ιουδαῖοι is the current expression, ῾Εβραῖοι the ancient.

Like Philo, too, Josephus uses ῾Εβραῖοι to describe what is peculiar to the Jewish people as a nation, i.e., such things as the language, script, measures, coins, or names of the month, which Jews of the diaspora no longer had.

We constantly find such expressions as καθ᾽ ῾Εβραίων γλῶτταν or διάλεκτον (e.g., Ant., 5, 323; 1, 36). When Joseph. spoke to the people of Jerusalem on the commission of Titus, διήγγελλεν τὰ τοῦ Καίσαρος ἐβραΐζων (Bell., 6, 96) in order to be the better understood. In the days of Isaiah Rabshakeh, the representative of the king of Assyria, speaks ἑβραϊστί (rather than συριστί) in order to be understood in the city (Ant., 10, 8). In his use of ἑβραϊστί it is obvious that Josephus does not always distinguish between Heb. and Aram., though he knew the distinction (→ 366). From the standpoint of the NT a variant on Bell., 1, 3 is interesting: Josephus παῖς γένει ῾Εβραῖος, as the son of a Jerusalem priest. As a Palestinian, Joseph. speaks Aram., but he is here called a ῾Εβραῖος because he comes of a Palestinian family.

Very occasionally ῾Εβραϊκά is used of distinctive Jewish customs (Ant., 18, 345). On the other hand ὁ ῾Εβραίων θεός is used in the common sense of ῾Εβραῖος elsewhere to denote the people in ancient times (Ant., 9, 20).

This historical use is also found in the poet Ezekiel. [92] It seems to be common to all his works so far as they are known. In his Exodus we always find ῾Εβραῖοι, not ᾿Ιουδαῖοι.

c. In the light of what has been said, we can interpret with relative certainty the use of ῾Εβραῖος on inscriptions. Here the use is contemporary, not historical. Hence the most obvious sense is that of a Jew from Palestine who also speaks Aramaic. This Jew is distinguished from other Jewish groups as a ῾Εβραῖος.

There are three references to a συναγωγὴ (τῶν) ῾Εβραίων [93] in Rome along with many others. Twice we read of leaders of this Hebrew synagogue in Rome. [94] Several

---

[92] REJ, 46 (1903), 48 ff., 161 ff.

[93] CIG, IV, 9909; Deissmann LO, 12 f., n. 8; J. Keil and A. v. Premerstein, "Bericht über eine dritte Reise in Lydien," Denkschriften der Akademie der Wissenschaften in Wien, phil.-hist. Kl., LVII (1914), No. 42.

[94] N. Müller-N. Bees, Die Inschr. der jüdischen Katakombe am Monteverde zu Rom (1919), No. 14 and 50.

suggestions have been made in interpretation of the name of this synagogue. [95] Common to all of them is the thought that these Ἑβραῖοι are more closely linked to Palestine than other Jews, whether by derivation or by language. This is particularly plain when a Jew named Μακεδόνις is more specifically described as ὁ Αἰβρέος Κεσαρεὺς τῆς Παλαιστίνης. [96] In three other cases those referred to are called Ἑβρέοι, Ἑβρέος. [97]

We may thus conclude that Ἑβραῖος is either used historically or to denote Palestinian nationality or language, especially when Jews are called Ἑβραῖοι in contradistinction from other Jews.

D. Ἰουδαῖος, Ἰσραήλ, Ἑβραῖος in the New Testament.

1. Ἰουδαῖος, Ἰουδαία, Ἰουδαϊκός, ἰουδαΐζω, Ἰουδαϊσμός.

i. Ἰουδαῖος in the Synoptists.

In the Synoptists Ἰουδαῖος, or Ἰουδαῖοι, is rare. Whereas in John (→ 377) οἱ Ἰουδαῖοι is the common term to describe those with whom Jesus has dealings, the Synoptists usually have the general expression ὁ ὄχλος or οἱ ὄχλοι, which is far less frequent in John. On the other hand, there is closer differentiation in the Synoptists. γραμματεῖς, πρεσβύτεροι, Φαρισαῖοι, Σαδδουκαῖοι, ἀρχιερεῖς are either more common in the Synoptists than in John (Φαρισαῖοι and ἀρχιερεῖς), or they do not occur in John at all (γραμματεῖς, Σαδδουκαῖοι, πρεσβύτεροι).

Ἰουδαῖος is never used in the Synoptists as a proper name for the people to whom Jesus comes. In this sense it is found only in the expression βασιλεὺς τῶν Ἰουδαίων. It should be noted, however, that this is never put on the lips of Jesus or the Evangelists themselves. It is always used by aliens. Thus the μάγοι ask (Mt. 2:2): ποῦ ἐστιν ὁ τεχθεὶς βασιλεὺς τῶν Ἰουδαίων; This is the question of a foreigner or a Gentile, not of a Jew. [98]

Materially we see here something which agrees with the usage outside the NT. A newly born βασιλεὺς τῶν Ἰουδαίων must obviously be sought in Palestine, and more specifically in Jerusalem. To this degree the term Ἰουδαῖος implies a national and even a geographical [99] basis. But in the first instance the emphasis in this formula is on the religious side. The Ἰουδαῖοι are the people to whom God has promised a king whom men come to worship. Herein this people is distinguished from all other peoples, and this king from all other kings. [100]

---

[95] Schürer, III, 83, n. 29; G. la Piana, "Foreign Groups in Rome during the First Centuries of the Empire" in *Harvard Theol. Review,* 20 (1927), esp. 356, n. 26. For bibl., cf. *ibid.,* also Keil and Premerstein, *op. cit.,* and cf. esp. Müller-Bees, *op. cit.,* 24, n. 1 (Deissmann) on organisation in terms of country of origin.

[96] Müller-Bees, No. 118.

[97] *Ibid.,* No. 117, 122; CIG, IV, 9922.

[98] Cf. Schl. Mt., *ad loc.*: "The Messianic concept in pre-Christian form as stated by Gentiles"; cf. also Trench, 83.

[99] Naturally not in the special sense of the province of Ἰουδαία, but of any parts of Palestine inhabited by Jews. In the NT Ἰουδαῖος is never limited to inhabitants of Judaea, nor is this general elsewhere (→ n. 27). Even Jn. 7:1 is no true exception, and Ac. 2:14 is questionable in the light of 2:5.

[100] Schl. Mt., *ad loc.*: "'Ἰουδαῖος is the name for the community which is united by the Law and by confession of the one God," though the term is hardly filled out in this way in the actual usage of Mt.

In the Synoptists βασιλεὺς τῶν Ἰουδαίων also occurs in the passion narrative, and again it is consistently put on the lips of a foreigner. At Mt. 27:11 and par. Pilate asks Jesus : σὺ εἶ ὁ βασιλεὺς τῶν Ἰουδαίων; According to Mt. Pilate also knows the term χριστός for this βασιλεὺς τῶν Ἰουδαίων (27:17, 22), but he takes neither term seriously (τὸν λεγόμενον χριστόν; though cf. Mk. 15:9, 12). Even if he does accept the fact that Jesus is this, he regards the one thus designated as a purely political figure who is to be destroyed rather than worshipped, and he seizes the opportunity to strike at Jewish Messianism, which he views only from the political angle, in the person of this harmless Jewish king. [101] Comparison of the two occasions when foreigners use βασιλεὺς τῶν Ἰουδαίων (Mt. 2:2 and 27:11) discloses the two possibilities contained in the term Ἰουδαῖος, namely, the religious and the political. Pilate for his part is well aware of the religious claim implicit in the title βασιλεὺς τῶν Ἰουδαίων. Hence the distinction in usage from that of the wise men who come to worship is not absolute ; it is a distinction of emphasis or priority.

The same point emerges in the other two instances at Mt. 27:29 (the soldiers) and 27:37 (the inscription on the cross).

In this connection it is noteworthy that the Jewish leaders adopt a different expression when they mock the Messianic claim of Jesus : Mt. 27:42 : βασιλεὺς Ἰσραήλ ἐστιν ... (Mk. 15:32 : ὁ χριστὸς ὁ βασιλεὺς Ἰσραήλ, Lk. 23:35 : ὁ χριστὸς τοῦ θεοῦ). This is the correct Palestinian form of the claim of Jesus.

Apart from this use Ἰουδαῖος is very rare in the Synoptists.

The only other instance in Mt. is at 28:15 : διεφημίσθη ὁ λόγος οὗτος (sc. that the disciples had stolen the body of Jesus) παρὰ Ἰουδαίοις μέχρι τῆς σήμερον [ἡμέρας]. The first point of interest here is that there is no article, so that we ought to render "among such as are Jews." [102] The use of Ἰουδαῖος resembles that which is fairly common in John (→ 378), for whom Ἰουδαῖος denotes a man who refuses to trust in Jesus. This single use certainly tells us nothing concerning the religion or nationality either of the author or of his readers. Nevertheless, it is so striking that we are tempted to see here the gloss of an early copyist [103] who in his day had heard this report among "Jews". At all events, it is not entirely satisfying.

Mk. 7:3 is interesting. Vv. 3 and 4 are a parenthetical note in the discussion of purification to explain the point at issue to outsiders : οἱ γὰρ Φαρισαῖοι καὶ πάντες οἱ Ἰουδαῖοι ... Mk. is thus writing for those who are not familiar with the Jewish Law and Jewish customs. The religious connotation of Ἰουδαῖος is plain. A man obeys these commandments as a Ἰουδαῖος, as one who is bound to the Law. This use of Ἰουδαῖος to explain matters to outsiders is much more frequent in Jn. (→ 377).

A certain exception from ordinary Synoptic use is to be found at Lk. 7:3 : The centurion sends πρεσβυτέρους τῶν Ἰουδαίων to Jesus. The probability in this instance is that we have here, not the actual statement, but rather the usage of Lk. himself, or consideration for his readers, as at Lk. 23:51, where Arimathea is called a πόλις τῶν Ἰουδαίων (cf. Mt. 10:23, the πόλεις [τοῦ] Ἰσραήλ).

In the Synoptists, then, we find substantially the same Palestinian usage as in 1 Macc. (→ 360). Ἰουδαῖοι is used for the Jewish people on the lips of non-Jews

---

[101] Cf. Schl. Jn. on 19:15.
[102] Cf. indirectly Schl. Mt., ad loc.
[103] Cf. Kl. Mt., ad loc.

or in the dealings of Jews with non-Jews, while Ἰσραήλ is the true designation not normally used by non-Jews.

ii. In John.

The use of Ἰουδαῖος in John has frequently called for notice, [104] especially in view of the sparse occurrence in the Synoptists (in Mt. 5 times, in Jn. 70). Yet we must be careful not to try to fix on a single meaning in Jn.; for the first point to be made is that in many passages we find a parallel to the Synoptists.

a. This is particularly true in the passion narrative, where we often find βασιλεὺς τῶν Ἰουδαίων or Ἰουδαῖος on the lips of non-Jews (18:33, 39; 19:3, 19, 21). Worth noting in this connection is 18:35, where Pilate answers Jesus : μήτι ἐγὼ Ἰουδαῖός εἰμι; In this saying we again see the religious and national aspects of the term.

Important, too, is a passage like 4:9, where Jesus is freely called a Ἰουδαῖος. We should certainly not overlook the fact that this is on the lips of a Samaritan.

In this context 4:22 can hardly be given a special sense. If σωτηρία is ἐκ τῶν Ἰουδαίων, this is said in opposition to the Samaritans. It does not mean that salvation is of the Jews because they are Jews, but because they are those who thus far are the community of God, and who may justifiably make this claim against the Samaritans.

In Rabbinic literature, too, the name Jew is used by Samaritans. [105] Hence Ἰουδαῖος is a normal term for Israel when dealing with them, as with Gentiles.

b. As distinct from the Synoptists, however, Jn. also uses Ἰουδαῖος to denote inhabitants of Palestine even when there is no non-Jewish reference. That is to say, he adopts a usage which is fitting when addressing non-Jews, as in the case of Josephus, or very occasionally the Synoptists (Mk. 7:3; Lk. 7:3). The purpose is to fix the time and place. There is thus a certain suggestion of remoteness, of distance in space and time. The general term οἱ Ἰουδαῖοι, and the individual differentiations, are a little formal and imprecise.

This is particularly so when Ἰουδαῖος is used in the many explanations of Jewish customs or expressions. These are much more common than in the Synoptists, where the only instance is Mk. 7:3. In Jn. 2:6 we read of pots κατὰ τὸν καθαρισμὸν τῶν Ἰουδαίων. This explanation is given for those who are not familiar with Jewish national and religious customs. At 4:9 there is an explanation which is quite superfluous for those who have some knowledge of Palestinian interrelations but which is essential for foreigners who do not. It concerns the hostility between Jews and Samaritans. Another explanation is given at 6:4, where τὸ πάσχα is described as ἡ ἑορτὴ τῶν Ἰουδαίων. We are also told that feasts are feasts of the Jews at 2:13; 5:1; 7:2; 11:55, and for other explanations which use the name Ἰουδαῖος cf. 19:40, 42.

We find the same objective and unemphatic use of Ἰουδαῖος elsewhere in John's Gospel. Thus we may cite 1:19 : ἀπέστειλαν πρὸς αὐτὸν (John the Baptist) οἱ Ἰουδαῖοι ἐξ Ἱεροσολύμων ἱερεῖς καὶ Λευίτας ἵνα ... Here it is possible to read into Ἰουδαῖος the sense of religious hostility (→ 378), but this is quite unnecessary, for Josephus can use the word in exactly the same way. It may well

---

[104] W. Lütgert, "Die Juden im JohEv." in *Festschr. f. Heinrici* (1914), 147 ff.; Bau. Jn., Exc. on 1:19.
[105] jSanh., 2d; v. Str.-B., II, 424.

be that the Baptist is set in antithesis to the Ἰουδαῖοι, but this is not decisive if we remember the national and spatial remoteness of at least the readers, if not the author. [106]

At 3:1 Nicodemus is called an ἄρχων τῶν Ἰουδαίων. His religious character, however, is to be sought in the designation Φαρισαῖος. Hence this phrase simply tells us that he had a leading position among the people. (It should be noted already that there can be no absolute distinction between the various nuances.) Even when the use is not emphatic, some regard is naturally had to the specific religious position of those called Ἰουδαῖος, as at 3:25, where the disciples of John the Baptist debate the question of purification with a Ἰουδαῖος. In the same sense οἱ Ἰουδαῖοι are often engaged in discussion with Jesus with no necessary implication of hostility to Him, e.g., 7:11; 8:31; 10:19; 11:19, 31, 33, 36; 12:9, 11. To be sure, the ultimate point is always one of understanding and faith, and often these Ἰουδαῖοι have neither. Yet they are not essentially different in this respect from others. If the Jews are often uncertain regarding Jesus in this Gospel, this is not a distinctive feature of the Jew *qua* Jew. Hence an inimical note is not necessarily contained in the name Ἰουδαῖος as such.

Since it is primarily a matter of national and temporal remoteness, there can also be reference to Ἰουδαῖοι who believe in Jesus (8:31; 11:45; 12:11). Again, they do not believe in spite of the fact that they are Jews. The emphasis in these passages is simply on the fact that they do believe, not on the fact that it is Jews who believe.

This all goes to show that Ἰουδαῖος can often be used in John to denote those with whom Jesus has dealings. In this sense it is used in exactly the same way as it would be by anyone who is distant in nationality and time.

This raises the question whether the remoteness is primarily that of the readers or of the author. But the usage cannot throw any light on this question, since the parallel of Josephus proves that even one who himself was born in Palestine could adopt the name Ἰουδαῖοι for Jews living in his own time (→ 371). The fact that John also uses Ἰσραήλ favours the view that he is himself a Jew (→ 371 f.).

c. Alongside the use to denote the people of Palestine we must also set the use which expresses the fact that those who bear this name refuse to believe in Jesus as the Christ, so that they are not merely His partners but His actual opponents in discussion. In this respect it is impossible to make a precise distinction. More depends on the emphasis which the context of the narrative imparts to the term Ἰουδαῖος than to anything implicit in the term itself. On the other hand, the great number of such contexts tends to create a certain fixity of usage in this direction.

The Jews oppose Jesus as Jews when to their eyes He seems to reject the temple. For them the temple is the place of God's presence. Hence their opposition arises from their essential Jewishness, from their attachment to the temple, 2:18, 20. The Jews complain as Jews when Jesus calls Himself the bread of life and says that only those who drink His blood can have life (c. 6, esp. v. 41 etc.). It is recounted

---

[106] Cf. the way in which we might speak of the attitude of the French to Voltaire, even though he himself was French.

in 10:31 that, when Jesus stated that He and the Father are one, ἐβάστασαν πάλιν λίθους οἱ 'Ιουδαῖοι ἵνα λιθάσωσιν αὐτόν, and this they do as Jews to whom such blasphemy is intolerable; they oppose Christ as 'Ιουδαῖοι. The same is true when they try to kill Jesus (5:16, 18; 7:1). Cf. also 8:48, 52, 57; 10:33; 13:33. Many who are themselves Jews either oppose Jesus, or take up an ambiguous attitude towards Him, for fear of the "Jews" (7:13; 9:22; 19:38). [107] These Jews are not a sharply defined group of legal zealots. [108] They are simply given this name — or this is at least the implication — because they oppose Jesus on the grounds of Jewish religion. They are found in the story of the man born blind (c. 9), where they appeal to Moses against Jesus (v. 29). They are also the opponents of the disciples at 11:8 and 20:19, not because they are faithful to the Law and the disciples are not, but because they resist the claim of Jesus to lordship, and are thus brought into opposition to the disciples.

In all this the author is separated from the Jews by a deep cleft which is much greater than the historical and national remoteness of his readers. In this usage may be discerned the cleft which was brought into being by the relationship between the Christian community and Judaism — a cleft which had its roots in the fact that Judaism rejected the Christ who had been sent to it, and that it based this rejection on its essential Jewishness, on its appeal to the religious possession proper to it as God's people.

The only point is that the relationship worked out in individual stories gives to John's use of οἱ 'Ιουδαῖοι an emphasis which obviously did not lie in the name previously, but which was made possible by the fact that it denoted the religious attitude of those who were thus designated. οἱ 'Ιουδαῖοι is a name for those who reject the claim of Jesus to lordship, and who remain Jews because they do so.

On the other hand, we must insist that there is no detachment of the name from the national foundation. A man is not called a 'Ιουδαῖος simply because he does not believe and rejects Christ. He has first to be a Jew by nationality. In fact, Jn. never uses 'Ιουδαῖος even for a proselyte. This is in keeping with the framework of the Gospel.

In the Johannine use of οἱ 'Ιουδαῖοι we may thus discern both a general historical remoteness, at least on the part of the readers, and also a cleavage which is due to the relationship between Christianity and Judaism exemplified in the Gospel.

iii. In Acts.

The usage in Acts is very similar to that of John. Acts, too, is recounting specific dealings with specific Jews, and is doing so for much the same kind of readers as John. A minor point is that 'Ιουδαῖος is applied in Ac. not only to Jews in Palestine but also to the Jews of the *diaspora*. The nature of the material accounts for this. The point is hereby emphasised that the Jews bear this name, not as inhabitants of Palestine, but as members of this people, of this religious community. On the other hand, the name is not extended in Ac. to those who belong to the religious fellowship as proselytes but who are not native Jews (Ac. 2:5 is the only possible exception). [109]

---

[107] On the obj. gen. cf. Bl.-Debr⁶ § 163.
[108] Lütgert, *op. cit.*, 152 f.
[109] Cf. the various interpretations in Wdt. Ac., *ad loc.*

'Ιουδαῖος is the normal term for this people on the lips of foreigners, e.g., Roman officials (18:14; 22:30; 23:27), or on the lips of Jews when dealing with non-Jews (21:39; 23:20; 24:5).

The religious connotation naturally varies in individual passages, and is difficult to evaluate. Thus at 16:20 the apostles are defamed as 'Ιουδαῖοι by the Roman Philippians, but here the reference seems to be national, though it is followed at once by mention of the ἔθη which they fear will be thrust upon them. On the other hand, the favourable testimony of the Jews to Cornelius at 10:22 has in view not merely his social attitude but also, and above all, his religious.

In Ac. 'Ιουδαῖος may also be a purely objective term for men of this people and religion. Thus Peter at Ac. 10:39 speaks of what Jesus did ἐν τῇ χώρᾳ τῶν 'Ιουδαίων. If Elymas is called a Jew at 13:6, this is a purely objective statement; it does not carry any unfavourable implication. Jews and Greeks are often mentioned together with no particular emphasis, 18:4; 19:10, 17. We can also be told quite simply that 'Ιουδαῖοι joined the community, 14:1.

When members of the community are called Jews, this is usually in explanation of the special circumstances or to denote that they are members by birth. At 16:1 Timothy is υἱὸς γυναικὸς 'Ιουδαίας πιστῆς. Paul says that he was a Jew of Tarsus, not merely before the chiliarch, but also in his address to the Jews (21:39; 22:3); cf. Apollos (18:24). At 18:2 Aquila is called a 'Ιουδαῖος to explain why he was in Corinth. He had to leave Rome whether or not he had become a Christian. (This is not ruled out, of course, by the fact that he is described as 'Ιουδαῖος.)

Naturally 'Ιουδαῖος is also used in Ac. for one who is Jewish in outlook, who is committed to the Law (10:28). Thus Paul circumcises Timothy because of the Jews (16:3; cf. 9:22; 18:28; 22:12). This can lead to a usage very like that of John; the 'Ιουδαῖοι are those who oppose Christ as preached by the apostles, and who oppose His community (9:23; 12:11; 13:50; 17:5, 13 etc.). Yet this aspect is not indissolubly linked with the term; Jewish members of the community are equally at odds with these 'Ιουδαῖοι (14:1 ff.). There are Jews who believe (14:2), and yet non-believers can be described simply as 'Ιουδαῖοι later on in the same passage.

iv. In Paul.

Even external observations indicate that there is in Paul a certain deviation from the use of 'Ιουδαῖος as hitherto established. Paul is almost unique in using the sing. 'Ιουδαῖος even when he is not thinking of an individual Jew. Along the same lines, he often uses 'Ιουδαῖος or 'Ιουδαῖοι without the article, which is infrequent in other writings. These facts suggest already that for Paul the 'Ιουδαῖος is a type, a spiritual or religious magnitude. When he speaks of the 'Ιουδαῖος, he does not have in view specific adherents of this nation and religion. He is thinking of a type abstracted from individual representatives. This naturally imparts to the term a new significance, and this development is primarily determined by the character of the Pauline literature.

Paul does, of course, use 'Ιουδαῖος in the common sense, e.g., at 1 Th. 2:14, where the Christian communities ἐν τῇ 'Ιουδαίᾳ have to suffer ὑπὸ τῶν 'Ιουδαίων, i.e., those who slew Jesus and the prophets. Yet even here it will be noted that, although 'Ιουδαῖοι denotes specific men in Palestine, the addition "and the prophets" gives a typical and supratemporal significance to the word. The 'Ιουδαῖοι are always those who decide against, and reject, both God and His community.

This aspect of the Jew, namely, that he rejects Christ, is not the only one which has typical significance. Nor is it consistently linked with the term. For the word has also abstract significance when it is used for the true Jew as distinct from the purely outward Jew, R. 2:28 f.: ὁ ἐν τῷ φανερῷ Ἰουδαῖος is distinguished from ὁ ἐν τῷ κρυπτῷ Ἰουδαῖος. According to the context, the true Jew is the one who does not merely know the Law, and boast in it, and proclaim it ; he is the one who keeps it (cf. R. 2:17). The reference here is not to specific individuals ; it is to the religious concept of the Jew.

A man is a Ἰουδαῖος for Paul on the basis of a specific relation, namely, his attachment to the Law. 1 C. 9:20 : ἐγενόμην τοῖς Ἰουδαίοις ὡς Ἰουδαῖος, ἵνα Ἰουδαίους κερδήσω. Here Paul continues : τοῖς ὑπὸ νόμον ὡς ὑπὸ νόμον. But this is simply to repeat the same point with a clearer indication of what is essentially at issue. The Ἰουδαῖοι for whose sake he becomes a Jew are naturally individual men with whom he has dealings. [110] But they are viewed under the aspect which subsumes them under the concept Ἰουδαῖος, namely, that of their commitment to the Law.

A particularly clear example of the fact that for Paul the Ἰουδαῖος is one who behaves as a Jew, i.e., as an adherent of the Law, is to be found at Gl. 2:13 : συνυπεκρίθησαν αὐτῷ (sc. Peter) [καὶ] οἱ λοιποὶ Ἰουδαῖοι, to whom, e.g., Barnabas also belongs. In quotation marks, as it were, Paul is here calling Christians Ἰουδαῖοι because they remain within the limits prescribed by the Law. Paul does not call himself a Ἰουδαῖος in this sense. But he naturally includes himself when the reference is to membership by birth : v. 15 ἡμεῖς φύσει Ἰουδαῖοι. He could not call himself simply a Ἰουδαῖος, with no supplementary explanation. This is proved by 2 C. 11:22 ff. Here he calls himself and his Christian opponents Ἑβραῖος and Ἰσραηλίτης. But then in v. 24, when he describes his sufferings, he calls those who condemned him to the lash Ἰουδαῖοι. The word implies the opposition to Christ which these people have displayed in their actions.

The same typical use of Ἰουδαῖος by Paul is to be found in the antithesis of Ἰουδαῖοι and Ἕλληνες or Ἰουδαῖοι and ἔθνη (both in essentially the same sense). In the first instance this distinction is not one of race or nationality. It is grounded in the divine revelation. The Ἰουδαῖος has as such an advantage over other men, R. 3:1 f.: τί οὖν τὸ περισσὸν τοῦ Ἰουδαίου; ... πολὺ κατὰ πάντα τρόπον (R. 9:4 f.). In this connection we might refer to the common Ἰουδαίῳ τε πρῶτον καὶ Ἕλληνι (R. 1:16; 2:9, 10). This advantage of the Jew, which is inherent in his being as such, consists in the fact that he has the Law, R. 3:2. It is thus posited by the will of God, and it is consequently valid.

> The Jew cannot boast of this advantage. For he does not keep the Law (R. 2:17 ff.). Hence he is not really better placed than the Gentile (3:9). Both are guilty. Furthermore, there is no absolute distinction between Jew and Gentile. God is one, and He is the God of the Gentile as well as the Jew. In Abraham all nations are to be blessed (Gl. 3:8). Only in the Christian community, however, is there no longer any radical distinction between the Ἰουδαῖος and the Ἕλλην (Gal. 3:28; Col. 3:11; R. 9:24; 10:12), though even here historical distinctions are still recognised (1 C. 7:17 ff.). [111]

In Paul, then, Ἰουδαῖος is almost always used in a sense which emphasises the essential, typical and suprapersonal aspect of the term, whether negatively in the

---

[110] Cf. Bl.-Debr.⁶ § 261, 1.
[111] Cf. W. Gutbrod, Die paul. Anthropologie (1934), 29 ff.

historical orientation towards rejection of Christ, or positively in the commitment to the Law which determines the being of a Jew as such.

This does not mean that the name Ἰουδαῖος is taken from Jews and transferred to some concept of a Jew apart from national membership of the Jewish people.

v. Ἰουδαῖος in Revelation.

In Rev. Ἰουδαῖος occurs only twice, at 2:9 and 3:9, and both times in the same sense. The reference is to Ἰουδαῖοι who proudly claim to be such but who are really the synagogue of Satan. If they were real Ἰουδαῖοι, we could say that they were the synagogue of God. Ἰουδαῖος is here used positively for one who is committed to God and to the will of God, and this is set in antithesis to what is Jewish only by name and derivation. This use is very close to that of Paul in R. 2:18 ff. But what is said does not justify us in arguing that Christians alone may be called genuine Ἰουδαῖοι.

In sum, the NT uses the word Ἰουδαῖος in two ways. The Ἰουδαῖος is either the Jew generally, whether by nationality, or more specifically in terms of his religious commitment to the Law and to God. Or, in the course of NT development, he is the Jew who, appealing to the Law, sets himself in opposition to Christ.

vi. Ἰουδαία, Ἰουδαϊκός.

Ἰουδαία as the name of a country is first used adjectivally (ἡ Ἰουδαία χώρα, Mk. 1:5; Jn. 3:22), but then also independently, though the constant use of the art. reminds us of the adj. derivation. [112] In the narrower sense Ἰουδαία is Judaea, esp. in the Syn., who often refer to Jerusalem as well when they mention Ἰουδαία, Mt. 3:5; 4:25 etc. At Mt. 19:1 we have ὅρια τῆς Ἰουδαίας πέραν τοῦ Ἰορδάνου, so called because one part of this territory was occupied by Jews alone as distinct from the Greek cities. But Ἰουδαία can also be used for the whole of Palestine, especially by foreigners who do not distinguish between the various parts. Hence Strabo Geogr., XVI, 21: ἡ δ' ὑπὲρ ταύτης (sc. Φοινίκης) μεσόγαια μέχρι τῶν Ἀράβων, ἡ μεταξὺ Γάζης καὶ Ἀντιλιβάνου Ἰουδαία λέγεται. Ἰουδαία seems to be used in this broader sense at R. 15:31; 2 C. 1:16; 1 Th. 2:14. Certainly no more precise delimitation is in view. [113]

Ἰουδαία never has any theological significance. It is a geographical term and has no inner connection with the events of the NT.

Ἰουδαϊκός. An adj. formed with the suffix -ικος denotes the species or class of the object of which it is an attribute, but with reference to the word from which it is derived, i.e., "related to this," "belonging to it," "bearing its nature." [114] In the only verse in which Ἰουδαϊκός is used in the NT, i.e., at Tt. 1:14, what is meant is not so much the nature of the fables as their derivation and connection. These μῦθοι circulate among Jews and are spread by them (cf. the ἐντολαὶ ἀνθρώπων); they are not Jewish by nature.

Cf. Plut. Is. et Os., 31 (II, 363d): Ἰουδαϊκὰ εἰς τὸν μῦθον παρέλκειν, Jewish stories, i.e., things known and confessed among the Jews, enter into the μῦθος which is under debate. These Ἰουδαϊκά are called such by virtue of their origin rather than their nature. According to Philo, 55 two of the five main portions of Alexandria are

---

[112] Cf. Bl.-Debr.⁶ § 261, 4.
[113] Ἰουδαία is not very clear in Ac. 2:9; cf. ZNW, 9 (1908), 253.
[114] Kühner-Blass, I § 334, 5.

called Ἰουδαϊκαί because they are primarily inhabited by Jews. Cf. Ep. Ar., 22, 24, 28, 121, 176; Ditt. Or., II, 543, 15/16; 586, 7; Philo Leg. Gaj., 170 and 245.

vii. ἰουδαΐζειν, Ἰουδαϊσμός.

Outside the NT ἰουδαΐζειν implies conversion to Judaism, especially by circumcision (Est. 8:17: πολλοὶ τῶν ἐθνῶν περιετέμοντο καὶ ἰουδάϊζον διὰ τὸν φόβον τῶν Ἰουδαίων; Jos. Bell., 2, 454: ἰκετεύσαντα (one Metellius) καὶ μέχρι περιτομῆς ἰουδαΐσειν ὑποσχόμενον διέσωσαν μόνον), or sympathy with Judaism which leads to the total or partial adoption of Jewish customs, Jos. Bell., 2, 463 : When the Jews are rooted out, τοὺς ἰουδαΐζοντας εἶχον ἐν ὑποψίᾳ (inhabitants of Syria); Plut. Cic., 7 (I, 864c): a man is ἔνοχος τῷ ἰουδαΐζειν. [115]

The word is to be taken in the latter sense in the one NT passage at Gl. 2:14. By such conduct one would force the Gentiles to live Ἰουδαϊκῶς. In this debate with Peter there is no question of the full Judaising which would lead to circumcision.

The term Ἰουδαϊσμός is found in the NT only at Gl. 1:14. Outside the NT it occurs esp. in 2 Macc. [116] in the sense either of the sum of Jewish being and life (obj.), as in 2:21: Manifestations from heaven τοῖς ὑπὲρ τοῦ Ἰουδαϊσμοῦ φιλοτίμως ἀνδραγαθήσασιν, [117] or of Jewishness and its representation in life and thought (subj.), e.g., in 14:38 : A worthy man called Rhazi is καὶ σῶμα καὶ ψυχὴν ὑπὲρ τοῦ Ἰουδαϊσμοῦ παραβεβλημένος.

Gl. 1:14 has the latter sense. Paul was above his contemporaries in Jewishness, and in the representation of this Jewishness in his whole life and thought.

2. Ἰσραήλ, Ἰσραηλίτης.

i. Of the Patriarch Israel.

Ἰσραήλ is never used directly for the patriarch in the NT. It is possible, however, that there is sometimes a reference to him. Thus at Phil. 3:5 Paul says ἐκ γένους Ἰσραήλ, and he then adds the more precise φυλῆς Βενιαμίν. In other words, he may be thinking of the race which descends from the patriarch. [118] On the other hand, although this is the ultimate basis of the expression γένος Ἰσραήλ (→ n. 3), it is unlikely that there was usually any conscious thought of the patriarch. The formula simply implied the people of Israel as we use the term, with no specific reference to the patriarch in person.

The same is true at R. 9:6: οὐ πάντες οἱ ἐξ Ἰσραήλ, οὗτοι Ἰσραήλ. Here proximity to the following sentence, which refers to the seed of Abraham, suggests a reference to the patriarch Ἰσραήλ. [119] Nevertheless, here too the οἱ ἐξ Ἰσραήλ really means those who are members of the people Israel by birth. Ἰσραήλ is an established term for the people. This is the more probable because the relation to

---

[115] On the two possibilities, ibid., § 328, 4.
[116] It is a Hellenistic Jewish term, → n. 49.
[117] This interpretation is not absolutely certain ; the second sense is also possible.
[118] At 3 Macc. 6:9, 13 there is reference to the race of Israel and then to the race of Jacob. Here it is fairly evident that we are to think of the patriarch.
[119] Schl. R., 297: "Here Israel is the name of the progenitor."

the patriarchs which is implied in this membership, and which gives it significance, is represented in terms of relationship to Abraham (σπέρμα and τέκνον).

At Hb. 11:22 Joseph is sure of the exodus of the children of Israel. But here, too, there is no direct reference to the patriarch. The expression is simply a technical term which implies no conscious awareness of its origin.

The same is true of similar phrases which might suggest such a reference, e.g., οἶκος Ἰσραήλ, Mt. 10:6; 15:24; [120], [121] λαός Ἰσραήλ, Lk. 2:32; γένος Ἰσραήλ, Phil. 3:5. [122] Along similar lines, there is also reference to a βασιλεύς Ἰσραήλ, Mt. 27:42 (Mk. 15:32; Jn. 1:49; 12:13) and to the φυλαὶ τοῦ Ἰσραήλ, Mt. 19:28; Rev. 7:4; 21:12.

ii. Israel as the People of God.

a. In the Synoptists, or, strictly, in Mt. and Lk. — Mk. hardly uses Ἰσραήλ, perhaps out of regard for his readers — Ἰσραήλ is the current designation of the people on the lips of Jews (for data outside the NT → 360). The emphasis is primarily on the religious side, though there is a more neutral use at Mt. 2:20 when Joseph is to return εἰς γῆν Ἰσραήλ. This corresponds to the normal designation of the country in Rabbinic literature: אֶרֶץ יִשְׂרָאֵל. [123] It does not occur elsewhere in the NT. Outside the NT the land is often called Palestine; [124] in the NT it is usually referred to by the individual provinces. In Mt. Ἰουδαία refers more strictly to Judaea (→ 382), which would include Bethlehem but not Nazareth; hence Mt. selects the more comprehensive γῆ Ἰσραήλ. [125] In other passages Ἰσραήλ can be used objectively for the people with no particular connotation of the people of God. Mt. 10:23: the πόλεις [τοῦ] Ἰσραήλ; Lk. 1:80: John the Baptist is in the wilderness ἕως ἡμέρας ἀναδείξεως αὐτοῦ πρὸς τὸν Ἰσραήλ. Something came to pass, or comes to pass, ἐν τῷ Ἰσραήλ, Lk. 4:25, 27; Mt. 9:33.

Normally, however, Ἰσραήλ carries the special sense that the people thus named is the people of God. There is thus emphatic reference to the God of Israel at Mt. 15:31; Lk. 1:68. It is not that God is limited to Israel. He is the God who has chosen Israel, who has revealed Himself in it. If Jesus is called βασιλεύς Ἰσραήλ in mockery, Mt. 27:42; Mk. 15:32, this is the true title of the divine King, for the One thus styled is the King of the people of God, not of a mere nation. For Jews the Messiah is not the King of the Jews (→ 375); He is the King of Israel. The same holds good with respect to other relations between the Messiah and Israel, Lk. 2:25, 32; 24:21.

It is because Ἰσραήλ is specifically the people of God that Mt. intentionally uses it in the saying of Jesus at 8:10 (cf. Lk. 7:9): παρ᾽ οὐδενὶ τοσαύτην πίστιν

---

[120] In the OT the term οἶκος Ἰσραήλ is often used for the 10 tribes, but this usage occurs in the NT only in a quotation at Hb. 8:10.

[121] On these formulae with Ἰσραήλ as a gen. without article, cf. Bl.-Debr.⁶ § 259, 2; 262, 3 (Hebraisms). Generally the art. is left off only in the nominative. It is used in other cases mainly because Ἰσραήλ is indeclinable and might cause difficulty. A strongly Gk. form like Ἰσράηλος (Jos. Ant., 4, 180) is not found in the NT.

[122] Thus a direct reference to the patriarch is unlikely in an expression like θεὸς Ἰσραήλ, Lk. 1:68; Mt. 15:31. It is to be noted that Jacob, not Israel, is used for the third patriarch in θεὸς Ἀβραὰμ καὶ Ἰσαὰκ καὶ Ἰακώβ, Mt. 22:32 par.; Ac. 3:13 (cf. Mt. 8:11 par.).

[123] Cf. Str.-B., I, 90 f.

[124] Cf. already Aristot. Meteor., II, 3, p. 359a, 17: "The Dead Sea is in Palestine."

[125] For the boundaries cf. Str.-B., I, 91. Zn. goes too far when he says (Mt., ad loc.) that "the Messiah belongs to the sacred land of Israel." This may be true, but it is not implied here.

ἐν τῷ Ἰσραὴλ εὗρον.[126] The fact that those in whom Jesus has hitherto sought faith are called Israel implies that they are expected and required as such to believe in Christ.

Jesus is aware that He is sent to the lost sheep of the house of Israel (Mt. 10:6; 15:24). This does not mean that the lostness of these sheep is the reason for His coming. This they share with the men of other nations. The point is that they belong to Israel, to the people of God. Israel is as such the people for whom God cares, Lk. 1:16. Through Christ it is brought into decision, Lk. 2:34. The disciples who follow Jesus will judge the 12 tribes (→ δώδεκα) of Israel in the παλιγγενεσία (Mt. 19:28). This is an indication of the loftiness of their promised position. To them will be committed judgment of the people of God.

We may thus conclude that in the Synoptists Ἰσραήλ mostly refers to the specific nature of this people as the people of God. This is what gives it its specific importance in the various passages. There is no apparent reference to others than members of the Jewish people, i.e., to members of the new community.

b. In John Ἰσραήλ (4 times) and Ἰσραηλίτης (once) are rare. Ἰουδαῖος (70 times) is much more common. On the other hand, Ἰσραήλ is used in a much more uniform and fixed sense (→ 377), Ἰσραήλ is the people of God. To be related to it is to be related to God's people, and consequently to God. At 1:49 Nathanael calls Jesus the Son of God and King of Israel. To be united with God as Son is to be King over God's people (cf. the acclamation at 12:13). John baptises in order that He whom he knew not, the Lamb of God, φανερωθῇ τῷ Ἰσραήλ (1:31). If we read τοῖς Ἰουδαίοις, this would refer to specific members of the people alive at the time. Ἰσραήλ is the people as a whole and in its essential being. Its essential being is that it is God's people. Ἰσραήλ is thus almost a supratemporal entity.

At 1:47 Nathanael is called an ἀληθῶς Ἰσραηλίτης, ἐν ᾧ δόλος οὐκ ἔστιν. Why he is described thus is unimportant.[127] The term shows that he is a member of God's people. But one can be an ostensible member of this people without being a genuine Ἰσραηλίτης. This is why we read that he is an ἀληθῶς Ἰσραηλίτης (cf. the material similarity to R. 9:6; also R. 2:28 f.).

Similarly, the address to Nicodemus: σὺ εἶ ὁ διδάσκαλος τοῦ Ἰσραήλ (3:10), gains its point from the contrast between being a doctor of Israel and ignorance of the work of God, the birth of the Spirit.

In John Ἰσραήλ always implies that this people, with its members, is God's people. It does not always denote the living members of to-day. It can also stand for the whole people almost as a supratemporal entity,[128] since Israel is a collective

---

[126] In this passage the emphatic ἐν τῷ Ἰσραήλ seems to give a particular stress, cf. Zn. Mt., ad loc.

[127] Possibly sitting under the fig tree denotes study of Scripture, cf. Str.-B., ad loc.

[128] Israel can be used in the same way in Rabb. literature, cf. S. Kaatz, Die mündliche Lehre und ihr Dogma, 1. Heft (1922), 43 f.: "The people of Israel is for it (sc. the Talmud) on the one side a historical concept, the sequence of generations, and on the other a supratemporal and suprahistorical, a community which was present in its comprehensive totality, including the last generations, at the Sinaitic revelation, where not only Israelites of the time, but the souls of those not yet born, were already present and entered into the Sinaitic covenant." But cf. Jos. (→ 372).

name.[129] On the other hand, we do not detect in John any extension of the name to the new people of God. The true Israelite is the man who is bound to the Law, and therewith to God.

c. In Acts it is striking that 'Ισραήλ is predominantly used in the first part, while 'Ιουδαῖος dominates the second. (We cannot deduce from this fact alone whether this is because of the actual contents of the narrative or literary and stylistic considerations.) Sometimes the use is neutral, e.g., at 5:21, where γερουσία τῶν υἱῶν 'Ισραήλ might just as well be γερουσία τῶν 'Ιουδαίων, though perhaps the theologically more significant term is chosen here because the leaders of God's people are now to decide whether or not to acknowledge Christ and His community.[130] On many occasions the people are addressed as ἄνδρες 'Ισραηλῖται (2:22; 3:12; 5:35; 13:16; cf. 4:8, if original), and here, too, the hearers are confronted with the responsibility that the act of God is now proclaimed to them as members of the people of God.[131, 132] Similarly, it is as Israel that Israel is summoned to see the way of God (2:36; 4:10; 13:24; cf. also 9:15).

For this reason 'Ισραήλ can also be used when there is reference to the distinction between the older people of God and the new, 4:27; 5:21. Yet this is no more implied in 'Ισραήλ than in 'Ιουδαῖος. For 'Ισραήλ can also be the name for the people of God to whom Christ will restore the βασιλεία, 1:6 (cf. also 28:20). Here the frontier of the people of God is not yet crossed, but there is an extension of the term to cover the new people of God.

'Ισραήλ can still be used in Acts for the people in the past (7:23, 37, 42; 13:17). And here again it implies the unity of the people across the ages. What is true of past Israel is no less true of present Israel. Between the two there is more than agreement; there is identity, 12:23: κατ' ἐπαγγελίαν ἤγαγεν (sc. ὁ θεὸς) τῷ 'Ισραὴλ σωτῆρα 'Ιησοῦν. The Israel which received the promise and the Israel for which it is fulfilled are one and the same. Israel is the one community of God.

d. In Paul 'Ισραήλ is mostly used in its specific sense as the people of God, especially in R. 9-11. This is no accident, for the issue here is one which arises out of the character of the Jews as the people of God. Can the new community trust God's Word when it seems to have failed the Jews (9:6)? The answer is complete only when it is given with reference to the Jews as Israel, because this is the name which implies that they are God's people. This is also true of passages where 'Ισραήλ is used in the historical sense (R. 9:27; cf. 2 C. 3:7), though no particular prominence may be given to the point. R. 11:1 is particularly important as regards the full significance of Israel. To the question whether God has rejected His people Paul make the reply: Not at all, καὶ γὰρ ἐγὼ 'Ισραηλίτης εἰμί. This makes sense only if, as an 'Ισραηλίτης, he is a member of God's people. Cf. also 9:4:

---

[129] Cf. Bl.-Debr.[6] § 262, 3.

[130] Especially as the phrase stands redundantly alongside συνέδριον, with which it is connected by an epexegetical καί. Cf. Str.-B., ad loc.; also Schürer, II, 245, n. 17.

[131] Hence this is not merely the style which would be most acceptable to the audience, Trench, 84.

[132] This could be the specific sense at 21:28, since the people are required as Israelites to prevent or to avenge any desecration of the temple. But Lk. is more likely using the form of address common in Jerusalem.

The Jews, Paul's kinsmen according to the flesh, are 'Ισραηλῖται; as such they enjoy all the blessings enumerated in v. 4 f. Even carnal Israel enjoys these blessings. Israel is bound to the Law. It seeks righteousness through the Law (R. 9:31 f.). But it misses the righteousness of God (R. 11:7). Now as previously Israel is in disobedience (R. 10:21; 11:2), and for this reason πώρωσις ἀπὸ μέρους τῷ 'Ισραὴλ γέγονεν (11:25). Yet Paul realises that πᾶς 'Ισραὴλ σωθήσεται by virtue of the promise made to the patriarchs (v. 28). It should be noted that this does not imply that πάντες οἱ 'Ιουδαῖοι σωθήσονται; [133] for Israel is not just the totality of its individual members; it is the bearer of the promise and the recipient of its fulfilment.

Eph. 2:12 is another clear example of the use of 'Ισραήλ for the people of God. In the time without Christ the Gentiles were far from the πολιτεία τοῦ 'Ισραήλ and ἄθεοι ἐν τῷ κόσμῳ.

In none of these passage do we find any extension of the term to cover the new people of God. Yet the thought is present, for the parable of the olive-tree in R. 11 suggests some such possibility.

There is also a step in this direction in R. 9:6, where membership of the people of God is not just equated with physical membership of the race of Israel. On the other hand, we are not told here that Gentile Christians are the true Israel. The distinction at R. 9:6 does not go beyond what is presupposed at Jn. 1:47, [134] and it corresponds to the distinction between 'Ιουδαῖος ἐν τῷ κρυπτῷ and 'Ιουδαῖος ἐν τῷ φανερῷ at R. 2:28 f., which does not imply that Paul is calling Gentiles the true Jews.

Nevertheless, the term 'Ισραήλ opens the way more readily for this extension, since it denotes the inner essence of the people of God. Hence Paul can use this word marginally and negatively for the new people of God when he speaks of 'Ισραὴλ κατὰ σάρκα at 1 C. 10:18. (He has in view the religious aspect, for the reference is to the worship of the former community, which is represented as an example.) On the other hand, there is no specific contrast between this 'Ισραὴλ κατὰ σάρκα and an 'Ισραὴλ κατὰ πνεῦμα. That there can be no transfer of the title to the new community at the expense of the old is shown particularly clearly by the image of the olive-tree in R. 11:17 ff.; Israel is the one community of God into which Gentiles are now engrafted.

The one passage where it is most probable that 'Ισραήλ has this new meaning is Gl. 6:16. Here 'Ισραὴλ τοῦ θεοῦ is used of those who follow the rule of Paul, to whom circumcision and uncircumcision are of no account, and for whom the world is crucified by Christ. It should be noted, however, that this statement is used against those who think that the heritage of ancient Israel, especially circumcision, is a necessary prerequisite of Christianity, and who believe that membership

---

[133] πᾶς 'Ισραήλ cannot mean every Israelite, for, while 'Ισραήλ is commonly used for the individual Israelite in Palestinian usage, it does not occur in this sense in the NT (→ 362). With Bl.-Debr.[6] § 275 we are rather to take this as a Hebraism for Israel as a whole. The context demands this.

[134] Cf. the common Rabbinical discussion whether physical descent constitutes a true Israelite. On the whole this was accepted (Str.-B., III, 263 f.). On the marks of the true Israelite, *ibid.*, 125; → n. 52.

of the people of God is only possible on this condition. Here too, then, the expression is in a sense to be put in quotation marks. [135]

Apart from this polemical passage and 1 C. 10:18, Paul does not seem to use Ἰσραήλ for the new community of God. For, as we may see from R. 9-11, he neither could nor would separate the term from those who belong to Israel by descent.

3. Ἑβραῖος, Ἑβραϊκός, ἑβραΐς, ἑβραϊστί.

i. The Derived Forms.

In the NT the derived forms ἑβραΐς and ἑβραϊστί are used only of the language. This is intrinsic to the very form of ἑβραϊστί, [136] and ἑβραΐς is found only in Ac. in the formula τῇ ἑβραΐδι διαλέκτῳ.

a. Ἑβραϊκός, the normal adjectival form, is not used in the NT except at Lk. 23:38 in the western and Byzantine texts as distinct from the Hesych. recension. The parallel in Jn. 19:20 seems to have had some influence here. Ἑβραϊκοῖς γράμμασιν, like the Roman and Greek, is used not merely for the characters but for the corresponding language. Outside the NT Ἑβραϊκός is often used for the language, but it can also denote that which belongs to Hebraic Judaism. For the former, cf. Preis. Zaub., I, IV, 3085, 8th Book of Moses; [137] Ep. Ar., 3; 30; 38; Jos. Ant., 12, 48 etc.; for the latter cf. Philo Vit. Mos., I, 240, 285; Jos. Ant., 13, 345.

b. On ἑβραΐς, cf. Jos. Ant., 2, 226. The term ἑβραΐς occurs at Ac. 21:40; 22:2, where we are told that Paul spoke Aramaic to the crowd, who did not expect it and who thus listened the more attentively. (Materially, cf. Jos. Bell., 6, 96; → 374.) Paul's acquaintance with Hebrew or Aramaic is suggested both by the brief sketch of his education in Ac. 22, by his theological principles, and indirectly by passages in which he calls himself a Ἑβραῖος (→ 390).

This is perhaps how we are to understand the obscure observation at 26:14. The voice from heaven comes to Paul τῇ ἑβραΐδι διαλέκτῳ. We might ask whether there does not lie behind this the view that Hebrew is the language of heaven, [138] or the fact that Aramaic is the earthly language of Jesus (Zn., ad loc.). More likely, Aramaic is the mother tongue of Paul himself. He knows it so well that this is the speech in which the voice is heard. [139] There is a possible parallel at this point in the fact that those who were in Jerusalem for the feast of Pentecost heard the language of the Spirit from the apostles in their native tongues (2:8). But we cannot be dogmatic regarding 26:14.

c. The term ἑβραϊστί occurs only in John's Gospel (5 times) and Rev. (twice). It is used either where a common or intelligible Greek expression is to be reproduced in the original, or where it is desired for some reason to give the original name of something.

When ἑρμηνεύειν and its derivatives are used (→ II, 661 ff.), the idea is to make something plain in the language which is being used, and this is naturally common in

---

[135] This impression is strengthened by the similarity of the statement to the conclusions of Jewish prayers, e.g., the Eighteen Benedictions, 19 : "Show mercy and peace upon us, and on Thy people Israel" (Str.-B., III, 579).

[136] Cf. Kühner-Blass, I, 303 β.

[137] A. Dieterich, Abraxas (1891), 177, 2; 182, 15.

[138] Hebrew is the sacred language of the Torah, which occupies God Himself, Str.-B., III, 160.

[139] Cf. K. Bornhäuser, Studien zur Ag. (1934), 18.

Jn. (1:38; 1:41 f.; 4:25; 9:7). But when ἐβραϊστί is used, the purpose is the very different one, not of interpretation, but of a greater historical precision which is sought for some reason. It is no accident that this occurs only in Jn. and not in the Synpt., for Jn. often displays an interest in the precise and careful establishment of important events (e.g., 1:39 : the time of day; cf. 19:35). The particular use in the passion narrative (19:13, 17, 20; 20:16; elsewhere only 5:2) is to be explained by the author's desire for accuracy at this point. 140 We see here, as in the use of οἱ Ἰουδαῖοι (→ 378), the greater distance in time and space which separated the author and his readers from the events narrated, and the proportionately greater interest in accuracy and precision of statement.

A rather different interest led to the use of ἐβραϊστί in Rev. 9:11 and 16:16. Yet we cannot say dogmatically what this interest was. Either what was intended by the alien Hebrew term that was also used was already known, or the point of introducing this term was to increase the element of strangeness and mystery.

It is worth noting that the terms introduced in Rev. are both Hebrew, whereas those in Jn. are almost without exception Aram. 141 The knowledgeable Josephus did not always distinguish between the two in his use of Ἑβραῖος etc. (→ 374). The same is true of the Rabbis ; consistent distinction is not always made in respect of עברית. 142

ii. Ἑβραῖος.

The word Ἑβραῖος occurs in the NT at only three passages : Ac. 6:1; Phil. 3:5; 2 C. 11:22. The paucity of examples makes it difficult to fix an established sense. We can only consider each passage in the light of the various possibilities already suggested by wider usage.

a. Ac. 6:1: There are in the community two groups ; one of these, to which the apostles belong, is called Ἑβραῖοι. The reported γογγυσμὸς τῶν Ἑλληνιστῶν πρὸς τοὺς Ἑβραίους is obviously linked with the characterisation of the second group by the term Ἑβραῖος. Otherwise it would be necessary to give some further reason. Yet it is hard to think that the widows of the Ἑλληνισταί (→ II, 511 f.) were neglected by the Ἑβραῖοι because of a mere linguistic difference, since in a bilingual country the native Aramaic of the one group would be no decisive obstacle in its relationship to the other. More likely is the suggestion that the Ἑβραῖοι were natives of the land who knew each other's ways and were in many cases old acquaintances ; on the other hand, the others were originally aliens, whether Jews or proselytes or even σεβόμενοι (cf. the Ἕλληνες of Jn. 12:20, and on this point Str.-B., II, 548), who could easily be passed over, not because of any ill-will, but simply because they were not known to the over-burdened leaders of the community (v. 2).

It thus seems that the Ἑβραῖοι of Ac. 6:1 are native Palestinians who naturally form a separate group and who are distinguished from those who have come to Palestine later, whether as Jews of the diaspora or as proselytes. That such people were in Jerusalem, and were in the community, is clearly implied in Ac. 2. It may be that there were linguistic problems between the two groups. Indeed, this is likely.

---

140 The suggestion of Holtzmann NT on Jn. 20:16 that the Evangelist conceives of his characters as speaking Gk. with a few Aram. glosses is quite untenable. Here, too, he is interested to give a "literal reproduction of speech and counter-speech" (B. Weiss, Erklärung des Joh.-Ev.9 [1902], ad loc.).
141 Zn. J. on 20:16 : "New Hebrew."
142 Cf. Str.-B., II, 442 ff.; Zn. Einleitung, I § 1, n. 12; Schl. J. on 5:2 (→ 366).

Nevertheless, it is not essential to interpretation, and we cannot be primarily guided by a linguistic understanding of Ἑβραῖος. [143]

b. At Phil. 3:5 Paul calls himself Ἑβραῖος ἐξ Ἑβραίων. Here again the reference is not primarily to language. He is speaking of his descent, which may also include language. As regards Phil. 3:5 we may agree with Lightfoot that there is a progressive argument. [144] One who was circumcised on the eighth day could still be of proselyte descent. But Paul is of the race of Israel. Some Israelites might not be able to display their genealogy. [145] But Paul could do this; he was of the tribe of Benjamin. As a Jew of the *diaspora* he might have been hellenized. Paul, however, is Ἑβραῖος ἐξ Ἑβραίων. By virtue of his Palestinian origin he has been safeguarded against hellenisation. [146] This line of argument suggests that Paul is claiming, not merely Jewish nationality, but descent from a Palestinian family. [147] This factor, along with the Pharisaic orientation of the family (Ac. 22:3), is the reason why Aramaic is his mother tongue; it is not because he speaks Aramaic that he calls himself Ἑβραῖος ἐξ Ἑβραίων. [148]

c. Ἑβραῖος is to be understood along similar lines at 2 C. 11:22. Here again we do not simply have three terms for one and the same concept of a full Jew. The variation of terms is not just for the sake of rhetorical effect. [149] There is again a progression, though now we may discern a progressive loftiness of designation. Like his opponents, Paul is a Jew of Palestinian descent. [150] As such he belongs to the people of God, is an heir of the promise given to the fathers, and is a servant of Christ. In the context, emphasis does not fall on the Aramaic mother tongue, though this may well be included in the designation.

d. This interpretation of the Ἑβραῖος passages in the NT sheds light on the title of the Epistle to the Hebrews, Πρὸς Ἑβραίους. This title can hardly imply merely that those addressed spoke Aramaic; the epistle is certainly not a translation from an Aramaic original. [151] It points rather to the fact that they are of Hebrew descent. This does not have to mean that they lived in Palestine. The title does not rule out the possibility that the letter was written to a group of Palestinian Jews living, e.g., in Italy (perhaps prisoners of war after 70 A.D.), as seems to be

---

[143] So also Cadbury, *op. cit.*, 65: "The word (Ἑβραῖος) is not commonly used elsewhere in a linguistic sense." From this, and from his understanding of Ἑλληνιστής at Ac. 6:1, Cadbury deduces that the Ἑβραῖοι are Jews and the Ἑλληνισταί Ἕλληνες. He thus arrives at a novel view of the development of the early community which allows for a number of Gentile Christians at this unlikely period. But this equation, and its implications, go far beyond what we may legitimately argue from Ac. 6:1; they also fail to give a satisfactory understanding of the situation in Ac. 6:1.

[144] J. B. Lightfoot, *Saint Paul's Epistle to the Philippians* (1903), ad loc.

[145] Cf. Jos. Ant., 11, 70, where we read of those who claim to be Israelites but cannot prove their descent.

[146] We cannot say, of course, how reliable is the later Jerome tradition that the family of Paul came from Giskala in Galilee, Jer. on Phlm. 23 (MPL, 26, p. 653); A. Deissmann, *Paulus* (1925), 71 ff.

[147] On both cf. Dib. Gefbr., *ad loc.*

[148] Cf. the alternative in Jos. Bell., 1, 3 (→ 374).

[149] Ltzm. K., *ad loc.*

[150] We cannot pursue in this context the important implications as concerns Paul's opponents in 2 C.

[151] Cf. F. Bleek, *Der Brief an die Hebräer* (1828), I § 2.

suggested at Hb. 13:24. But the title is later, and therefore it cannot lead us to a clear-cut decision concerning those to whom the letter is addressed.[152]

Gutbrod

† ἱστορέω (ἱστορία)

1. ἱστορέω is to be derived from ἵστωρ, a word which is found in the older Greek of several districts, and which is formed from the stem ϝιδ in the reduced grade with an ending -τωρ as a *nomen agentis*.[1] The meaning is "one who knows," "one who has seen," "one who is acquainted with the facts." The word is used both as noun and adjective.[2] It should not be overlooked that in the first instance it denotes an action, and only secondarily a state. The ἵστωρ is not merely one who knows; he is one who puts his knowledge to effect.

ἱστορέω and ἱστορία derive from ἵστωρ as ἀδικέω and ἀδικία from ἄδικος. The verb means to know in the special sense of to put knowledge to effect, and the noun this putting to effect, or its result. Study of the usage yields for ἱστορέω and ἱστορία the senses of "to investigate," "to enquire," and "investigation," "knowledge"; cf. the Ionians.[3] But ἱστορέω can also means "to bear witness to" in Hippocrates.[4] This sense arises naturally from the basic meaning. The man who knows puts his knowledge into effect *vis-à-vis* the ignorant by telling what he knows. But the sense of "to investigate" is also natural. For knowledge cannot be separated from enquiry. In many cases the

---

[152] The suggestion has been made that Ἑβραῖος is later substituted for Jewish Christians instead of Ἰουδαῖος, which now gives offence. But this is little help, since Ἑβραῖος is too general to denote Jewish Christians. On the later substitution of this name, cf. Zn. on Ac. 18:4 (though → n. 72).

ἱ σ τ ο ρ έ ω. W. Aly, *De Aeschyli Copia Verborum* (Diss. Bonn, 1904), 26 ff.; B. Snell, "Die Ausdrücke für den Begriff des Wissens in der vorplatonischen Philosophie" = *Philol. Untersuchungen,* ed. A. Kiessling and U. v. Wilamowitz, 29 (1924), 59 ff.; F. Müller, "De 'Historiae' Vocabulo atque Notione" in *Mnemosyne,* 54 (1926), 234 ff.; Liddell-Scott under ἵστωρ, ἱστορέω, ἱστορία; Pr.-Bauer under ἱστορέω; W. Schmid-O. Stählin, *Geschichte der griech. Lit.,* I, 1 (1929), 683-714; W. Kroll, Art. "Hekataios" in Pauly-W., VII (1912), 2667 ff.; F. Jacoby, Art. "Herodotus" in Pauly-W., Supplement II (1903), 205 ff.; E. Meyer, *Geschichte des Altertums,* I, 1² (1907), 223 ff.; E. Fraenkel, *Geschichte der griech. Nomina agentis,* I (1910), 218 f.; II (1912), 243 (Index); W. Nestle, "Griech. Geschichtsphilosophie" in *Archiv f. Geschichte der Philosophie,* 41 (1932), 80 ff.; R. Laqueur, *N. Jbch. f. Wiss. u. Jugendbildung,* 8 (1932), 1 ff.

[1] The question of aspiration is not treated by Aly, Snell, or Müller, and it is hardly solved by F. Sommer, *Griech. Lautstudien* (1905), 82 ff. The aspiration is the more surprising as we do not find it in similar forms of the stem ϝιδ, ἴσμεν, ἴστω.

[2] Thus the Muses are ἵστορες ᾠδῆς, Hom. Hymn., 32, 2, or the Amazons ἐγχέων ἵστορες κοῦραι, Bacchyl., 8, 44. Cf. also Hes. Op., 792: εἰκάδι δ' ἐν μεγάλῃ, πλέῳ ἤματι, ἵστορα φῶτα γείνασθαι· μάλα γάρ τε νόον πεπυκασμένος ἐστίν. Homer uses ἵστωρ in the sense of umpire, Il., 18, 501; 23, 486. It is obvious that one who is acquainted with both sides can be the umpire; we can hardly deduce the sense of umpire from that of witness. ἵστωρ or συνίστωρ can also be witness; thus the gods are invoked as witnesses at an oath, Thuc., II, 74: θεοί ... ξυνίστορές ἐστε, or at the pledge of allegiance of the Athenian ephebes, Poll. Onom., VII, 106: ἵστορες θεοί (cf. Ζεὺς ἵστω, Hom. Il., 7, 411; 10, 328).

[3] Aly, 27-29, n. 14.

[4] Aly, 28; 31; Snell, 61, n. 7.

activity of knowledge necessarily implies that of investigation. [5] The Ionian representatives of ἱστορίη, Thales, Heraclitus, Hecataios of Miletus, and Herodotus, surpassed their contemporaries as investigators. [6] The word ἱστορέω passed from Ionic into Attic tragedy in the sense of "to enquire." [7] With Ionic nature philosophy ἱστορία also passed into Attic philosophy in the sense of "enquiry," "science," "information." Plato knows the term, [8] and uses it as a target of witticisms. [9] He does not adopt it into his scholarly vocabulary. Perhaps the fact that Heraclitus uses it for a valueless smattering of many things [10] has some influence here. But Aristotle finds a place for it in his terminology. He speaks of ἡ ἱστορία ἡ περὶ τὰ ζῷα or ἡ ζῳικὴ ἱστορία. [11] Later Theophrastus speaks περὶ φυτῶν ἱστορία (ed. F. Wimmer, p. 1 ff.). Here ἱστορία is information resting on methodical and scientific research. The word does not necessarily imply that the method is inductive. In this general sense the word was used for a long time, and passed into Latin. Latin has the phrase *naturalis historia* for natural science. [12]

We cannot say exactly when ἱστορία came to be used for "history." This was certainly from the time of Aristotle, [13] and probably of Herodotus. [14] Thucydides does not use ἱστορία or ἱστορεῖν. He calls his work (I, 1, 1) συγγράφειν, not merely to differentiate himself from Herodotus, [15] but more likely because ἱστορία was not yet commonly used in the sense of history. As the title of a historical work ἱστορία is first found in Ephorus, then Polybius and others. [16] Why it took on this narrower sense, we

---

[5] Snell's (63) derivation of the sense "to investigate" from that of the noun: "umpire," is artificial, for Snell himself says that the ἵστωρ is umpire as one who knows, not as one who investigates.

[6] Cf. Fr., 332 of Hecataios (ed. R. H. Klausen [1831]): τάδε γράφω, ὥς μοι ἀληθέα δοκεῖ εἶναι· οἱ γὰρ Ἑλλήνων λόγοι πολλοί τε καὶ γελοῖοι ὡς ἐμοὶ φαίνονται εἰσίν.

[7] Aly, 31 f.; Snell, 62, n. 1.

[8] ἐγὼ (Socrates) ... νέος ὢν θαυμαστῶς ὡς ἐπεθύμησα ταύτης τῆς σοφίας ἣν δὲ καλοῦσι περὶ φύσεως ἱστορίαν: Phaed., 96a.

[9] Crat., 437b: ἡ ἱστορία ... ἵστησι τὸν ῥοῦν. Phaedr., 244c has ἱστορία as a par. of νοῦς in the sense of information or knowledge.

[10] Fr., 129 (I, 103, 13 ff., Diels): Πυθαγόρης, Μνησάρχου ἱστορίην ἤσκησεν ἀνθρώπων μάλιστα πάντων καὶ ἐκλεξάμενος ταύτας τὰς συγγραφὰς ἐποιήσατο ἑαυτοῦ σοφίην, πολυμαθείην, κακοτεχνίην, cf. Snell, 66, where there is a similar example from Hippocr.

[11] Part. An., III, 14, p. 674b, 16; III, 5, p. 668b, 30.

[12] Plin. (the Elder) Hist. Nat.

[13] Poet., 9, p. 1451b, 3. Here the ἱστορικός and the ποιητής are compared; ἱστορία is the work of Herodotus, i.e., historical narration. ἱστορέω can also mean "to narrate" in Aristot., De Plantis, I, 3, p. 818b, 28; De Mirabilibus Auscultationibus, 37, p. 833a, 12; Rhet., I, 4, p. 1360a, 36 f.: τὰς τῶν περὶ τὰς πράξεις γραφόντων ἱστορίας perhaps allows us to see something of the way in which ἱστορία came to mean "history," i.e., by a constriction of the general sense.

[14] In Hdt. ἱστορίη is first "investigation," II, 99, 1: μέχρι μὲν τούτου ὄψις τε ἐμὴ καὶ γνώμη καὶ ἱστορίη ταῦτα λέγουσά ἐστι, τὸ δὲ ἀπὸ τοῦδε Αἰγυπτίους ἔρχομαι λόγους ἐρέων κατὰ ἤκουον. Cf. II, 118, 1; 119, 3; I, 1, 1: ἱστορίης ἀπόδεξις, means "presentation of research." ἱστορέω is his own work, II, 19, 3; II, 34, 1; VII, 96, 1: οὐ γὰρ ἀναγκαίη ἐξέργομαι ἐς ἱστορίης λόγον is to be translated (with G. Stein, *Herodot erklärt*[6] [1908]), "I am not constrained with respect to the narrative," but this is an exception; ἱστορίη is elsewhere "investigation." Snell, 64, n. 4 tries to keep this sense by accepting the rendering of Maran: "I am not impelled ... to give any account of my inquiries on this head." But "account of my inquiries" is materially the same thing as "narrative," cf. Liddell-Scott: "written account of one's inquiries-narrative." If ἱστορίη already has the sense of "history" in Hdt., this cannot be derived from ἱστορεῖν, "to attest to" (cf. Aly, 31), since this sense is not found in Hdt.

[15] Cf. Snell, 65.

[16] Schmid-Stählin, I, 1 (1929), 685. Ephorus is a historian of the 4th century whose work is lost; cf. Pauly-W., VII (1912), 1 ff.

can only conjecture. It is not irrelevant that according to a later account Pythagoras called geometry ἱστορίη. [17] ἱστορία is an account of what happened on the basis of research, as distinct from poetic narration.

2. The significant results as regards ἱστορέω and ἱστορία fit in well with what we know of the rise of Greek historical writing. [18] For a long time epic poetry held the field which properly belonged to history. In the 6th century an attempt was made in Ionia, and then on the other side of the Aegean, to take down sagas relating to the founding of cities and other matters. This interest broadened; accounts were given of foreign countries, their inhabitants and history. These accounts often have the nature of saga or novel, as may be seen from the sections on barbarian countries and their history interwoven into Herodotus. The most important work in this field was done by Hecataios of Miletus. But the honour of having established historical writing among the Greeks belongs to Herodotus. [19] Herodotus is much influenced by Hecataios, and betrays many earlier characteristics. But if true history does not begin with him, it begins after and not before him.

The historical writing of the Greeks is obviously a result of their own history. They experienced and made world history in the true sense. They triumphantly withstood the world power of Persia. This event gave birth to their historical writing. Herodotus tells us in I, 1 that he writes history because he is filled with the greatness of what the Greeks and barbarians had achieved in their conflict. He works in order that this should not be forgotten. To arrive at a true evaluation of this greatness, he includes in his investigation a brief review of history prior to this conflict. [20] The joy of narration often causes him to work in many episodes which bear only a loose relation to his main theme. But he never loses sight of this theme. He is not impelled by the desire to romance, [21] but by a sense of the greatness of what was at issue, and of what was achieved, in the war between the Greeks and the eastern empires. This is even more true of Thucydides, who writes in order to bring out the greatness of what he has experienced, i.e., of the war between the two greatest Greek states at the height of their development, I, 1. [22]

Only with and through the Persian war did the Greek spirit reach the maturity which is the presupposition of historical writing. So long as man has not plumbed the depths of his life, partly through the greatness of experience and achievement and partly through consciousness of this, he will be more interested in the life of heroic periods [23] and distant countries than he is in his own life or in that of the immediate past. It is natural that this

---

[17] Iambl. Vit. Pyth., 89, referring to Nicomachos (2nd cent. A.D.): ἐκαλεῖτο δὲ ἡ γεωμετρία πρὸς Πυθαγόρου ἱστορία. This destroys all attempts to limit ἱστορία to empirical or inductive science.

[18] Cf. Schmid-Stählin, I, 1, 8, 683-714, also the arts. by Jacoby, "Hekataios" in Pauly-W., VII (1912), 2667 ff., and "Herodotus," Supplement, II (1903), 205 ff.; cf. Meyer, op. cit., 223 ff.; E. Howald, "Jonische Geschichtsschreibung" in Hermes, 58 (1923), 113 ff.

[19] With Meyer against Jacoby and Schmid. The scanty remains of the historical work of Hecataios do not justify us in reversing the judgment of antiquity that Herodotus is the father of history. Hecataios still made use of saga-like traditions in his historical work. His geography is scientific, but with elements of fantasy. Herodotus does not merely claim to be superior; he is superior, though not consistently.

[20] On this genuinely historical interest cf. K. A. Pagel, Die Bedeutung des ätiologischen Momentes für Hdts. Geschichtsschreibung (Diss. Berlin, 1927).

[21] Later writers who praised Herodotus for his ποικιλότης picked out his weakest side and were without historical sense. After Thucydides Greek history declined and came strongly under the domination of ethics and rhetoric.

[22] This also leads him to offer future generations the opportunity of learning from the past, cf. I, 22, 4. He expressly refuses to offer mere romance (μυθῶδες).

[23] In a ἡμεῖς τοι πατέρων μέγ᾽ ἀμείνονες εὐχόμεθ᾽ εἶναι (Hom. Il., 4, 405) we have a first flash of historical awareness.

distant life should seem to be more significant than one's own, and that literary art should be used to invest it with even greater significance, e.g., in the poetic form of an epic or novel. But the man who has truly plumbed the greatness of the life of his own time and world does not have the same interest in the past and is not so concerned to give poetic intensification to his account. Truth is interesting as such. There is for him nothing greater than the truth. If he has discovered himself, he needs nothing more than the truth of his life. He sets to work to investigate it. When he has discovered himself, and has thus attained the ability to write history, he then knows how to handle historical life and the truth of events even in remote ages and territories. Instead of merely presenting it, he can now see to the heart of it as an expression of human existence. But the beginning of historical understanding is in the time to which he himself belongs with his love and hate, with the hazarding of his own being, with the pride and pain of victory and defeat. He cannot see this as poetry. He can see it only as it happened. It may be judged that the task of history in this sense is insoluble. Historical truth is unattainable. It will be replaced by myth, the representation of a truth which cannot be comprehended scientifically. This will carry with it artistic exaggeration and compression. On this view it is interesting to see how poetry and truth intermingle in Herodotus. There is kindled a deeper interest in his predecessors. He is thought to have true greatness only in so far as he writes this kind of history.

Doubts have often been raised whether the Greeks really had any scientific history. [24] In my view, these doubts are settled by a mere reference to Thucydides. But the achievements of the Greeks in this field were limited. They did not have a historically orientated view of the world and of life. The total picture which they had of the world, and which they worked out speculatively in their philosophy, viewed the world as nature rather than as history. For this reason their history lacks the distinctive feature of modern history, namely, the insight that the men of different ages and cultures are different in nature as well as experience and acts, [25] and that it is consequently a presupposition of history that the historian should be willing and able to enter into the alien being of others. For this reason Greek history also lacks a methodical source criticism. It has no constructive source criticism whereby to replace a traditional and legendary picture, handed down from past generations, by one which is historically accurate. [26] But if the historical achievement of the Greeks is limited, [27] it is so important within these limits that it has pointed a later age in the right direction.

3.   a. The first Christian proclamation was proclamation of Jesus, the risen Lord, who was seated at the right hand of God, whose coming again was awaited, and whose historical activity as Teacher, Healer, Prophet and Messiah was recollected. [28] This proclamation was good news (→ εὐαγγέλιον, → κήρυγμα). But it was also witness (→ μαρτύριον). It was service of God and of the truth, even in respect of the historical element which had to be recounted. From the very first,

---

[24] U. v. Wilamowitz-Moellendorf, "Die griech. u. lat. Lit. u. Sprache" = *Kultur der Gegenwart,* I, 8³ (1912), 4; cf. also "Staat u. Gesellschaft d. Griechen u. Römer," *ibid.,* II, 4, 1 (1910), 203, n. 2: "The Greeks did not give birth to true historical science. Their thinking led them to abstract rules from observation, and to give to these the absolutely binding value of natural laws." This would be true if we were to read historical philosophy for historical science.

[25] The distinction between Greeks and barbarians does not mean that the latter are not men in the full sense (cf. esp. Herodotus), and the concept of humanity grows in importance.

[26] Cf. the work of B. Niebuhr on Roman history.

[27] Greek historical science seems naive by comparison with the more self-conscious historical work done since the Enlightenment.

[28] Cf. the speeches of Peter in Ac., and M. Dibelius, *Die Formgeschichte des Ev.*² (1933), 8 ff.

then, the early Christian tradition (→ παράδοσις) contained historical information concerning Jesus. From the meagre remains of the period when this tradition was merely oral (1 C. 15:3 ff.; 11:23 ff.), we can still be sure that great value was attached to the certainty and accuracy of this information. 1 C. 15:3 ff. introduces witnesses to whom the risen Lord appeared, and it mentions known persons who were still alive. 1 C. 15:4 and 1 C. 11:23 give relatively precise timings. All presuppose an early interest in the historical accuracy of the tradition. Each believer could not verify for himself what he believed. He had to accept the testimony of accredited witnesses. [29]

Though the tradition was concerned to maintain and pass on what was historically accurate and important, it was not influenced by Greek historical writing. Form criticism shows that the individual accounts of the sayings, acts, and experiences of Jesus are closely related to similar accounts of the sayings, acts, and experiences of the Rabbis preserved in Jewish literature. We find tersely related stories leading up to a characteristic utterance of the one who is thus presented. Similarly, the sayings and parables of Jesus are shown by form criticism to be closely related to those told of the Rabbis. [30] The first Gospel, i.e., Mark, arose as these individual accounts were collected and written down. It was unique in nature and origin. The material was collected and constructed as an account of the earthly activity of the Messiah who was now divinely exalted. Its standpoint was quite different from that of Greek biography, just as the formation of its individual parts was different. Nor was the writing of the Evangelists influenced or fructified by Jewish history in the Greek language and after Greek patterns, e.g., in the Books of Maccabees and on a bigger scale in Josephus.

b. The early Christian tradition first comes into contact with Greek historical writing in Luke. Luke gives clear evidence of literary culture in the sense of contemporary Hellenism. This is proved by the prologue to his two-part work. [31] It is particularly evident in Acts, e.g., in the great speeches which run through the whole book and which give both a comprehensive picture of the proclamation of the apostles and also an individualised picture of the person and situation of the speakers. In these addresses, which are very different in form from the series of sayings in the sermons of Jesus in the Gospels, we discern the cultivated ability of one who has read Greek history. The same is true of the account of Paul's journey from Caesarea to Rome. The work of Luke cannot be evaluated properly if we group it with inferior contemporary literature that treats of heroes, thaumaturges and other popular characters. [32] It is genuine history. [33] The nature of the material and the tradition which has to be presented do, of course, impose certain restrictions on the deployment of Luke's historical skill. In the Gospel he does not vary greatly from his predecessors. He is content simply to integrate the story of Jesus into world history (3:1-2; cf. 1:5; 2:1), to achieve a higher degree of perfection than previous writers in his investigation of the tradition, [34] to exclude

---

[29] Cf. also K. Holl, Ges. Aufsätze, II : Der Osten (1928), 50 ff.

[30] Cf. Schl. Gesch. d. Chr., 7; Dibelius, op. cit., 131 ff. On what follows cf. Bultmann Trad., 362 ff.

[31] Cf. the comm. of Zn., Hck., esp. Kl., ad loc.

[32] P. Wendland, Die urchristlichen Literaturformen (1912), 325 f.

[33] Meyer Ursprung, III, 7.

[34] Luke is the longest Gospel, and yet it cuts out doublets ; it is the richest in individual material.

popular narratives,[35] and to write better Greek. He neither desires, nor is he able, to make of the Gospel a biography of Jesus of Nazareth. And the story of the community of Jesus and His apostles is necessarily different from that of a state, people, war etc. On the other hand, here is a man who was acquainted with Greek historical writing. Hence we find in him the technical expressions of historical research and composition → αὐτόπτης, διήγησις (→ II, 909), → λόγος, → πρᾶγμα, → ἀσφάλεια, ἀνατάξασθαι (→ τάσσω), καθεξῆς, → γράψαι etc.

c. Paul took a great interest in the purity and accuracy of the tradition (1 C. 11:2, 23; 15:2, 3, 11; Gl. 1:9). He was not indifferent to the actual history of Jesus. He used to display Jesus before the eyes of the communities as crucified among them, Gl. 3:1.[36] But he had nothing in common with Greek historical writing, though he does use ἱστορέω at Gl. 1:18 — the only occurrence in the NT — in the common Hellenistic sense of "visit in order to get to know."[37] The same is true of John. The Fourth Evangelist is superior to the first three in skill of presentation. His subsidiary characters — Martha, Thomas, Mary Magdalene, Caiaphas, Pilate, the beloved disciple — are far more individual. In the conversations and addresses of Jesus the clash of opposites has a depth and force not found in the other Gospels. He can depict the mood of the crowd, 7:11-13; 11:55-57 etc., and succinctly sketch a situation, 13:30; 20:19 etc. But this is not based on Greek history or Greek drama. It is not the result of literary culture. It is the original power of a man of rare liveliness and gifts.[38]

As concerns the art of Greek historical writing, Luke is thus an exception in early Christianity.

Büchsel

---

[35] Cf. Mk. 7:31-37; 8:22-26; the healings with spittle are not found in Luke.
[36] Cf. F. Büchsel, *Der Geist Gottes im NT* (1926), 275 ff.
[37] Cf. Ltzm. Gl., *ad loc.*; he adduces Plut. Thes., 30 (I, 14c); Pompeius, 40 (I, 640b); Lucullus, 2 (I, 493a); De Curiositate, 2 (II, 516c); Epict. Diss., II, 14, 28.
[38] It is worth noting that Jn. claims to be an eye-witness (1:14; cf. 21:24), but does not use the technical αὐτόπτης; on the other hand he speaks of μαρτυρεῖν, 19:35; cf. 1:15 etc.

| ἰσχύω, ἰσχυρός, ἰσχύς, κατισχύω | → δύναμαι, II, 284 ff.

1. The word group ἰσχυ- has the meaning "to be able," "to be capable," "capacity," "power," "strength." It is largely co-extensive with δυνα-, and the derivatives overlap. In the case of ἰσχύ- there is more emphasis on the actual power implied in ability or capacity, [1] i.e., on the power which one possesses, for the stem is linked with ἰσχ - ἔχω.

ἰσχύω, [2] "to be strong or powerful" physically; in this context the meaning can be "to be healthy" as opposed to → ἀσθενέω, v. also → ὑγιαίνω; but also "to be able" in respect of psychic qualities.

κατισχύω, like ἰσχύω, a. "to be strong or able"; but also b. "to be superior to someone," "to master," "to overcome"; and c. "to strengthen." The word is found from the time of Soph. and occurs in the LXX, though it is rare in inscr. and pap.

ἰσχυρός, "strong," "powerful," both of men and things. Often used of God in the LXX, e.g., 2 Βασ. 22:32 f.

ἰσχύς, "power," "strength," "ability," also "military power." The word is common in older Greek, but tends to fade out later. It is rare in Hellenism, and hardly occurs at all in inscr. and pap. On the other hand, it is very common, and greatly liked, in the LXX. Here it is mostly used for כֹּחַ, and in this sense it occurs 98 times (+ 13 in Da. Θ); 16 times for מָעֹז; 28 for עֹז; 13 (+ 1 in Da. Θ) for גְּבוּרָה; also for עָצְמָה (Is. 47:9); גָּאוֹן (Is. 2:10); הוֹד (1 Ch. 29:11); גֹּדֶל (Dt. 3:24; 9:26); once each for חֹזֶק (ψ 17:1); חֵזֶק (Am. 6:13); מְאֹד (4 Βασ. 23:25); מַעֲרָצָה (Is. 10:33); מִשְׁעָן (Is. 3:1); תּוּשִׁיָּה (Job 12:16); תֹּקֶף (Da. 11:17 Θ). It is the most common word for "power" in the LXX. [3]

2. The words follow the common pattern in the NT. a. ἰσχύειν means "to be able," and it is particularly common in Luke (6:48; 8:43; 13:24, also Ac.). But it is also found at Mt. 8:28; 26:40; Hb. 9:17; Rev. 12:8. At Mt. 5:13 it is used of salt which has lost its savour: εἰς οὐδὲν ἰσχύει ἔτι; it is good for nothing. At Ac. 19:20 we read of the word of evangelical preaching: οὕτως κατὰ κράτος τοῦ κυρίου ὁ λόγος ηὔξανεν καὶ ἴσχυεν. [4] The Word of God which is preached acquires force through the effective power of the Lord. [5] The force which it acquires can overcome demons and create faith (19:13 ff.). At Gl. 5:6 we read: ἐν γὰρ Χριστῷ οὔτε περιτομή τι ἰσχύει οὔτε ἀκροβυστία, ἀλλὰ πίστις δι' ἀγάπης ἐνεργου-

---

ἰσχύω κτλ. W. Grundmann, "Der Begriff der Kraft in der nt.lichen Gedankenwelt" = BWANT, 4, 8 (1932), with bibl.; → δύναμαι, II, 284 ff.

[1] The concepts and problems related to the concept of power are worked out more fully under δύναμαι, so that we need only sketch the various meanings in this context. The art. on δύναμαι is a necessary prerequisite for full understanding of the present discussion.

[2] Examples in Pape, Pass., Liddell-Scott.

[3] This is dealt with under δύναμαι, → II, 290 ff.

[4] D reads .... ἐνίσχυσεν καὶ ἡ πίστις τοῦ θεοῦ ηὔξανε καὶ ἐπλήθυνε.

[5] → II, 309.

μένη. This is said with reference to the hope which, proceeding from faith and rooted in the Spirit, consists in δικαιοσύνη as the content of salvation, and forms the focus of the yearning expectation of the ἡμεῖς (v. 5): → ἀπεκδεχόμεθα. In Christ, i.e., in the sphere in which the expectant ἡμεῖς find themselves, it has become clear that in reference to this δικαιοσύνη a saving disposition which is effected by a human action like περιτομή has no power, nor is there any detriment in the lack of such a disposition, as ἀκροβυστία is from the Jewish standpoint. [6] In relation to δικαιοσύνη only πίστις δι' ἀγάπης ἐνεργουμένη has any power. It is important for early Christian thinking that the divine gift of πίστις works itself out in ἀγάπη. [7] Prayer is effective in relation to human obstacles and distresses, and to their overcoming: πολὺ ἰσχύει δέησις δικαίου ἐνεργουμένη (Jm. 5:16). The source of all Paul's capacity in face of the reality of human life is Christ: πάντα ἰσχύω ἐν τῷ ἐνδυναμοῦντί με (Phil. 4:13). [8] He who is in Christ partakes of a power which makes all things possible. Here, then, is the source of the Christian's power. δέησις is the means of this capacity in time, and with reference to eternity πίστις δι' ἀγάπης ἐνεργουμένη.

b. At Lk. 23:23 (κατίσχυον αἱ φωναὶ αὐτῶν) κατισχύω has the sense of "to be strong," "to penetrate," and at Lk. 21:36 (δεόμενοι ἵνα κατισχύσητε ἐκφυγεῖν ταῦτα πάντα τὰ μέλλοντα γίνεσθαι καὶ σταθῆναι ἔμπροσθεν τοῦ υἱοῦ τοῦ ἀνθρώπου) it means "to be strong," "to be able." The disciples are to ask for strength that they may not be overthrown in the approaching disasters of the last time and that they may be able to stand before the Son of Man. God's power will deliver them and bring them to the goal. In the saying at Mt. 16:18 we read of the community (→ ἐκκλησία): καὶ πύλαι ᾅδου οὐ κατισχύσουσιν αὐτῆς. The sense here is "to conquer," "to overcome." The realm of the dead cannot overcome the Church of God, since it is the Church of the stronger Man (→ 399 f.).

c. ἰσχυρός, "strong," "powerful," is used in the absolute in the NT, and can be applied either to men or things: Lk. 15:14; 1 C. 4:10; 10:22; 2 C. 10:10; Hb. 5:7; 11:34; Rev. 18:2, 21. At 1 C. 1:25 we have τὸ ἀσθενὲς τοῦ θεοῦ ἰσχυρότερον τῶν ἀνθρώπων with reference to the revelation of God's salvation in the cross of Christ. [9] Human efforts in ethics and religion, human knowledge and wisdom, have no power in respect of salvation. But what seems to be defeat and weakness to men, i.e., the cross, is more powerful and effective than man in his wisdom and might. Hb. 6:18 speaks of the fact that Christians have ἰσχυρὰν παράκλησιν, a consolation which is able and powerful because it is grounded in the saving act of Christ, which consists in the fact that He, our Forerunner, has entered into the Holiest as eternal High-priest. This act gives the strong consolation which can give stability to the soul. At 1 Jn. 2:14 the young men are called ἰσχυροί "because ... the Word of God abideth in you as living power, and you have overcome the devil." [10] At Rev. 18:8 we read of God: ἰσχυρὸς κύριος ὁ θεὸς ὁ κρίνας; [11]

---

[6] → II, 308.
[7] → II, 314 f.
[8] → II, 313.
[9] → II, 316.
[10] According to the paraphrase of Bü. J., 30.
[11] → II, 306.

He demonstrates His power against Βαβυλὼν ἡ πόλις ἡ ἰσχυρά (18:10). Rev. 5:2; 10:1; 18:21 speak of an ἄγγελος ἰσχυρός.

d. ἰσχύς, "ability of man," Mk. 12:30 : all human strength must be concentrated on the love of God. This is the teaching of the first commandment. The κράτος τῆς ἰσχύος of the Lord (Eph. 6:10) is the basis of the strength [12] to which the Christian community is summoned. The community is in Christ. This place is in some sense invested with the omnipotence which is Christ's. Hence the members are summoned to be strong. The following verses show how this strength is to be used (6:11 ff.). 2 Th. 1:9 speaks of the ἰσχύς which fulfils the glory of the returning Lord [13] and which plunges all the ungodly into eternal perdition — a power which can do what men cannot do (Lk. 12:4, 5). All ministry in the community is grounded in, and proceeds from, the power of Christ : [14] εἴ τις διακονεῖ, ὡς ἐξ ἰσχύος ἧς χορηγεῖ ὁ θεός (1 Pt. 4:11). For He is at work to build up the community. To a different degree angels share this strength, 2 Pt. 2:11. Doxologies which acknowledge and magnify God's eternal being and Godhead ascribe ἰσχύς to God and His Christ, Rev. 5:12; 7:12. [15]

3. A few verses demand more specific treatment. a. At Mt. 9:12, when the disciples are asked by the Pharisees why they eat with publicans and sinners, Jesus replies : οὐ χρείαν ἔχουσιν οἱ ἰσχύοντες ἰατροῦ ἀλλ' οἱ κακῶς ἔχοντες. He uses the term ἰατρός to describe His saving work. He is the Physician who has come to sick men to heal them. He is the One who brings life to sinners and sufferers. He is the One who restores the despairing. He does this by drawing them into fellowship with Himself, and by granting them fellowship with God thereby. In this fellowship they begin to see that the root of their sin and plight is separation from God. This is their sickness. This is why Jesus Christ is the Saviour. The ἰσχύοντες, the healthy or the strong, can make nothing of Him. They are not aware of this sickness. In this saying Jesus declares His mission, and tells us to whom it applies. He does not say whether the scribes and Pharisees are really ἰσχύοντες before God.

b. When John the Baptist is asked whether he is the Christ, he answers : ἐγὼ μὲν ὑμᾶς βαπτίζω ἐν ὕδατι εἰς μετάνοιαν· ὁ δὲ ὀπίσω μου ἐρχόμενος ἰσχυρότερός μού ἐστιν, οὗ οὐκ εἰμὶ ἱκανὸς τὰ ὑποδήματα βαστάσαι· αὐτὸς ὑμᾶς βαπτίσει ἐν πνεύματι ἁγίῳ καὶ πυρί (Mt. 3:11 par.). The Baptist thus distinguishes his work from the mission of Christ. His task is to administer the water baptism of repentance to sinners with a view to the coming kingdom of God. Christ is the ἰσχυρότερος to whom John is not worthy to render even the most menial service. Why He is the ἰσχυρότερος, John tells us when he declares that He will baptise with the Holy Ghost and with fire. → βαπτίζω; → πνεῦμα; → πῦρ.

Christ's own saying concerning the ἰσχυρότερος belongs to a different context and is most important. At Lk. 11:20-22 Jesus says of Himself : εἰ δὲ ἐν δακτύλῳ θεοῦ ἐκβάλλω τὰ δαιμόνια, ἄρα ἔφθασεν ἐφ' ὑμᾶς ἡ βασιλεία τοῦ θεοῦ. ὅταν ὁ ἰσχυρὸς καθωπλισμένος φυλάσσῃ τὴν ἑαυτοῦ αὐλήν, ἐν εἰρήνῃ ἐστὶν τὰ

---

[12] → II, 313.
[13] → II, 305.
[14] → II, 311.
[15] → II, 305, 306.

ὑπάρχοντα αὐτοῦ· ἐπὰν δὲ ἰσχυρότερος αὐτοῦ ἐπελθὼν νικήσῃ αὐτόν, τὴν πανοπλίαν αὐτοῦ αἴρει, ἐφ' ᾗ ἐπεποίθει, καὶ τὰ σκῦλα αὐτοῦ διαδίδωσιν. This saying occurs in the debate about His exorcisms. It is an answer to the query of the scribes and Pharisees whether He does not cast out demons in the name of Beelzebub, Jesus uses the illustration of the divided kingdom to show how ridiculous this suggestion is. He then goes on to utter this saying concerning His work. The ἰσχυρός is Satan, and He Himself is the ἰσχυρότερος who is at war with him. The metaphor compares Satan to a noble whose castle has been entered and despoiled. In the simpler version in Mt. and Mk. he is a householder. This version does not have ἰσχυρότερος, but the idea is there. It runs : ἢ πῶς δύναταί τις εἰσελθεῖν εἰς τὴν οἰκίαν τοῦ ἰσχυροῦ καὶ τὰ σκεύη αὐτοῦ ἁρπάσαι, ἐὰν μὴ πρῶτον δήσῃ τὸν ἰσχυρόν, καὶ τότε τὴν οἰκίαν αὐτοῦ διαρπάσει (Mt. 12:29 and Mk. 3:27). The ἰσχυρός has a certain dominion. The history of Christ is a history of the invasion of this dominion. Christ has successfully broken into it. He is thus the stronger. To understand the saying, we must consult some important testimonies from the religious world familiar to Jesus.

In the OT we read at Is. 49:25 : גַּם־שְׁבִי גִבּוֹר יֻקָּח. [16] The prisoners of the strong are to be taken away. This is a divine promise. In the song of the Suffering Servant, too, there is a verse which reminds us of this passage : [17] διὰ τοῦτο αὐτὸς κληρονομήσει πολλοὺς καὶ τῶν ἰσχυρῶν μεριεῖ σκῦλα, ἀνθ' ὧν παρεδόθη εἰς θάνατον ἡ ψυχὴ αὐτοῦ, Is. 53:12 (Mas.: לָכֵן אֲחַלֶּק־לוֹ בָרַבִּים וְאֶת־עֲצוּמִים יְחַלֵּק שָׁלָל תַּחַת אֲשֶׁר הֶעֱרָה לַמָּוֶת נַפְשׁוֹ). He will have a great inheritance and share booty with the strong because his soul was given up to death. The opponents of the Servant are the ἰσχυροί whose booty he shares. Now the influence of Dt. Is. on the interpretation of the mission of Jesus in the Gospels is very considerable. Hence there is good reason to believe that these passages underlie the saying. The answer to the scribes, who knew the Scriptures, is a claim that the OT promises are fulfilled in these exorcisms. I am the Servant of the Lord, says Jesus, who accomplishes the work of overthrowing demons and who divides the spoil. At Test. L. 18:12 we read : "And Beliar will be bound by him, and he will give power to his children to stride over evil spirits ;" [18] Test. Zeb. 9:8 (b d g): "And after that your God Himself shall shine forth as the light of righteousness and salvation and mercy on His wings. He will liberate all the prisoners of Beliar, and every spirit of error shall be scattered . . . ;" Jub. 10:8 : Mastema to God : "If some of them (i.e., the demons who were to be bound at the request of Noah) do not remain to me, I cannot exercise the dominion of my will on the children of men. For they are to be seduced and corrupted before my judgment, for great is the wickedness of the children of men." Cf. also in Rabbinic literature Pesikt. r., 36 (161a): "When he (Satan) saw it (the soul of the pre-existent Messiah), he was shaken, and fell on his face, and said : Truly this is the Messiah, who will one day plunge me and the angel princes of the nations into Gehinnom ; for it is written, He will swallow up death for ever, and the Lord Yahweh will wipe the tears from every face (Is. 25:8)." In the NT we may refer to Lk. 4:6, where Satan is the prince of this world, and to Lk. 13:16, where it is said of the woman whom Jesus healed : ταύτην δὲ θυγατέρα Ἀβραὰμ οὖσαν, ἣν ἔδησεν ὁ σατανᾶς ἰδοὺ δέκα καὶ ὀκτὼ ἔτη, οὐκ ἔδει λυθῆναι ἀπὸ τοῦ δεσμοῦ τούτου τῇ ἡμέρᾳ τοῦ σαββάτου;

---

[16] The LXX is garbled and cannot be used.

[17] Cf. K. F. Euler, "Die Verkündigung vom leidenden Gottesknecht aus Js. 53 in der griech. Bibel" = BWANT, 4, 14 (1934), 113.

[18] That these ideas and sayings are known in the NT may be seen from Lk. 10:19 : ἰδοὺ δέδωκα ὑμῖν τὴν ἐξουσίαν τοῦ πατεῖν ἐπάνω ὄφεων καὶ σκορπίων καὶ ἐπὶ πᾶσαν τὴν δύναμιν τοῦ ἐχθροῦ . . .

These references point to a closely knit circle of ideas. They speak of a satanic power under which men are bound. Satan exercises his dominion in the different forms of sin and sickness and possession and death. The demons are his agents. They view it as the mission of Christ to break Satan's fetters, to liberate the captives and to win the victory over Satan. The saying of Jesus belong to this circle. It speaks of Satan as an ἰσχυρός, a strong man who exercises rule. The σκεύη (Mt. 12:29 and Mk. 3:27) or τὰ ὑπάρχοντα (Lk. 11:21) and τὰ σκῦλα (v. 22) are the men whom he rules. [19] The mission of Christ means that the ἰσχυρό-τερος comes, that He overcomes and binds the ἰσχυρός when He has entered his house, and that He robs him of his spoil. This is how the exorcisms are to be understood. In these sayings, then, Jesus displays the background of His work. We see that His words and acts are based on the conviction that face to face with the strong man who exercises dominion He is the stronger who has overcome him and who inaugurates the rule of God in place of that of Satan. The mighty power of Jesus, displayed in His proclamation and miracles, [20] is the power of the kingdom of God, and it has vanquished the might of Satan. This saying undoubtedly pre-serves the most primitive tradition; it is prior to the theology of the community; it must come from Jesus Himself. In the theology of the community the death and resurrection of Jesus are the victory over satanic and demonic powers. [21] In this saying, however, the decisive victory is already presupposed. It consists in the triumph in temptation (Mt. 4:1 ff. par.). The whole work of Jesus is compared to seizing the spoils. This consists in taking from Satan those whom he has held and bound, in forwarding the kingdom of God, in disclosing the dominion of Satan, and in thus overcoming and destroying it. [22] But this yields a decisive insight for the understanding of the Synoptic history. For this saying, which on close examina-tion proves to be original, brings us face to face with Jesus' understanding of Him-self, with primitive Christology, which is quite simply grounded in the fact that Jesus is the ἰσχυρότερος who has overcome the ἰσχυρός and robbed him of his prey. The Synoptic picture of Jesus develops logically out of this early Chris-tological statement. [23] The verse behind the statement, i.e., Is. 53:12, forms a link with the death of the Servant of the Lord. Hence the saying may be connected with the later theological statements. Jesus Himself points in this direction at Mt. 20:28. The ministry which unites the life and death of Christ consists in the exposure and overthrow of the dominion of Satan and in the liberation of men for the kingdom of God. The λύτρον image belongs to the same circle of imprisonment and liberation. Thus Is. 53:12, Lk. 11:22 and Mt. 20:28 form a close-knit nexus which embraces the life, death and resurrection of Christ as the decisive act of liberation for men. This act is worked out in the service which Jesus renders them.

c. Eph. 1:18, 19: ... εἰς τὸ εἰδέναι ὑμᾶς ... τί τὸ ὑπερβάλλον μέγεθος τῆς δυνάμεως αὐτοῦ εἰς ἡμᾶς τοὺς πιστεύοντας κατὰ τὴν ἐνέργειαν τοῦ κράτους

---

[19] Kl. is mistaken when he suggests that the expelled demons are the σκεύη (Mk., *ad loc.*). OT and pseudepigraphical examples rule out this interpretation.

[20] → II, 299 ff. What is there said about the δύναμις of the fact of Christ reaches its climax in this statement. This statement sets it in correct focus.

[21] Cf. D. A. Frövig, "Das Sendungsbewusstsein Jesu und der Geist," BFTh, 29, 3 (1924), 145-168, esp. 162.

[22] Cf. Schl. Mt., 406 f. and Grundmann, 49 f., 68 f.

[23] This fact, which is rooted in the demonic conceptions of the NT, has been too long dis-regarded, to the detriment of Synoptic research, and with great effect on the solution of the problem of Jesus and Paul. Cf. Grundmann, 73, n. 25.

τῆς ἰσχύος αὐτοῦ. We have already given the exegesis of the first part.[24] The second part traces back the faith of the community to the mighty work of God. In this faith man finds the power of God at work. Noteworthy in this passage is the heaping up of words for power. This demands special consideration.

We find the beginnings of this kind of statement in the OT. Cf. Is. 40:26 : ἐν κράτει ἰσχύος, and Eph. 6:10 : ἐν τῷ κράτει τῆς ἰσχύος αὐτοῦ. The addition of κράτος to ἰσχύς expresses the mightiness. It is used for the adjective, as at Is. 40:26 Mas. (אַמִּיץ כֹּחַ). Cf. also Gr. En. 1:3, where we read of the appearance of God ἐν τῇ δυνάμει τῆς ἰσχύος αὐτοῦ, cf. 61:6. At Is. 44:12 the Targumist renders זרוע כהו by תקוף חיליה. Hence the combination of two words for power is not unusual in the world closest to the NT. In Eph., however, we have a threefold formula (cf. Col. 1:11). The closest analogy is in Tg. Is., where we often find the formula תקוף דרע גבורתיה (the might of the arm of his strength), in place of simple Mas. statements, e.g., Is. 40:10; 51:5 (twice); 53:1. The triple nature of the formula stands out. An interesting par. is to be found in the LXX, where there is threefold expansion of the Mas. at Dt. 9:26, 29; 26:8 : ἐν τῇ ἰσχύϊ σου τῇ μεγάλῃ καὶ ἐν τῇ χειρί σου τῇ κραταιᾷ καὶ ἐν τῷ βραχίονί σου τῷ ὑψηλῷ. In the Targum, the LXX and the NT, then, three rather than two expressions are heaped up to express the power of God. This is intentional, and corresponds to a favourite schema of composition. At Eph. 1:19, which is the basis of the discussion, it takes poetic form, and is occasioned by the preceding, threefold statement : ὁ πλοῦτος τῆς δόξης τῆς κληρονομίας αὐτοῦ.

Grundmann

| † ἴχνος | → ἀνεξιχνίαστος, I, 358. |

1. ἴχνος means "footprint,"[1] and may be used either for an individual impression on the ground or for a continuous line of such impressions, i.e., a trail.[2] Even when the word is used metaphorically, i.e., with reference to the spiritual side of human life, the plastic conception remains. ἴχνος is generally the trace left by someone's conduct or journey through life. It is a trail for others to mark and follow.[3] Thus Paul states at 2 C. 12:18 that his own conduct towards the community

---

[24] → II, 314.

ἴ χ ν ο ς. [1] Etym. uncertain, cf. Boisacq, *s.v.*; Walde-P., I, 9; 104; 196, and Class. Rev., 3 (1889), 45b.

[2] Poll. Onom., V, 11 links ἴχνος with a word group relating to the chase (so already Hom.: πρὸ δ' ἄρ' αὐτῶν ἴχνι' ἐρευνῶντες κύνες ἤϊσαν, Od., 19, 435 f., of human footprints, e.g., Il., 18, 321). Phot. Lex., *s.v.* suggests ὁδός, πορεία, βῆμα as similar words. Apart from secular examples, cf. ἴχνος at LXX ψ 76:19 (Heb. עָקֵב) par. ὁδός-τρίβοι; cf. also Prv. 5:5 for צַעַד and 30:19 for דֶּרֶךְ.

[3] So already Pind. Pyth., 10, 12 : τὸ δὲ συγγενὲς ἐμβέβακεν ἴχνεσιν πατρός, also Plat. Resp., VIII, 553a. Or in a votive inscr.: ... ἐπειδὴ 'Αρισταγόρας 'Απατουρίου, πατρὸς γεγονὼς ἀγαθοῦ καὶ προγόνων εὐεργετῶν καὶ ἱερημένων τῶν θεῶν πάντων, καὶ αὐτὸς στοιχεῖν βουλόμενος καὶ τοῖς ἐκείνων ἴχνεσιν ἐπιβαίνειν ..., Ditt. Syll.³, 708,

in the matter of money agrees with that of Titus, since they have both followed the trail which was set before them as responsible apostles, and which must be visible to the community as well: οὐ τῷ αὐτῷ πνεύματι περιεπατήσαμεν; οὐ τοῖς αὐτοῖς ἴχνεσιν; At R. 4:12 [4] Paul speaks very pregnantly, but figuratively, of ἴχνη τῆς ἐν ἀκροβυστίᾳ πίστεως τοῦ πατρὸς ἡμῶν Ἀβραάμ, with whom Gentile believers associate themselves (→ στοιχεῖν). The faith of Abraham did not pass without leaving a trace. It has left its impress. If we cannot perceive his actual faith in the ἴχνη, we can perceive its nature (cf. τῆς ἐν ἀκροβυστίᾳ πίστεως) and reality. These tracks left by the faith of Abraham serve as bearings to believers who come οὐκ ἐκ τῆς περιτομῆς. Through the ἴχνη the πίστις of Abraham becomes accessible in essence to the Gentiles. The ἴχνη are in a sense the place where the fellowship of faith arises irrespective of temporal distinction (→ n. 8; Abraham πατὴρ πάντων τῶν πιστευόντων). Linguistically it would be possible to render ἴχνη by "features" (→ infra), but it is better not to do this, since it might suggest special aspects of Abraham's life of faith whose imitative repetition will give the Gentiles a share in the fellowship of faith. It is unthinkable that anyone should reproduce the distinctive πίστις of the πατὴρ τῶν πιστευόντων. But it is quite understandable that all πίστις along the line of the fellowship of faith should follow that of Abraham both temporally and materially. [5] Finally, 1 Pt. 2:21: Χριστὸς ἔπαθεν ὑπὲρ ὑμῶν, ὑμῖν ὑπολιμπάνων ὑπογραμμὸν ἵνα ἐπακολουθήσητε τοῖς ἴχνεσιν αὐτοῦ. Here the context gives to the basic meaning of ἴχνος (→ ἐπακολουθεῖν, I, 215) the more precise sense of "example" which is also implicit at 2 C. 12:18 and R. 4:12. In this verse two questions arise. 1. In view of the parallel ὑπογραμμός (→ I, 772), is ἴχνος to be regarded as the concrete individual trait which we are called upon to imitate as closely as possible in ἐπακολουθήσητε? 2. Do we have in the following verses (22-24) a definitive definition of the content of the ἴχνη, i.e., do the ἴχνη left for the community by Christ point exclusively to the way of the cross and passion?

As regards the first question, there are instances of ἴχνη in the sense of an example to be followed as closely as possible, usually in the plur. and with reference to the fashioning of character by imitation of an earlier model. Thus it is said of Kimon with respect to his father Miltiades that he οὕτως εὖ καὶ καλῶς ... ἐμιμήσατο καὶ ὥσπερ ἰχνῶν εἴχετο τῶν ἔργων τοῦ πατρὸς ὥστ' εἰ μηδεὶς τῶν συγγραφέων ἐτύγχανεν εὑρηκὼς ὅτου παῖς ἦν, ἀπ' αὐτῶν εἶναι τῶν ἔργων εἰκάσαι τὸν πατέρα αὐτοῦ (Ael. Arist., 46, 160 [II, p. 214, Dindorf]). [6] Following in the tracks has now taken on the sense of keeping to, or attaching oneself to (εἴχετο), of → μιμεῖσθαι or → ὁμοιοῦν (→ n. 6). The track is now an example. This transition from a trail which one follows to an example which one imitates is linguistically possible in the case of ἴχνη as in that of → ἀκολουθέω. Yet the original sense is the track which is followed, not imitated. [7]

---

3 ff. Rare in this figur. sense in the LXX, e.g., Sir. 21:6: μισῶν ἐλεγμὸν ἐν ἴχνει ἁμαρτωλοῦ. Also rare in this sense in Philo, e.g., of the λόγος: πάντα καὶ λέγειν καὶ πράττειν ἐσπούδαζεν εἰς ἀρέσκειαν τοῦ πατρὸς καὶ βασιλέως, ἑπόμενος κατ' ἴχνος αὐτῷ ταῖς ὁδοῖς ..., Op. Mund., 144.

4 V. Schl. R., ad loc.

5 Here, too, there applies in some sense what is said under → n. 8.

6 Cf. ἡνίκα ἂν ποιῶ λόγους τῶν ἰχνῶν ἔχεσθαι τῶν Ἀριστείδου καὶ πειρᾶσθαι τοὺς ἐμοὺς ἀφομοιοῦν εἰς ὅσον οἷόν τε τοῖς ἐκείνου, Lib. Or., 64, 4.

7 The distinction may be easily grasped from a verse like Sir. 50:29: φῶς κυρίου τὸ ἴχνος αὐτοῦ ("the light of the Lord leads him," Luther).

2. At 1 Pt. 2:21 ἴχνος is really to be taken in its original sense. The πάσχειν of Christ took place ὑπὲρ ὑμῶν or ἡμῶν (v. 24). Hence we cannot construe the verse as a demand to imitate the features enumerated in the verses which follow. The ὑπέρ removes the whole process from the sphere of repetition or imitation. Once again the ἴχνη denotes the place at which the present sufferings of the readers are connected with the sufferings of Christ, or *vice versa*. Christian slaves must suffer as disciples of the Redeemer who has trodden the path of suffering (v. 24). They will then suffer in fellowship with Him (→ *infra*). This fellowship does not consist in the detailed imitation of individual traits. It consists in discipleship, which is primarily a matter of the direction (→ ὑπογραμμός and the plur. ἴχνη) in which we must go if we are to be related to the One who goes, or has gone, before: ἐπακολουθεῖν τοῖς ἴχνεσιν. [8]

The second question, which does not arise out of the mere word ἴχνος and which cannot be answered by linguistic investigation, is not finally solved by what we have already said. Even if ἴχνος is here taken in the literal sense of "footprint," it is still an open question whether the ἴχνη which Christ has left for the community denote exclusively the way of suffering. Is true discipleship always a discipleship of suffering, as in vv. 21-24 ? Like other general questions, this question seems at first sight to fly in face of the context. The immediate situation of the readers is one of suffering. Hence the author shows the community how it is to follow the Lord, how it is to walk in His steps, how it is to have fellowship with Him, in this situation. It must follow Him as the One who Himself was a sufferer like the community ; cf. 1 Pt. 4:1. This applies also to a number of similar passages outside 1 Pt. which, even though they do not use ἴχνος, speaks of disciples treading in the steps of the suffering Lord, e.g., Mt. 20:20 ff. par. But the disciples also receive commission and authority (Mt. 10:1 ff.) to do what Jesus Himself did according to Mt. 8 and 9. [9] And for Paul the σὺν Χριστῷ does not refer merely to suffering but also to δοξασθῆναι, R. 8:17; cf. especially R. 6:1-11. Nor does the Johannine καθώς (Jn. 13:15; 15:12) refer merely to a discipleship of suffering. Materially, we may also quote Jm. 5:10 f. in this connection (τὸ τέλος κυρίου εἴδετε) [10] (and on this whole issue → ἀκολουθέω, I, 210 ff.; → μιμέομαι).

3. Nowhere in the NT is there any explicit support for the view that the life of believers is to be in detail an imitation of the life of Jesus. This is true of Ac., even though in 7:58, 59, 60, in the account of the death of Stephen, there seem to be echoes of the passion narrative, as noted by the older catenae, *ad loc*. The healings and miracles of Ac. also remind us of the Synoptists, but this is natural enough. Again, Paul often holds up the figure of Jesus as an example to the churches in particular situations, Phil. 2:5 ff.; R. 15:1-3; cf. also 2 C. 8:9 in context, and passages like Col. 1:24; Phil. 3:10; Gl. 6:17. But we interpret Paul aright only if we see that in these passages he is seeking to stimulate discipleship rather than imitation. The two may merge in practice, but we

---

[8] ἴχνος rightly reminds us of the historical Jesus. As a genuine footprint, it testifies to a distance in time and place between the one who goes before and the one who follows (cf. οὐκ ἰδόντες, 1 Pt. 1:8). This NT understanding, from which has flowed and flows into Christianity all the blessing of practical imitation, is in danger of being lost if ἴχνος is construed as a trait to be imitated, and a non-existent contemporaneity is assumed (along the lines of Kierkegaard).

[9] In a fuller study we should have to consider all the passages in which Jesus sets His work in a ὡς-οὕτως relation to that of His disciples.

[10] Cf. ZNW, 7 (1906), 276 f.

must take our bearings from the ἐν and σύν statements if we are to achieve a correct understanding.

In the apocryphal Ac. we could hardly speak of a deliberate development of the concept of imitation. But here, too, the healings and miracles recall the Synoptic Gospels (e.g., the exorcism at Ac. Thom., 45), and we also find repetitions of details in the Gospel records, e.g., the slap in the face at Ac. Thom., 6 or the crucifixion at Ac. Pt. Verc., 36 ff.

The exegesis and practice of the early Church easily came to confuse discipleship and imitation, and to relate ἴχνη specifically to the passion, so that the martyr was primarily the one who trod in the steps of Christ or other martyrs.[11] In this respect varying degrees of importance were attached to individual features of the passion narrative. Cf. the catena on Jn. 21:18: "Αξιον καὶ ἐν τούτῳ θαυμάσαι τὴν τοῦ Κυρίου πρόγνωσιν πρὸ τοσούτων ἐτῶν προειπόντος αὐτῷ οὐ μόνον ὅτι μάρτυς γενήσεται, ἀλλ' ὅτι καὶ διὰ σταυροῦ ὑποστήσεται τὴν ἀναίρεσιν. ἡ γὰρ ἔκτασις τῶν χειρῶν, καὶ ὁ δεσμὸς τῆς ζώνης, οὐδὲν ἕτερον ἐδήλου ἢ τὸ σχῆμα τοῦ σταυροῦ. βούλεται δὲ αὐτὸν ἀκολουθεῖν αὐτῷ, μιμούμενον αὐτοῦ ἐν πᾶσι τὴν κατ' εὐσέβειαν πολιτείαν. οἱ γὰρ κατ' ἴχνος τῆς ἐκείνου βαίνοντες ἀρετῆς, καὶ κατὰ δύναμιν ὁμοιούμενοι αὐτοῦ τὴν τῆς δικαιοσύνης ἀκρίβειαν, οὗτοι αὐτῷ τὸ τηνικαῦτα ἀκολουθήσωσιν ὁδηγοῦντι εἰς τὴν κατ' οὐρανὸν βασιλείαν. ἴχνος is also used in the same specific sense at Ign. Eph., 12, 2: πάροδός ἐστε (to the community) τῶν εἰς θεὸν ἀναιρουμένων, Παύλου συμμύσται, τοῦ ἡγιασμένου, τοῦ μεμαρτυρημένου, ἀξιομακαρίστου, οὗ γένοιτό μοι ὑπὸ τὰ ἴχνη εὑρεθῆναι, ὅταν θεοῦ ἐπιτύχω.[12] Cf. also Mart. Pol., 22, 1: ἐμαρτύρησεν ὁ μακάριος Πολύκαρπος, οὗ γένοιτο ἐν τῇ βασιλείᾳ Ἰησοῦ Χριστοῦ πρὸς τὰ ἴχνη εὑρεθῆναι ἡμᾶς.

4. ἴχνος can also mean "sole" or "foot." The use is not common in class. Gk., where it is mostly poetic.[13] It is more common in the koine.[14] There are several instances in the pap.[15] It is worth noting that in the LXX ἴχνος is the common rendering of פַּ, e.g., ἴχνος τοῦ ποδός or ἴχνη τῶν ποδῶν at Dt. 11:24; 28:35, 65; Jos. 1:3; 2 Βασ. 14:25; 4 Βασ. 19:24; Da. 10:10 LXX; cf. ἴχνος κτηνῶν as a par. to πούς ἀνθρώπου at Ez. 32:13 (ἴχνος for Heb. פַּרְסָה); of the "foot" of God, Ez. 43:7. In this sense ἴχνος plays a role in religious history which has not yet been fully elucidated.[16] We find votive stones with engraven footprints (2 or 4), and stones which represent naked feet or feet shod with sandals. In some cases these are remembrance stones set up by pilgrims to commemorate their visit to a shrine, or to record their healing.[17] But in other cases the ἴχνος probably bears witness to the fact that a deity has visited the spot.[18] One such

---

[11] *Ibid.*, 4 (1903), 123.

[12] θεοῦ or Χριστοῦ ἐπιτυχεῖν is constantly used for martyrdom, *v.* W. Bau. on Ign. Eph., 12, 2.

[13] For examples v. Liddell-Scott, *s.v.*

[14] Cf. F. Blumenthal, "Der ägyptische Kaiserkult," APF, 5 (1913), 335, and n. 4.

[15] Preisigke Wört., *s.v.*

[16] Cf. A. Maury, "Sur un pied en marbre blanc, découvert à Alexandrie," *Revue Archéologique*, 7 (1850), 600 ff.; *Berichte über die Verhandlungen der Kgl. Sächs. Ges. d. Wiss. zu Leipzig*, Phil.-hist. Kl., 7 (1855), 103; G. Maspero in *Revue Archéologique*, NS, 43 (1882), 38; K. Graf Lanckoronski, *Städte Pamphyliens und Pisidiens*, II (1892), 220, No. 178; *Martyrium d. Dasius*, ed. F. Cumont in *Anal. Boll.*, 16 (1897), 11 ff., text and notes; O. Weinreich in *Ath. Mitt.*, 37 (1912), 36 f.; F. Blumenthal, *op. cit.*, 335; P. Roussel, "Les Cultes Égyptiens à Délos du 3e au 1er siècle avant J.-C." in *Annales de l'Est*, 29/30 (1915 f.), 115 f.; J. Hatzfeld, "Inscriptions de Panamara" in BCH, 51 (1927), 106; W. Drexler, Art. "Isis" in Roscher, II, 360 ff.

[17] Drexler, *op. cit.*; Weinreich, *op. cit.*

[18] In this connection Lanckoronski recalls Hdt., II, 91; IV, 82; Luc. Historiae Verae, I, 7. In interesting contrast cf. an observation of the (Docetic) Acta Johannis concerning Jesus: ἐβουλόμην δὲ πολλάκις σὺν αὐτῷ βαδίζων ἴχνος αὐτοῦ ἐπὶ τῆς γῆς ἰδεῖν εἰ φαί-

stone from Syria has on it an inscription which shows that it was dedicated to Serapis : ἴχνος ἔχων πόδ' ἂν ἴχνος ἔχων ἀνέθηκα Σεράπει. [19] Perhaps other stones of this shape are connected with the Serapis cult. But this circle of ideas has no influence at all on the NT. [20]

Stumpff

---

† Ἰωνᾶς

A. Jona, the Father of the Apostles Peter and Andrew.

At Mt. 16:17 Simon Peter is called Βαριωνᾶ (בַּר יוֹנָא) [1] while Jn. 1:42; 21:15-17; Ev. Hebr. Fr., 9 have Ἰωάννης (יוֹחָנָן) as the father's name. Apart from the name nothing is known of Jona-Johanan.

νεται· ... καὶ οὐδέποτε εἶδον. On this whole question cf. Maury, 602. In early Christianity this idea is found in the Quo vadis legend, which underlies the veneration of footprints of the Lord at two Roman shrines, San Sebastiano and Santa Maria della Piante. Here the steps have nothing to do with discipleship. They are visible signs of the appearance of Christ to Peter, and as such they are the basis of a local Christ cult (or even two) [Bertram].

[19] Weinreich, *op. cit.*, 36; Roussel, *op. cit.*, 115 f.; Hatzfeld, *op. cit.*, 106, No. 80.

[20] If the mythical motif of enduring footprints is not found in the NT, it influences the thought of discipleship in early Christian piety. The most important testimony to this is the famous Od. Sol. 39. Here we have the idea that the prints of the Lord are set in the waves and form an indestructible way on which believers can pass through the waves of death (cf. Ps. 18:4 and Gunkel on 2 S. 22:5 ff.). Ps. 77:16 ff. (v. 19 : "Thy way is in the sea, and thy path in the great waters, and thy footsteps are not known") shows us that this motif has a basis in salvation history, i.e., in the passage of Israel through the Red Sea (Ex. 14:16 ff.; cf. Jos. 3:10 ff.; 4:7). On the basis of Job 11:7 LXX ("Canst thou find the trace of the Lord?") Paul says : ἀνεξιχνίαστοι αἱ ὁδοὶ αὐτοῦ (R. 11:33). But Od. Sol. goes beyond this. It pictures the Lord's steps like posts set up imperishably in the water. This motif is alien to the biblical view of God. It derives from the cultic view of discipleship. It presupposes the development or transformation of OT revelation into a cultic religion of redemption. This transformation took place on the soil of Hellenistic Judaism. Many ideas of similar origin helped to shape the popular piety of the early Church [Bertram].

Ἰ ω ν ᾶ ς. On A.: Pr.-Bauer, *s.v.* Βαριωνᾶ and Ἰωνᾶς; Winer (Schmiedel) § 5, 26c; Dalman Gr., 179, n. 5; A. Merx, *Die vier kanonischen Ev. nach ihrem ältesten bekannten Texte*, II, 1: *Das Ev. Mt.* (1902), 169; II, 2 : *Das Ev. des Joh.* (1911), 466; Bl.-Debr.[6] § 53, 2. On B.: F. Zimmer, *Der Spruch vom Jonazeichen* (1881); Winer (Schmiedel) § 30, 10d; G. Runze, *Das Zeichen des Menschensohnes und der Doppelsinn des Jonâzeichens* (1897); the ensuing debate, P. W. Schmiedel, *Literarisches Centralblatt* (1897), 513-515; G. Runze, ZwTh, 41 (1898), 171-185; Schmiedel, *ibid.*, 514-525; S. L. Tyson, *The Biblical World*, 33 (1909), 96-101; C. Moxon, ExpT, 22 (1911), 566 f.; C. R. Bowen, *The American Journal of Theology*, 20 (1916), 414-421; J. H. Michael, JThSt, 21 (1920), 146-159; Str.-B., I, 642-649, 651; II, 705; IV, 266; Pr.-Bauer[2], 1201; J. Bonsirven, *Recherches de Science Religieuse*, 24 (1934), 450-455.

[1] So also acc. to the cod. (cf. E. Klostermann, *Apocrypha*, II[3] [1929], 9 = KlT, 8) Ev. Hebr. Fr., 11: *Simon, fili Jonae* (cf. Mt. 19:24).

In assessing the twofold tradition concerning the name we must remember that apart from the prophet Jonah (→ B.) there is no instance of Jona(h) as an independent man's name prior to the 3rd century A.D. At Jub. 34:20 it is a woman's name (= dove); in the LXX it is a variant of יוֹחָנָן (Ἰωάν[ν]ης), e.g., 4 Βασ. 25:23 B: Ιωνα for Heb. יוֹחָנָן; LXX 1 Ch. 26:3 A: Ιωναν, B: Ιωνας for Heb. יְהוֹחָנָן; 1 Εσδρ. 9:1 B: Ιωνα for Heb. יְהוֹחָנָן (Ezr. 10:6); 1 Εσδρ. 9:23 A: Ιωνας, B: Ιωανας.[2] No Tannaite bears the name. It occurs only in the 4th cent., and even here we find only two Palestinian[3] and one Babylonian[4] Amorean. Since there are in the 1st century no instances of Jona(h) as an independent name, but only as a variant of Ἰωάν(ν)ης, we may conclude that the יוֹנָא of Mt. 16:17 is a shorter form of יוֹחָנָן.[5]

But this is not certain, since the usual Palestinian abbreviation of יוֹחָנָן is יוֹחַי or יוֹחָא.[6] Hence there is the possibility that Jonah did occur occasionally in the NT period, and that Jn. 1:42; 21:15-17; Ev. Hebr. Fr., 9 replace this unusual name by the more common[7] John. We cannot make any final decision between the two alternatives.

B. The Prophet Jonah.

1. The Later Jewish View of Jonah.[8]

The story of Jonah provided plenty of opportunity for fantastic embellishment, and the figure of Jonah was greatly magnified in later Judaism. He was supposed to be the son of the widow of Zarephath whom Elijah restored to life.[9] According to the Haggada his flight (Jon. 1) occurred in the interests of Israel. He wanted to prevent the repentance of the Gentiles causing God to punish the impenitence of Israel.[10] With this in view, he offered his own life for that of his people. "R. Jonathan (c. 140 A.D.)[11] said: The only purpose of Jonah was to bring judgment on himself in the sea, for it is written: 'And he said to them, Take me and cast me into the sea' (Jon. 1:12). Similarly, you find that many patriarchs and prophets sacrificed themselves for Israel."[12] Jonah was perfectly righteous.[13]

---

[2] The variants carry no weight: Jn. 1:42 (א pl lat sy: Ιωνα for the original Ἰωάννου); 21:15, 16, 17 (א pl Ιωνα, sy^sin arm: יונן [Jaunan] for the original Ἰωάννου), since these are based on Mt. 16:17. יונן is undoubtedly an assimilation to Mt. 16:17, since it has nothing to do with יוֹחָנָן and is the Syrian rendering of Jona(h), Merx, II, 1, 169; II, 2, 466.

[3] Bacher Pal. Am., III, 220-231, 723; Strack, Einl., 146 f.

[4] Only in bChul., 30b (EJ, IX, 278).

[5] Winer (Schmiedel) § 5, 26c; Bl.-Debr.[6] § 53, 2; cf. Str.-B., I, 730.

[6] Dalman Gr., 179. A. Mayer, Die Muttersprache Jesu (1896) tries to avoid the difficulty by suggesting that Ιωνα is a Greek contraction (47, n. 3); cf. Michael, 151 f.

[7] There are 5 or 6 who bear this name in the NT. Cf. Ges.-Buhl, s.v. יוֹחָנָן; LXX concordance and index to Jos. and Ep. Ar., s.v. Ἰωάννης; Strack Einl., Index, s.v. Johanan; Bacher Tannaiten; Bab. Am.; Pal. Am., Indexes, s.v. Jochanan.

[8] Sources: In the OT only 2 K. 14:25 and Jon. 1-4. Tob. 14:4, 8 AB; 3 Macc. 8:8; Sib., 2, 248; Jos. Ant., 9, 206-214; Prophetarum Vitae Fabulosae, ed. T. Schermann (1907), Index. Rabbinic material in Str.-B., I, 642-649, 651; II, 280, 705; IV, 266; L. Ginzberg, The Legends of the Jews, IV (1913), 197, 246-253; VI (1928), 348-352; M. J. bin Gorion, Die Sagen der Juden. Juda und Israel (1927), 20, 202 f., 390-403; EJ, IX, 272-274.

[9] Prophetarum Vitae, 19, 7 par.; Gn. r., 98 on 49:13 (par. jSukka, 5, 55a); Midr. Ps. 26 § 7 on 26:9; PREl, 33 etc.

[10] M. Ex., 12, 1; jSanh., 11, 30b; PREl, 10.

[11] Str.-B., I, 643.

[12] M. Ex., 12, 1.

[13] Midr. Ps. 26 § 7 on 26:9.

2. The Prophet Jonah in the NT.

Two events from his life are mentioned in the NT, his stay in the belly of the great fish (Jon. 2; Mt. 12:40) and his successful preaching of repentance in Nineveh (Jon. 3; Mt. 12:41 and Lk. 11:32). [14]

> There are also echoes of Jonah (1:3, 4, 5, 6, 10, 11, 12, 16) in the story of the stilling of the storm (Mk. 4:35-41 par.).

a. The repentance of the men of Nineveh is held up to the Jews as a warning and a threat. At the judgment the men of Nineveh will raise up an accusation against [15] this generation and will bring it into condemnation, [16] because they repented at the preaching of Jonah, and a greater than Jonah is now present (Mt. 12:41, and word for word Lk. 11:32). Two facts give the threat its particular thrust. First, Gentiles on the one side are contrasted with Jews on the other; second, a prophet on the one side is contrasted with one who is above all the prophets on the other. [17]

b. The meaning of the sign of Jonah (Mt. 12:39; 16:4; Lk. 11:29 f.) has been the subject of much debate.

> There are grammatical as well as exegetical and critical differences. In the phrase τὸ σημεῖον Ἰωνᾶ some take the genitive as an appositive genitive (the sign which was given in the prophet Jonah), some as a subjective genitive (the sign which Jonah gave), and some as an objective genitive (the sign which Jonah experienced).

The following interpretations call for consideration. [18] 1. The saying referred originally to John the Baptist. As at Mt. 16:17, Ἰωνᾶ is an abbreviation of Ἰωάν(ν)ης. The misapplication to the prophet led to the introduction of Mt. 12:40; Lk. 11:30 into the context. [19] Now it is quite conceivable that Jesus saw in John

---

[14] Bonsirven (450-455) explains the combination of the two in Mt. 12:38-42 par. in terms of the fact that the repentance of the Ninevites was mentioned in the sermon summoning to repentance on fast days according to Ta'an, 2, 1, and Jonah's prayer for deliverance from the fish was mentioned in the fifth benediction of the prayer on fast days according to Ta'an, 2, 4. He concludes that Jesus is alluding to the liturgy of fast days in Mt. 12:38-42, and from Mt. 16:2 f.; Lk. 12:54 f. he also concludes that the sign from heaven which was demanded of Jesus (Mk. 8:11 par.) was that He should cause it to rain. But this is an importation into the text, and though allusion to the liturgy is possible, it is not very likely if the two sayings were first associated by the tradition (→ 409).

[15] ἀνίστασθαι μετά = Aram. עִם קָם, a. "to go with someone" (to court, either to accuse him or to bear witness against him), Well. Mt., 65; Dalman WJ, I, 51; P. Joüon, L'Évangile de Notre-Seigneur Jésus-Christ (1930), 83; b. (also possible in this passage) "to rise up with someone," Kl. Mt. on 12:41 in the exposition, though not the translation.

[16] κατακρίνειν = Aram. חַיֵּב, "to prove to be in the wrong," "to bring down condemnation," Well. Mt., 65; Dalman WJ, I, 51; P. Joüon, op. cit., 82 f.; Schl. Mt., 418.

[17] Cf. the similar twofold contrast in Midr. Lam., Intr. No. 31: "I sent one prophet to Nineveh, and he brought it to penitence and conversion. And these Israelites in Jerusalem — how many prophets have I sent to them!"

[18] We may also mention the conjecture of Runze, Das Zeichen des Menschensohnes 74 ff. that Jesus originally spoke of אוֹת יוֹנָה in the sense of "sign of the dove." For the most part, however, יוֹנָה in Aram. is used as a fem. with the status emphaticus יוֹנְתָא (e.g., Tg. J. I, Gn. 8:8, 11; Tg. Ps. 68:14 and Cant. 1:15). This rules out any confusion with the proper name יוֹנָה.

[19] C. Moxon, ExpT, 22 (1911), 566 f.; J. H. Michael, JThSt, 21 (1920), 146-159. Both are influenced by the writers mentioned in → n. 21.

the Elias proclaimed by Malachi (→ II, 937), and that He thus regarded John as the one sign given to the generation of His day (cf. Jn. 5:35). But the linguistic basis of this hypothesis is insecure (→ 407). 2. The context Lk. 11:29-32 caused earlier exegetes [20] to take the view that the sign is Jonah's preaching in Nineveh, which is renewed in the call of Jesus (or John the Baptist) [21] for repentance. But the Lucan context (par. Mt. 12:38-42) may well be secondary. [22] It arises from the combination of the rejection of the sign (Lk. 11:29 f.) with the threat of judgment (11:31 f. par.). The future ἔσται at 11:30 rules out the possibility that Lk. finds the renewed sign of Jonah in the present activity of Jesus as a preacher of repentance. Above all, it is highly unusual to describe the preaching of repentance as a → σημεῖον, since a sign consists, not in what men do, but in "the intervention of the power of God in the course of events." [23] 3. The sign of Jonah must refer to the miracle of the deliverance of Jonah from the belly of the great fish (Jon. 2). For the contemporaries of Jonah this event was the outstanding miracle in the life of Jonah. [24] The term "sign" is in fact used of this miracle. Thus PREl, 10, at the end of the story of the deliverance of the prophet, adds that "the sailors saw the signs (אותות) and great wonders which the Holy One — blessed be He — did to Jonah." Mt. 12:40 finds the *tertium comparationis* between the sign of Jonah and the sign of Jesus in the fact that Jonah stayed three days and three nights in the belly of the fish, the same period that the Son of Man will spend in the heart of the earth. [25] For Lk. 11:30, however, the *tertium comparationis* is that Jonah became a sign to the Ninevites, obviously as one who had been delivered from the belly of the fish, [26] and that Jesus will be displayed to this generation as the One who is raised up from the dead. According to Lk., then, both the old and the new sign of Jonah consist in the authorisation of the divine messenger by deliverance from death. [27] This is the original point of the saying. Mt. 12:40 might seem to be

---

[20] More recently Holtzmann NT, I, 144.

[21] W. Brandt, *Die Evangelische Geschichte u. d. Ursprung des Chrts.* (1893), 459, n. 2; "Die jüdischen Baptismen," ZAW, Beih., 18 (1910), 82-84; T. K. Cheyne, EB, II, 2502; B. W. Bacon, *The Sermon on the Mount* (1902), 232; *The Fourth Gospel in Research and Debate* (1910), 350; *Christianity, Old and New* (1914), 160; A. Blakiston, *John the Baptist and His Relation to Jesus* (1912), 220 f., n. 54. But cf. Bowen, 414-421.

[22] Well. Mt., 64 f.; Bultmann Trad., 124, n. 1; Kl. Mt. on 12:41 f.

[23] Schl. Mt., 416. The last objection also rules out the interpretation, on the basis of Lk. 11:30, that Jonah was a sign to the Ninevites because he came from a far country (Bultmann Trad., 124; cf. Hck. Lk. on 11:30). Coming from a far country is no σημεῖον.

[24] 3 Macc. 6:8 → n. 26; Jos. Ant., 9, 213; Str.-B., I, 645-649; also Ta'an., 2, 4; bSanh., 89ab. Cf. Schl. Mt., 416 f.

[25] I.e., in the world of the dead, → I, 148.

[26] It is not expressly said in the OT that the Ninevites heard of the deliverance of Jonah. But legend speaks of proclamation of the saving of the prophet. Thus PREl., 10 tells how the sailors who had thrown Jonah into the sea were moved by his deliverance to throw their idols into the sea and to embrace Judaism. 3 Macc. 6:8 also seems to assume that the prophet's hearers heard of his deliverance, for we read there : "On Jonah, who passed into the belly of the monster which lived in the depths, thou, O Father, didst direct thine eyes (ἀφιδών = ἀπιδών, cf. Thackeray, 125), and thou didst show him unharmed to all his hearers." Like Lk. 11:30, Justin Dial., 107, 2 also seems to assume that the Ninevites heard of Jonah's deliverance (τοῦ Ἰωνᾶ κηρύξαντος αὐτοῖς μετὰ τὸ ἐκβρασθῆναι (cast out on to the shore) αὐτὸν τῇ τρίτῃ ἡμέρᾳ ἀπὸ τῆς κοιλίας τοῦ ἀδροῦ ἰχθύος ὅτι μετὰ τρεῖς ἡμέρας παμπληθεὶ ἀπολοῦνται).

[27] Jalqut Jon., 4 calls the deliverance of Jonah a deliverance from she'ol. This helps us to see why Jesus could compare His destiny with that of Jonah.

original because it does not correspond exactly to the course of events. But the three days and three nights derive from a literal quotation of the LXX of Jon. 2:1, and we can only regard this as a secondary interpretation which draws attention to the time rather than to the actual deliverance from death.[28] To those who ask for a sign Jesus[29] replies with a riddle. The sign of Jonah will be renewed with the manifestation of the Son of Man returning from the dead.[30] This is the only sign which will be given them.[31] Materially, there is no discrepancy between the absolute refusal to give a sign (Mk. 8:11) and the intimation of the sign of Jonah. Both statements make it clear that God will not give any sign that is abstracted from the person of Jesus and that does not give offence.

Joachim Jeremias

---

[28] Prophetarum Vitae, 30, 15-17, Schermann: ὥσπερ γὰρ τὸ κῆτος (sea-monster) ἀδιάφθορον (unharmed) ἐξήμεσε (spewed out) τὸν Ἰωνᾶν, οὕτω καὶ ὁ τάφος τὸν δεσπότην ἐξήμεσε εἰς κρείττονα ζωήν. Here it is correctly perceived that the *tertium comparationis* is not the length of Jonah's stay in the belly of the fish (as Mt. 12:40 seems to suggest) but his deliverance from the monster. On the other hand, the eschatological reference of the passage is missed.

[29] It is no argument against the genuineness of the saying that Jesus expects His death and speaks of His *parousia,* for He does both elsewhere. A possible objection is that in Lk. 11:30 Jesus departs from His usual practice prior to the hearing before the Sanhedrin, describing Himself publicly as → ὁ υἱὸς τοῦ ἀνθρώπου and referring publicly to His *parousia.* Yet it should not be overlooked that He is speaking in *mashal* form, so that only initiates see that He is speaking of Himself.

[30] In the light of what we said earlier (→ 407), it is possible that Lk. 11:30 includes the thought of the self-offering of Jonah. If so, we should say: "The sign of Jonah will be renewed with the self-sacrifice and the manifestation of the Son of Man returning from the dead."

[31] Cf. Mt. 24:30: τὸ σημεῖον τοῦ υἱοῦ τοῦ ἀνθρώπου.

καθαιρέω, καθαίρεσις

† καθαιρέω.

This verb, found since Homer, has four main senses in secular Gk.: a. "to take down from above" (objects, the yoke, the moon; cf. Hom. Il., 24, 268; Od., 9, 149; Aristoph. Nu., 750); hence the expression καθαιρεῖν ὀφθαλμοὺς (ὅσσε) θανόντι, "to close the eyes of a dead person"; b. "to tear down" (buildings, houses, walls; cf. Thuc., I, 58; Xenoph. Hist. Graec., IV, 4, 13); c. "to destroy," "to vanquish," "to extirpate," "to condemn" (opponents, cities, also figur. δόγματα, ὕβριν etc.; cf. Hdt., 6, 41; Soph. Oed. Col., 1689 f., "to kill"; Plut. Pomp., 8 (I, 622e); P. Oxy., XII, 1408, 23; Epict. Diss., I, 28, 25); d. "to dethrone" (Jos. Ant., 8, 270; figur. Luc. Nigrinus, 4).

The LXX uses it for 11 Heb. equivalents: 1. דְּכָא pi; 2. הָרַס; 3. יָרַד; 4. כָּרַת[1]; 5. נָסַח; 6. נָצָה; 7. נָתַץ; 8. נָתַשׁ; 9. סוּר hi; 10. פָּרַץ; 11. רוּד hi. In sense a. Gn. 24:18, 46 (ὑδρίαν); 44:11 (μάρσιππον); Nu. 4:5 (καταπέτασμα); 2 K. 16:17 (the brazen sea from its place); Jdt. 13:6 (ἀκινάκην); Jer. 13:18 (στέφανον); 2 Macc. 12:35 (to hew off the arm from above). Cf. the special sense in Jos. 8:29; 10:27: "to take down those who are hanged from a post." Sense b. Ex. 34:13 etc. (altars); Prv. 21:22; Lam. 2:2; 1 Macc. 5:65; 8:10 (ὀχύρωμα); Lv. 14:45 etc. (houses); Ez. 26:4 (πύργους); Dt. 28:52 etc. (walls and parts of walls); Lv. 11:35 (polluted vessels); Ex. 23:24 (idols); 2 K. 10:27 (temples of idols). καθαιρέω is also used for striking the holy tent on decampment. The word is often used as the antonym of οἰκοδομεῖν, ψ 27:5; Is. 49:17; Ιερ. 24:6; 38:28; 49:10; 51:34; Ez. 36:36; 1 Macc. 9:62; esp. Sir. 34:23: εἷς οἰκοδομῶν καὶ εἷς καθαιρῶν.[2] Sense c. Ju. 9:45 (cities); 1 Macc. 11:4 (περιπόλια); 2 Macc. 10:2 (τεμένη). To express complete destruction, Lam. 2:17: καθεῖλεν καὶ οὐκ ἐφείσατο. Figur. Zech. 9:6: ὕβριν ἀλλοφύλων. Sense d. Sir. 10:14: θρόνους ἀρχόντων καθεῖλεν ὁ κύριος.

In the New Testament 1. we find sense a. for taking down from the cross, Mk. 15:36 (of the living); Mk. 15:46; Lk. 23:53; Ac. 13:29 (of the dead).

Outside the NT we find this use in Polyb., I, 86, 6; Philo Flacc., 83.[3] We cannot say anything more precise about the taking down of Jesus from the cross, since we do not know whether He was nailed or tied to the *patibulum,* or whether His head was fixed to the *patibulum* or free.[4] Many times, especially in mass crucifixions, the dead were

---

κ α θ α ι ρ έ ω. Pr.-Bauer, 602. The noun καθαιρέτης, found since Thuc. (cf. Dio C., 44, 1: καθαιρέται τοῦ Καίσαρος), does not occur in the NT. Mart. Pol., 12, 2 is the first instance in Christian lit.

[1] The Mishnah tractate כְּרִיתוֹת deals with sins which incur extirpation.

[2] Cf. the expression in Dalman Wört., 177: לֹא מַעֲלֶה וְלֹא מוֹרִיד, "he leaves out of account," lit. "he does not set either high or low in value."

[3] Mt. 27:59 has the simple λαβών instead of καθελών.

[4] H. Fulda, *Das Kreuz u. d. Kreuzigung* (1878); V. Schultze, Art. "Kreuz u. Kreuzigung," RE³, XI, 90 ff.; F. Hitzig, Art. *crux,* Pauly-W., IV (1901), 1728-31. The most important sources on crucifixion are Artemid Oneirocr., I, 76; II, 53; Apul. Met., III, 17; Cic. Verr., IV, 11, 26; Lucanus Pharsalia, VI, 538 ff.; Plin. Hist. Nat., XXVIII, 4, 11; Philo Flacc., 83; Polyb., I, 86, 6; Suet. Galba, 9; Xenophon Ephesius Ephes., IV, 281 f.

left on the cross either to rot or to be eaten by predatory birds.[5] Regard for the passover did not allow this in the case of Jesus and the two thieves.

καθαιρέω is appropriate since those who were crucified hung up on high; ὑψηλὸς ὁ σταυρωθείς (Artemid Oneirocr., II, 53; hence it is good for a poor man to dream of crucifixion). The express account of a crucifixion in Xenophon Ephesius Ephes., IV, p. 281 f. does not help us, since in this case the cross and its victim slip into the Nile because of the soft earth.

2. Sense b. is found literally at Lk. 12:18 : τὰς ἀποθήκας.[6] The folly of the rich farmer is emphasised by the fact that in spite of his uncertain future he tears down what he already has.

3. Sense c. is found at Ac. 13:19 on the basis of Dt. 7:1; Jos. 3:10; 24:11.[7] The apostle is trying to show God at work in a concrete section of history, even though His action takes the form of destruction. Figuratively at 2 C. 10:4 (λογισμούς, → infra).

4. Sense d. is found literally in the quotation at Lk. 1:52. The basis is Sir. 10:14, cf. also Job 12:19. In the OT one of the clearest proofs of God's work in history is that He overthrows the powerful who do not fulfil His will; the history of Saul is an example. With the increasing incursion of eschatology into the theology of history the Messiah now takes the place of God, and the overthrow of rulers is eschatological (En. 46:5). Since the Magnificat is an eschatological hymn, this passage, too, is to be taken eschatologically. Figuratively at Ac. 19:27 : μέλλειν τε καὶ καθαιρεῖσθαι τῆς μεγαλειότητος αὐτῆς (the silversmiths fear that the Ephesian Artemis will be deprived of her majesty).[8]

Allusion is here made to a cultic formula of Ephesus (cf. Xenophon Ephesius Ephes., I, 11: τὴν πάτριον ἡμῖν θεὸν τὴν μεγάλην Ἐφεσίων Ἄρτεμιν).[9]

† καθαίρεσις.

The noun occurs from the time of Thuc. in the same senses as the verb, esp. the tearing down of buildings, or figuratively destruction or overthrow (antonym οἰκοδομή, or from the time of Aristot. Phys., III, 6, p. 206b, 29, 31 αὔξησις). In the LXX it occurs only twice for forms of הָרַס Ex. 23:24 : tearing down, and 1 Macc. 3:43 : destruction of the people.

In the NT we find it at 2 C. 10:4 : καθαίρεσιν ὀχυρωμάτων, and here it is taken up again in the καθαιροῦντες which follows.[1] Paul is mounting an offensive;[2]

---

[5] Horat. Ep., I, 16, 48. The return of the corpse to relatives, Philo Flacc., 83; Ulpianus Digest., XLVIII (Mommsen, II, 863).

[6] Cf. S. Krauss, Talmudische Archäologie, II (1911), 195.

[7] Only six nations are mentioned in Dt. 20:17.

[8] Grammatically the verse is uncertain. Bl.-Debr.[6] § 180, 1 regards it as impossible and prefers ἡ μεγαλειότης αὐτῆς or αὐτῆς ἡ μεγαλειότης. Yet it could be a dialect phrase in which the subject is missing and has to be supplied from what has gone before (Artemis).

[9] As regards the forms of καθαιρέω, the future καθελῶ, derived from εἷλον, is worth noting, cf. Radermacher², 96 and 226.

κ α θ α ί ρ ε σ ι ς. [1] "Development through the nom. absol.," Ltzm. K., ad loc.

[2] H. Windisch, Der mess. Krieg u. das Urchr. (1909), 66 ff.; Paulus und Christus (1934), 200-214.

with the help of true Christian *gnosis* he will attack and pull down the bulwarks of human sophistry (λογισμούς) to the glory of Christ.

The image is first used of the true sage; Paul is building on Prv. 21:22. Closely related is Philo Conf. Ling., 129 ff.: The wise man is set πρός γε τὴν τοῦ ὀχυρώματος τούτου καθαίρεσιν; ungodly ὀχύρωμα is τῶν λόγων πιθανότης. Cf. also Epict. Diss., III, 22, 94 ff.; IV, 1, 86 f. [3]

At 2 C. 10:8 and 13:10 καθαίρεσις is the opposite of οἰκοδομή. Here, as often, Paul thinks of his own warfare as constructive. His opponents destroy; he builds up. Even his controversies serve the final purpose of edification. Perhaps Paul is alluding to his earlier activity as a persecutor. Once he tore down; now he knows that Christ wants him to build up. Jer. 1:10 and 24:6 form a basis.

Carl Schneider

> καθαρός, καθαρίζω, καθαίρω,
> καθαρότης, ἀκάθαρτος,
> ἀκαθαρσία, καθαρισμός,
> ἐκκαθαίρω, περικάθαρμα

† καθαρός, καθαρίζω, † καθαίρω, † καθαρότης.

Contents. A. The Usage. B. Clean and Unclean outside the NT: Part I: 1. In Primitive Religion; 2. In the Greek World; 3. In OT Religion. C. Clean and Unclean outside the NT: Part II: Judaism: 1. Cultic Uncleanness; 2. Cultic Cleansing; 3. The Attitude of the Rabbis to the Law; 4. Inward Purity. D. Clean and Unclean in the NT: 1. Physical Cleanness; 2. Cultic Cleanness and Cleansing; 3. Moral Purity.

---

[3] For other instances, Wnd. 2 K., *ad loc.*

κ α θ α ρ ό ς κ τ λ. RE[3], XVI, 564 ff.; XXIV, 382 ff.; RGG, IV, 1839 ff.; 1847 ff.; ERE, X, 455 ff.; J. Benzinger, *Hbr. Archäologie,*[3] *Angelos Beih.,* 1 (1927), 395 ff.; W. Brandt, *Die jüdischen Baptismen* (1910), *ZAW Beih.,* 18; *Jüdische Reinheitslehre u. ihre Beschreibung in den Evv.,* *ZAW Beih.,* 19 (1910); J. Döller, "Die Reinheits- und Speisegesetze des AT in religionsgeschichtlicher Beleuchtung," *At.liche Abh.,* 7, 2 and 3 (1917); B. Stade-A. Bertholet, *Bibl. Theol. d. AT,* I (1905), esp. 134 ff.; II (1911), 50 ff.; W. Eichrodt, *Theol. d. AT,* I (1933), 60 ff.; Trench, 299, 375; Hamburg, Art. καθαρμός in Pauly-W., X (1919), 2513 ff.; F. Pfister, Art. "Katharsis," *ibid.,* Suppl. VI (1935), 146 ff.; E. Fehrle, "Die kultische Keuschheit im Altertum," RVV, 6 (1910); T. Wächter, "Reinheitsvorschriften im griech. Kult," RVV, 9, 1 (1910); E. Williger, "Hagios" in RVV, 19, 1 (1922); *Reallex. d. Vorgesch.,* XI (1927/28), 80 ff. Art. "Reinheit"; P. Stengel, *Griech. Kultaltertümer*[3] (1920), 156 ff.; G. Wissowa, "Religion u. Kultus der Römer"[2] in *Handbuch d. kl. Altert.-Wissenschaft,* V, 4 (1912), 390 ff.; J. Horst, "Die Worte Jesu über d. kult. Reinheit u. ihre Verarbeitung in den ev. Berichten," ThStKr, 87 (1914), 429 ff.; H. Wenschkewitz, *Die Spiritualisierung der Kultusbegriffe* (1932), *Angelos Beih.,* 4; I. Scheftelowitz, "Die Sündentilgung durch Wasser," ARW, XVII (1914), 353 ff.

A. The Usage.

The term is used of physical, religious (ritual and cultic) and moral purity. It is an important concept which accompanies religious thought through its various stages.

1. καθαρός a. "clean" (from dirt), opp. ῥυπαρός. b. "clean," "free," opp. πλήρης, μεστός : ἐν καθαρῷ, Hom. Il., 23, 61; c. "morally free" from stain, shame etc. : ἀδικίας, Plato Resp., VI, 496d, καθαρὸς χεῖρας, Hdt., I, 35; d. "clean," "free from adulteration": χρυσίον καθαρώτατον, Hdt., IV, 166. καθαρίζειν, a later Hellenistic form from καθαίρω,¹ a. literally, "to cleanse" (from dirt etc.): τὸ γεώργιον P. Lips., I, 111, 12; b. figur., esp. of the cultic restoration of violated cleanness : [μηδένα] ἀκάθαρτον προσάγειν (sc. to the temple). καθαριζέστω δὲ ἀπὸ σ[κ]όρδων κα[ὶ χοιρέων] κα[ὶ γ]υναικός, Ditt. Syll.³, 1042, 2 ff. (2/3 cent. A.D.); 736, 37 (92 B.C.); Jos. Ant., 10, 70 τὴν χώραν. καθαρότης, already in class. Gk. both literally and figur.: Plato Leg., VI, 778c; Iambl. Vit. Pyth., 13 : ψυχῆς καθαρότητα; Ep. Ar., 234 : μέγιστον ... τὸ τιμᾶν τὸν θεόν· τοῦτο δ' ἐστὶν οὐ δώροις οὐδὲ θυσίαις, ἀλλὰ ψυχῆς καθαρότητι καὶ διαλήψεως ὁσίας.

2. In the LXX καθαρός is predominantly used for טָהוֹר; like → a. Ez. 36:25; ὕδωρ, like → c. of ritual (Lv. 7:19; 10:10) and moral purity (Ps. 51:10; Hab. 1:13), like → d. Ex. 25:11: χρυσός. Much less often it is used for בַּר (basic meaning "to be free") (Ps. 24:4) or for נָקִי (from נקה, "to be emptied," hence "clean"), "clean," "innocent" (Job 4:7), or for זָךְ (subsidiary form of זכה, "to be shining, clean," hence ethically "innocent" (Job 15:15; 25:5). καθαρίζω is used predominantly for טהר qal and pi (pass. hitp) (Gn. 35:2; Lv. 12:7, 8; 14:4, 7 f.), occasionally for נקה pi (pass. ni) (Ex. 20:7; 34:7; Dt. 5:11; ψ 18:12 f.). Often it is also used for כפר pi (Ex. 29:37; 30:10) and sometimes for חטא pi (Ex. 29:36; Lv. 8:15).² καθαρίζω and ἐξιλάσκεσθαι are synonyms : Lv. 14:18; 12:8; 16:30. Declarative of pronouncing clean by the priest, Lv. 13:13. καθαρότης³ in Ex. 24:10 A for טהר; cf. also Wis. 7:24; ψ 88:45 Σ.

B. Clean and Unclean outside the NT : Part I.

1. In Primitive Religion.

On the level of primitive religion man thinks in terms of what is filled with power (taboo). The numen is to be shunned (→ ἅγιος, I, 88 f.). To come into contact with what is filled with power is to be oneself charged with power, and hence to be dangerous to those around. Only cleansing can fit one for ordinary intercourse again. On the primitive view, birth, death and sexual intercourse are linked with what is filled with power. Hence they make unclean, and on contact with them cleansing becomes necessary.

---

¹ Ion. form καθερίζω, Bl.-Debr.⁶ § 29, 1; in the *koine* καθαίρω has the narrower sense "to wipe," "to brush," cf. ἐκκαθαίρω. καθαίρω occurs in the NT only at Jn. 15:2.

² Along the lines of OT sacrificial typology (Lv. 16:29 f.), the LXX also uses the verb at Is. 53:10 etc. Under Aram. influence it is taking דכא, "to destroy," as זכה, "to be clean," unless we accept the view of F. Wutz, *Die Transkriptionen von der LXX bis zu Hieronymus,* I (1925), 85, that there is an error in transcription. On the theological interpretation, cf. K. F. Euler, "Die Verkündigung vom leidenden Gottesknecht aus Jes. 53," BWANT, 4, 14 (1934), 75 ff. and 120 [Bertram].

³ Cf. also καθαριότης, Ex. 24:10 B; 2 S. 22:21, 25; ψ 17:20, 24; Sir. 43:1.

The numen, however, may be friendly and benevolent as well and hostile and dangerous. On further development, it is not just demon; it is also deity. To be able to enter into dealings with deity, man must set himself in a fitting, higher state. He must accept purifications to remove or wash away what is unclean. That is unclean which conflicts with the deity, which is related to alien or supplanted cults and powers (demons). Cleanness and uncleanness are thought of in a quasi-material way. Uncleanness can cling like dirt, or be washed away with water etc. By associating what is holy and what is clean (→ I, 89) religion fashions a starting-point for the ultimate moral spiritualising of the concept of purity. Clean becomes a moral rather than a cultic or ritual term, and the deity itself is regarded as a moral force.

2. In Greek Religion.

This general development is obviously followed in Greek religion. [4] The primitive stage is plainly reflected in ancient ideas of a dangerous force which makes unclean and which is connected with the mysterious processes of birth, sex, sickness and death. [5] Historical Greek religion is plainly at the second stage. The gods are regarded as exalted forces which are friendly to man. The demand for cultic purity is dominant. The man who dares to approach deity must be careful not to violate it by anything contradictory. [6] The whole field of the demonic becomes alien to deity, and must be kept at bay by the cultus. Rules originally designed as a protection against the demonic threat now become cultic regulations for the proper respecting of the holy nature of the gods. Hence a mass of cultic rules is fashioned, and the purity of the one concerned is assured by preparatory dedications (ἁγνεῖαι). Only in a state of cleanness can a man draw near to the deity. On the other hand, we have rules for καθαρμοί which are designed to remove any uncleanness incurred. [7] In the first instance, this system of purification is purely cultic. It is not moral. But along with cultic purification the Greek world has also a private system which diligently seeks by purification and abstinence etc. to ward off demonic influences. There is here, e.g., in the Orphics and Pythagoreans, a sublimation of

---

[4] F. Pfister, *Die Religion der Griechen u. Römer* (1930), 114 ff.; Stengel, *op. cit.,* 156 ff.; Wächter, *op. cit.,* 2 ff. The question of purity is central in Persian religion, cf. Chant. de la Saussaye, II, 239 ff.

[5] Examples in Wächter, 7 ff., e.g., the mother is unclean, and so, too, are the new baby and those present at its birth, 26 f.; if birth takes place in a sanctuary, this is defiled, 31; madness is caused by alien forces, and requires purifications, 41; on the purification of the raving Proitides in the river Anigros at Elis, cf. Paus., V, 5, 10; a corpse is unclean, and to touch it, or to take part in its burial, defiles, Wächter, 43 ff.

[6] Hes. Op., 336 f.: ἔρδειν (do, bring, sacrifice) ἱερ' ἀθανάτοισι θεοῖσιν ἁγνῶς καὶ καθαρῶς; Leges Graecorum Sacrae, II, 1 (1906), n. 49, 2 f. (ed. L. Ziehen): Access to the sanctuary: [μηδένα] ἀκάθαρτον προσάγειν. On vessels (περιρραντήρια) at the entrance to the sanctuary for purification, Wächter, 7. Washings before sacrifice, 12; clean hands at prayer, Hom. Od., 2, 261; Stengel, 156.

[7] On purifications and expiations, Stengel, 155 ff.; Diog. L., VIII, 33: τὴν δ' ἁγνείαν εἶναι ... καθαρεύειν ἀπό τε κήδους (funeral) καὶ λέχους (marriage bed) καὶ μιάσματος παντός. Hesych., *s.v.* ἁγνεύειν· καθαρεύειν ἀπό τε ἀφροδισίων καὶ ἀπὸ νεκροῦ. Plat. Leg., IX, 865a b. καθαρός and → ἁγνός are synon. Williger, *op. cit.,* 46 thinks καθαρός is the older term for cultic purity. The word is already a religious term in Hom. Il., 16, 228 ff. The most serious defilement is by shedding blood. Even the unintentional murderer needs expiation (Il., 23, 85 ff.; Demosth., 23, 61 [p. 639]): so Stengel, 157, though Rohde, *Psyche,* I[9, 10] (1925), 271, contests this as regards the Homeric period.

the concept of purity. Positive purity of life can be sought as well as freedom from demons. [8] Philosophical thinking in particular helps to separate the concept of cleanness from the cultic sphere and to set it in the spiritual sphere of personal morality. [9] Even in the cultic sphere the demand for moral purity is finally recognised as a presupposition for drawing near to deity. [10]

3. In OT Religion.

The OT, too, reflects the same general development. Traces of primitive thinking may be found in the view that birth, [11] death, [12] and sex life [13] are linked with the demonic and bring defilement (טָמֵא and טֻמְאָה; → ἀκάθαρτος). Uncleanness is not just a lack of cleanness. It is a power which positively defiles. In particular, anything associated with a foreign cult, or hostile to Yahweh, is unclean. This is the primary origin of the OT law of meats. Animals are disqualified which were once totem animals or animals dedicated to a god. [14] In only a few cases do aesthetic and hygienic considerations underlie the declarations of uncleanness. [15] Palestine is Yahweh's own land ; hence it is clean. [16] Other countries belong to other gods and are unclean. The laws of cleanness reflect the conflict of the religion of Yahweh against earlier or surrounding paganism. Because the religion of Israel emphasises so strongly the holiness of God (→ ἅγιος), it develops the concept of purity with corresponding energy. The Law works out a whole series of regulations. Some purifications are preparatory. They set man in the necessary state of holiness for encounter with God. [17] Some are expiatory. They restore forfeited purity by lustrations. [18] The washings are of particular importance. [19] Where there is severe impurity, a burnt offering may be used, or the water of purification may

---

[8] On the Orphics and Pythagoreans, Stengel, 681 f.

[9] Pind. Pyth., 5, 2 : καθαρὰ ἀρετή ; Plat. Resp., VI, 496d : καθαρὸς ἀδικίας τε καὶ ἀνοσίων ἔργων ; Xenoph. Cyrop., VIII, 7, 23 : ἔργα καθαρὰ καὶ ἔξω τῶν ἀδίκων. Acc. to Plat. Leg., IV, 716e τὴν ψυχὴν ὁ κακός is unclean. Acc. to Epict. Diss., II, 18, 19 κάθαρσις ψυχῆς consists in the acceptance of ὀρθὰ δόγματα ; IV, 11, 8 ; II, 22, 34 ff.

[10] Leg. Gr. Sacr. (→ n. 6), n. 91, 9 ff.: [παρ]ιέναι εἰς τὸ ἱερὸν . . . [χε]ρσὶν καὶ ψυχῇ καθα[ρᾷ]. Inscr. on the temple of Aesculapius in Epidaurus : Only he who is clean may enter the fragrant temple ; but he alone is clean who thinks on holy things (ἁγνείη δ' ἐστὶ φρονεῖν ὅσια, cf. J. Bernays, Theophr. Schrift über die Frömmigkeit (1866), 67. Initiation into the Eleusinian mysteries required purifications which are very similar to those of the guilty, Stengel, 180. But here, too, moral purity seems not to have been demanded until a later period, Orig. Cels., III, 59 : . . . ὅστις ἁγνὸς ἀπὸ παντὸς μύσους καὶ ὅτῳ ἡ ψυχὴ οὐδὲν σύνοιδε κακὸν καὶ ὅτῳ εὖ καὶ δικαίως βεβίωται, Wächter, 9 f.

[11] Lv. 12.

[12] Nu. 19:11 ; Dt. 26:14 ; Jer. 16:5 ff. Cf. Stade-Bertholet, I, 138 ; Döller, 125 ff.

[13] 1 S. 21:4 ff.; 2 S. 11:4 ; Lv. 12 ; 15:18 ; Stade-Bertholet, I, 140 ; Döller, 10 ff.; 64 ff.

[14] Lv. 11 ; Dt. 14:7 ff.; Stade-Bertholet, I, 136, 138 ; Döller, 168 ff. The pig is an ancient Canaanite domestic and sacrificial animal. It was sacred in Babylon, Cyprus and Syria (Aphrodite, Luc. Syr. Dea, 54). Mice, snakes and hares were used in magic and were thought to bear demonic powers, Eichrodt, op. cit., I, 61. The camel was typhonic for the Egyptians, and the dog was a sacred animal in Phoenicia, Babylon, Egypt and Persia, Döller, 190 f.

[15] E.g., reptiles, Lv. 11:29 f.; J. Hehn, RGG, IV, 1844.

[16] Am. 7:17 ; Ez. 4:12 f.

[17] Ex. 19:10 ; Nu. 8:15 ; 2 Εσδρ. 6:20.

[18] Lv. 16:1 ff., 19, 23 ff.; Ez. 39:12 ; 2 Ch. 29:15 ; 34:3, 8 ; Stade-Bertholet, I, 142 f.; Eichrodt, I, 60 ff.

[19] Lv. 11:32 ; 15:7, 16 ff. Flowing water has greater power, Lv. 14:5 ; 15:13.

be replaced by sacred things.[20] The impurity may be transmitted to an animal which takes it away.[21] As the holiness of Yahweh acquires moral content, so the ritual purity demanded of believers becomes a symbol of inner moral purity.[22] To be distinguished from the unclean thing indwelt by autonomous power is the profane thing (חֹל, → κοινόν) which is open to general use.[23]

While the concept of ritual purity is strong in the cultus, the ethical side is developed by the prophets. This can give rise to a clash of values. The prophets rate ethical purity far above that which is purely cultic.[24] Hence the prophets prepare the way for the religion of Jesus. The requirement of cultic purity had inner value and justification as a symbol pointing to something more profound. The fault of later Jewish religion was to give this requirement preference over the more inward concerns of religion,[25] and to prove incapable of expelling the primitive element. This led to a fatal distortion and ossification.

In Hellenistic Judaism there is an inclination to spiritualise the older cultic concept of purity. The importance of the ritual is depreciated in favour of the ethical and spiritual. Contact with the Gk. world influenced this development. The older ritual demand was not rejected. There was common consent, however, that the true value of purity is within. Hence in the LXX καθαρός is often used both for terms which primarily express ritual cleanness (e.g., טָהוֹר, Gn. 7:2; Lv. 4:12) and yet also for those which denote moral innocence (e.g., זַךְ, Gn. 44:10; Job 4:7). Josephus accepts as justifiable the older requirements.[26] But the purity which God requires goes deeper; it is a purity of soul and conscience.[27] This true purity is achieved through uprightness.[28]

The same observation applies to Test. XII[29] and Ep. Ar.[30] In Philo especially there is a complete ethical spiritualising of the concept of purity. The OT requirements are still upheld,[31] but their significance is now predominantly symbolical. Inward, moral purity is God's demand.[32]

Hauck

---

[20] Ashes of a red heifer, Nu. 19:9 ff.; fire and water, 31:22 ff. Water, fire and blood are originally counter-magic, Döller, op. cit., 261.
[21] Lv. 14:7 (sacrifice of birds for the leper); 15:13 ff.; 16:21 ff. (goat on the Day of Atonement).
[22] Both in Dt. (21:6 ff.) and the Holiness Code (Lv. 17-26).
[23] Ez. 22:26; 42:20; → ἅγιος, I, 89.
[24] Is. 1:15 ff.; Ps. 51:2; Jer. 33:8 (Ιερ. 40:8).
[25] Cf. esp. the Essenes, who are καθαροὶ ἄνδρες, 8th Book of Moses, 66 f., in A. Dieterich, *Abraxas* (1891), 141, 143; on their rites cf. Jos. Bell., 2, 128 ff.; Schürer, II, 566 ff.
[26] μὴ καθαρός of the leper, Ant., 9, 74; σάρκας ποιῆσαι καθαράς (to purify from blood), 6, 120; Ap., 1, 282; Ant., 4, 298 (στρατός); expiation of the temple, Bell., 1, 153; of the city, 6, 110 (opp. μίασμα); cf. Schl. Theol. d. Judt., 130 f.
[27] Bell., 6, 48: (ψυχαὶ) τὰ μάλιστα κηλίδων (spots) ἢ μιασμάτων ... καθαραί. Even the μνήμη of sin represents a μίασμα and must be blotted out, Ant., 9, 261 f. Jos. prefers καθαίρειν to καθαρίζειν, though he has the latter, e.g., at Ant., 10, 70; 12, 286.
[28] This is why Jos. praises John the Baptist, who describes his baptism as pleasing to God only when it is used, not as a prayer for the averting of sins (1 P. 3:21; Wnd. Pt., 73), but for the washing of the body. The soul must first be cleansed by uprightness, Ant., 18, 117 (μὴ ἐπί τινων ἁμαρτάδων παραιτήσει χρωμένων, ἀλλ᾽ ἐφ᾽ ἁγνείᾳ τοῦ σώματος, ἅτε δὴ καὶ τῆς ψυχῆς δικαιοσύνῃ προεκκεκαθαρμένης, Brandt, op. cit., 80 f., 87).
[29] Test. B. 6:5: ἡ ἀγαθὴ διάνοια ... ἔχει καθαρὰν διάθεσιν; 8:2: καθαρὸς νοῦς οὐκ ἔχει μιασμόν, 8:3; Test. R. 4:8: (καθαρίζειν) τὰς ἐννοίας ἀπὸ πάσης πορνείας.
[30] Ep. Ar., 2: ψυχῆς καθαρὰ διάθεσις; 234: καθαρότης ψυχῆς.
[31] Det. Pot. Ins., 20; Vit. Cont., 66; Spec. Leg., IV, 110.
[32] Deus Imm., 132; βελτιοῦσθαι τὰ ἔνδον καὶ ἐξ ἀκαθάρτων καθαρὰ γίνεσθαι; Ebr., 143; Plant., 64: ὁ τελείως ἐκκεκαθαρμένος νοῦς; Ebr., 125 (τοῦ συνειδότος); Leg. Gaj., 165; Vit. Mos., II, 24 (διάνοια); Ebr., 28.

C. Clean and Unclean outside the NT : Part II : Judaism.

In the Talmudic and Midrashic literature, as in the OT, the terms "clean" and "unclean" are used in both a cultic and an ethical sense. Most of the statements can be grouped accordingly, though the distinction between the cultic and the ethical is fluid.

The Palestinian ideal of the sanctifying of the everyday [33] is the impulse behind the creation of the ritual prescriptions which, on the basis of the OT laws of purity, affect the total life of the Jew.

1. Cultic Uncleanness.

a. For Judaism Levitical uncleanness [34] is something which clings to the unclean man or thing and which can be transferred to others. Distinction is made between the source of uncleanness (אַב הַטֻּמְאָה) [35] and what is infected (וְלַד הַטֻּמְאָה), Toharot, 1, 5. Among the unclean are reptiles, those defiled by the dead, [36] fallen beasts, normal sexual issues, those afflicted with issues, their excretions, couches and beds, also lepers and dead bones, Kelim, 1, 1-4. The corpse is partly a simple centre of uncleanness and partly the principal source (אֲבִי אֲבוֹת הַטֻּמְאָה). [37] According to distance from the source there are first, second, third and fourth degrees of uncleanness (רִאשׁוֹן לְטֻמְאָה etc.). Men, vessels and clothes are only infected directly, and are of the first degree. Hands (Jad., 3, 1), profane meats and drinks (חֻלִּין), are susceptible to second degree infection, consecrated things of lesser rank, e.g., first-fruits to the priests (תרומה) to the third degree, and sacrifices to the fourth. [38] The intensity of infection weakens a stage with each transmission. If a man or object is defiled only to the degree that he no longer infects his own class but a Levitically more susceptible class, he is called "unfit" (פָּסוּל). [39]

b. Transmission of uncleanness is by touch (מַגָּע), carrying (מַשָּׂא), pressing (sitting or lying etc., מִדְרָס), the entry of what is unclean into the empty space (אֲוִיר) [40] of a vessel,

---

[33] Cf. Bousset-Gressm., 127.

[34] טֻמְאָה; cf. esp. the sixth Mishnah ordinance ; S. Lv., 11-15; S. Nu., 1 on 5:1-4; 125-130 on 19:11-22; 157 f. on 31:19-24; cf. K. G. Kuhn, *S. Nu. übers.* (1933 ff.); Schürer, II, 560 ff.; Moore, II, 74 ff.

[35] The translation "principal uncleanness" (cf. Levy Wört., I, *s.v.* אָב; Schürer, II, 561) is misleading.

[36] He who has touched a dead man is אַב הַטֻּמְאָה. Vessels, except earthen, which touch a dead man have the same effect as the corpse. Hence he who touches them is also אַב הַטֻּמְאָה. Articles which come into contact with someone defiled by a dead man, or by vessels which are infected by a dead man, are אַב הַטֻּמְאָה. But earthen vessels, or eating vessels, which come into contact with a dead man are infected only to the first degree. The corpse is then אַב הַטֻּמְאָה and the infected objects רִאשׁוֹן לטמאה; cf. Ohalot, 1, 1-3, Obadia of Bertinoro (cf. Strack Einl., 159) on Kelim, 1, 1.

[37] So Rashi, e.g., bBQ, 2b : מי שנגע במת הוי אב הטומאה דמת עצמו אבי אבות הטומאה הוא, but → n. 36.

[38] Cf. E. Baneth, *Mischna,* II (1927), 171, n. 24 f.

[39] E.g., if a man has eaten unclean bread, he is unfit to eat the flesh of sacrifice or consecrated food ; he must bathe in order to be fit again (כָּשֵׁר). On eating unclean meats, *v.* Er., 8, 2 and Baneth, *Mischna,* II, 110, n. 18.

[40] Also אֲוִיר, Gr. ἀήρ.

or of a leper into a house (בִּיאָה),[41] of being under the same roof as a corpse (אָהִיל).[42] In addition the seven liquids (מַשְׁקִין or מַכְשִׁירִין), and dry, and as such immune, means of nourishment, if mingled with them, can also make capable of defilement.[43]

c. The degree of uncleanness means exclusion from the corresponding consecrated thing, if of lesser degree, and sacrifice as well as the prescribed purifications, if of higher. There is a systematic presentation in Kelim, 1, 5. Here are ten stages of uncleanness. 1. If the prescribed interval for purification has run out,[44] but the required sin offering has not been brought (מְחֻסַּר כִּפּוּרִים), a priest may not partake of the offering (אָסוּר בַּקֹּדֶשׁ), though he is allowed teruma and tithes. 2. If one has taken a bath and the required interval of purification (up to evening) has not expired (טְבוּל יוֹם), only tithes are allowed.[45] 3. One who has incurred nightly pollution (בַּעַל קְרִי) is barred from all consecrated things.[46] 4. One who has lived with a woman in her period (בּוֹעֵל נִדָּה) is himself a source of uncleanness.[47] 5. One who is afflicted with an issue, and who defiles his bed and seat[48] after two discharges, must wash in flowing water, but does not have to sacrifice. 6. After three discharges he must also sacrifice. 7. One who is cast out by the priest under suspicion of leprosy (Lv. 13:4-5, 21, 26, 31-33) defiles the house if he enters (בִּיאָה). But he need not let his hair be wild, or tear his clothes, or shave, or offer birds. 8. A confirmed leper must do these things. 9. A member which can be regarded as a dead bone brings defilement if touched or carried.[49] 10. If, however, there is so much flesh on it that healing might have been possible on the original body, it defiles like a corpse anything under the same roof with it (אֹהֶל). Even Palestine, which is more holy than Gentile countries, is divided into ten degrees of holiness, so that the unclean may be refused entry according to the holiness of a place, Kelim, 1, 5-9. Thus lepers are shut out of walled cities ; a dead body may be taken out of a city but not brought in again ; those afflicted with issues, also menstruous women and women after child-birth, may not approach the temple hill ; Gentiles[50] and those defiled by a corpse may not come into the inner courts of the temple ; a טְבוּל יוֹם is not allowed to enter the court of women ; one who has gone through the prescribed ritual but omitted the sin offering may not enter the court of Israelites etc.

d. To what extent an object can be defiled depends not only on the kind of infection but also on the make and material. Thus shallow vessels of wood, leather, bone or glass cannot be defiled, whereas deeper ones can, Kelim, 2, 1. Both shallow and deeper metal vessels can be defiled, 11, 1. The extent of defilement also varies. Deep vessels of wood, leather, bone and glass are made unclean on all sides, whereas earthen or bitumen

---

41 "House" in the broadest sense, v. Obadia of Bertinoro on Kelim, 1, 4. On leprosy cf. Strack-B., IV, 745 ff. (Exc.).

42 אֹהֶל, "tent," in the broadest sense, e.g., even the foliage of a tree.

43 Makshirin, 6, 4 : dew, water, wine, oil, blood, milk, honey. On the strength of defilement through liquids, cf. Baneth, Mischna, II, 171 f., n. 26.

44 E.g., one cured of leprosy ; cf. Obadia of Bertinoro, ad loc. Or one who has been defiled by a corpse (Nu. 19:11).

45 טְבוּל יוֹם defiles to the third degree, and thus makes unfit for teruma. What is meant by tithes is מַעֲשֵׂר רִאשׁוֹן, which applies like חֻלִּין, and which is allowed to one unclean to the second degree : Tebul jom, 4, 1 and Obadia, ad loc.

46 For he is רִאשׁוֹן לְטֻמְאָה, Obadia, on Kelim, 1, 1.

47 He defiles his whole bed to the first degree by lying on it, Kelim, 1, 3 and Obadia, ad loc.

48 Infection as in the case of בועל נדה (→ supra) by מִדְרָס (→ supra).

49 מַגָּע and מַשָּׂא.

50 Cf. Ac. 21:28 and the prohibition on the temple gate, Ditt. Or., II, 598.

vessels are made unclean only on the inside, 2, 1. The hollow at the base is defiled, but the exterior is immune. On the other hand, in the case of vessels which are defiled on all sides, distinction must be made between the exterior and the handle.[51] Thus we read in Kelim, 25, 8 that if someone has taken up such a vessel, he need not fear his hands becoming unclean so long as he has taken it by its handle. To guard against uncleanness, one must take note of the material and lid of vessels. Kelim, 10, 1: "The following vessels, which may be sealed with a good lid,[52] protect their contents : vessels of cowdung, bitumen, stone, earth, clay, fish-bone or fish-skin, the bone or skin of a sea animal, and pure vessels of wood protect (against uncleanness)."

Other objects in common use may differ according to form, material and use. Thus Kelim, 24, 1 distinguishes three kinds of shield : 1. the round shield, which can be defiled by pressure, since soldiers use it to sit on as well as to fight with ;[53] 2. the jousting shield, which can be defiled by contact with a corpse (→ n. 36); 3. the small Arabian shield, which is immune.

The question of clean and unclean also plays a role in economic life. Raw leather can become capable of defilement according to the use to which the owner decides to put it. It takes on the qualities of the object which it is to become. But it is not yet subject to the laws of defilement while in the possession of the tanner, since he is not the final owner, Kelim, 26, 8.

e. Apart from the Essenes, other Jewish and half-Jewish groups were deficient from the standpoint of the Pharisaic view of purity.[54] The clothes of an 'am ha' arez defile a Pharisee if he sits on them :[55] Chag., 2, 7. The wife of a Chaber may help the wife of an 'am ha' arez in baking only so long as she does not add water to the flour,[56] Shebi, 5, 2 (Git., 5, 9). Samaritan women are unclean from childhood, Nidda, 4, 1.[57] Their men have the degree of impurity of those who co-habit with a menstruous woman, loc. cit. (→ n. 47). The wives of Sadducees are like those of Samaritans if they live in the old way ; if they change, they are like full Jewesses, ibid., 4, 2.

The Gentile is unclean. He cannot visit the temple (→ 419). Vessels and objects used in idolatry are forbidden to Jews (e.g., AZ, 2, 3 ff.). Houses must not be built in close proximity to a temple (AZ, 3, 6) etc. Intercourse with non-Jews is defined as follows (AZ, 5, 12): "If a Jew buys a vessel from a Gentile, he must cleanse it by washing what is usually washed, by scalding what is usually scalded, by heating what is usually heated."

f. In apparent opposition to what we have said is the Rabbinic statement that the Holy Scriptures defile the hands, Jad, 3, 5. The term is a technical one for the Canon. The idea of defilement is supposed to have arisen as follows.[58] The scrolls were kept with the teruma, but there was a fear of their being eaten by mice. Hence, to separate them from the teruma, they were declared unclean, bShab., 14a par. This later story is a legendary explanation of an older fact. The original point is different. Clean and un-

---

[51] בֵּית הַצְּבִיעָה.

[52] בְּצָמִיד פָּתִיל; on this cf. Kuhn, S. Nu. übers., 481, n. 70.

[53] E.g., if the soldier has an issue, he defiles it by מִדְרָס, → 418.

[54] Schürer, II, 664; Bousset-Gressm., 460; EJ, III, s.v.

[55] Chag. works out a cultic order : 1. 'am ha'arez ; 2. Pharisee ; 3. priest ; 4. priest offering sacrifice ; each group defiles the next higher by מִדְרָס.

[56] Water makes the flour capable of receiving the uncleanness of the wife of the 'am ha'arez and of thus affecting the wife of the Chaber, → n. 43.

[57] They are always נִדָּה.

[58] So Levy Wört., II, s.v. טמא; also Str.-B., IV, 433 f. But cf. Kuhn (→ I, 100) for a more correct interpretation.

clean originally express the same situation, namely, that something is devoted to the deity, taboo. Later, with less gloomy views of deity, the taboo concept comes to express distance. An unclean man is banned from the sanctuary. But only in a few cases does this come through consecrated things.[59] This is why the Scriptures can cause defilement. Already Jochanan b. Zakkai is ignorant of the true point of this; hence his helplessness in face of the vexing question of the Sadducees, Jad., 4, 6. We can thus understand why a later generation advanced a legendary, but rational, explanation based on temple practice. That this is in fact a secondary explanation is shown by the persistence of the taboo concept in bMeg., 32 a par: "He who takes up a book of the Torah with bare hands[60] will be buried naked."[61]

2. Cultic Cleansing.

To restore Levitical cleanness it is necessary to cleanse by water. Distinction is made between 1. washing (נְטִילָה); 2. sprinkling (הַזָּיָה); 3. bathing (טְבִילָה). In certain cases d. a sin-offering is also required (כַּפָּרָה). Vessels are cleansed by water; they are dipped, scalded or heated. But some utensils may also have to be destroyed, e.g., Kelim, 2, 1; 11, 1. In this case the damage is so great that further use is impossible, Kelim, 17 passim. In the act of purification regard must also be had to the period of impurity (7 days in the case of death, Nu. 19:11).

Since water is the most important means of purification, we may briefly review the six stages of water purification according to Miq., 1, 4-8. 1. Water from ponds, cisterns and hollows, stagnant reservoir water or bath water, if less than the prescribed 40 seahs, is adequate, if not defiled, for preparing the gift of dough (חַלָּה) and for ritual washing of the hands; 2. replenished reservoir water may be used for the priestly tribute (תְּרוּמָה) and for washing the hands; 3. bath water of more than 40 seahs cleanses both men and vessels; 4. a little spring to which drawn water has been added is like a bath if collected, but otherwise like a pure spring which cleanses vessels irrespective of the amount of water; 5. מַיִם מוּכִין (meaning uncertain, perhaps "water from mineral springs") cleanses if flowing; 6. flowing water is the most effective of all; it can cleanse those who have an issue, can be used to sprinkle the leper, and is suitable for replenishing the water of expiation.

The most common act of cultic cleansing is washing the hands (נְטִילַת יָדַיִם).[62] This takes place before grace at meals. The water used before the opening grace is called מַיִם רִאשׁוֹנִים, and that used before the closing grace מַיִם אַחֲרוֹנִים. According to R. Idi b. Abin the first is a Rabbinic command (מִצְוָה), the second is commanded in the Torah (חוֹבָה). There can also be a cleansing of the hands during the meal, but this is not commanded; it is thus voluntary (רְשׁוּת).[63] Levitical cleansing of the hands is also necessary at times of prayer. Perfectly correct recitation of the schema', according to R. Jochanan (→ n. 61), should take place as follows. After the discharge of necessary tasks, one should wash the hands, put on the tefillin,

---

[59] Bousset-Gressm., 147. Cf. Lv. 16:4, 24.

[60] עָרוֹם: a play on words; Raschi expounds: בלא מטפחת סביב ספר תורה, "one should rather take the Torah in the cover into one's hand." cf. J. Leipoldt, Gegenwartsfragen in der nt.-lichen Wissenschaft (1935), 22.

[61] Author, Jochanan b. Nappacha, c. 250 A.D.

[62] Hands can be defiled to the second degree.

[63] bChul., 105 a par.; cf. also the material in Str.-B., I, 697.

and then say the "Hear, O Israel" and pray, bBer., 15a. If water were not available in Palestine, sand could be used, and the custom was not commonly practised in Babylon, *loc. cit.*

If in the moment of prayer a Jew finds himself in a state of Levitical impurity, he should not pray as usual, Ber., 3, 4 : "If someone has defiled himself over night, he recollects (merely) the 'Hear O Israel' in his heart. At meals he says (merely) the grace after ;" 3, 5 : "If someone is saying the prayer of eighteen petitions, and he is defiled by a discharge, he breaks (it) off." [64]

Levitical purity is also required for the study of the Law, but the Rabbis are not agreed as to the rules, bBer., 22a. As may be seen from the conduct of a pupil of Jehuda b. Bathyra (*c.* 110 A.D.), there was hesitation to pronounce the words of the Torah in a state of Levitical uncleanness, bBer., 22a. [65]

3. The Attitude of the Rabbis to the Law.

The attitude of the Rabbis to the laws which burden and affect the whole of life is summed up by Jochanan b. Zakkai in Pesikt., 40b (Buber): "In your life, it is not the corpse that defiles (מְטַמֵּא) and not the water that cleanses (מְטַהֲרִים); it is an ordinance of the King of all kings. God has said : ... No man has the right to transgress my statutes ..." [66] We must suppose, however, that this attitude was reached by only a few. The more common, popular opinion was that all uncleanness belongs to the realm of death and demons, and that apotropaic means may be used to remove it.

Sometimes, if only in a few places, there is a freer attitude to the Law. According to bBer., 19b it is customary, for the honour of a mourner who is in the lead, to follow even on an unclean way [67] if this is taken by him. It is told of Eleazar b. Zaddoq (*c.* 110 A.D.) that in his day one would have leapt to meet Jewish kings even over coffins with corpses. According to Chaninah, the priestly leader (*c.* 70 A.D.), sorrow for the destruction of God's house must be so great that one should be ready to forego a bath and to endure Levitical uncleanness, bTaan., 13a. In general, however, the stringency of the Law, and inner obligation to it, are hereby shown to be all the stronger. A pupil who sat under Jehuda b. Bathyra was afraid to read because of Levitical uncleanness. The Rabbi said that he should not be afraid, and should let his words shine forth, since the words of the Law, like fire, cannot be defiled, bBer., 22a. The pupil represented the common view. The teacher was more liberal, but only in so far as he ascribed to the Law the same purifying force as fire. He did not reach the religious height of Jochanan b. Zakkai. This can be seen from a second incident. In contrast to the strict Aqiba, who would not allow anyone defiled by pollution to enter the house of instruction, Jehuda b. Bathyra would at least allow the study of practical wisdom (דֶּרֶךְ אֶרֶץ). When he himself was Levitically unclean, his students asked him to lecture on

---

[64] If possible one should have cleansed himself from Levitical impurity in the morning, cf. Ber., 3, 5b.

[65] This is the common practice.

[66] Cf. the material in Str.-B., I, 719. On the meaning and interpretation of the saying, cf. esp. A. Schlatter, "Jochanan Ben Zakkai," BFTh, 3, 4 (1899), 41 ff. and K. G. Kuhn, *S. Nu. übers.*, 591, n. 53.

[67] What is meant is a way on which there is a grave ; Rashi : [דרך] שישבה קבר.

practical wisdom. "He descended, bathed, and only then taught them. They turned to him : Did not our teacher instruct us that he who is affected by a sexual issue should study *halakhoth* of practical wisdom ? He replied : If I lighten the Law for others, I make it heavier for myself," bBer., 22a. The saying displays the inner bondage to the Law for which any movement of liberation is too great a burden of conscience.

4. Inward Purity.

We should give a distorted picture if we did not mention the concept of moral purity in Rabbinic Judaism. The fact that we can give only a summary presentation should not deceive us as to the breadth of this stream in the writings of the Talmud and Midrash.

Man has received his soul pure from God, and he is responsible for keeping it so, e.g., bNidda, 30b, also bShab., 152b : "As God hath given thee the spirit in purity, thou must give it back in purity." [68] Hence Rabba b. Nachmani (bBM, 86a) is lauded by a heavenly voice at his death : "Hail to thee ..., that thy body was pure (טָהוֹר), and that thy soul has departed with (the word) טָהוֹר." [69] Joab is extolled in bSanh., 49a : "As the wilderness is pure (מְנֻקֶּה) from robbery and forbidden marriage, so the house of Joab was pure (מְנֻקֶּה) from robbery and forbidden marriage."

The demand for inner purity covers the whole of life. R. Meïr (c. 150 A.D.) said : "Keep thy mouth from every sin, and purify and sanctify thyself from all sin and guilt; for I shall be with thee everywhere," bBer., 17a. [70] One should draw to oneself the spirit of purity, not of impurity, bSanh., 65b. As Scripture speaks of intimate things without giving offence, so man should speak only in pure expressions (בְּלָשׁוֹן נְקִיָּה), bPes., 3a ; [71] for the sin of unclean speech (בְּעֲווֹן נַבְלוּת פֶּה) brings many evils and constantly renewed oppressions, and the young men of the haters of Israel [72] die, and widows and orphans cry and are not heard," bShab., 33a. [73] It should be noted finally that a court of justice must be pure (מְנֻקִּין), both in respect of righteousness and of origin, bSanh., 36b.

Rudolf Meyer

D. Clean and Unclean in the NT.

It is of the essence of NT religion that the older, ritual concept of purity is not merely transcended, but rejected as non-obligatory. The idea of material impurity

---

[68] Cf. Str.-B., I, 719.

[69] But cf. bSanh., 68a : "He was pure (טהור), and his soul departed in purity (בטהרה).

[70] Cf. Str.-B., I, 719.

[71] → n. 70; לָשׁוֹן נְקִיָּה, euphemism, in the sense of more decorous mode of expression.

[72] שׂוֹנְאֵי יִשְׂרָאֵל is used instead of the usual יִשְׂרָאֵל. When it is necessary to say something unfavourable or hostile or menacing concerning Israel, the opposite of Israel ("haters of Israel") is often used in Rabbinic lit. in order apotropaically to avoid the dangerous force of such a word. The meaning here is that the punishment for the sin of unclean speech is that the men of Israel will not grow old, but will die in early manhood and leave widows and orphans [K. G. Kuhn].

[73] Eleazar b. Jehuda of Bartotha ; on the textual tradition cf. Bacher, *Tannaiten*, I², 441, n. 4.

drops away. Religious and moral purity replaces ritual and cultic. Hellenistic Judaism presses on to a spiritual concept of purity, but it still recognises and maintains the ancient demands. Jesus, however, opposes the older view of cleanness (cf. the prophets). The full implications of this new position are worked out in the apostolic period, especially by Paul. The NT use of the word καθαρός reflects this new development. Since the battle for a new and spiritual view of purity is still being fought, we have to test the meaning of the term at every point.

1. Physical Cleanness.

This sense is present in passages which follow the traditional view, regarding that which is physically clean as adapted for cultic (Hb. 10:22 : ὕδωρ), ritual (Mt. 23:26 : ποτήριον), or generally respectful (Mt. 27:59 : σινδών) use. In the context of NT thought the statements which stand closest to Jewish use are those of Rev. regarding the new Jerusalem. What is physically clean is fit and adapted for sacred use and for intercourse with God.[74] On the other hand, that which is profane (κοινόν) and ungodly (ὁ ποιῶν βδέλυγμα καὶ ψεῦδος) is kept out of the sacred city (Mt. 21:27).

2. Cultic Cleanness and Cleansing.

The term has this sense when used of the ritual cleansing of vessels according to Pharisaic ordinance (Mt. 23:25), of cleansing from leprosy, which restores the person cured as a full member of the community of salvation (Mt. 8:2, 3 par.; 10:8 par.; 11:5 par.; Lk. 4:27; 17:14, 17), or of blood as a recognised means of cultic cleansing (Hb. 9:22). In the conflict concerning abstinence from meats in the Christian community Paul asserts the basic and general religious cleanness of all created things (R. 14:20 : πάντα μὲν καθαρά; cf. v. 14 : οὐδὲν κοινὸν δι' ἑαυτοῦ). Nothing is able of itself to separate man from God. From the religious standpoint of the NT, then, the righteous may eat any kind of food. Peter's experience in Ac. yields the same insight. God Himself declares unclean animals to be clean (καθαρίζει declarative) and demands that they be enjoyed (Ac. 10:15; 11:9). In the new time of salvation God Himself removes the ancient distinction between clean and unclean. Peter has to draw the deduction as concerns animals on the one side and the religious position of the Gentiles on the other. The purification of the righteous is not through ritual measures. It is through faith in the sphere of personal life, Ac. 15:9 : τῇ πίστει καθαρίσας τὰς καρδίας αὐτῶν. Perhaps the Evangelist Mark — or a glossator — ascribes this advance to Jesus Himself in the difficult verse Mk. 7:19 (καθαρίζων πάντα τὰ βρώματα). As the verse stands, it certainly implies that Jesus declared all meats clean.[75] In the Past., which draw up rules for the community on the basis of the insights of Paul, the principle that all things are clean by creation is formulated in such a way as to apply to those who are religiously clean, i.e., to members of the salvation community who have put their whole lives under the rule of God, Tt. 1:15. To the heretics who are opposed, and to unbelievers, whose inner being (διάνοια, νοῦς) is stained, nothing is clean, i.e., fit for God. Purity, then, is in the person, not the thing. In 1 Tm. 4:5

---

[74] The material used for the new Jerusalem (Rev. 21:18, 21); the material of which the garments of the saints (19:8, 14) and angels (15:6) are made.

[75] Cf. Kl. Mk., 80.

meats are sanctified (ἁγιάζεται) by the grace pronounced at meals, and we need not fear to enjoy them.

3. Moral Purity.

According to the judgment of Jesus the ritual or cultic purity sought by the Jews is quite inadequate, since it is concerned only with externalities, Mt. 23:25 f.; Lk. 11:41. [76] The purity of the NT community is personal and moral by nature. It consists in full and unreserved self-offering to God which renews the heart and rules out any acceptance of what is against God. Those who are pure in heart in this way are called to participate in the kingdom of God, Mt. 5:8. This purity of heart is far above the cleanness of hands which was so greatly valued by the Pharisees. It alone counts before God. Neither in the Synoptists [77] nor in Paul, however, is Jesus' new concept of purity made a positive guiding motif of the new piety. Jesus speaks of obedience, Paul of sanctification, and neither of purity of life. This motif first comes to the fore in the Past., Hb., Jn., also Jm. and 1 Pt., i.e., in writings which were strongly influenced either by opposition to the OT cultus (Hb.) or by the terminology of Hellenistic Judaism. Opposition to the inadequacy of purely cultic purity is found in the admonitions of Jm. when he describes practical love and the avoidance of worldliness as true, pure and unspotted religion (1:27) and when he says that the sinner must cleanse his hands and sanctify his heart if he is truly to draw near to God (4:7, 8; cf. Is. 1:16 f.). In a general exhortation 1 Pt. 1:22 demands sanctification of soul and love out of a pure heart. [78] In Eph. 5:26 the symbolism of baptism is impressively used to portray the basic moral purification by Christ which binds our whole conduct (καθαρίσας τῷ λουτρῷ τοῦ ὕδατος ἐν ῥήματι, nowhere else in Pl.). [79] In particular, the death of Christ is seen from the standpoint of an efficacious sacrifice which expiates sin and creates a new purity for those who are pledged thereto. In virtue of the sacrificial death of Christ, Christians are a new and purified people for God's possession, able and willing to perform the corresponding works (Tt. 2:14; cf. 1 Jn. 1:7, 9). Like Hellenistic Judaism, the Past. speak of a pure heart (1 Tm. 1:5; 2 Tm. 2:22) and conscience (1 Tm. 3:9; 2 Tm. 1:3), i.e., the inward life of believers as cleansed from past sin and wholeheartedly directed to God. The word expresses the unreserved nature of the return to God and also the inner unity of a conscience which is no longer disturbed by the sense of guilt (cf. Ac. 18:6; 20:26).

---

[76] The form of the saying in Lk. may be due to a misreading of the Aram. original (Wellh. Lk., *ad loc.*): δότε ἐλεημοσύνην = וכי, whereas the καθάρισον of Mt. gives us דכו. According to Lk. only the benevolent giving away of what we have (τὰ ἐνόντα) gives a comprehensive and true purity. Cf. Dalman WJ, I, 50 f.

[77] Apart from Past. and Eph., the root καθαρός, καθαρίζειν is found in Pl. only in the principle enunciated in R. 14:20 and in 2 C. 7:1. The Pauline authorship of the whole section 2 C. 6:14-7:1 is hotly debated, cf. A. Jülicher-E. Fascher, *Einleitung in d. NT*[7] (1931), 87 f. The terminology of spotting the flesh and spirit is generally alien to Paul, though it is common, e.g., in Herm. (s., 5, 7, 2 and 4; 6, 5 f.; m., 5, 1, 3). Naturally, only the human spirit can be stained in 2 C., by lack of love, contentiousness etc., Wnd. 2 K., 218.

[78] Acc. to the reading of א* C ℵ, as against BA vg : καθαρᾶς.

[79] ἐν ῥήματι, to be taken with τῷ λουτρῷ τοῦ ὕδατος, is a brief reminder (cf. 2:15) that it is the formula pronounced in baptism (→ ῥῆμα, efficacious word) which gives baptism its supramaterial efficacy. H. J. Holtzmann (A. Jülicher, W. Bauer), *Nt.liche Theologie*[2], I (1911), 455; W. Bousset, *Kyrios Christos*[2] (1921), 226 f., 287.

Hb. emphasises the superiority of the new covenant to the old. It uses the concept of purity in this connection. In contrast with the older ritual purity, the new moral purity is true and perfect purity (9:13). As in cultic religion, the cleansing power of blood is maintained (9:22). Cleansing and remission are synonymous. The author ventures to state that even the heavenly sanctuary needs to be cleansed (9:23). [80] But the blood of animals is obviously useless for this purpose. Cultic thinking thus demonstrates the necessity of the death of God's Son. The result of this supreme sacrifice is above temporal limitations (10:2 : ἅπαξ, valid once and for all). Materially, too, this is the supreme cleansing. Unlike that of the old covenant, it does not apply only to the body (9:13); it applies also to the conscience (9:14). The death of Christ accomplishes this cleansing from sins (1:3) and liberation from sinful impulses (9:14 : νεκρὰ ἔργα, which defile as contrasted with those done in the service of God). It thus gives access to holiness and enables man truly to live in the presence of God.

In the Johannine writings, too, the concept of purity is a leading motif (Jn. 3:25; 13:10 f.; 15:2 f.; 1 Jn. 1:7, 9). It is a basic thesis that the disciples of Jesus are clean (15:3; 13:10). The question arises what is the basis of this purity, whether it is absolutely valid, and whether it can be restored. According to the Gospel the disciples are clean because of their life-association with Jesus (15:3). His Word causes His Spirit, His higher divine mode of life, to enter into them effectively. They are thus made clean by the Word (15:3; 17:14 ff.). In 1 Jn. the death of Christ has power to wash away sin (1:7). In both Jn. and 1 Jn. the question of the full purity of Christians is discussed. It is affirmed absolutely in theory (Jn. 15:3; 1 Jn. 2:10; 3:6), but it is denied in relative and practical reality (1 Jn. 1:7 ff.; 2:1 ff.; Jn. 13:10 f.). In Jn. 13 the foot-washing has two meanings. On the one hand it is a parabolic action (6-11), on the other an example (12-17). The former sense expresses the fact that the full bath (ὁ λελουμένος, v. 10) of baptism accomplishes full cleansing. He who is baptised is clean (v. 10, cf. 3:6). [81] In distinction from other washings, baptism need not and cannot be repeated. The foot-washing (νίπτεσθαι of partial washing), however, symbolises the loving service which Jesus performs for His own by the daily forgiveness of minor offences (cf. 1 Jn. 5:16 : ἁμαρτία μὴ πρὸς θάνατον). The link with Jesus must be upheld if the disciple is to receive this service from his Master. In Rev., too, the purity of the new community is a leading motif. Here material and ritual cleanness is a symbol of perfect inward sanctity.

---

[80] Wnd. Hb., 85 assumes that by the law of correspondence (8:5) the sins of the people defiled the heavenly sanctuary too ; H. Strathmann (NT Deutsch, III, 113), however, thinks that the point of comparison is simply the general thought of the dedication or opening of the sanctuary. There is certainly no suggestion of defilement by warring angels (Col. 1:20) or by Satan (Lk. 10:18).

[81] The reading in ℵ vg Or : εἰ μὴ τοὺς πόδας, must be regarded as an erroneous attempt at harmonisation with ὅλος, cf. E. Hirsch, Das 4 Ev. (1936), 331 f. Brandt, op. cit., 121; A. Merx, Das Ev. des Joh. (1911), 350 f.; Zn. J., 539.

† ἀκάθαρτος, ἀκαθαρσία.

Of "physical,[1] cultic and moral impurity"[2] (→ καθαρός). According to antiquity these aspects are closely intertwined. Physical uncleanness takes cultic effect. ἀκάθαρτος can also signify an "unexpiated" state which leads to cultic difficulty.[3] The law demands cleansing by the expiation of wrong.[4] Moral uncleanness implies more broadly the defilement of the soul by all kinds of wrongdoing,[5] and more narrowly sexual profligacy.[6]

In the LXX ἀκάθαρτος and ἀκαθαρσία are used predominantly for טָמֵא and טֻמְאָה. They mostly signify cultic impurity (→ καθαρός), Lv. 5:3; 15:24; Ju. 13:7. On the older view, uncleanness clings to something like an infection, and renders it cultically unserviceable, e.g., objects, Lv. 7:21; animals, 11:1 ff.; places, 14:40, 45; Am. 7:17; vessels, Lv. 15:26; people, e.g., lepers, 13:11, 46; women after child-birth, 12:5; corpses, Nu. 9:6. Uncleanness comes by contact with something unclean, Nu. 19:13, 22. Sexual processes are a particular cause of defilement Thus Bathsheba must cleanse herself from her ἀκαθαρσία (not her adultery) after sinning with David, 2 S. 11:4. This view that the sexual makes cultically unclean is expressed in the rendering of נַבְלוּת (womanly shame), Hos. 2:12,[7] and נִדָּה (sexual discharge), Lv. 20:21, as ἀκαθαρσία. In addition, ἀκάθαρτος is particularly used for things connected with idolatrous cults, Ez. 36:17; Ιερ. 39:34; 2 Εσδρ. 6:21. It is the task of the priest to distinguish between clean and unclean, Lv. 10:10; Ez. 22:26, and by the prescribed rites to restore persons or things (e.g., the sanctuary, Lv. 16:16) to the cleanness which they have lost. Whereas the ritual and the moral are intertwined in the older period, in prophetic religion ἀκαθαρσία is purified and deepened to express the religious and moral inadequacy of unholy man before the holy God, Is. 6:5. This spiritualised concept of purity also occurs in Prv.; here ἀκαθαρσία is often used for תּוֹעֵבָה (e.g., 6:16); every παράνομος is ἀκάθαρτος before God, 3:32; 16:5; 20:10(13).

Hellenistic Judaism is characterised by the fact that on the one side it maintains the

---

ἀ κ ά θ α ρ τ ο ς κτλ. Bibl. → καθαρός, 413 n.

[1] P. Oxy., VI, 912, 26 : refuse, dung ; P. Lips., 16, 19 : letting of a house including θύραις καὶ κλεισὶ καὶ ἀπὸ πάσης ἀκαθαρσίας. Geoponica, XV, 3, 4 (ed. H. Beckh): of blossoms with δυσώδης; Plut. De Placitis Philosophorum, V, 6 (II, 905d): ἀκαθαρσία τῆς μήτρας; Luc. Lexiphanes, 19 : χρόνου ἤδη ἀκάθαρτον εἶναι αὐτῷ τὴν γυναῖκα.

[2] Demosth. Or., 21, 119; 25, 63 : with ὠμός, ἀσεβής, συκοφάντης; 37, 48 : with μιαρός; Suid., s.v. ἀκάθαρτος· ἁμαρτητικός. Epict. Diss., IV, 11, 5 (περὶ καθαριότητος), πρώτη οὖν καὶ ἀνωτάτω καθαρότης ἡ ἐν ψυχῇ γενομένη καὶ ὁμοίως ἀκαθαρσία ... IV, 11, 8 : ὥστε ψυχῆς μὲν ἀκαθαρσία δόγματα πονηρά, κάθαρσις δ' ἐμποίησις οἵων δεῖ δογμάτων.

[3] Plat. Leg., IX, 868a : ὅστις ἂν ἀκάθαρτος ὢν τὰ ἄλλα ἱερὰ μιαίνῃ.

[4] Ibid., 854b : ἐκ παλαιῶν καὶ ἀκαθάρτων ἀδικημάτων.

[5] Ibid., IV, 716e : ἀκάθαρτος τὴν ψυχὴν ὅ γε κακός, καθαρὸς δὲ ὁ ἐναντίος; Tim., 92b : τὴν ψυχὴν ὑπὸ πλημμελείας πάσης ἀκαθάρτως ἐχόντων; Plut. Lib. Educ., 17 (II, 12 f.): τοῦτον (sc. τὸν λόγον) δὲ ἀκάθαρτον ἡ πονηρία ποιεῖ τῶν ἀνθρώπων. Porphyr. of defilement through eating flesh, Abst., II, 45 : παθῶν ὄντες πλήρεις καὶ πρὸς ὀλίγον ἀπεχόμενοι τῶν ἀκαθάρτων (sc. animal) βρώσεων, μεστοὶ ὄντες ἀκαθαρσίας, δίκας τίνουσιν.

[6] Plut. De Othone, 2 (I, 1067ab): αὐτάς τε τὰς ἀνοσίους καὶ ἀρρήτους ἐν γυναιξὶ πόρναις καὶ ἀκαθάρτοις ἐγκυλινδήσεις.

[7] At Na. 3:6 ἀκαθαρσία is used for the verb נבל pi, "to vilify." The LXX alters the sense. The Mas is speaking of a monstrous and outrageous act, but the LXX speaks of the uncleanness (ἀκαθαρσία, א ἁμαρτία — on account of which the act is outrageous. It thus finds the cause of God's act in the conduct of man (→ I, 288) [Bertram].

cultic connection of the term. [8] This is shown in the use of the expression πνεῦμα ἀκάθαρτον for demons. Used in the LXX only at Zech. 13:2 (for רוּחַ הַטֻּמְאָה), this phrase is very common elsewhere. As beings which are outside the recognised cultus, demons are unclean (→ καθαρός). [9] On the other hand, Hellenistic Judaism gives evidence of a broadening and deepening of the concept along moral lines. [10] This is to become the dominant usage in Christianity. As in the NT, ἀκαθαρσία often denotes licentiousness. [11]

The NT uses ἀκάθαρτος and ἀκαθαρσία

1. in the sense of cultic impurity, e.g., Mt. 23:27 (the contents of graves). It adopts the common Jewish phrase πνεῦμα ἀκάθαρτον (Mt., Mk., Lk., Ac. and Rev.) [12] for demons. According to Ac. 10:14, 28; 11:8 Peter draws the decisive practical deduction from the insight which is basically attained in the preaching of Jesus. The distinction between profane (κοινόν) or unclean (ἀκάθαρτος) and clean, which is maintained by Judaism, ceases to have any divine validity for the conduct of the community. The community ventures to undertake dealings with those who are "unclean" (Cornelius the Gentile, 10:28; Simon the tanner, who is unclean by virtue of his calling, 9:43; Gl. 2:11 ff.). It no longer feels under any obligation to engage in ritual purification after such dealings. It thus grows away from the Jewish community.

The NT also uses the words 2. of moral impurity which excludes man from fellowship with God (opposite ἅγιος). Paul adopts ἀκαθαρσία from Judaism as a general description of the absolute alienation from God in which heathenism finds itself. But for him the term no longer has ritual significance, R. 1:24; Eph. 4:19 (with ἀσέλγεια and πλεονεξία). The quotation at 2 C. 6:17 (Is. 52:11) demonstrates clearly the transition from the OT material view of uncleanness (ἀκαθάρτου μὴ ἅπτεσθε) to the NT moral and spiritual view. Gentile ἀκαθαρσία is the direct opposite of the righteousness of Christian sanctification (R. 6:19; 2 C. 12:21). Unclean motives (πλεονεξία, v. 5) are completely ruled out in the work of Paul (1 Th. 2:3). At 1 Th. 4:7 again ἀκαθαρσία denotes the immoral state of the pre-

---

[8] Jos. Bell., 4, 562 : τὴν πόλιν πᾶσαν ἐμίαναν ἀκαθάρτοις ἔργοις; Ap., 1, 307; Test. L. 15:1: ὁ ναὸς ὃν ἐκλέξεται κύριος ἔρημος ἔσται ἐν τῇ ἀκαθαρσίᾳ ὑμῶν; Ep. Ar., 166 : ἀκαθαρσίαν ... ἐπετέλεσαν μιανθέντες αὐτοὶ ... τῷ τῆς ἀσεβείας μολυσμῷ. En. 10:20, 22, with ἀδικία, ἁμαρτία, ἀσέβεια; Philo Deus Imm., 132; Virt., 147; Spec. Leg., IV, 106.

[9] Test. B. 5:2 : ἐὰν ἦτε ἀγαθοποιοῦντες καὶ τὰ πνεύματα τὰ ἀκάθαρτα φεύξονται ἀφ' ὑμῶν. Jub. 10:1: in the same sense as πνεύματα πονηρά, cf. 11:4; 12:20; Test. S. 6:6; 4:9; Str.-B., IV, 503. The demonic is unclean in Persian religion, Yasna, 30 (Chant. de la Saussaye, II, 220, 239 ff.). δαίμονες ἀκάθαρτοι, Schol. Aeschin. Tim., 48, 11 (Oratores Graeci, III, 724, ed. J. Reiske [1771]).

[10] Ep. Ar., 166 : of the mind; cf. esp. Philo : Spec. Leg., III, 209 : ἀκάθαρτος γὰρ κυρίως ὁ ἄδικος καὶ ὁ ἀσεβής, I, 150; of ἐπιθυμία (opp. ἀρετή) with βέβηλος and ἀνίερος, Leg. All., III, 139 : ἀκάθαρτος οὖν καὶ ὁ τῷ ἑνὶ (sc. πάθει) χρώμενος τῇ ἡδονῇ, II, 29 : πάθος and ἡδονή defile, the λόγος purifies. Plant., 99, 109.

[11] Test. Jos. 4:6 : οὐχὶ ἐν ἀκαθαρσίᾳ θέλει κύριος τοὺς σεβομένους αὐτόν, οὔτε τοῖς μοιχεύουσιν εὐδοκεῖ, ἀλλὰ τοῖς ἐν καθαρᾷ καρδίᾳ καὶ στόμασιν ἀμιάντοις αὐτῷ προσερχομένοις, Test. Jud. 14:5.

[12] Mk. 1:23, 26 f.; 3:11, 30; 5:2, 8, 13; 6:7; 7:25; 9:25; Mt. 10:1; 12:43 p (only twice in Mt.); Lk. 4:33 (here πνεῦμα δαιμονίου ἀκαθάρτου); 4:36; 6:18; 8:29; 9:42; Ac. 5:16; 8:7; Rev. 16:13; 18:2 (here with ὀρνέου ἀκαθάρτου on the basis of Is. 34:11: ravens and owls).

Christian life ; [13] the primary allusion is to πορνεία and πλεονεξία, as at Eph. 4:19 and 5:3, 5 (opp. ἁγιασμός). Young Christianity regards the sexual immorality of the Hellenistic world as ungodly ἀκαθαρσία (R. 1:24 ff.; with πορνεία, 2 C. 12:21; Gl. 5:19; Eph. 5:3, 5; Col. 3:5; cf. Rev. 17:4). ἀκαθαρσία is ἔργον τῆς σαρκός (Gl. 5:19), i.e., it is an expression of the nature of the unregenerate man whose action is determined by commitment, not to God, but to natural ἐπιθυμίαι. Early Christianity accepts at this point the usage and judgment of Hellenistic Judaism. [14] In Judaism impurity is a clinging and infectious force ; in Paul the holiness which indwells Christians is of the same character. This holiness covers their children, presumably unbaptised, and lifts them out of their state of Gentile impurity, 1 C. 7:14. [15]

† καθαρισμός.

καθαρισμός, "purification," is a later construction which occurs along with the Attic καθαρμός in Hellenistic usage. [1] It means "physical" [2] and then "cultic cleansing." [3]

In the LXX it is used for the restoration of cultic purity, predominantly for טָהֳרָה (Lv. 15:13), though also for כִּפֻּרִים (expiatio, Ex. 29:36) and אָשָׁם (Prv. 14:9). At Ex. 30:10 (P) the annual expiation of the great Day of Atonement is described as a purification from sins by means of blood. [4] This combines a ritual and a moral concept of sin. It is in keeping with cultic religion that καθαρισμός (→ καθαρός) is a single cultic act (unlike → ἁγιασμός).

In the NT καθαρισμός is used for cultic cleansing in a few passages, e.g., Mk. 1:44 par. (leprosy), Lk. 2:22 (the new mother and child), [5] Jn. 2:6 (purification prior to a meal). But in line with the NT view of purity it is also used for moral cleansing. The link with the earlier cultic view is seen in the fact that this καθαρισμός still seems to refer essentially to a single act of purification. It is in keeping with the double impulse of NT religion that this basic purification is found on the one hand in baptism (Jn. 3:25; Eph. 5:26; 2 Pt. 1:9) and on the other in the atoning

---

[13] They were ἐν ἀκαθαρσίᾳ; but it was not for this (ἐπί) that God called them, i.e., in order that He might sanction impurity, but under (ἐν) holiness, Dob. Th., 170 f.

[14] Post-NT development follows Hellenistic asceticism in regarding all sexual intercourse as to some degree ἀκαθαρσία, Act. Pl. et Thecl., 17.

[15] Perhaps this is Paul's only use of ἀκάθαρτος; 2 C. 6:17 is a quotation, and some regard Eph. 5:5 as deutero-Pauline, → καθαρισμός. ἀκάθαρτος is also absent from Jn. and Hb.

κ α θ α ρ ι σ μ ό ς. [1] T. Wächter, "Reinheitsvorschriften im gr. Kult," RVV, 9, 1 (1910); Leg. sac. (Ziehen), VII, 117 (→ 415, n. 6).

[2] E.g. in husbandry, P. Lond., II, 168, 11 (oliveyard), cf. Jn. 15:2.

[3] Test. L. 14:6 (reading β): θυγατέρας ἐθνῶν λήψεσθε εἰς γυναῖκας καθαρίζοντες αὐτὰς καθαρισμῷ παρανόμῳ. Jos. does not have καθαρισμός, but he uses κάθαρσις and καθαρμός. κάθαρσις and καθάρσια are common in Philo.

[4] Ex. 30:10: καὶ ἐξιλάσεται ἐπ᾽ αὐτὸ (sc. θυσιαστήριον) ᾽Ααρὼν ἐπὶ τῶν κεράτων αὐτοῦ ἅπαξ τοῦ ἐνιαυτοῦ· ἀπὸ τοῦ αἵματος τοῦ καθαρισμοῦ τῶν ἁμαρτιῶν τοῦ ἐξιλασμοῦ ἅπαξ τοῦ ἐνιαυτοῦ καθαριεῖ αὐτὸ εἰς τὰς γενεὰς αὐτῶν.

[5] Sy[s] דתדכיתה = καθαρισμοῦ αὐτῆς, D : αὐτοῦ, a b c e ff² : eius, the Greeks αὐτῶν. Jewish law demands only the cleansing of the mother. The plur. αὐτῶν is perhaps due to the fact that on the popular Gk. view the newborn child and those present at the birth are unclean as well as the mother, cf. Wächter, 26; on the textual problem, A. Merx, Die 4 kanon. Evv., II, 2 (1905), 191.

death of Christ (Hb. 1:3; cf. 1 Jn. 1:7 ff.). In both cases it is a cleansing from sin (cf. 1 Pt. 3:21). The more inward concept of sin gives it greater depth than in the OT. For both baptism and the death of Christ Paul prefers other images than that of cleansing. Hence he does not use καθαρισμός. But we do find ἁγιασμός, which is more in keeping with non-cultic religion and which denotes an ongoing and dynamic process (1 C. 1:30; 1 Th. 4:7, 3; R. 6:19).

† ἐκκαθαίρω.

a. "To clean out," "to cleanse thoroughly," τί τινος; ἑαυτὸν ἀπό τινος, Epict. Diss., II, 23, 40; 21, 15. b. "To purge out," "to root, out," Lib., 36: ἐκκαθαῖρε ... τῆς σῆς καρδίας τὴν λύπην; Philo Vit. Mos., I, 303: τὸ μίασμα τοῦ ἔθνους ἐκκαθαίρουσι διὰ τῆς ... τιμωρίας. Ebr., 28: ἕψεται δίκη πάντα μοχθηρὸν τρόπον ἐκκαθαίρουσα διανοίας; Luc. Vit. Auctio, 8: στρατεύομαι δὲ ὥσπερ ἐκεῖνος ἐπὶ τὰς ἡδονὰς ... ἐκκαθᾶραι τὸν βίον προαιρούμενος.

In the LXX only Dt. 26:13; Ju. 7:4: "to separate," "to pick out from a greater number," Jos. 17:15: "to prepare ground" (i.e., by rooting out trees). [1]

At 1 C. 5:7 ἐκκαθάρατε τὴν ... ζύμην is a translation of the technical Rabbinic term בִּעֵר חָמֵץ (cf. Str.-B., III, 359 f.): "to purge out the leaven." Paul uses this metaphor of the purging out of everything leavened prior to the passover to show that all heathen sins and abominations must be set aside if Christ, our passover Lamb, is to reign. The word is also used at 2 Tm. 2:21 of the setting aside of shameful things (opp. ἡγιασμένος).

† περικάθαρμα.

περικάθαρμα is a more intensive form of κάθαρμα, which is common in secular Gk.[1] It has the same sense a. the sacrifice, laden with guilt,[2] which makes expiation and thus cleanses those who offer it. κάθαρμα is particularly used of human sacrifices which either regularly or in special emergencies are offered to make expiation for a community (people or city). The sacrifice had to be voluntary to be effective. Since the victims were well cared for prior to the sacrifice, only those in want, the hungry, cripples etc., usually offered, and therefore κάθαρμα or περικάθαρμα became b. a term of contempt for the unworthy and destitute.[3] According to ancient notions, the purifying object (e.g., wool) materially absorbs the impurity, and is thus thrown out.

ἐ κ κ α θ α ί ρ ω. [1] ἐκκαθαρίζειν is found at Dt. 32:43; Jos. 17:15, 18; Is. 4:4.

π ε ρ ι κ ά θ α ρ μ α. H. Usener, Kl. Schriften, IV (1914), 255 ff.; E. Rohde, Psyche [9], [10], II (1925), 78 f.; F. Schwenn, "Die Menschenopfer bei d. Griech. u. Römern," RVV, 15, 3 (1915), 26 ff.; 57 f.; Ltzm. K., Exc. on 1 C. 4:13.

[1] The fact that περί is often used with stems which denote catharsis (περικαθαίρω etc.) is due to the fact that transformation plays a great part in it, F. Pfister (Pauly-W., Suppl. VI [1935], 149 f.).

[2] Schol. in Aristoph. Ra., 745 (ed. Dindorf), 370: φαρμάκοισι: καθάρμασι· τοὺς γὰρ φαύλους καὶ παρὰ τῆς φύσεως ἐπιβουλευομένους εἰς ἀπαλλαγὴν αὐχμοῦ ἢ λιμοῦ ἤ τινος τῶν τοιούτων ἔθυον, οὓς ἐκάλουν καθάρματα. — Suid., s.v. κάθαρμα: ὑπὲρ δὲ καθαρμοῦ πόλεως ἀνήρουν ἐστολισμένον τινά, ὃν ἐκάλουν κάθαρμα. Aesch. Choeph., 98; Eur. Herc. Fur., 225; Iph. Taur., 1316.

[3] Poll. Onom., V, 163: τῶν ἐν ταῖς τριόδοις καθαρμάτων ἐκβλητότερος. Philo Virt., 174; Epict. Diss., III, 22, 78: Πρίαμος ὁ πεντήκοντα γεννήσας περικαθάρματα.

Hence κάθαρμα can also mean c. that which is to be thrown out after purification. [4] Three different strands meet in κάθαρμα, namely, the expiatory offering, that which is contemptible, and that which is to be thrown out. [5]

All three senses are apposite in 1 C. 4:13, where Paul describes himself as περικάθαρμα τοῦ κόσμου [6] (used with → περίψημα).

Hauck

| καθεύδω | → ὕπνος, → ἐγείρω.

Contents: A. The General Usage: 1. Of Men; 2. Of Gods and Heroes. B. Sleep in the OT and Judaism: 1. Of Men; 2. Of Idols which Sleep, and God who does not Sleep. C. καθεύδειν in the NT; 1. In the Literal Sense; 2. In the Metaphorical Sense. D. In Church History.

A. The General Usage.

1. Of Men.

a. καθεύδειν (from Homer onwards) has the same sense as the simple form εὕδειν, [1] which is rare in Attic and non-Attic prose. It means "to sleep," primarily in the literal sense. Vergil (Aen., IX, 224 f.) describes the common human experience of sleep as that which unravels care and gives refreshment:

> *Cetera per terras omnis animalia somno*
> *laxabant curas et corda oblita laborum ...*

An inscription in honour of the god Hypnos bears testimony to the same high evaluation among the Greeks (→ 197, n. 6). The figurative use points to some extent in the same direction. On the other hand, the activism of antiquity finds sleep distasteful. Both the Greeks and Romans were early risers. They went to sleep at sundown, but woke up with the first crow of the cock. In late autumn and winter this gave some hours to sunrise, 3 to 4 in Rome. These so-called lucubrations (from the lamp, *lucubrum,* which has died out) are the main period of intellectual activity. [2] In order to avoid pettiness, Plato in his Laws is not prepared to limit the hours of sleep, but he regards it as scandalous if the master or mistress of the house sleeps the whole night (ὅλην διατελεῖν νύκτα εὕδοντα) and has to be wakened by slaves. καθεύδων γὰρ οὐδεὶς οὐδενὸς ἄξιος, οὐδὲν μᾶλλον τοῦ μὴ ζῶντος. Those who really wish to live and to

---

[4] Ammonius, p. 143: καθάρματα τὰ μετὰ τὸ καθαρθῆναι ἀπορριπτούμενα.

[5] The word occurs in the LXX only at Prv. 21:18: περικάθαρμα δὲ δικαίου ἄνομος, which is to be taken in the sense of 11:8. Here, too, the three meanings are all implied. 'A has κάθαρμα twice (Dt. 29:16 and Ez. 6:4) for גִּלּוּל in a derogatory sense [Bertram].

[6] Instead of ὡς G 69 read ὡσπερεὶ καθάρματα, an assimilation to more common usage.

κ α θ ε ύ δ ω. [1] The etymology is uncertain acc. to Prellwitz Etym. Wört. and Boisacq. The words are not listed at all in the index of Walde-Pok.

[2] Cf. O. Roller, "Das Formular der paul. Briefe," BWANT, IV, 6 (1933), 311 ff., and bibl.

do intellectual work must be awake as long as possible (Leg., VII, 807e ff.). Among his possessions Plato had an alarm-clock which he had had made. [3] Nevertheless, it is a sign of greatness if one can sleep peacefully in a situation of danger, e.g., at the approach of death. Thus, when Socrates is in prison before he drinks the hemlock, Crito says to him : ἀλλὰ καὶ σοῦ πάλαι θαυμάζω αἰσθανόμενος ὡς ἡδέως καθεύδεις (Plat. Crito, 43b). Sleep may thus be judged differently according to circumstances. This duality has wider repercussions.

b. The state of sleep in human life is regarded as an incursion of the suprasensual. Later antiquity in particular pays special attention to dreams, and seriously believes that it can put their interpretation on a regular scientific basis. Artemidorus's book of dreams is typical. We certainly seek here in vain for any deeper religious impulse. Health, long life, appearance, wealth, love, posterity, and their counterparts, are the theme of these revelations with monotonous uniformity. This type of thinking revolves on its own axle. More significant are the nocturnal phenomena where a specific god appears with concrete expressions of his will and power. Zoilos receives from Sarapis ἐν ὕπνοις a command to see to the erection of a Sarapeion in the place where he lives, and he is repeatedly afflicted with sickness when he leaves the actual execution of the command to the Egyptian financial official Apollonius. [4] The devotee of a related Egyptian mystery religion receives in the same way increasingly urgent directions to translate a cultic script which unfortunately has not survived. [5] Mandulis-Aion grants to a nocturnal pilgrim to his shrine a long and earnestly sought assurance concerning him. [6] The temple sleep, incubation, is of some antiquity among the Greeks. It is found especially in the temples of Aesculapius, where it is a vehicle of significant religious experiences (→ 209). It is in keeping with the dignity of a temple that there should be certain distinctions and restrictions in this respect, e.g., the separation of the sexes, cf. the cultic statute of the Amphiareion in Oropus (4th cent. B.C., Ditt. Syll.³, III, 1004, 43 ff.): ἐν τοῖ κοιμητη-ρίοι καθεύδειν χωρὶς μὲν τὸς ἄνδρας, χωρὶς δὲ τὰς γυναῖκας.

c. Yet all this does not prevent the figurative use from being derogatory. The term serves to indicate defective concentration and deficient force of action. A member of the Platonic circle must accept the by no means flattering address : If another poet than Homer is recited, καθεύδεις τε καὶ ἀπορεῖς ὅτι λέγῃς (Plat. Ion, 536b). The general rouses his soldiers : ἐμοὶ οὖν δοκεῖ οὐχ ὥρα εἶναι ἡμῖν καθεύδειν οὐδ' ἀμελεῖν ἡμῶν αὐτῶν, ἀλλὰ βουλεύεσθαι ὅ τι χρὴ ποιεῖν ἐκ τούτων (Xenoph. An., I, 3, 11). The greatest orator in Athens cries to his fellow-citizens : τίς ὁ συσκευάζεσθαι τὴν Ἑλλάδα καὶ Πελοπόννησον Φίλιππον βοῶν, ὑμᾶς δὲ καθεύδειν; (Demosth. Or., 19, 303). Epictetus ironically commends a purely vegetative life to Epicurus if his low regard for human society is right : "Lie down and sleep, and follow the pursuits of a worm of which you judge yourself worthy ; eat and drink, mate, go to the privy, and snore" (Diss., II, 20, 10). For Plutarch καθεύδειν and προσέχειν τοῖς πράγμασι are opposites (Pomp., 15 [I, 626d]); so, too, are καθεύδειν and ἐνεργεῖν for Aristot. (Eth. Nic., VIII, 6, p. 1157b, 8). The dramatist uses a bold image for those who trample to the earth the glory of waiting, i.e., who cannot keep themselves from dallying : οὐ καθεύδουσιν χερί (Aesch. Ag., 1357). Similarly, inactive things are said to sleep, e.g., walls in the earth (Plat. Leg., VI, 778d), or laws which are not put into effect (Plut. Ages., 30, I, 613a). ἐλπίδες οὔπω καθεύδουσι (Eur. Phoen., 634).

d. From all this it may be seen finally that the term embraces the whole ambivalence of human life and death. Plato discusses the question whether life is but a sleep and all

---

[3] U. v. Wilamowitz-Moellendorff, Platon, I² (1920), 715 [J. Leipoldt].
[4] Deissmann LO, 121 ff.
[5] P. Oxy., XI, 1381.
[6] A. D. Nock, "A Vision of Mandulis-Aion," Harvard Theol. Review, 27 (1934), 53-104.

our activity a dream (Theaet., 158b). The Platonic Socrates considers the hypothesis that death is a only a deep and dreamless sleep, and he thinks that it would be a benefit even in this case : εἴτε μηδεμία αἴσθησίς ἐστιν, ἀλλ' οἷον ὕπνος, ἐπειδάν τις καθεύδων μηδ' ὄναρ μηδὲν ὁρᾷ, θαυμάσιον κέρδος ἂν εἴη ὁ θάνατος (Ap., 40d/e). But this is not the real view of the Platonic circle. If death were a sleep, with no reawakening (ἀνεγείρεσθαι ἐκ τοῦ καθεύδοντος), then the story of Endymion, to whom Zeus gave eternal sleep, immortality and youth, would be a pointless fable, since sleep would be the common lot of all (διὰ τὸ καὶ τἆλλα πάντα ταὐτὸν ἐκείνῳ πεπονθέναι, καθεύδειν, Plat. Phaed., 72b/c). In the story, however, immortality is deduced from the equation of sleep and death. The origin of the metaphor is not to be sought in philosophical deliberation. External resemblance suggested it at once to popular perception. It is based on the peacefulness of the dead, and therefore most Greeks find → κοιμᾶσθαι (related to κεῖσθαι) a more suitable term than καθεύδειν in such contexts. The use of καθεύδειν is based on a more complex imagery. Yet it does occur, and it is also applied euphemistically, e.g., on the Roman burial inscription of a certain Popilia : καὶ λέγε Ποπιλίην εὔδειν, ἄνερ· οὐ θεμιτὸν γὰρ | θνήσκειν τοὺς ἀγαθούς, ἀλλ' ὕπνον ἡδὺν ἔχειν. [7]

2. Of Gods and Heroes.

a. The sturdy anthropomorphism of Homer finds it natural that gods should sleep, and that this sleep should be as secure and comfortable as that of heroes. The Iliad says of Zeus : ἔνθα καθεῦδ' ἀναβάς, παρὰ δὲ χρυσόθρονος Ἥρη (Il., 1, 611). The Odyssey speaks in similar terms of Nestor and his spouse (Od., 3, 402 f.). But in spite of its canonical aspect Homeric superstition is only an episode in Greek religion. Prior to and along with the piety of Homer we also find the numinous where life and death touch and separate. The more fully philosophical speculation takes charge of the concept of God, the more theoretical this becomes. For the physical and cosmological allegorising of the Stoics the Homeric gods are simply personifications of the forces of nature. Whether we are dealing with these, or with the divine in the supreme sense, the literal idea of God sleeping is meaningless. Thought has outgrown this.

b. Yet in no period is pure thinking the only normative function of the spirit, nor does it scorn stimulation by myth and legend. Hence the idea of sleeping gods and heroes persists until late in the Greek world, yet in such a way that it always implies the problem of death. Bion sings of the dead Adonis (at the end of the 2nd cent. B.C., ed. U. v. Wilamowitz-Moellendorff [1900], 71: καὶ νέκυς ὢν καλός ἐστι, καλὸς νέκυς, οἷα καθεύδων. Attis lies as though lifeless in the cave, but he is incorruptible, his hair grows, and his little finger moves (Arnobius, ed. A. Reifferscheid [1875], V, 7): he sleeps. Both gods merge into Endymion, who is depicted by later artists as lying asleep with his eyes open. Licymnios of Chios explains this on the ground that Hypnos fell in love with the youth and left his eyes open so as to be able to see them. [8] The same phenomenon may be noted on the oldest known sarcophagus of Adonis. [9] It is narrated of the Cretan thaumaturge Epimenides, who was a historical figure, though the subject of many legends, that he slept for 40 years (Paus., I, 14, 4), or, according to some accounts, for 57. The first number corresponds to a whole generation. Hence the problem of the generations is present on the margin. There is a perhaps a connection between this legend and the Cretan cult of the dying and reborn Zeus. The circles concerned lay great store by ancient dream oracles and states of incubation. [10]

---

[7] Epig. Graec., 559, 2nd cent. A.D.
[8] O. Gruppe, Griech. Mythologie u. Religionsgeschichte, I (1906), Handbuch der klass. Altertumskunde, V, 2, p. 280, n. 5.
[9] Angelos, 3 (1930), 163 ff.
[10] Gruppe, op. cit., 778.

B. Sleep in the OT and Judaism.

1. Of Men.

a. The Israelite, too, values sleep for its refreshing and revitalising power (Jer. 31:26). It is a great burden when one cannot find sleep because of sickness or care or the gnawing of conscience (Ps. 32:4; Sir. 31[34]:1; 40:5). The Law of Yahweh protects the sleep of the poor, for the upper garment must not be kept as a pledge beyond sundown, since it also serves as a covering by night (Ex. 22:25 f.; Dt. 24:12 f.). On the other hand, the prophets inveigh against the luxury of the beds of the wealthy (Am. 6:4). Too much sleep involves a culpable indolence which leads to poverty (Prv. 10:5; 19:15 Heb.). Not to sleep by night is a mark of the faithful and diligent servant (Gn. 31:40). But this is exceptional. "Ten measures of sleep have come into the world; slaves have taken nine, and the rest of the world one" (bQid., 49b; Str.-B., II, 48). The righteous man stays awake, or even in sleep he meditates on the Torah (Ps. 1:2; Dt. 6:7; Jos. 1:8; Prv. 6:22). With divine wisdom and knowledge in his heart, he can sleep sweetly (Prv. 3:24). Under divine protection he sleeps securely and peacefully (Ps. 3:5; 4:8). For his Keeper does not sleep (Ps. 121:3; → 435). Everything rests on the blessing of Yahweh. Piety is thus an antidote to false busyness and unnecessary care. "He giveth his beloved sleep" (Ps. 127:2; LXX [126:2] mistakenly has: ὅταν δῷ τοῖς ἀγαπητοῖς αὐτοῦ ὕπνον). Jonah, however, sleeps the sleep of culpable indifference during the storm (Jon. 1:5).

b. Sleep can also become stupefaction, and in this case it is a judgment of Yahweh on those who sleep and a help to those who remain awake (Is. 51:20; 1 S. 26:12, cf. v. 7). Yet Yahweh also gives revelations in sleep. Abraham and Jacob receive the promises of God while they are asleep (Gn. 15:12 : תַּרְדֵּמָה, LXX ἔκστασις, cf. 2:21; Gn. 28:10 ff.). While asleep in the sanctuary at Shiloh, the young Samuel is called by Yahweh, who declares to him His judgment on the house of Eli (1 S. 3:1 ff.). Dream oracles, especially in association with Bethel, are implied in the stories of the patriarchs, and the story of Samuel shows that incubation was not wholly alien to the Israelites.

Strabo writes of Moses: ἐγκοιμᾶσθαι καὶ αὐτοὺς ὑπὲρ ἑαυτῶν καὶ ὑπὲρ τῶν ἄλλων ἄλλους τοὺς εὐονείρους (XVI, 761). [11] He is perhaps interpreting the ancient tradition of Israel in terms of Hellenism, but materially he is near the mark. Indeed, it is possible that his words reflect contemporary Jewish trends. Did men sleep in the synagogues, or was the overnight stay in the hostels associated with them regarded as incubation? [12] Inscriptions on the synagogue of Delos offer obvious parallels to the Aesculapius dedications. [13] In this light, sleeping in the sanctuary is not too remote.

Visions are often regarded as divine revelations in the OT. As such, they stand in need of divine interpretation. The best known examples are Jacob's ladder (Gn. 28:10 ff.), Joseph's dream (Gn. 37:5, 9), the dreams interpreted by Joseph

---

[11] I owe this reference to J. Leipoldt.

[12] Cf. the Theodotos inscr. in Deissmann LO, 378 ff.

[13] Cf. Ἀγαθοκλῆς καὶ Λυσίμαχος ἐπὶ προσευχῇ, or: Λυσίμαχος ὑπὲρ ἐμαυτοῦ θεῷ ὑψίστῳ χαριστήριον, or: Λαωδίκη θεῷ ὑψίστῳ σωθεῖσα ταῖς ὑφ' αὐτοῦ θαραπήαις εὐχήν. Mélanges Holleaux, Recueil de Mémoires concernant l'Antiquité Grecque. Offert a M. Holleaux (1913), 201 ff.

(Gn. 40:5 ff.; 41:1 ff.), Solomon's dream (1 K. 3:5 ff.), the dreams of Nebuchadnezzar interpreted by Daniel (Da. 2:1; 4:1 ff.), Daniel's dream (7:1 ff.), and rather more broadly the visions of Zechariah (1:7-6:8). Dreams are a regular means of prophetic revelation and a sign of divine favour, but they are not the highest or most trustworthy form of the declaration of God's will and may often be deceitful and dangerous (Nu. 12:6 f.; 1 S. 28:6; Jl. 2:28; Jer. 28:28, 32; 29:8; Zech. 10:2).

The view of later Judaism is similar. Dreams are indispensable in apocalyptic (En. 13:8 ff.; 4 Esr. 11:1-12:3; Gr. Bar. 36:1 ff.; Test. Jos. 19 etc.). They are regarded favourably by some Rabbis (cf. bBer., 57b: "The dream is a sixtieth part of a prophecy"), but others are more sceptical and explain them psychologically.[14] Philo explains Jacob's sleep at Bethel as follows. He who seeks virtue (ἀσκητής) rests on uprightness (καθεύδει); while the life of the senses lies still (κοιμᾶσθαι), that of the soul is awake (ἐγρηγορέναι, Som., I, 174).

c. Figuratively, καθεύδειν is not used in the OT for laziness, though cf. νυστάζειν at Na. 3:18 and ὑπνοῦν. But it is often used for death, and this use is neutral, without euphemism (ψ 87:5; Da. 12:2).

2. Of Idols which Sleep, and God who does not Sleep.

The fact that the term is expressly not applied to God marks a delimitation of the religion of revelation from paganism. Elijah ironically encourages the priests of Baal in their futile efforts to stir their god to action: "Cry aloud: for he is a god; either he meditateth, or he is pursuing, or he is in a journey, or peradventure he sleepeth, and must be awaked" (ἢ μήποτε καθεύδει αὐτός, 3 Βασ. 18:27; → ἐγείρειν τὸν θεόν, II, 333, n. 1). By contrast, "he that keepeth Israel shall neither slumber nor sleep" (ἰδοὺ οὐ νυστάξει οὐδὲ ὑπνώσει ὁ φυλάσσων τὸν Ἰσραήλ, ψ 120:4).

There are apparent exceptions at Ps. 44:23 (43:23) and Ps. 78(77):65. But here only the mode of expression, not the conception, is mythological. The same is true of Gn. 2:2 f., where the mythological basis is that of rest rather than sleep.

C. καθεύδειν in the NT.

For NT piety the very question of God sleeping is pointless from the very first. Only with the greatest caution — in the light of the technique of parable exposition — can we find the last dying echoes of mythological conceptions at Lk. 11:5 ff. The strict transcendence of God is here upheld, and use is made only of that which can serve to stimulate the life of prayer. In the NT, then, the term applies exclusively to men.

1. In the Literal Sense.

a. In the NT we seek in vain for general reflections on the nature and significance of sleep. This shows us at a specific point how little the NT is concerned with a full-orbed religious view of the world and of life. It presupposes sleep as a self-evident fact (Mt. 13:25; Mk. 4:27). It can tell us without agitation that during a long sermon by Paul a young man fell into such a deep sleep that he fell

---

[14] Cf. Str.-B., I, 53 ff. on Mt. 1:20.

from the roof (Ac. 20:9). On the whole, however, it is more interested in waking than sleeping. Jesus spends whole nights in prayer, or rises early in the morning to converse with His Father in heaven (Lk. 6:12; Mk. 1:35). The apostle Paul works night and day so as not to be a burden to any (1 Th. 2:9). The earliest community [15] regarded the sleepiness of the few witnesses of the wrestling in Gethsemane as almost demonic (Mt. 26:40 ff. par.). Jesus roused them with the exhortation to watch (Mt. 26:41 ff. par.). He then spoke about sleeping on; we are to take this either as an ironical demand or a reproachful question (Mt. 26:45a par.). Yet though the life of Jesus is one of energetic action, we also have the striking picture of Jesus asleep in the raging storm (Mk. 4:38 par.). From the physical standpoint this sleep bears witness to the disciplined concentration of nervous energy rather than to its ceaseless dissipation. But the secret lies deeper. Jesus knows that He is safe in His Father's care even in the violence of the elements. The fear of the disciples is due to their little faith (Mk. 4:40 par.). The serene assurance of Jesus, whether waking or sleeping, is grounded in His unbroken fellowship with God.

b. The NT also tells us that God gives directions to men in sleep, e.g., to Joseph (Mt. 1:20; 2:13, 19, 22), to the wise men (Mt. 2:12), to the wife of Pilate (Mt. 27:19), to Paul (Ac. 16:9; 18:9). The prophecy of Joel, which we have quoted already, is applied to the Pentecost experience. In this respect we have to take into account the distinctive nature of the dream life of simple men, especially in the Orient. By and large, the religious evaluation of dreams is only on the margin of NT piety. The essential point of revelation is not to be found here. It lies in the historical self-demonstration of God, → ἀποκαλύπτω. The dreams of Gnostics are dangerous and morally suspect delusions (Jd. 8).

2. In the Metaphorical Sense.

a. The term is used, though less frequently than κοιμᾶσθαι (→ 14, n. 60), as a euphemism for death (1 Th. 5:10). There is nothing specifically Christian in this usage. A case apart is Mt. 9:24 par. The Evangelists are undoubtedly narrating a true raising from the dead. Yet the question has been raised whether the Lord's saying, if authentic, might not originally bear a different sense. In terms of antique ideas, the most likely meaning is that the soul of the girl had left the body but was still in the vicinity and in the strength of God could be recalled by Jesus' word of power. The saying certainly does not teach that death in general is simply sleep.

b. A typical specialised use of καθεύδειν is for a spiritual, or unspiritual, attitude which is the direct opposite of the concentration and energy of the life of faith which are to be expected and even demanded of believers, especially in view of the approaching parousia. The demand μὴ καθεύδωμεν (1 Th. 5:6) is not just a piece of general wisdom. Nor is it a mere word of encouragement in face of a particular situation. As the context shows quite plainly, the image is eschatological (cf. v. 7). The same is true of Mt. 25:5, though with a difference. Sleeping is not the fault here, for we are told that the wise virgins also slept. The fault is not to have made preparations so as to be ready in the right place at the right time. We are saved, not by mere waiting for the coming Lord, but by enduring to the end.

---

[15] Cf. G. Bertram, "Die Leidensgeschichte Jesu u. der Christuskult," FRL, NF, 15 (1922), 45.

A momentary relaxation of expectation will not condemn us; inability to bestir ourselves at the decisive point will. For Eph. 5:14 → II, 336.

D. In Church History.

καθεύδω does not occur in the immediate post-NT writings. An incursion of ancient ideas is to be seen in the various legends of saints who slept for decades or for centuries and then woke up again. The best known is the story of the seven sleepers, which is linked with Ephesus in accordance with the tradition concerning John. At the very earliest it arose in the second half of the 5th century. It is dependent not only on the myths already mentioned but also on Jewish models (Ass. Mos. 9 ?). [16]

Oepke

---

† καθήκω (τὸ καθῆκον)

1. Popular Usage.

a. "To come down," then more generally "to come to," in various connections: Thuc., II, 27: ὁδὸς καθήκουσα ἐπὶ θάλατταν; Aeschin., 2, 25 : καθῆκεν εἰς ἡμᾶς ὁ λόγος; Xenoph. Hist. Graec., IV, 7, 2 : ὁπότε καθήκοι ὁ χρόνος; cf. Polyb., 4, 7, 1: καθηκούσης αὐτοῖς ἐκ τῶν νόμων συνόδου κατὰ τὸν καιρὸν τοῦτον, since according to law a gathering fell at this time ; Demosth. Or., 19, 185 : εἶτ' ἐκκλησίαν ποιῆσαι, καὶ ταύτην ὅταν ἐκ τῶν νόμων καθήκῃ ; cf. Plut. Fab. Max., 18, 2 (I, 184e). Hence τὰ καθήκοντα (πράγματα) "the present state of things," Hdt., I, 97; V, 49 etc. Polyb., 4, 14, 1 etc.: ἡ καθήκουσα σύνοδος, "the regular assembly" ; Demosth. Or., 59, 80 : αἱ καθήκουσαι ἡμέραι, "the set days"; Ditt. Syll.[3], 487, 1 ff.: καὶ τοῖς ἄλλοις θεοῖς, οἷς πάτριον ἦν, ἔθυσαν ... ἐν ταῖς καθηκούσαις ἡμέραις καλῶς καὶ φιλοτίμως; cf. 1 Macc. 12:11. b. "To be meet or proper," in the general sense of *convenire* and with various shades of meaning, especially "it is fitting," "it is seemly," "it is necessary," "it is (my) obligation or duty" : [1] P. Tebt., I, 5, 39 : οἱ τὴν πλείω γῆν ἔχοντες τῆς καθηκούσης, he who has more land than is fitting ; Xenoph. Cyrop., VIII, 1, 4 : οὕτω καὶ αὐτοὶ πειθώμεθα, οἷς ἂν ἡμᾶς καθήκῃ; Xenoph. An., I, 9, 7: οἷς καθήκει ἀθροίζεσθαι; Ep. Ar., 149 : οὐδ' ἅψασθαι καθῆκε τῶν προειρημένων; Ac. 22:22 : οὐ ... καθῆκεν αὐτὸν ζῆν; Inscr. Priene, 114, 32 : καθῆκόν ἐστιν αὐτὸν ἐπαινεῖσθαι; P. Tebt., I, 38, 7: καταστῆναι, ἐφ' οὓς καθήκει, "to lay before competent judges." BGU, IV, 1200, 10 ff.: τὰς καθηκούσας θυσίας καὶ σπονδάς, "the appropriate sacrifices and offerings," cf. 2 Macc. 14:31; Ditt. Syll.[3], 687, 27: τὴν καθή-

---

[16] J. Koch, *Die Siebenschläferlegende, ihr Ursprung und ihre Verbreitung* (1883); M. Huber, *Die Wanderlegende von den Siebenschläfern* (1910); cf. also RGG[2], V, 482 f.; Gruppe, *op. cit.,* II, 934, n. 10; 1525, n. 1; 1652 f.

κ α θ ή κ ω. Pass., Preisigke Wört., Anz Subsidia, 332 f.

[1] While in 1. a. καθήκω is usually construed with ἐπί, πρός, or εἰς and the acc., it is here used with the dat., synon. with προσήκει, πρέπει [Debrunner].

κουσαν ἐπιμέλειαν ἐποιήσατο; 1 Macc. 10:39 : καθήκουσα δαπάνη; Ditt. Syll.³, 709, 14 : καθήκουσαι τιμαί cf. 1 Cl., 1, 3; P. Amh., 90, 14; P. Flor., I, 16, 17 etc.: ἔργα ὅσα καθήκει. The neuter noun is also used in the same way, Hdt., VII, 104 : τὰ καθήκοντα Σπαρτιήτῃσι; Ditt. Syll.³, 717, 25 f.: καὶ ἔθυσαν τῷ Αἴαντι καὶ τἆλλα καθήκοντα ποιήσαντες ἀνεστράφησαν εὐτάκτως; 1042, 9 f.: παρέχειν δὲ καὶ τῷ θεῷ τὸ καθῆκον, δεξιὸν σκέλος καὶ δορὰν καὶ κεφαλήν κτλ. In the absolute, Xenoph. Cyrop., I, 2, 5 : τὰ καθήκοντα ἀποτελεῖν; Menand. Fr., 575 : ἐμὲ δὲ ποιεῖν τὸ καθῆκον οὐχ ὁ σὸς λόγος, εὖ ἴσθ' ἀκριβῶς, ὁ δ' ἴδιος πείθει τρόπος; Polyb., 6, 6, 7: τῆς τοῦ καθήκοντος δυνάμεως καὶ θεωρίας; cf. 12, 12; Diod. S., XVI, 1, 1; P. Oxy., VI, 939, 16 : τοῦτο τοῦ καθήκοντος ἀπαιτοῦντος. Adverbially, Polyb., 5, 9, 6 : δικαίως καὶ καθηκόντως. τὸ καθῆκον denotes the kind of requirement which gives evidence of custom and general morality.

2. Philosophical Usage.

From popular use the term is adopted by Zeno (according to Diog. L., VII, 108) into the vocabulary of philosophy, where its use is varied and sometimes not wholly perspicuous. [2] In general one may say that τὸ καθῆκον (or τὰ καθήκοντα) denotes that which is fitting or suitable for man, namely, the demands and actions which arise out of the claims of environment and which critical reason sees to be in harmony with his nature, cf. Diog. L., VII, 107 ff.; Stob. Ecl., II, 85, 12 ff. καθῆκον is here to be distinguished from κατόρθωμα as the middle-point between κατόρθωμα and ἁμάρτημα. As such a μέσον it does not occupy morally neutral ground where actions are morally indifferent (Stob. Ecl., II, 86, 10 f.: πᾶν δὲ τὸ παρὰ τὸ καθῆκον ἐν λογικῷ ζῴῳ γινόμενον ἁμάρτημα εἶναι, cf. II, 93, 14 ff.; 96). On the contrary, it denotes obligations which both the wise and the unwise recognise to be binding and fitting, though each from his own standpoint (cf. Epict. Diss., II, 17, 31: θέλω δ' ὡς εὐσεβὴς καὶ φιλόσοφος καὶ ἐπιμελὴς εἰδέναι, τί μοι πρὸς θεούς ἐστιν καθῆκον, τί πρὸς γονεῖς, τί πρὸς ἀδελφούς, τί πρὸς τὴν πατρίδα, τί πρὸς ξένους (cf. Ench., 30).

As actions, καθήκοντα are κατόρθωμα (full duties) for the wise, who alone can properly fulfil them (ὡς δεῖ and εὐκαίρως, Epict. Diss., III, 2, 2; 21, 14; Sext. Emp. Math., XI, 200; Philo Leg. All., III, 74). For the φαῦλος, who cannot do καθῆκον ἀφ' ἕξεως καθηκούσης (Philo Leg. All., III, 210), they are ἁμάρτημα. It is in keeping that καθῆκον in a narrower sense denotes the sphere of natural and traditional human duties, ὡς ἔχει τὸ γονεῖς τιμᾶν, ἀδελφούς, πατρίδα, συμπεριφέρεσθαι φίλοις, Diog. L., VII, 108. Chrysipp., for example, speaks of piety towards the dead in his work περὶ τοῦ καθήκοντος, Sext. Emp. Math., XI, 194, cf. 189. In a wider sense it embraces the whole range of obligatory actions. Thus there are three kinds of καθῆκον in Epict.: first, duties in respect of natural needs and for the advantage of man; second, duties which law and custom have made generally valid; and third, duties which may conflict with the ordinary moral sense, e.g., self-sacrifice on behalf of friends, Diss., II, 14, 18, or love of others, Diss., IV, 10, 12 etc. But Epict. also gives us an older description of the sphere of καθῆκον which demonstrates the breadth of the concept, Diss., III, 7, 25 : οὐκοῦν καὶ καθήκοντα τρισσά· τὰ μὲν πρὸς τὸ εἶναι, τὰ δὲ πρὸς τὸ ποιά εἶναι,

---

[2] Cf. for what follows E. Wellmann, "Die Philosophie des Stoikers Zenon," *Jbch. klass. Phil.,* 19 (1873), 441 ff.; A. Schmekel, *Die Philosophie der mittleren Stoa in ihrem geschichtlichen Zshg.* (1892), 214 f., 358 f.; A. Bonhöffer, *Die Ethik des Stoikers Epiktet* (1894), 193-233; A. Dyroff, *Die Ethik der alten Stoa* (1897), 133-145; A. Bonhöffer, "Epiktet u. d. NT," RVV, 10 (1911), 154, 157 ff.; G. Nebel, "Der Begriff des καθῆκον in der alten Stoa," *Hermes,* 70 (1935), 439 ff.

τὰ δ᾽ αὐτὰ τὰ προηγούμενα, i.e., καθήκοντα which relate to the fact and nature of existence and to moral decision within it (cf. Cic. Off., III, 20). In virtue of this broader and narrower use, it is understandable that καθῆκον should tend to replace κατόρθωμα. Thus κατόρθωμα occurs only once in Epict, in the ancient Stoic antithesis to ἁμάρτημα, Diss., II, 26, 5; καθήκειν and κατορθοῦν can also be used interchangeably, cf. Diss., II, 26, 5 with Ench., 42; Diss., I, 7, 1 with II, 3, 4. Chrysipp. already has τέλειον καθῆκον for κατόρθωμα (Stob. Ecl., II, 85, 18; cf. IV, 5). If τέλειον καθῆκον is in some sense contrasted with μέσα καθήκοντα, it denotes neutral obligations like γαμεῖν, πρεσβεύειν, διαλέγεσθαι, cf. II, 96. The μέσον καθῆκον is what Epict., like Chrysipp., calls ἐκλογὴ κατὰ φύσιν, and what he distinguishes from moral καθῆκον, which is for him προηγούμενον.

3. In the LXX [3] we find only the popular use of τὸ καθῆκον or καθήκω. The various shades of meaning are present : 1 Macc. 10:36 : καὶ δοθήσεται αὐτοῖς ξένια, ὡς καθήκει πάσαις ταῖς δυνάμεσιν τοῦ βασιλέως (as is fitting); Tob. 1:8; 6:12 f.: ὅτι σοὶ ἐπιβάλλει ἡ κληρονομία αὐτῆς; 1:13 : ὅτι τὴν κληρονομίαν σοὶ καθήκει λαβεῖν ἢ πάντα ἄνθρωπον; 7:10; Ez. 21:32; 2 Macc. 2:30 : τὸ ... ἐμβατεύειν (entry, penetration [figur.]) ... τῷ τῆς ἱστορίας ἀρχηγέτῃ καθήκει (is a matter of ...); 11:36 : ἵνα ἐκθῶμεν ὡς καθήκει ὑμῖν (as is advantageous for you); cf. Epict. Diss., III, 22, 43 : λυσιτελὲς καὶ καθῆκον, I, 18, 2 : συμφέρον καὶ καθῆκον; 3 Macc. 1:11: τῶν δὲ εἰπόντων μὴ καθήκειν γίνεσθαι τοῦτο (this need not happen), cf. Jdt. 11:13; Hos. 2:7: τῶν ἐραστῶν μου τῶν διδόντων μοι ... πάντα ὅσα μοι καθήκει (which I need); cf. Ex. 16:21: ἕκαστος τὸ καθῆκον αὐτῷ, [4] Ex. 36:1: ποιεῖν πάντα τὰ ἔργα κατὰ τὰ ἅγια καθήκοντα (all the work necessary for the erection of the sanctuary).

It is worth noting that καθήκει or (τὸ) καθῆκον is the rendering of three Heb. terms from which it takes its meaning : דֶּרֶךְ, Gn. 19:31: καὶ οὐδείς ἐστιν ἐπὶ τῆς γῆς, ὃς εἰσελεύσεται πρὸς ἡμᾶς ὡς καθήκει πάσῃ τῇ γῇ (after the manner of all the earth); דָּבָר, Ex. 5:13 : συντελεῖτε τὰ ἔργα τὰ καθήκοντα καθ᾽ ἡμέραν (daily work), cf. 5:19; מִשְׁפָּט, Lv. 5:10 : καὶ τὸ δεύτερον (turtledove) ποιήσει ὁλοκαύτωμα ὡς καθήκει (according to the Law), Dt. 21:17: καὶ τούτῳ (the firstborn) καθήκει τὰ πρωτοτόκια (is fitting according to the Law); cf. Lv. 9:16; Ez. 21:32; 3 Βασ. 2:16 (יוֹ); 1 Esr. 1:13; 2 Macc. 6:21; 14:31. Cf. also Sir. 10:23 :

> οὐ δίκαιον ἀτιμάσαι πτωχὸν συνετόν
> καὶ οὐ καθήκει δοξάσαι ἄνδρα ἁμαρτωλόν,

where the standard of what is fitting is presupposed general moral conviction rather than a specific command or order. The same is true at 2 Macc. 6:4 : τὸ μὲν γὰρ ἱερὸν ἀσωτίας καὶ κώμων ὑπὸ τῶν ἐθνῶν ἐπεπλήρουτο ῥαθυμούντων (make merry) μεθ᾽ ἑταιρῶν καὶ ἐν τοῖς ἱεροῖς περιβόλοις γυναιξὶ πλησιαζόντων, ἔτι δὲ τὰ μὴ καθήκοντα ἔνδον εἰσφερόντων, and 3 Macc. 4:16 : εἰς δὲ τὸν μέγιστον θεὸν τὰ μὴ καθήκοντα λαλῶν.

4. In the NT τὸ καθῆκον occurs only once, in the plural, at R. 1:28 : καὶ καθὼς οὐκ ἐδοκίμασαν τὸν θεὸν ἔχειν ἐν ἐπιγνώσει, παρέδωκεν αὐτοὺς ὁ θεὸς εἰς ἀδόκιμον νοῦν, ποιεῖν τὰ μὴ καθήκοντα, πεπληρωμένους πάσῃ ἀδικίᾳ ... From the negative form, and the content of what is called unseemly, it is evident that the term is not used here in its specific philosophical sense. In philosophical usage

---

[3] Of the 30 instances 16 are in the OT Apocrypha.
[4] Acc. to Anz Subsidia, 333 the καθήκοντες of Ex. 16:16(18): συναγάγετε ἀπ᾽ αὐτοῦ (manna) ἕκαστος εἰς τοὺς καθήκοντας are to be understood as *propinqui*. Cf. P. Par., 13, 17: τῶν ἐκείνης ἐμοὶ καθηκόντων; Act. Thom., 40 : τῆς γενεᾶς εἰμι ἐκείνης ... ἧς καὶ ὁ κύριός σου ... εἰς τὸν καθήκοντά μοι κατὰ γένος ἐκάθισεν.

what is contrary to καθῆκον is always τὸ παρὰ τὸ καθῆκον, Diog. L., VII, 108; also Epict. Diss., I, 7, 21; 28, 5 etc.; Philo Leg. All., II, 32, though cf. Cher., 14. What Paul means by this undefined μὴ καθήκοντα is that which is offensive to man even according to the popular moral sense of the Gentiles, i.e., what even natural human judgment regards as vicious and wrong. In accordance with the decision which they have made against the Creator, God finally abandons them to a blunted sensibility. Religious indifference is followed by moral. Perverted by a wrong basic attitude, the Gentile is possessed by destructive passions and overthrown by all kinds of vices. He thus loses all vestiges of the humanity which even the healthy pagan respects.

The language of 1 Clement is more philosophical. This may be seen, not so much from the τιμὴ ἡ καθήκουσα and καθηκόντως of 1, 3 but rather from the παρὰ τὸ καθῆκον of 41, 3 and the πολιτεύεσθαι κατὰ τὸ καθῆκον τῷ Χριστῷ of 3, 4, where καθῆκον has the specific sense of *officium*.

Schlier

| † κάθημαι, † καθίζω, † καθέζομαι | → θρόνος. |

κάθημαι (LXX almost always for יָשַׁב, יְתֵב, infrequently for סָכַן, הֲלַךְ; הָיָה hi ; רָכַב; שָׁכַב), both intr. "to sit," and, esp. in the *koine* and LXX, reflexive "to sit down," in the NT, quoting ψ 109:1, at Mt. 22:44; Mk. 12:36; Lk. 20:42; Ac. 2:34; Hb. 1:13; cf. also Jm. 2:3; Mk. 4:1; Mt. 28:2; 26:58; Jn. 6:3; and again Mt. 13:1 f.; 15:29; Lk. 22:55. The Atticist 2nd sing. κάθῃ is used at Ac. 23:3, the imp. κάθου in quoting ψ 109:1 and at Jm. 2:3. [1] The imperf. ἐκαθήμην corresponds to other augmented forms. [2] The fut. καθήσομαι (Mt. 19:28; Lk. 22:30 א A) replaces the Attic καθεδοῦμαι.

καθίζω (LXX almost always for יָשַׁב q and hi ; יְתֵב; infrequently for הָיָה; רָכַב; גּוּר; נוּחַ; נָפַל hi ; פָּגַר pi ; צוּר), trans. "to set down," causative "to seat oneself" and reflexive "to sit down," in the *koine* occasionally intr. "to sit." Fut. καθίσω (Mt. 25:31); imp. aor. κάθισον (Mk. 12:36 B); perf. κεκάθικα (Hb. 12:2). [3] The class. καθίζω εἰς is incorrectly changed to κάθημαι at Mk. 13:3. [4]

The rare ἐκαθέζετο (for ἐκάθητο) from καθέζεσθαι is found only at Mt. 26:55; Jn. 4:6; 11:20; καθεζόμενος for καθήμενος occurs at Lk. 2:46; Jn. 20:12; Ac. 20:9 and in most MSS of Ac. 6:15. [5]

κ ά θ η μ α ι κτλ. Pr.-Bauer, 606-608. Wilke-Grimm, 218.
[1] Bl.-Debr.[6] § 100.
[2] *Ibid.*, § 69, 1; Radermacher[2], 68 ff.
[3] Bl.-Debr.[6] § 101 *s.v.*; J. H. Moulton, *Grammar of NT Greek*, II (1929), 242.
[4] Bl.-Debr.[6] § 205.
[5] *Ibid.*, § 101 *s.v.*; Moulton, *op. cit.*, I, 118; II, 242. It always has durative significance in the NT.

1. It means "to sit," "to sit down" or "to set down" in the neutral sense, Hom. Il., 3, 68 etc.; LXX Gn. 18:1; 19:1; Lv. 15:6; Zech. 5:7; Gn. 8:4; 1 S. 5:11; ψ 25:4 etc.). Usually one sits on a stool (כִּסֵּא, δίφρος, Aram. כּוּרְסְיָא). [6] which is found even in the simplest room (2 K 4:10). Or the Greek and Egyptian custom is followed [7] and one sits on a κλίνη (Gn. 48:2; Ez. 23:41). Outdoors one may sit on stones (Ex. 17:12), preferably under trees (Ju. 4:5; 1 K. 13:14 etc.), on hill tops (2 K. 1:9), or on the edge of a well (Ex. 2:15; cf. Jn. 4:6). Jesus likes to sit in the open, especially by the shore (Mt. 13:1; Mk. 4:1) and on mountains (Mt. 5:1; 15:29; 24:3; Mk. 13:3; Jn. 6:3). We see here His love for nature. [8] The courtyard is a favourite sitting place, especially for slaves and underlings (Est. 5:13). Thus Peter sits down in the court (Mt. 26:58, 69; Lk. 22:55 f.) [9] to get news of the fate of his Master. It is unusual for soldiers to sit while on guard (Mt. 27:36), but Petronius presupposes much worse in a similar situation. [10]

One often sat at meals in the East (Ez. 44:3; Gn. 27:19; 37:25; Ex. 32:6 [cf. 1 K. 10:7]; Ju. 2:14; 1 S. 20:5; Prv. 23:1), [11] but the Hellenistic Greek custom of reclining is followed in the NT (Mt. 9:10; 26:7 ff.; Jn. 13:23 etc.).

2. Sitting is also a mark of particular distinction.

a. Gods. Archaeological material from Egypt, the Near East and the Greek Hellenistic world shows that sitting is a distinctive sign of deity. The god often sits while men stand to pray before him. [12] In the earlier period of Israel's history the ark represented God's throne; [13] κύριος καθήμενος (ἐπὶ τῶν) χερουβίμ (1 Βασ. 4:4; 2 Βασ. 6:2; 4 Βασ. 19:15; 1 Ch. 13:6; ψ 79:1; 98:1; Is. 37:16; 2 Βασ. 22:11; Da. 3:55 [LXX + Θ]) is thus a common name for God. Isaiah sees God enthroned (6:1 ff.), and liturgical language took up this idea (ψ 46:8 etc.). A cloud may take the place of the throne (Is. 19:1). For Jesus, too, the throne is a liturgical

---

[6] For the OT stool, which has no back, cf. P. Volz, *Bibl. Altertümer*[2] (1925), 294; J. Benzinger, *Hbr. Archäologie*[3] (1927), 106, 221. For a later period cf. S. Krauss, *Talmudische Archäologie*, I (1910), 61 f.

[7] Volz, *loc. cit.*; Krauss, I, 390 ff. For sitting in the Hellenistic world, J. Müller-A. Bauer, *Die griech. Privat- und Kriegsaltertümer*,[2] *Handbuch der klass. Altertumskunde*, IV, 1 (1893), 55, 59, 265; H. Blümmer, *Die röm. Privatsaltertümer*[3] (1911), 112-123.

[8] On this pt. cf. J. Leipoldt, *Jesus oder Paulus, Jesus und Paulus* (1936), 29-36; L. Friedländer, *Sittengeschichte Roms*[9], I (1921), 461-490; C. Schneider, *Nt.liche Zeitgeschichte* (1934), 66 ff.

[9] αὐλή is the *atrium*, not the palace itself, to which he would not have had access. Cf. Kl. Mk. on 14:54.

[10] Satir., 111 ff., ed. F. Bücheler (1882). But we must consider whether the κάθημαι of Mt. 27:36 is not just an Aram. pleonasm.

[11] Benzinger, 106. Also in older Greece; κλίνη is not yet found in Hom. and Hes.

[12] E.g., Hom. Il., 4, 1; Od., 16, 264; Aesch. Suppl., 101; Eur. Tro., 884; Paus., V, 17, 9. There are illustrations in J. Leipoldt, *Bilderatlas z. Religionsgeschichte*, 9-11: *Die Religionen in d. Umwelt des Urchr.* (1926); cf. also H. Möbius, "Form u. Bdtg. der sitzenden Gestalt," *Ath. Mitt.*, 41 (1916), 199 ff. It should be remembered that Isis has the hieroglyphic throne. In the OT to stand before the sitting God is to "serve" (1 K. 17:1; 18:15).

[13] On the ark cf. M. Dibelius, *Die Lade Jahwes* (1906); H. Gunkel, "Die Lade Jahwes als Thronsitz," ZMR, 21 (1906), 1 ff.; H. Gressmann, *Die Lade Jahwes u. das Allerheiligste des salomon. Tempels* (1920); G. v. Rad, "Zelt u. Lade," NKZ, 42 (1931), 476-98. The New Year festival was probably a festival of divine enthronement, cf. P. Volz, *Das Neujahrsfest Jahwes* (1912).

expression of divine dignity (Mt. 5:34 f.; 23:22). The seer of Rev. in particular follows Is. 6 in his vision of God on the throne [14] (4:2 ff.; 5:1 ff.; 6:16; 7:10 ff.; 19:4; 20:11; 21:5). But God's opponent, Antichrist, can also sit on a throne (2 Th. 2:4).

b. Rulers. Throughout antiquity there is a close connection between the god and the ruler, whether in personal or institutional terms. [15] This helps us to see why in archaeology and in literature rulers are enthroned like the gods. [16] Even in the OT the throne is the particular prerogative of the ruler (Ex. 11:5; 12:29 of Pharaoh; 1 K. 1:17 ff.; 3:6; 8:25 etc. of the king); also the queen (1 Esr. 4:29) and particular favourites of the king (1 Esr. 4:42; cf. Mt. 20:21 ff.) are accorded the same dignity. The king may even sit in the presence of God (Ps. 110:1; 1 Ch. 17:16). In the making of thrones, as we learn from the description in 1 K. 10:18 ff. and from excavations, certain traditional forms were followed in order that the ornamentation should symbolise royal power. [17] Ac. 2:30 is wholly OT in this respect.

In the NT the Messianic King especially is enthroned along with God and His community (Rev. 3:21). This conception explains the frequent allusion to ψ 109:1 (apart from the passages mentioned under a. cf. also Mt. 26:64; Mk. 14:62; Lk. 22:69; Col. 3:1; Hb. 1:3; 8:1; 10:12; 12:2). Da. 7:13 had some influence too (cf. Rev. 14:14 ff.). But the world powers which are hostile to God and His Christ are also enthroned in Rev., e.g., Rome as a symbol of world dominion (17:1, 9, 15; 18:7).

c. Judges. Part of the orderly process of a judicial hearing is that the judge should sit in accordance with his dignity. Egyptian gods sit for judgment in the Book of the Dead. So do the three judges of the dead in Greek depictions of the underworld, which follow the practice of earthly courts. In Rome all higher legal officials speak from the *sella curulis* (βῆμα) by right. [18] Similarly, the procurators of the NT conduct judicial proceedings from the *sella curulis* (Mt. 27:19; Jn. 19:13; [19] Ac. 25:6, 17). Herod Agrippa I (Ac. 12:21) and the high-priest (Ac. 23:3) follow the same custom. The Judge of the Last Judgment in the NT is also viewed as sitting, as in other apocalyptic writings (Mt. 19:28; 25:31). [20]

---

[14] C. Schneider, *Die Erlebnisechtheit der Apk. d. Joh.* (1930), on Rev. 4.

[15] F. Kampers, *Vom Werdegang der abendländischen Kaisermystik* (1924); E. Lohmeyer, *Christuskult und Kaiserkult* (1919); O. Weinreich, "Antikes Gottmenschentum" in *N. Jbch. Wiss. u. Jugendbildung*, 2 (1926), 633-651.

[16] When the king seats himself on the throne, he definitively takes power, 1 K. 1:35, 46. Cf. the German practice of sitting on the high throne at Aachen, and English coronation on "Jacob's stone" in Westminster Abbey, which is one of the most essential parts of the ceremonial.

[17] A. Wünsche, "Salomos Thron u. Hippodrom Abbilder des babyl. Himmelsbildes," *Ex Oriente Lux*, II, 3 (1906); H. Gressmann, *Der Messias* (1929), 21, n. 7.

[18] On the *sella curulis*, a portable chair of ivory, cf. T. Mommsen, *Röm. Staatsrecht*[3], I (1887), 395 ff., *Handbuch der röm. Altertümer*, I, 2; H. Schiller-M. Voigt, *Röm. Staats-, Kriegs- u. Privataltertümer*[2] (1893), 39; *Handbuch der klass. Altertumskunde*, IV, 2; Blümner, *op. cit.*, 122 f. Lower officials sat on simpler seats.

[19] But this passage is not unambiguous, cf. P. Corssen, ZNW, 15 (1914), 339 f. Here it is taken intransitively. Jesus is mockingly set on the βῆμα by Pilate. But this could not be the *sella curulis*.

[20] Cf. Volz Esch., 260-264; Bousset-Gressm., 257.

d. Teachers. Most depictions of the schools of antiquity show the teachers sitting. [21] Jesus almost always sits to teach (Mt. 5:1; 13:1 f.; 15:29; 24:3; 26:55; Mk. 4:1; 9:35; 13:3; Lk. 5:3; Jn. 6:3; 8:2). We see from Mt. 23:2; Mk. 2:6; Lk. 5;17 that in so doing He follows Rabbinic custom, though with no desire to emphasise any particular dignity.

e. Assemblies. In Hom. the Greeks sit at assemblies (Od., 2, 69 etc.). The Senate sits (Plut. Otho, 9 [I, 1071a etc.]). So does the Sanhedrin. [22] So do the elders of the congregation when they meet (Ju. 4:1 ff.; 2 K. 6:32 etc.). So do Christian synods. Apocalyptic speaks of a heavenly senate (Rev. 20:4), though this image merges into that of heavenly worship (→ 444).

f. On orders of precedence in sitting → δεξιός.

3. Sitting as a Psychological Attitude.

a. Sitting as a Gesture of Grief. In the OT, as also to-day in the East, sitting is a sign of mourning; it is psychologically the attitude of apathetic abandonment. One sits to bewail one's own grief or that of others (Job 2:8 ff.; 1 Macc. 1:27 etc.); καθήμενος ἐν σκότει (ψ 106:10; Is. 9:1 A [= Mt. 4:16; Lk. 1:79]; Is. 42:7) is the technical term for the mourner. Usually beggars also sit (2 K. 7:3; Mt. 20:30; Mk. 10:46; Lk. 18:35; Jn. 9:8; Ac. 3:10; 14:8). Sitting is a gesture of religious mourning among women who bewail the gods of the mysteries; thus the mourning Isis sits, [23] and so do the women who bewail Adonis (Ez. 8:14). The women who weep for Jesus also sit (Mt. 27:61). Penitents sit to express their grief (Jon. 3:6; Lk. 10:13).

b. Sitting for practical reasons. We are to regard it as purely practical that scholars usually sit (Mk. 3:32; 5:15; Lk. 2:46; 8:35). Some people have to sit because of their occupation, e.g., tax-gatherers (Mt. 9:9), fishermen (Mt. 13:48), money-changers (Jn. 2:14) and those who do office work (Lk. 16:6). Even to-day in the South one can often see children sitting down to play (Mt. 11:16; Lk. 7:32).

4. Sitting at Divine Service.

Standing was usual in the temples of antiquity. At the most ἱκέται sat on altars, or one sat while waiting for an oracle. [24] The lengthy services of the mystery religions first made sitting necessary. Whether it became general, we do not know, but the stone seats on the walls of Mithra shrines bear witness to it. In the worship of Isis either standing or sitting seems to have been allowed. [25] In the synagogue women sit as well as the teacher and the leader. There seems to have been also a number of seats for men on the side-benches, and men often sat on mats (ציפי). [26] Jesus (Lk. 4:20) and Paul (Ac. 13:14; 16:13) sat at synagogue

---

[21] Cf. the well-known relief at Trèves, Blümner, op. cit., 321.

[22] Schürer, II, 165; Sanh., IV, 3 f.

[23] Examples in H. Bonnet, Ägyptische Religion, Bilderatlas z. Religionsgeschichte, 2-4 (1924).

[24] E.g., Aristoph. Nu., 254; Plut. Def. Orac., passim.

[25] In the two depictions of the worship of Isis at Herculaneum, in the Museo Nazionale at Naples, only one figure is sitting and the rest are standing. But these are pictures of high points in the service.

[26] bBB, 8b/9a; J. Elbogen, Der jüd. Gottesdienst u. seine geschichtl. Entwicklung² (1924), 475 f.; S. Krauss, Synagogale Altertümer (1922), 384-398.

worship. Sitting was general in the early Christian Church (Ac. 2:2; 20:9; 1 C. 14:30; Jm. 2:3; also Rev. 4:4; 11:16 if these passages are modelled on divine service and not on an enthronement scene).

5. Figurative Meanings.

a. "To stay," Aristoph. Ra., 1103; Thuc., IV, 124, very common in the LXX, and often in the NT, Mt. 26:36; Lk. 24:49; Ac. 18:11. b. "To dwell," Thuc., III, 107, 1; Hdt., V, 63; common in the LXX, Gn. 23:10; Ju. 6:10 etc.; in the NT only at Lk. 21:35; Rev. 14:6. c. Frequently with suitable nouns for "to ride," "to journey," Mk. 11:2, 7; Lk. 19:30; Jn. 12:14 f.; Ac. 8:28, 31; Rev. 6:2, 4 f., 8; 9:17; 17:3; 19:11, 18 f., 21. d. "To instal," in two NT passages with a hint of the literal sense: 1 C. 6:4 as judges and Eph. 1:20 as head (reminiscent of the enthronement of a ruler, cf. Phil. 2:9 ff.). e. "To sit to consider," in the parables in Lk. 14:28, 31. f. Finally, at Pentecost the community has a vision of the Holy Spirit in fiery tongues lighting on each of them, Ac. 2:3 → πνεῦμα.

Carl Schneider

> καθίστημι, ἀκαταστασία
> ἀκατάστατος

† καθίστημι.

From the basic sense of "to set down," "to put in place," there derive the following meanings which are significant in the NT.

1. "To conduct," "to bring," "to lead to," Hom. Od., 13, 274; Hdt., I, 64; BGU, I, 93, 22; Jos. 6:23; 2 Ch. 28:15 (בוא hi); Ac. 17:15.

2. "To set in an elevated position, in an office," "to instal," a. with simple acc. of person, P. Hibeh, 29, 21 (3rd cent. B.C.); ἐπίτροπον: P. Ryl., II, 121, 15; 153, 18; πρεσβυτέρους: Tt. 1:5; pass. Hb. 5:1; 8:3; Diod. S., XVII, 62; Philo Mut. Nom., 151; b. with acc. and ἐπί and gen., Jos. Ant., 2, 73; Gn. 39:4; Mt. 24:45; Lk. 12:42; ἐπὶ πολλῶν σε καταστήσω: Mt. 25:21, 23; Ac. 6:3; 7:27; pass. ἐπὶ τῆς Αἰγύπτου κατασταθείς, APF, II (1902), 429,12; with acc. and ἐπί and dat.: ἐπὶ πᾶσιν τοῖς ὑπάρχουσιν: Mt. 24:47; Lk. 12:44; with acc. and ἐπί and acc.: Xenoph. Cyrop., 8, 1, 9; Isoc., 12, 132; καταστήσεις ἐπὶ σεαυτὸν ἄρχοντα οὐκ ἀλλότριον: Philo Spec. Leg., IV, 157; Ps. 8:6; 1 Βασ. 8:5; c. with double acc.: Hdt., VII, 105; P. Hibeh, 82, 14; τινὰ ἀρχιερέα: Diog. L., IX, 64; Jos. Ant., 12, 360; Ex. 2:14; Gr. Sir. 32(35):1; ἀνθρώπους ἀρχιερεῖς, Hb. 7:28; partly combined with b.: Lk. 12:14; Ac. 7:10, 27, 35; d. with final inf., also in the gen. or with εἰς: δικάζειν, 1 Βασ. 8:5; τοῦ δοῦναι, Mt. 24:45; Lk. 12:42; εἰς τὴν ἀρχήν: Jos. Ant., 17, 232; εἰς τὸ προσφέρειν δῶρα: Hb. 8:3.

κ α θ ί σ τ η μ ι. Cr.-Kö., *s.v.*; Khl. and Zn. R. on 5:19; Hck., Dib., Wnd. Jk. on 3:6; 4:4; J. de Zwaan, "R. 5:19; Jk. 3:6; 4:4 en de Κοινή," ThSt, 31 (1913), 85-94.

3. With double accusative : "To make someone something," "to put him in a certain position or state," pass. "to be instituted as something," "to become something," perf. "to be something." There is no philological ground for the common suggestion that the element of judgment predominates rather than the actual fact. The state itself is always presupposed.

All secular usage supports this. κλαίοντά σε καταστήσει : Eur. Andr., 635; ἔρημον καὶ ἄπορον κατέστησεν; Plat. Phileb., 16b; (Monobazos) κατέστησεν ἐγκύμονα (made Helen pregnant): Jos. Ant., 20, 18. Cf. also the combinations of καθιστάναι with εἰς or ἐν : εἰς ἀνάγκην : Lys., 3, 3; εἰς ἀγῶνα : Plat. Ap., 24c; τὴν πόλιν ἐν πολέμῳ, Plat. Menex., 242a. Cf., too, the mid. and pass. : ἀνάγκη τὴν ναυμαχίαν πεζομαχίαν καθίστασθαι : Thuc., II, 89 (the battle at sea is forced into a battle on land); οἱ μὲν ὀφθαλμῶν ἰητροὶ κατεστέασι, οἱ δὲ κεφαλῆς : Hdt., 2, 84 (not "they are reckoned," but "they are"); Kronos, Ares, Aphrodite ἐπιτάραχοι καὶ ἐπίδικοι καθίστανται : Vett. Val., I, 22 (43, 22 f., Kroll). The word is distinguished from ποιεῖν with the acc. or from γίγνεσθαι only to the degree that there is the suggestion of a spectator confirming the situation which has arisen : ψευδῆ γ' ἐμαυτὸν οὐ καταστήσω πόλει : Soph. Ant., 658. There is no thought of a distinction between judgment and reality.

The best examples of *koine* usage are in the pap. [1] Particularly instructive is P. Oxy., II, 281, from the time of Paul, 20-50. Syra, daughter of Theon, complains before the judge Heracleides concerning her husband, whom she once took into her house without any means of support (λειτὸν παντελῶς ὄντα): οὐ διέλειπεν κακουχῶν με καὶ ὑβρίζων καὶ τὰς χεῖρας ἐπιφέρων καὶ τῶν ἀναγκαίων ἐνδεῆ καθιστάς, ὕστερον δὲ καὶ ἐνκατέλιπέ με λειτὴν καθεστῶσαν. διὸ ἀξιῶ συντάξαι καταστῆσαι αὐτὸν ἐπὶ σέ. In the first two cases the reference is to the actual state of affairs ; καθιστάς has the sense of *reddens*, καθεστῶσαν of οὖσαν. In the third case we have a technical form of sense 1., "to lay before the judge." But this does not justify us in claiming that the forensic concept of affirmation affects the ordinary usage.

Theologically the most significant verse is R. 5:19 : ὥσπερ γὰρ διὰ τῆς παρακοῆς τοῦ ἑνὸς ἀνθρώπου ἁμαρτωλοὶ κατεστάθησαν οἱ πολλοί, οὕτως καὶ διὰ τῆς ὑπακοῆς τοῦ ἑνὸς δίκαιοι κατασταθήσονται οἱ πολλοί. Here, too, there is hardly any linguistic or material difference between κατεστάθησαν and ἐγένοντο. [2] The meaning is that "as the many became sinners through the disobedience of the one man, so the many become righteous through the obedience of the one." This does not imply that the forensic element is absent. 2 C. 5:21 and Gl. 3:13 show that in Paul ποιεῖν and γίνεσθαι do not necessarily bear an effective sense ; they may also have an affective. The context decides. In R. 5 the forensic element is evident at v. 18 (κατάκριμα — δικαίωσις). Vv. 13 f. also show that in the judgment of God the thing which counts is not exclusively the nature of the individual but the dominant character of the old (or the new) creation (→ ἐν, II, 541 f.). [3] According to the current Jewish view God decides qualitatively in the sense that the quality ultimately decides His sentence and our destiny. Borrowing from other Jewish conceptions, [4] Paul boldly reverses the relation. God's sovereign sentence decides both destiny and quality. To be sure, guilt is involved. Yet it is

---

[1] J. de Zwaan, *loc. cit.*
[2] The observations of Zn. and Khl. R. are philologically unsound.
[3] All expositions which reject this (e.g., Khl.) are suspect, however we expound the phrase ἐφ' ᾧ πάντες ἥμαρτον.
[4] Cf. B. Murmelstein, "Adam," WZKM, 35 (1928), 242 ff.

in Adam that the many, and virtually all, became sinners. Conversely, the many, again virtually all, but in fact believers, become righteous in Christ in spite of their own sin (δικαιοῦντα τὸν ἀσεβῆ, R. 4:5). They will stand forth as righteous in God's judgment. Pronounced righteous, they will then normally become righteous in fact as well (R. 8:3 f.). Here, however, the emphasis is on the judicial sentence of God, which on the basis of the act of the head determines the destiny of all. The subtleties which have rightly been found in the passage lie in the teaching rather than the wording. The suggestion that Paul has united senses 1. and 2. into a pregnant eschatological riddle is too artificial. [5]

4. The other NT passages lead us to a similar result. Thus true realisation is implied at 2 Pt. 1:8 : ταῦτα . . . οὐκ ἀργοὺς . . . καθίστησιν. At Jm. 4:4 : ἐχθρὸς τοῦ θεοῦ καθίσταται is more pregnant than a mere ἐστίν: [6] he proves himself to be, he is in God's eyes, an enemy, and he really is this. Jm. 3:6 : καὶ ἡ γλῶσσα πῦρ. ὁ κόσμος τῆς ἀδικίας ἡ γλῶσσα καθίσταται ἐν τοῖς μέλεσιν ἡμῶν, ἡ σπιλοῦσα ὅλον τὸ σῶμα, [7] "and the tongue is a fire; it is present among our members as a world of iniquity, and it corrupts the whole man." The sense would allow of ἐστίν, but the aspect of affirmation is expressed more strongly by καθίσταται.

† ἀκαταστασία.

"Disorder," "unrest," a. "political turmoil," "revolution," Polyb., 1, 70, 1 (synon. ταραχή); 14, 9, 6. In the plur. 32, 21, 5; Dion. Hal. Ant. Rom., VI, 31, 8; v. Arnim, III, 99, 31; Vett. Val., I, 1 (4, 18 Kroll); IV, 18 (191, 3, 15 Kroll) etc.; Catal. Cod. Astr. Graec., VII, 226, 13 f.; 227, 17; 228, 27; VIII, 3, 182, 8 figur. of the cosmic sphere : κοσμικαὶ ἀκαταστασίαι, φθορὰ καρπῶν, νόσος τε καὶ ἀκαταστασία. b. "personal unrest," Vett. Val., IV, 18 (190, 23 Kroll): ταραχαὶ οἰκείων τε ἀκαταστασίαι καὶ θηλυκῶν ἐπιπλοκαί; Prv. 26:28 : στόμα ἄστεγον ποιεῖ ἀκαταστασίας; Tob. 4:13, synon. ἀπώλεια.

Sense a. Lk. 21:9 : πολέμους καὶ ἀκαταστασίας. Sense b. 2 C. 6:5 : ἐν ἀκαταστασίαις. Another sense c. is peculiar to the NT, i.e., disruption of the peace of the community either by disputes, Jm. 3:16 : ὅπου γὰρ ζῆλος, . . . ἀκαταστασία καὶ πᾶν φαῦλον πρᾶγμα, cf. the list of vices at 2 C. 12:20 : ἔρις . . . ἀκαταστασίαι, or by orgiastic impulses in the gatherings of the congregation, 1 C. 14:33 : οὐ γάρ ἐστιν ἀκαταστασίας ὁ θεὸς ἀλλὰ εἰρήνης.

There is a material par. in the mystery script of Andania, Ditt. Syll.³, II, 736, 42 : ὅπως εὐσχημόνως καὶ εὐτάκτως (cf. 1 C. 14:40) . . . πάντα γίνηται, also the inscr. Ditt. Syll.³, III, 1109, 63 ff. οὐδενὶ δὲ ἐξέσται ἐν τῇ στιβάδι (at the festal gathering) οὔτε ᾆσαι οὔτε θορυβῆσαι οὔτε κροτῆσαι (to clap), μετὰ δὲ πάσης εὐκοσμίας καὶ ἡσυχίας τοὺς μερισμοὺς (the allotted role) λέγειν καὶ ποιεῖν.

---

[5] J. de Zwaan, op. cit., 92 : Interplay of the meanings "to be brought forth as a wrongdoer" and "to be set forth as righteous."
[6] Cf. v. 4a, Hck. Jk.
[7] Following the arrangement of B. Weiss and Hck. Jk. Spitta (Zur Gesch. u. Lit. des Urchr., II [1896] 96 f.) erases καὶ ἡ — τῆς ἀδικίας and ἡ σπιλοῦσα — σῶμα, Dib. Jk., ad loc. ὁ κόσμος — ἡμῶν. Wnd. Jk., ad loc. assumes that there are lacunae in the text.

† ἀκατάστατος.

"Restless," a. "exposed to unrest," Ditt. Syll.³, III, 1184, 10; LXX of individuals, Is. 54:11 (Σ Gn. 4:12; Lam. 4:14; Hos. 8:6); b. "restless," "unsettled," slander ἀκατάστατον δαιμόνιόν ἐστιν, μηδέποτε εἰρηνεῦον, Herm. m., 2, 3; "fickle," Polyb., 7, 6, 4; Plut. Def. Orac., 50 (II, 437d).

In the NT we find only sense b. Jm. 1:8 (in spite of the pass. figure in v. 6): ἀνὴρ → δίψυχος, ἀκατάστατος ἐν πάσαις ταῖς ὁδοῖς αὐτοῦ, reprehensibly "unstable" or "fickle." The man who doubts as he prays does not give himself wholeheartedly to God. Jm. 3:8 of the tongue: ἀκατάστατον κακόν v. l. ἀκατάσχετον, "unable to be tamed").

Oepke

Κάϊν → Ἄβελ, I, 6.

καινός, καινότης, ἀνακαινίζω, ἀνακαινόω, ἀνακαίνωσις, ἐγκαινίζω

† καινός.

1. Linguistic.

Of the two most common words for "new" since the classical period, namely, → νέος and καινός, [1] the former signifies "what was not there before," "what has only just arisen or appeared," the latter "what is new and distinctive" as compared with other things. νέος is new in time or origin, i.e., young, with a suggestion of immaturity or of lack of respect for the old (→ νέος for examples). καινός is what is new in nature, different from the usual, impressive, better than the old, superior in value or attraction, e.g., Xenoph. Cyrop., III, 1, 30: καινῆς ἀρχομένης ἀρχῆς ἢ τῆς εἰωθυίας καταμενούσης; Mem., IV, 4 and 6: πειρῶμαι καινόν τι λέγειν ἀεί (opp. τὰ αὐτὰ ... περὶ τῶν αὐτῶν), cf. previously: ἐκεῖνα τὰ αὐτὰ λέγεις ἃ ἐγὼ πάλαι ποτέ σου ἤκουσα; Demosth. Or., 35, 1: οὐδὲν καινὸν διαπράττονται οἱ Φασηλῖται, ... ἀλλ'

κ α ι ν ό ς. On 1: Cr.-Kö., 550 ff.; Moult.-Mill., 314 f.; Liddell-Scott, 858; Preisigke Wört., I, 720; Pr.-Bauer³, 655. On 2: P. Gennrich, *Die Lehre v. d. Wiedergeburt* (1907), 13 ff.; A. v. Harnack, "Die Terminologie d. Wiedergeburt u. verwandter Erlebnisse in d. ältesten Kirche," TU, 42, 3 (1918), 101 ff., 135 ff.

[1] Cf. J. H. H. Schmidt, *Synonymik d. griech. Sprache*, II (1878), 94 ff., esp. 112 ff.; *Handbuch d. lat. u. griech. Synonymik* (1889), 490 ff.; Trench, 133 ff. Etym. νέος (Lat. *novus*) is an Indo-European word from the adv. *nu* (νύ), now, of the moment. The deriv. of καινός is uncertain, probably from a root *ken-*, freshly come or begun [Debrunner].

ἅπερ εἰώθασιν; Isoc., 5, 84 : οὔτε γὰρ ταὐτὰ βούλομαι λέγειν ... οὔτ' ἔτι καινὰ δύναμαι ζητεῖν; Aeschin., 3, 208 : ὅτι τῷ πολλάκις μὲν ἐπιορκοῦντι, ἀεὶ δὲ μεθ' ὅρκων ἀξιοῦντι πιστεύεσθαι, δυοῖν θάτερον ὑπάρξαι δεῖ, ... ἢ τοὺς θεοὺς καινοὺς ἢ τοὺς ἀκροατὰς μὴ τοὺς αὐτούς; Plat. Euthyphr., 3b : φησὶ γάρ με (i.e., Socrates) ποιητὴν εἶναι θεῶν, καὶ ὡς καινοὺς ποιοῦντα θεοὺς τοὺς δ' ἀρχαίους οὐ νομίζοντα ἐγράψατο τούτων αὐτῶν ἕνεκα; cf. Ap., 24b (on this Just. Ap., 5, 3 : καινὰ εἰσφέρειν αὐτὸν δαιμόνια, also Epit., 10, 5); Ap., 27c : οὐκοῦν δαιμόνια μὲν φῇς με καὶ νομίζειν καὶ διδάσκειν, εἴτ' οὖν καινὰ εἴτε παλαιά; Philo Spec. Leg., I, 28 (the authors of myths) θεοὺς καινοὺς ... εἰσαγαγόντες; Plut. Cato Maior, 1 (I, 336b): εἰωθότων δὲ τῶν Ῥωμαίων τοὺς ἀπὸ γένους δόξαν οὐκ ἔχοντας, ἀρχομένους δὲ γνωρίζεσθαι δι' αὐτῶν καινοὺς προσαγορεύειν ἀνθρώπους; Jos. Ap., 2, 182 : (the reproach levelled against the Jews), τὸ δὴ μὴ καινῶν εὑρετὰς ἔργων ἢ λόγων ἄνδρας παρασχεῖν. Both terms are found in the sense of "unfamiliar," "unexpected," "striking," "wonderful," "unheard of," e.g., Eur. Hec., 689 : ἄπιστ' ἄπιστα καινὰ καινὰ δέρκομαι (I see); Xenoph. Mem., I, 1, 1: ἕτερα δὲ καινὰ δαιμόνια; Hippocr. De Morbis Internis, 17: οὐ καινόν (it is not surprising); Luc. Nigrinus, 22 : τὸ καινότατον (the most astonishing); 1 Cl., 42, 5 : καὶ τοῦτο οὐ καινῶς (and that was nothing very new); Just. Apol., 15, 9 : εἰ ἀγαπᾶτε τοὺς ἀγαπῶντας ὑμᾶς, τί καινὸν ποιεῖτε (cf. Mt. 5:46); ibid., 10 (cf. Lk. 6:34); Philo Migr. Abr., 50 : καινός (unheard of) δ' ὢν (sc. Scripture) ἐν ἅπασι τὴν ἐπιστήμην; Plut. Cic., 14 (I, 867d): ὁ δὲ πολλοὺς οἰόμενος εἶναι τοὺς πραγμάτων καινῶν (res novae, revolution) ἐφιεμένους ἐν τῇ βουλῇ; cf. Apophth. Lac., 52 (II, 212c): περὶ πραγμάτων καινῶν καὶ μεταστάσεως τοῦ πολιτεύματος; Ael. Var. Hist., 2, 14 : ὁ Ξέρξης ... ἑαυτῷ δὲ εἰργάζετο καινὰς ὁδοὺς (unaccustomed ways) καὶ πλοῦν ἀήθη; Achill. Tat., III, 16 : ὦ τροφῶν καινὰ (new-styled) μυστήρια. The distinction becomes less stringent as time passes, cf. the use of the adjectives together to strengthen the basic concept, Polyb., 1, 68, 10 : καθόλου δ' [ἀ]εί τι νέον [καὶ] καινὸν προσεξεύρισκον; 5, 75, 4 : καινοί τινες αἰεὶ καὶ νέοι πρὸς τὰς τοιαύτας ἀπάτας πεφύκαμεν; Cl. Al. Paed., I, 5, 14, 5 : λαὸν νέον καὶ λαὸν καινόν; ibid., 20, 3 : ἀεὶ νέοι καὶ ἀεὶ ἤπιοι καὶ ἀεὶ καινοί. In modern Greek καινός is the literary, νέος the popular word. [2]

The LXX regularly uses καινός for חָדָשׁ, Dt. 32:17; ψ 32:3; Ez. 11:19; Ἰερ. 38:31 etc., and only at Is. 65:15 for אַחֵר. Often [3] the misreading of the radical חרשׁ as הרשׁ introduces καινός into the LXX, e.g., 1 Βασ. 23:15 ff. In Ἰωβ א and A often misread the Gk. κενός as καινός, which thus has much the sense of "unheard of." Cf. the λόγος τοῦ νόμου at Dt. 32:47.

In the NT καινός means "not yet used" at Mt. 9:17 par.; Mk. 2:21; Lk. 5:36; Mt. 27:60; Jn. 19:41, and "unusual" or "interesting" at Ac. 17:21; [4] Mk. 1:27; [5] Ac. 17:19, cf. v. 20 : ξενίζοντα, but especially "new in kind," Mt. 13:52 : καινὰ καὶ → παλαιά, [6] Eph. 2:15; [7] Jn. 13:34; 1 Jn. 2:8; cf. v. 7 and 2 Jn. 5 : ἐντολὴν καινήν, and able and ordained as such to replace and excel the old, Hb. 8:13, cf. v. 6 ff.: the καινὴ διαθήκη [8] etc. The antithesis καινός/παλαιός is wholly one of kind. But cf. Eph. 4:22 ff. Yet the

---

[2] Cf. Moult.-Mill., op. cit.

[3] From here to the end of the paragraph by Bertram.

[4] Cf. Pr.-Bauer, ad loc.; K. Lake-H. J. Cadbury, ad loc. in F. J. F. Jackson-K. Lake, The Beginnings of Christianity, I, 4 (1933).

[5] Cf. P. Oxy., X, 1224, Fr. 2 verso (from an unknown gospel): π[ο]ίαν σέ [φασιν διδα]χὴν καιν[ὴν] δι[δάσκειν ἢ τί β]ά[πτισ]μα καινὸν [κηρύσσειν].

[6] Cf. Jülicher GlJ, II, 132 f.; Zn. Mt., ad loc.; Schl. Mt., 450 f. The Rabb. material in Str.-B., I, 677 is unrewarding in respect of Mt. 13:52.

[7] Cf. Chrys. Hom. in Eph. (MPG, 62, 40): ὁρᾷς οὐχὶ τὸν Ἕλληνα γενόμενον Ἰουδαῖον, ἀλλὰ καὶ τοῦτον κἀκεῖνον εἰς ἑτέραν κατάστασιν ἥκοντας;

[8] On the antithesis παλαιά — καινὴ διαθήκη cf. S. Dt., 33 on 6:6 (G. Kittel [1922], 1, 60): "an old order which no one observes ..., a new which all run to meet."

aspect of time is also present, 2 C. 5:17; Hb. 8:13 : καινὴν … τὴν πρώτην κτλ.; cf. v. 7 and 9:15; 1 Jn. 2:7: οὐκ ἐντολὴν καινὴν …, ἀλλ' … ἣν εἴχετε ἀπ' ἀρχῆς, v. 2 Jn. 5. Cf. Oecumenius on Rev. 21:1 (p. 232, ed. H. C. Hoskier): καινὸν γὰρ ἅπαν καλεῖται τὸ μὴ ὂν μὲν τοιοῦτον πρότερον, νῦν δέ γενόμενον.

2. Theological.

καινός is the epitome of the wholly different and miraculous thing which is brought by the time of salvation. Hence "new" is a leading teleological term in apocalyptic promise : a new heaven and a new earth, Rev. 21:1; 2 Pt. 3:13 (Is. 65:17); [9] the new Jerusalem, Rev. 3:12; 21:2 (Test. D. 5:12); [10] the new wine of the eschatological banquet, Mk. 14:25 par. (→ II, 34); the new name, Rev. 2:17; 3:12 (Is. 62:2; 65:15), cf. 19:12; the new song, 5:9; 14:3 (cf. Is. 42:10; ψ 95:1 etc.); [11] "Behold, I make all things new," 21:5 (Is. 43:19). [12] New creation is the glorious end of the revelation of God's salvation. It is the supreme goal of early Christian hope, and it is reflected from the future salvation in the present existence of Christians on the old earth because it has become present salvation in Christ, 2 C. 5:17: εἴ τις ἐν Χριστῷ, καινὴ → κτίσις· τὰ ἀρχαῖα (→ I, 487) παρῆλθεν, ἰδοὺ γέγονεν καινά, cf. Gl. 6:15; [13] the new aeon, which has dawned with Christ, brings a new creation, the creation of a new man. Christ Himself is the new man (so expressly for the first time in Ign. Eph., 20, 1, though this is the implication of Jesus' own description of Himself as ὁ → υἱὸς τοῦ ἀνθρώπου, cf. Paul in R. 5:12 ff., 1 C. 15:21 f., 45 ff.), the initiator of the new creation of the last time. [14] Thus καινός becomes a slogan of the reality of salvation which we know already in Christ (→ II, 700). In Christ Jews and Gentiles have been made εἰς ἕνα καινὸν ἄνθρωπον (Eph. 2:15; → I, 365). The Church is the new humanity. For the individual the new man is both a gift and a task, Eph. 4:24 : ἐνδύσασθαι τὸν καινὸν ἄνθρωπον τὸν κατὰ θεὸν → κτισθέντα. [15] God's saving will has worked itself out in history in the καινὴ διαθήκη which was promised for the last days in Jer. 31:31 ff. and which has been established by Jesus (→ II, 129), 1 C. 11:25 (Lk. 22:20); Hb. 8:8 ff.; 9:15. This is essentially different from the old divine order,

---

[9] Cf. from Jewish apocal. Eth. En. 91:16 f.; 45:4 f.; 72:1: "The new creation which lasts to eternity"; Jub. 1:29 : "… day of the new creation …, when heaven and earth and all creatures will be renewed"; 4:26; S. Bar. 32:6; 44:12; "the new world"; 57:2; 4 Esr. 7:75; cf. Str.-B., III, 840 ff.

[10] Cf. Eth. En. 90:29; S. Bar. 4:1 ff.

[11] Cf. Loh. Apk. on 5:9. The new song which was sung at OT feasts in praise of the new divine gifts of salvation (Ps. 33:3 etc.) was a song of the last time of salvation in the Rabbis too, cf. Str.-B., III, 801 f. Philo Vit. Mos., I, 255 : ᾆσμα καινόν, refers to the "song of the well" in Nu. 21:17 f.

[12] Cf. in Rabb. Judaism the expectation of the new Torah which the Messiah will bring, Str.-B., IV, 1 f.

[13] On the externally similar but essentially different concept of the new creation [בְּרִיָּה חֲדָשָׁה] in Rabb. Judaism, cf. Str.-B., II, 421 ff., III, 217 f., IV, 1243 (s.v. Kreatur). The closest to Paul is S. Dt., 30 on 3:29 (Kittel, 49): "Lo, you are now new ; the old is already put off." Very different is the Stoic concept of the renewal of the world, cf. Wnd. 2 K., ad loc.

[14] → I, 366; J. Jeremias, Jesus als Weltvollender = BFTh, 33, 4 (1930), 56 f.

[15] The par. Col. 3:10 : τὸν νέον (sc. ἄνθρωπον), and the context of Eph. 4:22 ff., show that the ideas of the new mode and the new time (→ 447 f.) of the Christian are closely related and complementary.

2 C. 3:6 : οὐ γράμματος, ἀλλὰ πνεύματος (→ I, 766). [16] It is better (Hb. 7:22).
It is founded on higher promises (8:6). It is infallible (8:7). It is of everlasting
validity (13:20). It is the perfect counterpart of its predecessor, which has now
been superseded and is doomed to perish, 8:13; cf. 7:18 f. [17] The parables of the
new which cannot be mixed with the old (Mk. 2:21 f. par.) point to the *totaliter
aliter* of the content of the message of Jesus. [18] The καινὴ ἐντολή of love which
Jesus gives (Jn. 13:34) is distinguished by the fact that the duty of the disciples
to love is grounded in the love of Jesus which they must experience (→ II, 553). [19]
That the same commandment is both old and new (1 Jn. 2:7 f.; 2 Jn. 5) is due to the
fear of heretical novelties, though we cannot expound these in detail (→ II, 555). [20]
In the promise of Mk. 16:17: γλώσσαις λαλήσουσιν καιναῖς, καινός indicates
the heavenly nature of the miraculous speech; in *glossolalia* we have one of the
marks of future existence in heaven (→ I, 726; II, 702).

> In post-apost. and apologetical writings καινός is still used to characterise and
> evaluate the revelation of salvation. But it is now primarily understood from within and
> legalistically. Jesus Christ is the new gate into the kingdom of God, Herm. s., 9, 12, 1 ff.
> He is the καινὸς ἄνθρωπος, Ign. Eph., 20, 1 in whom God has pointed to a new and
> eternal life (19, 3) and who has prepared for Himself τὸν λαὸν τὸν καινόν (Barn., 5, 7;
> 7, 5; cf. Dg., 1, 1: καινὸν τοῦτο γένος). To be a Christian is to be made new, Barn.,
> 16, 8; to become a new man, Dg., 2, 1: γενόμενος ὥσπερ ἐξ ἀρχῆς καινὸς ἄνθρωπος,
> ὡς ἂν καὶ λόγου καινοῦ ... ἀκροατὴς ἐσόμενος. [21] There comes a time μηκέτι
> οὔσης τῆς ἀνομίας, καινῶν δὲ γεγονότων πάντων ὑπὸ κυρίου, Barn., 15, 7. The
> content of the NT revelation is ὁ καινὸς νόμος τοῦ κυρίου ἡμῶν Ἰησοῦ Χριστοῦ,
> Barn., 2, 6, cf. Just. Dial., 11, 4; 12, 3, καινὴ διαθήκη καὶ νόμος αἰώνιος, 122, 5 etc.
> Christ Himself is this divine order and law in person, 11, 4 : οὗτός ἐστιν ὁ καινὸς
> νόμος καὶ ἡ καινὴ διαθήκη, cf. 51, 3 etc. or ὁ καινὸς νομοθέτης, 14, 3; 18, 3. [22]

† καινότης.

> "Newness," e.g., of invention in the field of speech, Thuc., III, 38, 5 : μετὰ καινό-
> τητος ... λόγου; Isoc., 2, 41: οὐκ ἐν τοῖς λόγοις χρὴ τούτοις ... ζητεῖν τὰς
> καινότητας, ἐν οἷς οὔτε παράδοξον οὔτ' ἄπιστον οὔτ' ἔξω τῶν νομιζομένων
> οὐδὲν ἔξεστιν εἰπεῖν, ἀλλ' ἡγεῖσθαι τοῦτον χαριέστατον, ὃς ἂν τῶν διεσπαρμέ-
> νων ἐν ταῖς τῶν ἄλλων διανοίαις ἀθροῖσαι τὰ πλεῖστα δυνηθῇ καὶ φράσαι κάλ-
> λιστα περὶ αὐτῶν. It often has the secondary sense of what is unusual and astonishing,
> Anaxandrides, 54, 5 f. (CAF, II, 159): χρὴ γὰρ εἰς ὄχλον φέρειν ἅπανθ' ὅσ' ἄν τις
> καινότητ' ἔχειν δοκῇ; Plut. Mar., 16 (I, 414d): ἡγεῖτο γὰρ πολλὰ μὲν ἐπιψεύ-

---

[16] Cf. Wnd. 2 K., *ad loc.*
[17] That it is also the διαθήκη νέα (12:24) results from its temporal relation to the old
(→ 447).
[18] Cf. Hck. Mk., 38; J. Schniewind, *Das Evangelium nach Mk.* (*NT Deutsch²*, 1 [1935],
61).
[19] Cf. Zn. J., *ad loc.*; Schl. J., 288 f.; Holtzmann NT, II, 1026.
[20] Cf. Bü. J., 27 f.
[21] We read of the new man in the NT sense in Preisigke Wört., 2266, 9 f. (middle of the
4th cent.): θεωροῦμεν σὲ τὸν δεσπότην καὶ κενὸν (= καινὸν) ἄ<ν>[θ]ρωπ[ον], unless we are to follow Deissmann LO, 183 in reading πάτρωνα for ἄνθρωπον.
[22] Cf. J. Behm, *Der Begriff* διαθήκη *im NT* (1912), 102 ff., 98 ff.

κ α ι ν ό τ η ς. J. H. H. Schmidt, *Synonymik d. griech. Sprache,* II (1878), 118; Liddell-
Scott, 858; Pr.-Bauer³, 655 f.

δεσθαι τῶν οὐ προσόντων τὴν καινότητα τοῖς φοβεροῖς (opp. συνήθεια); Philo Vit. Cont., 63 : εὐπαράγωγα ... ταῦτα πάντα, δυνάμενα τῇ καινότητι τῆς ἐπινοίας τὰ ὦτα δελεάζειν; Ign. Eph., 19, 2. For the LXX cf. 3 Βασ. 8:53a; Ez. 47:12.

In the NT it is found only in Paul. In accordance with the use of καινός (→ 449), it denotes the fulness of the reality of salvation which Christ has given to Christians in comparison with the worthlessness of their former condition, R. 6:7: δουλεύειν ἐν καινότητι → πνεύματος καὶ οὐ → παλαιότητι γράμματος (→ I, 766); R. 6:4 : ἐν καινότητι ζωῆς περιπατήσωμεν. ¹ Where there is καινὴ κτίσις (→ 449), law and sin are left behind. The Spirit is the completely different force which determines the new life.

Cf. Ign. Eph., 19, 3 : εἰς καινότητα ἀϊδίου ζωῆς; Mg., 9, 1: εἰς καινότητα ἐλπίδος.

† ἀνακαινίζω → ἀνακαινόω, → ἀνανεόω.

The simple καινίζω, "to make new," "to produce something new," "to bring into use," "to dedicate," is variously used from the time of the tragic dramatists, e.g., Aesch. Ag., 1071: καίνισον ζυγόν; Soph. Trach., 867: καί τι καινίζει στέγη; Eur. Tro., 889 : εὐχὰς ὡς ἐκαίνισας θεῶν, Ditt. Or., 669, 47: οὐκ ἐξὸν τοῖς βουλομένοις εὐχερῶς καθολικόν τι καινίζειν (cf. 62); Vett. Val., VII, 2 (p. 270, 24 f., Kroll): πολλὰ τῷ βίῳ καινίζει. In the LXX it is used for חָדָשׁ, Is. 61:4 "to restore," cf. 1 Macc. 10:10 "to introduce new customs," 2 Macc. 4:11; "to renew" in the religious sense, Wis. 7:27: (ἡ σοφία) τὰ πάντα καινίζει, Zeph. 3:17: κύριος ὁ θεὸς ... καινιεῖ σε ἐν τῇ ἀγαπήσει αὐτοῦ. ἀνακαινίζω, "to renew," "to give new life to something already there," "to restore," Isoc. Areop., 3 : τῆς ἔχθρας τῆς πρὸς βασιλέα πάλιν ἀνακεκαινισμένης; Jos. Ant., 9, 161: τὸν ναὸν ἀνακαινίσαι τοῦ θεοῦ (cf. 13, 57 and Test. L. 17:10 : ἀνακαινοποιήσουσιν οἶκον κυρίου); Plut. Marcellus, 6 (I, 300d): ἀνακαινίσαι τὸν πόλεμον; Appian Mithr., 37 (I, 475, 19 Mendelssohn): ἀνακαινίζων ... τὸ ἔργον ἀεί. In the LXX for חָדָשׁ, "to renew," "to make new" (of God), ψ 103:30; Lam. 5:21; 2 Ch. 15:8 B; cf. ψ 102:5. Pass. of a constantly returning mood, ψ 38:2, Mas. עָכַר ni; 1 Macc. 6:9.

Hb. 6:6 : (ἀδύνατον τοὺς ἅπαξ φωτισθέντας) πάλιν ἀνακαινίζειν εἰς μετάνοιαν, "to bring to conversion again." The seriousness of the distinctive teaching of Hb. that there is no second repentance is here shown from the standpoint of the Christian teacher who is speaking. He and his fellow-teachers cannot bring complete apostates to a new beginning which will lead to conversion. ¹ The miracle of becoming a καινὴ κτίσις (→ 449) occurs only once.

In early Christian writings ² ἀνακαινίζω is a common word in connection with regeneration and baptism, Barn., 6, 11: ἀνακαινίσας (sc. God) ἡμᾶς ἐν τῇ ἀφέσει τῶν ἁμαρτιῶν; Chrys. Hom. in R., 20 (MPG, 60, 598): ἀνακαίνισον αὐτὴν (sc. τὴν ψυχήν) μετανοίᾳ, Liturgia Marci (F. E. Brightman, Liturgies Eastern and Western [1896], 126, 1): ἀνεκαίνισας διὰ τοῦ φρικτοῦ καὶ ζωοποιοῦ καὶ οὐρανίου μυστηρίου τού-

---

¹ On the gen., which is good Gk., and which emphasises the newness better than πνεῦμα καινόν or ζωὴ καινή, cf. Winer § 34, 3; Bl.-Debr.⁶ § 165; Khl. R., 227 f.

ἀνακαινίζω. Pass., I, 1541, cf. 176; Cr.-Kö., 552; Pr.-Bauer³, 92 f.; Moult.-Mill., 34; Liddell-Scott, 107, cf. 858; Rgg. Hb. on 6:6; A. v. Harnack, "Die Terminologie der Wiedergeburt ...," TU, 42, 3 (1918), 101 ff.

¹ In the context of Hb. 5:11 ff., esp. 6:3, a Christian διδάσκαλος, like the author, is the subj. of ἀνακαινίζειν, not God (so Cr.-Kö.) or the individual apostate (so Orig. Comm. in Joh. on 8:40, p. 341, Preuschen). Cf. Rgg. Hb. and Wnd. Hb., ad loc.

² Cf. also the caricature in Luc. Philopatris, 12 : Γαλιλαῖος ..., ἐς τρίτον οὐρανὸν ἀεροβατήσας καὶ τὰ κάλλιστα ἐκμεμαθηκώς, δι' ὕδατος ἡμᾶς ἀνεκαίνισεν.

του, cf. O. Sol. 11:11: "The Lord renewed me by His vesture and created me by His light"; 17:4 : "I received the countenance and form of a new being, I entered therein and was redeemed"; Act. Thom. 132 (baptismal hymn): σοὶ δόξα ἀνακαινισμὸς δι' οὗ ἀνακαινίζονται οἱ βαπτιζόμενοι οἱ μετὰ διαθέσεως σοῦ ἁπτόμενοι. Of the angel of repentance in Herm. s., 8, 6, 3 : τοῦ ἀνακαινίσαι τὰ πνεύματα αὐτῶν, cf. s., 9, 14, 3; v., 3, 8, 9.

† ἀνακαινόω   → ἀνακαινίζω, → ἀνανεόω.

The basic word καινόω corresponds to καινίζω (→ 451) in the meanings "to make new," "to produce something new," "to renew," Thuc., III, 82, 3 : καινοῦσθαι τὰς διανοίας (there arose mentalities of a kind not previously found), Dio C., 47, 4(3): ἐς τὸ καινῶσαί πως τὰ ἐπιβουλεύματα in the sense of "to dedicate," Hdt. II, 100 : ποιησαμένων γάρ μιν οἴκημα περίμηκες ὑπόγαιον καινοῦν τῷ λόγῳ. Hence ἀνα-καινόω "to renew," pass. 2 C. 4:16; Col. 3:10; Athanasius contra gentes, 2 (MPG, 25, 8): ἀνακαινούμενος ἐπὶ τῷ πρὸς τοῦτον (τὸν πατέρα) πόθῳ etc., in the Church fathers. The verb need not be newly coined by Paul, though outside ecclesiastical authors it is first found only in the Byzantine period, cf. Heliodorus Prusanus, Paraphrasis in Eth. Nic. (Comm. in Aristot. Graeca, 19, 2 [p. 221, 12 ff., G. Heylbut]): καὶ γὰρ ἀνάπαυσίς τις ἢ παιδιὰ τοῖς ἀγωνιζομένοις, συνεχῶς οὐ δυναμένοις πονεῖν, ἢ τὴν δύναμιν αὐτοῖς ἀνακαινουμένη, τοῖς πόνοις ἀκμῆτας ἀποδίδωσιν.

The daily renewal of the inner man which Paul discusses in the light of the sufferings of the apostolic vocation at 2 C. 4:16 : ὁ ἔσω ἡμῶν (ἄνθρωπος) ἀνα-καινοῦται ἡμέρᾳ καὶ ἡμέρᾳ (→ I, 365; II, 699) is for him a consoling compensa-tion for the perishing of the outward man (→ II, 576), whose forces are dissipated in the tribulations of the earthly life of the apostle (v. 16a). Paul does not touch on the rise of the ἔσω ἄνθρωπος or on his relation to the καινὸς ἄνθρωπος (→ 449). He is not thinking of a process of moral alteration or a progressive course of sanctification or glorification in his use of ἀνακαινοῦσθαι. He is simply ex-pressing the glad certainty that each day he is renewed and strengthened as a Christian and lifted above all external pressures. [1] That it is the Spirit of God who accomplishes this renewal is shown both by the express reference to the presence of the Spirit at 4:13 and 5:5 and also by Paul's total conception of the → πνεῦμα. [2] Col. 3:10 refers to moral renewal : [3] ἐνδυσάμενοι τὸν → νέον (ἄν-

---

ἀ ν α κ α ι ν ό ω. Pass., I, 176, cf. 1543; Cr.-Kö., 552 f.; Pr.-Bauer[3], 93; Moult.-Mill., 34; Liddell-Scott, 107, cf. 859; J. H. H. Schmidt, Synonymik d. gr. Sprache, II (1878), 118 f.; Trench, 138; Bchm. and Wnd., 2 K. on 4:16; Haupt. Gefbr., Dib. Gefbr. and Loh. Kol. on Col. 3:10; A. v. Harnack, cf. Bibl. → 451.

[1] A different thought (cf. Lam. 3:23; Midr. Ps. 25, Str.-B., I, 897) is that of the worker who at night wearily commits his soul into the hand of God and then "in the morning it returns into his body as a new creature," cf. Gn. r., 14 on 2:7: "And in the hour when man sleeps the soul mounts upwards and creates for him life (i.e., new life) from above," also Jos. Bell., 7, 349: ὕπνος ..., ἐν ᾧ ψυχαὶ ... θεῷ ... ὁμιλοῦσαι κατὰ συγγένειαν ... Different again is the idea of the self-renewal of the soul or spirit in Philo Agric., 171: ἡ δ' (sc. ψυχή) ἐφ' ὅσον πρόεισιν, ἐπὶ μήκιστον ἡβᾷ καὶ ἐπακμάζει τὸ ἀειθαλὲς εἶδος φαιδρυνομένη καὶ ταῖς συνεχέσιν ἐπιμελείαις καινουμένη, Vit. Mos., II, 140: τὸ δὲ τῆς διανοίας (sc. κάλλος) ... μὴ χρόνου μήκει μαραινόμενον, ἀλλ' ἐφ' ὅσον ἐγχρο-νίζει καινούμενον καὶ νεάζον.

[2] The conceptions of nature mythology, e.g., the ancient Egyptian belief in the daily renewal of the sun or the earth serpent (Wnd. 2 K., ad loc.), are remote from the thought of Paul.

[3] In Rabb. lit. we first find the thought of renewal in this sense in Ex. r., 15 on 12:1 f., cf. Str.-B., III, 601.

θρωπον) τὸν ἀνακαινούμενον εἰς ἐπίγνωσιν κατ' εἰκόνα τοῦ κτίσαντος αὐτόν. The new man (→ 449) is present and he is also in constant process of becoming (pres. part.) as he continually receives the new life which is given. This renewal of being is moral by nature. [4] Its standard is the image of God manifested in Christ (→ II, 397). The Christian is to become a new man as Christ is the new man (→ 449).

† ἀνακαίνωσις.

"Renewal." The *koine* seems first to have coined abstract nouns from the verbs (ἀνα-)καινόω, (ἀνα-)καινίζω. Thus καίνωσις is found in Jos. Ant., 18, 230 : καίνωσίν τινα γεγονέναι τῶν λόγων; καίνισις in Jos. Ant., 18, 9 : ἡ τῶν πατρίων καίνισις καὶ μεταβολή; καινισμός, P. Lond., II, 354, 16 : ἀποστάσεως καινισμὸν παραλογιεῖσθαι; Vett. Val., IV, 19 (p. 192, 15, Kroll). ἀνακαίνωσις is first found in Paul at R. 12:2 and Tt. 3:5; then Herm. v., 3, 8, 9 : ἡ ἀνακαίνωσις τῶν πνευμάτων ὑμῶν. In the same sense (Suid., *s.v.*) ἀνακαίνισις is more common in early Christian lit., cf. Act. Joh., 78 : ἐπὶ δὲ τὴν ἰδίαν ... ἀνακαίνισιν βίου; Orig. Orat., 22, 4 : τῇ ἀνακαινίσει τοῦ νοός (cf. R. 12:2), also ἀνακαινισμός, Act. Thom., 158 : ἀνακαινισμὸν τῆς ψυχῆς ... καὶ τοῦ σώματος; Bas. Ep., I, 8, 11 (MPG, 32, 264): ἦν ... Παῦλος ... ἐξανάστασιν εἴρηκε, ταύτην Δαβὶδ ἀνακαινισμὸν προσηγόρευσε (cf. ψ 103:30); Didym. Trin., II, 23 (MPG, 39, 557): ἡμεῖς χρῖσμα δεχόμεθα ἐν τῷ ἀνακαινισμῷ (= baptism, cf. Act. Thom., 132 → 452).

R. 12:2 : → μεταμορφοῦσθε τῇ ἀνακαινώσει τοῦ → νοός, refers to the renewal of thought and will which Christians constantly need if they are to show by their moral conduct that they belong to the new aeon and are members of the new humanity (cf. Col. 3:10, → 452). The subj. of this inward renewal, which affects the centre of personal life, is the Spirit of God (R. 8:9-13, cf. 1 C. 12:13) who dwells and works in the Christian. The saying in Tt. 3:5 : ἔσωσεν ἡμᾶς διὰ → λουτροῦ → παλιγγενεσίας καὶ ἀνακαινώσεως πνεύματος ἁγίου, [1] refers to the unique and basic beginning which the Spirit makes in man at baptism. Without any human co-operation there arises in baptism the καινὴ κτίσις (2 C. 5:17, → 449) by the miracle of renewal through the Holy Spirit, who created a life that was not there before (→ 447 f.; 449).

† ἐγκαινίζω. [1]

Rare outside the Gk. Bible, cf. Archigenes, acc. to Oribasius, Collectionum Medicarum Reliquiae (CMG, VI, 1, 1 [1928]), VIII, 46, 16 : ἔλαιον, οὗ ... ἀποχυθέντος εἰς χύτραν ἐγκεκαινισμένην, IG, XII (fasc. 5), 712, 58 : ἐνκενί<σ>[θη ὁ] ἱ[ερὸς](?) ... ναὸς τοῦ ἁ[γίου ... "To make new," "to renew," Is. 16:11; 1 Βασ. 11:14; 2 Ch. 15:8; ψ 50:10 (quoted in 1 Cl., 18, 10): πνεῦμα εὐθὲς ἐγκαίνισον ἐν τοῖς ἐγκάτοις

---

[4] Cf. Dib. Gefbr. and Loh. Kol., *ad loc.*

ἀνακαίνωσις. Pass., I, 1541, 1543; Cr.-Kö., 553; Pr.-Bauer³, 93; Nägeli, 52, 86; Liddell-Scott, 107, cf. 858 f.; Zn. R. and Ltzm. R. on 12:2; Schl. R., 334; Dib. Past. on Tt. 3:5; P. Gennrich, *Die Lehre v. d. Wiedergeburt* (1907), 7 ff.

[1] On the constr. cf. J. Behm, *Die Handauflegung im Urchr.* (1911), 165, n. 4.

ἐγκαινίζω. Cr.-Kö., 552; Pr.-Bauer³, 355; Liddell-Scott, 469; Moult.-Mill., 215; Rgg. Hb. and Wnd. Hb. on 9:18 and 10:20.

[1] Later also ἐγκαινιάζω, cf. CIG, IV, 8660 : ἐγκαινιάσθη ὁ ναὸς οὗτος.

μου (for שׁ֫דֵּשׁ); Sir. 36:5. "To dedicate," Dt. 20:5; 3 Βασ. 8:63; 2 Ch. 7:5 (for חָנַךְ);
1 Macc. 4:36, 54; 5:1. Hence ἐγκαίνισις, Nu. 7:88 A (v.l. ἐγκαίνωσις) and ἐγκαι-
νισμός, Nu. 7:10 f., 84; 2 Ch. 7:9; Da. 3:2; 1 Esr. 7:7; 1 Macc. 4:56, 59; 2 Macc. 2:9, 19,
"dedication," as τὰ ἐγκαίνια, "feast of dedication," 2 Εσδρ. 22:27; Da. 3:2 Θ; Philo
Congr., 114, esp. "feast of the dedication of the temple," 2 Εσδρ. 6:16 f., Jn. 10:22.

If in the difficult saying at Hb. 10:19 f. the reference is to "access to the
sanctuary" as the "new way which Jesus has made for us" : ... τὴν εἴσοδον τῶν
ἁγίων ..., ἣν ἐνεκαίνισεν ἡμῖν ὁδὸν πρόσφατον, then ἐγκαινίζειν ὁδόν could
just as well mean "to make a way which was not there before" as "to use a way
for the first time," "to open it," "to dedicate it." [2] The way to God which Jesus
has newly opened and trodden is the way on which Christians can now find access
to God. Hb. 9:18 : οὐδὲ ἡ πρώτη (sc. διαθήκη) χωρὶς αἵματος (→ I, 175)
ἐγκεκαίνισται, refers to the διαθήκη, and here ἐγκαινίζειν means "solemnly to
bring something new into effect," "to consecrate." It is natural that a διαθήκη,
which is a divine ordinance in salvation history, [3] should be consecrated by blood
and put in effect by death. This is also true of the first διαθήκη, the ordinance
at Sinai (Ex. 24:6 ff.).

Behm

---

[2] So Chrys. Hom. in Hb., 19 (MPG, 63, 139): ἣν ἐνεκαίνισεν ... τουτέστιν, ἣν κατεσκεύασε, καὶ ἧς ἤρξατο· ἐγκαινισμὸς γὰρ λέγεται ἀρχὴ χρήσεως λοιπόν· ἣν
κατεσκεύασε, φησί, καὶ δι᾽ ἧς αὐτὸς ἐβάδισεν, cf. Theodoret, ad loc. (MPG, 82, 752):
ἐγκαινισμὸν δὲ ὁδοῦ, τὸ πρῶτον διὰ τούτων ὁδεῦσαι.
[3] The thought of consecration could hardly be linked with διαθήκη in the sense of
"testament," → II, 131.

```
καιρός, ἄκαιρος, ἀκαιρέω,
εὔκαιρος, εὐκαιρία,
πρόσκαιρος
```

† καιρός.

A. The non-biblical Use.

There is no certainty as to the original meaning. Etymological research has produced differing conclusions. [1] Nevertheless, the linguistic development of the term clearly suggests that the basic sense is that of the "decisive or crucial place or point," whether spatially, materially or temporally.

1. In the spatial sense the word is rare. In the Il. the adj. καίριος is used in this way, while in the Od. ὥρα denotes a propitious point in time. [2]

2. The word develops its decisive sense when used materially. a. In the period after Hesiod, [3] primarily in a positive sense, and for poets [4] and philosophers almost equivalent to the literal meaning of σωφροσύνη in the sense of "norm," it is "wise moderation" : μηδὲν ἄγαν· καιρῶι πάντα πρόσεστι καλά. [5] Thus καιρός is used in Plato along with μέτριον, πρέπον, δέον for something which εἰς τὸ μέσον ἀπῳκίσθη τῶν ἐσχάτων (Polit., 284e). [6] b. From another angle it means that which is "materially decisive." Here καιρός takes on the sense of fateful. Basic to this concept is that *Moira* forces man to a decision by putting him in a specific situation. Here καιρός can be quite neutral, e.g., in the ancient sentence : καιρὸν γνῶθι : [7] Know the critical situation in your life, know that it demands a decision, and what decision, train yourself to recognise as such the decisive point in your life, and to act accordingly. In most cases the sense is positive ; its ἐπιστήμη varies according to different callings (Aristot. Eth. Nic., I, 4, p. 1096, a, 32). But the negative implication is also common ; it often means "danger" in Polyb. The "situation," "circumstances," Thuc., VI, 85, 1; Demosth. Or., 1, 2, and hence "effect" (Thuc., I, 36, 1), "favour" (Orph. Fr., 237, 9), "opportunity" (Philo Mut. Nom., 196), "advantage" (Plat. Leg., XI, 926e), harmful or profitable "success," "further development" (Aristot. Eth. Nic., III, 1, p. 1110a, 14), and finally "goal" (Demosth. Or., 23, 182).

3. a. This leads us to the temporal sense of the "decisive moment" (plain from the time of Soph.). Here again there is the threefold orientation, neutral, positive and negative. [8] The positive is the most common ; hence the definitions of Aristot. :

κ α ι ρ ό ς. J. H. H. Schmidt, *Synonymik d. griech. Sprache,* II (1878), 60 f., 63, 65, 71 f.; Trench (1901), 196 ff.; D. Levi, "Il καιρός attraverso la letteratura greca," *Rendiconti della Reale Academia Nazionale dei Lincei Classe di scienzia morali* RV, 32 (1923), 260 ff.; "Il concetto di καιρός e la filosofia di Platone," 33 (1924), 93-118.

[1] Boisacq, *s.v.*; Levi (1923), 261 ff.; K. Brugmann, *Indogerm. Forsch.,* 17 (1904/5), 363 ff.

[2] Levi, *op. cit.,* 264.

[3] Levi contests the authenticity of Hes. Op., 694 (*op. cit.,* 265).

[4] Often in Pindar; καιρὸν χάριτος, Aesch. Ag., 787 (cf. Levi, 266); Eur. Hipp., 385 (Levi, 272).

[5] Kritias Fr., 7 (Diels, II, 315, 29); similarly Theogn., 401 (Diehl, I, 137): μηδὲν ἄγαν σπεύδειν· καιρὸς δ' ἐπὶ πᾶσιν ἄριστος ἔργμασιν, and Soph. Oed. Tyr., 1516 (πάντα γὰρ καιρῷ καλά).

[6] Cf. also Aristot. (in the banal sense): ψυχροτέρα ... τοῦ καιροῦ (*ultra modum* ; Probl., XXX, 1, p. 954b, 35).

[7] Diels, II, 216, 10. On γινώσκειν in this connection → I, 691.

[8] This is rare, v. Plato Leg., XII, 945c : πολλοὶ καιροὶ πολιτείας λύσεώς εἰσιν.

τἀγαθὸν ... λέγεται ... ἐν χρόνῳ καιρός (Eth. Nic., I, 4, 1096a, 23 ff.) and Philo (Op. Mund., 59): καιρός = χρόνος κατορθώσεως ("time of favourable execution"). [9] Here, too, the idea of fate is present, and it is obviously impossible to make a clear-cut distinction from sense b. : (Eur. Fr., 745, TGF, 593, Nauck) a fateful moment decides — use it boldly : τολμᾶν δὲ χρεών· ὁ γὰρ ἐν καιρῷ μόχθος πολλὴν εὐδαιμονίαν τίκτει θνητοῖσι τελευτῶν; he who grasps the helm firmly in the moment of fate, forces fortune ; therefore believe in thy destiny. That there can sometimes be a religious nuance may be seen from the Aristotelian statement [10] : ὁ καιρὸς οὐκ ἔστι χρόνος δέων· θεῷ γὰρ καιρὸς μὲν ἔστι, χρόνος δ᾽ οὐκ ἔστι δέων διὰ τὸ μηδὲν εἶναι θεῷ ὠφέλιμον. καιρός is not identical with the χρόνος δέων, the propitious situation, since God has only one (momentary) καιρός (no χρόνος δέων); καιρός, then, is the ever new point of time at which God must work creatively. The Pythagoreans gave to καιρός a firm and obviously important place in their system. [11] Within their basic doctrine, which substituted numbers for the current → ἀρχαί of the cosmos, καιρός was represented by the number seven. [12] More precisely, in Pythagorean teaching καιρός is the πάθος of a number. [13]

In this connection καιρός is often linked with τύχη, not as an alternative, but in clear differentiation. τύχη is characterised by contingency. It is fortuna as depicted by Dürer. Man is passively subjected to it. καιρός, however, is the destiny which demands decisive action from man. It thus determines the life of man by its challenge. [14, 15] To meet this demand is καιρὸν λαμβάνειν, καιρῷ χρῆσθαι, even καιρὸν ἁρπάζειν; to shrink from it is καιρὸν παριέναι. He who does the latter destroys his existence (ἐάν τίς τινος παρῇ ἔργου καιρόν, διόλλυται, Plat. Resp., II, 370b). By the web of fate [16] ethical decision is demanded of man in the

---

[9] The echo of the previous sense is often strong, e.g., when καιρός is the "arising circumstance" (Aristot. Rhet., 6, p. 1427b, 26) or the "acute significance" (Plat. Ep., 7, 339c). Cf. E. Curtius, Archäol. Zeitung, 33, NF, 8 (1876), 1b (= Ges. Abh., II [1894], 188): "As regards Kairos and Chronos, the one denotes time as the external framework within which all human action takes place, the other time in so far as it is ours, ... time in relation to the content which we give it, the moment which is decisive for each action."

[10] An. Pri., I, 36, p. 48b, 35 ff. The statement does not wholly tally with that quoted above (p. 1096a, 23 ff.). καιρός is also used for a propitious hour in the religious sense in the hymn to Demetrius Poliorketes, Athen., VI, 63, p. 253d.

[11] Iambl. Theol. Arithm., 44; cf. Philo Spec. Leg., II, 56 ff.

[12] Stob. Ecl., I, 21, 27 ff.: Πυθαγόρας ... ἐπωνόμαζεν ... τὴν δὲ ἑβδομάδα Καιρὸν καὶ ᾽Αθηνᾶν, Schol. on Arist. Metaph., I, 5, p. 985b, 26; 540a, 26 f.

[13] Arist. Metaph., I, 5, p. 985b, 30; W. H. Roscher (ASG, 24, 1 [1904], p. 31): "Because according to an ancient popular view which passed into ancient medicine the seventh day is the decisive one (= καιρός)," cf. Iambl. Theol. Arithm., 53. The ethical evaluation naturally varies. Sometimes it is the right moment to which we must measure up (e.g., Democr. Fr., 226 [II, 106, 8, Diels]; Fr., 229 [II, 107, 2, Diels]). But sophistry could also use the καιρός concept in a dialectical levelling of all ethical standards : any action is beautiful if done at the right moment, and any action is infamous if done at the wrong (Diels, II, 338, 9).

[14] καιροῦ παρακαλοῦντος, Epict. Ench., 33, 2; καιροῦ καλοῦντος, Epict. Diss., II, 1, 34.

[15] Plat. Ep., 9, 358a : πολλὰ δὲ καὶ τοῖς καιροῖς δίδοται τοῖς τὸν βίον ἡμῶν καταλαμβάνουσι. Cf. H. Lamer in Pauly-W., X (1919), 1519 : To Kairos belong attributes which presuppose the "decisive power of the human will."

[16] συνῆκτο γὰρ αὐτῷ τὰ πράγματα, ὥσπερ ἐκ τύχης, εἰς καιρὸν τοιοῦτον ..., Demosth. Or., 19, 317. Levi, op. cit., 32 : per volonta del destino.

καιρός. Naturally this concept of καιρός can play an important role in an ethics which is openly aware of responsibility, e.g., in Stoicism. But this is evident only in Epict. When the καιρός is manifested (φανῇ), then in a self-conquering battle against ἡδονή, or desire, one must obey its claim (Ench., 34). God calls man to account whether he has exerted himself to meet the demands of the καιρός (Diss., III, 10, 8; cf. IV, 4, 30; 12), demands which contribute to the everyday formation of character (IV, 4, 45 f.). Hence καιρός can finally be the moral necessity (II, 7, 3) which is known in virtue of reason (I, 1, 6).

This is the place to mention the religious veneration of Καιρός, who is (later) numbered among the gods [17] and to whom a religious hymn of praise is composed (Paus., V, 14, 9).

There is only one written attestation of the cultus ; an altar to Kairos stood at the entrance of the stadium at Olympia. [18] But we learn more from inscr. One tells us that the person honoured owed his successes to Kairos (IG, XII, 5, 939), another that the one who makes his vows awaits his duties from Kairos. [19] Again, the monuments [20] show us that "at a later period the cult of the god must have been widespread." [21] These depictions are copies of the statue of Kairos by Lysippus, [22] for whom he was "a young, naked ephebe with winged feet poised ... His only attribute apart from the winged feet was a striking hair-style, a lock at the front with short hair behind." [23] The latter characteristic confirms the fact that even religiously Kairos originally had the character of decision, since the lock of hair is a symbol that one must take the favourable opportunity by the forelock, [24] that one is summoned to action by Kairos. [25]

In the Eighth Book of Moses Kairos is next to the supreme God, endowed with all power, the bearer of good fortune ; [26] ibid., 584 f. he is the angel of the aeon, and man's relation to him is that of δοῦλος.

b. From sense a. — for the opposite development, which has sometimes been assumed, is linguistically impossible — καιρός acquires the greatly weakened sense of a mere term for time. (i) It denotes a "short space of time" (Hippocr. Praeceptiones, 1: καιρός [ἐστιν] ἐν ᾧ χρόνος οὐ πολύς; he gives the example that healing mostly takes place χρόνῳ, ἔστι δὲ ἡνίκα καὶ καιρῷ; a "point of time" (in the phrase ἐν τούτῳ τῷ καιρῷ, cf. τὰ κατὰ καιρούς for historical events described by the historian, Polyb., 5, 33, 5), hence δέων καιρός, the "favourable moment" (Menand. Sam., 294 f.; Polyb., 1, 61, 7; 2, 26, 1); "regularly recurring time" (IG, V, 1, Inscr., 1390, 101: καιρὸν τάσσειν). (ii) It then comes to mean more generally a "stretch of time" (Strabo, XVII, 46 [C 816]: μετὰ τὸν τῆς παλλακείας καιρόν, when the time had run its course):

---

[17] Stob. Ecl., I, 22, 4, listed with Athene, not Tyche (→ n. 12).

[18] Paus., V, 14, 9. The related hypothesis of Curtius (→ n. 9), 3 ff., 191 ff., that Kairos belongs originally with Agon and Hermes, leans one-sidedly on this passage and is open to question.

[19] Ditt. Syll.³, 852, 42. If τύχη here is the city tyche (Ditt., ad loc.), Kairos is perhaps the deity. Cf. also Athen., VI, 63 (p. 253d).

[20] Philo Poster. C., 121 f. is further evidence that the cult is widespread.

[21] Lamer in Pauly-W., X (1919), 1509.

[22] c. 270 B.C.; Lamer, 1511.

[23] Lamer, 1518 f., though cf. Jahresh. des österr. archäol. Inst., 26 (1930), 4.

[24] Lamer, 1516.

[25] Cf. the reproduction in Jahresh. des österr. archäol. Inst., 26 (1930), Plate I, also Roscher, II, 1, 899, E. Curtius, Plate IV (→ n. 9); v. A. Baumeister-B. Arnold, Denkmäler des klass. Altert., II (1887), Ill. 823.

[26] Preis. Zaub., XIII, 508 ff., unless we should read Κρόνος (A. Dieterich, DLZ, 38 [1917], 1431).

"age" (Aristot. Pol., VII, 16, p. 1334b, 35); "time of the year" (IG, V, 2, Inscr. 169: XIV, Inscr., 1018, 3; also mosaics and coins).[27]

B. The Use in the Septuagint.

In the LXX καιρός is mostly used for עֵת (198 times apart from Da. Θ);[28] also (in the Pentateuch) for מוֹעֵד, which denotes esp. the point of time (25 or 27 times apart from Da. Θ); also in bibl. Aram. for זְמָן ("specific time"), once in 2 Εσδρ. and 5 times in Da. LXX, and for עִדָּן ("time in general"), 6 times in Da. LXX. עֵת covers all the special nuances of these other terms. We also find יוֹם three times and קֵץ five to seven times. LXX usage is not greatly affected by these equivalents; indeed, later Rabb. literature did not feel that any of them gave the true sense of καιρός and it therefore adopted the rare loan word קירוס (cf. Levy Wört., s.v.). In the LXX we can see plainly the continuation of the development already sketched above. The spatial sense drops out, and the material is rare: "circumstances," 1 Macc. 8:25, 27; "situation," Sir. 18:26; 29:5b; "advantage," Sir. 6:8; "end," Est. 4:14; "lack," Sir. 29:2; "help" (of the gods), Nu. 14:9; plur. "expectation," Job 28:3 A; finally "judgment," divine punishment, ψ 80:16, here absol. in the light of the very broad temporal meaning, which embraces the following senses.

1. The "decisive point of time." The ethical (and in the LXX religious) background of the term is rarely in evidence, as in non-biblical usage. Even where it is present emphasis falls less on the demand which the καιρός makes than on its divine appointment. God is the One who seizes the καιρός (ὅταν λάβω καιρόν, ψ 74:2; → 456); cf. Job 39:18 : κατὰ καιρόν, when God's time is come; Nu. 23:23; ψ 118:126); αὐτὸς (God) ἀλλοιοῖ καιρούς, Da. 2:21; the reference is to God's καιρός, not to καιρός in general (Qoh. 3:11; Sir. 51:30[38]; ψ 20:9); the καιρός, the religiously "decisive time" (here the last time of blessedness) will be given by God.[29] The hour of death is also appointed by God (Qoh. 7:17). In this context καιρός has obviously become an established term in salvation history. In itself, without an explanatory addition, it denotes the "time of judgment" and the "last time" (especially the former) which God brings (Lam. 1:21; perhaps καιρός here stands in analogy to ἡμέρα, → II, 949; 951), cf. Ez. 22:3; 7:12; Gn. 6:13 (for קֵץ); Lam. 1:21; 4:18 (even ὥρα καιροῦ at Da. LXX 8:17). Finally, God Himself is boldly compared to καιρός.[30]

Thus the righteous of the OT, like the author of Ecclesiastes, can see the direction of God in the series of καιροί through which he passes (Qoh. 3:10-14); the καιρὸς τοῦ κλαῦσαι and τοῦ γελάσαι, that τοῦ φιλῆσαι and τοῦ μισῆσαι, that τοῦ τεκεῖν and τοῦ ἀποθανεῖν etc. — they are all given by God (3:2-8).

As we have said, the religious note is not always prominent. Thus at 1 Ch. 12:33; Sir. 22:16(20) καιρός is the "critical situation" when a right decision must be made. In the practical wisdom of Wisdom poetry the "right moment" for which we must be apt (συντήρησον καιρόν, Sir. 4:20) plays a certain role (cf. Sir. 27:12; 20:6 f.). In such

---

[27] Roscher, II, 1, 897.

[28] καιρός is the usual rendering of עֵת, other translations are rare [Debrunner]. Cf. the other terms for time.

[29] ἐδόθη in the prophetic aor., Da. LXX 7:22; cf. Jdt. 13:5(7).

[30] καθὼς καιρός, Ju. 13:23 B; cf. → supra, Nu. 14:9 and Philo Mut. Nom., 265.

cases the sense is usually that of the propitious hour; the καιρὸς συνεργεῖ for man, 1 Macc. 12:1. Cf. generally Hag. 1:2. Occasionally we find a *sensus ad malum* (the hour of death, 1 Macc. 9:10. Cf. also Jer. 27[50]26).

2. The purely temporal sense is by far the most common, but is of less theological interest. a. When used for a point of time, [31] καιρός is often influenced by 1. and means a set term (as elsewhere in the *koine*), [32] whether one that has been definitively fixed (by God, Sir. 48:10; Da. LXX 4:26; cf. also Gn. 17:21, 23; 18:10; so also ἕως καιροῦ to an appointed moment which God will fix, *v.* Da. Θ 11:24) or one that regularly recurs. It is used especially for festivals, Ex. 34:18; Lv. 23:4; Nu. 9:3, 7, 13; weekly, 1 Ch. 9:25; and then for the regular times of biological (Ez. 16:8; Lv. 15:25; Job 39:1; 1 Βασ. 1:20; technical term, 4:20), metereological (Lv. 26:4; Dt. 28:12) or other natural events (Ps. 1:3; Job 38:32).

b. The original sense is quite lost when καιροί is used for "stretches of time" (cf. the moon, ψ 103:19; cf. Gn. 1:14; πολλοὶ καιροί for a "long time" at 1 Macc. 12:10; cf. Ez. 12:27; Tob. 14:5 καιροί for the "duration of the world" in combination with → πληροῦσθαι), or when it occurs with a *gen. mensurae* (ἐνιαυτοῦ, Da. LXX 11:13 : μιᾶς ἡμέρας, 2 Macc. 7:20; 3 Macc. 4:14), or when it denotes the duration of life (Wis. 2:5; Sir. 17:2[3]; [33] → 457 f.) or some portion of it (3 Βασ. 11:4; 15:23; ψ 70:9). In Da. it can be used for a span of time in eschatological reckoning (the seven "times," Da. Θ 4:16, 23, 25, 32; cf. 7:25; 12:7; LXX 7:25; 9:27; 12:7). Finally it is used in the same way as → ἡμέρα either in general indication of time (with ἐν and ἐκεῖνος, esp. Dt. 1-3; Ju.; 3 and 4 Βασ.; 1 and 2 Ch.) or to denote a particular section of the life of the individual or nation according to the nature of the experiences undergone (with attributive gen. or [more rarely] part., esp. καιρὸς θλίψεως, and other combinations particularly in Sir.). At Wis. 7:18 etc. it means the "time of the year."

C. καιρός in the NT. [34]

It does not occur in the spatial sense in the NT, and the material is found only at Hb. 11:15 : "the (divinely given) opportunity." The temporal use, however, is widespread.

1. a. The "fateful and decisive point," with strong, though not always explicit, emphasis (except at Ac. 24:25) on the fact that it is ordained by God. In accordance with the NT concept of God, however, there is now a clearer grasp of the rich and incalculable and gracious goodness of God in the gift of the καιρός and of the judicial severity of its once-for-all demand. Thus Jerusalem did not recognise the unique καιρός when Jesus came to save it (Lk. 19:44), [35] and there can be no second chance. The reproach which Jesus must bring against the mass of the Jewish people, the ὄχλοι (Lk. 12:54), is that they did not think it worth the

---

[31] For a short space of time cf. esp. 1 Ch. 11:11, 20 : ἐν καιρῷ ἑνί.

[32] Cf. Preisigke Wört., I, 721.

[33] Cf. κατὰ τὸν καιρόν τινος, Jdt. 16:21.

[34] In relation to the use of καιρός it should be noted in advance that in many verses we cannot be absolutely sure as to the precise sense. In particular the instances treated under 1. a. might have a purely temporal significance, though this is unlikely. Our decision will largely depend on how far we think the author has a sense of the niceties of Greek. That this was possible for Semites may be seen from our earlier observation concerning קירוס (→ 458).

[35] This is a good reason for believing that καιρός is here used in its specialised sense, cf. also the technical term ἔγνως (→ 455 and n. 7), which forms a fixed formula when used with καιρός.

trouble to try to discern the decisive character of the καιρός of religious decision implied in His Messianic character (Lk. 12:56; cf. Mt. 16:3). According to Mk. 1:15 the fact that this καιρός is now present as God's gift in fulfilment of OT prophecy (πεπλήρωται) [36] is the first startling declaration of the primitive Gospel of Jesus.

Thus the seriousness of decision, already present in the Greek concept of καιρός, is given an intensity which we find strange both in the religious proclamation of Jesus and in the moral demands of Paul. The more fully the end is viewed together with present fulfilment, the more urgent is the demand of the καιρός, which recurs with each moment of the Christian life, and which in its instantaneousness requires of the Christian that he should recognise it and concretely fulfil its demand (R. 13:8-10) in the exercise of brotherly love (R. 13:11; → I, 51). For the Christian is in possession of this καιρός. That is, he has the ability, as a pneumatic man, to recognise it and to fulfil its command (Gl. 6:10). Thus each of its claims must be met (Eph. 5:16; Col. 4:5; → I, 128). In relation to non-Christians, too, there is a special compulsion for Christians. Cf. also R. 12:11 (D* G 5 it).

Not merely the life of Christians, but also the earthly life of Jesus Himself, stands under the claim of the divine καιρός. Jesus looks for this in individual decisions (Jn. 7:6, 8; → ὥρα). In accordance with the strict sense of καιρός, it seems that Jesus does not know it in advance. He discerns it as such only at the moment when it comes (πεπλήρωται). He then decides in accordance with its divine claim. Jn. 7:6, 8 makes it plain how fundamentally this divinely given καιρός differs from a cosmic or human. Those who do not realise that they stand under the καιρός of God think that they see a cosmic or human καιρός in all the opportunities which seem to be favourable for the realisation of their cosmic plans (Ac. 24:25). But this is not a true, divinely given καιρός. At this point we see again the decisive distinction between Greek religion and the NT. When autonomous man speaks of his καιρός, he sees it in what he believes to be independent decision — and he remains blind. When Jesus waits for His καιρός, He allows the Father to show it to Him, and He thus attains to genuine certainty. The end of Jesus especially stands under this καιρός, and we are left with the impression that Jesus Himself fixes it by His own decision in accordance with the will of God, cf. Mt. 26:18 : ὁ καιρός μου ἐγγύς ἐστιν. For the host (τὸν δεῖνα) the saying would be obscure, but it shows how consciously Jesus grasps and subjects Himself to the καιρός which is given by God's will. That this resolve to be ready for death, and to die, is taken in accordance with the καιρός, with the demand of God for decision, i.e., with the time of decision concerning the success of the work of Jesus, may be seen also from R. 5:6 (καιρός = the "propitious moment" [μεταλαβών, → 456], Ac. 24:25).

b. "The specific and decisive point, especially as regards its content." Here again there is a strong emphasis on the fact that the καιρός is divinely ordained, but the original implication of a decision to be made by man is greatly weakened. On the other hand, the thought of God's fixed and predetermined plan of salvation

---

[36] We cannot be sure that in this formulation the statement belongs to the earliest preaching of Jesus. D it did not understand this meaning of πληροῦσθαι and they therefore read καιροί, i.e., the periods of time which were to pass until Jesus came. When Jos. Ant., 6, 49 speaks of a πληροῦσθαι καιρόν (ἐξεδέχετο τὸν καιρὸν γενέσθαι, πληρωθέντος δ' αὐτοῦ ...), it is hard to decide whether he means the fulfilment of the divinely appointed time or the elapsing of the time.

is very clear. According to a schedule of relative development God lays down in advance the main points in the history of salvation. He gives them their content, and believers may await them with confident assurance. In Pauline writings καιρός is first found with ἴδιος (mostly in the plural) in a *dat. temporis* as the time which God has ordained and filled with content, whether it be the time of the manifestation of the Logos in Jesus (Tt. 1:3) and of the attestation of the divine love (μαρτύριον) by Jesus in His crucifixion (1 Tm. 2:6), or the time of the epiphany of Christ (1 Tm. 6:15) and of the ensuing felicity of believers in the βασιλεία (Gl. 6:9). But naturally the other decisive points in the development of salvation history, within which NT believers are conscious of standing (1 Pt. 4:17; cf. 2 Th. 2:6), also come under this divine ordination, and can thus be called καιρούς, οὓς ὁ πατὴρ ἔθετο ἐν τῇ ἰδίᾳ ἐξουσίᾳ (Ac. 1:7), e.g., the commencement of Messianic power over demons (Mt. 8:29), the beginning of the immanent judgment executed in the persecutions of believers (1 Pt. 4:17), the removal of the power of the κατέχον (2 Th. 2:6), the time of the final judgment of believers (1 C. 4:5) and of the general judgment of the dead (Rev. 11:18). In spite of the attempts of OT prophets (1 Pt. 1:11), Christians cannot calculate these times (Mk. 13:33; 1 Th. 5:1 f.; Ac. 1:7). God Himself will put them in an absolute schedule in accordance with the requirements of salvation history, and a prior fixing of the year or the day would be opposed to the divine sovereignty (Ac. 1:7). καιρός then becomes a technical term for the last judgment or the end; there is here an influence of LXX piety (→ 459); cf. Lk. 21:8 (in the gospel of pseudo-messiahs); 1 Pt. 5:6; Rev. 1:3; 22:10; cf. ἐν καιρῷ ἐσχάτῳ, 1 Pt. 1:5. [37]

But the believer also regards decisive points in individual life as divinely appointed καιρός (2 Tm. 4:6), cf. the time of the fulfilment of a personal divine promise (Lk. 1:20). It is in this light (cf. what was said concerning ἕως καιροῦ in the LXX → 459) that we are to understand ἄχρι καιροῦ (Lk. 4:13; Ac. 13:11): until the time appointed by God.

2. a. A "short space of time": ἐν παντὶ καιρῷ (also in the LXX), Lk. 21:36; Eph. 6:18: the Christian is to be always in an attitude of prayer. A specific "term": once, R. 9:9 (based on Gn. 18:10 → 459), regular: the giving of food, Mt. 24:45; Lk. 12:42; the delivery of the fruits of harvest, Mk. 12:2 par.; natural events, Mt. 13:30; 21:34; Mk. 11:13; Ac. 14:7; feasts, Gl. 4:10, cf. LXX. b. "Stretch of time," with *gen. mensurae,* 1 Th. 2:17; appointed by men, 1 C. 7:5; indefinite, Lk. 8:13; at disposal (divinely appointed), Lk. 21:24; 1 C. 7:29; [38] Rev. 12:12. "Portion of life," Hb. 11:11; "historical epoch," Ac. 17:26, cf. Eph. 1:10; καιρὸς ἐκεῖνος of the pre-Christian part of life, Eph. 2:12; the "present time," Mk. 10:30 par., cf. ὁ νῦν καιρός (→ I, 205 f.), R. 3:26; cf. 8:18; 11:5; 2 C. 8:14, ἐνεστὼς καιρός, Hb. 9:9; apocalyptic measure of time, Rev. 12:14 (cf. Da. LXX). A general indication of time ("about that time") in stories from the life of Jesus (ἐν ἐκείνῳ τῷ καιρῷ, Mt. 11:25; 12:1; 14:1) and Christian missionary history (κατ' ἐκεῖνον τὸν καιρόν, Ac. 12:1; 19:23); more exactly ἐν αὐτῷ τῷ καιρῷ "just after" (Lk. 13:1); ἐν ᾧ καιρῷ of the time of Moses (Ac. 7:20); ἐν ὑστέροις καιροῖς of indefinite later periods (1 Tm. 4:1). With attributive gen.: πειρασμοῦ, Lk. 8:13; ἐπισκοπῆς, Lk. 19:44, cf. LXX Wis. 3:7; Jer. 6:15; 10:15; ἀναψύξεως, Ac. 3:20

---

[37] Pr.-Bauer would also adduce here Mk. 13:33; Mt. 8:29; 1 C. 4:5; Eph. 1:10; Mt. 16:3. Eph. 1:10 does not seem to me to fit here. On the other hand, an eschatological understanding would be possible, though not very likely, Mk. 1:15; R. 13:11.

[38] In exposition cf. G. Delling, *Paulus' Stellung zu Frau u. Ehe* (1931), 77.

→ I, 391; διορθώσεως, Hb. 9:10; cf. 2 Tm. 4:6 → 459; adj. (2 C. 6:2; 2 Tm. 3:1; Ac. 14:17 → 459). Temporal clause, 2 Tm. 4:3.

† ἄκαιρος, † ἀκαιρέω, εὔκαιρος, † εὐκαιρία.

In the opposites of → καιρός and καίριος, ἀκαιρία and ἄκαιρος, [1] we find much of the same flexibility. Thus a. can mean "excessive," "not corresponding to the Greek ideal of moderation" (Democr. Fr., 71), [2] "opposed to χρή (ἀκαιρότερον ὄντα ἢ χρῆν, Plat. Polit., 307e); similarly ἀκαιρία denotes "that which does not belong" (with ἀδικία, Plat. Symp., 182a). b. "Unwelcome," or ἀκαιρία, "unwelcome event" or "sad condition." [3] c. ἄκαιρος, "unseasonable," ἀκαιρία, "inopportune time." d. ἀκαιρία, "lack of time."

In this connection we should mention ἀκαιρέω or the mid. "to have no time" (late and rare).

In the LXX we find only ἄκαιρος (ως) in Sir. (3 times) in the sense of "untimely" (though → n. 1). This is paralleled by the no less remarkable fact that in the pap. we find only ἄκαιρος, and this only once and late.

In accordance with the development of καιρός (→ esp. 457), the flexibility of the term led to a need for clear terms for the "propitious time." This was met in the post-classical period by the late εὔκαιρος, εὐκαιρία, εὐκαιρέω. [4] καιρός and καίριος could still be used in this sense, though καίριος more rarely (in the LXX only at Prv. 15:23). Finally εὐκαιρία itself was weakened, cf. Suid., s.v. σχολή : σχολή ... ἦν οἱ πολλοὶ ἀκύρως καλοῦσιν εὐκαιρίαν (correct rather εὐκαιρία ... τάττεται ... ἐπὶ καιροῦ τινος εὐφυΐας καὶ ἀρετῆς), → also LXX.

In the LXX εὐκαιρία means the "propitious time" (Sir. 38:24; though here, too, it might mean "rich possession"); "favourable opportunity" (1 Macc. 11:42); "appropriate time, or point of time" (ψ 144:15); but also "time" (of need), Ps. 9:9; ψ 9:21. εὔκαιρος can also mean "at the right time" (ψ 103:27; adv. Sir. 18:22) and also "favourable" or "suitable" (in a non-temporal sense in 2 and 3 Macc.).

In the NT, 2 Tm. 4:2 : ἐπίστηθι εὐκαίρως ἀκαίρως, "exercise your office, deal with members of the community who need your official help when in your judgment it is your duty to do so, whether it be convenient for them [5] (or for you ?), or not." Hb. 4:16 : εἰς εὔκαιρον βοήθειαν, "so that we may find divine help at the divinely appointed time." Here the time of help is left to the judgment of God, but the human ὁμοιότης of the high-priest (v. 15) ensures that the coming of this time does not stretch the patience of Christians too far.

εὐκαιρία is found only at Mt. 22:16 = Lk. 22:6 : "favourable opportunity," "propitious moment" (cf. the ἄτερ ὄχλου of Lk. 22:6). The passage shows how dangerous was the rise of the influence of Jesus in the last days. Fervent expectation of a decisive Messianic act meant that Jesus was constantly accompanied by enthusiastic crowds.

ἀκαιρέω (mid.) is found only at Phil. 4:10.

ἄκαιρος κτλ. [1] ἀκαίριος is very rare, cf. the lexicons and 2 Macc. 6:25, where it is a mistaken reading of A for the unknown ἀκαριαῖος.

[2] Diels, II, 77, 5. In our rendering we follow Pass.(-Cr.) against Diels. Cf. the other instances in Pass.(-Cr.).

[3] Examples of b.-d. in Pass.(-Cr.), s.v.

[4] Plat. Phaedr., 272a : εὐκαιρίαν—ἀκαιρίαν. Elsewhere in Plat. only εὔκαιρος, Phaed., 78a (derivatives of ἀκαιρ- are more common).

[5] In this case there is gentle irony. It is more likely.

† πρόσκαιρος.

All the examples are late.[1] a. (rare) "temporally conditioned," "suggested by the situation of the moment" (ῥῆμα, Aristoph. Schol. Ach., 275; ἀδικία, Ditt. Or., 669, 14; ἑορτή, Ditt. Syll.[3], 1109, 44). b. (most common) "temporally limited" (hence in the pap. esp. of taxes), "unusual,"[2] "auxiliary" (τεῖχος, Jos. Bell., 6, 32), "passing" in contrast with the abiding fame of the athlete, Dion. Hal. Art. Rhet., 7, 4 (36, 7, Usener): τοῖς μὲν γὰρ (spectators at gymnastic games) πρόσκαιρος ἡ τέρψις, τοῖς δὲ ἀθάνατος ἡ δόξα, and 7, 6 (39, 7, Usener): τὰ μὲν [χρήματα] πρόσκαιρα, ἡ δὲ [δόξα] ἀθάνατος. In contrast to ἀΐδιος, Dio C., XII, Fr. 46, 1: οὐ γὰρ πρόσκαιρόν τινα ἀνοχὴν ("temporary" alleviation) ἀλλ᾽ ἀΐδιον φιλίαν ... (lasting peace); cf. LVI, 39, 3 : μικράν τινα ἰσχὺν καὶ ταύτην πρόσκαιρον ... (only "for a limited time").

In moral discussions πρόσκαιρος is a concept of value : Aristoph. Schol. Nu., 360 : [τῇ ἀρετῇ] ... καὶ τοὺς ἐκείνης ἱδρῶτας προκρῖναι τῶν προσκαίρων τῆς κακίας ἡδονῶν, cf. the similar statement in Jos. Ant., 2, 51 (προσκαίρῳ τῆς ἐπιθυμίας ἡδονῇ in contrast to marital fidelity).

In the anthropological dualism of the Neo-Platonist Iambl. Protr., 21 (p. 110, 14, Pistelli) πρόσκαιρος is obviously used as a qualitative concept : ἡμῖν μὲν ἅτε σωματικοῖς ὑπάρχουσι γενητοῖς τε καὶ φθαρτοῖς (→ I, 479) καὶ προσκαίροις, the knowledge of God is more difficult for us since we have become corporeal and are thus temporal and transitory. πρόσκαιρος does not here mean short-lived ; it marks man as temporal in relation to the sensual world. He is subject not merely to the durative but also to the qualitative limitation of temporality in contrast to the absolute freedom of the eternal in the metaphysical sense (→ infra).

The term is used in the LXX only at 4 Macc. 15, in an absolute contrast between the temporal and the eternal. It denotes that which belongs to this world, v. 2 : δυεῖν προκειμένων, εὐσεβείας καὶ τῆς ... σωτηρίας προσκαίρου ... τὴν εὐσέβειαν μᾶλλον ἠγάπησεν; v. 8 : διὰ τὸν πρὸς τὸν θεὸν φόβον ὑπερεῖδεν τὴν τῶν τέκνων πρόσκαιρον σωτηρίαν; v. 23 : τὰ σπλάγχνα αὐτῆς ὁ εὐσεβὴς λογισμός ... ἐπέτεινεν τὴν πρόσκαιρον φιλοτεκνίαν παριδεῖν. Values which are first affirmed in themselves (physical σωτηρία and φιλοτεκνία)[3] are shown to lose their value as compared with such higher values as εὐσέβεια (or φόβος πρὸς τὸν θεόν).

The sense in the NT is purely durative at Mt. 13:21 = Mk. 4:17, for πρὸς καιρόν.[4] Reminiscent of the non-biblical moral usage, and especially of the LXX. is Hb. 11:25 : here, too, we have the favourite contrast in which πρόσκαιρος denotes the lower value which becomes the very opposite (ἁμαρτίας ἀπόλαυσιν !) when compared with that which we should choose ; πρόσκαιρος has thus the implication of an ethical norm (cf. 2 C. 4:17 D* G lat sy^p).

2 C. 4:18, if seen in the light of Jewish apocalyptic, simply maintains that the content of our present existence is transitory, that we have not yet reached the final state. In Jewish thought the defect of our present life is not that it is limited in time, but that it is variable in content, i.e., transitory. It is thus a burden not merely for those who go to torment after this life (S. Bar. 44:11) but also for the

---

π ρ ό σ κ α ι ρ ο ς. [1] Derivation : "what is πρὸς καιρόν," i.e., 1. "what relates to the right moment" (so πρὸς καιρόν in Soph.); 2. "what is appointed only for a limited time" (so πρὸς καιρόν in the NT). The lexicons often suggest the sense of "favourable," but this is never securely attested.

[2] Cf. Preisigke Wört., s.v.

[3] The latter is emphatically a good in Judaism.

[4] Cf. Ditt. Syll.[3], 1109, 44; Hck. Mk. on 4:17.

heirs of glory. In Greek thought, on the other hand, τὰ βλεπόμενα and πρόσκαιρα were strictly correlative concepts. The world of sense is necessarily tied to time, and this fact of bondage to time is the oppressive thing for all men (→ Iambl. *supra*). In Paul the Greek view seems to have imposed itself on the Jewish. The Christian does not fix his gaze on the destiny of the outward man in the sphere of the sensual world,[5] for (γάρ) this is temporal. In πρόσκαιρος we have both the sense of "corruptible," "transitory," "non-definitive," and also the sense of "temporal," "rooted in time," "non-transcendent."

> It is astonishing how rare are πρόσκαιρος and related expressions in the corresponding discussions in Gk. philosophy.[6] Plat. Phaed., 79b, d equates the invisible with the ἀεὶ ὄν, but there is no similar term for temporality, and even the ἀεὶ ὄν becomes less prominent in what follows ; θνητός (or θεῖος) is more common. This is not due to any lack of linguistic possibilities, for Plot. Enn., IV, 7, in a discussion of the immortality of the soul, still prefers the antithesis mortal-immortal (or divine); εἰς χρόνον τινὰ δοθείς (temporal) is found once at VII, 1 (II, 120, 24 f., Volkmann), and ἀίδιος occurs a few times. The case is similar in Stoic writings.[7]

Delling

καίω

καίω, "to kindle," "to burn," occurs 13 times in the NT. Of these instances, only two are theologically significant, namely, Lk. 24:32 and 1 C. 13:3.

1. Lk. 24:32 : οὐχὶ ἡ καρδία ἡμῶν καιομένη ἦν ἐν ἡμῖν; "did not our heart burn within us ?"[1] There are examples of this common expression in both Latin and Greek literature. But in this case the main influence is probably that of biblical and Jewish usage :[2] ψ 38:3 : ἐθερμάνθη ἡ καρδία μου ἐντός μου, καὶ ἐν τῇ μελέτῃ μου ἐκκαυθήσεται πῦρ; ψ 72:21: ἐξεκαύθη ἡ καρδία μου. The word καίω is found in Test. N. 7:4 : ἐκαιόμην τοῖς σπλάγχνοις.

> The reading κεκαλυμμένη in D, which makes sense, is perhaps an error for κεκαυμένη rather than καιομένη. Of more weight is the reading *jaqir* in the Syr. versions (sy^cs); this corresponds to βαρεῖα, and *jaqid* to καιομένη. Here, too, there might have been some confusion. Or perhaps *jaqir,* which is assumed in the older it MSS, e.g., *exterminatum* in e, corresponds to the original Gk. reading βεβαρημένη in the sense : "How lacking in judgment we have been !"[3]

---

[5] This is characterised by βλεπόμενα. Similarly Plato briefly uses τὸ ὁρατόν when he has more precisely described the sphere of the outward man in terms of the various sensual perceptions (Phaed., 79a).
[6] Cf. the material collected in Wnd. 2 K. on 4:18b.
[7] Cf. II, 223 ff., v. Arnim.
κ α ί ω. [1] Cf. Kl. Lk., *ad loc.* and Str.-B., *ad loc.*
[2] Wellh. Lk., *ad loc.* : "Our heart burned corresponds to the biblical נכמרו רחמי".
[3] Cf. the textual discussion in Kl. Lk., *ad loc.;* also W. C. Allen, JThSt, 2 (1901), 299.

2. 1 C. 13:3 : ἐὰν παραδῶ τὸ σῶμά μου ἵνα καυθήσομαι, [4] "if I give my body to be burned." Various interpretations have been suggested, namely, martyrdom by fire, [5] burning of self, [6] and branding as a slave. [7]

a. Martyrdom by fire would certainly have been familiar to Paul from the background of Judaism, though we cannot be sure whether there had been any examples of Christians executed in this manner.

The verse Hb. 11:34 : ἔσβεσαν δύναμιν πυρός, shows that endurance and victory in the flames were regarded as a supreme proof of faith. The men in the burning fiery furnace survived this test (Da. 3:23 ff.), and there are brief allusions to them in 2 Macc. 7:3 ff. and 1 Cl., 45, 7.

In Rabb. literature, too, martyrdom by fire is a favourite theme. We read of the fiery martyrdom of Chanina b. Teradion, bAZ, 18a par. The legend of Abraham's martyrdom in the fiery oven was soon fashioned after the model of Da. 3:23 ff.; it is found already in Ps.-Philo (Basel, 1527, 6D-7B). Abraham is taken with 11 companions because he refused to co-operate in building the tower of Babel. The leading prince Jectam wishes to liberate them. Abraham alone stands fast : *ecce ego fugio hodie in montana : et si evasero ignem, exient de montibus ferae bestiae et comedent nos, aut escae nobis deficient, et moriemur fame, et inveniemur fugientes ante populum terrae, cadentes in peccatis nostris. Et nunc vivit in quo confido : quia non movebor de loco meo, in quo posuerunt me, et si fuerit aliquod peccatum meum, et consumens consumar, fiat voluntas dei.* The legend of Abraham's martyrdom and deliverance enjoyed a great vogue in Judaism. This is a sign of the popularity of heroism of faith. The Arabs took over the legend from the Jews and embellished it with fantasy. 2 Macc. 7 (the martyrdom of the mother and her seven sons) also had a great influence in Rabb. literature, Eka r., I § 50 on 1:16 (Vilna, 1887, 17d/18a) and par. (though without death by fire). [8]

There are explicit depictions of martyrdom by fire in 2 Macc. 7:3 ff. and 4 Macc. *passim.* [9] 4 Macc. was probably not written long before Paul, perhaps even in his own lifetime. Hence he may have known the book. At any rate, in the Jewish persecutions under Caligula at this period Jews were burned to death in Egyptian Alexandria, and this made a painful impression on the whole Jewish world. [10] These Jews were martyred

---

[4] The reading καυχήσωμαι is supported by 𝔓 69 pc Or and A. v. Harnack (SAB [1911], 142) regards this as original. But cf. Ltzm., *ad loc.*: "The only trouble is that it (sc. καυχήσωμαι) seems to make the antithetical ἀγάπην δὲ μὴ ἔχω superfluous." Cf. also F. J. Dölger, *Antike und Christentum,* I (1929), 254 : "The variant καυχήσωμαι is probably due to mishearing, which is quite conceivable in the case of slovenly speech. But we may also conjecture that it was originally put in the margin by an expositor in elucidation and explanation of καυθήσομαι, and that it then penetrated into the text and replaced the similar καυθήσομαι. The term καυχήσωμαι, "that I may boast," would define the ultimate purpose of καυθήσομαι, "that I may be burned," since the burning would be for self-glory." A. Deissmann, *Paulus*² (1925), 76, n. 6 : "The alteration of καυθήσομαι was prompted by the later consideration that the martyrdom of Paul was not by fire." E. Preuschen, ZNW, 16 (1915), 129 : "The reading καυχήσωμαι will have to be accepted as a softening so long as a satisfactory explanation of καυθήσομαι can be found." Joh. W. 1 K., *ad loc.*: "καυχήσωμαι was substituted because καυθήσομαι was no longer understood." Nestle is wrong to adduce Clement of Alexandria in favour of καυχήσωμαι, since the relevant passage runs as follows : ἔστι γὰρ καὶ ὁ λαὸς ὁ τοῖς χείλεσιν ἀγαπῶν, ἔστι καὶ ἄλλος <ὁ> παραδιδοὺς τὸ σῶμα, ἵνα καυθήσεται (Cl. Al. Strom., IV, 18 § 112, 1).

[5] Deissmann, *loc. cit.*
[6] Joh. W. 1 K., *ad loc.,* also Dölger, *op. cit.,* 254 ff.
[7] E. Preuschen, *op. cit.,* 127 ff.
[8] This paragraph is by R. Meyer.
[9] Cf. Kautzsch Apkr. u. Pseudepigr., II, 149 ff. (A. Deissmann).
[10] Cf. Schürer, I, 498.

because they resisted emperor worship. Here, as in the case of the Maccabean martyr-doms, we have a fate which was voluntarily accepted and which might have been evaded if the martyrs had been willing to fall in with the wishes of the authorities. [11]

Paul is sceptical in relation to such heroism if it is finally orientated to self rather than to God. In 1 C. the apostle is contending against such various -isms as libertinism, asceticism, perfectionism and individualism, and he finds the enthusiasm of the martyr suspect if it simply expresses the charismatic endowment which can be, even though it does not have to be, an outlet for human hybris. Heroic religious achievements can become a false righteousness of works in which grace is no longer all in all. The desire for one's own cross in martyrdom can obscure the cross of Christ. Paul's refusal to adopt any -ism is a rejection of even the most noble and inspired attitudes and actions which are so dear to man, even to the Christian. It is a desire to be empty and obedient in order that God alone may rule and in order that He may display His grace in Christ when He judges man. [12] The usual interpretation of 1 C. 13 exalts ἀγάπη as brotherly love over all else, even over faith. The final statement of the apostle gives some support for this view, but it is a misunderstanding which misses the decisive point. [13] For the ἀγάπη of which Paul is thinking is no antithesis to πίστις.

Tertullian in his work against Praxeas (ch. 1) rightly speaks of the *dilectio dei*, and he is right in his understanding of 1 C. 13:3 : (Praxeas) *insuper de iactatione martyrii inflatus ob solum et simplex et breve carceris taedium ; quando, et si corpus suum tradidisset exurendum, nihil profecisset, dilectionem dei non habens, cuius charismata quoque expugnavit*. Thus the reference is to the *dilectio dei* and the *charismata dei*. [14] Even the martyr piety of the Maccabees is suspect in this connection. Bravely accepted and suffered, death by fire is for the Stoics the most painful and the most glorious test. Seneca demands an equable spirit even in face of stake or cross. [15] These Stoic ideas are also found in Hellenistic Judaism, as may be seen plainly from 4 Macc. [16] If Paul knew this work, he was rejecting its heroic ideal of the *vir bonus et impavidus*.

---

[11] This disposes of the objection of Joh. W. 1 K., *ad loc.*, that "Paul presumes a voluntary giving of the body, and this rules out an interpretation in terms of martyrdom" ; E. Preuschen has the similar objection (*op. cit.*, 131) that "if we think in terms of martyrdom it is hard to maintain voluntariness." Dölger, *op. cit.*, 258 f. is exaggerating when he says : "The saying of Paul is stronger. If we think in terms of martyrdom, we have to assume a voluntary surrender to the authorities who then pass and execute the sentence of punishment by fire."

[12] Cf. K. L. Schmidt, "Der Apostel Paulus u. die antike Welt," *Vorträge der Bibliothek Warburg* (1927), 59 ff.

[13] → I, 51 f., where it is rightly recognised that ἀγάπη stands under the sign of σταυρός and τέλος, but where there is still too strong an orientation to brotherly love, whereas 1 C. 13 deals with the ἀγάπη θεοῦ — a gen. which is too complex to be subjected to the schema subjective gen. or objective gen.

[14] Dölger, 259 takes a different view : "Even if there had been burnings of Christians prior to 1 C., a self-sought martyrdom at the stake does not seem to me to do justice to the text of Paul. Paul would not have denied that there is love in the zealous faith which seeks martyrdom. This could be done only by a temperamental man like Tertullian in his battle against heretics." This objection fails to see that Paul resists the righteousness of works even in its more subtle forms. Furthermore, Paul might have been as temperamental as Tertullian, and he surely had to deal with heretics in 1 C. Finally, even if there were no Christian martyrdoms by fire, there were certainly Jewish.

[15] Dölger, 258 refers to Sen. in Lact. Inst., VI, 17 § 28.

[16] A. Deissmann (→ n. 9) quotes E. Norden, *Die antike Kunstprosa ...,* I (1898), 417: "The Stoic principle that reason is mistress of the emotions" is well illustrated in 4 Macc.

b. The situation is much the same in respect of the burning of self, which was reckoned a particularly glorious act in the Graeco-Roman world. [17]

The best-known example and model from Greek mythology is the self-burning of Heracles, cf. Soph. Trach., 1195 ff.; Soph. Phil., 728; Apollodor., II, 7, 7 (J. G. Frazer [1921], 270); Diod. S., IV, 38, 4. Such an act is the τηλαυγὲς πρόσωπον for the heroic end and deification of man, whose whole life, including death, is toil and trouble (πόνος). [18] Tertullian (Apol., 50, 4, 5) sees in these actions, which were undertaken by great men and women of antiquity, famae et gloriae causa, a model for Christians facing martyrdom. This does not rule out the possibility that if Paul had the burning of self in view he had a different estimate of it. In the evaluations of writers of antiquity, Indian self-burning occupies a special position (cf. the story of Alexander the Great and Kalanos). Philo tells us of this in Omn. Prob. Lib., 96. This account of the true inner freedom of the philosopher even in face of death by fire was widely known in Christian antiquity, and there were warnings against seeking martyrdom along the lines of this self-immolation. Acc. to Cl. Al. Strom., IV, 4 § 17, 1-3 "such Christians give themselves up to a futile death like the gymnosophists of India, who delivered themselves to a pointless death by fire." An imitator of this Indian practice, and of Heracles, was Peregrinus Proteus, whose voluntary death on the funeral pyre is recounted in Luc. Pergr. Mort., 39. By his self-immolation and his subsequent heavenly ascent he stamped himself as a νέος Ἡρακλῆς. In this connection we may also mention the burning of Indian widows, which was known to antiquity. In Stoic philosophy this is all regarded as a particularly effective illustration of the doctrine of ἀπάθεια, ἀταραξία, καρτερία. If Paul was acquainted with this material and its evaluation, he regarded the much vaunted voluntary death by fire as useless without ἀγάπη. [19]

The question whether Paul is thinking of martyrdom at the stake or of self-immolation cannot be answered with precision, as though we had here an inescapable either — or. Possibly he is thinking of both. Such a view is suggested by the results of our investigation, since martyrdom at the stake and self-immolation both have their final basis in the same enthusiasm. In both the Stoic finds opportunity for self-advertisement. Neither is a demonstration of the true Christian.

c. We can deal with the theory of branding more by way of an appendix. On this view v. 3 would read : "If I give my body to receive the mark of slavery." Reception of this mark would imply self-giving to slavery in order to help others. But this would involve ἀγάπη, which is for Paul the higher thing. It should also be noted that the mark of slavery and branding are not necessarily identical. Branding was mostly used for runaway slaves and criminals. Tattooing was the normal way of marking slaves. [20]

Apart from these difficulties 1 C. 13:3 is more effective if we link it with the first two interpretations.

K. L. Schmidt

---

[17] Cf. Dölger, 259 ff. for examples.

[18] These two sentences are by H. Kleinknecht.

[19] Dölger, 269 concludes his presentation with the words : "The lit. of the time was full of the praise of personages who had voluntarily given themselves up to death by fire."

[20] In this respect we must agree with Dölger's criticism (255 ff.) of Preuschen (127).

---

† κακολογέω

A rare word (from the time of Lys. and Gorg.; the noun κακολογία from the time of Hdt., the basic adj. κακολόγος from that of Pind.), "to abuse," "to calumniate," "to speak evil of." In the LXX for קלל pi and hi : "to curse," though this is more often rendered καταρᾶσθαι. More common, too, is the better Attic κακῶς ἐρεῖν or εἰπεῖν.

In the NT Mt. 15:4; Mk. 7:10 in the negative version of the fifth commandment : "Whoso curseth father or mother shall die the death," almost literally quoting LXX Ex. 21:16, [1] cf. Lv. 20:9; Dt. 27:16; Prv. 20:9a; Ez. 22:7. According to the Rabbinic interpretation the punishment, which was theoretically by stoning, [2] fell only on those who cursed their parents in the name of God. [3] Jesus rejects all such casuistry and gives the commandment new breadth and depth and strictness. Even those who keep back from their parents their due on a religious pretext transgress the commandment of God. [4]

At Mk. 9:39 Jesus says of the strange exorcist : "If a man does a miracle in my name, he will not lightly speak evil of me." [5] According to the conjecture of J. Weiss, [6] there is a subtle humour in this proverbial type of saying, for which there are formal parallels. [7] The earlier view revived by Loisy, namely, that the saying is an attack on the primitive Jerusalem community which Paul regarded as "false exorcists," is most improbable. [8] It is in conflict with 1 C. 12:3, whose ultimate implication is that anyone who acknowledges the Lord does so under the impulsion of the Holy Spirit.

At Ac. 19:9 the Jews publicly deride the message of Paul (ὁδός, as at Ac. 9:2) in the synagogue ; here κακολογεῖν obviously means "to calumniate," not "to curse."

Carl Schneider

κακοπάθεια, -θέω → πάσχω.

κ α κ ο λ ο γ έ ω. Pr.-Bauer, 619 ([3]660); Wilke-Grimm, 222; Bl.-Debr.[6] § 151, 1; Helbing, *Kasussyntax*, 20; L. Brun, "Segen u. Fluch im Urchr.," *Skrifter utgitt av det norske Videnskaps Akademi, Hist.-Filos. Kl.* (1932).

[1] The lack of possessives in the NT is perhaps Galilean-Aram., cf. Zn. Mt., ad loc., but may also be good Gk.

[2] Sanh., VII, 4; M. Ex., 21, 17 (88a); Str.-B., I, 709.

[3] Sanh., VII, 8; Str.-B., loc. cit.

[4] In the context one might conjecture that, as at LXX Dt. 27:16, we ought to have ἀτιμάζειν rather than κακολογεῖν. But κακολογεῖν is demanded by Rabb. tradition, → n. 3. ἀτιμάζειν is broader than κακολογεῖν, cf. A. H. MacNeile, *The Gospel according to St. Matthew* (1915), ad loc. Jesus is characterising the narrowness of His opponents.

[5] κακολογεῖν is used similarly at 2 Macc. 4:1.

[6] Schr. NT, I² (1907), ad loc.

[7] Str.-B., II, 19.

[8] A. Loisy, *L'Evangile selon Marc* (1912), ad loc.; cf. also Kl. Mk., ad loc.

κακός, ἄκακος, κακία, κακόω, κακοῦργος, κακοήθεια, κακοποιέω, κακοποιός, ἐγκακέω, ἀνεξίκακος	→ ἀγαθός, I, 10 ff.; → ἁμαρτάνω, I, 267 ff.; → πονηρός.

κακός.

Contents. A. κακός in the Greek World ; B. κακός in Hellenism ; C. The Evil Principle in Parseeism ; D. κακός in the Old Testament (LXX): 1. τὸ κακόν as Evil ; 2. As an Ethical Concept ; E. κακός in the New Testament.

The word κακός, already considered in relation to → ἀγαθός, expresses the presence of a lack. It is not positive ; it is an incapacity or weakness. Like "evil," it has more than purely moral significance. The wealth of the term is expressed in the developing concepts χείρων, κακίων, ἥττων. Thus κακός means a. "mean," "unserviceable," "incapable," "poor of its kind," e.g., κακοὶ νομῆες, Hom. Od., 17, 246; κακὸς ἰατρός, Aesch. Prom., 471. Greater precision is attained by additions : πάντα γὰρ οὐ κακός εἰμι (not in every respect . . .), μετ' ἀνδράσιν ὅσσοι ἄεθλοι, Hom. Od., 8, 214; κακοὶ γνώμαισιν, Soph. Ai., 964; εἶδος μὲν ἔην κακός, Hom. Il., 10, 316; κακὸς μανθάνειν, Soph. Oed. Tyr., 545. It also means b. "morally bad," "wicked," e.g., ἐν νόστῳ ἀπόλοντο κακῆς ἰότητι γυναικός, Hom. Od., 11, 384; οὐχ ὁ χρηστὸς τῷ κακῷ (κακός and χρηστός opposites) λαχεῖν ἴσα, Soph. Ant., 520; κακὸς πρὸς . . . Thuc., I, 86, 1. It then means c. "weak," e.g., κακὸς καὶ ἄθυμος, Hdt., VII, 11; κακὸς καὶ δειλός, Plat. Menex., 246e; κακοὺς ὄντας πρὸς αἰχμήν, ἐν δὲ τοῖς λόγοις θρασεῖς, Soph. Phil., 1306. Cf. also the linking of κακοσκελής with weak bones, e.g., Xenoph. Mem., III, 3, 4. A final meaning d. is "unhappy," "bad," "ruinous," "evil," e.g., κακὸς δαίμων, Aesch. Pers., 346; κακὴ τύχη, Aesch. Ag., 1203; Soph. Ai, 323; ἄτη κακή, Soph. Ai, 123; κακὸν ἔπος ἀγγελέοντα, Hom. Il., 17, 701; ὁδὸς δύσποτμός τε καὶ κακή, Soph. Oed. Col., 1432 f. This fixes the meaning of the noun τὸ κακόν, τὰ κακά, "evil," "suffering," "misfortune," "ruin," e.g., τὰ πολλ' ἐκεῖν' ὅτ' ἐξέχρη κακά, Soph. Oed. Col., 87 etc.

The question of lack or incapacity, which in the most varied forms affects all spheres of life in terms of κακός, has always been particularly significant in relation to life and religion. It provokes a question of supreme significance, namely,

---

κ α κ ό ς. F. Billicsich, Das Problem der Theodizee im philosophischen Denken des Abendlandes (= Philos. Abh. der österreichischen Leo-Gesellschaft), I (1936); W. Capelle, "Zur antiken Theodizee," Archiv d. Geschichte der Philos., 20 (1907), 173 ff.; O. Dittrich, Geschichte d. Ethik, I/II (1926), Index s.v. böse, schlecht, Übel ; P. Günther, Das Problem d. Theodizee im Neuplatonismus, Diss. Leipzig (1906); H. Hommel, "Das Problem des Übels im Altertum," Neue Jahrbücher f. Wissenschaft u. Jugendbildung, 1 (1925), 186 ff.; F. A. Märcker, Das Prinzip des Bösen nach den Begriffen der Griechen (1842); C. Ritter, "Platons Gedanken über Gott und das Verhältnis der Welt u. des Menschen zu ihm," ARW, 19 (1919), 232 ff.; 466 ff.; E. Schröder, Plotins Abhandlung πόθεν τὰ κακά (Enn., I, 8), Diss. Leipzig (1916); W. Sesemann, "Die Ethik Platos u. das Problem des Bösen" in Philos. Abh. H. Cohen dargebracht (1912), 170 ff.; A. Titius, "Platons Gottesgedanke u. Theodizee" in R. Seeberg-Festschr., I (1929), 141 ff. For additional bibl. cf. → n. 23. In the case of the OT and NT the problems related to κακός do not arise independently but fall under the question of sin. Cf. bibl. → ἁμαρτάνω, I, 284; → ἀγαθός, I, 10.

that of the origin and purpose of evil, of the meaning of the world, of the plan and purpose of God. This is the problem of theodicy, and it involves the moral question of the overcoming of evil.

A. κακός in the Greek World.

In the earliest Greek period there developed two answers to the problem of evil [1] which constantly recur in new variations. The older is to the effect that by a divine necessity κακόν also comes from and is posited by deity: ἀτὰρ θεὸς ἄλλοτε ἄλλῳ Ζεὺς ἀγαθόν τε κακόν τε διδοῖ· δύναται γὰρ ἅπαντα, Hom. Od., 4, 236 f. (cf. also Il., 24, 525 ff.). A later view distinguishes between the misfortune which we bring on ourselves and that which is sent by God. In the assembly of the gods Zeus proclaims: ὢ πόποι, οἷον δή νυ θεοὺς βροτοὶ αἰτιόωνται. ἐξ ἡμέων γάρ φασι κακ' ἔμμεναι· οἱ δὲ καὶ αὐτοὶ σφῇσιν ἀτασθαλίῃσιν ὑπὲρ μόρον ἄλγε' ἔχουσιν, Hom. Od., 1, 32 f. In the example which then follows (1, 37 f.) Zeus shows that evil can come through disregarding divine warnings: εἰδὼς αἰπὺν ὄλεθρον, ἐπεὶ πρό οἱ εἴπομεν ἡμεῖς, Ἑρμείαν πέμψαντες. Greek tragedy is built on this twofold foundation. Guilt and fate intersect in both Aeschylus and Sophocles. [2] In Oed. Col. Sophocles builds on the belief expressed by the chorus prior to the carrying off of Oedipus: νέα τάδε νεόθεν ἦλθέ μοι [νέα] βαρύποτμα κακὰ παρ' ἀλαοῦ ξένου, εἴ τι μοῖρα μὴ κιγχάνει. μάτην γὰρ οὐδὲν ἀξίωμα δαιμόνων ἔχω φράσαι. ὁρᾷ ὁρᾷ ταῦτ' ἀεὶ χρόνος, ἐπεὶ μὲν ἕτερα, τὰ δὲ παρ' ἦμαρ αὖθις αὔξων ἄνω, Oed. Col., 1448 ff. According to this belief, everything that the gods do is meaningful and attains its goal. Even fate is teleologically directed by them. The fact that this belief is expressed in a miracle of rapture is indicative of its character as a mere sense or inkling of the truth. In the time allotted to man between birth and death there is no final solution to the problem. On the basis of his consideration of the political Greek, Solon in his elegy ἡμετέρα δὲ πόλις discusses the question of the evil which he sees approaching his city. For him it is not a divinely sent fate but a self-incurred misfortune which according to the law of δίκη fulfilled in time is now inevitable because the people would not listen to the warning which Solon himself delivered in place of the warning deities of Homer and tragedy: ταῦτα διδάξαι θυμὸς Ἀθηναίους με κελεύει. [3] "His instruction falls into two distinct parts, a negative (vv. 1-32), the warning of the disastrous consequences of unrighteousness, and a positive (v. 33 to the end), praise of the blessings of εὐνομία." [4] The presupposition of this elegy is the genuinely Greek view developed by Socrates and Plato, namely, that κακόν arises through ignorance and ἀγαθόν through knowledge.

The philosopher works out reflectively the impulse behind the poet and the politician. The question of evil, of its origin, nature and purpose, was already being discussed in the earliest days of Greek philosophy.

For the Pythagoreans formless ἄπειρον is the source of κακόν: τὸ γὰρ κακὸν τοῦ ἀπείρου ὡς Πυθαγόρειοι εἴκαζον, τὸ δὲ ἀγαθὸν τοῦ πεπερασμένου, Aristot. Eth.

---

[1] → ἁμαρτάνω, I, 296 ff.
[2] → I, 298 f.
[3] Cf. W. Jaeger, "Solons Eunomie," SAB (1926), 69 ff. (quoting from p. 76).
[4] *Ibid.*, 77.

Nic., II, 5, p. 1106b, 29 f. Theirs is thus from the very outset a dualistic solution. The limitless is confronted by the limitation which creates cosmic order. For Heraclitus evil is the necessary opposite of the good ; there is no good without evil : νοῦσος ὑγιείην ἐποίησεν ἡδύ, κακὸν ἀγαθόν, λιμὸς κόρον, Fr., 111 (Diels, I, 99, 8). In him we find the aristocratic judgment : οἱ πολλοὶ κακοί, ὀλίγοι δὲ ἀγαθοί, Fr., 104 (Diels, I, 98, 8 f.). [5] Yet behind the antitheses is a hidden but wonderful harmony. Empedocles found a very different solution : πάντα τὸν καθ᾽ ἡμᾶς τόπον ἔφη κακῶν μεστὸν εἶναι καὶ μέχρι μὲν σελήνης τὰ κακὰ φθάνειν ἐκ τοῦ περὶ γῆν τόπου ταθέντα, περατέρω δὲ μὴ χωρεῖν, ἅτε καθαρωτέρου τοῦ ὑπὲρ τὴν σελήνην παντὸς ὄντος τόπου, Fr., 163 (Diels, I, 210, 27 ff.). [6] In the background lies the view that the souls which inhabit men were ejected from the supraterrestrial sphere of good and felicity because of a fault, and that they were thus plunged into the miserable state of earthly existence from which they must now rise back again. The state of evil and evils is thus a punishment. Democritus finds the source of evil in man and says : ἂν δὲ σαυτὸν ἔνδοθεν ἀνοίξῃς, ποικίλον τι καὶ πολυπαθὲς κακῶν ταμιεῖον εὑρήσεις καὶ θησαύρισμα, Fr., 149 (Diels, II, 88, 28 ff.). Like Empedocles, he sharply opposes the implication of the gods in evil. Evil is in man, and its source is human ignorance : ... ὁκόσα κακὰ καὶ βλαβερὰ καὶ ἀνωφελέα, τάδε δ᾽ οὔ<τε> πάλαι οὔτε νῦν θεοὶ ἀνθρώποισι δωροῦνται, ἀλλ᾽ αὐτοὶ τοίσδεσιν ἐμπελάζουσι ("approach") διὰ νοῦ τυφλότητα καὶ ἀγνωμοσύνην, Fr., 175 (Diels, II, 96, 8 ff.). This conviction is particularly strong in Socrates. For him the evil one does is the result of ignorance of virtue, and suffering evil is the result of ignorance of the providence of deity. Knowledge of virtue leads men to do good and makes them moral. It also brings them under the protection of divine providence, which directs all things for the good of those who are moral. Socrates had to confirm this doctrine by his death, and he maintained it even in face of death : "One thing we must recognise as true, namely, that there is no evil for the good man, whether in life or in death. What now happens to me is no accident. So much is clear to me, that death and redemption are now the best for me," Plat. Ap., 41c. [7]

Here are the seeds of future thought. Here are also the two possibilities which are always present either in isolation or in various combinations. On the one side evil is a metaphysical principle whose origin and purpose must then be discussed and will receive very different answers. On the other side the basis of evil is to be found in the ignorance of men as they actually are.

In relation to evil Plato accepts and develops the thought which was first proposed by Democr. and then carried further by Socrates. He states the insight which Democr. first stated and Socrates developed, namely, that men do evil involuntarily through ignorance : οὐδεὶς τῶν σοφῶν ἀνδρῶν ἡγεῖται οὐδένα ἀνθρώπων ἑκόντα ἐξαμαρτάνειν οὐδὲ αἰσχρά τε καὶ κακὰ ἑκόντα ἐργάζεσθαι, ἀλλ᾽ εὖ ἴσασιν, ὅτι πάντες οἱ τὰ αἰσχρὰ καὶ τὰ κακὰ ποιοῦντες ἄκοντες ποιοῦσιν, Prot., 345d e. Hence knowledge

---

[5] We find the same judgment in Plato : ... ὁρᾶν αὐτῶν τοὺς μὲν ἀχρήστους, τοὺς δὲ πολλοὺς κακοὺς πᾶσαν κακίαν ... τί ποθ᾽ οἱ πολλοὶ κακοί, Resp., V, 490d, cf. also οἱ κακά, II, 379c; πολὺ γὰρ ἐλάττω τἀγαθὰ τῶν κακῶν ἡμῖν, also X, 609a; in Stoicism : τῶν δὲ ἀνθρώπων οἱ πλεῖστοι κακοί ..., Alex. Aphr. Fat., 28 (Bruns Suppl. Aristot., II, 2, p. 199).

[6] Cf. τὰ δὲ κακά φησι καὶ οὗτος (sc. Aristot.) κατ᾽ ἐναντίωσιν τῶν ἀγαθῶν γενέσθαι καὶ εἶναι ὑπὸ τὸν περὶ σελήνην τόπον, ὑπὲρ δὲ σελήνην μηκέτι, Hipp. Philos., 20, 16 (Diels, Doxographi Graeci [1879], 570, 31 ff.); τὴν γὰρ κακίαν ἐνθάδε δεῖν οἰκεῖν εἶπον, ἐν τῷ ἑαυτῆς χωρίῳ οὖσαν· χωρίον γὰρ αὐτῆς ἡ γῆ, οὐχ ὁ κόσμος, ὡς ἔνιοί ποτε ἐροῦσι βλασφημοῦντες, Corp. Herm., IX, 4b. The restriction of evil to certain spheres is expressed in the idea that it belongs to the planets, is received by souls on their descent to earth, and put off on their reascent, ibid., I, 25.

[7] Cf. Billicsich, 13 f.

leads to the doing of good : ἐάνπερ γιγνώσκῃ τις τἀγαθὰ καὶ τὰ κακά, μὴ ἂν
κρατηθῆναι ὑπὸ μηδενὸς ὥστε ἄλλ' ἄττα πράττειν ἢν ἂν ἐπιστήμη κελεύῃ, ἀλλ'
ἱκανὴν εἶναι τὴν φρόνησιν βοηθεῖν τῷ ἀνθρώπῳ, Prot., 352c. [8] But Plato then goes
on to ask wherein evil consists, and he arrives at the definition : τὸ μὲν ἀπολλύον καὶ
διαφθεῖρον πᾶν τὸ κακὸν εἶναι, τὸ δὲ σῷζον καὶ ὠφελοῦν τὸ ἀγαθόν (Resp., X,
608e). In this definition he thus sees that ἀπολλύον καὶ διαφθεῖρον, or κακόν, is a
cosmic and psychic power. He has thus moved on to the view that evil is not grounded
merely in ignorance but in materially rooted passions which influence the life of the
soul, so that the involuntariness of evil is true only of the rational part of the soul, not
the emotional. For moral life evil is more closely defined : ψυχῇ ἆρ' οὐκ ἔστιν ὃ
ποιεῖ αὐτὴν κακήν; καὶ μάλα ... ἀδικία τε καὶ ἀκολασία καὶ δειλία καὶ ἀμαθία,
Resp., X, 609b c. [9] This psychic evil finds its counterpart in cosmic κακά, disruptive
and destructive forces (cf. Resp., X, 608e ff.). This leads Plato to the question of the
cause of evil. He sharply rejects the thesis that it comes from the gods. Deity wills only
good, καὶ τῶν μὲν ἀγαθῶν οὐδένα ἄλλον αἰτιατέον, τῶν δὲ κακῶν ἄλλ' ἄττα
δεῖ ζητεῖν τὰ αἴτια, ἀλλ' οὐ τὸν θεόν, "as the author of good one should seek only
God, whereas for evil one should seek all possible causes except God" (Resp., II, 379c). [10]
He thus argues for the dialectical necessity of evil which underlies the conflict with it :
οὔτ' ἀπολέσθαι τὰ κακὰ δυνατόν ... — ὑπεναντίον γάρ τι τῷ ἀγαθῷ ἀεὶ εἶναι
ἀνάγκη — οὔτ' ἐν θεοῖς αὐτὰ ἱδρῦσθαι, τὴν δὲ θνητὴν φύσιν καὶ τόνδε τὸν τόπον
περιπολεῖ ἐξ ἀνάγκης, Theaet., 176a. Attempting a positive answer to the question of
its origin, he proposes two ways. First, he takes up the view of the Pythagoreans and
their definition of evil, and he finds the cause of evil in σωματοειδές (Polit., 273b ff.),
i.e., in the "not very precisely defined corporeal, the source of all evil," [11] in the matter
which the creator found and used in fashioning the world, since in Greek thought creation is strictly the imposition of order. He thus worked through to a metaphysical dualism
of spirit and matter which finds its ethical counterpart in the dualism of soul and body.
Later, however, he arrived at another view, namely, that of an evil world soul alongside
the good (Leg., X, 896a ff.). This implies cosmological dualism. [12] In life extraordinary
importance is attached to confident heroism against κακόν. This may be discerned
already in Socrates, is proclaimed by Plato, and reaches a new climax in Plotinus.
ὑποληπτέον περὶ τοῦ δικαίου ἀνδρός, ἐάντ' ἐν πενίᾳ γίγνηται ἐάντ' ἐν νόσοις ἢ
τινι ἄλλῳ τῶν δοκούντων (!) κακῶν, ὡς τούτῳ ταῦτα εἰς ἀγαθόν τι τελευτήσει
ζῶντι ἢ καὶ ἀποθανόντι, Resp., X, 613a. [13] Plato seems to have been most strongly
influenced here by his dying teacher, Socrates. The faith which builds on divine providence and goodness is heroically translated in life into the good and the beautiful, and
into victory over evil.

---

[8] We thus find in Prot. a rejection of the principle : γινώσκων ὁ ἄνθρωπος τὰ κακὰ
ὅτι κακά ἐστιν, ὅμως αὐτὰ ποιεῖ, 355c. This experience is found throughout the Gk.
world, e.g., Eur. Med., 1078 ff.: καὶ μανθάνω μὲν οἷα δρᾶν μέλλω κακά· θυμὸς δὲ
κρείσσων τῶν ἐμῶν βουλευμάτων, ὅσπερ μεγίστων αἴτιος κακῶν βροτοῖς, also
Xenoph. Cyrop., VI, 1, 41: οὐ γὰρ μία γε οὖσα ἅμα ἀγαθή τέ ἐστι καὶ κακή ... ἀλλὰ
δῆλον ὅτι δύο ἐστὸν ψυχαί ...
[9] Cf. esp. Leg., V, 731d e : πάντων δὲ μέγιστον κακῶν ἀνθρώποις τοῖς πολλοῖς
ἔμφυτον ἐν ταῖς ψυχαῖς ἐστιν ... τοῦτο δ' ἔστιν ὃ λέγουσιν ὡς φίλος αὐτῷ πᾶς
ἄνθρωπος φύσει τέ ἐστιν καὶ ὀρθῶς ἔχει τὸ δεῖν εἶναι τοιοῦτον. Self-love is here seen
as κακόν which destroys both the soul and fellowship. The spiritual forces mentioned in
Resp., 609b c are evils just as much as corporeal (νόσοι, πενία, Resp., X, 613a) and cosmic
κακά.
[10] Cf. Resp., II, 379c ff.; Tim., 29c f.; also Resp., III, 391e: ἐκ θεῶν κακὰ γίγνεσθαι
ἀδύνατον. Cf. Ritter in ARW, 481 ff. and Titius, 147.
[11] Cf. Schröder, op. cit., 29; Sesemann, op. cit.
[12] Cf. Schröder, 21-33; Billicsich, 28 ff.
[13] → ἀγαθός, I, 17 and n. 19; Billicsich, 25 f.

Such thoughts are remote from Aristot. He rejects the Platonic idea that evil is a metaphysical principle linked with matter. [14] "Evil is not outside things," Metaph., IX, 9, p. 1011a, 15 f. The possibility of the bad lies in human freedom: ἐφ' ἡμῖν δὲ καὶ ἡ ἀρετὴ ὁμοίως δὲ καὶ ἡ κακία, Eth. Nic., III, 7, p. 1113b, 6 f. To this freedom either to do or not to do belongs the ignorance which is the source of the bad. Ignorance is itself guilt. Apart from the assumption of freedom, no legislation would be possible. Hence: ὁμοίως γὰρ (sc. τῷ ἀγαθῷ) καὶ τῷ κακῷ ὑπάρχει τὸ δι' αὐτὸν ἐν ταῖς πράξεσι καὶ εἰ μὴ ἐν τῷ τέλει, Eth. Nic., III, 7, p. 1114b, 20 f.

Stoicism goes beyond Aristot. and further develops κακόν in sharp antithesis to ἀγαθόν. There are κακὰ τὰ περὶ ψυχήν (sc. κακίαι σὺν ταῖς μοχθηραῖς ἕξεσι καὶ καθόλου αἱ ψεκταὶ ἐνέργειαι), τὰ δ' ἐκτός (sc. οἱ ἐχθροὶ σὺν τοῖς εἴδεσιν) and τὰ δ' οὔτε περὶ ψυχὴν οὔτ' ἐκτός (sc. οἱ φαῦλοι καὶ πάντες οἱ τὰς κακίας ἔχοντες), Stob. Ecl., II, 70, 8 ff. Elsewhere ethical κακά are expressly enumerated as ἀφροσύνη, of which it is sometimes said: ἣν μόνην φασὶν εἶναι κακὸν οἱ ἀπὸ τῆς Στοᾶς (Sext. Emp. Math., XI, 90), ἀκολασία, ἀδικία, δειλία καὶ πᾶν ὅ ἐστι κακία ἢ μετέχον κακίας, Stob. Ecl., II, 57, 19 ff. The character of κακόν as such appears as βλάβη ἢ οὐχ ἕτερον βλάβης, Sext. Emp. Math., XI, 40 and may be known from the synonyms: τὰ δὲ κακὰ ἐκ τῶν ἐναντίων πάντα βλαβερὰ καὶ δύσχρηστα καὶ ἀσύμφορα καὶ ἀλυσιτελῆ καὶ φαῦλα καὶ ἀπρεπῆ καὶ αἰσχρὰ καὶ ἀνοίκεια, Stob. Ecl., II, 69, 13. Stoicism follows Aristot. by refusing to find a metaphysical explanation either for the evil that we do or the evil that we suffer, cf. Chrysipp.: οὐ γὰρ ἥ γ' ὕλη τὸ κακὸν ἐξ ἑαυτῆς παρέσχεν· ἄποιος γάρ ἐστι, καὶ πάσας ὅσας δέχεται διαφορὰς ὑπὸ τοῦ κινοῦντος αὐτὴν καὶ σχηματίζοντος ἔσχε, Plut. Comm. Not., 34 (II, 1076c d), and also by attributing the evil that we do to freedom, e.g., Cleanthes: οὐδέ τι γίγνεται ἔργον ἐπὶ χθονὶ σοῦ δίχα, δαῖμον, | οὔτε κατ' αἰθέριον θεῖον πόλον οὔτ' ἐνὶ πόντῳ | πλὴν ὁπόσα ῥέζουσι κακοὶ σφετέρησιν ἀνοίαις, Stob. Ecl., I, 26, 4 ff.; also: αὐτίκα ὁ μὲν κακὸς φύσει, ἁμαρτητικὸς διὰ κακίαν γενόμενος, φαῦλος καθέστηκεν, ἔχων ἣν ἑκὼν εἵλετο, Cl. Al. Strom., VI, 12, 98, 2; and finally Epictet.: ποῦ ζητήσω τὸ ἀγαθὸν καὶ τὸ κακόν; ἔσω ἐν τοῖς ἐμοῖς, Diss., II, 5, 5. Zeno taught that God is the cause of evil, but from Cleanthes onwards all the Stoics contradicted this. [15] The upshot, as may be seen clearly from Epictet., is a Platonic psychological dualism. In the structure of Stoic philosophy, whose starting-point is a humanistic monistic understanding of existence, there is fundamentally no place for evil, and attempts are made to relativise it and to integrate it into the system, whether by explaining it as a necessary counterpart to ἀγαθόν (e.g.: ... οὐκ ἀχρήστως γίνεται πρὸς τὰ ὅλα· οὔτε γὰρ τἀγαθὰ ἦν, Plut. Stoic. Rep., 35 [II, 1050 f.]), by viewing it as a punishment (e.g.: ταῦτα [sc. κακά] ἀπονέμεται κατὰ τὸν Διὸς λόγον, ἤτοι ἐπὶ κολάσει, ἢ κατ' ἄλλην ἔχουσάν πως πρὸς τὰ ὅλα οἰκονομίαν, ibid., 35 [II, 1050e]), or by deriving it from a false understanding of the world (e.g.: τοῦτο γάρ ἐστι τὸ αἴτιον τοῖς ἀνθρώποις πάντων τῶν κακῶν, τὸ τὰς προλήψεις τὰς κοινὰς μὴ δύνασθαι ἐφαρμόζειν τοῖς ἐπὶ μέρους, Epict. Diss., IV, 1, 42). It is taught that the perfection of the whole excludes rather than includes that of the individual, [16] though this seems to imply a dubious restriction of the divine omnipotence. Stoic eschatology furnishes at one point the insight ὅταν ἐκπυρώσωσι τὸν κόσμον οὗτοι, κακὸν μὲν οὐδ' ὁτιοῦν ἀπολείπεται, τὸ δ' ὅλον φρόνιμόν ἐστι τηνικαῦτα καὶ σοφόν, Plut. Comm. Not., 17 (II, 1067a).

---

[14] Schröder, 34.
[15] Billicsich, 44 f.
[16] Ibid., 37 f.

B. κακός in Hellenism.

Philo is wholly Greek in his thinking when he says of the Godhead : τὸ πάντων μὲν ἀγαθῶν αἴτιον, κακοῦ δὲ μηδενὸς νομίζειν εἶναι τὸ θεῖον, Omn. Prob. Lib., 84, and declares : παντὸς μὲν ἀμέτοχος κακοῦ, Spec. Leg., II, 53, attributing it to man : ἐν ἡμῖν αὐτοῖς . . . οἱ τῶν κακῶν εἰσι θησαυροί, Fug., 79, concentrating it on earth : τὸ κακὸν ἐνταυθοῖ καταμένει, πορρωτάτω θείου χοροῦ διῳκισμένον, περιπολοῦν (revolving around) τὸν θνητὸν βίον καὶ μὴ δυνάμενον ἐκ τοῦ ἀνθρωπίνου γένους ἀποθανεῖν, Fug., 62, and regarding it as the sharpest antithesis of the good : φύσει δὲ μάχεται ἀγαθῷ κακόν, Poster. C., 32.

On Philo's view, evil is from birth a possibility for man as well as good : παντὸς ἀνθρώπου κατ' ἀρχὰς ἅμα τῇ γενέσει κυοφορεῖ δίδυμα ἡ ψυχή, κακὸν καὶ ἀγαθόν, Praem. Poen., 63. The soul is naked, and it clothes itself either with good or evil, Leg. All., II, 53. It thus has two possibilities of existence. It is led to evil by ἐπιθυμία, which is ἁπάντων πηγὴ τῶν κακῶν and ἀρχίκακον, Spec. Leg., IV, 84 f. [17] κακόν reaches its ultimate depth in ἀσέβεια, the μέγιστον κακόν, Congr., 160. [18] Philo describes the way to this as follows : διὰ λαγνείας (excess) καὶ ἀκολασίας, μεγάλου κακοῦ, πρὸς μεῖζον κακόν, ἀσέβειαν, ἄγειν αὐτοὺς ἐσπούδασεν (sc. Balaam the Israelites) ἡδονὴν δέλεαρ (means of enticement) προθείς, Vit. Mos., I, 295. Even though man selects and seizes the possibility of good (→ ἀγαθός), in earthly life, he is always in conflict with κακόν. Hence death is greeted as κακῶν ἁπάντων ἀπαλλαγὴ καὶ ὡς ἀληθῶς τελευτή, Spec. Leg., II, 95. For Philo evil is a reality which is linked with man and the earth, which is intracosmic, which withstands God. But it is not a metaphysical principle. In contrast to Greek philosophy Philo has a more religious and ethical emphasis. Evil is overcome in union with God, and it is related to the concept of sin (→ ἁμαρτία, I, 291).

Elsewhere in Hellenism κακόν is a metaphysical principle.

Plut. takes up a possibility considered by Plato. The evil world soul is the cause of evils in the world : [19] ὁ γὰρ Πλάτων μητέρα μὲν καὶ τιθήνην (nurse) καλεῖ τὴν ὕλην, αἰτίαν δὲ κακοῦ τὴν κινητικὴν τῆς ὕλης καὶ περὶ τὰ σώματα γινομένην μεριστήν, ἄτακτον καὶ ἄλογον, οὐκ ἄψυχον δὲ κίνησιν, ἣν ἐν Νόμοις, ὥσπερ εἴρηται, ψυχὴν ἐναντίαν καὶ ἀντίπαλον τῇ ἀγαθουργῷ προσεῖπε. ψυχὴ γὰρ αἰτία κινήσεως καὶ ἀρχή . . ., De Animae Procreatione, in Timaeo Platonis, 7 (II, 1015d). [20] An absolute distinction such as was never made in Gk. or Hellenistic philosophy is found in some tractates of the Corp. Herm. Here the κόσμος as πλήρωμα τῆς κακίας (V, 4a) is distinguished from the deity as πλήρωμα τοῦ ἀγαθοῦ (loc. cit.): ὥσπερ γὰρ οὐδὲν τῶν κακῶν ἐν τῇ τοιαύτῃ οὐσίᾳ (sc. the deity), οὕτως ἐν οὐδενὶ τῶν ἄλλων τὸ ἀγαθὸν εὑρεθήσεται. ἐν πᾶσι γὰρ τοῖς ἄλλοις πάντα ἐστὶ κακὰ καὶ ἐν τοῖς μικροῖς καὶ ἐν τοῖς μεγάλοις . . . παθῶν γὰρ πλήρη τὰ γενητά, αὐτῆς τῆς γενέσεως παθητῆς οὔσης. ὅπου δὲ πάθος, οὐδαμοῦ τὸ ἀγαθόν, VI, 2a. Only with

---

[17] ἀδικία (Rer. Div. Her., 163) and ἀναρχία (Som., II, 289) are also roots of κακόν.
[18] Cf. also Fug., 61; described as κακά are ἀλαζονεία, Migr. Abr., 147; ἀπληστία, Spec. Leg., IV, 100; κακία καὶ αἱ κατὰ κακίαν ἐνέργειαι, Op. Mund., 75; as μέγιστον κακόν φιλαυτία, Congr., 130.
[19] Cf. the depiction of the evil principle Typhon : Τυφῶν δὲ τῆς ψυχῆς τὸ παθητικὸν καὶ τιτανικὸν καὶ ἄλογον καὶ ἔμπληκτον (the ill-considered)· τοῦ δὲ σωματικοῦ τὸ ἐπίκλητον καὶ νοσῶδες καὶ ταρακτικὸν αἰθρίαις καὶ δυσκρασίαις καὶ κρύψεσιν ἡλίου καὶ ἀφανισμοῖς σελήνης, Plut. Is. et Os., 49 (II, 371b).
[20] Cf. esp. ibid., 46 ff. (II, 369 ff.). But these ideas are only the presupposition for the moral philosophy which quickly follows, cf. Schröder, 58-60.

the help of the revelation of the νοῦς can there be access (→ I, 13) to the ἀγαθόν and escape from evil : κακίαν δὲ τῷ νοῦν ἔχοντι διεκφυγεῖν ἔστι, XII, 7. To have νοῦς implies union with the deity, i.e., with the good ; to be separated from it is the root of all evil : νόσος δὲ μεγάλη ψυχῆς ἀθεότης· ἐπεὶ ταῖς τῶν ἀθέων δόξαις πάντα τὰ κακὰ ἐπακολουθεῖ, καὶ ἀγαθὸν οὐδέν, XII, 3. Here, then, the metaphysical principle of evil has become a cosmological dualism which speaks of the absolute badness of everything that does not belong to the sphere of deity.

Plotin. tackles the problems in his treatise περὶ τοῦ τίνα καὶ πόθεν τὰ κακά, [21] and he deals with them systematically. As an essentially religious man he views the question of evil from a particular standpoint, and he devotes to it the most searching and comprehensive investigation in all ancient philosophy. The treatise which we have just mentioned is the heart of this enquiry. [22]

For him philosophy points the way to union with God. In his whole approach he is very near to Plato. But he also adopts the arguments of Stoicism and weaves them into a systematic outlook. An understanding of Plato which is mediated by Neo-Pythagoreanism leads him to find in matter the principle of evil, which he defines as follows : ἀμετρίαν εἶναι πρὸς μέτρον καὶ ἄπειρον πρὸς πέρας καὶ ἀνείδεον πρὸς εἰδοποιητικὸν καὶ ἀεὶ ἐνδεὲς πρὸς αὔταρκες, ἀεὶ ἀόριστον, οὐδαμῇ ἑστώς, παμπαθές, ἀκόρητον, πενία παντελής, Enn., I, 8, 3. This is matter : τὴν δὴ ὑποκειμένην ... κακὸν εἶναι πρῶτον καὶ καθ᾽ αὐτὸ κακόν (loc. cit.). Here is the source of all badness. Matter is at the end of a development from the One, which is the supreme good. As light becomes increasingly fainter, and a ray loses itself in the opposite of light, in darkness, so the power of the One becomes increasingly smaller, and ends in matter, which is the non-good : "One may grasp the necessity of evil as follows. Since the good is not alone, necessarily, by emanation from it, or, if one may put it thus, by constant emanation and increase of distance, there arises the final thing beyond which there can be nothing more. This is evil ... and this is the necessity of evil," I, 8, 7. For all Greek-Hellenistic thought evil is a lack : ὅταν παντελῶς ἐλλείπῃ (sc. τοῦ ἀγαθοῦ), ὅπερ ἐστὶν ἡ ὕλη, τοῦτο τὸ ὄντως κακὸν μηδεμίαν ἔχον ἀγαθοῦ μοῖραν, I, 8, 5. The necessity of evil in both its forms is dialectically grounded as the necessity of distinction and antithesis, and it is made supportable by reference to the harmony of the whole and the power of deity "to make fine use even of κακόν," III, 2, 5. We thus read in Plotin. : τὸ δὲ κακὸν οὐ μόνον ἐστὶ κακὸν διὰ δύναμιν ἀγαθοῦ καὶ φύσιν, ἐπείπερ ἐφάνη ἐξ ἀνάγκης περιληφθὲν δεσμοῖς τισι καλοῖς ... κρύπτεται τούτοις, ἵνα οὖσα [κακὴ] μὴ ὁρῷτο τοῖς θεοῖς καὶ ἄνθρωποι ἔχοιεν μὴ ἀεὶ τὸ κακὸν βλέπειν, I, 8, 15. The soul, which is a part of the world soul, is more closely related to νοῦς and the One. Even though it has sunk into matter, it has kept itself unspotted by the evil which clings to it. It is still divine. And it has an impulse towards union with the deity which it attains in ecstasy and in death. The most penetrating theodicy in the Greek-Hellenistic world thus ends with an insight which is implicit in the meaning of the term from the very outset, namely, that evil is a reality, but that as such it is simply a lack of true being.

---

[21] Max. Tyr., who belongs to Hell. philosophy, dealt expressly with this question : τοῦ θεοῦ τὰ ἀγαθὰ ποιοῦντος πόθεν τὰ κακά. But he did not achieve any profound insights ; in Stoic fashion he sought to eliminate κακόν. He discerned two causes, τὰ ὕλης πάθη, which he compared to σπινθῆρες ἐξ ἄκμονος (sparks from the anvil), and of which he judged : ἃ δὲ ἡμεῖς καλοῦμεν κακὰ καὶ φθοράς, καὶ ἐφ᾽ οἷς ὀδυρόμεθα, ταῦτα ὁ τεχνίτης καλεῖ σωτηρίαν τοῦ ὅλου (41, 4e-g), and ψυχῆς ἐξουσία, man's freedom in the choice of his way.

[22] Cf. the recent account in Billicsich, 56-97.

C. The Evil Principle in Parseeism. [23]

In Zoroastrian religion the evil principle takes a special form. The metaphysical dualism of two material principles is here replaced by that of two contending wills which are regarded as deities.

Of these two spirits that which favoured *drug* (falsehood) chose the doing of supreme wickedness, while the most holy spirit chose *aša* (truth). The question of the origin of good and evil in the world is answered as follows. The two spirits fight for mastery in the world and in man. "The two spirits at the beginning, revealed in a vision to be twins, are the better and the worse in thought, word and deed, between which men of understanding have made a right choice," Yasna, 30. [24] Thus men have a free choice between two possibilities of existence. This is made in essential, pre-temporal existence, and it is worked out in life. [25] All evil comes from the wicked spirit. He effects it through his demons. "Between the two even the Daevas have not made a right decision, because, when they deliberated, delusion overtook them, so that they chose the most wicked thinking. They then went over together to Aešma, through whom they make the life of man sick" (*loc. cit.*). Parsee eschatology envisages a division of men into good and evil. They will be assigned to heaven or hell according to their works. "When these two spirits met, they first agreed concerning life and non-life, and that at the end of things the adherents of *drug* should have the worst existence and those of *aša* the best" (*ibid.*, 30, 4). This led to the idea of a final conflict and an ultimate destruction of evil and the wicked. "Evil (sc. *drug*) will perish, and the chief captain (Ahriman) will pass away ... the evil mind will be overcome, the good conquers it. Falsely spoken speech will be overcome, that which is rightly spoken conquers it. Perfection and immortality will overcome hunger and thirst. Perfection and immortality will overcome evil hunger and thirst. The evil-doer Ahriman will weakly yield and vanish," Yašt, 19, 90, 96. [26]

D. κακός in the Old Testament (LXX).

In the whole of biblical literature the questions relating to the terms κακός and κακόν in the Greek and Hellenistic world are not orientated to these words but rather to → ἁμαρτία, → ἀδικία, → ἁμαρτωλός, → ἄδικος, and to some extent → πονηρός. [27] It is only in part that the term κακός sheds light on the ideas which developed in this field.

κακός is one of the LXX words which in the main correspond to a specific Heb. stem, namely, רַע. In numerous cases it is used for synonymous or generally related terms. If it thus misses the particular nuances of the original, it brings out even more strongly the one-sidedness and impressiveness of the moral and religious judgment which Judaism pronounces on evil and wickedness. The translator of Prv. in particular works along these lines. If here the term רַע is already frequent in the Mas., the number of κακός

---

[23] Cf. E. Lehmann in Bertholet-Leh., II⁴, 220 ff., 250 ff.; J. Reiner-C. Schmitt, *Zarathustra* (*Die Unsterblichen,* VI [1930]), 91 ff., 126 ff.; H. Lommel, *Die Religion Zarathustras* (1930), esp. 17 ff., 36 ff., 111 ff. O. G. Wesendonck, *Das Weltbild der Iranier* (1933), 71-89, 212-218.

[24] In C. Bartholomae, *Die Gathas der Awesta* (1905), 13 ff.

[25] Cf. Lommel, 148 ff.

[26] Acc. to K. F. Geldner, "Die zoroastrische Religion," *Religionsgeschtl. Lesebuch,* I (1926), 45 f.; cf. also the transl. of the Bundahesh, 47 ff.

[27] For the view of the bad, cf. esp. this term. The question of the bad is developed by Judaism in terms of πονηρός.

passages in the LXX is almost doubled. There are 371 [28] instances of κακός in the LXX. In 227 cases it is a rendering of רַע (293 times in the Mas.) or רָעָה (346 in the Mas.), for which κακία or more often πονηρός (266) is also used. On 33 occasions κακός is used for other Heb. terms. In 20 cases the Mas. has a different text, in 32 there is no Mas. original, and in 61 we have passages in books which have been preserved only in Gk.

1. τὸ κακόν as Evil.

In the whole complex of historical books the LXX uses the term only in the sense of "evil" or "disaster" (τὸ κακόν, τὰ κακά). [29] In so doing it brings together two thoughts, of which the first is that evils are God's punishment for sin when He withdraws His hand : καὶ εὑρήσουσιν αὐτὸν κακὰ πολλὰ καὶ θλίψεις, καὶ ἐρεῖ ἐν τῇ ἡμέρᾳ ἐκείνῃ· διότι οὐκ ἔστιν κύριος ὁ θεός μου ἐν ἐμοί, εὕροσάν με τὰ κακὰ ταῦτα ... διὰ πάσας τὰς κακίας ἃς ἐποίησαν, ὅτι ἐπέστρεψαν ἐπὶ θεοὺς ἀλλοτρίους, Dt. 31:17 f.; cf. 4 Βασ. 21:11 f.; 22:16 f. Here evil is a divine act of punishment. The reason for it is to be sought in idolatry and apostasy. Hence the Wisdom poet can say comprehensively : ἡ γὰρ τῶν ἀνωνύμων εἰδώλων θρησκεία παντὸς ἀρχὴ κακοῦ, Wis. 14:27. The thought is prophetic : ἄκουε, γῆ· ἰδοὺ ἐγὼ ἐπάγω ἐπὶ τὸν λαὸν τοῦτον κακά, τὸν καρπὸν ἀποστροφῆς αὐτῶν, Jer. 6:19; cf. 11:10 f.; 16:10 ff.; Mi. 1:12 f. Here, too, idolatry and apostasy are the cause of evil. But this leads us to the second thought, namely, that God is the Redeemer from evil. Thus Jeremiah can call on God and pray to Him in relation to the results of ungodliness : κύριε, ἰσχύς μου καὶ βοήθειά μου καὶ καταφυγή μου ἐν ἡμέρᾳ κακῶν, 16:19. [30] His prophetic preaching, in accordance with God's gracious will, is directed to the goal : καὶ νῦν βελτίους ποιήσατε τὰς ὁδοὺς ὑμῶν καὶ τὰ ἔργα ὑμῶν, καὶ ἀκούσατε τῆς φωνῆς κυρίου, καὶ παύσεται κύριος ἀπὸ τῶν κακῶν, ὧν ἐλάλησεν ἐφ᾽ ὑμᾶς, ᾽Ιερ. 33(26):13, cf. v. 3 and 19. This corresponds to the nature of God, which Jeremiah discloses in the words : καὶ λογιοῦμαι ἐφ᾽ ὑμᾶς λογισμὸν εἰρήνης καὶ οὐ κακὰ τοῦ δοῦναι ὑμῖν ταῦτα, 36(29):11. [31] The question of evil is here projected into the national and political life of the people. God and the people — the great theme of the OT — are involved in the question. κακά are the political blows which fall on the people. They come from God as the Lord of history, and they are a punishment for sin, which consists in apostasy and relapse into idolatry. They are the fruit of a walk (Jer. 6:19) which leads away from God. The way from God leads to destruction. God allows men and nations to tread this way to the end. He speeds up the way in order to give knowledge of error and destruction and thereby to move the individual and the nation to turn from the wrong way. The ruin which consists in κακά, and which is a punishment arising out of God's permission and precipitation, is also a visitation from God, who has thoughts of peace even when He causes and sends κακά, and who pursues these thoughts, which are the ultimate impulses of His nature. Human guilt and divine action are thus combined in the question of the

---

[28] The statistics are based on Hatch-Redp. and Mandelkern. This par. is by Bertram.
[29] E.g., Gn. 19:19; ποιεῖν κακόν (to do hurt), Gn. 26:29; 44:34; 48:16; 50:15; also 3 Βασ. 22:8, 18, 23 etc.
[30] Cf. the confident statement of the Psalmist : ἐὰν γὰρ καὶ πορευθῶ ἐν μέσῳ σκιᾶς θανάτου, οὐ φοβηθήσομαι κακά, ὅτι σὺ μετ᾽ ἐμοῦ εἶ, ψ 22:4.
[31] Cf. ψ 120:7; Wis. 16:8; 2 Macc. 1:25; 2:18.

origin of evil. Evils are the response of God's righteousness to the guilt of the people. But as visitations they are also an expression of the merciful seeking of God. This leads us to a highly significant feature which controls the whole view of God in the Bible. God is both One who sends evils and also the One who delivers from them. In His hand they are means to recall individuals and people to true worship. At this point the concept of God acquires a solemn and mysterious character; it becomes a *mysterium tremendum*. The question of the origin of evil finds its answer, not in a metaphysical dualism, but in an ethical monotheism, in knowledge of the God to whom the evil of man is guilt, and who punishes it accordingly. This insight underlies the attitude of Job: εἰ τὰ ἀγαθὰ ἐδεξάμεθα ἐκ χειρὸς κυρίου, τὰ κακὰ οὐχ ὑποίσομεν; 2:10. The prophet relates it to the further insight that the depth of God's being is peace and love. Here are the impulses which lead Him to make evils a visitation. The nature of God is thus *mysterium fascinosum* as well as *mysterium tremendum*. At this point we reach the lonely peak of prophetic proclamation and the prophetic view of history.

2. As an Ethical Concept.

κακόν is an ethical concept in the prophets. Micah speaks of λογιζόμενοι κόπους καὶ ἐργαζόμενοι κακὰ ἐν ταῖς κοίταις αὐτῶν, 2:1; cf. 7:3; 'Ιερ. 7:24; 9:13; 51(44):7, 9. We find the same view in the Psalms, ψ 27:3; 33:13 ff. The seat of evil is the human heart, the centre of human existence: κακὴ καρδία, Jer. 7:24; κακὰ ἐν ταῖς καρδίαις, ψ 27:3.

This usage of the prophets and the Psalms is also found occasionally in the Wisdom literature, especially in Proverbs.

The term κακός occurs 95 times in Prv. In 43 cases it is used for רַע, רָעָה; in 21 for very different Heb. words; in 13 cases the Mas. has a different text; in 18 cases there seems to be nothing corresponding in the Mas. We have here a deliberate contribution of the translator which has to be evaluated exegetically and in terms of religious history. To some degree the translator allows his own moral and religious principles to affect his work. A few examples will show how this levels down the distinctive and colourful thinking of the Heb. original. At Prv. 1:18 the Mas. speaks of those who, trying to trap the innocent, "lie in wait for their own blood and lurk secretly for their own lives"; the LXX substitutes a formulation which is in general correspondence: αὐτοὶ γὰρ οἱ φόνου μετέχοντες θησαυρίζουσιν ἑαυτοῖς κακά, ἡ δὲ καταστροφὴ ἀνδρῶν παρανόμων κακή. Again, at 2:16 we read that wisdom can protect a young man from a strange and seductive woman who "flattereth with her words, who forsaketh the guide of her youth, and forgetteth the covenant of her God"; the LXX, which is an exposition rather than a translation, and which has influenced interpretation right up to our own times, sees in the strange woman Lady Folly, κακὴ βουλή, the evil counsellor, ἡ ἀπολείπουσα διδασκαλίαν νεότητος καὶ διαθήκην θείαν ἐπιλελησμένη. That the LXX here has in view a personification of the opposite of wisdom is shown by what follows, which quite independently of the Mas. maintains that she has her dwelling in death and Hades. At 3:31 the Mas. refers to the אִישׁ חָמָס whom we should not envy and whose ways we should not choose; [32] the free rendering of the LXX is μὴ κτήσῃ κακῶν

---

[32] It has been proposed by BHK [2, 3], Steuernagel, *ad loc.*, F. Wutz, *Die Transskriptionen von der Septuaginta bis zu Hieronymus* (1933), 288 f. that, following the LXX and Prv. 24:19 and Ps. 37:1, we should change תִּבְחַר to תִּתְחַר, hitp of חרה, "to be provoked," "to compete with (?)"; but this conjecture is not supported by the continuation: "For he who follows false paths is an abomination to Yahweh." We have here a warning against choosing wrong paths. Cf. C. Steuernagel in Kautzsch (1923).

ἀνδρῶν ὀνείδη (do not heap up blame like evil men [gen. qual.]), μηδὲ ζηλώσῃς τὰς ὁδοὺς αὐτῶν. Again, at 4:27, where the Mas. simply has יט, the LXX speaks of the ὁδὸς κακή, and adds the familiar contrast between the two ways. [33]

Good and evil are the two possibilities for man. With the help of wisdom he may seize good and keep himself from evil. This is the message of the teacher of wisdom. Related to the ethical understanding of κακόν is the understanding in terms of suffering. Good brings good and evil evil in a rigid theory of retribution. What was in the prophets a living interpretation of history based on a living faith in God has here become a fixed and distorted schema into which everything must be forced. Evil is a possibility for man : εἰσὶν ὁδοὶ κακαὶ ἐνώπιον ἀνδρός· ἀποστρέφειν δὲ δεῖ ἀπὸ ὁδοῦ σκολιᾶς καὶ κακῆς, Prv. 22:14; it has its source in ungodliness and ignorance : πλανώμενοι τεκταίνουσι κακά ... οὐκ ἐπίστανται ἔλεον καὶ πίστιν τέκτονες κακῶν, Prv. 14:22; separation from it is the point of the admonition : ἀπόστρεψον δὲ σὸν πόδα ἀπὸ ὁδοῦ κακῆς, Prv. 4:27; its realisation involves the human will : κακὸς μεθ' ὕβρεως πράσσει κακά, Prv. 13:10; it leads to evil consequences : μὴ ποίει κακά, καὶ οὐ μή σε καταλάβῃ κακόν, Sir. 7:1, cf. Prv. 1:18; 25:19. The term κακός is used in a much more general way than in the Mas. Thus at Prv. 9:7-12 the original contrast is between mockers and the wise, whereas in the LXX it is between the bad and the wise.

In many verses the term is used in place of various Heb. terms or it is quite new. Thus strife and contention can be brought under this common denominator, e.g., at 13:10; 16:28; 18:6, where it is used equally for various Heb. terms. It has been introduced by the translator de novo at 19:6, 27; 21:26; 22:8, 14; 24:34 ff. (30:11 ff.); 27:21; 28:20.

While the term itself is weak and non-committal, it is significant as an expression of the moral attitude of later Judaism with its hasty, general and infallible judgments. The difference between Hellenistic Judaism and the Mas. as this is reflected in the translator of Prv. is true of readers of the whole LXX. The moral judgment of the Judaism of the period is just as superficial and schematic as appears in this translation. The dualism of world outlook invades the moral and religious realm and leads to contempt for all that is not proper to the "righteous." To say that a thing is "bad" is to exclude it from the sphere of the righteous, who must not have anything to do with evil in either of its forms. There thus develops the rigidity of moral attitude which tends to characterise the legalistic piety of Judaism. [34]

E. κακός in the New Testament.

The term κακός is of no great significance in the NT. The question of theodicy, which agitates Greek and Hellenistic thinking in face of κακά, loses its point when confronted by the good news proclaimed by Christ and attested by the apostles — the good news of the approaching and victorious dominion of God which is already present in Christ. The problem has found its solution in the history of Christ. Furthermore, κακός as a moral concept is far less important than → ἁμαρτία and → πονηρός. We may gather the most significant references under five main headings.

1. Jesus regards the human heart as the seat of evil : ἔσωθεν γὰρ ... οἱ διαλογισμοὶ οἱ κακοὶ ἐκπορεύονται ... πάντα ταῦτα τὰ πονηρὰ ἔσωθεν, Mk. 7:21,

---

[33] P. de Lagarde, Anmerkungen z. griech. Übersetzung der Proverbien (1863), 19, suggests a Christian glossator, but this can hardly be correct.

[34] The first and the last two par. of this small-print section are by Bertram.

23 par. [35] Evil comes from man. He is its author, though behind man the → πονηρός is its final centre. In Jm. God is separated from everything evil: θεὸς ἀπείραστός ἐστιν κακῶν, 1:13. Evil does not affect God. A similar restriction to the human sphere is apparent in 1 Tm. when love of money is called the ῥίζα πάντων τῶν κακῶν (6:10), and Jm. points to the tongue as ἀκατάστατον κακόν, μεστὴ ἰοῦ θανατηφόρου, 3:8. [36]

2. The NT uses τὰ κακά for the ruin which comes on man, whether in his temporal existence or his eternal. In the parable of Dives and Lazarus Abraham says: τέκνον, μνήσθητι ὅτι ἀπέλαβες τὰ ἀγαθά σου ἐν τῇ ζωῇ σου, καὶ Λάζαρος ὁμοίως τὰ κακά· νῦν δὲ ὧδε παρακαλεῖται, σὺ δὲ ὀδυνᾶσαι, Lk. 16:25. This story is significant inasmuch as it carries beyond the boundaries of earthly life the disturbing question of the destiny which brings ruin. Earthly loss and heavenly salvation, earthly salvation and eternal loss, correspond to one another. The point of the story, which is perhaps based on earlier material, is completely misunderstood if we try to see in it a human theory of retribution. This parable, too, bears witness to the lordship of God. This lordship decides salvation and perdition. But it is not fully worked out in this life. Hence we are left without an answer if we put the question of salvation and perdition solely in terms of this life. The important question of the parable, however, is how τὰ ἀγαθὰ καὶ τὰ κακά arise out of the divine lordship, i.e., not by mechanical retribution but by a decision which we make in earthly life when confronted by God's claim for obedience and the commandment of love. The suffering Lazarus puts his trust in God, and, as his name shows, [37] he is comforted. But the rich man does not ask concerning God and he ignores the command to love. Hence he is rejected and goes to perdition. [38] The parable illustrates the discourse in Mt. 25:31 ff. and the Beatitudes in Mt. 5:3 ff.

3. Paul finds in the state the divinely appointed order which has the task of restraining the evil in the world: οἱ ἄρχοντες οὐκ εἰσὶν φόβος τῷ ἀγαθῷ ἔργῳ, ἀλλὰ τῷ κακῷ ... ἐὰν ... τὸ κακὸν ποιῇς, φοβοῦ· οὐ γὰρ εἰκῆ τὴν μάχαιραν φορεῖ· θεοῦ γὰρ διάκονός ἐστιν ἔκδικος εἰς ὀργὴν τῷ τὸ κακὸν πράσσοντι, R. 13:3, 4. The NT soberly recognises that there is evil in the world. In face of this the genuine state receives from God a diaconal responsibility and dignity in the total context of the divine government of the world.

4. The revelation of Christ, the ἐν Χριστῷ εἶναι, yields a radical view of κακόν which is equally remote from pessimism and idealistic optimism. In this light evil is seen to be man's only and continually actualised possibility without the πνεῦμα, and human optimism is exposed as an illusion which certainly points to God's will for man but which counts on a possibility that can never be put into effect, i.e., an impossibility: οὐ γὰρ ὃ θέλω ποιῶ ἀγαθόν, ἀλλὰ ὃ οὐ θέλω

[35] Mt. 15:9 has διαλογισμοὶ πονηροί.

[36] Cf. παυσάτω τὴν γλῶσσαν ἀπὸ κακοῦ at 1 Pt. 3:10, quoting Ps. 34:13-17.

[37] It is to be noted that this is the only instance of a name in the parables. Like all names in the ancient world (→ ὄνομα), the name is significant. Lazarus derives from Eliezer and means "divine help." Lazarus is thus a πτωχὸς τῷ πνεύματι to whom Jesus promises the kingdom of God. But Jesus adds this to the original material.

[38] Cf. the exposition in Schl. Lk., 374 ff. As a commentary on this parable, cf. the saying at Lk. 17:26-31.

κακόν, τοῦτο πράσσω ... εὑρίσκω ἄρα τὸν νόμον τῷ θέλοντι ἐμοὶ ποιεῖν τὸ καλόν, ὅτι ἐμοὶ τὸ κακὸν παράκειται, R. 7:19, 21. This is the reality of man before God. And since God judges according to the principle : θλῖψις καὶ στενοχωρία ἐπὶ πᾶσαν ψυχὴν ἀνθρώπου τοῦ κατεργαζομένου τὸ κακόν (R. 2:9), it means that he is at the end of his tether. But what is κακόν for Paul ? It is closely related to what → ἁμαρτία is for him (→ I, 308 ff.). Sin is for him the action of the man who is separated from God, who asserts himself against God, who wills to be autonomous before Him and without Him. This finds expression in his refusal to give God the glory, in his opposition to Him. It is also expressed in vices (cf. R. 1:18 ff.). [39] Hence κακόν has more than moral significance. It is not merely moral evil. It has embracing significance for the whole of life. It is godlessness. Paul unmasks the contradiction in which man finds himself. He agrees to the Law of God, which summons him to relationship to God and to moral goodness. He wants to do good, to honour and obey God, to live a moral life. His longing for God and his striving after virtue prove this. This inner consent shows that man is the creature of God, and that he cannot forget his origin. On the other hand, it is equally plain that man cannot put into effect his obvious consent to the Law of God. In fact, he continually breaks away from God and falls into moral evil. He never gets beyond the stage of intention. Thus the Law of God pronounces judgment on him : ὅτι ἐμοὶ τὸ κακὸν παράκειται (R. 7:21). All his striving ends in death. Recognition of this leads to the cry : ταλαίπωρος ἐγὼ ἄνθρωπος· τίς με ῥύσεται ἐκ τοῦ σώματος τοῦ θανάτου τούτου; (7:24). κακόν thus includes the end of κακόν as moral evil, namely, death. The law of κακόν is the law of death. The fact that all life leads to death shows the truth of the saying : ἐμοὶ τὸ κακὸν παράκειται (7:21). The question is how man can be delivered from this law of death. "Man's separation from sinning is effected only when he is united by faith with Christ, who not only forbids him to sin but who has borne his guilt. What separates the believer from sin is not a prohibition, but God's saving power." [40]

5. Through faith in Christ, the ἐν Χριστῷ εἶναι, the previous impossibility becomes a genuine possibility which the Christian can and should grasp : νεκρώσατε ... ἐπιθυμίαν κακήν, Col. 3:5 (cf. 1 C. 10:6). The new reality of life enjoyed by Christians implies : θέλω δὲ ὑμᾶς σοφοὺς εἶναι εἰς τὸ ἀγαθόν, ἀκεραίους δὲ εἰς τὸ κακόν (R. 16:19). Turning from evil is fulfilled in love : μὴ νικῶ ὑπὸ τοῦ κακοῦ, ἀλλὰ νίκα ἐν τῷ ἀγαθῷ τὸ κακόν, R. 12:21; ἡ ἀγάπη τῷ πλησίον κακὸν οὐκ ἐργάζεται, R. 13:10; (ἡ ἀγάπη) οὐ λογίζεται τὸ κακόν, 1 C. 13:5, cf. also R. 12:17; 1 Th. 5:15; 1 Pt. 3:9. In this light evil is also a force which disrupts human fellowship (cf. R. 1:30 : ἐφευρετὰς κακῶν) — an insight which only attains its full significance in the NT. True fellowship is possible only in virtue of the ἀγάπη which derives from Christ.

---

[39] R. Bultmann, "R. 7 u. die Anthropologie des Pls." in *Imago Dei, Festschr. f. G. Krüger* (1932), 53 ff. → ἁμαρτάνω, I, 308 ff.
[40] Schl. R., 243 f.

† ἄκακος.

The meaning of the word is obvious ; it implies "the one who does not do evil, who is upright" (cf. Thes. Steph., I, 1142 : ἀκάκους esse μὴ προεννοοῦντας τὰ κακά, acc. to Dionysius Areopagita, Ep. 8 [ad Demophilum] v.l.), "the one whom evil does not touch, who is innocent" (cf. Ps.-Ammon. Adfin. Vocab. Diff., s.v. [Valckenaer, p. 147] : κακὸς πονηροῦ διαφέρει ὥσπερ ὁ ἄκακος τοῦ ἀγαθοῦ). The second and passive sense predominates.

The term occurs already in Aesch. Pers., 661: Βάσκε (come) πάτερ ἄκακε Δαριάν. Plat. Tim., 91d speaks of ἄκακοι ἄνδρες, cf. also Polyb., 3, 98, 5 : τοῦτον ἄκακον ὄντα τὸν ἄνδρα καὶ πρᾷον τῇ φύσει. In Plut. θαυμασικοὶ καὶ ἄκακοι are contrasted with καταφρονητικοὶ καὶ θρασεῖς (De Recta Ratione Audiendi, 7 [II, 41a]). Philo uses it, e.g., of children who have just come into life : νηπίοις ἄρτι παρεληλυθόσιν εἰς φῶς καὶ τὸν ἀνθρώπινον βίον ... ἀκακωτάτοις οὖσιν, Spec. Leg., III, 119 (cf. Virt., 43 : ζωγρήσαντες [take alive] παρθένους, ἄκακον ἡλικίαν οἰκτισάμενοι). Philo uses ἀκακία and ἁπλότης for the state in Paradise : τοιοῦτος μὲν ὁ βίος τῶν ἐν ἀρχῇ μὲν ἀκακίᾳ καὶ ἁπλότητι χρωμένων, Op. Mund., 170. The fall brings a state of πανουργία : τοῦτ' ἐξαπιναίως ἀμφοτέρους ἐξ ἀκακίας καὶ ἁπλότητος ἠθῶν εἰς πανουργίαν μετέβαλεν, ibid., 156. Cf. Dionysius Areopagita, Ep. 8 (MPG, 3, 1196): Christ is ἄκακος (alluding to Hb. 4:15).

In the LXX Job is called ἄκακος : ἄνθρωπος ἄκακος, ἀληθινός, ἄμεμπτος, θεοσεβής, ἀπεχόμενος ἀπὸ παντὸς κακοῦ, ἔτι δὲ ἔχεται ἀκακίας (2:3). It is said of the ἄκακος : κύριος οὐ μὴ ἀποποιήσηται τὸν ἄκακον (36:5; 8:20). The ἄκακος is he who can stand before God. The Mas. has תָּם. ἄκακος, then, means "unsullied," "pure." The word is particularly common in Prv., where the sense of "unsullied by evil" is carried a stage further to "ignorant or simple in relation to evil" (e.g., 21:11). Jeremiah once calls himself an ἀρνίον ἄκακον (Jer. 11:19).

In the NT the word occurs at R. 16:18. Paul warns against those who cause divisions and contentions : οἱ γὰρ τοιοῦτοι τῷ κυρίῳ ἡμῶν Χριστῷ οὐ δουλεύουσιν ἀλλὰ τῇ ἑαυτῶν κοιλίᾳ, καὶ διὰ τῆς χρηστολογίας καὶ εὐλογίας ἐξαπατῶσιν τὰς καρδίας τῶν ἀκάκων. The reference to means of deception fixes the sense as "guileless," "simple." The usage is thus similar to that of the LXX and Philo.

The word is also found at Hb. 7:26 : τοιοῦτος γὰρ ἡμῖν καὶ ἔπρεπεν ἀρχιερεύς, ὅσιος, ἄκακος, ἀμίαντος, κεχωρισμένος ἀπὸ τῶν ἁμαρτωλῶν, καὶ ὑψηλότερος τῶν οὐρανῶν γενόμενος. If → ὅσιος denotes His religious qualification — being ὅσιος, He is the true priest before God — and → ἀμίαντος the cultic — no μίασμα attaches to Him to cause cultic disqualification —, ἄκακος is the moral. As High-priest, He is one who has done no evil. The sense here is active ; ἀμίαντος expresses the passive side. The two statements which follow denote His majesty. With their contrast to all earthly priesthood, the negative statements are better adapted than positive to express His fitness.

κακία.

This word is related to κακόν as → ἀρετή is to ἀγαθόν. It is the quality of a κακός, and it can also signify the outworking of this quality, sometimes in the plural.

κακία can also be used synon. with τὸ κακόν, e.g., Corp. Herm., IX, 4b : τὴν γὰρ κακίαν ἐνθάδε δεῖν οἰκεῖν ...; Plat. Resp., X, 609a ff.: τὸ σύμφυτον ἄρα κακὸν ἑκάστου καὶ ἡ πονηρία ἕκαστον ἀπόλλυσιν ... ὥσπερ σῶμα ἡ σώματος πονηρία νόσος οὖσα τήκει καὶ διόλλυσι καὶ ἄγει εἰς τὸ μηδὲ σῶμα εἶναι, καὶ ἃ νυνδὴ ἐλέγομεν ἅπαντα ὑπὸ τῆς οἰκείας κακίας ... εἰς τὸ μὴ εἶναι ἀφικνεῖται. But it is usually distinct, either as an actual outworking of κακόν or as the principle of evil, e.g.: κακία ... ποιητικὸν κακοῦ, ἀλλ' οὐ τὸ κακὸν ἡ κακία ἔσται ... ἀπὸ τῆς κακίας καταβαίνοντι τὸ κακὸν αὐτό, ἀρξαμένῳ μὲν ἀπὸ τῆς κακίας [καὶ] θεωροῦντι μὲν ᾗ θεωρία τίς ἐστι τοῦ κακοῦ αὐτοῦ, γινομένῳ δὲ ᾗ μετάληψις αὐτοῦ, Plot. Enn., I, 8, 13. Here κακία is limited to the ethical field. The same is true in Stoicism, where there are two classes of κακά: τῶν κακῶν τὰ μὲν εἶναι κακίας, τὰ δ' οὔ· ἀφροσύνην μὲν οὖν καὶ ἀδικίαν καὶ δειλίαν καὶ μικροψυχίαν καὶ ἀδυναμίαν κακίας εἶναι· λύπην δὲ καὶ φόβον καὶ τὰ παραπλήσια οὐκ εἶναι κακίας, Stob. Ecl., II, 58, 14 ff. [1] On κακία in the absolute Plato expresses himself to the effect that knowledge that God is δικαιότατος, and that there is οὐκ αὐτῷ ὁμοιό-τερον οὐδὲν ἢ ὃς ἂν ἡμῶν αὖ γένηται ὅτι δικαιότατος, is ἀρετὴ ἀληθινή; ἡ δὲ ἄγνοια ἀμαθία καὶ κακία ἐναργής, Theaet., 176c. Here the word takes on a religious sense and is guilt before deity. But it can also denote "uselessness" or "incompetence" with no ethical emphasis, e.g.: κακίας καὶ ἀρετῆς ψυχῆς τε πέρι καὶ σώματος, Plat. Symp., 181e; ... κακίᾳ ἡνιόχων πολλαὶ μὲν χωλεύονται, πολλαὶ δὲ πολλὰ πτερὰ θραύονται, we read in the myth, Plat. Phaedr., 248b. Familiar from Prodicos is the story of Hercules at the cross-roads, where he has to choose between Ἀρετή and Κακία (Xenoph. Mem., II, 1, 21-23).

In Philonic ethics the κακίαι play an important part; Stoic influence may be seen here. Philo defines them as ἀλαζονεία ψυχῆς, Virt., 172; as ὅλης τῆς ψυχῆς ἀρρώστημα, Sobr., 45; as ἡ τῶν παθῶν ἡγεμονίς, Leg. All., III, 38. It is a possibility of human life: ... τοῦ βίου διττὴ ὁδός, ἡ μὲν ἐπὶ κακίαν, ἡ δ' ἐπ' ἀρετὴν ἄγουσα, Spec. Leg., IV, 108. The man who takes the first way is the bad and foolish, the man who takes the other is the wise: ὁ ... σοφὸς τεθνηκέναι δοκῶν τὸν φθαρτὸν βίον ζῇ τὸν ἄφθαρτον, ὁ δὲ φαῦλος ζῶν τὸν ἐν κακίᾳ τέθνηκε τὸν εὐδαίμονα, Det. Pot. Ins., 49. In content the κακίαι are defined as ἀφροσύνη, ἀκολασία, δειλία, ἀδικία, Conf. Ling., 90, as λήθη καὶ ἀχαριστία καὶ φιλαυτία καὶ ἡ γεννητικὴ τούτων κακία, οἴησις, Sacr. AC, 58. He also speaks of a τῶν κακιῶν ἀμήχανον πλῆθος, Op. Mund., 79. They are religiously defined as ἐχθρὸν θεῷ κακία, Mut. Nom., 30. Because God is πάσης κακίας ἀμέτοχος, Spec. Leg., II, 11, they cannot stand in His presence: τῶν ὅρων οὐρανοῦ μακρὰν κακία πεφυγάδευται, Op. Mund., 168.

In the LXX κακία is on the one hand a single wrong act, whether of an individual or the people: of an individual, Solomon to Shimei: σὺ οἶδας πᾶσαν τὴν κακίαν σου ἣν ἔγνω ἡ καρδία σου, ἃ ἐποίησας τῷ Δαυὶδ τῷ πατρί μου· καὶ ἀνταπέδωκεν κύριος τὴν κακίαν σου εἰς κεφαλήν σου, 3 Βασ. 2:44; of the people: πάσας τὰς κακίας αὐτῶν ἐμνήσθην (Hos. 7:2; cf. the whole context, vv. 1-3). In this sense it is used synon. with πονηρία (cf. Ju. 9:56 f. A κακία, B πονηρία). The term is used religiously. All κακία is κακία before and to God: καὶ λαλήσω πρὸς αὐτοὺς μετὰ κρίσεως περὶ πάσης τῆς κακίας αὐτῶν, ὡς ἐγκατέλιπόν με καὶ ἔθυσαν θεοῖς ἀλλοτρίοις καὶ προσεκύνησαν τοῖς ἔργοις τῶν χειρῶν αὐτῶν, Jer. 1:16 (cf. 2:13, where these κακίαι are πονηρά). On the other hand κακία can also be synon. with κακόν in the sense of "disaster," "misfortune," "ruin," e.g., συντετέλεσται ἡ κακία παρ' αὐτοῦ, 1 Βασ. 20:7; διὰ τοῦτο ἰδοὺ ἐγὼ ἄγω κακίαν πρὸς σὲ εἰς οἶκον Ἱεροβοάμ, 3 Βασ. 14:10 f.

In the NT it is used once for "trouble," "evil." At Mt. 6:34 Jesus says: ἀρκετὸν τῇ ἡμέρᾳ ἡ κακία αὐτῆς. "Measured by the striving which has God's kingdom and righteousness as its goal, the work which caters for natural needs is a burden."

κ α κ ί α. [1] Plat. Resp., IV, 444b: τὴν τούτων ταραχὴν καὶ πλάνην εἶναι τήν τε ἀδικίαν καὶ ἀκολασίαν καὶ δειλίαν καὶ ἀμαθίαν καὶ συλλήβδην πᾶσαν κακίαν.

It is so ... intrinsically, since it binds the disciples to that which nature demands."[2] When we know God as the Father who cares for His children, this burden is supportable, and the disciple need not be hampered by it.

Elsewhere κακία has ethical significance. It might denote a single iniquity, like the grasping desire of Simon Magus: μετανόησον ... ἀπὸ τῆς κακίας σου, Ac. 8:22, or it might be used more generally for the evil that men do among one another. As the force which destroys fellowship, κακία is the reality of this cosmos. For Paul it is a curse and a punishment consequent upon original sin and godlessness. Disruption of fellowship with God brings disruption of fellowship with men: παρέδωκεν αὐτοὺς ὁ θεὸς ... πεπληρωμένους πάσῃ ἀδικίᾳ, πονηρίᾳ, πλεονεξίᾳ, κακίᾳ, R. 1:28 f. Tt. speaks of this: ἐν κακίᾳ καὶ φθόνῳ διάγοντες, 3:3. The creation of the Christian community provides the chance to throw off this force: ἀποθέμενοι οὖν πᾶσαν κακίαν καὶ πάντα δόλον καὶ ὑποκρίσεις καὶ φθόνους καὶ πάσας καταλαλιάς, 1 Pt. 2:1; cf. Jm. 1:21; Eph. 4:31; Col. 3:8. There is a warning in 1 Pt. not to turn Christian liberty into licence: μὴ ὡς ἐπικάλυμμα ἔχοντες τῆς κακίας τὴν ἐλευθερίαν ἀλλ᾽ ὡς θεοῦ δοῦλοι, 2:16. Paul also admonishes: τῇ κακίᾳ νηπιάζετε, 1 C. 14:20. As ἀρετή is not used in the NT in the sense of the Stoic doctrine of virtue, so κακία is not used in the sense of the Greek doctrine of vice. As we have seen, κακία is a force which destroys fellowship.

† κακόω.

κακόω always means "to do hurt," "to maltreat," "to cause injury," Hom. Il., 11, 690; Od., 4, 754; Plat. Leg., XI, 928c: ἀμελείᾳ ... κακῶσαι τὸν ὀρφανόν, but also later in popular speech a father to his daughter: εὖ ποιήσεις μὴ κακώσασα ..., P. Tebt., II, 407, 9 (2nd cent. A.D.).

It is common in the LXX, being used for the fate of the Israelites: ἐκάκωσαν ἡμᾶς οἱ Αἰγύπτιοι, Nu. 20:15, cf. Ex. 5:22 f.; Dt. 26:6; Jos. 24:5, and also of the Servant of the Lord in Is.: διὰ τὸ κεκακῶσθαι οὐκ ἀνοίγει τὸ στόμα (53:7).

In the NT, apart from 1 Pt. 3:13: τίς ὁ κακώσων ὑμᾶς ἐὰν τοῦ ἀγαθοῦ ζηλωταὶ γένησθε; ἀλλ᾽ εἰ καὶ πάσχοιτε διὰ δικαιοσύνην, μακάριοι, it is found only in Ac., of the sufferings of Israel in Egypt at 7:6, 19; of the sufferings of the Christian community under Jewish persecution at 12:1; 14:2; of the danger of an attack on Paul which God averts at 18:10.

† κακοῦργος → λῃστής.

κακοῦργος, "the one who does evil," "the malefactor," "the villain," e.g.: ... τάχ᾽ ἂν κακοῖς γελῶν ἃ δὴ κακοῦργος ἐξίκοιτ᾽ ἀνήρ, Soph. Ai., 1042 f.; ... κακοῦργος ἐρευνῆσαι, Xenoph. Cyrop., I, 2, 12. It is common in legal and popular speech, cf. Ditt. Or., II, 669, 17; P. Oxy., XII, 1408, 19; BGU, I, 325, 3; III, 935, 4.

It is used in the same sense in the LXX at Prv. 21:15; Sir. 11:33: πρόσεχε ἀπὸ κακούργου, πονηρὰ γὰρ τεκταίνει. Cf. also Jos. Ant., 1, 270.

It occurs in the NT at Lk. 23:32, 33, 39. Jesus is crucified between two malefactors. His saving word of forgiveness extends to one of them. At 2 Tm. 2:9 Paul writes of himself: ἐν ᾧ (sc. εὐαγγελίῳ) κακοπαθῶ μέχρι δεσμῶν ὡς κακοῦργος. There is thus fulfilled the likeness between the master's fate and that of the disciple to which the NT often refers.

---

[2] Schl. Mt., 236.

† κακοήθεια.

Ps.-Ammon. Adfin. Vocab. Diff., *s.v.* (Valckenaer, p. 148) defines the word as κακία κεκρυμμένη. Aristot. says of it: ἔστι γὰρ κακοήθεια τὸ ἐπὶ τὸ χεῖρον ὑπολαμβάνειν πάντα, Rhet., II, 13, p. 1389b, 20 f.; Plat.: ... ἀσχημοσύνη καὶ ἀρρυθμία καὶ ἀναρμοστία κακολογίας καὶ κακοηθείας ἀδελφά, Resp., III, 401a. It is also found in popular speech, e.g., B. Grenfell, *An Alexandrian Erotic Fragment* (1896), 60, 13.

In the LXX, apart from Est. 8:12 f., it occurs only in 3 and 4 Macc. Cf. esp. 4 Macc. 3:4 : κακοήθειάν τις ἡμῶν οὐ δύναται ἐκκόψαι, ἀλλὰ τὸ μὴ καμφθῆναι τῇ κακοηθείᾳ δύναιτ᾽ ἂν ὁ λογισμὸς συμμαχῆσαι. It always means "wickedness," "malice."

In the NT it occurs only at R. 1:29: ... μεστοὺς φθόνου, φόνου, ἔριδος, δόλου, κακοηθείας ... The series shows that it is here conscious and intentional wickedness.

† κακοποιέω, κακοποιός.

κακοποιέω means "to act badly," "to do evil," e.g.: ... ὅπως ὅτι πλεῖστοι κακοποιῶσιν, Xenoph. Cyrop., VIII, 8, 14; b. "to treat badly," "to do evil to," "to ruin," e.g.: οὐ δυναμένου δὲ τοῦ πλήθους ἀπέχεσθαι τῆς χώρας ... κακοποιοῦντες αὐτὴν καὶ λυμαινόμενοι διῇεσαν, Polyb., 4, 6, 10, cf. 8, 14, 1; πολλὰ τὸν Ἀλέξανδρον ἐκακοποίουν, Plut. Alex., 59 (I, 698c).

κακοποιός is "the one who does evil," "who acts badly," or "that which has harmful effects," e.g., the κακοποιόν of the ὕλη, Aristot. Phys., I, 9, p. 192a, 15; Σωσίβιος ... ἐδόκει γεγονέναι σκεῦος ... κακοποιόν, Polyb., 15, 25, 1. Like → ἀγαθοποιός, ἀγαθοποιέω, it is also an astrological term: ... Χαλδαῖοι ... τῶν πλανητῶν ... δύο μὲν ἀγαθουργούς, δύο δὲ κακοποιούς, μέσους δὲ τοὺς τρεῖς ἀποφαίνουσι καὶ κοινούς, Plut. Is. et Os., 48 (II, 370c).

In the LXX it mostly has the sense of "to do evil to someone"; it is equally distributed in the history books and the Wisdom literature. In the prophets it is found once in Is. and twice in Jer. Examples: Gn. 31:7: οὐκ ἔδωκεν αὐτῷ ὁ θεὸς κακοποιῆσαί με, also v. 29; ... πόδες ἐπισπεύδοντες κακοποιεῖν, Prv. 6:18; ἐὰν εὕρῃ καιρόν, κακοποιήσει, Sir. 19:28; σοφοί εἰσιν τοῦ κακοποιῆσαι, Jer. 4:22; κακοποιός only Prv. 12:4 (γυνὴ κακοποιός) and 24:19 : μὴ χαῖρε ἐπὶ κακοποιοῖς. In the Mas. we almost always have forms of the stem רעע.[1]

In the NT the two words are found especially in 1 Pt.[2] κρεῖττον ... ἀγαθοποιοῦντας, εἰ θέλοι τὸ θέλημα τοῦ θεοῦ, πάσχειν ἢ κακοποιοῦντας, 3:17. In this connection: μὴ γάρ τις ὑμῶν πασχέτω ὡς ... κακοποιός, 4:15;[3] also : τὴν ἀναστροφὴν ... ἔχοντες καλήν, ἵνα ἐν ᾧ καταλαλοῦσιν ὑμῶν ὡς κακοποιῶν, ἐκ τῶν καλῶν ἔργων ἐποπτεύοντες δοξάσωσιν τὸν θεὸν ἐν ἡμέρᾳ ἐπισκοπῆς, 2:12. Sufferings will break over the community and they will experience the truth of the saying of Jesus that they would be treated like malefactors (2:12). The admonition of Peter is that they should suffer as those who do good and not evil, so that their suffering will truly be to God's glory and will cause men to praise God (1 Pt. 4:15).[4] We may also refer to 1 Pt. 2:14 with reference to the task of

---

κ α κ ο π ο ι έ ω κτλ. [1] 2 Εσδρ. 4:13, 15, κακοποιεῖν for רעע; 2 Βασ. 24:17 for עוה hi.
[2] Cf. also ἔξεστιν τοῖς σάββασιν ἀγαθὸν ποιῆσαι ἢ κακοποιῆσαι ..., Mk. 3:4, cf. Lk. 6:9.
[3] κακοποιός, 4:15, can hardly mean "magician," as Windisch suggests, since the word does not elsewhere bear this sense in 1 Pt.
[4] Cf. Mt. 5:16: ... ὅπως ἴδωσιν ὑμῶν τὰ καλὰ ἔργα καὶ δοξάσωσιν τὸν πατέρα ὑμῶν τὸν ἐν τοῖς οὐρανοῖς.

rulers. Obedience is to be rendered to all authority ὡς δι' αὐτοῦ (sc. κυρίου) πεμπομένοις εἰς ἐκδίκησιν κακοποιῶν ἔπαινον δὲ ἀγαθοποιῶν.

At 3 Jn. 11 we read: ὁ ἀγαθοποιῶν ἐκ τοῦ θεοῦ ἐστιν· ὁ κακοποιῶν οὐχ ἑώρακεν τὸν θεόν. The distinction is basic. The world without God knows no ἀγαθοποιεῖν, no love or pity. In contemplation of God, in Jesus Christ love and pity arise as the power of heaven in this world. He who has seen God can no longer κακοποιεῖν. The turn of thought is distinctively Johannine. When we see God the divine nature arises through new birth to divine sonship. Without this vision it is not present. It arises necessarily from this vision. But the vision of God is attained when we see His Christ: ὁ ἑωρακὼς ἐμὲ ἑώρακεν τὸν πατέρα (Jn. 14:9).

ἐγκακέω.

ἐγκακέω, "to act badly," "to treat badly": ... ἐγκακηθέντα τὸν ἐμὸν πατέρα, P. Lond., III, 1708, 92b; "to leave off (wickedly)": Λακεδαιμόνιοι δὲ τὸ μὲν πέμπειν τὰς βοηθείας κατὰ τὴν διάταξιν ἐνεκάκησαν, Polyb., 4, 19, 10.

In the NT we find it at Lk. 18:1: ἔλεγεν δὲ παραβολὴν αὐτοῖς πρὸς τὸ δεῖν πάντοτε προσεύχεσθαι αὐτοὺς καὶ μὴ ἐγκακεῖν. The context provides us with a clear meaning. In the preceding discourse Jesus dealt with the question of the approaching end. The discourse "firmly forbids all apocalyptic calculations, whether those of the Rabbis or those that might arise among the disciples."[1] The attitude of disciples consists in δεῖν πάντοτε προσεύχεσθαι καὶ μὴ ἐγκακεῖν. In the tension which expectation creates for them Jesus demands that they should "not grow weary" (μὴ ἐγκακεῖν) in prayer. This is a term whose sense is eschatologically determined.

It bears the same meaning in Paul, who uses it of the discharge of his ministry. καθὼς ἠλεήθημεν, οὐκ ἐγκακοῦμεν, 2 C. 4:1. From the mercy shown to him proceeds the power μὴ ἐγκακεῖν. The continuation shows that the Greek sense of "to act badly" is subsumed under the sense of "to fail," "to grow weary." Paul will not allow any failure to terminate his ministry or to cause him to grow tired in it. The emphasis given by eschatology is particularly clear in Eph. 3:13: αἰτοῦμαι μὴ ἐγκακεῖν ἐν ταῖς θλίψεσίν μου ὑπὲρ ὑμῶν, ἥτις ἐστὶν δόξα ὑμῶν. θλῖψις is the pressure caused by the tension between the Already and the Not Yet of the eschatological situation. Paul's request in prayer is that he should not fail to discharge his ministry in this situation. Paul demands the same μὴ ἐγκακεῖν of his communities in the exercise of love, which is the possibility of action that Christ has given them in this very situation: τὸ δὲ καλὸν ποιοῦντες μὴ ἐγκακῶμεν, Gl. 6:9; μὴ ἐγκακήσητε καλοποιοῦντες, 2 Th. 3:13.

† ἀνεξίκακος.

This word is attested in Herodotus Medicus Apud Oribasium, V, 30, 7; Luc. Judicium Vocalium, 9. In Joseph. we find ἀνεξικακία, cf. also LXX Wis. 2:19. It means "tolera-

---

ἐ γ κ α κ έ ω. [1] Schl. Lk., 369. The term does not occur in Joseph. Lk. perhaps takes it from Paul, who uses it in various ways in exhortation.

tion of evil," "long-suffering." ἀνεξίκακος means "tolerant of evil or calamity," "long-suffering."

In the NT it occurs only at 2 Tm. 2:24, where it is demanded of the δοῦλος κυρίου that he should not be contentious but long-suffering and patient in relation to those who withstand him : ἤπιον εἶναι πρὸς πάντας, διδακτικόν, ἀνεξίκακον, ἐν πραΰτητι παιδεύοντα τοὺς ἀντιδιατιθεμένους.

Grundmann

καλέω, κλῆσις, κλητός, ἀντικαλέω, ἐγκαλέω, ἔγκλημα, εἰσκαλέω, μετακαλέω, προκαλέω, συγκαλέω, ἐπικαλέω, προσκαλέω, ἐκκλησία

ἀνέγκλητος → I, 356 f., → παρακαλέω, παράκλητος, → συμπαρακαλέω.

---

† καλέω.

1. Data.

In the case of so common a word as καλέω, "to call," which is of frequent occurrence in the NT, it is as well to survey the NT usage, and in connection therewith to try to fix some of the shades of meaning.

καλέω is found in almost all the NT writings. It is particularly common in Lk. and Ac. That this should be so in these more historical works is perhaps due to the fact of its widespread use. It is fairly common in Mt., but less so in, Mk., perhaps because there are fewer sayings of Jesus in Mk. The less frequent use in Jn. is surprising; it is perhaps explained by the fact that Jn. has his own distinctive vocabulary as compared with the Synoptists. Paul, Hb. and 1 and 2 Pt. use καλέω fairly frequently, and usually with a special nuance which corresponds to a similar nuance in some Synoptic passages and in quotations from the OT. We may always translate "to call," though the special nuance suggests the more distinctive sense of "vocation," and this gives rise to the main question from the standpoint of biblical theology.

a. The act. is followed by the accus. of object and the vocative : Lk. 6:46 : τί με καλεῖτε· κύριε κύριε; "why do you call me, Lord, Lord ?"

More commonly the act. takes the accus. of object and predicative accus. In this sense it often has to the sense of "to name" : Mt. 10:25 : τὸν οἰκοδεσπότην Βεελζεβοὺλ καλοῦσιν, or ἐκάλεσαν (v.l. ἐπεκάλεσαν, → ἐπικαλέω); 22:43 : καλεῖ αὐτὸν κύριον; cf. 22:45. In this connection we may also refer to 23:9 : καὶ πατέρα μὴ καλέσητε ὑμῶν ἐπὶ τῆς γῆς, which we should translate as though there were a μηδένα for μή; Lk. 1:59 with the addition ἐπὶ τῷ ὀνόματι; 20:44 (= Mt. 22:45, λέγει in Mk. 12:37); Ac. 14:12; R. 4:17: θεοῦ ... καλοῦντος τὰ μὴ ὄντα ὡς ὄντα, 9:25 (= Hos. 2:25); Hb. 2:11; 1 Pt. 3:6. The idea of naming is particularly clear when the accus. of object linked with a predicative accus. is τὸ ὄνομα ...: Mt. 1:21, 23 (= Is. 7:14), 25; Lk. 1:13, 31.

The pass. "to be called" is linked with a nomin. of subject and predicative nominative, or with a corresponding double case in part. constructions. Mt. 2:23 : (Ἰησοῦς) Ναζωραῖος κληθήσεται; 5:9 : οἱ εἰρηνοποιοί ... υἱοὶ θεοῦ κληθήσονται. Cf. 5:19 (twice); 21:13 (= Is. 56:7); 23:7, 8 (v.l. μηδένα καλέσητε ῥαββί or διδάσκαλον ἐπὶ τῆς γῆς, as F. Blass conjectures in Nestle); 23:10; 27:8; Mk. 11:17 (= Mt. 21:13); Lk. 1:32, 35, 36 (τῇ καλουμένῃ στείρᾳ); 1:60 (D adds τὸ ὄνομα αὐτοῦ); 1:62, 76; 2:4, 21b (with the addition τὸ ὄνομα αὐτοῦ, D has ὠνομάσθη); 2:21c, 23 (= Ex. 13:2 ff.); 6:15; 7:11; 8:2; 9:10 (D reads λεγομένην); 10:39; 15:19, 21; 19:2 (with preceding ὀνόματι; D G al lat syr omit καλούμενος as superfluous); 19:29; 21:37; 22:25; 23:33; Jn. 1:42; Ac. 1:12, 19, 23; 3:11; 7:58; 8:10 (v.l. λεγομένη; other MSS and versions omit καλουμένη); 9:11; 10:1; 13:1 (D reads ἐπικαλούμενος); 15:22 (ἐπικαλούμενον is also attested here); 15:37 (ditto); 27:8, 14, 16; 28:1; R. 9:26 (= Hos. 2:1); 1 C. 15:9; Hb. 3:13; Jm. 2:23; 1 Jn. 3:1; Rev. 1:9; 11:8; 12:9; 16:16; 19:11, 13 (with the addition τὸ ὄνομα αὐτοῦ).

b. "To call" in the sense of "to call to," "to invite," is found with reference to men at Mt. 2:7; 20:8; 22:3 : καλέσαι τοὺς κεκλημένους εἰς τοὺς γάμους (to call those invited to the wedding); 22:4 : τοῖς κεκλημένοις (those invited ...); 22:8, 9; 25:14; Mk. 3:31 (A follows Mt. here and has ζητοῦντες; other MSS read φωνοῦντες); Lk. 7:39 (for ὁ Φαρισαῖος ὁ καλέσας αὐτόν; D has ὁ Φαρισαῖος παρ' ᾧ κατέκειτο); 14:7, 8 (twice), 9, 10 (twice), 12, 13, 16, 17 (א D al add ἔρχεσθαι); 14:24; 19:13; Jn. 2:2; 10:3 (φωνεῖ is as well attested as καλεῖ); Ac. 4:18; 24:2 (in both cases a legal term); 1 C. 10:27.

c. In some passages in the Gospels, and comparatively frequently in Paul, it is God or Christ who calls. These are the statements which have theological significance. According to Mt. 2:15 God says : ἐξ Αἰγύπτου ἐκάλεσα τὸν υἱόν μου (Hos. 11:1; LXX reads μετεκάλεσα, while Θ reinterprets : ἐκάλεσα αὐτὸν υἱόν μου, "I have called him my son"). Jesus called His disciples, Mt. 4:21 = Mk. 1:20. Jesus was conscious that He had come to call sinners rather than the righteous, Mt. 9:13 = Mk. 2:17 = Lk. 5:32 (which appropriately adds εἰς μετάνοιαν). In Paul we often read that God calls to Himself or to the blessings of salvation, R. 8:30 (twice) along with → προορίζω, or προγινώσκω, → δικαιόω and → δοξάζω, which give us the unmistakeable feel of καλέω. 9:7: God has called the seed of Abraham in Isaac (= Gn. 21:12), cf. Hb. 11:18. R. 9:12 : God is the καλῶν, cf. Gl. 5:8; 1Th. 5:24; 1Pt. 1:15; R. 9:24: God has called from both Jews and Gentiles. 1 C. 1:9 : God has called Christians to κοινωνία with His Son. 7:15 : He has called us ἐν εἰρήνῃ, cf. Col. 3:15. 1 C. 7:17: Each should walk as he is called ἐν κυρίῳ, cf. 7:18 (twice), 20, 21, 22 (twice), 24; Eph. 4:1. Gl. 1:6 : God has called the Galatians ἐν χάριτι (Ἰησοῦ) Χριστοῦ (v.l. θεοῦ), 1:15 : διὰ τῆς χάριτος αὐτοῦ, 5:13 : ἐπ' ἐλευθερίᾳ. Eph. 1:11 : ἐν ᾧ ἐκλήθημεν or ἐκληρώθημεν, 4:4 : ἐν μιᾷ ἐλπίδι, Col. 1:12 : εἰς τὴν μερίδα τοῦ κλήρου τῶν ἁγίων ἐν τῷ φωτί (perhaps we ought to read ἱκανώσαντι for καλέσαντι), 1 Th. 2:12 : εἰς τὴν ἑαυτοῦ (sc. θεοῦ) βασιλείαν καὶ δόξαν, 4:7 : οὐκ ἐπὶ ἀκαθαρσίᾳ, ἀλλ' ἐν ἁγιασμῷ, 2 Th. 2:14 : ἐν ἁγιασμῷ πνεύματος καὶ πίστει ἀληθείας, εἰς ὃ (καὶ) ἐκάλεσεν ὑμᾶς (or ἡμᾶς) διὰ τοῦ εὐαγγελίου ἡμῶν εἰς περιποίησιν δόξης τοῦ κυρίου ἡμῶν Ἰησοῦ Χριστοῦ, 1 Tm. 6:12 : εἰς τὴν αἰώνιον ζωήν, 2 Tm. 1:9 : σῴζειν καὶ καλεῖν κλήσει ἁγίᾳ, Hb. 5:4 : Christ, like the Christian, καλούμενος ὑπὸ τοῦ θεοῦ, καθώσπερ Ἀαρών; 9:15 : Christians are κεκλημένοι in the absolute, 11:8 : Abraham as our type is καλούμενος. 1 Pt. 2:9 : God calls us ἐκ σκότους εἰς τὸ θαυμαστὸν αὐτοῦ φῶς, 2:21: We are called to suffering (2:20), 3:9 : εἰς τοῦτο ... ἵνα εὐλογίαν κληρονομήσητε, 5:10 : εἰς τὴν αἰώνιον αὐτοῦ δόξαν ἐν Χριστῷ, 2 Pt. 1:3 : ἰδίᾳ (sc. θεοῦ) δόξῃ καὶ ἀρετῇ (Bא al : διὰ δόξης καὶ ἀρετῆς), Rev. 19:9 : μακάριοι οἱ εἰς τὸ δεῖπνον (τοῦ γάμου) τοῦ ἀρνίου κεκλημένοι.

In general we may say of our calling by God in Christ that the uniform view of Paul and his disciples is that God calls men in Christ through His own means and for His own purpose. If in the Synoptic Gospels Jesus of Nazareth is represented as the καλῶν, He herewith fulfils the divine function. The response of the man who is called can only be → πιστεύειν in the sense of → ὑπακούειν. As already said, the translator has to express all this in the word "to call." The fact that God is the καλῶν and that Christians are the κεκλημένοι, with no qualifying addition, makes it clear that in the NT καλεῖν is a technical term for the process of salvation. Since God is always the subject, it makes no difference whether the process is directly related to God or plerophorically described in terms of the means and end, e.g., in 2 Th. 2:14. On the basis of this conclusion we may and must assume that there is an element of technical usage even in passages where it is not obvious. [1] If God or Christ calls a man, this calling or naming is a *verbum efficax*. God, or Christ, always calls righteously, bringing judgment and grace. Related to this is the fact that ἐκάλεσεν is used of God as well as καλεῖ. The two terms can occur together. At 1 Th. 2:12 καλέσαντος is attested as well as καλοῦντος.

2. Parallels.

In the case of so common a secular word as καλέω, it is obvious that there should be older and later parallels to NT usage in Greek literature, in the LXX and in early Christian works. The LXX exerted an influence quite apart from the technical use for the process of salvation.

a. The phrase for "to name" : καλεῖν τὸ ὄνομά τινος, with the name added, is found at Gn. 17:19 : καλέσεις τὸ ὄνομα αὐτοῦ Ἰσαάκ, cf. 1 Βασ. 1:20 : ἐκάλεσεν τὸ ὄνομα αὐτοῦ Σαμουήλ, also 1 Macc. 6:17 : ... Εὐπάτωρ. This construction corresponds to the Heb. קָרָא אֶת־שְׁמוֹ. For the ancient world of Heb. religion the name is not just "sound and fury," but something real, so that to be called something is tantamount to being it. We can thus see that Lk. 1:32 : υἱὸς ὑψίστου κληθήσεται, is parallel to the preceding ἔσται μέγας. We can also understand why 1 Jn. 3:1 adds to τέκνα θεοῦ κληθῶμεν the words καὶ ἐσμέν, though these are not found in all MSS. There are also parallels in the pap. and ostraka for the practice (Lk., Ac., Rev.) of putting a present participle passive before the name of a person or thing, and esp. a place. [2]

b. "To call" in the sense of "to invite" (cf. *voco* = *invito*) is found from the time of Hom. and is common in the pap. and the LXX, cf. P. Oxy., XII, 1487, 1: καλῖ σε Θέων ... εἰς τοὺς γάμους; Est. 5:12 : ... εἰς τὴν δοχήν. Much favoured is the absolute use in the same sense, e.g., 2 Βασ. 13:23 : ἐκάλεσεν Ἀβεσσαλὼμ πάντας τοὺς υἱοὺς τοῦ βασιλέως. The κεκλημένοι are those who are invited, guests. Cf. Damoxenos in Athen., III, 59 (p. 102c). The legal use assumed at Ac. 4:18 and 24:2, "to summon," is common in the pap. [3]

κ α λ έ ω. [1] Cr.-Kö. tries to explain it the other way round with the conjecture : "The use in the parables at Mt. 22 and Lk. 14 (cf. Rev. 19:9 : οἱ εἰς τὸ δεῖπνον τοῦ γάμου τοῦ ἀρνίου κεκλημένοι) perhaps gives us the specifically Christian application of this word, namely, to summon or invite or call to participation in the kingdom of God ..." (*s.v.*). But it is then rightly supposed that there is "another point of contact to which these images attach themselves." This is found by Cr.-Kö. in what is said under 3. concerning the OT and Jewish origin of the technical use in the NT.

[2] Cf. Pr.-Bauer, *s.v.*; Moult.-Mill., *s.v.*, IV, 318.

[3] Class. Rev., 12 (1898), 194 f.; 15 (1901), 199; APF, 9 (1928-1930), 69; Preisigke Wört., *s.v.*, I, 728, 7: καλεῖν εἰς τὴν δίκην, "to summon to judgment."

c. That God calls with a view to man obeying finds a human par. in P. Hamb., I, 29, 3 (89 A.D.): κληθέντων τινῶν ... καὶ μὴ ὑπακουσάντων. The existence of such a par. in the human sphere makes is clear that the God of the Bible is a person confronting persons: Prv. 1:24: ἐκάλουν καὶ οὐχ ὑπηκούσατε, as the word of wisdom, the hypostasis of God. Both in general and in detail we find the same usage in the post-apostolic fathers. 1 Cl., 32, 4: διὰ θελήματος αὐτοῦ (sc. θεοῦ) ἐν Χριστῷ Ἰησοῦ κληθέντες; 59, 2: ἀπὸ σκότους εἰς φῶς. Cf. 2 Cl., 9, 5; 10, 1; and at 5, 1 Christ the καλέσας. 1 Cl., 65, 2: Christians are κεκλημένοι ὑπὸ τοῦ θεοῦ δι' αὐτοῦ (sc. Ἰησοῦ Χριστοῦ). Cf. Herm. s., 9, 14, 5; m., 4, 3, 4 (κληθέντες). The statement concerning God in 2 Cl., 1, 8: ἐκάλεσεν ἡμᾶς οὐκ ὄντας, suggests that we might render "to call" rather than "to name" at R. 4:17 (→ 487), and it reminds us of Philo Spec. Leg., IV, 187: τὰ γὰρ μὴ ὄντα ἐκάλεσεν εἰς τὸ εἶναι. There is a similar religious usage in the religion of Isis, concerning which we have information in Apuleius and Pausanias. Apul. Met., XI, 21 tells us that the initiate to be consecrated by the priest neque vocatus (κεκλη-μένος) morari nec non etc. And in Paus., X, 32, 13 we read: οὔτε ἔσοδος ἐς τὸ ἄδυτον ἄλλοις γε ἢ ἐκείνοις ἐστὶν οὓς ἂν αὐτὴ προτιμήσασα ἡ Ἶσις καλέσῃ σφᾶς δι' ἐνυπνίων. [4]

3. Origin.

a. A richer and more illuminating field in respect of NT usage is to be found in the LXX, and it is here that we are to seek the origin. Most rewarding is the second part of Is. At Is. 41:9 ἐκάλεσά σε finds significant exposition in the words which follow at once: καὶ εἶπά σοι· παῖς μου εἶ, ἐξελεξάμην σε. καλεῖν is thus equivalent to ἐκλέγεσθαι. Cf. 42:6: ἐγὼ κύριος ὁ θεὸς ἐκάλεσά σε ἐν δικαιο-σύνῃ ... καὶ ἔδωκά σε εἰς διαθήκην γένους. Cf. also 46:11 and 48:12: Ἰσραὴλ ὃν ἐγὼ καλῶ; 48:15: ἐγὼ ἐλάλησα, ἐγὼ ἐκάλεσα; especially 50:2: ἐκάλεσα, καὶ οὐκ ἦν ὁ ὑπακούων; 51:2: ἐκάλεσα αὐτὸν καὶ εὐλόγησα αὐτὸν καὶ ἠγά-πησα αὐτόν. In this context even naming takes on particular significance: 43:1: ἐκάλεσά σε τὸ ὄνομά σου, ἐμὸς εἶ σύ; 45:3: ἐγὼ κύριος ὁ θεὸς ὁ καλῶν τὸ ὄνομά σου, θεὸς Ἰσραήλ. [5]

b. The corresponding Heb. word in the OT is usually קָרָא, for which we have at Dt. 20:10 the more pregnant rendering ἐκκαλεῖν. The objective force of καλεῖν in the LXX may be seen from the fact that other Heb. correlatives are לָקַח ("to take") and הָיָה ("to be"). קָרָא can also be translated ἀνακαλεῖσθαι as well as ἐκκαλεῖν, Ex. 31:2. Tg. O. alters the sense here as follows: "I have glorified and honoured Bezaleel by name," and there is a similar emendation at 35:30. [6]

c. The idea of invitation or summoning to the blessings of salvation is familiar to the Rabbis. We thus find Rabb. parables which are reminiscent of Mt. 22:2-14 both in the

---

[4] Cf. A. Oepke, Die Missionspredigt des Ap. Pls. (1920), 56; R. Reitzenstein, Die hellen. Mysterienreligionen (1910), 26, 99. Cf. also R. Perdelwitz, "Die Mysterienreligion u. das Problem des I. Petrusbriefes," RVV, 11, 3 (1911), 78: "We may assume that the concept of calling was common and widespread in the speech of the mysteries; the god or goddess calls those who are to be initiated into the mystery."

[5] For further instances and discussion of καλεῖν in relation to God's action in the history of nations and individuals in the OT, cf. G. Bertram, Art. "Berufung (biblisch)" in RGG², I, 743 f.

[6] Cf. Str.-B., III, 1 f. This is not unusual. קָרָא (בְּ)שֵׁם is often rendered רַבִּי (בְ)שׁוּם in the Targums even when God as subject קָרָא (בְּ)שֵׁם of a man (thereby honouring him). Cf. in addition to the passages mentioned Is. 43:1; 45:3; Jer. 11:16; 20:3 etc. Also when God as subject יָדַע בְּשֵׁם of a man, this is rendered by רַבִּי in the Targums, Ex. 33:12, 17 [K. G. Kuhn].

general thought and in details. [7] For קָרָא we often find יָמַר, which corresponds to the → τάττω of Ac. 13:48 : τεταγμένος εἰς ζωὴν αἰώνιον. [8]

In the OT and Judaism we can see plainly that קָרָא or יָמַר, like καλεῖν in the LXX and NT, is an ordinary word which acquires special significance through the naming of salvation as the basis and goal and especially of God as the Author and Consummator. God calls His own by grace and to grace. He does this finally and definitively through Jesus Christ, who is the fulness of grace. [9]

† κλῆσις.

1. Data.

R. 11:29 : κλῆσις τοῦ θεοῦ, the "call" which goes out from God, the divine "calling," elucidated by the words χαρίσματα (v. 29) and → ἐκλογή (v. 28). 1 C. 1:26 : βλέπετε ... τὴν κλῆσιν ὑμῶν ... ὅτι οὐ πολλοὶ σοφοί κτλ, "consider the state of your calling, that there are not many wise etc." In v. 27 we have instead of κλῆσις the stronger → ἐκλέγεσθαι. 7:20 : ἕκαστος ἐν τῇ κλήσει ᾗ ἐκλήθη, ἐν ταύτῃ μενέτω, "each should remain in the state of the calling in which he was called," because in any case he is ἐν κυρίῳ κληθείς (v. 22), because you τιμῆς ἠγοράσθητε, were brought back, redeemed (v. 23), because this κλῆσις is παρὰ θεῷ (v. 24). [1] Eph. 1:18 : ἡ ἐλπὶς τῆς κλήσεως αὐτοῦ, "the hope to which

---

[7] Str.-B., I, 878 ff.
[8] Ibid., II, 726 f.; cf. Dalman WJ, I, 97.
[9] On the distinction between καλέω (κλῆσις) and → ἐκλέγω (→ ἐκλογή) cf. E. v. Dobschütz, ThStKr, 106 (1934/35), 9 ff.

κ λ ῆ σ ι ς. [1] Ltzm. K., ad loc. : "As may be seen from the context and v. 24, κλῆσις here means the state of circumcision or uncircumcision ; it thus corresponds to 'state'." Cr.-Kö., s.v. rightly observes : "As regards 1 C. 7:20 ... the unnecessary sense of externa conditio has been invented ..." It may be admitted that calling in this sense would fit v. 20. But the context is in the main against this, and v. 24 does not turn the scales in its favour. It is also hard to see why the word should have at 1 C. 7:20 a different sense from 1 C. 1:26, where it could mean calling, but where even Ltzm. rightly translates : "Consider your calling to be Christians." Finally, it should be pointed out that the sense of calling as a state is ruled out elsewhere in the NT. We may thus conclude that a special sense should not be assumed in one verse so long as the normal sense is possible. K. Holl, "Die Geschichte des Worts Beruf," SAB (1924), XXIX ff. = Gesammelte Aufsätze z. Kirchengeschichte, III (1928), 189 ff. supports Ltzm.: "From this strict usage (κλῆσις as Christian calling) there is only one deviation, i.e., at 1 C. 7:20, where Paul writes that each is to remain in the calling in which he was called. Our present state of linguistic knowledge does not enable us to decide with confidence whether Paul with this bold thought is boldly coining a word, namely, that the calling of Christians includes the divine ordination of the state of life in which they find themselves, or whether he is adopting a rare and mostly popular usage whereby κλῆσις is that from which we take our name, i.e., our state or calling. The latter is more probable. In any case, it is significant that in at least one passage in the NT a sense which bears on secular life is suggested to Christians" (190). Holl, whose statements are quite untenable, then goes on to emphasise quite correctly that "this suggestion was at first without effect. The further development of the term followed up the primary emphasis, the idea of a special calling of the Christian" (loc. cit.). "The adoption of the title of vocation by the monks was for many years in the West an obstacle to the development of a cor-responding religious evaluation of secular states, and to the use of vocatio for them. 1 C. 7:20 has been almost completely without influence in this respect in the East" (199). There is a change in the Middle Ages. Meister Ekhart finds that according to 1 C. 7:20 not all are called to the same path to God (205). Interpreted along these lines the verse began to

he (God) has called." 4:1: ἀξίως περιπατῆσαι τῆς κλήσεως ἧς ἐκλήθητε; 4:4 like 1:18. Phil. 3:14 : τὸ βραβεῖον τῆς ἄνω κλήσεως (codd apud Orig : ἀνεγκλησίας) τοῦ θεοῦ ἐν Χριστῷ 'Ιησοῦ, "the reward of the high (heavenly) calling through God in Christ Jesus." 2 Th. 1:11: ἵνα ὑμᾶς ἀξιώσῃ τῆς κλήσεως ὁ θεός. 2 Tm. 1:9 : (θεοῦ) τοῦ σώσαντος ἡμᾶς καὶ καλέσαντος κλήσει ἁγίᾳ, οὐ κατὰ τὰ ἔργα ἡμῶν ἀλλὰ κατὰ ἰδίαν πρόθεσιν καὶ χάριν. Hb. 3:1: ἀδελφοὶ ἅγιοι, κλήσεως ἐπουρανίου μέτοχοι. 2 Pt. 1:10 : σπουδάσατε βεβαίαν ὑμῶν τὴν κλῆσιν καὶ ἐκλογὴν ποιεῖσθαι.

These 11 passages, which are given in extenso, show that κλῆσις is in the NT a technical Pauline or deutero-Pauline term. Here, too, we may adopt the simple rendering "call." But it is better (cf. καλέω l.c.) to adopt the more emphatic "calling." It is always God who calls in Christ. Hence the direct attributes are the corresponding ἄνω, ἁγία, ἐπουράνιος, and the related nouns and verbs are also in correspondence, viz. χαρίσματα, χάρις, ἐκλογή, πρόθεσις, and ἐκλέγεσθαι, σῴζειν. The fullest expression at 2 Tm. 1:9 brings out particularly clearly that our concern here is with a pure act of grace on the part of God. [2]

2. Parallels.

In the Greek literature known to us κλῆσις is found in Aristophanes, Xenophon, Plato, the papyri, the LXX and early Christian writings.

a. There are a few instances of the sense of naming (cf. καλέω 2. a.) or name. [3] More common is that of invitation or summons (καλέω 2. b.). [4] We should mention here the three instances found in the LXX. Jdt. 12:10 : οὐκ ἐκάλεσεν εἰς τὴν κλῆσιν (A ;

---

exert an influence. Then Luther more than any others before him came to identify vocatio with one's state of life or office rather than with Christian calling as such. Deviating from the September Bible, he translated 1 C. 7:20 along these lines (Beruf rather than Berufung). This innovation of Luther, who still made the equation of call and calling, was adopted in the Augsburg Confession, which dealt with vocation in Articles 16, 26 and 27. One has the impression that the one passage 1 C. 7:20 which might mean vocation in the modern sense, but which Luther had hesitated to render as such, was now overemphasised as compared with the view of early Christianity. The vocation of a man in the sense of his state or office was not so important for Paul as it was for Luther, who had to demonstrate and prove that not only the monk has a vocation, but every Christian in the world and in secular employment as well. It appears that Holl imports this Reformation view into his exposition of 1 C. 7:20. E. Norden, "Antike Menschen im Ringen um ihre Berufsbestimmung," SAB (1932), XXXVIII ff. gives the following equivalents : vocation = ἔργον or πρᾶγμα, types of vocation = βίοι, choice of vocation = προαίρεσις. On κλῆσις = classis → 493. M. Weber, "Die protestantische Ethik u. d. Geist des Kapitalismus," Archiv f. Sozialwissenschaft u. Sozialpolitik, 20/21 (1904/5) = Gesammelte Aufsätze z. Religionssoziologie, I (1920), 63, n. 1, has drawn attention to the fact that "in Greek there is no equivalent for the German word Beruf with its ethical implication." Before Holl, Weber has much the best and most comprehensive discussion of this question which is so far-reaching and so complicated both linguistically and materially. His exposition of Luther's view of vocation and of the need for investigation on pp. 63-83 is well adapted to correct Holl, who does not adequately deal with Weber either materially or methodologically, and to show that distinction must be made between NT κλῆσις and Lutheran vocation. At the heart of Weber's presentation there rightly stands the fact that Luther deviates from all earlier translations by using Beruf for ἔργον and πόνος at Sir. 11:20 f.: ἐν τῷ ἔργῳ σου παλαιώθητι and ἔμμενε τῷ πόνῳ, which he knew only in the Greek.

[2] Wilke-Grimm, s.v.: ". . . divina invitatio ad amplectandam salutem in regno dei."
[3] Pape, s.v.; Moult.-Mill., s.v., IV, 348. Preisigke Wört., s.v., I, 808; Liddell-Scott, s.v.
[4] Ibid.

B reads χρῆσιν) οὐδένα, refers to Holofernes' feast. 3 Macc. 5:14 : ὁ πρὸς ταῖς κλήσεσιν τεταγμένος, "he who is entrusted with invitations (plur.)." 'Ιερ. 38(31):6 : ὅτι ἔστιν ἡμέρα κλήσεως ἀπολογουμένων is a mistranslation of the Heb. כִּי יֶשׁ־יוֹם קָרְאוּ נֹצְרִים.

c. Elsewhere κλῆσις is used almost exclusively in a religious sense, i.e., for "calling" (καλέω 2. c.). There seems to be a parallel to the NT view in Epict. Diss., I, 29, 49 : κλῆσις ἥν κέκληκεν (ὁ θεός). But this is only a formal parallel. In contrast to the Hellenistic religion of redemption, and in complete contrast to the NT faith in redemption, "κλῆσις means for the Stoic that he is set a difficult and critical task in which he must bear witness to the truth and power of his principles." [5] Materially the post-apostolic fathers are in agreement with the statements of the NT ; in this as in other matters they maintain the Pauline or deutero-Pauline view. Cf. Barn., 16, 9 : κλῆσις τῆς ἐπαγγελίας, "the calling which consists in the promise" ; Herm. m., 4, 3, 6 : μετὰ τὴν κλῆσιν ἐκείνην τὴν μεγάλην καὶ σεμνήν, "according to the great and august calling," i.e., baptism ; cf. Herm. s., 8, 11, 1.

Quite distinct is the statement in Dion. Hal. Ant. Rom., IV, 18, 2 : ἐγένοντο δὴ συμμορίαι ἕξ, ἃς καλοῦσι 'Ρωμαῖοι κλάσσεις, [κατὰ] τὰς 'Ελληνικὰς κλήσεις παρανομάσαντες. The κλήσεις or καλέσεις here are the Roman *classes*. [6]

3. Origin.

Since κλῆσις, as a verbal noun (ending -σις) in the sense of calling, is equivalent to καλεῖν "to call" or καλεῖσθαι "to be called," its origin is substantially the same as that of the verb (→ καλέω 3.). The fact that κλῆσις is a technical term in the NT implies a strengthening of what was said concerning the matter and form of καλεῖν in connection with corresponding statements in the OT and Judaism. That the verbal noun does not occur in the LXX in the sense of "calling" may be a statistical accident, though it could be related to the fact that the LXX as a translation is influenced by the Hebrew, which has fewer verbal nouns than verbs.

---

[5] So rightly A. Oepke, *op. cit.* (→ καλέω n. 4).

[6] It does not seem to be legitimate to find support here for the Lutheran view of 1 C. 7:20. Ltzm. K. (→ n. 1), who is in favour of *Beruf*, admits that there are no parallels. Cr.-Kö., *s.v.* points out that "in connection with the usage of Epictetus it is worth noting that A. Bonhöffer ('Epikt. u. d. NT,' RVV, 10 [1911], 208) does not believe that κλῆσις is anywhere used in the sense of the German *Beruf*." Pr.-Bauer, *s.v.* regards Ltzm's interpretation of 1 C. 7:20 as "daring in view of the complete absence of parallels." Among more recent lexicographers a different view of the passage from Dion. Hal. is taken by F. Zorell, *Lexicon Graecum Novi Testamenti*² (1931), *s.v.* on 1 C. 7:20 : *in eo vitae genere seu statu in quo* (ad fidem christianam) *vocatus est ... fort. etiam 1 C. 1:26 huc revocari potest*. According to A. Debrunner the Dion. Hal. passage is a mistaken etymological explanation of the Lat. *classis* and an invention of the author, like the word καλέσεις (κάλεσις). The etymology is disputed by two such authoritative works as A. Walde-J. B. Hofmann, *Lat. etym. Wörterbuch*³ (1931), 3, p. 228 and A. Ernout-A. Meillet, *Dictionnaire étymologique de la Langue Latine* (1932), 187. Cf. also M. Weber, *op. cit.*, 67; T. Siegfried, Art. "Beruf (Christentum u. Beruf)" in RGG², I, 930 ff.

† κλητός.

1. Data.

a. This verbal adjective is found 10 or 11 times in the NT. C 𝕶 D pl latt syr append the saying: πολλοὶ γάρ εἰσιν κλητοί, ὀλίγοι δὲ ἐκλεκτοί, to Mt. 20:16 in addition to Mt. 22:14, where it is generally attested. At R. 1:1 the statement κλητὸς ἀπόστολος is expounded in the ensuing ἀφωρισμένος εἰς εὐαγγέλιον θεοῦ and then further in vv. 2-5. The same statement at 1 C. 1:1 (A D do not have κλητός here) is elucidated by διὰ θελήματος θεοῦ. Elsewhere, as at Mt. 22:14, κλητός refers to believers or Christians, and explanations are again added: R. 1:6: κλητοὶ ᾿Ιησοῦ Χριστοῦ, "those who are called by Jesus Christ"; 1:7: κλητοὶ ἅγιοι, "called saints"; 8:28: κατὰ πρόθεσιν κλητοί, "called according to the decree (of God)"; 1 C. 1:2: κλητοὶ ἅγιοι, defined by the preceding ἡγιασμένοι ἐν Χριστῷ ᾿Ιησοῦ; 1:24, κλητοί as distinct from unbelieving Jews and Gentiles (v. 22 f.). At Jd. 1 the κλητοί are described as ἐν θεῷ πατρὶ ἠγαπημένοι (𝕶: ἡγιασμένοι) καὶ (or ἐν) ᾿Ιησοῦ Χριστῷ τετηρημένοι. Rev. 17:14: οἱ μετ᾽ αὐτοῦ (sc. κυρίου ᾿Ιησοῦ Χριστοῦ) κλητοὶ καὶ ἐκλεκτοὶ καὶ πιστοί.

This review shows that κλητός is sometimes used as a verb (κεκλημένος) and sometimes as a noun for Christians (R. 1:6; 1 C. 1:24; Jd. 1; Rev. 17:14). The use as a noun shows very clearly that we have here a technical term which is to be explained in the same way as καλέω (1. c.) and κλῆσις (1.).

b. There is something of a new development in the expression κλητὸς ἀπόστολος, since this suggests calling to an office. But this is no true novelty, since to be a Christian and to become and be an apostle could not be separated for Paul. We may thus suggest the rendering, or at least the exposition, Christian apostle. [1]

c. A *crux interpretum* is Mt. 22:14. This distinguishes between κλητοί and ἐκλεκτοί. In this respect is differs from all other passages. Thus κλητοί, ἐκλεκτοί and πιστοί are full equivalents in Rev. 17:14. We neither can nor should conceal this contradiction,[2] but two considerations prevent us from making too much of it. The first is that we do not know the Aram. original used by Jesus.

Attempts at retranslation have led to no very assured results.[3] The basic contrast in the saying is obviously that between the many and the few. This emerges in both Jewish and Greek proverbs, e.g., 4 Esr. 8:3: "Many are created but few are saved"; [4] 8:1: "The Most High has created this world for the many but the future world for the few"; S. Bar. 44:15: ". . . the world to come is given to these but the abode of the many others will be in the fire": and the Orphic saying in Plat. Phaed., 69c: ναρθηκοφόροι μὲν πολλοί, βάκχοι δέ τε παῦροι. [5]

κ λ η τ ό ς. [1] In Pr.-Bauer and also in Cr.-Kö. κλητός as a designation of the apostle is too woodenly separated from κλητός as a designation of Christians. Cf. G. Bertram, Art. "Berufung (biblisch)," RGG², I, 941 ff.

[2] Cf. the initially correct observation of Wilke-Grimm, *s.v.*: . . . *quae distinctio non est e mente Pauli*. On the other hand, too little justice is done to this distinction by the limping exposition of Cr.-Kö., *s.v.*

[3] Str.-B., I, 883 refers to Dalman WJ, I, 97, who suggests סַגִּיאִין זְמִינִין זְעֵירִין בְּחִירִין, but it it doubtful whether זמן and בחר could be contrasted in this way.

[4] H. Gunkel, *ad loc.* (in Kautzsch Apkr. u. Pseudepigr., II, 378) refers expressly to Mt. 22:14 and 20:16.

[5] Cf. Kl. Mt. on 22:14.

The second is that Mt. 22:14 is to be understood in a dialectical sense. Many are called and yet few are called; many are elected and yet few are elected. Paradoxical expression is here given to the important thought that our calling or election can never be taken for granted but is continually to be set afresh under the judgment and grace of God. In this light is it not possible that κλητός and → ἐκλεκτός are here to be given the same sense?

The material inner paradox is found elsewhere in Jesus' preaching. Thus, emphasising the personal nature of man in personal confrontation with God, He calls for prolonged and earnest prayer. Yet, emphasising the dependence of man on God, He also seems to maintain the very opposite, namely, that our prayers to God are not necessary. The paradox finds resolution in the thought that the omniscient God does not need our prayers and yet that man must wrestle through to God in prayer like Paul in 2 C. 12:1 ff. or Christ Himself in Gethsemane. A further paradox is to be seen in the fact that Jesus calls the obstinate Jews of Mt. 8:12 υἱοὶ τῆς βασιλείας, for they are this, and yet they are not. Cf. again Mt. 9:12 f., where Jesus calls the Pharisees ἰσχύοντες and even δίκαιοι, which they both are and are not. Mt. 22:14 is to be interpreted along the same lines. We are called and chosen, and yet we are not if we deduce therefrom a claim on the God of sovereign judgment and grace. There constantly applies to us the admonition of 2 Pt. 1:10 : σπουδάσατε βεβαίαν ὑμῶν τὴν κλῆσιν καὶ ἐκλογὴν ποιεῖσθαι. God is gracious only ἐὰν ἐπιμένῃς τῇ χρηστότητι (sc. θεοῦ), ἐπεὶ καὶ σὺ ἐκκοπήσῃ, R. 11:22. Or 1 C. 10:12 : ὥστε ὁ δοκῶν ἑστάναι βλεπέτω μὴ πέσῃ, and Gl. 5:4 : κατηργήθητε ἀπὸ Χριστοῦ ... τῆς χάριτος ἐξεπέσατε. [6]

2. Parallels.

There are not too many parallels in other Greek works.

Most dictionaries trace the word back to the time of Homer. a. As derived from καλέω "to name," it occurs in a number of LXX verses : Ex. 12:16 : ἡ ἡμέρα ἡ ἑβδόμη κλητὴ ἁγία ἔσται; cf. Lv. 23:2, 3, 4 (here κληταί in F for καὶ αὐταί), 7, 8, 21, 24, 27, 35, 36, 37; Nu. 28:25; b. from καλέω "to call," "to invite," it is found in Hom. Od., 17. 386 in the sense of "invited," "welcome"; cf. Il., 9, 165. The sense of "summoned to judgment" is found in Greek prose. [7] The LXX sometimes uses it for "invited," e.g., to a meal : Ju. 14:11; 2 Βασ. 15:11; 3 Βασ. 1:41, 49; Zeph. 1:7; 3 Macc. 5:14.

c. In Greek literature there is attestation for the sense of "called by God" only where Paul has exerted an influence. Cf. the inscription to 1 Cl., in which Christians are addressed as κλητοὶ ἡγιασμένοι ἐν θελήματι θεοῦ διὰ τοῦ κυρίου ἡμῶν Ἰησοῦ Χριστοῦ. Mt. 22:14 is quoted in Barn., 4, 14. [8]

---

[6] Cr.-Kö. is ultimately correct in his appeal to such Pauline passages for a correct understanding of Mt. 22:14. He implicitly detects the material dialectic, but fails to do justice to the formal dialectic of the saying. More recent lexicographers and exegetes miss the dialectic altogether. Thus Wilke-Grimm does not go beyond his initially (but only initially) correct statement. Zorell (→ 493, n. 6) says concerning ἐκλεκτός : *Multi, quidem, immo Israëlitae ad regnum meum messianum intrandum vocantur ; sed, pro dolor! pauci huic vocationi parebunt.* J. Wellhausen, *Das Ev. Mt.* (1904), 112 : "The κλητοί are not the κεκλημένοι of 22:3, 4, but the guests brought in from the hedgerows, i.e., members of the Church, who will to some degree be sifted at the judgment." Moult.-Mill., IV, 348 *s.v.* notes a similar patristic view according to which there is a distinction between κλητοί and κεκλημένοι : "We may cite Cl. Al. Strom., I, 18, 89, 3 (p. 57, ed. Stählin): πάντων τοίνυν ἀνθρώπων κεκλημένων οἱ ὑπακοῦσαι βουληθέντες ʽκλητοὶʼ ὠνομάσθησαν.

[7] Cf. Preisigke Wört., I, 808, *s.v.*

[8] Just before in Barn., 4, 13 we read : ἵνα μήποτε ἐπαναπαυόμενοι ὡς κλητοὶ ἐπικαθυπνώσωμεν ταῖς ἁμαρτίαις ἡμῶν, but this does not force us to distinguish between the called and the elect. On the contrary, it favours the above exegesis of Mt. 22:14, since κλητοί would fit just as well as ἐκλεκτοί.

3. Origin.

For the origin of the NT κλητός it is only necessary to consider what was said concerning that of κλῆσις in the NT. For מִקְרָא (Is. 48:12), which corresponds to κλητός at R. 8:28 and 1 C. 1:24, the LXX has ὃν ἐγὼ καλῶ. The fact that κλητή (called) ἁγία is found at Ex. 12:16 and Lv. 23:2 ff. (for מִקְרָא קֹדֶשׁ) may have favoured the combination of κλητός and ἅγιος in the NT. [9]

It may be because κλητός is a technical religious and biblical term that it is unusual in modern Greek, which uses καλῶ for "to name, call, invite or summon," κάλεσις or κάλεσμα for "invitation," καλεστής for "host," and κλῆσις for "call" (ὀνομαστικὴ κλῆσις, "roll-call"), "invitation" or "summons."

ἀντι-, ἐγκαλέω, ἔγκλημα, εἰς-, μετα-, προ-, συγκαλέω.

Two points distinguish the use of compounds of καλέω in the NT. 1. ἀνα-, ἀπο-, ἐκ-, and κατακαλέω are not found in the NT. 2. ἐγκαλέω, "to accuse," is found in the legal sense 6 times in Ac. and elsewhere only once at R. 8:33; the corresponding noun ἔγκλημα occurs only twice in Ac. [1] For → ἀνέγκλητος, which has a religious as well as a legal and ethical character, → I, 356 f. μετακαλέομαι, "to have brought to one," is found only in Ac. (4 times). συγκαλέω, "to call together," occurs at Mk. 15:16; Lk. 15:6, 9; Ac. 5:21; συγκαλέομαι, "to call to oneself," Lk. 9:1; 23:13; Ac. 10:24; 28:17. [2] εἰσκαλέομαι (only the mid.), "to summon to," "to invite," only Ac. 10:23 (D reads differently). That the words are mostly used only by Lk. may be attributed to the fact that they belong to the more elevated koine. Acquaintance with legal terms may be compared with the knowledge of medical terms in the Lucan writings. ἀντικαλέω, "to invite back," occurs only at Lk. 14:12, and προκαλέομαι (mostly mid.), "to call forth," only at Gl. 5:26.

In biblical exegesis and theology only ἐπικαλέω and προσκαλέομαι are of any importance apart from ἐκκλησία (→ 501 ff.), from ἐκκαλέω, and → παρακαλέω with its derivatives παράκλησις, παράκλητος and συμπαρακαλέω.

† ἐπικαλέω.

1. Data.

a. ἐπικαλέω [1] is used act. and pass. like καλέω in the sense of "to name" (→ καλέω 1. a.). In NT MSS the simple and compound are interchangeable. Act. only at Mt. 10:25 (D καλοῦσιν; ἀπεκάλεσαν, not found elsewhere in the NT, is also attested). Pass.

---

[9] Moult.-Mill., s.v. shows that the lack of parallels refutes a derivation of NT κλητός from the Gk. sphere : "Slaten (Qualitative Nouns, p. 57) throws out the conjecture that κλητός was a cult term adopted by the Christians from the terminology of the Greek mysteries, but he offers no evidence."

ἀ ν τ ι κ α λ έ ω κτλ. [1] On the legal character of ἐγκαλέω and ἔγκλημα cf. Preisigke Fachwörter, where ἐγκληματίζω, ἐγκληματικός, ἐγκλημάτιον, ἔγκλησις, ἔγκλητος are also noted ; Liddell-Scott also mentions ἐγκληματογράφω, ἐγκληματόομαι, ἐγκλήμων.

[2] Bl.-Debr.[6], § 316, 1: συγκαλεῖν and -εῖσθαι ("to oneself") is everywhere rightly separated if with DF at Lk. 15:6, and with ADEG al at 9, we read συγκαλεῖται instead of -εῖ.

ἐ π ι κ α λ έ ω. [1] The controversy concerning "The Meaning of ἐπίκλησις" (which does not occur in the NT and post-apost. fathers) between J. W. Tyrer and R. H. Connolly, JThSt, 25 (1924), 139 and 337 ff. involves a discussion of the verbs ἐπικαλέω and ἐπικαλέομαι.

Mt. 10:3 v.l.; Lk. 22:3 (BD καλούμενον); Ac. 1:23; 4:36; 10:5, 18, 32; 11:13; 12:12, 25; 15:17 (= Am. 9:12); 15:22 (also καλούμενον); Hb. 11:16; Jm. 2:7; but not under a. Ac. 9:14, 21; 1 C. 1:2. [2]

b. The mid. ἐπικαλέομαί τινα, "to appeal to someone" (on one's behalf or in one's favour) is a common legal term in the NT (Lat. *provocare* [ad]).

Παῦλος ἐπικαλεῖται Καίσαρα, "Paul appeals to," "makes an appeal to Caesar," Ac. 25:11, 12, 25 (here, instead of Καίσαρα, τὸν Σεβαστόν, Augustus); 26:32; 28:19. The absolute use is also found in this sense at Ac. 25:21: Paul appeals to be reserved to the decision of Augustus. A similar, though less technical, use is found at 2 C. 1:23: μάρτυρα τὸν θεὸν ἐπικαλοῦμαι ἐπὶ τὴν ἐμὴν ψυχήν, "I call God to witness against my soul (i.e., against me)." [3]

Often in the NT the believer calls on God or Christ, or the name of God or Christ, in prayer: Ac. 2:21: ὃς ἐὰν ἐπικαλέσηται τὸ ὄνομα κυρίου (= Jl. 3:5); cf. R. 10:13; Ac. 7:59: ... τὸν Στέφανον ἐπικαλούμενον καὶ λέγοντα· κύριε Ἰησοῦ (in this absolute verbal use the vocative replaces the accusative of object); 9:14: τοὺς ἐπικαλουμένους τὸ ὄνομά σου (sc. Χριστοῦ, or less likely θεοῦ); 9:21: ... τὸ ὄνομα τοῦτο; 22:16: ... τὸ ὄνομα αὐτοῦ (sc. θεοῦ); R. 10:12: .. αὐτόν (sc. Χριστόν rather than θεόν); cf. 10:13 (→ 499) and 14; 1 C. 1:2: ... τὸ ὄνομα τοῦ κυρίου ἡμῶν Ἰησοῦ Χριστοῦ; 2 Tm. 2:22: ... τὸν κύριον (A reads ἀγαπώντων for ἐπικαλουμένων, and this offers a useful commentary); 1 Pt. 1:17: ... πατέρα (cf. ψ 88:26).

2. Parallels.

There are parallels to the NT usage in Gk. literature, where ἐπικαλέω occurs from the time of Homer.

a. The act. sense "to name" is found, e.g., in Hdt., VIII, 44: ἐπεκλήθησαν (v.l. ἐκλήθησαν) Κεκροπίδαι, and then in most Gk. authors and also in inscr., the pap. and the LXX. [4] b. The legal term ἐπικαλέομαι, "to appeal," is attested in Plut. De

---

[2] Rightly Cr.-Kö., *s.v.*: "It is completely impossible to see how the expression at 1 C. 1:2: σὺν πᾶσιν τοῖς ἐπικαλουμένοις τὸ ὄνομα τοῦ κυρίου, can be taken in this sense, 'who are called by the name of the Lord,' " and at Ac. 9:14, 21 "the mid. is much more likely and corresponds to a sense current in the primitive community ... At 1 Cl., 64, 1, also, it seems to be unnecessary and strained: πάσῃ ψυχῇ ἐπικαλουμένῃ τὸ μεγαλοπρεπὲς καὶ ἅγιον ὄνομα, since it is only with difficulty that the accus. τὸ ὄνομα can be construed as an accus. of inner object. On the other hand, the dat. in Herm. s., 9, 14, 3: ἐπὶ πᾶσι τοῖς ἐπικαλουμένοις τῷ ὀνόματι αὐτοῦ (cf. 8, 6, 4) makes such an understanding more probable." Pr.-Bauer, *s.v.* translates this last passage "who are called by his name," and refers to Is. 43:7: ὅσοι ἐπικέκληνται τῷ ὀνόματί μου.

[3] Cf. Deissmann LO, 258, where we have the material par. from Ditt. Or., II, 532, 28 ff.: ἐπαρῶμαι αὐτός τε κατ' ἐμοῦ καὶ σ[ώμα]τος τοῦ ἐμαυτοῦ καὶ ψυχῆς καὶ βίου κτλ.

[4] The meaning ἐπικαλέω τί τινι, "to charge someone with something," "to bring an accusation against him" (cf. ἐγκαλέω), is found in the Bible only at 3 Βασ. 13:2: ἐπεκάλεσεν πρὸς τὸ θυσιαστήριον ἐν λόγῳ κυρίου καὶ εἶπεν κτλ., where it is used for קָרָא, which in this sense is normally rendered κράζω. Cf. Str.-B., II, 769: "Instead of ἐπικαλοῦμαι the Midr. once uses ἐγκαλοῦμαι אֲנִקְלִין in the same sense. Dt. r., 9 (205d) on 31:14: Wickedness does not deliver those who exercise it, Qoh. 8:8. No man may level a reproach אֲנִקְלִיטִין (ἔγκλητον) against him (God); no man may say before him: I make an appeal אַנְקְלוּמָא!"

Marcello, 2 (I, 299a): τοὺς δημάρχους, and Plut. Tib. Gracch., 16 (I, 832b): τὸν δῆμον ἀπὸ τῶν δικαστῶν. More common is ἐπικαλέομαί τινα μάρτυρα, σύμμαχον, βοηθόν, Hdt., Plat., Polyb., Diod. S., Plut., Heliodor. There is an exact par. to 2 C. 1:23 in Jos. Ant., 1, 243 : (Abraham and Eliezer) ἐπικαλοῦνται τὸν θεὸν μάρτυρα τῶν ἐσομένων. There are many par. to ἐπικαλέομαι for calling on God in prayer, Hdt., Xenoph., Plat., Polyb., Diod. S., Epict., inscr., pap. The following examples are taken from the Hellen. period : P. Leid., II W, p. 9a, 35 : ἐπικαλοῦ τὸν τῆς ὥρας καὶ τὸν τῆς ἡμέρας θεόν; P. Oxy., VI, 886, 10 : ἐπικαλοῦ μὲ[ν?] τὸν (ἥλιον) κὲ τοὺς ἐν βυθῷ θεοὺς πάντας. [5] Cf. the beginning of the vengeance prayers of Rheneia : [6] ἐπικαλοῦμαι καὶ ἀξιῶ τὸν θεὸν τὸν ὕψιστον τὸν κύριον τῶν πνευμάτων καὶ πάσης σαρκός, ἐπὶ [7] τοὺς δόλῳ φονεύσαντας κτλ. LXX formulations are found in the Christian as well as the Jewish world, cf. 1 Cl., 52, 3 (ψ 49:15); 57, 5 (Prv. 1:28); 60, 4. To the same context belongs Jos. Ant., 4, 222 : ἐπικαλεῖσθαι ἵλεω τὸν θεόν, and Bell., 2, 394 : ἐπικαλεῖσθαι τὸ θεῖον (instead of τὸν θεόν). The phrase ἐπικαλεῖσθαι τὸ ὄνομα θεοῦ is particularly common in the LXX.

3. Origin.

Since there are so many Greek parallels, of which we have adduced only a few, the NT usage might be regarded as similar to that of the Greek world generally. Nevertheless, something more specific can and should be said about its origin. Many features, and especially the many OT quotations, reveal a strong influence of the LXX.

a. This is true of the sense "to name." Thus Ac. 15:17: πάντα τὰ ἔθνη ἐφ' οὓς ἐπικέκληται τὸ ὄνομά μου ἐπ' αὐτούς, quotes from Am. 9:12 (cf. 2 Ch. 7:14). And this brings us up against the common OT practice of naming the name of God over a man, who is in this way God's possession, because God has revealed and made Himself known to him : ἐπικαλεῖται τὸ ὄνομα θεοῦ ἐπί τινα = נִקְרָא שֵׁם יְהֹוָה עַל־. [8]

So 2 Βασ. 6:2 (τὴν κιβωτὸν τοῦ θεοῦ, ἐφ' ἣν ἐπεκλήθη τὸ ὄνομα κυρίου); 2 Ch. 6:33 (ἐπικέκληται τὸ ὄνομά σου ἐπὶ τὸν οἶκον τοῦτον); Jer. 7:30; Bar. 2:15; Da. 9:19; 1 Macc. 7:37 (א has the gen. here). In other verses ἐπί is combined with the dat. or gen. or it is used instead of the part. construction of the dat.

Apart from Ac. 15:17 [9] we may refer to Jm. 2:7, where the same is said of the name of Jesus: οὐκ αὐτοὶ βλασφημοῦσιν τὸ καλὸν ὄνομα τὸ ἐπικληθὲν ἐφ' ὑμᾶς; If there is here no direct quotation from the OT, there is an obvious influence of OT modes of expression.

---

[5] Cf. Moult.-Mill., III, 239, s.v.

[6] Cf. the detailed discussion of these texts in Deissmann LO, 351-362, esp. 355 : "The prayer for vengeance begins with the verb ἐπικαλοῦμαι, which is also found very commonly in the LXX and early Christian texts (Note : individual instances are unnecessary), and often in the formulae of prayer in magical texts (Note : often in those edited by Wessely)."

[7] On this use of ἐπί cf. 2 C. 1:23.

[8] The formula נִקְרָא שֵׁם יְהֹוָה עַל־ comes from the sphere of secular law and denotes a relationship to property, including a protective relationship (2 S. 12:28; Is. 4:1). Applied to the relationship between God and man the emphasis is on the legal claim which God has [v. Rad].

[9] Cf. also Str.-B., II, 729.

LXX influence is equally clear in the case of ἐπικαλέομαι in the sense of calling on God (in prayer → 497).

1 Cl., 52, 3 and 57, 5 are OT quotations, and 60, 4 is perhaps under LXX influence even though not an actual quotation. We may mention many passages in the Psalms: ψ 49:15; 13:4; 30:17; 52:4; 85:5; 88:26; 90:15; 101:2; 114:4 etc. The vengeance prayers of Rheneia also show signs of Jewish origin in view of the many reminiscences of the LXX. For the expression ἐπικαλοῦμαι τὸν θεὸν ὕψιστον cf. Sir. 46:5 : ἐπεκαλέσατο τὸν ὕψιστον δυνάστην; 47:5 : ἐπεκαλέσατο ... κύριον τὸν ὕψιστον; 2 Macc. 3:31: ἐπικαλέσασθαι τὸν ὕψιστον. [10] It is worth noting that the phrase ἐπικαλεῖσθαι τὸν θεόν, which is comparatively infrequent in the Heb. canon (Am. 4:12; Jon. 1:6), is more common in the Hellenistically influenced LXX, which also defines God as δυνάστης or παντοκράτωρ as well as κύριος. Hellenistic influence may also be seen in the use of τὸ θεῖον for ὁ θεός by Joseph. at Bell., 2, 394.

This could lead to the conclusion that in their use of the expression ἐπικαλεῖσθαι τὸν θεόν the LXX and NT belong to the more general sphere of Hellenistic religious history.

c. While the number of such passages is relatively small in the NT, and in the LXX so far as it corresponds to the Heb., ἐπικαλεῖσθαι τὸ ὄνομα κυρίου occurs much more frequently. The NT usage suggests that this is a technical term, and this impression is heightened and confirmed when we turn to the LXX.

Cf. Gn. 13:4; 21:33; 26:25; ψ 78:6; 79:18; 104:1; 115:4; Is. 64:6; Jer. 10:25; Zeph. 3:9; Zech. 13:9; Jl. 2:32. The corresponding Heb. phrase is קָרָא בְּשֵׁם יְהוָה. In Semitic style בְּשֵׁם is not rendered τὸ ὄνομα but ἐν τῷ ὀνόματι (3 Βασ. 18:24 ff.; 4 Βασ. 5:11; 1 Ch. 16:8; ψ 19:7 — μεγαλυνθησόμεθα or ἀγαλλιασόμεθα is attested as well as ἐπικαλεσόμεθα — and ψ 115:8 v.l.) or ἐπὶ τῷ ὀνόματι, Gn. 12:8 (E reads τὸ ὄνομα). There is a particular stress on the fact that believers like the patriarchs and Elijah call on the one, true and eternal God and on His name : Θεὸς αἰώνιος = יְהוָה אֵל עוֹלָם Gn. 21:33; this God and not the Canaanite Baal is the true God : ἐγὼ (Elijah) ἐπικαλέσομαι ἐν ὀνόματι κυρίου τοῦ θεοῦ μου = וַאֲנִי אֶקְרָא בְּשֵׁם־יְהוָה as compared with ἐπεκαλοῦντο (the priests of Baal) ἐν ὀνόματι τοῦ Βάαλ = וַיִּקְרְאוּ בְשֵׁם־הַבַּעַל, 3 Βασ. 18:24 + 26.

It is certainly no accident that in the world of the (Greek) apocrypha the polemical aspect of calling on the true God of Israel is less evident ; only at Bar. 3:7 and Jdt. 16:1 do we find ἐπικαλεῖσθαι τὸ ὄνομα κυρίου.

d. The Heb. original of the LXX ἐπικαλεῖσθαι is mostly קָרָא. This common word for prayer is not always translated ἐπικαλεῖσθαι, but very often → κράζειν.

As קָרָא, which can take the accus. (Ps. 14:4; 17:6; 88:9; 91:15) can be linked with לְ (Ps. 57:3) or more commonly אֶל (Ps. 4:3; 28:1; 30:8; 55:16; 61:2; Hos. 7:7), [11] so we usually have κράζειν πρός (Ps. 4:4; ψ 21:5; 27:1; 29:8; 54:16; 56:3; 60:2; 87:9). Materially ἐπικαλεῖσθαι and κράζειν mean the same ; the reason why קָרָא is so often rendered κράζειν is perhaps because there is some similarity between the Heb. and the Gk., as in other cases. [12]

---

[10] Deissmann LO, 355.
[11] The LXX has here the Semitic ὁ ἐπικαλούμενος πρός με.
[12] → I, 225 f.

That קָרָא, like ἐπικαλεῖσθαι and κράζειν, is a technical term for the attitude of prayer may be seen from the fact that in the OT, as in the NT, these verbs can be used in the absolute, i.e., without object.

קָרָא, Ps. 4:1; 22:2; 34:6; 69:3; ἐπικαλεῖσθαι, Ps. 4:2; κράζειν, ψ 21:2; 33:6; 68:3. Cf. ἐπικαλεῖσθαι at Ac. 7:59 and R. 10:4.

e. The fact that in the LXX ἐπικαλεῖσθαι means "to call on in prayer," and ἐπικαλεῖσθαι τὸ ὄνομα (or other constructions) κυρίου "to call on the name of the Lord in prayer," and that קָרָא and קָרָא בְּשֵׁם יְהֹוָה are previously used in the same way in the Mas., sheds a distinctive light on the NT passages from the standpoint of faith in the → κύριος. What is said of the κύριος (יְהֹוָה) in the OT is said of the κύριος Ἰησοῦς Χριστός in the NT. In some verses the object of ἐπικαλεῖσθαι is God the Father (Ac. 2:21; 1 Pt. 1:17; and 2 C. 1:23 is almost a prayer); but in other verses it is God the Son (Ac. 7:59; 9:14, 21; 22:16; R. 10:12-14; 1 C. 1:2; 2 Tm. 2:22). The formula in 1 C. 1:2: οἱ ἐπικαλούμενοι τὸ ὄνομα τοῦ κυρίου ἡμῶν Ἰησοῦ Χριστοῦ, describes those whom we call Christians; [13] the use of → Χριστιανός is rare in the NT. "In this light (sc. of the OT) the relating of ἐπικαλεῖσθαι to Christ in the NT is the characteristic element of faith in the Messiah. The directing of prayer to Jesus is a mark of faith in the Messiah, like the קָרָא בְּשֵׁם־יְהֹוָה of the patriarchs, Elijah etc." [14]

† προσκαλέω.

1. Data.

In the NT and the LXX we find only the middle. Most passages are of no great importance from the standpoint of biblical theology.

In the parable of the wicked servant it is said of the master at Mt. 18:32: προσκαλεσάμενος αὐτόν, "he called him to him." At Jm. 5:14 a sick man calls others to him; Mk. 15:44 Pilate; Lk. 7:18 John the Baptist; 15:26 the elder son; 16:5 the unjust steward; Ac. 5:40 the members of the Sanhedrin; 6:2 the Twelve; 13:7 Sergius Paulus; 20:1 (μεταπεμψάμενος and μεταστειλάμενος are also attested); 23:17, 18 Paul; 23:23 a chiliarch. Some of these verses suggest a legal term.

God is the προσκαλούμενος at Ac. 2:39 and 16:10, and the Holy Spirit at Ac. 13:2. Jesus is often called the προσκαλούμενος τοὺς μαθητὰς αὐτοῦ, or τὸν ὄχλον, Mt. 10:1; 15:10, 32; 18:2; 20:25; Mk. 3:13, 23; 6:7; 7:14; 8:1, 34; 10:42; 12:43; Lk. 18:16. In themselves these passages might be taken to mean that God, the Holy Spirit and Jesus call to themselves. It is a matter of judgment how much weight we set on them.

2. Parallels.

Parallels from Greek writings show that the act. is rare, as in the Gk. Bible, and that the mid. is preferred. Indeed, προσκαλεῖσθαι is a technical legal term for "to bring to judgment." [1]

---

[13] Cf. Ltzm. on 1 C. 1:2.

[14] Cr.-Kö. finely concludes his art. on ἐπικαλέω with these words. Cf. J. Horst, "Proskynein, zur Anbetung im Urchr. nach ihrer religionsgeschichtlichen Eigenart," Nt.liche Forschungen, 3, 2 (1932), 193 f.

προσκαλέω. [1] For detailed instances cf. Pape, s.v.

3. Origin.

In one verse, Ac. 2:39, LXX influence is proved by the quoting of Jl. 2:32 (οὓς κύριος προσκέκληται), and it is plain that προσκαλεῖσθαι has here the significance of καλεῖν (→ καλέω, 1. c.).[2] The same is true of Ac. 16:10 : προσκέκληται ἡμᾶς ὁ θεὸς εὐαγγελίσασθαι αὐτούς, and 13:2 : τὸ πνεῦμα ... εἰς τὸ ἔργον ὃ προσκέκλημαι αὐτούς.

Cf. 1 Cl., 22, 1: αὐτὸς (sc. Χριστός) διὰ τοῦ πνεύματος τοῦ ἁγίου οὕτως προσκαλεῖται ἡμᾶς, and Ign. Tr., 11, 2 : δι' οὗ (sc. τοῦ σταυροῦ) ἐν τῷ πάθει αὐτοῦ προσκαλεῖται (the subject is Christ) ὑμᾶς.

When in Mt. and Mk. Jesus calls men, and especially the disciples, to Himself, we may certainly think of the divine calling as it is fulfilled by Jesus as the Christ.

This understanding is supported by a consideration which is stylistic rather than lexical. ('Ιησοῦς) προσκαλεσάμενος τοὺς μαθητὰς αὐτοῦ, or something similar, is a fixed opening to stories. As such it is christological and suggests the divine calling, Mt. 10:1 = Mk. 3:13, 23; 6:7; Mt. 15:10 = Mk. 7:14; Mt. 15:32 = Mk. 8:1 (the second Evangelist has here his distinctive πάλιν); Mt. 18:2; 20:25 = Mk. 10:42; Mk. 8:34; 12:43. While Mt. and Mk. almost always have much the same expression, the more literary third Evangelist has ὁ δὲ 'Ιησοῦς προσεκαλέσατο αὐτά (sc. τὰ παιδία) only at 18:16, and elsewhere he avoids the opening.[3]

† ἐκκλησία.

Contents. A. Introduction. B. The New Testament : 1. Acts ; 2. Pauline Epistles, I ; 3. Pauline Epistles, II : Colossians and Ephesians ; 4. The Rest of the New Testament. C. The Greek World. D. Parallel Expressions. E. Matthew 16:18 and 18:17: 1. The Problem ;

---

[2] Wilke-Grimm, s.v.: ... deus dic. προσκαλεῖσθαι gentiles ab ipso alienos ad sui in messiano regno consortium ope praedicationis evangelii invitans et perducens.

[3] Cf. K. L. Schmidt, Der Rahmen der Geschichte Jesu (1919), 122, 163, 197, 232, 245.

ἐ κ κ λ η σ ί α. Bibliography : O. Linton (Swedish scholar), Das Problem der Urkirche in der neueren Forschung, eine kritische Darstellung, Uppsala Universitets Arsskrift (1932), I (Linton), with a list of volumes and articles in various languages since 1880 on 378 (cf. for a review, F. Kattenbusch, ThStKr, 105 [1933], 97 ff.); L. Kösters (Roman Catholic), Die Kirche unseres Glaubens (1935); F. Kattenbusch, "Der Quellort der Kirchenidee," Festgabe f. A. v. Harnack (1921), 143-172 (Kattenbusch, I); "Die Vorzugsstellung des Petrus u. d. Charakter der Urgemeinde zu Jerusalem," Festg. f. K. Müller (1922), 96-131 (Kattenbusch, II); "Der Spruch über Petrus u. d. Kirche bei Matthäus," ThStKr, 94 (1922), 96-131 (there is in these three essays a wealth of material and insight which has not yet been fully exploited); K. L. Schmidt, "Die Kirche d. Urchristentums, eine lexikograph. u. biblisch-theolog. Studie," in Festg. f. A. Deissmann (1927), 258-319 (2nd impress., with preface, 1932) (K. L. Schmidt, Die Kirche); "Das Kirchenproblem im Urchristentum," ThBl, 6 (1927), 293-302 (cf. Deutsche Theologie, 1, 1928, 13-26 for an account of this address and the ensuing discussion); Forschungen u. Fortschritte, 3 (1927), 277 f. F. J. A. Hort, The Christian Ecclesia (1897); E. Lohmeyer, "Von urchristlicher Gemeinschaft," ThBl, 4 (1925), 135 ff.; Vom Begriff d. religiösen Gemeinschaft (1925); H. E. Weber, "Die Kirche im Lichte d. Eschatologie," NKZ, 37 (1926), 299 ff.; W. Macholz, "Um die Kirche," ThBl, 7 (1928), 323 ff.; E. Peterson, Die Kirche (1929), G. Holstein, Die Grundlagen des evangelischen Kirchenrechts (1928); W. Michaelis, "Taüfer, Jesus, Urgemeinde," Nt.liche Forschungen, 2, 3 (1928); G. Gloege, "Reich Gottes u. Kirche im NT," Nt.liche Forschungen, 2, 4 (1929); E. v. Dobschütz, "Die Kirche im Urchristentum," ZNW, 28 (1929), 107 ff.; A. Juncker, "Neuere Forschungen z. urchristlichen Kirchenproblem," NKZ, 40 (1929), 126 ff., 180 ff.;

2. The Relation of the Two Passages; 3. Textual and Literary Criticism; 4. Material Criticism: a. Statistics; b. Eschatology; c. Church History; d. Psychology; 5. Hebrew and Aramaic Equivalents. F. The Old Testament and Judaism: 1. Greek Judaism; 2. The Hebrew Text. G. Etymology? H. The Post-Apostolic Fathers and Early Catholicism. I. Conclusion.

A. Introduction.

General dictionaries like Passow, Pape, K. Jacobitz-E. E. Seiler (1839-41), Benseler [15](1931), give the two senses 1. "assembly" and 2. "church"; they call the former secular and the latter biblical or ecclesiastical. Following the general scheme, Liddell-Scott refers also to the LXX and gives us the following senses: 1. "assembly duly summoned, less general than σύλλογος," 2. a. in the LXX "the Jewish congregation," b. in the NT "the Church as a body of Christians."

NT lexicons follow the same arrangement, but go on to make a distinction between the Church a. as the whole body of believers and b. as the individual congregation, e.g., the house church. This raises the question whether a. or b. comes first, i.e., in what sense we have a succession as well as co-existence of the two meanings. Various answers are given. Wilke-Grimm has as the *christianus sensus* the *coetus Christianorum* in the following order: ... *qui alicubi regionum, urbium, vicorum eiusmodi coetum constituunt atque in unam societatem coniuncti sunt,* and *universus Christianorum coetus per totam terram dispersus.* The Roman Catholic F. Zorell (Lexic. Graec. Novi Testamenti [2][1931]) has the opposite order, *coetus religiosus ... universitas eorum qui ad societatem religiosam a Christo institutam pertinent,* and *ecclesia aliqua particularis, i.e. alicuius regionis vel civitatis Christi fideles suo episcopo subditi, fere = dioecesis.* Pr.-Bauer accepts the former order: "The congregation as the gathering of Christians living in a given place, and universally the Church in which all those who are called are together"; he goes on to speak accordingly of the local and the universal ἐκκλησία. The dictionaries vary in their distinction between the congregation and the Church. In some passages it is hard to tell which is really meant according to our current use of the terms.

Die Kirche im NT in ihrer Bdtg. für die Gegenwart, ein Gespräch zwischen lutherischen, reformierten u. freikirchlichen Theologen, ed. by F. Siegmund-Schultze (1930); H. D. Wendland, "Der christliche Begriff d. Gemeinschaft," ThBl, 9 (1930), 129 ff.; *Die Eschatologie des Reiches Gottes bei Jesus* (1931); H. W. Beyer, "Die Kirche des Evangeliums u. d. Loslösung des Katholizismus von ihr," in the symposium *Der römische Katholizismus u. das Evangelium* (1931); A. Médebielle, *Dictionnaire de la Bible,* Suppl. II (1934), 487 ff. On A: the lexicons mentioned in the text. On B: K. Holl, "Der Kirchenbegriff des Pls. in seinem Verhältnis zu dem der Urgemeinde," SAB (1921), 920 ff. = *Ges. Aufsätze zur Kirchengeschichte,* II (1928), 44 ff.; W. Koester, "Die Idee der Kirche beim Apostel Pls.," *Nt.liche Abhandlungen,* 14, 1 (1928); H. Schlier, "Zum Begriff der Kirche im Eph.," ThBl, 6 (1927), 12 ff.; *Christus u. d. Kirche im Eph.* (1930). On C: C. G. Brandis, 'Εκκλησία in Pauly-W., V (1905), 2163 ff. On E: A. Dell, "Mt. 16:17-19," ZNW, 15 (1914), 1 ff.; "Zur Erklärung von Mt. 16:17-19," ZNW, 17 (1916), 27 ff.; R. Bultmann, "Die Frage nach dem messianischen Bewusstsein Jesu u. das Petrusbekenntnis," ZNW, 19 (1919/20), 165 ff.; J. Sickenberger, "Eine neue Deutung der Primatsstelle (Mt. 16:18)," *Theol. Revue,* 19 (1920), 1 ff.; D. Völter, "Mt. 16:18," *Nieuw Theol. Tijdschrift,* 10 (1921), 174 ff.; S. Euringer, "Der *locus classicus* des Primats ...," *Festg. f. A. Ehrhard* (1922), 141 ff.; H. Dieckmann, "Neuere Ansichten über die Echtheit der Primatsstelle," *Biblica,* 4 (1923), 189 ff.; T. Hermann, "Zu Mt. 16:18 u. 19," ThBl, 5 (1926), 203 ff.; G. Krüger, "Mt. 16:18-19 u. d. Primat des Petrus," ThBl, 6 (1927), 302 ff.; K. G. Goetz, "Petrus als Gründer u. Oberhaupt d. Kirche u. Schauer von Gesichten nach altchristlichen Berichten u. Legenden," UNT, 13 (1927), K. Guggisberg, "Mt. 16:18 u. 19 in der Kirchengeschichte," ZKG, 54 (1935), 276 ff. On H: E. Foerster, "Kirchenrecht vor dem ersten Clemensbrief," in *Harnack-Ehrung* (1921), 68 ff.; F. Gerke, "Die Stellung des ersten Clemensbriefes innerhalb der Entwicklung der alt-christlichen Gemeindeverfassung u. des Kirchenrechts," TU, 47, 1 (1931).

The distinctions mentioned are mostly those of denomination or school rather than of lexical or biblical and theological enquiry. Thus an Anglican may speak of the ἐκκλησία as the one Church, "the body of Christians." A Roman Catholic will begin with the universal *ecclesia* on the basis of Mt. 16:18, [1] and he will then go on to emphasise the subordination of the individual congregation to the bishop. The orthodox Protestant will refer first to the whole community, while the liberal Protestant will think of the local congregation, and some confusion may be caused by earlier territorial church government (*alicubi regionum*). The translations and commentaries reflect this. As always, Cr.-Kö. is a notable exception. This digs deeper, and from the standpoint of biblical theology reaches more valuable lexical conclusions. On the basis of the OT use of ἐκκλησία for the total community of Israel, it speaks of the "saved community of the NT" which finds expression first as the total community and then as the same community in "local circumscription" (a carefully selected phrase). Express reference is made to the fact that there is not always a hard and fast distinction between the local community and the universal community. In this respect the remark of Zorell is apposite : *Cum primo tempore 1 et 2 (sc. ecclesia universalis et ecclesia particularis) coinciderent, ad utrumvis licebit referre A.* (Ac.) 2:47; 5:11 *al.*

In translation and exposition of ἐκκλησία there is no point in the pedantic piling up of different expressions. This is primarily shown by the simple but cogent fact that the NT always uses the same word even where we usually distinguish between the "Church" and the "congregation." The further fact that the same word is used in secular Greek on the one side and the OT and NT on the other is an additional reason why we should try to find a single rendering. We must first ask whether we might not always use either "Church" or "congregation" in the NT. This concern for a single, unequivocal rendering leads us further and raises the decisive questions of church government in the NT : How is the so-called Church related to the so-called congregation ? What is the bearing of Mt. 16:18 ? Is the primitive community at Jerusalem Church or congregation ? What is its relation to other communities throughout the Roman Empire ? What does ἐκκλησία mean in Jewish Christianity (Peter), in Gentile Christianity (Paul), in primitive Catholicism ? We must also ask whether a single translation, Church or congregation, can be adopted for the whole range of biblical usage. This enquiry also leads us further and raises the question of the interrelation of the OT and the NT. As a Heb. term lies behind the LXX ἐκκλησία, [2] it is also necessary to find the Aram. equivalent which would be used by Jesus and the first congregation in Jerusalem. This is another question which plunges us at once into material problems. Finally, we must ask whether a single rendering cannot be found to cover all Gk. usage, secular as well as sacred. "Community" or "assembly" might be suggested. But this again leads us a step further and raises the question of the special term which the NT community had for itself. Why did it avoid a cultic term and choose instead a secular one ?

In both the secular and the biblical use of ἐκκλησία the dictionaries distinguish between the assembling of men and the men thus assembled. Hence a *prima facie* case

---

[1] There is a certain exception in L. Kösters' art. "Kirche," in the Roman Catholic Lex. ThK.², V, 968 ff., when he writes : "In the NT used at an early date by Hellenists in Jerusalem for the (assembled) local Christian congregation, then for the total Christian community."

[2] E. Peterson, *Die Kirche*, 19 : "It is not enough to derive the technical meaning of ἐκκλησία from the NT ; one must rather expound it in the light of the new situation which arose for the apostles." It is true that the LXX is not enough ; we have to go back to the Heb. But Peterson weakens his case by his lack of interest in either the Gk. or the Heb. OT. His thesis that the Church is essentially a Gentile Church (*op. cit.*, 1) is shattered by the fact that the same word is used in the LXX, in Jewish Christianity and in Gentile Christianity. Peterson fails to see that it is for him to show that the same expression does not mean the same thing in each case. Cf. also his "Die Kirche aus Juden u. Heiden" in *Bücherei d. Salzburger Hochschulwochen*, II (1933).

can be made out for a word like "assembly," which has both an abstract and a concrete sense.

B. The New Testament.

A survey of the use of ἐκκλησία in the NT shows that it does not occur in Mk., Lk., Jn., 2 Tm., Tt., 1 Pt., 2 Pt., 1 Jn., 2 Jn. or Jd. [3] No importance need be attached to its absence from 1 and 2 Jn., since it is found in 3 Jn. The same applies to 2 Tm. and Tt. in view of its use in 1 Tm. Jd. is so short that we may discount its absence here as a matter of statistical probability. More surprising is its non-occurrence in 1 and 2 Pt. 1 Pt. deals most emphatically with the nature and signifi-cance of the OT community and uses OT expressions, so that we may ask whether the matter is not present even though the term is missing. The same question arises in respect of the non-occurrence of the word in the two Synoptists Mk. and Lk., and also in Jn.

1. Acts.

Since the threefold occurrence in Mt. 16:18 and 18:17 is disputed, and raises problems of its own, it is best to begin with the frequent and varied usage in Ac. The very first passages (2:47; 5:11; 7:38; 8:1; 8:3; 9:31) are highly significant. We first read of the ἐκκλησία in Jerusalem, which is explicitly referred to as such in 8:1. At 7:38 the people of Israel, led through the desert by Moses, is called ἐκκλησία. This is not a literal quotation, though there is allusion to Dt. 9:10 (Mas. קָהָל, LXX ἐκκλησία). At 9:31 the word is used not merely for the Jerusalem community but for that of all Judaea, Galilee and Samaria. [4] Whereas the ἐκ-κλησία was first a single congregation, it now covers several congregations, so that we do better to translate "Church" rather than "congregation." It should be noted that the textual evidence supports the plural as well as the singular at 9:31, so that ἡ ἐκκλησία = αἱ ἐκκλησίαι. [5] The plural is better attested at 15:41 (διήρχετο δὲ τὴν Συρίαν καὶ Κιλικίαν ἐπιστηρίζων τὰς ἐκκλησίας), where only B D pc have the singular. It is unchallenged at 16:5 (αἱ μὲν οὖν ἐκκλησίαι ἐστε-ρεοῦντο τῇ πίστει). Elsewhere the singular is predominant, whether used for the community at Jerusalem at 11:22; 12:1 (D pc add ἐν τῇ ᾽Ιουδαίᾳ), 5; 15:4, 22, for that at Syrian Antioch, 13:1; 11:26; 14:27; 15:3, for that at Caesarea, 18:22, or for that at Ephesus, 20:17, 28. The expression κατ᾽ ἐκκλησίαν at 14:23 means "church-wise" and perhaps presupposes the plural (cf. Luther: "in the congregations," AV: "in every church"). A particularly pregnant saying is 20:28: ποιμαίνειν τὴν ἐκ-κλησίαν τοῦ θεοῦ (vl. κυρίου), ἣν περιεποιήσατο διὰ τοῦ αἵματος τοῦ ἰδίου. Nestle recalls the OT parallel in ψ 73:2, though here we have συναγωγή rather than ἐκκλησία: μνήσθητι τῆς συναγωγῆς σου (Ps. 74:2: עֲדָתְךָ) ἧς ἐκτήσω ἀπ᾽ ἀρχῆς.

The distinctiveness of the NT concept of the Church or community comes out plainly in these verses from Ac. It must be emphasised that the congregation in different places is simply called ἐκκλησία with no question of precedence or

---

[3] In Cr.-Kö., and all earlier editions of Cr., 1 and 2 Pt. are overlooked.

[4] Although the art. is not repeated at 9:31 — this is possible in the *koine,* though its use at 1 C. 1:2 and 2 C. 1:1 is better Gk. — we probably have an attributive rather than a pre-dicative (e.g., Luther) definition.

[5] While Bruder prints the plur. and lists the sing. readings, Nestle, who chooses the sing., unfortunately fails to note the important plur. readings.

correlation. The local connection is not the decisive point. This is shown by the further references to the ἐκκλησία in Judaea, Galilee and Samaria. It must also be emphasised that the singular and plural are used promiscuously. It is not that the ἐκκλησία divides up into ἐκκλησίαι. Nor does the sum of the ἐκκλησίαι produce the ἐκκλησία. The one ἐκκλησία is present in the places mentioned, nor is this affected by the mention of ἐκκλησίαι alongside one another. We must always understand and translate either "congregation" and "congregations" or "Church" and "churches." Of the two, the former is preferable, though we cannot entirely dispense with the latter because congregation is now commonly used to differentiate the local congregation from the community as a whole. An important point is that the same word is used for the Jewish Christian congregation at Jerusalem and the Gentile congregation at Antioch. We never find ornamental epithets. The only attribute, if we may call it such, is the genitive τοῦ θεοῦ. This genitive is of OT origin. Even when it does not occur, we should understand it, since otherwise the full significance of ἐκκλησία cannot be appreciated. The congregation or Church of God always stands in contrast and even in opposition to other forms of society. This is clear in the very first reference in Ac. 2:47, which makes prior mention of the λαός or κόσμος (D).

In three verses very close to one another (19:32, 39, 40) ἐκκλησία is used of a gathering of the people, i.e., a secular assembly. Here ἐκκλησία is a secular term in the full sense. If we follow the fundamentally necessary and reasonable principle that the same word should be rendered consistently in the same author, this excludes the use of "Church." On the other hand, it also excludes the English "congregation," and even the German Gemeinde (cf. "convention") is normally used ecclesiastically unless there is some such preceding adjective as "political." This leaves us with very little option but the simple rendering "assembly" or "gathering." [6] On this basis we can then differentiate between secular and ecclesiastical assemblies even though we use the same term. This word also enables us the better to understand the obvious conjunction of the singular and the plural. The plural implies assembly in the sense of assembling. The decisive point is not that someone or something assembles; it is who or what assembles. The explicit or implicit addition τοῦ θεοῦ or τοῦ κυρίου tells us who assembles, or who causes men to assemble. And when it is said of the ἐκκλησία: ἥν περιεποιήσατο ... (20:28), it is plain that God assembles His own. To the ἐκκλησία belong all those who are His. At 5:11 and 15:22 ὅλη is explicitly added; this corresponds to the idea of assembling or assembly. It does not add anything specifically new. It simply underlines that which is implied in ἐκκλησία τοῦ θεοῦ. In contrast to secular ἐκκλησίαι, this is not a quantitative term; it is a qualitative. A national assembly is just what it is and is meant to be, and the bigger the more so. For the assembly of God's people, however, size is of no account. It is in being when God gathers His own. How many there are depends first on the One who calls and gathers it, and only then on those who answer the call and gather together. "Where two or three are gathered together in my name, there am I in the midst of them" (Mt. 18:20).

---

[6] This does not mean that we should banish the words "Church" and "congregation" from our vocabulary. Apart from the impossibility of such an undertaking, there would be no sense in forfeiting the wealth of meaning proper to these terms. What is needed is that we should grasp the precise significance of the word ἐκκλησία, since at this point linguistic sobriety will help us to the true meaning and bearing from the standpoint of biblical theology.

2. Pauline Epistles, I.

In the epistles of Paul we find the same usage as in Ac. Jewish Christians and Gentile Christians do not differ in the way they look at this matter and speak of it. That individual congregations stand alongside one another may be seen from the use of the plural, especially 2 C. 11:8 : ἄλλας ἐκκλησίας, 12:13 : τὰς λοιπὰς ἐκκλησίας, and Phil. 4:15 : οὐδεμία ἐκκλησία. Yet this juxtaposition is not the decisive point. The decisive point is the integration of the "congregations" into the "congregation." To the suggested idea of an assembly corresponds ἡ ἐκκλησία ὅλη at R. 16:23; 1 C. 14:23 and πᾶσαι αἱ ἐκκλησίαι at R. 16:4, 16; 1 C. 7:17; 14:33; 2 C. 8:18; 11:28; once also πᾶσα ἐκκλησία at 1 C. 4:17, where the expression used (πανταχοῦ ἐν πάση ἐκκλησία) corresponds fairly exactly to ἐν ταῖς ἐκκλησίαις πάσαις. [7] Elsewhere, too, it is easy to pass from the singular to the plural and *vice versa*. This is proved by the cleavage in textual readings at 1 C. 14:35. Immediately before (14:33 f.) we have the plural. At Gl. 1:13 (cf. 1 C. 15:9 and Phil. 3:6) Paul tells us that he persecuted the ἐκκλησία, but then at 1:22 he describes this as the ἐκκλησίαι τῆς Ἰουδαίας. There is a similar relation of singular and plural at 1 C. 10:32 and 11:16, where the two seem to be fully interchangeable.

Often the place is mentioned, e.g., Cenchrea at R. 16:1; Corinth at 1 C. 1:2; 2 C. 1:1; Laodicea at Col. 4:16; Thessalonica (the Θεσσαλονικεῖς) 1 and 2 Th. 1:1. Sometimes we have the district, e.g., Asia at 1 C. 16:19; Galatia at 1 C. 16:1; Gl. 1:2; Macedonia at 2 C. 8:1; Judaea at Gl. 1:22 (→ *supra*); 1 Th. 2:14.

In many cases there is no article, but there is no discernible difference between ἡ ἐκκλησία and ἐκκλησία, cf. 1 C. 14:4 (the article occurs at 14:5, 12); 14:19, 28, 35; 1 Tm. 3:5, 15. Obviously ἐκκλησία is almost a proper name, so that the article may be left out. It can also be omitted in the plural, e.g., 2 C. 8:23, with the article just before (v. 19) and just after (v. 24). [8]

Even so small a fellowship as a house church can be called ἐκκλησία, R. 16:5. Such a fellowship may be numbered with larger communities, 1 C. 16:19. Col. 4:15 is important, since here the name is given to a house church even in the context of a profound discussion of the nature and significance of the ἐκκλησία; Phlm. 2.

We have pointed out that the sum of the individual congregations does not produce the total community or the Church. Each community, however small, represents the total community, the Church. This is supported by 1 C. 1:2 : τῇ ἐκκλησία ... τῇ οὔση ἐν Κορίνθῳ, and also by 2 C. 1:1. The true rendering here is not "the Corinthian congregation," which would stand side by side with the Roman etc., but "the congregation, church, assembly, as it is in Corinth." If anyone is despised in such a gathering (1 C. 6:4), if people come together in it (1 C. 11:18; cf. 14:23 and Ac. 14:27), if women are to keep silent in it (1 C. 14:34), if it is not to be burdened (1 Tm. 5:16), these things apply to the Church as a whole and not merely to the local congregation.

When Paul gives an attributive or predicative definition of ἐκκλησία, he uses primarily the genitive τοῦ θεοῦ, which is added both to the singular (1 C. 1:2;

---

[7] As in other cases, Paul loves such hyperbole, but he has good ground for it.

[8] Bl.-Debr.[6] § 254 points out that the art. is omitted with personal designations such as θεός, κύριος, νεκροί, ἔθνη. It is perhaps the same with ἐκκλησία.

10:32; 11:22; 15:9; Gl. 1:13; 1 Tm. 3:5, 15) and to the plural (1 C. 11:16; 1 Th. 2:14; 2 Th. 1:4). That it is used with both is more important than might appear. We normally distinguish between the total Church and the individual congregation. We are thus accustomed to speaking of the Church of God, but not of the congregations of God. The fact that such distinction is impossible for Paul is an indication that he does not make the differentiation which later came into use. On the other hand, the words τοῦ θεοῦ are implied even when they are not specifically added, just as βασιλεία in the NT always means the βασιλεία τοῦ θεοῦ unless some earthly kingdom is expressly mentioned (→ I, 582 f.). It is worth noting that in some MSS the words have been appropriately added, cf. 1 C. 14:4; Phil. 3:6 (in both cases G vg al). The One who is at work in and with the ἐκκλησία is always God, cf. 1 C. 12:28: ἔθετο ὁ θεὸς ἐν τῇ ἐκκλησίᾳ πρῶτον ἀποστόλους κτλ.

Since God acts ἐν Χριστῷ, Christ is also mentioned in some places. The richest and all-comprehensive example is 1 Th. 2:14 : τῶν ἐκκλησιῶν τοῦ θεοῦ τῶν οὐσῶν ἐν τῇ Ἰουδαίᾳ ἐν Χριστῷ Ἰησοῦ. Gl. 1:22 simply has ἐν Χριστῷ (without τοῦ θεοῦ); R. 16:16 has only τοῦ Χριστοῦ, the genitive having the same sense as the formula ἐν Χριστῷ.[9] Certainly we cannot render τοῦ Χριστοῦ by the colourless adjective "Christian." Paul is not speaking merely of a Christian Church or congregation beside which there may be others. He is referring to the assembly of God in Christ. We have only one example of the addition τῶν ἁγίων, and this is in the plural (1 C. 14:33). But while this attribute is found only once, it is quite a natural one, since Paul explicitly equates the ἐκκλησία and the ἡγιασμένοι ἐν Χριστῷ Ἰησοῦ at 1 C. 1:2.[10]

Before we turn to the passages in Col. and Eph., whose greater richness and fulness have led some to deny their Pauline authorship, we must first consider the relation of the statements adduced to the data in Ac. In view of the debate and conflict between Paul and the primitive community in Jerusalem, the affinity which our review of what is said about the ἐκκλησία has demonstrated is statistically and lexically surprising. The fact that Paul uses τοῦ θεοῦ fairly frequently brings him particularly close to the single instance in Ac. at 20:28; this quotation from ψ 73:2 refers to what is called the assembly of God in the OT, and therefore to something whose importance is specially emphasised by Paul. Paul goes beyond Ac., however, by specifically mentioning Jesus Christ along with the ἐκκλησία, as Ac. does not do explicitly.[11] But this is not a material difference ; it is only a formal difference of expression. Materially, Paul develops in his conception of the Church that which he shares in common with the early disciples, and his practical attitude is in keeping with this. The new thing about the ἐκκλησία τοῦ θεοῦ ἐν Χριστῷ Ἰησοῦ, i.e., the fulfilment of the OT prophecy of the new covenant, is given with the fact that a specific number of selected disciples of Jesus experienced the resurrection of Jesus Christ from the dead and received special authorisation

---

[9] A. Deissmann, *Paulus*² (1925), 126 f. has rightly pointed out that the ἐν formula and the gen. are equivalent in many other passages. He has suggested the term *genetivus communionis* or *mysticus,* but this is open to criticism and it is in any case superfluous.

[10] Cf. on this point R. Asting, "Die Heiligkeit im Urchr.," FRL, NF, 29 (1930), 134, 147, 204, 269; cf. also → I, 107.

[11] It may be noted in passing that the very terseness of the ἐκκλησία sayings in Ac. is an argument for their early dating. The intrinsic possibility that a later writer is reproducing very old sources without alteration is unlikely in this case, since such a writer would inevitably have introduced the richer statements of his own age concerning the Church.

thereby. The divine assembly of the new covenant which was first constituted by
the resurrection of Jesus Christ did not derive its claim or commission from the
enthusiasm of pneumatics and charismatics. It derived it solely from a specific
number of specific appearances of the risen Lord. [12] This may be seen not only in
Ac., which is contested at many points, but also in the account of Paul himself
in 1 Cor. 15:3 ff., where the apostle to the Gentiles attaches supreme value to the
fact that the appearance of Christ to him on the Damascus road belongs to the
same series as the resurrection appearances to the original disciples. Paul was a
pneumatic and a charismatic. He had visions, auditions, raptures and transports
(cf. 2 C. 12:1 ff.). But he did not find in these the source of his apostolate as
service of the divine assembly. He found it solely and simply in the Damascus
vision as a resurrection appearance which he shared with the original disciples.

From this standpoint Paul had the same view of the Church as the primitive
community at Jerusalem. [13] It is in keeping that he recognised the special authority
and privileges of this community and its leaders. In this regard we cannot overemphasise the importance of his collection for the poor saints at Jerusalem. The
accent is to be placed on the fact, not that they are *poor saints* at Jerusalem, but
that they are poor saints at *Jerusalem*. Paul saw here an obligation. He did not act
merely out of *caritas*, though this is undeniable. Nor are we to speak merely of
his diplomacy or tact. The point is that he is conscious of an obligation to those
at Jerusalem who represented the first assembly of God in Christ. That this was
no mere personal matter is shown by the fact that the same Paul did not hesitate
to speak ironically of the "pillars" in Jerusalem and that he finally accused Peter
publicly of hypocrisy when he was guilty of double dealing in relation to Gentile
Christians (Gl. 2). Though Peter was entangled in sin, he was still raised up and
marked off from the multitude in Paul's eyes. What matters is not the individual as
such; it is the fellowship as God's assembly in Christ. This assembly is not the
object of unbridled will and speculation. It is posited by God and beyond the
control of us men. Psychological value-judgments are irrelevant in the case of a
man who was a greater enthusiast and pneumatic than all those who try to label
him thus, and who finally censure him because he did not sufficiently break free
from the view of the Church found in the primitive community. [14]

Paul himself placed a preliminary sign before all his statements concerning the
Church. Or, more accurately, there was already placed before them a sign which
he could not ignore or expunge. It was Jerusalem Christians who were engaged
in destroying this sign with their over-emphasis on authoritative persons (the
original disciples) and a holy place (Jerusalem), in short, with their tendency to
fall victim to a rank theocratic perversion against which all the prophets, from the
great writing prophets to John the Baptist and Jesus Himself, had uttered warnings,
never wearying of pointing to the call of God to His people. Paul is in this tradition. He speaks more purely than the first disciples of the assembly of God in
its promise and fulfilment. He never thinks — he cannot think — of founding a
new view of the Church as compared with that of Jerusalem. He is not the in-
novator. It is the first disciples who, while they cannot be regarded as innovators,

---

[12] Following A. Schlatter, K. Holl among modern writers has specially emphasised this
point in his uncommonly valuable treatment of Paul's view of the Church (→ Bibl.).

[13] Failure to see this seems to me to be the decisive fault in Holl's conclusions.

[14] Cf. the criticism of Paul by H. Weinel, RGG[1], III, 1130.

have yet allowed innovations to become predominant. Like the first and true disciples, who must be particularly on guard at this point, Paul believes that the assembly of God stands or falls with its sole foundation and continuance in the Messiah Jesus, with its recognition of Christ alone as Lord, and not of men in theocratic pretension, even though these men be specially endowed with the gift of revelation. The fact that Paul can sometimes speak of the ἐκκλησία(ι) (τοῦ θεοῦ) as gathering(s) ἐν Χριστῷ Ἰησοῦ or Χριστοῦ is perhaps aimed against the tendency of the first disciples to concentrate on persons or places. The words ἡ δὲ πέτρα ἦν ὁ Χριστός at 1 C. 10:4 may well contain a similar polemic. [15]

In all this, of course, Paul does not give us a true doctrine of the ἐκκλησία any more than Ac. His reference is to an assembly of men as the assembly of God in Christ. To understand how God deals with men in Christ is to understand the implicit nature and significance of the assembly of God even though the Church is not explicitly furnished with attributes and predicates. The only passage where we seem to have something more is 1 Tm. 3:15, where the ἐκκλησία is described as the → οἶκος θεοῦ, and the thought of its edification, of the → οἰκοδομὴ τῆς ἐκκλησίας (1 C. 14:4 f., 12) seems to be present. But → οἶκος is an even more colourless word than ἐκκλησία. And again everything depends on the emphasis and understanding of the addition τοῦ θεοῦ.

3. Pauline Epistles, II : Colossians and Ephesians. [1]

Explicit statements concerning the ἐκκλησία are to be found in Colossians and especially Ephesians. A specific doctrine of the Church is to be found for the first time in these epistles. At Col. 1:24 the ἐκκλησία is the σῶμα Χριστοῦ; at 1:18 Christ is the κεφαλή of this σῶμα. Similar statements are to be found in Eph. 1:22 and 5:23. It is worth noting that in 3:21 and 5:32 Christ and the ἐκκλησία are mentioned in juxtaposition. The reference is to co-ordination and subordination (this is why the καί is not found in many MSS): 5:24 : ἡ ἐκκλησία ὑποτάσσεται τῷ Χριστῷ; 5:25 : Χριστὸς ἠγάπησεν τὴν ἐκκλησίαν; 5:29 : Χριστὸς τὴν ἐκκλησίαν (ἐκτρέφει καὶ θάλπει). At 5:27 the ἐκκλησία is called ἁγία καὶ ἄμωμος. This direct designation as ἁγία is not found elsewhere in Paul, though it is common in later writings of the primitive period. Statements of this kind are almost too full and rich. Thus at 3:10 we read : ἵνα γνωρισθῇ ... διὰ τῆς ἐκκλησίας ἡ πολυποίκιλος σοφία τοῦ θεοῦ. Even strict examination does not enable us to get a clear grasp of these statements in Eph. The figurative language does not seem to be logical. Christ is the ἐκκλησία itself, for this is the σῶμα Χριστοῦ. Yet Christ is also above the Church as its κεφαλή. Obviously the statements are closely interwoven. Christology and ecclesiology are reciprocally related. If there is obscurity, it is not merely because we cannot understand correctly sayings which are intrinsically clear, but because these things are obscure in the thinking of the apostle, because human statements are here circling around a mystery (3:4 f.). This does not imply a flight to the sphere of the numinous.

---

[15] Cf. H. Lietzmann's foot-note in K. Holl Ges. Aufsätze, II, 63 : "Is there perhaps a certain edge in the saying ἡ δὲ πέτρα ἦν ὁ Χριστός at 1 C. 10:4 ? For him (sc. Paul) it is certainly obvious that Christ is the πέτρα." Cf. also 1 C. 3:11. We shall have to return to both passages when we discuss Mt. 16:18.

[16] On what follows cf. N. Glubokowsky, W. F. Howard, K. L. Schmidt : "Christus u. die Kirche (Eph. 5:25-32)," ThBl, 9 (1930), 327 ff. (reports of the Conference between Eastern and Western Theologians at Berne, 1930).

Rather, that which is always a mystery to human eyes is a revelation from God. What concerns Christ and the ἐκκλησία is conceived, created and sustained by God. It all culminates in the concluding hymn in 5:25-32. The familiar house-table means simply that the relation between husband and wife should be based on that between Christ and the ἐκκλησία, and that the latter relation is clarified by that between husband and wife.

The images used derive from the mythological language of the age. H. Schlier has maintained [17] "that in the statements of Ephesians concerning Christ and the Church a consistent world of ideas finds expression, and that the author of Ephesians speaks the language of specific Gnostic circles. The Redeemer who ascends to heaven overcomes the heavenly powers on His way (Eph. 4:8 ff.) and breaks through the wall which divides the world from the divine kingdom (2:14 ff.). He thereby returns to Himself as the higher *anthropos* (4:13 ff.) who lives independently in the heavenly kingdoms. Yet He is also the → κεφαλή of the → σῶμα. In this He raises up His μέλη, creates the 'new man' (2:15) and builds up His body to the heavenly building of His ἐκκλησία (2:19 ff.; 4:12 ff., 16) in which the work of God is manifest (3:10 f.). The *Soter* loves and cherishes His Church; He cleanses and saves it. It is His γυνή and He is its ἀνήρ. They are bound to one another in obedience and love (5:22-32)." These detailed sequences of thought (1. the ascension of the Redeemer; 2. the heavenly wall; 3. the heavenly *anthropos*; 4. the Church as the body of Christ; 5. the body of Christ as the heavenly building; 6. the heavenly marriage) obviously correspond only in a limited way to generally accepted Christian affirmations. The constantly emphasised view that the Church is the body of Christ can hardly be explained by transferring the relationships of the natural body to Christ and the Church. The body of which Eph. speaks is strictly only a torso. But all growth is to the head, and conversely this growth is from the head. Christ is the κεφαλή, and yet He is also the whole σῶμα, i.e., the body including the head. This complicated notion can hardly have been developed from the statements of Paul in R. 12:4 ff. and 1 C. 12:12 ff. Above all, the equation σῶμα = σάρξ = γυνή = ἐκκλησία cannot be deduced from Pauline usage elsewhere. 1 C. 12 speaks of the mutual relations of Christians; Eph. describes Christians as the body of Christ. This world of ideas is found fairly plainly in Valentinian Gnosticism, in the Odes of Solomon etc. [18]: the Redeemer leads up the

---

[17] → Bibl. In Mandaean liturgies (M. Lidzbarski, Mand. Liturg. [1920]) we read of a heavenly building which is the great place of light and which is also the ἄνθρωπος, the ἀνὴρ τέλειος, this ἄνθρωπος being interchangeable with his σῶμα.

[18] Cf. the statement of Theodotus, the pupil of Valentinian, in Cl. Al. Exc. Theod., 58, 1: ὁ μέγας ἀγωνιστὴς Ἰησοῦς ἐν ἑαυτῷ δυνάμει τὴν ἐκκλησίαν ἀναλαβών, τὸ ἐκλεκτὸν καὶ τὸ κλητόν ... ἀνέσωσεν καὶ ἀνήνεγκεν ἅπερ ἀνέλαβεν. On the idea that believers constitute the body of the (heavenly) *anthropos,* cf. O. Sol. 17:14 ff.: "They received my blessing and lived; they gathered around me and were redeemed. For they became my members and I their Head. Praise be to Thee, our Head, Lord Christ." Further examples from Christian apocryphal, Gnostic and Mandaean writings may be found in Schlier. It is impossible to deny these connections, even though the details are debatable. Yet it would be a mistake to think that this way of looking at the matter involves a surrender of Paul to Gnostic mythology. Schlier might have given stronger emphasis to the fact that in Eph., as elsewhere in the NT, the christological language is polemical, and that the unique dignity of Jesus Christ is thereby safeguarded, since He remains the logical subject no matter what new predicates are used. This is equally true when the predicates κύριος, σωτήρ and especially λόγος are applied to Him. The point is, not that Christ is the *Logos,* but that *Christ* is the Logos, → n. 19 and n. 20.

redeemed on high as His σῶμα. Christ is the ἄνθρωπος of which believers are the σῶμα and He Himself the κεφαλή. The ἐκκλησία as the σῶμα of the ἄνθρωπος exists only through Him and in Him. On the one side, the Church is identical with the σῶμα of the ἄνθρωπος, i.e., with the ἄνθρωπος Himself ; on the other, this ἄνθρωπος is interchangeable with His feminine counterpart, which is usually called σοφία. It is in terms of this figure of marriage that we are to interpret the distinctive statements in 5:25-32, which culminate in the affirmation : Χριστὸς ἐκτρέφει καὶ θάλπει τὴν ἐκκλησίαν. One has the impression that in such a complicated and sweeping view there are present speculations in which confession of God and His assembly in Christ is subjected to an interpretative pattern. But this impression, however strong, must be suppressed. The whole of the way in which Paul speaks of σοφία shows that what we have here are neither freely ranging speculations nor esoteric insights. In Eph. the wisdom and knowledge of God are not theoretical. They are practical. They are a knowledge of the "heart" (1:18) attained in obedience towards God, i.e., in faith. [19]

To see the source of the world of ideas of Eph. is not yet to answer the question of its nature and purpose. We may suggest two things which are closely related : a. that the Gnostic terminology and ideology used in Eph. are adapted to express the strict interrelationship between Christ and the Church, and are thus made to serve a christological ecclesiology ; and b. that the Gnostic background is calculated to safeguard a necessary exalted Christology in a difficult situation in the Church (the assault of false teaching, the conflict between Jewish and Gentile Christians), and is thus set in the service of a lofty Christology. In this respect Eph. is wholly Pauline in substance, whether written by Paul himself or one of his disciples. When one considers the external and internal difficulties which confronted an early Christian apostle in his attempt to clarify the true nature and significance of the assembly of God in Christ, one can hardly share the general critical certainty that the apostle himself could not have been the author of (Col. and) Eph. At any rate, Paul himself had to struggle both against Jewish Christian or Judaistic deflation on the one side and also against a certain Gentile Christian or even Gnostic exaggeration on the other. Hence he had to use strong and lofty terms, as in Eph. This outward struggle was a struggle within the Christian community, which was always in danger of corrupting what the ἐκκλησία is and should be. In face of the Jewish desire for privilege, which threatened to give a decisive central position to personalities and to a place among the early Christians, it was both possible and necessary to speak of the ἐκκλησία which is ἄνωθεν. In face of strange Gnostic speculations about the marriage of Christ as the masculine principle with σοφία as the feminine, it was both possible and necessary to speak of the ἐκκλησία which alone represents the feminine aspect. The Paul who speaks to us in undoubtedly genuine epistles is in so sense remote from these disputes. He stands at the very heart of them. In respect of what we have just said about the feminine principle, we need only think of 2 C. 11:2, where Paul tells us that his purpose for

---

[19] This may serve to show that H. Schlier was wrong in supposing that in my work *Die Kirche des Urchristentums*, 313, 315 I failed to see "that the mythology of Eph. is not used for its own sake, i.e., in the service of speculation." In any case, I wholly agree with Schlier when he says that the mythology of Eph. "is the conceptual possibility in which the author and his hearers may naturally express themselves." On p. 315 of my book I was simply speaking of the "limits of speculation concerning the Church."

Christians is ἑνὶ ἀνδρὶ παρθένον ἁγνὴν παραστῆσαι τῷ Χριστῷ. And if in R. 12:4 ff. and 1 C. 12:12 ff., as we have said, Christians as the σῶμα stand in relation to one another, not to Christ, this is only a formal and not a material antithesis — one need only think of the co-existence and co-inherence of love for God and love for neighbour. The difficulty of ascribing to Paul what is said about the Church in Col. and Eph. is one of form rather than matter. While we can understand quite well that in a specific polemical situation Paul would develop the kind of teaching about the Church which is found in Col. and Eph., it is difficult to assume that he would have made such uncritical use of the language of Gnostic mythology. [20] Yet clear expression is certainly given to the fact that the ἐκκλησία as the σῶμα Χριστοῦ is no mere human fellowship. In terms of a sociologically defined concept of society one can never grasp the nature or meaning of the assembly of God in Christ. The decisive point is fellowship with Christ. Epigrammatically, a single individual could be — and would have to be — the ἐκκλησία if he has fellowship with Christ. Only on this basis do we have a fellowship of men with one another as brothers. [21] In face of all sociological attempts to understand the question of the Church, it must be considered that in Paul, in his disciples and then in the Fourth Evangelist ecclesiology is simply Christology and *vice versa*. Paul speaks emphatically of the fact that among Christians, i.e., in the ἐκκλησία as the σῶμα Χριστοῦ, all human distinctions are set aside : Col. 3:11 = Gl. 3:28. The very next verse in Gl. says : "And if ye be Christ's, then are ye Abraham's seed, and heirs according to the promise" (v. 29). If we understand Paul correctly, we must speak of the body of Christ with caution and restraint. If we follow Paul, we must not speak too loudly or too fulsomely of the organism which the body of Christ has to represent. The figurative language must not be exaggerated and misunderstood as if we had here a higher growth in the sense of a natural growth. To be God's organ is to hearken to God's call. There can be no unrestrained Christology and ecclesiology in the sense of a Christ or Church mysticism, since the God who speaks in Christ is the God of the old covenant who has established the new covenant, and the NT assembly of God in Christ is none other than the fulfilled OT assembly of God. One and the same God has spoken and speaks to Israel with the word of promise and to Christians with the word of the fulfilment of this promise. As the God of the OT remains for all the so-called Christ mysticism, so the OT community of God remains for all the so-called Christ cult. ἁγιότης is ascribed to the ἐκκλησία, but not as a quality. In other words, a true conception of the Church, the community, the assembly of God in Christ, stands or falls with a true conception of justification. This is the

---

[20] This is the crux of the much agitated question of authenticity, and it involves also the peculiar relationship between Col. and Eph. There are traditionalist theologians who regard Eph. as genuinely Pauline because they credit the apostle with development even to the length of Gnostic ways of thought. In this respect a case for authenticity like that of T. Schmidt, *Der Leib Christi* (1919), 255 can contain the following argument : "In fact, nowhere but here does Paul rise to the height of so comprehensive a view of the world and of history, embracing heaven and earth, past, present and future." On the other hand, there are critical theologians who, because Gnostic terms are used but not Gnostic ways of thought, deny the Pauline authorship and yet maintain the substantially Pauline character of Eph.

[21] This is well brought out in the lecture by the Old Catholic theologian E. Gaugler, "Die Kirche, ihr Wesen und ihre Bestimmung," *Internat. Kirchl. Zschr.*, 17 (1927), 136 ff., esp. 146.

point at issue, as it is in the whole conflict of Paul, whether against Judaisers or Gnostics.

4. The few passages concerning the ἐκκλησία in the rest of the NT add nothing new to what has been said. In Rev. we have statements concerning the ἐκκλησία only in the framework. The plural occurs 13 times, and once each we read of the ἐκκλησία of Ephesus, Smyrna, Pergamon, Thyatira, Sardis, Philadelphia and Laodicea. 3 Jn. mentions the ἐκκλησία 3 times, twice with and once without the article, though there is no discernible distinction. Jm. 5:14 speaks of the πρεσβύτεροι τῆς ἐκκλησίας. The reference is not to a single congregation, but to the community as a whole, since this is a catholic epistle. Hb. 2:12 says: ἐν μέσῳ ἐκκλησίας ὑμνήσω σε, a literal quotation from ψ 21:22 ═ Ps. 22:22: בְּתוֹךְ קָהָל אֲהַלְלֶךָּ. At Hb. 12:23 there is reference to the ἐκκλησία πρωτοτόκων ἀπογεγραμμένων ἐν οὐρανοῖς. This is the only verse in which the term ἐκκλησία occurs with reference to the heavenly Jerusalem. It is doubtful, however, whether the word is here used technically as elsewhere in the NT. It is accompanied by πανήγυρις, so that we are to think of a festal gathering which takes place in heaven as there are also festal gatherings on earth. [22]

C. The Greek World.

That ἐκκλησία is also used in secular Gk., and denotes a popular assembly, is clear from the NT itself, Ac. 19:32, 39 f. The biblical sense in the OT and NT is furnished only by the addition τοῦ θεοῦ, and the specific NT sense by the further addition ἐν Χριστῷ ᾿Ιησοῦ, irrespective of whether the addition is present in a given case, or present in whole or in part. What is the significance of the fact that later Gk. Judaism and early Gk. Christianity adopted this particular term? May it be that this is already a cultic expression in secular Greek?

From the time of Thuc., Plat. and Xenoph., and especially in inscriptions, ἐκκλησία is the assembly of the δῆμος in Athens and in most Greek πόλεις. The etymology is both simple and significant. The citizens are the ἔκκλητοι, i.e., those who are summoned and called together by the herald. [23] This teaches us something concerning the biblical and Christian usage, namely, that God in Christ calls men out of the world. [24]

It is open to question whether or how a cultic society or union ever called itself an ἐκκλησία, thus forcing us to speak of a cultic term. [25] There is good reason to raise this question, since an affirmative answer would enable us to see why, in the light of

---

[22] Wnd. Hb., *ad loc.* rightly avoids the term *Gemeinde* and translates *Festschar und Versammlung* ("festal host and assembly").

[23] W. Koester (→ Bibl.) follows others in pointing to the form ἐκλησία (ἐκ-λαός), which is not listed even in more recent dictionaries, but this is so rare that no deductions can be made from it.

[24] Cf. Deissmann LO, 90.

[25] An affirmative view is taken by Joh. W. 1 K., XVII, who follows W. Liebenam, *Zur Geschichte u. Organisation des römischen Vereinslebens* (1890); E. Ziebarth, *Das griech. Vereinswesen* (*Preisschr., gekrönt u. hsgg. v. d. Fürstl. Jablonowskischen Gesellschaft zu Leipzig,* 1896), though he does not give any instances of the use of ἐκκλησία; F. Poland, *Geschichte des griech. Vereinswesens* (*ibid.,* 1909), 332. More recent dictionaries such as Pr.-Bauer and Moult.-Mill do not list this usage, and Ltzm. K., 4 says expressly that the word ἐκκλησία "does not occur as a term for cultic unions, and the three apparent exceptions (Poland, 332) prove this rule, since ἐκκλησία is here used, not for the union, but after the analogy of ordinary use for its 'business meeting.'"

social and cultic usage, a Christian congregation regarded itself as an ἐκκλησία and thereby as a cultic union. In this respect we are to think particularly of the relations at Corinth as depicted by Paul in 1 C. But apart from the fact that there is insufficient evidence to argue a cultic use of ἐκκλησία in the Greek world, Paul would have rejected this term and usage as an abuse. What mattered for him was simply and solely the OT and NT assembly of God in Christ. Some Gentile Christian circles, which were not so well, or not at all, acquainted with the OT context, might have understood the term in the light of its immediate derivation and possible recollections of Greek fellowships. It is quite possible, and wholly natural, that many matters of organisation in Christian congregations should have been regulated according to the pattern of contemporary societies. 26

Constitutive for the Christian ἐκκλησία within Greek usage is the line from the Septuagint to the NT. Only on this line does the word take on its particular significance. Once the correspondence between the OT and the NT ἐκκλησία had become clear to those who derived from Judaism and yet who also transcended it, this connection provided direction and force. The ἐκκλησία of the ancient δῆμος is a formal parallel from the secular world, but it corresponds only in the sense of an analogy, no more and no less, 27 just as κύριος Καῖσαρ is a (polemical) parallel to κύριος Χριστός, not its prototype. This is not altered by the fact that at least in the classical period the ἐκκλησία in the sense of a popular assembly is not without a religious undertone and is one of the main institutions of the divinely given *polis* and its order. We can see this from the prayers which were usually offered by the → κήρυξ before the ἐκκλησία and then by each individual speaker before his address in the assembly. 28 It is quite a different matter, however, that at a later date, already in the early Church, transition, continuation and imitation should be deduced from these similarities. This leads us to the sphere of Roman and Byzantine Church history.

---

26 Cf. G. Heinrici, "Zum genossenschaftlichen Charakter der paulinischen Christengemeinden," ThStKr, 54 (1881), 505 ff. It has rightly been argued against Heinrici that the reference here is to things which are common to the formation of all societies and which are not peculiar to societies of this particular age. For details cf. Joh. W. 1 K., XX ff.

27 A different view is taken by E. Peterson (→ Bibl.), 19, n. 19: "That the λαός of the Christian ἐκκλησία is a successor of the ancient δῆμος can be shown in various ways. I do not think merely of the acclamations which passed over from the δῆμος to the λαός. I would also draw attention to the link discovered by J. Partsch, namely, that manumission in the Christian ἐκκλησία in the form of proclamation may be traced to a practice of the secular ἐκκλησία (J. Partsch, "Mitteilungen aus der Freiburger Papyrussammlung, 2: Juristische Texte d. röm. Zeit," SAH VII, 10 [1916], 44 f.)." Now it may be rightly recognised that in a single instance there has been such transmission. But an isolated case is not enough to prove Peterson's thesis that the Christian ἐκκλησία is heir to the Gentile. Peterson himself writes rather more cautiously in the text, which should be quoted with the note (14 f.): "The secular ἐκκλησία of antiquity is acknowledged to be an institution of the πόλις. It is the assembly of full citizens of a πόλις meeting for the execution of legal acts. Analogously one might call the Christian ἐκκλησία the assembly of full citizens of the heavenly city meeting for the execution of certain cultic acts ... In the public legal character of Christian worship is reflected the fact that the Church is much nearer to political constructs like the kingdom and πόλις than to voluntary unions and societies."

28 Cf. G. Busolt-H. Swoboda, Griech. Staatskunde³ (Handbuch der Altertumswissenschaft, IV, 1, 1), I (1920), 518 f.; II (1926), 996. Examples of prayers in the Athenian ἐκκλησία may be found in Aristoph. Eq., 763 ff.; Demosth. Or., 18, 1; Plut. Pericl., 8 (I, 156c); Praec. Ger. Reip., 8 (II, 803 f.) [Kleinknecht].

That the Gk. word ἐκκλησία had direction and force in the sense described is due to the fact that it held the field when the Christian community had to be described by a technical term. The Latins hardly felt the need to translate ἐκκλησία into Latin, even if they had been able to do so. Tertullian, who exercised so great an influence on ecclesiastical Latin, uses the word *curia* in his Apologeticum (39), and this is an accurate rendering of ἐκκλησία, but it did not become technical.[29] The same is true of Augustine's *civitas dei*.[30] Other translations which occurred here and there demand consideration, e.g., *contio* or *comitia*.[31] *Convocatio* would also have been a literal rendering. But none of these words ever became a technical term for the Church. And the various Romance peoples followed the Romans in this regard. It is perhaps less striking that modern Greeks have kept ἐκκλησία. The English "Church," like the German *Kirche*, almost certainly comes from the adj. κυριακός, not from ἐκκλησία, but a kind of popular etymology constantly connects it with the latter. Why is this? Why has the Gk. loan word persisted? We may refer to the fact that even in non-Christian usage there was a dominant sense that Latin had no word exactly corresponding to ἐκκλησία.[32] But intrinsically interesting and attractive analogies are not the decisive point. The decisive thing is the genealogical derivation of ἐκκλησία from the Gk. Bible. No new term was used for the Church, just as κύριος was no new term for God. These considerations do not make it mathematically certain that the Gk. Bible is alone decisive in respect of ἐκκλησία or ecclesia. But there is a high degree of probability that when the Latins adopted the Greek term they felt the need not merely for a term which Greek Christians had taken from their own vocabulary but for one which had a sacred history in the sacred Book.

Thus, although ἐκκλησία is from the very first a secular and worldly expression, it expresses the supreme claim of the Christian community in face of the world. Intrinsically a Christian cultic society — and many Gentile Christians must have regarded themselves as such, like many modern students of the history of religion — might well have selected various other words to describe themselves. The world of societies and mystery groups offered a wealth of such terms.

Pagan writers did in fact use such titles for the Christian community. Lucian regards the Christians as a θίασος when he calls their leaders θιασάρχης.[33] Celsus calls the disciples of Christ θιασῶται.[34] More striking is the fact that Eusebius twice calls

---

[29] Cf. A. v. Harnack, *Die Mission und Ausbreitung des Christentums in den ersten drei Jahrhunderten*, I⁴ (1924), 420, n. 1.

[30] Kattenbusch, I, 144, n. 1 claims that this is "the first attempt at a translation which gives the material sense." On the other hand, Kleinknecht argues that "*civitas dei* in Augustine reproduces the (Platonically influenced) political concept πολιτεία in its ancient wealth of meaning, but certainly not ἐκκλησία." The relevant question of the use of terms with a political or legal or cultic and sacral emphasis which are taken from secular Gk. or used analogously will be dealt with in connection with the word group → πόλις, πολίτευμα, πολιτεύομαι. Cf. also → παρεπίδημος, II, 64 f. and → πάροικος, παροικία.

[31] Cf. Deissmann LO, 90.

[32] Deissmann LO, 90 f. recalls that the younger Pliny already uses the Latinised *ecclesia* (Letter to Trajan, Ep., X, 110 [111]: *bule* [sc. βουλῇ] *et ecclesia consentiente*). It is also found on a bilingual inscription from Ephesus (103/104 A.D.) in which the Gk. word ἐκκλησία is simply transcribed.

[33] Luc. Pergr. Mort., 11: τὴν θαυμαστὴν σοφίαν τῶν Χριστιανῶν ἐξέμαθε ... προφήτης καὶ θιασάρχης καὶ συναγωγεύς ...

[34] Orig. Cels., III, 23: ὁ δὲ ἡμέτερος Ἰησοῦς ὀφθεὶς τοῖς ἰδίοις θιασώταις — χρήσομαι γὰρ τῷ παρὰ Κέλσῳ ὀνόματι — ὤφθη μὲν κατ' ἀλήθειαν. Origen was evidently struck by the fact that Celsus should use the term. There is a corresponding example in the Latin church when in Minucius Felix (Octavius, 8 f., MPL, 3) a Gentile speaks of the

Christians θιασῶται and once even uses the pagan religious term θίασος for the Church. [35] This is all the known material to this effect. Hence we must be radically on guard against the exaggeration of regarding Christianity as a cultic society. [36] In order to form a just appreciation of the extent to which θίασος and ἐκκλησία are parallel, we must remember how extremely widespread was the use of θίασος and related terms (ἔρανος, κοινόν, σύνοδος, σύλλογος etc.) for the various societies of antiquity. None of these titles ever came to be adopted by Christians. Individual names, derived from the names of gods or historical figures, were also in common use. [37] But no attempt was made to form a title from the name Jesus, and it was only gradually that the term Χριστιανοί, which is very rare in the NT (only Ac. 11:26; 26:28; 1 Pt. 4:16) came into prominence, and in the form Χρηστιανοί was connected with the proper name Χρηστός. Christians are partisans of Christ, i.e., of a man with the supposed proper name Christ, just as the Herodians are of Herod (Mk. 3:6; 12:13; Mt. 22:16). Christians represent one particular movement among others.

The distinctive element in Christianity is much better expressed, however, by the emphasising of ἐκκλησία (τοῦ θεοῦ) than by the selection of a cultic word which might then be individualised by a personal name. The so-called Christ cult neither was nor desired to be one cult among others. It stood out against all cults in the sense that it stood out against the whole world, even the whole of the so-called religious world. This is all guaranteed by the choice of the self-designation ἐκκλησία, which, as we must constantly emphasise, implies the addition τοῦ θεοῦ (ἐν Χριστῷ).

It may be asked, and has been asked, who was the first in the early Christian movement to use ἐκκλησία. Was Paul, the earliest Christian writer, the chosen vessel whose example was followed by other Christians who spoke and wrote in Greek? [38] But it seems difficult in this case to fix on a single individual. More probably the term was used by Greek-speaking Jewish Christians, who came from the Hellenistic Synagogue and who attached to themselves Gentile Christians, thus forming congregations after the pattern of the Hellenistic Synagogue. [39] Originally Jews, these Hellenistic Christians knew the LXX. They no longer called themselves συναγωγή — we shall have to discuss this term later — but ἐκκλησία. As Christians, they adopted an expression which was no longer used very much by Jews. In contrast to LXX usage, συναγωγή was increasingly acquiring a restricted and local sense. This was an argument in favour of ἐκκλησία. In Greek terms, this

---

Christian community as a *factio, coitio, consensio* (terms of somewhat dubious connotation). → n. 40.

[35] Eus. Hist. Eccl., I, 3, 12 : (Χριστὸς) αὐτὰς γυμνὰς ἀρετὰς καὶ βίον οὐράνιον αὐτοῖς ἀληθείας δόγμασιν τοῖς θιασώταις παραδούς; cf. I, 3, 19. The word θίασος is used for Church at X, 1, 8.

[36] A striking example of such exaggeration and misconception may be found in K. J. Neumann, *Der römische Staat u. d. allgemeine Kirche bis auf Diocletian* (1890), 46 f., where the author claims that "it would have needed explanation if Greek Christians had not seen religious fellowships or thiasoi in their new associations." The *abusus* which we may assume on the part of some Gentile Christians is in so sense an *usus legitimus*.

[37] Cf. on this point the detailed researches of F. Poland (→ n. 25).

[38] Kattenbusch, I, 144, n. 1 is inclined to this view. Cf. F. Torm, *Hermeneutik des NT* (1930), 80. The thesis of H. Dieckmann, *De Ecclesia,* I (1925), 280 : *Nomen Ecclesiae ad ipsum Christum ut auctorem reducitur*, is rejected even by Roman Catholic scholars, since Jesus would hardly have spoken Greek ; cf. K. Pieper, *Jesus u. d. Kirche* (1932), 11.

[39] Cf. K. L. Schmidt, *Die Stellung des Apostels Paulus im Urchristentum* (1924), 16.

was also a more significant word. [40] It is worth noting that in the LXX ἐκκλησία is given emphasis by laudatory predicates. [41]

But why should LXX Jews almost always render the Hebrew קָהָל by ἐκκλησία? Apart from the significance of the basic verbal stems in both languages, there is much to be said for the conjecture that the similarity in sound between קָהָל and ἐκκλησία played some part. [42] This conjecture can be supported by reference to the fact that Greek and Latin Jews liked to add similarly sounding Greek and Latin names to their Hebrew and Aramaic names. [43]

D. Parallel Expressions.

If in the Jewish Christian ἐκκλησία we have a combination of OT and NT matter and a Greek term, it is not surprising that the matter does not stand or fall with a specific word. Hence there are many cases in the NT when ἐκκλησία is infrequent or absent, and yet the thing itself is under discussion. Most important in this regard is 1 Peter, which is Pauline in content, but unlike Paul does not use ἐκκλησία, [44] and yet offers a particularly rich exposition of what the ἐκκλησία τοῦ θεοῦ is. 2:9 presents us with a catena of OT designations: γένος ἐκλεκτόν, βασίλειον ἱεράτευμα, ἔθνος ἅγιον, λαὸς εἰς περιποίησιν. Cf. also 2:5: οἶκος πνευματικός, 2:10: → λαὸς θεοῦ. Paul's emphasis in Phil. 3:3 is important here: ἡμεῖς γὰρ ἐσμεν ἡ περιτομή. The following self-designations from the OT should also be noted: → Ἰσραήλ (R. 9:6: οὐ γὰρ πάντες οἱ ἐξ Ἰσραήλ οὗτοι Ἰσραήλ); Ἰσραὴλ τοῦ θεοῦ (Gl. 6:16); Ἰσραὴλ κατὰ πνεῦμα (implied at 1 C. 10:18: Ἰσραὴλ κατὰ σάρκα); σπέρμα Ἀβραάμ (Gl. 3:29: εἰ δὲ ὑμεῖς Χριστοῦ, ἄρα τοῦ Ἀβραὰμ σπέρμα ἐστέ, κατ' ἐπαγγελίαν κληρονόμοι cf. Hb. 2:16); δώδεκα φυλαί (Jm. 1:1). The fact of the diaspora (→ διασπορά, II, 101 ff.) holds a special place in this connection. Christians as the ἐκκλησία are παρεπίδημοι διασπορᾶς (1 Pt. 1:1) and the δώδεκα φυλαὶ αἱ ἐν τῇ διασπορᾷ (Jm. 1:1).

Other terms which are connected with the OT only loosely or not at all do not stand in contradiction to the title ἐκκλησία. They describe the faith or conduct of Christians (οἱ ἅγιοι — this term is closely linked with the OT — or οἱ πιστοί, οἱ ἀδελφοί, ἡ ἀδελφότης). Sometimes we have terms which are suggested by a

---

[40] Wellh. Mt., 84 believes that "in Greek ἐκκλησία is the better word." The passage from Tertullian quoted on → 515 (Apologeticum, 39) is also to be regarded as an emphatic paraphrase of the emphatic word ἐκκλησία: Hoc sumus congregati quod et dispersi, hoc universi quod et singuli ... cum probi, cum boni coëunt, cum pii, cum casti congregantur, non est factio dicenda, sed curia. Relevant, too, is the fact that in Enarr. in Ps. 82:1 Augustine suggests that the reason why ἐκκλησία is used for the Christian community and συναγωγή for the Jewish is that convocatio (ἐκκλησία) is a nobler expression than congregatio (συναγωγή), since the former properly signifies the calling together of men and the latter the driving together of cattle. Cf. also Trench, s.v.

[41] Ltzm. K. on 1 C. 1:1 draws attention to this. Cf. also K. Pieper, 20 (→ n. 38), and earlier A. v. Harnack, 419 f. (→ n. 29), though his thesis that the choice of ἐκκλησία was a master-stroke is questionable, if not completely erroneous.

[42] Cf. Cr.-Kö., s.v., 566; also G. Stählin, "Skandalon," BFTh, II, 24 (1930), 44 → I, 225 on ἀκροβυστία.

[43] The best known example is Saul-Paul; cf. also Jesus-Jason, Silas (obviously שְׁאִילָא, Aram. form of שָׁאוּל)-Silvanus. Modern examples are Luser (Lazar, El'azar)-Lewis, Moses-Maurice, Isaac-Isidore (or Ignatius).

[44] Cf. T. Spörri, Der Gemeindegedanke im ersten Petrusbrief (1925), esp. 271 ff.

particular situation and then fall into disuse (οἱ μαθηταί, οἱ πτωχοί). The word "disciple" applies to the first followers of Jesus, is then widened, and finally narrowed again, so that it fades into the background as a term for Christians. This is due to the fact that the first followers of Jesus stood in a unique relation to Jesus as His immediate disciples. The theory of a development from one term to another, and finally to ἐκκλησία, has no basis. [45]

The term synagogue is a special case; it will be discussed here only in its relation to ἐκκλησία. A widespread, but superficial, view is that ἐκκλησία is the Christian Church, συναγωγή the Jewish Synagogue. This clear-cut distinction only became normative in later centuries, and has continued to this day. But Jm. 2:2 compared with 5:14 seems to show that the Christian community can also call itself συναγωγή. [46] More secure and unequivocal is the fact that Jewish Christians in Trans-Jordan used συναγωγή both for their fellowship and for their building. [47] Apart from this more or less isolated instance, however, Jewish Christians did not at first call themselves συναγωγή, but ἐκκλησία. In contrast, we read expressly of a συναγωγή of Marcionites. [48] As Jewish Christians came to be more and more clearly separated from the Great Church, it is probable that they called both their assemblies and their places of assembly συναγωγή. In the very earliest period all Christians, both Jew and Gentile, used both expressions, ἐκκλησία and συναγωγή. It must also be remembered that there are examples of the second term for the societies of antiquity. [49] In spite of these analogies, however, the derivation of Christian usage from the OT is even more palpable in the case of συναγωγή than in that of ἐκκλησία. And the depicted association of the two words is particularly important in relation to the question which expression was used by the first Aramaic speaking Christians and before that by Jesus of Nazareth. The question is whether and how the Greek ἐκκλησία was influenced by a Semitic counterpart.

E. Matthew 16:18 and 18:17 (Heb. קָהָל, Aram. כְּנִישְׁתָּא, Syr. kʼnuštā, ἐκκλησία).

1. The Problem. Mt. 16:18 and 18:17 are burdened by several difficulties. Neither may be co-ordinated easily with the ἐκκλησία passages already discussed. Even from this standpoint the door seems to be opened at once to radical criticism. Even those who do not assume their inauthenticity, and they especially, are faced by great difficulties of exposition. Exposition is equally difficult whether we work with the present Greek or with the original used by Jesus. The effect of subsidiary questions is extremely complicated when they come to impinge on the main question. Only when we have expounded the Greek text can we fix on the Semitic equivalent for ἐκκλησία. But only when we have fixed on this equivalent can we engage in true exposition. Again, only when we have expounded the original can

---

[45] This is the assumption of Harnack, op. cit., p. 416 ff.

[46] Cf. Zn. Mt.⁴ (1922), 546.

[47] Epiph. Haer., 30, 18, 2 : πρεσβυτέρους γὰρ οὗτοι (sc. Jewish Christians of Transjordan) ἔχουσιν καὶ ἀρχισυναγώγους· συναγωγὴν δὲ καλοῦσιν τὴν ἑαυτῶν ἐκκλησίαν καὶ οὐχὶ ἐκκλησίαν.

[48] συναγωγὴ Μαρκιωνιστῶν : le Bas-Waddington, Inscr. Grecques et Latines, III (1870), No. 2558, p. 582; cf. A. v. Harnack, op. cit., 421, 659.

[49] Cf. W. Koester (→ Bibl.), 1, n. 12.

we give a definite answer to the question of authenticity. And conversely, only when this question has been answered on other grounds can we proceed to exposition. Intrinsically cogent expositions are possible both on the assumption of authenticity and on that of inauthenticity. All this influences our conception of the word ἐκκλησία as used in Mt. Material critical questions of various kinds thus affect the lexical problem, and *vice versa*. This interaction must be perceived and admitted. In the case of ἐκκλησία word, concept and thing are uncommonly complex. In mathematical terms, they are a combination of imaginary and real quantities. They are complicated and difficult, but not confused, as the vacillation of interpretation has shown, and continues to do so.

2. The Relation of the Two Passages. A peculiar difficulty is first raised by the fact that the two passages concerned (16:18 and 18:17) do not seem to be consonant with one another. If we assume that both verses are inauthentic, 16:18 suggests the Church as a world-wide entity and 18:17 suggests the individual congregation. There is no doubt that the customary — but not for that reason correct — differentiation between Church and congregation has affected the exposition of both verses in terms of inauthenticity. If we assume that they are authentic, however, exposition is particularly difficult, for 16:18 refers to the קָהָל and 18:17 to the synagogue. How, then, are we to explain the use of ἐκκλησία in both cases? We are at least forced to think through the mutual relation between the קָהָל and the synagogue. Is it certain that קָהָל underlies 16:18?

3. Textual and Literary Criticism. On textual grounds there are no objections to either 18:17 or especially 16:18. We have no Gk. MSS or ancient versions which do not contain 16:17-19 or at least 16:18. So far as the fathers are concerned, it may be accepted to-day that no argument can be brought against the verse from the way in which the contested passage occurs or does not occur from the time of Justin Martyr onwards. [50]

If attempts at textual criticism are still made, this is partly due to Protestant or Modernist efforts to excise the *locus classicus* for the Papal primacy, [51] but more particularly to literary criticism, which impresses many scholars by reason of the fact that 16:18 occurs in a passage which is not found in either Mk. or Lk. Two conclusions may be drawn from this: 1. that Mt. 16:17-19 has been interpolated into the text of Mt.; 2. that Mt. himself, or a predecessor whom he followed, interpolated these inauthentic words into an original text which is found in Mk. and Lk. and which goes back to Jesus, or is at least earlier. The first deduction is too crude to be taken very seriously. When a verse is so important, great caution is demanded. In other cases, a passage is not declared to be inauthentic because it is

---

[50] For details cf. K. L. Schmidt, *Die Kirche,* 283 ff. It must be particularly stressed that the later attempt of Harnack to discredit the text on the basis of a passage in Ephraem has been refuted by Roman Catholic scholars. Cf. C. A. Kneller, *Zeitschr. f. kath. Theol.,* 44 (1920), 147 ff.; J. Sickenberger (→ Bibl.); S. Euringer (→ Bibl.); J. Geiselmann, "Der petrinische Primat" in *Bibl. Zeitfr.,* XII, 7 (1927); K. Pieper (→ n. 38), 37 ff. Cf. also J. Jeremias, *Golgotha* (1926), 68 ff.

[51] Cf. K. L. Schmidt, *op. cit.,* 300 f. in reply to J. Schnitzer, *Hat Jesus das Papsttum gestiftet?*[2] (1910) and F. Heiler, *Der Katholizismus* (1923), 25 ff., 39 ff.

only attested in one Gospel. [52] But even the second and more cautious conclusion does not have the cogency which is often ascribed to it. It may be that the saying has been interpolated by Mt. or by a predecessor whom he follows. But this does not settle the question of the authenticity of the saying. We have to take into account the possibility that an interpolation follows a genuine tradition which is not known elsewhere and the validity of which must be tested apart from its present setting. The fact that the nature of the Gospel tradition does not permit us successfully to pursue chronological and psychological questions does not alter the fact that a saying without a context is to be expounded as such. [53]

4. Material Criticism. Literary criticism is in any case so uncertain that the cautious critic must direct his attention to material criticism. Basically all objections to the ἐκκλησία sayings in Mt. lead to the discussion of material questions. We may state first that Mt. 16:17-19 has a thoroughly Semitic flavour, so that we are forced to set the verse in the context of the original Palestinian community. [54] To say this is not to prove the authenticity of Mt. 16:18 as a saying of Jesus. The difficulties in material criticism [55] which remain relate to two questions: 1. Jesus and the Church, and 2. the position of Peter in primitive Christianity. Each of these questions contains 2 subsidiary questions, thus giving four in all: a. the statistical, why ἐκκλησία occurs only twice in the Gospels; b. the eschatological, whether Jesus, the preacher of the βασιλεία τοῦ θεοῦ, could found an ἐκκλησία; c. the historical, whether Peter really had the authoritative position ascribed to him in Mt. 16:18; and d. the psychological, whether the man Peter really proved to be a rock.

a. Statistics. The statistical data have no more cogency here than in 1 Pt., where the slogan ἐκκλησία does not occur, but what the ἐκκλησία stands for is richly described by other expressions from the OT. There are similar synonyms [56] in the Gospel tradition. At Mt. 26:31 and Jn. 10:16 we read of the → ποίμνη, which in 1 C. 9:7 is rightly equated with the ἐκκλησία. Cf. also ποίμνιον at Lk. 12:32; Ac. 20:28; 1 Pt. 5:2 f.; ἡ αὐλὴ τῶν προβάτων at Jn. 10:1; ἀρνία μου at Jn. 21:15; τὰ προβάτιά μου at Jn. 21:16 f. We even find a μου corresponding to the μου used of the ἐκκλησία at Mt. 16:18. As the ποιμὴν καλός (pastor bonus) is the same as the κύριος, so His ποίμνη is the same as His ἐκκλησία. In the first instance, this flock or assembly is the college of the twelve disciples of Jesus (→ II, 325). From the multitude of the Jewish people He separated a small company which stood in sharp contrast to the Pharisaic scribes and ultimately to the whole stiff-necked people, and which represented the true people of God, i.e.,

---

[52] Linton (→ Bibl.), 158 rightly says of literary objection to the authenticity of the verse: "But this alone is not enough, since the special material of the Evangelists is not so sharply judged in other instances."

[53] Cf. on this pt. K. L. Schmidt, Der Rahmen d. Geschichte Jesu (1919), 217 ff. Bultmann Trad., 277 on Mk. 8:27-30 gives a different analysis. Against this analysis in Bultmann's first edition (1921), cf. K. L. Schmidt, Die Kirche, 282, n. 1.

[54] Cf. Str.-B., ad loc.; Bultmann Trad., 277; J. Jeremias (→ n. 50).

[55] These are finely stated by Linton, 175 ff.

[56] Cf. Linton, 176. The problem of the Church in John's Gospel is treated by E. Gaugler in his Berne dissertation (1925) "Die Bedeutung d. Kirche in d. johanneischen Schriften," Intern. Kirchl. Zschr., 14 (1924), 97 ff., 181; 15 (1925), 27 ff. On synonyms for ἐκκλησία cf. esp. 15 (1925), 28.

the ἐκκλησία. Hence Mt. 16:18 is not an isolated incident in the life of Jesus as the history of the Christ. The existence of this circle of disciples in the lifetime of Jesus is not thrown in doubt by the imprecision of the different lists or the lack of individual features. The personal concrete element was missing even in the time when lists of the δώδεκα must have arisen, i.e., in that of the primitive community. The missing details are first found in the apocryphal Acts of the Apostles, which have all the characteristics of the Hellenistic novel. [57] In the days of the first community, however, it was more important that Jesus had the twelve with Him than that there should be precise information about each of the twelve. But if this is so, there is no compelling reason why we should not see this connection between Jesus and His disciples in His lifetime. [58] This is given a deeper and broader basis when the question is raised whether and in what sense Jesus regarded Himself as the Son of Man, and whether and in what sense He instituted the Lord's Supper. If Jesus viewed Himself as the Messiah in terms of Da. 7, new vistas are opened up as regards the nature and significance of His founding of the Church. The Son of Man in Da. is no mere individual. He is the Representative of the people of the saints of the Most High, who has set Himself the task of representing this people of God, i.e., the ἐκκλησία. [59] In this light the so-called institution of the Lord's Supper is shown to be an act in establishment of the Church. [60] The insight that materially Mt. 16:18 does not stand alone is thus given a more solid basis. It is also important, however, that this view of the complex Jesus, Messiah, Son of Man, Disciples, Community, Lord's Supper, leads directly to the Pauline and deutero-Pauline understanding of the ἐκκλησία, which is ἄνωθεν on the one hand and yet also σῶμα Χριστοῦ on the other, just as Christ is both exalted on the one hand and yet also present in the community on the other. The question of the founding of the Church by Jesus Himself is really the

---

[57] Cf. K. L. Schmidt, "Die Stellung der Evangelien in der allgemeinen Literaturgeschichte," Festschr. f. H. Gunkel (1923), II, 80.

[58] R. Schütz, Apostel u. Jünger (1921) follows J. Wellhausen and R. Bultmann on the one side : "The historical college of the twelve cannot be much earlier than the time when Paul became an apostle" (75), but on the other he has to admit that "the possibility that Jesus Himself already referred to the symbolical significance of the twelve cannot be ruled out a limine" (72).

[59] If I am right, three modern scholars have independently drawn attention to this aspect of the founding of the Church by Jesus : T. Schmidt (→ n. 20), 217 ff. ("Analogie von Messias und Gemeinde"); Schl. Gesch. d. Chr., 375 ("The very title of Christ required that He should establish the perfected community"); and mostly profoundly Kattenbusch, I, 143 ff. (145 : "Christ has His individual existence no less than those who are His, but He is Himself only in the σῶμα. Without this He would not be what His name declares"; 160 : Christ "had to fashion His personal life in such sort that He should really become, and might claim to be, the type of the people of the saints of the Most High, and He had to constitute or create this people as such among men"). These scholars are followed by Gloege (→ Bibl.) 218, 228 ("The Saviour is Saviour only as the Creator of a new redeemed and justified people." "Just as the ποιμήν is no real shepherd without the ποίμνιον, so the Χριστός is no true Christ without the ἐκκλησία") and Linton, 148 ("The Messiah is not a private person. A community belongs to Him. The flock belongs to the Shepherd").

[60] We again owe our deepest insights to Kattenbusch. I, 171: "In His founding of the ἐκκλησία, of a community in His name, by the Lord's Supper, He does not leave out of account, but brings to a climax, His self-designation according to Daniel (incorporating the prophecy of Is. in interpretation of the nature of the Son of Man)." This explanation would perhaps be more cogent than it is if Kattenbusch's analysis of the passages relating to the Last Supper were more convincing. Cf. K. L. Schmidt, Art. "Abendmahl im NT," RGG², I, 6 ff.

question of His Messiahship.[61] The detailed problems of when and where, which by their very nature the Gospel records do not solve, are subordinate to this main question.[62]

b. Eschatology. Does this all fit in with eschatology as Jesus presented it in His preaching of the kingdom of God? In the light of what has been said, we may deal with this question more briefly. That the ἐκκλησία, too, is an eschatological entity is proved by the eschatological events of the self-witness of Jesus as Son of Man and the institution of the Lord's Supper. But the βασιλεία τοῦ θεοῦ and the ἐκκλησία are not the same. They are not the same in the primitive community, which certainly regarded itself as the ἐκκλησία but which continued the proclamation of the βασιλεία. Nor are they the same in the preaching of Jesus, who promises the βασιλεία τοῦ θεοῦ to His ἐκκλησία, i.e., to the ἐκκλησία founded by Him. In this sense the post-Easter ἐκκλησία, too, regarded itself as eschatological. In this sense the individual is to be understood eschatologically as a justified sinner.[63]

---

[61] Cf. the short treatment of this question, which is to be answered in the affirmative in spite of J. Wellhausen, W. Wrede and R. Bultmann, in the art. "Jesus Christus" by K. L. Schmidt, RGG², III, 149 f.

[62] For this reason we must question H. D. Wendland's intrinsically attractive depiction of stages (→ Bibl.).

[63] Bultmann's construction (Trad., 149 f.) misses the points to which we have alluded; cf. also his review of Wendland's work in DLZ, 55 (1934), 2019 ff. The opinion is here expressed that "the true problem of the ἐκκλησία ... is that the ἐκκλησία constitutes itself in place of the βασιλεία τοῦ θεοῦ imminently expected by Jesus." This corresponds to an earlier formulation of the question in terms of historical development, which does not enable us properly to appreciate the transition from Jesus to the community, the community of Peter as well as Paul. Ascribing a "radically eschatological significance" to the ἐκκλησία, which he allows that the early community took itself to be, Bultmann fails to answer the question how the kingdom and the Church are distinguished in this community as eschatological magnitudes. → I, 589; also the preface to the second impression of K. L. Schmidt, Die Kirche; Linton, 179 f. J. Haller, Das Papsttum, I (1934) declares that "sober investigation, which considers individual sayings in the context of the whole teaching of the Saviour, cannot believe that Jesus spoke the words which are put on His lips by Mt. (16:18) ... We are dealing here with a later prediction which presupposes its fulfilment" (4). In exposition we read: "Whether it (sc. Mt. 16:18 f.) embodies an authentic saying of Jesus has not yet been decided. In my view, the vote can only go against authenticity unless we treat the saying in a different way from that demanded by the generally accepted canons of criticism. This is done, of course, by many, e.g., Kattenbusch ... To be judged similarly, in spite of its learning and perspicacity, is the lengthy and pretentious essay of K. L. Schmidt" (442). So far as concerns the "generally accepted canons of criticism" which Haller invokes in favour of "sober investigation," it may be noted amongst other things that the jurist G. Holstein, Die Grundlagen d. ev. Kirchenrechts (1928) and the historian E. Caspar, Geschichte d. Papsttums (1930/33) (cf. also "Primatus Petri" in Zschr. der Savigny-Stiftung, 47 [1927], 253 ff.) take an essentially different view both in general and in detail. Of Caspar Haller simply says: "For the rest our ways are so far apart, and the divergences in the estimation and use of sources are so radical in nature, that I think it right to abstain from critical discussion except at a few points. There are different ways of writing history, and every man must do as seems best to him" (441). This attitude seems to justify us in not pursuing the debate with Haller further. Cf. also K. Pieper, Die angebliche Einsetzung des Petrus? (1935); Jesus und die Kirche (1932). A more recent writer, W. G. Kümmel, "Die Eschatologie d. Evangelien," ThBl, 15 (1936), 225 ff. does not seem to clarify the question of the distinctive eschatological character of the ἐκκλησία as compared with the βασιλεία τοῦ θεοῦ. He writes: "K. L. Schmidt has tried to support by linguistic research the idea that Jesus planned to found a special community, and the saying to Peter in Mt. 16:18 f.,

c. Church History. The historical argument against Mt. 16:18 is that Peter did not occupy in early Christianity the authoritative position ascribed to him in this verse. This argument is supported by appeal to 1 C. 3:11; 10:4 (cf. Eph. 2:20) in opposition to the authenticity of Mt. 16:18 (→ 509, n. 15).[64] It may be met as follows. On the one hand, even when judged by Paul Peter played a bigger role than the Protestant side will admit in the controversy between Protestantism and Roman Catholicism. Since historical and psychological reasons cannot be provided for this special position, the riddle finds its easiest solution if the distinction of Peter rests on a saying of Jesus. If, on the other hand, Peter was challenged in the early Church — and in this respect we have to consider especially the Johannine tradition as well as Paul (cf. particularly the rivalry between Peter and the ἄλλος μαθητής at Jn. 20:2 ff.) — it is hard to see how Mt. 16:18 could have arisen post festum in view of this conflict. The theory of a vaticinium ex eventu is shattered by the fact that the eventus for Peter has a very different aspect from that which would have to be assumed on the basis of Mt. 16:18. The disputed passage is thus to be accepted as authentic as the lectio difficilior.[65]

d. Psychology. The psychological objection that the man Peter did not prove to be a rock involves a radical misunderstanding of the nature of the ἐκκλησία. The special position of Peter is a riddle which must be accepted as such. The various psychological solutions of this riddle may be more or less illuminating, but they do not really solve it. We neither can nor should answer the question why God chose the people of Israel as His people, His Church. Peter is chosen in a special sense; he proves obdurate, but he is still chosen, for he has become the fundamentum ecclesiae. Israel, too, is chosen, and is obdurate, but is still chosen, for a remnant is converted.[66]

---

regarded as authentic, is used in proof. It is characteristic of this whole discussion that exegetical formulation is wrested by systematic construction. In contrast, serious biblical theology must begin with the question of the exegetical data" (231). In reply we may simply say that the present enlarged exposition of the locus classicus ecclesiae does not start with "systematic construction" but with "exegetical formulation," and therefore that the author has attempted "serious biblical theology" in accordance with "the exegetical data."

[64] According to H. Windisch, ThR, NF, 5 (1933), 251 "only the third (sc. objection) has any real weight to-day."

[65] In relation to the many attempts to depreciate Peter more than is permissible, we should not follow the exegesis of Luther, who sees in Mt. 16:18 no more than in Mt. 5:3; cf. K. L. Schmidt, Die Kirche, 289 ff. The attempt of Str.-B., I, 732 to translate 16:18 back into Hb. is also prejudiced by the desire to depreciate Peter. Bultmann Trad., 148 regards this attempt as "absurd." Linton, 170 thinks it "worthy of attention."

[66] Cf. W. Leonhard in Una Sancta, 3 (1927), 485: "... the vacillating rock man, the confessor prone to denial, the prop who needs support, this as the first man in Christianity is in fact one of the most striking paradoxes of the Gospel; it is a part of the passion story and it finds its reflection in every Christian life. Peter must not depreciated, as K. L. Schmidt convincingly states." It is another matter that Leonhard is elsewhere dissatisfied with K. L. Schmidt on the ground that "he cannot refrain from concluding that the singling out of the personality of Simon Peter is the very thing that shatters all the claims of the Roman hierarchy"; this is for him a "Protestant surtax." K. Heim, Das Wesen des ev. Christentums[5] (1929), 36 gives a fine statement on the other side: "It is a remarkable irony of universal history that on the papal basilica there is inscribed in gigantic letters the very saying of Christ which, understood in its original sense, excludes and forbids the Papacy in every form because more than anything else it assigns to the apostle a unique and absolutely unrepeatable position in the spiritual edifice of God." W. G. Kümmel (→ n. 63), 232 can only say: "It is finally quite inconceivable that Jesus should have committed to a man

More by way of appendix, we may refer to a difficulty which is often emphasised, namely, that ἐκκλησίαν does not fit in very well as the object of the verb → οἰκο-δομεῖν. [67] The figure of building is common in Judaism and early Christianity, especially of the world in the sense of its creation. [68] In this light we may assume that an οἰκία lies behind the ἐκκλησία of Mt. 16:18. [69]

5. Hebrew and Aramaic Equivalents. Our arguments thus far are valid if at Mt. 16:18 and 18:17, and elsewhere in the NT, the Hebrew equivalent of ἐκκλη-σία is קָהָל. But it is an open question whether we are to think in terms of Hebrew or of Aramaic. It is also an open question whether the only terms to come into consideration are the Heb. קָהָל or the Aram. קְהָלָא (a loan word from biblical Heb.).

That Jesus and His disciples spoke Aram. does not justify us in assuming too easily that they used this familiar speech alone in the sphere of divine worship. [70] It may be presupposed that they must have had some acquaintance with Heb. as the ancient ecclesiastical language of their people. [71] But even so קָהָל is not the only term to call for notice. Perhaps we cannot take קְהִלָּה too seriously, the term used by F. Delitzsch at Mt. 16:18 in his Heb. translation of the NT (1880), since there are few examples of it either in the OT or in Rabbinic literature. But serious attention must be given to עֵדָה, [72] which is not particularly distinguished from קָהָל in the OT.

On the whole the Rabbis do not use either קָהָל or עֵדָה very frequently. More common is צִבּוּר, which is once used in the sense of "heap" in the OT (2 K. 10:8), and can be regarded as the proper term for the later Jewish congregation, whether national or local. [73] Fairly common, too, is the expression כְּנֶסֶת יִשְׂרָאֵל,

---

control over admission into the kingdom of God." In answer we may point out, as → supra in the text, that it is even more inconceivable that Mt. 16:18 should be a creation of the community. From the Roman Catholic standpoint K. Pieper engages in express controversy with Schmidt and Heim, op. cit. (→ n. 38), 60 ff. It is typical that according to him (67) J. Geiselmann (→ n. 50), 27 points out that "we must bear in mind the limits of the demonstration from Scripture alone of what the Petrine primacy was according to the Lord's promise," and that J. Sickenberger, "Leben Jesu," V (Bibl. Zeitfragen, 13 [1929], 16 ff.), in his discussion of the Messianic confession at Caesarea Philippi, does not raise at all the question of the bearing of Mt. 16:18 on the successors of Peter, while K. Adam, Das Wesen des Katholizismus⁷ (1934), 118 takes the view that the reference to Peter's successors "can be denied by those who stick to the biblical text alone and do not put it in the context of the divine-human person of Jesus and His purposes."

[67] It is on this ground that Holtzmann, NT, I, 165 f., decides against authenticity : ". . . one would expect of Jesus a figurative object consonant with οἰκοδομεῖν, such as τὴν οἰκίαν μου."

[68] Cf. Str.-B., I, 732 f.; Zn. Mt., 547; Schl. Mt., 506 f.

[69] Cf. the careful and solid essay by T. Hermann (→ Bibl.), whose thesis does not seem in the least to be "completely superfluous" (Bultmann Trad., 149), since there is real value in recognising the special affinity between ἐκκλησία and οἰκία in OT and NT usage. K. Pieper fails to support his objection (→ n. 38) that Hermann's proposal so empties ἐκ-κλησία or its Aram. equivalent of meaning that nothing remains but a religious society of a more general nature.

[70] Cf. G. Dalman, Jesus-Jeschua (1922).

[71] G. Dalman, op. cit., 34 : "That Jesus had not learned in vain is shown by the fact that in the synagogue of His native city He came forward to read the prophetic passage (Lk. 4:16). This implies a good acquaintance with Hebrew."

[72] O. Procksch argued in favour of this at the first German Theologentag ; cf. the account by A. Titius in Deutsche Theologie, I (1928), 23 and the reply by K. L. Schmidt, 26.

[73] Str.-B., I, 734; cf. also Dalman Wört., s.v.

of which the OT uses only the verb כנס ("to gather," "to assemble"). This phrase carries a special emphasis in the sense that it suggests a personification of the whole of believing Israel. [74] We cannot make any essential material distinction between צִבּוּר, עֵדָה, קָהָל, and כְּנֶסֶת, so that no firm deductions can be drawn from Hebrew usage.

If we assume that an Aram. equivalent is to be sought for ἐκκλησία, we may first suggest קְהָלָא, which is found in the Targumim, not as native Aram., but as a loan word from biblical Heb. The Targumim do not use the Aram. עֶדְתָּא for עֵדָה. [75] We therefore do well to rule out עֶדְתָּא. On the other hand, צִבּוּרָא occurs. But the most common expression is כְּנִישְׁתָּא. [76] And special significance attaches to this word because it is used for ἐκκλησία or συναγωγή in Syriac versions, i.e., in those versions which are closest to Palestinian Aram.

While the Syra Curetoniana (3rd cent.), the Peshitta (beginning of the 5th) and the Syra Philoxeniana (beginning of the 6th) use 'ēdtā for the ἐκκλησία as the Christian Church and k'nuštā for συναγωγή as the Jewish Synagogue, the Syra Sinaitica (3rd cent., and older than the Curetoniana) has k'nuštā for both. (The Sinaitica does not have Mt. 16:18, but retains 18:17.) In this respect it is followed by the Palestinian-Syriac, which is chiefly known to us through the so-called Evangeliarium Hierosolymitanum. [77] Though we do not know the date of this translation, it gives an impression of being older than the others. The dialect in which it is written varies quite widely from ordinary Syriac, and may be relatively closer to that spoken by Jesus and His disciples. [78] Here, too, the Aram. k'nuštā = כְּנִשְׁתָּא is actually used both for the Christian ἐκκλησία and for the Jewish συναγωγή. [79]

In the light of this, it seems highly probable that Jesus spoke of the כְּנִישְׁתָּא. [80] If for the Christian community קָהָל or קְהָלָא emphasises the significance and claim of the divine community of the OT, there is also the possibility that כְּנִישְׁתָּא, too, refers to this community in its totality. We have certainly to consider that in the first instance this Aram. term, like its normal Greek equivalent συναγωγή, refers to

---

[74] Str.-B., I, 734; cf. Schürer, II, 504: "When viewed as religious, the community is called כְּנֶסֶת."

[75] Dalman has this word in his Wört., but it is not listed in Levy Chald. Wört. Wellh. Mt., 84, says: "Edta is not Palestinian, but Syriac."

[76] Cf. Levy, s.v. Dalman also has כְּנִישְׁתָּא (ס for שׁ, cf. כְּנֶסֶת) is found for synagogue as a building.

[77] Ed. P. de Lagarde, Bibl. Syr. (1892). Cf. F. Schwally, Idioticon des christlich-palästinischen Aram. (1893) and F. Schulthess, Lexicon Syropalaestinum (1903). For all other Syr., cf. O. Klein, Syrisch-griech. Wörterbuch zu den vier kanonischen Ev. (1916).

[78] So E. Nestle, Einführung in das gr. NT³ (1909), 115; F. Schulthess, Gramm. d. christlich-palästinischen Aram., ed. E. Littmann (1924), 3.

[79] Cf. Schürer, II, 504: "In Christian Palestinian Aram. כנישתא, which corresponds to the Gk. συναγωγή, seems to have been the usual word for 'church'." Wellh. Mt., 84: "The original Aram. word k'nishta denotes the Jewish as well as the Christian community. Palestinian Christians retained it without distinction, and used it for the Church as well as the Synagogue."

[80] Cf. Zn. Mt., 546 and A. Merx, Die vier kanonischen Ev. nach der syrischen im Sinai-kloster gefundenen Palimpsesthdschr., Mt. (1902), 268. J. Jeremias (→ n. 50), 69 argues for "probably צִבּוּרָא, or at any rate כְּנִישְׁתָּא."

the narrower synagogue defined in local or personal terms, or in terms of a particular trend. It thus suggests a separate כְּנִישְׁתָּא. Does this mean, then that the primitive Christian community is a sect within Judaism? In fact official Judaism did often treat it as such. But the Christian community itself took the view that it was a synagogue with a special claim to represent true Judaism or the true Israel. There had been similar synagogues in Judaism before. If there is not much evidence to prove this, there is enough. We may refer to 1 Macc. 2:42: συναγωγὴ Ἀσιδαίων; 7:12: συναγωγὴ γραμματέων. Though these synagogues separated themselves on more scholastic grounds, they seem to have asserted the same exclusive claim. [81] We may also refer to the Jewish community of the New Covenant at Damascus, which in its document, found in the Genizah (= lumber-room) of the synagogue at Cairo, sometimes calls itself עֵדָה (7, 20; 10, 4 and 8; 13, 13), sometimes קָהָל (7, 17; 11, 22), and also feels itself to be the remnant of Israel (שְׁאֵרִית לְיִשְׂרָאֵל). [82] The idea of the קְהַל יְהוָה is not only not abandoned; it acquires special significance. For such a separate group represents the remnant of Israel on which depends the continued life of all Israel as the people of God. Similarly the community of God is embodied in the synagogue of Jesus the Messiah. In the apparent paradox of this *pars pro toto* arrangement lies the very essence of the genuine synagogue and of the genuine community of Jesus Christ. The founding of the ἐκκλησία by Jesus at Mt. 16:18, to which appeal is so often made, consists solely and simply in this process of separating and concentrating His band of disciples. All that we know of the attitude of Jesus to the קְהַל יְהוָה gains breadth and depth and colour when we recognise His concern for the כְּנִישְׁתָּא. [83]

This finally clarifies the inter-relation between Mt. 16:18 and 18:17. If in the second of these two verses the necessary admonition of an erring brother is finally to take place publicly before the ἐκκλησία, this cannot be explained merely as part of an early Christian catechism. [84] It is to be understood in terms of a reference to the Synagogue, the OT community, which Jesus does not deny, but expressly affirms, which He and He alone fulfils, since as the Messiah He here and elsewhere places Himself under the Law. [85]

---

[81] Bultmann Trad., 150 thinks it "hardly credible" that a special synagogue should claim to represent the קְהַל יְהוָה, His objections, which overemphasise the teaching aspect of the synagogue, are not convincing.

[82] For the text cf. S. Schechter, *Documents of Jewish Sectaries*, I (1910), from which the references are taken. L. Rost, *Die Damaskusschrift, KlT*, 167 (1933) gives Schechter's arrangement together with another. He emends the readings and works over the various proposals and the bibl. up to 1933. The various attempts at dating differ by centuries. Acc. to A. Bertholet in RGG², I, 1775 f. (Art. "Damaskusschrift") we are to think in terms of a Maccabean, or more accurately a Hasmonean, if not a Roman origin (1st cent. B.C. ?). G. Hölscher, *Geschichte d. israelitischen u. jüdischen Religion* (1922), 189 thinks with others (cf. Rost, *op. cit.*, 4) that it comes from the "sons of Zadok," who are mentioned by Kirkisani (10th cent.) as forerunners of the Karaites.

[83] This is completely missed by Bultmann Trad., 149 ff. when he states that "it is wholly irrelevant to Mt. 16:18 f. whether the equivalent of ἐκκλησία is קָהָל, עֵדָה or כְּנִישְׁתָּא."

[84] We need hardly give examples of this common critical view.

[85] Cf. K. L. Schmidt, "Die Verkündigung des NT in ihrer Einheit und Besonderheit," ThBl, 10 (1931), 120; "Das Christuszeugnis der synoptischen Ev.," *Kirchenblatt f. d. reformierte Schweiz*, 89 (1933), 403 (= "Jesus Christus im Zeugnis der Heiligen Schrift u. der Kirche," *Sammelband* [1936], 22).

F. The Old Testament and Judaism.

1. Greek Judaism.

a. The word ἐκκλησία occurs about 100 times in the LXX, and also a few times in Aquila, Symmachus and Theodotion. When there is a Heb. equivalent, it is almost always קָהָל. The only exceptions in the LXX may be listed as follows : 1 Βασ. 19:20 = 1 S. 19:20 הֵקָה לְ; Neh. 5:7 קְהִלָּה; ψ 25:12 = Ps. 26:12 מַקְהֵלִים; ψ 67:27 = 68:27 מַקְהֵלוֹת. The usage in translation is thus consistent and unequivocal. The Heb. equivalents mentioned are from the stem קהל. In the case of הֵקָה,לְ the same radicals are found in a different sequence. Either we are to assume that this is also a derivative of קהל or it may be that we have dittography in relation to לָקַחַת, which comes shortly before. [86]

In the LXX ἐκκλησία is a wholly secular term ; it means "assembly," whether in the sense of assembling or of those assembled (for the first, cf. Dt. 9:10; 18:16 : ἡμέρα τῆς ἐκκλησίας, יוֹם הַקָּהָל, the day of assembling : Luther Versammlung ; A.V. "assembly"; for the second cf. 3 Βασ. 8:65 : Σαλωμὼν ... πᾶς 'Ισραὴλ μετ' αὐτοῦ, ἐκκλησία μεγάλη = 1 K. 8:65 : קָהָל גָּדוֹל, a great assembly : Luther Versammlung, A.V. "congregation"). The real point is who assembles, or who constitutes the assembly. In 1 Βασ. 19:20 we have an assembly of prophets (A.V. the "company of the prophets"), whereas at Sir. 26:5 ἐκκλησία ὄχλου might be rendered according to the context as a riotous assembly of the mob. [87] Only the addition κυρίου makes it plain that the ἐκκλησία is the people or congregation of God : ἐκκλησία κυρίου = קְהַל יְהוָה, Dt. 23:2 ff.; 1 Ch. 28:8; Neh. 13:1; Mi. 2:5 (A.V. the "congregation of the Lord" or "of God"); cf. ἐκκλησίαν σου = קְהָל לָךְ, Lam. 1:10; also τοῦ ὑψίστου, Sir. 24:2; τοῦ λαοῦ τοῦ θεοῦ, Ju. 20:2. Often 'Ισραήλ is added, 3 Βασ. 8:14, 22, 55; 1 Ch. 13:2; 2 Ch. 6:3, 12 f.; Sir. 50:13; 1 Macc. 4:59. Less common are the attributes υἱῶν 'Ισραήλ, Sir. 50:20; 'Ιούδα, 2 Ch. 20:5; 30:25; ἁγίων, ψ 88:5; ὁσίων, Ps. 149:1; ἐν 'Ιερουσαλήμ, 1 Macc. 14:19. Mention might also be made of the addition τῆς ἀποικίας = הַגּוֹלָה to denote the congregation of the exile. In many cases there is no addition, since the context makes it plain that the ἐκκλησία is the community of God. These instances are so common in 1 and 2 Ch., Ps. and some apocryphal books that we might almost speak of a technical term. Now and then, however, there is room for doubt. In any case, the addition τοῦ θεοῦ is either explicit or implicit. To express the significance of the community as an assembly the word πᾶσα is a frequent addition. At ψ 25:12; 67:27 we have the plur., and at 106:32 the MSS vary between the sing. and the plur. How intrinsically insecure is the technical use of ἐκκλησία may be seen from the rendering of Prv. 5:14 : ἐν μέσῳ ἐκκλησίας καὶ συναγωγῆς. The translator is not sure how to handle two terms which obviously mean the same thing (cf. A.V. "congregation and assembly").

The verb ἐκκλησιάζω (ἐξεκκλησιάζω) is found in the sense "to gather" at Lv. 8:3; Nu. 20:8; Dt. 4:10; 31:12, 28; 3 Βασ. 8:1; 12:21; 1 Ch. 13:5; 15:3; 28:1; 2 Ch. 5:2 for the hiph'il of קהל, for which συναθροίζω is also used at Ex. 35:1, συνάγω at Nu. 1:18;

---

[86] So Ges.-Buhl, s.v.

[87] Cf. V. Ryssel in Kautzsch Apkr. u. Pseudepigr., I, 363 : "ἐκκλησία, lit. 'assembly'; ἐκκλησία is not (cf. O. F. Fritzsche, Libri apocryphi Veteris Test. Graece, 1871, ad loc.) an incorrect rendering on the ground of an original קְלָלָה rather than קְהֵלָה, (i.e., malediction or calumniation, which would be essentially the same as the par. term in v. 5a). Sir. links the two : 'murmuring of the assembly in the multitude of the people,' perhaps because he fails to see anything wrong in the second — an argument in favour of קְהֵלָה being original." Yet Fritzsche may well be right, for elsewhere in Sir. ἐκκλησία is always a technical term for the congregation of Israel.

8:9; 10:7 and ἐπισυνίστημι at Nu. 16:19. The verb ἐξεκκλησιάζομαι is found in the sense of "to assemble" (reflexive) at Jos. 18:1; Ju. 20:1; 2 Βασ. 20:14 for the niphal of קָהֵל, for which we find συνίσταμαι ('ΑΘ: ἐκκλησιάζομαι) at Ex. 32:1 and συναθροίζομαι at Jos. 22:12.

Things are much the same in respect of the more or less technical use of → συναγωγή. Often in Gn. συναγωγή or συναγωγαί is coupled with ἐθνῶν ⹀ קְהַל עַמִּים or קְהַל גּוֹיִם: 28:3; 35:11; 48:4 (Luther Haufe; A.V. "multitude"); ψ 21:16 (Ps. 22:16) συναγωγὴ πονηρευομένων, עֲדַת מְרֵעִים (A.V. "assembly of the wicked"); ψ 67:30 (Ps. 68:30): συναγωγὴ τῶν ταύρων, עֲדַת אַבִּירִים (A.V. "company of the bulls"); ψ 85:14 (Ps. 86:14): συναγωγὴ κραταιῶν, עֲדַת עָרִיצִים (A.V. "assemblies of violent men"). Cf. also 'Ιερ. 51:15 = Jer. 44:15; 'Ιερ. 27:9 = Jer. 50:9. On the other hand we find συναγωγὴ κυρίου as well as ἐκκλησία κυρίου, Nu. 20:4; 27:17; 31:16; ψ 73:2 (Ps. 74:2); this corresponds to קְהַל יְהוָה or עֲדַת יְהוָה (A.V. "congregation of the Lord").

Parallel discussion of ἐκκλησία and συναγωγή makes it plain 1. that the two words mean much the same and often correspond to the same Heb. word קָהָל; and 2. that both words are used both technically and non-technically, as underlined by the fact that translation varies between "assembly," "company" and "congregation."

b. The position is much the same in Philo and Josephus except that the technical use now seems to be more pronounced under the influence of secular Gk. A related factor is that there is now more frequent reference to national assemblies in the secular sphere.

Philo combines ἀγοραὶ καὶ ἐκκλησίαι, Spec. Leg., II, 44, or βουλαὶ καὶ ἐκκλησίαι, Omn. Prob. Lib., 138, cf. ὁ μὲν φαῦλος ... δικαστήρια βουλευτήριά τε καὶ ἐκκλησίας καὶ πάντα σύλλογον καὶ θίασον ἀνθρώπων ... μετατρέχει, Abr., 20. Philo also speaks of the ἐκκλησία θεοῦ or κυρίου, following Dt. 23: οἷς ἄντικρυς ἀπείρηται εἰς ἐκκλησίαν θεοῦ φοιτᾶν, Leg. All., III, 8; οὐκ εἰσελεύσονται, φησὶ Μωϋσῆς, <εἰς ἐκκλησίαν> κυρίου, ibid., 81; τῶν τοιούτων οὐδενὶ ἐπιτρέπει Μωϋσῆς εἰς ἐκκλησίαν ἀφικνεῖσθαι θεοῦ, Ebr., 213; cf. ὄργανον θεοῦ νομοθετοῦντος ἐκκλησίαν, Poster. C., 143. Instead of θεοῦ it is also described as τοῦ πανηγεμόνος, Mut. Nom., 204. A mark of the Hellenist in Philo is that he furnishes the ἐκκλησία with the epithet θεία, Conf. Ling., 144; cf. also ἐκκλησίας καὶ συλλόγου θείας, Leg. All., III, 81; also καλεῖν τε εἰς ἐκκλησίαν καὶ μεταδιδόναι λόγων θείων. To speak of θεῖον εἶναι in connection with the ἐκκλησία is alien to the LXX and NT. The same is true of the attribute ἱερός. [88] Yet Philo speaks of the ἐκκλησία ἱερά, Som., II, 184 and 187; Deus Imm., 111; Migr. Abr., 69; cf. Aet. Mund., 13.

Josephus, who likes to avoid ἅγιος and prefers θεῖος or ἱερός, might well have spoken of the ἐκκλησία as Philo did. But as his use of βασιλεία is secularised generally rather than cultically [89] (→ I, 576), so it is here. A certain Simon, one of the leaders in Jerusalem, summons an assembly of the congregation to exclude Agrippa from the temple, πλῆθος εἰς ἐκκλησίαν ἁλίσας, Ant., 19, 332. Herod repeatedly summons the community συνήγαγεν ἐκκλησίαν πάνδημον, Ant., 16, 62; ἐξεκκλησίασεν εἰς τὸ θέατρον, Ant., 17, 161; the community assembled in Tiberias, τὸ πλῆθος, decides political issues of the city, Vit., 37. [89] Cf. also Ant., 14, 150; οὐδεὶς ἀπεστάτει τῆς ἐκκλησίας, Bell., 4, 255: ἀθροίσαντες εἰς ἐκκλησίαν τοὺς 'Ιουδαίους, Bell., 7, 412.

2. The Hebrew Text.

We have already discussed all essential points concerning קָהָל and materially related words, esp. עֵדָה (→ 527 f.). Our only remaining task is to define them in terms of the

---

[88] Cf. θεῖος and ἱερός in Cr.-Kö.
[89] Cf. Schl. Mt., 508; Schl. Theol. d. Judt., 90 f.

Hebrew text, i.e., to take the way, not from the Greek to the Hebrew, but *vice versa*. While ἐκκλησία is almost always a rendering of קָהָל, קָהָל is not always translated ἐκκλησία. In Jos., Ju., S. (apart from 1 S. 19:20), 1 and 2 K., 1 and 2 Ch., Ezr., and Neh. we always find ἐκκλησία for קָהָל. The same is true of Dt. except for 5:22 (συναγωγή). Elsewhere in the Pentateuch, i.e., Gn., Ex., Lv. and Nu., συναγωγή is the word for קָהָל though it is normally used for עֵדָה. (At Lv. 4:14, 21 Ἄλλος has ἐκκλησία instead of συναγωγή, cf. also Ἰερ. 33:17; Ἀ Ἰερ. 51:15; ΑΘ Ez. 26:7; Θ Ez. 27:27; 32:22 [Bertram].) In Ex., Lv. and Nu. עֵדָה is more common than קָהָל. עֵדָה is almost always rendered συναγωγή and never ἐκκλησία. Jos. and Ju. use עֵדָה more frequently. In the following books, however, עֵדָה yields increasingly to קָהָל. In the Psalter it is only at 40:10 (= ψ 39:10; ΑΘ have ἐκκλησία) that קָהָל is translated συναγωγή; elsewhere we always find ἐκκλησία. This unevenness makes it clear that neither word is intrinsically a technical term. Everything depends on the addition יהוה or יִשְׂרָאֵל as עַם יהוה, whether explicit or implicit. This is even clearer when קָהָל is rendered ὄχλος, Jer. 31:8 (= Ἰερ. 38:8); Ez. 16:40; 23:46 f. (ΑΘ ἐκκλησία), or πλῆθος, Ex. 12:6; 2 Ch. 31:18; σύστασις, Gn. 49:6; συνέδριον, Prv. 26:26. [90]

---

[90] For a different view cf. M. Noth, "Das System d. zwölf Stämme Israels," BWANT, 4. *Folge, Heft* 1 (1930), 102 f., n. 2 : "... it seems to me that there is little doubt that ... the words עדה and קהל ... derive from the usage of the ancient amphictyony of Israel, and it is no surprise that words which are essentially linked with a sacral institution should first recur in the priestly writings, apart from a few places in the OT which come down directly from the amphictyonic tradition itself ... קהל obviously denotes the assembly and עדה the people united in such an assembly, called עם האלהים at Ju. 20:2 on the basis of the fact that the bond which united the tribes and their members was the covenant God and His cultus." After the conclusion of the present art., L. Rost, who saw it in proof, placed the following statement at my disposal : "As roots of the ἐκκλησία it is usual to appeal to עֵדָה and קָהָל; Yet the former belongs to the early stages of the συναγωγή and only the latter calls for consideration. קָהָל, a noun related to קוֹל, of which the denominative hiph'il and niph'al are in common use, originally signifies the summoning of the עַם, i.e., of the men, for council or for war. This is the usage in Gn. 49:6; Nu. 22:4. At Nu. 16:33 קָהָל seems to be the national community in a sense on which light is cast by Mi. 2:5. Here Mi. speaks of the קְהַל יהוה, the whole people of Yahweh ; Yahweh is the One who calls them together in unity. Dt. (23:2 ff.) uses קְהַל יהוה in exactly the same way when it lays down conditions for the reception of the maimed or of aliens. In Dt. (5:19; 9:10; 10:4; 18:16) we can also see why the combination קְהַל יהוה is justified. For the קָהָל which originally established the relation between Yahweh and His people is the assembly at Sinai, and the day when Yahweh and Israel were brought together is the יוֹם הַקָּהָל. In consequence, the worshipping community at the dedication of Solomon's temple is the קָהָל (1 K. 8:14 ff.) and later the same word is used for the gathering for the feast of tabernacles in 444, when Ezra read the Law to men, women and children. If קָהָל is thus used on these special cultic occasions, we still find instances of the older secular use. קָהָל is the mobilisation of the people for war, cf. 1 S. 17:47 and also genuine and augmented passages in Ez. (23:24, 46 etc.). A different kind of summons is the call to an extraordinary national assembly, e.g., Jer. 26:17; 44:15, the former without women and children, the latter including them. We may comprehensively define קָהָל as the assembly summoned on special occasions, whether of men alone (e.g., mobilisation for war or the sudden convening of a judicial session), or of the whole people (as in Ezr.). As the assembly thus convened, קָהָל can then be used for those who are qualified to take part in it (Dt. 23:2 ff.). In relation to the development of the term into the NT ἐκκλησία, we have to take into account the fact that the word is used for those who took part in the conclusion of the covenant at Sinai and also for those who pledged themselves afresh

G. Etymology?

The preceding history of the term ἐκκλησία is more important than the etymology, concerning which we must now say a few words in conclusion. If by way of the LXX the NT ἐκκλησία is the fulfilment of the OT קָהָל, and if קָהָל בְּנֵי שֵׁת, which represents this קָהָל, has also to be considered as an equivalent, there is no point in laying particular stress on the derivation of the noun ἐκκλησία from the verb ἐκκαλεῖν and the related adjective ἔκκλητος. In this respect it is significant that neither ἐκκαλεῖν nor ἔκκλητος occurs in the NT.

> In the LXX the first word is found only at Gn. 19:5 and Dt. 20:10 (Heb. קָרָא) and the second only at Sir. 42:11. In Gk. generally both are common, and ἔκκλητος is even a technical term in connection with the ἐκκλησία as a political national assembly, cf. Xenoph. Hist. Graec., II, 4, 38, where οἱ ἔκκλητοι are the members of the national council which takes the place of the ἐκκλησία in Sparta and in aristocratic states; cf. Eur. Or., 949 and ἔκκλητος ὄχλος, 612.

Whether Paul and other Greek speaking Christians were thinking of those "called forth" when they used the word ἐκκλησία, we cannot tell. It is not impossible, but not probable. Statements like Eph. 5:25 ff.; 1 Tm. 3:15 or Hb. 12:23 might well have given occasion to draw attention to ἐκκαλεῖν. [91] If we are to grasp the true sense, we cannot indulge in arbitrary or fanciful etymologising; we must

---

to the Law under Ezra. Thus קָהָל is a term for those who bear the covenant, and therewith the divine promise. Also significant is the fact that at least from the time of Ezra (cf. already Jer. 44:15) women and children belong to the קָהָל. This is why קָהָל, rendered ἐκκλησία in the LXX, commended itself to the Christian community, which admitted women and children as fully qualified, whereas συναγωγή did not commend itself, since its validity was linked with the presence and participation of men alone. Cf. my forthcoming publication (1937): *Die at.lichen Vorstufen von Kirche und Synagoge.*"

[91] A. Jehle rightly draws attention to these passages in his little art. "ΕΚΚΛΗΣΙΑ, eine bescheidene Anfrage an die Exegeten," *Evang. Kirchenblatt f. Württemberg,* 95 (1934), 78, and he correctly emphasises the doubtfulness, if not the total irrelevance, of the etymology of ἐκκλησία. But when he says that he wrote "in the hope of getting a decisive answer through Prof. Kittel's work" — he means the present art. — it should be stated that this answer had already been given in recent studies (Kattenbusch, K. L. Schmidt etc.). It is worth noting that Christians who still speak Greek obviously do not feel that there is any need to give an etymological explanation of the development of the special sense of ἐκκλησία as now used by them. P. Bratsiotis (Π. Μπρατσιώτης) of Athens has, by request, written the author of the present art. as follows: "As concerns the use of ἐκκλησία in modern Greek, I may inform you that apart from the special sense (ἐκκλησία = ναός), ἐκκλησία has all the meanings of your word *Kirche* (church). For your word *Gemeinde* (congregation) we use either ἐκκλησία or ἐνορία (strictly 'parish'). Unfortunately there is no work on ἐκκλησία in modern Greek except what may be found in handbooks of dogmatics, and these do not contain specific material on the philological sense of the term." As the Israelites in the case of קָהָל, and Greek Christians in that of ἐκκλησία, appropriated what was originally a political relationship, so the same thing happens to-day when newly converted Christians from non-Christian cultures seek and find expressions for their position as Christians from their own language and culture. This is made clear by an example from a letter of the missionary E. Peyer of St. Gallen: "Among the Duala people Christians are called *bona-Kristo*, i.e., kinsmen of Christ. The word *bona* means family, kin, clan. *Mwemba* was chosen for 'congregation.' This word originally denotes an age-group, i.e., those born in the same year or half-year. In youth, and especially in adolescence, these have to perform various rites together. It thus indicates a clearly defined group to which not everyone will be admitted."

study the *usus* and *abusus* of the word. There are theologians who emphasise the similarity between *Sünde* and *Sonderung* to show that sin is separation from God, and this makes sense in German. There are also philosophers who interpret *Zufall* (chance) existentially as *Zu-fall* (what befalls), which is quite artificial even in German. But at root these are more or less pseudo-philological considerations though they may convey sound ideas (as we often see in the strange allegorising of Paul). Ἐκκλησία is in fact the group of men called out of the world by God even though we do not take express note of the ἐξ. The original קְהַל יְהֹוָה already bears the same sense, and it does not give linguistic expression to the "out of".

How much depends on the history of a word, with its *usus* and *abusus,* may be seen from the following consideration regarding ἐκκλησία. Accurately to reproduce the biblical use of the word and concept, we ought always to say "assembly (of God)." If we cannot do this, it is because a dictatorial standard cannot be established in the linguistic field, and especially because we need both the term "church" and the term "congregation" in view of the wide range in significance of ἐκκλησία (→ n. 6). Both these words have advantages and disadvantages. "Church" has the advantage of emphasising the aspect of totality in the sense of the universal Church, and it has the disadvantage of stressing the Catholic-hierarchical element. "Congregation" has the advantage of emphasising the small fellowship which is already the Church, and it has the disadvantage of giving prominence to the individual congregation in a Congregational and even sectarian sense. Intrinsically "church" is to be preferred on etymological grounds. The "church" is the company which belongs to the Lord, the κυριακόν or κυριακή. On the other hand, "church" is now so loaded a term that we cannot make do with it alone. Perhaps "church community" might be recommended as a term to describe the "assembly (of God)." [92]

---

[92] Luther's dislike of the word *Kirche* is well-known. Less well-known is the fact that in the revised Luther Bible, and in the corresponding concordance, we do not find the term at all, whereas Luther himself used it in his own translation, though mostly in relation to pagan shrines in the OT, and in the NT only in connection with the dedication at Jn. 10:22 (as a rendering of τὰ ἐγκαίνια, "the dedication of the temple," cf. 2 Macc. 2:9). On this subject, cf. the fine presentation by W. Rotscheidt, "Das Wort 'Kirche' in Luthers Bibel-übersetzung," *Deutsches Pfarrerblatt,* 34 (1930), 506 f. Incidentally, the derivation of *Kirche* from κύριος is not absolutely certain, cf. R. Hildebrand, *Deutsches Wörterbuch,* V, 790, *s.v.* : "The derivation is much disputed ; it is certainly foreign, and came to us with Christianity. J. Grimm, Gramm., 3, 156 favoured derivation from the Lat. *circus* (as Lipsius etc. before him), which took such early forms as *chirih, chirch,* etc. This is supported by a gloss in Kero *ûzzana chirih : foris oratorio,* but this was corrected by H. Hattemer, 1 (1844), 94 to *ûzzana chirihhûn.*" Possibly connected with this reference to *circus,* which is unanimously rejected by German experts, is the view expressed by Karl Barth in his *Credo* (1935), 120 : "*Ecclesia* is a gathering assembled by a summons. The Germanic equivalent, *Kirche, Kerk,* Church, is not in my view a garbled reproduction of the Greek adjective κυριακή (ἐκκλησία), as is commonly supposed. It derives from the stem to which, e.g., the Latin terms *circa, circum, circare, circulus,* etc. also belong. It thus denotes a definite, restricted, and to this extent emphatic place." How wholly non-essential for the explanation of the matter etymologising is, may be illustrated by the fact that the word for "church" in Rhaeto-Romanic is *baselgia,* in Roumanian *biserica* and in Albanian *bijeske* — terms which all come down in architectural history from *basilica, v.* W. Meyer-Lübke, *Roman. Etymolog. Wörterbuch*³ (1935), *s.v. basilica* ; J. Jud, *Zur Geschichte der bündner-roman. Kirchensprache* (1919), *passim.* The thing itself is there even without the etymology. Finally, there is an etymological curiosity in the *Larger Catechism* of Luther, II, 3 (J. T. Müller, *Die symbol. Bücher der ev.-luth. Kirche* [1860], 457): "Thus the little word 'church' is strictly no more than an ordinary assembly, and is not really German but Greek (like the word *ecclesia*), for in Greek it is *kyria,* which is called *curia* in Latin." What Tertullian intended as a material explanation (→ n. 40) has thus become etymology in Luther. In-

H. The Post-Apostolic Fathers and Early Catholicism.

Side by side with, and subsequent to, the writings of the NT there took place in the post-apostolic fathers and early Catholicism a distinctive shift in the understanding of ἐκκλησία. [93] Whereas in the NT adjectival predicates are never attached to the Church as titles, these become very common in later writings. Furthermore, we can only speak of marginal speculation about the Church in the NT, but later these various predicates give rise to thorough-going speculation in the true sense.

In the very earliest writings outside the NT ἐκκλησία is not common except in Hermas. Here it is an individual, a person, whom the author meets in his visionary conversations — the κυρία alongside the κύριος, who is adorned by the epithet ἁγία, v., 1, 1, 6; [94] 1, 3, 4; 4, 1, 3. The lady, who is called πρεσβυτέρα because of her appearance, is described as the μορφή of a "holy spirit" who for his part is identical with the "Son of God." The Pauline and Deutero-Pauline concept of the Church as the ἓν σῶμα is symbolically expressed in the πύργος ἐξ ἑνὸς λίθου γεγονώς s., 9, 18, 3.

---

structed by pertinent modern German dictionaries (F. L. K. Weigand[5], ed. and rev. by Hirt, Vol. I, 1909; K. Kluge[11], rev. A. Götze, 1934; H. Paul[4], ed. K. Euling, 1935), and after consulting W. Altwegg of Basel and A. Debrunner of Berne, I turned to A. Götze of Giessen as the most learned and reliable authority, and he sent me the following communication : "We German students are now beginning to see our way a little more clearly as regards *Kirche*. Luther's derivation from the Latin *curia*, obviously a figment suggested by his journey to Rome, and Grimm's proposal of the Latin *circus*, have both been discarded. The only possible starting-point is the Greek κυρικόν, 'God's house,' a popular 4th century form of the older κυριακόν. In the ecclesiastical sphere Latin loanwords (e.g., *Papst* and *Propst*) did not undergo any shift in the final consonant ; this proves that they did not come into the Germanic sphere prior to 600. (*Kelch* came in with viniculture, while the 'z' in Kreuz is not due to a shift of sound, but reproduces the 'ts' sound of the second 'c' in the Latin *crucem*.) *Kirche*, on the other hand, has the ordinary 'ch' for 'k' (Swiss-German even changes the first 'k', *chilch*). It was thus present prior to 600 and was brought to us by an earlier missionary wave than words like *Papst* etc. Which wave this was is open to dispute. Kluge's view, which I have stated in the 11th ed. of his *Etymolog. Wörterbuch* (1934; art. *Kirche*, 1931, p. 301), and which he defended in an art. which is still well worth reading, 'Gotische Lehnworte im Althochdeutschen,' *Beiträge z. Geschichte d. deutschen Sprache u. Lit.*, 35 (1909), 124 ff., assumes a Gothic *kyrikō* and an early Gothic-Arian wave of missionary endeavour which must have reached S. E. Germany when the kingdom of Theoderic the Great (d. 526) was contiguous with the duchy of Bavaria. Modern scholarship now recognises that during this period Arian missionaries carried a number of ecclesiastical terms up the Danube and down the Rhine. Whether *Kirche* was one of these is questioned, however, by T. Frings, 'Germania Romana' in *Teuthonista, Ztschr. f. deutsche Dialektforschung u. Sprachgeschichte, Beiheft* 4 (1932), 24, 31, 37 f., 46, 50, 120. He suggests that κυρικόν, becoming a fem. under the influence of *basilica*, journeyed by way of Marseilles and Lyons to Trèves, and he lists *Kirche* with other Christian words in the Rhineland. He makes out a good case for these, but hardly explains why *Kirche* should be included when no examples are given. It is true that we have no instances of the Gothic *kyrikō*, for Ulfilas died before its arrival, but the Old Slavonic *crukŭ* and the Russian *cerkovĭ* bear witness to its presence. Thus the question of route is not yet settled ; W. Betz, who is writing the art. *Kirche* in the *Trübner Deutsches Wörterbuch* which I am now editing, will have to reach a decision on this question."

[93] The fullest statistics and best material are to be found in Kattenbusch, I, 146 ff., building on his *Das apostolische Symbol*, II (1900), 683 ff.

[94] The view here expressed that the world was created for the sake of the Church corresponds to the Jewish idea that the people Israel is the goal of creation, cf. M. Dibelius, *Der Hirt des Hermas* (1923), ad loc.

1 Cl. uses ἐκκλησία only in three places. In the introduction we read of the ἐκκλησία τοῦ θεοῦ ἡ παροικοῦσα 'Ρώμην or Κόρινθον. This is in keeping with 1 Pt. 1:1 and Jm. 1:1 (→ 517). συνευδοκησάσης τῆς ἐκκλησίας πάσης at 44, 3 and ἀρχαίαν Κορινθίων ἐκκλησίαν at 47, 6 are also in line with the NT.

Ign. soberly describes the ἐκκλησίαι to which he writes as οὖσα ἐν 'Εφέσῳ etc., but on the other hand he also uses most imposing epithets: ἀξιομακάριστος (Eph., cf. R.); εὐλογημένη ἐν χάριτι θεοῦ κτλ. (Mg.); ἁγία, ἐκλεκτὴ καὶ ἀξιόθεος (Tr.); ἠλεημένη ἐν μεγαλειότητι πατρός κτλ. κτλ. (R.; here Ign. can hardly seem to heap up enough titles — he has about a dozen); ἠλεημένη καὶ ἡδρασμένη κτλ. (Phld.); ... πεπληρωμένη ἐν πίστει κτλ. (Sm.). The language he uses concerning the Church is quite extravagant. Many of the epithets are dogmatic and typical, |many are pragmatic and individual. Some refer only to the congregation concerned; others transcend these limits. Distinctive is Eph., 5, 5, where we read of ἐνκεκραμένοι (joined) αὐτῷ (sc. τῷ ἐπισκόπῳ) ὡς ἡ ἐκκλησία 'Ιησοῦ Χριστῷ καὶ ὡς 'Ιησοῦς Χριστὸς τῷ πατρί, ἵνα πάντα ἐν ἑνότητι σύμφωνα ᾖ. God, Christ and the Church form one entity for believers. This is in line with the NT. But the introduction of the monarchical bishop goes beyond it. In Sm., 8, 2 the predicate καθολική occurs for the first time. In the first instance it probably means only μία μόνη, una sola, [95] but later it takes the sense of οἰκουμενική, universalis, universa. Ecclesiastical Latin kept catholica as well as ecclesia as a loanword.

Polycarp greets the Philippians as Cl. does the Corinthians, namely, as ἐκκλησία παροικοῦσα. The congregation of Smyrna uses the same term for itself in Mart. Pol., and it addresses the congregation in Philomelium καὶ πάσαις ταῖς κατὰ πάντα τόπον τῆς ἁγίας καὶ καθολικῆς ἐκκλησίας παροικίαις. It belongs to the dignity of self-assessment, and to the dignity which each congregation owes the others, that it is one and holy. On the one side the Church belongs to the world in which it still lives and of which it is still a part. On the other side it belongs to God. [96]

In the Did. the ἐκκλησία is mentioned only 4 times: 4, 14; 9, 4; 10, 5; 11, 11. ἐν ἐκκλησίᾳ ἐξομολογήσῃ τὰ παραπτώματά σου at 4, 4 is reminiscent of Mt. 18:17. At 9, 4 (cf. 10, 5) the Church is now scattered, but συναχθήτω ἀπὸ τῶν περάτων τῆς γῆς εἰς τὴν σὴν βασιλείαν. This is in keeping with what the NT says about the relation between the Church and the kingdom. The expression μυστήριον κοσμικὸν ἐκκλησίας at 11, 11 is hard to interpret. It is reminiscent of Col. and Eph., but in the Did. it seems to have further implications in the direction of an esoteric knowledge on the part of believers.

This esoteric element in the sphere of the μυστήριον is even more pronounced in the so-called Second Ep. of Clement. At 14, 1 the ἐκκλησία is here understood as ἡ πρώτη, ἡ πνευματική, ἡ πρὸ ἡλίου καὶ σελήνης ἐκτισμένη, and in the following verses this is worked out in detail in relation to the exposition of γραφή verses.

The idea of a pre-existent Christian Church which is prior to the Synagogue rests on Pauline (R. 4:9 ff.; Gl. 4:21 ff.) and Deutero-Pauline (Eph. 1:3 ff.) statements, and in Valentinian Gnosticism it is developed into speculation concerning the aeon of the ἐκκλησία. Similarly, the confession that the Church is ἄνωθεν becomes a far-reaching speculation [97] which gives comfort to the representatives of a theologia gloriae when they try to understand the antithesis between an empirical Church and an ideal. There

---

[95] So Kattenbusch, I, 148.
[96] We see from Barn. that, as in the NT, ἐκκλησία is not a kind of catchword to cover everything. Barn. never refers to Christians as the ἐκκλησία but often as the → λαός, i.e., as the people whom God has betrothed to His beloved Son, 5, 7; 7, 5, and elsewhere as the ναὸς τοῦ θεοῦ (4, 11) or the πόλις (16, 5).
[97] As Kattenbusch finely says (I, 155): "It is true that from a certain period the idea that the Church is ἄνωθεν became speculation; it was not so at first ..."

rises an awareness of the twofold nature of the Church as the Church militant and the Church triumphant. Such speculations introduce a distinctive ambiguity into statements concerning the Church. This is equally true of both the Greek and the Latin fathers. The greatest of them, Augustine, whose comprehensive thinking set the Church in the centre of Roman Catholic life and thought, is the very one in whom the relation between the empirical and the ideal Church is not made clear. If genuinely Gnostic speculation was held at bay, speculation still established itself in the form of Platonism, though this could be evaluated very differently according to the emphasis placed on the gulf between reality and idea. Protestantism, with its distinction between the invisible and the visible Church, has its own share in this unrealistic Platonism.

J. Conclusion.

Where, when, and how does Catholicism begin as distinct from early Christianity? The transition is nowhere so palpably clear as in the conception of the Church. It took place already in the sphere of early Christian writings outside the NT Canon. Speculations increased even to the point of Gnosticism. A latent, and often acute, Platonism split up the ἐκκλησία, which as a *corpus mixtum* ought not to have been divided.

The Church is never triumphant. It is always militant, i.e., under pressure. Triumphant, it would be the βασιλεία τοῦ θεοῦ, and no longer the ἐκκλησία. Moreover, this ἐκκλησία as the assembly of God in Christ is not invisible on the one side and visible on the other. The Christian community, which as the individual congregation represents the whole body, is just as visible and corporeal as the individual man. δικαιοσύνη and ἁγιότης are ascribed both to the community and to the individual without any implication that righteousness (justification) and holiness (sanctification) belong either to the ἐκκλησία or to the κλητός as qualities. If Luther distinguished between the invisible and the visible Church, especially in controversy with Rome, he did so without accepting the Platonism of his successors. The very fact that in his translation of the Bible he does not speak of the Church, but of the congregation of the saints as the people or company of God, the קְהַל יְהֹוָה, shows that the visible ἐκκλησία is the object of faith and not an essentially invisible *civitas Platonica*. This return of Luther to the OT is Pauline. [98] The strong bulwark against free speculations concerning the Church is

---

[98] Worth noting here are the agreement and conclusion of R. Sohm, *Kirchenrecht*, II (1923), 135: "Early Christianity had not yet won through to recognition of the invisibility of the people of God. This is how it became Catholic. But Luther's discovery that the Church is invisible implied the overthrow of Catholicism." Against this erroneous reading and judgment one must set the verdict of Kattenbusch (II, 351) that Paul "remains far superior to all who have taught concerning the Church, including Luther." On the debate as to the visible and invisible Church, cf. K. L. Schmidt, "Kirchenleitung u. Kirchenlehre im NT" in *Christentum u. Wissenschaft*, 8 (1932), 241 ff., esp. 254 ff. in reply to E. Foerster, "Kirche wider Kirche," ThR, NF, 4 (1932), 155 f. Justifiable caution in respect of the distinction between the visible and the invisible Church, which became so widespread and exercised such unfortunate influence amongst the Reformation churches, characterises the contribution of C. H. Dodd to *Essays Congregational and Catholic* (1931), in which he discusses the whole question of the Church in the light of early Christianity and in relation to the modern Church or churches. (In this connection we may note that Luther himself equated the *ecclesia invisibilis* with the *ecclesia (spiritualis) sola fide perceptibilis* [the earliest reference from the year 1521, Weimar ed., VII, 710].) A completely different view is taken by J. Böni, *Der Kampf um die Kirche, Studien z. Kirchenbegriff des christl. Altertums* (1934), 130: "When there is reference to the Church in the NT, one has the impression of dealing only

the ineffaceable significance of the primitive community, which Paul also recognised. [99]

As the Church of the NT cannot be understood by playing off idea against reality, so it cannot be understood by playing off the whole Church against the individual congregation. Questions of practical theology and sociology arise at this point, but these are secondary. Every true early Christian congregation was just as good a representation of the whole body as the primitive congregation at Jerusalem. The fact that individual congregations gradually formed larger organisations leaves an impression of development from the individual to the corporate. But we must not be dominated by this impression. What counts is that the congregation took itself to be representative of the whole Church. It is from this standpoint that we should approach the much discussed and controversial issue of the so-called development of the Church's constitution. We should not make too much of self-evident constitutional matters. The NT makes it quite plain that at the outset there was a stronger pneumatic and charismatic ministry than later, and that this was replaced by presbyters and bishops. But the way in which Paul thinks and speaks of the Church, and especially the way in which he maintains the link with the first community, shows that we are not justified in speaking of an essential constitutional change from a pneumatic to a juristic form. It was only

---

with an invisible Church." (Böni's work, which runs to 326 pages, is the most recent and comprehensive exegetical and historical discussion of the concept of the Church, and comes from the pen of a Swiss Reformed pastor, formerly a Roman Catholic priest, who is less concerned to advance scholarly discussion of the problems than to give an account of the way in which, in connection with the fruits of many years of reading, he moved from a traditionalist and conservative position to a modernist and liberal.)

[99] Cf. A. Schlatter, "Die Kirche Jerusalems vom Jahre 70-130," BFTh, 2 (1898), 90 : "When Israel died, the primitive Church died also. And its death was detrimental to the whole Church, for sectarian Christianity filled the gap, Mohammed on the one side, bishop, monk and pope on the other." Startling and exaggerated though this statement is, it is true none the less. It is true and important in spite of E. Peterson. Peterson himself rightly observes (op. cit. → n. 2, 69): "Those who view the relation of the Church to the Synagogue merely as a historical and not as a theological problem will necessarily revive the Gnostic outlook, which seeks to eliminate the OT and the Messiah 'according to the flesh.' To this extent it is no accident that theologically the historian Harnack is favourably inclined to the Gnostic Marcion." What is not so clear, however, is the standpoint from which Peterson is speaking as a theologian, not a historian, when he writes : "In the ecclesia they (i.e., the fathers) perceived, in distinction from the Synagogue, an ἐκκαλεῖν, an evocatio, a calling out of the world with its natural orders and natural sociological constructs" (24 f.), and when he formulates the following note : "Cf. C. Passaglia, De ecclesia Christi, I (1853), p. 10. I regard this patristic understanding of the word ἐκκλησία, which helps to differentiate between the institutional forms of the Ecclesia and the Synagogue, as far more significant than modern arguments that ἐκκλησία and συναγωγή are used promiscue in the LXX. The meaning of a word is decided, not by a quotation, but by the concrete situation in which it is uttered" (70). But surely the link between the OT and the NT is more than a simple quotation. And emphasis on the concrete situation runs counter to biblical theology by producing history rather than theology. Peterson combined and augmented his three Salzburg lectures on "Die Kirche aus Juden u. Heiden" into a single paper in Schweiz. Rundsch., Jan. 1936, 875 ff. This contains helpful but unclarified insights into the relation and antithesis between the Church and the Synagogue. In the NT, at any rate, ἐκκλησία and συναγωγή are not so distinct as Peterson thinks necessary. The fathers whom he follows, consciously accepting early and mediaeval exegesis, argued from R. 9-11 for their view that the true (spiritual) and false (carnal) Israel are the ἐκκλησία and the συναγωγή. But in the concrete form in which they finally worked it out this distinction could hardly be what the NT as a whole really has in view. → 518.

when *res iuris humani* became *res iuris divini*, largely under the impulse and influence of lofty speculations concerning the Church, that the step could be taken from primitive Christianity to early Catholicism — a step which, rightly understood, denotes the cleavage between Protestantism and Roman Catholicism.

K. L. Schmidt

καλοδιδάσκαλος → II, 159 f.

| καλός | → ἀγαθός, κακός, πονηρός. |

Contents : A. The Meaning of καλός. B. καλός καὶ ἀγαθός. C. καλός and τὸ καλόν in the Greek World and Hellenism : 1. Plato; 2. Aristotle; 3. Philo; 4. Plotinus; 5. Hermetica. D. καλός in the OT (LXX) and Judaism. E. καλός in the NT : 1. Synoptists ; 2. καλὰ ἔργα; 3. John ; 4. Paul ; 5. Pastoral and Catholic Epistles. F. καλός in Christological Statements in the Early Church : 1. The Influence of Is.|53 on the Early Church View of an Ugly Christ ; 2. The Concept of a Beautiful Christ in the Early Church.

κατὰ τὴν ἀρχαίαν παροιμίαν τὸ καλὸν φίλον εἶναι, Plat. Lys., 216c.[1] This ancient Greek proverb adopted by Plato brings out the significance of the term καλός for human life.

A. The Meaning of καλός.

In origin καλός is to be grouped with the Sanskrit *kalja* "sound," "powerful,'' "vigorous," "excellent." A linguistic relation has been indicated to the Old German *hoele*,[2] which means a "hero" or "strong man." This sense is to be found, e.g., in Homer's καλός τε μέγας τε.[3] We are thus led to the basic sense of καλός a. "organically healthy," "fit," "useful," "serviceable." E.g., καλὸς λιμήν, Hom. Od., 6, 263, "a serviceable harbour" ; σῶμα καλὸν ... πρὸς δρόμον πρὸς πάλην, Plat. Hi., I, 295c ; καλὴ γῆ, "good land," Mt. 13:8, 23. It can also be used of metal in the sense of

---

κ α λ ό ς. Bibl. → ἀγαθός and also κακός. J. Jüthner, "Kalokagathia" in *Charisteria Alois Rzach z. achtzigsten Geburtstag dargebracht* (1930), 99 ff.; W. Jaeger, *Paideia*, I (1934); J. Jeremias, "Die Salbungsgeschichte Mk. 14, 3-9," ZNW, 35 (1936), 75-82; Str.-B., IV, 536-610.

[1] The proverb is found in Theogn., 17: ὅττι καλόν, φίλον ἐστί· τὸ δ' οὐ καλὸν οὐ φίλον ἐστί; cf. also Eur. Ba., 881: ὅτι καλὸν φίλον ἀεί; Philo Agric., 99 : παντὶ τῷ σοφῷ τὸ καλὸν φίλον, ὃ καὶ πάντως ἐστὶ σωτήριον.

[2] F. Specht in *Zeitschrift f. vergleichende Sprachforschung*, 62 (1935), 258, n. 1.

[3] Others think that καλός is related to the Gothic *hails* ("hale," "healthy") and to the Old Saxon *hêl* ("whole"), but this is disputed.

"genuine" or "sterling," χρυσός ... καλός, Theogn., 1106; cf. also Xenoph. Mem., III, 1, 9. "Flawless," μαργαρῖται καλοί, Mt. 13:45. When τόπῳ is added to ἐν καλῷ it denotes a suitable or convenient place : κεῖσθαι τὴν Κέρκυραν ἐν καλῷ τοῦ Κορινθιακοῦ κόλπου, Xenoph. Hist. Graec., VI, 2, 9. When χρόνῳ is added, it denotes the right time : νῦν γὰρ ἐν καλῷ φρονεῖν, Soph. El., 384. καλὰ ἱερά are successful sacrifices in which everything is in order and there is the promise of good fortune, Xenoph. An., I, 8, 15 : οὐ γὰρ σφάγια γίνεται καλά; Aesch. Sept. c. Theb., 379. This sense of "in order" and therefore "auspicious" is also found in an expression like ἀεὶ καλὸς πλοῦς ἐσθ' ὅταν φεύγῃς κακά, Soph. Phil., 641. But if a thing or person is healthy, sound or fit, this means that we can also apply the epithet b. "beautiful" in respect of sensual impression. καλός ... δέμας means beautiful in form, Hom. Od., 17, 307; ἰδέᾳ καλός, Pind. Olymp., 10, 103; καλοὶ τὰ σώματα, Xenoph. Mem., II, 6 and 30. The opposite is αἰσχρός : εἶθ' ... αἴσχιον εἶδος ἀντὶ τοῦ καλοῦ ἔλαβον, Eur. Hel., 263. In this connection καλός takes on the sense of "pleasant," "attractive," "lovely." c. When applied to the inward disposition of a man, the term acquires the sense of "morally good," e.g.: καλὸς γὰρ οὑμὸς βίοτος ὥστε θαυμάσαι, Soph. El., 393; ἐργμάτων ἀκτὶς καλῶν ἄσβεστος, Pind. Isthm., 3(4), 60(43). From Critias we have the admonition concerning man's attitude and mode of life : μηδὲν ἄγαν καιρῷ πάντα πρόσεστι καλά, Fr., 7 (II, 315, 29, Diels). In Homer this sense is found only in the neut. : οὐ καλὸν ὑπέρβιον εὐχετάασθαι, Hom. Il., 17, 19. Cf. καλόν τοι, Il., 9, 615 : "it is fine, suitable." The expression καλόν ἐστι often occurs in this sense in every age and in all Gk. usage. E.g., οὔτ' ἐμοὶ τοῦτ' ἔστιν οὔτε σοὶ καλόν, Soph. Phil., 1304; καλόν μοι τοῦτο ποιούσῃ θανεῖν, Soph. Ant., 72. In this connection καλός may be grouped with δίκαιος, ἴσος, and the opposite is αἰσχρός as well as πονηρός.

In Gk. thinking the term καλός is coupled with τάξις and συμμετρία. From the Pythagoreans comes the statement : τὴν μὲν τάξιν καὶ τὴν συμμετρίαν ἀποφαίνομεν αὑτοῖς καλά, τὰ δὲ τούτων ἐναντία, τήν τε ἀταξίαν καὶ τὴν ἀσυμμετρίαν αἰσχρά (I, 368, 28 ff., Diels). Democritus defines the καλόν : καλὸν ἐν παντὶ τὸ ἴσον' ὑπερβολὴ δὲ καὶ ἔλλειψις οὔ μοι δοκέει (Fr., 102 [II, 81, 1 f., Diels]). As such it is found throughout the whole world acc. to the Pythagoreans : τὸ κάλλιστον καὶ ἄριστον μὴ ἐν ἀρχῇ εἶναι, διὰ τὸ καὶ τῶν φυτῶν καὶ τῶν ζώων τὰς ἀρχὰς αἴτια μὲν εἶναι, τὸ δὲ καλὸν καὶ τέλειον ἐν τοῖς ἐκ τούτων (Aristot. Met., XII, 7, p. 1072b, 32). The three senses stated above, namely, organically sound, beautiful in appearance and morally good, may thus be brought under the comprehensive meaning of that which is "ordered," i.e., which has τάξις and συμμετρία. This basic sense, developed into what are for us three distinct and separate spheres, gives to the Gk. καλός a unique and classical significance. On this basis καλός could acquire central importance in the Gk. world. When speaking of καλός, the Gk. had in view the total state of soundness, health, wholeness and order, whether in external appearance or internal disposition. For the Gk., then, the term applies particularly to the world of the divine — τῷ μὲν θεῷ καλὰ πάντα καὶ ἀγαθὰ καὶ δίκαια, Heracl. Fr., 102 (I, 98, 1 f., Diels). It is true that according to Democritus only those who are predisposed thereto have access to the καλόν : τὰ καλὰ γνωρίζουσι καὶ ζηλοῦσιν οἱ εὐφυέες πρὸς αὐτά Fr., 56 (II, 75, 6 f., Diels). Of these it is said : θείου νοῦ τὸ ἀεί τι διαλογίζεσθαι καλόν, Fr., 112 (II, 82, 6 f., Diels).

The noun τὸ καλόν, τὰ καλά follows the adj. in sense, and means that which is ordered or whole or healthy in the sense of a. "the good," "virtue," and b. "the beautiful," "beauty." τὸ κάλλος is also found in the latter sense. The noun, too, acquires great significance in Gk. and Hellenistic life and thought.

B. καλὸς καὶ ἀγαθός.

The combination καλὸς καὶ ἀγαθός, which also occurs in the forms καλός τε καὶ ἀγαθός, καλὸς κἀγαθός and καλός τε κἀγαθός, and from which there derives the noun καλοκαγαθία, [4] plays a most important role in Gk. life.

1. The combination is found from the fifth century. Two meanings are clearly recognisable, a political and social on the one side and an ethical and spiritual on the other. The latter derives from Socrates. Both terms must be considered to grasp the full significance. "Of the two terms the second raises no great difficulties. From the time of Homer the ἀγαθοί are those who stand out from the common herd by reason of their worth (ἀρετή), culture, breeding or possessions ... they constitute the best and most noble class ..." But what does καλός mean when combined with ἀγαθός? Jüthner examines thoroughly this by no means simple question, and in respect of the earliest period he comes to the conclusion that καλός expresses "the element by which the born 'gentleman' is distinguished from the worthy citizen, the καλὸς κἀγαθός from the ἀγαθὸς πολίτης." [5] But this sense was soon replaced. A few examples will best illustrate the meaning and the change in meaning. In the first instance καλὸς καὶ ἀγαθός is a political concept, which quickly moves over into the social sphere. For Thuc. the καλοὶ καὶ ἀγαθοί are the leading citizens in contrast to the δῆμος : τούς τε καλοὺς κἀγαθοὺς ὀνομαζομένους οὐκ ἐλάσσω ... σφίσι πράγματα παρέξειν τοῦ δήμου, VIII, 48, 6. The political comedies of Aristoph. point in the same direction : τῶν πολιτῶν οἱ καλοί τε κἀγαθοί, Eq., 227. From 186 ff. we learn that the καλοὶ κἀγαθοί should have some elementary musical instruction and an honourable character. Cf. esp. Ra., 727 ff.: τῶν πολιτῶν θ' οὓς μὲν ἴσμεν εὐγενεῖς καὶ σώφρονας ἄνδρας ὄντας καὶ δικαίους καὶ καλούς τε κἀγαθοὺς καὶ τραφέντας ἐν παλαίστραις καὶ χοροῖς καὶ μουσικῇ προσελοῦμεν, τοῖς δὲ χαλκοῖς καὶ ξένοις καὶ πυρρίαις καὶ πονηροῖς κἀκ πονηρῶν εἰς ἅπαντα χρώμεθα. Here it is plain that a certain qualitative superiority is linked with higher sociological rank — a superiority which is proper to those of this higher rank. The superiority of aristocratic political leadership is interwoven with that of character and culture. The political and sociological sense is still clearly present in Xenoph., e.g., ὁ δὲ Θηραμένης ἀντέκοπτε λέγων, ὅτι οὐκ εἰκὸς εἴη θανατοῦν, εἴ τις ἐτιμᾶτο ὑπὸ τοῦ δήμου, τοὺς δὲ καλοὺς κἀγαθοὺς μηδὲν κακὸν εἰργάζετο, Hist. Graec., II, 3, 15. In Cyrop., IV, 3, 23 — οὐδεὶς ἂν τῶν καλῶν κἀγαθῶν ἑκὼν ὀφθείη Περσῶν οὐδαμῇ πεζὸς ἰών — the expression is used for the leading class among non-Greeks as well.

2. We can see from Xenoph., however, how the change in meaning came about from a predominantly political and social sense to a spiritual and ethical, so that καλὸς κἀγαθός became an expression for the Greek ideal of life. In Oec., 6, 12 ff. Xenoph. tells us how Socrates, who was responsible for the change, investigated the content of the καλὸς κἀγαθός. In his search for a καλὸς κἀγαθός, he argued that outward beauty is not the distinguishing feature. Finally he met a man who was called καλὸς κἀγαθός in his neighbourhood. He was the landowner Ischomachos, who was in every respect a model landlord, who had a well-ordered family, and who discharged his duties to the *polis*. It thus became clear that one may become a καλὸς κἀγαθός by correct teaching and instruction. The καλὸς κἀγαθός whom Socrates encountered was given the title because of his worth and the social position which he enjoyed in consequence. But Socrates found in δικαιοσύνη the essence of the καλοκαγαθία in which he sought to instruct men (Sym., 3, 4). Socrates himself did not belong to the leading political and social caste, but Xenophon calls him a καλὸς κἀγαθός : οἶδα δὲ καὶ Σωκράτη

---

[4] Cf. Jüthner, 99 f.
[5] Jüthner, 113, 119.

δεικνύντα τοῖς συνοῦσιν ἑαυτὸν καλὸν κἀγαθὸν ὄντα καὶ διαλεγόμενον κάλλιστα περὶ ἀρετῆς καὶ τῶν ἄλλων ἀνθρωπίνων, Mem., I, 2, 17. In Mem., I, 1, 16 we have a description of the ἀνθρώπινα which one must learn to become καλὸς κἀγαθός and not πονηρός, which is from the very first the opposite, and which undergoes the same change in sense (→ πονηρός). The pupil who wishes to become καλὸς κἀγαθός (Mem., I, 2, 7) is instructed by Socrates in "what is pious and impious, beautiful and ugly, righteous and unrighteous, in moderation and folly, bravery and cowardice, in the nature of the state and the statesman, of rule over men and the qualifications for it, and in other things whose knowledge will justify us in calling men καλοὶ κἀγαθοί in outward appearance." [6] In time the καλοκαγαθία of the inward man will reflect itself in the outward. One takes more pleasure in the aspect of men, δι' ὧν τὰ καλά τε κἀγαθὰ καὶ ἀγαπητὰ ἤθη φαίνεται, ἢ δι' ὧν τὰ αἰσχρά τε καὶ πονηρὰ καὶ μισητά (Mem., III, 10, 5). καλὰ κἀγαθά are the works and qualities of καλοὶ κἀγαθοί (cf. Mem., I, 2, 23; 5, 1). For Socrates, then, the καλὸς κἀγαθός is a man who is pious and righteous, wise and understanding, and moderate and virtuous in his actions. His whole life is orderly in every respect. Socrates laid his impress on all subsequent Gk. thought. καλοκαγαθία finds its content in δικαιοσύνη and becomes a matter of παιδεία. When Socrates is asked concerning the felicity of the Persian king, of which καλοκαγαθία is a presupposition, he enquires as to his παιδεία and δικαιοσύνη, Plat., Gorg., 470e. The ideal of life is also an ideal of education. Happiness is only possible with καλοκαγαθία: τὸν μὲν γὰρ καλὸν κἀγαθὸν ἄνδρα καὶ γυναῖκα εὐδαίμονα εἶναί φημι, τὸν δὲ ἄδικον καὶ πονηρὸν ἄθλιον, loc. cit. In the political writings of Plato it is evident that the only true statesmen are men who are trained in mind and body and of high moral stature [7] (cf. Resp., III, 425d; Gorg., 518a-c). As thus deepened in terms of ethos and character, the term returns to the political sphere. In Aristotle it is still used in the older political sense (e.g., Pol., II, 9, p. 1270b, 23 f., 1271a), but we also find penetrating discussions concerning the nature of a καλὸς κἀγαθός (Eth. M., II, 9, p. 1207b, 20 ff.; Eth. Eud., VII, 15, p. 1248b, 8 ff.). [8] Aristotle finds this in the moral perfection which includes happiness: ἔστιν οὖν καλοκαγαθία ἀρετὴ τέλειος, Eth. Eud., VII, 15, p. 1249a, 16.

3. The influence of philosophical reflection and reconstruction on the political sphere may be seen from the orators. Thus Isaeus regards καλοὶ κἀγαθοί who come to the courts as witnesses, not merely as γνωριμώτατοι but also as ἐπιεικέστατοι τῶν πολιτῶν (3, 20). A mark of the καλὸς κἀγαθός for Isocrates is as follows: τὴν δὲ δικαιοσύνην καὶ σωφροσύνην ἴδια κτήματα τῶν καλῶν κἀγαθῶν ὄντα, 3, 43 (cf. 13, 6; 12, 183). In Demosthenes the καλὸς κἀγαθός is "the ideal politician who does not consider his private interests or personal enmities, but only the welfare of the state" (18, 278). [9] For Aeschines, the opponent of Demosthenes, καλοκαγαθία is again an ethical concept (I, 30 f.). This demonstrates the influence of philosophical thought on political life and the mutual relation between life and thought on the one side, e.g., in Socrates, and thought and life on the other, e.g., in the orators. [10]

---

[6] Ibid., 104.
[7] Ibid., 106.
[8] H. v. Arnim, "Das Ethische in Aristot. Topik." (Sitzungsber. Akad. Wien phil.-hist. Kl., 205, 4 [1927]), 100 ff.
[9] Jüthner, 110.
[10] We find the same influence in inscr., where καλοκαγαθία is used to express esteem, e.g., ... ἀξίους αὐτοὺς κατεσκεύακαν τῆς τε ἰδίας καλοκαγαθίας καὶ τῆς τῶν προγόνων ἀρετῆς, IG, IX, 2, 1108, line 13; ὁ δῆμος Μοσχίωνα Κυδίμου ἀρετῆς ἕνεκεν καὶ εὐνοίας καὶ καλοκαγαθίας καὶ φιλοδοξίας τῆς εἰς ἑαυτὸν καὶ εὐσεβείας τῆς εἰς τοὺς θεούς, Inscr. Priene, 108, p. 90, line 326. Cf. Jüthner, 111 f.

4. The phrase becomes stereotyped later, but the main lines established by Socrates and Plato remain. For Epict. καλοὶ κἀγαθοί are philosophers of whom it may be said: ὕλη τοῦ καλοῦ καὶ ἀγαθοῦ τὸ ἴδιον ἡγεμονικόν, ... ἔργον δὲ καλοῦ καὶ ἀγαθοῦ τὸ χρῆσθαι ταῖς φαντασίαις κατὰ φύσιν (Diss., III, 3, 1). The instruction to be received by a would-be καλὸς κἀγαθός, i.e., by a pupil of the philosophers, extends to the relation between desire and renunciation, between impulse and disinclination, and includes teaching on duty and on knowledge and judgment in moral questions (III, 3, 2). According to Epict. the καλὸς κἀγαθός by will and thought integrates himself into the will of deity (III, 24, 95). The judgment of Philo is the same as that of older philosophy: τὸ μέγιστον καὶ τιμιώτατον τῶν ἐν τῇ φύσει, καλοκαγαθία, Virt., 117. [11]

C. καλός and τὸ καλόν in the Greek World and Hellenism.

1. In the Greek world the concept of καλός and τὸ καλόν received from Plato a significant and characteristic impress which persisted to the time of Plotinus. For Plato the καλόν is very closely related to the idea of the ἀγαθόν (→ I, 11), the central idea which unites us with the divine. [12] This central idea of the good was made up of κάλλος, ξυμμετρία and ἀλήθεια (Phileb., 65a), and is πάντων ... καλῶν αἰτία (Resp., VII, 517c). But the καλόν is not merely a result of the good. It is also an aspect of the good. Hence it can be identified with the ἀγαθόν. It is a form of the ἀγαθόν. The ἀγαθόν takes form in the καλόν. πᾶν δὴ τὸ ἀγαθὸν καλόν, τὸ δὲ καλὸν οὐκ ἄμετρον· καὶ ζῷον οὖν τὸ τοιοῦτον ἐσόμενον σύμμετρον θετέον, Tim., 87c. It is the moving force of the Greek spirit, for which, in a rare harmony, supreme intellectual knowledge is a vision of the breadth and multiplicity of the καλόν. It is the eternal thrust of the Greek striving for self-fulfilment. For Plato, the basis of παιδεία is the hunger of the soul for the καλόν. The soul strives for a higher image of man by letting itself be led to the καλόν as a prototype. This is classically formulated in the prayer of Socrates: δοίητέ μοι καλῷ γενέσθαι τἄνδοθεν, Phaedr., 279b/c, [13] and in the περιποιεῖσθαι ἑαυτῷ τὸ καλόν of Aristotle, Eth. Nic., IX, 8, p. 1168b, 27.

Individual passages will help to make this clear. The καλόν reveals itself as the form of the good in the world which has come into being. It does so because it is fashioned in accordance with the eternal and invisible idea of the καλόν, the form of eternal being and the eternal good: εἰ μὲν δὴ καλός ἐστιν ὅδε ὁ κόσμος ὅ τε δημιουργὸς ἀγαθός, δῆλον ὡς πρὸς τὸ ἀΐδιον ἔβλεπεν ... ὁ μὲν γὰρ κάλλιστος τῶν γεγονότων, ὁ δ' ἄριστος τῶν αἰτίων. οὕτω δὴ γεγενημένος πρὸς τὸ λόγῳ καὶ φρονήσει περιληπτὸν καὶ κατὰ ταὐτὰ ἔχον δεδημιούργηται, Tim., 29a (cf. 30b c). Man can perceive the καλόν because he has looked clearly into the stage which precedes embodiment: κάλλος δὲ τότ' ἦν ἰδεῖν λαμπρόν, ὅτε σὺν εὐδαίμονι χορῷ μακαρίαν ὄψιν τε καὶ θέαν ... εἴδόν τε καὶ ἐτελοῦντο τῶν τελετῶν ἣν θέμις λέγειν μακαριωτάτην, Phaedr., 250b c. Man's ability to perceive the καλόν in this world is ἔρως. Ἔρως δ' ἐστὶν ἔρως περὶ τὸ καλόν, Symp., 204b. In the well-known

---

[11] In the Roman period καλὸς κἀγαθός is used as an adulatory epithet and even as a title, e.g., ἄνδρες καλοὶ κἀγαθοὶ καὶ φίλοι παρὰ δήμου καλοῦ κἀγαθοῦ καὶ φίλου συμμάχου, IG, IX, 2, 89, 16. Cf. Jüthner, 113.

[12] In addition to the examples given under → ἀγαθός, cf. esp. C. Ritter, "Platons Gedanken über Gott und das Verhältnis der Welt u. d. Menschen zu ihm," ARW, 19 (1916-19), on the idea of the good, 260 ff., 467 ff.

[13] Ritter, 492.

Diotima speech at table Socrates shows how man comes to have experience of the καλόν through ἔρως, [14] an experience which consists no less in a μάθημα than an ἰδεῖν: ... ἀρχόμενον ἀπὸ τῶνδε τῶν καλῶν ἐκείνου ἕνεκα τοῦ καλοῦ ἀεὶ ἐπανιέναι, ὥσπερ ἐπαναβασμοῖς χρώμενον, ἀπὸ ἑνὸς ἐπὶ δύο καὶ ἀπὸ δυοῖν ἐπὶ πάντα τὰ καλὰ σώματα, καὶ ἀπὸ τῶν καλῶν σωμάτων ἐπὶ τὰ καλὰ ἐπιτηδεύματα, καὶ ἀπὸ τῶν ἐπιτηδευμάτων ἐπὶ τὰ καλὰ μαθήματα, καὶ ἀπὸ τῶν μαθημάτων ἐπ' ἐκεῖνο τὸ μάθημα τελευτῆσαι, ὅ ἐστιν οὐκ ἄλλου ἢ αὐτοῦ ἐκείνου τοῦ καλοῦ μάθημα, καὶ γνῷ αὐτὸ τελευτῶν ὅ ἔστι καλόν ... τί δῆτα ... οἰόμεθα, εἴ τῳ γένοιτο αὐτὸ τὸ καλὸν ἰδεῖν εἰλικρινές, καθαρόν, ἄμεικτον, ἀλλὰ μὴ ἀνάπλεων σαρκῶν τε ἀνθρωπίνων καὶ χρωμάτων καὶ ἄλλης πολλῆς φλυαρίας θνητῆς, ἀλλ' αὐτὸ τὸ θεῖον καλὸν δύναιτο μονοειδὲς κατιδεῖν; Symp., 211c d e. From this knowledge of the καλόν, and from the vision of the καλόν to which ἔρως leads us by way of love for man, come virtue and immortality: ἆρ' οἴει ... ὁρῶντι ᾧ ὁρατὸν τὸ καλόν, τίκτειν οὐκ εἴδωλα ἀρετῆς, ἅτε οὐκ εἰδώλου ἐφαπτομένῳ, ἀλλὰ ἀληθῆ, ἅτε τοῦ ἀληθοῦς ἐφαπτομένῳ· τεκόντι δὲ ἀρετὴν ἀληθῆ καὶ θρεψαμένῳ ὑπάρχει θεοφιλεῖ γενέσθαι, καὶ εἴπερ τῳ ἄλλῳ ἀνθρώπων; ἀθανάτῳ καὶ ἐκείνῳ, Symp., 212a. Such a man is καλὸς κἀγαθός because he has the excellence of virtue by reason of which his concern for the beautiful is also a concern for the καλόν or ἀγαθόν (cf. Resp., III, 401e). The καλόν is also an object of art. In art the beautiful is objictified as follows: τὰ μὲν ἀρετῆς ἐχόμενα ψυχῆς ἢ σώματος, εἴτε αὐτῆς εἴτε τινὸς εἰκόνος σύμπαντα σχήματά τε καὶ μέλη καλά, Leg., 655b.

This question of the καλόν is a centre and climax in Platonic philosophy and therewith in Greek thought, and indeed in human thought generally. The καλόν, which as eternal idea belongs to the realm of the divine, is the form of the good which fuses deity, world and man into an ideal unity. In art and virtue it brings meaning, fellowship and eternity into human existence.

2. For Aristotle the καλόν is divided into τὸ ἡδύ — that which is naturally beautiful, differentiated into the καλὸν ἐν τοῖς τῆς φύσεως ἔργοις ἢ ἐν τοῖς τῆς τέχνης (Part. An., I, 1, p. 639b, 20) — and τὸ καθ' αὑτὸ αἱρετόν — that which is morally beautiful (Rhet., I, 7, p. 1364b, 27 f.). Either way, the beautiful is more precisely defined in terms of τάξις καὶ συμμετρία καὶ τὸ ὡρισμένον, which he calls μέγιστα εἴδη τοῦ καλοῦ (Metaph., XIII, 3, p. 1078a, 36 f.). It is distinguished from the ἀγαθόν: τὸ ἀγαθὸν καὶ τὸ καλὸν ἕτερον (τὸ μὲν γὰρ ἀεὶ ἐν πράξει, τὸ δὲ καλὸν καὶ ἐν τοῖς ἀκινήτοις), Metaph., XIII, 3, p. 1078a, 31 f., a distinction controlled by rejection of the Platonic doctrine of ideas (→ ἀγαθός). The same distinction may be seen clearly in the statement: τὸ μὲν γὰρ συμφέρον αὐτῷ ἀγαθόν ἐστι, τὸ δὲ καλὸν ἁπλῶς, Rhet., II, 13, p. 1389b, 37 f. The καλόν is the good absolutely. [15] More explicitly Aristot. speaks of the καλόν as τὸ καθ' αὑτὸ αἱρετόν. The καλόν is the τέλος τῆς ἀρετῆς, Eth. Nic., III, 10, p. 1115b, 12. Its realisation is experienced in καλοκαγαθία, in ἀρετὴ τέλειος, Eth. Eud., VII, 15, p. 1249a, 16. καλοκαγαθία is thus defined and delimited as follows: καλὸς δὲ κἀγαθὸς τῷ τῶν ἀγαθῶν τὰ καλὰ ὑπάρχειν αὐτῷ δι' αὐτά, καὶ τῷ πρακτικὸς εἶναι τῶν καλῶν καὶ αὐτῶν ἕνεκα. καλὰ δ' ἐστὶν αἵ τε ἀρεταὶ καὶ τὰ ἔργα τὰ ἀπὸ τῆς ἀρετῆς ... ὁ δ' οἰόμενος τὰς ἀρετὰς ἔχειν δεῖν ἕνεκα τῶν ἐκτὸς ἀγαθῶν κατὰ τὸ συμβεβηκὸς καλὰ πράττει, ibid., p. 1248b, 34 ff., 1249a, 14 f. The idea of the good is split, and hence the comprehensive Platonic view is lost. Pre-Platonic concepts are adopted, and primary emphasis is laid on the moral side of the καλόν. A lasting impress is thus made on the term. Stoicism follows the same course

---

[14] On the experience of *eros* in respect of the καλόν, cf. esp. Plat. Phaedr., 249 ff.

[15] Comparison with the definitions of Aristot. given under ἀγαθός shows that the ἀγαθόν and the καλόν are fundamentally akin, so that we cannot attach absolute significance to these distinctions.

as Aristotelianism. Diogenes Laertius sums up the Stoic outlook: καλόν δὲ λέγουσι τὸ τέλειον ἀγαθόν ... ἢ τὸ τελείως σύμμετρον. εἴδη δὲ εἶναι τοῦ καλοῦ τέτταρα, δίκαιον, ἀνδρεῖον, κόσμιον, ἐπιστημονικόν· ἐν γὰρ τοῖσδε τὰς καλὰς πράξεις συντελεῖσθαι ... λέγεσθαι δὲ τὸ καλὸν μοναχῶς μὲν τὸ ἐπαινετοὺς παρεχόμενον τοὺς ἔχοντας ἀγαθὸν ἐπαίνου ἄξιον· ἑτέρως δὲ τὸ εὖ πεφυκέναι πρὸς τὸ ἴδιον ἔργον. ἄλλως δὲ τὸ ἐπικοσμοῦν, ὅταν λέγωμεν μόνον τὸν σοφὸν ἀγαθὸν καὶ καλὸν εἶναι, VII, 100. The καλόν is wholly ethical.[16] The occasional exception expressed in the view: φύσει τοῦτο (sc. τὸ καλόν) αἱρετόν ἐστι καὶ ἀπὸ τῶν ἀλόγων ζῴων, Sext. Emp. Math., XI, 99) is warded off by the perception οὐ γὰρ φύσει, μαθήσει δὲ οἱ καλοὶ κἀγαθοὶ γίνονται, Cl. Al. Strom., ,I, 6, 34, 1. On this ethical understanding the main sense is that of the "virtuous," "orderly," "right," and the concept is that of a norm or standard: οὐδὲ ὁ πλεῖστα κιθαρῳδήσας, ἢ ῥητορεύσας, ἢ κυβερνήσας, ἀλλ᾽ ὁ καλῶς ἐπαινεῖται. Τὸ γὰρ καλὸν οὐκ ἐν μήκει χρόνου θετέον, ἀλλ᾽ ἐν ἀρετῇ καὶ τῇ καιρίῳ συμμετρίᾳ· τοῦτο γὰρ εὔδαιμον καὶ θεοφιλὲς εἶναι νενόμισται ... Μέτρον γὰρ τοῦ βίου τὸ καλόν, οὐ τὸ τοῦ χρόνου μῆκος, Plut. Cons. ad Apoll., 17 (II, 111a b d).

3. The religious character which the καλόν had in Plato's doctrine of ideas is found again in later Hellenistic philosophy. Philo adopts Stoic motifs on the one hand,[17] but on the other, influenced both by the OT and by religious Hellenism and Plato, he gives the καλόν religious significance. The divine is encountered in vision: τὸ ἀγένητον καὶ θεῖον ὁρᾶν ... τὸ πρῶτον ἀγαθὸν καὶ καλὸν καὶ εὔδαιμον καὶ μακάριον ... τὸ κρεῖττον μὲν ἀγαθοῦ, κάλλιον δὲ καλοῦ ..., Leg. Gaj., 5. The divine is the καλόν: οὐδὲν γάρ ἐστι τῶν καλῶν, ὃ μὴ θεοῦ τε καὶ θεῖον, Sacr. AC, 63. The world is conjoined with this divine καλόν: ὁ θεός ... τὸ ἴδιον μεταδεδωκὼς ἅπασι τοῖς ἐν μέρει τῆς τοῦ καλοῦ πηγῆς, ἑαυτοῦ· τὰ γὰρ ἐν κόσμῳ καλὰ οὔποτ᾽ ἂν ἐγεγένητο τοιαῦτα, μὴ πρὸς ἀρχέτυπον τὸ πρὸς ἀλήθειαν καλὸν τὸ ἀγένητον καὶ μακάριον καὶ ἄφθαρτον ἀπεικονισθέντα, Cher., 86. The way to the beautiful is threefold: ... τὸν μὲν ἐκ διδασκαλίας (Abraham), τὸν δ᾽ ἐκ φύσεως (Isaac), τὸν δ᾽ ἐξ ἀσκήσεως (Jacob) ἐφιέμενον καλόν, Abr., 52. On it, it is necessary ἀποστρέφεσθαι τὰ θνητά, ἐπιστρέφειν πρὸς τὸν ἄφθαρτον, Poster. C., 135, ἀδιάστατος περὶ τοῦ θεοῦ μνήμη καὶ ἡ κατάκλησις τῆς ἀπ᾽ αὐτοῦ συμμαχίας (to the unceasing battle of life), which is called τοῦ μεγέθους καὶ πλήθους τῶν καλῶν ἀρχὴ καὶ τέλος, Migr. Abr., 56. He who seeks the καλόν in this way, and actualises it in moral action, is one of the sons of God, Spec. Leg., I, 318.

4. The end of Greek and Hellenistic development is reached in Plotinus. In his Enn. he speaks περὶ τοῦ καλοῦ (I, 6) and renews at the very end of antiquity the thinking of Plato. He begins with the beautiful which is sensually perceptible: τὸ καλόν ἐστι μὲν ἐν ὄψει πλεῖστον, ἔστι δ᾽ ἐν ἀκοαῖς κατά τε λόγων συνθέσεις καὶ ἐν μουσικῇ ἀπάσῃ· καὶ γὰρ μέλη καὶ ῥυθμοί εἰσι καλοί· ἔστι δὲ καὶ προϊοῦσι πρὸς τὸ ἄνω ἀπὸ τῆς αἰσθήσεως καὶ ἐπιτηδεύματα καλὰ καὶ πράξεις καὶ ἕξεις καὶ ἐπιστήμαί τε καὶ τὸ τῶν ἀρετῶν κάλλος, I, 6, 1. Seeking the root of moral beauty, he criticises the usual aesthetics and ethics which finds it in συμμετρία and presses on to the idea of the beautiful as true being: ... τὰ ὄντα ἡ καλλονή ἐστιν, I, 6, 6. This gives us an answer to the question: πῶς δὲ καλὰ κἀκεῖνα καὶ ταῦτα (sc. the above and the earthly); μετοχῇ εἴδους φαμὲν ταῦτα. πᾶν μὲν γὰρ τὸ ἄμορφον πεφυκὸς μορφὴν καὶ εἶδος δέχεσθαι ἄμοιρον ὂν λόγου καὶ εἴδους αἰσχρὸν καὶ ἔξω θείου λόγου, I, 6, 2. "The beauty of the things of this world thus reveals the glory, power

---

[16] For Stoicism ἀγαθόν and καλόν are synonyms, cf. v. Arnim, III, 9-11.

[17] Stoic features are the dominant moralising of the concept, its synonymity with ἀγαθός (Spec. Leg., II, 73; Migr. Abr., 86), Stoic expressions like τέλειον ἀγαθὸν ... τὸ καλόν (Poster. C., 95) and δι᾽ ἑαυτὸ αἱρετόν (Som., II, 20), and the statement: ὁ σπερματικὸς καὶ γεννητικὸς τῶν καλῶν λόγος ὀρθός (Leg. All., III, 150).

and goodness of the spiritual world, so that there is an imperishable bond between all things, between the spiritual and the sensual," IV, 8, 6. [18] True beauty belongs to the world above. It is the transcendent beauty which is expressed in the beautiful of this world, V, 8, 8. To see it is man's greatest possible experience : τί δῆτα οἰόμεθα, εἴ τις αὐτὸ τὸ καλὸν θεῷτο αὐτὸ ἐφ᾽ ἑαυτοῦ καθαρόν, μὴ σαρκῶν, μὴ σώματος ἀνάπλεων, μὴ ἐν γῇ, μὴ ἐν οὐρανῷ, ἵν᾽ ᾖ καθαρόν; This experience is the ἀρίστη θέα, of which Plotinus says ἧς ὁ μὲν τυχὼν μακάριος ὄψιν μακαρίαν τεθεαμένος, I, 6,7; hence this vision brings supreme felicity. It is the goal of life. This is possible because the beautiful is also the good and the good is the beautiful, as the bad is the ugly, I, 6, 6. How does man attain to it ? The presupposition is beauty of soul : οὐ γὰρ ἂν πώποτε εἶδεν ὀφθαλμὸς ἥλιον ἡλιοειδὴς μὴ γεγενημένος, οὐδὲ τὸ καλὸν ἂν ἴδοι ψυχὴ μὴ καλὴ γενομένη. γενέσθω δὴ πρῶτον θεοειδὴς πᾶς καὶ καλὸς πᾶς, εἰ μέλλει θεάσασθαι τἀγαθόν τε καὶ καλόν, I, 6, 9. To attain to beauty of soul is possible only through purification. It is found in the virtues of self-discipline, in which man avoids contact with the lusts of the body, of courage, which is fearlessness in face of the death that separates body and soul, of magnanimity, which is an ability to look away from the things of earth, and of wisdom, which turns from what is below and directs the soul to what is above, I, 6, 6. In this reflection of Plotinus on the καλόν the Greek spirit thus re-arises in all its greatness.

5. In the Hermetic literature the καλόν appears alongside the ἀγαθόν as the beautiful, and it belongs to the world of God : ἡ δὲ τοῦ θεοῦ οὐσία τίς ἐστιν; τὸ ἀγαθὸν καὶ τὸ καλόν, Corp. Herm., XI, 3. The ideal cosmos in accordance with which the visible cosmos is fashioned is called καλὸς κόσμος, I, 8b. The way to the καλόν is by νοεῖν : τολμητέον γὰρ εἰπεῖν ... ὅτι ἡ οὐσία τοῦ θεοῦ ... τὸ καλόν ἐστι καὶ τὸ ἀγαθόν· ὑπὸ δὲ τούτων οὐδέν ἐστι καταλάμπεσθαι τῶν ἐν τῷ κόσμῳ ... ὥσπερ ὀφθαλμὸς οὐ δύναται τὸν θεὸν ἰδεῖν, οὕτως οὐδὲ τὸ καλὸν καὶ τὸ ἀγαθόν· ταῦτα γὰρ μέρη τοῦ θεοῦ ἐστιν, ἴδια αὐτοῦ μόνου ... εἰ δύνασαι νοῆσαι τὸν θεόν, νοήσεις τὸ καλὸν καὶ (τὸ) ἀγαθὸν τὸ ὑπερλαμπόμενον ὑπὸ τοῦ θεοῦ ... ἐὰν περὶ τοῦ θεοῦ ζητῇς, καὶ περὶ τοῦ καλοῦ ζητεῖς, μία γάρ ἐστιν εἰς αὐτὸ ἀποφέρουσα ὁδὸς ἡ μετὰ γνώσεως εὐσέβεια, VI, 4b-5. Here the καλόν has become a wholly transcendental quantity, like deity itself. Cosmological dualism denies to man any possibility of contemplating it. It can be reached only through the νοεῖν which arises with revelation and which takes concrete shape in ἡ μετὰ γνώσεως εὐσέβεια. Cosmological dualism shatters the Platonic unity. Yet the essential point in these writings is that the idea of the beautiful is still found, and that it is evaluated religiously.

D. καλός in the OT (LXX) and Judaism.

In the LXX καλός is mostly the rendering of 1. יָפֶה, e.g., Gn. 12:14; 29:17; 39:6; 41:2 etc., often with the addition τῷ εἴδει (יְפַת מַרְאֶה) and thus denoting "beautiful in respect of outward appearance"; and 2. טוֹב in terms of which it bears the senses a. more rarely "useful," "serviceable," e.g., Gn. 2:9, and b. more commonly "morally good," e.g., Prv. 17:26; 18:5 etc.

1. In the light of Greek thought we are first struck by the meagreness of the role played by the term in the OT (LXX). There is no reference to the καλόν in the Platonic and Hellenistic sense. The problem of the beautiful is outwith the

---

[18] Cf. F. Billicsich, "Das Problem der Theodizee im philosophischen Denken des Abendlandes" in *Philos. Abh. d. österreich. Leo-Gesellschaft* (1936), 70 f.; cf. Plot. Enn., II, 9 and 17: "This exists through the former. If this is not beautiful, neither is that. Hence the one is beautiful in accordance with the other."

range of biblical thinking, for these facts apply to the NT as well. What Plato and Hellenism mean by the καλόν as an idea may well be contained in biblical statements concerning the כָּבוֹד of Yahweh (→ δόξα), which are, of course, very differently fashioned in accordance with the personal concept of God. The ideal of life and education expressed in the καλὸς κἀγαθός [19] has no place in an ethics which is determined by the will of God revealed in the Law, since this combination has finally a humanistic character. Where καλός, καλόν occur in a moral connection (→ under 2.), they are a translation of טוֹב and denote that which corresponds to the will of God. Finally, καλόν does not occur at all as an aesthetic quantity; this is linked with the low estimation of art in biblical religion. Only at one point do we perhaps see a connection with the Greek view of beauty, namely, in the creation story (P). The concluding verdict in Gn. 1:31: וַיַּרְא אֱלֹהִים אֶת־כָּל־אֲשֶׁר עָשָׂה וְהִנֵּה־טוֹב מְאֹד, which sums up the verdicts in 1:4, 10, 12, 18, 21, 25, is translated in the LXX: καὶ εἶδεν ὁ θεὸς τὰ πάντα, ὅσα ἐποίησεν, καὶ ἰδοὺ καλὰ λίαν, and so, too, in the other verses. In this context טוֹב has the sense of successful accomplishment, i.e., "well done." By using καλός, the translator introduces the idea of the beauty of the world, and this recurs in the Wisdom literature at Wis. 13:7: καλὰ τὰ βλεπόμενα. [20]

2. In most cases καλός, καλόν mean "morally good" in the framework of OT and Jewish ethics. They are used synonymously with ἀγαθός. This is suggested already by טוֹב.[21] In this sense we read: καλὸν ἐνώπιον κυρίου Mal. 2:17; καλὸν ... ἔναντι κυρίου, Nu. 24:1; also in combination ποιεῖν τὸ ἀρεστὸν καὶ τὸ καλὸν ἐναντίον κυρίου, Dt. 6:18; 12:28 etc.; τὸ καλὸν καὶ τὸ εὐθὲς ἐνώπιον κυρίου, 2 Ch. 14:1. It is similarly used in the prophets, e.g., in the clear-cut statement of Amos: ἐκζητήσατε τὸ καλὸν καὶ μὴ τὸ πονηρόν, ὅπως ζήσητε ... μεμισήκαμεν τὰ πονηρὰ καὶ ἠγαπήκαμεν τὰ καλά, 5:14 f.; the saying of Micah: εἰ ἀνηγγέλη σοι, ἄνθρωπε, τί καλόν; ἢ τί κύριος ἐκζητεῖ παρὰ σοῦ ἀλλ' ἢ τοῦ ποιεῖν κρίμα ...; 6:8; the demand of Is.: μάθετε καλὸν ποιεῖν, 1:17. The Wisdom literature also uses it in this sense: προνοοῦ καλὰ ἐνώπιον κυρίου καὶ ἀνθρώπων, Prv. 3:4.

3. In the basic confession הוֹדוּ לַיהוָה כִּי טוֹב [22] we find καλόν as well as ἀγαθόν: εὐλόγουν εἰς οὐρανὸν ὅτι καλόν, 1 Macc. 4:24. In parallelism it is used for נָעִים in the sense of "lovely," "pleasing," at ψ 134:3: αἰνεῖτε τὸν κύριον, ὅτι ἀγαθὸς κύριος· ψάλατε τῷ ὀνόματι αὐτοῦ, ὅτι καλόν.

---

[19] The combination καλὸς καὶ ἀγαθός is found in the apocr. writings, but with no particular significance, cf. Tob. 5:14; 2 Macc. 15:12. καλός and ἀγαθός are par. at Tob. 12:7 f.

[20] Further examples: 13:5: ἐκ γὰρ μεγέθους καὶ καλλονῆς κτισμάτων ἀναλόγως ὁ γενεσιουργὸς αὐτῶν θεωρεῖται; Sir. 43:9, 11, 18: κάλλος οὐρανοῦ ... ἴδε τόξον καὶ εὐλόγησον τὸν ποιήσαντα αὐτὸ σφόδρα ὡραῖον ... κάλλος λευκότητος (χιόνος). In Qoh. 3:11 and Sir. 39:16 καλός means both excellent and useful in connection with Yahweh's works in history and nature. The meaning is determined by the thought of the superior wisdom of Yahweh. The presupposition is the term's basic sense of what is ordered.

[21] On this pt. → ἀγαθός, I, 14.

[22] Cf. → ἀγαθός, I, 13 f.

E. καλός in the NT.

1. Synoptists. In the preaching of the Baptist we find the statement: ἤδη δὲ ἡ ἀξίνη πρὸς τὴν ῥίζαν τῶν δένδρων κεῖται· πᾶν οὖν δένδρον μὴ ποιοῦν καρπὸν καλὸν ἐκκόπτεται καὶ εἰς πῦρ βάλλεται, Mt. 3:10; Lk. 3:9.[23] The image of the tree and the fruit is also found in Jesus: πᾶν δένδρον ἀγαθὸν καρποὺς καλοὺς ποιεῖ, Mt. 7:17 ff.; cf. 12:33. What are καλοὶ καρποί? Lohmeyer in a study of Mt. 3:10[24] has grasped the decisive point: "Fruits are good only if they grow and ripen on this basis of divine repentance, and they can ripen only in the man for whom this repentance has become through baptism the divine norm and power of his growth, so that he is 'converted' in this sense."[25] The same decisive view underlies the sayings of Jesus. These images do not merely present us with good and bad trees and fruits. They are a summons to man to participate in the kingdom of God by μετάνοια, and thus to be a good tree with good fruit. The statements in the parables are to be viewed from the same standpoint. The καλὸν σπέρμα which the man sows in his field is the word concerning God's rule (Mt. 13:24, 27, 37, 38).[26] The καλοί caught in the net and gathered in vessels are those who have attained to this lordship of God by μετάνοια. In the Synoptic *kerygma*, then, the adjective καλός is orientated to the word of the kingdom of God.

2. The καλὰ ἔργα referred to by Jesus demand special consideration from this angle. Jesus issues a call to καλὰ ἔργα, e.g., in Mt. 5:16: οὕτως λαμψάτω τὸ φῶς ὑμῶν ἔμπροσθεν τῶν ἀνθρώπων, ὅπως ἴδωσιν ὑμῶν τὰ καλὰ ἔργα καὶ δοξάσωσιν τὸν πατέρα ὑμῶν τὸν ἐν τοῖς οὐρανοῖς, or again in His parable of the Last Judgment, namely, that we should feed the hungry, give drink to the thirsty, receive strangers, clothe the naked and visit the sick (Mt. 25:35-45). These καλὰ ἔργα correspond to the works of love (מַעֲשִׂים טוֹבִים), which as works of mercy play a great role in Judaism.[27]

> The prophets, too, were concerned about good works. Is. 58:6-7 mentions as such the freeing of prisoners, the feeding of the hungry, the reception of the homeless and the clothing of the naked. We may compare Tob. 1:17 f. and Test. Jos. 1 in later Judaism. Later Judaism distinguishes between alms prescribed by the Law and good works, T. Pea, 4, 19: "Almsgiving and works of love are equal in importance to the fulfilment of all the commands of the Torah. But almsgiving is only to the living, works of love are to the living and the dead; almsgiving only to the poor, works of love to the poor and the rich; almsgiving only through money, works of love with one's own person as well as money."[28] The Rabbis had this to say in evaluation of almsgiving and works of love: "He who exercises charity is as he who fills the whole world with (God's) love, for it is said: He who loves benevolence and right fills the whole world with the love of

---

[23] Cf. Schl. Mt., 76: הָיוּ עוֹשִׂין פֵּירוֹת יָפִין Tanch. תצוה 6 (Buber, p. 50a). It is an old Heb. concept that the tree "makes" fruit, Jer. 17:8; Ez. 17:23.

[24] E. Lohmeyer, "Von Baum u. Frucht" in ZSTh, 9 (1931/32), 377 ff.

[25] *Op. cit.*, 396.

[26] In the exposition at v. 38 the καλὸν σπέρμα is equated with the υἱοὶ τῆς βασιλείας. Here the result and the cause, the fruit and the seed, are viewed together. In the parable of the sower what is sown is the λόγος τῆς βασιλείας, v. 19.

[27] Cf. the excursus on the private philanthropy of ancient Judaism in Str.-B., IV, 536-558, and that on works of love in ancient Judaism in IV, 559-610; cf. also J. Jeremias, "Die Salbungsgeschichte Mk. 14, 3-9" in ZNW, 35 (1936), 77 ff.

[28] Str.-B., IV, 537.

Yahweh" (cf. Ps. 33:5 acc. to this Rabbinic exegesis, bSukka, 49b). In the same passage
we read : "Alms are repaid according to the measure of love contained in them, for it
is written : 'Sow your alms and you will reap according to the measure of love' " (cf.
Hos. 10:12 according to this Rabbinic exegesis). [29] The latter saying safeguards against
misuse and against unrestricted lending which corrupts all benevolence and makes a
business of it. The Rabbis expressly considered what the reward of good works will
be, and they expected a rich reward in this world as well as in the hereafter. "He who
does works of love attains possessions on earth and his enemies fall before him, he is
kept from punishment and finds refuge in God's protection. Works of love bring the evil
impulse under man's control ; they atone for sin ; they are man's advocate before God ;
they establish peace between God and Israel ; they save from death, they shelter from
the woes of the Messiah, and they make him who does them equal in God's eyes to a
redeemer of Israel." [30]

Finally, the basis of works of love is found in the divine prototype : ". . . one should
act according to the manner of God. As He clothed the naked, as it is written : 'Yahweh-
Elohim made for Adam and his wife coats of skins and clothed them therewith' (Gn. 3:21),
so do thou clothe the naked. God visited the sick, as it is written : 'Yahweh appeared
unto him (Abraham, just after circumcision according to Gn. r., 48 on 18:1 passim) by
the terebinths of Mamre' (Gn. 18:1), so do thou visit the sick. God comforted the mourning, as it is written : 'After the death of Abraham God spoke words of comfort over
Isaac' (Gn. 25:11 as understood by the writer), so do thou comfort the mourning. God
buried the dead, as it is written : 'God buried him (Moses) in the valley' (Dt. 34:6),
so do thou bury the dead," bSota, 14a. [31] Here already we are given a list of highly
esteemed works of love, namely, clothing the naked, [32] also giving food and drink to those
in need, [32] visiting the sick [33] — this is specially emphasised in bNed. 39b Bar : "The
reward for this is without measure' [34] — laying out and burying the dead, [35] and comforting those who mourn, i.e., the bereaved. [36] We might also mention hospitality, [37]
which is the most important after visiting the sick, [38] adopting orphans, releasing captive
Israelites, supporting teachers, acting surety for the oppressed, helping poor brides and
taking part in wedding processions. [39]

Jesus expressly approves and demands works of love. He puts to the scribes and
Pharisees the requirement which underlies His own mission and which is derived
from the prophets : "I will have mercy and not sacrifice" (Mt. 9:13; 12:7). For
this reason He turns to sinners and the sick. In His incarnate life He does works
of love — He is God's work of love towards men. To be sure, His works of love
are not according to a rigid law. The decisive point for Jesus is the divine lordship

---

[29] Str.-B., IV, 540 and 543.

[30] Ibid., 562.

[31] Ibid., 561. The performance of works of love is also rooted in the examples of
Abraham, Moses and Daniel, and in the two commandments at Ex. 18:20 and Mi. 6:8. Cf.
Str.-B., IV, 560-562.

[32] Ibid., 566-8; Tob. 1:17; 4:16; Test. Jos. 1; Str.-B., IV, 6 and 12.

[33] Ibid., 573-8.

[34] Ibid., 577.

[35] Ibid., 578-592. Burying the dead is one of the works which will also bring a reward
in this world (interest on the capital), though the chief reward (capital) will be left for the
future world.

[36] Ibid., 592-607.

[37] Ibid., 565-572.

[38] Ibid., 560, quoting bShab., 127a.

[39] Ibid., 572 f.; cf. also the summary and many examples in J. Jeremias (→ n. 27).

into which these works are integrated as true works of love and which transcends all formalism. Thus on one occasion a man wants to follow Jesus and yet first to bury his father, i.e., perform an outstanding work of love. But Jesus says to him brusquely and unequivocally: "Let the dead bury their dead: but go thou and preach the kingdom of God" (Lk. 9:59; cf. Mt. 8:21 f.). This is for the Jews an unheard of demand which strikes at the heart of Jewish piety and cuts off at the root the idea of reward — cf. the high estimation of burying the dead. In this light it is worth noting that in the parable of the Last Judgment all the works of love are actual works of love and mercy to living men and are part of the action of the divine lordship (Mt. 25:35 f.). We might also add the adoption of children (Mt. 18:5; cf. Mk. 9:37; Lk. 9:48). But both Mt. 25:35 ff. and Mt. 18:5 introduce a completely new and decisive insight in the saying: "Inasmuch as ye have done it unto one of the least of these my brethren, ye have done it unto me" (Mt. 25:40; cf. 18:5; also Mk. 9:41; Mt. 10:40-42; → δέχομαι, II, 53 f.). Jesus Himself is in the NT our Advocate with the Father (1 Jn. 2:1; R. 8:34), and He shews Himself to be such (Lk. 13:8; 22:32; cf. works of love as an advocate, TPea, 4, 21). In this respect we may think especially of the high-priestly prayer in Jn. 17. But this "being for us" before God is also a "being for us" before one another. Jesus has learned to know His own. He is there for them in such a way that they can no longer see their fellowmen without seing the *Kurios* behind them. What they do to one another, whether good or bad, and also what they do not do, they either do or do not do to Christ, who comes to men in the form of the needy, and seeks to pursue His saving work through them. Here, then, is the decisive question of the Christian life. Here is the question which will be asked at the judgment. God wills the work of love. Faith is to take fire in this work and to become the praise of God: οὕτως λαμψάτω τὸ φῶς ὑμῶν ἔμπροσθεν τῶν ἀνθρώπων, ὅπως ἴδωσιν ὑμῶν τὰ καλὰ ἔργα καὶ δοξάσωσιν τὸν πατέρα ὑμῶν τὸν ἐν τοῖς οὐρανοῖς (Mt. 5:16). καλὰ ἔργα are no longer tied to the idea of reward. Done in faith in the Father, they have the magnifying of the Father, and faith in Him, as their goal. How radically the idea of reward is shattered may be seen from the direction in Lk. 14:12-14. This demands that we should ask to our table the poor, the halt, the lame and the blind rather than rich friends and relatives "... lest they also shall bid thee again, and a recompense be made thee ... for they (the poor etc.) cannot recompense thee: for thou shalt be recompensed at the resurrection of the just." This recompense is the inheriting of the "kingdom prepared for you from the beginning of the world" by those who are "the blessed of the Father" (Mt. 25:34; cf. v. 41). It does not allow of any table of rewards, as may be seen from the parable of the labourers in the vineyard. [40] Jesus gives us the prototype of this divinely willed mercy, which acts spontaneously and seeks no reward, in the parable of the Good Samaritan (Lk. 10:30 ff.). [41] Such men belong to the kingdom of God, for μακάριοι οἱ ἐλεήμονες, ὅτι αὐτοὶ ἐλεηθήσονται (Mt. 5:7).

---

[40] Similar Rabbinic parables contain the idea of rewards which Jesus transcends, cf. Schl. Mt., 590 f.

[41] This parable is particularly challenging to Jews when one considers that according to the judgment of a full Jew the Samaritan, who is the example, is a non-Jew, and when one realises that there are Jewish directions not to accept alms from non-Jews. All merits earned by Gentiles delay the redemption of Israel, cf. Str.-B., IV, 538 and 543 f.

Of particular interest is the story of the anointing in Mk. 14:3 ff., [42] where Jesus says : ἄφετε αὐτήν· τί αὐτῇ κόπους παρέχετε; καλὸν ἔργον ἠργάσατο ἐν ἐμοί. πάντοτε γὰρ τοὺς πτωχοὺς ἔχετε μεθ᾽ ἑαυτῶν, καὶ ὅταν θέλητε δύνασθε αὐτοῖς εὖ ποιῆσαι, ἐμὲ δὲ οὐ πάντοτε ἔχετε. ὃ ἔσχεν ἐποίησεν· προέλαβεν μυρίσαι τὸ σῶμά μου εἰς τὸν ἐνταφιασμόν. ἀμὴν δὲ λέγω ὑμῖν, ὅπου ἐὰν κηρυχθῇ τὸ εὐαγγέλιον εἰς ὅλον τὸν κόσμον, καὶ ὃ ἐποίησεν αὕτη λαληθήσεται εἰς μνημόσυνον αὐτῆς, Mk. 14:6 ff. and par. The train of thought in these words shows that the woman has performed a work of love (καλὸν ἔργον ἠργάσατο ἐν ἐμοί), that this work is more important than the almsgiving for which the disciples would have used the money spent on the ointment (14:4, 5), since there will be no further opportunity for this work, whereas alms will always be needed, and that it is a burial of the dead which by anointing is proleptically performed for one who faces a criminal's death and who thus faces the threat of being cast into a criminal's grave without anointing.

3. In John καλός occurs in a significant context in the address on the Good Shepherd : ἐγώ εἰμι ὁ ποιμὴν ὁ καλός, Jn. 10:11, 14. The word has nothing to do with the Romantic conception of the Good Shepherd. It expresses the absolute claim of Jesus to uniqueness. ὁ ποιμὴν ὁ καλός is the true shepherd who really has a right to the title. The primary point of the passage is the contrast of this right with the many contemporary claims to be shepherds, e.g., those of the many shepherd gods of Hellenism [43] on the one side, and those of the leaders of the people, who were regarded as shepherds, on the other. [44] The basis of this right is the fact that He gives His life for the flock : ὁ ποιμὴν ὁ καλὸς τὴν ψυχὴν αὐτοῦ τίθησιν ὑπὲρ τῶν προβάτων. He overcomes the wolf and saves the sheep from being lost : ὁ λύκος ἁρπάζει αὐτὰ καὶ σκορπίζει. On the basis of His fellowship with the Father, He takes up His people into this fellowship through the mutual → γινώσκειν of flock and shepherd, i.e., through the fellowship based on this γινώσκειν. The fact that He brings this fellowship and gives His life to overcome the lostness makes Him the true Shepherd, competent [45] and good and worthy of praise [46] — for all these concepts are expressed in the term καλός.

In the debate with the Jews which threatens to turn into stoning by the mob, Jesus says : πολλὰ ἔργα ἔδειξα ὑμῖν καλὰ ἐκ τοῦ πατρός· διὰ ποῖον αὐτῶν ἔργον ἐμὲ λιθάζετε; the answer of the Jews is : περὶ καλοῦ ἔργου οὐ λιθάζομέν σε ἀλλὰ περὶ βλασφημίας καὶ ὅτι σὺ ἄνθρωπος ὢν ποιεῖς σεαυτὸν θεόν, 10:31 f.

---

[42] Cf. on this pt. J. Jeremias, op. cit.

[43] E.g., Attis, Anubis, Dionysus, Hermes etc. → ποιμήν. This application seems to be particularly suggested by the conclusion in v. 16 : καὶ γενήσεται μία ποίμνη, εἷς ποιμήν — a saying which looks beyond the frontiers of Israel.

[44] Cf. Ez. 34, esp. v. 1 ff.

[45] Cf. Philo : φαῦλος μὲν γὰρ ὢν ὁ ἀγελάρχης οὗτος καλεῖται κτηνοτρόφος, ἀγαθὸς δὲ καὶ σπουδαῖος ὀνομάζεται ποιμήν, Agric., 29; also Themist., I, 9d-10b : ποίμνιον ἐκεῖνο εὔκολον τοῖς λύκοις, ὅτῳ ὁ ποιμὴν ἀπεχθάνοιτο ... κακὸς βουκόλος ... αὐτὸς δὲ ἔσται μισθωτὸς ἀντὶ βουκόλου ... ὁ δὲ ἀγαθὸς νομεὺς, πολλὰ μὲν ὀνίναται ἐκ τοῦ ἔργου. Cf. Bau. J., ad loc. for further passages.

[46] Schl. J., 237: "Because the gaze of Jesus is directed to the end, He calls Himself the καλὸς ποιμήν, the Shepherd to whom praise belongs. For the cross is a scandal by men's judgment. But for Him who is the true Shepherd it is καλόν." The use of καλός for "worthy of praise" develops naturally from the sense of "what is right," Plut. Cons. ad Apoll., 17 (II, 111d): μέτρον ... τοῦ βίου τὸ καλόν.

The καλὰ ἔργα ἐκ τοῦ πατρός — τὰ ἔργα τοῦ πατρός μου, v. 37 — are the works of God which Christ does. In them there is an open claim to be the Messiah. The Jews would accept the Messianic work, but not the Messianic claim. These works are καλά because they are true Messianic works (→ σημεῖον).[47]

4. In Paul the first use is absolute and the term is synonymous with → τὸ ἀγαθόν. At R. 7:18, 21 it denotes the good which we wish to do inwardly but which conflicts with the law of the flesh so that we cannot achieve the καλόν. In the same sense, it is also used for the new possibility of the Christian life : ... ἵνα ὑμεῖς τὸ καλὸν ποιῆτε, 2 C. 13:7. This possibility is to fill their whole life : τὸ δὲ καλὸν ποιοῦντες μὴ ἐγκακῶμεν, Gl. 6:9 (cf. R. 12:17, where the καλόν is also that which receives praise). On the other hand, the word is also used (καλόν ἐστι with inf.) for that which is "right," "good," "praiseworthy," "valuable," e.g., 1 C. 7:1, 8, 26, namely, marital restraint or virginity,[48] but cf. also Gl. 4:18 of zeal for the good, R. 14:21 of refraining from eating for the sake of one's brother. As an adjective it is used of the Law at R. 7:16 (→ ἀγαθός) and of the boasting of the Corinthians at 1 C. 5:6. No precise sense can be distinguished in Paul. Paul demands of the churches good works in the sense of works of love (→ 545-548), e.g., meeting the wants of the needy (R. 12:20), hospitality (R. 12:13; 1 C. 16:11). These are also demanded elsewhere in the apostolic period, especially in James, cf. 1:27; 2:15, 16, but also 1 Pt. 4:9; Hb. 13:2 f.; 3 Jn. 5 ff. The expression καλὰ ἔργα is not used, however, in these passages.

5. Special note should be taken of the data concerning the Pastorals. Jülicher maintains in his *Einleitung* : "It is no accident that καλός alone is used twenty-four times in the Past. and only sixteen times in the ten Pauline Epistles, and furthermore that Paul almost always uses it as a noun (τὸ καλόν, καλά, καλόν ἐστι), whereas in the Past. it is used twenty times as an adjective, especially with ἔργα (four times in Tt.)."[49] Let us consider the facts. There is reference to καλὰ ἔργα at 1 Tm. 5:10, 25; 6:18; Tt. 2:7, 14; 3:8, 14; also καλὸν ἔργον at 1 Tm. 3:1. καλὰ ἔργα are in the mind of Christ (Tt. 2:14). They are works of love and mercy as we have already seen. What is at issue is a mode of life fashioned by love on the basis of faith (cf. esp. 1 Tm. 5:10 f.). Tt. (3:8) says of καλὰ ἔργα : ... ἵνα φροντίζωσιν καλῶν ἔργων προΐστασθαι οἱ πεπιστευκότες θεῷ· ταῦτά ἐστιν καλὰ καὶ ὠφέλιμα τοῖς ἀνθρώποις. Intercession is demanded for all men, for the state and those in authority, and for a peaceful life. This is καλόν. The summons thereto closes with the words : τοῦτο καλὸν καὶ ἀπόδεκτον ἐνώπιον τοῦ σωτῆρος ἡμῶν θεοῦ, 1 Tm. 2:3. Here, as in the LXX, καλόν takes its distinctive flavour from the will of God. Military images are also linked with the term. The recipient is summoned : ἀγωνίζου τὸν καλὸν ἀγῶνα τῆς πίστεως, 1 Tm. 6:12; συγκακοπάθησον ὡς καλὸς στρατιώτης Χριστοῦ Ἰησοῦ, 2 Tm. 2:3, and ταύτην τὴν παραγγελίαν παρατίθεμαί σοι ... ἵνα στρατεύῃ ... τὴν καλὴν στρατείαν ..., 1 Tm. 1:18 f. The writer says of himself : τὸν καλὸν ἀγῶνα ἡγώνισμαι, 2 Tm. 4:7. The recipient is reminded of the καλὴ ὁμολογία which he made before many witnesses,

---

[47] καλὰ ἔργα are not here works of love but, as we have expounded, works of God which set man in fellowship with God. This is the point of σημεῖα.

[48] Cf. G. Delling, *Paulus Stellung zu Frau und Ehe* (1931), 69, esp. n. 93.

[49] A. Jülicher-E. Fascher, *Einleitung in das NT*[7] (1931), 169.

and this immediately recalls Jesus Himself: τοῦ μαρτυρήσαντος ἐπὶ Ποντίου
Πιλάτου τὴν καλὴν ὁμολογίαν, 1 Tm. 6:12 f. There is reference to the καλὸς
νόμος, i.e., the OT (1 Tm. 1:8), the καλὴ μαρτυρία which a bishop must have
(3:7), the βαθμὸς καλός which the deacons must earn by καλῶς διακονεῖν (3:13),
the καλός διάκονος which the recipient will be if he rightly instructs the community, the καλὴ διδασκαλία which is the Gospel (4:6), the καλὸς θεμέλιος εἰς
τὸ μέλλον which one achieves by good works (6:19) and the καλὴ παραθήκη
which the recipient has received through the Gospel (2 Tm. 1:14). Finally, we read
that πᾶν κτίσμα θεοῦ is καλόν (1 Tm. 4:4). What is the origin of this use, which
is so distinctive in relation to the rest of the NT, and especially the Pauline
Epistles? The only explanation which can be given is that, except in the Jewish
καλὰ ἔργα, which comes from Hellenistic Judaism, the term derives from the
popular usage influenced by Stoic ethics, [50] and that it bears much the same sense
as we found in Plutarch. καλός denotes what is "good, excellent, orderly and
right." In the Past. it is orientated to the Gospel as understood by the second
generation. This is well brought out in the observation: "... We best explain the
situation in terms of the fact that regard for external appearance and the demonstration of Christian conduct became increasingly imperative as the opening stage
passed and the world position of Christianity had to be considered." [51] Within
this situation there arose the question of correct doctrine as well as right conduct,
of a proper attitude to the surrounding world as well as true wrestling with the
various streams and movements which opposed Christian faith and conduct and
brought it into a situation of conflict, so that the Christian life had to be understood as a warfare. The term καλός occupies a significant role in this struggle.
It shows us the position of the second generation churches faced by the great
question of confirmation. It makes clear to us how they answered this question.

> Finally the usage of the Catholic Epistles and Hb. is along the same lines: καλοὶ
> οἰκονόμοι, 1 Pt. 4:10; καλὸν ὄνομα τὸ ἐπικληθὲν ἐφ᾽ ὑμᾶς, Jm. 2:7; καλὴ ἀναστρο-
> φή, 3:13, cf. 1 Pt. 2:12; καλὴ συνείδησις, Hb. 13:18. Though the phrase itself does not
> occur, good works as works of love are the subject of admonition especially in Jm.
> (1:27; 2:15, 16), and cf. also 1 Pt. 4:9; Hb. 13:2 f. and 3 Jn. 5.

In sum, the word did not achieve any distinctive sense in biblical literature. Its
use is in agreement with ordinary usage. Any special significance it has derives
from the fact that it is combined with concepts and ideas of distinctive NT content.

Grundmann

F. καλός in Christological Statements in the Early Church.

1. The Influence of Is. 53 on the Early Church View of an Ugly Christ.

In the development of the conception of Christ a significant role is played by
two passages in the Greek Bible which contain the concept of beauty or its opposite. These passages are Ps. 45 and Is. 52 and 53. In the latter the decisive state-

---

[50] For popular usage, cf. the examples in Preisigke Wört.
[51] Cr.-Kö., 576.

ments are 52:14 : ... ἀδοξήσει ἀπὸ ἀνθρώπων τὸ εἶδός σου καὶ ἡ δόξα σου ἀπὸ τῶν ἀνθρώπων, 53:2 : οὐκ ἔστιν εἶδος αὐτῷ οὐδὲ δόξα. καὶ εἴδομεν αὐτὸν καὶ οὐκ εἶχεν εἶδος οὐδὲ κάλλος, and 53:3 : ἀλλὰ τὸ εἶδος αὐτοῦ ἄτιμον.

At 53:2b. the Mas. is וְלֹא מַרְאֶה וְנֶחְמְדֵהוּ "and with no appearance to please us." No reference is made to beauty as such, though the LXX rightly deduces it from the sense. In 'A there is only one word, διαπρέπεια, which corresponds to the Mas. הדר and the LXX δόξα. This term is used elsewhere in 'A for הדר e.g., ψ 44:3. Σ has a rendering which is closer to the Mas.: οὐκ εἶδος αὐτῷ οὐδὲ ἀξίωμα, ἵνα εἴδωμεν αὐτόν, οὐδὲ θεωρία, ἵνα ἐπιθυμήσωμεν αὐτόν, ἐξουδενωμένος καὶ ἐλάχιστος ἀνδρῶν, whereas there is nothing corresponding in Θ. [52] As in the case of Is. 53 as a whole, it is the wording of the LXX which sets its imprint on the conception of Christ in early Catholic Christianity.

a. The two relevant terms, i.e., → εἶδος and κάλλος as used in Is. 53, do not play any role in the NT itself. Here the earthly figure of Christ is characterised, not by lack of beauty, but by humility, by acceptance of the form of a servant, by being made in the image of sinful flesh, by bearing suffering [53] and temptation. [54] In any case, the NT statements do not have Christ's outward appearance in view when they either describe Him as the image of God (2 C. 4:4; Col. 1:15) [55] or apply to Him the terms Son of Man or man (Ps. 8 and Hb. 2:6 f.). Similarly, when 1 Cl., 16 quotes Is. 53 the passage is not referring to His external appearance but thinking in terms of His humble mind. The same is true of the quotation from ψ 21:6-8 which immediately follows: ἐγὼ δέ εἰμι σκώληξ καὶ οὐκ ἄνθρωπος, ὄνειδος ἀνθρώπου καὶ ἐξουθένημα λαοῦ. According to 1 Cl. the humiliation and shame of Christ are linked, not with His incarnation, but with His suffering.

b. Substantially the same view is found in Justin, who often uses Is. 53 in this sense.

Thus in the introduction to the explicit quotation of the passage in Apol., 50, 1 ff. we read : παθεῖν καὶ ἀτιμασθῆναι ὑπέμεινε. It is true that Justin applies the concepts of Is. 53 to the incarnation and human life of Christ in general. Thus he writes in Dial., 100, 2 : διὰ τῆς ἀπὸ γένους αὐτῶν (τῶν πατριαρχῶν) παρθένου σαρκοποιηθείς, καὶ ἄνθρωπος ἀειδής, ἄτιμος καὶ παθητὸς ὑπέμεινε γενέσθαι, and again in Dial., 32, 2 : τὸ εἶδος αὐτοῦ ἄδοξον καὶ τὸ γένος αὐτοῦ ἀδιήγητον. Of the derivation of Christ he writes in Dial., 43, 3 : ὅτι ἀνεκδιήγητόν ἐστιν ἀνθρώποις. According to 88, 8 this might refer to the supposed descent of Jesus from Joseph. Thus error concerning His origin is just as much a part of His humiliation as is His lack of majestic presence (εἶδος): τοῦ 'Ιησοῦ ... νομιζομένου 'Ιωσὴφ τοῦ τέκτονος υἱοῦ ὑπάρχειν, καὶ ἀειδοῦς ... φαινομένου. Nevertheless, Justin does not understand these statements in terms of human appearance and majesty. He is thinking in terms of renunciation of the divine glory which is proper to Christ. Thus the expressions of Is. 53 characterise the first appearance of Christ in humility. They are a counterpart to His future second appearance in glory. Acc. to Apol., 52, 3 the first appearance is that of a dishonoured man delivered up to suffering. Acc. to Dial., 14, 8 Christ was here without honour,

---

[52] K. F. Euler, Die Verkündigung vom leidenden Gottesknecht aus Jes. 53 in der griechischen Bibel (1934), 13 ff.

[53] Phil. 2:5 ff.; 2 C. 5:21; R. 8:3; Gal. 3:13; Hb. 4:15.

[54] J. H. Korn, Peirasmos, die typische Darstellung der Versuchung des Gläubigen in der griechischen Bibel (1937, in BWANT).

[55] → εἰκών, II, 395; → μορφή.

without presence, subject to mortality. There are similar statements in Dial., 48, 3; 49, 2; 110, 2; 121, 3. Justin believes that the *parousia* in humility is supported not merely by Is. 53 and Ps. 22 but by the whole of the OT (Dial., 85, 1). Obviously in all these passages he is thinking more in terms of majesty and glory than of mere appearance. Yet there is a reference to His appearance in Dial., 36, 6 : οἱ ἐν οὐρανῷ ἄρχοντες ἑώρων ἀειδῆ καὶ ἄτιμον τὸ εἶδος καὶ ἄδοξον ἔχοντα αὐτόν. Because of His un-assuming and ugly figure the heavenly powers did not recognise Christ. On His ascension, therefore, they asked the puzzled question : "Who is this King of Glory ?" (Ps. 24:10). The assumption that the intermediary powers did not recognise Christ corresponds to the teaching of Paul in 1 C. 2:8 : ἣν (θεοῦ σοφίαν ἐν μυστηρίῳ) οὐδεὶς τῶν ἀρχόντων τοῦ αἰῶνος τούτου ἔγνωκεν· εἰ γὰρ ἔγνωσαν, οὐκ ἂν τὸν κύριον τῆς δόξης ἐσταύρωσαν. [56]

c. The mythological concept underlying Paul's statement finds sharpest focus in Act. Thom., 45 (II, 2, p. 162, 17 ff.), where the enemy, the devil, is speaking : οὐ γὰρ ᾔδειμεν αὐτόν· ἠπάτησεν δὲ ἡμᾶς τῇ μορφῇ αὐτοῦ τῇ δυσειδεστάτῃ καὶ τῇ πενίᾳ αὐτοῦ καὶ τῇ ἐνδείᾳ. [57] Here is express reference to the ugliness of Christ ; He appeared in an ugly form, in poverty and need, and thereby He deceived the demons. Yet here, too, the opposite is divine glory rather than human beauty. The same contrast is found in Act. Pt. Verc., 24 (I, p. 72), where Peter quotes Is. 53 in debate with Simon Magus. [58] In this sense Christian preaching has to take account of the μικρότης and ταπείνωσις of the Lord, to use the expressions of Euseb. in his account of the preaching of the disciple Thaddeus before Abgar of Edessa (Hist. Eccl., I, 13, 20). General depreciation of man lies behind the statements of the Sibyl regarding the incarnation of Christ. Acc. to 8, 256 f. Christ came ὡς βροτὸς εἰς κτίσιν ... οἰκτρὸς ἄτιμος ἄμορφος, and 458 says : οὐρανόθεν δὲ μολὼν βροτέην ἐνεδύσατο μορφήν. [59]

Here the biblical view of man as the image of God is completely forgotten. The optimistic view of creation found in Hellenistic Judaism, e.g., in Philo (cf. Op. Mund., 145 : τοῦ ... πρώτου φύντος ἀνθρώπου κάλλος, also 136 ; or Spec. Leg., I, 10; III, 108 : ζῴων τὸ κάλλιστον ἄνθρωπος) has been replaced by a pessimistic outlook based on dualistic philosophy.

d. The more the Church attempted to assert against docetic leanings the natural corporeality and historical reality of Jesus, the more strongly it sought to find in Is. 53 a description of His physical appearance. Hence Jesus was thought to have been ugly and unimposing from the external standpoint. Celsus, for example, could scorn His σῶμα μικρὸν καὶ δυσειδὲς καὶ ἀγεννές, [60] and many Christians were prepared to accept this, arguing that He intentionally did not appear in a beautiful form in order not to distract from His preaching. [61]

Origen, however, discounts the significance of Is. 53 as regards the outward figure of Jesus, and turns instead to Ps. 45:2 ff. [62] Among other fathers there is

---

[56] G. Bertram, *Die Leidensgeschichte Jesu und der Christuskult* (1922), 20, 58.

[57] J. Kroll, *Gott und Hölle. Der Mythus vom Descensuskampfe* (1932), 31, 43, 58 f. Further material and bibl. will be found here.

[58] K. F. Euler, op. cit., 134 ff.: "Der hässliche Christus."

[59] J. Geffcken, "Komposition und Entstehungszeit der Oracula Sibyllina," TU, II, 8, 1 (1902), 44 : vv. 456-479 are "a fine piece of Christology."

[60] Orig. Cels., VI, 75; cf. A. Miura-Stange, *Celsus u. Origenes, das Gemeinsame ihrer Weltanschauung* (1926), 144 f.

[61] Cl. Al. Paid., I, 10, 89. Cf. W. Bauer, *Das Leben Jesu im Zeitalter der nt.lichen Apokryphen* (1909), 312 ff.

[62] → n. 60. J. Ziegler, *Untersuchungen z. Septuaginta des Isaias* (1934), 128 considers the possibility of a dependence of the κάλλος of Is. 53:2 on ψ 44:2, whose influence on the translator of Is. 53 is also to be noted in the παρὰ τοὺς υἱοὺς τῶν ἀνθρώπων (B).

disagreement at this point. Some appeal to Is. 53, whereas others weaken the force of this passage, and yet others vacillate between the two views. Finally, there arises a certain consensus that Is. 53 certainly refers to the lowliness and passion of Christ, but that no conclusions can be drawn from it as to His human appearance. [63]

2. The Concept of a Beautiful Christ in the Early Church.

a. In many cases the outstanding beauty of the Lord is asserted in face of Is. 53. [64] Sometimes this view is championed by theologians in opposition to the idea of an ugly Christ on the basis of Is. 53. Assertion of Christ's beauty corresponds to a theological theory which Hellenistically regarded beauty as intrinsic to deity.

That this view could establish itself in the biblical sphere may be seen already from statements in the Gk. Bible about the beauty of creation and the Creator. Thus the conclusion of Wis. 13:5 : ἐκ γὰρ μεγέθους καὶ καλλονῆς κτισμάτων ἀναλόγως ὁ γενεσιουργὸς αὐτῶν θεωρεῖται, is one of the bases of Hellenistic Jewish and Christian theology and apologetics. Again, we read in Sir. 43:9, 11, 18 : κάλλος οὐρανοῦ ... ἰδὲ τόξον καὶ εὐλόγησον τὸν ποιήσαντα αὐτὸ σφόδρα ὡραῖον ... κάλλος λευκότητος (χιόνος), and Sir. 39:16 : τὰ ἔργα κυρίου πάντα ὅτι καλὰ σφόδρα. Here, as in Eccles. 3:11 : σὺν τὰ πάντα ἐποίησεν καλὰ ἐν καιρῷ αὐτοῦ, and ψ 95:5, 6 : ὁ δὲ κύριος τοὺς οὐρανοὺς ἐποίησεν, ἐξομολόγησις καὶ ὡραιότης ἐνώπιον αὐτοῦ, there is obvious allusion to the creation story at Gn. 1:4 etc. [65] The same is true at ψ 49:2 : ἐκ Σιὼν ἡ εὐπρέπεια τῆς ὡραιότητος αὐτοῦ, ὁ θεὸς ἐμφανῶς ἥξει, [66] at ψ 89:17 : Σ : καὶ ἔστω τὸ κάλλος (Mas. נעם, LXX ἡ λαμπρότης) κυρίου τοῦ θεοῦ ἡμῶν ἐπάνω ἡμῶν, and at ψ 26:4 Σ : ὥστε ὁρᾶν τὸ κάλλος ΠΙΠΙ [67] (LXX : τὴν τερπνότητα τοῦ κυρίου, Ἀ : ἐν εὐπρεπείᾳ κυρίου). Philo, too, expresses the same thought speculatively, e.g., in Op. Mund., 139 : θεοῦ δὲ λόγος καὶ αὐτοῦ κάλλους, ὅπερ ἐστὶν ἐν τῇ φύσει κάλλος, ἀμείνων, οὐ κοσμούμενος κάλλει, κόσμος δ' αὐτός, εἰ δεῖ τἀληθὲς εἰπεῖν, εὐπρεπέστατος ἐκείνου. [68] Among Christian apologists Athenagoras lays greatest stress on it. Thus we read of God in Suppl., 10, 1 : φωτὶ καὶ κάλλει ... περιεχόμενον, and 5, 2 : τὴν τοῦ θεοῦ φύσιν τοῦ κάλλους τοῦ ἐκείνου πληρουμένην (οὐρανὸν καὶ γαῖαν). But the basic apologetic idea is expressed in 16, 1 : καλὸς μὲν γὰρ ὁ κόσμος ... ἀλλ' οὐ τοῦτον, ἀλλὰ τὸν τεχνίτην αὐτοῦ προσκυνητέον (cf. Aetius, plac., 1, 6, 2-6, Diels), and the continuation in 16, 2 reads : πάντα γὰρ ὁ θεός ἐστιν αὐτὸς αὐτῷ, φῶς ἀπρόσιτον, κόσμος τέλειος, πνεῦμα, δύναμις, λόγος ... θαυμάζων αὐτοῦ τὸ κάλλος τῷ τεχνίτῃ πρόσειμι. If the reference in these passages is to the beauty of creation, 1 Cl., 49, 1 is referring to redemption and sanctification when it speaks of the pre-eminent nature of the beauty of

---

[63] For detailed evidence cf. W. Bauer, loc. cit. and N. Müller, Art. "Christusbilder" in RE, IV (1898), 63 ff.

[64] Cl. Al. Strom., II, 5, 21, 1: ὁ σωτὴρ ἡμῶν ὑπερβάλλει πᾶσαν ἀνθρωπίνην φύσιν. καλὸς μὲν ...

[65] Cf. also ψ 103:1; 144:5; ὄνομα καλόν; ψ 134:3 vl. in Aʳ ἡδύ, cf. 1 Macc. 4:24; Jm. 2:7 and Philo Abr., 156 : φῶς, ὃ καὶ τῶν ὄντων ἐστὶ κάλλιστον καὶ πρῶτον ἐν ἱεραῖς βίβλοις ὠνομάσθη καλόν. We also find the idea of the beauty of creation continued in Rabb. Judaism. Thus in bYoma, 54b, in an exposition of Ps. 50:2, the beauty of the cosmos has attained its perfection, beginning with Jerusalem. To the same context belong speculations on the measure of beauty which Yahweh has granted to the world. Thus we read in bQid., 49b : "Ten measures of beauty have come down upon the world ; Jerusalem has received nine, and the whole of the rest of the world one." [R. Meyer]

[66] Though cf. Ἀ : ἐκ Σιὼν τετελεσμένης κάλλει ὁ θεὸς ἐπεφάνη. Here the beauty refers to Sion.

[67] For the inexpressible יהוה.

[68] For further examples cf. Leisegang, 427 ff.

the bond of divine love : τὸ μεγαλεῖον τῆς καλλονῆς αὐτοῦ (δεσμὸς τῆς ἀγάπης τοῦ θεοῦ). The *eros* passages in Plato's Symp. are rightly adduced as an analogy for this spiritualised concept of beauty (197 c e): Ἔρως πρῶτος αὐτὸς ὢν κάλλιστος καὶ ἄριστος ... συμπάντων τε θεῶν καὶ ἀνθρώπων κόσμος, ἡγεμὼν κάλλιστος καὶ ἄριστος. [69] This spiritual view of beauty obviously makes the sensual representation of an ugly Christ quite impossible.

b. The spread of this view helps to make more comprehensible the Messianic interpretation of what the Gk. Bible says about beauty. ψ 44:2, 3 is to the fore in this connection. Here the LXX says of the Messiah King : ὡραῖος κάλλει παρὰ τοὺς υἱοὺς τῶν ἀνθρώπων, and : περίζωσαι τὴν ρομφαίαν σου ... τῇ ὡραιότητί σου καὶ τῷ κάλλει σου.

The other translators [70] have similar renderings : Ἀ v. 3 : κάλλει ἐκαλλιώθης ἀπὸ υἱῶν ἀνθρώπων, v. 4 : ... ἐπιδοξότητί σου καὶ διαπρεπείᾳ σου; Σ v. 3 : κάλλει καλὸς εἶ παρὰ τοὺς υἱοὺς τῶν ἀνθρώπων, v. 4 : [71] περίθου ὡς μάχαιράν σου ... τὸν ἔπαινόν σου καὶ τὸ ἀξίωμά σου; Ε᾽ v. 3 : κάλλει ὡραιώθης παρὰ τοὺς υἱοὺς τῶν ἀνθρώπων; Allos v. 4 : ... ἡ δόξα σου καὶ εὐπρέπειά σου. Messianic interpretation of Ps. 45 is found not only in the Christian [72] but also in the Jewish world. [73] With this psalm the author of a work ascribed to Origen [74] sets the type of handsome Moses (Ex. 2:2) as an indication of the beauty of Christ. In this verse the Mas. has טוֹב, LXX ἀστεῖος, Ἀ ἀγαθός and Σ καλός. In addition to the type of Moses is also that of Joseph, who is described as handsome at Gn. 39:6. [75] Other statements concerning beauty are also referred to Christ. Thus the Mas. at Is. 33:17 reads : "Thine eyes shall see the king in his beauty" (בְּיָפְיוֹ, literally rendered by Ἀ, Σ and Θ as ἐν τῷ κάλλει αὐτοῦ). The LXX has δόξα rather than the more secular κάλλος, [76] and thus thinks in terms of heavenly glory. The Vulgate has *regem in decore suo videbunt,* but Luther follows the Mas. and the A.V. has "beauty." The image in Dt. 33:17: πρωτότοκος ταύρου τὸ κάλλος αὐτοῦ, is referred to the mysterious power of the cross in Just. Dial., 91, 1. Very common is the Messianic interpretation of the Song of Songs. Christ is the Bridegroom (cf. Mk. 2:19; Mt. 25:1; Jn. 3:29; Eph. 5:25). 1:16 speaks of Him : ἰδού, εἶ καλός, ὁ ἀδελφιδός μου, καί γε ὡραῖος, and cf. the express depiction of His beauty in 5:10-16. [77]

---

[69] Kn. Cl., *ad loc.*

[70] Field, *ad loc.*

[71] On the paraphrase in Σ cf. the Rabb. interpretation of weapons as adornments, Shab., 63a, cf. Str.-B., III, 680 on Hb. 1:8, 9.

[72] For material in the fathers cf. W. Bauer, *op. cit.* and N. Müller, *op. cit.*

[73] Esp. in the Targum, cf. Str.-B., III, 679 on Hb. 1:8, where are also other instances. For the type of Abraham, cf. O. Schmitz, "Abraham im Spätjudentum u. im Urchristentum," *Aus Schrift u. Geschichte, Festschr. f. Adolf Schlatter* (1922), 122 and A. Schlatter, "Das Alte Testament in d. johann. Apokalypse," BFTh, 16, 6 (1912), 41.

[74] Tractatus Origenis, VII (ed. Batiffol [1900], p. 80). The Tractatus Orig. de libris ss. Scripturarum is usually ascribed to Gregory of Elvira, a Spanish opponent of Arianism. It consists of 20 homilies on mainly OT texts and comes from the 2nd half of the 4th century. Cf. O. Bardenhewer, *Geschichte d. altkirchlichen Literatur,* II (1914), 139, 632; III (1912), 400 f.

[75] A. Jeremias, *Das AT im Lichte des Alten Orients* (1916), 317, 332 and Index, *s.v.* "Schönheit." He thinks that beauty is here a Tammuz motif.

[76] → δόξα. Cf. G. Kittel, *Die Religionsgeschichte u. das Urchristentum* (1932), 82 ff. In the Gk. OT the term denotes esp. "the divine majesty and the radiance of divine glory."

[77] Cf. Hippolytus' Comm. on the Song of Songs (ed. G. N. Bonwetsch, TU, II, 8, 2 [1903], 51), and cf. W. Bauer, *op. cit.,* 313. The Targum gives evidence of a Messianic interpretation of the Song of Songs in Judaism. This was adopted by the fathers from the time of Hippolytus and Origen. Cf. W. Riedel, *Die Auslegung des Hohenliedes in d. jüdischen Gemeinde u. in d. griechischen Kirche,* 1898.

c. There is no clear line of descent from these OT texts to the description of a beautiful Christ in the apocryphal Acts of Gnosticism. These refer to the figure of the exalted Lord conceived in wholly human terms. Eternal beauty and eternal youth belong necessarily to the picture of the hereafter which is held in these circles.

Thus Christ appears as a child or a youth whose beauty is explicitly emphasised : Act. Andr. et Matth., 18 (II, 1, p. 87): [78] γενόμενος ὅμοιος μικρῷ παιδίῳ ὡραιοτάτῳ εὐειδεῖ; 33 (115, 6 f.): γενόμενος ὅμοιος μικρῷ παιδίῳ εὐειδεῖ, Mart. Mt., 13 (II, 1, p. 232, 1): παιδίον εὔμορφον ἐξ οὐρανοῦ καταβαίνον, vl. : ἐν ὁμοιώματι παιδίου ὡραιοτάτου; 24 (II, 1, p. 250, 10): τὸν Ματθαῖον ... χειραγωγούμενον ὑπὸ παιδίου εὐμόρφου; 26 (II, 1, p. 255, 1): τὸ παιδίον τὸ εὔμορφον; Act. Thom., 109 (II, 2, p. 220, 21 f.): παῖδα εὐχαρῆ καὶ ὡραῖον, υἱὸν μεγιστάνων. [79] Jesus is depicted as a youth : Act. Joh., 73 (II, 1, p. 186, 14): νεανίσκον εὔμορφον μειδιῶντα; Mart. Mt., 17 (II, 1, p. 238, 4 ff.): 'Ιησοῦς ... ἐμφανισθείς μοι ὅλος ἐξαστράπτων ὥσπερ τις νεανίσκος εὔμορφος; [80] Act. Thom., 154 (II, 2, p. 263, 13): ὁ νεώτερος οὗτος. In the Vita et Passio S. C. Cypriani per Pontium, 12 (ed. P. T. Ruinart in Acta Martyrum [1859]) Christ is described as iuvenis. In the Passio Perpetuae et Felicitatis, 12 (ibid.) the exalted Lord is described as follows : Niveos habentem capillos et vultu iuvenili. Many passages speak of His beauty in self-manifestation, cf. Act. Thom., 129, 149, 160 : ὡραῖος, 36 : κάλλος, εὐπρέπεια, 80 : εὐπρέπεια, Act. Andr., I (II, 1, p. 38, 12): ἐσμὲν τοῦ καλοῦ, δι' ὃν τὸ αἰσχρὸν ἀπωθούμενα (vl. : -μεθα). By contrast we read of the devil in Act. Thom., 44 : ὁ δυσειδής, ὁ τοὺς εὐειδεῖς ὑποτάσσων. ὁ καλός is used to describe and to address Christ in Act. Joh., 73, 74. Here we see especially the docetic character of this whole conception. Christ appears to one as a child and to another as a youth, to one as beautiful and to another as ugly (88, 89). He appears to each as he may grasp Him (Act. Pt. Verc., 20 [I, p. 67, 6]). [81] Thus the presentation of Christ in these Acts lacks historical concreteness. No earthly form can really express the heavenly beauty which is in the minds of the authors.

d. We should finally mention in this connection the artistic representations of a youthfully beautiful Christ in the catacombs and on glasses. [82] From what has been said, these depictions can hardly be linked with the conception of Christ in the apocryphal Acts. [83] Here is an independent conception which stands primarily under the influence of the image of the Good Shepherd.

This depiction of Christ is common in the catacombs, on sarcophagi and in independent pieces. It is debatable, however, whether the representation is based on Jn. 10:11 ff.

---

[78] Cf. also R. A. Lipsius, Die apokryphen Apostelgeschichten u. Apostellegenden, I (1883), II (1884, 1887), I, 269, 464 f., 542, 551, 554; II, 2, 111 f.

[79] W. Bousset, Hauptprobleme der Gnosis (1907), 252 ff. In the hymn the reference is primarily to the Gnostic Redeemer. The beautiful boy is to be regarded as His alter ego.

[80] Cf. also Act. Pt. Verc., 5 (I, p. 51, 5).

[81] We are to think here of the Gnostic doctrine of the Redeemer who takes many shapes. Cf. Act. Thom., 48 (II, 2, p. 164, 15); Act. Archelai, 59, 3, GCS, XVI, and cf. W. Bousset, "Manichäisches in den Thomasakten," ZNW, 18 (1918), 14 ff. Origen finds a biblical basis for the doctrine and exploits it theologically in his debate with Celsus, cf. Miura-Stange, op. cit., 152 ff.

[82] F. X. Kraus, Geschichte der christlichen Kunst, I (1896), 176 f. RE d. christl. Altertümer, II (1886), 15 ff.; W. Künstle, Ikonographie d. christl. Kunst, I (1928), 593 ff.

[83] J. E. Weis-Liebersdorf, Christus- und Apostelbilder, Einfluss d. Apokryphen auf die ältesten Kunsttypen (1902), though cf. Künstle, op. cit., 594 f.

(ὁ ποιμὴν ὁ καλός) [84] or whether it is to be traced back to "Messianic prophecies of the divine Shepherd." [85] We may certainly refer to OT passages like Ez. 34:23; 37:24; Is. 40:11, and the image of the shepherd in Zech. 11:7-10 (ἡ ῥάβδος "κάλλος"). The divine Shepherd is "an ideal embodiment of the Christian view of salvation." [86] Here also is the material basis of the beauty of the depiction, though formally we are naturally to see some influence of religious and secular models in the contemporary world.

In the Messianic reference of biblical verses to the beauty of Christ, in the docetic portrayal of the apocryphal Acts, and in the artistic conception of the figure of Christ, we may see finally the influence of popular ideas of the beauty of Christ such as are common in popular Christian piety in every age. This may be seen in the traditional picture of Christ, which has been subject to many changes and various influences, and which even the Gothic conception of the passion could not finally alter. [87] This understanding finds expression particularly in the popular spiritual song, or the hymn. A good example is the well-known Christian hymn by an unknown author which was circulating already in 1695 : "Fairest Lord Jesus ... All fairest beauty, Heavenly and earthly, Wondrously, Jesus is found in thee ..." And Johann Scheffler sings in the 17th century : "Oh, I will love thee, High-extolled beauty ..." [88] Here, as already in the NT, the image of the earthly Jesus merges into that of the exalted Lord.

Bertram

> καλύπτω, κάλυμμα, ἀνακαλύπτω,
> κατακαλύπτω, ἀποκαλύπτω,
> ἀποκάλυψις

† καλύπτω.

The basic meaning, which may be traced back to Indo-European, is possibly that of hiding, [1] or burying, [2] in the earth. This gave rise to the more general sense, "to conceal,"

---

[84] C. M. Kaufmann, *Handbuch d. christl. Archäologie* (1922), 322, draws attention to the literary tradition, which on the basis of the Gospels (Jn. 10; 21:15 ff.; Mt. 15:24; Lk. 15:4 f.) turns readily to the beautiful allegorical picture, cf. Herm. and Cl.

[85] Künstle, *op. cit.,* 402.

[86] Kaufmann, *op. cit.,* 322.

[87] Cf. N. Müller, *op. cit.,* 63 ff.; H. Preuss, *Das Bild Christi im Wandel d. Zeiten* (1932).

[88] The text has been altered in some recent editions. The Brandenburg Hymnal (1904) substitutes "Saviour" for "beauty" and the Hessian (1924) "love." For further material cf. G. Brock, *Evangelische Liederkonkordanz* (1926), 327 f.

κ α λ ύ π τ ω. [1] Indo-Europ. base *kelu, from *kel, Lat. celo, Old High German *helan,* whence *Hel,* New High German *Höhle* and *Hölle,* Eng. "hell." Like Hel and Nehalennia, Kalypso was from the very first a goddess of the underworld along with Hecabe or Hecate, cf. H. Güntert, *Kalypso, Bedeutungsgeschichtliche Untersuchungen auf dem Gebiet d. indogermanischen Sprachen* (1919). Severe objections to the method and detailed findings of Güntert are made by W. Porzig, "Indogerm. Forschungen," *Anzeiger,* 42 (1924), 16 ff.

[2] There are several examples in Güntert, 31 ff. Cf. also Anth. Pal., VII, 604 of a dead girl : μοῖρα ... σε καλύπτει.

"to cover." The term probably came into *koine* from Ionic. [3] It is predominantly poetic, very common in Homer and the tragic and lyric poets, also in Ionic (Ditt. Syll.[3], 1218 : Keos, 5th cent. B.C.) and Aeolic (*ibid.*, 999, 10 : Lycosura, 2nd cent. B.C., → 562, n. 3) inscriptions, and in Ionic prose writers (Hdt., II, 47; Hippocr. Mul., II, 146). The simple form is rare in Attic prose, and the noun κάλυμμα does not occur at all in Plato, though cf. Xenoph. Cyrop., V, 1, 4; Eq., 12, 5. It is more common later (Aristot. Hist. An., II, 13, p. 505a, 6 → *infra* ; Plut., Paus., Ael. Arist., Pap.). [4]

The word is used 1. lit., Hom. Il., 10, 29 : Menelaus conceals his broad back in the gaily coloured skin of a panther ; Aristot. Hist. An., II, 13, p. 505a, 6 : καλυπτόμενα καλύμματι [βράγχια]; Jos. Ant., 13, 208 : the snow covering the paths (τὰς ὁδοὺς καλύψασα). Even when the idea of burying is not present, a connection with death often suggests the basic meaning. Hom. Il., 5, 553 : τέλος θανάτοιο κάλυψεν; 13, 425 : ἐρεβεννῇ (obscure) νυκτὶ καλύψαι "to kill." But cf. Hom. Il., 5, 23 : σάωσε δὲ νυκτὶ καλύψας, of the saving intervention of Hephaistos. καλύπτω is particularly common in the LXX, in a purely neutral sense at Ex. 27:2; 1 Βασ. 19:13 etc., but with the subsidiary sense of "to bury" at Ex. 14:28. There is a numinous ring when it is said that the cloud of Yahweh covered Mount Sinai or the tent of revelation (Ex. 24:15 f.; Nu. 9:15 f.). Numinous awe is expressed on the human side in the fact that the priests at the altar of the burnt offering wore linen clothes down to their ankles (Ep. Ar., 87). 2. The fig. sense is sometimes found in secular Gk. (Eur. Hipp., 712), more commonly in the OT (=כסה pi), ψ 31:5 : "Mine iniquity have I not hid" (τὴν ἀνομίαν μου οὐκ ἐκάλυψα), though cf. ψ 84:2 : "Thou didst cover, forgive, all their sins" (ἐκάλυψας πάσας τὰς ἁμαρτίας αὐτῶν, synon. ἀφῆκας). On Test. L. 10:3 → 558, n. 11.

In the NT καλύπτω is used 1. literally. Mt. 8:24 : ὥστε τὸ πλοῖον καλύπτεσθαι ὑπὸ τῶν κυμάτων, Lk. 23:30, perhaps with a hint of "to bury" (quoting Hos. 10:8 LXX): ἄρξονται λέγειν τοῖς ὄρεσιν· πέσατε ἐφ' ἡμᾶς, καὶ τοῖς βουνοῖς· καλύψατε ἡμᾶς, Lk. 8:16 in the parable of the light : οὐδεὶς λύχνον ἅψας καλύπτει αὐτὸν σκεύει.

It is also used 2. figuratively. Mt. 10:26 : οὐδὲν γάρ ἐστιν κεκαλυμμένον ὃ οὐκ ἀποκαλυφθήσεται, καὶ κρυπτὸν ὃ οὐ γνωσθήσεται, is a general statement [5] which in the context (v. 24 f., 27 f.) is designed to emphasise the fact that God will publicly establish the message of the kingdom of God in spite of all appearances to the contrary and all opposition.

2 C. 4:3 : εἰ δὲ καὶ ἔστιν κεκαλυμμένον τὸ εὐαγγέλιον ἡμῶν, ἐν τοῖς ἀπολλυμένοις ἐστὶν κεκαλυμμένον. Opponents raise the objection that Paul's Gospel is covered, i.e., that the message lacks the perspicuous force of true divine revelation (cf. 3:12 ff.) and that the one who proclaims it lacks the simple candour of a true divine messenger (3:1 ff.; 4:2). Paul ironically accepts this and makes a humorous application. His Gospel is certainly hidden for unbelievers who are on the way to destruction. The god of this aeon, i.e., Satan, has blinded their eyes so that they cannot see the light of the Gospel of the glory of Christ. This thought links up with → κάλυμμα in 3:15 f. and → ἀνακεκαλυμμένῳ προσώπῳ in 3:18.

---

[3] Nägeli, 27.
[4] Anz Subsidia, 271 f.
[5] Rabbinic par. (Str.-B., I, 578 f.) suggest a proverb : "Nothing is so finely spun, that we do not finally see the sun," i.e., everything comes to light in the end.

Jm. 5:20 : He who helps to restore a sinner σώσει ψυχὴν αὐτοῦ ἐν θανάτου καὶ καλύψει πλῆθος ἁμαρτιῶν. 1 Pt. 4:8 : ἀγάπην ἐκτενῆ ἔχοντες, ὅτι ἀγάπη καλύπτει πλῆθος ἁμαρτιῶν.

Both passages go back to Prv. 10:12 Heb.: וְעַל כָּל־פְּשָׁעִים תְּכַסֶּה אַהֲבָה: love establishes peace (LXX, following another reading [לֹא פְשָׁעִים?]) or incorrectly, has πάντας δὲ τοὺς μὴ φιλονεικοῦντας καλύπτει φιλία). [6] 1 Pt. 4:8 is literally repeated in 1 Cl., 49, 5; 2 Cl., 16, 4, and is quoted as a saying of the Lord in Didasc., 2, 5. [7] No light has yet been shed on the literary relationships. [8] We shall not be mistaken if we assume that it was a current saying. This is supported by its uniform understanding in the Christian writers. Prv. 10:12 is seldom quoted in Rabb. literature, and it is variously referred to the love of God, the prayer of Moses, and the Torah (5:19 : love = Torah). [9]

The fathers generally agree that love covers the sins of those who exercise it. [10] This exposition also fits the two NT passages. They are not to be understood in terms of 1 C. 13:7 nor of divine forgiveness for one's neighbour. The point is that genuine love assures access to divine forgiveness. [11] This positive understanding, which seems almost to suggest a righteousness of works (for predominantly negative formulations, cf. Mt. 18:35; 6:15, though cf. also v. 14 and Mk. 11:25), seems a little strange in the NT world of thought. But is expresses the general view of the NT that the free grace of God, while it excludes the thought of merit, leaves intact the basic norm of punishment and reward.

† κάλυμμα.

1. Like the verb, the noun is mainly poetic in earlier literature. Of the many meanings, [1] the only one that has theological significance is that of "head-covering" or "veil."

---

[6] There may be here an influence of Ez. 28:17: διὰ πλῆθος ἁμαρτιῶν σου ἐπὶ τὴ; γῆν ἔρριψά σε, Sir. 5:6 : τὸ πλῆθος τῶν ἁμαρτιῶν μου ἐξιλάσεται, and ψ 84:2 : ἐκάλυψας πάσας τὰς ἁμαρτίας αὐτῶν.

[7] A. Resch, Agrapha², = TU, II, 15, 3/4 (1906), 310 f.

[8] There seems to be general evidence for the direct dependence of one epistle on the other. For the dependence of Jm., cf. H. Appel, Einl. in d. NT (1922), 118. More recent opinion favours the reverse, e.g., A. Meyer, D. Rätsel des Jkbriefes (1930), 75 ff.; A. Jülicher-E. Fascher, Einl. in d. NT⁷ (1931), 213. Dib. Jk., 29 f. and Hck. Jk., 14 f. consider the possibility that both drew on the same traditional material. Kn. on 2 Cl., 16, 4 regards the connection with Prv. 10:12 as unlikely. He thinks the saying may come from a lost apocryphon in which it was originally designed to promote almsgiving.

[9] Str.-B., III, 766.

[10] Cf. 1 Cl., 50, 5; 2 Cl., 15, 1.

[11] Wnd. Kath. Br., ad loc. Test. L. 10:3 is instructive : ἀνομήσετε ἐν τῷ Ἰσραήλ, ὥστε μὴ βαστάζειν τὴν Ἱερουσαλὴμ ἀπὸ προσώπου τῆς πονηρίας ὑμῶν, ἀλλὰ σχισθῆναι τὸ καταπέτασμα τοῦ ναοῦ, ὥστε μὴ καλύψαι (vl. : κατακαλύπτειν) ἀσχημοσύνην ὑμῶν.

κάλυμμα. O. Rühle, Art. "Masken," RGG², III, 2038 f. (Bibl. on masks in magic); A. Jeremias, "Der Schleier von Sumer bis heute," AO, 31, 1/2 (1931); J. Göttsberger, "Die Hülle des Moses nach Ex. 34 u. 2 K. 3," BZ, 16 (1924), 1-17. For full materials on the ecclesiastical use of the screen, cf. C. Schneider, "Studien zum Ursprung liturgischer Einzelheiten östlicher Liturgien." I. ΚΑΤΑΠΕΤΑΣΜΑ. Kyrios, Vierteljahresschrift f. Kirchen- und Geistesgeschichte Osteuropas, 1 (1936), 57 ff.

[1] "Cover" e.g., for the tent of revelation, Ex. 26:14 (B); "curtain" on the gate of the forecourt, Ex. 27:16, also before the Holy of Holies, Ex. 40:5; protective harness, 1 Macc. 4:6; 6:2; also the wooden cover on a roof, Ditt. Syll.³, 969, 57: καλύμματα etc.

The covering of the head is an expression of sorrow, e.g., Soph. Ai., 246 : κάρα καλύμμασι κρυψάμενον. It is probably to be traced back to animistic ideas. Covering the head or body is a common magico-religious custom among all peoples, but it has no single meaning. Thus, when the head of a corpse is covered, this serves to ward off the dangerous influences of the object on its surroundings.[2] But it can also protect the bearer against demonic forces, as in the initiation of the Mysteries. Since these rites have points of contact with marriage, the veiling of the bride (→ infra) should perhaps be mentioned here. The motif of fruitfulness is also old and significant. In the case of the Babylonian Ištar the (bridal ?) veiling denotes life and unveiling death.[3] With this veiling of the bride may be linked an image concerning revelation in Aesch. Ag., 1178 : ὁ χρησμὸς οὐκετ' ἐκ καλυμμάτων ἔσται δεδορκὼς νεογάμου νύμφης δίκην, "the oracle of the seer is no longer perceived from within a veil, like a newly married bride (but is given freely)." Here the half-concealed communication is a preparatory stage of revelation, and complete unveiling is the climax. Numinous inaccessibility is suggested by the famous inscription of the veiled Isis-Athene image at Sais (Plut. Is. et Os., 9 [II, 354c]): ἐγώ εἰμι πᾶν τὸ γεγονὸς καὶ ὂν καὶ ἐσόμενον καὶ τὸν ἐμὸν πέπλον οὐδείς πω θνητὸς ἀπεκάλυψεν. Cf. also Procl. in Tim., 21e (ed. E. Diehl, I [1903], p. 98, 17): τὰ ὄντα καὶ τὰ ἐσόμενα καὶ τὰ γεγονότα ἐγώ εἰμι· τὸν ἐμὸν χιτῶνα οὐδεὶς ἀπεκάλυψεν. Here, in accordance with the original sense, the true reference is to the prying removal of the veil of the goddess, i.e., to the violation of her virginity, as suggested by the articles of clothing mentioned (cf. the continuation in Procl., loc. cit.: ὂν ἐγὼ καρπὸν ἔτεκον, ἥλιος ἐγένετο). Finally, the veil is sometimes related to the mask. Mysteriously emphasising both presence and unreality, the mask indicates the combined proximity and distance of the numinous.[4] Putting on a divine mask confers divine powers on the wearer. In particular, it enables the priest to give an oracle in the name of the deity. Hence covering the face serves to reveal rather than to conceal the divine.

2. Whether or how the account in Ex. 34:33-35 can be fitted into this background in religious history is highly debatable. We read here (P) that in daily life Moses wore a mask because of the supernatural radiance of the skin of his face (already mentioned in v. 29 f.). He took off this mask (מַסְוֶה, LXX κάλυμμα) only when he stood before Yahweh or spoke to the people in His name.

Attempts have been made to reconstruct the original story in terms of presuppositions from religious history. The suggestion is that he wore a mask, the teraphim, when he spoke to the people in the name of Yahweh. A later age took offence at this, but wished to keep the story.[5] But if this is true, the reconstruction must have involved deliberate alteration of the text. It is unlikely that the teraphim have anything to do with it, since this puzzling word can hardly denote a cultic mask, but is more probably a scornful term ("good-for-nothings") for wooden household gods.[6] The story comes from a time when Yahweh religion no longer has anything to do with cultic masks. It is more likely, indeed, that the κάλυμμα motif has been added later. As the account now stands, we cannot say with certainty whether — apart from divinely given vision at special points — the people is to be protected against the glory of Yahweh which can bring death even in its reflection, or the glory of Yahweh is to be protected against profanation by

---

[2] In this connection we should also mention the mouth-covering of the Parsee priest to protect the sacred fire against pollution. There are isolated par. in Greece.

[3] Jeremias, op. cit., 7 ff.

[4] Esp. in Dionysus worship. Cf. W. F. Otto, "Dionysos, Mythos u. Kultus," Frankfurter Studien z. Religion u. Kultur d. Antike, IV (1933).

[5] H. Gressmann on Ex. 34:29 ff. in Die Schriften des AT, ed. H. Gunkel, I, 2 (1914), 76 f.

[6] I. Löw, WZKM, 10 (1896), 136, and MGWJ, 73 (1929), 314; L. Köhler, RGG², V, 1051.

spectators. The former seems to be the older view, but the two possibilities are not mutually exclusive. God's glory can be seen only as God gives it to be seen. The account forcefully expresses both the distance between God and man and also the fact that this can be bridged by God's will to reveal Himself.

3. In 2 C. 3:7-18 Paul uses this story to illustrate in Midrash style the superiority of apostolic proclamation over that of the OT. κάλυμμα is used literally in v. 13 for Moses' veil. The allegorical interpretation is developed in two directions. a. Paul introduces the thought that the veil was to stop the people noting the gradual fading of the glow (v. 13). There is here an intimation of the transitory nature of the glory of the OT ministration (cf. already v. 7: τὴν καταργουμένην). But this ministration possessed such a glory that the Israelites could not look on the radiant face of Moses (v. 7). Hence it follows that the glory of the imperishable ministration of the NT must be much greater (vv. 8-11). The office-bearer of the NT can thus proceed with supreme confidence. He has nothing to hide (v. 12 f.). b. In an abrupt transition the apostle then speaks (v. 14a) of the blindness of the wilderness generation, which is not mentioned in the κάλυμμα story but which is often spoken of in the Torah. He applies this to the unbelieving Judaism of his own time. Right up to the present, when it reads the old covenant in which Moses is in a sense constantly active as revealer (v. 15 : ἡνίκα ἂν ἀναγινώσκηται Μωϋσῆς), the same veil is present (in terms of an allegorical identity of type and antitype). This application might seem to suffer the weakness that the δόξα which Israel ought to see is that of Jesus Christ, not that of the OT God reflected in the face of Moses. For Paul, however, there is no doubt that the redeeming God of the OT and the NT is one and the same. Hence the glory of Christ is to be seen also in the OT covenant when this is properly understood (v. 18 : δόξα κυρίου referred to Christ). The idea of the veil resting on Moses [7] might also seem to threaten the point of the image. This is why Paul gives the allegory a new turn in v. 15. The veil is really on the hearts of obdurate Judaism. There is some justification for this in the fact that the veil comes between the glory of God and the eyes of the Israelites, and prevents the latter from seeing. This will be changed when Israel is converted. Paul finds this, too, in the OT passage (Ex. 34:34a), though he has to introduce a threefold application to achieve this end : 1. he understands the literal and external εἰσεπορεύετο (he went into the tent of revelation) in terms of conversion (was there perhaps an ἐπέστρεψεν in his version of the LXX ?); 2. he transfers what is said of Moses (here understood as the revealer of Christ) to the unbelieving people ; 3. he moves the whole statement from the past to the future. He thus achieves the sense that when Israel repents the veil will be taken away. [8] → ἀνακαλύπτω, and materially cf. R. 10:2 ff.; 11:25 ff.; 2 C. 4:3.

† ἀνακαλύπτω.

From the time of Eur., later more common in prose. "To uncover," a. with impersonal or personal object, "to unveil," lit. P. Oxy., X, 1297, 9 : "to undo a package"; Ditt. Syll.³, 1169, 62 (healing vision of a woman at Epidauros): ἐδόκει αὐταῖ [τὰν] νηδὺν (womb)

---

[7] It is unlikely that there is any reference to the covering or (antithetically ?) the uncovering of the scroll of the Torah in synagogue worship.
[8] Cf. Wnd., Ltzm. 2 K., ad loc.

ὁ θεὸς ἀγκαλύψαι, to procure for her the blessing of children (4th cent. B.C.); ψ 17:15 (on the appearance of Yahweh in a thunder-storm): ἀνεκαλύφθη τὰ θεμέλια τῆς οἰκουμένης. Philo speaks allegorically of the fact that virtue veils itself (ἐγκαλυψαμένη τὸ πρόσωπον) like Tamar at the cross-roads (Gn. 38:14 f.) in order that curious wayfarers may see her virgin beauty when she unveils it (ἀνακαλύψαντες), Congr., 124. Fig.: τι πρός τινα (Polyb., 4, 85, 6), "to reveal something to someone"; τινά, "to disclose the character of someone," Philochorus Fr., 20 (FHG, I, 387); νοῦν ἀνθρώπων, Job 33:16. b. with inner object: "to remove (a veil)," βλεφάρων μὴ ἀνακαλυφθέντων (Aristot. De Sensu et Sensili, 5, p. 444b, 25): without the eyelids being raised; Test. Jud. 14:5 (of whoredom with Tamar): ἀνεκάλυψα κάλυμμα ἀκαθαρσίας υἱῶν μου.

In the NT the word is found only in 2 C. 3:14, 18. At v. 14 we have sense b.: ἄχρι τῆς σήμερον ἡμέρας τὸ αὐτὸ κάλυμμα ἐπὶ τῇ ἀναγνώσει τῆς παλαιᾶς διαθήκης μένει, μὴ ἀνακαλυπτόμενον, ὅτι ἐν Χριστῷ καταργεῖται, "until this day the same veil remains, untaken away, because it is taken away (only) in (and through) Christ." [1] V. 18: ἡμεῖς πάντες ἀνακεκαλυμμένῳ προσώπῳ τὴν δόξαν κυρίου κατοπτριζόμενοι τὴν αὐτὴν εἰκόνα μεταμορφούμεθα, "we all, with uncovered face beholding the glory of the Lord (→ κατοπτρίζω, II, 696), are changed into the same image (or form)." Here we have a. in the literal sense, though applied metaphorically. The expression is in contrast to v. 13 and especially v. 15. It gives concise and forceful expression to the immediacy and absoluteness of revelation and fellowship with God in the NT.

† κατακαλύπτω.

1. Outside the NT the word is found in the sense of "to veil" or "to veil oneself" from Homer, esp. in the poets, but also in inscr. (Ditt. Syll.[3], 1218, 10 f.: τὸν θανό[ν]τα [φέρειν κ]ατακεκαλυμμένον σιωπῆι μέ[χ]ρι [ἐπὶ τὸ σ]ῆμα, a burial order from Iulis on Keos, 5th cent. B.C.) and in Plato. In the OT it acquires a sacral sense not only as used anatomically in sacrificial regulations (Ex. 29:22 etc.) but also in the command that Moses should place the ark within the Holy of Holies and hide it from sight behind the curtain (Ex. 26:34). Is. says of the seraphim before the throne of Yahweh that they respectfully covered their faces and feet with their wings (κατεκάλυπτον, Is. 6:2). The veiling of women is a custom in Israel. A disgraced woman comes veiled to judgment (κατακεκαλυμμένη, Sus. 32 Θ). Yet one may also suspect that a woman muffled up (κατεκαλύψατο τὸ πρόσωπον) and lurking by the wayside is a harlot (Gn. 38:15). This opens up the way for an understanding of the relevant NT passage.

2. The veiling of women in the NT and the contemporary world. In the NT κατακαλύπτειν occurs only in 1 C. 11:6 f. in the mid. In support of his requirement that women should not pray or prophesy with uncovered heads (→ I, 787), Paul appeals to the following considerations of natural law: εἰ γὰρ οὐ κατακαλύπτεται γυνή, καὶ κειράσθω· εἰ δὲ αἰσχρὸν γυναικὶ τὸ κείρασθαι ἢ ξυρᾶσθαι, κατα-

---

ἀ ν α κ α λ ύ π τ ω. [1] Cf. Wnd., Ltzm., 2 K., ad loc. It is better not to combine μένει μὴ ἀνακαλυπτόμενον ("remains untaken away") on account of the pregnancy of μένει. There are serious obstacles to taking μὴ ἀνακαλυπτόμενον as an abs. acc. on which the ὅτι clause is dependent. In face of all editions, we ought to put commas after μένει and ἀνακαλυπτόμενον.

κ α τ α κ α λ ύ π τ ω. G. Delling, Paulus' Stellung zu Frau und Ehe (1931), 96-109; A. Jeremias, "Der Schleier von Sumer bis heute," AO, 31, 1/2 (1931); R. P. R. de Vaux, "Sur le voile des femmes dans l'orient ancien," Rev. Bibl., NS, XLIV (1935), 395 ff.

καλυπτέσθω. ἀνὴρ μὲν γὰρ οὐκ ὀφείλει κατακαλύπτεσθαι τὴν κεφαλήν, εἰκὼν καὶ δόξα θεοῦ ὑπάρχων· ἡ γυνὴ δὲ δόξα ἀνδρός ἐστιν. Rightly to evaluate these principles, we must ask concerning the dominant practice in the world of Paul's day. [1]

It used to be asserted by theologians that Paul was simply endorsing the unwritten law of Hellenic and Hellenistic feeling for what was proper. But this view is untenable. To be sure, the veil was not unknown in Greece. It was worn partly as adornment and partly on such special occasions as match-making and marriage (→ 559), mourning (→ 559, cf. also Penelope), and the worship of chthonic deities (in the form of a garment drawn over the head). [2] But it is quite wrong that Greek women were under some kind of compulsion to wear a veil in public. Plut. may seem to suggest this. Quaest. Rom., 14 (II, 267a): συνηθέστερον ταῖς μὲν γυναιξὶν ἐγκεκαλυμμέναις, τοῖς δ' ἀνδράσιν ἀκαλύπτοις εἰς τὸ δημόσιον προϊέναι; [Plut.] Apophth. Lac., Charilli, 2 (II, 232c): ... διὰ τί τὰς μὲν κόρας (spinsters) ἀκαλύπτως, τὰς δὲ γυναῖκας (married women) ἐγκεκαλυμμένας εἰς τοὔμφανὲς ἄγουσιν ... But the first passage refers to the Roman custom, concerning which Plut. may not have been too well informed, and the second reflects special Laconic customs. Passages to the contrary are so numerous and unequivocal that they cannot be offset by two sayings of the sage of Chaironeia which are not apodictic and which may have been occasioned by a special trend. The mysteries inscription of Andania (Ditt. Syll.[3], 736), which gives an exact description of women taking part in the procession, makes no mention of the veil. Indeed, the cultic order of Lycosura seems to forbid it. [3] Empresses and goddesses, even those who maintain their dignity, like Hera and Demeter, are portrayed without veils, whereas hetaerae occasionally wear hoods. Helen appears before Paris with the upper part of her body uncovered, but with a veil. At the time of Tertullian Jewesses were prominent on the streets of North Africa because they wore veils (De Corona, 4, ed. F. Oehler, I [1853], 424 ff.; De Oratione, 22 [CSEL, 20, 193]). Hence veiling was not a general custom; it was Jewish. If the veiling of Jewish women was common in the West, we may presume that it was an accepted rule in the East. [4] The Jew regarded it as typical of Gentile women that they should go about unveiled (Nu. r., 9 on 5:18, Str.-B., III, 429). Philo describes the headband (ἐπίκρανον) as τὸ τῆς αἰδοῦς σύμβολον, ᾧ ταῖς εἰς ἅπαν ἀναιτίοις ἔθος χρῆσθαι, Spec. Leg., III, 56. Yet, though the custom was applied with particular stringency by the Jews, [5] it was oriental rather than distinctively Jewish. The home city of Paul, i.e., Tarsus, is the frontier. Evidence of the veil in Tarsus is provided by Dio Chrys. Or., 33, 46 and coins bearing the image of Tyche of Tarsus. There are exceptions. But Tarsus is stricter than the rest of Asia Minor. In general one may say that etiquette as regards the veil becomes stricter the more one moves east. This rule is brought out clearly by the provisions of an old Assyrian code. [6] Married

---

[1] There is a good collection of material, with bibl., in Delling, op. cit.

[2] Veiling was customary among the Romans at sacrifices (with the exception of the honos sacrifice, Plut. Quaest. Rom., 13 [II, 266 f., 267a]), but this did not apply to the Gks. In neither case was there any distinction of sexes. Hence Paul was not thinking of these customs.

[3] Ditt. Syll.[3], 999, 9 ff.: μηδὲ τὰς τ[ρί]χας ἀμπεπλεγμένας, μηδὲ κεκαλυμμένος. The explanation of Leonardo that the second part applies to men is grammatically correct but unlikely in the context.

[4] I. Benzinger, Hbr. Archäologie[3] (1927), 85 and S. Krauss, Talmudische Archäologie, I (1910), 189 emphasise that veiling was not always the custom in Israel and that there was no compulsion even in NT times. But this does not tell us much about the actual state of affairs.

[5] Cf. the anecdote in Str.-B., II, 430 concerning Qimchith, the high-priest's mother, who was always veiled, even in the house. There is a full description of the hair and veil of the Jewess, ibid., 428.

[6] Jeremias, op. cit., 14.

women and widows must be veiled when in public places. On the other hand, the head of the harlot, here equated with the slave, must remain unveiled under threat of severe penalties. When a man wishes to make one of these his legitimate wife, a special act of veiling is demanded.

Paul is thus attempting to introduce into congregations on Greek soil a custom which corresponds to oriental and especially Jewish sensibility rather than Greek. In principle the demand ought to extend to all women in all situations. In practice, however, Paul applies it to married women in the churches, and in the first instance he restricts it to the sphere of life which stands directly under the jurisdiction of the congregation, i.e., divine worship. → ἐξουσία, II, 573.

3. The veiling of women in Church history. From our account we may well understand that the apostle's ruling met with resistance not only in Corinth but in other places too, and was not universally obeyed. Orantes in the catacombs are only partially veiled. Mary and other holy women are often depicted without veils. Tertullian had to write a work De Virginibus Velandis (ed. F. Oehler, I [1853], 883 ff.). In Ps.-Ambrosius the veil is an obligatory adornment only for the dedicated virgin, so that a distinction can be mode between *velata* and *nondum velata*. This is how matters remained in the Church at large. But the veil has come to be characteristic of the nun, and some women, e.g., at Herrnhut, have made a point of wearing a head-covering, at least in public worship. Many Roman Catholics, too, will place at least a handkerchief on their heads when entering a church so as to obey at least the outward form of the apostolic injunction: κατακαλυπτέσθω.

† ἀποκαλύπτω, † ἀποκάλυψις.

Contents: A. The Idea of Revelation in Religious History Generally. B. Revelation in the Greek World and Hellenism: 1. Popular Religion; 2. Unbelieving and Believing Criticism; 3. The Turning to History; 4. The Rationalisation of the Idea of Revelation;

ἀποκαλύπτω κτλ. RGG², IV, 654 ff.; E. Thurneysen, "Offenbarung in Religionsgeschichte u. Bibel," ZdZ, 6 (1928), 453 ff.; P. Tillich, "Die Idee der Offenbarung," ZThK, NF, 8 (1927), 403 ff.; K. Stavenhagen, "Offenbarung u. Erlebnistheologie," ibid., 323 ff.; Deutsche Theologie, 3 (Bericht über den Breslauer Theologentag [1931]), 14 ff.; R. Bultmann, "Das Wort Gottes im NT," ibid., 24 ff.; H. Schmidt, "Das Wort Gottes im AT," ibid., 30 ff.; H. Bornkamm, "Äusseres u. inneres Wort in der reformatorischen Theologie." E. Brunner, Der Mittler (1927), 3 ff.; Philosophie u. Offenbarung (1925); Natur u. Gnade (1934); K. Barth, Nein! Antwort an Emil Brunner (1934); P. Barth, Das Problem der natürlichen Theologie bei Calvin (1935); G. Gloede, "Theologia naturalis bei Calvin," Tübinger Studien z. Syst. Theologie, 5 (1935). On A: Chant. de la Saussaye, Index, s.v. "Offenbarung"; G. van der Leeuw, Phänomenologie der Religion (1933). On B: F. Pfister, Die Religion d. Griech. u. Römer = Jahresbericht über die Fortschritte der klassischen Altertumswissenschaft, ed. K. Münscher, Suppl. 229 (1930), esp. 9, 20 ff., 146 ff.; Reitzenstein Poim., Hell. Myst.; A. J. Festugière, L'Idéal religieux des Grecs et L'Évangile (1933); E. Wechssler, Hellas im Evangelium (1936); → γνῶσις. On C: OT biblical theologies by B. Stade-A. Bertholet, I (1905), II (1911), predominantly in terms of the history of religion; W. Eichrodt, I (1933), II (1935), theological; E. Sellin, I (1933), history of religion, II (1935), theological; L. Köhler (1936), passim (cf. Index, s.v. "Offenbarung"); → ἔκστασις, προφήτης; J. Hempel, "Gott u. Mensch im AT,"² BWANT, III, 2 (1936); J. Hänel, "Das Erkennen Gottes bei den Schriftpropheten," ibid., NF, 4 (1923); "Prophetische Offenbarung," ZSTh, 4 (1926/7), 91 ff.; E. Sachsse, Die Propheten des AT u. ihre Gegner (1919); W. Staerk, "Das Wahrheitskriterium der at.lichen Prophetie," ZSTh, 5 (1927/8), 76 ff.; G. v. Rad, "Die falschen Propheten," ZAW, 51 (1933), 109 ff. On D: Jew. Enc., 10 (1905), 396 ff.; Bousset-Gressm., Index, s.v. "Offenbarung," "Apokalyptik"; RGG², I, 401 ff.;

5. Mysticism and Gnosticism ; 6. The Use of Terms. C. Revelation in the OT : 1. The Basis in Religious History ; 2. The Revelation of the Living God ; 3. The Delimitation of Revelation ; 4. Revelation and Eschatology ; 5. The Usage. D. The Attitude of Judaism to Revelation : 1. General Points ; 2. Apocalyptic ; 3. Natural Revelation. E. Revelation in the NT : 1. Revelation in the Synoptists ; 2. The Understanding of Revelation in the Primitive Community ; 3. Revelation in the NT Epistles ; 4. Revelation in the Johannine Literature ; 5. The Limitation and Confirmation of Revelation ; 6. The Terms in the NT ; 7. Theological Summary. F. Historical Review.

Unusual difficulties of method confront this lexical investigation. Because of ecclesiastical dogmatics, or some philosophy of the period, an unclarified pre-understanding of the subject is often imported into the normal translations "to reveal" and "revelation." We must ask whether this pre-understanding conforms to the data of the NT, whether it does not threaten to undermine these data from the very first. On the other hand, we cannot take refuge in a purely philological exposition of the relevant passages, e.g., by employing such literal renderings as "to disclose" or "to unveil." For this would imply evasion of the theological issue. Again, linguistic enquiry will show that, while the words do not bear a wholly unequivocal sense, there is nevertheless a large measure of inner unity. The term "revelation" correctly indicates in what direction this is to be sought. It is thus as well to take our bearings from it. In order not to miss anything essential, we must first lay the foundation of a broad understanding which will necessarily be somewhat imprecise. Revelation is a manifestation of deity. But to grasp the true essentials, we shall then have to achieve a closer definition in the course of our enquiry. This mounting precision is a result which we must seek to attain on the basis of the relevant data.

A. The Idea of Revelation in Religious History Generally.

The latest stage of general religious enquiry is characterised by a movement towards the objective. Investigation without presuppositions, i.e., under the general influence of the Enlightenment, led only to phenomena which were explained subjectively, so that they could be discounted as more or less illusory. But modern research, while it does not neglect the phenomena, sees behind them an ultimate objective element which the investigator will naturally set in the light of his own religion, e.g., of Christianity if he is a Christian, but which he will also discern in other religions, perhaps in a distorted form. [1]

All religion is concerned in some way with the manifestation of deity. [2] This consists in the removing of concealment. There can be no direct access to deity as to objects or men. In the first instance, deity is hidden. Even primitive man knows this. On the

---

Moore, I, 219 ff.; M. Wiener, "Zur Geschichte des Offenbarungsbegriffs" (Judaica, Festschr. f. H. Cohen [1912], 1 ff.); further bibl., RGG², IV, 661. On E : NT biblical theologies by P. Feine⁶ (1934) and H. Weinel⁴ (1928), s.v. "Offenbarung"; R. Bultmann, Der Begriff d. Offenbarung im NT (1929); H. E. Weber, 'Eschatologie' u. 'Mystik' im NT (1930); G. Kuhlmann, "Theologia naturalis bei Philon u. bei Pls.," Nt.liche Forschungen, I, 7 (1930); H. Daxer, R. 1:18-2:10 im Verhältnis zur spätjüdischen Lehrauffassung (Diss. Rostock, 1914); G. Bornkamm, "Die Offenbarung des Zornes Gottes," ZNW, 34 (1935), 239 ff. On F : relevant passages in histories of dogma.

[1] This point is most impressively made in the work of van der Leeuw, e.g., 613 : ". . . from a consciously Christian standpoint . . ."

[2] Border-line cases like Buddhism may be ignored in the present context.

other hand, there could be no dealings, let alone fellowship, with a God who remained permanently hidden. In the broadest sense, then, all religion depends on revelation. Nevertheless, we must ask how far the concealment is regarded as essential. The general view of man is that it belongs to the nature of deity to manifest itself. What really counts is the correct method of causing or even compelling it to do so.

Hence primitive man experiences revelation through powerful sacred objects (fetishes, trees, animals) or persons (medicine men, chieftains). The insatiable desire to learn the secret of the suprasensual, to discern the will of the gods, and above all to lift the veil of the future, leads continually to the employment of new methods of attaining revelation. These are unequally distributed, but they cannot be restricted to a single place. Dreams are universally accepted as intimations of another reality. The oracle, too, is widespread. Germans use wood-shavings dipped in the blood of animals for this purpose. Norsemen settle where the supports of the family seat go ashore. Germans believe that women have mantic powers. In the Orient there flourishes the art of reading revelation from the stars. This is the distinctive feature of the astral religion of Babylon. Auspices and haruspices are particularly prominent in Rome. Occasionally we find rational criticism, but this is unusual.

At first individual, these experiences become institutions (cultic and oracular shrines, rites and priests). Thus on the one side revelation is more sharply distinguished from non-revelation and thereby enhanced, but on the other it is exposed to the danger of hardening into a tradition. A counterpoise is found in the spontaneous emergence of ecstatically and prophetically gifted individuals unconnected with the shrines. For them the main agency of revelation is the word. Revelation thus acquires a concrete content which goes beyond the mere benevolence or malevolence of higher forces. Here too, however, there is still the danger of institutionalising or ossification. The prophetic word is written down as a word of revelation, primarily to control its later fulfilment, but increasingly for the purpose of codifying revelation. The Sibylline books in Rome are typical. There follows the historically significant mediator of revelation or founder of religion. Outside the Bible we might mention Zoroaster and particularly the less original and authentic figures of Mani and Mahomet. The impulse of mediation is towards complete codification. As the element of revelation loses its *ad hoc* character, the great religions of revelation become increasingly religions of the book, though naturally to varied degrees.

B. Revelation in the Greek World and Hellenism.

1. Popular Religion.

While Roman religion lays special emphasis on the element of regularity in its piety, and thus creates functional gods, though without excluding extraordinary revelation (auspices, haruspices, prophecy of disaster), the Greek encounters his gods primarily in the unusual.

He detects the numinous in rain and storm, in sickness and plague, in the secrets of mother earth. [3] He uses common means to declare the forces of destiny. Traces of oracular practice remain at Delphi. Delphic tradition speaks of the "bones of Dionysus," and these are probably the ancient oracle. [4] That the sacrificial animal should tremble all over when the drink-offering is poured over it is an almost indispensable sign of

---

[3] The patrons of sailors, the Dioscori (Ac. 28:11), are shown on horses in a storm in a dedicatory relief to the "great gods" above the altar at Larissa in Thessalonica (c. 200 B.C., Louvre, Haas, No. 13/14). Zeus Meilichios is often depicted as a snake (*ibid.*, 23, 24). On Apollo as the god of pestilence → I, 397.

[4] → II, 452, n. 14.

divine favour even as late as Plutarch's day (Def. Orac., 46 [II, 435c]). Dreams are often regarded as significant. A dream of healing during incubation is the primary means of revelation of Aesculapius (→ 209). Interpretation of dreams was so widespread in Hellenism that Artemidorus of Ephesus (c. 170 A.D.) himself composed five books of dreams, from the only one of which to survive we may gain a fairly complete picture of the culture and customs of the time.[5] Mantic and ecstatic prophecy was more common among the Gks. than the Romans (→ ἔκστασις, 448; προφήτης). It is in keeping with the Hellenistic regard for children that revelation is also received through the voices of children at play.[6] Astrology increasingly flows in from the Orient as a source of revelation which may not always be desirable but is constantly sought after.[7]

Particularly distinctive of Greek piety, however, is the oracle. Of the many Greek oracles[8] the Delphic is easily the most prominent.[9]

The names Δήλιος (lit. of Delos), Φαναῖος etc. are linked with the main functions of the Delphic god (Plut. Ei Delph., 2 [II, 385b]). Delphi had ceased to play any great part in Greek politics in the Hellenistic period. Plut. (Def. Orac., 7 [II, 413b]) — perhaps something of a *laudator temporis acti* — explains that in his day Apollo was investigated like a sophist, being particularly questioned on account of the heaping up of treasures and endowments and also in respect of illegitimate marriages. The lively interest in revelations of this kind may be seen from the operations of the adventurer Alexander of Abonuteichos, whose income Lucian estimated at 60,000 marks per annum (Alex., 23).

Does belief in revelation stand at the centre of Greek religion? Yes and no.[10] The Greek language has many expressions for revelation, but rather oddly these do not include ἀποκαλύπτειν. It is usual to speak of God's ἐπίδειξις or σημαίνειν. This suggests that the concealment removed by revelation is not regarded as essential. This is chiefly so, perhaps, in the case of the chthonic deities, among whom we may reckon Dionysus (→ II, 451f.). In general the Greeks regard the gods as basic forms of reality. They are as open and hidden as being itself. One may either see this or miss it. Which we do will be disclosed in the mainly tragic future. Yet is also of the essence of deity to reveal itself. Sometimes we have the thought of step-like progress, as in the saying in Xenophanes Fr., 18 (I, 61, 10 f., Diels):

οὔτοι ἀπ' ἀρχῆς πάντα θεοὶ θνητοῖσ' ὑπέδειξαν,
ἀλλὰ χρόνῳ ζητοῦντες ἐφευρίσκουσιν ἄμεινον.

But there is, of course, no question of a unique and central act of revelation. The Greek has no knowledge of any facts of salvation. In general, the god does not

---

[5] S. Laukamm, "Das Sittenbild des Artemidor von Ephesus," *Angelos*, 3 (1930), 32 ff. (Theol. Diss., Leipzig, 1928).

[6] Plut. Is. et Os., 14 (II, 356e) gives an aetiological derivation: It is from children that Isis receives word of the coffin of Osiris. ἐκ τούτου τὰ παιδάρια μαντικὴν δύναμιν ἔχειν οἴεσθαι τοὺς Αἰγυπτίους καὶ μάλιστα ταῖς τούτων ὀπτεύεσθαι (to see, to attain to revelation) κληδόσι (call) παιζόντων ἐν ἱεροῖς καὶ φθεγγομένων ὅ τι ἂν τύχωσιν. In modern Greece children whose parents are both alive still officiate at the oracle of love (A. Oepke, ARW, 31 [1934], 47 ff.). Ael. Arist. (I, 452d., Dindorf) in the morning in the sanctuary of Aesculapius hears the song of children like a revelation.

[7] E. Pfeiffer, "Studien zum antiken Sternglauben," ΣΤΟΙΧΕΙΑ, *Studien z. Geschichte d. antiken Weltbildes u. d. griech. Wissenschaft*, ed. F. Boll, *Heft* II (1916); F. Boll, *Sphaira* (1903); *Sternglaube u. Sterndeutung*² (1926).

[8] We are given an impression of their great number by the enumeration of the Boeotian alone in Plut. Def. Orac., 5 (II, 411e ff.).

[9] → II, 451 f.

[10] What follows I owe in part to the suggestions of H. Kleinknecht.

manifest himself. Certain hints are given, and these have to be deciphered by human reason, which must be free from *hybris* for this purpose. Heracl. Fr., 93 (I, 96, 12, Diels) says of the lord of the oracle at Delphi : οὔτε λέγει οὔτε κρύπτει, ἀλλὰ σημαίνει. The god neither speaks openly nor conceals himself, but gives hints. The Greek knows his Apollo only too well, and for this very reason he is never sure how he stands with him. Deity is as fickle as fortune. Neither for god nor man is there the standard of an inviolable moral will. To be sure, certain elementary moral principles, e.g., the sanctity of an oath (→ ὅρκος), are related to the gods. For Greek religion in its loftiest forms καλοκαγαθία is also an object of prayer. But this has nothing to do with revelation. Greek religion is familiar with revelations, but it is not a religion of revelation.

2. Unbelieving and Believing Criticism.

The ancient world can also be critical of revelations. Myth is not generally accepted as credible history. Materially objectionable features are either allegorised or refashioned. Miraculous signs are contested, whether in respect of their reality or their significance.

Particularly critical of miracles and signs are the Epicureans, who deny, not the existence of the gods, but their relationship to the world of man. The Platonists, Pythagoreans and Stoics still maintain a belief in miraculous communications and signs. Epictetus emphasises, however, that one should be guided by the sense of duty (Diss., II, 7; I, 1, 17; III, 1, 37; IV, 4, 5). Most interesting is the believing criticism of Plutarch, since it anticipates to some extent later conflicts as to the inspiration of the Bible. The question why the Pythian no longer answers in verses is the occasion of an exact definition of the process of revelation. One is not to believe that Apollo himself originally produced verses or that he now whispers oracles to the Pythian as though speaking through a mask. As the body uses many instruments, so the soul uses the body as an instrument. But it is itself an instrument of deity. Now the instrument should imitate the one who uses it. But this imitation is imperfect. The idea never manifests itself in its intelligible purity. It is admixed with the nature of the organ which serves it (Pyth. Or., 20 f. [II, 404b c]). The deity uses the nature of inspired men (*ibid.*, 21 [II, 404 f.]; for an essentially different view cf. Philo, → II, 453 f.). It adapts itself to the relative tastes and human needs of its servants (*ibid.*, 24 [II, 406b ff.]; 26 [II, 407d ff.]). Nothing is more inane than to think that the god enters bodily into the speakers and uses them as involuntary instruments (Def. Orac., 9 [II, 414e]). The vapours which rise up from the earth in different forms according to time and place excite in very different ways the mantic capacity which is always ready in the soul (*ibid.*, 40 ff. [II, 432c ff.]). Even demons can be mediators of revelation (*ibid.*, 38 [II, 431b]). Though natural conditions are to be taken into account, however, the Pythian deserves our full confidence, Pyth. Or., 29 (II, 408 f.): ἡ τῆς Πυθίας διάλεκτος ... οὐ ποιοῦσα καμπήν (contortion) ... οὐδ' ἀμφιβολίαν (uncertainty), ἀλλ' εὐθεῖα πρὸς τὴν ἀλήθειαν οὖσα, πρὸς δὲ πίστιν ἐπισφαλὴς καὶ ὑπεύθυνος (conscientious), οὐδένα καθ' αὑτῆς ἔλεγχον ἄχρι νῦν παραδέδωκεν.

3. The Turning to History.

The doctrine of the θεῖος ἄνθρωπος marks a certain turning to history on the part of the Greek idea of revelation. [11] To be sure, magical conceptions of inspiration and incarnation form the starting-point. Yet we are still dealing with bearers of revelation who are significant historically, i.e., for what are usually longer periods of time.

---

[11] H. Windisch, *Paulus und Christus* (1934), 24 ff.

The idea finds mythical embodiment in figures like Triptolemos, the missionary of the Eleusinian cult, and Orpheus, around whose name there clustered a revelation literature which even the ancient world knew to be pseudepigraphical. [12] Historically, the type finds expression in the ruler or outstanding statesman on the one side (→ κύριος, σωτήρ) and in the great intellectual leader, whether poet (→ II, 453), physician, scholar or philosopher on the other. The physician Menecrates of Syracuse (4th cent. B.C.) claims to be Zeus and gathers around him a following of healed patients who bear the names of saviour gods. Empedocles (c. 494-434) lives and disappears like a god, though he does not leave behind any school. Pythagoras, however, leaves such a deep impression of being a divine figure that even persecution and martyrdom cannot finally suppress his community (500 B.C.). Several centuries after his death it can still take on a new lease of life. Apollonius of Tyana comes forth from it in the 1st century A.D., and he himself is a bearer of revelation, whose life is described by Philostrat. in the 3rd century in a formal counterpart to the Christian Gospels and Acts. On into the 4th cent. Iamblichus could still honour Pythagoras as a good daemon, so that we can trace the influence of this outstanding figure for a thousand years. Socrates with his daimonion († 399) was also a divine revealer for his followers, and his interpreter Plato (427-347) was soon encircled by a halo of pious legend. Paradoxically Epicurus († 270), who was opposed to all revelation, himself founded a community after the religious pattern, and this celebrated his birthday with a memorial feast, and lingered on into the 4th cent. A.D. He found an inspired prophet among the Romans in the poet Lucretius. We have here the strange phenomenon of the opposition to revelation itself becoming "revelation."

4. The Rationalisation of the Idea of Revelation.

From the very first Greek philosophy has a strong bias towards a purely causal and immanent explanation of the world. In the case of Thales, Anaximander and Heraclitus the existence of the Creator is denied and the world is traced back to an original basic material. In that of Empedocles, Anaxagoras, Leucippus and Democritus it has its source in a contingent fusion of elements or atoms. But either way there seems to be no place whatever for any kind of revelation. Nevertheless, there takes place here one of the most influential turns in the intellectual history of the race, namely, the projection of thought into nature, the equation of individual thinking and cosmic reason. [13] In spite of everything, the world has meaning, and thought embraces this meaning. Being and thinking are superimposed on one another. At root they are one. For Heraclitus and the Stoics this ultimate unity is → λόγος, for Anaxagoras it is → νοῦς, for Plato ἰδέα (→ II, 373 ff.). In the present context, however, these distinctions are unimportant. The main point is that the cosmos is regarded as the manifestation of thinking spirit, even if not everywhere that of one thinking spirit. When the intelligence of the Greeks was fructified by the religious genius of the East, as especially in Poseidonius, no further impulse was needed to create the mood which later found its most influential expression in the idea of natural revelation.

Cicero (Tusc., I, 68 ff.) considers the objection how the soul can exist without a body, and he advances the following arguments which seem to have been borrowed from Poseidonius. [14] "When we consider the form and radiance of heaven, the sensually

---

[12] Orph. (Abel), Orph. Fr. (Kern).

[13] Related, but characteristically different, esp. in respect of the position of the visible world, is the Atman-Brahman teaching of India.

[14] We are following the translation in E. Norden, *Agnostos Theos* (1913), 25 f., which simply picks out the main points.

inapprehensible swiftness of its revolution, the alternation of day and night, the fourfold change of the seasons, which are so adapted to the ripening of fruits and the well-being of bodies, the sun which orders and leads all these operations, the moon . . ., the planets . . ., the star-spangled heaven at night, the ball of earth rising from the sea, anchored in the centre of the universe and habitable in two opposing zones, the host of animals which serve partly to nourish and till the fields and partly to transport and clothe our bodies, and finally man himself, the spectator of heaven and worshipper of the gods, together with the land and sea which supply his needs — when we contemplate these and countless other things, can we doubt that there is one to direct this mighty structure of the universe, a creator if it had a beginning as Plato thinks, or a governor if it has always existed according to the view of Aristotle? The case is the same with the spirit of man. You cannot see it, as you cannot see God. But as you know God from His works, so you know the divine power of the spirit from the power of memory, the capacity for discovery, the swiftness of movement and the whole glory of its endowment." Hidden from the senses, deity may still be grasped by *ratio,* the Νοῦς. No special revelation is needed. The natural revelation always and everywhere available is enough.

5. Mysticism and Gnosticism.

At a first glance things seem to be different in mysticism. Here it appears that the mystery of essentially hidden deity is acknowledged fully on the one side, and may be revealed in special instances on the other. Extremely instructive is the interpretation of the ostensible inscription of the veiled image at Sais (→ 559) in Plut. Is. et Os., 9 (II, 354b-d). In the basic and primitive meaning of the inscription, as in the rudiments of Egyptian religion in general, may be found something of the genuine sense of the remoteness of deity. But what is made of this? A secret theology of priests into which kings who come from a warrior caste are initiated by virtue of their office. Hence the dividing line is not really between God and man. It is between God and the uninitiated, in other words, between those who are initiated and those who are not.

> For the former deity is no longer hidden even though its secrets are only disclosed step by step. And for the latter deity is veiled only because of their lack of initiation, not by essence. Mysticism rests on the expressed or tacit assumption that man can control the divine. The roots of mysticism are in magic. Breaking free from sacral magic, myth is designed to illustrate the natural union of man with the divine, and to make this fruitful for the enhancement of life. This enhancement of life by divinisation is always and everywhere possible in principle. We have only to use the right formulae and methods. Mysticism is opposed in essence to singularity in the strict sense. It bears no true relation to definite facts of salvation, to a specific historical and cultic complex of revelation. All mystery religions are fundamentally akin. This is the surest proof that in them we do not have a genuine religion of revelation.

Mysticism goes through a partial process of spiritualisation. The sacral action becomes incidental. It may finally be left out altogether. Vision of the godhead is no longer a cultic climax. It takes place in visions. By purifications and contemplation — and many strange means are used, as may be seen from the Mithras Liturgy — man mounts up to the vision of deity. This vision may be purely inward. It does not have to be accompanied by feelings. It may be cognitive or speculative. For mysticism makes a compact with Gnosticism, and indeed with philosophy. The word becomes more strongly than ever before the bearer of revelation. [15]

---

[15] There is a brilliant depiction of this development in Reitzenstein Hell. Myst., 32 ff.

At the beginning of the Christian era this threefold alliance finds clear expression in the sublimely religious Hermetic writings. These rest on the esoteric knowledge (→ γνῶ-σις, I, 689 ff.) which was entrusted to Hermes Trismegistos, behind whom stands the Egyptian god of writing and wisdom, Toth or Tat, together with half-divine prophetic bearers of revelation, including not only Aesculapius (Imhotep), but rather strangely Tat again, now as the son of Hermes (cf. the discussion of revelation by the two, Corp. Herm., XIII). Hermes has now inscribed this knowledge in powerful written revelations. The technical expressions for the giving and receiving of revelation are παραδιδόναι (Corp. Herm., XIII, 1 etc.) and (παρα)λαμβάνειν (I, 26b; 30) or διδάσκειν (pass., I, 27) and μανθάνειν (XIII, 1) and occasionally our verb (→ infra). God reveals Himself; He wills to be known (γνωσθῆναι βούλεται). The word of revelation helps to regeneration. The λόγος τῆς παλιγγενεσίας must be received with reverent silence. It then moves to the λογικαὶ θυσίαι of thanksgiving. It must never be desecrated by betrayal to the public, but is to be kept secret. Yet it impels to witness (κηρύσσειν) which culminates in the summons: μετανοήσατε. These are the heights on which the conclusion of Poimandres moves (I, 27 ff.). This esoteric religion of mystical philosophy comes to fulfilment in later Neo-Platonism (→ II, 454).

Here, too, we can speak of revelation only with reserve, and not in the same sense as it bears in the Bible. God does not actively move out from Himself. He does not offer Himself for fellowship once for all and all-sufficiently. The handing over of knowledge to the bearer of revelation is little more than a stylistic device. In fact, we have here an Egypto-Hellenistic religious philosophy. The object of revelation is the ground of the world which is only factually and not intrinsically hidden from the non-Gnostic, and which may be personal but also impersonal. When knowledge of this underlying basis is attained, it may be passed on, not through mechanical learning, and only to the accompaniment of certain inner processes like repentance and regeneration, yet still as knowledge, not as news or gospel.

6. The Use of Terms.

When the Greek feels the need to speak of something analogous to revelation, he selects other terms (→ 566). Our words are rare, and outside the Bible their theological usage dates only from a later period.

ἀποκαλύπτειν ("to uncover") is found lit. in Hdt., I, 119 (τὴν κεφαλήν), fig. in Luc. Icaromenipp., 21 (shameful things), P. Masp., 295, II, 8 (Byz., facts), both close together in Plat. Prot., 352a (τὰ στήθη, τόδε τῆς διανοίας), mid. "to come forth publicly with one's view" (Diels, Doxographi Graeci, 298a, 9). The word takes on theological meaning in Corp. Herm. (XIII, 1) in a difficult and perhaps corrupt text which treats of σωθῆναι and the handing over of the λόγος τῆς παλιγγενεσίας : οὐκ ἀπεκάλυψας (syn. with αἰνιγματωδῶς καὶ οὐ τηλαυγῶς ἔφρασας), cf. also Iambl. Myst., III, 17 (ed. Parthey, 142, 9), in a passage which, superstitiously glorifying the crudest methods of manticism, says of the deity : τὰ πάσης γνώσεως προέχοντα νοήματα ἀποκαλύπτει. For the illegitimate betrayal of the mysteries by men, cf. ibid., VI, 7 (248, 11), where it is said that the demons tremble at the threat of a man to unveil the secrets of the cosmos (τὰ κρυπτὰ τῆς Ἴσιδος ἐκφανεῖν, VI, 5). Everything is intact and in order, ἐπειδὴ τὰ ἐν Ἀβύδῳ ἀπόρρητα (the mysteries of Abydos, where according to Egyptian teaching the head of Osiris is to be buried) οὐδέποτε ἀποκα-λύπτεται (VI, 7). It is typical that such human threats are taken seriously by the demons. The ἀποκαλύπτειν of mysteries by one man to another is always regarded as worthy of cursing. Collection des anciens Alchimistes Grecs, ed. M. Berthelot-C. E. Ruelle, Texte (1888), p. 296 § 14 : ἰδοὺ τὸ μυστήριον τῶν φιλοσόφων, καὶ περὶ αὐτοῦ ἐξώρκισαν ὑμῖν οἱ πατέρες ἡμῶν τοῦ μὴ ἀποκαλύψαι αὐτὸ καὶ δημοσιεῦ-σαι. Sopater, a rhetorician of the 5th century A.D., can still write : αὐτὰ τὰ μυστήρια διατυπώσεις καὶ ἐρεῖς, οὐδὲν ἀποκαλύπτων ὁμοίως τῶν μυστικῶν (Rhet. Graec., ed. E. C. Walz [1832 ff.], VIII, p. 123, 19 ff.). But there can also be a beneficial exposition. Iambl. Vit. Pyth., 103 speaks of the correctness and truth which the symbols of the Pythagoreans contain, ἀποκαλυφθεῖσαι καὶ τοῦ αἰνιγματώδους ἐλευθερωθεῖσαι τύπου.

The noun ἀποκάλυψις is found lit. for the non-covering of the head, Philodem. Philosophus (c. 110-28 B.C.), Vitia, 22 (p. 38, 15, ed. C. Jensen [1911]), the uncovering of the body (= γύμνωσις), Plut. Cato Maior, 20 (I, 348c), the discovery of hidden springs, Plut. Aem., 14 (I, 262b), fig. ἀποκάλυψις ἁμαρτίας (ἀνακάλυψις is a better reading) the disclosure of a fault (= νουθέτησις), Plut. Adulat., 32 (II, 70 f.). Acc. to Synesius († before 415 A.D.) ἀποκάλυψις is a technical term of soothsayers (Ep., 54, R. Hercher Epistolographi Graeci [1873], 662). It occurs frequently in later astrological and alchemistic texts. Catal. Cod. Ast. Graec., VII, 4, p. 164, 18 : ὀνείρων ἀποκαλύψεις, p. 145, 26; VIII, p. 99, 7: τὴν τῶν μυστηρίων ἀποκάλυψιν. It can also signify the revealing of secret matters in a cultic context, Berthelot, 219 § 1, more Gnostic, 112 § 6 : ἀποκάλυψις κεκρυμμένων ῥήσεων εἰς φανερὸν γινομένων. But neither term occurs in the mystical vocabulary of Philo.

These data show beyond question that the terms bear no dogmatic impress and that their theological use is fundamentally alien to the Gks. This use was imported from the Orient. In face of Jewish influences in the magic pap. and hardly contestable reminiscences of the OT in Hermes mysticism, the question arises whether the non-biblical use of the terms in the technical sense derives directly or indirectly from the Gk. Bible. [16] It is philologically debatable, but makes good theological sense, when Jerome says of the word ἀποκάλυψις : *proprie Scripturarum est ... a nullo sapientium saeculi apud Graecos usurpatum* (ad Gal., 1, 11 ff., VII, 1, 387, ed. Vallarsi).

C. Revelation in the Old Testament.

1. The Basis in Religious History.

OT religion knows and uses many means of revelation similar to those in other religions, e.g., signs and intimations, Gn. 24:12 ff.; 25:21 ff.; Ju. 6:36 ff.; 1 S. 15:27 ff.; the art of the spiritually endowed man of God and seer, 1 S. 9:6 ff.; 9:15 ff.; 2 S. 24:11; 1 K. 22:6 ff.; Am. 7:12; Is. 29:10; 30:10; → II, 454 f.; dreams and their interpretation (→ 438), incubation (→ 437), the oracle of the Urim and Thummim, 1 S. 14:37 ff., also as ordeal; [17] oracular sayings, Gn. 25:23; priestly directions, Dt. 17:9, 12; ecstasy and prophecy (→ II, 454). In preparation for the reception of revelation we read of fasting and mortification in Da. 9:3; 4 Esr. 5:20.

2. The Revelation of the Living God.

Under these forms, and to some extent bursting and transcending them, a new and unique revelation is given to Israel. The OT finds the distinctive point in the fact that Yahweh, the God of Israel, is the living God (אֵל חַי) Jos. 3:10; אֱלֹהִים חַי Is. 37:4; אֱלֹהִים חַיִּים Dt. 5:23; Jer. 10:10 etc., in distinction from empty idols, אֱלִילִים Is. 2:8; Ps. 96:5; 97:7 etc.).

---

[16] P. Tillich (→ Bibl.), 403 states : "Revelation as an idea is as old as religion ... the concept of revelation is a creation of Hellenistic philosophy." This formulation brings idea and concept into far too abstract antithesis. It does not sufficiently regard the differences within the idea of revelation nor the oriental origin of the later Hellenistic view of revelation. Rightly seeking to warn us against a historical hardening and dogmatic narrowing of revelation, it goes to the opposite extreme. It is thus in danger of regarding as pagan the biblical and ecclesiastical belief in a concrete content of revelation, and of replacing it by a subjectivistic revelation mysticism.

[17] For details cf. R. Press, "Das Ordal im alten Israel," ZAW, NF, 10 (1933), 121 ff., 227 ff.

There are different views as to the time when this new factor first appeared in the history of Israel. Older historical criticism dated it from 8th century prophecy, but more recent voices favour the thesis that the seeds of this new understanding were sown in Israel's history when it became a nation under Moses. [18] The epoch-making insight was certainly not explicit in the sense that the reality of Yahweh and the vanity of heathen gods were exclusively asserted from the very outset. They were established only after many serious crises. But biblical religion built on them as faith in one God who is God in the true sense as distinct from all other numinous experience (→ 87).

This does not mean, however, that this God unites Himself with men, or with His people, by continuous and palpable revelation. [19] As true God, He is the hidden God (אֵל מִסְתַּתֵּר Is. 45:15). He is the God of mystery who reveals Himself only when He wills to do so (→ κρύπτω). But this means that our concern here is with revelation in the strict sense. This revelation is worked out supremely in three directions. Yahweh reveals Himself as the Lord of history, as holy and gracious, and as the Creator of the world.

a. Yahweh reveals Himself as the Lord of history. The liberation of Israel from Egypt, the house of bondage, is always fundamental to OT religion. When Pharaoh and his power resisted Yahweh, He revealed Himself overwhelmingly as the Lord of glory ("they shall know that I am Yahweh," Ex. 14:18). By this powerful action He drew Israel uniquely to Him out of all the nations (Ex. 19:4 ff.). The prophets constantly refer to this fact (Am. 2:10; Hos. 11:1 etc.; Jer. 7:22; 32:20; cf. Dt. 4:34 etc.). Yet steps are also taken to prevent the illusion that Israel is thereby given some kind of claim (Am. 9:7). Intrinsically all nations are alike before Yahweh. He rules over them all and guides them to the place which He has appointed for them. Rightly understood, however, Yahweh's rule in history is constitutive for His covenant relationship with Israel.

Because Israel's religion is nourished by history, it is characterised by a historical orientation. The essential thing in the biblical view is not to be found in what always is, but in what happens. History, i.e., that which happens, is the work of Yahweh.

With His mighty hand He directs not merely the history of His people but also the history of all peoples. He causes empires to rise and fall. He frustrates the arrogant plans of kings (Is. 7:1-9; 8:1-4). World kingdoms must carry out His orders. He calls, and like flies and bees they swarm to execute His much threatened judgment on Israel (Is. 7:18 f.). But when the rod turns against the one who wields it, when the stick turns against the one who smites therewith, when the axe threatens the one who hews down with it, when the saw rises up against the one who uses it, they are each and all destroyed, and those who were smitten are wonderfully sustained (10:5 ff., 12 ff.). The pride of Assyria is broken on the walls of Jerusalem when God so determines (10:28 ff.). As flying birds He will protect the armies of Jerusalem (31:5). He calls Cyrus by name, so that he carries out His command and brings back Israel into the land of its fathers (45:1 ff.). The nations see this and are astonished (52:10, 15; 60:3, 5 etc.). The whole world is to do homage to Yahweh (Ps. 98).

---

[18] Cf. P. Volz, *Mose und sein Werk*[2] (1932); O. Procksch, *Der Staatsgedanke in der Prophetie* (1933), 4 ff. A. Alt would go back even earlier in "Der Gott der Väter," BWANT, Folge 3, 12 (1929).

[19] W. Baudissin, " 'Gott schauen' in der at.lichen Religion," ARW, 18 (1915), 173 ff. points out that OT religion "adapts the originally alien concept of seeing God to the basic idea of the majesty of God," thus excluding again its essentially alien sense (233).

Here at once we see the nature of revelation on the OT view. Revelation is not the impartation of supernatural knowledge or the excitement of numinous feelings. Knowledge can certainly come through revelation, and the revelation of God will be accompanied by numinous feelings (Ex. 19:16; Is. 6:5 etc.). But revelation is not to be identified with these. In the proper sense, it is the action of Yahweh. It is the removal of His essential concealment, His self-offering for fellowship. The distinctive feature of this fellowship, however, is that it rests on a moral foundation.

b. Yahweh reveals Himself as holy and gracious. He is holy in the moral sense. This is brought out very clearly in the Ten Commandments. Here the elementary bases of all morality are demands of Yahweh. The same truth may be seen throughout the history of the centuries which follow. The people is continually exposed to the danger of corrupting the insight given to its leaders along the lines of natural or cultic religion. With pitiless consistency, however, Nathan, Elijah, Amos, Hosea, Isaiah, Micah and Jeremiah assert the holy will of Yahweh. The cultus is not what Yahweh demands, whether alone or along with a modest amount of moral action. He simply demands obedience. The cultus without obedience is an abomination to Him. He will completely destroy His elect instruments and elect people rather than allow even the smallest portion of His holy moral will to be abrogated (2 S. 12:7 ff.; 1 K. 17:1; 18:1 ff.; 21:17 ff.; Am. 2:6 ff.; 4:1 ff.; 5:21 ff.; 8:4 ff.; Hos. 6:6; Is. 1:10-17; 3:16 ff.; 5:8 ff. etc.; Mi. 2:1 ff.; 6:8; Jer. 7:3 ff. etc.).

In His holiness Yahweh is concerned for His glory (Ex. 20:5; Is. 42:8). OT religion does not begin with an abstract idea of the good by which even God is measured. Yahweh's will is good. But its nature is not always clear to man. God's rule sometimes threatens to take on sub-moral features (2 S. 22:27 = Ps. 18:26; Ex. 20:5, cf. with Jer. 31:29 f.; Ez. 18:2 ff.). And even though one might speak here of just retribution, it must still be pointed out that the moral justice of divine retribution is not always plain. It is well known what severe problems this created for OT piety (cf. Ps. 37; 73; Job). Faith is always wrestling through from the hidden God to the revealed God.

Yahweh is gracious. He exercises mercy and forgives sins (Ex. 34:6 f.; Ps. 32:5; 103:8 ff.). The revealing Word of Yahweh which always accompanies His revealing act is to this effect — that His overruling leads through judgment to blessing. In this witness it reaches supreme heights almost comparable with the NT (Is. 40:1 ff.; 53; 61:1 ff.). But behind all this, as an indispensable background, is the transcendent power of the Creator over the world.

c. Yahweh reveals Himself as the Creator and Sustainer of the world. He has made heaven and earth (Is. 37:16). This insight is not the starting-point of Israel's belief in God. Yahweh is not one of the shadowy originator gods[20] familiar to us in religious history. In the first instance He is the One who acts in power to-day. But the insight that the origin of the world is to be sought in His will and Word arises with inner necessity and increasing clarity. The cosmogonies of surrounding peoples such as the Phoenicians and Babylonians cannot be used by Israel in their mythological form. Only after a radical process of purification can they provide basic material for the biblical creation story. The theme of this is not the battle between deity and chaos. The world exists by the Word of Yahweh, by His al-

---

20 This term derives from N. Söderblom, *Das Werden des Gottesglaubens* (1916), esp. 114 ff.

mighty will. The close connections between this insight and the moral and historical overruling of the world by Yahweh are brought out with particular clarity in Ps. 33. The glory of Yahweh in creation gives to poetry and prophecy a profitable theme which is often developed along similar lines, cf. Ps. 18:7 ff.; 19:1-7; 29; 96:10 ff.; 97:1 ff.; 98:7 ff.; 104; 148; Is. 40:12 ff., 22 ff.; 42:5; 45:12, 18; 48:13; Am. 5:8; 9:5 f.; Job 9:5 ff.; 38; 39.

From this standpoint the theological physics of the Greeks may seem to be similar in many respects. But the basic attitude is completely different. The Greek is trying to master the world by thought. For this purpose the ego is cosmically extended (→ 568). But the righteous man of the OT, even when he extols in the highest terms the revelation of God in creation and man's place of dominion on earth, is always conscious that this dominion is God-given and that there is distance between Creator and creature. Nothing is more instructive than to compare and contrast the famour choral song in the Antigone of Sophocles (332 ff.): πολλὰ τὰ δεινὰ κοὐδὲν ἀνθρώπου δεινότερον πέλει, with Ps. 8. On the Greek view, man unveils God; on the biblical, God reveals Himself to man. On the one side we have proofs of God and the praise of man, on the other the praise of God.

3. The Delimitation of Revelation.

The Greek understanding of revelation moves between the two extremes of compression into a mystery on the one side and humanistic and cosmopolitan extension on the other. Both are equally remote from the OT. The worship of Yahweh is no mystery. Nor is it in any direct sense a world religion. Yahweh is the God of His people. He is this because in free, prevenient grace He has elected the people Israel as His possession, as a kingdom of priests, as a holy nation (Ex. 19:4 ff.). Yet He is also the living God, the Creator and Lord of the world. Hence the covenant relationship obviously does not mean that Yahweh has formally abandoned the idea of manifesting Himself to other peoples. He declares Himself to all nations in His judgments (Is. 13 ff.; Jer. 25:12 ff.; Am. 1:3-2:3; Na. 1-3; Zeph. 2:8 ff.), but also in His blessings (Am. 9:7). The OT can even admit the thought that Yahweh summons other peoples to repentance by prophetic preaching (Jon. 3:4 ff.; 4:11). One day all nations will share the revelation of salvation (Is. 2:2-4; Mi. 4:1-3). Above all, Yahweh will then reveal Himself by definitively leading His people to salvation. This is the true theme of the prophecy of Dt. Is. (esp. 41:1 ff., 8 ff.; 45:4 ff., 14-25; 49:1 ff.; 51:4 ff.; 52:13 ff.). The cosmic breadth of the sphere of revelation does not alter the fact that the covenant revelation belongs to the chosen people and that in the first instance the self-offering for fellowship (→ supra) is strictly within the confines of this people. In the strict sense revelation is always and everywhere the act of God. No one has a right to it simply because he is a man. Even the Israelite has no right to it because he is an Israelite. The right thus granted can be withdrawn because of guilt. We oversimplify if we regard the Israelite and the non-Israelite worlds as respective spheres of revelation and non-revelation, of true revelation and false. On the one side God is not limited to Israel, and on the other we find the contrast between true and false revelation in Israel too.

It is one of the paradoxical depths of the OT view of God that deluding false revelation in Israel can also be ascribed to Yahweh (1 K. 22:19 ff.). This does not rule out the aspect of human responsibility. This aspect is predominant in the assessment of false prophecy.

The Heb. OT has no word for false prophets. [21] But the conflict with them may be followed like a red thread for over two centuries (1 K. 22:5 ff.; Mi. 3:5 ff.; Jer. 2:26; 6:13 ff.; 14:13 ff.; 18:18 ff.; 23:9-22, 30 ff.; 26:7 ff.; 27-29; Ez. 13:15 f.). Though there is no word, the concept is so distinct that we are right to suspect an institutional phenomenon. [22] The reference seems to be primarily, though not exclusively, to cultic prophets who are professionally engaged for money to make intercession and to issue prophecies. [23]

The OT itself wrestled seriously with the question where true prophecy is to be found and how it is to be differentiated from false (Dt. 18:21).

The following criteria are considered.

a. The personality and motivation of the bearers of revelation. False prophets cry "Salvation" when their teeth have something to bite, but they declare war against those who put nothing into their mouths (Mi. 3:5, cf. 11). The true prophet is independent (Am. 7:14), though the prophet's chamber is a warning that this principle is not to be applied schematically (2 K. 4:8 ff.; cf. 1 K. 17:7 ff.).

b. The result of the reception of revelation. "The prophet that hath a dream, let him tell a dream; but he that hath my word, let him speak my word faithfully" (Jer. 23:28, cf. v. 32). This disqualification of dreams — and we might also add ecstatic and visionary phenomena (cf. Is. 8:19) — is most significant. In face of all methodology of revelation, the decisive factor is the Word which is received. This does not mean, however, that these possibilities are completely excluded from genuine prophecy. In some cases they can be linked in various ways with the reception of the Word (Is. 6; Am. 7-9; Zech. 1:7-6:8 etc.). The OT itself shows us that the direct reception of revelation is an ideal which is truly fulfilled only in Moses (Ex. 33:11; Nu. 12:6 ff.; Dt. 34:10). The important thing is the direct and overmastering power of true reception of the Word (Am. 3:8; Is. 5:9; Jer. 20:9; 23:29), though even this may be to some degree equivocal.

c. Fulfilment or non-fulfilment of the prophecy (1 S. 3:19; 1 K. 8:56; Dt. 18:22; Jer. 28:9 : "By fulfilment of the word shall the prophet be known, that the Lord has truly sent him"; and esp. Dt. Is. : 41:21 ff.; 42:9; 44:7 ff.; 44:26; 45:21; 46:10; 48:15 f.; 55:10 f.). The only point is that even in the case of acknowledged messengers of God there may be some oracles that are not fulfilled as well as the many that are. Is. 29:5 f. is right rather than Mi. 3:12. The prophets themselves explain that the Word of Yahweh is not an unalterable decree. The divine rule adjusts itself elastically to the prevailing situation (Is. 28:23 ff.).

d. The content of the message is the safest sign. False prophets cry "Peace" when the true man of God is a herald of judgment (1 K. 22:5 ff.; Mi. 3:5; Jer. 28). Or false prophets speak of judgment when the true proclaim salvation (Mi. 3:5; Jer. 29:11; Am. 9:11 ff.; Hos. 14:5 ff.; [24] Is. 7:1-9; 9:1-6; Dt. Is. passim). The true distinction is that false prophets speak to please men except in so far as their carnal egotism leads them otherwise, whereas true bearers of revelation are ineluctably committed to the sacred will of Yahweh even though it mean destruction for the people and for themselves.

---

[21] ψευδοπροφήτης in the LXX at Ιερ. 6:13; 33(26):7 ff.; 34:9; 35:1 (Heb. נְבִיאִים).

[22] v. Rad, op. cit. Cf. S. Mowinckel, "Kultprophetie und prophetische Psalmen," Psalmenstudien, III (1923).

[23] The view that Dt. 18:18-22 is written from the standpoint of cultic prophecy in opposition to the prophets of woe who are recognised elsewhere (v. Rad), is not wholly convincing. W. Staerk, 92 regards v. 21 f. as "temporally conditioned embroidery" which is in no sense essential.

[24] We may now take it that there is no more question as to the authenticity of the concluding promises of prophetic books.

The proclamation is thus shown to be valid by its moral orientation (Jer. 23:21 f.). But this does not mean that it is moralistic. Man does not bring an existing concept of the good to revelation and on this basis make a judicial decision concerning its quality. It is man himself who is under judgment and decision. The true revelation of God hales corrupt and sinful human nature mercilessly to judgment, and then leads on through judgment to grace and salvation. This content is binding on prophecy. "It can do nothing in opposition to the truth of the living God. Otherwise it is broken by it." [25] Obviously we do not have here the rational application of an infallible criterion of truth. God makes Himself known to His messengers as the holy and gracious God both inwardly and in the march of history. They venture out on this declaration. Their sense of mission must have been frequently shaken. This is particularly true, as we may see, in Jeremiah (20:7-18). But their shattered confidence is restored. Revelation carries the day.

4. Revelation and Eschatology.

The distinctiveness of OT revelation is most clearly expressed in its reference to the future. The Greek idea of revelation, in its best forms, refers to that which is at all times, even though concealed behind empirical being. OT belief in revelation is directed to that which is to be.

In this regard we are to think of the popular expectations of a coming age of salvation which were current in the Orient from ancient times. These expectations bear a predominantly transcendent character when they correspond to Utopian depictions of the original state of man. [26] Prophecy, however, rejects sharply the unbroken natural optimism of these expectations. When the people speaks enthusiastically of the day of Yahweh, Amos sees that this will be a day of darkness and terror (5:18 ff.). Yet this pitiless No does not prevent Amos and other prophets from crowning their warnings of judgment by intimations of a great and final age of salvation (Am. 9:11 ff.; Hos. 2:16 ff.; Mi. 4:1 ff.).

> Is. especially uses popular colours to portray this time (9:1 ff.; 11:1 ff.). In Dt. Is. and Tr. Is. the Messianic age of salvation is the true theme of the prophecy (Is. 40-66 passim). In what is in part a more inward form, future expectation is also found in Jer. (31:31 ff.). We see it again in Ez. (36:24 ff.). From a priestly point of view the latter also gives a prophetic sketch of the new Jerusalem and its temple (40-48). This brings us close to Apocalyptic. The idea of revelation is now in process of change. The focus shifts from the Word of demand, warning, interpretation and comfort to the actual disclosure of the future glory which already exists in hidden form in the counsel of God and the heavenly world. The more evil the course of this world, the more fervently hope is set on the time when Yahweh will enter upon His world dominion and show Himself to be the King of all peoples. The so-called coronation psalms (46; 47; 96-99) celebrate this moment in dithyrambic transports.

5. The Usage.

ἀποκαλύπτειν is never used for יָדַע hi. In the LXX it is mostly used for the materially similar גָּלָה (pi), Aram. גְּלָא, comonly in the lit. sense "to uncover" (Ex. 20:26;

---

[25] Staerk, 86.

[26] The influence of these ideas on the West is best illustrated in Vergil's 4th Eclogue. Cf. E. Norden, *Die Geburt des Kindes* (1924). But these connections have no very profound significance for the Hellenistic view of revelation.

Lv. 18:6 ff.), though often fig., in the first instance as a Hebraism with no theological significance: ἀποκαλύπτειν τὸ ὠτίον τινός, "to initiate someone into a matter" (1 Βασ. 20:2; 22:8, 17), also with the obj. of what is imparted: ἀποκαλύπτειν (only here = הִגִּיד) τοὺς λόγους τούτους (Jos. 2:20). The term takes on theological significance when Yahweh is the subj. (Is. 52:10 is instructive: חָשַׂף יְהֹוָה אֶת־זְרוֹעַ קָדְשׁוֹ לְעֵינֵי כָּל־הַגּוֹיִם LXX ἀποκαλύψει κύριος τὸν βραχίονα αὐτοῦ, Heb. "to uncover," Gk. more fig. "to reveal"); 2 Βασ. 7:27: ἀπεκάλυψας τὸ ὠτίον τοῦ δούλου σου, similarly τοὺς ὀφθαλμούς of seeing in a vision, Nu. 22:31; 24:4, 16; pass. of the self-revelation of God with the πρός of person, 1 Βασ. 2:27; 3:21 (synon. δηλωθῆναι), or when the obj. is religious or moral (ῥῆμα θεοῦ, 1 Βασ. 3:7, ῥίζα σοφίας, Gk. Sir. 1:6). When the word is used for the impartation of knowledge, this is not intellectual knowledge, but intuitive contact with what is concealed in transcendence (cf. → δηλοῦν, II, 61). We see this esp. in Da. Θ. This Jewish translator is fond of the word. LXX prefers ἀνακαλύπτω, ἐκφαίνω or δείκνυμι (2:19, 22, 28, 29, 30, 47; 10:1). The concept of revelation has not yet been fixed dogmatically. Though it is central to the whole of OT piety, there is as yet no settled term for it. The concept takes an interesting and fateful turn when used for the becoming immanent of transcendentally pre-existent realities. Tr. Is. announces the day of salvation with the divine call: ἤγγισεν τὸ σωτήριόν μου παραγίνεσθαι καὶ τὸ ἔλεός μου ἀποκαλυφθῆναι (לְהִגָּלוֹת) Is. 56:1.

Here "to be revealed" means much the same as "to appear." In the interests of brevity of definition we may call this the "eschatological" use as distinct from the "mystical." The quotation marks show that these are only schematic terms. The LXX uses ἀποκάλυψις in the figurative sense, but not in the more narrowly theological, of the betrayal of human secrets (Gr. Sir. 22:22; in 41:26 [42:1] we should read ἀπὸ καλύψεως) and of the judicial disclosure of man's nature by God (Gr. Sir. 11:27).

D. The Attitude of Judaism to Revelation.

1. General Points.

In general Judaism does not expect any direct revelation from God in its own day. Prophecy is over (1 Macc. 4:46; 9:27; 14:41). Isolated ecstatic phenomena (→ II, 455) count for little. Attention is focused all the more on the past and the future. Israel has in the Torah a revelation which is valid for all ages (→ νόμος). In lesser measure the prophets and the writings share the character of revelation (→ κανών). There is an almost complete codification of revelation. Oral tradition (→ II, 172) is not meant to be more than a more precise exposition of the written will of God. The understanding of revelation is intellectualistic.[27] However wonderful the rule of God at the time of the giving of the Law, the essential point is that Israel knows the will of God and can earn merit by fulfilling it. New revelation is expected in the last time. Here everything seems to depend on God's action. But it is typical that the concept of revelation should again be intellectualised. What is expected from revived prophecy is the elucidation of individual difficulties, especially in casuistry. The idea that the Messiah will give a new exposition of the Law is interwoven with the further idea that he will give a new Torah. Qoh. r., 11, 8, p. 52a (Str.-B., III, 577): "The Torah which a man learns in this world is as nothing compared with the Torah of the Messiah." גָּלָא is a technical term for

---

[27] It still is so in modern Judaism. Cf. M. Wiener, "Zur Geschichte d. Offenbarungsbegriffs," Judaica, Festschrift f. H. Cohen (1912), 1: a knowledge "which does not owe its origin to the natural forces of the human spirit which are generally manifested in the business of life, but which is thought to flow from the inspiration that has its source directly in God." Cf. also J. Hänel, ZSTh, 4 (1926/27), 91.

revelation particularly in the expression: "The kingdom of God will be manifest (איתגליאת)," i.e., in the ἔσχατον (→ I, 573). In general, however, Torah is the technical word for revelation. Even in Hellenistic Judaism ἀποκαλύπτειν and ἀποκάλυψις are not very common outside the LXX. Neither occurs at all in Philo. This is connected with his general usage and with the lack of any precise concept of revelation in his theology. Nor does Josephus display any central interest in revelation. He is content to show that Jewish monotheism is the fulfilment of philosophy and the Torah the crown of Stoic morality.

2. Apocalyptic.

Judaism forged a certain substitute for living revelation in apocalyptic.

This genre is named after the last book of the NT, which calls itself ἀποκάλυψις (Rev. 1:1) and which has many affinities with the literature to which we now refer, though it cannot be simply classified with it. The earliest apocalypse, i.e., Daniel, was written in Heb. (Aram.), and most apocalypses have Heb. originals. Hence the genre is distinctively Palestinian. Yet it is hard to fix precisely either its popular setting in Palestine or its relation to Rabbinic Judaism. The suggestion that apocalyptic followed the secret tradition of the Rabbis [28] is unlikely in view of the strong material differences between the two strands and the wide distribution of apocalyptic in Hellenistic Judaism and Christianity. The champions of apocalyptic are to be sought especially in the less prominent but undoubtedly present group of the "quiet in the land." It is not impossible that its origins are linked with Pharisaism and that something of the legacy of esoteric Rabbinic tradition is incorporated into it.

In accordance with the current view of revelation Jewish apocalyptic is completely pseudepigraphical. The revelation was supposedly to great figures of the past. It was sealed (cf. Is. 8:16) and remained secret until the end of the days. Now it is disclosed. A more important point materially is the strong emphasis on the transcendence of God (→ II, 422), partly under foreign influences (→ I, 368 f. ἀνίστημι, bibl.). The present world is God's creation, but through the fall of Adam and the prevailing sin of all men it is now corrupt. God, however, has created, not one aeon alone, but two. The new aeon already exists in the upper world. When corruption has reached its supreme climax here — and the apocalyptist thinks that this has already happened — the final cosmic catastrophe will come and the new aeon will break in with power (→ I, 206). The powerful experience of the apocalyptist, or of his fictional sponsor, is to have looked already into the upper world of God. Hence he can proclaim imminent redemption to the struggling servants of God and encourage them to persevere. The curtain between this world and the world to come is lifted for a moment. With trembling joy the seer watches forceful visions whose meaning is for the most part disclosed to him by an interpreting angel. These are accompanied by a complicated series of apocalyptic calculations which are designed to meet objections and to prove that the time of salvation is near. Justice is also done to a primitively romantic cosmology. Thus large portions of Eth. En. are filled with astronomical or angelological revelations and descriptions from heaven.

The intricate visions which result seem to have little to do with genuine prophecy, which displays the rule of God in history and emphasises His moral will. Nevertheless, the aim is to strengthen the severely tried community in faith in the living God. The loftiest questions are treated with great seriousness. This finds striking confirmation in a passage in 4 Esr. which reminds us of Paul, though naturally it is not on the same plane as the NT. In the whole cultural life of

---

[28] J. Jeremias, Jerusalem z. Zeit Jesu, II B, 1, "Die gesellschaftliche Oberschicht" (1929), 107.

humanity, apart from some first beginnings in Babylonian and Persian thought, the idea of world history occurs for the first time in Jewish apocalyptic from the time of Daniel. [29] In an age when Jewish thinking seemed likely to be choked by chauvinistic fervour, and when revelation was hardening into intellectualistic casuistry, apocalyptic, even if it failed to purge out all the dross, did at least provide a broad cosmic vision and maintain to some degree an understanding of the active character of the divine self-impartation.

3. Natural Revelation.

Whereas Palestinian Judaism tended to place a one-sided emphasis on the divine transcendence, Hellenistic Judaism moved in the direction of immanence. Even pre-exilic Wisdom literature was not closed to the influence of the intellectual life of paganism. [30] The later *diaspora* was in constant touch with Hellenism, and partly for apologetic, partly for polemical reasons, it naturally inclined to combine the biblical belief in God with Hellenistic physico-theology.

Philo and Wis. are the main representatives of this natural theology. Thoughtful men may discern the existence of a Creator in the beauty and purposiveness of the world. "Coming into this world like visitors to a well-regulated city ... they yield to admiration and astonishment, and by means of what is laid before them they perceive that so much beauty and such pre-eminent order could not arise of themselves, but only at the hand of a cosmic architect, and that providence must exist; for it is a general law of nature (νόμος φύσεως) that what is created bears the impress of him who made it" (Philo Praem. Poen., 41 f.). Wis. 13:3 ff. demonstrates the folly of idolatry as follows: "When, charmed by the beauty of certain natural phenomena, they find in them gods, they ought to have known how much better than these is the Lord of the same ... And if they were astounded at the force and power, these ought to have led them to the consideration how much mightier is the one who has prepared them. For from the greatness and beauty of the creatures it is possible analogically to see their Creator. But lesser blame rests on them, since perhaps they (merely) err as they would seek and find God ... On the other hand they cannot be wholly excused ... But those who call the works of men's hands their gods are deserving of pity and set their hope on dead things." Religion stands behind all this. We are not concerned with mere theoretical knowledge. The practical deduction is drawn that man owes worship and obedience to the God self-revealed in creation. Now a genuine religion of revelation does find the self-revealing God in creation too. Here, however, the God of revelation is sought in the cosmic basis to which Greek thought was led. Philo rightly says that the thinking of philosophers moves from below upwards (κάτωθεν ἄνω προῆλθον οἷα διά τινος οὐρανίου κλίμακος, ἀπὸ τῶν ἔργων εἰκότι λογισμῷ στοχασάμενοι τὸν δημιουργόν, aiming at the cosmic architect by fitting consideration, Praem. Poen., 43). A new and second principle has been introduced into the knowledge of God. It is little help that Philo uses every possible method to ward off the threatening pantheism, that he attributes semi-personal characteristics to his Logos, and that in mystical vision he tries to set an ἄνωθεν κάτω alongside the κάτωθεν ἄνω. This does not prevent him from attaining great popularity and significance in Christian apologetics, Scholasticism and the Enlightenment. More recent research has recognised with increasing clarity that two quite different things are here brought into an untenable compromise. In a broader sense one can also speak of natural revelation where it is

---

[29] J. Behm, *Gott u. d. Geschichte: Das Geschichtsbild der Offenbarung Johannis* (1925); "Johannesapk. u. Geschichtsphilosophie," ZSTh, 2 (1924/25), 323 ff.

[30] A. Erman has discovered that in Prv. 22:17-23:11 we have a translation and revision of part of the Egyptian wisdom teaching of Amenemope (OLZ, 27 [1924], 241 ff.).

argued that the revealed moral law is coincident with natural law in the sense of Stoic morality, cf. Joseph. Ap., II, 173 ff.

E. Revelation in the New Testament.

The NT inherits OT revelation. The God of the NT is the same as that of the OT, not in the sense of an absolute identity of conception, but in the sense of a continuity of salvation history. The NT constantly presupposes the OT. This connection is basic to its view of revelation. To a large extent the NT ignores Judaism and goes back direct to the OT itself, especially to the prophets, and very especially to Jer. and Dt. Is. If this involves negative relations with Judaism, there are also some positive relations. In the first instance apocalyptic had a strong influence on Christianity from the very outset, and to a very large extent furnished it with its basic concepts. This is important for an understanding of revelation. It means that the meaning of the words in the NT has its true locus in eschatology. The NT adopts especially the previously mentioned sense of "to appear" for ἀποκαλύπτεσθαι (→ 577). Linked with this is the strong preponderance of the passive (→ infra; 583). It would be too much to say that the NT knows nothing of a present revelation effected here and now. This would fit neither the use of the terms nor the actual matter. The distinctive dynamic of the NT understanding of revelation arises from the alternating relationship between history and eschatology.

1. Revelation in the Synoptists.

The witness of the Baptist by word and deed (Mt. 3:2 and par.), and especially the initial preaching of Jesus (Mk. 1:15 and par.), imply that God is now coming out of His previous concealment and that He will manifest His kingdom and usher in the promised time of salvation. It is necessary to prepare for this. Hence NT piety is from the very first orientated to, and dependent upon, revelation as the act of God. In the course of the work of Jesus it becomes increasingly plain that He does not merely proclaim the coming kingdom of God. He Himself is this kingdom in person (→ I, 588 f.). In Him it is already present as an eschatological reality. He has full power to reveal the Father to whom He will (Mt. 11:27 and par.). He is the corporeal revelation of God, though at first concealed as everything divine is in this aeon. He is the heavenly Son of Man who will come on the clouds (Mk. 8:38; 14:62 etc.). [31] The meaning of ἀποκαλύπτειν in respect of Jesus is basically that He Himself will be revealed, that He will appear, at the parousia (Lk. 17:30). The previous concealment is now replaced by Messianic doxa. But this future doxa may be seen already in the present doxa. The only point is that enlightened eyes are needed to see it. Peter sees in Jesus the Anointed and the Son of God, but this is revealed to him, not by flesh and blood, but by the Father of

---

[31] W. Wrede's well-known thesis (Das Messiasgeheimnis in den Evangelien, 1901) that the theology of the community uses the Messianic secret to conceal the lack of Messianic self-declarations on the part of the earthly Jesus involves an exaggeration of correct insights. Mk. may well have allowed his love of the numinous to heighten the secrecy motif. But there can be little doubt as to the historicity of the fact that Jesus regarded Himself as the Messiah and that, in order to avoid popular misunderstanding, He concealed His Messiahship until it should be manifested. In this regard A. Schweitzer, Gesch. d. Leben-Jesu-Forschung[4] (1926), 390 ff. gives a truer picture. Cf. R. Otto, Reich Gottes u. Menschensohn (1934), 127 ff.

Jesus in heaven (Mt. 16:17). His knowledge comes, not by rational means or human impartation, but by revelation from above. Hence revelation is not understood in terms of a fixed historical or eschatological objectivism. The making known of present revelation is itself part of the act of revelation.

Human knowledge is a hindrance rather than an advantage for the reception of this knowledge which is from God. Even the one who of all those born of woman seemed to be the best equipped for receiving it had to be gently rebuked by Jesus : "Blessed is he, whosoever shall not be offended in me" (Mt. 11:6 and par.). The sovereign sway of God may at first have caused pain to Jesus Himself in virtue of its paradoxical character. But it was then adored and revered. It finds expression in the fact that the knowledge of salvation is denied to the wise and understanding, i.e., to those who are models of piety in Rabbinic and Pharisaic eyes. It is closed to these and concealed from them. Instead, it is given by revelation to the ignorant, i.e., to the despised 'amme ha'areç (Mt. 11:25 and par.). Yet revelation is equivocal for the people too. It is likely enough that in a moment of discouragement Jesus reproached the unreceptive multitude in terms of Is. 6:9, 10 (Mk. 4:11 f. and par.; in the best attested text Mt. softens the harsh ἵνα to ὅτι, but when the passage is reproduced in full this makes little material difference). [32] This saying cannot be one-sidedly construed as a rigid theory, whether in respect of the parables or of the whole work of Jesus. The manner of Jesus is neither radically esoteric nor forbiddingly paradoxical. He speaks in order that He may be understood, in order that God may be, not concealed, but revealed in all His zeal and love. He fulfils the revelation of the prophets, bringing it to its goal.

There is no problem of natural revelation or natural theology in the Synoptists. Jesus discerns the rule of His heavenly Father in the world (Mt. 6:26 ff.). He addresses His moral demands directly to the wills of His hearers. There is no new theoretical or casuistic instruction concerning the good, nor does He provide any dogmatic soteriological basis for a new ethics. "He never admitted the sincerity of ignorance of the good." [33] He can sometimes simplify and sum up the content of the Law and the prophets in what seems to be almost rationalistic fashion (Mk. 12:28 ff.). We also find isolated wisdom sayings (Lk. 14:7 ff.). [34] His parables are adapted to be understood in terms of general human presuppositions and are often a protest against the distorted Rabbinic theology of revelation. But these are not the first beginnings of a natural theology. For there is no question of the living God being crowded out by the cosmic basis or of His holy will being replaced by morality. It is simply that the understanding of nature and of man leads to the God of revelation. The same Jesus who teaches us to consider the lilies of the field and the fowls of the air points also to Scripture, and especially to the Ten Commandments. The teaching of Jesus does not consist of a rational foundation and a supra-

---

[32] Cf. J. Kögel, "Der Zweck d. Gleichnisse Jesu im Rahmen seiner Verkündigung," BFTh, 19, 6 (1916).

[33] Schl. Gesch. d. Chr., 177.

[34] Cf. Mt. 11:19. The resemblance of the saying in Mt. 11:25 ff. to Sir., esp. c. 51 and 24, has often been noted from the time of D. F. Strauss. In spite of E. Norden, *Agnostos Theos* (1913), 277 ff. this probably indicates direct dependence. What part the community played in its formulation is another question. Hermes mysticism is hardly original in relation to the saying. Both may well be dependent on oriental modes of speech.

natural superstructure. It is not like an ellipse with two foci — God and man. At its single centre stands only the living God of revelation. The vocation of Jesus is first to restore honour to the genuine revelation of the covenant God in face of human commandments (Mk. 7:8 ff.; 11:15 ff. and par.), and secondly to bring it to its fulfilment and goal in every direction (Mt. 5:17; 26:54) and in respect of all men. In spite of a few sayings which seem to be to the contrary (Mt. 10:5 f.; 15:24; Lk. 19:9b) Jesus is not a Jewish particularist; He is a universalist (Mt. 8:11 etc.). But He is this in the sense of a concrete self-offering of God to all sinners. To understand Jesus humanistically is grossly to misunderstand Him. Jesus rejects the intellectualistic Jewish understanding of revelation and brings the OT view to fulfilment.

2. The Understanding of Revelation in the Primitive Community.

The understanding of revelation in the primitive community is even more orientated to the future than that of Jesus Himself. More correctly, perhaps, we should say that it is so in a radically different way. The community believes that the Messiah who has come is the One who will come. Now concealed in heaven, He will one day be manifested (Ac. 3:21). The earthly work of Jesus, His death and resurrection are the fulfilment of OT promise, but in such a way that the message concerning them is caught up into revelation, so that the Gospel of Jesus Christ is now the Gospel about Jesus Christ (Ac. 10:36-43). It is only with the manifestation of the crucified and risen Lord in Messianic glory that the goal and crown of all revelation will be reached, i.e., the salvation of penitent sinners from all peoples and the restoration of creation (Ac. 2:38; 10:34 f.; 3:21). The link between past and future revelation is the impartation of the Spirit, which is conditioned by what is past and which points forward to what is future. This view of revelation can be gathered from the speeches in Acts even if they are not to be regarded as exact records of what was said. On the other hand, in the absence of source materials we have no means by which to differentiate the various shades of understanding within early Palestinian Christianity. [35] Certainly there are no serious grounds on which to interpose between the Jerusalem community and Paul a primitive Hellenistic community which replaced the relationship of revelation to history by a mystic and orgiastic ecstaticism or *gnosis*. [36] The earliest Gentile churches arose under the influence of Hellenistic Jewish Christianity (Ac. 11:19 ff.). As this encounters us in Stephen, it certainly had a freer attitude to the cultic and ritual parts of the OT. But it was essentially one with Palestinian Christianity in its faith in Christ, i.e., in its central understanding of revelation. In general, Jewish and Jewish Christian Gnosticism belong to a later period. [37]

3. Revelation in the New Testament Epistles.

In the period which followed, revelation was again understood, not as an impartation of supernatural knowledge, but as the coming of God, as the disclosure

---

[35] E. Lohmeyer, *Galiläa und Jerusalem* (1936), makes a discerning but not finally convincing attempt to relate faith in the Messiah Christ to Jerusalem and faith in the Son of Man who has yet to be manifested to Galilee.

[36] W. Heitmüller, ZNW, 13 (1912), 320 ff.; W. Bousset, *Kyrios Christos*[3] (1926).

[37] B. W. Bacon, *The Gospel of the Hellenists* (1933), 81 ff., tries to show that Hellenistic Christianity as a whole bore a Gnostic character in the first decades, but his arguments are not convincing. We certainly cannot appeal to the Mandaeans (→ I, 536 f.).

of the world to come, which took place in a historical development up to the person and death and resurrection of Jesus in the last time (1 C. 10:11; Hb. 1:1 f.) and which will culminate in the cosmic catastrophe at the end of history. The OT, the sacred letter of revelation, is consciously or otherwise expounded with great freedom in allegorical terms (Gl. 4:24; 1 C. 9:9 f. → I, 260). It is set in the service of the new revelation of the present (R. 4:23 f. etc.). We are here at the commencement of a centuries long struggle with Judaism for the revelational legacy of the past. Hb. especially is to be understood from this angle. It is hardly an accident, nor is it due to mere linguistic development (→ 590), that Scripture is never indicated by our present terms in the NT. Revelation is not a material possession which we have in black and white. It is a divine act, the unveiling of what is hidden.

In the epistles, too, its true *locus* is in eschatology. This gives us the basic sense of ἀποκάλυψις 'Ιησοῦ Χριστοῦ (1 C. 1:7; 2 Th. 1:7; 1 Pt. 1:7, 13).[38] The gen. is shown to be objective by the parallel ἀποκάλυψις τῶν υἱῶν τοῦ θεοῦ in R. 8:19. Both are elucidated by the use of φανεροῦσθαι in Col. 3:4. At the *parousia* the exalted Christ, who is still hidden in God, will be revealed in glory, and believers with Him. Hence there may be reference to the ἀποκάλυψις of the δόξα of Christ or of believers, or to that of their σωτηρία (1 Pt. 4:13; 1:5; 5:1; R. 8:18). This will be preceded by the revelation of the righteous judgment of God (ἀποκάλυψις δικαιοκρισίας τοῦ θεοῦ, R. 2:5). The day of judgment will be manifested in fire (ἐν πυρὶ ἀποκαλύπτεται, 1 C. 3:13), and it will put every man's work to the test. It can even be said that the hellish counterpart of the Messiah, Antichrist, will be revealed (2 Th. 2:3, 6, 8). This, too, is an eschatological happening, though it takes place in history. It is the final intimation of the end. The whole eschatological drama is now ready and is simply waiting for the curtain to be drawn. And this is slowly taking place. The wrath of God is revealed (R. 1:18), not by preaching, at any rate not by preaching alone,[39] but by the act of God from heaven. God exacts terrible retribution by giving up idolaters, who are already enmeshed in the lusts of their hearts, to the uncleanness of shameful vices. The question whether this has not happened for centuries does not concern Paul. Previously the world stood under the ἀνοχή of God (R. 3:26). But now wrath is unleashed up to the day of judgment. Yet righteousness is also revealed at the same time. This is the righteousness with which believers can stand before God and before the Judge whom He has appointed, namely, Jesus Christ (R. 1:16 f.). The simultaneity is no accident. The disclosure of this righteousness is also an eschatological event. The totality of the final revelation is expressed in the fact that wrath and grace accompany, or more correctly succeed, one another.

For believers grace is the decisive factor. This is a mystery which was hidden from eternal ages but which is now revealed (R. 16:25 f.). It is basically disclosed to called messengers such as Paul (Eph. 3:3, 5). This took place when God revealed His Son, the risen Lord, to Paul (→ II, 539). In other words, it took place through the self-revelation of Jesus Christ (ἀποκάλυψις 'Ιησοῦ Χριστοῦ, subj. gen.). This is how Paul received his Gospel (Gl. 1:12, 16). This does not mean

---

[38] Cf. Wnd. Pt., *ad loc.*
[39] To supplement the ἀποκαλύπτεται of v. 18 by the ἐν τῷ εὐαγγελίῳ of 16 f. (P. Feine, *Der Römerbrief* [1903], 86 ff.; A. Pallis, *To the Romans* [1920] 40) is a mistake.

that the content of Christian preaching was previously unknown to him. He is not saying that all that he has to say concerning Jesus was imparted to him by direct, ecstatic revelation. [40] No, God used revelation to convince him of the resurrection of the Crucified. This altered at a stroke his whole attitude to what he already knew of Jesus. The lying message became the message of salvation, and Paul's task was now to pass it on.

The operation of the divine summons (→ κήρυγμα) is also eschatological. The aim of the divine overruling of history is that faith should be revealed as a saving principle (Gl. 3:23). It is to be revealed by divine action and divine-human preaching (1 Th. 2:13 : λόγον ἀκοῆς παρ' ἡμῶν τοῦ θεοῦ). Like the message, the effective delivery and reception of the message are part of revelation. Its transmission is not simply a matter of natural psychology. There can be a παραδιδόναι and παραλαμβάνειν (1 C. 15:1 ff.), a διδάσκειν and διδάσκεσθαι (or μανθάνειν) or παραδίδοσθαι (R. 6:17; 16:17; Col. 2:7; Eph. 4:20), at least in the sense of living interchange rather than mere didactic formulation. But the essential thing cannot finally be learned. The psychic man does not understand this core. He rejects it (1 C. 2:14). Believers, on the other hand, confess it : ἡμῖν ἀπεκάλυψεν ὁ θεὸς διὰ τοῦ πνεύματος (1 C. 2:10). The apostle's sense of revelation reaches a giddy height in this passage. The depths of the hidden life of God are opened up (v. 11 f.). Some have thought that there is here reproduced in Paul the self-awareness of the Hellenistic pneumatic. [41] But even the statements which sound most mystical, if we put them in context (1 C. 2:6 ff., cf. with 1:18 ff.: the word of the cross), are orientated and related to the historical self-offering of God. [42] The extent to which Paul regards the distinctively Christian facts of salvation as basic facts of revelation may be seen from the fact that in R. 8, when he has spanned all the depths and heights of pneumatic experience, he finally comes back to the death and resurrection of Christ (8:31 ff.; cf. also R. 5:6 ff.; Gl. 2:20).

So far as we can see, Paul never used the term ἀποκάλυψις of the earthly life of Jesus. Like the Synoptists, he set the earthly life more under the category of concealment (→ 580; R. 8:3 : ἐν ὁμοιώματι σαρκὸς ἁμαρτίας; Phil. 2:7: μορφὴν δούλου λαβών; Gl. 4:4 : γενόμενον ἐκ γυναικός, γενόμενον ὑπὸ νόμον; cf. 2 C. 8:9; 1 C. 2:8). But it is the manner of God to reveal Himself by way of concealment. God's self-impartation stands as yet under a paradox (1 C. 1:18 ff.). The disclosure which corresponds to the concealment begins with the resurrection and exaltation of Christ, continues through the Messianic *kerygma,* and will culminate with the *parousia.*

Even in concealment, the whole earthly life of Jesus bears the character of eschatological revelation. This is confirmed by a concept which first appears in Paul but which is then found throughout the NT epistles, so that we must attribute it to the community in general. This is the concept of the pre-existence of Christ [43]

---

[40] Against this common view cf. Joh. W. 1 K.; Bchm. 1 K. on 11:23; 15:3; A. Oepke, *Galaterbrief* (1937), esp. 31 f.

[41] Reitzenstein Hell. Myst., 333 ff.

[42] Cf. the way in which this is developed in refutation of Reitzenstein by K. Deissner, *Pls. u. d. Mystik seiner Zeit*[2] (1921), 21 ff.

[43] E. Barnikol (*Mensch u. Messias* [1932]; *Phil. 2, der marcionitische Ursprung des Mythos-Satzes Phil. 2:6-7* [1932]) is quite unsuccessful in his attempt to deny that Paul taught the pre-existence of Christ.

(1 C. 8:6; 2 C. 8:9; Gl. 4:4; R. 8:3; Phil. 2:5 ff.; Col. 1:15 ff.; Hb. 1:3). The Christology of Paul is preponderantly Messianic. The accent falls on Christ's post-existence. To this belongs the ὄνομα τὸ ὑπὲρ πᾶν ὄνομα (Phil. 2:9). Yet His pre-existent being is depicted in analogical terms (ἐν μορφῇ θεοῦ ὑπάρχων = τὸ εἶναι ἴσα θεῷ, Phil. 2:6;[44] cf. the correspondence between Col. 1:15 ff. and 1:18 ff.). The Pre-existent is linked with the creation of the world. Thus the prospective Messianic consideration has a retrospective cosmic counterpart. For this reason, the very birth of Christ has for Paul the character of revelation. God sent His Son. Christ became poor for us, that we might be rich through His poverty (Gl. 4:4; 2 C. 8:9; R. 8:3).

We find a direct connection between pre-existence and revelation when the thought of an immanent pre-existence of Christ is underlined. Thus in 1 C. 10:4 Christ accompanied Israel through the wilderness as the pneumatic and sacramental rock which dispensed water. This interpretation, which is not worked out in detail, implies that the whole of salvation history prior to Christ is really the work of Christ. The close connection between Kyrios and Pneuma enables us to grasp at once the insight of 1 Pt. 1:11 f. that it was the Spirit of Christ[45] who inspired the prophets and bore witness to them beforehand concerning the sufferings which Christ should endure and the glorification which awaited His people. The prophets received this revelation because they ministered, not to themselves, but to believers of the last time, to whom the same facts, now accomplished, are proclaimed by the messengers of the Gospel in the same Holy Spirit, now sent down from heaven in fulness.

Thus the whole of salvation history in both OT and NT stands in the morning light of the revelation which will culminate in the *parousia* of Christ. It is impossible, however, to find a narrower eschatological sense for our terms in every passage. The "mystical" use (→ 577) exerts an influence and combines with the "eschatological." Paul is acquainted with ἀποκαλύψεις (κυρίου) which are ecstatic and visionary by nature and which have no immediate significance for salvation history (2 C. 12:1, 7). It is on the basis of an ἀποκάλυψις after the manner of Ac. 16:9 f. that he goes to Jerusalem to confer with the apostles (Gl. 2:2). He presupposes that other members of the community have similar direct revelations, and he classifies these with γνῶσις, προφητεία, and διδαχή, and sets them in juxtaposition with glossolalia (1 C. 14:6, 26, 30). He promises his readers, and desires for them, that by special revelation they will come to deeper knowledge (Phil. 3:15; Eph. 1:17). It is here very evident that in the NT the term "revelation" does not have, or does not always have, the specific sense which it came to have in later ecclesiastical dogmatics.[46] Things are different, however, in the case of → ἐπιφάνεια, λόγος (τοῦ θεοῦ). The NT always uses the latter for the central message of Jesus Christ, or for Jesus Christ Himself, as in Jn. (→ 587). Only in two passages can there be any question of the Word of God coming directly to a man (Lk. 2:29; 3:2), and here we are in the pre-Christian period[47] and ῥῆμα is used rather than the technical λόγος. Our terms, however, have not yet achieved

---

44 Dib. Gefbr. on Phil. 2:6 Excursus ; → I, 473, κενόω.
45 The absence of Χριστοῦ in B is due to dogmatic emendation.
46 Cf. G. Kittel and K. Barth, *Ein theologischer Briefwechsel²* (1934), 9 f.
47 I owe this point to G. Kittel, → λόγος.

this precision. Even later their development is less uniform, probably because pagan views of inspiration influenced the Church in the middle of the 2nd century (→ 567), and there thus arose an intellectualistic view of Christian proclamation which was applied to the Canon and which combined with the biblical concept of ἀποκάλυψις.

Nevertheless, it is highly significant that the broader use of the term in the NT is integrated into the narrower and affected by it. In the passages to which we have referred we have revelations of the risen Lord to His apostle which can confirm his apostleship, which can guide him in his apostolic calling, and which can further the edification of the community. There is no justification at all for revelations which produce mere sensation or confusion. Whatever seems to be revelation in the community must be tested by the criteria of Christ, of love and of the edification of the community.

b. The question of natural revelation in Paul demands careful treatment. It cannot be contested that the apostle repeatedly says that God has made Himself known ἀπὸ κτίσεως κόσμου even to those who have not been reached by His special biblical revelation. Without the latter there is a γνωστὸν τοῦ θεοῦ, a γινώσκειν τὸν θεόν (R. 1:19 ff.). Furthermore, the Gentiles know the will of God without special revelation. It is not merely that they know it to some degree (1:32). Even in detail they do φύσει that which is demanded by the Law, thus showing that the work of the Law is written in their hearts (2:14 ff.). In face of all attempts to escape this fact, [48] it must be insisted that these statements are made in a missionary context and that real Gentiles are thus in view. [49] The witness of Ac. is to the same effect (14:15-17; 17:22 ff.). [50] As has often been shown, [51] Paul is here dependent on Jewish physico-theology, and this means that indirectly from the linguistic standpoint, and directly from the literary, he is dependent on that of Greece. [52] On the other hand, Paul also denies that the Gentiles can know God (1 C. 1:21; Gl. 4:8; 1 Th. 4:5) and fulfil the Law (R. 1:32; Gl. 2:15). If a logical contradiction results, this is not a contradiction between Paul and Acts, as though the latter were purely rational and Paul christocentric. [53] It derives from the matter itself as Paul sees it. Hence we cannot solve it by arguing that the positive judgment

---

[48] Danger arises when it is strongly emphasised that God is known in creation only by those whose eyes have been opened (E. Brunner) or who have been given spectacles (Calvin) by revelation (cf. P. Barth, 9 ff.). This formulation has in view a Christian and theological knowledge of God. In this case the phrase of Calvin is better. But Paul is emphasising the possibility of an extra-Christian and pre-theological knowledge of God.

[49] Since there is an obvious missionary context in the case of the other passages, a similar assumption is helpful as regards R. 1 and 2. In spite of Zn., Schl., Feine, the whole section R. 1:18-3:20 has a propaedeutic and pre-evangelical character. It considers Gentiles and Jews from a Christian standpoint, but in terms of the theology of mission, i.e., as those who are not yet reached by revelation, or by the Gospel. To some extent it may well reflect the missionary preaching of Paul. Cf. A. Oepke, *Die Missionspredigt des Ap. Pls.* (1920), 7, and the bibl. there given. Feine once referred R. 2:14 ff. to Gentile Christians (*Das gesetzesfreie Ev. d. Pls.* [1899], 113 ff.; *Römerbrief* [1903], 93 ff.), but he later abandoned this view (*Theologie des NT⁶* [1934], 202).

[50] On the historical reliability, esp. of the Areopagus address, cf. Oepke, 178 ff.

[51] Cf. Bornkamm, 242 ff., with bibl.

[52] Cf. Wis. 12:27 ff. (→ 579).

[53] The general christocentric attitude of Ac. is shown by Oepke, 179 ff.

is an occasional concession which Paul makes to common sense in spite of his religious theory, so that his true assessment is negative. [54] The point is that Paul differentiates between what God has given to man and what man has made of it. The abiding self-witness of God in the world and in the human heart — even beyond the circle of saving revelation — is a fact. If man were to handle this divine self-offering aright, the world "in the wisdom of God could know the wisdom of God" (1 C. 1:21). This direct and unbroken knowledge of God would correspond to the original plan of God. The only trouble is that humanity has frustrated this purpose by its resistance. In so doing it has not merely forfeited the knowledge of God accessible to it; God has judicially withdrawn this knowledge. His revelation is now that of the broken line, of the paradox of divine folly and weakness (1 C. 1:21). If potentially there remains a relic of the direct knowledge, it constitutes the most terrible indictment of those who have fallen away from it: εἰς τὸ εἶναι αὐτοὺς ἀναπολογήτους (R. 1:20). Nor does the moral knowledge of the Gentiles help them (1:32). On the contrary, it is an accusation against those who think that the mere possession of the Torah confers on them an unconditional advantage (2:12 ff.). In fact, these statements of Paul do not go beyond the general biblical view that God has nowhere left Himself without a witness (→ 574), and that moral decision is possible even outside saving revelation — decision which may be positive, since otherwise it would not be real decision. It should be noted, however, that the apostle does not make theological or apologetic use of these statements. His use of them is missionary, or more accurately polemical. He shows not the slightest interest in systematically combining them with revelation. Indeed, he sees an immediate danger at this point. His judgment on natural theology is to be found in 1 C. 2:14. Only when natural thinking has passed through the judgment of the cross is it possible to attempt a synthesis under the slogan σοφία (cf. 1 C. 1:21 with 2:6 ff.). Prior to that, one must hold strictly aloof from such efforts. Paul always speaks, even in R. 1, from within the knowledge of the God of revelation. He does not need rational supports. When he refers to what the Gentiles either know or could know of God, he uses φανεροῦν (R. 1:19), but he never uses our present terms. What is revealed or disclosed from heaven is the wrath of God, and in the Gospel the righteousness of God for the salvation of him who believes. Paul knows of no other revelation which would set man at the centre as well as God. He does not want to know of any such.

4. Revelation in the Johannine Literature.

a. The Gospel and Epistles. Johannine theology does not use the terms (→ 590 f.). Yet it is a theology of revelation to the supreme degree, though in a different sense. Referring the Logos concept to Jesus, it gives most comprehensive expression to the absolute claim of Christianity to revelation. [55] The point of this usage is not to bind revelation to natural thought and being, but conversely to bind all creation in its total range to revelation in Christ. The Evangelist prefers the biblical "Word" (cf. Gn. 1:3 etc.) to the Hellenistic "reason." In Jn. the Logos concept has a strong cosmic reference (Jn. 1:3). But in contrast to Hellenism it is also strongly personal.

---

[54] So A. Bonhöffer, "Epiktet u. d. NT" (RVV, 10 [1911]), 152.

[55] Jn. 1:1, 14; 1 Jn. 1:1. The exposition which follows presupposes that the technical use of the designation Logos in Jn. is not to be explained exclusively in terms of biblical presuppositions but stands in some relationship to Hellenism. For details → λόγος.

Hence all being is strictly subordinate to the Logos as the divine Mediator. And the statement ὁ λόγος σὰρξ ἐγένετο (1:14), which would be intolerable to Hellenists, transfers the dignity of the personal, cosmic Mediator to the historical Mediator of salvation, i.e., Jesus. This leads, not to natural revelation, but to the universalism of revelation, yet in such way that in the person of Jesus satisfaction is also promised to the just concerns of Hellenistic thought. On this basis it is easy to understand the further course of the Evangelist. With fine insight he considers all the religious longings of his age, whether they be the concerns of the Messianic belief of the Jews or those of Gnosticism and mysticism (light, life, joy, salvation, the power of grace, pneumatic union with God), and he shows that they are all fulfilled in the only-begotten of the Father (1:14). How he transcends both Judaism and Hellenism in his Christian synthesis is instructively shown in c. 6. The address concerning the bread of life seems at first to attach itself one-sidedly to the sacramental materialism of Hellenism (esp. v. 52 ff.), but then there is a last minute switch and justice is done to the Jewish fear of crude conceptions of the divine. Hence we have here both a realistic and also a spiritual understanding of the sacrament. Yet we can no more think in terms of syncretism than of natural theology. Nowhere is there a stronger view of the absoluteness of the historical revelation. The Evangelist is not seeking new lights ; he finds the one sun reflected in myriads of drops. He is not sounding new notes ; he seeks to give full resonance to the one note which God has sounded. This note is primarily and supremely the note of love. In view of the Evangelist's presuppositions, it is quite understandable that the whole emphasis should be on the present. In spite of all assertions to the contrary, [56] eschatology is neither excluded, nor transmuted, nor even preserved in traditional form. But it does not control the understanding of revelation. If for Paul possession rests on hope, for John hope rests on possession. [57] This carries with it a shift in Christology. Pre-existence and post-existence are balanced against one another (cf. 1:1 f. with 17:5). Pre-Christian salvation history is unequivocally related to the Pre-existent (e.g., 8:58). [58] The earthly work of Jesus is no longer seen predominantly from the angle of concealment, but from that of revelation : ὁ λόγος σὰρξ ἐγένετο καὶ ἐσκήνωσεν ἐν ἡμῖν, καὶ ἐθεασάμεθα τὴν δόξαν αὐτοῦ (1:14; cf. 1 Jn. 1:1 ff. etc.). Yet this is only to make explicit the deepest significance of the self-witness of Jesus in the Synoptists (Lk. 4:21; Mt. 12:6). Dividing, and in this sense already judging, yet supremely saving and blessing, the reality of the living God shines into this world of sin and death in the person of Jesus Christ (Jn. 3:14 ff.). Faith in the incarnate Logos is the victory which has overcome the world (1 Jn. 5:4; cf. Jn. 16:33).

b. Revelation. The Revelation of John calls itself ἀποκάλυψις Ἰησοῦ Χριστοῦ. Here things are very different. There are, of course, puzzling agreements between this work and the other Johannine writings. The use of the term Logos in Rev. 19:13 is one of these. But the sure possession represented by the Logos concept in the Gospel and Epistles is of less interest to the Apocalyptist. His understanding of

---

[56] Cf. G. Stählin, "Zum Problem der johanneischen Eschatologie," ZNW, 33 (1934), 225 ff.

[57] H. E. Weber has an illuminating discussion of this point in Jn., op. cit., 167 ff. → ἔχω, II, 825.

[58] It is better not to refer 1:9-13 and 16-18 to the Pre-existent, though the expressions and the train of thought seem to point in this direction. The writer has before his eyes the incarnate Logos. His thinking takes a spiral form. On the other hand, 1:1-4 is plain enough.

revelation relates to the future. The heavenly world is unveiled for the divine because God wills to show to his servants ἃ δεῖ γενέσθαι ἐν τάχει (1:1). In this eschatological orientation and the related visionary apparatus the last book of the NT shows great affinity to the Jewish apocalyptic to which it has given its name. But it is closer to genuine prophecy and has more of the content of biblical revelation. It is probably not pseudepigraphical,[59] and is comparatively rich in authentic visionary experience.[60] Above all, it is wholly committed to the great end of strengthening the Church, the bearer of revelation, in its first severe clash with the self-absolutising power of the state, of preparing the Church for martyrdom. Above the creation which writhes in the woes of the Messiah, above the race which becomes increasingly obstinate in spite of divine judgments, above the community which is surrounded by the horrors of death and yet which waits in faith for its coming Lord, there is disclosed with shattering greatness the world of eternity. "Be thou faithful unto death, and I will give thee a crown of life" (2:10).

5. The Limitation and Confirmation of Revelation.

Fulfilling the OT covenant, the NT revelation is on the frontier between national restriction and full universalism. This does not mean that the former is wholly at fault. As God the Lord of the whole world has not left Himself without a witness among all nations (Ac. 14:16 f.; 17:23 ff.; R. 3:29 f.), so the people of Israel is the saving *locus* of His revelation. "Salvation is of the Jews." This is said by the Christ of the Fourth Gospel, which is certainly not guilty of overestimation of the Jews (Jn. 4:22). It is said, not to advance national claims, but to confirm the divine economy. Nowhere does the NT leave the slightest doubt as to the historical character of the divine revelation. But nowhere does it leave the slightest doubt that it is directed finally to all who bear the face of man. This is equally true of the Synoptic Jesus and the primitive community (Mk. 13:10; 14:9). Particularly in Paul and John are all restrictions removed, though we cannot now prove this in detail. Universalism in this sense is also expressed in other parts of the NT, e.g., Ac. 1:8; 2:39 and Lk. 2:32 (cf. Is. 42:6 and 49:6: ἀποκάλυψις ἐθνῶν either gen. poss. "revelation for the Gentiles," or gen. obj. on the analogy of ἀποκαλύπτειν τὸ ὠτίον, τοὺς ὀφθαλμούς τινος → 577, and materially 2 C. 3:14 ff.).

But the NT is also concerned with the question of the confirmation of revelation against false revelation. The NT consistently teaches that miracles and signs can be an indication of genuine revelation (Mt. 11:5 f.; 12:28; Jn. 5:36; 20:31; Ac. 2:43; R. 15:18 f.; 1 C. 2:4; 1 Th. 1:5). But these are not in themselves infallible marks. Demonic miracles also exist. The false prophets and messiahs of the last time, including Antichrist, will perform them, and if possible deceive even the elect (Mk. 13:22 f.; 2 Th. 2:9 f.). Satan can take the form of an angel of light (2 C. 11:14). Even the coming of an angel from heaven is no unconditional guarantee that the message which he brings is genuine revelation (Gl. 1:8). Indeed, faith in

---

[59] The attempt of B. W. Bacon, *The Gospel of the Hellenists* (1933), 21 ff. to show that Revelation is the pseudepigraphical work of a woman, the Ephesian daughter of Philip the evangelist, is hardly likely to find much support. E. Hirsch divides the Apocalypse into two mechanically related books, but he attributes both to the Ephesian John (*Studien z. vierten Evangelium* [1936], 156 ff.).

[60] C. Schneider, *Die Erlebnisechtheit der Apokalypse des Johannes* (1930).

divine miracles which reposes on them alone is no true saving faith. On the contrary, it is unbelief and impenitence (Mt. 12:39 and par.; Jn. 4:48; 20:29). True and false revelation may be distinguished by their fruits or products, whether in the individual or the community (Mt. 7:15 ff.). [61] The presupposition of right judgment is the Christian maturity of the one who judges. Paul counts ability to discern the spirits among the charismata effected by the Holy Spirit in the community (1 C. 12:10), but even a young community has the duty of distinguishing between true and false prophecy (1 Th. 5:20-22). The situation is simpler than in the OT, since the person of Jesus Christ provides a definite criterion by which to discern. He who in ecstasy, and therewith sincerely, cries : "Accursed be Jesus !" is not speaking by the Holy Spirit. But he who cries : "Jesus is Lord !" is speaking by the Holy Spirit (1 C. 12:3). [62] Furthermore, faith and confession are genuine only when they are accompanied by love (1 C. 13:1 ff.). The picture is the same in the Johannine literature. Testing of the spirits is essential, and confession of the incarnate Logos is the decisive mark (1 Jn. 4:1 ff.). The distinctive office of the Paraclete in the community is to glorify Christ (Jn. 16:13 ff.). Hence everything which claims to be revelation must verify itself by this commitment to the person of Jesus. Again, confession of God and of Christ is false when it is not backed up by love (1 Jn. 4:8 etc.; cf. Jn. 13:35). Rightly understood, the two criteria are not contradictory ; they are complementary. The test of life protects the confession of Christ against false dogmatic ossification, and the latter protects the former against moralistic degeneration.

6. The Terms in the NT.

To describe divine manifestations the NT uses esp. 4 stems : from $\sqrt{}$ γνω γνωρίζειν (→ I, 718), from $\sqrt{}$ δηλ δηλοῦν (→ II, 61), from $\sqrt{}$ φαν → φανεροῦν and → ἐμφανίζειν, and finally ἀποκαλύπτειν and ἀποκάλυψις. These synonyms are materially interrelated in the form of an ascending order, like the English "impart," "declare," "make manifest," and "disclose." The frequency of their secular use is a measure of their solemnity. In the case of γνωρίζειν this is much less than on the religious side, but still relatively high. When we turn to δηλοῦν, the only instances are 1 C. 1:11; Col. 1:8 and perhaps Hb. 12:27. φανεροῦν is much more common, and its use is almost exclusively religious. Only occasionally is the secular use reflected in more general expressions, and these are always combined with religious themes and never presuppose a human subject (cf. Mk. 4:22; 2 C. 2:14; Rev. 3:18). Statistics present a different picture in the case of the related ἐμφανίζειν, but this is a rare and colourless term. ἀποκαλύπτειν is again exclusively religious, though not always in the central sense. Materially this is true at Mt. 10:26, and Lk. 2:35 refers to the judicial disclosure of the thoughts of the heart. φανεροῦν and ἀποκαλύπτειν seem at a first glance to be completely synonymous (cf. the ἀπεκαλύφθη of Eph. 3:5 with the ἐφανερώθη of Col. 1:26, though in the former passage there is a rise in concreteness from γνωρίζειν, and in 1 Pt. 1:11 f. from δηλοῦν). With both terms the passive is predominant. A distinction becomes apparent when we consider the distribution of the words. In the Synoptics, apart from the conclusion to Mk., we find φανεροῦν only at Mk. 4:22, where Mt. and Lk. have ἀποκαλύπτειν. It does not occur at all in Gl., Phil., Th., Jm. and 2 Pt. On the other hand, it is common in Jn. and 1 Jn., 2 C., Col. and Past. ἀποκαλύπτειν, however, is common in the Synoptics, in most of Paul's epistles and in 1 Pt., but it is never found in Jn. (12:38 is a quotation), in 1-3 Jn. or in Col. Even when we allow for the contingent element in

---

[61] Cf. Schl. Mt., ad loc.
[62] In spite of Bchm. 1 K., ad loc. we are to think of differences within the community.

the use of words, we are led to a clear result. ἀποκαλύπτειν is basically Jewish and early Christian, while φανεροῦν is either neutral or has a Gnostic tinge. In contrast to the more intellectual γνωρίζειν and δηλοῦν, both words carry an intuitive element, but with a noteworthy distinction. For Gnosticism, what is seen is in principle immanent and accessible, if not to all perception, at least to that which is particularly chosen and prepared. It is revealed to this. In apocalyptic, however, what is seen is fundamentally supratemporal and inaccessible. It is disclosed only by a special act of divine will. In the former case the emphasis is on the suprasensual aspect, in the latter on the suprahuman, understood radically and not just mystically. The *gnosis* which arises by way of φανεροῦν is to some degree under our control, but this can never be said of ἀποκάλυψις. Hence the latter term corresponds better to the strict biblical concept of revelation. The adoption of the other word into the vocabulary of the NT is partly due to the missionary encounter. It is designed to show that the concerns of justifiable *gnosis* are fully met in Christianity. If some of the outer Jewish shell is thereby peeled off, there is no surrender of the inner core, namely, the essential hiddenness of that which is to be revealed. The fact is that within the NT the content of ἀποκαλύπτειν more or less absorbs the synonyms.

7. Theological Summary.

A theological summary can be attempted only along the lines of simplification and systematisation. In the NT, too, revelation denotes, not the impartation of knowledge, but the actual unveiling of intrinsically hidden facts, or, theologically, the manifestation of transcendence within immanence. What is meant cannot be expressed in purely formal terms, e.g., the crisis of the finite in the light of the infinite etc. Revelation in the narrower sense acquires a specific content which is then accessible to perception. It is the turning of the holy and gracious God to men who are lost in sin and death. This is prepared in the salvation history of the OT and actualised in the incarnation, crucifixion and resurrection of Jesus Christ. It now awaits its consummation at the *parousia*. By derivation, however, revelation is also the message which transmits this content. It is the effective tranmission of it to the hearer. This does not imply that revelation does not become revelation until this takes place, until it is received as such. It thereby becomes revelation for individuals, but from the very first it comes with the claim to be heard in the name of God, and with divine power it creates for itself the organ of reception unless culpably prevented. In brief, revelation in the NT is the self-offering of the Father of Jesus Christ for fellowship.

F. Historical Review.

The terms are comparatively common in the post-apostolic and early catholic period. They are particular favourites of Hermas. But in Hermas they are used exclusively of visionary experiences (the title of Herm. v., 5 = ὅρασις) or their interpretation, without which the revelation is not complete (ὁλοτελής, v., 3, 10, 9). There is no more precise relation to revelation in the central NT sense. Even the word "apocalyptic" would be a little too exalted for these well-meaning but tepid outpourings of a limited soul. [63] Justin uses the words, but he, too, thinks primarily of individual directions such as those given in a dream to Joseph or to the wise men from the East (Dial., 78, 2. 4. 7). He quotes Mt. 11:27, but with the

---

[63] Reitzenstein Poim., 11 ff., 33 ff. shows that it is very likely there were literary connections between Hermas and Hermetic Gnosticism.

well-known inversion, attested by Irenaeus, of the second and third clauses, and with other deviations from the usual text (Apol., 63, 3. 13; Dial., 100, 1 [106, 1]). Here ἀποκαλύπτειν undoubtedly has central significance. The more striking, then, is the intellectualistic understanding. Jesus ἀπαγγέλλει ὅσα δεῖ γνωσθῆναι, καὶ ἀποστέλλεται μηνύσων ὅσα ἀγγέλλεται (Apol., 63, 5). ἀπεκάλυψεν ἡμῖν πάντα ὅσα καὶ ἀπὸ τῶν γραφῶν διὰ τῆς χάριτος αὐτοῦ νενοήκαμεν (Dial., 100, 2). The prophets revealed all that they had to say in parables in order to make understanding more difficult (παραβολαῖς καὶ τύποις ἀπεκάλυψαν, ὡς μὴ ῥᾳδίως τὰ πλεῖστα ὑπὸ πάντων νοηθῆναι, κρύπτοντες τὴν ἐν αὐτοῖς ἀλήθειαν, ὡς καὶ πονέσαι τοὺς ζητοῦντας εὑρεῖν καὶ μαθεῖν, Dial., 90, 2). Even this one-sided presentation does not deviate from an intellectualistic view. Ignatius is closer to the NT when he uses the verb for deeper entry into knowledge of the divine economy with respect to the new man Jesus Christ (Eph., 20, 1). Even nearer is Dg., 8, 11: ἐπεὶ δὲ ἀπεκάλυψε διὰ τοῦ ἀγαπητοῦ παιδὸς καὶ ἐφανέρωσε τὰ ἐξ ἀρχῆς ἡτοιμασμένα, πάνθ' ἅμα παρέσχεν ἡμῖν, καὶ μετασχεῖν τῶν εὐεργεσιῶν αὐτοῦ καὶ ἰδεῖν καὶ νοῆσαι, ἃ τίς ἂν πώποτε προσεδόκησεν ἡμῶν; According to Origen [64] ἀποκάλυψις is ὅταν ὁ νοῦς ἔξω γίνεται τῶν γηΐνων καὶ ἀποθῆται πᾶσαν πρᾶξιν σαρκικὴν δυνάμει θεοῦ. At all events, he thinks, the knowledge of future things may be thus designated. It is to be noted, however, that this is not a general definition of revelation. It is an exegetical note on 1 C . 14:6. In general the early Church — we see this particularly clearly in theologians like Irenaeus and Athanasius, and dogma is basically seeking to express it — was very conscious of the cleft which runs across the creation of God, and of the fact that only God's saving action in Christ can bridge it. It was perhaps more conscious of this than the modern expositor who waxes eloquent on the "Hellenisation of the Gospel." [65]

Oepke

---

† κάμηλος

The camel was the oldest animal to be ridden and the most common beast of burden in the Near East. Its home was perhaps in Arabia, but it was known in Babylon and Assyria, and in the later Roman period was introduced into Egypt. It is mentioned in Aesch., Hdt., on inscr. and pap., and esp. in the OT.[1] According to the OT it was

---

[64] JThSt, 10 (1908/9), 36.
[65] Cf. E. Brunner, Der Mittler (1927), 219 ff.
κ ά μ η λ ο ς . [1] M. Ebert, Reallexikon d. Vorgeschichte, VI (1926), 196 : "The camel is the first animal to have been used expressly for riding, and historically it follows the ass, though this never had any military significance"; 197: "For many centuries, right up to the Roman period, Egypt effectively resisted the spread of the dromedary into the African continent. Only after the collapse of the Roman Empire do we read of camel nomads and their ravages in North Africa." On the other hand camels were used by Alexander in his march to the oasis of Ammon (Quintus Curtius Rufus, Historiae Alexandri, IV, 7, 12, ed. E. Hedicke [1919]). When the camel came into Palestine and Syria we do not know, but G. Schumacher has reported finding camels' teeth and bones in the excavations at Megiddo (20th cent. B.C. ?). Cf. G. Schumacher, Tell el-Mutesellim, I (1908), 15 and 158.

particularly loved by bedouins (Ju. 6:5; 7:12; 8:21; 1 S. 15:3; 27:9; 30:17; Jer. 49:29; 1 Ch. 5:21; 1 K. 10:2). It is also used by the patriarchs on their journeys (Gn. 24:10 ff.; 31:17 ff.).

1. In the NT we find (ὁ) κάμηλος only in the Synoptic tradition. John the Baptist wears a garment of camel's hair (τρίχες καμήλου) according to Mk. 1:6; Mt. 3:4; Ev. Eb. acc. to Epiph., 30, 13 (Hennecke, 44, 4). This is a cheap and hardwearing garment (ἔνδυμα) and not the apron of so much Christian art. [2] Even externally the prophet stands out from his contemporaries, and especially from the leaders in Jerusalem (cf. Mt. 11:8; Lk. 16:19; Jm. 2:2). He is under a special biblical discipline marked by freedom in respect of needs, though cf. the distinction between χιτών and ἱμάτιον in Mt. 5:40. Those who have insight and faith, however, discern the true prophet behind the externally unassuming and rigorous garb (cf. the rough garment of Zech. 13:4; Is. 20:2). Indeed, Ahaziah knew Elijah by his hairy garment and leathern girdle (2 K. 1:8). Was John trying even in this way to make it plain to believers that he was the returning Elijah? [3] John wears desert clothing and eats desert food. Unlike Jesus, he appears only in the desert, and calls men to the desert. The desert motif of ancient prophecy is obviously revived. In the last time as in the former time God speaks to His people in the wilderness (Hos. 2:16). [4]

2. After the interview with the rich young ruler who will not give up his possessions and who is unfit for discipleship (Mt. 19:16-22), Jesus in addressing His disciples (διδασκαλία) uses a paradoxical figure of speech: "It is easier for a camel to go through the eye of a needle than for a rich man to enter into the kingdom of God" (Mt. 19:24; Mk. 10:25; Lk. 18:25). As later in Mt. 23:24, the camel is here taken to be the largest animal on Palestinian soil. The Talmud reproduces a proverbial saying about an elephant going through the eye of a needle (Ber., 55b; BM, 38b). Jesus is using a typical oriental image to emphasise the impossibility of something by way of violent contrast: "Entry into the kingdom of God is completely impossible for the rich." [5] This rule of the kingdom corresponds to the first beatitude (Mt. 5:3; Lk. 6:20), though it is bounded by the miraculous action of God Himself (Mk. 10:27). It is erroneous to try to substitute

---

[2] A mixture of camel's hair and wool is softer (Kil., 9, 1). On different types of wool cf. Gn. r., 20 on 3:21.

[3] Cf. Jn. 1:21; Mk. 9:13; Mt. 11:14. Zn. Mt., 132 gives the following judgment: "Even Jn. 1:21 is no contradiction, for in 1:31 John ascribes to himself the task which on the Jewish view was to be that of Elijah ... and Jn. 3:28 is reminiscent of Mal. 3:1; 4:5. John is simply denying personal identity with Elijah, cf. Mt. 16:14."

[4] → II, 659. For the relation of John and Jesus to the desert tradition of the prophets cf. O. Michel, "Prophet u. Märtyrer," BFTh, 37, 2 (1932), 65-66; also J. Schniewind, Das Ev. nach Mk., NT Deutsch, 1 (1933), 43: "Perhaps John realises that he is directed to the desert by the saying about the one who cries (Jn. 1:23). That he is like one of the old prophets is shown at once by his withdrawal from the world, and by his rough food and clothing."

[5] Schl. Mt., ad loc. We thus have a similar rule to that of the ἀδύνατον of Hb. 6:4. There are forces and obstacles which hamper and destroy faith.

κάμιλον for κάμηλον or to take διὰ τρήματος ῥαφίδος figuratively. There is no reference either to a hawser or to a narrow gate in the city walls. [6]

3. In His prophetic denunciation of the scribes and Pharisees, Jesus calls them blind guides who strain out a gnat from their drinks and swallow a camel (Mt. 23:24). We again have the contrast between what is smallest and what is largest. The anxious scrupulosity of Pharisaic piety is contrasted with its utter lack of scruple. The Pharisee strains his drinks so that no dead insect should touch his lips, but he forgets righteousness, mercy and faith (23:23) and even incurs the guilt of extortion (ἁρπαγή) and excess (ἀκρασία) (23:25). He has lost all sense of what is great and what is little in the Law. The judgment of God on Pharisaic piety is manifest in this loss.

Michel

† κάμπτω   (→ γόνυ, προσκυνέω).

In the NT κάμπτω is found only in combination with γόνυ (γόνατα), and in this connection it is used trans. with γόνυ (γόνατα) as obj. (R. 11:4; Eph. 3:14) and intrans. with γόνυ as subj. (R. 14:11; Phil. 2:10).

κάμπτειν γόνυ (γόνατα) is the gesture of full inner submission in worship to the one before whom we bow the knee. Thus in R. 14:11 bowing the knee is linked with confession within the context of a judgment scene, and in Phil. 2:10 it again accompanies confession with reference to the worship of the exalted *Kyrios* Jesus

---

[6] Cf. Schniewind, 131: "Both camel and the eye of a needle are meant literally." For the elephant cf. Ber., 55b: R. Shemuel b. Nachman (c. 260) said, R. Jonathan (c. 220) said: "One (God) lets a man see (in dreams) only the thoughts of his heart"; v. Da. 2:29. Rabba (d. 352) said: "You can see this from the fact that one does not let a man see (in dreams) a palm of gold or an elephant which goes through the eye of a needle." BM, 38b (Rab Shesheth c. 260 to Rab Amram): "You are of Pumbeditha where they cause an elephant to go through the eye of a needle." For the eye of a needle: Midr. Cant. 5:2: "'Open to me, my sister'; R. Jose (c. 350) has said: God spake to the Israelites: Open to me an opening of penitence as big as the eye of a needle, and I will open to you gates through which wagons and carriages can pass" (also Pesikt., 163b). There are further examples in Str.-B., I, 828. κάμιλον is found for κάμηλον (η was pronounced ι in the post-Christian period) in some MSS and versions of Mt. 19:24; Mk. 10:25; Lk. 18:25, but elsewhere only in a schol. on the Vesp. of Aristoph. (1035) and in Suid., s.v. Up to c. 400 we find only κάμηλον in this passage (cf. the fathers); then uncertainty arises. A Ps.-Orig. schol. (Ev. Mt., ed. Matthaei [1788], 300, cf. Zn. Mt., ad loc.) asserts: "Some take κάμηλος to be τὸ σχοινίον τῆς μηχανῆς, others the animal, and the first is correct" (also Theophylact. Euthymius). Acc. to Herklotz, BZ, II (1904), 176 f. the Armenian Bible has *malh* (hawser, cable) for κάμηλος. In the Koran (S., 7) we have the threat: "They shall not enter into Paradise until a camel goes through the eye of a needle." On the exegesis of Mt. 19:24, cf. G. Aicher, *Kamel u. Nadelöhr* (1908); E. Rostan, *Les Paradoxes du Jésus* (1908), 11 ff.; R. Lehmann and K. L. Schmidt, "Zum Gleichnis vom Kamel u. Nadelöhr u. Verwandtes," ThBl, 11 (1932), 336-340; E. Böklen, *Deutsch. Pfarrerbl.*, 37 (1933), 162-165; and on the whole question cf. Zn. Mt., 598 f. and Pr.-Bauer[3], 667.

by the cosmos. At R. 11:4 κάμπτειν γόνυ τῇ Βάαλ signifies surrender to Baal, and at Eph. 3:14 the formula κάμπτω τὰ γόνατα πρὸς τὸν θεόν is a solemn description of the attitude of submission to God in prayer. The figurative use of the expression κάμπτειν τὰ γόνατα in connection with the demand to cast oneself down and repent [1] makes it clear that κάμπτειν τὰ γόνατα may also be understood as a gesture of humble obedience.

Paul takes both formulae from the LXX. We see this at R. 14:11, where he is quoting almost verbatim from Is. 45:23. The ὅτι ἐμοὶ κάμψει πᾶν γόνυ is a translation of the Heb.: כִּי־לִי תִּכְרַע כָּל־בֶּרֶךְ. כָּרַע (lit. "to squat," "to cower down," also "to sink down," 4 Βασ. 9:24) is rendered κάμπτειν ἐπὶ τὰ γόνατα at Ju. 7:5, 6, but elsewhere we have ἀνα- (προ-) πίπτειν (Gn. 49:9; ψ 21:29), κατακλίνεσθαι (Nu. 24:9), ὀκλάζειν (1 Βασ. 4:19; 3 Βασ. 8:54). Apart from Is. 45:23 the formula κάμπτειν γόνυ (γόνατα) is fairly common in the LXX, always in connection with prayer : 1 Ch. 29:20 : καὶ εὐλόγησεν πᾶσα ἡ ἐκκλησία κύριον τὸν θεὸν τῶν πατέρων αὐτῶν καὶ κάμψαντες τὰ γόνατα προσεκύνησαν τῷ κυρίῳ καὶ τῷ βασιλεῖ (κάμπτειν τὰ γόνατα = Heb. קָדַד); 1 Esr. 8:70 : κάμψας τὰ γόνατα καὶ ἐκτείνας τὰς χεῖρας πρὸς τὸν κύριον ἔλεγον ...; 3 Macc. 2:1: the high-priest Simon κάμψας τὰ γόνατα καὶ τὰς χεῖρας προτείνας εὐτάκτως ἐποιήσατο τὴν δέησιν τοιαύτην. In R. 11:4 Paul alters the LXX reading (3 Βασ. 19:18) from πάντα γόνατα, ἃ οὐκ ὤκλασαν γόνυ τῷ Βάαλ (כָּל־הַבִּרְכַּיִם אֲשֶׁר לֹא־כָרְעוּ לַבַּעַל) to οἵτινες (ἄνδρες) οὐκ ἔκαμψαν γόνυ τῇ Βάαλ. This is a sign that he was familiar with the common LXX use of κάμπτειν in this connection. The LXX has the trans. as well as the intrans. form : 4 Βασ. 1:13 : καὶ ἔκαμψεν ἐπὶ τὰ γόνατα αὐτοῦ κατέναντι Ἠλίου καὶ ἐδεήθη αὐτοῦ καὶ ἐλάλησεν, Da. 6:11 Θ : ἦν κάμπτων ἐπὶ τὰ γόνατα αὐτοῦ καὶ προσευχόμενος καὶ ἐξομολογούμενος ... In the same sense we find κάμπτειν alone at 2 Ch. 29:29 : ἔκαμψεν ὁ βασιλεὺς καὶ πάντες οἱ εὑρεθέντες καὶ προσεκύνησαν. Parallel to this we read in v. 30 : ἔπεσον καὶ προσεκύνησαν ..., cf. 2 Ch. 6:13 : καὶ ἔστη ἐπ' αὐτῆς καὶ ἔπεσεν ἐπὶ τὰ γόνατα ἔναντι πάσης ἐκκλησίας Ἰσραήλ (וַיִּבְרַךְ עַל־בִּרְכָּיו).

In secular Gk. κάμπτειν ("to bend," "to bow," "to crook") is found trans. with γόνυ (γόνατα) in the sense of bending one's knees to sit down and rest. Cf. Hom. Od., 5, 453; Il., 7, 118; 19, 72; Aesch. Prom., 32 : οὗ κάμπτων γόνυ, "never resting"; Eur. Hec., 1150: ἵζω ... κάμψας γόνυ. It has the same meaning without γόνυ (γόνατα), Soph. Oed. Col., 84 f.: εὖτε νῦν ἕδρας πρώτων ἐφ' ὑμῶν τῆσδε γῆς ἔκαμψ' ἐγώ. There seems to be no occurrence of κάμπτειν γόνυ (γόνατα) as a formula of prayer.

Schlier

κ ά μ π τ ω. [1] Cf. also 1 Cl., 57, 1: Ὑμεῖς οὖν οἱ τὴν καταβολὴν τῆς στάσεως ποιήσαντες ὑποτάγητε τοῖς πρεσβυτέροις καὶ παιδεύθητε εἰς μετάνοιαν, κάμψαντες τὰ γόνατα τῆς καρδίας ὑμῶν. μάθετε ὑποτάσσεσθαι ...

---

† κανών

Contents : A. κανών outside the New Testament. B. κανών in the New Testament. C. κανών in the Christian Church.

A. κανών outside the New Testament.

1. κανών is formed from κάνη like κάνης, κάννα, which signifies a cover woven from reeds, and κάνα, κάνεον, κάνειον, which is a basket woven from reeds. κάνη is a loan word from the Semitic ; [1] the basic meaning is "reed." The stem is found in Assyrian, Hebrew, Aramaic, Syriac, Arabic and modern Hebrew. [2] In Heb. קָנֶה is used for the bulrush, calamus or stalk, then, as in Assyrian, for a measuring reed or rod or staff, and finally for a scales or the arm of a candlestick. [3] It is never translated κανών in the LXX; κάλαμος, καλάμινος, πῆχυς and other Gk. words are used. κανών is found only 3 times in the LXX. At Jdt. 13:6 it denotes the bed-post, at Mi. 7:4 it seems to be an error and has no clear meaning, and at 4 Macc. 7:21, obviously under Gk. influence, the reference is to one who πρὸς ὅλον τὸν τῆς φιλοσοφίας κανόνα φιλοσοφεῖ. At Job 38:5 Aquila has κανών in the literal sense of measuring-line instead of the σπαρτίον of the LXX and the σχοινίον μέτρου of Symmachus. At Ps. 19:4 Aquila again has the literal ὁ κανὼν αὐτῶν for קַו (A.V. "line"), whereas LXX (ψ 18:4) seems to have read קוֹלָם ("voice") for קַוָּם and has the rendering ὁ φθόγγος αὐτῶν (cf. R. 10:18). [4] Philo often uses κανών for "rule," "statute," "law," very much in the same sense as νόμος. [5] Joseph. has σκοπός and κανών ("model and measure") at Ant., X, 49.

2. In secular usage the basic Semitic sense of "reed" yielded to the figurative use of κανών for a "straight rod or staff."

a. Thus it is used of sticks for stretching the rim of a shield, or of the weaver's beam, or of scales, as in Heb.

The word first takes on a more general sense when used for a measuring rod or ruler, e.g., as used in architecture.

κ α ν ώ ν. Pr.-Bauer[3], 669; Cr.-Kö., 579 ff.; Moult.-Mill., 320 f.; RE[3], VI, 682 ff.; IX, 742 ff., 769 ff.; Suic. Thes., II, 37 ff.; C. A. Credner, *Zur Geschichte des Kanons* (1847), 1 ff.; F. C. Baur, "Bemerkungen über die Bedeutung des Wortes Κανών," ZwTh, 1 (1858), 141 ff.; C. A. Credner, *Geschichte d. nt.lichen Kanon* (1860), 98 ff.; B. F. Westcott, *A General Survey of the History of the Canon of the New Testament*[6] (1889), 504 ff. App. A; T. Zahn, *Grundriss d. Geschichte d. nt.lichen Kanons*[2] (1904), 1 ff. On the formation of the Canon in Judaism → ἀπόκρυφος (→ κρύπτω).

[1] H. Lewy, *Die semitischen Fremdwörter im Griechischen* (1895), 133 (cf. also 99). Boisacq, 406 f. tries to derive the stem κάννα from the Sum.-Accad. *gin* by way of the Babyl.-Assyr. *kannu*. Prellwitz Etym. Wört., 207 also refers to the Phoenician *kaneh*. Cf. also T. Benfey, *Griech. Wurzellexikon* (1842), II, 156 f. It cannot be said for certain whether the form κανών is borrowed from the Sem. or is a Gk. construction from κάνη, cf. Zahn, 1, n. 1.

[2] Ges.-Buhl, *s.v.*; Levy Wört., *s.v.*; Levy Chald. Wört., *s.v.*

[3] For examples cf. Ges.-Buhl, *s.v.*

[4] Cf. F. Wutz, "Die Transskriptionen von der Septuaginta bis zu Hieronymus," BWANT, NF, 9 (1933), 205. But cf. Ges.-Buhl, *s.v.* Σ has ἦχος.

[5] Cf. Leisegang, *s.v.*

κανόνι ... καὶ τόρνῳ (an implement for marking out circles) χρῆται (sc. ἡ τεκτο-
νικὴ τέχνη) καὶ διαβήτῃ (plumb line) καὶ στάθμῃ (level) καί τινι προσαγωγίῳ
κεκομψευμένῳ (a kind of screw), Plat. Phileb., 56b/c; ὥσπερ γὰρ ἐν τῇ τεκτονικῇ,
ὅταν εἰδέναι βουλώμεθα τὸ ὀρθὸν καὶ τὸ μή, τὸν κανόνα προσφέρομεν, ᾧ δια-
γιγνώσκεται, Aeschin., 3, 199. τὸν κανόνα προσάγειν, "to use the plumb line," is a
common expression, e.g., Luc. Historia Quomodo Conscribenda Sit, 5; cf. also Epict.
Diss., II, 11, 20.

b. This type of expression soon acquired a figurative as well as the original
technical application, being used in the most varied spheres of life. Hence ὁ κανών
becomes the "norm," whether the perfect form and therefore the goal to be sought
on the one hand, or the infallible criterion (κριτήριον) by which things are to be
measured on the other. The Greek seeks what is perfect, balanced and harmonious,
i.e., the ideal. This is his measure for the assessment of empirical phenomena.
What corresponds to the canon attains the desired highest measure of perfection.

c. It is common knowledge that in the sphere of sculpture the spearman Polycletus
was regarded as the canon or perfect form of the human frame which is equal in all its
proportions, Plin. (the elder) Hist. Nat., XXXIV, 8, 55. He himself is supposed to have
described Doryphoros thus, and to have written a book on the "canon": Gal. de Placitis
Hippocratis et Platonis, V, 3 (ed. Kühn, V, 449). Cf. also Eur. Hec., 602 : κανόνι τοῦ
καλοῦ μαθών (or μετρῶν ?).

d. In music the monochord, by which all other tonal relationships are controlled, is
called the κανὼν μουσικός : Nichomachus Gerasenus (ed. R. Hoche [1866]), Introductio
Arithmetica, II, 27, 1.

e. Alexandrian grammarians spoke of a canon of writers whose Greek was accepted
as a model : Quint. Inst. Orat., X, 1, 54 and 59.

f. We need not be surprised that in the Greek world the concept of the canon
stood in close relationship to aesthetic and ethical beauty in the world of conception. But it was also carried over into the moral sphere. Law, as that which binds
us, is the κανών, and specific ideals are κανόνες.

Cf. Demosth. Or., 18, 296 : ... τὴν δ' ἐλευθερίαν καὶ τὸ μηδέν' ἔχειν δεσπότην
αὐτῶν, ἃ τοῖς προτέροις Ἕλλησιν ὅροι τῶν ἀγαθῶν ἦσαν καὶ κανόνες. Plut. (or
Ps.-Plut. ?) Cons. ad Apoll., 4 (II, 103a) speaks of τῆς φρονήσεως καὶ τῶν ἄλλων
ἀρετῶν κανόνες. Luc. Hermot., 76 says that one needs a κανὼν καὶ γνώμων (compass) to judge the moral life. Chrysipp. Fr. (in L. Spengel, Συναγωγὴ τεχνῶν sive
Artium Scriptores [1828], 177, n. 17): ὁ νόμος πάντων ἐστὶ βασιλεὺς θείων τε καὶ
ἀνθρωπίνων πραγμάτων· δεῖ δὲ αὐτὸν προστάτην εἶναι τῶν καλῶν καὶ τῶν
αἰσχρῶν ... καὶ κατὰ τοῦτο κανόνα τε εἶναι δικαίων καὶ ἀδίκων. It is obvious
that the concept can also be applied to the moral man who corresponds to the law of
perfection in his life. Thus Plut. Aud. Poet., 8 (II, 25e) calls the wise and righteous of
whom the poets sing κανόνες ἀρετῆς ἁπάσης καὶ ὀρθότητος. Cf. also Aristot. Eth.
Nic., III, 6, p. 1113a, 33; Epict. Diss., III, 4, 5.

g. The term κανών is given a specific emphasis by Greek philosophy, especially
by the Epicureans. Epicurus himself wrote a (lost) book called περὶ κριτηρίου ἢ
κανών. [6] He calls logic and method canonics. For him it is the task of thought to
find a basis (κανών) by which to know what is true and false, what is worth
seeking and what should be avoided. Epictetus makes a similar use of the term.

---

[6] Diog. L., X, 27, 30, 31; Epict. Diss., II, 23, 21; Cic. Nat. Deor., I, 16, 43; Sen. Ep., 89, 11.

He, too, regards κανόνες as the logical criteria by which one may judge the truth of a statement and the practical value of things.[7] The first step in philosophy is to find the canon, the rule of the knowledge of what is true as distinct from mere appearance, Diss., II, 11, 13. "To philosophise is simply to seek and to establish standards," *ibid.,* 14. These criteria are given to man directly by nature (I, 28, 28), but they must be extended and made applicable by philosophical reflection (II, 20, 21). The κανόνες are then the basic rules for the right use of free will.

h. Finally, the word κανόνες is used very formally for a "list" or "table," whether in mathematics and astronomy or in historical science. χρονικοὶ κανόνες are timetables to fix historical events.[8]

B. κανών in the New Testament.

1. In the NT only Paul uses this word κανών which later came to have such great and varied significance in the Christian, or, more specifically, the Roman Church. Even in Paul it is rare. For Paul it signifies a measure of assessment. He is hardly thinking of the original literal meaning. In him, as often in secular Greek, it has the double sense of the norm of one's own action and also the standard by which to judge that of others. This is plain in Gl. 6:16. Here Paul sums up not merely the content of the epistle but the whole doctrine of true Christian behaviour. Redemption through the crucifixion of Christ takes the one who accepts it out of the world by whose concepts and standards he has previously lived and sets him in a new creation or a new reality. To the old concepts belong especially those which are instituted by the Law, e.g., circumcision and uncircumcision. Also included is the concept "Israel" if this is understood genealogically or politically and if it is thus thought to constitute a claim before God. These things lose all significance for the Christian. For the Christian there is only one canon, namely, that these concepts of the old world have become meaningless and that he allows his whole life to be determined by the new reality of the freedom given in Christ. This is the significant meaning which the term "canon" has in the context in which it appears for the first time in Christian utterance. It denotes the ground by which Paul may know whether a man is a Christian, whether he belongs to the Israel of God in the new sense which is no longer tied to earthly distinctions, whether Paul can truly promise him mercy and peace. Luther described this Christian rule as follows:[9] "That he be a new man, made in the image of God, in righteousness and true holiness, inwardly righteous in spirit and outwardly holy and pure in the flesh ... The rule of which Paul speaks here is alone to be blessed (in contrast to all monastic orders), in which we live in Christian faith and become a new creature, i.e., truly righteous and holy through the Holy Ghost and not by deceit and hypocrisy."

The word is used in the same sense in some readings of Phil. 3:16. Some MSS add κανόνι to the brief τῷ αὐτῷ στοιχεῖν and then make the further addition: τὸ αὐτὸ

---

[7] A. Bonhöffer, *Epiktet u. d. NT* (1911), 119 f.

[8] Cf. already Plut. De Solone, 27 (I, 93b); the 2nd part of the Chronicle of Eusebius, which is preserved only in the form of tables, bears the title χρονικοὶ κανόνες (GCS, V, 5 [1911], ed. J. Karst), p. XXXIII and 156 ff.

[9] W.A., 40, II, 179 f.

φρονεῖν. [10] If this is a later gloss, it corresponds nevertheless to the usage of Paul in Gl. 6:16.

2. Less unambiguous is the meaning of the term in 2 C. 10:13-16, where Paul uses it three times in a linguistically difficult passage. [11] Paul defends his apostolic authority at Corinth against those who have come later to an already flourishing community and tried to oust Paul from the leadership by producing letters of commendation, perhaps from Jerusalem. Paul describes their claim as self-vaunting and irregular, whereas he himself judges his own κατὰ τὸ μέτρον τοῦ κανόνος [12] οὗ ἐμέρισεν ἡμῖν ὁ θεὸς μέτρου, ἐφικέσθαι ἄχρι καὶ ὑμῶν. He thus has a canon or standard for his work and for the associated claim to apostolic validity which he has not conferred on himself but received from God. In what does this canon consist? Its content is indicated by the ἐφικέσθαι ἄχρι καὶ ὑμῶν, which is dependent on ἐμέρισεν μέτρον. He is given the standard that he needs by the fact that it was given to him to press forward to Corinth and to establish the community there. On this ground some commentators have tried to explain κανών in terms of the sense of measuring line. It is the "space defined by the measuring line of God," [13] i.e., the sphere of work assigned to Paul, [14] the "delimitation of his work, a line on the map." [15] If we accept this geographical understanding, the question naturally arises when God gave to Paul this allotted sphere on the map. Heinrici [16] and Windisch [17] suggest that Paul was appointed the ἀπόστολος εἰς τὰ ἔθνη outside Damascus, and that this was then recognised at Jerusalem. But it is quite impossible that Paul should have deduced from this a claim to exclusive authority in the Gentile world, that the temporal sphere assigned to him should have been the whole world outside Palestine. A geographical distinction of this kind was in any case impossible because almost everywhere in the world there was also περιτομή. [18] In 2 C. 10:13 ff. Paul does not appeal to an exclusive right to come to Corinth as a missionary, but to the historical fact that it was granted to him to do this. [19] And he has the right to extend his work further only when the faith of the Corinthians has become strong, i.e., only when his missionary work has been successful.

The measure given to Paul is not, then, a sphere marked out in space in which he alone is to work. It is the orientation laid upon him, the χάρις granted to him (Gl. 2:9; R. 15:15 ff.) and the blessing which God has caused to rest on his missionary activity. [20]

---

[10] ℵc K L P syP and in a different arrangement vg go.

[11] "Hacked fragments of sentences," Ltzm. 2 K., ad loc. The text is "remarkably difficult, intolerable, almost untranslatable," Wnd. 2 K., ad loc.

[12] Sub. gen.: "The measure determined by the norm."

[13] Heinr. 2 K., 336.

[14] Pr.-Bauer, s.v.

[15] Wnd. 2 K., 310.

[16] Heinr. Sendschr., II, 432 f.

[17] Wnd. 2 K., 310 refers to Gl. 2:9; R. 1:5, 14.

[18] Cf. my exposition of Gl. 2:9 in NT Deutsch², II (1935), 453 f.

[19] It makes no difference if we accept the view of Heinr. 2 K., 337 that the correct translation of ὡς μὴ ἐφικνούμενοι is not (with Luther, Beza etc.): ut si non pervenissemus, but: "as though we were among those for whom attaining to you had not taken place." Wnd. 2 K., 310 suggests that ἐφικνεῖσθαι might mean" to come to someone with right and authority," but this is not very convincing.

[20] Wnd. 2 K., 310 takes a different view: "Charismatic endowment is included, but it is a secondary element." Moult.-Mill. are right when they say (320) that there is no strict parallel to this sense of an assigned sphere at 2 C. 10:13. The fact is that κανών never bears this sense.

God has given the apostle his mission and brought him to Corinth before any other disciple of Christ ever conceived of this possibility. He has also granted success to his preaching. This is for Paul τὸ μέτρον τοῦ κανόνος. If his work in Corinth ends when the community becomes inwardly strong in faith, then the canon which he is given will lead him further. His task is that of mission, not of caring for the self-developing life of the community. When he found out in Corinth that the faith of the community had increased, there was no further place for Paul in the Orient, and he directed his gaze to Spain. He planned to visit Rome only in transit. For the Gospel was already known there, and it would be for him boasting ἐν ἀλλοτρίῳ κανόνι (2 C. 10:16) if he tried to gain any credit for this community as his opponents did for Corinth when he had already evangelised it. He found in Is. 52:15b the law of the canon which had been given him. He expounds this in R. 15:20 f.: "I did not seek my glory by preaching the Gospel where Christ was already named, lest I should build upon the foundation of another."

C. κανών in the Christian Church.

1. In one passage alone (Gl. 6:16) is the word κανών used in the NT for the norm of true Christianity. In Church history, however, it is used in the most varied senses to denote what is ecclesiastically normative, whether with reference to the totality of Christian faith or to individual spheres of Church life. The reason for this is to be sought in the history of the Church itself. Very early disputes arose as to what was genuinely Christian. Hence the Church was constantly forced to set up norms, e.g., for doctrine, for life, for accepted Scripture, for worship. It thus felt the need for a word which would unmistakeably denote that which is valid and binding in the Church. The terms κανών and κανονικός, which easily passed into Latin in their journeying from East to West,[21] seemed well adapted for this purpose. For the Roman Church in particular they took on decisive significance.

In the post-apost. fathers we find κανών only in 1 Cl., where it is used in 7, 2 for the glorious and majestic rule of the tradition by which a Christian should live, with particular regard for what is good and well-pleasing and acceptable to the Creator. The term is thus ethical, as also in 1 Cl., 1, 3. In 41, 1, however, it denotes the measure of service which is allotted to each office-bearer in the community.

In the first three centuries ὁ κανών serves generally to emphasise what is for Christianity an inner law and binding norm. It is hardly ever used in the plural.

In three combinations it plays an increasingly significant role in the ancient Church: a. as ὁ κανὼν τῆς ἀληθείας; b. as ὁ κανὼν τῆς πίστεως; and c. as ὁ κανὼν τῆς ἐκκλησίας or ἐκκλησιαστικὸς κανών.

ὁ κανὼν τῆς ἀληθείας is binding truth as this is proclaimed by the Church and as it has taken shape in its preaching. Hence Iren., I, 9, 4 f. can use the expressions ἡ ὑπὸ τῆς ἐκκλησίας κηρυττομένη ἀλήθεια and τὸ τῆς ἀληθείας σωμάτιον along with κανὼν τῆς ἀληθείας. Very close materially is κανὼν τῆς πίστεως, which corresponds to the Latin regula fidei. From the standpoint of the Church as subject the phrase κανὼν τῆς ἐκκλησίας includes the other two. Acc. to Eus. Hist. Eccl., VI, 13, 3 Cl. Al. wrote a work περὶ τοῦ ἐκκλησιαστικοῦ κανόνος. This ecclesiastical canon includes the baptismal confession of Iren., I, 9, 4 regarded as regula veritatis, the whole sum of Christian doctrine in Cl. Al. Strom., VII, 15, 90, 2 and the right execution of ecclesiastical actions. For the 3rd century, then, the rule of faith was the canon of the Church long before this title was ever used of Scripture. Naturally the content of the rule is accepted

---

[21] Cf. Cic. Fam., XVI, 17: tu qui κανών esse meorum scriptorum soles.

as biblical. Thus Cl. Al. (Strom., VI, 15, 125) could describe as the canon of the Church the harmony (ἡ συμφωνία) between the Law and the prophets on the one side and the covenant instituted by the incarnation of the Lord on the other.

In sum we may say with Jülicher : [22] "The canon is the norm by which everything is directed in the Church ; to canonise is to recognise to be part of this norm. For the Christian of c. 400 the word canonical denoted much the same as we have in view when we say that something is divine, sacred, infallible, or unconditionally normative." The Greeks often use ἐκκλησιαζόμενος in place of or along with κανονιζόμενος. This denotes what belongs to, or is acknowledged by, the Church.

2. After the 4th century the general use was supplemented by the description of certain things in the Church as κανών or κανονικός.

i. Most significant is the fact that from the middle of the 4th century the term canon came to be used for the collection of the sacred writings of the OT, which had been taken over from the Synagogue, [23] and of the NT, which had already taken essential shape from c. 200. The Council of Laodicea in Phrygia (c. 360) lays down in can. 59 : ὅτι οὐ δεῖ ἰδιωτικοὺς ψαλμοὺς λέγεσθαι ἐν τῇ ἐκκλησίᾳ οὐδὲ ἀκανόνιστα βιβλία, ἀλλὰ μόνα τὰ κανονικὰ τῆς καινῆς καὶ παλαιᾶς διαθήκης. [24] Shortly after 350 Athanasius says of Hermas that it is not ἐκ τοῦ κανόνος. [25] Amphilochius of Iconium concludes at the end of his iambic catalogue of the Scriptures : οὗτος ἀψευδέστατος κανὼν ἂν εἴη τῶν θεοπνεύστων γραφῶν. [26] The use of κανών in this sense was not influenced by the fact that Alexandrian grammarians had spoken of a canon of writers of model Greek. Nor is the decisive point the equation of κανών and κατάλογος, [27] formal though the use of the term may be. What really counted was the concept of norm inherent in the term, i.e., its material content as the κανὼν τῆς ἀληθείας in the Christian sense. [28] The Latins thus came to equate canon and biblia.

ii. An older use of the word is for the resolutions of Church councils, which we find after Nicaea (325). [29] This was a logical development of the use of κανὼν τῆς ἐκ-κλησίας for what is valid in the Church. [30]

iii. From this developed the comprehensive sense of ius canonicum. [31] From the 5th century synodal decisions were gathered in collections of canons. [32] From the beginning

---

[22] A. Jülicher, Einleitung in das NT⁷ (1931), 555.
[23] On the Jewish concept of Scripture and the Canon → κρύπτω, ἀπόκρυφος and what is said there concerning קבב.
[24] F. Lauchert, Die Kanones der wichtigsten altkirchlichen Konzilien (1896), 78; J. D. Mansi, Sacrorum Conciliorum . . . collectio, II (1759), 574.
[25] De decretis Nicaenae synodi, 18, 3 (ed. H. G. Opitz, II, 1 [1935], 15).
[26] Iambi ad Seleucum, MPG, 37, 1598a; T. Zahn, Geschichte d. nt.lichen Kanons, II, 1 (1890), 214 ff.
[27] This view of F. C. Baur, 149 has found constant advocates.
[28] In express form this is first found in Isidore of Pelusium, ep., IV, 114, MPG, 78, 1185b. Cf. Jülicher, 555.
[29] Cf. can. 2 of Constantinople (381) concerning the resolutions of Nicaea and the validity of κανόνες, Lauchert, 84. Socrates Hist. Eccles., I, 13, 11 (I, 95, R. Hussey [1853]): Τότε δὲ οἱ ἐν τῇ συνόδῳ ἐπίσκοποι καὶ ἄλλα τινὰ ἐγγράψαντες, ἃ κανόνας ὀνομά-ζειν εἰώθασιν, ... ἀνεχώρησαν. Cf. Sozomenos Hist. Eccles., I, 23, 1 (I, 97, R. Hussey [1860]).
[30] Retrospectively the phrase Canones Apostolorum was also coined. Cf. Suic. Thes., s.v κανών, ad III.
[31] Cf. Socrates, II, 8, 4 (I, 189, Hussey): καίτοι κανόνος ἐκκλησιαστικοῦ κελεύοντος μὴ δεῖν παρὰ τὴν γνώμην τοῦ ἐπισκόπου Ῥώμης τὰς ἐκκλησίας κανονίζειν.
[32] RE³, X, 1 ff.

of the 9th century the term came to be used also of papal decretals, which had for a long time claimed equal rank. [33] In the Middle Ages every decision of the Church was called a canon, νόμος and lex being reserved for the secular sphere. [34] The comprehensive *Concordantia discordantium canonum* was the work of Gratian between 1139 and 1142. It is the basis of accepted canon law in the Church of Rome. Canonical has thus become an expression for anything prescribed in Church law, e.g., the canonical age of a priest.

iv. The formal sense of κανών = κατάλογος explains the fact that can. 16 of the Synod of Nicaea speaks of office-bearers in the Church as πρεσβύτεροι ἢ διάκονοι ἢ ὅλως ἐν τῷ κανόνι ἐξεταζόμενοι. [35] To prove ordination and appointment to a specific office all clergy were put on a list. [36] This ἱερατικὸς κατάλογος was called κανών. [37] Monks and nuns were put on similar lists.

v. The ethical sense is linked with this. The κανονικός is the spiritual man who fashions his life according to the rule of the Church. This is particularly true of the monk, the regular who lives according to the rule of the order. In the interests of order, however, Chrodegang of Metz drew up for secular clergy too a *vita canonica* with canonical hours of prayer, fasts etc. [38] But this could be observed only by the clergy of a cathedral or college living in established fellowship. Hence these especially came to be called canons. [39]

vi. In the Roman Mass the fixed central portion has been called the canon from the time of Gregory the Great. [40] Celebrated with great reverence, it comprises introductory prayers, intercession for the living, invocation of saints, the consecration and elevation, the anamnesis and epiclesis, the remembrance of the departed with further invocation of saints, and a doxology. [41]

vii. It is open to question with which of the preceding senses the canonising of saints is most closely related. For this official recognition a solemn process is necessary. Only then can there be paid to the saint the cultic honour of vi. The first attested canonisation took place in 993. Since the time of Alexander III the papacy has made an exclusive claim to this right.

Beyer

---

[33] Gratian Dist. III, c. 2 (*Corpus iuris canonici*, ed. Lipsiensis secunda, I [1876], 4): *Porro canonum alii sunt decreta pontificum, alii statuta conciliorum.*

[34] Gratian Dist. III, § 1 (*op. cit.*, 4): *Ecclesiastica constitutio nomine canonis censetur.* Cf. RE³, X, 1 ff. So also C. D. du Cange (ed. G. A. L. Henschel), *Glossarium Mediae et Infimae Latinitatis, s.v.*

[35] Lauchert, 41. So, too, can. 17 and 19. Cf. Antiochia (341), can. 2, 6, 11 (Lauchert, 44 ff.).

[36] Cf. N. München, "Über d. erste Konzil von Arles," *Zschr. f. Philosophie u. kath. Theologie*, 26 (1838), 64 ff.

[37] κανονικοί occurs first in Cyr. Procatechesis, 4 (MPG, 33, 340a). Can. 15 of Laodicea, e.g., speaks of the ministry τῶν κανονικῶν ψαλτῶν (Lauchert, 74).

[38] His rule in J. D. Mansi, XIV, 313 ff.

[39] Cf. du Cange, *s.v. canonicus.*

[40] Epistularum, IX, 12 (MPL, 77, 956).

[41] In the Gk. cultus ὁ κανών is a system of hymns called ᾠδαί, cf. Sophocles Lex, *s.v.* Examples of the use of κανών for cultic songs in the ancient eastern Church may be found in Suic. Thes., *s.v.* κανών, ad IV.

† καπηλεύω

1. The Greek Usage.

καπηλεύειν comes from κάπηλος, the "retailer" who sells on the market wares which he has bought from the ἔμπορος ("wholesaler"), and it means "to engage in retail trade." Both words carry with them the suggestion of trickery and avarice. κάπηλος (adj.) means "deceitful," "false"; καπηλεύειν, "to sell, to hawk, deceitfully, at illegitimate profit," or "to misrepresent a thing, i.e., wares"; hence καπηλικός means "deceitful." [1]

Intellectually, the word is used in the polemic of philosophers against inauthentic sophists or philosophers who sell their teaching for money.

Plat. Prot., 313c d : ἆρ' οὖν ... ὁ σοφιστὴς τυγχάνει ὢν ἔμπορός τις ἢ κάπηλος τῶν ἀγωγίμων, ἀφ' ὧν ψυχὴ τρέφεται; ... οὕτω καὶ οἱ τὰ μαθήματα περιάγοντες κατὰ τὰς πόλεις καὶ πωλοῦντες καὶ καπηλεύοντες τῷ ἀεὶ ἐπιθυμοῦντι. Soph., 231d, 2, where the σοφιστής is characterised as 1. νέων καὶ πλουσίων ἔμμισθος θηρευτής, 2. ἔμπορός τις περὶ τὰ τῆς ψυχῆς μαθήματα, 3. περὶ αὐτὰ ταῦτα κάπηλος, and 4. αὐτοπώλης (self-vendor) περὶ τὰ μαθήματα. Luc. Hermot., 59, where philosophy is drastically compared to wine : ὅτι καὶ οἱ φιλόσοφοι ἀποδίδονται τὰ μαθήματα ὥσπερ οἱ κάπηλοι, κερασάμενοί γε οἱ πολλοὶ καὶ δολώσαντες (cf. 2 C. 4:2) καὶ κακομετροῦντες. According to Philostr. Vit. Ap., I, 13 Euphrates opposed Apollonius of Tyana : ἐπειδὴ πάνθ' ὑπὲρ χρημάτων αὐτὸν πράττοντα ἐπέκοπτεν οὗτος καὶ ἀπῆγε τοῦ χρηματίζεσθαί τε καὶ τὴν σοφίαν καπηλεύειν — even Apollonius was regarded as a mercenary sophist. Aristides, 46, 144 (II, 193, 1 ff., G. Dindorf [1829]): ἀλλὰ καὶ τὴν Σωκράτους εἴτε χρὴ σοφίαν εἴτε φιλοσοφίαν λέγειν, ἢ καὶ τι ἄλλο, καὶ τοῦτ' ἄγαμαι, τὸ μὴ καπηλεύειν μηδ' ἐπὶ τοῖς βουλομένοις ὠνεῖσθαι ποιεῖν ἑαυτόν.

2. The Usage in the Septuagint and Philo.

καπηλεύειν is not found in the LXX, though we find κάπηλος twice in the characteristic sense : Is. 1:22 : τὸ ἀργύριον ὑμῶν ἀδόκιμον· οἱ κάπηλοί σου μίσγουσι τὸν οἶνον ὕδατι, and Sir. 26:29 : μόλις ἐξελεῖται ἔμπορος ἀπὸ πλημμελείας καὶ οὐ δικαιωθήσεται κάπηλος ἀπὸ ἁμαρτίας — every merchant stands under the suspicion of being a deceiver, a sinner ; the word has an evil ring about it like → τελώνης. [2]

κ α π η λ ε ύ ω. Heinr. 2 K.⁸ (1900), 107 f.; Wnd. 2 K., 100 f.; Schl. K., 499; Ltzm. K., 109; Wettstein on 2 C. 2:17; Str.-B., III, 499.

[1] Cf. the accounts of earlier lexicographers in Wettstein, etc.

[2] The OT is also opposed to trade, cf. the oracle against Tyre in Is. 23:1 ff. Here the LXX has μεταβόλος for סחר. Eschatological expectation looks for the destruction of traders, Zech. 14:21: "And in that day there shall be no more the trader (כְּנַעֲנִי) in the house of the Lord of hosts." The LXX has the literal Χαναναῖος, but Jerome follows Aquila and has mercator. Cf. Zeph. 1:11: "A cry from the fish gate ... for all the merchant people are cut down." The reference is to Canaanite-Phoenician traders located at the fish gate in Jerusalem and causing the people to desecrate the Sabbath (Neh. 10:32; 13:16 ff.). Θ has μεταβόλος here, while Mas. and LXX keep to the national "Canaan." These foreign traders seem to have had charge of the temple trade in money and sacrifices. If this continued to the time of Jesus, as is quite possible, there is no difficulty in understanding the cleansing of the temple by Jesus. Jesus is fulfilling a sign of the time of salvation in accordance with Zech. 14:21. Cf. K. Marti in Kautzsch, ad loc.; also J. Jeremias, Jerusalem z. Zeit Jesu, I (1923), 22, 54 f. [Bertram.]

In Philo we find only καπηλεία (retail business), which is used to describe the conduct of the Essenes in Omn. Prob. Lib., 78: ἐμπορίας γὰρ ἢ καπηλείας ἢ ναυκληρίας οὐδ' ὄναρ ἴσασι, τὰς εἰς πλεονεξίαν ἀφορμὰς ἀποδιοπομπούμενοι (abhorring). On the other hand, Philo uses other words to describe the avaricious and deceitful merchandising of sophists and false prophets, e.g., Gig., 39: πῶς γὰρ οὐκ ἐναργῆ καὶ πρόδηλα τὰ ὀνείδη τῶν λεγόντων μὲν εἶναι σοφῶν (cf. R. 1:22), πωλούντων δὲ σοφίαν καὶ ἐπευωνιζόντων (to sell cheaply), ὥσπερ φασὶ τοὺς ἐν ἀγορᾷ τὰ ὤνια προκηρύττοντας, τοτὲ μὲν μικροῦ λήμματος, τοτὲ δὲ ἡδέος καὶ εὐπαραγώγου λόγου, τοτὲ δὲ ἀβεβαίου ἐλπίδος ἀπὸ μηδενὸς ἠρτημένης ἐχυροῦ, ἔστι δ' ὅτε καὶ ὑποσχέσεων, αἵ διαφέρουσιν ὀνειράτων οὐδέν; cf. also Vit. Mos., II, 212: οὐχ ὅπερ μεθοδεύουσιν οἱ λογοθῆραι καὶ σοφισταὶ πιπράσκοντες ὡς ἄλλο τι τῶν ὠνίων ἐπ' ἀγορᾶς δόγματα καὶ λόγους, and again Spec. Leg., IV, 51. It is significant that Paul's contemporary in Alexandria knows the Platonic tradition and adopts it into his philosophy and theologico-philosophical understanding.

3. καπηλεύειν in the New Testament.

In the NT the word occurs only once in Paul in a combination which reminds us of Plato, 2 C. 2:17: οὐ γάρ ἐσμεν ὡς οἱ πολλοὶ[3] καπηλεύοντες τὸν λόγον τοῦ θεοῦ, ἀλλ' ὡς ἐξ εἰλικρινείας, ἀλλ' ὡς ἐκ θεοῦ κατέναντι θεοῦ ἐν Χριστῷ λαλοῦμεν. "We do not belong to the many preachers who make merchandise of the Word of God, but in sincerity (honesty, unselfishness, objectivity), (empowered and inspired) by God, before the face of God, we speak of Christ." The saying is a protestation of Paul's integrity (cf. Ac. 20:33), a defence against defamatory accusations, a demarcation from all the false and self-seeking missionaries and propagandists who either make life difficult for him or with whom he is falsely associated, 1 Th. 2:3-5; 2 C. 11:12 ff. A parallel expression is found in the apologetic and polemical section which comes immediately after in 4:1 ff.: μηδὲ δολοῦντες τὸν λόγον τοῦ θεοῦ.[4] In his battle with opponents and rivals, with Jewish Christian, Gnostic, Jewish and Greek wandering preachers, Paul thus uses a term which has been given its impress by the Greek philosophers in their conflict with sophists. It is likely enough that he knew the origin of the expression, since he must often have run across Sophists in the Greek sphere, and the philosophers themselves had often become "peddlers of words" in his day.[5]

Acc. to Ac. 17:18: τί ἂν θέλοι ὁ → σπερμολόγος οὗτος λέγειν, he himself is accused of being such a philosopher by those professionally qualified. → σπερμολόγος is a similar term of opprobrium to καπηλεύων or δολῶν τὸν λόγον (τοῦ θεοῦ).

On the lips of Paul καπηλεύειν τὸν λόγον τοῦ θεοῦ means 1. to offer for money the word concerning God which is entrusted to the missionary,[6] so that even a legitimate custom supported by a known saying of the Lord, i.e., ἐκ τοῦ

---

[3] A variant of the koine: λοιποί.

[4] The Vulg. has adulterantes verbum dei for καπηλεύοντες and δολοῦντες. Cf. Wnd., 2 C., 333 ff.

[5] Cf. Luc. Hermot., loc. cit.; Philostr. Vit. Ap., loc. cit.; Just. Dial., 2, 3 (of a peripatetic): καί μου ἀνασχόμενος οὗτος τὰς πρώτας ἡμέρας ἠξίου με ἔπειτα μισθὸν ὁρίσαι, ὡς μὴ ἀνωφελὴς ἡ συνουσία γίνοιτο ἡμῖν. καὶ αὐτὸν ἐγὼ διὰ ταύτην τὴν αἰτίαν κατέλιπον, μηδὲ φιλόσοφον οἰηθεὶς ὅλως. Wendland Hell. Kult., 91 ff.

[6] Did., 12, 5 describes the missionary who peddles Christ for money as a χριστέμπορος, cf. Kn. Did., 34. The two expressions are combined in Ign. Mg., 9 (MPG, 5): οἱ χριστέμποροι, τὸν λόγον καπηλεύοντες καὶ τὸν Ἰησοῦν πωλοῦντες κτλ.

εὐαγγελίου ζῆν (1 C. 9:14), is defamed. It also means 2. to falsify the word [7] (as the κάπηλος purchases pure wine and then adulterates it with water) by making additions (cf. 4:2 : μηδὲ δολοῦντες τὸν λόγον τοῦ θεοῦ). This refers to the false Gospel of the Judaizers, 2 C. 11:4.

At this point, then, the rule which Jesus Himself laid down for missionary work (Mt. 10:10; Lk. 10:7) seems in Paul to conflict with the basic principle accepted by the best philosophers, namely, that philosophy is not to be taught for money. [8] Paul knows the saying of the Lord (1 C. 9:14; 1 Tm. 5:18), but, if we may put it thus, he keeps it after the manner of Socrates. He personally does not accept support by the community and blames those who seek payment for their preaching of the Word. One of his reasons is undoubtedly the avarice, lashed by Plato, of wandering philosophers and sophists, whom he must often have met and with whom unfavourable critics classified him. [9] καπηλεύειν τὸν λόγον τοῦ θεοῦ is thus a striking phrase for a terrible abuse of the sacred Word. Hence Paul immediately contrasts with this the right attitude, his own, i.e., that of selflessness, commitment to God's own Word, a sense of responsibility towards God, and allegiance to Christ.

Windisch †

καρδία, καρδιογνώστης, σκληροκαρδία

καρδία.

Contents : A. לֵב, לֵבָב in the Old Testament. B. καρδία among the Greeks. C. The LXX, and Hellenistic and Rabbinic Judaism. D. καρδία in the New Testament.

This article offers only the linguistic foundations and the historical presuppositions for an understanding of the concept καρδία. From the standpoint of biblical theology it is

---

[7] This secondary thought is here rejected by many expositors, but the continuation shows that it is apt.

[8] There is, of course, a saying of the Lord for this rule too, Mt. 10:8 : δωρεὰν ἐλάβετε, δωρεὰν δότε = τὸν λόγον τοῦ θεοῦ μὴ καπηλεύσητε.

[9] Dob. Th., 106 f.

κ α ρ δ ί α. On A : Mandelkern, *s.v.*; Ges.-Buhl, *s.v.*; C. A. Briggs, "A Study of the Use of לֵב and לֵבָב in the Old Testament," *Semitic Studies in Memory of A. Kohut* (1897); P. Joüon, "Locutions hébraïques avec la préposition עַל devant לֵבָב, לֵב, *Biblica*, 5 (1924), 49 ff.; H. Kornfeld, "Herz u. Gehirn in altbiblischer Auffassung," *Jbch. f. jüd. Geschichte u. Lit.*, 12 (1909), 81 ff. On B.-D. : Pass., I, 1585; Liddell-Scott, 877; Cr.-Kö., 581 ff.; Pr.-Bauer³, 670 ff.; Moult.-Mill., 321; Levy Wört., II, 463 f.; Levy Chald. Wört., I, 399 f.; E. Hatch, *Essays in Biblical Greek* (1889), 94 ff.; A. Schlatter, "Herz u. Gehirn im 1. Jhdt.," *Studien z. systematischen Theologie, T. v. Haering ... dargebracht* (1918), 86 ff.; Schl. Theol. d. Judt., 20 f.

treated with other leading terms, e.g., ψυχή, νοῦς, διάνοια, πνεῦμα etc., in the article ψυχή.

A. לֵב, לֵבָב in the OT.

The use of לֵב and לֵבָב[1] is not *promiscue*. C. A. Briggs[2] has shown that "the earliest documents use לב." "לבב appears first in Isaiah." For details cf. Briggs and Holzinger.[3]

1. "Heart" in the literal sense. a. in men and animals, the "neighbourhood of the heart," "breast," *passim* ; סְגוֹר לֵב the "caul of the heart," Hos. 13:8. b. "Seat of physical vitality," vitalising (סעד) by nourishment, e.g., Gn. 18:5; "physical brokenness," כָּל־לֵבָב דַּוָּי Is. 1:5.

2. Fig. the "innermost part of man." Men look on the outward appearance, God looks on the heart," 1 S. 16:7; par. to קֶרֶב Jer. 31:33; to talk to oneself, to think (אמר, דבר passim, חשׁב Zech. 7:10, ברך Dt. 29:18; Job 1:5). The heart is the seat of mental or spiritual powers and capacities.

a. The heart stands firm in bravery and courage (עמד Ez. 22:14): לֵב par. בֹּחַ Da. 11:25, מָצָא אֶת־לִבּוֹ to find the heart, 2 S. 7:27, יִגְבַּהּ לִבּוֹ his courage arose, 2 Ch. 17:6, אַבִּירֵי לֵב the stouthearted, Ps. 76:5. The failure of courage (לֵב): רכך e.g., Dt. 20:3, מסס e.g., Dt. 20:8, חרד e.g., 1 S. 4:13, יצא Gn. 42:28, עזב Ps. 40:12, נפל 1 S. 17:32, מוג Ez. 21:20, דִּבֶּר עַל־לֵב to encourage, e.g., Gn. 34:3. Joy : שִׂמְחַת לֵב e.g., Dt. 28:47. Of merriness of heart : יטב e.g., Ju. 19:9, טוב e.g., 2 S. 13:28, שׂמח e.g., Zech. 10:7, רנן Job 29:13, רחשׁ Ps. 45:1, עלץ 1 S. 2:1. Trouble and sorrow (כְּאֵב לֵב Is. 65:14) lurk in the sides of the heart (קִירֹת לֵב Jer. 4:19). Of sorrow of heart : רעע Dt. 15:10 (רֹעַ לֵב Neh. 2:2), שֹׁבֶר ni e.g., Ps. 34:18, חִיל Ps. 55:4, הפך ni Lam. 1:20, חמם hitp. Ps. 73:21, כאב Prv. 14:13, סְחַרְחַר Ps. 38:10, זעק Is. 15:5. Pride : זָדוֹן לֵב Jer. 49:16, רָם לֵב Jer. 48:29, גֹּבַהּ לֵב 2 Ch. 36:26. Of arrogance of heart, רום e.g., Dt. 8:14, גבה e.g., Ez. 28:17, נשׂא 2 K. 14:10. Inclination of heart, הָיָה לֵב אַחֲרֵי 2 S. 15:13, הֵטָה (הֵסֵב) לֵב e.g., 1 K. 8:58; Ezr. 6:22, הֵשִׁיב לֵב עַל Mal. 3:24, נָטָה לֵב מֵעִם 1 K. 11:9. Anxious concern : שִׂים אֶת־לֵב ל or אֶל 1 S. 9:20; 1 S. 25:25. Sympathy : נֶהְפַּךְ לִבִּי Hos. 11:8. Incitement : חמם e.g., Dt. 19:6, קנא pi Prv. 23:17; dereliction : לֵב מַרְפֵּא Prv. 14:30. Desire : תַּאֲוַת לִבּוֹ Ps. 21:2; lusts : לֵב par. to עֵינַיִם e.g., Nu. 15:39, אַחַר עֵינַי הָלַךְ לִבִּי Job 31:7.

b. The heart as the seat of rational functions. The heart is given by God לָדַעַת Dt. 29:3. Those who have won understanding (קנה לב Prv. 19:8) are אַנְשֵׁי לֵבָב Job 34:10 or חַכְמֵי לֵב e.g., Job 37:24, with far-reaching insight (רֹחַב לֵב 1 K. 5:9). To them belongs לֵב נָבוֹן וְנָבוֹן 1 K. 3:12; of them may be said לֵב נָבוֹן יִקְנֶה־דַּעַת Prv. 18:15; they speak out of the treasures of their knowledge (מִלִּבָּם Job 8:10). Accordingly לִבּוֹ חָסֵר : his understanding fails him, Qoh. 10:3, חֲסַר־לֵב (or חֹסֶר־לֵב, cf. BHK[2, 3]) folly, Prv. 10:21, חֲסַר־לֵב : lacking in understanding, e.g., Prv. 6:22, אֵין לֵב without understanding, e.g., Hos. 7:11, גָּנַב אֶת־לֵב : to deceive someone, e.g., Gn. 31:20, wine takes away understanding יִקַּח לֵב

---

[1] לִבָּה Ez. 16:30, acc. to E. König, *Hbr. u. aram. Wörterbuch z. AT* (1910), is "linguistically incontestable as a later fem. form of לב" but since it does not occur elsewhere it is best explained as a textual corruption (cf. C. H. Cornill, *Das Buch d. Propheten Ezechiel* [1886], 265). From לב or לבב we have the denom. לבב ni, "to attain insight" (Job 11:12) and pi, "to rob of understanding" (Cant. 4:9).

[2] Briggs, *op. cit.*, 94 ff.

[3] H. Holzinger, *Einleitung in d. Hexateuch* (1893), 185. Cf. also Joüon, *op. cit.*

Hos. 4:11, תִּמְהוֹן לֵבָב confusion of mind, Dt. 28:28. Thoughts dwell in the heart רַעְיוֹנֵי לְבָב
Da. 2:30; חִקְרֵי־לֵב Ju. 5:16, including evil thoughts מַשְׂכִּיוֹת לֵבָב Ps. 73:7, fantasies תַּרְמִית לֵב
e.g., Jer. 14:14, self-invented visions חֲזוֹן לֵב Jer. 23:16, artistic sense חָכְמַת־לֵב Ex. 35:35
(חֲכַם־לֵב artist, e.g., Ex. 28:3). עָלָה עַל־לֵב to come into the mind, e.g., Is. 65:17, הֵשִׁיב אֶל־לֵב
to remember, e.g., Lam. 3:21, שִׂים (שִׁית) לֵב to direct attention to, e.g., Hag. 1:5; Jer. 31:21.

c. From the heart comes planning and volition (מְזִמּוֹת לֵב e.g., Jer. 23:20): בִּלְבָבוֹ it is in
his purpose, Is. 10:7, הָיָה עִם־לְבָב to have a purpose, e.g., 1 K. 8:17, עָשָׂה בְלִבּוֹ וּבְנַפְשׁוֹ to act
according to the will, 1 S. 2:35 (כַּלְבָב) 1 S. 13:14 etc.), נָתַן לֵבָב לְ 1 Ch. 22:19 or הֵכִין לֵבָב לְ
Ezr. 7:10, to direct one's purpose to, שִׂים עַל־לֵב to purpose, Da. 1:8, עָלְתָה עַל־לִבִּי it has
been my purpose, e.g., Jer. 7:31. Inner impulse comes from the heart : כָּל־אִישׁ אֲשֶׁר נְשָׂאוֹ לִבּוֹ
each whose heart moved him thereto, e.g., Ex. 36:2 (with מָלֵא Est. 7:5), נְדִיב לֵב one who
is willing, e.g., Ex. 35:5. לֹא מִלִּבִּי not of one's own impulse, e.g., Nu. 16:28. Attitude of
will, or character, is rooted in the heart (comprehensively כְּלָיוֹת וָלֵב Jer. 11:20). If the will
(דֶּרֶךְ לֵב Is. 57:17; יֵצֶר מַחְשְׁבֹת לֵב Gn. 6:5) is inclined in the right direction (הִטָּה לֵב Ps.
119:36, הֵכִין לֵב e.g., Job 11:13), this is renewal of heart (לֵב חָדָשׁ e.g., Ez. 18:31). The
whole man with his inner being and willing is comprised in לֵב: full committal בְּכָל־לֵב
(par. to בְּכָל־נֶפֶשׁ e.g., Jos. 22:5, בֶּאֱמֶת 1 S. 12:24, בְּכָל־רָצוֹן 2 Ch. 15:15, בְּכָל־מְאֹד Dt. 6:5) or
בְּלֵב שָׁלֵם e.g., 1 Ch. 29:9 (par. to בְּנֶפֶשׁ חֲפֵצָה 1 Ch. 28:9, בֶּאֱמֶת 2 K. 20:3). Thus לֵב can be
used for "person," e.g., Ps. 22:26 (along with כְּלָיוֹת Prv. 23:15 f., כָּבֵד Ps. 16:9, [4] שְׁאֵר
Ps. 73:26, בָּשָׂר Ps. 84:2), though with a slightly different nuance.

d. Religious and moral conduct is rooted in the heart. With the heart one serves
God (1 S. 12:20; par. to בֶּאֱמֶת 1 S. 12:24; "with the whole heart" *passim*). In it dwells
the fear of God, Jer. 32:40. The heart (לוּחַ לֵב) accepts the divine teachings, Prv. 7:3
(תּוֹרָתִי בְלִבָּם Is. 51:7). The heart of the righteous (יִשְׁרֵי־לֵב e.g., Ps. 7:10) trusts in God,
Prv. 3:5, is faithful to Him לֵבָב נֶאֱמָן (Neh. 9:8), and is without fear אמץ hi, Ps. 27:14.
We read of the defection of the heart : רחק pi, Is. 29:13, סור e.g., Dt. 17:17, סוג e.g.,
Ps. 44:18, פנה e.g., Dt. 29:17, פתה Dt. 11:16, זנה Ez. 6:9; of the hardening of the heart,
חזק q and pi, e.g., Ex. 4:21; 7:13, כבד q and hi, e.g., Ex. 9:7, 8:11, קשׁה hi, e.g., Ex. 7:3,
אמץ pi, e.g., Dt. 2:30; the hardened : חִזְקֵי לֵב Ez. 2:4 (par. to קְשֵׁי פָנִים), אַבִּירֵי לֵב Is. 46:12;
obduracy : שְׁרִירוּת לֵב e.g., Dt. 29:18, מְגִנַּת לֵב Lam. 3:65. The heart of the sinner (sin
is written עָרְלַת לֵב e.g., Dt. 10:16, עַרְלֵי לֵב Jer. 17:1) is uncircumcised : עַל לוּחַ לִבָּם
Jer. 9:25. Circumcision of the heart (מול e.g., Dt. 10:16) comes with conversion of heart :
שׁוּב Jl. 2:12, הֵשִׁיב אֶל־לֵב 1 K. 8:47, לֵב נִשְׁבָּר Ps. 51:17. וַיַּךְ לֵב is used for conscience smiting
us at 1 S. 24:5, and מִכְשׁוֹל לֵב for a scruple of conscience at 1 S. 25:31. The righteous is
pure in heart, בַּר־לֵבָב Ps. 24:4, אֹהֵב טְהוֹר־לֵב Prv. 22:11; cf. יְשַׁר לֵבָב Dt. 9:5, תָּם־לֵבָב Gn.
20:5, לֵב טָהוֹר 1 K. 3:6, יְשַׁרַת לֵבָב Ps. 51:10. He speaks the whole truth, אֶת־כָּל־לִבּוֹ Ju. 16:17.
The ungodly man has a corrupt heart, עִקְּשֵׁי־לֵב Prv. 11:20, חַנְפֵי לֵב Job 36:13; he speaks
with a double tongue, בְּלֵב וָלֵב Ps. 12:3.

3. Figur. בְּלֶב־יָם "in the midst of the sea," *passim*.
The various nuances are reproduced in the LXX. The most common renderings apart
from καρδία or στῆθος are διάνοια, ψυχή, ἐνδεὴς φρενῶν, νοῦς.

Baumgärtel

---

[4] As we should emend Ps. 16:9, cf. the comm.

B. καρδία[5] among the Greeks.

The word is primarily used 1. lit. for the heart in a physiological sense as the central organ of the body of man or beast, e.g., Hom. Il., 10, 94 : κραδίη δέ μοι ἔξω στηθέων ἐκθρῴσκει; 13, 442 : δόρυ δ᾽ ἐν κραδίῃ ἐπεπήγει; Aesch. Eum., 861: καρδίαν ἀλεκτόρων; P. Leid., V, XIII, 24 (Preis. Zaub., XII, 438): καρδία ἱέρακος; Gal. passim; cf. also Plat. Symp., 215d : ἡ καρδία πηδᾷ (also Aristoph. Nu., 1391; Plut. Aud. Poet., 10 [II, 30a]); P. Lond., I, 46, 157 (Preis. Zaub., V, 156 f.): ὄνομά μοι καρδία περιεζωσμένη ὄφιν.

It also occurs 2. figur., especially in the poets, infrequently in prose, for the heart as the seat of moral and intellectual life : a. the seat of emotions and passions : anger, Hom. Il., 9, 646 : ἀλλά μοι οἰδάνεται κραδίη χόλῳ; Eur. Alc., 837: ὦ πολλὰ τλᾶσα καρδία, courage or fear, Hom. Il., 21, 547: ἐν μέν οἱ κραδίη θάρσος βάλε; I, 225 : κυνὸς ὄμματ᾽ ἔχων, κραδίην δ᾽ ἐλάφοιο, joy or sadness, Od., 4, 548 : κραδίη καί θυμὸς ἀγήνωρ; 17, 489 : ἐν μὲν κραδίῃ μέγα πένθος ἄεξεν; Epict. Diss., I, 27, 21: τὸν δὲ τρέμοντα καὶ ταρασσόμενον καὶ ῥηγνύμενον ἔσωθεν τὴν καρδίαν, love, Sappho, 2, 5 f. (Diehl, I, 329): τό μοι μὰν καρδίαν ἐν στήθεσιν ἐπτόαισεν, Aristoph. Nu., 86 : ἐκ τῆς καρδίας μ᾽ ὄντως φιλεῖς; Theocr. Idyll., 29, 4 : οὐχ ὅλας φιλέειν μ᾽ ἐθέλησθ᾽ ἀπὸ καρδίας; M. Ant., II, 3 : ἀπὸ καρδίας εὐχάριστος τοῖς θεοῖς. b. The seat of the power of thought, Hom. Il., 21, 441: ἄνοον κραδίην ἔχες; Pind. Olymp., 13, 16 ff.: πολλὰ δ᾽ ἐν καρδίαις ἀνδρῶν ἔβαλον ὧραι ... ἀρχαῖα σοφίσμαθ᾽ ...; Corp. Herm., VII, 1: ἀναβλέψαντες τοῖς τῆς καρδίας ὀφθαλμοῖς (cf. IV, 11); VII, 2 : ἀφορῶντες τῇ καρδίᾳ εἰς τὸν <οὕτως> ὁραθῆναι θέλοντα, οὐ γάρ ἐστιν ... ὁρατὸς ὀφθαλμοῖς, ἀλλὰ νῷ καὶ καρδίᾳ. c. Seat of the will and resolves, Hom. Il., 10, 244 : πρόφρων κραδίη καὶ θυμὸς ἀγήνωρ; Soph. Ant., 1105 : καρδίας δ᾽ ἐξίσταμαι τὸ δρᾶν.

In philosophical terminology we find in Plato a weak trend toward ascribing to the καρδία functions of the soul, cf. Symp., 218a : δεδηγμένος τε ὑπὸ ἀλγεινοτέρου καί τὸ ἀλγεινότατον ὧν ἄν τις δηχθείη — τὴν καρδίαν γὰρ [ἢ ψυχὴν] ἢ ὅτι δεῖ αὐτὸ ὀνομάσαι πληγείς τε καὶ δηχθεὶς ὑπὸ τῶν ἐν φιλοσοφίᾳ λόγων, Resp., VI, 492c : ἐν δὴ τῷ τοιούτῳ τὸν νέον, τὸ λεγόμενον, τίνα οἴει καρδίαν ἴσχειν; Tim. Locr., 100a : τῷ δ᾽ ἀλόγῳ μέρεος τὸ μὲν θυμοειδὲς περὶ τὰν καρδίαν, τὸ δ᾽ ἐπιθυματικὸν περὶ τὸ ἧπαρ. But the basic physiological concept is maintained, cf. Tim., 65c : τὰ φλέβια (veins), οἷόν περ δοκίμια τῆς γλώττης τεταμένα ἐπὶ τὴν καρδίαν. Aristotle, for whom the heart is primarily the centre of the blood-stream, and hence the centre of physical life in general (e.g., De Somno et Vigilia, 3, p. 456b, cf. 458a; Mot. An., 10, p. 703a), locates the emotions in the neighbourhood of the καρδία on the basis of his physiology of the senses, cf. De Sensu et Sensili, 2, p. 439a, 1 f.: καὶ διὰ τοῦτο πρὸς τῇ καρδίᾳ τὸ αἰσθητήριον αὐτῶν, τῆς τε γεύσεως καὶ τῆς ἁφῆς, Part. An., II, 10, p. 656a, 28 ff.: ἀρχὴ τῶν αἰσθήσεών ἐστιν ὁ περὶ τὴν καρδίαν τόπος, διώρισται πρότερον ἐν τοῖς περὶ αἰσθήσεως· καὶ διότι αἱ μὲν δύο φανερῶς ἠρτημέναι πρὸς τὴν καρδίαν εἰσίν, ἥ τε τῶν ἁπτῶν καὶ ἡ τῶν χυμῶν, ibid., 656b, 22 ff.: ἔχει δ᾽ ἐν τῷ ἔμπροσθεν τὸν ἐγκέφαλον πάντα τὰ ἔχοντα τοῦτο τὸ μόριον, διὰ τὸ ἔμπροσθεν εἶναι ἐφ᾽ ὃ αἰσθάνεται, τὴν δ᾽ αἴσθησιν ἀπὸ τῆς καρδίας, ταύτην δ᾽ εἶναι ἐν τοῖς ἔμπροσθεν, καὶ τὸ αἰσθάνεσθαι διὰ τῶν ἐναίμων γίνεσθαι μορίων, φλεβῶν δ᾽ εἶναι κενὸν τὸ ὄπισθεν κύτος; ibid., III, 4, 666a, 11 ff. (after a physiological discussion of the heart): ἔτι δ᾽ αἱ κινήσεις τῶν ἡδέων καὶ τῶν λυπηρῶν καὶ ὅλως πάσης αἰσθήσεως ἐντεῦθεν ἀρχόμεναι φαίνονται καὶ πρὸς ταύτην περαίνουσαι. In Stoicism the heart is in some sense the central organ of intellectual

---

[5] On variant forms of the word in dialects and poetry (καρδίη, κραδίη, etc.) cf. Pass. and Liddell-Scott ; Walde-Pok., I, 423.

life, the seat of reason, from which feeling, willing and thinking proceed, cf. Chrysipp. [6] acc. to v. Arnim, II, 245, 34 ff.: τούτοις πᾶσι συμφώνως καὶ τοὔνομα τοῦτ' ἔσχηκεν ἡ καρδία κατά τινα κράτησιν καὶ κυρείαν, ἀπὸ τοῦ ἐν αὐτῇ εἶναι τὸ κυριεῦον καὶ κρατοῦν τῆς ψυχῆς μέρος, ὡς ἂν κρατία λεγομένη, ibid., 246, 1 f.: ὁρμῶμεν κατὰ τοῦτο τὸ μέρος καὶ συγκατατιθέμεθα τούτῳ καὶ εἰς τοῦτο συντείνει τὰ αἰσθητήρια πάντα, cf. ibid., 246, 13 f.: Χρύσιππος δὲ τοῦ ψυχικοῦ πνεύματος πλήρη φασὶν εἶναι τὴν κοιλίαν ταύτην (sc. τὴν ἀριστερὰν τῆς καρδίας), ibid., 244, 18 ff.; 248, 33 ff.; 247, 26 ff., 34 ff.; 249, 5 ff.; 236, 15 and 25 ff., esp. 34 f.: ἐν τῇ καρδίᾳ τὸ λογιστικὸν ὑπάρχειν; [7] also Diogenes of Babylon, the pupil of Chrysipp., ibid., III, 216, 16 f.: ὃ πρῶτον τροφῆς καὶ πνεύματος ἀρύεται, ἐν τούτῳ ὑπάρχει τὸ ἡγεμονικόν, ὃ δὲ πρῶτον τροφῆς καὶ πνεύματος ἀρύεται, ἡ καρδία; ibid., line 9 f.: ἡ διάνοια ἄρα οὐκ ἔστιν ἐν τῇ κεφαλῇ, ἀλλ' ἐν τοῖς κατωτέρω τόποις, μάλιστά πως περὶ τὴν καρδίαν, and other Stoics, cf. v. Arnim, II, 228, 4 f.: οἱ Στωϊκοὶ πάντες ἐν ὅλῃ τῇ καρδίᾳ ἢ τῷ περὶ τὴν καρδίαν πνεύματι (sc. εἶναι τὸ ἡγεμονικόν); Diog. Laert., VII, 159 (ibid., line 1 ff.): ἡγεμονικὸν δὲ εἶναι τὸ κυριώτατον τῆς ψυχῆς, ἐν ᾧ αἱ φαντασίαι καὶ αἱ ὁρμαὶ γίνονται καὶ ὅθεν ὁ λόγος ἀναπέμπεται· ὅπερ εἶναι ἐν καρδίᾳ. On the whole, however, this discussion does not go beyond the question of the seat of the spiritual life in the body. [8] There is no strict transposition of the concept καρδία into the spiritual realm (cf. v. Arnim, II, 248, 33 ff.: καθ' ἣν ἔτι φορὰν καὶ τὰ τοιαῦτα λέγεται πάντα· "ἡψάμην σου τῆς καρδίας" ὥσπερ τῆς ψυχῆς ... τῇ δὲ καρδίᾳ καθάπερ ἂν τῇ ψυχῇ χρώμεθα, cf. ibid., 249, 5 ff., 247, 26 ff. and 36 ff.). That is to say, the process of thought is not specifically identified with the καρδία.

3. Figur. of nature, the "inward part," the "core" of a plant or "kernel" of a tree, e.g., Theophr. Historia Plantarum, I, 2, 6 : καλοῦσι δέ τινες τοῦτο καρδίαν, οἱ δ' ἐντεριώνην· ἔνιοι δὲ τὸ ἐντὸς τῆς μήτρας αὐτῆς καρδίαν, οἱ δὲ μυελόν, P. Leid., V, XIII, 24 (Preis. Zaub., XII, 438): ἀρτεμισίας (wormwood) καρδία; P. Leid. W., VI, 50 f. (Preis. Zaub., XIII, 262 f.): λαβὼν βάϊν (palm branch) χλωρὰν καὶ τῆς καρδίας κρατήσας σχίσον εἰς δύο.

C. The LXX, and Hellenistic and Rabbinic Judaism.

1. In the LXX καρδία is the true equivalent of the Heb. לֵב or לֵבָב, more rarely translated διάνοια and ψυχή, and very rarely φρένες, νοῦς and στῆθος. Only in a few verses is καρδία used for קֶרֶב (ψ 5:9; 61:5; 93:19; Prv. 14:33; 26:24), for מֵעִים (Lam. 2:11; ψ 39:8 B), for רוּחַ (Ez. 13:3), for בֶּטֶן (Prv. 22:18; Hab. 3:16 vl.), or for דֶּרֶךְ (2 Παρ. 30:8 B). Nowhere in a certain LXX text does καρδία correspond to נֶפֶשׁ (cf. Dt. 12:20 A; ψ 93:19 S; 130:2 A). The wealth of nuances in the underlying Heb. words is reflected in καρδία in the LXX. Thus καρδία is first the principle and organ of man's personal life. It is the focus of his being and activity as a spiritual personality (cf. Prv. 4:23 : πάσῃ φυλακῇ τήρει σὴν καρδίαν· ἐκ γὰρ τούτων ἔξοδοι ζωῆς, cf. ψ 21:26). Hence it is also the source and seat of his moral and religious life, Dt. 6:5; 1 Βασ. 12:20, 24; 'Ιερ. 39:40; Prv. 7:3; 3:5; Jl. 2:12 etc. καρδία is often interchangeable

---

[6] Zeno and Cleanthes refer only the emotions to the heart, v. Arnim, I, 51, 28 f.: τοὺς φόβους καὶ τὰς λύπας καὶ πάνθ' ὅσα τοιαῦτα πάθη κατὰ τὴν καρδίαν συνίστασθαι.

[7] Religious functions, to the best of my knowledge, are ascribed to the καρδία in Hell. texts only in the Berlin magic pap., 5025 (Preis. Zaub., I, 21): ἔσται τι ἔνθεον ἐν τῇ σῇ καρδίᾳ → I, 646 f.

[8] Cf. Lucret. De Rerum Natura, III, 136 ff. (ed. J. Martin [1934]); Plut. De Placitis Philosophorum, IV, 5 (II, 899a/b); Claudius Ptolemaeus De Judicandi Facultate et Animi Principatu, 26 ff. (p. XIV f., ed. F. Hanow, in Programm d. Gymnasiums Küstrin [1870]). On the Stoic doctrine of ἡγεμονικόν v. J. Schneider, Πνεῦμα ἡγεμονικόν, ZNW, 34 (1935), 64 ff.

with ψυχή, διάνοια, πνεῦμα, νοῦς etc., but in contrast to even these synonyms it relates to the unity and totality of the inner life represented and expressed in the variety of intellectual and spiritual functions, → ψυχή.

2. When it follows OT lines of thought, Hellenistic Judaism uses καρδία in the same sense as the LXX, e.g., Test. L. 13:1: φοβεῖσθε κύριον τὸν θεὸν ὑμῶν ἐξ ὅλης τῆς καρδίας ὑμῶν; Test. Jos. 10:5 : εἶχον τὸν φόβον τοῦ θεοῦ ἐν τῇ καρδίᾳ μου; Test. S. 5:2 : ἀγαθύνατε τὰς καρδίας ὑμῶν ἐνώπιον κυρίου; Test. D. 5:11: ἐπιστρέψει καρδίας ἀπειθεῖς πρὸς κύριον; Test. S. 4:5 (cf. Test. R. 4:1 etc.): ἐν ἁπλότητι καρδίας; Test. R. 6:10 : ἐν ταπεινώσει καρδίας ὑμῶν; Test. Iss. 3:1: ἐν εὐθύτητι καρδίας; Test. N. 3:1: ἐν καθαρότητι καρδίας; Test. Jos. 4:6 : κύριος ... εὐδοκεῖ ... τοῖς ἐν καθαρᾷ καρδίᾳ ... αὐτῷ προσερχομένοις; 17:3 : τέρπεται ... ὁ θεὸς ... ἐπὶ προαιρέσει καρδίας ἀγαθῆς; Test. S. 4:7: ἀγαπήσατε ἕκαστος τὸν ἀδελφὸν αὐτοῦ ἐν ἀγαθῇ καρδίᾳ; Test. G. 5:3 : (the righteous and humble) ... οὐχ ὑπ' ἄλλου καταγινωσκόμενος ἀλλ' ὑπὸ τῆς ἰδίας καρδίας; 6:7: ἄφες αὐτῷ ἀπὸ καρδίας; Test. S. 2:4 : ἡ γὰρ καρδία μου ἦν σκληρά; Test. Jud. 20:5 : ἐμπεπύρισται ὁ ἁμαρτωλὸς ἐκ τῆς ἰδίας καρδίας; Test. Zeb. 2:5 : ἐβόμβει ἡ καρδία μου; Test. Jos. 15:3 : ἡ καρδία μου ἐτάκη; Test. D. 4:7: συναίρονται ἀλλήλοις ἵνα ταράξωσι τὴν καρδίαν; Test. Jos. 7:2 : πόνον καρδίας ἐγὼ ἀλγῶ; Test. L. 6:2 : συνετήρουν τοὺς λόγους τούτους ἐν τῇ καρδίᾳ μου; 8:19 : ἔκρυψα ... τοῦτο ἐν τῇ καρδίᾳ μου; Test. D. 1:4 : ἐν καρδίᾳ μου ἐθέμην; Gk. En. 14:2 : νοῆσαι καρδίᾳ; Ep. Ar. 17: ἐπεκαλούμην τὸν κυριεύοντα κατὰ καρδίαν etc.; cf. 4 Esr. 3:1: "My thoughts pierced to my heart" (cf. Is. 65:17 etc.); 3:30 : "Then my heart (I) was startled"; 3:21: Adam had an "evil heart," hence he sinned (cf. 4:30); similarly his descendants have an evil heart, which "has turned them from life and led them to destruction and to the way of death" (3:20, 26; 7:48).

Similarly Philo, directly following the OT, can speak of ἀπερίτμητοι τὴν καρδίαν, Spec. Leg., I, 304 (cf. Lv. 26:41), or demand with the Law, τὰ δίκαια ... ἐντιθέναι ... τῇ καρδίᾳ, Spec. Leg., IV, 137 (cf. Dt. 6:6). He constantly refers to Dt. 30:14: ἔστιν σου ἐγγὺς τὸ ῥῆμα σφόδρα ... ἐν τῇ καρδίᾳ σου, Poster. C., 85; Virt., 183; Mut. Nom., 237 f.; Som., II, 180; Omn. Prob. Lib., 68; Praem. Poen., 79 f. But the biblical idea that the heart is the centre of the inner life is alien to Philo. To him καρδία is an inexact term. It is merely a symbol of διάνοια or βουλαί (βουλεύματα). In Mut. Nom., 124 the name Caleb is explained in terms of πᾶσα καρδία, but in the allegorical exposition ψυχή replaces καρδία, which Philo knows only in a physiological context. The καρδία, seated in the στήθη (Leg. All., I, 68; cf. also the image in Vit. Mos., I, 189), is one of the 7 inner parts of the body, the entrails (Op. Mund., 118; Leg. All., I, 12). Its significance is as the centre of the blood-stream, Spec. Leg., I, 216 and 218. He has learned of the action of the heart [9] from doctors and scientists : δοκεῖ τοῦ ὅλου σώματος προπλάττεσθαι ἡ καρδία, θεμελίου τρόπον ἢ ὡς ἐν νηὶ τρόπις (keel), ἐφ' ᾗ οἰκοδομεῖται τὸ ἄλλο σῶμα — παρὸ καὶ μετὰ τὴν τελευτὴν ἔτι ἐμπηδᾶν φασιν αὐτὴν ὡς καὶ πρώτην γινομένην καὶ ὑστέραν φθειρομένην, Leg. All., II, 6. If there may be seen here the influence of Gk. philosophy on his understanding of καρδία, acquaintance with the anthropology of Hellenistic philosophers (→ 608 f.) may be seen in his frequent mention of the problem whether the ἡγεμονικόν is located in the heart or the brain. [10] Though he occasionally equates καρδία and ἡγεμονικόν (Spec. Leg., I, 305), he leaves the question open (Spec. Leg., I, 214; Som., I, 32; Poster. C., 137; Det. Pot. Ins., 90) even when referring to the Torah of sacrifices, which says nothing about offering the mind or heart, though this would be specially sanctified if the ἡγεμονικόν could be assumed in one or the other according to the will of the legislator, Sacr. AC, 136; cf. Spec. Leg., I, 213 ff. Once with reference to the tree of life in

---

[9] For Stoic teaching cf. v. Arnim, II, 214, 1 ff., 6 ff., 12 ff.
[10] On this pt. cf. J. Schneider, op. cit. (→ n. 8), 66 ff.

Paradise he mentions the view of those who regard the heart as the ἡγεμονικόν, Leg. All., I, 59 : τὴν καρδίαν ξύλον εἰρῆσθαι ζωῆς, ἐπειδὴ αἰτία τε τοῦ ζῆν ἐστι καὶ τὴν μέσην τοῦ σώματος χώραν ἔλαχεν, ὡς ἂν κατ' αὐτοὺς ἡγεμονικὸν ὑπάρχουσα. On another occasions he adopts the strange argument for circumcision that it is designed to conform the organ of generation to the heart, the more valuable inward organ which produces thought, Spec. Leg., I, 6 : τὴν πρὸς καρδίαν ὁμοιότητα τοῦ περιτμηθέντος μέρους· πρὸς γὰρ γένεσιν ἄμφω παρεσκεύασται, τὸ μὲν ἐγκάρδιον πνεῦμα νοημάτων, τὸ δὲ γόνιμον ὄργανον ζῴων. But his own opinion, in connection with his religious criticism of reason, is that the seat of the ἡγεμονικόν is not to be found in the human body, and that the heart, the physical organ which alone he has in view, cannot be the seat of the higher life. Joseph. mentions the καρδία exclusively as an organ of the body of men and beasts, after the manner of the Greeks, e.g., Ant., 5, 193 : πλήξας δ' αὐτὸν ... εἰς τὴν καρδίαν, 7, 241: τοξεύσας κατὰ τῆς καρδίας ἀπέκτεινεν; 9, 118 : τοῦ βέλους διὰ τῆς καρδίας ἐνεχθέντος; cf. 19, 346 : διακάρδιον ἔσχεν ὀδύνην. The movement towards a figurative understanding in εὐκαρδίως, "of good heart or courage," [11] Ant., 12, 373 : σφόδρα εὐκαρδίως ἐπ' αὐτὸν (sc. τὸν ἐλέφαντα) ὁρμήσας; Bell., 7, 358 : φέρειν εὐκαρδίως (sc. τὸν θάνατον), is again in accordance with Gk. usage, [12] and there is no analogy to it in the LXX. Where the OT has heart, Joseph. uses διάνοια or ψυχή.

3. Rabb. Judaism follows the OT in its use of לֵב, לֵבָב, Aram. לְבָּא, cf. e.g., Ber., 2, 1: כּוּן לבו, "he thinks of, is aware of"; [13] S. Dt., 33 on 6:6 : תֵן הדברים האלה על לבבך; S. Dt., 24 on 1:27 (p. 34, Kittel): (proverb) "what you have in your heart against your friend is the same as what he has in his heart against you"; Midr. Qoh. on 1:16 : [14] the heart as the centre of life ; Ab., 2, 9 : "What is the good way to which a man should keep ? ... A good heart ... What is the evil way which he must avoid ? ... An evil heart"; [15] S. Dt., 41 on 11:13 (p. 95, Kittel): "Is there a service (of God) in the heart ? ... This is prayer"; M. Ex., 20, 21: כל גבהי לבב קרוים תועבה, "all the proud are called an abomination." "So long as the Jew spoke of the heart, he had in view the inner life as a unity with all its willing, feeling and thinking." [16]

D. καρδία in the New Testament.

The NT use of the word agrees with the OT use as distinct from the Greek. Even more strongly than the LXX it concentrates on the heart as the main organ of psychic and spiritual life, the place in man at which God bears witness to Himself.

1. The thought of the heart as the central organ of the body and the seat of physical vitality is found only in Lk. 21:34 and the select poetic expressions of Ac. 14:17: ἐμπιπλῶν τροφῆς ... τὰς καρδίας ὑμῶν, and Jm. 5:5 : ἐθρέψατε τὰς καρδίας ὑμῶν (cf. 1 K. 21:7; ψ 101:5; 103:15).

2. That the heart is the centre of the inner life of man and the source or seat of all the forces and functions of soul and spirit is attested in many different ways in the NT.

---

[11] Cf. also Jos. Ap., 2, 85 : nisi cor asini ipse potius habuisset et impudentiam canis.
[12] E.g., Eur. Hec., 549; Dion. Hal. Ant. Rom., V, 8, 6.
[13] Often used in Rabb. thinking for the conscious and intentional resolve to keep the commandments [Kuhn].
[14] Str.-B., I, 721.
[15] Ibid., II, 14.
[16] Schl. Theol. d. Judt., 21.

a. In the heart dwell feelings and emotions, desires and passions.

Joy, Ac. 2:26 (cf. ψ 15:9); Jn. 16:22 (cf. Is. 66:14); Ac. 14:17; pain and sorrow, Jn. 16:6; 14:1, 27 (cf. ψ 54:4; 142:4; Lam. 2:11; Job 37:1); R. 9:2; 2 C. 2:4; Ac. 2:37 (cf. ψ 108:16); 7:54; 21:13; Lk. 4:18 א (cf. Is. 61:1; ψ 33:18), love, 2 C. 7:3; 6:11; Phil. 1:7; [17] desire, R. 10:1; Lk. 24:32 (cf. ψ 72:21; 38:3), [18] of God, Ac. 13:22 : ἄνδρα κατὰ τὴν καρδίαν μου (cf. 1 Βασ. 13:14); lust, R. 1:24; Jm. 3:14; Mt. 5:28; 6:21 and par.

b. The heart is the seat of understanding, the source of thought and reflection.

Mk. 7:21 and par.; Mt. 12:34 and par.; 13:15b; Jn. 12:40b and Ac. 28:27b (Is. 6:10); Lk. 1:51 (cf. 1 Ch. 29:18); 24:38 (cf. Da. 2:29 Θ'); 2:35; 9:47; Ac. 8:22; Hb. 4:12; Ac. 7:23 : ἀνέβη ἐπὶ τὴν καρδίαν αὐτοῦ, "it came into his mind," v. 1 C. 2:9 (cf. 'Ιερ. 3:16; 51:21; Is. 65:16; 4 Βασ. 12:5); Lk. 2:19, 51 (cf. Da. 7:28 Θ'); Mt. 9:4 (cf. Da. 1:8); Mk. 11:23; λέγειν ἐν τῇ καρδίᾳ αὐτοῦ, "to think," Mt. 24:48 and par.; R. 10:6; Rev. 18:7 (cf. Is. 47:8; ψ 13:1; Dt. 8:17; 9:4; 1 Βασ. 27:1); R. 1:21; Lk. 24:25.

c. The heart is the seat of the will, the source of resolves.

2 C. 9:7; Ac. 11:23; 1 C. 4:5 (cf. Sir. 37:13); 1 C. 7:37; Lk. 21:14 : θέτε οὖν ἐν ταῖς καρδίαις ὑμῶν, "then propose," v. Ac. 5:4 (cf. Hag. 2:15; Mal. 2:2; Da. 1:8 Θ'); [19] Jn. 13:2; [20] Rev. 17:17 (cf. 2 Esr. 17:5); Ac. 5:3; Col. 4:8; Eph. 6:22.

Thus καρδία comes to stand for the whole of the inner being of man in contrast to his external side, the πρόσωπον, 1 Th. 2:17; 2 C. 5:12 (cf. 1 Βασ. 16:7), to his mouth and lips, Mk. 7:6 and par. (Is. 29:13); Mt. 15:18; R. 10:8 ff. (Dt. 30:14); 2 C. 6:11; R. 2:29 : περιτομὴ καρδίας [21] in contrast to the ἐν τῷ φανερῷ ἐν σαρκὶ περιτομή, v. 28; Ac. 7:51 (cf. 'Ιερ. 9:25; Ez. 44:7, 9; Lv. 26:41). Ac. 4:32 : καρδία ... μία (cf. 2 Ch. 30:12). The heart, the innermost part of man, represents the ego, the person, Col. 2:2; 1 Jn. 3:19 f.; 1 Pt. 3:4 : ὁ κρυπτὸς τῆς καρδίας ἄνθρωπος.

καρδία phrases are often used for personal or reflexive pronouns, e.g., Mk. 2:6 : ἐν ταῖς καρδίαις αὐτῶν = v. 8 : ἐν ἑαυτοῖς; cf. Jn. 16:22; Col. 4:8; Jm. 5:5. [22]

d. Thus the heart is supremely the one centre in man to which God turns, in which the religious life is rooted, which determines moral conduct.

Lk. 16:15 (cf. 1 Βασ. 16:7; 1 Ch. 28:9); R. 8:27; 1 Th. 2:4 (cf. 'Ιερ. 11:20); Rev. 2:23 (cf. ψ 7:9; 'Ιερ. 17:10); Gl. 4:6; R. 5:5; 2 C. 1:22; Eph. 3:17; Hb. 8:10; 10:16 ('Ιερ. 38:33); 2 C. 3:3 (cf. Prv. 7:3); R. 2:15; Lk. 8:15; Mt. 13:19; 2 C. 4:6; Eph. 1:18; [23] Ac. 16:14 (cf. 2 Macc. 1:4); Ac. 15:9 (cf. Sir. 38:10); Hb. 10:22b; 2 Pt. 1:19; R. 10:9 f.; 1 C.

---

[17] Cf. Ovid. Tristia, V, 4, 23 f.: te tamen ... in toto pectore semper habet.
[18] Cf. P. Lond., I, 121, 472 (Preis. Zaub., VII, 472): καιομένην τὴν ψυχὴν καὶ τὴν καρδίαν.
[19] We find the same expression at Lk. 1:66 (cf. 1 Βασ. 21:13; 2 Βασ. 13:20) in the sense "to take into the heart," "to store up in the memory."
[20] Cf. Zn. J. and Bau. J., ad loc.
[21] Cf. Od. Sol., 11, 1 f. (Hennecke, 447): "My heart was circumcised ... The Most High circumcised me by His Holy Spirit," cf. Dt. 30:6; 10:16; 'Ιερ. 4:4; 39:39; Ez. 11:19 f.; 36:26.
[22] But cf. Winer (Schmiedel) § 22, 18b. In the LXX the reflexive stands for the Heb. לב, Ex. 4:14; ψ 35:1; Est. 6:6 etc.
[23] Cf. Corp. Herm., 11b; VII, 1a (→ 608). Cf. also the agraphon P. Oxy., I, 1, 17 ff. verso : πονεῖ ἡ ψυχή μου ἐπὶ τοῖς υἱοῖς τῶν ἀνθρώπων, ὅτι τυφλοί εἰσιν τῇ καρδίᾳ αὐτῶ[ν].

14:25; Mk. 12:30 and par. (Dt. 6:5); [24] Mt. 18:35 (cf. Is. 59:13; Lam. 3:33); R. 6:17; 1 Pt. 1:22. The heart of natural sinful man, Mk. 7:21 and par.; Mt. 13:15a and Ac. 28:27a (Is. 6:10); Mk. 3:5; 6:52; 8:17; Jn. 12:40; Eph. 4:18; Jm. 1:26; Ac. 8:21 (though cf. ψ 7:10; 10:2); 2 C. 3:15; Hb. 3:12; R. 1:21, 24; 2:5; 1 Jn. 3:20 (→ 610); 2 Pt. 2:14; Ac. 7:39. The heart of the redeemed as it ought to be, Mt. 11:29 (cf. Da. 8:37); 5:8 (cf. ψ 23:4); 1 Tm. 1:5; 2 Tm. 2:22 (cf. ψ 50:10); Hb. 10:22a (cf. Is. 38:3); Lk. 6:45; Ac. 2:46; 1 Th. 3:13; Col. 3:22; Eph. 6:5; 1 Pt. 3:15; Jm. 4:8 (cf. Sir. 38:10); 5:8 (cf. ψ 30:24; 111:8; Sir. 22:16); Hb. 13:9; Col. 3:15; Phil. 4:7; 2 Th. 3:5 (cf. 1 Παρ. 29:18; 2 Παρ. 19:3; Sir. 49:3).

3. Mt. 12:40 : ἐν τῇ καρδίᾳ τῆς γῆς, "in the inward part, the bosom, of the earth," cf. Jon. 2:4; Ez. 27:4, 25 f.; 28:2; 4 Esr. 13:3 etc.

† καρδιογνώστης.

Only in the NT and early Christian lit., Herm. m., 4, 3, 4; Act. Pl. et Thecl., 24; Act. Thaddaei, 3; Didasc., 7; 15; 18; 24 (cf. Const. Ap., II, 24, 6; III, 7, 8; IV, 6, 8; VI, 12, 4); Const. Ap., VIII, 5, 6. In explanation of the word Cl. Al. Strom., V, 14, 96, 4 adduces Thales : τὸ "καρδιογνώστην" λέγεσθαι πρὸς ἡμῶν ἄντικρυς ἑρμηνεύει. ἐρωτηθείς γέ τοι ὁ Θάλης, ... εἰ λανθάνει τὸ θεῖον πράσσων τι ἄνθρωπος "καὶ πῶς," εἶπεν "ὅς γε οὐδὲ διανοούμενος;"

The designation of God as ὁ καρδιογνώστης, "the One who knows the heart," expresses in a single term (Ac. 1:24; 15:8) something which is familiar to both NT and OT piety (Lk. 16:15; R. 8:27; 1 Th. 2:4; Rev. 2:23 of Christ, cf. 1 Βασ. 16:7; 3 Βασ. 8:39; 1 Παρ. 28:9; ψ 7:9; Ἰερ. 11:20; 17:10; Sir. 42:18 ff.), [1] namely, that the omniscient God knows the innermost being of every man where the decision is made either for Him or against Him (→ 609; 612).

† σκληροκαρδία → σκληρός, σκληρότης, σκληρύνω.

"Hardness of heart," "obduracy." Coined in the LXX for the Heb. עָרְלַת לֵבָב, Dt. 10:16; Ἰερ. 4:4; cf. Sir. 16:10 (3:26 f.: καρδία σκληρά); [1] the adj. to which it corresponds is σκληροκάρδιος, Prv. 17:20; Ez. 3:7 (cf. σκληρὸς τὴν καρδίαν, Prv. 28:14); analogous is σκληροτραχηλία, Test. S. 6:2 (vl.) from σκληροτράχηλος, Ex. 33:3, 5; Dt. 9:6, 13; Prv. 29:1 etc.; Ac. 7:51. Philo Spec. Leg., I, 305 adduces Dt. 10:16 and refers σκληροκαρδία to the περιττεύουσαι φύσεις τοῦ ἡγεμονικοῦ, ἃς αἱ ἄμετροι τῶν παθῶν

---

[24] Cf. APF, 5 (1913), 393, No. 312, 9 : ἐκ ψυχῆς καὶ καρδίας. There is a similar formula in Plaut. Captivi, II, 3, 27: *corde et animo atque auribus.*

κ α ρ δ ι ο γ ν ώ σ τ η ς. Cr.-Kö., 588; Pr.-Bauer³, 672; Moult.-Mill., 321; Pr. Ag., 9.

[1] Ps. Sol. 14:8 : ταμίεια καρδίας ἐπίσταται (sc. God) πρὸ τοῦ γενέσθαι, is valuable because of the reference to the heart as the place where resolves are made that issue in conduct. In Jos. Ant., 6, 263 we find : (God) οὐ τὰ ἔργα μόνον ὁρᾷ τὰ πραττόμενα, ἀλλὰ καὶ τὰς διανοίας ἤδη σαφῶς οἶδεν, ἀφ' ὧν μέλλει ταῦτα ἔσεσθαι. For Rabb. materials cf. Str.-B., II, 595; III, 748. As the Johannine Christ knows the hearts (Jn. 2:25; 21:17), so does the Mandaean redeemer, cf. Lidz. Liturg., 258 : "Thou knowest all hearts and penetratest all senses," cf. also Lidz. Ginza R., V, 4, 193 (p. 194, 14 f.): "Thou knowest hearts and penetratest senses. Hearts, livers and kidneys are spread out before thee like the sun."

σ κ λ η ρ ο κ α ρ δ ί α. Cr.-Kö., 588; Pr.-Bauer³, *s.v.*; Moult.-Mill., 578 (*s.v.* σκληροτράχηλος); Bl.-Debr. § 120:4.

[1] Cf. the καρδία λιθίνη, Ez. 11:19 f.; 36:26 (Ἰερ. 39:39 f.).

ἔσπειράν τε καὶ συνηύξησαν ὁρμαὶ καὶ ὁ κακὸς ψυχῆς γεωργὸς ἐφύτευσεν, ἀφροσύνη. The term is also found in the OT pseudepigrapha (e.g., Gr. En. 16:3; Test. S. 6:2), but apart from this it occurs only in the NT and early Christian authors, Herm. v., 3, 7, 6; Just. Dial., 18, 2; 45, 3; 46, 7; 137, 1; Act. Thom., 166 etc.

At Mk. 10:5 and par.; 16:14 (here with ἀπιστία, cf. R. 2:5 : τὴν → σκληρότητά σου καὶ → ἀμετανόητον καρδίαν), σκληροκαρδία denotes the persistent un-receptivity of a man to the declaration of God's saving will, which must be accepted by the heart of man as the centre of his personal life (→ 612).

Behm

> ### καρπός, ἄκαρπος, καρποφορέω

καρπός.

In secular Gk. a. lit. "fruit," [1] esp. of trees or the earth, Hom. Il., 6, 142 : ἀρούρης, also the fruit as seed ; figur. of the young of animals, Xenoph. Cyrop., I, 1, 2. b. generally "fruit," "product," "result," "gain," esp. of the working out of a matter for good or evil, M. Ant., IX, 42, 11: πράξεως, Jos. Ant., 20, 48 : τῆς εὐσεβείας, Philo Fug., 176 : ἐπιστήμης. Inscr. Priene, 112, 14 : μόνη μεγίστους ἀποδίδωσιν ἡ ἀρετὴ καρποὺς καὶ χάριτας. Proverbially Gregorius Cyprius = Corpus Paroemiographorum Graecorum (ed. v. Leutsch-Schneidewin), II (1851), p. 57: καρπὸν ὃν ἔσπειρας θέριζε. In the Stoic view of life καρπός is often used in a metaphorical sense. [2]

In the LXX we find a., as above, lit. in translation of פְּרִי, for the fruits of the earth, Nu. 13:27; Dt. 1:25 (τῆς γῆς); Lv. 25:3 (תְּבוּאָה); Dt. 11:17; Ez. 36:8, and fig. for children as the fruit of the body, ψ 131:11; 126:3 (γαστρός); Gn. 30:2 (κοιλίας); b. generally, and in the spiritual realm, for "fruit" or "result," χειλέων, Prv. 31:31 vl., στόματος, 12:14, δικαιοσύνης, Am. 6:12; of the result of an action : ἔδονται τῆς ἑαυτῶν ὁδοῦ τοὺς καρπούς, Prv. 1:31; Hos. 10:13; Jer. 17:10; ψ 103:13 (τῶν ἔργων, i.e., the works of God); more rarely works themselves are called fruits, Prv. 19:22.

In Iranian (as in Persian and Mandaean literature) the soul is often described as a tree or plant which is planted by the messenger of life with a view to bringing forth fruit. Paradise is the garden, planted by God, in which the souls of the perfect are plants that bear rich and precious fruits. [3]

Later Judaism also likes to call the result of an action its fruit, bQid., 40a (→ n. 5), or to speak of the actions of men as their fruits. [4] Since פְּרִי in the sense of interest is

---

κ α ρ π ό ς. [1] Etym. cf. *carpere, Herbst,* harvest (cf. Prellwitz, Boisacq, *s.v.*).

[2] M. Ant., IX, 10, 1: φέρει καρπὸν καὶ ἄνθρωπος καὶ θεὸς καὶ ὁ κόσμος; VI, 30, 4 : καρπὸς τῆς ἐπιγείου ζωῆς; IV, 23, 2 : πᾶν μοι καρπός, ὃ φέρουσιν αἱ σαὶ ὧραι, ὦ φύσις· ἐκ σοῦ πάντα, ἐν σοὶ πάντα, εἰς σὲ πάντα. Epict. Diss., IV, 8, 36.

[3] Cf. Reitzenstein Ir. Erl., 138 ff.

[4] Gn. r., 30 on 6:9 : "What are the fruits of the righteous, פירותיו של צדיק? Fulfilments of the Law and good works. Tanch. אמור 173a : On Ps. 36:6 : "Thy righteousness is like the mountains of God ; thy judgments are a great *tehôm,*" the midrash gives the exposition

also a financial term, the figure can also be worked out in this direction, and in this field it helps to bring home the thought of retribution. The earlier view that retribution for an act is to be expected in this life became more subtle with the development of belief in the hereafter. Reference was now made to the interest (פְּרִי) which would accrue to an act in terms of consequences in this world, but the capital (קֶרֶן) remained with God and would be credited only in the day of judgment. [5]

In the NT we find 1. the literal sense at Jm. 5:7, 18; Mt. 21:19 and par.; 13:8 and par., 26; 21:34 and par.; Mk. 4:29; Rev. 22:2; figuratively of children as fruit, Lk. 1:42 (κοιλίας, of woman); Ac. 2:30 (ὀσφύος, of man); Hb. 13:15 (χειλέων).

2. We also find the general figurative sense of "consequence," "result," "profit." Thus John the Baptist and Jesus speak of the acts of men as their fruits. The decisive requirement is that they should bring forth good fruits, Mt. 21:43. Good works are a test of the genuineness of μετάνοια, Mt. 3:8 and par. The acts of men, as their fruits, are signs by which to know (ἐπιγνώσεσθε) their inner nature, Mt. 7:16 f. As the value of a tree is estimated by its products, so the righteousness displayed in acts is a decisive standard for divine judgment, Mt. 3:10; 7:19. The man who is unfruitful is threatened with rejection, Lk. 13:6.

In the Synoptic statements there is no reflection on the power which produces fruits. In Jn., however, this power is fellowship with Christ, Jn. 15:2 ff., and in Paul it is the Holy Spirit, Gl. 5:22; Eph. 5:9. Sanctification of life is the fruit which the Christian experiences as one who bears the Spirit, R. 6:22. Conversely, the pre-Christian man is under the power of sin and brings forth the corresponding fruits, R. 6:20 f. [6]

καρπός is then applied in many different ways to the work of the apostle. The results of the missionary are his fruit, R. 1:13; Phil. 1:22. The apostle is like the γεωργός who may partake of the fruit which he has produced by his work, 2 Tm. 2:6; 1 C. 9:7. The collection for the Jerusalem community is a fruit of the Pauline congregations, R. 15:28. [7] Paul desires that the reward of blessing (καρπόν, cf. καρπός in the sense of consequence) may accrue to the Philippians because of the support which they have given him, Phil. 4:17. Again, in Hb. 12:11 righteousness is the blessed result (καρπός) which the divine παιδεία accomplishes in the pious affected thereby. According to Jm. 3:18 God grants the fruit of righteousness to those who seek the wisdom which is from above. [8]

---

that as the mountains, i.e., dry land, can be planted and bring forth fruits, so the righteous bring forth fruits (i.e., good works); and as the tehôm, i.e., the ocean, cannot be planted and brings forth no works, so the ungodly have no good works and bring forth no fruits (Str.-B., I, 466).

[5] T. Pea, 1, 2-4 (18): Merit has both capital and interest (פירות). In respect of sin, however, the case is as follows. A sin which bears fruit, i.e., which results in another sin, has, apart from the capital, i.e., punishment in the future world, fruits as well, i.e., the interest of punishment on earth; on the other hand, a sin which bears no fruit has no fruits, but is punished only in the world to come (Str.-B., I, 638). There is a par. passage in bQid., 40a (Str.-B., I, 466); cf. Str.-B., IV, Index s.v. "Kapital."

[6] Cf. Ab RN, 16 (6a) in Str.-B., IV, 474.

[7] σφραγίζειν τὸν καρπόν, the sack of corn is sealed, Deissmann NB, 65 f.; BGU, I, p. 250, 21: σφράγεισον τὸ σειτάριον; M.-J. Lagrange, Épître aux Romains = Études Bibliques, 13 (1922) on R. 15:28 : to seal is to bring to a close, to close. Ltzm. R., 123.

[8] A. Meyer, Das Rätsel des Jk. = ZNW Beih., 10 (1930), 263; Ep. Ar., 232; Herm. s., 9, 19, 2.

In Jn. Christ Himself is compared with the seed. His death is the decisive precondition of a rich harvest of fruit, Jn. 12:24. [9]

† ἄκαρπος.

a. Lit. "unfruitful," in the LXX only at Jer. 2:6 : γῆ; Herm. s., 2, 3; of the elm which does not bear any edible fruit; Jos. Ant., 2, 213 : of Sarah ; Epict. Diss., I, 17, 9 : ξύλον. In the NT Jd. 12 : δένδρα. Figur. "bearing no profit" : Wis. 15:4 : πόνος σκιαγράφων; Plat. Phaedr., 277a : λόγοι.

In the NT it is always fig. except at Jd. 12 (→ infra). The fruitfulness of the Christian, i.e., the translation of his commitment to God and to Christ into righteousness of life, is the presupposition of his acceptance in the last judgment (2 Pt. 1:8 : ἄκαρπος with ἀργός; → καρπός). Hence the righteous must not be unfruitful (Tt. 3:14, with καλῶν ἔργων προΐστασθαι). It is a mark of heretics that they are unprofitable in what is good, Jd. 12. Bad works can be described as unfruitful, Eph. 5:11, since they are not accompanied by the salvation of him who does them, → 614 f. In the prayer of those who speak with tongues the νοῦς is unfruitful, 1 C. 14:14. Mt. 13:22 and par. refer to the unfruitfulness of preaching.

† καρποφορέω.

a. Lit. "to bear fruit," in the LXX only at Hab. 3:17 (συκῆ) and Wis. 10:7. In the NT Mk. 4:28 : ἡ γῆ. b. Figur. Philo Som., II, 272 : ὧν ἐκαρποφόρησεν ἡ ψυχὴ καλῶν; II, 173 : αὕτη (ἡ ψυχὴ) δ᾽ ἐστὶν ἀμπελὼν ἱερώτατος, τὸ θεῖον βλάστημα καρποφορῶν, ἀρετήν; Cher., 84 : ἀρετάς.

In the NT, except at Mk. 4:28 (→ supra), it is always figurative, → καρπός. It is used of the righteous, Mk. 4:20 and par. Works are the fruit of the righteous, Col. 1:10. The righteous bring fruit to God (R. 7:4) as sinful passions do to death (7:5). The evangelical word of truth brings forth fruit in those who receive the epistle, as it does in all the world (Col. 1:6). [1]

Hauck

---

[9] Cf. the image in 1 C. 15:36 ff.; Epict. Diss., IV, 8, 36; there is no connection with the Eleusinian mysteries, for there the idea of bringing forth fruit is not central, Clemen, 280; G. Anrich, *Das antike Mysterienwesen in seinem Einfluss auf das Christentum* (1894), 146, n. 1.

κ α ρ π ο φ ο ρ έ ω. [1] Mid., the only instance apart from BMI, 918. The same thought occurs in 4 Esr. 3:20; 9:31: "For lo, I sow in you my law, and it shall bring forth in you the fruits of righteousness."

> καρτερέω, προσκαρτερέω,
> προσκαρτέρησις

† καρτερέω.

a. "To be strong," "to be courageous," "to endure," e.g., ῥᾷον παραινεῖν ἢ παθόντα καρτερεῖν, Eur. Alc., 1078, θαρρῶν καὶ καρτερῶν, Plat. Theaet., 157d, ἐπὶ τῇ ζητήσει ἐπιμείνωμέν τε καὶ καρτερήσωμεν, Plat. La., 194a, πῶς ἐσιώπας; πῶς ἐκαρτέρεις; Epict. Diss., I, 26, 12. b. "To endure steadfastly," "to bear": τὰ δ' ἀδύναθ' ἡμῖν καρτερεῖν οὐ ῥᾴδιον, Eur. Iph. Aul., 1370, ... σώματός τε καὶ ψυχῆς κακώσεις ... καρτερήσουσιν, Philo Agric., 152. The word is a term used in Gk. ethics with reference to the right attitude and conduct of the wise.

In the LXX it is used for חזק hi, "to hold fast to," Job 2:9: עֹדְךָ מַחֲזִיק בְּתֻמָּתֶךָ; μέχρι τίνος καρτερήσεις, where καρτερεῖν means "to endure," "to suffer," and פָּעָה "to groan," "to cry": ἐκαρτέρησα ὡς ἡ τίκτουσα, Is. 42:14, where the groaning of a woman in labour is changed into the patient endurance of a woman in labour. At Sir. 2:2 καρτέρησον is an admonition along with several others which are to be observed in the service of God. As a term familiar in Gk. ethics, it recurs frequently in 4 Macc. (9:9, 28; 10:1, 11; 13:11; 14:9) in the context of martyrdom, and in this connection it has the undoubted sense of "endure." In the sense of "to persevere" cf. also 2 Macc. 7:17. At Sir. 12:15 it is used for התכלכל (from כּוּל), "to restrain oneself." [1]

In the NT καρτερεῖν occurs only at Hb. 11:27 in the chapter on faith: πίστει κατέλιπεν Αἴγυπτον, μὴ φοβηθεὶς τὸν θυμὸν τοῦ βασιλέως· τὸν γὰρ ἀόρατον ὡς ὁρῶν ἐκαρτέρησεν: "In faith Moses left Egypt, and did not fear the wrath of the king. Having him who is invisible before his eyes, he endured." [2] Faith is the presupposition of endurance in a difficult situation. Faith makes it possible. We cannot be sure whether the leaving of Egypt relates to the wrath of the king, to the flight of Moses after the slaying of the Egyptian, or to the exodus under Moses. The basis of the endurance which has faith as its presupposition is: τὸν ἀόρατον ὡς ὁρῶν. The faith which makes endurance possible reaches through to Him who is invisible and grasps Him as something visible and present. The general elucidation of the faith which orientates itself to God (ἔστιν δὲ πίστις ... πραγμάτων ἔλεγχος οὐ βλεπομένων ... πιστεῦσαι γὰρ δεῖ τὸν προσερχόμενον [τῷ] θεῷ ὅτι ἔστιν, Hb. 11:1, 6) finds here a concrete illustration. What gives faith its distinctive quality is God's invisibility, not His grace, as in Paul. [3] It is thus essential to the NT concept of faith that man should have, and that in difficult situations he should be empowered for action by, a faith in the invisible but efficacious existence of God. This faith, which is exemplified in the OT, stands alongside faith in the God who is revealed and who has given Himself to us in Jesus Christ. Indeed, it is the presupposition of this specifically NT faith. [4]

κ α ρ τ ε ρ έ ω. Pape, Pass., s.v. Wnd. Hb. on 11:27.

[1] In Σ we find the verb at Mi. 7:18 for חוק (LXX συνέχειν), in 'A Zech. 12:5, which reads pi of אמץ whereas LXX assumes מצא [Bertram].

[2] G. H. Whitaker in ET, 27 (1915/16), 186 appeals to passages in Plut. in favour of "to direct one's eyes to ..."

[3] Wnd. Hb. on 11:27.

[4] Cf. R. 3:27 and 4:16-21.

† προσκαρτερέω.

The verb προσκαρτερέω is common in Gk.; it occurs in Gk. and Hellen. inscr. and pap. (e.g., Ditt. Syll.³, 717, 84; Or., 383, 130 and 168 etc.). Its basic meaning is "to stay by," "to persist at," "to remain with." 1. In connection with persons it means "to be loyal to someone," e.g.: θεραπαίνας τὰς Νεαίρᾳ τότε προσκαρτερούσας, Ps.-Demosth. Or., 59, 155. Cf. προσεκαρτέρει τῷ Τίτῳ, Polyb., 24, 5, 3; Diog. L., VIII, 11, 14. 2. In connection with objects it means a. "to occupy oneself diligently with something," "to pay persistent attention to" : ... προσεκαρτέρουν ταύτῃ (τῇ πολιορκίᾳ) κατὰ τὸ δυνατόν, Polyb., 1, 55, 4; τῇ καθέδρᾳ, Jos. Ant., 5, 130; τῇ γεωργίᾳ, P. Amh., 65, 3; νηστείαις, Pol., 7, 2; b. "to hold fast to something" : τῇ κατὰ τὴν δίαιταν ἐπιμελείᾳ προσκαρτερῶν, Polyb., 1, 59, 12; τῇ ἐλπίδι, Pol., 8, 1; c. "continually to be in," οὗτοι προσεκαρτέρουν ἐν τῇ οἰκίᾳ 'Ιωακίμ, Sus. (Θ) 6.

In the LXX it is the rendering of the hitp of רהב, "to pluck up courage," Nu. 13:20 : וְהִתְחַזַּקְתֶּם וּלְקַחְתֶּם מִפְּרִי הָאָרֶץ; προσκαρτερήσαντες λήμψεσθε ἀπὸ τῶν καρπῶν τῆς γῆς. Here προσκαρτερεῖν, without obj., is a stronger form of καρτερεῖν to express the hitp of the Heb. Cf. also — without Heb. original — Tob. 5:8 (only S) in the sense of μένειν, ὑπομένειν ("to expect someone").

In the NT προσκαρτερεῖν occurs in sense 2. c. at Mk. 3:9 : καὶ εἶπεν τοῖς μαθηταῖς αὐτοῦ, ἵνα πλοιάριον προσκαρτερῇ αὐτῷ διὰ τὸν ὄχλον, "to be continually ready." At Ac. 2:46 : καθ' ἡμέραν τε προσκαρτεροῦντες ὁμοθυμαδὸν ἐν τῷ ἱερῷ, it is again to be taken in 2. c., "to be continually in." It occurs in sense 2. a. at R. 13:6 : λειτουργοὶ γὰρ θεοῦ εἰσιν εἰς αὐτὸ τοῦτο προσκαρτεροῦντες; rulers are God's servants and in all their work and demands, even in their demands for taxes — the statement ends with an insistence on the obligation to pay taxes — they must have regard to the fulfilment of their ministry. They are God's servants and wait continually on their task. In this connection it is significant that Paul refers to a divine service in the earthly sphere which is discharged by Gentiles too, for the authorities of which he speaks are Gentiles. Finally, προσκαρτερέω is used in sense 1. at Ac. 8:13 with reference to the attachment of the baptised Simon Magus to Philip the deacon: καὶ βαπτισθεὶς ἦν προσκαρτερῶν τῷ Φιλίππῳ, and at Ac. 10:7 : στρατιώτην εὐσεβῆ τῶν προσκαρτερούντων αὐτῷ, with reference to the soldier's waiting upon the centurion.

The term is theologically significant when used in sense 2. b. for "to hold fast to," with prayer, and in two passages the teaching of the apostles, as the object of this clinging. When the disciples were waiting for the Spirit, we read concerning them : οὗτοι πάντες ἦσαν προσκαρτεροῦντες ὁμοθυμαδὸν τῇ προσευχῇ, Ac. 1:14. The reference is to common prayer, and this underlies the apostolic election of which we have an account in Ac. 1:15 ff. προσευχή (→ II, 807 f.) is prayer in concert, whether it be the prayer of thanksgiving, petition, or adoration. Every great decision in the apostolic period, and in the whole life of early Christianity, is sustained by persistent prayer. In this prayer Christians with thanksgiving and worship brought their decisions and their cause as petitions to God, seeking guidance and direction and clarity from Him. This persistence in prayer, which is just as natural as prayer itself, is determined — we can trace the sequence exactly — by looking to Jesus. Jesus, often in night-long prayer, brought His decisions, His cause, and those connected with it, before God. As the Son, He sought to do the

---

π ρ ο σ κ α ρ τ ε ρ έ ω. E. Schürer, SAB (1897), 214 f.; Moult.-Mill., s.v.

Father's work in an ever new experience of unity with the will and intention and nature of the Father, to receive power for this purpose, and to realise that He was hidden in the Father's hand (→ εὔχομαι, II, 803 f.). He not only directed His disciples to pray in this way (Lk. 11:1-13); He also told them to persist in prayer (Lk. 18:1-8). But this involves a different attitude and manner of prayer from those customary in contemporary Judaism, which had fixed hours and patterns of prayer. [1] The disciples continued the type of prayer which they had seen in Jesus and which He commanded them. And they in turn passed it on to primitive Christianity. In this they stood apart from both the Jewish and the Gentile world around them. The distinction in the nature and attitude of prayer is grounded in the new relationship to God which Jesus granted to His followers and which He Himself enjoyed, namely, unity with the Father in the divine sonship which makes Christians too the children of God and which leads them to the filial obedience that does the Father's will and to the filial confidence that trusts the Father's care. Prayer seeks the Father's will and guidance in human need and indecision. Hence when the apostles, as leaders of the community, hand over to others the tasks imposed by care and charity, they confess : ἡμεῖς δὲ τῇ προσευχῇ καὶ τῇ διακονίᾳ τοῦ λόγου προσκαρτερήσομεν, Ac. 6:4. Thus the Christian communities are admonished : τῇ προσευχῇ προσκαρτεροῦντες, along with joy in hope and patience in tribulation, R. 12:12, and τῇ προσευχῇ προσκαρτερεῖτε ..., Col. 4:2. Luke sketches the Christian community for us in Ac. 2:42 : ἦσαν δὲ προσκαρτεροῦντες τῇ διδαχῇ τῶν ἀποστόλων καὶ τῇ κοινωνίᾳ, τῇ κλάσει τοῦ ἄρτου καὶ ταῖς προσευχαῖς. With assembly for prayer we find the common meal, fellowship and apostolic doctrine. Persistence in these things is a practical fulfilment of the direction of the Lord to "continue in my word" (Jn. 8:31). [2] Hence the word προσκαρτερεῖν, used to describe the life of the community, expresses one aspect of the power and vitality of primitive Christianity.

† προσκαρτέρησις.

The word προσκαρτέρησις, found in Eph. 6:18, also occurs in two inscr. discovered at Panticapaeum on the Black Sea, in which there is reference to the manumission of slaves and which stand under Jewish influence. [1] A condition of manumission is (No. 52): χωρὶς ἱς τὴν προσευχὴν θωπείας τε καὶ προσκαρτερήσεως (with the reservation of a reverent attachment to the place of worship, cf. No. 53). The inscr. date from a period after 80 A.D., and in them προσκαρτέρησις has the sense of continuation, persistence, attachment. Cf. also [2] Philodem. Philos. Περὶ Ῥητορικῆς (ed. S. Sudhaus [1892], p. 11, 36).

In the NT προσκαρτέρησις occurs only at Eph. 6:18 : προσευχόμενοι ἐν παντὶ καιρῷ ἐν πνεύματι, καὶ εἰς αὐτὸ ἀγρυπνοῦντες ἐν πάσῃ προσκαρτερήσει καὶ δεήσει περὶ πάντων τῶν ἁγίων ... Part of the spiritual warfare which the

---

[1] Str.-B., II, 237 f.

[2] Cf. Tanch. נח 9a : "... in order that they may continue in their doctrine at Babylon from that day until to-day."

π ρ ο σ κ α ρ τ έ ρ η σ ι ς. Deissmann LO, 80; Schürer, III⁴, 24, 93.

[1] Inscriptiones Antiquae Orae Septentrionalis Ponti Euxini Graecae et Latinae, ed. Basilius Latyschev, II (Petropoli, 1890).

[2] Liddell-Scott, s.v.

Christian has to wage in daily life is the prayer which must be constantly offered in faith. The particular admonition is that in this prayer we are to see to it that along with intercession for all the saints (and for the apostle) who are engaged in this battle there should also be endurance or perseverance in prayer. Prayer knits together the Church militant with a firm bond. It establishes the community in the power of God. The bond should not be broken. Indeed, it should become increasingly close. The roots should go deeper and deeper into the sphere of God's life and power. To this end, there is need of persistence — ἐν παντὶ καιρῷ, ἐν πάσῃ προσκαρτερήσει. Prayer is not just a pious exercise. It is serious work. It is part of the battle, of our spiritual warfare.

Grundmann

καταβαίνω → I, 522.

> **† καταβολή**

"Laying down," "casting down," in the case of plants a tt. for the casting of seed into the bosom of the earth: σπέρματα εἰς γῆν ἢ εἰς μήτραν καταβαλλόμενα, M. Ant., IV, 36, applied also to the sexual function of the male, Luc. Amores, 19: τοῖς μὲν ἄρρεσιν ἰδίας καταβολὰς σπερμάτων χαρισαμένη, τὸ θῆλυ δ' ὥσπερ γονῆς τι δοχεῖον ἀποφήνασα. Gal. De Naturae Potent., I, 6, 11 (ed. Marquardt-Müller-Helmreich, Script. Min., III [1893]), Philo Op. Mund., 132 etc. Plut. Aquane An Ignis Sit Utilior, 2 (II, 956a): ἅμα τῇ πρώτῃ καταβολῇ τῶν ἀνθρώπων (of the begetting of individuals); of the "sowing" of a war, Jos. Bell., 2, 409 and 417; of the laying of the foundations of a building or government, Polyb., 13, 6, 2: καταβολὴν ποιεῖσθαι τυραννίδος, cf. Hb. 6:1; ἐκ καταβολῆς, from the basis up, i.e., fundamentally, Polyb., I, 36, 8. The verb καταβάλλειν is common in the LXX, e.g., Prv. 25:28, but the noun occurs only at 2 Macc. 2:29: ἀρχιτέκτονι τῆς ὅλης καταβολῆς.

In the NT the word is used 1. for the "foundation of the world,"[1] in the phrase ἀπὸ (πρὸ) καταβολῆς κόσμου, often to denote time, Mt. 13:35; Lk. 11:50; Hb. 4:3; 9:26, but predominantly in the context of salvation history. Thus ἀπὸ καταβολῆς κόσμου expresses the eternity of the divine plan of salvation, which was conceived before all ages and which is fulfilled in the last time, Mt. 25:34; Rev. 13:8; 17:8. In the form πρὸ καταβολῆς κόσμου the phrase expresses the pretemporality of the divine action, Jn. 17:24 (love for the Son), 1 Pt. 1:20 (the election of the Son), Eph. 1:4 (the election of believers). The Rabbis speak similarly of the divine foreordination from the beginning of creation.[2]

κ α τ α β ο λ ή. [1] Schl. Mt., 444, J., 325 translates "from the sowing of the human race," but this figure is alien to the Bible and the parallel of κτίζειν suggests that the image is that of laying foundations.

[2] מִתְּחִלַּת בְּרִיָּתוֹ שֶׁל עוֹלָם (= ἀπ' ἀρχῆς κτίσεως), Pesikt., 21, 145a; Midr. Est., 1, 1 (82a). From the beginning of the creation of the world God has prepared for each what is allotted to him. The same thought occurs with the variation "before" in Tanch. וירא 48a: "This portion was assigned to them before the world was created." Tanch. מצורע 26a: "Before God made man, He appointed every chastisement for him," Str.-B., I, 982.

2. In Hb. 11:11 δύναμιν εἰς καταβολὴν σπέρματος is used of the sexual function of the male. Though his ability to procreate had failed (v. 12 : νενεκρωμένου), Abraham received the power to do so through faith in God's promise. On the Jewish view, καταβολὴ σπέρματος can also be referred to the woman,[3] but in this verse the context, and especially the continuation (v. 12 : ἀφ᾽ ἑνός sc. Abraham ; νενεκρωμένου), forces us to take Abraham as the subject in v. 11. An early corruption of the text seems to be responsible for καὶ αὐτὴ Σάρρα. Westcott-Hort (Nestle) and Rgg. Hb. conjecture αὐτῇ Σάρρᾳ, "in sexual intercourse with Sarah"; others regard καὶ αὐτὴ Σάρρα as a gloss.

Hauck

καταγγελεύς, καταγγέλλω → I, 70 ff.

καταγελάω → I, 658 ff.

καταγωνίζομαι → I, 135 n. 7; 137 f.

καταδικάζω, καταδίκη

† καταδικάζω.

A. καταδικάζω outside the New Testament.

1. In the act. καταδικάζω is used for "to condemn," esp. in law. a. It is first used absol. : Plat. Leg., XII, 958c, of the judicial authority ; Philo Flacc., 54; Deus. Imm., 75. b. It is also related to persons and objects, so that we have two main types. The older use is with the person in the gen. and the object — denoting the punishment — in the acc. Hdt., I, 45 : ἐπειδὴ σεωυτοῦ καταδικάζεις θάνατον (to death); Jos. Bell., 4, 274 : καταδικάζοιεν ὅλου τοῦ ἔθνους ἀτιμίαν (to ignominy). Instead of the acc. of object we also find the inf., Jos. Ant., 10, 204 act. : μὴ ζῆν; Luc. Historiae Verae, I, 29 pass. : ἀποθανεῖν.[1] Yet in later Gk. καταδικάζειν is always used with acc. of person. LXX Lam. 3:36 : καταδικάσαι ἄνθρωπον ἐν τῷ κρίνεσθαι αὐτόν (עִנָּה pi); Da. 1:10 Θ : μήποτε καταδικάσητε τὴν κεφαλήν μου τῷ βασιλεῖ (חוב); Wis. 11:10 : ἐκείνους καταδικάζων; Prayer of Man. (LXX):13 (Odae 12): μηδὲ καταδικάσῃς με. In this case the dat. is normally used to denote the punishment : θανάτῳ : Plut. Instituta Laconica, 42 (II, 239 f.); Wis. 2:20; Test. Sol. D, IV, 2. Instead of the dat. we also find ἐπί c. dat.: Jos. Ant., 16, 369 : ἐπὶ θανάτῳ. εἴς τι, Preisigke Sammelbuch, I, 4639, 3 (3rd. cent. A.D.): εἰς ἀλαβαστρῶνα, Corp. Herm., II, 17a. Acc., Dio C., 68, 1: θάνα-

---

[3] Cf. bNidda, 31a : "His father gives the white seed ..., his mother gives the red seed ..., the Holy One, blessed be He, gives the spirit, the soul ..."; ibid., 31b : R. Ami (c. 280): "If the seed of the woman comes first, a boy is born, but if that of the man comes first, a girl is born, as we read in Lv. 12:2 ..." We have here a primitive view of the sexual act according to which there is separated from the woman in the orgasm a "red seed" (blood) corresponding to the male process ("white seed") [Kuhn].

κ α τ α δ ι κ ά ζ ω. [1] For the pap. cf. Preisigke Wört., s.v.

τον. c. The ground of condemnation is in the gen.: Polyb., 22, 4, 7: ἱεροσυλίας; Jos. Ant., 1, 75 : τῆς κακίας, though we also find ἐπί c. dat.: Diod. S., IV, 76, 4 : ἐπὶ φόνῳ (pass.).

2. In the pass. καταδικασθείς is esp. common. Plat. Leg., XII, 958c (→ 621); Philo Leg. All., III, 199 : ὑπὸ τοῦ θεοῦ καταδικασθείς; Deus Imm., 112 : ἐν δικαστηρίῳ καταδικασθέντας, of judicial condemnation ; Plant., 175 : ἐξ ἐρήμου καταδικασθέντος, of judgment by default. [2] Cf. Luc. de Calumnia, 8; Wis. 17:10 : πονηρία καταδικαζομένη. In the pap. the pass. καταδικάζομαι means "to lose the case." [3]

3. Mid.: "As a plaintiff to aim at or to achieve the condemnation of the opponent in one's favour, to win one's case," τινός; Demosth. Or., 47, 18 : ἐμοῦ ἀδίκως κατεδικάσατο. [4] Hence ὁ καταδικασάμενος is the plaintiff, Plat. Leg., IX, 857a. In the LXX it is a rendering of ‏רשע‎ hi : ψ 93:21: αἷμα ἀθῷον καταδικάσονται, "they seek to their own advantage the condemnation of innocent blood" ; Job 34:29 : καὶ τίς καταδικάσεται;

B. καταδικάζω in the New Testament.

Apart from Mt. 12:7: οὐκ ἂν κατεδικάσατε τοὺς ἀναιτίους (on the acc. of person → 621), καταδικάζειν, καταδικασθῆναι is always used in the absol. in the NT. The ἐκ in Mt. 12:37: ἐκ τῶν λόγων σου καταδικασθήσῃ — opp. δικαιωθήσῃ [5] — not only serves to denote the ground of condemnation (though → supra) but also refers to the proof adduced by the judge. [6] The forensic meaning of δικαιόω is also confirmed here by the contrast (→ II, 217). In Lk. 6:37: καὶ μὴ καταδικάζετε, καὶ οὐ μὴ καταδικασθῆτε (→ supra) the antonym is ἀπολύειν, "to acquit," rather than δικαιοῦν. At Jm. 5:6 we find κατεδικάσατε in the summons to the hard-hearted rich who secure the condemnation of the innocent poor by an abuse of justice.

† καταδίκη. [1]

1. "Condemnation." a. Normally it is used concretely in the judicial sense, e.g., condemnation to banishment and exile : Plut. Coriolanus, 20 (I, 223d), cf. 29 (I, 227d). To crucifixion, Jos. Bell., 4, 317; cf. Epict. Diss., II, 1, 35 (with δεσμωτήριον, ἀδοξία). b. More generally it is used for the sentence of moral condemnation passed on an action : Philo Spec. Leg., III, 116 (on parents who are lacking in love).

2. More commonly καταδίκη means "punishment": Wis. 12:27: τὸ τέρμα τῆς καταδίκης on the Egyptians. It is used a. preferably for a financial penalty, Thuc., V, 49, 1; Demosth. Or., 47 and 52; also in the pap. for the sum which a plaintiff can

---

[2] Ibid., s.v. ἔρημος.
[3] Ibid., s.v., with bibl.; Moult.-Mill., 326.
[4] In the pap., Preisigke Wört., s.v.
[5] Elsewhere in classical Gk. we also find ἀποδικάζειν as antonym : Aristot. Pol., II, 8, p. 1268b, 18. In the pap. it is used in the sense "to dismiss a case by acquittal," cf. Preisigke Wört. and Fachwörter, s.v. Rabb. par. for the antithesis καταδικάζειν—δικαιοῦν may be found in Schl. Mt., 412.
[6] For Rabb. material cf. Schl. Mt., loc. cit.

κ α τ α δ ί κ η. [1] Constructed from καταδικάζω.

claim, P. Hibeh, I, 32, 7 etc. [2] Cf. Jos. Ant., 17, 338 : punishment by financial loss. b. The word is also used in the imaginative depiction of punishment, e.g., Luc. Dialogi Mortuorum, 10 (of the judgment of the dead with the punishments of wheels, boulders and vultures); Test. Sol. 13:4 : στομάτων καταδίκη, as judicial torment; Corp. Herm., X, 8a : ψυχῆς κακῆς.

In the NT it occurs only in Ac. 25:15 : αἰτούμενοι κατ' αὐτοῦ καταδίκην. [3] When Festus explains to Agrippa the case against Paul, he says that the Jewish authorities were seeking his condemnation.

Schrenk

καταδουλόω → II, 279.

κατάθεμα, καταθεματίζω → I, 354 f.

καταισχύνω → I, 189 ff.

κατακαυχάομαι → καυχάομαι.

κατακληρονομέω → κλῆρος.

κατάκριμα, κατακρίνω, κατάκρισις
→ κρίνω.

κατακυριεύω → κύριος.

καταλαλέω, -λαλία, -λαλος
→ λαλέω.

καταλαμβάνω → λαμβάνω.

καταλείπω, κατάλειμμα → λείπω.

καταλιθάζω → λιθάζω.

καταλλάσσω, καταλλαγή → I, 254 ff.

καταλύω, κατάλυμα → λύω.

καταμανθάνω → μανθάνω.

καταμαρτυρέω → μαρτυρέω.

κατανπάω, ὑπανπάω, ὑπάνπησις	→ ἀπάνπησις, I, 380 f.

† κατανπάω.

The word is commonly attested, esp. in later literature and ordinary speech (Polyb., Diod. S., inscr., LXX). In the NT it is found only in Ac. (9 or 10 times) and figur. in Paul (4 times including Eph.). The simple ἀντᾶν (from ἄντα "over against") is common from the time of Hom., but does not occur in the NT or LXX. κατανπᾶν means lit. "to come down to a meeting," but the normal sense is simply "to reach a goal." The goal is set, the end determined, and κατανπᾶν simply denotes the meeting of this set goal and prescribed conclusion.

1. "To reach an external goal (εἰς)" : cod D Ac. 13:51 (εἰς Ἰκόνιον); 16:1 (εἰς Δέρβην); 18:19 and 18:24 (εἰς Ἔφεσον); 20:15 (ἄντικρυς Χίου); 21:7 (εἰς Πτολεμαΐδα); 25:13 (εἰς Καισάρειαν); 27:12 (εἰς Φοίνικα); 28:13 (εἰς Ῥήγιον). Ac. uses κατανπᾶν for reaching the goal of a journey.

2. "To reach the goal ordained or set for a man (εἰς)," Ac. 26:7: ἐπαγγελίας ... εἰς ἥν ἐλπίζει κατανπῆσαι. The twelve tribes serve God day and night in the

---

[2] Cf. further Preisigke Wört. and Fachwörter, s.v.; P. M. Meyer, Jurist. Pap. (1920), 71, Col. II, 32, n. and p. 258.

[3] Textus receptus has δίκην in view of Ac. 25:3 (correction).

hope of reaching the promise. God establishes the goal by His Word and act, and He does not do things without end or purpose. In faith man embraces God's Word, fixing his hope on the goal set thereby. This hope demands the commitment of the whole man (Phil. 2:12-13), and Paul recognises Israel's total and enduring commitment to the promise (Ac. 26:7). Yet this zeal for God does not achieve true knowledge of God, as we are told expressly in R. 10:2. With Ac. 26:7 we may compare Phil. 3:11: εἴ πως καταντήσω εἰς τὴν ἐξανάστασιν τὴν ἐκ νεκρῶν. This, too, is eschatological. By suffering Christ draws Paul into His death and fashions him in His own likeness with a view to resurrection from the dead. He draws the apostle into His death in order to lead him beyond death. The work of Christ, too, has a goal for which we hope with fear and trembling, namely, the resurrection. What is in doubt is not the attainment of this goal, but our personal share in it.[1] The divine goals always transcend individuals, though they include individual participation.

According to Eph. 4:13 the goal of the community is the unity of faith and of knowledge of the Son of God; it is perfection and maturity in the fulness of Christ (μέχρι καταντήσωμεν οἱ πάντες εἰς τὴν ἑνότητα τῆς πίστεως καὶ τῆς ἐπιγνώσεως τοῦ υἱοῦ τοῦ θεοῦ). Here, too, God sets for the community a task and destiny which is orientated to the end of history and which no believer can evade, namely, the growth of the community to unity and ripeness of knowledge. Because the Son of God is a unity, unity is also determined for our faith and knowledge. Once again the movement of καταντᾶν denotes the way to a goal and a totality beyond the immediate situation or generation. The unity guarantees the security and solidity of faith. But its one basis is the unity and historicity of the person of Christ.[2] The goal is certain knowledge of divine truth in contrast to the vacillation and variety of human opinion (Harless). Here, too, the goal is eschatological. But it is also a task of the divine word and the Church's ministry, to which is committed care for the body of Christ (Eph. 4:11-12).[3] Linked with unity is totality, maturity, perfection, undividedness. In Eph. and Hb. unity and perfection, ἑνότης and τελειότης, belong together. There is one knowledge in the community only when the Son of God dwells undividedly in our hearts (Harless). Unity and perfection are the goal of the community, and Christ gives individuals a share in this unity and perfection. By the movement of καταντᾶν initiated by the Word of God the individual grows to the goal of totality.[4]

κ α τ α ν τ ά ω. [1] "Paul has no control over the final goal, as some think. Resurrection in the glory of Christ — the reference is to this alone and not to resurrection to judgment — can only be hoped for with fear and trembling" (G. Heinzelmann, NT Deutsch, II² [1935], 528).

[2] In Eph. and Hb. unity and uniqueness, unity and absoluteness, and unity and perfection are all interwoven into close patterns of thought. Hence the theology of ἑνότης (Eph. 4:4-5) is closely linked with that of ἐφάπαξ (Hb. 9:12) in the NT.

[3] G. C. A. v. Harless, Commentar über den Brief Pauli an die Ephesier³ (1858), 380: "The ἀνὴρ τέλειος, the community as a great totality which has attained to maturity, is the goal which all human teachers have thus far been seeking to achieve; hence Calvin is right when he notes: hic admonet, usum ministerii non esse temporalem, sed perpetuum, quam diu in mundo versamur."

[4] Op. cit., 379: "The fruit of faith and knowledge is the unity in which Christ dwells undividedly in our hearts. To knowledge He gives unshakable truth, to faith inward love, and all this by the Spirit in whom He dwells within us" (cf. 3:16-17).

In a comparison 1 Cl., 23, 4 says : ἐν καιρῷ ὀλίγῳ εἰς πέπειρον καταντᾷ ὁ καρπὸς τοῦ ξύλου. As in a short time the fruit of the tree ripens, so the counsel of God will suddenly be consummated. Here the teleological significance emerges even in a figure. 1 Cl., 63, 1 points to the common goal of the Church which is to be reached without reproach : ὅπως ἐπὶ τὸν προκείμενον ἡμῖν ἀληθείᾳ σκοπὸν δίχα παντὸς μώμου καταντήσωμεν. In primitive Christianity, then, καταντᾶν often denotes the goal which is set by God, which is appointed for the whole community, and which points to the end of history. That the familiar image of a course may be linked with καταντᾶν is shown in 1 Cl., 6, 2 : ἐπὶ τὸν τῆς πίστεως βέβαιον δρόμον κατήντησαν. The goal of faith is perfect fidelity even to death, after the example set by Christ. Pol., 1, 2 describes the passion of Christ in these words : ὃς ὑπέμεινεν ὑπὲρ τῶν ἁμαρτιῶν ἡμῶν ἕως θανάτου καταντῆσαι. In the post-apostolic period καταντᾶν acquires increasing significance in terms of the theology of martyrdom.

3. "To come, to attain to, man." In 1 C. 10:11 (εἰς οὓς τὰ τέλη τῶν αἰώνων κατήντηκεν) it is presupposed that the former period and fashion of the world passes away (1 C. 7:31) and that this passing is discernible to the community (cf. Hb. 1:2 : ἐπ' ἐσχάτου τῶν ἡμερῶν τούτων; 9:26 : ἐπὶ συντελείᾳ τῶν αἰώνων). In a surprising way visible only to faith the end of the old aeon and the dawn of the new has come upon the community (κατήντηκεν). [6] From eternity there thus comes to the community a divine action which carries within it a purpose and meaning for men (καταντᾶν). The same movement towards the community from an unspecified starting-point may be seen in 1 C. 14:36 : ἢ εἰς ὑμᾶς μόνους (sc. ὁ λόγος τοῦ θεοῦ) κατήντησεν; The Word of God neither went out from (ἐξῆλθεν) Corinth nor has it come (κατήντησεν) to the Corinthians alone. There are older churches than Corinth, and others which live by the Word of God independently of it. Hence the church has a duty to listen to the word of its brothers and to test its own knowledge.

† ὑπαντάω, † ὑπάντησις.

"Encounter" (συνάντησις and → ἀπάντησις are also found in the LXX). The term occurs elsewhere in Gk. and Hellen. literature (Appian Bell. Civ., IV, 6; Jos. Ant., 11, 327; Bell., 7, 100; Ditt. Syll.³, 798, 16, 23). ὑπάντησις is found in the LXX only in variant readings : 1 Ch. 14:8 (cod A); Prv. 7:15 (cod B); Jdt. 2:6 (cod א); 1 Macc. 9:39 (cod א). Following similar LXX expressions (ἐκπορεύεσθαι, ἐξέρχεσθαι εἰς συνάντησιν), the NT has ἐξέρχεσθαι εἰς ὑπάντησιν (Mt. 8:34; 25:1; Jn. 12:13), "to go towards someone" (τινί or τινός). We see here the Sem. trend which characterises the first and fourth Gospels (cf. Bik., 3, 3 : יוֹצְאִים לִקְרָאתָם?). [1]

The related term ὑπαντᾶν (with συναντᾶν and ἀπαντᾶν also in the LXX) is found in Gk. literature from the time of Pindar (cf. inscr. and pap.). In the NT it occurs at

---

[5] Pr.-Bauer,³ s.v. : "It is not that man attains to something, but that something attains to him." Cf. the property which accrues by the law of inheritance, BGU, IV, 1169, 21; also P. Oxy., I, 75, 5; II, 248, 11; 274, 19. Cf. too 2 S. 3:29 LXX : καταντησάτωσαν ἐπὶ κεφαλὴν Ἰωάβ καὶ ἐπὶ πάντα τὸν οἶκον τοῦ πατρὸς αὐτοῦ. Cf., too, 2 Macc. 6:14 cod A : μέχρι τοῦ καταντήσαντος αὐτοὺς πρὸς ἐκπλήρωσιν ἁμαρτιῶν κολάσαι; Job 29:13 Σ : εὐλογία ἀπολλυμένου ἐπ' ἐμὲ κατήντα; ψ 31:6 'Α; Ez. 7:12 'Α; and esp. Is. 53:6 Σ : κύριος δὲ καταντῆσαι ἐποίησεν εἰς αὐτὸν τὴν ἀνομίαν πάντων ἡμῶν.

[6] On αἰών I, 197-209; W. Staerk, Soter (1933), 143 ff.; R. Löwe, "Kosmos und Aion," Nt.liche Forschungen, III, 5 (1935).

ὑ π α ν τ ά ω κτλ. [1] Schl. Mt., 294 f.

Mt. 8:28; 28:9; Mk. 5:2; Lk. 8:27 (17:12 ?); Jn. 4:51; 11:20, 30; 12:18; Ac. 16:16. There is considerable interchange between ὑπαντᾶν and ἀπαντᾶν in the MSS (e.g., Lk. 17:12).[2] ὑπαντᾶν is also found in Mart. Pol., 8, 2 and Herm. v., 4, 2, 1. Normally ὑπαντᾶν simply means "to meet," in a hostile sense at Lk. 14:31.[3]

Michel

---

† κατανύσσω, † κατάνυξις

This word is found only once in the NT in a quotation from the OT (R. 11:8, cf. Is. 29:10 and Dt. 29:3). The related verb, a hapax legomenon, is also borrowed from a verse in the Ps. (Ac. 2:37; cf. ψ 108:16). Paul finds in the words of Is. confirmation for his contention that the hardening of so many Jews is no less God's work than the election of Israel. The context allows us only one rendering of πνεῦμα κατανύξεως, namely, "spirit of stupefaction." This corresponds to the sense of the reference in Is.

Elsewhere in the LXX κατανύσσεσθαι is used for various states in which the free will of the one concerned is more or less obliterated, e.g., horror (Gn. 34:7), contrition (Sir. 14:1), silence (ψ 29:12) and senseless passion (Sus. 10 LXX and Θ). Apart from the LXX κατάνυξις appears only in Christian lit.[1] The simple νύσσω, "to stab," gives to κατανύσσω[2] the sense "to pierce through," "to transfix." But it is hard to believe that this is newly coined by the LXX. The word is already used metaphorically with no very close connection with the sense of piercing. This suggests a prior history for the figurative sense, which would explain why the LXX translator is not aware of the original meaning.

Greeven

καταξιόω → I, 380.   καταπατέω → πατέω.

---

[2] ἀπαντᾶν seems in general to be more common than ὑπαντᾶν (also in the LXX).
[3] Pr.-Bauer, s.v. : " 'To encounter' also in the hostile sense (Xenoph.), Lk. 14:31."
κ α τ α ν ύ σ σ ω κτλ. C. F. A. Fritzsche, *Pauli ad Romanos epistola,* II (1839), 558 ff.
[1] Cf. Thes. Steph., IV, 1160 and Pr.-Bauer, 649 s.v.
[2] A non-biblical instance adduced by Liddell-Scott, 903 s.v. (Phlegon, 36, 4, obj. τοὺς ὀφθαλμούς) has unfortunately not been traced.

| καταπαύω, κατάπαυσις | → ἀναπαύω, ἀνάπαυσις, ἐπαναπαύω. |

† καταπαύω.

"To cause to cease," referred to all kinds of conditions and actions : a. "to end," "to prevent" : Aesch. Suppl., 586 (sicknesses); Hom. Od., 4, 583 (wrath of the gods); ψ 84:4 (the wrath of God). It is also related to persons : b. "to bring someone to the point where he breaks off what he is doing," "to restrain," "to dismiss" : Hdt., I, 130; "to kill," Hom. Il., 16, 618. If καταπαύειν affects me in this sense, it is a painful invasion of my sphere. Yet in relation to persons the same word can bear a very different sense : c. "to bring someone to the point where he ceases to suffer something" (e.g., at the hands of his enemies, Ex. 33:14; Dt. 3:20, and sometimes without mentioning the source), "to give rest to someone," "to bring someone to rest." The fact that a basically negative term can also be used in this positive sense is not to be traced to a passive and quietistic view of life but to recognition of the fact that the way of man, if it is to be purposive, is characterised by a superior encroachment, by a pitiless οὐκ ἐπιθυμήσεις. Hence it is no accident that this usage is essentially known to us only from the LXX, that God alone is the subject of this καταπαύειν, and that the reference is to rest in the promised land (Dt. 3:20; Jos. 1:13 etc.). d. Also linked with this is the fact that the trans. "to cause to cease" and the intrans. "to cease" to some extent impinge upon one another, and the same mood of the same verb is also used in this sense, [1] whether linked with the part. (Gn. 49:33 : κατέπαυσεν ἐπιτάσσων) or in the absol. (Gn. 8:22 : θέρος καὶ ἔαρ οὐ καταπαύσουσιν). Accordingly, it often means (cf. c.) "to rest," Ex. 20:11: κατέπαυσεν τῇ ἡμέρᾳ τῇ ἑβδόμῃ, cf. Gn. 2:2. Outside the LXX the word is very rare in this intrans. sense in the act.; [2] it is more common in the mid. and pass. (occasionally in the LXX, Ex. 16:13; Job 21:34).

In the NT we find b. "to restrain," at Ac. 14:18 : μόλις κατέπαυσαν τοὺς ὄχλους τοῦ μὴ θύειν αὐτοῖς. In Hb. 4 two distinctive OT statements are interrelated, namely, that Joshua had the task of bringing the people to rest in the promised land (κατέπαυσεν, c.), v. 8, and that God rested on the seventh day (κατέπαυσεν, d.), v. 4. Comprehensive reflection on these two facts leads to the conclusion that here, too, the OT points beyond itself, and that the rest is still in the sphere of promise. A true fulfilment of the task of Joshua, as Ps. 95:7 ff. also demonstrates, v. 7, will take a different form from the historical. Since it is from God, it will and must bring a καταπαύειν which corresponds to that of God Himself (cf. 1 C. 15:28). To-day (Hb. 3:7, 15) the μέτοχοι τοῦ Χριστοῦ (3:14) are summoned to be ready for this rest (→ κατάπαυσις). The distinctive LXX use of the term is the normative linguistic instrument by which to describe the way from the OT via the to-day of the NT to the final ends of God.

κ α τ α π α ύ ω κτλ. G. v. Rad, "Es ist noch eine Ruhe vorhanden dem Volke Gottes," ZdZ, 11 (1933), 104-111.

[1] Cf. on this linguistic point Philo Leg. All., III, 5 f.; L. Cohn, Schriften d. jüd.-hell. Lit. in deutscher Übers., III (1919), 18, n. 1.

[2] Cf. Pr.-Bauer καταπαύω, No. 2.

† **κατάπαυσις.**

a. Act. "resting," "being set in a state of rest," figur. "deposition," Hdt., V, 38 (τυράννων). b. Pass. "rest," Theophr. De Ventis, 18 : καταπαύσεις τῶν πνευμάτων. In this sense it is common in the LXX (a. does not occur), → καταπαύω c. and d. : 3 Βασ. 8:56, of the rest of the people ; Ex. 35:2 etc. of the Sabbath ; Is. 66:1: ποῖος τόπος τῆς καταπαύσεώς μου (the rest of God in the sense of His presence with the people). Even without τόπος, κατάπαυσις can also mean the place of rest, e.g., ψ 94:11.

In the NT Ac. 7:49 follows Is. 66:1 in using it of God : "What is the place of my rest ?" Hb. 3:11, 18; 4:1, 3, 5, 10 f., on the basis of Ps. 95:11, refer to the rest (or resting-place ?) of the people. As the promise of Scripture undoubtedly points beyond the servant Moses to fulfilment by the Son (3:1-6), so the rest mentioned on the very first page (Gn. 2:2) points beyond Joshua (4:8) and David (4:7) to the last things. The movement from which flowed the life of creation in the first week will lead to the sacred rest of the Creator, to the seventh day. The people of God waits for this.

Bauernfeind

---

† **καταπέτασμα**

A. **καταπέτασμα outside the New Testament.**

1. The word, lit. "that which is spread out downwards," is rare outside the biblical literature, since "curtain" is usually παραπέτασμα or αὐλαία (from αὐλή, originally the curtains which closed the doors to the court), or as a Lat. loan word βῆλον = *velum.* Nevertheless, it seems even in the Gk. world to have been a tt. for a kind of temple curtain, with παραπέτασμα. Thus as early as 346/5 we find it in an inventory of the temple of Hera at Samos. [1] In the Gk. world curtains of all kinds were used in private homes as well as in temples. In houses and public buildings they could be found on doors, between pillars, on walls, under the ceiling, in front of windows. [2] They were usually thick and gaily coloured, and often of Asiatic origin. [3] In temples they served to cover images which were displayed only on high festivals. [4] They were absolutely essential to the cultic action in the shrines of Hellenistic religions, as in Eastern churches. [5] Apuleius has left a graphic picture of this in the case of Isis. [6] They could also have symbolical significance. [7]

κ α τ α π έ τ α σ μ α. Pr.-Bauer³, 691 f.; Wilke-Grimm, 233 f.; T. Zahn, "Der zerrissene Tempelvorhang," NkZ, 13 (1902), 729-756; H. Laible, *ibid.,* 35 (1924), 287-314; also in Str.-B., III, 733-736; P. Fiebig, "Der zerriss. Tempelvorhang," *Neues Sächs. Kirchenbl.,* 40 (1933), 227-236; C. Schneider, "Studien z. Ursprung liturgischer Einzelheiten östlicher Liturgien, I : Καταπέτασμα," in Κύριος, *Vierteljahrschr. f. Kirchen- u. Geistesgeschichte Osteuropas,* I (1936), *Heft* 1; H. Wenschkewitz, "D. Spiritualisierung der Kultusbegriffe Tempel, Priester u. Opfer im NT," "Αγγελος, 4 (1932), 70-230.

[1] Deissmann LO, 80; O. Hoffmann, *D. griech. Dialekte,* III (1898), 72.
[2] C. Daremberg-E. Saglio, *Dictionnaire des Antiquités Grecques et Romaines* V (1912/17), s.v. *velum,* with rich source material.
[3] L. de Ronchaud, *La tapisserie dans l'antiquité* (1884).
[4] CIG, II, 2886.
[5] Ovid. Fast., II, 563; Cl. Al. Paed., III, 2, 1 ff.
[6] Met., XI, 20.
[7] This seems at least to be suggested in Philo Vit. Mos., II, 87 f., 101. Cf. further Wenschkewitz, *op. cit.*

2. In the LXX καταπέτασμα always denotes a curtain of the temple or tabernacle (פָּרֹכֶת or מָסָךְ). This may be the curtain between the holy place and the holiest of all (Ex. 26:31-35; 27:21; 30:6; 35:12; 37:3 ff.; 40:3, 21-26; Lv. 4:6, 17; 16:2, 12-15; 21:23; 24:3; Nu. 4:5; 2 Ch. 3:14; 1 Macc. 1:22) or it may be that between the temple (tabernacle) and the forecourt (Ex. 26:37; 35:15 [Εξ. 35:12 f.]; 37:5 f., 16; 38:18; 39:4, 19; 40:5; Nu. 3:10, 26; 4:32; 18:7; 3 Βασ. 6:36; Sir. 50:5). Ep. Ar., 86 uses it for the outer curtain, Jos. Ant., 8, 75 for both, and Philo Vit. Mos., II, 101 for the inner (the outer is κάλυμμα). From all accounts the outer curtain has no true cultic significance. It simply replaces the doors when they are opened by day. Joseph. tells us that it was 55 by 16 ells: πέπλος ἦν Βαβυλώνιος, ποικιλτός ἐξ ὑακίνθου καὶ βύσσου, κόκκου τε καὶ πορφύρας, θαυμαστῶς μὲν εἰργασμένος.[8] The colours symbolise totality, and each material represents an element. The inner curtain, on the other hand, is the only dividing line between the holy place and the holiest of all, since the latter has no door.[9] Traditionally it depicts the two cherubim and is made of the finest wool shot through with purple and scarlet.[10] According to one not very secure tradition it was made by 82 maidens who were paid from temple taxes.[11] According to Prot. Ev. Jc., 10, 2 Mary was one of them. The only main point of dispute is whether we have a single curtain (Joseph.) or a double (Mishnah and Talmud in the main).[12] Its size is supposed to have been 40 by 20 ells.[13]

3. The supreme cultic significance of the inner curtain is that it alone conceals the holiest of all, that the high-priest alone may pass through it on the Day of Atonement,[14] and that on the Day of Atonement it, too, is sprinkled with blood.[15] The Talmudic legend of the bleeding curtain shows how easily magical notions could be connected with it.[16] According to the same tradition it was carried in the triumphal procession of Titus. It is not to be seen, however, on the relief on the Titus arch.

4. It is unlikely that synagogues had similar curtains, since one might only represent and not copy the furnishings of the temple. On the other hand, we do not know how binding or even how ancient this prohibition was.[17] There must have been curtains in the synagogues from an early period, and they would be placed before the ark of the Torah (וילון, = velum).[18]

B. καταπέτασμα in the New Testament.

1. In the NT τὸ καταπέτασμα τοῦ ναοῦ was torn on the moment of the death of Jesus (Mt. 27:51; Mk. 15:38; Lk. 23:45). The Evangelists are almost certainly thinking of the inner curtain, since the other had no great significance.[19] The

---

[8] Jos. Bell., 5, 212.
[9] Joma, 5, 1 is almost certainly wrong (→ n. 12).
[10] Cf. also Sheq., 8, 5; bJoma, 54a; Jos. Ant., 8, 75.
[11] Sheq., 8, 5, though the reading is uncertain. bKet., 106a.
[12] Joma, 5, 1; bKet., 106a; bJoma, 54a. Laible's attempt at harmonisation on the basis of Mt. 27:51 is a little too bold, cf. NkZ, 35 (1924), 288.
[13] Jos. Bell., 5, 219; Sheq., 8, 5.
[14] Lv. 16:2, 12-15.
[15] Lv. 4:6, 17; Joma, 5, 4.
[16] bGit., 56b. When Titus cut the curtain with his sword, blood spurted out. R. Eleazar bJose (180) is reported to have seen it full of drops of blood in Rome (T. Joma, 3, 8). Cf. Str.-B., I, 1043-1046.
[17] K. H. Rengstorf, "Zu den Fresken der Villa Torlonia," ZNW, 31 (1932), 33-60.
[18] S. Krauss, Synagogale Altertümer (1922), 373-381. Jüd. Lex., s.v. Parochet.
[19] Though cf. Fiebig and Zahn, op. cit., who argue for the outer, since this alone could be seen by the people. Cf. also G. Dalman, Orte u. Wege Jesu³ (1924) 323. Cf. also W. Bauer, D. Leben Jesu im Zeitalter d. nt.lichen Apokryphen (1909), 230 ff.

underlying conception is that the death of Jesus opened up access to the holy of holies.

Acc. to a fragment of the Naz. Ev. what happened was that the earthquake cracked the upper lintel (*superliminare templi infinitae magnitudinis fractum esse atque divisum*).[20] E. Nestle[21] suggests confusion between פְּרֹכֶת and כַּפְתֹּר, head of the pillar, but this hardly seems likely.[22] The basis is probably a story found also in Joseph., Tacitus and the Talmud to the effect that the temple itself gave warning signs of its approaching destruction.[23] This is how the early Church commonly understood the verses.[24]

2. In three verses Hb. interprets the curtain theologically (6:19; 9:3; 10:20). In each case the reference is to the inner curtain.[25] The heavenly sanctuary, which is in all things a higher prototype of the earthly, has also a curtain, but the true Highpriest, Christ, passes through this. Nor does He do so alone or for His own sake. He does so as the πρόδρομος (6:20) of His people. In 10:20 this veil through which Christ has passed, and through which we pass with Him, is identified with His flesh. The difficult symbolism of this passage suggests that the earthly existence of Jesus has a twofold sense. On the one hand (cf. 2 C. 5:16) it is a veil between the holy of holies and the congregation, but on the other it is the only possible way to the holy of holies.[26]

On the basis of this verse the Eastern Church has found a place for the καταπέτασμα in its liturgy. Even when ousted from its true place on the ciborium pillars of the altar or the triumphal arch, it remains to this day in the three curtains on the three doors of the iconostasis, and it often serves to announce a change of pictures.[27]

Carl Schneider

καταπίνω → πίνω.

καταπίπτω → πίπτω.

κατάρα, καταράομαι
→ I, 448 ff.

καταργέω → I, 452 ff.

καταρτίζω, κατάρτισις, καταρτισμός
→ I, 475 f.

κατασκηνόω → σκῆνος.

κατασκοπέω, κατάσκοπος → σκοπέω.

καταστέλλω, καταστολή → στέλλω.

---

[20] Fr., 23 (Hennecke, 31), quoted in Hier., In Mt. 27:51 (MPL, 26, 236 f.); Ep. ad Hedybiam CXX, 8 (CSEL, 55, 489 ff.).

[21] *Ev. Kirchenbl. f. Württemberg*, 56 (1895), 290 ff.; ZNW, 3 (1902), 167 f.; Nov. Test. Graec. Suppl. (1896), 79.

[22] Cf. Dalman WJ, I, 45; Zn., *op. cit.*, 753. Attempts at harmonisation by Zahn and Laible are too simple. It is possible that the author of Ev. Naz has rationalised with the help of Is. 6:4. The cracking of the lintel is a more likely result of the earthquake than the tearing of the curtain.

[23] Jos. Bell., 6, 290 ff.; bJoma, 39b; jJoma, 43c; Tacitus Hist., V, 13.

[24] Ev. Eb., 52 (Hennecke, 48); Tertullian Marc., IV, 42. Cf. Chrys. Hom. in Mt., 88, 2 (MPG, 58, 826).

[25] τὸ ἐσώτερον τοῦ καταπετάσματος (Lv. 16:2, 12) or τὸ δεύτερον καταπέτασμα.

[26] Cf. Wenschkewitz, 207 f.

[27] F. E. Brightman - C. E. Hammond, *Liturgies Eastern and Western*, I (1896), 590 f.; RE³, II, 226 f., *s.v.* "Bilderwand"; Schneider, *op. cit.*

† καταστρηνιάω

This word, found only at 1 Tm. 5:11,[1] has not been discovered thus far in secular Gk., though it occurs in the LXX. The simple στρηνιάω occurs in the sense of ἀτακτεῖν or τρυφᾶν, "to burn fiercely," "to be covetous," "to be sensually stimulated," cf. later comedy,[2] also Rev. 18:7, 9. The noun στρῆνος occurs in secular literature,[3] and once for תַּעֲנֻג in the sense of "pride" or "arrogance" (LXX 4 Βασ. 19:28), cf. also Rev. 18:3. Early Christian comm. construe 1 Tm. 5:11 in terms of ἀκκισθῶσιν ("to be vain") or θρύπτωνται (θρύψωνται).[4] Etym. it is related to the Lat. *strenuus,* "industrious," "valiant." The ending -ιάω is that of verbs of sickness.[5]

The gen. τοῦ Χριστοῦ is to some extent dependent on κατά. Hence the meaning of 1 Tm. 5:11 is that "they become lascivious against Christ," or that "they burn with sensual desire in opposition to Christ."[6]

The author demands that no widow under 60 should be put on the official list of χῆραι or allowed to serve as a deaconess in the narrower sense,[7] since he fears that younger widows will marry again and will thus be untrue to their office and therewith to Christ. This principle does not rest on dogmatic or ethical considerations, nor does it express an ascetic impulse. It simply arises from the experience of the community, as may be seen from the verses which both precede and follow.

Carl Schneider

κατασφραγίζω → σφραγίς.   κατατομή → τέμνω.

καταφρονέω, καταφρονητής
περιφρονέω

† καταφρονέω.

With the gen. or double gen., sometimes with the acc., more rarely with ἐπί, "to despise someone on account of something," or "to despise something," "to disparage," "to regard in unseemly fashion," "not to be concerned about," "not to fear" : τῶν

κ α τ α σ τ ρ η ν ι ά ω. Pr.-Bauer³, 697; Wilke-Grimm, 235; Thes. Steph., IV, 1254.
[1] Ps.-Ign. Ad Antiochenos, 11 is simply a free quotation from 1 Tm. 5:11.
[2] Suid., *s.v.*; Phryn. Ecl., 357, p. 475; Athen., III, 101 (p. 127d).
[3] Palladas in Anth. Pal., VII, 686, 6; Lycophron Alexandra, 438 (ed. C. v. Holzinger [1895]).
[4] Chrys. Ad Tim., I Hom. XV, *ad loc.* (MPG, 62, 634); Theophylact., *ad loc.* (MPG, 125, 578); Cramer Cat., *ad loc.*
[5] Debr. Gr. Wortb. § 184.
[6] Bl.-Debr.⁶ § 181.
[7] On this whole problem cf. L. Zscharnack, *Der Dienst d. Frau in d. ersten Jahrhunderten d. christl. Kirche* (1902), 100 ff.

κ α τ α φ ρ ο ν έ ω. Pr.-Bauer³, 699; Wilke-Grimm, 236; Helbing Kasussyntax, 184.

θεῶν; [1] τοῦ ἀποθανεῖν; [2] αἰσχροκερδείας; [3] μὲ καὶ Θήβας; [4] τῆς ἡλικίας. [5] In the LXX it is used for בּוּז and בָּזָה, also in independent paraphrase for בָּגַד, חָבַל and תָּעַע pi : Hos. 6:7 (God); Gn. 27:12 (father); Prv. 23:22 (mother); Jdt. 10:19 (τοῦ λαοῦ); 2 Macc. 7:24; 4 Macc. 5:10 (Antiochus IV); Zeph. 1:12; Tob. 4:18 (commandments, good advice); Prv. 19:16 (τῶν ὁδῶν τοῦ νόμου); Wis. 14:30 (ὁσιότητος); Prv. 18:3; 4 Macc. 4:26 (δόγματα); Hab. 1:13 absolute, related to the thought of hybris, → ὕβρις.

The NT warns especially against despising the riches of God's kindness (R. 2:4) in much the same fashion as the Jew of Wis. thinks unworthily of God. [6] It also warns against the contempt of the community in the form of unseemly and unsocial conduct at the *agape* (1 C. 11:22). [7] Jesus commands that we should not despise even the little ones (Mt. 18:10); this command stands against the background of the Hellenistic love of children. [8] 1 Tm. 4:12 warns us not to disparage a leader of the Church because of his youth; [9] special demands are also made of younger men in this connection. With the possibility of the emancipation of Christian slaves, 1 Tm. 6:2 warns slaves not to despise their masters but on the contrary to regard them as worthy of double honour after the pattern of the δοῦλος Christ.

Hb. 12:2 uses the word positively. Jesus despises the shame of crucifixion. [10]

A common proverbial use of καταφρονέω [11] may be seen at Mt. 6:24, par. Lk. 16:13. He who has become the slave of riches will despise God, and *vice versa*. 2 Pt. 2:10, which is based on Jd. 8, is uncertain. In all probability the κυριότης (cf. Herm. s., 5, 6, 1; Did., 4, 1) is the lordship of Christ which opponents despise. But at a pinch it might denote (cf. En. 61:10; Col. 1:16; Eph. 1:21) a class of angels. In this case opponents are warned against despising angels. But the indefinite sing. makes this unlikely, and the context does not demand it.

† καταφρονητής.

The most common sense is "despiser," so Plut. Brutus, 12 (I, 988 f.), Phil. Leg. Gaj., 322 (τῶν θείων); Jos. Ant., 6, 347; Bell., 2, 122; in the LXX for forms of בָּגַד, Hab. 1:5 (obj. God); 2:5; Zeph. 3:4 (subj. false prophets; obj. God).

At Ac. 13:41, Hab. 1:5 is quoted in a missionary address. Jews and proselytes are the subjects (Ac. 13:26) and the object is the message of Christ and remission of sins apart from the Law.

---

[1] Eur. Ba., 199.
[2] Epict. Diss., IV, 1, 70.
[3] Xenoph. Venat., XIII, 16.
[4] Eur. Ba., 503.
[5] P. Gen., 6, 13.
[6] Ltzm. R., *ad loc.*
[7] Ltzm. K., *ad loc.*
[8] Cf. J. Leipoldt, *Gegenwartsfragen in der nt.lichen Wissenschaft* (1935), 55 ff.
[9] σου belongs either to καταφρονείτω or to νεότητος; it makes no difference to the sense.
[10] Wnd. Hb., *ad loc.*
[11] For several instances of the proverb cf. Str.-B., I, 433 and Kl. Mt., *ad loc.*

† περιφρονέω.

With acc. or gen. originally "to weigh," "to consider," [1] then "to dismiss something," "to ignore someone," "to despise," [2] but also intr. "to be wise or understanding." [3] In the LXX "to despise" (4 Macc. 6:9 : τῆς ἀνάγκης; 7:16 : τῶν βασάνων; 14:1 : τῶν ἀλγηδόνων).

It is used in the NT only at Tt. 2:15 in the same sense as καταφρονέω at 1 Tm. 4:12, though here the youth of Titus is not mentioned as a special reason for scornful disparagement.

Carl Schneider

---

† καταχθόνιος

This word is found from the time of Hom. Il., 9, 457, where Hades is described as Ζεὺς καταχθόνιος. Formed from κατὰ χθονός, "he who is under the earth" in contrast to ἐπιχθόνιος = ἐπὶ χθονὶ ὤν, it bears the sense of "under the earth" and is synon. with the more common χθόνιος [1] for divine beings localised in the underworld. Thus in relation to feminine deities Apoll. Rhod., 4, 1412 f. distinguishes between οὐράνιαι θεαί, καταχθόνιαι, and οἰοπόλοι νύμφαι, i.e., nymphs living at a single spot on earth. θεοὶ καταχθόνιοι are mentioned on numerous burial insc., sometimes with individual names, e.g., IG, III, 2, 1423 : παραδίδωμι τοῖς καταχθονίοις θεοῖς τοῦτο τὸ ἡρῷον φυλάσσειν, Πλούτωνι καὶ Δήμητρι καὶ Περσεφόνῃ καὶ Ἐριννύσιν καὶ πᾶσιν τοῖς καταχθονίοις θεοῖς. If the gods of the underworld are here invoked as guardians of the grave and protectors of its peace, in IG, XIV, 1660 a wife erecting a memorial to her deceased husband seeks their care for the soul of the dead : περὶ οὗ δέομαι τοὺς καταχθονίους θεοὺς τὴν ψυχὴν εἰς τοὺς εὐσεβεῖς κατατάξαι. Of the many other inscr. which mention these deities as gods of the dead we may adduce IG, III, 2, 1424; Ditt. Or., I, 382, 1. The expression θεοὶ καταχθόνιοι corresponds to the Lat. *di manes*. There is reference to δαίμονες καταχθόνιοι in Hierocl. Carm. Aur., I, p. 419; ἄγγελοι καταχθόνιοι are mentioned in Audollent Def. Tab., 74, 1.

In the NT καταχθόνιος occurs only at Phil. 2:10 : ἵνα ἐν τῷ ὀνόματι Ἰησοῦ πᾶν γόνυ κάμψῃ ἐπουρανίων καὶ ἐπιγείων καὶ καταχθονίων, καὶ πᾶσα γλῶσσα

π ε ρ ι φ ρ ο ν έ ω. Pr.-Bauer³, 1090; Wilke-Grimm, 353.
[1] Aristoph. Nu., 741 (τὰ πράγματα).
[2] *Ibid.*, 225; Thuc., I, 25, 4; Luc. Demosthenis Encomium, 8; Ps.-Plat. Ax., 372a; Plut. Thes., 1, 4 (I, 1c); Pericl., 31 (I, 169a); P. Oxy., I, 71, II, col. 16.
[3] Ps.-Plat. Ax., 365b. The noun περιφρόνησις is not found in the NT.

κ α τ α χ θ ό ν ι ο ς. Liddell-Scott, Pr.-Bauer, *s.v.*; on the cult of θεοὶ καταχθόνιοι cf. E. Rohde, *Psyche*, I¹⁰ (1925), 119 ff.
[1] Originally only "belonging to the earth," "standing in relation to the earth" (opp. οὐράνιος), χθόνιος seems quite early to have come to be used synon. with καταχθόνιος [Debrunner].

ἐξομολογήσηται. Those in heaven, on earth and under the earth represent the sum of spiritual beings, cf. Ign. Tr., 9, 1, where it is said of the crucifixion of Christ that it took place βλεπόντων τῶν ἐπουρανίων καὶ ἐπιγείων καὶ ὑποχθονίων, and Rev. 5:13, where the sum of all creatures is mentioned in place of the totality of spiritual beings : πᾶν κτίσμα ὃ ἐν τῷ οὐρανῷ καὶ ἐπὶ τῆς γῆς καὶ ὑποκάτω τῆς γῆς καὶ ἐπὶ τῆς θαλάσσης, ² καὶ τὰ ἐν αὐτοῖς πάντα, ἤκουσα λέγοντας (the song of praise then follows). It is no longer possible to say for certain who the καταχθόνιοι were for Paul, or for the author of the carmen Christi in Phil. 2:6 ff. The point of the expression is in any case comprehension rather than classification. Such formulae do not yield to strictly logical analysis, as may be seen from Rev. 5:13, where the concept of rational creatures (λέγοντας) merges into that of created things (τὰ ἐν αὐτοῖς πάντα). It is a mistake, and betrays misunderstanding of the liturgical and poetic nature of the language in Phil. 2:6 ff., to classify the beings mentioned in 2:10 f. and to see in the καταχθόνιοι only the dead who rest in the earth. ³ This is refuted by Greek usage, in which the καταχθόνιοι are always θεοί or δαίμονες.

Sasse

κατείδωλος → II, 379.

| † κατεργάζομαι |

κατεργάζεσθαι, found from the time of Soph., means a. "to bear down to the ground," "to overcome," maintaining the older local sense of κατά; b. "to work at," "make." Refined by constant use, it gradually takes on the sense of the simple, so that the verb signifies working at, and finally accomplishing, a task. It is used in agriculture and in the making of materials, and occurs in the LXX in this sense at Dt. 28:39 (עבד) and Ez. 36:9 pass.(עבד ni); Ex. 35:33 (חֲרֹשֶׁת); 3 Βασ. 6:36 (כְּרֻתוֹת); in the sense "to prepare," "to equip" for פָּעַל, Ex. 15:17 A; ¹ ψ 67:28 א ᶜ· ᵃ; for עָשָׂה, Ex. 39:1 (38:24); for מִשְׁרָה, Nu. 6:3.

The term has religious significance only at ψ 67:28, where it refers in some sense to God's furnishing of salvation. Elsewhere in the LXX κάτεργον = עֲבֹדָה is used in relation to the cultus or to work for the temple (Ex. 30:16; 35:21). ² 'A often has

---

² On the fourfold division of the κόσμος → I, 678 f.
³ So Ew. Gefbr., ad loc.; cf. Loh. Phil., ad loc.
κ α τ ε ρ γ ά ζ ο μ α ι. Pr.-Bauer³, s.v.; Moult.-Mill., 336 f.; Preisigke Wört., 775; Bachm. K. on 2 C. 4:17; 5:5.
¹ Philo Plant., 50 refers this verse, and hence τὸ κατειργάσθαι, to the creation of the world.
² The latter is more likely in spite of the reference in P. Petr., II, 4 (2), 8 adduced by Moult.-Mill.

κατεργάζεσθαι, κάτεργον, κατέργασμα and κατεργασία for the stem פעל; ψ 10:2; 27:3, 4, 5; 45:8; 91:4, 7, 9; Prv. 8:22; Is. 40:10; 'Ιωβ 11:8; 24:5. Here, as often in Hellenism, it is no longer possible to distinguish between the compound and the simple; the LXX usually has ἐργάζεσθαι, ἔργον in these verses. On the other hand, in the Gk. OT as in secular Gk. κατεργάζεσθαι often means "to overcome," "to subdue," cf. Ez. 34:4 for רדה, also for רדד in the vl. at Lv. 25:53 along with κατατείνω and παιδεύω of the slave, cf. also the vl. at Lv. 25:39 for עבד with δουλεύειν. At Jos. 18:1 we have "to subdue" of the land along with κρατεῖν and ὑποτάσσειν. Perhaps this is the sense of 'Ιωβ 11:8 'Α; it is a softening of the Mas. צוק, "to oppress," at Ju. 16:16 A. In the Hellenistic part of the LXX κατεργάζεσθαι occurs only once at 1 'Εσδρ. 4:4 in the sense "to subdue," "to overcome." The word also bears this sense in Philo, e.g., Sacr. AC, 62: ἀτίθασον καὶ ὠμὸν πάθος κατειργάσαντο ὥσπερ τροφὴν λόγῳ πεπαίνοντι (τροφὴν κατεργάζεσθαι == "to digest").

In the NT the word is used particularly in R. and 2 C. Elsewhere it occurs only once each in 1 C., Eph., Phil. and 1 Pt., and twice in Jm. In all these passages it has a religious and ethical sense. It is used *in malam partem* at R. 1:27: κατεργάζεσθαι ἀσχημοσύνην; 2:9: τὸ κακόν; [3] 1 C. 5:3: κατεργάζεσθαι, "to commit an offence" in an obviously negative sense. 1 Pt. 4:3: τὸ βούλημα τῶν ἐθνῶν with reference to a wrong action ("to fulfil"); R. 4:15: ὀργήν; 7:13; 2 C. 7:10: θάνατον, with reference to evil consequences ("to cause"). The subject of sinful human action is the sin which causes ἐπιθυμία (R. 7:8, 15, 17, 20).

The opposite use of κατεργάζεσθαι *in bonam partem* is found in R. 7:18: κατεργάζεσθαι τὸ καλόν; 5:3; Jm. 1:3: ὑπομονήν; 2 C. 7:10a: μετάνοιαν εἰς σωτηρίαν; cf. 7:11: σπουδήν, ἀπολογίαν κτλ.; Phil. 2:12: σωτηρίαν; 2 C. 9:11: εὐχαριστίαν; 4:17: βάρος δόξης; in a warning sense, Jm. 1:20: δικαιοσύνην. [4] Whether Eph. 6:13: ἅπαντα κατεργασάμενοι, refers to full preparation for the battle or to the overcoming of all opposition is an open question. [5] That the final subject behind κατεργάζεσθαι, as behind → ἔργον, ἐργάζεσθαι, is God or Christ, may be seen in R. 15:18 and 2 C. 12:12 with reference to the work of the apostle. The latter verse refers to the validation of the message and person of the apostle by the wonderful acts of power wrought by God. We should thus supply διὰ θεοῦ along with κατειργάσθη. [6] Self-evidently God is also the One who effects all the gifts of salvation of which we read in the passages mentioned. θεὸς γάρ ἐστιν ὁ ἐνεργῶν (Phil. 2:12, 13) stands behind all κατεργάζεσθαι. God it is who has fashioned us to salvation, for the glory of the heavenly body: [7] 2 C. 5:5. In this passage the aor. part. κατεργασάμενος refers to the new creation which has taken place in baptism, [8] and the pres. κατεργαζόμενος of the vl. D G lat to present θλίψεις (cf. 4:17; R. 5:3).

Bertram

κατέχω → II, 829 f.

[3] Cf. 'Α ψ 27:3; 91:7, 9 (פֹּעֲלֵי אָוֶן); → ἔργον, II, 644.
[4] Cf. in Philo ἐργάζεσθαι ἀδικημάτων παραίτησιν (Poster. C., 48), πρὸς θεὸν οἰκείωσιν (*ibid.*, 135), τελειότητα (Gig., 26).
[5] Cf. Dib. Gefbr., *ad loc.*
[6] For a different view, Wnd. 2 K., *ad loc.*
[7] Bachm. K., *ad loc.*
[8] Cf. also Wnd. 2 K., *ad loc.*

κατήγορος, κατήγωρ,
κατηγορέω, κατηγορία

† κατήγορος, κατήγωρ.

κατήγορος = ὁ ἀγορεύων κατά τινος (cf. προσήγορος, "addressing," κακή-γορος, "speaking evil"), "speaking against someone," "accusing someone," as a noun "accuser," found in the NT only in a judicial sense, mostly of the human accuser before a human tribunal: (Jn. 8:10) Ac. 23:30, 35; 25:16, 18; of the devil as accuser at the divine judgment: Rev. 12:10 (all MSS but A).

At Rev. 12:10 A alone reads κατήγωρ; though poorly attested this is to be preferred as the more difficult reading. It may be explained as popular Gk. or as a Semitism. The only example of κατήγωρ is on a magic pap. of the 4th or 5th cent. A.D., P. Lond., I, 124, 25: ποιεῖ πρὸς ... κατήγορας. [1] But it is undeniable that similar changes in Gk. words are found earlier. διάκων for διάκονος occurs on a pap. dated 75 A.D., BGU, II, 597, 4. It cannot be said for certain that κατήγωρ must be a Semitism, but it is equally mistaken to deny the possibility. In Rabb. terminology we find κατήγωρ, like συνήγωρ, as the loan word קַטִּיגוֹר, and it is used for the devil as in Rev. 12:10. [2] The decisive considerations are those which relate to the language of Rev. This is only rarely to be classified as popular Gk. [3] Rev. is undoubtedly one of the most Semitic books of the NT, [4] and cc. 11 and 12 are amongst the most Jewish in the book. All the names for the devil in 12:9 are of Jewish origin. It is thus overwhelmingly probable that κατήγωρ in 12:10 is a Semitism, even though it represents popular usage in P. Lond., I, 124, 25.

The idea of the devil as the accuser of sinful man before God is found in the OT at Job 1:6 ff.; Zech. 3:1 ff. It is widespread in Judaism. [5] The NT has it only here and perhaps in part at Jn. 12:31. [6] Paul in R. 8:33 refers only to accusation, not to the accuser. The idea of the devil is only peripheral in the true NT doctrine of salvation.

κ α τ ή γ ω ρ. Deissmann LO, 72 ff.; Bl.-Debr.[6] § 52. On Radermacher, 19 cf. Debrunner GGA, 188 (1926), 137 ff.; cf. also the comm. on Rev. 12:10.

[1] Deissmann, loc. cit.

[2] Str.-B., I, 141-144, esp. Ex. r., 18 (80c): "To whom are Michael and Sammael like? The defender and the accuser in the judgment." Cf. Dalman Gr. § 37. The pointing acc. to Dalman Wört., s.v. is קְטִינוֹר, acc. to Str.-B., I, 141 קַטִּיגוֹר. It is worth noting that there is no known συνήγωρ corresponding to the סְנֵיגוֹר of the Rabb.; the only attested form of the Gk. word is συνήγορος.

[3] Deissmann, loc. cit.

[4] Bl.-Debr.[6], § 4.

[5] Cf. Str.-B., I, 141 f., also En. 40:7; Test. L. 5:6; Test. D. 6:2.

[6] Unfortunately we cannot fix the sense of ἐκβληθήσεται more precisely at Jn. 12:31.

† κατηγορέω.

From κατήγορος, as φιλοσοφέω from φιλόσοφος, ἀδικέω from ἄδικος, hence "to be an accuser," "to accuse." [1] The person accused is in the gen., the object in the acc. or with περί or κατά. Like many intr. verbs it is also found in the pass. [2] It is also used in a wider, extra-judicial sense. [3] Broader meanings are "to betray," "to make known," [4] "to maintain," "to declare." [5] This final sense occurs from the time of Aristot. [6] and is common is Philo. [7]

In the NT κατηγορεῖν has mostly the judicial sense "to accuse," Mk. 3:2 (Mt. 12:10; Lk. 6:7); Mk. 15:3, 4 (Mt. 27:12; Lk. 23:2); Lk. 11:54 D; 23:10, 14; Jn. 5:45 (8:6); Ac. 22:30; 24:2, 8, 13, 19; 25:5, 11, 16; 28:19; Rev. 12:10. A broader sense is found also at R. 2:15, [8] but there are no NT instances of "to make known" or "to declare." ἐγκαλεῖν is a par. at R. 8:33.

† κατηγορία.

This is formed from κατήγορος like ἀδικία from ἄδικος etc., and it means "accusation in the judicial sense," being found from the time of Aristot. In gramm. it denotes the "predicate" and in logic it is used for "category." [1]

Only the sense of "accusation" is found in the NT, Lk. 6:7 (𝔎); Jn. 18:29; 1 Tm. 5:19; Tt. 1:6. [2]

Büchsel

κ α τ η γ ο ρ έ ω. Pape, Passow, Pr.-Bauer, *s.v.*
[1] For examples cf. Pape, Passow.
[2] Bl.-Debr.[6] § 312.
[3] Examples in Pape, Passow.
[4] Aesch. Ag., 271: εὖ γὰρ φρονοῦντος ὄμμα σοῦ κατηγορεῖ.
[5] Plat. Theaet., 167a : οὐδὲ κατηγορητέον ὡς ὁ μὲν κάμνων ἀμαθής, ὁ δὲ ὑγιαίνων σοφός.
[6] Cf. Bonitz, Aristot. Index.
[7] Cf. Leisegang, *s.v.*
[8] Cf. 1 Cl., 17, 4.
κ α τ η γ ο ρ ί α. [1] Cf. Aristot. Index.
[2] In the two last verses κατηγορία seems to be a tt. in the exercise of ecclesiastical discipline.

---

† κατηχέω

1. This is a late and rare word in secular Gk. which is not found at all in the LXX. Its basic meaning is "to sound from above," cf. Luc. Jup. Trag., 39, where it is said of poets addressing their hearers from a stage : μέτροις κατάδουσι καὶ μύθοις κατηχοῦσιν. Cf. also Philostratus Imagines, I, 19 (ed. O. Benndorf-C. Schenkl [1893]). In common use we find two senses developing. The first of these a. with double acc. is "to recount something to someone," "to inform," Plut. Fluv., 7, 2 (II, 1154a); 17, 1 (II, 1160a); 8, 1 (II, 1154 f.): κατηχηθεὶς δὲ περὶ τῶν συμβεβηκότων ὁ Εὔηνος. Jos. Vit., 366 quotes a letter from Agrippa II in which the king writes after reading the *Jewish War* that, while the author obviously needs no further instruction, on a visit he will tell him many things that happened to him : καὶ αὐτός σε πολλὰ κατηχήσω τῶν ἀγνοουμένων. Cf. also Philo Leg. Gaj., 198.[1] Much more sharply, however, the word also means b. "to instruct someone," "to teach," esp. in respect of the rudiments of a subject or skill. Thus Suid. renders the term προτρέπομαι or παραινέω.[2] The noun κατήχησις is found occasionally in Stoicism, Diog. L., VII, 89; cf. also Gal. De Placitis Hippocratis et Platonis, V, 290, 33 (ed. Kühn, V, p. 463); Cic. Att., XV, 12. The word κατηχέω is often used for "to impart instruction" in the post-NT period, cf. Ps.-Luc. Asin., 48, where it is used for training an ass to do tricks.

2. In the NT κατηχέω is used in sense a. "to tell about something," also pass. "to receive news of something." Thus in Ac. 21:21 James tells Paul that amongst the Jewish Christians in Jerusalem there is a rumour concerning him (κατηχήθησαν περὶ σοῦ) that he teaches the Jews of the *diaspora* to forsake the Law, and that his assistance in purification from Nazirite vows will make it clear to all that the rumour is false (21:24): ὅτι ὧν κατήχηνται περὶ σοῦ οὐδέν ἐστιν. Now there can be no doubt that the report in question had been deliberately, and not wholly without cause, propagated by the opponents of Paul because of their theological views. On the other hand, what had been reported in this way was an account of historical actions, not of doctrine.[3]

Paul himself uses κατηχέω exclusively in sense b. "to give instruction concerning the content of faith." He can use it already with reference to pre-Christian Judaism. Thus the true Jew is κατηχούμενος ἐκ τοῦ νόμου, R. 2:18. When the congregation is assembled, Paul himself would rather speak five words with an understandable sense, ἵνα καὶ ἄλλους κατηχήσω, than ten thousand words in

---

κ α τ η χ έ ω. Thes. Steph., IV, 1348 f.; Cr.-Kö., 480 f.; Moult.-Mill., 337; Pr.-Bauer[3], 704; Meyer Ursprung, I, 7; F. Vogel, "Zu Lk. 1:4," NkZ, 44 (1933), 203 ff.; J. Mayer, *Geschichte d. Katechumenats u. d. Katechese in d. ersten 6 Jahrhunderten* (1868), 1 ff.; C. A. G. v. Zezschwitz, *System d. christl. kirchl. Katechetik*, I (1863), 17 ff.; E. C. Achelis, *Lehrbuch der praktischen Theologie*[3], II (1911), 281 ff. Cf. also the bibl. under → διδάσκαλος, II, 148 and the art. → διδάσκω, II, 135 ff.

[1] P. Lips., I, 32, 1 = P. Strassb., I, 41, 37 probably uses κατηχέω in the sense "to inform," "to acquaint with," rather than in that of "to convince," as Preisigke renders it. At any rate, it stands in correspondence to διδάσκω.

[2] Ed. A. Adler, III, 77.

[3] Meyer Ursprung, I, 7 brushes this aside when he claims that κατηχέω always means instruction in the NT. He does not quote Ac. 21:21, 24 among the examples, and in exposition of Ac. 21:21 in n. 1 he exploits the twofold sense of the German word "unterrichten."

tongues, 1 C. 14:19. This is the high value he attaches to the significance of κατηχεῖν, for he realises that faith comes through preaching. Gl. 6:6 draws a contrast between the κατηχῶν who gives instruction in Christian doctrine and the κατηχούμενος who receives this instruction. It thus establishes the claim of the teacher to support, and therewith confirms the validity and necessity of a professional teaching ministry in the congregation.[4] The κατηχοῦντες of Gl. 6:6 are to be equated with the διδάσκαλοι of 1 C. 12:28 and Eph. 4:11. Hence Paul uses not only the common διδάσκειν but also this much rarer word, hardly known at all in the religious vocabulary of Judaism, as a technical term for Christian instruction. He desires thereby to emphasise the particular nature of instruction on the basis of the Gospel. The word selected was in fact very apt to assume the exclusive sense of Christian instruction, and it finds an echo to-day in the word "catechism." This was particularly true when κατηχέω was specifically used for the instruction given before baptism, and the one preparing for this sacrament was called a catechumen. Clear evidence of this use of κατηχεῖν is to be found already in 2 Cl., 17, 1. Catechumens first appear as a distinct class in Tertullian.[5] A model for the high significance attached to the religious teacher was to be found, not in the philosophical διδάσκαλος of the Greeks, cf. a particularly forceful example like Epict. (→ II, 150), but in the → ῥαββί of Judaism.[6] Yet Paul chooses a word which was alien to Judaism. It had been part of the office of Jesus to be a unique and outstanding teacher (→ II, 153). Similarly in early Christianity teaching was a decisive part of the missionary task and of congregational life (→ II, 144). Ac. 18:25 sums up the scope of this teaching in a phrase when it says of Apollos that he was — we cannot say how — κατηχημένος τὴν ὁδὸν τοῦ κυρίου[7] and that he himself taught (ἐδίδασκεν) ἀκριβῶς τὰ περὶ τοῦ Ἰησοῦ.[8] If the content of the teaching of Jesus was the will of God with its claim and promise, early Christian teaching bears witness to this will as it was revealed in Christ, in the totality of His manifestation. The early Church, of course, did not have a special class of teachers. The function passed to bishops and other clergy.[9]

     c. The use of κατηχεῖν in the dedication of Lk., and the declaration of its purpose : ἵνα ἐπιγνῷς περὶ ὧν κατηχήθης λόγων τὴν ἀσφάλειαν (1:4), raises a special problem. If it bears a more general sense, then we must translate : "In order that you may know the reliability of the stories which have been reported to you." But if it bears a more specific sense, we must render : "In order that you may have certainty concerning the doctrines in which you have been instructed."[10] This question is decisive, because on it depends the problem whether we are to see in Theophilus a non-Christian who has heard of Jesus but who only in this Gospel receives a connected account which

---

[4] I accept this exposition as against A. Oepke, Der Brief d. Paulus an die Galater (1937), 114 f.

[5] Praescr. Haer., 41; De Corona, 2; Marc., V, 7. Perhaps Tertullian is following a usage of Marcion.

[6] Schürer, II, 372 ff., 491 ff., → II, 154.

[7] Cod. D : ὃς ἦν κατηχημένος ἐν τῇ πατρίδι τὸν λόγον, though in spite of the similarity to Gl. 6:6 this does not reach the profundity of the form attested elsewhere.

[8] Here already it seems that κατηχεῖν denotes elementary instruction in the Christian faith and διδάσκειν the teaching constantly given to believers.

[9] Cf. Did., 15, 1.

[10] Vogel favours the former, Meyer Ursprung the latter (I, 7). But Meyer falsely assumes that the sense in the NT is always "instruction in religion" (→ n. 3). Zahn Einl., II, 359 f., 384 and Lk., ad loc., also Kl. Lk., ad loc. support Vogel, and Pr.-Bauer³, 705 Meyer.

interprets the appearance of Christ, or whether he was a Christian already instructed in the doctrine of the Lord. Linguistically both are possible, and the author of Lk. and Ac. shows acquaintance with both. Hence we can only decide from the substance of what is said. It seems more likely in this respect that λόγοι means "reports" or "accounts" rather than "doctrines." Theophilus has heard these, and the point is to show him that these stories about Jesus are true. Hence κατηχεῖν is to be taken in the more general sense.

Beyer

κατιόομαι → 334 ff.   κατισχύω → 397 ff., esp. 398.

κατοικέω, κατοικίζω, κατοικητήριον,   κατοπτρίζομαι → II, 696 f.
κατοικία → οἶκος.

> κάτω, κατωτέρω,
> κατώτερος

† κάτω, † κατωτέρω.

κάτω is an adv. of place, "below" and "downward." In the NT, "below," Mk. 14:66; Ac. 2:19; "downward," Mt. 4:6; [1] 27:51 and par.; Lk. 4:9; Jn. 8:6 (12:31 vl.); Ac. 20:9.

"Below" and "above" denote on the one side earth, the sphere of (sinful) man, and on the other heaven, the sphere of (the holy) God, e.g., Ac. 2:19, and as the noun τὰ κάτω, Jn. 8:23, cf. 3:31; → I, 376-8.

In Rabb. lit.,[2] too, we find מַעְלָה (above) and מַטָּה (below) for heaven and earth, cf. jJoma, 44b: כשירות של מעלן כך שירות של מטן: "As is the heavenly service of God, so is the earthly service of God" (Chija bAbba); bBer., 16b: שתשים שלום בפמליא של מעלה ובפמליא של מטה: "Thou wouldest establish peace in the heavenly household (familia) and in the earthly household" (from the final prayer of R. Safra); bTem., 3a f.: בית דין של מעלה אין מנקין אותו אבל בית דין של מטה מלקין אותו ומנקין אותו: "The heavenly court does not pardon him (the perjuror), but the earthly court punishes and releases him" (exposition of Ex. 20:7 by R. Meir). מעלה can be used for God, e.g., MEx. 22:6: כביכול הגנב עשה את העין של מעלה כאלו אינו רואה: "The thief has imagined that the eye of God cannot see" (from a haggada of Jochanan b. Zakkai).

κατωτέρω at Mt. 2:16 means "from two years and under."[3]

† κατώτερος.

Comp. of κάτω as ἐξώτερος of ἔξω; in Attic we only have the relevant adv.[1] In the NT the comp. is also the superlative.[2]

κ ά τ ω κτλ. [1] Cf. also the addition to Mt. 20:28 in D Φ: ... ἔτι κάτω χώρει ...
[2] This paragraph is by R. Meyer.
[3] Cf. Bl.-Debr.[6] § 62.
κ α τ ώ τ ε ρ ο ς. Haupt, Ew., Dib. Gefbr. on Eph. 4:7-10.
[1] Bl.-Debr.[6] § 62.
[2] Ibid., § 60.

It is found in the NT only at Eph. 4:9 : κατέβη εἰς τὰ κατώτερα μέρη τῆς γῆς. What is meant has long been the subject of exegetical debate. ³ To-day the phrase is usually interpreted in relation to the Gnostic myth of the heavenly Redeemer who comes down from the height above. ⁴ Hence the κατώτερα μέρη τῆς γῆς are either Hades, into which He penetrates as Victor, or the earth, to which He comes in His incarnation. ⁵ The second alternative is the more commonly accepted. ⁶ Now καταβαίνειν may well be a tt. for descent into the underworld. ⁷ But its use is highly varied, and its presence does not prove that behind Eph. 4:7-10 are motifs from the myth of the victorious descent of a heavenly being into the underworld. The basis of the Eph. statement is that Christ's exaltation was His resurrection from the dead (1:20). ⁸ His descent among the dead in death is thus the presupposition. This corresponds to the common proclamation of the primitive Church, 1 C. 15:3-4 (ἐτάφη).

Almost all exegetes allow that τὰ κατώτερα μέρη τῆς γῆς can mean a. the lower parts, i.e., the earth, γῆς being gen. appos., ⁹ or b. the lowest parts of the earth, γῆς being gen. partitivus. ¹⁰ It must be conceded that exposition in terms of b. is essentially simpler, for a gen. with μέρη most naturally denotes the whole to which the parts belong, esp. if this whole has not yet been named.

Another consideration, however, is of greater exegetical cogency. Τὸ κατέβη εἰς τὰ κατώτερα μέρη τῆς γῆς there obviously corresponds ὁ ἀναβὰς ὑπεράνω πάντων τῶν οὐρανῶν. If He mounted up above all heavens, the obvious antithesis is that He descended under the earth, not to the earth. This is confirmed by the definition of His purpose : ἵνα πληρώσῃ τὰ πάντα. The κατέβη κτλ. and ὁ ἀναβὰς κτλ. denote the outer limits of His journey, and between them lies the all which He fills. But if the one limit is the supreme height of heaven at the right hand of God (1:20), the other will not be earth, but the lowest depths of earth, i.e., the sphere of the underworld, the place of the dead. ¹¹ Hence κατέβη κτλ. is entry into the sphere of the dead by death, which was not immediate exaltation to heaven, but which was followed by this only after a period in the grave (1 C. 15:4). Only as He who had been among the dead did Christ come to the right hand of God above all heavens, assuming over all spirits a position of power in which

---

³ Haupt Gefbr., 134-142 has the best treatment of the various theories and their history.
⁴ So W. Bousset, *Kyrios Christos*³ (1926), 32 f.; H. Schlier, *Christus u. d. Kirche im Eph.* (1930); Schneider → I, 522 f. When it is seen that the reference of Eph. 4:7-10 is to the incarnation of the Son of God rather than to the descent into Hades, it is more usual to speak of the earthly journey of the Redeemer, in order to make it clear that motifs from the journey into the underworld are transferred to this in Eph. → I, 523.
⁵ → I, 680 (Sasse).
⁶ Dib. Gefbr.; Pr.-Bauer, *s.v.* κατώτερος, Schneider, *op. cit.*; Rendtorff, *NT Deutsch,* II, also Ew. Gefbr. E. Haupt was the pioneer of this view.
⁷ → I, 523.
⁸ Note that He is raised, not from death, but from the dead whose dwelling is in Hades.
⁹ Bl.-Debr.⁶ § 167, cf. 2 C. 5:5 : τὸν ἀρραβῶνα τοῦ πνεύματος, the pledge which consists in the Spirit.
¹⁰ The earlier view that κατώτερος is only a comp. and not a superlative is wrong. Appeal to the LXX at ψ 62:9; 138:15 : τὰ κατώτατα τῆς γῆς, is not decisive, since the LXX quotation in v. 8 does not have καταβὰς εἰς κτλ. τῆς γῆς could be a gen. of comp., but this is unlikely.
¹¹ For the readers of Eph. τὰ πάντα, as well as the depths reached by Christ, undoubtedly stretched beyond earth to the sphere of the dead beneath it.

He is the Head of the community and the One who fills all things (1:20-23). In Eph. the saving significance of Christ rests in His death (1:20; 2:16; 5:2, 25) in combination with His resurrection (1:20-23; 2:5), not in His mere descent to earth or penetration to Hades.[12] "He led captivity captive" does not mean that He victoriously invaded Hades and liberated the dead there. Eph. does not speak in these terms. The point is that He who is raised from the dead (1:20) and exalted to the right hand of God has subdued all the spirits (1:21) which previously ruled over men and kept them captive in sins, as expressly stated in 2:1-7. We cannot say that Eph. 4:9 borrows from the idea of the victorious journey of a heavenly being to the underworld.

In 4:7-11 we learn that the descent and ascent of Christ are the presupposition of His distribution of the gifts (v. 14, cf. 6:12 and 1:20-23) which equip Christians for contending against seduction by teachers (v. 14) behind whom stand evil spirits, 6:12. The distinctive function (the μέτρον, v. 7) of the gifts of Christ is to mediate His superiority over these spirits. This superiority rests on the fact that He has traversed, and therefore fills, all things from the highest heights of heaven to the lowest depths of earth (1:20-23), whereas the spirits are restricted to the air (2:12)[13] or some other sphere, and are certainly subordinated to Him who is exalted to God's right hand. Through these gifts of Christ Christians will finally attain in the community to the fulness of Christ (4:13) which He has as the One who fills all things (1:23), since through death and exaltation He has traversed all things from the place of the dead to the right hand of God (1:20). To Christ alone belongs cosmic greatness. With Pauline boldness and passion this is here claimed on the basis of His cross,[14] of His death and His exaltation by resurrection from the dead.

Büchsel

| καῦμα, καυματίζω |

† καῦμα.

"Burning heat," esp. the burning or heat of the sun (Epigr. Graec., 649, 5 : οὐ χειμὼν λυπεῖ σ', οὐ καῦμα, οὐ νοῦσος ἐνοχλεῖ), fig. the "heat of fever" (e.g., Thuc., II, 49, 6 : ὑπὸ τοῦ ἐντὸς καύματος), Hippocr. Vet. Med., 19 (καῦμα καὶ φλογμὸς ἔσχατος), the "burning of frost" (Athen., III, 53 [p. 98b]; so also Σ ψ 147:16 [LXX and ᾽Α ψῦχος]), the "fire of love" (Anth. Pal., XII, 87). In Plat. Critias, 120b it is used with ὁρκωμόσια (assurances by oath): τὰ τῶν ὁρκωμοσίων καύματα. In the

---

[12] The objection that κατέβη ... γῆς is a peculiar paraphrase for the death of Jesus carries no weight. It is chosen in view of the ἀναβὰς εἰς ὕψος, and this derives from the verse in the Ps., which is quoted because of the linking of ἀναβὰς κτλ. and ἔδωκεν δόματα κτλ.

[13] At 2:2 the devil is called the ruler of the air to show that his dominion does not affect the higher regions which Christ fills, 1:23, cf. 4:10 and to which Christians are raised up with Christ, 2:6.

[14] 1 C. 1:17; 2:2; Gl. 6:14.

pap. we also find the meaning "inflammable material," e.g., P. Lond., III, 1166, 6 : γυμν[ασί]ω[ι βα]λανεῖον τὰ αὐτάρκη καύματα ..., fuel to heat the gymnasium.

In apocalyptic usage great heat is one of the final manifestations of divine wrath (Rev. 16:9). In the age of consummated salvation the redeemed of the nations will be protected against sun and heat (the blast of hot winds), [1] Rev. 7:16. The external conditions of their existence will be completely changed.

καυματίζω.

"To wither up," "to torture by heat," fig. mid, "to suffer from the heat of fever" (e.g., Plut. De Virtute et Vitio, 1 [II, 100b]); Quaest. Conv., VI, 6, 2 [II, 691e]); Soranus Gynaeciorum, I, 108 (ed. V. Rose [1882], 283); M. Ant., VII, 64, 3.

For the most part the NT uses the word only in the original concrete sense, e.g., of plants wilting in the heat. At Rev. 16:8, 9 the reference is to the judgment of divine wrath which burns up men like fire and heat.

J. Schneider

> ### καῦσις, καύσων, καυσόομαι, καυστηριάζομαι

† καῦσις.

"Burning," "consuming." On inscr. and pap. also "fuel" (P. Lond., III, 1177, 74 : τιμῆς ἐλαίου κα[ύ]σεως λύχνων, [1] "oil for lamps ;" P. Lond., III, 1121b, 4 : τιμὴ ἀχύρου καύσεως βαλανείου, straw for heating the bath). Cf. also Inscr. Magn., 179, 11: ὑπὲρ τῆς καύσεως τῆς βαίτης (heating the bath). [2] In Mitteis-Wilcken, I, 70, 10 we have interesting information on the cult of an Egyptian temple : τυγχάνομεν ἀδιαλείπτως τάς τε θυσίας καὶ σπονδὰς καὶ καύσεις λύχνων ... Cf. LXX Ex. 39:16 : λύχνοι τῆς καύσεως. The cultic use of the term also occurs in Hdt., II, 40 : καῦσις τῶν ἱρῶν, the burning of the sacrifices. In medicine it is a surgical term for the cauterising of sores (e.g., Plat. Resp., 406d). Fig. cf. 'Α ψ 101:4 (Σ ἀπόκαυμα). Technically we find it for the smelting of metals (Strabo, 14, 6, 5).

In the NT it occurs only at Hb. 6:8. The unfruitful earth falls victim to the divine curse and will finally be given up to fire. It is an image for Christians who allow a place for sin. They fall victim to the curse of God and will finally be consumed by the fire of divine wrath. [3]

κ α ῦ μ α. [1] So Bss. Ap., 287: "The reference of οὐδὲ πᾶν καῦμα is particularly to the heat of a scorching wind (καύσων)." Cf. Sir. 43:2 ff., which refers to the irresistible and consuming heat (καῦμα) of the sun. The idea of deliverance from heat is found in the LXX at Prv. 10:5 (cf. also Is. 4:6; Jer. 17:8).

κ α ῦ σ ι ς. [1] On this cf. G. Plaumann, "Der Idioslogos" (AAB, 1919), 37.

[2] Cf. Inscr. Magn., 179, 11, note on βαίτη : part of a spa ?

[3] Hb. 6:8 : κατάρας, ἧς τὸ τέλος εἰς καῦσιν. ἧς is not to be linked with κατάρα, as Pr.-Bauer³, s.v. believes, but with γῆ, so Rgg. Hb., 159, n. 21. Pr.-Bauer translates : "Whose end (i.e., that of the curse) leads to burning," "which ends with burning." On the expression εἰς καῦσιν, cf. Is. 40:16; 44:15; Da. 7:11.

† καύσων.

A late word ; in relation to καῦσος "(fever) heat" (Hipp., Aristot., etc.) a more individual word ; lit. "the hot one." "Heat," "burning of the sun"; in this sense it is found in the physician Diphilos of Siphnos (c. 300 B.C.), quoted in Athen., III, 2 (p. 73a): καύσωνος ὥρα, LXX Gn. 31:40 A; Sir. 18:16. In the NT Mt. 20:12; Lk. 12:55. A specific use is for a "scorching hot wind," and this is predominant in the LXX.

The exposition of Jm. 1:11: ἀνέτειλεν ὁ ἥλιος σὺν τῷ καύσωνι, is a matter of debate. The sun brings heat, but not the scorching east wind. [1] Hence strictly we are to think of the heat of summer rather than the hot wind which blows into Palestine from the Arabian steppes. The verb also suggests "heat" as the sense. On the other hand, we cannot wholly reject the translation : "The sun arises, accompanied by the hot wind." [2]

† καυσόομαι.

Strictly "to be beset by burning or fever heat," "to suffer from great heat." In the doctors (Diosc., Gal.) it is a tt. for "to burn with fever." It does not occur in the LXX.

It is rare in the NT. We find it in an apocalyptic sense at 2 Pt. 3:10, 12. Consumed by heat, the elements of the world will melt and dissolve (v. 10 : λυθήσεται; v. 12 : τήκεται). In the background stands the idea of a cosmic conflagration commonly found in the history of religion. [1]

† καυστηριάζομαι.

From καυστήριον (P. Lond., II, 391, 7, 10, 11 "kiln") = καυτήριον, "branding iron" (Eur., LXX, Luc. [vl. καυστήριον] etc.). Act. "to burn with glowing iron," "to supply with a branding mark." A very rare word. It is found in Strabo, 5, 1, 9 (καυτηριάσαι) and perhaps also in BGU, III, 952, 4 (Wilcken suggests the following reconstruction of the destroyed passage : κονιά]ζουσι or καυστηριά]ζουσι τὴν γύψον.

In the NT the word occurs only once in a figurative sense. At 1 Tm. 4:2 the false teachers are described as men who have been branded in their consciences, i.e., who bear the mark of slaves. The meaning is that they are in bondage to secret sin. Proclaiming a doctrine which makes strong ascetic demands, they are themselves controlled by self-seeking and covetousness. They are secretly the slaves of satanic and demonic powers which make them their instruments. [1]

In the background stands the custom of branding slaves and criminals. [2] Among the Greeks branding was mainly a punishment for runaway slaves. [3] But at his

---

κ α ύ σ ω ν. [1] So also Pr.-Bauer³, s.v. καύσων. Cf. also Hck. Jk., ad loc.
[2] Cf. W. Michaelis, Das NT II (1935), 402.

κ α υ σ ό ο μ α ι. [1]Cf. R. Reitzenstein, "Weltuntergangsvorstellungen, eine Studie zur vergleichenden Religionsgeschichte," Kyrkohistorisk Årsskrift, 24 (1924), 129 ff.

κ α υ σ τ η ρ ι ά ζ ο μ α ι. [1] Cf. Dib. Past. (13), 40. J. Jeremias, NT Deutsch, III (1935), 19. Wbg. Past., 146 : "They live in sins which mark their consciences like branding irons."
[2] Cf. Pauly-W., II, 3 (1929), 2520 ff., s.v. Στιγματίας and Ltzm. Gl. on 6:17, with bibl.
[3] Aristoph. Av., 760; Aeschin. Fals. Leg., 79; Luc. Tim., 17; cf. also Cl. Al. Paed., III, 10.

own whim the owner could punish other offences in the same way.[4] The mark was usually put on the forehead with an iron. It was called a → στίγμα, though ἐγκαύματα was another term for such marks.[5] Branding might also be used in the case of free men who committed particularly heinous offences. Plato still demands the punishment of branding in his *Laws*.[6] Sometimes prisoners of war were also branded.[7] Those condemned to the mines were branded to make escape difficult.[8] In the imperial period recruits and munition workers were distinguished by a mark on the arm for the same reason.[9] Even innocent people were sometimes branded. Thus Ptolemy caused Alexandrian Jews to be marked with an ivy leaf.[10] We also read of branding as part of martyrdom during the Christian persecutions.[11]

J. Schneider

> καυχάομαι, καύχημα, καύχησις,
> ἐγκαυχάομαι, κατακαυχάομαι

† καυχάομαι, καύχημα, καύχησις.

Contents: A. Greek Usage. B. OT, LXX and Judaism: 1. OT; 2. The Judaism of the LXX; 3. The Rabbis; 4. Philo. C. NT and Early Christianity: 1. Paul: a. The Basic Christian Attitude to Boasting; b. Apostolic Self-Boasting; 2. Early Christianity after Paul.

A. Greek Usage.

καυχᾶσθαι, first attested in Sappho (Fr., 26 [Diehl, I, 338]), Pindar and Herodot., is proved by the comic dramatists to be an everyday word in Attic.[1] Hom. uses εὔχεσθαι instead, and the tragic poets αὐχεῖν. Orators also use this and avoid καυχᾶσθαι (it is found only once in Lycurg. acc. to Suid., Lyc. Fr., 81). In the philosophers, too, it occurs only occasionally in Aristot. Pol., V, 10, p. 1311b, 4. The Stoics avoid it, though it occurs in Philodem. Philos. (De Vitiis, X, ed. C. Jensen [1911], col. 20, p. 35,

---

[4] Cf. Diog. L., IV, 46.
[5] Plat. Tim., 26c; Luc. Cataplus, 24.
[6] Plat. Leg., IX, 854d.
[7] Plut. Pericl., 26 (I, 166d); Ael. Var. Hist., II, 9. Acc. to Hdt., VII, 233 Xerxes caused the Thebans to be branded with the royal mark.
[8] Suet. Caes., IV, 27.
[9] For details cf. Pauly-W., *loc. cit.*
[10] 3 Macc. 2:29.
[11] E.g., Prud., X, 1080; Pontius Vita C. Cypriani, 7 (Hartel CSEL, III, 3, XCVII).

κ α υ χ ᾶ σ θ α ι κτλ. R. Asting, *Kauchesis* (1925); P. Genths, NkZ, 38 (1927), 501-521; Helbing, *Kasussyntax*, 260 f.; A. Fridrichsen, Symb. Osl., VIII (1929), 81; R. Steiger, *Die Dialektik d. paulin. Existenz* (1931), 100-103.
[1] Examples in Asting. Instances of its common use later may be found in Theocr. and the pap. (Asting, Pr.-Bauer). Conjectured non-Greek cognates suggest the meaning "to cry," "to call" (Walde-Pok., I, 529). There may well be a duplication of sound (Debrunner).

22 f.), who also has καύχησις (col. 15, p. 27, 21). This is also found in Epic. Fr., 93 (Usener, p. 130, Diog. L., X, 7); καύχημα also occurs once or twice in Pindar (as also καυχή).[2]

The sense of καυχᾶσθαι is "to boast," usually in a bad sense, which also attaches to καύχημα and καύχησις. If there are occasions for the expression of legitimate pride, to Greek sensibility too loud a trumpeting of one's own renown is a violation of → αἰδώς and the sign of an ἀνελεύθερος.[3] Warning against self-glory, and the ridiculing of it, are common themes in popular philosophers and satirists, though we usually find ἐπαινεῖν ἑαυτόν or ἀλαζονεύεσθαι rather than καυχᾶσθαι. Theophr. Char., 23 describes the ἀλαζών, who is typified in the *miles gloriosus* of Plautus.[4] Plut. wrote a whole treatise Περὶ τοῦ ἑαυτὸν ἐπαινεῖν ἀνεπιφθόνως (Qua quis ratione se ipsa sine invidia laudet, II, 539 ff.).[5] Warning ἐπὶ ῥώμῃ μὴ καυχῶ is among the ὑποθῆκαι of the sage, Sosiades (Stob. Ecl., III, 127, 9), and it occurs among other hortatory sayings in the Delphicorum praeceptorum titulus Miletopolitanus (Ditt. Syll.[3], 1268, 23).

B. OT, LXX and Judaism.

1. OT. The LXX uses καυχᾶσθαι for different verbs which have the sense of self-glorying or exulting, e.g., הלל hitp (10 times), עלז (twice) רנן and פאר (once each). Apart from verses in Sir. for which there is no Heb., it occurs without equivalent in Da. 5:1, 6; 3 Macc. 2:17. Ἐγκαυχᾶσθαι occurs 4 times (ψ 51:2; 96:7 for הלל hitp; ψ 73:4 for שאג; ψ 105:47 for שבח hitp); κατακαυχᾶσθαι 3 times (for הלל hitp 'Iερ. 27:38; Zech. 10:12 [MT erroneously has הלל)], for עלז 'Iερ. 27:11). καύχημα is used for תְּהִלָּה (6 times), καύχησις for תִּפְאֶרֶת (9 times).

In the OT there are many proverbs against self-glorying or boasting (1 K. 20:11; Prv. 25:14; 27:1; cf. 20:9), though place is also found for justifiable pride (Prv. 16:31; 17:6). Self-glorying, however, is not merely a casual fault. In many passages it is regarded as the basic attitude of the foolish and ungodly man (Ps. 52:1; 74:4; 94:3). For in it we see that man desires to stand on his own feet and not to depend on God, that he builds on that which he himself can accomplish and control. Hence "to boast" (התהלל) can be synonymous with "to trust" (בטח), Ps. 49:7.[6] God, however, is the Almighty before whom all human boasting is to be stilled, Ju. 7:2; 1 S. 2:2 f.; cf. Jer. 50:11; Ez. 24:25). Paradoxically there is opposed to self-confident boasting the true boasting which consists in self-humbling before God (Jer. 9:22 f.) who is the praise of Israel (Dt. 10:21) and who deals with Israel to His own glory (Dt. 26:19; Jer. 13:11; Zeph. 3:19 f.). Hence the righteous, or the cultic community, can boast of acts of divine succour (Ps. 5:11; 32:11; 89:17 f.; 1 Ch. 16:27 f.; 29:11; Dt. 33:29; Jer. 17:14). Hence "to boast" (καυχᾶσθαι in the LXX) can have the same cultic sense as verbs like "to rejoice," "to exult," with which it is often

---

[2] Examples in Asting. In Plut. Ages., 31 (I, 613d) we have αὔχημα rather than καύχημα (Pr.-Bauer, *s.v.*).

[3] Soph. Ai., 758 ff. shows from the example of Ajax how the deity overthrows the arrogant boaster who relies on his spear and not on God, cf. 127 ff. and the recently discovered fr. of the Niobe of Soph. with its warning against θρασυστομεῖν (O. Schadewald, SAH, 24 [1933/34], 3).

[4] O. Ribbeck, *Alazon* (1882).

[5] Wnd. 2 K. on 11:16.

[6] E.g., Ps. 97:7, to "boast" of idols, Jer. 42:17, to "trust" in them.

combined (in the LXX καυχᾶσθαι is often combined with → ἀγαλλιᾶσθαι, → εὐφραίνεσθαι, opp. αἰσχύνεσθαι → I, 189). But occasionally it also has eschatological significance, since this glorying is finally actualised in the time of salvation (Zech. 10:12; Ps. 149:5; 1 Ch. 16:33). A constituent element in all such glorying is that of confidence, joy and thanksgiving, and the paradox is that the one who glories thus looks away from himself, so that his glorying is a confession of God.

2. Judaism maintained this view, as may be seen in the LXX, which rightly chooses the verb καυχᾶσθαι to denote the basic attitude expressed in the various Heb. words, and which sometimes introduces the view in a rendering which does not correspond exactly to the Heb. ('Ιερ. 12:13; Prv. 11:7; so also Sir. 11:4). The older sense of the boasting of the ungodly is found in 3 Macc. 2:17, and there are in Sir. many references in terms of the old proverbial saying (30:2; 31:10; 38:25; 48:4). But Sir. thinks primarily of the glorying which is rooted in God and His lofty acts (17:9; 50:20). To some degree the high-priest reflects God's glory in the splendour of his cultic adornment (45:12; 50:11). [7] But Sir. transfers the thought from the cultic and eschatological sphere to that of legal righteousness with his emphasis on the fact that the fear of God is true glorying (1:11; 9:16; 10:22) and his coining of the expression that the wise man (i.e., one who is learned in the Law) makes his boast in the Law (39:8). Hence wisdom, which for Sir. is embodied in the Law, glories in itself (24:1 f.). There are similar expressions elsewhere. If Judith is lauded as καύχημα μέγα τοῦ γένους ἡμῶν (Jdt. 15:9), her hymn (16) at once ascribes the glory to God. The Test. XII reckon among evil spirits the πνεῦμα ὑπερηφανείας which brings man to the point ἵνα καυχᾶται (vl. κινῆται) καὶ μεγαλοφρονῇ, Test. R. 3:5, e.g., the spirit of drunkenness, Test. Jud. 14:8; cf. Δα. 5:1 (addition of the LXX). Self-glorying leads to sin, Test. Jud. 13:3), and young people are warned not to boast of their acts or their might (ibid. 13:2).

3. The thoughts of Sir. are echoed in the Rabbis. Israel's ornament and crown (καύχημα in the LXX) is the Torah. [8] Abraham's glory is to have fulfilled the Law. [9] Sometimes, of course, we find warnings not to fulfil the Law in our own interests, [10] and there are many warnings against pride [11] and admonitions to humility [12] (→ ταπεινοφροσύνη). It is characteristic that in the Rabbis the boasting rooted in God's action, which is a rejoicing and thanksgiving, can also take on the sense that the righteous rejoices in sufferings and gives thanks for them as the chastisement which makes him aware that God regards him as his own son, which atones for his sins and increases his merits. [13]

4. Warning against self-glorying is a characteristic theme in Philo, though καυχᾶσθαι κτλ. do not play any special role. [14] Instead we find φιλαυτία, οἴησις, ἀλαζονεία, ὑπεροψία, κενοδοξία, τῦφος, φυσᾶσθαι etc. Since's Philo's statements are closest to those of Paul, we must give a brief sketch of his view.

---

[7] The LXX here has καύχημα for הוֹד and תִּפְאֶרֶת.
[8] Str.-B., III, 115 ff.
[9] Ibid., 187.
[10] Ibid., 401 (on 1 C. 9:16).
[11] Str.-B., II, 101 ff.; III, 47 (on R. 1:22), 298 (on R. 12:16), 768 (on 1 Pt. 5:5).
[12] Str.-B., I, 192 ff., 197 (on Mt. 5:4e), 568. Humility as the greatest of virtues, I, 789 f. (on Mt. 18:15e). C. G. Montefiore, Rabbinic Literature and Gospel Teachings (1930), 7 f. Cf. the passages quoted in n. 8.
[13] Str.-B., II, 274 ff. (esp. M. Ex., 20, 23, 277); III, 222; A. Marmorstein, The Old Rabbinic Doctrine of God (1927), 185 ff.; W. Wichmann, "Die Leidenstheologie im Spätjudentum" (BWANT, 5, 3 [1930]).
[14] Leisegang does not list καυχᾶσθαι etc.; καύχησις is found in Congr., 107.

Self-glorying is regarded as μέγα (μέγιστον) κακόν. [15] It occurs in lists of vices, [16] and Cain is particularly τὸ φίλαυτον in opposition to Abel as φιλόθεον. [17]

The true sin of self-glorying is man's failure to acknowledge God as the Author and Lord of all being and Giver of all good things. [18] It is his forgetfulness of God [19] and ungrateful [20] usurpation of His glory. [21] It is the opposite of εὐσέβεια; [22] it is ἀθεότης; [23] in it we see man's desire to be as God. [24] The righteous man avoids such boasting. [25] He seeks to serve God alone, [26] for he knows himself, [27] his ἀσθένεια, [28] and he realises that he is dust and ashes. [29] He recognises God as the Lord of life and death, [30] and he knows that he has received his soul and all that he has only as a loan entrusted to him by the Creator. [31] In this humble submission he attains to God's grace [32] and true glory, [33] for the humble stand high with God; [34] He is their only glory : ἔστω δή ... μόνος θεὸς αὔχημά σου (Dt. 10:21, the LXX has καύχημα) καὶ μέγιστον κλέος, καὶ μήτ' ἐπὶ πλούτῳ μήτε δόξῃ μήτε ἡγεμονίᾳ μήτε σώματος εὐμορφίᾳ μήτε ῥώμῃ μήτε τοῖς παραπλησίοις, ἐφ' οἷς εἰώθασιν οἱ κενοὶ φρενῶν ἐπαίρεσθαι, σεμνυνθῇς (Spec. Leg., I, 311).

C. NT and Early Christianity.

1. Paul.

a. The Basic Christian Attitude to Boasting. In the NT καυχᾶσθαι (καύχημα, καύχησις) is characteristically used almost exclusively by Paul alone, in whom it is very common. [35] For Paul καυχᾶσθαι discloses the basic attitude of the Jew

---

[15] φιλαυτία, Spec. Leg., I, 333; οἴησις, Cher., 57; Vit. Mos., I, 286; ἀλαζονεία, Spec. Leg., IV, 170; Virt., 161.

[16] Cher., 71; Sacr. AC, 32; Poster. C., 52; Jos., 143.

[17] Sacr. AC, 3; Det. Pot. Ins., 32; 68; 78; Poster. C., 21.

[18] Leg. All., I, 52; III, 29 f., 33; Cher., 65; 71; 74 f.; 83; 113-123; Sacr. AC, 52; Agric., 173; Conf. Ling., 127 f.; Som., II, 219; Decal., 72; Virt., 161-170.

[19] Sacr. AC, 52-58; Spec. Leg., I, 344; Virt., 163; 165.

[20] Sacr. AC, 54; 58; Virt., 165.

[21] Spec. Leg., I, 195 f.

[22] Praem. Poen., 12; cf. Leg. All., III, 137.

[23] Leg. All., I, 49; III, 33.

[24] Virt., 172; Leg. All., I, 49 : φίλαυτος δὲ καὶ ἄθεος ὁ νοῦς οἰόμενος ἴσος εἶναι θεῷ καὶ ποιεῖν δοκῶν ἐν τῷ πάσχειν ἐξεταζόμενος.

[25] Vit. Mos., II, 96. Reference is made to circumcision, Spec. Leg., I, 10-12, and to the laming of Jacob, Praem. Poen., 47.

[26] Spec. Leg., IV, 131.

[27] Migr. Abr., 136-138; Spec. Leg., I, 10; → γινώσκω, I, 702 f.

[28] Spec. Leg., I, 293; Virt., 165.

[29] Sacr. AC, 55 f.; Som., I, 211 f.; Spec. Leg., I, 264 f., 293.

[30] Som., II, 296 f.

[31] Rer. Div. Her., 106; Congr., 130; Mut. Nom., 221.

[32] Spec. Leg., I, 265; Congr., 107: ἵλεως ... εὐθὺς γίνεται (God) τοῖς ἑαυτοὺς κακοῦσι καὶ συστέλλουσι καὶ μὴ καυχήσει καὶ οἰήσει φυσωμένοις.

[33] Poster. C., 136.

[34] Vit. Mos., II, 240 f.: The ἀλαζόνες should learn : ὅτι οὕτω ταπεινοὶ καὶ ἀτυχεῖς εἶναι δοκοῦντες οὐκ ἐν ἐξουθενημένοις καὶ ἀφανέσι τάττονται παρὰ τῷ θεῷ.

[35] The distinction between the trans. and intr. use of καυχᾶσθαι does not affect the basic attitude thereby denoted. For even when καυχᾶσθαι trans. is construed with the acc. of obj. (e.g., 2 C. 7:14; 9:2; 11:30), the boaster is really glorying in himself. On the model of the LXX the object of this boasting is denoted by ἐπί (R. 5:2) or (usually) ἐν (Bl.-Debr.⁶ § 196). For this is how we are to take the ἐν in, e.g., R. 5:3; 1 C. 3:21; 2 C. 10:15; 12:9;

to be one of self-confidence which seeks glory before God and which relies upon itself. For this reason he sets in contrast to καυχᾶσθαι the attitude of → πίστις which is appropriate to man and which is made possible, and demanded, by Christ. It is worth noting that the first question after the first dogmatic exposition of χωρὶς νόμου and διὰ πίστεως (R. 3:21-26) is: ποῦ οὖν ἡ καύχησις; — ἐξεκλείσθη (v. 27). And the proof from Scripture begins with the statement that Abraham has no καύχημα before God (4:1 f.). [36]

Paul notes that the boasting in God and the Law which Judaism requires has been perverted into an ἐπαναπαύεσθαι νόμῳ (R. 2:17, 23). This καυχᾶσθαι is in truth a πεποιθέναι ἐν σαρκί (Phil. 3:3 f.). For Paul then, as for the OT and Philo, the element of trust contained in καυχᾶσθαι is primary. [37] This means that self-confidence is radically excluded from καυχᾶσθαι ἐν τῷ θεῷ, and there is only one legitimate καυχᾶσθαι ἐν τῷ θεῷ, namely, διὰ τοῦ κυρίου ἡμῶν Ἰησοῦ Χριστοῦ (R. 5:11). For in Christ God has brought to nothing all the greatness of both Jews and Gentiles (1 C. 1:25-31): ὅπως μὴ καυχήσηται πᾶσα σὰρξ ἐνώπιον τοῦ θεοῦ (v. 29; cf. 2 C. 10:17); the saying in Jer. 9:22 f. is thus fulfilled (v. 31). [38] Hence the believer strictly knows only a καυχᾶσθαι ἐν Χριστῷ Ἰησοῦ (Phil. 3:3), and this means that he has abandoned all self-boasting (Phil. 3:7-10), that he has accepted the cross of Christ, and that he says: ἐμοὶ δὲ μὴ γένοιτο καυχᾶσθαι εἰ μὴ ἐν τῷ σταυρῷ τοῦ κυρίου ἡμῶν Ἰησοῦ Χριστοῦ, δι' οὗ ἐμοὶ κόσμος ἐσταύρωται κἀγὼ κόσμῳ (Gl. 6:14).

Faith implies the surrender of all self-glorying. But for those who stand in faith there may open up a new possibility of boasting, namely, in terms of their achievements in the propagation of faith (Gl. 6:13). For it is not they themselves who work in their labours, but the grace of God (1 C. 15:10; 3:5 ff.). Each can stand before God only as one who has received: τί δὲ ἔχεις ὃ οὐκ ἔλαβες; εἰ δὲ καὶ ἔλαβες, τί καυχᾶσαι ὡς μὴ λαβών (1 C. 4:7). This divine endowment certainly lifts them above the sphere of human dependence and obligation: ὥστε μηδεὶς καυχάσθω ἐν ἀνθρώποις· πάντα γὰρ ὑμῶν ἐστιν (1 C. 3:21), but it does so only on the presupposition: ὑμεῖς δὲ Χριστοῦ, Χριστὸς δὲ θεοῦ (v. 23). Boasting

---

on the other hand, the ἐν in R. 15:17; 1 C. 15:31; Phil. 1:26 (not 3:3) indicates the sphere in which self-glorying moves. Where we have ὑπέρ c. gen., καυχᾶσθαι is to be taken as "speaking about" (e.g., 2 C. 7:14, where the dat. indicates the one to whom it is directed, whereas in 1 C. 1:29 we have ἐνώπιον; Bl.-Debr.⁶ §§ 187, 4; 231, 1). καύχησις denotes boasting as an act; καύχημα is what is said in boasting (2 C. 9:3), or the object of pride or boasting. In Paul καύχημα is almost always used for the possibility of καύχησις (R. 4:2; 1 C. 9:16; 2 C. 1:14; Phil. 1:26). But the distinction between the two is not hard and fast (cf. R. 3:27 with 4:2), for καύχημα can denote the act of boasting (2 C. 5:12) and καύχησις the possibility (2 C. 1:12).

36 The text and exposition of R. 4:1 f. are uncertain in detail, but there can be no doubt that Abraham is allowed no boasting before God. I regard the text of v. 1 as hopelessly corrupt. The conditional clause in v. 2 is probably unreal, and the ἀλλ' οὐ πρὸς θεόν is then a strengthened denial.

37 Phil. 3:3 f. shows how καυχᾶσθαι and πεποιθέναι are synon. So are πεποιθέναι ἑαυτῷ Χριστοῦ εἶναι and καυχᾶσθαι περὶ τῆς ἐξουσίας, 2 C. 10:7 f.; the καυχᾶσθαι in v. 8 also corresponds to the πεποίθησις in v. 2. The καύχησις in 2 C. 1:12 and the πεποίθησις in 3:4 correspond similarly.

38 God has demonstrated this truth in the election of those called to be members of the community at Corinth, 1 C. 1:26-29; → n. 34.

is not grounded in what is seen (ἐν προσώπῳ) but in what is not seen (ἐν καρδίᾳ), 2 C. 5:12. [39]

Paul does not merely develop more radically the OT paradox that man can truly boast only when he looks away from himself to God's acts. [40] He also takes up and expands to the point of paradox the Rabbinic view (→ 647) that the believer boasts of his afflictions and sufferings: καυχώμεθα ἐν ταῖς θλίψεσιν, R. 5:3. This finds illustration in 2 C. 4:7-11 as well as in the list of sufferings in the section on self-glorying in 2 C. 11:23-29: εἰ καυχᾶσθαι δεῖ, τὰ τῆς ἀσθενείας μου καυχήσομαι (2 C. 11:30). Nor does this imply that self-glorying is negatively grounded, i.e., by an endurance which has the character of ascetic achievement. [41] For sufferings do not bear their meaning within themselves. They are simply the envelope of the δύναμις of God which comes to fulfilment in ἀσθένεια (2 C. 12:9), of the ζωὴ τοῦ Ἰησοῦ which is manifest in them (2 C. 4:10 f.). For this reason, he who boasts also looks away from himself in the sense that he looks to the future, since he enjoys no possession in the present. For this reason καυχᾶσθαι ἐν ταῖς θλίψεσιν is also καυχᾶσθαι ἐπ᾽ ἐλπίδι τῆς δόξης τοῦ θεοῦ (R. 5:2). But this looking to the future is different from that of the pious Jew. For sufferings have for Paul not merely the negative sense of a means of discipline (→ 647) but also the positive sense that in them God's δύναμις and eschatological ζωὴ τοῦ Ἰησοῦ are shown to be already at work for the one who suffers (2 C. 4:16) as well as for those to whom the sufferings are of advantage (2 C. 4:12).

b. Apostolic Self-Boasting. The basic rejection of self-glorying is not contradicted by passages in which Paul boasts of his work. When he boasts of the strength of a congregation as compared with others (2 C. 7:4, 14; 8:24; 9:2 f.), this is not really self-glorying. There is simply expressed in it his confidence in the congregation. [42] Such mutual trust is not ruled out by faith; on the contrary, it is promoted in the fellowship of faith. It is not the self-glorying of self-established man. The καυχᾶσθαι in which it finds expression stands in no contradiction to the καυχᾶσθαι ἐν Χριστῷ Ἰησοῦ. Paul is well aware that the καύχησις which his apostolic activity confers on him is grounded only in what Christ does through him (R. 15:17 f.; 1 C. 15:10). He does not earn God's favour by the results of his missionary work, but vice versa. For this reason, on the one occasion when he speaks with emotion of his καύχησις, [43] he adds at once: ἣν ἔχω ἐν Χριστῷ

---

[39] The καυχᾶσθαι ἐν προσώπῳ of 2 C. 5:12 corresponds to the καυχᾶσθαι κατὰ σάρκα of 11:18 and also to the πεποιθέναι ἐν σαρκί of Phil. 3:4 (→ n. 37). The κατὰ σάρκα of 2 C. 11:18 is the opposite of the κατὰ κύριον of 11:17, which corresponds to the ἐν καρδίᾳ of 5:12, cf. Phil. 3:3, ἐν Χριστῷ Ἰησοῦ. On the antithesis of πρόσωπον and καρδία cf. 1 Βασ. 16:7; R. 2:28 f.

[40] Paul's rejection of boasting is not motivated, as is that of the Gks. (→ 646), by the fact that boasting violates dignity and makes a man an ἀνελεύθερος, bringing him into dependence on others (Wnd. 2 K. on 11:16), but by the fact that it violates the divine glory and brings man into dependence on the σάρξ.

[41] Boasting on the basis of ascetic achievement would be expressly ruled out by Paul if the reading ἵνα καυχήσωμαι were original at 1 C. 13:3, but this is most unlikely, cf. the comm. and the bibl. in Pr.-Bauer.

[42] Cf. 2 C. 2:3: πεποιθὼς ἐπὶ πάντας ὑμᾶς, ὅτι ἡ ἐμὴ χαρὰ πάντων ὑμῶν ἐστιν, also 2 C. 1:15; 8:22: πεποιθήσει πολλῇ τῇ εἰς ὑμᾶς.

[43] 1 C. 15:31; as shown by the ἣν ἔχω ... which follows, the ὑμετέραν in νὴ τὴν ὑμετέραν καύχησιν is in place of the obj. gen., so that the meaning is: "by the renown which I have (won) in you."

'Ιησοῦ τῷ κυρίῳ ἡμῶν. Hence the καύχησις is strictly limited to the divinely imposed confines of his activity, 2 C. 10:13. That self-confidence is not herein expressed may be seen clearly from the fact that Paul does not attain to this boasting by comparing his work with that of others. It is not, then, the boasting of the arrogance which has more to show than others, 2 C. 10:12-16. As Paul rejects συνιστάνειν ἑαυτόν, 2 C. 3:1; 5:12; 10:18, and as he sees himself to be recommended by the fact that Christ works through him, 2 C. 3:2 f., and God commends him, 2 C. 10:18, as he can commend himself only by his proclamation of the truth, 2 C. 4:2, or paradoxically by the sufferings which envelop the greatness of his ministry, 2 C. 6:4-10, so he opposes the καυχᾶσθαι of his opponents which takes its strength from comparison with others. He argues that he measures himself only by himself, and therewith by the measure which God Himself has given him, 2 C. 10:12 f. This is no contradiction.[44] It is a genuinely Pauline thought which underlies the whole discussion in 2 C. 2:14 — 7:4. This thought is that the judgment of an apostle must be by the standard of his commission or office. Measuring by oneself is thus comparison of achievement with the divinely given task. But the measure of this is the δύναμις which works in the apostle, 2 C. 6:7; 13:4, and which may be seen in the results of his activity. Thus measuring by oneself implies assessment of καυχᾶσθαι in terms of the effective δύναμις, and it leads to καυχᾶσθαι of the δύναμις of God, 2 C. 4:7, i.e., to thanksgiving. In this sense Paul warns us in R. 11:18 against comparison with the unbelieving Jews : μὴ κατακαυχῶ τῶν κλάδων· εἰ δὲ κατακαυχᾶσαι (then consider), οὐ σὺ τὴν ῥίζαν βαστάζεις, ἀλλὰ ἡ ῥίζα σέ. And in the same sense he warns us in Gl. 6:4 that none can attain to his καύχημα by comparison with others, but only by self-scrutiny, by measuring his achievement in terms of the task which he is set. As the context shows, to do this also implies self-criticism. If, then, occasion is given to glory, this glorying is also thanksgiving.[45]

We recall that glorying had been connected with thanksgiving and exultation in the OT (→ 647), and this helps us to see why Paul often expresses the hope that his communities will be his boast at the *parousia* of the Lord (1 Th. 2:19 f.: χαρά, στέφανος καυχήσεως and δόξα; 2 C. 1:14 and Phil. 2:16 : καύχημα). Obviously boasting in the grace of God which gives, if it is to be more than dogmatic and theoretical, must include the thankful joy of the boasting recipient. The Corinthians, then, must realise that Paul is their καύχημα, 2 C. 1:14.[46] They must thank God that He has given Paul to them, cf. 1:11; 5:12. And in this sense the καύχημα of the Philippians, their possibility of being able to boast, must increase as their faith grows stronger thanks to the work of Paul, Phil. 1:26.

Similarly, we can understand the boasting of Paul that he does not exercise his apostolic ἐξουσία to be supported by the churches, 1 C. 9:15 f.; 2 C. 11:10. By this καύχημα he makes it plain that all his achievements and ἐξουσία are no ground

---

[44] So Ltzm. K. on 2 C. 10:12. Here it seems to be that we must omit the οὐ συνιᾶσιν, ἡμεῖς δέ with DG Ambst. The ἀλλὰ αὐτοί can be referred only to Paul. He has already refused to compare himself with others. Hence measuring oneself by oneself can only be characteristic of him and not of his opponents.

[45] 2 C. 1:12 shows that even this thanksgiving can be misunderstood. In v. 11 Pl. had said that there was a duty to give thanks for what God had done for him. Because he must expect this claim to be interpreted as boasting, he then goes on to speak of καύχησις in v. 12 f.

[46] At 2 C. 1:14 we are to take the ὅτι as "that" with Ltzm., not as "because" with Wnd.

for καύχημα. It is simply laid upon him, or given to him, by God that he does not merely accept the divine ἀνάγκη as constraint, but freely endorses it. He demonstrates this by his abnegation, which is not designed to accredit him before God but before himself, and which is meant to show, not that he is greater than others, but that he is less than others. His opponents boast of their ἐξουσία, and Paul does not wish to stand on the same level with them, 2 C. 11:12.

Finally, however, we have the paradoxical situation that this boasting of God's grace and power takes the form of self-boasting. Paul is forced into this by the Corinthians when they contest his ἐξουσία. This ἐξουσία is not his own cause ; it is that of Christ, in whose service he has received it. Hence he is forced to boast of it, and concretely this means that he must boast of himself. That there is danger in this may be seen clearly from the ἐάν τε γὰρ περισσότερόν τι καυχήσωμαι of 2 C. 10:8. Basically, however, Paul is forced into this self-glorying, and he brings out its paradoxical character by calling it a καυχᾶσθαι ὡς ἐν ἀφροσύνῃ, 2 C. 11:16 f., 21; 12:1, 11.[47] It is worth noting how he develops the theme (ἐν ταύτῃ τῇ ὑποστάσει τῆς καυχήσεως, 11:17). When he has listed all the things which might generally be a reason for boasting, 11:22, his glorying κατὰ σάρκα, i.e., on the basis of demonstrable advantages, 11:22-23, changes into a paradoxical boasting of his sufferings, of ἀσθένεια, vv. 23-30, and therewith of the χάρις and δύναμις of God, 12:8 f.; cf. 4:7 ff. Indeed, that which might be the basis of καύχημα in the eyes of his opponents, i.e., ὀπτασίαι or ἀποκαλύψεις, is expressly ruled out as a theme of boasting (v. 5). It is reversed and broken off. Glorying in ἀσθένεια becomes the dominant theme. Hence Paul abandons the motif of comparison, and ἀφροσύνη is strictly abandoned even though Paul still maintains the role of ἄφρων, vv. 11-13.

2. Early Christianity after Paul.

The basic theme of Paul is also found in Eph. 2:8 f.: τῇ γὰρ χάριτί ἐστε σεσωσμένοι διὰ πίστεως· καὶ τοῦτο οὐκ ἐξ ὑμῶν, θεοῦ τὸ δῶρον· οὐκ ἐξ ἔργων, ἵνα μή τις καυχήσηται, and at 2 Th. 1:4 we have a variation on the theme of apostolic self-glorying on the basis of the community : ὥστε αὐτοὺς ἡμᾶς ἐν ὑμῖν ἐγκαυχᾶσθαι. Outside the Pauline corpus the OT boasting of trust in God finds Christian expression in Hb. 3:6 : ἐὰν τὴν παρρησίαν καὶ τὸ καύχημα τῆς ἐλπίδος μέχρι τέλους βεβαίαν κατάσχωμεν.[48] The familiar OT paradox of boasting occurs in Jm. 1:9 f.: καυχάσθω δὲ ὁ ἀδελφὸς ὁ ταπεινὸς ἐν τῷ ὕψει αὐτοῦ, i.e., that he is or will be blessed by God, ὁ δὲ πλούσιος ἐν τῇ ταπεινώσει αὐτοῦ, i.e., that he humbles himself and glories in God alone.[49] The second part of the statement is made clear in 4:(13-)16, where νῦν δὲ καυχᾶσθε ἐν ταῖς ἀλαζονείαις ὑμῶν· πᾶσα καύχησις τοιαύτη πονηρά ἐστιν is contrasted with the submission

---

[47] This paradox is plainly brought out if Paul is consciously repudiating the style of laudation, of the *cursus honorum*, as conjectured by A. Fridrichsen, *Symb. Osl.*, VII (1928), 25 ff.

[48] παρρησία is here combined with καύχημα. Like πεποίθησις, this is used in Pl. for the self-awareness of the apostle (2 C. 3:12 → n. 37) or for trust in the community (2 C. 7:4 → n. 42). In Hb. it denotes the situation of the community before God (→ παρρησία). Hence, like καύχημα, it takes on a cultic sense which, with καύχημα, it bears in 1 Cl., 34, 5; Act. Andr., 1 (→ 653).

[49] This thought is OT and Jewish. We are not to see in it the ironic admonition suggested in Dib. Jk., *ad loc.*, namely, that the rich man should boast of his (imminent) downfall.

to and confidence in God which spring from a sense of the uncertainty of life, and legitimate boasting is expressed in the ἐὰν ὁ κύριος θελήσῃ.

In later literature we find the OT and NT warning against boasting and admonition to humility. 1 Cl., 13, 1 bases the ταπεινοφρονήσωμεν οὖν ... on a quotation from Jer. 9:22 f., and 1 Cl., 21, 5 speaks of ἄνθρωποι ἄφρονες καὶ ἀνόητοι καὶ ἐπαιρόμενοι καὶ ἐγκαυχώμενοι ἐν ἀλαζονείᾳ τοῦ λόγου αὐτῶν. We also find καύχησις with ὑψηλοφροσύνη and ὑπερηφανία in a list of vices in Herm. m., 8, 3. Ign. in Eph., 18, 1 has a variation of the saying of Pl. in 1 C. 1:20; he asks : ... ποῦ καύχησις τῶν λεγομένων συνετῶν; Ign. also follows Pl. (2 C. 10:12 f.) in Tr., 4, 1: πολλὰ φρονῶ ἐν θεῷ, ἀλλ' ἐμαυτὸν μετρῶ, ἵνα μὴ ἐν καυχήσει ἀπόλωμαι, and in Pol., 5, 2 he has the admonition : εἴ τις δύναται ἐν ἁγνείᾳ μένειν, εἰς τιμὴν τῆς σαρκὸς τοῦ κυρίου ἐν ἀκαυχησίᾳ μενέτω· ἐὰν καυχήσηται, ἀπώλετο. In this sense the Act. Thom., 86 say of Jesus : ἡ δὲ πραότης καύχημα αὐτοῦ ἐστιν. Similarly in Just. Dial., 101, 1 Jesus is characterised as οὐ τῇ αὐτοῦ βουλῇ ἢ ἰσχύϊ πράττειν τι καυχώμενος. The corresponding thought that the righteous boast in God is found in 1 Cl., 34, 5 : τὸ καύχημα ἡμῶν καὶ ἡ παρρησία ἔστω ἐν αὐτῷ (sc. τῷ θεῷ). If the community is here the subject of boasting, the boasting has a cultic sense (→ 646), and this is even plainer in Act. Andr., 1 (εὐχαριστίαν ἢ παρρησίαν ἢ ὕμνον ἢ καύχημα ... εἰπεῖν εἰς τὸν ... θεόν → n. 48). In this sense Jesus says of Himself in Mart. Mt., 2 (cod F): τὸ καύχημα τῶν χειρευόντων ἐγώ. [50]

† ἐγκαυχάομαι.

This word is sparsely attested [1] and can hardly be distinguished from καυχᾶσθαι in meaning. It is found a few times in the LXX → 646. In the NT we find it at 2 Th. 1:4 (vl. καυχᾶσθαι) → 652, and in post-apostolic writings at 1 Cl., 21, 5 → supra.

† κατακαυχάομαι.

Except for an inscr., [1] this is found only in biblical and Christian writings. It brings out strongly the element of comparative superiority expressed in boasting, "to boast in triumphant comparison with others." This sense is not prominent in the LXX, where the word is simply a stronger form of καυχᾶσθαι, but it is plain in R. 11:18 (→ 651) and in the figurative expression at Jm. 2:13 : κατακαυχᾶται ἔλεος κρίσεως, cf. also Jm. 3:14 : μὴ κατακαυχᾶσθε (in pride at one's own wisdom) καὶ ψεύδεσθε κατὰ τῆς ἀληθείας. [2] With whom the comparison is made

---

[50] The verb and nouns also occur in a few passages which are of no particular interest : καυχᾶσθαι in Ign. Phld., 6, 3; Ps.-Pls. ad Cor., 15 (KlT, 12 [1905], 17); Just. Dial., 86, 2; Tat. Or. Graec., 17, 1; καύχημα, Just. Apol., 41, 2; Tat. Or. Graec., 2, 1; καύχησις, Just. Dial., 141, 3.

ἐ γ κ α υ χ ά ο μ α ι. ¹ Cf. Liddell-Scott.

κ α τ α κ α υ χ ά ο μ α ι. ¹ SAB, 1932, 355.

² If the κατὰ τῆς ἀληθείας depends not only on ψεύδεσθε but also on κατακαυχᾶσθε (the κατά being repeated), we have a hendiadys : "Do not falsely boast in defiance of the truth," or : "Do not boastfully lie against the truth." Basically, of course, the contemptuous look of the boaster is not directed on the ἀλήθεια, but, as the context shows (vv. 13-18), on brethren less endowed with wisdom. This comes out more clearly if κατακαυχᾶσθε is taken in the absolute (cf. R. 11:18) and κατὰ τῆς ἀληθείας is dependent only on ψεύδεσθε.

may be learned from the context in R. 11:18 (unbelieving Jews), and it is expressed by the gen. in Jm. 2:13 (3:14).

Bultmann

κεῖμαι, ἀνά-, συνανά-, ἀντί-,
ἀπό-, ἐπί-, κατά-, παρά-,
περί-, πρόκειμαι

κεῖμαι.

The use of κεῖμαι is greatly varied. The basic sense "to lie" can either denote the fact as such or the results,[1] and a fig. as well as a spatial reference is possible. The word is not common in the LXX. In the NT it usually has the spatial sense "to lie" or "to be laid or set," Lk. 2:12, 16; Mt. 5:14; 28:6; Rev. 4:2; Phil. 1:16 etc. Fig. κεῖσθαι εἰς means "to be appointed" at Lk. 2:34; 1 Th. 3:3, κεῖσθαι "to be laid down or given" at 1 Tm. 1:9,[2] and finally κεῖσθαι ἐν "to lie in" at 1 Jn. 5:19.[3]

ἀνάκειμαι, συνανάκειμαι.

The verb first means "to be laid up," esp. of votive offerings etc., then ἀνάκειται εἴς τι, "something rests on ...,"[1] and finally "to recline at table."

In the NT it occurs only in the Gospels in the sense "to recline at table,"[2] Mk. 14:18; 16:14; Mt. 9:10; 22:10, 11; 26:7, 20; Lk. 22:27; Jn. 6:11; 12:2; 13:23, 28;[3] συνανάκειμαι, Mk. 2:15 and par.; 6:22 and par. The custom of reclining at table on cushions was common in the time of Jesus among the Jews and other civilised Mediterranean peoples.[4] But only those who were served could recline. Women, children and slaves usually ate standing or in other ways. In contrast to the διακονῶν, then, the ἀνακείμενος is one who enjoys himself because he can afford it;

κ ε ῖ μ α ι. Pape, Pass., Cr.-Kö., Pr.-Bauer, Liddell-Scott, *s.v.*

[1] κεῖμαι is used as a perf. pass. for τίθημι, cf. 1 C. 3:11.

[2] νόμος κεῖται, νόμος κείμενος are legal tt. from the time of Eur. and Thuc., cf. Pr.-Bauer, *s.v.* 2b.

[3] ἐν τῷ πονηρῷ is to be taken personally of the devil (cf. v. 18). The κεῖται ἐν ... is perhaps par. to the μένειν ἐν ἐμοί of Jn. 15:1-10 : As the believer abides in Christ, so that he is nourished and fruitfully sustained by Him, so the world lies in the devil, by whom it is controlled and rendered helpless and powerless, and finally killed (1 Jn. 3:14), cf. also Pr.-Bauer, *s.v.* 2d.

ἀ ν ά κ ε ι μ α ι κτλ. [1] Pape, Pass., *s.v.*

[2] At Mk. 5:40 : ὅπου ἦν τὸ παιδίον (the daughter of Jairus), the best MSS have no part. and lesser MSS have ἀνακείμενον or κατακείμενον.

[3] We can often render ἀνακείμενος as "guest," Mt. 22:10, 11. Elsewhere we have the gen. abs. "at table," Mk. 16:14; Str.-B., IV, 618.

[4] Str.-B., IV, 56 f.

he is the "greater" of Lk. 22:27. It was customary to lie on the left side so that the right hand would be free for eating. Reclining at the passover was meant to signify that after the Exodus the Israelites were free men and not slaves. It was thus regarded as essential, cf. Mk. 14:18 and par.

† ἀντίκειμαι.

This means "to confront," then "to be opposed or hostile to." [1] In the NT it occurs only in the second sense, Gl. 5:17; 1 Tm. 1:10. Elsewhere we have only the part. ὁ ἀντικείμενος, "the enemy," [2] Lk. 13:17; 21:15; 1 C. 16:9; Phil. 1:28; 2 Th. 2:4; 1 Tm. 5:14. [3]

† ἀπόκειμαι.

This means basically "to lie, to be laid aside," then "to be laid up so that it can be counted on," then "to come upon someone as destiny," and finally even "to be despised, rejected." [1]

In the NT Lk. 19:20; Col. 1:5; 2 Tm. 4:8 in the sense of "to be laid up," Hb. 9:27 in the sense of "there is awaiting man," it is appointed for him by the divine ordination to which he is subject. [2] At Col. 1:5; 2 Tm. 4:8; Hb. 9:27 the word expresses the certainty of man's future as this is established in the will of God. Whether for good or evil, this is already fixed and cannot be changed.

† ἐπίκειμαι.

"To lie, to be laid over," fig. "to be ordained," also "to oppress," also used in the pass. "to have laid on one," "to have on."

In the NT it is used in the sense "to lie on," Jn. 11:38; 21:9, then "to beat upon" of the storm, Ac. 27:20, "to throng" of the crowd, Lk. 5:1; 23:23, and finally "to be imposed," of legal ordinances, Hb. 9:10, of constraint, 1 C. 9:16.

† κατάκειμαι.

"To lie down," "to lie," esp. of the sick, sleepers, those at meals, denoting their relaxed attitude. It is often used of the sick in the NT, Mk. 1:30; 2:4 (Lk. 5:25);

ἀ ν τ ί κ ε ι μ α ι. Pr.-Bauer, s.v.; Nägeli, 39.

[1] Pape, Pass., s.v.

[2] ἀντικείμενος already has this sense in the LXX and P. Par., 45, 6 : Μενέδημον ἀντικείμενον ἡμῖν.

[3] Here ὁ ἀντικείμενος is generic ; it does not refer to Satan, who is only mentioned for the first time in v. 15.

ἀ π ό κ ε ι μ α ι. Pr.-Bauer, s.v.; Nägeli, 55; F. Pfister, "Zur Wendung ᾽Απόκειταί μοι ὁ τῆς δικαιοσύνης στέφανος," ZNW, 15 (1914), 94-96.

[1] Pape, Pass., s.v.

[2] Epigr. Graec., 416, 6: ὡς εἰδώς, ὅτι πᾶσι βροτοῖς τὸ θανεῖν ἀπόκειται, 4 Macc. 8:11: ἀποθανεῖν ἀπόκειται.

ἐ π ί κ ε ι μ α ι. Pape, Pass., Pr.-Bauer, s.v.

κ α τ ά κ ε ι μ α ι. Pape, Pass., Pr.-Bauer, s.v.

Jn. 5:3, 6; Ac. 9:33; 28:8, also of those reclining at table, Mk. 2:15 (Lk. 5:29); 14:3; 1 C. 8:10.

† παράκειμαι.

"To lie, or to be set, beside," "to be before someone for selection," also "to be a neighbour of." In the NT only at R. 7:18, 21: "to lie ready," "to lie at disposal," "to stand in the power of someone" (denoting human power and impotence).

    Cf. P. Greci e Latini, 542, 12 (3rd cent. B.C.): ἐμοὶ οὔπω παράκειται κέρμα, "I have no money ready to hand."

† περίκειμαι.

"To lie around," "to surround," also pass. "to have round one" (of clothes).

In the NT "to be hanged around," Mk. 9:42; Lk. 17:2; pass. Ac. 28:20 : "I have this chain around me." Fig. Hb. 12:1; pass. Hb. 5:2 : He is beset by weakness (cf. 7:28) Vulg : *circumdatus est infirmitate.*

† πρόκειμαι.

"To lie before," i.e., before another object or man, also "to be on public display," "to be settled," also of the subject of deliberation.

In the NT it means "to lie before all eyes," Jd. 7, or with the dat. of person "to be before someone," 2 C. 8:12; Hb. 12:2, denoting what is prescribed, Hb. 12:1 or what is promised, Hb. 6:18.

Büchsel

---

† κέλευσμα

    Noun of κελεύω, from the stem *kel* = "to impel," with the basic sense of "that by which one impels." An older form is κέλευμα. There is much vacillation between these forms in older MSS. The word is found equally in prose and poetry from Hdt. and Aesch.

    It has the detailed meaning a. "order," "command," "behest," always with a distinctive content, e.g., Soph. Ant., 1219 f.: τάδ' ἐξ ἀθύμου δεσπότου κελευσμάτων ἠθροῦμεν (vl. ἐδρῶμεν). It is used esp. of the command of a deity, Eur. Iph. Taur., 1483 and Andr., 1031. Rather weaker, a "demand" (often much the same as a command , Hdt., VII, 16. It also has the sense b. "call," "summons," "signal," "command," the substance

---

π α ρ ά κ ε ι μ α ι. Pape, Pass., Pr.-Bauer, *s.v.*
π ε ρ ί κ ε ι μ α ι. Pape, Pass., Pr.-Bauer, *s.v.*
π ρ ό κ ε ι μ α ι. Pape, Pass., Pr.-Bauer, *s.v.*

of the summons not being stated because it is already known to the one concerned (in the case of "command" it is not easy to make a clear-cut distinction from a.), Hdt., IV, 141: ἐπακούσας τῷ πρώτῳ κελεύσματι. The word takes on the sense of a "cry of encouragement" in relation to animals (horses or dogs), Plat. Phaedr., 253d : a well-trained horse can be guided κελεύσματι μόνον καὶ λόγῳ (opp. "whip"), of dogs, Ps.-Xenoph. Cyn., 6, 20. In the same connection κέλευσμα is used for the call of the κελευστής on a ship, who sets the rhythm for the rowers, [1] Aesch. Pers., 397: ἔπαισαν ἄλμην βρύχιον (the deep sea) ἐκ κελεύματος, also Eur. Iph. Taur., 1405. The word is here a tt., and as such it became a loan word in Latin, celeusma, celeustes. A fixed expression is (ὥσπερ, καθάπερ) ἐξ or ἀφ' ἑνὸς κελεύσματος, "(as) at a word,' "at a stroke," "at once," "to a man," e.g., Thuc., II, 92, 1; Diod. S., III, 15, 5; Sophron in Athen., III, 33 (p. 87a). κέλευσμα is used in this sense on its one appearance in the LXX at Prv. 30:27 (24:62). Finally the word can simply mean c. "cry," with an implied element of the imperative, Aesch. Choeph., 751: καὶ νυκτιπλάγκτων ὀρθίων (loud, high-pitched) κελευμάτων (of the crying of the little Orestes at night), cf. also Eur. Hec., 929, where κέλευσμα, with κέλαδος (928), is an equivalent of βοή, κραυγή.

In sum, the meaning can range from a specific command, through a terse order, to an inarticulate cry.

Joseph. and Philo both use the word in all these senses (LXX → supra).

Joseph. : a. "command" of Herod., Ant., 17, 199; "requirement" to take part in a conspiracy, ibid., 140; b. an "order" or "command," 19, 110; [2] c. "war-cry" (ἐγκέλευσμα καὶ κραυγή), Bell., 2, 549. Philo Praem. Poen., 117 of God's power to command; Abr., 116, the obedience of a ship's company to the authority of the κυβερνήτης as a comparison for the well-ordered household.

In ordinary speech, however, κέλευσμα seems to be replaced by κέλευσις (or ἐγκέλευσις).

κέλευσις is found for the first time in Plut. Aud. Poet., 11 (II, 32c), occurs along with κέλευσμα in Plot. (Enn., IV, 8, 2), and is very common in inscr. and pap., where κέλευσμα seems to be attested only once (Preisigke Sammelbuch, 4279, 3 : κελεύσμασιν, inscr. at a quarry, Egypt, c. 90 A.D.), but Liddell-Scott and Preisigke give many instances of κέλευσις and ἐγκέλευσις. It seems to have become a tt. in government, and denotes an official "order," "decree" or "resolve," whether issued by the lowest of officials or the emperor himself (in this case with θεῖος or ἱερός), [3] Preisigke Sammelbuch, 4284, 8; P. Masp., 32, 23 etc. Of the order of a God, Ditt. Or., 589 : κα[τ]ὰ κέλευσι[ν] θεοῦ (there follows the name of the god) ... εὐχαριστῶν ἀνέθηκα (a votive inscr. from Syria). [4]

In the NT the term is found only at 1 Th. 4:16, where it denotes a shout of command : ὅτι αὐτὸς ὁ κύριος ἐν κελεύσματι, ἐν φωνῇ ἀρχαγγέλου καὶ ἐν

κέλευσμα. [1] Cf. Suid., s.v. κελευστής : οἱ κελευσταὶ καθ' ἑκάστην ναῦν τὸ ἐνδόσιμον (the beat) τοῖς ἐρέταις ἐνέδοσαν. In special cases the human voice is replaced by something else, e.g., Xenoph. Hist. Graec., V, 1, 8 : λίθων τε ψόφῳ (sound) τῶν κελευστῶν ἀντὶ φωνῆς χρωμένων. On the idea of "Christ as the helmsman or κελευστής on the ship of the Church," cf. F. J. Dölger, Sol Salutis = Liturgiegeschichtliche Forschungen, 4/5² (1925), 277 ff., esp. 280 f. [Bertram].

[2] In this and the following verse Joseph. uses ἐγκέλευσμα. The compound is also found in Ps.-Xenoph. Cyn., 6, 24. Ant., 19, 110 has παρακελευσμός as well as ἐγκέλευσμα, and διακελευσμός occurs in Ant., 3, 53.

[3] Cf. δόγμα, Lk. 2:1. We seem to have both in Ditt. Or., 455, 3 : [... κατὰ δόγμα τι κ]αὶ κέλευσιν (Asia, 1st cent. B.C.).

[4] Other constructions with κέλευσμα and κέλευσις and compounds are κελευσμός and compounds and κελευσμοσύνη (Ionic), → n. 2.

σάλπιγγι θεοῦ καταβήσεται ἀπ' οὐρανοῦ, καὶ οἱ νεκροὶ ἐν Χριστῷ ἀναστήσονται πρῶτον ... Though it is easy to fix the meaning of the term, it is not so easy to gain a clear picture of the course of events at the *parousia*. Various questions arise. First, the ἐν does not seem to be temporal or instrumental, as though the κέλευσμα marked the decisive point for the καταβαίνειν (as a signal). It seems rather to express the accompanying circumstances of the καταβαίνειν (with a word of command). Who gives the order? God? Christ? Or the archangel? The last possibility is linked with the further question whether the three things introduced by ἐν are three different events or whether the φωνὴ ἀρχαγγέλου and σάλπιγξ θεοῦ are more concrete indications of the κέλευσμα, so that in effect we have only two events, i.e., κέλευσμα by means of the voice of the archangel and then by means of the trumpet of God (but who blows this?). This is suggested by the lack of a gen. in the case of κέλευσμα and by the καί between the second and third members. But no certain answer can be given to these questions.[5] Such depictions introduce traditional features of the apocalyptic world which are designed, not to describe the events in detail, but to set the mood for the commencement of the end. To attempt an analysis is thus futile. A final question arises: What is the point of the κέλευσμα, the φωνή and the σάλπιγξ? Simply to announce the end, the *parousia*? But the passage refers to the awakening of the dead, and we find elsewhere the view that the dead will be summoned from their graves (cf. Jn. 5:28).[6] The answer may thus be given that the κέλευσμα, φωνή and σάλπιγξ are a signal for the resurrection. It must be noted, however, that the various aspects of the *parousia* cannot be neatly distinguished. Hence the κέλευσμα, φωνή and σάλπιγξ are both a signal for the resurrection and an accompanying mark and intimation of the end in general.[7] Everything takes place ἐν ῥιπῇ ὀφθαλμοῦ (1 C. 15:52). In the strict sense a process is thus excluded. When the time is fulfilled, the *parousia* of the Lord will take place with the word of command, the voice of the archangel and the sound of the trumpet, and at the same moment the dead will rise.

This view is not contradicted by the πρῶτον-ἔπειτα of vv. 16-17. This has qualitative rather than chronological significance. The περιλειπόμενοι will not take precedence of the κοιμηθέντες (v. 15). The πρῶτον-ἔπειτα might seem to denote two successive acts, but the ἅμα of v. 17 shows that they are finally one. Similarly the καταβαίνειν on the one side and the ἁρπαγῆναι εἰς ἀέρα on the other serve the one goal of the

---

[5] The reference in Reitzenstein Poim., 5, n. 3 to a passage in the Ἀποκάλυψις τῆς ὑπεραγίας Θεοτόκου περὶ τῆς κολάσεως, Descensus Mariae (H. Pernot, "Descente de la Vierge aux enfers," in *Revue des Études Grecques*, XIII [1900], 233 ff.), which dates from the 8th or 9th cent. (op. cit., p. 239), is of little exegetical help. Here (in one form) Michael is addressed by Mary: χαῖρε, Μιχαὴλ ἀρχιστράτηγε, τοῦ ἁγίου πνεύματος τὸ κέλευμα (c. 3, p. 240), and just before (c. 2, p. 240) angels had addressed Mary (within a Trinitarian scheme): χαῖρε, τοῦ ἁγίου πνεύματος τὸ κέλευσμα (in three of four forms). Of interest here is also the further address of Mary to Michael (c. 3, p. 240): χαῖρε, Μιχαὴλ ἀρχιστράτηγε, ὁ μέλλων σαλπίζειν καὶ ἐξυπνίζειν τοὺς ἀπ' αἰῶνος κεκοιμημένους.

[6] In the par. passage in 1 C. 15:52 the sound of the trumpet and the resurrection of the dead are closely related: σαλπίσει γάρ, καὶ οἱ νεκροὶ ἐγερθήσονται ἄφθαρτοι, → n. 5.

[7] Cf. the varied use of the sound of the trumpet in the OT and later Judaism. It accompanies the revelation of Yahweh at Sinai (Ex. 19:13, 16, 19). It also accompanies the manifestation of Yahweh at the last day, it proclaims the end, serves to gather the dispersed (cf. Mt. 24:31), and also serves to awaken the dead. Cf. Volz Esch. and Str.-B., Index, *s.v.* "Posaune"; → σάλπιγξ.

ἀπάντησις τοῦ κυρίου. The ultimate goal of all events at the *parousia* is the πάντοτε σὺν κυρίῳ εἶναι of believers (v. 17; cf. Phil. 1:23). Other points have no independent significance ; they are simply means to an end or embellishing details which may fluctuate. This insight is essential to a true understanding of the eschatological statements of Paul.

Lothar Schmid

κενός, κενόω, κενόδοξος, κενοδοξία

---

† κενός.

A. κενός outside the NT.

1. Lit. "empty," "without content," opp. πλήρης or μεστός, common from the time of Hom., in inscr., pap., LXX, Philo, with gen. or abs., usually of things : οἶκος, P. Flor., 294, 52 (6th cent. A.D.), a cistern, Gn. 37:24, but also of persons : δακρύων, Eur. Hec., 230, esp. in expressions like ἥκεις οὐ κενή, Soph. Oed. Col., 359, ἀναπέμπειν or ἐξαποστέλλειν τινὰ κενόν (T. Reinach, *Papyrus grecs et démotiques* [1905], 55, 9, Gn. 31:42), to let someone go "with empty hands," οὐκ ὀφθήσῃ ἐνώπιόν μου κενός, "without sacrificial gift," Ex. 23:15; 34:20; Dt. 16:16.

2. Fig. a. of persons, "hollow," "vain," Pind. Olymp., 3, 45. The transition is formed by κενὸς τοῦ νοῦ, Soph. Oed. Col., 931, φρενῶν, Soph. Ant., 754, the latter common in Philo, Virt., 179 etc., as an address, ὦ κενοὶ φρενῶν, Migr. Abr., 138; Spec. Leg., IV, 200 etc., ἀνόητος καὶ κενός, Aristoph. Ran., 530, Plut. Qua quis ratione se ipse sine invidia laudet, 5 (II, 541a), cf. Epict. Diss., II, 19, 8. The judgment is primarily intellectual, but the suggestion of a pretended content gives it a moral nuance (cf. the English "vain"); διαπτυχθέντες ὤφθησαν κενοί, Soph. Ant., 709. In biblical Gk. the moral element becomes stronger. ἄνδρες κενοί are not just foolish and vain but useless and careless persons (Ju. 11:3 B; 9:4; Heb. אֲנָשִׁים רֵיקִים synon. פֹּחֲזִים "frothy," "frivolous," LXX B : δειλοί, A : θαμβούμενοι (neither quite accurate). b. Of things, if there is no true content to correspond to the form : κενὸς φόβος ═ ψοφοδέεια, v. Arnim, III, p. 99, 7; "empty," "futile," with the stress sometimes on the lack of content and sometimes on the resultant lack of successful impact. κενὴ δόξα, "erroneous" opinion, Epic., 74, 16; 78, 2, 5; 295, 15 and 28; κενὰ εὔγματα (boastings), Hom. Od., 22, 249; κενοὶ λόγοι, Plat. La., 196b, [1] Ex. 5:9; φάσει κενῇ, P. Par., 15, 68 (120 B.C.). Here there is a suggestion of lying : κενὴ πρόφασις καὶ ψευδής, Demosth., 18, 150; μεγαλαυχίας κενὸν φύσημα, Philo Ebr., 128; κεναὶ ἐλπίδες Aesch. Pers., 804; Philo Vit. Mos., I, 195; Wis. 3:11; Σιρ. 34:1; κενὴ ὄρεξις, Philo Decal., 149; αἱ τοῦ θνητοῦ βίου κεναὶ σπονδαί, Ebr., 152; τόξον Ἰωναθαν οὐκ ἀπεστράφη κενὸν εἰς τὰ ὀπίσω, καὶ ῥομφαία Σαουλ οὐκ ἀνέκαμψεν κενή, 2 Βασ. 1:22; with an ethical thrust, ῥήματα κενά, Job 6:6; 15:3 A (דָּבָר לֹא יִסְכּוֹן, "useless speech"). We often find phrases like εἰς κενόν, "in vain," P. Petr., II, 37, 1b, 12 (3rd cent. B.C.); Jos. Ant., 19, 96; Is. 29:8; Jer. 6:29; 18:15 (לַשָּׁוְא), or διὰ κενῆς : Aristot. Probl., V, 881a, 39 (with ῥίπτειν); Job 2:3; 6:5. → 660.

κ ε ν ό ς. [1] A fine par. to 1 C. 1:17 ff. is found in Corp. Herm., XVI, 2 : Ἕλληνες ... λόγους ἔχουσι κενοὺς ἀποδείξεων [ἐνεργητικούς]. καὶ αὕτη ἐστὶν (ἡ) Ἑλλήνων φιλοσοφία, λόγων ψόφος (noise, tinkling). ἡμεῖς δὲ οὐ λόγοις χρώμεθα, ἀλλὰ φωναῖς με[γί]σταις τῶν ἔργων. There are many variant readings, but the sense is clear.

B. κενός in the NT.

1. Sense 1. is found in Mk. 12:3; Lk. 20:10, 11: (ἐξ)απέστειλαν κενόν, and more profoundly Lk. 1:53: πεινῶντας ἐνέπλησεν ἀγαθῶν καὶ πλουτοῦντας ἐξαπέστειλεν κενούς. The thought of the Magnificat is OT and Jewish [2] (cf. 1 S. 2:7 f.; Gr. Sir. 10:14; Job 12:17 ff.; 20:6 ff.; Ps. 107:9; 34:10; Ps. Sol. 2:31; 10:6 → πτωχός, also the Jewish interpretation of the very widespread image of the wheel of life). [3] In a much spiritualised form, however, it is also Christian (cf. Mt. 5:3 ff.; Lk. 6:20 ff.; 1 C. 1:26; 2 C. 6:10; Jm. 2:5).

Sense 2. a. occurs in Jm. 2:20, with a Greek rather than a Jewish flavour. It can hardly be contested that ὦ ἄνθρωπε κενέ is linguistically comparable with the ῥακά of Mt. 5:22. [4] Equally incontestable, however, is the more intellectual or Greek understanding.

2. In most of the NT references — and apart from a quotation these are almost all Pauline — we have various nuances of sense 2. b. If the usage itself is not distinctively Christian, the content is. Closest to general use are Jm. 4:5, Eph. 5:6: μηδεὶς ὑμᾶς ἀπατάτω κενοῖς λόγοις, and Col. 2:8: συλαγωγῶν διὰ τῆς φιλοσοφίας καὶ κενῆς ἀπάτης. We are here in the ethical and religious sphere. There is a suggestion of futility (cf. Ac. 4:25 = Ps. 2:1) in 1 C. 15:10: ἡ χάρις … οὐ κενὴ ἐγενήθη, 15:58: ὁ κόπος οὐκ ἔστιν κενός, as in expressions like εἰς κενόν, 2 C. 6:1 (δέξασθαι); Gl. 2:2 (τρέχω); Phil. 2:16 (ἔδραμον, ἐκοπίασα), 1 Th. 3:5 (μή … εἰς κενὸν γένηται ὁ κόπος ἡμῶν). All these passages express a strong sense of responsibility in face of the greatness of the divine gift and of the task thereby imposed, yet also a strong confidence in the gracious power of God which normally guarantees success. By way of antithesis rather than mere contradiction κενός and οὐ κενός are decisive predicates for that which is against God and that which is of God (cf. λατρεῦσαι τοῖς κενοῖς for idolatry in 3 Macc. 6:6). In this respect there can be no strict differentiation between content and effect. When Paul calls his readers to witness that his εἴσοδος to them was not κενή (1 Th. 2:1), he is repudiating all false human motives such as deceit, cunning or self-seeking (vv. 3-7), but he is also rejecting any suggestion that his work was metaphysically impotent or factually unsuccessful (cf. 1:5), and he is thus teaching us to see the divine power (1:6; 2:4) at work behind human achievements accomplished in affliction (2:2). When Paul says that preaching and faith are κενός if Christ is not risen (1 C. 15:14), the antithesis in v. 20 may be applied both to the divine content and to the divine efficacy in the broadest possible sense, the latter with reference to deliverance from ἀπόλλυσθαι (→ I, 395). Hence κενός means both without content and also ineffective. → μάταιος in v. 17 is synon. (cf. μάταιος λόγος, Plat. Leg., II, 654e; κενὸς καὶ μάταιος, Hos. 12:2; Job 20:18; Is. 59:4; 1 Cl., 7, 2).

---

[2] W. Sattler, "Die Anawim im Zeitalter Jesu," Festgabe f. A. Jülicher (1927), 1-15.

[3] Kittel Probleme, 141 ff.; Wnd. Kath. Br., Dib. Jk. on 3:6; → τροχός.

[4] ῥακά = רֵיקָא "empty simpleton." Cf. Str.-B., Kl., Schl. Mt., ad loc. No great light is shed by the equation of רֵקָא with "slave" or "youth," which Zn. suggests on the authority of Chrys.

† κενόω.

"To make empty," a. "to deprive of content or possession," mostly with a gen. of obj., more rarely of person, or absolute : ἀνδρῶν τάνδε πόλιν κενῶσαι, Aesch. Suppl., 660; cf. Athen., IV, 17 (p. 139 f.); Jos. Bell., 1, 355; 2, 457; τᾶς συοπλουτοσύνας : God can quickly deprive the wealthy man of his sordid possessions, Kerkidas P. Oxy., VIII, 1082, Fr. 1, col. II, 9; Philo Leg. All., III, 226, medically "to empty," κενώσω τὸν κάμνοντα. Fig. Somn., I, 198 : κενοῖ ψυχὴν ἁμαρτημάτων. Pass. "to be desolate," Jer. 14:2 (Ez. 12:20 and 26:2 Σ); Jer. 15:9 : ἐκενώθη (אֻמְלְלָה) ἡ τίκτουσα ἑπτά, "the mother of seven sons languished, i.e., became desolate"; cf. Soph. Ai., 986 : κενός of a lioness robbed of her young, Bion., 1, 59 (ed. U. v. Wilamowitz-Moellendorff [1900]) of the Erotes robbed of Adonis. b. "To nullify, destroy" (→ κενός 2. b.), ὑπάρξεις (goods), Vett. Val., II, 22, p. 90, 7; pass. "to come to nothing."

In the NT sense a. is used only in Phil. 2:6 f. of Christ : ὃς ἐν μορφῇ θεοῦ ὑπάρχων οὐχ ἁρπαγμὸν ἡγήσατο τὸ εἶναι ἴσα θεῷ, ἀλλὰ ἑαυτὸν ἐκένωσεν μορφὴν δούλου λαβών, ἐν ὁμοιώματι ἀνθρώπων γενόμενος κτλ. Here sense b. "he negated himself, deprived himself of his worth, denied himself" (→ I, 474), is ruled out by the resultant weak tautology of ἐταπείνωσεν ἑαυτόν. We are rather to supply τοῦ εἶναι ἴσα θεῷ as an omitted object, and we thus have the equivalent of ἐν μορφῇ θεοῦ ὑπάρχων. There is no suggestion of a temptation of the Pre-existent to aspire beyond His existing state. [1] What is meant is that the heavenly Christ did not selfishly exploit His divine form and mode of being (→ I, 474), but by His own decision emptied Himself of it or laid it by, taking the form of a servant by becoming man. The subject of ἐκένωσεν is not the incarnate [2] but the pre-existent Lord. There is a strong sense of the unity of His person. The essence remains, the mode of being changes — a genuine sacrifice. Docetism is excluded. The best commentary is to be found in the par. 2 C. 8:9 : ἐπτώχευσεν πλούσιος ὤν, "he became a beggar even though (of himself, and up to this point) he was rich."

Sense b. is found with καύχημα, act. at 1 C. 9:15 and pass. at 2 C. 9:3. If anyone induced the apostle to ask for support, this would invalidate his materies gloriandi (and therewith his gloria). If the collection in Corinth did not come up to his hopes, then the boasted expectations of Paul would be brought to nothing. Neither of

---

κ ε ν ό ω. RE³, X, 246 ff., XXIII, 752 f.; RGG², III, 725-7; Haupt, Ew., Dib. Gefbr., Loh. Phil. on Phil. 2:5 ff.; NT theologies by Holtzmann, II² (1911), 96, Feine⁶ (1934), 179 f., Weinel⁴ (1928), 313 and 318; Schl. Theol. d. Ap., 340 ff.; W. Beyschlag, Christologie des NT (1866), 235; O. Michel, ZNW, 28 (1929), 324-333; I. A. Dorner, Ges. Schriften (1883), 188 ff.; E. W. Weiffenbach, Zur Auslegung d. Stelle Phil. 2:5-11 (1884); T. Zahn, ZWL, 6 (1885), 243-266; O. Bensow, Die Lehre von der Kenose (1903), esp. 174 ff.; J. Kögel, "Christus der Herr," BFTh, 12, 2 (1908), W. Warren, JThSt, 12 (1911), 461 ff.; H. Schuhmacher, Christus in seiner Präexistenz u. Kenose nach Phil. 2:5-8 (1914/21); W. W. Jäger, Herm., 50 (1915), 537 ff.; F. Loofs, Wer war Jesus Christus? (1916), 208 ff. and ThStKr, 100 (1927 f.), 1-102; A. Jülicher, ZNW, 17 (1916), 1 ff.; E. Lohmeyer, "Kyrios Jesus," SAH, 13 (1927/28); K. Barth, Philipperbrief (1928), 54 ff.; W. Foerster, ZNW, 29 (1930), 115-128; E. Barnikol, Phil. 2, der marcionitische Ursprung des Mythossatzes Phil. 2:6-7 (1932), an unsatisfactory attempt to prove that the kenosis passage is an interpolation.

[1] Lohmeyer, op. cit., 29, with an appeal to Persian cosmogony; for a more accurate understanding cf. Dib. Gefbr.², ad loc.

[2] Loofs, op. cit. has amassed considerable patristic evidence in support of this older dogmatic view, and has tried to show that it is exegetically correct.

these things must happen. At R. 4:14 the words κεκένωται ἡ πίστις are elucidated in the par. κατήργηται ἡ ἐπαγγελία: if the people of the Law are heirs, this logically implies the invalidation of faith as a principle of salvation; it is made of none effect and the promise loses its force. In this light we can understand 1 C. 1:17: οὐκ ἐν σοφίᾳ λόγου, ἵνα μὴ κενωθῇ ὁ σταυρὸς τοῦ Χριστοῦ. Paul must avoid preaching which involves false synthesis in content and empty technique in form, lest the cross of Christ should lose its searching and saving content, lest it should be robbed of its offence and therewith of its divine force and efficacy to save, lest it should become impotent and meaningless (cf. 1:18 ff.). [3]

† κενόδοξος.

One who is able or who tries to establish an unfounded opinion (κενὴ δόξα), one who talks big, who is boastful and vainglorious, Polyb., 27, 6, 12; Epict. Diss., III, 24, 43 (synon. ἀλαζών); Jul. Or., 6, 180c; Vett. Val., VII, 2 (p. 271, 2): κενόδοξος κληρονομία, a "dazzling inheritance," Did., 3, 5 : μηδὲ φιλάργυρος μηδὲ κενόδοξος.

Paul admonishes us in Gl. 5:26 : μὴ γινώμεθα κενόδοξοι, "let us not be boasters."

† κενοδοξία.

a. "Delusion," a favourite word of Epicurus, p. 78, 7; = κενὴ δόξα, cf. p. 74, 16; 78, 2 and 5 etc.; cf. also Philodem. Philos., ed. Sudhaus (1892), I, p. 332, 14 f.; Diod. S., 17, 107 of the Indian Karanos who gives himself to the flames ; Polyb., 10, 33, 6; Philo Mut. Nom., 96; Leg. Gaj., 114; Wis. 14:14. b. "Boasting," "vainglory," Vett. Val., 358, 31; Polyb., 3, 81, 9 (synon. τῦφος); 4 Macc. 2:15 (synon. ἀλαζονεία etc.); 9:19.

Sense a. is not found in the NT, though it is common in the post-apostolic fathers : Ign. Mgn., 11: τὰ ἄγκιστρα τῆς κενοδοξίας, "the hook of delusion"; Herm. s., 8, 9, 3 : πειθόμενοι ταῖς κενοδοξίαις τῶν ἐθνῶν. Sense b. occurs at Phil. 2:3 : μηδὲν κατ' ἐριθείαν μηδὲ κατὰ κενοδοξίαν, cf. Ign. Phld., 1, 1; 1 Cl., 35, 5; Herm. m., 8, 5.

Oepke

---

[3] Cf. Joh. W., Bchm. 1 K., *ad loc.*

κ ε ν ο δ ο ξ ί α. For bibl. cf. *Rheinisches Museum f. Philologie*, NF, 70 (1915), 188; 72 (1917/18), 383.

---

† κέντρον

A. κέντρον outside the NT.

The basic meaning is "anything which pierces." The usual verb is κεντέω (only ἐκκεντέω in the NT [→ II, 446], Jn. 19:37; Rev. 1:7).[1]

It is used 1. of the claws of animals, being common in the zoological writings of Aristot., e.g., Part. An., IV, 6, p. 682b, 33 ff., cf. Plut. Fort., 3 (II, 98d), esp. of the sting of bees, Aristot. Gen. An., III, 10, p. 759b, 4, cf. Hist. An., V, 21, p. 553b, 4, or of wasps, Hist. An., IX, 41, p. 628b, 4, naturally also in Aristoph. Vesp., 225, 407, 420 etc. For the κέντρον of the scorpion, Part. An., IV, 6, p. 683a, 12. Cf. also the quill of the porcupine, the spur of the cock, etc. (examples in Liddell-Scott).

It is also 2. a human instrument. a. "Spur," "whip," "goad" (wooden stick with metal points) to drive horses, oxen and other beasts of burden etc.; cf. already Hom. Il., 23, 387: ἄνευ κέντροιο θέοντες (horses in a chariot race), cf. 430: κέντρῳ ἐπισπέρχων, in both cases = μάστιξ. More common in Eur.: ἐπῆγε κέντρον εἰς χεῖρας λαβὼν πώλοις, Hipp., 1194 f., cf. Iph. Aul., 220; Herc. Fur., 882 and 949. Also in prose writers, Plat. Phaedr., 253e: μάστιγι μετὰ κέντρων μόγις ὑπείκων, cf. 254a,[2] Xenoph. Cyrop., VII, 1, 29; Philostr. Imagines (ed. O. Benndorf-C. Schenkl [1893]), II, 23, 1. In relation to oxen, Plut. Mar., 27 (I, 421b). It often happened that the ox esp. resisted the goad; hence the fig. expression πρὸς κέντρα λακτίζειν (→ 664). b. The "scourge" was also used on men either for chastisement or for torture, so Hdt., III, 130: μάστιγάς τε καὶ κέντρα, cf. Schol. Aristoph. Nu., 450 (ed. F. Dübner [1842] and Suid., s.v. κέντρων). c. The word can also be used for a nail, rivet or bracket, Paus., X, 16, 1: περόναις (clamps) ἢ κέντροις. Cf. also the receipt of a metal-worker from the Fayyûm in the time of Antoninus, BGU, II, 189, No. 544, lines 12-13: κέν[τ]ρου σιδηροῦ κίστην μίαν ταλάντων δύο.[3] Perhaps we should mention in this connection the verse in Soph. Oed. Tyr., 1318: κέντρων ... τῶνδ' οἴστρημα (rage), since κέντρα may be the περόναι (buckles) with which Oed. pierced his eyes (1268 ff.). Point of a spear, Polyb., 6, 22, 4.

3. Fig. κέντρον is used in many ways in relation to the life of the soul. The underlying metaphor may be that of the scourge or goad or that of the poison tip. Two passages are plain in this connection: ὄνειδος ... ἔτυψεν δίκαν διφρηλάτου (charioteer) μεσολαβεῖ (holding the middle) κέντρῳ (as with the charioteer's whip) ὑπὸ φρένας, Aesch. Eum., 155 ff.; (Pericles) μόνος τῶν ῥητόρων τὸ κέντρον ἐγκατέλιπε τοῖς ἀκροωμένοις, Eupolis Δῆμοι (Schol. Aristoph. Ach., 530, ed. F. Dübner [1842]), cf. Plat. Phaed., 91c on the lips of Socrates: ὥσπερ μέλιττα τὸ κέντρον ἐγκαταλιπών. In other passages the specific derivation of the figure is not so plain. The two basic concepts may merge to the degree that two essential features are common to both, namely, that the point is painful and that it acts as a spur. As the emphasis falls either on the one or the other aspect, the figurative use flows into two streams: a. "pain" or "torment," whether of body or of soul, and b. "spur," "incitement," "longing," both in a good sense and a bad. The senses naturally overlap. Pain brings dissatisfaction and is thus a goad, sometimes driving us to despair, while incitement by the κέντρον usually carries with

---

κ έ ν τ ρ ο ν. [1] κεντέω occurs in the LXX only at Job 6:4; ἐκκεντέω is more common.
[2] Greatly favoured is the combination κέντρα καὶ μάστιγες, e.g., Plat. Leg., VI, 777a.
[3] What kind of needle or nail or point is referred to we can only conjecture from the immediate context (λεπίδας (small plate) σιδηρᾶς, ἥλου χαλκοῦ, ἥλου σιδηροῦ, περονῶν χαλκῶν etc.).

it the thought of pain. Pain arises especially when the impulse is towards an objectively perverted or a subjectively undesired goal, and longing for that which is unattainable is naturally painful.

In the tragic poets we find the following examples : a. Aesch. Prom., 597: θεόσυτον (divinely caused) ... νόσον ..., ἃ μαραίνει με χρίουσα κέντροισι φοιταλέοισι (causing to wander), cf. 692; b. Aesch. Eum., 427: ποῦ γὰρ τοσοῦτο κέντρον ὡς μητροκτονεῖν, cf. Soph. Phil., 1039 : τὶ κέντρον θεῖον ... ἐμοῦ, Eur. Herc. Fur., 20 f.: Ἥρας, ὕπο κέντροις δαμασθείς. There is frequent reference to the κέντρα ἔρωτος, e.g., Eur. Hipp., 39, cf. 1301 ff.: τῆς ... ἐχθίστης θεῶν (Aphrodite) ... δηχθεῖσα κέντροις, [4] where the senses of pain and attraction are very closely linked. In these passages it is interesting to note how strongly the believing Greek sees all human life determined by the destructive or saving rule of the gods. There are many instances in the prose writers too, a. Plat. Phaedr., 251e : κέντρων τε καὶ ὠδίνων ἔληξεν, b. Plat. Resp., IX, 573a : πόθου κέντρον, cf. 573e : the κέντρα of ἐπιθυμίαι, esp. ἔρως. [5] Of the attraction of the appearance of Cleopatra, Plut. Anton., 27 (I, 927e); more generally κέντρον τι θυμοῦ, Plut. De Cleomene, 1 (I, 805b), cf. Ael. Arist. Or., 28, 104 (Keil). Of the inflaming effect of music, Plut. Inst. Lac., 14 (II, 238a), cf. De Lycurgo, 21 (I, 53a). Of the power of the word (in many nuances): Eupolis Schol. Aristoph. Ach., 530 (→ 663), Plat. Phaed., 91c (→ 663), [6] Ael. Arist. Or., 28, 115 (Keil): κέντρων τῶν λόγων. Esp. of the tongue: Eur. Herc. Fur., 1288 : γλώσσης πικροῖς κέντροισι, cf. Aesch. Fr., 169 (TGF): κέντημα γλώσσης, σκορπίου βέλος λέγω. [7]

4. He who has a κέντρον at his disposal has power ; hence κέντρον in the human sphere can be linked with the thought of authority. But since it is only he whose authority does not rest on inner superiority that resorts to the κέντρον to ensure his dominion by the use of naked force, κέντρον usually carries with it the undertone of tyranny (κέντρον is not, then, a neutral equivalent of σκῆπτρον). Wicked men make use of the κέντρον. Cf. the verse of Solon : κέντρον δ᾽ ἄλλος ὡς ἐγὼ λαβών, κακοφραδής (of evil intent) τε καὶ φιλοκτήμων ἀνήρ, οὐκ ἂν κατέσχε δῆμου, Solon, 24 (Diehl, I,37). [8] Also Soph. Fr., 622, TGF : κωτίλος (garrulous) δ᾽ ἀνὴρ λαβὼν πανοῦργα χερσὶ κέντρα κηδεύει πόλιν, [9] and Plat. Leg., VI, 777a : κατὰ δὲ θηρίων φύσιν κέντροις καὶ μάστιξιν ... ἀπεργάζονται δούλας τὰς ψυχὰς τῶν οἰκετῶν. Scoundrels have δεινὰ κέντρα (Plat. Resp., VIII, 552c and e).

In this connection we may quote the proverbial saying πρὸς κέντρα λακτίζειν (→ 663; 666) as an expression of futile and detrimental resistance to a stronger power, whether it be that of a god, of destiny, or of man. The saying occurs often from Aeschylus to Libanius ; we also have the variant κῶλον ἐκτείνειν instead of λακτίζειν. The most

---

[4] Cf. the representation of the god of love with an arrow.

[5] Non-literary examples, Preis. Zaub., IV, 2908 ff.: ἄξον τὴν δεῖνα ... φιλότητι καὶ εὐνῇ, οἴστρῳ ἐλαυνομένην, κέντροισι βιαίοις ὑπ᾽ ἀνάγκη (magic of love). On the other hand, longing for one who is dead (burial inscr., Byzantium, 3/4 cent. A.D.): σῆς γλυκερῆς ψυχῆς κέντρον ἄπαυστον ἔχων (Epigr. Graec., 534, 8, cf. Moult.-Mill., s.v.).

[6] Cf. the well-known sentence in Plat. Apol., 30e where Socrates sees himself as προσκείμενον τῇ πόλει ὑπὸ τοῦ θεοῦ, ὥσπερ ἵππῳ μεγάλῳ μὲν καὶ γενναίῳ, ὑπὸ μεγέθους δὲ νωθεστέρῳ καὶ δεομένῳ ἐγείρεσθαι ὑπὸ μύωπός τινος.

[7] We also read of κέντρον in relation to the eye : οἷον ὀφθαλμῷ κέντρον ... ἐνθεῖσα, Philostr. Imagines, II, 1, 2, and indeed : πολλὰ ... αὐτοῦ (sc. ὄμματος) πρὸς τὸν αὐλὸν τὰ κέντρα, I, 21, 2. Finally κέντρον can even be used of the mirror : κατόπτρῳ ἐοικυῖαν παρασχέσθω τὴν γνώμην ἀθόλῳ (bright) καὶ στιλπνῷ (shining) καὶ ἀκριβεῖ τὸ κέντρον, Luc. Quomodo Historia conscribenda sit, 51.

[8] Cf. Ael. Arist. Or., 28, 138 (Keil). The exegesis of Ael. Arist. is incorrect : ἄλλος δ᾽ ἂν τοῦτο τὸ κέντρον εἰς τοὺς λόγους εἰσενεγκάμενος οὐκ ἂν τοσοῦτο σωφροσύνης εἰσηνέγκατο (ibid., 139).

[9] In illustration cf. 1 K. 12:11, 14.

important and typical examples from the earlier period are : Pind. Pyth., 2, 94 ff. (173 ff.): ποτὶ κέντρον δέ τοι λακτιζέμεν τελέθει ὀλισθηρὸς οἷμος (a slippery path);[10] Aesch. Ag., 1624 : πρὸς κέντρα μὴ λάκτιζε, μὴ πταίσας μογῆς (to suffer misfortune); Prom., 322 f.: οὔκουν ἔμοιγε χρώμενος διδασκάλῳ πρὸς κέντρα κῶλον ἐκτενεῖς, ὁρῶν ὅτι τραχὺς μόναρχος οὐδ' ὑπεύθυνος (responsible, accountable) κρατεῖ, Eur. Ba., 794 f.: θύοιμ' ἂν αὐτῷ μᾶλλον ἢ θυμούμενος πρὸς κέντρα λακτίζοιμι θνητὸς ὢν θεῷ, Eur. Fr., 604, TGF : πρὸς κέντρα μὴ λάκτιζε τοῖς κρατοῦσί σου, Iph. Taur., 1396 : πρὸς κέντρα λακτίζοντες.[11]

5. κέντρον has a special sense in mathematics. Here it first denotes the point on a set of compasses, or the compasses themselves. But by extension it then comes to denote the point at which we fix one side of the compasses while making a circle with the other. κέντρον is thus the centre of a circle (Lat. *centrum*), then the centre of any surface or body, and even the centre of the universe, e.g., Aristot. An. Pri., I, 24, p. 41b, 15, Meteor., II, 5, 362b, 1, Probl., XV, 4, p. 911a, 5, Plut. De Placitis Philosophorum, III, Prooem. (II, 892e), Epict. Diss., I, 29, 53; for further passages from mathematical literature, and on the use of the word in astronomy,[12] *v.* Liddell-Scott. In the fig. sense we find in the Moralia of Plut. the fixed expression : (ὡς, καθάπερ) κέντρῳ καὶ διαστήματι περιγράφειν τι, De Garrulitate, 21 (II, 513c), De Cupiditate Divitiarum, 4 (II, 524 f.) etc. The origin of the expression is to be seen in Quaest. Plat., V, 2 (II, 1003e): ὁ κύκλος γράφεται κέντρῳ καὶ διαστήματι (radius). Cf. also De Romulo, 11 (I, 23d): ὥσπερ κύκλον κέντρῳ περιέγραψαν τὴν πόλιν.[13]

The LXX, Philo and Joseph. know and use the word.

It occurs 5 times in the LXX, twice for a goad, Prv. 26:3 : ὥσπερ μάστιξ ἵππῳ καὶ κέντρον (Heb. מֶתֶג "rein") ὄνῳ, οὕτως ῥάβδος ἔθνει παρανόμῳ, Sir. 38:25 : τί σοφισθήσεται ὁ κρατῶν ἀρότρου καὶ καυχώμενος ἐν δόρατι κέντρου, βόας ἐλαύνων . . . ; (here the δόρυ κέντρου is also meant ironically as a symbol of dominion, cf. under 4.). At 4 Macc. 14:19 it is used for the sting of a bee : μέλισσαι . . . ἐπαμύνονται τοὺς προσιόντας καὶ καθάπερ σιδήρῳ τῷ κέντρῳ πλήσσουσιν. It occurs twice in Hos. in a fig. sense : 5:12 : καὶ ἐγὼ . . . ὡς κέντρον (Heb. רָקָב, damage done by worms) τῷ οἴκῳ Ἰουδα. The meaning of κέντρον may be seen from the fine depiction of its operation in v. 13 : καὶ εἶδεν . . . Ἰουδας τὴν ὀδύνην αὐτοῦ. κέντρον

---

[10] Shortly before (88): χρὴ δὲ πρὸς θεὸν οὐκ ἐρίζειν.

[11] Lat. examples in A. Otto, *Die Sprichwörter . . . d. Römer* (1890), 331 f. For Lib. cf. E. Salzmann, *Sprichwörter u. sprichwört. Redensarten bei Lib.,* Diss. Tübingen (1910), 75. JHS, 8 (1887), 261 gives the following example from an inscr. : λακτίζεις πρὸς κέντρα, προ[σα]ντία κύματα μοχθεῖς (quoted from Zn. Ag., II, 801, n. 23). Cf. also Jul. Or., 8, 246b : χρὴ δὲ καὶ οὗ γεγόναμεν τιμᾶν, ἐπειδὴ τοῦτο θεῖός ἐστι νόμος, καὶ πείθεσθαί γε οἷς ἂν ἐπιτάττῃ καὶ μὴ βιάζεσθαι μηδέ, ὅ φησιν ἡ παροιμία, πρὸς κέντρα λακτίζειν· ἀπαραίτητον γάρ ἐστι τὸ λεγόμενον ζυγὸν τῆς ἀνάγκης. On the understanding of the saying, cf. the formulation in Ael. Arist., 45, 53 (Dindorf): πρὸς νόμον καὶ ταῦτα ἀνθρώπων ἅμα καὶ θεῶν βασιλέα μάχεσθαι with reference to Pindar, also Schol. Pind. Pyth., 2, 173a (ed. A. B. Drachmann [1903 ff.]) and Schol. Aesch. Prom., 323 (ed. G. Dindorf, III [1851]).

[12] Cf. here the passage in A. Souter, "Greek Metrical Inscr. from Phrygia," VI, line 4 (Class. Rev., 11 [1897], p. 136a, and n. on p. 137a. Interesting, too, is the use of the term in relation to time, a "point in time," "moment," Stob., I, 105, 1 (κέντρου μονή).

[13] The image of the circle, and of the κέντρον as its centre, has a place in the language of mysticism, Plot. Enn., VI, 9, 10 : ἕν ἐστιν ὥσπερ κέντρῳ κέντρον συνάψας (of the unity of him who sees and what is seen). On the margin we may adduce two peculiar uses. Soph. Fr., 734 TGF (ῥακτηρίοις κέντροισιν) has it for κῶπαι, "oar," with the twofold suggestion of the oar cleaving the sea and of sticking the oar into the sea. Sotades in Plut. Lib. Educ., 14 (II, 11a) uses it as a euphemism for πόσθη (penis): εἰς οὐχ ὁσίην τρυμαλιὴν τὸ κέντρον ὠθεῖς.

is a painful and disturbing instrument of chastisement in the hand of Yahweh. 13:14 : ἐκ χειρὸς ἅδου ῥύσομαι αὐτούς ... ποῦ τὸ κέντρον σου (Heb. קֶטֶב, corruption, wasting) ᾅδη ; ῞Αιδης is here represented as a personified force which has a κέντρον as the symbol of its dominion and which uses it painfully against men. It is worth noting that in the three verses in which there is a Heb. basis the original has nothing to correspond exactly to κέντρον. This is true only in another verse, Qoh. 12:11: λόγοι σοφῶν ὡς τὰ βούκεντρα (Heb. דָּרְבֹנוֹת).

Philo : in Som., II, 294 God is the charioteer who holds the reins of the world, keeping the world on a tight rein and with the whip (μάστιξι καὶ κέντροις) reminding it of His δεσποτικὴ ἐξουσία, which it is inclined to forget. In two passages we have the meaning "centre," Conf. Ling., 5 : the earth as the centre of the universe, 156 : κέντρον as the centre of a circle. In other passages we have a fig. use corresponding to the examples under 3. : Det. Pot. Ins., 46 : ἡδονῆς ἢ λύπης ἤ τινος ἄλλου πάθους κέντροις, Congr., 74 : κέντροις φιλοσοφίας, Leg. Gaj., 169 : to add a bitter point (κέντρον ὑποκακόηθες) to jests.

Joseph. speaks of the κέντρον of passion, Ant., 7, 169 : τῷ ... ἔρωτι καιόμενος καὶ τοῖς τοῦ πάθους κέντροις μυωπιζόμενος (Ammon for Tamar), and of the κέντρον of attraction, Bell., 2, 385 : ἀποστάσεως κέντρον, 3, 440 : κέντρον ἑτέρων ... συμφορῶν.

We also find the word in Ps. Sol. God stirs man from the sleep of death : ἐνυξέν με ὡς κέντρον ἵππου ἐπὶ τὴν γρηγόρησιν αὐτοῦ (16:4).

B. κέντρον in the NT.

1. In the NT κέντρον occurs in 3 verses. In Ac. 26:14 Paul, in his defence before Agrippa, says that when Christ appeared to him on the Damascus road He spoke the words : σκληρόν σοι πρὸς κέντρα λακτίζειν. [14] He also notes specifically that the words were spoken τῇ ῾Εβραΐδι διαλέκτῳ. This raises at once the question whether what we have seen to be a common Greek and Latin expression (→ 664 f.) was also current in Hebrew or Aramaic. Now the OT has שֵׁבֶט הַנֹּגֵשׁ at Is. 9:3 (LXX : ἡ ῥάβδος τῶν ἀπαιτούντων), the Jew is familiar with the stick for oxen (מַסָּע, מַרְדֵּעַ) and its point (דָּרְבָן, Aram. זִקְתָּא), [15] and in Qoh. 12:11 the reference to the sayings of the wise which are as דָּרְבֹנוֹת == βούκεντρα (→ supra) gave the Rabbis occasion for exegetical reflection, [16] but the fact remains that the common Greek and Roman saying πρὸς κέντρα λακτίζειν does not occur at all in the Jewish sphere. [17] It thus seems that Christ's warning to Paul not to attempt futile and harmful resistance takes the form of a suitable Greek proverb. [18] To be quite blunt, Paul or Luke puts a Greek proverb on the lips of Jesus. It is, of course, no accident that this proverb should occur in the account of Paul's conversion

---

[14] → λακτίζειν is found only here in the NT. E and some lat and syr put this saying also behind v. 4 or v. 5 in chapter 9, and a few behind v. 7 in chapter 22.

[15] Str.-B., II, 769 f.

[16] Loc. cit.

[17] Allusion might be made to a saying like Mal. 3:8 : LXX εἰ (vl. μήτι) πτερνιεῖ (Heb. קבע or עקב) ἄνθρωπος θεόν. But 1. πτερνίζειν here means "to outmatch" and 2. the image of the κέντρον does not occur. Cf. also ψ 40:9 and Jn. 13:18. The word λακτίζειν is not found at all in the LXX.

[18] Cf. the interesting discussion of the problem in the Diss. Critico-phil. of Hager and Kapp, Leipzig, 1738 [Hanse].

which is given to the Hellenist Agrippa. If it comes from Paul himself, this means that he cleverly adapts himself to the situation, as on other occasions. Out of regard for his particular hearers, he works in a suitable proverb which it is most unlikely that he himself should not have known. If Luke is responsible, he is exercising his literary skill to find an expression, familiar to him as an educated man of the age, which will be suitable both to the situation on the Damascus road and to the situation of the address. There is little point in labouring the minor flaw that a Greek proverb is put on the lips of one who speaks Hebrew or Aramaic.

Yet some scholars have not let the matter rest at this, but have tried to prove a direct literary dependence of Lk., in this case on the Ba. of Eur. (→ 665). In favour of this it is argued that the situations in Ba. and Ac. are similar. In both cases we have resistance to a (new) deity, in the former of Pentheus to Dionysus, in the latter of Paul to Christ (cf. Ac. 5:39 : θεομάχος); in both cases the new worship is regarded as folly ; and in both cases the disputed god himself uses the saying as a warning. Further appeal is made to the plural, which is required by the metre in Eur. but which Lk. does not have to use, and which is thus to be explained only in terms of quotation. [19] Now there can be little doubt that Lk. would know the Ba. of Eur., and the situations are certainly similar. It might well be, then, that there is at least an allusion to the famous play. But this cannot be proved, since quite apart from Ba. the proverb had passed into the common stock of quotations of the educated Greek. The plural is in no sense decisive, since examples from a later period show that the proverb was current in this form. [20]

2. In his chapter on the resurrection (1 C. 15) Paul in v. 55 freely combines two OT verses (Is. 25:8 and Hos. 13:14) to give the quotation : κατεπόθη ὁ θάνατος εἰς νῖκος. ποῦ σου, θάνατε, τὸ νῖκος; ποῦ σου, θάνατε, τὸ κέντρον; (according to the most likely reading), and he then adds his own elucidation in v. 57: τὸ δὲ κέντρον τοῦ θανάτου ἡ ἁμαρτία, ἡ δὲ δύναμις τῆς ἁμαρτίας ὁ νόμος — there are no solid reasons to justify the many attempts to strike out this verse as a later gloss. We may here leave aside the much debated question of the relation of the Hos. passage to the Heb. original, and also the related question of the meaning of this verse in the original. [21] It is enough to say that there κέντρον is no direct equivalent of the Heb. (קָטְבְךָ → 666). For our present purpose, we must study the version in Paul. What does Paul mean when he speaks of the κέντρον θανάτου ? Is he thinking of the goad, so that we have a personification of death

---

[19] Cf. W. Nestle in Philol., 59 NF, 13 (1900), 46 ff.: "Anklänge an Eur. in d. Ag." The conclusion of Nestle (57) is that it is highly probable that Lk. "could not help some reminiscences of similar happenings in the sphere of secular Greek literature, and that in particular he was influenced by the most read of all Greek dramatists, and specifically by his last play, the Ba." Cf. also F. Smend in Angelos, I (1925), 34 ff., esp. 41 ff., where there is great stress on the plur. κέντρα. Cf. H. Windisch, ZNW, 31 (1932), 9 ff., who concludes (14) that "the 'saying of Jesus' is a Greek proverb, in all probability a quotation from Eur."

[20] On the plur. cf. W. G. Kümmel, R. 7 u. d. Bekehrung des Pls. (1929), 155 ff. His conclusion is that "we cannot say more than that the author of Ac. has adopted a common Greek proverb" (156 f.). The question is left open by A. Oepke, "Probleme d. vorchristl. Zeit d. Pls.," ThStKr, 105 (1933), 387 ff.: "The expression πρὸς κέντρα λακτίζειν is taken either directly from Eur. or from the popular legacy of Hellenism" (402, n. 3).

[21] Cf. Sellin in Seebergfestschrift, I (1929), 307 ff. The problem of the relation to the LXX is not important. LXX reads : ποῦ ἡ δίκη σου, θάνατε; ποῦ τὸ κέντρον σου, ᾅδη; (→ 666). The variations (νῖκος for δίκη and θάνατε for ᾅδη) are easily explained from the context of Paul's use of the saying.

with the goad in his hand to rule and torture man?[22] Or is he thinking of the poisonous tip, so that death is a dangerous beast which gives man a mortal prick? Both metaphors may play some part, but it is difficult to carry either of them through with logical consistency. We come closest to Paul's meaning if, combining v. 56 with the saying, we interpret it as follows. Death rules over the race. The reality of its awful rule rests on the reality of sin (cf. R. 5:12). What gives death its power (→ δύναμις, II, 308 and → 664)[23] is sin. When sin is overcome, death is robbed of its power. Like an insect which has lost its sting, it is helpless, just as he who drives a beast is helpless without his goad. But sin is conquered by Christ. Hence Paul can cry out in triumph: "O death, where is thy sting? Thanks be to God who gives us the victory through our Lord Jesus Christ" (v. 57).[24]

3. The third κέντρον verse is Rev. 9:10 in connection with the depiction of the visionary processes on the sounding of the 5th trumpet, which are strongly reminiscent of similar descriptions in Joel. From the abyss rise ἀκρίδες; καὶ ἐδόθη αὐτοῖς ἐξουσία ὡς ἔχουσιν ἐξουσίαν οἱ σκορπίοι τῆς γῆς (v. 3). They are given power to torment those who do not have the seal of God on their forehead; καὶ ὁ βασανισμὸς αὐτῶν ὡς βασανισμὸς σκορπίου, ὅταν παίσῃ ἄνθρωπον (v. 5b). From v. 7 on there follows the imaginative description of this terrible being, and finally we read in v. 10: καὶ ἔχουσιν οὐρὰς ὁμοίας σκορπίοις (short for ὁμοίας οὐραῖς σκορπίων) καὶ κέντρα (i.e., in their οὐρά), that is, they have stings like scorpions. This is what makes them dangerous: καὶ ἐν ταῖς οὐραῖς αὐτῶν ἡ ἐξουσία αὐτῶν ἀδικῆσαι τοὺς ἀνθρώπους (10b). We are thus dealing with fabled demonic creatures, the product of oriental fantasy,[25] half locust, half scorpion, whose dangerous weapon is the κέντρον, the poisonous sting, which is what orientals feared in the scorpion.

Lothar Schmid

---

[22] Also possible is the image of an armed man with his striking lance or mortal arrow (cf. death as the man with the scythe), but this can hardly derive from κέντρον and is of later attestation, cf. death with the (broken) lance in the Uta-Evangeliarium at the beginning of the 11th cent., W. Molsdorf, *Christl. Symbolik d. mittelalterl. Kunst*[2] (1926), 241. For death with arrows, *ibid.*, 243 [Bertram].

[23] Not that which makes death painful.

[24] On the grouping Law-sin-death suggested in v. 56, cf. the exposition in R. 7:7 ff. On the thanksgiving in v. 57 cf. R. 8:1 ff.

[25] Cf. the fabled Indian monster μαρτιχόρας depicted by Ktesias in Aristot. Hist. An., II, 1, p. 501a, 25 ff., of which we read at the end (30 ff.): τὴν δὲ κέρκον (tail) ὁμοίαν τῇ τοῦ σκορπίου τοῦ χερσαίου (living on land), ἐν ᾗ κέντρον ἔχειν καὶ τὰς ἀποφυάδας (shoots) ἀπακοντίζειν (sc. φασίν).

---

† κέρας

A. The Horn outside the NT.

This word in common in all Greek.[1] It is used for the horn of an animal. In Rev. 13:11 of the animal like a lamb: εἶχεν κέρατα δύο. Of the horns of the altar, i.e., the horn-like corners,[2] Rev. 9:13 on the basis of OT usage, Ex. 27:2 etc.

Horns are commonly mentioned in religion to depict the strength and might of the gods[3] and also as an apotropaic means and symbol of human strength and bravery.[4] But the word κέρας does not seem to be used by the Gks. for physical bravery. In Hom. it is an expression for rigidity of the eyes.[5] Proverbially it is a symbol of courage.[6] Aristot. regards it as a weapon of defence like the sting, claw or tusk.[7] The book of dreams of Artemid. contains no suggestion that horns are linked with power.[8]

In the OT, however, the horn is not only an expression for physical power in symbolical prophetic action (3 Βασ. 22:11) or in visionary depiction of the might which has scattered Israel[9] (Zech. 2:1-4); it is a direct term for power (קֶרֶן). In this sense (as also for the horn of the altar) the LXX always has the rendering κέρας (up to Job 16:15, → infra): Dt. 33:17: κέρατα μονοκέρωτος τὰ κέρατα αὐτοῦ, "his power is as that of an unicorn"; 2 Βασ. 22:3 = ψ 17:2, where the par. expressions ὑπερασπιστής μου, κέρας σωτηρίας μου and ἀντιλήμπτωρ μου are used. The symbolism is always apparent, ψ 21:21: σῶσόν με ἐκ στόματος λέοντος καὶ ἀπὸ κεράτων μονοκερώτων τὴν ταπείνωσίν μου. But while teeth, mouth and claws are always an image for the violent exercise of force (Mi. 4:13: τὰ κέρατά σου θήσομαι σιδηρᾶ καὶ τὰς ὁπλάς σου θήσομαι χαλκᾶς), κέρας, even when there is no reference to the original horn of an animal (esp. the bull), is used simply to denote physical might and power: Sir. 49:5: the kings of Judah ἔδωκαν γὰρ τὸ κέρας αὐτῶν ἑτέροις καὶ τὴν δόξαν αὐτῶν ἔθνει ἀλλοτρίῳ. A very common OT expression is to exalt or to destroy a horn. The original figure may still be seen in Job 16:15: וְעֹלַלְתִּי בֶעָפָר קַרְנִי (LXX: τὸ

κ έ ρ α ς. I. Scheftelowitz, "Das Hörnermotiv in den Religionen," ARW, 15 (1912), 451-487; S. A. Cook, *The Religion of Ancient Palestine in the Light of Archaeology* (1930), 29 ff.; Comm. on Lk. 1:69; Rev. 5:6; 12:3; 13:1; 17:12. A. Schlatter, "Das AT in d. joh. Apk.," BFTh, 16, 6 (1912), 88-90; L. Brun, "D. römischen Kaiser in d. Apk.," ZNW, 26 (1927), 128-151; W. Foerster, "Die Bilder in Apk. 12 f. u. 17 f.," ThStKr, 104 (1932), 279 ff., esp. 291-300; Str.-B., I, 9 f., 70; II, 110 f.

[1] On the relation of κέρας/cornu to קֶרֶן v. F. Delitzsch, *Studien über indogermanisch-semitische Wurzelverwandtschaft* (Diss. Leipzig, 1873), 88 f.; H. Möller, *Vergleichendes indogermanisch-semitisches Wörterbuch* (1911), 121 and 142; H. Bauer and P. Leander, *Historische Grammatik d. hbr. Sprache d. AT* (1922), 12.

[2] These were originally real horns, Scheftelowitz, 473; P. Volz, *D. biblischen Altertümer*² (1925), 25, though cf. K. Galling, *Bibl. Reallexikon* (1934 ff.) 17 ff. Ill. in Cook, IV, 2; Galling, 19.

[3] Scheftelowitz, *passim*.

[4] *Ibid.*, 465.

[5] Od., 19, 211.

[6] Diogenianus Paroemiographus, VII, 89 in Paroemiographi Graeci, ed. E. L. Leutsch and F. G. Schneidewin, I (1839): πρὸ τούτου σε ᾤμην κέρατα ἔχειν· ἐπὶ τῶν ἀνδρείας ὑπόληψιν ἐχόντων.

[7] Part. An., III, 1, p. 661b, 31.

[8] Oneirocr., I, 39 relate horns in a dream to sudden death if borne by ζῷα βίαια, since animals with horns were usually slaughtered.

[9] There is a suggestion of the beast which pushes on all sides.

δὲ σθένος μου ἐν γῇ ἐσβέσθη). It is for God to exalt or to trample down the horn; when ὑψοῦν κέρας is used of men, it denotes arrogance, ψ 74:4, 5. We find (ἀν)ὑψοῦν 12 times, and ἐπαίρειν and (ἐξ)ἀνατέλλειν twice each; for the opp. we have συγκλᾶν 3 times and once each συντρίβειν, συγκόπτειν and καταγνύναι. κέρας ἐγείρειν never occurs. The meaning is always that of the winning or loss of power.

In later Judaism we still find the imagery of the horn. In Eth. En. 90:9 the growing of horns on lambs denotes their growing power; in 90:37(39) the Messiah is a white bullock with big, black horns, his power and royal dignity being thus suggested. [10] In S. Bar. 66:2 it is said of Josiah that he lifted up the horn of the saints and exalted the righteous and honoured the wise. Rabbinic examples are to the same effect. [11] The image is particularly frequent in prayers for the ending of Israel's subjection to the Gentiles, e.g., in the 15th petition of the Babylonian form of the Prayer of Eighteen Petitions: קַרְנוֹ תָרוּם בִּישׁוּעָתֶךָ ... בָּרוּךְ אַתָּה יְ"י מַצְמִיחַ קֶרֶן יְשׁוּעָה, in the prayer Abinu malkenu etc. [12] The hi of צמח is used as well as the verb רום. This expresses rather more clearly the fact that the reference is not just to the strengthening of an existing power, but to the creation of a power which does not yet exist.

B. The Horn in the NT.

1. In this sense we can quote the expression (Lk. 1:69): ἤγειρεν κέρας σωτηρίας ἡμῖν ἐν οἴκῳ Δαυὶδ παιδὸς αὐτοῦ. The distinctive feature of the verb ἐγείρειν is that it never seems to be linked with κέρας in the LXX (not even at Ex. 29:31; ψ 131:17). ἐγείρειν is used of God as the Governor of history, as the One who causes a thing to happen, who brings historical events into being. κέρας σωτηρίας is taken from 2 Βασ. 22:3 = ψ 17:2 and signifies a power of salvation, a power of help and blessing. If the Rabbis speak of the horn of the Messiah, this is not quite the same as the horn of help. But in Lk. the addition "in the house of David, thy servant" shows that Zacharias has the Messiah in view when he speaks of the power of salvation. In content, this passage does not transcend the OT form of the hope.

2. The symbol of the horn occupies a special position in the figurative language of Rev. The two horns of the other beast of 13:11 are simply meant to denote that it has the external appearance of a lamb. There is allusion here to the saying of Jesus concerning wolves in sheep's clothing. Whether we are also to see a reference to the two horns of the ram in Da. 8:3 [13] is highly doubtful. Elsewhere the image of the horn is used allegorically. It stands in no organic relation to the animals which carry it, but has independent symbolical significance. The Lamb has seven horns in 5:6, the dragon and the beast have ten in 12:3; 13:1; 17:3, 7, 12, 16. In accordance with the symbolical meaning of the number seven (→ ἑπτά) and of the figure of the horn, the seven horns of the Lamb express the divine plenitude of power. The great serpent has ten horns as well as the beast. In the case of the latter the horns

---

[10] The horns do not of themselves denote royal dignity, as R. H. Charles suggests in ICC on Rev. 5:6.

[11] M. Ex. 15:14; Str.-B., II, 110, with further instances. That the horn gradually dropped out of use as an image of power is perhaps indicated by the rendering of קֶרֶן as תּוּקְפָּא in Tg. O. Dt. 33:17; cf. W. Grundmann, Der Begriff der Kraft in d. nt.lichen Gedankenwelt (1932), 72, n. 23.

[12] Str.-B., I, 10; II, 111.

[13] Bss. Apk. on 13:11.

are mentioned before the seven heads, and they bear the crowns which in the case of the serpent adorn the heads. These minor differences can hardly be without significance, but it is no longer possible to say with any certainty what the significance is. In 17:12 ff. Rev. itself tells us that the ten horns are ten kings who have yet to come, who with the beast will receive power as kings for one hour, who will give their power to the beast, who with the beast will destroy Babylon and who will venture to make war on the Lamb. In respect of the number 10 Rev. follows Da. 7:7, and in respect of the reference to kings it follows Da. 7:24 and 8:20 ff. Once in Rabbinic literature the ten horns, or some of them, are referred to specific kings of the 3rd century A.D.[14] We find the same in the Hebrew Elias Apocalypse.[15] The Syrian Ezra Apocalypse[16] refers to the Omayyad rule in terms of a serpent with 12 horns on its head and 9 on its tail. In Barn., 4, 4 f. we again have allusion to the Daniel prophecy of 10 horns, but the interpretation is uncertain.[17] If the beast is historically linked with Nero redivivus, it is natural to refer the horns of Rev. to contemporary princes, most likely Parthian satraps, who would help the returning Nero and destroy Rome in revenge. Another possibility, however, is to see in the 10 horns, along with the 7 heads, a second list of the Roman emperors from Caesar onwards.[18] Some commentators have also suggested demonic powers,[19] though these are represented by the beast.[20] The interpretation in terms of Parthian satraps or a second list of emperors is almost certainly mistaken. For the true function of the horns is not to destroy Babylon. It is to put their power at the disposal of the beast in the war against the Lamb, and what is the role of Parthian satraps in this connection? The meaning of the 10 horns is determined by the fact that as 10 kings they are identical with the kings of the whole world (16:14, 16) who are provoked by spirits from the serpent and the beasts to fight against Christ at Armageddon. What Rev. says about the 10 horns implies, then, that all the rulers of the last time and their subjects (cf. 19:17 ff.) are at the disposal of Antichrist in the final open battle against Christ. The picture of the serpent with 10 horns is a picture of Satan as the one who will turn the power of the whole race against Christ. Other interpretations cannot explain the fact that Satan, too, bears the image of the 10 horns.

In this regard it is to be noted that, although Judaism applied the 4th beast of Da. to Rome, neither in the war of 66-70 nor in that of 132-135, so far as we know, was any part played by the reference of the 10 horns to Roman emperors. Finding the beast with 10 horns unserviceable as a contemporary symbol, 4 Esr. replaced it by that of the eagle with a series of feathers. Remaining Rabbinic exegesis either refers the last of the 10 horns to personages of the 3rd cent. A.D. (→ supra) or offers only a very confused interpretation.[21]

Foerster

[14] Gn. r., 76 on 32:12; Str.-B., I, 95 f.
[15] M. Buttenwieser, Die hbr. Elias-Apk., I (1897), 18, line 5; 63; 68 ff.
[16] W. Bousset, Der Antichrist (1895), 47.
[17] Wnd. Barn., ad loc.
[18] So Brun.
[19] Bss. Apk., 416; Charles on Rev. 17:14.
[20] Foerster, op. cit., 299, n. 3.
[21] Midr. Ps. 75 § 5 on 75:11; Str.-B., II, 110 f.

---

† κέρδος, † κερδαίνω

κέρδος, "gain," "advantage," "profit," from the time of Hom., [1] e.g., Aesch. Choeph., 825 : ἐμὸν ... κέρδος αὔξεται τόδε, Eum., 991: μέγα κέρδος ὁρῶ τοῖσδε πολίταις, Thuc., VII, 68, 3; Polyb., 6, 46, 3 : νομίζειν τι κέρδος, Xenoph. Cyrop., IV, 2, 43 : κέρδος ἡγεῖσθαι, Plat. Polit. 300a : κέρδους ἕνεκά τινος, Epict. Diss., I, 28, 13; III, 22, 37 etc.; Philo Spec. Leg., IV, 121: οὐ διὰ κέρδος ἄδικον, Leg. Gai., 242 : οὐχ ὑπὲρ κέρδους, ἀλλ' ὑπὲρ εὐσεβείας ἐστὶν ἡ σπουδή· ... τί γὰρ ἂν εἴη κέρδος λυσιτελέστερον ὁσιότητος ἀνθρώποις; Ditt. Syll.[3], 249, 19 : κέρδους καὶ χάριτος ἕνεκα. A derived sense is that of the "desire for gain or profit," e.g., Pind. Pyth., 3, 54, quoted in Athenag. Suppl., 29, 1, cf. 31, 2 : ἢ κέρδους ἢ ἐπιθυμίας ἐλάττους γενομένους ἁμαρτεῖν, Soph. Ant., 222; Eur. Heracl., 3. κέρδος is often used in the plur. (Hom.) in the sense of "crafty counsels," "cunning" etc. Esp. in relation to life or death we find the following formulations : Plat. Ap., 40e d : καὶ εἴτε ... μηδεμία αἴσθησίς ἐστιν, ἀλλ' οἷον ὕπνος, ἐπειδάν τις καθεύδων μηδ' ὄναρ μηδὲν ὁρᾷ, θαυμάσιον κέρδος ἂν εἴη ὁ θάνατος, Soph. Ant., 464 : πῶς ὅδ' οὐχὶ κατθανὼν κέρδος φέρει; Eur. Med., 145 : τί δέ μοι ζῆν ἔτι κέρδος; Aesch. Prom., 747 ff.: τί δῆτ' ἐμοὶ ζῆν κέρδος ... κρεῖσσον γὰρ εἰσάπαξ θανεῖν ἢ τὰς ἁπάσας ἡμέρας πάσχειν κακῶς, Jos. Ant., 15, 158 : κέρδος δ' εἰ θνῆσκοιεν ἐν συμφορᾷ τὸ ζῆν ποιούμενοι.

The antonym is → ζημία, not usually in the narrower sense of punishment, but in the more general sense of "disadvantage," "detriment." Soph. Fr., 738, TGF : ζημίαν λαβεῖν ἄμεινόν ἐστιν ἢ κέρδος κακόν, Plat. Leg., VIII, 835b : οὐδ' αὖ ... μέγα τῇ πόλει κέρδος ἢ ζημίαν ἂν φέροι, Xenoph. Cyrop., II, 2, 12 : μήτε ἐπὶ τῷ ἑαυτῶν κέρδει, μήτ' ἐπὶ ζημίᾳ τῶν ἀκουσάντων, μήτ' ἐπὶ βλάβῃ μηδεμιᾷ, Isoc., 3, 50 : μὴ τὸ μὲν λαβεῖν κέρδος εἶναι νομίζετε, τὸ δ' ἀναλῶσαι ζημίαν, Gal. De Hippocratis et Platonis Decretis, IV, 6 (ed. J. v. Müller [1874], p. 376): ὁ μὲν δειμῶν ἐπιγινομένων ἀφίσταται, ὁ δὲ κέρδους ἢ ζημίας φερομένης ἐξελύθη καὶ ἐνέδωκεν, ὁ δὲ καθ' ἕτερα τοιαῦτα οὐκ ὀλίγα (v. Arnim, III, 123, 28 ff.); Epict. Diss., III, 26, 25 : ἀλλὰ σκεῦος μὲν ὁλόκληρον καὶ χρήσιμον ἔξω ἐρριμμένον πᾶς τις εὑρὼν ἀναιρήσεται καὶ κέρδος ἡγήσεται, σὲ δ' οὐδείς, ἀλλὰ πᾶς ζημίαν. Nevertheless, ζημία (ζημιοῦσθαι) can often have the sense of punishment as an antonym of κέρδος without altering the sense of the latter. Eur. Med., 454 : πᾶν κέρδος ἡγοῦ ζημιουμένη φυγῇ, Aristot. Eth. Nic., V, 7, p. 1132a, 12.

κερδαίνειν, "to procure gain, advantage or profit," either abs. or with indication of the source. Hdt., VIII, 5; Aristoph. Av., 1591; P. Oxy., XII, 1477, 10; Jos. Ant., 5, 135; Hdt., IV, 152 : μέγιστα ἐκ φορτίων κερδαίνειν, Soph. Ant., 312 : ἐξ ἅπαντος, Xenoph. Mem., II, 9, 4 : ἀπὸ παντός, Soph. Trach., 231: χρηστὰ κερδαίνειν ἔπη, Plat. Resp., 343b : ὁ δὲ πολλὰ κερδαίνει, Jos. Bell., 2, 590 : πολλὰ παρὰ τῶν πλουσίων ἐκέρδανεν. Cf. Aristot. Eth. Nic., V, 7, p. 1132, 13 : τὸ μὲν γὰρ πλέον ἔχειν ἢ τὰ ἑαυτοῦ, κερδαίνειν λέγεται· τὸ δ' ἔλαττον τῶν ἐξ ἀρχῆς, ζημιοῦσθαι. A more general sense of κερδαίνειν, and just as common, is "to win, to attain something." Pind. Isthm., 5, 27: λόγον (fame) ἐκέρδαναν, Jos. Bell., 5, 74 : Ῥωμαῖοι ... κερδήσουσιν ἀναιμωτὶ τὴν πόλιν, 2, 324 : κερδήσειν αὐτοὺς τὴν πατρίδα καὶ τὸ μηδὲν παθεῖν πλέον. In some contexts this can lead to the sense "to save oneself something," Philem. (ed. T. Kock in CAF, 92, 10): μεγάλα κακά, Jos. Ant., 2, 31: τό γε μὴ μιανθῆναι τὰς χεῖρας αὐτῶν, Diog. L., VII, 14 : μέρος τῆς ἐνοχλήσεως.

Neither κέρδος nor κερδαίνειν occurs in the LXX. κέρδος is found in Σ (κερδαίνω at Job 22:3), but in the LXX this is χρήσιμον (= Θ) at, e.g., Gn. 37:26 (יֶבֶצַע‎), ὠφέλεια at ψ 29:9 (בֶצַע‎), cf. Θ Job 22:3, and μισθὸς ἀγαθός at Eccl. 4:9 (noun for שָׂכָר‎).

κ έ ρ δ ο ς κτλ. [1] Cf. Pass., Liddell-Scott, *s.v.*

In the NT Tt. 1:11 refers to the αἰσχρὸν κέρδος for the sake of which members of the community teach what they ought not. In Phil. 1:21 Paul says that for him to live is Christ, and therefore death, in which this life finds fulfilment in sight, is advantage or gain. For the sake of Christ who is his life all the natural and historical advantages that belong to the Jews by divine ordination, and especially their moral superiority and blamelessness, which might otherwise seem to be κέρδη, advantages, are now regarded as a disadvantage, ζημία (Phil. 3:7). [2] In the light of the all-transcending knowledge of Christ the life which trusts in, and appeals to, descent, the Law and achievement, is not just fruitless exertion but harmful in the absolute sense.

κερδαίνειν occurs in the NT in the sense 1. "to get (commercial) gain" (Jm. 4:13), 2. "to spare oneself something" (Ac. 27:21), and 3. "to win something," ἄλλα πέντε τάλαντα (Mt. 25:16, 17, 20, 22), but also Χριστόν (Phil. 3:8). In the main, however, κερδαίνειν is a missionary term. [3] Thus in 1 C. 9:19 ff. it means "to make a Christian," and is interchangeable with σῴζειν, 9:22. Cf. 1 Pt. 3:1: ἵνα καὶ εἴ τινες ἀπειθοῦσιν τῷ λόγῳ, διὰ τῆς τῶν γυναικῶν ἀναστροφῆς ἄνευ λόγου κερδηθήσονται. Mt. 18:15 speaks of winning the erring brother who can perhaps be restored to the right path by another's word. The concrete sense is disputed at Mt. 16:26, where the antithesis is ζημιωθῆναι [4] : τί γὰρ ὠφεληθήσεται ἄνθρωπος, ἐὰν τὸν κόσμον ὅλον κερδήσῃ, τὴν δὲ ψυχὴν αὐτοῦ ζημιωθῇ; Either winning the world means lordship over it as the sphere of natural goods and earthly possibilities, or κόσμος (עוֹלָם) implies men [5] as the object of missionary endeavour. The former is more likely in view of Rabbinic parallels, [6] which have הִשְׂתַּכֵּר for κερδαίνειν and אָבֵד for ζημιωθῆναι, and also in view of the context (v. 25).

Schlier

κεφαλή, ἀνακεφαλαιόομαι

Contents: A. κεφαλή outside the NT: 1. Secular Usage; 2. The LXX: 3. Jewish Literature; 4. Hellenistic Gnostic Usage. B. κεφαλή in the NT: 1. Theologically Unimportant Usage; 2. 1 C. 11:3 ff.; 3. κεφαλή in Ephesians and Colossians.

A. κεφαλή outside the NT.

1. As regards the history of the term κεφαλή in its theological significance, the first important point in secular usage is that it denotes what is first, supreme, or extreme. Thus from Hom. it is commonly used for the "head" of a man or animal in many different connections, but also for the "point," the "top," the "end," or the "point of departure." It may be the prow of a ship, Theocr. Idyll., 8, 87, the head of a pillar, CIG, II, 2782, 31; Poll. Onom., VII, 121; cf. LXX 3 Βασ. 7:21, the top of a wall, Xenoph.

---

[2] → II, 890.
[3] J. Weiss on 1 C. 9:19.
[4] → II, 891.
[5] Schl. Mt., 521 f.
[6] Str.-B., I, 749 f.

κ ε φ α λ ή. Pass., Liddell-Scott, Moult.-Mill., *s.v.*

Cyrop., III, 3, 68; Hist. Graec., VII, 2, 8, the mouth of a river, Callim. Aetia (P. Oxy., XVII, 2080, 48), but also its source, Hdt., IV, 91, the start of an epoch, Aetius, Placita Philosophorum (ed. H. Diels in Doxographi Graeci [1879], 2, 32, 2; Joh. Lyd. De Mensibus (ed. R. Wünsch [1898]), 3, 4, or a month, 3, 12. Worth noting is the phrase in Aristoph. Pl., 649 f.: τὰ πράγματα ἐκ τῶν ποδῶν εἰς τὴν κεφαλήν σοι πάντ᾽ ἐρῶ, also κεφαλὴν ἐπιθεῖναι, κεφαλὴν ἀποδοῦναι τοῖς εἰρημένοις, to add a conclusion to what has been said, Plat. Tim., 69b, Phileb., 66d, Gorg., 505d etc. κεφαλή then occurs with τέλος, e.g., Philo Sacr. AC, 115 : κεφαλὴ δὲ πραγμάτων ἐστὶ τὸ τέλος αὐτῶν; Vit. Mos., II, 290 : τὸ τέλος τῶν ἱερῶν γραμμάτων, ὃ καθάπερ ἐν τῷ ζῴῳ κεφαλὴ τῆς ὅλης νομοθεσίας ἐστίν; Som., I, 66 : τῆς ἀρεσκείας κεφαλὴν καὶ τέλος τὸν θεῖον λόγον.

But this leads us already to the second aspect, i.e., not merely what is first, or supreme, at the beginning or the end, but also what is "prominent," "outstanding" or "determinative." Thus man's head is not just one member among others, Xenoph. Cyrop., VIII, 8, 3. It is also the first and chief member which determines all the others. Philo is reproducing popular ideas when in Op. Mund., 118 he enumerates the seven outward parts of the body, and then says in 119 : τὸ ἡγεμονικώτατον ἐν ζῴῳ κεφαλή; cf. Spec. Leg., III, 184 etc. But the κεφαλή is τὸ ἡγεμονικώτατον because, as some Stoics say (v. Arnim, III, 217, 19): τὸ ἡγεμονικὸν ἐν τῇ κεφαλῇ. Thus, in relation to the tradition that Athena (ἡ τοῦ Διὸς σύνεσις) was born from the head of Zeus, Cornut. Theol. Graec., 20 says : τάχα μὲν τῶν ἀρχαίων ὑπολαβόντων τὸ ἡγεμονικὸν τῆς ψυχῆς ἡμῶν ἐνταῦθ᾽ εἶναι, ... τάχα δ᾽ ἐπεὶ τοῦ μὲν ἀνθρώπου τὸ ἀνωτάτω μέρος τοῦ σώματος ἡ κεφαλή ἐστι, τοῦ δὲ κόσμου ὁ αἰθήρ, ὅπου τὸ ἡγεμονικὸν αὐτοῦ ἐστι καὶ ἡ τῆς φρονήσεως οὐσία· κορυφὴ δὲ θεῶν, κατὰ τὸν Εὐριπίδην, ὁ περὶ χθόν᾽ ἔχων φαεννὸς αἰθήρ. Rather different is the physiologically based theory of Galen's De Remediis, I prooem. (ed. Kühn, XIV, p. 313): αὕτη γὰρ (sc. ἡ κεφαλή) καθάπερ τις ἀκρόπολίς ἐστι τοῦ σώματος καὶ τῶν τιμιωτάτων καὶ ἀναγκαιοτάτων ἀνθρώποις αἰσθήσεων οἰκητήριον. When the idea of that which is determinative is linked with the point of departure κεφαλή can easily take on the sense of ἀρχή, cf. examples in the LXX and Gnosticism (→ 675; 678).

Thirdly, κεφαλή is used in secular speech for the "whole man," the "person." In the κεφαλή we meet the man. This is clear in certain maledictions : Aristoph. Ach., 833 : ἐς κεφαλὴν τράποιτ᾽ ἐμοί, Nu., 40 : ἐς τὴν κεφαλὴν ἅπαντα τὴν σὴν τρέψεται, cf. Pax, 1063; Pl., 526; Plat. Euthyd., 283e : εἰ μὴ ἀγροικότερον ἦν εἰπεῖν, εἶπον ἄν· Σοὶ εἰς κεφαλήν, Demosth. Or., 18, 290 : ἃ σοὶ καὶ τοῖς σοῖς οἱ θεοὶ τρέψειαν εἰς κεφαλήν, 18, 294 etc. In the κεφαλή is man's life. Hence the term can be used for "life" : Hom. Il., 17, 242 : ἐμῇ κεφαλῇ περιδείδια, cf., 4, 162; Od., 2, 237: σφὰς γὰρ παρθέμενοι κεφαλάς, corresponding to ψυχὰς παρθέμενοι in 3, 74; Hdt., VIII, 65 : ἀποβαλέεις τὴν κεφαλήν. Finally the κεφαλή is the "man himself," Hom. Il., 11, 55 : πολλὰς ἰφθίμους κεφαλάς, 18, 82 : ἴσον ἐμῇ κεφαλῇ (not less than I myself); Hdt., IX, 99 : πεντακοσίας κεφαλὰς τῶν Ξέρξεω πολεμίων, Hom. Il., 8, 281: φίλη κεφαλή, 23, 94 : ἠθείη (dear, beloved) κεφαλή, Pind. Olymp., 7, 67: ἑᾷ κεφαλᾷ, Plat. Phaedr., 264a : φίλη κεφαλή, Eur. Rhes., 226 : Ἄπολλον, ὦ δία κεφαλά, Demosth. Or., 21, 117: ἡ μιαρὰ καὶ ἀναιδὴς αὕτη κεφαλή, 18, 153; Vett. Val., II, 16 (p. 74, 7): μεγάλη κεφαλή (a great man); VII, 5 (p. 292, 12, 14); Jul. Or., 7, 212a : τῆς θείας κεφαλῆς. We may also refer to the phrase κατὰ κεφαλήν (man for man), in which we see the beginning of the fig. significance, e.g., Aristot. Pol., II, 10, p. 1272a, 14; Jos. Ant., 7, 109 : φόρους ὑπέρ τε τῆς χώρας καὶ τῆς ἑκάστου κεφαλῆς etc. [1]

It will be seen that in secular usage κεφαλή is not employed for the head of a society. This is first found in the sphere of the Gk. OT.

---

[1] Cf. examples of ἡ ἁγία κεφαλή (dear head) for "honoured person" in F. J. Dölger, Antike u. Christentum, 3 (1932), 81, n. 3.

2. The LXX adopts the Gk. use. Here, too, in almost exclusive rendering of the Heb. רֹאשׁ, [2] it denotes the "head" of man or beast, Gn. 28:11; 40:16; 48:14 etc.; Gn. 3:15; Ex. 12:9; 29:10 etc., also of an idol, Ep. Jer., 8. We also find the related sense of "point," "limit," "top" etc., Gn. 8:5 : αἱ κεφαλαὶ τῶν ὀρέων; Ju. 9:25, 36; Gn. 11:4 : κεφαλή of the πύργος of Babel ; 28:12, of the κλῖμαξ; 2 Βασ. 2:25 : ἔστησαν ἐπὶ κεφαλὴν βουνοῦ ἑνός; cf. also Job 2:7: ἀπὸ ποδῶν ἕως κεφαλῆς. In various expressions a man is often described in terms of his κεφαλή, e.g., κατὰ κεφαλήν (לְגֻלְגֹּלֶת), Ex. 16:16; Nu. 1:2 etc., cf. Gn. 49:26 : The εὐλογίαι ... ἔσονται ἐπὶ κεφαλὴν Ἰωσήφ, καὶ ἐπὶ κορυφῆς ὧν ἡγήσατο ἀδελφῶν; 4 Βασ. 25:27: ὕψωσεν ... τὴν κεφαλὴν Ἰωακίμ, ψ 3:3 : δόξα μου καὶ ὑψῶν τὴν κεφαλήν μου; Prv. 10:6 : εὐλογία κυρίου ἐπὶ κεφαλὴν δικαίου; 11:26; Is. 35:10; 51:11 etc.; Lam. 3:5 : ἀνῳκοδόμησεν κατ᾿ ἐμοῦ καὶ ἐκύκλωσεν κεφαλήν μου καὶ ἐμόχθησεν; Ju. 9:57 B : καὶ τὴν πᾶσαν πονηρίαν ἀνδρῶν Συχὲμ ἐπέστρεψεν ὁ θεὸς εἰς κεφαλὴν αὐτῶν : 1 Βασ. 25:39; Jl. 3:4, 7; 3 Βασ. 8:32 : δοῦναι τὴν ὁδὸν αὐτοῦ εἰς κεφαλὴν αὐτοῦ; Ez. 9:10; 11:21; 16:43 etc.; 1 Esr. 8:72 : αἱ γὰρ ἁμαρτίαι ἡμῶν ἐπλεόνασαν ὑπὲρ τὰς κεφαλὰς ἡμῶν; 2 Esr. 9:6; Jdt. 8:22; Job 29:3 etc. Common, too, is the phrase which recurs in Mt. 27:25 and Ac. 18:6, cf. 2 Βασ. 1:16 : τὸ αἷμά σου ἐπὶ τὴν κεφαλήν σου; 3 Βασ. 2:32 f.; 3:1; Ez. 33:4; ψ 7:16. Worth noting is Is. 43:4 : καὶ δώσω ἀνθρώπους πολλοὺς ὑπὲρ σοῦ καὶ ἄρχοντας ὑπὲρ τῆς κεφαλῆς σου. It is the only verse in which κεφαλή stands for נֶפֶשׁ; κεφαλή has here the sense of life.

The implied element of what is superior or determinative is expressed in the LXX along with the sense of "man" or "person." κεφαλή is used for the head or ruler of a society. At Dt. 28:13 the antithesis κεφαλή/οὐρά is an obvious starting-point for this sense. To be sure, there is no express reference to Israel as the κεφαλή over others. But v. 13 in comparison with v. 43 f. shows that headship over someone (προσήλυτοι) is at issue : καταστήσαι σε κύριος ὁ θεός σου εἰς κεφαλὴν καὶ μὴ εἰς οὐράν, καὶ ἔσῃ τότε ἐπάνω καὶ οὐκ ἔσῃ ὑποκάτω, ἐὰν ἀκούσῃς τῶν ἐντολῶν κυρίου τοῦ θεοῦ σου ... 43 : ὁ προσήλυτος ... ἀναβήσεται ἐπὶ σὲ ἄνω ἄνω, σὺ δὲ καταβήσῃ κάτω κάτω ... 44 : ... οὗτος ἔσται κεφαλή, σὺ δὲ ἔσῃ οὐρά. In Is. 9:13 f. κεφαλή καὶ οὐρά refer in proverbial fashion to the μέγας and μικρός among the people, though a glossator introduces the thought of honourable men and lying prophets. It is worth noting that in v. 14 κεφαλή is interchangeable with ἀρχή. Apart from the antithesis κεφαλή/οὐρά, κεφαλή is used for "head," "ruler," "leader" of others or of a society at Ju. 10:18 : καὶ ἔσται (who ventures to fight the Ammonites) εἰς κεφαλὴν πᾶσιν τοῖς κατοικοῦσιν Γαλααδ, cf. 11:8, 9; 11:11 : καὶ κατέστησαν αὐτὸν (Jephthah) ἐπ᾿ αὐτῶν εἰς κεφαλὴν εἰς ἡγούμενον. In 10:18; 11:8, 9 B avoids κεφαλή and has ἄρχων instead, though it has it κεφαλή in 11:11: εἰς κεφαλὴν καὶ εἰς ἀρχηγόν. Cf. 3 Βασ. 20:12 : καὶ ἐκάθισαν τὸν Ναβουθαι ἐν ἀρχῇ τοῦ λαοῦ, where A has : ἐν κεφαλῇ τοῦ λαοῦ; 2 Βασ. 22:44 : καὶ ῥύσῃ με ἐκ μάχης λαῶν, φυλάξεις με εἰς κεφαλὴν ἐθνῶν· λαὸς ὃν οὐκ ἔγνων ἐδούλευσάν μοι (= ψ 17:43); Is. 7:8 f. ἡ κεφαλὴ Αραμ Δαμασκός ..., καὶ ἡ κεφαλὴ Εφραιμ Σομορων, καὶ ἡ κεφαλὴ Σομορων υἱὸς τοῦ Ρομελιου. This use does not have the further thought that those ruled by the κεφαλή are in the relation to it of a σῶμα. This is particularly clear in Is. 1:4 ff., cf. 7:20, where comparison of the people with a human body is implicit in the background. Cf. also Da. 2:31 ff., where the four empires appear under the image of a man, but only the first under the image of the κεφαλή as the highest part of man, 2:38.

---

[2] Though κεφαλή is almost exclusively used for רֹאשׁ, in many passages in the LXX רֹאשׁ is rendered differently, esp. by ἀρχή, ἄρχων, ἀρχηγός, ἡγεῖσθαι, προηγεῖσθαι, χιλίαρχος and κορυφή. The most varied Gk. words can be used according to context ; in all about 30 are used for רֹאשׁ, e.g., ἀριθμός at Nu. 1:49; ἀρχή (vl. ἀρχαῖος) at Is. 41:4; ἀρχιπατριώτης at Jos. 21:1; πατριάρχης at 2 Παρ. 19:8; 26:12; μέγας at 2 Παρ. 24:11; πρωτότοκος (variant) at 1 Παρ. 5:12; 11:11; πρῶτος in 9 passages etc. Aquila, however, always seems to have κεφαλή, even at Dt. 29:18(17); 32:33, where רֹאשׁ means poison. [Bertram.]

3. Dt. 28:13 is sometimes quoted or used in Jewish lit.[3]: Jub. 1:16: "And I will change them into a plant of righteousness ... and they shall be a blessing and not a curse, the head and not the tail"; cf. En. 103:11; Ab., 4, 15b. For the antithesis κεφαλή/ οὐρά cf. Philo Praem. Poen., 125: καθάπερ γὰρ ἐν ζῴῳ κεφαλὴ μὲν πρῶτον καὶ ἄριστον, οὐρὰ δ' ὕστατον καὶ φαυλότατον, οὐ μέρος συνεκπληροῦν τὸν τῶν μελῶν ἀριθμόν, ἀλλὰ σόβησις τῶν ἐπιποτωμένων ([means to] the driving off of flies), τὸν αὐτὸν τρόπον κεφαλὴν μὲν τοῦ ἀνθρωπείου γένους ἔσεσθαί φησι τὸν σπουδαῖον εἴτε ἄνδρα εἴτε λαόν, τοὺς δὲ ἄλλους ἅπαντας οἷον μέρη σώματος ψυχούμενα ταῖς ἐν κεφαλῇ καὶ ὑπεράνω δυνάμεσιν. Man's head is mentioned in Test. Zeb. 9 with reference to the divinely willed unity of Israel: "Do not divide into two heads; for everything which the Lord has made has only one head. He has given two shoulders, hands and feet, but all the members obey one head." But this comparison does not go beyond the LXX view. This is true only of much later and relatively infrequent combinations like "head of the priesthood," Slav. En. App. 3:37; Cave of Treasures, 2, 22: "O Adam, behold, I have made thee king, priest and prophet, and lord and head and leader of all created things"; 3, 1: the "head of the lower order"; Heb. En. 5:6 (Odeberg, p. 16): "the head of all the world's idolaters"; 45, 2 (p. 142): "the head of each generation" etc. ראש or κεφαλή has here only a very refined sense, cf. the title ראש הכנסת for the ἀρχισυνάγωγος: Sota, 7, 7 f.; Yoma, 7, 1; T. Meg., 4, 21 etc.

4. The term κεφαλή took on a special sense in Hellenistic and Gnostic circles influenced by speculations concerning the aeon and the first man — redeemer.[4] The sources which give us insight into these views are often late, but other, pre-Christian sources show that they embody ancient traditions.

In Indian cosmogony the cosmos is viewed as the gigantic body of the supreme god.[5] Persian cosmology is also dominated by this view. In this context we can only give this general indication. Yet it is also important for us that we find the idea of an eternal cosmic god of the universe in the Orph. Fr., 168 (Kern, 201 f.): Ζεὺς πρῶτος γένετο, Ζεὺς ὕστατος ἀργικέραυνος, Ζεὺς κεφαλή, Ζεὺς μέσσα, Διὸς δ' ἐκ πάντα τέτυκ-ται ... Ζεὺς βασιλεύς, Ζεὺς αὐτὸς ἁπάντων ἀρχιγένεθλος. The aeon which is here called Zeus embraces in its head and body the totality which in turn arises from it.

The same idea lies behind Fr., 167 and also the Gk. writing Περὶ Ἑβδομάδων c. 6 § 1 (ed. W. H. Roscher [1913]). Its outriders are found in the Sarapis oracle to king Nicocreon of Cyprus (Macrob. Sat., I, 20, 17):

εἰμὶ θεὸς τοιόσδε μαθεῖν, οἷόν κ' ἐγὼ εἴπω·
οὐράνιος κόσμος κεφαλή, γαστὴρ δὲ θάλασσα,
γαῖα δέ μοι πόδες εἰσί, τὰ δ' οὔατ' ἐν αἰθέρι κεῖται,
ὄμμα τε τηλαυγὲς λαμπρὸν φάος ἠελίοιο.

This has rightly been compared with a passage from the Leiden magic pap. (P. Leid., V, Preis. Zaub., XII, 243),[6] where we read of the παντοκράτωρ: οὗ καὶ ὁ ἥλιος, οὗ ἡ γῆ ἀκούσασα ἑλίσσεται, ... καὶ οὐρανὸς μὲν κεφαλή, αἰθὴρ δὲ σῶμα, γῆ

---

[3] Cf. later Const. Ap., II, 14, 12 (VIII, 47, 34): The bishop is κεφαλή, he should not οὐρᾷ προσέχειν.

[4] Cf. on what follows R. Reitzenstein and H. H. Schaeder, *Studien z. antiken Synkretismus aus Iran u. Griechenland* (1926); H. Schlier in *Religionsgeschtl. Untersuchungen z. d. Ignatiusbriefen* (1929), 88 ff.; *Christus u. d. Kirche im Epheserbrief* (1930), 37-60; E. Käsemann, *Leib u. Leib Christi* (1933), 59-97; 137 ff. For detailed bibl. cf. Schlier.

[5] E.g., Rgveda, X, 90, where heaven is the head, the sun the eyes, the parts of heaven the ears, the atmosphere the body and the earth the feet.

[6] A. Dieterich, *Abraxas* (1891), 195; Reitzenstein, op. cit., 99 f. We are quoting from Preis.; there are many variants in Dieterich and Reitzenstein.

πόδες, τὸ δὲ περί σε ὕδωρ ὠκεανός ... σὺ εἶ κύριος, ὁ γεννῶν καὶ τρέφων καὶ αὔξων τὰ πάντα. [7] The individual parts (elements) of the world are members of the god which bears the whole cosmos in itself. The κεφαλή is thus one member among others, though as the οὐρανός it is supreme and decisive.

This aeon myth, which is cosmologically fashioned, undergoes a significant change in Gnosticism. Its concepts and vocabulary are here put in the service of the first man — redeemer myth, which is soteriologically orientated.

We cannot list the resultant modifications in detail. But in the interests of our study of κεφαλή we must indicate the general change. Because of the anthropological concern, the aeon god becomes the man god or the first man, who comprises in himself the substance of the cosmos, the powers of soul. But the world god aeon also becomes the man god or redeemer, in whom is concentrated the remaining substance of a fallen world, the purified powers of soul. The first man and the redeemer are identical in respect of the substance enclosed in them, but different in respect of the destiny (or development) which they undergo. The first man (= aeon) who bears the cosmos (of men) in himself recovers from the fall in the redeemer (= aeon) who gathers and establishes the cosmos (of men) in himself.

In this connection the κεφαλή of the aeon plays a twofold part. On the one side it is the κεφαλή apart from the σῶμα, to which it belongs, but which is now a torso, the body which is the fallen and scattered cosmos. On the other side, it is within the σῶμα, which is the regathered and reestablished, i.e., the redeemed cosmos. Here, then, the concept of κεφαλή contains both an element of basic superiority over the body and also an element of unity with it.

Elements of this view, though naturally without integration into the scheme of redemption, may be found already in a passage in Philo's commentary on Exodus. [8] To the question where is the head if the breast in the official regalia of the high-priest represents heaven and the stars, Philo answers : *verbum est sempiternum sempiterni dei caput universorum ; sub quo pedum instar aut reliquorum quoque membrorum subjectus iacet universus mundus, supra quem transiens (?) constanter stat, ... quia necessarium est mundo ad perfectam plenitudinem pro cura habenda exactissimae dispensationis atque pro propria pietate* (χρηστότης) *omnis generis ipsius, divini verbi, sicut et animantia opus habent capitis, sine quo vivere non possunt.* The *logos,* here viewed in Stoic fashion as διοικητής and not in Gnostic as σωτήρ, is the head which rules the cosmos that is totally subject to it, and which maintains its life. In this κεφαλή the cosmos, even though it is *universus mundus,* finds its fulness. [9] The distinctiveness of this κεφαλή is expressed more clearly, because within the schema of redemption, in the very complicated text of the so-called Naassene sermon. [10] Acc. to § 20 there are two anthropoi, the higher or Adamas (the ἀχαρακτήριστος ἄνθρωπος) and the lower (the κεχαρακτηρισμένος ἄνθρωπος). These are identical in substance but different in form. The latter is the fallen first man who is brought back to himself, to the higher first man, by the former. But acc.

---

[7] Cf. also Corp. Herm., X, 10b, 11, where Platonic motifs (Tim., 44d ff.) seem to be mixed with the idea of the aeon. At any rate, this theory explains many peculiar features of the text (Scott, II, 249). In Stob. Excerpt., XXIV (Scott, I, 500 f.) the earth, which is in the centre of the universe, is ὥσπερ ἄνθρωπος <πρὸς> οὐρανὸν βλέπουσα.

[8] Cf. § 117 in R. Reitzenstein, *Die Vorgeschichte d. christlichen Taufe* (1929), 118.

[9] There is a similar relation of κεφαλή to the remaining σῶμα in the letter mysticism of Marcus, Hipp. Ref., VI, 44. The κεφαλή of ἀλήθεια is formed from α and ω, and its remaining members each from two other letters at the beginning and end of the alphabet. But α and ω are on the one side letters of the whole series and on the other the two basic and inclusive letters, → I, 1 ff.

[10] For the text cf. Reitzenstein (→ n. 4), 161-173.

to § 14 the higher anthropos is ὁ ἀκρογωνιαῖος <ὁ> εἰς κεφαλὴν γωνίας (the corner stone), which is then elucidated as follows : ἐν κεφαλῇ γὰρ εἶναι τὸν χαρακτηριστικὸν ἐγκέφαλον, τὴν οὐσίαν (the character = the world soul = the self = the descending Adamas). In the κεφαλή is the substance which loses itself as world. He himself, the higher Adamas, remains the κεφαλή, as may be seen also in § 20, though here we find κορυφή for κεφαλή. The lower man, who is only a torso, returns to this κεφαλή, i.e., to his κεφαλή. In Exc. Theod. (in Cl. Al.), 42, 1-3 it is said in the context of horos-stauros theology that through the cross Christ the κεφαλή brings the σπέρμα, the Church, into the πλήρωμα. The explanation is offered : ὤμοι ... τοῦ σπέρματος ὁ 'Ιησοῦς λέγεται, κεφαλὴ δὲ ὁ Χριστός. Christ, the heavenly anthropos, the κεφαλή, brings His body to itself, the higher anthropos, in Jesus, the first man — redeemer. We find further traces of this κεφαλή-σῶμα idea in passages which do not develop it. Cf. Exc. Theod., 33, 2 : καὶ ἔστιν ὡσπερεὶ ῥίζα καὶ κεφαλὴ ἡμῶν, ἡ δὲ ἐκκλησία καρποὶ αὐτοῦ. In Act. Thom., 7 (II, 1, p. 110, 20) the πατὴρ τῆς ἀληθείας represents the κεφαλή of the first man Σοφία, which is his body. [11] In Ephr. Hymn., 55, II (ed. Assemani, Rome [1732 ff.], 558 n.) [12] the κόρη (Achamoth-Sophia) cries out in the words of Ps. 22:1: "My God and head, why dost thou forsake me ?" The κεφαλή concept of the first man — redeemer myth is also found in the Od. Sol., though it is not very clear, since the interest of the Od. is more in the relation of the redeemed to the Redeemer. In 17:14 ff. we read : "They received my blessing and were brought to life, they gathered to me and were redeemed. For they became my members and I their head. Blessed be thou, our head, Christ." The new man is constituted by the unity of the assembling members and the redeeming head. The obscure passage 23:14 also speaks of this head, the Redeemer Christ : "The head came down to the foot, the wheel to the feet (foot)." [13] Cf. v. 18 : "Then appeared ... a head which was revealed, the Son of truth from the Father," and 24:1: "The dove (wisdom) flew on to the head of our Lord, the Messiah, because He was its head." Not very different is the view of the Mandaean writings, which in part enshrine ancient Gnostic conceptions. Certainly we do not find here the "concretely pictorial consistency" of the κεφαλή-σῶμα myth. But this is simply to say that the description of the first man — redeemer (Adam, Hibil, Mandā d' Haijē) as the "head of the race" or "head of the age" (Lidz. Ginza R., I, 26 [p. 27]; II, 1, 49 [45] etc.) is not related to the κεφαλή-σῶμα myth or evolved out of the thought of the aeon, but stands closer to Jewish usage. [14] The development of the formulae in these writings is certainly related to the first man — redeemer myth. When Adam, the head of the race, rises up, he is followed by his whole race, the souls of the good, L., I, 2, 16 f. (p. 435 f.); I, 2, 19 f. (p. 437), and when Mandā d' Haijē, the head of initiates or believers, treads the path "from the place of darkness to the place of light," he is followed by believers, Ginza, L., III, 10, 86 ff. (p. 522 ff.). The same is true of Hibil, R., XI, 257 (p. 256 f.). If it is not said that the head assembles its members and becomes a heavenly man with them, this is implied. In Iren. Haer., I, 5, 3 we find a counterpart to the description of the redeemer or first man as κεφαλή, since we read here that the Achamoth wished to make the demiurge the κεφαλὴν μὲν καὶ ἀρχὴν τῆς ἰδίας οὐσίας, κύριον δὲ τῆς ὅλης πραγματείας. Cf. Hipp. Ref., VII, 23, 3 (200, 25 f.), where the great Archon is called ἡ κεφαλὴ τοῦ κόσμου; cf. VII, 27, 9 (207, 14 ff.); X, 14, 6 (275, 16).

As regards the formal sense of the term, we thus learn first that in this Gnostic usage it is very close to ἀρχή, and secondly that it involves a reference to the being of those who are determined by the κεφαλή.

---

[11] Though cf. G. Bornkamm, *Mythus u. Legende in d. apokryphen Thomasakten* (1933), 105 f.

[12] R. A. Lipsius, *D. apokryphen Apostelgeschichten und Apostellegenden,* I (1883), 305.

[13] Cf. Act. Thom., 6 (II, 1, p. 105, 6 f.): ἔγκειται δὲ ταύτης τῇ κεφαλῇ ἀλήθεια, χαρὰν δὲ τοῖς ποσὶν αὐτῆς ἐμφαίνει.

[14] In this way we may do justice to the doubts of E. Käsemann (→ n. 4), p. 74.

B. κεφαλή in the NT.

1. In the NT we often read of the κεφαλή of men or animals or demonic manifestations when the term has no theological significance. It may be noted that the same is true of the κεφαλή of Jesus, though apart from Mt. 8:20; Lk. (7:46;) 9:58 we read of this only in the passion narrative : Mt. 26:7; 27:29; Jn. 19:2; Mt. 27:30; Mk. 15:19; Mt. 27:37; Jn. 19:30; 20:7; 20:12. Reference is made to the head of the risen Lord in Rev. 1:14; 14:14; 19:12.[15]

2. In 1 C. 11:3, in relation to the question of the veiling of women in divine service, Paul says : θέλω δὲ ὑμᾶς εἰδέναι, ὅτι παντὸς ἀνδρὸς ἡ κεφαλὴ ὁ Χριστός ἐστιν, κεφαλὴ δὲ γυναικὸς ὁ ἀνήρ, κεφαλὴ δὲ τοῦ Χριστοῦ ὁ θεός. From 11:7: ἀνὴρ μὲν γὰρ οὐκ ὀφείλει κατακαλύπτεσθαι τὴν κεφαλήν, εἰκὼν καὶ δόξα θεοῦ ὑπάρχων· ἡ γυνὴ δὲ δόξα ἀνδρός ἐστιν, we learn that to the direct subjection of the man to Christ corresponds the fact that the man is εἰκὼν καὶ δόξα θεοῦ, and to the position of man as κεφαλή of the γυνή corresponds the fact that she is the δόξα ἀνδρός. εἰκὼν καὶ δόξα have here the sense of image and reflection; this is fixed by the allusion to Gn. 1:27. The same point emerges from v. 8 f., where the being of woman as δόξα, and indirectly of man as εἰκὼν καὶ δόξα, is explained by the fact that the origin and *raison d'être* of woman are to be found in man. Hence man is the image and reflection of God [16] to the degree that in his created being he points directly to God as Creator. Woman is the reflection of man to the degree that in her created being she points to man, and only with and through him to God. In this relation of man and woman we are dealing with the very foundations of their creaturehood. In formal terms, we have a determination of their being and not just of the mode of their historical manifestation. This may be seen from the reference to Adam in v. 7 ff., from the reference to the Christian life in the appendix in v. 11 f., and from the reference to the mode of historical existence in v. 12. In relation to this we read : ὥσπερ ... ἡ γυνὴ ἐκ τοῦ ἀνδρός, οὕτως καὶ ὁ ἀνὴρ διὰ τῆς γυναικός, so that in the Lord neither is without the other, but each is referred to the other, and through him to the κύριος.

Not merely as a Christian, nor historically, but ontologically and by nature woman lives of man and for him. If this is true, the use of κεφαλή rather than κύριος in v. 3 is not accidental. It is not that Paul is, as it were, individualising the κεφαλή-σῶμα concept of Gnosticism. He is using the term κεφαλή as it is familiar to him, and in respect of one element at least its root is in the LXX. κεφαλή implies one who stands over another in the sense of being the ground of his being. Paul could have used ἀρχή if there had not been a closer personal relationship in κεφαλή.

We may thus understand the passage. Paul presupposes that man and woman are distinct by nature. This is rooted in the fact that woman is by nature referred to man as her basis (in a twofold sense). This distinction is expressed in the veiling of her κεφαλή, [17] in the non-exposure of her head before God and Christ, whose

---

[15] On Jesus as κεφαλὴ γωνίας → ἀκρογωνιαῖος, I, 792 f.

[16] → εἰκών, II, 396 f.; cf. also H. Willms, EIKΩN I : "Philon v. Alexandreia" (1935), 48 f.

[17] On ἐξουσία in 11:10 → ἐξουσία II, 573 f. On the whole passage cf. Bchm. K., *ad loc.*; G. Delling, *Paulus' Stellung z. Frau u. Ehe* (1931), 96-105.

presence in worship is indicated by angels. [18] It would be for Paul an abandonment of the foundations of creation if charismatically gifted women — the reference is to such in contrast to 1 C. 14:33 ff. — were to pray or prophesy with their heads uncovered like men. It would be an offence against their head (in the twofold sense) is they were not to cover themselves. As the Corinthians themselves may see, the necessity of covering is indicated by nature or custom (φύσις), which regards long hair as suitable in women for a covering.

3. The term κεφαλή takes on decisive theological significance when referred to Christ and the Church in Eph. and Col. The passages at issue are Eph. 1:22 f.; 4:15 f.; 5:23; Col. 1:18; 2:10; 2:19.

a. It is obvious from these passages that the term refers first to Christ, the exalted Lord, as the Head of His body, the Church. He is the Head of His body, the Church, in the sense that from this Head the body grows up to this Head, Eph. 4:15 f.; Col. 2:19, so that body and Head form the ἀνὴρ τέλειος or the καινὸς ἄνθρωπος, Eph. 4:13; 2:15. The schema itself make it clear that we have here more than a figurative application of the relationship of the human body to Christ and the Church. We are in the sphere of the Gnostic redeemer myth as a development of the aeon conception. To describe Christ as the Head of the Church against this background is to emphasise the unity between Christ and the Church. He is the Head which has its body in the Church, and which is thus present in earthly and bodily form in the Church. And the Church is the κεφαλή which has its Head in Christ, and which is present in heavenly form in Christ. The Head is not present without or apart from the body, nor the body without or apart from the Head. [19] The Church is the earthly body of the heavenly Head.

In this unity of Christ and the Church the headship of Christ is manifested in the fact that He directs the growth of the body to Himself. The κεφαλή determines not merely the being of the body but also the fulfilment of its life. As the κεφαλή Christ is the ἐξ οὗ of the αὔξησις of the σῶμα to οἰκοδομή. He is the effective "whence" of the activity of the body whereby it edifies itself through the gifts given to its members. As the κεφαλή He is thus the concrete principle of the bodily growth of the Church. He is the ἀρχή, Col. 1:18.

His description as the κεφαλή of His body, the Church, contains finally the element of an eschatological orientation of the Church. The body grows up to the heavenly Head, Eph. 2:15; 4:12, 15 f. It does so in such a way that the κεφαλή is always the heavenly goal of this body, and this goal cannot be attained except in the body sustained by faith and knowledge. For this reason the basis of the relation of the body to the Head is always the obedience of subjection, Eph. 5:23 f. κεφαλή draws attention to the eschatological reservation under which the body always stands.

b. From these passages, however, it is also clear that Christ is the κεφαλή in another sense. In Col. 2:20 He is also called ἡ κεφαλὴ πάσης ἀρχῆς καὶ ἐξουσίας. Note should be taken of the parallel statements in 1:15 ff. To His being as Head of the body and first-begotten from the dead corresponds (καὶ αὐτός ἐστιν) that

---

[18] In my view this is how we are to understand the ἄγγελοι of 11:10, not as the guardians of order, and certainly not as hostile powers.

[19] As Ign. says in Tr., 11, 2, the ἔνωσις of God does not allow the members to separate themselves from the Head.

which is called His being before all things and τὰ πάντα ἐν αὐτῷ συνέστηκεν, or πρωτότοκος πάσης κτίσεως, 2:9, 10. In Christ the Head is grounded, not merely the Church, but creation. Here we see both the ideas and terminology of the Gnostic myth. Christ is not merely the Redeemer; He is also the First Man. These are not alongside one another. In the Redeemer the First Man is at work. The body of creation is known in the body of the Church. The totality has its consistence in the Christ who is Head of the body of the Church. Outside Christ, i.e., outside His body, creation is the world. Like the Church, creation is present only under the Head. Hence it is worth noting that in Eph. 1:22 we read : καὶ αὐτὸν ἔδωκεν κεφαλὴν ὑπὲρ πάντα τῇ ἐκκλησίᾳ. As the Head is given to the Church, so the Lord is given to the totality (πάντα without the art. because of the quotation). The same point is more clearly made in Eph. 4:15 : ἵνα ... ἀληθεύοντες ... ἐν ἀγάπῃ αὐξήσωμεν εἰς αὐτὸν τὰ πάντα, ὅς ἐστιν ἡ κεφαλή, Χριστός. When we speak the truth in love, we cause the totality to grow into Christ. Hence in Eph. 3:9 f. the mystery hidden before time (the aeons) in God the Creator is disclosed by apostolic proclamation. This is none other than the unsearchable riches of Christ. It is also the manifold wisdom of God. This mystery, Christ or the wisdom of God in creation, is known to the world διὰ τῆς ἐκκλησίας. In the Church as the body of Christ the hidden wisdom of God in creation is disclosed. Finally we may refer to Eph. 1:23b. The σῶμα τοῦ Χριστοῦ is τὸ πλήρωμα τοῦ τὰ πάντα ἐν πᾶσιν πληρουμένου. In His body, which represents the pleroma, the heavenly sphere of His presence, Christ draws all things into the pleroma.

This is to say, however, that the term κεφαλή, referred to Christ in this sense and context, expresses the claim of Christ and the Church to the world. Christ is from the very first the Lord of the world. For from the very first (πρὸ πάντων) the world consists in Him. When as the risen Lord He takes control of the world in His body, He is simply actualising His real power over creation. Hence the Church as His body, when it relates the world to itself, is simply in process of taking over what truly belongs to it. For this reason the Church is relevant to each and all things. It is fundamentally a kind of cosmos. It is thus forced to organise itself, not as a private society, but as a public body.

That the created world comes to fulfilment in Christ, the Head of the body, the Church, is also intimated by the distinctive term → ἀνακεφαλαιοῦσθαι in Eph. 1:10. The statement of v. 9 is that God has made known to us the secret of His will : ... ἀνακεφαλαιώσασθαι τὰ πάντα ἐν τῷ Χριστῷ, τὰ ἐπὶ τοῖς οὐρανοῖς καὶ τὰ ἐπὶ τῆς γῆς.

† ἀνακεφαλαιόομαι.

This term is rich in allusion and significance. It is rare in secular Gk. and unknown outside literary sources. [1] In accordance with its meaning it signifies "to bring something to a κεφάλαιον," "to sum up," "to give a comprehensive sum," also "to divide into the main portions." [2] The first sense predominates. It is hardly distinguishable from κεφαλαιοῦν. Ps.-Aristot. Mund., 4, p. 394a, 8 : αὐτὰ τὰ ἀναγκαῖα κεφαλαιούμενοι, Dion. Hal. Ant. Rom., I, 90 : τὴν ἀνακεφαλαίωσιν τῶν ἐν ταύτῃ δεδηλωμένων τῇ βίβλῳ, De Lysia, 9; Iren. Haer., I, 9, 2 : ἀνακεφαλαιούμενος ... περὶ τοῦ εἰρημένου, Orig. Comm. in Jn. 5:6 (103, 26 f.): νῦν δέ φησι πάντα μίαν κεφαλίδα, τῷ ἀνακεφα-

---

ἀνακεφαλαιόομαι. [1] Moult.-Mill., s.v.; Ew. Gefbr., ad loc.
[2] E. Fraenkel, Griech. Denominativa (1906), 135.

λαιοῦσθαι τὸν περὶ ἑαυτοῦ εἰς ἡμᾶς ἐληλυθότα λόγον εἰς ἕν, cf. Thuc., VIII, 53, 1: λόγους ἐπιοῦντο ἐν τῷ δήμῳ κεφαλαιοῦντες ἐκ πολλῶν, Heliodor. Aeth., 5, 16 : τὰ ... λεχθέντα ... ἐπιτεμνόμενος καὶ ὡσπερεὶ κεφαλαιούμενος. In this connection we may also quote R. 13:9. Cf. Orig. Orat., IX, 3 (CSEL, Orig., II, p. 319, 10). Nor is it used only of summing up in reflection or speech, but also of the gathering together of things. This is how we are to understand Θ and the Quinta at ψ 71:20 : ἀνεκεφαλαιώθησαν προσευχαὶ Δαυίδ (LXX : ἐξέλιπον; 'Α : ἐτελέσθησαν; Mas.: יֹכֻּלוּ); "the prayers of David are gathered together." Cf. also Barn., 5, 11: οὐκοῦν ὁ υἱὸς τοῦ θεοῦ εἰς τοῦτο ἦλθεν ἐν σαρκί, ἵνα τὸ τέλειον τῶν ἁμαρτιῶν ἀνακεφαλαιώσῃ τοῖς διώξασιν ἐν θανάτῳ τοὺς προφήτας αὐτοῦ. To be sure, in these passages it might be asked whether the sense is not that of "to bring to a conclusion."[3] Iren. Haer., V, 29, 2 : Et propter hoc in bestia veniente recapitulatio fit universae iniquitatis et omnis doli, ut in ea confluens et conclusa omnis virtus apostatica, in caminum mittatur ignis ... Recapitulans autem et omnem ... errorem, presupposes ἀνακεφαλαίωσις, ἀνακεφαλαιοῦσθαι in the sense of gathering together, summation. Since every summation implies a kind of repetition, the word may sometimes have the direct sense of "to repeat." The ἀνα- thus assumes an iterative sense which it does not have elsewhere. Cf. Aristot. Fr., 123, p. 1499a, 33 : ἔργα δὲ ῥητορικῆς ... προοιμιάσασθαι πρὸς εὔνοιαν, διηγήσασθαι πρὸς πίστιν, ἀγωνίσασθαι πρὸς ἀπόδειξιν, ἀνακεφαλαιώσασθαι πρὸς ἀνάμνησιν, Quint. Inst. Orat., VI, 1, 1: Rerum repetitio et congregatio, quae Graece dicitur ἀνακεφαλαίωσις, a quibusdam Latinorum enumeratio, et memoriam judicis reficit et totam simul causam ponit ante oculos. Apsines, Ars rhetorica (ed. Rhet. Graec.), 532 f.: ἀνακεφαλαίωσις is ἀθρόα ἀνάμνησις τῶν διὰ πολλῶν εἰρημένων. But also Prot. Ev. Jk., 13 : μήτι εἰς ἐμὲ ἀνεκεφαλαιώθη ἡ ἱστορία τοῦ 'Αδάμ; with reference to the repetition of an event. The recapitulare of Iren. is also to be understood in the first instance as repetition, though it is to be noted that this sums up the original and is thus qualitative : Iren. Haer., III, 21, 10; 22, 1; IV, 38, 1; V, 1, 2 (IV, 40, 3). In this summation, however, the prominent element may be, not that of repetition, but that of the affirmation and confirmation implied in repetition. Cf. Hipp. Ref., VI, 16, 4 : ὥσπερ γὰρ ἡ ἀφὴ τὰ ὑπὸ τῶν ἄλλων αἰσθήσεων ὁραθέντα θιγοῦσα ἀνακεφαλαιοῦται καὶ βεβαιοῖ, σκληρὸν ἢ θερμὸν ἢ γλίσχρον δοκιμάσασα, οὕτως τὸ πέμπτον βιβλίον τοῦ νόμου ἀνακεφαλαίωσίς ἐστι τῶν πρὸ αὐτοῦ γραφέντων τεσσάρων, Const. Ap., I, 1, 4 : λέγει γὰρ ἐν τῷ Εὐαγγελίῳ, ἀνακεφαλαιούμενος καὶ στηρίζων καὶ πληρῶν τὴν δεκάλογον τοῦ Νόμου, ὅτι ἐν τῷ Νόμῳ γέγραπται ...

In Eph. 1:10 it is difficult to choose between these various possible senses of ἀνακεφαλαιοῦσθαι. This may be seen from the variations in translations and commentaries. In these circumstances the context must decide. The ἀνακεφαλαιοῦσθαι τὰ πάντα ἐν τῷ Χριστῷ obviously consists in the διδόναι αὐτὸν κεφαλὴν ὑπὲρ πάντα τῇ ἐκκλησίᾳ (1:22). The summing up of the totality takes place in its subjection to the Head. The subjection of the totality to the Head takes place in the co-ordinating of the Head and the Church. As the Church receives its Head the totality receives its κεφάλαιον, its definitive, comprehensive and (in the Head) self-repeating summation. In the Head, in Christ, the totality is comprehended afresh as in its sum.[4] To be sure, ἀνακεφαλαιοῦσθαι is to be derived from κεφάλαιον rather than κεφαλή. But it is most likely that what is meant by the designation of Christ as κεφαλή led the author of Eph. to choose this relatively infrequent but rich and varied term which agrees so well with his intention.

Schlier

---

[3] Wnd. Barn. on 5, 11.

[4] The Valentinians overlook this "afresh," and the eschatological or qualitative sense of ἀνακεφαλαιοῦσθαι, when they quote Eph. 1:10 in favour of their thesis : Σωτῆρα τὸν ἐκ πάντων ὄντα τὸ πᾶν εἶναι, cf. Iren. Haer., I, 3, 4.

κῆρυξ (ἱεροκῆρυξ), κηρύσσω,
κήρυγμα, προκηρύσσω

---

† κῆρυξ (ἱεροκῆρυξ).

Contents : A. The κῆρυξ in the Greek World : 1. The Dignity and Social Position of the Herald ; 2. The Qualities demanded in a Herald ; 3. The Religious Significance of the Herald : a. His Inviolability on Diplomatic Missions ; b. His Participation in Cultic Life ; 4. The Herald of the Gods. B. The Herald in the Jewish World : 1. Josephus and Philo ; 2. The Septuagint ; 3. The Rabbis : a. The Derivation of the Word כרז ; b. The Significance of the כרוז. C. The κῆρυξ in the New Testament.

A. The κῆρυξ in the Greek World.

1. The Dignity and Social Position of the Herald.

¹ κῆρυξ ² is a very common word in Hom. as compared with κηρύσσειν. ³ We can easily see from him what was the position of the herald in the ancient world and what significance was attached to him. He had a place at the royal court. Every prince had a

---

κ ῆ ρ υ ξ. H. Ebeling, *Lexicon Homericum,* I (1885), *s.v.*; C. F. v. Nägelsbach, *Homerische Theologie*³ (1884), 451 f.; H. Loewner, "Die Herolde in den Homerischen Gesängen," *Programm des k.k. Staats-Ober-Gymnasiums zu Eger* (1881), with additional older bibl.; E. Buchholz, *Die Homerischen Realien,* II, 1 (1881), 48 ff.; Schn. Euang., 247 ff.; J. Oehler, "Keryx" in Pauly-W., XI (1922), 349 ff.; E. Pottier, "Praeco" in C.Daremberg and E. Saglio, *Dictionnaire des Antiquités Grecques et Romaines,* IV (1905), 607 ff.; G. F. Schoemann, *Griechische Altertümer,* I⁴ (1897), rev. by J. H. Lipsius, 36 f., 469 f.; II² (1863), 8 ff., 60 f., 366, 399 ff.; G. Gilbert, *Handbuch d. griechischen Staatsaltertümer,* I² (1893), Index ; G. Busolt and H. Swoboda, "Griechische Staatskunde," Index, in *Handbuch d. Altertumswissenschaft,* ed. W. Otto, IV, 1, 1 (1926). K. F. Hermann, "Lehrbuch der gottesdienstlichen Altertümer d. Griechen," Index, in *Lehrbuch d. griechischen Antiquitäten,* II (1846); P. Stengel, *Die griechischen Kultusaltertümer*³ (1920), Index ; W. Dittenberger, "Die eleusinischen Keryken," *Hermes,* 20 (1885), 1 ff.; F. Poland, *Geschichte d. griechischen Vereinswesens* (1909), 395; S. Krauss, *Griechische u. lateinische Lehnwörter in Talmud, Midrasch u. Targum,* I (1898), II (1899); W. Bacher, *Die exegetische Terminologie d. jüdischen Traditionslit.,* II (1905); R. Bultmann, "Der Begriff des Wortes Gottes im NT" in *Glauben u. Verstehen* (1933), 275; O. Schmitz, "Die Bedeutung des Wortes bei Paulus" in *Nt.liche Forschungen,* I, 4 (1927); J. T. Spangler, "New Testament Conception of Preaching," *Bibliotheca Sacra,* 91 (1934), 442.

¹ The debat whether κηρυξ should take an acute or a circumflex is as good as decided, since κῆρυξ is now more or less universally accepted. Even P. Buttmann, *Ausführliche Griech. Sprachlehre,* I (1819), 170, n. 12, who takes the opposite view, must admit that "the pronounciation of ιξ and υξ gradually, but quite early, became shorter," cf. II, 399. The υ in κηρυκ is long. But acc. to the rule of older grammarians a long ι or υ can be shortened before ξ, and hence the form κῆρυξ. Cf. Bl.-Debr., 10 and Kühner-Blass-Gerth, § 74, n. 3.

² Etym. Gud. (ed. Sturz), 320, 42 gives the following derivation : κῆρυξ, ὡς παρὰ τὸ πτέρω γίνεται πτερῶ, καὶ πτερύσσω, οὕτω παρὰ τὸ ἐρῶ, ὁ δηλοῖ τὸ λέγω, ἐρύσσω, καὶ ἠρύσσω, καὶ πλεονασμῷ τοῦ κ κηρύσσω, ὁ μέλλων κηρύξω, ἀποβολῇ τοῦ ω κῆρυξ. The etym. is naturally different. In κῆρυξ, Doric κᾶρυξ, Sansk. *kāru,* the "singer," the "poet," we have the stem *qar-, qarặ* : To cry out loud, the extol, to laud, cf. Prellwitz, *s.v.* and Walde-Pok., I, 353.

³ It is worth noting that whereas we find the noun some 90 times in Hom. the verb occurs only about 10 times, cf. Ebeling, *s.v.*

herald, in many cases several. [4] To him was ascribed both political and religious significance. He was very highly regarded. Heralds were thus called ἀγαυοί (Il., 3, 268; Od., 8, 418), δῖοι (Il., 12, 343). They were counted among the δημιοεργοί (Od., 19, 135) and their cleverness and wisdom were extolled. [5] They had sceptres in their hands in token of their royal dignity and majesty. [6] In spite of this, they performed menial tasks like servants, killing bullocks, preparing meals with the maids (Il., 18, 558), mixing wine and serving the guests (Od., 1, 143 ff.; 17, 334). When the king rides out, the herald harnesses the horses (Il., 24, 281 f.) and drives the chariot (Il., 24, 149; cf. Soph. Oed. Tyr., 802). When Achilles returns from battle, his heralds prepare his bath (Il., 23, 39). These things are all part of their duties. They often run very ordinary errands. [7] Hence they are sometimes called θεράποντες. [8] Yet it would be a mistake to regard them as simple servants. [9] As we have seen, they are free men, not slaves. ἐνδοξότεροι θεραπόντων, οἱ κήρυκες. βασιλικοὶ μὲν γὰρ ἄνδρες καὶ θεῖον γένος οἱ κήρυκες, Eustath. Thessal. Comm. in Od., 1, 109 § 1397, 56. They stand to their lords almost in a position of friendship. They are their companions, comrades and fellows. [10] One might call them adjutants of their princes; they are at their personal service. [11]

The office continued in the post-Homeric period. But heralds now came to serve the state rather than the king. Several writers tell us what they understand by a herald. Hesych., s.v. calls him an ἄγγελος, διάκονος, πρεσβευτής. Cf. also Poll. Onom., IV, 94 : τάχα δ᾽ ἄν τις τοὺς κήρυκας καὶ ἑρμηνέας καὶ σπονδοφόρους καὶ ἐκεχειροφόρους (→ infra) καὶ ἀγγέλους ὀνομάσειεν. But this is only to describe one side of the office. Poll. Onom., IV, 91 says of the activity of heralds : τὸ δὲ κηρύκων γένος ἱερὸν μὲν Ἑρμοῦ, κατεκήρυττε δ᾽ ἡσυχίαν ἔν τ᾽ ἀγῶσι καὶ ἱερουργίαις καὶ σπονδὰς περιήγγελλε καὶ ἐκεχειρίαν (armistice) ἐπήγγελλε καὶ τοὺς ἀγωνιστὰς ἀνεκήρυττεν. Like Aeschin. Schol. on Or., 1, 20, [12] Poll. Onom., VIII, 103 divides heralds into 4 classes. There are the heralds of mysteries, of the games, of festivals, and of the market. Even this classification is not complete. It is enough, how-

---

[4] Hom. gives some names. Thus Talthybius (Il., 1, 321; 3, 118; 4, 192; 7, 276; 19, 196, 250; 23, 897) is in the service of Agamemnon and Idaeus accompanies Priam (Il., 3, 248; 7, 276).

[5] δαΐφρων, Il., 24, 325; πεπνυμένος, 7, 276; 9, 689; πεπνυμένα εἰδώς, Od., 4, 696 and 711; 22, 361; 24, 442; πεπνυμένα μήδεα εἰδώς, Il., 7, 278; Od., 2, 38; πυκινὰ φρεσὶ μήδε᾽ ἔχοντες, Il., 24, 282 and 674.

[6] Il., 7, 277; 18, 505; 23, 567; Od., 2, 38.

[7] Od., 8, 256 ff., 399; 16, 328 ff.; 18, 291. Thus they bring the singer to the prince's court, Od., 8, 47 and 62, and serve him, Od., 1, 153; 8, 69, 107, 471. Hector gives the alarm through heralds, Il., 8, 517. The herald is sent for a doctor, Il., 4, 192. He summons reinforcements, Il., 12, 351.

[8] It is said of Eurybates and Talthybius in Il., 1, 321: τώ οἱ ἔσαν κήρυκε καὶ ὀτρηρὼ θεράποντε, cf. also Od., 18, 423 f.

[9] Heralds and servants are set in contrast in Od., 1, 109. But their work is not essentially different. Heralds mix the wine with water, while servants clean and set the tables and serve meat. More important is Od., 18, 423 :

τοῖσιν δὲ κρητῆρα κεράσσατο Μούλιος ἥρως
κῆρυξ Δουλιχιεύς· θεράπων δ᾽ ἦν Ἀμφινόμοιο.

Here the herald is called θεράπων, but the added ἥρως shows that he is more a companion than a servant, for Achilles calls Patroclus θεράπων (Il., 16, 244) and Agamemnon calls the Greek captains θεράποντες Ἄρηος, Il., 19, 78.

[10] The herald of Odysseus is called ἑταῖρος, Od., 19, 247 f.:

Εὐρυβάτης δ᾽ ὄνομ᾽ ἔσκε· τίεν δέ μιν ἔξοχον ἄλλων
ὧν ἑτάρων Ὀδυσεύς, ὅτι οἱ φρεσὶν ἄρτια ᾔδη.

[11] When Odysseus throws off his garment, his herald quickly picks it up (Il., 2, 183).

[12] Aeschin. Schol., 1, 20 (ed. F. Schultz [1865]): κηρύκων ἐστὶν ἐν Ἀθήναις γένη τέσσαρα, πρῶτον τὸ τῶν πανάγνων τῶν ἐν τοῖς μυστηρίοις, οἵ εἰσιν ἀπὸ Κήρυκος τοῦ Ἑρμοῦ καὶ Πανδρόσου τῆς Κέκροπος, δεύτερον τὸ τῶν περὶ τοὺς ἀγῶνας, τρίτον τὸ τῶν περὶ τὰς πομπάς, τέταρτον τὸ τῶν περὶ τὰς ἀγορὰς καὶ τὰ ὤνια.

ever, to show that we must distinguish between heralds. For closer definition, there are often added adj. like δημόσιος, Ael. Var. Hist., II, 15 and κοινός, Dio C., 46, 14, or genitives, to show which institution the one concerned serves as a herald. We read of the κῆρυξ τῆς πόλεως (e.g., GDI, I, 311, 46), [13] κῆρυξ τῆς βουλῆς (IG, XII, 8, 53, 17), κῆρυξ τῆς βουλῆς καὶ τοῦ δήμου (IG, II/III,[2] 678, 8), κῆρυξ ἄρχοντος (Ditt. Syll.[3], 711, n. 15), κῆρυξ βουλῆς τῆς ἐξ Ἀρείου πάγου (Ditt. Syll.[3], 728), κῆρυξ Ἀμφικτυόνων (GDI, II, 2520, 7), κῆρυξ τῶν λογιστῶν (Aeschin. Or., 3, 23), κῆρυξ τῶν ἕνδεκα (Demosth. Or., 25, 56), [14] ἱεροκῆρυξ τῶν ἱερομναμόνων (Ditt. Syll.[3], 445), κῆρυξ τῶν συνέδρων (IG, VII, 190, 35), κῆρυξ τοῦ μουσικοῦ (Inscr. Magn., 89, 76), κῆρυξ τῶν μυστῶν (Xenoph. Hist. Graec., II, 4, 20), ὁ τῶν ἱερῶν κῆρυξ (Ditt. Syll.[3], 845), κῆρυξ τοῦ Ἀπόλλωνος (Ditt. Syll.[3], 773, 5), κῆρυξ τοῦ θεοῦ (Ditt. Syll.[3], 728 B, 7), ἱεροκῆρυξ τῶν ἱερέων ζακόρων σαώτηρος Ἀσκληπίω (GDI, I, 255, 21). [15]

At a first glance it seems as though the herald has completely lost the status which he had in the royal period. Only the poor and lazy, who hope to earn money this way, push into the office. [16] Non-citizens seem to have been accepted. [17] Obviously a herald was not highly regarded. He was simply an official (Plat. Polit., 290b). Poll. Onom., VI, 128 reckons him among the βίοι, ἐφ᾽ οἷς ἄν τις ὀνειδισθείη, and mentions him in the same breath with the keeper of brothels or inns, the small shopkeeper and others. The judgment of Theophrast. is to the same effect. [18] It is probable, however, that the herald's official status was better, and that only the popular opinion was so unfavourable. [19] Acc. to Aeschin. Or., 1, 20 any reproach of ἀτιμία must be far from him. We read in Ditt. Syll.[3], 145, 13 that he was under oath; hence he could not be ὑπηρέτης, but had to be an official. In the historical period as well as Hom. he was sent on diplomatic missions (→ 688). These could not be entrusted to the worst of men. It also appears that κήρυκες could be proposed as judges. Thus Athenian law lays down that they should not be chosen as judges when out of the country. [20] Heralds belong to the ἄσιτοι (IG, II/III², 1773, 57). Inscr. Priene, 111, 194, reckons the κῆρυξ τῆς πόλεως among the better classes of the city. We read of many honours being given to heralds because of their services. [21] They receive the προεδρία (Ditt. Syll.[3], 915, 6) and are

---

[13] Oehler, 351 ff., gives many instances, but there are so many mistakes and misprints that he is not very reliable.

[14] Demosth. Or., 25, 56 has the verb, not the noun: ἐκήρυττον οἱ ἕνδεκα.

[15] On the different heralds of specific cultic unions, v. Oehler, 357 and Poland; cf. Ditt. Syll.[3], 57, 40 ff., the herald of the Eleusinian singers' guild.

[16] Demosth. Or., 44, 4 speaks of κηρύττειν. τοῦτο δ᾽ ἐστὶν οὐ μόνον ἀπορίας ἀνθρωπίνης τεκμήριον, ἀλλὰ καὶ ἀσχολίας τῆς εἰς τὸ πραγματεύεσθαι.

[17] This is concluded from Ditt. Syll.[3], 186, where the fact that the πρόσοδος was awarded to Eucles suggests that he was not a citizen, cf. A. Kirchhoff, Hermes, 1 (1866), 20.

[18] Of the ἀπονενοημένος (the morally lost and desperate man) he says in Char., 6: δεινὸς δὲ πανδοκεῦσαι καὶ πορνοβοσκῆσαι καὶ τελωνῆσαι καὶ μηδεμίαν αἰσχρὰν ἐργασίαν ἀποδοκιμάσαι, ἀλλὰ κηρύττειν, μαγειρεύειν, κυβεύειν.

[19] Eur. Tro., 424:
... τί ποτ᾽ ἔχουσι τοὔνομα
κήρυκες; ἓν ἀπέχθημα πάγκοινον βροτοῖς
οἱ περὶ τυράννους καὶ πόλεις ὑπηρέται.

Eur. Or., 895:
τὸ γὰρ γένος τοιοῦτον· ἐπὶ τὸν εὐτυχῆ
πηδῶσ᾽ ἀεὶ κήρυκες· ὅδε δ᾽ αὐτοῖς φίλος,
ὃς ἂν δύνηται πόλεος ἔν τ᾽ ἀρχαῖσιν ᾖ.

[20] Cf. U. v. Wilamowitz-Moellendorff, Aristoteles u. Athen, I (1893), 202 f.

[21] Ditt. Syll.[3], 444, n. 10: στεφανῶσαι δάφνης στεφάνωι παρὰ τοῦ θεοῦ καὶ εἶναι αὐτῶι καὶ ἐκγόνοις προδικίαν, ἀσφάλειαν, ἀσυλίαν, ἀτέλειαν καὶ προεδρίαν ἐμ πᾶσι τοῖς ἀγῶσιν. Ditt. Syll.[3], 445: αὐτῶι καὶ ἐκγόνοις προξενίαν, προμαντείαν, προεδρίαν, προδικίαν, ἀσυλίαν, ἀτέλειαν πάντων.

adorned with a sash of honour in the theatre (IG, II/III², 5043). It matters a great deal which authority the herald serves. His status depends on that of the one who commissions him, and on the nature of the commission. κῆρυξ is certainly not just a term of reproach as the previous quotations might suggest. It can also be a title of honour. In the Roman period the herald of the Areopagus is a highly regarded personage. He is in the higher ranks with the στρατηγός and the βασιλεύς (IG, II/III², 3616, 5 f.). Far from being poor, he is well endowed, so that he can give costly gifts. [22] He is not among the lower officials but has precedence in the Areopagus [23] and is responsible for the execution of its decisions (Ditt. Syll.³, 796 B, 15 ff.).

2. The Qualities demanded in a Herald.

An external attribute is required in a herald. He has to have a good voice.

τίς κῆρυξ μὴ Στεντόρειος; Aristot. Pol., VII, 4, p. 1326b, 6. If a herald does not have a powerful voice, he is useless. This condition is related to his task. In Hom. he summons men to the assembly [24] and warriors to battle (Il., 2, 437 ff.). In the assembly itself he is responsible for peace and order. [25] In trials he has to pacify the people if they become too excited and if those present try to give vocal support to one side or the other (Il., 18, 503). Obviously he can do this only if he is λιγύφθογγος (clear), [26] ἠερόφωνος (loud) (Il., 18, 505), καλήτωρ (24, 577), ἀστυβοώτης (24, 701), ἠπύτα (7, 384), θεῷ ἐναλίγκιος (like) αὐδήν (19, 250), as Homer says. Even later it is a prime requisite in a herald that he should have a loud and resonant voice which carries well. [27] Among the Lacedaemonians the office was hereditary and passed down from father to son even if the son did not have a good voice. [28] Elsewhere those seeking to be heralds had to submit to a voice examination. [29] For even later the duties were much the same as in Homer. [30] The herald had to declare official decrees and announcements. [31]

---

[22] IG, II/III², 2773, 2 ff.: ὁ κῆρυξ τ[ῆς ἐξ Ἀρείου πάγου βου]λῆς καὶ ἀρ[χιερεὺς Σεβαστῶν ... [ἐκ τῶν ἰδίων ἔδωκε] τῷ σεμνοτά[τῳ συνεδρίῳ τῶν Ἀρε]οπαγειτῶ[ν πάσας τὰς ὑπογραφεί]σας δωρ(ι)εά[ς].

[23] Ditt. Or., 505, 1: Ἡ ἐξ Ἀρείου πάγου βουλὴ καὶ ὁ κῆρυξ αὐτῆς ... Αἰζανειτῶν ἄρχουσι, βουλῆι, δήμωι χαίρειν.

[24] Hom. Il., 2, 50; 9, 10; Od., 2, 7; 8, 8 ff.

[25] Eustath. Thessal. Comm. in Il., 2, 278 § 220, 11: ἔργον κηρύκων οὐ μόνον κηρύσσειν ἐλθεῖν εἰς ἀγορὰν τὸν λαόν, ἀλλὰ καὶ κελεύειν ἐν ἀγορᾷ τὸν λαὸν σιωπᾶν. In Aristoph. Acharn., 123 someone is called to order in the assembly : σῖγα, κάθιζε.

[26] Hom. Il., 2, 50 and 442; 9, 10; 23, 39; Od., 2, 6.

[27] Poll. Onom., IV, 94 : τὸ δὲ φθέγμα αὐτῶν μέγα, ἁδρόν, ὑψηλόν, πρόμηκες, ἐπίμηκες, σαφές, ἀρτίστομον, συνεχές, διηνεκές, ἀποτάδην φθεγγόμενον, ἀπνευστί.

[28] Hdt., VI, 60: οἱ κήρυκες ... ἐκδέκονται τὰς πατρωίας τέχνας ... οὐ κατὰ λαμπροφωνίην ἐπιτιθέμενοι ἄλλοι σφέας παρακληίουσι (exclude), ἀλλὰ κατὰ τὰ πάτρια ἐπιτελέουσι.

[29] Demosth. Or., 19, 338 : λογίζεσθ' ὅτι δεῖ, κήρυκα μὲν ἂν δοκιμάζητ' εὔφωνον σκοπεῖν.

[30] He must keep order in the assembly. When instructed by the chairman he opens it for discussion and invites contributions : τίς ἀγορεύειν βούλεται; Demosth. Or., 18, 191; Aristoph. Acharn., 45. Cf. Aeschin. Or., 3, 4 : τίς ἀγορεύειν βούλεται τῶν ὑπὲρ πεντήκοντα ἔτη γεγονότων καὶ πάλιν ἐν μέρει τῶν ἄλλων Ἀθηναίων; When the session is to end, he closes it with the words : οἱ γὰρ πρυτάνεις λύουσι τὴν ἐκκλησίαν, Aristoph. Acharn., 173. He plays a similar role in trials. He declares the result when the court is dismissed (Aristot. Res Publica Atheniensium, ed. H. Oppermann [1928], 64, 3; 66, 1). Before the judges vote, he loudly asks whether perchance there are still complaints against false witness. If not, he summons the judges to decide. It is τὸ ἐκ τοῦ νόμου κήρυγμα, Aeschin. Or., 1, 79. Aristot., op. cit., 68, 4 reads : ἡ τετρυπημένη τοῦ πρότερον λέγοντος, ἡ δὲ πλήρης τοῦ ὕστερον λέγοντος. In Aristoph. Vesp., 752 ff. the herald asks : τίς ἀψήφιστος; ἀνιστάσθω.

[31] Thus in P. Hamb., 29, 6 ff. the prefect makes it known through his herald that if the accused does not appear in court he will be judged in absentia. The later practice was to

He could do this only if he had the voice. He is like the heralds who up to recently went through smaller villages with a bell and publicly read official proclamations with a loud voice. Accompanied by a crowd of children (Aristot. Rhet., III, 8, p. 1408b, 24 f.), he went to the market place and published official and private news. [32] When an official or a private individual wished to sell something, he told the herald, who saw to it that others knew. He stood on the market place (Ps.-Luc. Asin., 35) and cried (Luc. Vit. Auct., 2 : τὸν ἄριστον βίον πωλῶ, τὸν σεμνότατον, τίς ὠνήσεται; in c. 6 he is asked : πόσου τοῦτον ἀποκηρύττεις; and he answers : 10 minas). [33] When the herald went through the streets or opened the assembly, he seems sometimes to have used a trumpet to gain a hearing. [34] But a good herald regarded it as a point of honour to manage without an instrument. At great festivals in honour of the gods heralds took part in contests. A number of lists have come down to us which mention not only the victors in gymnastic contests but also heralds, poets, flute-players, players on horns, zithers etc. [35] These contests were to test the strength and diction of heralds. Those who were victorious had the privilege, as the games proceeded, of summoning other contestants and announcing the victors. [36] Once again we see that the best herald was the one with the best voice.

Apart from the predominant question of the voice, certain qualities of character were required (→ 685). In many cases heralds are very garrulous [37] and inclined to exaggerate. They are thus in danger of giving false news. [38] It is demanded, then, that they deliver their message as it is given to them. [39] The essential point

---

publish things by posted notices. Claudius was praised in Dio C., 60, 13, 5 for announcing the games in this way rather than by heralds. If secret murder was committed and the killer could not be found, the herald in the market place declared sentence on the unknown to the effect that he should be debarred from temples and outlawed from the country, and that, if discovered, he should be seized and put to death (Plat. Leg., IX, 874a).

[32] Luc. Char., 2 and Demosth. Or., 25, 56 : the flight of a slave is proclaimed. Ditt. Syll.³, 47, 19 ff.: it is arranged that any who wish to return from Naupactos to the Epicnemidian Locrians should have this proclaimed by the herald on the market place of Naupactos and of the Locrian city. Aesch. Sept. c. Theb., 1005 :
δοκοῦντα καὶ δόξαντ' ἀπαγγέλλειν με χρὴ
δήμου προβούλοις τοῖσδε Καδμείας πόλεως.
[33] Poll. Onom., X, 18 : πρᾶσις ... ὑπὸ κήρυκι γενομένη, Demosth. Or., 51, 22 : ὑπὸ κήρυκος πωλεῖν. Cf. Ditt. Syll.³, 251, III, 20 ff. Dio C., 46, 14, 1. A κῆρυξ can be called a vendor or auctioneer.
[34] Aesch. Eum., 566 :
κήρυσσε, κῆρυξ, καὶ στρατὸν κατειργαθοῦ
ἥ τ' οὖν διάτορος Τυρσηνικὴ
σάλπιγξ, βροτείου πνεύματος πληρουμένη.
[35] There are many such lists in IG, VII, e.g., 3197.
[36] Poll. Onom., IV, 92 :
'Υβλαίῳ κήρυκι τόδ' 'Αρχία Εὐκλέος υἱῷ
δέξαι ἄγαλμ' εὔφρων Φοῖβ' ἐπ' ἀπημοσύνῃ
ὃς τρὶς ἐκάρυξεν τὸν 'Ολυμπίᾳ αὐτὸς ἀγῶνα
οὔθ' ὑπὸ σαλπίγγων οὔτ' ἀναδείγματ' ἔχων.
In Bacchyl., 9 (10), 25 ff. the κήρυκες who declare the victors are called προφῆται.
[37] Aesch. Sept. c. Theb., 1043 : αὐδῶ σε μὴ περισσὰ κηρύσσειν ἐμοί. In Soph. Trach., 319 the herald gives the assurance : σιγῇ τοὐμὸν ἔργον ἥνυτον. In Eur. Suppl., 426 he is called παρεργάτης λόγων.
[38] Eur. Heracl., 292 :
πᾶσι γὰρ οὗτος κήρυξι νόμος
δὶς τόσα πυργοῦν τῶν γιγνομένων.
[39] Aesch. Suppl., 931: καὶ γὰρ πρέπει κήρυκ' ἀπαγγέλλειν τορῶς ἕκαστα. Cf. Plat. Leg., XII, 941a. Aeschin. Or., 3, 189 : δεῖ γὰρ τὸν κήρυκα ἀψευδεῖν, ὅταν τὴν ἀνάρρησιν (proclamation) ἐν τῷ θεάτρῳ ποιῆται πρὸς τοὺς Ἕλληνας.

about the report which they give is that it does not originate with them. Behind it stands a higher power. The herald does not express his own views. He is the spokesman for his master. Plat. Polit., 260d : τὸ κηρυκικὸν φῦλον ἐπιταχθέντ' ἀλλότρια νοήματα παραδεχόμενον αὐτὸ δεύτερον ἐπιτάττει πάλιν ἑτέροις. Heralds adopt the mind of those who commission them, and act with the plenipotentiary authority of their masters. [40] It is with this authority that the κῆρυξ, like the πρέσβυς, conducts diplomatic business. Hence κῆρυξ and πρέσβυς are often used synonymously. Yet there is a distinction between the herald and the envoy (→ 689). In general one may say that the latter acts more independently and that he is furnished with greater authority. It is unusual for a herald to act on his own initiative and without explicit instructions. [41] In the main the herald simply gives short messages, puts questions, and brings answers. Sometimes he may simply hand over a letter (Diod. S., XIV, 47, 1). He is bound by the precise instructions of the one who commissions him (Eur. Suppl., 385). The good herald does not become involved in lengthy negotations but returns at once when he has delivered his message (ibid., 459, cf. 388). In rare cases he may be empowered to decide on his own. But in general he is simply an executive instrument. Being only the mouth of his master, he must not falsify the message entrusted to him by additions of his own. He must deliver it exactly as given to him (Plat. Leg., XII, 941a). In the assembly and in court he is the voice of the chairman, and in other aspects of his work as well he must keep strictly to the words and orders of his master.

3. The Religious Significance of the Herald.

a. His Inviolability on Diplomatic Missions.

Among the Greeks religion and politics cannot be separated. They are too closely linked. It is natural, then, that religious significance should attach to the political herald. When a κῆρυξ goes to a foreign land, he is not only under the protection of the country which he represents should anything befall him. [42] He is also under the special protection of the deity.

Hom. calls heralds ἄγγελοι Διός (Il., 1, 334; 7, 274), διίφιλοι (8, 517), θεῖοι (4, 192; 10, 315). They are holy and inviolable. An offence against them is ἀσέβεια [43] and brings down the wrath of the gods. To them one may not apply the ancient principle : As the message, so the reward (→ II, 722). One may be angry at those who send them, but they themselves are not to be punished. They are inviolable because they are under divine protection. Even if their news is unwelcome, they must be hospitably received. [44]

---

[40] This is why we find in this connection verbs like παρακαλεῖν and κελεύειν, Thuc., IV, 30, 5 etc. → κηρύσσειν.

[41] Thuc., IV, 68, 3 : ξυνέπεσε γὰρ καὶ τὸν τῶν Ἀθηναίων κήρυκα ἀφ' ἑαυτοῦ γνώμης κηρύξαι τὸν βουλόμενον ἰέναι Μεγαρέων μετὰ Ἀθηναίων θησόμενον τὰ ὅπλα.

[42] Plut. Pericl., 30 (I, 168c ff.): When the Megarians murdered an Athenian herald, the Athenians resolved never again to send a herald to Megara, and to treat the Megareans with implacable hostility. Any Megarean was an outlaw, and Athenian generals had to undertake to conduct two predatory campaigns against Megara each year.

[43] Demosth. Or., 12, 4; cf. Suid., s.v. κηρύκειον : οὐκ ἐξῆν αὐτοὺς ἀδικεῖν.

[44] Even the angry Achilles respects them, Il., 1, 334 :
χαίρετε, κήρυκες, Διὸς ἄγγελοι ἠδὲ καὶ ἀνδρῶν,
ἆσσον ἴτ'· οὔ τί μοι ὔμμες ἐπαίτιοι ἀλλ' Ἀγαμέμνων,
ὃ σφῶϊ προΐει Βρισηῖδος εἵνεκα κούρης, cf. 1, 391.

If offences are committed in an excess of passion, [45] the gods must be appeased. When the Persian king had sent heralds to the Spartans to summon them to surrender, they flung them into a well. But fearing the wrath of Talthybius, the patron of heralds, they then sent two Spartans voluntarily to the Persian king to make atonement for the death and the transgression (Hdt., VII, 131-136). Violation of a herald is an offence against the gods, for ἰστέον δὲ ὅτι ἄσυλοι ἐς τὸ παντελὲς ἦσαν οἱ κήρυκες οἷα θεῖον γένος νομιζόμενοι ... καὶ ἦσαν μέσοι θείου τε γένους καὶ ἀνθρωπίνου καὶ οὐκ ἦν θεμιτὸν κακοῦσθαι αὐτούς, Eustath. Thessal. Comm. in Il., 1, 321 § 110, 14. This is why the herald can travel unmolested in a foreign country. [46] He can speak openly, having nothing to fear. Eur. Heracl., 49, 271 and 648 are instructive in this connection. The herald tries to achieve by violence what he has failed to achieve by negotiation. He speaks almost threateningly to the ruler. When he goes so far as even to violate the sanctity of the altar, the ruler is about to oppose him. But the chorus calls to the prince : μὴ πρὸς θεῶν κήρυκα τολμήσῃς θενεῖν. Although the herald is in the wrong, and the king has a mandate from Zeus to protect the sanctity of the altar (238), a herald is still immune. Because he enjoys this divine protection, the herald accompanies envoys. [47] He secures for them the same immunity from attack. In particularly dangerous situations a herald precedes the envoys to procure a safe conduct for them. [48] Even in war a herald can dare to go into the camp of the enemy. When he has his herald's staff and crown — the sign that he is dedicated to the gods and has their special protection — he is recognised and respected. [49] He opens negotiations for a truce and for the burial of the dead (Xenoph. Hist. Graec., IV, 3, 21 etc.). When Suid., s.v. says : κῆρυξ ἐν πολέμῳ, πρέσβυς ἐν εἰρήνῃ, the statement does not contain the full truth, but it emphasises a correct distinction between the κῆρυξ and the πρέσβυς. The κῆρυξ establishes preconditions for the negotiations of the πρέσβυς, or he breaks off diplomatic relations by declaring war on a city or nation (e.g., Thuc., I, 29, 1 etc.). In both cases he undertakes this dangerous mission because he enjoys immunity as a herald.

b. His Participation in Cultic Life.

Because of the close relation between politics and religion, religious rites have a place in all national institutions. On the meeting of the assembly, the session of the council or the mustering of the army, sacrifice is offered and there is prayer by the herald. The same herald who must keep peace and order also discharges this cultic function. We may thus perceive the sacral significance of the political herald.

At the opening of the assembly, when the rites of purification are over, the κῆρυξ summons those present to reverent silence [50] in order that he may engage in a solemn opening prayer in which he prays for the welfare of the city and curses all traitors. The

---

45 Paus., IX, 25, 4, where Heracles maims the envoys by cutting off their noses.

46 Poll. Onom., VIII, 139 : ἄσυλοι δ' ἦσαν καὶ ἐξῆν αὐτοῖς πανταχόσε ἀδεῶς ἰέναι.

47 Demosth. Or., 18, 165; Aeschin. Or., 2, 13; 3, 62 and 63. For personal protection the men sent to the angry Achilles are accompanied by two heralds (Il., 9, 170).

48 Demosth. Or., 19, 163 : ὅτε γὰρ τὴν προτέραν ἀπῄρομεν πρεσβείαν τὴν περὶ τῆς εἰρήνης, κῆρυχ' ὑμεῖς προαπεστείλατε, ὅστις ἡμῖν σπείσεται, cf. Polyb., IV, 72, 3 : πέμψαντες οὖν κήρυκα πρὸς τὸν βασιλέα καὶ λαβόντες συγχώρημα περὶ πρεσβείας.

49 Xenoph. Hist. Graec., IV, 7, 3 : ἔπεμψαν ὥσπερ εἰώθεσαν ἐστεφανωμένους δύο κήρυκας ὑποφέροντας σπονδάς.

50 Aristoph. Thes., 295 ff.: εὐφημία ἔστω, εὐφημία ἔστω εὔχεσθε ... ἐκκλησίαν τήνδε καὶ σύνοδον τὴν νῦν κάλλιστα καὶ ἄριστα ποιῆσαι, πολυωφελῶς μὲν (τῇ) πόλει τῇ Ἀθηναίων ..., Aeschin. Or., 1, 23 : ἐπειδὰν τὸ καθάρσιον περιενεχθῇ καὶ ὁ κῆρυξ τὰς πατρίους εὐχὰς εὔξηται.

gods are asked to bless those who give good counsel [51] and to curse those who deceive the people and the state, [52] who consciously speak to the hurt of the state, who accept bribes, [53] break oaths, alter decisions and laws, betray state secrets, treat with the Persians, [54] falsify weights and measures and plan to introduce tyranny (Aristoph. Thes., 331 ff.). [55] The herald says grace at meals in the Prytaneion, [56] and we also read that on the sailing of the fleet he prays for the success of the undertaking. [57]

The herald also plays a part in the preparation and execution of great sacrifices.

He makes all things ready for the sacrifice. In the mystery of Andania he shares responsibility for the correct performance of the sacrificial ceremonies (Ditt. Syll.³, 736, 115). With the priest he looks out the animals (IG, XII, 5, 647, 14), slaughters them, and skins and quarters them (Athen., XIV, 79, [p. 660a-c]), so that he can be called μάγειρος (X, 26 [p. 425e]). There is an exact description of his duties in Ditt. Syll.³, 1025 (from Cos, 4th or 5th cent. B.C.). [58] The reference is to a feast in honour of Zeus Polieus. When the beast has been chosen and the preliminary sacrifices offered, [κᾶρυξ δ]ὲ καρυσσέτω ἑορτάζ[εν Ζηνὸς Π]ο[λιῆ]ο[ς] ἐνιαύτια ὡραῖα ἑο[ρτάν]. Only then does the feast proper begin (1025, 35 ff.). The κήρυκες choose a σαφεύς from their midst. Naturally they take part in the banquet; the tongue is specifically reserved for them. [59] After the sacrifice one of them sells the skins in the presence of the priest

---

[51] Aristoph. Thes., 332 :
εὔχεσθε τοῖς θεοῖσι τοῖς ᾿Ολυμπίοις
....
εἴ τις ἐπιβουλεύει τι τῷ δήμῳ κακὸν
....
κακῶς ἀπολέσθαι τοῦτον αὐτὸν κᾠκίαν
ἀρᾶσθε, ταῖς δ᾿ ἄλλαισιν ὑμῖν τοὺς θεοὺς
εὔχεσθε πάσαις πολλὰ δοῦναι κἀγαθά.

[52] Demosth. Or., 23, 97: διόπερ καταρᾶται καθ᾿ ἑκάστην ἐκκλησίαν ὁ κῆρυξ ... εἴ τις ἐξαπατᾷ λέγων ἢ βουλὴν ἢ δῆμον ἢ τὴν ἡλιαίαν.

[53] Dinarch., II, 16 : καθ᾿ ἑκάστην (ἐκκλησίαν) δημοσίᾳ κατὰ τῶν πονηρῶν ἀρὰς ποιούμενοι, εἴ τις δῶρα λαμβάνων μὴ ταὐτὰ λέγει καὶ γιγνώσκει περὶ τῶν πραγμάτων, ἐξώλη τοῦτον εἶναι.

[54] Aristoph. Thes., 356 ff.:
... ὁπόσαι δ᾿
ἐξαπατῶσιν παραβαίνουσί τε τοὺς
ὅρκους τοὺς νενομισμένους
κερδῶν εἴνεκ᾿ ἐπὶ βλάβῃ,
ἢ ψηφίσματα καὶ νόμον
ζητοῦσ᾿ ἀντιμεθιστάναι,
τἀπόρρητά τε τοῖσιν ἐ-
χθροῖς τοῖς ἡμετέροις λέγουσ᾿,
ἢ Μήδους ἐπάγουσι τῆς
χώρας οὔνεκ᾿ ἐπὶ βλάβῃ,
ἀσεβοῦσ᾿ ἀδικοῦσί τε τὴν πόλιν. Cf. Isoc., 4, 157.

[55] Cf. Ditt. Syll.³, 976, 15 ff.: ὅταν δὲ [ἡ] χειροτονία μέλλῃ γίγνεσθαι, ὁ τῆς πόλεως κῆρυξ ἐπε[υ]ξάσθω etc. In educational endowment, ibid., 577, 35 ff. we read : τὸν δὲ ἱεροκήρυκα ἐπεύξασθαι τοῖς ἐκκλησιάζουσιν, ὅστις χειροτονοίηι παιδοτρίβας καὶ τοὺς τὰ γράμματα διδάξοντας, οὓς ἄριστα νομίζει τῶν παίδων ἐπιστατήσειν καὶ μηδεμιᾶι φιλοτιμίαι παρὰ τὸ δίκαιον προσνέμοι τὴν αὐτοῦ γνώμην, ἄμεινον αὐτῶι εἶναι.

[56] Athen., IV, 32 (p. 149e): κατακλιθέντες ἐπανίστανται εἰς γόνατα τοῦ ἱεροκήρυκος τὰς πατρίους εὐχὰς καταλέγοντος συσπένδοντες.

[57] Thuc., VI, 32 : εὐχὰς δὲ τὰς νομιζομένας πρὸ τῆς ἀναγωγῆς οὐ κατὰ ναῦν ἑκάστην, ξύμπαντες δὲ ὑπὸ κήρυκος ἐποιοῦντο.

[58] Cf. M. P. Nilsson, Griechische Feste von religiöser Bedeutung (1906), 17 ff.

[59] Aristoph.Pl., 1110 : ἡ γλῶττα τῷ κήρυκι τούτων τέμνεται. Cf. the schol. on this (ed. F. Dübner [1842]) and P. Stengel, Opferbräuche der Griechen (1910).

(IG, IX, 2, 1110, 4). At sacrifices, too, the herald leads in prayer. He asks for solemn silence,[60] and beseeches health, well-being and peace for the state.[61] An inscr. tells us that when the successor to the throne was declared to be of age a city would pray for his σωτηρία through the ἱεροκῆρυξ at the sacrificial feasts.[62]

In all these cases the herald speaks to the deity on behalf of the assembled community. He brings before God the wishes and requests of men in words which are fixed and well known to all.[63] He is the liturgical minister in Greek worship who utters the great prayer of intercession. He is well-equipped for this by reason of his loud and audible and resonant voice.[64] When prayer was offered at the great festivals, all wished to hear it in order to participate. It should be noted, however, that the herald plays a further part in the sacrifices, that he also participates in oaths,[65] and that he has a role in the religious act of making treaties between two nations.[66] Hence we may rightly conclude that it is not for external reasons alone that he prays publicly on behalf of the people. Beyond this, he is a sacral person.

At this point we should mention specifically the κήρυκες who announce the festivals and the games, thought it is not clear whether theirs is a political or a cultic function. The great Greek festivals in honour of the gods were state institutions with great political significance. Whenever such a feast was held, heralds were sent out to intimate it. They invited all to take part, whether as citizens or guests (Ditt. Syll.[3], 1045, 5 ff.; IG, XII, 7, 35, 5). All Greece was to assemble for it. During it wars and enmities were all suspended. Hence the heralds who announced it were also called σπονδοφόροι (Pind. Isthm., 2, 23). To declare the feast they brought ἐκεχειρία and σπονδαί. At the feast

---

[60] Ael. Arist. Or. Sacr., 4, 17 ff. (Keil), cf. Hom. Il., 9, 171 ff.

[61] Two examples may be given, Ditt. Syll.[3], 589, 20 ff.: ἐν τῶι ἀναδείκνυσθαι τὸν ταῦρον κατευχέσθω ὁ ἱεροκῆρυξ μετὰ τοῦ ἱέρεω καὶ τῆς ἱερείας καὶ τοῦ στεφανηφόρου καὶ τῶμ παίδων καὶ τῶν παρθένων καὶ τῶμ πολεμάρχων καὶ τῶν ἱππάρχων καὶ τῶν οἰκονόμων καὶ τοῦ γραμματέως τῆς βουλῆς καὶ τοῦ ἀντιγραφέως καὶ τοῦ στρατηγοῦ ὑπέρ τε σωτηρίας τῆς τε πόλεως καὶ τῆς χώρας καὶ τῶμ πολιτῶν καὶ γυναικῶν καὶ τέκνων καὶ τῶν ἄλλων τῶν κατοικούντων ἔν τε τῆι πόλει καὶ τῆι χώραι ὑπέρ τε εἰρήνης καὶ πλούτου καὶ σίτου φορᾶς καὶ τῶν ἄλλων καρπῶν πάντων καὶ τῶν κτηνῶν. Ditt. Syll.[3], 695, 37 ff. at the feast of Artemis Leucophryene: τὸν δὲ ἱεροκήρυκα [τὸν] νῦν καὶ τὸν κατ' ἐνιαυτὸν ἀεὶ τοῦδε τοῦ μηνὸς ἐν τῆι ἀποδεδειγ[μέ]νηι ἱερᾶι ἡμέραι πληθυούσης ἀγορᾶς συμπαρόντων ἐν ἐσθῆσ[ιν] ἐπισή- μοις καὶ δάφνης στεφάνοις πολεμάρχων, οἰκονόμω[ν, γραμ]ματέως βουλῆς, στρα- τηγοῦ ἱππάρχων, στεφανηφόρου, ἀν[τιγρα]φέως, εὐφημίαν καταγγείλαντα πρὸ τοῦ βουλευτηρίου μετὰ [τῶν παίδ]ων κατευχὴν καὶ παράκλησιν παντὸς τοῦ πλήθους ποιεῖσ[θαι τὴν]δε· παρακαλῶ πάντας τοὺς κατοικοῦντας πόλιν καὶ χώρ[αν τὴν Μα]γνήτων ἐπὶ καλοῖς Ἰσιτηρίοις κατὰ δύναμιν οἴκου κεχ[αρισμένην θυ]σίαν συντελεῖν Ἀρτέμιδι Λευκοφρυηνῆι τῆιδε τῆ ἡμέ[ραι, εὔχεσθε δὲ] καὶ Μάγνησιν αὐτοῖς τε διδόναι καὶ γυναιξὶν ὑγ[ί]ει[αν καὶ πλοῦτον ῎Αρ]τεμιν Λευκοφρυηνήν, καὶ γενεὰν τήν τε ὑπά[ρχουσαν σώιζεσθαι] καὶ εὐτυχεῖν καὶ τὴν ἐπιγονὴν μακαρίαν [γίνεσθαι].

[62] American Journal of Archaeology, 2. Ser., 18 (1914), 323, 12: κατευχὰς ποιεῖσθαι διὰ τῶν ἱεροκηρύκων ὑπὲρ τῆς σωτηρίας αὐτοῦ.

[63] Aeschin. Or., 1, 23 → n. 50; Athen., IV, 32 (p. 149e) → n. 56; Thuc., VI, 32 → n. 57.

[64] → 686.

[65] E.g., Ditt. Syll.[3], 633, 105 ff.: οἱ δὲ ἀποδειχθέντες ὁρκισάτωσαν μετὰ τοῦ ἱεροκή- ρυκος τοὺς πρεσβευτὰς τοὺς ἥκο[ν]τας παρὰ Ἡρακλεωτῶν καὶ εἰς Ἡράκλειαν παραγενόμενοι τὸν δῆμον. In the Dionysus cult the herald supports the consort of the basileus at the swearing of the 14 worthy and noble matrons prior to the sacred wedding. Demosth. Or., 59, 78: βούλομαι δ' ὑμῖν καὶ τὸν ἱεροκήρυκα καλέσαι, ὃς ὑπηρετεῖ τῇ τοῦ βασιλέως γυναικί, ὅταν ἐξορκοῖ τὰς γεραιρὰς ἐν κανοῖς πρὸς τῷ βωμῷ, πρὶν ἅπτεσθαι τῶν ἱερῶν.

[66] Cf. Hom. Il., 3, 116, 245, 268, 274; Ditt. Syll.[3], 633, 20 ff.

the κῆρυξ proclaimed the worth of outstanding men and awards of wreaths were published (→ 698).

Some heralds must be regarded more specifically as sacral persons because they served a cultic society, a sanctuary or something similar. Ditt. Syll.³, 773, 5 speaks of a κῆρυξ τοῦ Ἀπόλλωνος. These κήρυκες or ἱεροκήρυκες are hard to distinguish from other heralds, since they often fulfil the same tasks. The only distinction is that they are employed, not by a political institution, but by a cultic society.

In the Eleusinian mysteries the herald is highly regarded. Along with the hierophant, the most important and prominent priest of the mysteries, the daduchos and the priest of the altar, he has the greatest influence. In Plut. Alcibiades, 22 (I, 202e), where it is told how Alcibiades imitates the Eleusinian mysteries, he is simply called κῆρυξ. In Xenoph. Hist. Graec., II, 4, 20 he is κῆρυξ τῶν μυστῶν, and he is also said to be εὔφωνος. Elsewhere he is called ἱεροκήρυξ. He calls the assembly to worship, leads in prayer, helps in the sacrifice and makes the most important announcements. He thus fulfils the same function as other heralds, but it is to be noted that he is one of the most prominent and influential men in the whole cult. Ditt. Syll.³, 845, 2 refers to a philosopher who was an Eleusinian herald.

4. The Herald of the Gods.

Every herald is strictly κῆρυξ τῶν θεῶν; he stands under their protection and enjoys their special favour. But the gods have also their own special heralds to whom they entrust specific messages in the same way as earthly kings. The heralds to whom we referred earlier, e.g., in relation to prayer (→ 689), are heralds of men to the gods rather than of the gods to men. Hermes is a divine herald in the specific sense.[67] He has the same task at the assembly of the gods as do heralds in popular assemblies.[68] The gods send him to men when they have something to impart.[69] But birds are also heralds of the gods to men (Plut. Pyth. Or., 22 [II, 405d]). The divine will may be discerned from their flight and cries, Eur. Ion, 159 and 180; cf. Aristoph. Av., 561. Furthermore, when the gods wish to communicate with men, they use not only Hermes and birds but also selected men who are commissioned to deliver the message to their fellowmen.[70]

The Stoic philosopher is a divine herald of this kind. In Diss., III, 21, 13-16 Epictet. compares the Eleusinian _keryx_ to the philosopher. In the age of Hellenism philosophers liked to play an active part in the cults.[71] For Epictet. the philosopher

---

[67] Pind. Olymp., 6, 78 : κῆρυξ θεῶν; Hes. Theog., 939; cf. also Epigr. Graec., 772 : κῆρυξ ἀθανάτων; Aesch. Choeph., 164 : κῆρυξ μέγιστε τῶν ἄνω τε καὶ κάτω.

[68] Luc. Jup. Trag., 18 : Hermes must τὸ κήρυγμα κηρύσσειν; then he cries : "Ακουε, σίγα, μὴ τάραττε. τίς ἀγορεύειν βούλεται τῶν τελείων θεῶν;

[69] Cornut. Theol. Graec., 16 : Hermes, the Logos, is sent by the gods in heaven to men : παραδέδοται δὲ καὶ κῆρυξ θεῶν· καὶ διαγγέλλειν αὐτὸν ἔφασαν τὰ παρ' ἐκείνων τοῖς ἀνθρώποις, κῆρυξ μέν, ἐπειδὴ διὰ φωνῆς γεγωνοῦ παριστᾷ τὰ κατὰ τὸν λόγον σημαινόμενα ταῖς ἀκοαῖς, ἄγγελος δέ, ἐπεὶ τὸ βούλευμα τῶν θεῶν γινώσκομεν ἐκ τῶν ἐνδεδομένων ἡμῖν κατὰ τὸν λόγον ἐννοιῶν. It is characteristic of the herald that in a loud voice he should declare a message entrusted to him.

[70] Epict. Diss., III, 1, 37: ἀλλ' ἂν μὲν κόραξ κραυγάζων σημαίνῃ σοί τι, οὐχ ὁ κόραξ ἐστὶν ὁ σημαίνων, ἀλλ' ὁ θεὸς δι' αὐτοῦ. ἂν δὲ δι' ἀνθρωπίνης φωνῆς σημαίνῃ τι, τὸν ἄνθρωπον ποιήσει λέγειν σοι ταῦτα.

[71] Philostr. Vit. Soph., II, 33, 4 : Νικαγόρου τοῦ Ἀθηναίου, ὃς καὶ τοῦ Ἐλευσινίου ἱεροῦ κῆρυξ ἐστέφθη; Ditt. Syll., 845 : Νικαγόρας ὁ τῶν ἱερῶν κῆρυξ καὶ ἐπὶ τῆς καθέδρας σοφιστής, Πλουτάρχου καὶ Σέξτου τῶν φιλοσόφων ἔκγονος.

is a sacred herald even though he does not do this. [72] His proclamation is something sacral. It replaces all other cults. Philosophy has become a religion, and religion has become philosophy. The Stoic has a profound sense of having a special God-given task among men. The deity has revealed the secret to him, and he must now bear witness to it. [73] Through him God Himself speaks. His teaching is revelation, his preaching the word of God. To despise his word and refuse to follow his teaching is to do despite to God. [74] It is with this claim to be heard that he comes before men. As κῆρυξ τοῦ θεοῦ he goes through the world and accepts all kinds of sufferings. He knows neither family, home nor country. [75] With only a scrip and a staff, he proclaims that there is no lack, comforting the weak, warning the wealthy, concerned for the salvation of all. On the streets and market-places he teaches men concerning good and evil, chiding errors and summoning to emulation. He even dares to compete with the imperial cult. The peace which the philosopher proclaims is higher than that which the emperor can grant. [76]

The relationship between these preachers and early Christian missionaries has often been noted. [77] Both are divine messengers. Both have a higher mission. Both bring to men a new message which offers salvation. There is little distinction as regards the mode of their activity. Their work consists in κηρύσσειν, in the loud publication of the message entrusted to them. The similarity is so strong that in Thessalonica Paul is suspected of being a wandering Cynic or Epicurean philosopher, and he refutes the idea in 1 Th. 2:3 ff. When the Stoic calls himself ἄγγελος καὶ κατάσκοπος καὶ κῆρυξ τῶν θεῶν (Diss., III, 22, 69), it is the word κατάσκοπος which best distinguishes him from the early Christian missionary. His task is to observe men, to inspect them, and then to declare his message on the basis of these observations. The Christian missionary, however, is not a κατάσκοπος of human relations. He is a preacher of the Word of God. Though certain parts of the

---

[72] Diss., III, 21, 13 : τί ἄλλο ποιεῖς, ἄνθρωπε, ἢ τὰ μυστήρια ἐξορχῇ καὶ λέγεις 'οἴκημά ἐστιν καὶ ἐν Ἐλευσῖνι, ἰδοὺ καὶ ἐνθάδε ... ἐκεῖ κῆρυξ· κἀγὼ κήρυκα καταστήσω. ἐκεῖ δᾳδοῦχος· κἀγὼ δᾳδοῦχος. ἐκεῖ δᾷδες· καὶ ἐνθάδε. αἱ φωναὶ αἱ αὐταί. τὰ γινόμενα τί διαφέρει ταῦτα ἐκείνων';

[73] Diss., I, 29, 46 f.: ὡς μάρτυς ὑπὸ τοῦ θεοῦ κεκλημένος. ἔρχου σὺ καὶ μαρτύρησόν μοι· σὺ γὰρ ἄξιος εἶ προαχθῆναι μάρτυς ὑπ' ἐμοῦ'. → μαρτυρεῖν and Diss., III, 22, 23 : εἰδέναι δεῖ, ὅτι ἄγγελος ἀπὸ τοῦ θεοῦ ἀπέσταλται καὶ πρὸς τοὺς ἀνθρώπους περὶ ἀγαθῶν καὶ κακῶν ὑποδείξων αὐτοῖς ...

[74] Diss., III, 1, 36 f.: ταῦτά μοι Ἐπίκτητος οὐκ εἴρηκεν· πόθεν γὰρ ἐκείνῳ; ἀλλὰ θεός τίς ποτ' εὐμενὴς δι' ἐκείνου ... ἄγε οὖν τῷ θεῷ πεισθῶμεν, ἵνα μὴ θεοχόλωτοι ὦμεν.

[75] Diss., III, 22, 46 ff.: ἰδοὺ ἀπέσταλκεν ὑμῖν ὁ θεὸς τὸν δείξοντα ἔργῳ ὅτι ἐνδέχεται. ἴδετέ με, ἄοικός εἰμι, ἄπολις, ἀκτήμων, ἄδουλος· χαμαὶ κοιμῶμαι· οὐ γυνή, οὐ παιδία, οὐ πραιτωρίδιον, ἀλλὰ γῆ μόνον καὶ οὐρανὸς καὶ ἓν τριβωνάριον. IV, 8, 31: ἰδοὺ ἐγὼ ὑμῖν παράδειγμα ὑπὸ τοῦ θεοῦ ἀπέσταλμαι μήτε κτῆσιν ἔχων μήτε οἶκον μήτε γυναῖκα μήτε τέκνα ἀλλὰ μηδ' ὑπόστρωμα μηδὲ χιτῶνα μηδὲ σκεῦος. [76] Diss., III, 13, 9 ff.: ὁρᾶτε γάρ, ὅτι εἰρήνην μεγάλην ὁ Καῖσαρ ἡμῖν δοκεῖ παρέχειν, ὅτι οὐκ εἰσιν οὐκέτι πόλεμοι, οὐδὲ μάχαι οὐδὲ λῃστήρια μεγάλα οὐδὲ πειρατικά, ἀλλ' ἔξεστιν πάσῃ ὥρᾳ ὁδεύειν ... μή τι οὖν καὶ ἀπὸ πυρετοῦ δύναται ἡμῖν εἰρήνην παρασχεῖν, μή τι καὶ ἀπὸ ναυαγίου ...; οὐ δύναται. ἀπὸ πένθους; οὐ δύναται. ἀπὸ φθόνου; οὐ δύναται. ἀπ' οὐδενὸς ἁπλῶς τούτων. ὁ δὲ λόγος ὁ τῶν φιλοσόφων ὑπισχνεῖται καὶ ἀπὸ τούτων εἰρήνην παρέχειν ... ταύτην τὴν εἰρήνην τις ἔχων [οὐχὶ] κεκηρυγμένην οὐχ ὑπὸ τοῦ Καίσαρος (πόθεν γὰρ αὐτῷ ταύτην κηρύξαι;) ἀλλ' ὑπὸ τοῦ θεοῦ κεκηρυγμένην διὰ τοῦ λόγου οὐκ ἀρκεῖται.

[77] Wendland Hell. Kult. → I, 409 ff.

preaching may be similar, the starting-point is quite different. What constrains the Christian to speak is not the wickedness of men, nor their wealth nor debauchery. It is the presence of God in Jesus Christ. If Christians call themselves God's envoys and preachers in the same way as the Stoics, there is a distinction between them. This is the distinction that Zeus, whose messenger Epictetus is, is a very different god from the Father of Jesus Christ, whose apostle Paul is. What counts is whose herald one is. The Stoic appeals to Socrates; he detects in himself the same sense of mission. The Christian missionary starts with the realisation that the prophetic word has been fulfilled in Jesus Christ. Philosophical preaching does not usher in the new age which involves the radical conversion and renewal of man. It simply aims at the change which will initiate development into a healthy man. It has to instruct. It must lead to self-instruction. The lists of vices and virtues serve this purpose. The Stoic has to be constantly scolding. As the doctor removes the ulcer with the sharp cut of the knife, so the doctor of the soul delivers man with hard words. The divine seed which slumbers in man is thus released and is henceforth able to grow. The philosopher does not proclaim the βασιλεία τοῦ θεοῦ; he preaches morality. His concern is not with God's wrath and grace; it is with man's wickedness and goodness. He declares, not the forgiveness of sins, but the development of the good. In place of the incarnation of God, he sets the divinisation of man.

B. The Herald and the Jewish World.

1. Josephus and Philo.

So long as we do not have an index or a complete vocabulary of Joseph., no definitive judgment is possible. It may be assumed, however, that in his works the herald is more commonly mentioned in connection with war and diplomacy (Ant., 10, 75). [78] In the other Gk. writings of Judaism κῆρυξ is very rare. Leisegang, *s.v.* does not list a single passage in Philo. We may refer to Agric., 112, where what happens at the games in the arena is transferred to the ethical sphere. In the struggle against wickedness it is honourable to go down. μὴ ἐπιτρέψῃς μηδὲ κήρυκι κηρῦξαι μηδὲ βραβευτῇ στεφανῶσαι τὸν ἐχθρόν, ἀλλ' αὐτὸς παρελθὼν τὰ βραβεῖα καὶ τὸν φοίνικα ἀνάδος καὶ στεφάνωσον.

2. The Septuagint.

In the LXX we find κῆρυξ only 4 times at Gn. 41:43; Da. 3:4; Sir. 20:15 and 4 Macc. 6:4. It may be noted that in Gn. 41:43 there is no Heb. equivalent. κῆρυξ is simply an addition of the LXX, which has κῆρυξ κηρύσσει for קָרָא. Since the other 3 instances are of no consequence we may conclude that the herald as we have learned to know him in the Gk. sphere finds no place in the biblical world. In Sir. 20:15 the term occurs in a comparison. The ἄφρων does not give much, but makes much of it: ἀνοίξει τὸ στόμα αὐτοῦ ὡς κῆρυξ (→ 686; 687). In the other passages the reference is to a herald at a foreign court. In Gn. 41:43 Pharaoh causes Joseph to ride in the second chariot καὶ ἐκήρυξεν ἔμπροσθεν αὐτοῦ κῆρυξ. At Da. 3:4 the herald of Nebuchadnezzar commanded the people to worship the image. At 4 Macc. 6:4 the herald of Antiochus tries to persuade Eleazar to eat swine's flesh. How alien the idea of the herald is to the Bible may be seen from the fact that there is no true word for it. At Da. 3:4 we have the Aram. כָּרוֹזָא. Where this word comes from we shall see in the next section.

---

[78] Cf. also Jos. Bell., 2, 624 : Josephus διὰ κηρύκων ἀπειλήσας, and 3, 92 : ὁ κῆρυξ δέξιος τῷ πολεμάρχῳ παραστάς, εἰ πρὸς πόλεμόν εἰσιν ἕτοιμοι.

3. The Rabbis.

a. Derivation of כרז. In contrast to Philo and the LXX, the Rabbis make frequent reference to the herald. The herald is כרוז, to proclaim is כרז (→ 702), proclamation is אכרזה or אכרזתה and הכרזה (→ 715). Most scholars agree that כרז is a loan word.[79] But there is some obscurity as to where it is borrowed from. The usual solution was to look to Greece, but then division arose as follows. Some argued that כרוז = κῆρυξ was the primary term, since loan words from the Greek are usually persons or things. The verb כרז was then derived from כרוז. Others, however, argued for the priority of the verb, with כרוז as a derived form.

H. H. Schaeder[80] has rendered this whole discussion superfluous by showing that כרז is a Persian loan word deriving from the old Persian *xrausa. Middle Persian has it in the form xros, xroh, and modern Persian in the form xuros, xuroh. It means crier, and is used for the cock who summons the faithful to wakefulness in the morning.[81]

b. The Meaning of כרוז. 1. כרוז is used very generally for the crier who goes through the town and makes something known.[82] 2. Heralds are used in courts. They have to declare decisions of the council to the people.[83] 3. Criers are used in the temple to waken the priests for the sacrifice.[84] 4. The rabbi uses a herald to declare his judgments, jSheq., 48d, 53 : In the presence of the school of R. Shilo Rab expounded (the words of the Mishnah קריאת הגבר): The man has cried ; then R. Shilo caused it to be proclaimed by a herald (אכריז כרוזא): Tell him (Rab, that the meaning of the Mishnah is): The cock has crowed. 5. Earthly relations are transferred to heaven.[85] The angel who is set over

---

[79] Schn. Euang., 221; G. Dalman, *Gramm. d. jüdisch-palästinischen Aram.*[2] (1905), 183; E. Kautzsch, *Gramm. des Biblisch-Aramäischen* (1884), § 64, 4; Ges.-Buhl, *s.v.*; Krauss (→ bibl.), I, 146; II, 296 f. For a different view cf. T. Nöldecke, GGA (1884), 1019 : "That כרז derives from κῆρυξ or κηρύσσειν does not seem quite certain to me." Cf. K. Marti (1901) on Da. 3:4 : „כָּרוֹזָא, herald, is a normal Aram. construction ... hence it can hardly be a direct borrowing from the Gk. κῆρυξ, but derives from the verb כְּרַז...., which does not necessarily relate to the Gk. κηρύσσειν, since a fairly old Aram. inscription has the stem."

[80] H. H. Schaeder, "Iranische Beiträge," I, *Schriften der Königsberger Gelehrten Gesellschaft, Geisteswissensch. Klasse,* 6. Jahr, Heft 5 (1930), 254 : "It is astonishing that this etymology, which is like a fossil from earlier periods of linguistic development, should still be maintained without any search for a better alternative ... In fact the word has nothing to do with κῆρυξ." [K. G. Kuhn.]

[81] For the cock as herald because he wakens men, cf. Aristoph. Eccl., 30.

[82] Pesikt., 78a; 82b; jShab, 15d, 38; Lv. r., 6 on 5:1; Tg. O. Ex. 36:6 and *passim.*

[83] Sanh., 6, 1 (cf. Str.-B., I, 1023, 5b; bSanh., 43a): A condemned man is led out to execution. The herald כרוז goes before him to the market-place and cries : NN, son of NN, is led out to be stoned because he has committed such and such a crime. NN and NN are witnesses. Anyone who can say anything in his favour should declare it.

[84] bJoma, 20b : What did the crier Gebini (most widely renowned because of his voice and often mentioned, e.g., Tamid, 3, 8; Sheq., 5, 1) proclaim ? Priests to your ministry, Levites to your dais and Israelites to your attendance (a proportion of the people which had to be present at the daily sacrifice). His voice could be heard for three parasangs.

[85] Dt. r., 11 on 31:14 : The angel which is set over proclamation (הכרזה) has the name Achreziel (אכרזיאל). Heb. Enoch 10:3 : "The herald went forth into each heaven and said ..." Beth ha Midrash (ed. A. Jellinek), 3 (1855), 88, line 7 from the bottom : "The herald comes forth from Araboth Raqia' (the highest heaven), proclaims and says in the court of the upper heaven : ..." H. Odeberg (Heb. Enoch 10:3 [II, p. 28]) refers to a passage in Jalkut Re'ubeni, II, 66b : "Gallisur stands behind the curtain, and asks to know the decisions of the Holy One, and proclaims them ... and the herald entrusts them to Elias, and Elias

proclamation is called אַכְרִזִיאֵל (Jalkut Shimeoni, I, 303a). He declares the resolves of the Most High. 6. God also charges men with His message that they should be heralds among their fellow-men. "Abba bKehana (c. 310) has said : God had a herald כרוז in the generation of the flood, this was Noah (inasmuch as he summoned his contemporaries to repentance)," Gn. r., 30, 7 on 6:9 (Str.-B., III, 645). 86

C. The κῆρυξ in the New Testament.

The herald who plays so important a part in the Greek world is of little account in the NT. The word occurs only 3 times, and always in later writings. Jesus is never called the κῆρυξ θεοῦ, though Paul is κῆρυξ καὶ ἀπόστολος καὶ διδάσκαλος in 2 Tm. 1:11. Cf. also 1 Tm. 2:7 and some MSS of Col. 1:23. 87 Noah, who is regarded as God's herald in Judaism (→ supra), is called κῆρυξ δικαιοσύνης in 2 Pt. 2:5 because by word and deed he summoned his contemporaries to repentance some 120 years before the coming of the flood. 88 Noah is also described as a herald in 1 Cl., 7, 6 and 9, 4. 89

How are we to explain the reserve with which the Bible views the term ? In many respects κῆρυξ seems to be a very suitable word to describe the Christian preacher. It has many links with → ἀπόστολος 90 (→ 685) and is also at many points an equivalent of εὐάγγελος (→ 711). 91 Nevertheless, the NT manifestly avoids it. Why ? The point is that it does not really fit the person of the one who proclaims the Word. For the true preacher is God or Christ Himself (→ 707). Hence there is little place for the herald. The Bible is not telling us about human preachers ; it is telling us about the preaching. Furthermore, the prior Greek history gives too specific a meaning to κῆρυξ. The NT knows nothing of sacral personages who are inviolable in the world (→ 688). The messengers of Jesus are like sheep delivered up to wolves (Mt. 10:16). As the Lord was persecuted, so His servants will be persecuted (Jn. 15:20). The servants of Christ are, as it were, dedicated to death (Rev. 12:11). But the message does not perish with the one who proclaims it. The message is irresistible (2 Tm. 2:9). It takes its victorious course through the world (2 Th. 3:1). Hence κηρύσσειν is more important than the κῆρυξ in the NT.

---

stands as a herald on Mt. Horeb." But this does not really throw light on the Rabb. use of כרוז, since Jalkut Re'ubeni is a collection of cabbalistic expositions of the Pentateuch deriving from R. ben Höschke Kohen, a rabbi of Prague († 1673). [K. G. Kuhn.]

86 Cf. Sib., I, 128 : Νῶε, δέμας θάρσυνον ἐὸν λαοῖσί τε πᾶσι κήρυξον μετάνοιαν, ὅπως σωθῶσιν ἅπαντες.

87 1 Cl., 5, 6 : Paul κῆρυξ γενόμενος ἔν τε τῇ ἀνατολῇ καὶ ἐν τῇ δύσει; Herm. s., 9, 15, 4 : ἀπόστολοι καὶ διδάσκαλοι τοῦ κηρύγματος; 9, 16, 5; 9, 25, 2 : ἀπόστολοι καὶ διδάσκαλοι οἱ κηρύξαντες.

88 The gen. here denotes the content of the message, not the one who commissions the herald (→ 685). Noah is a preacher of righteousness in the κόσμος ἀσεβῶν, Gn. 6.

89 1 Cl., 7, 6 : Νῶε ἐκήρυξεν μετάνοιαν; 9, 4 : Νῶε πιστὸς εὑρεθεὶς διὰ τῆς λειτουργίας αὐτοῦ παλιγγενεσίαν κόσμῳ ἐκήρυξεν.

90 ἀπόστολος and κῆρυξ are used synon. in Hdt., I, 21: ἔπεμπε κήρυκα εἰς Μίλητον ... ὁ μὲν δὴ ἀπόστολος ἐς τὴν Μίλητον ἦν ...

91 Cf. R. 10:5 : πῶς δὲ κηρύξωσιν ἐὰν μὴ ἀποσταλῶσιν; καθάπερ γέγραπται· ὡς ὡραῖοι οἱ πόδες τῶν εὐαγγελιζομένων ἀγαθά.

† κηρύσσω.

Contents: A. κηρύσσω in Greek: 1. Shades of Meaning and Synonyms; 2. κηρύσσω in Passages of Religious Significance: a. The Games; b. Aretalogies; c. The Corpus Hermeticum. C. κηρύσσω in the Old Testament. C. כרז in the Rabbis. D. κηρύσσω in the New Testament: 1. κηρύσσω and Other NT Words for Proclamation; 2. The Use of κηρύσσω; 3. The Secular Meaning of κηρύσσω in Lk. 12:3; 4. Proclamation by Different Preachers: a. The Jews; b. John the Baptist; c. Jesus Christ, Incarnate, Crucified and Risen; d. Those Healed; e. Disciples and Apostles; f. An Angel; 5. The Content of the Specific Message of the NT; 6. The Hearers; 7. Sending and Proclamation; 8. Teaching and Proclamation in the Synoptists; 9. Miracles and Proclamation.

A. κηρύσσω in Greek.

1. Shades of Meaning and Synonyms.

κηρύσσω, made up of κηρυκ-jω,[1] from κῆρυξ, does not have the same significance in the Greek world as we have noted in respect of κῆρυξ. Even numerically it is much less common not only in Homer (→ 683, n. 3) but also in other authors.

Very rarely we find κηρύσσειν in the absolute in the sense "to be a herald," "to discharge the office of a herald."[2] Usually it is trans. and describes the activity of the herald in the discharge of his office. Since this activity varies (→ 684), κηρύσσειν has a varied meaning. Yet, since the main quality demanded of a herald is that he should have a good voice (→ 686), it always carries the basic meaning "to cry out loud," "to proclaim," "to declare," "to announce." In Hom. it repeatedly has the sense of → καλεῖν and means "to call to something."[3] It is also synon. with καλεῖν in Ditt. Or., 218, 26: "to summon someone to something,"[4] and Eur. Hec., 146: "to appeal to, to implore someone."[5] But usually the obj. of person is in the dat. rather than the acc., and the object of the call is given in the acc. or a subordinate clause (→ 704). In accordance with what is declared by the herald κηρύσσειν can mean "to offer," "to forbid,"[6] "to order,"[7] "to ask."[8] When it is a matter of crying wares we must give the rendering "to offer for sale," "to auction."[9] But κηρύσσειν, with its compounds (Poll. Onom., IV, 93) ἀνακηρύττειν, ἀποκηρύττειν, διακηρύττειν, ἐπικηρύττειν, ἀντεπικηρύττειν, κατακηρύττειν, προκηρύττειν, προσκηρύττειν, ὑποκηρύττειν, is not the only

---

κ η ρ ύ σ σ ω. [1] Kühner-Blass-Gerth § 328.
[2] Hom. Il., 17, 323 f.: Περίφαντι ἐοικὼς κήρυκ' Ἠπυτίδη, ὅς οἱ παρὰ πατρὶ γέροντι κηρύσσων γήρασκε; cf. Demosth. Or., 44, 4 and Theophr. Charact., 6.
[3] Hom. Il., 2, 443, the Achaeans πολεμόνδε; Od., 2, 7 ἀγορήνδε; cf. Il., 2, 50 f.:
αὐτὰρ ὁ κηρύκεσσι λιγυφθόγγοισι κέλευσεν
κηρύσσειν ἀγορήνδε κάρη κομόωντας Ἀχαιούς.
and 9, 10:
κηρύκεσσι λιγυφθόγγοισι κελεύων
κλήδην εἰς ἀγορὴν κικλήσκειν ἄνδρα ἕκαστον.
[4] Ditt. Or., 218, 26: ἐν τοῖς ἀγῶ[σι] εἰς π[ρο]εδρίαν [κηρύ]σσεσθαι, IG, VII, 190, 35 etc.
[5] Eur. Hec., 146: κήρυσσε θεοὺς τούς τ' οὐρανίδας τοὺς θ' ὑπὸ γαίαν.
[6] Thuc., IV, 38; 116; Eur. Phoen., 47.
[7] Soph. Ant., 32, 447, cf. 449 and Plut. Apophth. Lac. Agesilaos, 72 (II, 214a).
[8] Demosth. Or., 43, 5; Hdt., II, 134.
[9] Hdt., I, 194; Plut. Apophth. Sebastos, 1 (II, 207a): ἐκήρυττε τὰ πατρῷα καὶ ἐπίπρασκεν. Ptolemaeus De Vocum Differentiis (Hermes, 22 [1887], 397, 20): κηρῦξαι μὲν καὶ ἀποκηρῦξαι λέγουσιν ἐπὶ τοῦ ὑπὸ κήρυκα ἀποδίδοσθαί τι. Jos. Ant., 19, 145: τῶν κηρυσσόντων τὰ πωλούμενα.

word for declaration by a herald. [10] A whole series of other terms and expressions is used for this purpose, e.g., κήρυγμα ποιεῖν, Hdt., III, 52; κηρύγματι δηλοῦν, Xenoph. Ag., I, 33; ἀγορεύειν, Hdt., VI, 97; ἀναγορεύειν, Ditt. Syll.³, 305, 33; ἀνάρρησιν, Aeschin. Or., 3, 189, and ἀναγόρευσιν ποιεῖν, Demosth. Or., 18, 120; → ἀγγέλλειν, Pind. Pyth., 1, 32; → ἀναγγέλλειν, Ditt. Syll.³, 282, 25 ff.; ἀναγγελίαν ποιεῖν, *ibid.*, 656, 31; ἀπαγγέλλειν, Aesch. Suppl., 931; ἐπαγγέλλειν and περιαγγέλλειν, Poll. Onom., IV, 91; βοᾶν, Hom. Il., 2, 97; κράζειν, Epict. Diss., I, 16, 11 f. etc. Comparison with these synon. shows that κηρύσσειν is less prominent than κῆρυξ and has a much weaker sense. In fact, it can be used very generally for "to make known" with no reference to the person or work of the herald.

2. κηρύσσω in Passages of Religious Significance.

Significant in relation to the early history of the NT term is the Hellenistic religious employment of κηρύσσειν a. in relation to the games, b. in aretalogies and c. in the Hermetic writings. For κηρύσσειν in Epict. → 693.

a. In the first instance we may refer to the sacral proclaiming of the games, of honours and of victors. Along with other words which are significant in the NT, κηρύσσειν is a tt. for the proclaiming of contests and divine festivals (→ 691). The herald announces the victor in a contest, and the honours or wreaths which a city confers on worthy men are proclaimed in the theatre or the assembly. [11] An example of this effectual κηρύσσειν, which reminds us of the NT, is to be found in Plut. Apophth. Titus Quinctius, 2 (II, 197b): νικήσας δὲ μάχῃ τὸν Φίλιππον ἐκήρυξεν ἐν Ἰσθμίοις, ὅτι τοὺς Ἕλληνας ἐλευθέρους καὶ αὐτονόμους ἀφίησιν. The moment this is announced at the games, the Greeks are free. The NT takes its terms, not from contemplative philosophical reflection, but from public life.

b. As an instance of κηρύσσειν in aretalogies we may quote P. Oxy., XI, 1381. The author wanted to translate into Gk. an ancient Egyptian pap. roll which had been found in the temple and which treated of the honouring of Imouthes-Aesculapius and sang of the great acts of the gods. In this work he learned κηρύσσειν, v. 35. He did not dare continue, for (v. 40) "it is permitted to gods alone, not mortals, to describe the mighty acts of the gods." As a punishment for his hesitation, first his mother falls sick, then he himself. In a vision he is given the task of completing the work, though at first he still resists. He is then cured, and in v. 144 ἐκήρυσσον αὐτοῦ [τ]ὰς εὐεργεσίας. In v. 183 he finishes the translation "according to thy favour, not according to my purpose." This aretalogy is in many respects worth noting. The devotee of Imouthes-Aesculapius recognises that we cannot understand κηρύσσειν of ourselves. We learn it when we put ourselves in the service of the deity and occupy ourselves with its demonstrations of power. Like Moses (Ex. 4:10), Jeremiah (1:6) and Jonah (→ 701), he first resists the divine command. But when he has learned to know the greatness of God in his own life, he declares it. He tells of what God has done for him. He thus becomes a missionary for his religion. With κηρύσσειν τὰς εὐεργεσίας in v. 144 cf. τὰς θεῶν διηγεῖσθαι δυνάμεις in v. 41, προφητεύειν ἐπίνοιαν in v. 169, διήγημα λαλεῖν in v. 177, ἀπαγγέλλειν ἐπ[ι]φανείας δυνάμεως τε μεγέθη εὐε[ρ]γετημάτων <τε> δωρήματα in v. 214.

---

[10] Poll. Onom., VIII, 138 : ἀπὸ δὲ κηρύκων κηρῦξαι ἐρεῖς καὶ ἀποκηρῦξαι καὶ ἐπικηρῦξαι καὶ προκηρῦξαι, ἀνακηρῦξαι, ἀνειπεῖν καὶ ἀναγορεῦσαι, ἐπικηρυκεύσασθαι, διακηρυκεύσασθαι, ἐκεχειρίαν ἀπαγγεῖλαι.

[11] Soph. Ai., 1240 : ἀγῶνας κηρύσσειν. Lys., 19, 64 : ἐνίκησεν ... ὥστε τὴν πόλιν κηρυχθῆναι καὶ αὐτὸν στεφανωθῆναι. Aeschin. Or., 3, 246 : κηρύσσεταί τις ἐν τῷ θεάτρῳ, ὅτι στεφανοῦται ἀρετῆς ἕνεκα καὶ ἀνδραγαθίας. P. Oxy., XV, 1827: κηρύττεσθαι τῇ δε [π]ολει τὸν τούτων [στ]εφανον.

c. Corp. Herm., I, 27 ff. On the basis of revelation the prophet begins his proclamation : καὶ ἦργμαι κηρύσσειν τοῖς ἀνθρώποις τὸ τῆς εὐσεβείας καὶ γνώσεως κάλλος. "ὦ λαοί, ἄνδρες γηγενεῖς, οἱ μέθῃ καὶ ὕπνῳ ἑαυτοὺς ἐκδεδωκότες [καὶ] τῇ ἀγνωσίᾳ τοῦ θεοῦ, νήψατε, παύσασθε δὲ κραιπαλῶντες [καὶ] θελγόμενοι ὕπνῳ ἀλόγῳ ... Τί ἑαυτούς, ὦ ἄνδρες [γηγενεῖς], εἰς θάνατον ἐκδεδώκατε, ἔχοντες ἐξουσίαν τῆς ἀθανασίας μεταλαβεῖν; μετανοήσατε, οἱ συνοδεύσαντες τῇ πλάνῃ καὶ συγκοινωνήσαντες τῇ ἀγνοίᾳ. ἀπαλλάγητε τοῦ σκότ[ειν]ου<ς, ἅψασθε τοῦ> φωτός· μεταλάβετε τῆς ἀθανασίας, καταλείψαντες τὴν φθοράν." καὶ οἱ μὲν αὐτῶν καταφλυαρήσαντες ἀπέστησαν, τῇ τοῦ θανάτου ὁδῷ ἑαυτοὺς ἐκδεδωκότες· οἱ δὲ παρεκάλουν διδαχθῆναι, ἑαυτοὺς πρὸ ποδῶν μου ῥίψαντες. ἐγὼ δὲ ἀναστήσας αὐτοὺς καθοδηγὸς ἐγενόμην τοῦ γένους, τοὺς λόγους διδάσκων, πῶς καὶ τίνι τρόπῳ σωθήσονται. καὶ ἔσπειρα ἐν αὐτοῖς τοὺς τῆς σοφίας λόγους. IV, 4 : δοὺς κήρυκα, καὶ ἐκέλευσεν αὐτῷ κηρύξαι ταῖς τῶν ἀνθρώπων καρδίαις τάδε· "βάπτισον σεαυτὴν ἡ δυναμένη εἰς τοῦτον τὸν κρατῆρα, γνωρίζουσα ἐπὶ τί γέγονας καὶ ἡ πιστεύουσα ὅτι ἀνελεύσῃ πρὸς τὸν καταπέμψαντα τὸν κρατῆρα ἡ γνωρίζουσα ἐπὶ τί γέγονας." ὅσοι μὲν οὖν συνῆκαν τοῦ κηρύγματος καὶ ἐβαπτίσαντο τοῦ νοός, οὗτοι μετέσχον τῆς γνώσεως καὶ τέλειοι ἐγένοντο ἄνθρωποι, τὸν νοῦν δεξάμενοι· ὅσοι δὲ ἥμαρτον τοῦ κηρύγματος, οὗτοι οἱ τὸν μὲν οἱ λογικὸν ἔχοντες, τὸν δὲ νοῦν μὴ προσειληφότες.

The terminology of this sermon is similar to that of the NT. There is hardly a word for which we do not find NT parallels. The prophet has a commission to preach (R. 10:15). He sows τοὺς λόγους (Mk. 4:14, 15 : τὸν λόγον) and instructs men how they can be saved. They are entangled in error (Jm. 5:20; 2 Pt. 2:18), given up to sleep (R. 13:11; Mt. 25:5) and to drunkenness (Lk. 21:34; R. 13:13), and overcharged with surfeiting (Lk. 21:34). To the συγκοινωνήσαντες (Eph. 5:11; Rev. 18:4) of ignorance (1 Pt. 1:14; Eph. 4:18) who know not God (1 C. 15:34) and yield themselves up to death (R. 6:16; 1:32) he appeals : Be sober (1 C. 15:34 : ἐκνήψατε ... ἀγνωσίαν γὰρ θεοῦ τινες ἔχουσιν; 1 Th. 5:6, 8; 1 Pt. 5:8); leave that which is corruptible (2 Pt. 1:4 : ἵνα διὰ τούτων γένησθε θείας κοινωνοὶ φύσεως, ἀποφυγόντες τῆς ἐν τῷ κόσμῳ ἐν ἐπιθυμίᾳ φθορᾶς); you have the ἐξουσία (Jn. 1:12) to attain to immortality (cf. 2 Pt. 1:4 : θεία φύσις). → μετανοήσατε, → βάπτισον, → ἀπαλλάγητε τοῦ σκότους. From darkness they should come to the light (Ac. 26:18; Eph. 5:8; 1 Pt. 2:9). The goal of the sermon is → σωτηρία, → γνῶσις. Men are to become τέλειοι (1 C. 14:20; Mt. 5:48) and to receive the νοῦς (cf. R. 12:2). Not all follow the call of the preacher. Some make light of it (3 Jn. 10; Ac. 17:32; 2:12), go their way and become victims of death. Others fall at his feet (Ac. 16:29) and wish to hear more, and he instructs them and they are saved (Ac. 17:34). When we read of πιστεύειν and ἁμαρτάνειν in this connection, we are again reminded of the NT — and yet we are in another world. The words are the same. Whole sentences have a biblical ring. But what matters is the meaning rather than the words. Words are vessels which the speaker fills with content. In Hermes-mysticism man is not liberated from sin — ἁμαρτάνειν here has nothing to do with the biblical term but is the counterpart of συνίημι. He is liberated from bondage through the earthly body. The kerygma promotes divinisation. σωτηρία does not come to men through the summons of an event in which God has invaded history. It comes through a sacramental act. It is by baptism that one attains γνῶσις, receives the νοῦς and becomes τέλειος. Preaching is not an act of God; it is instruction in what to do (πῶς καὶ τίνι τρόπῳ). It shows the way (καθοδηγός) on which one comes from error to knowledge. The presupposition of NT repentance is missing, namely, the imminence of the rule of God (Mt. 3:2). Hence there is no βάπτισμα μετανοίας εἰς ἄφεσιν ἁμαρτιῶν (Mk. 1:4). Hearers must be exhorted : ἀπαλλάγητε, break free from darkness. The Christian knows : . . . ἀπαλλάξῃ (Hb. 2:15): "He has delivered those who through fear of death were all their lifetime subject to bondage." The Christian comes out of darkness into light ; for he knows the Light of the world which has said (Jn. 8:12): "He that followeth me shall not walk in darkness, but shall have the light of life." In spite of external similarities, the content of the preaching is quite different, and κηρύσσειν itself is different from what it is in the NT.

B. κηρύσσω in the Old Testament.

In the Gk. OT the word κηρύσσειν occurs 33 times. There is no single Heb. equivalent ; it is used for a number of verbs and expressions that denote "loud crying." In 18 cases, i.e., more than half, the Heb. is קרא, "to cry," "to call" — a word which elsewhere is rendered καλεῖν, ἐπι- and ἐγκαλεῖν, βοᾶν and ἀναβοᾶν etc. In 4 instances [12] κηρύσσειν is used for רוע, "to make a noise," "to exult." [13] In Ex. 36:6 and 2 Ch. 36:22 it is used for הֶעֱבִיר קוֹל, at Jon. 3:7 for זעק, at 2 Ch. 24:9 for נָתַן קוֹל, at Da. 5:29 Θ for כרז and at Jer. 20:8 Σ for דבר.

As the linguistic basis varies, so does the meaning. The changes in translation show that it is not a fixed expression for a specific form of proclamation in the OT.

It is used of the activity of the herald who runs before the royal chariot to draw the attention of the people to the one who approaches (→ 702), i.e., Joseph in Gn. 41:43 and Mordecai in Est. 6:9, 11. [14] The κηρύσσειν of Da. 5:29 Θ is to be taken in much the same way. When Daniel has interpreted the mysterious writing to King Belshazzar, ἐκήρυξεν περὶ αὐτοῦ εἶναι αὐτὸν ἄρχοντα τρίτον ἐν τῇ βασιλείᾳ. Daniel is proclaimed to be the third ruler in the kingdom. In Da. 3:4 the herald makes known to the assembled officials the will of the king. We often read of the κηρύσσειν of various orders and statutes. Now it is the king (2 Ch. 24:9; 4 Βασ. 10:20), now another person in authority such as Moses (Ex. 36:6) or Aaron (Ex. 32:5), who makes known to the whole people what is to be done. In most cases the reference is to cultic decrees. Ἑορτὴ τοῦ κυρίου is proclaimed in Ex. 32:5 and νηστεία in 2 Ch. 20:3; Jon. 3:5. [15] These proclamations may also be in writing, 2 Ch. 36:22. [16] Here there is no thought of the person of a herald. The word has completely lost the sense of "to cry," "to proclaim orally." The written word has replaced the spoken, and the publication of the written word is a κηρύσσειν (→ II, 735). [17]

---

[12] Hos. 5:8; Jl. 2:1; Zeph. 3:14; Zech. 9:9.

[13] Many Gk. words are used for רוע: Jos. 6:16 : κράζειν; 1 S. 4:5 : ἀνακράζειν; Ezr. 3:13 : κραυγάζειν; Jos. 6:10 : βοᾶν and ἀναβοᾶν; Ju. 15:14; Ps. 81:1: ἀλαλάζειν; Ps. 41:11: ἐπιχαίρειν; Nu. 10:9 : σημαίνειν; Is. 44:23 : σαλπίζειν etc.

[14] At Gn. 41:43 we have κηρύσσειν in the absol. The Mas. gives the content of the cry : אַבְרֵךְ. It is hard to say what is the precise meaning of this word, cf. Ges.-Buhl, s.v. and H. Holzinger in Kautzsch, ad loc. The content is given in direct speech in Est. 6:9, 11. The LXX adds a λέγων : So will be done to the one whom the king delights to honour.

[15] Other verbs can naturally be used for κηρύσσειν, e.g., ἐξεκκλησιάζειν νηστείαν (Jer. 36:9 [43:9]) or καλεῖν καιρόν (Lam. 1:21).

[16] 2 Ch. 36:22 : Cyrus παρήγγειλεν κηρύξαι ἐν πάσῃ τῇ βασιλείᾳ αὐτοῦ ἐν γραπτῷ λέγων. The Mas. distinguishes between הֶעֱבִיר קוֹל and the written declaration : וְגַם בְּמִכְתָּב לֵאמֹר.

[17] Cf. Just. Dial., 89, 2 : αἱ γραφαὶ κηρύσσουσιν, that Christ must suffer ; cf. also 88, 8.

Against all expectation κηρύσσειν is seldom used of the proclamation of the prophets. [18] The reference in Mi. 3:5 is to false prophets who proclaim peace when they get something to eat. The true preacher is bound to his divine commission. Jonah receives the order: ἀνάστηθι καὶ πορεύθητι εἰς Νινευη τὴν πόλιν τὴν μεγάλην καὶ κήρυξον ἐν αὐτῇ (1:2). He hesitates to do this, for he knows how difficult is the preacher's task. [19] Jeremiah, too, resists the will of God: ὅτι ἀφ' οὗ κηρύσσω, ὦ ἀδικία, ὦ ταλαιπωρία, βοῶ (20:8 Σ). A fresh commission is given to Jonah (3:2) and Jonah ἐκήρυξεν καὶ εἶπεν: Ἔτι τρεῖς ἡμέραι καὶ Νινευη καταστραφήσεται (3:4). The preaching of Is. 61:1 is rather different. The prophet is to proclaim liberty to the captives and — according to the LXX rendering or emendation of לַאֲסוּרִים פְּקַח־קוֹחַ — τυφλοῖς ἀνάβλεψιν. In so doing he brings what he proclaims. He proclaims freedom, and the prisoners are free; he proclaims sight, and the blind see. His word is efficacious because he is sent by God and the Spirit of God rests on him. His word is God's Word, which does not demand, but gives. According to the NT the prophet who has proclaimed this word is Jesus, who said: This day is this scripture fulfilled, Lk. 4:21.

Is. 61:1 refers to an eschatological event. In Hos. 5:8 κηρύσσειν (for רוע) means to cry out, to sound the alarm, because the enemy is near. Such alarms are demanded in Jl. 2:1 because the Day of the Lord is immediately at hand: σαλπίσατε σάλπιγγι ἐν Σιων, κηρύξατε ἐν ὄρει ἁγίῳ μου καὶ συγχυθήτωσαν πάντες οἱ κατοικοῦντες τὴν γῆν, διότι πάρεστιν ἡμέρα κυρίου, ὅτι ἐγγύς, ἡμέρα σκότους καὶ γνόφου. κηρύσσειν is the warning and disturbing cry which declares the imminence of the Day of God. In face of this situation the נְאֻם־יְהוָה runs: שֻׁבוּ עָדַי בְּכָל־לְבַבְכֶם (2:12). But the word is used differently in Jl. 3:9. Messengers are here sent out to summon the nations to a holy war against Jerusalem. In Zeph. 3:14 and Zech. 9:9 רוע is again the Heb. equivalent, and κηρύσσειν is to be understood in the light of it. [20] It denotes the joyful exultation of the redeemed community:

---

[18] The distinction between prophetic proclamation and what we call preaching may be seen, e.g., in Is. 58:1: ἀναβόησον ἐν ἰσχύι καὶ μὴ φείσῃ, ὡς σάλπιγγα ὕψωσον τὴν φωνήν σου καὶ ἀνάγγειλον τῷ λαῷ μου τὰ ἁμαρτήματα αὐτῶν καὶ τῷ οἴκῳ Ιακωβ τὰς ἀνομίας αὐτῶν. Many people have wrong ideas about references to preaching in the OT. We recall that in the Luther Bible Abraham preached (Gn. 12:8; 13:4 etc.), and we think of the prophets as preachers. We thus conclude that preaching plays a great part in the vocabulary of the OT. But this is not so. A concordance of the Luther Bible will certainly yield a whole list of references, but when we examine them we note 1. that Luther often has "preach" for קרא when the LXX more correctly renders ἐπικαλεῖσθαι (e.g., Gn. 4:26; 12:8; 13:4; Ps. 105[104]:1 etc.), 2. that Luther often has "preach" for the חזה of the prophets (Ez. 13:8, 9, 16, 23; 22:28), and 3. that many OT references are to the preaching of false prophets (Jer. 14:14, 15; 20:6; 23:16). Apart from places which fall under these heads, there are comparatively few texts in which the reference is to preaching, though we could suggest others where Luther has a different translation.

[19] Cf. Is. 53:1; Jos. Bell., 6, 288 says of the people in another connection: τῶν τοῦ θεοῦ κηρυγμάτων παρήκουσαν.

[20] Sometimes the LXX has ἀλαλάζειν for רוע, e.g., Ju. 15:14: When the enemy advances, the host raises the war-cry which encourages the individual soldier and puts the enemy to flight. But רוע can also be used for rejoicing over a conquered foe (Jer. 50:15 = Ἰερ. 27:15: κατακροτέω, and Ps. 108:9), or for the exultation of the people on the election of a king (1 S. 10:24). The same jubilation will occur when God redeems Israel (Is. 44:23). All nature joins in the song of rejoicing. The reference in Ps. 81:1 is to the cultic magnifying of God for His wonderful acts.

χαῖρε σφόδρα, θύγατερ Σιων, κήρυσσε, θύγατερ Ιερουσαλημ, εὐφραίνου καὶ κατατέρπου ἐξ ὅλης τῆς καρδίας σου (Zeph. 3:14). Punishment is set aside ; God, the King of Israel, is in the midst (3:15); His reign of peace has begun (Zech. 9:9).

When we survey the use of κηρύσσειν in the OT we may conclude that it does not have here the predominant place which it comes to have in the NT. Mention of the most important references enables us to see the similarity and the difference between OT and NT κηρύσσειν. The preacher's call for repentance, the announcement of the Day of God, the word which brings fulfilment and the proclaiming of the ruler — all these remain in the NT. But nowhere do we find κηρύσσειν in the sense of Zeph. 3:14 and Zech. 9:9.

C. כרז in the Rabbis.

The verb כרז adds little new to what we have already learned of the various duties of heralds from כרוז. It is a tt. for the crying of the one who clears the way for an important personage (→ 700). [21] The word is also important in legal terminology. By Jewish law some things which have been found must be made public (BM, 2, 1 ff.). They are "cried." When this takes place, the findings attain general legal validity. [22] There is naturally a sacral use as well as a secular. Rabbis use a herald to publish their decisions and intimations concerning the cultus. [23] In synagogue worship the preacher was often accompanied by another speaker who made these known in a loud voice to the assembled congregation. "The Rabbi ordered . . . his Amora (speaker): Make known to the congregation (כרז): If one desires to pray the evening prayer, so long as it is still day, the prayer is in order" (jBer., 7c, 51). [24] כרז can here take on the sense of preaching. bAZ, 19b : "R. Alexander מכריז: Who desires life ? who desires life ? Then the whole world gathered round him and said (אמר): Give us life. Then he said to them (אמר): 'Ps. 34:12 : Who is the man who desires life etc. ? Keep thy tongue from evil etc., avoid evil and do good etc. Perhaps someone will say, I have kept my tongue from evil and my lips from deceitful speech, I will now give myself to sleep, but it then says : Avoid evil and do good, and by good is meant the knowledge of the Law, for it is said in Prv. 4:2 : For I gave you good doctrine, do not disregard my direction.' " This sermon is given in detail to bring out the difference between it and the NT. We have here the preaching of the Law, or moral preaching, directed to such men as the Jews of R. 2:21 (→ 705). כרז can also be a term for the revelation of God by the voice from heaven ; [25] indeed, it is said of God Himself that He cries out. [26] כרז is a favourite word of the Rabbis. Hence it occurs in many passages. It is even an exegetical term. When

---

[21] bKet., 77b : Elias caused to be proclaimed before him : Make way for the son of Levi. Midr. Ps. on 17:7: When man is on the way somewhere, angelic figures go before him and cry out and say : Make way for the image of God.

[22] jJeb., 10b, 1: A bill of divorce secured from a Jewish court is valid, but one secured from a Gentile court is not. Shemuel said : It is not valid, and disqualifies the woman from marrying a priest. And Mar Shemuel said : This has been proclaimed.

[23] bRH, 21a.

[24] The Rabb. passages have for the most part been checked by K. G. Kuhn and W. Gutbrod, who have translated some of them.

[25] Ab., 6, 2 : Each day a voice goes out from Mt. Horeb and proclaims (וּמַכְרֶזֶת): Woe to men on account of the hurt which they do the Torah. Cf. also Midr. Ps. on 79:2 and S. Dt., 357 on 34:5.

[26] bPes., 113a : The virtue of three classes of men God proclaims each day.

a text is quoted, it is often introduced by the words : God or Scripture מַכְרִיז וְאוֹמֵר. [27] This is how we are to take Cant. r. on 2:13, where Is. 52:7 is quoted after מַכְרִיז וְאוֹמֵר (→ 712). כרז often replaces the biblical קרא. Thus, where the OT has קרא, Rabbinic interpretation substitutes כרז. [28] This shows how later usage made a favourite term of כרז even though it occurs only once in the OT.

D. κηρύσσω in the New Testament.

1. κηρύσσειν and other NT Words for Proclamation.

When we to-day speak of the proclaiming of God's Word by men, we almost necessarily think of preaching, and with few exceptions Luther always uses this word (predigen) in translation of κηρύσσειν. [29] The NT is more dynamic and varied in its modes of expression than we are to-day. In addition to κηρύσσειν it uses [30] → λέγειν, → λαλεῖν, → ἀποφθέγγεσθαι, → ὁμιλεῖν, → διηγεῖσθαι, ἐκδιηγεῖσθαι, ἐξηγεῖσθαι, → διαλέγεσθαι, → διερμηνεύειν, → γνωρίζειν. Sometimes it has → ἀγγέλλειν, → ἀναγγέλλειν, → ἀπαγγέλλειν, → διαγγέλλειν, → ἐξαγγέλλειν, → καταγγέλλειν, → εὐαγγελίζεσθαι, and sometimes again → παρρησιάζεσθαι, → μαρτυρεῖν, → ἐπιμαρτυρεῖν, διαμαρτύρεσθαι, → πείθειν, → ὁμολογεῖν. We find → κράζειν, → προφητεύειν, → διδάσκειν, → παραδιδόναι, → νουθετεῖν, τὸν λόγον ὀρθοτομεῖν, → παρακαλεῖν, → ἐλέγχειν, and → ἐπιτιμᾶν. Naturally there are differences between these verbs. But our almost exclusive use of "preach" for all of them is a sign, not merely of poverty of vocabulary, but of the loss of something which was a living reality in primitive Christianity.

Even if we disregard the other terms, and restrict ourselves to "preach" in translation of κηρύσσειν, the word is not a strict equivalent of what the NT means by κηρύσσειν. κηρύσσειν does not mean the delivery of a learned and edifying or hortatory discourse in well-chosen words and a pleasant voice. It is the declaration of an event (→ 710). Its true sense is "to proclaim". And it is because κηρύσσειν has this sense that we may understand why, like → εὐαγγέλιον and → εὐαγγελίζεσθαι (cf. also → καλεῖν), it does not occur in the Johannine writings except at Rev. 5:2. John prefers → μαρτυρεῖν. From the standpoint of his eschatology [31] μαρτυρεῖν is better adapted than the dramatic and efficacious herald's cry to describe witness to that "which was from the beginning, which we have heard, which we have seen with our eyes, which we have looked upon, and our

---

[27] E.g., Pesikt. r., 199b; Midr. Ps. on 18:41; 7:8; cf. W. Bacher, Die exegetische Terminologie der jüd. Traditionslit., II (1905), 89 f.

[28] bBer., 55a in Str.-B., III, 1 [K. G. Kuhn]: R. Jochanan has said : Three things God Himself proclaims publicly (מַכְרִיז), and these are : Famine, abundance and a good overseer. Famine, 2 K. 8:1: God proclaimed (קָרָא) a famine ; abundance, Ez. 36:29 : I call (קָרָאתִי) for the corn and increase it ; a good overseer, Ex. 31:1 f.: And Yahweh said to Moses, See, I have called Bezaleel by name (קָרָאתִי).

[29] For the reason why Luther does not use predigen at Mk. 1:45; 5:20; 7:36; Lk. 8:39, → 708. At Mk. 13:10 he uses verkündigen (to proclaim) for κηρύσσειν τὸ εὐαγγέλιον, though he has predigen in Mk. 14:9; 16:15 and other verses (→ 704). At Lk. 4:19 and Rev. 5:2 predigen is impossible. The Vulgate always has praedicare (whence predigen) for κηρύσσειν.

[30] διαφημίζειν is intentionally not mentioned.

[31] G. Stählin, "Zum Problem der joh. Eschatologie," ZNW, 33 (1934), 225 ff.

hands have handled" (1 Jn. 1:1; cf. Jn. 3:11; 15:27). It is in keeping with the content of Jn. and Hb. that κηρύσσειν is not used. We find it 9 times in Mt., 14 in Mk., 9 in Lk., 8 in Ac. (with another 4 in D at Ac. 1:2; 16:14; 17:15 and 19:14), 17 in Paul, another 2 in Past., once in 1 Pt. and once in Rev. The verb occurs 61 (65) times in all in the NT. If we compare these figures with those for → κῆρυξ and → κήρυγμα, we are led already to some conclusion as to the theological significance of the terms. Emphasis does not attach to the κήρυγμα, as though Christianity contained something decisively new in content — a new doctrine, or a new view of God, or a new cultus. The decisive thing is the action, the proclamation itself. For it accomplishes that which was expected by the OT prophets. The divine intervention takes place through the proclamation. Hence the proclamation itself is the new thing. Through it the βασιλεία τοῦ θεοῦ comes.

2. The Use of κηρύσσω.

κηρύσσειν is usually act. We find passive constructions at Mt. 24:14 par. Mk. 13:10; Mt. 26:13 par. Mk. 14:9; Lk. 12:3; 24:47; 1 C. 15:12; 2 C. 1:19; Col. 1:23; 1 Tm. 3:16. Usually the content is denoted by a subst. in the acc., e.g., πολλά at Mk. 1:45; αὐτόν, i.e., Moses at Ac. 15:21; περιτομήν, Gl. 5:11; ἄλλον Ἰησοῦν, 2 C. 11:4; cf. also τὸ βάπτισμα, Ac. 10:37; βάπτισμα μετανοίας εἰς ἄφεσιν ἁμαρτιῶν, Mk. 1:4 par. Lk. 3:3; μετάνοιαν εἰς ἄφεσιν ἁμαρτιῶν, Lk. 24:47; ἄφεσιν καὶ ἀνάβλεψιν, Lk. 4:18; ἐνιαυτὸν κυρίου δεκτόν, Lk. 4:19; τὸν Ἰησοῦν, Ac. 9:20; 19:13 (cf. 19:14 D); τὸν Χριστόν, Ac. 8:5; Phil. 1:15; cf. 1 C. 1:24 and 1 C. 15:12 (also 1 Tm. 3:16); Χριστὸν ἐσταυρωμένον, 1 C. 1:23; Χριστὸν Ἰησοῦν, 2 C. 1:19; 4:5; τὴν βασιλείαν, Ac. 20:25; τὴν βασιλείαν τοῦ θεοῦ, Lk. 8:1; 9:2; Ac. 28:31; τὸ εὐαγγέλιον, Mk. 13:10; 14:9; 16:15; Gl. 2:2; Col. 1:23 (Ac. 1:2 D); τὸ εὐαγγέλιον τοῦτο, Mt. 26:13; τὸ εὐαγγέλιον τοῦ θεοῦ, Mk. 1:14; 1 Th. 2:9; τὸ εὐαγγέλιον τῆς βασιλείας, Mt. 4:23; 9:35; τοῦτο τὸ εὐαγγέλιον τῆς βασιλείας, Mt. 24:14; τὸν λόγον, 2 Tm. 4:2 (cf. Ac. 17:15 D); τὸ ῥῆμα τῆς πίστεως, R. 10:8. κηρύσσειν can also be used with an infinitive, R. 2:21, with ὅτι, Ac. 9:20; 10:42; 1 C. 15:12, or with ἵνα, Mk. 6:12. The content can also be given in a relative clause, Mt. 10:27; Mk. 5:20; Lk. 8:39; 12:3, or in direct speech, Mt. 4:17; Rev. 5:2. Sometimes a λέγων is used to indicate the content, Mt. 3:1 f.; Mt. 10:7; Mk. 1:7, and κηρύσσειν here denotes the activity of the herald in his crying of the message, i.e., the act of declaration. We find the absol. at Mt. 11:1; Mk. 1:39; Lk. 4:44; 1 Pt. 3:19, of Jesus; Mk. 1:38, of Him in indirect speech; Mk. 3:14; 16:20, of the disciples; Mk. 7:36, of those healed by Jesus; 1 C. 9:27; 15:11 (R. 10:14, 15), of Paul.

The person to whom the proclamation is addressed is always in the dat.: [32] Ac. 8:5: αὐτοῖς, 1 C. 9:27: ἄλλοις, Lk. 4:18: αἰχμαλώτοις καὶ τυφλοῖς, 1 Pt. 3:19: τοῖς πνεύμασιν, Ac. 10:42: τῷ λαῷ (cf. 1 C. 1:24: τοῖς κλητοῖς, Ἰουδαίοις τε καὶ Ἕλλησιν), Mk. 16:15: πάσῃ τῇ κτίσει.

The place at which the proclamation occurs is indicated by a preposition. Usually this is ἐν, Mt. 3:1: ἐν τῇ ἐρήμῳ, Mk. 5:20: ἐν τῇ Δεκαπόλει, Mt. 11:1: ἐν ταῖς πόλεσιν, Ac. 9:20: ἐν ταῖς συναγωγαῖς, [33] Gl. 2:2 (cf. 1 Tm. 3:16): ἐν τοῖς ἔθνεσιν, 2 C. 1:19: ἐν ὑμῖν, Col. 1:23: ἐν πάσῃ κτίσει, Mt. 24:14: ἐν ὅλῃ τῇ οἰκουμένῃ, Mt. 26:13: ἐν ὅλῳ τῷ κόσμῳ. εἰς can also be used instead of ἐν without any change in meaning. [34] Cf. Mk. 1:39; Lk. 4:44: εἰς τὰς συναγωγάς, [35] Mk. 13:10; Lk. 24:47:

---

[32] On the construction κηρύσσειν ἐν and εἰς → infra.

[33] It is of no great account at Mt. 4:23 and 9:35 whether ἐν ταῖς συναγωγαῖς belongs to κηρύσσειν or whether the κηρύσσειν and θεραπεύειν followed on the journey through Galilee.

[34] Cf. Bl.-Debr. § 205.

[35] At Lk. 3:3 εἰς πᾶσαν τὴν περίχωρον τοῦ Ἰορδάνου is not to be linked with κηρύσσειν as Zn. Lk. suggests, but with ἐλθεῖν.

εἰς πάντα τὰ ἔθνη, 1 Th. 2:9 : εἰς ὑμᾶς (cf. Ac. 17:15 D : εἰς αὐτούς), Mk. 14:9 : εἰς ὅλον τὸν κόσμον. We may also note Lk. 8:39 : καθ' ὅλην τὴν πόλιν, 36 and Mt. 10:27; Lk. 12:3 : ἐπὶ τῶν δωμάτων.

3. The Secular Meaning of κηρύσσω in Lk. 12:3.

ὅσα ἐν τῇ σκοτίᾳ εἴπατε ἐν τῷ φωτὶ ἀκουσθήσεται, καὶ ὃ πρὸς τὸ οὖς ἐλαλή-σατε ἐν τοῖς ταμιείοις κηρυχθήσεται ἐπὶ τῶν δωμάτων.

This verse does not refer to the activity of the disciples, 37 as a first glance might suggest. It refers to the preceding address concerning the Pharisees. The disciples are warned in v. 1 to "beware of the leaven of the Pharisees, which is hypocrisy." No matter how cunning the Pharisees are as hypocrites, in the last resort that which they think cannot be concealed. They will be unmasked, for "there is nothing covered that shall not be revealed ; neither hid, that shall not be known." To give force to this, a popular saying is adduced : 38 "Whatsoever you have spoken in darkness shall be heard in the light, and that which you have spoken in the ear in closets shall be proclaimed upon the housetops." This is how it will be with the Pharisees and their hidden designs. Their purposes will be brought to light and made public. Hence the "you" in v. 3 does not refer to the disciples, to whom it is addressed. It is to be understood as part of a quoted saying, and refers to the Pharisees. 39 Only in v. 4 : "And I say unto you my friends," does Jesus turn specifically to His disciples and speak to them and of them. 40

4. Proclamation by Different Preachers.

a. The Jews. The Jew preaches the Law (→ 702). As the philosopher summons to a moral way of life (→ 693), so the Jewish missionary 41 demands of his hearers : Thou shalt not steal (R. 2:21). In Ac. 15:21 the weekly reading of the OT Law in the synagogue is called a preaching 42 of Moses. 43

b. John the Baptist. John is a herald of the Messianic age 44 (Mk. 1:4 par. Mt. 3:1 and Lk. 3:3) who preaches in the desert. ἐν τῇ ἐρήμῳ κηρύσσειν does

---

36 In spite of the proposal in Hck. Lk., κατὰ πόλιν καὶ κώμην in Lk. 8:1 belongs to διοδεύειν, not κηρύσσειν.

37 This is the customary exposition, though cf. Dausch Synpt.

38 Cf. the proverb : "Murder will out," or the German : "Nothing is so finely spun, It is not brought to light by the sun."

39 Many proverbs are in this form.

40 Mt. 10:27 is rather different, since here the proverb is reorientated to the relation between Jesus and His disciples.

41 On the mission of the Jews → I, 418 and Str.-B., I, 926. Just. Dial., 108, 2 : of the Jews ἄνδρας ... εἰς πᾶσαν τὴν οἰκουμένην ἐπέμψατε, κηρύσσοντας, that the disciples had stolen Jesus.

42 The oldest term for synagogue preaching is למד, cf. 2 Ch. 17:9. By nature this cannot be proclamation, since it consists in exposition of the passage read. Later דרש was increasingly used, Ezr. 7:10. Thus synagogue preaching comes to be called דרשא and the preacher דרשן or דרושא. The fact that the sermon might often end with an edifying word of comfort or an eschatological reference does not change its character. It did not declare the presence of eschatology like NT preaching (→ 704). Str.-B., IV, 171 ff. and J. Elbogen, Der jüdische Gottesdienst in seiner geschichtlichen Entwicklung² (1924), 194 ff.

43 The connection of Ac. 15:21 with what precedes is much debated. Cf. the review in Wdt. Ag., ad loc. The verse is probably to the effect that we do not wish to burden Gentile Christians with the Law (v. 19). There are enough preachers of Moses. We desire to preach the Gospel. So Schl. Erl., Zn. Ag., ad loc.

44 Just. Dial., 49, 3, John the Baptist the herald of Jesus. Cf. also 88, 2 : μέχρις οὗ προελήλυθεν Ἰωάννης κῆρυξ αὐτοῦ τῆς παρουσίας.

not seem to make much sense, for what use is a herald in a place where no one lives? But John goes into the desert and preaches there because the dominion of God is near and the time of salvation will begin in the desert (→ II, 659). He does not come before the congregation as a teacher expounding the Scriptures in divine service. He shakes men from their slumbers and draws attention to what is to come like the prophets (→ 701). Like a herald he cries aloud so that all who wish to hear may do so, and his summons is: "Repent." He bases this summons on the nearness of the kingdom of heaven, Mt. 3:1. He is no preacher of the Law demanding that men should simply amend their lives. His preaching of repentance is also prophecy. He points beyond himself to one who is coming, to a figure of the future, to the Messiah, Mk. 1:7. Ancient prophecy comes to life again in John. Its greatest longing and supreme hope were for the remission of sins, the royal dominion of God and the coming of the Messiah. The word of the Baptist was still a word of promise. But it was sustained by the certainty of immediately imminent fulfilment. In this certainty that the Messianic age was just about to dawn John proclaimed the remission of sins. The baptism to which he summoned (Ac. 10:37) was a sealing of those who waited for the rule of God. It was an anticipation of the Messianic remission: προκηρύσσειν βάπτισμα μετανοίας, Ac. 13:24.

c. Jesus Christ.

Incarnate. In Mk. 1:38 Jesus describes preaching as His task on earth. He has come from the Father to men in order to proclaim the message. This is His mission, Lk. 4:18, 19, 43, 44. In Jn. Jesus is the Word in person; in the Synoptists He is the herald who proclaims the Word. He seems to be parallel to the Baptist. When the latter is put in prison, He takes up His work and preaches as he did: "Repent, for the kingdom of heaven is at hand" (Mt. 4:17; cf. Mk. 1:14 f.). This is not new. He is simply repeating what John said. Yet there is something new. Jesus is no longer speaking as a prophet of one to come. [45] He speaks as a prophet of the fulfilment of expectation and promise. He does not announce that something will happen. His proclamation is itself event. What He declares takes place in the moment of its declaration. At Lk. 4:18 ff. He proclaims, like a herald, the year of the Lord, the Messianic age. When heralds proclaimed the year of jubilee throughout the land with the sound of the trumpet, the year began, the prison doors were opened and debts were remitted. The preaching of Jesus is such a blast of the

---

[45] E. v. Dobschütz, "Matthäus als Rabbi und Katechet," ZNW, 27 (1928), 338 ff., opposes the view that Jesus took over the preaching of the Baptist. If we learn from Mt. 3:2 and 4:17 that the preaching of the Baptist and the first preaching of Jesus used the same formula, this is linked with the fact that Mt. likes similarity and when he has found a formula uses it again. Where we have exact agreement in Mt., we have his own formulations rather than reliable tradition. As Dobschütz sees it, the intimation of the heavenly kingdom was not an original part of the Baptist's message. John preached repentance, judgment, catastrophe and flight from the world, whereas Jesus preached faith, affirmation of the world and the Gospel. Now there is certainly a distinction between John and Jesus, but not along these lines. The preaching of the kingdom of God is a also a proclamation of judgment. The two are not mutually exclusive. Furthermore Jesus demands repentance in other places as well as Mt. 4:17 (→ μετανοέω), and John is not just a gloomy preacher of disaster, but also an evangelist, Lk. 3:18. We accept the view of W. Michaelis, "Täufer, Jesus, Urgemeinde," Nt.liche Forschungen II, 3 (1928), 11: "This theme fits in so well with the picture we form of the Baptist's preaching elsewhere that we conclude that the formula goes back to the Baptist and that it was then taken over by Jesus."

trumpet. Its result is that the Word proclaimed becomes a reality. For the divine Word is a creative force. It gives what it declares.

The Crucified. Between Good Friday and Easter Day Jesus brought the message of remission to the sinful generation of Noah. A share in the Messianic salvation was allotted to unbelievers before the flood. Because they had been especially disobedient, they were put in a special prison. When Jesus went down to them, and preached the Gospel, He showed Himself to be the unbounded Victor over all powers and dominions. His Word has force even in the realm of the dead, 1 Pt. 3:19 f. Nothing is said concerning the result of this preaching. No doubt it brought deliverance to some and final rejection to others, for all preaching is decision, and hence *praeludium iudicii universalis* (Bengel on 1 Pt. 3:19).

Exegesis of 1 Pt. 3:19 has to answer 5 questions : 1. Who are the πνεύματα ? 2. What is meant by φυλακή ? 3. When did the πορευθείς take place ? 4. Who is the preacher ? 5. What is the content of the preaching ?

1. Who are the πνεύματα ? V. 20 rules out the view of Calvin that they are the righteous of the old covenant, especially the contemporaries of Noah. Modern scholarship inclines for the most part [46] to see in them the fallen angels of Gn. 6, with appeal to Eth. En. 10-15. But acc. to Jub. 5 (cf. Eth. En. 10) these angels and their offspring were judged already in the days of Noah when he built the ark, so that there could be no salvation for them. It was the men of that time who were disobedient to the long-suffering of God. Acc. to Pr.-Bauer³, 1126 (cf. Kn. Pt., *ad loc.*) the πνεύματα may also be souls of the dead, and we accept this view.

2. What is meant by φυλακή ? For Calvin it is either the watch-tower on which the pious stand and look for salvation, or, if we have to render it "prison," it is the Law which walls them in like a prison. Acc. to Augustine (Ep., 164, 16) it has a spiritual sense : *animae, quae tunc* (of the contemporaries of Noah) *erant in carne atque ignorantiae tenebris velut carcere claudebantur* (MPL, 33, p. 715). Those who regard the πνεύματα as angelic beings locate the φυλακή in the heart of the earth (cf. Jd. 6; 2 Pt. 2:4; Jub. 5; Eth. En. 10). Acc. to K. Gschwind [47] spirits are not to be located in the underworld but in the successive strata of heaven. Probably φυλακή is a special prison in Hades.

3. When did the πορευθείς take place ? Augustine, Calvin, Spitta and Wohlenberg assume that the time of the preaching is that of Noah. Wohlenberg than takes ἐν φυλακῇ to be a description of the state of Noah's contemporaries at the time of the epistle. This is highly artificial. In any case, πορευθείς seems to be in temporal antithesis to ἀπειθήσασίν ποτε. Acc. to Gschwind the preaching is at the ascension (cf. 1 Tm. 3:16; Phil. 2:10; Eph. 1:20 f.). Since it comes between v. 18 (death), v. 21 (resurrection) and v. 22 (ascension), we are compelled to accept the order of the creed : He descended into hell ; the third day he rose again from the dead ; he ascended into heaven.

4. Who is the preacher ? If the preaching was to Noah's contemporaries at the time of the building of the ark, then the preacher is the pre-existent Christ using Noah (Wohlenberg and Augustine) or Enoch (Spitta) as His spokesman. If our previous answers are correct, the true preacher is the crucified, but still living, Christ.

---

[46] F. Spitta, *Christi Predigt an die Geister, 1 Pt. 3:19 f.* (1890), 22 ff.; H. Gunkel, *Zum religionsgeschichtlichen Verständnis des NT* (1903), 72 f.; *Schr. NT, ad loc.*; W. Bousset, ZNW, 19 (1919/20), 50 ff.; R. Reitzenstein, *Das mandäische Buch des Herrn der Grösse* (1919), 30; Kn. Pt. and F. Hauck in *NT Deutsch, ad loc.*
[47] C. Gschwind, *Die Niederfahrt Christi in die Unterwelt* (1911), 118 ff.

5. What is the content of the preaching? This is not given, but it is the same as elsewhere in the NT. If Jesus descended, the aim of His declaration of victory was not to increase the torments of the damned. The Gospel was the content of His κηρύσσειν. This is supported by the section vv. 18 ff., which speaks of the benefits of the death and resurrection and ascension of Christ.

Risen. Christ also speaks to men as the risen Lord. He is present in the word of His messengers, so that preaching is both the Word of God and the word of man, as Jesus, too, is very God and very man. Hence true proclamation is not just speaking about Christ. It is Christ's own speaking. Did He not say to His disciples: "He that heareth you heareth me" (Lk. 10:16)? But this speaking is a secret, just as the fact that Jesus was the Son of God was concealed from many during His days on earth. Only the believer hears God's call in the word of man, and worships God. "How shall they call on him in whom they have not believed? and how shall they believe in him of whom they have not heard? and how shall they hear without a preacher?" (R. 10:14). Christ Himself is the Preacher in the word of man. It is He who is heard in preaching, in Him that men believe, on Him that they call. That this is the bearing of the passage may be seen clearly in v. 17: "So then faith cometh by hearing, and hearing by the word of Christ." Christ is the Preacher, preaching is the Word of God and God's Word implies God's presence. Thus Paul can say of his preaching in Corinth: "As God is true, our word to you was not yes and no. For the Son of God, Jesus Christ, who was preached among you by us ... was not yes and no," 2 C. 1:18 f. Paul is bold to bring his word and Jesus Christ into the closest relationship. Through his preaching the Son of God is actively present, so that the Corinthians know that the yes was actualised in Him ("in him was yes"). Because God Himself speaks in preaching, a correct reproduction of the NT message is not proclamation by a long way. The impartation of the word of the NT must become an act of God. This takes place when He speaks.

d. Those Healed. It is part of aretalogy that those who are healed go away and extol and proclaim the great acts and miracles of God. In the miracle stories of the NT, too, we read that the healed tell what has happened to them in spite of the express order of Jesus that they should tell no one (Mk. 1:44 par. Mt. 8:4 and Lk. 5:14 and Mk. 7:36). [48] This proclaiming of the acts of Jesus is not NT preaching even though we find the word κηρύσσειν in this connection. [49] It does not take place by commission (→ 712) but against the will of Jesus. Hence we are not to compare it with the preaching of the disciples after their sending. As preaching it has no more significance than the fact that the demons name the name of Jesus and make Him known to those around. [50] At Mk. 1:44 f. the command not

---

[48] Cf. also Mt. 9:30; 12:16; Mk. 5:43 par. Lk. 8:56; Mk. 8:26. On the reasons for the prohibition cf. the quotations from older lit. on the question in W. Wrede, Das Messiasgeheimnis in den Ev. (1901), 254 ff.

[49] Thus Luther does not render κηρύσσειν "to preach," but uses "to speak much about" in Mk. 1:45 and "to publish abroad" in Mk. 7:36.

[50] Mk. 1:24 par. Lk. 4:34: ὁ ἅγιος τοῦ θεοῦ; Mk. 3:11; Mt. 8:29; Lk. 4:41: ὁ υἱὸς τοῦ θεοῦ; Mk. 5:7 par. Lk. 8:28: ὁ υἱὸς τοῦ θεοῦ τοῦ ὑψίστου, cf. also Ac. 16:17 and 19:15. Ac. 16:17: οὗτοι οἱ ἄνθρωποι δοῦλοι τοῦ θεοῦ τοῦ ὑψίστου εἰσίν, οἵτινες καταγγέλλουσιν ὑμῖν ὁδὸν σωτηρίας. The demons naturally do not wish to preach, but try to assert themselves by naming the name. Cf. O. Bauernfeind, Die Worte der Dämonen im Mk.-Ev. (1927).

to tell anyone and the order : Show thyself to the priests εἰς μαρτύριον αὐτοῖς, are in direct juxtaposition. There is a distinction between a witness and a herald.[51] The herald goes through countries and publishes what he has to say so that all may hear. The place of the witness is in a lawsuit.[52] There he is summoned, and on the basis of his personal acquaintance with the facts he supports the one party and opposes the other. The healed person is a witness in the conflict between Christ and the priests. He goes off and acts as a herald.[53] But in so doing he goes beyond his commission. At Mk. 5:19 f. par. Lk. 8:39 the command of Jesus is different. Jesus normally forbids preaching about Himself because He seeks, not astonishment, but faith. To many His deeds are not a revelation of the Messianic secret. They are simply marvels which may easily be detached from their true purpose. At Mk. 5:20, however, there is no danger of a false estimation of the miracle. Those present do not rejoice at what has happened. They ask Jesus to go away. Jesus must accede to this request. But, although the healed man asks to be allowed to go with Him, He leaves him behind as a preacher, and the man goes through Decapolis like a herald, proclaiming what Jesus has done for him.[54]

e. Disciples and Apostles. The disciples who are sent out by Jesus to preach proclaim the same message as that of Jesus and John the Baptist. We again have the brief formulation : repentance, Mk. 6:12, and the proximity of the kingdom of God, Mt. 10:7. As compared with the Baptist, however, there is the distinction that their proclamation is accompanied by healing. This takes place because the kingdom is near, nearer than it was in the case of John, namely, present. Jesus Himself has not publicly announced His title as the Christ. He has revealed the secret only to the innermost circle of disciples. But what the disciples have heard from Him, they are fearlessly to proclaim in public so that all may hear, Mt. 10:27.[55] For the Gospel is not an esoteric doctrine nor the concern of a secret society. It belongs to the public. The message is to ring out on the streets and from the roof-tops. In season and out of season (2 Tm. 4:2), it must be boldly and constantly proclaimed to all men and situations. When the whole world has heard the Word of Christ, the commission of the risen Lord will be executed and the end will come (Mt. 24:14). The preaching of the apostles is part of God's saving plan for men, like the death and resurrection of Christ.[56] It is not enough that Christ has lived and died,

---

[51] This does not exclude the possibility of μαρτυρεῖν and κηρύσσειν being synon., cf. Lk. 24:47 f.; 1 C. 15:14 f.

[52] Cf. Schl. Mt. on 8:4.

[53] The construction would allow us to relate the κηρύσσειν of Mk. 1:45 to Jesus, but par. in similar stories suggest that the reference is to the healed man. Cf. Kl. Mk., *ad loc.*

[54] This man, too, exceeds his commission. He is told to ἀπαγγέλλειν (Mk. 5:19) or διηγεῖσθαι (Lk. 8:39) the miraculous healing at home to his relatives. This would have satisfied Jesus. But he makes it known throughout the whole region. Luther has "declare" at Mk. 5:20 and "proclaim" at Lk. 8:39. Through the preacher whom He leaves behind Jesus is Master of the devilish powers even though He Himself must leave. Cf. K. Bornhäuser, *Das Wirken des Christus durch Taten und Worte* (1924)², 84 and Bauernfeind (→ n. 50), 44 f.

[55] We cannot decide whether the altered form of the saying in Lk. 12:3 contains an allusion to the Jewish custom whereby the preacher at synagogue worship does not speak directly to the congregation but uses a special speaker whose task is to proclaim out loud what is whispered in his ear (→ 702), or whether the reference is to certain secret doctrines which the teacher whispered only in the ear of his most trusted disciples (Str.-B., I, 579).

[56] Lk. 24:46 f.: "And he said unto them, Thus it is written, and thus it behoved Christ to suffer, and to rise from the dead the third day : and that repentance and remission of sins should be preached in his name among all nations."

and that He is risen. These saving facts must be proclaimed in order that they may become saving reality for individuals. Hence the NT speaks not only of the cross in 1 C. 1:18, but also of the λόγος τοῦ σταυροῦ which is the δύναμις θεοῦ. It speaks not only of reconciliation in 2 C. 5:19, but also of the λόγος τῆς καταλλαγῆς. [57] Sinful men are commissioned by God to declare this message to men. These men are neither miracle-workers nor philosophers. They are neither profound scholars who can convince all by their learning nor skilled orators who can bind men by their powerful speech. They are heralds — no more (1 C. 1:22 f.; 2:4). It is not their moral blamelessness nor their Christianity which decides the worth or efficacy of their preaching. Otherwise the Word of God would be dependent on men. Even through preaching inspired by impure motives (Phil. 1:15) the attention of men can be drawn to Christ. Christ is greater than the one who proclaims Him. We do not preach ourselves, our ethical qualities or our experiences, but Christ (2 C. 4:5). Nevertheless, the life of the preacher is not negligible. There should not be a discrepancy between the message and the conduct of the preacher, as there was in the case of Jewish missionaries who taught: "Thou shalt not steal," and yet who stole themselves (R. 2:21). Rather, "I keep under my body, and make it a slave, in order that I should not preach to others and myself be rejected" (1 C. 9:27). The messenger does not act for himself or in his own interests. He does not attach men to himself, but to Christ. Christ is the Lord. He proclaims Christ, not himself (2 C. 4:5). [58]

f. An Angel. At Rev. 5:2 the κηρύσσειν of the angel is a question to the whole world. In a loud voice, so that he may be heard in heaven, on the earth and under the earth, the herald asks who is worthy to open the book.

5. The Content of the Specific Message of the New Testament.

When we say (→ 704) that the main concern of the NT is with the act of proclamation, this does not mean that the content is subsidiary. Just because the action has this significance, namely, that what is proclaimed is actualised, regard must be had to the content. The content is not determined, of course, by the situation of those who hear or read (→ 693). Nor is it dependent on the view of the preacher on religious questions. It is fixed in advance. At the heart of the NT *kerygma* stands the lordship of God. [59] Preaching is not a lecture on the nature of God's kingdom. It is proclamation, the declaration of an event. If Jesus came to preach, this means that He was sent to announce the βασιλεία τοῦ θεοῦ, and therewith to bring it. The other items of content mentioned are to be understood in the light of the βασιλεία τοῦ θεοῦ. The summons to repentance (Mt. 3:1 f.; Mt. 4:17) stands

---

[57] 2 C. 5:18 distinguishes already between God's reconciliation through Christ and the office of reconciliation. The establishment of this office means that Paul can call himself in 1 C. 4:1 οἰκονόμος μυστηρίων θεοῦ (→ 717, n. 17). Note should be taken of the order of σῴζειν and καλεῖν in 2 Tm. 1:9. The word gives actuality to the σωτηρία accomplished on Golgotha, Ac. 11:14 → εὐαγγέλιον, II, 731.

[58] We do best to fill out the ἑαυτοὺς δὲ δούλους with λογίζεσθαι (Ltzm. K., ad loc.) rather than κηρύσσειν. Dio. Chrys. Or., 13, 11 f.: οἱ μὲν γὰρ πολλοὶ τῶν καλουμένων φιλοσόφων αὐτοὺς ἀνακηρύττουσιν ὥσπερ οἱ Ὀλυμπίασι κήρυκες. Synesius, De Dono Astrolabii, MPG, 66, p. 1580 A: τὸ κηρύττειν ἑαυτὸν καὶ πάντα ποιεῖν ὑπὲρ ἐπιδείξεως οὐ σοφίας ἀλλὰ σοφιστείας ἐστίν. Heinr. Sendschr., II, ad loc.

[59] Mt. 3:1; 4:17 par. Mk. 1:14 f.; Mt. 4:23; 9:35; Lk. 8:1; Mt. 10:7 par. Lk. 9:2; Mt. 24:14; Ac. 20:25; 28:31. κηρύσσειν does not occur in Jn. and βασιλεία τοῦ θεοῦ is found only at Jn. 3:3, 5; cf. 18:36.

in closest relationship to the preaching of God's kingdom. The reason and cause of μετάνοια is not the badness of man; it is the imminence of the βασιλεία. Man must amend himself because God is coming, because His rule is near. Repentance does not bring in the kingdom. It creates the possibility of participation in it. As the herald goes before the chariot of the king (→ 700) and announces the approach of the ruler, so the preacher hastens through the world and cries: Make ready, the βασιλεία is already near. It is no contradiction that the disciples, too, proclaim the imminence of God's rule (Mt. 10:7; Lk. 9:2) and preach repentance (Mk. 6:12). The message of the kingdom is always a preaching of repentance, and all true preaching of repentance speaks of the kingdom of God. Repentance is preached εἰς ἄφεσιν ἁμαρτιῶν (Lk. 24:47, cf. Mk. 1:4 par. Lk. 3:3). In the βασιλεία there is remission of sins. The word proclaimed is a divine Word, and as such it is an effective force which creates what it proclaims. Hence preaching is no mere impartation of facts. It is event. What is proclaimed takes place. Forgiveness of sins is always judgment, which calls the sinner sinful. But in this judgment forgiveness of sins is granted to believers. The message of the apostles, which has the Judge of the quick and the dead as its content, proclaims with the prophets that all who believe in Him "shall receive remission of sins," Ac. 10:42. Judgment and grace are contained in the same word. The proclamation of the message of salvation involves separation and division. To some it is deliverance, to others judgment. To some the Christ who is preached is σκάνδαλον and μωρία, to others He is the δύναμις θεοῦ and σοφία θεοῦ, 1 C. 1:23 f. Intrinsic to the βασιλεία is the βασιλεύς. One cannot speak of the kingdom without mentioning the King: κύριος Χριστός. Through preaching Jesus is proclaimed as the Messiah (Ac. 8:5), as the Son of God (9:20). Whether one speaks of the crucified (1 C. 1:23) or the risen Lord (1 C. 15:12), the reference is always to the total Christ who has become the Lord by death and resurrection, and who is proclaimed as such, 2 C. 4:5. The incarnate and the exalted Christ cannot be separated. One does not preach the myth of a dying and rising god, nor a timeless idea, but a once-for-all, factual event, the life of Jesus, His historical manifestation, Ac. 9:20; 19:13 (→ Ἰησοῦς). But the proclamation of Jesus is more than historical instruction concerning the words and acts of Jesus. Stories about Jesus, however edifying, are of themselves empty, 1 C. 15:14. If they are not understood in the light of faith in the risen Lord, they are simply stories of things that happened in the past and are more or less valueless for the present. The reality of the resurrection constitutes the fulness of the early Christian kerygma. This is a fact which cannot be apprehended like other historical events. It has to be continually proclaimed afresh. It is not a human dogma which we are to teach to others. It is salvation history which must be preached, and the preaching of salvation history is itself an event of salvation. What is at work in this word is not just the content of what is proclaimed; it is God Himself. The message does not lose its significance. Yet it must be proclaimed again and again, not just to the world, but to the community, 2 Tm. 4:2. It is δύναμις θεοῦ, 1 C. 1:24. The preaching of the NT will not brook any admixture, Gl. 5:11. Its radicalism causes offence and repulsion, and brings persecution and affliction on the preachers. On κηρύσσειν τὸ εὐαγγέλιον → εὐαγγέλιον.

In the NT κηρύσσειν and εὐαγγελίζεσθαι are often synon. (→ II, 715, n. 90), and κηρύσσειν is sometimes linked with εὐαγγέλιον (→ 704). Is this accidental in the NT, or do we find the same combination elsewhere, so that it may be understood in terms of linguistic development? In the Gk. world the εὐάγγελος and the κῆρυξ have much in common. Even outwardly they are very similar. The herald resembles the messenger of victory, his head crowned with a laurel wreath. Ael. Arist., I, 285, 5 (Dindorf): κῆρυξ παρὰ τῶν Θηβαίων ὡς ἐπ᾽ εὐαγγελίοις ἐστεφανωμένος. Herodian Hist., VIII, 6, 18 : κήρυκες δαφνηφόροι. Cf. Xenoph. Hist. Graec., IV, 7, 3 and Aesch. Ag., 493. Indeed, he may himself announce victories over enemies, Aesch. Ag., 577. Friendly greetings are given to the herald who brings good news, Soph. Trach., 227: χαίρειν δὲ τὸν κήρυκα προυννέπω, χρόνῳ πολλῷ φανέντα, χαρτὸν εἴ τι καὶ φέρεις. When he has good news, the herald hastens to tell it as quickly as possible ; he does not delay, for he knows that he will receive rewards and thanks if he is the first to bring it (Soph. Trach., 189 ff.), → II, 722 f. On the synon. nature of the verbs v. Luc. Tyrannicida, 9 : θαρρεῖν ἤδη προκηρύττων ἅπασι καὶ τὴν ἐλευθερίαν εὐαγγελιζόμενος. εὐαγγέλιον is news of victory in battle, but it can also be used for news of victory in the games (→ II, 722). The κήρυγμα is the announcement of the victor on the scene of the contest. On εὐαγγέλιον and κήρυγμα in the imperial cult v. IG, II/III², 1077. At Is. 61:1 κηρύσσειν is a more concrete form of εὐαγγελίζεσθαι. At Cant. r. 2:13 כרן is to be understood in terms of exegetical terminology (→ 703). But the fact that it is quoted of the מבשׂר gives it significance for us. At Ps. Sol. 11:1 we read : κηρύξατε ἐν Ιερουσαλημ φωνὴν εὐαγγελιζομένου, ὅτι ἠλέησεν ὁ θεὸς Ισραηλ ἐν τῇ ἐπισκοπῇ αὐτῶν.

6. The Hearers.

The goal of proclamation in the hearers is faith rather than understanding, 1 C. 2:4 f. Jesus does not bring a new doctrine which claims the intellect. He brings a message which demands faith. The content of the proclamation is intolerable to men of all races, since it treats of the Crucified. This satisfies neither the Greek urge for knowledge nor the Jewish demand for religious certainty, 1 C. 1:21 f. Only the believer, to whom this word means everything, accepts it. This is why preaching is so important in the NT. For the Bible is not concerned primarily with the vision of God nor with action. What counts is the faith which arises through the hearing of the word, and this faith is content with the simple word. It accepts preaching in spite of its foolishness, and this is salvation for men. The true hearing of preaching involves more than listening ; it is also obedience. This act of obedience is not a work of man. It is effected by God's Word. The faith which the Word demands of man is also a gift of the Word, R. 10:8. Since faith comes by preaching, faith and proclamation have the same content, 1 C. 15:14.

7. Sending and Proclamation.

πῶς δὲ κηρύξωσιν ἐὰν μὴ ἀποσταλῶσιν; R. 10:15. This statement is decisive for our understanding of the preaching office. The fact that ἀποστέλλειν is linked with κηρύσσειν elsewhere in the NT [60] is no accident. It belongs to the very nature of things. Without commissioning and sending there are no preachers, and without preachers there is no proclamation. True proclamation does not take place through Scripture alone, but through its exposition, Lk. 4:21. God does not send books to men ; He sends messengers. By choosing individuals for this service, He institutes the office of proclamation (→ 716). Not every Christian is called to preach. In the lifetime of Jesus only the innermost circle is given this commission (Mt. 10:7 par. Lk. 9:2; Mk. 3:14). In the first instance the office is of limited duration. [61] The

---

[60] Mk. 3:14; Lk. 4:18, 43 f.; 9:2. κῆρυξ καὶ ἀπόστολος, 1 Tm. 2:7; 2 Tm. 1:11. Cf. the short Marcan ending, also ἐπιταγή, Tt. 1:3; κελεύειν, Ac. 1:2 D and the imperatives in Mt. 10:7; Mk. 16:15.

[61] Bengel on Mt. 10:7: *Hic erant discipuli, ut studiosi theologiae, qui rudimenta ministerii ponunt, vicariasque praestant operas, postea in scholam reversuri.*

commission is renewed after the resurrection of Jesus, Mk. 16:15. Without the resurrection there would be no preaching office. It exists only because the risen Lord has charged His disciples to declare the message : παρήγγειλεν ἡμῖν κηρῦξαι τῷ λαῷ, Ac. 10:42. This time the risen Lord, who is Lord of the world, does not send His disciples to Israel alone. He naturally sends them to Israel, Ac. 10:42. But He now sends them to all nations. The mission is to start in Jerusalem, Lk. 24:47, and from there to embrace the whole world. All peoples without distinction are to hear the message, Col. 1:23; Mk. 13:10; Mk. 16:15, 20. The ἀποστέλλειν cannot be separated from the κηρύσσειν. Indeed, the κηρύσσειν itself contains an element of sending (→ 687 f.). Sending implies on the one side a restriction, but on the other an enhancement, of the power of the herald. The one who sends gives him the content of the message and authority. The disciples do not proclaim their own discoveries or insights. They proclaim what they have heard from another, and what they have been commissioned to tell, Mt. 10:27. A preacher is not a reporter who recounts his own experiences. He is the agent of someone higher whose will he loudly and clearly makes known to the public. Without calling and sending[62] preaching is a self-contradiction and even a deception. It holds out something which has no reality. If there is no sending, the preaching of Christ is propaganda, not mission.

8. Teaching and Proclamation in the Synoptists.

In the NT, especially the Synoptists, we often find κηρύσσειν and διδάσκειν together, Mt. 4:23; 9:35; 11:1; Ac. 28:31 (cf. R. 2:21). Teaching is usually in the synagogue, whereas proclamation takes place anywhere in the open.[63] Different hearers are present. → διδασκαλία is the exposition of Scripture in synagogue worship ; it is for the righteous with a view to increasing their knowledge. κήρυγμα is the herald's cry ringing out in the streets and villages and in houses. The herald goes to all, to publicans and sinners ; he attracts the attention of those who are without (Lk. 18:13) and who do not attend the gatherings of the righteous. To them, too, the call comes. But the NT also speaks of a κηρύσσειν in the synagogue (→ 704). Jesus did not give theoretical teaching when He spoke in the synagogue. He did not expound Scripture like the rabbis. He did not tell people what they must do (→ 705). His teaching was proclamation. He declared what God was doing among them to-day : This day is this scripture fulfilled (Lk. 4:21). His exposition was a herald's cry. His teaching concerning the coming of the kingdom of God was an address demanding decision either for it or against it. Hence His preaching was very different from that of the scribes at synagogue worship.[64] ἦν γὰρ διδάσκων αὐτοὺς ὡς ἐξουσίαν ἔχων καὶ οὐχ ὡς οἱ γραμματεῖς αὐτῶν, Mt. 7:29.[65]

9. Miracles and Proclamation.

The activity of Jesus is comprehensively depicted : "He went about all Galilee, teaching in their synagogues, and preaching the gospel of the kingdom, and healing

---

[62] Rather surprising in this respect is the fact that in the Fourth Gospel, which speaks a great deal about the sending of Jesus, κηρύσσειν does not occur at all.

[63] We are never told that John the Baptist taught.

[64] In Mk. 3:14 f. the disciples are sent out κηρύσσειν καὶ ἔχειν ἐξουσίαν ἐκβάλλειν τὰ δαιμόνια. When they return, we read in Mk. 6:30 : ἀπήγγειλαν αὐτῷ πάντα ὅσα ἐποίησαν καὶ ὅσα ἐδίδαξαν. Here it is obvious that κηρύσσειν and διδάσκειν can be used synon.

[65] Luther has here the well-known "he preached powerfully" (er predigte gewaltig).

all manner of sickness," Mt. 4:23 par. Mk. 1:39, cf. Mt. 9:35. When Jesus sent out His disciples, He charged them to preach and to heal, Lk. 9:2 par. Mk. 3:14 f. and Mt. 10:7 f., cf. Mk. 6:12 f. If preaching is true proclamation in which God is at work, so that His rule is a reality, then signs and wonders occur. It is not that miracles usher in the new age. Miracles take place because the efficacious Word of God has declared the divine rule, and in it everything is sound and well. Hence the miracle is not the important thing. The important thing is the message which effects it. Signs accompany the Word. Their office is simply to confirm what is proclaimed, Mk. 16:20, cf. Hb. 2:3 f., Ac. 4:29 f., 14:3. [66] Miracles, as σημεῖα, are a *verbum visibile* like the sacraments. As there is no sacrament without the Word, so there is no miracle without the preacher of God's act. Hence the NT crowd is not simply astonished at the miracles, as in the miracle stories of Hellenism. It is also astonished at the doctrine or word proclaimed. [67] For believers, who see the act already in the Word, miracles demonstrate the reality of what is proclaimed. But those who reply to preaching and its demand for faith by asking for a sign are refused a sign, 1 C. 1:22 ff. The miracle is not an event compelling those who see it to believe. It is exposed to the same ambiguity as Christian preaching. [68] Jesus does not lay too great stress on His miracles, Mk. 5:43; 8:26. He refuses to see in them a proof of His mission. [69] Those healed by Him are to keep silence. They are not living documents of His power which He takes round with Him as exhibits. When He had made many sick people well in Mk. 1:32 ff., and the disciples wished to exploit His reputation as a miracle-worker, He did not fall in with their plan. He had not come to work miracles; He had come to preach, v. 38, cf. Lk. 4:18. Proclamation is the main thing. Miracles have no independent value. They are simply signs that through the proclamation of the Word the kingdom of God has come, Mt. 11:5.

† κήρυγμα.

A. κήρυγμα outside the New Testament.

1. Among the Greeks. The subst. κήρυγμα arose like the words πρᾶγμα, δεῖγμα or βούλευμα by the affixing of the suffix μα to κηρυκ. [1] It has a twofold sense like the word proclamation, signifying both the result of proclamation (what is proclaimed) and the actual proclaiming. In other words, it denotes both the act [2] and the content. [3] In many cases it is hard to say where the emphasis falls. In correspondence with κη-

---

[66] Mk. 6:12 f.: ἐκήρυξαν ... καὶ δαιμόνια πολλὰ ἐξέβαλλον καὶ ἤλειφον ... καὶ ἐθεράπευον. Exorcism, anointing and healing are in the imperf., proclamation in the aor. "Thus preaching seems to be the main part of the apostolic mission, while the three other aspects of their work have more of the character of accompanying phenomena," Wbg. Mk., ad loc.

[67] Cf. E. Peterson, ΕΙΣ ΘΕΟΣ (1926), 213.

[68] Mt. 7:22; 9:34; Mk. 3:22 par. Mt. 12:24 and Lk. 11:15; Mk. 9:38 par. Lk. 9:49; Mt. 12:27 par. Lk. 11:19; Mt. 24:24 par. Mk. 13:22; 2 Th. 2:9; Rev. 13:13.

[69] Mt. 4:3 ff.; 27:40; Mk. 8:11 f. par. Mt. 12:38 ff.; Mt. 16:1; Lk. 11:16.

κ ή ρ υ γ μ α. [1] Debr., Griech. Wortb. § 310 and 311; Kühner-Blass-Gerth § 329, 30.

[2] Ditt. Syll.³, 1045, 8 : παρήγγειλεν ἐν τῆι ἀγορᾶι μετὰ κηρύγματος. Eur. Iph. Aul., 94: ὀρθίῳ κηρύγματι εἰπεῖν; Xenoph. Ag., I, 33 : κηρύγματι δηλοῦν; Barn., 12, 6 : κηρύγματι καλεῖν.

[3] Eur. Iph. Taur., 239: καινὰ κηρύγματα; Suppl., 382 : διαφέρων κηρύγματα; Ditt. Syll.³, 443, 39 ff.: τὸ κήρυγμα κηρύττειν. Thuc., IV, 105 : κήρυγμα τόδε ἀνειπῶν. IG,

ρύσσειν it can mean "news," [4] "declaration," [5] "enquiry," "demand," [6] "order," "decree," "command," [7] "proclamation of the victor," [8] "intimation of honours." [9]

2. In Philo. Whereas κῆρυξ is found only once in Philo (→ 694), and κηρύσσειν is very rare, [10] κήρυγμα is used a great deal both for the herald's cry [11] and for the declaration or decree. [12] Predominant in Philo is its use of the publication of honours or victors, Som., I, 130 : βραβεῖον and κήρυγμα; Agric., 117: στέφανοι καὶ κηρύγματα; Leg. Gaj., 46 : τιμὰς καὶ στεφάνους μετὰ κηρυγμάτων λαμβάνειν. Philo is acquainted with Gk. usages and customs at the games, and he turns these to his own purposes. The declaration is a figure, Spec. Leg., II, 246; gymnastic contests are also used figur. in the ethical sphere, Agric., 112. Athletes of virtue receive βραβεῖον and κήρυγμα, Praem. Poen., 6. Noah is praised as a victor : ἐπιστεφανῶν δ᾽ αὐτὸν ὡς ἀγωνιστὴν ἐκνενικηκότα κηρύγματι λαμπροτάτῳ προσεπικοσμεῖ φάσκων, ὅτι "τῷ θεῷ εὐηρέστησεν," Abr., 35.

3. The LXX. In the LXX κήρυγμα is the rendering of קֹל at 2 Ch. 30:5 and of קְרִיאָה at Jon. 3:2. This is the only occurrence of קְרִיאָה in the OT. 2 Ch. 30:5 : ἔστησαν λόγον, διελθεῖν κήρυγμα ἐν παντὶ Ισραηλ ... ποιῆσαι τὸ φασεκ. 1 Εσδρ. 9:3 : καὶ ἐγένετο κήρυγμα ἐν ὅλῃ τῇ ᾿Ιουδαίᾳ καὶ Ιερουσαλημ πᾶσι τοῖς ἐκ τῆς αἰχμαλωσίας συναχθῆναι εἰς Ιερουσαλημ. Prv. 9:3 : ἀπέστειλεν τοὺς ἑαυτῆς δούλους συγκαλοῦσα μετὰ ὑψηλοῦ κηρύγματος ἐπὶ κρατῆρα λέγουσα ...

4. In the Rabbis. The Rabbis use הכרזה for proclamation in court (bSanh., 26b) and as a tt. in connection with property (bKet., 100b).

B. τὸ κήρυγμα in the New Testament.

At Mt. 12:41 par. Lk. 11:32 κήρυγμα has been correctly rendered cohortatio, exhortatio, praedicatio. [13] The preaching of Jonah was followed by the repentance

---

XII, 5, 653, 47 ff.: ἀναγορεύειν ... κήρυγμα τόδε; Ditt. Syll.[3], 402, 21: ἀνειπεῖν τὸν ἱεροκήρυκα ... τόδε (τὸ) κήρυγμα. The phrase "formulated message" has been suggested to combine the ideas of the act and the content of proclamation [Debrunner].

[4] Eur. Iph. Taur., 239; Suppl., 382.

[5] Ditt. Syll.[3], 741, 20 ff.: κήρυγμα ποιῆσαι, ὅπως ἐάν τις ζῶν[τας ἀ]γάγῃ Χαιρήμ[ο]να λάβ[ῃ τάλαν]τα τεσσαράκοντα, Demosth. Or., 34, 36 : κήρυγμα γὰρ ποιησαμένου Παρεισάδου ἐν Βοσπόρῳ, ἐάν τις βούληται ᾿Αθήναζε εἰς τὸ ᾿Αττικὸν ἐμπόριον σιτηγεῖν, ἀτελῆ τὸν σῖτον ἐξάγειν, Hdt., III, 52.

[6] Aeschin. Or., 1, 79 : ἐπηρώτα ὑμᾶς τὸ ἐκ τοῦ νόμου κήρυγμα. 3, 4 : σεσίγηται μὲν τὸ κάλλιστον καὶ σωφρονέστατον κήρυγμα τῶν ἐν τῇ πόλει· "τίς ἀγορεύειν βούλεται ...;" cf. 3:23 : τίς βούλεται κατηγορεῖν;

[7] Soph. Ant., 453 ff.:
οὐδὲ σθένειν τοσοῦτον ᾠόμην τὰ σὰ
κηρύγμαθ᾽ ὥστ᾽ ἄγραπτα κἀσφαλῆ θεῶν
νόμιμα δύνασθαι θνητὸν ὄνθ᾽ ὑπερδραμεῖν.
Aristot. Oec., II, p. 1349b, 36 : κήρυγμα ἐποιήσατο τὰ ἡμίσεα, ὧν ἔχει ἕκαστος ἀναφέρειν, cf. 1350a, 5 : ἐκέλευσε πάλιν τὰ ἡμίσεα ἀναφέρειν. Athen., IV, 19 (p. 141 f.): πάντα ἀπὸ κηρύγματος πράσσεται.

[8] Dio C., 63, 14, 3.

[9] Aeschin. Or., 3, 178 : δωρεαὶ καὶ στέφανοι καὶ κηρύγματα, cf. 3, 210 and IG, XII, 9, 236, 46.

[10] Cf. Leisegang, Index.

[11] Phil. Spec. Leg., IV, 4 : By the κοινῷ κηρύγματι the slave is declared free in the 7th year.

[12] Vit. Mos., I, 9 : Parents disregarded τὰ τοῦ τυράννου κηρύγματα that all male children should be killed. Conf. Ling., 197: γράψαντός τε καὶ βεβαιώσαντος τὸ κήρυγμα, God draws up and confirms the decree that those who have fled for no reason should return.

[13] So J. Schleusner, Novum lexicon graeco-latinum in NT (1819), s.v.

of the Ninevites. [14] At 1 C. 2:4 κήρυγμα is the act of proclaiming. Christian preaching does not persuade the hearers by beautiful or clever words — otherwise it would only be a matter of words. Preaching does more. It takes place in the spirit and in power. It is thus efficacious. In the short Markan ending, however, the reference of κήρυγμα is to content: τὸ ἱερὸν καὶ ἄφθαρτον κήρυγμα τῆς αἰωνίου σωτηρίας. The sacred and incorruptible *kerygma* is in some sense a doctrine which treats of eternal salvation. Yet this does not exclude the possibility that the message which thus treats of salvation, or proclaims it, may also effect it. This is at least the meaning in 1 C. 1:21: The foolish message of Jesus crucified saves those who believe. [15] At 1 C. 15:14 the resurrection of Jesus from the dead is the content of the *kerygma*. At R. 16:25, too, the reference is to the message with a very definite content. The gospel of Paul is identical with that which Jesus Himself preached during His earthly life. [16]

In Tt. 1:3 the κήρυγμα is *actus praedicandi*. By preaching is manifested the λόγος which brings to man the eternal life that was promised. God could have made His Word known to men in other ways, but men could not have borne this. Hence God would not have been the σωτήρ who gives life ; His declaration would have spelled death. He thus chose men to be His preachers. By them His Word becomes flesh just as the Son came to sinners in human form. The κήρυγμα is the mode in which the divine Logos comes to us. This κήρυγμα is entrusted to the apostle Paul. The relative clause ὃ ἐπιστεύθην ἐγὼ κατ᾽ ἐπιταγήν makes of the *actus praedicandi* the *munus praeconis*, the apostolic office of preaching, which is entrusted to Paul and to which he is commissioned. The meaning κηρύσσειν = "to discharge the office of a herald" (→ 697) is not found in the NT. But we have the material presuppositions of this sense (→ 712). The primary emphasis,

---

[14] Jos. Ant., 9, 214 : Jonah σταθεὶς εἰς ἐπήκοον ἐκήρυσσεν ὡς μετ᾽ ὀλίγον πάλιν ἀποβαλοῦσι τὴν ἀρχὴν τῆς Ἀσίας καὶ ταῦτα δηλώσας ὑπέστρεψε, 1 Cl., 7, 7 : ᾿Ιωνᾶς Νινευίταις καταστροφὴν ἐκήρυξεν, οἱ δὲ μετανοήσαντες ἐπὶ τοῖς ἁμαρτήμασιν αὐτῶν ἐξιλάσαντο τὸν θεὸν ἱκετεύσαντες καὶ ἔλαβον σωτηρίαν, Just. Dial., 107, 2 : τοῦ ᾿Ιωνᾶ κηρύξαντος αὐτοῖς μετὰ τὸ ἐκβρασθῆναι (cast on the shore) αὐτὸν τῇ τρίτῃ ἡμέρᾳ ἀπὸ τῆς κοιλίας τοῦ ἁδροῦ ἰχθύος, ὅτι μετὰ τρεῖς ἡμέρας παμπληθεὶ ἀπολοῦνται.

[15] In no sense is κήρυγμα here only *modus tradendi religionem christianam, qui, quia omni eruditionis et subtilitatis specie caret, plerisque stultus videtur :* an unlearned and unskilled address, so Schleusner, *s.v.* It is worth considering whether the reference in 1 C. 1:21 might not be to the act, namely, that it pleased God through something foolish, i.e., human preaching, to save men. But the context (v. 18 : ὁ λόγος ὁ τοῦ σταυροῦ ... μωρία ἐστίν, and v. 23 : ἡμεῖς κηρύσσομεν Χριστὸν ἐσταυρωμένον ... ἔθνεσιν μωρίαν) favours the sense of content in v. 21.

[16] The phrase τὸ κήρυγμα ᾿Ιησοῦ Χριστοῦ raises several exegetical questions which admit of no easy answer. Even if we accept the fact that the κήρυγμα is the content of preaching rather than the act of proclamation, we have still to ask what is meant by the gen. Is ᾿Ιησοῦ Χριστοῦ a subj. gen., the preaching which Jesus Himself proclaims, or an obj. gen., the preaching which speaks of Him ? Again, is it the historical or the risen Christ who is meant ? Comparison with εὐαγγέλιόν favours the subj. gen., and ἀποκάλυψις μυστηρίου can hardly be adduced against this, for εὐαγγέλιον and κήρυγμα are linked by a καί, whereas something different is introduced by ἀποκάλυψις. κήρυγμα ᾿Ιησοῦ Χριστοῦ might be the preaching of the risen Lord who is present in the community in the words of His messengers. But we have this already in εὐαγγέλιόν μου. Christ Himself speaks in the gospel of Paul. Paul is not referring to his gospel added to the preaching of the risen Lord. He is emphasising the agreement of his preaching with that of the earthly Jesus. Hence τὸ κήρυγμα ᾿Ιησοῦ Χριστοῦ can only mean the message which Jesus Christ proclaimed.

however, is on the act rather than the office. [17] At a later period of early Christian development more stress came to be laid on the office, and we thus find the preaching office. [18] κήρυγμα has this sense in 2 Tm. 4:17. In 2 Tm. 4:5 Paul admonishes Timothy: τὴν διακονίαν σου πληροφόρησον, "faithfully fulfil thine office," and he says of himself in 2 Tm. 4:7: "I have finished the course, I have kept πίστις (the faith or faith ?)." For (2 Tm. 4:17): ὁ κύριος ... ἐνεδυνάμωσέν με, ἵνα δι' ἐμοῦ τὸ κήρυγμα πληροφορηθῇ. God has strengthened him so that even in hours of affliction and isolation he has fully discharged his office as a preacher. Before judges and listeners, before the whole court, he did not stand as a defendant but as a herald. Thus all nations heard the message through him. Representatives of peoples who knew nothing of Christ had the opportunity to hear his preaching. In this way he faithfully fulfilled his office.

† προκηρύσσω.

In Gk. words with προ can have two meanings. The original sense of προ is "forth," as in προΐημι or προδίδωμι. [1] Along these lines προκηρύσσειν means "to speak forth," "to declare publicly," "to set forth audibly." Even in early Gk., however, this first sense is to a large degree replaced by the temporal sense of προ, i.e., "before." On the other hand, in the instances we have of προκηρύσσειν the sense "to proclaim something in advance" is very rare. For the most part it is either used in the older way or else in Hellenistic fashion as a virtual equivalent of the simple κηρύσσειν. Soph. El., 683 : ὅτ' ᾔσθετ' ἀνδρὸς ὀρθίων κηρυγμάτων δρόμον προκηρύξαντος, Ant., 461: the publishing of a decree, also Luc. Tyrannicida, 9. Like κηρύσσειν, προκηρύσσειν is often used for "to offer publicly," "to auction." Poll. Onom., VIII, 103 : οἱ δὲ κατ' ἀγορὰν τὰ ὤνια προ (vl. ἀπο-) κηρύττοντες. Preisigke Sammelbuch, 4512, 7 f. : προτεθέντων εἰς πρᾶσιν καὶ προκηρυχθέντων. προκήρυξις is a tt. for "auctioning." Philo, who prefers the compound to the simple, writes in Gig., 39 : οἱ ἐν ἀγορᾷ τὰ ὤνια προκηρύττοντες, and in Agric., 17: ταῦτ' οὖν ἡ ψυχῆς ἐπαγγελλομένη γεωργικὴ προκηρύττει. Here we might render it "to promise." Jos. Ant., 10, 79 : οὗτος ὁ προφήτης καὶ τὰ μέλλοντα τῇ πόλει δεινὰ προεκήρυξεν ἐν γράμμασι καταλιπών, is important in this connection. Jeremiah prophesied misfortune that was still to fall on the city.

In the NT προκηρύσσειν occurs only at Ac. 13:24. At Ac. 3:20 it is a mistaken reading of the *textus receptus* for προχειρίζεσθαι. Ac. 13:24 reads : προκηρύξαντος Ἰωάννου πρὸ προσώπου τῆς εἰσόδου αὐτοῦ βάπτισμα μετανοίας παντὶ τῷ λαῷ Ἰσραήλ. It is not surprising that προκηρύσσειν in the sense of "to proclaim in advance" in rare in the NT. The proclamation of Jesus and the apostles does not deal so much with events that are still to take place. The proclamation itself is event. The NT message does not proclaim what is to happen. It is fulfilment, not promise. There is good reason why προκηρύσσειν should be used of John the Baptist, the last of the prophets (→ 705 f.), though even in this connection it does not mean "to foretell." By reason of the imminence of the βασιλεία τοῦ

---

[17] At 2 C. 3:9 Luther translates διακονία τῆς δικαιοσύνης "the office which preaches righteousness"; at 2 C. 5:18 he has for διακονία τῆς καταλλαγῆς "the office which preaches reconciliation"; at Col. 1:25 οἰκονομία τοῦ θεοῦ is "the divine office of preaching"; at Ac. 6:4 διακονία τοῦ λόγου is "the office of the word." → II, 87.

[18] κήρυγμα has this sense only in the Past., where we also find κήρυξ.

π ρ ο κ η ρ ύ σ σ ω. [1] Cf. J. Wackernagel, *Vorlesungen über Syntax*, II² (1928), 237 ff. [Debrunner]

θεοῦ John's preaching of baptism for the remission of sins was more than promise. It was an anticipation of what was to come.

Friedrich

κεφαλὴ γωνίας → I, 792.
Κηφᾶς → Πέτρος.

┌─────────────────────────┐
│ **κινέω, μετακινέω** │
└─────────────────────────┘

κινέω.

Hom. κίω ("to go"), Lat. *cieo*. "To set something in motion," "to propel forward." [1] Fig. "to stir," "to cause" : a. in the sphere of the soul : "to touch," "to make an impression on," "to disturb," e.g., καρδίαν : Eur. Med., 99 : μήτηρ κινεῖ κραδίαν, κινεῖ δὲ χόλον, τὸ πνεῦμα; Da. 2:3 : ἐκινήθη μου τὸ πνεῦμα (Heb. פעם ni), "my spirit was unsettled." b. In that of the mind, "to move," "to cause," e.g., P. Oxy., VIII, 1121, 16 : τίνι λόγῳ ἢ πόθεν κεινηθέντες, cf. also P. Flor., 58, 15 : δέομαι κεινηθέντα σε [ἐ]πεξελ[.], also Dg., 11, 8 : θελήματι τοῦ κελεύοντος λόγου ἐκινήθημεν ἐξειπεῖν μετὰ πόνου. c. In that of politics, "to instigate" : πολέμους, Plat. Resp., VIII, 566e; ταραχήν, Jos. Bell., 2, 175; θόρυβος ἐκινήθη, P. Bar., 68, n. 6; στάσεις, Ac. 24:5. d. A mixture of outer and inner disturbance, e.g., Ac. 21:30 : ἐκινήθη ἡ πόλις ὅλη, "the whole city (Jerusalem) was set in motion (against Paul)."

In 6th and 7th cent. pap. "to set a wish in motion," "to make demands," "to proceed against someone (at law)," "to bring an action against," "to make a complaint against." [2]

There is a special sense, "to shake one's head" : κινεῖν τὴν κεφαλήν, Hom., LXX : 4 Βασ. 19:21; Jer. 18:16; Lam. 2:15; Job 16:4; Da. 4:19; Sir. 12:18; 13:7; NT : Mt. 27:39; Mk. 15:29 (as a sign of contempt, so also ψ 21:7); *v.* also 1 Cl., 16, 16.

In the NT the word serves at Mt. 23:4 to express vividly the inner contradiction in the nature of the Pharisees and their attitude to the Law. They lay heavy burdens on the righteous without lifting even a finger of their own to help them.

A deep seriousness underlies the figure at Rev. 2:5. The community at Ephesus, which is represented by the candlestick, receives a severe sentence from the Lord of the Church. It will be rejected by Christ (κινήσω τὴν λυχνίαν σου) if it does not repent.

Theologically significant is Ac. 17:28 : ἐν αὐτῷ (θεῷ) γὰρ ζῶμεν καὶ κινούμεθα καὶ ἐσμέν, "in him we live and move and have our being." In his preaching at Athens Paul makes use of the pantheistic sense of God common to the Greeks, and attempts on this basis to open up to them the way to a full belief in God. The verse is not to be regarded as an expression of Pauline theology. For in terms of his own basic principles Paul could only say (in a dynamic sense) that all men

---

κ ι ν έ ω. [1] For details cf. Liddell-Scott, 952.
[2] For examples *v.* Moult.-Mill. and Preisigke Wört., *s.v.*

live and move and have their being through God.[3] Hence this statement is to be regarded merely as an acknowledged starting-point for his missionary preaching, not as a confession of his own theological convictions.

Paul is using Stoic terms and concepts.[4] It is difficult to say whether Paul himself or the author of Ac. is the first to link the words ζῶμεν, κινούμεθα and ἐσμέν in a formal triad. In the literature known to us we never find more than two of the words together, either movement and being[5] or life and movement.[6] The thought common to the Stoic statements is that the world is full of the deity, which permeates all things as the reason and soul of the world. It sustains the world with the power of divine life and movement.[7]

These Stoic views go back to Plato. Plato says of the world soul in Tim., 37c : ὡς δὲ κινηθὲν αὐτὸ καὶ ζῶν ἐνόησεν τῶν ἀϊδίων θεῶν γεγονὸς ἄγαλμα ὁ γεννήσας πατήρ. All movement presupposes that which is self-moved. This is the soul, which is from the beginning of the world, and which Plato calls ἀρχὴ κινήσεως in Phaedr., 245c. Hence all movement comes from this. Plato develops the idea of the world soul more fully in Leg., X, 896 ff. There are two world souls which work against one another in the cosmos. The orderly course of all movements in heaven and on earth, in the whole process of the universe, has its basis in the ἀρίστη ψυχή. In Plato's view of the cosmos as we find it in the Laws the concept of the world soul finally merges "into mystical unity with the souls of the stars."[8] Plato gives the following definition of the world soul in Leg., X, 896a : ψυχὴν ταὐτὸν ὂν καὶ τὴν πρώτην γένεσιν καὶ κίνησιν τῶν τε ὄντων καὶ γεγονότων καὶ ἐσομένων καὶ πάντων αὖ τῶν ἐναντίων τούτοις, ἐπειδή γε ἀνεφάνη μεταβολῆς τε καὶ κινήσεως ἁπάσης αἰτία ἅπασιν.[9]

Philo, who follows Stoic ideas, gives us the statement that God, who is Himself unmoved,[10] is the Master by whom all things are set in movement (Cher., 128 : τεχνίτης, ... ὑφ' οὗ πάντα κινεῖται).[11] It is worth noting that in Philo there is a pantheistic element along with the transcendent view of God. An example may be seen in Sacr. AC, 68, where it is said of God that He is τονικῇ χρώμενος τῇ κινήσει. Here Philo obviously has in view the Stoic notion that God is a kind of pneuma which extends through all things and which permeates all bodies with varying tension (τόνος).[12]

---

[3] This view is well worked out by D. A. Frøvig, "Das Aratoszitat der Areopagrede des Paulus," Symb. Osl., 15/16 (1936), 44 ff., esp. 51 ff., 53 : "If nevertheless we find these statements in the Areopagus address, they are to be viewed as an accommodation to Stoicism; Paul is here depicted as the discerning missionary who knows the religious assumptions of his hearers and puts them to use."

[4] Cf. on this whole question E. Norden, Agnostos Theos (1913), 19 ff. Norden thinks (20) that the combination ζῆν, κινεῖσθαι, εἶναι expresses "the graded sequence of organic life."

[5] Stob. Ecl., I, 106, 8 : (Chrysipp.:) καὶ κατὰ μὲν τὸν χρόνον κινεῖσθαί τε ἕκαστα καὶ εἶναι.

[6] Plut. Tranq. An., 20 (II, 477d): οἷα νοῦς θεῖος αἰσθητὰ νοητῶν μιμήματα, φησὶν ὁ Πλάτων, ἔμφυτον ἀρχὴν ζωῆς ἔχοντα καὶ κινήσεως ἔφηνεν ..., Corp. Herm., XI, 17c : τοῦτο γὰρ ὥσπερ ζωὴ καὶ ὥσπερ κίνησίς ἐστι τοῦ θεοῦ, κινεῖν τὰ πάντα καὶ ζωοποιεῖν.

[7] Cf. Sext. Emp. Math., IX, 75f., where among proofs of the existence of God we have the fact that God as the δύναμις αὐτοκίνητος (76) permeates the world and shapes all things by movement.

[8] J. Stenzel, "Über zwei Begriffe der platonischen Mystik : ζῷον und κίνησις," Jahresbericht d. Joh.-Gymn. zu Breslau, 1914, 17.

[9] Cf. on this whole section F. Überweg, Philosophie d. Altertums, I[12] (1926), 321 f. and U. v. Wilamowitz-Moellendorff, Plato II (1920), 317 ff.

[10] Cf. Poster. C., 29.

[11] Cf. also Leg. All., I, 6 : What is created by God's wisdom is in constant motion.

[12] Cf. L. Cohn, Die Werke Philos III (1919), 242, n. 2.

† μετακινέω.

A not very common word meaning a. "to set aside," "to replace," "to displace," "to remove" (Hdt., IX, 74). Mid. "to go from one place to another" (Hdt., IX, 51). Pass. "to be displaced," Hdt., I, 51; Plat. Leg., X, 894a : μεταβάλλον ... καὶ μετακινούμενον γίγνεται πᾶν, Aristot. Gen. Corr., I, 2, p. 315b, 14. b. Fig. "to alter," e.g., τὴν πολιτείαν, Aristot. Eth. Nic., VII, 11, p. 1152a, 30 : ῥᾷον γὰρ ἔθος μετακινῆσαι φύσεως; Theophr. Hist. Plant., 4, 11, 5 : ἡ τομὴ μετεκινήθη. Common on inscr., cf. IG, V, 1, 1390, 186 (Andania): μὴ μετακινοῦντες ἐπὶ καταλ[ύ]σει τῶν μυστηρίων μ[η]θὲν τῶν κατὰ τὸ διάγραμμα and Ditt. Syll.³, 736, 186; 1238, 4; 1239, 12/13 and 25.

LXX : "to remove a landmark" (ὅρια μετακινεῖν), Dt. 19:14; Pr. 23:10 Σ : "to put to flight," Dt. 32:30. Pass. "to be put to flight," Is. 22:3 Θ (μετεκινήθησαν, LXX πεφεύγασιν); Is. 54:10, of hills which are to be "removed" (οὐδὲ οἱ βουνοί σου μετακινηθήσονται).

In the NT it is found only fig. at Col. 1:23 : μὴ μετακινούμενοι ἀπὸ τῆς ἐλπίδος [1] τοῦ εὐαγγελίου. The Colossians are admonished to persist steadfastly in faith and not to be pushed away from the hope which they derive from the message of salvation. [2]

J. Schneider

---

† κλάδος

"The shoot, bud, branch on a tree or plant." So in the NT at Mt. 13:32; 24:32; Mk. 13:28; Lk. 13:19; κλάδους ποιεῖν, "to put forth branches," Mk. 4:32; κλάδους κόπτειν, "to hew down branches," Mt. 21:8. [1] "Shoots of the olive," Hdt., VII, 19 (τῆς ἐλαίης τοὺς κλάδους); Aesch. Eum., 43 (ἔχοντ' ἐλαίας θ' ὑψιγέννητον κλάδον). [2] Fig. of the poor who hang on our shoulders (like branches), Emped. Fr., 29, 1 (I, 238, 1, Diels): οὐ γὰρ ἀπὸ νώτοιο δύο κλάδοι ἀίσσονται (to swing or hang). In the pap. it is also used for the "wooden platter" or "board" (P. Oxy., XIV, 1738, 4 etc.).

κλάδος is often applied fig. to men. [3] Thus we find a touching example of pious recollection on the gravestone of a young girl, Epigr. Graec., 368, 7: Θεοδώρα, κλάδος ἐλέας, τάχυ πῶς ἐμαράνθης; at Sir. 23:25 the children of the adulteress are called κλάδοι αὐτῆς, and at Sir. 40:15 we read of the posterity of the wicked that they shall not have many κλάδοι, i.e., children.

Paul in R. 11:16-21 speaks metaphorically of the root and branches of the olive. [4] The root is the people of the promise, namely, Israel. The branches which are

---

μ ε τ α κ ι ν έ ω. [1] Hope includes patient expectation, cf. → ἐλπίς, II, 533.
[2] Cf. also → εὐαγγέλιον, II, 732 : Hope is already the portion of Christians through the message concerning it.
κ λ ά δ ο ς. [1] So also Hermes s., 8, 1, 2.
[2] Cf. also Aesch. Suppl., 23; Soph. Oed. Tyr., 143.
[3] For details cf. Liddell-Scott, 955, s.v. κλάδος (5).
[4] On the idea of the root and branches cf. Menand. Fr., 716 (CAF): ὁ μὴ τρέφων τεκοῦσαν ἐκ τέχνης νέος, ἄκαρπος οὗτός ἐστιν ἀπὸ ῥίζης κλάδος.

grafted from the wild olive (the Gentile nations) into the genuine tree (the saved community of God) are Gentile Christians. Thus Paul emphasises the close organic connection which exists between the saved community of the OT and that of the NT. [5]

In Jewish thought the idea of the saved community is very closely linked with the fact of the blood relationship of the living descendants of Abraham. It is thus natural that the saved community should be equated with Israel. Paul disrupts this equation by enunciating the principle that the promise which Abraham received on the basis of faith applies to "the seed" (Gl. 3:16), i.e., Christ. Hence believers who belong to Christ and are one in Him (Gl. 3:28) are heirs of Abraham's promise. For Paul, then, the equation is not that of the saved community with 'Ισραὴλ κατὰ σάρκα but that of the saved community with 'Ισραὴλ κατὰ πνεῦμα. Paul maintains the continuity of the community, but in him its structure is completely changed. To the divine community of salvation there now belong only those Jews who believe as Abraham did. [6] In the Christ situation, however, to believe is to acknowledge Jesus as the Messiah and to accept His sacrifice as God's all-sufficient act of salvation for man. He who will not do this has no valid place in the community. Now that Christ has ended the period of the Law and brought the Abrahamic promise into force there is only one qualification for membership of the community, namely, faith in Christ and in God's saving work in Him. Hence Gentiles who believe in Christ are incorporated into God's people of salvation as fully accredited members. The relationship of blood is replaced by one of faith. In terms of the figure, the tree remains, but God breaks off those branches which no longer belong in the situation inaugurated by Christ and puts in new branches which originally stood in a very different organic relationship. Thus Paul clings to the idea and reality of the divine community of salvation. He declares, however, that its character and structure have been completely changed by Christ. [7]

Ign. Tr., 11, 2 describes Christians as κλάδοι τοῦ σταυροῦ. This expresses the inner relation of Christians to the crucified (and risen) Christ. [8] Here is a conception which became an important motif in early and medieval Christian art. [9]

In this connection we may also recall the allegory of the willow-tree in Herm. s., 8, 1 ff. This tree symbolises the Law, i.e., the Son of God (8, 3, 2). From it branches are

---

[5] The picture of the root and branches (R. 11:16 ff.) perhaps rests originally on a purely Jewish image in which the organically developed tree represents the family unity of the Jewish world which as such is also the Israel of God's saved community. The inserted branches are proselytes from the Gentile nations who enter into the divine community of salvation by circumcision and who then in subsequent generations are incorporated into the blood relationship of the community of Israel. Paul changes the image by viewing Gentile Christians instead of proselytes as the engrafted branches [Kuhn].

[6] Cf. on this pt. Ltzm. on R. 11:16b : The branches are the totality of Israel ; the ancestors of the people, i.e., the patriarchs, are the root ; Jewish believers are the branches which remain as distinct from those which are broken off.

[7] The parable does not conform to natural history, which teaches us to graft good shoots into wild and not vice versa, cf. Ltzm. R. on 11:16b. Even to-day, however, there is a method of renewing old vines by engrafting young wild shoots (described by Columella, De re rustica, V, 9, 16 [Ress]; W. M. Ramsay, Exp., VI, 11 [1905], 16 ff., 152 ff.; S. Linder, Paläst. Jbch., 26 [1930], 40 ff.). Whether Paul would have known this is open to question. Deissmann LO, 235, is of the opinion that Paul intentionally introduces into the metaphor something which is against nature.

[8] Cf. J. Schneider, Die Passionsmystik des Paulus (1929), 128 f. Cf. also L. v. Sybel, "Zu Ξύλον ζωῆς," ZNW, 20 (1921), 93 ff.; also A. Deissmann, Paulus² (1925), 157 f.

[9] Cf. Deissmann, loc. cit.

chopped off and given to the people of God which is gathered in the shade of the willow. The staves are then demanded back and engrafted. The main point of the allegory is the testing of the engrafted staves, i.e., the testing of Christian sinners. [10]

Finally, we may refer to a par. in Justin, who in Dial., 110, 4 has the parable of the vine and its continual shoots.

J. Schneider

κλαίω, κλαυθμός

κλαίω.

From Hom. intr. "to cry" (Il., 18, 340), also trans. "to bewail" (Od., 1, 363), so in the LXX, usually for בכה, [1] and in Joseph. Common in the NT with various nuances, e.g., to express grief at parting (Ac. 21:13, cf. Τωβ. 5:18, 23), or strong inner emotion (Phil. 3:18, cf. 1 S. 1:7), esp. shame or remorse (Lk. 7:38; Mt. 26:75 and par., cf. Lam. 1:15), or finally weeping for the dead (Mk. 5:38 f. and par.; Lk. 7:13, 32; Jn. 11:31, 33; 20:11, 13, 15; Ac. 9:39, cf. Gn. 50:1; Dt. 21:13; 2 S. 3:32). On the other hand weeping may also be a sign of strong and overwhelming joy (cf. Gn. 46:29; 2 Εσδρ. 3:12), though not in the NT.

The term has theological significance in the NT only in a few materially related passages, i.e., Lk. 6:21, 25; 23:28; Jn. 16:20; Jm. 4:9; 5:1; Rev. 18:9 ff. In all these it is used with reference to the present to describe a typical attitude of men of God, or, when applied to the future, to denote that which awaits the ungodly when God manifests His right and rule to the whole world. Thus Jesus blesses the κλαίοντες νῦν, and promises them: γελάσετε, whereas conversely He holds out for the γελῶντες νῦν the prospect: πενθήσετε καὶ κλαύσετε (Lk. 6:21, 25; cf. esp. Jm. 4:9; 5:1). For the Gk. Bible and the Rabbis as well as the NT, [2] laughter is an attitude which expresses human self-confidence in face of God. [3] Indeed, it is almost a tt. for the affirmation of man as an autonomous being in face of the Creator and Lord of all things. [4] κλαίειν is opposed to it as the attitude which

---

[10] Cf. Dib. Herm., 586 ff.

κλαίω. [1] Ju. 9:7 B (A: καλέω); 15:18 B; 16:28 B (in both cases A: βοάω) for קרא (cf. also → 723). At 'Ιερ. 41 (34):5 κλαίομαι is used for שרף; we may well surmise that an ancient custom, later felt to be heathen and discontinued, has here been intentionally dropped out of the text, namely, that of burning sweet-smelling plants (cf. 2 Ch. 16:14; 21:19).

[2] → I, 658 ff.

[3] In this respect, and with further reference to γελάω, we should also note the Tannaitic rule: If a man dies laughing (מתוך השחוק), it is a good sign (סימן יפה) for him; if he dies weeping (מתוך הבכי), it is a bad sign (סימן רע) for him (bKet., 103b Bar.). The laughter of one who is dying shows that he has not done, or left undone, anything which will cause him to be afraid of the divine judgment. Is there here Gk. influence (→ I, 660 f.)?

[4] Rather in the sense of Plutarch in his linguistically quite unbiblical: γέλως ἑταῖρος ὕβρεως, Quaest. Conv., I, 4 (II, 622b).

expresses the assurance of being, not autonomous, but for good or ill dependent on God, so that all things must, yet also can, be awaited from Him. This kind of weeping arises when man recognises his total inadequacy in face of God and when he sees that he cannot evade this, whether it be in respect of his life and its duration, of his human powers and capacities, or of his service of God, including the moral life. Thus in weeping God is acknowledged as God and His sway is fundamentally accepted (cf. Lk. 7:29 with 17:15; 18:11). This secures to the κλαίοντες God's grace and fellowship in the future when God will manifest Himself as such. But for those who now set aside God's claim this self-revelation will mean the disclosure of their lostness before Him, and it will thus bring κλαίειν, and the more so the more confident they have felt (cf. esp. Jm. 5:1 ff.; Lk. 16:19 ff.; 18:14). The complete transvaluation of all values, which is just as certain as that God exists and that He ushers in His day (cf. Lk. 1:51 ff.),[5] will leave no doubt whatever as to the place of true security and false.

This usage is common in the OT.[6] When Hezekiah on his bed of sickness hears from Isaiah of his approaching death, ἔκλαυσεν κλαυθμῷ μεγάλῳ = וַיֵּבְךְּ בְּכִי גָדוֹל (2 K. 20:3; Is. 38:3) and this gives God cause to extend his life (2 K. 20:5 f.; Is. 38:5). Even though the tears are caused by fear of death, the story makes it clear that it was his κλαίειν which made God change His resolve. It should be noted that Hezekiah does not ask for an extension of life. He appeals to God's righteousness and accepts His will. This is why he weeps. We have here the very opposite of the attitude of those who treat God as the partner in a business transaction. Things are much the same in 2 K. 22:19 f. Here king Josiah is faced with a prophecy of disaster on the nation, the city and the temple because of apostasy against God and disobedience to His will. He personally, however, is promised a peaceful death because, after reading the newly discovered book of the Law of God (22:8 ff.), he wept before God (ἔκλαυσας ἐνώπιον ἐμοῦ, v. 19), and this was accepted as a sign of humiliation before Him. It should be noted that the reference is to v. 11, where it is simply said that he rent his clothes in sign of grief, not that he actually shed tears (cf. also 2 Εσδρ. 18:9 ff.; Tob. 3:1). But esp. we should mention the three passages referred to in → n. 1, where κλαίειν is used three times for קרא in B. The κλαίειν of Ju. 9:7 B is readily understandable in view of Jotham's situation, though it seems that these are tears of anger rather than of sorrow. At Ju. 15:18 and 16:28 B, however, the word clearly denotes a cry to God for help in a situation in which God alone can help (A ἐβόησεν). Even plainer is Hos. 12:5, for here the ultimate victory of Jacob over the angel in their wrestling by night (Gn. 32:22 ff.) is grounded in the fact that he wept (בכה, κλαίειν) and begged for mercy (התחנן, δεῖσθαι).[7] Since there is no reference to Jacob's tears in the story, this can only refer to the attitude expressed in what he says in v. 11 ff. and v. 27. The crying of Ps. 126:5 f. (בכה, κλαίειν) may be mentioned in this connection if it is correct that we are to see in weeping at sowing a widespread[8] cultic rite.[9, 10]

---

[5] Cf. K. H. Rengstorf in NT Deutsch, ad loc.
[6] Here is also the source of the NT antithesis κλαίειν/γελᾶν (Qoh. 3:4).
[7] LXX has the plur., and thus sees in Jacob the representative of his people, as also suggested by the context.
[8] Esp. in connection with the worship of Osiris in Egypt, though also elsewhere, cf. examples in H. Gunkel, Die Psalmen⁴ (1926), 552.
[9] Cf. Gunkel, op. cit.; A. Weiser, Die Psalmen (1935), ad loc.
[10] Cf. also ψ 83:6 f. and Lk. 6:21, 23; also ψ 94:6, where σκληρύνειν τὰς καρδίας (v. 8) is the antithesis, and esp. ψ 68:10 (LXX καὶ συνέκαμψα..., 'Α : καὶ ἔκλαυσα ἐν νηστείᾳ ψυχήν μου, καὶ ἐγενήθη εἰς ὀνειδισμόν ἐμοί; cf. Σ). The pious attitude of κλαίειν provokes scorn (cf. v. 9, 19 f.). [Bertram.]

This is the point where the κλαίειν of shame and remorse (→ 722) links up with the previous figure, since God is hereby vindicated. This is also the point where the biblical use necessarily diverges from that of the world outside the Bible. For the idea of manifested remorse which is occasionally present in κλαίειν is quite alien to the Greek world, just as the whole idea of guilt before God is alien (→ I, 296 ff.). Thus the tears shed by the blinded Oedipus are for the fate of the daughters begotten by him in incest, not for his deed. For the deed was not due to an evil will; it was possible and indeed inevitable by reason of his own deficient knowledge (→ I, 298). Thus his own measureless grief is the object of his sorrow. [11] It is a fearful thing for man to be in the hands of the gods and not to be able to determine either himself or his relationships. [12] κλαίειν has here as little place in his description of his own situation as, e.g., in Eur. Alc., 100 ff., where the sorrow is for the dead Alcestis. Here πένθος is a comprehensive term for the grief of those who are left. κλαίω seems to be used more for outward grief than for grief in general. It thus seems to refer to manifested grief of a physical rather than a spiritual kind. For this reason κλαίειν is often linked with tears, [13] though it does not have to be. [14] When it threatens, κλαίειν can conjure up the thought of painful punishment or affliction. Hence κλαύσει (= κλαύσῃ) can have much the same sense as "it will go ill with you," [15] and κλαίειν τινὰ λέγειν can mean "to wish evil to someone." [16] The full distinction between the non-biblical and the biblical use may be seen when we consider the metaphorical use in both cases. For on the one side it is a powerful description of the need to endure a painful situation which we may well have brought on ourselves; on the other it denotes the acceptance and affirmation of dependence on God. The basis of the distinction is that non-biblical κλαίοντες, in and with their grief, stand in no relation to a God who according to an eternal plan directs the destinies of men to their salvation.

In NT usage the occurrence of κλαίειν in declarations of judgment on the worldly has theological significance in the sense of denoting the awakening of knowledge of God and of insight into the consequences of earlier ungodliness in the form of a future of eternal separation from God. In keeping with this is the fact that in such contexts κλαίειν is always accompanied by a softer word designed to express lamentation in the narrower sense, especially πενθεῖν (Lk. 6:25; Jm. 4:9; Rev. 18:11, 15, 19), [17] also θρηνεῖν (Jn. 16:20), [18] ταλαιπωρεῖν (Jm. 4:9), [19]

---

[11] Soph. Oed. Tyr., 1486 f.:
    καὶ σφὼ δακρύω . . .
    νοούμενος τὰ λοιπὰ τοῦ πικροῦ βίου,
    οἷον βιῶναι σφὼ πρὸς ἀνθρώπων χρεών.

[12] Cf. also Soph. Fr., 513, 1 (TGF): εἰ μὲν ἦν κλαίουσιν ἰᾶσθαι κακά — ὁ χρυσὸς ἧσσον κτῆμα τοῦ κλαίειν ἂν ἦν. [Kleinknecht.]

[13] Sometimes κεκλαυμένος has the sense of streaming with tears (= δεδακρυμένος), Aesch. Choeph., 457 and 731.

[14] Already in Hom. κλαίειν can also express joy and emotion. The usage stems from the same source. The rule of fate is accepted, but in this case it is joyous and surprising, not shattering.

[15] Cf. Eur. Cyc., 554: Polyphem. to Silenus, who has let himself be kissed by Dionysus because he secretly drank of the wine of Odysseus: κλαύσει φιλῶν τὸν οἶνον οὐ φιλοῦντά σε. The κλαύσει suggests coming blows.

[16] Cf. Hdt., IV, 127: σοὶ δὲ ἀντὶ μὲν δώρων γῆς τε καὶ ὕδατος δῶρα πέμψω τοιαῦτα οἷα σοὶ πρέπει ἐλθεῖν, ἀντὶ δὲ τοῦ ὅτι δεσπότης ἔφησας εἶναι ἐμός, κλαίειν λέγω.

[17] On Rev. 18:11 ff. cf. Ez. 27:30 ff. πενθεῖν also occurs with κλαίειν at 2 Εσδρ. 18:9.

[18] Cf. Tob. 10:4, 7 א. On Jn. 16:20 → n. 24; the passage is only partially relevant here.

[19] But cf. Jm. 5:1, where we have ταλαιπωρία.

ὀλολύζειν (Jm. 5:1), κόπτεσθαι (Rev. 18:9), ²⁰ λυπεῖσθαι (Jn. 16:20). ²¹ Only this combination yields the full severity of what is intimated in the sayings. For the men concerned the disclosure of God ²² will entail subjection to Him in acknowledgment, but it will also entail grief, since they will now see what they have done in resisting His will and rejecting His offer of fellowship (cf. Lk. 13:23 ff.; esp. v. 28).

In Lk. (23:28) we have a special account of the saying of Jesus to the weeping women of Jerusalem, and this, too, is illuminated by the distinctive use of the term. When it is said of the women: ἐκόπτοντο καὶ ἐθρήνουν (23:27), this shows us how great was the grief which filled them, and it is also an indication of the irreversibility of the way of Jesus to the cross (→ n. 20 on κόπτεσθαι). They weep because they do not understand how God can permit what is happening to Jesus. But Jesus will not allow them to weep over Him and His fate. If anyone should be an object of tears, it is not He; it is rather those who weep and their children. In His way to the cross He fulfils the plan of God, ²³ and He should be glorified. ²⁴ By crying over Him, the women of Jerusalem show the tragedy of their people in respect of His execution; for by their tears they finally bear witness that they do not understand what it is all about. ²⁵ Because their children will have to bear the consequences, Jesus tells them to weep for these. He thus issues once again His call to repent, just as He issued it when, on His royal entry into Jerusalem, He Himself broke into tears when He saw the city because it saw in Him an enemy, whereas He was the only One who could bring it lasting peace (Lk. 19:41f.).

† κλαυθμός.

Like κλαίειν, it is used from the time of Hom. (Od., 4, 212 etc.) as a term for "weeping," or for "lamentation for the dead" (cf. Od., 4, 168 ff.). In the LXX it normally stands for בְּכִי and it is thus combined with θρῆνος, 'Ιερ. 38:15 f. (cf. Jos. Ant., 20, 112), πένθος, Bar. 4:11, 23, κραυγή, Is. 65:19, κοπετός, ¹ ξύρησις and ζῶσις σάκκων, Is. 22:12. In addition to the strict sense, we also find an emphatically religious use. In the prophet's call to repentance at Jer. 3:21 we find: φωνὴ ἐκ χειλέων ἠκούσθη κλαυθμοῦ καὶ δεήσεως υἱῶν 'Ισραήλ, ὅτι ἠδίκησαν ἐν ταῖς ὁδοῖς αὐτῶν. If the beginning of conversion is here perceived in κλαυθμός, at 'Ιερ. 38:9 κλαυθμός finds its answer and fulfilment in παράκλησις by God. 2 Macc. 13:12 describes the attitude of the people in its prayer to God for assistance and help. It prays for three days μετὰ

²⁰ Cf. 'Ιερ. 41:5. The two words are found together at Lk. 8:52 (so also Jos. Ant., 13, 399; Schl. Lk., 90), κλαίειν is used for weeping over the dead girl, and κόπτεσθαι for the customary lamentation.
²¹ Cf. Tob. 7:6.
²² At Lk. 6:25 the reference is to the βασιλεία τοῦ θεοῦ, at Jm. 5:3 to the ἔσχαται ἡμέραι, at Rev. 18:1 ff. to the day of judgment.
²³ Cf. Lk. 17:1 f.
²⁴ Jn. 16:20 is designed to show this to the disciples. God will expose both their weeping at the death of Jesus and the world's rejoicing, since both the disciples and the κόσμος overlook the fact that God is for Jesus the → πατήρ, and they thus completely misunderstand the situation created by His death. This death is neither meaningless nor is it a righteous judgment. In God's plan for Jesus it is a necessary part of the way to His public demonstration as the Son (cf. Jn. 17:1 f.).
²⁵ Cf. the material par. in Jer. 22:10.
κ λ α υ θ μ ό ς. ¹ Cf. also 'Ιερ. 9:9 'Α (LXX κοπετός).

κλαυθμοῦ καὶ νηστειῶν καὶ προπτώσεως. In these and other instances [2] κλαυθμός denotes readiness to submit to God's will in the assurance that He wills only that which is to the salvation of His people.

In the NT κλαυθμός occurs in the literal sense at Mt. 2:18 (quoting Jer. 31:15) and Ac. 20:37. Elsewhere it is found only in the phrase ἐκεῖ ἔσται ὁ κλαυθμὸς καὶ ὁ βρυγμὸς τῶν ὀδόντων (Mt. 8:12; 13:42, 50; 22:13; 24:51; 25:30; Lk. 13:28). The formula describes the fate of those who receive the summons to the joy of God's kingdom but who do not come to partake of it. [3] The twofold article forbids us to see in it an extravagant expression of the painful, bitter or even embittered feelings of those who are thus excluded. The specific use of κλαίειν (→ 722) in similar contexts gives content here to this definite κλαυθμός. It implies the mortal terror which God's self-revelation entails for those who thus far have more or less made God in their own image. The terror is at the frivolously rejected goodness of God which is now irretrievably lost. Hence we read not only of the κλαυθμός of those excluded but also of their βρυγμὸς τῶν ὀδόντων, [4] which suggests the despairing remorse that shakes their whole body.

The sentence ἐκεῖ ἔσται ὁ κλαυθμὸς καὶ ὁ βρυγμὸς τῶν ὀδόντων is regarded by many [5] as an addition of Matthew to the older tradition. [6] But this cannot be proved. The idea that the ungodly will at that time sing songs of lamentation (קִינִים!) is also found in Rabb. Judaism. [7]

Rengstorf

---

† κλάω, † κλάσις, † κλάσμα

Contents : A. General Usage. B. Breaking of Bread as a Term for the Lord's Supper. C. The Lord's Supper in Primitive Christianity : 1. Sources : a. Review ; b. Appraisal ; 2. The Last Supper : a. The Passover Setting ; b. The Jewish Passover of the Time ;

---

[2] E.g., Mal. 2:13; Is. 38:3 (→ 723). Important, too, is Job 30:31: ὁ δὲ ψαλμός μου εἰς κλαυθμὸν ἐμοί, "my praise is turned to invocation of God with weeping."
[3] Cf. Schl. Mt., 280 on 8:12.
[4] → I, 641 f.
[5] E.g., Bultmann Trad., 352.
[6] As a par. to Mt. 8:12, Lk. 13:28 does not create any difficulties.
[7] S. Nu. § 103 on 12:8 (ed. K. G. Kuhn [1934], 271 f.). Cf. also Job 30:31 (→ n. 2), where Job's κλαυθμός expresses his inner grief at seeing himself rejected by God like one of the ungodly.

κλάω κτλ. on A : Pass., Liddell-Scott, Cr.-Kö., Pr.-Bauer³, Moult.-Mill., *s.v.*; J. Jeremias, *Die Abendmahlsworte Jesu* (1935), 66 f. (with bibl., 10 ff.). On B : T. Schermann, "Das 'Brotbrechen' im Urchristentum," BZ, 8 (1910), 33 ff., 162 ff.; Wdt. Ag. on 2:42; Zn. Ag. on 2:42 ff. and 20:7; F. Cabrol, Art. *Fractio panis* in *Dictionn. d'archéologie chrétienne,* V, 2103 ff.; K. Völker, *Mysterium und Agape* (1927), 28 ff.; Jackson-Lake, I, 4 (1933), 28 f. On C : In general F. Loofs, Art. "Abendmahl," II, RE³, I, 38 ff., XXIII, 2 ff.; P. Drews, Art. "Eucharistie," *ibid.* V, 560 ff., XXIII, 432 ff.; F. Kattenbusch, Art. "Messe," *ibid.,* XII, 669 ff.; K. L. Schmidt, Art. "Abendmahl im NT," RGG², I, 6 ff.; H. Lietzmann, Art. "Abendmahl, liturgiegeschichtlich," *ibid.,* I, 31 ff.; R. A. Falconer-D. Stone, Art. "Lord's Supper," DCG, II, 63 ff.; G. H. Clayton, Art. "Eucharist" and "Love-feast," DAC, I, 373 ff., 717 f. NT Theologies : H. J. Holtzmann² (1911), esp. I, 364 ff., II, 200 ff., 558 ff. (older

c. Traces of the Passover in the Tradition ; 3. The Meaning of the Sayings of Jesus at the Supper : a. The Groups of Sayings in the Oldest Texts ; b. The Passover Sayings ; c. The Sayings concerning the Bread and Wine ; d. Alterations and Additions in Paul and the Synoptists ; e. Maranatha ; 4. The Lord's Supper in Paul : a. Relation to the Lord's Supper of the Primitive Community ; b. The Lord's Supper according to 1 C. 11 and 10 ; c. Pauline Thinking in respect of the Lord's Supper ; 5. The Lord's Supper in John : a. The Discourse in Jn. 6 ; b. John's Understanding of the Lord's Supper ; 6. The Lord's Supper in the Post-Apostolic Age : a. Didache ; b. Ignatius ; c. Apocryphal Acts.

A. General Usage.

1. κλάω, "to break," "to break off," e.g., shoots or branches from a tree, Hom. Od., 6, 128 : ἐκ πυκινῆς δ᾽ ὕλης πτόρθον κλάσε, R. 11:19 f. vl.; Ez. 17:4 ᾽Α : τὰ ἄκρα τῆς

---

bibl.); H. Weinel[4] (1928), esp. 64 ff., 157 f., 203 ff., 246 ff., 468; P. Feine[6] (1934), esp. 117 ff., 315 ff., 385 ff. (more recent bibl.); Schl. Gesch. d. Chr., 485 ff.; Theol. d. Ap., 39 ff., 519 ff., 558; T. Zahn, Grundriss d. nt.lichen Theologie (1928), 53 ff.; F. Büchsel (1935), 56 ff., 132 f. From the rich specialised literature, esp. A. Jülicher, "Zur Gesch. d. Abendmahlsfeier in d. ältesten Kirche," in Theol. Abh. C. v. Weizsäcker gewidmet (1892), 217 ff.; A. Merx, Die vier kanonischen Ev. nach ihrem ältesten bekannten Texte, II, 1 (1902), 371 ff., II, 2 (1905), 416 ff.; K. G. Goetz, Die heutige Abendmahlsfrage in ihrer geschichtlichen Entwicklung[2] (1907); Das Abendmahl eine Diatheke Jesu oder sein letztes Gleichnis? (1920); Der Ursprung des kirchlichen Abendmahls (Rektoratsprogramm Basel, 1929); "Der Einfluss des kirchlichen Brauches auf die Abendmahlstexte des NT" in Vom Wesen u. Wandel d. Kirche (Zum 70. Geburtstag von E. Vischer) (1935), 21 ff.; R. Seeberg, Das Abendmahl im NT[1] (1905), [2](1907) = Biblische Zeit- u. Streitfragen, I, 2;[3] in R. Seeberg, Aus Religion u. Geschichte, II (1909), 293 ff. (quoted as R. Seeberg, Abendmahl); Lehrbuch der Dogmengeschichte, I[3] (1922), 164 ff.; Christl. Dogmatik, II (1925), 443 ff.; Wellh. Mk.[2], 108 ff.; Einleitung in die drei ersten Ev.[2] (1911), 130 ff.; W. Heitmüller, "Taufe u. Abendmahl im Urchristentum," Religionsgeschichtliche Volksbücher, I, 22/23 (1911), 39 ff.; G. Loeschcke, "Zur Frage nach d. Einsetzung u. Herkunft d. Eucharistie," ZwTh, 54 (1912), 193 ff.; G. Beer, Pesachim (1912), 92 ff.; A. Seeberg, "Das Abendmahl" in R. Seeberg, D. Alfred Seeberg ... Arbeiten aus seinem Nachlass (1916), 91 ff.; J. Weiss, Urchr. (1917), 41 ff., 502 ff.; B. Frischkopf, "Die neuesten Erörterungen über die Abendmahlsfrage," Nt.-liche Abh., IX, 4/5 (1921); E. Meyer, Ursprung u. Anfänge des Christentums, I (1921), 173 ff., III (1923), 229 ff.; G. Dalman, Jesus-Jeschua (1922), 80 ff., 98 ff. (Dalman, I); Ergänzungen u. Verbesserungen zu Jesus-Jeschua (1929) (Dalman, II), 8 ff.; Clemen, 174 ff.; H. Lietzmann, Messe u. Herrenmahl (1926), 211 ff., 249 ff.; A. Oepke, "Ursprung u. ursprünglicher Sinn des Abendmahls im Lichte der neuesten Forschung," AELKZ, 59 (1926), 12 ff., 37 ff., 54 ff., 79 ff.; C. A. Anderson Scott, Christianity acc. to St. Paul (1927), 181 ff.; K. Völker, Mysterium u. Agape (1927); Str.-B., IV, 41 ff.: "Das Passahmahl" ; F. Hamm, "Die liturgischen Einsetzungsberichte, im Sinne vergleichender Liturgieforschung untersucht," Liturgiegeschichtl. Quellen u. Forschungen, 23 (1928); A. Loisy, "Les origines de la cène eucharistique" in Congrès d'Histoire du Christianisme, I (1928), 77 ff.; H. Huber, Das Herrnmahl (Diss. Bern) (1929); G. H. C. Macgregor, Eucharistic Origins (1929); A. Schweitzer, Das Abendmahl im Zusammenhang mit dem Leben Jesu ..., Heft 1[2] (1929), [1](1901); Die Mystik des Ap. Pls. (1930), 222 ff. etc.; C. N. Moody, The Purpose of Jesus in the First Three Gospels (Bruce Lectures, 1929), 114 ff. etc.; H. v. Soden, "Sakrament und Ethik bei Paulus," Marburger Theol. Studien, 1 (R. Otto Festgruss, 1931), 1 ff.; H. D. Wendland, Die Eschatologie des Reiches Gottes bei Jesus (1931), 187 ff.; W. Goossens, Les Origines de l'eucharistie (1931); G. van der Leeuw, Phänomenologie der Religion (1933), 341 ff.; R. Otto, Reich Gottes und Menschensohn (1934), 223 ff.; O. Gauss, "Die nt.liche Grundlegung d. Lehre vom Heiligen Abendmahl" in Monatsschrift f. Pastoraltheologie, 30 (1934), 176-185, 201-212, 256-264; J. Jeremias, "Das Brotbrechen beim Passahmahl u. Mk. 14:22 par.," ZNW, 33 (1934), 203 f.; Die Abendmahlsworte Jesu (1935) (Jeremias Abendmahlsworte); M. Goguel, Das Leben Jesu (1934), 295 ff.; R. Hupfeld, Die Abendmahlsfeier (1935), 46 ff.; L. Fendt, Die Abendmahlsnot des Gegenwartsmenschen (1936), 17 ff.; W. Niesel, "Das Abendmahl u. die Opfer des alten Bundes," Theol. Aufsätze K. Barth zum 50. Geburtstag (1936), 178 ff.; J. Leipoldt, Der Gottesdienst der ältesten Kirche jüdisch? griechisch? christlich? (1937).

ἁπαλότητος ἔκλασεν, esp. the superfluous shoots of the vine, Longus, 3, 29 (Erotici Scriptores Graeci, ed. R. Hercher, I [1858], 301): ἐγὼ ... οἶδα καλῶς ... κλᾶν ἄμπελον, Gal. De Sanitate Tuenda, 2 (ed. Kühn, VI [1823], 134): κλᾶν ἀμπέλους. Theophr. De Causis Plantarum, I, 15, 1 etc.; *v.* also Epigr. Graec., 538, 5 f.: ματέρι πένθος ἔφυς, λύπα πατρί· [οἶ]α δὲ δένδρου | κλῶν [νῦ]ν ἐκλάσθης ἔ[κτ]ομος εἰς Ἀίδαν. In the LXX κλᾶν ἄρτον for פָּרַס לֶחֶם, Jer. 16:7: οὐ μὴ κλασθῇ ἄρτος, Lam. 4:4 Α : νήπια ἤτησαν ἄρτον, καὶ ὁ κλῶν (διακλῶν B א) οὐκ ἔστιν αὐτοῖς [1] (the expression is not found in secular Gk. [2] or in Philo or Joseph. [3]). "To break," "to shatter," "to destroy," Ἰερ. 27:23 B; Ju. 9:53 B; 4 Macc. 9:14; Jos. Bell., 5, 407: (God) τοὺς ... Ἀσσυρίους ... ἔκλασεν, *ibid.*, 2, 327: πνιγόμενοι ... καὶ κλώμενοι πλήθει τῶν ἐπιβαινόντων ἠφανίζοντο (cf. 152). P. Lips., I, 39, 12 f.: τύψας με [ἀν]ελεῶς κλά[σας] καὶ χεῖράν μου. Fig. at ψ 146:3 Σ : ὁ ἰώμενος τοὺς κεκλασμένους τὴν καρδίαν; Philo Gig., 43 : αὐτομολῆσαι πρὸς τὴν ἄνανδρον καὶ κεκλασμένην ἡδονήν; Sacr. AC, 21: κεκλασμένῳ τῷ βαδίσματι ὑπὸ τρυφῆς τῆς ἄγαν καὶ χλιδῆς, Jos. Bell., 3, 187: κλάσαι τὴν ἐλπίδα ταύτην αὐτῷ προαιρούμενος, Jos. Vit., 212 : ἐκλάσθην πρὸς ἔλεον.

κλάσις means "breaking," Plat. Tim., 43d : πάσας ... κλάσεις καὶ διαφορὰς τῶν κύκλων ἐμποιεῖν, esp. (→ *supra*) of the breaking off of luxuriant shoots of the vine, Theophr. De Causis Plantarum, II, 14, 4 : αἱ ... κλάσεις τῶν ἀμπέλων, cf. III, 14, 1 etc. This word does not occur in the LXX, nor is it anywhere in Jewish-Greek literature a substantive for κλᾶν ἄρτον (→ *supra*). In Philo κλάσις φωνῆς is a musical term for modulation of the voice, Deus Imm., 25; Poster. C., 106, Sacr. AC, 23. [4]

κλάσμα means "fragment," inventory of the temple at Delos (C. Michel, *Recueil d'inscr. grecques* [1900], 833, 39 ff.): στεφάνων κλάσματα χρυσᾶ ... στλεγγίδων κλάσματα καὶ ἄλλα παντοδαπὰ χρυσία κτλ., Ps.-Xenoph. Cyn., 10, 5 : ἔσται δὲ καὶ τοῖς κυνηγέταις πολλὰ δῆλα αὐτοῦ, ἐν μὲν τοῖς μαλακοῖς τῶν χωρίων τὰ ἴχνη, ἐν δὲ τοῖς λασίοις τῆς ὕλης κλάσματα, Ju. 9:53 Α : κλάσμα μύλου, cf. 2 Βασ. 11:21 f.; Diod. S., XVII, 13, 4 : οἱ δὲ κλάσματι δόρατος ἐρειδόμενοι συνήντων τοῖς ἐπιφερομένοις, cf. Plut. Tib. Gracch., 19 (I, 833b); Vett. Val., II, 36 (p. 110, 31) ; Test. Sol. 5:13 : μετὰ κλάσματος στύρακος (lance). Esp. a "bite" or "piece" of bread, Ju. 19:5 Α ; Ez. 13:19, cake 1 Βασ. 30:12, meat-offering, Lv. 2:6; 6:14 (Heb. פַּת or פִּתּוֹת) cf. Anth. Pal., VI, 304 (Phanias): αἴσιον αὐδάσεις με τὸν οὐ κρέας, ἀλλὰ θάλασσαν | τιμῶντα ψαφαροῦ κλάσματος εἰς ἀπάταν, *ibid.*, 11, 153 (Lucillius): ἂν δὲ παραρπάζῃς ἄρτους καὶ κλάσματ' ἀναιδῶς ...

2. The word group is used in the NT of the breaking of bread or bread thus broken in pieces. There was an ancient custom in Palestine (Jer. 16:7; Lam. 4:4) of breaking bread with the hands rather than cutting it with a knife. At meals, whether ordinary family meals, special meals with guests or ritual feasts, e.g., the Passover or the beginning of the Sabbath, the head of the house gives thanks,[5] then breaks bread and hands the pieces to those who sit at table with him (→ I, 477).[6] The breaking of bread is simply a customary and necessary part of the

---

[1] At Is. 58:7 the LXX has διαθρύπτειν τὸν ἄρτον for פָּרַס לֶחֶם.

[2] Cf. Schermann, *op. cit.*, 39 f.; Jeremias Abendmahlsworte, 66, n. 6. The exception in the Paris magic pap. (Preis. Zaub., IV, 1392 ff. [p. 118]): καταλιπὼν ἀπὸ τοῦ ἄρτου, οὗ ἐσθίεις, ὀλίγον καὶ κλάσας ποίησον εἰς ἑπτὰ ψωμούς, is not important because the usage stands under strong Jewish Hellenistic and Christian influence.

[3] In the sense of "break to distribute," Jos. Ant., 10, 244 : φαρές· καὶ τοῦτο κλάσμα δηλοῖ καθ' Ἑλλάδα γλῶτταν· κλάσει τοιγαροῦν σου τὴν βασιλείαν καὶ Μήδοις αὐτὴν καὶ Πέρσαις διανεμεῖ (cf. Da. 5:28). *V.* on this pt. Schl. Mt., 465.

[4] Cf. on this pt. L. Cohn-I. Heinemann, *Schriften d. jüd.-hell. Lit.*, 4 (1923), 30, n. 3.

[5] Cf. bBer., 39a b, 47a.

[6] Cf. Str.-B., I, 687; II, 619 f.; IV, 70, 621 ff.; G. Beer, *op. cit.*, 96; E. D. Goldschmidt, *Die Pessach-Haggada* (1936), 27, 70.

preparation for eating together. It initiates the sharing of the main course in every meal. [7] Thus Jesus faithfully follows the custom as head of the house and as host when He breaks bread for the multitude which is miraculously fed (Mk. 6:41 and par.; [8] 8:6 and par., cf. v. 19), for the disciples at the Last Supper (1 C. 11:24; Mk. 14:22 and par.), or for the two whom He joins on the way to Emmaus (Lk. 24:30, 35). Cf. also Paul in Ac. 20:11; 27:35; [9] and cf. 1 C. 10:16. It is from this breaking of bread at the commencement of the common meal in Palestinian Judaism [10] that the common meal of the members of the primitive community in Jerusalem receives its name, Ac. 2:42: ἡ κλάσις τοῦ ἄρτου, v. 46: κλᾶν ἄρτον, also 20:7: the evening meal of Paul and his companions with the Christians of Troas. At Mk. 6:43 and par.; 8:8 and par. (cf. v. 19 f.); Jn. 6:12 f. the κλάσματα are the fragments of broken bread which according to custom [11] Jesus causes to be gathered up when the meal is over.

B. Breaking of Bread as a Term for the Lord's Supper.

In the NT, as in contemporary Judaism, breaking of bread at the beginning of a meal is not a cultic act, not even in connection with thanksgiving or praise (בְּרָכָה), the grace of the righteous (→ II, 760, 764). This is true in Mk. 6:41 and par., 8:6 and par.; Lk. 24:30, 35; [12] Ac. 27:35. [13] Even in the accounts of the institution of the Lord's Supper in 1 C. 11:24; Mk. 14:22 and par., and of the common meals of the first communities in Ac. 2:42, 46; 20:7, 11; 1 C. 10:16, the breaking of bread has no particular significance as an isolated act; [14] in these meals as in others it is simply a part of the accepted introductory process. The technical use of κλᾶν ἄρτον and κλάσις τοῦ ἄρτου for the common meals of primitive Christianity is to be construed as the description of a common meal in terms of the opening action,

---

[7] Zn. Mt. on 26:26; Dalman, I, 125 f. As a term the breaking of bread may cover both the distribution and the preceding grace, cf. bBer., 46a, 47a; jBer., 10a, 12a. But to suppose that κλᾶν thus has for Paul the significance of sacrificial offering: "to bless in sacrifice, to consecrate" (K. G. Goetz, Die heutige Abendmahlsfrage, 186 ff., Das Abendmahl eine Diatheke Jesu ...?, 14) is to go far beyond the usage of פָּרַס.

[8] Mk. 6:41 and Lk. 9:16 have κατακλᾶν as a synonym of κλᾶν, cf. Ez. 19:12; Job 5:4 Σ.

[9] V. Theophylact. on Ac. 27:35 (MPG, 125, 836d): κλῶμεν τὸν ἄρτον ἐπὶ τὸ μετασχεῖν τροφῆς, and Jeremias Abendmahlsworte, 47, n. 5.

[10] S. Krauss, Talmudische Archäologie, I (1910), 104 f., III (1912), 51. R. Otto, op. cit., 264 is wrong here.

[11] Cf. Str.-B., I, 687; IV, 625 ff.

[12] On ἐγνώσθη αὐτοῖς ἐν τῇ κλάσει τοῦ ἄρτου cf. linguistically Bl.-Debr. § 220, 2 and Jn. 13:35, materially → n. 7; → II, 762; Str.-B., IV, 74; A. Seeberg, op. cit., 107. For a different, though less satisfactory, view cf. J. Jeremias, Jesus als Weltvollender, 78 and Abendmahlsworte, 47, n. 4.

[13] Cf. also the account in the Gospel of the Hebrews of the appearance of the risen Lord to James, who had sworn not to eat bread from the last meal with Jesus to the resurrection: tulit panem et benedixit, ac fregit et dedit Jacobo iusto et dixit ei: frater mi, comede panem tuum, quia resurrexit filius hominis a dormientibus (Hier., De viris illustribus, 2), and also the παράδοσις of a meal of Jesus with the disciples in prison in Epiphanius (Fr. of an epistle, ed. K. Holl, Gesammelte Aufsätze z. Kirchengeschichte, 2 [1928], 206, lines 19 ff.): ἔκλασεν ἄρτον ψιλὸν καὶ συνεγεύσατο μετ' αὐτῶν ἐν τῇ φυλακῇ.

[14] The often repeated idea that the breaking of bread symbolises the slaying of the Lord's body is a theologumenon alien to the NT which appears for the first time in the impossible addition of κλώμενον to τὸ σῶμα τὸ ὑπὲρ ὑμῶν, 1 C.11:24 ℵ Gd. To follow Goetz, Die heutige Abendmahlsfrage, 155 f., 187 f. and Das Abendmahl eine Diatheke Jesu?, 16 ff. in referring τὸ ὑπὲρ ὑμῶν κλώμενον to τοῦτο (sc. the bread) is to offer a defence of κλώμενον which does violence both to language and to the tradition.

the breaking of bread (→ 728). Hence the phrase is used for the ordinary table fellowship of members of the first community each day in their homes (Ac. 2:42, 46), and also for the common meals of the Gentile Christian communities (Ac. 20:7, cf. 1 C. 10:16). In the former table fellowship is one of the forms in which the early Christian sense of fellowship finds expression. It has no liturgical character, but is full of religious content because of the recollection of the table fellowship which Jesus had with His followers during His earthly ministry (Ac. 2:46 : μετελάμβανον τροφῆς ἐν ἀγαλλιάσει καὶ ἀφελότητι καρδίας). In the latter, however, within the context of the Pauline mission, [15] the breaking of bread, which is on the Lord's Day in Ac. 20:7, is a cultic meal, elsewhere described by Paul (1 C. 11:20) as → κυριακὸν δεῖπνον (→ II, 34) (cf. Ac. 20:7: συνηγμένων ἡμῶν κλάσαι ἄρτον with 1 C. 11:33 : συνερχόμενοι εἰς τὸ φαγεῖν = v. 20 : συνερχομένων ὑμῶν ... κυριακὸν δεῖπνον φαγεῖν). As we learn from Did., 14, 1: κατὰ κυριακὴν δὲ κυρίου συναχθέντες κλάσατε ἄρτον (cf. the designation of the Lord's Supper as κλάσμα in 9, 3 f.) and Ign. Eph., 20, 2 : συνέρχεσθε ... ἕνα ἄρτον κλῶντες, the ancient Palestinian term "breaking of bread" is one of the titles, perhaps the oldest, for the new liturgical meal of fellowship in primitive Christianity, i.e., the Lord's Supper. [16]

Both the use and the title continue in the Church. Cf. Ps. Clem. Hom., 14, 1: τὸν ἄρτον ἐπ᾽ εὐχαριστίᾳ κλάσας, 11, 36; Act. Pt. (TU, II, 9, 1 [1903], 10; Act. Pl. et Thecl., 5; Act. Joh., 106 : τὴν κλάσιν τοῦ ἄρτου (p. 203, 17, Bonnet); 109 : κλῶντες τὸν ἄρτον τοῦτον, 110; 72; 85; [17] Act. Thom., 27; 29; 50; 121; 133; 158; [18] Epiph. Haer., 37, 5, 7 (Ophites). [19] But the favourite name for the Lord's Supper soon becomes → εὐχαριστία (Did., 9, 1; Ign. Eph., 13, 1; Phld., 4; Sm., 8, 1; Just. Apol., 66, 1 etc.), which later became a tt. in the Gk. Church. In later liturgies the breaking of bread became an independent rite which was accompanied by prayers and which was a symbol of the violent death of Jesus. [20]

C. The Lord's Supper in Primitive Christianity.

1. Sources.

a. Review. Along with the four accounts in 1 C. 11:23-25; Mk. 14:22-25; Mt. 26:26-29 and Lk. 22:15-20, we have also to consider 1 C. 10 and 11; 1 C. 16:20b,

---

[15] The setting of the we-passage Ac. 20:5 ff. is the same as that of 1 C.

[16] Jeremias Abendmahlsworte, 47 f. suggests that breaking of bread in Lk. is a title designed to conceal the *arcanum* of the cultic meal from non-Christians. Against this we must set the non-cultic use of κλᾶν or κλάσις τοῦ ἄρτου in Lk. 24:30, 35; Ac. 27:35, and the improbability that Luke, a Gentile Christian, would adopt a Palestinian Jewish expression.

[17] The presence of breaking of bread in burial meals finds an analogy in the representation of the *fractio panis* in the Priscilla catacomb at Rome, cf. J. Wilpert, Fractio panis (1895), and *Die Malereien der Katakomben Roms* (1903), 285 ff., but also the explanation in Schermann, *op. cit.*, 178 and H. Leclercq, art. "Agape," *Dictionn. d'archéologie chrétienne*, I, 797 f. It should be noted, however, that burial meals (on the model of the Roman *parentalia* ?) usually took the form of celebrations of the Lord's Supper cf. Drews, RE[3], V, 571 f. No connection can be established between the Lord's Supper and pre-Christian burial meals, cf. against Leclercq, 775 ff., K. Völker, *op. cit.*, 48 f.

[18] *V.* R. A. Lipsius, *Die apokryphen Apostelgeschichten,* I (1883), 338 ff.

[19] Cf. also F. J. Dölger, ΙΧΘΥΣ, II (1922), 536 ff. and Index, *s.v.* κλάσαι τὸν ἄρτον; *Antike u. Christentum,* I (1929), 29 f.

[20] Cf. the material in Schermann, 182 f., cf. 33 ff. and Cabrol, *op. cit.*, 2105 ff., also B. Stephanides, "Ein Überrest d. alten Agapen in der gr. Kirche," ZKG, 3, F. 3 (1933), 610 ff.

22b; Ac. 20:7, 11; Jn. 6, especially v. 51 ff. (→ 4. and 5.),[21] and outside the NT some passages in Did., Ign. and Just. (on these → 6.). Ac. 2:42, 46 refers to the daily fellowship of the first Christians in Jerusalem (→ 730) and has nothing to do with liturgical celebration of the Lord's Supper, though the primitive community may well have celebrated the Lord's Supper as the Christian Passover each year on the evening of the 14th Nisan.[22]

b. Appraisal. In the accounts of the institution[23] there are three types, that of Paul, that of Mark (Matthew) and that of Luke. The Pauline text is the oldest and in 1 C. 11:23 claims to represent a tradition which goes back directly to Jesus.[24] It agrees with the Markan text in its main features and may be traced back to an original Aramaic form of great antiquity which is part of the original tradition of the passion story.[25] To this original belong the features shared by Paul and Mark : 1. the narrative setting, that Jesus took bread, prayed, broke it and spoke an interpretative word, and that He then took the cup, blessed it and spoke an interpretative word ; 2. the formulated words of interpretation in respect of the bread and wine ; and probably 3. a saying of eschatological content, cf. Mk. 14:25 and 1 C. 11:26. It should be noted that the word of interpretation is the same in respect of the bread : This is my body, but that there is wide variation in Mk. in respect of the cup : This is my blood of the new (divine) order, as compared with Paul : This cup is the new (divine) order by virtue of my blood.[26] The autonomous form in Paul as compared with the first saying could not easily be invented and is thus an argument in favour of its originality.[27] Mark,[28] on the other hand, balances the two sayings by assimilating that about the cup to Ex. 24:8. The lesser or greater additions to the original in Paul, Mark and Matthew[29] do not disturb the tradition ; in some cases they bear powerful witness to ideas and practices which clustered around the Lord's Supper even in the early apostolic period, though in each case we have to ask whether they offer an authentic interpretation of the institution of

---

[21] We are not considering passages like 1 C. 12:13; 1 Pt. 2:3 (→ I, 676); Hb. 13:10 (→ III, 183); Rev. 3:20 (→ II, 34); Jn. 15:1 ff. (→ I, 342); 21:9 ff.; 1 Jn. 5:6 (→ I, 175), which have been incorrectly or very doubtfully linked with the Lord's Supper.

[22] Cf. T. Zahn, Forschungen z. Geschichte d. nt.lichen Kanons, 4 (1891), 283 ff.; Einleitung in d. NT³, II (1907), 463 f., 473, 518 ff., 532; Grundriss d. nt.lichen Theologie (1928), 54; Zn. Ag. on 2:42, 46. So also Afrahat, cf. P. Schwen, Afrahat, seine Person u. sein Verständnis d. Christentums (1907), 106.

[23] Cf. esp. Kl. Mk., Mt. and Lk., ad loc.; Lietzmann, op. cit., 213 ff.; M. Dibelius, Die Formgeschichte des Evangeliums² (1933), 207 ff.; Otto, op. cit., 223 ff.; Jeremias Abendmahlsworte, 42 ff.

[24] → II, 171, 172 f.; also Jeremias, 72 ff.

[25] That the account of the institution is not an aetiological legend but belongs to the context of the passion story is shown by the time reference in 1 C. 11:23, 25, cf. J. Finegan, Die Überlieferung der Leidens- u. Auferstehungsgeschichte Jesu (1934), 67 f.

[26] → I, 174; II, 133.

[27] So also Kattenbusch RE³, XII, 670; M. Dibelius, op. cit., 208; Huber, op. cit., 49 f.; cf. J. Behm, Der Begriff διαθήκη im NT (1912), 60 and bibl. in n. 2. Without good reason Mk. is often regarded as the older, and it is still given priority in Jeremias Abendmahlsworte, 59 f., 64.

[28] And even more strongly the short form in Just. Apol., 66, 3 : τοῦτό ἐστι τὸ αἷμά μου.

[29] Mk. (Mt.): intimation of the situation by ἐσθιόντων αὐτῶν; distribution of bread and wine to the disciples : λάβετε (φάγετε); all (are to) drink of the cup ; expansion of the second saying by adding τὸ ἐκχυννόμενον ὑπὲρ πολλῶν (τὸ περὶ πολλῶν ἐκχυννόμενον εἰς ἄφεσιν ἁμαρτιῶν). Pl.: addition to the first saying of τὸ ὑπὲρ ὑμῶν; the repeated command : τοῦτο ποιεῖτε (+ ὁσάκις ἐὰν πίνητε in the second saying) εἰς τὴν ἐμὴν ἀνάμνησιν.

Jesus. The genuine Lucan text 22:15-19a D it [30] differs strikingly from that of Paul and Mk. both by abbreviation and by expansion. On the one side, it ends the account of the Lord's Supper with the words : This is my body. But on the other it adds an earlier section which presents the last Passover of Jesus with His disciples (v. 15, 17) in the context of eschatological expectation of consummation in the kingdom of God (v. 16, 18). Luke's deviations from the Markan original are both deliberate. He describes what took place at the institution only to the point where initiates would know what it was about but pagan readers would not be allowed to look into the innermost sanctuary of the Gospel. [31] On the other hand, he describes concretely the Passover, which is only briefly indicated in Mark. As often in his historical work, Luke in vv. 15-18 offers an ancient independent tradition [32] from a Palestinian Jewish source which is designed to supplement the account in Mk. This credible tradition confirms the fact that Jesus uttered at the Last Supper the eschatological saying of Mk. 14:25, and that He uttered it prior to the eucharistic sayings in the narrower sense. [33] It thus gives us a more concrete picture of what took place at this last solemn meal which Jesus celebrated with the inner circle of His disciples.

2. The Last Supper.

a. Traces of the Passover Setting. In all probability the Last Supper was the Passover. Certain decisive features in the oldest account are satisfactorily explained only on the assumption that the external forms of the Passover were observed at the meal. The objections which have been brought are too slight to throw any doubt on the Passover setting of the table fellowship which Jesus here enjoyed with His disciples. [34]

b. The Jewish Passover of the Time. According to Jewish sources, especially Pes., 10, and features of the Jewish rite confirmed by the NT, the course of the Passover at this period was as follows. [35] The meal was to take place on the evening of the 14th Nisan in Jerusalem. At least 10 persons had normally to be

---

[30] For the textual problem cf. the literature in n. 23. I see no reason to dismiss vv. 17 and 19a as not original (so K. L. Schmidt, RGG², I, 8).

[31] Cf. Zn. Lk., ad loc.; Schl. Theol. d. Ap., 520; Jeremias Abendmahlsworte, 45 ff.

[32] Cf. Bultmann Trad., 286, 300, 302; Schl. Lk., 420 f., cf. 137; Jeremias, 61 ff.; also W. Bussmann, Synoptische Studien, I (1925), 191 f.

[33] Cf. the illuminating note in Jeremias, 62 f.

[34] For detailed arguments, which we need not repeat here, cf. esp. Merx, op. cit., II, 2, 416 ff.; D. Chwolson, Das letzte Passahmahl Christi (1908); Dalman, I, 80 ff.; 98 ff.; II, 8 ff.; Str.-B., IV, 41 ff.; II, 812 ff.; Jeremias Abendmahlsworte, 5 ff. For the weak counter-arguments cf. Wellh. Mk., 108 ff.; Einleitung, 130 ff.; Beer, op. cit., 92 ff.; Lietzmann, op. cit., 211 f.; Huber, op. cit., 49, 71, 79 ff.; Hupfeld, op. cit., 54 ff. It is most unlikely that the Last Supper was a Sabbath Kiddush meal (so F. Spitta, Zur Geschichte u. Literatur des Urchristentums, I [1893], 247; Drews, RE³, V, 563; G. H. Box, "The Jewish Antecedents of the Eucharist," JThSt, 3 [1902], 357 ff., and more recently Lietzmann, op. cit., 202 ff., cf. also Otto, 240 f. and Büchsel, op. cit., 56). Equally improbable is the suggestion that it was a Chabura meal (so Lietzmann, 228 and Otto, 235 ff.). Cf. Jeremias Abendmahlsworte, 18 ff. Again, there is no connection between the Last Supper and the common meals of the Essenes (cf. Jos. Bell., 2, 129-133, also Bousset-Gressm., 460 f.; W. Bauer, Art. "Essener," Pauly-W. Suppl., IV [1924], 424 etc.).

[35] Cf. Merx, II, 2, 416 ff.; Beer, op. cit., 60 ff.; Str.-B., IV, 56 ff.; Jeremias, 40. On the prayers cf. also E. Freiherr v. d. Goltz, "Tischgebete u. Abendmahlsgebete," TU, II, 14, 2b (1905), 5 ff.

present. When the meal had been prepared, those participating took their places at the table. [36] The head of the house opened the feast with two blessings, first of the festival [37] and then of the wine : "Blessed be Thou, Yahweh our God, King of the world, who hast created the fruit of the vine." [38] Then the first cup was drunk. The food was then brought in, consisting of unleavened bread, bitter herbs, stewed fruit and roast lamb. [39] The son then asked what distinguished this night with its special customs and food from every other night. [40] The father answered by giving instruction concerning the redemption out of Egypt. Particular reference was made to the passing over ("because God passed over the houses of our fathers in Egypt"), to the unleavened bread ("because they were redeemed" so fast that there was no time for the dough to be leavened, cf. Dt. 16:3), [41] and to the bitter herbs ("because the Egyptians made the life of our fathers in Egypt bitter"). The miracles of the divine guidance from bondage to freedom were to be displayed to all who celebrated the festival together at table. "In every age man is under obligation to regard himself as if he had been delivered out of Egypt." "Hence it is our bounden duty to thank, to praise, to magnify, the glorify, to extol and to exalt the One ... who has redeemed us, and who has redeemed our fathers out of Egypt, and who has brought us to this night." Beyond the experience of salvation in past and present a glance full of eschatological longing was also directed to future salvation : "So may Yahweh, our God and the God of our fathers, cause us to enjoy the feasts that come in peace, glad of heart at the upbuilding of Thy city and rejoicing in Thy service ..., and we shall thank Thee with a new song for our redemption." [42] After singing the first part of the Hallel, which embraced Ps. 113-118, the second cup was drunk. Then the head of the house took bread and pronounced over it the blessing : "Blessed be Thou, Yahweh our God, King of the world, who hast caused bread to come forth out of the earth. [43] He then broke the bread in pieces and handed these to those who were at table, who ate them with bitter herbs and stewed fruit. Only then did the meal really begin with the eating of the Passover lamb, and this was not to extend beyond midnight. [44] When the meal was over, the head of the house blessed the third cup in a con-

---

[36] Pes., 10, 1.

[37] We do not have the exact form of the first blessing. A form for all festivals may be found in Str.-B., IV, 62 based on bBer., 49a.

[38] Pes., 10, 2. For the wording of the thanksgiving cf. Ber., 6, 1; bPes., 103a, 106a. The sequence of the blessing was a point of dispute between the schools of Shammai and Hillel, cf. Pes., 10, 2 (Str.-B., IV, 61); the school of Shammai put the blessing of the festival first (as above).

[39] Pes., 10, 3.

[40] Pes., 10, 4.

[41] Another ancient interpretation based on the "bread of affliction" of Dt. 16:3 may be found in Jos. Ant., II, 316 f. Cf. S. Dt., 130 on 16:3 (v. Jeremias, 23, n. 5), also the formula from the Yemenic Siddur : "Behold, the bread of affliction which our fathers ate who came out of Egypt. He who is hungry, let him come and eat ; he whose duty it is to keep the passover, let him come and discharge it" (v. Dalman, I, 127 f.). On the significance of the constituent parts of the meal as a fixed part of the Passover ritual, cf. Jeremias, 22 ff.

[42] Pes., 10, 4-6. On eschatological ideas in the Passover, v. also Dalman II, 9 f. The hope of redemption with which the Passover is celebrated is expressed in the words of the ancient Jewish Passover liturgy : "This year here, the next in the land of Israel ; this year as servants, next year as free men" (Dalman, I, 166 quoting Seder Rab Amram Gaon, I, 38).

[43] Cf. Ber., 6, 1.

[44] Pes., 10, 9.

cluding prayer of thanksgiving [45] — hence this cup was called כּוֹס שֶׁל בְּרָכָה, the cup of thanksgiving. [46] There then followed the second part of the Hallel and the fourth cup. [47]

c. Traces of the Passover in the Tradition. In the oldest parts of the account of the Last Supper the following features show that it was a Passover meal : 1. the drinking of wine (1 C. 11:25; Mk. 14:23, 25; Lk. 22:17), which would not apply to the daily table fellowship of Jesus and His disciples (Mt. 11:19 can hardly refer to this), and which the order of the Passover prescribed even for the poor ; [48] 2. the linking of interpretative sayings which draw their content from salvation history with constituent parts of the meal (1 C. 11:24 f.; Mk. 14:22 ff.); [49] 3. the eschatological glance from the meal to the kingdom of God (Mk. 14:25; Lk. 22:16, 18); 4. the express description of the meal as the Passover in Lk. 22:15, and the fact that the rite of v. 17 is the Passover rite. Confirmation may be found in the following aspects of the NT accounts and their established setting : 1. The meal takes place in the evening (1 C. 11:23; Mk. 14:17 and par.), which agrees with the Passover but not with common habit ; [50] 2. whereas on other evenings He left the city, for this meal He now remained in Jerusalem (Mk. 14:13 and par.) even though it was thronged with pilgrims, for the Passover had to be eaten in Jerusalem ; [51] 3. Jesus had the meal carefully prepared by two disciples (Mk. 14:12 ff.); 4. there is emphasis on reclining at table (Mk. 14:18 and par.; Jn. 13:23), which is not in keeping with the ordinary practice of Jesus and His age, but which the Passover ritual prescribes even for the "poor in Israel" ; [52] 5. Luke mentions two cups, that of 22:17 and that tacitly presupposed after v. 19, again in agreement with the Passover ritual ; 6. Jesus gives thanks for the cup and causes it to be passed round μετὰ τὸ δειπνῆσαι (1 C. 11:25), cf. the third cup at the Passover, and also the expression τὸ ποτήριον τῆς εὐλογίας in 1 C. 10:16, → II, 763; 7. the ἀνάμνησις of Jesus (→ I, 349) which acc. to 1 C. 11:24 f. is to take place at the Lord's Supper corresponds to the recollection of the Passover in the repetition of the Passover Haggada by the head of the house ; 8. at Mk. 14:26 and par. the meal ends with a hymn, and this reminds us of the concluding Hallel. [53] Even though some of these traits may have been added by the community, they still rest on the correct historical assumption that the Last Supper was a Passover meal.

In the early Christian tradition there is no reference to the Paschal lamb which was the main feature of the Passover. But this does not invalidate the Paschal character of the Last Supper, as is shown by a consideration of the words which Jesus spoke in the course of the evening.

---

[45] Pes., 10, 7.

[46] This name is also given to any cup over which the long thanksgiving is pronounced after a festal meal, cf. Dalman, I, 138; Str.-B., IV, 628.

[47] Pes., 10, 7. It is uncertain whether there was this fourth cup in the time of Jesus.

[48] Pes., 10, 1. Cf. Jeremias, 21 f.

[49] Jeremias, 22 f.

[50] Jub. 49:12 etc. Cf. Oepke, op. cit., 58; Jeremias, 16 f.

[51] Cf. Dalman, I, 99; Jeremias, 14 f.

[52] Pes., 10, 1. Cf. Jeremias, 17 ff. → ἀνάκειμαι, 654 f.

[53] Cf. Dalman, I, 120 ff.; Str.-B., IV, 75 f.; Jeremias, 22.

3. The Meaning of the Sayings of Jesus at the Supper. [54]

a. The Groups of Sayings in the Oldest Texts. The sayings attested by the oldest texts (→ 730 f.) fall into two groups : those which concern the Passover now and in the future (Lk. 22:15 ff.; Mk. 14:25); and those which interpret the bread and wine (1 C. 11:24 f.; Mk. 14:22 ff. [Mt. 26:26 ff.]; Lk. 22:19a). In the context of the Passover ritual the sayings in the first group are linked with the opening blessings of the festival and the first cup (→ 733). [55] The latter occur before and after the main meal, and are also attached to the customary blessings, the saying about the bread on the occasion of the distribution of the broken bread, and that about the cup at the end with the sharing of the third cup. [56]

b. The Passover Sayings. The very first Passover saying (Lk. 22:15 f.) sounds the double note which characterises this feast of Jesus with the disciples, namely, joy at the fellowship of this sacred festal day and the sense of approaching death, the solemnity of parting and the glad certainty of coming consummation. This is the last Passover in which Jesus shares in recollection of the saving acts of God in history ; only in the divine banquet of the last time, which brings the fulfilment of salvation (→ II, 34, 695), will it be renewed for Him in its perfect form. How strongly this eschatological thought fills Jesus may be seen from its repetition in the second Passover saying (parallel to v. 16) in Lk. 22:18 and par., which is connected with the wine in the cup and which again indicates the dividing line which Jesus sees to be drawn for Himself between past and present, between the celebration of redemption now and in the future. He will no more drink of the festal wine ; He will no more partake of the Passover. This implies that the disciples will. He knows and desires that they should hold table fellowship in the future. That they will repeat this without Him is just as self-evidently presupposed in the Passover sayings of Jesus as that they will again be united with Him in the consummating banquet. [57]

c. The Sayings concerning the Bread and Wine. It is to the Master who thus departs, and whom the disciples will now have to do without when they keep the Passover meal together, that the interpretative sayings refer which Jesus speaks concerning the bread and the wine in the third cup : This is my body, and : This cup is the new divine order in virtue of my blood. These are figurative sayings after the manner of the parables of Jesus. [58] But they differ from the parables by reason of the fact that they accompany an action of Jesus, the distributing of bread and wine to the disciples. Nor do the disciples merely hear the words of Jesus and see a parabolic action. They actually partake of the bread and wine which Jesus hands to them with these words of explanation. [59] The words and the actions of Jesus and the disciples are closely interrelated and form an indissoluble whole.

---

[54] Cf. R. Seeberg, Abendmahl, 304 ff.; Dogmengeschichte, 165 ff.; Dogmatik, 444 ff.

[55] According to the sequence in the use of the school of Shammai (→ n. 38), v. Jeremias, 62, cf. 40.

[56] Cf. Dalman, I, 128 ff., 141 ff.; Str.-B., IV, 75; Jeremias, 39 ff.

[57] So also M. Dibelius (→ n. 23), 209, cf. Hck. Lk. on 22:19, also F. Büchsel, op. cit., 56. Lk. 22:18 and par. is echoed in the Coptic Epistula Apostolorum, VIII, 12 ff. (TU, III, 13 [1919], 55, 57), where the disciples ask : "Is there then a continuing need that we should take the cup and drink ?" and Jesus answers : "Yes, there is a need until the day when I shall come with those who have been put to death for My sake," cf. also Just. Dial., 51, 2.

[58] Hence the parabolic understanding of the Lord's Supper in Jülicher, op. cit., 234 ff., 239 ff.; Schweitzer, Das Abendmahl, 41 ff.; Goetz, Die heutige Abendmahlsfrage ..., 248 ff. and Das Abendmahl eine Diatheke Jesu ...?, 53 ff.

[59] Cf. Otto, 255 ff.; Jeremias, 86 ff.

It should be noted, however, that in the course of the Passover the sayings do not come closely together. The main body of the meal lies between them. Originally they are separate and independent. Hence we must consider and expound them separately.

If on the lips of Jesus the saying about the bread was probably גּוּפִי [הוּא] דֵּין, [60] a more important point than the absence of the copula (by Aram. usage) is that the word which He probably used for "body," i.e., גּוּף, means not only "body" but also "self" or "person" [61] (→ σῶμα). In the figure Jesus was hardly referring to His body as such. There is no point of comparison for the equation of bread and body. [62] The obvious sense is that "this (the bread) I am myself." [63] When the disciples repeat the meal without Him, He will still be bodily with them. The bread is the pledge of His personal presence in their fellowship. As certainly as they eat the bread which He hands them, so certainly will He be truly present at the meal. Even in the time between the present and the future meal — this is the disciples' consolation in separation — their table fellowship with Him will not cease. The bread is a guarantee that He is present in person.

The saying on the occasion of the third cup [64] relates the cup (with the red wine) to the new διαθήκη. The cup represents the new divine order on the basis of the blood of Jesus. The blood which is shed, His violent death (→ I, 173, 174), makes the cup a vessel of the new divine order. As certainly as the disciples drink the cup whose wine represents the blood of Jesus, so certainly they share in the new divine order which is brought into being by the death of Jesus. The cup is a pledge that their Master who goes to death is present with the fulness of salvation accomplished by this death (→ II, 133).

Independently, then, the two sayings at this festival of remembrance of the saving acts of God contain the same new content and direct attention away from the past to Jesus Himself as the One who fulfils the divine will to save. Though they are linked with different parts of the meal, they come together in the same basic thought that Jesus is present in the table fellowship of the disciples. The promise of the saying about the bread is simply that He will be there, and the promise of the saying about the cup is that He will be there as the Saviour who establishes the new διαθήκη by His death. The first saying reveals already in all its fulness the gift of salvation which Jesus gives to His people in the Supper, i.e., His personal presence. The second saying does not add anything new. But it

---

[60] Cf. Dalman, I, 129 ff.

[61] Loc. cit.; Levy Chald. Wört.; Levy Wört.; Dalman Wört., s.v. גּוּף; also Str.-B., III, 366 f.; I, 827 on Mt. 19:23 No. 2.

[62] The usual reference of the broken bread to the violent death is not in accord with the situation. For the saying is not about the breaking of the bread but about its distribution. The state of brokenness is not peculiar to this bread. It is a result of the ordinary daily action of breaking bread (→ 728). Hence it is too slender for the elucidation of an important new truth.

[63] So F. Kattenbusch RE³, XII, 670; "Der Quellort d. Kirchenidee" in Festgabe f. A. v. Harnack (1921), 169 f.; "Die Vorzugsstellung des Petrus u. d. Charakter d. Urgemeinde" in Festgabe f. K. Müller (1922), 347; R. Seeberg, Abendmahl, 306; T. Schmidt, Der Leib Christi (1919), 38; J. Schniewind, Das Evangelium nach Markus, NT Deutsch, 1² (1935), on 14:22; cf. also Büchsel, op. cit., 57; H. Seesemann, Der Begriff κοινωνία im NT (1933), 38.

[64] For retranslation back into Aram. cf. Dalman, I, 147. Cf. Peshitta: הנא כסא איתוהי דיתיקא חדתא בדמי (1 C. 11:25).

stresses the unique significance of the gift. [65] He is present who offers up His life in order that God's will to save may be accomplished in a new relationship between Himself and men. By giving a new sense to these parts of a meal which the disciples continued to hold, Jesus thus sets up a new institution which consists in the fact that He makes the bread and wine of table fellowship a sign of His presence to His people during the period up to the establishment of perfect fellowship with Him in the eschatological banquet.

d. Alterations and Additions in Paul and the Synoptists. The original meaning still shines through the alterations and additions in Paul and the Synoptists (→ 731 and n. 29). The first part of the saying about the cup in Mk. says in other words the same as the original form, namely, that the blood of Jesus which is poured out in death and which establishes the διαθήκη is represented in the wine. The second part explains the death of Jesus in terms of Is. 53:12. [66] The expansion in Mt. combines with this a leading thought from the prophesying of the new divine order (Jer. 31:34). τὸ ὑπὲρ ὑμῶν in 1 C. 11:24 underlines the idea of the presence of salvation. The forms of distribution in Mk. and Mt. emphasise the handing out of the elements for actual reception. The command to repeat the action in Pl. expresses the unspoken presupposition of the sayings and acts of Jesus at the Last Supper (→ 735). The feast of remembrance of 1 C. 11:24 f. has its roots in the Passover which Jesus too, in the Passover Haggada, must have celebrated as a recollection of salvation history (→ 739).

e. Maranatha. The fact that the presence of Jesus was for primitive Christianity the gift of the Lord's Supper is shown again by → μαραναθά = מָרַנָא תָא, "Our Lord, come" (1 C. 16:22; Did., 10, 6; cf. Rev. 22:20), which intrinsically is a cry of longing to the Lord of the *parousia*, but which in the context of 1 C. and Did. is a petition at the Lord's Supper and part of the liturgy of the Supper. [67] In the Supper one looks and prays for the coming of the Lord. One experiences His true presence there, and has a pledge of fellowship with Him in spite of separation, and a foretaste of endless union with Him in glory. The meaning of the institution thus lives on here in its original force.

4. The Lord's Supper in Paul. [68]

a. Relation to the Lord's Supper of the Primitive Community. We have no direct information on the Lord's Supper in the primitive community or in Christianity before Paul. The daily table fellowship of the Christians in Jerusalem (Ac. 2:42, 46) has no connection with the institution of Jesus (→ 730). But the nature of the account of the Last Supper in Pl. and the Synoptists makes it clear

---

[65] "These are not two co-ordinated factors in one action. The relation is as follows. There is strictly one institution, and a more precise elucidation is added," R. Seeberg, Abendmahl, 306.

[66] Cf. G. Kittel, "Jesu Worte über sein Sterben," DTh, 3 (1936), 184 ff.

[67] Cf. R. Seeberg, Abendmahl, 311 ff.; "Kuss u. Kanon" in *Aus Religion u. Geschichte,* I (1906), 120 ff.; *Dogmengeschichte,* 166; T. Schmidt, *op. cit.,* 38 f.; F. J. Dölger, "Sol salutis" in *Liturgiegeschichtliche Forschungen,* 4/5² (1925), 198 ff.; H. Lietzmann, RGG², I, 32. In Act. Thom., 50 we have the request to Jesus: ἐλθὲ καὶ κοινώνησον ἡμῖν.

[68] Cf. the comm. on 1 C. 10 and 11, NT theologies, and histories of early Christianity, also R. Seeberg, Abendmahl, 313 ff.; E. v. Dobschütz, "Sakrament u. Symbol im Urchristentum," ThStKr, 78 (1905), 9 ff.; G. P. Wetter, *Altchristliche Liturgien:* "Das christliche Mysterium" (1921), 146 ff.; Clemen, 180 ff.; Lietzmann, *Messe u. Herrenmahl,* 222 ff., 251 ff., Völker, *op. cit.,* 75 ff.; K. L. Schmidt, RGG², I, 12 ff.; Huber, *op. cit.,* 26 ff.; H. E. Weber, *"Eschatologie" u. "Mystik" im NT* (1930), 156 ff.; Schweitzer, *op. cit.,* 246 ff.; v. Soden, *op. cit.,* 26 ff.; E. Käsemann, *Leib u. Leib Christi* (1933), 174 ff.; H. D. Wendland, *Die Briefe an die Korinther,* NT Deutsch, 7 on 1 C. 11.

that from the very first the disciples held the Supper according to the institution of Jesus. Neither the term "breaking of bread" (→ 729 f.), which indicates a common meal no matter whether there is eating alone or also drinking, nor the occasional traces from the 1st century on of celebrations without wine, [69] can justify the assumption that communion in bread alone was the original form of the Lord's Supper. [70] Freedom in respect of the instituted use of bread and wine is an illegitimate application of the true insight that the meaning of the feast is truly fulfilled in the reception of bread alone.

b. The Lord's Supper according to 1 C. 11 and 10. The evening [71] feast of the → κυριακὸν δεῖπνον (→ II, 34) in 1 C. 11:20 (cf. the breaking of bread in Ac. 20:7), which took place on Sunday, the new Christian day of rest, Ac. 20:7; 1 C. 16:2; 11:20 ff., no longer has any connection with the Passover. This detachment of the institution of Jesus from the setting of the Passover must have taken place before Paul on Gentile Christian soil (Antioch?). It would be facilitated by the fact that Jesus did not link His institution with the main part of the Passover meal, the eating of the lamb, but with the bread and wine, which are elements in all festal meals in the Orient. In 1 C. 11:20 ff. the Lord's Supper seems to be combined with a common meal shared by members of the congregation. It takes place within the setting of the Agape, to use the later term (→ I, 55). Serious abuses arose out of this link at Corinth. Thus the rich made it an occasion for gormandising before the starving poor etc. It was because of these scandals that Paul spoke of the holy seriousness of the Lord's Supper in 1 C. 11:23 ff. By its institution (vv. 23-25) the feast is a remembrance of the death of Christ (v. 26). It demands a corresponding frame of mind on the part of those partaking (v. 27). The bread is no ordinary bread; it is the Lord's body. He who ignores this and profanes the feast falls victim to God's judgment. This is shown by the fact that there has been sickness and even death in the congregation (vv. 28 ff.). In his discussion of idol meats Paul refers with the same sharpness to the absolute opposition between the Lord's Supper and idol feasts, 1 C. 10:14 ff. The → κοινωνία τοῦ αἵματος and τοῦ σώματος τοῦ Χριστοῦ which the Christian enjoys in the Lord's Supper (v. 16) does not permit cultic fellowship with demons (→ II, 17), v. 20 f. The discussions of the Lord's Supper in 1 C. 10 and 1 C. 11 are occasional in character, but they enable us to discern the basic elements in Paul's thinking on the matter.

c. Paul's Thinking in Respect of the Lord's Supper. For Paul, too, the meaning of the Supper is personal fellowship with Christ. [72] This may be seen in 1 C. 16:22 (→ 737) and also in 1 C. 10:3 f., where the miraculous gifts of manna and water from the rock given to Israel in the wilderness are types of the Lord's Supper, and

---

[69] Cf. already 1 C. 11:25 : ὁσάκις ἐὰν πίνητε (Schl. K., 324 f.; Schl. Lk., 422) and the insistence that all should drink, Mk. 14:23; Mt. 26:27 (cf. Kl. Mk. and Hck. Mk., ad loc.). For water instead of wine cf. Act. Pt. Verc., 2; Act. Thom., 121; Cyprian Ep., 63 (CSEL, III, 2 [1871]); Epiph. Haer., 30, 16, 1; 47, 1, 7; cf. A. v. Harnack, "Brod u. Wasser : Die euchar. Elemente bei Justin," TU, I, 7, 2 (1891), 117 ff.; T. Zahn, Brot u. Wein im Abendmahl d. alten Kirche (1892); Jülicher, op. cit., 217 ff.; Lietzmann, Messe u. Herrenmahl, 246 ff.; L. Fendt, Gnostische Mysterien (1922), 29 ff.

[70] So Heitmüller, op. cit., 51 ff.; J. Weiss, op. cit., 42 f., 502 f., A. Seeberg, op. cit., 101 ff. and esp. Lietzmann, 239 ff., 249 ff. On the other hand, cf. Clemen, 175 ff.; Huber, 72 ff.; Jeremias Abendmahlsworte, 45; Hupfeld, 63, 67 ff.

[71] There is no basis for the statement of Schweitzer, 248 f. that the celebration took place in the morning.

[72] Cf. R. Seeberg, Abendmahl, 313 ff.

the rock that followed is Christ now present. The community which blesses the cup of blessing and breaks the bread is inwardly related to Christ now present (1 C. 10:16). [73] But partaking of one bread (v. 17) creates fellowship between the members too; it merges them into one body, the → σῶμα Χριστοῦ, the Church. Here again we have the thought of table fellowship by the institution of Jesus. If Paul regards the death of Christ as the central content of the eucharistic sayings (1 C. 11:26) — the community declares or proclaims it as something which has happened [74] when it repeats the words of institution concerning the cup — he also takes up the thought of the new διαθήκη established by Christ's death — an idea which Jesus Himself used to bring out the meaning of His presence in the Supper. Paul also sees that the celebration takes place between the times, with a backward look to the Lord's incarnate ministry (v. 24b, 25b), and a forward look to His parousia (v. 26: ἄχρι οὗ ἔλθῃ). Here, then, we have the same tension as that which Jesus showed to His disciples on the night of the institution. Paul is thus true to the original essence of the institution. In accordance with the changed character of the feast, however, he has also introduced some new thoughts. 1. Now that the Supper is taken out of the framework of the Passover, the two distinct but related acts appointed by Jesus are naturally merged in a single action. The two main elements of bread and wine are received immediately after one another. And since the main point of the Supper was the presence of the person of Christ, it was natural that the elements should be seen to represent elements in His person in recollection of the body and blood of the words of institution. [75] Bread as a figure of the body and wine as a figure of the blood are the constituent factors representing the two aspects of the presence of the whole Christ. In Paul 1C. 10:16 f. and 11:27 bear witness to this shift of meaning in eucharistic terminology under the influence of anthropological conceptions. This shift does not affect Paul's basic view of the Supper. But it has the consequence of focusing attention on the elements and to that degree obscuring the original meaning of the institution. 2. The Lord's Supper is for Paul a feast of remembrance (1 C. 11:24 f.), not, however, in the sense of the antique memorial meal for the dead, [76] which was designed to foster the memory of loved ones now deceased (→ I, 349), but in the sense of the Jewish Passover (→ 733), which was designed to proclaim as a present reality the saving acts of God on which the faith of those participating was founded. The death of the Lord is thus made present (v. 26) as an event of divinely effected history which has created and sealed the new order in the relation between God and man. In virtue of the fact that it is thus embedded in history and strictly related to the historical Jesus and the unique historical event of His death, Paul's view of the Lord's Supper is distinguished from the mythological ideas linked with sacred feasts in Hellenistic syncretism. [77] For Paul the source of the Christian sacrament

---

[73] Cf. H. Seesemann, Der Begriff κοινωνία im NT (1933), 34 ff.

[74] On καταγγέλλειν → I, 72; Käsemann (→ n. 68), 178.

[75] → I, 172 ff., → σάρξ, → σῶμα. There is no need to postulate an early Christian formula like the Jewish "flesh and blood" which Paul has modified by substituting "body" for what was on his anthropology the less suitable "flesh" (Käsemann, op. cit., 176, cf. Goetz, Abendmahlsfrage ..., 265 ff.).

[76] So Lietzmann K., ad loc. Cf. → n. 17.

[77] For material and bibl. → II, 34, 690 f.; I, 176, 645, 646 f.; III, 13; also F. Pfister, Art "Kultus" in Pauly-W., XI (1922), 2171 ff. Cf. also → κοινωνία, → οἶνος, → πίνω, πόμα, πόσις, ποτήριον, → τράπεζα, → τρώγω.

is salvation history — like its OT type it offers → πνευματικὸν βρῶμα (→ I, 643) and πνευματικὸν → πόμα, 1 C. 10:3 f. — whereas the soil of syncretistic mysteries is non-historical myth. 3. The Lord's Supper is a solemn cultic action of the community. Though it may be linked externally with a meal, it is essentially distinct from it, 1 C. 11:20 ff., esp. 26 ff.; separation of the Eucharist from the Agape is here intimated. The cultic meal of Christians stands in antithesis to pagan feasts, 1 C. 10:20 f. The latter offer fellowship with demons, the former offers fellowship with the Lord. Paul is not thinking here in terms of a religious analogy. He sees an absolute antithesis. The heathen sacrifice to demons and not to God. Hence pagan worship is wholly different from the worship of God. The Lord's Supper has nothing to do with pagan feasts. The absence of sacrificial ritual or thinking from Paul's treatment of the Lord's Supper (→ 184) is an indication of the essential difference between the Christian feast and supposed analogies. Moreover, the idea of *communio* in the cultic meals of Hellenistic mysticism is crassly sensual. In the form of the sacrificed animal the deity itself is eaten. By eating, initiates are incorporated into the God in order that they themselves may be gods. [78] This is on a completely different plane from Paul's conception of partaking of the table of the Lord (v. 21) and of the → κοινωνία τοῦ αἵματος or τοῦ σώματος τοῦ Χριστοῦ (v. 16). Paul never speaks of eating the body or drinking the blood of Christ. He does not bind the presence of the Lord in the Supper to the material elements. He binds it to the whole action as a repetition, at the Lord's command, of what took place at the Last Supper. In the Supper Christians do become one with their Lord in intimate table fellowship. They do participate in His life and death. But this is a spiritual reality of personal union (cf. 10:3 f.), in which, according to His presence, the fruit of His historical work of salvation is proffered to them in vital presence. If in the sacramental meals of the religious syncretism of later antiquity we have the mechanico-magical operation of *opus operatum,* in the Lord's Supper, as Paul sees it, we have the true personal action of Christ, who by the word and act of His own institution guarantees the saving gifts of the life as Saviour which He recently lived and which He crowned on the cross. The wholly realistic but spiritual and historical understanding of the Lord's Supper which we find in Paul is equally distinct both from a spiritualising which makes the sacrament a mere symbol and from a materialising which sanctifies things and deifies nature. 4. The Lord's Supper, as one of the two original sacraments (cf. 1 C. 10:1 ff.) and as a liturgical celebration in which the Lord Himself is present, demands of those who participate in it a corresponding attitude which is to be tested by self-examination ; an unseemly attitude is a fault which God punishes (1 C. 11:27 ff.). [79] The exhortation against Corinthian indiscipline (vv. 20 ff.) does not represent the Lord's Supper as a *mysterium tremendum* at which salvation can be easily lost nor as a magical sacrament whose holy food may sometimes be deadly poison. [80] The → κρίμα which Paul descries in the cases of sickness and death found among the community is a divine means of correction designed to disturb the frivolous and to protect them from damnation at the last assize (v. 31 f.). What Paul desires is

---

[78] → I, 176; II, 34, 690 f., though cf. E. Reuterskiöld, *Die Entstehung der Speisesakramente* (1912), 126 ff.

[79] → I, 380, 493; II, 260, 828.

[80] Cf. W. Heitmüller, *Taufe u. Abendmahl bei Paulus* (1903), 50 f.; W. Bousset (*Die Schriften des NT,* 2³ (1917), *ad loc.*; H. Windisch, *Paulus u. Christus* (1934), 225. For another view cf. Schl. K., 328 f.

simply that Christians, before meeting the Lord in the Supper, should put to themselves the serious question whether they are as they should be, not according to some moral law, but according to the Gospel which is both indicative and imperative (→ II, 734). This is the starting-point for the practice of penance prior to Holy Communion.

5. The Lord's Supper in John. [81]

a. The Discourse in Jn. 6. Instead of an account of the institution in c. 13, where Jesus' demonstration of love in the foot-washing is a pictorial representation of the spirit of the early Christian celebration, John's Gospel offers us reflections on the Supper in connection with the story of the feeding (c. 6). [82] The discourse on the bread of life which Jesus gives to believers (vv. 32-58) culminates in the paradoxical thesis that the bread which He will give is His flesh for the life of the world (v. 51). The eating of His flesh and drinking of His blood mediates eternal life. His flesh is in truth food and His blood drink. Whosoever eats His flesh and drinks His blood has abiding fellowship with Him. Whosoever partakes of Him owes divine life to Him as He does to the Father (vv. 53-58). The paradox is resolved, however, by the antithesis that it is the Spirit who gives life; the flesh profits nothing (v. 63). In spite of the polemically exaggerated Capernaitic statements [83] about real eating (→ τρώγω) and drinking of the flesh and blood of Christ, which might well raise the objection of anthropophagy, there can be no doubt as to John's true view of the Lord's Supper.

b. John's Understanding of the Lord's Supper. In the Lord's Supper, when bread and wine are received, Christ is personally present. On the Jewish and early Christian view, the human person as perceived is made up of → σάρξ and αἷμα (→ I, 172). If flesh and blood similarly constitute the person of Christ, we may thus speak of the presence of His flesh and blood at the Supper. These elements of His person are represented by the elements of bread and wine. Like Paul (→ 739), John follows an early anthropologising reinterpretation of the words of institution. But he goes beyond Paul by substituting σάρξ for → σῶμα in eucharistic terminology.

The gift of the Lord's Supper is → ζωή. The flesh and blood of Christ mediate eternal life. They are true food and drink, and are to be enjoyed. Christ Himself wills to be eaten (v. 57: ὁ τρώγων με). He who eats His flesh and drinks His blood enters into the closest fellowship with Him and comes to partake of the eternal life which He has in Himself. But this does not mean that reception by sense effects union with Christ and filling with life — ἡ σάρξ οὐκ ὠφελεῖ οὐδέν

---

[81] Cf. the comm. and NT theol., also R. Seeberg, *Abendmahl*, 319 ff.; *Dogmengeschichte*, 168 f.; *Dogmatik*, 451 f.; Heitmüller (→ bibl.), 77 ff.; Wetter (→ n. 68), 145 ff.; Völker, 84 ff.; F. Büchsel, *Johannes u. d. hellenistische Synkretismus* (1928), 49 ff.; Huber, 92 ff.; Schweitzer, *Mystik*, 352 ff.

[82] In Jn. 21:12 f. (2:1 ff.), as in Lk. 24:30 and in the Synoptic accounts of the feeding, which are not "proleptic forms of later communions" (Hupfeld, 58), there is nothing to refer us to the Lord's Supper. There are few to-day who dispute the connection of Jn. 6 with the Lord's Supper, though cf. H. Odeberg, *The Fourth Gospel* (1929), 259 ff. On the history of exegesis cf. V. Schmitt, *Die Verheissung der Eucharistie (Jn. 6) bei den Vätern*, I (1900); Zn. J. [5], [6], 350, n. 57; Bau. J.[3], Excursus after 6:59.

[83] We need not discuss the question whether these are directed against the charge of Thyestean feasts (→ II, 35; Feine, 386, n. 1) or against docetic Gnosticism (cf. J. Behm, "Die joh. Christologie als Abschluss der Christologie des NT," NkZ, 41 [1930], 583 f., 597 ff.).

(v. 63a). The operation which does this is spiritual in nature. The living, pneumatic Christ imparts Himself in the Supper and grants life and salvation through fellowship. The exalted Christ, who is the same as the man of flesh and blood, i.e., Jesus, is spiritually present and active. Of all the work of the Johannine Christ, whether it be the sayings about becoming flesh (v. 63b) or the self-impartation of the risen Lord in the bread and wine of the Lord's Supper, the statement is true: τὸ → πνεῦμα ἐστιν τὸ ζῳοποιοῦν (v. 63a). [84] In the Lord's Supper the basic truth of the Johannine understanding of salvation is continually renewed: ὁ → λόγος σὰρξ ἐγένετο, 1:14.

With his concept of the spiritual presence of the living Christ, to which the hard sayings about eating and drinking Christ's flesh and blood refer, John is wholly in line with the teaching of Jesus Himself on the Supper. The linking of the sayings about the meaning of the Supper with the great miracle of bread and the theme of Jn. 6, "Jesus the Bread of life," obviously rests on meditation concerning the institution of Jesus, which linked the basic promise of His presence with the bread. The fact that the Supper also refers to the saving death of Jesus echoes through 6:51c. The thought of fellowship with Christ in 6:56 is connected with the oldest tradition of the institution. And the realism of the Johannine view, which is equally remote from both a purely symbolical and a magico-sacramental view, is genuinely primitive. What confers the gift of salvation is not the eating and drinking of the participants, but the actual presence of the pneumatic Christ. More strongly than in Paul, however, there threatens in Jn. the danger that the unity of the historico-superhistorical person of Christ will be split into the duality of the elements of flesh and blood represented by the bread and wine, so that each alone will take on saving significance as a material element. The anthropological misunderstanding of terms, which lurks in Jn. even though the dangerous implications are avoided, became a basis for serious errors in the history of the Lord's Supper.

6. The Lord's Supper in the Post-Apostolic Age. [85]

a. Didache. According to the rules given in the Didache [86] the Lord's Supper is to take place on Sunday (14, 1) in the context of a common meal (10, 1), and certain prayers and customs are laid down (9, 1 and 5). The celebration is to be approached with eschatological expectation (10, 6, cf. 9, 4; 10, 5), for here the Lord comes to His people. Hence there is to be the cry Maranatha (→ 737) and the greeting Hosanna (10, 6). In the blessing of the cup thanks are offered ὑπὲρ τῆς ἁγίας → ἀμπέλου Δαβὶδ τοῦ παιδός σου, ἧς ἐγνώρισας ἡμῖν διὰ 'Ιησοῦ τοῦ παιδός σου (9, 2). In that of the bread the thought of fellowship is worked out eschatologically and expanded into a prayer for the gathering of the scattered Church from the ends of the earth into the kingdom of God (9, 4, cf. 10, 5). The description of the divine gifts of the Supper as πνευματικὴ τροφὴ καὶ ποτὸς καὶ ζωὴ αἰώνιος (10, 3) has a Johannine ring. If there is no reference to the words of institution or to the death of Christ this may be due to the partial nature of the rules; they do not cover the whole celebration. But in

---

[84] Because word and sacrament are essential means to mediate the activity of Christ, partaking of the Lord's Supper is necessary to salvation in Jn. (v. 53).

[85] Cf. the histories of dogma, Harnack, I⁴ (1909), 231 ff., 291, 462 ff.; Seeberg, I³ (1922), 169 ff., 305 ff., 354 etc.; Loofs⁴ (1906), 101, 145 f., 212 f.; also Goetz, *Abendmahlsfrage . . .*, 149 ff., 158 ff., 197 ff., 225 ff., 287 ff.; Heitmüller, 76 ff.; Kn. Did. and Bau. Ign. on the relevant passages; Lietzmann, *Messe u. Herrenmahl*, 230 ff., 256 ff., Völker, 99 ff.

[86] On the liturgical problems cf. Lietzmann, 230 ff.; Völker, 99 ff.; Hupfeld, 73 ff.

the Did. there are also alien elements among those which are genuinely primitive. The gifts of the revelation of God in Christ for which prayers are offered include not only ζωή and πίστις but also ἀθανασία and γνῶσις (9, 3; 10, 2). The term "sacrifice" is also found (14, 1 ff.), though in the first instance only with reference to the eucharistic prayer (→ 189). Qualifications for partaking are given. Only the baptised and holy are to do so (9, 5; 10, 6), and confession of sin and reconciliation of differences will guarantee the purity of the offering (14, 1 ff.).

b. Ignatius. In the short and often obscure references which he makes to the Lord's Supper (εὐχαριστία, Eph., 13, 1; Phld., 4; Sm., 7, 1; 8, 1; ἀγάπη R., 7, 3; Sm., 8, 2; cf. 7,1), Ignatius [87] reminds us of Jn. but also of Paul. The heretics who do not confess τὴν εὐχαριστίαν σάρκα εἶναι τοῦ σωτῆρος ἡμῶν ᾽Ιησοῦ Χριστοῦ τὴν ὑπὲρ τῶν ἁμαρτιῶν ἡμῶν παθοῦσαν, ἣν τῇ χρηστότητι ὁ πατὴρ ἤγειρεν and who thus resist the gift of God fall victim to death; they do not attain to the resurrection, to life incorruptible (Sm., 7, 1). The bread of the eucharist is φάρμακον ἀθανασίας (→ 23 f.), ἀντίδοτος τοῦ μὴ ἀποθανεῖν, ἀλλὰ ζῆν ἐν ᾽Ιησοῦ Χριστῷ διὰ παντός (Eph., 20, 2). Ign. depicts the bliss of the martyr in terms of the eucharist: οὐχ ἥδομαι τροφῇ φθορᾶς οὐδὲ ἡδοναῖς τοῦ βίου τούτου. ἄρτον θεοῦ θέλω, ὅ ἐστιν σάρξ ᾽Ιησοῦ Χριστοῦ, τοῦ ἐκ σπέρματος Δαβίδ, καὶ πόμα θέλω τὸ αἷμα αὐτοῦ, ὅ ἐστιν ἀγάπη ἄφθαρτος (R., 7, 3). Like Jn., he believes that the risen Christ is at work in the Supper, and for him, too, the gift of the sacrament is abiding life in fellowship with Christ. But the elements are linked more closely with the elements in Christ's person, the concept of life is hellenised, and the idea of the medicine of immortality which is an antidote to death suggests a natural operation of the eucharistic bread. [88] Even though these be liturgical expressions which are not coined by Ign., [89] for whose pneumatic understanding of the flesh and blood of Christ one may appeal to Tr., 8, 1 (faith = σάρξ, τοῦ κυρίου, love = αἷμα ᾽Ιησοῦ Χριστοῦ), they prepare the way for a progressive materialisation of the concept of the Supper whose next step is to be found in Just. Apol., 66, 2, where the flesh and blood of Jesus are εὐχαριστηθεῖσα τροφή, ἐξ ἧς αἷμα καὶ σάρκες κατὰ μεταβολὴν τρέφονται ἡμῶν. [90] Ign. speaks of the unifying power of the eucharist for participants (cf. 1 C. 10:17) in Phld., 4: μία ... σάρξ τοῦ κυρίου ἡμῶν ᾽Ιησοῦ Χριστοῦ καὶ ἓν ποτήριον εἰς ἕνωσιν τοῦ αἵματος αὐτοῦ (through His blood), ἓν θυσιαστήριον (cf. Eph., 5, 2; Tr., 7, 2; Mg., 7, 2 → 190, n. 41). The unity of the Church is represented in the celebration, which as in Did. is thought of as a sacrifice of prayer (cf. Sm., 7, 1; Eph., 13, 1 → 190), and at which, according to Ign.'s view of the Church, the bishop ought to preside (Sm., 8, 1 f.).

c. Apocryphal Acts. In their understanding of the Lord's Supper the Did. and Ign. still observe the frontier which marks off the Christian view from magical sacramentalism and Hellenistic cult mysticism. [91] But this is no longer true of the apocr. Acts, which make the eucharist into a Gnostic mystery. Cf. Act. Joh., 109; Thom., 27; 49 f., 121; 133; 158. [92]

Behm

κλαυθμός → 725 f.

---

[87] Cf. E. Freiherr v. d. Goltz, "Ignatius von Antiochien als Christ u. Theologe" TU, I, 12, 3 (1894), 71 ff.; 121 f.; Schweitzer, *Mystik*, 264 ff.; Weber (→ n. 68), 189 ff.; C. C. Richardson, *The Christianity of Ignatius of Antioch* (1935), 20, 55 ff., 72.

[88] Bau. Ign., 219; Reitzenstein Hell. Myst., 83; 393; 400; Richardson, 102 f., n. 101.

[89] Lietzmann, 257 thinks they are quotations from the liturgy of Antioch.

[90] In exposition of this passage cf. the histories of dogma and Goetz, *Abendmahlsfrage ...*, 295 f.; Völker, 141 ff.

[91] The same is true of Mart. Pol., 14, 2; cf. Lietzmann, 257.

[92] Cf. L. Fendt (→ n. 69), 44 ff., 50 ff., 59 ff.

† κλείς   (→ θύρα, πύλη).

Contents : A. The Different Applications of the Image of the Keys in the NT : 1. The Keys of Heaven ; 2. The Keys of the Underworld ; 3. The Key of (to) Knowledge ; 4. The Eschatological Use : a. The Key of David ; b. The Keys of the Royal Dominion of God. B. The Power of the Keys : 1. Mt. 16:19; 2. The Extension of the Power of Binding and Loosing to the Apostles ; 3. The Exercise of the Power of Binding in Primitive Christianity ; 4. The Power of Loosing.

"Keys" are not mentioned in the everyday sense in the NT.[1] The term always has figurative significance.

A. The Different Applications of the Image of the Keys in the NT.

1. A common view in the ancient world was that heaven is closed off by doors → θύρα, III, 176, and that certain deities or angelic beings dispose of the power of the keys to heaven. In Babylon Shamash has the key to heaven in his left hand ;[2] in Greece there may be traced back to the 7th cent. B.C.[3] the notion that Dike keeps the key ;[4] in Italy Janus has the key,[5] in Mithraism Aion-Kronos[6] and in a Neo-Platonic author Helios.[7]

In later Judaism there are only a few references to the key of heaven as a mark of dignity. In Gr. Bar. 11 the angelic prince Michael is called ὁ κλειδοῦχος (keeper of the keys) τῆς βασιλείας τῶν οὐρανῶν;[8] in Heb. En. 18:18 the angelic prince 'Anaphiel

---

κ λ ε ί ς. L. A. Ahrens, *Das Amt d. Schlüssel* (1864); G. E. Steitz, "Der nt.liche Begriff der Schlüsselgewalt," ThStKr, 39 (1866), 435-483; Dalman WJ, I, 176 f.; H. Gunkel, *Zum religionsgesch. Verständnis des NT²* (1910), 73; J. Grill, *Der Primat des Petrus* (1904); A. Sulzbach, "Die Schlüssel des Himmelreichs," ZNW, 4 (1903), 190-192; W. Köhler, "Die Schlüssel des Petrus," ARW, 8 (1905), 214-243; A. Dell, "Matthäus 16:17-19," ZNW, 15 (1914), 1-49, esp. 27-38; K. Adam, "Zum ausserkanonischen u. kanonischen Sprachgebrauch von Binden u. Lösen," *Theol. Quart.*, 96 (1914), 49-64; 161-197 (also K. Adam, *Gesamm. Aufsätze zur Dogmengeschichte u. Theologie der Gegenwart* [1936], 17-52); Str.-B., I, 33, 151, 437, 523, 736 f., 741; III, 3 f., 790, 795; IV, 1087, 1089 f.; J. Jeremias, *Golgotha* (1926), 71 f.; K. Bornhäuser, "Zum Verständnis von Mt. 16:18-19," NkZ, 40 (1929), 221-237; "Anathema esto !" in *Die Reformation*, 26 (1932), 82 f.; J. Kroll, *Gott u. Hölle. Der Mythos vom Descensuskampfe* (Studien der Bibliothek Warburg, 20 [1932]), 10, 89 f., 121, 476 f.; V. Burch, "The 'Stone' and the 'Keys' (Mt. 16:18 ff.)," JBL, 52 (1933), 147-152; Pr.-Bauer³, 720 f.; F. Heiler, *Urkirche u. Ostkirche* (1937), 48-61; H. v. Campenhausen, "Die Schlüsselgewalt d. Kirche," *Evangelische Theologie*, 4 (1937), 143-169. On the declension of κλείς v. bibl. in Pr.-Bauer³, 720.

[1] On the technical aspect of keys in antiquity cf. H. Diels, *Parmenides* (1897), 117-151; S. Krauss, *Talmudische Archäologie*, I (1910), 41; I. Benzinger, *Hb. Archäologie³* (1927), 103 f.

[2] H. Gressmann, *Altorientalische Texte z. AT²* (1926), 243; *Altorientalische Bilder z. AT²* (1927), 91; A. Jeremias, *Handbuch z. altorientalischen Geisteskultur²* (1929), 367.

[3] Diels, 153.

[4] *Ibid.*, 28 f., 51 (on Parm., 1, 14); Köhler, 226 f.; H. Fränkel, NGG (1930), 153 ff.

[5] Ovid. Fast., I, 99, 125, 139.

[6] F. Cumont, *Textes et Monuments figurés relatifs aux mystères de Mithra*, I (1899), 74 ff.; Mithr. Liturg., p. 8, 18 and p. 66 f.; A. Dieterich, *Abraxas* (1891), 48; Köhler, 227 f.; Reitzenstein Ir. Erl., p. XII, and 238 f.

[7] Procl. Hymni (Orph. [Abel], 276 f.), I, 2 f.: πηγῆς (from which flows "the rich stream of harmony from above," I, 4) αὐτὸς ἔχων κληῖδα.

[8] → 749.

Yahweh is the keeper of the keys to the palaces of the 7th heaven ; in 48 C 3 it is said of Enoch Metatron that God has given him the keys to all the treasure chambers of heaven. Acc. to Pirqe R. Eli'ezer, 34, God Himself carries the key to the chambers of souls. [9] We also have a reference to the doors of heaven, though to those of the lower heaven, when it is said of God that He Himself keeps the key of rain [10] and that He gave it only temporarily to Elijah. [11]

Lk. 4:25 is alluding to the so-called heavenly key of rain when it says that heaven was closed in the days of Elijah the prophet. As often in the Gospels the passive is used for the name of God, so that we ought to render : "God closed heaven." God has the key of heaven in His hand ; it is His goodness when He gives the gift of rain to the world and His judgment when He withholds it. But God can entrust this key to His messengers. The two witnesses of the last time (→ II, 939) "have full power to close heaven in order that no rain should fall in the days of their prophecy" (Rev. 11:6).

2. The Keys of the Underworld.

On the common ancient view the underworld, too, is thought to be barred by gates (→ πύλη). [12] He who has the keys to these has power over the underworld.

For the Babylonians Nedu is the keeper of the underworld who guards the lock. [13] In Greece Pluto, [14] Aiacos, [15] Persephone [16] and Selena-Hecate [17] hold the keys to Hades, and in the religion of Mithras Kronos. [18] In magic lit. conjuration of the deities which hold the key to Hades, among which we find Anubis, [19] plays an important part. [20] The Isis-Osiris mysteries honour Isis as mistress of the *inferum claustra*. [21] In later Judaism there are only isolated refs. to the keys of the underworld, e.g., Slav. En. 42 Rec. B : "And I saw the keepers [22] of the key (sing.) of Hades standing before the

---

[9] The reference is to the souls of the dead ; the chambers (treasuries) in which the souls of the righteous dead are kept are to be found in the heavenly world (Qoh. r. 3:21) or the 7th heaven (bChag., 12b).

[10] bTaan., 2a (par. in Str.-B., I, 437, 523, 737; III, 3 f.).

[11] bSanh., 113a. Acc. to Slav. En. heavenly beings dispose of the key of thunder and lightning (40:9), of the keys of the treasuries of snow and the depositories of ice and frosty winds (v. 10), and also of the keys of the winds (v. 11).

[12] Köhler, 222 ff.; Dell, 27 ff.

[13] A. Schollmeyer, "Sumerisch-babylonische Hymnen u. Gebete an Šamaš," *Studien z. Geschichte u. Kultur des Altertums*, ed. E. Drerup-H. Grimme-J. P. Kirsch, 1st Suppl. Vol. (1912), 130 f.; Dell, 28.

[14] Hom. Il., 8, 367; Plut. Is. et Os. (II, 364 f.), 35; Paus., V, 20, 3.

[15] Köhler, 223.

[16] *Loc. cit.*

[17] *Loc. cit.*; Kroll, 476 f.

[18] Cumont, I, 84.

[19] Köhler, 223.

[20] In the Paris mag. pap. (Preis. Zaub., IV, 2290 ff.) the magician says threateningly to Selena-Hecate :

    ἄκουσον . . .
    τὸ σάνδαλόν σου ἔκρυψα καὶ κλεῖδα κρατῶ
    ἤνοιξα ταρταρούχου κλεῖθρα (locks) Κερβέρου.

[21] Apul. Met., XI, 21.

[22] Cf. LXX Job 38:17: πυλωροὶ ᾅδου (Heb. שַׁעֲרֵי read by LXX as שֹׁעֲרֵי); bChag., 15b : "The keeper of the door of the (intermediate) gēhinnōm," i.e., the realm of the dead.

gates [23] like great serpents." Reference is often made to the Rabb. tradition that God Himself bears "the key of the quickening of the dead," [24] and it is likely, though not certain, that this is the key of the underworld. [25] What is beyond doubt is that later tradition taught that the keys to the 40,000 gates of the last hell are in God's hand. [26]

Rev. mentions the key to the well of the (→ I, 10) abyss, i.e., to the prison of spirits depicted as a well-like shaft (Rev. 9:1; 20:1). This key is in the hand of God [27] or an angel. [28] Prior to the end God will cause the abyss to be opened and demonic locusts will be a terrible plague on the earth (9:1 ff.). Then again at the parousia God will cause it to be opened in order that Satan, chained by the angel, may be shut up in it during the millennial reign (20:1-3).

We must distinguish from this key to the prison of spirits the keys of death and of Hades which are in the hands of the exalted Christ (Rev. 1:18). The expression τὰς κλεῖς τοῦ θανάτου καὶ τοῦ ᾅδου is to be understood, not as a gen. obj. ("keys to death and the world of the dead"), [29] but as a gen. poss. ("keys of — personified — death and Hades"). [30] For the spatial idea of θάνατος (as "realm of the dead") is alien to the NT, and when θάνατος and ᾅδης appear together they are always [31] viewed in personal terms. [32] Hence Rev. 1:18 refers to the keys which death and Hades carry as lords of the underworld. But if death and Hades are personified, it is quite plain that the possession of their keys implies a preceding battle between them and Christ. As shown by His resurrection (1:18a), Christ overcame death and Hades on His descensus ad inferos. [33] Death, then, has lost its terror for His community. Possessing the keys [34] of death and Hades, Christ has

---

[23] The powerful gates and locks of the entries to Hades are depicted in Sib., 2, 227 f.; cf. also an anon. apoc. ed. by G. Steindorff (TU, NF, 2, 3a [1899], 6, 18-20).

[24] bTaan., 2a par.

[25] Cf. the vl. "key to the graves" in Tanch. וירא, 35 (ed. S. Buber, p. 106) and Midr. Ps. 78 § 5; cf. also Tg. Qoh. 9:10, where בית קבורתא stands for the שׁאוֹל of the text.

[26] Alphabeth-Midr. of R. 'Aqiba : "In that hour the Holy One, blessed be He, takes the keys of gēhinnōm and gives them to Michael and Gabriel before the eyes of all the righteous, and says to them : Go and open the gates of gēhinnōm ... Forthwith Michael and Gabriel go and open the 40,000 gates of gēhinnōm" (A. Jellinek, Beth ha-midras 3 [1855], 28, 9); par. Neue Pesiqta (ibid., 6 [1877], 63, 23).

[27] Rev. 9:1: ἐδόθη; the pass. is probably for God's name (→ 745). Cf. the Prayer of Man., 3, where it is said of God : ὁ κλείσας τὴν ἄβυσσον.

[28] Rev. 20:1. Cf. 9:1; the star is personified in this verse (acc. to E. B. Allo, St. Jean. L'apocalypse³ [1933], ad loc. the star of 9:1 is Abaddon [→ I, 4]).

[29] So Had. Apk.; Allo (→ n. 28); J. Behm, NT Deutsch, ad loc.

[30] W. Bousset, Die Offenbarung des Joh.⁶ (1906), ad loc.; Kyrios Christos² (1921), 30; Kroll, 10, 447.

[31] Kroll, 10.

[32] NT examples : Rev. 6:8; 20:13 f.; 1 C. 15:55 vl. On the personification of θάνατος, cf. Pr.-Bauer³, 585 f., of ᾅδης, ibid., 27.

[33] Bousset; Kroll; Loh. Apk., ad loc.; W. Staerk, Soter, I (1933), 128. We also read of the bars of the earth (in the sense of the underworld) in Jon. 2:7: κατέβην εἰς γῆν, ἧς οἱ μοχλοὶ αὐτῆς κάτοχοι αἰώνιοι. The figure in Is. 45:2 is also that of God's battle with Hades, and Messianic interpretation has to take it this way : μοχλοὺς σιδηροῦς συγκλά-σω. This idea is also present in Job 26:13 LXX, except that here the reference is to the gates of heaven : κλεῖθρα δὲ οὐρανοῦ δεδοίκασιν αὐτόν. Yet the verse still speaks of powers which are hostile to God. Cf. v. 6 : γυμνὸς ὁ ᾅδης ἐνώπιον αὐτοῦ, καὶ οὐκ ἔστιν περιβόλαιον τῇ ἀπωλείᾳ [Bertram].

[34] Plur. because the underworld has many gates, cf. Mt. 16:18 : → πύλη, also → n. 26.

the power to open the doors of the world of the dead and to summon the dead to resurrection.

The older *descensus* doctrine, which answers the question what happened to Christ between His death and resurrection on the basis of Scripture (Ps. 16:8-11 = Ac. 2:25-28, cf. 13:35),[35] is genuinely primitive. Only in 1 Pt. 3:19 f.; 4:6, which explains that the purpose of the descent was to preach in the prison of spirits (3:19), do we find traces of the *descensus* myth.[36,37] These recur in Rev. 1:18 with its further explanation that the aim of the descent was to overcome the rulers of the underworld in battle.

Against the background of the later Jewish view[38] that the key of quickening the dead is one of the three keys which are in the hand of God and which He entrusts only to plenipotentiaries, to describe the risen Christ as Lord of the sphere of the dead is to ascribe to Him a divine predicate.

3. The Key of (to) Knowledge.

Lk. reports the Woe of Jesus against the scribes : οὐαὶ ὑμῖν τοῖς νομικοῖς, ὅτι ἤρατε τὴν κλεῖδα τῆς γνώσεως· αὐτοὶ οὐκ εἰσήλθατε καὶ τοὺς εἰσερχομένους ἐκωλύσατε (11:52).[39]

In the phrase τὴν κλεῖδα τῆς γνώσεως, τῆς γνώσεως is either gen. appos. or gen. obj. a. If we take it as gen. appos. ("You have taken away the key to God's kingdom, namely, knowledge"),[40] the image is that of the door to the kingdom of God. The kingdom of God is the supreme good, while knowledge is the key which opens up access to it. Since "entry into the royal dominion of God" is a specifically Palestinian image,[41] on this interpretation knowledge must also be taken in the Palestinian sense, namely, as the obedient knowledge of Scripture (→ I, 706). In fact, the comparison of knowledge with a key is Rabb.[42] b. On the other hand, if τῆς γνώσεως is a gen. obj. ("you have taken away the key to knowledge"), the metaphor is different. The reference now is to the door to knowledge,[43] and knowledge is the supreme good. This would demand a Hellenistic understanding of γνῶσις as the vision of God (→ I, 692 f., 706).

---

35 Also R. 10:7.

36 On this cf. esp. Kroll, bibl. in Wnd. Pt. on 1 Pt. 3:20 and Pr.-Bauer³, 1126.

37 Cf. F. Hauck, *NT Deutsch* on 1 Pt. 3:19.

38 bTaan., 2a par.

39 Cf. the apocr. Ev.-Fr., P. Oxy., IV, 655, 41: [τὴν κλειδα] τῆς [γνωσεως ε]κρυψ [ατε· αυτοι ουκ] εισηλ[θατε και τοις εισερ[χομενοις ου]κ αν[εωξατε].

40 So Ps.-Clem. Hom., 3, 18 : τὴν κλεῖδα ἧς βασιλείας ... ἥτις ἐστὶν γνῶσις, ἣ μόνη τὴν πύλην τῆς ζωῆς ἀνοῖξαι δύναται. 18, 15 : παρ' αὐτοῖς (sc. the σοφοί) γὰρ ἡ κλεὶς τῆς βασιλείας τῶν οὐρανῶν ἀπέκειτο, τουτέστιν ἡ γνῶσις τῶν ἀπορρήτων. Ps.-Clem. Recg., 2, 30 (MPG, 1): Jesus condemns the scribes and Pharisees *quod clavem scientiae quam a Moyse traditam susceperunt, occultarent, per quam possit ianua regni coelestis aperiri ;* 2, 46.

41 → II, 677; III, 178.

42 bShab., 31a b : "Rabbah bar Huna (c. 300) has said : 'He who has knowledge of the Torah but no fear of God is like the treasurer to whom one gave the key of the inner rooms without giving him the key to the outer. How can he enter ?' " Hence knowledge of the Torah is possession of the key. Cf. S. Dt. § 321 on 32:25 of the decisions of the scribe : "When he has opened, no one shuts" (i.e., his decisions are of absolute validity). The teaching of the scribes is thus an exercise of the power of the keys. Cf. Lk. 24:32, 45 : διανοίγειν τὰς γραφάς, Ac. 17:3 without obj.

43 This image is found in Corp. Herm., VII, 2a : ζητήσατε χειραγωγόν, τὸν ὁδηγήσοντα ὑμᾶς ἐπὶ τὰς τῆς γνώσεως θύρας, ὅπου ἐστὶ τὸ λαμπρὸν φῶς. Interpol. Phld., 9, 1 of Christ : ἡ θύρα τῆς γνώσεως, *ianua scientiae et agnitionis.*

The original would almost certainly be a gen. appos. This is shown by the second half of the verse: αὐτοὶ οὐκ εἰσήλθατε καὶ τοὺς εἰσερχομένους ἐκωλύσατε. For the Synoptic use of εἰσέρχεσθαι (→ II, 677; III, 178) shows that the original reference of 11:52b is to entry into God's kingdom, and this implies that the key of 11:52a is the key to this kingdom. [44] In fact the par. in Mt. 23:13 reads: οὐαὶ δὲ ὑμῖν, γραμματεῖς καὶ Φαρισαῖοι ὑποκριταί, ὅτι κλείετε τὴν βασιλείαν τῶν οὐρανῶν ἔμπροσθεν τῶν ἀνθρώπων. On Hellenistic soil, however, it would be more natural to see here an objective gen.: "You have taken away the key to knowledge."

Either way the reference is to the theological knowledge of the scribes. This is the key either to the kingdom of God or to knowledge of God. Jesus has in view the claim of the theologians of His day to have the power of the keys in virtue of their knowledge of Scripture. [45] He does not pronounce on this claim as such. But He does raise the charge that, instead of opening the door of salvation to men, they have hidden the key, [46] keeping their knowledge secret and barring the way of salvation to the crowd by keeping from them the true will of God. [47]

4. The Eschatological Use.

a. The Key of David.

In Rev. 3:7 the exalted Christ is called ὁ ἔχων τὴν κλεῖν Δαυίδ, ὁ ἀνοίγων καὶ οὐδεὶς κλείσει, καὶ κλείων καὶ οὐδεὶς ἀνοίγει. The description is based on Is. 22:22, where the appointment of Eliakim as royal treasure is announced with the words: "And the key of the house of David will I lay upon his shoulder; so he shall open, and none shall shut; and he shall shut, and none shall open." The Messianic interpretation of this verse in unknown in Judaism. [48] It rested on the words "key of the house of David." Is. 22:22 had in view the royal palace in Jerusalem, [49] but the Apocalyptist was thinking of the Davidic line [50] whose representative is Christ (Rev. 22:16). Hence the key of David is now (3:7) the key which Christ has in His hands as the promised shoot of David. This is the key to God's eternal palace. [51]

The meaning of the description is that Christ has unlimited sovereignty over the future world. He alone controls grace and judgment. He decides irrevocably

---

[44] So already the Ps.-Clem. Hom. and Recg., → n. 40.

[45] → n. 42.

[46] The reading ἐκρύψατε D (Θ) 157 it sy^sc arm Tat P. Oxy. (→ n. 39) for ἤρατε is materially sound, cf. also Ps.-Clem. Hom. (→ n. 47) and Recg. (→ n. 40 and 47).

[47] Ps.-Clem. Hom., 18, 15 (→ n. 40): The wise possessed γνῶσις τῶν ἀπορρήτων, but 18, 16: ἀπέκρυβαν τὴν γνῶσιν τῆς βασιλείας ...˙ ... ὡς ἀπέκρυψαν αὐτοὶ τὰς ὁδοὺς ἀπὸ τῶν θελόντων, οὕτω καὶ ἀπ' αὐτῶν ἀπεκρύβη τὰ ἀπόρρητα (sc. as a punishment, cf. Mt. 11:25). Ps.-Clem. Recg., 1, 54 of the scribes and Pharisees: velut clavem regni coelorum verbum veritatis tenentes er Moysis traditione susceptum, occultarunt auribus populi. On esotericism among the Rabb. → I, 741, also J. Jeremias, Jerusalem zur Zeit Jesu, II, B (1929), 106 ff.; Die Abendmahlsworte Jesu (1935), 51 f.

[48] As against W. Bousset (→ n. 30, Had. on Rev. 3:7, also Staerk, Soter, I (1933), 118. Is. 22:22 is mentioned only infrequently in Rabb. lit. Tg., ad loc. renders "key of the house of David" as "key to the sanctuary and dominion over the house of David"; S. Dt. § 321 in 32:25 refers Is. 22:22 to the decisions of the scribes (→ n. 42); bSanh., 44b says of Gabriel, with allusion to Is. 22:22, that he was called Siggaron, "because, when he closes (סוגר), (the gates of grace) none can open them."

[49] So also Tg. Is. 22:22 → n. 48.

[50] Cf. Lk. 1:69: ἐν οἴκῳ Δαυίδ.

[51] → 178 and n. 70.

whether a man will have access to the salvation of the last age or whether it will be withheld from him.

b. The Keys of the Royal Dominion of God.

In Mt. 16:19 Jesus says to Peter: Δώσω σοι τὰς κλεῖδας τῆς βασιλείας τῶν οὐρανῶν. There are no non-Christian instances of the phrase "keys of the kingdom (royal dominion) of God." [52] The antithesis to the gates of hell in 16:18 might suggest that the κλεῖδες τῆς βασιλείας τῶν οὐρανῶν are the keys to the door of heaven (→ 744), [53] especially if we compare the phrase with the description of the archangel Michael as ὁ κλειδοῦχος (the doorkeeper) τῆς βασιλείας τῶν οὐρανῶν (Gr. Bar. 11), which means that he has full authority in the heavenly world. Against this view, however, there is the severe objection that, like the phrase in Gr. Bar. 11, which was probably under Christian influence [54] and which is thus of no help in the interpretation of Mt. 16:19, it demands an equation of the βασιλεία τῶν οὐρανῶν with the heavenly world and is thus out of step with the usage of the Gospels elsewhere. If we keep this point in mind, we shall reject the idea of the door to heaven and construe the βασιλεία τῶν οὐρανῶν, whose key Peter holds, as the royal dominion of God in the last time. [55] Materially, then, the keys of the kingdom of God are not different from the key of David (a.). This is confirmed by the fact that in Mt. 16:19, as in Rev. 3:7, Jesus is the One who controls them. But in what sense is the power of the keys given to Peter?

B. The Power of the Keys.

1. Mt. 16:19.

In answering the question what authority is given to Peter with the keys of the kingdom of God, many factors have to be considered.

a. First, it must be stated that Mt. 16:17-19 has a strong Semitic character linguistically. This is proved by the vocabulary, [56] by the style (three groups of three members, on the pattern: theme (1st member) and antithetical parallelism (2nd and 3rd members), [57] and by the rhythm (3 x 3 beats of four when translated back into Aram.). [58] This point is important both in relation to questions of authenticity (→ 518 ff.) and also in respect of detailed exegesis. Nor should it be overlooked that the basis of the Gr. δώσω (16:19) is the Aram. impf. אֶיהַב or אֶתֵּין, [59] which

---

[52] On Gr. Bar. 11 → infra and 744 (also n. 54). It is significant, however, that κλείειν τὴν βασιλείαν τῶν οὐρανῶν is found in Mt. 23:13.

[53] Köhler, 214 ff.; Dell, 37 f.

[54] W. Lueken, Michael (1898), 125. The ed. of Gr. Bar., M. R. James (TSt, 5, 1 ([1897]), is even prepared to regard it as a Christian Apoc. of the 2nd cent. (p. LXXI). It is more likely that the work is basically Judaistic but that the material has undergone Christian revision. The assertion of Köhler that the term "key of the kingdom of heaven" is not found in Jewish lit. (218) is still valid.

[55] If a concrete image lies behind the phrase τὰς κλεῖδας τῆς βασιλείας τῶν οὐρανῶν, we should think of the gates of the future city of God.

[56] J. Jeremias, Golgotha, 69, n. 5. Esp. on v. 19 cf. ἡ βασιλεία τῶν οὐρανῶν (the substitution for the name of God and the plur. οἱ οὐρανοί are both Semitic); ἐν τοῖς οὐρανοῖς (plur.); δεῖν and λύειν, → II, 60 and infra.

[57] J. Leipoldt, Vom Jesusbilde der Gegenwart² (1925), 11.

[58] C. F. Burney, The Poetry of our Lord (1925), 117.

[59] Cf. the Syr. translations (syᶜ ᴾ ᵖᵃˡ : 'attäl).

has here voluntative significance ("I will to give"). [60] This means that the handing over of the keys is not just future. It is regarded as taking place now.

b. We should also note that in the usage of the Bible and later Judaism handing over of the keys does not have the sense of appointing as porter. [61]

> There are numerous instances to show that in biblical and later Jewish usage handing over the keys implies full authorisation. He who has the keys has full authority. [62] Thus when Eliakim is given the keys of the palace he is appointed the royal steward (Is. 22:22, cf. 15). When Jesus is said to hold the keys of death and Hades (Rev. 1:18) or the key of David (3:7), this means that He is, not the doorkeeper, but the Lord of the world of the dead and the palace of God. In the same sense there is reference to the three keys in the hand of God, that of rain, that of conception (i.e., the key which opens the closed womb of the mother), [63] and that of quickening the dead; [64] a fourth was also added in Palestine, that of nourishment [65] or harvest. [66] Mention might also be made of the key of rain which the coming Elijah will have (Rev. 11:6), of the keys of a king [67] or treasurer, [68] and of the keys which priests have in their hands as rulers of the sanctuary. [69] In Gr. Bar. 11 Michael is the keeper of the keys of the kingdom of heaven (→ 749), not as porter, but as angelic prince.

Hence handing over the keys implies appointment to full authority. He who has the keys has on the one side control, e.g., over the council chamber or treasury, cf. Mt. 13:52, and on the other the power to allow or to forbid entry, cf. Rev. 3:7.

c. Mt. 23:13 leads us a step further. This passage is particularly important for an understanding of Mt. 16:19 because it is the only one in the NT which presupposes an image not found elsewhere, namely, that of the keys of the kingdom (royal dominion) of God (→ n. 52). Mt. 23:13 shows us that the scribes of the time of Jesus claimed to possess the power of the keys in respect of this kingdom (→ also n. 42). They exercised this by declaring the will of God in Holy Scripture in the form of preaching, teaching and judging. Thereby they opened up for the congregation a way into this kingdom (→ 747), i.e., by acting as spiritual leaders of the congregation. Jesus complained that they did not fulfil their task and that they thus barred entry into the kingdom of God rather than opening it up. As Lord of the Messianic community He thus transferred the keys of God's royal dominion, i.e., the full authority of proclamation, to Peter.

---

[60] The Aram. impf. has only limited future significance (W. B. Stevenson, *Grammar of Palestinian Jewish Aramaic* [1924] § 18, 8).

[61] So Köhler, 236 ("in answer to pagan and Gnostic speculations the Church had its porter"); Reitzenstein Ir. Erl., XII (only "the idea of the Aion as servant and doorkeeper" can explain Mt. 16:18 f.); F. Kattenbusch, "Der Quellort der Kirchenidee," *Festgabe f. A. v. Harnack* (1921), 167, n. 1 ("doorkeeper, guardian of the house").

[62] Ahrens, 7 ff.; Steitz, 437 ff.; A. Wünsche, *Neue Beiträge z. Erläuterung d. Ev.* (1878), 195, 447; Wellh. Mt., 85; Str.-B., I, 736 f.; Jeremias, 71 f.; Dalman, 176 f.; Schl. Mt., 510.

[63] So the vl. which Tanch. וירא, 35 (ed. S. Buber, p. 106) offers; Dt. r., 7 on 28:12 : "Key of the unfruitful"; Midr. on Ps. 78:25 ff.: "Key of the mother's womb."

[64] bTaan., 2a etc. (par. in Str.-B., I, 437, 523, 737; III, 3 f.). The meaning is that only God can perform these miracles.

[65] bTaan., 2b.

[66] Tanch. וירא, 35 (ed. S. Buber, p. 106).

[67] Pesikt., 5 (ed. S. Buber [1868], 53b) and par.

[68] bShab., 31a b.

[69] S. Bar. 10:18; Paral. Jerem. 4:3 f.; Ab R. Nat., 4 (Str.-B., I, 737; par. 33 and 151).

Mt. 16:19 has, therefore, a polemical implication. This explains what is at first sight a surprising fact, namely, that a present function of Peter should be described as control of the keys of the kingdom of God. Jesus is simply adopting a current expression. [70]

d. Finally we should recall that the three verses Mt. 16:17-19 are so constructed that in each a theme is elucidated by antithetical parallelism. V. 19a is thus to be seen in the light of v. 19b c, where we have a new image. The power of the keys consists in full authority to bind and to loose.

Linguistically it should be noted of 16:19b c (ὃ ἐὰν δήσῃς ἐπὶ τῆς γῆς ἔσται δεδε-μένον ἐν τοῖς οὐρανοῖς, καὶ ὃ ἐὰν λύσῃς ἐπὶ τῆς γῆς ἔσται λελυμένον ἐν τοῖς οὐρανοῖς) 1. that we have a twofold substitution for the divine name, the passive and *shemajjā,* [71] and 2. that *jehē 'asīr* and *jehē sherē* are *futura exacta.* We may thus render : "What you bind on earth God will recognise to be bound (at the Last Judgment), and what you loose on earth God will recognise to be loosed (at the Last Judgment).

In Rabb. lit. binding and loosing are almost always used in respect of halakhic decisions (→ II, 60). The scribe binds (declares to be forbidden) and looses (declares to be permitted). But this special use of the antonyms, which is grounded in the juridical character of Rabb. lit., should not cause us to overlook the fact that originally [72] they are used of the authority of the judge [73] to imprison or to release, to impose or to withhold the ban, [74] and that they then take on the figurative sense of executing the divine judgment or averting it (by intercession). [75] Restriction to the teaching office is hardly in accord with the sense of Mt. 16:19, as shown by the understanding of binding and loosing in primitive Christianity → 752, and even more so by what we read of the authority that Jesus gives to those authorised by Him elsewhere, e.g., in Mt. 10:13 ff., where they bring peace to those who receive them and leave divine judgment on those who do not.

In Mt. 16:19, then, we are to regard the authority to bind and to loose as judicial. [76] It is the authority to pronounce judgment on unbelievers and to promise forgiveness to believers.

---

[70] Hence we ought not to conclude that in Mt. 16:18 f. ἐκκλησία and βασιλεία τῶν οὐρανῶν are to be equated (as against H. J. Holtzmann, *Handkomm. z. NT, Die Synopt.*³ [1901], 259; Wellh. Mt., 85; Meyer Ursprung, I, 112, n. 1; Kl. Mt., *ad loc.*; even Jeremias, *op. cit.*, 72 f. is in need of correction here) → 522. Nevertheless, it is true that Mt. 16:18 f. points to the close connection between the two, which rests on the fact that the ἐκκλησία is a preliminary stage of the βασιλεία (Bultmann Trad., 147, n. 1), since its members have the promise that if they persevere to the end (Mk. 13:13) they will share in God's royal dominion (H. Windisch, ZNW, 27 [1928], 186).

[71] Cf. Str.-B., I, 741.

[72] Schl. Mt., 511.

[73] *Ibid.*, 510 f. for examples.

[74] bMQ, 16a, and later Tosafoth on Men., 34b (Str.-B., I, 739).

[75] Dt. r., 2 on 3:23 ("Also I besought Yahweh at that time"): "With what may this be compared ? With an *eparchos* who was in his territory and who apart from the king passed ordinances which the king executed (i.e., acknowledged). He released (פודה) whom he would and bound (חובש) whom he would ... So also Moses. So long as he was in his own territory, he bound whom he would, for it is written (Nu. 16:33): 'They (Korah and his company) went down alive with all that they possessed,' and he released whom he would, for it is written (Dt. 33:6): 'Let Reuben live, and not die.'" (Schl. Mt., 511 quotes this passage.) Cf. also Damasc., 13, 9 f. (of the leader of the camp → II, 618): "And he shall have mercy on them as a father on his children. And he shall ... all their ... faults. As a shepherd his flock, he shall loose all the bands of their imprisonment."

[76] → II, 60 f., though here restriction of binding and loosing to excommunication is a little too narrow.

In sum we may say that the power of the keys is authority in the dispensing of the word of grace and judgment.

2. The Extension of the Power of Binding and Loosing to the Apostles.

There can be no doubt that Mt. 18:18 refers back to 16:19, and probably also the analogously constructed [77] antithetical double saying in Jn. 20:23. Both show that the apostolic age did not regard the power of binding and loosing as a special prerogative of Peter. [78] In Jn. 20:23 it is extended to the eleven. A more difficult question is raised by Mt. 18:18. Who holds the power of binding and loosing here?

> The verse before (17) seems to support the view that it is the congregation. But this can hardly be the writer's meaning. For 1. the whole discourse in Mt. 18 is addressed to the μαθηταί (18:1), which usually denotes the twelve; [79] 2. in 18:12 ff. he gives us directions of Jesus to the twelve in their capacity as shepherds of the flock of Jesus, and vv. 15-18 seem to be a direct continuation designed to show that the exercise of discipline as well as love is part of the office of leadership; 3. in Tt. 3:10, where an analogous disciplinary process to that of Mt. 18:15-17 is laid down, it is the authorised apostle rather than the congregation who excommunicates, infra.

We may thus conclude that in both Jn. 20:23 and Mt. 18:18 the apostles have the power to bind and to loose.

3. The Exercise of the Power of Binding in Primitive Christianity.

In accordance with the present context of Mt. 18:18 the power of binding was interpreted by the Palestinian and Syrian churches as the power to exclude from the congregation. This was preceded by a disciplinary process in three courts for which there is no precise analogy in the Synagogue: [80] reprimand (→ II, 474) with just the two present, then in the presence of witnesses, and then before the congregation. Only when public rebuke was in vain did excommunication follow (Mt. 18:15-17). We find a similar process in Tt. 3:10: "A heretic reject (→ παραιτέομαι, I, 195) after a first and second admonition." [81] This suggests that the excommunication of Mt. 18:17 would take place in the congregation. The process would not only prevent overhasty decisions but also guarantee that no means should be left untried to restore the erring brother to the right path. [82]

> Excommunication might take very different forms, e.g., rejection of fellowship with execration (Ac. 8:20 f.), with cursing (Gl. 1:8-9; 1 C. 16:22), [83] with handing over to

---

[77] The only point is that Mt. puts the binding first (δεῖν—λύειν), Jn. the power to forgive (ἀφιέναι—κρατεῖν).

[78] It is hardly of material significance that only the power to bind and to loose, not the power of the keys, is given to the wider circle.

[79] Bultmann Trad., 369, 381.

[80] Str.-B., I, 787.

[81] It should be noted that Titus speaks the decisive word as the fully authorised representative of the apostle.

[82] It is significant that the Past., which more than any other NT writings insist on discipline in the form of admonition, prohibition and if necessary excommunication, also lay great stress on the fact that the true servant of the Lord will do all that can be done by way of love and patience that God may free those who go astray from the snares of Satan and bring them to repentance (2 Tm. 2:24-26).

[83] That the meaning of anathema is expulsion from the fellowship and congregation is rightly emphasised in Schl. K., 459 f. A different view is taken by K. Bornhäuser, Die Reformation, 26 (1932), 82 f., who links anathema with the sharper interdict (on this cf. Str.-B., IV, 327-329), which did not imply excommunication from the synagogue (IV, 330).

Satan (1 C. 5:3-5; 1 Tm. 1:20 → II, 170). It took place when there were serious moral lapses (1 C. 5:1 ff.; Mt. 18:15; Ac. 8:18 ff.) or when the Gospel was falsified (Gl. 1:8-9; Tt. 3:9 f.). [84]

In Jn. 20:23b : "If you retain the sins of any, [85] God has retained them (i.e., to the Last Judgment)," [86] the reference seems to be to intimation of judgment to the unbelieving world, cf. the words of the risen Lord in Lk. 24:47 and in the false Marcan ending, 16:16b.

4. The Power of Loosing.

In the present context, the power of loosing in Mt. 18:18 is the power to promise forgiveness. The same view is found in Jn. 20:23a, which derives from a pre-Johannine tradition. [87] Here the risen Lord says : ἄν τινων ἀφῆτε τὰς ἁμαρτίας, ἀφίονται [88] αὐτοῖς, "when you forgive men their sins, God [89] will [90] forgive them," i.e., He will confirm the promised remission at the Last Day. The corresponding words of the risen Lord in Mt. (28:16 ff.), Lk. (24:47) and the false Marcan ending (16:16a) make it likely that the forgiveness of Jn. 20:23a is in the first instance that associated with baptism. It is important that the power of remission in Jn. 20:22 rests on reception of the Spirit. Since Jn. distinguishes between the impartation of the Spirit to the apostles at Easter (20:22) and that to other believers at Pentecost (7:39), this means that the power rests on reception of the Spirit who is imparted to the apostles when they are sent out (20:21) and who equips them for their task. [91] Through the Spirit, whom He sends as His authorising messenger, Christ Himself is directly at work as the One who forgives.

J. Jeremias

---

[84] We must distinguish between excommunication and the refusal of intercourse (μὴ συναναμίγνυσθαι, 2 Th. 3:14; 1 C. 5:9, 11), esp. of table fellowship (1 C. 5:11). This means of discipline was exercised by the congregation on unruly members (2 Th. 3:14) or those living unclean lives (1 C. 5:9-13). It did not mean a full break, but was an attempt to bring the guilty back to the right path by fraternal means (2 Th. 3:15).

[85] κρατεῖν τὰς ἁμαρτίας is a Semitism (examples in Str.-B., II, 585 f.).

[86] Here we have the passive for the divine name.

[87] Jn. 20:23 is the only passage in the Fourth Gospel which speaks of ἀφιέναι τὰς ἁμαρτίας.

[88] So B, ἀφίενται א Θ pm. The perf. ἀφέωνται (A D al) is an assimilation to κεκράτηνται (Jn. 20:23b).

[89] → n. 86.

[90] On the future significance of the present here, cf. P. Joüon, L'Évangile de Notre-Seigneur Jésus-Christ (Verbum Salutis, V) (1930), 593.

[91] "The ordination of the disciples," J. Wellhausen, Das Ev. Johannis (1908), 94.

---

† κλέπτω, † κλέπτης

κλέπτω. a. "To steal," "secretly and craftily to embezzle and appropriate," Hom. Il., 5, 268; 24, 24. No blame is attached in these passages ; indeed, the cunning and skill displayed are recognised, hence gods, demi-gods and heroes steal (Epict. [Diss., III, 7, 13] deduces from Epicurean ethics that stealing is justifiable for this philosophy so long as it takes place κομψῶς καὶ περιεσταλμένως, "with craft and secrecy"). Later it is condemned as no less wrong than robbery, murder and other serious offences. κλέπτω denotes the secret and cunning act as compared with ἁρπάζω, which is characterised by violence (βίᾳ), Soph. Phil., 644; Aristoph. Pl., 372; Xenoph. Oec., 20, 15 (κλέπτων ἢ ἁρπάζων ἢ προσαιτῶν διανοεῖται βιοτεύειν). The objects may be articles of value, Aesch. Prom., 8 (τὸ πῦρ); Eur. Rhes., 502 (ἄγαλμα); Hdt., V, 84; Xenoph. An., VII, 6, 41 (χρήματα), animals, P. Oxy., I, 139, 19, or men (in the sense "to abduct"), Pind. Pyth., 4, 445 (Μήδειαν). The ref. might also be to places, Xenoph. An., IV, 6, 11 ("to seize with cunning, unnoticed") or to circumstances, Aristot. Rhetorica ad Alexandrum, 36, p. 1440b, 21 ("to provide for oneself surreptitiously"). b. More generally the word can mean "to deceive," "to cheat," "to bewitch (by flattery)": Hom. Il., 1, 132 (νόῳ); Hes. Theog., 613; Aesch. Choeph., 854 (οὔτοι φρέν' ἂν κλέψειεν . . .); Soph. Ant., 681; 1218; Aeschin. Or., 3, 35 (κλέπτοντες τὴν ἀκρόασιν); Sext. Emp. Math., ed. Bekker, 39 (τὰς τῶν θεωμένων ὄψεις, of conjurers). c. A further meaning is "to hold secretly," "to put away," "to conceal," "to hide": Pind. Olymp., 6, 60 (θεοῖο γόνον); Aeschin. Or., 3, 142 (τοῖς ὀνόμασιν κλέπτων καὶ μεταφέρων τὰ πράγματα). d. "To do something in a secret or furtive manner": Soph. Ai., 189 (ὑποβαλλόμενοι κλέπτουσι μύθους); Plato contrasts this secret action with βιάζεσθαι: Leg., XI, 933e (κλέπτων ἢ βιαζόμενος); Resp., III, 413b.

κλέπτης is a. "the thief": Aesch. Prom., 946 (τὸν πυρὸς κλέπτην); Eur. Iph. Taur., 1026; P. Greci e Latini, 393, 18 (3rd cent. A.D.); Plat. Resp., I, 344b, with emphasis on the ἀδικεῖν; 351 c with ληισταί; Epict. Diss., I, 9, 15. κλέπτης is also b. "one who acts with subterfuge and secrecy," Soph. Ai., 1135 : κλέπτης γὰρ αὐτοῦ ψηφοποιὸς ηὑρέθης, "you are found as one who secretly stole the voices which otherwise would have been for him" (i.e., a deceitful judge).

In the LXX κλέπτειν is one of the chief sins with murder, adultery and false witness, Jer. 7:9. The commandment οὐ κλέψεις is unconditional (Ex. 20:14; Dt. 5:19; cf. Lv. 19:11 [plur.]; Is. 1:23; cf. Philo Decal., 135; 138; 171). The things stolen may be objects of value like silver and gold, Gn. 44:5, 8; Ex. 22:6 f., or animals, Gn. 30:33; Ex. 21:37; cf. Philo Spec. Leg., IV, 12; men, Gn. 40:15; Ex. 21:17; Dt. 24:7 etc.; cf. Philo Spec. Leg., IV, 13; things devoted to God, Jos. 7:11; idols, Gn. 31:19, 30, 32; or genuine words of God (stolen by false prophets), Jer. 23:30. κλέπτειν is a crime which meets with corresponding punishment, Ex. 22:2 (21:37) ff.; Dt. 24:7; cf. Sir. 5:14; 20:25; Zech. 5:3 f. [1] It is a sin against God, Ex. 20:14; Dt. 5:19. Even when due to need and poverty, it is to dishonour God, Prv. 30:9 (24:32); cf. 6:30. Philo Leg. All., III, 32 f. calls it thieving even to ascribe to man something which is the work of God. Violent tyranny is also stealing, Decal., 136. In Tob. 1:18 κλέπτειν means "to do something secretly." In the LXX, as elsewhere, κλέπτων or κλέψας always refers to a concrete instance of stealing or to the act of stealing, Prv. 6:30; Ex. 22:7 (8); cf. Plat. Leg., XI, 933e; Xenoph. Oec., 20, 15; Eur. Rhes., 502; κλέπτης, however, can be used of this class of men, Dt. 24:7;

κλέπτω κτλ. [1] Cf. A. Jirku, Das weltliche Recht im AT (1927); H. Schmökel, Das angewandte Recht im AT (Diss. Breslau, 1930). The severest penalty, i.e., death, is the punishment for one who abducts a fellow-citizen (Dt. 24:7) or who steals goods dedicated to God (Jos. 7:1, 25).

Job 24:14; Hos. 7:1; Jl. 2:9 etc. God's activity is never compared with that of the thief. Only once, in Ob. 5, do we find a degree of comparison when it is said that Yahweh's work of destruction will be even more radical than that which takes place in burglary. In Jl. 2:9 the locusts which descend like a plague are compared with thieves breaking through the windows. Thieving is distinguished by the following characteristics: the use of the night, Job 24:14; Ιερ. 30:3 (49:9); Philo Spec. Leg., IV, 10; breaking in by force, Job 24:16; the use of unlawful means of entry (windows), Jl. 2:9; cf. Hos. 7:1; ruthless self-seeking, Ιερ. 30:3 (49:9). Secrecy (cf. Philo Spec. Leg., I, 127) and violence are also essential features.

The NT knows of a new being of the Christian in the Spirit which works itself out in love. This new being embraces the whole man with his whole duty and capacity, with everyday obligations and the most self-evident moral demands. All the commandments are summed up and fulfilled in love. This means that the requirements of the Decalogue are taken with unconditional seriousness, and the validity of the οὐ κλέψεις as God's will is thus posited also [2] (Mk. 10:19; Mt. 19:18; Lk. 18:20; R. 13:9; cf. R. 2:21). What the proclamation of the Law could not do, i.e., overcome inordinate greed, should now be self-evident for believers in virtue of their possession of the Spirit. Hence the thief should not steal any more, but work with his hands, so that he will be in a position to give to those in need and to help them (Eph. 4:28). κλέπτειν is condemned as a selfish and loveless breaking of fellowship. It is to be replaced by work and service in the new disposition of love. [3] Jn. 12:6 characterises the κλέπτης as a betrayer of fellowship. 1 Pt. 4:15 groups him with murderers, receivers and criminals. A similar judgment is found in 1 C. 6:10. In Mt. 27:64 the Jews fear that there might be a κλέπτειν of the body of Jesus by the disciples, and in 28:13 they maintain that this has in fact taken place.

In the NT κλέπτης (κλέπτειν) is often used in parables or parabolic sayings for the breaking in of the Messianic age. As the householder prevents the thief from breaking in by watching, so the disciples must be ready for the coming of the Lord by watching, Mt. 24:43 = Lk. 12:39. The only point of comparison in this pure parable is the element of the sudden and unexpected which is common both to the coming of the Messiah and to that of the thief. But the entry of the thief is marked also by a violent element (διορύσσω), [4] as in Mt. 6:19 f. with its warning that earthly treasures may only too easily fall victim to the thief. Paul uses the same comparison in 1 Th. 5:2-4 when he is answering a question as to the time of the day of the Lord. He obviously builds on the dominical saying that the day of the Messiah will come as a thief at an unexpected hour. But if unbelievers are suddenly surprised thereby as by a thief, this ought not to be so with members of the community. For they realise that the coming of the Messianic day is imminent. Again, they live already in the bright radiance of the new age of salvation.

---

[2] → II, 547 ff.; H. Preisker, *Geist u. Leben, Das Telos-Ethos des Urchristentums* (1933), 51 ff.

[3] Lv. r., 3 on 2:1; Midr. Qoh. on 4:6: "Better is he who goes and works and gives alms of his substance than he who goes and robs and extorts and gives alms of that which belongs to others." Eph. 4:28 is rather different, since here we do not have a comparison between two men, one of whom gives alms of what he has won honestly and the other of what he has stolen, but a great change is demanded in the thief himself, so that instead of being a disruptive element he becomes a useful member of society.

[4] διορύσσω as in Job 24:16: חָתַר; מַחְתֶּרֶת, Ex. 22:1.

They are not groping in uncertain night. Hence they cannot be surprised by the *parousia*.[5] The sudden and unexpected element in the day of the Lord is also brought out by the same figure in 2 Pt. 3:10. Allegorically the comparison is applied to the Lord Himself in Rev. 3:3; 16:15.[6] The Lord will come unexpectedly like a thief in the night, and this should startle the community into watchfulness.[7]

In the figurative discourse on the Good Shepherd in Jn. 10, all those who claimed lordship over the community before Jesus — is the reference to the Herodians, the Rabbis, party heads,[8] or is it linked with Eth. En. 89 ff.? — and who came with self-seeking and caused disruption, are condemned by the example of the thief (10:8, 10). Hence the community should be directed only by those who have their ministry and authority from the κύριος; all others, in their selfish seeking after power, are compared to thieves (10:1).[9] Here the thought of selfish violence is the point of comparison.

The common use of this metaphor for the suddenness of the coming of the Messianic day or the Messiah, or in opposition to a false conception of the pastoral office in the community, shows a. that in a parable the moral nature of an object of comparison is not important, but only one point of comparison is decisive, and b. that there is a greatness, transcendence and freedom in primitive Christian faith in the κύριος which liberates it from fear of such comparisons, in contrast to the timidity and uncertainty of Jewish faith, which dare not use such a figure for the unexpected coming of the day of Yahweh, but is forced to look elsewhere for similes.[10] Even in such minor details one may see the "liberty of the children of God" with its bold outlook: "All things are yours" (1 C. 3:21).

Preisker

---

[5] This keeps the unity of the train of thought. The reading ὡς κλέπτας in A B bo introduces a very different idea, namely, that those who are still in the night of unbelief will be caught by the coming day like thieves; the day of the Lord will surprise them as daylight overtakes thieves (G. Foerster, ZNW, 17 [1916], 169 ff.). But the decisive ideas of the passage have nothing to do with unbelievers. The concern is with Christians. Hence we should accept ὡς κλέπτης (אּ DFG) in v. 4. Otherwise "the harmony with v. 2 would be completely destroyed" (A. Steinmann, *Th.-Briefe*[2] [1921]). Dib. Th., *ad loc.* points out that the history of the image also favours the above interpretation.

[6] 16:15 is to be seen in the light of 3:3a, Loh. Apk., *ad loc.*

[7] In 3:3 we should not read ἐπὶ σέ (אּא vg^cl). Hence the idea of destructive violence is not part of the comparison. In 16:15 the figure of "walking naked" is a fixed technical phrase meaning "condemned in the judgment." Hence it does not introduce the idea of violence, as Foerster tries to argue, *loc. cit.*

[8] Schl. J., *ad loc.*

[9] Cf. Ep. Jer., 57: κλεπτῶν ... λῃστῶν; 1 Esr. 4:23: λῃστεύειν καὶ κλέπτειν; 1 Esr. 4:24: κλέπτειν καὶ ἁρπάζειν.

[10] bSanh., 97a: "When R. Ze'ira (c. 300) found the rabb. occupied therewith (i.e., the question of the coming of the Messiah), he said to them: I ask you not to put it in the remote future, for I have learned that three things come unexpectedly, the Messiah, a discovery and a scorpion."

† κλῆμα¹

"Shoot," "young twig," which is broken off to be replanted, "slip," Xenoph. Oec., 19, 8 : ὁ βλαστὸς τοῦ κλήματος (cf. 9), or "branch" generally, Aristot. Hist. An., V, 18, p. 550b, 8 f.; Ez. 15:2; 17:23; Mal. 3:19; Jl. 1:7, specifically "shoot of the vine," e.g., Plat. Resp., I, 353a : ἀμπέλου κλῆμα, Theophr. Historia Plantarum, 2, 5, 5; De Causis Plantarum, 3, 14, 6; Nu. 13:23; ᾽Ιερ. 31:32; Ez. 17:6 f.; 19:11; ψ 79:11; Polyb., 29, 27, 5; Jos. Ant., 2, 64 and 67; ibid., 12, 75; P. Flor., 148, 9 : συλλέξατε δὲ κλήματα Θηβαϊκὰ καὶ λευκά (cf. 14);² Jn. 15:2, 4, 5, 6;³ v. also Poll. Onom., 1, 237: ἰδίως δὲ καλεῖται ὁ τῆς ἀμπέλου (sc. κλάδος) κλῆμα. Fig. Aeschin., 3, 166 : ἀμπελουργοῦσί τινες τὴν πόλιν, . . . τὰ κλήματα τὰ τοῦ δήμου ὑποτέτμηται.

In the LXX κλῆμα is used for זְמוֹרָה, Nu. 13:23; Ez. 15:2, דָּלִית, Ez. 17:6 f., 23; 19:11, קָצִיר, Ps. 80:11, שָׂרִיג, Jl. 1:7, עָנָף, Mal. 3:19, נְטִישָׁה, Jer. 48:32. These Heb. words denote a branch or shoot, and when they occur they are fairly regularly translated κλῆμα. Only in the case of עֲנָף (עֲנָף, עָנָף) is there greater variety, and this is explained in part by the combination of synonymous words. κλάδος is used for דָּלִית along with κλῆμα. κλῆμα is most often used in the OT for the shoot of the vine, esp. in connection with the figure of the vine, e.g., in relation to Israel in Jl. 1:7; Nah. 2:3; Ez. 17:6 ff. and to other nations in Mal. 3:19. ⁴

In Jn. 15:1ff. (→ I, 342) the organic relationship between the vine and the branches is used metaphorically to show the inner living relationship which Jesus has established between Himself and the disciples. In order to fulfil their purpose of bearing fruit, branches must abide in the vine which nourishes them with sap. So it is essential for the disciples, if they are to fulfil the task which is laid upon them, that they should abide in fellowship with Jesus, who gives them their vitality (v. 4 f.). Again, when the harvest is past, branches must either be pruned by the vinedresser or taken away.⁵ Similarly the disciples, when they have shown the vitality of their fellowship with Jesus (v. 12 f.), must be subjected to the serious discipline or the crushing judgment of God, who rules over all things (2, 6). In this allegory in John's Gospel we have a new and distinctive application of the organic connection between the vine and the branches as a picture of the closest possible union. There is nothing exactly comparable in the many oriental parallels (→ I, 342 f.).

Behm

κ λ ῆ μ α. Liddell-Scott, Cr.-Kö., Pr.-Bauer³, s.v.; Zn. J., Bau. J. and F. Büchsel, *Das Ev. nach Joh.* (*NT Deutsch*, 4³ [1937]) on Jn. 15:1 ff.

¹ Like κλάδος (Mt. 4:32 and par.; Mt. 21:8; Mk. 13:28 and par. etc.), to be derived from κλάω (→ 727), v. Walde-Pok., I, 437.

² Cf. M. Schnebel, *Die Landwirtschaft im hellen. Ägypten*, I, *Münchener Beiträge zur Papyrusforschung usw.*, 7 (1925), 248.

³ We also have reference to κλήματα (Lat. *palmites*) in the agraphon, attested to by Papias, of the wonderful fruitfulness of vines in the kingdom of God (preserved in Latin in Iren. Haer., V, 33, 3 f.).

⁴ This paragraph is by Bertram.

⁵ On this pt. cf. G. Dalman, *Arbeit u. Sitte in Palästina*, IV (1935), 330 ff.

κλῆρος, κληρόω, προσκληρόω,
ὁλόκληρος, ὁλοκληρία, κληρονόμος,
συγκληρονόμος, κληρονομέω,
κατακληρονομέω, κληρονομία

---

† κλῆρος.

Contents : 1. The Greek Usage ; 2. κλῆρος and its Relation to κληρονομία in the LXX ;
3. κλῆρος in Later Judaism ; 4. κλῆρος in Philo ; 5. κλῆρος in the NT.

1. The Greek Usage.

The basic meaning of κλῆρος is "lot." Even in the Homeric period, however, this
divides into the two main senses of the "lot which is drawn" and the "lot of land." This
duality, which is also found in Heb. and English, is linked with the ancient system of
economic settlement.

κλῆρος [1] means first the "lot" in drawing lots [2] (κλήρῳ λαγχάνειν, Hdt., III, 83) or
the "act of drawing lots" (Plut. Cons. ad Apoll., 4 [II, 102e]: ἐν δημοκρατίᾳ κλῆρός
ἐστι τῶν ἀρχῶν). It then means the "portion of land which is assigned by lot" [3] (Hdt.,
II, 109 : κλῆρον ἴσον ἑκάστῳ τετράγωνον διδόντα), and then simply a "portion of
land," a "lot" (Ditt. Syll.[3], 169, 59 ff.: κλῆρον ἐπρίατο). The idea of patrimony
plays a role in inheritance. Thus Plat. Leg., XI, 923d lays down that when a son is going
to a colony his father may give him what he wills, πλὴν τοῦ πατρῴου κλήρου καὶ
τῆς περὶ τὸν κλῆρον κατασκευῆς πάσης. κλῆρος can then come to be the equivalent
of "inheritance" (Demosth. Or., 43, 3 : ἐπεδικάσατο τοῦ κλήρου, came into judgment
in respect of inheritance). The parcelling out of land leads also in Egyptian pap. to
the sense of "land in fee," [4] i.e., a piece of land which from the beginning of the Roman
period belonged to the crown and which was made over to soldiers to work. In the first
instance this was not hereditary, but could be assigned only to a son able to serve in the
army. Later, however, it was hereditary in fact, though not in law (from the 2nd cent.
B.C.). This helps us to understand the further sense of "allotted sphere" (Ael. Arist. Or.,
43, 14 [Keil]: Zeus ἅμα δὲ τῇ ποιήσει ... διῄρει ... ἕκαστα καὶ κλήρους ἀπένε-
μεν, ποιῶν μὲν ζῷα τὰ πρέποντα ἑκάστοις τόποις τάς τε γιγνομένας οἰκήσεις
τε καὶ λήξεις τοῖς γεννηθεῖσιν ἀποδιδούς, where λῆξις shows how easy is the
transition from "lot" to "allotted share," and then to "allotted portion" in a more general
sense. Always in secular Gk., in these contexts, the spatial conception of κλῆρος is
maintained. [5]

κ λ ῆ ρ ο ς. In general cf. T. Lenschau in Pauly-W., XI (1922), 810-813, s.v. κλῆρος;
V. Ehrenberg, ibid., XIII (1927), 1451-1504, s.v. Losung; also Str.-B., II, 596 f. and the
comm., esp. on Col. 1:12 and 1 Pt. 5:3; Cr.-Kö., 603 f.
[1] The linguistic explanations are mostly taken from Liddell-Scott, s.v.
[2] Ehrenberg, loc. cit., with further bibl.
[3] Lenschau, loc. cit. and Ehrenberg, loc. cit.
[4] H. Kreller, Erbrechtliche Untersuchungen (1919), 6 ff.
[5] Cf. a similar spatial view in the astrologer Vett. Val., v. Index in Kroll. But we have
more than this in Cornut., Theol. Graec., 15 (p. 19, 3 ff., Nock), where the Charites are said
by some to descend from Eurynome, and this proves ὅτι χαριστικώτεροί πώς εἰσιν ἢ
ὀφείλουσιν εἶναι οἱ μεγάλους κλήρους νεμόμενοι.

2. κλῆρος and its Relation to κληρονομία in the LXX.

Used for גּוֹרָל, κλῆρος in the LXX means the "lot," e.g., Jon. 1:7: βάλωμεν κλήρους. The term for casting lots is usually βάλλειν but cf. also ἐμβάλλειν, Jos. 18:10, ἐκφέρειν, Jos. 18:6, 8; for the decision we have ἐξῆλθεν ὁ κλῆρος, Jos. 18:11 or ἔπεσεν ὁ κλῆρος ἐπί τινα, Jon. 1:7. Casting lots is done specifically by victors in dividing the spoil, Jl. 3:3; Ob. 11; Nah. 3:10; Sir. 37:8 and ψ 21:18 : διεμερίσαντο τὰ ἱμάτιά μου ἑαυτοῖς καὶ ἐπὶ τὸν ἱματισμόν μου ἔβαλον κλῆρον. κλῆρος is also used of the lot by which God's rule was exercised in Israel, and in the partition of Canaan, [6] Nu. 26:52 ff.; 33:53 ff.; Jos. 18:1 ff.; Ez. 47:22; 48:29 etc., cf. also the assigning of duties in the temple, 1 Ch. 25:8 f.; 26:13 f.; 2 Ἐσδρ. 20:35, cf. 21:1, and also the choice between the two goats in Lv. 16:8-10. Sometimes the image of casting lots is used for the determination of destiny by God, Is. 34:17; Ἐσθ. 10:3 g h.

κλῆρος then denotes, as in secular Gk. the "lot of land," 1 Ἐσδρ. 4:56 : the king πᾶσι τοῖς φρουροῦσι τὴν πόλιν, ἔγραψε δοῦναι αὐτοῖς κλήρους καὶ ὀψώνια, Nu. 16:14 : ἔδωκας ἡμῖν κλῆρον ἀγροῦ καὶ ἀμπελῶνας.

κλῆρος is found 129 times in the LXX, 62 times for גּוֹרָל, 49 for נַחֲלָה, 11 for words of the stem ירשׁ, two for פּוּר, which means the same as גּוֹרָל, two for derivates of the stem חלק, and one each for חֶבֶל and קָרְבָּן. גּוֹרָל is twice rendered κληρονομία (ψ 15:5; Is. 17:14), and 4 times in Jos. its equivalent is ὅριον in the sense of the portion of the tribes.

To clarify the meaning of κλῆρος in the LXX it is necessary to explain why it can be used for נַחֲלָה and also to show its relation to κληρονομία. From different angles — κληρονομία means inheritance — κλῆρος and κληρονομία coincide when the form in which the Israelites took possession of Canaan, and the land itself as their own special, God-given possession, are described. Cf. Jos. 17:4 : ὁ θεὸς ἐνετείλατο ... δοῦναι ἡμῖν κληρονομίαν ἐν μέσῳ τῶν ἀδελφῶν ἡμῶν. καὶ ἐδόθη αὐταῖς ... κλῆρος ἐν τοῖς ἀδελφοῖς τοῦ πατρὸς αὐτῶν (in both cases נָתַן נַחֲלָה). In a whole series of similar phrases there is a similar interchangeability. The land is given to the Israelites ἐν κλήρῳ, Ex. 6:8 (מוֹרָשָׁה) and it is said to them : ὑμῖν ... δέδωκα τὴν γῆν αὐτῶν ἐν κλήρῳ. καὶ κατακληρονομήσετε τὴν γῆν αὐτῶν ἐν κλήρῳ, Nu. 33:53 f., though in Jos. 12:6 we read : καὶ ἔδωκεν αὐτὴν Μωϋσῆς ἐν κληρονομίᾳ Ρουβην, cf. Dt. 2:9 with Jos. 24:4 A; Mal. 1:3. In Nu. 18:24 we have κληρονομεῖν κλῆρον, and the verse before, in the same connection, [7] κληρονομεῖν κληρονομίαν. Both terms are used for the concrete portion of land assigned to Israel, to a tribe, to a family or to an individual. Joshua is buried πρὸς τοῖς ὁρίοις τοῦ κλήρου αὐτοῦ, Ιησ. 24:31 [MT (Jos. 24:30) נַחֲלָה,], and the 3½ tribes will not return home ἕως ἂν καταμερισθῶσιν οἱ υἱοὶ Ισραηλ ἕκαστος εἰς τὴν κληρονομίαν αὐτοῦ, Nu. 32:18. The Lord is the κλῆρος of the Levite, Dt. 10:9; 18:2; He is also their κληρονομία, Nu. 18:20. Again, the καρπώματα κυρίου are the κλῆρος of the Levites, Dt. 18:1, or their κληρονομία, Sir. 45:20. In Dt. 18:1 we have the fixed phrase : οὐ ... μερὶς οὐδὲ κλῆρος, but cf. Gn. 31:14; 3 Βασ. 12:16, 24 and 2 Ch. 10:16 : μερὶς καὶ κληρονομία; the Heb. is always חֵלֶק and נַחֲלָה. There are even traces of κληρονομία taking on senses of κλῆρος originally alien to it (→ 777). Hence it is not easy to say what ideas the translator and readers linked with the two terms in the passages cited. But we are helped by the fact that the words are not absolute equivalents. Thus it may be said that the whole land of Canaan ἔσται ὑμῖν εἰς κληρονομίαν, Nu. 34:2, but we never find a similar phrase with κλῆρος. On the other side, we find κλῆροι in the plur., Nu. 32:19; 34:14 f. (Heb. נַחֲלָתָם in the sing.); Hos. 5:7

[6] διὰ κλήρων, Nu. 26:55; ἐκ τοῦ κλήρου, Nu. 26:56; ἐν κλήρῳ, Nu. 33:54; κατὰ κλήρους, Jos. 14:2; μετὰ κλήρου, Nu. 34:13; κληρωτί, Jos. 21:8.
[7] And by the same translator.

(קְלָל); Jer. 12:13; Gn. 48:6; Jos. 19:1 B, but never κληρονομίαι in the plur. In such passages κλῆρος means a portion of land, i.e., that which is allotted by God, whereas κληρονομία emphasises the fact that it is given as a firm and lasting patrimony. Thus we read of a κλῆρος τῆς κληρονομίας ἡμῶν in Nu. 36:3 : the inheritance consists in a κλῆρος, it is a portion which constitutes a patrimony ; but we never find κληρονομία τοῦ κλήρου. Again we find κλῆροι κατασχέσεως, Nu. 35:2 (the lots of the tribes) and κατάσχεσις κληρονομίας, Nu. 27:7, cf. Ez. 46:16 (possession which is an inheritance), but we never find κληρονομία κατασχέσεως (inheritance which is a possession). A more difficult question is what the translators and readers have in view when we read of the land being given ἐν κλήρῳ. We might think of the sense of land in fee, which was particularly common in Egypt, but the idea that the land is really God's possession seems to be later, and in any case it would not explain the parallel use with κληρονομία. The thought of patrimony plays some part, rather in the sense of what is to be inherited than of what is inherited, and at this point κλῆρος and κληρονομία tend to merge, though κλῆρος is preferred in ordinary Gk. Also important is the idea that each people is allotted its land. In passages in which this thought occurs κληρονομία is used, Jos. 24:4 A; Mal. 1:3, and κληρονομεῖν, Dt. 2:9; Jos. 24:4; Ju. 11:24, but does not δέδωκα τὴν γῆν ἐν κλήρῳ suggest the share of the people of Israel in the earth ? Again, διδόναι ἐν κλήρῳ has in view the apportionment of the land into individual κλῆροι, Nu. 36:2 : ἀποδοῦναι τὴν γῆν τῆς κληρονομίας ἐν κλήρῳ τοῖς υἱοῖς Ισραηλ, cf. Jos. 11:23 : καὶ ἔδωκεν αὐτοὺς (the Anakim or their land) Ἰησοῦς ἐν κληρονομίᾳ Ισραηλ ἐν μερισμῷ κατὰ φυλὰς αὐτῶν. That the land is assigned gives confidence in the legitimacy of possession.

Both κλῆρος and κληρονομία indicate that Israel did not conquer the land by its own achievements or indeed plan its conquest, but that God's free disposition gave Israel the land as its share, and that it has thus been conquered and possessed by Israel as a legitimate portion. In this whole matter κλῆρος emphasises the aspect of allotment and κληρονομία the sure and lasting nature of the possession. The giving of the land to the people finds a parallel in the apportionment of individual κλῆροι to the tribes, clans and families. What God's promise is in respect of the whole land, the lot is in respect of individual κλῆροι; it expresses the will of God.

From what has been said it is not surprising that a figurative use of the terms develops in which they mean much the same thing. And if thus far the use of κλῆρος remains close to the Gk., since we are still thinking of spatial allotment, there is a marked divergence from this in the figurative use. The spatial concept fades, and there remains only that of allotment, par. with μερίς. Only twice is it said that Israel is God's κλῆρος, Dt. 9:29 and Est. 4:17 h; cf. Dt. 32:8 f.: ὅτε διεμέριζεν ὁ ὕψιστος ἔθνη ... ἐγενήθη μερὶς κυρίου λαὸς αὐτοῦ Ιακωβ, σχοίνισμα κληρονομίας αὐτοῦ Ισραηλ, the nations are a portion of the ἄγγελοι θεοῦ (v. 8), Israel's is God's portion ; the sense is obviously very different when it is said that Israel is God's κληρονομία (→ 780). In Israel destiny is also assigned, and here again the two terms differ, for only in a play on words is κληρονομία used at Is. 17-14 : αὕτη ἡ μερὶς τῶν ὑμᾶς προνομευσάντων καὶ κληρονομία (= בְּגוֹד) τοῖς ὑμᾶς κληρονομήσασιν (= "win," → 777), and apart from this we may adduce only Job 31:2 and ψ 15:5 f.[8] In this sense κλῆρος becomes the fixed rendering of גוֹרָל in the non-historical books of the OT. The par. with μερίς makes it plain that the sense is "what is allotted" : Is. 57:6 : ἐκείνη σου ἡ μερίς, οὗτός σου ὁ κλῆρος, cf. Jer. 13:25 : οὗτος ὁ κλῆρός σου καὶ μερίς. Thus in the later books there develops the idea of a κλῆρος assigned to each individual : τὸν ... σὸν

---

[8] These passages show that it is hard to distinguish sharply between the two terms.

κλῆρον βάλε ἐν ἡμῖν ("share thy life with us," "make common cause with us"), is the demand of the ungodly to the righteous in Prv. 1:14, and in Wis. 2:9 the ungodly say that merriness is their μερὶς καὶ κλῆρος. Of the righteous it may be said : ἐν ἁγίοις ὁ κλῆρος αὐτοῦ ἐστιν, Wis. 5:5; Sir. 25:19 desires that the κλῆρος ἁμαρτωλοῦ should fall on the woman. Transitions to this usage may be seen in 2 Εσδρ. 20:35 : decision was made περὶ κλήρου ξυλοφορίας (on the share of the individual in the supply of wood), Wis. 3:14 : to the faithful eunuch is given κλῆρος ἐν ναῷ κυρίου θυμηρέστερος, and 1 Μαcc. 2:54 S* : Phinehas acquired κλῆρον διαθήκης ἱερωσύνης, where κλῆρος is no longer a part of something concrete. Cf. also ψ 124:3 : οὐκ ἀφήσει τὴν ῥάβδον τῶν ἁμαρτωλῶν ἐπὶ τὸν κλῆρον τῶν δικαίων, and the MS tradition at ψ 30:15. Of special significance is the fact that with the rise of hope in the resurrection גּוֹרָל and κλῆρος came to be applied to the portion allotted to man after death : Da. 12:13 : וְתַעֲמֹד לְגֹרָלְךָ לְקֵץ הַיָּמִין, Θ : καὶ ἀναστήσῃ εἰς τὸν κλῆρόν σου (LXX : ἐπὶ τὴν δόξαν σου) εἰς συντέλειαν ἡμερῶν.

Ultimately this use of κλῆρος is rooted in the OT awareness of a God who exercises concrete control of history, leading the people into the land of Canaan and thus giving it its portion. Israel learned thereby that it is God who generally assigns to man his portion.

3. κλῆρος in Later Judaism.

In later Judaism, as in the NT and the post-apostolic fathers, κλῆρος is important only in two senses, first as the lot with which lots are drawn, and then as the specific portion appointed for man, usually in eschatological terms.

In NT the lot stills plays a sacral role in the temple. Lots are still drawn over the two goats. Priestly duties are assigned by lot. [9] In 67 A.D. the Zealots choose a new high-priest by lot on appeal to the ancient tradition (of the Law), Jos. Bell., 4, 153-155. Both Jos. and Philo recognise this use, though Philo is alien and sceptical in terms of a piety which dissolves the singularity of history. [10] From a different angle Jub. expands the biblical record by telling us that Noah apportioned the earth to his sons by lot, 8:11 ff.; 10:28, 31. They then draw further lots, and Canaan falls to Shem, not to Canaan. The point of the story is obvious. It is designed to show that God has legitimately assigned Canaan to Israel, for God speaks through the lot. The emphasis is predominantly negative, namely, that Palestine does not belong to the Hamite Canaan. But the midrash threatens the particularity of the conquest of Canaan by the Israelites, which becomes only one instance of the general history of all nations. Jos. also accepts the LXX meaning of κλῆρος as "portion" when he tells us how Philip went to Rome κλήρου τινὸς ἀξιωθῆναι, "to acquire a share (in the inheritance)," Bell., 2, 83.

Of the pseudepigrapha Test. XII uses κλῆρος in the general sense of portion at L. 8:12a : Levi's descendants were divided into three ἀρχαί, καὶ ὁ πρῶτος κλῆρος ἔσται μέγας : the first portion, also at Zeb. 1:3 : ὅτε ἐν ταῖς ποικίλαις ῥάβδοις εἶχεν (εἶχον) τὸν κλῆρον, "when he acquired his portion through the coloured rods," and at D. 7:3 : the Danites are once ἀλλοτριωθήσονται γῆς κλήρου αὐτῶν (the land of their portion). Ass. Mos. 2:2 is important : (Moses to Joshua): stabilibis eis (the Israelites) sortem in me : the Israelite has a portion (sors = κλῆρος = חֵלֶק) in Moses by the fact that he is a member of the people and its history, and by the fact that he affirms this in faithfulness to the Torah. To have a portion in Moses is to have a portion in all the blessings associated with him. In other pseudepigrapha the position is not so

---

[9] There are examples in Str.-B., II, 596 f. on Ac. 1:26.

[10] Jos. Ant., 6, 61 κλήρους βάλετε in expanded repetition of 1 Βασ. 10:20 f. Philo Spec. Leg., IV, 151: εὐτυχίαν ... ἀλλ᾽ οὐκ ἀρετὴν ὁ κλῆρος ἐμφαίνει. Rer. Div. Her., 179 : The lot ἄδηλος καὶ ἀτέκμαρτος τομεύς.

clearly indicated by the linguistic relations. But Eth. En. uses the corresponding term to κλῆρος in a varied eschatological sense along the line which begins with Da. 12:13 Θ. This may be seen in 48:7: The Son of man maintains the lot of the righteous. The lot here is a positive good, i.e., the portion of the righteous. This lot consists in eternal life at 37:4, cf. 58:5 : The saints will seek out in heaven the mysteries of righteousness, the portion of faith. A spatial sense may easily accrue at this point, as in 39:8 : "Here I wished to dwell ... here my inheritance has already been earlier." [11]

The pseudepigraphical passages must supply the lack of Rabbinic examples. With the NT they show the use of the period. Neither in respect of גורל nor of פור are there any parallels in the Rabb. writings which have come down to us. [12] The term used by the Rabb. for the fact that each man is allotted a portion is חֵלֶק = μερίς, μέρος. bShab., 118b preserves a series of sayings of R. Jose (beginning of the 2nd cent. A.D.) which all begin with יהא חלקי מן. These sayings relate to retribution in this world, as two of them plainly show. [13] The basic thought is that, as each man receives his portion, so the portion of those who act alike may be regarded as the same. The desire of R. Jose is that his portion may be that of various saints. Similarly, in the Prayer of Eighteen Petitions, Bab. Rec., the 13th petition runs : שים חלקנו עמהם. A voice from heaven says of people like R. Akiba : חלקם בחיים (bBer., 61b), and R. Eleazar prays (ibid., 16b): תשים חלקנו בגן עדן, "may thou establish our portion in Paradise." The use of מחיצה shows that spatial conceptions are not far off, Str.-B., II, 266 C.

4. κλῆρος in Philo.

Philo is important, for although he diverges in content from the line which runs from the OT to the NT, he stands linguistically on the soil of the OT.

The senses "lot" (Mut. Nom., 151), "inheritance" (Leg. Gaj., 143), "portion" (Spec. Leg., II, 168) and "patrimony" (Vit. Mos., I, 304) are ordinary enough, though it should be noted that, in contrast to the OT and NT, Philo is sceptical as regards the lot, which he calls πρᾶγμα ἀβέβαιον (Mut. Nom., 151 → n. 10). Connection with the OT sense of "allotted portion" may be seen in Op. Mund., 64 : ὕδατος καὶ ἀέρος τὰ προσήκοντα τῶν ζῴων γένη καθάπερ τινὰ κλῆρον οἰκεῖον ἀπειληφότων. Fig. κλῆρος means lot in life at Conf. Ling., 177: incorporeal souls τὸν ἀκήρατον καὶ εὐδαίμονα κλῆρον ἐξ ἀρχῆς λαχοῦσαι; [14] sometimes the sense is almost "gift" (Decal., 112; Congr., 108). On this basis Philo erects a distinctive religious usage in which the righteous are God's κλῆρος and God is the κλῆρος of the righteous. This may be seen plainly in Plant., 47-72 in which Philo expounds Ex. 15:17: ὄρος κληρονομίας σου. In Plant., 48 and 50 κληρονομία = κλῆρος is par. with κτῆμα and οἶκος. In 55 ff. the parable of the king to whom all the possessions of his subjects belong and yet who has his own specifically royal possessions makes it plain that here, too, κλῆρος is for Philo an allotted portion or possession. The portion which God κληρονομεῖ (possesses) is, along with the world, the θίασος of the righteous. In a further development Philo then shows that God can also be called the κλῆρος of the Levites. He explains this allegori-

---

[11] Cf. also Eth. En. 71:16 (with "dwelling"); 99:14 (with "measure"); Slav. En. 9; 55:2; though sometimes we are to think in terms of κληρονομία (→ 781), without a spatial conception, Ps.-Phil. Antiquitates, 23, 13 (P. Riessler, Altjüd. Schrifttum ausserh. der Bibel [1928], 783).

[12] Remotely related is perhaps jBer., 7d, 65 = bBer., 16b : R. Jochanan (or R. Eleazar) prayed : May it be thy will, God, that thou causest to come into our lot love, friendship, peace ... שתשכן בפוריינו אהבה.

[13] He desires a portion with those who die under certain circumstances, Str.-B., III, 625 on Col. 1:12.

[14] The combination of κλῆρος and λαγχάνειν is more common, Cher., 51; Det. Pot. Ins., 140.

cally interpreted concept by pointing out that art is the κλῆρος of the artist (71); we have something of the same here, not a γήινον κτῆμα, but an ὀλύμπιον ἀγώνισμα, which ὠφελεῖ τοὺς ἔχοντας. "Being" is κλῆρος ὡς ὠφελιμώτατον καὶ μεγίστων τοῖς θεραπεύειν ἀξιοῦσιν ἀγαθῶν αἴτιον (72). If in Philo Leg. All., II, 52 we can have the combination : γίνεται δὴ τοῦ μὲν φιλοπαθοῦς κλῆρος τὸ πάθος, τοῦ δὲ (φιλο-θέου) τοῦ Λευὶ κλῆρος ὁ θεός, if in Som. I, 159 Philo can say : ἵνα τὸν αὐτὸν ὅ τε κόσμος ἅπας καὶ ὁ φιλάρετος ἔχῃ κλῆρον and if finally we see that he can call nobility the κλῆρος of the soul (Virt., 189; Det. Pot. Ins., 140), it is evident that this is a spiritual participation which is not without a natural basis, just as the two merge into one another in → κληρόω.

5. κλῆρος in the NT.

In the NT κλῆρος first means "lot," as in the Passion story in Mk. 15:24 and par. What is in the OT a poetic expression of defeat and impotence (→ 759) is here a sign and part of the powerlessness of Christ in His humiliation. Shortly after, however, the same lot expresses diligent seeking of the will of God. The means of selection sanctified by the cultus is employed by the early community in Ac. 1:26 to choose a successor to Judas. On Palestinian soil we find no trace of Philo's scepticism as regards the lot.

Linguistically κλῆρον βάλλειν in Mk. 15:24 corresponds to the Greek and Hebrew expression, and ἔπεσεν ὁ κλῆρος ἐπὶ Μαθθίαν in Ac. 1:26 corresponds to Jon. 1:7.

In the main, however, κλῆρος is used in the NT for the "portion allotted to someone." As in the OT, this is something which is given rather than won ; it is given by God. Judas ἔλαχεν τὸν κλῆρον τῆς διακονίας ταύτης (Ac. 1:17); this ministry is something which was assigned. κλῆρος and λαγχάνειν both emphasise the freedom of the divine will.

For the Jews the decisive question was whether they had a portion in Moses (Ass. Mos. 2:2 → 761). For Christians, however, the decisive question is whether they have a portion in the Word or gift of God, Ac. 8:21: οὐκ ἔστιν σοι μερὶς οὐδὲ κλῆρος ἐν τῷ λόγῳ τούτῳ. [15] As in the Rabb. חלק, so in two passages in the NT and in several in the post-apostolic fathers κλῆρος is used to denote the eschatological portion assigned to man : Ac. 26:18 : (ἀποστέλλω σε) ἀνοῖξαι ὀφθαλμοὺς αὐτῶν ... τοῦ λαβεῖν αὐτοὺς ... κλῆρον ἐν τοῖς ἡγιασμένοις πίστει τῇ εἰς ἐμέ, and Col. 1:12 : εὐχαριστοῦντες τῷ πατρὶ τῷ ἱκανώσαντι ὑμᾶς εἰς τὴν μερίδα τοῦ κλήρου τῶν ἁγίων ἐν τῷ φωτί. [16] In both cases a portion is given to believers among the saints. Whereas the Rabbis desired and prayed for this, there is a stronger assurance in the NT. Ignatius and Polycarp expand the NT passages and elucidate their meaning. The latter (Pol., 12, 2) writes : deus ... det vobis sortem et partem inter sanctos suos ; he thus keeps close to the NT passages. Ignatius has four references to κλῆρος. The clearest is in Eph., 11, 2. Here Ignatius desires to have a part in the prayer of the Ephesians, ἵνα ἐν κλήρῳ Ἐφεσίων εὑρε-θῶ τῶν Χριστιανῶν, οἳ καὶ τοῖς ἀποστόλοις πάντοτε συνῆσαν ἐν δυνάμει Ἰησοῦ Χριστοῦ. He wishes to share in the eternal portion of the Ephesians, who are faith-

---

[15] In view of the Semitic style, κλῆρος along with μερίς (חֵלֶק) must correspond to גּוֹרָל or פּוּר.

[16] This verse is characteristic of the rich style of Col., for μερίς and κλῆρος mean the same thing (Loh. Kol., ad loc.), though not in the sense of inheritance (loc. cit. and Pr. Ag. on 26:18), but in that of portion, Abbott in ICC, ad loc.

ful to the apostles. In the three other passages he speaks of his own κλῆρος. Tr., 12, 3 : I need your love εἰς τὸ καταξιωθῆναί με τοῦ κλήρου, οὗ περίκειμαι ἐπιτυχεῖν, ἵνα μὴ ἀδόκιμος εὑρεθῶ, R., 1, 2 : ἡ μὲν γὰρ ἀρχὴ εὐοικονόμητός ἐστιν, ἐάνπερ χάριτος ἐπιτύχω εἰς τὸ τὸν κλῆρόν μου ἀνεμποδίστως (unhindered) ἀπολαβεῖν, Phld., 5, 1 : ἡ προσευχὴ ὑμῶν εἰς θεόν με ἀπαρτίσει, ἵνα ἐν ᾧ κλήρῳ ἠλεήθην ἐπιτύχω. Here one might render "lot" and take it that he is thinking of his martyrdom ; [17] the Tr. passage could be adduced in support : martyrdom will prove his δοκιμότης. But what Ignatius seeks to attain to is always God ; hence the κλῆρος which he would attain to in Phld., 5, 1 is not martyrdom, but his allotted portion. He would attain to this portion without hindrance, for now is his unique opportunity θεοῦ ἐπιτυχεῖν, R., 2, 1. Tr., 12, 3 fits this sense.

In these passages κλῆρος denotes the heavenly gift which God has allotted to each called believer in fellowship with all the saints, not so much as a "lot," but as a present benefit which God apportions to each, thus giving him a share, his individual share, in that which is prepared for the community.

Much contested is 1 Pt. 5:2 f.: ποιμάνατε τὸ ἐν ὑμῖν ποίμνιον τοῦ θεοῦ, μὴ ἀναγκαστῶς, ἀλλὰ ἑκουσίως ... μηδ᾽ ὡς κατακυριεύοντες τῶν κλήρων ἀλλὰ τύποι γινόμενοι τοῦ ποιμνίου. We are off the track if with Wohlenberg, ad loc., we think of taxes or bounties for the community and the elders, for offerings to the Levites were never called κλῆρος or κλῆροι, but are their κλῆρος, their share in the land of Canaan. Nor is it natural to take the κλῆρος as a personal possession at one's own disposal in contrast to the flock entrusted to one. [18] Here, too, the κλῆρος is the portion allotted to each individual elder. [19]

† κληρόω.

"To appoint someone by lot," Aristot. Pol., 4, 9, p. 1294b, 7 ff.: δοκεῖ δημοκρατικὸν μὲν εἶναι τὸ κληρωτὰς εἶναι τὰς ἀρχάς, τὸ δ᾽ αἱρετὰς ὀλιγαρχικόν, also of drawing lots, Eur. Ion, 416 : οὓς ἐκλήρωσεν πάλος (lot), in the mid. "to draw lots," Lys., 6, 4 : ἐὰν ... ἔλθῃ κληρωσόμενος τῶν ἐννέα ἀρχόντων καὶ λάχῃ βασιλεύς, in the pass. "to be appointed by lot," in the act. and mid. "to cast lots," Aesch. Sept. c. Theb., 55 : κληρουμένους ἔλειπον, "leave behind as those who cast lots," in the mid. also "to receive by lot" : Eur. Tro., 29 : αἰχμαλωτίδων ... δεσπότας κληρουμένων, then purely fig. "to acquire," Ael. Nat. An., 5, 31: The serpent τὴν καρδίαν κεκλήρωται ἐπὶ τῇ φάρυγγι ("throat"), with later an ἔχει corresponding to the κεκλήρωται. Finally κληρόω means "to appoint", "to apportion" : Thuc., VI, 42 : τρία μέρη νείμαντες ἐν ἑκάστῳ ἐκλήρωσαν, also in the pass.: Eur. Hec., 100 : ἐκληρώθην καὶ προσετάχθην.

The LXX has κληρόω plainly only at 1 Βασ. 14:41: κληροῦται Ιωναθαν καὶ Σαουλ, pass. "to be taken by lot" = נִלְכַּד; Is. 17:11, where the Heb. and Gk. are both uncertain. [1]

---

[17] So Bau. Ign. on Phld., 5, 1. Bau. relates the following part. clause προσφυγών κτλ. to ἠλεήθην and thus makes his interpretation easier.
[18] Cr.-Kö., 603 f.
[19] Here we differ from Procksch → I, 107. The basic difference is that Pr. deduces the further development of κλῆρος from its equation with נַחֲלָה whereas → 760 we have argued that the equation with גּוֹרָל determines the development which underlies NT usage.
κ λ η ρ ό ω. Cr.-Kö., 604 f.
[1] The compound κατακληρόω is found in the pass. in the sense "to be taken by lot" = נִלְכַּד at 1 Βασ. 10:20 f.; 14:42b; and in the act. sense in mid. form at 1 Βασ. 14:42a = "to appoint someone by lot" (of God). It also occurs in 1 Βασ. 14:47: Σαουλ κατακληροῦται ἔργον ἐπὶ Ισραηλ, where the LXX reads מְלָאכָה for מְלוּכָה and the sense is "to acquire."

Philo's usage is linguistically connected with the Ael. passage. In Philo the term always relates to orderly apportionment in the natural and moral world : Op. Mund., 57: the sun κεκλήρωται τὴν ἡμέραν, Sacr. AC, 104 speaks of the ἄλογον, ὅπερ αἱ αἰσθήσεις κεκλήρωνται, Fug., 126 of the ἀμείνων γενεά, ἣν ἀρεταὶ κεκλήρωνται, Det. Pot. Ins., 145 of the ἐπιστασία and ἀρχὴ φυσική which parents have had assigned to them over their children (κεκλήρωνται), Deus. Imm., 34 of the Creator, the ἔννοιαν καὶ διανόησιν ... κληρωσάμενος καὶ χρώμενος.

In the post-apost. fathers κληρόω occurs twice. In Mart. Pol., 6, 2 there is mention of the eirenarch Herod ὁ κεκληρωμένος τὸ αὐτὸ ὄνομα Ἡρώδῃ, and in Dg., 5, 4 Christians inhabit Greek and barbarian cities ὡς ἕκαστος ἐκληρώθη. We cannot say with certainty how far the author of κληροῦν is in view in these passages, but the concept is at least implicit in the expression. The matter is quite plain in the apocr. Acts : in Act. Phil., 94 a sphere of work is assigned to the apostles, *ibid.*, 142 ἐκληρώθη is said of the dying Mariamne (Lipsius-Bonnet, II, 2, p. 78, 5), and in the pers. pass. it is said in Act. Thom., 24 : (prayer goes up) ἵνα ... κληρωθῶ ἄξιος γενέσθαι τῶν ὀφθέντων μοι. Naturally this is all along with senses relating to the use of the lot (Jos. Ant., 6, 62; Mart. Andr., I, 2 [Lipsius-Bonnet, II, 1, p. 46, 18]). Cf. the Ps.-Clem. Recg., 9, 35 : *uxorem ... sortitus est.*

In the NT κληρόω occurs only at Eph. 1:11: ἐν αὐτῷ, ἐν ᾧ καὶ ἐκληρώθημεν προορισθέντες κατὰ πρόθεσιν τοῦ τὰ πάντα ἐνεργοῦντος κατὰ τὴν βουλὴν τοῦ θελήματος αὐτοῦ, εἰς τὸ εἶναι ἡμᾶς εἰς ἔπαινον δόξης αὐτοῦ.[2] With Cr.-Kö. we are to take εἰς τὸ εἶναι κτλ. as supplementary to the main verb. κληρόω does not denote a pre-temporal act. It is an "appointment" or "determination" which affects men in their being. It is also the goal which is assigned to them in their calling. Materially, then, it is related to ἐκλήθημεν, but with the nuance, implicit in κλῆρος, that the call imparts something to the called, namely, a life's goal.

† προσκληρόω.

"To distribute by lot," then just "to distribute" : Jos. Bell., 2, 567: προσκεκλήρωτο δ' αὐτῷ Λύδδα καὶ Ἰόππη καὶ Ἀμμαοῦς, esp. of things which destiny has ordained or which just are : Luc. Amores, 3 : τούτῳ τῷ βίῳ ἡ τύχη προσεκλήρωσέ σε; Plut. Quaest. Conv., IX, 3 (II, 738d): ἡ ... ἐννεὰς δήπου ταῖς Μούσαις ... προσκεκλήρωται; Philo Leg. Gaj., 279 : (Herod. Agrippa I of himself) ἔθνει δὴ τοιούτῳ προσκεκληρωμένος καὶ πατρίδι καὶ ἱερῷ. Also of the education one has received, P. Par., 63, VIII, 18 (164 B.C.): παιδήᾳ (*sic*) προσκεκληρωμένον. As mid./pass. "to join oneself to," Ditt. Or., 257, 5 (109 B.C.): Σελευκεῖς ... τῷ πατρὶ ἡμῶν προσκληρωθέντας, Philo Leg. Gaj., 68 : τῶν μὲν τούτῳ τῶν δὲ ἐκείνῳ προσκληρουμένων, ἐξ ὧν ταραχαὶ ἐμφύλιοί τε καὶ ξενικοὶ πόλεμοι συνίστανται. Common in Philo of the natural ordering of powers of soul, virtues, men, festivals etc. to God or to the creature, to virtue or vice, and the corresponding self-ordering of the righteous and the wicked : act. Conf. Ling., 111: διέλωμεν ... ἑκάστας τῶν ἐν ψυχῇ δυνάμεων προσκληρώσαντες τὰς μὲν λογικῇ, τὰς δὲ ἀλόγῳ μερίδι, Cher. 85 : ἑαυτῷ γὰρ τὰς ἑορτὰς προσκεκλήρωκε (sc. θεός), perf. pass. (to express the fact of being ordered) Op. Mund., 65 : ψυχῆς γὰρ ἡ μὲν ἀργοτάτη ... τῷ γένει τῶν ἰχθύων προσκεκλήρωται, ἡ δ' ... ἀρίστη τῷ τῶν ἀνθρώπων, Leg. All., I, 24 : τὸ αἰσθητὸν τῷ ἀλόγῳ μέρει ψυχῆς προσκεκλήρωται, Poster. C., 92 : ὁ γὰρ ὁρῶν τὸν θεὸν ... τῷ ὁρωμένῳ προσκεκλήρωταί τε καὶ μεμέρισται;[1] of conscious self-attachment προσκληροῦν

---

[2] Cod ADG it ἐκλήθημεν is certainly the *lectio facilior.*

π ρ ο σ κ λ η ρ ό ω. [1] = חלק? Cf. jBer., 7d (Schl. K., 227, n. 1), where it is said of God that he apportions to man knowledge and good works (חלק לי דיעה ומעשה טוב).

ἑαυτόν, Mut. Nom., 127: τὸ δέ γε εὔχεσθαι καὶ εὐλογεῖν οὐκ ἔστι τοῦ τυχόντος, ἀλλ' ἀνθρώπου τὴν πρὸς γένεσιν μὴ ἑωρακότος συγγένειαν, προσκεκληρωκότος δὲ ἑαυτὸν τῷ πάντων ἡγεμόνι καὶ πατρί.

In the NT we only have Ac. 17:4 : καί τινες ἐξ αὐτῶν ἐπείσθησαν καὶ προσε-κληρώθησαν τῷ Παύλῳ καὶ τῷ Σιλᾷ, where the sense is either "they joined themselves to"[2] or "they were assigned (by God)."[3] If Lk. often traces back adherence to the community directly to God's working (2:41; 5:14; 11:24; 13:48; 14:27; 16:14), 17:34 : τινὲς δὲ ἄνδρες κολληθέντες αὐτῷ ἐπίστευσαν, shows that this is no mere formula, and the preceding ἐπείσθησαν in 17:4 (cf. also 28:24 : οἱ μὲν ἐπείθοντο — οἱ δὲ ἠπίστουν) rules out the passive understanding of προσε-κληρώθησαν. We may thus translate : "They attached themselves to."

† ὁλόκληρος → ὑγιής.

ὁλόκληρος denotes completeness in extent or compass, and is thus a term of quantity rather than quality.

"Whole," of vessels : Epict. Diss., III, 26, 25 : σκεῦος ... ὁλόκληρον καὶ χρήσιμον ἔξω ἐρριμμένον πᾶς τις εὑρὼν ἀναιρήσεται καὶ κέρδος ἡγήσεται, of the house, P. Lond., 935, 7: ὁλόκληρος οἰκία, in the LXX of whole, i.e., unhewn stones, Dt. 27:6; Jos. 9:2b; 1 Macc. 4:47; of the vine, Ez. 15:5. Of time : ἔτεσιν δύο οὐχ ὁλοκλήροις, IG, 14, 1386, in not quite two whole years, cf. also the LXX Lv. 23:15; Dt. 16:9. While ἀσθενής or νοσῶν negates the qualitative concept ὑγιής, ὁλόκληρος, when referred to man, denotes the unmutilated state whose opp. in Plut. Quaest. Conv., II, 3 (II, 636 f.) is πεπηρωμένος, cf. Epict. Diss., III, 26, 7: σὺ δ' ὁλόκληρος ἄνθρωπος χεῖρας ἔχων καὶ πόδας. There is thus an evident distinction from ὑγιής and it is clear why ὑγιής is more easily used of the soul and ὁλόκληρος of the body, Luc. Macrobii, 2 : εἰς μακρὸν γῆρας ἀφικέσθαι ἐν ὑγιαινούσῃ τῇ ψυχῇ καὶ ὁλοκλήρῳ τῷ σώματι, Mithr. Liturg., 14, 4 f.: (ἀφιέντες) ἐμοὶ ... ὑγίειαν καὶ σώματος ὁλοκληρίαν ἀκοῆς τε καὶ ὁράσεως εὐτονίαν, cf. Plut. Stoic. Rep., 30 (II, 1047e): μαίνεσθαι τοὺς τὸν πλοῦτον καὶ τὴν ὑγίειαν καὶ τὴν ἀπονίαν καὶ τὴν ὁλοκληρίαν τοῦ σώματος ἐν μηδενὶ ποιουμένους (Chrysipp.). Of animals in the LXX Zech. 11:16 as the opp. of συντετριμμένος. In the sense of lack of bodily defect (not sickness) being ὁλόκληρος is a necessary prerequisite for the priesthood, Ditt. Syll.[3], 1009, 10; 1012, 9; Jos. Ant., 14, 366, and also for the sacrificial animal, Jos. Ant., 8, 118, but not with this reference in the LXX. Plat. Phaedr. (250c) uses it for the uncorrupted state of the soul prior to its coming into the world. The word also indicates the presence of all the constitutive elements of something : Ditt. Or., 519, 14 : δῆμος ὁλόκληρος, a people in the true sense, a real people ; so also ὁλόκληρος πήρωσις (maiming), Democr. Fr., 296 (II, 121, 8 Diels), and with a wider reference in the LXX at Wis. 15:3 : τὸ γὰρ ἐπίστασθαί σε ὁλόκληρος δικαιοσύνη, full or true righteousness, and 4 Macc. 15:17: ὦ μόνη γύναι τὴν εὐσέβειαν ὁλόκληρον ἀποκυήσασα. Here, as always, the point of ὁλόκληρος is that something is quantitatively complete.

In Philo it is often used with παντελής; God, virtue, the good and the world are both. But the common use of ὁλόκληρος is no accident ; it denotes the world of God completely unadulterated by the evil of the sensual world. A man is ὁλόκληρος who from the first has and expresses completeness naturally, cf. the definition of the τέλειος,

---

[2] Pr.-Bauer and Cr.-Kö., s.v.
[3] Wdt. Ag., ad loc.
ὁ λ ό κ λ η ρ ο ς. Trench, s.v.

the μετατεθειμένος and the ἐλπίζων in Abr., 47: ὁ μὲν γὰρ τέλειος ὁλόκληρος ἐξ ἀρχῆς, ὁ δὲ μετατεθειμένος ἡμίεργος, τοῦ βίου τὸν μὲν πρότερον χρόνον ἀναθεὶς κακίᾳ, τὸν δ' ὕστερον ἀρετῇ … ὁ δὲ ἐλπίζων … ἐλλιπής, ἐφιέμενος μὲν ἀεὶ τοῦ καλοῦ, μήπω δ' ἐφικέσθαι τούτου δεδυνημένος.

There are only two instances in the NT. 1 Th. 5:23: ὁλόκληρον ὑμῶν τὸ πνεῦμα καὶ ἡ ψυχὴ καὶ τὸ σῶμα ἀμέμπτως ἐν τῇ παρουσίᾳ τοῦ κυρίου ἡμῶν Ἰησοῦ Χριστοῦ τηρηθείη. As often in Gk. the τηρηθείη ἐν … unites movement towards the goal with being at the goal (cf. in German bewahrt sein, not werden). The predicative ὁλόκληρον, which embraces all three nouns, expresses the hope that the Thessalonians, each as a totality, may remain unaffected by evil in every respect. Since σῶμα is also mentioned we cannot rule out the idea that the Thessalonians will attain to the imminent parousia (1 Th. 4:15: ἡμεῖς οἱ ζῶντες οἱ περιλειπόμενοι) unaffected at least by physical death, though the thought is also present that even in respect of the body man has a work to do which will either stand or not stand at the judgment, cf. 1 C. 5:5 for a specific instance. In v. 23 Paul expects the fulfilment of his wish from the θεὸς τῆς εἰρήνης; εἰρήνη here embraces the bodily and spiritual salvation ("wholeness") which comes from God alone (→ II, 413 ff.). Before God no man is simply a ἡμιτελής. This God can take even a man who is broken in body and soul, make of him a new whole man, and preserve him as such.

Jm. 1:4: ἡ δὲ ὑπομονὴ ἔργον τέλειον ἐχέτω, ἵνα ἦτε τέλειοι καὶ ὁλόκληροι, ἐν μηδενὶ λειπόμενοι. Here, too, the quantitative aspect remains. We learn from 3:1 ff. why James uses this singular concept. The goal of our manifold temptations, the aim of God's direction of the readers, is the attainment of whole men who can achieve even the hardest part of all, the curbing of their tongues.

† ὁλοκληρία.

"Completeness," "intactness," Plut. Stoic. Rep., 17 (II, 1041 f.): the Stoic separates us τοῦ ζῆν καὶ τῆς ὑγιείας καὶ τῆς ἀπονίας καὶ τῆς τῶν αἰσθητηρίων ὁλοκληρίας, cf., ibid., 30 (1047e); Comm. Not., 11 (II, 1063 f.). In the LXX it occurs only at Is. 1:6 in Cod LC and 'A.

In the NT we find it at Ac. 3:16 of the physical wholeness which is restored to the lame man.

† κληρονόμος, † συγκληρονόμος, † κληρονομέω, † κατακληρονομέω, † κληρονομία.

Contents: A. The Greek Usage of the Word Group κληρονόμος. B. נַחֲלָה and נָחַל in the OT. C. The Word Group in the LXX: 1. Linguistic; 2. Material. D. The Word Group in Later Judaism: 1. Linguistic; 2. Material. E. The Word Group in the NT: 1. The Usage; 2. The Theological Usage.

κληρονόμος κτλ. Note: For material reasons the terms κληρονόμος, συγκληρονόμος, κληρονομέω, κατακληρονομέω, κληρονομία are gathered into a single art., with detailed elucidations at the beginning of the various sections. B. F. Westcott, The Epistle to the Hebrews (1889), 167-169; J. B. Mayor, The Epistle of St. James (1892), 80; E. Lohmeyer, Diatheke (1913), 140-142; Cr.-Kö., 606-609; E. de Witt Burton, The Epistle to the Galatians (ICC [1921]), 185 f.; 224-227; 503; Str.-B., III, 545-553; Dalman WJ, I, 102-104; Volz Esch., 341; A. Halmel, Über römisches Recht im Galaterbrief (1895); F.

A. The Greek Usage of the Word Group κληρονόμος.

In Greek the word group κληρονόμος circles around the concept of inheritance and never moves very far away from it.

κληρονόμος, the "heir" in the sense of the natural heir and the one named by a will or by legal provisions, Ditt. Syll.[3], 884, 52 ff. (early 3rd cent. A.D.): εἰ δ[έ τις μὴ καταλιπὼν δια]θήκας τελευτήσαι, ᾧ μή εἰσιν νόμιμοι κληρονόμοι, [ὁ]π[αρχέτω κατ' ἀμφ]ότερα κληρονόμος τοῦ ἑαυτῆς κτήμ[ατ]ος ἡ πόλις. Also of the inheritance of non-material items, Isoc., 5, 136 : τῆς δ' εὐνοίας τῆς παρὰ τῶν πολλῶν ... μηδένας ἄλλους καταλείπεσθαι κληρονόμους πλὴν τοὺς ἐξ ἡμῶν γεγονότας. Wholly fig. in Demosth. Or., 21, 20 to show that we must bear the consequences of our actions : τῆς δ' ὑπὲρ τῶν νόμων (sc. δίκης), οὓς παραβὰς οὗτος κἀκείνους ἠδίκει καὶ νῦν ἐμὲ καὶ πάντας τοὺς ἄλλους, ὑμεῖς ἐστε κληρονόμοι. The point of κληρονόμος here is that the Athenians must accept the result of their actions even though they did not intend this as a goal ; actions leave behind an inheritance which is not envisaged. κληρονόμος is used for the one who actually possesses or controls entrusted goods in Plut. Cicero, 41, 3 (I, 881 f.): τὴν οὐσίαν αὐτῆς ὁ Κικέρων ἐν πίστει κληρονόμος ἀπολειφθεὶς διεφύλαττεν.

συγκληρονόμος, the "fellow-heir," always in the literal sense. Apart from the two instances in Deissmann LO, 71 f. we may quote an inscr. from ancient Capitolias on which a Μ. Ἄρριος Σαβεῖνος ἀδελφὸς καὶ συγκληρονόμος erected an οἶκος and an ἄγαλμα ἐκ διαθήκης Ἀντωνείνου Οὐάλεντος Ἀρδαίου (in the time of Commodus).[1]

κληρονομέω, "to be heir," "to inherit something" (gen. or acc.), "to be the heir of someone" (gen. and more often acc.), also of non-material things, Isoc., 1, 2 : πρέπει γὰρ τοὺς παῖδας ὥσπερ τῆς οὐσίας οὕτω καὶ τῆς φιλίας τῆς πατρικῆς κληρονομεῖν. There does not have to be any kinship, Dio C., 45, 47: τῶν μὲν ἐκείνου (of his father) χρημάτων οὐκ ἐκληρονόμησεν, ἄλλων δὲ δὴ καὶ πάνυ πολλούς, τοὺς μὲν ..., τοὺς δὲ καὶ νῦν ἔτι ζῶντας, nor a will, Luc. Dialogi Mortuorum, 11, 3 : "I have never prayed in life that he should die, ὡς κληρονομήσαιμι τῆς βακτηρίας αὐτοῦ, nor even death, as shown by the passage in Dio C.; the decisive point is the actual transition of the possesssion from the one to the other. It can also be used fig., Polyb., 15, 22, 3; 18, 55, 8 : τὴν ἐπ' ἀσεβείᾳ δόξαν or φήμην κληρονομεῖν. What links this usage with true inheritance is that a corresponding action is a reason for acquiring δόξα, but that this is an involuntary acquisition which we can no more describe as the direct and planned result of the action than we can inheritance.

κατακληρονομέω → C.

κληρονομία "the portion which is to be, or is, inherited," "inheritance," and then simply "possession" : Aristot. Eth. Nic., VIII, 14, p. 1153b, 33 : ἡδοναί are not the same for all, but εἰλήφασιν τὴν τοῦ ὀνόματος κληρονομίαν αἱ σωματικαὶ ἡδοναί.

Sieffert, Das Recht im NT (1900), 17 f.; M. Conrat, ZNW, 5 (1904), 204-227; F. v. Woess, Das römische Erbrecht u. d. Erbanwärter (1911), 77; 266 ff.; O. Eger, "Rechtswörter u. Rechtsbilder in den paul. Briefen," ZNW, 18 (1917/18), 84-108; "Rechtsgeschichtliches z. NT," Rektoratsprogramm Basel (1918/19), 31-37; H. Kreller, Erbrechtliche Untersuchungen (1919); W. M. Calder, "Adoption and Inheritance in Galatia," in JThSt, 31 (1930), 372-374. On B : H. Breit, Die Predigt des Deuteronomisten (1933); K. Galling, Die Erwählungstraditionen Israels (1928); J. Herrmann, "Das zehnte Gebot," Sellin-Festschrift (1927), 69-82; F. Horst, Das Privilegrecht Jahwes (1930); G. v. Rad, Das Gottesvolk im Dt. (1929); G. Westphal, Jahwes Wohnstätten nach den Anschauungen der alten Hebräer (1908), 91 ff.; L. Rost, "Die Bezeichnungen für Land u. Volk im AT," Festschr. f. O. Procksch (1934), 125-148.

[1] Bulletin of the American Schools of Oriental Research, 46 (April, 1932), 13 f.

In general it is important that Roman law recognised a full freedom of testamentary disposition, so that the son did not have to be the heir, whereas in Greek, Egyptian and Hellenistic [2] as well as Jewish law [3] the son, sons or children were the heirs *eo ipso*. It may also be noted that in the pap. κληρονόμος denotes specifically the heir of real property or goods, whereas he who simply receives movable property is never called by this name. [4] In other words, the term is linked with essential possession.

Foerster

B. נַחֲלָה and נָחַל in the OT.

1. Review of the Hebrew Equivalents to the Word Group κλῆρος etc. When we study this word group in the LXX we find that two or three Hebrew stems are predominant.

In its 129 appearances κλῆρος is used 62 times for גּוֹרָל, 49 for נַחֲלָה, 11 for words of the stem ירשׁ (ירשׁ, יְרֵשָׁה, מוֹרָשָׁה). κληρόω occurs only 3 times, once for נַחֲלָה. προσκληρόω is not used. κληρονόμος is found 4 times, always for ירשׁ. There are 163 instances of κληρονομία, in 143 cases for נַחֲלָה, in 16 for words of the stem ירשׁ (ירשׁ, יְרֵשָׁה, יְרֵשָׁה, מוֹרָשָׁה, מוֹרֶשֶׁת), and twice for גּוֹרָל. κληρονομέω also occurs 163 times, 111 times for ירשׁ (103 q, 8 hi), 27 for נחל (19) and נַחֲלָה (8). In 59 instances of κατακληρονομέω it is used 28 times for ירשׁ (27) and מוֹרָשׁ (1), 25 for נחל (24) and נַחֲלָה (1). συγκληρονόμος does not occur, but we have συγκληρονομέω once at Sir. 22:23 without Heb. equivalent. Also found in the LXX is κατακληρόω (pass. for לכד ni 4 times, q once, with no equivalent once). We might also mention κληροδοτέω (2 Εσδρ. 9:12 for ירשׁ hi, ψ 77:55 for נפל hi) and κληροδοσία (ψ 77:55 and Qoh. 7:11 in AS for נַחֲלָה, Da. 11:21, 34, original doubtful).

The Greek terms are mostly used for נַחֲלָה and נחל; then comes ירשׁ (with derivatives), and much further behind גּוֹרָל. If we consider other renderings, נַחֲלָה and נחל are well ahead of ירשׁ. ירשׁ and גּוֹרָל both stand in a close material relation to נַחֲלָה and נחל. Theologically, too, investigation of the whole group finds its focus in נַחֲלָה and נחל.

2. The Promise of Possession of Canaan to the Patriarchs. The stories of the patriarchs begin (Gn. 12:1) with the command of Yahweh to Abraham to go into the land which God will show him. There God will make him a great people (12:2). When he comes to Canaan without knowing that this is the land intended, the first thing that Yahweh says to him is: "I will give this land to your descendants" (12:7). In Gn. and throughout the Bible there is constant reference to this promise. On it rests the belief of Israel that possession of Palestine by Israel is based on the promise to Abraham, [5] and therefore on divine ordination. Cf. in Gn. J and E 13:14-17; 15:18; 24:7; 26:3-5. For this reason the land is for Jacob the

---

[2] Kreller, *op. cit.*, *passim*. Mitteis-Wilcken, II, 363, 21 f.: ... εἶναι δ' αὐτὸν καὶ τῶν ἐμῶν πραγμάτων κληρονόμον, υἱοθετηθέντα μοι ὡς προείρηται: the υἱοθεσία establishes the position as κληρονόμος (381 A.D.), cf. ZNW, 18 (1917/18), 95.

[3] Str.-B., *loc. cit.*

[4] Kreller, 58.

[5] In this enquiry it makes no difference that Gn. 28:13 does not seem to refer back to 12:7.

"land of thy fathers," 31:3 J, and for Joseph and his brethren it is the "land of your fathers," 48:21 E. Since the promise to Abraham is renewed to Isaac and Jacob, Joseph, addressing his brothers, also calls it the "land which God has sworn to Abraham, Isaac and Jacob," 50:24 E. Similar expressions are found in P, with no essential differences for our purpose, e.g., 17:8; 28:4; 35:12; 48:4. נַחֲלָה and נחל are not used in any of these passages. [6]

3. The Promise of the Possession of Canaan in the Moses Stories. In the story of the call of Moses Yahweh says : "I have seen the affliction of my people ... and I have come down ... to bring them up out of this land into a land ... which flows with milk and honey," Ex. 3:7 f. E and cf. 3:17 J. At the very commencement of Yahweh's dealings with Moses and the Israel of his time we thus see this promise of possession of the land of Palestine. If there is in this passage no reference to the promise to Abraham and the patriarchs, this is perhaps an indication of the originally independent origin of the Moses traditions, cf. the present conclusion of the book of the covenant in Ex. 23:20-33 J E, also Ex. 12:25 and possibly 20:12. In the present form of the pre-Palestinian history of Israel the stories of the patriarchs and of Moses are linked by and with the Joseph stories, so that in Ex. reference to the original promise to the fathers accompanies and finally absorbs the new promise which is given to Moses on behalf of his people, cf. Ex. 13:5 J Eˢ, 32:13 J Eˢ, 6:8 P. The land which Yahweh swore to their fathers is to be given to the people as an inheritance (נחל, Ex. 32:13) and possession (מוֹרָשָׁה, 6:8), even though the generation of Moses never sees it because of their unbelief (Nu. 14:23 J E), and the last word of Yahweh to Moses as He shows him the whole land from Nebo just before he dies is as follows : "This is the land which I swore to Abraham, Isaac and Jacob, saying, I will give it to your descendants. I have caused thee to see it with thine eyes, but thou shalt not go over thither" (Dt. 34:4 J E).

4. Canaan as Israel's Nachala in Exodus to Numbers. When Israel entered Canaan after the death of Moses, it was always referred to as the land which Yahweh had sworn to give either to the patriarchs or to the generation of the age of Moses. This may be seen in the use of נחל at Ex. 32:13 J Eˢ ; it is their חֶלְקָה (Nu. 16:14 J E; 34:2 P). Yet while it is true that quite commonly in Ex. to Nu., esp. in P texts, we read that Israel receives Canaan in possession, that Yahweh gives them the land, it is only rarely that we find נחל and נַחֲלָה. This is because נחל does not seem to denote the inheritance as such, but one's share in it, the lasting possession which one receives by apportionment and distribution. Hence נחל and נַחֲלָה come into prominence when the reference is not to the possession of all Canaan by all Israel but to the possession of the portions of individual tribes, and within these of individual families and persons. For as the people as such holds the whole land, so portions of the people hold portions of the land, by divine ordination. Once the reference is to the possessions of the tribes we find נחל and נַחֲלָה, e.g., Gn. 48:6 P, and esp. in Nu. at 26:52-56; 33:50-54; 32:18 f.; 34:14-18; 36:2-12; 34:29; 18:20 ff.; 26:62; 27:1 ff.

5. Canaan as Israel's Nachala in Dt. Since in Ex. to Dt. entry into the "affianced" (promised) land seems to be the goal of the people led by Moses out of

---

[6] The use in Gn. 48:6 P is with reference to the inheritance of one of the 12 tribes. In Gn. 31:14 E the daughter's share of the inheritance is in question.

Egypt, it is hardly surprising that in Dt. we find specific reference to the promises to this effect from the time of Abraham, for the law of Deuteronomy with its introductory and concluding addresses is the last discourse of Moses to the people when on the plains of Moab, at the very gates of Canaan. In accordance with the divine order, Israel is to take possession of Canaan as the land which Yahweh, the God of their fathers (Dt. 1:21), of Abraham, Isaac and Jacob, swore to give to them and their descendants at Horeb. Cf. Dt. 1:7, 8, 21, 35, 38; 2:12, 29; 3:18, 20, 28; 4:1, 5, 14, 21, 26, 38, 40; 6:1, 10, 23; 7:1, 13; 8:1, 10; 9:4, 5; 10:11; 11:9, 21, 25, 29, 31; 12:1, 9, 10; 15:4; 17:2, 14; 18:9; 19:1, 2, 3, 8, 10, 14; 20:16; 21:1, 23; 24:4; 25:19; 26:1, 3, 9, 10, 15; 27:2, 3; 28:8, 21, 63; 30:5, 16, 20; 31:7, 20, 21. If נַחֲלָה is used here, it is not just of the whole land, but also of the portion of the individual tribe or citizen, as plainly shown by, e.g., 19:14. It is Joshua's task to lead Israel in taking the land as נַחֲלָה (נחל hi, which is used in Dt. 21:16 of the distribution of the patrimony among sons), Dt. 1:38; 3:28; 31:7; Jos. 1:6 (Dt.), and if the Israelites conquer and possess (ירשׁ) the land, this is only because Yahweh has given it to them (e.g., 3:20) as נַחֲלָה, and it can be successful only as Yahweh, fulfilling His sworn oath to the fathers, drives the ungodly Canaanites before them (9:4, 5) and makes them afraid of them (11:25).

6. Canaan as Israel's Nachala in Jos. The Book of Joshua begins with God's command to Joshua: "Go over into the land which I will give to the Israelites" (1:2 J E). Joshua repeats the command to the officers (1:10, 11) and they pass it on to the people (3:2, 3), and the first part of the book then tells how with God's help the people takes Palestine in possession under the leadership of Joshua. The ageing Joshua then concludes his life's work by dividing (חלק pi) the land as נַחֲלָה among the tribes (13:1, 7). This division takes place by lot (גּוֹרָל), i.e., by divine decision, for Joshua throws the lot (ירה; 18:6) before Yahweh. That the tribes came into possession of their נַחֲלָה in this way is the view not only of J E but also of P (cf. also Nu. 26:52 ff.; 33:54; 34:13), to whom we are largely indebted for accounts of the partition in Jos. 13-21, and of D (Jos. 23:4, Dt.). In so far as the נַחֲלָה is determined by lot, the portion itself is often called גּוֹרָל (e.g., Jos. 14:2; 15:1; 16:1). In Jos. נַחֲלָה is not just the portion of the tribes but also of families and individuals (24:28, cf. also 24:32 J E), including Joshua himself (19:49; 24:30; Ju. 2:9). The lasting significance of this view of the division of the promised land by Moses and Joshua by the divine commission may be seen in a later casuistical P passage (supplement to the law of inheritance, Nu. 27), where it is insisted that the נַחֲלָה of the individual tribes must not be fundamentally changed, and that provision must be made lest even the נַחֲלָה of an individual family be lost to the tribe.

7. Canaan as Israel's Nachala in Ju., S., K., Ezr., Neh., Ch. Even though we have been able to present only a fraction of the material, we have seen already how varied and important in the whole Hexateuch is the belief, and the historical theory, that the possession of Palestine was promised to Abraham, Isaac and Jacob for their descendants, that it was then assigned to the generation of Moses, and that it was then undertaken, and with God's help successfully accomplished, by Joshua and his generation. In the historical books of the Canon which follow the material is much more sparse. In Ju. we seem to have in the ancient record in 1:3 the divergent suggestion that each individual tribe was assigned its portion before the conquest, and that it was therewith given the task of occupying it. On the other hand, the Deuteronomic redactor of Ju. repeats Jos. 24:28 in Ju. 2:6. Even in the

ancient story of the migration of the Danites in Ju. 17-18 each tribe receives its allotted נַחֲלָה, though 18:1 does not seem to tally with the presentation in Jos. 19:40 ff. In the other story appended in Ju. 19-21 the whole territory of the tribes is called "all the country of the נַחֲלָה of Israel" (20:6). In the Books of Samuel we are reminded in 1 S. 12:8 of the exodus from Egypt and the entry of the people into Palestine. In the Books of Kings Solomon in his Deuteronomic prayer at the dedication of the temple refers to Canaan as the land which Yahweh has given to His people as נַחֲלָה (1 K. 8:36, cf. 34 and 48), cf. also 1 K. 9:7; 14:15; 2 K. 21:8 (none of these verses is pre-Deuteronomic). The great festival prayer of Ezra in Neh. 9 gives evidence of the same conviction (Neh. 9:8, 15, 23, 35, 36). Similarly, David in Ch. admonishes the people to keep the commandments of God in order that they may remain in possession of the land and that their sons may inherit it for ever (נחל hi, 1 Ch. 28:8).

8. The Land of Canaan and the People of Israel the נַחֲלָה of Yahweh. In a prayer in 2 Ch. 20:11 Jehoshaphat speaks of Canaan as "thy possession (יְרֻשָּׁה) which thou hast given us to inherit. Similarly in a late passage in Jos. (22:19 Ps) the land west of Jordan is called "the land, the אֲחֻזַּת of Yahweh." Already in early times the whole land is called the נַחֲלָה of Yahweh, as in S. in older (2 S. 21:3) as well as younger strata (1 S. 26:19). In 1 K. 8:36 it is "thy land, which thou hast given to thy people as נַחֲלָה." In the hymn in Ex. 15 the hill country of Palestine is called "the mountain of thy נַחֲלָה (15:17).

More commonly than the land the people of Israel is called the possession, the portion, the נַחֲלָה of Yahweh. According to Ex. 19:5 (J Es) Israel is to be for Yahweh, to whom the whole earth belongs, His possession (סְגֻלָּה) out of all peoples. Dt. alludes to this passage with its promise that Israel shall be for Yahweh „עַם סְגֻלָּה, out of all peoples that are upon the face of the earth," Dt. 7:6; 14:2; 26:18; cf. also 4:20 (עַם נַחֲלָה); 9:26, 29 ("thy people and thy נַחֲלָה": 1 K. 8:51, 53; 2 K. 21:14 (D). In the Books of Samuel Israel is described as the נַחֲלָה of Yahweh or God in the later source (2 S. 14:16) and also in the older (1 S. 10:1) and the very oldest (2 S. 20:19). In the so-called Song of Moses in Dt. 32 the divine ordination of Israel as His נַחֲלָה is put in the remote past, since God appointed the frontiers of the nations and gave to each its נַחֲלָה (Dt. 32:8, 9).

9. נַחֲלָה and נחל in the Prophetic Writings. The 8th century prophets yield little material. Isaiah and Hosea may be left out of account. Amos reminds us that God destroyed the Amorites before the Israelites and that He led the latter out of Egypt and caused them to wander 40 years in the wilderness that they might take the land of the Amorites in possession (Am. 2:9, 10). [7] In Micah Yahweh calls the land of Israel חֵלֶק עַמִּי "the portion of my people," 2:4. This is all. The situation is very different in Jeremiah, the contemporary of the Deuteronomic reform. Yahweh wished to give to Israel a pleasant land, the most precious נַחֲלָה among the nations (3:19). He commanded the people in the time of Moses, when He had brought them out of Egypt, to obey the words of the covenant that He might keep the oath sworn to their fathers and give them the land flowing with milk and

---

[7] The authenticity of Am. 9:15 is greatly contested.

honey, as they have possessed it to this day (11:4, 5), and will possess it to all eternity if they do the will of Yahweh (7:7, cf. 25:5). But they have made His land and His נַחֲלָה an abomination (2:7), and so Yahweh has forsaken His house, rejected His נַחֲלָה, and given up the dearly beloved of His soul into the hands of her enemies, many shepherds having destroyed His vineyard (12:7-10).[8]

For Ezekiel, too, Canaan, the land which Abraham already possessed (33:24), is the נַחֲלָה of the house of Israel (35:15). Yahweh, who also calls it "my land" (38:16), promised it by oath to the patriarchs (20:5, 6, 42) and gave it to His servant Jacob (37:25; 28:25; cf. also 20:15, 28, 42). When brought back from exile, the people is to settle it afresh and to possess and inhabit it as נַחֲלָה for ever (36:12; 37:25). Ez. 40-48 looks ahead to this prophetic future of the people. As in the days of Joshua, the tribes will again divide the land (נחל hitp), so that each will acquire its נַחֲלָה by lot (47:13, 14; 48:29; 45:1). This distribution must not be altered in any respect. This is particularly plain in 46:16-18, where the prince is neither to take away any of the נַחֲלָה of the people nor to surrender any of his own נַחֲלָה for ever.[9] In Dt. Is., too, Yahweh will re-establish the land in the day of salvation. He will again apportion (נחל hi, 49:8) the devastated נְחָלוֹת as נַחֲלָה. Here again Yahweh calls Canaan His נַחֲלָה (47:6). In Tr. Is. the land or people is called Yahweh's נַחֲלָה at 63:17. The future people of Jerusalem, which will consist only of the right-eous, will possess the land for ever (60:21).[10] In Zechariah Yahweh will take Judah in נַחֲלָה as His חֵלֶק (2:16) and cause the remnant of His people to inherit all Judaea (נחל hi, 8:12). According to a gloss in Zephaniah (2:9) the remnant of Israel is also to take Moab and Ammon as נַחֲלָה. Joel calls Israel the people and נַחֲלָה of Yahweh, and Palestine the land of Yahweh (1:2; 2:17, 18, 26, 27; 3:3, 16). In another post-exilic verse in Isaiah Yahweh calls Israel my נַחֲלָה (19:25).

Thus the concepts linked with נַחֲלָה, even though they are rare in the 8th century prophets, persist throughout the whole period and range of the prophetic writings. They are most vital in the works of Jeremiah and Ezekiel.

10. נַחֲלָה and נחל in the Psalms. In the Psalter נַחֲלָה is fairly common in passages which recall traditions concerning the age of the patriarchs, Moses and Joshua. Edification is found in a grateful review of the great acts of God in these days. It is a source of comfort that Yahweh constantly remembers the covenant which He made with Abraham, Isaac and Jacob when He said: "To thee will I give the land of Canaan as thine allotted נַחֲלָה" (105:9-11). Happy is the people which is chosen by Yahweh for נַחֲלָה (33:12), for סְגֻלָה (135:4). One may ask God to be mindful of His people which He won (קנה) in the time of Moses and redeemed (גאל) as the tribe of His נַחֲלָה (74:2). Then Judah became His sanctuary and Israel His dominion (114:1, 2). With His own hand Yahweh drove the heathen out of Palestine and caused the fathers of Israel to take the land (44:2-4). The land of the Canaanite kings, the נַחֲלָה of the heathen (111:6), He chose for His people as

---

[8] Cf. also Jer. 17:4. Further material may be found in secondary passages at 3:18; 10:16 = 51:19; 12:14, 15; 16:14, 15, 18; 32:21, 22; 35:15; 50:11.

[9] We need not go into the question of the authorship of these sections; they are certainly exilic and bear significant testimony to the continued existence of ancient views.

[10] 58:14 and 57:13 seem to be later additions.

נַחֲלָה (47:4) and gave it to them (135:12; 136:21, 22) as an allotted נַחֲלָה (78:55). When they were unfaithful, He gave them into the hand of their enemies and burned in wrath against His נַחֲלָה (78:62, the reference is to the events of 1 S. 4). But He then chose His servant David and fetched him from the flock to feed Israel, His נַחֲלָה, (78:70, 71).

As may be seen from these passages, the people is often called the נַחֲלָה of Yahweh in the Psalms (cf. also 28:9; 94:5, 14; 106:5, 40). But it is realised that strictly all nations belong to Yahweh as נַחֲלָה, and this can be the ground of the request that Yahweh will rise up to judge the earth (82:8). The land is only once called the נַחֲלָה of Yahweh (79:1); it is the נַחֲלָה of Israel (37:18; 47:4; 69:36; 105:11; 135:12; 136:21, 22), not only in the past from the very earliest times, but also in the last days (37:18; 69:36) as an object of eschatological expectation. In spiritualising piety the Psalmist can even call Yahweh Himself the נַחֲלָה which is apportioned to him by lot (16:5, 6), and a later psalm can speak in the same way of the self-attestations of Yahweh in His commandments (119:111). Even in these expressions the vitality of the ancient נַחֲלָה concept is displayed.

11. Conclusion. In the preceding discussion we have for the time being refrained from translating נַחֲלָה and we have rendered נחל by English verbs in combination with נַחֲלָה in order not to anticipate the difficult matter of a definition. Not much help is gained from comparison with other Semitic languages. Ges.-Buhl, *s.v.*, relates the modern Hebrew "to possess," the Arabic "to give, to apportion as a possession, " and the South Arabian "to enfeoff," to נחל. The OT material gives us the following general characteristics.

a. We gather from נַחֲלָה and נחל that something is allotted to one, and possessed only on this basis. Hence the terms are well adapted to express a deeply rooted OT conviction that Palestine was allotted to Israel by Yahweh and that the conquest could succeed only on this basis. Israel possesses its land only by divine ordination.

b. נַחֲלָה and נחל also contain the thought of apportionment. Hence the words are apt to express the fact that at the conquest the land was divided among the tribes by sacred lot, and that families and even individuals came to their portions in the same way. On this view the shares of the tribes, families and individuals are also fixed by divine ordination.

c. There can be no doubt that נַחֲלָה refers originally and almost exclusively to the possession of land. The divinely ordained portion is to be a lasting possession of the family etc. The extraordinary interest of Israel in maintaining the family portion intact is expressed not only in material already adduced but also very significantly in the fact that one of the Ten Commandments of Ex. 20, the tenth, is devoted to ensuring this.[11] Concern for safeguarding possessions for ever in the hands of the owner also lies behind one of the most remarkable of the social laws of Israel, that of the year of jubilee in Lv. 25. Isaiah, too, invokes woes on the rich who drive the peasants from their land, Is. 5:8,[12] and his contemporary

---

[11] J. Herrmann, *op. cit.*, 69-82.
[12] For details cf. O. Procksch, *Jesaja*, I (1930), 92; Herrmann, 78.

Micah inveighs similarly against those who "covet fields, and take them by violence; and houses, and take them away : so they oppress a man and his house, even a man and his נַחֲלָה" 2:2. [13]

d. It is thus plain that נַחֲלָה and נחל are very well suited to describe the possession in so far as it comes from the fathers, i.e., the patrimony or inheritance. If we take a. and b. together we might perhaps hesitate to speak of inheritance, since possession of Israel was not primarily based on the fact that the land was inherited from the patriarchs or from the generation of Moses. The patriarchs and the generation of Moses did not yet possess it. It was promised to them for their descendants, who would not acquire it in virtue of a civil law of inheritance but in virtue of God's faithfulness to the promise which He had given (cf. Ex. 32:13 J Es). On the other hand, when they had come into possession of the land in virtue of these promises to the fathers, it was to be their inheritance for all generations, and to the degree that the content of God's promises is a reality as soon as they are uttered the land can be viewed retrospectively as an inheritance (נַחֲלָה) even at the time when they received it. A few more passages may be adduced to show that נַחֲלָה can refer to the inherited portion of land and that it can then come to denote the inheritance. In the ancient narrative in 1 K. 21 Naboth refuses to yield his vineyard to the king in the words : "The Lord forbid it me, that I should give the נַחֲלָה of my fathers unto thee" (21:3). In the no less ancient story in Ju. 11:2 נחל q means "to inherit," and in the Deuteronomic Law (Dt. 21:16) נחל hi means "to assign portions of the inheritance (to sons)," the inheritance here being, not merely land, but all that the testator has, cf. Prv. 13:22; נחל hitp is also used at Lv. 25:46 when the reference is not just to landed property. נַחֲלָה is the portion of sons (Prv. 17:2) or daughters (Job 42:15) and can embrace house and goods (Prv. 19:14), though it refers primarily to land inherited by the sons, and in special cases the daughters, Nu. 27:1-11; 36:2 ff.; cf. also Rt. 4:5 ff. How closely linked are the beliefs that Palestine is Israel's inheritance and Israel's possession may be seen in the case of נַחֲלָה in Jer. 3:19 and in that of נחל hi in 1 Ch. 28:8. Careful exegetical consideration, however, will show that in neither instance is it necessary to translate "inheritance" or "to inherit." The strict sense of inheritance is unmistakably secondary to the other ideas which we have seen to be associated with נחל and נַחֲלָה.

e. From what has been said in a.-d., it may be seen why Palestine or Israel is called Yahweh's נַחֲלָה. נַחֲלָה is the share which Yahweh allots to Himself and which will always be His. Thus pious Israelites, in faith regarding their people and land as Yahweh's נַחֲלָה, could link with this conviction all the feelings of love, loyalty and concern associated elsewhere with the נַחֲלָה of the fathers.

f. Finally נַחֲלָה like חֵלֶק and גּוֹרָל denotes the portion which is allotted to man (his "lot") in the sense of his destiny, Job 20:29; 27:13; 31:2.

The religious concepts associated with נַחֲלָה are developed in a way which is particularly vital and far-reaching in a passage like Ps. 16:5, 6. In the blessedness of his assurance of faith the righteous man dares to say that the God who maintains

---

[13] Herrmann, 73.

his גּוֹרָל is allotted to him as חֵלֶק; hence the line has fallen on a fair ground and this נַחֲלָה pleases him well. [1]

It will be seen how important are the convictions associated with נַחֲלָה for the religion of the OT saints, and their imperishable influence may be perceived not only in Judaism but also in Christianity.

J. Herrmann

C. The Word Group κληρονόμος in the LXX.

The Greek word group mentioned on → 768 undergoes further development in the Bible primarily on the basis of the meaning of the Hebrew equivalents but more particularly by reason of the fact that the word group came to be used for a specific train of religious thought.

1. Linguistic.

That the range of meaning of the Gk. terms was influenced by the Heb. equivalents may be seen from the example of κληρονόμος. We must lay particular emphasis on the fact that in the LXX this word plays no part in the trains of religious thought which we shall have to discuss later. It means "heir" in 2 Βασ. 14:7; Sir. 23:22 and "owner" in Ju. 18:17 B and Mi. 1:15. [15] It is always used for יוֹרֵשׁ.

συγκληρονόμος does not occur in the LXX.

κληρονομέω means "to inherit something," Tob. 14:13 : ἐκληρονόμησεν τὴν οὐσίαν αὐτῶν; there is also a play on this sense at Sir. 10:11, a man on dying κληρονομήσει ἑρπετά ... καὶ σκώληκας. The obj. [16] is always in the gen. (Is. 63:18) or the acc., "to be the heir of someone," or "to inherit something," Gn. 15:3 f.; Nu. 27:11; Tob. 3:15; 6:12 S; 14:13. The abs. "to be heir" is found at Ju. 11:2. The causative "to give to possess" is found with the dat., Nu. 34:17; 2 Εσδρ. 9:12 A V, with the double acc., "to let someone take in possession," Jos. 17:14 (נָתַן נַחֲלָה); Ju. 11:24 B; Prv. 13:22; Sir. 46:1 B. "To hold in possession," Ez. 33:25 A; 1 Ch. 28:8. The class. use "to inherit a reputation etc." is followed in the Wisdom lit., which speaks of what the wise or the righteous will inherit : δόξαν σοφοὶ κληρονομήσουσιν (נחל), Prv. 3:35; cf. 11:29; Sir. 4:13 etc.

κληρονομεῖν goes rather beyond secular usage in 3 Βασ. 20:15-19 (יָרַשׁ) when we read that Ahab "took" Naboth's vineyard on the death of the latter; in Is. 34:17 it is used of wild beasts (יָרַשׁ) which take Edom in possession. At Tob. 3:17; 6:12 S it is used of marrying, cf. also Hos. 9:6; 1 Macc. 2:57. The word is used of violent appropriation, e.g., at Gn. 24:60, where the blessing of her relatives desires for the parting Rebekah : thy seed κληρονομησάτω τὰς πόλεις τῶν ὑπεναντίων, cf. Gn. 22:17; Ju. 3:13; 4 Βασ. 17:24; Is. 14:21; 17:14 (for בזו!); Ez. 7:24 B; 35:10; 1 Macc. 1:32; 2:10. Of lasting possession, "to hold," "to have," Ju. 11:24 : οὐχὶ ὅσα κατεκληρονόμησέν σοι Χαμὼς ὁ θεός σου, αὐτὰ κληρονομήσεις; (A), so also perhaps ψ 118:111, Ez. 33:25 f. A and 1 Ch. 28:8, where David gives the warning : "Keep God's commandments ἵνα κληρονομήσητε τὴν γῆν τὴν ἀγαθήν."

---

[14] At this point we may mention the argument that the Levites were not to receive a portion (נחל) like the other tribes because Yahweh was their נַחֲלָה, Nu. 18:20, 21, 24, 26; Dt. 10:9; 18:2; Jos. 13:14, 33. That there was a real basis for this may be seen in Jos. 18:7 and esp. Dt. 18:1.

[15] In this case the translator may not have understood the verse correctly. Jer. 13:25 א reads κληρονόμος, but this makes no sense.

[16] On the construction cf. Helbing, *Kasussyntax*, 138-141.

κατακληρονομέω. Relatively common in the LXX, often with κληρονομέω and κατακληροδοτέω as *vl*. In meaning it is close to the simple, though the causative sense is more common. "To take in possession," of the conquest and of any invasion by force (Hab. 1:6), obj. nations and gods (Dt. 12:2, 29); of the wisdom which man acquires, Sir. 4:16; of an eternal name, Sir. 15:6; with God as subj. ψ 81:8. Esp. common in the causative, "to divide the inheritance," "to cause someone to inherit," Dt. 21:16; 1 Ch. 28:8; of the inheritance of the land, Ez. 46:18; "to cause someone to take possession of," with double or single acc., Zech. 2:16; Sir. 36:10; 46:1; "to give to someone in possession," dat. and acc., Dt. 3:28; of the throne of glory which God gives to the poor, 1 Βασ. 2:8. In the pers. pass., "it will be given to me in possession," Dt. 19:14; Sir. 24:8.

In κληρονομία, too, there is advance beyond the ordinary Gk. meaning.[17] Apart from lines of thought to be considered later, it means "inheritance" (Gn. 31:14; Job 42:15), "possession" (Mi. 2:2 : διήρπαζον ἄνδρα καὶ τὸν οἶκον αὐτοῦ, ἄνδρα καὶ τὴν κληρονομίαν αὐτοῦ, Lam. 5:2 : κληρονομία ἡμῶν μετεστράφη ἀλλοτρίοις, οἱ οἶκοι ἡμῶν ξένοις, Qoh. 7:11 B : ἀγαθὴ σοφία μετὰ κληρονομίας, and esp. Sir. 9:6; 22:23; 33:24). Of possession of a wife, Tob. 6:13, of children, ψ 126:3, of wisdom, Sir. 24:20. The merging with κλῆρος mentioned above (→ 759) may be seen in the fact that it can also denote "share," "portion," Is. 17:14 (par. μερίς) as a rendering of גּוֹרָל; ψ 15:5b f. (par. σχοινίον), נַחֲלָה and גּוֹרָל. At Sir. 24:7, too, one would rather expect κλῆρος. Ps. Sol. 14:5 (par. μερίς).

2. Material.

Any attempt to grasp clearly the sense borne by the word group in the LXX must be preceded by a full review of the main words κληρονομέω and κληρονομία and of their main equivalents יָרַשׁ, נָחַל, and נַחֲלָה. In 163 appearances κληρονομέω is used 111 times for יָרַשׁ, 27 for נָחַל and נַחֲלָה, 2 for אָחַז (Gn. 47:27; Jos. 22:9), 1 for יָדַע (Nu. 14:31), 1 for לָכַד (Ju. 1:18), בּוֹז, Is. 17:14 (?) and חֵלֶק, Is. 53:12. On the other hand, יָרַשׁ (q, ni, hi) is not only rendered κληρονομεῖν and κατακληρονομεῖν but also 8 times ἀπολλύναι, 4 ἐκβάλλειν, 13 ἐξαίρειν, 3 each ἐκτρίβειν, παραλαμβάνειν, ἐξολεθρεύειν, 2 each κατασχεῖν, κυριεύειν, πτωχεύειν, and 1 each ἀγχιστεύειν, διαδιδόναι, ἐκβιάζειν, ἐκζητεῖν, κατακυριεύειν, κατοικεῖν, κτῆσις, λαμβάνειν, προνομεύειν, πτωχίζειν, περιτιθέναι, ὀλεθρεύειν, ἐξέλκειν and ἐξαναλίσκειν. Similarly נָחַל is translated 4 times μερίζειν and καταμερίζειν, 2 each κληροδοτεῖν, κατέχειν, κτᾶσθαι, and 1 each διέρχεσθαι, ἐμβατεύειν, ἐξολεθρεύειν, διαμερίζειν (apart from Jos. 1:6). In 163 instances κληρονομία is used 143 times for נַחֲלָה, 16 for words of the stem יָרַשׁ, 2 each for גּוֹרָל, גְּבוּל and אֲחֻזָּה, and once for חֵלֶק. On the reverse side נַחֲלָה is also rendered 5 times κατάσχεσις, 1-2 times κληρονομέω, 2 times κληροδοσία and κτῆμα, 3-4 times μερίς, and once each διαίρεσις, ἔγκληρος (εὔκληρος), κληρουχία, μερίζειν, οἶκος, τόπος.

The meaning attached by the LXX to κληρονομέω and κληρονομία in the passages mentioned under B is not immediately evident either from the usual meaning of the Greek — we have seen already that the LXX goes beyond this — or from the OT context. In the Greek the concept of inheritance is basic, but, as in the case of נַחֲלָה, it is not now the decisive point. This is not merely because the idea of inheritance arises in the OT only in respect of family and individual possessions after the conquest but also because the LXX makes lavish use of κληρονομεῖν — usually for יָרַשׁ — in the stories of the patriarchs, e.g., Gn. 15:7:

---

[17] For the sense of "property," "possession," Liddell-Scott, *s.v.* gives only LXX examples.

ἐγὼ ὁ θεὸς ὁ ἐξαγαγών σε ἐκ χώρας Χαλδαίων ὥστε δοῦναί σοι τὴν γῆν ταύτην κληρονομῆσαι (שׁרי); Dt. 30:5 : εἰσάξει σε κύριος ὁ θεός σου εἰς τὴν γῆν, ἣν ἐκληρονόμησαν οἱ πατέρες σου, καὶ κληρονομήσεις αὐτήν. The taking of the land is κληρονομεῖν, cf. Gn. 28:4; Dt. 1:8; 10:11. When we read in Nu. 34:2 : ὑμεῖς εἰσπορεύεσθε εἰς τὴν γῆν Χανααν· αὕτη ἔσται ὑμῖν εἰς κληρονομίαν, the future ἔσται shows that the implication of κληρονομία is not that even before the actual seizure of the land Israel has by God's promise a right to the land similar to that of an heir prior to his entering into the inheritance — true though this may also be. The common feature in the verb κληρονομεῖν and the noun κληρονομία, and the aspect which characterises these terms in the present theological context and elsewhere, is the element of lasting possession. In the case of the verb this is clear in Joshua's question in Jos. 18:3 : ἕως τίνος ἐκλυθήσεσθε κληρονομῆσαι τὴν γῆν, ἣν ἔδωκεν κύριος ὁ θεὸς ἡμῶν; cf. also Ex. 23:30; Nu. 14:24. κληρονομεῖν denotes the actual taking of the land in possession. The verb is no less clearly used of violent seizure in passages which do not refer to the conquest (→ 776, esp. 3 Βασ. 20:15-19), particularly where neither ירשׁ nor נחל underlies the choice of κληρονομέω, Gn. 47:27 of the stay of Israel in Goshen : ἐκληρονόμησαν ἐπ' αὐτῆς (= אחז ni), cf. also Ju. 1:18 (לכד) and 2 Ἐσδρ. 19:25; in Zech. 9:4 κληρονομεῖν is stated of God. The fact that so many other words denoting violent seizure, expulsion and extermination can also be used for ירשׁ and נחל shows that the parallel κληρονομεῖν is also meant to denote taking possession, for the other verbs selected are always found with reference to the conquest, e.g., Nu. 32:39; 33:52, 53; Jos. 15:63; 16:10; 23:5 (ἀπολλύναι); Nu. 21:32 (ἐκβάλλειν); Jos. 1:11 (κατασχεῖν); Ju. 1:21 ff. (ἐξαίρειν). We may compare κληρονομεῖν with a personal object, e.g., Dt. 9:1; 11:23; Ju. 1:19b A. Thus נתן לרשׁת is rendered διδόναι κληρονομῆσαι at Dt. 21:1 but διδόναι ἐν κτήσει at Lv. 20:24. As regards the noun, comparison with κλῆρος (→ 759 f.) shows us already that the decisive point is that of enduring possession. That it can mean inheritance or the inheritance, and that these are linked in the OT, is illustrated in the story of the daughters of Zelophehad in Nu. 27:8. There are also examples under B. But this is not the chief meaning. Here, too, we may see this from the fact that the substantive can be used of the possession of alien peoples, Ez. 25:4 : παραδίδωμι ὑμᾶς τοῖς υἱοῖς Κεδεμ εἰς κληρονομίαν (מורשׁה), cf. v. 10 and Mi. 1:14. Even when the greater part of the land of Canaan could no longer be referred to as the patrimony of Israel, it was still κληρονομία Ἰσραηλ, and the religio-political aim of the Maccabees was to recapture the land in the entirety in which God gave it to Israel as a lasting possession ; thus Simon says to Athenobios in 1 Macc. 15:33 f.: οὔτε γῆν ἀλλοτρίαν εἰλήφαμεν οὔτε ἀλλοτρίων κεκρατήκαμεν, ἀλλὰ τῆς κληρονομίας τῶν πατέρων ἡμῶν, ὑπὸ δὲ ἐχθρῶν ἡμῶν ἀκρίτως ἔν τινι καιρῷ κατεκρατήθη· ἡμεῖς δὲ καιρὸν ἔχοντες ἀντεχόμεθα τῆς κληρονομίας τῶν πατέρων ἡμῶν. The fact that κατάσχεσις occurs 5 times in the passages in question (Nu. 32:32; 33:54 [twice]; 36:3; Ez. 36:12) points in the same direction.

What has been said seems to make it rather enigmatical that this word group should have been selected when the essential Greek element of inheritance is pushed so much into the background. The reason is perhaps to be sought in the Hebrew, for the thought of inheritance is present in ירשׁ and נחל though less so in the former. Yet we must also emphasise another aspect which also applies to the Hebrew. The MT never speaks of the conquest in terms of קנה, and the LXX never calls the land κτῆσις, nor speaks of its κτᾶσθαι. קנה or κτᾶσθαι describes a process whereby one possession changes owner in exchange for another possession, so that the process can be reversed if desired. κτᾶσθαι confers possession, but not of a lasting kind. In the happenings in the history of Israel and other nations for which the LXX uses κληρονομεῖν, we do not have reversible processes.Only with force can a people be removed from the territory which it ἐκληρονόμησεν. This type of acquisition confers a lasting right of ownership. This is expressed in the extension of the right to families and individuals, and in the legislation of the year of jubilee. Inheriting is linked with this type of possession inasmuch as it denotes a process which cannot be reversed at will.

If this is the decisive aspect of the LXX terms κληρονομεῖν and κληρονομία, it is evident that the LXX has maintained an essential element in the Hebrew נַחֲלָה. It is no longer possible to say how far the LXX is here adopting a special use which may perhaps be Egyptian but of which we no longer have any instances. One aspect of Greek usage may have worked in this direction → 768.

In view of the definition now attained it is easily seen how κληρονομεῖν and κληρονομία could be integrated into the more developed religious usage of the OT. To call both Israel and Canaan God's κληρονομία, and to apply the term in eschatological contexts, was both meaningful and possible because we have here a lasting possession which rests, not on the basis of a reversible transaction, but on the gift of God.

D. The Word Group in Later Judaism.

1. Linguistic. In the Mishnah נחל and ירש commonly denote "to inherit," "to be heir to," in terms of the juridical interest of the work. The religious usage of the OT still exerts an influence, and in accordance with developing concepts there is a stronger tendency towards the transcendental aspect. The pseudepigrapha may be treated along with Rabb. Judaism. Here κληρονομεῖν is used of violent appropriation, Test. XII, N. 5:8; in Test. Job, 18 (ed. M. R. James, TSt, V, 1 [1897], 104 ff.) it means "to take in possession," cf. also 4 Esr. 7:6 ff.

2. Material. Materially κληρονομεῖν is used of the conquest and κληρονομία of the promised land (נחלה), but in such a way that there is an eschatological reference beyond the historical conquest, as in ψ 36:9. The community of the new covenant in Damascus, with its eschatological expectations, looks back to its beginnings with the words ויצמח מישראל ומאהרון שרש מטעת לירוש את ארצו, Damasc., 1, 7 f., cf. Eth. En. 5:7: "The elect ... shall inherit the land." But we must make special mention of Jub., which as a midrash on Gn. paraphrases the promises to the fathers. In 22:14 Abraham's blessing of Jacob is to the effect that he shall inherit the whole earth, as Abraham has inherited Canaan, for ever (22:27; 17:3 the earth). The blessing of Jacob confirms this prospect (32:19): "I will give thy seed the whole earth which is under heaven, and they shall rule over all peoples, and they shall then inherit the whole earth and possess it for ever" (cf. 25:17), v. also Ps. Sol. 12:6 : ὅσιοι κυρίου κληρονομήσαισαν ἐπαγγελίας κυρίου. In Apc. Sedrach, 6 (ed. M. R. James, TSt, II, 3 [1893]) Adam is κληρονόμος οὐρανοῦ καὶ γῆς. Rabb. testimonies agree with this expectation of the fulfilment of the extended promises of Abraham. Leqach Tob., 1, 72a on Gn. 28:14 [18] notes expressly that Gn. 28:14 will be fulfilled in the days of the Messiah. [19] Even in their eschatological

---

[18] Str.-B., III, 209.

[19] *Loc. cit.* The passages quoted here from Nu. r., 12 and 14 use קנה for Abraham's inheriting of heaven and earth, cf. 4 Esr. 5:27: *adquisisti.*

expansion and in their extension to the whole world the patriarchal promises of inheriting the land still refer to this earth, cf. the expression נחל ארץ ירש (Qid., 1, 10), ירש ארץ (Sanh., 11, 1 [= Is. 60:21], cf. Nu. r., 11 on Nu. 6:26b, where salvation [שלום] is meant as in Ps. 37:11). The view that the conquest itself is an event of salvation is jeopardised by the midrash in Jub., acc. to which Canaan is divided among the Israelites by lot, 8:10 ff.; 9:1 ff.; 10:28 ff. We see something of the same in the theologically significant passage 4 Esr. 6:55 f. Here Ezra asks : The first world was created for the sake of Israel, and the nations were regarded as nought ; why, then, do the nations scatter Israel and why has not Israel come to possess this world ? (haereditatem possidere = κληρονομεῖν). This question points to the extension of the patriarchal promises to the whole earth and yet it also threatens the specifically OT conception of κληρονομεῖν, for if the world was created for Israel's sake, then it is Israel's possession from the very first and is κτῆμα rather than κληρονομία. The answer is given in a twofold comparison, and in the second κληρονομία is used. Israel is like a man to whom a city has been given as his portion, but to get to it he has to go along a narrow path between fire and water. The path is this aeon, which was created for Israel's sake but which was judged through Adam's fall (7:11 f.). Hence 4 Esr. takes the fulfilment of the promise to inherit the earth right out of this aeon, though apart from this there is also a limited fulfilment, restricted to Palestine (9:8) and to 400 years (7:28) which will be enjoyed only by those who live when this time comes.

Hence alongside the inheriting of the earth there is an inheriting of eternal life. This becomes a fixed expression, Ps. Sol. 14:10; Eth. En. 40:9; Sib. Fr., 3; [20] Test. Job 18 (→ 779), cf. also the coming aeon, (4 Esr. 7:96; [21] S. Bar. 44:13; Slav. En. 50:2; 66:6), or the glory of God. [22] In the Rabb. ירש and נחל (Aram. ירת and חסן) are found without distinction, and as obj. העולם הבא or חיי העולם הבא|, גן עדן‎ also גיהנום (Ab., 1, 5; Test. Job 43). [23] Nowhere in this context do we find God as Father or Israel as son or any other expression which would suggest "inheriting." In 4 Esr. 6:55 ff. (v. 58) Israel is the first born son of God, and the parable of the heir is used in 7:9, but if there had been here a real connection between sonship and inheritance ought we not to have expected an introduction of the parable that a king made over to his son a city as his portion, cf. the introduction of many Rabb. parables ?

κληρονομία or נחלה in the sense of "inheritance." In Ab., 2, 12 יְרֻשָּׁה is the inheritance which falls into our lap with no co-operation on our part. This is contrasted with the winning of knowledge of the Torah. Elsewhere in the Rabb. נחלה and ירשה are often used juristically for "inheritance," cf. also Ps. Sol. 15:11. Instances of the noun for the heavenly inheritance may be adduced from the pseudepigrapha, 4 Esr. 7:9, 17; Eth. En. 39:8; 71:16; 99:14; Slav. En. 9; 55:2; Ps. Sol. 14:9 f. It is, of course, difficult to decide whether κλῆρος or κληρονομία is the right word for inheritance. In the first two passages from Eth. En. the par. is "dwelling." Thus one might suppose that there is a transcendentalising of the promise of inheriting the earth and think of κληρονομία. In Eth. En., however, the par. is "measure" and we are thus to think of κλῆρος. Gehenna can also be the obj. of ירש, cf. Slav. En. 10:6, where the place of hell is prepared as the eternal portion of the ungodly, cf. Ps. Sol. 14:9; 15:10. The pseudepigraphical writings make it plain — cf. the whole form of ascensions — that the in-

---

[20] P. 232, 47, Geffcken.

[21] Cf. Gunkel in Kautzsch Pseudepigr., ad loc. Cf. also the common use of possidere etc. for κληρονομεῖν in it and Vg (W. Matzkow, De vocabulis quibusdam Italae et Vulgatae christianis quaestiones lexicographae [1933], 45 f.).

[22] Apc. Elias in Cl. Al. Prot., X, 94, 4.

[23] Cf. the convenient review of examples in Volz Esch., 341. In these contexts κληρονομεῖν has a spatial aspect which facilitates its further use in Rabb. Judaism. "To inherit both worlds," e.g., bBer., 51a.

heritance is regarded as spatial. This is supported by the factual description of future torment and bliss.

That Israel is God's possession is an indispensable thought in later Judaism. Yet κληρονομία is not used by the Rabb. in this sense. In the 18th petition of the Palestinian recension of the Prayer of Eighteen Petitions: שים שלומך על ישראל עמך ועל עירך ועל נחלתך, נחלה is Canaan as well as the people and city, as in Ps. Sol. 7:2; 9:1; 17:23; in Test. B. 9:2 Α κληρονομία is the temple. The term occurs in Jub. 1:19, 21; 16:18; 22:9 f., 15, 29; 33:20; 4 Esr. 8:16; Apc. Abr. 20, and, as in the OT, it carries with it both comfort and commitment. Thus in Jub. 22:29 Abraham prays for Jacob: "That thou mayest sanctify him as a people of thine inheritance"; Ps. Sol. 14:5 : ἡ μερὶς καὶ κληρονομία τοῦ θεοῦ ἐστιν Ισραηλ. As the possession acquired at a specific moment, κληρονομία can express the idea of election, though in Rabb. Judaism this tends to yield before the thought of merit, or to be coloured by it. Hence it is not surprising that we do not find נחלה in this sense in the Rabb.

Israel has acquired the Torah as a precious possession. Hence in Damasc., 1, 16 this is נחלה, and in Asc. Is. 1:13 Is. is haereditatis Dilecti haeres, i.e., like all the prophets in Ab., 1, 1, he is a link in the unbroken chain which passed on the Torah from Moses to the scribes. [24]

E. The Word Group in the New Testament.

1. The Usage.

κληρονόμος ("son and) heir," Mk. 12:7 and par.; Gl. 4:1; in a religious sense, R. 8:17; Gl. 3:29; 4:7; Hb. 1:2; of the recipients of God's promises and of those who wait for what is promised, with no emphasis on the link with sonship and inheritance, R. 4:13 f.; Tt. 3:7; Hb. 6:17; 11:7; Jm. 2:5.

συγκληρονόμος, "he who receives, or will receive, something along with another," R. 8:17; Eph. 3:6 (adj.); Hb. 11:9; 1 Pt. 3:7.

κληρονομέω, "to inherit," in the strict sense, of children, Gl. 4:30; of Christ, Hb. 1:4. Of the receiving of God's promises and gifts, Mt. 5:5 (τὴν γῆν); Mk. 10:17, cf. Lk. 18:18; [25] Mt. 19:29; Lk. 10:25 (ζωὴν αἰώνιον); Mt. 25:34; 1 C. 6:9 f.; 1 C. 15:50a; Gl. 5:21 (τὴν βασιλείαν τοῦ θεοῦ); Mk. 16:14 Cod. W (δόξαν); Hb. 1:14 (σωτηρίαν); 12:17; 1 Pt. 3:9 (εὐλογίαν); 1 C. 15:50b (τὴν ἀφθαρσίαν); Rev. 21:7 (ταῦτα); Hb. 6:12 (τὰς ἐπαγγελίας).

κατακληρονομέω, Ac. 13:9, "to give in possession," of the conquest (OT).

κληρονομία, "inheritance," Mk. 12:7 and par.; Lk. 12:13; in the religious sense, Gl. 3:18; [26] "possession" (of the land), Ac. 7:5; 13:33 D (par. κατάσχεσις = ψ 2:8); Hb. 11:8, all 3 passages with reference to the OT promises to the fathers; the "eternal inheritance," Ac. 20:32; Eph. 1:18; 5:5; [27] Eph. 1:14; Col. 3:24; Hb. 9:15; 1 Pt. 1:4.

2. The Theological Usage.

The special sense acquired by the group in the NT is to be found almost entirely in the parable of the wicked husbandmen in Mk. 12:1-12 and par. The heir is the Son, and the inheritance is God's kingdom. A firm link is established between son-

---

[24] Cf. also Apc. Sedrach (ed. M. R. James, TSt, II, 3 [1893], 130 ff.), 6, where Adam is made κληρονόμος of heaven and earth.

[25] In the par. Mt. has ἵνα σχῶ for ἵνα κληρονομήσω.

[26] Not "inheriting" (Zn. Gl., ad loc.), since in what follows it is the obj. of κεχάρισται.

[27] In the last 3 passages the sense approximates to that of κλῆρος, cf. Ac. 26:18 and Col. 1:12 → 763.

ship and inheritance such as we hardly ever find in the OT and later Judaism, and this runs through the whole of the NT. Thus Paul, although he never calls Christ κληρονόμος, refers to Christians as συγκληρονόμοι Χριστοῦ in R. 8:17 and attributes the inheritance of Christians expressly to their υἱοθεσία, R. 8:17: εἰ δὲ τέκνα, καὶ κληρονόμοι· κληρονόμοι μὲν θεοῦ, συγκληρονόμοι δὲ Χριστοῦ; Gl. 3:29; 4:7: ὥστε οὐκέτι εἶ δοῦλος ἀλλὰ υἱός· εἰ δὲ υἱός, καὶ κληρονόμος διὰ θεοῦ. In the careful introduction to Hb. it is said of the Son ὃν ἔθηκεν (sc. θεός) κληρονόμον πάντων. [28] According to the common Greek and Oriental view, sonship is the basis of inheritance (→ 769). In the parable of the wicked husbandmen inheritance does not mean actual inheritance but expectation of it. The Son does not come as the Lord of the vineyard with the full power of one who is already in possession. Albeit foolishly, the husbandmen think that they can kill the Son without penalty. Only the risen Lord has entered upon His inheritance, Mt. 28:18 : ἐδόθη μοι πᾶσα ἐξουσία ἐν οὐρανῷ καὶ ἐπὶ γῆς. One might apply Paul's parable in Gl. 4:1 f. to the earthy activity of Jesus : ὁ κληρονόμος ... οὐδὲν διαφέρει δούλου κύριος πάντων ὤν, cf. Phil. 2:7: μορφὴν δούλου λαβών. Jn. strongly emphasises the κύριος πάντων ὤν; hence κληρονόμος is not used. Indeed, the Johannine writings (apart from Rev. 21:7) avoid the word group as a whole, since they set the earthly life of Jesus and His disciples in the light of the supratemporal fulfilment. To be heir does not now include a title which may be claimed by law, since sonship is not exhausted by descent from the Father but finds fulfilment in the fact that the Son does what He sees the Father doing. [29] Hence κληρονόμος is an eschatological concept.

This leads us to the further point that the inheritance is the kingdom of God. In the parable of the husbandmen only Mt. says this expressly (21:43), and for him the kingdom is active in all Israel's history. But he has grasped the true sense of the parable. While Judaism did not speak of inheriting the kingdom of God, and the rich young ruler did so only when, like the Rabbis, he asked : τί ποιήσω, ἵνα ζωὴν αἰώνιον κληρονομήσω; (Mk. 10:17), the combination κληρονομεῖν τὴν βασιλείαν θεοῦ is firmly established in the NT, → 781. When Jesus in His earthly lowliness describes Himself as υἱὸς καὶ κληρονόμος, the concept of the kingdom of God and of the inheritance is freed from all earthly limitations and qualifications. The kingdom or inheritance is the new world in which God reigns alone and supreme.

If Christ as Son is heir, His people as those set in sonship are συγκληρονόμοι. Whereas the element of inheritance is discounted in later Judaism by exploiting the full range of meaning of נָחַל and יָרַשׁ, this aspect is given full weight in the NT. Yet there is an important nuance. The children are heirs, but this sonship is not based on physical descent, nor on the origin of all natural life in the creative power of God, nor on derivation from Abraham, but on the divine call and appointment. The "sons of the kingdom" are excluded, and many are invited from the East and the West, Mt. 8:11 f. Hence neither Israel, Palestine, the temple nor the Torah can now be called κληρονομία θεοῦ. We read : σὰρξ καὶ αἷμα βασιλείαν θεοῦ κληρονομῆσαι οὐ δύναται, 1 C. 15:50; sonship and inheritance are grounded in a new creation, or, to change the figure, in υἱοθεσία. Paul can regard this as future,

---

[28] The reference is to the ascension (Wnd. Hb. and Rgg. Hb., ad loc.).
[29] Strongly emphasised by F. Büchsel, *Theologie des NT* (1935), 61 ff.

R. 8:23, and in the same way, although more exclusively, the κληρονομία of Christians is an object of hope. [30] The things associated with κληρονομεῖν, and the genitives dependent on κληρονομία, show what is the content of the inheritance: σωτηρία, Hb. 1:14; δόξα, R. 8:17 (i.e., ἀπολύτρωσις τοῦ σώματος ἡμῶν); Eph. 1:18; Mk. 16:14 Cod W; χάρις, 1 Pt. 3:7; εὐλογία, 1 Pt. 3:9; in sum, eternal life, Tt. 3:7. [31] This means that spatial conceptions are less significant. We still read in Mt. 5:5: μακάριοι οἱ πραεῖς, ὅτι αὐτοὶ κληρονομήσουσιν τὴν γῆν, but the earth is not the epitome of the inheritance, [32] nor is a lot or portion in the heavenly regions. It is God's rule or reign, which lavishes on man the inconceivable riches of the divine life. Nor is this an abstraction. As life from God, it implies commission, service and lordship, cf. Mt. 25:21; Lk. 19:17. Paul and Rev. can speak of reigning: R. 5:17: ἐν ζωῇ βασιλεύσουσιν, cf. 1 C. 4:8: χωρὶς ἡμῶν ἐβασιλεύσατε· καὶ ὄφελόν γε ἐβασιλεύσατε, ἵνα καὶ ἡμεῖς ὑμῖν συμβασιλεύσωμεν, also Rev. 5:10; 20:4; 22:5, cf. 1:9: συγκοινωνὸς ἐν τῇ ... βασιλείᾳ. In Rev. 21:2 ff. the divine sees the new Jerusalem coming down from heaven and he is told that it is ἡ σκηνὴ τοῦ θεοῦ μετὰ τῶν ἀνθρώπων (v. 3), so that men should be His people and He should dwell with them. Death and pain are abolished and all things are made new. Then we read in v. 7: ὁ νικῶν κληρονομήσει ταῦτα καὶ ἔσομαι αὐτῷ θεὸς καὶ αὐτὸς ἔσται μοι υἱός. This tells us what is meant by the βασιλεία τοῦ θεοῦ, by ζωή, by σωτηρία and εὐλογία. In short, it tells us what the inheritance includes. In the light of this passage the apparent contradiction of 1 Pt. 1:3 f. is easily explained: θεὸς ... ἀναγεννήσας ἡμᾶς εἰς ἐλπίδα ζῶσαν ... εἰς κληρονομίαν ἄφθαρτον ... τετηρημένην ἐν οὐρανοῖς εἰς ὑμᾶς. This passage, and that in Rev., might suggest a spatial conception, and added support seems to be given by verses in which κληρονομία is used in much the same way as κλῆρος (→ 780). Nevertheless, the decisive point is the absence of any idea of spatially distinct portions of heaven. [33] We may add in conclusion that it is no accident that the common Rabbinic idea of inheriting hell does not occur. In the Rabbis נָחַל (יָרַשׁ) means to "acquire," "attain to"; in the NT it is inheritance on the ground of a filial relationship to God.

The NT view sheds new light on that of the OT, especially in Paul and Hebrews.

In Gl. (and R. 4) Paul found himself confronted by a Jewish Christian thesis which may be reconstructed as follows. Promises are made to Abraham and his

---

[30] F. J. A. Hort, The First Epistle of St. Peter (1898) on 1:4 doubts whether κληρονομία is eschatological, cf. E. de Witt Burton, Gl. (ICC) on 3:29; Zn. Gl. on 3:29 (²[1907], 190) and Ew. Gefbr. on Eph. 5:5. In respect of the Gl. passages there is justification for this verdict, but its general validity is open to question.

[31] In this verse it makes no material different how we take ζωῆς; even if it is combined with κατ' ἐλπίδα, it is a development of the κληρονόμοι γενηθῶμεν.

[32] Dalman WJ, I, 103 favours a fig. interpretation, since Sanh., 10 (11), 1 uses Is. 60:21 ("they shall take the land in possession for ever") in proof of the statement that all Israel has a share in the future world, and in Qid., 1, 10 "to inherit the land" is an eschatological phrase. The question is, however, whether the Rabbis took עוֹלָם הַבָּא so transcendentally that Is. 60:21 had to be interpreted fig., cf. Str.-B., IV, 817. Cr.-Kö., 607, Zn. Mt. and Schl. Mt., ad loc. are against a fig. interpretation.

[33] J. Weiss, Die Offenbarung des Johannes (1904), 102 differentiates between two aspects of the idea of God's reign according to the more spatial or the more abstract emphasis. In the case of the former we might see an influence of the type of entry into the promised land or of the simile of possession of the land (κληρονομεῖν τὴν γῆν); in the latter the main influence is that of Daniel's world dominion. In fact, however, the κληρονομεῖν is linked specifically with βασιλεία.

σπέρμα (e.g., Gn. 13:15 : πᾶσαν τὴν γῆν, ἣν σὺ ὁρᾷς, σοὶ δώσω αὐτὴν καὶ τῷ σπέρματί σου ἕως τοῦ αἰῶνος). These promises are to be fulfilled in the Messianic age. Who may refer them to themselves ? That is, who is this σπέρμα of Abraham ? Or, in Paul's words in this connection, who are the υἱοὶ 'Αβραάμ or the κληρονόμοι of the promise ?³⁴ The answer of the Judaisers is that the sons of Abraham are his physical descendants who keep the Law and the men of other nations who are incorporated into sonship by accepting the Law. ³⁵ In this way the promise to Abraham ἐνευλογηθήσονται ἐν σοὶ πᾶσαι αἱ φυλαὶ τῆς γῆς (Gn. 12:3) will be fulfilled. There thus arises the thesis which in Gl. 3:18 Paul calls ἡ κληρονομία ἐκ νόμου. κληρονομία here is the portion assigned to Abraham and his seed, the fulfilment of the promise in the Messianic time. Paul has several arguments to bring against this thesis. 1. The promise given as a testament to Abraham and his seed is in force long before the giving of the Law. It is in force because God has uttered it. Hence God does not add to it just as a man does not add to a testament once it is legally in force. ³⁶ The inheritance allotted to Abraham and his seed cannot be won, then, ἐκ νόμου. It is given ἐξ ἐπαγγελίας. Similarly, the status of heir cannot be attained by fulfilment of the Law. 2. What made Abraham a recipient of the promise was πίστις. Hence οἱ ἐκ πίστεως are also υἱοὶ 'Αβραάμ (Gl. 3:7). 3. He who belongs to the Messiah is of the σπέρμα 'Αβραάμ, for the σπέρμα to whom the promise was given, as denoted by the singular, is not a group consisting of those who keep the Law ; it is the one Christ Himself (Gl. 3:16, 19). 4. The disputed comparison in Gl. 4:1-7 is also relevant. This speaks of a father who under his will has placed his son, a minor, under a guardian and trustee until a time which the father himself has set. ³⁷ In two respects the heir is a δοῦλος. First, he is not his own master ; the ἐπίτροπος is this. Secondly, he does not have control of his property or inheritance ; this is the function of the οἰκονόμος. On the other hand, he is potentially the κύριος πάντων. This is the position of the heirs of Abraham to whom the blessing of Gn. 12:3 applies, whether Jews or Gentiles. Until the πλήρωμα τοῦ χρόνου both are δοῦλοι (Gl. 4:3, 8), and both have received their sonship through Christ. The starting-

---

³⁴ Cf. Philo Rer. Div. Her., title : Περὶ τοῦ τίς ὁ τῶν θείων ἐστὶν κληρονόμος ;

³⁵ Though the Judaisers attach importance to descent from Abraham, there is a shift of emphasis as compared with Judaism. For the Rabb. the proselyte is not incorporated into sonship of Abraham ; his relation to God is determined only by the Law ; he cannot speak of "our fathers," Bik., 1, 4 (Str.-B., I, 119, No. 4; cf. also the later passage from Nu. r., 8, loc. cit.). The Judaisers were ready to accept full incorporation to sonship on the condition of fulfilment of the Law.

³⁶ Hellenistic law did not define the age of majority, hence we have clauses about this in the pap., O. Eger, ZNW, 18 (1917/18), 107 f. Paul can hardly be thinking of any general prohibition of adding to a will, since we do not find this in the pap. The impossibility here arises from the fact that the will is assumed to be in force. Paul's point is that what God has said is already in force by the mere fact that He has said it. Hence we need not assume with Halmel, op. cit. that the ἐρρέθησαν in v. 16 is a term from Roman law (dicere as distinct from promittere).

³⁷ We cannot appeal to Roman law with its distinction between the tutor and the curator, since this applied to Roman citizens, not to the Galatians. Paul has in view a kind of unwritten koine law (Eger, 4 f.; Kreller, op. cit., 201 f. mixed Greek and Egyptian law). There are no instances in the pap. of the distinction between ἐπίτροπος and οἰκονόμος ; Burton, op. cit., 214 on Gl. 4:2 adduces the twofold office of Lysias in 1 and 2 Macc. to raise (τρέφειν) the young Antiochus as ἐπίτροπος and to be ἐπὶ τῶν πραγμάτων, 1 Macc. 3:32 f.; 2 Macc. 10:11; 11:1; 13:2; 14:2.

point and the goal of Paul's expositions is a new understanding of the place of Abraham and the promises made to him in salvation history. In the light of Christ the promises which in Judaism are overshadowed by the Law shine out independently of the Law. κληρονόμος now becomes a term belonging to salvation history. For it raises the question who is integrated into this history of salvation which began with Abraham. The absence of the corresponding Rabbinic terminology is evidence of the new orientation. Here too, where it refers back to the OT, κληρονόμος has an eschatological content. But the initiation of fulfilment is stronger now. In Christ the blessing of Abraham has already come to the Gentiles. To the same circle of thought belong R. 4:13 f.: οὐ γὰρ διὰ νόμου ἡ ἐπαγγελία τῷ ᾿Αβραὰμ ἢ τῷ σπέρματι αὐτοῦ, τὸ κληρονόμον αὐτὸν εἶναι κόσμου, [38] ἀλλὰ διὰ δικαιοσύνης πίστεως. εἰ γὰρ οἱ ἐκ νόμου κληρονόμοι, κεκένωται ἡ πίστις, and Eph. 3:6 : εἶναι τὰ ἔθνη συγκληρονόμα καὶ σύσσωμα καὶ συμμέτοχα τῆς ἐπαγγελίας ἐν Χριστῷ ᾿Ιησοῦ διὰ τοῦ εὐαγγελίου.

In Hb. κληρονομία is the content of the OT promise, 9:15 : διὰ τοῦτο διαθήκης καινῆς μεσίτης ἐστίν, ὅπως ... τὴν ἐπαγγελίαν λάβωσιν οἱ κεκλημένοι τῆς αἰωνίου κληρονομίας. [39] In Hb. 6:17 the κληρονόμοι τῆς ἐπαγγελίας are Christians, who are heirs in the twofold sense that they have taken over the promises and that they have attained to what is promised. [40] In Hb., however, κληρονομεῖν is much closer to the simple "acquire," like the Heb. נָחַל and יָרַשׁ in the Rabb. By his attitude of faith Noah became τῆς κατὰ πίστιν δικαιοσύνης κληρονόμος (11:7), [41] and with the fathers in view the readers are admonished that they be μιμηταὶ ... τῶν διὰ πίστεως καὶ μακροθυμίας κληρονομούντων τὰς ἐπαγγελίας (6:12). In the context this cannot mean "attain the promise," [42] for the aim of the author is to spur on the readers to πληροφορία τῆς ἐλπίδος ἄχρι τέλους (6:11), and to this end the sworn assurance of God is held out before them. God gave a similar assurance to the fathers, especially to Abraham, and by πίστις and μακροθυμία Abraham attained to what was promised, i.e., the birth of Isaac. In the same way, the promise is set before the readers in order that by patience and longsuffering they may receive what is promised. The further development of comparison with the fathers in c. 11 interposes the thought (v. 8) that Abraham did not finally attain to what is promised and that throughout his life he is thus an example for the readers. He was to receive the land as κληρονομία, in firm possession, [43] and the same promise applied to Isaac and Jacob, the συγκληρονόμοι τῆς ἐπαγγελίας τῆς αὐτῆς, those who with him received the same promise (v. 9). They did not attain to what was promised, τὰς ἐπαγγελίας (v. 13). [44] In Hb., then, OT history is an impressive illustration of the tension of the "not yet" of the inheritance, its eschatological aspect.

The father-son relation is an evident element in Hb. 12:17: Esau θέλων κληρονομῆσαι τὴν εὐλογίαν ἀπεδοκιμάσθη.

Foerster

κλῆσις, κλητός → 491-496.

---

[38] The expansion of the inheritance to the world is Rabb., → 779 and Str.-B., ad loc.
[39] τῆς ... κληρονομίας is to be referred to ἐπαγγελίαν.
[40] In 6:18 what is promised is what is hoped for.
[41] Noah is the first to be called δίκαιος in Scripture, cf. esp. Rgg. Hb., ad loc.
[42] Cf. the comm.
[43] Not promised possession, for Abraham is to acquire the land in firm possession, 11:8.
[44] On ἐπαγγελία as promise and what is promised → II, 583, n. 59.

---

† κοιλία

A. κοιλία outside the NT.

1. Lit. "hollow," esp. with reference to the human (or animal) body. a. The "hollow of the body" in general, Hippocr. De Articulis, 46 (IV, 196 ff., Littré); Paris mag. pap. (Preis. Zaub., IV, 3141 ff.): βάλε δὲ ἐν τῇ κοιλίᾳ αὐτοῦ (sc. the magical image) καρδίαν μαγνητίνην (of magnetic stone). καὶ εἰς πιττάκιον ἱερατικὸν (hieratic tablet) γράφε τὰ ὀνόματα ταῦτα καὶ ἔνθες αὐτοῦ εἰς τὴν κοιλίαν. Within this a distinction is sometimes made between the ἄνω κοιλία, "breast," and the κάτω κοιλία, "belly," Gal. Comm. in Hippocr. Acut., IV, 94 (XV, 896, Kühn). b. "Belly," "lower part of the body," Hdt., II, 87: τοῦ νεκροῦ τὴν κοιλίην, cf. 40; 86; 92; Hippocr. Aphorismi, VI, 14 (IV, 566, Littré); Wilcken Ptol., I, 81, II, 16 : πεσόντα ἐπὶ κοιλίαν; P. Magd., 33, 4; P. Par., 18b, 13; "entrails," i.e., "stomach," Aristot. Hist. An., I, 2, p. 489a, 2 and "intestines," Aristoph. Eq., 280 : κενῇ τῇ κοιλίᾳ, Vesp., 794 : ἀλεκτρυόνος (cock) μ' ἔφασκε κοιλίαν ἔχειν, Thuc., II, 49, 6 : ἐπικατιόντος τοῦ νοσήματος ἐς τὴν κοιλίαν, distinguished as ἡ ἄνω κοιλία, Plat. Tim., 85e; Aristot. Part. An., II, 3, p. 650a, 13 f. and ἡ κάτω κοιλία, Hippocr. De Ulceribus, 3 (IV, 404, Littré); Plat. Tim., 73a, 85e; Aristot. Part. An., loc. cit.; Plut. Quaest. Conv., VII, 1 (II, 698b); Gal. (→ supra). For ancient views of the κοιλία, Plut. Carn. Es., II, 1 (II, 996e): Αἰγύπτιοι τῶν νεκρῶν τὴν κοιλίαν ἐξελόντες, καὶ πρὸς τὸν ἥλιον ἀνασχίζοντες ἐκβάλλουσιν, ὡς αἰτίαν ἁπάντων ὧν ὁ ἄνθρωπος ἥμαρτεν (cf. the adjoining discussion), also Plut. Sept. Sap. Conv., 16 (II, 159c); Diog. L., VI, 69 (of Diogenes): "εἴθε ἦν," ἔλεγε, "καὶ τὴν κοιλίαν παρατριψάμενον τοῦ λιμοῦ παύσασθαι." Rarely c. the belly as the seat of the sexual organs, i.e., the womb, Hippocr. Mul., I, 38 (VIII, 94, Littré); Epict. Diss., III, 22, 74 : ἐκ τῆς κοιλίας ἐξελθόντα; II, 16, 44 : ἐν βοὸς κοιλίᾳ. d. Other hollows in the body, for the brain, the heart, etc., Plut. De Placitis Philosophorum, IV, 5 (II, 899a): acc. to Herophilus the seat of the ἡγεμονικόν is ἐν τῇ τοῦ ἐγκεφάλου κοιλίᾳ and acc. to Diogenes ἐν τῇ ἀρτηριακῇ κοιλίᾳ τῆς καρδίας, ἥτις ἐστὶ πνευματική. e. Of hollows in the earth, Aristot. Meteor., I, 13, p. 350b, 22 ff.: οὐ δεῖ νομίζειν οὕτω γίνεσθαι τὰς ἀρχὰς τῶν ποταμῶν ὡς ἐξ ἀφωρισμένων κοιλιῶν, gaps in the clouds, ibid., II, 9, p. 369b, 1 f.: παντοδαποὶ δ' οἱ ψόφοι (roll of thunder) ... γίνονται ... διὰ τὰς μεταξὺ (sc. the clouds) κοιλίας etc.

2. In the LXX it is the equivalent of בֶּטֶן (Nu., Dt., Ju., and mostly Prv. and Is.) [1] or מֵעִים, more rarely קֶרֶב (only Gn., Ex., Lv.), רֶחֶם (only Job) or כָּרֵשׂ (only Jer. 51:34). Of the senses mentioned in 1. it occurs in sense b. (Gn. 41:21; Jon. 2:1 f.; Ιερ. 28:34; Ez. 3:3; 2 Παρ. 21:15) and c. (frequently), "mother's womb" (Gn. 25:24; Dt. 28:4, 11; Job 1:21; 3:11; Rt. 1:11 etc.); of the male sex organ, e.g., ψ 131:11: ἐκ καρποῦ τῆς κοιλίας σου, 2 Βασ. 7:12; 16:11; Sir. 23:6 : κοιλίας ὄρεξις, elsewhere fig. of the "innermost part," e.g., of the underworld, Jon. 2:3, v. v. 4 : βάθη καρδίας θαλάσσης, → 607, 613, and esp. the "hidden recesses of man," the inner state of his thoughts and feelings, Job 15:35; Prv. 20:30, 27; 18:20; Job 30:27; Lam. 1:20; Is. 16:11; ψ 39:8; [2] Sir.

κ ο ι λ ί α. Pass., I, 1766; Pr.-Bauer³, 726; Liddell-Scott, 966 f.; Moult.-Mill., 349.

[1] In Ps., Job, Qoh. γαστήρ is always used for בֶּטֶן [G. Bertram].

[2] In the first 4 passages the Heb. is בֶּטֶן, rendered σπλάγχνα in LXX Prv. 26:22 (LXX and Mas. diverge at Prv. 18:8). In the second 4 the original is מֵעִים. On בֶּטֶן = κοιλία, cf. W. Brandt, ZNW, 14 (1913), 105, n. 1.

19:12; 51:21, synon. and interchangeable with καρδία → 609, cf. Lam. 1:20 and textual variants in ψ 39:8 and Hab. 3:16, Mas. בֶּטֶן, also the rendering of בֶּטֶן as καρδία in Prv. 22:18.

For Philo the κοιλία, which is one of the seven μέλη σώματος, Leg. All., I, 12, is the digestive system, cf. Spec. Leg., I, 217; IV, 107. He follows the Gk. philosophers, esp. Plato and Posidonius, in the view that desire has its seat περὶ τὸ ἦτρον (lower part of the body) καὶ τὴν κοιλίαν, Leg. All., III, 115; cf. Spec. Leg., I, 148, where we have the Platonic image of the manger (Plat. Tim., 70e): κοιλίαν δὲ φάτνην ἀλόγου θρέμματος (irrational beast), ἐπιθυμίας, εἶναι συμβέβηκεν, Migr. Abr., 66 : τὸ δὲ ἐπιθυμίας εἶδος ἐν κοιλίᾳ; Quaest. in Gn., IV, 191: terrenis nimirum cupiditatibus, quae circa ventrem voluptates sunt, and sees in Gn. 3:14; Lv. 11:42; 9:14; 1:9 etc. Gk. ideas as to the lowliness and moral inferiority of the body, Leg. All., III, 138-159; Migr. Abr., 65 f.; Spec. Leg., I, 206.

Joseph.[3] uses κοιλία only to denote the diseased lower part of the body, Ant., 19, 346: ἄθρουν δ' αὐτῷ (Agrippa) τῆς κοιλίας προσέφυσεν ἄλγημα, 3, 273 : τὴν κοιλίαν ὑδέρου (dropsy) καταλαβόντος, cf. Nu. 5:27.

3. In Rabb. writings[4] the Heb. and Aram. equivalents maintain their three OT meanings. a. "Belly," esp. the digestive system, e.g., S. Dt., 40 on 11:12 (p. 88, Kittel) of food : ירד בתוך מעיו; bChul., 93a : ריש מעיא the beginning of the intestines, T. Maas., 2, 6 : אני אמלא כריסי "I eat my fill" (not in a bad sense), Tanch. B מסעי § 5 (82b): "We have the desire to fill our bellies, i.e., to slake our thirst) with the waters of the land of Israel," cf. also[5] S. Nu., 88 on 11:6 (p. 236 f., Kuhn): acc. to R. Shim'on manna was a food which was fully assimilated by the body, so that there was no excrement ; hence the Israelites feared that "the manna would swell in their stomachs (בתוך כריסינו) so that they would die." b. "Womb," e.g., S. Dt., 147 on 17:1: ממעי אמו (as the OT Is. 49:1; Ps. 71:6 etc., cf. אם בֶּטֶן, Ps. 22:10; Job 1:21; Ju. 16:17 etc.), Pesikt., 22 (p. 149a, Buber): אשרי הבטן שיצא ממנו (sc. the Messiah). c. Fig. Gn. r., 68 on 28:12 : "count 20 beams כברסא דביתך, i.e., in the frame or vault of your house."

B. κοιλία in the NT.

1. The same three meanings of κοιλία occur in the NT. a. "Belly" as that part of the body which digests food, Mk. 7:19 and par.; Mt. 12:40 (Jon. 2:1 f.); Lk. 15:16 : ἐπεθύμει γεμίσαι τὴν κοιλίαν ἐκ ..., a popular expression for "to eat one's fill" (→ supra); 1 C. 6:13; Rev. 10:9 f.[6] (Ez. 3:3). b. "Womb," Mt. 19:12;[7] Lk. 1:15, 41, 42 (cf. Mi. 6:7; Lam. 2:20), 44;[8] 2:21; 11:27; 23:29; Jn. 3:4; Ac. 3:2; 14:8; Gl. 1:15.[9] c. "The inward part," Jn. 7:38.

2. In Mk. 7:14 ff. Jesus explains the nature of sin in terms of the distinction between κοιλία and καρδία, between the comparatively lowly and inferior sphere of corporeal life whose task is the digestion of food (v. 19) and the central organ

---

[3] Schl. Lk., 162; Schl. J., 88.
[4] Cf. Levy Wört., I, 212 ff.; II, 410 ff.; III, 184 f.; Levy Chald. Wört., I, 389 f.; II, 56 f.; Schl. Mt., 485 f., 573; Schl. Lk., 302, 359.
[5] [K. G. Kuhn]. Cf. also Schlatter, Sprache u. Heimat des vierten Evangelisten (1902), 91.
[6] vl. for κοιλίαν at v. 9, καρδίαν A 1678 (Gregory). Cf. Andrew of Caesarea, ad loc. (MPG, 106, p. 308): πικρανεῖ δέ σου ὅμως τὴν κοιλίαν, δηλαδὴ τὴν καρδίαν τὴν τῶν λογικῶν τροφῶν χωρητικήν.
[7] On the Semitism ἐκ κοιλίας μητρός → 786 f.; Bl.-Debr. § 259, 1.
[8] For instructive par. to Lk. 1:41, 44 cf. jJoma, 45 and bJoma, 82b, → σκιρτάω, → τέκνον, → πνεῦμα.
[9] Ac. 2:30 vl.: ἐκ καρποῦ τῆς κοιλίας αὐτοῦ corresponds to ψ 131:11 (→ supra).

of the spiritual life which determines man's conduct on the religious and ethical level (v. 20 ff. → 612). What disrupts man's relation to God is not to be found in the sphere of the external and physical — the superficial view of the Jewish casuistry of purification. Evil is rooted in the innermost being of man. The cause of all sin in thought and word and act is his evil heart and ungodly nature. In 1 C. 6:13, [10] too, the κοιλία, or digestive system, is depreciated, but with a different purpose from that of the dominical saying in Mk. 7:19. To justify sexual freedom the libertines of Corinth were pleading the moral indifference of the body and its functions. Paul takes up their slogan in order to overthrow it. The belly, as a creaturely organ which is necessary to maintain earthly life, is corruptible. When we are transfigured and the conditions of earthly life no longer obtain, it will not be needed (cf. 1 C. 15:50, cf. 35 ff.; 2 C. 5:1; R. 8:21 ff.; 14:17). But the belly is not the same as the body. The body (→ σῶμα) still belongs to the risen and living Lord. Hence it must not be abandoned to licentiousness (v. 13b f.). Paul's view of the κοιλία is not based, like that of the Greek world, on the idea that it is the home of sensuality (→ 787, cf. 786). The point is that the κοιλία is part of the perishing creaturely world, cf. Mt. 22:30. Only because of this, and not because it is sinful, is it doomed to destruction. When we turn to the polemical and sarcastic expressions in R. 16:18 : οἱ γὰρ τοιοῦτοι τῷ κυρίῳ ἡμῶν Χριστῷ οὐ δουλεύουσιν ἀλλὰ τῇ ἑαυτῶν κοιλίᾳ, and Phil. 3:19 : ὧν ὁ θεὸς ἡ κοιλία, it is hard to say what the reference is. If, in contrast to 1 C. 6:13, Paul is here using κοιλία in the common Greek sense, [11] he is speaking of unbridled sensuality, whether gluttony or sexual licentiousness. [12] But the context in both instances seems to point to Judaisers rather than libertines. [13] Hence the older view is more plausible that Paul is alluding to the observance of laws of food and that he is pouring bitter scorn on the Judaisers with their belly god. [14, 15]

3. In the deeper sense of the "inward part," or the "heart," [16] which is a distinctive feature of the LXX, → 786, the term is used with no unfavourable implications in Jn. 7:38 : ὁ πιστεύων εἰς ἐμέ, καθὼς εἶπεν ἡ γραφή, ποταμοὶ ἐκ τῆς κοιλίας αὐτοῦ ῥεύσουσιν → ὕδατος ζῶντος (→ II, 872). The believer whose

---

[10] Cf. Joh. W. 1 K.; Bchm. 1 K.; Schl. K., ad loc.

[11] Cf. the words κοιλιοδαίμων (Eupolis Fr., 172 [CAF, I, p. 306]; Ael. Fr., 109; Athen., III, 52 [p. 97c]: κοιλιόδαιμον ἄνθρωπε), κοιλιόδουλος and κοιλιολάτρης (the two last only in later ecclesiastical authors), also the par. in Wettstein and Loh. Phil. on 3:19.

[12] Cf. Dib. Gefbr. on Phil. 3:19; Khl. R. and Schl. R. on 16:18.

[13] Cf. Ew. Phil., ad loc.; P. Feine, "Die Abfassung des Phil. in Ephesus," BFTh, 20, 4 (1916), 26 ff.; K. Barth, Erklärung des Phil.² (1933), ad loc. But cf. also Dib. Gefbr. and Mich. Ph. on Phil. 3:19.

[14] Theod. Mops. (MPG, 66, p. 875 and 926), Ambrosiaster (MPL, 17, p. 417, cf. 118), Pelagius (p. 124, 409 f., A. Souter in TSt, IX, 1/2, 1922/26).

[15] Quite outside the history of the term is the explanation of Loh. Phil. on 3:19, namely, that for those who despise martyrdom the highest concern is not the cause of God but their own physical life.

[16] From the time of Chrys., ad loc. (MPG, 59, p. 283): κοιλίαν ἐνταῦθα τὴν καρδίαν φησί (with allusion to ψ 39:8) most commentators have taken it in this sense. The explanation of Zn. J., ad loc. "carnal body," "the body in its present constitution in this world," rests on an incorrect understanding of the decisive LXX passages. Since the saying is a quotation, there is nothing surprising in the avoidace of John's customary καρδία. The OT origin of this sense makes it superfluous to explain it as the right or wrong translation of an Aram. term, cf. Str.-B., II, 492; C. F. Burney, The Aramaic Origin of the Fourth Gospel (1922), 109 ff.; "The Aram. Equivalent of ἐκ τῆς κοιλίας in Jn. 7:38," JThSt, 24 (1923), 79 f.

thirst is quenched by Jesus is promised that his refreshed inward being will become a source of wider refreshing, and that he is to share with others in overflowing abundance that which he himself has received from Jesus. [17] Whatever may be the OT (or apocr.?) passage which the Evangelist has in view (Is. 58:11; Zech. 14:8; Ez. 47:1 ff.; Sir. 24:30 ff. etc.), the basic thought is that he who is touched by Jesus in the innermost recesses of his personal life will from thence send forth saving powers in superabundant measure (cf. v. 39, also Mt. 5:13 ff.). [18]

Behm

κοιμάομαι → 14, n. 60.

κοινός, κοινωνός, κοινωνέω,
κοινωνία, συγκοινωνός, συγκοινωνέω,
κοινωνικός, κοινόω

---

† κοινός.

Contents : A. κοινός in Secular Greek. B. κοινός in the OT and Judaism. C. The Individual and Society. Theories and Forms of Society. D. κοινός in the NT.

A. κοινός in Secular Greek.

"Common" [1] 1. of things, a. "common," opp. ἴδιος, esp. to express a legal relationship, e.g., common ownership, Hes. Op., 723, ἐκ κοινοῦ; P. Eleph., 2, 10, τὰ ὑπάρχοντα

---

[17] The thesis that the αὐτοῦ refers to Jesus, and hence that the saying speaks of the saving powers which flow from the body of the Redeemer (Ps.-Cyprian, De Rebaptismate, 14 and De Montibus Sina et Sion, 9, CSEL, 3, 3 [1871], p. 87 and 115; J. Grill, *Untersuchungen über die Entstehung des 4. Ev.,* I [1902], 16; J. Jeremias, "Golgotha u. der heilige Felsen," *Angelos,* 2 [1926], 121 f.; H. Bornhäuser, *Sukka* [1935], 35 ff.; Bau. J., *ad loc.,* with par. from the history of religion ; also E. Hirsch, *Studien z. vierten Ev.* [1936], 70), has the text very definitely against it, though it suggests the Johannine view that the works of Jesus and those of His disciples are one, 14:12.

[18] Schl. J., *ad loc.* and H. Odeberg, *The Fourth Gospel,* I (1929), 284 f., who rightly refer to Akiba's exposition of Prv. 5:15 f., S. Dt., 48 on 11:22 (p. 124, Kittel): "Lo, it says : 'Drink water from thy cistern' : at first the cistern cannot bring forth a drop of water of itself, but only what is in it. So it is with the scholar who at first has learned nothing. There is nothing in him but what he has learned. 'And what flows from thy well.' He uses the comparison of the well. What is the nature of the well ? It causes living water to flow on all sides. So scholars and disciples flow forth from him. And so it is also said : 'Thy springs spread forth, thy streams on the streets.'" Cf. also Str.-B., II, 493.

κοινός. J. H. Schmidt, *Synonymik,* III (1879), 467; Preisigke Wört., I 812 ff.; Pauly-W. Suppl., IV (1924), 914-941; XI (1922), 1053 ff.; Hastings DB, I, 460 ff.; A. Carr, "The Fellowship (κοινωνία) of Acts 2:42 ...," Exp. 8th Ser., Vol. V (1913), 458 ff.; C. A. Scott, Exp. T., 35 (1923/1924), 567; W. S. Wood, "Fellowship (κοινωνία)," Exp. 8th Ser., XXI (1921), 31 ff.; E. P. Groenewald, ΚΟΙΝΩΝΙΑ (*Geemeenschap*) *bij Paulus* (Delft, 1932); J. Y. Campbell, "κοινωνία and its Cognates in the NT," JBL, 51 (1932), 352-380; H. Seesemann, *Der Begriff* κοινωνία *im NT* (1933); S. Krauss, *Gr. u. lat. Lehnwörter im Talmud,* II (1899), 532 on κοινωνία; Helbing, *Kasussyntax,* 136, 252; A. Bonhöffer, *Epictet u. d. NT* = RVV, 10 (1911), 51 ff.; P. J. T. Endenburg, *Koinoonia en Gemeenschap van Zaken bij Grieken in den klassieken Tijd* (1937). For further bibl. *v.* in the art.

[1] Found from the time of Hesiod, etym. linked with σύν, ξύν, *cum,* Walde-Pok., I, 458.

ἔστω κοινὰ πάντων τῶν υἱῶν; of the common property of a married couple, P. Amh., 78, 11, κοινὰ ὑπάρχοντα; of common ownership in equal parts, P. Strassb., 29, 37, κοινῶς ἐξ ἴσου. [2] Philosophy speaks of ideas and phenomena common to all men, κοιναὶ ἔννοιαι, κοινὸς λόγος etc. [3] While the current proverb κοινὰ τὰ φίλων [4] does not enunciate a theory or law, but only a guiding principle for the thinking and conduct of true friends, in politics and philosophy the common ownership of goods is of great significance in the question of a true social order, → 791. b. "That which concerns all"; τὸ κοινόν, of the state, Thuc., I, 90, 5; οἳ εἰσιν ἐν τῷ κοινῷ τῶν ʿΡωμαίων, Polyb., 7, 9, 14; of unions, e.g., cultic unions, Σωτηριαστᾶν ʾΑσκλαπιαστᾶν ... ʿΕρμαιστᾶν Ματρὸς Θεῶν κοινόν (in Rhodes), Ditt. Syll.[3], 1114, 5 f., or guilds, τὸ κοινὸν τῶν σιδηροχαλκέων (cf. Ac. 19:24, 38); [5] τὰ κοινὰ χρήματα of public monies, Xenoph. Hist. Graec., VI, 5, 34; κοινὸν δόγμα, of a public resolve, Polyb., 25, 8, 4. c. "Common," "of little worth," χρυσόν, P. Oxy., X, 1273, 6; καλὸν γὰρ ἡ φιλία καὶ ἀστεῖον, ἡ δὲ ἡδονὴ κοινὸν καὶ ἀνελεύθερον, Plut. Amat., 4 (II, 751b).

2, Of men : "participants," "fellows," Soph. Oed. Tyr., 240, "affable" in disposition, Plut. Anton., 33 (I, 930d); κοινῶς καὶ φιλικῶς ... ἔπραττον, Isoc., 4, 151.

B. κοινός in the OT and Judaism.

1. "Common." The term occurs in the OT only a few times in Prv., e.g., in 1:14 of the common (Mas. אֶחָד) chest of a band (cf. Jn. 12:6, the common purse of the disciples of Jesus), 15:23 (no Mas.) in the sense of public life, 21:9 and 25:24 of the common house (ἐν οἴκῳ κοινῷ or οἰκίᾳ κοινῇ), in both cases for בֵּית חָבֶר. We find it more often in the apocr. writings, e.g., Wis. 7:3 (ἀήρ), 2 Macc. 8:29 (κοινὴν ἱκετείαν ποιησάμενοι), 9:21 (τῆς κοινῆς πάντων ἀσφαλείας), Tob. 9:6 (ὤρθρευσαν κοινῶς) etc. For Joseph. cf. Ap., 2, 196 (σωτηρία κοινή), Ant., 4, 137: τὰς τροφὰς ὑμῖν ἰδιοτρόπους εἶναι καὶ τὰ ποτὰ μὴ κοινὰ τοῖς ἄλλοις. On Jewish soil Joseph. lauds the community of goods among the Essenes and Philo among these and the Therapeutae (→ 795 f.). In the LXX the Jewish community is the συναγωγή or ἐκκλησία. In Greek fashion Joseph. lumps government and people together under the title τὸ κοινόν (τῶν ʿΙεροσολυμιτῶν). [6] This corresponds to the חבר היהודים on coins; we are to read חֶבֶר and refer it to the whole national community. [7]

Analogous to the secular Greek use for unions or guilds (→ supra) is the Rabb. use of חֶבֶר (synon. חֲבוּרָה). Thus חֶבֶר עִיר is the civic union which organises almsgiving. This is responsible for working out individual burdens in equitable proportion and also for just and fair distribution (cf. Str.-B., IV, 607 ff. for examples).

2. "Profane," "accessible and permissible to all." In this sense κοινός corresponds to the Heb. חל "given up to general use," from the root חלל pi, "to free,"

---

[2] Cf. Preisigke Wört., s.v.; Pauly-W., XI (1922), 1078 ff.; Suppl. IV (1924), 914 ff.

[3] E.g., Epict. Diss., III, 6, 8 (νοῦς); F. Ueberweg-K. Praechter, Die Philosophie d. Altertums[12] (1920), 418.

[4] E.g., Gregorius Cyprius, II, 54; Apostolius, IX, 88 (Leutsch-Schneidewin, Corpus Paroemiographorum Graecorum, II [1851], 76 and 481).

[5] P. Oxy., I, 84, 3 f.; τῶν χαλκοκολλητῶν, 85, col. 2, 3 f.; synon. ἡ σύνοδος. Examples M. San Nicolò, Ägyptisches Vereinswesen (1913), I, 48 and 50; F. Poland, Geschichte d. griech. Vereinswesens (1909), 163 ff.

[6] Vit., 65, 72, 190, 254 etc.; Schürer, II [3, 4], 246.

[7] Schürer, I[3, 4], 269, n. 25; also the inscr. of Leontopolis in S. Krauss, Synagogale Altertümer (1922), on the Jewish community there as κοινὸν τῶν ἐν τῷ τεμένει (sc. of Leontopolis) κατοικούντων ʿΙουδαίων.

"to hand over to common use." The opposite is that which is sanctified or dedicated and hence withdrawn from ordinary use (→ ἅγιος). The LXX, however, consistently uses βέβηλος for חֹל (→ I, 604), e.g., Lv. 10:10.

In Rabbinic literature, too, חֹל denotes what is profane in contrast to what is holy, to things devoted to God. Hence חֹל is often used for the working day as distinct from the Sabbath, and חֹל מוֹעֵד is found for the working days in the octave of a festival, i.e., between the first feast day and the last a week later. חֹל is also used for profane ground as compared with the temple precincts, or for profane money as compared with that of the second tenth which may be used only for specific (sacred) purposes. In particular חֻלִּין, pl. חֻלִּין is found for profane foods which any one may eat as distinct from foods of corn and fruits which, as dues to the priests (heave offerings etc.), are holy, and may be eaten only by the priests and their dependents. [8] Finally חֻלִּין is a tt. for animals slaughtered for common use as distinct from sacrificial beasts. Detailed regulations for the killing of these animals may be found in the tractate Chullin. חֹל is never used of men. [9]

Only in the apocr. is κοινός used for חֹל instead of βέβηλος, e.g., 1 Macc. 1:47: θύειν ὕεια καὶ κτήνη κοινά; 1:62 : φαγεῖν κοινά. We find the same usage in Jos. Ant., 11, 346 : αἰτία κοινοφαγίας (cf. Gl. 2:12 ff.); 3, 181 : βέβηλον καὶ κοινόν τινα τόπον; 12, 320 (desecration of the temple); 13, 4 : κοινὸς βίος (of apostate Jews). In general κοινός, like חֹל, is used only of things like these, but in Ep. Ar., 315 it is also used of men : τὰ θεῖα ... εἰς ἀνθρώπους κοινοὺς (non-Jews) ἐκφέρειν. Philo does not have κοινός in the sense of "profane." This sense seems to have developed on Jewish soil. At any rate, there are no instances in non-Jewish secular Greek.

C. The Individual and Society. Theories and Forms of Society. [10]

1. In contrast to the Orient, the Greeks discovered the individual (ἴδιος) with his personal life and rights. Yet they had a strong sense of the duty of the individual towards society. The individual lives by and for society. The freeing of the individual from society disturbs society. This orderliness runs through the whole of reality. It is valid in the κόσμος and in nature, in the relation of men and gods, in the relation to the state. If the individual is not to perish, he must be firmly bound to the κοινόν. This leads to theories and forms of society which are in some measure communistic, but we are to distinguish these quite radically from modern communism with its economic orientation.

Among the Greeks as among all other civilised peoples the beginning and basis of development are the common possessions of the tribe. The individual has a right to use these. Gradually private ownership emerges, since this gives a better economy. The Greeks had already reached this stage at the time of Homer. Heads of families had their share (→ κλῆρος) in the land and worked it in common with

---

[8] Examples in Levy Wört., s.v., also Strack Einl., 56.

[9] A. Merx, Die 4 kanonischen Evv., II, 2 (1905), 67.

[10] Cf. W. Nestle-E. Zeller, Grundriss der Geschichte d. gr. Philosophie⁷ (1923), I, 402; R. Pöhlmann, Geschichte d. antiken Kommunismus u. Sozialismus, I (1893), II (1901); Handwörterbuch d. Staatswiss., by Conrad-Lexis-Elster-Loening, VII³ (1911), 604 ff.; F. Hauck, Die Stellung des Urch. zu Arbeit u. Geld (1921), 38 ff.

the members of the family. [11] They could treat the ground as their own property and divide it if they so desired. [12] This led to the distinction between the rich and the poor (πολύκληροι, ἄκληροι). A constitutional economy also prevailed later on the Lipari Islands, where one part of the inhabitants had to see to the common working of the land while the other was charged with defence against pirates. This development was unique in Greece and obviously arose out of the need to protect the land. [13] Some degree of communal economy was also introduced in Sparta and Crete. In both states the citizens were supported in συσσίτια at the cost of the general public. But here again this "socialism" was an organic part of the military structure. [14] The inalienable apportionment of κλῆροι to heads of families was designed to prevent the disruption of the people into rich and poor. To a later age the Spartan ἰσότης and κοινότης seemed to be an ideal order and Lycurgus the social saviour who made Sparta the abode of justice and who extirpated πλεονεξία. [15] Economic development led to the blossoming of the Greek city states, but also to sharper distinctions between rich and poor. The control of property also became a problem. Critical and hypercritical thinking was devoted to the question of a true social order. Theories of society arose which purported to solve the problem by communal ownership. According to his story, Pythagoras was supposed to have seen in the cosmic order a model of the order of human life. The original state when there was no private property, but all things were held in common, was the ideal. [16] Hence Pythagoras fashioned a communal order for the narrower circle of his disciples. These parted from their relatives and renounced their personal possessions, putting them under the control of the fellowship (οὐσίας κοινάς). In the common life of the order they thus achieved the divinely willed ideal of society. [17] Heraclitus bound the individual very closely to society with his admonition ἕπεσθαι τῷ κοινῷ, Fr., 2 (I, 77, 12, Diels); cf. Fr., 89 (I, 95, 10, Diels), and the Delphic god ordered κοινὸς γίνου (Ditt. Syll.³, 1268, I, 19). In Athens the movement of ethical reform after Socrates had as its goal the discovery of a correct theory on which to establish a happy order of society and state. Plato (→ 799 f.), who was influenced by the Pythagorean Timaeus, projected a model and ideal of the best state in the πολιτεία. He was strongly motivated by an ethical

---

[11] Hom. Il., 6, 243 ff., Od., 3, 412 ff.

[12] Od., 14, 208 ff.

[13] Diod. S., V, 9, 4 f.: οἱ μὲν ἐγεώργουν τὰς νήσους κοινὰς ποιήσαντες, οἱ δὲ πρὸς τοὺς λῃστὰς ἀνετάττοντο· καὶ τὰς οὐσίας δὲ κοινὰς ποιησάμενοι καὶ ζῶντες κατὰ συσσίτια, διετέλεσαν ἐπί τινας χρόνους κοινωνικῶς βιοῦντες. Pöhlmann, op. cit., I, 46 ff.

[14] Pöhlmann, I, 58 ff. Plat. Leg., I, 633a.

[15] Polyb., 6, 45 and 48; Pöhlmann, I, 126 f.

[16] Iambl. Vit. Pyth. (ed. M. T. Kiessling, I [1815], 5, 29; 6, 30 and 32; 16, 69; the original state : κοινὰ γὰρ πᾶσι πάντα καὶ ταῦτα ἦν, ἴδιον δὲ οὐδεὶς οὐδὲν ἐκέκτητο. καὶ εἰ μὲν ἠρέσκετο τῇ κοινωνίᾳ, ἐχρῆτο τοῖς κοινοῖς κατὰ τὸ δικαιότατον, εἰ δὲ μή, ἀπολαβὼν ἂν τὴν ἑαυτοῦ οὐσίαν καὶ πλείονα, ἧς εἰσενηνόχει εἰς τὸ κοινόν, ἀπηλλάττετο, 168. The earliest writers on Pyth. are Epicur. (in Diog. L., X, 6 [11]) and Timaeus of Tauromenium (ibid., VIII, 8 [10]). F. W. A. Mullach, Fragmenta Philosophorum Graecorum, I, (1860), 408 ff. The accounts in Iambl., Philostrat. and Porphyrius, if not a later reconstruction, are based on Tim., cf. E. Rohde, Rheinisches Museum, 26 (1871), 554 ff.; 27 (1872), 33 ff.; W. Bertermann, De Jamblichi vitae Pyth. fontibus, Diss. Königsbg. (1913), 75 ff.; J. Levy, La Légende de Pyth. (1927), 30 ff.

[17] Iambl. Vit. Pyth., 5, 29; 19, 92. From Pyth., acc. to Tim., comes the statement : κοινὰ τὰ φίλων εἶναι καὶ φιλίαν ἰσότητα, Diog. L., VIII, 8 [10].

concern to overcome the natural egotism of those responsible for the state and to make them willing servants of the common good. Plato regarded private property as the root of all evil, since it leads inevitably to a selfish desire for gain (πλεο-νεξία) which disrupts society. Hence the two chief classes in the state, the guardians (φύλακες) and the soldiers, should renounce private property in order to be free from all desire or concern for gain. They should be fed communally from the national' store and at public expense. [18] By the establishment of community of wives and children the guardians should be freed from private wedlock and domestic concerns and thus committed the more fully to concerns of state. [19] Hence the truly "social" (φιλοπόλιδες) should rule in place of the "a-social" (δυσκοινώ-νητοι), Resp., VI, 503a, cf. 486b. The young should be instructed from the very first in social thinking. Summoned by Dionysius to Syracuse as counsellor and legislator, Plato suffered severe disillusionment. He discovered that the actuality of life hardly allows a complete balancing of social and individual principles. Only gods and the sons of gods can accept the community of goods, wives and children, Leg., V, 739d. In the Leg., then, Plato settles for the second best rather than the best state. Here social principles are kept within the bounds of the practical. It seems advisable to put the government of the state in the hands of those who by virtue of their own rights of possession are interested in the economic welfare of the whole. Agriculture should be the basis of the state. All land is to be regarded as a common possession of the state. Individuals will receive by lot equal and inalienable shares to which they have the right of use. [20] There are to be no workers without land, and there are also to be no excessive holdings. For remuneration the peasants must make firmly specified contributions to the working population (VIII, 849b). Even over movables the individual has only a limited control (XI, 923a). Private rapacity is to be restricted as much as possible by economic super-vision.

Aristotle is a far more realistic and individualistic thinker than Plato. In his sketch of the ideal state in the 2nd book of the Pol. he seeks a balance between individual and communal interests. [21] One portion of the land should be held in common to support the *syssitia* (II, 9, p. 1271a, 28 ff.). Apart from this, there is to be the nearest possible equality of ownership among citizens. No citizens should be without the minimum necessary for subsistence. [22] But social harmony (συμ-φωνία) in the state prevents striving after too great unity (II, 5, p. 1263b, 35). Against Plato he judges that community of wives and goods involves too great a truncation of the individual. Its disadvantages far outweigh the advantages (II, 2, p. 1261a, 10 ff.). Experience shows that communal ownership leads to neglect and to all kinds of dissensions (II, 5, p. 1263a, 21 f.). Hence private ownership is to be

---

[18] Plat. Resp., III, 416d : οὐσίαν κεκτημένον μηδεμίαν μηδένα ἰδίαν, ἂν μὴ πᾶσα ἀνάγκη· ἔπειτα οἴκησιν καὶ ταμιεῖον μηδενὶ εἶναι μηδὲν τοιοῦτον ... 416e: ... κοινῇ ζῆν. Pöhlmann, I, 184 ff., 269 ff.; E. Salin, *Platon u. die griech. Utopie* (1921), 14 ff.

[19] Plat. Resp., IV, 321, 424a, 451, 452, 464, 464a d : law-suits will disappear διὰ τὸ μηδὲν (sc. αὐτοὺς) ἴδιον ἐκτῆσθαι πλὴν τὸ σῶμα, τὰ δ' ἄλλα κοινά. 457c : τὰς γυναῖκας ταύτας τῶν ἀνδρῶν τούτων πάντων πάσας εἶναι κοινάς, ἰδίᾳ δὲ μηδενὶ μηδεμίαν συνοικεῖν καὶ τοὺς παῖδας αὖ κοινούς.

[20] Leg., V, 740a : δεῖ τὸν λαχόντα τὴν λῆξιν ταύτην νομίζειν μὲν κοινὴν αὐτὴν τῆς πόλεως συμπάσης κτλ. 741b; Praechter (→ n. 3), 318 f.

[21] Aristot. Pol., II, 2, p. 1260b, 37 ff.; Pöhlmann, 581 ff.; Salin, 163 ff.

[22] II, 9, p. 1271a, 26 ff.; IV, 9, p. 1295a, 25 ff., 1295b, 27 ff.; II, 2, p. 1263b, 22 ff.

preserved. But there must be an ethical softening of the concept of private owner-ship. Possessions are to be common by common usufruct. [23] For the sake of virtue there must be an actualisation by the citizens of the proverb κοινὰ τὰ φίλων (II, 5, p. 1263a, 29 f.). There can be no enforcement of community and unity in the state ; they are to be fashioned by education. [24]

The poets were also concerned with the question. Hesiod (Op., 109 ff.) depicts the glory of the golden age in which the earth freely lavished inexhaustible gifts on her children under the rule of Kronos and there was general equality and brotherly love. The achievement of life in society is here seen romantically in the primitive past. In Critias Plato himself gives a fictional depiction of the achieve-ment of his ideal state. In this original Athens there is no private property, gold or silver. In perfect community of goods the people lives contentedly on the labour of all. The antithesis is the state-colossus of Atlantis in which the whole aim is the increase of wealth and enjoyment. Here evil πλεονεξία destroys all sense of community (φιλία κοινή, Critias, 121a), and therewith corrupts everything. In Av. and Eccl. Aristoph. ridicules the communistic ideal, and esp. the idea of a community of women (Eccl., 589 ff., 608 ff., 690 ff.). Theopomp. sets the actualisa-tion of perfect communal life in the distant Meropic country, [25] Hecataeus in the Cimmerian city, [26] Iambulos in the distant state of the sun with its natural wealth, [27] while Euhemeros depicts in the sacred chronicle the ideal social order on the island of Panchaea. Here everything apart from house and garden is held in common. Individuals produce for society. Fruits must be brought to priestly officials who are in charge of their distribution. Trade and money are superfluous. [28]

To various degrees the view that common possession is the true social order lives on in the Cynic, Stoic and Neo-Pythagorean schools. But while Plato re-garded this as the best arrangement, a basis was now found for it in nature. We see this first in the Cynics, [29] who were keen critics of society. Divine φύσις is contrasted with human νόμος. [30] The justice of God has created all things for all and has thus designed a common use of the gifts of nature. The Cynic, who is a friend of God, draws the conclusion that among friends all things are common (Crates, p. 208, 2). Land and sea are the sack from which the Cynic draws nourish-ment (Diog., p. 241, 26). He does not ask as a beggar ; he demands back (ibid., p. 238, 10). For the human order of property has no just basis. Property is theft from the community. The foundations of natural law are thus laid by the Cynics. Even marriage is to be abandoned. Wives and children should be in common. [31]

---

[23] II, 5, p. 1263a, 26 f.: δεῖ γάρ πως μὲν εἶναι κοινάς, ὅλως δ' ἰδίας . . ., 38 f.: βέλτιον εἶναι μὲν ἰδίας τὰς κτήσεις, τῇ δὲ χρήσει ποιεῖν κοινάς. 5, p. 1263b.
[24] II, 2, p. 1263b, 36 f.: διὰ τὴν παιδείαν κοινὴν καὶ μίαν ποιεῖν.
[25] Philippica, VIII, Fr., 76 (FHG, I, p. 289 f.); Pöhlmann, II, 47 ff.
[26] In Diod. S., II, 47. Pöhlmann, II, 53 ff. Pauly-W., VII (1912), 2752, 2755 f.
[27] Diod. S., II, 55-60; Pöhlmann, II, 70 ff.
[28] In Diod. S., V, 45. Pöhlmann, II, 55 ff.
[29] Praechter, 159 ff., 432 ff. Mullach, II, 259-395; Crates (Epistolographi Graeci, ed. R. Hercher [1873], p. 208 ff.; Diog., ibid., p. 235 ff. This epistolary pseudepigr. literature is mostly from the 1st cent. A.D. but it presents what are essentially the views of ancient Cynicism, Praechter, 528. Pauly-W., s.v. "Antisthenes," 10 (I [1894], 2538 ff.); s.v. "Dio-genes," 44 (V [1905], 765 ff.).
[30] Diog. in Diog. L., VI, 4 (29), 6 (38), 6 (72), 11 (79), 6 (33).
[31] Diog. L., VI, 6 (72): γάμον μηδένα νομίζων (the true reading acc. to Praechter, 168, instead of μηδὲν ὀνομάζων).

Later Cynicism withdraws these extreme, abstract demands and sketches for its state a positive social programme which will create better conditions for the poor of the population by giving them uncultivated lands. [32]

Stoicism, whose founder, Zeno, was dependent on Cynicism, proceeds from criticism to a positive consideration. The well-integrated universe is a model for the ideal state and civic life. The world is the common state of all men. [33] The original state of nature, in which there was a *consortium* between men, is the ideal. [34] Then all natural gifts were ready to be enjoyed by all (Sen. Ep., 90, 36). Only human greed made things private and alien (90, 38). As children of the same God all men are brothers (Epict. Diss., I, 13, 2 ff.). Hence they must act toward one another with brotherliness in order to realise so far as possible the golden age which has now been lost for ever (Sen. Ep., 90, 39). Stoicism, which deals with reality as it is, does not advocate for the present any community of goods, but is content to require a common spirit of brotherhood. Hence it does not reject the owning of money, like Cynicism; it permits its use. For to use all things is a law of nature. [35]

In the Neo-Pythagorean school, which arose in the 1st century B.C., [36] Philostratus in his novel-like *Vita* of Apollonius of Tyana renews the Pythagorean ideal of an order of life in full community. Here, too, the community of goods is based on nature. The common enjoyment of all the gifts of nature is the ruling principle. The earth is the common mother of all (I, 15) and animals are the instructors of men (IV, 3). Property arises only by injustice. In the inner freedom of ownership which the Pythagorean seeks, he possesses nothing and yet is the owner of all things (III, 15, cf. 2 C. 6:10).

2. Apart from the Pythagorean societies, the question of common ownership is never more than a matter of theory in the Greek world. On Jewish soil, however, we find communistic societies, though only in limited circles. Both Josephus and Philo describe with enthusiasm the achievement of community of goods in the order of the Essenes. [37] The ascetic renunciation of earthly possession which was here demanded led to the establishment of religious societies of those like-minded. The individual placed his private property at the disposal of the group when he

---

[32] Dio Chrys. Or., 7; cf. Demonax, who abandons community of wives and children, Praechter, 510 f.

[33] M. Ant., IV, 4: τὸ νοερὸν ἡμῖν κοινόν, καὶ ὁ λόγος ... κοινός· ... ὁ νόμος κοινός· εἰ τοῦτο, πολῖταί ἐσμεν· εἰ τοῦτο, πολιτεύματός τινος (Phil. 3:20) μετέχομεν· εἰ τοῦτο, ὁ κόσμος ὡσανεὶ πόλις ἐστίν. τίνος γὰρ ἄλλου φήσει τις τὸ τῶν ἀνθρώπων πᾶν γένος κοινοῦ πολιτεύματος μετέχειν; Plut. Stoic. Rep., 34 (II, 1050b): ἡ κοινὴ φύσις; v. Arnim, III, p. 4, 8 f., III, p. 80, 35: no other principle of justice ἢ τὴν ἐκ τοῦ Διὸς καὶ τὴν ἐκ τῆς κοινῆς φύσεως. On natural law in Stoicism cf. P. Barth, *Die Stoa* [3, 4] (1922), 136 ff.

[34] Sen. Ep., 90, 3. Luc. Saturnalia; the Saturnalia festival renews each year the original equality and community of goods.

[35] Sen. Ad Gallionem De Vita Beata, 22 ff.; Hauck, 50 ff.

[36] Praechter, 513 ff.; Mullach, I, 388 ff.; Hauck, 41 ff.

[37] Jos. Bell., II, 122 f.: καταφρονηταὶ δὲ πλούτου καὶ θαυμάσιον αὐτοῖς τὸ κοινωνικόν, ... τῶν δ᾽ ἑκάστου κτημάτων ἀναμεμιγμένων μίαν ὥσπερ ἀδελφοῖς ἅπασιν οὐσίαν εἶναι. 139: πρὶν δὲ τῆς κοινῆς ἅψασθαι τροφῆς ..., Ant., 18, 20: τὰ χρήματά τε κοινά ἐστιν αὐτοῖς, ἀπολαύει δὲ οὐδὲν ὁ πλούσιος τῶν οἰκείων μειζόνως ἢ ὁ μηδ᾽ ὁτιοῦν κεκτημένος. Philo Omn. Prob. Lib., 75-91 (→ 803, n. 46). Pauly-W., Suppl., IV (1924), 386 ff.

joined it, and the work of his hands (agriculture and handicrafts) as a member of the order also belonged to the order. The members of the order had meals together from the common store. Wealth was despised by them. With its full community of consumption and production, the order lasted at least two centuries. It is possible that its singular views and arrangements were influenced by Pythagoreanism. [38]

The society of the Therapeutae, which lived communistically according to Philo, practised monastic isolation specifically for the purpose of a pious study of Scripture. [39]

D. κοινός in the NT.

1. "Common," Tt. 1:4 πίστις; Jd. 3 σωτηρία, esp. Ac. 2:44 (εἶχον ἅπαντα κοινά), 4:32 (οὐδὲ εἷς τι τῶν ὑπαρχόντων αὐτῷ ἔλεγεν ἴδιον εἶναι, ἀλλ' ἦν αὐτοῖς πάντα κοινά), of the "religious communism of love" (Troeltsch) found in the primitive community. On the one hand this is a continuation of the common life of Jesus and the disciples (Lk. 8:1-3; Jn. 12:4 ff.; 13:29), on the other it is a representation of the conditions promised for the last days (Dt. 15:4). This subjective sense of fellowship (ἔλεγεν, Ac. 4:32) is a spontaneous expression of the disposition of love created by Christ and the Spirit. It is not economic in the sense of a planned communistic economy, nor is it legal in the sense of a constitutional socialisation of property (the Essenes, cf. Ac. 5:4; 4:36 f., where we have individual and voluntary acts), nor is it philosophical in the sense of an imitation of the order of nature (Cynicism, etc.). Brotherly love is willing to forego its legal claim to ownership (4:32: ἴδιον εἶναι). All egotistic striving (πλεονεξία) is submerged by readiness to renounce earthly goods in obedience to the saying of Jesus (Lk. 12:33; 14:33; Mt. 6:19 ff.) [40] and for the sake of helping brothers in need (Ac. 2:45; 4:35: καθότι κτλ.). The formula πάντα κοινὰ εἶχον which Luke uses in an ideal (2:44: πάντες; 4:34: ὅσοι, though cf. 4:36; 5:1, 4) depiction of the perfect common life in this early period, is Hellenistic rather than biblical. It is found neither in the OT, nor in the Gospels, nor elsewhere in the NT, whether as requirement or depiction. [41] The Hellenist Luke, influenced by the Greek ideal (→ 791), uses it to express the fact that the ideal which the Greeks sought with longing was achieved in the life of the primitive community. [42]

---

[38] Schürer, II⁴, 659 f. Levy (→ n. 16), 264 ff.

[39] Vit. Cont., 32 and 40.

[40] The words of Jesus are essentially stronger in Lk. than Mt. Perhaps there is a later softening in Mt. On the other hand, if Lk. derived his material from poor Jewish Christians in Palestine, there may be here a sharpening. As a Hellenist, Lk. himself seems to have been influenced by a Greek ideal which would renounce private ownership, cf. Hck. Lk., 205 f.

[41] The almost hesitant demand for a collection (1 C. 16:1 ff.; 2 C. 8:9; R. 15:26 κοινωνίαν τινὰ ποιήσασθαι) and the detailed instructions for arranging it (1 C. 16:2) show that the maintaining of private property was pretty well taken for granted in the Pauline congregations.

[42] J. Weiss, Urchristentum (1917), 49 ff.; J. Behm, "Kommunismus u. Urchr.," NkZ, 31 (1920), 275 ff.; E. Troeltsch, Die Soziallehren der chr. Kirchen u. Gruppen (1912) (= Ges. Schr., I), 49 f.; E. v. Dobschütz, Probleme d. apost. Zeitalters (1904), 39 ff.; F. Meffert, Der "Kommunismus" Jesu u. d. Kirchenväter (1922); O. Schilling, Naturrecht u. Staat nach d. Lehre d. alten Kirche (1914); K. Kautsky, Ursprung d. Christentums¹² (1922), 347 ff.; EB, I, 877; RE³, X, 657 ff.; RGG², III, 1159 f.

2. "Profane" (→ 790) as distinct from ἄγιος. The holy city will be clear of everything profane (Rev. 21:27). [43] The sacred blood of the covenant must not be profaned, Hb. 10:29 (κοινὸν ἡγεῖσθαι, opp. ἁγιάζειν). [44] In Mk. 7:2 κοιναῖς χερσίν, "with cultically unclean hands," elucidated by the ἀνίπτοις, corresponds to the Heb. אֲמָא, so that ἀκαθάρτοις would be a more precise translation. [45]

A material concept of purity is transcended in the NT. The common religious purity of all that God has created (Ac. 10:15; 11:9 → καθαρός) is now recognised. Hence the community has neither the right nor the obligation to declare that certain animals or men are κοινός and are to be avoided as unclean, Ac. 10:28. There is no longer any such thing as the objectively or materially profane, R. 14:14. Only the subjectively backward judgment of individuals can still cling to older views, R. 14:14b. Those who still distinguish between foods because they cling to the older judgment are soon forced into a defensive position in the community. They are regarded as "weak," R. 14:2.

† κοινωνός, † κοινωνέω, † κοινωνία, † συγκοινωνός, † συγκοινωνέω.

Contents : A. The Meaning and Construction of the Term. B. κοινων- in Secular Greek : 1. In Human Life ; 2. In Sacral Speech. C. κοινων- in the Israelite-Jewish Sphere : 1. In the OT : Man ; 2. In the OT : God ; 3. In Rabbinic Literature ; 4. Philo. D. κοινων- in the NT.

A. The Meaning and Construction of the Term.

κοινωνός means "fellow," "participant." It implies fellowship or sharing with someone or in something. It is thus construed a. often in the absol., Plat. Tim., 20d : ταῦτα χρὴ δρᾶν, εἰ καὶ τῷ τρίτῳ κοινωνῷ Τιμαίῳ συνδοκεῖ, [1] b. often with gen. of obj., Plat. Resp., V, 450a : κοινωνὸς τῆς ψήφου ταύτης, c. much less frequently, following κοινωνέω, with dat. of person and gen. of obj., Plat. Resp., II, 370d : τέκτονες δὴ καὶ χαλκῆς καὶ τοιοῦτοί τινες πολλοὶ δημιουργοί, κοινωνοὶ ἡμῖν τοῦ πολιχνίου (small city) γιγνόμενοι, συχνὸν αὐτὸ ποιοῦσιν, d. with prep., e.g., εἰς (Plat. Resp., I, 333b), περί (Plat. Leg., VII, 810c), ἐπί (Plat. Leg., XII, 969c).

Sometimes κοινωνός is accompanied by a second noun indicating the nature of the participation, Xenoph. Cyrop., IV, 2, 21: συμμάχους καὶ κοινωνούς, Plat. Resp., II, 369c : κοινωνούς τε καὶ βοηθούς, cf. 2 C. 8:23. By stem (κοινός) the participation is differently orientated from that of e.g., φίλος, where the bond is that of relationship or love, ἑταῖρος, which implies sharing a common enterprise, συνεργός (fellow-worker), or the colourless μέτοχος (participant). The main element in κοινωνός is that of fellowship. Hence the word is esp. adapted to express inner relationship.

κοινωνέω, from κοινωνός, means 1. "to share with someone (to be κοινωνός) in something which he has," "to take part," 2. more rarely, "to have a share with someone (to be fellow) in something which he did not have," "to give a part," "to impart," Demosth., 25, 61: μὴ πυρός, μὴ λύχνου, μὴ ποτοῦ, μὴ βρωτοῦ, μηδενὸς μηδένα τούτῳ κοινωνεῖν; Philo Spec. Leg., II, 107 with μεταδιδόναι. This usage is infre-

---

[43] The basic verse in Is. 52:1 has ἀπερίτμητος.

[44] Vulg.: pollutum, d syP : communem, r z : immundum.

[45] Cf. A. Merx, Die 4 kanon. Ev. nach ihrem ältesten bekannten Text, II, 2 (1905), 66 f.; though cf. → 791; Ep. Ar., 315.

κοινωνός κτλ. [1] The use with gen. of person seems to be found only in Jewish and Christian writings, e.g., Prv. 28:24; Is. 1:23; H. Seesemann, Der Begriff κοινωνία im NT (1933), 19.

quent because the common μεταδιδόναι can be used instead. But this does not carry the idea of "making a fellow," cf. Sextus Pythagoreus Sententiarum, 266 (ed. A. Elter, Index Lect. Hib., 1891/2): τροφῆς παντὶ κοινώνει.

κοινωνέω is found 1. in the absol., Aristot. Pol., I, 2, p. 1253a, 27 f.: ὁ δὲ μὴ δυνάμενος κοινωνεῖν; 2. with gen. of obj., Isoc., 7, 31: πατρίδος; 3. with dat. of person, Eur. Heracl., 299 f.: ὃς δὲ νικηθεὶς πόθῳ κακοῖς ἐκοινώνησεν ("gave himself to fellowship"), or of obj., Epict. Diss., IV, 6, 30 : ἔργον ἔργῳ οὐ κοινωνεῖ; 4. with dat. of person and gen. of obj., Polyb., 3, 2, 3 : κοινωνεῖν Καρχηδονίοις τῶν αὐτῶν ἐλπίδων; 5. with prep. εἰς, πρός, ἐν. [2]

κοινωνία, an abstract term from κοινωνός and κοινωνέω, denotes "participation," "fellowship," esp. with a close bond. It expresses a two-sided relation (κοινωνία πρὸς ἀλλήλους, Epict. Diss., II, 20, 6; Plat., Resp., V, 426b : οὐκοῦν ἡ μὲν ἡδονῆς τε καὶ λύπης κοινωνία συνδεῖ). As with κοινωνέω, emphasis may be on either the giving or the receiving. It thus means 1. "participation," 2. "impartation," 3. "fellowship."

It is constructed 1. in the absol., "fellowship," Iambl. Vit. Pyth., 30, 168 (→ κοινός, n. 16), in law a contract of partnership, BGU, 586, 11, community of possession or communal possession, P. Lond., 311, 12 : τ[ρεφόμενα κοι]νων[ία] (cf. Preisigke, s.v. κοινωνία); 2. with obj. gen. of the thing shared, Plat. Soph., 250b : ἡ τῆς οὐσίας κοινωνία; Tim., 87e : τῶν πόνων; 3. with subj. gen. of the person or thing sharing, the recipient being in the dat. or with prep. (εἰς, μετά, πρός), [3] Aristoph. Thes., 140 : τίς ... κατόπτρου (ladies' toilet) καὶ ξίφους (men's arms) κοινωνία, cf. 2 C. 6:14; 4. with obj. gen. of the person in whom there is sharing, Plat. Soph., 264e : τῆς τοῦ σοφιστοῦ κοινωνίας (not subj. gen., in spite of Cr.-Kö.). In Plat. Resp., V, 466c ἡ τῶν γυναικῶν κοινωνία τοῖς ἀνδράσιν means "the common sharing of men in women" (cf. the construction of κοινωνέω).

B. κοινων- in Secular Greek.

1. In Human Life.

The group κοινων- is applied to the most varied relationships, the common share in a thing, e.g., πᾶσιν ὅσοι φύσεως κοινωνοῦντες ἀνθρω[πί]νης, [4] common enterprises, [5] and esp. legal relations. κοινωνός is a tt. for a business partner or associate. [6] κοινωνία is used esp. of a close life partnership. Marriage (κοινωνία παντὸς τοῦ βίου) is closer and more comprehensive (οἰκειοτέρα, μείζων) than all other forms of fellowship. [7]

For the Gk. world, however, friendship is also a supreme expression of fellowship. In Gk. thinking this includes a considerable readiness to share material possessions. [8] Sharing the same city underlies the fellowship of equal citizens, Aristot. Eth. M., I, 34,

---

[2] Cf. Seesemann, 10 f. for examples.

[3] For examples cf. Seesemann, 16 f.

[4] Inscr., 1st cent. B.C., K. Humann and O. Puchstein, Reisen in Kleinasien u. Nordsyrien Textbd. (1890), 371, 46.

[5] Polyb., 1, 6, 7 : κοινωνήσαντας Πύρρῳ τῶν πραγμάτων; P. Oxy., XII, 1408, 25 (3rd cent. A.D.): οἱ ... κοινωνοῦντες τῶν ἀδικημάτων.

[6] P. Flor., 370, 2 f. (2nd cent. A.D.): ὁμολογῶ ἔσεσθαί σοι κοινωνὸς ... γεωργίας; P. Amh., 100, 4 : προσελάβετο τὸν Κορνήλιον κοινωνὸν τῆς αὐτῆς λίμνης κατὰ τὸ ἕκτον μέρος ἐπὶ φόρῳ.

[7] Isoc., 3, 40; Plat. Leg., IV, 721a : ἡ τῶν γάμων σύμμειξις καὶ κοινωνία; Resp., V, 466c; BGU, IV, 1051, 8 (1st cent.): συνεληλυθέναι ἀλλ[ήλοις] πρὸς βίου κοινωνίαν.

[8] V. Arnim, III, p. 27, 3 : φιλίαν δ᾽ εἶναι κοινωνίαν βίου (Stob. Ecl., II, 74, 4). Aristot. Eth. Nic., VIII, 11, p. 1159b, 31 : ἡ παροιμία "κοινὰ τὰ φίλων" ὀρθῶς· ἐν κοινωνίᾳ γὰρ ἡ φιλία; Pol., IV, 11, p. 1295b, 24 : ἡ γὰρ κοινωνία φιλικόν; Iambl. Vit. Pyth., 5, 29; 6, 32; 16, 69; 30, 168 (→ n. 16 κοινός).

p. 1194b, 9. In Platonism (→ 792 f.) κοινωνία acquires its greatest systematic significance. κοινωνία is the basis of → σωτηρία, the preservation not merely of individuals, but of the whole cosmos, which includes both men and gods. [9] This is what underlies Plato's projected political ideas on the community of goods and wives (→ 793). [10] To Stoicism (→ 794 f.) the small city state is alien, but the concept of fellowship is still dominant. The world is the state for Stoics. [11] Hence they value the model harmony and fellowship which is found in the universe and which is the basis of its preservation. [12] The idea of an unbroken relationship of fellowship between God and man is thought to be wholly Gk. [13]

2. In Sacral Speech. The group κοινων- is important in sacral speech. According to primitive ideas there is an inward reception of mysterious divine power (mânâ) in eating and drinking. [14] This notion of direct union with the deity is at least a basic impulse in later cults as well, e.g., that of Dionysus etc. [15] On the level of popular polytheism the sacrificial meal then becomes a communion of the deity with men. In Homer sacrifices are cheerful feasts in which the gods take part. [16] Man and god are companions at table. [17] Nor is this true only of the naive primitive age. In the Hellenistic period, too, the gods arrange and conduct sacrificial meals. Men are invited as companions (κοινωνός) to the table of the gods. [18] In

---

[9] Plat. Gorg., 507e, 508a : The man who lives by ἐπιθυμία is pleasing neither to man nor God, κοινωνεῖν γὰρ ἀδύνατος· ὅτῳ δὲ μὴ ἔνι κοινωνία, φιλία οὐκ ἂν εἴη. φασὶ δ' οἱ σοφοί ... καὶ οὐρανὸν καὶ γῆν καὶ θεοὺς καὶ ἀνθρώπους τὴν κοινωνίαν συνέχειν καὶ φιλίαν καὶ κοσμιότητα καὶ σωφροσύνην καὶ δικαιοσύνην. Hence the universe is called κόσμος and not ἀκοσμία and ἀκολασία. L. Schmidt, Die Ethik d. alten Griechen, II (1882), 275 f.; E. Salin, Platon u. d. griech. Utopie (1921), 20 ff.
[10] → κοινός, n. 18, 19.
[11] → κοινός, n. 33.
[12] Dio. Chrys. Or., 40, 35 f. of the ἁρμονία of the στοιχεῖα : αὐτά τε σῳζόμενα καὶ σῴζοντα τὸν ἅπαντα κόσμον. 36 on the other hand ταύτης δὲ τῆς κοινωνίας διαλυθείσης their own incorruptibility would be destroyed; 40, 39 : καὶ ταῦτα μὲν οὕτως ἰσχυρὰ καὶ μεγάλα τὴν πρὸς ἄλληλα κοινωνίαν ἀνέχεται καὶ διατελεῖ χωρὶς ἔχθρας. Ael. Arist. Or., 45, 33 (Keil): Sarapis is the κοινὸν ἅπασιν ἀνθρώποις φῶς. Comprehensive κοινωνία is also felt Stoically in Bas. Hom. in Hexaemeron, 2, 2 (MPG, 29, p. 33a): ὅλον δὲ τὸν κόσμον ... ἀρρήκτῳ τινὶ φιλίας δεσμῷ εἰς μίαν κοινωνίαν καὶ ἁρμονίαν συνέδησεν, cf. W. W. Jaeger, Nemesios v. Emesa (1914), 113; cf. also Phil. Migr. Abr., 178.
[13] Plat. Symp., 188b; Ael. Arist. Or., 45, 27 (Keil); v. Arnim, III, p. 83, 5 and 8.
[14] Pauly-W., XI (1922), 2171 f., art. "Kultus"; P. Stengel, Opferbräuche der Griechen (1910), 73 f.; O. Gruppe, Griech. Mythologie u. Rel.-Geschichte (1906), 730 ff.; E. Reuterskiöld, Die Entstehung der Speisesakramente (1912).
[15] Reuterskiöld, 126 ff.; ERE, III (1910), 746 ff. ("Communion with Deity"); Rohde, II [9, 10], 11 ff.
[16] Hom. Od., 3, 51 ff. and 436; 8, 76; Il., 1, 67, 423 ff.; 9, 535; Paus., IV, 27, 1 f.; P. Stengel, Gr. Kultusaltertümer³ (1920), 97.
[17] Demosth. Or., 19, 280 : κρατήρων κοινωνοὺς πεποίησθε (sc. τοὺς ἥρωας); Eur. El., 637: ὅθεν γ' ἰδών σε δαιτὶ κοινωνὸν καλεῖ. The passage shows that κοινωνός is an old term for the companion at a sacrificial meal. Dit. Syll.³, 1106, 6 f.: ἐπι[μ]ελέσθων [δ]ὲ αὐτῶν τ[οὶ τῶ]ν ἱερῶν κοινωνεῦντες. Plat. Symp., 188b: ἔτι τοίνυν καὶ αἱ θυσίαι πᾶσαι καὶ οἷς μαντικὴ ἐπιστατεῖ — ταῦτα δ' ἐστὶν ἡ περὶ θεούς τε καὶ ἀνθρώπους πρὸς ἀλλήλους κοινωνία — ...
[18] P. Oxy., I, 110 (2nd cent. A.D.): Ἐρωτᾷ σε Χαιρήμων δειπνῆσαι εἰς κλείνην τοῦ κυρίου Σαράπιδος ἐν τῷ Σαραπείῳ αὔριον; P. Oxy., III, 523; Ael. Arist. Or., 8 (I, 93 f., Dindorf): καὶ θυσιῶν μόνῳ τούτῳ θεῷ διαφερόντως κοινωνοῦσιν ἄνθρωποι τὴν ἀκριβῆ κοινωνίαν, καλοῦντές τε ἐφ' ἑστίαν καὶ προϊστάμενοι δαιτυμόνα (guest) αὐτὸν καὶ ἑστιάτορα (host) ... παραπλήσια δὲ καὶ ἡ κατὰ τὰ ἄλλα πρὸς αὐτὸν κοινωνία ὁμότιμος. G. Anrich, Das antike Mysterienwesen (1894), 37; ERE, III, 766 f.; Seesemann, 54; Ltzm. Exc. on 1 C. 10:20; G. P. Wetter, ZNW, 14 (1913), 202 f.

θεοξένια, the *lectisternia* of the Romans, the gods take a lively part in the common festivities through their statues.[19] With union by eating and drinking in the sacred meal we may also mention sexual union with the deity.[20] Greek philosophy (Plato) lifts the thought of divine fellowship above the cultic experience and extols it as the highest and most felicitous form of fellowship.[21] Stoic thinking regards the universe as a dynamic and integrated totality, and on this basis it arrives at the concept of mutual κοινωνία between men and of their κοινωνία with God.[22] For Epict. κοινωνός is equivalent to fellow-man.[23] Hellenistic mysticism conceives of a general κοινωνία ψυχῶν between gods, men and irrational creatures.[24] By its very nature, however, it seeks union with the deity rather than communion.

C. κοινων- in the Israelite-Jewish Sphere.

1. In the OT: Man. In the OT the group κοινων- is not prominent.[25] The LXX selects it for the Heb. group חבר. But it is not the uniform equivalent, since κοινωνός has a different orientation (*cum*); hence חבר is far more common. κοινωνία occurs only at Lv. 6:2 for תְּשׂוּמֶת יָד, "that which is deposited." While this is not literal, it agrees with the rendering of the Targums as שׁוּתָּפוּת יְדָא, "in community of hand," i.e., something which is at the disposal of various shareholders.[26] The verb II חבר means "to bind" (Assyr. *ebru*, "fellow"). It is used of objects at Ex. 26:6 (LXX συνάπτω); 28:7; 26:4, 10: חֹבֶרֶת, joining or coupling of two parts (LXX συμβολή), of nations joining together at Gn. 14:3 (LXX συνεφώνησαν), of all kinds of legal or semi-legal unions, Prv. 21:9, of the common house (LXX οἴκῳ κοινῷ), Prv. 25:24, of joining in a common task, e.g., the fishers in Job 40:30 (חַבָּר,[27] cf. Lk. 5:7: μέτοχος). In Qoh. 9:4 the qere יְחֻבַּר (for יבחר) simply means "association" (πρὸς ... τοὺς ζῶντας). חָבֵר means esp. "companion" or "fellow," partly in the sense of the one who is linked in a common life or

---

[19] P. Stengel, 124; E. Huber, *Das Trankopfer im Kulte d. Völker* (1929), 228 ff.

[20] Cf. ERE, III, 763 f.; F. J. Dölger, *Ichthys,* II (1922), 378, n. 6; Servius Grammaticus Commentarius in Verg. Aen., I, 79 (ed. G. Thilo-H. Hagen, I [1881]: "*Tu das epulis accumbere divum" hoc est, tu me deum facis. Duplici enim ratione divinos honores meremur : dearum conjugio et convivio deorum. Unde et in bucolicis : "nec deus hunc mensa, dea nec dignata cubili est.*" [Bertram.]

[21] Plat. Symp., 188b (→ n. 17). On the other hand, the philosophy of Epicurus denies any communion with deity.

[22] Epict. Diss., I, 9, 5 : κοινωνεῖν τῷ θεῷ of men as rational creatures. II, 19, 27: τῆς πρὸς τὸν Δία κοινωνίας. M. Ant., XI, 8, 4 : κοινωνία Διός. Cic. Leg., I, 7, 23 : *Lege quoque consociati homines cum diis putandi sumus ... Universus hic mundus una civitas communis deorum atque hominum existimanda <sit>.* Nat. Deor., II, 62; Dio. Chrys. Or., 36, 23; v. Arnim, III, 82, 8.

[23] Epict. Diss., I, 1, 9 : κοινωνοῖς τοιούτοις; I, 12, 16; 22, 10 and 13; II, 14, 8; III, 1, 21 in address to Socrates : κοινωνός μου ὢν καὶ συγγενής. A. Bonhöffer, *Epict. u. d. NT* (1911), 51 ff.

[24] Corp. Herm., X, 22b (Stob. Ecl., I, 303, 15). Anrich, 37; Reitzenstein Hell. Myst., 245 ff. "Liebesvereinigung mit Gott"; ἱερὸς γάμος.

[25] κοινωνικός 3 times in the OT, 3 in the Apocr.; κοινωνέω 5 times in the OT, 7 in the Apocr.; κοινωνία once in the OT, once in the Apocr.

[26] Levy Chald. Wört., *s.v.*; Seesemann, 29 f. No partnership (שׁוּתָּפוּת, κοινωνία) is possible for the Jew in pagan enterprises, bSanh., 63b par. אסור לאדם שיעשה שותפות עם העכו״ם.

[27] LXX ἐνσιτοῦνται ἐν αὐτῷ derives the Heb. יִכְרוּ from III כרה, "to give a meal," rather than from II כרה, "to deal," "to negotiate."

undertaking (Qoh. 4:10 of the helpful comrade [LXX μέτοχος], 2 Ch. 20:35 f., association in building ships), but more often of legal, social or professional association (Cant. 1:7; 8:13, LXX ἑταῖρος). In Mal. 2:14 the spouse is חֲבֶרֶת, the "life companion" (LXX κοινωνός σου καὶ γυνὴ διαθήκης σου); the ideas of a companionship of life and in law are intermingled here (→ διαθήκη בְּרִית). The righteous know that they are closely linked with others who worship God, Ps. 119:63 (ψ 118:63 : μέτοχος πάντων τῶν φοβουμένων σε). חָבֵר is used esp. of the ignoble but close association of accomplices in wickedness, Is. 1:23 (κοινωνοὶ κλεπτῶν), Prv. 28:24 (κοινωνὸς ἀνδρὸς ἀσεβοῦς). So also the abstr. חֶבֶר, Hos. 6:9 (not the LXX) and חֶבְרָה, Job 34:8 (LXX : ὁδοῦ κοινωνήσας μετὰ ποιούντων τὰ ἄνομα) of evil companionship.

In all these instances חָבֵר refers to the relation of man with man. It can also be used on occasion for union with gods, but never for that with God. Hos. 4:17 condemns strongly those who, in adultery against the God of salvation, join themselves to gods in alien cults (חבר, LXX μέτοχος εἰδώλων), and Is. 44:11 scornfully calls the worshippers of idols their fellows [28] (LXX ; Θ : πάντες οἱ κοινωνοῦντες αὐτῷ). For members of the people of salvation this close relationship is religiously offensive, and indeed impossible (cf. 1 C. 10:18, 20).

In the Apocr. κοινωνός is often used for close fellowship, e.g., at table (Sir. 6:10 : φίλος κοινωνὸς τραπεζῶν), or in sharing and co-operating in unlawful acts, Sir. 41:19, also in the abs. for "companion," "comrade," (Sir. 42:3 : חוֹבֵר). [29]

κοινωνέω denotes close comradeship with the wicked or the rich, Sir. 13:1: ὑπερηφάνῳ; 13:2: πλουσιωτέρῳ; proverbially it is used of impossible fellowship between opposites, 13:2, 7 → 798). [30]

κοινωνία is used of material participation, Wis. 8:18 with gen. of obj. (λόγων αὐτῆς, sc. σοφίας), 3 Macc. 4:6 (πρὸς βίου κοινωνίαν γαμικόν) and Wis. 6:23 with dat. of obj. (σοφίᾳ).

2. In the OT : God. The most significant point in our OT findings is that neither חבר nor κοινων- is used for the relation to God, as so often in the Gk. world. Herein is expressed the sense of distance which the righteous Israelite feels from God, as distinct from the Greek. The righteous man of the OT regards himself as עֶבֶד in a relationship of dependence upon God and of belonging to Him. This can be deepened into a relationship of trust (cf. עֶבֶד יהוה), But he never regards himself as the חָבֵר of God. This he never ventures to say. Similarly, in the LXX, even though this is influenced by Greek usage and thinking, we never find κοινωνία for the relation between God and man (Philo differs in this respect → 803). This is a surprising fact. For there can be little doubt that in ancient Israel sacrifice, or the sacrificial meal, was widely regarded as sacral fellowship between God and man. [31] In this respect Israel shares ancient Semitic ideas which can be proved elsewhere. [32] In Israel, too, the common meal implies a close relationship which binds the participants to one another. This applies not merely to the men who

---

[28] חֲבֵרִיו Kittel : חֹבְרִיו Ps. 58:5; Dt. 18:11 ("to charm") "charmer."
[29] Kautzsch Apkr., 439, ad loc.
[30] Proverbially, cf. Macarius, VIII, 34, Apostolius, XVI, 60a (Leutsch-Schneidewin, Corpus Paroemiographorum Graecorum, II [1851], 219, 677), cf. 2 C. 6:14.
[31] W. Eichrodt, Theol. d. AT, I (1933), 72.
[32] W. R. Smith, The Religion of the Semites³ (1894), 213 ff., 251 ff., 269 ff.

partake of it; it is equally true of the believed participation of God. The public cult expresses and represents this fellowship, which involves commitment on both sides. The entry of God into sacral fellowship is herein expressed by the sprinkling of blood on the altar. Only to the serious detriment of the one responsible can the fellowship thus established be broken. [33] Yet in respect of the close sharing and fellowship actualised in the sacrificial meal the word group חבר κοινων- is avoided. Conscious theology is hesitant to express what participants in the feasts know by experience. Dt. 12 paints the joy of these festivals in glowing terms, yet even here we find the לִפְנֵי of distance rather than the *cum* (κοινων-) of fellowship (v. 7, 12, 18). Nor do we read of a חֲבוּרָה with God, but rather of a בְּרִית, of a legal order established by the sacrifice of the covenant (Ex. 24:1 ff.). [34] When the description seems to be veering towards an expression of the closest and truest fellowship with God in the cultic meal (Ex. 24:9 ff.), it suddenly breaks off with the unrelated "and did eat and drink" (v. 11; → διαθήκη, II, 121). Even at this climax there is no express statement concerning fellowship with God in the cultic meal.

3. In Rabbinic Literature. Here חֶבֶר has a. the basic sense of "fellow," "friend," "participant," e.g., Ab., 2, 9, a good or evil "companion," cf. the Aram. חַבְרָא, e.g., bBB, 28b. [35] Also of the wife. [36] חֲבֵרִים, e.g., S. Nu., 181 on 25:1 [37] of rebellious cities. b. In legal terminology the word can then take on the more general sense of "one who stands in some relation to another." Thus the debtor is חָבֵר, in relation to his creditor (S. Nu., 3 on 5:7), or the seducer in relation to the seduced (adulteress, S. Nu., 15 on 5:21), or the unclean in relation to someone else who is unclean. [38] Thus in the Golden Rule of Hillel, bShab., 31a, "What is not acceptable to you, do not do to another (לחברך). [39] c. From at least the 1st cent. B.C. חָבֵר is also used as a tt. for members of the Pharisaic Chaber society (→ Φαρισαῖος) who personally pledged that they would pay the full tithe, observe scrupulously the laws of purity, and faithfully keep the Jewish Law. [40] Uncertainty as to the fidelity of ordinary Jews meant that those who were strict in their observance ran constant risks of making themselves unclean by contact with them, and of sinning thereby. The חֲבֵרִים thus felt that they must separate themselves rigidly from the עַמֵּי הָאָרֶץ (Jn. 7:49). The strictly segregated αἵρεσις of the Pharisees developed out of the movement of fidelity to the Law in the Maccabean period. *In nuce* this technical use of חָבֵר is found already in Ps. 119:63, where the righteous man is a חָבֵר of those who live in the fear of God and who inwardly keep His commandments, as distinct from other members of the people, i.e., the ungodly in Israel, to whom he is not a חָבֵר.

d. With the consolidation of the status of the rabbi (→ ῥαββί) by the second half of the 1st century (or the 2nd?), we find another technical use quite independent of c., namely, that the rabbis think of one another as חֲבֵרִים and call one another by this name.

---

[33] Eichrodt, I, 72.

[34] Etym. בְּרִית is dependent on ברה, "to eat," though cf. → διαθήκη, II, 107.

[35] In Levy Wört., *s.v.*

[36] Examples in Levy Wört., *s.v.*

[37] K. G. Kuhn, S. Nu. tr. (1933 ff.), 507.

[38] S. Nu., 130 on 19:22 (Kuhn, 501).

[39] Str.-B., I, 460 under a.

[40] Demai, 2, 3: "He who undertakes to be a Chaber may not sell to an '*Am ha'arec* any fresh or dried fruits, nor may he buy from him any fresh fruits, nor may he dwell with him as a guest, nor may he take him home in his robe as a guest." Cf. also Kuhn, 423, n. 23; Schl. Gesch. Isr., 138; Str.-B., II, 500 ff.; Schürer⁴, 452, 454 (identity of Pharisee and חָבֵר).

With the development of the organisation of the rabbinic office there arises a ladder of academic grades. The תַּלְמִידִים are those who aspire to the office. The most suitable of these are then ordained and instituted into the office and dignity of a rabbi (חָכָם). For תַּלְמִידִים who by age and education might have become חכמים, but who did not attain to ordination for other reasons, חָבֵר in the narrower sense ("colleague") became an established title. [41]

In the first instance חֲבוּרָה, "fellowship," "union," is also a very general term (v. חָבֵר a, supra). Yet it takes on a varied semi-religious and religious content. A חֲבוּרָה arises esp. in table fellowship. Those who share in the Passover meal — acc. to Ex. 12:4 there have to be at least 10 persons — are called בְּנֵי חֲבוּרָה (bPes., 89a b). In the post-exilic period the custom arises of meeting with friends in the house (cf. Ac. 2:46 κατ' οἶκον) on Friday afternoon and holding a common meal to introduce the Sabbath (Seder evening, Sabbath qiddush). [42] These times of table fellowship are also called חֲבוּרָה. We have here in some sense a preliminary stage towards the semi-cultic Christian feasts (the Lord's Supper, the agape), in which the early community κλῶντες κατ' οἶκον ἄρτον (Ac. 2:46) experienced and celebrated its fellowship of faith. [43]

4. Quite distinctive is the usage of the Hellenistic Jew, Philo. In contrast to the LXX he adopts κοινωνία, κοινωνέω and κοινωνός for the religious sharing and fellowship between God and man. [44] The distance maintained in Israelite theology is in him transformed into the proximity of the Greek world. Thus Philo speaks of a close fellowship between the righteous and God in the cultus, esp. in the sacrificial meal. [45] These expressions, so different from OT usage, are undoubtedly influenced by corresponding expressions in Hellenism. Philo also depicts as κοινωνία the ideal common life of the Essenes (→ 795) with its full community of goods. [46] Joseph. uses κοινωνία for the living relationship with one's fellow-man which the Jew regarded as so important (cf. Gl. 2:11-14). [47]

In Philo κοινωνέω and κοινωνία are also used in the sense of "giving a share" or "imparting," which is rare in secular Gk. [48]

---

[41] Schürer, II⁴, 468 ff.; Jew. Enc., VI, 121 ff.; EJ, V, 121 ff.

[42] W. O. E. Oesterley, *The Jewish Background of the Christian Liturgy* (1925), 167 ff.; I. Elbogen, *Der jüdische Gottesdienst³* (1931), 107.

[43] It cannot be shown that the primitive community was directly called חֲבוּרַת יֵשׁוּ, κοινωνία 'Ιησοῦ, as C. A. Scott assumes (Exp. T., 35 [1923/4], 567). Cf. Seesemann, 90.

[44] Vit. Mos., I, 158 : οὐχὶ καὶ μείζονος τῆς πρὸς τὸν πατέρα τῶν ὅλων καὶ ποιητὴν κοινωνίας ἀπέλαυσε προσρήσεως τῆς αὐτῆς ἀξιωθείς;

[45] Spec. Leg., I, 221: ὃς (sc. God) εὐεργέτης καὶ φιλόδωρος ὢν κοινωνὸν ἀπέφηνε τοῦ βωμοῦ καὶ ὁμοτράπεζον τὸ συμπόσιον τῶν τὴν θυσίαν ἐπιτελούντων. I, 131 of the priests : κοινωνοὶ τῶν κατ' εὐχαριστίαν ἀπονεμομένων γίνονται θεῷ.

[46] Omn. Prob. Lib., 84 : τοῦ δὲ φιλανθρώπου (δείγματα παρέχονται) εὔνοιαν, ἰσότητα, τὴν παντὸς λόγου κρείττονα κοινωνίαν ... 85 : οὐδενὸς οἰκία τίς ἐστιν ἰδία, ἣν οὐχὶ πάντων εἶναι κοινὴν συμβέβηκεν ... 86 : ταμεῖον ἓν πάντων καὶ δαπάναι <κοιναί>, καὶ κοιναὶ μὲν ἐσθῆτες, κοιναὶ δὲ τροφαὶ συσσίτια πεποιημένων ... οὐκ ἴδια φυλάττουσιν, ἀλλ' εἰς μέσον προτιθέντες κοινὴν τοῖς ἐθέλουσι χρῆσθαι ... παρασκευάζουσιν ὠφέλειαν.

[47] Ap., I, 35 : τὴν πρὸς ἀλλόφυλον κοινωνίαν ὑφορώμενοι. Bell., 7, 264 : τὴν πρὸς ἀνθρώπους ἡμερότητα καὶ κοινωνίαν οὐκ ἐτήρησεν.

[48] Spec. Leg., II, 107 with μεταδιδόναι; Virt., 84 κοινωνία with χρηστότης, 80 with φιλανθρωπία → κοινωνικός.

D. κοινων- in the NT.

1. κοινων- = "to share with someone in something."

a. In Lk. 5:10 κοινωνοὶ τῷ Σίμωνι is used of partnership in work which may even be taken as a legal partnership. [49] The next sense is that of sharing in a nature which has been received or which is to be attained. Thus in Hb. 2:14 children share in the common mortality of man (τὰ παιδία κεκοινώνηκεν αἵματος καὶ σαρκός). Since Christ acquired a share herein (μετέσχεν, synon. κοινωνέω), He entered into a full fellowship of flesh and blood in order that He might vanquish death thereby. In 2 Pt. 1:4 redemption is presented along these lines as a liberation from the natural corruption of earth to participation in the divine nature (θείας κοινωνοὶ φύσεως). [50] In R. 11:17 the συγκοινωνός (τῆς ῥίζης τῆς πιότητος τῆς ἐλαίας) denotes the close participation of the engrafted branch in the total life of the cultivated olive. Partaking of the sins of others is to be strictly avoided (1 Tm. 5:22; 2 Jn. 11 → 801; Prv. 28:24; Is. 1:23), since it entangles one in a fatal fellowship of guilt and judgment with those who commit them (Mt. 23:30, cf. 27:25). The participation of the righteous in what is holy has an exclusive character (2 C. 6:14: τίς κοινωνία φωτὶ πρὸς σκότος;). It demands separation. As children of light Christians cannot possibly have a part in sin (Eph. 5:11: μὴ συγκοινωνεῖτε τοῖς ἔργοις τοῖς ἀκάρποις τοῦ σκότους). Hence the people of God must leave Babel lest they share in its sins and the resultant judgment (Rev. 18:4).

b. The κοινων- group is most common in Paul, for whom it has a directly religious content. Paul uses κοινωνία for the religious fellowship (participation) of the believer in Christ and Christian blessings, and for the mutual fellowship of believers. [51] According to 1 C. 1:9 Christians are called to fellowship (participation) with the Son (ἐκλήθητε εἰς κοινωνίαν τοῦ υἱοῦ, constr. 4. → 798). They are lifted up to be His fellows. They enter into a spiritual communion with the risen Lord. This description of the Christ relationship is to be distinguished from Paul's distinctive ἐν Χριστῷ (→ II, 541) and also from his common image of the believer as a member in the body of Christ, 1 C. 12:12 ff. The σύν verbs, which are peculiar to Paul (cf. R. 8:17: συμπάσχειν — συνδοξασθῆναι), develop the content of this fellowship with Christ as regards both present and future (→ 806). Since there is no question of mystical absorption into Christ, this participation in Christ and fellowship with Him arise only through faith, which implies the identification of our life with His. By the very nature of the case this participation in the Son is a present possession of the Christian to salvation. Yet it is to be consummated in the future (1 Th. 4:17: σὺν κυρίῳ). As there is personal participation in Christ, so there is participation in the Gospel (1 C. 9:23) [52] or in faith. Since in his salutations

---

[49] Cf. v. 7 μέτοχος. Deep sea fishing was carried on by many partners working together and helping one another from different boats, G. Dalman, Orte u. Wege Jesu³ (1924), 145; F. M. Willam, Das Leben Jesu im Land u. Volk Israel³ (1934), 154 f.

[50] Cf. Philo Decal., 104: τῶν ... θείας καὶ μακαρίας καὶ εὐδαίμονος φύσεως μετεσχηκότων, Leg. All., I, 38: ἀντιλαβέσθαι θεοῦ φύσεως, cf. Abr., 107.

[51] Paul does not venture to speak of a direct κοινωνία θεοῦ. In the NT this is mediated through Christ, in the OT, e.g., through the altar, 1 C. 10:18.

[52] By faithful work for the Gospel Paul here hopes to be a partaker of the blessings of salvation which it promises (ἵνα συγκοινωνὸς αὐτοῦ [sc. τοῦ εὐαγγελίου] γένωμαι). Joh. W., 1 K., 246; Ltzm. K., 44; Seesemann, 79, n. 4.

Paul is usually thinking of the good standing of the readers in faith, the thanksgiving ἐπὶ τῇ κοινωνίᾳ ὑμῶν εἰς τὸ εὐαγγέλιον ἀπὸ τῆς πρώτης ἡμέρας ἄχρι τοῦ νῦν (Phil. 1:5, constr. 3. → 798) refers to the inward and undisturbed (ἀπό — νῦν) participation of the Philippians in the saving message of Christ (→ II, 732).[53] The ἡ κοινωνία τῆς πίστεώς σου of Phlm. 6 ("thy close union with faith," constr. 2. → 798)[54] refers similarly to the vitality of the faith of Philemon which is now to work itself out further in knowledge.

c. Paul then makes highly significant use of κοινωνία for the fellowship which arises in the Lord's Supper (→ 730 ff.). Participation in Christ, which is known basically and perfectly in faith, is achieved and experienced in enhanced form, with no dogmatic implication, in the sacrament, 1 C. 10:16 ff.[55] In the first instance Paul classifies the Lord's Supper with Jewish and pagan festivals. In terms of the common belief of antiquity it is self-evident for him that those who partake of the cultic meal become companions of the god.[56] Hence those who partake of the sacrificial feasts of the Jews become κοινωνοὶ τοῦ θυσιαστηρίου (v. 18); θυσιαστήριον is obviously used for God. The altar represents and guarantees the presence of God.[57] It is equally self-evident for him that those who partake of pagan feasts become κοινωνοὶ τῶν δαιμονίων (v. 20). By analogy, those who partake of the Lord's Supper are Christ's companions. The real fellowship which arises here entails for Christians the very natural religious conclusion that they should avoid the cultic meals of alien deities (v. 21). Thus the nature of the Lord's Supper is expounded by Paul in terms of fellowship with the person of Christ, namely, κοινωνία with His body and blood (v. 16, constr. 2. → 798). For Paul the bread and wine are vehicles of the presence of Christ, just as the Jewish altar is a pledge of the presence of God. Partaking of bread and wine is union (sharing) with the heavenly Christ. To Paul the exalted Christ is identical with the earthly and historical Christ who had body and blood.[58] κοινωνία is here expressive of an inner union. This is for Paul the important thing in the celebration. It is self-evident that for Paul real union with the exalted Lord should include the blessing of forgiveness which He won by His death. How this union takes place in the cultic meal Paul does not tell us either in respect of demonic or of Christian

---

[53] Seesemann, 73 ff., though Zahn (Zschr. f. kirchl. Wiss. u. kirchl. Leben, 6 [1885], 185 ff.; Einl. i. d. NT, I³ [1906], 380) takes the κοινωνία here to refer to the co-operation displayed by the Philippians in their gift to Paul, cf. also Dib. Phil., 53.

[54] Seesemann, 79 ff. Loh. Phlm., however, refers the πίστεως as gen. auct. to the fellowship in which Philemon has come to participate with other believers through faith.

[55] H. Lietzmann, Messe u. Herrenmahl (1926), 223 ff.; W. Heitmüller, Taufe u. Abendmahl bei Pls. (1903), 27; K. G. Goetz, Das Abendmahl eine Diatheke Jesu oder sein letztes Gleichnis? (1920); A. Schweitzer, Die Mystik des Ap. Pls. (1930), 260 ff.; K. L. Schmidt, art "Abendmahl," RGG², I, 12 ff.

[56] → n. 14; 45.

[57] For instances cf. H. Gressmann, "Ἡ κοινωνία τῶν δαιμονίων," ZNW, 20 (1921), 224 ff.; Bousset-Gressm., 308 ff.; W. Reichel, Über vorhellenische Götterkulte (1897), 40 ff.

[58] The question whether we are to think in terms of the earthly or the ascended body is meaningless for Paul, since the two are identical, Seesemann, 35 ff.; T. Schmidt, Der Leib Christi (1919), 20 ff., 106 ff. Both the Gk. σῶμα and the corresponding Aram. גוף mean person as well as body, cf. G. Dalman, Jesus-Jeschua (1922), 130 f. Paul mentions the blood as well because this was handed down in the traditional eucharistic words. E. v. Dobschütz, ThStKr, 78 (1905), 11 ff. suggests that κοινωνία τοῦ σώματος καὶ αἵματος Χριστοῦ means a "society of Christ's body and blood" which arises through common eating and drinking, but in this case v. 17 is superfluous.

fellowship. The point that matters for Paul is the fact, not the nature, of this close communion.[59] In the interjected statement in v. 17 Paul declares that at the Lord's Supper, as at sacrificial feasts, there is also fellowship between the participants. This is not apart from Christ. It arises out of common union with Him, as Christ is represented by the one loaf.

d. According to Paul fellowship with Christ also means that the Christian participates in the detailed phases of the life of Christ. There is a συζῆν (R. 6:8; 2 C. 7:3), συμπάσχειν (R. 8:17), συσταυροῦσθαι (R. 6:6; Gl. 2:19), συναποθανεῖν (2 C. 7:3), συνθάπτειν (R. 6:4; Col. 2:12), συνεγείρειν (Col. 2:12; 3:1; Eph. 2:6), συζωοποιεῖν (Col. 2:13; Eph. 2:5), συνδοξάζειν, συγκληρονομεῖν (R. 8:17), συμβασιλεύειν (2 Tm. 2:12). These terms are often arranged in antithetical pairs (R. 6:4 ff.; 8:17). Fellowship with Christ means that present participation in one phase, namely, that of humility and suffering, assures us of winning through to participation in the other, namely, that of glory.[60] The spiritual union with Christ which characterises the whole life and work of Paul is especially described in terms of a spiritual fellowship in suffering with Him (Phil. 3:10 : κοινωνίαν παθημάτων αὐτοῦ).[61] This is not just a living again of Christ's sufferings. Nor is it a mere personal conformity. Nor is it a retrospective passion dogmatics. By spiritual participation in Christ the sufferings of the apostle are a real part of the total suffering which is laid on Christ (Col. 1:24). By participation in Christ's sufferings Paul has hope of analogous participation in His glory (Phil. 3:10 : συμμορφιζόμενος τῷ θανάτῳ αὐτοῦ, εἴ πως καταντήσω κτλ., R. 8:17: εἴπερ συμπάσχομεν, ἵνα καὶ συνδοξασθῶμεν). The same thought is picked up in 1 Pt. 4:13 : καθὸ κοινωνεῖτε τοῖς τοῦ Χριστοῦ παθήμασιν χαίρετε, ἵνα καὶ κτλ., and it is also in the background in 5:1. The whole life and work of the apostle, with the suffering which it entails, is a witness to the sufferings of Christ (μάρτυς τῶν τοῦ Χριστοῦ παθημάτων). Hence the apostle may have certainty here and now that he will partake of the coming glory (ὁ καὶ τῆς μελλούσης ἀποκαλύπτεσθαι δόξης κοινωνός).[62] For Paul fellowship with Christ's sufferings is not restricted to individual believers. It broadens out into the spiritual fellowship in suffering of the whole community both within itself and with Christ. As the body of Christ the community has to bear a certain degree of His sufferings. For Paul the sufferings which he has to endure as an individual are a gladly accepted shouldering of part of the burden which lies on the whole (Col. 1:24). Similarly in 2 C. 1:5, 7 Paul deduces from the participation of the Corinthians in his sufferings that they will also be fellow-participants in the divine comfort allotted to him (ὅτι ὡς κοινωνοί ἐστε τῶν παθημάτων οὕτως καὶ τῆς παρακλήσεως). Here, too, he expects a fulfilment of the law of fellowship.

---

[59] On the pagan side this is often construed highly realistically as the entry of the deity into the celebrants as they eat the sacrifice, e.g., Porphyrius in Eus. Praep. Ev., IV, 23. But it is questionable whether Paul was thinking in such realistic terms.

[60] It may be accepted that Paul was to some degree influenced by similar ideas and statements in current Hellen. cults, e.g., that of Osiris, cf. J. Leipoldt, *Sterbende u. auferstehende Götter* (1923); J. Schneider, *Die Passionsmystik des Pls.* (1929), 75 ff.

[61] Schneider, 31 ff.; 48 ff.

[62] Cf. Wbg. Pt., 144. Interpretation is affected by problems of authorship. It is hardly enough to see a mere reference to first hand witness of the sufferings of Jesus (cf. the title τοῦ Χριστοῦ), but it is too much to find a reference to Peter as a confessor (μάρτυς) who already shares in the glory (κοινωνός), cf. A. v. Harnack, *Die Chronologie d. altchr. Lit.*, I (1897), 451 f.

e. Partaking of the Spirit is also a mark of the Christian. In the triadic formula in 2 C. 13:13 : ἡ χάρις τοῦ κυρίου 'Ιησοῦ Χριστοῦ καὶ ἡ ἀγάπη τοῦ θεοῦ καὶ ἡ κοινωνία τοῦ ἁγίου πνεύματος, it should be noted, however, that the third member is not quite parallel to the first two. The Holy Spirit is not distinguished in quite such clear-cut fashion as God and Christ. In the Spirit Christ comes to believers. Hence the κοινωνία τοῦ ἁγίου πνεύματος does not quite seem to suggest a person and a gift as do the first two. What we have here is rather an objective genitive (constr. 2. → 798), i.e., participation in the Spirit. [63] Similarly in Phil. 2:1 κοινωνία πνεύματος, like σπλάγχνα καὶ οἰκτιρμοί, is something present in man, i.e., fellowship in the Spirit (constr. 2. → 798), [64] not a fellowship which the Spirit Himself effects (gen. auct., subj.). [65]

f. Fellowship with Christ necessarily leads to fellowship with Christians, to the mutual fellowship of members of the community. For this Paul uses κοινωνέω in various connections, and in accordance with the meaning the idea of "having a share" may often pass over into that of "giving a share." In Phlm. 17 Paul appeals to the close link between Philemon and himself, and on this ground he asks him to show mercy to the delinquent slave, now a newly won brother in the faith. The κοινωνέω here can hardly refer to the mere bond of friendship ; at the very least it includes spiritual union in the same faith. [66] Similarly Titus, who in 2 C. 8:23 is called κοινωνὸς ἐμός as Paul's fellow-worker in the work of Christ, especially in relation to the Corinthians (καὶ εἰς ὑμᾶς συνεργός), has a claim to be honourably received by the congregation. According to Paul there is a particularly close bond of union between Jewish and Gentile Christians, since Gentile Christians have acquired a share in the spiritual blessings of the original community (R. 15:27: τοῖς πνευματικοῖς αὐτῶν ἐκοινώνησαν) and are thus under obligation to help the latter with material goods (15:26, → 808). Particularly in R. 12:13 living participation in the needs of the saints (ταῖς χρείαις τῶν ἁγίων κοινωνοῦντες) already includes thoughts of active assistance. [67] The union and communion of Christians is quickened and expressed specifically under the pressure of sufferings and persecutions from without. Sharing in the sufferings of Paul, the Philippians are said by him to share also in his grace (Phil. 1:7), i.e., the distress which God has laid on him to salvation. And Paul thanks them for their willing sharing in his affliction (4:14: συγκοινωνήσαντές μου τῇ θλίψει). Here, too, shared feeling moves over into the sharing of active assistance, and in this verse Paul is thanking them for the gift which he has received. Similarly in Hb. 10:33, where we have the two classes of those who suffer persecution and those who are indirect companions of the sufferers, the thought is that of active help (giving a share) as well as sympathetic disposition (having a share). [68]

g. In 1 Jn. κοινωνία is a favourite term to describe the living bond in which the Christian stands. Here, too, the word implies inward fellowship on a religious

---

[63] Seesemann, 56 ff.; H. Windisch, 2 K., Exc. on 13:13; O. Schmitz, *Die Christusgemeinschaft des Pls. im Lichte seines Gen.-Gebrauchs* (1924), 209; E. v. Dobschütz, "Zwei- und dreigliedrige Formeln im NT," JBL, 50 (1931), 117 ff., 141 ff.

[64] Seesemann, 58 ff., 61.

[65] Ew. Phil.³, 105 f.; Loh. Phil., 138 f.

[66] Dib. Gefbr., 81 f.

[67] So most commentators ; Zn. R., 551 f. prefers the reading ταῖς μνείαις (D*G lat Ambst Or) and suggests sharing in the collection.

[68] Rgg. Hb., 332.

basis. [69] To be a Christian is to have fellowship with God. This fellowship is with the Father and the Son, 1:3, 6. [70] It issues in the brotherly fellowship of believers, 1:3, 7. The believer's communion with God or Christ consists in mutual abiding (→ μένειν, 3:24; 4:13), which begins in this world and reaches into the world to come, where it finds its supreme fulfilment, 3:2.

2. κοινων- = "to give someone a share in something."

The sense "to give a share," which is rare in secular Greek, is more common in the NT, especially in Paul. The two-sided meaning is obviously present in Phil. 4:15, where Paul commends the community for demonstrating its fellowship with him (ἐκοινώνησέ μοι) εἰς λόγον δόσεως καὶ λήμψεως. [71] Between apostle and community there is a reciprocal relation. The community shares in the spiritual gifts of the apostle and it grants him a share in its own material goods. Paul demands the same reciprocity in Gl. 6:6. The pupil, who receives valuable spiritual goods in his course of instruction, ought to give the teacher a share in his material possessions, cf. 1 C. 9:11. [72] Hence Paul also uses κοινωνία in connection with the collection. This is not just a financial matter, cf. the term λογεία in 1 C. 16:1, 2. It expresses at the deepest level the fellowship between the original Jewish Christian congregation and the Gentile missionary congregations. Thus the collection has for Paul a religious significance. The fellowship ἐν Χριστῷ between the two parts of Christianity (Gl. 2:9) is given a definite form in the collection on behalf of the mother church at Jerusalem. The abstract κοινωνία becomes for Paul the concrete collection, cf. R. 15:26. [73] On the other hand in 2 C. 9:13 the ἁπλότητι τῆς κοινωνίας εἰς αὐτοὺς καὶ εἰς πάντας has the active and abstract sense of sincere and ready sharing (constr. 3. → 798). [74] In 2 C. 8:4 κοινωνία is again used in connection with the collection. Alongside the lofty χάρις ("they asked of us the grace") it can hardly have the weak sense of "participation." Here, too, it bears the religious meaning of "fellowship and union" in service to the saints. [75] Again the gathering of money is not the main thing for the apostle. What really counts is the fellowship of Christians expressed in the collection. In Hb. 13:16, too, κοινωνία with εὐποιΐα is obviously active sharing or imparting.

3. κοινωνία in the absolute, = "fellowship."

In Gl. 2:9 (ἔδωκαν δεξιὰς κοινωνίας) shaking hands is an expression of the full fellowship established by common faith in Christ. Paul is in this way acknow-

---

[69] John's Gospel does not have κοινωνία, κοινωνέω or κοινωνός. Instead it uses verbal phrases like μένειν ἐν, εἶναι ἐν, e.g., 14:20, 23; 15:4 ff.; 17:21; Seesemann, 94 f.

[70] Paul has only the second, → supra.

[71] A commercial term, "to the account of expenditure and income," instances in Moult.-Mill., s.v., Loh. Phil., 185, n. 2.

[72] Cf. Barn., 19, 8 (κοινωνήσεις ἐν πᾶσιν τῷ πλησίον σου καὶ οὐκ ἐρεῖς ἴδια εἶναι); Did., 4, 8 (οὐκ ἀποστραφήσῃ τὸν ἐνδεόμενον, συγκοινωνήσεις δὲ πάντα τῷ ἀδελφῷ σου καὶ οὐκ ἐρεῖς ἴδια εἶναι). Just. Apol., I, 15, 10; Seesemann, 25 f.

[73] The combination κοινωνίαν ποιήσασθαι forces us to take the noun concretely. The added τινά indicates that it is not used strictly. Against deriving κοινωνία, "collection," from תְּשׂוּמֶת יָד (Lv. 6:2, Heb. 5:21, Str.-B., III, 316), cf. Seesemann, 29 f.

[74] Seesemann, 26 ff. "kindness which shares"; Epict. Gnom. Stob., 43: χρηστότητι κοινωνίας λαμπρύνειν φιλοκάλου ἅμα καὶ φιλανθρώπου (Stob. Ecl., III, 110, 3).

[75] The χάρις with κοινωνία is either hendiadys, "grace of sharing," or the καὶ indicates that κοινωνία is meant to give greater precision ("namely"), cf. Ac. 1:25.

ledged to be a genuine κοινωνός of Christ and therefore of the earlier believers represented by the apostles. [76] In Ac. 2:42 κοινωνία does not denote the concrete community or society of Christians [77] which, while it had not yet separated itself legally and cultically from the Jewish community, already represented a circle of the closest fellowship. Nor can it signify the community of goods (cf. v. 44: εἶχον ἅπαντα κοινά). It is rather an abstract and spiritual term for the fellowship of brotherly concord established and expressed in the life of the community. [78]

† κοινωνικός.

a. "Belonging or appointed to society," Aristot. Eth. Eud., VII, 10, p. 1242a, 25: κοινωνικὸν ἄνθρωπος ζῷον; Pol., III, 13, p. 1283a, 38: κοινωνικὴν ... ἀρετὴν εἶναι ... τὴν δικαιοσύνην; Epict. Diss., III, 13, 5 (with φιλάλληλος); Philo Det. Pot. Ins., 72 (δικαιοσύνη). b. "He who gladly gives others a share" (→ κοινωνέω, 798, → κοινωνία, 798). Polyb., 2, 44, 1: κοινωνικὴ ἡ φιλικὴ διάθεσις; 18, 48, 7: κοινωνικῶς χρῆσθαι τοῖς εὐτυχήμασιν; Luc. Tim., 56: ἀνὴρ τῶν ὄντων κοινωνικός. This sense of community is the basis of kindly action. Philo Omn. Prob. Lib., 13: φθόνος ἔξω θείου χοροῦ ἵσταται, θειότατον δὲ καὶ κοινωνικώτατον σοφία; Jos. Bell., 2, 122, of the communal life of the Essenes: καταφρονηταὶ δὲ πλούτου καὶ θαυμάσιον αὐτοῖς τὸ κοινωνικόν. Philo Congr., 71.

The word is not found in the LXX.

In the NT it occurs only at 1 Tm. 6:18 (with εὐμετάδοτος) in sense b.

† κοινόω.

"To make common," "to share," found from the time of Aesch., Aristot. Pol., II, 5, p. 1263b, 40 ff.: τὰ περὶ τὰς κτήσεις ἐν Λακεδαίμονι καὶ Κρήτῃ τοῖς συσσιτίοις ὁ νομοθέτης ἐκοίνωσεν.

It does not occur in the LXX, which uses → βεβηλοῦν for "to profane," and in the Apocr. the only instance is 4 Macc. 7:6 א: οὐδὲ τὴν θεοσέβειαν καὶ καθαρισμὸν χωρήσασαν γαστέρα ἐκοίνωσας μιαροφαγίᾳ, "to profane cultically," "to deprive of the capacity for fellowship with God" (→ κοινός, 790 f.).

It has three senses in the NT.

1. In connection with the OT idea of material holiness it is used in Ac. 21:28 for the profaning of the temple by bringing in the uncircumcised and in Hb. 9:13 for ritually unclean things (cf. 4 Macc. 7:6) which can be made capable of cultic use by lustrations. In both cases the opposite is → ἅγιος.

2. In connection with the NT view of personal holiness it is found in Mt. 15:11, 18, 20 and par., where we read that the capacity for fellowship with God is destroyed, not by material uncleanness (foods, hands), but only by personal sin.

3. In Ac. 10:15; 11:9 it means "to declare unclean or profane." The opposite → καθαρίζειν can also have this declarative sense.

Hauck

---

[76] Ltzm. Gl., 13.
[77] C. A. Scott, Exp. T., 35 (1923/1924), 567; cf. Seesemann, 90 f.
[78] Cf. also of the communal life of the Pythagoreans, Iambl. Vit. Pyth., 30, 167 f. → κοινός, n. 16.

κ ο ι ν ω ν ι κ ό ς. → κοινός.

κόκκος, κόκκινος

† κόκκος.

This word means "seed" and is found in Gk. from the time of Hom. Hymn., also Hdt. and Ditt. Syll.³, 1173, 12; in the LXX it is used for תּוֹלֵע, Sir. 45:10; Lam. 4:5 (A : κόλπων).

1. In the NT κόκκος σινάπεως is first found in the metaphors and parables of Jesus (Mt. 13:31; 17:20; Mk. 4:31; Lk. 13:19; 17:6) for the grain of mustard seed.

Proverbially this is the least of all seeds. We often hear of it in the Rabb. writings (חַרְדָּל), e.g., "as big (or as little) as a grain of mustard seed." [1]

The parable (מָשָׁל) of the mustard seed in Mt. 13:31 f.; Lk. 13:19; Mk. 4:31 f. is grouped with that of the leaven in Mt. and Lk. and with that of the seed which grows by itself in Mk. It represents the tiny seed of the preaching of Jesus in comparison with the comprehensive significance of the kingdom of God. With the seed of the Word of God there is presented the heavenly rule itself, which embraces all men and all peoples. The unassuming and insignificant event of the preaching of Jesus carries with it the secret of the action of God embracing and enclosing the world. The sower and the field (Mt. ἀγρός, Lk. κῆπος) are stock elements in parables. They conceal the mysterious reference to Jesus Himself and His proclamation in the world. The picture of the tree in whose branches the birds of heaven nest is found in the OT prophets (Ez. 17:22 f.; 31:6; Da. 4:9, 18). It points to a kingdom which will embrace all peoples. In Lk. 17:6 a paradoxical metaphor of Jesus is followed by the comparison between the mustard seed and the "sycamine" (συκάμινος). The seed is small, unassuming and outwardly weak ;

κ ό κ κ ο ς. [1] חַרְדָּל is the lowest limit of sexual defilement, so bBer., 31a : "R. Se'era has said : Jewesses have made things difficult for themselves, for even when they see a drop of blood the size of a mustard seed they sit on it the seven days of purification" (cf. Lv. 15:28), also jBer., 8d : "If a woman perceives a drop (of blood) as big as a mustard seed, she sits and awaits the seven days of purification." As regards male issues, the rule of Nidda, 5, 2 is used : "(Sexual issues) defile no matter how small, even though they be as small as a mustard seed or smaller." The passage in Lv. r., 31 on 24:2 is difficult : "R. Hoshaya b. Shimlai of Caesarea has said in the name of Yizchak b. Se'era : No one goes under the wheel of the sun without becoming like a drop of blood the size of a mustard seed." The usual explanation is that just before setting the sun is like a drop of blood the size of a mustard seed, Levy. Wört., II, 107; Bacher Pal. Am., III, 722; Str.-B., I, 669. But the texts adduced from Ps. 19:5 and Gn. 18:11 seem to show that the uncleanness rather than the smallness of the blood is the *tertium comparationis*. Cf. also Midr. Ps., 19, 5 (§ 12) = Jalkut Shim'oni, II, 673 : "As the bridegroom goes in (into the bridal chamber) clean and comes out unclean, so the sun arises clean and sets unclean." The reason is that it is spotted by the sight of wicked human works.

the tree (שִׁקְמָה) is firmly rooted and has grown out of the soil. [2] Related is the saying about the faith which moves mountains (Mt. 17:20; 21:21; Mk. 11:23; 1 C. 13:2). "To root out" or "to tear up" mountains is a proverbial expression meaning "to make possible what appears to be impossible" (Str.-B., I, 759). Faith is small and weak in face of the promise which Jesus gives it. The first impression made by the saying is that Jesus is recognising even the smallest and weakest faith. In reality, however, He is showing that faith should cease to think about itself. He is pointing to the kingdom of God, which is not proportionate to the faith of the disciples. The impossible becomes possible when faith looks away from itself. [3]

2. Paul and John find in the corn of wheat (κόκκος σίτου, 1 C. 15:37; Jn. 12:24) a parable of the rule of divine action and creation. The corn is set in the ground and dies, and then it comes to life again and bears fruit. Paul is expounding the resurrection and the connection between the old corporeality and the new, John the necessity of the death and passion of Jesus. The image of the seed which falls naked into the ground and is buried and then emerges with a new robe or body seems to have been traditional in the doctrine of the resurrection, bSanh., 90b. It reveals the wealth and mystery of the divine creation to which faith may entrust itself. It has no connection with the modern idea of evolution. [4] In Jn. 12:24 the image of the corn of wheat which must die to bring forth fruit is one of the discipleship sayings. In hidden form it describes the necessity of the death of Jesus and also the divine law which unites master and disciple. God creates only through death and dying. Only negation of one's own life wins the promise. What is elsewhere an eschatological picture takes on Christological immediacy and depth in John.

3. Outside the NT κόκκος is also used for the scarlet berry and the colour scarlet (Dromo in Athen., 6, 38 [p. 240d]; Sir. 45:10). In 1 Cl., 8, 3 we find the saying : "Though your sins reach from earth to heaven, and though they be redder than scarlet (πυρρό-τεραι κόκκου) and blacker than sackcloth, and you turn to me with all your heart and say 'Father,' I will hear you as a holy people." This apocr. quotation is in form a prophetic call to repentance (μετανοήσατε, οἶκος 'Ισραήλ) and uses an image found

---

[2] Cf. Str.-B., II, 234 : "The rootage of the sycamine (שִׁקְמָה) was reckoned to be particularly strong ; it was thought that the tree could stand 600 years in the earth. On the advice of the scribes Barkochba made the uprooting of a cedar from the horse a proof of the military power of his men." Cf. jBer., 14a, line 27: "R. Chanina bJaqqa has said in the name of R. Jehuda (d. 299): The roots of corn go 50 ells deep into the earth, the roots of the fig-tree, which are tender, go into a rock." In Gn. r., 13 on 2:5 we read that the roots of the sycamine and the carob-bean tree go down into the primal depths, cf. Str.-B., II, 234 for further examples.

[3] Cf. J. Schniewind, NT Deutsch, I, 141 on Mk. 11:23 : "The saying is parabolic. Faith can lift burdens like mountains, for faith is 'comforted despair' (Luther) of everything human and committal to God who created the mountains (Ps. 65:6; 90:2) and who is from eternity to eternity before the mountains were."

[4] Cf. bSan., 90b (Str.-B., II, 551): "Queen Cleopatra (Bacher Tannaiten, II, 68, n. 2 conjectures "the patriarch of the Samaritans") asked R. Meir (c. 150) and said : I know that those who have fallen asleep shall rise again, for it is written in Ps. 72:16 : 'They shall bloom out of the city as the grass of the earth.' But when they arise, will they do so naked or in clothes ? He answered her : We learn this from the corn of wheat by the deduction of the harder from the easier. If the corn of wheat (חִטָּה), which comes into (is buried in) the earth naked, rises again in who knows how many different robes, how much more is it true that the righteous, who are buried in their clothes, will rise again in their clothes !" The parable of the corn of wheat is thus traditional in discussion of the resurrection of the dead.

elsewhere (ὡς φοινικοῦν, ... ὡς κόκκινον, Is. 1:18 = 1 Cl., 8, 4). But the motif that sin is as red as (or redder than) scarlet is linked with the religious and cultic significance of this colour. [5]

† κόκκινος.

"Scarlet" (→ κόκκος, 3.). It is common in Hellenism, so Herond., 6, 19; Mart., 2, 39; Plut. Fab. Max., 15 (I, 182e); Epict. Diss., III, 22, 10 (ἐν κοκκίνοις περιπατεῖν); IV, 11, 34 (φορεῖν κόκκινα); P. Hamb., 10, 24; P. Lond., 191, 5; 193, 22; also often in the LXX for כַּרְמִיל, שָׁנִי, תּוֹלָע and תּוֹלֵעָה. [1]

In the furnishing of the OT sanctuary we find enumerations like that of Ex. 25:4: καὶ ὑάκινθον καὶ πορφύραν καὶ κόκκινον διπλοῦν καὶ βύσσον κεκλωσμένην καὶ τρίχας αἰγείας (Ex. 26:1, 31, 36; 27:16; 28:5, 8, 15, 33; 31:4; 35:6, 25, 35; 36:9, 10, 12, 31; 37:3). Among the means of atonement in Lv. 14:4, 6, 49, 51, 52 we find κεκλωσμένον κόκκινον (cf. also Nu. 19:6). κόκκινον is normally a term for a red garment or cloth. Purple and scarlet are found together. In David's lament for Saul in 2 Βασ. 1:24 we read: τὸν ἐνδιδύσκοντα ὑμᾶς κόκκινα μετὰ κόσμου ὑμῶν.

In the prophets scarlet is often linked with ungodly and sinful conduct. With something of a cultic background, its opposite is white wool: ἐὰν δὲ ὦσιν (sc. αἱ ἁμαρτίαι ὑμῶν) ὡς κόκκινον, ὡς ἔριον λευκανῶ (Is. 1:18). In the call to repentance we find the divine promise that God will hear His people even though its sins be redder than scarlet and blacker than sackcloth, 1 Cl., 8, 3-4. Related is the petition in Ps. 51:7: "Wash me, and I shall be whiter than snow," which perhaps derives from the same cultic circles as Is. 1:18. Scarlet cloth is also a sign of ungodly and worldly luxury. Thus Is. in his preaching of repentance describes the extravagant attire of the daughters of Zion: καὶ τὰ βύσσινα καὶ τὰ ὑακίνθινα καὶ τὰ κόκκινα καὶ τὴν βύσσον σὺν χρυσίῳ καὶ ὑακίνθῳ συγκαθυφασμένα καὶ θέριστρα κατάκλιτα ... (3:23), and in Jer. 4:30 we find the reproach against Jerusalem: καὶ σὺ τί ποιήσεις, ἐὰν περιβάλῃ κόκκινον καὶ κοσμήσῃ κόσμῳ χρυσῷ καὶ ἐὰν ἐγχρίσῃ στίβι τοὺς ὀφθαλμούς σου. Scarlet and purple are obviously the colours of particularly costly garments and in prophetic preaching they are a sign of ungodly extravagance and worldly desire.

Joma, 6, 6 and 8 may be cited in respect of the cultic background of the colour red. When the goat for Azazel was driven out, a crimson strip was divided, one part being bound to the rock and another put between the horns of the goat. When the goat reached the wilderness, this strip became white, according to the saying: "Though your sins be as crimson, they shall be as white as snow" (Is. 1:18). [2]

---

[5] Cf. on Is. 1:18 and Ps. 51:7 the old cultic expiatory customs cited, e.g., by R. Press, "Das Ordal im alten Israel, II," ZAW, NF, 10 (1933), 227-255. The staying red and becoming white of the crimson threads obviously played a special part in expiation, bJoma, 67a; Joma, 6, 6 and 8.

κ ό κ κ ι ν ο ς. [1] -ινος forms adj. of material (Debr. Griech. Wortb. § 319) up to the Hell. period (E. Schwyzer, Zschr. f. vergl. Sprachforschung, 63 [1936], 64): κόκκινος, made of scarlet berries, cf. πράσινος, κίτρινος, λευκόϊνος (pap.).

[2] Acc. to Joma, 6, 8 a scarlet ribbon was tied earlier to the temple door; this tradition emphasises the cultic derivation. During the period of Simeon the Just the ribbon lost its colour at the same time as the goat lost its life. Later this did not happen regularly and the people became unsettled. Hence the strip was cut in two, one part being tied to the rock and the other to the horns of the goat. 40 years before the second destruction of Jerusalem the red ribbon was no longer supposed to have become white, nor the lot for the goat לַיהוה to have come into the right hand of the high-priest, and this was taken to be a bad sign, J. Meinhold, Traktat Joma, Giess. Mischna, II, 5 (1913), 64 f. On the whole question of the cultic background cf. R. Press, ZAW, NF, 10 (1933), 227-255. Cf. Dt. 21:6-9; Lv. 14:6; Nu. 19:6.

In the NT κόκκινος is connected 1. in the passion narrative with Roman custom and costume. Red is the colour of war. The red mantle (*paludamentum*, χλαμύς) is the mark of the field-marshal and emperor outside Italy. [3] The reference is to a cloak fastened over the left shoulder and denoting the warrior. According to Mk. 15:17 Jesus was clothed in a purple robe (ἐνδιδύσκουσιν πορφύραν) to mock His Messianic claim, while in Mt. 27:28 it was a scarlet mantle (χλαμύδα κοκκίνην περιέθηκαν αὐτῷ). [4] In Mt. a soldier's cloak is obviously used in place of the true kingly or imperial garb. The King of gentleness and peace (Mt. 21:5) is clothed in the warlike garb of a Roman soldier because His claim is misunderstood and misconceived. "According to the view of the soldiers, to be the King of the Jews Jesus must lead His hosts against the Roman cohorts" (Schl. Mt., 778).

2. In its depiction of the blood sacrifice on the conclusion of the OT covenant, Hb. adds other means of cultic atonement drawn from another part of the Bible, namely, water, scarlet-coloured wool and hyssop, Hb. 9:19, cf. Lv. 14:4, 6, 49, 51, 52; Nu. 19:6. This enumeration shows us the varied nature of the OT statutes and of the pre-Christian rites of expiation.

> Acc. to Chrys. the red wool is to arrest fluidity, but it may have had independent expiatory significance (→ n. 2). [5] Barn. perceives in the sending away of the scapegoat (Lv. 16:7-10) a logical reference to Jesus Christ. As the goat bears the scarlet wool round its head, so Jesus Christ bears the scarlet mantle (τὸν ποδήρη τὸν κόκκινον, 7, 9), and as the wool was laid between thorns (7, 8 and 11), so the community must accept afflictions and hardships (7, 11). The suffering Jesus is typified in the accursed goat. [6]

3. Purple and scarlet indicate the worldly pomp of the demonic power Βαβυλών in Rev. The woman sits on a scarlet beast (θηρίον κόκκινον, 17:3), and she is herself arrayed in purple and scarlet (περιβεβλημένη πορφυροῦν καὶ κόκκινον, 17:4). [7] The divine emphasises this similarity in colour between the beast and the woman. He obviously distinguishes between fiery red in 6:4 and 12:3 (πυρρός) and scarlet in 17:3, 4; 18:12, 16 (κόκκινος), and scarlet and purple are linked together (πορφυροῦς, Jn. 19:2, 5; Rev. 17:4; 18:16; πορφύρα, Rev. 18:12). Only purple and scarlet fit the deeds of this woman, namely, licentiousness, seduction by the wine of unchastity, blasphemies, abominations, and murder of the saints and witnesses of Jesus, 17:1-6. Here red epitomises demonic abomination, ungodly lasciviousness and the power which is hostile to God. The army of the Messiah is clothed in white linen and rides on white horses, 19:11-14. The Messiah is spattered with blood (dipped in blood, 19:13, cf. Is. 63:1), but Jn. is referring here to the cleansing and atoning blood of the Lamb, 7:14; 1:5. The sign of faith is washing and being made white in the blood of the Lamb, 7:14. The white of the

---

[3] E. Wunderlich, *Die Bedeutung d. roten Farbe im Kultus d. Griechen u. Römer* = RVV, 20 (1925/6), 74 ff.

[4] We may ignore the reading ἱμάτιον πορφυροῦν καὶ χλαμύδα κοκκίνην, cod D it sys Orig.

[5] Rgg. Hb. 2, 3, 278, n. 57.

[6] Acc. to Barn., 7, 8 the one who has to send off the goat takes the wool from it and lays it on a shrub called the bramble, whose fruits we are accustomed to eat when we find them in the fields, for this is the only thorn whose berries are so sweet.

[7] Loh. Apk., 138 : "Scarlet refers, not to the hide, but to the trappings of the beast. It is a sign of luxury and rank. It is also the colour of Roman triumphs, of the flags of Roman horsemen, and of warriors and heroes generally." White, on the other hand, indicates the nature and glory (δόξα) of heaven and the victory over, and vanquishing of, evil.

heavenly rider and the heavenly community is an effective contrast to the red of the beast and the woman. The cultic concept may be seen again behind the imagery of the seer. That in this mention of demonic scarlet the seer also has in view the ancient prophetic preaching of repentance may be seen in 17:4; 18:12, 16: "Alas, alas, that great city, that was clothed in fine linen, and purple, and scarlet, and decked with gold, and precious stones, and pearls," 18:16. All extravagance is of antichrist and will perish in the last divine judgment.

Michel

κολάζω, κόλασις

† κολάζω.

From κόλος (Hom.) "mutilated," this means "to cut short," "to lop" or "to trim." It is used fig. for a. "to impede," "to restrain"; b. "to punish," "to chastise" (in the tragic poets, cf. also Ditt. Syll.[3], 108, 42; 305, 80; 454, 18; 1199, 10; Ditt. Or., 90, 28; P. Greci e Latini, 446, 14 etc.). The word seems to be linked with κολάζω, "to maim," "to cut off." The sense of punishing probably comes by way of trimming, i.e., cutting off what is superfluous. Punishment is designed to cut off what is bad or disorderly. It may be, however, that the idea of punishment is originally identical with that of maiming. It is often used of the punishment of slaves, cf. Herm. s., 9, 28, 8: εἰ τὰ ἔθνη τοὺς δούλους αὐτῶν κολάζουσιν.

For the pass. cf. BGU, I, 341, 14: π]αρεστάθησαν καὶ ἐκολάσθησα[ν; P. Ryl., II, 62, 9: ἀγρυπνεῖται καὶ κολάζεται [καὶ τι]μωρεῖται καὶ παρηγορεῖται. Fig. the term then means "to be robbed by cutting off," or gen. "to be cut off from something," "to suffer loss," so BGU, I, 249, 4: λείαν [= λίαν] ἐκολάσθημεν [αὐτῶν] (sc. ἀρταβῶν σειταρίου), "we suffer serious loss" (of corn), or "we have great need." Cf. the similar use in P. Fay., 120, 5: ἐπὶ (ἐπεὶ) κ[ο]λάζωμαι (-ομαι) αὐτῶν, "since I have lack of them (the objects of economic necessity)," and ibid., 115, 19: κολάζεται ὁ ζευγηλάτης (the coachman needs a thong). [1]

In the LXX κολάζω, like κόλασις, is most common in Wis. in connection with the punishment of the ungodly, of idolaters, and esp. of the Egyptians. Only in Ez. is the noun more common (mostly κόλασις ἀδικίας [ἀδικιῶν]). Both verb and noun are elsewhere very rare in books with a Mas. basis. In other Gk. renderings there are only occasional instances: a. κολάζω, 'Α 2 Βασ. 8:1 (= כנב hi, "to subjugate"); Σ Prv. 22:23 (= קבע "to rob"); b. κόλασις, 'Α Jer. 11:20; 20:10, LXX ἐκδίκησις, Heb. נקמה, "revenge," Θ Ez. 7:19, LXX βάσανος, 'ΑΣ σκάνδαλον, Heb. מכשׁול, "offence," so also 4 times in the LXX.

The idea of divine punishment and chastisement is widespread in antiquity. From pagan expiatory inscr. we note that κολάζειν and κόλασις were fixed terms in sacral jurisprudence. [2]

κ ο λ ά ζ ω. [1] Cf. also B. Olsson, *Papyrusbriefe aus d. frühesten Römerzeit* (1925), 42, 4; 57, 19; 62, 5.
[2] Cf. BCH, 25 (1901), 422, n. 1.

Particularly conclusive are the inscr. given by Steinleitner [3] from Phrygian and Lydian monuments of the imperial period. Typical examples are No., 3, 9 : ὁ θεὸς ... ἐκόλασεν τὸν Ἑρμογένην καὶ ζημίας αὐτῷ ἐπόησεν; 6, 11: κολ[α]σθέντος οὖν τοῦ Σκόλλου ὑπὸ τῶν θεῶν ἰς θανάτου λόγον; 9, 15 : ἐκολάσετο καὶ διέφθειρε τοὺς ἐπιβουλεύσαντας αὐτοῖς ὁ θεός; 12, 2 : ἐκολάσθη Ἀμμιὰς οἰπὸ Μητρὸς Φιλεῖδος ἰς τοὺς μαστοὺς δι' ἁμαρτίαν λόγον λαλήσασα; 22, 5 : κολαθέσα ἐπὸ τοῦ θεοῦ; 23, 4 : κολασθεὶς ὑπὸ τοῦ θεοῦ; 26, 4 : κολαθὶν ἐπὸ τὸ θεοῦ; 27, 2 : [Ἀσκλ]ηπιάδης Ἀττά[λου ἱ]ερὸς κολασ[θεὶς ὑ]πὸ τοῦ ἐπιφ[ανεστ]άτου θεοῦ [Ἀπόλ]λωνος Λαρ[μηνοῦ. [4]

In these inscriptions the sins punished by deity are those against the deity itself, e.g., violations of the sacred cultic laws. [5] The deity smites the offender with sickness and infirmity, or even punishes himself and his family with death. The sinner can win back the grace of the deity only by open confession of his guilt. In this way alone can he be liberated from sickness and misfortune.

The question of the justice of divine punishment occurs in the context of the problem of theodicy.

In his work Περὶ θεῶν (Plut. Stoic. Rep. 35 [II, 1050e]) Chrysipp. addresses the question how evil in the world can be reconciled with belief in God. It is to be regarded as divine punishment and retribution. Plut. himself took up the same position in chapters 9 and 11 of his work Ser. Num. Pun. (II, 553 f., 555d).

Philo made a valuable contribution to the problem of theodicy in this respect when he stated that the punitive power of God is one of the first powers of being. In Rer. Div. Her., 166 he differentiates two powers in being, the beneficent power (χαριστικὴ δύναμις) with which God made the world and which is called God, and the judicial power (κολαστικὴ δύναμις) in virtue of which He rules and directs what is created, this power being called Lord. Cf. also Spec. Leg., I, 307; Abr., 129; Leg. Gaj., 6. [6] We should also note Sacr. AC, 131 with its reference to the legislative power of God (νομοθετικὴ δύναμις). This power divides into two branches, the one for the rewarding of the good and the other for the punishment of sinners. [7] Philo's view of God includes the insight that in God mercy is older than punishment (Deus Imm., 76) and that God would rather forgive than punish (Spec. Leg., II, 196 : τοῦ συγγνώμην πρὸ κολάσεως ὁρίζοντος). Punishment is for those who are not amenable to reason (Agric., 40). Thus punishment may seem to be the greatest evil, but it is to be regarded as the greatest blessing for fools, loc. cit. This is a Stoic view.

Already in Gorg., 476a ff. Plato had advanced the view that he who punishes aright does good, and that he who is punished is blessed, since he is liberated from his false frame of soul. At the conclusion of the Gorg. Plato depicts judgment in Hades in a myth in which he makes free use of Orphic ideas of judgment. Here is fulfilled the punishment of the wicked (ἐὰν δέ τις κατά τι κακὸς γίγνηται, κολαστέος ἐστί [527b]).

---

[3] Steinleitner, 10 ff.

[4] Cf. also 10, 7: ὁ θεὸς ἐκολάσετο; 14, 6 : κολασθείς; 15, 6 : κ[ολά]σεσθε; 19, 2 : κολασθεῖσα; 29, 4 : ἐκολάσθην; 31, 6 : κολαθίς; in 33, 2 the sinner prays ὑπὲρ τοῦ κολ[ασθ]έντος βοός (he was punished in respect of his property).

[5] Cf. Steinleitner, 92.

[6] Cf. L. Cohn, Die Werke Philos, I (1909), 19, where there is ref. to the two supreme qualities of God, His goodness and His power.

[7] Cf. Fug., 65 : κόλασις ἁμαρτημάτων; Spec. Leg., I, 55 : κολάσει ἀσεβῶν; Leg. Gaj., 7; Praem. Poen., 67: ... τὰς προτεθείσας τοῖς πονηροῖς κολάσεις. The legal punishment of sinners is also part of the task of the ruler, Vit. Mos., I, 154 : κολάσει ἁμαρτανόντων.

The NT uses the verb κολάζειν twice, in Ac. 4:21 [8] and 2 Pt. 2:9. Only the latter is theologically important with its reference to divine punishment: οἶδεν κύριος ... ἀδίκους δὲ εἰς ἡμέραν κρίσεως κολαζομένους τηρεῖν, "the Lord knoweth how to reserve the unjust under chastisements until the day of judgment." The phrase εἰς ἡμέραν κρίσεως has in view the time between death and judgment. For the ungodly this time is filled with punishments. They remain in this dreadful state until the day when their fate will be finally decided.

To the same milieu belong the statements in Apc. Pt. (→ infra). In hell are the angels who execute punishment (οἱ κολάζοντες ἄγγελοι, 21b) and the men who are punished for their deeds on earth (οἱ κολαζόμενοι ἐκεῖ, 21a). 2 Cl., 17, 7 refers to punishment in the last judgment (κολάζονται δειναῖς βασάνοις πυρὶ ἀσβέστῳ), Dg., 2, 8; 5, 16 to the punishment of Christians by the heathen, i.e., by heathen governments (κολαζόμενοι χαίρουσιν ὡς ζωοποιούμενοι), cf. also 6, 9; 7, 8; 10, 7; Mart. Pol., 2, 4 (ἄλλαις ποικίλων βασάνων ἰδέαις κολαζόμενοι).

† κόλασις.

"Chastisement," "punishment," found from the time of Hippocr. and Plato, common in Diod. S. (I, 77, 9; IV, 44, 3); Plut. (Ser. Num. Pun., 9 and 11 [II, 553 f., 555d]); Ael. (Var. Hist., VII, 15); Philo (Leg. Gaj., 7; Vit. Mos., I, 96 etc.). In the LXX cf. esp. Ez. and Wis., [1] also of divine punishment in 2 Macc. 4:38 : κυρίου τὴν ἀξίαν αὐτῷ κόλασιν ἀποδόντος, "the Lord has repaid him (Andronicus) with the merited punishment," v. also 4 Macc. 8:9 : δειναὶ κολάσεις, "severe punishments which precede execution." δειναὶ κολάσεις is used in Mart. Pol., 2, 4 of the punishments and torments which martyrs had to endure, οἱ εἰς τὰ θηρία κριθέντες ὑπέμειναν δεινὰς κολάσεις. Joseph. makes frequent use of the term, e.g., of the punishment of Cain, Ant., 1, 60.

It is found only twice in the NT. Speaking to the disciples about the Last Judgment in Mt. 25:31-46, Jesus says in v. 46 that on those who have neglected the practical ethical task the sentence is pronounced: ἀπελεύσονται εἰς κόλασιν αἰώνιον. [2]

κόλασις αἰώνιος occurs in Test. XII, Test. R. 5:5. In Apc. Pt. 21 hell is τόπος κολάσεως. κόλασις alone is used for hell in modern Gk. [3]

αἰώνιος κόλασις also occurs in Mart. Pol., 2, 3 : τὴν αἰώνιον κόλασιν ἐξαγοράζεσθαι; 2 Cl., 6, 7: There is no salvation from eternal punishment if we are disobedient to the commands of Christ. Cf. also 1 Cl., 11, 1: God plunges gainsayers into punishment and torment, εἰς κόλασιν καὶ αἰκισμόν; Dg., 9, 2 : Punishment and death are the reward of unrighteousness; Herm. s., 9, 18, 1: He who does not know God and who does wrong receives a punishment for his wickedness, ἔχει κόλασίν τινα τῆς πονηρίας αὐτοῦ. [4] Ep. Ar., 208 contains the general truth that human life consists of sorrows and punishments.

---

[8] Ac. 4:21 has the mid. (πῶς κολάσωνται αὐτούς), cf. also Aristoph. Vesp., 406; Plat. Prot., 324c; 3 Macc. 7:3.
κ ό λ α σ ι ς. [1] → 814.
[2] Cf. Jos. Bell., 2, 163, where Jos. states as a Pharisaic doctrine : τὰς δὲ (ψυχὰς) τῶν φαύλων ἀϊδίῳ τιμωρίᾳ κολάζεσθαι (quoted in Schl. Mt., 728). There is an interesting par. to Mt. 25:46 in P. Oxy., 840, 6 (fragm. of a non-canonical gospel): οἱ κακοῦργοι τῶν ἀν(θρώπ)ων ... κόλασιν ὑπομένουσιν καὶ πολ[λ]ὴν βάσανον.
[3] Already in the Byzantine period κόλασις = γέεννα, v. Sophocles Lex., s.v. κόλασις (Apophthegmata Zen., 6; Isidor, 6; Macarius, 38).
[4] Dg., 2, 8 f. is ironical : the savour of sacrifice is a punishment for the heathen.

Ign. in R., 5, 3 mentions among other tortures the κακαὶ κολάσεις τοῦ διαβόλου which may come over him if only he attains to Christ.

Of greater theological significance is 1 Jn. 4:18 : ὁ φόβος κόλασιν ἔχει, "fear contains punishment in itself." [5] This means that the man who lives in fear (before God) is already punished by this fear. His fear is his punishment. This thought may be linked with the express statement in Jn. 3:18 that the unbeliever is judged already. The opposite of fear is love. Perfect love is free from every fear, because perfect love for God drives out fear before Him. [6]

J. Schneider

(κολακεύω) † κολακία

κολακεύω (from κόλαξ), "to flatter," from Aristoph. [1] In the LXX it occurs only 3 times, 1 Εσδρ. 4:31; Job 19:17; [2] Wis. 14:17. It is comparatively frequent in Philo, e.g., Leg. Gaj., 116; Det. Pot. Ins., 21; Spec. Leg., I, 60. In Migr. Abr., 111 Philo depicts the nature of the flatterer. He torments day and night those whom he would flatter, insinuating into their ears, nodding to all they say, making long addresses, singing songs of praise, wishing good things with the lips but cursing in the heart. The flatterer is also a dissembler. [3]

The word does not occur at all in the NT. In the post-apost. fathers we find it in Ign., R., 4, 2; 5, 2; Pol., 2, 2 in the sense of "to allure by flattery." Cf. also the Apologists, Just. Apol., 2, 3; Tat. Or. Graec., 2, 1.

From κολακεύω we have κολακεία, [4] "flattery," found from Democr. In the pap. also "overreaching by flattery" (P. Lond., V, 1727, 24, etc.). [5] The LXX does not have

---

[5] Most expositors think of the punishment in terms of future judgment and future damnation, e.g., H. J. Holtzmann, Handkomm. z. NT, IV² (1893), 259 f.; Schl. Erl., ad loc. ("looking to the day of judgment awakens fear"); F. Hauck, NT Deutsch ("fear stands under the continuous thought of threatening judgment"). Cf. also, though not so firmly, W. Michaelis, Das NT, II (1935), 442 ("fear has punishment always before its eyes"). For a middle position cf. de Wette, Erkl. d. Ev. u. d. Ep. Joh.⁵ (1863), 397: "Fear already has punishment as this will be revealed on the day of judgment," cf. also F. Büchsel, Die Johannesbriefe (1933), 75 : "Punishment with its pain is not just future, but may be discerned already in fear." For the phrase κόλασιν ἔχειν cf. Herm. s., 9, 18, 1 (→ 816). On the connection between κόλασις or κολάζειν and φόβος cf. the instructive chapters 9 and 11 in Plut. Ser. Num. Pun., II, 553 f., 555d. This link is also found frequently in Philo. Thus fear teaches man to accept the ruling and commanding power of God in order to avoid punishment (Abr., 129, cf. Agric., 40), and punishment imbues fear (δέος γὰρ ἐμποιοῦσιν αἱ κολάσεις), Spec. Leg., IV, 6.

[6] For Rabb. material cf. R. Sander, "Furcht u. Liebe im rabb. Judentum," BWANT, IV, 16 (1935), Index, s.v. "Züchtigung."

κ ο λ α κ ε ί α. [1] For examples in class. Gk. cf. Liddell-Scott, 971 s.v.

[2] The LXX of Job 19:17 does not agree with the Mas. The Heb. is : וְחַנֹּתִי לִבְנֵי בִמְנִי, "I am loathsome to my brethren," while the LXX runs : προσεκαλούμην δὲ κολακεύων υἱοὺς παλλακίδων μου, "I summoned the sons of my concubines and spoke flatteringly to them."

[3] Cf. also P. Greci e Latini, 586, 4.

[4] On the orthography cf. Bl.-Debr. § 23. ει and ι were often confused in the early Hellen. period. Cf. also Mayser, I, 87 f.

[5] For further examples cf. Preisigke Wört., s.v.

the term. On the other hand, we find it several times in Philo, e.g., Sobr., 57; Leg. All., III, 182 : νόσος γὰρ φιλίας ἡ κολακεία, "flattery is a perversion of friendship." In Sacr. AC, 22 it occurs in a list of vices in which the friends of lust are enumerated, including flattery. In Abr., 126 Philo declares that men fear dissembled flattery (τὴν προσποίητον κολακείαν) and friendship as something harmful.

Cf. also Jos. Bell., 4, 231: πρὸς ὀλίγην τε κολακείαν τῶν δεομένων. Ditt. Syll.³, 889, 29 ff. gives us a statement of profound practical experience and wisdom, namely, that there is no means by which man can pass the limits set for him by fate : εἰδότας ὅτι οὔτε χρημάτων οὔτε κολακείᾳ οὔτε ἱκετείᾳ οὔτε δάκρυ[σιν] ἄνθρωπ[ος τ]ῆς εἱμαρμένης ὅρον ὑπερβῆναι δυνηθήσεταί ποτε.

The word is found only once in the NT at 1 Th. 2:5 (λόγος κολακ[ε]ίας). Paul can say with pride that in his preaching he has never used base methods, including flattery. His preaching thus stands in marked contrast to the practice of many Hellenistic rhetoricians. [6]

J. Schneider

---

† κολαφίζω

This is a relatively rare word found only a few times in the NT and elsewhere only in early Christian authors with very few exceptions. In a pagan letter from the Roman period we read : εἰ δέ τις ... ἀντιλέγει, σὺ ὀφείλεις αὐτοὺς κολαφίζει[ν], Preisigke Sammelb., III, 6263, 22-24. Cf. also Test. Jos. 7:5 vl.: κολαφίσει τὰ τέκνα σου. There are no instances in the LXX, though the noun κόλαφος ("box on the ear," "buffet") is fairly frequent, and κολαφίζω ("to box on the ear," "to buffet") is derived from it in the normal way. [1] Though comparatively rare, the terms must have been in general use, for the noun is very early and later the verb passed into Latin and then into some Romance languages. The word κόλαφος was used in common speech. [2] In detail it is

---

[6] On this pt. cf. the fine discussion of the art of flattery in ancient rhetoric in Moult.-Mill., *s.v.* On the work of the Epicurean Philodemus, Περὶ κολακείας, cf. the short account of W. Crönert, "Neues über Epikur u. einige Herkulanensische Rollen," *Rhein. Museum,* NF, 56 (1901), 623. κολακεία is also found in the lists of vices of antiquity, cf. A. Vögtle, *Die Tugend- und Lasterkataloge im NT* (1936), 201.

κ ο λ α φ ί ζ ω. [1] Thes. Steph., *s.v.* gives the following pedantic definition from Theophylact. on Mt. 26:67: "κολαφίζειν ἐστὶ τὸ διὰ χειρῶν πλήττειν συγκαμπτομένων τῶν δακτύλων, καὶ ἵνα ἀφελέστερον εἴπω, διὰ τοῦ γρόνθου (ὁ γρόνθος = ὁ κόνδυλος, clenched fist) κονδυλίζειν. Pape and Pass. mention not only κόλαφος and κολαφίζω but also κολάφισμα, κολαφισμός, κολαφιστικός, but only with a vague reference to the NT and the fathers. Liddell-Scott is a little more explicit. There are several patristic ref. in Thes. Steph., but material is scanty in E. A. Sophocles, *Gk. Lexicon of the Roman and Byzantine Periods* (1888) and there is nothing in C. du Cange, Glossarium ad Scriptores Mediae et Infimae Graecitatis, I (1688).

[2] Cf. Thes. Ling. Lat., *s.v.* Cf. also Itala and Vulgata on the NT passages. In Portuguese we find *colaphizár,* "to box on the ear," fig. "to torment," "to provoke," but it is now very rare. So, too, is the Italian *colafizzare,* which is not listed in modern dictionaries. On the French cf. F. Godefroy, *Dictionnaire de l'ancienne langue française,* II (1883), *s.v.* colaphiser ; K. Sachs-C. Villatte, Suppl. (1894), *s.v.* colaphisation. W. Meyer-Lübke, *Romanisches etym. Wörterbuch*³ (1935), *s.v. colaphus* draws attention to the development κόλαφος, *colaphus, colpus, coup,* Ital. *colpo,* Span. *golpe* etc. The dictionaries suggest that in

not always easy to say with precision whether the verb is used lit. or fig., i.e., in respect of body or soul. In many case the sense "to ill-treat," "to revile," is apposite.

In the passion story in Mt. 26:67 [3] = Mk. 14:65 [4] it occurs in the context of maltreatment and there can be no doubt that it is meant literally. [5] In martyrdom, however, the bodily pain is also spiritual. We can see this from Paul's account of his sufferings in 1 C. 4:11: κολαφιζόμεθα [6] καὶ ἀστατοῦμεν, and also from the admonition to Christians in 1 Pt. 2:20 [7] that they should suffer maltreatment patiently, not for their faults, but even when they have committed no faults: κολαφιζόμενοι ὑπομενεῖτε. [8] In this passage there may well be allusion to Ἰησοῦς Χριστὸς κολαφιζόμενος, whose innocent suffering has already been recalled in 1 Pt. 2:21 ff. Christ and His people are smitten by the fists of evil and deluded men. He who truly smites is the Evil One, Satan himself. In his comprehensive list of sufferings in 2 C. 12:7 Paul understands his sickness as the work of the ἄγγελος σατανᾶ, ἵνα με κολαφίζῃ. [9]

Does this usage help us to diagnose the sickness? [10] Older expositors found the explanation of v. 7 in v. 10 and suggested persecutions, the ἄγγελος σατανᾶ being interpreted as a human opponent. The traditional Roman Catholic view is that we have here temptations to licentiousness. But both these explanations founder on the fact that it is here plainly thought that evil demons, and particularly their chief, cause sicknesses which are hard to diagnose. A particular nuance is given to the whole statement by the fact that Paul's sickness may be linked with his visionary states, one of which is vividly

---

Latin and the Romance languages this is for the most part a biblical or ecclesiastical expression. We may note, however, that H. Georges, *Ausführl. lat.-deutsch Handwörterbuch,* I[8] (1913), gives an example of *colaphizare* from Terence (cf. also Wilke-Grimm on κολαφίζω) and of *colaphus* from Plautus, in whom a slave has this nickname. Here is the common speech of comedy. Similarly there are par. between the NT lists of vices and Plautus, cf. Deissmann LO, 269. It is in keeping with the popular nature of the terms that an imprecise foreign heritage was carried with them. As *colaphus* comes from the Gk., κόλαφος may well come from the Semitic sphere, cf. J. M. Stobwasser, *Lat.-deutsch Schulwörterbuch*[2] (1900).

[3] It Cod δ : *colophitzaverunt eum ;* Vulg : *colaphis eum ceciderunt.*

[4] Vulg : *colaphis eum caedere.*

[5] That hitting with the fist תָּקַע ... is an insult (Str.-B., on Mt. 26:67) is obvious. For hitting on the cheek cf. 1 K. 22:24 : הִכָּה עַל־הַלֶּחִי = πατάσσειν ἐπὶ τὴν σιαγόνα (LXX), also Mi. 4:14. D. F. Strauss, *Das Leben Jesu,* II (1836), 488 refers to the Mi. passage and also to Is. 50:6 f. and 53:7. It may be noted that in the Babylonian New Year festival, in a ceremony of repentance, the king is smitten on the cheek by the priest and submits to other degrading rites [v. Rad]. It seems likely from L. Dürr, *Ursprung u. Ausbau d. isr.-jüd. Heilandserwartung* (1925), 133 ff. that there are connections here with the עֶבֶד concept in Dt. Is.

[6] It Codd d g Ambst : *colaphizamur ;* Vulg : *colaphis caedimur.*

[7] Vulg : *colaphizati.*

[8] The reading κολαζόμενοι (e.g., P it syP) prefers a more common word, unless it is a simple mistake. On the other hand, in Mart. Pol., 2, 4 the well-grounded κολαζόμενοι is replaced by κολαφιζόμενοι in some MSS.

[9] Vulg : *colaphizet.*

[10] Cf. the excurs. on 2 C. 12:7 ff. in the Comm., esp. Wnd. 2 K. and Ltzm. K., also → II, 457, and from the theological and medical angle Pr.-Bauer[3], *s.v.*, and esp. F. Fenner, "Die Krankheit im NT," UNT, 18 (1930), 30-40, where κολαφίζειν is regarded as a popular term for → πυκτεύειν, → ὑπωπιάζειν and Paul is interpreted as a hysterical visionary who received the stigmata (Gl. 6:17 → στίγμα) by autosuggestive reaction to the passion of Jesus (2 C. 4:10, → νέκρωσις).

portrayed just before in v. 1 ff. The history of religion and medicine shows that visions and ecstatic experiences may be accompanied by pain, weakness and sickness. This may be seen from the account of Paul's conversion in Ac. 9:9, 18. For three days he could not see and refused nourishment, and it was only gradually that he recovered. "In this regard we may also refer to the story of Jacob's wrestling with Yahweh and his laming by God (Gn. 32), as suggested already by the exposition of Philo, which is very close to the thinking of Paul. In this case it is God Himself who does the injury to the visionary, but in the sphere of Jewish and early Christian ideas the notion that God gives the angel of Satan power over the visionary is quite a possible one. If in bChag., 15b ministering angels were ready to throw Akiba down, in Paul's case an angel of Satan might well be given leave to buffet the visionary. Visions may well be linked with conditions of acute pain which Paul felt to be blows of Satan ... It cannot be ruled out that he actually had to pay for his visions and revelations with new outbreaks of sickness." [11] The few hints as to his sickness in Gl. 4:13-15 fit in with this, since the temptation of the Galatians in face of Paul might well be interpreted as an apotropaic action against demonic influences. Attempts at diagnosis are complicated, of course, if we assume that Gl. forces us to think in terms of an eye affliction, so that the blows of the angel of Satan affected the eyes. But this conclusion is by no means certain. For the fact that the Galatians would willingly have plucked out their eyes and given them to Paul need mean no more than that they were willing to give even the most precious things they had on behalf of their esteemed but sorely afflicted apostle. More significant and rewarding is that in 2 C. 12:7 we also read : ἐδόθη μοι σκόλοψ τῇ σαρκί. Now this might mean → σκόλοψ, "thorn" in the general sense of tormenting affliction. But it probably has the more precise meaning of an illness which causes stabbing pains. And this illness is chronic, since attacks recur. This description of stabbing pains and the blows of Satan's angel seems to fit in best with epilepsy. [12] This would also explain the eye affliction, since epileptic attacks can result in temporary blindness or weakness of the eyes, and this would fit Ac. 9:9, 18 as well as Gl. 4:13-15. Doctors in all ages bear witness that even men who are capable of such great activity and mental lucidity as Paul may well be epileptics. On the other hand, if the names of great historical characters like Frederick the Great or Napoleon are suggested, it is open to doubt whether these were really epileptics. An even more serious difficulty is that in his account Paul seems to suggest a frequent series of attacks, and this would hardly be consistent with the total picture of his life and work. For this reason many doctors [13] incline to think in terms of an affliction which is outwardly related to epilepsy but which on more precise diagnosis proves to be hysteria in perhaps a particularly severe form. In the case of Paul this is supported both by his undeniable capacity for action on the one side and also by his obvious depression on the other. These are characteristics of hysteria or neurasthenia. There may be pains, lassitude, the sense of being bruised, then terrible visions and auditions, conversations with hallucinary persons, yet with no impairment of intellectual power. In such attacks Paul might well have seen an angel of Satan and yet not have been so gravely affected as in genuine epilepsy. Hysteria, like epilepsy, is accompanied by physical and mental changes, by muscular spasms and temporary disruptions of consciousness, so that its victim, like the epileptic, might well give the impression of devil possession. [14] Yet along with hysteria and its manifestations we have

---

[11] Wnd. 2 K., 386.

[12] Cf. M. Dibelius, *Die Geisterwelt im Glauben des Pls.* (1909), 46 : "These individual cases may be compared with the effect of blows. That antiquity viewed epilepsy in this way is proved by Krenkel's catena of quotations from ancient physicians."

[13] So in Ltzm., *ad loc.* the psychiatrist O. Binswanger, who in his *Lehrbuch d. Epilepsie* (1899), 314, thinks Paul was perhaps an epileptic, but in his *Lehrbuch d. Psychiatrie²* (1907, 2nd ed.) is more cautious, cf. also K. Bonhöffer in a letter to Ltzm.

[14] Acc. to Wnd. 2 K., *ad loc.* radical students derive the *Paulus-Saulus epilepticus* motif from the OT, where king Saul is presented as an epileptic. But this is to explain one *X* by

also to consider other sicknesses which are similarly accompanied, e.g., types of nightmare, [15] headache causing severe migraine of the eyes, [16] periodic depressions, malaria, severe sciatica or rheumatism, poor hearing with serious resultant manifestations, even leprosy, [17] or a speech defect such as stammering. [18]

In the long run we cannot give any certain diagnosis. [19] More assured and important, however, is the fact that Paul regards himself as κολαφιζόμενος ὑπὸ τοῦ ἀγγέλου σατανᾶ and that in prayer he comes to see the profound meaning of his condition. Christ, too, was a κολαφιζόμενος; His κολαφίζοντες were those who crucified Him, but finally Satan and his minions. Only Christ can and will defeat Satan and his work in the apostle.

K. L. Schmidt

---

another, and the idea of a motif is contradicted by the objectivity of Paul's statements. To what follies this method can lead is humorously shown in Wnd. 2 K. on 5:13 (179, n. 1): "Radical students might be referred to ψ 67:28 : ἐκεῖ Βενιαμεὶν νεώτερος ἐν ἐκστάσει. Perhaps the younger Benjamin is the Benjaminite Paul, and ψ 67:28 the source of the motif of *Paulus ecstaticus.*"

[15] Ltzm. claims this in the case of a man who acc. to Eus. Hist. Eccl., V, 28, 12 was seduced into a heretical group and had in the night the experience of being beaten by angels, also in the case of Jerome, who reports in Ep., 22, 30 (CSEL, 54 [1910]) that he had the same experience when he read Cicero and other pagan authors too avidly.

[16] Acc. to Wnd. 2 K., *ad loc.* this is the view which, on the basis of his own experience, Uhle-Wettler graphically advances in an essay "Der Pfahl im Fleisch u. die Fausthiebe Satans bei Paulus," *Evang. Kirchenzeitung* (1913), 9/10.

[17] Cf. Wnd. 2 K., *ad loc.* and Fenner, *op. cit.* for references.

[18] Cf. W. K. L. Clarke, Exp. T., 39 (1927/1928), 458-460.

[19] We need hardly consider earlier explanations in terms of spiritual conflicts, e.g., opponents, conscience etc. (cf. Pr.-Bauer³, *s.v.*). Cf. also A. Forcellini, Totius Latinitatis Lexicon, II³ (1861), *s.v.: Dicunt quidam Apostolum saepe dolore capitis esse vexatum. Melius autem puto ita accipi, ut colaphizatus in illis passionibus intelligatur, quas enumeravit ipse dicens : ter virgis caesus sum, semel lapidatus sum,* etc. (2 C. 11:25). *Stimulum ergo carnis appellat tribulationem carnis ; et angelum Satanae illum, quo, quasi immissore, tanta illa pateretur, ostendit. Weidenauer in Lex Bibl. ad h.l. haec habet: Ingeniose autem et verecunde Apostolus haec libidinis irritamenta colaphos appellavit, qui detrimenti nihil, doloris non parum, pudoris vero plurimum sibi afferrent.*

κολλάω, προσκολλάω

† κολλάω.

In the NT we find only the mid. or pass. The act. of the verb, which is found in older and later Greek texts, means "to glue together," "to join together," "to bind." κολλᾶσθαι means "to cleave to."

1. Lk. 10:11: τὸν κονιορτὸν τὸν κολληθέντα ἡμῖν. The word is used fig. here in the sense of "to touch," cf. Rev. 18:5: ἐκολλήθησαν (vl. ἠκολούθησαν) αὐτῆς (sc. Βαβυλῶνος τῆς μεγάλης) αἱ ἁμαρτίαι ἄχρι τοῦ οὐρανοῦ, cf. Ιερ. 28:9: ἤγγισεν εἰς οὐρανὸν τὸ κρίμα αὐτῆς.[1] In the sense of "to attach oneself closely to" κολλάομαι is often used with the dative of object or person.[2] In Ac. 8:29 Philip attaches himself firmly to the chariot of the Ethiopian eunuch. In R. 12:9 Christians are admonished to hold fast to what is good. In Lk. 15:15 the Prodigal Son attaches himself to another person. In Ac. 5:13; 9:26; 10:28 we might very well render "to seek closer intercourse with someone." In Ac. 17:34 this takes the form of discipleship. Cf. 2 Βασ. 20:2; 1 Macc. 3:2; 6:21.[3]

2. On this basis we can see how κολλᾶσθαι comes to be used for intimate association in the form of sexual intercourse. Thus we read in Mt. 19:5: κολληθή-σεται τῇ γυναικὶ αὐτοῦ. This is a quotation from Gn. 2:24, except that the LXX has προσκολληθήσεται. According to the best authorities this is quoted literally in Eph. 5:31, while on the other side the *textus receptus* has προσκολληθήσεται, like the LXX, at Mt. 19:5 (→ προσκολλάω). P. Lond., 1731, 16 (6th cent. A.D.) has κολλᾶσθαι ἑτέρῳ ἀνδρί in the sense of "marriage."[4] In this connection we may also refer to 1 C. 6:16: ὁ κολλώμενος τῇ πόρνῃ ἓν σῶμά ἐστιν. At root this κολλᾶσθαι, like the corresponding דבק[5] in Gn. 2:24; 34:3 (וַתִּדְבַּק נַפְשׁוֹ בְּדִינָה = καὶ προσέσχεν τῇ ψυχῇ Δινας) and 1 K. 11:2 (דָּבַק שְׁלֹמֹה לְאַהֲבָה = ἐκολλήθη Σαλωμων τοῦ ἀγαπῆσαι), does not have the sexual sense, but it acquires this, just as the word copulation is used particularly for marriage.

> There is a distinctive and comprehensive application of Gn. 2:24 in the Halacha (bSanh., 58b): "If a son of Noah lives with his wife in an unnatural way, he is culpable, because we read in Gn. 2:24: 'He shall cleave,' but not in an unnatural way. Raba (d. 352) has said: Is there then something for which an Israelite is not culpable but a non-Israelite is (as R. Chanina thinks)? Rather Raba has said: If a son of Noah lives with the wife of another in an unnatural way, he is not culpable. Why not? It says: To his wife (shall he cleave), but not to the wife of another; he shall cleave, but not in an unnatural manner."[6]

κ ο λ λ ά ω. [1] Loh. Apk., *ad loc.*: "There is an obvious reminiscence of Jer. 28:9"; hence κολλᾶσθαι is simply "to reach to."
[2] Cf. Bl.-Debr. § 193, 3.
[3] Pr.-Bauer³, *s.v.*
[4] Preisigke Wört., *s.v.*
[5] Ges.-Buhl, *s.v.*
[6] Str.-B., I, 803 on Mt. 19:5.

In opposition to κολλᾶσθαι τῇ πόρνῃ, we read in 1 C. 6:17: ὁ δὲ κολλώμενος τῷ κυρίῳ ἓν πνεῦμά ἐστιν. [7]

† προσκολλάω.

1. At Ac. 5:36, instead of the best attested reading προσεκλίθη (Θευδᾶς ... ᾧ προσεκλίθη ἀνδρῶν ἀριθμὸς ὡς τετρακοσίων, "whom a number of about 400 men followed"), we find the less well attested προσεκλήθη, προσεκλήθησαν, προσετέθη, and also προσεκολλήθη, προσεκολλήθησαν. This parallelism makes it perfectly plain that προσκολλάομαι has the same meaning as κολλάομαι 1. The preposition πρός may strengthen the degree of attachment, though this is not wholly certain in view of the fact that the koine tends to prefer compounds to simple forms.

2. Mt. 19:5 text. rec. and Eph. 5:31 [1] use it according to sense 2. of κολλάομαι to denote sexual intercourse. In the second passage this shows how close is the relation between Christ and His → ἐκκλησία. Mk. 10:7 text. rec. amplifies from the par. Mt. 19:5 or the LXX Gn. 2:24 to complete the quotation καταλείψει ἄνθρωπος τὸν πατέρα αὐτοῦ καὶ τὴν μητέρα αὐτοῦ by adding (καὶ) προσκολληθήσεται πρὸς τὴν γυναῖκα (vl. τῇ γυναικὶ) αὐτοῦ.

There are instances of the same usage in P. Oxy., XVI, 1901, 26, 41; 43; 63.

K. L. Schmidt

---

† κολοβόω

"To maim" (from the time of the comic writer Araros, early in the 4th cent. B.C., Fr., 3, CAF, II, p. 216, then Aristot. etc.), [1] mostly limbs, with acc. of that affected or of the one concerned. In the LXX only 2 Βασ. 4:12: κολοβοῦσι τὰς χεῖρας αὐτῶν. [2]

In the NT [3] we find it only in the Mk. Mt. Apc. God has already [4] (Mk. 13:20; in Mt. 24:22 there is less emphasis on the fact that for God it is already done) "cut short" the time of the tribulation in Judaea. That is, He has made it shorter than it would normally have been in terms of the purpose and power of the op-

---

[7] On 1 C. 6:17 cf. 4 Βασ. 18:6: ἐκολλήθη τῷ κυρίῳ, with the comment: οὐκ ἀπέστη ὄπισθεν αὐτοῦ, καὶ ἐφύλαξεν τὰς ἐντολὰς αὐτοῦ, cf. also Sir. 2:3: κολλήθητι αὐτῷ καὶ μὴ ἀποστῇς, also ψ 62:8.

π ρ ο σ κ ο λ λ ά ω. [1] Cf. H. Schlier, Christus u. die Kirche im Epheserbrief (1930), 60-75: "Die himmlische Syzygie."

κ ο λ ο β ό ω. [1] [Debrunner].

[2] The other renderings often have "to be (too) short" for קצר, of the camp, Is. 28:20 (ΣΘ), of the hand of God, Is. 59:1 ('ΑΣ), esp. fig. of the ψυχή or πνεῦμα, Ju. 16:16 ('Α), Job 21:4 ('ΑΣ), Zech. 11:8 ('Α): "to be fainthearted" [Bertram].

[3] Perhaps under the influence of Heb. usage, Str.-B. and Schl. Mt. on 24:22.

[4] This cannot just be a prophetic aor. (B. Weiss[10] [1910] on Mt. 24:22) because of the other tenses in the passage.

pressors. [5] If He had not done so, even those who prove themselves to be the elect by their faithfulness, and who have been wonderfully kept thus far, would be brought to physical destruction.

This interpretation is supported not only by the πᾶσα σάρξ of Mk. 13:20 and par. but also by the whole Mk. Mt. Apc. In the preceding section we read only of physical oppressions which Christians are to escape so far as possible. To be sure, false Messiahs seek to confuse them (Mk. 13:22 and par.), but they will obviously have no success (Mt. 24:24) against the ἐκλεκτοί. Perhaps with the assistance of the πνεῦμα (Mk. 13:11 and par.) and in contrast to the πολλοί (Mt. 24:12), these will remain steadfast up to the parousia, and they will thus remain alive (Mk. 13:13 and par.) up to their final gathering (Mk. 13:27; even those who have fled acc. to Mk. 13:14). The explanation given in → I, 627, n. 12 may perhaps be linked with this.

Delling

---

† κόλπος

a. "Bosom," "lap," Hom. Il., 14, 219; Pind. Olymp., 6, 31; Callim. Hymn., 4, 214 ("mother's womb"); also medically: Philo Spec. Leg., I, 7. For motherly love, Hom. Il., 6, 400; Epigr. Graec., 292, 1. At a meal the place of the guest of honour, Plin. Ep., IV, 22, 4, hence fig. to express an inward relationship, Plut. Cato Minor, 33 (I, 775e). The κόλπος of mother earth is the grave, Epigr. Graec., 56, 1; we read of the κόλπος of the sea in Hom. Il., 18, 140 and 398 (κόλπος of Thetis), and of the κόλπος of the underworld in Epigr. Graec., 237, 3. b. The "fold" of a loose garment used as a pocket, Hdt., VI, 125; it can also be used to hide things, Luc. Hermot., 37, hence fig. in Theocr. Idyll., 16, 16 of the miser: ὑπὸ κόλπου (vl. -ῳ) χεῖρας ἔχων. c. Generally any "arch" or "hollow," e.g., of the bosom of the sea, Pind. Pyth., 4, 49; Ditt. Syll.³, 92, 19, or of the floor of a valley, Pind. Olymp., IX, 131, also medically "fistula."

In the LXX it is mostly used for חיק: [1] a. to express marital fellowship, Dt. 13:7; 28:54; Sir. 9:1, of the fact that the wife belongs and gives herself to her husband, Gn. 16:5; 2 Βασ. 12:8, [2] and also that the husband belongs to the wife, Dt. 28:56. To express loving concern for a child, Nu. 11:12; 3 Βασ. 3:20; 17:19; Ju. 4:16; Is. 49:22 (חֵיק), for a lamb, 2 Βασ. 12:3. b. "Fold of a garment," Ex. 4:6 f.; ψ 73:11; 128:7 (Ps. 129:7 חֵצֶן); Prv. 16:33; 17:23; 6:27. As the place of retribution, Is. 65:6 f.; Ιερ. 39:18; ψ 78:12. c. Generally "hollow" of a chariot, 3 Βασ. 22:35, or of the altar, Ez. 43:13:

---

[5] Eth. En. 80:2; S. Bar. 20:1 contribute little to exposition, esp. if Bar. 20:1 is to be expounded acc. to En. 80:2. Barn., 4, 3 is later. On the other hand cf. Gr. Bar. 9 (T. St., V, 1 [1899]): Originally the moon shone always, but as a punishment God cut short the time of its shining (ἐκολόβωσεν τὰς ἡμέρας αὐτῆς).

κ ό λ π ο ς. Thes. Steph., Pape, Pass.(-Cr.), Liddell-Scott, Moult.-Mill., Pr.-Bauer, *s.v.* On 2. H. Gressmann, "Vom reichen Mann u. armen Lazarus," AAB (1918), No. 7; E. Schwyzer, "Der Götter Knie — Abrahams Schoss" in *G. Wackernagel-Festschrift* (1923), 283 ff.; M. Mieses, OLZ, 34 (1931), 1018 ff.; B. Heller, *ibid.*, 36 (1933), 146 ff.; Str.-B., II, 225; Kl. Lk., *ad loc.*

[1] κόλπος is used for צַחַת at Prv. 19:24; 26:15, for חֹפֶן at Prv. 30:4.

[2] Str.-B., II, 160 wrongly has "to pay back in the good sense."

κόλπωμα (though cf. v. 14, 17). d. κόλπος as the seat of the reins and hence of the feelings, Job 19:27; ψ 34:13; 88:50; Qoh. 7:9.

In Rabb. lit. we find חֵיק, חֵב for κόλπος (Job 31:33), Aram. חובא, חיקא. עובא.[3] a. "Bosom," "lap," bMQ, 24a : an infant who dies before the age of 30 days is carried to the grave in his mother's breast. The sanctuary was in the bosom of the world : בחיקו של עולם: Eka r. on 3:64 par.[4] He who leaves his homeland (Palestine) leaves the bosom of his mother, j MQ, 81c, line 46.[5] חיק refers to the marriage act in T. Jeb., 9, 4. b. "Fold of a garment," Shab., 10, 3; Joma, 7, 1. c. Also generally, bBQ, 81a (branches), 119b (band, hem), bErub., 4a (foundation of the altar, Ez. 43:13 = יסוד).

1. In the NT we find κόλπος as a. "bosom," "lap" in Jn. 13:23 : ἦν ἀνακείμενος εἷς ἐκ τῶν μαθητῶν αὐτοῦ ἐν τῷ κόλπῳ τοῦ Ἰησοῦ, "at supper he took the place of honour on Jesus' breast" (→ ἀνάκειμαι, 654). Applied fig. to membership of the community, we find the same motif in 2 Cl., 4, 5 in an unknown saying of the Lord : Ἐὰν ἦτε μετ' ἐμοῦ συνηγμένοι ἐν τῷ κόλπῳ μου καὶ μὴ ποιῆτε τὰς ἐντολάς μου, ἀποβαλῶ ὑμᾶς. Without the idea of a meal it expresses closest fellowship in Jn. 1:18 : ὁ ὢν εἰς τὸν κόλπον τοῦ πατρός.[6] b. As the "fold of a garment," Lk. 6:38 : μέτρον καλὸν ... δώσουσιν εἰς τὸν κόλπον ὑμῶν. c. As a "bay," Ac. 27:39 : κόλπον ... ἔχοντα αἰγιαλόν.

2. Lk. 16:22 f. has religious significance : ἐγένετο δὲ ἀποθανεῖν τὸν πτωχὸν καὶ ἀπενεχθῆναι αὐτὸν ... εἰς τὸν κόλπον Ἀβραάμ· ἀπέθανεν δὲ καὶ ὁ πλούσιος καὶ ἐτάφη. καὶ ἐν τῷ ᾅδῃ ... ὁρᾷ Ἀβραὰμ ἀπὸ μακρόθεν καὶ Λάζαρον ἐν τοῖς κόλποις[7] αὐτοῦ. In the first instance we are to think in terms of the feast of the blessed at which Lazarus takes the place of honour. But we have also to consider the possibility that v. 22 f. are simply denoting the loving fellowship of Abraham with Lazarus quite apart from the feast of the blessed. Both ideas are found in Rabb. Judaism.[8]

Reception into Abraham's bosom is found in the legend of the martyrdom of the mother and her 7 sons in Eka r. (ed. Buber, 1899, I, p. 43a). The mother says to her youngest son : "And you will be brought to the bosom of our father Abraham : ואתה ניתן בתוך חיקו של אברהם אבינו;[9] Pesikt r., 43 (180b): "Do you wish that all your brothers (without

---

[3] Sometimes paraphrased in the Tg. lit., e.g., Tg. O. Dt. 13:7: אֵשֶׁת חֵיקֶךָ = אִיתַּת קְיָמָךְ.

[4] Ibid. of circumcision : מילה שנתו[נ]נה בחיקו של אדם, cf. Tanch. Buber תצא § 10 (20a). Pesikt. r., 12 (51b): מילה שנתונה בחיק, cf. ibid., 13 (53b). Pesikt. Buber, 25b : בחיקו של אדם הראשון; Bub. (n. 79) suggests we read only אדם Cod. Oxford (cf. Bub., n. 79) חיקו של אברהם. From this isolated reading and Rashi's interpretation of bQid., 72b Heller (148) concludes that "originally to lie in Abraham's bosom meant to be circumcised." → n. 10.

[5] אחיו של אותו האיש הניח חיק אמו וחיבק חיק נכריה.

[6] Cf. the formal par. in bJeb., 77a : Rehoboam sat in David's bosom : היה רחבעם יושב בחיקו של דוד (cf. Str.-B., II, 363); cf. also Cl. Al. Paed., II, 10, 105, 1, where we read of Lazarus: ἀνέθαλλεν ἐν κόλποις τοῦ πατρός.

[7] On the plur. Bl.-Debr.[6] § 141, 5.

[8] The future banquet, e.g., Ex. r. 25 on 16:4 : Yahweh will recline at table, the patriarchs and the righteous at His feet : כביכול מיסב למעלה מן האבות ואבות וכל צדיקים בתוכו. Cf. Mt. 8:11. With no reference to the feast, 3 Macc. 13:17 : οὕτω γὰρ θανόντας ἡμᾶς (the 7 brothers) Ἀβρααμ καὶ Ισαακ καὶ Ιακωβ ὑποδέξονται. Mieses, 1019 quotes an ed. of Jos. which has εἰς τοὺς κόλπους αὐτῶν before ὑποδέξονται (not noted by A. Rahlfs); this is probably a Christian interpolation.

[9] Not in most editions, or in Str.-B.; bGit., 57b (= Seder Elijahu r., 28 [153]) and Eka r. on 1:16 simply have the idea of the reception of the martyrs by Abraham, without the κόλπος motif.

you) should in the future world lie in Abraham's bosom ?" ‏מה אתה מבקש שיהיו כל אחיך‏
‏נתונים בחיקו של אברהם לעתיד לבא‏. bQid 72a/b gives us what purports to be a vision of
the dying patriarch Jehuda I, and in it we read of a certain rabbi that to-day he sits in
Abraham's bosom : ‏היום יושב בחיקו של אברהם‏. The κόλπος motif belongs to a wider
circle of legends about Abraham's work in the hereafter. This was probably taken over
by Judaism, and it includes the motif of the meal, of rest, and of Abraham's judging the
dead (cf. Plat. Resp., X, 614b), bErub., 19a; Gn. r., 48 on 18:1b, though this in a form
which no longer allows us to establish any connection with the κόλπος motif. [10]

Although the κόλπος motif is well adapted to serve as a burial inscr., the Jews were
content with general formulae, e.g., Ἐνθάδε κῖτε Ἰακώβ. Μετὰ τῶν ὁσίων ἡ
κ[ύ]μησις [α]ὐτ<ι>οῦ, [11] often μετὰ τῶν δικέων. So, too, were Christians, both
in services and on tombstones : μετὰ τῶν δικαίων ἀνάπαυσον τὸν δοῦλόν σου or τὴν
δούλην σου. [12] On the other hand, in a prayer in Const. Ap., VIII, 41, 2 the righteous
rest in the bosom of Abraham, Isaac and Jacob. This later and more obscure formula,
which may have been influenced by Mt. 8:11, finds a par. in Semachoth, VII (p. 7b,
line 26): With two steps you will lie in the bosom of the righteous : ‏בחיקם של צדיקים‏.
The formula from the prayer in Const. Ap., VIII, 41 is common on Saïdic [13] and on
Greek tombstones in Nubia and Egypt in the Christian period, e.g., Preisigke Sammelb.,
2034 : Ὁ θεός ... ἀνάπαυσον τὴν ψυχὴν τοῖς δούλοις (!) σου πιστὰ (!) ἐν κόλποις
Ἀβράμ καὶ Ἰσὰκ καὶ Ἰακώβ. Examples take us into the 12th century, and show
how popular the motif was. The reason why Lk. 16:22 f. had this influence in Egypt is
that it corresponds to ancient Egyptian ideas. Abraham's bosom is a place of pleasant
coolness. Fresh water is available for Lazarus, v. 24. The rich man, however, languishes
in the heat of Hades. This idea of refrigerium, of the quickening of the dead in the
hereafter, is deeply rooted in Egyptian religion [14] — so much so that even in Rome
followers of the Egyptian gods have written on their tombstones: "May Osiris grant
thee cool water." [15] We have to assume, therefore, that the κόλπος motif became so
widespread in Egypt because it represented the distinctive idea of refrigerium in a new
Christian form.

Rudolf Meyer

---

[10] Attempts to trace back lying in Abraham's bosom to a sponsorship rite conducted by
Abraham on entrance to Hades (Heller) are simply an inspired guess and have no foundation. Only later do we find a link between the κόλπος motif and sponsorship. The connecting of Abraham's office as porter with circumcision is also the Haggadic assimilation
to Jewish thinking of an originally alien motif.

[11] N. Müller-N. A. Bees, *Die Inschriften d. jüdischen Katakombe am Monteverde zu
Rom* (1919), No. 62.

[12] *Ibid.*, p. 65. To some degree the κόλπος motif was no longer understood even c. 200 :
Tertullian Marc., IV, 34 (CSEL, 47, p. 537): *unde apparet sapienti cuique, qui aliquando
Elysios audierit, esse aliquam localem determinationem, quae sinus dicta sit Abrahae, ad
recipiendas animas filiorum eius, etiam ex nationibus.* On the other hand we read in Orig.
Comm. in Lc., 77 on 16:23 : ὅτε δυνατόν ἐστι μυρίους ἐν τῷ κόλπῳ τοῦ Ἀβραὰμ
ἅμα ἀναπαύεσθαι. There is a humorous depiction of Abraham's bosom as the abode of
the blessed in the princes' entrance to Bamberg cathedral, c. 1240, and cf. *Atlantis*, 8 (1936),
753 [J. Leipoldt].

[13] I owe the reference to Coptic inscr. to J. Leipoldt.

[14] This is the basis of the view that Eth. En. 22:2, 9, also jChag., 77d, lines 55 ff., are
under Egyptian influence, cf. F. Cumont, *Die orient. Religionen im röm. Heidentum* (1910),
276, n. 90.

[15] Δοίη σοι ὁ Ὄσιρις τὸ ψυχρὸν ὕδωρ, Cumont, *loc. cit.*

† κονιάω

From κονία, "dust," also "plaster." The word is found in literature from the time of Aristot. [1] It means "to daub with lime," "to plaster." It occurs in this sense in temple accounts, e.g., C. Michel, *Recueil d'Inscriptions Grecques* (1900), 594, 95 ff. (Delos): τὴν θυμέλην τοῦ βωμοῦ τοῦ ἐν τῆι νήσωι κονιάσαντι Φιλοκράτει. Cf. also Ditt. Syll.³, 695, 87 ff.: τοῖς κατασκευάσασιν [κα]τὰ δύναμιν βωμοὺς πρὸ τῶν θυρῶν καὶ κονιάσασιν. In the LXX Dt. 27:2, 4 (of whitewashing the stones in memory of the Law) and Prv. 21:9 (a saying of popular wisdom): κρεῖσσον οἰκεῖν ἐπὶ γωνίας ὑπαίθρου (under the free heaven) ἢ ἐν κεκονιαμένοις μετὰ ἀδικίας καὶ ἐν οἴκῳ κοινῷ. [2]

In Ac. 23:3 Paul uses the graphic metaphor of the whited wall (τοῖχε κεκονιαμένε) to characterise the laboriously concealed wickedness of Ananias, the high-priest. Along the same lines, Jesus calls the scribes and Pharisees τάφοι κεκονιαμένοι [3] because of their hypocrisy (Mt. 23:27). The image used by Jesus is particularly impressive when one recalls that in Palestine graves were whitewashed in the new year for cultic reasons, and this made it possible for the Pharisees to hold aloof from them as places of impurity. Not least, the biting irony of the saying lies in the fact that the Pharisees represent in themselves the very thing which they studiously avoid. [4] Thus two points are made : 1. the Pharisees are not what they appear to be ; and 2. they are to be avoided as unclean ; intercourse with the "clean" defiles.

J. Schneider

† κόπος, † κοπιάω

In secular Gk. κόπος means a. "beating," [1] "weariness as though one had been beaten," [2] and b. the "exertion" or "trouble" which causes this state. [3] In prose it is the proper word for physical tiredness induced by work, exertion or heat. Expressing

---

κ ο ν ι ά ω. [1] Cf. Liddell-Scott, *s.v.*
[2] The 2nd half of the verse has no Heb. original ; it is found only in the LXX.
[3] For the pass. there is a par. in non-biblical Gk. in CIG, I, 1625, 16 : ἐπισκε[υ]ασθῆναι καὶ κονι[α]θῆνα[ι].
[4] Cf. on this pt. Str.-B., I, 936 f. V. also K. H. Rengstorf on T. Jeb., 3, 4 (*Rabb. Texte*, 34 f., esp. n. 24 and 25). In T. Jeb., 3, 4 we have the questions : "How about the white-washing of the house ?" and : "How about the whitewashing of the grave ?" Rengstorf points out (p. 35, n. 24) that after the destruction of Jerusalem whitewashing of the house was often omitted in sorrow for the overthrow of the sanctuary. Whitewashing graves was not ordered by the Law but was a useful safeguard against defiling contact with them, cf. Rengstorf, *loc. cit.* and also E. L. Rapp on MQ, 1, 2 (*Giessener Mischna*).

κ ό π ο ς κ τ λ. A. v. Harnack, ZNW, 27 (1928), 1 ff.; Trench, 352 f.; Deissmann LO, 265 f.; H. T. Kuist, *Biblical Review*, 16 (1932), 245-249.
[1] Etym. cf. Lithuanian *kapóti*, "to chop up small," Old Slavic *kopati*, "to bury," Boisacq, 492; Walde-Pok., I, 559 ff. Similarly κόπος seems to be used esp. of heavy work on the land.
[2] Hippocr. Aphorismi, 2, 5; Plat. Resp., VII, 537b (with ὕπνοι); Jos. Ant., 1, 336; 2, 257; 3, 25; 8, 244; P. Masp., 32, 50 (with σκυλμός) for the shattering effects of travel.
[3] Aesch. Suppl., 209; with a play on words in the proverbial saying in Makarius Paroimiographus, V, 22 (Leutsch-Schneidewin, Corpus Paroem. Graec., II [1851], p. 180): κόπος κόπον λύει; Test. Iss. 3:5 : διὰ τοῦ κόπου ὁ ὕπνος μοι περιεγένετο; En. 7:3; 11:1.

severe labour, it is synon. with πόνος, which signifies the most tense or strenuous effort, e.g., of the soldier in battle, [4] or the exertions of messengers or manual workers. [5] πόνος is the express term for the strenuous wrestling of the hero. [6] Another slightly different term is μόχθος, which is used for the physical or mental toil that is the lot of men on earth, but with no necessary suggestion of actual labour. [7] A further synon. is κάματος; this refers more specifically to the weariness bound up with strenuous or diligent work. [8]

Along the same lines κοπιᾶν means a. "to tire," Jos. Bell., 6, 142 : οὔτ' εἶκον οὔτ' ἐκοπίων (in battle), and b. "to make great exertions," "to wear oneself out," whether through physical or mental effort, e.g., in burial inscr. of severe and strenuous work : μετὰ τὸ πολλὰ κοπιᾶσαι, [9] spiritualised by Philo in Mut. Nom., 254; Cher., 41: (Rebekah) κοπιῶσα ἐπὶ τῇ συνεχείᾳ τῆς ἀσκήσεως.

In the LXX κοπιᾶν is used esp. for יגע in sense a. of "tiring," e.g., in battle, 2 Βασ. 23:10, but also of the physical and spiritual weariness of the afflicted in their groans and cries (ψ 6:6), and also in sense b. of "exertion" (יגיע), e.g., in connection with work on the land (Jos. 24:13 cf. ψ 126:1), with labouring for wealth, Job 20:18; Sir. 31:3, or with the diligent efforts of the Servant of the Lord on behalf of His people, Is. 49:4. The noun κόπος is mostly used in the LXX for עמל, "toil." [10] It is often used with πόνος, Jer. 20:18; Hab. 1:3. The OT is inclined to view life with realistic pessimism. Life consists very largely of oppressive labour and sorrow, ψ 89:10. Man is born to trouble as the birds to soaring aloft, Job 5:7. Hence κόπος is a fixed term in OT piety. It depicts the trouble which is allotted to man, esp. to the righteous man, in the world, and from which he is delivered by God (ψ 24:18 with ταπείνωσις; 87:15; 106:12; Job 11:16). Thus κοπ- is an important antonym of eschatological hope. The toil of the present and the refreshing rest of the age of salvation (→ ἀνάπαυσις) are contrasted. In the age of salvation there will be no more futile striving, Is. 65:23. As God knows no weariness, Is. 40:28 ff., so the man who is so hard beset by sorrows will never grow tired or weak then, Is. 33:24 (חלה).

In the NT κοπ- is used in the sense 1. "to weary," literally in Jn. 4:6 (ἐκ τῆς ὁδοιπορίας), [11] fig. of the confessing community which has not fainted under assault (Rev. 2:3, with → ὑπομένω).

It is also used in the sense 2. "to tire oneself out," lit. in Mt. 6:28 and par.; Lk. 5:5; Eph. 4:28 (κοπιάτω ἐργαζόμενος ταῖς ἰδίαις χερσίν); 2 Tm. 2:6 (τὸν

---

[4] πόνος μάχης, Hom. Il., 16, 568; 6, 77; 17, 718; synon. with πόλεμος, 12, 348 and 361.
[5] Ps.-Plat. Ax., 368a/b of βάναυσος : πονουμένων ἐκ νυκτὸς εἰς νύκτα.
[6] Esp. of Heracles. πόνος is then a favourite term of the Stoics, e.g., Epict. Diss., I, 2, 15; II, 1, 10 and 13 f. As in Paul, often with ἀγρυπνεῖν, I, 7, 30 : οὐ πονήσομεν οὐδ' ἀγρυπνοῦμεν ἐξεργαζόμενοι ...; Harnack, 4 suggests that for this reason Paul may have intentionally avoided the secular πόνος. In the NT πόνος occurs only 4 times (Col. 4:13; Rev. 16:10 f.; 21:4 : in the New Jerusalem οὔτε πένθος οὔτε κραυγὴ οὔτε πόνος). Along the lines of secular Gk. 1 Cl., 5, 4 uses πόνος for the exertions and sufferings of the apostles.
[7] Eur. Phoen., 784 : πολύμοχθος Ἄρης; Job 2:9 : ὠδῖνες καὶ πόνοι, οὓς εἰς τὸ κενὸν ἐκοπίασα μετὰ μόχθων. 20 times in Qoh. (1:3; 2:10, 11, 18, 19, 20, 21 etc.). 3 times in the NT, always with κόπος, 2 C. 11:27; 1 Th. 2:9; 2 Th. 3:8.
[8] Theophr. Fr., 7, 13 : τῷ δὲ βραχίονι κοπιαρώτερον διὰ κενῆς ῥίπτειν ἢ λίθον ἢ ἄλλο τι βάρος, διότι σπασματωδέστερον καὶ καματωδέστερον. Hom. Od., 9, 126 of shipbuilding.
[9] In Deissmann LO, 265, n. 1. Cf. also burial inscr., CIG, 9552, Rome : τεὶς [= ὅστις] μοι πολλὰ ἐκοπίασεν, cf. R. 16:6.
[10] In the minor prophets for און (perversity, evil, distress), Mi. 2:1; Hab. 3:7; Zech. 10:2; of Jacob, Hos. 12:4 (און).
[11] Cf. Jos. Ant., 2, 321: ὑπὸ τῆς ὁδοιπορίας κεκοπωμένοι, from κοπόω (κοπόομαι = κοπιάω, cf. Liddell-Scott); cf. Is. 40:31.

κοπιῶντα γεωργόν), fig. and with an eschatological reference in Mt. 11:28 f.: Jesus, who ushers in the time of salvation, will bring refreshing rest to those who thus far have fainted under the burden of the legal requirements of Judaism. [12] In the expression κόπους παρέχειν, [13] κόπος has the general sense of "to trouble," Mk. 14:6 and par.; Lk. 11:7; 18:5; Gl. 6:17. κόπος is used in Rev. 2:2 (with ὑπομονή and ἔργα) and 14:13 (ἀναπαήσονται ἐκ τῶν κόπων αὐτῶν) in eschatological connection with the piety of suffering which expects heavenly refreshment in place of earthly toil. Here, too, the actualisation of salvation ends earthly distress and turns it into its opposite. Paul, who as an apostle is a favoured servant of Christ, regards it as normal and fitting (Mt. 5:11 f.) that many troubles should come upon him (2 C. 6:5 : ἐν ἀκαταστασίαις, ἐν κόποις, ἐν ἀγρυπνίαις; 2 C. 11:27: κόπῳ καὶ μόχθῳ, ἐν ἀγρυπνίαις πολλάκις). Indeed, the fact that he has to bear more κόποι than the others strengthens him in his apostolic awareness and assurance (2 C. 11:23). κόποι take precedence in his appeal to the experiences which show that he is a servant of Christ (2 C. 11:23). Here the passive and active senses shade into one another ("toil" and "trouble").

A final and distinctive NT use of κοπ- is for Christian work in and for the community. [14] This use is found first and most frequently (19 times) in Paul, and it seems to have been then adopted by the community (Harnack). Paul is first referring to his own work (1 C. 15:10). As the term for manual labour, κόπος was well adapted to describe this (1 C. 4:12; 2 Th. 3:8). But like all his work for the community, this wins for him the deeper sense of a burden which he takes up for Christ (1 Th. 2:9). As an apostle, Paul had no obligation to work with his hands. But as a former persecutor of the Church he goes beyond the call of duty and engages in this work for which he expects a special reward from God (1 C. 9:18 → μισθός) and which is for him personally a ground of "boasting" (→ καύχημα), 9:15. Paul uses κόπος to show that his work for Christ is a severe and exhausting burden. Yet it is also his pride and joy (2 C. 11:23; 1 C. 15:10). The goal which he energetically seeks in this work is that he may present mature Christians to Christ (Col. 1:29 : κοπιῶ ἀγωνιζόμενος). Like the man who, working for reward, receives no payment for poor work, he has always the accompanying concern (Gl. 4:11) and the constant spur of anxiety that his work will not finally be acknowledged (1 C. 3:8) or that he will lose the reward of his labour through hostile circumstances (1 Th. 3:5). The reward is consistently thought of in eschatological terms (Phil. 2:16).

Paul uses κοπ- not only for his own work but also for the missionary and pastoral work of others (1 C. 15:58; 2 C. 10:15). Since their work is labour in the Lord (R. 16:12) and for the Lord and the community (R. 16:6), it is worthy of the highest esteem (1 C. 16:16; 1 Th. 5:12). The mainspring of this laborious toil is love (1 Th. 1:3 : κόπου τῆς ἀγάπης, labour of love). In the τοὺς κοπιῶντας ἐν ὑμῖν (with προϊστάμενοι) of 1 Th. 5:12 the reference is to office-bearers of the congregation, though voluntary efforts do not seem to be in any sense excluded. [15]

The same distinctive Pauline usage is found in the Past. (1 Tm. 4:10; 5:17), and then again in Jn. (4:38) and Ac. (20:35). On the other hand, it is less prominent

---

[12] J. Jeremias, "Jesus als Weltvollender," BFTh, 33, 4 (1930), 73.
[13] Deissmann B, 262 ff.; P. Tebt., 21, 10.
[14] Harnack, 1 ff.
[15] Dob. Th., 215 f.

in the 2nd cent. (Barn., 19, 10). With increased esteem for the officers of the Church it was perhaps felt that κοπιᾶν, with its sense of manual work, was not wholly fitting. [16] 1 Cl., 5, 4 again speaks of the πόνοι of Christian heroes and martyrs.

Hauck

κοπετός, κόπτω, ἀποκόπτω,
ἐγκοπή, ἐγκόπτω, ἐκκόπτω

---

† κοπετός, † κόπτω.

Contents : A. The General Custom of Mourning : 1. Beating oneself in Mourning ; 2. The Noisy Lamentation of the East ; 3. The Posture at κοπετός ; 4. The Origin of Loud Lamentation. B. Mourning in the Greek and Roman World : I. Popular Mourning : 1. Age and Origin of the Custom ; 2. Attacks on the part of the State and Philosophy ; 3. The Change in Meaning and the Constructions of κόπτομαι ; 4. The Roles of the Sexes in κοπετός. II. Mourning in the Cultus : 1. The East ; 2. The Greeks. C. Mourning in the OT : I. Popular Mourning : 1. Linguistic ; 2. The Form of κοπετός ; 3. The Mourners ; 4. The Content of κοπετός ; 5. The Prohibition of κοπετός. II. The Lamentation of the Prophets : 1. Form and Content ; 2. Examples ; 3. The Prophetic Renunciation of Popular Mourning ; 4. The Prophetic Declaration of κοπετός ; 5. κοπετός in Prophecies of Salvation. D. Mourning in Judaism : 1. Sources and Usage ; 2. Customs and Times of κοπετός : a. Before Burial ; b. After Burial ; 3. The Mourners : a. Mourning Women ; b. Relatives and Men ; c. National Mourning ; 4. Significance and Motifs of Mourning. E. Mourning in the NT : I. Popular κοπετός : 1. Mourning in the Stories of Raising Again : a. Before Burial ; b. After Burial ; 2. The Burial Game of Children (Mt. 11:17) ; 3. κοπετός in the Passion : a. Before Burial ; b. After Burial ; 4. Mourning in the Early Church : a. Men as

---

[16] Harnack, 7.

κ ο π ε τ ό ς κ τ λ. Pr.-Bauer³, 735 f.; Trench, 151 f.; Buttmann § 131, 4. On A.-B. : Rohde ⁹, ¹⁰ (1925), I, 220 ff.; C. Sittl, *Die Gebärden d. Griechen u. Römer* (1890), 65-78 (c. 4 : "Totenklage"); K. F. Ameis-C. Hentze, *Anhang zu Homers Ilias*, VIII³ (1886), 136 ff. (on Il., 24, 677 ff.; with additional bibl.); *Handbuch d. klass. Altertumswiss.*, IV, 1, 2; I. v. Müller-A. Bauer, *Die griech. Privat- u. Kriegsaltertümer*² (1893), 214; *ibid.*, IV, 2, 2; H. Blümner, *D. röm. Privatsaltertümer*³ (1911), 486; J. G. Frazer, *The Golden Bough*, IV : *Adonis, Attis, Osiris*, I³ (1914), II³ (1927). On C. : RE³, XX, 83, 36-90, 50 (R. Zehnpfund, "Trauer u. Trauergebräuche bei d. Hebräern"); Hastings DB, III, 453 ff. (T. Nicol, "Mourning"), with further bibl. in both these art.; K. F. Keil, *Handbuch d. bibl. Archäologie*, II (1859), 101 ff.; W. Nowack, *Hbr. Archäologie*, I (1894), 192 ff.; J. Benzinger, *Hbr. Archäologie*³ (1927), 133 ff.; A. Bertholet, *Kulturgeschichte Israels* (1919) = *A History of Hebrew Civilization* (1926); H. J. Elhorst, "Die israelit. Trauerriten," ZAW, Beih. 27 (1914), 115 ff.; W. Baumgartner, "Die Klagegedichte des Jeremia," ZAW, Beih. 32 (1917); H. Jahnow, "Das hbr. Leichenlied im Rahmen d. Völkerdichtung," ZAW, Beih. 36 (1923); P. Heinisch, "D. Totenklage im AT" (= *Bibl. Zeitfragen*, XIII, 9/10 [1931]), quoted as Heinisch Totenklage; also "Die Trauergebräuche bei den Israeliten" (*Bibl. Zeitfragen*, XIII, 7/8, 1931), quoted as Heinisch Trauergebräuche. On D. : J. Hamburger, *Realencyklopädie des Judt.* I and II (1896), s.v. "Trauer," "Kaddisch"; M. Guttmann, מפתח תלמוד, Clavis Talmudis, I (1906), s.v. אבל, II (1907), s.v. אונן; S. Krauss, *Talmudische Archäologie*, II (1911), 54 ff.; Str.-B., I, 521 ff., IV, 578 ff.

Mourners ; b. Relationship of Jews and Christians ; 5. The Further History of Mourning in the Church. II. Mourning in the Life, at the Death and on the Coming Again of Christ : 1. Jesus and the κοπετός of His Times ; 2. κοπετός for the Dying Christ ; 3. Eschatological κοπετός : a. The Prophecy of Zech. 12:10; b. Mourning for Babylon ; 4. Summary.

A. The General Custom of Mourning.

1. It is common to Gk. and many other languages of East and West that verbs with the basic sense of "to beat" take on the secondary sense "to mourn." The Heb. ספד, [1] the Lat. plangor, [2] the Gothic flōkan all have senses par. to those of the mid. [3] of κόπτω. κόπτομαι, orig. "to beat oneself," has in the NT [4] only the one sense of "to mourn," "to lament," and the noun κοπετός [5] has everywhere the derived sense of "mourning," "lamentation for the dead." These linguistic relationships are enough to show that some kind of beating is one part of mourning, if not the part. In fact, when death entered a house, one would see "women sorrowfully beating on their breasts, wan and with their hair unloosed," not merely on the border between East and West as in Schiller's Siegesfest, but on both sides of the border, and on the eastern side almost everywhere right up to our own times.

Men beat themselves primarily in reaction to two strong feelings, remorse (→ n. 128) and pain. Pain for pain ! Pain of soul is so overwhelming that man pays no heed to physical pain. By wounding himself — this is often a secondary motif in remorse as well as suffering — he bears witness to the genuineness of his sorrow. This explains the scratching of the cheeks [6] or the breast, [7] the rending of other parts of the body [8] etc. which we find in many different cultures. It may be that for many peoples it was essential that blood should flow, even though we cannot assume in every case that we have here an original blood sacrifice which was meant to take the place of primitive human sacrifice — a sacrifice which would either placate the particularly evil spirits which infest the house of death, or satisfy the demand of the dead for blood, or protect the dead themselves against demons. [9] Particularly in later times it is more likely that the explanation lies in a direct demand that grief should be expressed outwardly and that it should be made visible on one's own body. Certainly the beating of the breast [10] or cheeks [11] or head [12] cannot be interpreted in terms of such sacrifice, though here, too, we cannot wholly reject the idea of a cultic background ; for here, too, some influence

---

[1] Cf. Jer. 22:18 with Is. 32:12, also under C.

[2] Cf. Aug. Confessions, III, 11, where the verb refers to weeping, with a play on the mortuos plango of the bell.

[3] Only once (Aesch. Choeph., 423) in a fig. etym. do we find the act.: κόπτειν κομμόν; elsewhere it, too, is mid., e.g., LXX Gn. 50:10; Zech. 12:10.

[4] The act. in the original sense "to strike (off)" occurs only at Mk. 11:8 and par.

[5] Other forms with the same sense are κομμός (Bion, ed. U. v. Wilamowitz-Möllendorff in Bucolici Graeci [1905], 1, 97, → n. 3) and κόπος Aesch. Suppl., 209; Eur. Tro., 794 : κόπος στέρνων. Already in the class. period κομμός loses the original concrete sense and comes to mean a "lament," synon. with → θρῆνος (cf. Aristot. Poet., 12, p. 1452b, 18 and 24).

[6] Cf. Nonnus Dionys., 24, 182 etc.; cf. Sittl, 68.

[7] Hom. Il., 19, 284 f., cf. AOB, No. 665 (Byblos); Statius Thebais (ed. A. Klotz [1908], 6, 178; Heinisch Trauergebräuche, 58.

[8] Cf. Jer. 16:6; 41:5 (LXX 48:5 : κοπτόμενοι, → C. (I, 1); 48:37 (Moab ; LXX, 31:37; κόψονται q.v.); 47:5 (Philistia ; LXX 29:5 : κόψεις in another connection and sense → n. 56), also B. Meissner, Babylonien u. Assyrien, I (1920), 425.

[9] Heinisch Trauergebräuche, 60-66.

[10] E.g., Is. 33:12; Lk. 23:48; Luc. De Luctu, 12.

[11] LXX Ez. 6:9; 20:43; cf. P. Kahle, "Die Totenklage im heutigen Ägypten," Eucharisterion f. H. Gunkel, I (1923), 346 ff.

[12] Cf. Il., 22, 33 (→ n. 25), perhaps also Jer. 2:37; cf. Lk. 23:48 D; → n. 105.

may well have been exerted by the ancient belief that "to the invisibly present soul of the departed the most extreme expressions of grief for his loss are the most dear." [13]

2. What is true of κοπετός in the narrower sense is also true of it in the broader sense of lamentation for the dead. This is very seldom quiet grief. It normally shows sign of violent exaggeration. And we might almost venture the generalisation that the further east one goes the more uncontrolled and persistent the wailing is and the longer the laments continue. [14] The ancient peoples of the East, and in some cases their modern successors, show remarkable unanimity as regards mourning. In Egypt the day of death is the day of lamenting for the dead [15] by the women of the house helped by paid women mourners. Violent and persistent outcries alternated with laments, and between individual laments or strophes there would again be loud cries : "Alas for the misfortune," "O sweet father, my lord" etc. [16]

In Babylon mourning was even more graphic and pompous. We read of a great host of mourners who came into action when the need arose. [17] The peoples between Egypt and Babylon, e.g., Syrians, Arabs and Israelites, [18] yield the same essential features as the two dominant states.

3. The common posture at mourning in both the wider and the narrower sense was the typical posture of grief, i.e., that of sitting on the ground [19] in the dust from which man is taken and to which he returns, and of beating on the breast and cheeks. This was done as long as the corpse was in the house and then again at pauses in the burial procession. [20] In relation to modern Palestine and Syria, and especially ancient and modern Egypt, we also read of a dance of death by the wailing women in which the women (in Egypt) beat their cheeks to the rhythm of the tambourine. [21]

4. The origin of noisy lamentation is to be explained along the same lines as that of κοπετός in the narrower sense. "Violent lamentation is already a part of the cult of the departed," says Rohde. [22] It is perhaps of a piece with this that the gestures of grief are so often depicted in Egyptian temples. [23] But among many peoples the origin may be the exact opposite. Like self-mutilation, the loud outcries, along with various other noises (cf. Mk. 5:38 f.) which may accompany lamentation for the dead, are designed to frighten away the evil spirits which particularly threaten the house of death or even to frighten away the spirit of the dead man himself. [24] But this explanation hardly fits

---

[13] Rohde, I, 222 f.
[14] For the violence of Oriental and esp. here Indian κοπετός, cf. the impressive depiction in Nonnus Dionys., 24, 181 ff.:

καὶ γόος ἄσπετος ἔσκε· φιλοθρήνων δὲ γυναικῶν
πενθαλέοις ὀνύχεσσι χαράσσετο κύκλα προσώπου,
καὶ μεσάτου στέρνοιο διεσχίζοντο χιτῶνας
στήθεα γυμνώσαντες, ἀμοιβαίῃσι δὲ ῥιπαῖς
τυπτομένων παλάμῃσιν ἴτυς φοινίσσετο μαζῶν
αἱμοβαφής.

[15] In the so-called harpist song, AOT, I, 29.
[16] Cf. A. Erman-H. Ranke, Ägypten u. ägypt. Leben im Altertum (1923), 364 f.
[17] Cf. Meissner, II (1925), 67 and 95; AOT, 275.
[18] → C. I, 3; D. 3a.
[19] Cf. Lam. 2:10; Job 2:13; Ez. 8:14; 26:16; also Heinisch Totenklage, 19 f.; Trauerge-bräuche, 36 ff.; Meissner, I, 425; Erman-Ranke, 364.
[20] → D. 3a.
[21] On the dance cf. A. Wiedemann, Das Alte Ägypten (1920), 368, 372 f.; Blümner, 493; P. Kahle, FRL, 19, 1 (1923), 349; Heinisch Totenklage, 19 f.; Trauergebräuche, 57 ff.
[22] Rohde, I, 222 f.; cf. also the bibl. notes of O. Weinreich, ibid., p. IX ff.; on the OT, Bertholet, 96 and 269.
[23] Cf. C. J. Ball, Light from the East (1899), 119.
[24] Cf. Heinisch Trauergebräuche, 95 ff.

those cases in which the laments bear direct witness to the love of those who mourn, e.g., the cries cited from Egypt (→ n. 16) or the laments of Israel. Here the main themes of lamentation are the grief of the bereaved, the honouring of the dead and the awakening of sympathy among acquaintances present (→ B. I. 4.).

B. Mourning in the Greek and Roman World.

I. Popular Mourning.

1. Both forms of κοπετός, i.e., beating the body and loud crying, are found from the earliest period of Gk. culture. Hom. depicts the custom of true κοπετός not merely among the Trojans (Il., 22, 33 of Priam : κεφαλὴν²⁵ δ' ὅ γε κόψατο χερσὶν ὑψόσ' ἀνασχόμενος) but also among the Greeks (Il., 19, 284 f. Briseïs²⁶ when she sees the dead Patroclus χερσὶ δ' ἄμυσσεν στήθεα, "with her hands tore her breast"). It may be conjectured that these violent customs, like some excesses in certain cults, had their home in the East, which seems in every respect to have been more inclined to the strong expression of emotion (→ n. 14). At any rate, in Gk. civilisation κοπετός seems to have been most passionate later in Hellenised portions of the Orient, and it is worth noting that the Orient was always the model for this type of utterance. Thus Electra (Aesch. Choeph., 418 ff.) compares her κομμός (→ n. 3 and 5) with Persian lamentation for the dead to stress the intensity of her grief (cf. also Aesch. Pers., 683).

2. This helps us to understand why Solon found it necessary to take measures against these violent customs, which Greek sensibility found excessive, Plut. Sol., 21 (I, 90c): ἀμυχὰς κοπτομένων ἀφεῖλεν, "he abolished the practice of scratching in mourning."²⁷ His legal enactments were copied in other codes and even in the Roman Law of the Twelve Tables. Nevertheless, κόπτεσθαι ἐπὶ τεθνηκότι continued, as may be seen from many depictions on vases, and it maintained its place at two points in the solemnities, namely, the showing (πρόθεσις) of the corpse in the house and the actual interment.²⁸ In Rome the Law of the Twelve Tables and the restrictions of Sulla did not prevent increasing extravagance, and members of all classes laid value on the greatest possible pomp at burial. To meet the high costs, not least for the many professional mourners (B. I. 4.), burial societies were formed which collected regular contributions and then bore the burial expenses of members.²⁹ For a description of κοπετός in the Roman period, with all the essential features, cf. Luc. De Luctu, 12 : Οἰμωγαὶ δὲ ἐπὶ τούτοις καὶ κωκυτὸς γυναικῶν καὶ παρὰ πάντων δάκρυα καὶ στέρνα τυπτόμενα καὶ σπαραττομένη κόμη καὶ φοινισσόμεναι παρειαί, καί που καὶ ἐσθὴς καταρρήγνυται καὶ κόνις ἐπὶ τῇ κεφαλῇ πάττεται.

No more effective than the attacks of the state on the custom of κοπετός were those of popular Hellenistic philosophy, which obviously perceived the oriental character of the custom and which rejected as abhorrent the exaggerated laments and outcries.³⁰ But

---

²⁵ On vases we often see men too. Their hair is shaved off in token of grief and they beat their heads, cf. Sittl, 66; Heinisch Trauergebräuche, 42 ff.; Rohde, I, 221, n. 2; O. Benndorf, Griech. u. sicilische Vasenbilder (1868 ff.), 6 (in Rohde).

²⁶ We can hardly agree with Sittl, 65⁶ that the grief of Briseïs is only at her own misfortune. Nor does his historical judgment seem to be in accord with the facts when he argues that there was a palpable first Gk. period which excluded violent gestures.

²⁷ Cf. ibid., 12 (I, 84d): At burials Solon softened τὸ σκληρὸν καὶ τὸ βαρβαρικὸν ᾧ συνείχοντο πρότερον αἱ πλεῖσται γυναῖκες (cf. Rohde, 225, n. 3).

²⁸ Cf. Rohde, 224 f.; J. Müller, 214; Blümner, 486. In some places like Delphi, Keos etc. lamentation was forbidden outside the house, and in particular profound silence had to be observed during the procession to the grave (Rohde, 225).

²⁹ Cf. Blümner, 488 f.

³⁰ Plut. Consolatio ad Uxorem suam, 4 (II, 609b): ἡ θρήνων ἄπληστος ἐπιθυμία καὶ πρὸς ὀλοφύρσεις ἐξάγουσα καὶ κοπετούς ("who proceeds both to loud outcries and to a wild beating of the breast") αἰσχρὰ μὲν οὐχ ἧττον τῆς περὶ τὰς ἡδονὰς ἀκρασίας.

κοπετός in the strict sense had for too long been an essential part of mourning in the popular view, as may be seen from the change of meaning of κοπετός, to be abolished either by force or reason.

3. We have already mentioned (→ 831) that by synecdoche κοπετός, as a chief part of mourning, very early came to be used as a general term for mourning. Perhaps the verb is already to be construed this way in Aesch. Pers., 683 : (πόλις στένει, κέκοπται), and cf. Plat. Resp., X, 619c : (κόπτεσθαί τε καὶ ὀδύρεσθαι τὴν αἵρεσιν); Eupolis Fr., 347 = CAF, I, p. 349 (ὅσος δ᾽ ὁ βρυγμὸς καὶ κοπετὸς ἐν τῇ στέγῃ); Anth. Pal., XI, 135, 1: μηκέτι, μηκέτι, Μᾶρκε, τὸ παιδίον, ἀλλ᾽ ἐμὲ κόπτου etc. κόπτομαι and κοπετός are used generally in the NT period and later (cf. Plut. Sol. [→ 833]; Liban., ed. J. J. Reiske, IV [1797], p. 149, 4 ff.) in this sense. Cf. also Schol. on Aristoph. Lys., 397 (ed. G. Dindorf [1823], II, p. 103): κόπτεσθαι δὲ κεφαλὴν χερσίν, ὅτι ἐντελῶς λέγεται, κόπτεσθαι κατὰ μόνας ἀτελῶς. καὶ κόπτεσθαι τὸ πενθεῖν. ὅθεν κοπετός, τὸ πένθος, ὁ θρῆνος. Hesych.: κοπετός· θρῆνος μετὰ ψόφου χειρῶν.

A change in the construction of the verb corresponds to the shift in meaning. Like the par. τύπτειν, [31] it was originally combined with the acc. of the part of the body affected, cf. Hom. Il., 22, 33; Schol. on Aristoph. Lys., 397 (→ supra); also Ev. Pt., 8, 28 : κόπτεσθαι τὰ στήθη. [32] But it is found either in the absol., Aesch. Pers., 683; Plat. Phaed., 60a; Mt. 11:17; 24:30, or with the acc. of the person deceased, Aristoph. Lys., 396; Anth. Pal., XI, 135, 1; Lk. 8:52; [33] cf. also Luc. Syr. Dea, 6 : μνήμην, sc. of Adonis τύπτονται, or, under Heb. influence, with ἐπί and the acc., e.g., Rev. 1:7; → n. 126, or with ἐπί and the dat., Zech. 12:10 vl.; Rev. 18:9 vl.

4. A question which calls for separate treatment is that of the part of the sexes in κοπετός. As in the case of other religious customs which originated in the Orient, e.g., the Thracian mysteries, it is striking that women especially are the mourners, and that even in early times these seem to have been paid women, sometimes with hired men as well. In Egypt crowds of women accompanied the deceased to the grave and sang their laments, interrupted from time to time by individual cries. [34] In Babylon the lamentation of wailers [35] became proverbial. [36] They even appear in the Descent of Ishtar in connection with mourning for Tammuz. [37] Similar customs are found in Syria, Palestine and elsewhere. [38] The task of these women was 1. to express the grief of relatives more fully and dramatically than they could do themselves, 2. to magnify the praise of the dead in their songs, [39] 3. to stir up in all who hear admiration for the deceased, sympathy with the bereaved and participation in the mourning (hence the frequent introduction of the words "weep," "bewail," "mourn," etc.), and 4. to ease the pain of relatives by comforting thoughts. [40]

In Greece we find mourning women in the mourning for Patroclus (Il., 19, 284) and Hector (24, 722 : ἐπὶ δὲ στενάχοντο γυναῖκες). Further evidence for the early ex-

---

[31] Cf. Luc. De Luctu, 12 : στέρνα τυπτόμενα; Lk. 23:48 : τύπτοντες τὰ στήθη; also 18:13.

[32] The LXX construes Is. 32:12 differently : ἐπὶ τῶν μαστῶν κόπτεσθε.

[33] → n. 99.

[34] Cf. AOB Abb. 195 f. etc. (→ 832).

[35] Meissner, I, 424, 427.

[36] AOT, 275.

[37] Cf. AOT, 210; Meissner, II, 67 and 95; → 835.

[38] For Syria cf. AOB, 665; generally cf. Heinisch Totenklage, 10 f., where we are also told of modern practices in Arabia, Egypt, Corsica etc. in which the ancient ceremonial still lives on.

[39] Ibid., 31 ff.

[40] For grounds of comfort, ibid., 36 ff.

istence of the custom may be found on vases such as that described in Rohde (224), where a whole host of women follows the bier with its company of men, wailing and beating their heads. Whether in very early days the Greeks had paid mourners as well as singers (→ θρηνέω, 149) may be doubted, though perhaps popular customs are reflected in poetic and artistic representations, e.g., when the nine Muses appear as mourning women in Hom. Od., 24, 60 f., or when the Sirens appear in a similar capacity on a burial relief, with one hand rumpling their hair and with the other beating their breasts. [41]

Solon (→ 833) wished to restrict the right of mourning to the nearest women relatives, yet in Athens, too, there still seems to have been a company of hired men and women mourners who sounded their native notes. This is further evidence of the fact that the Orient was felt to be a model in κοπετός. [42] Plato, too, bears witness to the existence of κοπτόμενοι in respect of epic and tragic poetry (Resp., X, 605d). Socrates, of course, did not wish to hear the wailing of even his own spouse; at his request ἐκείνην ἀπῆγόν τινες τῶν τοῦ Κρίτωνος βοῶσάν τε καὶ κοπτομένην (Plat. Phaed., 60a). But on the whole women remained in the forefront, not only in the classical period, but also in the Hellenistic and Roman, in which there was a new flood of oriental influences. Plut. Fab. Max., 17 (I, 184d) speaks of κοπετοὶ γυναικεῖοι, Luc. De Luctu, 12 of κωκυτὸς γυναικῶν, Statius (Thebais, 6, 178 → n. 7) of women who mourn, not sparing their hair and breasts, and the well-known burial relief of the Haterii [43] shows women esp. with the hair unloosed beating on their breasts. [44] Nevertheless, in a few cases, esp. in Hellenistic parts of the Orient, there is no clear distinction between the roles of the sexes. Both beat on their breasts, rumple their hair, scratch their cheeks etc. [45] Above all, we find professional mourners of both sexes in both East and West.

II. Mourning in the Cultus (→ θρηνέω, 149).

1. Apart from private mourning with its originally cultic origins the most violent κοπετός in both the oriental and the Greek worlds is to be found in religious ceremonies, namely, in cults whose central point is the death and rising again of a deity.

The OT mentions (Ez. 8:14) ritual mourning for one of the oriental gods, i.e., the Babylonian Tammuz, to whom many religious songs were dedicated. [46] Along with many individual details the cult of Tammuz shared its decisive characteristic with the cults of the Syrian Adonis, the Phrygian Attis and the Egyptian Osiris. As Ishtar weeps for Tammuz, so does Astarte for Adonis, Cybele for Attis [47] and Isis for Osiris, [48] and as these goddesses of ancient legend weep for their divine loved ones, so do their human followers in the days of the great annual feasts devoted to the memory of the dying god, with all the expressive actions with which the Orient gives itself to lamentation. [49]

---

[41] Sittl, 75.

[42] Cf. Plat. Leg., VII, 800e and the Schol. (Rohde, 225, n. 1); → 833.

[43] Cf. Blümner, 486, n. 4; Sittl, 70.

[44] Cf. Dion. Hal. Ant. Rom., XI, 31, 3 (though this is not mourning for a dead person) and → 838; 842; 846.

[45] Cf. Sittl, 67.

[46] Cf. the examples in A. Ungnad, D. Religion d. Babylonier u. Assyrer (1921), 231 ff. and AOT, 270 ff., esp. the 2nd song, which is obviously put on the lips of Ishtar; cf. also Frazer, I, 9 f. and the bibl., ibid., 10, n. 1.

[47] Cf. Frazer, I, 272.

[48] Cf. "the lament which became the model of all laments" in A. Erman, Die Religion d. Ägypter (1934), 73.

[49] Luc. De Sacrificiis, 15 tells of a distinctive form of mourning which is obviously specifically Egyptian, namely, of πένθος and κοπετός for sacrificial beasts: αἱ δὲ θυσίαι καὶ παρ' ἐκείνοις αἱ αὐταί, πλὴν ὅτι πενθοῦσι τὸ ἱερεῖον καὶ κόπτονται περιστάντες ἤδη πεφονευμένον, οἱ δὲ καὶ θάπτουσι μόνον ἀποσφάξαντες.

2. The corresponding Greek mystery rites based on the myth of the dying and rising god stand under oriental influence or derive directly from the Orient. A central part of the myth is loud lamentation for the cultic god who is so dreadfully snatched away from life, for Persephone and Dionysus as well as for Adonis and Osiris, and then when there is the great turning back to life we have corresponding jubilation at the salvation of the god. The rite follows the myth. Mourning and rejoicing accompany the climaxes of the annually repeated cultic drama, cf. Hier. in Ez. 8:14 (MPL, 25, p. 83a): ... interfectionem et resurrectionem Adonidis planctu et gaudio prosequens. If the joy of the devotees finds wild expression at the end, the presupposition is the equally wild lamentation to which the same devotees have given themselves in mourning for the god.[50] Ecstatic gestures in which the whole passion of the Orient found expression accompanied, first the θρῆνοι, then the διθύραμβοι, which echoed the two main acts of the mysteries. κοπετός in the original sense corresponded esp. to the → θρῆνος, and the playing of the flute to the jubilation. This counterplay of cultic actions is perhaps reflected in the probably Gnostic hymn which has found its way into c. 95 of the Act. Joh.: αὐλῆσαι θέλω· ὀρχήσασθε πάντες ... θρηνῆσαι θέλω· κόψασθε πάντες. This two-membered prose verse with its obvious reminiscence of the saying of Jesus Himself in Mt. 11:17 and par. is interwoven into a parting hymn of Christ; but its true provenance is to be sought elsewhere, namely, in the Attis mysteries with their loud lamentation and jubilation, which were perhaps both accompanied by orgiastic dancing (→ 832) and playing on the flute (→ n. 96). The first act of this drama with its weeping, beating on the breast and self-wounding,[51] is usually described by the comprehensive tt. κόπτομαι (or τύπτομαι), e.g., in Aristoph. Lys., 396 (κόπτεσθ' "Αδωνιν) and Luc. Syr. Dea, 6 (→ θρηνέω, 149), both with reference to the cult of Adonis.[52]

In a broader sense we may also refer to the mourning for the cultic hero Achilles, which acc. to the report of Pausanias (VI, 23, 3) took place every year in Elis at his cenotaph: αἱ γυναῖκες αἱ Ἠλεῖαι ἄλλα τε τοῦ Ἀχιλλέως δρῶσιν ἐς τιμὴν καὶ κόπτεσθαι νομίζουσιν αὐτόν ("the women of Elis, in addition to other occasions in honour of Achilles, are accustomed to hold a mourning feast for him").

C. Mourning in the OT.

I. Popular Mourning.

1. Linguistic. The exact equivalent of κόπτομαι in the strict sense is the Heb. ספד, which in Syriac still has the sense "to beat," and which even in the OT, where it normally has the fig. sense "to mourn," still occurs in the phrase ספד על שדים (Is. 32:12).[53] In the broader sense, however, the words κόπτομαι and κοπετός [54] correspond to the Heb. terms for mourning, esp. the verbs אבל, e.g., Is. 3:26; Jer. 4:28; Jl. 1:9, esp. in the

---

[50] Cf. W. M. Ramsay in Hastings DB, Extra Vol. (1904), 124: "The mourning over Attis in the Phrygian worship of Cybele was succeeded by the Hilaria, as the lamentation for Adonis or 'Thammuz yearly wounded' in Syria was followed by the rejoicing over his rejuvenation." Cf. also Wendland Hell. Kult., 130; Frazer, I, 224 f., esp. 224, n. 2.

[51] H. Schlier, Religionsgeschichtliche Untersuchungen zu d. Ignatiusbriefen (1929), 164, n. 3.

[52] Many — F. Hitzig the first — have tried to see in Zech. 12:11 the κοπετός for Adonis (= sun-god of Hadad-Rimmon), cf. the θρῆνος for Tammuz in Ez. 8:14 → 835, but a ref. to the death of Josiah at Megiddo is intrinsically more likely (cf. the comm., ad loc.). On the other hand, κοπετός for Adonis may well underlie the weeping of the priests in Ep. Jer. 30 f. (cf. Heinisch Totenklage, 6 f.).

[53] Cf. Ges.-Buhl, s.v. ספד; Bertholet, 139, n. 16.

[54] Though in the Gk. translation these are not always used for the Heb. terms mentioned (→ 837). The LXX customarily uses κόπτομαι and κοπετός for derivatives of the stem ספד (even in the broader sense), → supra.

hitp, Gn. 37:34; 2 S. 13:37; 19:2; 2 Ch. 35:24; Is. 66:10; אנה, Is. 3:26; and ספד, in the general sense, e.g., Gn. 23:2; 1 S. 25:1; 2 S. 11:26; 1 K. 14:13, 18; Zech. 12:12, and the nouns אֵבֶל, Gn. 27:41; 50:11; 2 S. 11:27; Am. 5:16; Ez. 24:17; בְּכִית, Gn. 50:4; and מִסְפֵּד e.g., Am. 5:16 f.; Mi. 1:8. In Gn. 50:10 we find the fig. etym. ספד מסֵפֵד.

In the LXX κόπτομαι and κοπετός are mostly used for ספד and מספד. In most of these cases these exact equivalents are general terms for mourning, esp. where κόπτομαι is used in stereotyped phrases, or in parallelism, with κλαίω (2 Βασ. 1:12; Ιερ. 41:5; Ez. 24:16, 23), ἀλαλάζω (Jer. 4:8; Ιερ. 32:34), πενθέω (Jer. 16:5; 1 Macc. 9:20); θρηνέω (Mi. 1:8; Jl. 1:13), θάπτω (1 Βασ. 25:1; 3 Βασ. 13:29 f.; Jer. 8:2; 16:4) or κοπετός with κλαυθμός (Is. 22:12; Jl. 2:12), πένθος (Am. 5:16; Mi. 1:8; Jer. 6:26; Est. 4:3), θρῆνος (Jer. 9:9), or with all three (Sir. 38:16 f.), with γόοι (3 Macc. 4:3) etc. The same is true of cases in which κοπετός is used in antithesis to expressions of joy (e.g., ψ 29:11) and of the fig. etym. κόπτομαι κοπετόν, Gn. 50:10; 1 Macc. 2:70; Zech. 12:10; → n. 3.

The verb [55] was one of the commonest expressions for weeping or sorrowing, as may be seen from the fact that it is used for various other Heb. words which are not strictly synon., namely, those which for the translators perhaps denote less common gestures of sorrow, e.g., גדד hitpoel, [56] "to cut oneself" (in sign of mourning, Ιερ. 48:5 [41:5], → 831) and the corresponding noun גְּדוּדָה (Ιερ. 31:37 [48:37]), or פלש hitp, "to roll in the dust" (Ιερ. 32:34 [25:34]), and אסף ni of the bringing together of bones, Jer. 8:2. Rather surprisingly the original meaning of κόπτομαι often emerges in such cases, e.g., Ιερ. 31:37 (48:37): καὶ πᾶσαι χεῖρες κόψονται, cf. also Ez. 6:9: κόψονται πρόσωπα αὐτῶν, 20:43: κόψεσθε τὰ πρόσωπα ὑμῶν, where the gesture of mourning is a graphic expression of self-repugnance. The basic sense is also discernible when κόπτομαι is accompanied by concrete actions such as cutting off the hair (Is. 22:12; Jer. 16:6) or the beard (Ιερ. 48:5 [41:5]), tearing the clothes (loc. cit.), putting on sackcloth (Is. 22:12; Ιερ. 30:19 [49:3]; Jl. 1:13), cutting oneself (Jer. 16:6), etc.

The technical terms for instituting mourning are the fig. etym. κόπτομαι κοπετόν, which corresponds in the Mas. (Gn. 50:10; cf. Zech. 12:10) to ספד מספד, and later (bAZ, 18a; bMQ, 21b) to הספיד הספד, κοπετὸν ποιοῦμαι or ποιῶ (Jer. 6:26; Mi. 1:8; Ac. 8:2), κοπετὸν λαμβάνω (-νομαι) (Jer. 9:9; cf. θρῆνον λαμβάνω, loc. cit.; Am. 5:1; Is. 14:4; Jer. 9:17; Ez. 26:17; 27:2, 32; 28:12), and κοπετὸν κλαίω (acc. to Rahlfs' conjecture in the original recension of Ez. 27:31).

2. The linguistic data and the accounts of customs, e.g., in Jer. 16:6 f. and Ez. 24:16 f., 22 f., yield the following practices : going barefoot ; stripping off one's clothes ; rumpling or cutting the hair and the beard ; cutting oneself ; the scattering of ashes ; fasts ; banquets ; cries of sorrow and laments. In addition, beating the breast (cf. Is. 32:12), the face (Ez. 6:9; 20:43) or the hip (Ez. 21:17; cf. Ιεζ. 24:17; Jer. 31:19 Mas.; → n. 105) is an established part of mourning. Nevertheless, it is also apparent that in the LXX the terms κοπετός and κόπτομαι are predominantly used for mourning in general. We may also add that in Israel, as in the Orient generally, mourning comes from the very earliest times ; we read of it in the days of the patriarchs (Gn. 23:2; 37:34; 50:3 f., 10).

As with the Greeks, it began immediately [57] or very soon after the coming of death (cf. Mt. 9:23 and par.) and continued on the way to the grave and during the committal.

---

[55] The noun κοπετός is used once in Jer. 9:9 for בְּכִי and נְהִי, but elsewhere for מספד.
[56] In Ιερ. 29:5 (47:5) we have the act. κόπτω, but this is combined with μάχαιρα (v. 6) and thus takes on a different sense. On the other hand, יתגדד in Jer. 16:6 is correctly rendered ἐντομίδας ποιεῖν, and the nearby ספד is correctly rendered κόπτομαι.
[57] There is perhaps a ref. in Qoh. 12:5; cf. H. Menge in his transl., ad loc.; Heinisch Totenklage, 12.

Even elsewhere there would be lamentation when the sad news was heard, cf. 2 S. 1:11 ff.; 1 Macc. 12:52. The day of burial, which would often be the day of death, was followed by a seven day mourning period of fasts and laments, cf. Gn. 50:10; 1 S. 31:13 = 1 Ch. 10:12; Jdt. 16:24; Sir. 22:12, though cf. 38:17. In the case of great men this period might be extended, cf. Gn. 50:3; Nu. 20:29; Dt. 34:8. [58] In addition, the memory of some, e.g., Jephthah's daughter (Ju. 11:40) or Josiah (2 Ch. 35:25) might be celebrated by an annual period of mourning. [59]

3. In accordance with universal custom the mourners were first the immediate relatives, the husband (Gn. 23:2), the wife (2 S. 11:26), the bride (Jl. 1:8), the father (Gn. 37:34), the friend (2 S. 1:17 ff.) etc. This is reflected in such stereotyped cries as "O my brother" (1 K. 13:30; Jer. 22:18), "Alas, sister" (Jer. 22:18 Mas.), cf. Ishtar's "O my good wife," "O my good husband" in her mourning for Tammuz. [60] In comparisons (cf. the mother's comfort in Is. 66:13 or the anxious love of the hen in Mt. 23:37) the epitome of κοπετός is mourning for a firstborn and perhaps an only son, Am. 8:10; Jer. 6:26: [ὡς] πένθος ἀγαπητοῦ, Zech. 12:10: κοπετὸν ὡς ἐπ' ἀγαπητὸν καὶ ... ὀδύνην ὡς ἐπὶ πρωτοτόκῳ (→ 849 f.). The circle of mourning relatives is quickly enlarged to include others, cf. 2 S. 1:12; 1 K. 13:30, and it is a mark of Israelite life that the whole nation might finally be involved in the case of prominent men, especially national leaders, e.g., Moses in Dt. 34:8; Samuel in 1 S. 25:1; Abner in 2 S. 3:31 ff.; Abijah, son of Jeroboam I in 1 K. 14:13, 18, Josiah in 2 Ch. 35:24 f., the Maccabean leaders in 1 Macc. 2:70; 9:20; 12:52, and cf. the mourning of the Egyptians for Jacob in Gn. 50:3.

In Israel, as elsewhere, women are prominent at mourning. [61] Sometimes there are choruses of women and sometimes all the women of a city or country are summoned to mourn, cf. Ju. 11:40; 2 S. 1:24; Na. 2:8; Is. 32:12; Ιερ. 30:19 (49:3); Ez. 32:16, also Zech. 12:12-14. But men are not excluded, even in large groups, cf. 2 S. 1:12; Zech. 12:12 ff.

In Israel, too, it was often felt that lay mourning was not enough, and professional mourners [62] were hired, esp. women, cf. Jer. 9:16: αἱ σοφαί in the special sense of those versed in laments, cf. v. 19; on θρηνοῦσαι → 150; 2 Ch. 35:25: οἱ ἄρχοντες καὶ αἱ ἄρχουσαι, male and female singers of laments. The second quotation shows that men were not excluded, and we are led to the same conclusion by Am. 5:16: εἰδότες θρῆνον, and Qoh. 12:5: οἱ κοπτόμενοι, the mourners who throng the street outside the house of the dying to be hired when death supervenes.

4. The main expression of both spontaneous and professional κοπετός was formless cries which were the precursors of structured θρῆνοι, cf. Am. 5:16: ἐν πάσαις ὁδοῖς ῥηθήσεται· οὐαί, οὐαί (הֹו-הֹו; Lam. 1:1; 2:1; 4:1: אֵיכָה). Later the simple cry was accompanied by an apostrophe of the departed, cf. 3 Βασ. 13:30: καὶ ἐκόψαντο αὐτόν· οὐαὶ ἀδελφέ; 12:24: καὶ τὸ παιδάριον κόψονται· οὐαὶ κύριε; Jer. 22:18: [63] οὐ μὴ κόψωνται αὐτὸν ὦ ἀδελφέ, οὐδὲ μὴ κλαύσονται αὐτόν· οἴμμοι κύριε; Ιερ. 41:5 (34:5): κλαύσονται καὶ σὲ καὶ 'ὦ αδων' (= οἴμμοι κύριε) κόψονταί σε. [64]

---

[58] Cf. also Jer. 22:10: μὴ κλαίετε τὸν τεθνηκότα μηδὲ θρηνεῖτε αὐτόν, sc. Josiah, who had fallen three months before.

[59] Cf. the festival of Achilles in Elis, Paus., VI, 23, 3; → 836.

[60] Cf. Ungnad, 236.

[61] Cf. Heinisch Totenklage, 7 f. → θρηνέω, 150.

[62] Heinisch Totenklage, 8 f. → θρηνέω, 150.

[63] Here the Mas. brings together various cries; the LXX reduces them to two.

[64] These passages show that κοπετός consisted in these cries and also that they had become very formal, a stranger (3 Βασ. 13:30) or king (Jer. 22:18) being addressed "Ah brother" and a little boy "Ah lord" (3 Βασ. 12:24). The same use of bridegroom, bride, father etc. as titles is to be found in Rabb. writings, cf. Semachoth (→ 842), 3, 7 f.; cf. also c. 11.

Similar cries are still found in post-NT Judaism,[65] but they are mostly an introduction to the developed θρῆνος and they take on a fixed character — ὦ αδων,[66] Oh! oh!, Alas! alas! etc. — as the response of the main body to individual strophes or to the recurrent rhymes with which the professional mourners seek to excite the sympathy of those around.[67] The same cry 'hō' may still be heard in Palestine as the answer of the chorus to the words of the chief singer.

Mourners, who were to be found in rural areas as well as in the city, cf. Am. 5:16: πλατεῖαι—γεωργός, were not paid primarily to utter formless cries, though it might well be necessary to supplement members of the family in this respect. Their main task was to sing → θρῆνοι or laments, and they were specially trained for this. For the most part their songs were homespun productions, but real poems might also be found, like that which Jeremiah composed on the death of Josiah in battle, 2 Ch. 35:25; → θρηνέω, 150, and these became models for future authors, cf. the words added to the lament of Ez. (c. 19) for the royal house of Judah (v. 14): εἰς παραβολὴν θρήνου ἐστὶν καὶ ἔσται εἰς θρῆνον (cf. also 32:16). Like the profession of κοπτόμενοι, these songs came down from generation to generation and were later gathered in written collections from which suitable pieces could be chosen at funerals acc. to the status of the deceased and the circumstances of his death. Sometimes the songs were sung responsively[68] by male or female soloist and choir, cf. 2 Ch. 35:25, or antiphonally by two choirs, cf. Zech. 12:10-14.[69] The deceased is often addressed in the 2nd person, Ez. 27:3 ff.; 19:2, 10; 2 S. 1:26; 3:34, and the mourners speak in the 1st person of the bereaved relatives, cf. Lam. 1:12-22; 2:21 f., where the mother, Jerusalem, is weeping for her children. But sometimes the lament is put on the lips of the deceased, cf. Jer. 9:18,[70] or the two forms are combined, as in northern Arabia to this day,[71] and the deceased and the bereaved express their grief in alternation.

In Israel, as in Greece and Rome, abuses also crept in[72] (→ 833, also n. 30). Violence of outcry was regarded as more important than the beauty of the songs. In particular, money became the criterion of the popularity of the deceased and the sincerity of grief for him (cf. Sir. 38:17: χάριν διαβολῆς). In time, then, it was necessary to make similar restrictions to those in the Greek and Roman sphere (→ 843).

5. It is a distinctive feature of the OT, however, that the full practice of κοπετός is regarded as a sign of normal conditions and esp. of a healthy relationship of the nation to God. If God's peace departs from the land, if a curse falls on it, then κοπετός has to cease and ordinary burial customs are abandoned. The dead become food for the fowls and dung for the earth, cf. Jer. 8:2; 16:4, 6 f.; Ez. 24:22 f. The curse of not being buried and lamented is pronounced by Jeremiah (22:18) on the disobedient king, Jehoiakim, and by Job (27:15) on the children of the ungodly. Jeremiah explains what is meant by this dying without grave or mourning. It is humiliation to the status of a beast. The king

---

[65] Cf. Str.-B., I, 523, 1; IV, 582 and 583b.

[66] Cf. the recurrent rhyme on Adonis: αἰάζω τὸν "Αδωνιν· ἀπώλετο καλὸς "Αδωνις in Bion's 'Αδώνιδος ἐπιτάφιος (Bucolici Graeci, ed. U. v. Wilamowitz-Moellendorff [1905], 122 ff.).

[67] Cf. Heinisch Totenklage, 7.

[68] Cf. Heinisch Totenklage, 18.

[69] Ritual κοπετός sometimes takes this form, e.g., that for Tammuz in Babylon, cf. Ungnad, 236 f.

[70] Heinisch Totenklage, 5; 25; 39 f.; 51.

[71] *Ibid.,* 41.

[72] As in pagan antiquity there is hypocritical lamentation (that of Herod in Jos. Ant., 15, 60) and also conventional (cf. also Heinisch Trauergebräuche, 92 on 2 S. 1:11 f. and 3:31). The NT itself gives a striking example of the deep, inner unconcern of most mourners, and esp. of the paid professionals, in Mt. 9:24 and par. (cf. also Jn. 11:46 with v. 19 and 31); → 844.

will be cast out like an ass (22:19). This fate will also strike members of the family of Jeroboam I for their ungodliness. Only the young Abijah will have the honour of κοπετός, "because in him there is found some good thing toward the Lord" (1 K. 14:13, 18). Cf. also the case of Zedekiah, Ιερ. 41:5 (34:5).

II. The Lamentation of the Prophets (→ θρηνέω, 151).

1. In the OT world, as in that of Greece and Rome, there is a specifically religious form of lamentation. In the OT, however, this is quite different from cultic κοπετός. Lamentation is here a task of the prophets. In public acts and also in written form they give it expression both for their own times and for the future.

Formally, the prophets keep closely to popular mourning. They employ the motifs and expressions of the usual laments, and they adopt their rhythm (qina) and monotony, cf. Ez. 32:19-32. In some cases simple, popular laments are introduced into prophetic lamentation, e.g., in Jer. 9:20 f. and Ez. 27:32b-34. In content and purpose, however, prophetic κοπετός is very different. Mourners sought to bring comfort and relief; the prophets aimed to startle. The former wished to excite sympathy, the latter repentance. The former were expressing the feelings of their hearers for the deceased, the latter the judgment of God on their hearers as on the dead. In fact, the κοπετός of the prophets shares the twofold character of prophecy, which both speaks in the name of God and also declares the future. Prophetic lamentation is normally for a future death rather than for one which has already taken place.[73] This death is the destruction of the nation and the nations. Basically, however, the prophets' concern is with rebellion against God rather than external catastrophe. In Israel and in the nations they bewail this as a mortal fate. For this reason κοπετός is integrated into the τέλος of prophecy as a whole. This is not prepared to accept death and corruption. It seeks to keep the people alive, or to lead it back to life, cf. Am. 5:14. Indeed, behind prophetic κοπετός stands the assurance of eventual restoration,[74] just as the hope of the resurrection underlies later Christian mourning.

2. The model of the genre of prophetic lamentation is to be found in the lament of Amos (5:1 f.) for the virgin daughter, Israel. "The virgin daughter" — this is designed to create the deepest sense of loss in the minds of the hearers, for the people would usually bewail a virgin even more than a young mother with small children. A virgin had not fulfilled the purpose of her life, and so it was with Israel. Amos speaks in the prophetic perfect (as distinct from 8:10), and his vision became history, cf. Jer. 9:9 etc. We may then refer to the lament of Micah for Samaria (1:8 Mas.),[75] to that of Jeremiah for Jerusalem (9:18), to the symbolical laments of Ezekiel for the royal house of Judah (c. 19) and for Tyre and its princes (c. 27 and 28:11-19), to the scornful lament of the same prophet for Pharaoh (c. 32), and to the ironical lament for the king of Babylon in Is. 14. What God causes the poet of the second part of Is. to proclaim in 40:6 f. is also fundamentally a lament, as the genius of Johannes Brahms perceived and emphasised. The beauty of the imagery makes it apparent that many of these laments are also true poetry.

---

[73] This is not true of Lamentations.

[74] Cf. the hope behind Ez. 19:13. The vine has not withered; there is still hope that it will be planted in fruitful soil.

[75] In the LXX Samaria itself is represented as a woman bewailing her own fate (→ θρηνέω, 150).

How graphically they present to the hearers the fruitful vine (Ez. 19:10-14), the meadows with the spring flowers (Is. 40:6 f.), Jerusalem as the mother (Lam. 1 f.), the virgin daughter of Israel (Am. 5:2), the proud lioness with its young (Ez. 19:1-9), the crocodile in the Nile (Ez. 32:2-10), and the magnificent spectacle of the merchantman of Tyre (Ez. 27)!

3. A distinctive subsidiary aspect of prophetic κοπετός is that the prophet may have to abstain from ordinary mourning. Thus κοπετός for his wife is expressly forbidden to the prophet Ezekiel (24:16) in order to illustrate the curse which has been resolved upon Jerusalem and the sanctuary there (v. 21), and among the dramatic restrictions placed on Jeremiah is the fact that he is not to take part in any mourning (16:5).

These symbolical actions are meant to draw attention to the terrible state (→ 839) when there will be no mourning in the whole land because the curse of God is on it, to the time when death will have a dreadful seriousness and no dead person will be bewailed or buried. The prophets proclaim this judgment also in words which accompany and supplement the symbolical actions (Jer. 16:4 ff.; 8:2; Ez. 24:22 ff.).

4. On the other hand, prophetic activity also includes the varied declaration of a κοπετός, i.e., the requirement of it. Prophetic lamentation is thus to be confirmed and repeated by the historical actuality. Through the prophets God summons to repentance and conversion, which must and will be accompanied by lamentation for sin, [76] especially the sin of idolatry (Jl. 2:12; also Ez. 6:9; 20:43 LXX). Through the prophets God proclaims terrible judgments, and with this proclamation He calls to lamentation over the affliction of Zion at the hands of the hosts which He has launched against it (Is. 22:12; Jer. 4:8; 6:26), over the destruction of Moab (Ιερ. 31:37 [48:37 f.]), over the precursors of the day of the Lord (Jl. 1:15), and over the day of the Lord itself (Am. 5:16 f.). In this form, too, the prophetic intimation of death is often combined with a dreadful scorn and irony. Under the comic picture of the howling rams (Ιερ. 32:34 [25:34]) a world-wide catastrophe is scornfully announced to the nations, and even plainer is the grim mockery with which the prophet (Ιερ. 30:19 [49:3]) summons the Ammonites to bewail the departure of the god Milkom.

5. But here, too, there is promise of salvation as well as intimation of disaster. God will one day put an end to κοπετός and turn sorrow into joy and the beating of the breast into joyful dancing: ἔστρεψας τὸν κοπετόν μου εἰς χορὸν ἐμοί (ψ 29:11; cf. Jn. 16:20). [77] In the prophets, however, intimation of mourning can also belong to the promise of salvation in the specific form of κοπετός for the Messiah (Zech. 12:10 ff.). [78] But this is sorrow which issues in life (cf. 2 C. 7:10).

D. Mourning in Judaism.

1. Sources and Usage. Apart from the NT (→ 844), several Mishnah, Talmud and Tosefta tractates bear witness to the mourning customs of Judaism, namely, the tractates

---

[76] Cf. Test. R. 1:10: πενθῶν ἐπὶ τῇ ἁμαρτίᾳ μου.

[77] Cf. the opp. in Am. 8:10: καὶ μεταστρέψω τὰς ἑορτὰς ὑμῶν εἰς πένθος καὶ πάσας τὰς ᾠδὰς ὑμῶν εἰς θρῆνον.

[78] → 849; on Rabb. exposition of Zech. 12:11 cf. bMQ, 28b (Str.-B., IV, 605 with n. 1).

Moed qatan and Ebel rabbati or Semachot (= Sem.), one of the little Talmud tractates. [79]
The Rabb. word corresponding to κόπτεσθαι proper [80] is טפח [81] pi and hitp (MQ,
3, 8 and 9; TMQ, 2, 17), "to beat with the hands on the breast," or "to beat the hands
together on the breast." [82] On the other hand, for κόπτεσθαι in the more general sense
of mourning we find either the same words as in the OT, esp. אבל (→ 836), cf. also
אָבֵל "mourner" (e.g., Sem., 6, 1) and בכה [83] (bMQ, 5b), or words which occur in OT
Heb. but are not rendered κόπτομαι (κοπετός) in the LXX, e.g., אנן and ילל pi with
derivatives. [84]

2. Customs and Times of κοπετός. a. One of the main parts of Jewish mourning is
the funeral procession, the carrying of the corpse to the place of burial, and the accompanying lamentation (bKet., 72a, Bar.; Str.-B., IV, 579h, with other par.), one of
whose main features is beating on the breast, cf. MQ, 3, 8 and 9; Jos. Ant., 16, 216.
Mourning proper takes place in the time between death and burial. It begins when the
corpse is put on the bier, cf. Mk. 5:38 and par., and reaches its climax in the rites of
interment.

b. At a later time a second period of mourning follows interment. The first period,
called אֲנִינָה (Eka r., Intr. § 7) or אֲנִינוּת (bQid, 80b) — the mourner in this period is אוֹנֵן
(bMQ, 14b) — and usually lasting only a single day (→ 837 f.; cf. Str.-B., I, 1047a on
Mt. 27:57), is followed after burial by the אֲבֵילָה (Eka r., Intr. § 7) or אֲבֵילוּת (MQ, 20b)
or אֵבֶל (jMQ, 82b, line 30) — the mourner in this period is called אָבֵל (MQ, 3, 7). This
second period is itself divided into two sections differentiated by different degrees of
strictness. In some cases (bMQ, 27b; Str.-B., IV, 596) the first three days are the time
of greatest strictness. Very common is a seven day period of mourning, as already in
the OT (→ 838). The Rabbis tried in various ways to deduce this custom, called
אבלות שבעה (bMQ, 20a), from the OT, cf. bMQ, 20a; bShab., 152a; Gn. r., 100 on 50:10;
jMQ, 92c etc.; Str.-B., IV, 596g. There then followed from the 8th to the 30th day after
burial a period of lesser severity, the so-called thirty days, cf. already Nu. 20:29; Dt. 34:8,
also bMQ, 27b; jMQ, 83c, line 21; Str.-B., loc. cit. On the death of parents there was a
whole year of mourning, cf. bMQ, 22b; Sem., 9.

In addition to these regular times of mourning there were sometimes extra commemorations which might be held long after the death and which were encouraged by wandering
orators who arranged them on behalf of the relatives for payment, cf. bMQ, 8a; Str.-B.,
IV, 587w. This custom reminds us of the commemorations of Achilles (→ 836), Josiah,
and Jephthah's daughter (→ 838), but it does not have their regularity.

3. The Mourners. a. κοπετός is chiefly carried on by hired women (מְקוֹנְנוֹת) who
accompany their cries and laments with the beating of two musical instruments [85] or

---

[79] For Sem. cf. ed. M. Klotz (Diss. Königsberg, 1890); Strack Einl., 73; A. Marmorstein,
Art. "Ebel Rabbati," EJ, VI, 147-149, with further bibl. In what follows we are much indebted to R. Meyer.

[80] From the stem of the OT tt. ספד we find in Rabb. writings הֶסְפֵּד, either in the general
sense of "lament" (cf. מִסְפֵּד in the OT, → 837), or, with a shift of meaning, in the special
sense of a "funeral oration" (cf. Str.-B., IV, 582, n. 1, → θρηνέω, 152).

[81] Cf. Syr. taphach "to beat with the fists" (Ges.-Buhl, s.v. טפח I); cf. Bertholet, 139
with n. 16.

[82] The transl. in Str.-B. (I, 522c e f), "to strike on the hands," "to beat the hands together
before the breast," is not quite accurate [K. G. Kuhn].

[83] Cf. Gn. 50:4 Mas. בְּכִית, LXX πένθος; Jer. 9:9 Mas. (ונהי) בְּכִי, LXX κοπετός.

[84] In later Jewish schematisation derivations from these roots are allotted to specific
sections of mourning, אנן to the time up to burial, אבל to the time which follows, cf. Eka r.,
Intr. § 7; jHor., 48a, lines 11 ff.

[85] Cf. Str.-B., I, 522g h; → θρηνέω, 152.

the beating of the breast, cf. TMQ, 2, 17; Str.-B., I, 522 f.; also MQ, 3, 8 f. Is. 32:12 is often adduced as the *locus classicus* for this in the Bible, e.g., TMQ, 2, 17. These women were mainly in evidence on the way from the house to the place of interment, and esp. during breaks in the procession, when they could sit on the ground, the prescribed posture of mourning (→ 832), as may be seen from Sem., 11 and MQ, 3, 8 (Str.-B., I, 522c), [86] and also from T. Kelim BB, 2, 8 (Str.-B., I, 522g). But definite restrictions were set on the activity of this class (→ θρηνέω, 151). In the so-called intervening days of feasts, i.e., the time between the first and last feast-days of the Passover and Tabernacles, κοπετός in the literal sense was forbidden and only lamentation (עינוי) was ordained (MQ, 3, 8). On the other hand עינוי and κοπετός were allowed on the days of the New Year, the Dedication and Purim, and only the lament proper (קינה) was prohibited, though κοπετός in both the narrower and the broader sense could not continue after burial on these days, MQ, 3, 9; Str.-B., I, 522e.

b. Beating the breast and lamentation were not restricted to professional women mourners. Members of the family, both women [87] and men, not only took part in the procession but also joined in the lamentation, cf. jSanh., 20b, line 42; bSanh., 20a, Bar.; Str.-B., IV, 581g. The men were particularly prominent; they accompanied their cries with all kinds of expressive gestures, e.g., stamping their feet, bMQ, 27b; Str.-B., I, 522 f.; Gn. r., 100 on 50:10; Str.-B., IV, 584c, wringing their hands, TMQ, 2, 17 and beating their breasts, as may be deduced from Gn. r., 100 on 50:10. [88] In fact, there seems to have been in Judaism a kind of εἰδότες θρῆνον (Am. 5:16, → 838), a male counterpart to mourning women, cf. bBer., 62a, Bar.; bMQ, 25b. Their foremost representative is the orator, who has the task of honouring the dead in his oration at the grave. [89]

c. As in OT times, the circle of mourners might be extended beyond relatives and professionals to the nation in the case of leading figures, cf. e.g., Jos. Bell., 3, 437, where the whole people is supposed to have mourned 30 days for the fallen leader, Josephus. The same is particularly true in the case of rabbis, cf. Sem., 9. Thus we read in bMQ, 25a, Bar. (Str.-B., IV, 599r): "When a scribe dies, then (in respect of mourning) all are his relatives," and there is no limit to the number of those who might take part in the obsequies of rabbis, bKet., 17b, Bar.; Str.-B., 581a; cf. Ned., 9, 10; Str.-B., 590o).

On the other hand, no public mourning was allowed in cases of execution, Sanh., 6, 6; bSanh., 47a; Str.-B., I, 1049; II, 686).

4. Significance and Motifs of Mourning. In Judaism mourning had great significance for many different reasons. It is a duty of love [90] which is proved from Ex. 18:20 [91] and Mi. 6:8 [92] and which even takes precedence of study of the Torah and worship. [93] Lamentation and burial also have atoning power on the basis of 1 K. 14:13 and Jer.

---

[86] This rule may be compared with the very similar but more general ordinance of the Labyadae of Delphi (BCH, 19 [1895], p. 11, 31 ff.) which prohibits putting the bier down on street-corners, obviously to prevent pauses for breath when loud outcries can break out unchecked.

[87] Female relatives are obviously in view in T. Kelim BB, 2, 8 (Str.-B., I, 522g), for only in relation to them, not to hired women, could there be a reference to "their" dead.

[88] Cf. Str.-B., IV, 584c.

[89] *Ibid.,* 583 β; 586 ff. (r-x); → θρηνέω, 152.

[90] At the burial of a wife it was a duty that there should be at least two flute-players and one woman mourner, Ket., 4, 4; Str.-B., I, 521a, with an orator too in many districts, T. Ket., 4, 2; Str.-B., IV, 586q.

[91] Cf. M. Ex. on 18:20; bBQ, 99b, Bar.; Str.-B., IV, 560 f. a.

[92] Cf. bSukka, 49b.

[93] Cf. bMeg., 3b; Str.-B., IV, 579d; also bBer., 18a, Bar.; Str.-B., I, 1048c; jChag., 76c, line 44; Ab. R. Nat., 4 (2d) etc.; Str.-B., IV, 580a.

16:4. [94] Finally and supremely the gestures and cries are made as violent and noisy as possible because it is believed that the deceased perceives everything (→ 832) until the stone is rolled before the tomb, bShab., 152b, Str.-B., 586t). This is why the bereaved can be called consolers of the deceased, bShab., 152a, Str.-B., 608u. Originally many customs may be based on fear of demons which are particularly potent and dangerous in the neighbourhood of tombs (→ 832, cf. also Mk. 5:5), cf. bBB, 100b; Str.-B., IV, 597k. In general one may say that the reason why mourning in Israel has a great deal in common with that of surrounding nations, and is not completely leavened by faith in Him who is the God of the living and dead, is because belief in the resurrection and the future life has not yet permeated the whole life of faith. Only in the NT is there a decisive change in this respect.

E. Mourning in the New Testament.

I. Popular κοπετός.

As many customs and condition of the age are reflected in the NT, so we find evidence of mourning customs. In two houses, that of Jairus and that of Lazarus, the NT brings us into close contact with contemporary Jewish mourning. The children's burial game throws light on the corresponding adult practice. Jesus Himself is shown on His way to the cross, the laments of His people in His ears. Indeed, we find evidence of the continuation of many Jewish mourning practices in the primitive Church.

1. In accordance with the basic difference between the stories of raising to life again in the Synoptists and in John, the case of Jairus introduces us to what the terminology of the Aramaean period (→ 842; → n. 84) calls the first period of mourning, the אנינה, whereas the case of Lazarus introduces us to the second, the אבילה.

a. When Jesus came to the house of Jairus, the latter's daughter had only been dead an hour, but already mourning was in full swing, Mk. 5:38; Mt. 9:23; Lk. 8:52. It thus began immediately after death, [95] and in addition to the relatives there were obviously present many condoling acquaintances (ὄχλος θορυβούμενος, Mt.; cf. θόρυβος, τί θορυβεῖσθε; Mk.), the flute-players, [96] and mourning women. The ἀλαλάζειν of Mk. probably refers to the latter, [97] and also, at least in the first instance, the κόπτομαι

---

[94] bSanh., 46b; cf. bKet., 111a; Str.-B., IV, 591c.
[95] Cf. in the OT esp. Qoh. 12:5 (→ n. 57; → 838); Hck. Lk., 118 on 8:52.
[96] It seems that to many people the flute of all musical instruments was most in accord with the heavy mood of mourning. In the East we read of mourning songs on the flute among the Babylonians; these were prayers of mourning accompanied by the flute, Heinisch Totenklage, 19. In the West the flute was played among the Romans for the laying out of both rich and poor, cf. Blümner, 491. That it was used in Israel too finds attestation in Jeremiah's "lament like the sound of a flute" in 48:36 (Ιερ. 31:36), and at a later time the flute introduced mourning songs (Jos. Bell., 3, 437; → θρηνέω, 151 f.) and accompanied the lamentation right up to the interment and even after, cf. occasional Rabb. observations in Ket., 4, 4; Sem., 14; Shab., 23, 4; BM, 6, 1 (Str.-B., II, 521a); TMQ, 2, 17 (Str.-B., II, 522d). But this characterisation of the flute as an instrument of mourning did not prevent its use for merry music at feasts, weddings etc., cf. 1 K. 1:40; Is. 5:12; Rev. 18:22; TMQ, 2, 17, and also its employment in the temple cultus, cf. Sukka, 5, 1; Str.-B., II, 806, also → 836.
[97] So, e.g., Pr.-Bauer, s.v.; J. F. Schleusner, Novum Lexicon Graeco-Latinum in NT, I⁴ (1819), s.v. ad loc.: de praeficis, naenias cantantibus, usurpatur.

of Lk. [98] (ἔκλαιον δὲ πάντες καὶ ἐκόπτοντο αὐτήν). [99] On the other hand, those who offer condolences are included in the πάντες, and the fact that their grief is just as external as that of the professional women [100] may be seen from the rapidity with which it could change into scornful laughter (Lk. 8:53 and par.). The same conventional emptiness may be seen in the change of mood among the Jews who after the death of Lazarus stay and weep with his sisters and then quickly yield to scorn and hatred (cf. Jn. 11:37, 46). [101]

b. In the house of Mary and Martha we see the second part of mourning when the grave was sealed. Jesus came four days after burial (Jn. 11:17, 39), i.e., after the three days of strictest mourning (→ 842), but in the middle of the official time for condolence, for the first seven days after burial, the main period of mourning (→ 837; 842), were for the most part filled with visits, which according to ancient Jewish ceremonial had to be made in the first seven days. [102] In relation to the mourners at Bethany (→ παρα-μυθέομαι, Jn. 11:19, 31) there is thus no mention of κοπετός, for weeping was their function, not κοπετός or θρῆνος in the narrower sense, cf. v. 33.

2. There is a reflection of burial customs in the burial game of the children with whom Jesus compares the corrupt generation of His day (Mt. 11:16 f. = Lk. 7:31 f. → 154). Their game, or rather their refusal to co-operate in it, illustrates the close connection between κοπετός and θρῆνος (→ 152) in Jewish mourning.

The reproach of the one side (Mt. 11:17 and par.) rests on the assumption that a soloist, both in the game and in reality, [103] strikes up the θρῆνος and the rest join in with κοπετός: ἐθρηνήσαμεν καὶ οὐκ ἐκόψασθε. We are obviously to think here of κοπετός in the original sense, [104] namely, movements of the hand which may have accompanied the θρῆνος rhythmically, though this did not have to be a real lament in the children's game. One may assume that even in NT times κοπετός included beating the forehead [105] as well as the breast; this is presupposed in the addition of Cod D at Lk. 23:48: τύπτοντες τὰ στήθη καὶ τὰ μέτωπα.

3. a. What Jesus here described as play He Himself experienced only a little later in the reality of His way to the cross. κοπετός and θρῆνος were practised

---

[98] Cf. Zn., ad loc.

[99] On the constr. with acc. cf. the ref. → 834 and also LXX Gn. 23:2; 50:10; 1 Βασ. 25:1; 3 Βασ. 13:30 f.; Mi. 1:11; Jer. 16:6 etc., probably also Lk. 23:27; cf. Buttmann § 131, 4; Bl.-Debr. § 148, 2; Pr.-Bauer, s.v. Cf. the similar constr. of θρηνέω, e.g., Ez. 32:16; Lk. 23:27, and κλαίω, 1 Macc. 9:20; Mt. 2:18.

[100] κλαυθμός and κοπετός supplement one another and are to be taken together, cf. the refs. → 837, also Rev. 18:9 and Ev. Pt. 12:52 and 54, and as a par. → θρηνέω, 153; cf. also Lk. 7:32 with Mt. 11:17.

[101] → n. 72.

[102] Str.-B., IV, 592; cf. the passages adduced, ibid., 596g, esp. jMQ, 82b, lines 32 ff.; bMQ, 23a, Bar., also detailed regulations for the comforting of the bereaved, ibid., 592-607.

[103] We find soloists among the Gks., cf. the θρήνων ἔξαρχοι of the Homeric world, Il., 24, 721, among the Romans, cf. praefica, if this means the one who strikes up or leads the lament, among the Israelites, cf. οἱ ἄρχοντες καὶ αἱ ἄρχουσαι, 2 Ch. 35:25, → 838, and so also in NT times.

[104] Cf. Kl. Mk., ad loc.; → θρηνέω, 152, n. 28; also Qoh. 3:4, where ὀρχέομαι is the counterpart.

[105] There is evidence of the same custom in the LXX in its rendering of Ez. 6:9; 20:43: κόπτεσθαι τὰ πρόσωπα. Rather different is the old Gk. practice by which men and women would beat their heads with the palms of their hands, cf. Hom. Il., 22, 33 (→ n. 12) and → n. 25. In Israel both before and during the Exile it seems to have been a gesture of sorrow to strike not only the breast and the forehead but also the hips, cf. Jer. 31:19; Ez. 21:17, and on this RE³, XX, 85; Bertholet, 139.

together by the Jews (and not by them alone, → n. 86), especially on the way to the place of burial, and more particularly where the bearers halted and put down the bier for others to take over. [106] In a distinctive prolepsis the women of Jerusalem provided this kind of procession for Jesus on the way to Golgotha: (γυναῖκες) ἐκόπτοντο καὶ ἐθρήνουν αὐτόν, Lk. 23:27. This passage and its counterpart in v. 48, [107] in which we read of the κοπετός of the same people on their return from this procession, shows how national mourning was accorded to Jesus as befitting One who was Rabbi (→ 843) or even King of His people (v. 38), in complete antithesis to the denial of all public mourning implicit in the sentence of death which had been passed on Him (→ 843). With this twofold emphasis on the general sorrow the Evangelist is trying to show that the Jews thus gave involuntary recognition to Jesus as their Lord and King, as did also Pilate in his own way (Jn. 19:19-22). It is also possible, however, that this was a conscious and courageous confession that Jesus was no malefactor. [108]

b. In the case of Jesus we have no record of the second period of mourning, which usually began after interment. Even the women maintain silence (cf. Lk. 23:55 f.), probably out of regard for the feast (→ 843). On the other hand the Pt. Ev. (12:50 ff.) causes the women to come to the tomb on Easter morning, not to see it (Mt. 28:1) and to anoint the body (Mk. 16:1; Lk. 24:1), [109] but to make up the lament which had been omitted, both at (or in) the grave, and then on the way back from the grave to the house (v. 54). From their conversation we learn that it was an unconditional duty (v. 53: τὰ ὀφειλόμενα) of Jewish women to weep and bewail close relatives both on their dying bed (v. 50: ἐπὶ τοῖς ἀποθνήσκουσι) and also at the tomb after burial (v. 52: κλαῦσαι καὶ κόψασθαι, → n. 100).

4. The primitive community took over the custom of κοπετός, among many other things, from the Jewish world. This may be seen in the first account of martyrdom, which contains the only verse in the NT in which the noun is used: συνεκόμισαν δὲ τὸν Στέφανον ἄνδρες εὐλαβεῖς καὶ ἐποίησαν κοπετὸν μέγαν ἐπ' αὐτῷ (Ac. 8:2). This verse is also interesting in other respects.

a. The κοπετός is the second part of mourning after burial, and the mourners seem to be exclusively men, whereas in the NT, as elsewhere (→ 834; 838; 842), women are usually predominant (cf. Lk. 23:27; Ac. 9:39; also Mk. 5:38; → 844; also Ev. Pt. 12:50 ff. [→ supra]). Yet in other places in the NT men are also numbered among the κοπτόμενοι (cf. πάντες in Lk. 8:52 [→ 844] and 23:48 [→ supra], also Jn. 11:19), and in contemporary Judaism there is evidence of a strong participation of men (→ 843).

Men are found at mourning from the earliest times. Priam on the one side (Il., 22, 33), Abraham (Gn. 23:2) and David (2 S. 1:12) on the other, θρήνων ἔξαρχοι in the one case (Il., 24, 721), εἰδότες θρῆνον in the other (Am. 5:16), attest to the voluntary and paid participation of men at mourning in both the Greek and the Israelite worlds. Pictorial representations give additional evidence in the case of the Gks. and Romans, [110] whereas in that of the Israelites there are noteworthy signs of the antiphonal singing [111]

---

[106] Cf. Str.-B., I, 521 and 522c; IV, 582 and 583a; → 843.

[107] Obviously in imitation of this verse (τύπτοντες τὰ στήθη) Ev. Pt. 8:28 records: ὁ λαὸς ἅπας γογγύζει καὶ κόπτεται τὰ στήθη κτλ.

[108] Cf. Heinisch Totenklage, 82.

[109] This purpose is undoubtedly surprising (cf. Kl. Mk., ad loc.) and may well be the basis of the divergent account by the author of Ev. Pt.

[110] Cf. the Gk. Prothesis vases (Rohde [9], [10], 221, n. 2; also 224), and the Roman Haterii relief (Blümner, 486, n. 4); cf. also → 835.

[111] The Heb. קינה was later understood as an antiphonal song (→ θρηνέω, 151).

of men and women, cf. 2 Ch. 35:25 (→ 838) and esp. Zech. 12:10, 14 : [112] κόψεται . . . φυλὴ καθ' ἑαυτὴν καὶ αἱ γυναῖκες αὐτῶν καθ' ἑαυτάς κτλ. A distinctive instance of the practice of κοπετός by men in the biblical world is that of the prophets (→ 840), who struck up lamentation both in deadly serious play and also in the seriousness of the reality of death, e.g., 2 Ch. 35:25.

b. In respect of Ac. 8:2 one might raise the question whether all the ἄνδρες εὐλαβεῖς were not Jews. [113] If this is so, it must have been at the very least secret believers [114] who made great lamentation, i.e., who held [115] public mourning [116] for the first Christian martyr and who thus did for Him what, wittingly or unwittingly, the women of Jerusalem did for Jesus (→ 846), protesting against his official condemnation by their public κοπετός. Except with respect to confession of Jesus as Christ, the boundaries between the two communities were still fluid, and even if this passage cannot be regarded as evidence, there can be no doubt that κοπετός passed over into the Christian Church with many other customs ; as regards the NT we need only refer to Ac. 9:39.

5. κοπετός as practised in the pre-Christian aeon has lost its essential point and justification in the Christian aeon with its assurance of resurrection, its joy in dying and its triumph over death. Yet the general tendency of Christian life to lag behind Christian faith is specifically displayed in the stubborn persistence of pre-Christian and fundamentally non-Christian burial customs. In this respect a distinctive contribution was made by the influence of the customs of the Hellenistic Roman world, which were similar to those of the Jews. Indeed, one must even say that mourning remained for a particularly long time a seat of tenacious paganism. John Chrysostom, who also attests to the continuation of a link between θρῆνος and κοπετός (Hom. in Ac. 21:3 [MPG, 60, p. 168]; → θρηνέω, 153), inveighs in his sermons, as against other vices of his age, so also against unchristian excess in mourning customs. He tells us that rumpling the hair and the κοπετός of women at the bier took place either out of vanity or coquetry (Hom. in Jn. 62 [61], 4 [MPG, 59, p. 346]). Even later the Venetian government of the Middle Ages had to take steps against exaggerated ancient practices in Greece. "Only at this late date did Church and state succeed in rooting out the paganism of the descendants of the Greeks and the Romans at this point." [117]

II. Mourning in the Life, at the Death and on the Coming Again of Christ.

1. What does Jesus do with κοπετός when and where He meets it in life and death ? He sets it aside. He resists it, whether it be expected of Him or offered on His behalf. He gives the power to overcome even κοπετός. For He is the Victor over death and the Lord of life. There is no place for lamentation with Him.

---

[112] Cf. O. Procksch, Die kleinen prophetischen Schriften (Erläuterungen z. AT, 6² [1929]), 114; Heinisch Totenklage, 18.

[113] This is the view of Zahn (Ag., 267 [81, n. 5]). It must be granted that εὐλαβής is often used by Lk. of the Jews (Ac. 2:5; 22:12; Lk. 2:25), whereas Christians are usually μαθηταί (Ac. 6:1 f.; 9:1 etc.). But the position of the verse between v. 1 and v. 3 does not prove anything (cf. M. Dibelius, ThR, 3 [1931], 234), and εὐλάβεια in Hb. 12:28 shows that → εὐλαβής does not have to refer to the Jews.

[114] So O. Zöckler, ad loc. (Strack-Zöckler, Kurzgefasster Komm. B., II [1886], 187).

[115] On this expression → 837.

[116] The expression κοπετὸς μέγας occurs already in the LXX at Gn. 50:10; 1 Macc. 2:70; 9:20; cf. also Est. 4:3 : κραυγὴ καὶ κοπετὸς καὶ πένθος μέγα, 1 Macc. 12:52 : καὶ ἐπένθησεν πᾶς Ισραηλ πένθος μέγα; also the equivalent גדול הספד in bAZ, 18a; bMQ, 21b, Bar.; Str.-B., II, 687 on Ac. 8:2. These are all references to public mourning.

[117] Sittl, 78.

The accounts of mourning in Mk. 5 and par. and Jn. 11 first confirm the fact that it was death which Jesus withstood and overcame. For He banishes mourning and turns it into the wonder of joyful awe (Mk. 5:42 and par.; Lk. 7:16), into grateful faith (Jn. 11:45; 12:11) and into cheerful praise of God (Lk. 7:16; Jn. 12:17). The spirits of grief must yield when He, the Master of joy, makes His entry.

It is thus nonsensical to expect mourning from Him who is Himself life, as the Jewish leaders do according to His parabolic saying in Lk. 7:32 and par. (→ θρηνέω, 154). The charge of Jesus is not just that of caprice, [118] or of the common attitude of expecting from spiritual leaders the observance of a particularly strict and exceptional ethics. The fundamental error is that they have their own human and nationalistic picture of the Messiah which they are trying, as it were, to force on God (→ 154), and that they are thus treating the will of God as though it were not valid for themselves. Jesus Himself gives this explanation of the parable in the saying which immediately precedes in Lk. 7:30 : οἱ δὲ Φαρισαῖοι καὶ οἱ νομικοὶ τὴν βουλὴν τοῦ θεοῦ ἠθέτησαν εἰς ἑαυτούς. According to their dogma there ought to be something about the Messiah which is severe, remote from the world and forbidding. No one may know whence He comes (Jn. 7:27). He must appear as Judge — this requirement is perhaps the basis of Jesus' saying about His judicial office in Jn. 3:17 ff. [119] He must keep the Sabbath commandment with pitiless severity, preferring to "kill" on the Sabbath rather than to heal (Mk. 3:4 etc.). He must be at least the equal of the Pharisees in fasting — in the question of the disciples in Mk. 2:18 and par. there lies concealed a reproach against Himself. Jesus seems to have this last demand in mind when in a transparent figure in Mt. 11:17 and par. He says that the men of this generation (v. 16) expect of Him a demeanour of grief which corresponds to their own. For in Israel, as elsewhere, fasting was an ancient mourning practice (cf. 1 S. 31:13, a seven day fast [→ 838]; 2 S. 1:12; 3:35 etc.). On the other hand, the Pharisees were not content with the very different demeanour of the precursor of the Messiah. At least, they did not want the direct antithesis of an ἄνθρωπος ἐν μαλακοῖς ἱματίοις ἠμφιεσμένος (Lk. 7:25 and par.), which was a standing reproach to their own manner of life. Instead of following John in serious penitence and bringing forth works meet for repentance (Lk. 3:8 and par.), they preferred ἀγαλλιαθῆναι πρὸς ὥραν (Jn. 5:35). Like the Baptist, Jesus does not do them the pleasure of acting otherwise than He should according to the will of God. He came, not as Judge, but as Saviour (Jn. 3:17; 12:47). He did not appear suddenly, but was brought up normally in a Galilean village. He helped and healed on the Sabbath too, and joined harmlessly in feasts (Jn. 2:1 ff.; Mk. 2:15). Perhaps this eating and drinking gave most pointed expression to the fact that He did the very opposite of what the θρηνοῦντες desired. His sayings about fasting (Mt. 6:16-18) also run directly contrary to what these demanded of Him.

Their answer to His joy in life is a mortal blow by which they conjure up a lamentation they had not desired (→ 850 on Rev. 1:7; Zech. 12:10 ff.). For finally they are the guilty ones who have forfeited life, whereas God and His messengers are justified (Lk. 7:29, 35 and par.).

---

[118] Zn. Mt. on 11:16 ff.

[119] Cf. E. Schwartz, "Aporien im vierten Evangelium," III (NGG, 1908), and on this G. Stählin, "Zum Problem d. joh. Eschatologie," ZNW, 34 (1934), 238, n. 7.

2. κοπετός for the Dying Christ. But before there is this exchange of mourning and this justification, Jesus Himself must go through κοπετός, for κοπετός precedes, not only His victories over death in the lives of others, but also His own decisive Easter victory (→ 845). It does so in the form of profound lamentation for the dying Messiah. In its proleptic form (Lk. 23:27) this was probably unconscious on the part of the majority. But once death supervened, many seem to have engaged in it with a full awareness of what they were doing (Lk. 23:48). We may see this from the confession of the centurion, especially as it has been handed down in Mk. (15:39) and Mt. (27:54).

In this there was perhaps seen a fulfilment of later prophecy, which included mourning for the dead Messiah in its depiction of the Messiah. This is particularly true in the much contested passage Zech. 12:10: "They look upon me (?) whom they have pierced, and they mourn for him, as one mourneth for his only son (LXX: καὶ κόψονται ἐπ' αὐτὸν κοπετὸν ὡς ἐπ' ἀγαπητόν), and are distraught for him, as one that is distraught for his firstborn (LXX: καὶ ὀδυνηθήσονται ὀδύνην ὡς ἐπὶ πρωτοτόκῳ).

In this verse, which is perhaps the most important κοπετός passage in the Bible, there is mourning for the wonderful figure who has been fittingly called the "martyr of God." [120] In the obscure picture there is a fusion of a retrospective prophetic view of the past, the painful experience of the prophet himself, ancient Messianic hopes, and a tentative preview of the mysterious salvation of God which is the theme of prophetic enquiry and reflection (1 Pt. 1:10).

This figure is first portrayed by Zech. (11:4-14) in prophetic action under the image of the good shepherd, possibly with king Josiah as the model (cf. 12:11 Mas., with its possible allusion to Josiah's death, → n. 52). It is then declared that he is smitten by the sword according to God's own counsel (13:7-9). [121] But now a miracle takes place. The one who has been laid low (12:8) and pierced through (v. 10) by the people rises again, and like David he becomes as an angel of God (v. 8). But rather strangely there begins at the same time a mourning of great intensity (as for an only son, v. 10, → 838, → supra) and of national scope (all the tribes take part, vv. 12-14), as for a beloved king (v. 11; → 838). Why does this κοπετός take place? Two factors are obviously involved, remorse at guilt for the death of the divine martyr, and grief at the misfortune which has come on the people of God by reason of this death (13:7-9; cf. Mk. 14:27 and par.). One point is decisive, however, namely, that the κοπετός is held against a background of light. [122] The mourning of penitence is possible only because the divine spirit of grace has already been received. Moreover, the reawakening of the good shepherd obviously implies the renewal of the Davidic monarchy, with which the restoration of Judah and Jerusalem is linked. It is thus a blessed κοπετός, and its gracious acceptance by God is confirmed by the welling up of a purifying fountain in Jerusalem (13:1).

Even to points of detail this passage has manifold significance for NT κοπετός for Christ. Jesus is the Son of David, the Good Shepherd and King of Israel, who by the counsel of God is smitten by His people. He is also in a unique sense the

---

[120] This is the title which Procksch, 107 gives to the section 11:4—13:9.

[121] As it seems to me, 13:7-9 more probably bears this reference than to the bad shepherd (11:15-17), cf. Procksch, 108.

[122] Cf. the similar connection between θρῆνος and prophecy of salvation in Mt. 2:17 and Jn. 16:20 (→ θρηνέω, 153 f.).

ἀγαπητός (LXX, v. 10), [123] and πρωτότοκος, cf. Hb. 1:6, and He is bewailed by the inhabitants of Jerusalem both out of repentance for His fate and out of concern for their own. This takes place against the background of divine salvation, which is in fact fulfilled in the very object of the lamentation.

Linked with this is the interpretation which Barnabas (7, 5) gives to a haggada on the Great Day of Atonement. He finds in the action τοῦ λαοῦ νηστεύοντος καὶ κοπτομένου ἐπὶ σάκκου καὶ σποδοῦ [124] (while the priests eat of the sin-offering) a typical representation of the offering of Christ and of mourning for Him. Finally, we may refer again to the Gnostic hymn in Ac. Jn., 95, which lays on the lips of Jesus Himself a lament for His death and a demand that His disciples should accompany it with κοπετός (θρηνῆσαι θέλω· κόψασθε πάντες, → 836). This is obviously at variance with history, for the Jesus of the Gospels, while He does sometimes speak of θρῆνος in the last afflictions (Jn. 16:20; → θρηνέω, 153), rejects any κοπετός for Himself (Lk. 23:28 ff.; → 153). Only in one instance is there a similar anticipation of His burial (Mk. 14:3-9) which He Himself interprets as such (v. 8).

Along the lines of the prophecy in Zechariah, Jesus admonishes those who bewail Him to weep rather for themselves and their approaching fate. In so doing He takes up the prophetic demand for κοπετός, [125] and yet at the same time He also demonstrates His self-forgetful pity (cf. Lk. 23:34) and love εἰς τέλος (Jn. 13:1). For κοπετός for Him can become a way to penitence and hence to escape from destruction.

3. But there is also a κοπετός which no longer leads to conversion, and the rest of the NT speaks of this eschatological κοπετός.

a. In spite of its fulfilment in the passion of Jesus, the primitive Church takes Zechariah 12:10 differently. It still regards it as a prophecy and refers it to the great κοπετός at the end, thus maintaining the prophetic intimation of general κοπετός for the Day of Yahweh (→ 841). In the so-called Synoptic and the Johannine apocalypses eschatological κοπετός takes place at the same point, namely, at the parousia. In Mt. 24:30 we read that when the sign of the Son of Man appears in heaven, i.e., to show that His coming is at the very doors, then κόψονται πᾶσαι αἱ φυλαὶ τῆς γῆς. Rev. 1:7, which combines Zech. 12:10 ff. with Da. 7:13, is to the same effect: ἰδοὺ ἔρχεται μετὰ τῶν νεφελῶν ... καὶ κόψονται ἐπ' αὐτὸν [126] πᾶσαι αἱ φυλαὶ τῆς γῆς. Seeing and lamenting are one, as concretely exemplified in both parts of the rhyme (ὄψονται [127] — κόψονται).

The words are the same as in Zech. 12:10 ff., but the meaning is new. ἡ γῆ means there (v. 12) the land of Judah and πᾶσαι αἱ φυλαί (restricted by αἱ ὑπο-

---

[123] Cf. Mk. 1:11; 9:7; 12:6 etc. → ἀγαπάω, I, 48: "The ἀγαπητὸς υἱός is the one Martyr at the turning point of the times whose death is an exercise of judgment on the whole world and lays the foundation of the new order of all things."

[124] On this rather enigmatic expression, which rests on the usual combination of wearing sackcloth, putting ashes on the head, lamentation and fasting, cf. 2 S. 3:31 f.; Est. 4:3; Jer. 6:26; 49:3 (30:19 LXX); Ez. 27:31 etc., cf. Pr.-Bauer, s.v.

[125] → 841; θρηνέω, 151; 153. Acc. to an addition to the text in Old Lat. (vae nobis) and Old Syr. at Lk. 23:48 the people of Jerusalem complied with this requirement, cf. Ev. Pt. 7:25; 8:28.

[126] On the constr. with ἐπί and acc. (→ 834) cf. not only Zech. 12:10 and Rev. 18:9 but also 2 Βασ. 11:26 (Orig. and Lucian); 1:12; cf. also Bl.-Debr. § 233, 2; and the par. expressions κλαίω ἐπί (acc.) in Lk. 19:41; 23:28 etc.; πενθέω ἐπί (acc.), Rev. 18:11; 2 Βασ. 13:37 etc.; θρηνέω ἐπί (acc.), 2 Ch. 35:25; Lam. 1:1 etc.

[127] In Rev. 1:7 ὄψονται is simply a vl. for ὄψεται.

λελειμμέναι, v. 14) means the tribes of Israel. In the NT, however, both have a general reference in keeping with the universal character of the *parousia*, when it will be irresistibly and irrefutably made known to all who Christ is and what it means to have rejected Him. As in the OT prophecy (→ 849), κοπετός is on the one side an outburst of remorse, but on the other side mourning for the death of Christ is far less prominent than grief at one's personal fate, at the immediately impending judgment of God, [128] concerning which the sign manifested in heaven precludes all further doubt. This is a fatal realisation, for already it is too late. The bright light which shines behind the κοπετός in Zechariah has now been extinguished. Eschatological κοπετός is mourning in the most specific and eternally valid sense. It is the world's mourning for itself in its final, hopeless distress.

b. A special form of the prophetic intimation of eschatological κοπετός is to be found in Rev. 18:9 in the ironical declaration of mourning for Babylon. The idea comes from Is. 14:4 ff. and the words are taken from Ez. 26:16; 27:30 ff.: καὶ κλαύσουσιν καὶ κόψονται ἐπ' αὐτὴν οἱ βασιλεῖς τῆς γῆς. In Is. the king of Babylon is the representative of the enemies of God on earth, and similarly in the NT his city is still the symbol of ungodliness, though its seat has shifted to the West. "Babylon must perish" is a τόπος of both OT and NT eschatology, and in keeping with its universal significance the whole world must raise a lament for it. Only the world, for the people of God rejoices at its destruction (v. 20).

> This is not, of course, a true lament (→ n. 128), for in the κόπτεσθαι of kings and the thrice repeated κλαίειν καὶ πενθεῖν (v. 11, 15) of merchants and seafarers there is also grief for themselves, who are sorely hit by the death of their good patron and protector.

4. Summary.

The Bible bears consistent witness to the fact that death, which came upon the earth through sin, belongs to the world which is against God. From the first pages to the last Scripture testifies that death cannot be where God is, the source of all life. Where death is, is distance from God and separation from this source, Gn. 3:19; 4:8 ff.; Rev. 21:4. Around death there is thus by nature an atmosphere of remoteness from God. That which is hostile to God, or heathen in the strict sense, thus finds its most congenial centre here. The history of mourning customs, even in the Bible, offers a vivid illustration. If the heathen are those who have no hope, this comes out most sharply in the face of death, in the hopelessness of reaction to this most elemental event of life, and it is striking how this almost essential feature of humanity is manifested in the mourning of the biblical world as well as the non-biblical. But it is also striking and significant that the sense that this is something which ought not to be is also found in both the non-biblical and the biblical world even though the war against the heathen element in mourning is waged under the cover of varied motifs. Finally, it is striking that neither in the non-biblical world nor in the biblical world can this battle be carried through to a successful issue until the separation of fallen and mortal man from God has been

---

[128] Like κοπετός in the prophets and Rev. 18:9, κόπτομαι is used here, i.e., in the absolute at Mt. 24:30; Zech. 12:12, to denote not merely a lament but also, at least as an undertone, grief at one's own wrong or destiny. Beating on the breast, and many other mourning practices like scattering ashes, fasting etc., can also express consciousness of sin, cf. κοπετός in Jl. 2:12; κόπτομαι in Barn., 7, 5; τύπτω τὰ στήθη, Lk. 18:13 etc.

overcome from within, or better, by God Himself. The Greek states and Roman law could not meet the situation with their prohibitions. The Hellenistic philosophers and Jewish rabbis exerted themselves more or less in vain to check the excesses of lamentation and mourning. Even until late in the Christian epoch one can still hear the voice of pre-Christian and non-Christian lamentation, and the voice of protest against it.

There is only one place where κοπετός is fully defeated. This is the cross. For at the cross man's remoteness from God is changed into nearness. In the light of the cross a profound change in the practice of mourning is possible. On the basis of the reality of Easter arises a faith which, hesitant at first, then bold as death itself, exercises a fundamental influence on the attitude of Christ's disciples to death (1 C. 15). From this time on true Christian grief for the departed has become a very different thing from κοπετός. Natural grief is no less than that which finds expression in κοπετός. But it is illumined by the certainty of a life in which all tears will be wiped away and there will be no more pain or crying (Rev. 21:4). In contrast to pagan κοπετός, Christian sorrow is thus quiet, and this quietness is itself a presentiment and anticipation of the blessed rest in which all sorrow and lamentation will be changed for ever into the fulness of joy.

† ἀποκόπτω (→ ἐκκόπτω, εὐνοῦχος, εὐνουχίζω, II, 765 ff.).

ἀποκόπτω, "to cut off," 1. lit. "to cut off," "to strike off," e.g., cutwaters, Hom. Il., 9, 241; tree-branches, Hom. Od., 23, 195; 9, 325; parts of the body, Hdt., VI, 91 and 114; Plut. G. Julius Caesar, 16 (I, 715b); Dion. Hal. Ant. Rom., III, 58; → infra; b. "to hew through," "to chop," e.g., cords, Hom. Il., 16, 474; anchor cables, Od., 10, 127; Xenoph. Hist. Graec., I, 6, 21; Ac. 27:32 : ἀπέκοψαν . . . τὰ σχοινία τῆς σκάφης. c. "to break," e.g., bridges, Plut. Nicias, 26 (I, 540c); d. "to hew down," esp. enemies, Xenoph. An., III, 4, 39; 2. Symbolically ἀποκόπτομαι = → κόπτομαι, "to mourn for," Eur. Tro., 627; 3. Fig. a. "to cut off," "to take away," "to remove," e.g., hope, Apoll. Rhod., IV, 1272 (ἐλπίδα); Plut. Pyrrhus, 2 (I, 383e) (τῆς ἐλπίδος), pity, ψ 76:8; the voice, Dion. Hal. Compos. Verb., 14; Plut. Demosthenes, 25 (I, 857d); b. in rhetorical usage of the abrupt termination of a period, Aristot. Rhet., III, 8, p. 1409a, 19; c. in grammatical usage of apocope, the omission of one or more letters, esp. at the end of a word, Aristot. Poet., 22, p. 1458b, 2. [1]

In the NT the word occurs in two important passages, in each of which it refers to the cutting off of members.

1. The Saying of Jesus concerning the σκάνδαλον of Members, Mk. 9:43, 45.

Members of the human body [2] are struck or hewn off a. in battle, e.g., Hom. Il., 11, 146 (αὐχένα); 13, 203 (κεφαλὴν . . . ἀπὸ δειρῆς κόψεν); 11, 261 (κάρη); cf. Aesch. Suppl., 841 (ἀποκοπὰ κρατός); in this connection cf. Jn. 18:10, 26 : ἀπέκοψεν . . . τὸ ὠτάριον [ὠτίον] (10 τὸ δεξιόν); b. in amputations, e.g., Archigenes in Oribasius Medicinalia (ed. Bussemaker-Daremberg, IV [1862]), 47, 13, 2; cf. § 3 (ἀποκοπή); c. as a punishment, esp. on prisoners of war as a continuation of the horrors of battle, e.g., Ju. 1:6 f. (thumbs and big toes), and cf. the proclamation of Ez. (23:25) to Jeru-

---

ἀ π ο κ ό π τ ω. Nägeli, 78 f.; A. Bischoff, "Exegetische Randbemerkungen," ZNW, 9 (1908), 169 f.; Zn. Gl.², 258, n. 82; A. Oepke, Der Brief des Pls. an die Galater (1937), 95 f.
[1] For further usage in secular Gk. cf. Liddell-Scott, s.v.
[2] Cf. also ἀποκόπτειν at sacrifice, e.g., Hom. Od., 3, 449 (the sinews of the neck).

salem : They will cut off your nose and ears, though there is here also the thought of punishment for infidelity to Yahweh (cf. Diod. S., I, 78 for this punishment on the adulterer). Odysseus proceeds rather differently in his punishment of the unfaithful goatherd Melanthios, Od., 22, 477: χεῖράς τ' ἠδὲ πόδας κόπτον (there is a preceding ἀπό in v. 475). [3] Related is the commandment in Dt. 25:11 f. that if a woman, to help her husband in a scuffle, seizes his opponent by the privy parts, her hand shall be struck off. Dillmann [4] says that this is the only place in the OT in which mutilation is laid down as a penalty, but we might also refer to the OT *ius talionis* (cf. Mt. 5:38), which occurs in almost exactly the same form in three passages, Ex. 21:23 f., with reference to the hurting of pregnant women ; Lv. 24:20 more generally with reference to various bodily injuries, and Dt. 19:21 in respect of false witnesses, who are to suffer the same as those who have been damaged by their witness. These regulations obviously presuppose mutilations. According to 2 S. 4:12 murderers were also mutilated, at least after execution. When Jesus uses the term διχοτομεῖν in Mt. 24:51 and Lk. 12:46 He also seems to be alluding to the legal practice of punishing malefactors by cutting off parts of the body. [5] On the problem of such punishments in Rabbinic writings → ἐκκόπτω, 859. Joseph. mentions such a case in Vit., 147: τὴν ἑτέραν τῶν χειρῶν ἀποκόψαι κελεύσας.

The prescription of cutting off members as a punishment obviously underlies the direction of Jesus in Mk. 9:43, 45. The meaning can hardly be that we are to make further temptation impossible by cutting off a hand or foot. The plucking out of the right eye in particular makes it plain that this is not the real purpose. What is at issue is self-punishment inflicted on the sinning member. [6] This may also weaken the sinful influence of this part of the body, [7] but above all it anticipates future punishment and is thus a prevention of eternal judgment (cf. the threefold ἤ ... βληθῆναι εἰς τὴν γέενναν), → ἐκκόπτω, 859 on Mt. 5:30; 18:8.

2. Paul's Saying about His Opponents, Gl. 5:12.

A special instance of the ἀποκόπτειν of members is emasculation (→ εὐνουχίζω, εὐνοῦχος, II, 765-768; cf. κατατομή, Phil. 3:2), e.g., Philo Spec. Leg., I, 325 : ἀποκεκομμένοι τὰ γεννητικά; Leg. All., III, 8 : ἀποκεκομμένοι τὰ γεννητικὰ τῆς ψυχῆς; Dio C., 79, 11: ἀποκόψαι αὐτό (sc. τὸ αἰδοῖον). In this sense ἀποκόπτω is also used absol. without explanatory object, esp. the pass., Luc. Eun., 8 : τοῦτον δὲ ἐξ ἀρχῆς εὐθὺς ἀποκεκόφθαι, whose part. (like that of the mid.) can have the sense of "eunuch" (οἱ ἀποκοπτόμενοι, Epict. Diss., II, 20, 19; ἀποκεκομμένος, Dt. 23:2), like the verbal adj. ἀπόκοπος, Strab., XIII, 4, 14; Oecumenius (MPG, 118) and Theophylact. (MPG, 124) on Gl. 5:12.

Eunuchs could be found in two places in the ancient world, [8] as chamberlains in oriental courts (→ εὐνοῦχος) and as servants of the deity in many oriental cults, e.g., the *Galli* of Cybele (cf. Ps.-Luc. Syr. Dea, 51).

The OT speaks of the first of these forms as a given fact not only in Babylon (cf. Is. 39:7) but also in Israel itself (cf. 1 S. 8:15; 3 Βασ. 22:9; 4 Βασ. 8:6; 9:32; 24:12, 15; also Ιερ. 36:2 [29:2]). [9] But it also excludes ἀποκεκομμένοι quite radically from the

---

[3] Cf. K. F. Ameis-C. Hentze, *Anhang z. Hom. Od.³* (1879), ad loc.
[4] A. Dillmann, "Nu., Dt. und Jos." in *Kurzgefasstes exeget. Hndbch. z. AT* (1886), ad loc.
[5] In Egypt the hands of robbers were cut off, cf. Hastings DB, I, 525, s.v. "Mutilation" (in the art. "Crimes and Punishments").
[6] Schl. Mt., 178 f. speaks of the "all-sacrificing bravery which Jesus demands for this conflict," but his case against the idea of self-punishment cannot be regarded as complete.
[7] Cf. G. Stählin, *Skandalon* (1930), 267 and 269, though the basic thought of self-punishment is not very clearly stated here.
[8] Cf. A. D. Nock, "Eunuchs in Ancient Religion," ARW, 23 (1925), 25 ff.
[9] In a few passages there is room for doubt whether we have real eunuchs or a mere title, cf. esp. 2 K. 25:19 = Ιερ. 52:25.

community of Yahweh, Dt. 23:2 : οὐκ εἰσελεύσεται θλαδίας καὶ ἀποκεκομμένος εἰς ἐκκλησίαν κυρίου. The reasons for this exclusion are as follows. a. Emasculation is an offence against the will of God as Creator. The body is divinely given ; hence it is a sin to mutilate it. In particular, only God who has given life, and the power to procreate it, has the right to take these away again. Man has no such right. b. Emasculation is an offence against monotheism and against the covenant of God with Israel. It is an imitation of heathen customs and is thus unworthy of a people which is so closely bound to God. It is alien to the way of life and the worship of this people, like making incisions and cutting off the forelock in mourning, Dt. 14:1; Lv. 19:28; → κόπτομαι. c. Finally, emasculation is an offence against pure worship. Only that which is without blemish is good enough for God, cf. the related regulations concerning priests with scrotal hernia (Lv. 21:20) or sacrificial animals with damaged testicles (Lv. 22:24). [10] He who has lost one of the most important powers does not belong to the cultic community of the people of God.

But the OT does not hold to this restrictive attitude [11] with full consistency. The victorious breakthrough of prophetic universalism makes a place for εὐνοῦχοι too. In Jer. (Ιερ. 48:16 [41:16]) we are told that Johanan took such along with him to Egypt, i.e., as a constituent part of the community, and acc. to Is. 56:3-5 the εὐνοῦχος who is faithful to the covenant has an honourable place in the community — a promise whose fulfilment is perhaps to be seen in Ac. 8:27.

Jesus Himself does not take up any position as regards the question of eunuchs in the community, not even in Mt. 19:12, since here He is probably thinking of the renunciation of sexual life (→ II, 767 f.). This is how Paul (and later Cl. Al. Strom., III, 59, 4) understands the saying, as may be seen from his own practice in 1 C. 7:7. If he had taken a different view, he could not have written with such savage scorn in Gl. 5:12. [12]

In Gl. 5:12 Paul is obviously expressing a sharp rejection of emasculation : Ὄφελον καὶ ἀποκόψονται οἱ ἀναστατοῦντες ὑμᾶς. What is he really wishing for these men who disrupt the peace of the Galatian churches ? Attempts have been made to show that ἀποκόπτομαι is here used in the figurative sense of "to separate themselves." This is how the Reformers and Erasmus took it. Not even as a curse could Paul envisage the supreme brutality and impiety of the literal act. [13] But if we concede that the apostle was not fastidious in his choice of linguistic media, and that at a time like this the strongest expressions in current speech seemed to be the best adapted to his purpose, [14] we must also grant that the overwhelming force of his argument is lost if we weaken the sense of this dramatic term to segregari. Above all the καί is deprived of all meaning, since it obviously points to a climax as compared with what has gone before. But this climax depends on the contrast between περιτέμνεσθαι (v. 2 ff.; cf. v. 11) and ἀποκόπτεσθαι, as Chrysostom already perceived and brought out when he expounded in terms of περικοπτέσθωσαν as the counterpart to περιτεμνέσθωσαν. [15] ἀποκόπτειν is a radical surpassing of περιτέμνειν which changes the legalism into contradiction of

---

[10] Rabb. exegesis also found a ref. to men in this passage, cf. Str.-B., I, 807.
[11] Cf. also the avoidance of the word εὐνοῦχος in Ιερ. 45:7 (38:7); 41:19; 34:19; → II, 766.
[12] Cf. also J. R. Willis in DRG, s.v. "Eunuch."
[13] A. Bischoff, 169 f.
[14] Nägeli, 78 f.
[15] Cf. the similar antithesis in Phil. 3:2 : κατατομή — περιτομή.

the Law, since it incurs the verdict of Dt. 23:2. This is the very point that Paul wishes to make. His opponents are in conflict with the will of God. In the light of Dt. 23:2 there is also a subsidiary thought of self-excommunication. By self-emasculation they would shut themselves out of the Church of God, as in truth they have already been outside for long enough. Indeed, self-emasculation is an acute relapse into paganism, for it was at the heart of the Cybele cult which had its home in Galatia. [16]

It might be asked whether the reference is to true self-emasculation [17] or to an operation (ἀποκόπτομαι = "to have oneself castrated") [18] such as seems to be envisaged also in Dt. 23:2, where there are, as it seems, two operations resulting in emasculation, the reference being to the θλαδίας as well as the ἀποκεκομμένος. In fact, however, the question is irrelevant, for Paul's cry is one of biting scorn and is obviously not meant to be taken literally. [19] What he is saying is simply that they ought to carry their error to its logical extreme and thereby make evident [20] something which is indubitably clear to him, namely, that they do not belong to the community of God.

The withdrawal referred to by Jesus (Mt. 19:12) and practised by Paul was sometimes found also among the rabbis, e.g., Ben Azzai (T. Jeb., 8, 4; Str.-B., I, 807). Self-emasculation among pagans, perhaps on religious grounds, was treated with contempt (cf. bShab., 152a, Midr. Qoh. on 10:7), for castration was unconditionally repudiated, cf. S. Lv. 22:24 (399a) and bShab., 110b, Bar.; Str.-B., I, 807.

Emasculation is also condemned outside the Bible and Judaism, e.g., by the Romans. Typical of the attitude of popular philosophy is the saying of Epictetus (Diss., II, 20, 19): καὶ οἱ ἀποκοπτόμενοι τάς γε προθυμίας τὰς τῶν ἀνδρῶν ἀποκόψασθαι οὐ δύνανται. [21]

† ἐγκοπή, † ἐγκόπτω (→ προσκοπή, πρόσκομμα).

The word group ἐγκοπή, ἐγκόπτω took on its main sense [1] of "obstacle" (e.g., Vett. Val., I, 1 [p. 2, 7]: ἐγκοπαὶ τῶν πρασσομένων; Diog. L., IV, 50 : οἴησις προκοπῆς ἐγκοπή, "conceit is an obstacle to progress") or "to impede," "to arrest" [2] (e.g., Polyb., 23, 1, 12) from the military practice of making slits in the street to hold up a pursuing enemy. Hence the basic meaning is "to block the way." [3] By derivation

---

[16] Cf. Oepke, 95; also G. S. Duncan, *The Epistle of Paul to the Galatians* (1934, Moffatt NT Commentary), 161.

[17] So J. C. K. v. Hofmann, *Die hl. Schrift NT's*, II, 1: *Der Brief Pauli an die Galater* (1863), ad loc. (ἑαυτὸν ἀποκόπτειν); C. Weizsäcker, *Das NT übers.* (1922) ("mutilate oneself"); W. Lütgert, BFTh, 22, 6 (1919), 31 ff.; W. M. Ramsay, Exp. 5th Ser., Vol. II (1905), 103 ff.; Liddell-Scott, Wilke-Grimm, s.v.

[18] Zn. Gl., ad loc.; cf. Bl.-Debr. § 317.

[19] Moulton, 255 f.; 318.

[20] Cf. Lütgert, 31 ff., 81, though he suggests a mystico-pneumatic error under the influence of the Cybele cult.

[21] This sounds like a reply to a possible development of Mt. 5:29 f. (cf. H. Windisch, ZNW, 27 [1928], 170, n. 1): εἰ δὲ τὸ μόριόν σου σκανδαλίζει σε, ἔκκοψον αὐτὸ καὶ βάλε ἀπὸ σοῦ.

ἐ γ κ ό π τ ω. On the constr. with inf. and μή (Gl. 5:7 ? → n. 6), cf. Bl.-Debr. § 429; with the gen. of inf. (R. 15:22), ibid., § 400, 4; also Kühner-Gerth, II, 215.

[1] In Ac. 24:4 ἐγκόπτω might be rendered "to burden" (Zn., ad loc.) or "to weary," so syr, Pr. Ag., ad loc.; Pr.-Bauer, s.v., with ref. to the expression ἔγκοπον ποιέω, "to weary" (Job 19:2), "to burden" (Is. 43:23); cf. also Qoh. 1:8, where the meaning of ἔγκοπος is not clear.

[2] Hesych. ἐμποδίζω, διακωλύω. But there is also an intr. use : Vett. Val., VI, 9 (p. 260, 24); cf. Moult.-Mill., s.v. ἐκκόπτω (ἐνκόπτω).

[3] Hence a dat. constr. is possible as well as the acc., cf. P. Alex., 4, 3 (→ 856).

only a temporary hold-up is suggested, in contrast to → πρόσκομμα, and this may still be discerned in NT usage, cf. R. 15:22 : ἐνεκοπτόμην τὰ πολλὰ ... νυνὶ δὲ ... But later the distinction faded, cf. M. Ant., XI, 1: In certain things ἀτελὴς γίνεται ἡ ὅλη πρᾶξις ἐάν τι ἐγκόψῃ, Pap. Ptolémaiques du Musée d'Alexandrie, 4, 3 = Bulletin de la Société Archéologique d'Alexandrie, 2 (1899), 65 : ἡμῖν ἐγκόπτεις καλὰ καὶ ἐν τοῖς λοιποῖς πρὸς τὸ μὴ γίνεσθαι ... τὸ χρήσιμον, and even in the NT the thought of a definitive obstacle predominates, [4] and the term is used in the metaphor of running on the race-track (→ ἀγών, I, 135 ff., ἀθλέω, 167 f., βραβεῖον, 638 f.; στέφανος, στάδιον, τρέχω); cf. esp. Gl. 5:7: ἐτρέχετε καλῶς· τίς ὑμᾶς ἐνέκοψεν; [5] but the same image lies behind 1 Th. 2:18 and R. 15:22.

1. The Concept of Religious Obstacles in the NT. The obstacles denoted by ἐγκοπή and ἐγκόπτω in the NT are always (on Ac. 24:4 → n. 1) of a religious nature, in contrast to κωλύω. This emerges at once when we ask what is hindered. It is the course of the apostle through the world (R. 15:22; 1 Th. 2:18), or the course of the Gospel itself (1 C. 9:12), or the walk (course) of Christians in obedience to the truth (Gl. 5:7), [6] or the ascent of prayers to God (1 Pt. 3:7).

2. The main question is : By whom and how are these obstacles brought into being ? The NT has two answers to this question.

a. By Satan. 1 Th. 2:18 : ἐνέκοψεν ἡμᾶς ὁ σατανᾶς. He it is who tries to hinder not merely the missionary work but also the joys of the apostle, e.g., in seeing again his spiritual children. [7] It is true that in this case there must be a special reason for Paul's statement, since he makes it only here (Chrys. Hom. in 1 Th., ad loc. [MPG, 62]), cf. 2 C. 1:15 ff.; R. 1:13, and esp. Ac. 16:6 f.: κωλυθέντες ὑπὸ τοῦ ἁγίου πνεύματος ... οὐκ εἴασεν αὐτοὺς τὸ πνεῦμα 'Ιησοῦ. It may be doubted whether Paul ascribes natural events, e.g., a storm at sea, to the devil. [8] To be sure, he calls the devil θεὸς τοῦ αἰῶνος τούτου (2 C. 4:4). But "the dominion of the devil over this world is primarily a dominion over men" (→ διάβολος, II, 79), not over creation. It is more likely that he is thinking of an illness, or (cf. Ramsay) [9] of a prohibition on the part of the Thessalonian authorities, in which Paul might well see a cunning stratagem of Satan. Satanas egit per homines malos, Bengel on 1 Th. 2:18. Along the same lines we might consider the proximity of v. 16, where the apostle says that it was the Jews who hindered him (κωλυόντων ἡμᾶς) τοῖς ἔθνεσιν λαλῆσαι ἵνα σωθῶσιν (cf. the similar reproach of Jesus in Lk. 11:52 and par.). For other instances of the devil acting through the Jews cf. 1 C. 2:8b; Jn. 13:27; 8:44. But these are not his only agents.

Though he is not mentioned specifically, the same ἐγκόπτων stands behind the Judaisers who arrest the fine progress of the Galatians (Gl. 5:7), [10] for he is the

---

[4] Formally the 3 phrases διδόναι ἐγκοπήν (1 C. 9:12), διδόναι προσκοπήν (2 C. 6:3) and τιθέναι πρόσκομμα (R. 14:13) can have the same sense.

[5] The text. rec. has here ἀνέκοψεν from ἀνακόπτω, "to arrest in course," to stop the course of a ship, e.g., Theophr. Char., 25, 2 (vl. ἀνακύπτειν).

[6] The connection of ἀληθείᾳ μὴ πείθεσθαι with ἐνέκοψεν is questionable, cf. Zn. Gl., ad loc.; Bl.-Debr. § 488, 1b, and on the other side A. Oepke, Der Brief des Pls. an die Galater, 1937, ad loc. In fact the image can be sustained only if we put the question mark after ἐνέκοψεν. Yet such direct transitions from the figure to the reality are not uncommon, cf. 1 Pt. 2:8b; Mt. 5:16; 7:6a.

[7] Cf. Dib. Th., 12; Die Geisterwelt im Glauben des Pls. (1909), 56.

[8] Wbg. Th., ad loc.

[9] Pls. in der Ag. (1898), 188 f.

[10] Cf. the similar charge against Diotrephes in 3 Jn. 10 : τοὺς βουλομένους κωλύει.

antithesis τοῦ καλοῦντος ὑμᾶς (v. 8), and he mixes the corrupting ζύμη (v. 9; cf. 1 C. 5:6 with v. 5; → II, 903 and 905) into the νέον φύραμα of God.

b. In accordance with the paradoxical tension in the assessment of evil, which the NT sometimes traces to the devil and sometimes to the heart of man (→ πονηρός), men, too, may be regarded as the authors of the ἐγκόπτειν which, since it is always opposed to the good in the NT (→ 856), is simply a specific instance of evil. Thus the apostle himself might become an ἐγκόπτων in respect of his own evangelistic work (1 C. 9:12) if he were to use his apostolic ἐξουσία (v. 4, 7 ff., 14) in a way which his conscience forbade. ἐγκοπή would arise to the Gospel of Christ if 1. the appearance were given that he was using his missionary work as a means of livelihood or gain, and 2. the fear of having to make a material contribution would frighten away the poor from entry into the community.[11] Either way there would be an attachment to money (Mt. 6:24) which would be an ἐγκοπή to the προκοπή τοῦ εὐαγγελίου (Phil. 1:12). The supreme concern of Paul is ἵνα μή τινα ἐγκοπήν[12] δῶμεν τῷ εὐαγγελίῳ τοῦ Χριστοῦ. The thought of the → προκοπή τοῦ εὐαγγελίου drives into the background any consideration for his own rights or wishes or sufferings.

As here sin can disturb and arrest God's work in the world, so in 1 Pt. 3:7 (εἰς τὸ μὴ ἐγκόπτεσθαι τὰς προσευχὰς ὑμῶν) it can hamper the relationship of individual Christians to God. The apostle is not thinking here merely of married couples praying together. To be sure, he does suggest that this might be made impossible by the husband if he does not honour his wife as equally justified, though physically weaker. But perversion in this most important and inward relation between men can disrupt[13] and even destroy the relation between these men and God, just as the converse is often true. The problem that sin bars the way to God in prayer[14] is one which has affected the whole race since the days of Cain, and it has been truly solved only in Christ.

The course of the Gospel, the apostle and Christians, and the ascent of prayer, are all movements which are effected by the Holy Spirit. Hence their hampering is one of the things which are to be avoided at all costs (→ σκάνδαλον).

ἐκκόπτω.

The radical quality of → ἀποκόπτω in the NT is also characteristic of ἐκκόπτω. The use of the two verbs is particularly close where it is a matter of radical decisions in the NT sense (→ 858 f.).

A. General Greek Usage.

a. ἐκ- in the literal sense gives the sense "to strike out," esp. eyes,[1] e.g., Aristoph. Av., 342 : ἤν ... τὼ ὀφθαλμὼ ἐκκοπῇς, "if both your eyes are struck out"; the noun

---

[11] Bchm. 1 K., ad loc.

[12] The reading ἐκκοπήν does not give a satisfactory sense.

[13] The ideas suggested in 1 C. 7:5 and Test. N. 8:8, to which Wnd. Kath. Br., ad loc. draws attention, are rather more distant, though that of Paul, namely, that the devil has free play when the relation with God is broken, is important in this connection.

[14] Contrast the promise given to the righteous (deduced from Dt. 7:14) in bBek., 44b; Str.-B., I, 455 : Thy prayer shall not be unfruitful (without result) before God. Cf. also the other passages in Str.-B., I, 450 ff. on the question of the hearing and answering of prayer in Judaism.

ἐ κ κ ό π τ ω. K. Bornhäuser, Die Bergpredigt² (1927), 90 ff.

[1] In the sayings of Jesus ἐξαιρεῖν (Mt. 5:29; 18:9) or ἐκβάλλειν (Mk. 9:47) is used instead.

ἐκκοπή is found in the same sense, e.g., Philodem. Philos. De Ira, Fr. 8b, Col. XIII
(C. Wilke [1914], p. 33); teeth, e.g., Phryn. Comicus, Fr. 68 (CAF, I, p. 387); of surgical
incisions (→ ἀποκόπτω, 852); Luc. Tyr., 24; also ἐκκοπή, Heliodor. in Oribasius
Medicinalia, ed. Bussemaker-Daremberg, III [1858], 44, 11 *titulus*; branches which are
pruned to make way for new grafts, R. 11:22, or to be themselves grafted in another
tree, v. 24; cf. P. Fay., 114, 14. Here, where ἐκκόπτω (with ἐκκλάω) is correlative to
ἐγκεντρίζω, the cutting out is not radical to the degree that it is not definitive, for
there is also a πάλιν ἐγκεντρίζειν (v. 23), though → 859. b. From sense a. there arises
the sense "to break open," i.e., by beating down doors, locks, bars etc., e.g., Lys., 3, 6
(θύρας), Polyb., 4, 3, 10 (οἰκίας). c. ἐκ- in the broader sense as a prep. of radical
separation gives the sense "to hew off," esp. trees, e.g., Ditt. Syll.[3], 966, 34 and 41
(ἐλάας); P. Oxy., VI, 892, 10 (cf. Moult.-Mill., *s.v.*); Zech. 12:11; Gr. En. 26:1: τοῦ
δένδρου ἐκκοπέντος, "even when the tree is hewn down" (sc. the branches remain and
sprout again); Jer. 22:7: καὶ ἐκκόψουσιν τὰς ἐκλεκτὰς κέδρους σου καὶ ἐμβαλοῦσιν
εἰς τὸ πῦρ. In form we are reminded of the similar sayings of the Baptist and Jesus,
Mt. 3:10 and par.; 7:19 : πᾶν δένδρον μὴ ποιοῦν καρπὸν καλὸν ἐκκόπτεται καὶ εἰς
πῦρ βάλλεται. Cf. the same thought in Jn. 15:2, 6 and, without the continuation about
fire, Lk. 13:7, 9 : ἐκκόψεις αὐτήν (sc. τὴν συκῆν). A counterpart may be seen in
Dt. 20:19 : αὐτὸ (sc. a tree bearing fruit) οὐκ ἐκκόψεις. The noun occurs in the same
expression, e.g., Polyb., 2, 65, 6. In respect of members of the human body (→ ἀποκόπτω, 852) we have as yet no instances outside the NT,[2] Mt. 5:30; 18:8 (→ 859).

Fig. the usage follows two main lines in accordance with the emphasis on separation
on the one side (d.e.) and complete removal or destruction on the other (f.).

From the thought of separation arises the sense d. "to drive out," e.g. Xenophon
Hist. Graec., VII, 4, 26, cf. 32; Plut. Cic. et Demosth., 4 (I, 887 f.) (τῆς πατρίδος) and
also the sense e. "to sunder," "to exclude," "to repel." Symmachus uses ἐκκόπτειν in
this sense in ψ 30:22; 87:5 to express the feeling of the righteous that he is cut off from
God, and in ψ 36:38 to state that the wicked is actually separated from God. Along
these lines the early Church uses ἐκκόπτειν of exclusion from the Church, i.e., excommunication, e.g., Canones Apostolorum, 29 (ed. F. Lauchert [1896]): οὗτος παντάπασιν ἐκκοπτέσθω τῆς ἐκκλησίας, 30 : ἐκκοπτέσθω τῆς κοινωνίας παντάπασιν.
f. Radical removal implies extirpation or destruction : of men, e.g., Hdt., IV, 110;
Demosth. Or., 7, 4 (λῃστάς); Ιερ. 51:7 (44:7); cf. v. 8 : ἵνα ἐκκοπῆτε καὶ ἵνα γένησθε
εἰς κατάραν; Barn., 12, 9 : ἐκκόψει ἐκ ῥιζῶν τὸν οἶκον πάντα τοῦ 'Αμαλὴκ ὁ
υἱὸς τοῦ θεοῦ.[3] Of cities or countries, e.g., Paus., III, 8, 6 (τὰς 'Αθήνας); Plut. Pomp.,
24 (I, 631a). For fig. usage in the same sense, with the idea of putting out (a.) or hewing
down (c.) in the background, cf. Job 19:10 : ἐξέκοψεν δὲ ὥσπερ δένδρον τὴν ἐλπίδα
μου (→ ἀποκόπτω, 852); often of the banishing of states of mind, impulses etc., e.g.,
Plat. Charm., 155c (θρασύτης), Philodem. Philos. Περὶ παρρησίας, Fr. 88, Col. XVI
(ed. A. Olivieri [1914], p. 56) (φαντασία); 4 Macc. 3:2 ff. (ἐπιθυμία, θυμός, κακοήθεια, cf. v. 5 → n. 3), 1 Cl., 63, 2 (τὴν ἀθέμιτον τοῦ ζήλους ὑμῶν ὀργήν), and of
evils of all kinds, e.g., Gal. Utrum Medicinae sit an Gymnastices Hygiene, 27 (V, 856,
Kühn); De Methodo Medendi, 10, 1 (X, p. 662, Kühn) (τὰς νόσους, τὴν αἰτίαν [τοῦ
πυρετοῦ]); Preisigke Sammelbuch, 4284, 8 (τὰ βίαια καὶ ἄνομα); Ditt. Or., 669, 64
(τὰ τοιαῦτα, sc. misuses); Vett. Val., VII, 2 (p. 268, 6) (τὰ πολλὰ τῶν φαύλων);
Epict. Diss., II, 22, 34 (ταῦτα τὰ δόγματα). In this list we should also place 2 C. 11:12 :
ἵνα ἐκκόψω τὴν ἀφορμὴν τῶν θελόντων ἀφορμήν. What the opponents of Paul

---

[2] Though cf. the note of A. Deissmann on 4 Macc. 3:3 (in Kautzsch Pseudep., 155, n. i)
on ἐκκόπτειν = "amputate" in contrast to βοηθεῖν = "cure."
[3] To be noted here is the ἐκ ῥιζῶν, which underlines the radical character of ἐκκόπτω.
Cf. also in 4 Macc. 3, after the threefold οὐ δύναται ἐκκόψαι (vv. 2-4), the comprehensive
statement in v. 5 : οὐ γὰρ ἐκριζωτὴς τῶν παθῶν ὁ λογισμός ἐστιν, ἀλλὰ ἀνταγω-
νιστής, and also the supplementary adverbs with ἐκκόπτω in Ditt. Or., 669, 64 (ὁλικῶς),
Canones Apostolorum (→ *supra*), 29 (παντάπασιν), etc.

seek is to do him mischief, to discredit him, and for the sake of his apostolic commission he does all he can to rule this out, to make it impossible.

B. Radical ἐκκόπτειν in the Sayings of Jesus.

At two points in the sayings of Jesus (and the Baptist) the verb serves to express the radical nature of His message.

1. In the repeated parable of the unfruitful tree (Mt. 7:19; Lk. 13:7, 9; Mt. 3:10 and par.) hewing down is a symbol of the complete separation of a man from life (cf. especially Jn. 15:2 ff.), of his irrevocable handing over to destruction. In the parable of the fig-tree (Lk. 13) this is obviously in punishment and it takes place within this aeon (and its years). In Mt. 7:19 and in the parallel saying of the Baptist in 3:10 the thought is that of eternal perdition. A parallel to Luke is to be found in the warning to arrogant Gentile Christians in R. 11:22: ἐπεὶ καὶ σὺ ἐκκοπήσῃ, "otherwise you will be cut off" (though cf. v. 24, → 858).

2. In the twice repeated saying (Mt. 5:30; 18:8) about cutting off the hand (the foot only at 18:8), ἐκκόπτω, which is synonymous with → ἀποκόπτω (→ 852), expresses the seriousness of the decision which Jesus requires of men.

a. For the basic OT punishment of cutting off the hand (Dt. 25:12), cf. ἀποκόπτω → 852. The same principle that punishment should affect the member which committed the act is to be found in the Rabbis. bNidda, 13b[4]: R. Tarphon (1st-2nd cent.) has said: The hand which seizes one's own privy member is to be hewn off upon the navel. bShab., 108b[5]: R. Muna (c. 180 A.D.; cf. Str.-B., I, 303, n. 1) says: The hand which is put in the eye, the nose, the mouth etc. (before washing or before morning prayer?)[6] should be cut off. Rashi comments: It is better that it be cut off, for an evil spirit rests on the hand which is not washed in the morning, and it blinds etc. (or, any action, however insignificant, is sinful before morning prayer). bNidda, 13b and bSanh., 58b; Str.-B., I, 302; R. Huna (d. 297; Strack Einl., 139) has said: Cut off the hand (i.e., which raises itself against one's neighbour), as it is written. The hand which is upraised shall be broken (Job 38:15). R. Huna did in fact have the hand of a man cut off who was in the habit of striking others.[7] bPes., 57b demands the cutting off of the hand without reference to the nature of the offence, namely, lese-majesty.

b. In externally similar fashion Jesus demands the cutting off of a member which becomes an occasion for stumbling (→ σκανδαλίζω), whether it be a matter of sexual temptation (Mt. 5:30) or of a threat to one's whole religious life.[8] A feature shared with the Rabbinic sayings is the close connection between the offence and the punishment. But while the Rabbis have in view a judicial punishment[9] and not just a curse,[10] Jesus is obviously thinking of rigorous self-punish-

---

[4] Cf. the exposition of this passage in E. Bischoff, Jesus u. die Rabbinen (1905), 45.
[5] Bischoff, op. cit., 108 (under Addenda).
[6] On the relevant regulations, cf. Str.-B., IV, 190 ff. and bBer., 14b; Str.-B., IV, 202 f. (k).
[7] H. Freedman in his rendering (The Babylonian Talmud translated, ed. J. Epstein, Sanhedrin, I [1935], 399, n. 4) has this note: "This is not actually permitted in the Torah. J. H. Weiss (Dor Dor Wedoreshaw, II, 14) holds that R. Huna was influenced by a Persian practice in this."
[8] On both passages cf. G. Stählin, Skandalon (1930), 265 ff.
[9] So bNidda, 13b and esp. bPes., 57b. Later the Rabb. lost the authority to inflict such punishments (already in the 6th cent. A.D.?, though cf. Str.-B., I, 1026 on Mt. 27:2, also bBer., 58a, Str.-B., II, 571 f., where it is testified that the Babylonian exilarch claimed the power of scourging, though not of execution). The note of Rashi on bShab., 108b reflects the problematical character of these laws in the time of the political dependence of Judaism.
[10] Cf. Bischoff, 46 f., and the story how such a curse was fulfilled in bTaan., 21a, Str.-B.,

ment (→ ἀποκόπτω, 852 on Mk. 9:43, 45). That the demand ἔκκοψον αὐτὴν καὶ βάλε ἀπὸ σοῦ is meant literally[11] is quite probable when we take into account the spirit of theocentric and eschatological radicalness which fills the sayings of Jesus, especially in the Sermon on the Mount.[12] The eschatological background is particularly evident in the present saying. The radical self-punishment which will sacrifice a hand or a foot has as its goal a radical removal of the danger of Gehenna. Better lose this life, or members which are important to it, if this is the only way to attain eternal life (Mt. 16:26).

Stählin

---

† κορβᾶν, † κορβανᾶς

1. κορβᾶν is the Heb. קָרְבָּן adopted as a loan word (Lv. 2:1 ff.; Nu. 7:12 ff.; Ez. 40:43; Ned., 1, 2; cf. already the Assyrian *kurbânu*); κορβανᾶς is the Graecised Aram. קָרְבָּנָא or קוּרְבָּנָא (Tg. O. Gn. 4:4; bZeb., 116b etc.). Josephus has the word in the form κορβᾶν, Ant., 4, 73; Ap., 1, 167 and in the form κορβανᾶς (-ωνᾶς), Bell. 2, 175. He seems to distinguish between the two forms in a way which must be in keeping with current usage. Ant., 4, 72 f. refers to the significance of certain advantages which accrue to the priests by reason of vows. We then read in 4, 73: καὶ οἱ κορβᾶν αὑτοὺς ὀνομάσαντες τῷ θεῷ, δῶρον δὲ τοῦτο σημαίνει κατὰ Ἑλλήνων γλῶτταν, βουλομένους ἀφίεσθαι τῆς λειτουργίας τοῖς ἱερεῦσι καταβάλλειν ἀργύριον, γυναῖκα μὲν τριάκοντα σίκλους, ἄνδρα δὲ πεντήκοντα. This obviously refers to Lv. 27:1 ff., which lays down the necessary rules for the vowing of men and for their redemption from the possession of God. The reference is to men who dedicate themselves to God by calling themselves κορβᾶν and by thus in a sense making themselves a present to God. This is underlined by Josephus' use of δῶρον to try to make this alien word clear to non-Jewish readers. The fact that he regards it as necessary to preserve κορβᾶν in the text even though his readers do not understand it brings out the technical character of the word which made it sometimes indispensable, namely, if the consecration to God was to be valid. In keeping with this is what Joseph. says about κορβᾶν in Ap., 1, 166 f. In support of the correctness of his assertion of the importance and prominence of his people in antiquity he here appeals to a statement of Theophrastus[1] in a work which has not

---

I, 779 f. Such passages show that we can hardly take the sayings adduced as merely conventional expressions of the time (cf. Bornhäuser, 91).

[11] As against Bornhäuser, 92; cf. G. Dalman, *Arbeit u. Sitte in Palästina,* I, 2 (1928), 477, n. 10. Again, an "as if" ethics ("Live as if you had neither eye nor hand if these are an occasion of sin," H. Huber, *Die Bergpredigt* [1932], 91) does not do justice to the absoluteness of the radical ethics of Jesus, which Huber himself emphasises (the "as if" in 1 C. 7:29-31 is rather different).

[12] Cf. H. Windisch, *Der Sinn der Bergpredigt* (1929), 65 ff., 69 ff.

κ ο ρ β ᾶ ν κτλ. Pr.-Bauer,[3] s.v., Dalman Gr., 174, n. 3; H. Oort, "De verbintenissen met 'Korban,'" ThT, 37 (1903), 289-314; J. H. A. Hart, "Korban," JQR, 19 (1907), 615-650; H. Laible, "Korban," AELKZ, 54 (1921), 597-599, 613 f.; Str.-B., I, 711 ff.; C. G. Montefiore, *The Synoptic Gospels,*[2] I (1927), 148-152; Comm., *ad loc.* On Philo → ὅρκος and 863.

[1] Theophrastus of Eresos on Lesbos (c. 372-287 B.C.), pupil of Aristotle.

survived, namely, his Περὶ νόμων, to the effect that the people of Tyre were forbidden to use strange formulations in their vows, including the form κορβᾶν, which, when translated from the Heb., is equivalent to δῶρον θεοῦ. The technical character of the term is again emphasised by its designation as ὅρκος. Its use makes it clear that there is no doubt as to the transference to God of things dedicated to Him. Worth noting is the fact that the word is used here in the form which it has in the Torah, the basis of all Jewish worship. On the other hand κορβωνᾶς in Bell. 2, 175 [2] denotes the temple treasury (ἱερὸς θησαυρός) in which everything offered as κορβᾶν, or its redemption, is collected. [3] So far no corresponding use of קָרְבָּנָא has been traced. [4]

2. Corban in the Old Testament and in Later Judaism.

a. In the OT קָרְבָּן (a derivative of הִקְרִיב/קרב, "to offer something," esp. used of sacrifice, Lv. 1:13 etc.) means "that which is offered," esp. to God or to the sanctuary, i.e., "sacrifice." The general sense is still discernible in Nu. 7:3 ff., though here, too, there is an evident transition to sacrificial usage. Perhaps the word had from the very first a religious nuance: If so, it contains a reminiscence of the time when all the relations between men and men, except for those of war-like hostility, took religious forms (cf. הִקְרִיב of the handing over of a gift as a sign of subjection in Ju. 3:17 f., or of the handing of food to an eminent guest in Ju. 5:25). In any case, the word [5] enables us to see the origin of the minutely re-gulated sacrificial worship of Israel in the custom of bringing voluntary gifts of all kinds to God on the basis of a sense of dependence on Him and orientation to Him. As compared with other OT words for sacrifice, e.g., מִנְחָה (→ n. 5), קָרְבָּן does not come to be linked with any specific kind. The general character of the term, and its inclusion of a reference to the initiative of the one who makes the offering, are the basis of the special use which develops in later Judaism. [6]

b. The general use of קָרְבָּן ("sacrifice") may still be seen in Rabbinic Judaism. Thus there are occasional references (bMen., 110a, Bar.; Shim'on ben 'Azzai, d. c. 135 A.D.) to פָּרָשַׁת קָרְבָּנוֹת, the portion of Scripture dealing with offerings, and elsewhere a distinction is drawn between קָרְבָּן יָחִיד, the offering of the individual,

---

[2] Μετὰ δὲ ταῦτα ταραχὴν ἑτέραν ἐκίνει (Pilate) τὸν ἱερὸν θησαυρόν, καλεῖται δὲ κορβωνᾶς, εἰς καταγωγὴν ὑδάτων ἐξαναλίσκων.

[3] K. Kohler, in the light of Mt. 27:6, leaves open the possibility that κορβανᾶς is used for the receptacle for alms (Jew. Enc., I, 436; VII, 561), but there are no known instances of this usage.

[4] Very rarely קָרְבָּנָא is used for "gift" (bChul., 8a, perhaps also bZeb., 116b; cf. also Tg. Hos. 12:2 [Mas. שֶׁמֶן, LXX, a theological interpretation of the original], which speaks of the paying of tribute [→ infra, with n. 5]).

[5] A good par. may be found in מִנְחָה, which denotes a gift that in certain circumstances is obligatory (cf. Gn. 32:14; 33:10), and which can thus be used for tribute to a ruling political power (Ju. 3:15; Hos. 10:6) as well as for sacrifice to deity (Gn. 4:3; 1 S. 2:17; 26:19). Priestly usage then restricted the term to non-bloody offerings (Lv. 2:1 ff.). According to context the Gk. Bible differentiates between מִנְחָה as δῶρα (Gn. 32:14; 33:10; Ju. 3:15) or ξένια (Hos. 10:6), both plur., and מִנְחָה as θυσία (Gn. 4:3; 1 S. 2:17; 26:19; Lv. 2:1 etc.).

[6] This cannot be discerned in the Septuagint, which always has δῶρον for קָרְבָּן. The other renderings seem to make regular use of προσφορά, Lv. 1:2; 2:1; Nu. 5:15. We also find θυσία, Lv. 2:1. These are all in the Hexapla. In LXX Lv. and Nu. δῶρον is reserved for קָרְבָּן (and לֶחֶם), but in the other transl. it also occurs for עֹלָה ('ΑΣ Lv. 1:9) and מִנְחָה ('ΑΘ Lv. 6:21 [Mas. 14]; 'ΑΣ Nu. 16:15) [Bertram.]

and קָרְבַּן צִבּוּר, that of the congregation (jJoma, 39d, lines 76 ff.). Only in the Mishnah do we find several examples of this usage. [7] The distinctive nature of the term in later Judaism as compared with earlier rests in the fact that it has become a vow formula used when something is dedicated to God, or, more precisely, a vow formula used when something is to take on the character of a sacrificial gift offered to God. This does not mean that there always has to be an actual offering in sacrifice. In some cases the implication is simply that that over which the formula is pronounced is withdrawn from the use originally intended. From this point the transition is easy to an ordinary word of protestation with no particular religious connotation, though with an original religious connection.

At a later period the usual formula is no longer קָרְבָּן, but קוֹנָם (Aram. קוֹנָמָא, קִינוּמָא [8], bNed., 10b), also קוֹנַח and קוֹנָס. These subsidiary forms [9] are conscious distortions of the original so that a word which is found so often in the sacred Torah should not have to be employed, even when needed. [10] The underlying principle is that all other terms for vows (נְדָרִים) are as vows themselves (כִּנְדָרִים), Ned., 1, 1. Similarly the terms for individual forms of sacrifice have the same value if used instead of קָרְבָּן on dedication, Ned., 1, 4. It should also be noted that קוֹנָם קָרְבָּן etc. as vow formulae (נְדָרִים) are sharply distinguished from oaths (שְׁבוּעוֹת). Thus, when it is a question of the non-observance of some מִצְוָה or statute of the Torah, e.g., the regulations for the feast of Tabernacles (Lv. 23:33 ff.), only a נֶדֶר is effective e.g., the cry קָרְבָּן, whereas a שְׁבוּעָה is not, "because one does not swear to transgress the commandments" (שֶׁאֵין נִשְׁבָּעִין לַעֲבוֹר עַל הַמִּצְוֹת, Ned., 2, 2; cf. bNed., 16b-17a). [11]

The Rabb. texts make it plain that in the vow קָרְבָּן קוֹנָם etc. there is no question of the actual transfer of certain things to God but only of their withdrawal from the control of certain persons. This is as clear as one could wish in Ned., 1, 3: "If someone says, This or that be as the lamb, [12] the sheds, [13] the wood, the fire, [14] the altar, the temple,

---

[7] Cf. Kassovsky, II, 1593 ff., s.v. קָרְבָּן. Cf. the common expression קָרְבַּן טְמְאָה (Nazir, 1, 2; 3, 5 etc.) for the sacrifice which the Nazarite has to bring when the time of his vow is prematurely interrupted by unforeseen defilement (cf. Nu. 6:10). This is a Rabb. expression. For the usual sense of קָרְבָּן along with the particular cf. Ned., 2, 5.

[8] The corresponding verb is קָנַם, "to make forbidden by קוֹנָם" (bNed., 10b). In the same way we have קָנַח with קוֹנַח, קָנַס with קוֹנָס (loc. cit., though only here and as a play on words; קָנַח is elsewhere "to wipe off" and קָנַס [κῆνσος] "to punish").

[9] Cf. Ned., 1, 2: "If someone says (to his fellow) קוֹנָם, קוֹנָח, קוֹנָס, these are equivalents of קָרְבָּן.

[10] We find the same procedure with the terms נָזִיר, חֵרֶם and שְׁבוּעָה, which belong materially to the same context (Ned., 1, 2; Nazir, 1, 1).

[11] On שְׁבוּעוֹת cf. Str.-B., I, 321 ff. and → ὅρκος. It should be noted in this connection that the oath was in the name of God, whereas it is not necessary to mention God's name in a vow. God Himself gave the Torah, hence there is no ground on which to appeal to Him for its non-observance.

[12] The daily burnt offering, morning and evening, is always a one-year old lamb (Ex. 29:38 ff.).

[13] The reference is to the sheds of the temple in which the sacrificial vessels and wood were stored, also the pen in which the necessary animals for the daily sacrifices — never less than six acc. to Ar., 2, 5 — were kept in readiness (cf. Tamid, 3, 3 f.; Mid., 1, 6; bJoma, 15b ff. and Schürer, II⁴, 324 and n. 25; A. Brody, Der Mišna-Traktat Tamid [1936], 118 f.).

[14] The sacrificial fire on the altar.

Jerusalem, and finally if he has vowed [15] by one of those who serve the altar, [16] this
is a vow by קָרְבָּן even though he has not mentioned קָרְבָּן. The decisive assumption of
the statement is that all the objects and persons named are קָדוֹשׁ/ἅγιος, that they belong
to God, and hence that they are withdrawn from all other use or service. Thus to say
קָרְבָּן of something means that, like everything which is קָדוֹשׁ/ἅγιος, it is now withdrawn
from all possibility of secular use. In connection with the קָרְבָּן formula we have no more
than this negative demarcation contained in קָדוֹשׁ; there is no expression of the primarily
positive goal. [17] This is brought out only externally in the fact that it is usually stated
to whose disadvantage or advantage the negative demarcation is. As a rule the renunciation is personal, and the common phrase is : "קוֹנָם, that I will have no further profit from
this or that." [18] The reference may be to a man, or to a group of men (Ned., 3, 6: sailors),
or to a whole nation (Ned., 3, 10 f.), or to specific objects (Ned., 4, 7 ff.), foods (Ned.,
6, 1 ff.) etc. The result is simply that they are of no further profit to the one concerned,
not that the persons or objects named are made over to the temple. This would no more
be possible in a קוֹנָם vow than in a vow to abstain for a year from wine (Ned., 8, 5).
The exclusive character of the expression comes out even more clearly when we see it
used to deny to others the use of one's own person or possessions. Philo Spec. Leg.,
II, 16 f. shows that such vows were current among the Jews in Egypt ; at any rate,
Philo issues a warning against them. In Rabb. sources it is said in such a case :
קוֹנָם=קוֹנָם שֶׁאַתָּה נֶהֱנֵיתָה לִי, that you have no profit from me (Ned., 8, 7). We can see from
the Mishnah that this was used when there was a desire to exert pressure on someone,
or to avenge oneself on him, or to deal him some other injury or annoyance. The results
of such a vow are always far-reaching and can lead to a complete breach of relations,
with all that this entails. In a patriarchal order such as that of later Judaism the effects
are particularly noticeable when the קוֹנָם is between husband and wife (cf. Ned., 8, 7;
9, 4 and 5) or parents and children (cf. BQ, 9, 10) or children and parents (Ned., 9, 1
and esp. 5, 6). [19]

Since such vows could be brought into effect without prior deliberation by the
mere utterance of קוֹנָם/קָרְבָּן [20] the Rabbis sought and found ways either to reverse
them or to rob them of their most drastic consequences. [21] But the sources show
that this was not always possible (→ n. 19). It is a much debated question [22] when
the Rabbis adopted this practice of alleviation, whether the administration of the
law in such matters was from the very first discharged only by one of the two
great Rabbinic schools, [23] or whether the possibilities of alleviation in certain cases,

---

[15] Cf. other equivalents in Ned., 2, 4.

[16] By a priest—access to the sanctuary and altar was forbidden to Levites on pain of
death, Nu. 18:3 → Λευίτης. The translation of L. Goldschmidt, Der babylonische Talmud,
V (1931), 389, is incorrect.

[17] Cf. on this bNed., 28b and Ned., 5, 6.

[18] E.g., Ned., 3, 11: קוֹנָם שֶׁאֵינִי נֶהֱנֶה לִבְנֵי נֹחַ. Instead of לִבְנֵי one might read מִבְּנֵי, cf. 3:11:
[קוֹנָם] שֶׁאֵינִי נֶהֱנֶה מִיִּשְׂרָאֵל. Here קָרְבָּן is simply a word of protestation, as the use of אֵין shows.

[19] Cf. Str.-B., I, 716 for this important passage and the account of such a case in Beth-
Horon. The passage is particularly instructive because it shows us that there were cases
in which the effects of a son's קָרְבָּן which separated father and son could not be set aside
even with the best will on the part of the son.

[20] Cf. the cases considered in Ned., 9, 1 f. and the account in 9, 4 of the קָרְבָּן vow of a
husband without prior deliberation in respect of his wife.

[21] Cf. the instances in Str.-B., I, 715; also Chag., 1, 8.

[22] Esp. between Jewish and Christian scholars.

[23] The followers of Shammai, as opposed to those of Hillel, generally decided in favour

as these may now be seen in Rabbinic literature, arose only after the time of Jesus.[24] The matter cannot be decided from the Rabbinic sources. The oldest known authority in this connection seems to be R. Sadok, who was held in high regard c. 70 A.D. (Ned., 9, 1, unless the reference is really to his grandson of the same name). If this is so, we shall have to pay closer attention to Mt. 15:3 ff. than has seemed good to many scholars.

The Damascus document, too, seems to have a section which deals with the קָרְבָּן vow. Unfortunately the text is badly damaged : על משפט ה]נדב[ות : אל ידור איש למזבח מאום אנום | וגם [הכ]הנים אל יקחו מאת ישראל[......ואל] יקדש איש את מאכל [פע]ל[ל]ו כ]י הוא אשר אמר איש את ע[ב]דו [ויצוד]ו חרם [25]: "And in respect of the regulation of vows, no one shall dedicate to the altar anything that has come into his possession by force, and the priests shall not take from an Israelite (by force?[26] nor) shall anyone declare holy the sustenance of his worker, for this is what (Scripture) says (cf. Mi. 7:2): This one and that takes his servant with *herem* "(Damasc., 16, 9 ff., ed. L. Rost, 28, lines 13-15).[27] Now it is true that we do not have here either קָרְבָּן or a corresponding term.[28] Yet the יִדּוֹר...לַמִּזְבֵּחַ and the יַקְדֵּשׁ...מַאֲכָל make it clear that we are dealing with the same question. In both cases the reference is to the קָרְבָּן vow. In what follows we find קדש at the beginning of line 17 and הנודר at the beginning of 18, and these suggest the same line of thought. In the first and second of the three prohibitions the principle seems to be advanced that only what is given voluntarily and joyfully befits the dignity of God's altar. It should be noted that the community concerned had separated from the temple and cultus (cf. 4, 12 ff.), but not in principle (cf. 11, 19 ff.). There is as yet no unanimity whether the parts which refer to the temple cultus really do refer to it or are to be taken to refer to the synagogue and its worship, so that the work does not presume the continued existence of the temple and its worship.[29] As concerns the third of the prohibitions, it is not clear whether the יַקְדֵּשׁ implies true transfer to the sanctuary[30] or a plot to cheat the workers of their reward.[31] The former interpretation would give us an earlier stage of the later קָרְבָּן vow, the latter the vow itself. Well-founded decision is not possible until more light is shed on the date of the work. But there can be no doubt as to the fundamental relationship between this passage and the custom of קָרְבָּן.[32]

---

of severity (cf. Hart, 616), but at almost all points the view of Hillel prevailed. Cf. also Montefiore, 149, who refers to Dt. 23:22 ff. and Nu. 30:2 f.

[24] So Laible, 613, who is inclined to see some effect of the preaching of Jesus on later practice. Cf. also with reservations Str.-B., I, 715, n. 1.

[25] Cf. Mi. 7:2 and also Dt. 23:25 f. in Rabb. exposition (BM, 7, 2 ff.) with W. Staerk, "Die jüdische Gemeinde des Neuen Bundes in Damaskus," BFTh, 27, 3 (1922), 84 (from Ginsberg).

[26] So Segal, Staerk.

[27] On the emendations cf. apparatus in Rost.

[28] Though חֵרֶם seems here to be deliberately used, not as "net," but as a formula of dedication (→ ἀνάθεμα, I, 354), thus in the practical sense which קָרְבָּן has as a vow formula.

[29] So G. Hölscher, "Zur Frage nach Alter u. Herkunft der sog. Damaskusschrift," ZNW, 28 (1929), 21 ff., esp. 23 ff. For a review of attempts to fix the date, *ibid.*, 21 ff., also L. Rost, Kl. T., 167 (1933), 4.

[30] חֵרֶם "net" in Mi. 7:2 is changed into the votive formula חֵרֶם "taboo," cf. Staerk, 84 *ad loc.* For the same play on words in reverse, cf. Ned., 2, 5.

[31] Cf. Jm. 5:4.

[32] Staerk and Rost also refer to Mk. 7:9 ff.

3. Corban in the New Testament.

a. In Mt. 27:6 the ἀρχιερεῖς take the view that the silver pieces which Judas had received for his betrayal (Mt. 26:15), and which he cast into the temple before hanging himself (27:5), were not suitable for the κορβανᾶς : οὐκ ἔξεστιν βαλεῖν αὐτὰ εἰς τὸν κορβανᾶν, ἐπεὶ τιμὴ αἵματός ἐστιν. Here κορβανᾶς means the temple treasury, as in Jos. Bell., 2, 175 (→ 860 f.).

The question discussed by the ἀρχιερεῖς was suggested by the fact that the money had been cast into the temple and thus transferred to it. Perhaps it originally came from the treasury, and this suggested its return. If the ἀρχιερεῖς would not allow this, it was because blood clung to the money and it could not be regarded as holy or fit for the temple. [33] There are no Rabb. par. for this use of the word.

b. κορβᾶν occurs only in Mk. 7:10 ff. in conflict with the scribes and Pharisees : Μωϋσῆς γὰρ εἶπεν· τίμα τὸν πατέρα σου καὶ τὴν μητέρα σου, καί· ὁ κακολογῶν πατέρα ἢ μητέρα θανάτῳ τελευτάτω. ὑμεῖς δὲ λέγετε· ἐὰν εἴπῃ ἄνθρωπος τῷ πατρὶ ἢ τῇ μητρί· κορβᾶν, ὅ ἐστιν δῶρον, ὃ ἐὰν ἐξ ἐμοῦ ὠφεληθῇς, οὐκέτι ἀφίετε αὐτὸν οὐδὲν ποιῆσαι τῷ πατρὶ ἢ τῇ μητρί, ἀκυροῦντες τὸν λόγον τοῦ θεοῦ τῇ παραδόσει ὑμῶν ᾗ παρεδώκατε.

Mark here explains κορβᾶν for his Gk. readers in the same way as Jos. did (→ 860). Mt. (15:3 ff.) avoids the alien term and uses δῶρον [34] in the sense of קָרְבָּן = "offering." Mt. is consistent in his use of δῶρον. Apart from 2:11 it is the equivalent of קָרְבָּן at 5:23 f.; 8:4; 23:18 f. But Mk. and Lk. avoid it in the par. to Mt. 8:4, probably because it was not familiar to their readers in the sense of "offering." Lk. has τὰ δῶρα at 21:1 (for קָרְבָּנוֹת, independently of Mk.) and at 21:4 (again independently of his original) in a sense which brings it close to γαζοφυλακεῖον or the κορβανᾶς of Jos. Bell., 2, 175 and Mt. 27:6. δῶρον is used for קָרְבָּן in Hb. (5:1; 8:3 f.; 9:9; 11:4). The combination of δῶρα and θυσίαι for unbloody and bloody sacrifices occurs 3 times in Hb. (5:1; 8:3; 9:9) and is also found in Jos. Bell., 2, 409 (→ n. 5). We thus see a Palestinian form of speech in Hb.

The words of Jesus presuppose that a case like that to which He alludes comes before a forum of scribes and that this decides that the declaration must stand and that those concerned must bear the consequences. But this situation is only possible when the son repents of his hard saying and when it is thus evident that it was spoken without proper deliberation, e.g., in anger — a case sufficiently well known to us from Rabbinic texts (→ 863 f.). The statement that the declaration removes all the claims which a father would normally have on his son finds both a verbal and a material equivalent in the expression קוֹנָם שֶׁאַתָּה נֶהֱנֵיתָה לִי (Ned., 8, 7; → 863). The renunciation of all profitability includes not only support but all the other things a son might do for a father, e.g., help in the performance of religious duties, care in sickness etc. [35] Even commercial dealings are forbidden in such a case (cf. Ned., 4, 6). If, on the basis of a vow, God's claims must be upheld even in face of those of the father, this rests on the Rabbinic principle that God's claims

---

[33] Cf. Schl. Mt., ad loc. Cf. also the earlier ref. (→ 864) to the Damascus document on the vowing of what is exacted.

[34] δῶρον as דּוֹרוֹן also became a loan word in the Rabbis for קָרְבָּן. It was mostly used for "gift," cf. the dictionaries s.v.

[35] Cf. the passages in Str.-B., I, 714.

are fundamentally higher than man's, and they have to take precedence, since God's relation to man is also expressed in legal categories. [36] An impregnable scriptural basis for this was found in Nu. 30:2 f. [37] In Mt. Jesus refers to Is. 29:13 in His rejection of the attitude of the Rabbis in such cases. The quotation comes first in Mk., but this makes no vital difference. For Jesus this is God's own judgment on the worship of the Rabbis and on its implications. But the quotation can be properly understood only if קָרְבָּן here signifies a true transference of paternal claims to God or to the temple in the sense of a good work. [38] Above all, we learn from the quotation that Jesus is not so much attacking a specific Rabbinic practice as He is showing that his opponents, the scribes, are in no true position to do justice to their concern for the fulfilment of the letter of the divine Law. They forget that God has given it, not for its own sake, but for the sake of men. For they forget that in Him righteousness and lovingkindness are one, and that His lovingkindness is not to be found only where satisfaction is done to His legal claim. In this debate Jesus is not opposing the untruncated validity of all Scripture. He is contending for it in opposition to a type of exposition which fixes on the letter and which is thus unable to see Scripture as a self-enclosed whole which derives from the same holy will and has the same goal of sanctification, but which also leads with sanctification to lovingkindness, since its Giver is absolutely good (Mk. 10:18 and par.). Seen in this way, the saying concerning the קָרְבָּן vow of the son over against his father, which was defended by the Rabbis, merges into His total conflict with the scribes of His own time, both as to His own attitude, and also the position which He repudiates. [39]

4. The early Church took the saying only along the lines presupposed in Lk. 21:4 (→ 865), though here we do not have κορβᾶν or κορβανᾶς, but τὰ δῶρα; cf. Const. Ap., II, 36, 8: εἰς τὸν κορβανᾶν ὃ δύνασαι βάλλων, κοινώνει τοῖς ξένοις ἓν ἢ δύο ἢ πέντε λεπτά. [40] Latinised, corban is used for the sacrificial chest or poor box in Cyprian, De Opere et Eleemosynis, 15 (CSEL, 3, 1): Locuples et dives dominicum celebrare te credis, quae [41] corban omnino non respicis. In this early usage, which later dropped away, [42] we find the idea that almsgiving is a sacrifice brought to God — a view which the early Church may well have developed under the influence of Judaism.

Rengstorf

---

[36] Cf. on this, and on the theological implications, R. Sander, *Furcht u. Liebe im palästinischen Judentum* (1935), 67 ff.

[37] Cf. S. Nu., 153 on 30:3 and Montefiore, 149, who argues against Mk. 7:12 that the work of Rabbinic tradition was the dissolution rather than the upholding of vows, and who thus finds here a saying against Scripture which He would not expect to find in Jesus ("Let us hope that 9-13 is not authentic," 152).

[38] Perhaps in the same sense as in the Damascus document (→ 864), but not acc. to Rabb. Judaism as we find it in Tannaitic sources, where קָרְבָּן became a formula of disjunction (→ 863).

[39] Cf. the exposition of the Law in Mt. 5:21 ff. and esp. the temptation story (Mt. 4:1 ff., esp. v. 8 ff.).

[40] An allusion to Mk. 12:42.

[41] This saying is under the influence of Rev. 3:17 ff.

[42] It cannot be derived directly from the original use (as against K. Kohler; → n. 3).

κοσμέω, κόσμος,
κόσμιος, κοσμικός

† κοσμέω.

This verb was used in class. Gk. from the time of Hom. Its meanings derive from the basic sense of κόσμος, i.e., order or adornment. In the sense "to order" κοσμέω is a technical military term for the placing of a host or the ordering of combatants, Hom. Il., 2, 554; 3, 1; 12, 87; 14, 379; cf. Od., 9, 157 (of hunters); Xenoph. Cyrop., II, 1, 26. The related sense "to order" or "command" [1] need not be considered in relation to biblical usage, but the general sense "to bring to order," "to regulate," is significant, e.g., τράπεζαν, Xenoph. Cyrop., VIII, 2, 6; Ditt. Syll.[3], 1038, 11; δεῖπνον, Pind. Nem., 1, 22; ἔργα, Hes. Op., 306; στέφανον, Eur. Hipp., 73 f. κοσμέω is very common in the sense "to adorn," esp. of women, Hom. Hymn., 6, 11; Hes. Op., 72. Often the means of adornment is given, e.g., κοσμεῖν πανοπλίῃ, Hdt., IV, 180, in which case the sense may be weaker, namely, "to furnish with," e.g., τριπόδεσσι κοσμεῖν δόμον, Pind. Isthm., I, 19. In the fig. sense κοσμεῖν means "to adorn" in expressions like λόγους κοσμεῖν, Eur. Med., 576; Plat. Ap., 17c. This sense may pass over into that of "to honour," e.g., when it is said of certain people that they adorn their country, e.g., Theogn., 947.

In the LXX κοσμεῖν occurs in the sense "to order" at Sir. 29:26: κόσμησον τράπεζαν, "set the table"; also 50:14: κοσμῆσαι προσφορὰν ὑψίστου παντοκράτορος. On the other hand, in ἐκόσμησεν καιροὺς μέχρι συντελείας at Sir. 47:10 it probably has the original meaning "to adorn." [2] It is commonly used in this sense in the LXX, esp. of women, e.g., Jer. 4:30 (κοσμεῖν κόσμῳ χρυσῷ); Ez. 16:11; 23:40 (κοσμεῖν κόσμῳ); Jdt. 12:15: ἐκοσμήθη τῷ ἱματισμῷ καὶ παντὶ τῷ κόσμῳ τῷ γυναικείῳ, also of the temple, 2 Ch. 3:6: ἐκόσμησεν τὸν οἶκον λίθοις τιμίοις; 2 Macc. 9:16: ἅγιον ... καλλίστοις ἀναθήμασι κοσμήσειν. It is found in the fig. sense at 3 Macc. 3:5: τῇ τῶν δικαίων εὐπραξίᾳ κοσμοῦντες τὴν συναναστροφήν, "as they adorned their common walk with the good conduct of the righteous"; 6:1: πάσῃ τῇ κατὰ τὸν βίον ἀρετῇ κεκοσμημένος, "adorned with every virtue of human life."

In the NT the sense "to put in order" occurs only at Mt. 25:7: ἐκόσμησαν τὰς λαμπάδας. Elsewhere the meaning is "to adorn." As in Gk. usage, the verb is used of women, also figuratively, Rev. 21:2; 1 Tm. 2:9; 1 Pt. 3:5. It is used of the house at Mt. 12:44 (par. Lk. 11:25), the temple at Lk. 21:5 (λίθοις καλοῖς καὶ ἀναθήμασιν κεκόσμηται, cf. 2 Macc. 9:16, and in pagan Hellenistic usage Ditt. Syll.[3], 725, 2 f.; 1100, 21 f.; 1050, 6), cf. Rev. 21:19; and graves at Mt. 23:29: κοσμεῖτε τὰ μνημεῖα τῶν δικαίων (cf. κοσμεῖν τάφον, Soph. Ant., 396 and Xenoph. Mem., II, 2, 13); also fig. at Tt. 2:10: ἵνα τὴν διδασκαλίαν τὴν τοῦ σωτῆρος ἡμῶν θεοῦ κοσμῶσιν ἐν πᾶσιν, "that they may adorn the doctrine." [3]

κ ο σ μ έ ω. Liddell-Scott, 984; Pr.-Bauer[3], 737 f.

[1] Cf. κόσμος → 868 and the use of διακοσμεῖν, διακόσμησις, → 870.

[2] Ryssel in Kautzsch Apkr., ad loc.

[3] For early Christian use outside the Canon, which is essentially the same as that of the LXX and NT, v. Pr.-Bauer.

κόσμος.

Contents: A. Non-biblical Usage: 1. κόσμος = That which is Well Assembled; 2. κόσμος = Order between Men; 3. κόσμος = Order generally; 4. κόσμος = Adornment; 5. κόσμος = World I, Development and Meaning of the Greek View of the Cosmos; 6. κόσμος = World II, God and the Cosmos for the Greeks; 7. κόσμος as World in the Sense of Earth, Inhabited World, Humanity. B. κόσμος in the LXX. The Concept of the Cosmos in Judaism. C. κόσμος in the NT: 1. General. κόσμος in the Sense Adornment; 2. κόσμος = World I, as the Universe, the Sum of all Created Being; 3. κόσμος = World II, as the Abode of Men, the Theatre of History, the Inhabited World, the Earth; 4. κόσμος = World III, as Humanity, Fallen Creation, the Theatre of Salvation History.

A. Non-biblical Usage.

Though the word had an established place in the vocabulary of the Greeks from the time of Homer, its etymology is uncertain.[1] In its original sense the idea of building or establishing (parallel with the twice-used ποίησις in Hdt., III, 22) it seems to be linked with that of order (cf. Heracl. Fr., 124 [I, 102, 1 f., Diels]): ὥσπερ σάρμα εἰκῇ κεχυμένον ὁ κάλλιστος [ὁ] κόσμος, "the most beautiful order of the world is like a heap of things tossed together at random"). This gives us the following senses.

1. "That which is well assembled or constructed from individual constituents."

ἵππου κόσμον, the structure of the horse, of the Trojan horse, Hom. Od., 8, 492; κόσμον ἐμῶν ἐπέων, the structure of my words, Parm. Fr., 8, 52 (I, 158, 10, Diels), cf. Democr. Fr., 21 (II, 67, 5, Diels); par. with ποίησις, Hdt., III, 22.

2. When the object of the building consists of individual men who are integrated into a whole, κόσμος is a term for the order between men.

Hom. Od., 13, 76 f. for the order in which rowers sit, Il., 12, 225 for the order of battle. From a military term κόσμος then becomes a common tt. in politics for the order of life and constitution which binds the citizens of a city-state, e.g., Plat. Leg., VIII, 846d: τὸν κοινὸν τῆς πόλεως κόσμον σῴζων καὶ κτώμενος, Prot., 322c: ἵν' εἶεν πόλεων κόσμοι τε καὶ δεσμοὶ φιλίας συναγωγοί, cf. also Thuc., III, 77; VIII, 48, 67, 72; Aristot. Pol., V, 7, p. 1307b, 6. κόσμος is a legal term for the state of the Spartans in Hdt., I, 65 and an official title in Crete, Ditt. Syll.³, 712, 57; 524, 1; Aristot. Pol., II, 10, p. 1272a, 6.

κ ό σ μ ο ς. Cr.-Kö., 619 ff.; Pr.-Bauer³, 739; Liddell-Scott, 985; W. Jaeger, *Paideia*, I (1934), 219 ff.; K. Reinhardt, *Parmenides u. die Geschichte d. griech. Philosophie* (1916), 174 f.; *Kosmos und Sympathie* (1926), 44 ff.; O. Gigon, *Untersuchungen zu Heraklit* (1935), 52 ff.; O. Gilbert, *Griech. Religionsphilosophie* (1911), *passim*, esp. 90 ff., 100, n. 1, 116, n. 1, 207, 358; G. Kittel, *Die Religionsgeschichte u. d. Urchristentum* (1932), 88 ff.; C. H. Dodd, *The Bible and the Greeks* (1935), Index, p. 253; R. Löwe, *Kosmos u. Aion* (1935); E. v. Schrenck, "Der Kosmosbegriff bei Johannes mit Berücksichtigung des vorjohanneischen Gebrauchs von κόσμος," *Mitteilungen u. Nachrichten f. d. evang. Kirche in Russland*, 51 (NF, 28) (1895), 1 ff.; F. Bytomski, "Die genetische Entwicklung des Begriffes ΚΟΣΜΟΣ in der Hl. Schrift," *Jbch. f. Philosophie u. spekulative Theologie*, XXV (1911), 180 ff., 389 ff.; Class. Rev., 3 (1889), 131a, 418b; 5 (1891), 416a.
[1] Cf. L. Meyer, "Kosmos" in *Zschr. f. vergleich. Sprachforschung*, 6 (1857), 161 ff. (ed. A. Kuhn); also K. Brugmann, *Indogerm. Forschungen*, 28 (1911), 358 ff., and the observations of P. Kretschmer, *Glotta*, 5 (1914), 309. More recently Walde-Pok., I, 403; 474.

3. κόσμος is very common in the general sense of "order."

Cf. the common expression κατὰ κόσμον, "according to right order," i.e., as is meet or fitting (the glossators usually suggest κατὰ τάξιν, κατὰ τὸ δέον, κατὰ τὸ πρέπον), e.g., in Hom. Il., 2, 214; 10, 472; Od., 8, 179 etc., with similar expressions in the poets (Pind., Aesch.) and prose writers (e.g., Hdt., II, 52; VIII, 86; IX, 59). In this sense κόσμος is often used with, and synon. with, τάξις, e.g., Hdt., IX, 59; Aristot. Metaph., I, 3, p. 984b, 16 f.; Cael., III, 2, p. 301a, 10, or with εὐταξία, Pol., VI, 8, p. 1321b, 7.

4. In so far as the concept of the beautiful is inseparable from that of the ordered, it is always implied in κόσμος and finds particular expression in the sense "adornment" (usually of women).

Hom. Il., 14, 187; Hes. Op., 76; Hdt., V, 92 η; γυναικεῖος κόσμος, Plat. Resp., II, 373b; also fig. like the Lat. decus in the sense "ornament," "glory" : γύναι, γυναιξὶ κόσμον ἡ σιγὴ φέρει, Soph. Ai., 293. Of the innumerable examples of this use we can only quote a few from the Hellenistic Orient, Ditt. Or., 383, 73; 131; 135; 223 (Antiochus of Commagene); 90, 40; 423, 5; 514, 3; 525, 13; 595, 6 (adornment of buildings, temples, walls, cultic actions etc.); P. Oxy., VI, 899, 12; XII, 1467, 11; P. Flor., 384, 8 and 78 (5th cent. A.D.); P. Lond., 198, 10. [2]

5. κόσμος = World I, Development and Meaning of the Greek View of the Cosmos.

The senses previously mentioned merge in that of the world (the cosmic order or system, the universe, also heaven). Here κόσμος becomes one of the most important terms in Greek philosophy. It has significance not merely in intellectual history but also in the history of ancient religion.

a. In the sense "world" κόσμος is for Plato (Gorg., 507e) part of the language of the σοφοί. This is confirmed by Xenoph., who in Mem., I, 1, 11 calls it a technical term of the σοφισταί. Acc. to a later tradition which is found c. 100 A.D., but which may go back to Theophrast., Pythag. was the first to use κόσμος for the universe : Πυθαγόρας πρῶτος ὠνόμασε τὴν τῶν ὅλων περιοχὴν κόσμον, ἐκ τῆς ἐν αὐτῷ τάξεως : cf. Plut. De Placitis Philosophorum, II, 1 (II, 886b) and Stob. Ecl., I, 186, 14. [3] Diog. L., VIII, 1, 25 (48) mentions a tradition which has it that Pythag. was the first to call heaven the κόσμος. O. Gigon, [4] however, makes the interesting suggestion that οὐρανός here is perhaps an incorrect rendering of τὴν τῶν ὅλων περιοχήν in the previous quotation.

There is no means to-day of evaluating this tradition. If Anaximenes Fr., 2 (I, 26, 18 ff., Diels) is genuine, [5] the statement οἷον ἡ ψυχὴ ἡ ἡμετέρα ἀὴρ οὖσα συγκρατεῖ ἡμᾶς, καὶ ὅλον τὸν κόσμον πνεῦμα καὶ ἀὴρ περιέχει, "as our soul is air, and holds us together thereby, so breath and air embrace the whole world," is the oldest instance of the designation of the world as κόσμος. We can no longer affirm with certainty any more than that κόσμος owes its new meaning to the Ionian natural philosophy of the 6th century. Materially the concept of the cosmos therein implied is found already in Anaximander Fr., 9 (I, 15, 26 ff., Diels): ἐξ ὧν

---

[2] For further examples cf. Preisigke Wört., s.v. κόσμος.

[3] H. Diels, Doxographi Graeci² (1929), 327, 8 ff.; cf. also the passages there adduced from Achill. Tat. and Cyr. Alexandrinus, also this quotation in Gal. De Hist. Philosophiae, 44, Diels, op. cit., 621.

[4] Op. cit., 54.

[5] Its authenticity is contested by K. Reinhardt, Parmenides (1916), 175; Kosmos u. Sympathie (1926), 209 ff.

δὲ ἡ γένεσίς ἐστι τοῖς οὖσι, καὶ τὴν φθορὰν εἰς ταῦτα γίνεσθαι κατὰ τὸ χρεών· διδόναι γὰρ αὐτὰ δίκην καὶ τίσιν ἀλλήλοις τῆς ἀδικίας κατὰ τὴν τοῦ χρόνου τάξιν, "whence is the origin of being, thither must also be its end according to the decree of fate. For the one must pay the other penalty and penance according to the verdict of time."[6] The meaning is that there is an order of things which corresponds to the order of law which exists between men. Individual things are at legal odds, and time will give the verdict (τάσσειν). But as in human life Δίκη (→ II, 178 f.), or immanent righteousness, creates a balance between contesting claims, so Anaximander finds "this eternal balance achieved not merely in human life but in the whole world and in all being."[7] What holds things together and integrates them into a whole is an immanent cosmic norm which obviously is not to be identified with the modern concept of natural law. "The world thereby shows itself to be a macrocosm, an ordered society of things."[8]

Though still in the mythological sphere, a preliminary form of this idea of a universal order of things may be found in Hes. Theog., 73 f., where it is told how Zeus after his victory εὖ δὲ ἕκαστα ἀθανάτοις διέταξεν ὁμῶς καὶ ἐπέφραδε τιμάς.

b. As regards the origin of the Greek view of the cosmos we thus reach the following conclusion. The κόσμος — sometimes διάκοσμος is used instead in this sense[9] — is in the first instance the order whereby the sum of individual things is gathered into a totality. In other words, it is the cosmic system in the sense of the cosmic order. Only later does κόσμος come to denote the totality which is held together by this order, i.e., the world in the spatial sense, the cosmic system in the sense of the universe.

When this second stage of development was reached we cannot say. If the fragment from Anaximenes quoted above is genuine, the origin of the concept of a spatial cosmos is to be located in the early stages of Milesian philosophy. But if, like K. Reinhardt (→ n. 5), one disputes its authenticity, one will be inclined to believe that the philosophers of the 6th and earlier 5th century used κόσμος only in the sense of cosmic order. Yet even if, as some believe, it is only in the age of the Peloponnesian War that κόσμος is used for the *universitas rerum* in the spatial sense,[10] and all earlier passages have to be understood in terms of cosmic order, a thought which remains predominant in the concept of the cosmos, there can be no overlooking the fact that the idea of a spatial totality played a great role even in early thinkers. They speak of the all as the epitome of all being in phrases like τὰ ὄντα (Anaximand. Fr., 9 [I, 15, 23, Diels]), πάντα (Xenophanes Fr., 25 [I, 63, 2, Diels]), τὰ πάντα, ἅπαντα (Heracl. Fr., 90 [I, 95, 12 f., Diels]). When acc. to De Placitis Philos., II, 1, 6,[11] Melissos and Diogenes of Apollonia taught: τὸ μὲν πᾶν ἄπειρον, τὸν δὲ κόσμον πεπεράνθαι, "the all is infinite, the

---

[6] Acc. to Jaeger, 217.

[7] Jaeger, 218.

[8] *Ibid.,* 219.

[9] Parm. Fr., 8, 60 (I, 159, 5, Diels), also Leucipp. Fr., 1 (II, 9, 37 f., Diels) and Democr. Fr., 5 (II, 58, 15 ff., Diels) in the titles of their works μέγας διάκοσμος and μικρὸς διάκοσμος. In Democr. Fr., 5 we also find διακόσμησις in the same sense; in Plato and others this is used for the legal or constitutional order etc. Cf. also Anaxag. Fr., 12 (I, 405, 2 ff., Diels): ὁποῖα ἔμελλεν ἔσεσθαι καὶ ὁποῖα ἦν ... καὶ ὅσα νῦν ἐστι καὶ ὁποῖα ἔσται, πάντα διεκόσμησε νοῦς; Aristot. Cael., I, 10, p. 280a, 21.

[10] F. Buecheler, *Kl. Schriften,* I (1915), 631.

[11] H. Diels, Doxographi Graeci² (1929), 328.

cosmos limited," [12] it is, of course, uncertain whether later tradition did not import the term κόσμος into the statements of these thinkers of the second half of the 5th century, but the matter itself, i.e., the idea of a cosmos in the spatial sense, is undoubtedly present, and the question which they raised, namely, that of the infinitude of the world and its relation to space, already occupied natural philosophy, as we know from authentic sources. [13]

c. The spatial sense of κόσμος, and its identification with the universe, are found in Plato, though the older idea of world order is still present. For Plato the cosmos is the universe, elsewhere called τὸ ὅλον [14] or τὸ πᾶν, [15] inasmuch as in it all individual things and creatures, heaven and earth, gods and men, are brought into unity by a universal order: φασὶ δ' οἱ σοφοὶ ... καὶ οὐρανὸν καὶ γῆν καὶ θεοὺς καὶ ἀνθρώπους τὴν κοινωνίαν συνέχειν καὶ φιλίαν καὶ κοσμιότητα καὶ σωφροσύνην καὶ δικαιότητα, καὶ τὸ ὅλον τοῦτο διὰ ταῦτα κόσμον καλοῦσιν ... οὐκ ἀκοσμίαν οὐδὲ ἀκολασίαν, Gorg., 507e-508a. This κόσμος, "the manifestation of the idea in space, the sensual and corruptible reflection of the eternal," [16] is to be described as a σῶμα, Phileb., 29e; Tim., 32c; indeed, it is a body with a soul, a rational creature: δεῖ λέγειν τόνδε τὸν κόσμον ζῷον ἔμψυχον ἔννουν τε τῇ ἀληθείᾳ διὰ τὴν τοῦ θεοῦ γενέσθαι πρόνοιαν, Tim., 30b. [17] Plato gives a summary of his views on the universe (περὶ τοῦ παντός) in the concluding words of the Tim. (92c): θνητὰ γὰρ καὶ ἀθάνατα ζῷα λαβὼν καὶ συμπληρωθεὶς ὅδε ὁ κόσμος οὕτω, ζῷον ὁρατὸν τὰ ὁρατὰ περιέχον, εἰκὼν τοῦ νοητοῦ θεὸς αἰσθητός, μέγιστος καὶ ἄριστος κάλλιστός τε καὶ τελεώτατος γέγονεν, εἷς οὐρανὸς ὅδε μονογενὴς ὤν, "furnished and filled with mortal and immortal living creatures, this cosmos has become a visible living creature, embracing the visible, the reflection of that which can be known only by reason, a sensually perceptible God, the greatest and the best, the most beautiful and the most perfect, this one and only-begotten world."

The theological content of this passage will be elucidated below (→ 875). Linguistically we are struck by the alternation of κόσμος and οὐρανός, which are used synon. While → οὐρανός is here used, as probably in older natural philosophers from the time of Anaximander, [18] for the spatial cosmos or universe, in other passages the sense of κόσμος merges into that of heaven, e.g., Phaedr., 246b c on the soul which wanders through terrestrial and celestial space: ψυχή ... πάντα δὲ οὐρανὸν περιπολεῖ ... μετεωροπορεῖ τε καὶ πάντα τὸν κόσμον διοικεῖ; cf. μετελθεῖν εἰς τὸν ἀέναον

---

[12] In the same place it is said of the Stoics that they distinguished between τὸ πᾶν and τὸ ὅλον: πᾶν μὲν γὰρ εἶναι σὺν τῷ κενῷ τῷ ἀπείρῳ, ὅλον δὲ χωρὶς τοῦ κενοῦ τὸν κόσμον. On this view the cosmos is surrounded by infinite empty space; both together constitute the all. → n. 18.

[13] De Placitis Philos., II, 3 in Diels, op. cit., 327.

[14] E.g., Phileb., 28d; Gorg., 508a.

[15] E.g., Polit., 270b, 272e; Tim., 28c, 30b, 69c, 92b; Crat., 412d.

[16] E. Zeller, D. Philosophie d. Griechen, II, 1⁵ (1922), 789, cf. Tim., 29, where the εἰκών of the ὅδε ὁ κόσμος is τὸ ἀίδιον. The world is created acc. to the idea of the most perfect living creature. Cf. → αἰών, I, 197 on the concepts time and eternity in Plato.

[17] Cf. Antipater in Diog. L., VII, 70 (139): ὁ κόσμος ζῷον ἔμψυχον καὶ λογικόν.

[18] K. Reinhardt, Parmenides (1916), 175 on Anaximand. Fr., 9 (I, 15, 21 ff., Diels), acc. to which Anaximand. did not declare water or any other element to be the basic material of the world, ἀλλ' ἑτέραν τινὰ φύσιν ἄπειρον, ἐξ ἧς ἅπαντας γίνεσθαι τοὺς οὐρανοὺς καὶ τοὺς ἐν αὐτοῖς κόσμους (I, 15, 25 f., Diels). As it has come down to us, the Fr. quoted above (→ 869 f.) is linked directly with this reference. The idea is that there is a plurality of κόσμοι each of which is surrounded by an οὐρανός. → n. 12.

κόσμον (of the soul after death), Ditt. Or., 56, 48. κόσμος is the sphere of the fixed stars in Ps.-Plat. Epin., 987b, and the starry heaven in general in Diog. L., VII, 70 (138): αὐτὴν δὲ τὴν διακόσμησιν ἀστέρων κόσμον εἶναι λέγουσιν (Posidonius?). Isoc., too, uses κόσμος for heaven when he speaks of the whole earth lying under heaven and divided into two parts (Asia and Africa): τῆς ... γῆς ἁπάσης τῆς ὑπὸ τῷ κόσμῳ κειμένης δίχα τετμημένης (IV, 179). Indeed, the stars, and esp. the planets, can be called κόσμοι (Iambl. Myst., VIII, 6; Corp. Herm., XI, 7), a usage which De Placitis, II, 13, 15 traces back to the Pythagoreans (H. Diels, Dox. Graeci² [1929], 343; cf. H. Diels, op. cit., 476, 8 [Theophr. Physicarum Opinionum Fr., 2]; 559, 17 [Hipp. Philos., 6, 1]). From this merging of the senses "cosmic space" and "heavenly space" resulted the uncertainty in distinguishing between οὐρανός and κόσμος which is attested for his whole age by Plato in Tim., 28b : ὁ δὴ πᾶς οὐρανὸς — ἢ κόσμος ἢ καὶ ἄλλο ὅτι ποτὲ ὀνομαζόμενος μάλιστ' ἂν δέχοιτο, τοῦθ' ἡμῖν ὠνομάσθω, "the whole structure of heaven, or the universe, or whatever other name one might prefer, we will accept it."

d. The same equation of κόσμος and οὐρανός occurs in Aristot. Thus in Cael., III, 2, p. 301a, 17 and 19 συστῆσαι τὸν οὐρανόν is synon. with συνέστηκεν ὁ κόσμος, cf. also the combination of the two words in Cael., I, 10, p. 280a, 21: ἡ δὲ τοῦ ὅλου σύστασίς ἐστι κόσμος καὶ οὐρανός, "the integration of the whole is the world and heaven." [19] The whole work Περὶ οὐρανοῦ presupposes — and it is made explicit in I, 9 f., — that οὐρανός means not only heaven in the narrower sense, the sphere of heavenly bodies, but the universe. This is specifically underlined in the phrase ὁ πᾶς οὐρανός, Cael., I, 9, p. 279a, 25 f.; II, 1, p. 283b, 26. Aristot. took over from Plato the understanding of the κόσμος as the spatial universe — he, too, uses it synon. with τὸ πᾶν and τὸ ὅλον — and he adapted this understanding in accordance with his scientific and metaphysical convictions. [20] The cosmos is for him a spherical body [21] at the heart of which, surrounded by the spheres of the world and heaven, is the spherical earth, which Aristot. regards as unmoved. The authority of this great scholar, supported here by the views of Plato and Stoicism, forced this geocentric picture on the West for 1800 years in spite of the superior insights of Aristarchus of Samos. For Aristot. the body of the world is no longer a σῶμα ἔμψυχον. He finds no place for the world soul of Plato. Only the heavenly spheres are controlled by soul and reason (ὁ δὲ οὐρανὸς ἔμψυχος καὶ ἔχει κινήσεως ἀρχήν, Cael., II, 2, p. 285a, 29). [22] The cosmos, which has no beginning or end in time, embraces everything bound to time and space : φανερὸν ἄρα ὅτι οὔτε τόπος (place) οὔτε κενὸν (empty space) οὔτε χρόνος ἐστὶν ἔξωθεν (Cael., I, 9, p. 279a, 17). The supracosmic or transcendent (τἀκεῖ) which knows neither place nor time — time is only for the cosmos — leads incorruptibly and impassibly (ἀπαθῆ) the most perfect life. [23] There can be no plurality of worlds, whether successively or simultaneously.

---

[19] Cf. the expression ὁ περὶ τὴν γῆν ὅλος κόσμος, Meteor., I, 2, p. 339a, 19 etc. The senses world and heaven merge into one another. The double meaning of κόσμος is reflected in the use of mundus in Cic. Nat. Deor., II, 12 : ex mundi ardore motus omnis oritur (mundus = heaven, ether). Cic. follows here the use of κόσμος in Pos.; cf. K. Reinhardt, Posidonius (1921), 227 f.

[20] Thus the criticism of the doctrine of ideas implies a shift in the understanding of the κόσμος, since that which Plato found in the sphere of ideas is now to be sought in the visible κόσμος. On the other hand, the rediscovery of Plato in Philo and Neo-Platonism led to a doctrine of the κόσμος νοητός which will be discussed below.

[21] σφαιροειδής, Cael., II, 2, p. 285a, 32; II, 4, p. 287b, 14.

[22] Cf. De Placitis Philos., II, 3, 4 in Stob., I, 186, 5, H. Diels, Dox. Graeci² (1929), 330, 7 ff.

[23] Cael., I, 9, p. 279a, 18 ff. Cf. W. Jaeger, Aristoteles (1923), 316 ff.

e. Classical Gk. thinking concerning the κόσμος reached its termination in Aristot. The further development of ancient cosmology in the Hellen. and Roman period from Stoicism to Neo-Platonism took place under increasing oriental influence and with mounting religious emphasis. We shall have to consider it later (→ 876 ff.). For the moment we may simply adduce the definition of the κόσμος in Ps.-Aristot. Mund., 2, p. 391b, 9, since it shows how, under the influence of later Stoicism (Posidonius), the accepted philosophical cosmology of the age of the NT appropriated the legacy of classical Gk. thinking concerning the world : κόσμος μὲν οὖν ἐστι σύστημα ἐξ οὐρανοῦ καὶ γῆς καὶ τῶν ἐν τούτοις περιεχομένων φύσεων. λέγεται δὲ καὶ ἑτέρως κόσμος ἡ τῶν ὅλων τάξις τε καὶ διακόσμησις, ὑπὸ θεῶν τε καὶ διὰ θεῶν φυλαττομένη. ταύτης δὲ τὸ μὲν μέσον, ἀκίνητόν τε ὂν καὶ ἑδραῖον, ἡ φερέσβιος εἴληχε γῆ, παντοδαπῶν ζῴων ἑστία τε οὖσα καὶ μήτηρ. τὸ δ' ὕπερθεν αὐτῆς πᾶν τε καὶ πάντη πεπερατωμένον· ἧς τὸ ἀνωτάτω θεῶν οἰκητήριον οὐρανὸς ὠνόμασται ("... The centre of this world system [= διακόσμησις], firm and unmoved, includes the life-dispensing earth, the home and mother of manifold living creatures. What is above it, is the all which extends on every side. What is highest above it, is the abode of the gods, which is called heaven.") On the typical Stoic view of the κόσμος as a σύστημα, cf. the definition of Chrysipp. in Stob. Ecl., 184, 8 (→ 880), also Philo Aet. Mund., 4 and Epict., I, 9, 4.

f. The concept of the κόσμος, whose development we have here sought to understand, is one of the great original creations of the Greek spirit. If it is asked how this concept differs from other views of the world, its uniqueness finds expression in the following features.

(1) Unity is of the nature of the κόσμος.

Even where there is a plurality of κόσμοι, as in Anaximander, Anaximenes, Xenophanes, Leucipp. or Democritus, it is still true that each conceivable cosmos is a perfect unity of many individual things or beings : ἐκ πάντων ἓν καὶ ἐξ ἑνὸς πάντα, as Heraclitus says in Fr., 10 (I, 80, 3 f., Diels), one of those who opposed the doctrine of many κόσμοι, [24] as did Plato, Aristot. and the Stoa after him ; cf. also the statement of Philolaos, Fr., 17 (I, 316, 25, Diels), which in many variations runs through Gk. thought right up to Neo-Platonism : ὁ κόσμος εἷς ἐστιν, cf. v. Arnim, I, p. 27, 5 and 7; II, p. 169, 15; 170, 3 and 5; 172, 13 etc.

(2) The κόσμος is a perfect unity by virtue of the immanent norm which integrates the individual things into a totality.

Anaximander sought to understand this norm by projecting the order of the *polis* on the universe ; it was thus a kind of universal norm of law. Pythagoras found it in number and in the proportions between numbers. The mathematical norms, which are also aesthetic, create the harmony of the cosmos. Heraclitus makes a further step with his discovery of the *logos* (→ λόγος), which is the supreme norm of the thinking and conduct of men and which is also the norm which integrates the varied and opposing elements into cosmic unity. It is no accident that after the magnificent concepts of Plato and Aristotle concerning the subjection of the universe to divine reason, Stoicism returned to the idea of the *logos* in its attempt to understand the divine nature of the immanent law of the world.

(3) The beauty of the world is a third feature of the Greek understanding.

From the earliest Milesian philosopher to the Enn. of Plotinus the beauty of the world is hymned with great power. The κόσμος is by nature καλός (cf. the superlative

---

[24] Cf. De Placitis Philosophorum, II, 1, 2; H. Diels, Dox. Graeci, 327, 10 ff.

κάλλιστος in the solemn concluding sentence of Plato's Tim., 92c, [25] and we may also recall the κάλλιστος of Heracl. Fr., 124 [I, 102, 1, Diels]). The mathematical and aesthetic view of the world, which is peculiar to the Gks., perceives in the κόσμος the epitome of all order and beauty. In its spherical form and circular movement it is the most perfect and therefore the most beautiful σῶμα. To contemplate this beauty is bliss. This is expressed, e.g., by Euripides when he calls the student blessed (ὄλβιος) who contemplates the never-changing cosmic order of immortal nature : ἀθανάτου καθορῶν φύσεως κόσμον ἀγήρων (TGF, 910).

(4) A fourth point which calls for mention is the unique relation of man to the cosmos.

Anaximander may understand cosmic order in terms of law, Stoicism may take the opposite course and derive the order of society from that of the cosmos, [26] Heraclitus may set both world occurrence and human life under the rule of the *logos,* Anaximenes may compare the cosmos with man, but in each and every case we find the same underlying conviction that there is a deep natural relation between the cosmos of the world, the cosmos of human society and the cosmos of man. According to the fundamental principle of Gk. epistemology : τὸ ὅμοιον ἐκ τοῦ ὁμοίου καταλαμβάνεσθαι πέφυκεν, this is the basis of the possibility of knowledge of the world by man as the μικρὸς κόσμος. [27]

6. κόσμος = World II, God and the Cosmos for the Greeks.

a. Among the cosmological questions debated by philosophy from the 6th century that of the origin of the world (ἡ τοῦ κόσμου γένεσις, Plat. Tim., 27a, 29e; cf. Gn. LXX A title : γένεσις κόσμου) and that of its duration are of theological significance.

In this regard we may leave aside the cosmogonic speculations of Hesiod and other early poets and thinkers in whom the philosophical and the mythological interfuse, since there is here nothing distinctively Greek.

b. Heraclitus rejects all doctrines of a beginning of the world, even those suggested on scholarly grounds by his philosophical predecessors. This may be seen in Fr., 30 (I, 84, 1 ff., Diels): κόσμον τόνδε, τὸν αὐτὸν ἁπάντων, οὔτε τις θεῶν οὔτε ἀνθρώπων ἐποίησεν, ἀλλ' ἦν ἀεὶ καὶ ἔστιν καὶ ἔσται πῦρ ἀείζωον, ἁπτόμενον μέτρα καὶ ἀποσβεννύμενον μέτρα, "this cosmic order, the same for all beings (i.e., there is none which does not belong to the cosmos), no god or

---

[25] In Tim., 29a the κόσμος is καλός and κάλλιστος τῶν γεγονότων, cf. also Proclus in Tim., II, 101d (ed. E. Diehl, I [1903], 332, 18 ff.): ὅτι δὲ ὅ τε κόσμος ὀρθῶς εἴρηται κάλλιστος καὶ ὁ δημιουργὸς τῶν αἰτίων ἄριστος, ῥάδιον καταμαθεῖν. πρῶτον μὲν καὶ τὸ φαινόμενον τοῦ οὐρανοῦ κάλλος καὶ ἡ τάξις τῶν περιόδων καὶ τὰ μέτρα τῶν ὡρῶν καὶ ἡ ἁρμονία τῶν στοιχείων καὶ ἡ διὰ πάντων διήκουσα ἀναλογία δείκνυσι τοῖς μὴ παντάπασιν ἐσκοτωμένοις, ὅτι κάλλιστον τὸ πᾶν.

[26] Cf. also the par. between *mundus* and *urbs,* Cic. Nat. Deor., II, 62. The implications of the view of man as a microcosm were worked out by the Stoics, esp. by Posidonius, who with great scholarly profundity understood man as the bond which binds the κόσμος together. Cf. W. Jäger, *Nemesios v. Emesa* (1914), 96 ff. and K. Reinhardt, *Kosmos u. Sympathie* (1926). F. Cumont, *Die orient. Religionen im römischen Heidentum*[3] (1931), 157 and 296, n. 41 traces back the doctrine of the microcosm and sympathy to the astrology of the "Chaldeans."

[27] First Democr. Fr., 34 (II, 72, 7 and 12, Diels), then Aristot. Phys., VIII, 2, p. 252b, 26, Gal. De Usu Partium Corporis Humani, III, 10 (III, 241, Kühn), Nechepso Fr., 25 (ed. E. Riess in Philol. Suppl., 6 [1891-93], 325 ff.) (Firm. Mat. Math. III prooem, 3 f.), Phot. Bibliotheca, 249 (MPG, 103, p. 1584d).

man has created (i.e., there is no creator), but it was always there, and it is and will always be living fire, by measure (i.e., according to set intervals) glowing bright and by measure dying down." [28] There is only one cosmos, and this is eternal, with neither beginning nor end. There is a periodic glowing and dying down, but this is within the one enduring order.

The mythological and philosophical speculations which Heraclitus is attacking are not to be taken in the sense of belief in creation. For the concept of creation in the true sense (→ κτίζω) is unknown in Greek thought. This knows only the idea of the world's coming into being (γένεσις) out of original matter or the ἄπειρον, together with the idea that that which is originally formless is ordered and fashioned into a κόσμος by a divine architect (δημιουργός, ἀρχιτέκτων).

c. Along these lines, and perhaps with the help of oriental materials, Plato in Tim., 28 ff. describes the making of the cosmos by a god (θεός, e.g., 30a) whom he designates δημιουργός (e.g., 28a, 29a), συνιστάς (29d) and whom he calls ποιητὴν καὶ πατέρα τοῦδε τοῦ παντός (28c, cf. ὁ γεννήσας πατήρ, 37c). This god formed the world in accordance with the idea of the perfect living being. He did this in empty space, the womb of all becoming (Tim., 49a), which is also a kind of plastic material. [29]

In this system we do not find the distinction which characterises genuine belief in creation, namely, between God the Creator and the creature which is not God. The demiurge is not God in the full sense, nor is the cosmos truly creation. Strictly Plato in Tim., 28 ff. is speaking of the creation of one god by another. If we ask how far on the Platonic view the κόσμος is a manifestation of god, we receive a twofold answer. First the κόσμος is a demonstration of god's existence — Plato is the father of the cosmological proof which is then further developed by Aristot. and the Stoa. [30] Secondly, the κόσμος is itself god. This wonderful being, as it is described at the end of Tim., is θεὸς αἰσθητός. Plato sees no contradiction between these answers because there are for him stages of the divine and the cosmos can be the lowest of these as god sensually perceptible. Yet the contradiction is just as evident as that which Aristot. [31] already censured, i.e., between the assertions that the cosmos came into being in time and that it is incorruptible.

---

[28] In interpretation cf. O. Gigon, *Untersuchungen zu Heraklit* (1935), 51 ff.

[29] On this *v.* F. Ueberweg-K. Praechter, *Grundriss d. Geschichte d. Philosophie*, I[12] (1926), 310.

[30] Plat. Leg., X, 886a gives the following reasons for the existence of the gods : πρῶτον μὲν γῆ καὶ ἥλιος ἄστρα τε καὶ τὰ σύμπαντα, καὶ τὰ τῶν ὡρῶν διακεκοσμημένα καλῶς οὕτως, ἐνιαυτοῖς τε καὶ μησὶν διειλημμένα· καὶ ὅτι πάντες Ἕλληνές τε καὶ βάρβαροι νομίζουσιν εἶναι θεούς, cf. XII, 966e, where the movements of the heavenly bodies are also seen as a proof that νοῦς ἐστιν τὸ πᾶν διακεκοσμηκώς. From the order of the world is deduced one who orders. Acc. to Aristot. Fr., 12, p. 1476a, 8 ff. (Sext. Emp. Math., IX, 20-22, p. 395, Bekker) contemplation of the stars leads to the belief εἶναί τινα θεὸν τὸν τῆς τοιαύτης κινήσεως καὶ εὐταξίας αἴτιον, i.e., to the conviction that there is a god who is the cause of the movement and order of the cosmos, cf. Fr., 17, p. 1477a, 7 (Philo Aet. Mund., 10). On the proofs of Aristot., *v.* Jaeger, *Aristoteles* (1923), 161 ff. For the cosmological argument in Stoicism cf. Chrysipp. acc. to Cic. Nat. Deor., II, 6 : *atqui res caelestes omnesque eae, quarum est ordo sempiternus, ab homine confici non possunt ; est igitur id, quo illa conficiuntur, homine melius. Id autem quid potius dixeris quam deum ?* Cf. on Stoicism H. Diels, Dox., 292 f.; v. Arnim, II, p. 299, 10. On the influence of these ideas in Hellen. Judaism and early Christianity cf. Ltzm. R. on 1:20.

[31] Cael., I, 10, p. 280a, 28 ff. and prob. the lost Περὶ φιλοσοφίας, III, cf. Jaeger, 320; 141.

Thus Plato's doctrine of the γένεσις τοῦ κόσμου is an unsuccessful attempt to unite the idea of creation, which must always presuppose *creatio ex nihilo* and the unbridgeable gulf between Creator and creature, and the Greek idea of a cosmos which is divine by nature, and hence eternal.

d. Aristotle is consciously the first (Cael., I, 10-12, p. 279b, ff.) to teach that the world is without beginning or end, even in opposition to Heraclitus, who, like the Stoics later, thought in terms of an eternal rejuvenating of the world. Cf. Cael., II, 14, p. 296a, 33 : ἡ ... τοῦ κόσμου τάξις ἀΐδιος, Fr., 17, p. 1477a, 10 : ἀγένητον καὶ ἄφθαρτον ἔφη τὸν κόσμον εἶναι, also Fr., 18, p. 1477a, 25 and the exposition of the problem whether the οὐρανός (universe) is ἀγένητος ἢ γενητὸς καὶ ἄφθαρτος ἢ φθαρτός in Cael., I, 10, p. 279b, 4 ff.

Since the time of the world is for Aristot. identical with eternity — for, as there is no space outside the world even though this be finite, so there is no time alongside or outside that of the world, since there is time only where there is movement — he can find no place, as Plato can, for a πρὶν γενέσθαι τὸν κόσμον (Cael., III, 2, p. 300b, 17). For Aristot. God is not an architect of the world ; he is pure νοῦς which thinks itself, pure form without matter, hence the πρῶτον κινοῦν, though not in the temporal sense. As there was always movement, so there was always the moved. The god of Aristot. "moves without fashioning or acting, himself unmoved, as the good and the goal which has no goal outside itself, but to which all things strive in virtue of the attraction which everything that is loved exercises on that which loves." [32] This god is by nature, and in his relation to the world, the opposite of the God of the Bible. He is not the Creator God, the active God : ἀνάγκη εἶναί τινα ἀΐδιον οὐσίαν ἀκίνητον, Metaph., XI, 6, p. 1071b, 4. He moves the world, not because he loves it, but because he is loved by it, i.e., as the object of its ἔρως : κινεῖ δὲ ὡς ἐρώμενον, κινούμενον δὲ τἆλλα κινεῖ, *ibid.*, XI, 7, p. 1072b, 3. For Aristot. God would no longer be God if he were to love man. [33]

e. Stoicism has yet another solution to the problem of God and the world. It speaks of a coming into being (γίνεσθαι δὲ τὸν κόσμον, ὅταν ἐκ πυρὸς ἡ οὐσία τραπῇ δι' ἀέρος εἰς ὑγρότητα [Diog. L., VII, 142]) and a passing of the κόσμος, but we have here the idea of the eternal recurrence of the same thing — a notion which came into Greek philosophy from the view of the world found in oriental astrology. [34]

The γένεσις τοῦ κόσμου is for the Stoics no true beginning of the world. It is simply the dawn of a new epoch, the restoration of what already was (→ ἀποκατάστασις, I, 389 f.; παλιγγενεσία, I, 686 f.). Similarly, the destruction of the world in an ἐκπύρωσις is no true end ; it is simply the presupposition of a new ἀποκατάστασις τοῦ παντός. This system can allow neither of the doctrine of the fashioning of the κόσμος by a creator god in the Platonic sense nor of the view of Aristotle which denies any divine action on or in the world. God and the cosmos are thought of together in pantheistic fashion. God is the world soul which permeates all things as ether, as breath

---

[32] Ueberweg-Praechter, 383.

[33] → θεός, 74.

[34] Nemesius De Natura Hominum, 38 (v. Arnim, II, p. 190, 10): οἱ δὲ Στωϊκοί φασιν ἀποκαθισταμένους τοὺς πλάνητας εἰς τὸ αὐτὸ σημεῖον ... ἔνθα τὴν ἀρχὴν ἕκαστος ἦν, ὅτε τὸ πρῶτον ὁ κόσμος συνέστη, ἐν ῥηταῖς χρόνων περιόδοις ἐκπύρωσιν καὶ φθορὰν τῶν ὄντων ἀπεργάζεσθαι· καὶ πάλιν ἐξ ὑπαρχῆς εἰς τὸ αὐτὸ τὸν κόσμον ἀποκαθίστασθαι ... ἔσεσθαι γὰρ πάλιν Σωκράτη καὶ Πλάτωνα καὶ ἕκαστον τῶν ἀνθρώπων ... καὶ πᾶσαν πόλιν καὶ κώμην καὶ ἀγρὸν ὁμοίως ἀποκαθίστασθαι· γίνεσθαι δὲ τὴν ἀποκατάστασιν τοῦ παντὸς οὐχ ἅπαξ, ἀλλὰ πολλάκις.

(πνεῦμα), as spiritual fire. [35] He is the reason which rules the cosmos. His πρόνοια is identical with the law of εἱμαρμένη which controls the world. [36] One can not only say ὅτι ... καὶ ζῷον ὁ κόσμος καὶ λογικὸν καὶ ἔμψυχον καὶ νοερόν (Chrysipp. acc. to Diog. L., VII, 70 [142 f.]; v. Arnim, II, p. 191, 34 ff.). On occasion one can also equate god and the world : νοερός ἐστιν ὁ κόσμος. νοερὸς δὲ ὢν καὶ θεὸς καθέστηκεν (Sext. Emp. Math., IX, 95; v. Arnim, II, p. 303, 34); οὐσίαν δὲ θεοῦ Ζήνων μέν φησι τὸν ὅλον κόσμον καὶ τὸν οὐρανόν, Diog. L., VII, 73 (148). This older Stoic pantheism marks the high-water mark of the apotheosis of the world among the Gks., though it should not be forgotten that alongside the Stoic system is the Epicurean, which resolutely denied the divine origin of the κόσμος and the direction of the κόσμος by divine πρόνοια.

Within Stoicism itself there begins with Posidonius a movement which we can follow through the philosophical writings of Cicero, then Philo, and then the work Περὶ κόσμου [37] which was contemporary with Paul. Apparently under the influence of a religious awakening which moves from East to West, pure pantheism yields to a new belief in a transcendental divine power, though faith in the *divinitas mundi* (Cic. Nat. Deor., II, 15) does not suffer any loss thereby. In Posidonius, then, we have an impressive combination of the views of the world found in Stoicism and in Plato's Tim. [38]

f. The story of the κόσμος concept, which began with the Ionian thinkers and reached its climax in the great Athenian schools, ended, like that of Greek philosophy generally, in Alexandria. Here both the term and the concept were adopted by Judaism and brought into the Greek Bible. But here, too, the last thinkers of Hellenism concluded philosophical work on the concept. Both these achievements of intellectual history are represented by Philo. No thinker of antiquity used the word more than he did. This is in itself a sign how significant the Greek concept was and how concerned he was to harmonise Jewish biblical faith and Greek philosophy in the understanding of the world and its relationship to God. His philosophical originality is nowhere more apparent than in the way in which, loyal both to the truth of the OT and to that of the main principles of (Platonic-Stoic) philosophy, he solves the problem of God and the world.

Whereas for previous thinkers the world had always been the empirical world or the plurality of material worlds, for Philo the term includes the world of ideas. He makes a distinction between the κόσμος νοητός (= ἰδέα τῶν ἰδεῶν καθ' ἣν ὁ θεὸς ἐτύπωσε τὸν κόσμον, Migr. Abr., 103), the spiritual model of the empirical world, on the one side, and this world, the κόσμος οὗτος (Rer. Div. Her., 75) or κόσμος αἰσθητός (Op. Mund., 25), κόσμος ὁρατός (Op. Mund., 16), on the other. Philo found an exegetical basis for this distinction in the LXX text of Gn. 1:1 f., where the ἡ δὲ γῆ ἦν ἀόρατος καὶ ἀκατασκεύαστος seemed to teach the creation of an invisible world. On the basis of Gn. 1:1-5 Op. Mund., 15 ff. describes the creation on the first day of a world of ideas, i.e., of an incorporeal earth, an invisible heaven, of the ideas of air and empty space, of the incorporeal substances of water and wind (πνεῦμα), and seventhly of the idea of light (Op. Mund., 29). The sensually perceptible world stands to this world in the relation of copy to original. Philo follows philosophical tradition in

---

[35] Cf. the quotations *s.v.* θεός, → 75.
[36] Cf. the definition of Chrysipp. (v. Arnim, II, p. 264, 18): εἱμαρμένη ἐστὶν ὁ τοῦ κόσμου λόγος.
[37] = Ps. Aristot. Mund.; cf. the citation → 873.
[38] On the κόσμος concept in Pos., v. W. Jaeger, *Nemesios v. Emesa*, 96 ff.; K. Reinhardt, *Kosmos u. Sympathie* (1926). Particularly important is the integration of man into the cosmos. The philosophical and religious influence of Pos. is best seen in Ps.-Aristot. Mund., 5 f., p. 396 ff. On the historical context cf. H. Lietzmann, *Geschichte d. Alten Kirche*, I (1932), 180 ff.

regarding this world as one of order (κόσμος as distinct from ἀταξία, ἀκοσμία etc.,
Aet. Mund., 32, 54 etc.; cf. Op. Mund., 28); as σύνοδός τε καὶ κρᾶσις τῶν στοιχείων,
i.e., the four elements of Greek natural philosophy, Det. Pot. Ins., 8; as the epitome of
all individual things and creatures : λέγεται τοίνυν ὁ κόσμος καθ' ἓν μὲν σύστημα
ἐξ οὐρανοῦ καὶ ἄστρων κατὰ περιοχὴν καὶ γῆς καὶ τῶν ἐπ' αὐτῆς ζῴων καὶ
φυτῶν, καθ' ἕτερον δὲ μόνος οὐρανός, Aet. Mund., 4. Philo is thus acquainted with
the meaning "heaven" for κόσμος. There is only one κόσμος and this is τέλειος, a
perfect work (e.g., Aet. Mund., 26; 50; 73), whose beauty Philo can extol with no less
enthusiasm than Greek thinkers. He again follows their example in regarding the κόσμος
as a living creature with a soul, a ζῷον or φυτόν (Aet. Mund., 95). Philo's thinking on
the relation between God and the world is informed by the concern to reconcile the
doctrine of the divine transcendence, which had been increasingly stressed since Plato
and Aristot. and which was now represented esp. by the Neo-Pythagoreans, with the
Stoic doctrine of the divine πρόνοια that governs the world and with the biblical belief
in God the Creator. It is by way of the → λόγος that he does this. The *logos* is the
mediator between God and the world. It is the εἰκὼν θεοῦ, δι' οὗ σύμπας ὁ κόσμος
ἐδημιουργεῖτο, Spec. Leg., I, 81 (cf. Conf. Ling., 97; Deus Imm., 57). In and through
it the transcendent God of philosophy is the Creator and Lord of the world as taught
by the OT : ὁ τοῦ κόσμου πατήρ, e.g., Vit. Mos., II, 134; πατὴρ καὶ ἡγεμὼν τοῦ
κόσμου, Decal., 90; πατέρα μὲν τὸν γεννήσαντα [τὸν] κόσμον, Det. Pot. Ins., 54;
γεννητὴν καὶ πατέρα καὶ σωτῆρα τοῦ τε κόσμου καὶ τῶν ἐν κόσμῳ θεόν, Spec.
Leg., II, 198; it is δημιουργός, ποιητής, κοσμοποιός, τεχνίτης, ἀρχιτέκτων, κυβερνήτης, ἡγεμών, βασιλεύς, as suggested by all the expressions which speak of the
positive relation of God to the world established in the *logos*. Worth noting is the fact
that in Philo, as in Plato, the images of father and architect are found together. Only
in the period of the Arian controversy did the Church come to make a precise distinction
between γεννᾶν and ποιεῖν. In Op. Mund. [39] Philo works out his doctrine of creation
in close dependence on Plato's Tim. and in conscious opposition to the Aristotelian view
that the world has no beginning. But while he maintains with Plato the ἀφθαρσία τοῦ
κόσμου (cf. Aet. Mund.), he deviates from the biblical doctrine of the world. For the
OT view of creation as an absolute beginning posited by God presupposes that there is
also an end of the world (→ αἰών, I, 202 ff.). Thus Philo, for all his attempt to be loyal
to biblical truth, is nearer to the Tim. than to Gn. What he really describes is not the
creation of the world by almighty God, who summons what is not into being by His
Word, but the fashioning of a cosmos by a superior spirit working on already existing
material. This given material is τὸ παθητὸν ἄψυχον καὶ ἀκίνητον ἐξ ἑαυτοῦ (Op.
Mund., 9). Hence creation, as in Wis. 11:17, is a κτίζειν τὸν κόσμον ἐξ ἀμόρφου
ὕλης, but not οὐκ ἐξ ὄντων, as in 2 Macc. 7:28. Even the use of τὰ μὴ ὄντα for τὸ
παθητόν (e.g., Op. Mund., 81) does not alter this. For in Philo τὸ μὴ ὄν does not mean
nothing ; it has rather the sense of formless matter. In his cosmology, as in other parts of
his teaching, other traditions are also at work as well as that of the Jewish OT and
that of Gk. philosophy. This may be seen in his development of the idea of God as the
father of the cosmos, which goes beyond the Tim. Ebr., 30 teaches the birth of the
κόσμος from God and ἐπιστήμη : ἡ δὲ παραδεξαμένη τὰ τοῦ θεοῦ σπέρματα ...
τὸν μόνον καὶ ἀγαπητὸν αἰσθητὸν υἱὸν ἀπεκύησε, τόνδε τὸν κόσμον, cf. Deus
Imm., 31, where the κόσμος is called υἱὸς θεοῦ (cf. also the μονογενής in Plat. Tim.,
92c). Here we may discern traces of the influence of oriental cosmogonies such as are
reflected in the Corp. Herm. [40]

---

[39] On the question of the interrelation of Op. Mund and Aet. Mund., cf. E. Zeller, *Philosophie d. Griechen*, III, 2⁵ (1923), 437, and R. Löwe, *Kosmos u. Aion* (1935), 55 f. If Philo
himself taught that the world has no beginning, and Aet. Mund. is not just an academic
exercise on a philosophical thesis (so K. Reinhardt, *Posidonius*, 212 f.), this is only a
provisional phase in his thinking.
[40] → 880; cf. Reitzenstein Poim., 41.

g. The history of the concept in ancient philosophy ends with Neo-Platonism. The final word is Plotinus' doctrine of the two worlds, the κόσμος ἐκεῖνος of the intelligible world and the κόσμος οὗτος of the phenomenal. The Platonic duplication of the κόσμος, which Aristot. already had criticised in his master's view of the ideas (Metaph., I, 9, p. 990a, 34 ff.), and which reappeared in Philo's differentiation of the κόσμος νοητός and the κόσμος αἰσθητός, finds now its culmination.

In striking words Plot. Enn., V, 1, 4 lauds the beauty of the κόσμος νοητός. If we praise the empirical world (κόσμον αἰσθητὸν τόνδε) for its greatness, beauty and orderly movement, how much more are we to magnify the κόσμος which is the ἀρχέτυπος of this world and ἀληθινώτερος than it! Plot. never wearies of glorifying the beauty, harmony and felicity of the κόσμος νοητός (e.g., in the work Περὶ τοῦ νοητοῦ κάλλους, Enn., V, 8). Among the advantages which the intelligible world has over the empirical may be listed not only the fact that there is in it nothing imperfect, finite or evil but also its perfect unity, a familiar feature in the Gk. view of the cosmos: ὑφίσταται γοῦν ἐκ τοῦ κόσμου τοῦ ἀληθινοῦ ἐκείνου καὶ ἑνὸς κόσμος οὗτος οὐχ εἷς ἀληθῶς, "from that true and one world, this world which is not truly one has its being" (Enn., III, 2, 2). The distinctively Gk. element in Plotinus' view may be seen in the way in which he tries to avoid the logical implications of this dualism. Although the κόσμος οὗτος is not the true world, although matter is not merely τὸ μὴ ὄν but also τὸ πρῶτον κακόν (Enn., I, 8, 3 ff.), Plotinus can still extol with enthusiasm the beauty of the phenomenal world (Enn., III, 2, 3 f.; 11 ff.). Its beauty resides in the fact that it is the copy, or, more precisely, the reflection of the κόσμος νοητός. Thus Plotinus, writing against Christian Gnostics, protests emphatically against their pessimistic appraisal of the world: Πρὸς τοὺς κακὸν τὸν δημιουργὸν τοῦ κόσμου καὶ τὸν κόσμον κακὸν εἶναι λέγοντας (Enn., II, 9, title). The objection which the Platonist raises against a view which denies the eternity and divinity of the κόσμος is primarily directed, of course, against the evaluation of the κόσμος οὗτος in Christian belief. [41]

h. The thousand-year story of the κόσμος concept from the Milesian thinkers to the last Neo-Platonists was not confined, of course, to the more specific sphere of philosophy. When Platonic and Stoic ideas of the cosmos began to influence the outlook and religion of wider circles, the word κόσμος made its way into religious and cultic speech. In relation to Hellenistic Judaism this process will demand separate treatment (→ 880). In relation to Hellenistic Roman paganism a few indications must suffice.

In earlier times the concept had vanquished the nature myths which controlled the view of early Greece (Hesiod, the Orphics). But the ancient theogonic and cosmogonic speculations were never completely banished. With the penetration of oriental religions into the Hellenistic Roman world, the nature speculations and creation myths of the Babylonians, Phoenicians, Egyptians and Persians came also. How powerfully these speculations, long since overcome by Greek learning, dominated the minds of the time, may be seen in the flowering of syncretistic Gnosticism. This adopts even the term κόσμος with its rich content and varied meaning, and brings it into the vocabulary of syncretistic nature mythology. Here the word is used for "universe," but the universe is a mythological personage, and thus becomes the subject of fantastic speculations. We can see something of this already in Philo's statements concerning the κόσμος as the

---

[41] A. Neander, "Über die welthistorische Bedeutung des 9. Buchs in der II. Enneade des Plotinos oder seines Buchs gegen die Gnostiker," ABB, 1843, 299 ff. (outdated); C. Schmidt, "Plotins Stellung zum Gnostizismus u. kirchlichen Christentum," TU, II, 5, 4 (1901); H. F. Müller, "Plotinos über die Vorsehung," Philol., 72 (1913), 338 ff.

son of God. It is found again in Corp. Herm.,⁴² in which the κόσμος is again called the son of God, e.g., VIII, 5; X, 14. Ideas found in Platonic and Stoic cosmology, e.g., that the κόσμος is a living creature with a soul, that it is the image of God and that man is its image, are carried to absurd lengths, e.g., Corp. Herm., X, 11. An older, widespread and perhaps originally Indo-Aryan view that the κόσμος is the body of a god, or of god, whose members are equated with the parts or basic elements of the world, is also adopted. ⁴³ The κόσμος is arranged in a ladder of being in which it is set alongside other concepts, e.g., Corp. Herm., XI, 2 : ὁ θεὸς τὸν αἰῶνα ποιεῖ, ὁ αἰὼν δὲ τὸν κόσμον, ὁ κόσμος δὲ τὸν χρόνον, ὁ χρόνος δὲ τὴν γένεσιν. The material reality from which the term cannot be separated did not stop the mythological game from being carried to the same lengths as in the case of αἰών.

7. κόσμος as World in the Sense of Earth, Inhabited World, Humanity.

As the meaning of κόσμος can be restricted to "heaven" or even "heavenly body," so the term can also be used for "earth" as one essential part of the universe, e.g., Stob. Ecl., I, 405, 1: ὁ ἐπιχθόνιος κόσμος as distinct from heaven, or Iambl. Vita Pyth., 27, 123 : ὁ ἄνω κόσμος as distinct from the underworld. The earth can also be linked with its inhabitants. Hence in the later *koine* κόσμος can be used in the sense of the "inhabited world," the "earth and its inhabitants," "humanity," e.g., Ditt. Or., 458, 40 : ἦρξεν δὲ τῷ κόσμῳ τῶν δι᾽ αὐτὸν εὐαγγελί[ων ἡ γενέθλιος] τοῦ θεοῦ, i.e., of Augustus ; Ditt. Syll.³, 814, 31: ὁ τοῦ παντὸς κόσμου κύριος (of Nero), cf. Inscr. Graecae ad res Romanas pertinentes (ed. R. Cagnat, IV [1908]), No. 982 (Samos). That κόσμος can also denote the totality of creatures existing in the world may be seen from the definition ascribed to Chrysipp. (Stob. Ecl., I, 184, 8): σύστημα ἐξ οὐρανοῦ καὶ γῆς καὶ τῶν ἐν τούτοις φύσεων· ἢ τὸ ἐκ θεῶν καὶ ἀνθρώπων σύστημα, cf. Epict. Diss., I, 9, 4. Often the sense of humanity is weakened to that of the "world" in the sense of the "whole world," the "people," P. Oxy., 1298, 8 (4th cent. A.D.): πᾶσαι αἱ λέσχαι τοῦ κόσμου, "the babblings of the whole world"; P. Lond., 1727, 15 (6th cent. A.D.).

B. κόσμος in the LXX. The Concept of the Cosmos in Judaism.

1. In the history of the word κόσμος there is no more incisive event than its adoption into the vocabulary of the LXX. From this point on we have to reckon with a biblical as well as a philosophical concept, and this is further developed in the NT. The story of the concept thus becomes the story of the interaction between two concepts which affect the future history of thought both in their antithesis and also in their relationship.

In the LXX κόσμος is used as follows.

(1) It is used for צָבָא, "host (of heaven)," Gn. 2:1; Dt. 4:19; 17:3; Is. 24:21; 40:26 (13:10); in resultant phrases like ὁ κόσμος τοῦ οὐρανοῦ it is understood by LXX readers in a sense which combines the ideas of order → 868 f. (A. 1.-3.), adornment, world, heaven and stars.

(2) It is used in the sense of "adornment" for many Heb. terms which either mean this or are understood in this sense : Ex. 33:5, 6; 2 Βασ. 1:24; Jer. 2:32; 4:30; Ez. 7:20; 16:11;

---

⁴² Reitzenstein Poim. (1904); J. Kroll, *Die Lehren des Hermes Trismegistos* (1914), 118 ff., 233 ff. On the cosmogonies of syncretism cf. also A. Dieterich, *Abraxas* (1891); Reitzenstein Ir. Erl.

⁴³ Cf. W. H. Roscher, "Die hippokratische Schrift von der Siebenzahl," *Studien zur Geschichte und Kultur des Altertums,* ed. E. Drerup, 6, 3/4 (1913); R. Reitzenstein-H. H. Schaeder, "Studien zum antiken Synkretismus ...," *Studien der Bibl. Warburg,* 7 (1926), 91 ff.

23:40 for עֲדִי; Prv. 20:29 for תִּפְאֶרֶת; Is. 3:24 for מַעֲשֶׂה; Is. 61:10 for כְּלִי; Prv. 29:17 for מַעֲדַנִּים; 2 Βασ. 1:24 for עֵדֶן; Na. 2:10 for תְּכוּנָה; Is. 3:18 f. for other words.

(3) It is also used for "adornment" (also fig.) where there is no specific Heb. original or in passages written in Gk.: Is. 49:18; Prv. 28:17; Jdt. 1:14; 10:4; 12:15 (παντὶ τῷ κόσμῳ τῷ γυναικείῳ); Sir. 6:30; 21:21; 22:17; 26:16; 32(35):5; 43:9; [44] 50:19 (κόσμος κυρίου of the service of the altar, → 870, A. 4.); 1 Macc. 1:22; 2:11; 2 Macc. 2:2; 5:3.

(4) The Heb. OT has no word for the universe. It normally speaks of heaven and earth, or occasionally of the "all" (כֹּל or הַכֹּל e.g., Ps. 8:6; Is. 44:24; Qoh. 3:1). Hence there is no specific reason why the translator should use the term κόσμος in the sense "world." It is Symmachus who later on one occasion has κόσμος rather than γῆ for אֶרֶץ, (Job 38:4). [45] On the other hand, the word is common in the books originally composed in Greek. Indeed, the Jewish Hellenistic writers, especially those influenced by Greek philosophy, seemed to have a liking for the term (→ 877 on Philo) and brought it into their religious and theological vocabulary. It denotes the world in the spatial sense and replaces the older "heaven and earth."

The process described in Gn. 1:1 ff. is now γένεσις κόσμου, [46] cf. ἐποίεις τὸν κόσμον, Wis. 9:9; thine almighty hand κτίσασα τὸν κόσμον ἐξ ἀμόρφου ὕλης, 11:17 (→ 878). God is Creator, Ruler and King of the world: ὁ τοῦ κόσμου κτίστης, 2 Macc. 7:23; 13:14; 4 Macc. 5:25 (cf. Wis. 13:3 S² ὁ γὰρ τοῦ κόσμου [ABS¹ κάλλους] γενεσιάρχης ἔκτισεν αὐτά); τὸν μέγαν τοῦ κόσμου δυνάστην, 2 Macc. 12:15; ὁ τοῦ κόσμου βασιλεύς, 2 Macc. 7:9. Other instances of the sense "universe" are: εἰδέναι σύστασιν κόσμου, "to know the system of the world," Wis. 7:17; [47] ὡς ῥοπὴ ἐκ πλαστίγγων ὅλος ὁ κόσμος ἐναντίον σου, "the whole world is before thee as a speck of dust in the balance," Wis. 11:22 (cf. Is. 40:15); πρυτάνεις κόσμου θεούς, "gods which rule the world," Wis. 13:2; ὑπέρμαχος ὁ κόσμος ἐστὶν δικαίων, "the world (nature) fights for the righteous," Wis. 16:17, cf. 5:20, where it is said of the κόσμος that in the eschatological conflict it will be on God's side against the corrupt; τὸν ὅλον κόσμον, 2 Macc. 8:18; ἐπὶ γὰρ ποδήρους ἐνδύματος ἦν ὅλος ὁ κόσμος, "the whole world was (represented) on his long robe," Wis. 18:24 (of Moses). [48] κόσμος means the "earthly world," "earth," in Wis. 9:3: "that man may rule over the creatures καὶ διέπῃ τὸν κόσμον ἐν ὁσιότητι and have dominion over the world in holiness"; τοῦ τετιμημένου κατὰ τὸν σύμπαντα κόσμον ἱεροῦ, "of the temple honoured in the whole world," 2 Macc. 3:12; to come into the world, εἰς τὸν κόσμον: of death, Wis. 2:24; of idolatry, 14:14; of all that lives, Wis. 7:6 S: μία δὲ πάντων εἴσοδος εἰς τὸν κόσμον [AB βίον]; μεταλαμβάνειν τοῦ κόσμου, "to have a share in the world," 4 Macc. 16:18; ἀποστεροῦμεν ἑαυτοὺς τοῦ γλυκέος κόσμου, "to remove us from the sweet world," 4 Macc. 8:23, here, as in the previous reference, par. to βίος. Finally, κόσμος is used for the "world of men": πρωτόπλαστον πατέρα κόσμου, "the first-formed father of the world," Wis. 10:1 of Adam; ἡ ἐλπὶς τοῦ κόσμου ἐπὶ σχεδίας καταφυγοῦσα, "the hope of the world taking refuge in the ark,"

---

[44] Here κόσμος means "adornment," but the idea of cosmic processes is suggested by the context: κάλλος οὐρανοῦ δόξα ἄστρων, κόσμος φωτίζων ἐν ὑψίστοις κυρίου.
[45] LXX: ποῦ ἦς ἐν τῷ θεμελιοῦν με τὴν γῆν; Σ: μὴ συμπαρῆς δημιουργοῦντι τῷ θεῷ τὸν κόσμον;
[46] So the heading of Gn. in A. In the σωτήριοι αἱ γενέσεις τοῦ κόσμου of Wis. 1:14 γενέσεις means creatures.
[47] Cf. Plato's συνιστάς for the cosmic architect (→ 875).
[48] Acc. to the Midrash, cf. K. Siegfried, *Philo v. Alexandria als Ausleger des AT* (1875), 188 f., 223, 227. In Philo we find the notion that the garment of the high-priest is ἀπεικόνισμα καὶ μίμημα τοῦ κόσμου, Vit. Mos., II, 117 and 133; Spec. Leg., I, 84 and 96.

Wis. 14:6; πλῆθος δὲ σοφῶν σωτηρία κόσμου, "the number of the wise is the salvation of the world," Wis. 6:24; ὁ δὲ κόσμος καὶ ὁ τῶν ἀνθρώπων βίος ἐθεώρει,
"the world and humanity were spectators," 4 Macc. 17:14 — κόσμος is here to be taken
as the sum of all spiritual beings.

2. Hence it is only in the final writings of the LXX, which are Greek in their
very conception, that κόσμος is found in the sense of "world." The fact that
κόσμος is so common in the later parts of the LXX (19 times in Wis., 5 in 2 Macc.
and 4 in 4 Macc.) supports the conclusion already suggested by its place in Philo,
namely, that it became a favourite word of Hellenistic Judaism, which adopted it
instead of the older terms for the universe. In this way Greek speaking Judaism
found a fixed expression for the world. The primary influence seems to have been
that of current Hellenistic usage, which even in the 4th century had adopted this
technical philosophical term. Yet amongst the more educated we may also assume
that the philosophical doctrine of the κόσμος was not without effect. In this respect
Philo played a mediatorial role. It is to be noted that the different nuances of the
sense "world" in Wis. and 2 and 4 Macc. correspond formally to those found in
the NT, i.e., "universe," "earth," "inhabited earth" and "humanity." The expression "to come into the world" is also stereotyped. The use of κόσμος in such
divine titles as Creator, Lord or King of the cosmos, which are alien to the NT,
enables us to conclude that among the Jews the word had found its way not only
into cultic speech but also into liturgical usage, and that it was beginning in some
cases to oust such terms as οὐρανὸς καὶ γῆ and αἰών.

3. One may assume that in the light of this use of κόσμος in Hellenistic Judaism
the Heb. עוֹלָם and Aram. עָלְמָא began to take on what had hitherto been an alien
spatial significance. This is confirmed by the adoption of the adj. κοσμικός as a
loan word in Rabb. Heb. (→ κοσμικός, 897).

To the εἰσέρχεσθαι εἰς τὸν κόσμον of Wis. 2:24 etc. (cf. Jn. 1:9; R. 5:12) corresponds
בָּא לְעוֹלָם, bJeb., 63a, 92b; Aram. אָתָא בְעָלְמָא, Tg. Qoh. 3:14; 4:2, cf. 5:15 [49] (→ 889).
The object of creation is עוֹלָם or עָלְמָא in the sense of the spatially extended universe,
e.g., Ed., 1, 13; Tg. O. Dt. 33:28; Tg. Is. 41:4. Finally, עוֹלָם and עָלְמָא are often used
in the sense of the spatial world or universe in phrases like מֶלֶךְ עָלְמָא, Tg. Zech. 14:17;
מֶלֶךְ הָעוֹלָם, Seder Rab. Amram, I, 1b; [50] אֵילָה עָלְמָא, Tg. O. Gn. 21:33; Tg. Is. 40:28; 42:5,
though these terms for God are originally eternity formulae (→ αἰών, I, 200 f.).

The temporal sense of עָלְמָא may be demonstrated at the end of the 1st century
A.D. (→ αἰών I, 203 f.) from the time of 4 Esr. and S. Bar. At this period the Greek
concept of the cosmos invaded Aramaic speaking Judaism and forced it to substitute a special term for the cosmos in place of older expressions. A few examples
will show how fixed the sense of עוֹלָם became and how clearly it reflected Greek
influence.

Tanch. פקודי § 3 (Horeb [1924], 172b) reads : "The setting up of the tabernacle has
such significance that it is equivalent in importance to the creation of the whole world
or to the creation of man, who is a little world" : המשכן שקול כנגד כל העולם וכנגד יצירת
האדם שהוא עולם קטן. Greek influence may also be discerned here in the idea of a man as

---

[49] Cf. on this and on what follows Dalman WJ, I, 140 ff.; → 889.
[50] Dalman WJ, 142.

a microcosm. It is also found elsewhere. Thus R. Meir (c. 150 A.D.) [51] says that the dust from which the first man was formed was brought together מִכָּל הָעוֹלָם, "from the whole world" (bSanh., 38a). An older contemporary, R. Jose of Galilee, [52] speaks to the same effect: "All that the Holy One, blessed be He, has created in His world, He has created (also) in man," AbRN, 31: כל מה שברא הקב"ה בעולמו ברא באדם.[53] Nu. r., 14 on 7:78 (Vilna, 1887, 62d) speaks of the 4 elements from which God created the עוֹלָם.

C. κόσμος in the NT.

1. General. κόσμος in the Sense Adornment.

In the NT κόσμος is never used in the sense "order," and it occurs for "adornment" only once at 1 Pt. 3:3 of women: ὁ ἔξωθεν ἐμπλοκῆς τριχῶν καὶ περιθέσεως χρυσίων ἢ ἐνδύσεως ἱματίων κόσμος, "the outward adorning of plaiting the hair, and of wearing of gold, or of putting on of apparel." This sense is elsewhere represented in the NT only by the derivatives → κοσμέω and → κόσμιος. In all other passages κόσμος means "world" in some sense. The references are very unevenly distributed. Over half are found in the Johannine writings, 78 times in Jn., 22 in 1 Jn., 1 in 2 Jn. and 3 in Rev. Paul comes next with 46 instances. The others are far behind, with 15 in the Synoptists (including parallels), 5 each in Hb., Jm. and 2 Pt., 2 in 1 Pt. and 1 in Ac. These statistics are in proportion to the significance of the term in the theology of the works concerned. In general, early Christian usage follows that of Hellenistic Judaism at this point. We have no means of telling how far a temporally understood עָלְמָא on the lips of Jesus Himself, or in primitive Aramaic speaking Christianity, may have been a first step in the development of the usage. [54] Jesus Himself constantly uses the OT "heaven and earth" (→ γῆ I, 678 f.) for the cosmos. Yet κόσμος could be used for the Aram. עָלְמָא in the Synoptic Gospels, esp. in Mt., where it occurs 7 times.

Whether the further sense of "totality," "sum," "epitome" is also to be found in the NT depends on the exposition of the difficult verse Jm. 3:6: ἡ γλῶσσα πῦρ, ὁ κόσμος τῆς ἀδικίας, ἡ γλῶσσα καθίσταται ἐν τοῖς μέλεσιν ἡμῶν, ἡ σπιλοῦσα ὅλον τὸ σῶμα.

In support of the rendering "epitome of unrighteousness" for κόσμος τῆς ἀδικίας Pr.-Bauer [55] points to Prv. 17:6a : τοῦ πιστοῦ ὅλος ὁ κόσμος τῶν χρημάτων, τοῦ δὲ ἀπίστου οὐδὲ ὀβολός (only LXX); Ditt. Syll.[3], 850, 10 : τὸν κόσμον τῶν ἔργων, "the sum of the works"; Mart. Pol., 17, 2 : τοῦ παντὸς κόσμου τῶν σῳζομένων. Nevertheless, the rendering "world of iniquity," i.e., "unrighteous, evil world," is

---

[51] Bacher Tannaiten, II, 65.

[52] Ibid., I[2], 365, cf. Pal. Am., I, 413, n. 3.

[53] Rudolf Meyer, to whom I owe the above passages on the microcosm, also points out that similar ideas passed from Judaism into Syr. Christianity, e.g., the depiction of the creation of Adam in Syr. Treasure Cave, II, 7 ff.: "God took a speck of dust from the whole earth, a drop of water from all waters, a breath of wind from all the air, and a little heat from all fire ... Then God formed Adam" (P. Riessler, Altjüd. Schrifttum ausserhalb der Bibel [1928], 944).

[54] Cf. on this question Dalman WJ, I, 137. Dalman believes that only with reference to κερδαίνειν τὸν κόσμον at Mk. 8:36 and par. can we assume with any certainty that Jesus used עלמא in the sense of "world."

[55] Pr.-Bauer[3], 742.

established by Eth. En. 48:7 and similar instances, and the σπιλοῦσα reminds readers of Jm. of the ἄσπιλον ἑαυτὸν τηρεῖν ἀπὸ τοῦ κόσμου of 1:27. Thus κόσμος is to be taken as a predicate noun related to the γλῶσσα καθίσταται which follows, and with M. Dibelius we may translate: "The tongue, which defiles the whole body, represents the evil world among our members." [56]

2. κόσμος = World I, as the Universe, the Sum of all Created Being.

a. In the sense "world," "universe," κόσμος is synon. with the OT "heaven and earth" (→ γῆ): ὁ θεὸς ὁ ποιήσας τὸν κόσμον καὶ πάντα τὰ ἐν αὐτῷ, οὗτος οὐρανοῦ καὶ γῆς ὑπάρχων κύριος, Ac. 17:24. It denotes here the universe which consists of heaven and earth and in which is found the totality of all individual creatures (πάντα τὰ ἐν αὐτῷ). It has the sense of the spatial, just as κόσμος, used of the world, carries that of the temporal. It suggests space in the sense of the greatest space that can be conceived in the sentence: οὐδ᾽ αὐτὸν οἶμαι τὸν κόσμον χωρήσειν τὰ ... βιβλία, "even the world itself, I think, could not contain the books," Jn. 21:25; cf. Herm. s., 9, 2, 1, which speaks of a rock that is so big ὥστε δύνασθαι ὅλον τὸν κόσμον χωρῆσαι, "that it could comprehend the whole world in itself." [57] The hyperbolical use of κόσμος to indicate immeasurably great space shows that the idea of cosmic space may to some degree be separated from that of the things which fill this space. The distinction between the κόσμος and πάντα τὰ ἐν αὐτῷ goes back to the OT view of the world which still persists in the NT; in relation to the τὸν κόσμον καὶ πάντα τὰ ἐν αὐτῷ of Ac. 17:24 cf. the synon. expressions τὸν οὐρανὸν καὶ τὴν γῆν καὶ τὴν θάλασσαν καὶ πάντα τὰ ἐν αὐτοῖς, Ac. 4:24; 14:15 (Ex. 20:11; cf. also ψ 145:6; ψ 23:1) and τὸν οὐρανὸν καὶ τὰ ἐν αὐτῷ καὶ τὴν γῆν καὶ τὰ ἐν αὐτῇ καὶ τὴν θάλασσαν καὶ τὰ ἐν αὐτῇ, Rev. 10:6 (cf. 14:7 and Neh. 9:6). The indication of the world by an enumeration of its constituent parts, like the distinction between the κόσμος and its contents, may be attributed to the influence on the NT of the older OT concept which did not yet envisage the world as a unity. [58] The concept of the κόσμος as the totality of all created things, of universal space and everything contained in it, comes to expression in statements concerning creation and the part of the Logos in it, e.g., Jn. 1:10: ὁ κόσμος δι᾽ αὐτοῦ ἐγένετο, cf. 1:3: πάντα δι᾽ αὐτοῦ ἐγένετο. In such statements ὁ κόσμος is used synonymously and interchangeably with [τὰ] πάντα, and this corresponds to NT usage elsewhere, cf. 1 C. 8:6; 15:27 f.; Phil. 3:21; Col. 1:16 f.; 1:20; Eph. 1:10; Hb. 1:2 f.; 2:8, 10; 1 Pt. 4:7, and also to Jewish usage, e.g., Wis. 9:9: ἐποίεις τὸν κόσμον, cf. 9:1: ὁ ποιήσας τὰ πάντα ἐν λόγῳ σου, which is analogous to the use of πάντα for the universe in Hellenistic philosophy [59] and to the meaning of כֹּל in later strata of the OT. [60] κόσμος means world in the sense of the sum of all created being at 1 C. 3:22, where the πάντα ὑμῶν ἐστιν is broken up into εἴτε Παῦλος εἴτε Ἀπολλῶς εἴτε Κηφᾶς, εἴτε κόσμος εἴτε ζωὴ εἴτε θάνατος, εἴτε ἐνεστῶτα εἴτε μέλλοντα.

Further examples from post-canonical literature are Herm. m., 12, 4, 2: ἔκτισε τὸν κόσμον ἕνεκα τοῦ ἀνθρώπου, v. 2, 4, 1: διὰ ταύτην (sc. τὴν ἐκκλησίαν) ὁ κόσμος

---

[56] V. Dib. Jk., ad loc.; also Hck. Jk., ad loc. On the meaning of κόσμος here → 893 f.
[57] So Dib. Herm., ad loc.; cf. the vision of the stone which ἐπλήρωσεν πᾶσαν τὴν γῆν in Da. 2:35 Θ.
[58] → γῆ, I, 678.
[59] Cf. the quotations → 870 and 871, cf. also Cleanthes' hymn to Zeus in Stob. Ecl., I, 25, 3 (v. Arnim, I, p. 121 f.).
[60] From the time of Is. 44:24, cf. Jer. 10:16; Ps. 8:6; 103:19; Sir. 36:1.

κατηρτίσθη, Dg., 10, 2 : ὁ γὰρ θεὸς τοὺς ἀνθρώπους ἠγάπησε, δι' οὓς ἐποίησε τὸν κόσμον. These statements answer the question why God created the κόσμος. This question, much discussed by Judaism, [61] is not raised in the NT and only begins to play a further role in the post-canonical writings of the early Church.

b. Like all that is created, the κόσμος has only limited duration. The time defined by creation and the end of the world is called → αἰών or αἰὼν τοῦ κόσμου τούτου, Eph. 2:2. The end of the world can be denoted by expressions which imply the end of time, e.g., συντέλεια τοῦ αἰῶνος (Mt. 13:40 → αἰών, I, 203). But formulae which denote the beginning of the world speak of its creation or commencement or foundation as the world in the spatial sense : ἀπ' ἀρχῆς κόσμου, "from the beginning of the world," Mt. 24:21 (par. ἀπ' ἀρχῆς κτίσεως, Mk. 13:19, cf. ἀπὸ τοῦ αἰῶνος, Jl. 2:2 and ἀφ' οὗ γεγένηται ἔθνος ἐπὶ τῆς γῆς, Da. 12:1 Θ); ἀπὸ κτίσεως κόσμου, "since the creation of the world," R. 1:20. The usual expression is ἀπὸ καταβολῆς [62] κόσμου, "from the foundation of the world," Lk. 11:50; Hb. 4:3; 9:26; cf. Barn., 5, 5 in the sense of "at (or immediately after) the foundation of the world," while in passages like Mt. 25:34; Rev. 13:8; 17:8 the meaning of ἀπὸ καταβολῆς κόσμου approximates to that of πρὸ καταβολῆς κόσμου, "before the foundation of the world," Jn. 17:24 (= πρὸ τοῦ τὸν κόσμον εἶναι, 17:5) in the sense of pre-existence, cf. also Eph. 1:4; 1 Pt. 1:20.

Transitoriness is of the very essence of the κόσμος as the sum of everything created. It is the locus of φθορά, 2 Pt. 1:4, and hence we read of it : ὁ κόσμος παράγεται, 1 Jn. 2:17; παράγει τὸ σχῆμα τοῦ κόσμου τούτου, 1 C. 7:31. Inasmuch as eschatological expectation is focused on an eternal and imperishable world, the κόσμος is by contrast κόσμος οὗτος [63] whose end has come. Paul uses the phrase κόσμος οὗτος along with αἰὼν οὗτος (1 C. 3:19; 5:10; 7:31; cf. Eph. 2:2) and in the same sense, as is shown by the alternation of σοφία τοῦ κόσμου, 1 C. 1:20, σοφία τοῦ κόσμου τούτου, 3:19 and σοφία τοῦ αἰῶνος τούτου, 2:6. In John κόσμος οὗτος in an expression like ὁ ἄρχων τοῦ κόσμου τούτου, Jn. 12:31; 16:11 (cf. τῶν ἀρχόντων τοῦ αἰῶνος τούτου, 1 C. 2:6, 8) is used instead of αἰὼν οὗτος, which does not occur. But in many places it is also used in place of the simple κόσμος, cf. Jn. 14:30 (ὁ τοῦ κόσμου ἄρχων) with 12:31; 16:11, also εἰς τὸν κόσμον τοῦτον ἦλθον at 9:39 with ἐλήλυθα εἰς τὸν κόσμον, 16:28; 18:37. There are further instances at 8:23; 11:9; 12:25; 12:31; 13:1; 18:36; 1 Jn. 4:17. If κόσμος is here used for αἰών to denote what Jewish apocalyptic calls עוֹלָם הַזֶּה, the NT avoids κόσμος when speaking of the world to come. The reason is undoubtedly to be found in the additional sense which κόσμος has taken on in the NT, and of which we shall have to speak below. For κόσμος is not just the universe as the sum of all created things. It is also the world which is now estranged from its Creator and Lord. Hence the linguistic sense of the early Church does not allow it to use this term for the eternal world of eschatological hope. [64]

---

[61] E.g., S. Bar. 14:18. The world is created for man. For many other references and answers cf. Str.-B., I, 732.

[62] → καταβολή, Polyb., 1, 36, 8; 24, 8, 9; Diod. S., XII, 32, 2 has ἀπὸ καταβολῆς in the sense "from the foundation or the beginning." ἀπὸ καταβολῆς alone for ἀπὸ καταβολῆς κόσμου is found in the NT at Mt. 13:35 (ψ 77:2).

[63] Cf. the concept of κόσμος οὗτος in Plot. → 879.

[64] Jn. 12:25 contrasts ἐν τῷ κόσμῳ τούτῳ and εἰς ζωὴν αἰώνιον. It is also no accident that οὐρανὸς καὶ γῆ is retained in place of κόσμος in the phrase "new heaven and new earth" at Rev. 21:1; 2 Pt. 3:13; → γῆ, I, 678.

This is still evident in post-canonical writings. Thus Herm. v., 4, 3, 2 ff. contrasts the κόσμος οὗτος in which Christians now live, and which is rushing to destruction, with ὁ αἰὼν ὁ ἐπερχόμενος, ἐν ᾧ κατοικήσουσιν οἱ ἐκλεκτοὶ τοῦ θεοῦ (5). The new world is spatial. It is a dwelling-place. But the temporal concept αἰών is used for it. Barn., 10, 11 uses οὗτος ὁ κόσμος and ὁ ἅγιος αἰών similarly. Barn., 15, 8, where the day of the Lord is called ἄλλου κόσμου ἀρχή, is the first indication of a change in this respect. The restriction of κόσμος to the universe which was created and which is now rushing to destruction safeguards the biblical view of the world against the speculative assumption of a plurality of simultaneous or successive worlds. Such theories, which are occasionally found even in Judaism, [65] imperil the concept of creation out of nothing, fail to take seriously the end of the world, and destroy the uniqueness of the world-process, the singularity of history and the ἐφάπαξ of salvation history (Hb. 7:27; 9:12; 10:10). If the plural αἰῶνες is to be understood spatially in passages like Hb. 1:2; 11:3 and is thus to be translated "worlds" or "spheres," the reference is to the spheres of the one cosmos. The only example of the plural use of κόσμος as world in early Christian lit. is 1 Cl., 20, 8 : ὠκεανὸς ... καὶ οἱ μετ' αὐτὸν κόσμοι, "the ocean and the parts of the world (earth) beyond it." But the reference here is obviously not to a plurality of worlds. κόσμος is used for the human race in 2 Pt. 2:5 and 3:6 (→ 890).

The same reason which led the early Church to avoid κόσμος for the future world made it impossible for the NT to use the word in descriptions of God. It is true that God is called ὁ ποιήσας τὸν κόσμον [66] at Ac. 17:24 in a passage which is perhaps influenced by the language of Jewish Hellenistic apologetics, but the NT does not follow Hellenistic Judaism in calling God the Lord and King of the κόσμος. In this case αἰών, which belongs to the liturgical sphere, is again preferred to what is felt to be the more secular κόσμος. Thus βασιλεὺς τῶν αἰώνων in 1 Tm. 1:17 is materially equivalent to ὁ τοῦ κόσμου βασιλεύς in 2 Macc. 7:9. A designation like κύριος τοῦ οὐρανοῦ καὶ τῆς γῆς, Mt. 11:25, par. Lk. 10:21; Ac. 17:24, never becomes κύριος τοῦ κόσμου in the NT, though the corresponding רִבּוֹנוֹ שֶׁל עוֹלָם is extremely common in Palestinian Judaism. [67]

It is the non-canonical writings, influenced in this as in other points by the usage of the Hellenistic synagogue, which first make this transition. Thus 1 Cl., 19, 2 calls God τὸν πατέρα καὶ κτίστην τοῦ σύμπαντος κόσμου. In Barn., 21, 5 God is called ὁ τοῦ παντὸς κόσμου κυριεύων, while in 5, 5 Christ is called παντὸς τοῦ κόσμου κύριος.

The NT realises that the fulfilment of God's rule over the κόσμος is the object of eschatological expectation. The world stands now under the power of the ἄρχων τοῦ κόσμου. Only when the victory over the κόσμος is fully won, and judgment is passed on the ἄρχων and ἄρχοντες of the world, will the triumph song peal out : ἐγένετο ἡ βασιλεία τοῦ κόσμου τοῦ κυρίου ἡμῶν καὶ τοῦ χριστοῦ αὐτοῦ, Rev. 11:15.

Cf. 2 Cl., 17, 5 : ἰδόντες τὸ βασίλειον τοῦ κόσμου ἐν τῷ Ἰησοῦ, "when they (i.e., unbelievers) see the royal government of the world in the hands of Jesus."

---

[65] The plur. עוֹלָמִים gives rise to such speculations, esp. in designations of God, when there is a spatial understanding ; for details → αἰών I, 204. There is ref. to several successive creations in Gn. r. 3 on 1:5 (→ I, 204). bAZ, 3b speaks of 18,000 simultaneous worlds, though these are the spheres which constitute the universe. Midr. Ps. 18 § 15 on 18:11 refers to many worlds עוֹלָמוֹת הַרְבֵּה.

[66] Cf. ὁ κτίσας τὸν κόσμον, Herm. v., 1, 3, 4; ἔκτισε τὸν κόσμον, m., 12, 4, 2.

[67] Thus in Taan., 3, 8 Onias addresses God : רִבּוֹנוֹ שֶׁל עוֹלָם. κύριε τοῦ κόσμου would correspond to this in Gk. (→ 881 f.).

c. On the question of the details of the NT view of the world the following points may be noted. The κόσμος as the universe is viewed as a system of spheres. As in the OT, it is divided into → γῆ and → οὐρανός. The tripartite division of the OT is also found; the sea or the underworld is here the third sphere. [68]

On the OT model (e.g., Neh. 9:6, cf. also the plur. שָׁמַיִם), and along the lines of later Judaism, and esp. of the oriental conception, heaven, too, is regarded as a system of spheres. It is in terms of cosmic or heavenly spheres that we are to construe the spatial αἰῶνες in passages like Hb. 1:2; 11:3. The meaning "heaven" in the sense of the sphere which stretches over the earth, and in which the stars pursue uninterruptedly their regular courses, occurs in 1 Cl., 60, 1, where we read in a liturgical prayer: σὺ τὴν ἀένναον τοῦ κόσμου σύστασιν ("the eternal, i.e., unbreakable, order of heaven") ... ἐφανεροποίησας· σύ, κύριε, τὴν οἰκουμένην ἔκτισας. Whether this is the meaning in Phil. 2:15, and φαίνεσθε ὡς φωστῆρες ἐν κόσμῳ is to be rendered: "Ye shine as stars in cosmic space," or whether the sense here is the same as at Mt. 5:14, is much debated. [69]

d. The statements of the NT concerning heaven and the stars, the hints found as to the powers which rule the κόσμος, and an expression like τὰ στοιχεῖα τοῦ κόσμου (Gl. 4:3; Col. 2:8, 20), "the elements, or elemental spirits, of the world" (→ στοιχεῖον), point us to a plenitude of individual cosmological conceptions which were linked with the term κόσμος in the minds of the NT authors. Concerning these the following basic points are to be noted.

(1) In the Bible these cosmological notions never become the object of proclamation as in other religions or even in Jewish apocalyptic (Eth. En., Slav. En., 4 Esr., S. Bar. etc.). [70] In the NT they are sometimes more or less clearly presented or indicated, as in depictions of eschatological events. But even here there is no express cosmological teaching.

(2) There are no distinctive NT cosmological conceptions. The NT shares all its views on the structure and external form of the world with the systems of the contemporary world. Hence it is possible to explain the details of NT cosmology only with the help of our knowledge of these systems. If it is asked, then, what is the cosmological or scientific content of various NT passages, the principle is no longer valid that Holy Scripture is its own interpreter.

(3) It is no doubt a worthy goal of historical research to explain the cosmology of detailed NT words and passages in the light of our knowledge of Hellenistic and oriental scientific conceptions. But even when this is done, it is impossible to integrate the pieces into a consistent scheme and to call this the world-view of the NT. For while it is true that certain notions are common to all the books, there are obvious differences in the various layers of the NT, e.g., between the cosmological statements of Mk. 13, 1 C. 15, Rev. and Jn. These differences make it quite impossible to present a coherent cosmology.

---

[68] Cf. Phil. 2:10; → καταχθόνιος. On the tripartite division → I, 678. The Rabb. achieve this by adding the air (אויר = ἀήρ), S. Nu. § 134 on Dt. 3:24 ("Where is there a god in heaven or on earth?"). Is there a god outside these two? (Answer: No, acc. to Dt. 4:39); not even in the air (ἀήρ) (is there a god apart from Yahweh). Cf. K. G. Kuhn, S. Nu. übers. u. erkl. (1933 ff.), 554, n. 118.

[69] Cf. Loh. Phil., ad loc.

[70] On the indissoluble connection between religious proclamation and cosmological theory in Mithraism, with an instructive note on Christianity, cf. F. Cumont, Die orientalischen Religionen im römischen Heidentum, Germ. tr. A. Burckhardt-Brandenberg³ (1931), 147.

(4) Already in the NT (Past., 2 Pt., 1 Jn., Jd.) we find an incipient demarcation from Gnosticism and its cosmological interests. This is carried a step further with the formation of the Canon, which excludes all apocalypses apart from Rev. This act of the early Church confirms the decision of apostolic proclamation that cosmology is no part of the message of the Gospel. The κόσμος is an object of proclamation, and therewith of Christian theology (Pl., Jn.), only in so far as it stands in relation to God as its Creator, Lord, Judge and Redeemer.

3. κόσμος = World II, as the Abode of Men, the Theatre of History, the Inhabited World, the Earth.

a. When the world is seen as the theatre of human life and earthly history, the meaning of κόσμος can be narrowed to "inhabited world," "earth."

In this respect the NT simply follows Hellenistic and Jewish usage. Two typical passages with the expression "the whole world" have been quoted already, i.e., Ditt. Syll.³, 814, 31, in which Nero is ὁ τοῦ παντὸς κόσμου κύριος [71] (cf. Ditt. Or., 458, 40) and the statement in 2 Macc. 3:12 that the Jerusalem temple is honoured κατὰ τὸν σύμπαντα κόσμον.

κόσμος is to be taken in this sense in passages like Mt. 4:8 : πάσας τὰς βασιλείας τοῦ κόσμου, "all the kingdoms of the world" (Lk. 4:5 τῆς οἰκουμένης); Lk. 12:30 : ταῦτα γὰρ πάντα τὰ ἔθνη τοῦ κόσμου (Mt. 6:32, simply τὰ ἔθνη) ἐπιζητοῦσιν, "the nations of the world" = עַמְמֵי הָאָרֶץ. [72] In relation to Mt. 4:8 there also belongs here the saying κερδαίνειν τὸν κόσμον ὅλον, "to gain the whole world" (i.e., to gain possession of everything that man can control), [73] Mk. 8:36; Mt. 16:26; Lk. 9:25, with which may be compared the saying ascribed to Shimᵉon b. Shetach c. 90 B.C. (jBM, 8c, 26) concerning the gaining of this whole olam. [74] In the promise to Abraham κληρονόμον αὐτὸν εἶναι κόσμου, R. 4:13, the sense of the inhabited world merges into that of the nations of the world (Gn.18:18; 22:18). The meaning "inhabited world" is also found at Mk.16:15: πορευθέντες εἰς τὸν κόσμον ἅπαντα, with which may be compared materially Ac. 1:8 and the statement concerning Paul in 1 Cl., 5, 7: δικαιοσύνην διδάξας ὅλον τὸν κόσμον, καὶ ἐπὶ τὸ τέρμα τῆς δύσεως ἐλθών ...; R. 1:8: ἡ πίστις ὑμῶν καταγγέλλεται ἐν ὅλῳ τῷ κόσμῳ; Mt. 26:13 : κηρυχθῇ τὸ εὐαγγέλιον τοῦτο ἐν ὅλῳ τῷ κόσμῳ (though cf. Mk. 14:9 → 890); Herm. s., 9, 17, 1 f.: δώδεκα φυλαί ... αἱ κατοικοῦσαι ὅλον τὸν κόσμον, "twelve tribes which dwell in the whole world"; 1 Pt. 5:9 : τῇ ἐν τῷ κόσμῳ ὑμῶν ἀδελφότητι, "to your brethren in the world."

b. κόσμος bears the same sense, though with a closer approximation to "humanity," in certain phrases which express the coming into, or being in, or going out of the world of a person or thing. For these there are exact parallels or models in the usage of the Rabbis.

---

[71] → 880; in Barn. 5:5 Christ is παντὸς τοῦ κόσμου κύριος, → 887.

[72] "One of the commonest Rabbinic terms for the human race outside Israel," Str.-B., II, 191, with many references, including what seems to be the oldest instance, bBB, 10b (Jochanan b. Zakkai, c. 80 A.D.); cf. also Str.-B., I, 204; Dalman WJ, I, 144 f.

[73] Schl. Mt. on 16:26 construes κόσμος here as humanity : "The disciples gain the world by winning men and gathering a following which ... embraces the whole race."

[74] Str.-B., I, 749; Dalman WJ, I, 136 ff. → I, 206.

"To come into the world," Heb. בֹּא לְעוֹלָם, Aram. אֲתָא בְּעָלְמָא, is used in the Talmud of certain persons (e.g., Abraham, Isaac, Jacob, S. Dt. § 312 on 32:9) or of men generally (בָּאֵי הָעוֹלָם, "who come into the world," i.e., "men," Pesikt., 172b; cf. "all who come into the world," M. Ex. 18:12 [67a]).[75] It is also used of events (e.g., Tg. Qoh. 3:14 : "punishment comes into the world") and of things (e.g., bJeb., 92b : "something which has not come into the world," בָּא לְעוֹלָם, i.e., which does not exist).[76] Corresponding phrases for "to go out of the world" (to die) are עֲבַר מִן עָלְמָא, Tg. J. I, Gn. 15:2; אֲזַל מִן עָלְמָא, Tg. J. II, Gn. 15:2; Tg. Qoh. 1:4; תפטר מן העולם, "to leave the world," S. Nu., 140 on 27:18 etc.[77] There are par. to Rabb. usage in Hell. Judaism, e.g., Wis. 2:24; 14:14; 7:6 Σ.

In the NT the following are named as subjects of (εἰσ)έρχεσθαι εἰς τὸν κόσμον : "every man," Jn. 1:9 (cf. 16:21: ἐγεννήθη εἰς τὸν κόσμον), unless ἐρχόμενον is here to be linked with τὸ φῶς; Christ or the Logos as "the light," Jn. 3:19; 12:46; perhaps 1:9; the "Son of God," Jn. 11:27, cf. the self-witness, Jn. 9:39; 16:28; 18:37; "the prophet," Jn. 6:14; "the Christ," Jn. 11:27; "Christ Jesus," 1 Tm. 1:15; "the Christ who speaks in the OT," Hb. 10:5; "sin and death," R. 5:12 f. (cf. Wis. 2:24 and the statement in bJeb., 63a and Tg. Qoh. 3:14 that punishment comes into the world, בְּעָלְמָא or לְעוֹלָם); "false prophets," 1 Jn. 4:1; "seducers" (πλάνοι), 2 Jn. 7. The subject of "in the world" (ἐν τῷ κόσμῳ) is the "Logos," Jn. 1:10; "Christ" according to His self-witness, Jn. 9:5; no longer so after going to the Father, Jn. 17:11; the "disciples," Jn. 13:1; 17:11; "Christians," 1 Jn. 4:17, cf. 1 C. 5:10; Christians in their walk, 2 C. 1:12 and according to their natural life, 1 Jn. 3:17; the "spirit of Antichrist," 1 Jn. 4:3; also γένη φωνῶν, 1 C. 14:10, and οὐδὲν εἴδωλον, 1 C. 8:4. "To go out of the world," ἐκ τοῦ κόσμου ἐξελθεῖν, is something Christians would have to do to avoid all contact with fornicators, 1 C. 5:10. Jesus goes "out of this world," ἐκ τοῦ κόσμου τούτου, to the Father, Jn. 13:1.

Cf. ἀπαλλάσσεσθαι τοῦ κόσμου, "to depart from the world," 1 Cl., 5, 7 and similar expressions in Ign. R., 2, 2; 3, 2.

In such phrases κόσμος is mostly used without emphasis to denote the theatre of human life. When it is said that man is born εἰς τὸν κόσμον, or that we bring nothing εἰς τὸν κόσμον (1 Tm. 6:7, cf. Philo Spec. Leg., I, 294), or when death is called a departing ἐκ τοῦ κόσμου, such expressions have no specific cosmological or theological content. Only in the passages in which we read of the coming of Christ into the world or of His being in the world, or in those which remind us of facts which belong intrinsically to salvation history, does any particular emphasis fall on κόσμος. When the term no longer denotes merely the dwelling-place of man or the theatre of human history, but the setting of God's saving work, then it takes on a new significance which is distinctive in the NT and for which there are no parallels either in the Greek world or in the Jewish.

4. κόσμος = World III, as Humanity, Fallen Creation, the Theatre of Salvation History.

a. As the "universe" becomes the "inhabited world" once we think of it as the theatre of human life, so the "inhabited world" can narrow down to the "humanity"

---

[75] For further examples → 882 in relation to Wis. 2:24; 14:14; Str.-B., II, 358.
[76] Cf. Str.-B., II, 358.
[77] Ibid., 556.

which inhabits it. The sense "human world," "humanity," has been found already in the *koine* [78] and in the LXX. [79] The Heb. עוֹלָם or Aram. עָלְמָא undergoes a similar change under the influence of the Greek term; thus the Rabbis often use כָּל־עָלְמָא and כָּל־הָעוֹלָם in the sense of "all the world," "everyone" (jBer., 4b, line 37; bSanh., 101b; bJeb., 46b). [80] How easily this transition can be made may be seen from attempts to express the idea of proclaiming a message to the whole world. The εὐαγγέλια about Augustus, to which the Inscr. of Priene [81] refers, apply τῷ κόσμῳ, i.e., to "all the dwellers on earth." The great commission in Mk. 16:15 runs: πορευθέντες εἰς τὸν κόσμον ἅπαντα κηρύξατε τὸ εὐαγγέλιον πάσῃ τῇ κτίσει, cf. παντὶ τῷ λαῷ, Lk. 2:10; πάντα τὰ ἔθνη, Mt. 28:19; ἕως ἐσχάτου τῆς γῆς, Ac. 1:8. According to Mt. 26:13 the Gospel, or this Gospel, is to be preached ἐν ὅλῳ τῷ κόσμῳ, cf. Mk. 14:9: εἰς ὅλον τὸν κόσμον. In the Mt. version κόσμος might be taken in a purely spatial sense, but in Mk. the main sense is that of humanity. Preaching to the whole world implies preaching to "all who dwell on earth."

How the meanings merge into one another may be seen also in Herm. s., 8, 3, 2: νόμος θεοῦ ἐστιν ὁ δοθεὶς εἰς ὅλον τὸν κόσμον. [82] ὁ δὲ νόμος οὗτος υἱὸς θεοῦ ἐστι κηρυχθεὶς εἰς τὰ πέρατα τῆς γῆς.

The sense "world of men," "humanity," occurs in several other NT passages, though one cannot always mark it off with precision from other meanings. Thus we find it three times in sayings of the Lord in the special material in Mt.: ὑμεῖς ἐστε τὸ φῶς τοῦ κόσμου, 5:14; [83] ὁ ἀγρός ἐστιν ὁ κόσμος, 13:38; οὐαὶ τῷ κόσμῳ, 18:7. It is also used of the race at the time of the flood: ἀρχαῖος κόσμος, "the ancient world," κόσμος ἀσεβῶν, "the world of the ungodly," 2 Pt. 2:5; ὁ τότε κόσμος, "humanity as it then was," ὕδατι κατακλυσθεὶς ἀπώλετο, 2 Pt. 3:6; cf. also κατέκρινεν τὸν κόσμον, Hb. 11:7. In Pl. this sense occurs in 1 C. 4:13: περικαθάρματα τοῦ κόσμου, "dregs of humanity," while at 1 C. 4:9 κόσμος embraces the world of angels and of men: θέατρον ἐγενήθημεν τῷ κόσμῳ, καὶ ἀγγέλοις καὶ ἀνθρώποις. This understanding of κόσμος as the totality of rational creatures corresponds exactly to the Stoic saying already adduced concerning the κόσμος as τὸ ἐκ θεῶν καὶ ἀνθρώπων σύστημα. [84] The sense "humanity" can be found along with another nuance still to be mentioned, namely, that of the "world which is in opposition to God," cf. τὰ μωρὰ τοῦ κόσμου, τὰ ἀσθενῆ τοῦ κόσμου, τὰ ἀγενῆ τοῦ κόσμου, "the weak and foolish and low-born things of the world," 1 C. 1:27 f. The same transition from simple "humanity" to the "world which is hostile to God" may be observed in Hb. 11:38: ὧν οὐκ ἦν ἄξιος ὁ κόσμος. To the same category belong many passages in Jn. to which we shall refer below.

---

[78] → 880.

[79] Wis. 10:1; 14:6; 4 Macc. 17:14; → 881 f.

[80] For further instances cf. Str.-B., II, 548.

[81] Ditt. Or., 458, 40; → 880.

[82] Cf. the saying of R. Aqiba, bSanh., 101b, that Hezekiah instructed כָּל־הָעוֹלָם, the "whole world," i.e. ,"everyone," in the Torah, Str.-B., II, 548.

[83] Cf. Midr. Cant., 1, 3: יִשְׂרָאֵל אוֹרָה לְעוֹלָם; Schl. Mt., 148; Str.-B., I, 237, with examples also on Jn. 8:12.

[84] Stob. Ecl., I, 184, 8 → 880; cf. also 4 Macc. 17:14 → 882.

b. It is obvious that in the sense of humanity the word κόσμος will necessarily acquire a particular nuance when the world of men is not only related to other creatures and to the universe, as in Greek thought, but also seen in its connection with the living God. It has been shown already that in the Bible the κόσμος is always regarded as the object of divine creation. Once the κόσμος is related to man as the theatre of history or dwelling-place of the race, the OT view of God as the שֹׁפֵט כָּל־הָאָרֶץ (Gn. 18:25; Ps. 94:2) necessarily comes to bear on the relationship between God and the κόσμος. The κρίνειν τὴν γῆν (Gn. 18:25) or τὴν οἰκουμένην (e.g., ψ 9:8) must become a κρίνειν τὸν κόσμον.

Nevertheless, Judaism is much more restrained than the NT in developing this sense. κόσμος is brought into connection with κρίσις and κρίνειν in Sib., 4, 40 f.; 184. In Rabb. lit. עוֹלָם is only rarely [85] the object of God's judgment. The idea that the world is the abode of sin, that it is under the dominion of evil and that it has thus fallen victim to divine judgment, is certainly found in Judaism, but not by a long way does it play the role which it is given in the NT. It figures most prominently where the present and the future αἰών are contrasted, as in apocalyptic. Against the radiant background of the future aeon, the present aeon, and the κόσμος whose time it is, are regarded not only as a world of sorrows (Slav. En. 66:6), a *corruptum saeculum* (in the sense of transitoriness, 4 Esr. 4:11), but also as a world of unrighteousness, as an unrighteous or ungodly world, Eth. En. 48:7, an aeon of ungodliness, Apc. Abr. 29:8, a world of falsehood (עוֹלָם הַשֶּׁקֶר, Lv. r., 26 on 21:1), a *locus ubi seminatum est malum*, 4 Esr. 4:29, where the first Adam fell into sin and guilt and all those born of him, 3:21, where sins abound by reason of the evil impulse, Tanch. נֹחַ, 13a. [86] The dominion of sin is also connected with the power of demons (e.g., Jub. 10:8) and of Satan, who has brought temptation and death into the world, Wis. 2:24.

If one tries to make a total picture out of the various Jewish sayings on the world in the age of the NT, the only conclusion is that Judaism does not have any single view. It maintains that the world is God's creation and also that it stands under judgment and needs redemption. But these two chief lines of thought are never brought together in a consistent picture. Hence the more optimistic openness of the Alexandrians and the profound pessimism of apocalyptic confront each other irreconcilably as two outlooks between which one may alternate but which one cannot unite. Both rest on biblical foundations, the former on belief in creation, the latter on the thought of judgment. Both incorporate alien elements in order to become systems, Hellenistic joy in the world in the first case, Persian dualism in the second. But if Judaism vacillates to some degree between these extremes in the NT age, it is not these extremes alone which express its uncertainty in assessment of the world. Even when the extremes pass from the scene, the uncertainty remains, as may be seen from the statements of the Talmud concerning the simultaneity of good and evil in the world. [87]

The NT presents a different picture. One can see from the use of the term κόσμος that a new and more consistent concept of the world arises in the early

---

[85] E.g., Midr. Prv. 11:8; S. Dt., 311 on 32:8; 326 on 32:36.

[86] "In Rabb. lit. the present world is depicted as an aeon in which the יֵצֶר הָרַע, the evil impulse, human passion, rules. Hence this world is a world of sin and impurity, of lying and falsehood. It is a world in which good and evil, salvation and ruin, are found together ...," Str.-B., IV, 847.

[87] *Loc. cit.*

Church. To be sure, there are still differences in usage. The Synoptists, especially Mt., use κόσμος only infrequently, and only in the senses which we have discussed already and which correspond to the Jewish use of עוֹלָם. There are also manifest differences between Paul and John. In these two writers, however, there develops out of the use of κόσμος the new concept of the world which is peculiar to the NT. The κόσμος is now understood as the theatre of salvation history, as the *locus* of revelation in Christ, and in consequence it appears in a wholly new light. With the preaching of the apostle ἡμεῖς τεθεάμεθα καὶ μαρτυροῦμεν ὅτι ὁ πατὴρ ἀπέσταλκεν τὸν υἱὸν σωτῆρα τοῦ κόσμου (1 Jn. 4:14) begins the Church's understanding of the world, which outside the Church, i.e., where a false σωτὴρ τοῦ κόσμου [88] or none at all is known, continually encounters opposition. The understanding of the κόσμος depends always on what is known of the σωτὴρ τοῦ κόσμου (Jn. 4:42; 1 Jn. 4:14).

c. In Paul's statements about the κόσμος we have noted already (→ 885) the identification of the κόσμος with the αἰὼν οὗτος. The influence of the doctrine of the two aeons may be discerned especially in the way in which Paul conceives of the distinction between God and the κόσμος. According to 1 C. 2:12 the πνεῦμα τοῦ κόσμου and the πνεῦμα τὸ ἐκ τοῦ θεοῦ are mutually exclusive opposites. The σοφία τοῦ κόσμου is μωρία παρὰ τῷ θεῷ, 1 C. 1:20 f.; 3:19, cf. 1:27, and the θεοῦ σοφία is not understood by the wise of the world, 1 C. 2:6 ff., 14. God's standards for assessing men are different from those of the world, 1 C. 1:26 ff. While ἡ κατὰ θεὸν λύπη brings repentance and leads to σωτηρία, ἡ τοῦ κόσμου λύπη brings death, 2 C. 7:10. The deep gulf between God and the κόσμος is traced back by Paul to sin, which came into the world through the first man and which brought with it death, R. 5:12. Since all men have become sinners, πᾶς ὁ κόσμος, "the whole race," is guilty before God, R. 3:19, and has fallen under God's judgement, which is thus a judgment on the κόσμος (κρίνειν τὸν κόσμον, R. 3:6; 1 C. 6:2, here also κρίνεται ὁ κόσμος) and which leads to the condemnation of the κόσμος, 1 C. 11:32. In R. 11:12 : εἰ δὲ τὸ παράπτωμα αὐτῶν πλοῦτος κόσμου καὶ τὸ ἥττημα αὐτῶν πλοῦτος ἐθνῶν ..., and 11:15 : εἰ γὰρ ἡ ἀποβολὴ αὐτῶν καταλλαγὴ κόσμου, Paul uses κόσμος synonymously with ἔθνη for the nations outside Israel. He thus follows Jewish usage, which distinguishes Israel from the ἔθνη τοῦ κόσμου. [89] In R. 3:19, however, Israel is expressly included in the "whole world" which is guilty before God. Only the ἅγιοι, the true people of God, are seen apart from the κόσμος on which judgment and condemnation fall, 1 C. 11:32. Of them it is written : οἱ ἅγιοι τὸν κόσμον κρινοῦσιν, 1 C. 6:2. The real depth of the antithesis between God and the κόσμος is shown by the fact that the ἄρχοντες τοῦ αἰῶνος τούτου crucified the Lord of glory, 1 C. 2:8. But as the antithesis between God and the world may be fully appreciated only with reference to Christ, so the removal of the antithesis by reconciliation is manifested only in Him : θεὸς ἦν ἐν Χριστῷ κόσμον καταλλάσσων ἑαυτῷ μὴ λογιζόμενος αὐτοῖς τὰ παραπτώματα αὐτῶν, 2 C. 5:19, cf. καταλλαγὴ κόσμου, R. 11:15. As the context shows, the reference of κόσμος here is to the world of men, humanity. Nevertheless, the comprehensive significance of the term, which includes angels at 1 C.

---

[88] On σωτὴρ τοῦ κόσμου as an imperial title (esp. under Hadrian, e.g., CIG, 4334, 4335, 4336, 4337, cf. W. Weber, *Untersuchungen zur Geschichte des Kaisers Hadrianus* [1907], 225 f., 229) → σωτήρ.

[89] Lk. 12:30, cf. Str.-B., II, 191, *ad loc.*

4:9, and the reference to superhuman powers which rule the κόσμος in connection with the sin of man (e.g., 1 C. 2:6, 8; 2 C. 4:4; Eph. 2:2), lead us necessarily to the conclusion that κόσμος means more than just humanity in this kind of statement concerning salvation history. Since κόσμος in the sense of universe is understood as the theatre of salvation history, this history transcends the framework of human history. The whole universe, πᾶσα ἡ κτίσις in the sense of R. 8:22, τὰ πάντα ἐν τοῖς οὐρανοῖς καὶ ἐπὶ τῆς γῆς, τὰ ὁρατὰ καὶ τὰ ἀόρατα, εἴτε θρόνοι εἴτε κυριότητες εἴτε ἀρχαὶ εἴτε ἐξουσίαι in the sense of Col. 1:16, takes part in this history, and yet this history does not cease to be true human history. The Christ who is πρωτότοκος πάσης κτίσεως, and of whom it is writen : αὐτός ἐστιν πρὸ πάντων καὶ τὰ πάντα ἐν αὐτῷ συνέστηκεν, [90] is the historical man Jesus. His crucifixion and resurrection, which are historical events on earth, are the beginning of the redemption which will be consummated when the crucified and risen Lord παραδιδοῖ τὴν βασιλείαν τῷ θεῷ καὶ πατρί, ὅταν καταργήσῃ πᾶσαν ἀρχὴν καὶ πᾶσαν ἐξουσίαν καὶ δύναμιν, 1 C. 15:24.

This view yields a full unity of concept. The universe and all individual creatures, the visible world and the invisible, nature and history, humanity and the spirit world, are all brought under the single term κόσμος. The κόσμος is the sum of the divine creation which has been shattered by the fall, which stands under the judgment of God, and in which Jesus Christ appears as the Redeemer.

When the κόσμος is redeemed, it ceases to be κόσμος. The reconciled and redeemed world is no longer κόσμος, αἰὼν οὗτος; it is βασιλεία τοῦ θεοῦ, αἰὼν ἐρχόμενος, οὐρανὸς καινὸς καὶ γῆ καινή (→ I, 678). While the new world is described in terms of these expressions taken from apocalyptic and the OT belief in the Creator, the term κόσμος, which derives from pagan philosophy, is reserved for the world which lies under sin and death. This is very clear in Paul. When Christ Jesus ἦλθεν εἰς τὸν κόσμον ἁμαρτωλοὺς σῶσαι (1 Tm. 1:15), then the sinners saved by Him are taken by God from the ἐξουσία τοῦ σκότους which rules the κόσμος and are set in the βασιλεία τοῦ υἱοῦ τῆς ἀγάπης αὐτοῦ, Col. 1:13, cf. Gal. 1:4. Hence the ἐκκλησία does not belong to the world. The ἅγιοι live in the κόσμος, 1 C. 5:10; Phil. 2:15, and cannot ἐκ τοῦ κόσμου ἐξελθεῖν. They gratefully honour the Creator of the κόσμος (Ac. 17:24) and receive His gifts (e.g., Ac. 14:15 ff.). In the interim of the time of this world they obey the orders which are set up by God (cf. θεοῦ διαταγή, Dei ordinatio, R. 13:2) and by which He upholds His creation. Indeed, they are forced τὰ τοῦ κόσμου μεριμ-νᾶν, "to care for the things of the world" and are thereby hampered in their attempt μεριμνᾶν τὰ τοῦ κυρίου (1 C. 7:32 ff.). They are forced χρῆσθαι τὸν κόσμον, "to have dealings with the world (7:31). [91] But they must do so as though they did not, for their true life is no longer a ζῆν ἐν κόσμῳ (Col. 2:20). Through the cross of Christ, says Paul in Gl. 6:14, the world is crucified to me and I to the world. Hence there arises the distinctive nuance which has ever after clung to the word κόσμος in the NT and the Church. The world is the epitome of un-redeemed creation. It has become the enemy of God. It is the great obstacle to the Christian life. As Jm. 1:27 maintains, in material agreement with Paul (R. 12:2; 1 C. 7:31), one of the duties of believers is ἄσπιλον ἑαυτὸν τηρεῖν ἀπὸ τοῦ κόσμου. φιλία τοῦ κόσμου, says Jm. 4:4, is ἔχθρα τοῦ θεοῦ. He who would be

---

[90] Col. 1:15, 17. On the meaning of πάντα → 884.
[91] Cf. Ltzm. K., ad loc.

a friend of the world becomes an enemy of God. The cleavage which is found between Christ and the world is also found between the ἐκκλησία and the world. And yet the world needs the ἐκκλησία as it also needs Christ.

d. The biblical view of κόσμος comes to fruition in the Johannine writings. These hardly contain a thought on κόσμος which is not at least implicit in Paul's doctrine of the world, but the seed thoughts of Paul are now developed, and the terminology is more fixed and clear-cut. Furthermore, the concept is at the centre of theological thinking in a way which is not true of any other NT writing or group of writings. The κόσμος is the setting of the drama of redemption which is recounted in the Gospel. All the meanings of κόσμος come together in the usage of the Fourth Gospel. Not just the Prologue uses κόσμος for the world in the sense of the universe. When Christ is called τὸ φῶς τοῦ κόσμου, 8:12; 9:5; cf. 3:19; 12:46; 1:9, and when He or the Evangelist speaks of His coming or being sent εἰς τὸν κόσμον, 3:17; 10:36; 11:27; 12:46 f.; 16:28; 17:18; 18:37; 1 Jn. 4:9, the reference is to the whole cosmos and not merely to the world of men. Christ is not ἐκ τοῦ κόσμου τούτου (8:23), like men. Nor is His βασιλεία (18:36). He is not ἐκ τῶν κάτω, like men; He is ἐκ τῶν ἄνω (8:23). Out of love for the world the Father sends the Son: οὕτως ἠγάπησεν ὁ θεὸς τὸν κόσμον, ὥστε τὸν υἱὸν τὸν μονογενῆ ἔδωκεν, not to judge the world, but to save it (3:16 f.; 12:47). Christ comes as the Lamb of God αἴρων τὴν ἁμαρτίαν τοῦ κόσμου, 1:29, cf. 1 Jn. 2:2, where Jesus is called ἱλασμὸς περὶ τῶν ἁμαρτιῶν ἡμῶν, οὐ περὶ τῶν ἡμετέρων δὲ μόνον ἀλλὰ καὶ περὶ ὅλου τοῦ κόσμου. He comes as σωτὴρ τοῦ κόσμου (4:42; 1 Jn. 4:14), as ζωὴν διδοὺς τῷ κόσμῳ (6:33, cf. 51), as φῶς τοῦ κόσμου (8:12; 9:5; cf. 3:19; 12:46; 1:9). But the world does not know Him (1:10). Hence it does not know God (17:25). Outwardly it might seem as though ὁ κόσμος, "all the world," goes after Him (12:19). In truth, however, the world does not believe in Him and meets Him with hatred (7:7; 15:18). Hence His mission εἰς τὸν κόσμον entails its judgment rather than its deliverance. This judgment begins with the death of Christ as judgment on the ἄρχων τοῦ κόσμου τούτου (12:31; 16:11; cf. 14:30: ὁ τοῦ κόσμου ἄρχων). Mention of this ἄρχων who does not belong to the human race makes it plain that we cannot restrict the meaning of κόσμος to "humanity" in these passages.[92] When Jn. says of the κόσμος that it does not know the Son of God, that it does not know God, that it does not believe, that it hates, the κόσμος is in some sense personified as the great opponent of the Redeemer in salvation history. It is as it were a powerful collective person which the ἄρχων τοῦ κόσμου represents. Christ and the world are opponents in the saying: οὐ καθὼς ὁ κόσμος δίδωσιν ἐγὼ δίδωμι ὑμῖν (14:27), or in the witness of 1 Jn. 4:4: μείζων ἐστὶν ὁ ἐν ὑμῖν ἢ ὁ ἐν τῷ κόσμῳ. By ὁ ἐν τῷ κόσμῳ is understood the → πονηρός — if πονηρός may be taken in the masculine as in 1 Jn. 5:18[93] — of whom it is said: ὁ κόσμος ὅλος ἐν τῷ πονηρῷ κεῖται (1 Jn. 5:19). As believers in Christ are ἐν Χριστῷ, so the unbelieving cosmos is ἐν τῷ πονηρῷ, and as Christ is ἐν ὑμῖν, so the ἄρχων τοῦ κόσμου τούτου, ὁ πονηρός, the wicked one, is ἐν τῷ κόσμῳ. The same is true of the *pneuma* of → ἀντίχριστος: νῦν ἐν τῷ κόσμῳ ἐστὶν ἤδη (1 Jn. 4:3). Hence salvation history is a

---

[92] There is much debate as to the meaning of שַׂר הָעוֹלָם in the Rabbis, whether it signifies the devil (A. Schlatter, *Sprache u. Heimat des 4. Evangelisten* [1902], 121) or "the angelic prince who presides over the natural life of all creation" (Str.-B., II, 552).

[93] Cf. Pr.-Bauer on πονηρός and on κεῖμαι.

conflict between Christ and the κόσμος, or the πονηρός who rules it. Jn. 16:33 speaks of Christ's victory in this struggle : ἐγὼ νενίκηκα τὸν κόσμον.

As in Paul the ἅγιοι, those who belong to the ἐκκλησία, are not part of the κόσμος, so in Jn. believers are not ἐκ τοῦ κόσμου (15:19; 17:14; 17:16). Christ has elected them ἐκ τοῦ κόσμου (15:19), and the Father has given them to Him ἐκ τοῦ κόσμου (17:6). If physically they are ἐκ τοῦ κόσμου, there applies to them what is said of the sons of God in 1:12 f., who ἐκ θεοῦ ἐγεννήθησαν (cf. γεννηθῆναι ἐκ τοῦ πνεύματος, 3:6; ἄνωθεν γεννηθῆναι, 3:3, 7). In them dwells, and in them there ought to be, τὸ πνεῦμα τῆς ἀληθείας, ὃς ὁ κόσμος οὐ δύναται λαβεῖν, ὅτι οὐ θεωρεῖ αὐτὸ οὐδὲ γινώσκει (14:17). In them the κόσμος is to see and believe that the Father has sent the Son and that He loves them (17:21, 23). The hatred of the world will be turned against them as it was against Christ (15:18 f.; 17:14; 1 Jn. 3:13). But in spite of all the θλῖψις which they are to have (16:33) as those who are still ἐν τῷ κόσμῳ (17:11, cf. 15) and who are sent by Christ εἰς τὸν κόσμον (17:18), they, too, will overcome the κόσμος : ὅτι πᾶν τὸ γεγεννημένον ἐκ τοῦ θεοῦ νικᾷ τὸν κόσμον. Indeed, this victory is already won : αὕτη ἐστὶν ἡ νίκη ἡ νικήσασα τὸν κόσμον, ἡ πίστις ἡμῶν (1 Jn. 5:4). He who believes that Jesus Christ is the Son of God is a νικῶν τὸν κόσμον (1 Jn. 5:5). For to believe in Christ and to be born of God is one and the same thing. Thus those who believe in Christ are ἐν τῷ κόσμῳ, "in the world" (17:11; cf. 13:1; 1 Jn. 4:17: ἐν τῷ κόσμῳ τούτῳ) as Christ in His days on earth was "in the world" (9:5). But they no longer belong to the world; they are no longer ἐκ τοῦ κόσμου. In John's teaching, as in that of Paul and James, the Church does not belong to the world, though the world is its sphere of operation. To the warning against φιλία τοῦ κόσμου ("friendship with the world") in Jm. 4:4 corresponds the stern command in 1 Jn. 2:15 : μὴ ἀγαπᾶτε τὸν κόσμον μηδὲ τὰ ἐν τῷ κόσμῳ· ἐάν τις ἀγαπᾷ τὸν κόσμον, οὐκ ἔστιν ἡ ἀγάπη τοῦ πατρὸς ἐν αὐτῷ. At a first glance this seems to contradict the command to love's one neighbour, and also the statement that the Father loves the κόσμος (IJn. 3:16). But the κόσμος of 1 Jn. 2:15 ff. is the world which has rejected Christ and on which judgment has already been passed. It is the world in which the ἐπιθυμία τῆς σαρκός, the ἐπιθυμία τῶν ὀφθαλμῶν and the ἀλαζονεία τοῦ βίου reign. Hence the admonition of 1 Jn. 2:15 is exactly the same as that of R. 12:2 : μὴ συσχηματίζεσθε τῷ αἰῶνι τούτῳ. The reason for this warning is also the same in Jn. and Pl. To the Pauline παράγει γὰρ τὸ σχῆμα τοῦ κόσμου τούτου of 1 C. 7:31 corresponds the saying in 1 Jn. 2:17: ὁ κόσμος παράγεται καὶ ἡ ἐπιθυμία αὐτοῦ· ὁ δὲ ποιῶν τὸ θέλημα τοῦ θεοῦ μένει εἰς τὸν αἰῶνα. This is not negation of the world or contempt for it. It is the faith which has overcome the world.

† κόσμιος.

In secular Gk. we find this in poetry from the time of Soph. and Aristoph. and in prose from that of Plato, Xenoph., Lys. It describes one who disciplines himself and who may thus be regarded as genuinely moral and respectable. An essential part of the Gk. ideal, namely, the element of the ordered, the controlled, the measured, or the balanced, is reflected in the idea of κοσμιότης. Primarily a philosophical term, in the course of

---

κ ό σ μ ι ο ς. Pape, Liddell-Scott, s.v.

time κόσμιος became a weaker social expression. Its philosophical sense may be seen in Plat. Resp., VI, 500c/d : θείῳ δὴ καὶ κοσμίῳ ὅ γε φιλόσοφος ὁμιλῶν κόσμιός τε καὶ θεῖος εἰς τὸ δυνατὸν ἀνθρώπῳ γίγνεται, "in dealing with divine things, the philosopher himself becomes divine and well-mannered to the degree that this is possible for a man." To the physiognomic traits, the κοσμίου σημεῖα, as Aristot. Physiognomica, 3, p. 807b, 33 ff. develops them in contrast to the ἀναιδοῦς σημεῖα, there belongs in the first instance that a man should be ἐν ταῖς κινήσεσι βραδύς, "measured in his movements" (as distinct from ὀξύς). Thus it is said of Chrysothemis when she runs quickly for joy (Soph. El., 872): τὸ κόσμιον μεθεῖσα, "neglecting decorum." The virtue of κοσμιότης (the noun occurs in Plato, Aristot., Isoc., Demosth.) is described as the opp. of ἀκολασία ("licence"), Plat. Gorg., 507e/508a; Aristot. Eth. Nic., II, 8, p. 1109a, 16 and also in terms of its association with other virtues, esp. σωφροσύνη, of which it is often the fruit and companion, cf. σωφροσύνη and κοσμιότης in Aristoph. Pl., 563 f.; κοσμιότητα καὶ σωφροσύνην καὶ δικαιότητα, Plat. Gorg., 508a; κόσμιος καὶ σώφρων, Lys., 21:19, cf. Plat. Leg., VII, 802e; Luc. Bis accusatus, 18; Inscr. Magn., 162, 6; also Ps.-Plat. Def., 412d : κοσμιότης ὕπειξις ἑκουσία πρὸς τὸ φανὲν βέλτιστον· εὐταξία περὶ κίνησιν σώματος, and Aristot. De virtutibus et vitiis, 4, p. 1250b, 11: παρέπεται δὲ τῇ σωφροσύνῃ εὐταξία, κοσμιότης, αἰδώς, εὐλάβεια. The concept always contains the idea of control of the body and its movements and impulses, cf. the antithesis of αἱ ἐρωτικαί τε καὶ τυραννικαὶ ἐπιθυμίαι and αἱ βασιλικαί τε καὶ κόσμιαι in Plat. Resp., IX, 587ab; ἐγκρατεῖς αὐτῶν καὶ κόσμιοι ὄντες, Phaedr., 256b; also the description of a quiet patient as κόσμιος, Hippocr. Acut., 65. Since κοσμιότης is mostly, though not exclusively, a virtue of noble women (cf. Aristot. Pol., III, 4, p. 1277b, 23; Epict. Ench., 40; Philo Spec. Leg., I, 102; III, 51, here equivalent to "modesty" of a woman, cf. σωφροσύνη, Jos. Ant., 18, 66), in later popular usage it is a common epithet for women, e.g., ἡ κοσμιωτάτη αὐτοῦ θυγάτηρ, P. Masp., 6, II, 7 (6th cent. A.D.); τὴν ἐμὴν κοσμ(ιωτάτην) ἐλευθέραν γυναῖκα, P. Greci e Latini, 97, 1. Derived from κόσμος in the sense of "order," then of "adornment," κόσμιος thus means "self-controlled," "disciplined," "well-mannered," "honourable." The secondary meanings [1] which the word takes on are of no significance in relation to the NT.

In the LXX the adj. κόσμιος is not found. In the incorrect rendering κόσμιον παραβολῶν for תִּקֵּן מְשָׁלִים ("he composed proverbs") at Qoh. 12:9, (τὸ) κόσμιον is the diminutive form of κόσμος in the sense of "adornment."

In the NT κόσμιος is used at 1 Tm. 3:2 of a person : δεῖ οὖν τὸν ἐπίσκοπον ... εἶναι ... νηφάλιον, σώφρονα, κόσμιον ..., "the bishop must be ... sober, well-behaved, honourable." [2] The term has the same sense of "honourable," "disciplined," in 1 Tm. 2:9, where it is used of the conduct of persons : [3] women are to adorn themselves ἐν καταστολῇ κοσμίῳ, μετὰ αἰδοῦς καὶ σωφροσύνης κοσμεῖν ἑαυτάς, "in a decorous manner, with modesty and sobriety." The reading κοσμίως for κοσμίῳ, found in D G H 33 Orig., is secondary. The virtue which is here demanded of bishops and Christian women is not specifically Christian. It is the κοιμιότης which we have found already in the classical Greek world and which is also found in the popular ethics of Hellenism along with αἰδώς and σωφροσύνη. [4]

---

[1] E.g., like the Lat. *modestus, moderatus,* it can denote "modest" of things, κοσμίας οἰκήσεις, "modest dwellings," Plat. Critias, 112c; κοσμίαν δαπάνην, Resp., VIII, 560d. On these secondary meanings cf. Liddell-Scott.

[2] Cf. ἄνδρα κόσμιον, Ditt. Or., 485, 3.

[3] Cf. κόσμιος ἀναστροφή, Inscr. Magn., 179, 4.

[4] Cf. Dib. Past. on 1 Tm. 2:9; 3:2.

† κοσμικός.

In secular Gk. the adj. κοσμικός, which derives from κόσμος in the sense "world," is found from the time of Aristot. and means "belonging or pertaining to the world," "cosmic." Aristot. Phys., II, 4, p. 196a, 25 speaks of views of the cause τοῦδε τοῦ οὐρανοῦ καὶ τῶν κοσμικῶν πάντων, "of this heaven (world) and of all that belongs to the universe." Philo Aet. Mund., 53 expounds time (χρόνος) as διάστημα ... κοσμικῆς κινήσεως, an interval (section) of the movement of the universe. Plut. Cons. ad Apoll., 34 (II, 119 f.) has together τὴν τῶν ὅλων πρόνοιαν καὶ τὴν κοσμικὴν διάταξιν, "the providence which governs the whole, and the order of the world." Luc. De Parasito, 11 says of the scholar who enquires περὶ σχήματος γῆς καὶ κόσμων ἀπειρίας καὶ μεγέθους ἡλίου : οὐ μόνον ἐν ἀνθρωπίναις ἀλλὰ καὶ ἐν κοσμικαῖς ἐστιν ἐνοχλήσεσιν, i.e., that the universe as well as men will cause him difficulty. The word also occurs in the jargon of astrology, e.g., κοσμικὰ κέντρα, Vett. Val., II, 17 (p. 79, 26).

As a loan word κοσμικός came into Rabb. Heb. in the form קוֹזְמִיקוֹן or קוֹזְמִיקוֹן. In the sense "applying to the whole world" it is found in jBer., 13d, lines 7 ff., where the "wind of Elijah" (1 K. 19:11) is described as קוֹסְמִיקוֹן, cf. Gn. r., 24 on 5:1; Midr. Qoh. on 1:6.[1]

In the usage of early Christianity the word denotes something "which belongs to this world," with a suggestion of the transitoriness or the hostility to God characteristic of the κόσμος. In the NT the tabernacle is called τὸ ἅγιον κοσμικόν, "the earthly sanctuary," in contrast to the τελειοτέρα σκηνὴ οὐ χειροποίητος, τοῦτ᾽ ἔστιν οὐ ταύτης τῆς κτίσεως (Hb. 9:1, 11).[2] κοσμικαὶ ἐπιθυμίαι, "worldly desires," which believers are to deny along with ἀσέβεια (Tt. 2:12) in order to live σωφρόνως καὶ δικαίως καὶ εὐσεβῶς in the present aeon, are identical with what is called in 1 Jn. 2:16 ἡ ἐπιθυμία τῆς σαρκὸς καὶ ἡ ἐπιθυμία τῶν ὀφθαλμῶν καὶ ἡ ἀλαζονεία τοῦ βίου, and with what is there said to be ἐν τῷ κόσμῳ and ἐκ τοῦ κόσμου, not ἐκ τοῦ πατρός.

In post-canonical writings we find the phrases κοσμικαὶ ἐπιθυμίαι, 2 Cl., 17, 3; τὰ κοσμικὰ ταῦτα ("these earthly things") ὡς ἀλλότρια ἡγεῖσθαι καὶ μὴ ἐπιθυμεῖν αὐτῶν, 5, 6; τῶν κοσμικῶν κατεφρόνουν βασάνων, διὰ μιᾶς ὥρας τὴν αἰώνιον κόλασιν ἐξαγοραζόμενοι, "they despised earthly torments, knowing that within the hour they would free themselves of eternal punishment," Mart. Pol., 2, 3 of the martyrs of Smyrna. In the difficult and much debated[3] passage in Did., 11, 11 ποιῶν εἰς μυστήριον κοσμικὸν ἐκκλησίας is to be rendered "acting according to the earthly mystery of the Church." The different interpretations do not affect the sense of κοσμικός, but only of μυστήριον ἐκκλησίας. It is hard to say whether the ref. is to actions of the prophets in which supratemporal truths are represented in the sphere of the earthly,[4]

κ ο σ μ ι κ ό ς. Liddell-Scott; Pr.-Bauer, s.v.
[1] Cf. Str.-B., III, 667.
[2] This distinction rests on the common Rabb. idea that all religious institutions and usages are found up in heaven as well as on earth (→ ἄνω, I, 376 f.). For the Rabb. academy (מתיבתא דארעא) there is the מתיבתא דרקיעא, bGit., 68a; cf. the many instances in Str.-B., II, 267. In Cant. r. on 4:4 (ed. Vilna [1921] fol. 25c, line 4) the בית המקדש של מעלה corresponds to the temple in Jerusalem [K. G. Kuhn].
[3] A. v. Harnack, Lehre d. zwölf Apostel (1884), 44 ff.; E. Hennecke, Handbuch zu d. NT.lichen Apokryphen (1904), 274 ff.; Kn. Did., ad loc.
[4] P. Bryennios, Διδαχὴ τῶν δώδεκα ἀποστόλων (1883), ad loc.; C. Taylor, The Teaching of the Twelve Apostles (1886), ad loc.; J. R. Harris, The Teaching of the Apostles (1887), ad loc.; F. H. Funk, Patres Apostolici, I² (1901), ad loc.; Zahn, Forsch. III (1884), 301; ThLBl, 5 (1884), 201 f.

or to an ascetic life in which the mystery of Eph. 5:32 finds symbolical earthly expression. [5] In Byzantine usage κοσμικός denotes the secular as distinct from the spiritual.

Sasse

κοσμοκράτωρ → κράτος.

| † κράζω, † ἀνακράζω, |
| † κραυγή, † κραυγάζω |

κράζω is a word like "croak." It uses kr + vowel + guttural to suggest a rough or raucous sound. It is based on the croaking of ravens. [1] The meaning is a. "to croak or cry with a loud and raucous voice": σὺ δ' αὖ κέκραγας κἀναμυχθίζῃ (or ἀναμυχθίζει) (groan deeply), Aesch. Prom., 743 vl.; ποίου κέκραγας ἀνδρὸς ὧδ' ὑπέρφρονα; Soph. Ai., 1239; Κάτων ... ἐδυσχέραινε (to be dissatisfied) καὶ ἐκεκράγει, Polyb., 31, 2, 5 vl. It is used of an ass in Job 6:5 and of childbirth in Is. 26:17. It is a warcry in Jos. 6:16: εἶπεν 'Ιησοῦς ... κεκράξατε (of the capture of Jericho). [2] A second sense is b. "to demand with cries": κέκραγεν ἐμβάδας (men's shoes), Aristoph. Vesp., 103; ἐκέκραξεν δὲ ὁ λαὸς πρὸς Φαραω περὶ ἄρτων, Gn. 41:55; cf. Ex. 5:8. [3]

The forms are mostly the perf. κέκραγα, which has a present sense, and the pluperfect, which has an imperfect. The fut. is κεκράξομαι, e.g., Aristoph. Eq., 487. The pres. is rare, [4] cf. Aristoph. Eq., 287; Aristot. Hist. An., IX, 1, p. 609b, 24; Ex. 32:17; Ju. 18:22. [5]

ἀνακράζω (mostly in the aor. II ἀνέκραγον), "to cry out": Xenoph. An., VI, 4, 22: ἀκούσαντες δ' οἱ στρατιῶται ἀνέκραγον. Jos. 6:5: ... ἀνακραγέτω πᾶς ὁ λαὸς ἅμα, καὶ ἀνακραγόντων αὐτῶν ...

κραυγή, "outcry": κραυγὴν ἔθηκας, Eur. Or., 1509, ... σε κραυγὴν στῆσαι, *ibid.*, 1529; Xenoph. Cyrop., III, 1, 4; Demosth. Or., 54, 5.

κραυγάζω (from κραυγή), "to cry," e.g., ... κύων ἐκείνη κραυγάζουσα ..., Plat. Resp., X, 607b.

A. The Use of the Terms outside the NT.

1. In the Gk. world κράζω and ἀνακράζω have religious significance in the sphere of the demonic. In Luc. Nec., 9 the magus calls on the gods of the underworld after a blood-offering: ὁ δὲ μάγος ... οὐκέτ' ἠρεμαίᾳ τῇ φωνῇ, παμμέγεθες δέ, ὡς οἷός

---

[5] Harnack (→ n. 3), *ad loc.*; H. Weinel, *Die Wirkungen des Geistes u. d. Geister* (1899), 131 ff.; Kn. Did., *ad loc.*

κ ρ ά ζ ω κ τ λ. [1] On the etym. cf. Walde-Pok., I, 413 ff. Croaking ravens, Job 38:41, their croaking being crying to God: τίς δὲ ἡτοίμασεν κόρακι βοράν; νεοσσοὶ γὰρ αὐτοῦ πρὸς κύριον κεκράγασιν πλανώμενοι τὰ οἶτα ζητοῦντες.

[2] Job 6:5: נָהַק; Is. 26:17: זָעַק; Jos. 6:16: רוּעַ hi.

[3] In both passages צָעַק.

[4] Bl.-Debr. § 75 and 77; Winer (Schmiedel) § 13, 2.

[5] Ex. 32:17: רֵעַ; Ju. 18:22: זָעַק.

τε ἦν ἀνακραγὼν δαίμονάς τε ὁμοῦ πάντας ἐπεβοᾶτο καὶ Ποινὰς καὶ Ἐρινύας καὶ νυχίαν Ἑκάτην καὶ ἐπαινὴν Περσεφόνειαν, παραμειγνὺς ἅμα καὶ βαρβαρικά τινα καὶ ἄσημα ὀνόματα καὶ πολυσύλλαβα. This loud invocation of the gods of the underworld is in long, unarticulated and mysterious words, cf. also Hipp. Ref., IV, 28, 3 : μέγα καὶ ἀπηχὲς κέκραγε καὶ πᾶσιν ἀσύνετον. There is similar crying in magic, which is closely related to such incantations, cf. Lucanus Pharsalia, ed. C. Hosius³ (1913), VI, 688 ff.: The voice of the witch is like the belling of hounds, the howling of wolves, the hooting of the howl, the hissing of the snake ... tot rerum una vox fuit. The demon itself cries out : ὁ δὲ ἀπελήλατο ὁ δαίμων, ἀνακραγὼν εὐλαβεῖσθαι μὲν τοὺς θεούς, αἰσχύνεσθαι δὲ καὶ αὐτόν, Damascius Vita Isidori, ed. A. Westermann (1862), 55 f.

The Greeks and Romans very largely felt that this kind of crying was barbaric and unworthy of the gods, e.g., Juv. Sat., XIII, 112 f., where there is mockery of a man who in his prayer to Jupiter is said to cry louder than Stentor and than Ares wounded by Diomedes : tu miser exclamas ... audis Juppiter haec. Apollonius of Tyana regarded as man's true converse with God, not the λόγος ... ὁ κατὰ φωνήν, but διὰ δὲ σιγῆς καθαρᾶς καὶ τῶν περὶ αὐτοῦ καθαρῶν ἐννοιῶν θρησκεύομεν αὐτόν, Porphyr. Abst., II, 34. ⁶

The verbs are found in the Gk. and Hell. world in the sense of proclamation. Thus the hierophant proclaims the great mysteries of Eleusis : ... βοᾷ καὶ κέκραγε λέγων, Hipp. Ref., V, 8. Cf. P. Oxy., IV, 717, 9 and 13 : ἐγὼ οὖν ἐβόων καὶ ἔκραζον ... βοῶν καὶ κράζων ὅτι τοῦτο ἔστιν, or Plut. Cato Minor, 58 (I, 787d): οὐχ ὑπέμεινεν ὁ Κάτων, ἀλλὰ μαρτυρόμενος καὶ κεκραγὼς ἐν τῷ συνεδρίῳ ...

2. The Gk. OT uses the words, especially κράζω, primarily in translation of צָעַק, זָעַק and קָרָא. The latter occurs predominantly in the Ps. in the context of crying or calling on God in some individual or national emergency. God hears such crying in His grace and delivers the oppressed : ἐὰν δὲ κακίᾳ κακώσητε αὐτοὺς καὶ κεκράξαντες καταβοήσωσι πρός με, ἀκοῇ εἰσακούσομαι τῆς φωνῆς αὐτῶν, Ex. 22:22 (of oppressed widows and orphans). καὶ ἐκέκραξαν οἱ υἱοὶ Ισραηλ πρὸς κύριον· καὶ ἤγειρεν κύριος σωτῆρα τῷ Ισραηλ καὶ ἔσωσεν αὐτούς, Ju. 3:9 (cf. 3:15; 4:3; 6:6, 7; 10:12; ψ 21:5 : πρὸς σὲ ἐκέκραξαν καὶ ἐσώθησαν, 33:6, 17; 106:6, 13, 19, 28 : καὶ ἐκέκραξαν πρὸς κύριον ἐν τῷ θλίβεσθαι αὐτούς, καὶ ἐκ τῶν ἀναγκῶν αὐτῶν ἐξήγαγεν αὐτούς ... in national history). But God may also refuse to hear : κεκράξονται πρὸς κύριον καὶ οὐκ εἰσακούσεται αὐτῶν, Mi. 3:4; cf. Zech. 7:13 and Jer. 11:11. He will not hear an ungodly people.

The crying of prayer takes on a distinctive sense in the Ps. Man turns in prayer to God in the various situations of life : φωνῇ μου πρὸς κύριον ἐκέκραξα, ψ 3:4; cf. 17:6; 87:2, 10, 14. This prayer is with the assurance : κύριος εἰσακούσεταί μου ἐν τῷ κεκραγέναι με πρὸς αὐτόν, ψ 4:3; 16:6; 21:24; 30:22. Because of this certainty the address takes the form : εἰσάκουσον, κύριε, τῆς φωνῆς μου, ἧς ἐκέκραξα, ψ 26:7. This form can express the strong assurance which can become a wrestling for the answer : πρὸς σέ, κύριε, ἐκέκραξα, ὁ θεός μου, μὴ παρασιωπήσῃς ἀπ' ἐμοῦ, ψ 27:1. The man whom God confronts as a living and free Thou is directed to His hearing and answering. We are here in a different world from that of Greek and Hellenistic usage. There is no magical forcing of the frontiers between God and man. Hence a twofold experience is possible, the one

---

⁶ Cf. on this H. Schmidt, "Veteres philosophi quomodo iudicaverint de precibus," RVV, 4, 1 (1907), 66 f.; O. Casel, "De philosophorum Graecorum silentio mystico," RVV, 16, 2 (1919).

heavy : κεκράξομαι ἡμέρας καὶ οὐκ εἰσακούσῃ, ψ 21:2, and the other joyful : ἐγὼ δὲ πρὸς τὸν θεὸν ἐκέκραξα, καὶ ὁ κύριος εἰσήκουσέν μου, ψ 54:16.

Special mention should be made of the heavenly praise of the angels in Isaiah's vision : καὶ ἐκέκραγον ἕτερος πρὸς τὸν ἕτερον καὶ ἔλεγον· "Αγιος, ἅγιος ... καὶ ἐπήρθη τό ὑπέρθυρον ἀπὸ τῆς φωνῆς, ἧς ἐκέκραγον, Is. 6:3, 4, and also of the statement of Dt. Is. concerning the quiet coming of the Servant of the Lord : οὐ κεκράξεται οὐδὲ ἀνήσει, Is. 42:2. The prophet Jeremiah is ordered by God : κέκραξον πρός με, καὶ ἀποκριθήσομαί σοι καὶ ἀπαγγελῶ σοι μεγάλα καὶ ἰσχυρά, and there is proclaimed to him the redemption from Babylon, the coming of the Messiah and the new covenant, Ιερ. 40:3 ff. (Jer. 33:3 ff.).

3. In Judaism the words κράζω and ἀνακράζω are found in different forms. Philo makes little use of them, but one instance is clearly Hellenistic : ἐκέκραγεσαν ἐν ἡμῖν αἱ ἄλογοι ὁρμαί, Ebr., 98. In the sense of proclamation the word is particularly used of the prophets : ὁ προφήτης Ἰερεμίας οὐχ ἡσύχαζεν, ἀλλὰ ἐκέκραγει καὶ ἐκήρυττε ..., Jos. Ant., 10, 117. In Rabb. Judaism, too, we find the expression : "Isaiah cried (צווח) before God," Tanch. תולדות, 19 (69b, Buber); "the prophet Jeremiah cried and said ...," Tanch. ויצא, 14 (77b, Buber). The phrase came to be used as a formula to introduce quotations adduced by the Rabbis in support of the views expounded and championed by them. This formula still suggests something of the element of proclaiming. In the light of it we can understand the type of expression found, e.g., in M. Ex. on 15:2 (p. 126, 11 Rabin): ורוח הקדש צווחת ואומרת, "and the Holy Spirit cries and says." This always introduces quotations which apply to the people and extol it as the chosen people. The Spirit who thus cries or proclaims is the inspired text. As the Spirit of inspiration the Holy Spirit worked in this way in the heroes of the past and in the prophets. M. Ex. on 14:31 (p. 114, 14, Rabin): "... for as a reward for their faith the Holy Spirit rested on them and they sang a song ..." [7] But we also find the same usage as that of the OT, esp. in apocalyptic, e.g., En. 71:11: "I cried with a loud voice, with the spirit of power ..." [8]

B. The Use of the Terms in the NT.

1. In the NT the terms are significant in the story of Christ. The demons which He drives out raise cries, whether unarticulated sounds and simple outcries (Mk. 5:5; 9:26; Lk. 9:39), or the clear expression in cries of their recognition of Christ and His will : Mk. 1:23 : καὶ ἀνέκραξεν λέγων· τί ἡμῖν καὶ σοί, Ἰησοῦ Ναζαρηνέ; ἦλθες ἀπολέσαι ἡμᾶς. οἶδά σε τίς εἶ, ὁ ἅγιος τοῦ θεοῦ, Mk. 3:11: ἔκραζον λέγοντα ὅτι σὺ εἶ ὁ υἱὸς τοῦ θεοῦ, Mk. 5:7: καὶ κράξας φωνῇ μεγάλῃ λέγει· τί ἐμοὶ καὶ σοί, Ἰησοῦ υἱὲ τοῦ θεοῦ τοῦ ὑψίστου; ὁρκίζω σε τὸν θεόν, μή με βασανίσῃς (cf. Mt. 8:29; Lk. 4:33; 8:28). [9] In these sayings of demons, which are magical incantations, [10] we have demonic resistance to Jesus, who on His way attacks the realm of the demons and overcomes it with His Word and work. [11]

---

[7] Cf. also Cant. r., 1, 6 on 1:1, which refers to the fact that the Spirit rested on Solomon and through him composed the three books, Proverbs, Qoheleth and Canticles.

[8] I owe the Rabb. refs. to K. G. Kuhn.

[9] Lk. 4:41: ἐξήρχετο δὲ καὶ δαιμόνια ἀπὸ πολλῶν, κραυγάζοντα καὶ λέγοντα ὅτι σὺ εἶ ὁ υἱὸς τοῦ θεοῦ.

[10] Cf. on this pt. the important work of O. Bauernfeind, *Die Worte der Dämonen im Markusevangelium* (1927).

[11] → ἰσχύω, 400 f.

Even the magical arts of this kingdom have no power in face of Him. To Jesus comes, too, the cry for help which springs from need or fear ; the sick turn to Him, like the two blind men : κράζοντες καὶ λέγοντες· ἐλέησον ἡμᾶς, υἱὸς Δαυίδ, Mt. 9:27; cf. 20:30, 31 and par., or the Canaanite woman on behalf of her daughter : ἔκραζεν λέγουσα· ἐλέησόν με, κύριε υἱὸς Δαυίδ· ἡ θυγάτηρ μου κακῶς δαιμονίζεται. ὁ δὲ οὐκ ἀπεκρίθη αὐτῇ λόγον. καὶ προσελθόντες οἱ μαθηταὶ αὐτοῦ ἠρώτων αὐτὸν λέγοντες· ἀπόλυσον αὐτήν, ὅτι κράζει ὄπισθεν ἡμῶν, Mt. 15:22, 23. In his perplexity of faith the father of the possessed boy cries out when Jesus says to him : τὸ εἰ δύνῃ, πάντα δυνατὰ τῷ πιστεύοντι. εὐθὺς κράξας ὁ πατὴρ τοῦ παιδίου ἔλεγεν· πιστεύω· βοήθει μου τῇ ἀπιστίᾳ, Mk. 9:23, 24. The disciples cry out for fear — ἀπὸ τοῦ φόβου ἔκραξαν, Mt. 14:26 (Mk. 6:49 : καὶ ἀνέκραξαν) — when they see Jesus walking toward them on the sea, and they think He is a ghost. Peter, when He hastens to Him on the water and begins to sink, ἔκραξεν λέγων· κύριε, σῶσόν με, Mt. 14:30. These cries are addressed to Jesus as He goes on His way to help and to save. In the story of Jesus we also read of the cries of jubilation on His entry into Jerusalem, Mt. 21:9, 15; Mk. 11:9. Jesus wills the rejoicing on this occasion, and when the Pharisees try to stop it He says : λέγω ὑμῖν, ἐὰν οὗτοι σιωπήσουσιν, οἱ λίθοι κράξουσιν, Lk. 19:40. But it is counterbalanced by the cries of hate which demand His death, Mt. 27:23; Mk. 15:13, 14 and which order the release of the murderer, Lk. 23:18.

Of Jesus Himself we read at the very end : πάλιν κράξας φωνῇ μεγάλῃ ἀφῆκεν τὸ πνεῦμα, Mt. 27:50. In accordance with the context, [12] and with the significance of the term elsewhere in the NT and the OT, this is not an inarticulate death-cry but a final prayer to God. This may be seen from the version in Lk. : καὶ φωνήσας φωνῇ μεγάλῃ ὁ Ἰησοῦς εἶπεν· πάτερ, εἰς χεῖράς σου παρατίθεμαι τὸ πνεῦμά μου. τοῦτο δὲ εἰπὼν ἐξέπνευσεν, 23:46. [13] The statement concerning the Servant of the Lord in Is. 42:2, → 900, is applied by Mt. to the way of Christ, though in a different form from that of the LXX : οὐκ ἐρίσει οὐδὲ κραυγάσει, Mt. 12:19.

2. In places where the Synoptists have κράζειν and ἀνακράζειν Jn. has κραυγάζειν : 12:13, the rejoicing on Christ's entry into Jerusalem for the feast : ἐκραύγαζον· ὡσαννά ..., 18:40 : ἐκραύγασαν οὖν πάλιν λέγοντες· μὴ τοῦτον, ἀλλὰ τὸν Βαραββᾶν, 19:6 : ἐκραύγασαν λέγοντες· σταύρωσον, also v. 12 to Pilate : ἐκραύγασαν λέγοντες· ἐὰν τοῦτον ἀπολύσῃς, οὐκ εἶ φίλος τοῦ Καίσαρος, v. 15 : ἐκραύγασαν οὖν ἐκεῖνοι· ἆρον ἆρον, σταύρωσον αὐτόν. κραυγάζειν is used of Jesus Himself on the raising of Lazarus : φωνῇ μεγάλῃ ἐκραύγασεν· Λάζαρε, δεῦρο ἔξω, 11:43. The strong verb κραυγάζειν, strengthened even more by the φωνῇ μεγάλῃ, is meant to express the greatness of the miracle. All resources have to be thrown in to rob death of its prey. The verb κράζειν occurs four times in Jn. and denotes a message which is declared in spite of contradiction and opposition. It is best rendered as crying in the sense of proclamation : Ἰωάννης

---

[12] The πάλιν points back to a first κράζειν. This is the prayer of Ps. 22, cf. v. 46 : ἀνεβόησεν ὁ Ἰησοῦς φωνῇ μεγάλῃ λέγων· ἠλὶ ἠλὶ λεμὰ σαβαχθάνι;
[13] To the κράξας φωνῇ μεγάλῃ of Mt. 27:50 (46 : ἀνεβόησεν ... φωνῇ μεγάλῃ) corresponds the φωνήσας φωνῇ μεγάλῃ ... εἶπεν· πάτερ ..., which gives the substance of the cry. Acc. to Lk. the second cry recorded in Mt. was also a saying from the Ps. like the first, which is found only in Mt. and Mk. Mk. has at this point ἀφεὶς φωνὴν μεγάλην ἐξέπνευσεν (15:37). Instead of the first cry Lk. has two other words from the cross.

μαρτυρεῖ περὶ αὐτοῦ καὶ κέκραγεν λέγων· οὗτος ἦν ὃν εἶπον· ὁ ὀπίσω μου ἐρχόμενος ἔμπροσθέν μου γέγονεν, ὅτι πρῶτός μου ἦν, 1:15; after the preceding dispute concerning His person ἔκραξεν οὖν ἐν τῷ ἱερῷ διδάσκων ὁ Ἰησοῦς καὶ λέγων· κἀμὲ οἴδατε καὶ οἴδατε πόθεν εἰμί· καὶ ἀπ' ἐμαυτοῦ οὐκ ἐλήλυθα, ἀλλ' ἔστιν ἀληθινὸς ὁ πέμψας με, ὃν ὑμεῖς οὐκ οἴδατε ... 7:28; ἐν δὲ τῇ ἐσχάτῃ ἡμέρᾳ τῇ μεγάλῃ τῆς ἑορτῆς εἱστήκει ὁ Ἰησοῦς καὶ ἔκραξεν λέγων· ἐάν τις διψᾷ ἐρχέσθω <πρός με>, καὶ πινέτω ὁ πιστεύων εἰς ἐμέ· καθὼς εἶπεν ἡ γραφή· ποταμοὶ ἐκ τῆς κοιλίας αὐτοῦ ῥεύσουσιν ὕδατος ζῶντος, 7:37 f.; [14] Ἰησοῦς δὲ ἔκραξεν καὶ εἶπεν· ὁ πιστεύων εἰς ἐμὲ οὐ πιστεύει εἰς ἐμὲ ἀλλὰ εἰς τὸν πέμψαντά με, καὶ ὁ θεωρῶν ἐμὲ θεωρεῖ τὸν πέμψαντά με, 12:44 ff. In each case there is reference to definite mysteries of His person and His work which He solemnly intimates and proclaims (κράζειν). Jn. reserves κράζειν for this and uses κραυγάζειν for the ordinary sense of the term. [15]

3. In Ac. κράζειν, ἀνακράζειν is used as in the Synoptists for the tumultuous out-cries of the mob, Ac. 19:28, 32, 34 (ἔκραζον λέγοντες· μεγάλη ἡ ᾿Αρτεμις ᾿Εφεσίων, v. 28); 21:28 (on the seizure of Pl.); 21:36 (κράζοντες· αἶρε αὐτόν); [16] 7:57 (on the stoning of Stephen). Lk. brings out the similarity of Stephen's end to that of Jesus: θεὶς δὲ τὰ γόνατα ἔκραξεν φωνῇ μεγάλῃ· κύριε, μὴ στήσῃς αὐτοῖς ταύτην τὴν ἁμαρτίαν. καὶ τοῦτο εἰπὼν ἐκοιμήθη, 7:60 (cf. Lk. 23:46 [cf. v. 34]). Here κράζειν is "to call on God." The verb is also used for calling out to make oneself heard in an uproar, 14:14, or for saying something decisive in a decisive hour, 23:6; 24:21, cf. Jn. It is used for the cries of one possessed in 16:17: αὕτη ... ἔκραζεν λέγουσα· οὗτοι οἱ ἄνθρωποι δοῦλοι τοῦ θεοῦ τοῦ ὑψίστου εἰσίν, οἵτινες καταγγέλλουσιν ὑμῖν ὁδὸν σωτηρίας, 16:17.

In Rev. κράζειν has the sense of calling on God, of calling for help (6:10), of jubila-tion (7:10), of proclamation on the lips of an angel (18:2), of a command on the lips of an angel (7:2; 19:17), of the call of an angel to the Son of Man by divine commission (14:15), and of the cry of an angel (10:3), of a woman with child (12:2) and of lamenta-tion for the fall of Babylon (18:18 f.).

In Jm. 5:4 it is used of the injustice which cries to heaven when labourers do not receive their reward.

4. Two concurrent passages call for special mention: R. 8:15: ἐλάβετε πνεῦμα υἱοθεσίας, ἐν ᾧ κράζομεν· ᾿Αββᾶ ὁ πατήρ, Gl. 4:6: ὅτι δέ ἐστε υἱοί, ἐξα-πέστειλεν ὁ θεὸς τὸ πνεῦμα τοῦ υἱοῦ αὐτοῦ εἰς τὰς καρδίας ἡμῶν, κρᾶζον· ᾿Αββᾶ ὁ πατήρ.

Both verses come at the end of a similar train of thought, more extended in R. (3-8), more compressed in Gl. In both cases the rather difficult argument is to the effect that

---

[14] Our punctuation of the text, which differs from that of Nestle, presupposes the follow-ing sense: "If any man thirsts, let him come (to me — not found in some authorities), and he shall drink who believes in me; as the Scripture says, streams of living water shall flow out of his body." On this view the verse is not a promise to those who drink, as traditional exegesis assumes on the basis of the accepted punctuation. It is to be taken as a Messianic promise and gives the reason for the call of the Saviour. Because, as the Scripture says, streams of living water flow out of His body, He can cry: If any man thirsts, let him come. Only thus is justice done to the rhythmic character of the saying. It is closely linked with Jn. 4. On its connection with the last day of the feast, cf. the comm.

[15] Cf. also R. 9:27: Ἡσαΐας δὲ κράζει ὑπὲρ τοῦ Ἰσραήλ. By reason of the term κράζειν the prophetic message takes on a similar character. Paul has the same usage as we earlier saw in Judaism.

[16] κραυγάζειν is found at Ac. 22:23 in the sense of tumultuous outcry.

the goal of Christ's work is divine sonship by the Spirit, and that this is a new life. Divine sonship finds expression in the prayer, Abba, our Father. G. Kittel (→ ἀββᾶ, I, 5 f.) has pointed out that "the use of the word in the community is linked with Jesus' term for God and thus denotes an appropriation of the relationship proclaimed and lived out by Him. Jewish usage shows how the Father-child relationship to God far surpasses any possibilities of intimacy assumed in Judaism, introducing indeed something which is wholly new." [17] This relationship of divine sonship is a → πνεύματι ἄγεσθαι, R. 8:14, as Jesus Christ is God's Son κατὰ πνεῦμα (R. 1:4). Similarly, the prayer "Abba, our Father" derives from the Spirit. The difference between Gl. 4:6, where the πνεῦμα is the subject of prayer, and R. 8:15, where ἡμεῖς is the subject, is more apparent than real, since in R. the ἡμεῖς can only pray thus through the Spirit, and in Gl. the Spirit is sent εἰς τὰς καρδίας ἡμῶν. The subject of the prayer "Abba, our Father" is thus the man who is apprehended by the Spirit.

But what is the meaning of κράζομεν or κρᾶζον in this connection? We cannot accept the view that it denotes ecstatic outcry after the manner of glossolalia. There is no suggestion that man's self-awareness is lost in such prayer. The reference is rather to the Spirit sent εἰς τὰς καρδίας, i.e., to the λαμβάνειν of the Spirit of sonship as distinct from that of bondage. In R. 8:15 an ecstatic understanding is also ruled out by the explanatory statement that the Spirit bears witness to our spirit, i.e., to our personal consciousness, that we are the sons of God. Thus the κράζειν of R. 8:15 is more akin to the calling on God of the Ps. and other parts of the NT. The Spirit, who effects divine sonship, impels us to this. In this calling on God (ἐν ᾧ κράζομεν and especially Gl. 4:6, where κράζειν can also mean "to proclaim") there is a revelation of the name (→ ὄνομα) [18] and nature of God by the Spirit. This revelation is first effected in and through the One who bears the Spirit, Jesus Christ. Probably Ἀββᾶ ὁ πατήρ is quoted from the opening verse of the prayer which Christ taught His disciples. [19] This suggests that formally Paul is following the Rabbinic usage to which we referred earlier (רוח צווחת = πνεῦμα κρᾶζον) but that he changes the content inasmuch as the Spirit is not understood in terms of the doctrine of inspiration but as a living reality. This is the basis of a new kind of prayer. "In calling is expressed the certainty and joy with which the one who is moved by the Spirit turns to God. The address of servants, on the other hand, is the murmured prayer prescribed by Jewish custom." [20] Prayer in the Spirit ("Abba, dear Father") and sonship by the Spirit are one and the same thing.

5. The noun κραυγή is found as a cry of joy in Elisabeth's greeting of Mary at Lk. 1:42, or in the greeting of the bridegroom at Mt. 25:6. It denotes clamour at Ac. 23:9 (after Paul's *apologia*), and Eph. 4:31 (as something which Christians are to avoid). It is an anxious cry in Rev. 21:4 (where it is banished from God's eternal kingdom) and Hb. 5:7 (of the prayer of Jesus on His way of suffering).

Grundmann

---

[17] → I, 5 f.
[18] The NT name of God revealed by Jesus is → ἀββᾶ, πατήρ, → ὄνομα.
[19] If it was the custom in the early Church first to repeat the Lord's Prayer to catechumens at the time of baptism, the apostolic and primitive understanding was thereby given cultic form.
[20] Schl. R., 265.

κράσπεδον

Prob. originally "tip of the head" from κρασ- (κάρη κάρα κάρηνα) and πεδον, [1] corresponding roughly to "front."

In general it is used for the "outer limit" of something with various subjects, a. "hem" or "edge" or "border" of a garment (Theocr. Idyll., II, 53; Athen., IV, 49 [p. 159d]; IX, 16 [p. 374a]), so often in the LXX, e.g., Zech. 8:23 : ἐπιλάβωνται τοῦ κρασπέδου ἀνδρὸς Ἰουδαίου, Preis. Zaub., VII, 371: ἐξάψας κράσπεδον τοῦ ἱματίου σου (as a magical provision before pronouncing the magical formula); b. "Border" or "coast" of a country, Soph. Fr., 545; Eur. Fr., 381 (TGF); c. the "outer wing" of an army, Xenoph. Hist. Graec., III, 2, 12 etc. It also occurs in medicine ; in Aret. De Causis et Signis Acutorum Morborum, I, 8, 2 it denotes a sick condition of the uvula (or of the "knot" of the soft palate). Ez. 8:3 ᾽ΑΘ : κράσπεδον τῆς κορυφῆς (for Σ μαλλός, "lock of hair"), LXX : ἀνέλαβέν με τῆς κορυφῆς μου, "he seized me by my hair" (Heb. בְּצִיצִת רֹאשִׁי).

In the Bible it denotes the "hem of a garment" or especially the "tassel" which the Jews bore an each of the four corners of their outer garment as a constant reminder of all the commandments (Nu. 15:38 f.; Dt. 22:12). κράσπεδον = צִיצִת. [2] In Mt. 23:5 Jesus lashes the Pharisees for their purely outward display of piety. Using wool of the prominent hyacinth blue and white, [3] they made their tassels as long as possible in order to gain a reputation for zealous prayer and strict observance of the commandments.

In the story of the healing of the woman with an issue of blood the hem of the garment plays an important role. The woman believes that by touching the κράσπεδον τοῦ ἱματίου of Jesus (Mt. 9:20; Lk. 8:44) [4] she will be the recipient of His healing power. [5] Even though her views border on the magical, Jesus perceives the faith of the woman and He therefore assures her of healing.

J. Schneider

κ ρ ά σ π ε δ ο ν. [1] Cf. Boisacq, 509, s.v.
[2] Cf. Str.-B., IV, 276-292; Schürer, II⁴, 566 (with sources and bibl.). At both passages in Tg. O. (Nu. 15:38 f.; Dt. 22:12) the Gk. word κράσπεδον is adopted as a loan word in the form כְּרוּסְפְּדָא (plur. כְּרוּסְפְּדִין), (cf. also Str.-B., IV, 277).
[3] Acc. to Str.-B., IV, 277 the earlier practice was to have 3 blue and one white thread, then 2 of each. But "the colour was not indispensable."
[4] Mk. (5:27) does not refer to the κράσπεδον : (ἥψατο) τοῦ ἱματίου αὐτοῦ.
[5] Cf. on Mt. 9:20 Schl. Mt., 317: "The easiest way to touch a garment secretly was to touch one of the tassels. If one of these was on the back, it could be reached with a quick grasp and no one would notice."

> κράτος (θεοκρατία), κρατέω,
> κραταιός, κραταιόω,
> κοσμοκράτωρ, παντοκράτωρ

---

† κράτος (θεοκρατία).

1. κράτος, more closely related to → ἰσχύς than → δύναμις, and thus denoting the presence and significance of force or strength rather than its exercise, is found in various areas of Gk. literature from the time of Homer.[1] Its first meaning is a. "might" or "strength" as a natural attribute, e.g., the physical strength which a man has, Hom. Il., 7, 142, or the toughness which constitutes the strength of iron, Od., 9, 393. A common expression is κατὰ κράτος, "powerfully," "impressively," "forcefully," esp. with military verbs, e.g., αἱρεῖν κατὰ κράτος, "to take by storm," Ditt. Or., 90, 26 (2nd cent. B.C.), P. Tebt., 27, 83 (2nd cent. B.C.), Ditt. Or., 654, 3 (1st cent. B.C.). We then find the sense b. of "power" which one has or attains, or with which one is invested; the power of the gods: τοῦ γὰρ κράτος ἐστὶ μέγιστον (of Zeus), Hom. Il., 2, 118, ἐλθέ μοι θεὰ θεῶν, κράτος ἔχουσα μέγιστον (invocation of Isis), P. Leid. U., col. 2a, 17 (2nd cent. B.C.); or the power which the gods have given to men, esp. rulers: ἀνθ᾽ ὧν δεδώκασιν αὐτῶι οἱ θεοὶ ὑγίειαν, νίκην, κράτος καὶ τἄλλ᾽ ἀγαθὰ πάντα, Rosetta stone, Ditt. Or., 90, 35 (2nd cent. B.C.), ὑγίειαν, [ν]ίκην, κράτος, σθένος, κυριείαν τῶν [ὑ]πὸ τὸν οὐρανὸν χώρω[ν], P. Leid. G., 14 (1st cent. B.C.), in the Egyptian royal style: ᾧ ὁ Ἥλιος ἔδωκεν τὸ κράτος, Mitteis-Wilcken, I, 109, 10 f. (3rd cent. B.C.). In this sense it is used esp. of political power: ἀρχὴ καὶ κράτος τυραννικόν, Soph. Oed. Col., 373, εἰς κράτος Ῥώμης, Ditt. Syll.[3], 1125, 5 (1st cent. B.C.). It also occurs in the plur., which is otherwise rare: κράτη καὶ θρόνους, Soph. Ant., 173. When applied politically, κράτος almost always denotes the legal and valid superior power which confers supremacy and legally, politically and physically turns the scale. In this connection we may note the compounds which denote the various constitutional forms and political groupings: ἀριστοκρατία (since Hdt.), δημοκρατία (Xenoph.), πλουτο-κρατία (Xenoph.); on θεοκρατία → 908. κράτος is not prominent as a tt. in the vocabulary of the imperial cult (though it occurs in Test. Sol. 4:10 and 6:2: τὸ σὸν κράτος as a title, "thy royal majesty"). With a gen. it takes on the sense c. of "power" or "control over something," Hdt., III, 69, τὸ κράτος εἶχε τῆς στρατιῆς, IX, 42, κράτος ἔχειν ἑαυτοῦ, Plat. Polit., 273a. Finally, it has also the sense d. of "supremacy," "victory," e.g., Hom. Il., 1, 509; 6, 387. It is not common as a tt. term in law (like → κρατέω and κράτησις), nor in the context of ancient ideas of power[2] or of stories of healing. Divine or demonic beings are not described in terms of it. The predominant singular use — it bears a primarily comparative sense of "superiority" — militates

---

κ ρ ά τ ο ς. Cf. the bibl. under → δύναμαι κτλ. Other NT derivat. of the stem κρατ- are κρείττων, κράτιστος, → προσκαρτερέω and προσκαρτέρησις, and the word group ἐγκρατ, → II, 339 ff. In the LXX we also find κρατιότης, κραταίωμα, κραταίωσις, κράτησις, κρατύνω (Symm. κρατερός). Etym. κρατ- and καρτ- correspond to a basic krt- (cf. kret- in κρείττων), Germ. hart, Eng. "hard" (Walde-Pok., I, 354) [Debrunner].

[1] Cf. Liddell-Scott, s.v.

[2] Cf. J. Röhr, "Der okkulte Kraftbegriff im Altertum" (Philol. Suppl.-Bd., XVII, 1 [1923], 20). In the magic pap. δύναμις is more common, Preis. Zaub., I, 211; IV, 1024 f., 2448 f., 2998; ἰσχύς, II, 182; σθένος, IV, 948 and 964 (cf. ἰσχὺν καὶ θάρσος καὶ δύναμιν, IV, 1665 f.).

against personification in a plurality of forces. It should also be noted that there are not many instances of its use in acclamations, which would be a step towards the adoption of the word in Christian doxologies. [3]

2. In the LXX κράτος occurs some 50 times, though only in 20 cases in works which are also in the Heb. Canon. [4] In the first instance it denotes natural "strength" or "might" such as is proper to man's hand (Dt. 8:17) or to man more generally (Job 21:23), or to the bow (ψ 75:3) or horse (Jdt. 6:3) or even the raging sea (ψ 88:9). The expression κατὰ κράτος occurs in Ju. 4:3 and as vl. in Is. 22:21 (for καὶ τὸ κράτος, which attests the currency of this adv. turn of speech); cf. also μετὰ κράτους, Gn. 49:24; 2 Macc. 12:28. In the overwhelming majority of instances the ref. is, however, to the power of God, e.g., 2 Εσδρ. 8:22; Job 9:19 B; 12:16; ψ 61:11, and esp. 2 and 3 Macc. [5] God can be called θεὸς πάσης δυνάμεως καὶ κράτους in Jdt. 9:14 (cf. τὸν πᾶν κράτος ἔχοντα, 3 Macc. 1:27). By the power of God man knows who he himself is and who God is (cf. Wis. 11:21; Sir. 18:5), hence εἰδέναι σου τὸ κράτος ῥίζα ἀθανασίας, Wis. 15:3 (cf. 15:2 and 12:17 vl.). Man can seek God's κράτος, ψ 85:16, and God's strength can be at work in man, even in the weak, cf. Jdt. 9:11: οὐ γὰρ ἐν πλήθει τὸ κράτος σου. Hence the LXX can cause the righteous to address God as τὸ κράτος μου, ψ 58:9. κράτος is linked with ἰσχύς in Job 12:16; Is. 40:26; Da. 4:30; 11:1 (cf. also the alternative readings at Job 9:19 and the variant renderings of LXX and Θ at Da. 4:30). κράτος is also linked with δύναμις, e.g., Jdt. 5:23; 9:14 (cf. 9:8, where we have ἰσχύς, δύναμις and κράτος, though with different references). The plur. occurs only at ψ 75:3. [6] The sense of victory is found at 4 Macc. 6:34. κράτος is not found in true acclamations or doxologies, but there are many examples of the use of the term in prayer.

3. κράτος occurs in Philo, but it is much less common than δύναμις and also less than ἰσχύς. Always in the sing., it means "strength," e.g., Poster. C., 28 : τὰ κινούμενα κράτει τοῦ ἑστῶτος ἐπέχεταί τε καὶ ἵσταται, "that which is in movement is restrained and arrested by the power of that which is fixed," cf. also Deus Imm., 85; Migr. Abr., 26; Det. Pot. Ins., 114; Praem. Poen., 39. The adv. κατὰ κράτος also occurs (Leg. All., III, 18), but ἀνὰ κράτος is more usual, e.g., Poster. C., 37. In many passages we also find the sense of "might," or "supremacy," Spec. Leg., III, 184, or "victory" (Conf. Ling., 34; Cher., 74), and the use with the gen. in the sense of "power over something," Deus. Imm., 26; Op. Mund., 56 (τῆς μὲν ἡμέρας τὸ κράτος ὁ πατὴρ ἀνεδίδου τῷ ἡλίῳ) and 79; Spec. Leg., IV, 177; Cher., 63. Philo speaks esp. of God's κράτος. In many cases he expresses this in terms of a phrase also used in other connections (e.g., Sobr., 57), namely, κράτος (τῆς) ἀρχῆς, "power of rule" or "ruling power," e.g., Gig., 47; Op. Mund., 45. In nine cases he has κράτος (τοῦ) θεοῦ. Epithets are often used to indicate the uniqueness and superiority of the divine power; it is ἀνίκητον, Som., II, 141; Gig., 47, αὐτεξούσιον, Plant., 46, ἀκαθαίρετον, Som., II, 290, φοβερόν, Som., II, 266; Gig., 47; there can thus be reference to the superabundance of the divine power: πρὸς τὰς ὑπερβολὰς τοῦ κράτους αὐτοῦ, Spec. Leg., I, 294. All is subject to it: τὸ ἐφ' ἅπασι κράτος, Plant., 58. Philo is obviously taking issue with the Stoic view that ἡδονή (→ II, 917) has power over all things, Op. Mund., 160. It is God who has this power, τῶν ὅλων τὸ κράτος, Spec. Leg., I, 307; He has reserved it for Him-

---

[3] The examples in E. Peterson, ΕΙΣ ΘΕΟΣ (1926), 168 f. yield the sense of political power.

[4] Among equivalents עֹז is predominant, cf. W. Grundmann, Der Begriff d. Kraft in der nt.lichen Gedankenwelt (1932), 125, though only with ref. to nouns.

[5] Once at 3 Macc. 2:6 κράτος is linked with the proof of God's power in the Exodus. Cf. → 912.

[6] Perhaps because of the plur. רְשָׁפֶיהָ. In the corrective addition in B this is rendered τὰ κέρατα (is κράτη a scribal error?).

self, οὕτως οὖν αὐτὰ συνθεὶς τὸ μὲν κράτος ἁπάντων ἀνῆψεν ἑαυτῷ; hence it follows that we men have ἑαυτοὺς καὶ ὅσα περὶ ἡμᾶς only from God as a loan, χρῆσιν ἔχομεν, that our power is only lent and derived, Cher., 113. [7] Knowledge of God's power impels man to fear and also leads him to trusting confidence : οὐκ ἀγνοῶ σου τὸ ὑπερβάλλον κράτος, ἐπίσταμαι τὸ φοβερὸν τῆς δυναστείας, δεδιὼς καὶ τρέμων ἐντυγχάνω καὶ πάλιν θαρρῶ, Rer. Div. Her., 24. God's power is linked with the fact that He is the Lord, cf. Spec. Leg., I, 307. In Philo we find κράτος with δύναμις, Poster. C., 9; Plant., 46, with δυναστεία, Leg. All., III, 73; Rer. Div. Her., 24, with ἰσχύς, Som., II, 90, with ἐξουσία, Spec. Leg., I, 294, and with ἡγεμονία, Poster. C., 129; Spec. Leg., III, 111 (cf. Leg. All., III, 73).

Elsewhere in Gk. Judaism we again find κράτος for God's power. Thus Apc. Mos., 23 has Adam say to God in Paradise : αἰδέσθην τὸ κράτος σου, δέσποτα. Joseph., too, uses κράτος as well as δύναμις, ἰσχύς and ἐξουσία for God's power. [8]

4. In the NT there is no place in which it is said of man that he either has or can gain κράτος (though cf. the use of → κραταιόω).

In one verse κράτος is linked with the devil. Thus we read in Hb. 2:14 that Christ became man ἵνα διὰ τοῦ θανάτου καταργήσῃ τὸν τὸ κράτος ἔχοντα τοῦ θανάτου, τοῦτ' ἔστιν τὸν διάβολον. This is the only NT instance of the gen. construction often found elsewhere (→ 905 f.) and denoting that over which one has power. The devil controls death. Death is subject to him. He uses it as an instrument. Death is in the devil's service and is his myrmidon, cf. Wis. 2:24. In other places, too, one finds the view that death is a demonic force which may be listed with the ἀρχαί, ἐξουσίαι and δυνάμεις, cf. 1 C. 15:24, 26, where death is the last and most deadly of these enemies of Christ (or men) who form the train of the devil. Cf. → II, 79 f.; III, 15. [9]

In all other passages κράτος refers always to God or the Lord. It should be noted, however, that in Ac. 19:20 the κατὰ κράτος is not to be linked with the τοῦ κυρίου which follows, but this belongs to the ὁ λόγος. κατὰ κράτος, "powerfully," "mightily," is the common adverbial phrase which is often found outside the NT (→ 905 f.); in it the κράτος has no article and carries no supplementation. [10]

The Synoptists, who often use → κρατέω, employ κράτος only once in the Magnificat, Lk. 1:51: ἐποίησεν κράτος ἐν βραχίονι αὐτοῦ. This statement has an OT orientation. [11] In the context of 1:51-53 it is designed to stress the power of God which none can withstand and which is sovereign over all.

---

[7] On χρῆσις in the sense of "loan" cf. Preis. Wört., s.v. and P. M. Meyer, Juristische Papyri (1920), s.v.

[8] E.g., Ant., 10, 263, τὸ πάντων κράτος ἔχων; Ap., 2, 165. Cf. Schl. Jos., 44; Theol. d. Judt., 28 : "κράτος is purely Greek, and cannot be equated with any Jerusalem term." Cf. → n. 10 : κατὰ κράτος in Joseph.

[9] In the background is the connection between sin and death, cf. Rgg. Hb., 56. The Jewish view of the angel of death (cf. Str.-B., III, 683; I, 144 ff.) is not wholly comparable.

[10] The expressions with the art. in Eph. 1:19, Col. 1:11 are not comparable (in spite of Zn. Ag., 685 f.). Schl. Lk., 619 points out that κατὰ κράτος is often found in Joseph. The reversal of order (ὁ λόγος τοῦ κυρίου) in many later MSS shows that κατὰ κράτος was taken in the common adverbial sense. Cf. also Wdt. Ag., 276.

[11] Zn. Lk., 106, n. 49 refers to עָשָׂה גְבוּרָה in 1 K. 16:27; 22:46 (LXX δυναστεία or δυναστείαι). A better suggestion is ψ 117:15 : δεξιὰ κυρίου ἐποίησεν δύναμιν (Kl. Lk., 19 f. and Schl. Lk., 170). Cf. also → I, 639.

In the rest of the NT κράτος is rare and the circle of meanings is restricted. In Eph. 1:19 we read that τὸ ὑπερβάλλον μέγεθος τῆς δυνάμεως αὐτοῦ, the overwhelming greatness of the power of God as this is demonstrated in believers, is along the same lines as the outworking of the power of His might κατὰ τὴν ἐνέργειαν τοῦ κράτους τῆς ἰσχύος αὐτοῦ, as this is expressed in the resurrection of Christ, 1:20. Notwithstanding the synonymous nature of the various terms, which is in keeping with the stylistic peculiarity of Eph., one may say that κράτος denotes more particularly the outer aspect of the divine strength, perhaps its supremacy.[12] κράτος τῆς ἰσχύος is again used in Eph. 6:10,[13] this time with reference to the Lord Christ: ἐνδυναμοῦσθε ἐν κυρίῳ καὶ ἐν τῷ κράτει τῆς ἰσχύος αὐτοῦ.[14] In Col. 1:11 we have κατὰ τὸ κράτος τῆς δόξης αὐτοῦ: the divine glory works effectually in the lives of believers.[15]

κράτος also occurs in doxologies.[16] It stands alone in 1 Pt. 5:11, is linked with τιμή and called αἰώνιον in 1 Tm. 6:16, occurs with δόξα in 1 Pt. 4:11; Rev. 1:6; 5:13 (with reference to the Lamb as well as God) and with ἐξουσία in Jd. 25. It denotes the superior power of God to which the final victory will belong.[17]

    5. By way of appendix a few words may be said about θεοκρατία. This does not occur in the NT, but the related problems have a bearing on it. We owe the term to Joseph. In Ap., 2, 164 f. he writes: ... οἱ μὲν γὰρ μοναρχίαις, οἱ δὲ ταῖς ὀλίγων δυναστείαις, ἄλλοι δὲ τοῖς πλήθεσιν ἐπέτρεψαν τὴν ἐξουσίαν τῶν πολιτευμάτων. ὁ δ' ἡμέτερος νομοθέτης (Moses) εἰς μὲν τούτων οὐδοτιοῦν ἀπεῖδεν, ὡς δ' ἄν τις εἴποι βιασάμενος τὸν λόγον θεοκρατίαν ἀπέδειξε τὸ πολίτευμα θεῷ τὴν ἀρχὴν καὶ τὸ κράτος ἀναθείς. Jos. does not use ἀριστοκρατία (ὀλιγαρχία) or δημοκρατία, substituting other words, but it is evident that in coining θεοκρατία he assumed that his readers would understand it analogously with the similarly formed political terms ἀριστοκρατία, δημοκρατία, πλουτοκρατία (→ 905). One may justly stress the fact that Jos. hardly represented the biblical truth in an adequate or felicitous manner when he grouped it without qualification with such constitutional forms as monarchy, aristocracy etc. The Mosaic theocracy makes much broader and deeper claims than any one of these, and its focus is so little political that in spite of its basic principle it has been able to unite with many forms of civil government during the course of the centuries.[18] On the other hand, it must be admitted that Jos. is making a deliberate comparison with other forms of government and that he intends θεοκρατία to be taken in this sense.

    This rules out the easy assumption that Jos. is simply using θεοκρατία as an alternative for βασιλεία τοῦ θεοῦ. This thesis of Schlatter is the main reason for the present discussion. Schlatter first argued that θεοκρατία is a parallel to the Palestinian מַלְכוּת שָׁמַיִם "in so far as it underlies the present state of the community."[19] But he finally came to the conclusion: "Jos. opposed the unlimited arrogance and unrestricted omnipotence of kings. This made the term 'king' unsuitable for God and led Jos. to drop the phrase βασιλεία τοῦ θεοῦ, with which those in Jerusalem described both the re-

---

[12] Cf. Haupt Gefbr., 41, Grundmann, op. cit., 109, n. 2 and → II, 314; III, 401 f.

[13] Cf. → 906 and n. 17.

[14] Cf. → II, 313, III, 399.

[15] → II, 314, Grundmann, 21, n. 20.

[16] → II, 306, III, 906. We include 1 Tm. 6:16 in spite of Wbg. Past., 215.

[17] Cf. κράτος in doxologies in the post-apost. fathers, 1 Cl., 64; 65; Mart. Pol., 20, 2; cf. also κράτος τῆς ἰσχύος, 1 Cl., 27, 5; with δόξα (and with ref. to Christ, elsewhere only to God), 2 Cl., 17, 5; cf. also 1 Cl., 33, 3; 61, 1.

[18] K. v. Orelli, Art. "Israel, Geschichte, biblische," RE³, IX (1901), 466.

[19] Schl. Jos., 12.

lationship to God already conferred on the people and also the glorious goal of the divine revelation, and to use instead the word θεοκρατία, which he himself had coined." [20] ("Theocracy is a suitable term to describe the constitution of the Jewish world.") [21] The non-occurrence of βασιλεία τοῦ θεοῦ in Jos., however, is not to be explained wholly in terms of his coining the new word, nor *vice versa*. It is primarily linked with the fact "that Jos. also avoided speaking of the eschatological and Messianic orientation of his people as this was linked with βασιλεία." [22] The use of θεοκρατία for the constitution of Judaism is to be explained independently of his non-use of βασιλεία τοῦ θεοῦ. It is a rather daring attempt, as he himself was aware, to explain to his readers the distinctive character of the Jewish constitution by using a term of similar construction to those used by them in such connections. βασιλεία τοῦ θεοῦ, even though it "underlies the present state of the community," could never be described by Joseph. or anyone else as a constitutional form. "Theocracy and the kingdom of God are two concepts which stand on very different planes." [23]

Now inasmuch as βασιλεία τοῦ θεοῦ in the course of its history was never wholly unrelated to "the present state of the community," and could never be completely divorced from the constitution of Judaism, it might seem that the above distinction is too rigid. Even if its correctness in the age of Joseph. and the NT were beyond debate, one might still ask whether there had not been closer links at an earlier stage. This brings us to the problem of the preparatory history of the NT concept βασιλεία τοῦ θεοῦ, which we cannot discuss in the present context. It seems that some distinction must be made according to the section of this history under consideration. A point of particular importance is whether we are thinking of the concept in its narrower usage [24] or whether we are thinking more broadly of the lordship of God. [25] In any case, it is advisable to restrict the term theocracy to the "constitutional positing of a spiritual lordship" [26] and to be correspondingly careful in its usage. Gloege's warning against the facile confusion of the divine lordship and Jewish theocracy [27] is not unjustified. It is directed particularly against A. v. Gall, [28] but has a wider reference. [29] Great caution is demanded in respect of M. Buber's use of the word "theocracy." [30]

When Joseph. coined the term, he was acting with the same creative independence as we do to-day when, without ancient precedents, we fashion such terms as nomocracy [31] or pneumatocracy. [32] Joseph. used it only in the passage adduced, so that it

---

[20] Schl. Theol. d. Judt., 26. Cf. K. L. Schmidt, → I, 576.

[21] Schl. Theol. d. Judt., 48.

[22] K. L. Schmidt → I, 576.

[23] G. Gloege, "Reich Gottes u. Kirche im NT," *Nt.liche Forschungen*, 2. *Reihe, Heft* 4 (1929), 26, n. 1.

[24] This is how I interpret v. Rad, → I, 565 ff.

[25] Cf. W. Eichrodt, "Gottes ewiges Reich u. seine Wirklichkeit in d. Geschichte nach at.licher Offenbarung," ThStKr, 108 (1937), 1 ff.; H. W. Wolff, "Herrschaft Jahwes u. Messiasgestalt im AT," ZAW, NF, 13 (1936), 168 ff., esp. 170 : "By lordship of God we thus understand neither a purely eschatological rule nor simply an enduring monarchy, but the mode of ruling which is proper to the God of Israel ; we might almost say the way in which Yahweh exercises His deity."

[26] Bertholet, Art. "Theokratie," RGG[2], V, 1112.

[27] Gloege, 26, n. 1.

[28] ΒΑΣΙΛΕΙΑ ΤΟΥ ΘΕΟΥ (1926); cf. esp. the equation, 200 : The thought "of theocracy or the βασιλεία τοῦ θεοῦ."

[29] Cf. P. Feine's title, *Theologie des NT*[6] (1934), 48 : "Gottessohnschaft Jesu im theokratischen oder messianischen Sinn"; Harnack Dg., I, 58 and n. 1.

[30] M. Buber, *Königtum Gottes* (1932), esp., 137 ff., Chapter 8 : "Um die Theokratie." Buber's direct theocracy of the earlier period is not pure theocracy, the combination with the kingdom of God (143) is open to question, the association with theopolitics is dangerous (146), and the derivation from the "anarchical basis" of the "bedouin soul" (142) may also be questioned. Cf. the observations of v. Rad, → I, 570.

[31] E. Salin, *Civitas Dei* (1926), 1; 218.

[32] Gloege, 320. Cf. also "bibliocracy" in E. Choisy, *La Théocratie à Genève au temps de*

obviously has no world-wide significance. In fact, the term was not immediately adopted. [33] Its true history began only in the languages in which it was adopted as a loan word unaffected by the problems discussed above, [34] and it is to be noted that other terms could also be used for theocratic phenomena.

The NT has neither the word nor the idea. That the βασιλεία τοῦ θεοῦ is not in any sense "theocracy" in the constitutional sense is obvious. The theocratic concept is also alien to thinking on the Church in primitive Christianity. [35] Only later, and first with Origen, do we find a theocratic understanding, or misunderstanding, of the βασιλεία. [36] Thus far no comprehensive history has been written of the concept "theocracy," which, it seems, has now lost the theological significance that it used to have for previous generations in respect of the OT data.

κρατέω.

1. The verb κρατέω (from → κράτος) is well attested from the time of Hom. It means "to be strong," "to possess power." It can be used in the abs., e.g., οἱ κρατοῦντες, Aesch. Choeph., 267; Soph. Oed. Tyr., 530; in the sense "to have power over, to be lord of, something" it is found with the gen.: αὐτοῦ Soph. Ai., 1099; ἡδονῶν καὶ ἐπιθυμιῶν, Plat. Symp., 196c, cf. in the Praecepta Delphica, Ditt. Syll.³, 1268, I, 5 : ἡδονῆς κράτει, I, 2 : θυμοῦ κράτει, II, 9 : ὀφθαλμοῦ κράτει, Orph. (Abel), 55, 5. Very common, with various constructions, is the sense "to gain the upper hand," "to conquer," e.g., τὰ κατὰ πόλεμον κρατούμενα τῶν κρατούντων εἶναί φασιν, Aristot. Pol., I, 6, p. 1255a, 6 f., τὰς φρένας τῶν ἀνθρώπων διὰ τοῦ λάρυγγος κρατῶ καὶ οὕτως ἀναιρῶ, Test. Sol. 10:3; pass. ὑπὸ τῶν ἡδονῶν, Plat. Leg., I, 633e. Also "to seize," "to win" (esp. with force), e.g., θρόνους Soph. Oed. Col., 1381, also "to arrest," "imprison," Polyb., 8, 18, 8; "to hold," P. Tebt., 61b, 229 (2nd cent. B.C.). As a legal tt., "to have the use of," οἱ κρατοῦντες τῶν ἱερῶν, P. Tebt., 5, 73 (2nd cent. B.C.); "to have the right of possession," esp. in the phrase κρατεῖν καὶ κυριεύειν, cf. Moult.-Mill., s.v., Preisigke Wort., s.v. (and the noun κράτησις), also "to attach," "distrain," cf. P. M. Meyer, Jurist. Pap. (1920), s.v.; pass. "to be pledged," cf. Preis. Fachwörter. Rare and late is the phrase "to hold in one's hand," Diosc., 3, 93; κράτει τῇ ἀριστερᾷ σου τὸν δακτύλιον, Preis. Zaub., V, 451 f. (4th cent. A.D.).

2. In the LXX it occurs some 170 times (very often for חזק hi). Most of the extrabiblical senses (apart from the legal) are found : "to be strong," ἐκράτησας καὶ ἠδυνάσθης, Jer. 20:7; ἡ δὲ ἀλήθεια μένει καὶ ἰσχύει εἰς τὸν αἰῶνα καὶ ζῇ καὶ κρατεῖ

Calvin (1897), 53; 168; 277; also "hierocracy" (e.g., M. Weber, "Wirtschaft u. Gesellschaft," *Grundriss d. Sozialökonomik,* III [1922], 780).

[33] Liddell-Scott, Pass. and Sophocles Lex. give only this one instance from the whole range of writings considered by them (Soph. up to 1100).

[34] This transition was late. C. D. du Cange, Glossarium mediae et infimae latinitatis (ed. G. A. L. Henschel), VIII² (1887), does not have the word. A. Sleumer, *Kirchenlateinisches Wörterbuch*² (1926) has it, but gives no examples. *A New English Dictionary on Historical Principles,* ed. Murray, Bradley, Craigie, Onions, Vol. IX, Part II (1919), 272 adduces "theocraty" from 1622 and "theocracy" from 1652. A. Hatzfeld and A. Darmesteter, *Dictionnaire général de la langue française . . .,* II⁶ (1920), 2145 find the earliest instance of "théocratie" in 1704. Calvin did not use it [P. Barth, Madiswil].

[35] On the danger of an uncontrolled development of theocracy in the primitive community cf. K. L. Schmidt, *Die Kirche d. Urchristentums*² (1932), 304, 306, n. 1 (and → 509); cf. also Gloege, 380 n.

[36] Cf. W. Vollrath, "Das Reich Gottes in d. altchristlichen u. mittelalterlichen Theologie," ThBl, 6 (1927), 125 ff. and R. Frick, "Die Geschichte d. Reich-Gottes-Gedankens in d. alten Kirche bis zu Origenes u. Augustin," Beih. ZNW, 6 (1928), 103. Even here we do not find the word.

εἰς τὸν αἰῶνα τοῦ αἰῶνος, 1 Εσδρ. 4:38; "to have power over something," Εσθ. 1:1 s; Prv. 16:32; "to rule," common in 4 Macc. in discussion of the theme εἰ τῶν παθῶν ὁ λογισμὸς κρατεῖ, 1:5; "to take control," e.g., τῆς ἀρχῆς, 1 Macc. 10:52; 2 Macc. 4:27; "to seize," Ju. 8:12; ψ 136:9; ὁ κρατῶν αὐτῆς ὡς ὁ δρασσόμενος σκορπίου, Sir. 26:7; ἐκράτησαν αὐτὸν οἱ ἀλλόφυλοι, Ju. 16:21 B (ἐπελάβοντο αὐτοῦ, A); "to hold," ἐκράτησα αὐτὸν καὶ οὐκ ἀφήσω αὐτόν, Cant. 3:4. We often find a phrase which recurs in the NT but is not found outside the Bible, κρατεῖν τῆς χειρός, Gn. 19:16; Is. 42:6; ἐκράτησας τῆς χειρὸς τῆς δεξιᾶς μου, ψ 72:23; τῆς δεξιᾶς, Is. 41:13; 45:1 (cf. also τὸν νεανίαν τὸν κρατοῦντα τὴν χεῖρα αὐτοῦ, Ju. 16:26 B and 1 Βασ. 15:27).

In Philo the circle of meanings is much smaller, "to rule," e.g., ἀδικία κρατεῖ, Leg. All., I, 73 and 100; ὅταν δὲ ἐπιθυμία κρατήσῃ, Rer. Div. Her., 269; pass. "to be ruled," e.g., νῦν ὅτε ζῶμεν κρατούμεθα μᾶλλον ἢ ἄρχομεν, Cher., 115; κρατηθεὶς ἐπιθυμίᾳ, Decal., 149; "to be lord over," e.g., μηδ' αὐτοῦ κρατεῖν ἱκανὸς ὤν, Poster. C., 42; "to conquer," Ebr., 105; act. and pass., Cher., 75; "to gain the upper hand," Leg. All., III, 92.

We also find κρατεῖν τῆς δεξιᾶς in Joseph. Bell., 1, 352; Ant., 14, 480.

3. Many of the senses of κρατέω are not found in the NT. The main meaning is "to seize," "to hold." In the Synoptics the term is often used of the attempts of the opponents of Jesus to arrest Him, to lay hands on Him, e.g., Mk. 12:12; 14:1. It is also used of the arrest of the Baptist, Mk. 6:17 = Mt. 14:3, and with reference to the flight of the young man, Mk. 14:51. It occurs again in the story of the attempt made by the family of Jesus to seize Him (Mk. 3:21), and this is also the sense in Ac. 24:6; Rev. 20:2. [1] In the stories of healing we often read of κρατεῖν τῆς χειρός,[2] Mk. 1:31 (= Mt. 8:15 : ἥψατο); Mk. 5:41 = Mt. 9:25 = Lk. 8:54; Mk. 9:27.[3] κρατέω is rare in Lk. (→ n. 1) but occurs at 24:16 in the expression : οἱ δὲ ὀφθαλμοὶ αὐτῶν ἐκρατοῦντο τοῦ μὴ ἐπιγνῶναι αὐτόν, "their eyes were 'held,' prevented from recognising" (opp. διηνοίχθησαν, 24:31).[4] In Ac. we find κρατέω in 2:24 ("hold," → II, 304); 3:11;[5] 27:13 : δόξαντες τῆς προθέσεως κεκρατηκέναι, in the sense of having obtained their purpose, i.e., of being able to carry it out.[6] If we have already mentioned passages in which the main idea is "to hold," most of the others amount to much the same thing. Rev. 2:1: ὁ κρατῶν τοὺς ἑπτὰ ἀστέρας ἐν τῇ δεξιᾷ αὐτοῦ, refers back to 1:16 : ἔχων ἐν τῇ δεξιᾷ χειρὶ αὐτοῦ ἀστέρας ἑπτά. The point in Rev. 2:25; 3:11 is holding on to a possession. The idea of holding a view, of taking one's stand on it, is found in connection with διδαχή in Rev. 2:14 f., though with παράδοσις at Mk. 7:3, 4, 8 and 2 Th. 2:15

κ ρ α τ έ ω. [1] It is doubtful whether one can say that κρατέω is a favourite word of Mk. (Hck. Mk.) or that Lk. avoids it as much as possible (Kl. Lk., 193 on 20:19, Bl.-Debr.⁶, 300, suppl. to § 170). In the case of Lk. the influence of OT expressions seems to be decisive, cf. Schl. Lk., 120, 139 (cf. also the Joseph. par., ibid., 135 and 140).

[2] Cf. Wbg. Mk., 167; F. Fenner, "Die Krankheit im NT," UNT, 18 (1930), 90 and → χείρ.

[3] On the constr. in these cases and generally, cf. Bl.-Debr.⁵, 102 § 170, 2 and ⁶, 300, on Mt. 28:9 cf. also Zn. Mt., 720. On the constr. in the pap., Mayser, II, 2, 216.

[4] Cf. Hck. Lk., 293, Schl. Lk., 458, Str.-B., II, 271 ff. and Bl.-Debr.⁵, 227 § 400, 4. The use in Rev. 7:1 is not directly related.

[5] Not so much "the lame man clung to them so that they could not get away" (Pr.-Bauer, s.v.) as "he did not leave their side."

[6] Cf. Bl.-Debr.⁵, 102 § 170, 2. Perhaps there is a suggestion here of gaining power over something.

[7] Wbg. Th., 162 rightly refers to 1 Tm. 6:20 φύλαξον. At Mk. 7:8 the antithesis to ἀφίημι supports this.

the sense is more that of keeping or following a tradition, [7] cf. Hb. 4:14 : κρατῶμεν τῆς ὁμολογίας ("hold fast"), whereas the sense in Hb. 6:18 : κρατῆσαι τῆς προκειμένης ἐλπίδος, is more "to grasp." [8] Also to be mentioned in this connection are Rev. 2:13: κρατεῖς τὸ ὄνομά μου and Col. 2:19: οὐ κρατῶν τὴν κεφαλήν. [9] In Mk. 9:10 τὸν λόγον ἐκράτησαν refers not so much to observing the silence enjoined by Jesus as to the careful keeping of the sayings which precede. [10] Finally, in Jn. 20:23 κρατέω stands in plain antithesis to ἀφίημι and denotes the nonremission or retention of sins. [11, 12]

† κραταιός. [1]

With κρατερός, which does not occur in the LXX or NT, this adj. is found from Hom. on in poetry and later in prose works. In the sense of "strong," "mighty," it is used of men in Hom. Od., 15, 242, animals, Il., 11, 119, events, κραταιὸς ἀγών, Polyb., 2, 69, 8 and things, κραταιὸν ἔπος, Pind. Pyth., 2, 81. In relation to deities Hom. Il., 16, 334 refers to μοῖρα κραταιή, and in magic texts and astrological writings, which also use the adj. in another connection, we find, e.g., θεοὶ κραταιοί, P. Lond., 121, 422, cf. also τῷ μεγίστῳ κραταιῷ θεῷ Σοκνοπαίῳ in Mitteis-Wilcken, I, 122, 1 (6th cent. A.D.). In connection with χείρ (or βραχίων) there are many occurrences, Soph. Phil., 1110, also Preis. Zaub., IV, 1279 f. In the LXX the word appears 68 times, of God in Dt. 7:21; 2 Εσδρ. 19:32; ψ 23:8; 70:7; Prv. 23:11. In 31 instances it is linked with → χείρ, in 2 with → βραχίων, and in most cases the reference is to the mighty hand of God, esp. in connection with His election and deliverance at the Exodus. [2] κραταιός occurs several times in Philo, but as a predicate of God only in Spec. Leg., I, 307. [3]

The only instance in the NT is at 1 Pt. 5:6 : ταπεινώθητε οὖν ὑπὸ τὴν κραταιὰν χεῖρα τοῦ θεοῦ, ἵνα ὑμᾶς ὑψώσῃ ἐν καιρῷ. The reference is to the blows and severe punishments which God sends and which man cannot and will not escape (cf. Job 30:21). [4]

† κραταιόω.

A late construction from → κραταιός, "to make strong," this word replaces κρατύνω, which is also not very common, and seems to be found [1] outside the Bible only in Philo, who uses the mid., e.g., Conf. Ling., 101 and 103 and the pass., e.g., Agric., 160. In the LXX, which has κρατύνω only at Wis. 14:16, it is found 64 times and occurs in the

---

[8] Rgg. Hb., 175, n. 71. On the gen. cf. Bl.-Debr.⁵, 102 § 170, 2.
[9] Cf. Ew. Gefbr., 401; Loh. Kol., 125, n. 2 f.; Haupt Gefbr., 108. Here, too, the antithesis to ἀφίημι is in the background (cf. → 911).
[10] Cf. Wbg. Mk., 246, as against Hck. Mk., 109. The addition of an οὐ and the conjectured sense "to understand" in A. Pallis, Notes on St. Mark and St. Matthew (1932), 29, are erroneous.
[11] Cf. Zn. J., 680, n. 54 f.; Schl. J., 360; → I, 511; III, 753, n. 85.
[12] On the use in the post-apostolic fathers, cf. Pr.-Bauer, s.v.
κ ρ α τ α ι ό ς. [1] On the constr. cf. Boisacq, 510, n. 1.
[2] Cf. W. Grundmann, Der Begriff d. Kraft in d. nt.lichen Gedankenwelt (1932), 14, 110, n. 2; K. Galling, Die Erwählungstraditionen Israels (1928), 7, n. 3 and → II, 291, n. 34.
[3] Cf. Leisegang, s.v.
[4] The ἐπί corresponding to the ὑπό in Ez. 3:14: χεὶρ κυρίου ἐγένετο ἐπ᾽ ἐμὲ κραταιά (cf. 1 Εσδρ. 8:60) relates, however, to God's help. There are 3 instances in the post-apost. fathers, all referring to God : Herm. v., 1, 3, 4, and with χείρ, 1 Cl., 28, 2; 60, 3.
κ ρ α τ α ι ό ω. [1] Cf. Liddell-Scott, s.v.

abs. (Job 36:22), trans. with acc. (Jdt. 13:7), with ὑπέρ or ἐπί (2 Βασ. 1:23; 11:23), or pass. (ψ 104:4). ²

In the NT it occurs only in the pass. κραταιοῦσθαι, "to become strong." In Lk. 1:80; 2:40 — combined in both cases with αὐξάνειν — it denotes growth in childhood, especially from the standpoint of mental independence. ³ In 1 C. 16:13 ἀνδρίζεσθε, κραταιοῦσθε is undoubtedly influenced by the concurrence of these two verbs in 2 Βασ. 10:12; ψ 26:14; 30:24 (cf. also 1 Βασ. 4:9 : κραταιοῦσθε καὶ γίνεσθε εἰς ἄνδρας). ⁴ The expression in Eph. 3:16 : δυνάμει κραταιωθῆναι διὰ τοῦ πνεύματος αὐτοῦ εἰς τὸν ἔσω ἄνθρωπον, has also a model in 2 Βασ. 22:33 : ὁ ἰσχυρός (i.e., God) ὁ κραταιῶν με δυνάμει, but it is to be set in the context of NT views on the working of divine power in the believer. ⁵

† κοσμοκράτωρ.

A rare and late word, whose history is hard to follow. It is relatively common in astrological writings, where it means the planets, orig. perhaps as the rulers of the heavenly spheres, then as the rulers of the universe who also ordain the destinies of men. ¹ It cannot be proved that this sense was already losing its prominence in the pre-Christian period. ² Nor is it likely that the word was being used as an imperial title before the 3rd cent. A.D. ³ Only later is the term used of the gods in the Gk. world (Orph. Hymn.), ⁴ but from the standpoint of religious history this is the root of the concept. ⁵ The term is also found in the mag. pap., Preis. Zaub., III, 135; IV, 166, 1599, 2198 f.; V, 400; XIII, 619; XVIIb, 1 (cf. IV, 1966 δέσποτα κόσμου), most frequently in address to Helios. The word does not occur in the LXX or Philo, but it passed as a loan word (קוזמוקרטור or קוזמוקראטור‎) into Rabb. writings, and this shows that it must have been in common use. ⁶

---

² κρατύνω is more common in other renderings, cf. Σ ψ 26:14; 30:24; 63:5; Is. 35:3. It is worth noting that in the LXX κραταιόω occurs only in the historical books Jos.-Jdt., Job, Ps., Lam., Da. and 1 Macc., not in the Pentateuch, Prophets or most of the hagiographa. It seems to gain prominence only in the later translations [Bertram].

³ Cf. Zn. Lk., 120; Schl. Lk., 181 mentions 1 Βασ. 30:6, but this is no true par.

⁴ Cf. Schl. K., 456; Nägeli, 64.

⁵ Cf. → II, 314; 699. κραταιόω and κρατύνω do not occur in the post-apost. fathers.

κ ο σ μ ο κ ρ ά τ ω ρ. Cf. Liddell-Scott, s.v.; M. Dibelius, Die Geisterwelt im Glauben des Pls. (1909), 163 f., 230; F. Cumont and L. Canet, "Mithra ou Sarapis ΚΟΣΜΟΚΡΑ-ΤΩΡ," Acad. des Inscr. et Belles-Lettres, Comptes rendus des séances de l'année 1918 (1919), 313-328; J. Schmid, "Der Eph. des Apostels Pls.," BSt, 22, 3/4 (1928), 145; H. Schlier, "Mächte u. Gewalten im NT," ThBl, 9 (1930), 289 ff. On -κράτωρ cf. E. Fraenkel, Gesch. d. gr. Nomina agentis, I (1910), 15, n. 5; ibid., 128 f.; also H. Frisk, "Zur indo-iranischen u. gr. Nominalbildung," Göteborgs Kungl. Vetenskaps- och Vittenhets-Samhälles Handlinger, 5. földjen, Ser. A, Vol. 4, No. 4 (1934), 67 ff. Probably -κράτωρ is formed from -κρατής (which is related to κράτος as εὐγενής to γένος etc.) by assimilation to sacral and political terms in -τωρ (ῥή-τωρ, πράκ-τωρ etc., αὐτοκράτωρ for αὐτοκρατής [Debrunner].

¹ Cf. the many instances in Cumont.

² As against Cumont, 318, n. 2; cf. also E. Peterson ΕΙΣ ΘΕΟΣ (1926), 173, n. 1.

³ Cf. Peterson, 173, n. 1 on the passages in Ps.-Callisth. So far the oldest attestation is in an Egyptian inscr. of 216 which calls Caracalla κοσμοκράτωρ (APF, 2 [1902], 449, No. 83). Cf. Preisigke Wört. for pap.

⁴ Cf. Pr.-Bauer, s.v. and the inscr. in Cumont Εἷς Ζεὺς Μίτρας (orig. Σάραπις) κοσμο-κράτωρ ἀνείκητος.

⁵ Cf. Cumont, 321, n. 1 and 4.

⁶ Cf. S. Krauss, Gr. und lat. Lehnwörter in Talmud, Midrasch u. Targum, II (1899), 502 and Str.-B., I, 149; II, 552 (here Satan is meant as the angel of death). The term is also a loan word in Syr., cf. Cumont, 324, n. 1.

In Eph. 6:12 there are interposed between the → ἀρχαί and → ἐξουσίαι not only the πνευματικὰ τῆς πονηρίας ἐν τοῖς ἐπουρανίοις but also the κοσμοκράτορες τοῦ σκότους τούτου. In this list we do not have different groups, but more or less synonymous designations of the forces of the devil with which believers have to contend. [7] These forces are called rulers of the world in order to bring out the terrifying power of their influence and comprehensiveness of their plans, and thus to emphasise the seriousness of the situation. [8]

> κοσμοκράτωρ does not occur in the post-apost. fathers, but it is found in Act. Joh. 23 (for Satan) and Act. Phil. 144. In Test. Sol. 8:2 the στοιχεῖα are called κοσμοκράτορες τοῦ σκότους and in 18:2 κοσμοκράτορες τοῦ σκότους τοῦ αἰῶνος τούτου; this usage is almost certainly influenced by Eph. 6:12 (cf. the vl. in א). The Mandaean phrase "lords of the world" (e.g., Lidz. Liturg., 79, 5) is no equivalent.

† παντοκράτωρ.

> παντοκράτωρ, "the almighty," "the ruler of all things" (fem. παντοκράτειρα) is used as an attribute of the gods, though it is not common, e.g., Epigr. Graec., 815, 11 (Hermes); CIG, 2569, 12 (Eriunios Hermes); IG, V, 2, 472 (Isis). More common are expressions like Διὶ τῷ πάντων κρατοῦντι καὶ Μητρὶ μεγάλη τῇ πάντων κρατούσῃ, Ditt. Syll.³, 1138, 2 ff. (2nd cent. B.C.). By contrast, the term is very common in the LXX as an equivalent of צְבָאוֹת as a divine name (cf. Shebu., IV, 13) or of שַׁדַּי, and the preference for it continues in later Jewish writings. [1] In Philo it occurs only in Sacr. AC, 63 and Gig., 64; Philo prefers πανηγεμών. Joseph. does not use it at all. [2] It is found in the magic pap., under Jewish influence, e.g., Preis. Zaub., IV, 968 and 1375. [3] We also find παντοκράτωρ in the inscr. of the σεβόμενοι θεὸν ὕψιστον of Gorgippia, where we read, e.g., θεῷ ὑψίστῳ παντοκράτορι εὐλογητῷ; this is the introductory dedication. [4] The title is also found in Jewish prayers, Const. Ap., VII, 33, 2; 38, 1; also Ep. Ar., 185. [5] The latter passage reads: πληρώσαι σε, βασιλεῦ, πάντων τῶν ἀγαθῶν ὧν ἔκτισεν ὁ παντοκράτωρ θεός. This liturgical usage has obviously influenced Rev. Yet the term has also a philosophical character, and in patristic lit. it was used to express the universalist claim of Christianity. With this eschatological orientation, it thus carries with it a strong religious accent. [6]

---

[7] Cf. Ew. Gefbr., 249 f. → I, 483.

[8] The ref. to the world is rather different from that in Jn. 12:31 (ἄρχων τοῦ κόσμου τούτου); τοῦ → σκότους τούτου here corresponds to the gen. in Jn. How to fit in the Eph. passage with other usage is hard to say. Cumont's suggestion that the word is "demoted" in Christianity to denote satanic powers is improbable, Cumont, 324 and cf. → n. 6. C. F. G. Heinrici, *Die Hermes-Mystik u. das NT* (1918), 185 f. also feels that the term is "distinctively weakened" as thus used in NT demonology.

π α ν τ ο κ ρ ά τ ω ρ. [1] Cf. Bousset-Gressm., 312, n. 2, where related expressions may be found; cf. also → II, 292.

[2] Cf. Schl. Jos., 44, n. 2; Theol. d. Judt., 26; in Ant., 10, 263 we find the paraphrase τὸ πάντων κράτος ἔχων.

[3] Cf. Deissmann B, 29, Hadrumetum tablet, line 9, and Test. Sol. 3:5, 7 vl.; 6:8; 3:3 D; 4:7 D.

[4] Cf. E. Schürer, "Die Juden im bosporanischen Reiche u. d. Genossenschaften der σεβόμενοι θεὸν ὕψιστον ebendaselbst," SAB, 13 (1897), 204 ff.

[5] Cf. H. Lietzmann, "Symbolstudien," ZNW, 22 (1923), 274. Corresponding to the LXX παντοκράτωρ we find both in older post-bibl. lit. and even to-day the common רִבּוֹן הָעוֹלָמִים for the divine name, which also passed over into Islam, cf. M. Lidzbarski, *Ephemeris f. semitische Epigraphik*, I (1902), 258.

[6] G. Bertram in F. Rosen-G. Bertram, *Juden u. Phönizier. Das antike Judentum als Missionsreligion u. d. Entstehung der jüdischen Diaspora* (1929), 507; 144. The last few lines and nn. 4-6 are by Bertram.

In the NT we find λέγει κύριος παντοκράτωρ in 2 C. 6:18 at the end of a collection of OT quotations. [7] Under LXX influence, and hence not indicative of a change in primitive Christianity, [8] κύριος ὁ θεὸς ὁ παντοκράτωρ is used in Rev. 1:8; 4:8; 11:17; 15:3; 16:7; 19:6; 21:22, and ὁ θεὸς ὁ παντοκράτωρ in Rev. 16:14; 19:15. [9]

The reference is not so much to God's activity in creation [10] as to His supremacy over all things. [11] The description is static rather than dynamic. Hence it has only a loose connection with the dogmatic concept of the divine omnipotence, which is usually linked with the omnicausality of God. [12]

Michaelis

κραυγή, κραυγάζω → 898 ff.

> † κρεμάννυμι (κρεμάω),
> † κρέμαμαι, † ἐκκρέμαμαι

Contents : 1. Mt. 18:6. 2. Gl. 3:13. 3. Mt. 22:40. 4. Lk. 19:48.

κρεμάννυμι, κρεμάω (formed from the aor. ἐκρέμασα), κρεμάζω and the popular κρεμνάω, are not common in the Gk. Bible. [1] The Heb. original is usually תלה or תלא. The range of meaning is the same in both Gk. and Heb. κρεμάννυμι, from the Indo-Germ. root *qer*, is commonly linked with the Gothic *hramjan*, "to crucify" (OHG *rama*, "frame"), though this is more likely connected with the Germanic *qrom*, "lattice-frame." [2]

---

[7] Cf. Wnd. 2 K., 217.

[8] As against Loh. Apk., 11; cf. Had. Apk., 30, 72, 232 and Zn. Apk., 178.

[9] The word is common in various connections in the post-apost. fathers, cf. Pr.-Bauer, s.v. It is common also in the Christian pap. of the 4th cent., Preisigke Wört., III, 403, and Moult.-Mill., s.v.

[10] The rendering "All-worker" (H. Frick, *Deutschland innerhalb d. religiösen Weltlage* [1936] 177) is wide of the mark. Nor does the rendering "All-ruler" (E. v. Dobschütz, "Das Apostolicum in biblisch-theologischer Bedeutung," *Aus d. Welt d. Religion, Bibl. Reihe, Heft* 8 [1932], 19) really do justice to the word. P. Feine, *Die Gestalt des apost. Glaubensbekenntnisses in d. Zeit des NT* [1925] 93, offers a good material par. with his ref. to the ὁ μακάριος καὶ μόνος δυνάστης of 1 Tm. 6:15.

[11] Not "power over all things" (= → κοσμοκράτωρ).

[12] The conventional character of παντοκράτωρ in the NT makes it difficult to give it a precise NT sense. This fact, and the paucity of instances, makes it likely that the adoption of the term in the creed was determined more by OT than NT usage. That the addition "Creator of heaven and earth" was later felt to be necessary shows that the specific ref. of παντοκράτωρ itself is not to God's power as Creator.

κρεμάννυμι κτλ. Thes. Steph.; Liddell-Scott; Pr.-Bauer; Comm. on Mt. 22:40, esp. Schl. Mt.

[1] Radermacher, 44; 98.

[2] Walde-Pok., I, 412, s.v. *qer*, 487, s.v. *qrom*-.

The word means "to hang (on or from)" (compounds with ἐπι-, ἐκ-), "to hang on the gallows," "to be suspended." The dep. κρέμαμαι is used intr. In the Gr. OT the ref. in Ez. 15:3 is to the hanging of all kinds of vessels, and in Cant. 4:4; Ez. 27:10, 11 to that of shields, helmets and quivers, cf. musical instruments in ψ 136:2 and amulets in Ez. 13:18 (Heb. Hexapla, not the Mas.). At Ez. 17:22 the verb is used for "to plant" in the Mas. In 1 Macc. 1:61 [3] and 2 Macc. 6:10 the children of Jewish women who are to be executed are hung on their breasts or around their necks. Acc. to Job 26:7 the earth hangs on nothing, and 2 S. 18:9, 10 tells how Absalom was hanging in the branches (הלה) and swung between heaven and earth (נתן). The κρεμάμενος of 18:10 led to the use of κρέμαμαι for הלה and נתן in 18:9. [4] In Ac. 28:4 the snake hangs from the hand of Paul (κρεμάμενον ... ἐκ τῆς χειρός).

1. Mt. 18:6.

In the sense of "to hang from or around" the verb occurs in the NT only at Mt. 18:6 with reference to the millstone. The saying does not have in view an earthly punishment, since there is none corresponding to this in Jewish law. The basis of the idea is perhaps to be found in a foreign custom, possibly Syrian or Greek.

So Aristoph. Eq., 1363: ἐκ τοῦ λάρυγγος ἐκκρεμάσας ὑπέρβολον (weight), cf. the note of the Schol. (ed. G. Dindorf, IV, 2 [1838]): ὅτε γὰρ κατεπόντουν τινάς, βάρος ἀπὸ τῶν τραχήλων ἐκρέμων. Cf. also Suet. (Aug.) Caes., II, 67 (ed. M. Ihm [1907]): superbe avareque in provincia grassatos oneratis gravi pondere cervicibus praecipitavit in flumen. That the custom was known and occasionally practised in Galilee may be seen from Jos. Ant., 14, 450, cf. also Ap. 1, 307, where we read of the weighting with lead of those about to be drowned. Here the βυθίζειν may well have a mythical connection too : ὡς τοῦ ἡλίου ἀγανακτοῦντος ἐπὶ τῇ τούτων ζωῇ (Ap., 1, 306). [5]

The saying in the Gospel tradition is a revelation of divine wrath. No human judge can establish by human law the fault mentioned, nor impose the corresponding punishment. [6] It is an open question whether the συμφέρει and the parallel expressions in Mk. and Lk. are to be taken comparatively : [7] it would be better for him to fall victim to this temporal destruction than to eternal damnation, or positively : it befits him [8] that he should fall victim to destruction — the depth of the sea is the kingdom of Hades. [9] In any case, the reference is probably to eternal salvation at the cost of life — the comparative understanding fits this best — just as in the following sayings about offences there is eternal salvation at the cost of a

---

[3] Cf. Jos. Ant., 12, 256 (ἀπαρτάω).

[4] Joseph. uses ἀνακρεμνᾶται (vl.) and κρεμάμενον in the story of Absalom, Ant., 7, 239; 241. The correction of the Mas. by the LXX at 2 Βασ. 18:9 is not to be recommended.

[5] Cf. 2 S. 21:6. Here too, as in Ap., 1, 307, the reference is to a famine. A. Jeremias, Das AT im Lichte d. Alten Orients³ (1916), 415, cf. 468 and 569, suggests a connection with the cult of the sun. Sinking in the sea as a means of expiation is known to Athens from the Poseidon cult.

[6] Zn. Mt., ad loc. (567, n. 31).

[7] Cf. Cramer Cat., ad loc.: τὸ δὲ 'συμφέρει' πρόσκειται, δεικνύς, ὅτι καὶ τούτου χαλεπωτέραν ὑποστήσονται κόλασιν οἱ τοιοῦτοι. Cf. also Mt. 5:29 and on this Str.-B., I, 302, and I, 775 on Mt. 18:6.

[8] So W. Michaelis, Das NT, I (1934), ad loc.

[9] In Christian symbolism the sea is a picture of death and of the sin in which man has sunk and from which he can be saved only by the apostles as fishers of men, cf. F. J. Dölger, Ichthys, II (1922), 32.

member. Those who despise the little ones that believe in Jesus can be saved only if their earthly life is destroyed.

Rabb. tradition is familiar with this thought. Thus we read in Sanh., 8, 7: The following are those who may be saved through their life : he who pursues his neighbour to kill him, or a man, or a betrothed maid. [10] Acc. to R. Simon b. Jochai there may be added the idolater, and acc. to R. Eleazar the one who desecrates the Sabbath. [11] Paul, too, speaks of salvation at the cost of life (1 C. 5:5). In the same connection the Rabbis raise the question whether the reference is to judicial punishment or to malediction. [12] The latter is the case with Paul. It is so with Jesus too. Jesus uses the image of drowning, which suggests the drowning of the sinful man in the depths of the waters of death in order that the spirit may be saved in the day of the Lord.

2. Gl. 3:13.

The verb is most commonly used in the Bible to denote judicial hanging.

In the OT Law this punishment is in general only a supplement to stoning. The reference is thus to the hanging of corpses. [13] This is so in the basic law of Dt. 21:22, 23, which even after the loss of national independence still controls inner Jewish relationships. This may be seen from the exposition of the Law in Joseph., in which the ordinance of Dt. 21:22, 23 is given in the following form (Ant., 4, 202): ὁ δὲ βλασφημήσας θεὸν καταλευσθεὶς (stoned) κρεμάσθω δι' ἡμέρας καὶ ἀτίμως καὶ ἀφανῶς θαπτέσθω. It is also shown by individual OT instances of the hanging of the dead acc. to the law of Israel, cf. Jos. 8:29; 10:26; 2 S. 4:12 (תלה); Jdt. 14:1, 11; 2 Macc. 15:33. To be sure, Jos. 8:29 does not say explicitly that the king of Ai was put to death first, but this is most likely in view of the usual practice and the original context. The LXX no longer makes a sharp distinction, however, between the OT law of hanging corpses and the more general practice of putting to death by hanging, impaling or crucifixion. In Jos. 8:29 : τὸν βασιλέα τῆς Γαι ἐκρέμασεν ἐπὶ ξύλου διδύμου, it seems to have had crucifixion in view ; this is why the διδύμου is independently added. In the translation traced back to Σ two other instances deserve mention. In Nu. 25:4 and 2 S. 21:6, 9, 13, the Mas. has the rare and difficult verb יקע. For this the LXX uses παραδειγματίζειν in Nu. but in Βασ. it has ἐξηλιάζειν, "to abandon or expose to the sun." Σ uses the present word, 'A has ἀναπήγνυμι in both instances. Perhaps they are confusing יקע with יקה, which means "to fasten to," "to affix," and which the LXX occasionally [14] renders πήγνυμι. It thus follows that κρεμάννυμι and ἀναπήγνυμι are used as equivalents of יקה, "to affix with nails," and both in the sense "to hang or affix on the cross," "to impale." Naturally, the translators could well be selecting the term which to them seemed best to fit the sense. In Nu. 25 and 2 Βασ. 21 neither the original nor the translations refer to the ancient Israelite punishment of exposing corpses, but to impaling as the main punishment. Σ uses the present verb for this even though it really has a different sense in the sphere of OT law. 'A seems to link ἀναπήγνυμι with the same conception. On Nu. 25 in Σ Thdrt. (MPG, 80, p. 396b) observes : τοῦ μέντοι λαοῦ ἡμαρτηκότος οἱ ἄρχοντες ἐκρεμάσθησαν, ὡς ὁ Σύμμαχος ἔφη, ὡς μὴ ἐξάραντες τὸ πονηρὸν ἐξ αὐτῶν. [15] A use fixed by the astral cult seems to underlie 2 Βασ. 21:6;

---

[10] S. Krauss, *Giessener Mischna* (1933), 248 f., *ad loc.* Cf. Str.-B., I on Mt. 5:29.
[11] bSanh., 73b, cf. L. Goldschmidt, *Der babyl. Talmud* (1925 ff.), *ad loc.*
[12] Str.-B., I, 302 on Mt. 5:29.
[13] *Ibid.*, 1034 on Mt. 27:26 : "The Jews were familiar with hanging on a tree, but this had nothing whatever to do with Roman crucifixion."
[14] Gn. 31:25; Ju. 4:21 vl.; 16:14 vl.; Jer. 6:3. The ref. in these verses is to tents or tent pegs.
[15] Cf. Field, *ad loc.*

the later Gk. translators then interpret this in the light of familiar penal practice. [16] In many OT passages the Heb. תלה does not refer to the supplementary Heb. punishment but to the customs of hanging, impaling and crucifixion customary elsewhere. Thus Egyptian practice underlies Gn. 40:19, 22; 41:13, and Mesopotamian practice underlies Lam. 5:12; 1 Εσδρ. 6:31 and the relevant verses in Est. In 1 Εσδρ. the translator is responsible for κρεμασθῆναι ἐπὶ ξύλου. The Mas. is יָקִים יִתְמְחֵא, which in 2 Εσδρ. 6:11 (the later transl. of the same book) is rendered ὠρθωμένος παγήσεται. [17] In both translations ξύλον is used for "beam," but in this context it must be given the sense of "stake." Thus the distinction between the Israelite and the non-Israelite practice of hanging, which is linguistically not very emphatic in the Mas., is completely obliterated in the Greek versions.

In this light one may see why it is that in the NT at Lk. 23:39 (Mt., Mk. σταυροῦσθαι); Ac. 5:30; 10:39 (cf. 2:23 προσπήγνυμι; [18] 2:36; 4:10 σταυρόω) the present verb is used for crucifixion (→ σταυρός), and why it is that both on the Christian and also on the Jewish side OT passages, esp. Dt. 21:23, can be adduced as material parallels in the polemical and apologetical discussion of the fact of the crucifixion.

The LXX rendering of Dt. 21:23 (κεκατηραμένος ὑπὸ θεοῦ πᾶς κρεμάμενος ἐπὶ ξύλου) is not wholly literal. Πᾶς and ἐπὶ ξύλου are not found in the Mas. and are thus marked with asterisks in the Hexapla tradition. The typologically significant addition ἐπὶ ξύλου (→ ξύλον) derives from the many passages in which it is found in the original Heb. A literal translation of the Mas. כִּי קִלְלַת אֱלֹהִים תָּלוּי is given by 'ΑΘ: κατάρα θεοῦ κρεμάμενος. Similarly, in Gl. 3:13a Paul first uses the noun κατάρα; the ἐπικατάρατος in 13b comes from Dt. 27:26, which has been quoted just before in Gl. 3:10. Σ takes a different line : διὰ τὴν βλασφημίαν τοῦ θεοῦ ἐκρεμάσθη. [19] This presupposes an obj. gen. and ὕβρις (mockery) θεοῦ or λοιδορία θεοῦ for קִלְלַת אֱלֹהִים, for which there are par. elsewhere. [20] On the other hand 'Α, Pl. and the Rabb. tradition (Sanh., 6, 4) take κατάρα θεοῦ as a subj. gen. The Rabb. tradition regularly applies the word תלה to Jesus. [21] This is obviously intentional. It places Jesus under the curse of Dt. 21:23, [22] and groups him with Haman, who was hanged, [23] and with Absalom, whose fate was equivalent to hanging. [24] It was the κρεμάννυμι of the LXX which made this understanding possible. Perhaps Gl. 3:13 shows that Paul had to meet this

---

[16] → n. 5.

[17] זקף means "to impale" in Aram., "to set up" in Heb. (Ps. 146:8, cf. ψ 145:8 : ἀνορθόω); we thus have a Hebraism in the LXX transl. in contrast to the Aram. text.

[18] Only here in the Gk. Bible.

[19] Jer. Gal., II, 435 (MPL, 26, p. 387a).

[20] Zn. Gl., ad loc., 158.

[21] bSanh., 43a (ed. princ.; Cod M 95); 67a (if it applies to Jesus, which is doubtful). Elsewhere to crucify is צלב.

[22] Cf. Just. Dial., 32, 1: οὗτος δὲ ὁ ὑμέτερος λεγόμενος Χριστὸς ἄτιμος καὶ ἄδοξος γέγονεν, ὡς καὶ τῇ ἐσχάτῃ κατάρᾳ τῇ ἐν τῷ νόμῳ τοῦ θεοῦ περιπεσεῖν· ἐσταυρώθη γάρ. Just. in his answer refers to Is. 53 and the 2nd coming, 89, 3; 90, 1; Tert. adv. Judaeos, 10 (MPL, 2, p. 665a): non esse credendum, ut ad id genus mortis exposuerit Deus filium suum quod ipse dixit : maledictus omnis homo, qui pependit in ligno.

[23] Zn. Gl., 157. In Est. Haman is hanged on a gallows, in Joseph. on a cross (σταυρός). It is said of Blandina in Martyr. Lugdunensium (Eus. Hist. Eccl., V, 1, 41): σταυροῦ σχήματι κρεμαμένη. The ref. here is obviously to a form of cross. Cf. also Jos. 8:29, the ξύλον δίδυμον.

[24] Euagrius, Altercatio Legis inter Simonem Judaeum et Theophilum Christianum, 2, 4 (ed. E. Bratke [1904], p. 25 f.).

kind of objection from the very first. The significance of Paul's answer is stated by Justin as follows : ἡμῶν τονοῖ τὴν ἐλπίδα ἐκκρεμαμένην ἀπὸ τοῦ σταυρωθέντος Χριστοῦ.²⁵ For Paul, and therewith for early Christianity, the curse was made a blessing, and the OT passages which refer to Christ point forward to this. Worth noting in this connection is the typology of a free rendering of נֶאֱחַז in Gn. 22:13, the story of the offering of Isaac ; this refers to the ram which was caught in a thicket. Hebr. and Syr. have κρεμάμενος for it, and Melito of Sardis notes that this rendering is to be introduced : ὡς σαφέστερον τυποῦν τὸν σταυρόν.²⁶

3. Mt. 22:40.

The verb is here used figuratively in the sense "to be dependent on."

Normally a prep. (ἐξ or ἐν) is used with κρεμάννυμι in this sense, e.g., Xenoph. Sym., 8, 19 : ὁ ἐκ τοῦ σώματος κρεμάμενος; Plat. Leg., VIII, 831c : ἐξ ὧν κρεμαμένη πᾶσα ψυχὴ πολίτου. A similar sense to that of Xenoph. is found in Philo Poster. C., 61, which derives the name Θαλαμειν in Nu. 13:22 from תלה, and which thus interprets κρεμάμενός τις. The following train of thought is linked with this etymology : ἀνάγκη γὰρ ψυχαῖς ταῖς φιλοσωμάτοις ἀδελφὸν μὲν νομίζεσθαι τὸ σῶμα, τὰ δὲ ἐκτὸς ἀγαθὰ διαφερόντως τετιμῆσθαι· ὅσαι δὲ τοῦτον διάκεινται τὸν τρόπον, ἀψύχων ἐκκρέμανται καὶ καθάπερ οἱ ἀνασκολοπισθέντες ἄχρι θανάτου φθαρταῖς ὕλαις προσήλωνται. In Agric., 97 Philo uses the compound : αἰσθήσεως καὶ σαρκῶν ἐκκρεμαμένης ζωῆς. In secular Gk. the present word is less common in this sense than ἀρτάω, ἀρτέω, which does not occur at all in biblical Gk. Aristot. esp. prefers ἀρτάω, cf. Metaph., III, 2, p. 1003b, 17: τὸ πρῶτον ... καὶ ἐξ οὗ τὰ ἄλλα ἤρτηται (sc. problems); cf. also Plat. Leg., X, 884a : ἐκ γὰρ δὴ τοῦ τοιούτου (disregard for the rights of one's neighbour) πάντα ἠρτημένα τά τε εἰρημένα κακὰ γέγονε καὶ ἔστι καὶ ἔσται.

Particularly important in the present connection is the well-known reference in Plut. Cons. ad Apoll., 28 (II, 116c): τὸ γνῶθι σαυτὸν καὶ τὸ μηδὲν ἄγαν· ἐκ τούτων γὰρ ἤρτηται τὰ λοιπὰ πάντα. This is a material parallel to Mt. 22:40. Moral conduct is shown to be dependent on two basic presuppositions, though these naturally differ from those of the Gospel. The common feature is the attempt to achieve a unity of the human spirit in face of the divisiveness of casuistical legalism. The OT has a similar orientation to a unifying epitome of the Law. Attempts in this direction may be found in Ps. 15; Is. 33:15; Mi. 6:8; Am. 5:4; Is. 56:1; Hab. 2:4.²⁷ In the Gk. OT, however, the word κρεμάννυμι is not found in this connection.

The following are the only linguistic par.: Jdt. 8:24 : ἐξ ἡμῶν κρέμαται ἡ ψυχὴ αὐτῶν, and Gn. 44:30 : ἡ δὲ ψυχὴ αὐτοῦ ἐκκρέμαται ἐκ τῆς τούτου ψυχῆς, Mas. קְשׁוּרָה; ᾿Α : συνδεδεμένη; Σ : ἐνδέδεται.²⁸ But the formula is found in the Rabb., though they do not make it clear how the 613 OT commandments can be summed up in one. Acc. to Shab., 31a Shammai refused to attempt this for a Gentile who wished to become a proselyte. Hillel, his younger contemporary, does it in the negative form of the Golden Rule.²⁹ The verb תלה is found in the formula in SDt, 41 on 11:13 : המעשה תלוי

---

²⁵ Just. Dial., 96, 1.
²⁶ Field on Gn. 22:13.
²⁷ H. Grotius, Adnotationes in Novum Testamentum, ed. C. E. v. Windheim (1755), ad loc. Cf. R. Simlai (c. 250) in Str.-B., I, 907.
²⁸ Cf. the passage from Just. Dial., 96, 1 quoted above.
²⁹ Cf. Str.-B., I, 357 on Mt. 5:43. The attempts of the older Synagogue to reduce the demands of the Torah to a single principle are summarised, ibid., 907 on Mt. 22:40.

בתלמוד ואין תלמוד במעשה: Conduct depends on doctrine, not doctrine on conduct. A compendium of the Law is introduced by the present term in Ber., 63a in a tradition traced back to bar Qappara (c. 220): "What is the smallest section of Scripture on which all the essential provisions of the Torah depend (תלויין)?" The answer is Prv. 3:6: "In all thy ways acknowledge him, and he shall smooth thy paths." [30] A similar emphasis is sometimes placed on the commandment to love God, e.g., Ber. 9, 5a: "One owes praise in evil things as in good; for it is written, Thou shalt love Yahweh, thy God, with all thy heart and with all thy soul and with all thy might." [31]

In the NT the law of love is singled out by Paul as well as Jesus. In R. 13:9 the apostle writes: τὸ γὰρ οὐ μοιχεύσεις ... οὐκ ἐπιθυμήσεις, καὶ εἴ τις ἑτέρα ἐντολή, ἐν τῷ λόγῳ τούτῳ ἀνακεφαλαιοῦται, and in Gl. 5:14: ὁ γὰρ πᾶς νόμος ἐν ἑνὶ λόγῳ πεπλήρωται, ἐν τῷ· ἀγαπήσεις τὸν πλησίον σου ὡς σεαυτόν. It is of no particular significance that Paul refers to love for one's neighbour while Jesus appeals to the twofold command of love for God and one's neighbour, or that the two commands are associated differently in the three Synoptists. Only in Lk. can one really speak of a twofold command; in Mk. the command to love one's neighbour is second, and in Mt. the two commands are set alongside one another as equal. But these are only peculiarities of tradition, just as the concluding statement in 22:40 is found only in Mt. and is perhaps to be regarded as an addition of Mt. like the endorsement of the Golden Rule in 7:12: οὗτος γάρ ἐστιν ὁ νόμος καὶ οἱ προφῆται. [32]

The particular significance of Mt.'s metaphor of hanging (ἐν not ἐξ) is as follows. As objects hang on a nail, and fall if the nail does not hold, so that they are essentially dependent on it, [33] so the details of moral conduct, or individual requirements of the Law, are dependent on the law of love. This does not mean that the Law is acknowledged to be a way of fulfilling the law of love for God and one's neighbour. [34] More particularly it does not mean that the different commandments are assessed "according to their closer or more distant relation to the two cardinal commandments." [35] It means rather that the love of God is seen to be the sustaining basis of all human attitudes and actions. But the love of God in men, and therewith also the love of men for God, is revealed and actualised in love for one's neighbour. [36] "God is the God of love, and he who would be a child of God must be embraced and impelled by the stream of divine love, and must reflect the love of God in his life." [37] The NT is not attempting a logical derivation of the many commandments from the one, or a logical reduction of the many to the one. It is recognising the basic law of all action in faith. κρέμαται, ἀνακεφα-

[30] Str.-B., loc. cit.; Schl. Mt., ad loc.

[31] O. Holtzmann, Giessener Mischna (1912), ad loc., 92 f.

[32] Bultmann Trad., 93.

[33] Cf. also the image of the vine and the elm in Herm. s., 2, 3, 4, and ἐπικρεμάννυμι in Hos. 11:7; Is. 22:24 Mas. "to hang" (from a nail, v. 25).

[34] H. Jacoby, NT Ethik (1899), 83.

[35] Zn. Mt., 646. Acc. to Schlatter the value of the statutes is no longer intrinsic; it lies in the fact that they provide means for love to do its work (Gesch. d. Chr., 282).

[36] G. Bertram in Die Entwicklung zur sittlichen Persönlichkeit im Urchr., ed. J. Neumann (1931), 59 ff., esp. 77. Cf. also → ἔργον, II, 649 ff.

[37] P. Feine, Theologie des NT² (1911), 95. This eliminates a purely ethical understanding such as we find in a particularly crass form in H. E. G. Paulus, Philol.-kritischer u. hist. Komm. über das NT² (1812), ad loc.: "All the individual duties will be self-evident for him who adopts the two universal."

λαιοῦται and πεπλήρωται are exact material parallels which have the same fact in view. The believer is not bound in his conduct by a multiplicity of demands. He acts in the power of love. He thus stands in the unity, purity and freedom of the children of God.

4. Lk. 19:48.

The general MS tradition has at Lk. 19:48 the compound ἐκκρεμάννυμι. Only D (and a minusc.) have the simple form. [38] The sense is that of fixed attention, of hanging on the lips. This is in keeping with a usage attested elsewhere. Cf. Aristot. Rhet., III, 14, p. 1415a, 12 : ἵνα προειδῶσι περὶ οὗ ἦν ὁ λόγος καὶ μὴ κρέμηται ἡ διάνοια. The LXX, too, occasionally uses κρέμαμαι in a similar sense, e.g., Dt. 28:66 : ἔσται ἡ ζωή σου κρεμαμένη ἀπέναντι τῶν ὀφθαλμῶν σου, καὶ φοβηθήσῃ ἡμέρας καὶ νυκτὸς καὶ οὐ πιστεύσεις τῇ ζωῇ σου. And Philo Poster. C., 24 and 25 judges with respect to the life of the ἄφρων : ζωὴ κρεμαμένη, βάσιν οὐκ ἔχουσα ἀκράδαντον. [39]

The observation of Lk. is in keeping with his historicising and psychologising style. He is depicting in this way the attitude of the people towards Jesus. With this special term he replaces the expression ἐξεπλήσσοντο (Mt. 22:33; Mk. 11:18) which is used elsewhere to sum up the impression made by Jesus on those around Him. [40] This small trait is interwoven into a more "human" picture of Jesus.

Bertram

κρίνω, κρίσις, κρίμα, κριτής, κριτήριον,
κριτικός, ἀνακρίνω, ἀνάκρισις, ἀποκρίνω,
ἀνταποκρίνομαι, ἀπόκριμα, ἀπόκρισις,
διακρίνω, διάκρισις, ἀδιάκριτος, ἐγκρίνω,
κατακρίνω, κατάκριμα, κατάκρισις,
ἀκατάκριτος, αὐτοκατάκριτος,
πρόκριμα, συγκρίνω

κρίνω.

Contents : A. Linguistic. B. The OT Term מִשְׁפָּט: 1. The Stem שׁפט; 2. God as the Giver and Guardian of מִשְׁפָּט; 3. מִשְׁפָּט as a Relationship ; 4. The Ethical and Religious Meaning of מִשְׁפָּט; 5. The Change in the Meaning of מִשְׁפָּט; 6. מִשְׁפָּט in its Relation to the Nations. C. The Concept of Judgment in the Greek World. D. The Concept of Judgment in Judaism.

---

[38] Ἐξεκρέματο vl. ἐξεκρέμετο, cf. Tisch. NT : *forma* κρέμομαι *pro* κρέμαμαι *a vulgari usu haud aliena videtur fuisse.*

[39] Cf. κρέμαμαι ἀπ᾽ ἐλπίδος, ἐπ᾽ ἐλπίδι, "to hover in expectation or uncertainty," Anacr., 92, 17 (Preisendanz, XVII, 17, p. 679); Porphyr. Abst., 1, 54. Sometimes the underlying image is plainly that of being stretched on the rack. Cf. the above quotation from Philo Poster. C., 61, where one may clearly see the interrelationship of the various meanings "to hang from," "to hang on the cross," "to be stretched on the cross."

[40] → θαῦμα, 36 ff.

κ ρ ί ν ω. In general : Cr.-Kö., *s.v.* A : Liddell-Scott, Pape, Pass., Pr.-Bauer, *s.v.* B : A. Alt., "Die Ursprünge des israelitischen Rechts," *Berichte d. Sächsischen Akademie d.*

E. The Concept of Judgment in the New Testament : 1. The Baptist ; 2. The Synoptic Preaching of Jesus ; 3. Paul ; 4. John, Epistles and Gospel ; 5. Revelation ; 6. Peter and Hebrews ; 7. Human Judgment ; 8. Conclusion.

A. Linguistic.

The word is related in root to the Lat. *cerno* : "to sunder." [1] In the basic sense "to part," "to sift," it occurs in Hom. Il., 5, 500 : ὅτε τε ξανθὴ Δημήτηρ κρίνῃ ... καρπόν τε καὶ ἄχνας (chaff). This leads to the sense "to divide out," "to select," Il., 1, 309 : ἐς δ᾽ ἐρέτας ἔκρινεν ἐείκοσιν, "to value," κρίνοντες τὸν Ἀπόλλω ... πρὸ Μαρσύου, Plat. Resp., III, 399e. The most common meaning is "to decide," νείκεα κρίνειν, Hom. Od., 12, 440; "to judge," "to assess," and in the mid. "to go to law, to dispute with," Τιτήνεσσι κρίναντο, Hes. Theog., 882; also "to seek justice," or "to be accused," θανάτου δίκῃ κρίνεσθαι, Thuc., III, 57, 3, also, from the sense "to assess," "to expound," ὁ γέρων ἐκρίνατ᾽ ὀνείρους, Hom. Il., 5, 150; ὀνειροκρίτης, the interpreter of dreams, and, from the more general sense of "judge," "to believe," "to decide," "to resolve," Isoc., 4, 46 : τὰ γὰρ ὑφ᾽ ἡμῶν κριθέντα τοσαύτην λαμβάνει δόξαν. Hence, though the word is most commonly found in legal terminology, it does not belong here either exclusively or by derivation.

Wissenschaften zu Leipzig, Phil.-hist. Klasse, 86 (1934), *Heft* 1; W. W. Graf Baudissin, *Kyrios als Gottesname im Judentum u. seine Stelle in d. Religionsgeschichte,* III (1929), 379-428; "Der gerechte Gott in altsemitischer Religion," *Festgabe A. v. Harnack dargebracht* (1921), 1 ff.; W. Cossmann, "Die Entwicklung des Gerichtsgedankens bei d. at.lichen Propheten," *Beih. ZAW,* 29 (1915); K. Cramer, "Amos, Versuch einer Theolog. Interpretation," BWANT, 15 (1930); H. Cremer, *Die paulinische Rechtfertigungslehre im Zusammenhang ihrer geschichtlichen Voraussetzungen* (1899); L. Diestel, "Die Idee d. Gerechtigkeit, vorzüglich im AT bibl.-theologisch dargestellt," *Jbcher. f. deutsche Theologie,* 5 (1860), 173 ff.; W. Eichrodt, *Theologie des AT,* I (1933), 121-126, 246-273; K. H. Fahlgren, צְדָקָה *nahestehende u. entgegengesetzte Begriffe im AT* (Diss. Uppsala, 1932); H. Fuchs, "Das at.liche Begriffsverhältnis von Gerechtigkeit (צדק) u. Gnade (חסד) in Profetie und Dichtung," *Christentum u. Wissenschaft,* 3 (1927), 101-118, 149-158; J. Hempel, "Gott u. Mensch im AT," BWANT 3. *Folge* 2 (1926); "Gottesgedanke u. Rechtsgestaltung in Altisrael," ZSTh, 8 (1931), 377-395; H. W. Hertzberg, "Die Entwicklung des Begriffes מִשְׁפָּט im AT," ZAW, 40 (1922), 256-287; 41 (1923), 16-76; "Die prophetische Botschaft vom Heil u. d. at.liche Theologie," NkZ, 43 (1932), 513-534; E. Kautzsch, *Über die Derivate des Stammes* צדק *im at.lichen Sprachgebrauch* (1881); F. Nötscher, *Die Gerechtigkeit Gottes bei d. vorexilischen Propheten* (1915); O. Procksch, "Die hbr. Wurzel d. Theologie," *Christentum u. Wissenschaft,* 2 (1926), 405-417, 451-461; H. Schultz, "Die Beweggründe zum sittlichen Handeln in d. vorchristlichen Israel," ThStKr, 63 (1890), 1 ff.; M. Weber, *Ges. Aufsätze z. Religionssoziologie,* III : "Das antike Judt." (1923). C : O. Gruppe, *Griech. Mythologie u. Rel. Gesch.* (1906); Rohde ; Bertholet-Leh., II, 280-417 (by M. P. Nilsson); O. Kern, *Die Religion d. Griechen,* I (1926), II (1935); U. v. Wilamowitz-Moellendorff, *Der Glaube d. Hellenen,* I (1931), II (1932); L. Rühl, "De Mortuorum Iudicio," RVV, 2, 2 (1903). D : Bousset-Gressm., 202 ff.; P. Volz, *Die Eschatologie d. jüdischen Gemeinde* (1934), 89-97, 272-309; Str.-B., IV, 1199-1212; A. Schlatter, "Jochanan ben Zakkai," BFTh, 3, 4 (1899), 72 ff. → ᾅδης, γέεννα, παράδεισος. E : H. Cremer, *Die paulin. Rechtfertigungslehre* (1899), 187 ff., 256 ff., 359 ff.; M. Kähler, Art. "Gericht," RE³, VI, 568 ff.; H. Braun, *Gerichtsgedanke u. Rechtfertigungslehre bei Pls.* (1930); P. Feine, *Theol. d. NT*⁴⁻⁷ (1923-36), 130-132, 246-250, 382-384; H. Weinel, *Biblische Theol. d. NT*⁴ (1928), 53 ff.; F. Büchsel, *Theol. d. NT* (1935), 35-40, 68-71, 122-123, 141-142; P. Althaus, *Römerbrief (NT Deutsch,* 2 [1935]), 19; W. Lütgert, *Joh. Christologie*² (1916), 157 ff., 235 ff.; P. Althaus, *Die letzten Dinge*⁴ (1933), 165 ff.

[1] This relationship of root is even clearer in the verbal forms and derivatives : κέ-κρικα, ἐ-κρί-θην, κρι-τής, κρί-σις etc. and *cre-vi, cre-tum, cri-men, cri-brum* (the sieve which separates).

The LXX uses κρίνειν for predominantly legal words, esp. שׁפט, more rarely דין and ריב. Hence κρίνειν means judging, even when this means deliverance or salvation for the oppressed, ψ 71:2 : κρίνειν τὸν λαόν σου ἐν δικαιοσύνῃ καὶ τοὺς πτωχούς σου ἐν κρίσει, Zech. 7:9 : κρίμα δίκαιον κρίνατε καὶ ἔλεος καὶ οἰκτιρμὸν ποιεῖτε. In keeping with the sense of שׁפט → infra κρίνειν can also have the more general meaning "to rule," Ju. 3:10; 4:4 etc.; 1 Βασ. 4:18; 4 Βασ. 15:5.[2] At this point the LXX goes beyond ordinary Gk. usage.

In the NT [3] κρίνειν means esp. "to judge," e.g., the judgment of God, R. 2:16; 3:6, of men, Ac. 23:3; Jn. 18:31 etc. It is used not merely for official judgment but also for personal judgments on others, Mt. 7:1, 2; Lk. 6:37; R. 2:1, 3; R. 14:3, 4, 10, 13; Jm. 4:11, 12. The mid. is used for "to be accused," Ac. 23:6; 26:6, "to seek justice," "to be engaged in a legal suit," Mt. 5:40; 1 C. 6:6. The sense "to resolve," "to determine," occurs at Ac. 16:4 : τὰ δόγματα τὰ κεκριμένα ὑπὸ τῶν ἀποστόλων, 20:16; 25:25; 27:1; 1 C. 2:2; 7:37: τοῦτο δὲ κέκρικεν ... τηρεῖν τὴν ἑαυτοῦ παρθένον. The sense "to value" is found at R. 14:5 : ὃς μὲν κρίνει ἡμέραν παρ' ἡμέραν, ὃς δὲ κρίνει πᾶσαν ἡμέραν, "the one esteems one day higher than another, the other esteems every day." We also find the meanings "to assess," "to regard as," Ac. 13:46; 16:15; 26:8, "to think," Ac. 15:19; 2 C. 5:14, in the aor. "to form an opinion or judgment," Lk. 7:43; Ac. 4:19; 1 C. 10:15; 11:13. The sense "to rule" rather than "to judge" occurs at Mt. 19:28; Lk. 22:30. [4] This usage goes back to the LXX and ultimately to the Heb. שׁפט. [5] Since it is alien to non-biblical Gk., we have here another instance of "biblical" Gk. From the theological standpoint the most important sense is "to judge," esp. of God.

Büchsel

B. The OT Term מִשְׁפָּט.

1. The Stem שׁפט. [6]

In the OT the stem שׁפט carries the double sense a. "to rule" and b. "judge." In passages like Gn. 16:5, in which the added בֵּין makes the legal sense quite incontestable, one may see that the main point is not so much to reach a decision as to restore the legal relationship which has been disrupted by the injury done to one of the partners. In Is. 2:4; Mi. 4:3 the emphasis again falls, not on deciding in the distributive sense (in spite of the בֵּין), but on the state of שָׁלוֹם which is established by the doing of שׁפט. Yet there are also passages in which the meaning is "to decide" in the distributive sense, e.g., 1 S. 24:13.

Because of the ambiguity of the word, the question arises whether the office of the ruler includes judging, or that of the judge includes ruling. [7] Ex. 2:14 runs : מִי שָׂמְךָ לְאִישׁ שַׂר וְשֹׁפֵט עָלֵינוּ. By assuming the office of אִישׁ שַׂר, Moses will also judge the people.

---

[2] It is most unlikely, though not absolutely impossible, that the LXX sense in these verses is simply "to judge" and not also "to rule."

[3] For an excellent review of NT usage, with many par. from Hellenistic usage, cf. Pr.--Bauer. The word is relatively common in Lk., Ac., Pl. and Jn.

[4] The Rabb. par. adduced in Schl. Mt., 583 on 19:28 seem to leave the possibility open that κρίνειν here means "to judge" rather than "to rule." But Zn. rightly points out that it would be no privilege for Israelites to judge, i.e., preponderantly to condemn, Israelites. Moreover, in Rev. 20:4 the activity of those who sit on the thrones and hold κρίμα is βασιλεύειν, "reigning."

[5] On the sense "to rule" for שׁפט cf. also the title *sufetes* for the leading officials in Carthage, Liv., 28, 37, 2; 30, 7, 5 etc.

[6] On LXX usage → δίκη.

[7] Cf. Hertzberg, 257.

Here judging is obviously part of ruling. Similarly, in 2 S. 15:4 Absalom can reach his goal of judging Israel only by seeking the office of the king. In keeping with this is the fact that the noun שֹׁפֵט is often found in lists which mention only those positions which exclusively involve the office of rule. [8] The interrelation between judging and ruling is perhaps seen best in 1 S. 8, where the people seeks liberation from the injustices of the sons of Samuel by asking Samuel to appoint a king. In 8:20 it says explicitly: "Our king will judge us." To do justice is part of the royal office. This presupposes the outward unity of the two acts expressed by the single stem. It is part of the ruler's office to establish justice by his decisions. Nor is it difficult to discover the point of unity between the two meanings. It lies in the will of a subject who in his governmental or judicial decisions asserts himself against an object and sets up a specific state, whether it be the restoration of a broken legal relation or the establishment of a sphere of dominion. Is. 2:4 and Mi. 4:3 show how the meanings can interfuse.

Comparison with other Semitic languages is not particularly rewarding. In Assyr. we find šapatu (with taw) in the sense "to judge" and šiptu (with tet) for penal judgment. It is worth noting that the sense "commander of a division" is also found for šapitu, [9] so that the same duality occurs as with the Heb. term.

The most common noun is that with the prefix מ, i.e., מִשְׁפָּט. It is found in the basic stages of meaning of nouns of the miqtal form, which denote a state or action by which the activity contained in the appropriate verbal form is expressed. If this is the most common sense, there are three possible meanings of these nouns. 1. They may denote the transition to a more concrete state, esp. when the noun signifies the instrument which serves the activity denoted. 2. Along with the state which expresses the activity contained in the verb, a series of words relates simultaneously, or exclusively, to the object of the activity. 3. Along with the first meaning, a third series also denotes the place at which the activity expressed by the verb takes place. [10]

Thus מִשְׁפָּט denotes "judgment" both in the concrete sense of a verdict or decision and also in the more abstract form of the process. Greater precision is expressed in the senses "legal use," "legal norm" and "legal claim." But along with these ordinary levels of meaning there is in the OT a distinctive transition to the sense, not merely of religion or truth, but of grace and salvation. To this transition, which is essentially grounded in the OT revelation to God, we shall have to return later.

2. God as the Giver and Guardian of מִשְׁפָּט.

It is an old Semitic belief that God is the Judge (→ δίκη). This belief may well go back to tribal religion in which God was regarded as both legislator and legal partner. His judging consisted in watching over the social relationship of the tribe and in intervening for it in war. Thus His מִשְׁפָּט applies to the society of which He is God. The twofold meaning of שפט is to be noted. As Ruler of the tribe, the God of the tribal religion is also Judge. His rule finds expression in judgment; His judgment shows that He is the Lord. The idea of rule is not ethically orientated. On the other hand, one cannot speak of the judgment of either God or man without some implication of justice or righteousness. It is obvious that there can thus be a tension between the power of God displayed in rule and the righteousness

---

[8] With שֹׁר or שׂרים, Ex. 2:14; Am. 2:3; Mi. 7:3; Zeph. 3:3; Ps. 148:11; Prv. 8:16; 2 Ch. 1:2; with מֶלֶךְ, Hos. 7:7; Ps. 2:10; with both, Hos. 13:10, cf. also Is. 33:22; 40:23.

[9] Cf. *Zschrf. f. Assyriologie*, 4 (1889), 278 ff.

[10] Cf. Hertzberg, 260 f.

of God displayed in judgment. The twofold sense of שָׁפַט expresses already a problem which always arises when legal terms are adopted as theological.

> The legal parts of the OT, in which it is particularly evident that the relationship to God is legally conceived, derive in their present form from a period when the tribes had already become a people. Nevertheless, they reflect the relationship of tribal religion. It is the unanimous witness of the OT that the people came into being through the conclusion of a covenant with Yahweh (→ διαθήκη). This covenant consisted in the fact that Yahweh entered into a legal relationship to Israel in which He was both legislator and legal partner. Yahweh's מִשְׁפָּטִים are the outworking of this covenant, in which Yahweh as supreme Lord and Judge so regulates the social relationships of the people of God that He Himself watches over the observance of His מִשְׁפָּטִים. Blessing and cursing reflect the direct reference of these מִשְׁפָּטִים to the Lord of the covenant. So, too, does the personal address "Thou shalt," in which the "I" of the covenant God speaks to His people.

In Israel, then, all law is referred to Yahweh as Lord and Judge. Herein is the distinctiveness of the OT relationship to God. The theological use of legal terms is possible only when faith in nature gods is vanquished by faith in the personal God who has established a historical relationship with the people which worships Him. Hence the attribute of judgment and justice cannot be native to a nature god; it can only be imported from without, as, e.g., in the case of the Babylonian Shamash. Because of the plurality of nature gods the only possibility is a casuistical law which establishes certain norms on the basis of long practice but which is quite unable to make rulings in the apodictic form: "Thou shalt." The distinctiveness of the OT belief in God may be discerned in the legal sections of the Canon because here ancient casuistical law is integrated into larger contexts controlled by the idea of a historical covenant concluded once and for all. It is thus possible to see the conflict between the casuistical law of Canaan and the apodictic law of Yahweh, which is to be found in particularly impressive form in the Decalogue. Here the introduction "I am thy God" plainly presupposes the historical situation of the making of the covenant. Yahweh Himself takes the initiative with His word. The provisions of the covenant are based upon the covenant promise. [11] The fact that the canonical writings of the OT trace back all the legal enactments to the conclusion of the covenant at Sinai shows the outcome of the conflict. There is fundamentally no place for secular law in Israel.

> The lexical evidence supports this. Not only does it show us that the theological use of legal terms controls all the concepts of faith. It also gives us the impression that in Israel all legal conduct is directly related to the supreme Lord and Judge. When שָׁפַט and מִשְׁפָּט are used in a secular context, it is only in a much weaker sense. [12]

If the social relations of the people of God are regulated by the revelation of Yahweh's will at the conclusion of the covenant, Yahweh also shows Himself to be the Guardian of מִשְׁפָּט by defending His people against military threats from without. It is worth noting that the victories of Israel are called צִדְקוֹת יהוה; they are thus an outworking of the judicial decisions of Yahweh. As Judge, Yahweh is also Helper of His people, Ju. 11:27; 2 S. 18:31; Dt. 33:21. The question of Abraham in Gn. 18:25: "Shall not the judge of all the earth do מִשְׁפָּט?", enables us to see how

---

[11] Cf. Alt., 68.
[12] Cf. Gn. 40:13; 1 S. 27:11; 2 K. 1:7 (?); 25:6; Jer. 32:7, 8.

this idea advances faith in God. The society which realises that it is unconditionally subject to the rule and therewith to the judgment of God gains confidence that the מִשְׁפָּט experienced in its own history is of universal validity. [13]

3. מִשְׁפָּט as a Relationship.

We have seen that the theological use of legal terms has its origin in tribal religion. We have also seen that in Israel the conclusion of the covenant was of decisive significance in the development of this line of thought. It is surely evident, then, that in the מִשְׁפָּט of Yahweh we do not have a legal principle or an absolute and abstract norm of morality which will control judicial decisions on earth. The OT view of מִשְׁפָּט has to be differentiated from the Roman concept of law and also from the abstract notion of an ethos or idea of virtue or law. Like צְדָקָה, מִשְׁפָּט is a term which expresses relationship. It regulates the relationships in a specific society. It can be understood only in the light of its validity in this society. The idea is that of a Judge who, on the basis of His ownership as the Lord, regulates the social relationships within His tribe. It is that of the God who in the covenant has bound Himself to the people as its Lord and Judge. It is that of the God who has thus revealed His will and who is just as concerned about the observance of this revealed will as He is about keeping the promise given in the covenant. This conception stands diametrically opposed to that of a judge who gives judgment according to a specific norm on the basis of a *iustitia distributiva*. Appraisals of the OT based on the idea of a *iustitia distributiva* which operates according to a fixed norm of absolute morality will necessarily miss the mark. They do not see the true meaning of the OT witness because they fail to note that the judicial decisions of Yahweh in the covenant people and its history serve a specific goal. The justice worked out in this judgment is not a *iustitia distributiva*; it is a *iustitia salutifera*. Only in this light can one understand what is in its own way the magnificent understanding of history in the Deuteronomic circle.

That מִשְׁפָּט is not originally an objective norm but a term which expresses relationship may be seen from the fact that one may read not merely of the מִשְׁפָּט of Yahweh but also of the מִשְׁפָּט and מִשְׁפָּטִים of other gods. Thus 1 K. 18:28 says that the priests of Baal cut themselves with swords and lances until the blood ran — כְּמִשְׁפָּטָם — i.e., according to the מִשְׁפָּט valid for the priests of Baal. It is evident that this מִשְׁפָּט is used to denote the manner of the dealings of these priests with their god, i.e., in the attempt to gain influence over him. The מִשְׁפָּט of Baal obviously stands in contrast with the מִשְׁפָּט of Yahweh, i.e., the way in which He is worshipped. Similarly it is recorded of the people settled in Samaria by the king of Assyria that they did not know the מִשְׁפָּט of the God of the land. The context makes it plain that the reference is to the worship of Yahweh. When they had been instructed concerning the מִשְׁפָּט of the God of the land, they worshipped Yahweh, but they also continued to worship their own gods acc. to the מִשְׁפָּט of the nations from whom they had been taken, 2 K. 17:24-28, 33. [14] The existence of the מִשְׁפָּט of other nations alongside that of the people of God raises the question of the relationship of Yahweh to the מִשְׁפָּטִים of other nations. The direction of the answer is given already in Gn. 18:25. Ezekiel then touches on it, and it is a specific theme of Dt. Is.

4. The Ethical and Religious Meaning of מִשְׁפָּט.

In the covenant Yahweh as Lord and Judge made His people His own. If the term מִשְׁפָּט is related to this relationship denoted by בְּרִית, the most general and com-

---

[13] Gn. 18:25 is perhaps in one of the latest sections of J.

[14] The ref. of כְּמִשְׁפַּט צְדֹנִים in Ju. 18:7 is primarily to the secular life of the Sidonians. But it is possible that here, too, religious customs are included.

prehensive definition of מִשְׁפָּט is perhaps to be found in the statement: "I will be your God and ye shall be my people." According to the witness of the canonical writings of the OT the מִשְׁפָּטִים comprised in the legal sections are the exposition of this מִשְׁפָּט. They present in detail the revelation of the will of Yahweh given at the conclusion of the covenant. They are thus a binding norm for the people. On the revelation of God's will, i.e., on His מִשְׁפָּט, there rests the obligation of the whole people and of each individual, and also the legal claim of each individual (e.g., the poor) and of the whole people.

Because this relationship is always the basis when the OT refers to מִשְׁפָּט and מִשְׁפָּטִים, the reference is never to the binding norm of a general morality. Yet the fact that the social relationship of the בְּרִית is established by God as the Judge carries an ethical implication, for, as we have seen, it is impossible to conceive of judging without a criterion of justice. It is not surprising, then, that not merely in the prophets the concept takes on ethical concreteness. Nor is this betrayed merely in the fact that צְדָקָה and מִשְׁפָּט are so constantly mentioned together as to suggest that these two words of very different origin came to be regarded as virtually synonymous. [15] It may be seen also in the fact that מִשְׁפָּט is defined in content as the capacity to make a basic and actual distinction between good and evil.

Thus in 1 K. 3:9 Solomon prays to Yahweh: "Give therefore thy servant a heart which is adapted to judge thy people, which discerns between good and evil, for who is able to judge this thy so great a people?" In Yahweh's answer in v. 11: "Thou hast asked for the understanding to hear מִשְׁפָּט," the ability to discern between good and evil is embraced in the term מִשְׁפָּט. The same ethical concreteness may be seen in the theological use of the term in Mi. 3:1 f.: "Is it not for you to know הַמִּשְׁפָּט? — you who hate the good and love the evil." If מִשְׁפָּט is here an obvious parallel to discerning between good and evil, the הַמְתַעֲבִים מִשְׁפָּט in v. 9 corresponds to the שֹׂנְאֵי טוֹב in v. 2. Is. 1:17 points in the same direction: "Learn to do good, seek after מִשְׁפָּט" (cf. Am. 5:15). There is also an ethical note in passages like Am. 5:7 and 6:12, in which we read of a turning of מִשְׁפָּט into wormwood or poison. Hos. 10:4 says similarly that "מִשְׁפָּט springs up like hemlock." If the meaning is more comprehensive here, these ironical sayings contain a positive estimation of מִשְׁפָּט. The ethical aspect may be clearly seen when the term מִשְׁפָּט is brought into relation to the poor and needy. In Dt. 10:18 it is said of Yahweh that He is a God who creates מִשְׁפָּט for widows and orphans. In keeping with this is the unanimous demand of the prophets that the cause of widows and orphans should be championed at the judgment (Is. 1:17; 10:2, cf. Am. 5:11, 15; 8:4 ff.; Jer. 5:28; 21:12; 22:15; Ez. 22:29). The poor is obviously regarded as the צַדִּיק, Am. 5:12. If he is not morally righteous, he is at least in the right against his oppressor. That Yahweh exercises מִשְׁפָּט for all the oppressed (Ps. 103:6; 140:12) is a conviction of faith which ultimately rests on Yahweh's relation to His people and to its individual members as this is grounded in the election. All the ways of Yahweh are מִשְׁפָּט, His jurisdiction is not crooked but straight. This finds expression in the fact that He exalts the humble and humbles the exalted. This is the witness of Is. 5:15 f.: "And man shall be brought down, and shall be humble, and the eyes of the great shall be humbled, and Yahweh of hosts shall be

---

[15] Procksch, 454 finds the distinction in the fact that מִשְׁפָּט is a legal term whereas צְדָקָה belongs strictly to the moral sphere. But this distinction cannot be pressed, since both words are used theologically.

exalted in מִשְׁפָּט and the holy God shall be sanctified in righteousness." [16] Here, as in Is. 3:13-15, there is also an ethical contrast. But the outworking of מִשְׁפָּט in uprightness has the further implication that everything which opposes the will of Yahweh, whether physically or ethically, is subjected to Him, cf. Is. 2. Thus in Ez. 34:16 no ethical basis is given for Yahweh's action: "I will bind up the broken and strengthen the weak, and I will destroy the fat and the strong, I will feed them בְמִשְׁפָּט."

The primary orientation of מִשְׁפָּט is religious rather than ethical. This finds plain expression in Hos. 6:5b, 6: "And my law (מִשְׁפָּט) shall go forth as light: I have pleasure in piety (חֶסֶד) and not in sacrifices, in the knowledge of God more than burnt offerings." [17]

The law of Yahweh as expressed in v. 6 has gone forth "as light" by the revelation of His will inasmuch as Yahweh has chastised His refractory people as their Judge. His מִשְׁפָּט is thus that man do מִשְׁפָּט. But for man to do מִשְׁפָּט is to exercise חֶסֶד and to know Yahweh, or, in the words of Jer. 5:1, to do מִשְׁפָּט and to seek after truth. Similarly, the religious aspect of מִשְׁפָּט appears again in Mi. 3:8: The prophet knows of himself that he is full of power and מִשְׁפָּט and courage to proclaim to Israel its misdeeds and to Jacob its sin. Of the three terms גְבוּרָה, מִשְׁפָּט and כֹּח, only מִשְׁפָּט denotes the content which makes possible the preaching of repentance, while כֹּח and גְבוּרָה are purely formal presuppositions. [18] מִשְׁפָּט is used in the same way in Zeph. 3:5: In face of the religious and moral corruption of the inhabitants of Jerusalem, the prophet bears witness: "Yahweh is righteous in her; he does no injustice; every morning he brings his מִשְׁפָּט to light; it does not fail ..." Because the people does not regard His מִשְׁפָּט, His justice entails judgment on the rebel, for מִשְׁפָּט can continue only if the proud are humbled and the lowly receive justice. Theological formulation is found in the thought of Jer. 9:23 f. Man's only boast should be that he knows Yahweh. But to know Yahweh is to know that He executes מִשְׁפָּט, חֶסֶד and צְדָקָה on the earth. That this knowledge also pledges man for his part to execute מִשְׁפָּט, חֶסֶד and צְדָקָה is not so clearly brought out here as in Hos. 12:7 and Mi. 6:8, but it is the obvious implication of the closing words of v. 24, cf. Jer. 22:15. [19] In any case, the religious aspect of the term מִשְׁפָּט is emphasised by combining it with חֶסֶד and צְדָקָה.

Only in the light of this deeper meaning of מִשְׁפָּט can one understand the prophetic preaching of repentance. It is where the formulated מִשְׁפָּטִים are understood essentially in terms of the revelation of the will of Yahweh that the terrifying seriousness of the implied commitment emerges. For the implication is that man is set under the blessing and cursing of God, and this means that there is the possibility, or penalty, of an actual breach of the covenant when it is seriously considered, as in the Deuteronomic literature, that the מִשְׁפָּטִים can be fulfilled. The extension of the concept מִשְׁפָּט in the prophets, which breaks through the universally demonstrable limits of the מִשְׁפָּטִים, means in fact that the relationship between God and the people of God is seriously called in question. If the day of Yahweh had

---

[16] Though vv. 15 and 16 do not fit the context in their present position, they are probably from Is., since they agree materially with the depiction of judgment in c. 2.

[17] Read וּמִשְׁפָּטִי כָאוֹר BH.

[18] The common deletion of אֶת־רוּחַ יְהוָה is open to doubt on this ground. If we keep רוּחַ יהוה the religious aspect of מִשְׁפָּט is even plainer, cf. Is. 42:1.

[19] The masc. אֵלֶּה relates to those who have true knowledge of God. The LXX reads: ὅτι ἐν τούτοις τὸ θέλημά μου.

originally been envisaged as a day of victory over Israel's foes, the concept changes
in the presentation of Am. 1 and 2, and the day of Yahweh now becomes a day of
judgment on Israel, cf. Hos. 4:1 ff.; Is. 1:2, 18 ff.; Mi. 1:2-4; Zeph. 3:8; Jl. 3:2; Mal.
3:2. Indeed, the judgment on Israel stands at the very heart of the general judgment
on the nations. Israel's only privilege of election at the judgment is to be judged
with particular severity, Am. 3:1 ff.; Is. 5:1 ff. This outworking of election may be
discerned already in the judgments which have fallen on the people of God during
the course of its history. But the sentence will now become so much more severe
that only a remnant of the people will be delivered, and finally this concept, which
still remains within rational categories, will be set aside and the "remnant" will
simply be an ironical term for a non-existent quantity, Am. 3:12. [20] Precisely in
the judgment of the covenant people the Judge shows Himself to be the Lord and
King (→ βασιλεύς) of heaven and earth who summons every force against the
elect people. [21] Thus judgment will mean the dissolution of the covenant insofar
as there is in the existence of the covenant people no point of contact for its
restoration. If nevertheless the covenant remains, it can do so only in the form
of a completely new institution. But the possibility of such a new creation lies only
in the constant חֶסֶד and אֱמֶת of Yahweh. We have seen that Yahweh is characterised
by the combination of מִשְׁפָּט, חֶסֶד and צְדָקָה. This raises the following question. If
Yahweh's מִשְׁפָּט has brought about the dissolution of the covenant, will not a new
institution of the covenant on the basis of חֶסֶד contradict His מִשְׁפָּט and צְדָקָה? Or is
the content of מִשְׁפָּט and צְדָקָה so orientated that they can be subordinated materially
to חֶסֶד, because the activity implied in them serves the same end? [22]

5. The Change in Meaning of מִשְׁפָּט.

That מִשְׁפָּט can take on the sense of grace and mercy may be seen from a passage
like Is. 30:18 ff.: "Therefore Yahweh waits to be gracious to you, and exalts himself to be merciful to you; for Yahweh is a God of מִשְׁפָּט, salvation for all who
wait on him. Yes, you people in Zion ... he will certainly bless you." [23] To understand this change of meaning, it is essential to note that the salvation which is the
outworking of the מִשְׁפָּט of Yahweh is promised to a people that has become a
remnant like a lonely pole on the top of a mountain. Yahweh's מִשְׁפָּט is thus for
an afflicted people. But this relationship of judgment to the needy and oppressed
is something which can be seen from the very first, since it is materially implicit
that the Judge should execute justice for those who have no rights. [24] Yet a
distinctive development of this thought may also be discerned, for, applied to

---

[20] In spite of the corrupt conclusion, there can be no doubt that this is the drift of the
saying. E. Sellin (*Das Zwölfprophetenbuch*[2-3] [1929]) in his exposition misses the point of
comparison.

[21] Am. 9:2; cf. 5:3, 16 ff.; 7:1 ff.; 8:8 ff.; Hos. 5:12 ff.; 9:6; 10:14; 13:8, 14 ff.; Is. 3:1 ff.;
5:9 ff.; 8:5 ff.; 29:2 ff.; Mi. 3:12; Jer. 4:5 ff.; 7:30 ff.; 9:9 ff.; Ez. 5:7 ff.; 7:1 ff.

[22] In this connection it should be noted that חֶסֶד denotes action which is orientated to legal
thinking. Yet the fact remains that there is in the first instance a profound difference between
חֶסֶד and מִשְׁפָּט.

[23] The meaning of this saying and its contextual significance are contested. O. Procksch
(*Komm.* [1930], *ad loc.*) basis his exposition on the premise that Yahweh's saving action
cannot be grounded in the fact that Yahweh is a God of מִשְׁפָּט. But the prophet, or the one
who combined vv. 18 and 19, did not share this premise.

[24] Cf. Ex. 23:6; Dt. 24:17; 27:19; Ps. 25:9; 146:7; Job 36:6; Is. 10:2; Jer. 5:28.

widows and orphans in Dt. 10:18, the מִשְׁפָּט is given a theological turn; an אהב (v. 19) corresponds to the עָשָׂה מִשְׁפָּט. If Yahweh executes justice for the helpless and needy, this is not merely out of His righteousness; it is also out of His love and mercy. Because the judgment of Yahweh, which establishes the right, means humiliation for the uplifted and exaltation for the lowly, the term מִשְׁפָּט carries no fears for the poor and the oppressed. For them judgment means help and deliverance.

This helps us to understand Ez. 34:16, where it is said that Yahweh feeds the sheep בְּמִשְׁפָּט. If this means destruction for the strong, it means binding up and strengthening for the broken and the weak. An essential point, however, is that the verse refers to Israel. For with the Exile Israel, too, is numbered among the poor, the broken and the oppressed. Hence it can await from the Judge who has punished it the מִשְׁפָּט which is the protection and salvation of the weak, because מִשְׁפָּט is the legal claim which belongs to the poor and needy. Dt. 32:4 has in view the acknowledgment of this legal claim by Yahweh when it says: "All his ways are מִשְׁפָּט." But v. 36 shows that the poor do not regard the meeting of this claim by Yahweh merely as an exercise of His justice: "For Yahweh will execute judgment (יָדִין) for his people and have mercy on his servants," cf. Dt. 10:18; Is. 30:18 ff. The more strongly it is emphasised that Yahweh's judgment means help and deliverance (e.g., Ps. 76:9; 82:2 f.), the clearer is the change in meaning of מִשְׁפָּט from judgment to salvation. Especially in places where מִשְׁפָּט includes the divine act which means remission of sins for men (Ps. 25:6 ff.; 103:6 ff.), we can see that this saving judgment of God springs not merely from His righteousness but also from His mercy and grace. [25]

This seems to overthrow the legal content of מִשְׁפָּט. For forgiveness is in tension with justice as this is expressed in the doctrine of individual retribution (cf. Ez. 18). It also seems to call in question the basic tenet that the prosperity of the people and the individual is linked with observance of the מִשְׁפָּטִים of Yahweh. We can see from the prayer of Solomon in 1 K. 8, however, that there is no contradiction if the OT righteous puts his confidence both in the righteousness of God and also in His grace.

While vv. 58 f. relate the prosperity of the people to the keeping of the מִשְׁפָּטִים of Yahweh (cf. v. 61), we have in vv. 49, 50 the petitions: "Execute מִשְׁפָּט for them," and then: "Forgive them their sins which they have committed against thee, and all the transgressions which they have transgressed against thee, and let them find mercy." Here then, and not merely in the fact that prayer is made for מִשְׁפָּט, there is an obvious interrelating of מִשְׁפָּט with forgiveness and mercy.

It has been suggested already that fundamentally the theological use of legal terms presents a challenge to these terms. Yahweh's lordship, which is grounded in His omnipotence, resists the objectification attempted by the use of legal terminology. The answer which the author of Job gives to the question of the righteousness of God's judicial action is that one cannot speak of Yahweh's מִשְׁפָּט when man begins with his מִשְׁפָּט, but that the execution of justice by Yahweh is something which defies comprehension and which thus calls for submission and trust. Dt. Is. bears similar witness to the omnipotence of Yahweh, who has mercy on His people and judges the nations, in 40:14: "With whom took he counsel, and who instructed him and taught him בְּאֹרַח מִשְׁפָּט?" But it is hardly adequate to ground the blessing of the people and of righteous individuals on Yahweh's omnipotence. What

---

[25] Ps. 33:5; 48:10-12; 89:14; 101:1; 119:149.

makes Israel God's people is the fact that it has experienced more from Yahweh than omnipotence. The covenant which is worked out in the revelation of the מִשְׁפָּט of Yahweh is a demonstration of God's gracious action in delivering His people. The unity of justice and grace rests on this. Israel's מִשְׁפָּט is grounded in the conclusion of the covenant, i.e., in God's gracious act. For Yahweh remains true to His covenant. This consistency of His saving action can be called Yahweh's מִשְׁפָּט (Dt. 32:4; Ps. 105:5-9; Ps. 111), and it is only in the light of this experience of God's gracious saving action that the people of God can bear its witness that Yahweh is Lord and Judge of the world.

Yet the elect people is judged by Yahweh because of its sins. This fact is not removed by the further fact that in exile Israel regards itself as the broken and the weak which is in the right against its oppressor. For the people now ranged with the poor and oppressed knows that it is a thoroughly sinful people. Its sins are a wall between itself and its God. "Therefore is מִשְׁפָּט far from us, and צְדָקָה does not reach us; we wait for light and behold darkness ... we wait for מִשְׁפָּט and there is none. For many are our transgressions before thee, and our sin accuses us; for our transgressions are with us, and as for our faults, we know them," Is. 59:9 ff. This is true of the people within which the prophet is obviously quite aware of a distinction between צַדִּיקִים and רְשָׁעִים. But just as in the religion of the Psalms protestation of one's own innocence or uprightness does not in the very least exclude a prayer for deliverance and grace, [26] so the presence of righteous men among the people does not invalidate the statement that there is none righteous before God. If, especially after the commencement of the Exile, the distinction between צַדִּיקִים and רְשָׁעִים within the people necessarily led to an individualising of the thought of judgment, e.g., in the doctrine of individual retribution and the idea of purification, this form of expectation of the future was challenged by the recognition of the general sinfulness of men. The more clearly the sin of the people was seen, especially with the judgment of the Exile, the more the hope of the future had to look away from the state of the people or of individuals and base itself on the saving action of Yahweh, whose grace and faithfulness alone could actualise the establishment of the divine rule. Hence the מִשְׁפָּט of Yahweh revealed itself not merely in the upholding of the covenant of grace but also in the cancelling of sins by judgment or by grace. Eschatological preaching could not stop even at this thought, however, when judgement was regarded as a radical abolition of the covenant. Jer. had to proclaim the new covenant (c. 30, 31). The kingdom of God can come only because Yahweh Himself will grant מִשְׁפָּט and צְדָקָה to the people. With אֱמוּנָה, רַחֲמִים, חֶסֶד and דַּעַת יהוה, צֶדֶק and מִשְׁפָּט are the bridal gifts of Yahweh to the people in a new betrothal (Hos. 2:21 f.). [27] If the kingdom of the future can stand only because Yahweh Himself lays a new corner-stone in Zion, this includes the fact that He will make מִשְׁפָּט the line and צְדָקָה the plummet (Is. 28:17). מִשְׁפָּט and צְדָקָה are the means whereby the Messiah establishes the coming kingdom of peace (Is. 9:6 f.). Yahweh's Spirit rests on the future Ruler raised up by Him, and this means that He will judge the poor בְּצֶדֶק (Is. 11:1-5). Ez. promises that the people will keep the מִשְׁפָּטִים of Yahweh

---

[26] Ps. 99:4 ff.; 106:1 ff.; cf. 33; 89:14; 101:1; 111.

[27] These testimonies to the *iustitia salutifera* of Yahweh are in danger of reinterpretation when exposition is controlled by the presupposition that the prophets were preachers of what is called an ethical monotheism. If this were so, the moral renewal of the people would be the condition of the coming of salvation. It is of vital significance that this rational schema is already transcended by the OT message itself.

because the Lord will put His Spirit in their hearts and will Himself see to the observance of the commandments (Ez. 36:27; cf. 37:24). Again, according to the witness of Jer. the coming kingdom consists in the fact that the Messianic King exercises מִשְׁפָּט and צְדָקָה. Thus Yahweh's action will manifest itself as the righteousness of the people (23:5, 6). In Is. 1:27, too, the action of Yahweh, which means redemption for Zion and the converted, is called מִשְׁפָּט and צְדָקָה. In this connection it should be noted that here, too, the judgment of the wicked is the reverse side of the saving act of God which is described as מִשְׁפָּט (v. 28). But a causal succession of judgment and salvation, or one which is logically controlled by the idea of purificatory judgment, is completely ruled out when the only basis of the coming of the time of salvation is the grace of Yahweh which brings salvation. [28] At the very point, then, where the legal aspect of מִשְׁפָּט seems to have faded completely into the background, we can still see the tension which is created by the fact that the twofold sense of grace and judgment is present from the very first in the terms בְּרִית, מִשְׁפָּט and צְדָקָה.

6. מִשְׁפָּט in its Relation to the Nations.

If judging is part of the office of a ruler, the sphere of God's rule is also that of His judgment. This means that מִשְׁפָּט applies to the nations too. This is expressed with unique force by Ez., who in 5:6 ff. not only speaks of the מִשְׁפָּטִים of the Gentiles along with the מִשְׁפָּטִים of Yahweh, but who also assumes that the מִשְׁפָּטִים of the Gentiles are in some way related to Yahweh. Similarly, in 20:25 he traces back to Yahweh the false מִשְׁפָּטִים by which the Israelites cannot live. The suggestion is that all מִשְׁפָּטִים go back to Yahweh. With this we may compare the view of Is. 40:14 that מִשְׁפָּט is an expression of Yahweh's universal action. Judgment on the nations, which seems to be a fixed part of OT eschatology, is the negative side of this world dominion. [29]

Yet the term מִשְׁפָּט is also used when there is reference to the positive relations of Yahweh to other peoples. Here, too, one may see the change in meaning of מִשְׁפָּט. Thus in the first Servant Song in Is. 42:1-4 it is part of the task of the Ebed to bring מִשְׁפָּט to the nations. [30] To equip Him for this task Yahweh has laid His Spirit on Him. Hence the מִשְׁפָּט is from Yahweh Himself. If special emphasis is laid on this extension to the Gentiles, it is because מִשְׁפָּט was previously given to Israel alone. Through the office which the Ebed will execute לָאֱמֶת these limits are now transcended. The bringing of מִשְׁפָּט means salvation for the nations, and mercy for the oppressed. It is a gracious revelation of Yahweh's will — the revelation upon which the covenant with Israel was founded. Hence the extension of מִשְׁפָּט to the Gentiles is the extension of the covenant to the world. [31] מִשְׁפָּט is used similarly in

---

[28] The idea that the ref. is to a purificatory judgment in which sin is judged but the sinner is saved has been read into the text by Hertzberg, 67. Nor can we explain Is. 4:4 along these lines, for here מִשְׁפָּט has the simple sense of penal judgment.

[29] Cf. Am. 1:3-2:16; Is. 1:2; Jer. 1:14 ff.; 25:15 ff.; Mi. 1:2 ff.; Zeph. 3:8 ff.; Jl. 3:2 ff.; Mal. 3:2 ff.

[30] One might compare the use of מִשְׁפָּט here with the Arab. din, which has the sense of law and religion.

[31] The distinctive sense of מִשְׁפָּט is expressed here esp. in the fact that it is used abs. and yet the ref. is also to the bearing of מִשְׁפָּט to the nations, so that it has historical definition.

Is. 51:4. But here the task which the Ebed received in 42:1-4 is fulfilled by Yahweh Himself. He will cause His מִשְׁפָּט to shine as a light to the nations. If it is said in v. 5 that His arm will judge the peoples, the terms "light," "salvation" and "help" show that this is a judgment which brings salvation. The comprehensive significance of מִשְׁפָּט is shown especially in the fact that the prophet uses it in the absolute. מִשְׁפָּט is a comprehensive term for the revelation of God on which is grounded not merely the relationship of Yahweh to His chosen people but also His relationship to the nations.

Herntrich

C. The Concept of Judgment in the Greek World.

Where the gods are worshipped, they are commonly accepted as the guardians of right and custom, and therefore as the judges of men. This is true in popular Greek belief, [32] though we do not have sufficient knowledge of the development of the concept to say for certain when this belief first appeared. It was certainly not a dominant thought in Greek religion. In the early period the gods were far too like superior men with human passions. Nor was this true in poetry alone. Prior to the great age of Greece it was really thought that the divine or the gods were envious, that they did not grant too great good fortune to men, that they would use any manifestation of independence to destroy them. [33] Various means of placation could be used, e.g., sacrifices or votive offerings, to appease their wrath and to gain their favour (→ ἱλάσκομαι, 311, 313). Basically, they were the mere executors of a fate whose decisions did not follow any rule of justice. [34] But the best of the Greeks outgrew and consciously opposed these views. They believed that Zeus, the most divine of the Greek gods, ruled as judge and caused the right to triumph. This belief was fostered by the intellectual upper classes. It was often stated with great earnestness and maintained in spite of experiences to the contrary. [35] Dike, right, is the daughter of Zeus and shares his throne. [36]

The Greeks expect divine judgment in this life. It may take its toll first, or also, on children and grandchildren. [37] This life is its sphere. There is no expectation of a future judgment of the world. [38] The early period seems not to have any belief in a judgment after death. The pitiable lot of shades in the underworld is not a penalty allotted by a divine judge. It is the general fate of men. The account of the journey of Odysseus through Hades [39] tells of individual famous examples of human wickedness and of the penal righteousness of the gods which is to be seen in the underworld. [40] The Eleusinian mysteries give preference to devotees in the underworld. [41] But the Orphics are the first to proclaim a judgment which is held on all men in the underworld and which determines their fate. [42] They do this in

---

[32] Gruppe, II, 1000.

[33] *Loc. cit.*; Kern, II, 261. The idea of the envy of the gods is expressly repudiated from the time of Plato.

[34] Gruppe, II, 989 ff. On Nemesis, cf. Pauly-W., 16, 2 (1935), 2338 ff.

[35] Esp. by Hesiod and Aesch., cf. Kern, I, 281; II, 156.

[36] Cf. Pauly-W., 5 (1905), 574 f.

[37] Rohde, II[9-10], 228, n. 1.

[38] The ἐκπύρωσις of the Stoics is not a world judgment but a natural cosmic catastrophe which destroys all things.

[39] On others who journey through Hades cf. Rohde, I[9-10], 302.

[40] Hom. Od., 11, 576 ff. This passage is mostly regarded to-day as a later addition, though on not very convincing grounds.

[41] Hom. Hymn. Cer., 482 f.

[42] In Hom. Od., 11, 568 ff. Minos is not the judge who apportions to newcomers their fate but the umpire of the dead to whom they bring their legal matters.

connection with their doctrine of the divine nature of the soul and of its migration through various earthly existences. [43] Their judgment in the underworld is not a final retribution. It is the apportionment of a transitional stage between one earthly existence and the next. [44] Through them belief in a judgment on souls in the hereafter achieved great influence. [45] It was championed by men like Pindar [46] and Aeschylus [47] in whom the life of Greece came to its finest flower and who helped to give direction to the age which followed. Through Plato it became an established part of the philosophical tradition. [48] The deep seriousness of the ethical outlook of this tradition finds expression in it. On the basis of it Plato combatted the disintegrating trend of Sophism. [49] The belief thus proved also to have productive power. [50]

Where the enlightenment prevailed it destroyed belief in divine judgment. Zeus was ridiculed. His bolts did not strike perjurers but the tops of the mountains. The doctrine of all-seeing and all-hearing gods who punish wickedness was declared to be an invention of cunning statesmen. [51] The ancient belief in destiny returned in new garb. But the enlightenment did not overthrow belief in divine judgment after death. This persisted both among the people [52] and also among the philosophically educated. [53] It is part of the legacy of antiquity. [54]

---

[43] Cf. W. Stettner, *Die Seelenwanderung bei Griechen u. Römern* (1934); K. Hopf, *Antike Seelenwanderungsvorstellungen* (Diss. Leipzig, 1934).

[44] Rohde, II, 129; Kern, II, 162.

[45] On the Orphics (from c. 600 B.C.), cf. Kern, II, 147-173. That their origin was non-Greek (oriental) is only a conjecture. In any case the Gk. spirit was much enriched and deepened by them.

[46] Rohde[9-10], II, 204-222. Esp. Pind. Olymp., 2, 57-60. U. v. Wilamowitz-Moellendorff (*Pindaros* [1922], 243) sees in Olymp., 2, 57-60 the belief of Theron, for whom the poem is composed, not of Pindar, but this is hardly correct even though the passage is poetry, not teaching.

[47] Suppl., 220 ff.; Eum., 269 ff.; Rohde, II, 232.

[48] In Apol., 40c ff. Plato advances the view of a judgment of the dead with the proviso that death may be a complete end which is not followed by any new existence. Since the judges of the dead are contrasted with "these supposed judges," they judge what men have done in life (as against Rohde, I, 310, n. 1). In Gorg., 523a-527a Plato espouses the idea of a judgment after death with full conviction, 523a, 524a. Cf. also Resp., X, 614b-615d and Axiochus, 371a-372a. In the three passages he gives three different forms to the belief, deliberately borrowing from the Greek, the Armenian and the Persian traditions, so that the external aspects are obviously regarded as mythical. But Plato would not have used the myths if he had not believed in judgment after death.

[49] The incisive polemic against the Sophists in Gorg, involves belief in judgment. Though the mythical form serves to adorn the dialogue, the conviction represented is Plato's own, which here wrestles with the inconceivability of the hereafter.

[50] It is worth noting that there is no fear of not being able to stand in the last judgment. A feeling of moral integrity prevails.

[51] Critias in his Sisyphos (Fr., 25 [II, 320, 14 ff., Diels]).

[52] Rohde, II, 366 ff., 382.

[53] In part these adopt the belief and form of popular religion, though they seek to "purify" or rationalise it. In part they seek new forms. Belief in the divine justice may be seen in the belief in providence, for an ordered world is not unjustly ordered. But the concept of divine justice is sterner than that of a friendly providence. Belief in the judgment of the dead is crowded out by that in present rewards. Both arouse sceptical questions which give rise to great debates on religious questions, cf. Cicero. Plut., the Neo-Pythagoreans and the Neo-Platonists display a new faith.

[54] Deism did not regard judgment after death as one of the truths of natural religion, since it did not find this belief in ancient (i.e., non-Christian) tradition. With the rejection of life and judgment after death the estimation not only of Christianity but also of antiquity is incisively altered, as may be seen in Rohde and his disciples.

D. The Concept of Judgment in Judaism.

It is one of the cardinal articles of faith in Judaism that God judges, that He does not just let evil occur without resisting it, that He upholds with punishments and rewards His holy Law and its demands and prohibitions, that He enforces it irresistibly in face of those who despise it. This belief, whose roots go back to the very earliest days of Israelite religion, was inseparably related to the Law, and was transmitted with it. The Jew saw God's judgment in all the evils and deliverances that came on men, and he was prepared to trace back a particular misfortune to a particular sin on the part of the one concerned. But this did not always work out, so that it entangled the belief in all kinds of problems. The surest form of belief in divine judgment was thus the expectation, early represented in Israel, of a future judgment on the world. This expectation related to sinners in the Jewish community and to Gentiles who enslaved the Jews. To this degree the Jew looked forward with hope and joy to the judgment which would bring redemption to Israel. Yet the final judgment could also apply to the individual Jew, for none could say whether God reckoned him among the sinners or the righteous.

This question was particularly difficult for the Pharisees, for they believed in a resurrection of the dead when men would stand before God's judgment even if it did not affect them in this life. [55] For this reason the unwearying concern of Pharisaic religion was to stand in the judgment, i.e., to achieve merits which would outweigh sins, → ἀποδίδωμι, μισθός. But the Pharisee found it hard to achieve any certainty in the matter. He tended to vacillate between an arrogant confidence in his good works, which blinded him to his sinfulness, [56] and a hopeless fear of God's wrath, though this is more rarely expressed. [57] His service of God was a struggle with a problem which was both unsolved and finally insoluble, so that his whole life was marked by strain. In the last resort, his religion was not the force which sustained his life; it was the open wound from which he suffered. To be sure, he sought forgiveness, and even counted on it. But he could have little assurance. The Messiah tended to be regarded, not as his Helper against sin, but as the Executor of divine judgment (Ps. Sol. 17, 18).

On the details of judgment, and especially on the relation between the general final judgment and that which each man undergoes immediately on death, the widest possible variety of views is to be found. [58] It is not possible to expound these in the present context, nor can we pursue the question of the historical origin of these views. [59]

---

[55] Belief in divine judgment was very much weaker among the Sadducees (Joseph. Bell., 2, 164; Ant., 13, 173); they rejected a judgment after death.

[56] Cf. Lk. 18:9-14.

[57] Cf. the moving story of the last days of Jochanan b. Zakkai, who died in inconsolable fear of God's judgment and attained to no assurance of salvation, bBer., 28b (Schlatter, "Jochanan b. Zakkai," BFTh, 3, 4 [1899], 72 ff.). Cf. also the hopeless lamenting of human sinfulness in 4 Esr. 3-4; 7-8. → ἐλπίς, II, 527.

[58] Cf. Volz, 256-309.

[59] Joseph.'s views of the divine judging and the last judgment are Pharisaic, although in Hellenistic garb, cf. Schlatter, Theol. d. Jdt., 38-45, 259-263. Philo believes in divine judgement, though eschatologically the national and cosmic aspects are less prominent than the individual, cf. Volz, 59-62.

E. The Concept of Judgment in the New Testament.

1. The Baptist. The preaching of the Baptist displays a more urgent expectation of judgment. The final judgment of God or His Christ is directly imminent, Mt. 3:10. No one is safe against it, Mt. 3:7-9. The only salvation is to repent, to confess one's sins in baptism, and to bring forth the righteous fruits of repentance. Then baptism effects remission. Then Christ the Judge becomes the Saviour.

2. The Synoptic Preaching of Jesus. Here the thought of judgment is central. Jesus' call to repentance is urgent because God's judgment hangs over every man. The task of Jesus is continually to impress on men the seriousness of this judgment and to awaken fear of the Judge, [60] cf. the Sermon on the Mount, Mt. 5:22, 26, 29 f.; 7:1 f., 21-23, 24-27, the address to the disciples, Mt. 10:28, 33, the parables of the kingdom, Mt. 13:30, 47-50, the parables of the return, Mt. 24:50, 51; 25:11 f., 30, 41-46, and the debates with the people, Mt. 11:20-24; 12:41 f.; 21:40 f.; 22:7; 23:38 and the Pharisees, Mt. 12:32; 23:13-35. The merits with which a man might seek to protect himself in the judgment are of no avail, Lk. 17:7-10. Nor are the vicarious merits of others, the patriarchs or other saints. It is constantly insisted that God is the Lord and that man is responsible, so that no human defences will be of any value in the judgment. The standard by which God judges is known ; it is the Law, i.e., the law of love. [61] With the details Jesus is not concerned. [62] It makes no odds whether the judgment will be by God, Mt. 10:32 f., or by Jesus, Mt. 7:22 f.; 16:27; 25:31-46; 26:64. [63] It does not even make any material difference whether those judged are Jews or Gentiles, Mt. 25:32. The only ground of deliverance in the judgment is God's remission, not man's achievement. But the believer may have assurance of this forgiveness. The divine forgiveness is wholly grace and miracle. But Jesus promises it to man (Mk. 2:9) notwithstanding the severity of his guilt, Lk. 7:36-50; Mt. 18:21-35; 21:31 f. He promises His disciples that He will confess them before the divine Judge and that He will thus assure them against condemnation, Mt. 10:32. Hence the last judgment will mean their deliverance, and they can look forward to it with longing, the more so as their discipleship entails persecutions, Lk. 21:28, cf. 18:6-8. The coming of the kingdom of God, or the last judgement, is the object of daily petition, Mt. 6:10. The forgiveness by which Jesus lifts men out from judgment and from the fear of it may be enjoyed only in personal fellowship with Him. It is not an actual possession. Hence there must be prayer

---

[60] It is in keeping that Jesus expressly recognises the validity of the Law (the law of love), Mt. 5:17 ff. To miss either the one aspect or the other in the Synoptic portrayal of Jesus is to cause serious distortion.

[61] Not, then, a sum of detailed commands and prohibitions. The relation to Jesus is finally decisive (Mt. 10:32 f.) only because Jesus proclaims the Law in its purity and embodies its fulfilment, so that any act of kindness to someone in need is an act of kindness to Him, Mt. 25:40. Cf. Kähler, 572, 23 ff.

[62] Jesus regards the judgment of God as a reality of the conscience, i.e., as something which is unconditionally accepted by those who are aware of moral responsibility even though the details of the when and the where and the how cannot be imagined, let alone expressed. Hence it is completely beside the point to argue that divine judgment is inconceivable, or to draw attention to the mythical character of all pictures of the last judgment, even that of Mt. 25:31-46. On the idea of the fire of judgment, which derives from the OT and is widely present in the NT, → πῦρ.

[63] The Word of Jesus always decides concerning man, whether He is thought of as Judge or as the Judge's Assessor. "Nothing and no one in the world of men comes to his end without his fate being decided by the person of Christ," Kähler, 570, 45 ff.

for it every day, Mt. 6:12. There must also be a new readiness to show mercy to others, Mt. 6:14; 18:21-35. In the preaching of Jesus reception of forgiveness from God and granting of forgiveness to one's brother are inseparably connected. Without the latter God's judgment reassumes its full validity. This does not mean, however, that the divine forgiveness effected by Jesus is only provisional, conditional, or experimental. For the pitilessness by which it may be forfeited is meaningless and nonsensical. Indeed, it is quite impossible for those who have been truly seized by God's forgiveness.

The preaching of Jesus about judgment comes to a head in His self-witness "I am he" (Mk. 14:62). The fact that the Preacher is also the Judge at the last judgment gives to His preaching a supreme impressiveness and urgency for those who hear it. As the Word of Him who passes eternal judgment it decides concerning man not merely in terms of the present but in terms of eternity. If this were merely the word of a last prophet before the judgment, it would be only a provisional Word of God, and it would have to be confirmed by Jesus as the Judge at the last judgment, as the word of the Baptist had to be and was confirmed by Jesus as the Judge at the last judgment, Mt. 11:7-19. And until it received this confirmation, i.e., so long as it was still read and heard by men in this life, there could be no certainty that it was the Word of God which would decide the eternal destiny of the hearer. When the Messiahship of Jesus is contested, His Word is robbed of its true relevance and therewith of its constructive historical power. [64]

The preaching of Jesus plumbs the very depths of the concept of judgment. By comparison, the Jewish understanding lacks true cogency because it lacks final clarity. This is particularly so because Judaism still leaves man with the hope that he can counterbalance his sins by merits, so that he does not have to admit his utter sin and guilt before God, and is not wholly cast back upon grace.

On the other side, however, Jesus gives real liberation from the divine judgement, since He brings the divine forgiveness from heaven to earth, Mk. 2:10. In Him the majesty of the divine judgment and the divine forgiveness is unreservedly vindicated, whereas in Judaism man still tries to vindicate himself with his achievements, and for this reason does not attain to freedom before the judgment of God. The problem which in Judaism is unsolved and insoluble is here solved, and religion thus becomes in truth the sustaining force of life. The Jews found it difficult to understand the forgiveness of Jesus. They could only reject as blasphemy the liberation before God's judgment which Jesus imparted, Mk. 2:7. They could only resist and destroy Jesus. [65] His death, then, was a condition on which His people received from Him liberation before God's judgment (→ λύτρον). This is not just a later assertion of the community. For all who are prepared to take His work as

---

[64] The Sermon on the Mount in Mt. brings out the significance of the Preacher by portraying Him as the Judge at the last judgment in the concluding parables, 7:22 f. It is only because He is this that due weight can be attached to His exposition of the Law, His criticism of the Pharisees, and His beatitudes. This is not just the Word of God spoken by one to whom 1 Cor. 13:10-12 might apply ; it is the Word of God spoken by the One to whom Mt. 24:35 applies. If we deprive the Word of Jesus of its Messianic character, we can no longer understand either His Word or the results of His work, His death, and the faith of the community in Him. Cf. R. Bultmann, *Jesus* (1926), 29 f.; *Erforsch. d. synpt. Ev.* (1925), 34; *Glauben u. Verstehen* (1933), 203.

[65] So alien was the fellowship with God which Jesus mediated to His disciples. It answered a question posed by Judaism, but not along acceptable lines.

it was, it belongs to the historical actuality of His forgiveness. His death is part of the total achievement by which He overcame the problem of Judaism and gave man peace with His Creator and Judge. Nothing can be deducted from this.

Understanding of the preaching and person of Jesus depends absolutely on understanding of His concept of judgment. If there is no judgment of God as Jesus bears witness, then Jesus and His preaching can have only a constantly diminishing historical significance. They can have no bearing on man's relation with God. Conversely, if there is such a judgment, man's life is hopeless and intolerable without the declaration of Jesus : Thy sins are forgiven thee. [66]

3. Paul. The preaching of Paul is dominated by expectation of the day of wrath and of the righteous judgment of God, who repays all men according to their works, R. 2:1-11. Works here are expressions of the personal attitude of a man. They are not independent externalities. For the Judge is the omniscient God who sees man through and through. All men without exception must come before God's judgment, including Christians, 2 C. 5:10. The suggestion that this concept of judgement is purely dialectical, applying only in controversy with the Jews, [67] is without foundation, for Christians themselves are to be judged, 2 C. 5:10. The concept has axiomatic significance, R. 3:6. As Paul views the wrath of God as a reality already revealed, R. 1:18 ff., for him God's κατάκριμα rests on the race from the time of Adam's sin, R. 5:16, 18, 19. The goodness and patience of God leave man time for repentance, R. 2:4. The final decision is still future. For this reason the question of justification is the main question of human life. It is answered by God's reconciling grace → καταλλάσσω, ἱλαστήριον. Paul is sure that believers will be saved in the last judgment, R. 8:31-39. This applies even to the incestuous man, 1 C. 5:5. Believers are justified. But he does not ground this confidence on the moral renewal which is associated with justification or which follows on possession of the Spirit. He grounds it on Christ alone, R. 5:9, 10; 8:33 f. For this reason He can expect salvation even for those whose work will not stand in the last judgment, 1 C. 3:15. [68]

4. John. In the Epistles and Gospel of John expectation of the day of judgment, 1 Jn. 4:17, when all the dead shall rise, Jn. 5:28 f., is a constant presupposition. Disciples as well as Jews are threatened with this judgment by Jesus Himself, Jn. 15:6. In all its range judgment is committed to the Son, 5:22, 27. In His historical life Jesus has come to save, not to judge, 3:17; 8:15; 12:47. But He cannot avoid judging, 8:16. In the last day His Word will judge, 12:48. Judgment has taken place already on those who do not believe, 3:18, 19. Along the same lines it can be said of believers that they will not come into judgment, but have passed already from death to life, Jn. 5:24; cf. 1 Jn. 3:14. They can thus have confidence in the judgment

---

[66] The question whether Jesus taught an individual judgment immediately after death, Lk. 23:43; 16:23, or whether He expected judgment only in the context of the general resurrection and His own coming, is quite irrelevant for those who accept His teaching as it was meant (→ ἄδης, → γέεννα, → παράδεισος).

[67] A. Ritschl, Rechtfertigung u. Versöhnung, II (1900), 319.

[68] Hence the doctrine of judgment by works is not opposed to that of justification by faith, nor is it a remnant of Judaism to which Paul clings. The doctrine of judgment by works is the constant presupposition of the doctrine of justification by faith. Without it, the latter loses its seriousness and depth. Self-evidently, the doctrine of justification apart from works cancels the thought of judgment by works, but only in such a way as to include its permanent validity, not in such a way as to rule it out as error and falsehood cf. F. Büchsel, Theol. d. NT (1935), 122 ff.

day, 1 Jn. 4:17, cf. 2:28; 3:21. Similarly, judgment has already been passed on the world, 12:31. Its ruler, the devil, is judged, 12:31; 16:11. This judgment took place in the hour when the Son of God resolved to sacrifice Himself to the glory of the Father, and God promised to glorify Him, 12:27-31. The distinctive feature of John's thinking on judgment, even by comparison with Paul, is to be found in this emphasis on the fact that on both sides judgment is already present. It expresses the certainty and definitiveness to which the faith of Jn. had attained. Before the revelation of God in His Son, which has supratemporal validity, the distinction between future and present fades. The eternal is present in time. [69]

5. Revelation. The Revelation of John gives a terrifying picture of judgment, 20:11-15, and also brings serious warnings to the community, 2:5, 16, 22 f.; 3:3, 16. Christ is the Judge of all. Here, too, one perceives the central significance of the concept of judgment for the NT.

6. Peter and Hebrews. 1 Pt. contains an impressive appeal for fear of God as the Judge, 2:17; 1:17. It emphasises that judgment must begin in the house of God, i.e., the community, 4:17. Hb. has an express warning against taking too lightly the judgment of God (10:26-31) which falls specifically on the people of God. It brings out sharply the fact that one can do God true service only with fear (μετὰ εὐλαβείας καὶ δέους, 12:28). For our God, too, is a consuming fire, 12:29.

7. Human Judgment. From the fact that God's judgment threatens man it is often deduced that no man has the right to judge another, Mt. 7:1 f.; Jm. 4:11; R. 14:4, 10; 1 C. 4:5. This does not imply flabby indifference to the moral condition of others nor the blind renunciation of attempts at a true and serious appraisal of those with whom we have to live. What is unconditionally demanded is that such evaluations should be subject to the certainty that God's judgment falls also on those who judge, so that superiority, hardness and blindness to one's own faults are excluded, and a readiness to forgive and to intercede is safeguarded. The emphatic way in which Jesus extended the law of love in this direction has far-reaching consequences. It means that the Church cannot practice discipline with merciless severity (2 C. 11:24). It means that the Church cannot take up a hard, contemptuous and supercilious attitude towards those whom it regards as sinners. It means that Church discipline must make predominant, if not exclusive, use of means which promote edification and pastoral care. Precisely the unreserved

---

[69] This does not imply a depreciation of the temporal. On the contrary, it is given supreme significance. The Word and work of Jesus, and the relation of man to Him, which are all events in time, decide man's eternal destiny. There is no justification for the view that the references to "judgment on the last day, 5:28, 29; 12:48," are an "accommodation to the popular conception" (Bau. Jn. on 3:18). Since it is not apparent to the world (1 Jn. 3:2) that unbelievers are already judged and that believers have already passed from death to life, there is need of a final judgment to make this clear. Judgment and the possession of life are not just a private affair between God and individuals. They are a public affair between individuals and those around. In this connection an exact parallel to the idea of the last judgment is to be found in that of the resurrection. Those who have life now still need a future resurrection, 5:24-29; 6:40, 44, 54, since death wipes out any distinction between them and others. The one is as little an accommodation to the popular conception as the other. To take this view is to import an alien element into Jn.'s depiction. The early Christian idea of the last judgment and of resurrection on the last day are the basis on which Jn. builds his own distinctive doctrine that the last judgment and the resurrection have occurred already.

seriousness with which the community takes the concept of judgment in the Gospel is that which enables it to overcome a mere legalism in its religious and moral life.

8. Conclusion. Understanding of the NT concept of judgment is confronted to-day by a rationalistic criticism which rejects the concept as mythical and un-ethical. In face of this we must stress the fact that in the NT judgment is not capricious or emotional, as so often in myths of judgment. It is an inwardly necessary consequence of the sin of man. All human acts are a sowing; God's judgment is the related and self-evident reaping, Gl. 6:7, 8. God's judgment is the inevitable repayment of what man does, R. 1:27. Before the judgment throne of God man is rewarded according to his work, 2 C. 5:10. There is an organic connection between the human act and its consequence in the divine judgment. That this connection is established by God's act means that it is not accidental. For the God of the NT is holy and righteous in His judgment. If what He does transcends man's understanding, He is no less worthy of our adoration, R. 11:33-36. The wrath in which He judges is holy. It is no mere passion (→ ὀργή). God's will for man, or, to put it in ethical terms, the moral order, is not just an order of demand; it is also an order of being. For God is not just the moral Legislator. He is also the Creator and Ruler of the world, without whom not even the most insignificant detail in the life of the world or of men takes place, Mt. 20:29-31, without whom there is no weal or woe in human life, R. 1:18-32. His demand upon man is simply that which is planned with the existence of man. It is that which underlies man's existence. Hence it ineluctably decides man's fate. On its fulfilment depends the rightness or wrongness of what man makes of his existence. Either the ordered nature of his existence, its integration into the totality of being, on the one side, or on the other the disordered nature of his existence, its friction with the existence of others, will be the unavoidable consequence of his obedience or disobedience to the divine requirement which is a constituent part of God's holy order in the world of His creating. Disobedience to God's order inevitably means the restriction of life, and finally death, R. 6:23. It entails the expulsion of man from the world, the house of God, Jn. 8:34, 35. Death is ultimately eternal. It is the exclusion of man from the renewing of his life to eternal abiding in the house of the Lord; as such it will prove to be permanent. Those who truly think in moral terms and not just naturalistic, those who see in the doing of good and the overcoming of bad, not just an incidental aspect, but the true content of human existence, cannot escape the truth of the NT witness to the divine judgment. It is a mistake to assume that the NT sets the judgment of God only in an unknown and mythical hereafter. Judgment begins in this life; it is simply consummated in the next. This is made perfectly clear by, e.g., the relationship between R. 1:18-32 and 2:3-10. The restriction of life which man knows already in virtue of God's judgment, and which is a first instalment of death, is not to be located primarily in the sphere of external life and its possessions. Its chief operation is in the sphere of the inward life, in the process of blinding and constriction whch leads to hollowness and self-seeking, as portrayed by Jesus in Lk. 16:19-31; 18:10-12; 12:16-20, or in the process of impoverishment and unsettlement of one's own life, as portrayed by Paul in R. 1:21-32. If the moral law is made a mere order of demand, existence is deprived of its true meaning. It is therewith depreciated, and the inevitable result is a purely negative relation between moral man and the existence which he has and which is around him. But the connection between the order of demand and the order of being is to be found in God alone, and so long as God is not regarded as absolutely holy and righteous, as in the NT, it might appear derogatory for

the man who is conscious of his moral worth to stand under the judgment of God. The plastic imagery associated with the divine judgment in the NT, the judgment throne, the right hand and the left, the fire, worm or darkness as penalty, are all traditional and non-essential. They do not justify us in speaking of a judgment myth. If it is argued that the NT witness to divine judgment involves a clouding of moral motives, the fault lies, not with the NT, but with the one who argues this way, since he is not taking the NT witness with sufficient seriousness. For what the NT tells us is that God's judgment is on the hypocrisy and outward piety which is acting only for the sake of external reward, Mt. 6:1-18; Mk. 7:6 etc. God's judgment lays bare the hidden essence of man, R. 2:16; 1 C. 4:5, 6; Rev. 2:23 etc. He who does good only for fear of the judgment has not attained to fulfilment of the first commandment, that he should love God with all his heart, Mk. 12:29 f. If the NT witness seeks to rouse man from his indifference and slackness with its reference to the divine judgment, it is in order that he should consider his duty to do the good as such, i.e., out of love for his Creator.

The concept of judgment cannot be taken out of the NT Gospel. It cannot even be removed from the centre to the periphery. Proclamation of the love of God always presupposes that all men are moving towards God's judgment and are hopelessly exposed to it. For this reason mysticism and the Enlightenment, which either set aside or restrict the thought of divine judgment, are directly opposed to the NT Gospel.

κρίσις.

Like other words formed from verbal stems with the suffix -σις, κρίσις denotes the action expressed by the verbal stem. It is much used outside the OT and NT, and in accordance with the meaning of κρίνειν it bears the sense a. "parting," "estrangement," "conflict," Hdt., V, 5; VII, 26, par. with ἔρις, Plat. Resp., II, 379e; b. "selection"; c. "decision of an umpire or judge," "judgment," Thuc., I, 131, 2; also "verdict" or "sentence," Xenoph. An., I, 6, 5; even "accusation," Lyc., 31; d. "decision in a battle," Thuc., I, 23, 1, or in an illness. [1]

1. In the NT it is the "decision of the judge," the "judgment." This may be either divine or human, and it is mostly penal judgment. The word is rare in Pl. but common in Jn. and the Catholic Epistles. [2]

2. In Jn. κρίσις is the world judgment of Christ, originally future, 5:28 f. and 1 Jn. 4:17, but also present already, 3:18-21; 5:24 f., 30; 12:31; 16:11, → 938. The sense of decision or separation is hinted at here. But this does not mean that for Jn. κρίσις is not judgment. World judgment always entails separation, cf. Mt. 25:31-46, esp. v. 32: ἀφορίσει αὐτοὺς ἀπ' ἀλλήλων.

3. The LXX uses κρίσις frequently, mostly for מִשְׁפָּט (→ 942; 923). It carries the sense of the right, especially the right of the oppressed which is vindicated by the

---

κρίσις. [1] For further examples v. Liddell-Scott, s.v.

[2] Jud. 9: Μιχαὴλ ... οὐκ ἐτόλμησεν κρίσιν ἐπενεγκεῖν βλασφημίας and 2 Pt. 2:11: ἄγγελοι ... οὐ φέρουσιν κατ' αὐτῶν παρὰ κυρίῳ βλάσφημον κρίσιν, use κρίσις in the sense of condemnation. Michael or the angels dare not undertake the judgment which condemns Satan or the δόξαι. Self-evidently this would take place, but κρίσις is not for this reason to be translated "verdict." In 2 Pt. 2:11 the παρὰ κυρίῳ makes the conception clear. The witness who proves guilt before the judge brings condemnation on the guilty, cf. Mt. 12:27, 41 → κριτής, n. 4. With this agree best the verbs ἐπενεγκεῖν, φέρειν, which are used in Jn. 18:29; Ac. 25:18 for accusing and in 2 Pt. 1:17 for bearing witness. κρίσις βλασφημίας, gen. qual., cf. βλάσφημον κρίσιν.

Judge. κρίσις is thus parallel to ἔλεος in ψ 100(101):1: ἔλεος καὶ κρίσιν ᾄσομαι, to ἐλεημοσύνη in ψ 32(33):5: ἀγαπᾷ ἐλεημοσύνην καὶ κρίσιν, to ἀλήθεια in ψ 110(111):7: ἔργα χειρῶν αὐτοῦ ἀλήθεια καὶ κρίσις. This LXX usage helps us to understand that of the NT at Mt. 23:23: ἀφήκατε τὰ βαρύτερα τοῦ νόμου, τὴν κρίσιν καὶ τὸ ἔλεος καὶ τὴν πίστιν, and Lk. 11:42: παρέρχεσθε τὴν κρίσιν καὶ τὴν ἀγάπην τοῦ θεοῦ. In both cases the reproach against the Pharisees is, not that they neglect judgment, but that they are indifferent to the right of the poor. In the quotations of Is. 42:1-4 at Mt. 12:18-21 and Is. 53:7 f. at Ac. 8:32 f. κρίσις is again used for מִשְׁפָּט in this sense.

κρίμα.

Originally κρεῖμα, Hellenistically κρίμα,[1] this word means the "decision" of the judge, a. as an action, Jn. 9:39; Ac. 24:25; R. 11:33; 1 C. 11:29, 34; Hb. 6:2; 1 Pt. 4:17; 2 Pt. 2:3; Rev. 20:4, b. as the result of the action, the sentence, as in most of the other NT passages apart from 1 C. 6:7; Rev. 18:20.[2] Usually the decision is unfavourable, and it thus bears the sense of condemnation. It may be used of human as well as divine judgment. Distinctive expressions are κρίμα λαμβάνειν, Mk. 12:40 and par. (Mt. 23:14); Lk. 20:47; Jm. 3:1; R. 13:2; κρίμα βαστάζειν, Gl. 5:10; κρίμα ἔχειν, 1 Tm. 5:12; ἐμπίπτειν εἰς κρίμα, 1 Tm. 3:6;[3] ἐν τῷ κρίματι εἶναι, Lk. 23:40;[4] in all these κρίμα is penal judgment → a.[5] In 1 C. 6:7: κρίματα ἔχετε μεθ' ἑαυτῶν, κρίμα bears the sense of a legal action or process; though there are no other known instances of this usage,[6] it arises naturally from b. Rev. 18:20 rests on LXX usage: ἔκρινεν ὁ θεὸς τὸ κρίμα ὑμῶν ἐξ αὐτῆς, "he has fulfilled your legal claim on her by his judgment." The LXX normally uses κρίμα for מִשְׁפָּט. It can thus have the sense of judicial decision. But it can also mean the right which someone has, namely, the oppressed.[7] Hence it is linked with δικαιοσύνη, ἔλεος, ἐλεημοσύνη. In dependence on κρίνειν it occurs in κρίμα δίκαιον (εἰρηνικὸν) κρίνατε, Zech. 7:9; 8:16; cf. Jer. 21:12; τὰ κρίματά μου κρινοῦσιν, Ez. 44:24; τὰ βραχέα τῶν κριμάτων κρινοῦσιν αὐτοί, Ex. 18:22; κρίνων καὶ ἐκζητῶν κρίμα, Is. 16:5; κρινεῖ ἡ συναγωγὴ ... κατὰ τὰ κρίματα ταῦτα, Nu. 35:24. There is no full parallel to Rev. 18:20 in the LXX.

† κριτής.

In the NT this is mostly used of the judge.[1] It denotes the human judge as an official person in Mt. 5:25 (Lk. 12:58); Lk. 18:2, 6;[2] Ac. 18:15; 24:10, and the man

κρίμα. [1] Cf. Bl.-Debr. § 13; 109, 3.

[2] It is impossible to distinguish sharply between the two senses.

[3] The διάβολος here is the human blasphemer, cf. v. 7, not the devil (→ II, 81).

[4] To this corresponds τὸ κρίμα τῆς πόρνης in Rev. 17:1, the only case with the obj. gen. in the NT. This obj. gen. has nothing to do with LXX usage, → n. 7.

[5] Materially κρίμα has in these expressions the sense of punishment, though it is strictly the vedict or sentence which brings on the punishment. Cf. Lk. 24:20: παρέδωκαν αὐτὸν ... εἰς κρίμα θανάτου.

[6] Though this sense is not found, κρίματα comes close to it at Ex. 18:22.

[7] Ex. 23:6; Job 13:18; 19:7; 31:13; 32:9 etc.

κριτής. Cr.-Kö., Pr.-Bauer, s.v.

[1] In true Attic and Ionic κριτής is only the umpire, not the penal judge (δικαστής). It becomes synon. with δικαστής from the time of Aesch. and Soph., E. Fraenkel, "Gesch. d. gr. nomina agentis ...," II, Untersuch. z. indogerm. Sprach- u. Kulturwissenschaft, 4 (1912), 32 f. δικαστής is found in the NT only at Ac. 7:27, 35 in dependence on LXX Ex. 2:14. κριτήν should be read at Lk. 12:14, not δικαστήν. There is no material distinction

who engages in judicial activity without being called thereto, Jm. 2:4; [3] 4:11. It can also denote the one through whom the wrong of another is manifested, Mt. 12:27 (Lk. 11:19). [4] OT judges are called κριταί in Ac. 13:20. [5] κριτής is used of God in 2 Tm. 4:8; Hb. 12:23; Jm. 4:12; 5:9, and of Jesus as Messiah in Ac. 10:42. [6]

† κριτήριον.

The adjective κριτήριος, which is formed from κριτήρ (= κριτής) as σωτήριος is from σωτήρ or ἱλαστήριος from ἱλαστής, [1] does not occur as such, [2] but only in the neuter as a noun. It denotes either the means of judging, i.e., the mark or criterion or proof-stone, [2] or the place of judgment, the court, [3] or judgment as the sum total of those who judge, [3] Jm. 2:6. [4] At 1 C. 6:2, 4 the only possible sense is "legal process." [5]

† κριτικός.

This is an adjectival construction from κριτής (or κριτός) and has the sense of one who has the manner of a judge, who is capable of judging, who has the right to judge, who is engaged in judging. It is also used with reference to judgment in general, especially literary judgment. [1] In Hb. 4:12 it is a predicate of the Word of God, which is able to judge the intents and thoughts of the heart. [2]

† ἀνακρίνω, † ἀνάκρισις.

This word means "to investigate," [1] and is used of judicial investigation, especially prior to the hearing proper. [2] It is rare in the LXX and in the NT is found only in Lk. and Pl. It refers mostly to the judicial interrogation of the accused, Lk. 23:14; Ac. 4:9; 12:19; 24:8; 28:18; 25:26 (ἀνάκρισις). It is also used of a

---

between the terms. δικαστής is generally less common. A. Schlatter, "Wie sprach Josephus von Gott?", BFTh, 14, 1 (1910), 56 attempts to make a distinction as regards Joseph.: κριτής has in view "the valid decision which is a norm for further conduct," whereas δικαστής suggests the protection of existing law by sentence and punishment. But this will hardly do.

[2] κριτής τῆς ἀδικίας is gen. qual., Bl.-Debr. § 165 (cf. ὁ μαμωνᾶς τῆς ἀδικίας, Lk. 16:19 = ὁ ἄδικος μαμωνᾶς, 16:11). The construction is thus Semitic.

[3] διαλογισμῶν πονηρῶν, gen. qual.: judges directed by evil thoughts.

[4] The expression is Jewish. The witness judges the accused if the latter is convicted on his witness. Cf. κατακρινοῦσιν in Mt. 12:41, and on this Str.-B., I, 650 and Schl. Mt., 418, ad loc.

[5] So also in the LXX, which seldom uses → κρίνω.

[6] The formula ζῶντας καὶ νεκρούς is ancient, cf. R. 14:9; it is found as an obj. of κρίνειν at 2 Tm. 4:1; 1 Pt. 4:5. It is of Jewish origin.

κ ρ ι τ ή ρ ι ο ν. [1] On the meaning of -τήριον cf. P. Chantraine, "La formation des noms en grec ancien," Collection Linguistique, 38 (1933), 62 ff.

[2] Cf. Liddell-Scott, s.v. The sense "court" in first found in the later Plato, cf. E. Fraenkel, op. cit. (→ κριτής, n. 1).

[3] So usually in the LXX and already in Plat. Leg., VI, 767b.

[4] ἕλκειν εἰς τὸ κριτήριον seems to be a current expression, cf. P. Tor., I, No. 1, p. 6, 11 (117 B.C.): ἑλκυσθέντων ἁπάντων εἰς τὸ κριτήριον.

[5] Cf. κρίμα in v. 7, and → 942. In Diod. S., I, 72, 4: προετίθεσαν (the priests) κατὰ νόμον τῷ τετελευτηκότι (the Egyptian king) κριτήριον τῶν ἐν τῷ βίῳ πραχθέντων, κριτήριον can only have the sense of judgment as a process. Cf. the description which follows in § 5.

κ ρ ι τ ι κ ό ς. [1] Cf. Liddell-Scott, s.v., P. Chantraine, op. cit., 385 ff.

[2] Cf. Rgg., Wnd. Hb., ad loc.

quasi-judicial investigation which the arrogant in Corinth mount against Paul, 1 C. 4:3 (opp. in 4:4: the true ἀνακρίνειν of the κύριος); 9:3; parallel with ἐλέγχειν, 1 C. 14:24; in a more general sense "to enquire into," 1 C. 10:25, 27; of the searching of the Scriptures by the Jews in Berea, Ac. 17:11; of the power of discrimination, and the superiority, of the πνευματικός, 1 C. 2:14 f. In the last reference there is a hint of judicial investigation, which is also judgment or appraisal, in respect of the things touched on by Paul in 4:3; 9:3. The extreme boldness of this statement is justified and explained in v. 16. The spiritual man is so united to Christ that his thinking is the thinking of Christ. Hence it is false to imagine that claims to this pneumatic awareness might disrupt the congregation. The man thus bound to Christ is a member of Christ's body, 1 C. 12:12-27. He is vitally linked to the congregation. On the other hand, he is subject only to the Lord, not to majority decisions or to other individuals, R. 14:4. For other Christians he is thus the servant of another. It was along these lines that Paul dealt with his churches and with the original apostles. To the degree that life from Christ was present in his churches, his desire was to be, not an authority, but a helper of their joy, 2 C. 1:24. He did not betray the imperiousness which "seeks with all its powers to enforce its own experience as a norm on others." [3] He wanted all to live according to their own consciences, R. 14 f. But where his congregations lived according to the flesh, 1 C. 3:3, he did not spare to correct them, 2 C. 12:19-13:10. For Paul the congregation is united only through Christ. Its common life derives from common union with Him, not from the common ties between believers. The community is not a pneumatic democracy; it is a pneumatic organism. [4] Its unity is love, not compulsion.

ἀποκρίνω, † ἀνταποκρίνομαι.

The usage is very varied. ἀποκρίνω means "to separate," also "to secrete," esp. of bodily secretions, or "to separate" in the sense "to dedicate." b. ἀποκρίνομαι in the pass. means "to separate oneself," "to incline to"; c. ἀποκρίνω act. "to condemn," "to reject." d. ἀποκρίνομαι mid. "to vindicate oneself"; e. ἀποκρίνομαι mid. "to answer," found from Herodot., though he usually has ὑποκρίνομαι for this. Atticists reject the pass. aor. of the mid., but it is found later. [1] The LXX uses ἀποκρίνομαι often, predominantly in forms of the pass. aor. It is usually the rendering of עָנָה, which means "to answer," "to commence," [2] also of הֵשִׁיב in the sense "to answer."

In the NT ἀποκρίνομαι occurs only in the mid. in the sense "to answer" etc. What is answered may be a request or a speech, not just a question. The aor. in the NT is 7 times mid. ἀπεκρινάμην and 195 times pass. ἀπεκρίθην. [3] In most cases in the Gospels ἀπεκρίθη is linked with λέγει, εἶπεν etc. In Jn. both are often verba finita: ἀπεκρίθη καὶ εἶπεν, Jn. 2:19; 3:3, 9, 10, 27; 4:10, 13; 6:26, 29, 43; 7:21;

ἀ ν α κ ρ ί ν ω κτλ. [1] Examples in Pape, Pass., Liddell-Scott, Pr.-Bauer.
[2] Demosth. Or., 48, 31: ὁ ἄρχων ... ἀνακρίνας εἰσήγαγεν εἰς τὸ δικαστήριον ..., 48, 43: ἐπειδὴ ἀνεκρίθησαν πρὸς τῷ ἄρχοντι ἅπασαι αἱ ἀμφισβητήσεις (doubtful questions) καὶ ἔδει ἀγωνίζεσθαι ἐν τῷ δικαστηρίῳ ...
[3] Reitzenstein, Hell. Myst., 378.
[4] F. Büchsel, Der Geist Gottes im NT (1926), 352.
ἀ π ο κ ρ ί ν ω κτλ. The dict., s.v.; Dalman, WJ, I, 19, 20.
[1] Liddell-Scott, Pape, Pass., s.v.
[2] Ges.-Buhl, s.v.
[3] Bl.-Debr. § 78; Pr.-Bauer, s.v.

14:23; 18:30 (plur.); 20:28 etc., but this is rare in the Synopt., ἀπεκρίθη καὶ λέγει, Mk. 7:28. Here we usually have the part. ἀποκριθείς with εἶπεν following, Mt. 11:25; 15:3; 17:4; 21:29 f.; 22:1; 25:12, 26, 40 (ἐρεῖ); 26:23, 25, 63 (vl.); 28:5; Mk. 9:5 (λέγει); 10:51; 11:14; 12:35 (ἔλεγεν); Lk. 1:60 (ἀποκριθεῖσα); 11:7 (εἴπῃ); 13:14 (ἔλεγεν), 25 (ἐρεῖ); 14:3; 15:29; Ac. 19:15; 25:9 etc. Combinations of ἀπεκρίθη with the part. of λέγειν are less common. ἀπεκρίθη λέγων is found at Jn. 1:26; Mk. 15:9; Ac. 15:13, ἀπεκρίθησαν λέγουσαι at Mt. 25:9, ἀποκριθήσονται λέγοντες at Mt. 25:37, 44, 45 (λέγων), ἀποκρίνεται λέγων at Jn. 12:23. The original form of the expression is probably the paratactic, which like the Heb. וַיַּעַן...וַיֹּאמֶר has two *verba finita*, i.e., the Johannine ἀπεκρίθη καὶ εἶπεν. The construction with a part. ἀποκριθείς is better Gk., hence secondary. Undoubtedly the usage of the Gospels rests on that of the LXX, where ἀποκριθεὶς εἶπεν is common, deriving from the Heb. וַיַּעַן...וַיֹּאמֶר. In the combinations of ἀποκρίνεσθαι with λέγειν, εἰπεῖν etc. we thus have an element of genuine biblical Gk. (ἀπεκρίθη καὶ εἶπεν). This comes out most clearly in the fact that in the Gospels, as in the LXX, ἀπεκρίθη is not always used in answer to something just said. It really means "he began," which is in accord, not with Gk. usage, but with the Heb. ענה. Worth noting is the fact that it is in Jn. that ἀπεκρίθη καὶ εἶπεν, which corresponds so closely to the ויען ויאמר of the OT, is so very common. The Heb. OT comes out particularly strongly in the language of this Gospel. "This form is common in 1 Macc., Tobit, Enoch, Apc. of Baruch, 4 Ezra, Ass. of Moses, strikingly rare in Jubilees and Judith, occasional in 2 Macc."[4]

The rule of Meïr (c. 150 A.D.): "Whenever it says (in the OT): He answered and said this, lo, the one concerned spoke in the Holy Ghost,"[5] is hardly applicable to the Gospels. But this is perhaps the point of Mt. 11:25: ἀποκριθεὶς ὁ Ἰησοῦς εἶπεν, in the light of the par. in Lk. 10:21: ἠγαλλιάσατο τῷ πνεύματι τῷ ἁγίῳ καὶ εἶπεν.

ἀνταποκρίνομαι is a stronger form which illustrates the love of later Greek for double compounds. It is found 3 times in the LXX for ענה.[6] It occurs in the NT at Lk. 14:6; R. 9:20 with the implied sense "to make unjustified accusations," "to dispute," "to grumble."

† ἀπόκριμα.

Deissmann can still call this word an obviously rare one.[1] It does not occur in the LXX or Philo. Nevertheless, it is found in Polyb., 12, 26b, 1; Jos. Ant., 14, 210; IG, XII, 1, 2, 4 (51 A.D.); Ditt. Syll.³, 804, 5 (and n. 3); Or., 335, 95 and 119; 494, 18; P. Tebt., II, 286, 1.[2] It is a tt. of official and legal speech and denotes an official resolution (on an enquiry or petition) which decides the matter.

It bears this sense in the only verse in which it occurs in the NT, namely, 2 C. 1:9: We received in ourselves the decision which spelled death (τὸ ἀπόκριμα

---

[4] Dalman, *op. cit.,* 19.
[5] Str.-B., I, 606, where Midr. Qoh. 7:2 (32b) is given as an example.
[6] ἀνταποκρίνομαι is also a mathematical term, cf. Nicomachus Arithmetica Introductio (ed. R. Hoche [1866], I, 8), cf. also Nägeli, 43.
ἀ π ό κ ρ ι μ α. [1] NB, 85.
[2] Cf. Wnd. 2 K., *ad loc.,* who also adduces Nägeli, 30, Moult.-Mill., I, 64 and S. R. Mantey, Exp. 9th Ser., Vol. I (1922), 376 f.

τοῦ θανάτου).³ By human judgment Paul could only reckon that his position was like that of a man condemned to death who had made a petition for mercy and received the answer that he must die.⁴ The gen. is to be taken as an appos. gen. (cf. Bl.-Debr. § 167), not a subj., as though death had imparted the decision to Paul. It is a fine point that Paul does not name the author of the decision.

† ἀκόκρισις.

This is common from an early period (Theognis), being found also in inscr., pap. and LXX. When derived from the act. of the verb it means a. "separation," "secretion," esp. in medicine, Ps.-Plat. Def., 415 f. When derived from the mid. of the verb it means b. "answer."¹

In the NT it is used only in sense b., cf. Lk. 2:47; 20:26; Jn. 1:22; 19:9, in Jn. in the phrase ἀπόκρισιν δοῦναι. On 1:22 Schl. J. refers to M. Ex., 18, 27: תְּשׁוּבָה שְׁנָתַן לוֹ, the answer which he gave him. ἀπόκρισιν is often used in the LXX for עָנָה and הֵשִׁיב.

† διακρίνω.

1. Since the simple κρίνω already means "to sunder," "to separate," δια-κρίνω is originally a stronger form (cf. dis-cerno). Much used, the word took on many senses.¹ The LXX uses it for several terms, mostly for שָׁפַט and דִּין.² In the NT it does not occur in its original spatial sense, only in the fig. "To make a distinction between persons," Ac. 15:9 : God has made no distinction between (us) Jews and the Gentiles ; also 11:12.³ "To distinguish," 1 C. 4:7: Who has distinguished you (as compared with others)? 11:29 : μὴ διακρίνων τὸ σῶμα, "because he does not distinguish the body of the Lord (from ordinary bread)."⁴ "To distinguish between persons" gives the further sense "to judge between two," 1 C. 6:5 διακρίνειν ἀνὰ μέσον τοῦ ἀδελφοῦ⁵ (here a tt. in

---

³ Less exact is the common transl.: "We had to pass sentence of death on ourselves" (Weizsäcker, Ltzm. K., H. D. Wendland, NT Deutsch, ad loc.). ἀπόκριμα is not a sentence. This inexactitude goes back to Theodoret : ἀπόκριμα δὲ θανάτου τὴν τοῦ θανάτου ψῆφον ἐκάλεσε (III, 291, MPG, 82, p. 380c).

⁴ Wnd. 2 K., ad loc. compares the ancient practice of petitioning an oracle in serious emergencies, also 2 K. 8:7 ff. and Is. 38:1. The nature of Paul's situation can only be conjectured. Perhaps it was a serious illness, since the sources make no reference to an imprisonment in Ephesus.

ἀπόκρισις. ¹ Cf. the dict., esp. Pr.-Bauer, s.v.

διακρίνω. Pass., Pape, Pr.-Bauer, s.v.; Schl. Mt. on 21:21; Hck., Wnd., Dib. on Jm. 1:6; 2:4; Joh. W., Bchm., Ltzm. on 1 C. 6:5; 11:29; Kn., Wbg., Wnd. on Jd. 22.

¹ Cf. Pape, Pass., s.v.

² Cf. Hatch-Redp., s.v.

³ Act. διακρίναντα, not mid. διακρινάμενον. Comparison with 15:9 is closer than with 10:20.

⁴ So with Bchm. and Ltzm. against Joh. W.: "does not correctly assess." Weiss has to supply "correctly," but this is not implied by the word as such, which has rather the sense of preference.

⁵ On the combination with ἀνὰ μέσον cf. Ez. 34:17, 20 : διακρινῶ ἀνὰ μέσον προβάτου καὶ προβάτου (προβάτου ἰσχυροῦ καὶ προβάτου ἀσθενοῦς). In spite of P. Schmiedel, Handkommentar z. NT, II, 1: Die Briefe an d. Thess. u. Korinth. (1893), ad loc.; Joh. W., ad loc., the sing. ἀδελφοῦ after ἀνὰ μέσον is not to be conjecturally set aside. If incorrect, it arose because the correct double ἀνὰ μέσον ἀδελφοῦ καὶ ἀδελφοῦ (cf. Ez. 34:17, 20) was probably felt to be clumsy. It is worth noting that in Sir. 25:18 ἀνὰ μέσον τοῦ πλησίον αὐτοῦ is a variant of ἀνὰ μέσον τῶν πλησίον, cf. Ryssel in Kautzsch Apkr., I, 360, ad loc., also 248. A non-collective sing. could follow ἀνὰ μέσον, but it was felt to be incorrect.

law), [6] and "to assess," used of a thing, Mt. 16:3 : τὸ πρόσωπον τοῦ οὐρανοῦ, as well as a person, 1 C. 11:31: ἑαυτοὺς διεκρίνομεν, [7] or without obj., 1 C. 14:29. [8] The mid. διακρίνομαι (with pass. aor.) means "to contend," [9] Jd. 9 : τῷ διαβόλῳ δια-κρινόμενος, Ac. 11:2 : διεκρίνοντο πρὸς αὐτὸν (Peter) οἱ ἐκ περιτομῆς, or "to doubt." This meaning, which is not known prior to the NT, occurs at Mk. 11:23; Mt. 21:21; Jm. 1:6; 2:4; R. 4:20; 14:23; Ac. 10:20. [10]

2. The attitude which the NT expresses by διακρίνεσθαι in the sense "to doubt" is seen in prayer and action, not in reflective thought. What is questioned in διακρίνεσθαι is not a human doctrine ; it is God's Word. Philosophical scepticism was known in the NT age. So, too, was the cultural sickness of the weakening of assurance and resolution by conflicting motives in personal life. But NT δια-κρίνεσθαι neither derives from the one nor is it a special instance of the other. It is a specifically religious phenomenon. In Mk. 11:23; Mt. 21:21 man has the promise of God and he clings to it when he speaks the word of faith to God, or to the mountain. But he still thinks it impossible, or at least not certain, that what he says should be done. He is at odds with himself. He believes, and yet he does not believe. For Jesus this attitude is the opposite of faith, as Mk. 9:14-29 and par. (cf. v. 19, 23) and Mk. 4:40 and par. also show. Jm. 1:6 gives a vivid description of the man of prayer who is a διακρινόμενος. He does not stand firm on the promise of God but moves restlessly like a wave of the sea. He is double-minded and inconstant in all his conduct, v. 8. The δίψυχος brings out very clearly the inner cleavage. In R. 4:20 Abraham has a divine promise which far exceeds the possibilities of natural fulfilment. He is full of the fact (πληροφορηθείς) that God will make a reality of this promise. Here the emphasis obviously falls on the unreserved nature of his confidence. He trusts with his whole heart, and overcomes everything that might impede this trust. This is οὐ διεκρίθη; one might almost translate : "He was not inwardly divided ..." In R. 14:23 we have the contrast between the διακρινόμενος and the one who does not need to condemn himself for doing what he regards as good. The διακρινόμενος is the one who has no certainty as regards either his judgment or his action, who does with a bad conscience what he cannot refrain from doing, who is inwardly at odds with him-

---

[6] Xenoph. Hist. Graec., V, 2, 10; Ditt. Syll.³, 545, 18; Or., 43, 4 and 11; Ep. Ar., 110.

[7] Joh. W. prefers the reading ἐκρίνομεν, but this is not well attested and it disturbs the movement from v. 29 to v. 31. The change in the meaning of the word between 29 and 31 should not worry us ; it is natural to such loose constructions. In 31 Paul demands self-judgment in general ; in 29 he simply demands that the sacramental bread should be distinguished from ordinary bread. Ltzm.'s rendering "to test" (with an appeal to δοκιμα-ζέτω in v. 28) and Bachmann's "to differentiate" fail to do justice to the necessary similarity of meaning between the verbs in the major and minor propositions and v. 31.

[8] The ref. is not so much to what the prophets say as to the spirits of the prophets, 12:10. The subjects are the charismatics mentioned in 12:10, or prophets who do not speak prophetically, not the congregation. There is no thought of congregationalism in the democratic sense.

[9] This sense is well attested outside the NT, cf. Pape, Pass., s.v.

[10] Jd. 22 is to be taken as a three-membered verse, with Wbg., Kn., Wnd., against Nestle (cf. the discussion in Kn., Wbg.): οὓς μὲν ἐλέγχετε διακρινομένους, οὓς δὲ σῴζετε ἐκ πυρὸς ἁρπάζοντες, οὓς δὲ ἐλεᾶτε ἐν φόβῳ κτλ. ἐλεᾶτε for ἐλέγχετε in the first member is an assimilation to the third. In the third ἐλεᾶτε is better than ἐκβάλετε (Wnd.) or ἐλάσατε (Wbg.). διακρινομένους can mean here 1. judged (Vulg. arguite iudicatos), 2. when they dispute, 3. when they doubt. The third sense fits best, the first is hardly possible.

self.[11] Ac. 10:20 is to the same effect. In Jm. 2:4 διακριθῆναι is to go to the assembly and thus to demonstrate one's faith, and yet at the same time to despise the poor, acting according to the standards of the world and not according to the promise which God has given the poor (v. 5). The inconsistency of this is sin.[12]

3. There is doubt so long as there is faith. Nevertheless, attention to doubt, and the condemnation of it, are later.

In the OT there is much reference to the rejection of God's Word (Gn. 18:12; Is. 7:1-25 etc.), but not to doubt, i.e., to half affirmation which is also half negation. This arises in the OT only in the form of a deliberate attitude, of hypocrisy, not as a failure to reach consistency in the personal affirmation of God's Word. Job is not called a doubter ; he is a fighter. There is no cleavage in his attitude. It is consistently directed against God. In later Judaism pusillanimity in prayer is censured (ὀλιγοψυχεῖν, Sir. 7:10). The demand here is similar to, though not quite the same as, that of Mk. 11:23 (Mt. 21:21); Jm. 1:6.

> In Apc. Elias 24:3 f. we read : "None should go to the holy place who doubts in his heart. He who doubts in prayer is his own enemy, and the angels do not add their assent. Hence be at all times of one heart in the Lord, that you may know all things." (The Sahidic text differs somewhat.) If this saying is Jewish and pre-Christian, it shows that Mk. 11:23 (Mt. 21:21) and Jm. 1:6 raise a demand which has Jewish roots. But in the text edited by Steindorff it is likely that there are Christian interpolations. Indeed, it is probable that the whole of this text is Christian, though this does not rule out Jewish *secreta Eliae prophetae* (cf. Schürer, III⁴, 361 ff.).

The attention paid to doubt in the NT is obviously the reverse side of the un-conditional promise which is given to faith. Both come from Jesus and are the consequence of the full fellowship with God which He enjoyed and brought. Because on man's part nothing is needed for fellowship with God except faith, doubt is from the very outset a breach of this fellowship. It is a sin which excludes from God's help. With the grace of God comes a direct intensification of God's demand on man. Since the community of Jesus, cf. especially Paul and James, accepts Jesus' estimation of faith, it also accepts His condemnation of doubt.

> 4. Linguistically διακρίνεσθαι in the sense "to doubt" is a product of Greek speaking Christianity. Gk. uses διστάζω, ἀμφισβητέω, ἀμφιβάλλω for "to doubt." Of these only διστάζω occurs in the NT at passages in Mt. which are not common to Mk. and Lk., 14:31; 28:17.[13] The NT also uses διαλογισμός for doubt. διακρίνομαι in this sense does not occur in the post-apost. fathers, but is found in Prot. Ev. Jc. 11:2; Ps.-Clem. Hom., I, 20; II, 40. The word was accepted only to a small degree ; it probably

---

[11] To translate διακρινόμενος : the one who makes a distinction between foods (Ltzm.), destroys the essential contrast between διακρινόμενος and πίστις (cf. R. 4:20). On the analogy of 1 C. 11:29; 4:7; Ac. 11:12; 15:9 it would also require the act. instead of the mid.

[12] The rendering : "Have you not of yourselves made distinctions (between the rich and the poor)" (Wnd., Hck., also Dib.) presupposes the act. διεκρίνατε and can make little sense of the ἐν ἑαυτοῖς, which fits in well with the sense "to doubt." It also demands some reason why making such distinction is wrong. But for believers (v. 1) the inconsistency of attitude is wrong, since it undermines faith. As vv. 2-4 support the statement in v. 1 that faith and respect of persons are mutually exclusive, so v. 4 speaks of the antithesis of faith, i.e., doubt.

[13] The post-apost. fathers use διστάζω more frequently, Did., 1 Cl., 2 Cl., Barn., Herm., cf. E. J. Goodspeed, *Index Patristicus* ... (1907). On the other hand, it does not occur in the LXX. Neither ἀμφισβητέω nor ἀμφιβάλλω is used for "to doubt" in the NT, LXX or post-apost. fathers.

could not overcome the competition of διστάζω. The Aram. equivalent is apparently פלג in pass. of reflex. constructions. This does not mean "to doubt," but מַלְכוּ פְּלִיגָה in Da. 2:41 is an inwardly divided kingdom (LXX: διμερής, Θ: διῃρημένη) and פְּלִיג denotes a man of divergent opinion or a divergent tradition, cf. Tg. J., II on Gn. 49:1; bBM, 5a; jKil., 32a, lines 18 ff. [14] פְּלִגוּ is cleavage, פְּלוּגְתָּא contention, and פְּלַג לָשׁוֹן "to make the tongue divided." [15] "Thou sayest this with a divided mouth" (בְּפַלְגוּת פּוּמָךְ) is the opp. of בְּכֹל פּוּמָךְ, "with the whole mouth," jPes., 32c, line 44. [16] The dividedness which Judaism found on the lips or in the opinions of a majority of men Jesus perceived in the relation of man to the divine promise. Hence for Him פְּלִיג and פְּלַגוּ take on a new significance. In this new sense פלג was rendered διακρίνομαι when the preaching of Jesus about faith moved from the Aram. sphere to the Gk. The Heb. equivalent is חלק, which in the part. q pass. and the ni means "to be of divided or different opinion," "to contend," of scholars who do not agree among themselves. [17] Confirmation that פלג is the Aram. equivalent is found in the Syr. translation of Mt. 21:21: וְלָא תֶתְפַּלְּגוּן. [18] The use of "to doubt" for this (cf. dubito from duo and διστάζω from δίς) tends perhaps to lay the emphasis on the two-ness rather than the dividedness, as in the case of διακρίνεσθαι; it was perhaps recognition of this which caused διακρίνομαι to be preferred to διστάζω in translation of the פלג sayings of Jesus. [19]

Certainly διακρίνομαι and its history, so far as it is known, illustrate the constructive force of the Gospel in the linguistic sphere.

† διάκρισις.

Like διακρίνειν, this bears several divergent meanings, "separation," "distinction," "strife," "appraisal," "exposition." [1] In the LXX it occurs only at Job 37:16, where the meaning is not clear.

In the NT it usually means "differentiation," at 1 C. 12:10 of the spirits of the prophets, at Hb. 5:14 between good and evil. R. 14:1: μὴ εἰς διακρίσεις διαλο-

---

[14] Levy Wört., IV, s.v.

[15] J. Fürst, Heb. u. chald. Handwörterbuch³ (1876), II, s.v.

[16] The meaning of בכל פּוּמָךְ and בפלגות פּוּמָךְ is difficult. Acc. to M. Jastrow, A Dict. of the Targumim (New York-Berlin, 1926), s.v. [I owe this to R. Meyer], "Do you say this with your whole mouth?" means "Are you the true author of this opinion?" and "dividedness of the mouth" implies that "the opinion expressed derives from another." But it is hard to derive this from the literal meaning of פְּלַגוּ, and it does not fit the context. It is better to take "with thy whole mouth" to mean "with full conviction (as to the truth of the opinion)" and "with divided mouth" as "with doubts (as to the truth of the opinion)," cf. Levy Wört., IV, s.v. פְּלַגוּ.

[17] Levy Wört., II, s.v.; Sanh., 110a : "Any man who נחלק against his teacher is as though he נחלק against God." Cf. also the passage with לֵב חָלוּק adduced by Schl. on Mt. 21:21.

[18] Cf. Schl., ad loc. The Syr. translation of Jm. 2:4 has the same ethpael of פלג. It thus achieves the right understanding which most translations miss, cf. Hck., ad loc., n. 97. For the Egyptian Christians who added to or composed the Apc. Elias (→ 948) the opposite of doubt is again the single heart, so that doubt is dividedness of heart.

[19] It cannot be proved that διακρίνομαι was used for פלג prior to Jesus (Da. 2:41 !), but it is possible. On the other hand, one cannot assume that the two words would then mean a divided attitude in face of the divine promise, the opp. of simple affirmation in faith.

διάκρισις. Pape, Pr.-Bauer, B. Weiss, Erklärung d. Römerbr.⁹ (1899), Zn. on R. 14:1.

[1] Cf. Pape for examples.

γισμῶν, is enigmatically brief and not very clear. Zahn's striking explanation: "Not for the sake of disputations about thoughts," suffers from the defect that one would expect περί with the gen. or something similar instead of the gen. δια-λογισμῶν. It is best to take διάκρισις here in the sense of "evaluation." [2] The weak man should be accepted as the Christian brother he claims to be. One should not judge the thoughts which underlie his conduct. This is for God alone to do, cf. v. 22. [3]

† ἀδιάκριτος.

This is found from the time of Hippocrates (d. 356 B.C.), also as an adverb. It is much used in various senses. [1] Basic distinction should be made between the passive senses: "indistinguishable," "imprecise," "obscure," and the act. "not differentiating," "impartial," "of one mind," "without distinction." [2]

The word occurs in the LXX only at Prv. 25:1: αἱ παιδεῖαι (παροιμίαι) Σαλω-μῶντος αἱ ἀδιάκριτοι, probably "uncertain" proverbs in distinction from those said to be genuinely by Solomon in 1-24. [3] Philo has it in Op. Mund., 38: εἰς μίαν ἀδιά-κριτον καὶ ἄμορφον φύσιν, "to an essence without form or distinction," Det. Pot. Ins., 118: ἀγωγαὶ δύο σφόδρα ἀδιάκριτοι καὶ σπουδῆς ἄξιαι, "two mutually agreed ... methods," and Spec. Leg., III, 57: ὧν (of animals) ἀδιακρίτους εἶναι καὶ ἀνεπιστά-τους τὰς ὀχείας συμβέβηκε, impulsive and unconscious. Hence it has for him a passive sense. Test. Zeb. 7:2 reads: ἀδιακρίτως πάντας σπλαγχνιζόμενοι ἐλεᾶτε, not "without doubts," but "without distinction."

Its only occurrence in the NT is at Jm. 3:17. Here it is used with ἀνυπόκριτος of the wisdom which is from above. It means "without doubts [4] and hypocrisy." A passive sense is not suitable, nor is "without division," i.e., undeviating in terms of the demand of 3:9 ff. [5] Again, the senses "impartial" and "simple" [6] are not ap-posite. [7] In the post-apostolic fathers the term is used only by Ign. It expresses the distinctive assurance and resolution of faith, and also the reliability of Jesus Christ. The best rendering is perhaps "without wavering," "unshakable." [8] Eph., 3, 2: Ἰησοῦς Χριστός, τὸ ἀδιάκριτον ἡμῶν ζῆν, "our life which is unshakable," Mg., 15, 1: ἀδιάκριτον πνεῦμα, "an unshakable spirit," Tr. 1, 1: διάνοιαν ... ἀδιάκριτον

---

[2] So Ltzm., cf. B. Weiss, also Chrysostom, Augustine.

[3] "Doubt" (Cr.-Kö.) is not the meaning of διάκρισις.

ἀ δ ι ά κ ρ ι τ ο ς. Pass.-Cr., Pr.-Bauer, Moult.-Mill., s.v.; Dib., Hck., Wnd. on Jm. 3:17; J. B. Lightfoot, The Apostolic Fathers, II, 1 (1885), p. 39, n. 5 on Ign. Eph., 3, 2; T. Zahn, Ignatius v. Antiochen (1873), 429, n. 1.

[1] Cf. Pass.-Cr., where there are many examples.

[2] P. Oxy., IV, 715, 36: κατακεχώ[ρικα] ἀδιακ[ρίτως], "I have recorded summarily (without material proof)," cf. U. Wilcken, APF, 4 (1908), 254.

[3] Hck.'s "proverbs in which there is no vacillation" (on Jm. 3:17) is not convincing.

[4] So also Wnd., who also allows "impartial." The sense "without doubts" depends on the corresponding use of διακρίνεσθαι, but this is well attested in Jm. (1:6; 2:4).

[5] J. H. Ropes in ICC, also Hck., op. cit.

[6] Though Dib. points to the "fluctuating character of Ignatian usage, he thinks the basic sense is "simple," "harmonious," which he derives from "impartial."

[7] Of older transl. the Vulg. has non diiudicans, cf. sa bo ff Corbeiensis, sine diiudicatione irreprehensibilis, the Pesh. דְּלָא פַלְגוּתָא, "without cleavage (of heart)," i.e., "without doubts." The Pesh. has the right translation because in the specific NT usage διακρίνεσθαι is a rendering of an Aram. reflexive פלג.

[8] Dib.'s "simple," "of one accord," does not fit Eph., 3, 2, nor is it very suitable in Tr., 1, 1.

ἐν ὑπομονῇ, "a mind which is unshakable in patience," superscription to R.: πεπληρωμένοις χάριτος θεοῦ ἀδιακρίτως, "unshakably filled by God's grace," and to Phld.: ἀγαλλιωμένη ἐν τῷ πάθει τοῦ κυρίου ἀδιακρίτως, "which is unshakable in its joy in the passion of the Lord." [9]

† ἐγκρίνω.

This is common in Attic Gk. from the time of Euripides, also inscr., not the LXX.

In the NT it is found only at 2 C. 10:12 : "to reckon or count in, to number with, to elect or admit to, a series, party or fellowship," cf. Plat. Resp., VI, 486d : ἐπιλήσμονα (forgetful) ... ψυχὴν ἐν ταῖς ἱκανῶς φιλοσόφοις μήποτε ἐγκρίνωμεν, CIG, II, 2715a, 11: ἐγκρίνειν εἰς τοὺς ἐφήβους.

κατακρίνω, † κατάκριμα, † κατάκρισις.

κατακρίνω, "to condemn," [1] of the divine and human judge, Mt. 12:41 f., par. Lk. 11:31 f., or the witness, → κριτής n. 4. When κατακρίνειν refers to human judgment there is a clear distinction between the condemnation and its execution, [2] but this is irrelevant in the case of divine κατακρίνειν, where the two can be seen as one, Mk. 16:16; 1 C. 11:32; 2 Pt. 2:6 : πόλεις Σοδόμων καὶ Γομόρρας τεφρώσας καταστροφῇ κατέκρινεν. Here τεφρώσας shows that both the sentence and its execution are meant. To understand the much discussed verse R. 8:3 : κατέκρινεν τὴν ἁμαρτίαν ἐν τῇ σαρκί, [3] it is best to take these words, which again see as one the pronouncement and execution of the sentence, [4] in the light of the ἠλευθέρωσέν σε of v. 2 and the οὐδὲν ἄρα νῦν κατάκριμα τοῖς ἐν Χριστῷ Ἰησοῦ of v. 1. One cannot seek a single historical fact in which the condemnation is pronounced and executed. Paul is obviously thinking of the totality of what God has done, and does, through His Son. He has in mind the whole movement from the incarnation to the impartation of the Spirit to believers, v. 4. The obedience of the Son to the death of the cross (Phil. 2:8) is obviously part of this κατέκρινεν τὴν ἁμαρτίαν ἐν τῇ σαρκί. [5] But in R. Paul's concern is with the whole

---

[9] Cl. Al. Paed., II, 3, 38 calls faith ἀδιάκριτος, "free from doubt," cf. also Orig. Comm. in Joh. XIII, 10, 63 on 4:17, where the faith of the woman of Samaria is ἀδιάκριτος.

ἐ γ κ ρ ί ν ω. Pape, Pass., Liddell-Scott, Pr.-Bauer, s.v.

κ α τ α κ ρ ί ν ω κτλ. [1] In class. Gk. constructed with the acc. of person and gen. of obj., or gen. of person and acc. or infinitive of punishment (examples in Pape, Pass., Liddell-Scott), in the LXX (only 7 instances) with the acc. of pers. and dat. of punishment (instead of θανάτῳ also εἰς θάνατον), cf. the same constr. in Jos. Ant., 10, 124; Diod. S. (Bl.-Debr. § 195, 2), inscr. (Ditt. Syll.³, 736, 160 ff.): τὸν μὴ ποιοῦντα κατακρινάντω εἴκοσι δραχμαῖς, also Hellenistic.

[2] Mk. 14:64.

[3] The exegetical difficulties may be conveniently studied in B. Weiss (1899) and Ltzm. R., ad loc.; cf. also Zn. R., ad loc.

[4] Also Zn. R. (1910), 383, who takes κατέκρινεν as a "sentence," and fills out the idea of God's pronouncement with that of a "basic beginning of the fulfilment of this will of God," 384. The only pt. not clarified — and it is the main one — is how this beginning is followed up.

[5] Materially the sinless life of Jesus cannot be separated from it. But these are all explications of the more succinct statement of Paul. They are unavoidable, however, if we are

of God's saving action in the Son, not with details. The κατέκρινεν is of unrestricted validity, but it is efficacious only for those who are ἐν Χριστῷ, i.e.,
believers, v. 1. It is identical with the reconciliation which is universal but which
finds completion only when man becomes the new creature (2 C. 5:17) which no
longer lives for itself but is controlled by the love of Christ (5:14 f.). It is the
setting aside of sin as the enmity between God and man (R. 8:7) which the Law
cannot overcome. The guilt and power of sin are as little separable here as in
reconciliation → καταλλάσσω, I, 255. The Law condemned sinners, and the result
was that man perished. Only God in Christ could so condemn sin that man was
made free, v. 2.[6]

κατάκριμα, "condemnation,"[7] in the NT only at R. 5:16, 18; 8:1, of the divine
condemnation, including its execution (→ 951), "damnation." R. 8:1 refers not
merely to the divine sentence but also to its actual results, cf. the ἠλευθέρωσέν σε
of v. 2 with its factual connotation.

κατάκρισις, "condemnation," a rare word, not found in the LXX, in the NT
only in Paul, 2 C. 3:9; 7:3. The ministry of the old covenant is one of condemnation
because, by reason of sin, it cannot bring on man anything but death, cf. 3:6, 7.

† ἀκατάκριτος, † αὐτοκατάκριτος.

Both words are formed from the verbal adj. of κατακρίνω, i.e., κατάκριτος. ἀκατάκριτος with α privativum means "uncondemned."

ἀκατάκριτος occurs in the NT only in a legal connection at Ac. 16:37 and
22:25, where Paul complains against the actual or threatened mistreatment of
illegal examination by punishment or torture. Elsewhere this is a very rare word.
αὐτοκατάκριτος, "self-condemned," is used in a moral connection of the man who
sins consciously. In Tt. 3:11 it refers to one who has been admonished twice and
who can have no doubts as to the wrongness of what he does.

In a Philo fragment from the Sacra Parallela of John of Damascus, ed. T. Mangey,
II (1742), 652: μηδενὶ συμφορὰν ὀνειδίσῃς ... μήποτε τοῖς αὐτοῖς αὐτοκατάκριτος ἐν τῷ συνειδότι εὑρεθῇς, the reference is to a man who falls into the sin which
he condemns in others. Otherwise a rare word.

---

not simply to repeat Paul's words but to clarify his meaning. Acc. to P. Althaus (*NT
Deutsch, ad loc.*) Paul is referring to Christ's death. This is hardly in keeping, however,
with the very general πέμψας. One would expect at least a παραδούς before περὶ
ἁμαρτίας.

[6] If we do not understand R. 8:3 in the light of Paul's doctrine of reconciliation (i.e.,
finally of what the preaching of the Word of the cross by Paul itself accomplished as reconciliation with God), then we are faced with the choice of either ending in futile exegetical scepticism or of asserting "a purely imaginative conception with a mythological
thrust" (A. Jülicher, *Schriften d. NT* [1908], II, 275). In the latter case it makes little
difference what ideas our own imagination reads into the imaginations of Paul.

[7] The term is first attested in Dion. Hal. Ant. Rom., 6, 61 (age of Augustus), also in pap.,
P. Oxy., II, 298, 4; Pap. Erzherzog Rainer, I, ed. C. Wessely (1895), 1, 15 ff.; 188, 14 ff.;
Mitteis-Wilcken, I, 2, 28, 12. At Sir. 43:10 we should not read κατάκριμα, but κατὰ
κρίμα, so Swete and Rahlfs. Deissmann NB (1897), 92 f. has drawn attention to the
meaning found in Pap. Erzherzog Rainer, *loc. cit.*: "legally imposed obligation which rests
on a piece of land."

ἀ κ α τ ά κ ρ ι τ ο ς κτλ. Dib. on Tt. 3:11.

† πρόκριμα.

This is a later term. πρόκρισις occurs in Plato. [1] The LXX has only the verb προκρίνω, Wis. 7:8. [2]

πρόκριμα occurs in the NT only at 1 Tm. 5:21. From the 2nd cent. A.D. it is attested as a legal tt. in pap. [3] It corresponds to the Latin *prae-iudicium*, a pre-judgment in the sense of a preceding sentence, "a prior, anticipatory decision which can or must serve as a norm for a later decision in another or the same case." [4] In 1 Tm. 5:21 it cannot be used in a strict legal sense. It bears a more general moral sense, just as the word pre-judgment has passed from the legal sphere into the moral. The meaning here is a pre-judgment or preconceived opinion in favour of the accused or accuser which would hinder judges from exercising the justice required in Church discipline, v. 19 f. Cf. the warning against πρόσκλισις (partiality) which follows.

† συγκρίνω.

This is common in secular Gk. from the time of Epicharmus. It is also found frequently in the LXX with its derivatives σύγκριμα and σύγκρισις.

In the NT the derivatives do not occur and the word itself is found only at 1 C. 2:13 and 2 C. 10:12. συγκρίνω is the antonym of διακρίνω ("to separate"). It is used in various ways: a. "to unite," "to compound"; b. "to compare"; c. "to measure," "to evaluate"; d. "to interpret." [1] At 2 C. 10:12 it means "to compare" with the suggestion that what is to be compared is in some sense of equal value. [2] Paul is ironically rejecting the idea that he can even be compared with the arrogant pseudo-apostles in Corinth (11:13). He alleges that they compare themselves only with themselves and measure themselves only by themselves, so that they are not aware of their own poverty. The detached words πνευματικοῖς πνευματικὰ συγκρίνοντες in 1 C. 2:13 are difficult to construe. They develop in some way the thought that Paul proclaims revelations given by the Spirit in words taught by the Spirit. The sense "to unite" (a.): "uniting Spirit-given content with Spirit-given form," is not very likely, since the word "unite" is too weak. The sense "to compare" (b.): "comparing spiritual gifts and revelations (which we already have) with spiritual gifts and revelations (which we receive ...), and evaluating and understanding them accordingly," [3] introduces an alien thought. There is no re-

---

π ρ ό κ ρ ι μ α. [1] Polit., 298e.
[2] This verb also occurs in the perf. pass. in Ign. Sm., 6, 1; Mg., 1, 2, in the sense "to have precedence."
[3] Cf. Preisigke Wört., *s.v.* with ref. to P. Flor., 68, 13; 16 f. (2nd cent. A.D.): χωρὶς προκρίματος; Sammelbuch, 6000, II, 19 (6th cent. A.D.): παθεῖν πρόκριμα; P. Masp., 6, II, 71 (6th cent. A.D.): προκρίματος μὴ γιγνομένου; Mitteis-Wilcken, II, 2, 88, Col. II, 30 (2nd cent. A.D.): μέχρι προκρίματος.
[4] K. E. Georges, *Lat. Handwörterbuch*, II (1918), *s.v.*, ref. to Quint. Inst. Orat., V, 2, 1.
σ υ γ κ ρ ί ν ω. Pape, Pass., Pr.-Bauer, *s.v.* and the Comm. of Ltzm., Joh. W., Bchm., Schl. on 1 C. 2:13.
[1] Examples in Pape and → n. 4.
[2] Cf. CIG, 5002: ὁ πατὴρ τῶν ἱερέων ... ᾧ οὐδεὶς τῶν ἱερέων συγκρίνεται.
[3] Reitzenstein Hell. Myst., 336, followed with qualifications by Ltzm.

ference here to comparison of different revelations, or to different revelations at all. Hence it is best to accept the meaning "to interpret," "to expound," "to explain" (d.), which is predominant in the LXX : [4] "expounding revelations of the Spirit."

That the πνευματικά need exposition is shown by the fact that they are the wisdom of God in a mystery, the hidden wisdom (v. 7). πνευματικοῖς is best taken personally as a dat. of remoter obj.: "for spiritual men." This interpretation has the advantage of fitting in with v. 14 : "The non-spiritual man does not receive the things of the Spirit." [5] On the other hand, the instrumental understanding of πνευματικοῖς is contrary to Paul's preceding use, not of an instrumental dat., but of a construction with ἐν (ἐν ... λόγοις).

Büchsel

> † κρούω

κρούειν means "to strike," "to knock," in the most varied connections and with a wide variety of meanings. In biblical Gk. it is found only in the sense "to knock at the door," whether with or without τὴν θύραν. This expression occurs in secular Gk., e.g., Plat. Symp., 212c; Prot., 310a; 314d, though Atticists prefer κόπτειν τὴν θύραν. In the Gk. OT compounds are used for all other senses, e.g., ἀνακρούειν for striking musical instruments (Philo in Mut. Nom., 139 has κρούειν τὸ φωνῆς ὄργανον), [1] ἐγκρούειν, κατακρούειν for ירה (to knock in nails, pegs), also ἐπι-, παρα-, προς-, and συγκρούειν in various senses. The simple occurs only 3 times in the LXX at Ju. 19:22 and Cant. 5:2 for דפק [2] q, hitp with על, and at Jdt. 14:14 with no Heb. original. The ref. is always to knocking at the door or the tent curtain (Jdt.). Significant is Cant. 5:2 : φωνὴ ἀδελφιδοῦ μου, κρούει ἐπὶ τὴν θύραν, on which Cod. S has the scenic note : ἡ νύμφη ἔσθετε (ᾔσθηται) τὸν νυμφίον. The passage influenced the specific NT usage and understanding.

In the NT, apart from the secular use [3] at Ac. 12:13, 16 : [τοῦ Πέτρου] ... κρούσαντος; ἐπέμενεν κρούων, the image of knocking at the door is used in two ways. In the one believers seek access ; in the other the Lord Himself seeks access to them.

---

[4] Gn. 40:8, 16, 22; 41:12, 13, 15; Δα. LXX 5:7; Θ 5:12, 16, always with ref. to the interpretation of divine revelations through dreams. The LXX also uses σύγκρισις and σύγκριμα in a similar sense. "Theodorus, too, knows this interpretation, though he does not accept it here : οὐκ ἀντὶ τοῦ 'παρεξετάζοντες' λέγει, Cramer Cat., 45, 14" (Ltzm. K., ad loc.).

[5] The reading πνευματικῶς B 33 misses this connection.

κ ρ ο ύ ω. Bibl. : Pr.-Bauer ; Liddell-Scott, s.v. → θύρα, 173.

[1] Cf. Aristot. De Audibilibus, p. 802a, 32; An., II, 12, p. 424a, 32; Probl., XIX, 39, p. 921a, 25.

[2] The verb is used in the Mas. only of the hard driving of cattle, Gn. 33:13.

[3] On the Jewish custom of knocking cf. Str.-B. on Mt. 7:7, I, 458, and on Rev. 3:20, III, 798.

1. In Mt. 7:7, 8 and Lk. 11:9, 10, [4] in the saying about asking, the material content of the first clause is heavily underscored by the images of seeking and knocking [5] in the second and third clauses. The saying does not express a popular belief in God which counts on answers to prayer. [6] It is one of the varied forms characteristically used in the Sermon on the Mount to proclaim salvation. [7] These imperatives do not demand achievements which are the presupposition of the fulfilment of God's promise. The promise itself, as God's creative Word, fashions the confidence on which all prayer rests. Only the man who believes the promise can turn to God, the heavenly Father, with the same spontaneous and natural requests as a child brings to its earthly father. As finding follows seeking, or the opening of the door knocking, so giving follows asking. This understanding is confirmed in v. 8. Like the language of the Bible elsewhere, this does not take into account all the varied possibilities of human experience. It envisages the normal case of knocking at a door — this is often merely an act of politeness [8] — in the justifiable expectation that it will be opened. The Word of the Saviour is designed to establish the sure expectation which we often have in earthly things [9] as a foundation for man's dealings with God. It is thus an integral part of Jesus' preaching of salvation with its declaration of the imminence of the kingdom and its impartation of confidence and hope.

The saying about useless knocking in Lk. 13:25 does not run counter to this exposition. It is linked with the θύρα, the "narrow gate," of v. 24, though the reference in the two verses is not to the same door. [10] It is also an introduction to the rejection of the contemporaries of Jesus in v. 26 f., though we are not to regard it as a mere transitional verse supplied by Lk. [11] Nor is the saying grammatically dependent on the οὐκ ἰσχύσουσιν of v. 24. [12] Materially the verse denotes the separation between those who partake of the banquet in the house of the Lord (the kingdom of God), Lk. 22:30; 14:1 ff. and par., and those who are shut out. [13] The knocking here is not just a matter of politeness. It is an attempt on the part of those who have despised the open door [14] to remedy their fault when the door is shut. At the right time they did not have the faith and confidence that opening would follow on knocking. They did not trust the One of whom it is said that He is ὁ ἀνοίγων καὶ οὐδεὶς κλείσει, καὶ κλείων καὶ οὐδεὶς ἀνοίγει. [15] They did

---

[4] The sayings are best construed as independent sayings for which the redactor has supplied the context. Hence there is no connection with the preceding parable in Lk. about the friend and his request, from which Zn. (Lk., ad loc.) tries to draw the figure of knocking.

[5] The Rabb. use the figure of knocking at the door of mercy in prayer (bMeg., 12b) and of knocking with ref. to study (Pesikt., 176a). For other instances cf. Str.-B., I, 458 on Mt. 7:7. Kl. Mt. 7:7 quotes from the Qolasta (ed. J. Euting [1867], p. 67): "For him who stands before a closed door thou wilt open the closed door."

[6] Bultmann Trad., 109.

[7] G. Bertram, "Bergpredigt und Kultur," Zschr. f. den Evangelischen Relig.-Unterricht, 43 (1932), 333 ff.

[8] → n. 3. Cf. also Sir. 21:22 f., and on this V. Ryssel in Kautzsch, ad loc.

[9] καὶ πάλιν δὲ τὸ "κρούειν" σημαίνει τὸ μετὰ σφοδρότητος προσιέναι καὶ θερμῆς διανοίας, διὰ τῶν ἀνθρωπίνων ὑποδειγμάτων συγκαταβαίνων τῇ ἀσθενείᾳ ἡμῶν (Cramer Cat. on Mt. 7:7 f.).

[10] Wellh., ad loc.

[11] Bultmann Trad., 137 f.

[12] Zn. Lk., ad loc.

[13] Hck., ad loc.

[14] Rev. 3:8. It is polite to knock even at an open door, cf. Str.-B., I, 458.

[15] Rev. 3:7.

not believe in this power of the keys. Hence they did not follow His injunction to knock, and they did not enter. The result is that they have judged themselves. They are shut out. The offer of salvation in Mt. 7:7 carries with it the possibility of rejection, and hence the threat of judgment, Lk. 13:25.

2. In Lk. 12:36 and Rev. 3:20 it is the Lord who knocks. The saying in Lk. belongs to the great complex of sayings and parables about watching (→ ἐγείρειν). It is closely parallel to Mt. 25:1-13, and there have been conjectures whether, with Lk. 13:25, it does not provide a basis for this parable, or whether we do not have here relics of the parable. [16] In any case, Lk. has assembled eschatological sayings in 12:35-59, and 12:36 contains an exhortation to watchfulness in the form of a parable. [17] Under the influence of the image of the Messianic Bridegroom, the Lord who returns from the feast (γάμος does not have to be a wedding) is understood as the returning Christ for whose return from the heavenly banquet the Church is waiting. [18] Hence the question whether this is a saying of the earthly Jesus or a saying about the revelation of the exalted Christ is irrelevant. The history of the Gospel tradition shows that the primitive community made no sharp distinction in its understanding at this point. [19] Certainly the saying does not come from a period of relaxed eschatological tension. It breathes manly readiness and suppressed excitement. [20]

It is the Risen Lord who speaks in Rev. 3:20. This saying, too, is one of the admonitions and warnings in primitive proclamation which owe their distinctiveness to the expectaton of Christ's imminent return to judgment and which also expresses the seriousness of the Christian attitude to life.

The saying is strongly influenced by the bride mysticism of the Song of Songs [21] and the NT image of the Bridegroom (cf. also Lk. 12:36). In the early Church already this came to be understood less in terms of the Church's expectation of Christ and more in terms of the longing of the individual for union with Him. [22] Thus in the catena tradition we read: τὴν θύραν τῆς καρδίας κρούω καὶ τοῖς ἀνοίγουσιν ἐπὶ τῇ ἑαυτῶν σωτηρίᾳ συνευφραίνομαι ... ὁ ἀγαθὸς καὶ πρᾷος κρούσας τὴν θύραν καὶ μὴ τυχὼν ἀνοίξεως ἄπεισιν ἀψοφητί, and then Cant. 5:2 (→ supra) is quoted. On this understanding, too, there is the possibility of the missed opportunity, Cant. 5:6: ἤνοιξα ἐγὼ τῷ ἀδελφιδῷ μου, ἀδελφιδός μου παρῆλθεν, or, as the catena says: καὶ εἰ μὲν ἀνοίξει τις αὐτῷ, εἰσέρχεται, εἰ δὲ μή, παρέρχεται. Hence the expected coming of the Lord can also imply judgment, and the mystical tradition merges with the eschatological, cf. Jm. 5:9: ἰδοὺ ὁ κριτὴς πρὸ τῶν θυρῶν ἔστηκεν. But this side of the matter is as little evident in Rev. 3:20 as is that of ἐλέγχειν καὶ παιδεύειν alluded to in v. 19. [23] We are rather to think in terms of the history of the church of Laodicea.

---

[16] H. J. Holtzmann, Erklärung d. Synpt.[3] (1901), ad loc. Bultmann Trad., 125, favours the second possibility.

[17] Bultmann Trad., 350.

[18] Kl. Lk., ad loc. and B. Weiss, Erklärung des Mk.- u. Lk.-Ev.[9] (1901), ad loc.

[19] G. Bertram, "Die Himmelfahrt Jesu vom Kreuz aus ...," Deissmann-Festgabe (1927), esp. 188 ff.

[20] Wellh., ad loc.

[21] 4 Esr. 5:25 attests to the Messianic interpretation of Cant. in the NT period; cf. on this verse H. Gunkel in Kautzsch.

[22] → θύρα, 178.

[23] Had. Apk., ad loc. Cf. Prv. 3:11 f. The ref. in the LXX here is to chastisement, not training. G. Bertram, "Der Begriff d. Erziehung in d. griech. Bibel," Imago Dei, Festschr. f. G. Krüger (1932), 38 f.

Thus the verse has been construed as a picture of the reconciliation between the wrathful Lord and the bishop of Laodicea, His penitent servant.[24] It is a mistake, however, to see here the experience of an individual, the granting to him of amendment,[25] and the resultant restoration of the congregation. The witness of the verse is to the wooing love of the Lord as this is revealed in the spread of the Gospel. The same image occurs in a similar sense in S. Dt. 33:2 § 343 (142b) with reference to the revelation of God in the OT:[26] "There was no nation among the nations to which he did not go forth and speak, at whose door he did not knock, whether they would accept the Torah." The ref. in the NT, however, is not to doctrine but to the power of life which flows from the constant experience of fellowship with Christ. Hence the saying transcends both eschatology and mysticism. It declares the timeless coming of Christ which is both present and future.[27] At one and the same time it is both a serious and disturbing admonition and a striking and encouraging message of grace. It awakens the individual and establishes the community. It is the Christian message in the comprehensive sense.

Bertram

---

† κρύπτω, † ἀποκρύπτω, † κρυπτός,
† κρυφαῖος, † κρυφῇ, † κρύπτη,
† ἀπόκρυφος

Contents: A. Occurrence and Meaning. B. Theological Significance of the Terms: I. The Greek and Hellenistic World: 1. Popular Religion; 2. Mysticism, Gnosticism and Philosophy. II. The Old Testament: 1. The Essential Distinction between Creator and Creature;

---

[24] Zn. Apk., *ad loc.*
[25] B. Weiss, *Das NT, Handausgabe*[1-2] (1902), *ad loc.*
[26] Cf. Str.-B., III, 39 on R. 1:20.
[27] Loh. Apk., *ad loc.*

κ ρ ύ π τ ω κ τ λ. Liddell-Scott, Pr.-Bauer³, Moult.-Mill., Preisigke Wört., Cr.-Kö., *s.v.*; RE³, 19, 663 ff.; RGG², II, 291 ff., 1355; V, 1130 ff.; Wettstein, esp. on Mt. 10:26 f. (I, 374) and 1 C. 4:5 (II, 112 f.); K. F. Nägelsbach, *Homerische Theologie*³ (1884), 26 ff., 144 ff.; *Nachhomerische Theologie* ... (1857), 23 ff.; A. S. Hunt, "A Greek Cryptogram," *Proceedings of the Brit. Academy*, 25 (1929), 4 ff., on this Preis. Zaub., LVII and the bibl., II, p. 184; J. Hempel, *Gott u. Mensch im AT*² (1936); R. Bultmann, ZNW, 29 (1930), 169 ff.; E. Fascher, "Deus invisibilis," *Marburger Theol. Studien,* I (1931), 41 ff.; R: Otto, *Das Heilige*[17-22] (1929); *Aufsätze das Numinose betreffend*⁴, I (1929), 11 ff. → 563. On C. I.: G. Hölscher, *Kanonisch u. apokryph.* (1905); H. Graetz, MGWJ, 35 (1886), 281 ff.; F. Buhl, *Kanon u. Text d. AT* (1891), H. L. Strack, RE³, IX, 741 ff.; E. Schürer, RE³, I, 622 ff.; F. Hamburger, *Realencyclopädie f. Bibel und Talmud*, II (1883), 66 ff.; Schürer, II⁴, 363 ff.; H. Eberharter, *Der Kanon d. AT z. Zt. des Ben Sira* (1911); on this N. Peters, OLZ, 16 (1913), 267 ff.; G. F. Moore, Jew Enc., II, 1 ff.; L. Blau-N. Schmidt, Jew Enc., III, 140 ff.; Bousset-Gressm., 142 ff.; Moore, I, 235 ff.; S. Bernfeld, EJ, IV, 485 ff.; J. Kaufmann, EJ, II, 1161 ff.; O. Eissfeldt, *Einl. in d. AT* (1934), 614 ff.; Str.-B., IV, 415 ff. On C. II.: RE³, I, 622 ff., 653 ff.; RGG², I, 407 ff., with older bibl.; IV, 1630 f.; Kautzsch Apkr. u. Pseudepigr., esp. introd.; Hennecke; Schürer, III⁴, 188 ff.; Zahn Kan., I (1888), 117 ff.; II (1890), *passim*; A. v. Harnack, *Gesch. d. altchristl. Literatur,* esp. I (1893), 845 ff., II, 1 (1897), 560 ff.; W. Reichardt, "D. Briefe d. Sextus Julius Africanus an Aristides u. Origenes," TU, 34, 3 (1909), 63 ff.

2. The Divine Omniscience; 3. Man in Flight from God; 4. The Righteous Conceals
Nothing from God; 5. His Situation is not Hidden from God; 6. Yahweh Gives Him a
Share in His Hidden Life; 7. God does not Conceal His Wisdom from His Instruments and
Community; 8. God can always Conceal Himself Judicially; 9. The Righteous Hides God's
Word in himself; 10. He is not to Keep it Hidden. III. Judaism: 1. Palestinian Judaism;
2. Hellenistic Judaism; 3. Gnosticism influenced by Judaism. IV. The New Testament:
1. The Synoptists; 2. John's Gospel; 3. The Other NT Writings; 4. Conclusion. V. Transition to Church History. C. Supplement on the Canon and the Apocrypha: I. The Canon
and the Apocrypha in Judaism: 1. The Term Canon; 2. The Early History of the Canon;
3. The OT in the 1st Century A.D.; 4. The Closing of the Canon by the Rabbis; 5. The
Influence of Non-Canonical Writings. II. Βίβλοι ἀκόκρυφοι in Christianity: 1. The LXX
and Hebrew Canon in the Early Church. 2. Apocryphal Quotations in the NT; 3. The
Apocrypha in the Fathers; 4. The Christian Preservation, Revision and Canonisation of
the Jewish Apocrypha; 5. Christian Apocrypha; 6. The Term Apocryphal.

A. Occurrence and Meaning.

κρύπτω can hardly be a secondary form of → καλύπτω.[1] It goes back to √ q̄rāu-, qru-,
"to lay one on the other," "to cover," "to conceal," Lith. *kráuti,* Old Slav. *kryti,* "to
heap," "to load," "to cover," "to conceal," Lett. with labial expansion *krâpju, krâpu,
krâpt,* "to steal," "to deceive."[2] The Gk. word, in distinction from → καλύπτω, whose
wider meaning has a more neutral sense, and κεύθω, which emphasises the depth of the
concealment, tends to lay a heavier stress on the subjective element: "to conceal," "to
hide," "to dissemble."

Literally, the sense in the oldest poetic sources is "to conceal protectively." Hom. Il.,
14, 372 f.: κεφαλὰς δὲ παναίθησιν κορύθεσσιν (helmet) κρύψαντες, 8, 272 (of
Ajax): ὁ δέ μιν σάκεϊ (shield) κρύπτασκε φαεινῷ, cf. Jos. 2:4, 6 (of Rahab the
harlot): ἔκρυψεν αὐτούς, cf. v. 16: κρυβήσεσθε, 6:25. Elsewhere more generally "to
conceal," cf. the difficult bilingual burial inscr. of a boy from Rome, IG, XIV, 1909:
πα]ῖδά με πενταέτη ὀλίγη ἐκρύψατο κρ(ω)σσό[ς (urn). There is a certain counterpart to this in the story of the mother of Moses in Ex. 2:3: οὐκ ἠδύναντο αὐτὸ ἔτι
κρύπτειν (cf. Hb. 11:23). At the command of Yahweh Jeremiah had to hide a linen cloth
by the Euphrates (ἔκρυψα αὐτὸ ἐν τῷ Εὐφράτῃ, Jer. 13:5, cf. v. 4: κατάκρυψον)
and then to dig it up again later in its corrupt state — a sign of judgment on arrogant
Judah. Test. B. 2:4 (vl.): κρύψαι τὸ ἱμάτιον. The concealment is often for selfish
reasons, e.g., to prevent others from using the object, to keep it for oneself. The oligarchs
have their robbers' nests where they conceal their treasures (οἵ θέμενοι ἂν αὐτὰ
κρύψειαν, Plat. Resp., VIII, 548a). The accusation of a provoked woman of the 4th
cent. A.D. charges her husband with keeping all the keys. He has taken an oath before
the bishop: οὐ μὴ κρύψω αὐτὴν πάσας μου τὰς κλεῖς, but in vain: ἔκρυψεν πάλιν
ἐμὲ τὰς κλεῖς, P. Oxy., VI, 903, 16 and 18. The parable of the kingdom tells of a
treasure κεκρυμμένῳ ἐν τῷ ἀγρῷ which the finder at once concealed again (ἔκρυψεν),
to fetch it later (Mt. 13:44). False prudence buries entrusted capital instead of putting it
to work (Mt. 25:18, 25). In rare cases the subjective element is less evident and the ref. is
simply to the result, the disappearing, e.g., to mix in: Lk. 13:21: ζύμη, ἣν λαβοῦσα
γυνὴ ἔκρυψεν (Mt. 13:33 ἐνέκρυψεν) εἰς ἀλεύρου σάτα τρία. But the expression is
chosen for a theological purpose → 973. The same is true in Mt. 5:14: οὐ δύναται
πόλις κρυβῆναι ἐπάνω ὄρους κειμένη, "a city on a hill cannot remain hidden, cannot
conceal itself." The meaning then takes two main directions: a. "to hide in the earth,"
"to bury," → καλύπτω, 556 f. Soph. Ant., 196, the order of Creon regarding Eteocles

[1] Cf. Prellwitz Etym. Wört., *s.v.*
[2] Walde-Pok., I, 477; also L. Meyer, *Handbuch d. gr. Etymologie,* II (1901), 415.

(τάφῳ τε κρύψαι καὶ τὰ πάντ᾽ ἀφαγνίσαι), cf. Plat. Leg., XII, 958e, and the pun in Ps.-Empedocl. Fr., 157 (I, 281, 15, Diels). Not just technically, but with ref. to conduct that shuns the light, Ex. 2:12 (Ac. 7:24 D) and Prv. 1:11, "to cover with earth"; b. astronomically etc., either pass. of the regular setting of the constellations, Anaxim. (I, 23, 26, Diels), or of eclipses, Theon Smyrnaeus, ed. E. Hiller (1878), p. 193, 2 ff.: ἡ μὲν σελήνη, προσγειοτάτη οὖσα, . . . πάντα τὰ πλανώμενα, τινὰ δὲ καὶ τῶν ἀπλανῶν, κρύπτει, ἐπειδὰν μεταξύ τινος αὐτῶν καὶ τῆς ὄψεως ἡμῶν ἐπ᾽ εὐθείας καταστῇ, αὐτὴ δὲ ὑπ᾽ οὐδενὸς ἄστρου κρύπτεται.

Figur., "to conceal something," "to keep it secret," a. with acc., Hom. Od., 4, 350 (Menelaos to Telemachos) οὐδέν τοι ἐγὼ κρύψω ἔπος οὐδ᾽ ἐπικεύσω, also mid., Soph. Trach., 474; b. with double acc., Soph. El., 957 (Electra to the chorus): οὐδὲν γάρ σε δεῖ κρύπτειν μ᾽ ἔτι; c. with prep.: τὶ πρός τινα, Soph. Phil., 588; τὶ ἀπό τινος, Gn. 18:17. Openness, which conceals nothing, is basic to society. One conceals things of which one is ashamed, Heracl. Fr., 95 (I, 97, 1 f., Diels): ἀμαθίαν γὰρ ἄμεινον κρύπτειν, Plat. Phileb., 66a, of sexual things: ἀφανίζοντες κρύπτομεν ὅτι μάλιστα, νυκτὶ πάντα τὰ τοιαῦτα διδόντες, ὡς φῶς οὐ δέον ὁρᾶν αὐτά. κεκρυμμένος thus has also the sense of "close," "cunning." The noxious person who adopts a mien of gentleness is for his fellow-men a κεκρυμμένη παγίς (Menand. Fr., 689 [CAF]). Cf. Jer. 18:22 : παγίδας ἔκρυψαν ἐπ᾽ ἐμέ. Andromache is blamed by Hermione for making her childless and hateful to her husband φαρμάκοις κεκρυμμένοις, Eur. Andr., 32. Secret agitation is the opp. of proper legal processes (κεκρυμμένη σκευωρία, Mitteis-Wilcken, II, 2, 31, Col. VI, 14). Test. R. 4:10 : πονηρὸς κεκρυμμένος θάνατος, evil, artful death. But κρύπτειν can also mean "to overlook something," "to let it go," "to pardon it." In Soph. El., 823 ff. the chorus answers Electra's complaint : ποῦ ποτε κεραυνοὶ Διός ἢ ποῦ φαέθων Ἅλιος, εἰ ταῦτ᾽ ἐφορῶντες κρύπτουσιν ἔκηλοι ("to look on calmly"). Of human forgiveness, Prv. 17:9 : ὃς κρύπτει ἀδικήματα, ζητεῖ φιλίαν· ὃς δὲ μισεῖ κρύπτειν, διίστησιν φίλους καὶ οἰκείους, though never with reference to divine forgiveness in the Bible. In a good sense κρύπτειν is used of the keeping of entrusted secrets, esp. the mysteries. Thus in the so-called catalogue of Delphic rules of life from Miletopolis, which seem for a long period to have played almost the role of a "decalogue" in antiquity, we read : ἀπόρρητα κρύπτε (Ditt. Syll.³, 1268, II, 16).

ἀποκρύπτω (only the aor. in Hom.) is less frequent than the simple form in the poets and LXX, more common in Attic prose. It has the same meaning, lit. "to conceal," "to cover," as in the famous saying of the Lacedaemonian Dienekes before the battle of Thermopylae : ἀποκρυπτόντων ("darken") τῶν Μήδων τὸν ἥλιον (scil. ὑπὸ τοῦ πλήθεος τῶν ὀιστῶν) ὑπὸ σκιῇ ἔσοιτο πρὸς αὐτοὺς ἡ μάχη καὶ οὐκ ἐν ἡλίῳ, Hdt., VII, 226. Cf. Eur. Fr., 153 (TGF); Mt. 25:18 vl.; pass. ψ 18:6. The special meanings of the simple are not developed, though → 961 (κατακρύπτω). Fig. "to keep secret," Plat. Leg., III, 702c : οὐ γὰρ ἀποκρύψομαι σφὼ τὸ νῦν ἐμοὶ συμβαῖνον, also P. Greci e Latini, 169, 13 (2nd cent. B.C.); Gr. Pap. d. Kaiserlichen Universitäts- u. Landesbibliothek zu Strassburg, ed. F. Preisigke, I (1906), 42, 17; Test. G. 2:3 "to suppress." In distinction from the simple, the perf. part. pass. seems to be used only in a favourable sense, though not always without irony, Plat. Phaedr., 273c : Tisias "seems to have discovered a secret craft (ἀποκεκρυμμένην τέχνην)," cf. Prot., 348e, Vett. Val., I, 3 (p. 15, 25 f.) (ζητητικαὶ τῶν ἀποκεκρυμμένων). In the LXX, the word is mostly fig.: Wis. 6:22 : οὐκ ἀποκρύψω ὑμῖν μυστήρια, Is. 40:27; Ιερ. 39:17 (32:17).

κρύπτω and ἀποκρύπτω occur from time to time in the act. intr. Thus in a set of rules for observing birds from the 6th cent. B.C. (Ditt. Syll.³, 1167, 7), it is a good sign if the bird disappears from sight without flapping its wings : ἢμ μὲν ἰθὺς ἀποκρύψει (= ἐὰν . . . ἀποκρύψῃ). Eur. Phoen., 1116 f. (of the shield of Hippomedon): τὰ μὲν σὺν ἄστρων ἐπιτολαῖσιν (rising) ὄμματα βλέποντα, τὰ δὲ κρύπτοντα (the eyes are covered, closed) δυνόντων μέτα, ὡς ὕστερον θανόντος εἰσορᾶν παρῆν. Perhaps the use of ἀποκρύπτειν for "to pass from sight" derives from this, e.g., Plat. Prot., 338a : φεύγειν εἰς τὸ πέλαγος . . . ἀποκρύψαντα γῆν.

κρυπτός, "covered," "hidden" : lit. κρυπτὴ διῶρυξ, an underground passage, Hdt., III, 146, ὀχετὸς κρυπτός, a covered canal, Ditt. Syll.³, 973, 5, κρυπτοὶ καρκίνοι, deep-seated ulcers, Hippocr. Aphorismi, 6, 38 (IV, 572, Littré). Fig. "secret." κρυπτή was used for the secret service which the Athenians maintained in subject states, κρυπτοί for those entrusted with it (Anecd. Graec., p. 273, 33 ff., s.v. κρυπτή : ἀρχή τις ὑπὸ τῶν Ἀθηναίων πεμπομένη εἰς τοὺς ὑπηκόους, ἵνα κρύφα ἐπιτελέσωσι τὰ ἔξω γινόμενα· διὰ τοῦτο γὰρ καὶ κρυπτοὶ ἐκλήθησαν). In Plato's state (Leg., VI, 763b) the κρυπτοί are secret police or rangers. Sparta is supposed to have given the κρυπτεία the task of stabbing superfluous helots from behind. The word is also used for a kind of military training during which youths were put under privations and had to support themselves by hunting, thieving and robbery, Plat. Leg., I, 633b. Like κεκρυμμένος, κρυπτός often has a bad connotation. κρυπτὸν πάθος (BGU, I, 316, 28, 4th cent. A.D.) is a vicious habit of a slave which is concealed at purchase and for which the seller shares responsibility for half a year. The word is commonly used by the tragic dramatists in the sense of "cunning." Philoctet. complains that low cunning steals bow and arrows from him : ἀλλά μοι ἄσκοπα κρυπτά τ᾽ ἔπη δολερᾶς ὑπέδυ φρενός (Soph. Phil., 1111 f.). But it can also denote a preference. Hera opens her chambers κληῖδι κρυπτῇ· τὴν δ᾽ οὐ θεὸς ἄλλος ἀνῷγεν (Hom. Il., 14, 168). The noun τὸ κρυπτόν is rare outside biblical lit. It is partly neut.; Thuc., V, 68, 2 tells us that the secret character of the Lacedaemonian state (τῆς πολιτείας τὸ κρυπτόν) ruled out exact figures of warriors. Partly it is used for distinction ; Preis. Zaub., LVII, 13, from an incantation addressed to a divine power which is not more precisely designated : ἀπάγγελλε τὰ κρυπτὰ (the mysteries) τῆς μυριωνύμου θεᾶς Ἴσιδος. Finally, it occurs in a bad sense ; Jos. Bell., 5, 402 : τὰ κρυπτὰ τῶν ἁμαρτημάτων, the abomination of sins. It can hardly be an accident that we do not seem to have instances of phrases like ἐν κρυπτῷ in non-biblical Gk. (except for Test. Jud. 12:5). They do not occur, of course, in the LXX, though cf. → ἐν ἀποκρύφῳ, 961. For the noun τὸ κρυπτόν cf. 4 Βασ. 21:7 vl. (Orig.; B etc.: τὸ γλυπτὸν τοῦ ἄλσους ἐν τῷ οἴκῳ), τὰ κρυπτά, Dt. 29:28; Sir. 1:30; 3:22; 4:18; Is. 22:9; 29:10; Ιερ. 30:4; Sus. 42 (Θ). In the NT τὸ κρυπτόν, Lk. 8:17, τὰ κρυπτά, R. 2:16; 1 C. 4:5; 14:25; 2 C. 4:2, ἐν τῷ κρυπτῷ, Mt. 6:4, 6, on v. 18 → κρυφαῖος, infra ; Jn. 7:4, 10; 18:20; R. 2:29. On Lk. 11:33 → κρύπτη, infra.

κρυφαῖος is a rare syn. adj. found from Pind. Isthm., I, 67, lit. in Plat. Tim., 77c, anatomically : ὀχετοὺς κρυφαίους, hidden canals, fig. Plat. Soph., 219e : τὸ δὲ κρυφαῖον αὐτῆς πᾶν θηρευτικόν. It does not seem to be used as a noun outside bibl. lit., LXX Jer. 23:24 : εἰ κρυβήσεται ἄνθρωπος ἐν κρυφαίοις, Lam. 3:10 : λέων ἐν κρυφαίοις. In the NT only Mt. 6:18 : ὅπως μὴ φανῇς τοῖς ἀνθρώποις νηστεύων ἀλλὰ τῷ πατρί σου τῷ ³ ἐν τῷ κρυφαίῳ· καὶ ὁ πατήρ σου ὁ βλέπων ἐν τῷ κρυφαίῳ ἀποδώσει σοι → 974.

κρυφῇ ⁴ adv. from the time of Soph. Ant., 85 etc.; Xenoph. Sym., 5, 8; P. Oxy., I, 83, 14 (κρυβῇ); Test. S. 8:2; Zeb. 1:6; G. 2:3 : "secret." In the NT only Eph. 5:12 : τὰ γὰρ κρυφῇ γινόμενα ὑπ᾽ αὐτῶν αἰσχρόν ἐστιν καὶ λέγειν, → 976.

κρύπτη, Callixenus, 1 (3rd cent. B.C., in FHG, III [1849], p. 56). Strabo, 17, 1, 37; Jos. Bell., 5, 330 (Niese : κρυπτήν), "vault," "covered way," "cellar." In the NT only Lk. 11:33, → 975.

---

³ There are no real reasons for rejecting the τῷ before ἐν τῷ κρυφαίῳ, Wellh. Mt., ad loc. The corresponding τῷ in Mt. 6:6 is also well attested. It is missing only in D Sysc, some Latins and the min. of the Lake group.

⁴ On the orthography, whether with or without the iota subscriptum, v. Bl.-Debr. § 26. That the word was later at least felt to be a dative η, not an instrumental η, is shown by the common ἐν κρυφῇ in the LXX (ψ 138:15; Is. 29:15; 45:19; 48:16; also Test. Jos. 4:2; Test. B. 12:3). Hence in the NT, whatever the linguistic position, it is better to write κρυφῇ; so also the ostracon, APF, 6 (1920), 220, No. 8, 2 f. (3rd cent. B.C.): ἀπόστειλον τοῖς ὑπογεγραμμένοις τὰς πεταλίας κρυφῆι καὶ μηθεὶς αἰσθανέσθω.

ἀπόκρυφος, first in Hdt., II, 35 : τὰ μὲν αἰσχρὰ ἀναγκαῖα ἐν ἀποκρύφῳ ἐστὶ ποιέειν. Eur. Herc. Fur., 1070; also Vita Philonidis Fr., 3, 1, ed. W. Crönert, SAB, 41 (1900), 943. The word is not found in Plato nor is it common in inscr. (on the Isis hymn of Andros → 963) and the pap., but it is a favourite term in some magic books and Vett. Val. and esp. among astrologers, → 965. Lit. "hidden" of treasure, Da. 11:43 (Θ); 1 Macc. 1:23; fig. "concealed," "secret," common in the LXX in phrases like ἐν ἀποκρύφῳ (→ 968): Dt. 27:15; ψ 30:20; Is. 4:6, or ἐν ἀποκρύφοις, ψ 9:29; 63:5; Sir. 16:21. Only as an adj. in the NT, Mk. 4:22; Lk. 8:17; Col. 2:3.

B. Theological Significance of the Terms.

In all true religion there is awareness of a reality which man cannot reach by ordinary perception. In the religious significance of the words this awareness finds specific expression in many different directions.

I. The Greek and Hellenistic World.

1. Popular Religion.

The deity is hidden. Even uncomplicated and this-worldly Homeric man is aware of this.

A veil of mystery (ἀχλύς) envelops it. No one sees it unless it chooses (Od., 10, 573; 16, 161). Often its presence may be discerned only by certain signs. Let man sense it and be silent, Od., 2, 400 ff.; 19, 29 ff. Most Greeks have an even stronger sense of the numinous. To see the gods at an unfavourable time means destruction. "Let us flee, mother," says Ion (Eur. Ion, 1549 ff.), "lest we see what is of the gods — unless it be the right time for us to see." The daughter of Zeus hides herself in heaven (οὐρανῷ κρύπτεται, Eur. Hel., 606).

The numinous element is strengthened by the riddle of death and the related cult of chthonic deities and heroes.

The word group is used technically for concealment in the often underground adytum ; this is understood as rapture and eternal life. [5] Paus., II, 3, 11 recounts the legend which gathered around the burial of the children of Medea near the Sicyon street in Corinth. Having first given the form which serves to establish a festival of child-heroes (cf. II, 3, 6 ff.), he then gives the version of Eumelos in his Corinthiaca. Acc. to this account, the Corinthians did not stone the children of Medea and then sacrifice their own children in expiation until the gruesome custom was replaced by an annual animal sacrifice, but Medea herself brought her children to the temple of Hera in the hope, which was not fulfilled, that she would thereby make them immortal. Μηδεία δὲ παῖδας μὲν γίνεσθαι, τὸ δὲ ἀεὶ τικτόμενον κατακρύπτειν αὐτὸ ἐς τὸ ἱερὸν φέρουσαν τῆς Ἥρας, κατακρύπτειν δὲ ἀθανάτους ἔσεσθαι νομίζουσαν (II, 3, 11). This is the version which with modifications underlies Eur. Med. Medea kills her children and buries them in the sanctuary of Hera that no enemy may disturb their rest. The legend is best understood if it is realised that in the adyta of temples, originally caves, which were accessible only to the priests, buried heroes were venerated who were thought to be set among the gods and hence to be immortal. The cult of Rhesos at Pangaion offers a particularly good example. In Eur.'s tragedy of this name the corpse of the hero, who was killed before Troy, is brought by his mother, a Muse, to Mt. Pangaion and buried, or concealed, there, at the later cultic site :

---

[5] F. Pfister in Pauly-W., XI (1922), 2141, s.v. "Kultus"; Rohde, I⁹⁻¹⁰, 136; F. Pfister, "Der Reliquienkult im Altertum," RVV, 5, 1 (1909), 313 f.; 5, 2 (1912), 570; H. Güntert, Kalypso (1919), 28 ff. [G. Bertram].

κρυπτὸς δ' ἐν ἄντροις τῆς ὑπαργύρου χθονὸς
ἀνθρωποδαίμων κείσεται βλέπων φάος,
Βάκχου προφήτης ὥστε Παγγαίου πέτραν
ᾤκησε σεμνὸς τοῖσιν εἰδόσιν θεός. (Eur. Rhes., 970 ff.).

κρυπτός has here almost the sense of "placed among the gods." On related motifs
→ καθεύδω, 433; 447.

Yet the numinous element should not be overestimated.

Xenophon fears the gods, but he can call the practice of natural covetousness a
ὑπηρετεῖν τοῖς θεοῖς so far as it rests on instinct. The wise man corrects it by making
friends with superfluous mammon (Xenoph. Cyrop., VIII, 2, 22; cf. Lk. 16:9). The ethical
movements touch, but only externally. They rest on basic religious attitudes which are
radically different.

The Greek deity was never a reality which had absolute control over man, even
in the sense that nothing could be hidden from it. The omniscience of the gods is
theoretically upheld, especially for purposes of oaths, but it is never acknowledged
in practice. [6]

Cf. on the one side Od., 4, 379 and 468 : θεοὶ δέ τε πάντα ἴσασιν, and on the other
numerous examples in Hom. (Il., 18, 185 f.: Iris, sent by Hera, comes to Achilles, οὐδ'
οἶδε Κρονίδης ὑψίζυγος, οὐδέ τις ἄλλος ἀθανάτων, οἳ Ὄλυμπον ἀγάννιφον
ἀμφινέμονται, 1, 540 ff. etc.), and later cf. Paus., VIII, 42, 2; IX, 3, 1, where the gods
are ignorant and are deceived. The gods, too, are subject to the impersonal power of
fate, and they do not know what it has ordained. The golden scales in the hand of Zeus
are not subject to his will or knowledge (Hom. Il., 22, 208 ff.). Time alone is omniscient
in the strict sense. Soph. Fr., 280 (TGF): πρὸς ταῦτα κρύπτε μηδέν· ὡς ὁ πάνθ'
ὁρῶν καὶ πάντ' ἀκούων πάντ' ἀναπτύσσει χρόνος.

It is no accident that the word group is in the first instance rare in religious
contexts.

The Greek is more familiar with his gods than the Oriental. The deity is more and
more divested of the reverence of the earlier period [7] and approximates more or less to
idealised man. [8] Plastic representation in works of art which were not primarily designed
for cultic use hastened the process of assimilation which it also documents. The feared
deity becomes the affable deity [9] and finally the impotent and helpless deity, an object

---

[6] The current opinion and the protest of a soaring spirit against it are reflected in Xen.
Mem., I, 1, 19 : ἐπιμελεῖσθαι θεοὺς ἐνόμιζεν (ὁ Σωκράτης) ἀνθρώπων οὐχ' ὃν τρόπον
οἱ πολλοὶ νομίζουσιν· οὗτοι μὲν γὰρ οἴονται τοὺς θεοὺς τὰ μὲν εἰδέναι, τὰ δ' οὐκ
εἰδέναι· Σωκράτης δὲ πάντα μὲν ἡγεῖτο θεοὺς εἰδέναι, τά τε λεγόμενα καὶ πραττόμενα καὶ τὰ σιγῇ βουλευόμενα. There is a par. from the political sphere in Dion. Hal.
Ant. Rom., 10, 10 : ἐπεὶ δὲ ἡ τοῦ δαιμονίου πρόνοια ... τὰ κεκρυμμένα βουλεύματα
καὶ τὰς ἀνοσίους ἐπιχειρήσεις τῶν θεοῖς ἐχθρῶν εἰς φῶς ἄγει ...
[7] E. v. Dobschütz, "Christusbilder," TU, II, 3 (1899), 18; L. Radermacher, Festschr. T.
Gomperz dargebracht (1902), 200 ff.; Weinreich, AH, 147; E. Williger, "Hagios," RVV,
19, 1 (1922), 5 f.
[8] There is hardly a more significant statue in this regard than the Apollo Sauroctonos
of Praxiteles (c. 350 B.C.), Roman copy in the Louvre, Haas 13/14 (1928), 61.
[9] Characteristic is a votive relief dating from the 5th cent. which shows Athena coming
to a workman at his table and graciously extending her hand (Phot. Alinari, 24, 605); cf.
also the well-known terra cotta relief of the Roman imperial period which shows Athena
giving instruction in shipbuilding, Brit. Museum.

of lewd ridicule to Phlyacic humour. [10] There are now no longer any hidden depths. In so far as the numinous remained in Gk. religion, the typical term for it was μυστήριον rather than κρυπτόν. But this means that the deity is accessible only to the initiate as δεικνύμενον, not to every one.

2. Mysticism, Gnosticism and Philosophy.

No sharp lines of differentiation can be drawn between popular religion, mysticism, Gnosticism and philosophy. But they may be justifiably distinguished for the purpose of classification.

a. The Greek mysteries in the narrower sense lay no great stress on the concept of hiddenness. In practice the majority of initiates found it absolutely necessary to make concessions. Thus the Eleusinians resemble private cultic societies with no mystery character, and they even have connections with the national cult. The situation is different where alien mysteries exert an influence.

Whether the distinction between concealed and revealed gods in the Dionysus mysteries is to be viewed from this angle is debated (→ II, 451 f.). That the secret character of the Bacchic mysteries was taken very seriously is shown by the fate of Pentheus in the legend, and also at Rome in Liv., 39, 8 ff. Egypt especially with its distinctive language and literature, and its ancient religion protected by a priestly caste, was for antiquity the land of hidden things, as India has been more recently. The Isis hymn of Andros (1st cent. B.C.) [11] sets the following words on the lips of Isis:

δειφαλέω δ' Ἑρμᾶνος ἀπόκρυφα σύνβολα δέλτων
εὑρομένα γραφίδεσσι κατέξυσα, ταῖσι χάραξα
φρικαλέον μύσταις ἱερὸν λόγον· ὅσα τε δᾶμος
ἀτραπὸν ἐς κοινὰν κατεθήκατο, πάντα βαθείας
ἐκ φρενὸς ὑφάνασα διακριδόν.

"I have found the clever Hermes' hidden signs of the tables and inscribed them with styles with which I have indicated the sacred doctrine which infuses the initiate with pious awe. And what has set the people on the common way, all that I have woven out of the depths of the heart." The underlying sentence in the inscr. of Kyme runs: ἐπαιδεύθην ὑπ[ὸ] Ἑρμοῦ καὶ γράμματα εὗρον μετὰ Ἑρμοῦ τά τε ἱερὰ καὶ τὰ δημόσια <γράμματα>, ἵνα μὴ ἐν τοῖς αὐτοῖς πάντα γράφηται (Peek, 122, 3, a. b). Here the invention of hieroglyphics is called the common act of Hermes-Toth and Isis, and the distinction between hieratic and demotic writing is traced back to the purpose of variation, or perhaps to the concealment of certain things. This view is nearer to the genuine Egyptian feeling for the matter. The Hellenistic redactor takes it that the great goddess penetrated into the secrets of the even greater god. We see here the beginning of the technical use of ἀπόκρυφος (→ 965) in Gnosticism. Plut. (Is. et Os., 9 [II, 354b ff.]) tells us that when an Egyptian king left the warrior caste he was adopted by the priests and "given a share in their philosophy, which was for the most part concealed behind myths and sacral words which have an obscure reflection of truth and enigmatic meanings" (μετεῖχε τῆς φιλοσοφίας ἐπικεκρυμμένης τὰ πολλὰ μύθοις καὶ λόγοις ἀμυδρὰς ἐμφάσεις τῆς ἀληθείας καὶ διαφάσεις ἔχουσιν). The sphinxes before the temples were symbols of this secret wisdom, ὡς αἰνιγματώδη σοφίαν τῆς θεολογίας αὐτῶν ἐχούσης. The Egyptian name for Zeus, Ammon, was given by Manetho of Sebennytos the meaning of concealment (τὸ κεκρυμμένον ... καὶ τὴν κρύψιν ὑπὸ ταύτης δηλοῦσθαι τῆς φωνῆς). Hecataios of Abdera, however, regarded

---

[10] For an example on a vase, cf. Haas, 66.
[11] *Der Isishymnus von Andros u. verwandte Texte erklärt*, W. Peek (1930), p. 15, lines 10 ff., p. 31 ff.

the word as an invocation by which the Egyptians sought to make the supreme god reveal himself (τὸν πρῶτον θεόν, ὃν τῷ παντὶ τὸν αὐτὸν νομίζουσιν, ὡς ἀφανῆ καὶ κεκρυμμένον ὄντα προσκαλούμενοι καὶ παρακαλοῦντες ἐμφανῆ γενέσθαι καὶ δῆλον αὐτοῖς Ἀμοῦν λέγουσιν).[12] The Isis mysteries were kept particularly secret. Paus., X, 32, 18 tells us that a Roman who had bought his way into the sanctuary of Isis with money told what he had seen and was punished by the goddess with death. Apuleius is very restrained in his account in Met., XI. But the concealment of the deity is not essential. The distinction is between initiates and non-initiates.

b. With Gnosticism we may already in some sense classify Orphism.

Very typical is a hymn to Zeus handed down by Porphyrius and Stobaeus (Orph. Fr., No. 168, Kern). Zeus is described as the universal body which embraces all being from the sun to Tartarus, and then the poem closes (lines 31 f.):

πάντα δ᾽ ἀποκρύψας αὖθις φάος ἐς πολυγηθὲς
μέλλεν ἀπὸ κραδίης προφέρειν πάλι, θέσκελα ῥέζων.

"After he had concealed all things, he wished to bring it forth again from the heart to gladdening light by doing marvels." The meaning of ἀποκρύπτω here is close to the sense of "bury" or "snatch away" mentioned earlier. The giving of new life is a second act. The reference is to the eternal polarity of death and birth (→ II, 451). The deity, understood as cosmic body, is fully visible in all things, but also hidden. For the doctrine of the universal body of the deity is an esoteric doctrine. There is, however, no essential concealment. It is emphasised as strongly as possible that nothing is hidden from the deity (lines 17 ff.):

νοῦς δέ οἱ ἀψευδὴς βασιλήϊος ἄφθιτος αἰθήρ,
ᾧ δὴ πάντα κλύει[13] καὶ φράζεται· οὐδέ τίς ἐστιν
αὐδὴ οὐδ᾽ ἐνοπὴ οὐδὲ κτύπος οὐδὲ μὲν ὄσσα,
ἣ λήθει Διὸς οὖας ὑπερμενέος Κρονίωνος.

"And he has an infallible royal intelligence, which is the imperishable ether, by which all things are heard and to which all things are reported; there is no sound or tone or stir or whisper which is hidden from the ears of the omnipotent son of Cronos." In spite of the anthropomorphic vesture, the presuppositions are wholly pantheistic. Materially the statement hardly goes beyond that given earlier (→ 962). The distinctively personal view of Socrates (→ 962, n. 6) is more or less isolated in the Greek world.

If influences from the East are already apparent in Orphism, they may be seen in full flood in Gnosticism in the narrower sense.

There is a strange mixture of Oriental, Egyptian and Greek influences in the Naassene sermon preserved by Hippolyt.:[14] διὰ τοῦτό φησιν ἀκίνητον εἶναι τὸ πάντα κινοῦν· μένει γὰρ ὅ ἐστι ποιοῦν τὰ πάντα καὶ οὐδὲν τῶν γινομένων γίνεται. τοῦτο εἶναί φησι τὸ ἀγαθόν, καὶ τοῦτ᾽ εἶναι τὸ μέγα καὶ κρύφιον τῶν ὅλων καὶ ἄγνωστον μυστήριον τὸ παρὰ τοῖς Αἰγυπτίοις κεκαλυμμένον καὶ ἀνακεκαλυμμένον. οὐδεὶς γάρ, φησίν, ἔστιν ἐν ᾧ ναῷ πρὸ τῆς εἰσόδου οὐχ ἕστηκε γυμνὸν τὸ κεκρυμμένον κάτωθεν ἄνω βλέπον καὶ πάντας τοὺς καρποὺς τῶν αὐτοῦ γινομένων στεφανούμενον. Acc to the conjecture of Reitzenstein this address was given in Alexandria. The continuation shows that it had phallic statues in view.[15] The *membrum erectum* which

---

[12] Cf. the ed. by G. Parthey (1850).

[13] As the context shows, κλύειν is here intr. or pass. Comparable is the intr. use of ἀκούειν in the tragic poets, Liddell-Scott, *s.v.*

[14] Quoted acc. to Reitzenstein Poim., 87.

[15] Examples in Haas, 13/14 (1928), 29, 30, 32, 67, 70.

is the cause of all life is compared with the deity as *causa causarum,* and the display of a member otherwise concealed, which is common in other places as well as Egypt, symbolises on the author's view the revelation of the divine. In the main Gnosticism prefers esoteric knowledge. This is particularly plain in the documents of decaying Gnosticism, the magic books and the works of astrologers. Leid. Pap., V introduces the account of a magic formula called the great Uphôr with the words : ἔχε ἐν ἀποκρύφῳ ὡς μεγαλομυστήριον. κρύβε, κρύβε (Preis. Zaub., XII, 321 f.). The word ἀπόκρυφος becomes technical for secret books or inscr. which are particularly valuable, *ibid.,* IV, 1115 : στήλη ἀπόκρυφος, XIII, 343 f., Μωϋσέως ἱερὰ βίβλος ἀπόκρυφος ἐπικαλουμένη ὀγδόη ἡ ἁγία, 731: Μωϋσέως ἀπόκρυφος η᾽, 1059 : Μωϋσέως ἀπόκρυφος Σεληνιακή. In spite of the name of Moses, this secret knowledge is pagan rather than Jewish in origin and nature. To keep the books secret they were written in secret writing, hence cryptogram, *ibid.,* LVII. [16] Although there is ref. here to the mysteries of Isis of a thousand names (→ 960), awe of the divine which is essentially hidden is extraordinarily remote. To cause a subordinate demonic power to yield up these secrets, the speaker makes use of these conjurations, among them : σὲ κατακρύψω ἐκ (protectively cover against) τῶν γιγάντων (lines 8 f.).

The word group is particularly liked by astrologers, esp. ἀπόκρυφος. ἀπόκρυφα [πράγματα] are dark affairs in the criminal or mantic sense (Vett. Val., IV, 11 [p. 176, 6]; II, 35 [p. 108, 3 f.]). In so far as the discovery of such things is a sign of perspicacity, a gift of combination and perhaps also a proof of supernatural assistance, the designation ἀποκρύφων μύσται becomes a mark of distinction. It is found in many lists of praiseworthy qualities along with φρόνιμοι (I, 2 [p. 7, 30]) and περίεργοι (magicians, I, 2 [p. 10, 16]). The term μύσται suggests that we have here degenerate theology, and this is fully borne out elsewhere. Cf. I, 21 (p. 37, 27 ff.): οὐκ ἀπόρους ... οὐδὲ ἀσυνέτους, πολυπείρους καὶ πολυΐστορας ἢ προγνωστικοὺς φιλομαθεῖς περιέργους, ἀποκρύφων μύστας, εὐσεβοῦντας εἰς τὸ θεῖον, δυσσυνειδήτους. [17] IV, 12 (p. 179, 22 ff.): ὁ φιλίας (scil. τόπος, an astrological term) ἀποδημίας ξένων ὠφελείας θεοῦ βασιλέως δυνάστου ἀστρονομίας χρηματισμῶν, θεῶν ἐπιφανείας, μαντείας, μυστικῶν ἢ ἀποκρύφων πραγμάτων κοινωνίας. Envious people curse (VIII, 5 [p. 301, 21 ff.]) διὰ τὴν τῶν μυστικῶν καὶ ἀποκρύφων φωταγωγίαν. The writer resists them with the required counter-curses. This degenerate theology becomes increasingly secular. Later astrologers group τῶν ἀποκρύφων μύστας with mathematicians and athletes (παλαίστρας ἡγεμόνας, Catal. Cod. Astr. Graec., VIII, 4, p. 151, 26). In such passages the ref. to *libri apocryphi* also recurs, e.g., in a certain Rhetorios (*ibid.,* 176, 16): ἐὰν Κρόνος ἐπίδῃ τινὰ αὐτῶν τῶν ε᾽ λαμπρῶν ἀστέρων ὁμονοοῦντα, ἰατρικῆς ἔμπειροι γίνονται καὶ προγνῶσται, ἀποκρύφων βίβλων καὶ τελετῶν πολυΐστορες. On Gnosticism under Jewish influence → III, 3.

c. Later periods believed they were honouring Greek philosophy when they traced back its origins to the secret knowledge of the Orient.

Suidas tells us that Pherecydes of Syros, the reputed teacher of Pythagoras, had no teacher ἀλλ᾽ ἑαυτὸν ἀσκῆσαι κτησάμενον τὰ Φοινίκων ἀπόκρυφα βιβλία (II, 199, 25 ff., Diels). That this tradition is old is shown by the account in Jos. Ap., I, 6-14, who calls Thales as well as Pherecydes and Pythagoras a pupil of the East, cf. in general also Cl. Al. Strom., I, 15, 77 ff.

---

[16] A. S. Hunt, "A Greek Cryptogram," *Proceedings of the British Academy,* 25 (1929), 127 ff.

[17] The meaning "with a bad conscience," which is always given by the dict. for δυσσυνείδητος, hardly fits the context. If we are not to assume that contradictory qualities are here brought together — which seems to occur — or that there is a scribal error, another meaning must be sought. Is there perhaps a ref. to the occult ability to eliminate the consciousness?

It is in fact true that Greek philosophy from Heraclitus to Neo-Platonism was subject to many oriental influences.[18] The new thing, however, is that it sought primarily a purely natural explanation of the world (the Ionic natural philosophers, the Eleatic school). Nevertheless, the inscrutability of nature is always to some degree a living factor.

Heracl. writes : ἡ φύσις κρύπτεσθαι φιλεῖ (Fr., 123, I, 101, 13, Diels). The enigmatic nature of being is shared by the gods (→ the quotation from Heracl., 567). One may grasp its meaning ; one may also miss it. Yet there is no essential hiddenness. In pure Gk. thought the conviction grows that true being contains the *logos* and may be grasped with the *nous*.[19] This unconditional rationalism retreats as antiquity declines. The decline of exact science, the weariness of an aging culture, the renewed influence of the Orient,[20] all combine to heighten the sense of the hidden and to waken the demand for revelation. But the word group does not seem to have taken on technical significance in these connections. It is rare in the Hermetic writings and in Neo-Platonism.[21] To be sure, emphasis is laid on the fact that God is remote from sensual apprehension. But He is also high above human thought. He is the basis of *nous,* but not Himself *nous.* Many terms are used which seem to be almost syn. of κρυπτός or ἀπόκρυφος, e.g., ἀόρατος, ἀθεώρητος, ἀκατάληπτος, ἀφανής, νοῦ κρείσσων.[22] The words themselves are hardly found at all in instructive contexts. This can hardly be an accident. Even later philosophy holds aloof from ordinary mysticism and Gnosticism. It maintained a certain speculative bent. Its principle is : ἅγιος ὁ θεός, ὃς γνωσθῆναι βούλεται, καὶ γινώσκεται τοῖς ἰδίοις (Corp. Herm., I, 31). Cf. I, 474, 15; 486, 30 ff.

The term "to conceal" takes a strongly ethical turn in later Stoicism. Epict. in his famous hymn περὶ κυνισμοῦ (Diss., III, 22, 14 ff.) claims that in distinction from others the Cynic has nothing to hide. Of others it may be said : τὰ κρύψοντα πολλὰ ἔχουσιν. κέκλεικε τὴν θύραν, ἔστακέν τινα πρὸ τοῦ κοιτῶνος· 'ἄν τις ἔλθῃ, λέγε ὅτι ἔξω ἐστίν, οὐ σχολάζει'. But the only cloak of the Cynic is his own sense of honour (αἰδώς). This is for him house and gate and watchman and darkness. οὔτε γὰρ θέλειν τι δεῖ ἀποκρύπτειν αὐτὸν τῶν ἑαυτοῦ (εἰ δὲ μή, ἀπῆλθεν, ἀπώλεσε τὸν Κυνικόν, τὸν ὕπαιθρον, τὸν ἐλεύθερον, ἦρκταί τι τῶν ἐκτὸς φοβεῖσθαι, ἦρκται χρείαν ἔχειν τοῦ ἀποκρύψοντος) οὔτε ὅταν θέλῃ δύναται. ποῦ γὰρ αὐτὸν ἀποκρύψῃ ἢ πῶς; (III, 22, 14 ff.). The life of the Cynic is before all men under the open sky. This fine passage is typical in its nearness to the Bible and remoteness from it.

---

[18] Cf. L. v. Schroeder, *Pythagoras und die Inder* (1884); R. Reitzenstein, "Plato und Zarathustra," *Vorträge d. Bibliothek Warburg,* 1924/25 (1927), 20 ff.

[19] → 568. Cf. also the description in E. Norden, *Agnostos Theos* (1913), 83 ff.

[20] On these A. Oepke, *Karl Barth u. die Mystik* (1928), 10 and bibl.

[21] Cf. the dict. and indexes of Porphyr. and Iambl., the indexes to J. Kroll, *Die Lehren d. Hermes Trismegistos* (1914), Norden, Reitzenstein Poim. and Hell. Myst. Iambl. Myst., II, 4 (75, 12, Parthey) uses τὸν οὐρανὸν ἀποκρύπτειν for to "darken" the heaven. *Ibid.,* I, 6 (19, 17): The race of heroes takes to itself the better thing which comes from above and which is to some degree inwardly hidden (ἄνωθεν ἐφεστηκότα καὶ οἷον ἀποκρυπτόμενα εἰς τὸ ἔσω τὰ βελτίονα παραδεχόμενον). The use approximates to that of Mt. 13:33 and par., but is not strictly theological. A technical use occurs in Corp. Herm., XIII, 16 : ὅθεν τοῦτο (the reward of regeneration) οὐ διδάσκεται, ἀλλὰ κρύπτεται ἐν σιγῇ. But acc. to Scott this sentence is from a later hand. κρυπτοὶ λόγοι as God's magic formula at creation (I, 468, 1, cf. 464, 20) can be regarded as the harmless echo of popular modes of expression. ἐκέκρυπτω (I, 462, 7) is not genuine.

[22] These terms recur constantly from the time of Plato. The Platonic counterpart was νοητός. God may be grasped by the *nous,* though not the senses. Hence He is not absolutely hidden. Even in the Κόρη κόσμου of Hermes Trismegistos ἄγνωστος occurs only once and with ref. to God before creation ; θεῷ τῷ ἔτι ἀγνώστῳ (perhaps not genuine, Corp. Herm., I, 458, 3 f.) (Kroll [→ n. 21]). νοῦ κρείσσων is found in Ps.-Archytas (Norden [→ n. 19] 84).

II. The Old Testament.

To express the idea of concealment, Greek in general and the Greek OT have only the present terms, along with compounds like ἐπι-, κατα-, συγκρύπτω, and → καλύπτω. In Hebrew, however, quite apart from textual corruptions, errors in translation and similar details, there are at least seven roots: עלם, סתר, כסה, כחד, טמן, חבה or חבא and צפן, and many other related expressions like חשׂךְ, לוט, מנע, כמס, נצר, ספן, חפשׂ and כנף are also found in the relevant stem forms. If there is not always a direct religious connection, in the case of most of the synonyms the wealth of connections in which "to hide" and "to be hidden" occur in OT religion gives a fulness which in the LXX has to be pressed into the far too narrow bed of a single stem. Yet the many subsidiary meanings of the Heb. terms are expressed in the many Gk. words which the LXX selects acc. to its understanding of the various contexts. Thus the element of λανθάνειν and ὑπεριδεῖν is found in עלם, of ἀφιστάναι, ἀποστρέφειν and ἀπαλλάσσειν in סתר, of κωλύειν, ἀφαιρεῖν etc. (in all 22 Gk. words) in מנע, of esp. ἀφανίζειν, ἐκλείπειν in כחד, of θησαυρίζειν etc. in צפן. כסה is predominantly rendered by καλύπτειν and its compounds and by περιβάλλειν. A certain perplexity may be discerned here in face of the many nuances of the Heb. [23]

The connections in which the word group is used in the OT are so varied and loose that no attempt at a history of theological use is possible. We can only say that the later writings, especially Psalms and the Wisdom literature, give the best insight. Our surest course is to give a systematic account of the data.

1. The words denote the essential distinction between Creator and creature. With all that belongs to Him, God is hidden. The concern here is not with epistemological considerations. It is possible that God should make Himself known to the senses. But because of the inaccessibility and consuming holiness of Yahweh, death would normally result (Is. 6:5 etc.). The accent falls on the fact that God alone disposes of Himself and of all being. In distinction from the Greek world, His hiddenness is here regarded as strictly essential and willed (→ 963 ff.).

Yahweh dwells in the concealment of the clouds (ἐν ἀποκρύφῳ καταιγίδος, ψ 80:7; synon. σκότος, γνόφος, θύελλα, Dt. 4:11; Ex. 20:21). He wills to dwell in darkness (1 K. 8:12; 2 Ch. 6:1). His works are κρυπτά (Sir. 11:4), ἀπόκρυφα (43:32), ἐν ἀποκρύφοις (16:21). To Him belong future things which are still hidden (τὰ ἀπόκρυφα par. τὰ ἐσόμενα, 48:25, τὰ κρυπτὰ κυρίῳ τῷ θεῷ ἡμῶν, Dt. 29:28). Divine wisdom is withdrawn from man's regard and hidden from the fowls of heaven, Job 28:21.

2. Nothing is hidden from this God who controls all being. The OT takes God's omnipresence and omniscience more seriously than any religion. Materially the obscure intimations of Socrates and Dion. Hal. (→ 962, n. 6) are here brought to fulfilment.

Yahweh uncovers everything secret (Da. 2:22 Θ: ἀποκαλύπτει βαθέα καὶ ἀπόκρυφα, 47 LXX: ὁ ἐκφαίνων μυστήρια κρυπτὰ μόνος, Sus. 42 Θ: ὁ τῶν κρυπτῶν γνώστης). Nothing can hide itself from Him, Σιρ. 39:19. [24] Not even the future can do this, 42:19, 48:25. His eyes are ten thousand times brighter than the sun and see through all things, Σιρ. 23:19. No sinner can hide from Him, Jer. 16:17; 23:24; Ιερ. 30:4 (49:10); Job 34:22; Σιρ. 1:30; 16:17; 17:15, 20. With a personal incisiveness which goes far beyond any pantheism, Ps. 139, for all its childlike understanding of the world, gives

---

[23] The last four sentences are by Bertram.
[24] Cf. also Ιερ. 39(32):17, 27. The LXX read יִפָּלֵא for יִכָּלֵא.

a most impressive picture of the way in which man is ineluctably accompanied by the divine knowledge.

3. Sinful man tries to flee, of course, from the omniscient God. In the OT, too, that which is hidden is reticent and afraid of the light. In the first instance, the concealment is from man. But this signification (→ 959 f.) is radicalised, for everything is now related to the living God. Those who flout His will try to escape Him in vain.

> The ungodly lurks like a lion in ambush (ἐν ἀποκρύφῳ, ψ 9:29) to rob the poor. His purpose is secretly to overthrow the righteous (ἐν ἀποκρύφοις, ψ 9:28; 63:4). They offend in secret, Ez. 8:12; Is. 29:15; they set up their idols ἐν ἀποκρύφῳ, Dt. 27:15. Aware of his sin, the sinner avoids the light of God: Adam after the fall, Gn. 3:8, 10; the murderer Cain, Gn. 4:14; the thief Achan, Jos. 7:19, 21, 22. When judgment falls, the guilty will try to hide in clefts of the rocks, but in vain, Is. 2:10; cf. 29:14; Jer. 4:29.

4. The righteous gives up this useless flight. He does not hide from God. He discloses everything. This is the prerequisite for the restoration of fellowship. Parallels which might be adduced from other religions can only serve finally to show with what unique intensity the moral relation to God was experienced on the soil of the OT revelation of God.

> The righteous, too, is in the first instance in danger of covering his sins, and he gives way to this temptation for a period. But then the hand of God is so heavy on him that he resolves to conceal his misdeeds no more. He now has a sense of relief and blessing (Ps. 32:1-5). He confesses to Yahweh even his innermost sin (ψ 68:5; 18:12: ἐκ τῶν κρυφίων μου καθάρισόν με. Materially the so-called penitential psalms are most relevant here (6; 32; 38; 51; 102; 130; 143). These display a close formal relation with the penitential psalms of Babylon ("the sin which I do not know") whose language is often no less striking but whose content is polytheistic and ritualistic and full of hopeless pessimism. [25] The penitential inscr. of Phrygia and Lydia [26] are no more successful in offering true parallels to the OT psalms.

5. On the basis of restored fellowship it is a comfort to the righteous that his way is not hidden from Yahweh and that his supplication is manifest to Him.

> The righteous need not hide from God's face, Job 13:20. He knows very well that his defects are not concealed, ψ 68:5. But he is also confident that his sighing before God is not hidden, ψ 37:9. Yahweh demands such confidence. The prophet reproachfully asks a people of little faith why it thinks and says that its destiny and cause are hidden from Yahweh, Is. 40:27. Rightly understood, it is an occasion of praise that God uncovers and judges what is hidden, 2 Macc. 12:41.

6. Yahweh gives the elect a share in His own hidden life. He covers them protectively and gives them hidden wisdom. If older thoughts of rapture are present here, it is particularly striking that what is meant applies to this life and is worked out in the sober light of day within God's historical direction. Indeed, there are warnings against excessive striving for what is hidden.

> Yahweh protectively conceals the righteous in His tent in the hour of trouble, ψ 26:5; 30:20: κατακρύψεις αὐτοὺς ἐν ἀποκρύφῳ τοῦ προσώπου σου ἀπὸ ταραχῆς

---

[25] H. Zimmern, *Babylonische Busspsalmen* (1885). On the questions raised esp. by F. Delitzsch, cf. Bertholet-Leh., I, 580 ff.; R. Kittel, *Die at.liche Wissenschaft*[5] (1929), 274 ff.
[26] Cf. Steinleitner, 10-61.

ἀνθρώπων. He shelters His servant under the cover of His hand, Is. 49:2. He is a cover for His people against storm and rain, Is. 4:6. His people may go into the chambers and hide until wrath is past, Is. 26:20. In Hades itself the righteous knows that he is hidden in God's hand, Job 14:13. Yahweh has hidden His goodness; He has reserved it for those who fear Him, ψ 30:19. The penitent addresses Him as follows : ἰδοὺ γὰρ ἀλήθειαν ἠγάπησας, τὰ ἄδηλα καὶ τὰ κρύφια τῆς σοφίας σου ἐδήλωσάς μοι, ψ 50:6. But occultism is rejected. What is hidden and future is in God's hand. Man must not be inquisitive. He must keep to the revealed will of God, Dt. 29:28. Put in the form of practical wisdom, this means that one is to consider that over which power is given, for what is hidden does not concern us : אֵין לְךָ עֵסֶק בַּנִּסְתָּרוֹת, ἃ προσετάγη σοι, ταῦτα διανοοῦ, οὐ γάρ ἐστίν σοι χρεία τῶν κρυπτῶν, Σιρ. 3:22.

7. God also comes forth from His hiddenness. He reveals Himself (→ ἀποκαλύπτω, 563 ff.). In the first instance He reveals Himself to His instruments, from whom He normally does not conceal anything. Increasingly, however, He reveals Himself to the whole community to the degree that it shows itself capable of receiving His revelation.

According to J Yahweh did not conceal anything He planned to do from Abraham, Gn. 18:17. It is customary for Israel's leaders, especially the prophets, to see what is hidden, Is. 29:10. [27] On the other hand, God's direction forces the enemies of God's people to confess that the God of Israel is for them a God who hides Himself, Is. 45:15. [28] Later, the living revelation of the present became less prominent. Past revelation was codified. But the boundaries were thereby extended. Every member of the community who could receive it now had access to the hidden wisdom of God, ψ 118:19; Σιρ. 39:3. The image of secret treasuries was now used, cf. 1 Macc. 1:23; Da. 11:43 Θ; Is. 45:3; Prv. 2:4.

8. Yahweh, however, keeps control over His revelation. If He wills, He may again conceal it in judgment. Even the righteous is not spared such experiences.

He often conceals His purposes even from His prophets, 2 K. 4:27. An increased incapacity to receive necessarily leads to a harmful and judicial self-concealment, Is. 29:10 (also the original → n. 27) and materially Is. 6:9 ff.; 28:11; 51:17; 57:17 etc.). Is. 8:16 belongs partly here, and partly under 9.: Keep the revelation, seal the doctrine among my disciples. Only with an appearance of justification could pseudepigr. writings appeal to this command of Yahweh. Esoteric tendencies in the strict sense are remote from the saying. Even the righteous knows the painful experience of God concealing His face or His ear from him. He prays that this may not happen, and often his prayer is heard, but only as free and unmerited grace, Job 3:23 Heb.; 13:24; 34:29; Lam. 3:56; in the Psalter the LXX uses other words for this, mostly ἀποστρέφειν = סתר Heb. hi, cf. ψ 9:31; 21:24; 43:24; 50:9; 68:17; 88:46; 101:2; 142:7. The hiddenness of Yahweh can become almost intolerable. He leads His people into the darkness, Lam. 3:6; He becomes for them a bear or lion in ambush, λέων ἐν κρυφαίοις, 3:10, → 967. But Yahweh's grace is not at an end. His mercy is new every morning. Hence the righteous is still ;

---

[27] Heb.: Because Yahweh has poured out a spirit of deep sleep on you and has closed your eyes (the prophets) and covered your heads (the seers). The words in brackets are glosses. LXX : ὅτι πεπότικεν ὑμᾶς κύριος πνεύματι κατανύξεως καὶ καμμύσει τοὺς ὀφθαλμοὺς αὐτῶν καὶ τῶν προφητῶν αὐτῶν καὶ τῶν ἀρχόντων αὐτῶν, οἱ ὁρῶντες τὰ κρυπτά. This transl. is very inaccurate, but it represents the common OT view.

[28] Heb. מִסְתַּתֵּר אֵל, LXX : σὺ γὰρ εἶ θεός, καὶ οὐκ ᾔδειμεν. H. Gressmann, "Der Messias," FRL, 26 (1929), 63 and 339 alters the מִסְתַּתֵּר into מַסְתִּיר, a protecting God (cf. Ehrlich).

perhaps there is hope, 3:22, 28 f. In prayer he flees from the hidden God to the revealed God. Such notes are never sounded outside the Bible.

9. Since God's Word is a supreme treasure, the immediate task of the righteous is to hide this treasure in himself. There is a similar demand in Hermes mysticism, but differently expressed.

Job confesses : I have not gone back from his statutes, ἐν δὲ κόλπῳ μου ἔκρυψα ῥήματα αὐτοῦ. Cf. the Psalmist : ἐν τῇ καρδίᾳ μου ἔκρυψα τὰ λόγιά σου, ὅπως ἂν μὴ ἁμάρτω σοι, ψ 118:11. The wise man puts at the head of his teaching of wisdom the statement : υἱέ, ἐὰν δεξάμενος ῥῆσιν ἐμῆς ἐντολῆς κρύ-ψῃς παρὰ σεαυτῷ, ὑπακούσεται σοφίας τὸ οὖς σου, Prv. 2:1. With this one may compare the dialogue at the beginning of Poimandres : God : τί βούλει ἀκοῦσαι καὶ θεάσασθαι, καὶ νοήσας μαθεῖν καὶ γνῶναι; ... The Seeker after Wisdom : μαθεῖν θέλω τὰ ὄντα καὶ νοῆσαι τὴν τούτων φύσιν, καὶ γνῶναι τὸν θεόν ... God : ἔχε νῷ σῷ ὅσα θέλεις μαθεῖν, κἀγώ σε διδάξω, Corp. Herm., I, 1 ff. In the psalm the interest is in the Torah as the Word of God historically given, in the wisdom literature it is in practical wisdom on a religious foundation, in Hermes mysticism it is in cosmic Gnosis.

10. In only apparent contradiction with what has gone before it is finally demanded that what God says and does is not to be kept hidden. Even in Hermes mysticism the esoteric side is accompanied by an exoteric, a missionary concern, though with a very different content.

We are reminded of a saying of Heracl. (→ 959) by the counsel of Sir., ἀποκρύπτειν τὴν μωρίαν. But this is in a context which takes us much beyond it : σοφία κεκρυμ-μένη καὶ θησαυρὸς ἀφανής, τίς ὠφέλεια ἐν ἀμφοτέροις; κρείσσων ἄνθρωπος ἀποκρύπτων τὴν μωρίαν αὐτοῦ ἢ ἄνθρωπος ἀποκρύπτων τὴν σοφίαν αὐτοῦ (Σιρ. 20:30 f.; cf. 41:14 f.). The author of Wis. also says of wisdom : τὸν πλοῦτον αὐτῆς οὐκ ἀποκρύπτομαι, 7:13. Above all the righteous does not conceal the righteous-ness and faithfulness of Yahweh, ψ 39:10; 77:4; cf. 21:22. The fate of those who evade the divine commission and try to hide the Word of God which has come to them is depicted in various ways. The most striking is in Jer. 20:9, cf. Jon. 1. The demand that God's words and deeds should be published is often repeated in rhetorical, almost dithyrambic form, Ιερ. 27:2; ψ 95:2, 3. Praise for grace received and preaching are also found together at the conclusion of Poim.: ἅγιος εἶ, ὁ κρείττων πάντων ἐπαίνων. δέξαι λογικὰς θυσίας ἁγνὰς ἀπὸ ψυχῆς καὶ καρδίας πρὸς σὲ ἀνατεταμένης, ἀνεκλάλητε, ἄρρητε, σιωπῇ φωνούμενε. αἰτουμένῳ τὸ μὴ σφαλῆναι τῆς γνώσεως τῆς κατ' οὐσίαν ἡμῶν ἐπίνευσόν μοι· καὶ ἐνδυνάμωσόν με, ἵνα τῆς χάριτος ταύτης τυχὼν φωτίσω τοὺς ἐν ἀγνοίᾳ τοῦ γένους μου, ἀδελφοὺς ἐμούς, υἱοὺς δὲ σοῦ (Corp. Herm., I, 31 f.; cf. also the continuation). But there is again a marked difference of content, as under 9.

III. Judaism.

With the insights of the OT, Judaism also adopts Hellenistic and Oriental features, and fashions an independent, though not wholly consistent, usage, with some tendency towards superficiality and ossification.

1. Palestinian Judaism.

In the main Judaism felt that present revelation had ceased.

Cf. → 577; also Ps. 74:9; S. Bar. 85:1, 3 : "The prophets have gone to sleep"; Jos. Ap., 1, 41: διὰ τὸ μὴ γενέσθαι τὴν τῶν προφητῶν ἀκριβῆ διαδοχήν, bSota, 48b, Bar. par.: "With the death of Haggai, Zechariah and Malachi, prophecy ceased in Israel, though they still used the resounding voice." Hillel the Elder and Samuel the Little were worthy that divinity should rest on them, but their generation was not worthy. Cf. also T. Sota, 13, 2 (Str.-B., II, 133; I, 127). [29]

Apocalyptic is a rather frenzied but popular attempt to meet the need. The discovery of something hidden, whether it be hidden guilt or the ultimate purposes of God, is here linked increasingly with eschatology.

Thus Enoch receives the intimation : "This is the Son of Man who has righteousness, with whom righteousness dwells, and who reveals all the treasures of what is hidden" (Eth. En. 46:3). [30] The Messiah and the kingdom of God are hidden until manifested, → 577 f. Secret books are very popular as we move to the NT period. This is proved by the rise of most apocalypses on Palestinian soil. Even the fictional Ezra of the 4th Book receives an order to publish, of the 94 books he has written, only the first 24, to cause only these to be read to worthy and unworthy alike, and to give the remaining 70 only to the wise of his people, because in them the spring of insight, the well of wisdom and the river of knowledge flows (4 Esr. 14:44 ff.). Joseph., however, displays a certain contempt for apocryphal literature (→ C. 1.).

Yet for all the love of what is hidden, the idea that Judaism must have had a strong sense of the *Deus absconditus* is not wholly correct.

While Rabb. Judaism on the one side laid strong emphasis on the majesty of Yahweh and generally opposed mystical union with God, on the other side it is fully conscious of Yahweh's presence in nature and history. Belief in God's presence can sometimes lead to strongly anthropomorphic ideas. Again, the revelation given with the Torah is increasingly understood in such a way that the numinous concealment of God is jeopardised. Nevertheless, the divine guidance is puzzling enough for the Jews and keeps their understanding alert. After the disaster of 70 A.D. the author of 4 Esr. made a penetrating attempt to understand the sway of the hidden God, cf. esp. c. 4.

The antithesis between secret and open takes on technical significance in casuistry and literal exegesis. This is a mark of the externalism of the Rabbis, though a wrestling for the internal is not completely lacking.

Distinction is made between what one does openly (בְּפַרְהֶסְיָא = ἐν παρρησίᾳ) and what one does in secret (Heb. בְּצִנְעָא; Aram. בְּצִנְעָא = ἐν κρυπτῷ), like the burial of the dead or the bringing of the bride under the nuptial canopy, and it is concluded that the command to walk secretly (Mi. 6:8) is to be observed with particular strictness in the latter case (bSukka, 49a, Str.-B., II, 485), or the Sabbath command is described as one which is given in secret, bBesa, 16a, *loc. cit.* Other antitheses are בפרהסיא...בַּסֵתֶר or בַּגָּלוּי...בסתר. Secret guilt is openly punished, and secret hallowing of the name of Yahweh is publicly recognised, Str.-B., II, 486. In the 3rd cent. there is discussion whether in times of persecution it is lawful to save one's life by idolatry even though this is not just secret, but public. A negative answer is given, bSanh., 74a, Str.-B., I, 414.

2. Hellenistic Judaism.

To the degree that the use of the terms is theologically significant, one may discern mystical influences in Hellenistic Judaism.

Thus in Test. XII Reuben, when dying, wants to declare to his brothers and sons the hidden things in his heart (ὅσα ἔχω ἐν τῇ καρδίᾳ μου κρυπτά, Test. R. 1:4). That these are secret revelations seems likely from Test. L. 8:19, where Levi, at the end of

---

[29] Bousset-Gressm., 394.

[30] This combination is well worth noting.

the account of the visions in which the priesthood of his tribe was revealed, continues: καὶ ἔκρυψα καί γε τοῦτο ἐν τῇ καρδίᾳ μου, καὶ οὐκ ἀνήγγειλα αὐτό τινι ἀνθρώπῳ ἐπὶ τῆς γῆς. κρύπτεσθαι also occurs in exhortations, but in such a way as to betray clearly the influence of mystical ontology, of the thought of the *coincidentia oppositorum*. Test. A. 5:1: δύο εἰσὶν ἐν πᾶσιν, ἓν κατέναντι τοῦ ἑνός, καὶ ἓν ὑπὸ τοῦ ἑνὸς κέκρυπται· ἐν τῇ κτήσει ἡ πλεονεξία, ἐν τῇ εὐφροσύνῃ ἡ μέθη, ἐν τῷ γέλωτι τὸ πένθος, ἐν τῷ γάμῳ ἡ ἀσωτία. There follow the antitheses life and death, honour and shame, day and night. Philo shows some awareness of the essential hiddenness of God. He describes God as ἀκατάληπτος and ἀόρατος, Poster. C., 15. But he does not use the present terms in such contexts. He emphasises God's omniscience in a way which is OT but which also fits a pantheistic background: ἄνθρωπος δ' ἂν ἤ τι τῶν γενομένων κρύπτεσθαι δυνηθείη θεόν; ποῦ; τὸν ἐφθακότα πάντῃ, τὸν ἄχρι περάτων ἀποβλέποντα, τὸν πεπληρωκότα τὸ πᾶν, οὗ τῶν ὄντων οὐδὲ τὸ βραχύτατον ἔρημον; καὶ τί παράδοξον, εἰ μηδενὶ τῶν γενομένων ἐφικτὸν κρύπτεσθαι τὸ ὄν; Det. Pot. Ins., 153. The terminology of the *disciplina arcana* serves to characterise the mystical knowledge which the philosopher reads into the OT: οἱ ἀλληγορίας καὶ φύσεως τῆς κρύπτεσθαι φιλούσης ἀμύητοι. Sacr. AC, 60: κεκρύφθαι δεῖ τὸν ἱερὸν περὶ τοῦ ἀγενήτου καὶ τῶν δυνάμεων αὐτοῦ μύστην λόγον, ἐπεὶ θείων παρακαταθήκην ὀργίων οὐ παντός ἐστι φυλάξαι. *Ibid.*, 62: (They did not tell of the grace imparted to them), ἀλλὰ ἐν ἀποκρύφοις ... ἐθησαυρίσαντο. The whole passage reads mystery rites into the OT. The term mystery is actually used. Very significant is the addressing of God as mystagogue, Som., I, 164: (Do not cease), ἕως ἐπὶ τὸ κεκρυμμένον ἱερῶν λόγων φέγγος ἡμᾶς μυσταγωγῶν ἐπιδείξῃς τὰ κατάκλειστα καὶ ἀτελέστοις ἀόρατα κάλλη. The basic mystical conception produces a predominantly negative ethics. To express this, too, the present terms are used. Thus Philo observes on Gn. 31:20 f.: φυσικώτατόν (full of a profound knowledge of nature) ἐστι τὸ κρύπτειν ὅτι ἀποδιδράσκει, Leg. All., III, 16. If endangered by beauty, one should flee from it and not declare it to the *nous*, i.e., here the understanding linked to the senses. Cf. also Gn. 35:4: ὁ γὰρ ἀστεῖος (the educated man) οὐδὲν λήψεται πρὸς περιουσίαν τῶν ἀπὸ κακίας, ἀλλὰ κρύψει καὶ ἀφανιεῖ λάθρα (*ibid.*, III, 23).

3. Gnosticism influenced by Judaism.

The Essenes are a preliminary step to Jewish Gnosticism.[31] Joseph. tells us that in their novitiate oath they had to promise μήτε κρύψειν τι τοὺς αἱρετιστὰς μήθ' ἑτέροις αὐτῶν τι μηνύσειν, Jos. Bell., II, 141. The full openness to members of the order which is here demanded is primarily in the field of discipline. But in virtue of the oath of secrecy towards those outside κρύπτειν acquires indirectly a theological significance. The reference is to esoteric knowledge. This is embodied in writings which are to be kept secret, συντηρήσειν ὁμοίως τά τε τῆς αἱρέσεως αὐτῶν βιβλία, *ibid.*, 142. It is only by chance that these are not called ἀπόκρυφα. In later Jewish Gnosticism the idea of the hidden certainly takes on technical significance. This is shown by the name of the founder of the Elkesaites.[32] The name is the equivalent of חֵיל כְּסַי = δύναμις κεκαλυμμένη or κεκρυμμένη. It is not a proper name, but a title of honour which the head of the sect claims or which his followers give him. This is at least highly probable in view of Ac. 8:10: οὗτός ἐστιν ἡ δύναμις τοῦ θεοῦ ἡ καλουμένη μεγάλη (of Simon Magus). The idea of hiddenness confers honour, as in Gnostic usage elsewhere (→ 965). The divine is as such the hidden, accessible only to a few elect. The

---

[31] On the nature and origin of Essenism, cf. esp. Schürer, II⁴, 668 ff.; W. Bauer in Pauly-W. Suppl., IV (1924), 386 ff.

[32] RGG², II, 116; Hennecke, 422 ff. Acc. to the prevailing view the name transmitted in different script is not that of a sacred book but of the author, who is to be regarded as a historical personage. The name of his supposed brother Yexai, however, arose by derivation from El and the interchanging of El and Yah = Yahweh.

usage of the Mandaeans fully supports this (→ I, 536 f.), e.g., Lidz. Ginza R., XV, 5, 314 (p. 316): "It granted to him the seven hidden, pure and preserved mysteries by which he is perfectly preserved"; 315 (p. 317): "We will offer thee hidden prayers." The inaccessibility of God is a popular theme in Mandaean writings, e.g., Lidz. Ginza R., I, 2, 7 (p. 6); I, 3, 15 (p. 7) etc. One may also compare the common designation of the beings beyond as alien, op. cit., I, 1, 1 (p. 5) etc. and the frequent use of the term secret or mystery, Lidz. Ginza, Index, s.v. The term Ginza may be cited in the same connection, → C. II. 6. A very different development is responsible for bringing a high evaluation of the hidden, and of the hidden book, into true Judaism, → C. I. 4. and 5.

IV. The New Testament.

Even where we cannot show this explicitly, the NT adopts the general presuppositions of the OT and in part those of Judaism, though with the difference that it bears witness to the fulfilment of eschatological expectation, even if the final fulfilment is still to come. The material is hardly adequate either to afford a history of the term in the NT or to permit a systematic development of the related concepts. We shall be content, then, simply to take the theologically significant verses in historical, and, if possible, material order. References to earlier sections will be made in an attempt to bring out the implications and qualifications.

1. The Synoptists.

Everything divine is primarily and essentially hidden (→ 967). It is accessible only to revelation. This is seldom brought out in the transmitted sayings of the Lord but it is always presupposed. God's kingdom in particular is in its beginnings in this world comparable with a hidden treasure (Mt. 13:44) or the leaven which disappears in a measure of meal (Lk. 13:21; Mt. 13:33: ἐνέκρυψεν). Its divine nature is thereby manifested. An esoteric tendency, as in Hellenism (→ 963, 971 f.) does not result just because the hiddenness is essential. For God reveals Himself. The treasure is found, the leaven begins to work. By means of a general principle (→ 557) Jesus impresses on His disciples the fact that the cause of God is entrusted to them, that it has emerged from its original concealment, and that God will publicly confess it, Mt. 20:26 f.; Lk. 12:2 f.; Mk. 4:22; Lk. 8:17; → 970. Revelation is closed, of course, to human unreceptivity. The disciples cannot understand at all Jesus' intimation of His passion: ἦν τὸ ῥῆμα τοῦτο κεκρυμμένον ἀπ' αὐτῶν. Lk. (18:34; cf. 9:45) underlines this aspect very strongly with his three different expressions, though he does not include the clash between Jesus and Peter (Mk. 8:32 f.; Mt. 16:22 f.), or the request of the sons of Zebedee (Mk. 10:35 ff. and par.). The chief concern of the Evangelist is the incomprehensible divine secret. Often a numinous element is interfused (24:16). This is perhaps linked with his Hellenism. More OT (→ 969) is the idea that God Himself judicially hides the knowledge of salvation from those who do not seek it seriously. This is at least included in the νῦν δὲ ἐκρύβη ἀπὸ ὀφθαλμῶν σου of Lk. 19:42. Jesus brings it out very plainly in Mt. 11:25 f. and Lk. 10:21. The heavenly Father has hidden the knowledge of salvation from the wise and the clever, i.e., from Rabbinic and Pharisaic scribes and models of piety (Mt. ἔκρυψας, Lk. ἀπέκρυψας), and has revealed them to babes, i.e., the 'Amme ha'ares. The thanksgiving relates to both halves of the interconnected statement, not to the second half alone. Jesus extols the divine direction even in its paradoxical character, which sets in the wrong all human arrogance. In this light we may understand the grim severity of the saying in Mk. 4:11 f. and par., → 581. On the other hand, the concluding observation of the Evangelist in Mk. 4:33 f. and par. reflects an esoteric tendency which is surprising in a Palestinian setting. Under the influence of this Mt. 13:35 introduces a quotation from Ps. 78:2, using the Heb. (אַבִּיעָה חִידוֹת מִנִּי־קֶדֶם) rather than the LXX (ψ 77:2 : φθέγξομαι προβλήματα ἀπ' ἀρχῆς): ἐρεύξομαι κεκρυμμένα ἀπὸ καταβολῆς. A right attitude in face of the reception of revelation is shown by the man who finds the treasure when he hides it again with joyous haste, i.e., to make it secure for himself (Mt. 13:44, → 958). The mode of expression is conditioned by the simile, but there is striking agreement with some material parallels in the OT (→ 969). A further contrast with Pharisaism results from the fact that the Pharisees display their achievements, whereas Jesus would have piety be modest. Almsgiving, prayer and fasting should take place in secret so that the heavenly Father, who sees in secret, may reward it (ἐν τῷ κρυπτῷ, ἐν τῷ κρυφαίῳ, Mt. 6:4, 6, 18, → 960).

Rabb. writings bear rich testimony to the theatrical nature of Pharisaic righteousness (→ ὑποκριτής, "actor"). While the means for the communal support of the poor was provided by assessment, [33] almsgiving over and above this rested on free gifts. These were made known to the congregation in the synagogues and at fasting services on the open street. Those who gave very generously were allotted special places alongside the rabbis. [34] Many later forgot to pay the sums promised. Obligatory prayer had to be offered up in the synagogue or wherever one was. The Rabbis gave detailed directions as to the proper demeanour in public prayer. [35] Many people let themselves be surprised on the streets and squares at the times of prayer in order to parade their piety. Beyond the fast prescribed in the Law for the Day of Atonement and other officially ordained fasts, fasts were often undertaken for personal reasons or for the sake of merit. Several accompanying ceremonies were prescribed, e.g., putting on sackcloth, sitting in ashes, the sprinkling of ashes on the head (Mt. 11:21), refraining from washing and anointing the body (Mt. 6:17), the putting off of sandals etc. [36] There was a great temptation to attract the attention of others by making a particularly sorry spectacle of oneself. This widespread attitude, which could even vaunt itself before God, finds living embodiment in the Pharisee of Lk. 18:11 f. These excesses are, of course, the reverse side of a serious and self-sacrificing piety. Judaism itself says many fine things against them. "He who gives alms in secret is greater than our teacher Moses" (proof from Dt. 9:19 and Prv. 21:14, bBB, 9b; Str.-B., I, 391). Joseph prays in his room to resist temptation by the wife of Potiphar (Test. Jos. 3:3 : εἰσερχόμενος εἰς τὸ ταμιεῖον [κλαίων] προσηυχόμην Κυρίῳ). When R. Aqiba prayed with the congregation, he prayed only briefly because of those around, but when he prayed alone, he kneeled from one side of the room to the other, T. Ber., 3, 5 (7). Warnings were issued against excessive public mortifications, T. Sota, 15, 11 ff., Str.-B., I, 195; bTaan., 14b, Str.-B., IV, 114. But opinions on these matters were mixed, and the outlook was rather different from that of the Sermon on the Mount. One should avoid putting the recipient of alms to shame, or wearying the congregation with long prayers, or exposing onself to scoffing if particularly zealous prayers are not answered. The practice tended on the whole to be as Jesus depicted it.

Jesus restores lost modesty to piety by directing it to the place of concealment. He does not forbid public prayer (Mt. 6:41). Nor does He seek to check other

---

[33] There are striking pictures in the tractate jPea, transl. J. J. Rabe (1781).

[34] For rich Rabb. material cf. Str.-B., I, 388; IV, 536 ff. Schl. Mt. on 6:2 thinks that we are perhaps to take the trumpets lit.

[35] Str.-B., I, 396 ff.

[36] Ibid., IV, 77 ff.

expressions of piety. On the contrary, selfishly and overanxiously to conceal a gift which has been received is reprehensible unfaithfulness (Mt. 25:18, 25 ff.; cf. Lk. 19:20 ff.). As the city set on a hill cannot by its very nature be concealed, so the light of the disciples of Jesus should so shine that men may see their good works and glorify their Father in heaven (Mt. 5:14, 16). The place for the lamp is not under the bushel or the bed, or in the cellar (→ κρύπτη, 960); it is on the candlestick, → λύχνος, λυχνία (Mt. 5:15; Lk. 11:33; cf. Mk. 4:21; Lk. 8:16; [37] → 970).

2. John's Gospel.

The Fourth Gospel refers to secret disciples of Jesus, e.g., Joseph of Arimathea (ὢν μαθητὴς τοῦ Ἰησοῦ κεκρυμμένος, 19:38). The sense seems to be the same when Nicodemus is called the one who came to Jesus by night (3:2; 7:50; 19:39). It should be noted, however, that the intention is not to blame the two men for their timidity. It is rather recognised and stressed that their reserve is understandable in a difficult situation and that they abandoned it at the decisive moment. Their example should be followed in the days of the Evangelist by Jews who honour Christ but are ashamed to confess Him. In this respect the Fourth Gospel is written with a view to winning the Jews. [38] The terms are used for the most part, however, to express the Evangelist's numinous conception of Christ. To unbelief it seems to be an offence that Jesus keeps Himself ἐν κρυπτῷ and yet also seeks to be ἐν παρρησίᾳ, i.e., to make a public impression (→ 971). But this is in keeping, at least at times, with the puzzling nature of His mission (7:4). For this reason, in spite of His prior intention, [39] Jesus exercises His sovereign freedom and resolves to visit the feast οὐ φανερῶς ἀλλὰ ὡς ἐν κρυπτῷ (7:10). When, after the excited controversy of Jn. 8, the Jews took up stones to kill Him, Jesus hid Himself (ἐκρύβη) and went to the temple (8:59). [40] He could escape from His enemies at any time. He disappeared almost as the deity which hastens away. In a second instance (12:36) the ἐκρύβη has almost a judicial quality, → 969. The Jews' time of grace is past. Only once again does the voice of Jesus ring out to the people like a sound from the other world, 12:44 ff. [41] But this numinous reserve is only one side of the matter. At the hearing before the high-priest Jesus assures him emphatically that He has spoken παρρησίᾳ before the whole world and not ἐν κρυπτῷ, 18:20. The readers of the Gospel, particularly the Jews, are to know that Christianity is not a hole-in-the-corner affair (→ 973). It has nothing to hide, → 960; 968.

---

[37] The recurrence of the saying in Lk. shows that as a single unit it was originally in both Mk. and Q. Mt.'s context is materially the most convincing. Mk. 4:21 and Lk. 8:16 are possible, but Lk. 11:33 with its continuation ad vocem λύχνος is very forced. Cf. on Mt. 5:14 the agraphon P. Oxy., I, 1 recto 15 ff.: λέγει Ἰησοῦς, πόλις οἰκοδομημένη ἐπ᾽ ἄκρον ὄρους ὑψηλοῦ καὶ ἐστηριγμένη οὔτε πεσεῖν δύναται οὔτε κρυβῆναι. This does not have the same imperative ring.

[38] K. Bornhäuser, Das Johannesevangelium eine Missionsschrift f. Israel (1928), 121 f., does not work this out clearly enough. He finds esoteric tendencies behind the coming by night, 26 f.

[39] At 7:8 the more difficult reading οὐκ, attested by א D and Lat. and Syr., is to be preferred to the more common οὔπω.

[40] C and א strengthen the paradox by additions.

[41] It is hardly in keeping with vv. 36 ff. that Jesus should have spoken again. E. Hirsch, Studien z. vierten Evangelium (1936), 27, 98, regards vv. 44-50 as a misplaced part of c. 8 "which has here become the last word ad vocem judgment." B. W. Bacon, The Gospel of the Hellenists (1933), 280 regards the section as the addition of a redactor. Comparison of the two analyses does not give us much confidence in their reliability.

3. The Other New Testament Writings.

In the rest of the NT we find something similar in 2 C. 4:2. Paul gives the assurance that he avoids secret scandal in the exercise of his office : ἀπειπάμεθα τὰ κρυπτὰ τῆς αἰσχύνης, μὴ περιπατοῦντες ἐν πανουργίᾳ μηδὲ δολοῦντες τὸν λόγον τοῦ θεοῦ, ἀλλὰ τῇ φανερώσει τῆς ἀληθείας κτλ. The natural man is afraid of the light (Eph. 5:12 : τὰ γὰρ κρυφῇ γινόμενα ὑπ' αὐτῶν αἰσχρόν ἐστιν καὶ λέγειν). He tries to hide from God the Judge, → 968. The divine of Rev. sees the time coming when the rulers of this world will hide in clefts of the rock and say to the mountains : Fall on us, and hide us from the One who sits on the throne, and from the wrath of the Lamb, 6:15 f.; cf. Hos. 10:8; Lk. 23:30. But in vain! It is basic to the NT too that no evil can conceal itself from God, → 967; 1 Tm. 5:25 : τὰ ἔργα τὰ καλὰ πρόδηλα, καὶ τὰ ἄλλως ἔχοντα κρυβῆναι οὐ δύνανται. The Judge who comes then will bring τὰ κρυπτὰ τοῦ σκότους to light and reveal the counsels of the hearts, 1 C. 4:5; R. 2:16; cf. 2 C. 5:10; Qoh. 12:14. Even now the one who stands afar off sees how under the impress of Christian prophecy τὰ κρυπτὰ τῆς καρδίας αὐτοῦ are made manifest (1 C. 14:25), and he perceives hereby the work of God in those who speak. [42] It is widely and strongly emphasised that the Deity for its part is hidden by nature, but that God gives to His people a share in His hidden life, → 968. An excellent key to the understanding of such statements is to be found in the promise found in the letter to the church of Pergamon : τῷ νικῶντι δώσω αὐτῷ τοῦ μάννα τοῦ κεκρυμμένου (Rev. 2:17). The prerogative of believers is, in brief, the fact that the hidden eschatological blessings of salvation are accessible to them by revelation, → ἀποκαλύπτω, 576 f.; 580; 582 f. The mystery which has been concealed for aeons and generations is now manifested to the saints of God, Col. 1:26; cf. Eph. 3:9. In Christ all the hidden treasures of wisdom and knowledge are present, Col. 2:3; cf. Is. 45:3; Prv. 2:3 f. Hence those who preach the Gospel, even though their message be offence and folly to the natural man, proclaim God's wisdom in a mystery, the hidden wisdom which God ordained before all eternity for the glorifying of believers. None of the rulers of this world recognised it. There applies to them the saying which is written (→ 988) that no eye has seen nor ear heard, nor has it entered the heart of man, what God has prepared for those who love Him, 1 C. 2:7 ff. It is no accident that such lines of thought are always found in Paul when he gets to grips with vaunting ideas of wisdom and *gnosis*. What he wants to say is that in so far as the concern of this frame of mind is justifiable it finds its fulfilment in Christ. One may thus understand why the mode of expression is coloured by the reference. Paul's view, however, is primarily rooted in the OT. There is a steep line of ascent from the sayings of the Prophets, the Psalms, and the Wisdom literature (→ 969) to what the apostle says about the hidden wisdom of God. Above all, his view is Christian. [43] The spiritual knowledge of hidden wisdom depends upon the divine plan of salvation historically fulfilled in Christ. This is its object, cf. 1 C. 2:6 ff. with 1:18, 24; Col. 1:26 with v. 27, 18 ff. This does not

---

[42] Acc. to the ancient view supernatural knowledge, esp. thought reading, is a mark of θεῖοι ἄνθρωποι : Euthyphron in Plato (Euthyphr., 3e); Apollonius of Tyana (Philostr. Vit. Ap., I, 19 : "I know all the languages of men, I even know the unexpressed thoughts of men"; *ibid.,* VII, 22 : Apoll. tells Damis what he wants to ask); G. P. Wetter, *Der Sohn Gottes* (1916), 69 f.; H. Windisch, *Paulus u. Christus* (1934), 27 f.; 54.

[43] Reitzenstein Hell. Myst., 333 ff. overlooks these aspects and he thus expounds Paul from a one-sided Hellenistic standpoint. → 584, n. 42.

mean that all piety which is not historically and eschatologically grounded is set aside and denied. There is a basic "mystical" element (→ 577) in NT religion. The "hidden man of the heart" turns the scale with God in contrast to all externalities (R. 2:29) or obtrusive display (1 Pt. 3:4). But the extent to which these general religious presuppositions are shot through with eschatology may be seen in Col. 3:3 : τὰ ἄνω φρονεῖτε ... ἀπεθάνετε γάρ, καὶ ἡ ζωὴ ὑμῶν κέκρυπται σὺν τῷ Χριστῷ ἐν τῷ θεῷ. The word is here a mark of the inwardness of an eschatological "mysticism" which is quite non-mystical in its historical concreteness and moral orientation (cf. Col. 3:5 ff.), which is, in effect, sui generis.

4. Conclusion. In sum, the emphatically low (→ 959 f.) and the emphatically high (→ 960; 963 f.) significance of the words in general usage are both reflected in the NT. Materially, the usage of the NT is predominantly rooted in that of the OT. All ten of the lines indicated above (→ II., 1.-10.) may be traced from the OT to the NT. If 4. and 5. are the least clear, this is only accidental. That echoes of Gnosticism may be heard is not to be denied. In genuine Gnosis, however, the true boundary is between Gnostics and non-Gnostics, pneumatics and psychics or hylics. In the Bible, it is between Creator and creature. The second line drawn between σῳζόμενοι and ἀπολλύμενοι is orientated to the first, and subordinate to it. God is essentially hidden and yet He reveals Himself to all. The concept of the hidden does not lead in the NT to esotericism. It leads to world mission. Individual tendencies towards disciplina arcana — perhaps discernible in Lk. — do not alter this in the very least. If the concept of election is undoubtedly present, it never takes the hardened form of an absolute decree, but stands in genuinely numinous tension and bears the character of decision.

V. Transition to Church History.

In the earliest ecclesiastical writings the terms occur mostly in biblical quotations (1 Cl., 12, 3; 18, 6; 28, 3; 56, 10; Barn., 11, 4). For the rest, it is stressed that God discloses what is hidden (καὶ τὰ κρυπτὰ ἡμῶν ἐγγὺς αὐτῷ ἐστιν, Ign. Eph., 15, 3). Nothing escapes Him ... οὔτε τι τῶν κρυπτῶν τῆς καρδίας (Pol., 4, 3). Of the Spirit it is said : τὰ κρυπτὰ ἐλέγχει (Phld., 7, 1, with an echo of Jn.). The thought of judgement is accompanied by that of revelation. Thus we read that the great High-priest πεπίστευται τὰ κρυπτὰ τοῦ θεοῦ (Phld., 9, 1). The Shepherd assures Hermas : οὐδὲν ὅλως ἀποκρύψω ἀπὸ σοῦ (s., 9, 11, 9). This is all within the biblical understanding, though there may be connections between The Shepherd and Hermes mysticism.[44] A singular usage is that of Dg., 9, 5, which describes the expiatory significance of the death of Jesus as κρυβῆναι of the ἀνομία πολλῶν. κρύπτειν never has this sense in biblical Gk., → 959.

Most illuminating for the different views of the hidden God in Christianity and Hellenism, and for the rivalry of religions, is an anecdote which is found in Apophthegmata patrum and which may well rest on a stratum of truth.[45] The abbot Olympios said : "There was once a priest of the heathen (τῶν Ἑλλήνων) who came to Sketis to my cell and stayed the night there. And when he saw the monastic way of life, he said to me : 'With such a manner of life, do you see nothing of your God?' I gave him the reply : 'No.' Then said the priest to me : 'When we serve our god so long, he conceals nothing from us, but discloses to us his secrets (οὐδὲν κρύπτει ἀφ' ἡμῶν, ἀλλὰ ἀποκαλύπτει ἡμῖν τὰ μυστήρια αὐτοῦ). And you go to so much trouble with watchings and silences and ascetic exercises, and you say : We see nothing? Surely, if you see

---

[44] Reitzenstein Poim., 11 ff.
[45] Ibid., 34.

nothing, you have evil thoughts in your hearts which separate you from God, so that His secrets are not manifest to you.' And I went and declared to the old men the words of the priest. And they were astonished and said: 'It is true, for unclean thoughts separate God from man.' "

Oepke

C. Supplement on the Canon and the Apocrypha. [46]

I. The Canon and the Apocrypha in Judaism.

1. The Term Canon.

As regards Judaism, one may speak of a Canon as a closed and normative record of revelation from the beginning of the 2nd cent. A.D.

Canonisation is preceded by the purely literary collection and editing of individual writings. Certain works or collections then take on special significance, e.g., because of their cultic relevance. The normative evaluation of writings then begins. Finally, by inner development and in reaction to the outside world, a selection is made from among the religious works available. Thus the Canon arises, and its counterpart is apocryphal literature. [47]

2. The Early History of the Canon.

The usual name for the OT is the Law, the Prophets and the Writings. [48] This shows us that the Canon is made up of different parts.

a. The Law (→ νόμος). The Torah was closed by c. 300 B.C. [49] It was carried over as a whole from the temple, where it was used on the Day of Atonement (Yoma, 7, 1), to the worship of the synagogue. This is shown by the lectionaries, [50] the continuous division into pericopes, [51] and the canonical order of the Rabb. (→ 985 f.). The Torah had from an early period a central place in the service. [52] With the process of decline, a Law which certainly rested on divine inspiration, but which could be replaced at any time by a new draft, gradually became a normative code on which there could only be commentaries. [53]

b. The Prophets (→ προφήτης). Acc. to the Rabb. order the Prophets embrace Jos., Ju., (1 and 2) S., (1 and 2) K., Jer., Ez., Is., and the Twelve. [54] Whether the present number is older than the Rabb. order (→ 985 f.) is open to question. Sir. is often quoted as a guarantor of the fixed number of the collection c. 200 B.C., [55] and he also mentions

---

[46] It may be noted that, although this supplement goes rather beyond the limits of a *TDNT* art., it is included at the request of many readers because of many special questions which are the subject of modern discussion.

[47] Harnack, Dg., I⁵, 372 ff.; Hölscher, *op. cit.*, 1 ff.

[48] bSanh., 90b: Gamaliel II (c. 90 A.D.).

[49] Eissfeldt, 621.

[50] Meg., 4, 4 : מדלגין בנביא ואין מדלגין בתורה : in reading the Torah, as distinct from the Prophets, it is forbidden to miss out anything.

[51] Meg., 4, 10.

[52] Cf., e.g., Ac. 15:21; I. Elbogen, *Der jüd. Gottesdienst in seiner geschichtl. Entwicklung*³ (1931), 159 ff.

[53] The first work on a part of the Pentateuch is Jub.; cf. Eissfeldt, 661 ff.

[54] In 2 Macc. 2:13 there also seems to be a recollection of the fact that the prophetic collection was composed of historical and prophetic books.

[55] Cf. Hölscher, 21; Eissfeldt, 621 ff. That Da. was not included among the prophets would be a proof that the Canon of the Prophets was closed in the days of Sir. only if it could be shown that the Rabb. order went back to 200 B.C. or that the Rabb. exercised literary criticism in drawing up their order. On the enumeration of Da. with the Prophets in NT times → 980 f.

Job [56] and ranks him with the 3 great prophets : 49:9. [57] He also uses the work of the Chronicler without differentiating it from the Prophets, → n. 56. The grandson of Sir. (c. 130 B.C.) speaks in his prologue of the Law, the Prophets, and their descendants, or the other books transmitted from the fathers. He thus bears witness to a preliminary stage of the later threefold Canon. But he shows no belief in the singularity of the Prophets as compared with the other writings. As Jesus b. Sir. feels called to continue the Prophets (24:33), so his grandson has no scruples in making the undoubtedly later work available to the Alexandrian congregation. In so doing, he makes it clear that he counts Jesus b. Sir. among the descendants of the Prophets. [58] The freedom of the 2nd cent. regarding the historical and prophetic lit. is reflected in the cultus of a later period. Only selected portions were used, [59] lectionaries were prepared, [60] and liberties could be taken in reading (→ n. 50). Many pericopes were forbidden altogether. [61] It may thus be seen that in the first instance the prophetic writings were cultically read only for edification.

c. The Writings (→ I, 751). From the books mentioned along with the Law and the Prophets in the prologue to Sir. there developed later the collection of Writings. The 11 fixed by the Rabb. (→ 986) do not belong together originally. Ru. and Lam. were regarded as supplements to Ju. and Jer. and put with the Prophets. This is shown by the silence of Sir., the order of the LXX, Joseph.'s theory of the Canon (→ 985), and the tradition regarding authorships in bBB, 14a/15b. Da. is regarded as a prophet by Joseph. and Mt. 24:15, and is also used as the equal of the prophets in Sib., 3, 390 ff. and 1 Macc. 2:59 f. Esther, which was highly regarded in Palestine as early as the time of Lysimachos, is counted among the historical and prophetic writings by Joseph. Job is a prophet for Sir. (→ supra) and Joseph. The work of the Chronicler is mentioned along with the Prophets by Jesus b. Sir. (→ supra). On the other hand, the Psalms, which have no historical or prophetic content, were always regarded as outside the Prophets, though this did not prevent them from being very highly esteemed. With the Ps., Prv., Qoh. [62] and Cant. belonged from the very outset to the "other books transmitted from the fathers."

There was still no closed Canon c. 130 B.C. Only the Torah had a secure place. It was accompanied by a literature of edification which divided into a historical and prophetic group on the one side and a poetic and instructive on the other. This literature did not yet have any fixed or dogmatic limits.

3. The Old Testament in the 1st Century A.D.

In the 1st century A.D., under the influence of the Rabbis, there arose the concept of a normative Scripture based on the Torah. Already Scripture could be regarded as a unity. But in distinction from the age of the closing of the Canon, the full consequences of this idea of the totality of the record of revelation were not yet drawn. There was no clear demarcation from literature which was religious but had not been declared normative.

---

[56] Hölscher, 20, n. 7.

[57] The text must read [?הגביא] וגם אזכיר את איוב. Instead of אזכיר Fr. B (Strack) reads הזכיר following Ez. 14:14, 20; cf. R. Smend, Die Weisheit d. Jesus Sirach (1906/1907), ad loc. and Ryssel in Kautzsch Apkr., 466.

[58] On the other hand it is to be noted that pseudepigr. prophetic writings had already appeared in Palestine in his days.

[59] Elbogen, 176.

[60] bGit., 60a : ספר אפטרתא.

[61] Thus acc. to Meg., 4, 10 it is forbidden to read Ez. 1 (→ 984).

[62] Said to be quoted already by Simon b. Shetach, jBer., 11b; obviously contested by Wis. 2:1 ff. → 985.

a. The Writings of the Later Canon. Philo and the NT writers bear witness to this early stage of the Canon. Philo is familiar with the idea of a totality, e.g., when he speaks of ἱεραὶ γραφαί, → I, 751. He is thinking esp. of the Torah, but the other writings are equally regarded. In contrast to the Rabb. Philo has a doctrine of inspiration orientated to Plato. [63] This means that he sees no point in the limitation of the prophetic literature which is to be regarded as normative, and that he deliberately ascribes the sway of the prophetic spirit to the present. [64] The authors of the NT presuppose Scripture as a totality. Paul, the former Pharisee, speaks of Scripture (γραφή), cf. also Jn., Ac., Jm., 1 and 2 Pt. [65] The concept corresponds to the Rabb. כתוב, [66] and cf. מקרא [67] = Aram. קרא. [68] The Synpt., Pl., Jn. and Ac. also use the plur. γραφαί (→ n. 65) = Rabb. כתבי הקדש (→ n. 66). Pl. and Jn. also use νόμος [69] = Rabb. תורה [70] for the whole of Scripture. In Synpt. and Pl. we also find ὁ νόμος καὶ οἱ προφῆται, [71] which corresponds to the rare Rabb. תורה ונביאים. [72] More common is תורה וקבלה, "law and tradition" (→ n. 72). At Lk. 24:44 the totality is denoted by three groups, as in the Rabb. Canon. [73] It is an open question whether Lk. is referring to this Canon. Equally open to debate is whether one may conclude from Mt. 23:35 that Ch. already stood at the end of the Canon when the Gospel was composed. [74] Individual collections mentioned in the NT are the Law, the Prophets, and the Twelve Minor Prophets. [75] Of refs. to individual works Mt. 24:15 is important as regards the history of the Canon, since here Da. is numbered with the prophets, as in Joseph. (→ 985).

b. The later Apocrypha. At the time of the NT the boundary between canonical and non-canonical writings was not yet fixed. This may be seen from the estimation of

---

[63] Hölscher, 23; Moore, I, 239.

[64] A similar view to that of Philo is held, though for different reasons, by the probably Sadducean author of 1 Macc. Here we read in 4:44-46 : καὶ ἐβουλεύσαντο περὶ τοῦ θυσιαστηρίου τῆς ὁλοκαυτώσεως τοῦ βεβηλωμένου, τί αὐτῷ ποιήσωσιν· καὶ ἔπεσεν αὐτοῖς βουλὴ ἀγαθὴ καθελεῖν αὐτό, μήποτε γένηται αὐτοῖς εἰς ὄνειδος ὅτι ἐμίαναν τὰ ἔθνη αὐτό· καὶ καθεῖλον τὸ θυσιαστήριον καὶ ἀπέθεντο τοὺς λίθους ἐν τῷ ὄρει τοῦ οἴκου ἐν τόπῳ ἐπιτηδείῳ μέχρι τοῦ παραγενηθῆναι προφήτην τοῦ ἀποκριθῆναι περὶ αὐτῶν. On the restoration of the temple by Judas Maccabeus the stones of the desecrated altar were set aside to be used only when a prophet arose to make the necessary intimation. This is usually regarded as a sign that there was no current prophecy, but this understanding is not quite correct. Exposition should rather assume that the author regards the present appearance of a prophet as possible (2 Macc. 10:1 ff. does not carry the prophecy motif). In terms of this basic religious attitude 1 Macc. agrees with Sir. and his grandson. It need be no surprise that such views were possible at a time when neo-prophecy was already emerging pseudepigraphically, for the differing outlooks did not cancel one another out, but existed together for a long time. The Rabb. theory that there is no present prophecy, as we shall see later (→ 982), did not prevail until the post-apost. period. Even the Pharisee Joseph. speaks quite freely of prophecy where later Rabb. avoid the term (→ n. 79). The existence of this line of thought which expects prophecy to appear is important in relation to the NT use of → προφήτης.

[65] E. Hühn, Die messian. Weissagungen des isr.-jüd. Volkes, II : Die at.lichen Zitate u. Reminiszenzen im NT (1900), 276. → also γραφή, I, 751 ff.

[66] W. Bacher, Die exegetische Terminologie d. jüd. Traditionslit., I (1899), 90 ff.

[67] Bacher, I, 117 ff.

[68] Ibid., II (1905), 195 f.

[69] Hühn, 277.

[70] Bacher, I, 197.

[71] Hühn, 277, cf. also Ac. 13:15.

[72] Str.-B., IV, 416.

[73] Cf. 2 Macc. 2:13, → n. 54; Kl. Lk., 241.

[74] On this cf. Kl. Mt., 189 f. For Joseph. Est. was probably the last of the prophetic collection, → n. 80.

[75] Hühn, 277.

works later declared to be non-canonical. Philo's theory of Scripture shows that for him, and for the Alexandrian congregation, there was no distinction within the literature of edification. Prv. and Sir. stand on the same level. Similarly, Christian authors of the 1st and 2nd cent. know no fixed Canon. Thus 1 C. 2:9 cites an apocryphon from Apc. Elias (?); Lk. 11:49 quotes an apocryphon which has perished; Jd. 14 describes Enoch as a prophet; 2 Tm. 3:8 presumes that the story of Jannes and Jambres is well known and uses it for the purpose of instruction, → 192.[76] In Palestinian Judaism, too, the limits of the Canon are not yet fixed. Joseph. (Ap., 1, 38 ff.) is a representative of the age which had developed the theory of the Canon but still maintained the earlier practice. Acc. to his theory all works written after Artaxerxes I (→ infra) are less trustworthy than those of the classical period. This does not exclude his using a work like 1 Macc. for the later period. But his use of LXX quotations from Ezr. and Est. in depiction of the classical age, and his assertion that he uses only ἱεραὶ βίβλοι for his antiquities (Ant., 20, 261), shows that a strong concept of the Canon has not yet taken root in him. [77] A further indication of the fluidity of the Canon is the attitude of Rabb. Judaism to Sir. Sir. is expressly ruled out by the later Rabb. theory of the Canon (→ 982), and this suggests that it found strong support in Rabb. circles. The Apocalypses, too, seem to have been highly regarded until the closing of the Canon. [78]

c. The LXX as a Preliminary Stage of the Canon. From what has been said it may be seen that in the time of Jesus there was no closed Canon either in Palestine or Alexandria. But the idea of a totality of Scripture based on the Torah is present. The Alexandrian collection belongs to this early stage of the Canon. Without qualification it still includes 1 Macc. with the historical books and Sir. with Prv.

4. The Closing of the Canon by the Rabbis.

a. The Restriction of the Prophetic Age.

The Canon owes its origin above all to the sense of decline in the post-exilic period. An awareness of separation from the classical period steadily grew. It is intimated already in Zech. 13:2 ff. The Wisdom of Jesus Sir. is the last book to bear the name of its author and to raise a certain prophetic claim. But already Da., which initiates neo-prophecy, is pseudepigraphical. The Rabb., of course, were the first to differentiate sharply between the prophetic past and the present. [79]

Thus Jos. Ap., 1, 38 ff. says: "There are not ten thousand contradictory and conflicting books among us, but only 22 books which contain a description of the whole period (of Jewish history). They are rightly regarded as trustworthy. To them belong the 5 books of Moses. These contain the Law and the tradition from the origin of man to the death of Moses ... The post-Mosaic prophets delineate the events of their time from the death of Moses to Artaxerxes I ... From Artaxerxes I to our time is also depicted, but it does not deserve the same credibility as the earlier work, since the prophets have no true successors." It has been shown already that this theory of Joseph. is accompanied by an older and freer attitude to the traditional literature.

---

[76] Cf. Hühn, 270 f., Hölscher, 66 ff. → I, 756 f.; also → III, 988 ff.

[77] To save a supposedly strict concept of the Canon in Palestine, Joseph. is made an Alexandrian, e.g., Buhl, 44.

[78] The 1st cent. certainly displays tension in relation to this lit. This rests on the antithesis traditionalism/neo-prophecy, not on a philosophical antithesis, as against Hölscher, 56 f. On the self-evaluation of the neo-prophets, cf. 4 Esr. 14:45 ff.

[79] The dogmatic differentiation finds expression, e.g., in the assessment of Hyrcanus I. Jos. Bell., 1, 68 says that he has a prophetic gift (προφητεία), while jSota, 24b, line 27 and par. refer only to a בת קול.

With slight exceptions, the theory of Joseph. is the same as that of the Rabb. acc. to Seder Olam r., 30: "Up to this point (the time of Alexander the Great) the prophets have prophesied in the Holy Spirit. From this point on incline your ear and listen to the words of the wise." [80] The limitation of the prophetic period contains the claim of the Rabbis that in the present they alone, as the bearers of oral tradition, have the right to formulate legal and philosophical pronouncements. The claim of Sir. and all other post-prophetic literature is thus invalidated, T. Jad., 2, 13: "Sir. and all books which were written from then on do not make the hands unclean." [81] This theory naturally aroused opposition in some circles, but towards the end of the 1st cent. it prevailed with the triumph of Rabbinism. Traces of opposition to the sharp differentiation between prophetic and post-prophetic writings even among the Rabb. are to be found as late as the 4th cent. In bSanh., 100b the Babylonians Joseph and Abaye discuss whether Sir. is extra-canonical. R. Joseph affirms the order that Sir. should not be read in the synagogue and the house of instruction. [82] Abaye finds the reason in the unsuitability of some of the things contained in it. [83] But R. Joseph replies: "If our fathers had not concealed the book, we should expound the excellent sayings contained in it." [84] He then gives an example. The way he handles the question shows that he was only bowing to the authority of an earlier period.

There was also differentiation against the pre-Mosaic period. Since the Torah was the source of all knowledge, there could be no work of greater antiquity if the system was to stand. This implied the rejection of any religious claim which the lit. of the patriarchal period might have. Where it was thought that the patriarchs had engaged in written work, it was explained that this work had been handed down and enshrined in the Torah. Thus bBB, 14b/15a shows how David wrote the Psalms acc. to the tradition of ten patriarchs, including Adam, Melchizedek and Abraham. The only exception was Job, which bore the name of a man whom legend regarded either as a contemporary of the patriarchs or as the adviser of Pharaoh. This highly esteemed work was saved for the Canon by calling Moses the author. Apart from minor variations, Moses, Joshua, Samuel, David, Jeremiah, Hezekiah, the men of the great synagogue and Ezra were regarded as the authors of the sacred Scriptures, bBB, 14a/15b.

b. The Sacramental Holiness of the Scriptures.

The defiling of the hands. The idea that a material holiness indwelled the Scriptures used in the cultus is perhaps linked in the first instance with the scrolls of the Torah which were kept in the temple. There is a reminiscence of this in T. Kel. BM, 5, 8 acc. to which the Torah of the forecourt which comes outside defiles the hands. Later this taboo (→ 420 f.) extended to all copies in the forecourt. The Pharisees carried over this idea of the sacramental holiness of Scripture to all OT books in current use. A canonical writing must now be used in rotation ‹מִטַּפַּחַת›. The taboo was strengthened

---

[80] Quoted from the Hamburg ed., 1757, 19b: עד כאן היו הנביאים מתנבאים ברוח הקודש. מכ[א]ן ואילך הט אזנך ושמע דברי חכמים. The historical difference between Jos. and the Rabb. is grounded in the fact that Jos. regarded Est. as the last book of the Prophets and equated אחשורוש with Artaxerxes Longimanus, Buhl, 35.

[81] On the defiling of the hands → infra, b.

[82] בספר בן סירא נמי אסור למיקרי; this is the actual practice, as opposed to Graetz, 287 f., who is followed by Hölscher, 44, n. 8.

[83] Acc. to Graetz Abaye's objection is to the alphabet of Sir. It is true that some of the passages adduced are not in Sir., but the ref. to 42:9 f. shows that Sir. is in his mind. The errors of Abaye are probably due to the fact that Sir. was regarded as a purveyor of popular wisdom, so that pseudepigraphical material could obtrude in free quotation.

[84] The expansion is a marginal reading in Cod. Mon. 95; in support of this reading cf. R. N. Rabbinovicz, Variae Lectiones in Mischnam et in Talmud Babylonicum, IX (1878), p. 304 and C. G. Montefiore, JQR, 3 (1891), 700, n. 30.

by the ascription of magical holiness to the tetragrammaton (אַזְכָּרוֹת). This was so strong that one could not handle freely even heretical works which contained the name of Yahweh, → *infra*. Since holiness was the most prominent difference between canonical and non-canonical writings, the defiling of the hands became a tt. for the concept of canonical validity. [85] How well this theory of the holiness of Scripture fitted in with popular feeling may be seen from Jos. Ant., 20, 115 ff. When a Roman soldier tore a Torah scroll on the occasion of plunder, the procurator Cumanus had to have him executed to prevent a riot.

The concealment of the Scriptures. The idea of the concealment of the Scriptures גֵז is closely linked with that of cultic holiness. [86] Acc. to bYoma, 12b Lv. 16:23 was taken to mean that the clothes worn by the high-priest on the Day of Atonement must be hidden. They were cultically unserviceable and had to be abandoned to natural corruption. On the other hand, they could not be put to secular use. The difference between throwing away and hiding is brought out in bMeg., 26b: Objects of use which are necessary for the fulfilment of commands are thrown away when they become unserviceable, but those which serve a sacred use are left to decay in a protected place: תשמישי מצוה נזרקין תשמישי קרושה נגנזין. The sacred Scriptures are treated in this way. Acc. to Sanh., 10, 6 that which belongs to Yahweh is not to be burned on the capture of an apostate town. The scribes conclude from this that that which is dedicated (ההקדשות) in the city should be released, that the priestly tribute (תרומות) should be allowed to lapse, but that the second tithe [87] and the sacred Scriptures should be concealed: ומעשר שני וכתבי הקדש יגנז. The combining of the Scriptures with the second tithe means that, as a possession of the apostates, they are desecrated and hence cultically unserviceable. [88] They are thus to be put in a protected place to perish.

The same procedure is to be followed in the synagogue with Scriptures which have become unusable or have a blemish. Acc. to Shab., 16, 1 sacred Scriptures in any language are to be hidden in case of unserviceability. They are put either in the lumber-room of the synagogue or the grave of a scribe, bMeg., 26b. Violent destruction is not fitting. That the concept of holiness is a powerful factor in this concealment is shown by T. Shab., 13, 5. Acc. to R. Jose of Galilee (c. 140 A.D.), if Gospels or heretical writings come into one's hands on a weekday, one should cut out and hide the tetra-

---

[85] E.g., Jad., 3, 5: כל כתבי הקדש מטמאין את הידים; the hagiographa in particular are also "holy scriptures," e.g., T. Shab., 13, 1.

[86] גנז (generally) means 1. "to gather" = θησαυρίζειν, e.g., bBB, 11a → 137; 2. "to keep," e.g., bPes., 119a; hence "treasure" גנז, גנזא, e.g., bChag, 12b: גנזי חיים; bPes., 119a: בית גנזיו של קרח, "treasure-house"; 3. "to conceal," "to withdraw from public access"; e.g., bYoma, 52b: משגנגז ארון נגנז עמו צנצנות המן, also Pes., 4, 9 (Bar. from bPes., 56a): חזקיהו המלך גנז ספר רפואות = king Hezekiah ... withdrew from the public a book of (magical) means of healing, cf. jSanh., 18d. The derivative גְּנִיזָה — an abstract construction — means gathering, keeping, concealing, hence bPes., 118b: בית גניזה = "treasure-chamber" and the expression טעון גניזה found, e.g., in Shab., 16, 1. Cf. Levy Wört., I, 346 f.; M. Jastrow, Dictionary ..., I² (1926), 258 f. Attempts to regard גנז, which occurs in Ab. R. Nat., 1 (1b) as a model for ἀπόκρυφος are to be found, e.g., in Zahn Kan., I, 123 ff. and (more cautiously) Hölscher, 59 ff. In so far as ἀπόκρυφος means "secret" it is to be related esp. to the roots סתם, Da. 8:26 etc. and סתר, Sir. 3:22 and bMeg., 3a (opp. גלה in the piel). The conservare of 4 Esr. 14:46 noted by Hölscher, 64 could easily be rendered סתם. Hence the question whether גנז has anything to do with secret lit. is still left open by Hölscher too.

[87] Lv. 27:30.

[88] Though cf. H. L. Strack, Sanhedrin-Makkoth (1910), 40, n. 23.

grammaton, [89] since it is something holy which has become unserviceable, but the rest may be burned as heretical. [90]

גנז has rather a different significance in T. Shab., 13, 2 f. R. Chalafta came upon Gamaliel II (c. 100 A.D.) in Tiberias reading an Aramaic translation of Job. "Then Chalafta said to him: 'I remember Rabban Gamaliel, your grandfather, sitting on a step on the temple hill, and someone brought him a targum of Job. And he spoke to the builder, and the latter built it in under the wall.' That hour Rabban Gamaliel II sent it away and caused it to be hidden." The story refers to a symbolical act whereby a book which is neither heretical nor unserviceable, but which is undesirable for some reason which we cannot now determine, is withdrawn from circulation. Since the Job targum implies a translation of Holy Scripture, which rules out any secular use, the symbolical act is equivalent to a general prohibition.

Where a secular use is conceivable, גנז implies removal from the sphere of the cultus, i.e., the synagogue and the house of instruction, so that religious study of the work concerned is completely forbidden. Thus we read in bSanh., 100b that Sir. is not to be read. In the further course of discussion this prohibition proves to be a forbidding of exposition. If the marginal reading in bSanh., 100b (→ 982) is correct, Sir. is a book which prior to the fixing of the Canon was regarded in the same way as Prv. but after the fixing of the Canon was declared to be profane. In the case of Ez., Qoh., Prv. and Cant., which were also disputed for a time, there was only an attempt at concealment, i.e., secularisation.

c. The Battle for Individual Writings.

The Rabbis of the 1st cent. A.D. agreed in principle on the theory of an ideal past and on belief in the sacramental character of Scripture. But the closing of the Canon was not without friction. Some effort was needed to close it against books like Sir. Furthermore, the dogma of the inner unity of the message of revelation, which is championed already in Jos. Ap., 1, 38 ff. (→ 981), worked against some writings which were unobjectionable from the standpoint of the historical theory concerning the prophetic age. Hence it came about that the struggle with other Jewish groups in respect of some books sanctified by tradition posed the question of agreement with Rabbinic religion. But this criticism came at a time when tradition was already too strong; hence it was bound to be fruitless.

Ezekiel. Acc. to bShab., 13b there were those of the school of Shammai who tried to exclude Ez. from the Canon. Acc. to Rab († 247), the charge brought against Ez. was that of contradicting the Law; for example, Ez. 46:7 was compared with Nu. 15:4 ff. [91] Another objection, based on a legend, bChag., 13a (Bar.), was that Ez. 1 provided a starting-point for cosmogonic and theosophical speculations. That this was a serious charge may be seen from the fact that the Mishnah does not allow Ez. 1 to be read in the synagogue, → n. 61. Nevertheless, Eleazar b. Chananya b. Chizkia, → n. 91, a contemporary of Paul, triumphed over his fellow-scholars when, accepting the principle that there is no inner contradiction in Scripture, he explained away the difficulties, and when he also met the charge that Ez. furthers Gnostic speculation by arguing that the secret knowledge contained in it is reserved for a few illustrious spirits.

---

[89] בחול קורא קורא (קודר .l : את האזכרות וגונו ושורף את השאר cf. jShab., 15c. By an incorrect grammatical connection ושורף + וגונו there results for Hölscher, 62 the reference of גנז to heretical writings.

[90] In T. Shab., loc. cit. Tarphon as a man of particular zeal shows little concern for cultic considerations. It is a testimony to the cultic veneration of the tetragrammaton that in T. Shab., 13, 5 it has to be mentioned specifically that in a fire heretical writings and their אזכרות shall not be saved.

[91] Cf. S. Dt. § 294 on 25:14. On the name of the Shammaite, v. R. Meyer, "Hellenistisches in d. rabb. Anthropologie," BWANT, IV, 22 (1937), 137, n. 1.

Qoheleth. Wis. 2:1 ff. already attacks the religion of Qoh., which runs contrary to Pharisaic and Rabbinic thought. On the other hand, Qoh. bears the name of Solomon and belongs to the classical period. Thus it is quoted by Jochanan b. Zakkai (c. 70 A.D.) notwithstanding the conflicting views of the Rabbis. [92] Acc. to Jad., 3, 5 the school of Shammai did not accept the canonicity of Qoh. The conflict was officially decided at Jamnia about 100 A.D. Echoes of it may still be heard throughout the 2nd cent., [93] but they did not affect the status of the book. Acc. to Rab inner contradiction was alleged against the book, bShab., 30b, and acc. to the statement of later Amoreans its antinomianism was censured. [94]

Proverbs. Acc. to Rab an attempt was made to declare this profane on the ground of inner contradictions, bShab., 30b, but tradition was too strong.

Canticles. With Qoh., this was the main target of attack. It was dealt with at the Council of Jamnia, Jad., 3, 5. Here, too, there are echoes of the debate in the 2nd cent. The chief objection seems to have been that of worldliness, and this not without reason, since it found corresponding application. Perhaps it was also used in mystical speculation. [95] To save Cant., for the Canon, Akiba († 135 A.D.) forbade its use at banquets and withheld any share in the future world from those who regarded it as a secular song, T. Sanh., 12, 10. He also established allegorical interpretation of the book by expounding Yahweh as the friend, Israel as the beloved, and the nations as the chorus of women. This allegory had a decisive influence on Christianity as well as Judaism. How strongly Akiba supported Cant. may be seen from the fact that he hyperbolically claimed that it had never been contested and that it was holier than all other hagiographa, Jad., 3, 5.

Esther. The objections to Est. were of a different kind. Its dogmatic integrity was uniformly accepted, and it had been used for a long time in the cultus as a single hagiographon, bMeg., 7a. The difficulties were political in nature. Because it was so nationalistic, the hatred of other nations was feared because of it. Joshua b. Chananya (c. 90 A.D.) fought against its canonicity on this ground. But he failed because Est. was too deeply rooted in the religious consciousness of the people. Eleazar of Modeïm rebutted Joshua, and Joshua's contemporary Eliezer b. Hyrcanos, Akiba and others regarded Est. as inspired and hence canonical. Occasional doubts later do not affect the actual canonicity of the book.

d. The Canon and Apocryphal Literature.

Attacks on individual books sanctified by tradition did not arrest the process of closing the Canon. Alongside the theory of the prophetic age and that of the sanctity of the books, there also grew up the theory of the compass of the Canon.

The canonical number. Joseph. in Ap., 1, 38 gives us the Rabb. theory of the number c. 60 A.D. He counts 5 books of the Pentateuch, 13 Prophets (Jos., Ju. [with Ruth], S., K., Is., Jer. [with Lam.], Ez., the Twelve, Job, Da., Est. [→ n. 80], Ezra and Ch.), and 4 "songs of praise to God and rules for the life of man" (Ps., Prv., Qoh., Cant.). The church fathers are acquainted with this view. [96] The Rabbis, however, tended to accept the older number of 24, with Ru. and Lam. as separate books, and this gave rise to many allegories. The oldest instance in 4 Esr. 14:18 ff. comes from the time of Jamnia. [97]

The canonical order. A new order was linked with the establishment of the canonical number. As distinct from the LXX, the view already represented by the grandson of

---

[92] Bacher Tannaïten, I², 41 f.
[93] Hölscher, 31 f.
[94] Pesikt., 8 (68b) par.
[95] Hölscher, 53.
[96] Hölscher, 26.
[97] On the canonical numbers, *ibid.,* 25 ff.

Sir. was accepted, namely, that there are three kinds of writings. The corpus of the Torah remained unaltered. Of the Prophets 8 were chosen to constitute the second collection, Jos., Ju., S., K., Jer., Ez., Is. and the Twelve. The other 7 were combined with the existing 4 to produce the hagiographa, Ruth, Ps., Job, Prv., Qoh., Cant., Lam., Da., Est., Ezr., Ch. (bBB, 14b). The reasons for the change are obscure. [98] Perhaps frequency of use in the synagogue had something to do with it. Sometimes in Rabb. lit. we also find the division תּוֹרָה וְקַבָּלָה, which reminds us of the enumeration in the LXX. The order implies degree of sanctity as well as inspiration as between the different groups. [99]

The excluded books. The final closing of the Canon was challenged not merely by heretical works but by intrinsically sound works which did not meet the theories of the Rabbis. The danger here, as may be seen from bSanh., 100b (→ 982), was that they would be made an object of religious study as well as secular use. It is in this light that we are to understand Sanh., 11, 1: Akiba reckons among those who have no share in the future world men who read in the excluded books: אַף הַקּוֹרֵא בַּסְּפָרִים הַחִיצוֹנִים. The סְפָרִים חִיצוֹנִים are non-canonical books. [100] There is something analogous in Nu. r., 18 on 16:35, where the judgment that is not accepted into the corpus of the Mishnah is called an excluded Mishnah: מִשְׁנָה חִיצוֹנָה; the more common term baraita: בְּרִיתָא, is simply the Aram. equivalent. Offence has been taken at the severity with which Akiba forbids the reading of non-canonical books, but one must remember that his principle arose out of the situation. As Akiba forbids the common secular use of Cant. on pain of eternal death, → 985, so he forbids the religious study of non-canonical writings. He does not have more than this in view, i.e., a general prohibition. His aim is to make a clean distinction between sacred literature and profane, and to prevent transition from the one to the other. Hence the Palestinian Gemara (jSanh., 28a) is quite right when it illustrates Akiba's statement from Sir. and another book not now extant, and when it allows the reading of Greek books, since we read these only as if they were letters. The Babyl. Gemara (bSanh., 100b) identifies the excluded books with heretical writings, [101] and it quotes a passage from a baraita which is not very relevant here. [102] But R. Joseph points out that the prohibition of religious study (מִיקְרֵי) applies also to an orthodox work like Sir. In Qoh. r., on 12:12 we read that anyone who brings more than the 24 canonical books into his house for religious study causes confusion. Extra-canonical writings may be used only for secular reading. [103]

5. The Influence of Non-Canonical Writings.

With the closing of the Canon at the beginning of the 2nd cent. A.D. the Apocrypha lost their place of equality alongside the canonical writings. Nevertheless, they still exerted an influence in Rabb. Judaism, and, in some cases corresponding very well to the religion of the Rabbis, they served as exposition of the canonical books. They were used in the same way as the Jewish and more generally oriental heritage, and even motifs from Greek saga and philosophy, were also used, namely, as a secular legacy.

---

[98] Apart from Ps. some of the Writings were seldom used in worship, some never. Their place was only in instruction. Hölscher, 29 maintains that the transferring of Ru. and Lam. to the Writings was due to the desire to unite the 5 Megillot, but it is only later that we read of the 5 Megillot used at festivals. The order of the books shows that this was not the reason.

[99] Cf. T. Meg., 4, 20.

[100] Hölscher, 42 ff. takes a different view, but not very convincingly.

[101] סְפָרֵי מִינִין: Rabbinovicz (→ n. 84), IX, p. 303; Str.-B., IV, 408.

[102] Cf. EJ, II, 1165.

[103] Cf. also Nu. r., 15 on 11:16 par.; less clearly, Pesikt. r., 3 (9a); Nu. r., 14 on 7:48.

A few examples may be given. From the non-canonical Wisdom lit., a series of quotations from Sir. was used by the Rabb., [104] often in a way which has led many students to assume that this book was canonical up to the 4th cent. [105] From apocalyptic the motif of the rapture and concealment of the Messiah [106] found an echo in Rabb. lit. in the comforting legend of the birth and rapture of the Messiah, Lam. r., 1 on 1:16 par. Speculations on heaven and its contents may be mentioned in this connection, bChag., 12b. From apocryphal history the motif of Bel at Babel may be adduced ; it is found in Gn. r., 68 on 28:12. The martyrdom of the mother and her seven sons (2 Macc. 7:1 ff.) also found its way as a motif into Rabb. lit., Lam. r., 1 on 1:16. The Jannes and Jambres motif is found in the Targum lit. (→ 192), while light is shed on many motifs in a comm. on Ex. 1:8 ff. (bSota, 11a ff.) by an apocryphal historical writing, Ps.-Philo, which has been preserved only in a secondary Lat. translation. [107]

R. Meyer

II. Βίβλοι ἀπόκρυφοι in Christianity.

The term βίβλοι ἀπόκρυφοι takes on technical significance in Church history. The usage which has become predominant in Protestantism is that those parts of the LXX not in the Heb. Canon are called the OT Apocrypha. As Luther put it, these are good and useful to read, but they are not God's Word. On this model, certain ancient Christian writings which were never canonised are then called the NT Apocrypha. But this usage is relatively late. The basis of the former description is to be found in Jer. (Pref. to the Books of Samuel, MPL, 28, p. 556a) and some medieval authors, but it was first formulated in Carlstadt's work *De Canonicis Scripturis* (Wittenbergae, 1520), then in the Frankfurt Bible of 1534, and the first edition of the Luther Bible the same year. In none of the canonical lists to be mentioned later (→ C. II. 6.) are these books called Apocrypha ; they are either disputed, or non-canonical, or books which are not read in church, but only before catechumens. The first to make a collection of NT Apocrypha was Michael Neander Soraviensis ; he added it to his *Catechesis Martini Lutheri Parva, Graeco-Latina* (1564, [2] 1567). The term "apocryphal" is found in the Church from the time of Irenaeus, but in the first instance in another sense. It has a complicated and much disputed history. Our best plan is first to sketch the actual use of the Apocrypha c. 200 with the help of early usage, and then to trace the history of the term.

1. The LXX and Hebrew Canon in the Early Church.

Since Christianity soon passed on to Greek-speaking territory, the LXX was its earliest Canon. Already in the NT the OT is with few exceptions quoted from the LXX. In patristic literature this is accepted procedure. It means that from the very first those parts of the LXX not in the Hebrew Canon come into the possession of Christians. One can hardly say that they are avidly used and quoted. There are no quotations from them at all in the NT. The post-apost. fathers know Wis., Sir., Est., Jdt. and Tob., but do not quote them as Scripture. There are echoes of Wis. in Justin. Iren. regards the additions to Da. as prophetic and quotes Bar. as Jer. The deviation from the Heb. Canon is apparently not clearly understood, or even considered. The Alexandrians use the whole LXX without reservation. Around this time, however, doubts arise which are later to become stronger and to lead to the formulae quoted above, though not to the exclusion of these sections. Of greater basic significance is an exchange of letters between

---

[104] Cf. Montefiore, 682 ff.

[105] Schürer, II⁴, 369, n. 14; EJ, II, 1167.

[106] Cf. 4 Esr. 13:1 ff.

[107] *Philonis Judaei Alexandrini Libri Antiquitatum* (Basel, 1527); E.T. M. R. James, *The Biblical Antiquities of Philo* (1917).

Julius Africanus and Origen c. 240 (MPG, 11, 41 f.). The occasion was a discussion between Origen and a certain Bassus in which Origen appealed to the story of Susanna. Africanus succinctly contests the canonicity of this "clearly invented" story on sound literary and historical grounds. Origen must concede that he has demonstrated many προβλήματα ἐν ὀλίγοις. His own lengthy expositions to the contrary are not very convincing, though they bear the mark of the expert and are typical of the Alexandrian position. That the situation of the Jews in exile is falsely depicted in Susanna could be shown only with the help of the Book of Tobit, which is absent from the Heb. Canon like Susanna and Judith, and which acc. to reliable accounts was not handed down among the Jews in Hebrew even ἐν ἀποκρύφοις. The Jewish scholars and elders probably suppressed the story of Susanna, which was present ἐν ἀπορρήτοις and historically reliable, lest they should be exposed before their own people. The writer ironically asks whether the Church should destroy its own copies of the Bible, admit that the Jews are right and accept from them pure texts without interpolations. Yet even in the heat of the fight for the Jewish secret books, the pseudepigrapha, this does not prevent him from asking whether these were in part falsified by the Jews to make them unserviceable to Christians. Many of these works are canonised for Christians by the fact that they are used in the NT. The historical basis of this argument demands separate investigation.

2. Apocryphal Quotations in the New Testament.

The aversion of the Jews to the hidden books, which slowly increased from the 1st century onwards (→ 985), did not affect Christianity at first. In the NT and the fathers up to the 3rd century these books are freely quoted, often as Holy Scripture, though not so commonly as sometimes assumed.

There is much debate as to the position in the NT. The surest instance is the latest, namely, Jd. 14: ἐπροφήτευσεν δὲ καὶ τούτοις ἕβδομος ἀπὸ Ἀδὰμ Ἑνὼχ λέγων (followed by Eth. En. 1:9). On the Enoch traditions → II, 556 ff., esp. 559. The same epistle (Jd. 9) alludes to the battle of the archangel Michael with Satan for the body of Moses, which acc. to Cl. Al. (Adumbrationes In Ep. Judae, 9, GCS, 17, p. 207, 23 ff.) and Orig. (Princ., III, 2, 1 [→ C. II. 3. b]) and others occurred in the Ass. Mos., though it was, of course, widespread elsewhere. [108] Hb. 11:37 perhaps contains an allusion to Asc. Is. 5:2, 11, 14, but there is no direct quotation. [109]

Perhaps the earliest instance of a NT quotation from the Apocrypha is 1 C. 2:9: ἀλλὰ καθὼς γέγραπται· ἃ ὀφθαλμὸς οὐκ εἶδεν καὶ οὖς οὐκ ἤκουσεν καὶ ἐπὶ καρδίαν ἀνθρώπου οὐκ ἀνέβη, ὅσα ἡτοίμασεν ὁ θεὸς τοῖς ἀγαπῶσιν αὐτόν, but this is much contested. If it is a true agraphon, the solemn formula of quotation is highly significant. In favour of this assumption is the fact that, though it is not in the OT, it is often found, e.g., in 1 Cl., 34, 8; Mart. Pol., 2, 3; also 2 Cl., 11, 7 between an unidentified quotation (11, 2 ff.) and one from the Gospel of the Egyptians (? 12, 2, Hennecke, 58); the Gnostic Act. Thom., 36; Act. Pt. Verc., 39; the Lat. text of Asc. Is. (11, 34, cf. Hennecke, 314); Lidz. Liturg., 77, 4. The Ophite Justin perhaps read it in a Book of Baruch which was highly esteemed by him (Hipp. Ref., V, 24, 1; 26, 16; 27, 2, 5) immediately alongside a Mandaean sounding statement which presupposes the drinking of the water of baptism (ibid., 27, 2). Acc. to Origen it was to be found in the Apc. El. (Comm. Series 117 in Mt. 27:9, GCS, 38, p. 250, 4 ff.): et apostolus scripturas quasdam secretorum profert, sicut dicit alicubi: "quod oculus non vidit nec auris audivit"; in nullo enim regulari libro hos positum invenitur, nisi in secretis Eliae prophetae, cf. also Series

---

[108] For details cf. Wnd. Kath. Br. on Jd. 9; Schürer, III⁴, 294 ff., esp. 301 ff. Neither citation occurs in 2 Pt. 2, perhaps because of scruples against the Apocrypha.

[109] Cf. Wnd. Hb., ad loc.; Schürer, III⁴, 386 ff.; Hennecke, 303 ff. For patristic quotations from Asc. Is. → C. II. 3.b.

28 in Mt. 23:37 (51, 5 ff.): *si autem aspiciat et quod ad Corinthios prima positum est*: (as above, but *quae*), *numquid poterit haec omnia* ｜*aliquis abdicare*? (cf. also "Secretum Esaiae," *ibid.*, 50, 28). [110] Jer. Comm. in Is. XVII on 64:4 (MPL, 24, p. 622b ff.) cannot contest the fact that the saying is found in the Apc. El. and the Asc. Is., but he regards *apocryphorum deliramenta* as secondary in relation to 1 C. 2:9, which he thinks he can understand as a paraphrase of Is. 64:3 f., cf. also Ep., 57, 9 (MPL, 22, p. 575 f.); Praefatio in Pent. (MPL, 22, p. 150). Cl. Al. has perhaps preserved the original of Apc. El. in his quotation in Prot., X, 94, 4: ὅθεν ἡ γραφὴ εἰκότως εὐαγγελίζεται τοῖς πεπιστευκόσιν· »οἱ δὲ ἅγιοι κυρίου κληρονομήσουσι τὴν δόξαν τοῦ θεοῦ καὶ τὴν δύναμιν αὐτοῦ«. ποίαν, ὦ μακάριε (address to an interpreting angel?), δόξαν; εἰπέ μοι· (answer) ἣν ὀφθαλμὸς οὐκ εἶδεν οὐδὲ οὖς ἤκουσεν, οὐδὲ ἐπὶ καρδίαν ἀνθρώπου ἀνέβη· καὶ χαρήσονται ἐπὶ τῇ βασιλείᾳ τοῦ κυρίου αὐτῶν εἰς τοὺς αἰῶνας, ἀμήν. The question whether Paul is quoting an apocryphon thus reduces itself to the question whether Apc. El. is Jewish and pre-Pauline. The former is likely enough, since Apc. El. is mentioned with Jewish pseudepigrapha in ancient accounts of the Canon. [111] But this does not force us to conclude that it is pre-Pauline and that Paul is dependent on it. Christian interpolation on the basis of 1 C. 2:9 (also Asc. Is. → *supra*) is quite conceivable. Or Pl. and the Apc. El. could have been dependent on an older tradition. Rabb. exposition of Is. 64:4 makes it probable that there was a connection with this passage. The basic text here is: "From the beginning of the world men have not perceived, nor heard, neither hath an eye seen, a God apart from thee, who worketh for him that waiteth upon him." LXX: ἀπὸ τοῦ αἰῶνος οὐκ ἠκούσαμεν οὐδὲ οἱ ὀφθαλμοὶ ἡμῶν εἶδον θεὸν πλὴν σοῦ καὶ τὰ ἔργα σου, ἃ ποιήσεις τοῖς ὑπομένουσιν ἔλεον. The Rabb. interpretation, which may be traced back to the Tannaitic period, took אֱלֹהִים as a vocative and supplied it again as the subject of יַעֲשֶׂה or vocalised this as ni. This gives the sense: "No eye has seen, O God, apart from thee, what God prepares for him that waits on him." [112] This interpretation might well have been known to Paul. It was perhaps a current saying [113] and was used by Apc. El. and then spread even further abroad, not without some help from 1 C. 2:9. It is thus misleading to cite the saying as evidence of pre-Christian Gnosticism. [114] The only point is that, naturally enough in view of its mysterious content, it found particular entry into Gnostic circles. This also explains its occurrence in Manichean MSS remains from Turfan: [115] "... in order that I may redeem you from death and destruction, I will give you what you have not seen with the eye nor heard with the ear nor grasped with the hand." That Paul was intentionally quoting an apocryphon as Scripture remains to be proved. Because of the similarity to Is. 64:4 he perhaps thought that he was quoting Scripture. [116]

Gl. 6:15: οὔτε γὰρ περιτομή τί ἐστιν οὔτε ἀκροβυστία, ἀλλὰ καινὴ κτίσις, is said in the list of quotations of Euthalius (MPG, 85, p. 721b, cf. Georgius Syncellus, ed. G. Dindorf, I [1829], p. 48, 6 ff., Photius, Quaestiones ad Amphilochium, 151 [183], MPG, 101, p. 813c) to have originated in a Μωϋσέως ἀπόκρυφον. The accounts are not very ancient and may be due to the fact that the saying was interpolated into the Ass. Mos. or that it was combined with a Jewish saying about בְּרִיאָה חֲדָשָׁה and then mis-

---

[110] In his comm. on Cor., written before he knew Apc. El. (Cramer Cat., V, p. 42, 12 ff.), Origen traces back the saying to Is. 52:15 or to an OT book lost at the Exile.

[111] Cf. Schürer, III⁴, 357 ff.

[112] First found under the name of R. Shim'on ben Chalaphta (c. 190), Qoh. r. 1:8, though without a name (S. Nu., 135 on 27:12 [Dt. 3:26], p. 558, Kuhn) probably much older, Str.-B., III, 327 ff.

[113] 1 Cl., 34, 8: ὅσα ἡτοίμασεν κύριος τοῖς ὑπομένουσιν αὐτόν, is closer to Is. 64:4. Elsewhere there seems to be dependence on 1 C. 2:9, but 1 Cl. shows a sense of the OT connection.

[114] Bau. J.³, 4 f.

[115] II, ed. F. W. K. Müller, AAB, 1904, App. 68, M. 789, cf. 67 f., M. 551, reverse side.

[116] Cf. Ltzm. 1 C. on 2:9; Zahn Kan., II, 801 ff.; Schürer, III⁴, 361 ff.

takenly ascribed to a Moses apocryphon. There seems to be little doubt that it is original in Pl. This is shown by the divergence from the par. Gl. 5:6; 1 C. 7:19 in spite of the agreement in content. 1 C. 9:10 : δι' ἡμᾶς γὰρ ἐγράφη, ὅτι (that) ὀφείλει ἐπ' ἐλπίδι ὁ ἀροτριῶν ἀροτριᾶν, καὶ ὁ ἀλοῶν ἐπ' ἐλπίδι τοῦ μετέχειν, is not a quotation from an unknown apocryphon but an expository addition after the Rabb. manner (cf. 1 C. 15:45) by means of which Paul transfers the quotation in v. 9 (Dt. 25:4) from the beast to man with a view to its further extension to the spiritual sphere. [117]

Eph. 5:14 : ἔγειρε, ὁ καθεύδων, καὶ ἀνάστα ἐκ τῶν νεκρῶν, καὶ ἐπιφαύσει σοι ὁ Χριστός, [118] is attributed by Epiph. [119] to Elias (an Apc. El.), by Hipp. [120] to Is. (60:1 ?), and by Euthalius [121] to a Jeremiah apocryphon. Since these accounts diverge so widely, little credence may be attached to them. The verse is undoubtedly a bit of ancient Christian poetry which is quoted as God's Word [122] because of its prophetic quality. The poem is in three lines with homoioteleuton. [123] If it had already received written form, the continuation is perhaps to be found in Cl. Al. (Prot., IX, 84, 2): ὁ τῆς ἀναστάσεως ἥλιος, ὁ πρὸ "ἑωσφόρου γεννώμενος," ὁ ζωὴν χαρισάμενος ἀκτῖσιν ἰδίαις, though this may well be a not unskilful addition. The content of the saying is specifically Christian, but Persian or Greek influences seem to have contributed to the form. [124] Hence the world of the βίβλοι ἀπόκρυφοι does here penetrate into the NT in the broader sense. 1 Tm. 3:16 is another hymn, not an apocryphon. But here again it would be difficult to contest a certain familiarity with apocryphal and apocalyptic traditions. [125]

2 Tm. 3:8 mentions the Egyptian magicians Jannes and Jambres who withstood Moses. The names do not occur in the OT (Ex. 7:8 ff.) and derive from apocryphal tradition. The oldest extant occurrence is in Damasc., v. 18 f.: [126] "In ancient times, when Moses and Aaron came forth in the power of the prince of lights, Belial caused Jachne and his brother to rise up in his evil plans, at the time when Israel was delivered for the first time." The legend is extremely common, not only in Jewish [127] and Christian literature, [128] but also in pagan authors : Plin. Hist. Nat., XXX, 1, 11; Apul. Apologia, 90 (ed. R. Helm [1905]); Numenius, in Eus. Praep. Ev., IX, 8. Because of the difference of the names it is unlikely that all these traditions go back to a single book "about Jannes and Jambres." [129] Such a book is mentioned by Origen → 193, Ambrosiaster on 2 Tm. 3:8 (MPL, 17, p. 521): Exemplum hoc de apocryphis est : Iannes enim et Mambres fratres erant magi (the story follows), and the Decretum Gelasii, → 193. A fragment is perhaps preserved

---

[117] Str.-B., III, 385 ff.

[118] D e Ambst nonnulli apud Chrys : ἐπιψαύσεις τοῦ Χριστοῦ.

[119] Haer., 42, 12, 3 (refutatio, 37) on the above citation : πόθεν τῷ ἀποστόλῳ τὸ "διὸ λέγει" ἀλλὰ ἀπὸ τῆς παλαιᾶς δῆλον διαθήκης; τοῦτο δὲ ἐμφέρεται παρὰ τῷ 'Ηλίᾳ. The ref. seems to be to a canonical quotation; perhaps we should emend to 'Ησαΐᾳ. Cf. Holl (GCS), ad loc. (II, 179, 25 ff.).

[120] Esp. Comm. in Da., IV, 56.

[121] MPG, 85, p. 721c.

[122] Dib. Gefbr., ad loc. One need not assume a lapse of memory.

[123] E. Peterson Εἷς Θεός (1926), 132.

[124] Cf. on the one side the Manichean Fr., 7 (Reitzenstein Hell. Myst., 58): "Shake off the drunkenness in which you slumber; awake and behold me"; Act. Thom., 110 : ἀνάστηθι καὶ ἀνάηψον ἐξ ὕπνου, καὶ τῶν ἐπιστολιμαίων ῥημάτων ἄκουσον, καὶ ὑπομνήσθητι υἱὸς βασιλέων ὑπάρχων (→ II, 336), and on the other Aristoph. Ra., 340 ff.: ἔγειρε· φλογέας λαμπάδας ἐν χερσὶ γὰρ ἥκεις τινάσσων, / "Ιακχ' ὦ "Ιακχε, / νυκτέρου τελετῆς φωσφόρος ἀστήρ. Clemen, 306 f.

[125] A certain kinship of style may be seen in O. Sol. 19:10 f. Dib. Past. on 1 Tm. 3:16.

[126] Transl. W. Staerk, BFTh, 27, 3 (1922), 24.

[127] Examples in Schürer, III⁴, 403; Str.-B., III, 660 ff.; Dib. Past. on 2 Tm. 3:8, → 192.

[128] Examples in Schürer, III⁴, 404; Dib., loc. cit.

[129] Schürer, III⁴, 403 decides for a pre-Christian origin of the book on this assumption.

in a Lat. tractate with Anglo-Saxon transl. in a MS of the 11th cent. [130] Whether the author of 2 Tm. drew on this book cannot be determined. He certainly did not quote it.

Jm. 4:5 : ἢ δοκεῖτε ὅτι κενῶς ἡ γραφὴ λέγει· πρὸς φθόνον ἐπιποθεῖ τὸ πνεῦμα ὃ κατῴκισεν ἐν ἡμῖν; contains a quotation of unknown provenance. The conjecture that it is from the book Eldad and Modad (→ C. II. 3. a.) [131] is untenable. If we read πνεῦμ' ὃ and κατῴκισ' ἐν the saying can be treated as a hexameter and is perhaps taken from a Jewish Hellenistic didactic poem. [132] Nevertheless, the author can regard it as a scriptural saying. The Rabbis occasionally quote conclusions from the Torah either intentionally or erroneously as the Torah. [133]

Also open to debate is Jn. 7:38 : ὁ πιστεύων εἰς ἐμέ, καθὼς εἶπεν ἡ γραφή, ποταμοὶ ἐκ τῆς κοιλίας αὐτοῦ ῥεύσουσιν ὕδατος ζῶντος. As Chrysostom and Ischodad noted already, there is no corresponding saying in the OT. The former concludes from this (Cramer Cat., II, p. 269, 11) that καθὼς εἶπεν ἡ γραφή belongs only to ὁ πιστεύων εἰς ἐμέ. But in this case the quotation would be so general as to be pointless. The difficulty arises in the concluding words, which contain the alleged quotation. Since in the context the ref. is to Christ as the One who dispenses living water, one might perhaps apply the quotation to Him and paraphrase : "He who believes in me (will learn that it is) as the Scripture says : Streams of living water will flow out of his (the Redeemer's) body." It is then suggested that this is a saying of unknown apocryphal origin which is given the status of Scripture. [134] Grammatically, however, it is more natural to link αὐτοῦ with ὁ πιστεύων εἰς ἐμέ, [135] cf. 6:39. The idea that blessing flows from the disciples analogous to that which flows from Jesus Himself is so common in Johannine thinking that it does not surprise us in this passage, cf. Jn. 4:14 with 4:36; 15:16; 17:18; 20:21 etc. κοιλία is perhaps a transl. of the Heb. נֶפֶשׁ, which means a hollow, then the cavity of the stomach, then the body, and finally and very generally the person. Hence ἐκ τῆς κοιλίας αὐτοῦ hardly means more than "from him," [136] and there is no serious obstacle to regarding the quotation as a paraphrase (→ supra) of OT passages like Is. 58:11: ἔση ὡς κῆπος μεθύων καὶ ὡς πηγὴ ἣν μὴ ἐξέλιπεν ὕδωρ, καὶ τὰ ὀστᾶ σου ὡς βοτάνη ἀνατελεῖ, or Sir. 24:30 ff.: κἀγὼ ὡς διῶρυξ ἀπὸ ποταμοῦ καὶ ὡς ὑδραγωγὸς ἐξῆλθον εἰς παράδεισον· εἶπα Ποτιῶ μου τὸν κῆπον κτλ. (cf. also Is. 43:20; 44:3; 55:1; Ez. 47:1 ff.; Jl. 2:23; 3:18; Zech. 13:1; 14:8; Cant. 4:15). The accounts of well miracles (Ex. 17:6 : καὶ ἐξελεύσεται ἐξ αὐτῆς [מִמֶּנּוּ] ὕδωρ, Nu. 20:11: καὶ ἐξῆλθεν ὕδωρ πολύ) may have influenced these formulae. Hence it cannot be proved that an apocryphon is here quoted as Scripture.

There is a slip at Mt. 27:9. [137] The Evangelist has Zech. 11:13 in mind, but because of the incorrect reading אֶל־הַיּוֹצֵר (potter) for אֶל־הָאוֹצָר (treasury) he confuses it with Jer. 18:3 and 32 (LXX 39):9. To imagine a Jer. apocryphon [138] is just as unfounded as to

---

[130] For details, Schürer, III⁴, 405.

[131] F. Spitta, Der Brief d. Jk. (z. Geschichte u. Lit. d. Urchr., II [1896], 121 ff.).

[132] Wnd. Kath. Br., ad loc.

[133] Examples in Str.-B., III, 297 on R. 12:14; 608 on Eph. 5:14.

[134] Bau. J., ad loc. Along these lines all kinds of analogies may be seen in other religions. For the Babylonians the gods of the rivers are the bringers of living water, even in the sense that the river wells up from the shoulder or body of the god. The Nile springs from the shank of Osiris. Hermes Psychopompos or a similar deity gives the blessed to drink from the speaking source (Rohde, 390). The Redeemer who dispenses living water is also Mandaean. But the OT analogies are much closer than these.

[135] Zn. J. etc.

[136] Examples in Str.-B., II, 492, e.g., to offend בְּגוּפָן, "personally."

[137] So already Aug. De Consensu Evangelistarum, III, 7, 29 f., CSEL, 43, p. 304 ff., though all prophets agree. In 22 the marginal reading of the revised Syr Ζαχαρίου, and the omission of the name in Φ 33 157 a b syr are forced attempts at solution.

[138] The Nazarenes acc. to Jer. Comm. in Mt. 27:9 (MPL, 28, 213). Cf. Zahn Kan., II, 696 f., 806.

assume that the words have been accidentally or intentionally expunged. [139] Lk. 11:49 might well be a quotation from an unknown passage of Heb. or Hellen. Wisdom lit., but it can also be explained in terms of a revelation of the plan of the divine government of the world (ἡ σοφία τοῦ θεοῦ = God in His wisdom), whether we refer to earlier sayings of Jesus or, preferably, to OT passages like Jer. 7:25 f. [140]

On examination the instances of apocryphal quotation in the NT prove to be very small, though one can hardly deny them altogether.

3. The Apocrypha in the Fathers.

a. The post-apostolic fathers. Passages like 1 Cl., 8, 3; [141] 26, 2; [142] 2 Cl., 13, 2; [143] Barn., 7, 4. [144] 8; [145] 11, 9, [146] are not to be taken as apocryphal quotations. As many allusions show, they are the inexact paraphrasing from memory of OT sayings or trains of thought. This explains the introductory formulae. We may assume an apocryphon when under the formula γέγραπται or the like we have a quotation which does not occur in the OT and which is original in content and form, e.g., 1 Cl., 17, 6: πάλιν λέγει· Ἐγὼ δέ εἰμι ἀτμὶς ἀπὸ κύθρας, [147] and 46, 2: γέγραπται γάρ· Κολλᾶσθε τοῖς ἁγίοις, ὅτι οἱ κολλώμενοι αὐτοῖς ἁγιασθήσονται, [148] or when one and the same quotation occurs in the same or almost the same form, e.g., 1 Cl., 23, 3 f. = 2 Cl., 11, 2 ff.: [149] ... ἡ γραφή ..., ὅπου λέγει (λέγει γὰρ καὶ ὁ προφητικὸς λόγος)·

---

[139] Eus. Dem. Ev., X, 4, 13. Orig. Comm. Series 117, ad loc. (GCS, 38, p. 249, 20 ff.), however, leaves us with a choice between an error scripturae and a secreta Hieremiae scriptura. Cf. Kl. Mt., ad loc.

[140] Kl. Lk., ad loc.

[141] Cf. Is. 1:16 ff.

[142] Cf. ψ 27:7; 87:10.

[143] Cf. Is. 52:5; Ign. Tr., 8, 2; Pol., 10, 3.

[144] τί οὖν λέγει ἐν τῷ προφήτῃ; Καὶ φαγέτωσαν ἐκ τοῦ τράγου τοῦ προσφερομένου τῇ νηστείᾳ ὑπὲρ πασῶν τῶν ἁμαρτιῶν. προσέχετε ἀκριβῶς· Καὶ φαγέτωσαν οἱ ἱερεῖς μόνοι πάντες τὸ ἔντερον ἄπλυτον μετὰ ὄξους. This quotation, esp. towards the end, is completely at odds with the OT but suggests the malicious legend, ascribed in Jos. Ap., II, 95 to Apion, that the Jews annually consumed the entrails of a slaughtered Greek and vowed enmity against the Greeks. Materially the author has in view OT legislation concerning the Day of Atonement (Lv. 16:7 ff.) and the sin offering (Lv. 6:19). Perhaps Ex. 29:32 f.; 12:8 f.; Nu. 29:7-11 also had some influence. It may be that Barn. was drawing on the oral tradition of Judaism. It is recorded in bMen., 99b/100a that the goat of the Day of Atonement, if this fell on the evening of a Sabbath, was eaten raw, contrary to Lv. 16:27, by the Babylonians, a term of opprobrium for the Alexandrian priests. Cf. Wnd. Barn., ad loc. The genesis of an apocryphal quotation may be very instructively observed here.

[145] The OT basis is to be found in Lv. 16:21; 14:4; Nu. 19:6. Here again Barn. seems also to draw ἐξ Ἰουδαϊκῆς ἀγράφου παραδόσεως (Eus. Hist. Eccl., IV, 22, 8, Hegesipp.). Cf. Yoma, 6, 4 f., where it is said that the Babylonians (→ n. 144) tore off the goat's hair. Cf. also Yoma, 6, 6: "He parted the red thread, binding one half to the rock (from which the goat was hurled) and the other between the horns of the goat." Barn., 7, 8 speaks of the thread being bound to a bramble. Perhaps this is a variant transl. (ῥαχία, ῥάχος confused with ῥάχις, Heb. צֶלַע or צוּר). Wnd. Barn., ad loc.

[146] Cf. Ez. 20:6.

[147] Perhaps from a book of Moses, e.g., the Ass. Mos., Kl. Cl., ad loc. R. Harris, JBL, 29 (1910), 190 ff., has shown, however, that the same expression occurs in the Targum-like Syr. transl. of 1 Ch. 29:15 and almost word for word in the Syr. transl. of 1 Cl. He is inclined to assume "a targumized Greek version of Ch." as the common source and a slip of memory on the part of the author of the epistle. Here, too, an OT explanation is possible.

[148] Origin indeterminate acc. to Kn. Cl., ad loc.

[149] Kn. Cl., ad loc. suggests an apocr. book which went under the flag of the OT and was probably of Jewish origin. The quotation is given in the 1 Cl. form. The deviations in 2 Cl. are noted in parentheses.

Ταλαίπωροί εἰσιν οἱ δίψυχοι, οἱ διστάζοντες τῇ ψυχῇ (καρδίᾳ), οἱ λέγοντες· Ταῦτα (+ πάλαι) ἡκούσαμεν καὶ ἐπὶ τῶν πατέρων ἡμῶν, καὶ ἰδοὺ γεγηράκαμεν καὶ οὐδὲν ἡμῖν τούτων συνβέβηκεν (ἡμεῖς δὲ ἡμέραν ἐξ ἡμέρας προσδεχόμενοι οὐδὲν τούτων ἑωράκαμεν). ῏Ω (—) ἀνόητοι, συμβάλετε ἑαυτοὺς ξύλῳ, λάβετε ἄμπελον· πρῶτον μὲν φυλλοροεῖ, εἶτα βλαστὸς γίνεται, εἶτα φύλλον, εἶτα ἄνθος, καὶ (—) μετὰ ταῦτα ὄμφαξ, εἶτα σταφυλὴ παρεστηκυῖα (+ οὕτως καὶ ὁ λαός μου ἀκαταστασίας καὶ θλίψεις ἔσχεν, ἔπειτα ἀπολήψεται τὰ ἀγαθά).

More solid instances of Jewish apocr. include Barn., 4, 3 : τὸ τέλειον σκάνδαλον ἤγγικεν, περὶ οὗ γέγραπται, ὡς Ἐνὼχ λέγει, where an Enoch prophecy concerning the tribulation of the end time is estimated as Scripture (En. 99:1 ff.; 100:1 ff.), [150] and Barn., 16, 5, where, among prophetic sayings, and introduced by λέγει ἡ γραφή, there is a non-literal reminiscence of Eth. En. 89:56, 66 : καὶ ἔσται ἐπ' ἐσχάτων τῶν ἡμερῶν, καὶ παραδώσει κύριος τὰ πρόβατα τῆς νομῆς καὶ τὴν μάνδραν καὶ τὸν πύργον αὐτῶν εἰς καταφθοράν. 16, 6 also seems to have been influenced by Eth. En. 91:13 (along with Da. 9:24 ff.). Barn., 6, 13 : λέγει δὲ κύριος· Ἰδοὺ ποιῶ τὰ ἔσχατα ὡς τὰ πρῶτα, is of unknown apocr. provenance ; passages like 4 Esr. 6:6 are not decisive. Perhaps it is a free composition of Barn. on the basis of passages like Is. 43:18 f.; 46:10; Da. 11:29 LXX Θ; Lam. 5:21; Ez. 36:11; Mt. 19:30; 20:16; Rev. 21:4 f. But it is also possible that the saying was already current and that it stood in some apocalypse. Related, but perhaps dependent on Barn., are Didasc., 26, p. 136, Didascalia Apostolica Latina, III (ed. E. Hauler [1900], p. 75, 30 f.), Hipp. Comm. in Da., IV, 37, 5. [151] Barn., 12, 1 introduces a quotation which echoes Ez. 47:1 ff. as the saying of an ἄλλος προφήτης : Καὶ πότε ταῦτα συντελεσθήσεται; λέγει κύριος· Ὅταν ξύλον κλιθῇ καὶ ἀναστῇ, καὶ ὅταν ἐκ ξύλου αἷμα στάξῃ. The saying is composed from 4 Esr. 4:33 : quo et quando haec? and 5:5 : et de ligno sanguis stillabit. Cf. Ps.-Hier. Comm. in Mk. 15:33 (MPL, 30, p. 639c): hic stillavit sanguis de ligno ; Greg. Nyss., Testim. adv. Judaeos, 7 (MPL, 46, p. 213d): but for τότε for πότε word for word the same. The meaning is originally that of a marvel of the last days. The reference to the cross is read in. The words ὅταν ξύλον κλιθῇ καὶ ἀναστῇ do not occur in the present text of 4 Esr. A material par. is Job 14:7: ἔστιν γὰρ δένδρῳ ἐλπίς· ἐὰν γὰρ ἐκκοπῇ, ἔτι ἐπανθήσει, καὶ ὁ ῥάδαμνος αὐτοῦ οὐ μὴ ἐκλίπῃ. [152] Herm. v., 2, 3, 4, after a warning to Maximus, continues : ἐγγὺς κύριος τοῖς ἐπιστρεφομένοις, ὡς γέγραπται ἐν τῷ Ἐλδὰδ καὶ Μωδάτ, τοῖς προφητεύσασιν ἐν τῇ ἐρήμῳ τῷ λαῷ. The book mentioned here refers to the narrative of Nu. 11:26 ff. Other quotations from this pseudepigr. work are not known (→ 991). Its compass is given as 400 lines in the Stichometria of Nicephorus. It is also mentioned in the so-called Synopsis Athanasii and in an anonymous canonical list in the Codex Coislinianus. The context there enables us to conclude that it is an apoc. of Jewish origin. [153] In Papias' account of the sayings of the Lord acc. to Iren. Haer., V, 33, 4 a quotation from S. Bar. 29:5 seems to have occurred which is supposedly quoted as a saying of the Lord and elaborated. Iren. Haer., V, 33, 3 traces it back, not just to the presbyters, but to John the son of Zebedee. The saying gives a fantastic description of the fertility of the earth in the other aeon, and is not in the least after the style of Jesus. [154]

b. The later fathers. In his description of the fall of the angels in Apol. II (appendix to Apol. I), Just. follows either the Book of En. (cf. Eth. En. 7) or a tradition close to

---

[150] Ref. to Eth. En. 89:61-64; 90:17 f., does not work out, since the thought here is that of judgment, not the τέλειον σκάνδαλον. The ὡς Ἐνὼχ λέγει is a more precise form of περὶ οὗ γέγραπται. A. D. Loman, ThT, 18 (1884), 192 regards it as a gloss, Wnd. Barn., ad loc., as a later addition of the author. The ref. to Da. 9:27; 12:11 fits better ; so the Lat. transl., though to avoid apocrypha.

[151] Wnd. Barn., ad loc.

[152] Ibid. on 12, 1.

[153] Schürer, III⁴, 358 ff.

[154] Hennecke, 544 f.

it, though he does not mention the book, let alone quote it. He is also familiar with the legend of the sawing asunder of Is. now found in Ass. Is. 5 and deriving from the originally Jewish Mart. Is. [155] (Dial., 120).

Iren. Haer., IV, 16, 2 assumes the authenticity of the story of the sending of Enoch to the angels found in Eth. En. 12-16. In III, 21, 2, in his account of the origin of the LXX, he follows, if not Ep. Ar., at least a Jewish legend which goes far beyond the account there in its emphasis on the miraculous. He also accepts the legend in 4 Esr. 14:37 ff. concerning the restoration of the Scriptures by Ezra (III, 21, 2). Iren. Fr., 17 (MPG, 7, p. 1239b), whose genuineness is, of course, disputed, [156] reminds us of the view of salvation history in Test. XII (in a Christian recension ? → 995).

In the Alexandrian theologians romantic curiosity and a weakening of ecclesiastical sense create a mood favourable to apocrypha. They not only quote them almost as canonical writings, but appeal to the NT for so doing. Cl. Al. knows several Jewish apocrypha : [157] a book of Moses, perhaps Ass. Mos. (τρίτον ὄνομα ἐν οὐρανῷ μετὰ τὴν ἀνάληψιν, ὥς φασιν οἱ μύσται, Strom., I, 23, 153, 1; VI, 15, 132, 2; Adumbrationes in Epist. Judae, 9 : Hic confirmat (= recognises as canonical) assumptionem Moysi); [158] a propheticum of Ham (quoted by the Gnostic Isidore acc. to Pherecydes, Strom., VI, 6, 53, 5); the Apc. El. → 988 f.; Eth. En. (6-8, Strom., I, 17, 81, 4; 7 ff. [cf. GCS, 17, p.152, 8 f.], esp. 8:3; Ecl. Proph., 53, 4; 16, 3 : Strom., V, 1, 10, 2); Slav. En. (40:1, 12 : Ecl. Proph., 2, 1; Adumbrationes in Ep. Jud., 14 : His verbis prophetam comprobat); an indeterminate propheticum of Parchor [159] (Strom., VI, 6, 53, 2); Sib. (e.g., Prot., VI, 70, 2, very common, but along with secular quotations); Apc. Sophonias [160] (Strom., V, 11, 77, 2, as an appendix to Plato's attack on costly offerings): ἆρ᾽ οὐχ ὅμοια ταῦτα τοῖς ὑπὸ Σοφονία λεχθεῖσι τοῦ προφήτου; "καὶ ἀνέλαβέν με πνεῦμα καὶ ἀνήνεγκέν με εἰς οὐρανὸν πέμπτον καὶ ἐθεώρουν ἀγγέλους καλουμένους κυρίους, καὶ τὸ διάδημα αὐτῶν ἐπικείμενον ἐν πνεύματι ἁγίῳ καὶ ἦν ἑκάστου αὐτῶν ὁ θρόνος ἑπταπλασίων φωτὸς ἡλίου ἀνατέλλοντος, οἰκοῦντας ἐν ναοῖς σωτηρίας καὶ ὑμνοῦντας θεὸν ἄρρητον ὕψιστον"; 4 Esr. (5:35 : Strom., III, 16, 100, 3 : Ἔσδρας ὁ προφήτης λέγει, 14:18-22, 37-47: Strom., I, 22, 149, 3 : τὰς παλαιὰς αὖθις ἀνανεούμενος προεφήτευσε γραφάς).

Origen is equally fond of apocr. works, though not wholly uncritical. He sometimes points out that many things are falsified in apocr., but only to emphasise the more strongly that they are not to be completely rejected but carefully tested on their individual merits. In Comm. Ser. 28 in Mt. 23:37 ff., GCS, 38, p. 51, 8 ff., Orig. seeks to prove that the apocr. are almost indispensable for the exposition and confirmation of the NT : Haec omnia diximus ... non ignorantes quoniam multa secretorum ficta sunt ab impiis ... et utuntur quidem quibusdam Ypythiani, aliis autem qui sunt Basilidis, oportet ergo caute considerare, ut nec omnia secreta quae feruntur in nomine sanctorum suscipiamus propter Judaeos, qui forte ad destructionem veritatis scripturarum nostrarum quaedam finxerunt confirmantes dogmata falsa, nec omnia abiciamus quae pertinent ad demonstrationem scripturarum nostrarum. magni ergo viri est audire et adinplere quod dictum est : "omnia probate, quod bonum est tenete." tamen propter eos, qui non possunt

---

[155] On the distinguishing of a Jewish original from the Christian revision cf. Schürer, III[4], 386 ff.; Hennecke, 303.

[156] On the descent of Christ from Levi and Judah, cf. Test. L. 2:11; 8:14; Test. Jud. 24. But this is not the usual view of Iren., cf. A. v. Harnack, Geschichte d. altchristlichen Literatur, I (1893), 853; II, 1 (1897), 521, 569.

[157] Assembled in O. Stählin, Cl. Al. Index, GCS, 39 (1936), 26 ff.

[158] Acc. to Harnack, op. cit., I, 852 the Ἀνάληψις Μωϋσέως often quoted by the fathers was the lost Christian supplement to the Jewish Ass. Mos., cf. also Schürer, III[4], 303.

[159] Perhaps identical with the prophet Barkob mentioned by Agrippa Castor (Hier. De Viris Illustribus, 21, MPL, 23), Harnack, I, 159. Acc. to legend Buddha had dealings with a prophet Πάρκος, A. Hilgenfeld, Die Ketzergeschichte d. Urchristentums (1884), 214.

[160] Schürer, III[4], 367 ff.

quasi trapezitae inter verba discernere utrum vera habeantur an falsa, ... nemo uti debet ad confirmationem dogmatum libris, qui sunt extra canonizatas scripturas. Origen knows and more or less highly values Mart. Is. (Ep. ad Africanum [→ 988], 9; Comm. in Mt., X, 18 on 13:57, GCS, 40, p. 24, 6 ff.: εἰ δέ τις οὐ προσίεται τὴν ἱστορίαν, διὰ τὸ ἐν τῷ ἀποκρύφῳ Ἡσαΐα αὐτὴν φέρεσθαι, πιστευσάτω τοῖς ἐν τῇ πρὸς Ἑβραίους ... γεγραμμένοις, → 988, Comm. Ser., 28 on Mt. 23:37, GCS, 38, p. 50, after a ref. to *libri secretiores qui apud Iudaeos feruntur : fertur ergo in scripturis non manifestis serratum esse Esaiam et Zachariam occisum* etc.); [161] a book of Jannes and Jambres → 990; Eth. (and Slav.?) En. (Cels., V, 54 : ἐν ταῖς ἐκκλησίαις οὐ πάνυ φέρεται ὡς θεῖα τὰ ἐπιγεγραμμένα τοῦ Ἐνὼχ βιβλία); [162] Ass. Mos. (Princ., III, 2, 1: *in ascensione Moysi, cuius libelli meminit in epistola sua apostolus Judas, Michahel archangelus cum diabolo disputans* etc.); Gr. (?) Bar. (Princ., II, 3, 6); Test. XII (Hom. in Jos., XV, 6 : *sed et in aliquo quodam libello, qui appellatur testamentum duodecim patriarcharum, quamvis non habeatur in canone, talem tamen quendam invenimus sensum, quod per singulos peccantes singuli Satanae intelligi debeant,* cf. Test. R. 2 f., many allusions in the Comm. in Joh.); the Prayer of Joseph (Comm. in Joh., II, 31, 188 : εἰ δέ τις προσίεται καὶ τῶν παρ' Ἑβραίοις φερομένων ἀποκρύφων τὴν ἐπιγραφομένην Ἰωσὴφ προσευχήν, he can even take from this the δόγμα [→ supra] of the conferring of privilege on certain pre-existent souls, *ibid.,* 192 : οὐκ εὐκαταφρόνητον γραφήν); [163] the Apc. Abr. (Hom. in Lk., 35, GCS, 35, p. 207: *legimus — si tamen cui placet huiuscemodi scripturam recipere — justitiae et iniquitatis angelos super Abrahae salute et interitu disceptantes);* [164] Apc. El. → 988 f.

After Origen the estimation of apocr. suffers a sharp decline. Priscillian c. 380 meets with general disapproval when he tries to follow the Alexandrian approach (Tractatus, III, 58 f., 68, ed. G. Schepss, CSEL, 18 [1889]). Writings like the apocrypha of Moses, Adam and Is. are regarded as sources of corruption and inimical to the truth, Const. Ap., VI, 16.

4. The Christian Preservation, Revision and Canonisation of the Jewish Apocrypha.

As the preface to Jerome's comm. on Da. shows, the Jews had then for a long time scorned the apocrypha read by Christians. The preservation of these works is thus in large measure due to Christianity rather than Judaism. This is proved by the many translations, often in remote languages. [165] To make them more suitable for Christian use, some not unimportant revisions were made. This may be most confidently affirmed in the case of Mart. Is. (now preserved in the Asc. Is.), Sib. (1, 2, 3, 4, 12, 13 ?); Gr. Bar. (c. 4); Test. XII, [166] Vit. Ad. [167] Many apocrypha passed into the Canon of barbarian churches, [168] and even for a long time *per nefas* into Western Bibles, though listed as apocrypha. [169] 4 Esr. may still be found in the Zürich Bible of 1524 ff.

---

[161] Further examples, *ibid.,* 390 f.

[162] *Ibid.,* 285. Origen's restriction is tactical.

[163] *Ibid.,* 359 f.

[164] *Ibid.,* 336 ff.; Harnack, I, 857 f.

[165] Latin, Greek, Syriac, Arabic, Coptic, Ethiopian, Old Slavic. For details cf. Schürer, III⁴, 268 ff., the introductions in Kautzsch Pseudepigr. and Harnack, I, 852 ff., II, 1, 560 ff.

[166] Finally, but incorrectly, contested by E. Lohmeyer, "Kyrios Jesus," SAH, 1927/28, 4 (1928), 69.

[167] On the question of Christian revision in general, cf. the bibl. in n. 165. Acc. to A. Meyer, *Das Rätsel des Jakobusbriefes* (1930), Jm. was already a Jewish pseudepigraphon (patriarchal) which underwent Christian revision.

[168] So En. and Jub. in the Abyssinian Canon, S. Bar. and 4 Esr. in a Peshitto MS from Milan.

[169] Cf. the Stichometria of Nicephorus, the canonical list of the Codex Coislinianus often added to the Quaestiones of Anastasius, and the Synopsis Athanasii. Cf. Schürer, III⁴, 357 ff., and more fully Zahn Kan., II, 289 ff.

5. Christian Apocrypha.

During the first centuries, Christianity itself produced not only the canonical Scriptures but also a varied literature which has been more or less correctly called apocryphal. In so far as this is a practical and colourless general term, we need not pursue the matter. [170] But apocryphal Gospels, Acts, Epistles and Revelations in the narrower sense demand brief consideration. We are not referring to sayings of the Lord quoted in the post-apostolic fathers and apologists — sayings which are Synoptic in type even though they cannot be assigned with certainty to any particular Gospel. [171] It would be methodologically wrong to deduce from these the existence of unknown apocryphal Gospels. Here, as in the case of quotations coloured by the OT (→ 991), it is more a question of in-exact reproduction. Of the Jewish Christian Gospels — if the distinction of several is apposite — the Gospel of the Hebrews at least deserves the title apocryphal. Genuinely apocryphal are the Protevangelium of James, the Gospel of Thomas, that of the Egyptians, that of Peter, the fragments of Gnostic Gospels and legends, many agrapha and the Oxyrhynchos sayings. To the same group belongs the Gospel fragment published in 1935. [172] All the post-canonical Acts are apocryphal. This is true even of the Acts of Paul, though these are the work of a presbyter who paid for his literary venture by losing his office. It is even more true of the others. [173] They contain Gnostic teachings in the form of romance. Attributing letters to apostolic men is of early origin. It is possible that Jude and 2 Peter in the NT belong already to this class, [174] though they are not apocryphal in tendency. The Epistle to the Laodiceans, a feeble compilation, is not genuinely apocryphal, nor is the correspondence of Paul with the Corinthians contained in Armenian in Ephraem's Commentary and deriving from the Act. Pl. [175] On the other hand, the so-called "Epistle of the Apostles," in spite of its orthodox trend, is to be described as apocryphal because it contains revelations of the future from the Risen Lord. Apocryphal Apocalypses are the Rev. of Peter, which is influenced by Orphic ideas, and the Shepherd of Hermas, which stands in some connection with the Hermetic writings, → 993.

The attitude of the Church to these writings is not consistent. Thus Hermas is often quoted as authoritative by the Alexandrians, sometimes along with prophetic or dominical sayings, e.g., Cl. Al. Strom., VI, 15, 131, 2; II, 12, 55, 3; Orig. Comm. in Joh., I, 17, 103; XXXII, 16, 187 ff. Tertullian recognised it in his pre-Montanist days, though later he energetically combatted it as apocryphal, Pud., 10 : *sed cederem tibi, si scriptura Pastoris, quae sola moechos amat, divino instrumento meruisset incidi, si non ab omni concilio ecclesiarum, etiam vestrarum, inter apocrypha et falsa iudicaretur.* Acc. to the Muratorian Canon, 73 ff. (ed. H. Lietzmann, KIT, 1² [1908]) it should be read, but not publicly. The Muratorian Fragment regards the Apc. Pt. as canonical along with Rev., but with the addition : *quam quidam ex nostris legi in ecclesia nolunt.* Cl. Al. seems unhesitatingly to accept the authenticity of the Gospel of the Egyptians as testimony to the sayings of the Lord ; he simply tries to protect it against the false exposition of the Encratites, Strom., III, 5, 45, 3; III, 9, 63, 1 ff.; Exc. Theod., 21, 2; 67, 2 ff. Origen, who is usually so accommodating, plainly regards it as a heretical work, Hom. in Lk., 1. The apocryphal

---

[170] → 987. Hennecke's collection is based on this usage.

[171] Cf. the index of passages in the editions.

[172] *Fragments of an Unknown Gospel and Other Early Christian Papyri,* ed. H. Idris Bell and T. C. Skeat (1935).

[173] Cf. → Abbreviations, *s.v.* Act., also Hennecke, 163 ff. There is no complete collection. M. R. James, TSt, V, 1 (1897) has published a version not identical with the current Act. Thom. Basic for all other work on the Act. Pl. is Πραξεις Παυλου, Acta Pauli, acc. to the Pap. of the Hamburg State and University Library, ed. C. Schmidt (1936).

[174] On this, and on other NT epistles whose authenticity is questioned, cf. the introductions to the NT.

[175] Cf. Zahn Kan., II, 592 ff. These and other texts may be found in Hennecke, either *in toto* or in the form of excerpts.

Acts were never regarded as canonical, and even less so the varied esoteric literature of the Gnostics and other heretics. Even Christian apocrypha which were acknowledged in the first instance never found their way into the Canon. The exclusion was much more radical than in the case of the Jewish apocrypha.

6. The Term Apocryphal.

According to the traditional view ἀπόκρυφος was from the very first a technical term for the books which could not be read at public worship but which mature church members were allowed or even recommended to read privately. This usage is not supposed to have developed independently in the Christian sphere, but in close relation to Judaism. ἀπόκρυφος was simply a transl. of the Heb. גנז. [176] Yet even in respect of Judaism this equation is not convincing → 983. For in the rare cases in Jewish lit. in which גנז does not denote the removal of copies of the Holy Scriptures which have become unserviceable, but refers to whole writings as such, its sense is not that of exclusion from public reading, but from any study at all. גנז thus signifies almost an index of prohibited books. In patristic lit., however, ἀπόκρυφος or secretus is the opp. of φανερός or manifestus, or of κοινὸς καὶ δεδημευμένος, vulgatus, publicus. [177] In fact, then, the reference is to public reading. No one disputes the actual connection between the Church and the Synagogue. A mutual interaction of usage may thus be accepted. The only point is that the root of the usage is not to be found in the Synagogue but in pagan Gnosticism (→ 965 f.). In patristic lit. the word first occurs, not in connection with the Canon, but in the struggle against false teachers. The βίβλοι ἀπόκρυφοι of Zoroaster, which the disciples of the Gnostic Prodikos boasted of possessing, [178] were obviously not given this title as works which were excluded from the Jewish or Christian lectionary, but as sources of esoteric wisdom, and from the standpoint of those who used them the title was an endorsement. The fathers used the term first in the sense of those who admired such lit., and then gave it a censorious stress from their own opposing standpoint. The statement of Iren. unmistakably refers to false teachers: πρὸς δὲ τούτοις (the false doctrines about God) ἀμύθητον πλῆθος ἀποκρύφων καὶ νόθων γραφῶν, ἃς αὐτοὶ ἔπλασαν, παρεισφέρουσιν εἰς κατάπληξιν τῶν ἀνοήτων καὶ τὰ τῆς ἀληθείας μὴ ἐπισταμένων γράμματα (Haer., I, 20, 1). Here the sense of "falsified," "of obscure origin," is already present. For Tert. apocrypha and falsa are interchangeable terms (→ 996). Hipp. (Ref., VII, 20) aims to show that Basilides, in appealing to λόγους ἀποκρύφους which Matthias supposedly received of the Lord, is traducing both Matthias and the Lord. Cl. Al. Strom., III, 4, 29, 1 exclaims at the crudities of those who follow Prodikos: ἐρρύη δὲ αὐτοῖς τὸ δόγμα ἔκ τινος ἀπο-

---

[176] Zahn Kan., I, 123 ff., Schürer RE³, I, 622 ff. rightly point out the different meanings of ἀπόκρυφος 1. "kept hidden," a. because of value, b. because the contents are objectionable ; 2. "of hidden origin," "interpolated," but they do not make a clear enough distinction and accept a Jewish origin. Hölscher, 59 ff., 69 ff. is on the point of striking off in a new direction, but maintains the equation with גנז and introduces an irrelevancy when he suggests that the Christian Scriptures were all βίβλοι ἀπόκρυφοι when seen from the standpoint of those outside. This is historically untrue, since only baptism and the Lord's Supper were the subject of the disciplina arcana in Christianity, not the Scriptures and preaching. It also obscures the original and specific use of the term in the fathers.

[177] Orig. Ep. ad African. (→ 988), 9 : ὧν τινα σῴζεται ἐν ἀποκρύφοις ... ἐν οὐδενὶ τῶν φανερῶν βιβλίων γεγραμμένα ... ἔν τινι ἀποκρύφῳ τοῦτο φέρεται. Comm. in Mt., X, 18 in 13:57: (Jesus gave witness in Mt. 23:35) γραφῇ οὐ φερομένη μὲν ἐν τοῖς κοινοῖς καὶ δεδημευμένοις βιβλίοις, εἰκὸς δ' ὅτι ἐν ἀποκρύφοις φερομένῃ. Comm. Ser., 28 in Mt. 23:37-39 : ex libris secretioribus = in scripturis non manifestis ; ibid., Ser., 46 in Mt. 24:23-28 : secretas et non vulgatas scripturas ; ibid., Ser., 117 in Mt. 27:3-10 : non in publicis scripturis, sed in libro secreto, GCS, 38, p. 250.

[178] Cl. Al. Strom., I, 15, 69, 6 : Ζωροάστρην δὲ τὸν Μάγον τὸν Πέρσην ὁ Πυθαγόρας ἐζήλωσεν, <καὶ> βίβλους ἀποκρύφους τἀνδρὸς τοῦδε οἱ τὴν Προδίκου μετιόντες αἵρεσιν αὐχοῦσι κεκτῆσθαι.

κρύφου, and he raises the question whether they concocted this nonsense themselves or whether, by misunderstanding and twisting, they took their wisdom from others. The quotation which follows points to the metaphysics of pagan Gnosticism. [179] All the apocryphal works mentioned are ἀπόρρητα to their admirers and *obscura* or νόθα to true fathers. The word is not used in the first instance of works which the Catholic Church uses.

In time the situation changes because the Church itself comes to use βίβλοι ἀπό-κρυφοι for Jewish apocalypses which were much loved and almost canonised. It is doubtful whether the Synagogue itself used the designation. It could do so only by borrowing from the Gnostic usage, not by a technical use of גנז. [180] This use of ἀπό-κρυφος is first found for certain in Origen (→ 994). But he finds it so natural that he can hardly be its inventor. [181] The Church probably liked to be able to oppose to the secret books of the Gnostics its own secret books, and it is striking that it took these exclusively from the Synagogue. Because of the position of the Jewish people in salvation history, these seemed to guarantee the genuineness of prophecy in so far as later generations of Jews had not falsified the books. This view made its way all the more easily because the Jews themselves had already weeded out and rejected their own apocrypha. It is attractive to pursue the parallels in the canonisation and reduction of the LXX (→ 987 f.). Applied specifically to the Jewish secret writings, ἀπόκρυφος again carries with it temporarily the ring of acknowledgment.

Reaction quickly follows. Even Origen did not dare to adduce the apocrypha as Scripture proof so freely as his great teacher had done (→ 994). Even in his qualified admiration for the apocrypha, however, he is fairly isolated. This admiration, along with his theology, will be discredited later. Other factors enter in, esp. the establishment of the idea of the Canon, which in spite of Eusebius moves increasingly from the orderly West to the East. The aloofness of the Synagogue is not without effect in the long run.

---

[179] C. Schmidt, TU, 20, 4a (1901), 54 thinks that Cl. read the words in a Jewish (?) Apc., but he is assuming too narrow a concept of ἀπόκρυφος. προφητεία ἁγία, Strom., III, 4, 29, 3 is naturally meant in the sense of false teachers, and is to be put in inverted commas.

[180] Eus. Hist. Eccl., IV, 22, 9 (on Hegesipp.): καὶ περὶ τῶν λεγομένων δὲ ἀποκρύφων διαλαμβάνων, ἐπὶ τῶν αὐτοῦ χρόνων πρός τινων αἱρετικῶν ἀναπεπλάσθαι τινὰ τούτων ἱστορεῖ, proves nothing as regards the Jewish designation of Apc. as apocrypha, since we do not know whether Hegesipp. is quoted literally or whether he follows Jewish usage (as against Zahn Kan., I, 135 f.). Rabb. lit. says little about the apocrypha, hence it yields neither proof nor counter-proof. The only passage which deserves serious considera-tion is 4 Esr. 14:45 ff.: "But when the 40 days were accomplished, the Most High spoke to me thus: The 24 books which you wrote first you shall publish to be read by the worthy and the unworthy; but the last 70 you shall keep back and give only to the wise of your people (*conservabis, ut tradas eos sapientibus de populo tuo*). For in them flows the fount of insight, the well of wisdom, the river of knowledge." The tacit equation of *con-servare* with גנז (Hölscher, 64) is not firmly grounded, → n. 86. The Syr. text (Translatio Syra Peschitto Vet. Test. ex cod. Ambr. photolithographice, ed. A. M. Ceriani, II, 4 [1883]) does not use g^enaz but has n^etar for *conservare* and s^elam *aph* for *tradere*. The passage only proves, then, that Judaism had an interest in esoteric lit., not that it used גנז in the technical sense for the removal of this lit. In other words, linguistically as well as materially the Church copied the Synagogue some centuries later. When the Mandaeans use Ginza for their sacred book, they give to גנז a sense which corresponds exactly to the Gnostic meaning of ἀπόκρυφος; it denotes secret lit. It is overhasty to conclude that the technical use of the term in the Synagogue is to be understood in this light. This can be explained in terms of the sense "to deposit" (→ n. 86) without the help of Gnostic terminology.

[181] The suggestion that Origen is influenced by Julius Africanus (→ 988) in henceforth using the concept of the apocryphon "after the Jewish model" (Hölscher, 70) does not fit chronologically. For he already uses the term in the later sense in Book II of the Comm. on Jn., which was probably written soon after 220 (II, 31, 188, GCS, cf. the intr. LXXVIII f.), whereas the correspondence with Julius cannot be before 240 (TU, 34, 3 [1909], 65).

Development in the Church follows the same lines as that within Judaism, though two or three centuries later. The derogatory sense of ἀπόκρυφος, now including the Jewish apocrypha, returns c. 400, and carries the day. Thus Aug. writes in Faust., 11, 2 : *de his qui appellantur apocryphi, — non quod habendi sint in aliqua auctoritate secreta, sed quia nulla testificationis luce declarati de nescio quo secreto, nescio quorum praesumptione prolati sunt.* So also Jerome → 989.

With the exclusion of apocrypha the term is free to be used for those parts of the LXX not in the Heb. Canon. But there are reasons for great reserve in respect of this new usage. In fact, it really establishes itself only in Protestantism (→ 987).

The later canonical lists instructively reflect the usage of the ancient Church, which is unequivocal enough in general, but not always consistent in detail. We may take as examples the Codex Coislinianus, or Baroccianus, the Synopsis Athanasii, the Stichometria of Nicephorus and the Decretum Gelasii in the pertinent sections. [182] Whether continuously, or punctuated by the second group, these all give first the canonical Scriptures of the OT and NT, the former acc. to the Heb. Canon though in the LXX order. The books preserved in the LXX alone are either simply included as sufficiently attested or added as non-canonical but acceptable (ὅσα ἔξω τῶν ξ′, [183] ὅσαι ἀντιλέγονται καὶ οὐκ ἐκκλησιαζονται, [184] οὐ κανονιζόμενα μέν, ἀναγινωσκόμενα δὲ μόνον τοῖς κατηχουμένοις). [185] In so far as there is a corresponding NT group of antilegomena, it is composed of Apc. Jn., Apc. Pt., Barn., Ev. Heb., but also Act. Pt., Jn., Thom., Ev. Thom., Did., 1 and 2 Cl. Finally, a list of apocrypha follows as a third group. The order itself makes it plain that this is not a list of books which, while not to be read publicly, are good and profitable for mature Christians. It is rather an index of prohibited works. The paraphrases and synonyms of the word "apocryphal" support this : νόθα καὶ ἀπόβλητα ... ἀποκρυφῆς μᾶλλον ἢ ἀναγνώσεως ὡς ἀληθῶς ἄξια, [186] *libri apocryphi, qui nullatenus a nobis recipi debent* [187] ... *Haec et his similia, quae ... haeretici haereticorumque discipuli sive schismatici docuerunt vel conscripserunt, quorum nomina minime retinemus, non solum repudiata, verum ab omni Romana catholica ecclesia eliminata atque cum huis auctoribus auctorumque sequacibus anathematis insolubili vinculo in aeternum confitemur esse damnata.* [188] Finally, the selection of the works listed is also in keeping. Where distinction is made between the apocrypha of the OT and the NT, the first group includes all the Jewish pseudepigrapha known to us (expressly described as such), but also an Apc. of Zacharias, the father of the Baptist, and the second all Gospels except the four canonical Gospels, namely, the Ev. Thom. and Acts. The facts are the same when the list is given without distinction and in lively confusion. Here, then, ἀπόκρυφος has the technical sense of גָּנַז, i.e., excluded from the Canon and placed on the index. This does not mean that it is a translation of גָּנַז. For the basic meanings which underlie the technical use of ἀπόκρυφος, namely, "esoteric" and "of obscure origin," do not apply to גָּנַז. The most we can say is that Jewish and Christian usage finally merge. But at this later date we can no longer assume that the Synagogue exerted so strong an influence.

---

[182] For the texts cf. Zahn Kan., II, 289 ff. and E. Preuschen, Analecta, II² (1910), 27 ff. The dates, which are earlier than existing MSS, are hard to fix. Probably the lists did not arise as they now are, but were gradually added to. This is generally recognised in the case of Decretum Gelasii. Here the works of Caecilius Cyprianus may be studied, while those of Thascius Cyprianus are apocrypha !

[183] Codex Baroccianus, Zahn Kan., II, 291.

[184] Stichometria of Nicephorus, 34, Zahn Kan., II, 299.

[185] Synopsis Athanasii, p. 128, Zahn Kan., II, 316.

[186] Ibid., 202 (Zn., II, 317).

[187] Decretum Gelasianum, Preuschen, 58, 31 f.

[188] Ibid., 61, 22; 62, 1 ff.

Attention must now be drawn, however, to a new vacillation of usage. Among the NT apocrypha there appeared in canonical lists 1 and 2 Cl., Did., Ign., Pol. and Herm. Serious exclusion can apply at most only to the last of these. In the case of the others the meaning is simply that they do not belong to the Canon. Here, then, the sense of ἀπόκρυφα approximates again to that of ἀντιλεγόμενα. We can explain this only by supposing that as the usage began to soften again new names were put on a list originally meant as an index. We are here on the path which leads to the later Protestant use, → 987.

In the Church rejection of the βίβλοι ἀπόκρυφοι has a different significance from that which it has in Judaism. By excluding apocalyptic, the latter robbed itself of all living prophecy and tended to ossify in a nomistic casuistry. On the other hand, the serviceable elements of apocalyptic were fused from the very first into Christian piety. For this reason, as has been recognised only in our own time, the apocrypha are of great importance in historical and theological research. But they have nothing to offer the Church in its practical task which is not to be had even better in the canonical writings of the OT and NT. From this standpoint exclusion of the apocrypha is the stopping up of a constant source of danger. Dogmatic consolidation, if it was not the final goal, was at least the necessary historical path.

Oepke

> † κτίζω, † κτίσις,
> † κτίσμα, † κτίστης

Contents: A. Historical Review. B. Belief in Creation in the OT : 1. The Development of the OT Belief in Creation ; 2. Creation Terminology and Conceptions in the OT ; 3. The OT Belief in Creation. C. The Doctrine of Creation in Later Judaism : 1. Terminology ;

κ τ ί ζ ω κ τ λ. On A.: L. Preller, "Die vorstellungen der alten, bes. d. Griechen, von dem ursprunge u. den ältesten schicksalen des menschlichen geschlechts," Philol., 7 (1852), 1-60; F. Lukas, *Die Grundbegriffe in d. Kosmologien d. alten Völker* (1893); O. Gruppe, *Griech. Mythologie u. Religionsgeschichte,* I (1906), 411-432; O. Dähnhardt, *Natursagen,* I (1907); W. Wundt, *Völkerpsychologie,* VI, 3² (1915), 268-290; K. Seeliger in Roscher, VI (1924 ff.), s.v. "Weltschöpfung," 430-505; K. Ziegler, *ibid.,* V (1916/24), 1469-1554; Bertholet-Leh., *passim* ; C. A. Scharbau, *Die Idee d. Schöpfung in der vedischen Lit.* (1932). On B : OT Theologies and Histories of Religion by A. Dillmann (1895), 284 ff.; R. Smend² (1899), 112, 348, 434 ff.; B. Stade-A. Bertholet (1905/11); E. König ³, ⁴ (1923), 202 ff.; E. Sellin (1933), 37-40; W. Eichrodt, I (1933), II (1935); L. Köhler (1936); B. Duhm, *Kosmologie und Religion* (1892); J. Hänel, *Die Religion der Heiligkeit* (1931), *v.* Index ; F. Strothmann, *Schöpfungsanschauungen u. Schöpfungsgedanke im AT* (unpublished diss., Münster, 1932); R. Hönigswald, *Erkenntnistheoretisches zur Schöpfungsgeschichte der Gn.* (1932); G. v. Rad in *Werden u. Wesen des AT,* ed. J. Hempel (1936), 138-147. On C : Weber, 196 ff.; L. Couard, *Die religiösen u. sittlichen Anschauungen der at.lichen Apkr. u. Pseudepigr.* (1907), 73 ff.; Bousset-Gressm., 358-360; Moore, I, 380 ff.; III, 119, No. 120; J. B. Frey, "Dieu et le monde d'après les conceptions juives au temps de Jésus-Christ," in Rev. Bibl., NS, 13 (1916), 33-60; R. Meyer, *Hellenistisches in d. rabb. Anthropologie* (1937). On E : Cr.-Kö., 640-642; Schl. Theol. d. Ap., *v.* Index ; H. Weinel, *Bibl. Theol. d. NT⁴* (1928), *v.* Index ; C. F. Burney, "Christ as the ἀρχή of Creation," JThSt, 27 (1925/26), 160-177; M. Teschendorf, "Der Schöpfungsgedanke im NT," ThStKr, 104 (1932), 337-372; W. Gutbrod, *Die paul. Anthropologie* (1934), 9-18; G. Bornkamm, *Gesetz u. Schöpfung im NT* (1934). On dogmatic aspects cf. W. Lütgert, *Schöpfung u. Offenbarung* (1934); E. Brunner, *Der Mensch im Widerspruch* (1937); E. Gerstenmaier, *Die Kirche u. die Schöpfung* (1937).

2. God as Creator of the World ; 3. The World as God's Creation ; 4. Man as the Creature of God. D. δημιουργέω and κτίζω in Greek and the Linguistic Contribution of the LXX. E. Creation in the NT : 1. Terminology ; 2. God the Creator of the World ; 3. Fallen Creation ; 4. Man as Creature and the New Creation.

The question of the "whence" [1] of the world and of man within it leads remorselessly to the limit of our thinking where it comes up against what is "above" it and what it necessarily finds to be the frontier imposed upon it from without — or where it threatens to lose itself as it plunges further and further into the void. The question is, then, whether it is in fact led to that limit which it can and must honour as the frontier imposed upon it.

The answer to the decisive questions of life is enclosed in the answer to this question of the origin of the world. The "whither" is indissolubly bound up with the "whence." So, too, is the "what," i.e., the meaning of the world and of man. It is not for nothing that creation plays a leading part in the modern philosophical debate.

A. Historical Review.

In the religion of many peoples chaos stands at the beginning of being and becoming. [2] It may be understood mythically as Tiamat, as the original water, [3] as the abyss, as night [4] or darkness. But the decisive point is that it is felt to be something supremely negative, abstracted and unqualified. Chaos is the world without its form in history, in space and time. It is unfashioned matter as a mythical quantity. [5] Hence it can also be described philosophically as ἄποιον, as that which is without quality, or as μὴ ὄν, as that which has no being in the true sense. [6] Man thus moves away as far as he can from the present being of the world. The world arises out of chaos because in it are seeds, [7] or an egg, [8] the cosmic egg, or a bud. Or there is reference to chaos as the "mother which fashions all things." [9] This implies a cosmic becoming after the analogy of becoming in nature. As the plant develops spontaneously out of the "lifeless" seed, so does the world out of unqualified chaos. There is a basic similarity when psychological processes are substituted for the organic processes of natural life, e.g., longing, desire, eros etc. [10] For behind these psychological processes are natural strivings (as distinct

---

[1] For this formulation cf. W. Lütgert, 74.

[2] Seeliger, 462-464; Bertholet-Leh., I, 106 f.; Hes. Theog., 116; Seeliger, 438, 462.

[3] Seeliger, 432. For the Egyptians cf. A. Erman, *Die Religion d. Ägypter* (1934), 61, 90.

[4] So, e.g., Eudemus ; Aristoph. Av., 695; acc. to Damascius the Orphics, though the age of this Orphic view is contested ; Seeliger, 433, 436, 465.

[5] Bertholet-Leh., II, 356 says already of Hesiod : "The mythical names of Hesiod are no more than a transparent robe for the first natural philosophy." Time is also an abstract quantity which in Iran and Greece is often set at the beginning, Seeliger, 474-479; Hönigswald, 16 ("Urzeit und Urraum in Ägypten").

[6] Cf. Indian speculations, Scharbau, 75 ff., 79 : "Hence the non-existent is not absolute nothing but . . . the metaphysical substance . . . in an uncrystallised state."

[7] In Brahmanism Prajapati, the creator of the world, is described as a golden seed, Bertholet-Leh., II, 59.

[8] So the Japanese, E. Lehmann, *Textbuch zur Religionsgeschichte* (1912), 29; the Egyptians, Lukas, 47; the Indians, Bertholet-Leh., I, 107; perhaps also the Orphics, *ibid.*, II, 371; cf. also Seeliger, 479-482.

[9] *Enuma eliš* (cf. A. Ungnad, *Die Religion d. Babylonier u. Assyrer* [1921], 27 ff.), 1; Hes. Theog., 126 ff.; Seeliger, 439 n.*

[10] Rigveda, X, 129, 4 : craving ; 3 : *tapas* = ardour (?), cf. Scharbau, 86 f.; *eros* in Hes. Theog., 120 and the Orphics, Seeliger, 482-485; Πόθος in the Phoenicians, Damascius, De Principiis (ed. C. A. Ruelle [1889]), 125 (p. 323); cf. also Seeliger, 485.

from conscious processes of will). In Indian thought the attainment of self-consciousness belongs here — the first movement of self-apprehension. [11] Natural categories are also evident when the embrace of a mythical divine couple [12] stands at the beginning of becoming. All these ideas are the final limits to which thought can go if it is to interpret the origin of the world in meaningful categories. [13] But if the cosmic egg almost develops of itself, and desire is natural and spontaneous, a final riddle remains which is harshly exposed in the Egyptian idea of the self-copulation of the original god. [14] The "beginning" in these trains of thought is only a relative one. [15]

In the course of this natural occurrence there arise figures of a different kind, forces of order which shape things consciously as compared with natural becoming and striving : δημιουργοί (on this → 1023). Arising ultimately out of chaos, [16] they are not absolutely free. Zeus is subject to fate. [17] At the death of the gods chaos swallows up its children again. Yet these figures have a measure of autonomy in relation to chaos. They are against it. They fight against their own ancestors. [18] Out of their corpses they fashion the world. [19] By these forces of shape and order man is formed, but out of the defeated power of chaos. [20] Hence man is pledged to the forces of order, and it is no accident that in this context there is reference to a goal of human life which is related to the gods. [21] These myths show that, while man is part of nature, he transcends it. The meaning and goal of his life are not in nature. He does not owe his existence to it alone. Those who have made him have a claim on him. They are his legitimate lords (→ κύριος). Nevertheless, in so far as the δημιουργοί who have fashioned men are secondary to the power of chaos, man's obligation to them is not final, nor can they give to man the ultimate goal of his being. Man is more or less resigned to fate, esp. in the form of death. [22]

If the ordering of matter and forms is here secondary to the conflict between the demiurge and the powers of chaos, there is another view which more or less equates the two. This view was developed by the Indians [23] and esp. the Greek philosophers,

---

[11] Scharbau, 10.

[12] Apsu and Tiamat, heaven (Zeus) and earth, Seeliger, 431, 434, 435, 439, 466; Oceanos and Tethys, Hom. Il., 14, 201; Orphic Verse in Plat. Crat., 402b c; Seeliger, 432, 435, 458, 463; Aer and Chaos in the cosmogony of the Phoenicians, Eus. Praep. Ev., I, 10, 1; Epimenides : ᾿Αήρ and Νύξ, Seeliger, 465 f.; 471 f.; cf. also Seeliger, 438 ff. More philosophically in Pherecydes : Αἰθήρ and Χθονίη (with Χρόνος), Gruppe, 427 f.

[13] Cf. Scharbau, 24 : "A metaphysical creation out of an absolute nothing transcends human experience and is thus questionable as a metaphysically dogmatic statement."

[14] Lehmann, 71. Cf. also the Babylonian hymn to Sin : Fruit which is born of itself ... mother's womb which bears all things, Bertholet-Leh., I, 548, and the copulation of the two feet of the giant Ymir, ibid., II, 593. For the Veda cf. Scharbau, 110 f., who correctly says of similar speculation : "Here is an attempt to observe the final inner divine processes, i.e., how creation arises by intellectual polarisation, tension and act, and to express these ideas or observations," cf. also 110 f.: "It is only a step from the primitive to the lofty philosophical concept." But the primitive picture can also show how inadequate is the lofty philosophical concept.

[15] Scharbau, 90 : " 'In the beginning' means here (in Vedic lit.) the state of reality before the beginning of this world."

[16] For Greece cf. → 69 f.

[17] → 70.

[18] Marduk-Tiamat ; Zeus-Kronos ; Indra, too, fights against mythical forces, Lehmann, 177.

[19] Examples from the epic Enuma eliš, Bertholet-Leh., II, 68 (Rigveda, X, 90); 212 (original cow); 497 (Mithras); 593 (Ymir.).

[20] Enuma eliš, 6. Orphics.

[21] Enuma eliš, 6 (Ungnad, 47). Another Babyl. Fr., ibid., 57.

[22] This is the teaching of the Babyl. Gilgamesh epic.

[23] Bertholet-Leh., II, 70 f., 147, 157.

beginning with the Hylozoists, [24] who found in original matter the original principle of all life, by way of the Eleatic School [25] and Empedocles [26] to Stoicism, which basically equated πάσχον, matter, and ποιοῦν, the guiding principle = Zeus = original fire = πρόνοια = είμαρμένη. [27] The world is for Stoicism a great circular movement which turns back upon itself. To integrate oneself into this movement, to play well the role assigned to man by nature, Zeus or providence, is the task which is set for man by his place in the cosmos, by his nature : ὁμολογουμένως τῇ φύσει ζῆν. As the world is directed by reason, so man should follow reason. As the world is a harmonious whole, so man should strive after harmony, ἀταραξία. As the demiurges are autonomous in relation to chaos and yet not completely free, so conversely Stoicism regards πρόνοια as material. And yet the Stoic can speak of Zeus and honour him in the most personal terms. [28] There is another inconsistency. The course of the world is ineluctable, and after an ἐκπύρωσις the same course repeats itself. Its only meaning and purpose is to do this. [29] What, then, is the source of the ethical passion of Epictetus ? How can man play badly his part in the cosmic drama ? The system has no answer to these questions, and the implied second inconsistency, along with the first one, is a sign that without a personal encounter between the Creator and man the creature there can be neither well-founded ethical instruction nor indeed a livable life.

Finally, matter and the forms can be brought into confrontation and the latter given at least logical precedence over the former. In this respect the meaning and import of the statements made are often doubtful. Thus we cannot decide here whether the idea of creatio e nihilo really stands behind the conception of creator-gods. [30] In many religions, however, there may be observed a tendency to pick out one god — he may alternate fairly freely within a polytheistic pantheon — as the creator, and to give him precedence as such over the others and over all things. Thus in a hymn [31] the moon-god Sin is called : Fruit which is born of itself, mother's womb which bears all things, father, begetter of gods and men, begetter of all things, lord, ruler of the gods, who alone is exalted in heaven and on earth, who decides in heaven and on earth, whose decree no man alters. It is also said of him that his word causes the green herb to spring forth, nourishes hearth and herd, and establishes truth and right. The nature formulae originally used of primitive chaos are here transferred to a demiurge, and he is thus the first god who is not restricted by any prior chaos and who has unlimited power over nature, humanity and the world of the gods. [32] The same is true in Egypt, [33] Assyria, [34] India. [35]

---

[24] Heracl. Fr., 30 : κόσμον τόνδε, τὸν αὐτὸν ἀπάντων, οὔτε τις θεῶν οὔτε ἀνθρώπων ἐποίησεν, ἀλλ᾽ ἦν ἀεὶ καὶ ἔστιν καὶ ἔσται πῦρ ἀείζωον (I, 84, 1 ff., Diels).

[25] Ξενοφάνης ... εἰς τὸν ὅλον οὐρανὸν ἀποβλέψας τὸ ἓν εἶναί φησι τὸν θεόν, Aristot. Metaph., I, 5, p. 986b, 21 ff.

[26] The 4 elements, and love and hate, as the bases of occurrence ; natural strivings play a part in love and hate (→ 1001).

[27] When Diog. L., VII, 68 (134) says of the Stoics : δοκεῖ δ᾽ αὐτοῖς ἀρχὰς εἶναι τῶν ὅλων δύο, τὸ ποιοῦν καὶ τὸ πάσχον. τὸ μὲν οὖν πάσχον εἶναι τὴν ἄποιον οὐσίαν, τὴν ὕλην, τὸ δὲ ποιοῦν τὸν ἐν αὐτῇ λόγον, τὸν θεόν, this simply shows that Stoic monism cannot free its statements from inner contradiction.

[28] E.g., in the hymn to Zeus of Cleanthes, v. Arnim, I, p. 121 f., No. 537.

[29] It is no accident that Epict. so often uses the image of playing a role.

[30] So W. Schmidt, Der Ursprung d. Gottesidee, VI, 2 (1935), 407 as the conclusion of his researches : The idea of creation out of nothing is most common in primitive Arctic-American cultures. Schmidt asks whether this was not the original view of this ancient race as a whole. Cf. also E. Johannsen, Geistesleben afrikanischer Völker im Lichte des Ev. (1931), 219-234 and Bertholet-Leh., I, 180-182; N. Söderblom, Das Werden des Gottesglaubens (1916), c. 4.

[31] Bertholet-Leh., I, 547 ff.; Ungnad, 165 ff.

[32] Cf., e.g., Bertholet-Leh., I, 544.

[33] Ibid., I, 436, 451.

[34] Ibid., I, 534.

[35] Ibid., I, 83 f., II, 31 f.

The most explicit in this connection is Aelius Aristides, who in his hymn to Zeus expressly contests the nature myths which subordinate Zeus to the forces of chaos and who consciously gives him a position of primacy: ἦν τε ἄρα ἐξ ἀρχῆς καὶ ἔσται εἰσαεί, Or., 43, 9 (Keil). He originated of himself, and the deduction is: οὕτω δὴ ἀρχὴ μὲν ἁπάντων Ζεύς τε καὶ ἐκ Διὸς πάντα. If Zeus and the world are then made simultaneous, ibid., 10, this is only to show the speed of Zeus' work (ποιεῖν); there was no ἀντικόψων. [36] In this connection we should also mention the many and varied attempts to understand creation as a miracle, as a personal act of power, whether it be creation by word or creation by certain psychic states of the creator, e.g., ecstasy. The point here is to emphasise that creation is an act which is beyond human conception. But if it is a magical act, the decisive force does not lie in the meaning of the word spoken but in the magical power of the word itself, which may at a pinch be divorced from the meaning. To understand creation as magic is to see at work in it a mysterious power which may be separated from the creator. It is not to see the creator as a person. These notions are all moving in the direction of a personal act of will, but they cannot reach this because creation alone is not enough to give a personal view of God. Hence these divine figures cannot be grasped as truly personal. The decisive personal element, action in history, is not stated of them. This is true in the Greek world. Philosophical reflection makes of Zeus an abstract quantity. We see this already in Anaxagoras, who perceives the rule of νοῦς in all things (διακοσμεῖν). [37] The world then owes its being to the idea of the good or to absolute being. In Plato's Timaeus, of course, a δημιουργός plays a not very clear role as a kind of intermediary between the world of ideas and that of phenomena. [38] Acc. to Diog. Laertes Plato's teaching is as follows: δύο ... ἀρχάς, θεὸν καὶ ὕλην, ὃν καὶ νοῦν προσαγορεύει, καὶ αἴτιον. The hyle is ἀσχημάτιστος καὶ ἄπειρος, ἀτάκτως κινουμένη, but God regards τάξις as better than ἀταξία, and He therefore fashions the hyle. [39] Elsewhere, however, emanation formulae and images are used. [40] This is consistently worked out in Neo-Platonism. Acc. to Plotinus the supreme God, who can be grasped only by way of negation, has within Himself the ladder of beings according to natural necessity, and He releases them from Himself, though not by way of emanation, since this would be a diminution of substance. [41] The result is on the one side the high estimation of the beauty of the cosmos, the reflection of the divine harmony, and on the other side aversion to earthly things and to matter, and an ascetic striving for the all and the one. How the many can flow from the one, evil from the all-good, and matter from that which is above being, is not clear even when the series and stages of emanation are greatly extended, and the result is that for man the goal of life can lie only in the impersonal. Man is a bundle of different parts which are destined to be dissolved again. Gnosticism developed this view of the world in many different ways. A particular place is occupied by the teaching of Zarathustra, which assumes the existence of two original powers of good and evil that

---

[36] Here we might also mention the Orphic Verse (Eus. Praep. Ev., III, 9, 2): Ζεὺς πρῶτος γένετο, Ζεὺς ὕστατος ἀργικέραυνος / Ζεὺς κεφαλή, Ζεὺς μέσσα, Διὸς δ' ἐκ πάντα τέτυκται. Elsewhere, too, the Greeks continually put Zeus at the head, Seeliger, 484, cf. also Soph. (Fr., 1017, TGF [Seeliger, 468]) of Helios: ὃν οἱ σοφοὶ λέγουσι γεννητὴν θεῶν καὶ πατέρα πάντων. Cf. also the Aton hymn of Amenophis IV (Erman, 111 ff., cf. also A. Oepke, Die Missionspredigt des Ap. Pls. [1920], 84 ff.).

[37] K. Prächter, Die Philosophie des Altertums[12] (1926), 100. Pherecydes (6th cent. B.C.) forms a kind of transition; for him Αἰθήρ, called Zas, is in confrontation with Χθονίη, Gruppe, § 171.

[38] → 74.

[39] Diog. L., III, 41 (69).

[40] The term πατήρ for the supreme god as distinct from δημιουργός as the ποιητής in Numenius (Prächter, 521, 602) points in the same direction.

[41] Prächter, 603, → 77.

are engaged in a conflict in which man is summoned to take sides. [42] Later all creation is divided between these powers. The first tractate of the Corp. Herm. solves the riddle of the world in the same way by assuming the existence of two original, though not simultaneous, forces, cf. also the Manichees.

B. Belief in Creation in the Old Testament.

1. The Development of the Old Testament Belief in Creation.

Pre-exilic statements concerning creation are not very common in the OT. Even if we assume from them, and from various indications, that belief in the creation of the world by God is very old in Israel, [43] the fact remains that the pre-exilic prophets made little use of this concept. Along with the story of the fashioning of man from the earth in J (Gn. 2:4b ff.; 6:6 f.; cf. 7:4), [44] the account of P in Gn. 1:1 ff. [45] and the conclusion of Gn. 14, which is very hard to date (vv. 19 and 22, blessing and oath by אֵל עֶלְיוֹן קֹנֵה שָׁמַיִם וָאָרֶץ), we may refer especially to the address of Solomon at the dedication of the temple, which in LXX 3 Βασ. 8:53a begins in the form: Ἥλιον ἐγνώρισεν ἐν οὐρανῷ κύριος. Here ἐγνώρισεν is used for a הֵכִין misread as הֵבִין; [46] in the original God has "established" the sun in heaven.

All the other statements bring us close to the exilic period. [47] In Jer. statements concerning creation are clearer: 5:22-24 speaks of Yahweh who has placed the sand as an eternal frontier for the sea; in 27:5 God says: "I have created the earth, men and the animals which there are on the whole earth, by my great power and outstretched arm, and I give them to whom I will"; 31:35-36 or 37 speaks of the eternal order of Yahweh that the sun should shine by day. [48] Finally, in Ez. 28:13 the word ברא is used with reference to the king of Tyre in a passage which is shot through with many mythological allusions.

These findings are related to the fact that the primary witness of the OT is to the God who is mighty in history, to the God of Abraham, Isaac and Jacob, to the God who led the people out of Egypt, through the Red Sea and across Jordan into the promised land, to the God who conducted the wars of Israel. The movement in the OT is not from creation to history but *vice versa*. It is not that the Creator is Yahweh but rather that Yahweh, the God of Israel, is Creator. The content of

---

[42] That with the idea of a personal God is linked the sense of man's complete dependence and his summons to action may be seen from the inscr. of Darius I, which begin: "A great [God is] Ahuramazda, who is supreme over all gods, who created heaven and earth and created men, who gave all blessings to the men who live on it, who made Darius king and invested him with dominion over this broad earth on which are many lands" (F. H. Weissbach, *Die Keilinschriften der Achämeniden* [1911], 85, 87, 99 etc.).

[43] Eichrodt, II, 47.

[44] Perhaps Gn. 2:4b: בְּיוֹם עֲשׂוֹת יְהוָה אֱלֹהִים אֶרֶץ וְשָׁמָיִם, is also a ref. by J to the making of heaven and earth, F. M. T. Böhl in *At.liche Studien f. R. Kittel* (1913), 59.

[45] G. v. Rad, *Die Priesterschrift im Hexateuch* (1934), 11-18; L. Rost, "Der Schöpfungsbericht der Priesterschrift," *Christentum u. Wissenschaft*, 10 (1934), 172-178.

[46] Cf. O. Eissfeldt in Kautzsch on 1 K. 8:12; Hänel, 211.

[47] Strothmann, 200 f. also regards as older 1 S. 2:8 ff.; Is. 17:7; Na. 1:4; Hab. 3:6 ff. In the last of these he finds an echo of the myth of the conflict with chaos. But the datings are all disputed.

[48] Cf. Jer. 38:16. The authenticity of Jer. 10:11 f., 16; 32:17 is open to question.

the word יהוה is primarily determined by His revelation in history. [49] In the patriarchal stories God does not make Himself known as the One who has made heaven and earth but as the God of the fathers. [50] The revelation in history, however, was from the very first of such a kind that it contained the seed for the development of affirmations concerning creation. [51] Yahweh is from the very first only the Subject of historical action. Beside Him there is no other divine subject. He is the Subject who acts personally. He engages in conscious volition (in contrast to the "strivings" of cosmogonic powers in the religions). He has a goal in view. Yahweh declares in advance what He will do — Dt. Is. exploited this theme later in his conflict with idols. It is not simply that events are later attributed with gratitude to the deity, as in the Achaemenid inscriptions (→ n. 42). Yahweh made and fashioned it "long ago," Is. 22:11, cf. 2 K. 19:25 = Is. 37:26. The absolute superiority of Yahweh over all the factors of history finds expression in the metaphor of the potter and the vessel in Jer. 18:1-6. [52] Historical action is action in time and space, and nature moves in time and space, so that what is mighty in history is mighty in nature. In the field of nature, too, there are only objects of God's action. The earth quakes and the mountains are moved at the very appearance of Yahweh, Ju. 5:4 f.; Hab. 3:3 ff. etc. A striking point in Am. 9:2-4 is that the outermost spheres of the cosmos, heaven, earth, the kingdom of the dead, the top of Carmel and the bottom of the sea are all accessible to Yahweh and may all be used by Him.

The concept of creation is further developed with the orders of nature which God has guaranteed according to Gn. 8:22 (J). In Jer. 5:22-24 (cf. 14:22) one of the motives for the fear of God, along with the giving of rain in its season and the assuring of the established order of harvest, is the fact that God has set (שִׂים) a limit to the sea as an eternal decree (cf. the reference to the sun in Solomon's address at the dedication of the temple). [53] Hence it is in Jer. (27:5) that there appears the first clear and comprehensive statement concerning creation : אָנֹכִי עָשִׂיתִי [54] אֶת־הָאָרֶץ אֶת־הָאָדָם וְאֶת־הַבְּהֵמָה אֲשֶׁר עַל־פְּנֵי הָאָרֶץ בְּכֹחִי הַגָּדוֹל וּבִזְרוֹעִי הַנְּטוּיָה וּנְתַתִּיהָ לַאֲשֶׁר יָשַׁר בְּעֵינָי. The absolute power of God over history is now for the first time traced back to His being as Creator. The connection between power in history and power as Creator is a very close one in the OT, for the shaping of history is also a creation, and the same words are used of it as are applied to the creating and fashioning of the world and man. Thus עשׂה and יצר are used of God's rule in history at Is. 22:11; 29:16 f.; Jer. 18:11, and פעל at Hab. 1:5. The people of Israel is likewise

---

[49] Eichrodt, I, 10 : "In Israel, on the other hand, knowledge of the covenant God and His act of redemption awakened the capacity to see and present historical occurrence, first in the context of the national destiny, but then in that of world history as an effect of the one divine will, so that even nature myth could be used in the service of this concept."

[50] Though cf. Jub. 32:18 : "I am the God who has made heaven and earth" (on His appearance to Jacob).

[51] Eichrodt, I, 115 f.: "The most influential presuppositions for the subjection of all natural life to the powerful sway of the one divine Lord are to be found in the ancient belief of Israel in the covenant God ..."

[52] Perhaps earlier in Is. 29:16, though the genuineness of this is contested.

[53] Cf. Jer. 31:35-36 (whether v. 37 is authentic is open to question).

[54] Authentic acc. to P. Volz, Der Prophet Jeremia (1922), 255 (though it is possible that a later hand has added basic religious ideas which are quite conceivable on the lips of Jer.) and Strothmann, 64-66, who gives the meaning of עָשָׂה as "to bring forth by work" (66).

fashioned. That is to say, it is by historical direction made into, not just a people, but the people of God, Is. 27:11 (עשה and יצר). This usage is firmly fixed in Dt. Is.: 43:7, 15, 21; 44:2, 21, 24; 45:11; 49:5. In this sense of the bringing forth of historical events there also occurs the word ברא, which then becomes a tt. for God's creating: Ex. 34:10 (J?): וְאָם בְּרִיאָה; Nu. 16:30 (JE): אֲשֶׁר נִפְלָאת אֶעֱשֶׂה לֹא־נִבְרְאוּ בְכָל־הָאָרֶץ וּבְכָל־הַגּוֹיִם. יִבְרָא יְהֹוָה וּפָצְתָה הָאֲדָמָה אֶת־פִּיהָ The reference here is to extraordinary historical events. The OT belief in creation thus achieves full clarity with Dt. Is. and P, with the word ברא and with the idea of almighty creation by the Word.

2. Creation Terminology and Conceptions in the OT.

We shall consider first the strict terms ברא, פעל, עשה, יצר, קנה, then fig. expressions linked with the ancient view of the world, סכך (= "to weave," Ps. 139:13), כון, יסד, נטה, הוליד (Ps. 90:2), and then finally allusions to creation myths.

קנה[55] of creation, Gn. 14:19, 22: אֵל עֶלְיוֹן קֹנֵה שָׁמַיִם וָאָרֶץ (in both cases LXX ἔκτισεν); Ps. 139:13: אַתָּה קָנִיתָ כִלְיֹתָי, with "weaving" in the mother's womb (LXX for קנה κτάο-μαι); Prv. 8:22: Wisdom says: יְהֹוָה קָנָנִי רֵאשִׁית דַּרְכּוֹ (LXX κτίζω); Dt. 32:6 (exilic): הֲלוֹא־הוּא אָבִיךָ קָנֶךָ הוּא עָשְׂךָ וַיְכֹנְנֶךָ (LXX in the same sequence κτάομαι, ποιέω, κτίζω). For these passages Ges.-Buhl suggests the sense "to establish," "to create," but we have to take them in connection with those which apply the term to God's relation with Israel, e.g., with Dt. 32:6, Ex. 15:16 (the Song of the Red Sea, later than J and E) זְכֹר עֲדָתְךָ קָנִיתָ קֶּדֶם גָּאַלְתָּ שֵׁבֶט נַחֲלָתֶךָ; Ps. 74:2: (LXX κτάομαι); יַעֲבֹר עַם־זוּ קָנִיתָ (LXX κτάομαι); Is. 11:11 (late): On that day God will stretch out His hand for the second time, לִקְנוֹת אֶת־שְׁאָר עַמּוֹ (LXX ζηλοῦν); Ps. 78:54 of the temple hill: הַר־זֶה קָנְתָה יְמִינוֹ (LXX κτάομαι). The meaning is always "to make for oneself."[56] God has acquired or made or prepared for Himself heaven and earth or the people Israel; the same terms are used for the fashioning of both. The word is older in Gn. 14, elsewhere it is used poetically. Even the LXX did not take it to mean "to create," for קנה does not have for the translators of Gn. the same sense as in other parts of the LXX, → 1027.

יצר denotes the activity of the potter as he shapes and fashions vessels and figures with his hands. It thus corresponds to the Gk. πλάσσειν, which is the usual LXX rendering.[57] The lit. sense of "shaping" is certainly present in Gn. 2:7, 8, 19, but in Jer. 1:5 (formation in the mother's womb) it is already a figure for God's invisible and omnipotent action. The plastic element gradually fades, and it is useless to ask to what degree the lit. sense is present in individual cases. In no other pre-exilic passage is יצר used for certain in the sense of "to make." In Is. 45:7 the obj. is light and it is used along with ברא — this also occurs in Is. 45:18; Am. 4:13; Is. 43:1. In Is. 27:11; 44:2; 45:18 it is found with עשה. Dt. Is. likes to use יצר of the people Israel which God has fashioned, 43:1, 21; 44:2, 21, 24; 45:9, 11; 49:5. One reason why the term is very suitable for expressing the relation of the creature to the Creator is that it brings out very forcefully the distinction, superiority and higher wisdom of the one who fashions in relation to what he fashions, just as the image of the vessel and the potter, even apart from creation in the strict sense, is well calculated to express the absolute dependence of

---

[55] On קנה Dillmann, 287; Hänel, 176 f.; L. Köhler, ZAW, 52 (1934), 160; Theol. d. AT (1936), 68; Eichrodt, II, 50; Burney, 166.

[56] Köhler, 68 f.: "laborious and painstaking action by which God gains possession of things."

[57] Exceptions in Is. 45:18: καταδείκνυμι (of the earth); 43:21: περιποιεῖσθαι (of Israel); 22:11; 46:11: κτίζω; 37:26: συντάττω (events); 45:7: κατασκευάζω (light); Am. 4:13: στερεόω (mountains, LXX: βροντήν); Is. 29:16 and 45:11: ποιέω.

man on God, cf. Is. 29:16 f.; Jer. 18:1 ff. Another point which applies particularly to Dt. Is. is that in this picture the creature owes not only its being but its nature, its concrete form, to God.

פעל and the noun פֹּעַל are used of the Creator only once (פָּעֳלִי, Job 36:3); elsewhere they often refer to God's acts in history. עשה is the most common term for creating, and ποιέω is used most frequently for it in the LXX. When J in Gn. 3:1 speaks of the "formation" of the beasts of the earth, cf. וַיִּצֶר יְהוָֹה אֱלֹהִים מִן־הָאֲדָמָה כָּל־חַיַּת הַשָּׂדֶה in 2:19, he uses the phrase כָּל־חַיַּת הַשָּׂדֶה אֲשֶׁר עָשָׂה יְהוָֹה. Here עשה is undoubtedly used in the sense of יצר; it thus signifies making from existing material. On the other hand, when P in Gn. 1:6 f. adds to the statement: "And God said, Let there be a firmament," the words: וַיַּעַשׂ אֱלֹהִים אֶת־הָרְקִיעַ, v. 7, we have evidence of an older stage of the narrative in which God makes the firmament and divides the waters directly,[58] but the redactor who joined the verses (also Gn. 1:14 f. with 16 f. and v. 24 with 25) was not aware of any disruptive distinction between calling into being and making. This is also true of ברא, for with the word of command which summons creeping things and fowls into being in 1:20 we find in v. 21: וַיִּבְרָא אֱלֹהִים אֶת־הַתַּנִּינִם, an older stage of the tradition, so that ברא must once have had a concrete significance related to יצר.[59] There are many references to the hands or finger with which God created (e.g., Ps. 8:3; Job 12:9), but these, too, are to be taken figuratively. Dt. Is. has a view of creation by fiat which it is impossible to contest, but he uses ברא, יצר, עשה and כּוֹנֵן alongside one another in 45:18.[60]

ברא is found in P Gn. 1:1, 21, 27 (twice); 2:3, 4; 5:1, 2 (twice); 6:7 (J, but interposed from P);[61] Dt. 4:32; 20 times in Dt. Is.; 6 in the Psalms; also Am. 4:13 (not authentic);[62] Is. 4:5 (not authentic: LXX reads בא for ברא); Jer. 31:22; Ez. 21:35; 28:13, 15; Mal. 2:10; Qoh. 12:1; also Ex. 34:10; Nu. 16:30 (→ infra). This word, too, obviously had an original concrete significance, but this cannot now be traced.[63] It is used exclusively for God's creating. In what source criticism suggests are perhaps the oldest passages, Ex. 34:10[64] and Nu. 16:30 (JE) it relates to a miraculous and powerful work of God in history. This is also the sense in Jer. 31:22 and a few other passages, Is. 45:7, 8; 48:7; 65:18. It is thus par. to the other terms. By this restriction to an act of God the word was given a special theological stamp and reserved for the belief in creation as this finds particularly clear expression in P and Dt. Is. The presupposition is that something falls to be said about God's creation for which there is no analogy in the sphere of human life and knowledge.

With these words is also a series of terms related to the peculiar way in which the Oriental conceived of the formation of the world. Thus God stretched out heaven like a tent (נטה, Is. 40:22;[65] 44:24; 45:12; 51:13; Zech. 12:1; Ps. 104:2; Job 9:8, cf. 26:7; Jer. 10:12 = 51:15;[66] or טפח, Is. 48:13). Or again, heaven is made fast like a metal

---

[58] Rost; v. Rad, 12 ff.

[59] Cf. also 1:26 and 27.

[60] Cf. also a passage like Gn. 2:8 f., where Yahweh planted a garden, cf. Gn. 3:21.

[61] So also Böhl, 47.

[62] Böhl, 48 f. defends the genuineness of the doxologies to the Creator in Am. 4:13; 5:8 f.; 9:5 f. But the rhythm reminds us of Dt. Is., and 9:5 f. does not form an apt conclusion to 1-4, since 2-4 adequately emphasise the almightiness of Yahweh without it.

[63] For details cf. Böhl, 42 f. On ברא cf. the OT Theologies of Dillmann, 286 f.; H. Schultz⁵ (1896), 449; Smend, 348, n. 1; Sellin, 37; Eichrodt, II, 51; Köhler, 69; cf. also Hänel, 249.

[64] The critical break-down is not certain here, cf. Böhl, 47 f.

[65] With מָתַח כָּאֹהֶל.

[66] Neither of these verses is by Jer.

mirror, Job 37:18. [67] Or again, the earth is based on pillars, יסד, in the Psalms, Dt. Is., Zech. 12:1; Job; Prv.; Am. 9:6 (not authentic, → n. 62); 1 S. 2:8, never for certain pre-exilic. Or the earth is made fast, הֵכִין (כּוֹנֵן), Ps. 93:1; 96:10 = 1 Ch. 16:30; Is. 45:18; Ps. 24:2; 119:90; Jer. 10:12 = 51:15 (not authentic). The stars, too, are made fast, Ps. 8:3, and also heaven, Prv. 3:19; 8:27, and the mountains, Ps. 65:6, and the orderly sequence of crops and rain, Ps. 65:9; 147:8, since creation and preservation merge into one another. Very different images are also found. Thus Ps. 90:2; Job 15:7; cf. 38:8 speak of the mountains being born, Ps. 139:13, 15; Job 10:11 of man being woven together, Ps. 104:3 etc. of God's balcony having its beams in the waters. These expressions are particularly common in the time of the Exile, i.e., in the time when creation was stated to be by the Word. Once this position was reached, anthropomorphic images could be used without fear. Thus Dt. Is. 48:13 can speak on the one side of God's hand having established the earth, His right hand having spread out the heaven, and on the other side of God's calling to them and their being there; ברא is in parallelism with יסד etc., cf. also Ps. 89:11 f.; Is. 45:18. By using human terms of reference, these images show that God's work far exceeds human terms of reference. The One whose hand has stretched out the heaven is not a giant man; He is quite other than man; He is God, the First and the Last, who will still abide when heaven and earth, the work of His hands (Ps. 102:25 f.), have perished and in face of whom it is nonsensical to fear men, Is. 51:13. The firmness with which earth is established is a guarantee of the faithfulness of God, Ps. 119:90. Finally, these fig. expressions point to the power and wisdom of God: Jer. 10:12 : עֹשֵׂה אֶרֶץ בְּכֹחוֹ מֵכִין תֵּבֵל בְּחָכְמָתוֹ וּבִתְבוּנָתוֹ נָטָה שָׁמָיִם cf. Prv. 3:19; 8:27; Job 38 f.; Ps. 65:6. [68]

A third and final series indicates the mythological background of the oriental view of the world [69] (→ 1002). According to this a battle between more or less personified powers of chaos preceded the true fashioning of the world. There are all kinds of references to this from the clear use of mythological names (Rahab, Leviathan) to the faintest echoes, e.g., Yahweh's chiding of the sea. But the myth itself does not occur. The allusions are all in lofty style, esp. in Ps., Dt. Is. and Job. This shows us at once their significance. It may be noted that different stages in the use of the myth are to be found in the same work. Thus Job 9:13 speaks of the helpers of Rahab who must bow to God, while Job 38:8 says only that God enclosed the sea by doors when it broke forth. In both cases the ref. is to the same thing, namely, creation as a battle with chaos, and a final echo of this myth may be found in Ps. 33:6 ff. along with creation by the Word. If one considers the way in which the myth is used, it will be seen that all the echoes and allusions assume that the mythical monsters are mere objects of the divine action. This is plainest in Ps. 89:10 : "Thou hast crushed Rahab as one who is mortally wounded." The forces of chaos are as impotent before God as those who are mortally wounded, who have received the *coup de grâce*. In other words, the mythical allusions are statements about God, not about the forces of chaos. [70]

3. The Old Testament Belief in Creation.

a. All the OT statements concerning the Creator are characterised by the fact that they do not constitute of themselves the picture of God but they relate to

---

[67] Cf. Strothmann, 53.

[68] It would be a plain indication of metaphorical use if at Prv. 8:23 we were to read נִסַּכְתִּי "I have been woven," of wisdom, so B. Gemser, *Sprüche Salomos* (1937), *ad loc.*

[69] For details cf. H. Gunkel, *Schöpfung u. Chaos²* (1921) and Strothmann.

[70] There is also an ancient mythical allusion in the rejoicing of the morning stars when God laid the corner-stone of the earth, Job 38:6 f., but it is hard to see an explicitly different view of creation from that of Gn. 1, as B. Duhm, 26 and Stade-Bertholet, II, 130 try to make out. The thought of the mountains being born in Ps. 90:2 and Job 38:28 ff. reminds us of the mythical notion of fruitful chaos.

the specific God Yahweh who declares Himself in historical events. The basic revelation is not creation. It is the historical action which began with the patriarchs. [71]

b. The OT belief in creation found its true expression in the creation story of P in Gn. 1. Here creation is an action. It arises out of nothing by the Word of God. The element in the OT which is related to mythical conceptions and to figurative expressions which denote artistic activity on God's part, so that it is in some sense at odds with the belief in creation of the first account in Gn., leaves full scope for the development of the OT belief, since the hostile powers of chaos and the material which God shapes are never more than objects of the divine action (→ 1006).

The narrative of Gn. 1 is summed up in Ps. 33:9 in the words : הוּא אָמַר וַיֶּהִי הוּא־צִוָּה וַיַּעֲמֹד. This statement contains a logical impossibility which Pl. makes even more evident in R. 4:17: (κατέναντι ... θεοῦ) καλοῦντος τὰ μὴ ὄντα ὡς ὄντα. One can call forth only that which already exists. [72] But God calls forth that which does not yet exist. He commands it, and in obedience to this command creation takes place. We must not try to evade the logical inconceivability of this statement by taking the μὴ ὄντα as though in some sense they were ὄντα. [73] This OT view also goes beyond the conception, attested elsewhere, that the process of creation is an act of magic. For the word spoken is not an incantation which has power irrespective of its meaning (→ 1004). The Word of creation is the command in its concrete wording. Nor can one object that the view is non-organic. As regarded in the OT, creation is a positing of the organic. As such it is a personal act, an act [74] to which the categories of organic and inorganic do not apply any more than they do (to some degree) to human acts of will. In this respect creation is not a final cause any more than human deeds or acts of human will can be brought under the category of causality. Thus the OT concept of creation is one which in the strict sense makes sense only with one reference, namely, to God. This makes it plain why בָּרָא is used in the OT only of a divine action (→ 1008). As Creator God is the Lord, → κύριος, and He confronts all created things as such. Creation is an act of absolute power. The Creator is here wholly personal will. There can be no limitation of His power.

In the sphere of earthly life there is an organic relation between father and son ; the son can become as the father. But between Creator and creature there is no natural connection ; the creature is and remains basically different from its Creator,

---

[71] Strongly emphasised by v. Rad, 138 ff. Cf. v. Rad in A. Alt, J. Begrich, G. v. Rad, *Führung zum Christentum durch das AT* (1934), 57; Eichrodt, → n. 49 and 51.

[72] Scharbau, 137: "The idea of a command presupposes the existence of ministering and obedient powers to carry out the will to create."

[73] Scharbau tries to do this, 17-28.

[74] Cf. Hönigswald, 18 f. To jolt too great a confidence in science one should recall the reflection of A. S. Eddington that while neither he nor most men would welcome the idea of a sudden beginning of the present natural order, and while even those who might do so would not regard a past divine intervention as a satisfying relation between God and His world, there seems to be no way out of this dilemma. Indeed, even if natural science were to come to similar conclusions in respect of the continuation of the world and the validity of natural laws as Eddington does in respect of the beginning of the cosmos, it would still not break through to the biblical proclamation of creation and preservation as a personal act, since personal categories are not at its disposal. At this point it can lead only to a vacuum.

and no time either removes or even diminishes this distinction. [75] The OT has a strong sense of the distance between Creator and creature. In Ex. 33:23 Moses may see God from behind, וּפָנַי לֹא יֵרָאוּ. Elijah conceals his face when he realises that God is passing by, 1 K. 19:13. Is. (6:5) cries out : "Woe is me, I perish, for my eyes have seen the king, Yahweh Sabaoth." In the OT, then, God is also the hidden God, Is. 45:15. His work is concealed, Ps. 139:15; Job 11:7; 42:1-6. As Creator, God is absolutely different from and superior to man and the whole of nature. This is why the OT is full of praise of the Creator. For man cannot laud and extol that which is part of himself. He can laud and extol only that which is above him and which has a right thereto. This is true of the Creator. [76] Thus in the OT He is magnified not only by man, e.g., Ps. 8; 95:1-5; 104, but also by all nature : "The heavens declare the glory of God." When it is said in Job 38:6 f. that the morning stars rejoiced when God laid the foundation of the earth, the view of creation may be different from that of Gn. 1 (→ n. 70), but by their praise these morning stars recognise the majesty and transcendence of God, and, even though it is not explicitly stated, they thus acknowledge His being as Creator. Hence there is an inner reason why Dt. Is., who constantly bears witness to God as Creator, should speak no less constantly of the glory which He will not give to another, 42:8; 45:23.

The Creator has the power to consign again to nothing the creature which He has called forth out of nothing, Ps. 102:26-28; 104:29; Dt. 32:39; cf. Job 34:14 f. Between calling forth out of nothing and sending back to it lies preservation. Whatever may be the significance of God's resting on the seventh day, Gn. 2:2 f., the fact is that the OT speaks of a continuing creative activity of God, Jer. 1:5. In Dt. Is. Israel is created or fashioned by God, and we have seen that the terms used for creation are also used for God's work in nature and history. This is particularly plain in Ps. 104 (esp. v. 27 f.) and Neh. 9:6. Even regular natural events are under God's command, Is. 40:26, cf. Gn. 8:22. While ancient Israel saw God's power particularly in more violent natural happenings, in storm and thunder, [77] at a later date it is the orderliness of nature which displays His glory. In distinction from the Greek world, however, Israel does not deduce from the regular course of the stars the planned and rational order of the κόσμος. When it contemplates nature, it thinks always of the חֻקִּים or decrees which God has imposed on nature. [78] Thus in becoming, being and perishing all creation is wholly dependent on the will of the Creator.

c. As distinct from the various images and expressions used to emphasise God's power in creation (→ 1009), the only theologically adequate concept (so far as this is possible) to express God's creation is that of creation by the Word. Creation by will might be considered, but it suffers from the defect that it can be misconstrued as natural impulse or positing from within oneself. Word alone safeguards creation against all emanationist misunderstanding and makes it clear that the Creator is a person. For word is the expression of one who wills and acts

---

[75] This is the basis of the prohibition of images, → II, 382.
[76] Eichrodt, I, 221: "The jubilant echo which Gn. 1 finds in many psalms shows the liberating effect which comes from a monotheistic concept of creation and which is experienced as supreme exaltation in absolute commitment."
[77] Ps. 29; cf. Eichrodt, II, 79.
[78] Eichrodt, II, 80 f.; Jer. 8:7; 31:35 ff.

consciously. What God wills (חֵפֶץ), He does (Ps. 115:3; 135:6). At the same time, creation by the Word brings out the miraculous and spiritual character of creation and also the absolute transcendence of the Creator over the creature, which cannot offer even the passive resistance that material might offer to being fashioned. Dt. Is. is the first to speak of creation by the Word: קרא (again both of creation at the first and of the determination of history) 41:4; 48:13; cf. 44:26 f. (אמר) and 45:12 (צוה) cf. also Am. 9:6 (קרא), cf. Job 37:5 f.) and esp. Ps. 33:6: בִּדְבַר יְהוָֹה שָׁמַיִם נַעֲשׂוּ, also v. 9; 148:5; Job 38:11; Jon. 4:6 f. Alongside Dt. Is. may be set the creation narrative of P with its clear-cut וַיְהִי כֵן — וַיֹּאמֶר אֱלֹהִים.[79]

Creation by the Word implies *creatio e nihilo*. This is not stated in Gn. 1:1 f., which selects the chaos of earth as the starting-point. Gn. 1:1 does not speak of the making of this chaos;[80] שָׁמַיִם וָאָרֶץ embraces the cosmos. But Gn. 1:1 is placed before the account as a title, and it thus controls v. 2 as well. On בְּרֵאשִׁית we may compare the saying of Dt. Is. that God is the first and the last, 44:6; 48:12, and it is to be noted that in the second of these verses the statement is closely related to the fact that God has created heaven and earth by His Word. In the beginning God is, but the creature comes into being. The beginning is thus the beginning of the creature, before which it did not exist. It is in keeping with the practical nature of the OT that it does not formulate creation out of nothing as a dogmatic principle but always, so far as we can see, makes about God only statements which do not subject Him to, or bring Him under the influence of, any pre-existent conditions.

The more clearly the concept of creation is worked out, the broader is the circle of ideas which are linked with it or based on it. Creation displays not only the omnipotence but also the wisdom and omniscience of God, Jer. 10:12 = 51:15; Ps. 104:24; Job 28:24-26; Prv. 3:19; 8:27. In particular, the creative act of God establishes His right to creation; because He has created them, heaven and earth belong to Him, Ps. 24:1 f.; 89:11; 95:5; Εθ. 4:17b c. The creative act of God is also the basis of His power in history, Jer. 27:5, of the duty of trust in Him, of His claim to trust and gratitude, Is. 17:7; 22:11; 40:26 ff.; 43:1; 44:2; Hos. 8:14; Dt. 32:6, 15; Ps. 103:22, and of the duty of obedience, Ps. 119:73. Tr. Is. is the first to deduce from the fact that they are created a kind of claim of creatures to pity (64:7). In Dt. Is. it is the Creator Himself who summons His creatures to trust, and on this basis, referring to His being as Creator, Dt. Is. seeks to call Israel to faith and confidence when confidence is crippled by doubt of God's power in face of the impotence of the people. For the same reason the righteous in his prayers remembers gladly the creative power of God. In the distress in which he prays, he sets before his eyes the power of God which can deliver him from it, 2 K. 19:15; Neh. 9:6. The creative act of God establishes the fact that the creature cannot escape its Creator nor hide from Him, Ps. 33:14; 94:9; 139. It establishes the fact that the creature is a vessel in the hands of the potter, Jer. 18:1 ff. (19:11);

---

[79] That the command תַּדְשֵׁא הָאָרֶץ in Gn. 1:11 or תּוֹצֵא הָאָרֶץ in Gn. 1:24 does not imply an appeal to the fertility of the earth (Strothmann, 81 f.) may be seen from Ps. 104:14: מַצְמִיחַ חָצִיר לַבְּהֵמָה. An appeal to the fertility of the earth is not enough; it is always at God's command that the earth produces plants.

[80] As against Hänel, 249. On Gn. 1 cf. the comm., also K. Budde, ZAW, 35 (1915), 65-97 (בְּרֵאשִׁית in Gn. 1:1 is prep., so also H. Schultz, 449); A. Bertholet, JBL, 53 (1934), 237-240; G. v. Rad, 11 ff.

Is. 29:16; 45:9. The fact that He has created heaven and earth distinguishes the God of Israel from idols, Jer. 10:12-16 (cf. 14:22); 51:15-19; Ps. 96:5; 115:3 f.; Jon. 1:9. This does not mean that God's being as Creator is added as a necessary qualification to a general concept of God. It means that witness is borne to the fact that Yahweh, the God of Israel, is the Creator, and none else. The uniqueness of God is indissolubly linked to the fact that He is the Creator, e.g., Is. 44:24. In good and evil Israel has to do only with this One "who fashions light and creates (בָּרָא) darkness, who makes salvation (שָׁלוֹם) and creates evil," Is. 45:7. Thus the message of the Creator leads again to the one mighty God of history in which it was enclosed as in a bud from the very first.

This belief in the Creator from whom everything, שָׁלוֹם and רַע, comes, before whom creatures are as the potter's vessel, also encloses the insight that God's ways and works are right. Elihu in Job 34:12 f. establishes the principle that the Almighty does not deviate from what is right with his question: "Who has entrusted the earth to his charge, and who has established the whole earth?" Cf. also Ps. 33:4 f.: 6 ff., where the constancy of the natural order is an indication of God's enduring faithfulness from generation to generation.

The formulation of Dt. Is. embraces all things, whether in creation or in history: 44:6; 48:12: אֲנִי רִאשׁוֹן וַאֲנִי אַחֲרוֹן וּמִבַּלְעָדַי אֵין אֱלֹהִים. This means that the goal of the world and man is enclosed in Him. To be sure, there are few statements which comprehensively state the final goal. It is said that Jeremiah was already sanctified a prophet in his mother's womb, 1:5, and there are similar sayings in Dt. Is. with reference to Israel, which is fashioned as a servant to bring light to the Gentiles, 42:1, 6; 44:21; 49:5 f. The confidence with which one can move from belief in the Creator of the world to purpose in the world may be seen in Dt. Is., which tells us that the earth is fashioned as a dwelling-place, and from the creation narratives, which both tell us that man has a divinely willed task on this earth, although in different forms. In the creation psalm 104 the fact that man may work is a reason for praising God, vv. 19-23, cf. Prv. 31:10 ff. But this can hardly be the final goal of creation. Is. 43:21 reads: "The people which I have formed for myself will tell my praise," and the goal and climax of history is similarly formulated in the confession in Is. 45:24: בַּיהוָֹה לִי צְדָקוֹת וָעֹז.

d. This is the point where we must raise the question of the form of the world, of fallen creation. In the first instance the two creation stories part company at this point. For J the aim set for man is to till the Garden of Eden, and after the fall man is expelled from Paradise. In the obscure saying to the serpent there is perhaps a glance into the distant future — after the flood, and the dark judgment on the thoughts and imaginations of the human heart, the promise is given that there will never again be a judgment like this on the earth. The story of the patriarchs, the exodus and the entry into the promised land must have some connection with the story of creation, but it is hard to discern. P does not have the story of Paradise and the fall, but the story of the flood occupies a similar place in his account. "This disaster corresponds negatively to the process of creation in Gn. 1. What is there built up and distinguished here collapses in chaos." [81] Hence the blessing of creation in Gn. 1:28 must be renewed, though not without reference to the changed situation, Gn. 9:2, 3, 6. Here again no final goal of history

---

[81] v. Rad, 172.

is stated. That the story which begins with the patriarchs has some purpose may be seen from the promise to Abraham that in him shall all the nations on earth be blessed, and Ex. 19:5 f. points in the same direction. But the seeds laid in these two stories for the development of the idea of a fallen creation are not yet brought to fruition in the OT. To be sure, Is. 11 looks forward to a removal of the situation depicted in Gn. 9:1 ff. In v. 7c the lion is to eat straw like an ox — a return to the original conditions of Gn. 1:30; cf. also the fact that Gn. 9:2 refers to the fear of man by animals. Again, Is. 66:22 speaks directly of a new heaven and a new earth which God will make. But if the clearest expression of the concept of a fallen creation is to be found in the hope of victory over death, the Book of Job shows how remote the concept is.

The legislation concerning meats has nothing to do with a dualistic outlook. The flesh of swine does not represent fallen creation in the OT. On the other hand, praise of creation (Gn. 1:31: טוֹב מְאֹד; Qoh. 3:11) can be so loud and clear in the OT because the subject of praise is never creation itself; it is always the Creator in His works. Hence there is no glorification of nature as such. Regard for the Creator gives to creation and man their rightful place.

e. The OT view of man is also determined by the belief in creation. If the decisive point in this is that the Creator confronts creation as personal will, this is also true in respect of man. In both accounts man is part of creation and yet he is also differentiated from it in virtue of his relation to God. In J both man and beast are נֶפֶשׁ חַיָּה, Gn. 2:7, 19, but only of man is it expressly said that this living soul is a breath from God, and man also names the animals and finds no עֵזֶר כְּנֶגְדּוֹ among them. What J expresses in terms of naming the animals is in P dominion over the whole earth and the animal world. P also coins an expression of un-fathomable depth when he says that God created man בְּצַלְמוֹ בְּצֶלֶם אֱלֹהִים. It must be noted at once that in P this divine likeness was not lost at the fall, since P does not offer any account of the fall. If P says of Adam in Gn. 5:3 וַיּוֹלֶד בִּדְמוּתוֹ כְּצַלְמוֹ. this image of the image of God does not imply a greater remoteness and progressive diminution of the divine likeness of man, since in relation to the creation of plants P emphasises the fact that they are to bring forth after their kind and in relation to both beast and man he refers to the divine blessing of fertility, so that no room is left for natural degeneration after the flood. In Gn. 9:6 we read of each man in particular that God made him בְּצֶלֶם אֱלֹהִים. Neither for P nor more generally are צֶלֶם and דְּמוּת separable from the figure of man, → II, 390-392. Yet for the whole of the OT and beyond this expression finds its fulness and significance in terms of the understanding of the אֱלֹהִים in whose image man is created. No matter how the relation of man to God is mediated, no matter how it is viewed, what is far more important is that man is therewith related to this Creator God of whom the narrative speaks of which Gn. 1:26 f. is a part. [82] As the Creator confronts nature as conscious personal will, so man — a part of nature and related to it — confronts and transcends it also. Because man in the OT knows that he confronts the personal God, he himself is established as a person. Because God has created man as a whole, he is a whole both body and soul. Because God's creation is an act, man,

---

[82] Cf. the bibl. on → εἰκών C. ff., also Eichrodt, II, 60-64; Köhler, 133; T. C. Vriezen, *Onderzoek naar de paradijsvoorstelling bij de oude semietische volken*, Diss. Utrecht (1937), 85 ff., 130.

too, is summoned to action. Because God the Creator is one, humanity also is one before Him. [83]

Since man is not just a part of nature, something else which is an enigma is brought to light. If an animal knows its master, how much more so should man, Is. 1:3. The "unnatural" character of the fact that he does not finds dramatic expression in Gn. 6:6. In the OT sin is never natural. It is a personal attitude, and at bottom it is a great mystery. [84] The seat of this mystery is the human heart, defiant and desperate (Jer. 17:9). J tells us that the imagination of the thought of the heart is wicked from youth up, Gn. 6:5, cf. 8:21. The prophets in their struggle for obedience from the heart on the part of the people come to the same conclusion, not as an inherited dogma, but as a finding to which they are forced by their own activity, Jer. 5:4 f. The seal of this is the promise of a new heart, Ez. 36:26 ff.; cf. Jer. 31:33 ff.; Ps. 51:10. In this connection it is stated that the final goal of God's history with the people Israel is that He will be their God and that the state of the world will then correspond to His will, Ez. 36:26 ff. We should not, of course, exaggerate the significance of these statements concerning the human heart. For example, P not only tells us that plants, animals and men are created with the capacity of reproduction and that death is posited from the very first; he also indicates that the same blessing rests on the creatures after the flood, though naturally the conditions have changed. He certainly does not say that the imagination of the thought of man is evil, nor does this teaching find any place in Ps. 8. [85]

C. The Doctrine of Creation in Later Judaism.

1. Terminology.

The most common terms for God's creating in the Rabbis are ברא [86] and עשה, [87] but we also find פעל [88] and frequently יצר, [89] which is used in 4 Esr. 3:4 of the earth and in 3:5 of Adam. קנה occurs, e.g., in the first petition of the Prayer of Eighteen Petitions (קונה שמים וארץ). [90] The metaphor of building a palace or city is also used of the creation of the world, [91] and so, too, is the older metaphor of stretching out a tent, e.g., Gn. r., 1, 3 on 1:1 (מתח, p. 1b, Vilna). A special term is the noun בְּרִיָּה, בְּרִיָּה, plur. בְּרִיּוֹת. [92] It means "what is created," "creation," whether rational or irrational, organic or inorganic. [93]

---

[83] The social implications of this are worked out in Prv. 17:5; Job 31:13-15.

[84] Cf., e.g., Is. 5:1-7.

[85] Köhler, 119 makes perhaps too sharp and irreconcilable an antithesis out of the resultant tension in the OT statements.

[86] A. Marmorstein, The Old Rabbinic Doctrine of God, I (1927), 74-76. ברא in Gn. 1 means "to call into life" as distinct from עשה "to prepare," jChag., 2, 77d, 5 ff.; Str.-B., III, 245.

[87] Cf., e.g., מעשה בראשית == "cosmos," Str.-B., III, 246. עשה for "to make" as distinct from נתן and שים, "to make" someone into something, Gn. r., 39 on 12:2 (p. 44b, Vilna). עֹשֶׂה == "Creator," Damasc., 2, 21 (Schechter).

[88] Tanch. בשלח 2 (p. 54, Buber); Marmorstein, 95, R. Eleazar b. R. Jose ha-Gelili.

[89] Tannaitic and Amorean, Marmorstein, 86 f.

[90] Cf. Chag., 2, 1, and further examples in Marmorstein, 98.

[91] M. Ex. on 15:11 (Str.-B., I, 733); Gn. r., 1 on 1:1 (p. 3, Vilna) (dispute between the schools of Shammai and Hillel) == bChag., 12a; Gn. r., 12 on 2:4.

[92] Str.-B., III, 245 f.

[93] Ab. R. Nat., 37 (Str.-B., III, 246c) calls, e.g., the festivals a בריה.

But it is very often used for "men," in the sing. בְּרִיָּה אַחַת "a man," [94] plur. "men," Ab., 1, 12 : (הוי) אוהב את הבריות ומקרבן לתורה (Hillel). An inscr. in the catacomb at Monteverde, Rome, reads : אֲנִיָּה חַתְנָּה דְּבַר כּוֹל־בְּרִיָּה.[95] In Rabb. lit. there is no instance of בְּרִיָּה = ἡ κτίσις as a comprehensive term for creation,[96] as in Damasc., 4, 21 (Schechter): יסוד הבריאה זכר ונקבה ברא אותם, where the context shows that בְּרִיאָה is used in this way ; cf. also 4 Esr. 7:75; S. Bar. 32:6; Ass. Mos. 10:1 and the NT.

In the pseudepigr., along with κτίζειν and ποιεῖν (both together in Apc. Sedr. [ed. M. R. James, TSt, 2, 3, 1893], 8 and Test. Abr. Rec. B, 12), we find πλάσσω (πλάσμα) used for the creation of man = יָצַר, Apc. Sedr., 3; 7; 13; Sib., 3, 24 f.; 8, 440 ff.; also Joseph. on the basis of Gn. 2:7;[97] τεχνίτης, Wis. 13:1; κτίσμα, Test. Abr. Rec. B, 13; Ep. Ar., 17; Sib., 4, 16.

κτίσις means "creation" in Ps. Sol. 8:7: ἀπὸ κτίσεως οὐρανοῦ καὶ γῆς; Sib., 8, 439; Ass. Mos. 1:2, 17; 12:4; Jos. Bell., 6, 437. Elsewhere, esp. LXX → 1028, it means "creation" in the sense of what is created, Ep. Ar., 136; 139; Test. R. 2:3, 9; L. 4:1; N. 2:3; cf. Eth. En. 18:1; 36:4; 75:1; 82:7; 84:2; 93:10; 4 Esr.; Ass. Mos. 1:13; 10:1; Apc. Esr. 7:5, though not Joseph.[98] God is often called "Creator" in the apocr. and pseudepigr.[99] Since in Heb. the part. בֹּרֵא has to take the place of the subst., it is not surprising that ὁ κτίσας is commonly used along with the more Gk. κτίστης; thus Joseph. does not use the subst. of God,[100] but often has ὁ κτίσας : Ant., 4, 314; Bell., 3, 354, 356, 369, 379; 5, 377. In contrast he does not call God the δημιουργήσας ἀνθρώπινα καὶ θεῖα, but δημιουργὸν ἀνθρωπίνων καὶ θείων, Ant., 7, 380; cf. 1, 155, 272. δημιουργός comes from the Gk. world ; with its derivatives it is also found in Test. N. 3:4; Test. Job (ed. M. R. James, TSt, 5, 1 [1897]), 39; Apc. Esr. (ed. C. Tischendorf, Apocalypses Apocryphae [1866]), p. 32 M.

2. God as Creator of the World.

In later Judaism, both in Rabb. and pseudepigr. writings, it is clearly stated that God alone created the world by His Word, i.e., that He called it into existence from nothing, that He is thus its Lord and King, and that He has appointed its beginning and end in omniscience and omnipotence. This faith in the Creator separates Israel from the Gentiles, Ep. Ar., 139.[101]

It is not always clear, of course, that creation is out of nothing. One cannot be sure what ideas lay behind the LXX translation of Gn. 1:2 : ἡ δὲ γῆ ἦν ἀόρατος καὶ ἀκατασκεύαστος, whether Gk. philosophical conceptions of the existence of what is unfashioned, or an interpretation of Gn. 1:1 in terms of the creation of chaos (in spite of v. 8). In the OT apocrypha we find two lines of thought. In Wis. 11:17 God's almighty hand is given the predicate κτίσασα τὸν κόσμον ἐξ ἀμόρφου ὕλης, whereas

---

[94] Cant. r., 1 on 1:3.

[95] N. Müller and N. A. Bees, Die Inschr. d. jüdischen Katakombe am Monteverde zu Rom (1919), No. 142. J. B. Frey, Corpus Inscriptionum Iudaicarum, I (1936), No. 290, reads אניה חתנה דבר קלבריה "Annia, gendre de Bar-Calabria."

[96] Str.-B., III, 246 n.

[97] Schl. Theol. d. Judt., 3, n. 2.

[98] Ibid., 3.

[99] Examples in Bousset-Gressm., 360, n. 2. On the whole question cf. the collection in R. Marcus, "Divine Names and Attributes in Hellenistic Jewish Lit.," Proceedings of the American Academy for Jewish Research, 1931-32 (1932), 43-120, esp. 86 f.

[100] Schl. Theol. d. Judt., 3. There is another use in Ap., 2, 39.

[101] The power of belief in the Creator of the world and in the God who acts in history is a reason why the authors of magic lit. adopted OT expressions in their search for conceptions of a god of power.

in 2 Macc. 7:28 we read : οὐκ ἐξ ὄντων [102] ἐποίησεν αὐτὰ (sc. τὸν οὐρανὸν καὶ τὴν γῆν καὶ τὰ ἐν αὐτοῖς πάντα) ὁ θεός. The Wis. verse shows clearly that the idea of creation out of nothing is remote, [103] but like the passage as a whole this ref. to the fashioning of the world is meant to display God's omnipotence ; 4 verses later we read : τὸ γὰρ μεγάλως ἰσχύειν σοι πάρεστιν πάντοτε, καὶ κράτει βραχίονός σου τίς ἀντιστήσεται; ὅτι ὡς ῥοπὴ ἐκ πλαστίγγων (the tip on the tongue of the scale) ὅλος ὁ κόσμος ἐναντίον σου (11:21 ff.). Remarkable speculations on creation out of non-being and out of the invisible are found in Slav. En. 24:2 ff. But creation out of nothing is plainly taught in S. Bar. 14:17; 21:4 ff. and 48:2 ff. The same is true of Sib., 3, 20 ff. when it says that the "mighty mother Tethys" and the nights were created by God, for Tethys and Νύξ were for the Gks. cosmogonic principles of chaos. Intentionally rejecting Gk. speculations, the verse thus maintains that God created chaos also. A similar strand may be seen in Eth. En. 69:16. By God's oath heaven was established before the world was created. If the very place of God's dwelling is created, no room is left for the idea of anything existing from the beginning. [104]

In the Rabb. writings, too, some passages seem to speak against creation out of nothing. Thus Resh Laqish [105] tells us that God said He would let the world relapse into chaos if Israel did not receive the Torah : אני מחזיר...לתהו ובהו. Weber adduces [106] other speculations in which a certain autonomy and even the possibility of disobedience against God are ascribed to the creature. But in the Rabb. these are only exegetical exercises without dogmatic significance, and Weber misunderstands the Rabb. view of the organic nature of cosmic bodies (→ ἀστήρ). More important is the fact that in Jub. 2:2, 4 Esr. 6:38 ff. and Jos. Ant., 1, 27 Gn. 1:1 is understood in terms of the creation of the first day, i.e., in terms of the creation of the chaos mentioned in v. 2. This is the point at issue in the debate between a philosopher and R. Gamaliel. [107] The philosopher grants that the Jewish God is a great artist (צַיָּר) but claims that He had good materials to help Him : רוח, מים, תהומות, תהו, בהו, חשך. Gamaliel proves from Gn. 1:1 that their creation (בריאה) is narrated in Scripture. Elsewhere, and already in the time of the Mishnah, speculations which go behind creation, like those which seek the time of the consummation or which ask what is above heaven or below earth, are sharply rejected. [108] This means that the Rabbis regarded such questions as useless and dangerous. It is enough to say that God created the world and all that therein is. How alien to the Rabbis was the idea of a pre-existence of matter may be seen from speculation on pre-existent things, which in part, e.g., the throne of God or the Torah, were really created, and in part arose in the thoughts of God. The significant thing here is not merely that there is no matter or chaos. The fact that even God's throne was created, though it was before the world, shows that the Rabb. distinguished between God and absolutely

---

[102] On the position of the negation v. Bl.-Debr.⁶ § 433, 3. Hence οὐκ ἐξ ὄντων = ἐξ οὐκ ὄντων, and the deductions of Scharbau, 25 are dubious.

[103] Couard, 74 f.; for a different view Frey, 36-39.

[104] Worth mentioning are some alterations of the Mas. in the LXX. At Is. 54:16 the adding of a negative expressly rejects the figure of a workman as a comparison of God's creating with man's. At ψ 88:48 the ref. to man's corruptibility in the Mas. is set aside with the question : μὴ γὰρ ματαίως ἔκτισας πάντας τοὺς υἱοὺς τῶν ἀνθρώπων; at ψ 92 the LXX adds the superscription εἰς τὴν ἡμέραν τοῦ προσαββάτου, ὅτε κατῴκισται ἡ γῆ· αἶνος ᾠδῆς τῷ Δαυιδ. The content of the psalm is that God has assumed His lordship ; this happened at creation. At 1 Εσδρ. 6:12 the "God of heaven and earth" of the Mas. (Ezr. 5:11) becomes κύριος ὁ κτίσας τὸν οὐρανὸν καὶ τὴν γῆν. The expansion is because of the opposition to polytheism.

[105] bShab., 88a; Cant. r. on 7:1.

[106] 200-203.

[107] Gn. r., 1 on 1:1 (p. 2a, Vilna).

[108] Chag., 2, 1; Gn. r., 1 on 1:1 (p. 2b, Vilna).

everything conceivable as between Creator and creature. The divine name קדמונו של עולם is also to be taken in this sense. [109]

Testimony to creation by the Word is to be found in the apocr. (Jdt. 16:14; Wis. 9:1; 11:25; Bar. 3:33) and pseudepigr. (Jub. 12:4; 4 Esr. 3:4; 6:38 ff.; S. Bar. 14:17; 21:4 ff.; 48:2 ff.; 56:4; Sib., 3, 20) as well as the Rabb. For the latter one may refer to the Tann. name of God: "He spake, and the world came into being" (מי שאמר והיה העולם), [110] or to Mishnah passages like Ber., 6, 2 (שהכל נהיה בדברו) and Ab., 5, 1. In M. Ex. on 15:17 [111] we read that when God created He did so only by the Word, and the meaning of Ps. 33:6 is explained by an Amorean to be that God tirelessly created לא בעמל ולא ביגיעה ברא הקדוש. [112] Joseph. agrees with this: [113] ברוך הוא את עולמו אלא בדבר השם וכבר שמים נעשו ταῦτα (light, heaven, earth etc.) θεὸς ἐποίησεν οὐ χερσὶν οὐ πόνοις οὔ τινων συνεργασομένων ἐπιδεηθείς, ἀλλ' αὐτοῦ θελήσαντος καλῶς ἦν εὐθὺς γεγονότα. [114]

As in the OT, no essential distinction is made between creation and preservation, cf. Sir. 42:15-43:33. Often with a view to exhortation reference is made to the fact that nature follows faithfully the original command of God, Sir. 16:26 ff.; Prayer of Man. 2 ff. (God has bound the sea); Ps. Sol. 18:10; Test. N. 3:4; Eth. En. 2:1 ff.; 5:2 ff.; 69:16 ff.; 83:11; 101:6-8; in the latter passages it is mentioned in the same connection that God withholds rain, and S. Bar. 48:2 ff. applies the creation terms "summon" and "obey" to the course of the times. In Eth. En. 5:2 we read that everything takes place, not as God has commanded, but as He commands, cf. 84:3: "Thou hast created and rulest all things." [115]

The thought occurs in the Rabb. that God renews the works of creation every morning; [116] a Rabb. name for God is שומר עולמים. [117] It is not surprising that one can allude to two opposing Rabb. statements: M. Ex. on 31:17: [118] God rests = He draws breath, from עבורה or דין (world government)? The answer is: יאין הדין בטל מלפניו לעולם On the other side, however, the Rabb. argue whether at the blessing of the bread one should use מוציא: "He who has brought forth bread out of the earth," or המוציא, which means the same thing but acc. to the Tannaite R. Nehemja is to be construed in the present — a view which did not prevail. [119] If there is an element of casuistry here, a later statement (Eka r. on 3:23) brings out the theological importance of the question for faith. That God creates afresh every morning shows that He will raise the dead or redeem Israel. Related is the statement of R. Jochanan (bTaan., 2a) that God has not entrusted the three keys (→ κλείς, 744 f.) of rain, birth and the resurrection of the dead to anyone else. This implies the presence of the divine operation in every act, and it is

---

[109] Marmorstein, 97 f. For the sake of completeness it should be mentioned that Rabb., too, found difficulty with Gn. 1:2. Gn. r., 1 on 1:1 (p. 1d, Vilna) records that R. Huna said in the name of Bar Qappara that if Gn. 1:2 were not written we could not state that the earth was created out of תהו ובהו.

[110] Str.-B., II, 310; Marmorstein, 89 and 7, n. 1.

[111] Str.-B., III, 671.

[112] Gn. r., 3 on 1:3 (cf. also the text, ad loc., ed. Theodor, p. 19, line 6); par. 12 on 2:4 etc. For other Rabb. instances of creation by the Word, v. Str.-B., III, 671; II, 304 f.

[113] Ap., II, 192.

[114] Creation by the Spirit is essentially the same, Ass. Mos., Fragment from Gelasius Cyzicenus in the ed. by C. Clemen (KlT, 10 [1904]), 15.

[115] Cf. Wis. 11:25; Ep. Ar., 16, 132 and 157.

[116] Prayer יוֹצֵר אוֹר (ed. W. Staerk, KlT, 58 [1910], 4).

[117] Marmorstein, 103.

[118] Bacher Tannaiten, I¹ (1884), 85, n. 1.

[119] bBer., 38a.

also an indication that in the Judaism of the time many angelic powers could interpose themselves between God and nature. [120]

The significance of belief in creation for the piety of later Judaism may be seen clearly from the role it plays. It is surprising how often the Creator figures in prayer, whether in the apocr. (Εσθ. 4:17c; Jdt. 9:5 f., 12; 13:18; 16:14; 3 Macc. 2:3; Prayer of Man. 2 ff.; Δα. 4:37), the pseudepigr. (Ps. Sol. 18:10 ff.; Eth. En. 81:3; 84:2 ff.; Jub. 25:11; S. Bar. 21:4 ff.), Joseph. (Ant., 1, 272; 7, 380) or the Rabb. (Prayer of Eighteen Petitions, Qaddish, etc.). Reference is made to the Creator both in praise and thanksgiving and also in petition and supplication — a sign that belief in the Creator was indispensable to the living piety of later Judaism. In distress and persecution by superior powers appeal was made to the One who in spite of all appearances is omnipotent because He is the Creator, and if the time of affliction provoked prayer for the coming of the end of the world, a particular appeal was then made to the Creator's power (S. Bar. 21:4 ff.), since it was firmly believed by Judaism that the Creator, who is also powerfully at work in history, has set creation its goal, Eth. En. 39:11; 4 Esr. 6:1 ff., esp. 6:6. The one who prays proves himself before the eye of the omniscient Creator, Εσθ. 4:17c d, and when salvation comes it looses the tongue to give thanks to the God who with His help has again displayed His creative power, Jdt. 16:14. But in particular the thought of creation establishes the obligation of obedience, Jdt. 16:14; 4 Macc. 11:5; Eth. En. 5:2 ff.; Damasc. 2:21 (Schechter). In Ab. R. Nat., 16, 5 the commandment: "Thou shalt love thy neighbour as thyself," is presented with the "great oath": "I am God who hath created thee"; the Creator is the One who may command obedience. Joseph. bases the biblical prohibition of suicide on the reference to God as the Creator of man, Bell., 3, 369 and 379; and jBer., 7d, line 61 states that we are created to do Thy will. [121] The fact that God is Creator is greatly emphasised as a ground of distinction from idols (Δα. 4:37; Βηλ 5; Ep. Ar., 136 and 139; Jub. 12:4, 19; Jos. Ant., 1, 155). Creation shows that God is the living God as distinct from dead idols. Acc. to legend (Jub. 12) Abraham can attain of himself to knowledge of the Creator. This is new, and is linked with the stress on righteous conduct. In the Prayer of Eighteen Petitions, however, the starting-point of all confession and prayer is still the God of the fathers rather than God the Creator. In 4 Esr. (5:33; 8:8 ff., 45, 47; 11:46; cf. Apc. Sedrach [ed. M. R. James, TSt, 2, 3, 1893], 13) appeal is often made to the fact that God loves His creature and will spare it as such. Similarly, Joseph. points out that God, the Creator of the Jews, will also be their Avenger if wrong is done them; [122] this is a development beyond the OT, though traces of it may be seen already in the LXX, → II, 638.

In the struggles which after the Syrian period often posed a radical threat to the continuation of the existence of the Jewish people, decisive help was found in faith in the God who as Creator confronts creation with absolute superiority in His living omnipotence and omniscience. [123] Hence the apocalyptic writings, which wrestle with the interpretation of history, emphasise the transcendence of the Creator, Eth. En. 84:2 ff.; Ass. Mos. 12:4.

3. The World as God's Creation.

That this world, as God's creation, is absolutely dependent on Him, and is known and directed by Him, has been seen already. [124] Created, creation is not God, and it is

---

[120] E.g., Gn. r., 10 on 2:1: R. Simon (Amorean): Every plant has in heaven its starry image (מזל) which causes it to grow.

[121] Str.-B., IV, 478bb. It is no accident that the obligation of obedience is based on God's name as Father, e.g., Ab., 5, 20.

[122] Bell., 5, 377. Hellen. influence on Joseph. may be seen in the use of δημιουργός and also in the impersonal γένεσις τῶν ὅλων of God, Ant., 7, 380.

[123] Cf. the previously mentioned verses from Da., Jdt., 4 Esr. and S. Bar.

[124] Cf. also Sir. 39:19; Wis. 11:25; Εσθ. 4:17c; Eth. En. 9:5.

not to be worshipped, for Judaism ascribes obedience, i.e., a personal function, to all parts of nature.

The nature of the world determines its meaning. Later Judaism spoke plainly of this. It lies in the Torah, i.e., in God's will. Acc. to bPes., 54a seven things were created before the world ; the first was the Torah. If later there is doubt as to the sequence and number, [125] the Torah always occupies the first place, and emphasis is thereby laid on the fact that, along with the throne of glory, it is really created, whereas the other things are only considered. It is already a Tannaitic tradition that without the Torah the world would not have been created [126] or come into being. [127] In Ass. Mos. 1:12 we read : *creavit enim orbem terrarum propter legem* [128] *suam*. In the pre-Maccabean period the same thought is recorded of Simon the Just in the form that the world rests (עמד) on three things, the Torah, the cultus, and demonstrations of love. [129] This is, then, a basic principle of Judaism. Along with it, in greatly varied form, is the further principle that the world was created for Abraham, [130] the patriarchs, [131] Israel, [132] Moses, [133] or the righteous. [134] The point of this speculation emerges in the consideration that the world was created only that Israel might receive the Torah, [135] or that God foresaw that Israel would receive the Torah and hence created the world. [136] Thus the Torah is the objective purpose of both the creation of the world and the history of the world. This purpose could not have been fulfilled if there had not been men to receive the Torah. Hence the patriarchs and Israel are among the things which pre-exist. The point of creation, then, is to provide a setting for the doing of God's will. [137] Only Slav. En. 65:2 ff. shows any basic divergence. Here this world and its temporality are created in order that man may know his time, count his life and consider his sins. In this passage one may see a rift in the world which the other statements overlook.

This raises the question whether the fall finds any place in this understanding. The six or seven pre-existent things, the Torah, the throne of God, the patriarchs, Israel, the earthly sanctuary, the name of the Messiah and penitence, accompany world history from its planning to its consummation in the Messianic kingdom. God's will is done already in this world and God's abode is on it. Bondage to Rome, which will be ended by the Messiah, still remains, and this is based on Israel's sin. If all Israel would grasp the envisaged possibility of repentance, the time of salvation would come. Such a con-sistent view of history hardly allows of any reference to a fallen creation. What man

---

[125] E.g., Gn. r., 1 on 1:1.

[126] *Loc. cit.*: R. Benaja : העולם ומלואו לא נברא אלא בזכות התורה.

[127] R. Eleazar (Tann.), bNed., 32a : אילמלא תורה לא נתקיימו שמים וארץ.

[128] MSS *plebem*.

[129] Ab., 1, 2.

[130] The oldest Rabb. example is Gn. r., 12 on 2:4 (R. Joshua b. Qorcha, c. 150): בהבראם in Gn. 2:4 is equal to באברהם (the same letters !) = בזכותו של אברהם (בזכות) not through the merit but for the sake of, → n. 126 : בזכות התורה.

[131] S. Bar. 21:24; Ex. r., 15 on 12:17.

[132] 4 Esr. 6:55, 59; 7:11; Jub. 16:26; Gn. r., 1 on 1:1, tradition in the name of R. Shemuel b. R. Jiçchaq.

[133] Gn. r., 1 on 1:1, R. Berechja.

[134] S. Bar. 15:7; Tann. bYoma, 38b, R. Eleazar : אפילו בשביל צדיק אחד עולם נברא.

[135] bShab., 88a.

[136] Ex. r., 40, 1 on 31:1 f., R. Tanchuma b. Abba (later Amor.).

[137] In face of this plenitude of witnesses the statement of the Tann. R. b. Jochaj, that the Torah was created for Israel's sake has little weight, esp. as it is modelled on a schema in elucidation of Qoh. 1:4 (Qoh. r. on 1:4). Furthermore, the fact that the world is created generally for man (4 Esr. 8:44; S. Bar. 14:18; Qoh. r. on 1:4; Josua b. Qorcha, Tann.) cannot alter the above conclusion. Men are those who should keep the Law, and acc. to the view sketched above the Torah and those who keep it cannot be separated from one another, so that occasionally it can be said that the Torah was made for Israel as well as *vice versa*.

has lost through the fall is simply radiance of countenance, length of life and greatness of stature, and what creation has lost is fertility of the earth and trees and intensity of the heavenly lights. [138] R. Shemuel says with ref. to the expression "became corrupt" (אתקלקל): "Although all things were created in fulness, when the first man sinned they were corrupted, and they will not return to their order (תקון) until the *ben-perez* comes." [139] But for the Rabbis this corruption of nature is more a state of sickness than an alteration of being. It is not surprising, then, that the word "healing" is used of the age of salvation. [140]

If the pseudepigr. are not unanimous on this point, they are at least significantly more profound. In the Rabb. the most penetrating statement on the difference between the two worlds is that the verse Is. 64:4 : "What no eye has seen . . .," is to be referred to the coming aeon. [141] This world is unable even to supply forms by which to conceive of the next. In 4 Esr. and S. Bar. the two worlds are contrasted, and this world is condemned to perish because the relation to sin is inherent in it ; it is the place of evil seed, and it cannot sustain the promises given to the coming aeon. [142] S. Bar. 30:3 and Slav. En. 65:7 believe that temporality itself, which is so tied to the present aeon that its cessation would involve a whole new form of existence, will have no place in the new aeon. The pseudepigr. enable us to speak with some justification of a fallen creation, and they give to Satan and demons a more radical place than do the Rabb. [143] The expression "new creation" is here given a place of emphasis. [144] Between the two aeons 4 Esr. believes that there will be a return of the world to the silence of primal time (7:30). But all this does not mean that the world is identified with sin. Test. N. 2:3 reads : σταθμῷ γὰρ καὶ μέτρῳ καὶ κανόνι πᾶσα ἡ κτίσις ἐγένετο. [145]

4. Man as the Creature of God.

It has been seen already (→ 1019) that as the creature of God man owes God obedience, and that the goal of his life has been appointed by the Creator. Our present task will be to discuss the influence of the OT idea of the divine likeness of man. It had a powerful effect on the Rabb. and pseudepigr. As in the OT, so here the *imago Dei* is a lasting determination of man (→ II, 393). Both man and woman are not without the שכינה, Gn. r., 8 on 1:26. The decisive point in the likeness is דְּיָצֶה; [146] speech is an expression of it which puts man on a level with, or even above, ministering angels. [147] At Gn. 2:7 Tg. O. and Tg. J. I have רוח ממללא for נפש חיה. Sometimes we find the view that the divine likeness embraces something mysterious and ineffable which is not exhausted in natural endowment but is won or lost in man's conduct: "If man is worthy, it is said to him, thou dost take precedence of ministering angels, but if not, then it is

---

[138] Str.-B., III, 247.

[139] Gn. r., 12 on 2:4; R. Shemuel c. 260.

[140] Amor. Gn. r., 10 on 2:1: Is. 30:26 : He shall heal the wound of his blow, is referred to the world : מחץ מכתו של עולם ירפא. Gn. r., 20 on 3:15 : לעתיד לבא הכל מתרפאין. Cf. also Str.-B., III, 247-255.

[141] Str.-B., IV, 828.

[142] 4 Esr. 4:27, 29. Creation was judged after Adam's fall, 7:11.

[143] → II, 12 ff.; 75 ff.

[144] 4 Esr. 7:75 (6:16); S. Bar. 32:6 (40:3); 44:12; 57:2; Jub. 1:29; 4:26; 19:25; Eth. En. 45:4 f.; 72:1; 91:16; Apc. Abr. 17; Sib. (3, 82); 5, 273; cf. Test. L. 4:1; 4 Esr. 13:26.

[145] Cf. also Couard, 75 f. and on the whole subject W. Foerster, "Die Erlösungshoffnung des Spätjudt." in *Morgenland, Heft* 28 (1936), 24-37.

[146] Ab. R. Nat., 37; Str.-B., III, 246.

[147] Gn. r., 8, 11 on 1:27; Pesikt., 34a, Str.-B., III, 681.

said to him, even a fly, a gnat, an earthworm, takes precedence of thee." [148] The divine likeness is a proof of God's love. [149]

The significance of the divine likeness is developed in two directions. On the one side it means that all men equally are confronted by the demands of God. None has any advantage. [150] If Israel accepts the Law and the Gentiles do not, if one Israelite keeps it and another does not, this is a free decision. On the other side, the divine likeness is an ethical motive in conduct towards one neighbour (cf. already the Wisdom lit. of the OT) and indeed all men. It is a reason for honouring men, Slav. En. 44:1 ff. Ben Azzai expressly says that Gn. 5:1 is a greater principle than the commandment of love. [151] If in 4 Esr. 6:8-10 and the Rabb. Esau is a name for Rome, it expresses both the relation of Israel to the Gentiles by creation and also their distinction in a free decision of the will either for God or against Him.

Acc. to the Rabb. the fall of Adam did not essentially alter man's existence. [152] This is clear in teaching on the evil impulse. This goes back to the time of Sir. (15:14 : אלהים מבראשית ברא האדם ויתנהו ביד יצרו; καὶ ἀφῆκεν αὐτὸν ἐν χειρὶ διαβουλίου αὐτοῦ). Already in the Mishnah there is ref. to the good and evil impulse, Ber., 9, 5. The best explanation is offered in Gn. r., 9 on 1:31: The words "and behold, it was very good," refer to the evil impulse, for if this were not present men would not build houses, marry, beget children or engage in business. We have here self-evident and natural human strivings which must be controlled and which, if not, will lead to sin. (The good impulse can be equated with the voice of conscience.) There is thus an evil impulse to idolatry, one to unchastity, or to resisting the commandments of God. The decisive pt. for the Rabb. is that God created the evil impulse [153] and that with it He also created the Law to counteract it. [154] Once again, as always in the Rabb., the uniformity of the total world view is thus maintained without a break. Creation as it now is does not differ essentially from God's creation. It has been disturbed, but not essentially altered, by the forces of evil. There is some contradiction in the expectation that one day God will destroy the evil impulse before the eyes of the righteous.

In the pseudepigr. a new mood is in many respects dominant. 4 Esr. begins with the teaching that God created Adam body and soul, but that Adam transgressed the one commandment given to him and that God thus passed sentence of death upon him. The cause of Adam's fall is an evil heart (3:21). It is not said that God created this until we come to 4:30 : "A little grain of evil seed was sown in Adam's heart at the beginning." But this is not quite the same as the creation of the evil impulse by God. The complaining question of 4 Esr. is why God did not prevent transgression (3:8) and take away the evil heart. An alteration of the heart is promised the dwellers on earth in the last time (6:26) when evil will be destroyed and corruption vanquished (6:27 f.; cf. 8:53). In the pseudepigr. generally the question of the origin of evil plays a role different from that which it has in the Rabb. The fall of Adam is always a torturing event, [155] the story of the fall of angels in Gn. 6:1 ff. is greatly elaborated, and in the depiction of judgment on them the sense of the burden which this fall has brought on men finds vivid expression.

---

[148] Gn. r., 8, 1 on 1:26; Moore, I, 452.

[149] Ab., 3, 14 (R. Aqiba); cf. Sir. 17:1 ff.

[150] T. Sanh., 8, 4, Str.-B., II, 744.

[151] S. Lv. קדושים 4, 12 on 19:18; Bacher Tannaiten, I¹, 420, n. 1; jNed., 41c M; Moore, I, 446 and n. 5.

[152] Moore, I, 479.

[153] S. Dt., 32 on 6:5; Gn. r., 14, 4 on 2:7.

[154] S. Dt., 45 on 11:19: God to Israel : בני בראתי לכם יצר הרע בראתי לכם תורה תבלין, Moore, I, 481, n. 2.

[155] The ref. to Adam, which is meant as consolation, is also tormenting for R. Johanan b. Zakkai, Ab. RN, 14, Str.-B., IV, 604.

Jub. 5 depicts the fall of angels. They are bound in the depths of earth and their children are extirpated, for God makes (5:12) "for all his creatures a new and righteous nature, that according to their whole nature they should no more sin to all eternity, and that they should be righteous." In terms of what follows, this does not imply the impossibility of sinning, but the possibility of not sinning. The fallen angels were obviously regarded as superior in strength, and in union with them the nature of man was changed. Hence one can speak of a fallen humanity. The consequences of this fall, however, have been set aside by a new creative act of God. But then for the second time (10:1 ff.) unclean demons come on the race with overwhelming power and begin to seduce it. At Noah's request these demons are bound, but the intercession of Mastema secure the freedom of one tenth of them. The power of Satan and demons is thus limited, and perhaps the whole point of the speculation is that only a small part of the race, Abraham and his seed, can free itself from the seducing power of demons. Even Abraham suffers many blows of fate on his way to full conversion (23:23-26), but these are then fully healed, and Satan and evil will be no more. [156] Only through special and painful experiences, then, will a portion of the race find its way to God. In spite of many differences, this answer of Jub. to the question of fallen humanity is similar to that of 4 Esr., for which the number of the righteous is painfully small, though there are such, and they are for this reason all the more precious, 4 Esr. 7:45-61.

Although a uniform view of the world and men prevailed among the Rabb., they, too, spoke of the renewal of man and of a new creation. Man is new, or a new creation, when the relation between him and God becomes new. This is primarily true of the proselyte, who on conversion is like a new-born child. [157] The image of creation is not far off. Thus in Cant. r., 1 on 1:3 we read that "he who has brought a man under the wings of the Shekinah, to him it is reckoned as if he had made (ברא), fashioned (יצר) and formed (רקם) him." It is then particularly true of the introduction of the sign of circumcision : By circumcision Abraham was made a new creature, Gn. r., 39 on 12:2, [158] and R. Berechja explains explicitly that the term is not נתן or שׂים, but עשׂה, The same is also true of any renewal of the relation of God and man by penitence and forgiveness. These go together. God's forgiveness is available for those who are converted. [159] The action of God and that of man are on the same plane. Hence the term "creation" is not to be taken literally. It shows, however, that the OT word of forgiveness was not an empty one.

Nevertheless, if there are certain indications of a dualistic division of man, in later Judaism there can be no question of a true dualism or of hostility to the body, bSanh., 91a b. [160]

D. δημιουργέω and κτίζω in Greek and the Linguistic Contribution of the LXX.

In LXX Gk. the main terms used to denote God's creative work are the simple ποιεῖν (= עשׂה) and words like πλάσσειν (= יצר) or θεμελιοῦν (= יסד) which cor-respond to Hebrew metaphors. In addition, the LXX had at its disposal esp. δημιουργός and its derivatives. This word group was constantly used by the pagan world to express

---

[156] The same hope occurs in Eth. En. 91:14 ff.; 92:5; 100:5; 107:1.

[157] R. Jose (c. 150) bJeb., 48a; bJeb., 22a. Cf. K. H. Rengstorf on Jeb., 11, 2a (Giessener Mischna, 1929), 138 f.

[158] Str.-B., II, 421.

[159] S. Dt., 30 on 3:29; Ex. r., 15, 6 on 12:1 f.; jRH, 59c, lines 60 f.; cf. also Str.-B., II, 422c. Ex. 4:12 : God gives Moses the power of speech, is expounded in Tanch. שמות § 18 on Ex. 4:12 (p. 5b, Buber) as אני עושה אותן בריה חדשה.

[160] Cf. on this R. Meyer.

its views on the formation of the world. [161] It is interesting, however, that not even on one occasion did the LXX use this group for the creative work of God (→ δημιουργός). Instead it chose a word group — κτίζω and its derivatives — whose use in this sense is new. To understand this, we must investigate the range of meaning and the social level of the two groups and their relation to the Greek and biblical views of creation.

The strict meaning of δημιουργός is "one who does something specific for the whole body." In Homer it is used of the seer, doctor, builder, herald and singer, then for the one who makes specific articles for common use, i.e., the craftsman, whether he be potter, sculptor, painter, shipbuilder, weaver, dyer, apothecary, or cook. The δημιουργός is the specialist as distinct from the layman, [162] the one who fashions or manufactures something. In course of time emphasis came to rest on the element of direct workmanship on a material already there. Hence Aristot. can say (Pol., VIII, 4, p. 1325b, 40-1326a, 1): ὥσπερ γὰρ καὶ τοῖς ἄλλοις δημιουργοῖς, οἷον ὑφάντῃ καὶ ναυπηγῷ, δεῖ τὴν ὕλην ὑπάρχειν ἐπιτηδείαν οὖσαν πρὸς τὴν ἐργασίαν ... Fig. the word is used of the author of a direct effect: κακία is the δημιουργός of a miserable life [163] as its direct cause, or the πολιτικός is δημιουργός εὐνομίας καὶ δίκης, which arise by reason of his activity. [164] The movements of the sun and moon are δημιουργοί of day and night. [165] Even when the sense can approximate to that of inventor, it implies the first to make. Thus Plut. [166] says that Athens had no celebrated δημιουργός of epic and lyric poetry, and if in another place [167] the same writer speaks of the δημιουργοί of feasts, he does not mean those who appointed them, but those who won victories which constituted the occasions for them. Their work made the feast, whereas the κτίστης appointed it by his will and command. It is thus plain in what sense Plato can describe μαντική as the φιλίας θεῶν καὶ ἀνθρώπων δημιουργός, [168] or Plutarch nature as δημιουργός of sicknesses. [169]

Later δημιουργός was restricted to artisans who were not so highly esteemed socially. There are many proofs of this. Aristot. says: [170] παρ' ἐνίοις οὐ μετεῖχον οἱ δημιουργοί τὸ παλαιὸν ἀρχῶν, πρὶν δῆμον γενέσθαι τὸν ἔσχατον. τὰ μὲν οὖν ἔργα τῶν ἀρχομένων οὕτως οὐ δεῖ τὸν ἀγαθὸν οὐδὲ τὸν πολιτικὸν οὐδὲ τὸν πολίτην τὸν ἀγαθὸν μανθάνειν, εἰ μή ποτε χρείας χάριν αὐτῷ πρὸς αὐτόν. Plato [171] divides citizens into γεωργοί and δημιουργοί, προπολεμοῦντες and ἄρχοντες. Plut. [172] refers to a constitution of Theseus in which the δημιουργοί come last, their only advantage being that they are most numerous; in other places, too, the scorn of the Gks. for the δημιουργός is evident. [173] The same attitude may be seen in Sir. 38:24 ff. It applies even to artists. Thus Aristodemus [174] admired, e.g., Polycletus because of his ἀνδριαντοποιία, but Plut. makes clear what is meant by differentiating [175] between

---

[161] Plat. Tim., → 1004, and then more commonly in Neo-Platonism.
[162] Plat. Ion, 531c: περὶ ὁμιλιῶν πρὸς ἀλλήλους ἀνθρώπων ἀγαθῶν τε καὶ κακῶν καὶ ἰδιωτῶν καὶ δημιουργῶν (laymen-experts). From the original sense of public activity δημιουργός (δημιουργέω) becomes also a sacral (e.g., CIG, 4415b, priests) and a political word (ὁ δημιουργῶν and ὁ στρατηγῶν as compared with the rest, Artemid., II, 22 [official person]).
[163] Plut. Ser. Num. Pun., 9 (II, 554b) (with τεκταίνεσθαι as verbal concept).
[164] Plut. Praec. Ger. Reip., 13 (II, 807c).
[165] Plut. Superst., 12 (II, 171a).
[166] Bellone An Pace Clariores Fuerint Athenienses, 5 (II, 348b).
[167] Suav. Viv. Epic., 18 (II, 1099 f.).
[168] Symp., 188d.
[169] Quaest. Conv., IX, 1 (II, 731b).
[170] Pol., III, 4, p. 1277b, 1-6.
[171] Praechter, 270.
[172] Thes., 25 (I, 11c d).
[173] Pericl., 1 (I, 152e f.).
[174] Xenoph. Mem., I, 4, 3.
[175] Pericl., 1 (I, 152e).

admiration of the works and contempt for those who created them. This applies not merely to players on the flute or those who make ointments, but also quite expressly to artists : οὐδεὶς εὐφυὴς νέος ἢ τὸν ἐν Πίσῃ θεασάμενος Δία γενέσθαι Φειδίας ἐπεθύμησεν ἢ τὴν Ἥραν τὴν ἐν Ἄργει Πολύκλειτος, οὐδ' Ἀνακρέων ἢ Φιλητᾶς ἢ Ἀρχίλοχος ἡσθεὶς αὐτῶν τοῖς ποιήμασιν. Οὐ γὰρ ἀναγκαῖον, εἰ τέρπει τὸ ἔργον ὡς χαρίεν, ἄξιον σπουδῆς εἶναι τὸν εἰργασμένον. [176] If δημιουργός is also used in Gk. religion and philosophy for the power which fashions the world, this is because the δημιουργὸς τοῦ κόσμου has made the world out of existing material as the ordinary δημιουργός does his products out of his materials. The essential thing for the Gks. is the bringing of the world out of ἀταξία into a κόσμος. Plut. again states his view : Βέλτιον οὖν Πλάτωνι πειθομένους τὸν μὲν κόσμον ὑπὸ θεοῦ γεγονέναι λέγειν καὶ ᾄδειν· ὁ μὲν γὰρ κάλλιστος τῶν γεγονότων, ὁ δὲ ἄριστος τῶν αἰτιῶν· τὴν δὲ οὐσίαν καὶ ὕλην ἐξ ἧς γέγονεν, οὐ γενομένην, ἀλλὰ ὑποκειμένην ἀεὶ τῷ δημιουργῷ, εἰς διάθεσιν καὶ τάξιν αὐτῆς, καὶ πρὸς αὐτὸν ἐξομοίωσιν ὡς δυνατὸν ἦν ἐμπαρασχεῖν. Οὐ γὰρ ἐκ τοῦ μὴ ὄντος ἡ γένεσις, ἀλλ' ἐκ τοῦ μὴ καλῶς μηδ' ἱκανῶς ἔχοντος, ὡς οἰκίας καὶ ἱματίου καὶ ἀνδριάντος. [177] Along similar lines Christian Gnosticism called the one who fashioned the world δημιουργός, in spite of the biblical tradition. The LXX avoided the word precisely because the God of the OT is not just the one who fashioned the world.

The verb δημιουργεῖν is similarly used for workmanship. The τέκτων makes (δημιουργεῖν) the spindle [178] or the πηδάλιον. [179]

κτίζω [180] is used by Hom. for "to make a land habitable," "to settle it," "to populate it" (affected object), Od., 11, 263 : Amphion and Zethos οἳ πρῶτοι Θήβης ἕδος ἔκτισαν ἑπταπύλοιο; Hdt., I, 149 : οἱ Αἰολέες χώρην μὲν ἔτυχον κτίσαντες ἀμείνω Ἰώνων. It then means "to build" or "establish" a city (effected object), Il., 20, 216 : Δάρδανος κτίσσε δὲ Δαρδανίην, Hdt., I, 168 : ἐνθαῦτα ἔκτισαν πόλιν Ἄβδηρα. It is common in this sense in NT times, e.g., in Plut. Thes., 2 (I, 1d); 20 (I, 9a); 26 (I, 12d); Romulus, 9 (I, 22d); 12 (I, 24a); Camillus, 20 (I, 139b); Nicias, 5 (I, 526b); Pomp., 39 (I, 639e); Praec. Ger. Reip., 17 (II, 814b); Col., 33 (II, 1126 f.) ("to build up again"). It is also used of the foundation or establishment of groves, temples, theatres, baths, cemeteries, or the institution of festivals or games. In contrast to δημιουργέω, the verb in this case does not denote the actual execution (building etc.), but the basic and decisive resolve to establish, found or institute, which is then followed by δημιουργεῖν. To be sure, κτίζω can also be used for the execution, esp. in the tragic dramatists, Soph. Trach., 898 : κτίσαι suicide ; Aesch. Choeph., 483 f.: οὕτω γὰρ ἄν σοι δαῖτες ἔννομοι βροτῶν κτιζοίατ'. In the poetry of Aesch. τροπὴν κτίσαι corresponds to the current τροπὴν ποιεῖν (ποιεῖσθαι) [181] of prose (Empedocles says of artists that they make = κτίζοντε trees, men and cattle). [182] But this use was never popular and it tended to fade out in course of time, whereas the other aspect underwent increasing development. κτίζω is also used for invention, i.e., the basic intellectual act, [183] and for the establishment, e.g., of philosophical schools.

In NT days the word group is used particularly for the founding of cities, houses, games, and sects, and for the discovery and settlement of countries. It denotes specifically the basic intellectual and volitional act by which something comes into being, in the first instance the city. This may also be seen in the derivatives : [184] ἐγκτίζω, "to build

---

[176] Pericl., 2 (I, 153a).
[177] De Animae Procreatione in Timaeo Platonis, 5, 3 (II, 1014a b); cf. → 74.
[178] Albinus, Intro. in Platonem (ed. C. F. Hermann, Plato, 6 [1892]), 7.
[179] Plut., Maxime Cum Principibus Viris Philosophis Esse Disserendum, 4 (II, 779a).
[180] Basic Indo-Eur. meaning : "to settle," "to dwell," Walde-Pok., I, 504 [Debrunner].
[181] W. Schadewaldt, Hermes, 71 (1936), 34 [H. Schöne]. Cf. also Pind. Olymp., 9, 444 f. of Deucalion and Pyrrha : ἄτερ δ' εὐνᾶς ὁμόδαμον κτισσάσθαν λίθινον γόνον.
[182] Emped. Fr., 23 (I, 235, 6 Diels).
[183] Cf. already Soph. Oed. Col., 715.
[184] I owe this mostly to H. Schöne and the examples to Liddell-Scott.

cities"; ἐϋκτίμενος, well laid out (houses etc.); ἔϋκτιτος, "finely built"; θεόκτιτος of Athens ; νεόκτιστος, "recently built," of cities ; νεόκτιτος, "newly awakened," of ἐπιθυμία, Bacchyl., 16, 126; αὐτόκτιστος in Aesch. of self-created grottos ; φιλόκτιστος, φιλοκτίστης, "desirous of building"; κτισμός, "establishment" of a city ; κτιστεῖον, "sanctuary" of a κτίστης; κτιστόν, "building"; κτιστήρ ═ κτίστης. κτίσις, κτίσμα, κτίστης, → 1027 f. Only a few compounds are based on the sense "to make," and they are all used poetically. ἐϋκτίμενος is used in Hom. of all that "on which man's labour has been bestowed," and Hom. also uses κτιστός for "made." If it might thus appear that the LXX chose κτίζω for "to create" because of the possible equation of κτίζω and ποιέω in poetry, everyday usage is against this. [185] If we start with the sense "to found," it is obvious that from the time of Alexander the Great the term took on a special nuance. Founding is a task for the ruler, esp. the Hellenistic ruler with his autonomous glory and his approximation to divinity. Thus Philo says in Op. Mund., 17: ἐπειδὰν πόλις κτίζηται κατὰ πολλὴν φιλοτιμίαν βασιλέως ἤ τινος ἡγεμόνος αὐτοκρατοῦς ἐξουσίας μεταποιουμένου ..., the founding of a city is a matter for the αὐτοκρατὴς ἐξουσία, for the ruler does not himself build the city with his own hands (this would be δημιουργεῖν), but it is his word or will or command which causes the city to be built, and behind his will stands his real power which brings obedience (another spiritual act), → II, 563. If newly founded cities were always linked in some way with something already present, [186] the nature and extent of this link could be decided by the founder, and often the link did not amount to more than a minor juxtaposition of the old settlement and the new πόλις. The city owed its existence as πόλις to the κτίστης, who as such is the recipient of divine honours within it. [187] The dependence of Hellenistic foundations on the κτίστης is often expressed in their names ; allusions to the founder are predominant in these. [188]

In this light it is clear why the LXX preferred the word group κτίζω to the more obvious δημιουργεῖν. δημιουργεῖν suggests the craftsman and his work in the strict sense, whereas κτίζειν reminds us of the ruler at whose command a city arises out of nothing because the power of the ruler stands behind his word. δημιουργεῖν is a technical manual process, κτίζειν an intellectual and volitional.

Avoidance of δημιουργεῖν also averts a second misunderstanding. Apart from the general estimation of the craftsman in antiquity, one might have thought that δημιουργός as artist would be quite an apt term for the Creator. But artistic work has in it a strong emanatic element [189] which is not present in the biblical belief in creation. Thus Philo gives a comprehensive explanation of the difference between δημιουργός and κτίστης in Som., I, 76 : ἄλλως τε ὡς ἥλιος ἀνατείλας τὰ κεκρυμμένα τῶν σωμάτων ἐπιδείκνυται, οὕτως καὶ ὁ θεὸς τὰ πάντα γεννήσας οὐ μόνον εἰς τοὐμφανὲς ἤγαγεν, ἀλλὰ καὶ ἃ πρότερον οὐκ ἦν, ἐποίησεν, οὐ δημιουργὸς μόνον ἀλλὰ καὶ κτίστης αὐτὸς ὤν. [190]

---

[185] For Plut. cf. D. Wyttenbach, Lex Plutarcheum (1843), s.v.; for Ep. Ar. v. 36; 115; on Jos. cf. Schl. Theol. d. Judt., 3; Schl. Jk., 137, n. 1. It is worth noting that the pass. κτίζεσθαι ("to arise") occurs only in Test. XII, R. 2:4, 7; 3:1.

[186] V. Tscherikower, "Die hell. Städtegründungen von Alexander dem Grossen bis auf die Römerzeit," Philol. Suppl.-Bd., 19, 1 (1927), 128, who should be consulted on this whole subject.

[187] Ibid., 132.

[188] Ibid., 115.

[189] Scharbau, 22.

[190] In general, of course, κτίζειν is less prominent in Philo than δημιουργεῖν. This is because in him the Jewish image of the foundation of a city for God's creation is intersected by Greek ideas of the fashioner of the world. The latter influenced his ideas even more than his terminology, so that we find in him a whole series of non-biblical ideas taken from the religions around, e.g., creation by thought (Op. Mund., 24 : the νοητὴ πόλις is nothing

Of the 46 passages in which the LXX read ברא in the sense "create" (not counting Is. 4:5), only 17 have κτίζειν, and none of these is in Gn., which always uses ποιέω. Indeed, only at Dt. 4:32 do we find κτίζειν for ברא in the Pentateuch. In the prophets, apart from Dt. Is., 5 of 6 passages have κτίζειν (not Ez. 21:35). There are 20 passages in Dt. Is., and here the distribution is: κτίζειν 4 times, ποιεῖν 6, καταδείκνυμι 3, κατασκευάζω and εἰμί 2 each, no equivalent 3 (45:12; 57:19; 65:18a). In Ps. (6 times) and Qoh. (once) κτίζειν is always used. In Sir. we find κτίζειν (40:10), ποιεῖν (15:14) and ὁ κύριος (3:16 בּוֹרא). Apart from ברא, for which it is used 17 times (and once in Sir.), κτίζειν is also used for קנה (Gn. 14:19, 22; Prv. 8:22; Ιερ. 39:15 B), יסד (Ex. 9:18), יצר (Is. 22:11; 46:11; Sir. 39:28 f.; 49:14), חלק (Sir. 38:1; 39:25; 44:2), and occasionally other words (Lv. 16:16; ψ 32:9; Sir. 10:18; 38:4).

Our review shows that κτίζω is used comparatively infrequently for the divine creation in the Pentateuch, namely, 4 times, or 5 with Dt. 32:6 (A). It does not occur in the historical books, but is found 15 times in the prophetic (apart from Da.), 9 in the hagiographa, and 36 in the Apocrypha (including Δα. 4:37). It is not used in either of the creation stories. Since the Pentateuch was translated first, and the other books at varied intervals after, it would appear that the equation ברא = κτίζω, and the giving of theological significance to this Gk. term, came only when the translation of the Torah was complete. For in Lv. 16:16: τῇ σκηνῇ τοῦ μαρτυρίου τῇ ἐκτισμένῃ ἐν αὐτοῖς (שכן), and Ex. 9:18: χάλαζαν ... ἥτις τοιαύτη οὐ γέγονεν ἐν Αἰγύπτῳ ἀφ' ἧς ἡμέρας ἔκτισται (= יסד), κτίζω is used quite lit. of establishing or founding even in the sense of making or setting up. Hence it is not surprising that in Gn. 14:19, 22 κτίζω is used for קנה and in Dt. 32:6 (A) כונן is rendered κτίζω (vl. πλάσσω). The obvious conclusion is that κτίζω did not yet have its full content for the translators of the Torah. It denoted actual handiwork, as in Hag. 2:9. In 1 Εσδρ. 4:53 κτίζω does not mean the foundation of a city by a ruler but its actual (re-)building by its inhabitants, cf. Ιερ. 39:15 B* S* (ἔτι κτισθήσονται ἀγροὶ καὶ οἰκίαι καὶ ἀμπελῶνες).

The Hexapla translators use the term differently and regularly employ it for ברא. Thus it occurs in Gn. 1:1 ('Α); 1:27 ('ΑΣΘ), cf. also 7 times in Dt. Is. in 'ΑΣΘ, 40:26; 41:20; 43:7; 54:16; 57:19; 65:17, 18. In ψ 50:10 'Α uses ἀνάκτισον for the (new) creation of the heart, LXX: καρδίαν καθαρὰν κτίσον ἐν ἐμοί. In Σ Is. 43:15 κτίστης is used for ברא part. In Ez. 2:10 'Α misunderstood the Mas. and reformulated the content of the scroll. Instead of קינים = θρῆνος, "complaint," he read קינִים and translated: καὶ γεγραμμένον ἦν αὐτοῦ κτίσις καὶ ἀντίβλησις καὶ ἔσται. The book which the prophet is to swallow thus contains a depiction of creation and of what opposes it (ἀντίβλησις is a hapaxlegomenon) and what will take place (ἔσται). It is thus the kind of apocalypse current in Hellen. Judaism. In Sir. 1:14 we find as a hapaxlegomenon συγκτίζειν (cf. ψ 50:10 'Α): μετὰ πιστῶν ἐν μήτρᾳ συνεκτίσθη αὐτοῖς (subj. φοβεῖσθαι τὸν κύριον): To fear the Lord is created for believers in the mother's womb. Perhaps the Heb. here was יצר (Hatch-Redp., III, 192) in allusion to Jer. 1:5; cf. also Sir. 49:6 Heb. [191]

κτίσις is used of the settling or founding of cities, Thuc., VI, 5, 3: ἔτεσιν ἐγγύτατα πέντε καὶ τριάκοντα καὶ ἑκατὸν μετὰ Συρακουσῶν κτίσιν. Poetically it also equals

_____

other than τοῦ ἀρχιτέκτονος λογισμός); God as αἴτιος and πατήρ, ὕλη as μήτηρ (Ebr., 61); creation from non-being as creation from that which is without quality (Spec. Leg., IV, 187: τὰ γὰρ μὴ ὄντα ἐκάλεσεν εἰς τὸ εἶναι τάξιν ἐξ ἀταξίας καὶ ἐξ ἀποίων ποιότητας ... ἐργασάμενος. On Philo's doctrine of creation cf. J. Horovitz, Untersuchungen über Philons u. Platons Lehre von der Weltschöpfung (1900), with older bibl.; E. Bréhier, Les Idées Philosophiques et Religieuses de Philon d'Alexandrie (1907), 78-82; Stade-Bertholet, II, 489; Bousset-Gressm., 441 f.; Praechter, 575; Frey, 39-45; → 77.
[191] This paragraph is by Bertram.

πρᾶξις, the action. [192] This verbal sense is also the only one in Plut. but it does not occur in the LXX, where κτίσις means a single created thing, [193] Tob. 8:5, 15; Jdt. 9:12; ψ 103:24 vl.; 104:21 vl.; Prv. 1:13 A; 10:15 א* (read κτῆσις); Sir. 43:25 (= גבורות), though the sing. κτίσις is also used for the totality of created things, creation, Jdt. 16:14 : σοὶ δουλευσάτω πᾶσα ἡ κτίσις σου, ψ 73:18 B; Wis. 2:6; 16:24; 19:6; Sir. 16:17 (how the LXX read the Heb. is not clear); 49:16 (=תפארת?); 3 Macc. 2:2, 7; 6:2.

κτίσμα, "what is founded," of cities, houses etc., Strabo, VII, 5, 5 : Tragurion Ἰσσέων κτίσμα, i.e., their foundation. In the LXX it occurs only in the Apocrypha (6 times) for a single creature. In Sir. 38:34 : κτίσμα αἰῶνος στηρίσουσιν (namely, artisans), κτίσμα can also mean something made, but only in the sense of an "order," for Sir. often says that God has created (κτίζειν) things, e.g., γεωργία (7:15), wine (31:27), the physician (38:1, 12) and the means of healing (38:4), indeed, everything for the χρεία of men, and the δημιουργός supports (B upholds) the whole complex of this creation. This is a common thought in Egypt, where the gods, esp. Isis, are the founders of culture (→ II, 648), and Hellenistic Judaism seems to have adopted it in its own way.

κτίστης means "founder" and is a common title in the Hell. period (cf. already Hdt., V, 46: συγκτίστης), [194] e.g., Plut. Camillus, 1 (I, 129b) or 31 (I, 144e); Mar., 27 (I, 421d): Camillus or Marius the second (third) κτίστης of Rome. A city owes, if not its very existence, at least the decisive thing about it, to the will or personality of the κτίστης. By his will and power the Hell. ruler also institutes a festival; he is its κτίστης (as distinct from δημιουργός, → 1026).

Like κτίσις and κτίσμα, κτίστης has no fixed Heb. equivalent, for in Heb. בָּרָא retains its verbal nature; thus God is not called Creator, but reference is made to His creation. κτίστης occurs 8 times in the LXX (7 in the Apocrypha) and here it becomes a divine attribute or designation : 2 S. 22:32 : מִי־אֵל מִבַּלְעֲדֵי יְהוָה וּמִי צוּר מִבַּלְעֲדֵי אֱלֹהֵינוּ : = 2 Βασ. 22:32 : τίς ἰσχυρὸς πλὴν κυρίου; καὶ τίς κτίστης ἔσται πλὴν τοῦ θεοῦ ἡμῶν; shows how in the LXX God's being as Creator was a demonstration of His power and differentiated Him from idols.

E. Creation in the New Testament.

1. Terminology.

The most common NT word for creation is κτίζειν and derivatives, followed at a fair distance by → ποιέω and ποίημα; ποίησις and ποιητής do not occur in this sense. Then follows πλάσσω with πλάσμα, while the noun δημιουργός occurs only once (δημιουργέω not at all), namely, at Hb. 11:10 with τεχνίτης. Κατασκευάζω occurs in Hb. 3:4 in a play on words, and θεμελιόω in Hb. 1:10 in a quotation.

In the NT κτίζω and derivatives are used only of God's creation. κτίζω, "to create"; κτίστης, "creator," occurs only at 1 Pt. 4:19, since the NT, like the Heb. and older parts of the LXX, prefers a part. to the noun (R. 1:25; Col. 3:10; Eph. 3:9; cf. Lk. 11:40; Ac. 4:24; 17:24; R. 9:20; Hb. 3:2) or uses a relative clause (Rev. 10:6; cf. Ac. 14:15). κτίσμα, "creature," the individual creature, 1 Tm. 4:4; Jm. 1:18; Rev. 5:13; 8:9; κτίσις a. "creation" as an act, R. 1:20; b. the "creature," R. 8:39; 2 C. 5:17; Gl. 6:15 (?); Col. 1:15; Hb. 4:13; 1 Pt. 2:13 (→ 1034); c. "creation," i.e., the totality of all created things as a comprehensive term, Hb. 9:11: οὐ ταύτης τῆς κτίσεως; Rev. 3:14; cf. also Mk. 10:6; 13:19; 2 Pt. 3:4 : ἀπ' ἀρχῆς κτίσεως. [195] Acc. to context the ref. is often to the

---

[192] Example in Liddell-Scott.
[193] → II, 637.
[194] Cf. E. Fraenkel, Gesch. d. Griech. Nomina agentis, I (1910), 44, 161, 180, 222. κτίστωρ (and κτίτωρ "inhabitant") seems to be older, cf. Fraenkel, II (1912), 246 (Index). [Debrunner.]
[195] Acc. to Gutbrod, 12 f. = actus creationis.

human race (as frequently in the Rabb. → 1016), Mk. 16:15; Col. 1:23, though it may also be to nature (R. 1:25; 8:19-22, both organic and inorganic).[196] This usage, which occurs also in the LXX, poses quite a riddle, since there are no par. in Gk. or Rabbinic usage.[197]

2. God as Creator of the World.

That God has created the world, i.e., heaven and earth and all that therein is, is found in a series of statements in the NT whose aim is not usually to make a declaration about the nature of creation. The more precise ideas behind these statements must be worked out from them. First, we must mention a common reference back to the beginning of the world, Mk. 10:6: ἀπὸ δὲ ἀρχῆς κτίσεως (= Mt. 19:4: ὁ κτίσας ἀπ' ἀρχῆς), cf. Mt. 19:8: ἀπ' ἀρχῆς and R. 1:20: ἀπὸ κτίσεως κόσμου, also Mk. 13:19: ἀπ' ἀρχῆς κτίσεως ἣν ἔκτισεν ὁ θεός (par. Mt. 24:21: ἀπ' ἀρχῆς κόσμου), 2 Pt. 3:4: ἀπ' ἀρχῆς κτίσεως, cf. Rev. 3:14: ἡ ἀρχὴ τῆς κτίσεως τοῦ θεοῦ, Hb. 1:10 = ψ 101:25: σὺ κατ' ἀρχὰς ... τὴν γῆν ἐθεμελίωσας, and Jn. 8:44: ἀνθρωποκτόνος ἀπ' ἀρχῆς, 2 Th. 2:13; 1 Jn. 1:1; 2:13 f.; 3:8, and the common expression ἀπὸ or πρὸ καταβολῆς κόσμου,[198] Mt. 13:35; 25:34; Lk. 11:50; Jn. 17:24; Eph. 1:4; Hb. 4:3; 9:26; 1 Pt. 1:20; Rev. 13:8; 17:8, cf. also 1 C. 11:9.

These phrases show that creation involves the beginning of the existence of the world, so that there is no pre-existent matter. Paul states this in R. 4:17 with his (θεοῦ) καλοῦντος τὰ μὴ ὄντα ὡς ὄντα (→ 1010). Here and in 2 C. 4:6: ὁ θεὸς ὁ εἰπών· ἐκ σκότους φῶς λάμψει, creation is by the Word. Hence creation out of nothing by the Word explicitly or implicitly underlies the NT statements.

Everything is created, τὰ πάντα, Eph. 3:9; Col. 1:16; Rev. 4:11, or specifically, Rev. 10:6: (ὃς ἔκτισεν) τὸν οὐρανὸν καὶ τὰ ἐν αὐτῷ καὶ τὴν γῆν καὶ τὰ ἐν αὐτῇ καὶ τὴν θάλασσαν καὶ τὰ ἐν αὐτῇ, cf. Ac. 4:24 and 14:15: τὸν οὐρανὸν καὶ τὴν γῆν καὶ τὴν θάλασσαν καὶ πάντα τὰ ἐν αὐτοῖς (cf. Rev. 5:13), or comprehensively, Ac. 17:24: τὸν κόσμον καὶ πάντα τὰ ἐν αὐτῷ, or according to a different enumeration, Col. 1:16: τὰ πάντα ἐν τοῖς οὐρανοῖς καὶ ἐπὶ τῆς γῆς, τὰ ὁρατὰ καὶ τὰ ἀόρατα, εἴτε θρόνοι εἴτε κυριότητες εἴτε ἀρχαὶ εἴτε ἐξουσίαι. That this excludes emanation as well as pre-existent matter is obvious, but is should be noted expressly that οὐρανός includes heaven in the sense of the third petition of the Lord's Prayer. This request also shows that in the NT, too, creation establishes a confrontation of Creator and creature: the will of the Creator is done in heaven. In adoration the four creatures render to the Creator worship, praise and thanksgiving, lauding Him as the Thrice Holy who is distinct from all creation, and in a clear symbolical action the four and twenty elders lay down their crowns before the throne of God, thereby confessing that they have them from God, and join in the worship of the creatures, declaring that it is right (ἄξιος) to render praise and honour and power to God because He is the Creator, Rev. 4:8-11. Even these who stand closest to the throne are nothing in and of themselves; they fulfil the purpose of their existence by offering worship and praise to God. This praise is a personal, voluntary action, an utterance as distinct from natural being. Thus the Son affirms the εὐδοκία of the Father, who as Creator is → κύριος, the legitimate Lord of heaven and earth, Mt. 11:25 f.: ἐξομο-

---

[196] Gutbrod, 15-18 incorrectly restricts κτίσις here to humanity.
[197] On the Rabb. → 1016.
[198] On the meaning of καταβολή here v. Pr.-Bauer³, s.v., as against Schl. Mt. on 13:35.

λογοῦμαί σοι, πάτερ, κύριε τοῦ οὐρανοῦ καὶ τῆς γῆς, ὅτι ἔκρυψας ταῦτα ἀπὸ σοφῶν καὶ συνετῶν, καὶ ἀπεκάλυψας αὐτὰ νηπίοις· ναί, ὁ πατήρ, ὅτι οὕτως εὐδοκία ἐγένετο ἔμπροσθέν σου. The confrontation of Creator and creature, which is inherent in the proclamation of the Creator, makes the creature a creature of will. To be a creature is to be willed, and to be willed is to be willed for a goal. It is to be summoned to will, to the willing for which the creature was created. [199] Thus Paul in his comprehensive statements is forced by the theme itself to conjoin the whence and the whither, and he sets himself with his doxology in the place of what was created εἰς αὐτόν, R. 11:36: ἐξ αὐτοῦ καὶ δι' αὐτοῦ καὶ εἰς αὐτὸν τὰ πάντα· αὐτῷ ἡ δόξα εἰς τοὺς αἰῶνας· ἀμήν (cf. 1 C. 8:6). For Paul the goal of all history is that the Son also should be subject to the Father; this subjection is a personal relationship, not an absorption, which enables us to understand the conclusion of the verse (1 C. 15:28): ὅταν δὲ ὑποταγῇ αὐτῷ τὰ πάντα, τότε καὶ αὐτὸς ὁ υἱὸς ὑποταγήσεται τῷ ὑποτάξαντι αὐτῷ τὰ πάντα, ἵνα ᾖ ὁ θεὸς πάντα ἐν πᾶσιν.

Important testimony is borne to God the Creator in Rev. Rev. 4 and 5 stand at the beginning of the revelation proper in a planned order. The vision of the glory of God's throne comes before the vision and interpretation of historical events. Over all the course of history is enthroned in eternal rest and radiance the One "who sits on the throne." If lightnings, voices and thunderings proceed from the throne (v. 5), the actual description is marked by majestic repose. He "who sits on the throne," and whom the divine does not dare to name more precisely, appears as ὅμοιος ὁράσει λίθῳ ἰάσπιδι καὶ σαρδίῳ (v. 3). In comparison with pseud-epigraphical [200] and Rabbinic writings, [201] it is striking that there is no reference to a consuming glory. The image proclaims "the message which we have heard ... that God is light, and that in him there is no darkness." The precious stones indicate this more clearly than the fiery brightness of the sun, for a precious stone is such only when its clarity and radiance are completely unspotted and unclouded. Since Rev. 4 sees in God the Creator (v. 11), the lesson is that no shadow of obscurity falls on God's glory as Creator. The vision also points to the One who alone is worthy to be described by the predicate ὁ καθήμενος [202] as the one Lord and King from whom all things derive their being and nature. But it also portrays Him as surrounded not only by representatives of organic nature (ζῷα) but also by elders, i.e., by those whom the One who sits on the throne has adjudged worthy of participation in his government of the world, who as elders, comparable to men, share therein freely and consciously as persons. [203] God the Creator creates personal being. Before His throne burn seven torches, i.e., seven spirits. God's Spirit of life (ψ 103:30) permeates and sustains all created things in the multiplicity of

---

[199] Cf. Lütgert, 93-95.

[200] E.g., Eth. En. 14:20 ff.: "His garment was brighter than the sun and whiter than pure snow. None of the angels could enter this house and look on his face for glory and majesty. No flesh could behold him. Burning fire was round about him; a great fire burned before him, and none of the angels drew near to him." Apc. Abr. 18 : "(The throne) was covered with fire, and fire flowed round about him, and, lo, indescribable light stood about a fiery host."

[201] PRE1, 4 : Animals do not know the place of glory, they stand there in anxiety and fear.

[202] He who sits is God, bChag., 15a; Heb. En. 16:3; → II, 572, n. 63.

[203] This must be seen against the background of contemporary Jewish transcendentalisation.

creation. All that God has created is life ; even so-called inorganic nature is full of life. The lightnings, voices and thunderings, however, remind us of fallen creation (4:5).

3. Fallen Creation.

Hb. 9:11 says that Christ διὰ τῆς μείζονος καὶ τελειοτέρας σκηνῆς (than that of the OT) οὐ χειροποιήτου, τοῦτ᾽ ἔστιν οὐ ταύτης τῆς κτίσεως, has entered into the sanctuary. Everything made with hands belongs to this creation. The opposite is αὐτὸς ὁ οὐρανός (Hb. 9:24), i.e., the place of God's presence. Paul in Eph. 2:11 calls Jewish circumcision χειροποίητος, and the implied contrast between the two circumcisions is explained in R. 2:28 f. in terms of the fact that one takes place ἐν τῷ φανερῷ ἐν σαρκί and the other is a περιτομὴ καρδίας ἐν πνεύματι, οὐ γράμματι. Behind this distinction is the Pauline antithesis of the flesh and the spirit, and flesh is here, in the terminology of Hb., what belongs to this creation. What is made with hands is in space, and what is in space belongs to this creation. In Rev. 20:11 John sees how heaven and earth vanish before the One who sits on the throne and no longer find any place, cf. 6:14. Hb. 1:10-12 had already said the same thing in OT phrases, contrasting the transitoriness of heaven and earth with the eternity of the Son of God (Hb. 1:12, cf. 13:8). What is in time also belongs to this creation. In the NT, then, heaven is used in a twofold sense, first, as the dwelling-place of God, and secondly, as רָקִיעַ, which shares this visibility and transitoriness. With this is linked the further fact that all things are created, including the angels and powers ; indeed, even in respect of the Son Hb. 3:2 speaks of God as ποιήσας αὐτόν. Nevertheless, the angels do not belong to this creation. The song of praise in Rev. 5:8-14 is sung by the four living creatures, the 24 elders, then innumerable angels, and finally πᾶν κτίσμα ὃ ἐν τῷ οὐρανῷ [204] καὶ ἐπὶ τῆς γῆς καὶ ὑποκάτω τῆς γῆς καὶ ἐπὶ τῆς θαλάσσης καὶ τὰ ἐν αὐτοῖς πάντα. The song attracts to itself concentrically widening circles, and the outermost of these is this creation, which embraces heavenly powers but not angels. What theosophy, anthroposophy etc. might classify as suprasensual belongs to the sphere of this creation because it is accessible to the media of time and space, in contrast to what is effected by the Spirit of God. It is also true, on the other hand, that Satan does not belong to this creation. R. 8:19 f. sets the same limits for this creation. κτίσις here refers to the whole of creation, [205] since this is properly subject to φθορά and ματαιότης; for from a natural perspective the only purpose of the plant and animal world is to produce descendants who will also produce descendants, an inconceivable miracle (Gn. 1:12) and yet also a gigantic circle of futility : ματαιότης; and alongside this is φθορά, death, which is implied in temporality. The κτίσις is subject to ματαιότης and φθορά διὰ τὸν ὑποτάξαντα. To see here a reference to Adam raises serious objections because it seems strange that the innocent should be punished for the guilty. Only on this view, however, does the statement cease to be a more or less independent declaration or digression and bear true reference to a remarkable fact, the first intimation of the ἐλευθερία τῆς δόξης τῶν τέκνων τοῦ θεοῦ. The result is that this creation is all that which on man's account (including man himself) was subjected to vanity. Hence it is better not to speak of a fallen creation but of a creation which is subjected to corruption. In this respect, too, Satan does not belong to this creation.

---

[204] = שָׁמַיִם, so that no ἐστίν is needed.
[205] As against Gutbrod, → n. 196.

Does the διὰ τὸν ὑποτάξαντα need further elucidation? The vanity to which creation is subjected on account of Adam is given with the form of temporality. Time, however, is a disjunction of cause and effect.[206] Hence there is space for the ἀνοχὴ τοῦ θεοῦ and for repentance. But the ἀνοχὴ τοῦ θεοῦ, the form of this world, also offers the possibility of offence. It raises the question: Where is now thy God? This means that temptation arises in this world; if we had no need of money, there would be no unrighteous mammon. This creation stands under the dominion of the god of this world. Perhaps the διὰ τὸν ὑποτάξαντα takes on particular significance in face of this fact. If the climax of the exposition of R. 1-11 is the statement in R. 11:32: συνέκλεισεν γὰρ ὁ θεὸς τοὺς πάντας εἰς ἀπείθειαν ἵνα τοὺς πάντας ἐλεήσῃ, and if this note runs through the whole of the first part of the epistle, one may perhaps understand it not merely of the historical direction of humanity but also of the form of this creation, which is designed to convict man ineluctably of his sin, so that it both displays the Godhead εἰς τὸ εἶναι αὐτοὺς ἀναπολογήτους (R. 1:20) and also tempts man as κόσμος. This creation, then, is always to be viewed in two ways. On the one hand, it is the *locus* of the revelation of God's glory. In the NT, too, the heavens declare the glory of God. On the other hand, the form of this world is σάρξ in the Pauline sense. Man can perceive God in nature only in Christ. Only in Him does the knowledge of God in nature find its norm and attain clarity and certainty. Only the Son can say: "Consider the lilies of the field ..." (Mt. 6:28), and in indissoluble connection with Christ the apostles lead us from the revelation of God in nature (Ac. 14:17; R. 1:19 f.) to the acknowledgment of the guilt of man before God (R. 1:20).[207]

In Rev. 5 Jn. sees the angel who cries through the heavens, on earth and under the earth, and asks who is worthy to open the book with seven seals. This book contains God's will for the world. But this will is sealed; there is a ban on creation which neither human nor angelic power can lift. If, however, victory over Satan is declared in the victory of the Lamb through His death, this implies that this creation lies under the power of Satan and that the Lamb has liberated it. Now the seals can be opened and the contents of the book seen, and this causes πᾶν κτίσμα in heaven and on earth, both organic nature and inorganic, to break out in rejoicing,[208] since the opening of the book means a new heaven and a new earth, Rev. 21:1; 2 Pt. 3:13. The ματαιότης which rests on all creation will be lifted. This will involve the lifting of all the orders which are imposed with time and space, Mk. 12:25 and par.; 1 C. 15:26, 42 ff.

From what has been said, it is plain that creation was created ἐν Χριστῷ with all the powers which rule it, 1 C. 8:6; Col. 1:16; Hb. 1:2, 10; Jn. 1:1 ff.;[209] Rev. 3:14. Its meaning is to be found in the redemption of humanity through Christ. He sustains all things, Hb. 1:3; the counsel of God is comprehended in Christ πρὸ καταβολῆς κόσμου, Eph. 1:4; 1 Pt. 1:20; cf. Jn. 17:24; Mt. 25:34; Rev. 13:8; 17:8.

The form of this world is on man's account both in the sense that man has fallen and also in the sense that he is called to glory. This form of the world gives man

---

[206] A. Schlatter, *Das christliche Dogma*[1] (1911), 52-54.
[207] On R. 1:20 v. G. Kuhlmann, Theologia naturalis *bei Philon u. bei Paulus* (1930), 39 ff. with further bibl.; H. Schlier, "Über d. Erkenntnis Gottes bei den Heiden," *Evangelische Theologie,* 2 (1935/36), 9-26.
[208] Earth is just as affected as heaven, cf. Rev. 12:12.
[209] Neither the ἐγένετο of Jn. 1:3 nor the ἐκ θεοῦ of 1 C. 8:6 is to be taken emanatically.

the time which he can and should utilise. He may use everything that sustains him as a member of this creation and he may receive with grateful heart everything that points him to the Creator. Of the things necessary to life nothing is common or unclean, as we learn both from Jesus (Mk. 7:14 ff. and par.), who sanctified all meats (Mk. 7:19 d), and also from Paul, who laid down the principle : οἶδα καὶ πέπεισμαι ἐν κυρίῳ Ἰησοῦ ὅτι οὐδὲν κοινὸν δι᾽ ἑαυτοῦ (R. 14:14), and who always applied this principle when ascetic tendencies arose, whether in relation to food (1 C. 8-10; esp. 10:25 f.; Col. 2:22a; 1 Tm. 4:3b-5; Tt. 1:14 f.; cf. Hb. 13:9) or in relation to marriage (1 C. 7; 1 Tm. 2:15; 4:3a; cf. 1 C. 11:9). What can be received with thanksgiving is not to be refused (1 Tm. 4:4). Thanksgiving means that the gift is received as a gift, creation is acknowledged as creation, and the Giver and Creator is honoured. This attitude keeps to the narrow ridge between the two precipices which are a constant threat in religious history, either to worship creation instead of the Creator, and thus to be absorbed in creation, or to reject it in asceticism (or despise it in libertinism). Both of these attitudes are unnatural since they both treat creation as something which it is not ; for in itself creation is neither a final norm nor is it evil. What distinguishes the ἀρχὴ κτίσεως (Mk. 10:6) from the present state is basically the σκληροκαρδία of men (Mk. 10:5).

4. Man as Creature and the New Creation.

From what has been said it is evident that man and his destiny are the goal of this creation. On his account it is subject to corruption, in him evil has its true starting-point and centre, while the evils of creation outside man, ματαιότης and φθορά, are only consequences.

Man as the creature of God is ψυχὴ ζῶσα, 1 C. 15:45, and the ψυχικὸς ἄνθρωπος, to follow the masterly translation of the A.V. (cf. Luther), is the natural man. The basis of his natural existence is the unfathomable mystery of natural life. This involves sharp tensions. The living breath of the eternal God is taken from man in death. He is created to have dominion over the world, and yet this aim is a final incomprehensible torment. [210] He is created as the image of God and as such he should subject himself to God's will as a free person, but he is the slave of impulses. The origin of evil in man is wrapped in impenetrable obscurity. How the creature of God could fall, how it can do so afresh with every sinful act, is quite incomprehensible to us, though even in principle we can see that it is human enough. Evil reaches right down into the hidden roots of our existence, and Satan is a pneumatic magnitude (Eph. 6:12) which cannot be grasped by flesh and blood. The only factual procedure is not to try to solve the riddle of evil.

Man is the creature of God. This means that he has no claim on God. Paul depicts this in the image of the vessel and the potter, R. 9:20 ff. The figure relates not merely to the historical situation of man [211] but to the total relationship of man to God. For this reason, the NT never advances the interrelation of Creator and creature as a basis of prayers for grace.

The phrase "this creation" is also applied to man. As ψυχὴ ζῶσα man belongs to this creation, for ψυχή is its principle of life. πνεῦμα is the principle of life of the

---

[210] To have to seek eternity on this earth is a torment because all incentive is thereby destroyed ; it makes no difference whether a discovery takes place in thousands or millions of years.

[211] As against Zn. R., ad loc.

world of God. Thus there is an antithesis between the ψυχικὸς ἄνθρωπος and the πνευματικός, between birth of flesh and birth of the Spirit, between the old man and the new creature. εἴ τις ἐν Χριστῷ, καινὴ κτίσις· τὰ ἀρχαῖα παρῆλθεν, ἰδοὺ γέγονεν καινά, 2 C. 5:17; οὔτε γὰρ περιτομή τί ἐστιν οὔτε ἀκροβυστία, ἀλλὰ καινὴ κτίσις, Gl. 6:15. The use of the verb shows that κτίσις here is not just a term for "being," "man," as in the Rabb., but that it bears the full signification of the word, cf. Eph. 2:10 : αὐτοῦ γάρ ἐσμεν ποίημα, κτισθέντες ἐν Χριστῷ Ἰησοῦ ἐπὶ ἔργοις ἀγαθοῖς, Eph. 2:15 : ἵνα τοὺς δύο κτίσῃ ἐν αὐτῷ εἰς ἕνα καινὸν ἄνθρωπον, Eph. 4:24 : ἐνδύσασθαι τὸν καινὸν ἄνθρωπον τὸν κατὰ θεὸν κτισθέντα ἐν δικαιοσύνῃ, Col. 3:10 : ἐνδυσάμενοι τὸν νέον τὸν ἀνακαινούμενον εἰς ἐπίγνωσιν κατ᾽ εἰκόνα τοῦ κτίσαντος αὐτόν, also Jm. 1:18 : βουληθεὶς ἀπεκύησεν ἡμᾶς λόγῳ ἀληθείας, εἰς τὸ εἶναι ἡμᾶς ἀπαρχήν τινα τῶν αὐτοῦ κτισμάτων. All God's work of creation is by His Word and Spirit, but this new creature has its existence in the Spirit ; the new life is now "hid with Christ in God," Col. 3:3. Man's existence is new in virtue of the new relation to God ; his position before God determines his being. The relation has been renewed by Christ. The decisive thing in the new creature, then, is not an alteration in man's moral conduct but the acceptance (in faith) of a new relation to God. This new relation is bound up with Christ, through whom it has entered into and become history. Naturally, the new relation neither can nor should be without effect on man's conduct, R. 6:1 ff.

With the entry of the πνεῦμα into this world in the person and work of Christ, Mt. 12:28, [212] the new world breaks into its course. [213] Wherever God's action is effective for man's salvation, God is creatively at work. The uniting of divided humanity into one new man, Eph. 2:15, is also a κτίζειν. The goal is a new creation in antithesis to the totality of this creation. The full revelation of the new creation, which will manifest the refashioning of both man and the world, will not come until Christ reveals Himself, Col. 3:4, when this heaven and earth will pass away, the new heaven and earth will appear, and death and corruption will be abolished. Then Christ will reveal Himself as πνεῦμα ζωοποιοῦν in the totality of the world, and the glorious liberty of the children of God, R. 8:21, will be displayed on the mortal bodies of those who belong to Christ, and on all κτίσις.

Special difficulties are created by 1 Pt. 2:13 : ὑποτάγητε πάσῃ ἀνθρωπίνῃ κτίσει διὰ τὸν κύριον. The main proposal is that κτίσις here means "order" [214] with special ref. to the order of the state represented by the βασιλεῖς and ἡγεμόνες. Thus far, however, this usage is not supported by any examples from secular Gk., the LXX, or the Rabb. The only remote par. is κτίσμα in Sir. 38:34. But here the ref. is to the order of culture whose material foundations are sustained by artisans, not to the order of the state. An attempt should first be made to explain the verse in Pt. in terms of known usage. In this respect, exposition of the context of the verse is of decisive importance. The πᾶς without article (πᾶσα ἀνθρωπίνη κτίσις = every kind of human κτίσις) points to wider connections. It is also plain that the slogan ὑποτάσσεσθαι is often deliberately adopted in a broader context, 2:18; 3:1; what is said to husbands in relation to their wives in 3:7; what is said comprehensively to all in 3:8 f., i.e., the admonition to serve one another, which implies a kind of free subjection to others. In

---

[212] In this formulation the ἐν πνεύματι θεοῦ is obviously a theological interpretation of the fig. expression ἐν δακτύλῳ θεοῦ preserved in Lk.

[213] Schl. considers the relation between the new creation and the miracles of Jesus in his Gesch. d. Chr., 242.

[214] E.g., Pr.-Bauer³, s.v.

this light 2:13 might well be the title of the whole section 2:13-3:9. If this is so, it is a mistake to construe κτίσις as the order of the state or any other order or ordinance. The ref. is not to an order ; it is to men. A linguistic par. for κτίσις in this sense is to be found in the Rabb. בְּרִיאָה (→ 1016), which could denote the individual without any danger of misunderstanding. ἀνθρώπινος is added here to ensure that the phrase is correctly understood in the Gk.-speaking world. Peter's admonition to the congregations is that they should be subject to men of every sort. He works this out in terms of the subjection of free men to authority, of slaves to their masters and of wives to their husbands, and also in terms of the regard that husbands should have for their wives and of the readiness of all humbly to subordinate themselves to one another, to be ταπεινόφρονες (3:8), which implies mutual subordination even to the point of blessing enemies who curse, cf. the fact that Paul in Phil. 2:3 uses as an exact par. the phrase τῇ ταπεινοφροσύνῃ ἀλλήλους ἡγούμενοι ὑπερέχοντας ἑαυτῶν.

Foerster

---

† κυβέρνησις

1. κυβέρνησις is the noun of κυβερνάω. This means "to steer a ship." The κυβερνήτης is thus the "helmsman," as the context makes perfectly clear, e.g., in Ac. 27:11 [1] and Rev. 18:17. The clarity of the image of the work of the helmsman made it obviously suitable for fig. use for the statesman. Plat. Euthyd., 291c says, ἡ πολιτικὴ καὶ ἡ βασιλικὴ τέχνη is πάντα κυβερνῶσα. Polyb., 6, 4, 2 speaks of a βασιλεία τῇ γνώμῃ τὸ πλεῖον ἢ φόβῳ καὶ βίᾳ κυβερνωμένη. Here κυβερνάω undoubtedly means "to rule." Pindar had already used the word in this sense for the work of the deity, Pyth., 5, 164 : Διός τοι νόος μέγας κυβερνᾷ δαίμον' ἀνδρῶν. This conception of the deity as κυβερνήτης became a favourite one, e.g., Plat. Symp., 197d e, where it is said of Ἔρως that he is ἐν πόνῳ, ἐν φόβῳ, ἐν πόθῳ, ἐν λόγῳ κυβερνήτης, ἐπιβάτης, παραστάτης τε καὶ σωτὴρ ἄριστος ... ἡγεμὼν κάλλιστος καὶ ἄριστος. In Polit., 272e God is called τοῦ παντὸς ... ὁ κυβερνήτης, and in the hymn to Zeus of Cleanthes νόμου μέτα πάντα κυβερνῶν (v. Arnim, I, p. 121, 35). The same idea occurs in 3 Macc. 6:2. Jos. Ant., 10, 278 is directed against the Epicureans, who deny that all world occurrence is steered by a blessed and lofty being high above all change and chance. Philo combines the images of the charioteer and the helmsman, Decal., 155 : ἡγεμὼν καὶ βασιλεὺς εἷς ὁ ἡνιοχῶν καὶ κυβερνῶν τὰ ὅλα σωτηρίως, or Ebr., 199 : ἡνιοχοῦντος καὶ κυβερνῶντος ... θεοῦ. The same line of thought is found in Epictet. Diss., II, 17, 25 etc.

The noun κυβέρνησις is less common. It, too, is used both lit. and fig. In Plat. Resp., VI, 488b d it is used for "steering" or the "art of the helmsman." The κυβερνήτης is ὁ ἐπιστάμενος τὰ κατὰ ναῦν, the one who knows the times of the day and the year, the sky, the stars, currents of air etc. He is also νεὼς ἀρχικός, the one who is qualified

---

κ υ β έ ρ ν η σ ι ς. Moult-Mill., 363; for bibl. on the constitution of the Church and the office of governing the congregation → ἐπίσκοπος, II, 608.

[1] It is to be noted, however, that the reference is not just to the man at the helm who carries out orders, but to the responsible captain under the owner who is also making the voyage, the ναύκληρος. Sometimes he engages only the κυβερνήτης and the κυβερνήτης the rest of the crew, Plut. Praec. Ger. Reip., 13 (II, 807b). The κυβερνήτης is thus νεὼς ἀρχικός, Plat. Resp., VI, 488d; → *infra*. Cf. the ἀληθινὸς κυβερνήτης, who is the man responsible for the ship's course, the captain. Cf. Class. Rev., 16 (1902), 386 f.

to direct the ship. The fig. use is directly connected with this. Pind. Pyth., 10, 112 calls the government of states πολίων κυβερνάσεις (note the plur.). Plut. Sept. Sap. Conv., 18 (II, 162a) calls the divine governance θεοῦ κυβέρνησις. P. Lond., 1349, 20 and 1394, 17 and 22, which belong to 710 A.D. and presuppose Arab connections, apply the metaphorical sense to the purposeful regulation of public service.

2. In the LXX κυβέρνησις occurs three times (in Prv.) for תַּחְבֻּלוֹת. The word is here closely related to σοφία and means "clever direction." 1:5: ὁ δὲ νοήμων κυβέρνησιν κτήσεται, by the proverbs of Solomon a wise man will increase his knowledge and one who has no understanding will find right direction to knowledge of the truth and to right conduct. 11:14: οἷς μὴ ὑπάρχει κυβέρνησις, πίπτουσιν ὥσπερ φύλλα. σωτηρία δὲ ὑπάρχει ἐν πολλῇ βουλῇ, where there is no right direction, men and nations fall. 24:6: μετὰ κυβερνήσεως γίνεται πόλεμος, only with wise direction can a successful war be fought, for the wise man is mightier than the strong.

3. The literal meaning and the attested usage make it clear what Paul has in view when in 1 C. 12:28, among the gifts of grace which God gives individuals in the Church, he mentions κυβερνήσεις along with → δυνάμεις, → χαρίσματα ἰαμάτων, → ἀντιλήμψεις and γένη → γλωσσῶν. The reference can only be to the specific gifts which qualify a Christian to be a helmsman to his congregation, i.e., a true director of its order and therewith of its life.[2] What was the scope of this directive activity in the time of Paul we do not know. This was a period of fluid development. The importance of the helmsman increases in a time of storm. The office of directing the congregation may well have developed especially in emergencies both within and without. The proclamation of the Word was not originally one of its tasks. The apostles, prophets and teachers saw to this. But these can hardly be possessors of the χάρισμα κυβερνήσεως in the specific sense, which comes only later in the list. The combination of ἀντιλήμψεις and κυβερνήσεις makes it certain that the ἐπίσκοποι (→ II, 615 ff.) and διάκονοι (→ II, 88 ff.), who are first mentioned in Phil. 1:1, are to be regarded as the bearers of this gift, or the → προϊστάμενοι of R. 12:8. No society can exist without some order and direction. It is the grace of God to give gifts which equip for government. A striking point is that when in v. 29 Paul asks whether all are apostles, whether all are prophets or whether all have gifts of healing, there are no corresponding questions in respect of ἀντιλήμψεις and κυβερνήσεις. There is a natural reason for this. If necessary, any member of the congregation may step in to serve as deacon or ruler.[3] Hence these offices, as distinct from those mentioned in v. 29, may be elective. But this does not alter the fact that for their proper discharge the *charisma* of God is indispensable.[4]

4. The early Church soon came to like the picture of the Church as a ship and Christ as the Helmsman:[5] Tertullian, De Idolatria, 24 (CSEL, 20, p. 58); Bapt., 8 (p. 208). Hippolyt. De Antichristo, 59 (GCS, ed. H. Achelis, I, 2, p. 39) says in exposition of Is. 18:1 f.: "The sea is the world in which the Church is surrounded by storms like a ship on the sea, but it does not founder beacuse it has on board the experienced pilot, Christ." Similarly on a sarcophagus from Spoleto Christ is depicted as the pilot with

---

[2] "The plur., like δυνάμεις, refers to specific expressions ... of κυβέρνησις, of government and rule," Joh. W., 1 K., 308. It is also found in secular Gk. (→ *supra*). Hesych., *s.v.* explains κυβερνήσεις as προνοητικαὶ ἐπιστῆμαι καὶ φρονήσεις.
[3] H. Lietzmann, ZwTh, 55 (1914), 108 f.
[4] On the development of offices of rule in the churches → II, 615 ff.
[5] This presupposes the concept of the κυβερνήτης in n. 1. On what follows cf. F. J. Dölger, "Sol Salutis" (*Liturgiegeschichtliche Forschungen*, 4-5² [1925]), 272 ff.

his left hand on the rudder and His right stretched out in command. [6] There are many examples in art and literature. [7]

The image does not derive just from the NT. The story of the calming of the storm certainly gives us the disciples in a ship and Jesus as the One who rules the wind and the waves, but Jesus is not the helmsman. Obviously OT conceptions helped to create the metaphor. Tertullian already compares the Church, not to the fishing boat on the lake, but to Noah's ark. This is one of the favourite themes of early Christian art. [8] God's act of saving the ark is extolled. Wis. 14:3 ff.: ἡ δὲ σή, πάτερ, διακυβερνᾷ πρόνοια, ὅτι ἔδωκας καὶ ἐν θαλάσσῃ ὁδὸν ... ἡ ἐλπὶς τοῦ κόσμου ἐπὶ σχεδίας (the ark) καταφυγοῦσα ... τῇ σῇ κυβερνηθεῖσα χειρί. God is here compared to the pilot. Cf. also Ps.-Clementines, 14 (ed. A. R. M. Dressel [1853], p. 20): "There is only one Lord of this ship, God, and the pilot is to be compared with Christ." Gradually bishops and clergy came to have a place in the picture. According to the symbolism Christ as the Pilot steers His Church through all perils and directs believers safely through all the storms of life which threaten them. The sea of sin engulfs man like one travelling over the sea on a ship, Prv. 23:34. But Christ steers the ship of life from the sea of time to the harbour of eternity. Cf. Andreas Gryphius: "Steer Thou Thy ship, direct its course," or Johann Daniel Falk: "As the waves in wild confusion roar ..."

Beyer

| † κύμβαλον |

This word occurs in the NT only at 1 C. 13:1. It comes from κύμβη, κύμβος (any hollow, esp. hollow vessel or dish) and denotes a shallow metallic basin which, when struck against another, gives out a resounding note. Such vessels were particularly used in the cultus. In later texts we often find τύμπανα and κύμβαλα together.

Jewish usage may be seen from many LXX passages in which κύμβαλα is the rendering of מְצִלְתַּיִם [1] (from צלל "to clash," "to clang"), cf. esp. 1 and 2 Ch., Ezr., Neh. In 1 Ch. 13:8 and elsewhere many musical instruments are mentioned together: ἐν ψαλτῳδοῖς καὶ ἐν κινύραις καὶ ἐν νάβλαις, ἐν τυμπάνοις καὶ ἐν κυμβάλοις καὶ ἐν σάλπιγξιν. Cf., with no Heb. original, 1 Macc. 4:54; 13:51; Jdt. 16:1. In Ps. 150:5 (cf. also Σ): αἰνεῖτε αὐτὸν ἐν κυμβάλοις εὐήχοις, αἰνεῖτε αὐτὸν ἐν κυμβάλοις ἀλαλαγμοῦ, κύμβαλα is used for צֶלְצְלִים, (from צלל). In 1 Βασ. 18:6 it stands for שָׁלִישׁ, perhaps a three-cornered harp, a plucking instrument, or a triangle, and in 2 Βασ. 6:5 for מְנַעַנְעִים (a shaking instrument, from נוע). Acc. to 1 Ch. 15:19 the מְצִלְתַּיִם were used by the three leaders of the choirs to direct the orchestra and were of bronze. They are striking instruments used in divine worship, [2] chiefly in connection with the temple orchestra. [3] In terms of the מְצִלּוֹת הַסּוּס of Zech. 14:20 one might think of bells, but it

---

[6] R. Garrucci, *Storia dell' Arte Cristiana*, V (1879), 395, 6.
[7] F. X. Kraus, *Realencyklopädie d. christ. Altertümer*, II (1886), 731.
[8] J. Wilpert, *Die Malereien der Katakomben Roms* (1903), 344 ff.
κ ύ μ β α λ ο ν. [1] V. Ges.-Buhl, *s.v.*
[2] Cf. H. Gressmann, "Musik u. Musikinstrumente im AT," RVV, 2 (1903). Further information is to be found in the older work, not mentioned by Gressm., by the Roman Catholic theologian J. Weiss, *Die musikalischen Instrumente in den heiligen Schriften des AT* (1895).
[3] The verb κυμβαλίζω occurs in 2 Εσδρ. 22:27.

should be recalled that horses are not only furnished with bells, but also that harness includes bosses, which in outward form are not unlike cymbals. Many Rabbis tell of cymbals in divine worship, their material, size, sound, use and origin. [4] Jos. Ant., 7, 306 records: κύμβαλά τε ἦν πλατέα καὶ μεγάλα χάλκεα.

These Jewish cultic instruments were familiar to Paul, and his contrast between the κύμβαλον ἀλαλάζον and ἀγάπη reminds us of a prophet of the old covenant speaking of the noisy, empty and futile nature of an external cultus.

Perhaps Paul was also thinking of the cultic equiment of paganism which would have been familiar to the Corinthian Christians, who in the main had been pagans. [5] As has been said, κύμβαλον often occurs with τύμπανον. This was used particularly in the worship of Cybele; it was struck like a drum. [6]

In P. Hibeh, 54, 12 f. [7] clappers are also mentioned with drums and cymbals: τύμπανον καὶ κύμβαλα καὶ κρόταλα. If Gk. cymbals were of bronze, it should be remembered that Corinthian bronze was particularly noted for its excellence. [8] And in this passage Paul also speaks of χαλκὸς ἠχῶν (= aes sonans). Beyond the cultic aspect in the narrower sense, it is to be noted that a sounding cymbal might well be a term for an empty-headed and boastful prattler. [9] Acc. to Plin. (the Elder) Hist. Nat. praef., 25 the emperor Tiberius calls the grammarian Apion the cymbalum mundi. With this we may also compare the fact that Tertullian in De Pallio, 4 (MPL, 2, p. 1098a) says of the philosopher in his doubtful capacity: Digne quidem, ut bacchantibus indumentis aliquid subtinniret, cymbalo incessit. [10] The vain philosopher is like a raving Bacchant; [11] worldly philosophy with its meaningless and futile noise is nothing other than the clanging cymbal in a procession of Bacchantes. [12] Many of the things so dear to the

---

[4] Cf. Str.-B. on 1 C. 13:1.

[5] E. Peterson in → ἀλαλάζω, I, 227 f. concentrates on this side of the background at the expense of the Jewish: "Here the 'ecstatic noise' in orgiastic cults is linked with the κύμβαλον used in these cults (esp. that of Cybele)."

[6] Cf. Pape, s.v.

[7] Cf. Deissmann LO, 131 f. on this pap.: "Paul in 1 C. 13:1 is thinking of such basins used as musical instruments."

[8] Cf. Weiss, 101.

[9] For examples and a discussion of this side of the matter cf. F. J. Dölger, Antike u. Christentum, I (1929), 184 f. on 1 C. 13:1.

[10] Cf. the judgment of Diogenes on Antisthenes in Dio Chrys. Or., 8, 2: ἔφη αὐτὸν εἶναι σάλπιγγα λοιδορῶν· αὐτοῦ γὰρ οὐκ ἀκούειν φθεγγομένου μέγιστον. A musical instrument (σάλπιγξ) describes a man whose imposing outward appearance is not sustained by corresponding inward qualities. Cf. on this A. Fridrichsen, ThStKr, 94 (1922), 73; Clemen, 327.

[11] Dölger, I, Plate 13 gives us a picture of one such Bacchant with a girdle of bells (relief in the Loggia scoperta of the Vatican Museum).

[12] For full material on the cymbal in this connection, with illustr., cf. C. Daremberg-E. Saglio, Dictionn. d. Antiquités Grecques et Romaines, I, 2 (1887), s.v. There is a vivid depiction of orgiastic cult-music, in which the cymbal had a part, in H. Hepding, "Attis," RVV, 1 (1903), 128, which quotes Firm. Mat. Err. Prof. Rel., 18, 1: De tympano manducavi, de cymbalo bibi et religionis secreta perdidici, quod graeco sermone dicitur ἐκ τυμπάνου βέβρωκα, ἐκ κυμβάλου πέπωκα, γέγονα μύστης Ἄττεως (ibid., 49). Wendland Hell. Kult., Plate VII (p. 424) shows the relief (at the Capitoline Museum at Rome) of a certain Archigallus — castrated Galli represent the Phrygian cult personnel of the mother of the gods, Cybele — on whose upraised right hand are a pair of cymbals, with a tympanum to match on the other side. On March 24 (dies sanguinis) the flutes united their sound with the clanging of the cymbals, the howling Galli whirled round in the dance, they whipped themselves until the blood ran, and then in supreme ecstasy the priests cut their arms with daggers and the disciples, frenzied by the presence of their deity, made the bloody self-sacrifice of castration. The same picture may also be found in J. Quasten, "Musik u. Gesang

Corinthian Christians, esp. speaking with tongues, are of a similar nature in comparison with ἀγάπη.

Certainly such references give added force to the mention of the κύμβαλον ἀλαλάζον. [13]

K. L. Schmidt

κυνάριον → κύων.

```
┌─────────────────────────────────────────────┐
│   κύριος, κυρία, κυριακός, κυριότης,          │
│        κυριεύω, κατακυριεύω                    │
└─────────────────────────────────────────────┘
```

κύριος.

Contents : A. The Meaning of the Word κύριος : 1. The Adjective κύριος; 2. The Noun ὁ κύριος. B. Gods and Rulers as κύριοι : 1. κύριος for Gods and Rulers in Classical Greece ; 2. Gods and Rulers as Lords in the Orient and Egypt ; 3. The Hellenistic κύριος.

in d. Kulten der heidnischen Antike u. christlichen Frühzeit," *Liturgiegeschichtliche Quellen und Forschungen,* 25 (1930), Table 18; on Table 22 there is also a picture of a sacred tree with cymbals hanging from it, cf. also Dölger, IV (1934), who appends to the discussion mentioned in → n. 9 a discussion of the bells on the garments of the Jewish high-priest as expounded in Jewish, pagan and early Christian authors, of bells in the worship of the Arval brethren, and of tinkling, dancing and hand-clapping in the worship of Christian Melitians in Egypt. It is clear that bells etc. were very important in Jewish, pagan and Christian worship and that cymbals were a particularly significant instrument in orgiastic cult music, cf. esp. 257 f.

[13] Dölger, I, 185 makes the qualifying observation that "while bells were much used in antiquity in children's play and to ward off evil and demons, it is likely that the apostle was thinking chiefly of the aimless tinkling of bells."

κ ύ ρ ι ο ς. In general, cf. the bibl. up to 1924 in W. Foerster, *Herr ist Jesus* (1924), 11-56; we may mention W. Bousset, *Kyrios Chrystos*[2] (1921); Deissmann LO, 298-310; Ltzm. R. on 10:9; Cr.-Kö., 644-655; cf. also E. Rohde, ZNW, 22 (1923), 43 ff.; Williger, Pauly-W., XII (1924), 176-183; K. Prümm, "Herrscherkult u. NT," *Biblica,* 9 (1928), 1 ff.; W. W. Graf Baudissin, *Kyrios als Gottesname* ... (1929); I. A. Smith in JThSt, 31 (1930), 155-160; A. D. Nock in *Essays on the Trinity and Incarnation,* ed. A. E. J. Rawlinson (1928), 51 ff.; C. H. Dodd, *The Bible and the Greeks* (1935), 8-11. On A : K. Stegmann v. Pritzwald, *Zur Geschichte der Herrscherbezeichnungen von Hom. bis Plat.* (1930), § 86; 110; 155. On B : W. Drexler in Roscher, *s.v.*; J. Leipoldt, *War Jesus Jude?* (1923), 24 ff., esp. 27 f.; 38; 42 f.; F. Doppler in *Opuscula Philologa,* I (1926), 42-47; O. Eissfeldt, "Götternamen u. Gottesvorstellung bei den Semiten," ZDMG, 83 (1929), 21-36. On C (→ θεός Bibl. B.): A. Alt, "Jahwe," *Reallexikon d. Vorgeschichte,* 6 (1926), 147 ff.; W. R. Arnold, "The Divine Name," JBL, 24 (1905), 107 ff.; F. B. Denio, "On the Use of the Word Jehovah in Translating the Old Testament," JBL, 46 (1927), 146-149; M. Buber, *Königtum Gottes*[2] (1936); M. Buber-F. Rosenzweig, *Die Schrift und ihre Verdeutschung* (1936), 184 ff., 332 ff.; A. Ganschinietz, "Jao," Pauly-W., IX (1916), 698 ff.; F. Giesebrecht, *Die at.liche Schätzung d. Gottesnamens* (1901); O. Grether, *Name u. Wort Gottes im AT* (1934); J. Hänel, "Jahwe," NkZ, 40 (1929), 608 ff.; J. Hempel, "Jahwegleichnisse d. israelit. Propheten," ZAW, NF, 1 (1924), 74 ff.; R. Kittel, "Jahve," RE³, VIII (1900), 529 ff.; H. Schmökel, *Jahwe u. d. Fremdvölker* (1934); C. Toussaint, *Les Origines de la religion d'Israel,* I : "l'ancien Jahvisme" (1931); K. G. Kuhn, יי, יהו, יהוה, *Oriental. Studien, E. Littmann-Festschr.* (1935),

C. The OT Name for God : 1. The Name for God in the LXX ; 2. "Lord" as a Designation for Yahweh ; 3. The Name Yahweh as a Concept of Experience ; 4. The Institution by Moses ; 5. The Origin of the Divine Name ; 6. The Form and Meaning of the Name Yahweh ; 7. The Reasons for Reticence in relation to the Name ; 8. The Name of God in the Account of Yahweh's Revelation to Moses in Ex. 3:14; 9. The Name Yahweh as the Basic Form of the OT Declaration about God ; 10. The Confession of Yahweh in Dt. 6:4. D. "Lord" in Later Judaism : 1. The Choice of the Word κύριος in the LXX ; 2. "Lord" in the Pseudepigrapha ; 3. "Lord" in Rabbinic Judaism. E. κύριος in the New Testament : 1. Secular Uusage ; 2. God the Lord ; 3. Jesus the Lord ; 4. Earthly κύριος Relationships.

In German the word "Herr" (lord) is the most common expression for a fact which is present only in the personal sphere, among men, and which constitutes an essential part of personal being. This is the fact that there is a personal exercise of power over men and things. In this man may be either the subject of the exercise of power (as lord), or its object (as servant), but either way he is its object as concerns his relation to God. In the concept of the lord two things are conjoined in organic unity : the exercise of power as such, and the personal nature of its exercise, which reaches beyond immediate external compulsion into the moral and legal sphere. The exercise of power as such is found also in the non-human sphere of existence as the expression of utilitarian order (the strongest animal as the leader). The decisive element in the exercise of power among men is that in principle it is validated not merely by some form of utility but by an element of law which transcends what is merely natural or expedient, which changes purely temporal possession into the moral concept of ownership, transforms the momentary superiority of the stronger into the authority of the ruler, and turns the superiority of parents over their children, which enforces subordination, and the social authority of masters over their servants, into a rank which demands obedience and imposes responsibility. It seems that in the course of human history, from the first beginnings recorded in language, there must have developed an awareness of the distinctive unity of the two elements. We find the most varied attempts to understand this aright, though in the general intellectual and religious history of humanity there has never yet been a full realisation that the two elements in their completeness are destined to permeate one another organically. This realisation has arisen only when man is confronted in God the Creator by One who posits, i.e., creates him in absolute power, and who also as such is the absolute authority before which it is freedom rather than bondage to bow. In other words, it has arisen only in the sphere of the biblical revelation. Here a humanity which has rejected subordination to its Creator is confronted by the One who with the authority of the ministering and forgiving love of God woos its obedience and reconstructs all the relations of lordship.

25 ff. On D (→ θεός, 93-95): Dalman WJ, 266-280; B. Stade-A. Bertholet, *Biblische Theologie des AT,* II (1911), 370-373; Str.-B., III, 672 on Hb. 1:2; Bousset-Gressm., 307-316; Moore, I, 423 ff.; A. Marmorstein, *The Old Rabbinic Doctrine of God,* I (1927): "The Names and Attributes of God"; Schl. Theol. d. Judt., 24-26; 61. On E: NT Theol. by B. Weiss[7] (1903); H. Weinel[4] (1928); P. Feine[6] (1934), 140 f., 175; F. Büchsel (1935), 84 f., 87, 103; E. Lohmeyer, SAH, 18 (1927/28), 4; ZNW, 26 (1927), 164-169; F. H. Stead, "The Chief Pauline Names for Christ," Exp., 3, Ser. 7 (1888), 386-395; B. Weiss, ThStKr, 84 (1911), 503-538; C. Fabricius, *R. Seeberg-Festschr.,* I (1929), 26-32; E. de Witt Burton, Gl. (1921, ICC), 393, 399-404; C. A. A. Scott, *Dominus noster* (1918); K. Holl, *Ges. Aufsätze,* II (1928), 115-122; O. Michel, ZNW, 28 (1929), 324-333; *ibid.,* 32 (1933), 10-12; E. v. Dobschütz, ZNW, 30 (1931), 97-123; W. Schmauch, *In Christus* (1935).

A. The Meaning of the Word κύριος.

ὁ κύριος is the noun form of the adj. κύριος, which for its part derives from the noun τὸ κῦρος. The root of this is an Indo-Germanic √ *keu*(*ā*), *kū,* with the sense "to swell" (cf. κυέω, ἔγκυος, ἐγκύμων, κῦμα), then "to be strong"; κύρ-ιος is linked with the Sansk. *sūra* (strong, brave, hero).[1] τὸ κῦρος, which is found from the time of Aesch., means "force," "power," Aesch. Suppl., 391: οὐκ ἔχουσιν κῦρος οὐδὲν ἀμφὶ σοῦ, also "cause": Soph. El., 918 f.: ἡ δὲ νῦν ἴσως πολλῶν ὑπάρξει κῦρος ἡμέρα καλῶν.

1. Hence the adj. κύριος means "having power," or "having legal power," "lawful," "valid," "authorised," "competent," "empowered"; also "important," "decisive," "principal." κύριος is used as an adj. from the class. to the NT period but does not occur as such in the NT or later Jewish lit. This must be connected with the fact that the Heb.-Aram. equivalent for the noun ὁ κύριος has no corresponding adj.

a. "Having power": Pind. Olymp., 1, 104: δύναμιν κυριώτερον: "higher in power"; cf. Fr., 260 (ed. W. Christ [1896]) of Palamedes: ὄντα μὲν αὐτὸν κυριώτερον τοῦ Ὀδυσσέως εἰς σοφίας λόγον; also Isthm., 5, 53: Ζεὺς ὁ πάντων κύριος; cf. Plut. Def. Orac., 29 (II, 426a): If there are several worlds, does it necessarily follow that there are also several Zeuses and not one, οἷος ὁ παρ' ἡμῖν κύριος ἁπάντων καὶ πατὴρ ἐπονομαζόμενος;[2] In general κύριος does not indicate the possession of physical strength; the closest to this is in Plut. Aristides, 6 (I, 322b): three emotions animate man in face of the divine, ζῆλος, φόβος, τιμή, ... ἐκπλήττεσθαι δὲ καὶ δεδιέναι κατὰ τὸ κύριον καὶ δυνατόν. The ref. is rather to the power of disposal. Demosth. Or., 50, 60 of the dying mother: οὐκέτι τῶν ὄντων κυρία οὖσα, 8, 69: a constitution in which πλειόνων ἡ τύχη κυρία γίνεται ἢ οἱ λογισμοί, 18, 194: οὐ ... τῆς τύχης κύριος ἦν, ἀλλ' ἐκείνη τῶν πάντων; ibid., 321: τούτου γὰρ ἡ φύσις κυρία τοῦ δύνασθαι δὲ καὶ ἰσχύειν ἕτερα. Often κύριος γενόμενος is used of the military capture of a city, Plut. Quaest. Conv., VI, 8, 2 (II, 694c). κύριος can also denote possession, e.g., of money, Demosth. Or., 21, 98; 27, 55 f. etc.; Plut. Fort., 1 (II, 97c). Esp. it denotes man's possession of control over himself, Plat. Ep., 7, 324b: εἰ θᾶττον ἐμαυτοῦ γενοίμην κύριος. Aristot. Eth. Nic., III, 6, p. 1113b, 32: κύριος τοῦ μὴ μεθυσθῆναι. Plut. Quaest. Conv., VIII, 9, 2 (II, 731c): αὐτοκρατὲς δὲ ἡ ψυχὴ καὶ κύριον, Apophth. praef. (II, 172d): τῶν μὲν λόγων ἔφη κύριος αὐτὸς εἶναι, τῶν δὲ πράξεων τὴν τύχην. It can have the general sense of "exhibiting the decisive factor," Plat. Resp., IV, 429b: whether a city is brave or cowardly is decided by its soldiers, the others in the city οὐ ... κύριοι ἂν εἶεν ἢ τοίαν αὐτὴν εἶναι ἢ τοίαν, "do not have it in their hands." Thus in Dio Chrys. Or., 25, 1 the δαίμων of a man is called τὸ κρατοῦν ἑκάστου, and the question whether it is something in man or something ἔξωθεν ὂν ἄρχον τε καὶ κύριον τοῦ ἀνθρώπου is answered in the affirmative, and the explanation is given that kings, leaders and generals have been good or evil daemons for their subjects. In other words, to be a κύριος is to exert a powerful influence. The κύριος does not exercise direct, brutal, external force. His power may be as impalpable and yet as ineluctable as that of fate. Hence κύριος is the right word for "valid," i.e., "having the force of law." The transition may be seen in Andoc., 1, 87: ψήφισμα δὲ μηδὲν μήτε βουλῆς μήτε δήμου νόμου κυριώτερον εἶναι. It means "valid" of laws which are in force. Demosth. Or., 24, 1 says of the law: κύριος εἰ γενήσεται. Cf. often in the pap. of treaties, agreements, signatures, e.g., P. Oxy., II, 261, 17 f.: κυρία ἡ συγγραφήι (a scribal error, read συγγραφή), 55 A.D. Of persons with infin. or part., "authorised," "entitled," "competent," Demosth. Or., 59, 4: κύριον δ' ἡγούμενος δεῖν τὸν δῆμον εἶναι περὶ τῶν αὐτοῦ ὅ τι ἂν βούληται πρᾶξαι; Eur. Suppl., 1189 f.: οὗτος κύριος, τύραννος ὤν, πάσης ὑπὲρ γῆς Δαναϊδῶν ὀρκωμοτεῖν (take an oath); with part.

---

[1] Walde-Pok., I, 365 f.

[2] In the Pindar ref. κύριος is still an adj., in that from Plut. it inclines more to be a noun.

P. Eleph., 1, 15 f. (marriage contract, 311/310 B.C.): κύριοι δὲ ἔστωσαν Ἡρακλείδης καὶ Δημητρία ... τὰς συγγραφὰς αὐτοὶ τὰς αὐτῶν φυλάσσοντες, Polyb., 6, 37, 8 : κύριος δ' ἐστὶ καὶ ζημιῶν ὁ χιλίαρχος καὶ ἐνεχυράζων (pledge); with infin., Andoc., 4, 9 : τοὺς δικαστὰς ἀπολέσαι μὲν κυρίους εἶναι. With gen., "having full power over," Antiphon Or., III, 1, 1 (ed. L. Gernet [1923]): ὑπὸ ... τῶν ψηφισαμένων, οἳ κύριοι πάσης τῆς πολιτείας εἰσίν, Isoc., 19, 34 : τὴν μητέρα καὶ τὴν ἀδελφὴν τῶν αὐτοῦ κυρίας ... κατέστησε, Plat. Leg., XI, 929d : if the father who has become sick or demented οἰκοφθορῇ ... ὡς ὢν τῶν αὐτοῦ κύριος : the law gives him full power to do as he pleases with his possessions. The νόμος is κύριος βασιλεύς, Plat. Ep., 8, 354c; the opp. is τύραννος. P. Eleph., 2, 4 f. (285/4 B.C., will): ἐὰν δέ τι πάσχῃ Καλλίστα Διονυσίου ζῶντος, κύριον εἶναι Διονύσιον τῶν ὑπαρχόντων. Hence τὰ κύρια denotes the legal power in the state, Demosth. Or., 19, 259 : τὰ κύρι' ἄττα ποτ' ἐστὶν ἐν ἑκάστῃ τῶν πόλεων.

b. "Decisive," "important," "principal." Pind. Olymp.: κυρίῳ δ' ἐν μηνί, Aesch. Ag., 766 : ὅτε τὸ κύριον μόλῃ (comes): the decision, Eur. Or., 48 f.: κυρία δ' ἥδ' ἡμέρα, ἐν ᾗ διοίσει ψῆφον Ἀργείων πόλις, Eur. Iph. Aul., 318 : οὑμὸς οὐχ ὁ τοῦδε μῦθος κυριώτερος λέγειν : "important," Aristot. Eth. Nic., VI, 13, p. 1143b, 34: (ἡ φρόνησις) τῆς σοφίας κυριωτέρα; Plat. Leg., I, 638d : λέγειν τι κύριον, "to say something right," Phileb., 67b : κύριοι μάρτυρες, "valid witnesses," Symp., 218d : οἶμαί μοι συλλήπτορα οὐδένα κυριώτερον εἶναι σοῦ, "appropriate support." Hence κυριώτατος often occurs with μέγιστος, e.g., Plat. Soph., 230d; Polit., VIII, 565a (with πλεῖστος); Tim., 84c; 87c; Aristot., v. Index. κύριος is used similarly as an adj. in, e.g., Epict. Diss., I, 20, 18, where Epicurus is asked : τί κυριώτερον ἔχεις than the body, while Epict. himself says in II, 10, 1 that man has nothing κυριώτερον προαιρέσεως. Of the three τόποι for the προκόψων the κυριώτατος is ὁ περὶ τὰ πάθη ("the most important," "the chief"), Diss., III, 2, 3. κυριώτατος is used with μέγιστος in Diss., I, 9, 4; 12, 15; III, 1, 37. Cf. also Plut., e.g., Praec. Ger. Reip., 15 (II, 811d); Sept. Saep. Conv., 21 (II, 163d); Stoic. Rep., 45 f. (II, 1055d e). [3]

2. The noun κύριος occurs occasionally, though hardly as yet distinct from a substantivised adj., in the Attic tragic dramatists : Aesch. Choeph., 658 : κύριοι δωμάτων, ibid., 688 f.: εἰ δὲ τυγχάνω τοῖς κυρίοισι καὶ προσήκουσιν λέγων, cf. also Soph. Ai., 734; Oed. Col., 1643 f., where the γῆς ἄναξ (1630) Theseus is called ὁ κύριος Θησεύς, ibid., 288 f., where Oedipus says to the chorus : ὅταν δ' ὁ κύριος παρῇ τις, ὑμῶν ὅστις ἐστὶν ἡγεμών, also Eur. Iph. Aul., 703, where the father who gives his child in marriage is κύριος, and Andr., 558, where Neoptolemus is κύριος to the captured Andromache. [4]

By way of comparison it may be noted that Eur. uses δέσποινα 62 times (Aesch. 5) and δεσπότης 106 times (Aesch. 17). In the pre-Socratics the only instance which calls for notice is the statement of Democritus : [5] τόλμα πρήξιος ἀρχή, τύχη δὲ τέλεος κυρίη, where the meaning is : "has to decide concerning the end."

κύριος first occurs as a noun with a precise sense in the first half of the 4th cent. B.C., and it begins to have two fixed meanings. The first is the "lord" as the lawful owner of a slave, Demosth. Or., 36, 28 and 43 f.; 37, 51; 47, 14 f. (as against δεσπότης some 16 times for this); Xenoph. Oec., 9, 16; Aristot. Pol., II, 9 (1269b, 9 f.), the lord of subject peoples, who τῶν ἴσων ἀξιοῦσιν ἑαυτοὺς τοῖς κυρίοις, the master of the

---

[3] For further expressions with the adj. which need not be mentioned here (e.g., κυρία ἐκκλησία, κύριος τόνος, κύριον ὄνομα etc.), cf. Liddell-Scott, s.v. and the Index to Aristot., s.v.

[4] κύριος is also the head of the family, P. Oxy., II, 288, 36 (1st cent. A.D.). On the other hand Plut. still has δεσπότης for this, Sept. Sap. Conv., 12 (II, 155d): The best house is that ἐν ᾧ τοιοῦτός ἐστιν ὁ δεσπότης δι' αὐτόν, οἷος ἔξω διὰ τὸν νόμον. For the class. period cf. G. Busolt, Gr. Staatskunde, Index of F. Jandebeur (1926), s.v. κύριος.

[5] Fr., 269 (II, 115, 8 f., Diels).

house, Demosth. Or., 47, 60 (→ n. 4). In the sense of one who "is there for something," who "is put in charge of certain things" and has them "under him," it occurs in Antiphon Or., II, 4, 7 (ed. L. Gernet, 1923) of a slave who was not tortured : οὐδὲν θαυμαστὸν ἔπαθεν ὑπὸ τῶν κυρίων, cf. Plat. Crito, 44a : φασί γέ τοι δὴ οἱ τούτων κύριοι. The second more fixed sense of κύριος is that of the legal guardian of a wife or girl, Isaeus, 6, 32; Demosth. Or., 46, 15 etc. (for pap. v. APF, 3 [1906], 409 f.; 5 [1913], 472 and esp. 4 [1908], 78-91). Both uses of the noun are connected with the adj. in the sense of "one who has full authority." The implied idea of "legitimate" may still be seen in P. Hibeh, 34, 3 (243/2 B.C.): an offer ἢ τὸ ὑποζύγιον ἀποδοῦναι τῷ κυρίῳ (the lawful owner) or to pay the price. How strongly this idea is present in the term in Athens c. 400 may be seen in Aristoph. Pl., 6 f., where the lot of the slave (his owner is δεσπότης in v. 2) is depicted in gloomy terms : τοῦ σώματος γὰρ οὐκ ἐᾷ τὸν κύριον κρατεῖν ὁ δαίμων, ἀλλὰ τὸν ἐωνημένον, fate does not allow the lawful owner, namely, the slave himself, to dispose of his own body, but the one who bought him ; if δεσπότην were used instead of ἐωνημένον, the distinction between κύριος and δεσπότης would be palpable.[6] In Attic κύριος derives from the adj. a restriction to legitimate power of disposal which is never wholly lost in the koine : Dio Chrys. in his addresses De Servitute (Or. 14 and 15) always uses δεσπότης for the owner of a slave. Or., 14, 22 is typical both of him and of Attic usage ; here Odysseus as a beggar οὐδὲν ἧττον βασιλεὺς ἦν καὶ τῆς οἰκίας κύριος. Lucian, too, uses δεσπότης where the koine has κύριος; in Dial. Mar., 7, 2 Zephyrus says of Io : ἡμῶν ἔσται δέσποινα, ὅντινα ἂν ἡμῶν ἐθέλῃ ἐκπέμψαι. Antatticistes (Anecd. Graec., I, p. 102, 20): κυρίαν οὔ φασι δεῖν λέγειν, ἀλλὰ κεκτημένη· τὸν δὲ κεκτημένον μὴ λέγεσθαι ἀντὶ τοῦ δεσπότου. Σατυρικοῖς (?) κεκτημένον λέγει, Φιλήμων κυρίαν — the latter is thus an exception. In the Fr. of the Attic comic poets δεσπότης occurs 56 times, and δέσποινα[7] 11. Where κύριος is used as a noun, it is normally where δεσπότης is unsuitable or where there is no clear distinction between the noun and the adj.: Philemon :[8] ἐμοῦ γάρ ἐστι κύριος μὲν εἷς ἀνήρ (said by the slave), τούτων δὲ καὶ σοῦ μυρίων τ' ἄλλων νόμος : κύριος == "has to say," which δεσπότης could not express so well ; Alexis Fr., 262 :[9] When thou marriest, οὐδὲ σαυτοῦ κύριον ἔξεστιν εἶναι, → 1041; Fr., 149 :[10] οὐκ ἀρχιτέκτων κύριος τῆς ἡδονῆς μόνος καθέστηκ', enjoyment of art does not depend on the artist alone. κύριος means owner only in Crito (CAF, III, 354, Fr. 3): μεγάλου κύριον βαλλαντίου ... ποιήσας. In Menand. κύριος as a noun is used for the guardian of a child, Epit., 89, the master of a slave, Peric., 186, and in Sam., 287 for Ἔρως (ὁ τῆς ἐμῆς νῦν κύριος γνώμης Ἔρως).[11] W. Schmid, Der Atticismus in seinen Hauptvertretern (1887-1897) has κύριος in his Index only as an adj. Eustath. Thessal. (Opuscula, ed. ThLF [1832], p. 40, line 90) reads : ὅπου γε ἡ εὐγενὴς ἀττικὴ γλῶσσα τὸν κύριον ἐπὶ ἀνδρὸς τίθησιν, ᾧ γυναῖκα ὁ νόμος συνέζευξε. Dion. Hal. Ant. Rom., II, 27, 2 : τὴν ἐλευθερίαν εὐράμενος (sc. ὁ θεράπων) αὐτοῦ τὸ λοιπὸν ἤδη κύριός ἐστιν, illustrates the usage described above. The later relations of κύριος and δεσπότης may be seen in Manuel Moschopulos (c. 1300 A.D.), Sylloge Vocum Atticarum, s.v. δεσπότης :[12] δεσπότης λέγεται πρὸς δοῦλον, κύριος δὲ πρὸς ἐλεύθερον, s.v. δέσποινα : δέσποινα λέγεται οὐ μόνον ἡ βασιλίς, ἀλλὰ καὶ ἡ τοῦ οἴκου δεσπότις, ἣν ἰδιωτικῶς κυρίαν φαμέν. The use of κύριος

---

[6] Stegmann v. Pritzwald, 105 f. states that "one must always count on κύριος having the sense of one who has full power or control ; that is, there is always a legal implication."
[7] Acc. to the ed. of A. Meineke (1839 ff.).
[8] CAF, II, 486, Fr. 31.
[9] Ibid., II, 393.
[10] Ibid., II, 351.
[11] The Menand. passage (ibid., III, 116, Fr., 403) demands conjectural emendation : κυρίαν τῆς οἰκίας καὶ τῶν ἀγρῶν καὶ τῶν πατρῴων ἄντικρυς ἔχομεν.
[12] On the editions v. K. Krumbacher-A. Ehrhardt-H. Gelzer, Geschichte d. byzantinischen Lit.[2] (1897), 547 f. The extract is from the Paris ed., 1532.

is thus very limited in Attic. The extension of usage found in the NT belongs to the *koine*; this is particularly true of the noun. [13]

In the *koine* δεσπότης and κύριος are to a large degree used alongside one another. The κύριος is the owner of slaves and property. In the treaty between Miletus and Heraclea [14] the (lawful) owners of runaway slaves are called κύριοι. A distinction may still be discerned, however, between the two terms. Epict. uses both for the master of slaves, often interchangeably, e.g., Diss., IV, 1, 116. But in elucidation of his concept of freedom he prefers κύριος because it is capable of wider application. In Diss., IV, 1, 59 πᾶς ὃς ἂν ἐξουσίαν ἔχῃ τῶν ὑπ' αὐτοῦ τινος θελομένων πρὸς τὸ περιποιῆσαι ταῦτα ἢ ἀφελέσθαι is κύριος, and in 1, 145 the rich are οἱ τὸν κύριον τὸν μέγαν ἔχοντες καὶ πρὸς τὸ ἐκείνου νεῦμα καὶ κίνημα ζῶντες. The distinction between the terms is often to be seen in the way they are alternated. Thus the senator asks who can force him εἰ μὴ ὁ πάντων κύριος Καῖσαρ, to which Epict. replies: οὐκοῦν ἕνα μὲν δεσπότην σαυτοῦ καὶ σὺ αὐτὸς ὡμολόγησας. The senator calls the emperor κύριος as the one who has the right and power to control all things, but in the light of Epict.'s concept of freedom he is still a slave who has his δεσπότης over him. For this reason there is a suggestion of hardness in δεσπότης, as may be seen in Plut. Lucull., 18 (I, 503a), where a woman taken captive in war bewails her beauty ὡς δεσπότην ... ἀντ' ἀνδρὸς αὐτῇ ... προξενήσασαν (procured). Plut. Apophth., Philippus, 4 (II, 177d) attributes to Philip, the father of Alexander, the saying: μᾶλλον πολὺν χρόνον ἐθέλειν χρηστὸς ἢ δεσπότης ὀλίγον καλεῖσθαι. Correlative is τύραννος, Phoc., 29 (I, 754e), also κτῆμα, Plut. Praec. Coniug., 33 (II, 142e): κρατεῖν δὲ δεῖ τὸν ἄνδρα τῆς γυναικὸς οὐχ ὡς δεσπότην κτήματος, ἀλλ' ὡς ψυχὴν σώματος. κύριος, however, is the one who has ἐξουσία. The element of legality intrinsic in the word can sometimes come out even more clearly, e.g., in Plut. Aratus, 9 (I, 1031b) of those who are exiled: κατελθόντες δὲ οἱ πλεῖστοι πένητες ὧν κύριοι πρότερον ἦσαν ἐπελαμβάνοντο. κύριοι τῆς ὁλκάδος are those who give commands on a ship, Plut. Mar., 37 (I, 427a). Arat. says to Philip of Macedonia, Arat., 50 (I, 1050e): "If you begin with

---

[13] It must be particularly emphasised that Demosth. does not call Philip κύριος; when he uses κύριος of him (always with the gen.) he is simply saying that he, the one, has control of that which Gk. law has put under the people, Or., 18, 235 f.: τὰ ... τοῦ Φιλίππου ... πρῶτον μὲν ἦρχε τῶν ἀκολουθούντων αὐτὸς αὐτοκράτωρ ὤν ... ἔπειτα ... ἔπραττεν ἃ δόξειεν αὐτῷ οὐ προλέγων ἐν τοῖς ψηφίσμασιν, οὐδ' ἐν τῷ φανερῷ βουλευόμενος, οὐδὲ γραφὰς φεύγων παρανόμων, οὐδ' ὑπεύθυνος (responsible, accountable) ὢν οὐδενί, ἀλλ' ἁπλῶς αὐτὸς δεσπότης ἡγεμὼν κύριος πάντων. (That κύριος is an adj. here is also shown by the continuation, where Demosth., comparing himself with Philip and alluding to the preceding formulation, asks: ἐγὼ δ' ... τίνος κύριος ἦν;) Or., 19, 64: τηλικούτων μέντοι καὶ τοιούτων πραγμάτων κύριος εἷς ἀνὴρ Φίλιππος γέγονε, Or., 6, 6: ἡλίκος ἤδη καὶ ὅσων κύριός ἐστι Φίλιππος, Or., 18, 201: ἡγεμὼν ... καὶ κύριος ᾑρέθη Φίλιππος ἁπάντων, Or., 1, 4: τὸ γὰρ εἶναι πάντων ἐκεῖνον (sc. τὸν Φίλιππον) ἕνα ὄντα κύριον καὶ ῥητῶν καὶ ἀπορρήτων, καὶ ἅμα στρατηγὸν καὶ δεσπότην καὶ ταμίαν (note that δεσπότης, but not the adj. κύριος, can dispense with the gen.). In contrast is the Gk. view that the people (or νόμος) gives full power, is κύριος ἁπάντων, Or., 13, 31: τότε μὲν ὁ δῆμος δεσπότης ἦν καὶ κύριος ἁπάντων ... νῦν δὲ τοὐναντίον κύριοι μὲν τῶν ἀγαθῶν οὗτοι, καὶ διὰ τούτων ἅπαντα πράττεται (here, too, only κύριος takes a gen.); Or., 20, 107: ἐκεῖ μὲν γάρ ἐστι τῆς ἀρετῆς ἆθλον τῆς πολιτείας κυρίῳ γενέσθαι μετὰ τῶν ὁμοίων, παρὰ δ' ἡμῖν ταύτης μὲν ὁ δῆμος κύριος, καὶ ἀραὶ καὶ νόμοι καὶ φυλακαὶ ὅπως μηδεὶς ἄλλος κύριος γενήσεται ..., cf. also Or., 23, 69 (the plaintiff, even though he is in the right, is not κύριος τοῦ ἀλόντος, ἀλλ' ἐκείνου μὲν οἱ νόμοι κύριοι κολάσαι καὶ οἷς προστέτακται ταῦτα). As a noun to denote the position of the king in relation to his subjects and subject cities and territories, Demosth. uses δεσπότης, Or., 5, 17; 6, 25; 15, 27; 18, 296; 19, 69; 20, 16 (= τύραννος, 20, 15), and some of the passages already cited. To be κύριος is to have the supreme power of state in one's hands, G. Busolt, *Griech. Staatskunde*, I (1920), 304, and n. 4.

[14] Ditt. Syll.[3], 633, 95. For further examples *v.* Preisigke Wört., *s.v.*

πίστις and χάρις (confidence and friendliness), τῶν μὲν (of the Cretans) ἡγεμών, τῶν δὲ (of the Peloponnesians) κύριος ἤδη καθέστηκας." He explains the two terms shortly before : "Although you, Philip, have not taken any fortresses, πάντες ἑκουσίως σοι ποιοῦσι τὸ προστασσόμενον." κύριος is the one whose authority is obeyed. Cf. Plut. Apophth. Lac., Pausanias Plistonactis, 1 (II, 230 f.): τοὺς νόμους . . . τῶν ἀνδρῶν, οὗ τοὺς ἄνδρας τῶν νόμων κυρίους εἶναι δεῖ. The master of slaves is called κύριος in Plut. Apophth., Agathocles, 2 (II, 176e). Finally, the gods are called κύριοι as those who can control a sphere, Lat. Viv., 6 (II, 1130a): τὸν δὲ τῆς ἐναντίας (in contrast to the sun) κύριον μοίρας . . . "Αιδην ὀνομάζουσιν, Def. Orac., 29 (II, 426a, → 1041); Quaest. Conv., V, 3, 1, 4 (II, 675 f.): Poseidon and Dionysus τῆς ὑγρᾶς καὶ γονίμου κύριοι δοκοῦσιν ἀρχῆς εἶναι. κύριος is the word which is often used by the inferior of the superior because it emphasises the authority and legitimacy of his position. Hence Cassius is greeted as βασιλεὺς καὶ κύριος in Rhodes, and the answer is incisive : οὔτε βασιλεὺς οὔτε κύριος, τοῦ δὲ κυρίου καὶ βασιλέως φονεὺς καὶ κολαστής (Plut. Brutus, 30 [I, 998b]), while Brutus himself says, ibid., 22 (I, 994c): οἱ δὲ πρόγονοι... ἡμῶν οὐδὲ πρᾴους δεσπότας ὑπέμενον.

κύριος is the one who can dispose of something or someone, δεσπότης the one who owns something or someone. This shows how the terms both intersect and diverge. The more popular the speech, and the nearer the time of the NT, the more κύριος replaces δεσπότης. The closer to literary speech, and the nearer the beginning of the Hellenistic era, the stronger is the authoritative and legal element. We may well conclude with the interesting passage from Luc. Nigrinus, 26 : The philosopher despises earthly goods, maintaining ὅτι τούτων μὲν φύσει οὐδενός ἐσμεν κύριοι, νόμῳ δὲ καὶ διαδοχῇ τὴν χρῆσιν αὐτῶν εἰς ἀόριστον παραλαμβάνοντες ὀλιγοχρόνιοι δεσπόται νομιζόμεθα. There can be no confusing κύριος and δεσπότης here.

Not everyone who controls a thing or person can without qualification be called κύριος. The term is generally used for the lawful owner (including the owner of slaves) apart from some special legal phrases. In particular, officials are not as such called κύριοι. But gradually the usage developed of addressing those of higher rank as κύριε (κυρία) and of referring to them as ὁ κύριος. In the case of officials the title of their office was often added. The letters of the general Apollonius from the beginning of the 2nd cent. A.D. enable us to see that he was addressed as κύριε not merely by his employees and slaves but also by the villagers, P. Giess., 61, 17 (119 A.D.), while a rich ναύκληρος alternates between φίλτατε and κύριε, ibid., 11, 12 and 20 (118 A.D.), but his family (with one exception, → infra) does not address him in this way. Apollonius for his part addresses his superiors as ἡγεμὼν κύριε P. Giess., 41, I, 4, 9, 13. This usage may be traced back into the 1st cent. A.D. In Epict. high officials (Diss., IV, 1, 57), celebrated philosophers (III, 23, 11 and 19), the physician (II, 15, 15; III, 10, 15) and the μάντις (II, 7, 9) are addressed as κύριε, and the Cynic as κύριε ἄγγελε καὶ κατάσκοπε (III, 22, 38). In Ench., 40 he says generally that wives of 14 years standing are addressed as κυρίαι by their husbands. Acc. to Dio C., 61, 20, 1 Nero as a flute-player addressed the audience as κύριοί μου, and already in 45 A.D. P. Oxy., II, 283, 18 speaks of the κύριος ἡγεμών, cf. P. Oxy., I, 37, II, 8 (49 A.D.): τὰ ὑπὸ τοῦ κυρίου ἡγεμόνος κριθέντα, and from the year 71/72 A.D. (P. Tebt., 302, 11, 20), over against ἡγεμών, we find the phrase σοῦ τε τοῦ κυρίου γράψαντος. What seems to be an isolated instance goes back into the 1st cent. B.C.: BGU, 1819, 2 (60/59 B.C.): τῷ κυρίῳ στρατηγῷ. If already in the 1st cent. A.D. (BGU, 665, II, 18) a son addresses his father, and probably Hermaios his brother, the general Apollonius (P. Giess., 85, 16, early 2nd cent. A.D.), as κύριέ μου, this may still imply a certain subordination. But finally the father can also address the son as κύριε, P. Oxy., I, 123, 1: κυρίῳ μου υἱῷ Διονυσοθέωνι ὁ πατὴρ χαίρειν, line 24 : κύριε υἱέ (3rd-4th cent. A.D.). For further details cf. Dölger, op. cit. → κυρία, 1095.

Even before the beginning of the age of Constantine δεσπότης begins to replace κύριος in every sphere. In P. Oxy., I, 67, 10 (338 A.D.) δεσποτία is used to denote legal ownership, but already in 266 A.D. we find the address δέσποτα ἡγεμών (P. Tebt., 326, 3), and in the letter of a father to his son already mentioned (P. Oxy., I, 123) the former calls the addressee δέσποτά μου in line 7 and speaks of δέσποινά μου μήτηρ ὑμῶν in line 22. In the imperial titles, too, κύριος is increasingly replaced by δεσπότης.

One may sum up the whole development by saying that κύριος, originally the one who is fully authorised and has the legal power of disposal, did not contain the element of arbitrariness which so easily clung to δεσπότης. Hence it was first used by slaves to their masters in a kind of subtle flattery [15] and then it gradually ousted δεσπότης in ordinary parlance. But just because δεσπότης emphasised more strongly the direct and unrestricted aspect of possession, it came into vogue again in the age of dawning Byzantinism.

At the commencement of the Hellenistic era, then, the noun κύριος was still comparatively rare, and it was used in a narrow sense for the lord, the owner, the one who has full authority. If gods and rulers were later called κύριοι, this usage must have developed in Hellenism. There are no instances of Philip of Macedonia, of Alexander the Great, or of any of the early Diadochoi being called κύριοι, just as there are no instances of gods being called κύριοι in this period. For the well-known passage in the paean which the Athenians sang to Demetrius Poliorketes (306 B.C.): [16] πρῶτον μὲν εἰρήνην ποίησον, φίλτατε, κύριος γὰρ εἶ σύ, is to be rendered: "For thou canst do it, thou hast it in thy hand" (→ 1041). The first example of κύριος used of deity is to be found in the LXX, and in the light of the above exposition it is most unlikely that this is following an accepted usage. [17] The oldest example in independent Hellenistic development is to be found in the treaty between Philip VI of Macedonia and Hannibal as recorded by Polyb.: [18] ἐφ' ᾧτ' εἶναι σῳζομένους ... κυρίους Καρχηδονίους καὶ Ἀννίβαν τὸν στρατηγόν. Chronologically this is then followed by the use of κύριος βασιλειῶν [19] and κύριος τριακονταετηρίδων [20] in the Greek translation of the titles of Pharaoh.

B. Gods and Rulers as κύριοι.

In all religions the concept of God must contain the element of legitimate power, i.e., the power to which man must concede authority and before whose sovereignty he knows that he must bow. If the element of legitimacy is lacking, religion yields before the fear of spirits against which man seeks to defend himself by every

---

[15] In the two letters given by Jos. Ant., 17, 137 and 139 the slave calls her mistress ἡ ἐμὴ κυρία, but Joseph. in 138 uses δέσποινα.

[16] Athen., VI, 63 (p. 253e); the whole passage, so far as it is relevant, may be found in Foerster, 110. For a different rendering v. Baudissin, II, 288, but to construe as an adj. seems to be supported by the context, cf. also W. Schubart, Die religiöse Haltung des frühen Hellenismus (1937), 19.

[17] An argument from silence (the lack of instances in the sources) is not in itself entirely convincing (though → 1049 f.), but it gains added weight in connection with linguistic considerations.

[18] 7, 9 and 5. Cf. on this U. Kahrstedt, NGG, 1923 (1924), 99 f.: To call the citizens of a city its lords is a Semitism; the choice of κύριος is Hellenistic.

[19] APF, 1 (1901), 480 ff. = Deissmann LO, 300, n. 2 (Ptolemy IV. Philopater, 221-205 B.C.): Ditt. Or., 90, line 1 = CIG, 4697 (196 B.C.).

[20] Ditt. Or., 90, n. 2 (→ n. 19). Cf. on both these notes Baudissin, II, 288, n. 2 and 3.

possible means, against which he fights. If the element of power is lacking, the deity is no more than an idea. But the two together, might and right as a single concept, are bound up with the personal being of their bearer. For right and its correlate, responsibility, are categories which apply only between persons. The concept of God in Greek religion is not entirely without the element of personal, legitimate power. This finds expression in the term "lord." δεσπότης (δέσποινα) is also used of the gods in classical Greek, and occasionally later. It denotes the relation of the gods to nature and to men. But in the whole sphere of human life, political as well as religious, what separates the Greeks from the barbarians is that the Greeks do not basically regard their gods as lords and themselves as δοῦλοι (→ δοῦλος, II, 261 ff.). This is connected with the fact that the fundamental personal act, the creative activity of God, finds almost no place at all in the Greek concept of God (→ 1002 f.).

1. κύριος for Gods and Rulers in Classical Greece.

It is true that the word κύριος is used of the Greek gods from the classical era right on into the imperial period, first as an adjective, then increasingly as a noun, and specifically when it is desired to state that the gods can control definite spheres.

Pind. Isthm., 5, 53 : Zeus ὁ πάντων κύριος, Plat. Leg., XII, 13 (966c): the φύλακες must know of the gods ὡς εἰσίν τε καὶ ὅσης φαίνονται κύριοι δυνάμεως, cf. Resp., VII, 517c; [21] Xenoph. Mem., I, 4, 9 : Against the proof of God from the νοῦς of man the objection is brought : οὐ γὰρ ὁρῶ τοὺς κυρίους, Oec., 6, 1: One must begin with the gods ὡς τῶν θεῶν κυρίων ὄντων οὐδὲν ἧττον τῶν εἰρηνικῶν ἢ τῶν πολεμικῶν ἔργων, Demosth. Or., 60, 21: ὁ πάντων κύριος δαίμων, Ep., 4, 6, of the gods : ἁπάντων τῶν ἀγαθῶν ἐγκρατεῖς ὄντας κυρίους εἶναι καὶ αὐτοὺς ἔχειν καὶ δοῦναι τοῖς ἄλλοις. Sosiphanes Fr., 3 (TGF):

ἢν δ' εὐτυχῆτε, μηδὲν ὄντες εὐθέως
ἴσ' οὐρανῷ φρονεῖτε, τὸν δὲ κύριον
Ἀίδην παρεστῶτ' οὐχ ὁρᾶτε πλησίον.

Dio Chrys. Or., 37 (Corinth), 11 calls Poseidon and Helios τὸν μὲν τοῦ πυρὸς κύριον τὸν δὲ τοῦ ὕδατος, Plut. Is. et Os., 35 (II, 365a): οὐ μόνον τοῦ οἴνου Διόνυσον, ἀλλὰ καὶ πάσης ὑγρᾶς φύσεως Ἕλληνες ἡγοῦνται κύριον καὶ ἀρχηγόν, Quaest. Conv., V, 3, 1 (II, 675 f.): ἀμφότεροι γὰρ οἱ θεοὶ (Poseidon and Dionysus) τῆς ὑγρᾶς καὶ γονίμου κύριοι δοκοῦσιν ἀρχῆς εἶναι, Def. Orac. (→ 1041); Lat. Viv. (→ 1045); Ael. Arist. Or., 37, 17 (Keil): Nike is not κυρία of Athene, but Athene of Nike, Plut. Is. et Os., 40 (II, 367a) calls Isis ἡ κυρία τῆς γῆς θεός, ibid., 12 (II, 355e) tells of a legendary voice which greeted Osiris as ἁπάντων κύριος at his birth, and ibid., 49 (II, 371a): ἐν μὲν οὖν τῇ ψυχῇ νοῦς καὶ λόγος ὁ τῶν ἀρίστων πάντων ἡγεμὼν καὶ κύριος Ὄσιρίς ἐστιν. Philo of Byblos says of Beelsamen (FHG, III, p. 566a): ὅ ἐστι παρὰ Φοίνιξι κύριος οὐρανοῦ, Ζεὺς δὲ παρ' Ἕλλησι. Along the same lines Epict. Diss., IV, 1, 12 speaks of ὁ πάντων κύριος Καῖσαρ. (For further details → n. 49 and → 1054.)

It should be noted, however, that in contrast to divine designations in the Orient and Egypt the gods are not here described strictly as the κύριοι of their spheres. In other words, they are not characterised by lordship. In Babylon and Egypt, on

---

[21] Plat. Ep., 6, 323d : τὸν τῶν πάντων θεὸν ἡγεμόνα τῶν τε ὄντων καὶ τῶν μελλόντων, τοῦ τε ἡγεμόνος καὶ αἰτίου πατέρα κύριον ἐπομνύντας. θεὸς ἡγεμών and πατὴρ κύριος correspond. Is κύριος meant to emphasise the position of the father as head of the family (→ n. 4)?

the other hand, they are named after that over which they are lords: "May the acts of Marduk, the lord of the gods, be seen by all the gods and goddesses, Anu, Enlil, the lord of the ocean, regnant Ea."[22] This fact is connected with the fundamental structure of the Greek concept of God, namely, that for the Greeks the gods are basically no more than the fundamental forms of reality (→ 68). Hence they do not confront the world and man personally as creators or designers. They are not the lords of the reality which comprehends all things, of destiny. This stands autonomously alongside the gods (→ 70). Because gods and men draw their breath from one mother (→ 70) they are organically related members of one reality, and their mutual relation cannot be described in terms of κύριος and δοῦλος.[23] At root, man has no personal responsibility towards these gods, nor can they personally encounter man with punishments. To pray to them is fundamentally illogical, as is also the fact that Zeus appears again as the lord of fate. But this simply shows that here, too, another factor comes to light, namely, that a concept of God in which the gods are only the basic forms of reality is bound to disintegrate.

In any age the concept of the lordship of the gods is indissolubly connected with the understanding of the relations of lordship in the whole sphere of reality. If the gods are the meaning of reality, there is need to find this meaning in the remaining spheres of reality. The political consequence of this is democracy, in which each individual makes his contribution towards the grasping of this meaning. When the Greek serves the laws (→ II, 262), he gives himself freely to that which binds him, for in his own reason he has seen that it is such, and he has contributed his own portion towards its construction and affirmation. On the other hand, right is not just something which the citizens decree. It also stands above them, as may be seen in the passage already quoted from Andoc., → 1042.

While it is true that the Hellenistic monarchies deviated widely from Greek democracy, and while the later Greeks always greeted with enthusiasm the proclamation of their freedom, it must be emphasised that the Hellenistic cult of the ruler had its roots in classical Greece. For the divine element which fills the world is deposited to a special degree in the ruler (→ 68). The ruler does not need the consent of the people, since their decisions will agree with those of the ruler, who participates to a special measure in virtue. The ruler is θεός, θεὸς ἐπιφανής, νέος Διόνυσος etc. But he is not κύριος. He does not stand apart from the people. He is simply inspired to a special degree by the divine element which indwells all Hellenes. The Hellenistic ruler is νόμος ἔμψυχος.[24]

2. Gods and Rulers as Lords in the Orient and Egypt.

For Orientals the gods are the lords of reality. Destiny is in their hands. The individual man is personally responsible to the gods who made him (→ 1002).

---

[22] A. Ungnad, Die Religion d. Babylonier u. Assyrer (1921), 174, etc. In Egypt the gods are not only called lords of towns (e.g., G. Roeder, Urkunden zur Religion des alten Ägypten [1915], 5: Amon-Re as lord of Karnak) but also of eternity, of what exists (ibid., 5), of justice, of grain (7), also of heaven and earth (Aton, 69). An imprecise use of "lord" (cf. בַּעַל in the OT) is also found, e.g., lord of worship (5). For details cf. A. Erman and H. Grapow, Wörterbuch d. ägypt. Sprache, II (1928), s.v. nb.

[23] A point worth considering is whether δεσπότης (δέσποινα) might have been used of deities in the class. period because it suggests the pater familias, i.e., the organic connection between the divine and the human.

[24] E. R. Goodenough, "The Political Philosophy of Hellenistic Kingship," Yale Classical Studies, I (1928), 55-102.

They intervene in his life with punishments. [25] From both these angles it is necessary that the gods be called lords. They are the lords of the world and all its component parts. They are the lords of destiny and the lords of men. That which is essential to the Greeks, namely, that reality show itself to be divine to man, and that man as a free agent take up a position in relation to it, is completely lacking here. As the gods lay down what is right, the ruler proclaims this to his subjects, and these have no option but to submit in silence. This is what the Greeks felt to be servile. In the Orient, however, there was a lively sense that the administration of law requires personal authorisation. This leads to the oriental cult of the ruler. Here the king is not regarded as a new form of manifestation of the divine. The power which he possesses and the justice which he administers set him above men and in the proximity of the gods to whom he owes his position. As king, as administrator of law, the ruler stands above men, and since the administration of law is committed to him by the gods he may issue unconditional commands to men and these owe to him the same unconditional obedience as they do to the gods. Everything is here based on the personal confrontation of God and man.

3. The Hellenistic κύριος.

For a discussion of the Hellenistic application of the title κύριος to gods and men it is first necessary that we review the data.

a. Chronology. Except for κύριος with the gen. → 1042; 1044, n. 13, κύριος is never used of gods or rulers prior to the 1st cent. B.C. [26] It is first used of Isis in Egypt, CIG, 4897a (99-90 B.C.): τὸ προσκύνημα ... παρὰ τ[ῇ κυρίᾳ "Ισιδι], also from the 1st cent. CIG, 4898; 4899; 4904; 4917; 4930b; 4931; Ditt. Or., 186, 8 f. Already in 81 B.C. we find the phrase προσκυνήσας τὴν κυρίαν θεὰν ⁵Ισιν, CIG, 4936d, addenda; all from Philae. Similarly we read of the god Soknopaios (Seknebtynis) in the 1st cent. B.C.: ὡς θέλει ὁ Σεκνεβτῦ[νις] ὁ κύριος θεός, P. Tebt., 284, 5 f. From Gizeh comes the dedication of a building τῷ θεῷ καὶ κυρίῳ Σοκνοπαίῳ, Ditt. Or., 655, 24 B.C. From the time of Augustus or Tiberius we have a Syrian inscr. with the formula θεὸς Κρόνος κύριος, Ditt. Or., 606.

For the ruler κύριος βασιλεύς is often used in Egypt between 64 and 50 B.C., BGU, 1767, 1; 1768, 9; 1816, 3; Ditt. Or., 186, 8. From 52 B.C. there is mention of feasts τοῖς κυρίοις θεοῖς μεγίστοις; the ref. is to Ptolemy XIII and his co-rulers, SAB (1902), 1096; cf. CIG, 4717, line 25, also line 29: θύειν τοῖς κυρίοις θεοῖς (45-37 B.C.), though Baudissin thinks this refers to gods, II, 285; BGU, 1834, 6 f., where the writer calls himself "chief keeper of the boots" τῶν θεῶν καὶ κυρίων βασιλέων (51-50 B.C.), cf. BGU, 1764, 8 (διὰ τὴν τύχην τοῦ θεοῦ καὶ κυρίου βασιλέως). In Egypt, too, Augustus is called θεὸς καὶ κύριος Καῖσαρ Αὐτοκράτωρ in 12 B.C., BGU, 1197, I, 15, in part amplified; BGU, 1200, 10 ff.: εἰς τὰς] ὑπὲρ τοῦ θε[οῦ] καὶ κυρίου Αὐτοκράτορος Κα[ίσαρος καθηκούσας] θυσίας καὶ σπονδάς; P. Oxy., VIII, 1143, 4: θυσίας καὶ σπονδὰς ὑπὲρ τοῦ θεοῦ καὶ κυρίου Αὐτοκράτορος (1st cent. A.D.); Herod the Great is called βασιλεὺς Ἡρώδης κύριος, in Ditt. Or., 415; cf. also Agrippa I and II, κύριος βασιλεὺς Ἀγρίππας, ibid., 418; 423; 426, and

---

25 Cf. the Babylonian penitential psalms, e.g., Ungnad, 220: "As though I did not fear my god, my goddess, so it befalls me. Sorrow, sickness, destruction and corruption are my portion."

26 Two Thracian inscr., one with (κυρ)ίῳ Διί, the other (κυ)ρίῳ Ἀσκληπιῷ, belong to the 3rd cent. B.C. acc. to J. J. E. Hondius, Supplementum Epigraphicum Graecum, III (1929), Nos. 510 and 511. But as may be seen from Revue des études anciennes, 26 (1924), 32, also n. 1 and 2, this is either a mistake or a misprint, since they date from the 3rd cent. A.D. There is an inscr. from Susa, c. 200 B.C., ibid., VII (1934), No. 18, but it is not certain how this should run: [ἀφιέρωσεν κυρίᾳ Ἀρτέμιδι (?) Ν]αναίᾳ.

βασιλεὺς μέγας Ἀγρίππας κύριος, 425; Hondius, VII (1934), 970 B; in Upper Egypt Queen Candace is ἡ κυρία βασίλισσα (13 B.C.), Mitteis-Wilcken, I, 2, 4. A Ptolemaic στρατηγός is called ὁ κύριος στρατηγός (60/59 B.C.), BGU, 1819, 2, and ὁ θεότατος καὶ κύριος στρατηγός (51/50 B.C.), 1838, 1.

In Egypt, then, κύριος appears within a life-span in this use for gods, rulers, and high officials. Since we have a not inconsiderable number of Greek documents of every kind from the preceding centuries in Egypt, in which κύριος is not used in this way, there is no reason to suppose that gaps in the sources give us an essentially false picture of the time when κύριος first began to occur in these connections, or that new findings would essentially alter the picture.

The situation might be different in Syria, since there we do not have sacral inscr. from the 3rd and 2nd cent. B.C. (Baudissin, II, 258). On the other hand, it is a fact that in Syria, too, the Gk. κύριος is not used of gods and rulers prior to the 1st cent. B.C. The oldest attestation of κύριος in this sense in Syria is the inscr. in Ditt. Or., 606 already quoted above, where the imperial house, as well as Chronos, is called ὑπὲρ τῆς τῶν κυρίων Σεβαστῶν σωτηρίας, lines 1 f. This seems to suggest that it was only in the 1st cent. B.C. that the counter-thrust from the Orient began which was to pour the eastern concept of the ruler into Greek forms.

It is worth noting that almost at once κύριος begins to be used in close connection with the nouns θεός, βασιλεύς, στρατηγός, with no intermediate καί. This usage cannot possibly mark the beginning; it is rather the sign of a final stage. But since this cannot be the final stage of Gk. usage, it must be an adaptation of an older Egyptian and Syrian development. Here the word corresponding to κύριος was used without copula along with terms like God or king (→ 1053).

b. Location. As regards the spatial distribution of the use of κύριος for gods, we begin intentionally with Egypt. The word is used once each of Ammon, Anubis, Apollo, Aesculapius, the Dioscuri, Horogebthios, Priotos, Rhodosternos and Sruptichis, twice of Soknopaios, 3 times of Pan, 4 of Bes, 9 of Mandulis, 16 of Hermes, and 38 each of Sarapis and Isis. [27] Outside Egypt it is used for Egyptian gods as follows: Sarapis, once in Asia Minor, twice in Crete, once in Italy; Helios, once in Spain; Isis, twice in Asia Minor, once in Rome. In addition, κυρεία is the official name for Isis in Heracliu Pelagos acc. to P. Oxy., XI, 1380, 61 f.; she is also addressed as κυρία Ἶσι, ibid., 142, and often as κυρία with the gen. of the sphere over which she reigns; cf. Horus and Hermes, 210 f. and 265 f. Plut speaks similarly of Osiris, 1046, 20 ff., and in the Isis hymn of Cyrene Isis 4 times calls herself κυρία with the gen. of a noun. [28] Of the 119 times which I have counted for κύριος in Egypt, in 95 it occurs in the phrase τὸ προσκύνημά τινος ποιεῖν παρὰ τῷ κυρίῳ (τῇ κυρίᾳ) with the name of the deity following, or in similar expressions which relate to a προσκύνημα.

In Syria κύριος is used once of Balmarkos, Ὀαου, Echo, Jupiter Heliopolitanus, Marnas, twice each for Atargatis, Dionysus, Chronos, Nemesis, 4 times for Artemis, 5 for Πατρίς, 7 for Athene, 12 for Zeus. We might also mention once each for Ameros and Athene from Arabia. Outside Syria the distribution for Syrian deities is once each for Athene (Allat) and Helios in Spain.

In Asia Minor κύριος (κυρία) is attested once each for Aesculapius, Hermes, Sarapis, Tiamos, Zeus, twice each for Helios, Isis, Sabazios and Apollo, 3 times for Nemesis, 4 for Πατρίς, 13 for Artemis. The Ephesian Artemis is once called κυρία in Italy, and in addition she is probably meant on two other Italian inscr. which have κυρία Ἄρτεμις (without Ἐφεσία).

---

[27] The statistics which follow make no claim to completeness, but they are taken from so wide a range of material that the conclusions based on them are hardly likely to be false. The figures are mainly based on the list of Drexler amplified from material in P. Amh., P. Fay., P. Giess., P. Hibeh, P. Oxy., I-XVII, P. Tebt., BGU, Hondius etc.

[28] W. Peek, Der Isishymnus von Andros u. verwandte Texte (1930), 122 ff.

κύριος (κυρία) is also found without a divine name 4 times in Syria and once in the phrase θεῷ οὐρανίῳ πατρῴῳ τῷ κυρίῳ, [29] also several times in the expression ὁ κύριος θεός in Egypt.

On the other hand, it should be pointed out that Jupiter Heliopolitanus is called κύριος only once, and Jupiter Dolichenus not at all.

The implication is that κύριος never became widespread as a predicate of the gods. It was in common use only in certain places where it corresponded to native, non-Greek usage, and it remained there. At root, then, the use of κύριος for the gods is the translation of an alien usage and no more. In keeping with this is the fact that, compared with the very common occurrence of אדן on Semitic inscr., the number of instances of κύριος we might expect on Syrian Greek inscr. ought to be very much greater. In fact, however, κύριος is used comparatively much less frequently in Syria than its Semitic equivalent. To a large extent, therefore, the authors of Gk. inscr. in Syria avoided κύριος. [30]

c. From what has been said, it follows that when κύριος is used of gods its meaning and content must be derived in the main from indigenous usage. Nevertheless, the Greek examples do enable us to discern a certain tendency.

In the first place the predicate κύριος is not designed to distinguish outstanding or sovereign gods from others who are subordinate. [31] There is certainly no such distinction in Syria, and in Egypt less important local gods are also called κύριος. [32] Again, the term is not used only for gods particularly venerated in the cultus. Our observations show that what κύριος expresses is the personal relation of an individual to a god. As concerns Egypt, this perhaps explains the very common use of κύριος in προσκυνήματα, which represent a prayer or petition. Then κύριος is found particularly in inscr. of thanksgiving ; thus Ephesian Artemis is called κυρία only in the phrase εὐχαριστῶ σοι, κυρία Ἄρτεμι, [33] and there are similar examples for Egyptian deities : εὐχαριστῶ τῷ κυρίῳ Σεράπιδι, ὅτι μου κινδυνεύσαντος εἰς θάλασσαν ἔσωσε εὐθέως, [34] of Mandulis : εὐχαριστῶ τῷ κυρίῳ, ὅτι (CIG, 5070), of Hermes [35] and Νέμεσις, [36]

---

[29] We might also note the figures for Thrace, where κύριος occurs once each for Artemis, Dionysus, the Dioscuri, Helios, Heracles, Pluto, twice for Sabazios, 3 times each for Apollo and Hera, 4 for Aesculapius, 5 for Zeus, 6 each for Ἥρως and the nymphs, also once κύριος θεός with no name. In Greece itself (Sparta) the only instance is κυρία once for Πατρίς. Gnostic instances are not adduced as in Baudissin, II, 270, n. 2, nor instances from magic lit., where much of the material is certainly old, but there is the interaction of the most diverse influences. E. Peterson, Byzantin.-Neugriech. Jbcher., 5 (1926/27), 224 thinks that the use of κύριος in astrological texts should be included, but these do not add anything, as will be seen in the course of the enquiry.

[30] A sample test will quickly prove this. In that portion of the great work of P. Le Bas/ W. H. Waddington, Inscriptions grecques et latines recueillies en Grèce et en Asie Mineure, III (1870), which contains the Syrian inscr. (No. 1826-2677), Zeus is called κύριος 6 times, but 5 times he is simply Ζεύς, once each θεὸς Ζεύς, Ζεὺς Κεραύνιος and Ζεὺς ὕψιστος, 5 times Ζεὺς ὕψιστος καὶ ἐπήκοος, 5 times other predicates are used. It is true that Athene is 5 times κυρία Ἀθηνᾶ and only once θεὰ Ἀθηνᾶ and twice Ἀθηνᾶ, but in all there are only 20 instances of κύριος as compared with 106 other titles.

[31] Baudissin, II, 271 ff.

[32] Cf. the earlier list.

[33] BMI, 578c; 580; 582a; 586a; 587b; 588; 588b; 590; Hondius, IV (1930), 535, 9 f.

[34] BGU, 423, 6 ff. (2nd cent. A.D.).

[35] P. Giess., 85, 6 f.: τοιοῦτό σοι μόνῳ εὐχαριστῶ παρὰ τῷ κυρίῳ Ἑρμῇ (Trajan/ Hadrian).

[36] Hondius, VII (1934), 804 : τῇ κυρίᾳ Νεμέσι ... ἀνέθηκα εὐχαριστῶν (1st-2nd cent.).

cf. also the Dioscuri. [37] In petitionary prayer Sarapis is addressed as κύριε Σάραπι, [38] and we find the same form in consultations of the oracle [39] and in demands for vengeance addressed to Helios. [40] There is also a personal relation to an unspecified god in the inscr. καθαρμοῖς κὲ θυσίαις ἐ[τίμησα τὸν κ]ύριον ἵνα μυ (= μοι) τὸ ἐμὸν σῶ[μα σῴζ]ει (= σῴζοι), [41] in the well-known invitation to the κλείνη τοῦ κυρίου Σαρά-πιδος, [42] and also to the ἐγκατοχήσας τῷ κυρίῳ Σαράπιδι. [43] In Syria κύριος is often used as a divine name in the dedication of votive monuments; it expresses the personal relation of the author of the monument to this god. On the other hand, κύριος is seldom used in contexts which do not obviously contain this personal relation to the deity. [44] Apart from some passages whose context is not clear, the only remaining group consists of inscr. in which the author describes himself as under the command of the deity named: Λούκιος ... πεμφθεὶς ὑπὸ τῆς κυρίας 'Αταργάτης; [45] κατ' ἐπιταγὴν τῆς κυρίας 'Αρτέμιδος; [46] ἐπικέκριταί μοι μὴ καταβῆναι ἕως τῆς κε, καὶ ὡς θέλει ὁ Σεκνεβτῦνις ὁ κύριος θεὸς καταβήσομαι ἐλευθέρως. [47]

κύριος, then, is particularly used in expression of a personal relationship of man to the deity, whether in prayer, thanksgiving or vow, and as a correlate of δοῦλος inasmuch as the man concerned describes as κύριος the god under whose orders he stands. Yet we cannot separate this whole complex of ideas from the power of the gods over nature or its components. It is no accident that in the case of Isis and Sarapis, the two who are most commonly called κύριος (κυρία), the idea of dominion over nature and destiny is most impressively present. As concerns Isis, we may refer to P. Oxy., XI, 1380, 121 ff., to the hymn of Cyrene (→ n. 28) and to Apul. Met., XI, 5; as concerns Sarapis, to the Sarapis Aretalogies. [48] Finally, the element of power in κύριος is predominant in the Hermetic writings. [49]

---

[37] L. Heuzey-H. Daumet, *Mission archéologique de Macédoine* (1876), 407, No. 185 (Drexler, 1760): πα]ρὰ [τ]οῖς κυρ[ίοις Διοσκού]ροις ἐμν[ήσθ]η Σωτήριχ[ος].

[38] κύριε Σάραπι, δὸς νείκην, the rest is uncertain. Cf. Drexler, 1763; CIG, 4710 (Lycopolis): κύριε Σάραπι, δὸς αὐτῷ τὴν κατεξουσίαν κατὰ τῶν ἐχθρῶν αὐτοῦ (burial inscr.); CIG, 4712b: ἀντιλαβοῦ, κύριε Σάραπι ...; an unknown god is addressed: κύριε, βοήθει τὸν δοῦλόν σου Βαρι ... H. Böhlig, *Die Geisteskultur v. Tarsos* ... (1913), 55, n. 8.

[39] P. Oxy., VIII, 1148, 1 (1st cent. A.D.): κύριέ μου Σάραπι "Ηλιε εὐεργέτα; P. Fay., 138 (1st-2nd cent. A.D., Dioscuri).

[40] JHS, 5 (1884), 253, No. 4; Hondius, VI (1932), 803.

[41] JHS, 8 (1887), 388, No. 17.

[42] P. Oxy., I, 110; III, 523; XII, 1484; XIV, 1755 (1st-2nd—2nd-3rd cent. A.D.).

[43] CIG, 3163 (Smyrna).

[44] E.g., Le Bas/Waddington, 1879: ἐθεμ[ελιώθη] ... ἐκ τῶν τοῦ κυρίου Διὸς (προσόδων), Hondius, II (1925), 830, 3 ff.: ᾠκοδομήθησαν ... ἐκ τῶν τοῦ κυρίου Διός; also 832 (3rd or 4th cent. A.D.). In all I have counted 13 passages in which there does not seem to be a personal relation of the speaker to the κύριος.

[45] Le Bas/Waddington, 1890.

[46] Hondius, III (1929), 691 (Mytilene).

[47] P. Tebt., 284, 2 ff. (1st cent. B.C.). Perhaps also the Nabatean inscr. with עלימי מראנא, *Rev. Bibl.*, 42 (1933), 415, No. 5.

[48] O. Weinreich, *Neue Urkunden z. Sarapis-Religion* (1919).

[49] The content of κύριος in the Corp. Herm. (I, 6; V, 2; XIII, 17 and 21) is not so plain as in the rest of the Herm. lit., in which it is linked with expressions of universality: ὁ τῶν ὅλων κύριος, Κόρη Κόσμου, 25; πάντων κύριος, Fr., 12, 23, 24, 29, 33; Lord and Creator of all: Ascl., I, 8; Fr., 32; *pater omnium vel dominus*, Ascl., III, 29b; *summa vero gubernationis summo illi domino paret*, III, 19c; esp. III, 20a: *deus etenim vel pater vel dominus omnium quocumque [alio] nomine ... nuncupatur ... Non enim spero totius maiestatis effectorem omniumque rerum patrem vel dominum uno posse quamvis e multis conposito nuncupari nomine.* We also find *pater* and *deus* together in III, 22b, 23b, 26a (*ille dominus et pater, deus primipotens et unius gubernator dei*). The quotations are acc. to the Corp. Herm., ed. W. Scott (1924).

The Greek side thus brings us to the same result as that which was reached by Baudissin in his express analysis of the meaning of the corresponding Semitic term. κύριος corresponds, not to the Semitic בעל, but to the Phoenician Canaanite אדון fem. רבת, and to the Aram. מרא. These words are commonly placed before the names of deities as epithets, like the Hellenistic κύριος. In many cases they were linked to a personal suffix which referred to the worshipper of the god and which was sometimes added as the gen. of a personal pronoun to the Greek κύριος as a divine name. [50] The personal relationship expressed in this personal suffix or personal pronoun is absent among the Greeks and the Romans. [51] This is linked with the general distinction between oriental and Greek religion already discussed. That the correlate of this term for lord is slave, in Greek δοῦλος, is shown by some inscr. (→ 1052) and in the Semitic sphere by the common use of עבד in theophorous personal names. Now it is not possible to discern in the term "lord," when linked with the name of a god, only the element of personal attachment and not also the element of personal authority which the worshipper ascribes to his god and which finds its counterpart in his own subjection of will. Furthermore, it is not possible to separate the elements of power and greatness as Baudissin once does. [52] If all Semitic personal names which contain the name of a god, and which are formed with some other word than servant, speak of something which the god either has done or will do to save his worshippers, or mention a quality which is the basis of the certainty or hope that the god will intervene on their behalf, [53] this implies that the god has the power to act for his servant in this way. Whether his sphere of power may extend only to that on which the development of the group or its members depends [54] is not essential, although in NT days it is important that the power of the god should be constantly expanded, and in Palmyra we find the divine designations מרא עלמא and מרא כל. [55] And if for Orientals the power of the ruler was in earliest times expressed in judging rather than in ruling, [56] the administration of justice presupposes an authority which will be obeyed, i.e., it is real power. "A superior position, as predominant, implies the power of him who occupies it." [57] Hence the linking of a personal suffix with the designation "lord" is an impressive reminder that "already in primitive conditions the relation of the slave to his master as the latter's property was a guarantee of protection against danger from others." [58]

The Heb. בעל denotes more the owner, while אדון is the lord as the one who has power. [59] Baethgen puts it as follows: "The master in relation to the slave is בעל as the owner of the slave and אדון as the one who can dispose of this possession as he wills." [60] The distinction between the terms is similar to that between δεσπότης and κύριος, and linguistically κύριος is the equivalent of אדון.

---

[50] ἐκ τῶν τοῦ κυρίου αὐτῶν θεοῦ Ἀμέρου, Hondius, VII (1934), 1069, 7 (Arabia); ἀπὸ τοῦ κυρίου ἡμῶν Ἑρμοῦ καὶ Ἀσκληπιοῦ (Thebes, 138 A.D., P. Par., 19, 5); κύριέ μου Σάραπι, → n. 39.

[51] Baudissin, III, 556 and n. 1.

[52] Ibid., 631: "In the designation of God as Lord is expressed the submission of man not so much to a power which he cannot resist as to a greatness in face of which only humble reverence is befitting."

[53] Ibid., 527.

[54] Ibid., 625.

[55] Ibid., 684 f.

[56] Ibid., 613 ff.

[57] Ibid., 620.

[58] Ibid., 526.

[59] Ges.-Buhl, s.v. אדון. G. Dalman, Der Gottesname Adonaj u. seine Geschichte (1889), 10 f.

[60] F. Baethgen, Beiträge z. semitischen Religionsgeschichte (1888), 41.

Perhaps the connection between the lordship of the deity over nature or its components, and the linguistic expression of this in the concept of lord, is rather more common in Egyptian. There can be little doubt that the transferring of κύριος to the gods on the basis of a native, non-Greek usage took place independently in Egypt and Syria. Baudissin's assumption that this use of κύριος as an epithet for the gods came from Syria to Egypt is most improbable. [61] In its favour Baudissin advances the erroneous idea that "in Egypt 'lord' is never an epithet which stands alone or which is linked with a personal suffix," [62] and he appeals to a statement of Erman which he has obviously misunderstood. [63] In fact the linking of nb (lord) and (less frequently) nb.t (lady) not only with a gen. but also with a personal suffix is "the normal use attested in every age." The use with the 1st person suffix "my lord" as an address, "O my lord Re," "O king, my lord," etc. is naturally very common, but nb or nb.t is also linked with all other suffixes : "thy lord," "his lords," "my lord," "your lady," etc. [64] The use of κύριος in Egypt in the 1st cent. B.C. (→ 1049) corresponds to an ancient native usage, but in keeping with Greek usage the personal suffix fell away with the transference into Greek. [65]

Though there is an obvious distinction, it is thus impossible to separate materially the κύριος [66] which is connected with a genitive of the sphere of lordship and the κύριος which is added to the divine name as an epithet, with a personal suffix which dropped away with the transference into Greek.

d. We have already considered the earliest examples of the application of κύριος to rulers. The phrases κύριος βασιλειῶν and κύριος τριακονταετηρίδων which derive from Egyptian titles, may be left on one side (→ 1046). They are adaptations of an alien usage which would not seem quite right to Greeks. The instances (→ 1049) of phrases like κύριος θεός, κύριος βασιλεύς, κύριος Καῖσαρ, θεός καὶ κύριος βασιλεύς etc. ceased at the very latest in the reign of Tiberius (Ditt. Or., 606 : ὑπὲρ [τ]ῆ[ς] τῶν κυρίων Σε[βαστῶν] σωτηρίας is from the time of Augustus or Tiberius). These expressions, which are found in the Orient, are translations of native usage, and there the parallels for them in the use of a similar style for the στρατηγός (→ 1050) or in the addressing of a priestly superior as ὁ θεὸς καὶ κύριος. [67] In the Semitic sphere there are also instances of אדן מלכם for the Ptolemies. [68]

Instead, in the imperial period κύριος is used, not in solemn and lengthy formulae, but as a brief summary of the emperor's position in unemphatic phrases, especially for the purpose of dating.

The oldest example is P. Oxy., I, 37, 5 f.: ζ(ἔτους) Τιβερίου Κλαυδίου Καίσαρος τοῦ κυρίου and a contemporary ostrakon. [69] P. Oxy., II, 246 offers an interesting

---

[61] Baudissin, II, 266-269.
[62] Ibid., 266.
[63] Ibid., 267, n. 1.
[64] I owe this to H. Grapow.
[65] The use of "lord" without gen. or personal suffix is relatively infrequent compared with the huge number of instances from every age of use with the gen. or suffix. It is limited to a. superiors, esp. in letters (from the time of the Middle Kingdom, later replaced in letters by "my lord"), b. the king (statue of the lord, to swear by the life of the lord, from the time of the Middle Kingdom), c. to the gods several times, though not frequently, from c. 500 B.C., esp. of Osiris [H. Grapow]. On this whole question cf. Erman-Grapow.
[66] Examples are particularly numerous in the case of Isis, → 1050.
[67] BGU, 1197, I, 1 (5/4th cent. B.C.); 1201, 1 (2nd cent. A.D.).
[68] Baethgen, 41.
[69] Deissmann LO, 301.

example in the case of Nero: A small farmer dates his report by the year Νέρωνος Κλαυδίου Καίσαρος Σεβαστοῦ Γερμανικοῦ Αὐτοκράτορος, and he uses the same form in the attestation of his information, lines 11 f., 24 f. But the three certifying officials date by the year Νέρωνος τοῦ κυρίου or Νέρωνος Καίσαρος τοῦ κυρίου, lines 30, 33, 36. This style of dating begins on ,the ostraka with Nero, and it becomes increasingly predominant. [70] In the longer official imperial names κύριος is occasionally found already under Nero: P. Lond., 280, 6: τοῦ κυρίου Νέρωνος Κλαυδίου Καίσαρος Σεβαστοῦ Γερμανικοῦ Αὐτοκράτορος, cf. Ditt. Syll.³, 814, 55: εἰς τὸν τοῦ κυρίου Σεβαστοῦ [Νέρωνος οἶκον]. But the addition of κύριος to the full imperial title is more common from the time of Trajan. ἡμῶν is then increasingly added to κύριος: Ditt. Or., 677, 1 ff.: ὑπὲρ τῆς τοῦ κυρίου Αὐτοκράτορος Καίσαρος Νέρουα Τραιανοῦ Ἀρίστου Σεβαστοῦ Γερμανικοῦ Δακικοῦ τύχης, P. Giess., 7, 10 ff.: ἐπεὶ οὖν ὁ κύριος ἡμῶν Ἀδριανὸς Καῖσαρ Σεβαστὸς Γερμανικὸς Δακικὸς Παρθικὸς ἐκούφισεν τῶν ἐνχωρίων τὰ βάρη ... Later we read: ἐκ τῶν τοῦ κυρίου ἐντολῶν προνοούμενος, lines 21 f.; ibid., 6, II, 11 ff.: κατὰ τὴν τοῦ κυρίου Ἀδριανοῦ Καίσαρος εὐεργεσίαν. This slow penetration of κύριος into the imperial style is independent of the fluctuating degree to which emperors assigned divine honours to themselves, or allowed them to be assigned. After the reigns of Nero and Domitian, which marked a climax in this respect, the use of κύριος does not disappear or decline in frequency. Although Domitian's dominus ac deus noster is shunned after his death, the brief formula with κύριος is still found on the ostraka and κύριος also occurs elsewhere in the full name. From Nero on a steady increase in the use of κύριος may thus be discerned.

In addition to κύριος with the name of the emperor κύριος is also used in the absolute; a first example of this is Ac. 25:26: περὶ οὗ ἀσφαλές τι γράψαι τῷ κυρίῳ οὐκ ἔχω. [71] The adj. κυριακός, "imperial," may also be mentioned in this connection. This is common in administrative terminology. [72]

At the beginning of the imperial period, however, the word dominus (κύριος) has also another role. If we may trust the formulation of Plut., Cassius was greeted in Rhodes as βασιλεὺς καὶ κύριος, and he rejected this in the words: οὔτε βασιλεὺς οὔτε κύριος, τοῦ δὲ κυρίου καὶ βασιλέως φονεὺς καὶ κολαστής (→ 1045), and Brutus is alluding to Caesar when he says: οἱ δὲ πρόγονοι ἡμῶν οὐδὲ πράους δεσπότας ὑπέμεινον (→ 1045). Here rejection of κύριος and δεσπότης implies rejection of an oriental-style monarchy. Thus Caesar's heir, Augustus, would not let himself be called dominus. Sueton. says: [73] Domini appellationem ut maledictum et opprobrium semper exhorruit. Cum spectante eo ludos pronuntiatum esset in mimo: O dominum aequum et bonum! et universi quasi de ipso dictum exultantes comprobassent, et statim manu vultuque indecoras adulationes repressit et insequenti die gravissimo corripuit edicto; dominumque se posthac appellari ne a liberis quidem aut nepotibus suis vel serio vel ioco passus est, atque eius modi blanditias etiam inter ipsos prohibuit. The attitude of Tiberius

---

[70] Loc. cit., also P. Viereck, Griech. u. griech.-demotische Ostraka d. Universitäts- u. Landesbibliothek zu Strassburg, I (1923), Index: for Nero 8 times the longer formula, 15 times Νέρων ὁ κύριος, for Vespasian 3 times only the name, once the longer formula, 8 times Οὐεσπασιανὸς (Καῖσαρ) ὁ κύριος, for Domitian 8 times only the name, 4-5 times Δομιτιανὸς ὁ κύριος, 3 times Δομιτιανὸς Καῖσαρ ὁ κύριος, for Nerva, 3 times Νέρουας (ὁ) κύριος, for Trajan, once each Τραιανός and Τραιανὸς Ἄριστος, 17 times each Τραιανὸς Καῖσαρ ὁ κύριος and Τραιανὸς ὁ κύριος, once Τραιανὸς Ἄριστος Καῖσαρ ὁ κύριος.

[71] Examples esp. from Syria: Le Bas/Waddington, 2640 (115 A.D., Durbah); 2186 (178 A.D., Djenîn); 2481 (Zor'a); F. Lukas, "Repertorium d. griech. Inschr. aus Gerasa," Mitteilungen u. Nachrichten des Deutschen Palästina-Vereins, 7 (1901), 68, No. 54 (Hadrian); 73, No. 71; cf. also Ditt. Syll.³, 880, 8 (Pizos, 202 A.D.); P. Giess., 3, 12 (Hadrian); 7, 21 f. (→ supra); P. Tebt., 286, 10 and coins and acclamations, → n. 76.

[72] For examples v. Foerster, 115, n. 3.

[73] Caes. (Augustus), 53.

was the same acc. to the account of Dio C., 57, 8, 2 : δεσπότης μὲν τῶν δούλων, αὐτοκράτωρ δὲ τῶν στρατιωτῶν, τῶν δὲ δὴ λοιπῶν πρόκριτός εἰμι. In these passages "lord" is a specific term for the absolute position of a monarch, and it has an obvious political aspect.

The peculiar feature of the situation in Roman Empire, however, is that under a constitutional cover there triumphed in fact the type of absolute monarchy constantly associated in the Orient with the term "lord." The scene under Augustus reported by Suetonius shows us already that the relevant word was also very much in the air at Rome. The above depiction of the introduction of κύριος as a brief expression for the emperor shows how, in spite of its official rejection by the majority of emperors, the word slowly but surely established itself. It also shows, however, that it received no specific emphasis. Neither κύριος nor κυριακός has in the first instance any connection with the imperial cult. There is no passage in which κύριος, when used of a Roman emperor, is sufficient of itself to describe the emperor as god. The imperial priest is practically never called ἱερεὺς τοῦ κυρίου. [74] The same holds good for the formula of swearing by the emperor, [75] for inscriptions on coins, and for acclamations. [76] κύριος is not found on the private domestic altars of Hadrian in Miletus, which apparently once stood in every citizen's house in Miletus. [77] Used of the emperor, κύριος has nothing whatever to do with the divine predicate of our earlier discussion.

The difficulty lies elsewhere. If the emperor is not κύριος as god, he can be god as κύριος.

In an epigram to Augustus :

Καίσαρι ποντομέδοντι καὶ ἀπείρων κρατέοντι
Ζανί, τῷ ἐκ Ζανὸς πατρός, Ἐλευθερίῳ
δεσπότᾳ Εὐρώπας τε καὶ Ἀσίδος, ἄστρῳ ἁπάσας
Ἑλλάδος, [ὃς] σωτ[ὴ]ρ Ζεὺς ἀν[έ]τ[ει]λ[ε] μέγας.

(CIG, 4923), all the epithets are bathed in a religious atmosphere. As Zeus rules over all, so Augustus is ποντομέδων and ἀπείρων κρατέων. As Helios shines brightly over all parts of the world, so Augustine is lord over the then known world. Divinity combined with universality of the sphere of rule is even more plainly expressed in an inscr. in honour of Nero : ὁ τοῦ παντὸς κόσμου κύριος Νέρων. [78] Of Hadrian we also read

---

[74] Foerster, 103. On the exception mentioned there in n. 1, ref. should be made to Le Bas/Waddington, No. 2606 : ἐπίτροπον [Σεβ]αστο[ῦ τοῦ κυρίου] (Palmyra, 263 A.D.).
[75] Foerster, 114 f.
[76] On coins κύριος is rare, and apparently not before the 2nd cent. A.D., cf. the list of refs. in B. Pick, Journal International d'Archéologie Numismatique, 1 (1898), 451-463. No instance of dominus is found in either W. Wruck, Die syrische Provinzialprägung von Augustus bis Trajan (1931) or P. L. Strack, Untersuchungen zur römischen Reichsprägung des 2. Jhdts., I (1931), II (1933). In Alexandria in the 2nd year of Hadrian we find ΤΡΑΙΑΝΟΣ ΣΕΒΑΣΤΟΣ ΠΑΤ ΚΥ, and in the 10th year of Gallienus ΔΕΚΑΕΤΗΡΙΣ ΚΥΡΙΟΥ, J. Vogt, Die alexandrinischen Münzen, II (1924), 40 and 155. Most coins offer κύριος in acclamation, cf. also Suet. Caes. (Domitian), 13 : domino et dominae feliciter ; Dio C., 72, 20, 2 (Commodus): καὶ κύριος εἶ καὶ πρῶτος εἶ καὶ πάντων εὐτυχέστατος. νικᾷς, νικήσεις. ἀπ' αἰῶνος, Ἀμαζόνιε, νικᾷς; P. Oxy., I, 41, 3; 11; 20; 30 (3rd/4th cent. A.D.), cf. on this E. Peterson, Εἷς θεός (1926), Index, s.v. "Acclamation" and κύριος. In imperial acclamations κύριος is usually a designation of the recipient and it has no more religious overtone than Ἰησοῦς in Phil. 2:10 — if this is an acclamation. Τὸ κύριος in Phil. corresponds a formula like εἰς αἰῶνας etc. in imperial acclamations. But when κύριος is the true acclamatory cry, as in the passage in Dio C., it is spoken with emphasis and can easily take on religious significance (→ infra).
[77] T. Wiegand, Milet, I, 7 (1924), 350 ff., No. 290-297.
[78] Ditt. Syll.³, 814, 31.

in Pergamos: (πάντων ἀνθρώπ)ων δεσπότης, βασιλεὺς δὲ (τῶν τῆς γῆς χω)ρῶν, [79] and of Antoninus Pius: ἐγὼ μὲν τοῦ κόσμου κύριος, ὁ δὲ νόμος θαλάσσης. [80] The mood behind this is shown in the homage which Tiridates paid to Nero. In Naples he greeted him as δεσπότης and offered him *proskunesis,* and in Rome he solemnly declared: ἐγώ, δέσποτα, Ἀρσάκου μὲν ἔκγονος, Οὐολογαίσου δὲ καὶ Πακόρου τῶν βασιλέων ἀδελφός, σὸς δὲ δοῦλός εἰμι. καὶ ἦλθόν τε πρὸς σὲ τὸν ἐμὸν θεόν, προσκυνήσων σε ὡς καὶ τὸν Μίθραν, καὶ ἔσομαι τοῦτο ὅ τι ἂν σὺ ἐπικλώσῃς· σὺ γάρ μοι καὶ Μοῖρα καὶ Τύχη. [81] If κύριος is not used, the fact remains that he who is Μοῖρα and Τύχη for another is his lord. There is a clear connection between *dominus* and divinity in Tacitus Annales, II, 87 (ed. K. Nipperdey-G. Andresen, I[11] [1915]) with ref. to Tiberius: *acerbeque increpuit eos, qui divinas occupationes ipsumque dominum dixerant.* In one place an emphatic *dominus* is actually used of the emperor at his own instigation. Domitian not only allowed himself to be proclaimed *dominus* in the theatre: *domino et dominae feliciter,* [82] but he caused official letters to begin: *dominus et deus noster hoc fieri iubet.* [83] Perhaps Caligula used this formula before him; [84] from Aurelian we certainly have some coins which bear the inscription: *dominus et deus (natus),* though these are from a provincial mint. [85] Whether the Greeks would have used κύριος and not δεσπότης for the *dominus* of Domitian is open to question. [86] *Dominus* and *dominus et deus* are richly attested in Statius and Martial. [87] From Martial we have a poem in which he later breaks free from his habit of calling Domitian *dominus et deus.* [88] The two titles are not a ἓν διὰ δυοῖν, [89] but they are very closely related. It is just because the *dominus* denotes the position of the ruler in relation to his subjects [90] that the bearer of this title is also *deus.* Neither title could be omitted. The thinking behind them is indicated by Domitian's great predecessor, Caasar, who, when a *haruspex* told him of an inauspicious omen, replied: *futura laetiora, cum vellet.* [91] A similar view is expressed by Tiridates with ref. to Nero. When uttered with this emphasis, the *dominus* binds a man as a god binds him. If he is willing to be bound thus, he must give up being bound to God. And he who thus binds him must take the place of deity or destiny.

On the other hand, there are good reasons for doubting whether κύριος usually bore this emphasis when used of the emperor. The steady increase in its use, to which we have referred above, can be explained only on the assumption that it did not. Tertullian makes a pertinent distinction between *dominus* and *dominus*: *dicam plane imperatorem dominum, sed more communi, sed quando non cogor, ut dominum dei vice dicam.* [92] It is not surprising that in the acts of Christian martyrs

---

[79] Inscr. Perg., 365.
[80] Justinianus, Digesta (in *Corpus Juris Civilis* rec. T. Mommsen-P. Krüger I[11] [1908]), 14, 2, 9. Caracalla as ὁ γῆς καὶ θαλάσσης δεσπότης, IG, XII, 3, 100.
[81] Dio C., 63, 1, 2 ff., esp. 63, 2, 4; 63, 5, 2.
[82] Suet. Caes. (Domitian), 13, 1.
[83] *Ibid.,* 13, 2.
[84] Sextus Aurelius Victor, Liber de Caesaribus (ed. F. Pichlmayr [1911]), 39, 4, cf. Foerster, 104.
[85] W. Kubitschek in *Numismatische Zeitschrift* 48 = NF, 8 (1915), 167-178.
[86] Dio C., 67, 4, 7 (preserved only in Zonaras): ἤδη γὰρ καὶ θεὸς ἠξίου νομίζεσθαι, καὶ δεσπότης καλούμενος καὶ θεὸς ὑπερηγάλλετο. ταῦτα οὐ μόνον ἐλέγετο, ἀλλὰ καὶ ἐγράφετο.
[87] F. Sauter, *Der römische Kaiserkult bei Mart. u. Statius* (1934), 31-40.
[88] X, 72, Sauter, 31.
[89] Ltzm. R. on 10:9.
[90] Mart., X, 72: *non est hic dominus, sed imperator;* this shows the constitutional significance of *dominus* even when Martial is breaking free from the formula *dominus et deus noster.* Cf. Sauter, 39.
[91] Suet. Caes. (Julius), 77.
[92] Apologeticus, 34.

opposition to the absolute claim of the Roman state, with its implication of deity, is also found in the form of the distinction between *dominus noster imperator* and *dominus meus, rex regum et imperator omnium gentium*. [93] But the use of *rex* and *imperator* along with *dominus* shows that the point at issue was not the mere title but the religious claim of the state, which Christians were forced to resist in demonstration of their loyalty to God and the state. A different picture is presented by the *sicarii*, who would not accept the emperor as such, i.e., as their supreme ruler, and who thus refused to call him δεσπότης. [94] For the Christian martyrs this was a conflict of religions ; for the *sicarii*, in the light of Mt. 22:21, the issue was political. Since the latter were in any case excused the duty of participating in emperor worship, there was no question of any particular stress on the word "lord." When applied to the emperor, κύριος bears a different content according to the context and the inner attitude of those who use it. In one of the pagan accounts of martyrdom in P. Oxy., I, 33, the condemned man, Appian, calls the emperor τύραννος, but when he makes a request of him he uses κύριε Καῖσαρ (III, 1). On the other hand, the address δέσποτα on the lips of Tiridates (→ 1057) expresses the religious veneration which he then demonstrates and declares to Nero. Again, the Jews, who rejected emperor worship, could still dedicate a synagogue ὑπὲρ σωτηρίας τῶν κυρίων ἡμῶν Καισάρων Αὐτοκρατόρων Λ. Σεπτιμίου Σεουήρου Εὐσεβοῦς Περτίνακος Σεβαστοῦ κτλ. [95] This shows incidentally how attenuated in 197 A.D. was the word Σεβαστός, which originally expressed the religious dignity of the emperor. But it shows particularly that the Jews had no hesitation in styling their rulers οἱ κύριοι ἡμῶν. [96]

Foerster

C. The Old Testament Name for God.

1. The Name for God in the LXX.

a. The word κύριος, "lord," as a name for God in the LXX is a strict translation only in cases where it is used for אָדוֹן or אֲדֹנָי (in the *ketib*). As a rule, however, it is used as an expository equivalent for the divine name יהוה. It is thus meant to express what the name, or the use of the name, signifies in the original. That it does not altogether succeed in this may be seen at once from the switching of the name to the general concept and also from the fact that in the Bible, as in common usage, κύριος cannot be restricted to the one function of being a term for God. On the contrary, it is also used of men as well as God, like the Heb. אָדוֹן ("lord"), e.g., in the respectful term of address אֲדֹנִי, plur. אֲדֹנָי (Gn. 19:2), of which there are 192 instances. בַּעַל, too, which can have the secular sense of "owner," is regularly translated κύριος (15 times). [97] The same is true of גְּבִיר, "master" (Gn. 27:29, 37), of the Aram. מָרֵא, "lord" (Da. Θ 2:47; 4:16, 21 [19, 24]; 5:23), which can also be used of God, and שַׁלִּיט, "ruler" (Da. Θ 4:14 [17]). On the other hand, when בַּעַל is used of a pagan deity, the LXX either uses (ὁ or ἡ) Βάαλ as a proper name or introduces εἴδωλον (Jer. 9:13; 2 Ch. 17:3; 28:2) or

[93] *Akten d. scilitanischen Märtyrer*, ed. R. Knopf, *Ausgewählte Märtyrerakten*² (1913), 33.

[94] Jos. Bell., 2, 118; 7, 418.

[95] R. Cagnat, *Inscr. Graecae ad res Romanas pertinentes*, III (1906), 1106.

[96] It is no doubt true, as Prümm, 134, says, that the richer and weaker senses of κύριος as applied religiously to the emperor were often present together, but the point is that the weaker sense was the normal one to which a fuller content was sometimes added.

[97] Cf. Gn. 49:23; Ex. 21 and 22 (11 times); Ju. 19:22 f.; Is. 1:3; Job 31:39.

αἰσχύνη (1 K. 18:19, 25). In the religious sphere, then, κύριος or ὁ κύριος is reserved for the true God, and, apart from unimportant periphrases of the name in figurative speech, it is used regularly, i.e., some 6156 times, for the proper name יהוה in all its pointings and in the combination יהוה צְבָאוֹת or in the short form יָהּ. Only by way of exception is κύριος used for the other terms for God : 60 times for אֵל, 23 for אֱלוֹהַּ. 193 for אֱלֹהִים, and 3 for אֱלֹהֵי צְבָאוֹת. The expressions κύριος θεός, κύριος ὁ θεός and ὁ κύριος θεός usually indicate a Mas. יהוה with or without the apposition אֱלֹהִים. δεσπότης corresponds to יהוה only in Jer. 15:11 (in the vocative); elsewhere δέσποτα κύριε is sometimes used for אֲדֹנָי יהוה (Gn. 15:2 [Swete], 8; Jer. 1:6; 4:10), though κύριος κύριος is the usual rendering of this.

b. The presence or omission of the art. before κύριος does not seem to be wholly without a bearing on the meaning of the Gk. term, though there is a strong element of caprice in the tradition. [98] For as a free rendering of יהוה κύριος is in some way meant to be an interpretation of the original, and the use of the article or not should enable us to see whether the singular nature of the name is implied. Unfortunately the text no longer presents us with a clear picture in this regard, though if the LXX use of the article with θεός gives evidence of some methodical order, [99] we may suspect that this was originally true of κύριος, at least so far as some of the translators are concerned. Certainly κύριος without the art. preserves the character of the Heb. original as a proper name better than the definite ὁ κύριος, which, like εὐεργέτης or σωτήρ, is simply an appellative title.

The consensus of the translators in the use of this title "lord" or "the lord" for יהוה is not quite satisfactorily explained by supposing that they were using a uniform original. This is particularly so if the original is sought in the *qerē* אֲדֹנָי, which is so common in the final Mas. version of the text. We should then have to presuppose that an early form of this tradition was widespread long before the Christian era in transcriptions in Greek, ἀντίγραφαί as Origen presumably calls them, in which αδωναι was read for the divine name. [100] But this is an insecure hypothesis, and it leaves room for the other and no less uncertain theory that when the Greek translators used κύριος for the divine name they did so in free creativity, applying the common use of κύριος as a divine epithet in terms of the insight into the nature of the OT God which was current in Hellenistic Judaism. There is certainly good reason to suspect that אֲדֹנָי as *qerē* first came into use under the influence of the Gk. text, [101] and that even as *ketib* it penetrated relatively late into the Heb. text, so that esp. in the prophetic books it can be accepted as an original expression of the authors only with the greatest reserve. [102]

The result is that the justification or otherwise of the use of κύριος as the OT term for God will be demonstrated less from the use of אָדוֹן or אֲדֹנָי than from an examination of the basis and significance of the name יהוה in the original.

---

[98] Cf. B. Weiss, "Der Gebrauch des Artikels bei den Gottesnamen," ThStKr, 84 (1911), 319 ff.

[99] → 90; Baudissin, I, 441 f. Generally κύριος is used without the art. only as a term for God, and it is found as such more often in the nominative than in other cases, where the art. may well have been occasioned by the Heb. לְ or אֵת, so A. Debrunner, "Zur Übersetzungstechnik der LXX," Festschr. K. Marti (= Beih. ZAW, 41) (1925), 69 ff.; cf. also Baudissin, I, 17 ff.

[100] So F. Wutz, Die Transkriptionen von d. LXX bis zu Hieronymus (1925/33), 145 f.

[101] The texts on which E. Stauffer, 121, bases his objections to this theory are hardly relevant to the problems of the biblical text, though they contribute to the uncertainty.

[102] This is the conclusion reached in the extensive researches of Baudissin, Kyrios, esp. II, 305. From the form δέσποτα κύριε e.g., for the Mas. אֲדֹנָי יהוה, Baudissin (I, 523) infers that the translator knew neither the Mas. ădonāi ĕlohīm nor ădonāi for the simple יהוה.

2. "Lord" as a Designation for Yahweh.

The fact should not be overlooked, of course, that in the history of the Bible and the effect of its message the rendering "lord" has been no less significant than the use of the name in the original. If the function of the two terms is not wholly identical, it overlaps to such a degree that the content of the statements, being equally orientated to the basic motif of the acknowledgment of the power of the divine will, can have a vital effect.

The difference between אֲדֹנָי and אָדוֹן is that the form distinguished by the affirmative is reserved for sacral use whereas the simple אָדוֹן may be used of human lordship too. The first point about אָדוֹן is that in the OT it is a very broad term for the one who has power over men (Ps. 12:4; of the king, Jer. 22:18; 14:5 [103]), and to a lesser degree over things (Gn. 45:8; Ps. 105:21 בַּיִת, which includes men). It is closely related to בַּעַל, "owner," but with a distinctive emphasis on the emotional rather than the legal aspect, as may be seen in the address אֲדֹנִי, "my lord," which predominates even in the legally established relation of a subject to his בַּעַל.[104] The slave speaks thus to his owner (Gn. 24:12; Ex. 21:5) or the wife to her husband (Gn. 18:12). It is also common in the language of court (אֲדֹנִי הַמֶּלֶךְ, e.g., 1 S. 26:17), of veneration (Nu. 11:28; Gn. 31:35), and of the politeness enjoined by custom (Gn. 23:6; Ju. 4:18).

A peculiarity of the word even in secular use is that it commonly takes the plur. form and plur. suffixes even when there is no ref. to several people.[105] Since the same is true of בַּעַל (e.g., Is. 1:3), a simple explanation is perhaps to be sought in the need to raise the expression to the totality of the concept.[106] This leaves only the difficulty of the extension of the ā in אֲדֹנָי, which is not demanded by any pause and which can thus be understood only as an intentional characteristic of the word in its function as a divine name and epithet. The hypothesis that this is not really an afformative as marked in the Mas., but that it is a part of the root and that the word is a non-semitic loan word,[107] considerably overestimates the philological value of the Mas., since Punic examples also show plainly the pronominal nature of the suffix.[108] On the other hand, אֲדֹנָי also occurs in we-texts (e.g., Ps. 44:24), so that it is impossible to take it as a possessive form "my lord" in the biblical texts unless one assumes that an original vocative has become ossified as a nominative.[109] Granted this assumption, one may assume, without detriment to the philological possibility already mentioned, that אֲדֹנָי as a divine name had its origin as an address in private prayer, of which there are in fact many examples in the Mas.[110] The extension of the ā may be traced to the concern of the Massoretes to mark

---

[103] The cry הוֹי אָדוֹן finds a formal analogy in the Phoenician Adonis lament αιαι Αδωνιν, cf. W. W. Graf Baudissin, *Adonis u. Esmun* (1911), 91.

[104] בַּעֲלִי occurs only in Hos. 2:18.

[105] Typical is אֲדֹנִים קָשֶׁה, "a hard lord," Is. 19:4.

[106] Ges.-K. § 124 i.

[107] H. Bauer and P. Leander, *Historische Grammatik d. hbr. Sprache ...*, I (1922) § 2h, 29t; in this case אָדוֹן is a "secondary sing." § 61i α (p. 469). The word is not part of the common Semitic heritage, but occurs only among the Israelites and Phoenicians. This, too, might suggest borrowing.

[108] Cf. e.g., אדני בעלשמם, "my lord Baalsamen" (Umm-el-'Awâmîd, *Corp. Inscr. Semiticarum*, ed. E. Renan, I, 1 [1881], 7, line 7; M. Lidzbarski, *Altsemitische Texte,* I [1907] 22). For further material cf. also Baudissin, *Adonis,* 66.

[109] For the transition of the vocative into other cases Baudissin, *Kyrios,* II, 35 ff. compares רַבִּי as a title, the Syr. מרי, also the Accadian *belti*.

[110] The table in Baudissin, *Kyrios,* 60 lists 55 instances, of which 31 are for אֲדֹנָי יהוה.

the word as sacred by a small outward sign. Since the fact that אֲדֹנָי was of four letters, corresponding to the tetragrammaton, was also probably of importance to them, [111] one can also, perhaps, understand why it was that the my-form established itself in use in place of the our-form אֲלֹנֵינוּ (Ps. 8:2, 9; 147:5; 135:5 etc.). [112]

Used of Yahweh, אָדֹון, like מֶלֶךְ, denotes His sovereign power. It is a title which corresponds to His nature. Only seldom does it indicate His position as lord of the land. This is to be seen, perhaps, in the appositional combination "the Lord Yahweh" in Ex. 23:17; 34:23, [113] since the ref. here is to harvest festivals. As אֲבִיר יִשְׂרָאֵל, "the strength of Israel," cf. Gn. 49:24, He is called אָדֹון in Is. 1:24. From this one may conclude that Is. probably uses the word elsewhere only in this sense [114] if it is really one of his own expressions in every case. [115] In the main, however, OT statements concerning Yahweh as Lord already go far beyond the idea that He is just the lord of the land or people and more or less clearly presuppose the prophetic belief in Yahweh as Lord of all. The phrase "Lord of the whole earth" (Mi. 4:13; Zech. 4:14; 6:5; Ps. 97:5; Jos. 3:11, 13) gives us clearest evidence of the enhancement of the sense to embrace everything. This is perhaps also the meaning when אָדֹון stands alone (only Ps. 114:7), [116] and the meaning of אֲרֹנָי, which is lengthened in form as well, admits of no doubt.

The uncertainty of the ketib אֲדֹנָי has already been recalled (→ 1059). It is a fact, however, that this ketib, even where it is grounded in the text as in Is. 6, in the majority of cases serves the purpose of avoiding the name of God, like the qerē which derived from it. In Is. 6:11 the prophet uses the vocative אֲדֹנָי spontaneously under the unweakened impression of the nearness of the majesty of the Holy One, and we could only ask whether אֲדֹנָי was not used there. The desire to avoid the name because the majesty which fills the whole earth encounters man is as clear here as it is rare elsewhere. On the other hand, the introduction of אֲדֹנָי at the beginning of the account in Is. 6:1 and then again in 6:8 [117] gives rise to the impression that there is a didactic desire to impress firmly on the reader the thought expressed in the hymn of the seraphs by choosing a word which will correspond to the reverent attitude of the prophet. The common formula of Ezekiel, אֲדֹנָי יהוה or יהוה אֲדֹנָי (212 times according to Baudissin's reckoning) is to be understood in the same way. It is in a sense an elucidation of the name as an expression for the divine majesty, and the moving of the accent from the name to the title is unmistakable. Thus the use of the ketib אֲדֹנָי seems to have started a development of the technique of transmission which finally in the qerē led to a complete exclusion of the divine name from the text. Such tendencies were probably strongly stimulated also by the Sodom stories in Gn. 18 f., which used the courtesy title "my lords" for the visitors to Abraham and Lot, among whom, as the reader learns only from the context, was the "judge of the whole earth" (18:25), who had come down (18:21). There can be no doubt that this usage was valued as most instructive by the Mas. [118]

The substitution of אֲדֹנָי, which is restrained in the ketib, but which is then carried through so radically in the qerē that the very sound of the divine name is completely

---

[111] Cf. A. Geiger, Urschrift u. Übersetzungen d. Bibel² (1928), 262.

[112] Baudissin, II, 27 regards adonēnu as a form derived from adonāi.

[113] Cf. Buber, 124.

[114] The full-sounding הָאָדֹון יהוה צְבָאֹת is confined to Is., where it occurs twice in the audition formula (1:24; 19:4) and 3 times in freer introductions to threats (3:1; 10:16, 33).

[115] The tradition is hesitant, cf. BHK² on the instances mentioned in → n. 114.

[116] הָאָדֹון could also be understood in this way in Mal. 3:1 in spite of Baudissin's doubts, II, 305.

[117] On these passages BHK² has the note: c. 100 MSS יהוה.

[118] The address to the three (18:3) is pointed as a divine designation because God must be one of them. Lot greets the two others with a secular form (19:2). Finally, the mythical motif of three men is dropped, and the ref. is to Yahweh alone (19:18).

excluded, implies no less than a total exegesis of the Holy Scriptures of Israel. In combination with the κύριος usage of the LXX it signifies an act of immeasurable consequence in the history of religion. The considerations which prepared and supported it can no longer be reconstructed with full certainty, → 1070. Even the question already mentioned (→ 1059) whether the LXX or the original gave the first impulse admits of no satisfactory answer. One can hardly adduce a definite missionary trend, at least as a leading motive, since the age of active missionary work had not yet dawned for Judaism when the LXX was completed and it had already passed when the last Massoretes established the qerē. On the other hand, missionary activity may be inferred from the wording of the LXX in many passages.

There is tremendous missionary force in the conclusion of Ps. 134 (135) when, after the house of Israel, Aaron and Levi, the φοβούμενοι τὸν κύριον are also summoned to praise the Lord. It stands beyond all doubt that this extension of the terminology used to denote God, which theologically derives from the prophets, played an essential part in the dissemination of the OT message. If it implied a weakening of the link with history, it did not break this link. If it softened its numinous dynamic for Israel, at the decisive point it surrendered the national character of the Canon and thereby interpreted its deepest meaning. The God to whom the Canon bears witness is called "Lord" because He is there shown to be the exclusive holder of power over the cosmos and all men, the Creator of the world and the Master of life and death. The term "Lord" is thus a summation of the beliefs of the OT. It is the wholly successful attempt to state what God is, what the Holy One means in practice for men, namely, the intervention of a personal will, with approximately the pregnancy and binding force which constitute the distinctive mark of the name Yahweh.

3. The Name Yahweh as a Concept of Experience.

The OT belief in God is grounded in historical experience and it developed in continuing contact with history. The most meaningful expression of this fact is the use of the name Yahweh in statements about God and in calling upon Him.

This name, like every other name for God, is a concept of experience. As such, it is gradually distinguished by the specific and concrete nature of its content from more general terms like אֵל, אֱלוֹהַּ and אֱלֹהִים (→ θεός, 81), which point in the direction of the abstract, and from the honorific title אָדוֹן. It denotes, not just any deity, but an unequivocally distinct divine person. It fills out the terms God and Lord with so strong a numinous content that the final result is that it completely overwhelms their general function. God is no longer an appellation which can be applied in many different ways, and Lord takes on the sense of "Lord of all." Thus, although the general terms occur less frequently in the Canon, they can still be used in many cases as synonyms of Yahweh, and אֲדֹנָי itself can also take its place. They have taken up the meaning of the personal name into themselves and have become unequivocal concepts of experience. Understanding of the translations must then orientate itself to such statements as "the Lord is God" (1 K. 18:39; cf. Jos. 24:15) or "the Lord is his name" (Ex. 15:3) if the clear focusing of the biblical usage on the figure of Yahweh is to be maintained. For the basic text never means that "God" or "Lord" is a name. The word Yahweh is exclusively integrated into the name with a very special emphasis. "Yahweh is his name" or "Yahweh of hosts (יהוה צְבָאוֹת) is his name" are expressions often used in hymns. [119] They demonstrate

---

[119] Cf. the full list of examples in Grether, 55; on the meaning Buber-Rosenzweig, 335.

primarily and fundamentally that the personal name of God is used with a strong sense of its significance as the confession of a specific experience of the divine. For His confessors as for others the God named by this name is a sharply defined figure, the *numen praesens* in person. "To call by the name of Yahweh" (קָרָא בְּשֵׁם יהוה, e.g., Is. 65:1 etc.) is to confess and to be ready for encounter with this person.[120] Only those who do not know Him, like the Gentiles (Ps. 79:6; Jer. 10:25), do not know what to make of the name Yahweh, which is the "Thou" whom one may address in prayer,[121] the symbol of all the will and power of deity. In the language of dogmatics one may put it thus : "*Shem* is always the name of the *deus revelatus*."[122]

Thus, whenever this proper name for God appears in the texts, quite independently of its meaning and solely in virtue of its linguistic nature as a concept of experience, it establishes an indissoluble linking of religion to history, namely, to the history in which the use of this name arose and developed as described above The name of Yahweh may have been used in some other way before (→ 1065 f.), but in the religion founded by Moses it became the form of revelation and it points back implicitly to this historical encounter between God and man and to all that resulted from it in causal sequence. It is as non-intellectual as a name for God can be. It leaves practically no room at all for speculation about the divine.[123] It reminds us tacitly and constantly of an active declaration of God which we know took place in the early days of Israel, and of encounters in the lives of prophetic men who were called to speak as mouthpieces of Yahweh with full authority : "Thus hath Yahweh spoken." Use of the name disclosed the essential and indelible features of the picture of God which the biblical tradition paints in its portrayal of the inner history of the people of God and the spiritual development of its religious leaders as an ineluctable demonstration of divine reality. The emotional power and convincing integrity of OT religion is rooted in the message about Yahweh, in whose clearly delineated divine person and insistent will man finds a standard and norm for the world and for life, now full of fear of the Holy as he senses his creatureliness, now satisfied with the vision of the "likeness" (Ps. 17:15) in whom all salvation is guaranteed. "The fact that in Yahweh the characteristics of the personal are so incomparably strong is part of His dignity and superiority over all the gods of the Gentiles."[124]

4. The Institution of Moses.

OT religion as the religion of Yahweh is an instituted religion. The declaration of the divine name by Moses did not imply only a "Yahwistic reformation of Canaanite animism."[125] It meant a new beginning of religious life which could not

---

[120] On the freeing of the phrase from magic cf. Grether, 21 f.

[121] This may well be the meaning of the almost untranslatable word וְאַתָּה־הוּא in Ps. 102:27, a stammering "Thou art He" with the accent solely on the "Thou." הוּא simply fills out the sound as in אֲנִי־הוּא, Is. 41:4 etc.; cf. Job 3:19. It follows that these passages have no bearing on the derivation of יהוה.

[122] Grether, 18; cf. 159 ff.

[123] Cf. the synon. זֵכֶר for שֵׁם, e.g., Ex. 3:15 and the cultic phrase "to bring the name to remembrance," Ex. 23:13.

[124] R. Otto, *Das Gefühl des Überweltlichen* (1932), 269.

[125] G. van der Leeuw, *Phänomenologie der Religion* (1933), 581. On the concept of "founder," cf. 618 ff. The functions of witness, prophet, teacher and even theologian all

be explained in terms of any theory of development or assimilation. Both earlier and later tradition have much to tell us, of course, about a history of belief in Yahweh in the pre-Mosaic generations of the patriarchs. The migration of Abraham from Mesopotamia to Canaan was undertaken in obedience to Yahweh and entailed renunciation of the worship of other gods (Jos. 24:2 f.; Gn. 12:8; 35:2; Jdt. 5:5-7). Nevertheless, the core of these traditions, whose significance for salvation history is brought out in a particularly impressive way in Gn. 12:1 ff., may be pared down to the fact that religious movements played some part, though not perhaps a decisive part, in developments in the early history of the tribes of Israel which we cannot now unravel in detail. [126] The distinctive feature of the J narrative, as compared with E and P, is that on the basis of a primitive revelation of God men already called on the name of Yahweh in the very earliest periods of human history (Gn. 4:26). But seeing that it would have been impossible to invent such precise statements as Hos. 12:9 ("I am Yahweh from the land of Egypt"; cf. also 13:4) or Ex. 6:3 ("But by my name Yahweh I was not known to them," P), there can be no serious questioning of the historical value of the tradition that Moses was the founder of Yahweh religion. From the standpoint of the history of religion, the attempt to integrate the name Yahweh into the early history of the race as a summary term for the Creator and Lord of the world, and especially the scholarly observation in Gn. 4:26, are only a faint reflection of a fact which it is almost impossible to pin down, namely, that the name of God was already present and had some location in primitive history before Moses introduced it to the children of Israel (→ 1065 f.).

It was in the age of Moses, however, that Yahweh religion first entered the stage of history, and possibly that it first came to birth. Certainly, as the religion of the national confederation of Israel, [127] it then began to exert a visible influence as the spur to political action and the binding norm of conduct. The story of the founding itself is concealed in a saga which is not wholly free from legendary details and which tells of a theophany granted to Moses. On the basis of the revelation which he had received Moses was the author of a relationship of loyalty sworn in the covenant (→ II, 114 ff.), of a treaty between the tribes of Israel and the God Yahweh as the One who should command and protect them. The religious legacy of these tribes, which seems thus far to have consisted of a wide variety of divine beings, [128] each with his own ἱερὸς λόγος, was from now on strictly orientated to the specific and concrete reality which Moses had seen. In consequence, a concept which had not previously existed now came to dominate all expressions of the life of the "people of Yahweh" (Ju. 5:11). This was confidence in the guiding power and will of the God who was under no natural constraint and who at the supreme crisis of the exodus of Moses' host out of Egypt had proved His transcendent majesty by overthrowing horse and rider in the Red Sea (Ex.

---

occur in the biblical tradition concerning Moses' work, and this saga-like plenitude is a guarantee that he was recognised to be the founder.

[126] Cf. R. Kittel, *Geschichte des Volkes Israel*, I⁶ (1923), 289 f. F. Böhl, *Das Zeitalter Abrahams* (1930), 41 f. uses the concept of monotheism, which is hardly pertinent here, to define the historical significance of the Abraham tradition; cf. further → 1079 f.

[127] This name, which occurs already c. 1223 B.C. on a stele of Merneptah, does not presuppose Yahweh religion but aptly denotes its underlying motif if the most likely meaning "God fights" is correct. Cf. W. Caspari, *Zschr. f. Semitistik*, 3 (1924), 194 ff.

[128] Cf. A. Alt, *Der Gott der Väter* (1929), 3 ff.; K. Elliger, ThBl, 9 (1930), 97 ff.; C. Steuernagel, *Festschr. G. Beer* (1935), 62 ff.

15:21). [129] The tradition of a common worship of Yahweh dates from the time of Moses. [130] The tribes left Egypt to celebrate a feast to Yahweh in the desert (Ex. 3:12 E ; 4:23 J). From this time, too, date theophorous personal names which represent a confession of Yahweh. יְהוֹשׁוּעַ is perhaps the earliest if we do not believe that יוֹכֶבֶד, the name of the mother of Moses (Ex. 6:20 P), contains the name Yahweh or has come down in authentic form. [131] This is also the time when the "wars of Yahweh" begin (Nu. 21:14; 1 S. 18:17). Under the leadership of their God the tribes which make up the confederacy now engage in attacks on the Canaanite states, not all of which are successful. "Rise up, Lord, and let thine enemies be scattered and let them that hate thee flee before thee" (Nu. 10:35) was the warcry when the standard [132] of Yahweh was carried before them, probably the holy shrine as the symbol of the presence of the cultic God. Victory is Yahweh's victory; defeat implies His anger. "Who is like unto thee, Yahweh, among the gods ? Thou art praised as the fearful one who doeth wonders" (Ex. 15:11). With acceptance of the name of Yahweh the religion of Israel began as a militant and exclusive confession of God the Leader, as active obedience to His will (cf. also Jos. 24:16 ff.).

5. The Origin of the Divine Name.

Where does the name of this powerful God come from ? The tradition in Ex. 3 replies that it comes from the lips of God Himself. It thereby shows how inexplicable is the process in which the divine finds expression in the form of human speech. But is this form newly created by the founder of the religion or did he take it from a tradition ? No one can give a sure and certain answer to this question. If we refuse the first alternative, the second can be established only in terms of probability, and thus far no one has been able to do even this with any cogency.

The question of a Yahweh outside and before Israel has attracted much attention. This was formerly due to some findings in Accadian proper names, [133] and it has been raised again by texts from Ras Shamra, the coastal town in Syria, which certainly date

---

[129] O. Eissfeldt, *Baal Zaphon* ... (1932), 66 ff. advances with all due caution the possibility that the help received was first attributed to the god of the locality and only later to Yahweh. This hypothesis is possible only if we completely miss the real meaning of Ex. 15. The Song of the Red Sea hymns something which took place at a decisive turning-point for the whole future of Israel and which was regarded as the essential basis of its poetic motifs, cf. A. Weiser, *Glaube u. Geschichte im AT* (1931), 3 f. A transposed saga can hardly acquire this kind of significance. Furthermore, the theory assumes that the revelation of Yahweh took place after the Exodus, but there is no account of any such revelation. Finally, the topographical conjecture may well be right.

[130] This forms the basis of the thesis that the social form of the Yahweh tribes is analogous to the amphictyonic league of ancient Greece, cf. A. Alt, RGG², III (1929), 438 f., and most explicitly M. Noth, *Das System der zwölf Stämme Israels* (1930), 61 ff.

[131] The name does not occur in Ex. 2:1 where we should expect it. It was perhaps introduced by P from another context and given to the mother of Moses. But cf. M. Noth, *Die israelitischen Personennamen* (1928), 111 and H. Bauer, ZAW, NF, 10 (1933), 92 f.

[132] So Ex. 17:15 : יהוה נִסִּי, though there may be also ref. to a throne, cf. כסיה as *ketib* in v. 16.

[133] Cf. the collection of material in J. Hehn, *Die bibl. u. die babylonische Gottesidee* (1913), 230 ff.; G. R. Driver, "The Original Form of the Name 'Yahweh'" (ZAW, NF, 5 [1928], 7 ff.); R. Kittel, I, 452 ff. Well-attested identity of theophorous elements with Yahweh is rare and does not as yet go back beyond the time of the prophets. On the esp. significant name *Ya'u-bi'di,* cf. M. Noth, 110.

back to a period before Moses (15th/13th cent. B.C.). [134] If it is true that there is evidence here of a deity יו whose name shows unmistakable affinity to the form of the name יהוה as used in proper names and also attested independently on inscr., this can hardly be explained in terms of a linguistic accident, [135] though there is at a first glance some likelihood of this. Attention might also be directed to Egyptian religion, and especially to Amon-Reʻ, the "king of the gods," who resided in Thebes, [136] if it were simply a matter of tracing a theological tradition which might conceivably have contributed some legacy to the Yahweh tradition or which might help to explain the derivation of the name. But such conjectures lead to no solid conclusions. [137]

The same is true of the so-called Kenite hypothesis, [138] which has had some importance as comparatively the most concrete attempt to fill the vacuum. This rests on the story that Moses became the son-in-law of Jethro, the priest of the Midianites (Ex. 3:1; a different name is given in 2:18), and how Jethro then helped to organise the government of the tribes of Israel (Ex. 18:1 ff.). It is then suggested that Yahweh was the God of the nomadic Kenite tribe, to which Moses was bound by oath acc. to Ju. 1:16 (cf. also 4:11). Through cultic fellowship with the Kenites Israel adopted the name. Some support for the thesis is found in the traditions concerning the habitation of Yahweh at Mount Sinai (J) or Horeb (E). The host of Moses is led there when it comes out of Egypt (Ex. 19:3 f.), and His τέμενος or "holy ground" is there (Ex. 3:5 J). Yahweh comes out from thence with the people to do battle for Canaan (בָּא מִסִּינַי, Dt. 33:2). Rather less precisely we read in the Song of Deborah (Ju. 5:4) that Yahweh went out from Seir and marched out of the field of Edom [139] to the battle. These texts thus locate Yahweh in territories on the southern frontiers of Canaan. Of Elijah, too, it is reported that he sought and found the presence of Yahweh at Horeb (1 K. 19:8 ff.). If we may conclude from this that Yahweh was really a God of nomads who pitched their tents in open country, then the history of His name emerged from the non-historical past of these tribes. [140]

In no respect is it possible to say anything certain which leads to definite conclusions, and to fill the gap with conjectures on the personal contribution of Moses [141] it utterly valueless. The only firm possibility is that Yahweh was one of the many cultic gods associated with specific places, so that the Mosaic institution was a reformation in the sense that it filled an ancient form of epiclesis with new content.

---

[134] Cf. the discussion of *yw* in Bauer, 92 ff. On the whole question cf. O. Eissfeldt, ZDMG, NF, 13 (1934), 173 ff.; A. Jirku, *ibid.*, 14 (1935), 372 ff.; R. Dussaud, *Les textes de Ras Schamra et l'Ancien Testament* (1937).

[135] So Bauer, *loc. cit.*

[136] K. Sethe, "Amun u. die acht Urgötter von Hermopolis," ABB (1929), No. 4, bases his conjecture of the possibility of an Egyptian model for the idea of Yahweh upon statements which connect Yahweh with רוּחַ (119 f.), among which the name Yahweh itself is listed, → n. 154. But these statements would have to be much more strongly emphasised in the proclamation of Yahweh, and would need much earlier attestation, to point to Amun as a basis. What Yahweh and Amun would really have in common would be the concealment of the divine name (*'imn*, "hidden") if the name Yahweh was concealed from the very first as it came to be later. But אֵל מִסְתַּתֵּר, "the God who hides himself," dates only from Is. 45:15 and has no connection with the idea of "spirit."

[137] For a collection of older and in some cases fantastic hypotheses cf. A. Schleiff, ZDMG, 90 (NF, 15) (1936), 683 ff.

[138] First put on a solid basis by B. Stade, ZAW, 14 (1894), 250 ff. and more recently stated with great confidence by H. Schmökel, "Jahwe u. d. Keniter," JBL, 52 (1933), 212 ff.

[139] Worth noting is the harmonising gloss in v. 5: "That is Sinai."

[140] A. Alt, 6, n. 2 adduces אהיו in Nabatean names of the 3rd cent.

[141] Cf. Schleiff, 696.

6. The Form and Manner of the Name Yahweh.

In these circumstances it would be of great importance to know the meaning of the name Yahweh, for, even if this was not always present to those who spoke and heard the name, it would probably enable us to come to important conclusions regarding the root and the original nuance of the view of God embodied in the name. The only trouble is that even in respect of the form of the name there are difficulties in the tradition which prevent us, or largely prevent us, from reading the word in its full phonetic form with no possibility of objections.

a. There is not even unanimity regarding the consonants. The so-called tetragrammaton יהוה, which occurs 5,321 times in the OT, alternates with the digrammaton יָהּ, which is found 25 times, and the relation between the longer and shorter forms is by no means clear, → 1068. The Elephantine pap. have יהו, and also, apparently in error, יהה. יהו, which is also attested epigraphically, alternates with יו at the beginning of proper names, cf. יוֹאֵל, יְהוֹיָקִים etc., or with יָה, at the conclusion of names, cf. יְשַׁעְיָה. אֵלִיָּהוּ etc. There can be no certainty which of these forms is original. The earliest attested is יהוה. This occurs on the 9th cent. stele of King Meša of Moab in old Semitic script, which completely excludes the doubts that may so easily arise in square script regarding the correct transmission of such precarious characters as jōd, wāw and hē.[142] The consonant grouping admits neither of certain reading nor unambiguous interpretation since even in the Mas. the vowels added to the tetragrammaton vary and in any case are obviously alien additions to the word. The most common form is יְהֹוָה, but along with this, in combination with אֲדֹנָי either before or after the tetragrammaton, we also find the reading יֱהֹוִה. In ancient and important MSS with Tiberian vocalisation, e.g., in Codex B 19a Leningradensis (sig. L), which underlies the third edition of Biblia Hebraica by R. Kittel and P. Kahle,[143] יְהוָה (without ḥōlem) occurs regularly,[144] while texts with the Babylonian pointing usually refrain altogether from any vocalisation of the divine name or else follow the Tiberian tradition.[145] From the fluctuating data one may conclude that the vocalisation is not intrinsic to the word in the one case or the other, but always indicates a periphrastic qerē. יְהוָה is to be read as אֲדֹנָי. "Lord of all," יֱהֹוִה as אֱלֹהִים, "God," יְהֹוָה. as שְׁמָא, "the Name," while the proper name of God itself disappears from reading and meditation.[146] It is שם המפורש, "express name."[147]

b. Thus attempts to achieve the full original form and meaning of יהוה cannot count on help from the biblical tradition. They are referred exclusively to philological combinations. Even Ex. 3:14, as will be shown (→ 1071), contributes nothing, so that from

---

[142] Meša-inscr., line 18; cf. M. Lidzbarski, Hndbch. d. nordsemitischen Epigraphik (1898), 415 and 286. In square script יהוה is also found in the pre-Mas. pap. Nash in the text of the Decalogue, cf. the facsimile in N. Peters, Die älteste Abschrift d. zehn Gebote (1905); J. Goettsberger, Eind. in d. AT (1928), Plate III.

[143] Cf. A. Harkavy and H. L. Strack, Catalog d. hbr. Bibelhandschriften d. Kaiserlichen Öffentlichen Bibliothek in St. Petersburg (1875), 263 ff.; P. Kahle, Masoreten des Westens, I (1927), 66 f.

[144] J. Fischer, Biblica, 15 (1934), 50 ff. establishes the pointing יְהוָה (without ḥōlem and with patah) in a scholastic source; a qames is completely unknown in the MS. Cf. "Werden und Wesen des AT," ZAW, Beih. 66 (1936), 198 ff.

[145] P. Kahle, Der masoretische Text d. AT nach d. Überlieferung d. babylonischen Juden (1902), 11.

[146] When the tetragrammaton occurs outside the Canon, e.g., in the Targums, the Massoretic version is assumed to be valid.

[147] Geiger, 264; Bousset-Gressm., 309, n. 2.

the very outset one can have no hope that any of the results of such deliberations will achieve the degree of certainty sufficient for conclusions as regards the interpretation of the usage of יהוה. At the same time, much perspicacity has been displayed in these attempts, and the two possibilities of (i) a root הוה as the basis, and (ii) a construction on some other basis, have both been pursued.

(i) The tetragrammaton יהוה without vowels has been viewed as either a verbal or a substantival form of the root הוה. The former seems to be more likely, especially if we may believe the report of Theodoret of Cyros [148] that the Samaritans said 'Ιαβέ, and that of Clement of Alexandria [149] that the name was 'Ιαουε. It is true that this at once raises the question of the subject of the verbal statement. On the analogy of many verbal proper names, e.g., יִצְחָק, יַעֲקֹב, one might suggest a *hypocoristicum* which has excluded the element officiating as the subject of the verbal statement. [150] If this is so, only half the meaning of the name is contained in the remaining form. It should be noted, however, that while this type of name construction is common in theophorous proper names, there are no sure instances of it in the names of gods. Hence it is better to turn from the verbal sense to the nominal. [151]

If, however, יהוה is a noun with a prefixed *jōd*, its meaning must depend on the root הוה, which seems to be less at home in Heb. than Aram. The two meanings found in the OT: a. "to fall," and b. "to be," are so little related that it is best not to mix them. [152] In Job 37:6 : הֱוֵא אָרֶץ, "fall to the earth," corresponds exactly to the Arab. הוא "to fall." [153] If יהוה is the one who falls, the ref. is perhaps to lightning or a meteorite, and the sphere of a storm-god is indicated. [154] But if we think in terms of the Aram. הוה "to be" (cf. Gn. 27:29 : הֱוֵה גְבִיר לְאַחֶיךָ; Is. 16:4), יהוה might signify "he who is" or "being in person," which is, however, much too abstract to be convincing.

(ii) Inconclusive though these suggestions are, the other possibility, namely, that of understanding יהוה from its shorter form, which displays the root הוה less clearly, yields no results. The independent shorter form attested in the Bible, chiefly in the liturgical formula הַלְלוּ־יָה, is יָה. [155] In the Elephantine pap. the divine name appears as יהו, which due either to caprice or to carelessness sometimes takes the form of יהה. [156] As an

---

[148] Quaestio 15 in Ex. 7 (MPG, 80, p. 244a b).

[149] Strom., V, 6, 34 (II, p. 348): τὸ τετράγραμμον ὄνομα τὸ μυστικόν, δ περιέκειντο οἷς μόνοις τὸ ἄδυτον βάσιμον ἦν· λέγεται δὲ 'Ιαουε.

[150] The once greatly misunderstood Accadian proper name *jawi-ilu* or *jawi-Dagan* (T. Bauer, *Die Ostkanaanäer* [1928], 56, 61, 63, 74), in which *jawi* is a verb, not a name, illustrates in a particularly impressive way the linguistic possibility. (H. Bauer, 93 now advocates again the old interpretation.)

[151] The question of *hi* or *q* is best left on one side. All attempts at a causative meaning seem to be artificial, and thus break down.

[152] E. König, *Hbr. u. aram. Wörterbuch z. AT* (1910), 76 f. *s.v.* הוה attempts a very violent combination, comparing the Lat. *cecidit* and *accidit*. He regards the meaning "to become," "to be," as a metaphysical and intellectualised version of "to fall." This is scarcely conceivable.

[153] Related is הַוָּה (also הֹוָה), "fall," which is common in the Psalms for the act which brings about a fall, i.e., wickedness.

[154] Derivation from the Arab. *hwy*, "to blow" has some significance in Sethe's conjectures, → n. 136, but unfortunately this is not "certain" (*op. cit.*, p. 120); it lacks the element of cogency, like all other attempts to find the meaning.

[155] Transcribed 'Ιά in Orig. Cels., VI, 32 vl., in Jerome (*Breviarium in Psalmos* on Ps. 146 [MPL, 26, p. 1253b]), also in Θ.

[156] E. Sachau, *Aram. Papyrus u. Ostraka aus einer jüd. Militärkolonie zu Elephantine* (1911), 9 f., 277.

ending in theophorous proper names (יְרְמְיָהוּ etc.) there corresponds to this the Mas. יָה,
and at the beginning of such names יְהוֹ (e.g., יְהוֹנָתָן) or with elision יוֹ (e.g., יוֹחָנָן). [157]
Mention should also be made of the transcription ᾽Ιαώ, [158] of which there are several
instances, some of them pre-Christian, [159] though many of these can be ruled out as
testimonies to the biblical name of God, since Iren. (Haer., I, 30, 5) and Origen (Cels.,
VI, 32) remind us already that Jao (or Jaoth) or ᾽Ιαώ was used by the Gnostics as the
name of a god or demon, obviously as a result of borrowing. Thus יהו can be pronounced
Jāhū as well as Jāhō. [160]

The relation of the longer form to the shorter presents an insoluble problem. If the
shorter form is taken to be an interjection, [161] a "cry to God," [162] such as is found in
Arabic, this rests on the sound consideration that proper names derive from a practical
need, namely, to be able to call on someone. [163] But this is of no help to interpretation
in face of the fact that יָה, like the tetragrammaton, is a name used of the divine person.
A mere call is colourless. It does not constitute a name, even if a הוּא ("he") is added
to fill it out. A He is not a Thou. [164] Furthermore, this would imply that the longer
form, the tetragrammaton, originated in a kind of scholarly development, [165] which is
disproved both by the early attestation of יהוה (→ n. 142) and also by the existence of
constructions with -jama, which derive from the longer form, in Accadian proper names
containing Yahweh. [166] The possibility that the present shorter and longer forms are
not originally the same word deserves consideration in view of the difficulty of explaining the relation between them. [167] But no sure path presents itself in this direction
either.

7. The Reasons for Reticence in Relation to the Name.

The data reveal that it is impossible to state indisputably what יהוה means. All
attempts at etymological interpretation, which are also attempts to convey the
religious content of the word and which are affected by particular theories about
this, suffer from ambiguity. The greatest difficulty in this respect is occasioned
by the fence which the biblical tradition has built around the divine name because
of its awareness of the dangers inherent in the fact of a proper name for the Deity.
This is partly rooted in a feeling of taboo and partly — we should not overlook
this aspect — in a mature perception of the nature of God.

---

[157] Cf. also the epigraphical data, Lidzbarski, 286.

[158] Diod. S., I, 94, 2.

[159] ᾽Ιαή is not clear (Orig. Comm. in Ps., ed. C. H. E. Lommatzsch, XI [1841], 396).
᾽Αϊά in Thdrt. (Comm. in Ex. interrogatio, 15 [MPG, 80, p. 244b]) is אֶהְיֶה, Ex. 3:14.

[160] Jer. (→ n. 155) on Ps. 8 (p. 838a) also has Jaho in a very instructive sentence : Nomen
domini apud Hebraeos quatuor litterarum est, jod, he, vau, he, quod proprie dei vocabulum
sonat : et legi potest Jaho, et Hebraei ἄρρητον, id est, ineffabile opinantur.

[161] Driver, 24.

[162] So F. Rosenzweig, Der Ewige (1929), 108.

[163] Cf. Buber, 236; R. Otto, 210 conjectures a dervish-cry, and refers to the nebiim.

[164] The name Jehu suggests that a הוּא is not contained in the name Yahweh, cf. T. Bauer,
31.

[165] This is the view of Kuhn, who regards Yahweh as a verbal inflexion of a nominal
plur. (?).

[166] V. the list in Driver, 13; cf. also O. Eissfeldt, ZAW, NF, 12 (1935), 65 ff., who
appeals to יהביה in Jewish-Babylonian names of the 7th cent. (= ייהוה!) in support of the
meaning of -jama as יהוה, and who also (74) assumes that the free pronouncing of the name
Yahweh was a practice which survived rather longer than previously believed.

[167] Cf. Schleiff, 699; H. Grimme, BZ, 17 (1926), 29 ff.

a. In those of naive sensibility the names of gods naturally kindle a certain awe which may be explained to some degree in terms of the significance inherent in the giving of names, especially in the world of antiquity. The name brings the person of its bearer into a serviceable formula. It embraces his nature. [168] "As his name is, so is he," can be said sarcastically and yet in all seriousness of a man (1 S. 25:25). The nature of God is thus compressed in the name of God. The name is both the quintessence of His person and the vehicle of His power. To name His name is to give concrete form to all that is perceptible in God. Not least, the specifically divine element, the element of the holy and the wonderful (פִּלְאִי, Ju. 13:18), is visible and efficacious in it. Thus the name of God is a numinous force; it is נִכְבָּד, "fraught with might," and נוֹרָא "feared" (Dt. 25:58), as is God Himself. [169]

b. It would be one-sided, however, to view the name only in this way. For in the God of Israel there are other attributes apart from the dynamic and terrifying. We must take full account of the fact that the overwhelming majority of the biblical writers, when they put the tetragrammaton on paper in their works, must have been familiar in both ear and mind with a usage which dared to utter the divine name just as it was, without restriction. This is certainly true of men of prayer who began with the word יהוה in the vocative as a most personal expression of confidence and hope. [170] There was strongly felt in the name, not merely the negative element which rejected or threatened man, but the positive element of the divine reality and power which protected him. In the authors of the Canon the inclination to avoid the use of the name is thus rare except in E and Qoh. [171] Even when ĕlohīm is used, the name is referred to as the power of God: "Save me, O God, by thy name, and judge me by thy strength" (Ps. 54:1). There can hardly be any question here of the numinous awe which was certainly dominant in the redactors when, e.g., in the story of the cursing of God in Lv. 24:11 they substituted the cursing of the name, [172] or the Greek translators of Ex. 4:24 LXX, who wrote ἄγγελος κυρίου for Yahweh. [173] To be sure, the sense of distance was strongly developed in Yahweh religion from the very first, and was even one of its basic elements, cf. Ex. 3:6, where Moses is afraid to look on God, and esp. Is. 8:13: "He it is who makes you afraid, and he who terrifies you." [174] Nevertheless, it was only as the result of a revival of the primitive dynamic conceptions of paganism, which perhaps came into Judaism through contact with cults involving adjurations, that the sense of distance grew to the inordinate proportions illustrated in the Masoretic treatment of the name of God and in the Samaritan use of שְׁמָא.

c. But a fundamental and intellectually powerful criticism of the name of God, a conscious challenging of the basis of its structure in mythical thinking, preceded these closely-channeled anxieties and perhaps involuntarily helped to further their

---

[168] Cf. J. Pedersen, Israel (1926), 245 ff.

[169] Because the name is feared, there is hesitation to utter it, Am. 6:10, cf. Zeph. 1:7; Hab. 2:20. Cf. also R. Hirzel, "Der Name," ASG, 36, 2 (1918).

[170] Cf. Ps. 27:4: The close proximity of Yahweh is bliss.

[171] Cf. Bousset-Gressm., 307 f.; B. Jacob, Im Namen Gottes (1903), 164 ff.

[172] Baudissin, Kyrios, II, 174 ff.

[173] For further details cf. Geiger, 264 ff.

[174] Cf. also Jos. 24:19; Lv. 10:3.

over-development. This criticism is to be found in the procedure which the so-called E recension of the Hexateuchal narrative adopts with reference to the name of God, and then by way of confirmation in the outworking of these ideas in the Elohistic Psalter (Ps. 42-83). [175]

Irrespective of the answer one might give to the open question of the literary independence of the E recension, [176] there can be no doubt that it is here that a first major attempt is made to break with the use of the proper name יהוה. [177] An obstacle to this attempt was the tradition that this name had decisive significance in the Mosaic institution. The claim of this tradition is met by gradually introducing the name of Yahweh in those parts of the narrative which come after the story of the theophany granted to Moses in Ex. 3. But this is not done with any regularity, and one might conjecture that the use of Yahweh in E is due to changes made by redactors, whereas the author himself used אֱלֹהִים throughout his work. [178]

Whatever may have been the reasons for what he did, he did at least show unmistakably that the divine person cannot be distinguished from other persons by the ordinary method of using names, since the divine nature is borne, not by many, but only by One. [179]

8. The Name of God in the Account of Yahweh's Revelation to Moses in Ex. 3:14.

a. This conscious restraint of E as regards the divine name Yahweh is particularly striking at the very point in his narrative where he is forced to use it, namely, in the account of the revelation of Yahweh to Moses in Ex. 3. [180] That the very heart of the account is the imparting of the divine name is taught not only by v. 15, which is easily seen to be an editorial addition, [181] but also by the P account of the same event in Ex. 6:2 f. Nevertheless, the words which touch on the heart of the matter in Ex. 3:14 do not contain the tetragrammaton. Instead, in reply to the question what information Moses is to give about the name of the God who speaks to him, God says: "I am that I am: and he said, Thus shalt thou say unto the children of Israel, I am hath sent me unto you." These puzzling words are designed either to explain the name יהוה by an alliterative paraphrase of its meaning or, by a close approximation to its form, to avoid the name and thus to call its use in question.

b. At a first glance it is tempting to take the common course and to understand the statement which presents God's answer as a bold and clever attempt to give the meaning of the hitherto unexplained name יהוה. If this is so, then the statement is to be judged in the same way as, e.g., the attempt to explain חַוָּה in terms of חַיִּים (Gn. 3:20) or אַבְרָהָם from הֲמוֹן (Gn. 17:5). That is to say, it is a very loose pro-

---

175 Cf. H. Gunkel, Einleitung in d. Psalmen (1933), 447 ff.

176 Cf. the discussion in P. Volz and W. Rudolph, Der Elohist als Erzähler — ein Irrweg der Pentateuchkritik? (1933), esp. 19 and 82 ff.

177 Baudissin, Kyrios, II, 171 takes a different view.

178 So J. Wellhausen, Die Composition des Hexateuchs² (1889), 72; O. Procksch, Das nordhebräische Sagenbuch ... (1906), 197 f.

179 R. Kittel, I, 258 sees in the E usage, not a monotheistic trend, but a pre-Yahwistic form which is dependent on Canaanite nomenclature. If E was really so correct from the standpoint of religious history, he must have had some educative purpose, but what was it?

180 Vv. 1, 4b, 6, 9-14 belong to E.

181 "And God said moreover unto Moses ..."

cedure which makes free use of the given form of the word — the kind of procedure which narrators love because it enables them to direct the attention of their audience to the symbolic content of names. The fact that there are many such linguistically inadequate etymologies in the biblical story is a strong argument in favour of the view that we have something similar here, and that it shares the naive earnestness of all attempts to arrive at the inner meaning of names, however different may be the spirit in which they are made. [182] In the present case the intention is clear. The name of God is meant to express something like existence (הָיָה). [183] But in what sense? Does not every name, including every divine name, self-evidently embrace a simple statement of existence in virtue of the very fact that it denotes a concrete phenomenon? And what purpose is served by the relative clause "that I am"?

> There is no certain answer to these questions, and this has led expositors from Raschi to our own time to exercise great profundity in the analysis of this אֶהְיֶה. The result may well be many true and incontestable statements about the concept of existence and reality, and various reflections on the freeing of belief from magic, [184] and on the *Deus revelatus* and *Deus absconditus*. But all this is just as speculative as the ἐγώ εἰμι ὁ ὤν of the LXX, [185] which strictly has very little to do with אֶהְיֶה אֲשֶׁר אֶהְיֶה. [186]

c. The speculative profundity of a ὁ ὤν is certainly not present in the Heb. The words lose their unfathomability as soon as we stop trying to construe them as aetiological etymology. For the view that this is what they are is largely called in question by strong formal and material weaknesses which cannot all be explained in terms of the general strangeness of OT etymologies.

> There are several arguments against the etymological interpretation. 1. The consonants forming the tetragrammaton are ignored, since the ref. is to הָיָה, not to הוה, as one would expect. But היה and הוה, while they are closely related, are two very different things for the ear. [187] 2. The imperf. form אֶהְיֶה sets aside the preformative י, which is essential to the structure of the tetragrammaton. The syntactical necessity of using the 1st person in a narrative would have prevented an author who wished to give an explanation of the form יהוה from attempting an explanation along these lines. 3. Nowhere else in the lit. of the OT is the root of יהוה sought in היה. For it is impossible to understand every occurrence of אֶהְיֶה or the like on the lips of God [188] as a reminiscence of Ex. 3:14. 4. The style of revelation is both the least adapted and the least common form for etymologies. "Etymologies are not revealed." [189]

---

[182] Cf. on יַעֲקֹב Gn. 27:36 with 25:26 and the satirical allusions to Edom and Seir in 25:25 or the hostile allusions to Moab and Ammon in 19:37 f. etc.

[183] Cf. Job 3:16 לֹא אֶהְיֶה, "I do not exist"; Gn. 1:2 (?); 2:18.

[184] Cf. Buber, 85. "I rule" is an explanatory periphrasis (J. Hempel, *Gott u. Mensch im AT²* = BWANT, 3. F. 2a [1936], 69).

[185] This could at a pinch be based on אֶהְיֶה אֲשֶׁר יִהְיֶה, cf. P. Haupt, OLZ, 12 (1909), 211 ff.; W. F. Albright, JBL, 43 (1924), 370 ff.

[186] For the *nota relationis* אֲשֶׁר is ambiguous, and there is only a slight possibility that אֲשֶׁר אֶהְיֶה could fulfil the static function of a participle like ὁ ὤν. For where Heb. wishes a verb to discharge this function in a relative clause, it everywhere uses the participle form, cf. אֲשֶׁר יוֹשֵׁב (Dt. 1:4) or אֲשֶׁר מְבַקְשִׁים (Jer. 38:16) etc. and there is in Heb. no part. corresponding to the speculative Gk. ὤν.

[187] In Is. 38:11 יָהּ is a vocative of the short form in litany-like repetition.

[188] Cf., e.g., Hos. 1:9; Ez. 14:11; 34:24 etc.

[189] H. Gunkel, *Genesis⁵* (1922), XXII.

d. The situation is, then, that the words אֶהְיֶה אֲשֶׁר אֶהְיֶה and the isolated אֶהְיֶה represent an intrusion into the original. They are what was later called a תִּקּוּן סוֹפְרִים, [190] and they simply denote a refusal to take up the question of the name of God. The only other possibility is that they refuse this question according to the express intention of the author himself.

(i) On the former view the present form must have arisen roughly as follows. Setting aside all individual reflection, the narrator simply followed the existing tradition and told how God named His name in self-authentication. But by authenticating Himself in this form God also authenticated quite unequivocally the polytheistic presupposition of the whole narrative, namely, the intrinsically dubious fact [191] that the children of Israel could have doubts as to which of the deities who might have been the God of their fathers (cf. Jos. 24:14 f.) had given Moses his commission. It is easy to imagine how objections would arise to so pointedly mythical a statement about the revelation of a divine name in the most crucial passage in the whole tradition of salvation history. This would seem to be almost an admission that the other gods of whom we read in Jos. 24 were also to be accepted as gods of the fathers. Hence a redactor who at the same time was following Elohistic tendencies might well have removed the name from God's answer, since in this particular verse, and in the context of a divine saying, the whole complex of questions associated with the name was felt to be too burdensome. [192] The violence of the correction is, of course, glossed over in masterly style by turning to good account a phrase already present in v. 12 : אֶהְיֶה עִמָּךְ ("I am beside thee") in the recapitulatory form : "I am he who I am." Almost imperceptibly the heightened form of היה has been given an existential function and the mystery of the divine nature presented as the deepest meaning in all invocation. The author of the tiqqūn is no longer concerned with the context.

(ii) More difficult than the theory of an early editorial insertion is the understanding of the phrase as the narrator's own rejection of the question which is put to God. For in this case the rejection takes the form of a pointless tautology : "I am I." The hypothesis is not completely impossible, [193] for the spirit who wrestled with Jacob at Jabbok refused to give him his name (Gn. 32:29): "Wherefore is it that thou dost ask after my name?" The divine messenger who came to Samson's parents gave a similar answer, and he also gave the reason that his name was פֶּלְאִי "belonging to the divine," and that it was thus inaccessible and dangerous to men (Ju. 13:18). But the assumption that the analogy of this motif of refusing a name may have influenced the narrator comes up against the difficulty that in the whole description of the encounter there is not a single phrase to suggest refusal on the part of God. On the contrary, v. 14b: "Thus shalt thou say unto the children of Israel, אֶהְיֶה hath sent me," seems to indicate that the request was granted. [194] The refusal, then, is expressed only in the word אֶהְיֶה, a stylistic difficulty which is very noticeable in this highly important passage, especially as it does not occur in the two stories which support the thesis. For this reason it may be assumed that the explanation advanced under (i) is in better accord with the facts.

---

[190] On this term cf. E. Ehrentreu, Untersuchungen über die Massora (1925), 8 f.

[191] Cf. on this Alt, 12 ff.

[192] שִׁילֹה in Gn. 49:10 is a possible analogy. Perhaps there was here a name for the Messiah which it seemed advisable to conceal for some reason.

[193] E. Meyer, Die Israeliten ... (1906), 6; H. Gressmann, Mose u. seine Zeit (1913), 35 f.; L. Köhler, Theologie des AT (1936), 234.

[194] Buber, 237 f.; Grether, 22.

9. The Name Yahweh as the Basic Form of the Old Testament Declaration about God (→ 79).

The statements of the OT concerning Yahweh take many forms, display varying degrees of intensity in consciousness of faith, and are given a differing impress by greater and lesser writers according to their ability and character. In some cases they are strangely enclosed in curious thinking, although in the main they are developed in clear and logical form. The link with history, with the here and now, can also work itself out in many different ways, though it can never break away from its basic theme that Yahweh is Lord. Man has no power over Him. If he can influence Him at all, it is only to the degree that a servant may influence his master. No one can invoke Yahweh by magic, and he who tries to do so has not felt even the slightest breath of His Spirit. Together, the statements give us a uniform picture of God which acquires its full significance from an understanding of the power of the Thou who speaks to man. Not so much that this power is felt to be total as that its vitality is orientated to salvation, to the fulness of the meaning of existence, is the revelation for whose sake the history of Yahweh with Israel, its commencement, its climax, and its transition into the history of God with the world, has been collected in the Canon of the OT. One might sum up the situation by saying that the name of Yahweh is the basic form of all OT statements about God, or that the figure of Yahweh is the original form of biblical revelation.

a. On a simple phenomenological consideration this verdict does, of course, come up against the difficulty that the God who bears the name of Yahweh is thereby set as God among the gods. In fact, such important early statements of the belief in God as the Decalogue in its two forms (Ex. 20:3 ff.; Dt. 5:7 ff.), psalms like 58 and 82, narratives like Jos. 24:14 f. and prophecies like Am. 5:26, confirm the fact that from an early period and over a wide area a distinction of Yahweh from the gods was made both with mind and heart (→ 88). As a rule this takes the form of the rejection of false gods, but there are also positive instances of mythical thinking. One cannot sing Yahweh's songs in a strange land (Ps. 137:4). In exile one is forced to serve other gods (1 S. 26:19). Rimmon is lord in Damascus (2 K. 5:18) and Chemosh in Moab (Ju. 11:24; 2 K. 3:27). A foreign land is an unclean land, Am. 7:17; Hos. 9:3 f. But the surest proof of the vitality of mythical thinking in the community of Yahweh is the fact that the rivalry of other gods did not cease to plunge the obedience of faith into a new crisis in each generation. The narrative of 1 K. 18:17 ff. tells of the trial which Elijah arranged to demonstrate the competence of his God for worshippers in the territory of Carmel. [195] Here, as almost always, the crisis was resolved by political development, in which shifts of power among the gods seemed to find expression. The state deities of alien powers, "the whole host of heaven" (2 K. 21:3), could sometimes find an official place alongside Yahweh. [196] Ishtar, the queen of heaven (Jer. 7:18) and Adonis, the Syrian Baal of vegetation (Is. 1:29 f.), attracted the women. "According to the number of thy cities are thy gods," Jeremiah could say (2:28). In the prophetic books one may read on almost every page that the meaning of faith in Yahweh is challenged and its definitiveness endangered.

---

[195] A. Alt, "Das Gottesurteil auf dem Karmel," Beer-Festschr. (1935), 1 ff. understands the event as a political coup d'état of the national God of Israel against the Phoenicians.
[196] Ez. 8:10 ff. seems to refer to Egyptian cults. An officially sponsored syncretism may be seen from the time of Solomon, cf. R. Kittel, II, 192 ff.

b. In addition to deviation into alien myths, a complete lack of numinous feeling is also to be noted. In times of peace and among the secure strata of the people Yahweh is acknowledged with a certain official factuality which found some support in the mythical conception. Especially in Northern Israel the political division of the people of Yahweh created a receptivity to alien myths which induced a fatal lack of insight and instinct in religious matters. "They sacrificed unto Baalim, and burned incense to graven images" (Hos. 11:2). They did not cry to Yahweh "with their heart" (7:14). They were incapable of meeting His demands (Jer. 6:10). The sacrifices of children in the days of Manasseh and Ahaz sound like the acts of despair of uprooted people. On the other hand, we find a common complacency to which the prophets can refer only with anger and disgust. The Holy One of Israel was spurned, there was apostasy from Him (Is. 1:4), because the will refused every appeal and men were guided by impulsive needs, so that the worship of symbolic gods seemed to be more natural. In the unruffled enjoyment of bourgeois prosperity they were like "wine on the lees" (Jer. 48:11), "settled on their lees" (Zeph. 1:12), untouched by any fear of God: "God does neither good nor evil," i.e., His activity is fundamentally in doubt. "God does not seek out" (Ps. 10:4; cf. Jer. 5:12). What is the "work of Yahweh"? (Is. 5:12). The subject arouses only scorn: "Let him make speed, and hasten his work, that we may see the counsel of the Holy One of Israel" (5:19). Thus the complacent bourgeois answers with ridicule the inspired speaker; he can even call him mad (Hos. 9:7; Jer. 29:26). The fear of God is simply a human precept taught and learned by rote (Is. 29:13). It is not an experience. Even those who told the stories of the patriarchs could not refrain from introducing a frivolous trait of this kind into the picture of Jacob, who in a crisis dares to support his deceit with the name of Yahweh, though he himself remains at a prudent distance ("Yahweh, thy God," Gn. 27:20).

It is true that such aberrations cannot be explained only in terms of mythical thinking, for which God is a fluctuating and hence a crippled authority. Nevertheless, the history of religion gives evidence that the indifferent attitude of cunning self-assurance is usually supported by a mythical conception of God. The god who is restricted by frontiers is also a limited lord. The decisive point for Yahweh religion is that the figure of Yahweh, who was thus endowed with many mythical traits, was not a specific god with a limited sphere but the God who claimed unconditional authority in every sphere of life. "Seek ye me, and ye shall live" (Amos 5:4), is the sum of His demands and promises, and mythical ways of thinking and speaking about Him lose the personal element and become monumental expressions of a dominant cosmic will.

c. For those who proclaim Him, then, Yahweh is no abstract concept or euphemeristic idea. He comes to them and forces Himself upon them as an audible, visible and palpable force. They do not think they are dreaming when His hand seizes them. Jeremiah has some sharp words to say about this supposed reception of revelation (Jer. 23:28). They see Yahweh, though they cannot describe Him. The picture which their inner eye perceives has none of the naivety of mythical conception. It is in every respect overwhelming and compelling. Particularly instructive is the description of the theophany in Ez. A remarkable picture is drawn consisting of a whirl of animals and wheels and beating wings, and only at the very end does the prophet come to the essential point and dare to say, in cautiously guarded terms, that it was something which had the appearance of an image of the majesty of Yahweh. The prophet is almost terrified that he has said before that what is seated on the throne-like structure has the appearance of a man. In self-correction, he thus repeats the whole statement, referring it to *kabōd*. *Kabōd*, the royal plenitude of power, is substituted for person, man (Ez. 1). [197]

In the light of statements like this, it is of no real help to emphasise the common human and mythological features in the portrait of Yahweh if our concern is to establish the meaning of the statement of faith concerning Him. It has only the value of a metaphor to say that Yahweh has a mouth or a heart, that His lips are full of wrath, that His arm is stretched out like a giant's. The need for plastic depiction, especially in religious poetry, has led to the use of forms which seem to be the only possible ones for the depiction of resolute and virile motifs in the experience of God. The astringent originality of personal experience finds expression in them without regard for possibilities of interpretation which might lead away from the central experience of revelation. The strong resolution of the prophets and the hymnic or tragic fervour of the poets have their origin in encounter with the personal will of Yahweh. This is the reason why even in the message concerning Him the concept of divine grandeur and power impresses itself with imperious force upon those who study the traditional manifestations, so that even from the most modest and fragmentary accounts of the founding of belief in Yahweh the question of reality arises spontaneously, and no reader can escape passing an existential judgment on the divine person and His will.

d. The great poetic attempts to discern the divine rule of Yahweh in the dimensions of time (Ps. 90) and space (Ps. 139) projected to infinity may well lead us to the limits of the human conception of personality, but they do not surrender the revealed knowledge of divine personality, and hence they, too, keep to the general line of biblical religion. The unusual speculative features of these discussions [198] are neither resigned nor quietistic. They arise out of the feeling of responsibility of the man whom God has addressed — a feeling which threatens to develop into purely numinous awe. When the poet seeks knowledge (Ps. 139:6) of the mystery of divine existence, he comes up against a "wonder" (פלא), and the realisation that Yahweh always sees and encloses him kindles in him a creaturely anxiety: "Whither shall I go from thy spirit? or whither shall I flee from thy presence?" The threatening words of Amos (9:2) surge up in him, and the motif of flight from God gives rise to a basic feeling of the "religion of holiness" [199] such as is portrayed in the poetry of Job in words of helpless anguish wrung from the dark depths of experience. It sounds like a bitter travesty of Ps. 8:4 when Job vainly seeks to elude God: "Let me alone; for my days are vanity. What is man, that thou shouldest magnify him? and that thou shouldest set thine heart upon him? and that thou shouldest visit him every morning, and try him every moment? How long wilt thou not depart from me?" (Job 7:16 ff.). Even the sense of guilt is choked by anxious panic: "Whether righteous, whether wicked, it is one; he destroyeth" (9:22). But Ps. 139 — and in this it is akin to Ps. 73:13 ff. — is an example of the way in which this crippling feeling of being subjected to demonic

---

[197] By speaking of the Ancient of days and His white hair, the apocalyptist of Da. 7 himself shows that he is unconsciously using a temporal concept for authority with this reference to age.

[198] Ps. 90:4: A thousand years as a day; Ps. 139:5: "Thou enclosest me behind and before"; for both motifs there are Indian par., cf. H. Gunkel, *Die Psalmen* (1926), 397, 590; H. Hommel, "Das religionsgeschichtliche Problem des 139. Ps.," ZAW, NF, 6 (1929), 110 ff.

[199] J. Hänel, *Die Religion der Heiligkeit* (1931), 1, 317 ff.

caprice can find its way back to the calm attitude of praise to the Lord and the final request : "Lead me in the way everlasting."

e. Naive conceptions are more evident in the statements of P concerning man as a plastic image or likeness of God (Gn. 1:26 f.; 9:6; → II, 390). They are also reflected in the We-style of God's speech and find very strong expression in the word צֶלֶם. It is also typical that the asyndetically added term כִּדְמוּתֵנוּ, "corresponding to our likeness," immediately seeks to turn the very factual expression a little in the direction of allegory. But in simple logic, understood without abstraction or spiritualisation, the statement : "We will make men as our plastic image corresponding to our likeness" tells us two things : 1. that the God who speaks, like all the gods, has a form which man can represent as צֶלֶם. which he can thus imagine ; and 2. that by looking at the human form one can arrive at the thought that "God looks something like this." [200] If we have to spiritualise the saying, this is not so much due to the statement which immediately follows, namely, that He created them man and woman, since man and woman are both man, [201] as it is to the context of the narrative, of which it may rightly be said, with this exception, that it "demythologises the material as much as it possibly can." [202]

f. The same observation may also be applied to the few relatively tangible testimonies to the early period of Yahweh religion. The emphatically masculine picture of God evoked by the tradition of the Mosaic institution shaped OT religion in its basic attitude not merely as obedience and loyalty but also as love, not because the myth was particularly imposing, but because in it the unrecognised dynamism of the Holy was transformed into the will of the Leader God directed to a specific goal and binding men to obedience and loyalty. Yahweh, the "man of war" (Ex. 15:3), is no berserk. He does not fight for fighting's sake. He fights for the triumph of His resolve to give to this people, which bears and is pledged to the name "God fights," an inheritance, the necessities of life, and happiness. To see that the loyalty between God and people, their mutual חֶסֶד, was not just theoretical, it is particularly important to note how strong is the impulsive feeling sensed in this powerful divine figure. In the Decalogue and elsewhere Yahweh is אֵל קַנָּא, the "jealous God" (Ex. 20:5 etc.). [203] This can even be His name (Ex. 34:14), a description of the mystery of His person, and the importance of the concept for the knowledge of Yahweh receives sharp emphasis in the tradition. Its significance for the whole of the biblical message concerning God must not be overlooked. Literally, [204] it tells us that Yahweh wills to be loved by those whom He loves,

---

[200] 5:3 shows that the ref. is to His physical form (→ II, 391). A silver coin from Gaza (5th [?] cent. B.C.) with the inscription יהו depicts a bearded man sitting on a winged chariot, cf. Haas, 9/10, Leipoldt (1926), No. 81, greatly magnified in J. Hempel, Die alt-hebräische Lit. ... (1930), 111. Is Jahu here meant to be the territorial God of a heathen province or a heathen god as the territorial god of an Israelite province ? Cf. H. Gressmann, ZAW, NF 2 (1925), 16 f.; Leipoldt, XI. [But the true reading is yhd, "Judah."]

[201] But cf. Köhler, 133.

[202] G. v. Rad, Die Priesterschrift im Hexateuch (1934), 168.

[203] The thought appears so spontaneously that it stands out strongly from its immediate context in the text of the Decalogue. It belongs to the oldest stratum of the Yahweh message, as rightly perceived by H. Schmidt, Eucharisterion f. H. Gunkel (1923), 86 ff. When it is turned to exhortatory use as a threat in Dt., its concealed kernel, the concept of love, is so suppressed that we are hardly aware of it.

[204] Thus without the "obscuring exposition" (Köhler, 50) which seems to be present esp. when the root of Yahweh's jealousy is found in holiness, ibid., 34. For in this case holiness

that loyalty to Him must be unconditional, because reciprocal. There could hardly be stronger expression for the personal and emotional attitude of God to man, which is only half seen if one looks at its character as a threat. A very inward sphere of the divine life is cautiously indicated when there is reference to an elemental feeling which moves into this sphere with irresistible force as a painful reaction against alien intrusion. As אֵל קַנָּא Yahweh is no static Baal. Love may be discerned in Him. It is part of the virile seriousness of this divine message that the statement is shrouded in negation and has to be detected. In man קִנְאָה is wounded love, a raging "gnawing at the bones" (Prv. 14:30). It is the correlative of נְקָמָה, "vengeance," the affronted sense of right and honour. The jealous and avenging God (Na. 1:2; Ps. 94:1) is thus vulnerable in soul. He is a person in the full sense as the bearer of sensitivity. He can be provoked [205] by contemptuous doubts of His imperious seriousness. He puts feeling into His directions and actions. He does this so fully and so unreservedly that He seems to require of the men whom He trusts that they should do as He directs. Hence one might say that אֵל קַנָּא is a young God, for only an old man like the rarefied Eliphaz finds jealousy foolish (Job 5:2). The passionate fulness of the concept comes out the more strongly, and its logical inadequacy emerges the more clearly, immediately one tries to develop its consequences in methodical fashion, as in the glosses on the text of the Decalogue which try to enlist its support for a theory of retribution. [206] To understand the concept, it is essential that it be set in the framework of the total picture of Yahweh, the man who is yet no man, but God. This means that the imponderable element of the dynamic and the demonic is structured as the imponderable element of the person of the Holy One. Referred to it, man is at a loss only when he tries to escape it. Then he falls victim to wrath. [207] But feeling still teaches man that it is better to fall into the hands of Yahweh than those of men, for "his mercies are great" (2 S. 24:14).

g. Yahweh is recognised and acknowledged as Lord in His directions. These are total; they embrace the whole of life. The basic classical text of the Torah, the Decalogue, [208] suggests this. The I of the speaking God turns to a Thou. It is not at first clear who is thus addressed as a Thou, whether a collective, the legally constituted community, or the individual. [209] What is clear, however, is that

---

has to be construed as an emotion, which is out of keeping. Jealousy is certainly rooted in an emotion, but the emotion is love.

[205] Cf. כַּעַס, Ps. 85:5 etc. and the verb הִכְעִיס.

[206] Ex. 20:5 f.; Dt. 5:9 f. is not fully worked out theologically, so that it has been subjected to explanatory additions ("which love me," "which hate me") which in turn are not too well-advised.

[207] Wrath, too, is a description of the operation of the Holy One which presupposes expression in personal feeling. In the OT wrath is not part of the essence of God as elsewhere, cf. R. Otto, 123. It denotes a specific emotional reaction. פַּחַד יִצְחָק (Gn. 31:42) is not Yahweh but a Baal of Beersheba.

[208] Against attempts to show that the Decalogue comes from Moses, it has been urged, e.g., by L. Köhler, ThR, NF 1 (1929), 161 ff. that they can lead to no evident results and that even a probable conclusion is outside the realm of possibility. The two texts are separate corpora. This means that they are in any case older than any of the great narrative sources of the Hexateuch, into which they have been introduced at a crucial point, namely, the account of the constitution of the national community.

[209] Yahweh is Israel's God; hence the Thou can refer to Israel collectively. This conclusion would be easier if it were quite so convincing in the statements which follow, but it is surely excluded in clauses which deal with conduct vis-à-vis the compatriot (רֵעַ). Another

the statement "I am Yahweh thy God" finds practical culmination in the phrase "there shall be no other gods for thee in despite of me." If there are other gods for thee, this implies, not the theoretical acceptance of their existence, but practical, willing appropriation of their powers, i.e., service in the widest sense. This must not happen "in despite of me." What we have here is not a didactic statement on the existence or non-existence of gods as distinct from God. The theologoumenon "monotheism" has only subordinate significance in relation to biblical religion since it has no practical outworking in life. The God who speaks to the Thou, who declares His will authoritatively and in a way which is intelligible to human powers of comprehension, is God for those who hear Him. That this authoritative relation excludes all other relations of the same or a similar kind is the principle which is felt to be self-evident and which ineluctably propels the biblical belief in God beyond all national and mythical frontiers. The prohibitive form: "There shall be no other gods for thee," which is implied also in most of the other clauses of the Decalogue, makes it clear that the legal character of the phrase exercises exclusive control as a way of life. Its significance as an attack on the creative mythical impulses of tribal religions, and indeed on the constant luxuriant growth of myth in religious thought, may now be assessed by modern man in a retrospective survey of the history of religion. But the men to whom the author of the statement spoke merely felt at first that they were authoritatively reminded of the reality of the will of their God Yahweh and saw themselves compelled to bow to His will. Here is the strongest germ-cell of the religious life, the contact of experience of God with the will.

But this shows us what the lordship of God is. Firmly grasped both in emotion and will, man receives unconditionally binding direction which gives meaning, measure and purpose to his life and which demands an obedience that is not exhausted in an elegiac cultivation of feeling but manifests itself in concrete action, especially towards others, in fulfilment of an imposed duty of loyalty. "We do and we hear" (Ex. 24:7) is the answer of those assembled on the Mount of God when they receive the Law. The recognition that the revelation of the divine engages man, not just theoretically or in principle, but for the most concrete action for which it gives the great and simple norms — this may be called the most valuable legacy of the whole OT to its readers. It is by its moral requirement that the experience of the community of Yahweh with its God is first seen to be universally valid. "He hath shewed thee, O man, what is good; and what doth Yahweh require of thee, but to do justly, and to love mercy, and to walk humbly with thy God" (Mi. 6:8). The collective term "man" is suggested spontaneously to the prophet by the dynamic of his divine commission. Similarly, the threats of Amos against Damascus and other foreign states (Am. 1:3 ff.) arise out of the sudden realisation that the nations cannot do or not do what they want, but must give an account to the same transcendent God whose threatening voice he heard from Sion (Am. 1:2; cf. 9:12).

10. The Confession of Yahweh in Dt. 6:4.

The historico-religious term "monotheism" can be justly used of OT religion only in so far as it implies a theoretical appraisal of its total contribution to religious

---

possibility is that the usage fluctuates, but if this is not acceptable it is also conceivable that in the very first statement individual members of the nation and cultus are addressed.

insight. A need to speculate is alien to Yahweh religion itself. [210] This is also true of the beginning of the so-called שְׁמַע in Dt. 6:4, which might be regarded as a speculative statement if the form of the confession and the context did not show that here, too, the intention is not to stimulate or justify thought but by means of emotional statements about God to energise the will of those who confess Him. Love for Yahweh is expressed in order to strengthen the community's love for Him. The rich cultic and theological exploitation of the four short words יְהֹוָה אֱלֹהֵינוּ יְהֹוָה אֶחָד justifies a special investigation of their much debated meaning.

They are introduced by a hortatory formula: "Hear, O Israel," which is used only in Dt. (5:1; 9:1; 20:3; 27:9). For this reason, they sound like a quotation from some existing formulation. This might well have been a hymn, since they have the pregnant brevity of hymnic motifs and this is not the usual style of Dt. They consist — and this is the difficulty — either of two sentences or of only one. Grammatically, it is easier to assume that there are two substantival clauses. The first: "Yahweh is our God," is a kind of basic confession of the people of God. It is monolatrous, like the first clause of the Decalogue. A second clause is then added. This, too, may well be hymnic, but it is much more strongly didactic and demanding: "Yahweh is one." If we understand it on the analogy of a very similar construction like Gn. 41:25: חֲלוֹם פַּרְעֹה אֶחָד הוּא, i.e., that one dream is at issue, not two, then its import is that Yahweh is a single person, not many. This would be a trite commonplace, though only if emphasis is laid on the אֶחָד to give a pointless mathematical statement. [211] The surprising and for this reason effective aspect of the mathematical climax, however, is to be found quite unmistakably in the definite emphasising of the name, which is thereby given the value of the denomination of a species. "Yahweh is one" means that in Yahweh everything that He is is absolutely exhaustively and exclusively present. [212] The second statement is thus analytic, not synthetic. It goes beyond the first, reminding us of a verse like Is. 45:6: אֲנִי יהוה וְאֵין־עוֹד and demanding interpretation along the lines of verses like Dt. 4:35: יהוה הוּא הָאֱלֹהִים אֵין־עוֹד מִלְבַדּוֹ or Dt. 7:9 etc., namely, that "none is what Yahweh is, God."

The difficulty which this understanding has to face, however, is that of the combination of the two clauses. The question why the more far-reaching statement is accompanied by a narrower one can be answered only if we suppose that the whole has a hymnic character. But if it is not accepted that the second clause goes beyond the first we are brought back to the fact that יהוה אֶחָד is a trite mathematical statement which is not made any the more tolerable by seeing in it a polemic against a poly-Yahwism which tried to import the multiformity of Baal into faith in Yahweh. [213]

---

[210] There is, perhaps, an exception in Qoh. in the obscure saying about the "one shepherd" (12:11).

[211] The author of Zech. 14:9 obviously read and understood it thus. The difficulty of the apparent futility of the verse corresponds to this; the author means to say something very different from what he actually says.

[212] Cf. a similar phrase like that in Job 12:2: אַתֶּם־עָם: "you are the species man wholly and exclusively."

[213] There may well have been something of this kind (cf. Gn. 16:13; 12:7; 18:1 ff.; 28, the divine triad in the temple of Yeb), but it is undoubtedly out of the question here, and in any case so doctrinaire a thought could not possibly have found expression in two short words.

On the other hand, to regard as one clause the words which we have hitherto construed as two does not yield any essentially different meaning. In this case אֱלֹהֵינוּ is in apposition to יהוה, after which the subject יהוה is repeated: "Yahweh, our God, Yahweh is one." [214] Though poor in style, this arrangement is preferable to that which would put יהוה אֶחָד in apposition to אֱלֹהֵינוּ. If it is felt that a numeral cannot be linked with a proper name, our only resort is paraphrase, e.g., "Yahweh is our God, Yahweh as the only one." This maintains the lofty monolatry, but at the price of linguistic clarity.

Analysis shows that it is not possible to determine the content of the words with a logical precision free from all possible objection. This fact, together with the rhythmical sweep of the language and the unmistakable majesty of the subject of the statement, makes the words a unique testimony to the sustained and yet restlessly onrushing power of faith in Yahweh. They seem to stand at a dividing line. The active dynamic of the national religion is using a mode of expression which it no longer finds adequate, and so a questionable spirit of reflection is beating against the mystery of the real content of the revelation of Yahweh. According to this confession, Yahweh as the sum and centre of all religious experience is the source of a single and unbroken historical revelation. It is certainly possible to ask how many, and what similar, revelations there may be. But what has been experienced is to be heard.

Quell

D. "Lord" in Later Judaism.

1. The Choice of the Word κύριος in the LXX.

Oud present task is to discuss the reasons for the choice of the word κύριος in the LXX. Baudissin [215] has argued that the meaning of κύριος is "the superior" rather than "the one who has power over something or someone." This superiority may find expression in the exercise of power, but it is to be differentiated from it. In the OT אָדוֹן is used of God in such as way as to describe Him as the superior being who belongs to the speaker in this capacity (Baudissin, II, 249). κύριος bears the same meaning in the LXX. But Baudissin's arguments are not convincing at this point. When Baudissin adduces in favour of his thesis the fact that in the OT the address אֲדוֹנִי is also used by independent persons who simply use it in order to convince the one addressed that they honour him and wish to enter into relationship with him (II, 246), he fails to see that in the context such an address entails the self-designation of the speaker as "servant," and that even if this is not meant in strict literalness it still involves the dependence of the speaker on the one whom he addresses. It expresses subservience. The fact that גְּבִירָה, used of the queen, is not rendered by κυρία, as elsewhere, but by expressions which unequivocally denote rule (II, 253), is not connected with the fact that κυρία simply expresses superiority and not rule, but with the circumstance that it is not used specifically for "queen." In most of the instances cited by Baudissin (loc. cit., n. 1), κυρία would not have been sufficiently explicit, since the queen is also κυρία in relation to her slaves.

It is better to start with the Greek meaning of the word in the time of the LXX. Since κύριος was not then used as an epithet for God in paganism, the ethnic use expounded

---

[214] So the LXX: κύριος ὁ θεὸς ἡμῶν κύριος εἷς ἐστιν. Dt. 6:4 does not seem to have had any influence on the ancient Christian formula εἷς θεός, unless some Gk. form of the schema which deviated from the LXX (1 C. 8:4 ff. [?]; Jm. 2:19) supplied the text; cf. E. Peterson, Εἷς θεός (1926), 293 ff.

[215] Op. cit., II, 241-257.

by Baudissin has no bearing on the LXX. At the time when the specifically Hellenistic usage was first emerging, κύριος denoted the one who has lawful power of disposal. The element of legality is to be emphasised because the rendering of the tetragrammaton by κύριος occurs throughout the LXX and thus goes back to the first stages of this translation. With its choice of κύριος rather than δεσπότης, which was also possible and perhaps more natural in terms of current usage, the LXX makes a strong and conscious affirmation of the fact that Yahweh's position as Lord is legitimate. This affirmation can be based on the historical fact of the election of Israel. He who re-deemed Israel from the "iron furnace" of Egypt had thereby a right to this people. But the affirmation can also be based on the fact that God is Creator. He who has made the universe and men is their legitimate Lord. Baudissin favours the first alternative. A main argument for this, apart from that already mentioned, is that κύριος is sometimes used for אֱלֹהִים with suffix (I, 449 ff.). Yet we cannot be absolutely sure of the reasons for occasional deviations from the Mas. like this. It is also open to doubt whether the LXX, **when** choosing an equivalent for יהוה (if, as Baudissin has argued in his detailed in-vestigation, the LXX was not influenced here by the substitution of אֲדֹנָי for יהוה), would have restricted itself to a word which simply means the superior, the one who gives himself to those who honour him. Above all, the meaning which Baudissin attaches to κύριος in the LXX arises neither from the Greek word nor even from its actual use in the LXX. Support in a specific pagan usage is especially lacking. Indeed, if there had been such a link with pagan usage, this would have been a good reason for the LXX to avoid the word. The consistent use of κύριος in the absolute suggests God's legitimate, unrestricted and invisible power of disposal over all things, His ἐξουσία. Even if we have not correctly understood the reasons why the LXX selected κύριος, even if it is true, e.g., that אֲדֹנָי is the term which underlies κύριος, the actual significance of this consistent translation remains. The one word κύριος, the word which corresponded without the addition of a divine name (as later in ethnic use, and as from time im-memorial in Egypt and Babylon), was of itself adequate to name a God, the one God. This must have suggested continually to its hearers God's unlimited control over all things. "In the one case (ethnic usage) the title is added to the name, and the name distinguishes its bearer from numerous other gods and men who may bear, or may have borne, the title ... In the other case (the LXX) the title is substituted for the name, and the implication is that the bearer is 'sovereign' in the absolute sense. There is no exact parallel to this in earlier or contemporary Greek." [216]

2. "Lord" in the Pseudepigrapha.

Baudissin has advanced many reasons against the widespread view that the use of אֲדֹנָי for the tetragrammaton was older than the LXX. He places the introduction of this artificial form in the 1st cent. B.C. or A.D. Indeed, except in the reading of Scripture the use of the tetragrammaton was not perhaps completely avoided until the 1st cent. A.D., esp. in view of the address *dominator domine* used in prayer in 4 Esr. (II, 189 ff.). The facts are as follows (→ also 93-95). A and Σ keep the tetragrammaton in Heb. characters in their Gk. renderings. For the Mas. אֲדֹנָי in the vocative A uses δέσποτα once, Σ more often, and elsewhere they have κύριος, which Θ uses for יהוה and אֲדֹנָי. The Mas. אֲדֹנָי יהוה is rendered in different ways by these translations (II, 98 ff.). κύριος is used fairly commonly in the apocr. up to 1, 3 and 4 Macc., also Ps. Sol., which holds the scales pretty evenly between κύριος or (more rarely) ὁ κύριος and κύριε on the one side and θεός or ὁ θεός (more commonly) and ὁ θεός as a vocative on the other. In the later Ass. Mos. *dominus* predominates strongly over *deus*; so, too, in Test. XII, though not to the same degree, while 4 Esr. consistently uses *altissimus*, occasionally *fortis*, and once *excelsus*. *Dominus* is here only a vocative and (occasionally with *meus*)

---

[216] Dodd, *op. cit.*, 11.

in contrast to angels. S. Bar. mostly has "the Almighty," and also common is "the Most High," while "Lord" occurs 8 times, "the exalted Lord" once, "God" (or "the almighty God") 6 times, "the Exalted" once. In the vocative, however, "Almighty" occurs only once, "Lord my God" 7 times, "my Lord" twice, and "Lord" 7 times. Eth. En. presents a variegated picture. In the oldest part, the vision of the animals in 83-90, God is "Lord of the sheep" in the parable, and we also find "Lord" in 83:2; 89:14, 15, 16, 18, 54; 90:17, 21, 34, in the vocative "my Lord" (84:6), and "God" once (84:1). In the similitudes God is usually called "Lord of spirits," infrequently the simple "Lord," "our Lord," "Lord of the world," "Lord of kings," "the Most High," 217 and even less frequently "God" (55:3; 61:10; 67:1). In the other parts of the same collection we find "God" and "Lord" more or less equally, several periphrases, esp. "the Most High" (11 times), "the Great One," "the Holy One" and "Lord" with many genitives, Lord of heaven, of the world, of creation, of glory, of judgment, of righteousness, cf. also "the God of glory," "the King of the world," "the King of glory." Finally, in Jub. the simple "God" is strongly predominant, along with compounds like "the Most High God," "the God of Abraham," "our God" etc. The simple "Lord" is hardly found 218 except as a vocative, but it occurs in compounds, e.g., God the Lord, the Lord our God (on the lips of the angel of revelation) etc. Damasc. usually has אֵל, once עֶלְיוֹן, 3 times הַיָּחִיד. In quotations from the OT יהוה is usually omitted or אֵל is substituted. Oaths with Aleph and Daleth (אדני) and with Aleph and Lamed (אלהים) are forbidden in 15:1 (Schechter).

These data may be given a different explanation from that of Baudissin, namely, that the authors of the pseudepigr. wanted their works to be regarded as sacred and therefore used the tetragrammaton as it was used in the OT even though they pronounced it אדני when reading the OT. This would in no way conflict with the assumption that the use of κύριος in the LXX was influenced by the fact that the tetragrammaton had already been commonly replaced by אדני (→ 93-95). The reasons for the choice of κύριος would not be affected. It must be admitted that there can be no absolute certainty as regards the dating of אדני, esp. as the use of "Lord" in the pseudepigr. displays such wide individual variations. On the other hand, the rich use of varied substitutes for the name of God in e.g., Eth. En., betrays strong apprehension in face of the simple terms. We can certainly see from Jos. 219 and also from the basic material of the Synoptic Gospels and from Jn., that אדני and יהוה had disappeared from everyday use. The substitute terms in the pseudepigr. give us a good picture of the divine characteristics which the authors felt to be important. In circles open to Hellenism, from which the authors of Ep. Ar., 3 and 4 Macc. and the Sib. 220 derive, the word κύριος is avoided, not out of religious awe, but because it could not be understood by Hellenism without the addition of divine names. Philo was confronted by the fact that in his Bible, the LXX, θεός and κύριος were used alongside one another as the two chief terms for God. In allegorical fashion he found in κύριος a ref. to the βασιλικὴ δύναμις and in θεός a ref. to the χαριστικὴ δύναμις. 221

---

217 Lord : 39:9, 13; 41:2; 62:1; 65:6; 67:3, 10; 68:4. Our Lord : 63:8; Lord of the world : 58:4. Lord of kings : 63:4. Lord of glory : 40:3; 63:2. The Most High : 46:7; 60:1; 62:7.
218 Exceptions : the introduction (vl.); 27:27; 49:22.
219 Jos. uses the adj. κύριος more frequently : Ap., 1, 19, 146; 2, 177, 200; he calls the Romans οἱ κύριοι νῦν Ῥωμαῖοι τῆς οἰκουμένης, 2, 41; he is also aware that κύριος corresponds to the Heb. אדון Ant., 5. 121. He does not use κύριος of God except in a prayer in Ant., 20, 90 (δέσποτα κύριε ... τῶν πάντων δὲ δικαίως μόνον καὶ πρῶτον ἥγημαι κύριον) and a quotation from Scripture in 13, 68. But δεσπότης is common, also δέσποτα in prayer, A. Schlatter, "Wie sprach Josephus von Gott?" BFTh, 14, 1 (1910), 8-11; Theol. d. Judt., 25 f.
220 Cf. the Jewish Hellenistic authors Artapanus etc.
221 Som., I, 163. For further instances v. Foerster, 119, n. 3 and → n. 222.

3. "Lord" in Rabbinic Judaism.

In Palestine in the days of Jesus the literal pronunciation of the tetragrammaton was restricted to very few cases (→ 93). The Rabbis, too, linked with the two chief terms for God in their Bible, יהוה and אלהים, speculations concerning the two "measures" of God, that of mercy and that of judgment, but they allotted them to the names differently from Philo. [222]

אדון had almost disappeared from ordinary speech. It occurs occasionally along with a title: אדני הרופא, [223] to the king אדני המלך, [224] to the high-priest; אדני כהן גדול, [225] אדנינו ורבינו, to the king. [226] It is said of Pharaoh that he called himself אדון העולם. [227] אדון is still used in various ways of God along with כל בריות, לכל באי עולם, לכל מעשים, העולמים, העולם (כל), [228] When the Rabbis raise the question who first called God אדון, [229] this is an indication of the importance attached to the name. The interconnecting of Lord and Creator is clearly to be seen here. [230] In general the Rabbis use for "lord" רב, רבא, רבון, רבונא, מרא, and later קיריס (κύριος) or קירי (= κύριε). מרא is "lord" in the most varied senses: the master of slaves, the owner of goods, the master of the soul, i.e., passions (like κύριος); as an address (always with the personal pronoun) it is the polite form for inferiors (servants and subjects) and also for equals (like אדון in the OT). [231] It is used of God along with שמיא [232] and עלמא. [233] מרי as an address to God is found, e.g., in Gn. r., 13, 2 on 2:5, [234] and the abstract מרותא דעלמא occurs in Gn. r., 55 on 22:2. [235]

רב is in general, even without the suffix, the teacher, [236] but it is most common as an address in the suffix form רבי. The suffix soon became fixed. [237] But רב can also be used for lord in other senses, e.g., the master of slaves. [238] רבי is in any case an "unusually respectful address." [239] Along with רב stands רבון (later רבון), which is used in address in the Gospels and also occurs in the Targums, [240] where it is used for the biblical אדון when it is not a term for God. Later, however, this word is almost exclusively used for God, especially in the phrases רבון של עולם, ר״ העולמים. [241]

בעל is not unimportant. It means "owner," [242] and in the phrase בעל הבית it often

---

[222] Cf. on this A. Marmorstein, "Philo and the Names of God," JQR, NS, 22 (1931/32), 295-306 with bibl.

[223] jBer., 9b; Dalman WJ, 399.

[224] Dalman, loc. cit.

[225] Lv. r., 3, 5 on 2:1; Dalman, loc. cit.; Schl. Mt. on 15:22.

[226] Loc. cit.

[227] Ex. r., 5, 14 on 5:2; Marmorstein, 63.

[228] Instances in Marmorstein, 62 f.

[229] First Simeon b. Jochai (middle 2nd cent. A.D.), bBer., 7b; Marmorstein, 62.

[230] R. Aha, Marmorstein, loc. cit.: "Thou art worthy to be called Lord, for thou art truly Lord over all thy creatures."

[231] Dalman WJ, 267, with examples. Cf. also on what follows Schl. Mt. on 6:24; 7:21; Schl. J. on 5:3.

[232] Sachau, No. 1, 15; Qoh. r. on 3:2; also Marmorstein, 93 f.; 94, n. 45; Schl. Mt. on 11:25.

[233] Gn. r., 99 on 49:27; Marmorstein, 94, n. 46; Schl. Mt. on 11:25.

[234] Schl. Mt. on 7:21.

[235] Marmorstein, 93, n. 44.

[236] Ab., 1, 6 and 16. On "Rabbi" cf. also Moore, III, 15-17.

[237] Dalman WJ, 274.

[238] bTaan., 25b; bGit., 23b.

[239] Dalman WJ, 275.

[240] Ibid., 266 f.; Str.-B., II, 25 on Mk. 10:51.

[241] For examples cf. Str.-B., III, 671 f.; Marmorstein, 98 f.

[242] בעל התאנה (Aram. מרא דתאינתא) jBer., 5c, line 16; Schl. Mt., 256 M.

denotes God in parables. [243] Note should also be taken of some divine names constructed with בַעַל, [244] though these are names, of course, only in a fig. sense. בַעַל דִין ("Accuser"), ב״ חוב ("Creditor"), ב״ מלאכה ("Master"), ב״ המשפט ("Judge"), ב״ הפקדון ("He to whom a pledge is entrusted," with ref. to good works); also ב״ הרחמים, ב״ הנחמות and ב״ העולם.

The Heb. and Aram. use of "lord" is distinguished from the Gk. by the fact that it is never used in the absolute without a dependent noun [245] or suffix and also by the fact that it is occasionally doubled when used as an address. [246]

In later Judaism the lordship of God is important in two directions. First, God is the Lord and Governor of the whole world and its history; secondly, He is the Lord and Judge of the individual. The significance of these lines of thought may be seen from the number of designations of God which carry this twofold reference. The former is particularly, though not exclusively, stated in the pseudepigr., which seek to convey the certainty that in spite of every hostile force world history has a divinely determined goal. [247] Typical expressions are those in Eth. En. 9:4 : σὺ εἶ κύριος τῶν κυρίων καὶ ὁ θεὸς τῶν θεῶν καὶ βασιλεὺς τῶν αἰώνων, and 25:3 : ὁ μέγας κύριος ὁ ἅγιος τῆς δόξης, ὁ βασιλεὺς τοῦ αἰῶνος, cf. also 25:7; 27:3; 91:13. The favouring of names like "the Most High" and "the Almighty" in 4 Esr. and S. Bar. points in the same direction. The second line of thought is denoted by names constructed with בַעַל, cf. also Eth. En. 83:11: "Lord of judgment." The lordship of God is absolute, but still concealed. It is still possible to "incur guilt" [248] and to be indolent before the "Lord of work" (Ab., 2, 19). It is still possible for the kings of the world to deploy their might against God and His people. This is a consequence of the sin of the people. If it would, e.g., keep only one Sabbath, it would be redeemed at once (jTaan., 64a, line 31 f.). The attitude of Judaism to the powers of this world stands under this sign.

The reason why God is absolute Lord of this world and its course, and also of individuals, is that He is the "Creator of all," [249] cf. Eth. En. 84:2 f.: "Blessed art thou, O Lord, King, great and mighty in thy greatness, Lord of all the creation of heaven, King of kings and God of the whole world. Thy power, dominion and greatness remain to all eternity, and thy lordship throughout all generations; all heavens are thy throne to eternity, and the whole earth is always the footstool of thy feet. For thou hast created all things and dost rule all things." [250] This reference to creation gives to the lordship of God its final inescapable foundation and also gives ineluctability to the ethical obligation, 4 Esr. 8:60 : "Creatures have dishonoured the name of him who created them and have shown ingratitude to him who gave them life. Hence my judgment is now about to fall upon them." jBer., 7d, line 61: [251] בראתנו לעשות רצונך. The motif of the election of Israel is now a far less prominent imperative than this, and its essential form is that God is the Creator of Israel, S. Bar. 78:3; 79:2; 82:2.

---

[243] Marmorstein, 77 f.

[244] *Ibid.*, 78 ff.

[245] Dalman WJ, 268. But there are exceptions : bBer., 61b; R. Abayye to Rab : לא שביק מר חיי לכל בריה, when the latter reckoned himself among the mediocre.

[246] King Jehoshaphat is supposed to have greeted every scholar with אבי אבי רבי רבי מרי מרי, bMak., 24a; Dalman WJ, 268.

[247] How strongly the tension was felt may be seen from, e.g., Eth. En. 89:57 f., 70 f., 75-77; 90:3.

[248] Cf. the saying of R. Aqiba, Ab., 3, 16.

[249] Cf. Jub. 2:21, 31, 32; 17:3; 22:4; 31:29; 45:5; also 22:27.

[250] *Ibid.*, 9:4 f. : σὺ εἶ κύριος τῶν κυρίων ... σὺ γὰρ ἐποίησας τὰ πάντα.

[251] Str.-B., IV, 478bb.

E. κύριος in the New Testament.

1. Secular Usage.

In the NT κύριος is used for the "lord" and "owner" of a vineyard, Mk. 12:9 and par., of an ass, Lk. 19:33, a dog, Mt. 15:27, the master of the (free) steward, Lk. 16:3, 5, 8 (?), unfree slaves, often in parables, cf. also Ac. 16:16, 19; Eph. 6:5, 9; Col. 3:22; 4:1, then the one who has the power to control and give the word, e.g., concerning the harvest, Mt. 9:38 and par. [252] or the Sabbath, Mk. 2:28 and par. It is probably with oriental politeness, so far as linguistic usage is concerned, that Elisabeth can call Mary the "mother of my Lord," Lk. 1:43. The superiority to which there must be submission is implied in κύριος when 1 Pt. 3:6 points out that Sarah calls Abraham "lord" (an allusion to Gn. 18:12 LXX) and also in the quotation from Ps. 110 in Mk. 12:36 f. and par.; Ac. 2:34. Festus calls Nero κύριος in Ac. 25:26 (→ 1055). κύριος is used in a stricter sense, closer to the adj. κύριος and with a suggestion of lawful, not actual, ownership, in Gl. 4:1: ἐφ' ὅσον χρόνον ὁ κληρονόμος νήπιός ἐστιν, οὐδὲν διαφέρει δούλου κύριος πάντων ὤν. With few exceptions (Mt. 18:25; 24:45; Lk. 12:37, 42; 14:23; cf. Jn. 13:13 f.) κύριος in this sense is always used in the Gospels and Acts with a gen., whether a noun or personal pronoun (also of objects in Lk. 20:13, 15). This is a sign of the influence of Palestinian usage, → 1085. But there is no corresponding gen. in the epistles, Eph. 6:5, 9; Col. 3:22; 4:1; 1 Pt. 3:6; also Ac. 25:26. On Palestinian soil the word corresponding to this κύριος can be רב, רבּוֹן or מָרֵא, → 1084. κύριε is common as an address. Slaves never use anything else in the Gospels. But the workers in the vineyard also use it towards the owner in Lk. 13:8, the Jews to Pilate in Mt. 27:63, the son to his father in Mt. 21:29 (this is a special case), [253] Mary to the unknown gardener in Jn. 20:15, and the Philippian gaoler to the prisoners in expression of his respect, Ac. 16:30. κύριε is also used to angels in Ac. 10:4 and Rev. 7:14 (with μου), and unknown apparitions in Ac. 9:5; 22:8, 10; 26:15; 10:14; 11:8. The double κύριε, κύριε of Mt. 7:21, 22; 25:11; Lk. 6:46 is in keeping with Palestinian usage, → 1085. κύριε in the Gospels corresponds to מָרִי with suffix, since the Evangelists rendered רַבִּי differently with ref. to Jesus, and as an address it was normally used only of scholars. On κύριε as an address to Jesus → 1093. This κύριε is never accompanied by a pers. pronoun, and the same is true of ἐπιστάτα and διδάσκαλε (apart from Jn. 20:28 and Rev. 7:14), although "lord" in the vocative always had a suffix in Palestinian usage. The address "lord" is applied to a much larger circle than the designation, and is thus the more quickly attenuated. The use of the nominative with art. instead of the vocative (Jn. 20:28; Rev. 4:11) is a Semitism. [254]

We find genitive combinations in 1 C. 2:8 : κύριος τῆς δόξης, and 2 Th. 3:16a : τῆς εἰρήνης. The latter is based on בַּעַל הַנֶּחָמוֹת, → 1085, while the former is an example of a Semitic gen. instead of an adj.

δεσπότης occurs in the Gospels only as a vocative in prayer to God or with ref. to the master of slaves (1 Tm. 6:1 f.; Tt. 2:9; 1 Pt. 2:18), or the lord and owner of the house (2 Tm. 2:21). It denotes a careful choice of words, → 1045.

2. God the Lord.

God is primarily called (ὁ) κύριος in the NT in OT quotations or allusions, which generally follow the LXX, e.g., Mk. 1:3 and par.; Mk. 12:11 and par.; Mk. 12:36 and

---

[252] Cf. on this Schl. Mt. on 9:38.

[253] Mt. 21:29. The other son does not use any form of address. The difference between the words and the deeds of the one who says yes is all the more incisive when we recall that at that time such an address from a son to a father emphatically stressed his subordination, → 1045.

[254] Cf. Bl.-Debr.[6] § 147, 3.

par. and Ac. 2:34 (here the LXX has ὁ κύριος, but in the NT passages the art. is omitted by B with some support from other witnesses); Mt. 27:10; Lk. 1:46; 4:18, 19; Mk. 11:9 and par.; Jn. 12:38 (twice); Ac. 2:20, 21, 25; 4:26; 13:10 (most MSS do not have the art. in spite of the LXX); 15:17 (in the LXX only A has τὸν κύριον, the others omit it altogether); R. 4:8; 9:28 (the LXX has ὁ θεός for κύριος, except B); 11:3 (κύριε is added to the LXX); 11:34 = 1 C. 2:16; R. 15:11; 1 C. 1:31 (the words ἐν κυρίῳ do not occur in this form in the LXX); 3:20; 10:22 (τὸν κύριον is not a quotation); 10:26; 2 C. 3:16; 8:21; 10:17; 2 Th. 1:9; 2 Tm. 2:19 (LXX has ὁ θεός instead of κύριος); Hb. 1:10; 7:21; 8:2 (LXX without, Hb. with art.); 8:8-10, 11; 10:30; 12:5, 6; 13:6; Jm. 5:11 (B without art.); 1 Pt. 1:25 (LXX τοῦ θεοῦ); 2:3; 3:12 (twice); Jd. 9 κύριος Σαβαώθ : R. 9:29; Jm. 5:4. κύριος ὁ θεός followed by gen. occurs in Mt. 4:7, 10 and par.; Mk. 12:29, 30 and par.; Ac. 3:22 (unlike the LXX no personal pronoun); 2:39 (adding ὁ θεὸς ἡμῶν to the LXX). ὁ κύριος (LXX + πάσης) τῆς γῆς is found in Rev. 11:4.

In the basic material of the Synoptic Gospels, i.e., the Marcan material and Q, God is never called ὁ κύριος except in Mk. 5:19 (peculiar to Mk.), where Jesus says to the healed (pagan) Gergesene demoniac : ἀπάγγειλον αὐτοῖς ὅσα ὁ κύριός σοι πεποίηκεν, and Mk. 13:20 : εἰ μὴ ἐκολόβωσεν κύριος τὰς ἡμέρας (Mt. and Lk. either change this or use different sources). In the Gospels κύριος is also used of God in the prologues to Mt. and Lk. and in the epilogue to Mt., [255] also in Lk. 5:17; 20:37, both peculiar to Lk. This shows that אֲדֹנָי was not in common use in the primitive Palestinian community. [256] The striking frequency of κύριος in the prelude to Lk. is in keeping with the intentional biblical phrasing and demonstrates dependence on the LXX rather than on living Palestinian usage. In keeping with this, no essential distinction can be made between κύριος with and without the art. LXX influence is also to be discerned in certain fixed expressions : χεὶρ κυρίου (Lk. 1:66; Ac. 11:21; 13:11); ἄγγελος κυρίου (Mt. 1:20, 24; 2:13, 19; 28:2; Lk. 1:11; 2:9; Ac. 5:19; 8:26; 12:7, 23); ὄνομα κυρίου (Jm. 5:10, 14); πνεῦμα κυρίου (Ac. 5:9; 8:39); and λέγει κύριος, which is added as a formula in R. 12:19; 2 C. 6:17 and Rev. 1:8, and which has replaced the φησὶν κύριος of the LXX in Hb. 8:8, 9, 10. In these cases there is no art., but we always find it in ὁ λόγος τοῦ κυρίου, Ac. 8:25; 12:24; 13:48, 49; 15:35, 36; 19:10, 20. [257] κύριος is also used for certain for God in 1 C. 10:9; 1 Tm. 6:15 (+ τῶν κυριευόντων); 2 Tm. 1:18; Hb. 7:21; 8:2; Jm. 1:7; 3:9 (+ καὶ πατήρ); 5:11a; 2 Pt. 3:8; Jd. 5, and in Rev., which in its lofty style often uses the OT κύριος ὁ θεός (+ ὁ παντοκράτωρ): 1:8; 4:8; 11:17; 16:7; 18:8; 19:6; 21:22; 22:5. There are no par. for the formulae in Rev. 4:11: ὁ κύριος καὶ ὁ θεὸς ἡμῶν; 11:15 (τοῦ κυρίου ἡμῶν) and 22:6 : ὁ κύριος ὁ θεὸς τῶν πνευμάτων.

This shows that on Palestinian soil particularly, though also in the community whose Bible was the LXX, κύριος was not a very common term for God apart from its basic attestation in the Bible. But at any time the content implicit in the word κύριος can be given its full weight. This takes place in certain highly important passages, primarily and especially in Mt. 11:25 (almost literally the same as Lk. 10:21): ἐξομολογοῦμαί σοι, πάτερ, κύριε τοῦ οὐρανοῦ καὶ τῆς γῆς, ὅτι ἔκρυψας ταῦτα ἀπὸ σοφῶν καὶ συνετῶν, καὶ ἀπεκάλυψας αὐτὰ νηπίοις· ναί,

---

[255] Mt. 1:20, 22, 24; 2:13, 15, 19; 28:2; Lk. 1:6, 9, 11, 15, 17, 25, 28, 38, 45, 58, 66; 2:9, 15, 22, 23, 24, 26, 39.

[256] Hence I cannot accept the observation of Schl. J., 42 that for Palestinians κύριος without art. = אֲדֹנָי and with art. = מרא = Jesus.

[257] In Ac. we find only ὁ λόγος τοῦ θεοῦ, but this is probably equivalent to ὁ λόγος τοῦ κυρίου. Whether Paul is thinking of the Word of God when he uses ὁ λόγος τοῦ κυρίου in 1 Th. 1:8 and 2 Th. 3:1 it is perhaps impossible to decide and makes no material difference. The main point to be noted here is the influence of LXX usage.

ὁ πατήρ, ὅτι οὕτως εὐδοκία ἐγένετο ἔμπροσθέν σου, where the solemn address is an organic part of free submission before the omnipotence of the divine εὐδοκία, and this has cosmic significance. The complete freedom of the divine decision is adoringly ascribed to the Lord of heaven and earth. Free assent to this εὐδοκία shows that submission to this Lord does not deprive of the power of will. The metaphorical expression κύριος τοῦ θερισμοῦ in Mt. 9:38 and par. stands in a similar context. The harvest is the great harvest of humanity and its lord is thus the Lord of all world history. With reference to the day whose hour is known to no man, not even the Son, Paul in 1 Tm. 6:15 calls God ὁ μακάριος καὶ μόνος δυνάστης, ὁ βασιλεὺς τῶν βασιλευόντων καὶ κύριος τῶν κυριευόντων. He thus describes Him as the One who, as the Governor of history, stands over all the men who make history on earth. In an important passage in Ac., the Areopagus address, Lk. tells us that Pl. adopted the word κύριος (Ac. 17:24), with the genitives οὐρανοῦ καὶ γῆς, to uproot heathen worship by means of the lordship of God. In this connection the lordship of God is traced back to the fact that He is the Creator. It is naturally no accident that the full formula κύριος ὁ θεὸς ὁ παντοκράτωρ plays so great a role in Rev. No less significant, however, is the fact that that in 4:11 the 24 elders, who are not unrelated to the whole of humanity as the creation of God, use the newly coined expression ὁ κύριος καὶ ὁ θεὸς ἡμῶν to describe their position before God. The address κύριε can also carry an emphatic stress in prayer, e.g., in Ac. 1:24: σὺ κύριε καρδιογνῶστα πάντων. Mention should also be made of Jm. 3:9, where κύριος underlies the obligation of worship. [258] Even when the word is not used, however, that for which it stands is often present in the NT, namely, the personal, legitimate and all-embracing sovereignty of God.

3. Jesus as Lord.

It is best to start our exposition with Paul, whose use of κύριος is clear. We can then turn to the other NT writings for support and confirmation, and to show the consistency of usage.

In 1 C. 12:3 Paul contrasts ἀνάθεμα Ἰησοῦς and κύριος Ἰησοῦς. The former expresses what Ac. calls βλασφημεῖν, i.e., for the sake of God to deliver Jesus to God's judgment as against God and as thus incurring God's judgment. It is a strictly religious attitude to be against something for the sake of God. There is no corresponding term for its opposite. It would perhaps be εὐλογητός = בָּרוּךְ, but in the NT this is reserved for God. Hence κύριος Ἰησοῦς is not exactly parallel to ἀνάθεμα Ἰησοῦς, for the latter can be used of many things or people, but not the former. Yet the former does include a religious affirmation of Jesus for the sake of God, even though this is possible and legitimate only in respect of the One.

Further light is shed by the well-known and inexhaustible passage in Phil. 2:6-11 (vv. 9 ff.): διὸ καὶ ὁ θεὸς αὐτὸν ὑπερύψωσεν καὶ ἐχαρίσατο αὐτῷ τὸ ὄνομα τὸ ὑπὲρ πᾶν ὄνομα, ἵνα ἐν τῷ ὀνόματι Ἰησοῦ πᾶν γόνυ κάμψῃ ἐπουρανίων καὶ ἐπιγείων καὶ καταχθονίων, καὶ πᾶσα γλῶσσα ἐξομολογήσηται ὅτι κύριος Ἰησοῦς Χριστὸς εἰς δόξαν θεοῦ πατρός. The name, which is characterised as a very specific one by the repetition of the art., can only be the name κύριος. It is

---

[258] We have here emphasised the passages in which κύριος receives a special emphasis when used of God and could not be replaced by θεός without altering the train of thought.

thus given to Jesus as the divine answer (διό) to His suffering of death in obedience. At the name which Jesus, who took the form of a servant, has received, i.e., before the historical Jesus who is now exalted, all the world bows the knee. Rev. (5:12) says similarly of the ἀρνίον ὡς ἐσφαγμένον that it is worthy to receive the book which contains the *dénouement* of world history and thus to take δύναμις, δόξα, and εὐλογία.²⁵⁹ The name of κύριος implies a position equal to that of God. Bowing the knee and acclaiming the κύριος Ἰησοῦς Χριστός are related actions, and while it is true that Phil. does not quote Is. 45:23 f. expressly, since the κύριος Ἰησοῦς Χριστός can hardly allude either to the ἐξομολόγησις of the LXX or to the Mas., nevertheless the ἐν τῷ ὀνόματι Ἰησοῦ takes the place of the ἐμοί (sc. κάμψει πᾶν γόνυ) on the lips of God. And the fact that this Jesus is confessed as κύριος is to the glory of God. The name of κύριος thus designates the position of the Risen Lord. It is hardly possible to decide whether the ὑπέρ in ὑπερύψωσεν refers to the ἐν μορφῇ θεοῦ ὑπάρχων or simply means "beyond all measure." If κύριος Ἰησοῦς here takes the form of an acclamation, this is no argument against its high material significance.²⁶⁰

That the risen Jesus is κύριος is stated throughout the NT. In R. 10:9 Paul rightly connects the confession of Jesus' lordship with the lips and the faith of the heart that God has raised Him from the dead. In Ac. 2:36, at the close of Peter's Pentecost sermon, Lk. quotes him as saying: ἀσφαλῶς οὖν γινωσκέτω πᾶς οἶκος Ἰσραὴλ ὅτι καὶ κύριον αὐτὸν καὶ χριστὸν ἐποίησεν ὁ θεός, τοῦτον τὸν Ἰησοῦν ὃν ὑμεῖς ἐσταυρώσατε. The greater Lk.'s contribution to the formulation of this passage, the more clearly it shows that for him the resurrection and the κυριότης of Jesus were related. Even when the word κύριος is not particularly prominent, the connection between the suffering, resurrection and divine position of Jesus finds varied expression. Thus in Hb. 2:6 ff. the quotation of Ps. 8:4 ff. is followed by the proof in v. 8 that it cannot apply to man generally but refers specifically (v. 9) to Jesus, who because He suffered death is crowned with δόξα and τιμή. Hence, even though the author does not expressly say that the πάντα ὑπέταξας ὑποκάτω τῶν ποδῶν αὐτοῦ is also fulfilled in Him, the lordship of Jesus is plainly indicated. The same relationship between resurrection and lordship is to be seen at Mt. 28:18 in the saying of the Risen Lord: ἐδόθη μοι πᾶσα ἐξουσία ἐν οὐρανῷ καὶ ἐπὶ γῆς: he who has ἐξουσία is κύριος (→ II, 568). But it is brought out especially in the use of Ps. 110:1. This verse is the only basis for the idea of session at the right hand of God. There is no other reference. In this psalm, however, session is linked with lordship, and specifically with being David's lord. With an οὖν Ac. 2:36 causes Peter to draw from this verse the deduction concerning Jesus. Session at the right hand of God means joint rule.²⁶¹ It thus implies divine dignity, as does the very fact of sitting in God's presence (bChag., 15a; Heb. En. 16:3).

Reminiscences of this psalm in the NT mostly bring out the connection between resurrection and exaltation (cf. also Ac. 5:31; R. 8:34; Col. 3:1; Hb. 1:3, 13; 8:1; 12:2; Rev. 3:21 [cf. R. 1:4]) and between exaltation and universal lordship (1 C. 15:25 ff. [where there is also ref. to Ps. 8:6], also Eph. 1:20 f.: ἐγείρας αὐτὸν ἐν νεκρῶν, καὶ καθίσας ἐν δεξιᾷ αὐτοῦ ἐν τοῖς ἐπουρανίοις ὑπεράνω πάσης ἀρχῆς καὶ ἐξουσίας

---

²⁵⁹ Rev. 5:12. Only the most pregnant terms are mentioned in the text.
²⁶⁰ Cf. F. J. Dölger, *Sol Salutis*² (1925), as against Peterson, 317.
²⁶¹ Jos. Ant., 6, 235; cf. Ges.-Buhl, *s.v.* יְקָר No. 5c.

καὶ δυνάμεως καὶ κυριότητος καὶ παντὸς ὀνόματος ..., 1 Pt. 3:22 : ὅς ἐστιν ἐν δεξιᾷ θεοῦ, πορευθεὶς εἰς οὐρανόν, ὑποταγέντων αὐτῷ ἀγγέλων καὶ ἐξουσιῶν καὶ δυνάμεων, also Hb. 10:12 f.).

In 1 C. 11:3 Paul refers to a series of higher and lower ranks : θέλω δὲ ὑμᾶς εἰδέναι ὅτι παντὸς ἀνδρὸς ἡ κεφαλὴ ὁ Χριστός ἐστιν, κεφαλὴ δὲ γυναικὸς ὁ ἀνήρ, κεφαλὴ δὲ τοῦ Χριστοῦ ὁ θεός. It can hardly be supposed that he is arguing that the woman is more distant from Christ than the man.[262] The point of the whole section is the natural superiority of the man. The total sphere of the reality of which the man-woman relation is a part has no direct reference to God ; it has only an indirect reference through Christ. Without Christ the world could not exist before God. Christ is the One by whom it can exist before God. He is the One who exercises God's sovereignty in relation to the world. As things in heaven, on earth and under the earth bow the knee to Him (Phil. 2:10), so He is the κεφαλὴ (Col. 2:10, the same term as in 1 C. 11:3) πάσης ἀρχῆς καὶ ἐξουσίας. He is πρὸ πάντων καὶ τὰ πάντα ἐν αὐτῷ συνέστηκεν, Col. 1:17. With reference to this cosmic[263] position of Christ which he has just outlined, Paul says comprehensively of Christ in Col. 2:6 (οὖν): ὡς οὖν παρελάβετε τὸν Χριστὸν Ἰησοῦν τὸν κύριον ... The emphatic κύριος (cf. the repeated article) gathers up all that Paul has previously said about Christ in Colossians. The reason why the world cannot exist before God without Him is because of its fallen state, Col. 1:20 : δι' αὐτοῦ ἀποκαταλλάξαι τὰ πάντα εἰς αὐτόν, εἰρηνοποιήσας διὰ τοῦ αἵματος τοῦ σταυροῦ αὐτοῦ, δι' αὐτοῦ εἴτε τὰ ἐπὶ τῆς γῆς εἴτε τὰ ἐν τοῖς οὐρανοῖς, cf. Eph. 1:20 f.; 1 Pt. 3:22 (→ II, 573). The Son exercises the Father's sovereignty in relation to the world in order that He may overcome all hostile forces and present the world and Himself at the Father's feet : ὅταν δὲ ὑποταγῇ αὐτῷ τὰ πάντα, τότε καὶ αὐτὸς ὁ υἱὸς ὑποταγήσεται τῷ ὑποτάξαντι αὐτῷ τὰ πάντα, ἵνα ᾖ ὁ θεὸς πάντα ἐν πᾶσιν (1 C. 15:28). The goal of the lordship of Jesus in exercise of the Father's sovereignty is thus to make the reconciled and judged world subject to God.

In this work, however, man is the crucial point. While the lordship of Jesus is cosmic in scope, its centre is lordship over men : εἰς τοῦτο γὰρ Χριστὸς ἀπέθανεν καὶ ἔζησεν, ἵνα καὶ νεκρῶν καὶ ζώντων κυριεύσῃ (R. 14:9). The usage of Paul makes this clear.[264] (ὁ) Χριστός is the One who was crucified and is risen, R. 5:6, 8; 6:4, 9; 14:9; 1 C. 1:23 f.; 5:7; 8:11; 15:3, 12 ff.; Gl. 3:13 etc.[265] The word appears when there is reference to the work of redemption, R. 8:35; 15:7; 2 C. 3:14; 5:14, 18 f.; Gl. 3:13. This work is in view when Paul admonishes by the πραΰτης καὶ ἐπιείκεια τοῦ Χριστοῦ, 2 C. 10:1, cf. 1 C. 11:1. It is τὸ εὐαγγέλιον τοῦ Χριστοῦ, R. 15:19; 1 C. 9:12; 2 C. 2:12; 4:4; 9:13; 10:14; Gl. 1:7; cf. 1 C. 1:6; 2 C. 3:3. It is being crucified and dead with Christ, R. 6:8; 7:4; Gl. 2:19. It is being baptised into Christ, Gl. 3:27. Christ has called the Galatians into grace, Gl. 1:6. Paul is sure that he will come to Rome in the fulness of the blessing of Christ, Rom. 15:29. Christ has sent him, 1 C. 1:17; R. 16:9; 1 C. 4:1; Gl. 1:10; 2 C. 11:13, 23. The community is one body in Christ, R. 12:5; Gl. 1:22.

From what has been said, however, κύριος refers to the exalted Lord who is authority, 1 C. 4:19; 14:37; 16:7 (Jm. 4:15). The service of believers must be

---

[262] Joh. W., 1 K., 270.
[263] "Cosmic" understood in such a way as to include men.
[264] Cf. Stead, Burton, Dobschütz, also H. E. Weber in NkZ, 31 (1920), 254-258.
[265] On what follows v. the tables in Foerster, 237 ff.

rendered to the Lord, R. 12:11; 1 C. 12:5; Eph. 6:7; Col. 3:23. Each stands or falls to his Lord, R. 14:4-8; cf. 1 C. 7:32-35; R. 16:12, 22; 2 C. 8:5. The same applies to private life, 1 C. 7:39. We are to walk worthy of the Lord (→ ἄξιος), 1 C. 11:27; R. 16:2. It is the exalted Lord who distributes to every man the measure of faith, 1 C. 3:5; 7:17. The Lord is the coming One (1 Th. 4:15 ff.; 1 C. 4:5; 11:26; Phil. 4:5) and the Judge (1 Th. 4:6; 2 Th. 1:9; 1 C. 4:4; 11:32; 2 C. 5:11; 10:18). In this life Paul is absent from the Lord, 2 C. 5:6 ff. He is the Lord of His servants, to whom He gives full powers, 2 C. 10:8; 13:10, and in His work the members of the community are to engage, 1 C. 15:58, as Timothy does, 1 C. 4:17; 16:10. The Corinthian congregation is Paul's work in the Lord, 1 C. 9:1, 2. At Troas a door is opened to Paul in the Lord, 2 C. 2:12. He is the one Lord of all, R. 10:12. Christ is proclaimed as Lord, 2 C. 4:5. This exalted Lord is the Spirit, 2 C. 3:17. Paul prays to the Lord for deliverance from his sufferings, 2 C. 12:8. All this is summed up in 1 C. 8:5 f.: εἴπερ εἰσὶν λεγόμενοι θεοὶ εἴτε ἐν οὐρανῷ εἴτε ἐπὶ γῆς, ὥσπερ εἰσὶν θεοὶ πολλοὶ καὶ κύριοι πολλοί, ἀλλ' ἡμῖν εἷς θεὸς ὁ πατήρ, ἐξ οὗ τὰ πάντα καὶ ἡμεῖς εἰς αὐτόν, καὶ εἷς κύριος Ἰησοῦς Χριστός, δι' οὗ τὰ πάντα καὶ ἡμεῖς δι' αὐτοῦ. There are many so-called gods in heaven and on earth — Paul remembers that rulers, too, are equated with gods. There are in fact, he adds, many gods — more than those who speak of gods in heaven and on earth are aware (cf. Phil. 3:19 : ὧν ὁ θεὸς ἡ κοιλία). There are also many lords, many things on which men are dependent, and these are real powers. Paul, then, does not make any distinction between θεός and κύριος as though κύριος were an intermediary god; there are no instances of any such usage in the world contemporary with primitive Christianity. [266] κύριος is here a concept of relationship. It denotes that on which men make themselves, or are in fact, dependent. For Christians there is only one God with whom they have to reckon and from and to whom are all things (cf. 1 C. 15:28, → 1090). Again, there is only one Lord on whom they are dependent and through whom are all things, through whom they have their very being as Christians. Here again it is plain that κύριος is the One through whom God has come into the world to work and to save.

Now there is no set pattern for the distribution of Χριστός and κύριος. [267] When Paul says εἰς Χριστὸν ἁμαρτάνετε (not εἰς τὸν κύριον) in 1 C. 8:12, he wants to make it clear that with their thoughtless attitude they are sinning against the One who died for them and for the brother. The situation is much the same in R. 14:18 : ὁ ... ἐν τούτῳ δουλεύων τῷ Χριστῷ. On the other hand, 1 C. 11:26 reads : τὸν θάνατον τοῦ κυρίου καταγγέλλετε, which runs contrary to current usage, perhaps because ἄχρι οὗ ἔλθῃ follows. In 1 C.7:22 there is alternation, most likely for stylistic reasons : ὁ γὰρ ἐν κυρίῳ κληθεὶς δοῦλος ἀπελεύθερος κυρίου ἐστίν· ὁμοίως ὁ ἐλεύθερος κληθεὶς δοῦλός ἐστιν Χριστοῦ.

In addition to the simple use of κύριος or (Ἰησοῦς) Χριστός the two are also combined in different ways. Here, too, there is a certain freedom of use. Of the

---

[266] Bousset, 99, states that "when the apostle with the help of the *kyrios* concept sets his Lord directly at the side of God on the one hand, and in some sense subordinates Him to God on the other, he thinks that he has analogies in Hellenistic religion for this gradation within the divine essence," but then in a note (n. 2) even he has to explain that it is not wholly clear "what the apostle had in mind when he presupposed a recognised distinction of rank between the terms θεός and κύριος."

[267] Schmauch's exposition does not take this sufficiently into account.

27 times in which ὁ κύριος (ἡμῶν) Ἰησοῦς occurs without Χριστός in the Pauline epistles, 10 are in the Thessalonian letters, and of the 18 instances outside Paul 14 are in Ac. The explanation is probably that the Thessalonian congregation was an early one and that Ac. bears a missionary character, → 288. The expression ὁ κύριος (ἡμῶν) Ἰησοῦς (Χριστός) is found as well as the simple (Ἰησοῦς) Χριστός or κύριος. Gl. 6:14: καυχᾶσθαι ... ἐν τῷ σταυρῷ τοῦ κυρίου ἡμῶν Ἰησοῦ Χριστοῦ, may be set alongside the many cases in which Χριστός stands alone in this context, cf. Eph. 3:11; R. 5:1; 6:23; 8:39; 1 C. 15:57; 1 Th. 5:9, and in contexts in which ὁ κύριος occurs elsewhere we also find the more explicit form in R. 15:30; 16:18; 1 C. 1:7, 8, 10; 2 C. 1:14; 1 Th. 2:15, 19; 3:13; 4:2; 5:23; 2 Th. 2:1; 1 Tm. 6:14. It is quite obvious that the more explicit form of the name of Jesus bears a certain emphasis or solemnity. This is particularly true in introductory and closing greetings and at decisive points in the line of argument: R. 5:1; 8:39; 1 C. 15:57; R. 15:30. A new element is introduced, however, by the addition of the personal pronoun, mostly ἡμῶν, to κύριος. The general significance is brought out clearly in Phil. 3:8 : ἡγοῦμαι πάντα ζημίαν εἶναι διὰ τὸ ὑπερέχον τῆς γνώσεως Χριστοῦ Ἰησοῦ τοῦ κυρίου μου. It is designed to express personal attachment. But it should be noted emphatically that this is not just the kind of attachment there is between the indolent slave and his master, or between any slave and even the harshest master, whom the slave inwardly despises. In the phrase ὁ κύριος ἡμῶν Ἰησοῦς Χριστός the ἡμῶν means more than a mere coupling together. "I never knew you" is the Lord's answer to the "many" in Mt. 7:23. Paul calls Him Χριστὸς Ἰησοῦς ὁ κύριός μου because he may call him his Lord, because He is the Lord who is for him, who "counts him faithful," 1 Tm. 1:12, cf. Rev. 11:8. The "our" which is always used elsewhere refers, not to a single congregation, but to the whole Christian community. In this connection it is worth noting that "your" is never used. The Christian community has all that it is and has in virtue of the fact that it is "His" and He is "its" Lord, This means that the "our" can sometimes carry a further implication, namely, that of the mutual interrelationship of the community itself, which imposes obligations, R. 15:30 : παρακαλῶ δὲ ὑμᾶς διὰ τοῦ κυρίου ἡμῶν Ἰησοῦ Χριστοῦ ... συναγωνίσασθαί μοι ἐν ταῖς προσευχαῖς ὑπὲρ ἐμοῦ (cf. 1 C. 1:10), which unites, 1 C. 1:2 : σὺν πᾶσιν τοῖς ἐπικαλουμένοις τὸ ὄνομα τοῦ κυρίου ἡμῶν Ἰησοῦ Χριστοῦ, but which also separates from others, R. 16:18 : οἱ γὰρ τοιοῦτοι τῷ κυρίῳ ἡμῶν Χριστῷ οὐ δουλεύουσιν.

b. In the NT epistles and Ac. κύριος is also used in a sense which we have not yet discussed, namely, for the historical Jesus: "I command, yet not I, but ὁ κύριος," 1 C. 7:10, followed by a dominical saying, cf. also 1 C. 9:14. In 1 C. 7:25, where Paul has no saying of the Lord on the point at issue, he says : ἐπιταγὴν κυρίου οὐκ ἔχω. The same situation lies behind 1 C. 7:12 : λέγω ἐγώ, οὐχ ὁ κύριος. Again, in 1 Th. 4:15 : τοῦτο γὰρ ὑμῖν λέγομεν ἐν λόγῳ κυρίου, Paul is probably referring to a dominical saying which has not come down to us. It might be supposed that Paul selects κύριος here to denote authority, but this theory does not explain Gl. 1:19; 1 C. 9:5 : James the brother, and the brethren, τοῦ κυρίου. Hb. 2:3 also refers to the historical Jesus: (σωτηρία) ἥτις ἀρχὴν λαβοῦσα λαλεῖσθαι διὰ τοῦ κυρίου, ὑπὸ τῶν ἀκουσάντων εἰς ἡμᾶς ἐβεβαιώθη. A lost saying of the Lord is reckoned by Paul among the λόγοι τοῦ κυρίου Ἰησοῦ at Ac. 20:35, and ἐμνήσθην δὲ τοῦ ῥήματος τοῦ κυρίου introduces a recorded saying at Ac. 11:16. There are also parallels for this usage in the Gospels. Luke has ὁ κύριος 13 times, [268] always in material peculiar to his Gospel or in his own formulations. Jn. has it 5 times. [269] The only other instances in the Gospels, except in address, are at Mk. 11:3 and par.: καὶ ἐάν τις ὑμῖν εἴπῃ· τί ποιεῖτε τοῦτο; εἴπατε· ὁ κύριος αὐτοῦ χρείαν ἔχει, and Jn. 21:7 on the lips of Peter: ὁ κύριός ἐστιν. At Mk. 11:3 there is, of course some doubt as to the significance. If it is a translation of the Aram. of the disciples, this demands a suffix, and the meaning is thus "our," "your" or "its" (the donkey's) lord. On the other hand, ὁ κύριος is perhaps meant to be a term for God, cf. Mk. 5:19. The par. Mk. 14:14 makes it likely that the original Aram. carried a suffix denoting "our" with reference to the disciples.

Address to Jesus demands separate treatment. In Mark only the Syro-Phoenician woman uses κύριε (7:28). The disciples, Pharisees and people all use διδάσκαλε. [270] Mt. in his reshaping of the Marcan material reserves διδάσκαλε for the Pharisees, Judas Iscariot and the uncommitted. Elsewhere he has κύριε. For him reservations about Jesus are thus clearly implicit in διδάσκαλε as a mode of address. Lk. in his Marcan material either keeps διδάσκαλε or substitutes ἐπιστάτα. Where there is no Marcan original he often uses κύριε, esp. on the lips of disciples. In Jn. κύριε is predominant. Mk. and Jn. have kept the original ῥαββί, Mk. 9:5; 11:21; 14:45 (= Mt. 26:49); Jn. 1:38, 49; 3:2; 4:31; 6:25; 9:2; 11:8 (Jn. 3:26 to the Baptist), ῥαββουνί, Mk. 10:51; Jn. 20:16. John expressly translates these διδάσκαλε. Lk. (always) and Mt. (usually) have κύριε (Mt.; Lk., e.g., at 18:41 for ῥαββουνί) and ἐπιστάτα for these foreign words. In Mt. 26:25, which is peculiar to Mt., Judas addresses Jesus as ῥαββί. As regards the meaning of this word, Mk. and Jn. must be regarded as its oldest and best exegetes. Even Lk.'s independent rendering (ἐπιστάτα) shows that a distinction was felt between רבי and מרי.

According to Mark, then, Jesus is addressed as κύριε only once by a Gentile woman, but elsewhere as ῥαββί (only, of course, when an address is used at all). This was the respectful address customarily used to scribes. The less frequent ῥαββουνί is closer to מרי, though Jn. regards it as identical in meaning with רבי. Luke, however, uses κύριε for this. It is open to question whether we should attach so much weight to the Marcan tradition as to conclude that Jesus was never addressed as מרי. For the double κύριε of Lk. 6:46; Mt. 7:21 f.; 25:11 is Semitic. At least, the doubling is Semitic, and why should not the word be as well? Moreover, in Jn. 13:13 Jesus expressly refers to both forms of address, i.e., ὁ διδάσκαλος and ὁ κύριος, and it was by no means impossible that a scribe should be addressed as מרי. [271] which was more common than רבי as a general mode of address. The fact that מרי was not one of the titles which Jesus forbade the disciples to use between themselves (Mt. 23:7 ff.) is linked with the practice of conferring the title of rabbi on those who had no real right to it.

διδάσκαλος is also a word which is used both by Jesus Himself and by others to describe the position of Jesus in relation to His disciples. It is used by Jesus Himself in Mk. 14:14 and par.; Mt. 10:24 f. and par.; (23:8); cf. Jn. 13:14, and by others in Mk. 5:35 and par. (the only instance in Mk.); Mt. 9:11; 17:24; Jn. 3:2;

---

[268] 7:13, 19; 10:1, 39, 41; 11:39; 13:15; 17:5, 6; 18:6; 19:8; 22:61 (twice); 16:8 and 24:34 are omitted.

[269] 4:1; 6:23; 11:2; 20:2, 13, not counting 20:18, 20, 25; 21:12, which refer to the Risen Lord.

[270] For details cf. Foerster, 216 ff.

[271] jKet., 28d, line 43, Dalman WJ, 267.

11:28. To an appreciable extent, then, Jesus was neither addressed as Lord during His days on earth, nor was He referred to as the Lord.

Nevertheless, there lies here the root of the later usage, namely, that of speaking of the historical Jesus as the κύριος. The designation of members of the family of Jesus as δεσπόσυνοι, Eus. Hist. Eccl., I, 7, 14, may be traced back in formulation to Palestine. Here is no μετάβασις εἰς ἄλλο γένος, but a development of the usage attested in the Gospels. If it is only later, in the special Lucan and Johannine material, that Jesus may be called κύριος in the narrative, this is connected with the fact that the material of the Gospels owes its formulation to the goals of mission. [272]

This κύριος, however, must be differentiated from what we find in the epistles. Perhaps it may be concluded from the addresses in Ac. at least that the name of Lord was not immediately used of the exalted Jesus; if Ac. 2:36 and 10:36 are against this, 3:20 shows that in early days the name of Messiah was still current. We are to seek, not the origin, but the roots of the use of κύριος which may be observed most clearly in Paul. The resurrection of Jesus is decisive. Without this the disciples might at any time have defined their relation to Jesus retrospectively by saying that He had been their Lord. But the real point now is that He still is the Lord. The relationship of personal attachment which had determined the dealings of the disciples with Him has now been renewed and sealed in a living way by the resurrection. The parables in which Jesus depicted His relationship to His disciples in terms of the master and his slaves or servants now acquired their deepest significance. The disciples themselves were the servants waiting for their Lord. Because the disciples knew that Jesus was at the right hand of God, their relationship to Him transcended every human analogy and had a strictly religious basis, i.e., a basis of faith. Another root of the ascription of the name of Lord to Jesus is to be found in the use which Jesus twice made of Ps. 110, at Mk. 12:35 ff. and par. and 14:62 and par. [273] We have seen already how strong was the influence of this psalm on the NT, → 1089. He who is David's Lord is also Israel's Lord, and in the faith of the first community He is Lord of the new Israel. Perhaps the primitive Palestinian community did not go further than this. For them the "Lord" would have a genitive or a personal suffix. "Our Lord" would be the name of Jesus. This may be seen from the Aram. word μαραναθα, which occurs twice in early Christianity, in 1 C. 16:22 and Did., 10, 6. The meaning is debated, also whether we should transcribe מָרַן אֲתָא or מָרַנָא תָא. [274] But there is no doubt that the reference is to "our Lord," and that Jesus is meant. We have no reason to suppose that the word does not come from the original Palestinian community, since all the Aram. words in the Gospels have their source there and the retention of alien words makes no sense unless they come, not from an Aramaic speaking church in Syria, but from the original community itself. In Greek speaking congregations the personal pronoun corresponding to the suffix (ἡμῶν) was dropped, as was often the case when κύριος was used by pagans for their gods (→ 1054). In the absolute κύριος could thus express the comprehensive lordship of Jesus. It could convey the truth that "the Father ... hath committed all judgment to the Son" (Jn. 5:22), that He has given Him "all ἐξουσία in heaven and in earth" (Mt. 28:18). If κύριος expressed all this, then LXX passages which spoke of the κύριος could be referred to Jesus. In Him God acts as is said of the κύριος in the OT.

---

[272] Foerster, 213 ff.
[273] So also Meyer Ursprung, III, 218, n. 1.
[274] Cf. on this Peterson, 130 f.; Fabricius, and the Comm.

4. Earthly κύριος Relationships.

Earthly relationships of superiority and subordination take on a new aspect in the NT. This is illustrated clearly by the relationship of slaves to their masters: Col. 3:22 : οἱ δοῦλοι, ὑπακούετε κατὰ πάντα τοῖς κατὰ σάρκα κυρίοις, μὴ ἐν ὀφθαλμοδουλίαις ὡς ἀνθρωπάρεσκοι, ἀλλ' ἐν ἁπλότητι καρδίας φοβούμενοι τὸν κύριον. ὃ ἐὰν ποιῆτε, ἐκ ψυχῆς ἐργάζεσθε ὡς τῷ κυρίῳ καὶ οὐκ ἀνθρώ-ποις, εἰδότες ὅτι ἀπὸ κυρίου ἀπολήμψεσθε τὴν ἀνταπόδοσιν τῆς κληρονομίας. The reference is to a total obedience to the master which avoids ὀφθαλμοδουλία, a mere show of service, and is thus wholehearted loyalty. This loyalty is possible only because the service rendered to their masters is service rendered to the Lord, their service of God. It is thus that, wholly free in respect of men, they can fully serve their masters in allegiance to Christ. In this one relationship of superiority and subordination there is thus reflected the radical solution of the whole problem involved in the word "lord," a problem which all peoples have tried to solve in their own way.

† κυρία.

Fem. of κύριος, i.e., "mistress" in relation to slaves, "proprietress," "lady of the house," Plut. Quaest. Rom., 30 (II, 271e), the young wife to her husband : ὅπου σὺ κύριος καὶ οἰκοδεσπότης, καὶ ἐγὼ κυρία καὶ οἰκοδέσποινα, then as an address to the lady (→ 1045) or mistress (Dio C., 48, 44, 3).

In the NT the only occurrences are ἐκλεκτῇ κυρίᾳ in 2 Jn. 1 and the address κυρία in v. 5. The reference is undoubtedly to the church to which the epistle is addressed, for the address moves over at once from the 2nd person sing. to the 2nd person plural, v. 6, and then back again to the 2nd person sing. the moment the symbolic usage is taken up again, v. 13. According to this symbolic usage the churches are sisters (v. 13) and their members are "children" (v. 4, 13). The same symbolism may be found in Rev. 12:17: οἱ λοιποὶ τοῦ σπέρματος αὐτῆς; it makes no difference whether the "woman clothed with the sun, and the moon under her feet, and upon her head a crown of twelve stars," is regarded as Israel κατὰ σάρκα or κατὰ πνεῦμα. Jn. does not simply call the church κυρία as the bride of the κύριος.[1] To use κυρία as a style or address was then a mark of respect, expressing the higher station of the one thus addressed (→ 1045). Jn. is thus making it clear that he has to honour, and does honour, the community as a work of God. Hence, even though in 2 Jn. he confronts the congregation as one who judges its conduct with joy and admonition (v. 4 : ἐχάρην λίαν; v. 8 : βλέπετε ... [imp.]), he is simply the servant of another's work. The use of the term κυρία is suggested to the πρεσβύτερος by the fact that he has not founded the church himself. This prevents him from using the image of the father and children, which Paul uses for his relation to the churches founded by him.

† κυριακός.

An adj. derived from the noun κύριος in the sense of "owner" and meaning "of the lord or owner" : πρὸς τὸν κυριακὸν λόγον, "to the debit of the proprietor."[1] In

---

κυρία. The Comm. on 2 Jn. 1, and Introductions, esp. Zahn Einl., II, 593 f. Cf. also Pr.-Bauer³, s.v. and F. J. Dölger, Antike u. Christentum, 5 (1936), 211-217.
[1] So Zahn, loc. cit.
κυριακός. T. Zahn, Geschichte des Sonntags (1878), 23 ff.; G. Loeschcke, Jüdisches u. Heidnisches im christl. Kult (1910), 1 ff.; J. Weiss, Das Urchristentum (1917), 502, n. 1; Deissmann LO, 304-309; S. V. McCasland, The Resurrection of Jesus (1932), 111-129.
[1] Example in Preisigke Wört., s.v.

official terminology it is used esp. as a tt. for "imperial," κυριακὸς λόγος, στρατιώτης, φόρος etc. ²

It occurs twice in the NT : 1 C. 11:20 : συνερχομένων οὖν ὑμῶν ἐπὶ τὸ αὐτὸ οὐκ ἔστιν κυριακὸν δεῖπνον φαγεῖν, and Rev. 1:10 : ἐγενόμην ἐν πνεύματι ἐν τῇ κυριακῇ ἡμέρᾳ. The adj. as thus applied arose on Greek soil, for there is no corresponding adj. in Semitic. κυριακὸν δεῖπνον may be compared with τράπεζα κυρίου in 1 C. 10:21, and κυριακὴ ἡμέρα with the double κυριακὴ κυρίου in Did., 14, 1. A gen. τοῦ κυρίου might have been used instead of the adj. But the choice of this adj. based on κύριος is not surprising, since of the Greek adjectives formed from the customary terms for Christ this was the only one which could denote the relation of a thing to Christ; Χριστιανός was used of people and σωτήριος had acquired a different sense from "belonging to the σωτήρ." If it is asked, then, why the two words δεῖπνον and ἡμέρα are combined with the adj. instead of the genitive τοῦ κυρίου, the answer is that this is an indirect relation to the Lord, e.g., as compared with λόγος τοῦ κυρίου, παρουσία τοῦ κυρίου etc.

The Lord's Day takes its significance from the resurrection of Christ. The κυριακὴ ἡμέρα soon became the day when the congregations assembled, Ac. 20:7; Did., 14, 1: κατὰ κυριακὴν δὲ κυρίου συναχθέντες. Jn.'s Gospel emphasises that Jesus rose on the first day of the week, Jn. 20:1, 19, 26, while the reference to the κυριακὴ ἡμέρα in Rev. 1:10 does not mention its importance as a day of assembly. The custom of not working on the Lord's Day was naturally impossible both for Jewish Christian congregations, which still kept the Sabbath, and for Gentile Christian congregations, which included slaves among their members and which were implicated in many different ways in the everyday life of paganism. The day could be distinguished only by coming together, although in 1 C. 16:2 Paul writes that something for the Jerusalem collection should be laid aside on this day (the actual expression does not occur). Whether this is connected with pay-day, as Deissmann suggests, ³ is not certain. Perhaps Paul takes the day when the congregation was assembling and when its thoughts would thus be occupied with church affairs. There is no proof, of course, that the Pauline churches assembled every Lord's Day, or only on the Lord's Day. But the first day of the week already enjoyed a certain prominence in Judaism, since it was the day when the creation of the world began. ⁴ For Christianity the resurrection of Jesus was the beginning of a new age. The fasts on the fourth and sixth days (Did., 8, 1) were also connected with the story of Jesus, since they were the days when counsel was taken to destroy Him (Mk. 14:1) and when He was crucified.

† κυριότης.

"Power or position as lord." In the NT its first use is for the members of a class of angels, Col. 1:16 : ἐν αὐτῷ ἐκτίσθη τὰ πάντα ἐν τοῖς οὐρανοῖς καὶ ἐπὶ τῆς γῆς ... εἴτε θρόνοι εἴτε κυριότητες εἴτε ἀρχαὶ εἴτε ἐξουσίαι, Eph. 1:20 f.: καθίσας ἐν δεξιᾷ αὐτοῦ ἐν τοῖς ἐπουρανίοις ὑπεράνω πάσης ἀρχῆς καὶ ἐξουσίας καὶ δυνάμεως καὶ κυριότητος καὶ παντὸς ὀνόματος ... These powers are always mentioned in the plural, Slav. En. 20:1; Eth. En. 61:10; Cave of Treas. 1:3; ¹

---

² Examples, *loc. cit.*
³ LO, 309.
⁴ Str.-B., I, 1052-1054.
κ υ ρ ι ό τ η ς. II, 251 f.; 568.
¹ In P. Riessler, *Altjüdisches Schrifttum ausserhalb der Bibel* (1928), 942.

Test. Sol. D 8:6. On material aspects → II, 571. Much debated is Jd. 8, where it is said of the false teachers : σάρκα μὲν μιαίνουσιν, κυριότητα δὲ ἀθετοῦσιν, δόξας δὲ βλασφημοῦσιν, par. 2 Pt. 2:10 : κυριότητος καταφρονοῦντας. The sing. shows that the reference is not to angels. [2] κυριότης denotes here the divine majesty and therefore God Himself, whom the false teachers wilfully despise with their libertinism. The inclination to substitute abstract for concrete terms is evident in Judaism, especially in terms for God. מרותא דעלמא is attested in the Rabbis → 1084, and we may also recall שכינה. A similar tendency may be observed in the Greek sphere, P. Oxy., II, 237, V, 6 (186 A.D.): γράφειν τῇ ἡγεμονίᾳ, cf. also "Your Majesty."

† κυριεύω.

"To be or become κύριος"; originally "to act as κύριος." Xenoph. Mem., III, 5, 11: ἀγωνιζόμενοι πρὸς τοὺς κυριεύοντας τῆς τε 'Ασίας πάσης κτλ. of political lords, Polyb., 2, 11 and 14 : ἐκυρίευσαν δὲ καὶ λέμβων εἴκοσι, "to seize." With the inf. Aeschin., 1, 35 : κυριευέτωσαν οἱ πρόεδροι μέχρι πεντήκοντα δραχμῶν ἐγγράφειν, "they ought to be authorised." Of the right of a lessor to the harvest of land on lease until the payments of the tithe, P. Tebt., 105, 47 (2nd cent. B.C.). Hence "to be lord" with the element of legality implicit in κύριος.

The word is common in the LXX, esp. for משׁל, whether of alien and oppressive rule or usurpation (e.g., 1 Macc. 10:76), of the self-elected king (Ju. 9:2), or of God in Ep. Ar., 16, 17, 18, 45, 269. Cf. Eth. En. 22:14.

In the NT it occurs at Lk. 22:25 in Luke's own formulation of a Synoptic saying : οἱ βασιλεῖς τῶν ἐθνῶν κυριεύουσιν αὐτῶν, καὶ οἱ ἐξουσιάζοντες αὐτῶν εὐεργέται καλοῦνται. The reference here is to the use of power as such (not its misuse), and to the associated outlook. Then it is used of the "powers" which rule human life : of death, whose sway has been broken once and for all by Christ, R. 6:9; of sin, from whose dominion Christians are released by the fact that they are no longer under Law, but under grace, R. 6:14 ; and of the Law, which cannot be arbitrarily evaded by the one who belongs to it any more than the wife can be separated from her husband by Jewish law, R. 7:1. Finally, it is used of the lordship of Christ as the goal of His passion and resurrection, R. 14:9. 1 Tm. 6:15 has in view earthly relationships of lordship, especially political, when it calls God ὁ βασιλεὺς τῶν βασιλευόντων καὶ κύριος τῶν κυριευόντων. Behind the use of κυριεύω in all these different connections is a human and secular understanding which does not view man as a free lord over himself but as subject to some lordship, whether to salvation or perdition.

In 2 C. 1:24 Paul finds it necessary to forestall misunderstanding of the statement he has just made, namely, that it was to spare the Corinthians that he did not come to Corinth. He does this by saying : οὐχ ὅτι κυριεύομεν ὑμῶν τῆς πίστεως, ἀλλὰ συνεργοί ἐσμεν τῆς χαρᾶς ὑμῶν· τῇ γὰρ πίστει ἐστήκατε. The first statement might have suggested that he was a lord graciously sparing his subjects. He guards against this misconception. As relationship to Christ liberates every slave from his master, and then binds him back again to his earthly master in freedom, for the Lord's sake (→ κύριος, E. 4), so the Corinthian Christians have their own relationship to Christ ; they themselves stand in faith, and it is Paul's task to be a fellow-helper of their joy.

---

[2] א has the plur. at Jd. 8, but the par. in 2 Pt. is against this.

† κατακυριεύω.

= κυριεύω, Diod. S., XIV, 64, 1: οἱ Συρακόσιοι ... κατακυριεύσαντες (sc. σιτη-γοῦ πλοίου) κατῆγον εἰς τὴν πόλιν; Apc. Mos. 14 : θάνατος κατακυριεύων παν-τὸς τοῦ γένους ἡμῶν. Later the force of the prep. was completely lost, and in the 6th cent. A.D. it came to mean "to have title to something."[1] In the LXX it is almost always used of the rule of an alien, e.g., of man over the earth, Gn. 1:28, or over animals, Sir. 17:4; of sin over man, ψ 118:133; of foreign conquest and domination, Jos. 24:33b (A); of God only at Jer. 3:14.

It occurs in the NT at Mk. 10:42 and par. : οἱ δοκοῦντες ἄρχειν τῶν ἐθνῶν κατακυριεύουσιν αὐτῶν καὶ οἱ μεγάλοι αὐτῶν κατεξουσιάζουσιν αὐτῶν. Here the κατά, which is used twice in the parallelism, is not without significance, and the word means the exercise of dominion against someone, i.e., to one's own advantage. Another instance is Ac. 19:16, where it occurs with reference to the man possessed of an unclean spirit : κατακυριεύσας ἀμφοτέρων ἴσχυσεν κατ' αὐτῶν, ὥστε ... τετραυματισμένους ἐκφυγεῖν. Similarly, the force of the κατά may still be seen in 1 Pt. 5:2 f.: ποιμάνατε τὸ ἐν ὑμῖν ποίμνιον τοῦ θεοῦ ... μηδ' ὡς κατακυριεύοντες τῶν κλήρων ἀλλὰ τύποι γινόμενοι τοῦ ποιμνίου, i.e., the elders, each over his portion (→ κλῆρος), are not to exercise their power for themselves and therewith against those entrusted to them.

Foerster

κυρόω, ἀκυρόω, προκυρόω

---

† κυρόω.

The chief meanings are a. "to enforce," "to confirm," "to validate," of legal actions of the most varied kinds, e.g., laws, Andoc., 1, 85 : τοὺς κυρωθέντας (sc. νόμους), cf. 84, Demosth. Or., 20, 93, decrees, IG, VII, 303, 45 : τὸ ψήφισμα τὸ κυρωθὲν περὶ τούτων (cf. also C. Michel, *Recueil d'Inscriptions Grecques* [1900], 478, 6 : κυρωθέντος τοῦδε τοῦ ψηφίσμ[ατο]ς, Ep. Ar., 26 : οὕτω δοχθὲν (sc. τὸ πρόσταγμα) ἐκεκύρωτο ἐν ἡμέραις ἑπτά, conditions of peace, Polyb., 1, 17, 1: τοῦ δήμου ... κυρώσαντος τὰς ... διαλύσεις, treaties, Gn. 23:20; Lv. 25:30 (Heb. קום);[1] Polyb., 5, 56, 1: τούτων (sc. τῶν συνθηκῶν) ... κυρωθέντων, P. Petr., II, 13, 18b, 15 : [περὶ] δὲ τοῦ κυρω-θῆναι τὰ ἔργα, wills, Gl. 3:15 (cf. the common clause in records of wills : ἡ διαθήκη κυρία, "the will is valid," P. Oxy., III, 491, 12; 493, 12; 494, 30; Preisigke Sammelbuch, 5294, 15 etc.), at auctions "to make a bid," BGU, 992, I, 9 etc. Rather more freely, 4 Macc. 7:9 : τὴν εὐνομίαν ἡμῶν διὰ τῶν ὑπομονῶν εἰς δόξαν ἐκύρωσας, Jos. Ant., 10, 254 :

κ α τ α κ υ ρ ι ε ύ ω. [1] An example in Preisigke, *s.v.*

κ υ ρ ό ω κ τ λ. Moult.-Mill., 366, 20; Pr.-Bauer³, 764 f., 55, 1181; Preisigke Wört., 855 f., 50 f.; Preisigke Fachwörter, 115; Liddell-Scott, 1014, 59, 1487; O. Eger, "Rechtswörter und Rechtsbilder in den paulinischen Briefen," *ZNW*, 18 (1917/18), 88 ff.; *Rechtsgeschichtliches zum NT* (1919), 31 ff.; Nägeli, 29; Zn. Gl.; Ltzm. Gl.; E. de Witt Burton, *A Critical and Exegetical Comm. to the Epistle to the Galatians* (1921) (ICC); M. J. Lagrange, *Saint Paul Épitre aux Galates*² (1926); A. Oepke, Gl. (1937) on 3:15, 17; Bchm. K., Ltzm. K., Wnd. 2 K., and Schl. K. on 2 C. 2:8; Zn. Mt. on 15:6; Hck. Mk. and J. Schniewind, *Das Evangelium nach Markus* (*NT Deutsch*, 1² [1935]), on 7:13.

[1] Cf. Σ Ez. 13:6 : κυρῶσαι λόγον (τοῦ κυρίου), where the Mas. has קום pi, the LXX ἀναστῆσαι, Θ στῆσαι [G. Bertram].

κυρώσειν τὴν προαίρεσιν αὐτῶν, Bell., 4, 362 : ἃ δὴ πάντα κατὰ τῶν ἀσεβῶν ἐκύρωσεν ὁ θεός, Mitteis-Wilcken, I, 2, No.122, 5 f.: ὑπόδειξόν μοι κα[ὶ] κύρωσ[όν] μοι τοῦτο τὸ γραπτόν (sc. the oracular question and request). b. "To stipulate," "to resolve," Hdt., VI, 86 β : ταῦτα ... ὑμῖν ἀναβάλλομαι κυρώσειν ἐς τέταρτον μῆνα ἀπὸ τοῦδε, VI, 126 : ὡς κυρώσοντος Κλεισθένεος τὸν γάμον ἐν ἐνιαυτῷ, VIII, 56 : ἔνιοι τῶν στρατηγῶν οὐδὲ κυρωθῆναι ἔμενον τὸ προκείμενον πρῆγμα, Thuc., VIII, 69, 1: ἡ ἐκκλησία οὐδενὸς ἀντειπόντος ἅμα κυρώσασα ταῦτα διελύθη, Polyb., 1, 11, 3 : κυρωθέντος δὲ τοῦ δόγματος ὑπὸ τοῦ δήμου (cf. 1; 4, 26, 1 f.); 6, 13, 9 : τὰ σφῶν πράγματα σχεδὸν πάντα τὴν σύγκλητον κυροῦν, 7, 5, 5 : τὰ μὲν τοῦ πολέμου τοῦ πρὸς ʿΡωμαίους ἐκεκύρωτο τὸν τρόπον τοῦτον, 5, 49, 6 : ἐκυρώθη τὸ διαβούλιον, Da. 6:10; Jos. Ant., 2, 18 : ταύτην κυρώσαντες τὴν βουλήν (ibid., 9, 76); IG, VII, 4133, 3 f.: τ]ιμαὶ καὶ δω[ρ]εαὶ κεκυρωμέναι, Preisigke Sammelbuch, 7457, 24 f.: τὰς διὰ τοῦ προκειμένου δόγματος κεκυρωμένας εἰκόνας δύο. c. Mid. "to bring into force," "to achieve one's resolution," Plat. Gorg., 451b: καὶ αὕτη (sc. ἡ λογιστικὴ τέχνη) ἐστὶν τῶν λόγῳ τὸ πᾶν κυρουμένων, 451c: καὶ αὕτη (sc. ἡ ἀστρονομία) λόγῳ κυροῦται τὰ πάντα, esp. 451d, where κυρουμένων is par. to διαπραττομένων, which is undoubtedly mid.

In the illustration from the legal sphere in Gl. 3:15 : ἀνθρώπου κεκυρωμένην διαθήκην (→ II, 129) οὐδεὶς → ἀθετεῖ ἢ ἐπιδιατάσσεται, κυρόω is used as a technical legal term for a will which has come into force (→ 1098). That the illustration does not quite fit the promise (→ II, 582) may be seen from its legally meaningless description as διαθήκη προκεκυρωμένη (→ 1100) ὑπὸ τοῦ θεοῦ, v. 17. Materially → II, 129. In 2 C. 2:8 : παρακαλῶ ὑμᾶς κυρῶσαι εἰς αὐτὸν ἀγάπην, "I admonish you to resolve on love for him,"[2] two alien concepts are combined, namely, ἀγάπη (→ I, 49 ff.), the basic ethical principle of the Pauline Gospel, and κυροῦν, the legal term of developing Church law, and an effective oxymoron is the by no means accidental result.[3] The congregation has now to make another decision in the case of the ἀδικήσας (7:12; cf. 2:5) whom it has punished (2:6) and who now sincerely repents of his fault (2:7). Paul desires a decision whose content is love. Right is to be replaced by right as pardoning love dictates and crowns the final legal dicision.

† ἀκυρόω.

"To make invalid," "to rob of force," a technical legal term, e.g., Dinarch., 1, 63 : αὐτὸς τὸ ψήφισμα ἀκυροῖς, 1 Εσδρ., 6:31;[1] Ditt. Syll.³, 742, 30 f.: ἠκυρῶσθαι τὰς κ[α]τ᾽ αὐτῶν ἐκγραφὰς καὶ ὀφειλήμ[ατα], Dion. Hal. Ant. Rom., 2, 72, 5 : εἰρήνην ... γεγενημένην ... ἀκυροῦν, BGU, 1167, 26 : κατὰ τὴ[ν] ἠκυρω[μένην] (sc. συγχώρησιν) (cf. 1053, II, 14), Jos. Ant., 20, 183 : ἐπιστολὴν ἀκυροῦσαν τὴν Ἰουδαίων πρὸς αὐτοὺς ἰσοπολιτείαν, Plut. De Lycurgo, 9 (I, 44d): ἀκυρώσας πᾶν νόμισμα χρυσοῦν καὶ ἀργυροῦν, P. Oxy., III, 491, 3 : ἐφ᾽ ὃν μὲν περίειμι χρόνον ἔχειν

---

[2] The possibility considered by Pr.-Bauer³, 765 that the meaning here is "to bring into force," like the mid. in Plat. Gorg., 451b-d (→ supra), is to be discounted in view of the use of the act. and the context of 2 C. 2:5 ff., in which Paul carefully safeguards the right of an autonomous congregation to make its own decision.

[3] On Gospel and Law in Pl. cf. J. Behm, Religion u. Recht im NT (Rectoral Address, Göttingen, 1931), 6 ff., 12 f.

ἀ κ υ ρ ό ω. [1] Cf. 2 Εσδρ. 6:11 ἀλλάσσειν = אשנ‎, haph. 1 Εσδρ. uses the two words παραβαίνειν καὶ ἀκυροῦν, ʾA has ἀκυρόω for פרר‎ and פור‎, "to break (a covenant)," "to frustrate (a plan)," at Nu. 30:13 (twice); Dt. 31:20; Job 5:12; ψ 32:10; 118:126 (τὸν νόμον); Is. 24:5. The LXX mostly uses διασκεδάζω [G. Bertram].

μ[ε] τὴν τῶν ἰδίων ἐξου[σί]αν ὃ ἐὰν βούλωμαι ἐπιτελεῖν ... καὶ ἀκυροῦν τ[ὴν διαθήκην] ταύτην, Preisigke Sammelbuch, 5676, 9 : ὁ ... ἡγεμὼν ... ἀκυρώσας ... τὴν οὐ δεόντως γενομένην ὑπο[θήκη]ν. Less frequent in the general sense, "to put out of action," "to render inoperative," "to frustrate," e.g., Diod. S., IV, 34, 4 : ἀκυροῦντες ... τὴν δωρεάν, Jos. Ant., 18, 304 : μηδαμῶς ἀκυροῦν αὐτοκράτορος ἀνδρὸς ἐντολάς, 4 Macc. 2:1, 3, 18; 5:18; 7:14; 17:2.

The word has a legal ring in the NT. Mk. 7:13 (Mt. 15:6): When the Jews place cultic obligations above the keeping of the command of God in the Decalogue, [2] they make the Word of God of none effect in favour of human decisions of doubtful religious value : ἀκυροῦντες (cf. v. 9 : → ἀθετεῖτε) τὸν → λόγον τοῦ θεοῦ τῇ παραδόσει ὑμῶν ᾗ παρεδώκατε (→ II, 171 f.). In Gl. 3:17 Paul uses the analogy of a valid will, which cannot be reversed (v. 15 → 1099), to show how unbreakable is the declaration of God's will in the promise made to Abraham and his seed (v. 16, 18, cf. 6 ff; → II, 130). Since this διαθήκη is of unconditional legal force, its validity cannot be altered by the Law, which came much later. The original and unshakable divine order is the gracious promise of the righteousness of faith.

† προκυρόω.

"To make valid in advance." The only pre-Christian instance thus far found is on an inscr. in Rhodes (2nd cent. B.C.) which refers to the execution of resolves of the κοινόν; cf. Suppl. Epigr. Graec. ... ed. J. J. E. Hondius, III (1929), No. 674, n. 28 f.: καθὼς ἐν τῷ προκεκυρωμένῳ ψαφίσματι ποτιτέτακται, ibid., 30 : τὰ ποτιτεταγμένα ἐν τῷ προκεκυρωμένῳ ψαφίσματι. Later it is found occasionally in the fathers, e.g., Eus. Praep. Ev., X, 4, 1.

In Gl. 3:17 Paul wishes to show that the Gospel is absolutely superior to the Law (→ II, 582) and he thus describes it as a will which God made valid before — i.e., long before the coming of the Law[1] — or in advance (διαθήκην προκεκυρωμένην ὑπὸ τοῦ θεοῦ). The image and the thought are here very contradictory, for whereas a human will comes into effect only with the death of the testator, the will and testament of God (v. 15 → II, 129), the promise of salvation to Abraham and his seed (v. 6 ff., 16, 18; cf. Gn. 12:3; 17:2 ff.; 18:18 etc.), is put into effect as soon as it is drawn up, and from this point on it is exclusively and incontrovertibly valid (→ 1099 f.).

Behm

---

[2] Cf. on this Str.-B., I, 717.

προκυρόω. [1] Cf. F. Sieffert, *Der Brief an d. Galater*⁹ (1899), ad loc.; Burton, ad loc.; Oepke, ad loc. For a different but rather far-fetched view based on Gn. 15:8 ff. (esp. 17 f.), Eger, "Rechtswörter u. Rechtsbilder ...," 91, n. 1.

[2] Cf. Zn. Gl., W. Bousset (in *Schr. NT*), ad loc.

κύων, κυνάριον

† κύων. [1]

1. "Dog," esp. the annoying and despised eastern dog of the streets, in the OT כֶּלֶב,
Aram. כַּלְבָּא. The word is used both lit. and fig. from the time of Homer, cf. also pap.
and the LXX. [2] Although there are Jews who speak of the faithfulness of the dog, in
the main it is regarded as "the most despicable, insolent and miserable of creatures"
(Str.-B., I, 722). Comparison with a dog is insulting and dishonouring (1 S. 17:43). The
description "dead dog" (ὁ κύων ὁ τεθνηκώς) is the last word in contempt or self-
abasement (1 S. 24:15; 2 S. 9:8; 16:9). This is the sense behind Hazael's question to
Elisha: Τίς ἐστιν ὁ δοῦλός σου, ὁ κύων ὁ τεθνηκώς, ὅτι ποιήσει τὸ ῥῆμα τοῦτο;
(4 Βασ. 8:13). [3] To be eaten by dogs on the streets or by fowls on the field is the sign
of a special judgment of God which is sometimes declared by the prophets (1 K. 14:11;
16:4; 21:24). Elijah prophesies to Ahab: "In the place where dogs licked the blood of
Naboth shall dogs lick thy blood" (1 K. 21:19; 22:38). It is a special indignity to be
delivered up to dogs. [4] Psalm 22 (LXX 21) refers to dogs surrounding the psalmist and
threatening his life (v. 16, 20); his ungodly opponents are here compared to bulls of the
steppes and ravenous dogs of the streets. The passionate complaint of Is. 56:10-11 is
that the rulers of the people are dumb dogs (κύνες ἐνεοί) who do not watch or warn,
but who are greedy and insatiable (ἀναιδεῖς) when it is a matter of their own advantage. How despised the dog is may be seen from the comparison in Prv. 26:11: "As
a dog returneth to his vomit, so a fool returneth to his folly." As hyenas and dogs,
wolves and sheep, lions and deer do not go together, neither do rich and poor or the
ungodly and the righteous (Sir. 13:17 ff.). Dt. forbids the hire of harlots or the price
of dogs (מְחִיר כֶּלֶב) to be brought into the sanctuary of God (23:18); this excludes both
female and male hierodules (the latter κύνες?) from the worship of Israel.

In later Judaism it is uncertain whether the dog is to be reckoned as a domestic
animal (בְּהֵמָה) or a wild animal (חַיָּה); Kil., 8, 6 says: "The dog is a wild animal, R. Meïr
says: a domestic animal." That it is faithful and will give its life for its master is stated
in Pesikt., 79b (Buber): נפשא דכלבא ("the memorial of the dog"). According to a commonly reported tradition (R. Shimeon, bLakish, R. Jakim) there are three obstinate things:
among animals the dog, among birds the cock, and among the nations Israel. This is not

---

κ ύ ω ν. A. Zeller, Das Pferd, der Esel u. der Hund in d. Hl. Schrift, Beitrag zur bibl.
Archäologie (1890).
[1] Old Indo-Eur. word, Lat. canis, Eng. hound, Germ. Hund. Walde-Pok., I, 465 f.
[2] A. Jeremias, Das AT im Lichte d. Alten Orients⁴ (1930), 438: "In the Orient scavenging
dogs are the plague of the land, but also the board of sanitary inspectors, Asurb. Ann.,
VII, 74 ff. (Vorderasiatische Bibliothek, ed. A. Jeremias and H. Winkler [1906 ff.], VII,
39). This illustrates the position in Babylonian cities and in many parts of the East to this
day. Dogs and pigs block the streets and fill the market-places, eating offal; cf. 1 K. 14:11;
2 K. 9:35 ff.; Ps. 22:16, 20; Jer. 15:3." On the later use of κύων, cf. Class. Rev., 4 (1890), 44a
and Class. Quarterly, 3 (1909), 281.
[3] A. Jeremias, 612, n. 1: "The self-designation 'thy servant, thy dog' (2 K. 8:13) is servile
abasement, like the Austrian servus. It is found in Assyrian letters, also in the Amarna
letters, e.g., Vorderasiat. Bibl., II, No. 71, 16 f. To call someone a dog (dead dog) is to
offer the strongest possible insult (2 S. 16:9)."
[4] The Midrash says contemptuously of Goliath: "He died like a dog" (Ex. r., 31, 3 on
22:25, p. 56d [Vilna]).

told in disparagement, but in praise, of Israel (bBeça, 25b and par.; Str.-B., I, 723). R. Jannai brings in a well-dressed man as his guest, but is astonished at his ignorance of Scripture and the Mishnah, and because of his ignorance calls him a dog (Lv. r., 9, 3 on 7:11, p. 13a [Vilna]; Str.-B., I, 724). This saying excludes the guest from the inheritance of Israel. Acc. to Ps. 110:2 God smites the ungodly with a rod because they are like dogs (cf. Ps. 59), Ex. r., 9, 2 on 7:9; Str.-B., I, 724. R. Aqiba calls his dogs Rufus and Rufina because the Gentiles are like dogs in their manner of life (Tanch. תרומה, p. 107b [Warsaw]; Str.-B., I, 725). A man is brought into contempt when he is either called a dog or a dog is named after him.

2. What makes Israel superior to the Gentiles is that it has the Torah. The Torah is a divine secret which must not be declared to the Gentiles. This is explicitly laid down in Midr. Cant. 2:7 (מסטרין = μυστήριον) and bKet., 111a (though not as Halacha). The loftiness of the Torah demands that it be kept aloof from anything common. R. Ammi deduces from Ps. 147:20 that the Torah is not to be delivered to a Kuthean = Goy (bChag., 13a). The Gentile world is inferior because it is thus excluded from the Torah. Jesus transcends the old Rabbinic restriction in Mt. 7:6 and describes the majesty of the Gospel in a new way. The disciple is not to judge (Mt. 7:1-5), but he is also not to believe that he can overcome all resistance by himself. "Jesus says that there are invincible obstacles which no missionary zeal can break through."[5] Mt. 7:6 is a self-contained word of admonition which speaks periphrastically and indirectly of the message itself in a twofold figure (κύνες, χοῖροι). The saying of Jesus shows reverence for the divine Word and thus differentiates itself from the dignity of human wisdom.[6]

The first figure: μὴ δῶτε τὸ ἅγιον τοῖς κυσίν, has formally a cultic ring, and is based on a well-known cultic rule in Judaism. τὸ ἅγιον[7] is sacrificial meat acc. to Ex. 29:33; Lv. 2:3; 22:10-16; Nu. 18:8-19 (not קָדֵשׁ, ear-ring); it is to the flesh of sacrifice that the much quoted saying refers: "What is holy is not to be released to be eaten by dogs" (bBek., 15a Bar. on Dt. 12:15; Tem., 6, 5; cf. bTem., 130b [or 30b]; bTem., 117a Bar.; bShebu., 11b [in the form of a question] and bPes., 29a [acc. to which the basic principle is not generally acknowledged]). Dogs and swine were often associated as unclean animals (2 Pt. 2:22; Horat. Ep., I, 2, 23 ff.; bShab., 155b; P. Oxy., V, 840, 33). They did not refer to distinct classes of men but to men of all classes who set themselves in opposition to the Gospel (cf. the term "cynical").

The majesty of the Gospel should protect the disciples against addressing the message to the wrong quarters. They are not to decide to whom the Gospel is to be addressed or from whom it is to be withheld. But they must see the limits of their

---

[5] Schl. Mt., 243.

[6] Bultmann Trad., 107 thinks that Mt. 7:6 is one of the secular *meshalim* which tradition later made into sayings of Jesus, and he reminds us of Lidz. Ginza R., VII, 217 (p. 218): "The words of the wise to fools are like pearls for a sow."

[7] τὸ ἅγιον acc. to LXX usage, and קֹדֶשׁ (קָדָשִׁים) in the Rabbis, mean a. animals appointed for sacrifice (also sacrificial meat), b. any animals dedicated to God, i.e., paid to the priests, whether literally or "in redemption," i.e., in the form of an equivalent payment; these might be animals which the owner has appointed to be sacrificed in connection with a vow, or the first-fruits of his cattle. Since the animal is τὸ ἅγιον, the owner ought not to have any more profit from it before it is sacrificed or before the redemption money is paid. Nor should he turn the corpse to any advantage, even by feeding it to dogs, but should have it buried. Nor may the owner later pay redemption money for the slain animal so as to gain free use of the corpse. Cf. K. G. Kuhn, S. Nu. bearb. u. erklärt (1933 ff.), 386, n. 28, also Str.-B., I, 447 on Mt. 7:6.

ministry. Faith is a fruit of the Holy Spirit, not an achievement of the disciples. The Holy Spirit is bound by no limits; in comparison our human ministry is small and restricted. The cultic form of the saying of Jesus suggests that it be applied also to the Church's worship, and it is along these lines that the Did. restricts participation in the eucharist (9, 5): "And let none eat or drink of your Eucharist, but they that have been baptised into the name of the Lord; for concerning this the Lord hath said: Give not that which is holy to the dogs."

In the parable of Dives and Lazarus (Lk. 16:19 ff.) it is told how the dogs came and licked the sores of Lazarus (16:21). This is hardly a reference to the sympathy of animals in contrast to the heartlessness of men. It is rather a sign of the supreme wretchedness of the poor beggar; he has to endure even contact with these unclean animals. [8] It seems as though Lazarus in his misery and death has come wholly under the divine judgment. The more striking is the sudden change in the situation after death.

3. Paul's warning in Phil. 3:2 has a polemical edge. Whereas the saying of the Lord in Mt. 7:6 is a figure of speech in which men who oppose the Gospel are compared to animals recognised to be unclean, Paul describes specific Jewish or Judaising opponents as "dogs" (κύνες). Is he turning their own weapon against themselves? As in Mt. 7:6 the reference is to the scorning of the message rather than ignorance of it. He has in view, not exclusion from salvation, but the disturbing of the community. Did he know the saying in Mt. 7:6 and refer it to his own situation? Or is he describing the hostile and obtrusive nature of his opponents? The Psalmist had a similar complaint about his enemies: "They return at evening, they make a noise like a dog, and go round about the city. Behold, they belch out with their mouth, swords are in their lips" (Ps. 59:6 f., 14). [9] How strong is the influence of OT themes in early Christian polemics may be seen from the quotation of Prv. 26:11 in 2 Pt. 2:22 and from the combination of dogs and pigs in a proverbial saying (παροιμία). The Christian who falls back into sin and error reassumes the filth which he put off at baptism; he is thus the fool (ἄφρων) of the proverb. [10] The uncleanness described in the proverb (παροιμία) is a metaphor for the defilement of the world and the corruption of sin.

κύνες remained a term of reproach in the proclamation of the Church, as may be seen from the conclusion of Rev. (22:15). He who washes his garments may enter the holy city (22:14), but dogs, sorcerers, whoremongers, murderers, idolaters, and those who love and make a lie are shut out. Here the term κύων (κύνες) is influenced by the OT and the tradition which stems from it, but it is also used generally for men who resist the will of God and entangle themselves in demonism and falsehood. [11] The final phrase πᾶς φιλῶν καὶ ποιῶν ψεῦδος characterises the whole verse. The reference is neither to Jews nor Gentiles as such, but to men who have fallen under the sphere of untruth and build up this sphere. Resistance to the message, hardening against the grace of God, allegiance to evil and falling back into evil are perhaps the various factors which evoke the apostle's outburst.

---

[8] For a different view cf. Zn. Lk. [3, 4] (1920), 585; Wettstein, ad loc.

[9] But cf. Loh. Phil., ad loc.: "But then all who are separated from the early Christian community are dogs" (125).

[10] Cf. on this Wettstein and Str.-B., III, 773.

[11] Not wholly clear in Bss. Apk., 458, Loh. Apk.: "A common term to express Jewish contempt for other peoples" (177).

Certainly, it is only metaphorically that Jesus compares men to unclean animals (Mt. 7:6), but Phil. 3:2 and Rev. 22:15 sound like apostolic exposition of this mysterious saying. At any rate, the NT reproach differs plainly from later Jewish usage.

In Ign. Eph., 7, 1 we have a distinctive part of the post-apostolic attack on heresy. Certain aspects of the earlier reproach are retained in this picture, but the colours are stronger: "They are mad dogs, biting stealthily, against whom you must be on your guard, for their bite is hard to heal." The community must avoid their attack, for it is dangerous. Error is depicted not merely as an intellectual deviation from the Church's truth but as an invasion of demonic powers which seize control of thought and action. The Church is still aware of the limit indicated in Mt. 7:6 and it speaks of only one Physician who can help, Jesus Christ, the Lord Himself (Eph., 7, 2).

† κυνάριον.

Plat. Euthyd., 298d; Xenoph. Cyrop., VIII, 4, 20; Epict. Diss., IV, 1, 111; also κυνίδιον, Euthyd., 298d; Philo Spec. Leg., IV, 91; diminutives of κύων for the "house dog" as distinct from the "yard dog" or the "dog of the streets."

In the NT κυνάριον occurs only in the figurative saying of Jesus at Mt. 15:26; Mk. 7:27. It is debatable whether Jesus is adopting the Jewish habit of calling the person of a different faith κύων (cf. the figurative saying at Mt. 7:6). The saying in Mt. 15:26; Mk. 7:27 brings the claims of children and house dogs into comparison. [1] The choice of κυνάριον shows that Jesus has in mind little dogs which could be tolerated in the house. [2] The metaphor of Jesus recognises the distinction which God demands between Jews and Gentiles, accepts the historical privilege of Israel (Dt. Is., Pl., Ac.) and limits the earthly work of Jesus (Jn. 12:20-26). [3] This is how Mk. 7:27 interprets the saying. The children of the house must be satisfied first (πρῶτον). The answer of the Gentile woman (Mt. 15:27; Mk. 7:28) shows that in obedience to the will of God she recognises the prerogative of Israel. She simply appeals to the readiness of Jesus to help, which knows no frontiers. The faith of the Gentile woman sets itself unconditionally under the Messianic lordship of Christ, and in this unconditional quality it receives the acknowledgment and promise of Jesus.

Michel

κυνάριον. [1] Cf. Zn. Mt., *ad loc.*

[2] bKet., 61b: A woman who plays with little dogs (Aram. גּוּרְיָיתָא קְטַנְיָיתָא) or with a chess-board; cf. also bShab., 155b; Str.-B., I, 722, 726.

[3] Cf. Schl. Mt., 490.